THE ANALYTICAL CONCORDANCE
to the
NEW REVISED STANDARD VERSION
of the
NEW TESTAMENT

Richard E. Whitaker and John R. Kohlenberger III

WILLIAM B. EERDMANS PUBLISHING COMPANY
GRAND RAPIDS, MICHIGAN / CAMBRIDGE, U.K.

OXFORD UNIVERSITY PRESS
NEW YORK   OXFORD

William B. Eerdmans Publishing Company

Grand Rapids · Cambridge

Oxford University Press

Oxford   New York

Athens   Auckland   Bangkok   Bogotá   Buenos Aires   Calcutta
Cape Town   Chennai   Dar es Salaam   Delhi   Florence   Hong Kong   Istanbul
Karachi   Kuala Lumpur   Madrid   Melbourne   Mexico City   Mumbai
Nairobi   Paris   São Paulo   Singapore   Taipei   Tokyo   Toronto   Warsaw

and associated companies in
Berlin   Ibadan

Published jointly 2000 by
Wm. B. Eerdmans Publishing Company
255 Jefferson Ave. S.E., Grand Rapids, Michigan 49503
and by
Oxford University Press, Inc.
198 Madison Avenue, New York, New York 10016

Oxford is a registered trademark of Oxford University Press

Printed in the United States of America
on acid-free paper

05 04 03 02 01 00   5 4 3 2 1

Library of Congress Cataloging-in-Publication Data

A catalog record for this book is available from the Library of Congress

Eerdmans ISBN 0-8028-3883-9
Oxford ISBN 0-19-528443-7

Table of Contents

Preface

This volume is based on the New Testament portion of *The Eerdmans Analytical Concordance to the Revised Standard Version of the Bible*, compiled and edited by Dr. Richard E. Whitaker.

Using software developed by Tim Hare of Telios Systems in Portland, Oregon, John R. Kohlenberger III first aligned the text of the Revised Standard Version (RSV) to that of the New Revised Standard Version (NRSV). This alignment was then run against the New Testament extracted from Whitaker's RSV concordance database to produce a preliminary NRSV concordance database, roughly similar in content to the RSV database with its English-Greek alignments and contexts. Kohlenberger then worked through the NRSV database word-by-word to verify the existing English-Greek alignments and contexts, and to add alignments and contexts for all unaligned words, including articles, adverbs, conjunctions, particles, and prepositions. A preliminary concordance was then proofed and corrected by Whitaker and Kohlenberger.

The Concordance and the Greek-English Index were then compiled by Kohlenberger with commercial software and the volume was typeset with Quark XPress for Windows 4.03.

Introduction

T he whole design of this volume, and all decisions in its development, have been aimed at making this an easy-to-use aid, not just a scholarly reference tool. It was designed primarily for the person with a lively interest in the New Testament but limited or no knowledge of the Greek language. It will also prove useful to those who are conversant with the Greek, particularly pastors and serious students. Scholars, too, will find it helpful for some types of study.

The New Testament, as treated in the present volume, includes the English text of the New Revised Standard Version (NRSV) and the Greek text of the United Bible Societies' *The Greek New Testament:* Fourth Revised Edition. Those who are not concerned with the original Greek can use the English concordance without interference from the "analysis." Apart from the exceptions noted below, all words in the English text are included. The words are listed by dictionary form in alphabetical order followed by every context in which any form of the word is found. A citation giving the book, chapter, and verse for the context is provided at the left margin of each context line.

The "analytical" feature of the concordance is that it provides information about what word in the original Greek is being translated in each context. Following the dictionary form of the English word is a listing in alphabetical order of all of the Greek words that the NRSV translators have translated by any form of the English word, with a reference number for each of the Greek words. At the right end of each context line is the reference number for the Greek word that is translated in that particular context.

Included and Omitted Words

In order to keep the volume down to a useable size, certain very frequent words have been omitted. These include the articles "a" and "the"; conjunctions "and," "but," "or," and "then"; all personal pronouns, including the personal reflexive pronouns (e.g., "I" and "myself"); most subordinating and demonstrative pronouns, such as "that," "who," "whoever," "what," "whatever," "which," etc.; all forms of the verbs "become" and "be" except "being" when it is a noun and "am" in the phrase "I am" spoken by God; all auxiliary verbs when used with a main verb, such as "do," "may," "shall," and "will"; and the adverbs "too," "also," and "not."

Many words normally omitted from concordances have been included wherever they directly translate a Greek word. These include the prepositions "about," "after," "against," "among," "as," "at," "before," "by," "even," "for," "from," "in," "into," "like," "on," "out," "over," "through," "to," "under," "with"; the verb "have" in the senses of possession and obligation ("have to"); the adverbs "how," "no," "nor," "there," "why," and "yet"; and the conjunctions "both," "if," "now," "so," "that," "though," "when," and "where."

Headings

In order to group English words into a more helpful arrangement, the various occurrences of a word are listed under a heading word that corresponds to the dictionary form of the word, e.g., all contexts in which "fills," "filling," and "filled" occur will be found under "fill." All of the -ing and -ed forms, e.g., "filling" and "filled," are listed under the verb even if they function in their particular contexts as adjectives or nouns. When, however, forms have become so fixed in English as nouns that they have lost their original verbal force, they are listed as separate nouns, e.g., "building" when it means "a structure" is a separate noun, but "building" as a verbal form would be under "build." Nouns are listed under their singular form. Proper names in the contexts have the same form as they have in the NRSV.

Ideally a concordance of this type would list each English word in the Bible with each context referenced

to a single corresponding word in the original Greek. This, however, is not possible, since many times a Greek word is translated by an English phrase, or a Greek phrase is translated by a single English word. Whenever possible, single English words are used in the headings, but it has often been necessary to include headings that are phrases. If a heading phrase is found, it indicates either that the phrase translates a single Greek word, or that the phrase translates a phrase in which there is no correspondence between the single words of the Greek phrase and the single words of the English.

Phrase Headings

Since phrases contain more than one word, and the order of words in the same basic English phrase may vary from one context to another, e.g., "know fully" versus "fully known," some decisions had to be made about where the phrases would be listed in the concordance. On the assumption that most users of the concordance would look up phrases by the word carrying the major meaning of the phrase, a system was developed to list by major or primary meaning. If a phrase contains a verb, it is usually listed after the verb in the concordance. If there are two verbs, it is listed after the verb carrying the primary meaning. If the phrase contains a linking verb and an adjective or noun, the phrase will be listed following the adjective or noun, since it carries the primary meaning of the phrase. A phrase containing the verbs "act" or "do" followed by an adverb will be listed after the adverb. Phrases containing nouns with prepositions or modifiers will normally be listed after the noun. Certain rather neutral nouns in English are regularly used with an adjective to translate adjectives in the Greek that are used as nouns (similar to the English use in expressions like "the poor"). Phrases containing a neutral noun plus an adjective are listed after the adjective. These nouns include "fellow," "man," "woman," "deed," "act," "thing," "person," "people," "one," "sort," "place," "kind," "part," "stuff," and "manner." Names of plants and animals are treated as units, even though following the principles listed above they might be listed otherwise. "Fig tree" will be found following "fig," not "tree." But so that each phrase could be found by any of its words, there is a generous system of cross references. These cross references list the complete heading phrase, e.g., "**abroad** *See* go abroad, scatter abroad, spread abroad." The cross references assume the heading phrase is alphabetized under its first word; otherwise, the alphabetizing word is italicized, e.g., "**abusive** *See also* abusive *language*." Words that are omitted in the concordance as a whole (e.g., "a," "and," "the") are not included as part of a phrase cross reference.

Headings with Superscript Numbers

Often English words or phrases that are spelled the same will have different meanings (e.g., "charge" meaning "have authority," "accuse legally," or "give a command"), or they will be in the same field of meaning but represent different parts of speech (e.g., "rain" as either a noun or a verb). When the field of meaning varies, there will be separate headings with superscript numbers, e.g., "charge[1]" (have authority), "charge[2]" (give a command), "charge[3]" (accuse legally), etc. But words representing the same field of meaning but different parts of speech will be listed under the same heading. Thus "charged against this generation" and "the charge against him" are both under "charge[3]." Sometimes it is difficult to determine whether a distinction in usage really constitutes a difference in field of meaning. The real test, of course, is whether the distinctions help the user see together the passages with related meaning.

Numbers as Headings

In the NRSV all numbers are spelled out as words, so all numbers in this concordance are alphabetized as words. Following the letter Z, however, there is a complete list of numbers in numerical order from 1/10 to 144,000 with cross references to their alphabetic entries, e.g., "1/10 *See* tenth" and "144,000 *See* hundred, forty-four, thousand."

Greek–English Numbering Systems

Each context has to its right a number, which refers to a Greek word or phrase. Each heading is followed by a list of one or more words or phrases in Greek, with one exception. Where the translators supplied or repeated a word for clarity in context, the English entry "Contextual: Not in Greek" is used in place of a Greek word or phrase. Single Greek words as well as phrases are in their dictionary forms. The forms listed are the forms used in the standard Greek dictionary *A Greek-English Lexicon of the New Testament and Other Early Christian Literature* by Bauer, Arndt, Gingrich, and Danker (University of Chicago / Zondervan, second edition: 1979).

Greek phrases are listed in their most common word order, but are not listed in their contextual, inflected form. This assists general users and beginning students of Greek in identifying each component of any phrase. To further assist readers, each Greek word is transliterated into English and is keyed to the Goodrick-Kohlenberger (G/K) numbering system for easier access to the Greek-English Index of this volume and to other biblical reference books.

The fact that a word or phrase in English is referenced to a word or phrase in Greek does not mean that they have the same meaning. Ways of expression vary from language to language. The focus of the concordance is on the English text of the NRSV and the words and expressions in the Greek that are behind the words in the NRSV. The Greek words are not to be seen as having the exact meaning of the English, but as the dictionary form of the word that is behind the English. Gender, for example, is often a matter of inflection or spelling and not part of the essential meaning of a word. The three entries "unmarried," "unmarried man," and "unmarried woman" all include the Greek word *agamos*. The word means "unmarried" regardless of gender, and only refers to an unmarried man or woman in a specific context.

Abbreviations

The citations of book, chapter, and verse for each context in which a word or phrase is found use the numbering of the NRSV. This varies at times from the numbering of texts in the United Bible Societies' *Greek New Testament*. Tables of abbreviations for the biblical books are found in the next section of the concordance, as is a complete listing of words and phrases in which the NRSV differs in versification from the Greek.

Greek–English Index

The Greek-English Index at the end of the book includes all of the Greek words and phrases that are cited in the concordance. As in the concordance, headings include G/K numbers and words and phrases in Greek and in English transliteration. The English words that follow are the headings of the concordance, followed by a number in square brackets. This number indicates how many times that Greek word or phrase was translated by that NRSV word or phrase. These English entries are listed in order of frequency and include every Greek and English word in the New Testament. Thus, even though "and" is not listed in the concordance, the index still offers the statistic that the Greek word *kai* is translated by "and" 5,802 times.

Greek phrases are listed by the first word in the phrase. However, each word in the phrase is cross referenced to the phrase heading by G/K number and English word or phrase. For example, the Greek words *eis* + *ho* + *aiōn* are translated "forever" 43 times in the NRSV. The phrase is alphabetized following the word *1650 eis*, and both words *ho* and *aiōn* have the cross reference "*see 1650* [forever]."

These indexes are not dictionaries of the languages and do not include any words that are not referenced in the concordances. That is why there are some gaps in the G/K numbers, for example, between *14* and *16*. No attempt is made to indicate the full translation of a word or phrase. For further insights on the range meaning in the New Testament vocabulary, consult the *Lexicon* of Bauer, Arndt, Gingrich and Danker, mentioned above, as well as the two-volume *Greek-English Lexicon of the New Testament Based on Semantic Domains* (United Bible Societies, 1988), the three-volume *Exegetical Dictionary of the New Testament* (Eerdmans, 1990-93), the three-volume *Theological Lexicon of the New Testament* (Hendrickson, 1994), the four-volume *New International Dictionary of New Testament Theology* (Zondervan, 1975-86), and the ten-volume *Theological Dictionary of the New Testament* (Eerdmans, 1964-76) with its one-volume abridgment (Eerdmans, 1985).

Abbreviations

The Books of the New Testament in Canonical Order

Mat.	Matthew	1Ti	1 Timothy
Mrk	Mark	2Ti	2 Timothy
Lke	Luke	Tit	Titus
Jhn	John	Phm	Philemon
Act	Acts	Heb.	Hebrews
Rom.	Romans	Jas.	James
1Co	1 Corinthians	1Pe	1 Peter
2Co	2 Corinthians	2Pe	2 Peter
Gal.	Galatians	1Jn	1 John
Eph.	Ephesians	2Jn	2 John
Php	Philippians	3Jn	3 John
Col	Colossians	Jde	Jude
1Th	1 Thessalonians	Rev	Revelation
2Th	2 Thessalonians		

The Books of the New Testament in Alphabetical Order

Act	Acts	Mat.	Matthew
Col	Colossians	Mrk	Mark
1Co	1 Corinthians	1Pe	1 Peter
2Co	2 Corinthians	2Pe	2 Peter
Eph.	Ephesians	Phm	Philemon
Gal.	Galatians	Php	Philippians
Heb.	Hebrews	Rev	Revelation
Jas.	James	Rom.	Romans
Jde	Jude	1Th	1 Thessalonians
1Jn	1 John	2Th	2 Thessalonians
2Jn	2 John	1Ti	1 Timothy
3Jn	3 John	2Ti	2 Timothy
Jhn	John	Tit	Titus
Lke	Luke		

S as a verse number refers to the so-called "Shorter Ending" to the Gospel of Mark

Differences in Versification between the NRSV and the UBS *Greek New Testament*

Bold text in the NRSV is in . . . . Greek verse

Mat 2:19 . . . an angel of the Lord suddenly appeared ... and **said,** 2:20
Mat 15:5 . . . **then that person need not honor the father** 15:6
Mat 20:4 . . . **So they went.** 20:5
Mat 22:23 . . and they asked him a question, **saying,** 22:24
Mat 25:16 . . The one who had received the five talents went off **at once** 25:15
Mrk 1:24 . . . **and he cried out,** 1:23
Mrk 3:19 . . . **And they went into a house.** 3:20
Lke 20:28 . . **and asked him a question,** 20:27
Jhn 4:36. . . . The reaper is **already** receiving wages. 4:35
Jhn 7:38. . . . and **let the one** who believes in me **drink.** 7:37
Jhn 19:25. . . **And that is what the soldiers did.** 19:24
Act 1:21 . . . one of these **must** become a witness with us to his resurrection." 1:22
Act 2:10 . . . visitors from Rome, **both Jews and proselytes,** 2:11
Act 10:36 . . **You know** the message he sent to the people of Israel, ... 10:37
Act 13:39 . . **from all those sins from which you could not be freed by the law of Moses** 13:38
Act 19:41 . . **When he had said this, he dismissed the assembly.** 19:40
Rom 1:9 . . . I remember you **always in my prayers,** 1:10
Rom 3:26 . . because **in his divine forbearance** he had passed over the sins 3:27
1Co 5:4 . . . . in the name of the Lord Jesus **on the man who has done such a thing.** 5:3
1Co 16:16 . . **I urge you** to put yourselves at the service of such people, ... 16:15
Gal 1:17 . . . , but I went away **at once** into Arabia, ... 1:16
1Ti 3:14. . . . I am writing these instructions to you **so that,** 3:15
1Pe 1:2 . . . . who have been **chosen** and destined by God the Father 1:1
1Pe 2:4 . . . . chosen and precious in God's sight, **and** 2:5
Rev 8:9 . . . . **A third of the sea became blood,** 8:8

ANALYTICAL CONCORDANCE

TO THE

NEW TESTAMENT

OF THE

NEW REVISED STANDARD VERSION

A

a Not Indexed

Aaron
1. Ἀαρών, *Aarōn, 2*

Lke	1: 5	His wife was a descendant of Aaron	1
Act	7:40	saying to Aaron, 'Make gods for us who will lead	1
Heb	5: 4	only when called by God, just as Aaron was.	1
	7:11	rather than one according to the order of Aaron?	1
	9: 4	Aaron's rod that budded	1

Abaddon
1. Ἀβαδδών, *Abaddōn, 3*

Rev	9:11	his name in Hebrew is Abaddon	1

abandon
1. ἀποβάλλω, *apoballō, 610*
2. ἀφίημι, *aphiēmi, 918*
3. ἐγκαταλείπω, *enkataleipō, 1593*
4. ἔκθετος, *ekthetos, 1704*
5. ἐκτίθημι, *ektithēmi, 1758*
6. ἐκχέω, *ekcheō, 1772*
7. παραδίδωμι, *paradidōmi, 4140*
8. περιαιρέω, *periaireō, 4311*

Mrk	7: 8	You abandon the commandment of God	2
Act	2:27	you will not abandon my soul to Hades	3
	2:31	'He was not abandoned to Hades	3
	7:19	forced our ancestors to abandon their infants	4
	7:21	when he was abandoned	5
	27:20	hope of our being saved was at last abandoned.	8
Eph	4:19	have abandoned themselves to licentiousness	7
Heb	10:35	Do not, therefore, abandon that confidence of yours;	1
Jde	1:11	abandon themselves to Balaam's error for the sake of gain	6
Rev	2: 4	you have abandoned the love you had at first.	2

Abba
1. ἀββά, *abba, 5*

Mrk	14:36	"Abba, Father, for you all things are possible;	1
Rom	8:15	a spirit of adoption. When we cry, "Abba! Father!"	1
Gal	4: 6	Spirit…into our hearts, crying, "Abba! Father!"	1

Abel
1. Ἀβελ, *Habel, 6*

Mat	23:35	from the blood of righteous Abel	1
Lke	11:51	from the blood of Abel to the blood of Zechariah	1
Heb	11: 4	Abel offered to God a more acceptable sacrifice	1
	12:24	that speaks a better word than the blood of Abel.	1

abhor
1. βδελύσσομαι, *bdelyssomai, 1009*

Rom	2:22	You that abhor idols, do you rob temples?	1

Abiathar
1. Ἀβιαθάρ, *Abiathar, 8*

Mrk	2:26	when Abiathar was high priest	1

abide
1. Contextual: Not in Greek
2. μένω, *menō, 3531*

Jhn	5:38	you do not have his word abiding in you	2
	6:56	who eat my flesh and drink my blood abide in me	2
	14:17	You know him, because he abides with you	2
	15: 4	Abide in me as I abide in you.	2
	15: 4	Abide in me as I abide in you.	1
	15: 4	unless it abides in the vine	2
	15: 4	neither can you unless you abide in me.	2
	15: 5	Those who abide in me and I in them	2
	15: 6	Whoever does not abide in me	2
	15: 7	If you abide in me, and my words abide in you	2
	15: 7	If you abide in me, and my words abide in you	2
	15: 9	so I have loved you; abide in my love.	2
	15:10	you will abide in my love	2
	15:10	just as I…abide in his love.	2
1Co	13:13	And now faith, hope, and love abide, these three;	2
1Jn	2: 6	whoever says, "I abide in him," ought to walk	2
	2:14	and the word of God abides in you	2
	2:24	Let what you heard from the beginning abide	2
	2:24	what you heard from the beginning abides in you	2
	2:24	then you will abide in the Son and in the Father.	2
	2:27	the anointing…abides in you	2
	2:27	just as it has taught you, abide in him.	2
	2:28	now, little children, abide in him	2
	3: 6	No one who abides in him sins;	2
	3: 9	do not sin, because God's seed abides in them;	2
	3:14	Whoever does not love abides in death.	2
	3:15	murderers do not have eternal life abiding in them.	2
	3:17	How does God's love abide in anyone	2
	3:24	All who obey his commandments abide in him	2
	3:24	and he abides in them.	1
	3:24	And by this we know that he abides in us	2
	4:13	By this we know that we abide in him and he in us	2
	4:15	God abides in those who confess that Jesus	2
	4:15	God abides in those…and they abide in God.	1
	4:16	God is love, and those who abide in love abide in God	2
	4:16	God is love, and those who abide in love abide in God	2
	4:16	and God abides in them.	2
2Jn	1: 2	because of the truth that abides in us	2

2Jn	1: 9	does not abide in the teaching of Christ,	2
	1: 9	whoever abides in the teaching has both the Father	2

Abijah

1. Ἀβιά, *Abia, 7*

Mat	1: 7	and Rehoboam the father of Abijah	1
	1: 7	and Abijah the father of Asaph	1
Lke	1: 5	who belonged to the priestly order of Abijah.	1

Abilene

1. Ἀβιληνή, *Abilēnē, 9*

Lke	3: 1	Lysanias ruler of Abilene	1

ability

1. ἀποφθέγγομαι, *apophthengomai, 710*
2. δύναμις, *dynamis, 1539*
3. εὐπορέω, *euporeō, 2344*

Mat	25:15	to each according to his ability.	2
Act	2: 4	as the Spirit gave them ability.	1
	11:29	according to their ability, each	3

Abiud

1. Ἀβιούδ, *Abioud, 10*

Mat	1:13	Zerubbabel the father of Abiud	1
	1:13	and Abiud the father of Eliakim	1

ablaze   *See* set ablaze

able

1. Contextual: Not in Greek
2. δύναμαι, *dynamai, 1538*
3. δυνατέω, *dynateō, 1542*
4. δυνατός, *dynatos, 1543*
5. ἔχω, *echō, 2400*
6. ἱκανός, *hikanos, 2653*
7. ἰσχύω, *ischyō, 2710*

Mat	3: 9	I tell you, God is able from these stones to raise	2
	9:28	"Do you believe that I am able to do this?"	2
	20:22	Are you able to drink the cup that I am	2
	20:22	They said to him, "We are able."	2
	22:46	No one was able to give him an answer	2
	26:61	'I am able to destroy the temple of God	2
Mrk	3:25	that house will not be able to stand.	2
	4:33	as they were able to hear it;	2
	9:22	if you are able to do anything, have pity on us	2
	9:23	Jesus said to him, "If you are able!	2
	9:27	lifted him up, and he was able to stand.	1
	9:39	will be able soon afterward to speak evil of me.	2
	10:38	Are you able to drink the cup that I drink	2
	10:39	They replied, "We are able."	2
Lke	3: 8	God is able from these stones to raise up children	2
	12:26	you are not able to do so small a thing as that	2
	13:24	many...will try to enter and will not be able.	7
	14:29	laid a foundation, is not able to finish	7
	14:30	began to build and was not able to finish.'	7
	14:31	whether he is able with ten thousand to oppose	4
	20:26	they were not able in the presence of the people	7
	21:15	will be able to withstand or contradict.	2
Jhn	9: 7	Then he went and washed and came back able to see.	1
	18:28	and to be able to eat the Passover.	1
	21: 6	now they were not able to haul it in	7
Act	5:39	you will not be able to overthrow them	2
	15:10	neither our ancestors nor we have been able to bear?	7
	20:32	a message that is able to build you up	2
	24: 8	be able to learn from him concerning everything	2
	27:16	scarcely able to get the ship's boat under control.	7
Rom	4:21	that God was able to do what he had promised.	4
	8:39	will be able to separate us from the love of God	2
	14: 4	for the Lord is able to make them stand.	3
	15:14	and able to instruct one another.	2
	16:25	Now to God who is able to strengthen you	2
1Co	10:13	so that you may be able to endure it.	2
2Co	1: 4	so that we may be able to console	2
	5:12	so that you may be able to answer	5
	9: 8	God is able to provide you with every blessing	3
Eph	3:20	is able to accomplish abundantly far more	2
	6:11	able to stand against the wiles of the devil.	2
	6:13	that you may be able to withstand on that evil day	2
	6:16	able to quench all the flaming arrows of the evil one.	2

2Ti	1:12	I am sure that he is able to guard until that day	4
	2: 2	who will be able to teach others as well.	6
	3:15	that are able to instruct you for salvation	2
Tit	1: 9	be able both to preach with sound doctrine	4
Heb	2:18	he is able to help those who are being tested.	2
	4:12	able to judge the thoughts...of the heart.	1
	5: 2	He is able to deal gently with the ignorant	2
	5: 7	to the one who was able to save him from death	2
	7:25	Consequently he is able for all time to save	2
	11:19	God is able even to raise someone from the dead	4
Jas	3: 2	perfect, able to keep the whole body in check	4
	4:12	who is able to save and to destroy.	2
2Pe	1:15	you may be able at any time to recall these things.	5
Jde	1:24	Now to him who is able to keep you from falling	2
Rev	3: 8	an open door, which no one is able to shut.	2
	5: 3	no one...was able to open the scroll or to look	2
	6:17	wrath has come, and who is able to stand?"	2

aboard   *See* go aboard

abolish

1. ἀναιρέω, *anaireō, 359*
2. καταλύω, *katalyō, 2907*
3. καταργέω, *katargeō, 2934*

Mat	5:17	not think that I have come to abolish the law	2
	5:17	I have come not to abolish but to fulfill.	2
Eph	2:15	He has abolished the law with its commandments	3
2Ti	1:10	who abolished death and brought life	3
Heb	10: 9	He abolishes the first	1

abomination

1. βδέλυγμα, *bdelygma, 1007*

Lke	16:15	an abomination in the sight of God.	1
Rev	17: 4	holding...a golden cup full of abominations	1
	17: 5	mother of whores and of earth's abominations."	1
	21:27	nor anyone who practices abomination	1

abound

1. Contextual: Not in Greek
2. περισσεύω, *perisseuō, 4355*
3. πλεονάζω, *pleonazō, 4429*

Rom	3: 7	if...God's truthfulness abounds to his glory	2
	5:15	the grace of God...abounded for the many.	2
	6: 1	continue in sin in order that grace may abound?	3
	15:13	may abound in hope by the power of the Holy Spirit.	2
2Co	3: 9	does the ministry of justification abound in glory	2
Col	2: 7	abounding in thanksgiving.	2
1Th	3:12	may the Lord make you increase and abound in love	2
	3:12	just as we abound in love for you.	1

abound all the more

1. ὑπερπερισσεύω, *hyperperisseuō, 5668*

Rom	5:20	where sin increased, grace abounded all the more	1

about[1]   *See also* blow about, bring about, bring about death, dispute about words, gad about, go about, move about, roll about, rush about, shine about, something to boast about, talk about, turn about, walk about, what about

1. διά, *dia, 1328*
2. εἰς, *eis, 1650*
3. ἐκ, *ek, 1666*
4. ἐν, *en, 1877*
5. ἐπί, *epi, 2093*
6. κατά, *kata, 2848*
7. περί, *peri, 4309*
8. πρός, *pros, 4639*
9. ὑπέρ, *hyper, 5642*

Mat	6:28	And why do you worry about clothing? Consider	7
	6:34	"So do not worry about tomorrow	2
	11: 7	began to speak to the crowds about John:	7
	11:10	This is the one about whom it is written	7
	15: 7	You hypocrites! Isaiah prophesied rightly about you	7
	16:11	that I was not speaking about bread?	7
	17:13	he was speaking to them about John the Baptist.	7
	18:19	agree on earth about anything you ask	7
	19:17	"Why do you ask me about what is good?"	7
	21:45	they realized that he was speaking about them.	7
	24:36	about that day and hour no one knows	7
	27:19	suffered...because of a dream about him."	1

Mrk	1:30 they told him about her at once.	7
	5:27 She had heard about Jesus	7
	6:52 for they did not understand about the loaves	5
	7: 6 "Isaiah prophesied rightly about you hypocrites	7
	7:25 immediately heard about him, and she came	7
	8:30 ordered them not to tell anyone about him.	7
	9:12 How then is it written about the Son of Man	5
	9:13 as it is written about him."	5
	10:10 the disciples asked him again about this matter.	7
	12:26 in the story about the bush	5
	13:32 about that day or hour no one knows	7
Lke	2:17 what had been told them about this child;	7
	2:33 amazed at what was being said about him.	7
	2:38 speak about the child to all	7
	4:14 and a report about him spread	7
	4:37 report about him began to reach every place	7
	4:38 they asked him about her.	7
	5:15 the word about Jesus spread abroad;	7
	7: 3 When he heard about Jesus	7
	7:17 This word about him spread	7
	7:24 Jesus began to speak to the crowds about John:	7
	7:27 This is the one about whom it is written	7
	9: 9 who is this about whom I hear such things?"	7
	9:11 and spoke to them about the kingdom of God	7
	9:45 they were afraid to ask him about this saying.	7
	11:53 and to cross-examine him about many things	7
	12:26 why do you worry about the rest?	7
	13: 1 who told him about the Galileans	7
	16: 2 'What is this that I hear about you?	7
	18: 1 about their need to pray always	8
	20:37 Moses himself showed, in the story about the bush	5
	21: 5 When some were speaking about the temple	7
	22:37 what is written about me is being fulfilled."	7
	23: 8 because he had heard about him	7
	24: 4 While they were perplexed about this	7
	24:14 talking with each other about all these things	7
	24:19 replied, "The things about Jesus of Nazareth	7
	24:27 he interpreted to them the things about himself	7
	24:44 everything written about me in the law of Moses	7
Jhn	1:22 What do you say about yourself?"	7
	2:25 and needed no one to testify about anyone;	7
	3:25 Now a discussion about purification arose	7
	3:31 to the earth and speaks about earthly things.	3
	5:31 "If I testify about myself	7
	5:46 you would believe me, for he wrote about me.	7
	6:41 Then the Jews began to complain about him	7
	6:61 his disciples were complaining about it	7
	7:12 complaining about him among the crowds.	7
	7:13 Yet no one would speak openly about him	7
	7:32 heard the crowd muttering such things about him	7
	7:39 Now he said this about the Spirit	7
	8:26 I have much to say about you and much to condemn;	7
	9:17 "What do you say about him?	7
	10:41 everything that John said about this man was true."	7
	11:13 Jesus, however, had been speaking about his death	7
	11:19 to console them about their brother.	7
	12: 6 (He said this not because he cared about the poor	7
	12:41 because he saw his glory and spoke about him.	7
	16: 8 about sin and righteousness and judgment:	7
	16: 9 about sin, because they do not believe in me;	7
	16:10 about righteousness, because I am going	7
	16:11 about judgment, because the ruler of this world	7
	18:19 about his disciples and about his teaching.	7
	18:19 about his disciples and about his teaching.	7
	18:34 did others tell you about me?"	7
Act	1: 1 I wrote about all that Jesus did and taught	7
	1: 3 speaking about the kingdom of God.	7
	5:24 they were perplexed about them	7
	8:12 proclaiming the good news about the kingdom of God	7
	8:34 "About whom...does the prophet say this	7
	8:34 about himself or about someone else?"	7
	8:34 does the prophet say this...about someone else?"	7
	9:13 I have heard from many about this man	7
	10:19 While Peter was still thinking about the vision	7
	13:29 everything that was written about him	7
	17:32 others said, "We will hear you again about this."	7
	18:15 a matter of questions about words and names	7
	19: 8 argued persuasively about the kingdom of God.	7
	21:21 They have been told about you	7
	21:24 nothing in what they have been told about you	7
	22:18 will not accept your testimony about me.'	7

	24:21 about the resurrection of the dead	7
	24:22 was rather well informed about the Way	7
	25: 5 if there is anything wrong about the man	4
	25:15 the chief priests...informed me about him	7
	25:19 disagreement...about their own religion	7
	25:19 disagreement...about a certain Jesus, who had died	7
	25:24 about whom the whole Jewish community petitioned	7
	25:26 nothing definite to write to our sovereign about him.	7
	26:26 the king knows about these things	7
	28:21 "We have received no letters from Judea about you	7
	28:21 reported or spoken anything evil about you.	7
	28:23 trying to convince them about Jesus	7
	28:31 teaching about the Lord Jesus Christ	7
Rom	8:31 What then are we to say about these things?	8
	15:14 feel confident about you, my brothers and sisters	7
1Co	3:21 So let no one boast about human leaders.	4
2Co	2: 3 I am confident about all of you	5
	5:12 giving you an opportunity to boast about us	9
	7: 4 I often boast about you; I have great pride	8
	7: 7 consolation with which he was consoled about you	5
	7:14 For if I have been somewhat boastful about you	9
	8:20 no one should blame us about this generous gift	4
	8:24 and of our reason for boasting about you.	9
	9: 1 to write you about the ministry to the saints	7
	9: 2 the subject of my boasting about you	9
	9: 3 boasting about you may not prove to have been empty	9
	12: 8 Three times I appealed to the Lord about this	9
Gal	4:20 I am perplexed about you.	4
	5:10 I am confident about you in the Lord	2
	6:13 so that they may boast about your flesh.	4
Php	1: 7 right for me to think this way about all of you	9
	1:27 see you or am absent and hear about you,	7
Col	4: 7 Tychicus will tell you all the news about me;	6
1Th	1: 9 report about us what kind of welcome we had	7
	3: 7 encouraged about you through your faith.	5
	4:13 uninformed...about those who have died	7
1Ti	1: 7 the things about which they make assertions.	7
	1:18 the prophecies made earlier about you	5
Heb	2: 5 the coming world, about which we are speaking	7
	4: 4 For in one place it speaks about the seventh day	7
	4: 8 God would not speak later about another day.	7
	5:11 About this we have much to say	7
	7:14 Moses said nothing about priests.	7
	11: 7 warned by God about events as yet unseen	7
	11:22 gave instructions about his burial.	7
1Pe	1:11 inquiring about the person or time	2
1Jn	2:27 as his anointing teaches you about all things	7
	5:16 I do not say that you should pray about that.	7
Jde	1: 3 to write to you about the salvation we share	7
	1: 9 Michael...disputed about the body of Moses	7
Rev	10:11 prophesy again about many peoples and nations	5

about²

1. Contextual: Not in Greek

2. μέλλω, mellō, 3516

Mat	2:13 Herod is about to search for the child, to destroy	2
	17:12 the Son of Man is about to suffer at their hands."	2
	20:22 to drink the cup that I am about to drink?"	2
Mrk	13: 4 these things are about to be accomplished?"	2
Lke	9:31 which he was about to accomplish at Jerusalem.	2
	21: 7 the sign that this is about to take place?"	2
Jhn	6:15 they were about to come and take him by force	2
	11:51 Jesus was about to die for the nation	2
	12: 4 (the one who was about to betray him), said	2
Act	3: 3 saw Peter and John about to go into the temple	2
	16:27 he drew his sword and was about to kill himself	2
	18:14 Just as Paul was about to speak,	2
	20: 3 He was about to set sail for Syria	2
	21:37 Paul was about to be brought into the barracks	2
	22:26 "What are you about to do?	2
	22:29 those who were about to examine him drew back	2
	23:27 and was about to be killed by them	2
	27: 2 that was about to set sail for the ports	2
	28:10 when we were about to sail	1
Rom	8:18 the glory about to be revealed to us.	2
Heb	8: 5 Moses, when he was about to erect the tent	2
Rev	2:10 Do not fear what you are about to suffer.	2
	2:10 devil is about to throw some of you into prison	2
	3:16 I am about to spit you out of my mouth.	2
	8:13 trumpets that the...angels are about to blow!"	2
	10: 4 I was about to write, but I heard a voice	2

Rev	12: 4	the woman who was about to bear a child	2
	17: 8	beast...is about to ascend from the bottomless pit	2

about³

1. Contextual: Not in Greek
2. ἤδη, *ēdē*, 2453
3. κατά, *kata*, 2848
4. περί, *peri*, 4309
5. πού, *pou*, 4543
6. ὡς, *hōs*, 6055
7. ὡσεί, *hōsei*, 6059

Mat	14:21	who ate were about five thousand men, besides	7
	20: 3	went out about nine o'clock, he saw others	4
	20: 5	When he went out again about noon	4
	20: 5	about noon and about three o'clock,	1
	20: 6	about five o'clock he went out	4
	20: 9	When those hired about five o'clock came	4
	27:46	about three o'clock Jesus cried	4
Mrk	5:13	herd, numbering about two thousand, rushed down	6
	8: 9	Now there were about four thousand people	6
Lke	1:56	Mary remained with her about three months	6
	3:23	Jesus was about thirty years old when he began	7
	8:42	an only daughter, about twelve years old,	6
	9:14	For there were about five thousand men.	7
	9:14	sit down in groups of about fifty each."	7
	9:28	Now about eight days after these sayings	7
	22:41	he withdrew from them about a stone's throw	7
	22:59	about an hour later	7
	23:44	It was now about noon,	7
	24:13	Emmaus, about seven miles from Jerusalem	1
Jhn	1:39	It was about four o'clock in the afternoon.	6
	4: 6	It was about noon.	6
	6:10	so they sat down, about five thousand in all	6
	6:19	When they had rowed about three or four miles	6
	7:14	About the middle of the festival	2
	19:14	it was about noon. He said to the Jews,	6
	19:39	myrrh and aloes, weighing about a hundred pounds	6
	21: 8	not far...only about a hundred yards off	6
Act	1:15	the crowd numbered about one hundred twenty persons)	7
	2:41	that day about three thousand persons were added.	7
	4: 4	they numbered about five thousand.	6
	5: 7	After an interval of about three hours	6
	5:36	a number of men, about four hundred, joined him;	6
	10: 3	One afternoon at about three o'clock	7
	10: 9	About noon the next day	4
	12: 1	About that time King Herod laid violent hands	3
	13:18	For about forty years he put up with them	6
	13:20	for about four hundred fifty years.	6
	16:25	About midnight Paul and Silas were praying	3
	19: 7	altogether there were about twelve of them.	7
	19:23	About that time no little disturbance broke out	3
	19:34	for about two hours all of them shouted	6
	22: 6	about noon a great light from heaven	4
	27:27	about midnight the sailors suspected	3
Rom	4:19	(for he was about a hundred years old)	5
	9: 9	the promise said, "About this time I will return	3
Rev	8: 1	silence in heaven for about half an hour.	6
	14:20	for a distance of about two hundred miles.	1
	16:21	hailstones, each weighing about a hundred pounds	6

about⁴

1. περί, *peri*, 4309

Act	22: 6	a great light from heaven suddenly shone about me.	1

above *See also* above *all*, above *reproach*, exalt *above*, from *above*, write *above*

1. Contextual: Not in Greek
2. ἄνω, *anō*, 539
3. ἀνώτερος, *anōteros*, 542
4. ἐπάνω, *epanō*, 2062
5. ἐπί, *epi*, 2093
6. ὅπου, *hopou*, 3963
7. πρό, *pro*, 4574
8. ὑπέρ, *hyper*, 5642
9. ὑπεράνω, *hyperanō*, 5645

Mat	10:24	"A disciple is not above the teacher	8
	10:24	nor a slave above the master;	8
Mrk	2: 4	they removed the roof above him;	6
Lke	6:40	A disciple is not above the teacher	8

Jhn	3:31	one who comes from above is above all;	4
	3:31	one who comes from heaven is above all.	4
	8:23	"You are from below, I am from above;	2
Act	2:19	I will show portents in the heaven above	2
Gal	4:26	Jerusalem above; she is free, and she is our mother.	2
Eph	1:21	and above every name that is named	1
	4: 6	who is above all and through all and in all.	5
Php	2: 9	the name that is above every name	8
Col	3: 1	seek the things that are above, where Christ is	2
	3: 2	Set your minds on things that are above	2
	3:14	Above all, clothe yourselves with love	5
2Th	2: 4	exalts himself above every so-called god	5
Heb	9: 5	above it were the cherubim of glory	9
	10: 8	When he said above	3
Jas	5:12	Above all, my beloved, do not swear	7
1Pe	4: 8	Above all, maintain constant love	7

far above

1. ὑπεράνω, *hyperanō*, 5645

Eph	1:21	far above all rule and authority and power	1
	4:10	who ascended far above all the heavens	1

Abraham

1. Contextual: Not in Greek
2. Ἀβραάμ, *Abraam*, 11

Mat	1: 1	Jesus the Messiah, the son of David, the son of Abraham.	2
	1: 2	Abraham was the father of Isaac	2
	1:17	So all the generations from Abraham to David	2
	3: 9	say to yourselves, 'We have Abraham as our ancestor';	2
	3: 9	from these stones to raise up children to Abraham.	2
	8:11	eat with Abraham and Isaac and Jacob	2
	22:32	'I am the God of Abraham, the God of Isaac	2
Mrk	12:26	'I am the God of Abraham, the God of Isaac	2
Lke	1:55	to Abraham and to his descendants forever."	2
	1:73	the oath that he swore to our ancestor Abraham	2
	3: 8	'We have Abraham as our ancestor';	2
	3: 8	these stones to raise up children to Abraham.	2
	3:34	son of Isaac, son of Abraham, son of Terah	2
	13:16	a daughter of Abraham whom Satan bound	2
	13:28	when you see Abraham and Isaac and Jacob	2
	16:22	carried away by the angels to be with Abraham.	2
	16:23	he looked up and saw Abraham far away	2
	16:24	He called out, 'Father Abraham, have mercy	2
	16:25	Abraham said, 'Child, remember	2
	16:29	Abraham replied, 'They have Moses and the prophets;	2
	16:30	He said, 'No, father Abraham;	2
	19: 9	because he too is a son of Abraham.	2
	20:37	where he speaks of the Lord as the God of Abraham	2
Jhn	8:33	They answered him, "We are descendants of Abraham	2
	8:37	I know that you are descendants of Abraham;	2
	8:39	They answered him, "Abraham is our father."	2
	8:39	said to them, "If you were Abraham's children	2
	8:39	you would be doing what Abraham did	2
	8:40	This is not what Abraham did.	2
	8:52	Abraham died, and so did the prophets;	2
	8:53	Are you greater than our father Abraham, who died?	2
	8:56	Abraham rejoiced that he would see my day;	2
	8:57	and have you seen Abraham?"	2
	8:58	I tell you, before Abraham was, I am."	2
Act	3:13	The God of Abraham, the God of Isaac, and the God	2
	3:25	saying to Abraham, 'And in your descendants	2
	7: 2	The God of glory appeared to our ancestor Abraham	2
	7: 8	so Abraham became the father of Isaac	1
	7:16	tomb that Abraham had bought for a sum of silver	2
	7:17	promise that God had made to Abraham	2
	7:32	the god of Abraham, Isaac, and Jacob.'	2
	13:26	brothers, you descendants of Abraham's family	2
Rom	4: 1	What then are we to say was gained by Abraham	2
	4: 2	For if Abraham was justified by works	2
	4: 3	"Abraham believed God, and it was reckoned to him	2
	4: 9	"Faith was reckoned to Abraham as righteousness."	2
	4:12	the faith that our ancestor Abraham had	2
	4:13	promise...did not come to Abraham...through the law	2
	4:16	but also to those who share the faith of Abraham	2
	9: 7	and not all of Abraham's children	2
	11: 1	I myself am an Israelite, a descendant of Abraham	2
2Co	11:22	Are they descendants of Abraham? So am I.	2
Gal	3: 6	Just as Abraham "believed God	2
	3: 7	those who believe are the descendants of Abraham.	2
	3: 8	declared the gospel beforehand to Abraham	2

3: 9	blessed with Abraham who believed.	2
3:14	that in Christ Jesus the blessing of Abraham	2
3:16	Now the promises were made to Abraham	2
3:18	God granted it to Abraham through the promise.	2
3:29	then you are Abraham's offspring	2
4:22	For it is written that Abraham had two sons	2

Heb 2:16 come to help…the descendants of Abraham. 2
6:13 When God made a promise to Abraham 2
6:15 thus Abraham…obtained the promise. 1
7: 1 met Abraham as he was returning from defeating 2
7: 2 to him Abraham apportioned "one-tenth of everything." 2
7: 4 Abraham…gave him a tenth of the spoils. 2
7: 5 though these also are descended from Abraham. 2
7: 6 collected tithes from Abraham 2
7: 9 Levi himself…paid tithes through Abraham 2
11: 8 By faith Abraham obeyed 2
11:17 By faith Abraham…offered up Isaac. 2
Jas 2:21 Was not our ancestor Abraham justified by works 2
2:23 "Abraham believed God, and it was reckoned to him 2
1Pe 3: 6 Thus Sarah obeyed Abraham and called him lord. 2

abroad See go abroad, scatter abroad, spread abroad

abrogation
1. ἀθέτησις, *athetēsis, 120*
Heb 7:18 There is…the abrogation of an earlier commandment 1

absence
1. ἀπουσία, *apousia, 707*
2. ὑστέρημα, *hysterēma, 5729*
1Co 16:17 because they have made up for your absence; 2
Php 2:12 in my presence, but much more now in my absence 1

absent
1. ἄπειμι[1], *apeimi[1], 582*
1Co 5: 3 For though absent in body, I am present in spirit; 1
2Co 10:11 what we say by letter when absent 1
13: 2 I warn them now while absent 1
Php 1:27 so that, whether I come and see you or am absent 1
Col 2: 5 For though I am absent in body 1

absolute
1. πᾶς, *pas, 4246*
1Ti 5: 2 younger women as sisters—with absolute purity. 1

abstain
1. ἀπέχω, *apechō, 600*
2. μή + ἐσθίω, *mē + esthiō, 3590 + 2266*
3. οὐ + ἐσθίω, *ou + esthiō, 4024 + 2266*
4. φυλάσσω, *phylassō, 5875*
Act 15:20 abstain only from things polluted by idols 1
15:29 you abstain from what has been sacrificed to idols 1
21:25 should abstain from what has been sacrificed to idols 4
Rom 14: 3 Those who eat must not despise those who abstain 2
14: 3 those who abstain must not pass judgment 2
14: 6 those who abstain, abstain in honor of the Lord 2
14: 6 those who abstain, abstain in honor of the Lord 3
1Th 4: 3 that you abstain from fornication; 1
5:22 abstain from every form of evil. 1
1Pe 2:11 to abstain from the desires of the flesh 1

abstinence
1. ἀπέχω, *apechō, 600*
1Ti 4: 3 demand abstinence from foods, which God created 1

abundance See also have abundance, have an abundance, provide in abundance
1. περισσεία, *perisseia, 4353*
2. περίσσευμα, *perisseuma, 4354*
3. περισσεύω, *perisseuō, 4355*
4. πληθύνω, *plēthynō, 4437*
Mat 12:34 For out of the abundance of the heart 2
Mrk 12:44 have contributed out of their abundance; 3
Lke 6:45 out of the abundance of the heart 2
12:15 not consist in the abundance of possessions." 3
21: 4 have contributed out of their abundance 3
Rom 5:17 those who receive the abundance of grace 1
2Co 8:14 your present abundance and their need 2
8:14 so that their abundance may be for your need 2

1Pe	1: 2 May grace and peace be yours in abundance.	4
2Pe	1: 2 May grace and peace be yours in abundance	4
Jde	1: 2 May mercy, peace, and love be yours in abundance.	4

abundant
1. περισσεία, *perisseia, 4353*
2. περισσεύω, *perisseuō, 4355*
3. περισσοτέρως, *perissoterōs, 4359*
4. πολύς, *polys, 4498*
Jhn 3:23 near Salim because water was abundant there; 4
2Co 1: 5 just as the sufferings of Christ are abundant for us 2
1: 5 our consolation is abundant through Christ 2
2: 4 to let you know the abundant love that I have 3
8: 2 their abundant joy and their extreme poverty 1

abundantly See also grow abundantly, produce abundantly, share abundantly
1. περισσεύω, *perisseuō, 4355*
2. περισσός, *perissos, 4356*
3. ὑπερεκπερισσοῦ, *hyperekperissou, 5655*
Jhn 10:10 they may have life, and have it abundantly. 2
Eph 3:20 is able to accomplish abundantly far more 3
Php 1:26 share abundantly in your boasting in Christ Jesus 1

abuse See also return abuse
1. ἐπηρεάζω, *epēreazō, 2092*
2. λοιδορέω, *loidoreō, 3366*
3. λοιδορία, *loidoria, 3367*
4. ὀνειδισμός, *oneidismos, 3944*
Lke 6:28 pray for those who abuse you. 1
Heb 10:33 being publicly exposed to abuse and persecution 4
11:26 He considered abuse suffered for the Christ 4
13:13 and bear the abuse he endured. 4
1Pe 2:23 When he was abused, he did not return abuse; 2
3: 9 Do not repay…abuse for abuse; 3
3: 9 Do not repay…abuse for abuse; 3
3:16 those who abuse you for your good conduct in Christ 1

abusive See also abusive *language*
1. βλάσφημος, *blasphēmos, 1061*
2Ti 3: 2 lovers of money, boasters, arrogant, abusive 1

abusive language
1. αἰσχρολογία, *aischrologia, 155*
Col 3: 8 malice, slander, and abusive language from your mouth. 1

abyss
1. ἄβυσσος, *abyssos, 12*
Lke 8:31 not to order them to go back into the abyss. 1
Rom 10: 7 "or 'Who will descend into the abyss?' " 1

accent
1. λαλιά, *lalia, 3282*
Mat 26:73 for your accent betrays you." 1

accept
1. ἀκούω, *akouō, 201*
2. δεκτός, *dektos, 1283*
3. δέχομαι, *dechomai, 1312*
4. ἔχω, *echō, 2400*
5. λαμβάνω, *lambanō, 3284*
6. παραδέχομαι, *paradechomai, 4138*
7. παραλαμβάνω, *paralambanō, 4161*
8. προσδέχομαι, *prosdechomai, 4657*
9. χωρέω, *chōreō, 6003*
Mat 11:14 if you are willing to accept it, he is Elijah 3
19:11 "Not everyone can accept this teaching 9
19:12 Let anyone accept this who can." 9
Mrk 4:20 hear the word and accept it and bear fruit 6
Lke 4:24 no prophet is accepted in the prophet's hometown. 2
14:18 please accept my regrets.' 4
14:19 please accept my regrets.' 4
Jhn 1:11 and his own people did not accept him. 7
3:32 yet no one accepts his testimony. 5
3:33 Whoever has accepted his testimony has certified 5
5:34 Not that I accept such human testimony 5
5:41 I do not accept glory from human beings. 5
5:43 you do not accept me; 5

Jhn	5:43	you will accept him.	5
	5:44	you accept glory from one another	5
	6:60	"This teaching is difficult; who can accept it?"	1
	8:43	It is because you cannot accept my word.	1
Act	8:14	Samaria had accepted the word of God	3
	11: 1	the Gentiles had also accepted the word of God.	3
	22:18	because they will not accept your testimony	6
	24:15	a hope that they themselves also accept—	8
2Co	6: 1	urge you also not to accept the grace of God	3
	8:17	For he not only accepted our appeal	3
	11: 4	a different gospel from the one you accepted	3
	11: 8	I robbed other churches by accepting support	5
	11:16	if you do, then accept me as a fool	3
1Th	2:13	you accepted it not as a human word	3
1Ti	5:19	Never accept any accusation against an elder	6
Heb	10:34	you cheerfully accepted the plundering	8
	11:35	Others were tortured, refusing to accept release	8
	12: 6	chastises every child whom he accepts."	6
3Jn	1: 7	accepting no support from non-believers.	5

accept a complaint

1. ἀνέχομαι, *anechomai, 462*

Act	18:14	justified in accepting the complaint of you Jews;	1

accept authority

1. ὑποτάσσω, *hypotassō, 5718*

1Pe	2:13	For the Lord's sake accept the authority	1
	2:18	Slaves, accept the authority of your masters	1
	3: 1	Wives…accept the authority of your husbands	1
	3: 5	women…accepting the authority of their husbands.	1
	5: 5	who are younger must accept the authority of the elders.	1

acceptable   *See also* acceptable *duty*

1. ἀπόδεκτος, *apodektos, 621*
2. δεκτός, *dektos, 1283*
3. εὐάρεστος, *euarestos, 2298*
4. εὐαρέστως, *euarestōs, 2299*
5. εὐπρόσδεκτος, *euprosdektos, 2347*

Act	10:35	anyone who fears him…is acceptable to him.	2
Rom	12: 1	as a living sacrifice, holy and acceptable to God	3
	12: 2	what is good and acceptable and perfect.	3
	14:18	one who thus serves Christ is acceptable to God	3
	15:16	the offering of the Gentiles may be acceptable	5
	15:31	my ministry…be acceptable to the saints	5
2Co	6: 2	"At an acceptable time I have listened to you	5
	6: 2	See, now is the acceptable time;	5
	8:12	if the eagerness is there, the gift is acceptable	5
Php	4:18	a sacrifice acceptable and pleasing to God.	2
1Ti	2: 3	is acceptable in the sight of God our Savior	1
Heb	12:28	by which we offer to God an acceptable worship	4
1Pe	2: 5	offer spiritual sacrifices acceptable to God	5

more acceptable

1. πολύς, *polys, 4498*

Heb	11: 4	a more acceptable sacrifice than Cain's.	1

acceptance

1. ἀποδοχή, *apodochē, 628*
2. πρόσλημψις, *proslēmpsis, 4691*

Rom	11:15	what will their acceptance be but life	2
1Ti	1:15	The saying is sure and worthy of full acceptance	1
	4: 9	is sure and worthy of full acceptance.	1

access

1. προσαγωγή, *prosagōgē, 4643*

Rom	5: 2	we have obtained access to this grace	1
Eph	2:18	for through him both of us have access in one Spirit	1
	3:12	access to God in boldness and confidence through faith	1

accompany

1. εἰμί + σύν, *eimi + syn, 1639 + 5250*
2. ἐξέρχομαι + σύν, *exerchomai + syn, 2002 + 5250*
3. ἐπακολουθέω, *epakoloutheō, 2051*
4. ἔρχομαι + σύν, *erchomai + syn, 2262 + 5250*
5. παρακολουθέω, *parakoloutheo, 4158*
6. περιάγω, *periagō, 4310*
7. πορεύομαι + σύν, *poreuomai + syn, 4513 + 5250*
8. σύν, *syn, 5250*
9. συνέπομαι, *synepomai, 5299*

10. συνέρχομαι, *synerchomai, 5302*

Mrk	16:17	⟦these signs will accompany those who believe:⟧	5
	16:20	⟦by the signs that accompanied it.⟧	3
Act	1:21	one of the men who have accompanied us	10
	10:23	some of the believers from Joppa accompanied him.	10
	11:12	These six brothers also accompanied me	4
	15:38	and had not accompanied them in the work.	10
	16: 3	Paul wanted Timothy to accompany him;	2
	18:18	accompanied by Priscilla and Aquila.	8
	20: 4	He was accompanied by Sopater son of Pyrrhus	9
	27: 2	we put to sea, accompanied by Aristarchus	1
1Co	9: 5	have the right to be accompanied by a believing wife	6
	16: 4	they will accompany me.	7

accomplish

1. γίνομαι, *ginomai, 1181*
2. ἐνεργέω, *energeō, 1919*
3. κατεργάζομαι, *katergazomai, 2981*
4. πληρόω, *plēroō, 4444*
5. ποιέω, *poieō, 4472*
6. συντελέω, *synteleō, 5334*
7. τελέω, *teleō, 5464*

Mat	5:18	will pass from the law until all is accomplished	1
Mrk	13: 4	these things are about to be accomplished?"	6
Lke	9:31	which he was about to accomplish at Jerusalem.	4
	18:31	everything…will be accomplished.	7
Act	19:21	Now after these things had been accomplished	4
Rom	15:18	except what Christ has accomplished through me	3
Eph	1:11	the purpose of him who accomplishes all things	2
	3:20	is able to accomplish abundantly far more	5

accord

1. ἀπό, *apo, 608*
2. αὐθαίρετος, *authairetos, 882*
3. αὐτόματος, *automatos, 897*

Jhn	10:18	I lay it down of my own accord.	1
Act	12:10	It opened for them of its own accord	3
2Co	8:17	he is going to you of his own accord.	2

full accord

1. σύμψυχος, *sympsychos, 5249*

Php	2: 2	having the same love, being in full accord	1

one accord

1. ὁμοθυμαδόν, *homothymadon, 3924*

Act	8: 6	The crowds with one accord listened eagerly	1

in accordance with

1. ἐν, *en, 1877*
2. ἐπί, *epi, 2093*
3. κατά, *kata, 2848*

Mat	22:16	teach the way of God in accordance with truth	1
Mrk	12:14	teach the way of God in accordance with truth.	2
Lke	20:21	teach the way of God in accordance with truth.	2
Rom	2: 2	God's judgment…is in accordance with truth	3
	15: 5	in harmony…in accordance with Christ Jesus	3
1Co	15: 3	Christ died…in accordance with the scriptures	3
	15: 4	he was raised…in accordance with the scriptures	3
2Co	4:13	spirit of faith that is in accordance with scripture	3
Eph	3:11	This was in accordance with the eternal purpose	3
1Ti	1:18	in accordance with the prophecies	3
	6: 3	the teaching that is in accordance with godliness	3
Tit	1: 1	the truth that is in accordance with godliness	3
	1: 9	word that is trustworthy in accordance with the teaching	3
Heb	9:19	told to all the people…in accordance with the law	3
	11: 7	righteousness that is in accordance with faith.	3
1Pe	4:19	let those suffering in accordance with God's will	3
2Pe	3:13	in accordance with his promise, we wait for new heavens	3

according   *See also* according to the *likeness*, according to the *rules*

1. Contextual: Not in Greek
2. ἐκ, *ek, 1666*
3. ἐν, *en, 1877*
4. καθό, *katho, 2771*
5. καθώς, *kathōs, 2777*
6. κατά, *kata, 2848*
7. ὡς, *hōs, 6055*

Mat	2:16	two years old or under, according to the time	6
	8:13	let it be done for you according to your faith."	7
	9:29	"According to your faith let it be done to you."	6
	25:15	to each according to his ability.	6
Mrk	7: 5	according to the tradition of the elders	6
	15: 8	Pilate to do for them according to his custom.	1
Lke	1: 6	blamelessly according to all the commandments	3
	1: 9	according to the custom of the priesthood	6
	1:38	let it be with me according to your word."	6
	1:55	according to the promise he made to our ancestors	5
	2:22	purification according to the law of Moses	6
	2:24	according to what is stated in the law of the Lord	6
	2:29	according to your word;	6
	23:56	they rested according to the commandment.	6
Jhn	8:44	When he lies, he speaks according to his own nature	2
	18:31	judge him according to your law."	6
	19: 7	according to that law he ought to die	6
	19:40	according to the burial custom of the Jews.	5
Act	2:23	handed over to you according to the definite plan	1
	7:44	according to the pattern he had seen.	6
	11:29	according to their ability, each	5
	15: 1	circumcised according to the custom of Moses	1
	22: 3	educated strictly according to our ancestral law	6
	22:12	Ananias, who was a devout man according to the law	6
	23: 3	sitting there to judge me according to the law	6
	23:31	according to their instructions, took Paul	6
	24:14	according to the Way, which they call a sect	6
	24:14	believing everything laid down according to the law	6
Rom	1: 3	descended from David according to the flesh	6
	1: 4	with power according to the spirit of holiness	6
	2: 6	he will repay according to each one's deeds:	6
	2:16	according to my gospel, God…will judge	6
	4: 1	Abraham, our ancestor according to the flesh?	6
	4:18	according to what was said	6
	8: 4	in us, who walk not according to the flesh	6
	8: 4	us, who walk…according to the Spirit.	6
	8: 5	For those who live according to the flesh	6
	8: 5	but those who live according to the Spirit	6
	8:12	not to the flesh, to live according to the flesh—	6
	8:13	if you live according to the flesh, you will die;	6
	8:27	Spirit intercedes…according to the will of God.	6
	8:28	who are called according to his purpose.	6
	9: 3	my own people, my kindred according to the flesh.	6
	9: 5	and from them, according to the flesh	6
	12: 3	each according to the measure of faith	7
	12: 6	gifts that differ according to the grace given	6
	16:25	to strengthen you according to my gospel	6
	16:25	according to the revelation of the mystery	6
	16:26	according to the command of the eternal God	6
1Co	3: 3	behaving according to human inclinations?	6
	3: 8	will receive wages according to the labor of each.	6
	3:10	According to the grace of God given to me	6
	12: 8	according to the same Spirit	6
2Co	1:17	make my plans according to ordinary human standards	6
	8: 3	they voluntarily gave according to their means,	6
	8:11	completing it according to your means.	2
	8:12	gift is acceptable according to what one has	4
	8:12	not according to what one does not have.	4
	10: 2	who think we are acting according to human standards.	6
	10: 3	we do not wage war according to human standards;	6
	11:18	since many boast according to human standards	6
Gal	1: 4	according to the will of our God and Father	6
	3:29	Abraham's offspring, heirs according to the promise.	6
	4:23	child of the slave, was born according to the flesh;	6
	4:29	who was born according to the flesh persecuted	6
	4:29	child who was born according to the Spirit	6
Eph	1: 5	according to the good pleasure of his will	6
	1: 7	according to the riches of his grace	6
	1: 9	according to his good pleasure	6
	1:11	destined according to the purpose of him	6
	1:11	according to his counsel and will	6
	1:19	according to the working of his great power.	6
	3: 7	according to the gift of God's grace	6
	3:16	according to the riches of his glory	6
	4: 7	grace according to the measure of Christ's gift.	6
Php	3:17	who live according to the example you have in us.	5
	4:19	according to his riches in glory in Christ	6
Col	1:25	its servant according to God's commission	6
	2: 8	according to human tradition	6
	2: 8	according to the elemental spirits	6
	2: 8	not according to Christ.	6

	3:10	according to the image of its creator.	6
2Th	1:12	according to the grace of our God	6
	3: 6	living…not according to the tradition	6
2Ti	1: 9	a holy calling, not according to our works	6
	1: 9	called us…according to his own purpose and grace	6
Tit	3: 5	but according to his mercy	6
	3: 7	become heirs according to the hope of eternal life.	6
Heb	2: 4	distributed according to his will.	6
	5: 6	a priest forever, according to the order of Melchizedek."	6
	5:10	a high priest according to the order of Melchizedek.	6
	6:20	according to the order of Melchizedek.	6
	7:11	priest arising according to the order of Melchizedek	6
	7:11	rather than one according to the order of Aaron?	6
	7:17	a priest forever, according to the order of Melchizedek."	6
	8: 4	priests who offer gifts according to the law.	6
	8: 5	make everything according to the pattern	6
	10: 8	(these are offered according to the law)	6
Jas	2: 8	fulfill the royal law according to the scripture	6
1Pe	1:17	judges all people…according to their deeds	6
2Pe	2:22	It has happened to them according to the true proverb	1
	3:15	Paul wrote…according to the wisdom given him	6
1Jn	5:14	if we ask anything according to his will, he hears	6
2Jn	1: 6	love, that we walk according to his commandments;	6
Rev	20:12	dead were judged according to their works,	6
	20:13	all were judged according to what they had done.	6
	22:12	to repay according to everyone's work.	7

accordingly

1. ἄρα + οὖν, *ara + oun, 726 + 4036*
2. δέ, *de, 1254*
3. κατά, *kata, 2848*

Jhn	11: 5	Accordingly, though Jesus loved Martha and her sister	2
Rom	7: 3	Accordingly, she will be called an adulteress	1
Heb	7:22	Accordingly Jesus has also become the guarantee	3

account[1] *See also* call to account, charge to an account, give an account

1. ἀπό, *apo, 608*
2. διά, *dia, 1328*
3. ἕνεκεν, *heneken, 1915*
4. ἐπί, *epi, 2093*

Mat	5:11	evil against you falsely on my account.	3
	13:21	persecution arises on account of the word	2
	14: 3	put him in prison on account of Herodias	2
Mrk	4:17	persecution arises on account of the word	2
	6:17	and put him in prison on account of Herodias	2
Lke	6:22	revile you…on account of the Son of Man.	3
	19: 3	but on account of the crowd he could not	1
Jhn	12:11	on account of him that many…were deserting	2
	15:21	do all these things to you on account of my name	2
Act	26: 6	on account of my hope in the promise made by God	4
2Co	7:12	not on account of the one who did the wrong	3
	7:12	nor on account of the one who was wronged	3
Col	3: 6	On account of these the wrath of God is coming	2
1Jn	2:12	your sins are forgiven on account of his name	2
Rev	1: 7	on his account all the tribes of the earth will wail.	4

account[2]

1. βίβλος, *biblos, 1047*
2. λογίζομαι, *logizomai, 3357*
3. λόγος, *logos, 3364*

Mat	1: 1	An account of the genealogy of Jesus the Messiah	1
	18:23	to settle accounts with his slaves.	3
	25:19	settled accounts with them.	3
Lke	16: 2	Give me an accounting of your management	3
Rom	8:36	we are accounted as sheep to be slaughtered."	2
Php	4:17	I seek the profit that accumulates to your account.	3
Heb	4:13	the eyes of the one to whom we must render an account.	3
	13:17	and will give an account.	3
1Pe	3:15	defense to anyone who demands from you an accounting	3
	4: 5	give an accounting to him who stands ready to judge	3

orderly account

1. διήγησις, *diēgēsis, 1456*
2. καθεξῆς, *kathexēs, 2759*

Lke	1: 1	many have undertaken to set down an orderly account	1
	1: 3	to write an orderly account for you	2

accountable

1. ἔνοχος, *enochos, 1944*
2. λόγος, *logos, 3364*
3. ὑπόδικος, *hypodikos, 5688*

Rom 3:19 the whole world may be held accountable to God. 3
     14:12 So then, each of us will be accountable to God. 2
Jas   2:10 whoever…fails in one point has become accountable 1

accumulate

1. ἐπισωρεύω, *episōreuō, 2197*
2. πλεονάζω, *pleonazō, 4429*

Php 4:17 I seek the profit that accumulates to your account. 2
2Ti 4: 3 will accumulate for themselves teachers 1

accurately

1. ἀκριβῶς, *akribōs, 209*

Act 18:25 taught accurately the things concerning Jesus 1

more accurately

1. ἀκριβῶς, *akribōs, 209*

Act 18:26 explained the Way of God to him more accurately. 1

accursed

1. ἀνάθεμα, *anathema, 353*
2. ἐπάρατος, *eparatos, 2063*
3. κατάθεμα, *katathema, 2873*
4. κατάρα, *katara, 2932*
5. καταράομαι, *kataraomai, 2933*

Mat 25:41 'You that are accursed, depart from me 5
Jhn   7:49 does not know the law—they are accursed." 2
Rom   9: 3 For I could wish that I myself were accursed 1
1Co 16:22 anyone be accursed who has no love for the Lord. 1
Gal   1: 8 let that one be accursed! 1
      1: 9 let that one be accursed! 1
2Pe   2:14 hearts trained in greed. Accursed children! 4
Rev 22: 3 Nothing accursed will be found there any more. 3

accusation *See also* basis for accusation, make an accusation, make an accusation against

1. ἐγκαλέω, *enkaleō, 1592*
2. κατηγορέω, *katēgoreō, 2989*
3. κατηγορία, *katēgoria, 2990*

Lke   6: 7 that they might find an accusation against him. 2
Jhn 18:29 "What accusation do you bring against this man?" 3
Act 26: 2 against all the accusations of the Jews 1
1Ti   5:19 Never accept any accusation against an elder 3

false accusation

1. συκοφαντέω, *sykophanteō, 5193*

Lke   3:14 not extort money from anyone by…false accusation 1

accuse

1. ἐγκαλέω, *enkaleō, 1592*
2. ἐν + κατηγορία, *en + katēgoria, 1877 + 2990*
3. κατηγορέω, *katēgoreō, 2989*

Mat 12:10 so that they might accuse him. 3
     27:12 when he was accused by the chief priests 3
Mrk   3: 2 so that they might accuse him. 3
     15: 3 the chief priests accused him of many things. 3
Lke 23: 2 They began to accuse him, saying, "We found this 3
     23:10 the scribes stood by, vehemently accusing him. 3
Jhn   5:45 that I will accuse you before the Father; 3
Act 22:30 what Paul was being accused of by the Jews, 3
     23:28 the charge for which they accused him 1
     23:29 he was accused concerning questions of their law 1
     24: 2 Paul…summoned, Tertullus began to accuse him 3
     24: 8 everything of which we accuse him." 3
     25: 5 let them accuse him." 3
     25:16 before the accused had met the accusers face to face 3
     26: 7 for this hope…that I am accused by Jews! 1
Rom   2:15 their conflicting thoughts will accuse…them 3
Tit   1: 6 not accused of debauchery and not rebellious. 2
Rev 12:10 who accuses them day and night before our God. 3

accuser

1. ἀντίδικος, *antidikos, 508*
2. κατηγορέω, *katēgoreō, 2989*
3. κατήγορος, *katēgoros, 2991*

4. κατήγωρ, *katēgōr, 2992*

Mat   5:25 Come to terms quickly with your accuser 1
      5:25 or your accuser may hand you over to the judge 1
Lke 12:58 you go with your accuser before a magistrate 1
Jhn   5:45 your accuser is Moses 2
Act 23:30 ordering his accusers also to state before you 3
     23:35 give you a hearing when your accusers arrive." 3
     25:16 before the accused had met the accusers face to face 3
     25:18 When the accusers stood up 3
Rev 12:10 the accuser of our comrades has been thrown down 4

accustom

1. εἴωθα, *eiōtha, 1665*
2. συνήθεια, *synētheia, 5311*

Mat 27:15 the governor was accustomed to release 1
1Co   8: 7 have become so accustomed to idols until now 2

Achaia

1. Ἀχαία, *Achaia, 938*

Act 18:12 when Gallio was proconsul of Achaia 1
     18:27 when he wished to cross over to Achaia 1
     19:21 to go through Macedonia and Achaia 1
Rom 15:26 for Macedonia and Achaia have been pleased 1
1Co 16:15 were the first converts in Achaia 1
2Co   1: 1 including all the saints throughout Achaia: 1
      9: 2 Achaia has been ready since last year; 1
     11:10 will not be silenced in the regions of Achaia. 1
1Th   1: 7 an example to all the believers…in Achaia 1
      1: 8 sounded forth from you…in Macedonia and Achaia 1

Achaicus

1. Ἀχαϊκός, *Achaikos, 939*

1Co 16:17 Stephanas and Fortunatus and Achaicus 1

achieve

1. κρατέω, *krateō, 3195*

Act 27:13 they thought they could achieve their purpose; 1

Achim

1. Ἀχίμ, *Achim, 943*

Mat   1:14 and Zadok the father of Achim 1
      1:14 and Achim the father of Eliud 1

acknowledge *See also* acknowledged *leader*

1. δοκέω, *dokeō, 1506*
2. ἐπιγινώσκω, *epiginōskō, 2105*
3. ἐπιδέχομαι, *epidechomai, 2110*
4. ἔχω + ἐν + ἐπίγνωσις, *echō + en + epignōsis, 2400 + 1877 + 2106*
5. ὁμολογέω, *homologeō, 3933*

Mat 10:32 "Everyone…who acknowledges me before others 5
     10:32 I also will acknowledge before my Father 5
Lke 12: 8 everyone who acknowledges me before others 5
     12: 8 the Son of Man also will acknowledge 5
Act 23: 8 the Pharisees acknowledge all three.) 5
Rom   1:28 since they did not see fit to acknowledge God 4
1Co 14:37 acknowledge that what I am writing to you 2
Gal   2: 2 in a private meeting with the acknowledged leaders) 1
      2: 9 Cephas and John, who were acknowledged pillars 1
3Jn   1: 9 Diotrephes…does not acknowledge our authority. 3

acknowledge justice

1. δικαιόω, *dikaioō, 1467*

Lke   7:29 the people…acknowledged the justice of God 1

acquaintance

1. γνωστός, *gnōstos, 1196*

Lke 23:49 all his acquaintances, including the women 1

acquire

1. κτάομαι, *ktaomai, 3227*

Act   1:18 acquired a field with the reward of his wickedness; 1

acquit

1. δικαιόω, *dikaioō, 1467*

1Co   4: 4 I am not thereby acquitted. 1

across *See also* drift across, go across, sail across

   1. ἐν, *en, 1877*
   2. πέραν, *peran, 4305*
   3. περιζώννυμι, *perizōnnymi, 4322*

Mat	4:15 Naphtali, on the road by the sea, across the Jordan	2
Jhn	1:28 This took place in Bethany across the Jordan	2
	3:26 the one who was with you across the Jordan	2
	6:17 started across the sea to Capernaum.	2
	10:40 He went away again across the Jordan	2
	18: 1 he went out...across the Kidron valley	2
Act	27:27 as we were drifting across the sea of Adria	1
Rev	1:13 and with a golden sash across his chest.	3
	15: 6 with golden sashes across their chests.	3

act *See also* act *consistently*, mighty act, shameless act

   1. Contextual: Not in Greek
   2. ἀναστρέφω, *anastrephō, 418*
   3. ἔργον, *ergon, 2240*
   4. περιπατέω, *peripateō, 4344*
   5. ποιέω, *poieō, 4472*
   6. πράσσω, *prassō, 4556*
   7. χράομαι, *chraomai, 5968*

Mat	7:24 who hears these words of mine and acts on them	5
	7:26 does not act on them will be like a foolish man	5
Lke	6:47 who comes to me, hears my words, and acts on them.	5
	6:49 one who hears and does not act	5
	16: 8 commended...because he had acted shrewdly;	5
Jhn	7: 4 who wants to be widely known acts in secret.	5
Act	3:17 now, friends, I know that you acted in ignorance	6
	17: 7 all acting contrary to the decrees of the emperor	6
Rom	14:23 because they do not act from faith;	1
2Co	3:12 we have such a hope, we act with great boldness	7
	10: 2 who think we are acting according to human standards.	4
1Ti	1:13 I received mercy because I had acted ignorantly	5
Heb	13:18 desiring to act honorably in all things.	2
Jas	1:25 being not hearers who forget but doers who act	3
	2:12 So speak and so act as those who are to be judged	5

act of charity

   1. ἐλεημοσύνη, *eleēmosynē, 1797*

Act	9:36 She was devoted to good works and acts of charity.	1

act of giving

   1. δόσις, *dosis, 1521*

Jas	1:17 Every generous act of giving...is from above	1

act of righteousness

   1. δικαίωμα, *dikaiōma, 1468*

Rom	5:18 one man's act of righteousness leads	1

generous act

   1. χάρις, *charis, 5921*

2Co	8: 9 you know the generous act of our Lord Jesus Christ	1

very act

   1. αὐτόφωρος, *autophōros, 900*

Jhn	8: 4 ⟦caught in the very act of committing adultery.⟧	1

action *See also* dress for action, prepare for action, sphere of action, take action

   1. ἔργον, *ergon, 2240*
   2. κατεργάζομαι, *katergazomai, 2981*
   3. πρᾶξις, *praxis, 4552*

Lke	23:51 had not agreed to their plan and action.	3
Rom	7:15 I do not understand my own actions.	2
Tit	1:16 they deny him by their actions.	1
1Jn	3:18 let us love, not in word...but in truth and action.	1

activate

   1. ἐνεργέω, *energeō, 1919*

1Co	12: 6 the same God who activates all of them in everyone.	1
	12:11 All these are activated by one and the same Spirit	1

active

   1. ἐνεργής, *energēs, 1921*

Heb	4:12 Indeed, the word of God is living and active	1

active along with

   1. συνεργέω, *synergeō, 5300*

Jas	2:22 faith was active along with his works	1

activity

   1. ἐνέργημα, *energēma, 1920*

1Co	12: 6 there are varieties of activities	1

actually

   1. Contextual: Not in Greek
   2. αὐτός, *autos, 899*
   3. καί, *kai, 2779*
   4. μᾶλλον, *mallon, 3437*
   5. ὅλως, *holōs, 3914*
   6. ποτέ, *pote, 4537*

Act	21:28 he has actually brought Greeks into the temple	1
Rom	5: 7 for a good person someone might actually dare to die.	3
1Co	5: 1 It is actually reported	5
Gal	2: 6 (what they actually were makes no difference to me;	6
	2:10 which was actually what I was eager to do.	2
Php	1:12 actually helped to spread the gospel	4

Adam

   1. Ἀδάμ, *Adam, 77*

Lke	3:38 son of Seth, son of Adam, son of God.	1
Rom	5:14 Yet death exercised dominion from Adam to Moses	1
	5:14 sins were not like the transgression of Adam	1
1Co	15:22 for as all die in Adam	1
	15:45 "The first man, Adam, became a living being";	1
	15:45 the last Adam became a life-giving spirit.	1
1Ti	2:13 For Adam was formed first, then Eve;	1
	2:14 Adam was not deceived, but the woman was deceived	1
Jde	1:14 Enoch, in the seventh generation from Adam	1

add

   1. Contextual: Not in Greek
   2. ἐπιδιατάσσομαι, *epidiatassomai, 2112*
   3. ἐπιτίθημι, *epitithēmi, 2202*
   4. λέγω, *legō, 3306*
   5. προστίθημι, *prostithēmi, 4707*
   6. συγκαταψηφίζομαι, *synkatapsēphizomai, 5164*

Mat	6:27 any of you by worrying add a single hour to your span	5
Lke	3:20 added to them all by shutting up John in prison	5
	12:25 add a single hour to your span of life?	5
Act	1:26 he was added to the eleven apostles.	6
	2:41 that day about three thousand persons were added.	5
	2:47 day by day the Lord added to their number	5
	5:14 more than ever believers were added to the Lord	5
	12:17 he added, "Tell this to James and to the believers."	4
Gal	3:15 no one adds to it or annuls it.	2
	3:19 It was added because of transgressions	5
Heb	10: 9 he added, "See, I have come to do your will."	4
	10:17 he also adds, "I will remember their sins"	1
Rev	22:18 if anyone adds to them, God will add to that person	3
	22:18 God will add to that person the plagues	3

add one's testimony

   1. συνεπιμαρτυρέω, *synepimartyreō, 5296*

Heb	2: 4 while God added his testimony by signs and wonders	1

Addi

   1. Ἀδδί, *Addi, 79*

Lke	3:28 son of Melchi, son of Addi, son of Cosam	1

addicted to wine

   1. πάροινος, *paroinos, 4232*

Tit	1: 7 addicted to wine or violent or greedy for gain;	1

in addition

   1. ἐπί, *epi, 2093*

2Co	7:13 In addition to our own consolation	1

address *See also* deliver a public address

   1. ἀποκρίνομαι, *apokrinomai, 646*
   2. ἀποφθέγγομαι, *apophthengomai, 710*
   3. διαλέγομαι, *dialegomai, 1363*
   4. προσφωνέω, *prosphōneō, 4715*

Lke	23:20 Pilate...addressed them again;	4

Act 2:14 Peter...raised his voice and addressed them   2
      3:12 When Peter saw it, he addressed the people   1
    21:40 he addressed them in the Hebrew language, saying: 4
    22: 2 him addressing them in Hebrew   4
Heb 12: 5 the exhortation that addresses you as children   3
Rev 7:13 Then one of the elders addressed me, saying

adherent   *See also* gain adherent
   1. ἐκ, *ek, 1666*
Rom 4:14 If it is the adherents of the law who are...heirs   1
     4:16 not only to the adherents of the law   1

adjourn
   1. ἀναβάλλω, *anaballō, 327*
Act 24:22 Felix...adjourned the hearing with the comment   1

adjure
   1. ὁρκίζω, *horkizō, 3991*
Mrk 5: 7 I adjure you by God, do not torment me."   1
Act 19:13 "I adjure you by the Jesus whom Paul proclaims."   1

Admin
   1. Ἀδμίν, *Admin, 98*
Lke 3:33 son of Amminadab, son of Admin   1

administer
   1. διακονέω, *diakoneō, 1354*
   2. ἐργάζομαι, *ergazomai, 2237*
2Co 8:19 while we are administering this generous undertaking   1
     8:20 this generous gift that we are administering   1
Heb 11:33 administered justice, obtained promises   2

admit
   1. ὁμολογέω, *homologeō, 3933*
Act 24:14 I admit to you...I worship the God of our ancestors   1

admonish
   1. νουθετέω, *noutheteō, 3805*
1Co 4:14 to admonish you as my beloved children.   1
Col 3:16 teach and admonish one another in all wisdom;   1
1Th 5:12 have charge of you in the Lord and admonish you;   1
     5:14 we urge you, beloved, to admonish the idlers   1

admonition
   1. νουθεσία, *nouthesia, 3804*
Tit 3:10 After a first and second admonition,   1

adopt
   1. ἀναιρέω, *anaireō, 359*
   2. παραδέχομαι, *paradechomai, 4138*
Act 7:21 Pharaoh's daughter adopted him   1
   16:21 not lawful for us as Romans to adopt or observe."   2

adoption
   1. υἱοθεσία, *huiothesia, 5625*
Rom 8:15 but you have received a spirit of adoption.   1
    8:23 groan inwardly while we wait for adoption   1
    9: 4 to them belong the adoption, the glory   1

adoption as a child
   1. υἱοθεσία, *huiothesia, 5625*
Gal 4: 5 so that we might receive adoption as children.   1
Eph 1: 5 adoption as his children through Jesus Christ   1

adorn
   1. κοσμέω, *kosmeō, 3175*
   2. κόσμος, *kosmos, 3180*
   3. χρυσόω, *chrysoō, 5998*
Lke 21: 5 how it was adorned with beautiful stones   1
1Pe 3: 3 Do not adorn yourselves outwardly   2
    3: 5 women who hoped in God used to adorn themselves   1
Rev 17: 4 and adorned with gold and jewels and pearls   3
   18:16 adorned with gold, with jewels, and with pearls!   3
   21: 2 prepared as a bride adorned for her husband.   1
   21:19 foundations...are adorned with every jewel;   1

adornment
   1. Contextual: Not in Greek

1Pe 3: 4 let your adornment be the inner self   1

Adramyttium
   1. Ἀδραμυττηνός, *Adramyttēnos, 101*
Act 27: 2 Embarking on a ship of Adramyttium   1

Adria
   1. Ἀδρίας, *Adrias, 102*
Act 27:27 as we were drifting across the sea of Adria   1

adrift
   1. ἐκπίπτω, *ekpiptō, 1738*
   2. ποιέω, *poieō, 4472*
Act 27:32 cut away the ropes of the boat and set it adrift.   1
2Co 11:25 a night and a day I was adrift at sea;   2

adult
   1. ἀνήρ, *anēr, 467*
   2. τέλειος, *teleios, 5455*
1Co 13:11 I became an adult, I put an end to childish ways.   1
   14:20 be infants in evil, but in thinking be adults.   2

adulterer
   1. μοιχαλίς, *moichalis, 3655*
   2. μοιχός, *moichos, 3659*
Lke 18:11 thieves, rogues, adulterers   2
1Co 6: 9 adulterers, male prostitutes, sodomites,   2
Heb 13: 4 God will judge fornicators and adulterers.   2
Jas 4: 4 Adulterers! Do you not know that friendship   1

adulteress
   1. μοιχαλίς, *moichalis, 3655*
Rom 7: 3 Accordingly, she will be called an adulteress   1
    7: 3 marries another man, she is not an adulteress.   1

adulterous
   1. μοιχαλίς, *moichalis, 3655*
Mat 12:39 "An evil and adulterous generation asks for   1
   16: 4 An evil and adulterous generation   1
Mrk 8:38 in this adulterous and sinful generation   1

adultery   *See also* commit adultery
   1. μοιχαλίς, *moichalis, 3655*
   2. μοιχεία, *moicheia, 3657*
   3. μοιχεύω, *moicheuō, 3658*
Mat 15:19 evil intentions, murder, adultery, fornication   2
Mrk 7:22 adultery, avarice, wickedness, deceit   2
Jhn 8: 3 ⟦a woman who had been caught in adultery;⟧   2
Rom 2:22 You that forbid adultery   3
2Pe 2:14 They have eyes full of adultery   1

advance   *See also* arrange in advance, prepare in advance, testify in advance
   1. αὐξάνω, *auxanō, 889*
   2. προκόπτω, *prokoptō, 4621*
Act 12:24 the word of God continued to advance and gain adherents.   1
Gal 1:14 I advanced in Judaism beyond many among my people   2

advantage   *See also* take advantage
   1. Contextual: Not in Greek
   2. καρπός, *karpos, 2843*
   3. περισσός, *perissos, 4356*
   4. συμφέρω, *sympherō, 5237*
   5. σύμφορος, *symphoros, 5239*
   6. ὠφέλεια, *ōpheleia, 6066*
Jhn 16: 7 it is to your advantage that I go away   4
Rom 3: 1 Then what advantage has the Jew?   3
    6:21 what advantage did you then get from the things   2
    6:22 the advantage you get is sanctification.   2
1Co 10:24 Do not seek your own advantage   1
   10:33 not seeking my own advantage, but that of many   5
Jde 1:16 speech, flattering people to their own advantage.   6

adversary
   1. ἀντίδικος, *antidikos, 508*
   2. ἀντίκειμαι, *antikeimai, 512*
   3. ὑπεναντίος, *hypenantios, 5641*
1Co 16: 9 there are many adversaries.   2

1Ti 5:14 give the adversary no occasion to revile us.   2
Heb 10:27 fire that will consume the adversaries.   3
1Pe 5: 8 Like a roaring lion your adversary the devil prowls   1

adverse

1. Contextual: Not in Greek

Mrk 6:48 against an adverse wind, he came towards them   1

advice

1. γνώμη, *gnōmē, 1191*

2Co 8:10 in this matter I am giving my advice: 1

advisable

1. ἄξιος, *axios, 545*

1Co 16: 4 If it seems advisable that I should go also   1

advise

1. παραινέω, *paraineō, 4147*
2. συμβουλεύω, *symbouleuō, 5205*

Jhn 18:14 Caiaphas was the one who had advised the Jews   2
Act 27: 9 Paul advised them   1

advocate

1. καταγγέλλω, *katangellō, 2859*
2. παράκλητος, *paraklētos, 4156*

Jhn 14:16 give you another Advocate, to be with you   2
     14:26 the Advocate, the Holy Spirit   2
     15:26 "When the Advocate comes, whom I will send to you   2
     16: 7 if I do not go away, the Advocate will not come   2
Act 16:21 advocating customs that are not lawful for us   1
1Jn 2: 1 we have an advocate with the Father, Jesus Christ   2

Aeneas

1. Αἰνέας, *Aineas, 138*

Act 9:33 There he found a man named Aeneas   1
     9:34 Peter said to him, "Aeneas, Jesus Christ heals you;   1

Aenon

1. Αἰνών, *Ainōn, 143*

Jhn 3:23 John also was baptizing at Aenon near Salim   1

affair

1. Contextual: Not in Greek
2. ὁ, *ho, 3836*
3. πραγματεία, *pragmateia, 4548*

1Co 7:32 is anxious about the affairs of the Lord   2
     7:33 married man is anxious about the affairs of the world   2
     7:34 are anxious about the affairs of the Lord   2
     7:34 married woman is anxious about the affairs of the world   2
1Th 4:11 to mind your own affairs   1
2Ti 2: 4 gets entangled in everyday affairs;   3

affection

1. σπλάγχνον, *splanchnon, 5073*

2Co 6:12 There is no restriction in our affections   1

mutual affection

1. φιλαδελφία, *philadelphia, 5789*

Rom 12:10 love one another with mutual affection;   1
2Pe 1: 7 and godliness with mutual affection   1
     1: 7 and mutual affection with love.   1

affirm

1. λέγω, *legō, 3306*

Eph 4:17 Now this I affirm and insist on in the Lord: 1

afflict

1. θλίβω, *thlibō, 2567*
2. συνέχω, *synechō, 5309*

Mat 4:24 those who were afflicted with various diseases   2
2Co 1: 6 If we are being afflicted, it is for your consolation   1
     4: 8 We are afflicted in every way   1
     7: 5 we were afflicted in every way   1
2Th 1: 6 to repay with affliction those who afflict you   1
     1: 7 give relief to the afflicted as well as to us   1
1Ti 5:10 washed the saints' feet, helped the afflicted   1

affliction

1. θλῖψις, *thlipsis, 2568*

Act 7:10 rescued him from all his afflictions   1
2Co 1: 4 who consoles us in all our affliction   1
     1: 4 able to console those who are in any affliction   1
     1: 8 the affliction we experienced in Asia;   1
     4:17 this slight momentary affliction   1
     6: 4 through great endurance, in afflictions   1
     7: 4 I am overjoyed in all our affliction.   1
     8: 2 for during a severe ordeal of affliction   1
Col 1:24 what is lacking in Christ's afflictions   1
2Th 1: 4 the afflictions that you are enduring.   1
     1: 6 to repay with affliction those who afflict you   1
Rev 2: 9 "I know your affliction and your poverty   1
     2:10 and for ten days you will have affliction.   1

aflame with passion

1. πυρόω, *pyroō, 4792*

1Co 7: 9 it is better to marry than to be aflame with passion.   1

afraid

1. δειλιάω, *deiliaō, 1262*
2. δειλός, *deilos, 1264*
3. μή, *mē, 3590*
4. τρέμω, *tremō, 5554*
5. φοβέομαι, *phobeomai, 5828*

Mat 1:20 do not be afraid to take Mary as your wife   5
     2:22 in place of his father Herod, he was afraid to go   5
     8:26 he said to them, "Why are you afraid   2
     10:31 So do not be afraid; you are of more value   5
     14:27 "Take heart, it is I; do not be afraid."   5
     17: 7 "Get up and do not be afraid."   5
     21:26 'Of human origin,' we are afraid of the crowd;   5
     25:25 so I was afraid, and I went and hid your talent   5
     28: 5 the angel said to the women, "Do not be afraid;   5
     28:10 Then Jesus said to them, "Do not be afraid;   5
Mrk 4:40 "Why are you afraid? Have you still no faith?"   2
     5:15 they were afraid.   5
     6:50 "Take heart, it is I; do not be afraid."   5
     9:32 were afraid to ask him.   5
     10:32 those who followed were afraid.   5
     11:18 for they were afraid of him   5
     11:32 they were afraid of the crowd   5
     16: 8 they said nothing to anyone, for they were afraid.   5
Lke 1:13 angel said to him, "Do not be afraid, Zechariah   5
     1:30 The angel said to her, "Do not be afraid, Mary   5
     2:10 the angel said to them, "Do not be afraid;   5
     5:10 Jesus said to Simon, "Do not be afraid;   5
     8:25 They were afraid and amazed,   5
     8:35 they were afraid.   5
     9:45 they were afraid to ask him about this saying.   5
     12: 7 not be afraid; you are of more value than   5
     12:32 "Do not be afraid, little flock   5
     19:21 I was afraid of you, because you are a harsh man;   5
     22: 2 they were afraid of the people.   5
Jhn 6:20 he said to them, "It is I; do not be afraid."   5
     9:22 because they were afraid of the Jews;   5
     12:15 "Do not be afraid, daughter of Zion.   5
     14:27 and do not let them be afraid.   1
     19: 8 he was more afraid than ever.   5
Act 5:26 they were afraid of being stoned by the people.   5
     9:26 they were all afraid of him   5
     16:38 were afraid when they heard that they were Roman   5
     18: 9 "Do not be afraid, but speak and do not be silent;   5
     22:29 the tribune also was afraid   5
     27:24 he said, 'Do not be afraid, Paul;   5
Rom 13: 4 if you do what is wrong, you should be afraid   5
2Co 11: 3 I am afraid that as the serpent deceived Eve   5
Gal 4:11 I am afraid that my work for you may have been wasted.   5
1Th 3: 5 afraid that somehow the tempter had tempted   3
Heb 11:23 they were not afraid of the king's edict.   5
     13: 6 "The Lord is my helper; I will not be afraid.   5
2Pe 2:10 they are not afraid to slander the glorious ones   4
Rev 1:17 "Do not be afraid; I am the first and the last   5

after *See also* day after day, house after house, one after another, town after town

1. ἀπό, *apo, 608*
2. διά, *dia, 1328*

3. ἐκ, *ek, 1666*
4. ἐν, *en, 1877*
5. ἐπειδή, *epeidē, 2076*
6. ἐπί, *epi, 2093*
7. ἔχω, *echō, 2400*
8. καθεξῆς, *kathexēs, 2759*
9. κατά, *kata, 2848*
10. μετά, *meta, 3552*
11. ὅθεν, *hothen, 3854*
12. ὄπισθεν, *opisthen, 3957*
13. ὀπίσω, *opisō, 3958*
14. ὅς, *hos, 4005*
15. ὅταν, *hotan, 4020*
16. ὅτε, *hote, 4021*
17. ὀψέ, *opse, 4067*
18. ὕστερος, *hysteros, 5731*
19. ὡς, *hōs, 6055*

Mat	1:12	after the deportation to Babylon: Jechoniah was	10
	3:11	one who is more powerful than I is coming after me;	13
	15:23	"Send her away, for she keeps shouting after us."	12
	17: 9	until after the Son of Man has been raised	14
	21:32	even after you saw it, you did not change your minds	18
	24:29	"Immediately after the suffering	10
	25:19	After a long time the master…came	10
	26: 2	"You know that after two days	10
	26:32	But after I am raised up	10
	26:73	After a little while the bystanders came up	10
	27:31	After mocking him, they stripped him of	16
	27:53	After his resurrection they came out of the tombs	10
	27:62	next day, that is, after the day of Preparation	10
	27:63	'After three days I will rise again.'	10
	28: 1	After the sabbath	17
Mrk	1: 7	who is more powerful than I is coming after me;	13
	1:14	Now after John was arrested	10
	2: 1	When he returned to Capernaum after some days	2
	8:31	be killed, and after three days rise again.	10
	9: 9	until after the Son of Man had risen	15
	9:31	three days after being killed, he will rise again."	10
	10:34	after three days he will rise again."	10
	13:24	in those days, after that suffering	10
	14:19	to say to him one after another, "Surely, not I?"	9
	14:28	after I am raised up, I will go before you	10
	14:70	after a little while the bystanders again said	10
	15:20	After mocking him, they stripped him of	16
	16:12	⟦After this he appeared in another form to two⟧	10
	16:19	⟦the Lord Jesus, after he had spoken to them⟧	10
Lke	1:24	After those days his wife Elizabeth conceived	10
	1:59	going to name him Zechariah after his father.	6
	2:21	After eight days had passed, it was time	16
	2:36	seven years after her marriage	1
	2:46	After three days they found him in the temple	10
	5:27	After this he went out and saw a tax collector	10
	7: 1	After Jesus had finished all his sayings	5
	9:28	Now about eight days after these sayings	10
	10: 1	After this the Lord appointed seventy others	10
	11: 1	after he had finished, one of his disciples said	19
	12: 4	after that can do nothing more.	10
	12: 5	fear him who, after he has killed, has authority	10
	15: 4	go after the one that is lost until he finds it?	6
	19:14	sent a delegation after him, saying, 'We do not	13
	21: 8	'The time is near!' Do not go after them.	13
	22:20	did the same with the cup after supper, saying,	10
Jhn	1:15	'He who comes after me ranks ahead of me	13
	1:27	one who is coming after me;	13
	1:30	'After me comes a man who ranks ahead of me	13
	2:10	inferior wine after the guests have become drunk.	15
	2:12	After this he went down to Capernaum	10
	2:22	After he was raised from the dead	16
	3:22	After this Jesus and his disciples went	10
	5: 1	After this there was a festival of the Jews	10
	6: 1	After this Jesus went to the other side	10
	7: 1	After this Jesus went about in Galilee.	10
	7:10	after his brothers had gone to the festival	19
	11: 6	after having heard that Lazarus was ill	19
	11: 7	Then after this he said to the disciples	10
	11:11	After saying this, he told them	10
	12:19	Look, the world has gone after him!"	13
	13:12	After he had washed their feet	16
	13:27	After he received the piece of bread, Satan	10
	19:28	After this, when Jesus…said…"I am thirsty."	10

	19:38	After these things, Joseph of Arimathea,	10
	21: 1	After these things Jesus showed himself again	10
Act	1: 3	After his suffering he presented himself alive	10
	3:24	from Samuel and those after him,	8
	5:37	After him Judas the Galilean rose up	10
	7: 4	After his father died, God had him move from there	10
	7: 5	to him…and to his descendants after him	10
	7: 7	after that they shall come out and worship me	10
	9:23	After some time had passed	19
	10:37	after the baptism that John announced:	10
	10:41	after he rose from the dead.	10
	12: 4	to bring him out to the people after the Passover.	10
	13:15	After the reading of the law and the prophets	10
	13:20	After that he gave them judges	10
	13:22	a man after my heart, who will carry out all my wishes.'	9
	13:25	No, but one is coming after me;	10
	15:13	After they finished speaking, James replied	10
	15:16	'After this I will return, and I will rebuild	10
	15:36	After some days Paul said to Barnabas, "Come	10
	18: 1	After this Paul left Athens and went to Corinth.	10
	19: 4	to believe in the one who was to come after him	10
	19:21	Now after these things had been accomplished	19
	19:21	"After I have gone there, I must also see Rome."	10
	20: 1	After the uproar had ceased	10
	20: 6	we sailed…after the days of Unleavened Bread	10
	20:15	the day after that we came to Miletus.	7
	20:29	that after I have gone, savage wolves will come	10
	21:15	After these days we got ready	10
	24:17	after some years I came to bring alms to my nation	2
	25: 1	Three days after Festus had arrived in the province	10
	26:19	"After that, King Agrippa, I was not disobedient	11
	28: 6	after they had waited a long time	6
	28:13	After one day there a south wind sprang up	10
Rom	4:10	Was it before or after he had been circumcised?	4
	4:10	It was not after, but before he was circumcised.	4
1Co	11:25	In the same way he took the cup also, after supper,	10
	15:24	after he has destroyed every ruler	15
	16: 5	visit you after passing through Macedonia	15
Gal	1:18	Then after three years I did go up to Jerusalem	10
	2: 1	Then after fourteen years I went up again	2
	2:12	but after they came, he drew back	16
Php	2:27	so that I would not have one sorrow after another.	6
Tit	3:10	After a first and second admonition,	10
Heb	7:27	he has no need…to offer sacrifices day after day	9
	8:10	with the house of Israel after those days	10
	9:25	as the high priest enters the Holy Place year after year	9
	9:27	to die once, and after that the judgment	10
	10: 1	are continually offered year after year	9
	10: 3	there is a reminder of sin year after year.	9
	10:11	every priest stands day after day at his service	9
	10:15	also testifies to us, for after saying	10
	10:16	after those days, says the Lord:	10
	10:26	after having received the knowledge of the truth	10
2Pe	1:15	I will make every effort so that after my departure	10
	2: 8	day after day, was tormented in his righteous soul	3
Rev	1:19	what is, and what is to take place after this.	10
	4: 1	After this I looked, and there in heaven a door	10
	4: 1	I will show you what must take place after this."	10
	7: 1	After this I saw four angels standing	10
	7: 9	After this I looked, and there was a great multitude	10
	11:11	after the three and a half days, the breath of life	10
	12:15	the serpent poured water…after the woman	13
	15: 5	After this I looked, and the temple…was opened	10
	18: 1	After this I saw another angel coming down from heaven	10
	19: 1	After this I heard what seemed to be the loud voice	10
	20: 3	After that he must be let out for a little while.	10

not after that

1. οὐκέτι, *ouketi, 4033*

Mrk 12:34   After that no one dared to ask him any question.   1

afternoon   See also four o'clock in the afternoon, one in the afternoon, three in the afternoon, three o'clock in the afternoon

1. ἡμέρα, *hēmera, 2465*

Act 10: 3   One afternoon at about three o'clock   1

afterward   See also soon afterward

1. δεύτερος, *deuteros, 1311*
2. μετά, *meta, 3552*

   3. ὕστερος, *hysteros, 5731*

Mrk 16: S	⟦afterward Jesus himself sent out through them,⟧	2
Jhn 13:36	you will follow afterward."	3
Jde 1: 5	afterward destroyed those who did not believe.	1

afterwards   *See also* soon afterwards

   1. πάλιν, *palin, 4099*
   2. ὕστερος, *hysteros, 5731*

Mat 4: 2	and forty nights, and afterwards he was famished.	2
Gal 1:17	afterwards I returned to Damascus.	1

Agabus

   1. Ἄγαβος, *Hagabos, 13*

Act 11:28	One of them named Agabus stood up	1
21:10	a prophet named Agabus came down from Judea.	1

again   *See also* alive again, ask again, crucify again, never again, once again, receive again, rise again, see again, threaten again, turn again

   1. Contextual: Not in Greek
   2. ἀλλά, *alla, 247*
   3. ἀπό + ἄρτι, *apo + arti, 608 + 785*
   4. εἰς + ὁ + αἰών, *eis + ho + aiōn, 1650 + 3836 + 172*
   5. ἔτι, *eti, 2285*
   6. πάλιν, *palin, 4099*
   7. πάλιν + ἄνωθεν, *palin + anōthen, 4099 + 540*

Mat 4: 7	Jesus said to him, "Again it is written, 'Do not	6
4: 8	Again, the devil took him to a very high mountain	6
5:33	"Again, you have heard that it was said to those	6
13:45	"Again, the kingdom of heaven is like a merchant	6
13:47	"Again, the kingdom of heaven is like a net	6
18:19	Again, truly I tell you, if two of you agree	6
19:24	Again I tell you, it is easier for a camel	6
20: 5	When he went out again about noon	6
21:19	"May no fruit ever come from you again!"	4
21:36	Again he sent other slaves, more than the first;	6
22: 4	Again he sent other slaves, saying	6
23:39	you will not see me again until you say	3
26:29	I will never again drink of this fruit	3
26:42	Again he went away for the second time and prayed	6
26:43	Again he came and found them sleeping	6
26:44	So leaving them again, he went away	6
26:72	Again he denied it with an oath	6
27:21	The governor again said to them	1
27:50	Jesus cried again with a loud voice	6
Mrk 2:13	Jesus went out again beside the sea;	6
3: 1	Again he entered the synagogue	6
3:20	and the crowd came together again	6
4: 1	Again he began to teach beside the sea.	6
5:21	Jesus had crossed again in the boat	6
7:14	he called the crowd again and said	6
8: 1	In those days when there was again a great crowd	6
8:13	he left them, and getting into the boat again	6
8:25	Then Jesus laid his hands on his eyes again;	6
10: 1	crowds again gathered around him;	6
10: 1	as was his custom, he again taught them.	6
10:10	in the house the disciples asked him again	6
10:24	Jesus said to them again	6
10:32	took the twelve aside again and began to tell	6
11:14	"May no one ever eat fruit from you again."	4
11:27	Again they came to Jerusalem.	6
12: 4	again he sent another slave to them;	6
14:39	again he went away and prayed	6
14:61	Again the high priest asked him	6
14:69	began again to say to the bystanders	6
14:70	again he denied it.	6
14:70	the bystanders again said to Peter	6
15: 4	Pilate asked him again, "Have you no answer?	6
15:12	Pilate spoke to them again, "Then what do you wish	6
Lke 6:43	nor again does a bad tree bear good fruit;	6
13:20	again he said, "To what should I compare the kingdom	6
23:20	Pilate…addressed them again;	6
Jhn 1:35	The next day John again was standing	6
4:13	who drinks of this water will be thirsty again	6
4:46	Then he came again to Cana in Galilee	6
6:15	he withdrew again to the mountain by himself.	6
8: 2	⟦Early in the morning he came again to the temple.⟧	6
8:12	Again Jesus spoke to them, saying, "I am the light	6
8:21	Again he said to them, "I am going away	6

9:17	So they said again to the blind man	6
9:27	Why do you want to hear it again?	6
10: 7	So again Jesus said to them, "Very truly	6
10:17	I lay down my life in order to take it up again.	6
10:18	I have power to take it up again.	6
10:19	Again the Jews were divided	6
10:31	The Jews took up stones again to stone him.	6
10:39	they tried to arrest him again	6
10:40	He went away again across the Jordan	6
11: 7	"Let us go to Judea again."	6
11: 8	are you going there again?"	6
11:38	Jesus, again greatly disturbed, came to the tomb.	6
12:28	"I have glorified it, and I will glorify it again."	6
14: 3	I will come again and will take you to myself	6
16:16	again a little while, and you will see me."	6
16:17	again a little while, and you will see me';	6
16:19	again a little while, and you will see me'?	6
16:22	you have pain now; but I will see you again	6
16:28	again, I am leaving the world	6
18: 7	Again he asked them, "Whom are you looking for?"	6
18:27	Again Peter denied it	6
18:33	Pilate entered the headquarters again	6
18:38	went out to the Jews again and told them	6
19: 4	Pilate went out again and said to them	6
19: 9	He entered his headquarters again and asked	6
19:37	again another passage of scripture says	6
20:21	Jesus said to them again, "Peace be with you.	6
20:26	later his disciples were again in the house	6
21: 1	After these things Jesus showed himself again	6
Act 10:15	The voice said to him again, a second time	6
11:10	everything was pulled up again to heaven.	6
13:42	speak about these things again the next sabbath.	1
17:32	others said, "We will hear you again about this."	6
27:28	a little farther on they took soundings again	6
Rom 10:19	Again I ask, did Israel not understand?	2
11:23	for God has the power to graft them in again.	6
14: 9	For to this end Christ died and lived again	1
15:10	and again he says, "Rejoice, O Gentiles	6
15:11	and again, "Praise the Lord, all you Gentiles	6
15:12	again Isaiah says, "The root of Jesse shall come	6
1Co 3:20	again, "The Lord knows the thoughts of the wise	6
7: 5	come together again, so that Satan may not tempt	6
12:21	nor again the head to the feet	6
2Co 1:10	set our hope that he will rescue us again	5
3: 1	Are we beginning to commend ourselves again?	6
5:12	We are not commending ourselves to you again	6
12:21	I fear that when I come again, my God may humble me	6
13: 2	if I come again, I will not be lenient—	6
Gal 2: 1	I went up again to Jerusalem with Barnabas	6
2:18	build up again the very things that I once tore down	6
4: 9	can you turn back again to the weak and beggarly	6
4: 9	you want to be enslaved to them again?	7
4:19	for whom I am again in the pain of childbirth	6
5: 1	do not submit again to a yoke of slavery.	6
5: 3	Once again I testify to every man	6
Php 1:26	when I come to you again.	6
2:28	that you may rejoice at seeing him again	6
4: 4	again I will say, Rejoice.	6
Heb 1: 5	Or again, "I will be his Father	6
1: 6	And again…he says,	6
2:13	And again, "I will put my trust in him."	6
2:13	again, "Here am I and the children whom God has given	6
4: 5	And again in this place it says	6
4: 7	again he sets a certain day—"today"	6
5:12	someone to teach you again the basic elements	6
6: 1	not laying again the foundation: repentance	6
6: 4	For it is impossible to restore again to repentance	6
10:30	And again, "The Lord will judge his people."	6
Jas 5:18	Then he prayed again, and the heaven gave rain	6
2Pe 2:20	again entangled in them and overpowered	6
Rev 10: 8	the voice…from heaven spoke to me again	6
10:11	"You must prophesy again about many peoples	6

again and again

   1. ἅπαξ + καί + δίς, *hapax + kai + dis, 562 + 2779 + 1489*
   2. πολλάκις, *pollakis, 4490*

1Th 2:18	I, Paul, wanted to again and again	1
Heb 9:25	Nor was it to offer himself again and again	2
9:26	he would have had to suffer again and again	2
10:11	offering again and again the same sacrifices	2

not again

1. μηκέτι, *mēketi, 3600*
2. οὐκέτι, *ouketi, 4033*

Jhn	8:11 [[Go your way, and from now on do not sin again."]]	1
Act	20:38 that they would not see him again.	2
2Co	1:23 it was to spare you that I did not come again	2

against *See also* beat against, bring a charge against, bring against, burst against, cast against, charge against, count against, fight against God, hold against, lie against, lift against, make an accusation against, rise against, sentence against, set against, speak against, testify against, thing against

1. ἀπό, *apo, 608*
2. διά, *dia, 1328*
3. εἰς, *eis, 1650*
4. ἐκ, *ek, 1666*
5. ἐν, *en, 1877*
6. ἐναντίος, *enantios, 1885*
7. ἐπί, *epi, 2093*
8. κατά, *kata, 2848*
9. μετά, *meta, 3552*
10. μή, *mē, 3590*
11. μή + προσεάω, *mē + proseaō, 3590 + 4661*
12. περί, *peri, 4309*
13. πρός, *pros, 4639*
14. ὑπεναντίος, *hypenantios, 5641*

Mat	4: 6 so that you will not dash your foot against a stone.' "	13
	5:11 utter all kinds of evil against you falsely	8
	5:23 that your brother or sister has something against you	8
	10:21 children will rise against parents	7
	10:35 For I have come to set a man against his father	8
	10:35 and a daughter against her mother	8
	10:35 a daughter-in-law against her mother-in-law;	8
	12:14 and conspired against him, how to destroy him.	8
	12:25 "Every kingdom divided against itself	8
	12:25 no city or house divided against itself	8
	12:26 he is divided against himself;	7
	12:30 Whoever is not with me is against me,	8
	12:32 Whoever speaks a word against the Son of Man	8
	12:32 but whoever speaks against the Holy Spirit	8
	14:24 for the wind was against them.	6
	18:15 "If another member of the church sins against you	3
	18:21 if another member of the church sins against me	3
	20:11 they grumbled against the landowner	8
	24: 7 For nation will rise against nation	7
	24: 7 kingdom against kingdom	7
	26:59 looking for false testimony against Jesus	8
	27: 1 elders…conferred together against Jesus	8
Mrk	3: 6 conspired with the Herodians against him	8
	3:24 If a kingdom is divided against itself	7
	3:25 if a house is divided against itself	7
	3:26 if Satan has risen up against himself	7
	3:29 whoever blasphemes against the Holy Spirit	3
	6:48 against an adverse wind, he came towards them	6
	9:40 Whoever is not against us is for us.	8
	10:11 and marries another commits adultery against her;	7
	11:25 forgive, if you have anything against anyone;	8
	12:12 he had told this parable against them	13
	13: 8 For nation will rise against nation	7
	13: 8 kingdom against kingdom;	7
	13:12 children will rise against parents	7
	14:55 looking for testimony against Jesus	8
	14:56 For many gave false testimony against him	8
	14:57 Some stood up and gave false testimony against him	8
	15:46 rolled a stone against the door of the tomb.	7
Lke	4:11 you will not dash your foot against a stone.' "	13
	9: 5 dust off your feet as a testimony against them."	7
	9:50 for whoever is not against you is for you."	8
	11:17 "Every kingdom divided against itself	7
	11:18 If Satan also is divided against himself	7
	11:23 Whoever is not with me is against me,	8
	11:51 it will be charged against this generation.	1
	12:10 who speaks a word against the Son of Man	3
	12:10 whoever blasphemes against the Holy Spirit	3
	12:15 Be on your guard against all kinds of greed;	1
	12:52 three against two and two against three;	7
	12:52 three against two and two against three;	7
	12:53 father against son and son against father	7
	12:53 father against son and son against father	7
	12:53 mother against daughter	7
	12:53 daughter against mother	7
	12:53 mother-in-law against her daughter-in-law	7
	12:53 daughter-in-law against mother-in-law."	7
	14:31 to oppose the one who comes against him with	7
	15:18 I have sinned against heaven and before you;	3
	15:21 I have sinned against heaven and before you;	3
	17: 4 same person sins against you seven times a day	3
	18: 3 saying, 'Grant me justice against my opponent.'	1
	20:19 he had told this parable against them	13
	21:10 he said to them, "Nation will rise against nation	7
	21:10 kingdom against kingdom;	7
	23: 4 no basis for an accusation against this man."	5
	23:14 guilty of any of your charges against him.	8
Jhn	7: 7 I testify against it that its works are evil.	12
	11:38 It was a cave, and a stone was lying against it.	7
	13:18 who ate my bread has lifted his heel against me.'	7
	18:29 "What accusation do you bring against this man?"	8
	18:38 "I find no case against him.	5
	19: 4 to let you know that I find no case against him."	5
	19: 6 I find no case against him."	5
Act	4:26 against the Lord and against his Messiah.'	8
	4:26 against the Lord and against his Messiah.'	8
	4:27 gathered together against your holy servant	7
	6: 1 the Hellenists complained against the Hebrews	13
	6:11 blasphemous words against Moses and God."	3
	6:13 saying things against this holy place and the law;	8
	7:57 with a loud shout all rushed together against him.	7
	8: 1 a severe persecution began against the church	7
	9: 1 murder against the disciples of the Lord	3
	13:11 now listen—the hand of the Lord is against you	7
	13:50 and stirred up persecution against Paul	7
	13:51 they shook the dust off their feet in protest	7
	14: 2 poisoned their minds against the brothers.	8
	19:38 the artisans…have a complaint against anyone	13
	21:28 against our people, our law, and this place;	8
	23:30 there would be a plot against the man	3
	23:30 to state before you what they have against him."	13
	24: 1 reported their case against Paul to the governor.	8
	24:19 if they have anything against me.	13
	25: 2 gave him a report against Paul.	8
	25: 3 requested, as a favor to them against Paul	8
	25: 8 in no way committed an offense against the law	3
	25: 8 or against the temple, or against the emperor."	3
	25: 8 or against the temple, or against the emperor."	3
	25:15 asked for a sentence against him.	8
	25:16 to make a defense against the charge	12
	25:27 without indicating the charges against him."	8
	26: 2 against all the accusations of the Jews	12
	26: 9 against the name of Jesus of Nazareth.	13
	26:14 It hurts you to kick against the goads.'	13
	27: 4 because the winds were against us.	6
	27: 7 and as the wind was against us	11
	28:17 though I had done nothing against our people	6
Rom	1:18 against all ungodliness and wickedness of those	7
	2:21 While you preach against stealing, do you steal?	10
	4:18 Hoping against hope, he believed	7
	8:31 If God is for us, who is against us?	8
	8:33 Who will bring any charge against God's elect?	8
	11: 2 of Elijah, how he pleads with God against Israel?	8
1Co	4: 6 puffed up in favor of one against another.	8
	6: 1 When any of you has a grievance against another	13
	6: 6 believer goes to court against a believer	9
	6:18 the fornicator sins against the body	3
	8:12 thus sin against members of your family	3
	8:12 you sin against Christ.	3
2Co	1:23 I call on God as witness against me:	7
	8: 8 your love against the earnestness of others.	2
	10: 5 proud obstacle raised up against the knowledge of God	8
	13: 8 For we cannot do anything against the truth	8
Gal	5:23 There is no law against such things.	8
Eph	6:11 able to stand against the wiles of the devil.	13
	6:12 struggle is not against enemies of blood and flesh	13
	6:12 against the rulers, against the authorities	13
	6:12 against the rulers, against the authorities	13
	6:12 against the cosmic powers of this present darkness	13
	6:12 against the spiritual forces of evil	13
Col	2:14 erasing the record that stood against us	14
	3:13 if anyone has a complaint against another	13
1Ti	5:19 Never accept any accusation against an elder	8

Heb	12: 3	who endured…such hostility against himself	3
	12: 4	In your struggle against sin	13
Jas	5: 9	Beloved, do not grumble against one another	8
1Pe	2:11	desires…that wage war against the soul.	8
	3:12	the face of the Lord is against those who do evil."	7
2Pe	2:11	do not bring against them a slanderous judgment	8
Jde	1:15	that ungodly sinners have spoken against him.	8
Rev	2: 4	But I have this against you	8
	2:14	But I have a few things against you:	8
	2:16	make war against them with the sword of my mouth.	9
	2:20	But I have this against you:	8
	7: 1	blow on earth or sea or against any tree.	7
	12: 7	Michael…angels fought against the dragon.	9
	13: 4	"Who is like the beast, and who can fight against it?"	9
	13: 6	to utter blasphemies against God, blaspheming	13
	18:20	For God has given judgment for you against her.	4
	19:19	to make war against the rider on the horse	9
	19:19	to make war against…and against his army.	9

agate
1. χαλκηδών, *chalkēdōn, 5907*

Rev	21:19	every jewel;…the third agate	1

age¹
1. Contextual: Not in Greek
2. ἔτος, *etos, 2291*
3. ἡλικία, *hēlikia, 2461*
4. ἡμέρα, *hēmera, 2465*

Mrk	5:42	(she was twelve years of age).	1
Lke	2:36	She was of a great age	4
	2:37	then as a widow to the age of eighty-four	2
Jhn	9:21	he is of age. He will speak for himself."	3
	9:23	his parents said, "He is of age; ask him."	3

age²
1. Contextual: Not in Greek
2. αἰών, *aiōn, 172*
3. αἰώνιος, *aiōnios, 173*
4. καιρός, *kairos, 2789*
5. χρόνος, *chronos, 5989*

Mat	12:32	either in this age or in the age to come.	2
	12:32	either in this age or in the age to come.	1
	13:39	the harvest is the end of the age	2
	13:40	so will it be at the end of the age.	2
	13:49	So it will be at the end of the age.	2
	24: 3	the end of the age?"	2
	28:20	I am with you always, to the end of the age."	2
Mrk	10:30	receive a hundredfold now in this age	4
	10:30	in the age to come eternal life.	2
Lke	16: 8	the children of this age are more shrewd	2
	18:30	who will not get back very much more in this age	4
	18:30	in the age to come eternal life."	2
	20:34	"Those who belong to this age marry	2
	20:35	who are considered worthy of a place in that age	2
Rom	16:25	the mystery that was kept secret for long ages	5
1Co	1:20	Where is the debater of this age?	2
	2: 6	though it is not a wisdom of this age	2
	2: 6	rulers of this age, who are doomed to perish.	2
	2: 7	which God decreed before the ages for our glory	2
	2: 8	None of the rulers of this age understood this;	2
	3:18	If you think that you are wise in this age	2
	10:11	on whom the ends of the ages have come.	2
Gal	1: 4	to set us free from the present evil age	2
Eph	1:21	not only in this age	2
	1:21	but also in the age to come.	1
	2: 7	so that in the ages to come	2
	3: 9	plan of the mystery hidden for ages in God	2
Col	1:26	mystery that has been hidden throughout the ages	2
1Ti	1:17	the King of the ages, immortal, invisible, the only God	2
	6:17	As for those who in the present age are rich	2
2Ti	1: 9	This grace was given to us…before the ages began	3
Tit	1: 2	that God, who never lies, promised before the ages	3
	2:12	in the present age to live lives that are self-controlled,	2
Heb	6: 5	the powers of the age to come	2
	9:26	he has appeared once for all at the end of the age	2
1Pe	1:20	He…was revealed at the end of the ages	5

old age
1. γῆρας, *gēras, 1179*

Lke	1:36	Elizabeth in her old age has also conceived a son;	1

same age
1. συνηλικιώτης, *synēlikiōtēs, 5312*

Gal	1:14	many among my people of the same age	1

agitate
1. ἀδημονέω, *adēmoneō, 86*

Mat	26:37	and began to be grieved and agitated.	1
Mrk	14:33	and began to be distressed and agitated.	1

agitator
1. κινέω + στάσις, *kineō + stasis, 3075 + 5087*

Act	24: 5	an agitator among all the Jews	1

ago   *See also* long ago
1. ἀπό, *apo, 608*
2. πρό, *pro, 4574*

Act	5:36	For some time ago Theudas rose up	2
	10:30	Cornelius replied, "Four days ago at this very hour	1
2Co	12: 2	who fourteen years ago was caught up	2

agony
1. βασανίζω, *basanizō, 989*
2. ὀδυνάω, *odynaō, 3849*
3. πόνος, *ponos, 4506*

Lke	16:24	for I am in agony in these flames.'	2
	16:25	now he is comforted here, and you are in agony.	2
Rev	12: 2	in birth pangs, in the agony of giving birth.	1
	16:10	people gnawed their tongues in agony	3

agree
1. Contextual: Not in Greek
2. εἷς, *heis, 1651*
3. εἷς + γνώμη, *heis + gnōmē, 1651 + 1191*
4. ἴσος, *isos, 2698*
5. προσέρχομαι, *proserchomai, 4665*
6. συγκατατίθημι, *synkatatithēmi, 5163*
7. σύμφημι, *symphēmi, 5238*
8. συμφωνέω, *symphōneō, 5244*
9. συντίθημι, *syntithēmi, 5338*
10. φρονέω, *phroneō, 5858*

Mat	18:19	truly I tell you, if two of you agree on earth	8
	20: 2	After agreeing with the laborers	8
	20:13	not agree with me for the usual daily wage?	8
Mrk	14:56	their testimony did not agree.	4
	14:59	even on this point their testimony did not agree.	4
Lke	22: 5	greatly pleased and agreed to give him money.	9
	23:51	had not agreed to their plan and action.	6
Jhn	9:22	the Jews had already agreed	9
Act	15:15	This agrees with the words of the prophets	8
	23:20	"The Jews have agreed to ask you to bring Paul	9
Rom	7:16	I agree that the law is good.	7
2Co	13:11	agree with one another, live in peace;	10
Gal	2: 9	agreeing that we should go to the Gentiles	1
1Ti	6: 3	does not agree with the sound words of our Lord	5
1Jn	5: 8	and these three agree.	2
Rev	17:17	by agreeing to give their kingdom to the beast	3

agree together
1. συμφωνέω, *symphōneō, 5244*

Act	5: 9	agreed together to put the Spirit…to the test?	1

agreement
1. ὁ + αὐτός + λέγω, *ho + autos + legō, 3836 + 899 + 3306*
2. συγκατάθεσις, *synkatathesis, 5161*
3. συμφώνησις, *symphōnēsis, 5245*
4. σύμφωνος, *symphōnos, 5247*

1Co	1:10	that all of you be in agreement	1
	7: 5	except perhaps by agreement for a set time	4
2Co	6:15	What agreement does Christ have with Beliar?	3
	6:16	What agreement has the temple of God with idols?	2

Agrippa
1. Ἀγρίππας, *Agrippas, 68*

Act	25:13	King Agrippa and Bernice arrived	1
	25:22	Agrippa said to Festus, "I would like to hear	1
	25:23	So on the next day Agrippa and Bernice came	1
	25:24	"King Agrippa and all here present with us	1
	25:26	especially before you, King Agrippa	1

Act	26: 1	Agrippa said to Paul, "You have permission	1
	26: 2	"I consider myself fortunate…King Agrippa	1
	26:19	"After that, King Agrippa, I was not disobedient	1
	26:27	King Agrippa, do you believe the prophets?	1
	26:28	Agrippa said to Paul	1
	26:32	Agrippa said to Festus	1

aground *See* run aground

aha

1. οὐά, *oua, 4025*

Mrk	15:29	shaking their heads and saying, "Aha!	1

Ahaz

1. Ἀχάζ, *Achaz, 937*

Mat	1: 9	and Jotham the father of Ahaz	1
	1: 9	and Ahaz the father of Hezekiah	1

ahead *See also* arrive ahead, go ahead, go on ahead, lie ahead, look ahead, run ahead, walk ahead

1. εἰς + ὁ + ἔμπροσθεν, *eis + ho + emprosthen, 1650 + 3836 + 1869*
2. ἔμπροσθεν, *emprosthen, 1869*
3. κατέναντι, *katenanti, 2978*
4. πρό, *pro, 4574*
5. πρό + πρόσωπον, *pro + prosōpon, 4574 + 4725*

Mat	11:10	'See, I am sending my messenger ahead of you,	5
	21: 2	to them, "Go into the village ahead of you	3
Mrk	1: 2	"See, I am sending my messenger ahead of you,	5
	11: 2	said to them, "Go into the village ahead of you	3
Lke	7:27	'See, I am sending my messenger ahead of you,	5
	9:52	he sent messengers ahead of him.	5
	10: 1	sent them on ahead of him in pairs	5
	19: 4	So he ran ahead	1
	19:28	After he had said this, he went on ahead	1
	19:30	saying, "Go into the village ahead	3
Jhn	1:15	'He who comes after me ranks ahead of me	2
	1:30	'After me comes a man who ranks ahead of me	2
	3:28	not the Messiah, but I have been sent ahead of him.'	2
	5: 7	my way, someone else steps down ahead of me."	4
	10: 4	he goes ahead of them, and the sheep follow him	2

ailment

1. ἀσθένεια, *astheneia, 819*

Lke	13:12	"Woman, you are set free from your ailment."	1
1Ti	5:23	your stomach and your frequent ailments.	1

aim *See also* make one's aim

1. ἵνα, *hina, 2671*
2. τέλος, *telos, 5465*

1Ti	1: 5	But the aim of such instruction is love	2
2Ti	2: 4	the soldier's aim is to please the enlisting officer.	1

aim in life

1. πρόθεσις, *prothesis, 4606*

2Ti	3:10	my aim in life, my faith, my patience, my love	1

aimlessly

1. ἀδήλως, *adēlōs, 85*

1Co	9:26	So I do not run aimlessly	1

air *See also* put on airs

1. ἀήρ, *aēr, 113*
2. οὐρανός, *ouranos, 4041*

Mat	6:26	Look at the birds of the air; they neither sow	2
	8:20	"Foxes have holes, and birds of the air have nests;	2
	13:32	so that the birds of the air come and make nests	2
Mrk	4:32	birds of the air can make nests in its shade."	2
Lke	8: 5	the birds of the air ate it up.	2
	9:58	"Foxes have holes, and birds of the air have nests;	2
	13:19	the birds of the air made nests in its branches."	2
Act	10:12	creatures and reptiles and birds of the air.	2
	11: 6	beasts of prey, reptiles, and birds of the air.	2
	22:23	their cloaks, and tossing dust into the air	2
1Co	9:26	nor do I box as though beating the air;	1
	14: 9	For you will be speaking into the air.	1
Eph	2: 2	following the ruler of the power of the air	1
1Th	4:17	together with them to meet the Lord in the air;	1
Rev	9: 2	the sun and the air were darkened with the smoke	1

	16:17	The seventh angel poured his bowl into the air	1

alabaster *See* alabaster *jar*

alarm

1. ἐκθαμβέω, *ekthambeō, 1701*
2. θορυβέω, *thorybeō, 2572*
3. θροέω, *throeō, 2583*
4. φοβέομαι, *phobeomai, 5828*
5. φόβος, *phobos, 5832*

Mat	24: 6	see that you are not alarmed;	3
Mrk	13: 7	do not be alarmed; this must take place	3
	16: 5	sitting on the right side; and they were alarmed.	1
	16: 6	But he said to them, "Do not be alarmed;	1
Act	20:10	"Do not be alarmed, for his life is in him."	2
2Co	7:11	what indignation, what alarm, what longing	5
2Th	2: 2	not to be quickly shaken in mind or alarmed	3
1Pe	3: 6	do what is good and never let fears alarm you.	4

alas

1. οὐαί, *ouai, 4026*

Rev	18:10	"Alas, alas, the great city, Babylon	1
	18:10	"Alas, alas, the great city, Babylon	1
	18:16	"Alas, alas, the great city	1
	18:16	"Alas, alas, the great city	1
	18:19	"Alas, alas, the great city, where all…grew rich	1
	18:19	"Alas, alas, the great city, where all…grew rich	1

alert *See also* keep alert

1. ἀγρυπνέω, *agrypneō, 70*
2. βλέπω, *blepō, 1063*
3. γρηγορέω, *grēgoreō, 1213*

Mrk	13:23	alert; I have already told you everything.	2
Lke	12:37	whom the master finds alert when he comes;	3
	21:36	Be alert at all times	1
Act	20:31	Therefore be alert	3
Col	4: 2	keeping alert in it with thanksgiving.	3
1Pe	5: 8	Discipline yourselves, keep alert.	3

Alexander

1. Ἀλέξανδρος, *Alexandros, 235*

Mrk	15:21	the father of Alexander and Rufus.	1
Act	4: 6	Caiaphas, John, and Alexander	1
	19:33	Some of the crowd gave instructions to Alexander	1
	19:33	Alexander motioned for silence	1
1Ti	1:20	among them are Hymenaeus and Alexander	1
2Ti	4:14	Alexander the coppersmith did me great harm;	1

Alexandria

1. Ἀλεξανδρεύς, *Alexandreus, 233*

Act	18:24	a Jew named Apollos, a native of Alexandria.	1

Alexandrian

1. Ἀλεξανδρεύς, *Alexandreus, 233*
2. Ἀλεξανδρῖνος, *Alexandrinos, 234*

Act	6: 9	Cyrenians, Alexandrians, and others	1
	27: 6	There the centurion found an Alexandrian ship	2
	28:11	an Alexandrian ship	2

alien

1. ἀπαλλοτριόω, *apallotrioō, 558*
2. πάροικος, *paroikos, 4230*

Eph	2:12	aliens from the commonwealth of Israel	1
	2:19	you are no longer strangers and aliens	2
1Pe	2:11	I urge you as aliens and exiles to abstain	2

resident alien

1. πάροικος, *paroikos, 4230*

Act	7: 6	resident aliens in a country belonging to others	1
	7:29	became a resident alien in the land of Midian.	1

alienate

1. ἀπαλλοτριόω, *apallotrioō, 558*

Eph	4:18	alienated from the life of God	1

sensual desires alienate

1. καταστρηνιάω, *katastrēniaō, 2952*

1Ti	5:11	their sensual desires alienate them from Christ	1

alight

1. ἔρχομαι, *erchomai, 2262*

Mat 3:16 saw the Spirit of God...alighting on him. 1

alike

1. Contextual: Not in Greek
2. ἀπό + εἷς, *apo + heis, 608 + 1651*
3. αὐτός, *autos, 899*

Lke 14:18 they all alike began to make excuses. 2
Rom 14: 5 while others judge all days to be alike. 1
1Co 15:39 Not all flesh is alike 3

alive *See also* make alive, make alive together

1. εἰμί, *eimi, 1639*
2. ζάω, *zaō, 2409*
3. μένω, *menō, 3531*

Mat 6:30 which is alive today and tomorrow is thrown 1
      27:63 what that impostor said while he was still alive 2
Mrk 16:11 ⟦heard that he was alive and had been seen by her⟧ 2
Lke 12:28 the grass of the field, which is alive today 1
      20:38 to him all of them are alive." 2
      24:23 a vision of angels who said that he was alive. 2
Jhn 4:51 his slaves...told him that his child was alive. 2
Act 1: 3 After his suffering he presented himself alive 2
      9:41 he showed her to be alive. 2
      20:12 they had taken the boy away alive 2
      25:19 who had died, but whom Paul asserted to be alive. 2
Rom 6:11 dead to sin and alive to God in Christ Jesus. 2
      7: 3 with another man while her husband is alive. 2
      7: 9 I was once alive apart from the law 2
1Co 15: 6 most of whom are still alive 3
2Co 6: 9 as dying, and see—we are alive; 2
1Th 4:15 that we who are alive, who are left 2
      4:17 Then we who are alive, who are left 2
Heb 9:17 as long as the one who made it is alive. 2
Rev 1:18 I was dead, and see, I am alive forever and ever; 2
      3: 1 you have a name of being alive, but you are dead. 2
      19:20 These two were thrown alive into the lake of fire 2

alive again

1. ἀναζάω, *anazaō, 348*

Lke 15:24 this son of mine was dead and is alive again; 1

all *See also* abound all the more, all *sides*, all *time*, at all, beyond all *measure*, by all *means*, even to all, first of all, go through all, have all one wants, last of all, look all around, lose all sensitivity, no *at* all, not *at* all, once for all

1. Contextual: Not in Greek
2. ἀμφότεροι, *amphoteroi, 317*
3. ἄνθρωπος, *anthrōpos, 476*
4. ἅπας, *hapas, 570*
5. ἀριθμός, *arithmos, 750*
6. ἕκαστος, *hekastos, 1667*
7. λόγος, *logos, 3364*
8. μόνον, *monon, 3667*
9. ὁ, *ho, 3836*
10. ὅλος, *holos, 3910*
11. ὅς, *hos, 4005*
12. ὅσος, *hosos, 4012*
13. ὅσος + ἄν, *hosos + an, 4012 + 323*
14. ὅστις, *hostis, 4015*
15. πάντως, *pantōs, 4122*
16. πᾶς, *pas, 4246*
17. πᾶς + ἄνθρωπος, *pas + anthrōpos, 4246 + 476*
18. τελείως, *teleiōs, 5458*
19. τίς, *tis, 5515*
20. τὶς, *tis, 5516*
21. τοσοῦτος, *tosoutos, 5537*
22. ψυχή, *psychē, 6034*

Mat 1:17 So all the generations from Abraham to David 16
      1:22 All this took place to fulfill what had been spoken 10
      2: 3 he was frightened, and all Jerusalem with him; 16
      2: 4 calling together all the chief priests and scribes 16
      2:16 he sent and killed all the children 16
      3: 5 Then the people of Jerusalem and all Judea 16
      3: 5 to him, and all the region along the Jordan 16
      3:15 proper for us in this way to fulfill all righteousness." 16
      4: 8 showed him all the kingdoms of the world 16

      4: 9 "All these I will give you, if you will fall down 16
      4:24 So his fame spread throughout all Syria 10
      4:24 all Syria, and they brought to him all the sick 16
      5:15 and it gives light to all in the house. 16
      5:18 will pass from the law until all is accomplished 16
      6:29 even Solomon in all his glory was not clothed 16
      8:16 and cured all who were sick. 16
      9:35 Jesus went about all the cities and villages 16
      10:22 you will be hated by all because of my name. 16
      10:30 even the hairs of your head are all counted. 16
      11:13 For all the prophets and the law prophesied 16
      11:28 all you that are weary and are carrying heavy burdens 16
      12:15 Many crowds followed him, and he cured all 16
      12:23 All the crowds were amazed and said 16
      13:32 it is the smallest of all the seeds 16
      13:33 until all of it was leavened." 10
      13:34 Jesus told the crowds all these things in parables; 16
      13:41 collect out of his kingdom all causes of sin 16
      13:44 sells all that he has and buys that field. 16
      13:46 went and sold all that he had and bought it. 16
      13:51 "Have you understood all this?" 16
      13:56 are not all his sisters with us? 16
      13:56 Where then did this man get all this?" 16
      14:20 all ate and were filled; 16
      14:35 and brought all who were sick to him 16
      14:36 and all who touched it were healed. 12
      15:37 all of them ate and were filled; 16
      18:25 his wife and children and all his possessions 16
      18:31 reported to their lord all that had taken place. 16
      18:32 'You wicked slave! I forgave you all that debt 16
      19:20 "I have kept all these; 16
      20: 6 'Why are you standing here idle all day?' 10
      21:12 drove out all who were selling and buying 16
      21:26 for all regard John as a prophet." 16
      22:10 gathered all whom they found, both good and bad; 16
      22:27 Last of all, the woman herself died. 16
      22:28 For all of them had married her." 16
      22:37 love the Lord your God with all your heart 16
      22:37 with all your heart, and with all your soul 10
      22:37 with all your soul, and with all your mind.' 10
      22:40 On these two commandments hang all the law 10
      23: 5 They do all their deeds to be seen by others; 16
      23: 8 you have one teacher, and you are all students. 16
      23:12 All who exalt themselves will be humbled 14
      23:12 all who humble themselves will be exalted. 14
      23:35 so that upon you may come all the righteous blood 16
      23:36 all this will come upon this generation. 16
      24: 2 he asked them, "You see all these, do you not? 16
      24: 2 one stone...all will be thrown down." 11
      24: 8 all this is but the beginning of the birth pangs. 16
      24: 9 hated by all nations because of my name. 16
      24:14 as a testimony to all the nations; 16
      24:30 then all the tribes of the earth will mourn 16
      24:33 So also, when you see all these things 16
      24:34 until all these things have taken place. 16
      24:39 the flood came and swept them all away 4
      24:47 put that one in charge of all his possessions. 16
      25: 5 all of them became drowsy and slept. 16
      25: 7 Then all those bridesmaids got up 16
      25:29 For to all those who have, more will be given 16
      25:31 all the angels with him 16
      25:32 All the nations will be gathered before him 16
      26:27 "Drink from it, all of you; 16
      26:31 Jesus said to them, "You will all become deserters 16
      26:33 "Though all become deserters because of you 16
      26:35 And so said all the disciples. 16
      26:52 all who take the sword will perish by the sword. 16
      26:56 But all this has taken place 10
      26:56 Then all the disciples deserted him and fled. 16
      26:70 he denied it before all of them, saying 16
      27: 1 all the chief priests and the elders 16
      27:22 All of them said, "Let him be crucified!" 16
      28:18 "All authority in heaven and on earth 16
      28:19 Go therefore and make disciples of all nations 16
Mrk 1: 5 and all the people of Jerusalem 16
      1:27 They were all amazed 4
      1:32 they brought to him all who were sick 16
      2:12 took the mat and went out before all of them; 16
      2:12 so that they were all amazed and glorified God 16
      3: 8 hearing all that he was doing, they came to him 12
      3:10 so that all who had diseases pressed upon him 12

Mrk	4:13 Then how will you understand all the parables?	16
	4:31 the smallest of all the seeds on earth;	16
	4:32 becomes the greatest of all shrubs	16
	5:26 spent all that she had;	16
	5:40 Then he put them all outside	16
	6: 2 "Where did this man get all this?	1
	6:12 and proclaimed that all should repent.	1
	6:30 told him all that they had done and taught.	16
	6:31 "Come away to a deserted place all by yourselves	1
	6:33 they hurried there on foot from all the towns	16
	6:39 he ordered them to get all the people to sit	16
	6:41 he divided the two fish among them all.	16
	6:42 all ate and were filled;	16
	6:50 for they all saw him and were terrified.	16
	6:56 all who touched it were healed.	13
	7: 3 (For the Pharisees, and all the Jews, do not eat	16
	7:14 "Listen to me, all of you, and understand:	16
	7:19 (Thus he declared all foods clean.)	16
	7:23 All these evil things come from within	16
	8:32 He said all this quite openly.	7
	9:35 "Whoever wants to be first must be last of all	16
	9:35 must be last of all and servant of all."	16
	10:20 "Teacher, I have kept all these since my youth."	16
	10:44 wishes to be first…must be slave of all.	16
	11:17 a house of prayer for all the nations'?	16
	11:32 for all regarded John as truly a prophet.	4
	12:22 Last of all the woman herself died.	16
	12:28 "Which commandment is the first of all?"	16
	12:30 shall love the Lord your God with all your heart	10
	12:30 with all your soul, and with all your mind	10
	12:30 with all your soul, and with all your mind	10
	12:30 with all your mind, and with all your strength.'	10
	12:33 and 'to love him with all the heart	10
	12:33 and 'to love him…with all the understanding	10
	12:33 and 'to love him…with all the strength,'	10
	12:33 much more important than all whole burnt offerings	16
	12:43 this poor widow has put in more than all	16
	12:44 For all of them have contributed…abundance;	16
	12:44 everything she had, all she had to live on."	10
	13: 2 all will be thrown down."	11
	13:10 good news must first be proclaimed to all nations.	16
	13:13 you will be hated by all because of my name.	16
	13:37 what I say to you I say to all: Keep awake."	16
	14:23 and all of them drank from it.	16
	14:27 Jesus said to them, "You will all become deserters;	16
	14:29 "Even though all become deserters, I will not."	16
	14:31 all of them said the same.	16
	14:50 All of them deserted him and fled.	16
	14:53 all the chief priests, the elders, and the scribes	16
	14:64 All of them condemned him as deserving death.	16
	16:15 ⟦"Go into all the world and proclaim the good news⟧	4
	16: S ⟦all that had been commanded them they told briefly⟧	16
Lke	1: 6 blamelessly according to all the commandments	16
	1:48 all generations will call me blessed;	16
	1:63 all of them were amazed.	16
	1:65 Fear came over all their neighbors	16
	1:65 all these things were talked about	16
	1:66 All who heard them pondered them and said,	16
	1:71 saved…from the hand of all who hate us.	16
	1:75 before him all our days.	16
	2: 1 all the world should be registered.	16
	2: 3 All went to their own towns to be registered.	16
	2:10 great joy for all the people:	16
	2:18 all who heard it were amazed	16
	2:19 Mary treasured all these words	16
	2:20 for all they had heard and seen	16
	2:31 have prepared in the presence of all peoples	16
	2:38 all who were looking for the redemption of Jerusalem.	16
	2:47 all who heard him were amazed	16
	2:51 His mother treasured all these things in her heart.	16
	3: 3 He went into all the region around the Jordan	16
	3: 6 all flesh shall see the salvation of God.' "	16
	3:15 all were questioning in their hearts concerning	16
	3:16 John answered all of them by saying, "I baptize	16
	3:19 because of all the evil things that Herod had done	16
	3:20 added to them all by shutting up John in prison	16
	3:21 Now when all the people were baptized	4
	4: 5 in an instant all the kingdoms of the world.	16
	4: 6 I will give their glory and all this authority;	4
	4: 7 If you…worship me, it will all be yours."	16
	4:14 spread through all the surrounding country.	10

4:20 The eyes of all in the synagogue were fixed on him.	16
4:22 All spoke well of him	16
4:25 there was a severe famine over all the land;	16
4:28 all in the synagogue were filled with rage.	16
4:36 were all amazed and kept saying to one another	16
4:40 all those who had any who were sick	4
5: 5 "Master, we have worked all night long but	10
5: 9 For he and all who were with him were amazed	16
5:26 Amazement seized all of them	4
6:10 looking around at all of them	16
6:17 a great multitude of people from all Judea	16
6:19 all in the crowd were trying to touch him	16
6:19 power came out from him and healed all of them.	16
6:26 "Woe to you when all speak well of you	17
7: 1 After Jesus had finished all his sayings	16
7:16 Fear seized all of them; and they glorified God	16
7:17 throughout Judea and all the surrounding country	16
7:29 (And all the people who heard this	16
7:35 wisdom is vindicated by all her children."	16
8:37 all the people of the surrounding country	4
8:40 for they were all waiting for him.	16
8:43 though she had spent all she had on physicians	10
8:45 When all denied it, Peter said, "Master	16
8:47 declared in the presence of all the people	16
8:52 were all weeping and wailing for her;	16
9: 1 gave them power and authority over all demons	16
9: 7 ruler heard about all that had taken place	16
9:10 the apostles told Jesus all they had done.	12
9:13 go and buy food for all these people.	16
9:15 They did so and made them all sit down.	4
9:17 all ate and were filled.	16
9:23 he said to them all, "If any want to become	16
9:43 all were astounded at the greatness of God.	16
9:43 everyone was amazed at all that he was doing	16
9:48 least among all of you is the greatest."	16
10:19 authority…over all the power of the enemy;	16
10:27 love the Lord your God with all your heart	10
10:27 with all your soul, and with all your strength	10
10:27 with all your soul, and with all your strength	10
10:27 with all your strength, and with all your mind;	10
10:40 sister has left me to do all the work by myself?	1
11:50 the blood of all the prophets	16
12: 7 But even the hairs of your head are all counted.	16
12:18 there I will store all my grain and my goods.	16
12:27 even Solomon in all his glory was not clothed	16
12:44 put that one in charge of all his possessions.	16
13: 2 worse sinners than all other Galileans?	16
13: 3 unless you repent, you will all perish as	16
13: 4 than all the others living in Jerusalem?	16
13: 5 unless you repent, you will all perish just as	16
13:17 all his opponents were put to shame;	16
13:17 crowd was rejoicing at all the wonderful things	16
13:21 until all of it was leavened."	10
13:27 go away from me, all you evildoers!'	16
13:28 Abraham and Isaac and Jacob and all the prophets	16
14:10 then you will be honored in the presence of all	16
14:11 For all who exalt themselves will be humbled	16
14:18 they all alike began to make excuses.	16
14:29 all who see it will begin to ridicule him	16
14:33 if you do not give up all your possessions.	16
15: 1 Now all the tax collectors and sinners	16
15:13 the younger son gathered all he had	16
15:29 'Listen! For all these years I have been working	21
15:31 and all that is mine is yours.	16
16:14 The Pharisees, who were lovers of money, heard all	16
16:26 Besides all this, between us and you a great chasm	16
17:10 when you have done all that you were ordered	16
17:27 the flood came and destroyed all of them.	16
17:29 destroyed all of them	16
18:12 I give a tenth of all my income.'	16
18:14 all who exalt themselves will be humbled	16
18:14 all who humble themselves will be exalted."	1
18:21 He replied, "I have kept all these since my youth."	16
18:22 Sell all that you own and distribute the money	16
18:34 they understood nothing about all these things;	1
18:43 all the people, when they saw it, praised God.	16
19: 7 All who saw it began to grumble and said,	16
19:26 to all those who have, more will be given;	16
19:37 for all the deeds of power that they had seen	16
19:48 for all the people were spellbound	4
20: 6 all the people will stone us;	4

	20:31 in the same way all seven died childless.	1
	20:38 for to him all of them are alive."	16
	20:45 In the hearing of all the people	16
	21: 3 this poor widow has put in more than all of them;	16
	21: 4 all of them have contributed out of their abundance	16
	21: 4 put in all she had to live on."	16
	21: 6 all will be thrown down."	11
	21:12 before all this occurs, they will arrest you	16
	21:17 You will be hated by all because of my name.	16
	21:22 as a fulfillment of all that is written.	16
	21:24 and be taken away as captives among all nations;	16
	21:29 "Look at the fig tree and all the trees;	16
	21:35 all who live on the face of the whole earth.	16
	21:36 Be alert at all times	16
	21:38 all the people would get up early in the morning	16
	22:31 Satan has demanded to sift all of you like wheat	1
	22:70 All of them asked, "Are you...the Son of God?"	16
	23: 5 teaching throughout all Judea	10
	23:48 when all the crowds who had gathered there	16
	23:49 all his acquaintances, including the women	16
	24: 9 returning from the tomb, they told all this	16
	24: 9 told all this to the eleven and to all the rest.	16
	24:19 before God and all the people	16
	24:21 Yes, and besides all this, it is now the third day	16
	24:25 to believe all that the prophets have declared!	16
	24:27 beginning with Moses and all the prophets	16
	24:27 the things about himself in all the scriptures.	16
	24:47 proclaimed in his name to all nations	16
Jhn	1: 4 and the life was the light of all people.	1
	1: 7 so that all might believe through him.	16
	1:12 to all who received him, who believed in his name	12
	1:16 From his fullness we have all received, grace	16
	2:15 he drove all of them out of the temple	16
	3:20 For all who do evil hate the light	16
	3:26 here he is baptizing, and all are going to him."	16
	3:31 one who comes from above is above all;	16
	3:31 one who comes from heaven is above all.	16
	4:45 had seen all that he had done in Jerusalem	16
	5:20 shows him all that he himself is doing;	16
	5:22 has given all judgment to the Son	16
	5:23 so that all may honor the Son	16
	5:28 all who are in their graves will hear his voice	16
	6:10 so they sat down, about five thousand in all	5
	6:39 lose nothing of all that he has given me	16
	6:40 all who see the Son and believe in him	16
	6:45 'And they shall all be taught by God.'	16
	7:21 performed one work, and all of you are astonished.	16
	8: 2 〚All the people came to him〛	16
	8: 3 making her stand before all of them	1
	10: 4 When he has brought out all his own	16
	10: 8 All who came before me are thieves and bandits;	16
	10:29 What my Father has given me is greater than all	16
	13:10 you are clean, though not all of you."	16
	13:11 this reason he said, "Not all of you are clean."	16
	13:18 I am not speaking of all of you;	16
	14: 9 to him, "Have I been with you all this time	21
	14:26 remind you of all that I have said to you	16
	15:21 they will do all these things to you	16
	16:13 he will guide you into all the truth;	16
	16:15 All that the Father has is mine.	16
	17: 2 you have given him authority over all people	16
	17: 2 to give eternal life to all	16
	17:10 All mine are yours, and yours are mine;	16
	17:21 they may all be one. As you, Father, are in me	16
	18: 4 Jesus, knowing all that was to happen to him	16
	18:20 where all the Jews come together.	16
	19:28 Jesus knew that all was now finished	16
Act	1: 1 I wrote about all that Jesus did and taught	16
	1: 8 in Jerusalem, in all Judea and Samaria	16
	1:14 All...were constantly devoting themselves to prayer	16
	1:18 all his bowels gushed out.	16
	1:19 This became known to all the residents	16
	1:21 during all the time that the Lord Jesus went	16
	2: 1 they were all together in one place.	16
	2: 4 All of them were filled with the Holy Spirit	16
	2: 7 "Are not all these who are speaking Galileans?	4
	2:12 All were amazed and perplexed	16
	2:14 "Men of Judea and all who live in Jerusalem	16
	2:17 I will pour out my Spirit upon all flesh	16
	2:32 of that all of us are witnesses.	16
	2:39 the promise is...for all who are far away	16

2:44 All who believed were together	16
2:45 distribute the proceeds to all, as any had need.	16
2:47 having the goodwill of all the people.	10
3: 9 All the people saw him walking and praising God	16
3:11 all the people ran together to them	16
3:16 in the presence of all of you.	16
3:18 what he had foretold through all the prophets	16
3:24 all the prophets, as many as have spoken	16
3:25 all the families of the earth shall be blessed.'	16
4: 6 and all who were of the high-priestly family.	12
4:10 let it be known to all of you	16
4:10 known...to all the people of Israel	16
4:16 is obvious to all who live in Jerusalem	16
4:21 all of them praised God for what had happened.	16
4:29 servants to speak your word with all boldness	16
4:31 they were all filled with the Holy Spirit	4
4:33 great grace was upon them all.	16
5: 5 great fear seized all who heard of it.	16
5:11 all who heard of these things.	16
5:12 they were all together in Solomon's Portico.	4
5:16 they were all cured.	4
5:17 took action; he and all who were with him	16
5:34 Gamaliel...respected by all the people	16
5:36 all who followed him were dispersed	16
5:37 all who followed him were scattered.	16
6:15 all who sat in the council looked intently at him	16
7:10 rescued him from all his afflictions	16
7:10 ruler over Egypt and over all his household.	10
7:14 all his relatives to come to him, seventy-five in all;	16
7:14 all his relatives to come to him, seventy-five in all;	22
7:22 instructed in all the wisdom of the Egyptians	16
7:57 with a loud shout all rushed together against him.	1
8: 1 all except the apostles were scattered	16
8:10 All of them, from the least to the greatest,	16
8:40 he proclaimed the good news to all the towns	16
9:14 to bind all who invoke your name."	16
9:21 All who heard him were amazed and said	16
9:26 they were all afraid of him	16
9:32 Peter went here and there among all the believers	16
9:35 all the residents of Lydda and Sharon saw him	16
9:39 All the widows stood beside him, weeping	16
9:40 Peter put all of them outside, and then he knelt	16
10: 2 devout man who feared God with all his household;	16
10:33 So now all of us are here	16
10:33 listen to all that the Lord has commanded you to say	16
10:36 peace by Jesus Christ—he is Lord of all.	16
10:38 healing all who were oppressed by the devil	16
10:39 We are witnesses to all that he did	16
10:41 not to all the people but to us	16
10:43 All the prophets testify about him	16
10:44 the Holy Spirit fell upon all who heard the word.	16
11:23 he exhorted them all to remain faithful to the Lord	16
11:28 there would be a severe famine over all the world;	10
12:11 from all that the Jewish people were expecting."	16
13:10 you enemy of all righteousness	16
13:10 full of all deceit and villainy	16
13:22 a man after my heart, who will carry out all my wishes.'	16
13:24 already proclaimed...to all the people of Israel.	16
13:39 set free from all those sins	16
14:15 the earth and the sea and all that is in them.	16
14:16 allowed all the nations to follow their own ways;	16
14:27 related all that God had done with them	12
15: 3 brought great joy to all the believers.	16
15: 4 they reported all that God had done with them.	12
15:12 as they told of all the signs and wonders	12
15:17 so that all other peoples may seek the Lord	1
15:17 all the Gentiles over whom my name has been called.	16
16: 3 for they all knew that his father was a Greek.	4
16:26 immediately all the doors were opened	16
16:28 "Do not harm yourself, for we are all here."	4
16:32 to him and to all who were in his house.	16
17: 7 all acting contrary to the decrees of the emperor	16
17:21 Now all the Athenians and the foreigners	16
17:26 From one ancestor he made all nations	16
17:30 now he commands all people everywhere to repent	16
17:31 of this he has given assurance to all	16
18: 2 Claudius had ordered all Jews to leave Rome	16
18: 8 Crispus...together with all his household;	10
18:17 all of them seized Sosthenes, the official	16
18:23 strengthening all the disciples.	16
19:10 so that all the residents of Asia...heard	16

Act	19:16	mastered them all, and so overpowered them	2
	19:17	this became known to all residents of Ephesus	16
	19:27	that brought all Asia and the world to worship	10
	19:34	for about two hours all of them shouted	16
	20:19	serving the Lord with all humility	16
	20:28	Keep watch over yourselves and over all the flock	16
	20:32	among all who are sanctified.	16
	20:35	In all this I have given you an example	16
	20:36	he knelt down with them all and prayed.	16
	20:37	There was much weeping among them all	16
	21: 5	all of them, with wives and children	16
	21:18	all the elders were present.	16
	21:20	they are all zealous for the law.	16
	21:21	you teach all the Jews living among the Gentiles	16
	21:24	Thus all will know	16
	21:30	Then all the city was aroused	10
	21:31	all Jerusalem was in an uproar.	10
	22: 3	zealous for God, just as all of you are today	16
	22:12	well spoken of by all the Jews living there	16
	22:15	you will be his witness to all the world	16
	23: 8	the Pharisees acknowledge all three.)	2
	24: 5	an agitator among all the Jews	16
	24: 9	asserting that all this was true.	1
	24:16	a clear conscience toward God and all people.	1
	25:24	"King Agrippa and all here present with us	16
	25:26	Therefore I have brought him before all of you	1
	26: 2	against all the accusations of the Jews	16
	26: 3	you are especially familiar with all the customs	16
	26: 4	"All the Jews know my way of life from my youth	16
	26:11	punishing them often in all the synagogues	16
	26:14	When we had all fallen to the ground	16
	26:29	not only you but also all who are listening	16
	27:20	all hope of our being saved was…abandoned.	16
	27:24	God has granted safety to all those who are sailing	16
	27:33	Paul urged all of them to take some food, saying	4
	27:35	giving thanks to God in the presence of all	16
	27:36	Then all of them were encouraged	16
	27:37	(We were in all two hundred seventy-six persons	16
	27:44	so it was that all were brought safely to land.	16
	28: 2	they kindled a fire and welcomed all of us	16
	28:10	they put on board all the provisions we needed.	1
	28:30	welcomed all who came to him	16
	28:31	teaching…with all boldness and without hindrance.	16
Rom	1: 5	among all the Gentiles for the sake of his name	16
	1: 7	To all God's beloved in Rome	16
	1: 8	I thank my God through Jesus Christ for all of you	16
	1:18	against all ungodliness and wickedness of those	16
	2:12	All who have sinned apart from the law	12
	2:12	and all who have sinned under the law	12
	2:16	God…will judge the secret thoughts of all.	3
	3: 9	all, both Jews and Greeks, are under…sin	16
	3:12	All have turned aside	16
	3:22	faith in Jesus Christ for all who believe.	16
	3:23	since all have sinned and fall short of the glory	16
	4:11	to make him the ancestor of all who believe	16
	4:16	and be guaranteed to all his descendants	16
	4:16	Abraham (for he is the father of all of us	16
	5:12	death spread to all because all have sinned—	17
	5:12	death spread to all because all have sinned—	16
	5:18	one man's trespass led to condemnation for all	17
	5:18	leads to justification and life for all.	17
	6: 3	all of us who have been baptized into Christ	12
	8:14	For all who are led by the Spirit of God	12
	8:32	not withhold his own Son, but gave him up for all	16
	8:36	we are being killed all day long;	10
	8:37	No, in all these things we are more	16
	8:39	nor depth, nor anything else in all creation	1
	9: 5	Messiah, who is over all, God blessed forever.	16
	9: 6	For not all Israelites truly belong to Israel	16
	9: 7	and not all of Abraham's children	16
	9:10	Nor is that all; something similar happened	8
	9:17	so that my name may be proclaimed in all the earth."	16
	10:12	the same Lord is Lord of all	16
	10:12	and is generous to all who call on him	16
	10:16	But not all have obeyed the good news;	16
	10:18	"Their voice has gone out to all the earth	16
	10:21	"All day long I have held out my hands	10
	11:26	so all Israel will be saved; as it is written	16
	11:32	For God has imprisoned all in disobedience	16
	11:32	so that he may be merciful to all.	16
	12: 4	and not all the members have the same function	16
	12:17	take thought for what is noble in the sight of all.	17
	12:18	If it is possible…live peaceably with all.	17
	13: 7	Pay to all what is due them	16
	14: 5	while others judge all days to be alike.	16
	14: 5	Let all be fully convinced in their own minds.	6
	14:10	For we will all stand before the judgment seat	16
	15:11	and again, "Praise the Lord, all you Gentiles	16
	15:11	and let all the peoples praise him";	16
	15:13	the God of hope fill you with all joy and peace	16
	15:14	filled with all knowledge, and able to instruct	16
	15:33	The God of peace be with all of you. Amen.	16
	16: 4	give thanks, but also all the churches of the Gentiles.	16
	16:15	Greet…all the saints who are with them.	16
	16:16	All the churches of Christ greet you.	16
	16:19	For while your obedience is known to all	16
	16:26	is made known to all the Gentiles	16
1Co	1: 2	together with all those who in every place	16
	1:10	that all of you be in agreement	16
	3:22	the present or the future—all belong to you	16
	5:10	not at all meaning the immoral of this world	15
	7: 7	I wish that all were as I myself am.	17
	7:16	Wife, for all you know	19
	7:16	Husband, for all you know	19
	7:17	This is my rule in all the churches.	16
	8: 1	we know that "all of us possess knowledge."	16
	9:19	For though I am free with respect to all	16
	9:19	I have made myself a slave to all	16
	9:23	I do it all for the sake of the gospel	16
	9:24	in a race the runners all compete	16
	10: 1	our ancestors were all under the cloud	16
	10: 1	all passed through the sea	16
	10: 2	all were baptized into Moses in the cloud	16
	10: 3	all ate the same spiritual food	16
	10: 4	all drank the same spiritual drink.	16
	10:17	for we all partake of the one bread.	16
	11:29	For all who eat and drink	9
	12: 6	the same God who activates all of them in everyone.	16
	12:11	All these are activated by one and the same Spirit	16
	12:12	all the members of the body, though many, are one	16
	12:13	in the one Spirit we were all baptized	16
	12:13	were all made to drink of one Spirit.	16
	12:19	all were a single member, where would the body be?	16
	12:26	If one member suffers, all suffer together	16
	12:26	if one member is honored, all rejoice together	16
	12:29	Are all apostles? Are all prophets?	16
	12:29	Are all apostles? Are all prophets?	16
	12:29	Are all teachers? Do all work miracles?	16
	12:29	Are all teachers? Do all work miracles?	16
	12:30	Do all possess gifts of healing?	16
	12:30	Do all speak in tongues? Do all interpret?	16
	12:30	Do all speak in tongues? Do all interpret?	16
	13: 2	and understand all mysteries and all knowledge	16
	13: 2	and understand all mysteries and all knowledge	16
	13: 2	if I have all faith, so as to remove mountains	16
	13: 3	If I give away all my possessions	16
	14: 5	Now I would like all of you to speak in tongues	16
	14:18	I speak in tongues more than all of you;	16
	14:23	church comes together and all speak in tongues	16
	14:24	if all prophesy	16
	14:24	outsider who enters is reproved by all	16
	14:24	called to account by all.	16
	14:31	For you can all prophesy one by one	16
	14:31	so that all may learn and all be encouraged.	16
	14:31	so that all may learn and all be encouraged.	16
	14:33	(As in all the churches of the saints	16
	15: 7	he appeared to James, then to all the apostles.	16
	15: 8	Last of all, as to one untimely born	16
	15:19	we are of all people most to be pitied.	16
	15:22	for as all die in Adam	16
	15:22	so all will be made alive in Christ.	16
	15:25	until he has put all his enemies under his feet.	16
	15:28	so that God may be all in all.	16
	15:28	so that God may be all in all.	16
	15:39	Not all flesh is alike	16
	15:51	We will not all die	16
	15:51	but we will all be changed	16
	16:14	Let all that you do be done in love.	16
	16:20	All the brothers and sisters send greetings.	16
	16:24	My love be with all of you in Christ Jesus.	16
2Co	1: 1	including all the saints throughout Achaia:	16
	1: 3	Father of mercies and the God of all consolation	16

	1: 4	who consoles us in all our affliction	16
	2: 3	I am confident about all of you	16
	2: 3	that my joy would be the joy of all of you.	16
	2: 5	not to exaggerate it—to all of you.	16
	3: 2	to be known and read by all;	17
	3:18	all of us, with unveiled faces, seeing the glory	16
	5:10	For all of us must appear before the judgment seat	16
	5:14	we are convinced that one has died for all;	16
	5:14	therefore all have died.	16
	5:15	he died for all, so that those who live	16
	5:18	All this is from God, who reconciled us	16
	7: 4	I am overjoyed in all our affliction.	16
	7:13	his mind has been set at rest by all of you.	16
	7:15	as he remembers the obedience of all of you	16
	8:18	the brother who is famous among all the churches	16
	9:13	your sharing with them and with all others	16
	11:28	my anxiety for all the churches.	16
	13: 2	who sinned previously and all the others	16
	13:12	All the saints greet you.	16
	13:13	communion of the Holy Spirit be with all of you.	16
Gal	1: 2	all the members of God's family who are with me	16
	2:14	I said to Cephas before them all	16
	3: 8	saying, "All the Gentiles shall be blessed in you."	16
	3:10	all who rely on the works of the law are under a curse;	12
	3:26	for in Christ Jesus you are all children of God	16
	3:28	for all of you are one in Christ Jesus.	16
	4: 1	though they are the owners of all the property;	16
	6: 4	All must test their own work;	6
	6: 5	For all must carry their own loads.	6
	6: 6	share in all good things with their teacher.	16
	6:10	opportunity, let us work for the good of all	16
Eph	1: 8	With all wisdom and insight	16
	1:15	your love toward all the saints	16
	1:21	far above all rule and authority and power	16
	1:23	the fullness of him who fills all in all.	16
	1:23	the fullness of him who fills all in all.	16
	2: 3	All of us once lived among them	16
	3: 8	Although I am the very least of all the saints,	16
	3:18	the power to comprehend, with all the saints	16
	3:19	you may be filled with all the fullness of God.	16
	3:20	abundantly far more than all we can ask or imagine	16
	3:21	to him be glory…to all generations	16
	4: 2	with all humility and gentleness	16
	4: 6	one God and Father of all, who is above all	16
	4: 6	who is above all and through all and in all.	16
	4: 6	who is above all and through all and in all.	16
	4: 6	who is above all and through all and in all.	16
	4:10	who ascended far above all the heavens	16
	4:13	until all of us come to the unity of the faith	16
	4:25	let all of us speak the truth to our neighbors	6
	4:31	Put away from you all bitterness and wrath	16
	4:31	wrangling and slander, together with all malice	16
	5: 9	fruit of the light is found in all that is good	16
	6:16	With all of these, take the shield of faith	16
	6:16	able to quench all the flaming arrows of the evil one.	16
	6:18	Pray in the Spirit at all times	16
	6:18	in supplication for all the saints.	16
	6:24	Grace be with all who have an undying love	16
Php	1: 1	To all the saints in Christ Jesus	16
	1: 4	in every one of my prayers for all of you	16
	1: 7	right for me to think this way about all of you	16
	1: 7	all of you share in God's grace with me	16
	1: 8	For God is my witness, how I long for all of you	16
	1:20	that by my speaking with all boldness,	16
	1:25	I will remain and continue with all of you	16
	2:17	I am glad and rejoice with all of you	16
	2:21	All of them are seeking their own interests	16
	2:26	for he has been longing for all of you	16
	2:29	Welcome him then in the Lord with all joy	16
	4: 7	the peace of God, which surpasses all understanding	16
	4:12	In any and all circumstances	16
	4:22	All the saints greet you	16
Col	1: 4	the love that you have for all the saints	16
	1: 9	knowledge of God's will in all spiritual wisdom	16
	1:11	May you be made strong with all the strength	16
	1:15	the firstborn of all creation;	16
	1:19	in him all the fullness of God was pleased to dwell	16
	1:28	teaching everyone in all wisdom	16
	1:29	For this I toil and struggle with all the energy	1
	2: 1	for all who have not seen me face to face	12
	2: 2	so that they may have all the riches of assured	16

	2: 3	in whom are hidden all the treasures of wisdom	16
	2:13	when he forgave us all our trespasses	16
	2:22	All these regulations refer to things that perish	16
	3:11	Christ is all and in all!	16
	3:11	Christ is all and in all!	16
	3:14	Above all, clothe yourselves with love	16
	3:16	teach and admonish one another in all wisdom;	16
	4: 7	Tychicus will tell you all the news about me;	16
1Th	1: 2	We always give thanks to God for all of you	16
	1: 7	you became an example to all the believers	16
	3: 7	during all our distress and persecution	16
	3: 9	for all the joy that we feel before our God	16
	3:12	abound in love for one another and for all,	16
	3:13	the coming of our Lord Jesus with all his saints.	16
	4:10	indeed you do love all the brothers and sisters	16
	5: 5	for you are all children of light	16
	5:14	help the weak, be patient with all of them.	16
	5:15	always seek to do good to one another and to all.	16
	5:18	give thanks in all circumstances;	16
	5:26	Greet all the brothers and sisters with a holy kiss.	16
	5:27	that this letter be read to all of them.	16
2Th	1: 4	and faith during all your persecutions	16
	1:10	marveled at on that day among all who have believed	16
	2: 9	Satan, who uses all power, signs, lying wonders	16
	2:12	so that all who have not believed the truth	16
	3: 2	for not all have faith.	16
	3:16	Lord of peace himself give you peace…in all ways	16
	3:16	The Lord be with all of you.	16
	3:18	The grace of our Lord Jesus Christ be with all of you.	16
1Ti	2: 1	First of all, then, I urge that…	16
	2: 2	for kings and all who are in high positions	16
	2: 2	peaceable life in all godliness and dignity.	16
	2: 6	who gave himself a ransom for all	16
	4:10	the living God, who is the Savior of all people	16
	4:15	so that all may see your progress.	16
	5:20	rebuke them in the presence of all	16
	6: 1	all who are under the yoke of slavery	12
	6: 1	regard their masters as worthy of all honor	16
	6:11	as for you, man of God, shun all this;	1
2Ti	1:15	all who are in Asia have turned away from me	16
	2:21	All who cleanse themselves of the things	20
	3:11	Yet the Lord rescued me from all of them.	16
	3:12	Indeed, all…will be persecuted.	16
	3:16	All scripture is inspired by God	16
	4: 8	also to all who have longed for his appearing.	16
	4:16	but all deserted me.	16
	4:17	all the Gentiles might hear it.	16
	4:21	and Claudia and all the brothers and sisters.	16
Tit	2: 7	in all respects a model of good works	16
	2:11	has appeared, bringing salvation to all,	16
	2:14	that he might redeem us from all iniquity	16
	2:15	exhort and reprove with all authority.	16
	3:15	All who are with me send greetings to you.	16
	3:15	Grace be with all of you.	16
Phm	1: 5	I hear of your love for all the saints	16
	1: 6	may become effective when you perceive all the good	16
Heb	1: 6	he says, "Let all God's angels worship him."	16
	1:11	they will all wear out like clothing;	16
	1:14	Are not all angels spirits in the divine service,	16
	2:11	those who are sanctified all have one Father.	16
	2:15	free those who all their lives were held in slavery	16
	3: 2	just as Moses also "was faithful in all God's house."	10
	3: 5	Now Moses was faithful in all God's house	10
	3:16	Was it not all those who left Egypt	16
	4: 4	God rested on the seventh day from all his works."	16
	4:13	all are naked and laid bare to the eyes of the one	16
	5: 9	the source of…salvation for all who obey him	16
	6:16	an oath given as confirmation puts an end to all dispute.	16
	8:11	'Know the Lord,' for they shall all know me	16
	9:19	had been told to all the people by Moses	16
	9:19	sprinkled both the scroll itself and all the people	16
	9:21	both the tent and all the vessels used in worship.	16
	10:25	all the more as you see the Day approaching.	21
	11:13	All of these died in faith	16
	11:39	all these, though they were commended for their faith	16
	12: 8	discipline in which all children share	16
	12:23	God the judge of all	16
	13: 4	Let marriage be held in honor by all	16
	13:24	Greet all your leaders and all the saints.	16
	13:24	Greet all your leaders and all the saints.	16
	13:25	Grace be with all of you.	16

Jas	1: 5	ask God, who gives to all generously	16
	1:21	rid yourselves of all sordidness and rank growth	16
	2:10	has become accountable for all of it.	16
	3: 2	For all of us make many mistakes.	4
	4:16	boast in your arrogance; all such boasting is evil.	16
	5:12	Above all, my beloved, do not swear	16
1Pe	1:13	set all your hope on the grace that Jesus Christ	18
	1:15	be holy yourselves in all your conduct;	16
	1:24	For "All flesh is like grass	16
	1:24	and all its glory like the flower of grass.	16
	2: 1	Rid yourselves…of all malice, and all guile	16
	2: 1	Rid yourselves…of all malice, and all guile	16
	2: 1	Rid yourselves, therefore, of…all slander.	16
	2:18	Slaves, accept the authority…with all deference	16
	3: 8	Finally, all of you, have unity of spirit, sympathy	16
	4: 8	Above all, maintain constant love	16
	5: 5	all of you must clothe yourselves with humility	16
	5: 7	Cast all your anxiety on him	16
	5: 9	your brothers and sisters in all the world	1
	5:10	the God of all grace, who has called you	16
	5:14	Peace to all of you who are in Christ.	16
2Pe	3: 9	but all to come to repentance.	16
	3:11	Since all these things are to be dissolved in this way	16
	3:16	speaking of this as he does in all his letters.	16
1Jn	1: 7	blood of Jesus his Son cleanses us from all sin.	16
	1: 9	and cleanse us from all unrighteousness.	16
	2:16	for all that is in the world	16
	2:20	and all of you have knowledge.	16
	3: 3	all who have this hope in him purify themselves	16
	3:10	all who do not do what is right are not from God	16
	3:15	All who hate a brother or sister are murderers	16
	3:24	All who obey his commandments abide in him	9
	5:17	All wrongdoing is sin	16
2Jn	1: 1	and not only I but also all who know the truth	16
3Jn	1: 2	Beloved, I pray that all may go well with you	16
Jde	1:15	to execute judgment on all, and to convict everyone	16
	1:15	to convict everyone of all the deeds	16
	1:15	all the harsh things that ungodly sinners have spoken	16
	1:25	before all time and now and forever. Amen.	16
Rev	1: 7	on his account all the tribes of the earth will wail.	16
	2:23	And all the churches will know that I am the one	16
	5: 6	seven spirits of God sent out into all the earth.	16
	5:13	every creature…and all that is in them, singing	16
	7: 9	multitude…from every nation, from all tribes	1
	7:11	all the angels stood around the throne	16
	8: 3	prayers of all the saints on the golden altar	16
	8: 7	and all green grass was burned up.	16
	11:18	all who fear your name, both small and great	1
	12: 5	who is to rule all the nations with a rod of iron	16
	13: 8	all the inhabitants of the earth will worship it	16
	13:12	exercises all the authority of the first beast	16
	13:13	making fire come down…in the sight of all;	3
	13:16	Also it causes all…to be marked	16
	14: 8	She has made all nations drink of the wine	16
	15: 4	All nations will come and worship before you	16
	18: 3	For all the nations have drunk of the wine	16
	18:12	all kinds of scented wood, all articles of ivory	16
	18:12	all articles of costly wood, bronze, iron,	16
	18:14	all your dainties and your splendor are lost to you	16
	18:17	And all shipmasters and seafarers, sailors	16
	18:17	sailors and all whose trade is on the sea	12
	18:19	all who had ships at sea grew rich by her wealth!	16
	18:23	and all nations were deceived by your sorcery.	16
	18:24	blood…of all who have been slaughtered on earth."	16
	19: 5	"Praise our God, all you his servants	16
	19: 5	his servants, and all who fear him, small and great."	1
	19:17	with a loud voice he called to all the birds	16
	19:18	flesh of all, both free and slave,	16
	19:21	and all the birds were gorged with their flesh.	16
	20:13	all were judged according to what they had done.	6
	21: 8	as for…sorcerers, the idolaters, and all liars	16
	22:21	The grace of the Lord Jesus be with all	16

above all

1. μάλιστα, *malista, 3436*

2Ti	4:13	also the books, and above all the parchments.	1

all along

1. πάλαι, *palai, 4093*

2Co	12:19	Have you been thinking all along	1

all around

1. κυκλόθεν, *kyklothen, 3239*

Rev	4: 8	are full of eyes all around and inside	1

all at once

1. ἐξαίφνης, *exaiphnēs, 1978*

Lke	9:39	a spirit seizes him, and all at once he shrieks.	1

all kinds

1. πᾶς, *pas, 4246*
2. ποικίλος, *poikilos, 4476*

Mat	5:11	and persecute you and utter all kinds of evil	1
	23:27	bones of the dead and of all kinds of filth.	1
Lke	11:42	you tithe mint and rue and herbs of all kinds	1
	12:15	Be on your guard against all kinds of greed;	1
Act	10:12	In it were all kinds of four-footed creatures	1
Rom	7: 8	sin…produced in me all kinds of covetousness.	1
1Ti	6:10	the love of money is a root of all kinds of evil	1
2Ti	3: 6	swayed by all kinds of desires	2
Heb	13: 9	carried away by all kinds of strange teachings;	2
Rev	18:12	all kinds of scented wood, all articles of ivory	1

all mortals

1. πᾶς, *pas, 4246*

Act	17:25	he himself gives to all mortals life and breath	1

all people

1. ἕκαστος, *hekastos, 1667*
2. πᾶς, *pas, 4246*

Jhn	2:24	because he knew all people	2
	12:32	I…will draw all people to myself."	2
1Co	9:22	I have become all things to all people	2
1Pe	1:17	If you invoke as Father the one who judges all people	1

all right

1. σῴζω, *sōzō, 5392*

Jhn	11:12	if he has fallen asleep, he will be all right."	1

all the more

1. μᾶλλον, *mallon, 3437*
2. μείζων, *meizōn, 3505*
3. περισσοτέρως, *perissoterōs, 4359*
4. περισσῶς, *perissōs, 4360*

Mat	27:23	they shouted all the more	4
Mrk	15:14	they shouted all the more, "Crucify him!"	4
Jhn	5:18	the Jews were seeking all the more to kill him	1
2Co	1:12	and all the more toward you.	3
	7:15	his heart goes out all the more to you	3
	12: 9	I will boast all the more gladly of my weaknesses	1
1Ti	6: 2	rather they must serve them all the more	1
Heb	13:19	I urge you all the more to do this	3
Jas	4: 6	But he gives all the more grace; therefore it says	2
2Pe	1:10	all the more eager to confirm your call and election	1

all the way

1. ἄχρι, *achri, 948*

2Co	10:14	we were the first to come all the way to you	1

all things

1. Contextual: Not in Greek
2. ἅπας, *hapas, 570*
3. πᾶς, *pas, 4246*

Mat	6:32	the Gentiles who strive for all these things;	3
	6:32	your heavenly Father knows that you need all these things	2
	6:33	all these things will be given to you as well.	3
	11:27	All things have been handed over to me by my Father;	3
	17:11	Elijah is…coming and will restore all things;	3
	19:26	but for God all things are possible."	3
	19:28	at the renewal of all things, when the Son of Man	1
	26: 1	Jesus had finished saying all these things	3
Mrk	9:12	"Elijah is indeed coming first to restore all things.	3
	9:23	All things can be done for the one who believes."	3
	10:27	for God all things are possible."	3
	13: 4	all these things are about to be accomplished?"	3
	13:30	until all these things have taken place.	3
	14:36	"Abba, Father, for you all things are possible;"	3
Lke	7:18	disciples of John reported all these things	3
	10:22	All things have been handed over to me by my Father;	3

	12:30 the nations...that strive after all these things	3
	21:32 until all things have taken place.	3
	21:36 may have the strength to escape all these things	3
	24:14 talking with each other about all these things	3
Jhn	1: 3 All things came into being through him	3
	3:35 and has placed all things in his hands.	3
	4:25 "When he comes, he will proclaim all things to us."	2
	13: 3 the Father had given all things into his hands	3
	16:30 Now we know that you know all things	3
Act	2:44 and had all things in common;	2
	7:50 Did not my hand make all these things?'	3
	17:25 gives to all mortals life and breath and all things.	3
Rom	8:28 We know that all things work together for good	3
	11:36 and through him and to him are all things.	3
1Co	2:15 Those who are spiritual discern all things	3
	3:21 For all things are yours	3
	4:13 the dregs of all things, to this very day.	3
	6:12 "All things are lawful for me,"	3
	6:12 not all things are beneficial.	3
	6:12 "All things are lawful for me,"	3
	8: 6 from whom are all things and for whom we exist	3
	8: 6 through whom are all things	3
	9:22 I have become all things to all people	3
	9:25 exercise self-control in all things;	3
	10:23 "All things are lawful,"	3
	10:23 not all things are beneficial.	3
	10:23 "All things are lawful,"	3
	10:23 not all things build up.	3
	11:12 but all things come from God.	3
	13: 7 It bears all things, believes all things	3
	13: 7 It bears all things, believes all things	3
	13: 7 hopes all things, endures all things.	3
	13: 7 hopes all things, endures all things.	3
	14:26 Let all things be done for building up.	3
	14:40 all things should be done decently and in order.	3
	15:27 For "God has put all things in subjection	3
	15:27 "All things are put in subjection,"	3
	15:27 one who put all things in subjection under him.	3
	15:28 When all things are subjected to him	3
	15:28 one who put all things in subjection under him	3
2Co	11: 6 in all things we have made this evident to you.	3
Gal	3:10 does not observe and obey all the things written	3
	3:22 imprisoned all things under the power of sin	3
Eph	1:10 to gather up all things in him	3
	1:11 the purpose of him who accomplishes all things	3
	1:22 he has put all things under his feet	3
	1:22 the head over all things for the church	3
	3: 9 hidden for ages in God who created all things;	3
	4:10 so that he might fill all things.)	3
Php	2:14 Do all things without murmuring and arguing	3
	3: 8 I have suffered the loss of all things	3
	3:21 to make all things subject to himself.	3
	4:13 I can do all things through him who strengthens me.	3
Col	1:16 in him all things in heaven and on earth were created	3
	1:16 all things have been created through him	3
	1:17 He himself is before all things	3
	1:17 in him all things hold together.	3
	1:20 God was pleased to reconcile to himself all things	3
	3: 8 now you must get rid of all such things—anger,	3
1Th	4: 6 the Lord is an avenger in all these things	3
1Ti	3:11 temperate, faithful in all things.	3
	6:13 God, who gives life to all things	3
2Ti	2: 7 will give you understanding in all things.	3
Tit	1:15 To the pure all things are pure	3
Heb	1: 2 a Son, whom he appointed heir of all things	3
	1: 3 sustains all things by his powerful word.	3
	2: 8 subjecting all things under their feet."	3
	2: 8 Now in subjecting all things to them	3
	2:10 for whom and through whom all things exist	3
	3: 4 but the builder of all things is God.)	3
	13:18 desiring to act honorably in all things.	3
1Pe	4: 7 The end of all things is near;	3
	4:11 so that God may be glorified in all things	3
2Pe	3: 4 all things continue as they were	3
1Jn	2:27 as his anointing teaches you about all things	3
Rev	4:11 for you created all things	3
	21: 5 "See, I am making all things new."	3

all this

1. τοσοῦτος, *tosoutos, 5537*

Rev	18:17 in one hour all this wealth has been laid waste!"	1

all together

1. παμπληθεί, *pamplēthei, 4101*

Lke	23:18 all shouted out together, "Away with this fellow!	1

allegory

1. ἀλληγορέω, *allēgoreō, 251*

Gal	4:24 Now this is an allegory:	1

allot

1. διαιρέω, *diaireō, 1349*
2. λαγχάνω, *lanchanō, 3275*
3. ὁρίζω, *horizō, 3988*

Act	1:17 allotted his share in this ministry."	2
	17:26 he allotted the times of their existence	3
1Co	12:11 who allots to each one individually	1

allow

1. ἀφίημι, *aphiēmi, 918*
2. δίδωμι, *didōmi, 1443*
3. ἐάω, *eaō, 1572*
4. ἔξεστι, *exesti, 2003*
5. ἐπιτρέπω, *epitrepō, 2205*
6. καθήκω, *kathēkō, 2763*

Mat	19: 8 Moses allowed you to divorce your wives	5
	20:15 Am I not allowed to do what I choose	4
Mrk	5:37 He allowed no one to follow him except Peter	1
	10: 4 "Moses allowed a man to write a certificate	5
	11: 6 and they allowed them to take it.	1
	11:16 he would not allow anyone to carry anything	1
Lke	4:41 would not allow them to speak	3
	8:51 he did not allow anyone to enter with him	1
Act	10:40 allowed him to appear	2
	14:16 allowed all the nations to follow their own ways;	3
	16: 7 the Spirit of Jesus did not allow them;	3
	22:22 he should not be allowed to live."	6
	27: 3 allowed him to go to his friends to be cared for.	5
	28: 4 justice has not allowed him to live."	3
	28:16 Paul was allowed to live by himself	5
Rev	9: 5 were allowed to torture them for five months	2
	13: 5 allowed to exercise authority for...months.	2
	13: 7 Also it was allowed to make war on the saints	2
	13:14 and by the signs that it is allowed to perform	2
	13:15 allowed to give breath to the image of the beast	2
	16: 8 and it was allowed to scorch people with fire;	2

allowance of food

1. σιτομέτριον, *sitometrion, 4991*
2. τροφή, *trophē, 5575*

Mat	24:45 to give the other slaves their allowance of food	2
Lke	12:42 to give them their allowance of food	1

almighty

1. παντοκράτωρ, *pantokratōr, 4120*

2Co	6:18 be my sons and daughters, says the Lord Almighty."	1
Rev	1: 8 who is and who was and who is to come, the Almighty.	1
	4: 8 sing, "Holy, holy, holy, the Lord God the Almighty	1
	11:17 singing, "We give you thanks, Lord God Almighty	1
	15: 3 amazing are your deeds, Lord God the Almighty!	1
	16: 7 the altar respond, "Yes, O Lord God, the Almighty	1
	16:14 for battle on the great day of God the Almighty.	1
	19: 6 For the Lord our God the Almighty reigns.	1
	19:15 of the fury of the wrath of God the Almighty.	1
	21:22 for its temple is the Lord God the Almighty	1

almost

1. μέλλω, *mellō, 3516*
2. πρός, *pros, 4639*
3. σχεδόν, *schedon, 5385*

Lke	24:29 almost evening and the day is now nearly over."	2
Act	13:44 The next sabbath almost the whole city gathered	3
	19:26 in almost the whole of Asia	3
	21:27 When the seven days were almost completed	1
Heb	9:22 almost everything is purified with blood	3

alms

1. ἐλεημοσύνη, *eleēmosynē, 1797*

Mat	6: 2 "So whenever you give alms, do not sound a trumpet	1
	6: 3 when you give alms, do not let your left hand know	1

Mat	6: 4	so that your alms may be done in secret	1
Lke	11:41	give for alms those things that are within;	1
	12:33	Sell your possessions, and give alms.	1
Act	3: 2	could ask for alms from those entering the temple.	1
	3: 3	he asked them for alms.	1
	3:10	the one who used to sit and ask for alms	1
	10: 2	gave alms generously to the people	1
	10: 4	"Your prayers and your alms have ascended	1
	10:31	your alms have been remembered before God.	1
	24:17	to bring alms to my nation and to offer sacrifices.	1

aloe

1. ἀλόη, *aloē, 264*

Jhn	19:39	came, bringing a mixture of myrrh and aloes	1

alone *See also* leave alone, let alone

1. εἷς, *heis, 1651*
2. κατά + μόνος, *kata + monos, 2848 + 3668*
3. μόνον, *monon, 3667*
4. μόνος, *monos, 3668*

Mat	4: 4	written, 'One does not live by bread alone	4
	14:23	When evening came, he was there alone	4
	17: 8	they saw no one except Jesus himself alone.	4
	18:15	point out the fault when the two of you are alone.	4
Mrk	2: 7	Who can forgive sins but God alone?"	1
	4:10	When he was alone	2
	6:47	he was alone on the land.	4
	10:18	you call me good? No one is good but God alone.	1
Lke	4: 4	"It is written, 'One does not live by bread alone.' "	4
	5:21	Who can forgive sins but God alone?"	4
	9:18	Once when Jesus was praying alone	2
	9:36	When the voice had spoken, Jesus was found alone.	4
	18:19	you call me good? No one is good but God alone.	1
Jhn	5:44	glory that comes from the one who alone is God?	4
	6:22	his disciples had gone away alone.	4
	8: 9	[[Jesus was left alone with the woman]]	4
	8:16	for it is not I alone who judge	4
	8:29	sent me is with me; he has not left me alone	4
	16:32	and you will leave me alone.	4
	16:32	I am not alone because the Father is with me.	4
Rom	4:23	the words…were written not for his sake alone	3
	11: 3	I alone am left, and they are seeking my life."	4
Php	4:15	no church shared with me…except you alone.	4
1Th	3: 1	we decided to be left alone in Athens;	4
1Ti	6:16	It is he alone who has immortality	4
Jas	2:24	justified by works and not by faith alone.	3
Rev	15: 4	who will not fear…For you alone are holy.	4

along *See also* active along with, all along, along the *coast*, bring along, carry along, come along, go along, pass along, region along, ride along, take along, walk along

1. ἅμα, *hama, 275*
2. ἐν, *en, 1877*
3. κατά, *kata, 2848*
4. μετά, *meta, 3552*
5. παρά, *para, 4123*
6. σύν, *syn, 5250*

Mat	12:45	it goes and brings along seven other spirits	4
	13:29	you would uproot the wheat along with them.	1
	15:29	he passed along the Sea of Galilee	5
Mrk	1:16	Jesus passed along the Sea of Galilee	5
Lke	9:57	As they were going along the road, someone said	2
Act	8:36	As they were going along the road	3
	21:16	disciples from Caesarea also came along	6
	25: 3	planning an ambush to kill him along the way.	3
	26:13	at midday along the road…I saw a light	3

along with

1. καί, *kai, 2779*
2. μετά, *meta, 3552*
3. σύν, *syn, 5250*

Mat	22:16	disciples to him, along with the Herodians	2
	27:41	the chief priests also, along with the scribes	2
Mrk	4:10	those who were around him along with the twelve	3
	15:31	the chief priests also, along with the scribes,	2
Jhn	4:53	he himself believed, along with his whole household.	1
Act	15:25	along with our beloved Barnabas and Paul	3
1Co	11:32	may not be condemned along with the world.	3
2Ti	2:22	along with those who call on the Lord from a pure heart.	2

aloud *See also* cry aloud, read aloud

1. Contextual: Not in Greek

Rev	18:15	fear of her torment, weeping and mourning aloud	1

Alpha

1. ἄλφα, *alpha, 270*

Rev	1: 8	"I am the Alpha and the Omega," says the Lord God	1
	21: 6	I am Alpha and the Omega, the beginning and the end.	1
	22:13	I am the Alpha and the Omega, the first and the last	1

Alphaeus

1. Ἁλφαῖος, *Halphaios, 271*

Mat	10: 3	James son of Alphaeus, and Thaddaeus;	1
Mrk	2:14	walking along, he saw Levi son of Alphaeus	1
	3:18	Matthew, and Thomas, and James son of Alphaeus	1
Lke	6:15	Matthew, and Thomas, and James son of Alphaeus	1
Act	1:13	James son of Alphaeus, and Simon the Zealot	1

already *See also* charge already, here already, proclaim already, suffer already, tell already, word already quoted, work already done

1. Contextual: Not in Greek
2. ἤδη, *ēdē, 2453*
3. παρέρχομαι, *parerchomai, 4216*

Mat	5:28	a woman with lust has already committed	2
	17:12	I tell you that Elijah has already come	2
Mrk	4:37	so that the boat was already being swamped.	2
	11:11	as it was already late	2
	15:44	Pilate wondered if he were already dead;	2
	16: 4	that the stone…had already been rolled back.	1
Lke	11: 7	door has already been locked, and my children	2
	12:49	how I wish it were already kindled!	2
	21:30	know that summer is already near.	2
	22:12	show you a large room upstairs, already furnished.	1
Jhn	3:18	those who do not believe are condemned already	2
	4:36	The reaper is already receiving wages	2
	9:22	the Jews had already agreed	2
	9:27	He answered them, "I have told you already	2
	11:17	Lazarus had already been in the tomb four days.	2
	11:39	"Lord, already there is a stench	2
	13: 2	The devil had already put it into the heart	2
	15: 3	You have already been cleansed by the word	2
	19:33	came to Jesus and saw that he was already dead	2
Act	4: 3	it was already evening.	2
	27: 9	because even the Fast had already gone by	2
Rom	4:19	his own body, which was already as good as dead	2
	15:20	not where Christ has already been named	1
1Co	4: 8	Already you have all you want!	2
	4: 8	Already you have become rich!	2
	5: 3	I have already pronounced judgment	2
	6: 7	to have lawsuits…is already a defeat for you.	2
	7:18	at time of his call already circumcised?	1
2Co	1:14	as you have already understood us in part	1
Gal	1:17	to those who were already apostles before me	1
Eph	3: 2	for surely you have already heard of the commission	1
Php	3:12	Not that I have already obtained this	2
	3:12	or have already reached the goal;	2
1Th	4: 6	just as we have already told you beforehand	1
2Th	2: 7	the mystery of lawlessness is already at work	2
1Ti	5:15	For some have already turned away to follow Satan.	2
2Ti	2:18	claiming that the resurrection has already taken place.	2
	4: 6	I am already being poured out as a libation	2
1Pe	4: 3	You have already spent enough time in doing	3
2Pe	1:12	you know them already and are established in the truth	1
1Jn	2: 8	and the true light is already shining.	2
	4: 3	coming; and now it is already in the world.	2

also Not Indexed

altar *See also* sacrifice on an altar

1. αὐτός, *autos, 899*
2. βωμός, *bōmos, 1117*
3. θυσιαστήριον, *thysiastērion, 2603*

Mat	5:23	So when you are offering your gift at the altar	3
	5:24	leave your gift there before the altar and go;	3
	23:18	'Whoever swears by the altar is bound by nothing	3
	23:18	whoever swears by the gift that is on the altar	1
	23:19	which is greater, the gift or the altar	3
	23:20	So whoever swears by the altar	3

	23:35	murdered between the sanctuary and the altar.	3
Lke	1:11	at the right side of the altar of incense.	3
	11:51	perished between the altar and the sanctuary.	3
Act	17:23	I found among them an altar with the inscription	2
Rom	11: 3	"Lord…they have demolished your altars;	3
1Co	9:13	those who serve at the altar	3
	10:18	who eat the sacrifices partners in the altar?	3
Heb	7:13	from which no one has ever served at the altar.	3
	13:10	We have an altar from which those who officiate	3
Jas	2:21	when he offered his son Isaac on the altar?	3
Rev	6: 9	I saw under the altar the souls of those	3
	8: 3	angel with a golden censer…stood at the altar;	3
	8: 3	prayers of all the saints on the golden altar	3
	8: 5	censer and filled it with fire from the altar	3
	9:13	a voice from the four horns of the golden altar	3
	11: 1	"Come and measure the temple of God and the altar	3
	14:18	Then another angel came out from the altar	3
	16: 7	I heard the altar respond, "Yes, O Lord God,	3

altar of incense

1. θυμιατήριον, *thymiatērion, 2593*

Heb	9: 4	In it stood the golden altar of incense	1

although

1. Contextual: Not in Greek
2. δέ, *de, 1254*
3. εἰ, *ei, 1623*
4. καίπερ, *kaiper, 2788*
5. καίτοιγε, *kaitoige, 2793*

Jhn	4: 2	although it was not Jesus himself…who baptized	5
	12:37	Although he had performed so many signs	1
	20:26	Although the doors were shut	1
Rom	3: 4	Although everyone is a liar, let God be proved true	2
2Co	7:12	So although I wrote to you	3
Eph	3: 8	Although I am the very least of all the saints,	1
Heb	5: 8	Although he was a Son, he learned obedience	4
1Pe	1: 8	Although you have not seen him, you love	1
2Jn	1:12	Although I have much to write to you	1

altogether

1. πᾶς, *pas, 4246*

Act	19: 7	altogether there were about twelve of them.	1

always

1. Contextual: Not in Greek
2. ἀεί, *aei, 107*
3. διά + πᾶς, *dia + pas, 1328 + 4246*
4. πάντοτε, *pantote, 4121*
5. πᾶς, *pas, 4246*
6. πᾶς + ὁ + ἡμέρα, *pas + ho + hēmera, 4246 + 3836 + 2465*

Mat	26:11	For you always have the poor with you	4
	26:11	you will not always have me.	4
	28:20	I am with you always, to the end of the age."	6
Mrk	5: 5	on the mountains he was always howling	3
	14: 7	For you always have the poor with you	4
	14: 7	but you will not always have me.	4
Lke	15:31	father said to him, 'Son, you are always with me	4
	18: 1	their need to pray always and not to lose heart.	4
Jhn	6:34	said to him, "Sir, give us this bread always."	4
	7: 6	your time is always here.	4
	8:29	I always do what is pleasing to him."	4
	11:42	I knew that you always hear me	4
	12: 8	You always have the poor with you	4
	12: 8	but you do not always have me."	4
	18:20	always taught in synagogues and in the temple	4
Act	2:25	'I saw the Lord always before me	3
	24:16	I do my best always to have a clear conscience	3
Rom	1: 9	I remember you always in my prayers	4
1Co	1: 4	I give thanks to my God always for you	4
	15:58	always excelling in the work of the Lord	4
2Co	1:19	not "Yes and No"; but in him it is always "Yes."	1
	2:14	who in Christ always leads us in triumphal procession	4
	4:10	always carrying in the body the death of Jesus	4
	4:11	always being given up to death for Jesus' sake	2
	5: 6	So we are always confident;	4
	6:10	as sorrowful, yet always rejoicing;	2
	9: 8	so that by always having enough of everything	4
Gal	2: 5	the truth of the gospel might always remain	1
Eph	6:18	To that end keep alert and always persevere	5
Php	1:20	Christ will be exalted now as always in my body	4

	2:12	my beloved, just as you have always obeyed	4
	4: 4	Rejoice in the Lord always;	4
Col	1: 3	we always thank God, the Father of our Lord Jesus	4
	4: 6	Let your speech always be gracious	4
	4:12	always wrestling in his prayers on your	4
1Th	1: 2	We always give thanks to God for all of you	4
	3: 6	told us also that you always remember us kindly	4
	5:15	always seek to do good to one another and to all.	4
	5:16	Rejoice always	4
2Th	1: 3	We must always give thanks to God for you	4
	1:11	To this end we always pray for you	4
	2:13	we must always give thanks to God for you	4
2Ti	3: 7	who are always being instructed	4
	4: 5	As for you, always be sober, endure suffering	5
Tit	1:12	"Cretans are always liars, vicious brutes	2
Phm	1: 4	I always thank my God	4
Heb	3:10	'They always go astray in their hearts	2
	7:25	since he always lives to make intercession	4
	12:11	discipline always seems painful rather than pleasant	5
1Pe	3:15	Always be ready to make your defense to anyone	2

amaze

1. ἐξίστημι, *existēmi, 2014*
2. θαμβέω, *thambeō, 2501*
3. θάμβος, *thambos, 2502*
4. θάμβος + περιέχω, *thambos + periechō, 2502 + 4321*
5. θαυμάζω, *thaumazō, 2513*

Mat	8:10	When Jesus heard him, he was amazed	5
	8:27	They were amazed, saying, "What sort of man	5
	9:33	who had been mute spoke; and the crowds were amazed	5
	12:23	All the crowds were amazed and said	1
	15:31	so that the crowd was amazed	5
	21:20	When the disciples saw it, they were amazed,	5
	22:22	When they heard this, they were amazed;	5
	27:14	so that the governor was greatly amazed.	5
Mrk	1:27	They were all amazed	2
	2:12	so that they were all amazed and glorified God	1
	5:20	and everyone was amazed.	5
	6: 6	he was amazed at their unbelief.	5
	10:32	they were amazed	2
	15: 5	so that Pilate was amazed.	5
Lke	1:63	all of them were amazed.	5
	2:18	amazed at what the shepherds told them.	5
	2:33	amazed at what was being said about him.	5
	2:47	who heard him were amazed at his understanding	1
	4:22	amazed at the gracious words	5
	4:36	were all amazed and kept saying to one another	3
	5: 9	For he and all who were with him were amazed	4
	7: 9	When Jesus heard this he was amazed at him	5
	8:25	They were afraid and amazed,	5
	9:43	everyone was amazed at all that he was doing	5
	11:14	mute spoke, and the crowds were amazed.	5
	11:38	The Pharisee was amazed to see	5
	20:26	amazed by his answer, they became silent.	5
	24:12	he went home, amazed at what had happened	5
Act	2: 7	Amazed and astonished, they asked,	1
	2:12	All were amazed and perplexed	1
	4:13	they were amazed	5
	7:31	When Moses saw it, he was amazed at the sight;	5
	8: 9	and amazed the people of Samaria	1
	8:11	for a long time he had amazed them with his magic.	1
	8:13	was amazed when he saw the signs	1
	9:21	All who heard him were amazed and said	1
	12:16	opened the gate, they saw him and were amazed.	1
	13:41	'Look, you scoffers! Be amazed and perish	5
Rev	17: 6	When I saw her, I was greatly amazed.	5
	17: 7	But the angel said to me, "Why are you so amazed?	5
	17: 8	inhabitants…will be amazed when they see the beast	5

amaze utterly

1. ἐκθαυμάζω, *ekthaumazō, 1703*

Mrk	12:17	And they were utterly amazed at him.	1

amazement *See also* overcome with amazement

1. ἔκστασις, *ekstasis, 1749*
2. θαυμάζω, *thaumazō, 2513*

Mrk	16: 8	terror and amazement had seized them;	1
Lke	5:26	Amazement seized all of them	1
Act	3:10	they were filled with wonder and amazement	1
Rev	13: 3	In amazement the whole earth followed the beast.	2

amazing

1. θαυμαστός, *thaumastos, 2515*

Mat 21:42 it is amazing in our eyes'?   1
Mrk 12:11 it is amazing in our eyes'?"   1
Rev 15: 1 another portent in heaven, great and amazing: 1
    15: 3 "Great and amazing are your deeds, Lord God   1

amazing thing

1. θαυμάσιος, *thaumasios, 2514*

Mat 21:15 the amazing things that he did   1

ambassador

1. πρεσβεύω, *presbeuō, 4563*

2Co 5:20 So we are ambassadors for Christ   1
Eph 6:20 for which I am an ambassador in chains.   1

selfish ambition

1. ἐριθεία, *eritheia, 2249*

Php 1:17 the others proclaim Christ out of selfish ambition   1
    2: 3 Do nothing from selfish ambition or conceit   1
Jas 3:14 if you have…selfish ambition in your hearts   1
    3:16 For where there is envy and selfish ambition   1

ambush   *See also* lie in ambush

1. ἐνέδρα, *enedra, 1909*

Act 23:16 the son of Paul's sister heard about the ambush;   1
    25: 3 planning an ambush to kill him along the way.   1

amen

1. ἀμήν, *amēn, 297*

Rom 1:25 the Creator, who is blessed forever! Amen.   1
    9: 5 who is over all, God blessed forever. Amen.   1
    11:36 To him be the glory forever. Amen.   1
    15:33 The God of peace be with all of you. Amen.   1
    16:27 Jesus Christ, to whom be the glory forever! Amen.   1
1Co 14:16 say the "Amen" to your thanksgiving   1
2Co 1:20 it is through him that we say the "Amen,"   1
Gal 1: 5 to whom be the glory forever and ever. Amen.   1
    6:18 be with your spirit, brothers and sisters. Amen.   1
Eph 3:21 to all generations, forever and ever. Amen.   1
Php 4:20 glory forever and ever. Amen.   1
1Ti 1:17 be honor and glory forever and ever. Amen.   1
    6:16 to him be honor and eternal dominion. Amen.   1
2Ti 4:18 To him be the glory forever and ever. Amen.   1
Heb 13:21 to whom be the glory forever and ever. Amen.   1
1Pe 4:11 glory and the power forever and ever. Amen.   1
    5:11 To him be the power forever and ever. Amen.   1
2Pe 3:18 glory both now and to the day of eternity. Amen.   1
Jde 1:25 before all time and now and forever. Amen.   1
Rev 1: 6 glory and dominion forever and ever. Amen.   1
    1: 7 Look! He is coming…So it is to be. Amen.   1
    3:14 words of the Amen, the faithful and true witness   1
    5:14 the four living creatures said, "Amen!"   1
    7:12 singing, "Amen! Blessing and glory and wisdom   1
    7:12 might be to our God forever and ever! Amen."   1
    19: 4 worshiped God…saying, "Amen. Hallelujah!"   1
    22:20 I am coming soon." Amen. Come, Lord Jesus!   1
    22:21 grace…be with all the saints. Amen.   1

amethyst

1. ἀμέθυστος, *amethystos, 287*

Rev 21:20 the eleventh jacinth, the twelfth amethyst.   1

Aminadab

1. Ἀμιναδάβ, *Aminadab, 300*

Mat 1: 4 Aram the father of Aminadab   1
    1: 4 Aminadab the father of Nahshon   1

Amminadab

1. Ἀμιναδάβ, *Aminadab, 300*

Lke 3:33 son of Amminadab, son of Admin   1

among   *See also* from among, walk among

1. ἀνά + μέσος, *ana + mesos, 324 + 3545*
2. διά, *dia, 1328*
3. εἰς, *eis, 1650*
4. εἰς + ὁ + μέσος, *eis + ho + mesos, 1650 + 3836 + 3545*
5. ἐκ, *ek, 1666*

6. ἐν, *en, 1877*
7. ἐν + μέσος, *en + mesos, 1877 + 3545*
8. ἐντός, *entos, 1955*
9. ἐπί, *epi, 2093*
10. κατά, *kata, 2848*
11. κύκλῳ, *kyklō, 3241*
12. μέσος, *mesos, 3545*
13. μετά, *meta, 3552*
14. παρά, *para, 4123*
15. πρός, *pros, 4639*

Mat 2: 6 are by no means least among the rulers of Judah;   6
    4:23 disease and every sickness among the people.   6
    7: 9 Is there anyone among you who, if your child   5
    10: 5 "Go nowhere among the Gentiles   3
    11:11 Truly I tell you, among those born of women   6
    13: 7 Other seeds fell among thorns   9
    13:22 As for what was sown among thorns   3
    13:25 an enemy came and sowed weeds among the wheat   1
    18: 2 whom he put among them   7
    18:20 I am there among them."   7
    20:26 It will not be so among you;   6
    20:26 whoever wishes to be great among you   6
    20:27 whoever wishes to be first among you   6
    22:25 Now there were seven brothers among us;   14
    26: 5 or there may be a riot among the people."   6
    27:56 Among them were Mary Magdalene   6
    28:15 story is still told among the Jews to this day.   14
Mrk 2: 8 discussing these questions among themselves;   6
    4: 7 Other seed fell among thorns   3
    4:18 others are those sown among the thorns: 3
    5: 3 He lived among the tombs;   6
    5: 5 Night and day among the tombs   6
    6: 4 among their own kin, and in their own house."   6
    6: 6 he went about among the villages teaching.   11
    9:19 how much longer must I be among you?   15
    9:36 he took a little child and put it among them   7
    10:43 it is not so among you;   6
    10:43 whoever wishes to become great among you   6
    10:44 whoever wishes to be first among you   6
    15:31 the scribes, were also mocking him among themselves   15
    15:40 among them were Mary Magdalene…and Salome.   6
Lke 1: 1 that have been fulfilled among us   6
    1:25 the disgrace I have endured among my people."   6
    1:42 "Blessed are you among women   6
    2:14 on earth peace among those whom he favors!"   6
    2:44 they started to look for him among their relatives   6
    2:46 sitting among the teachers   7
    7:16 "A great prophet has risen among us!"   6
    7:28 among those born of women no one is greater   6
    7:49 began to say among themselves   6
    8: 7 Some fell among thorns   7
    8:14 As for what fell among the thorns   3
    9:46 An argument arose among them   6
    9:48 least among all of you is the greatest."   6
    11:11 anyone among you who, if your child asks   5
    17: 7 "Who among you would say to your slave   6
    17:21 in fact, the kingdom of God is among you."   8
    20:14 saw him, they discussed it among themselves   15
    21:24 and be taken away as captives among all nations;   3
    22:17 "Take this and divide it among yourselves;   3
    22:24 A dispute also arose among them   6
    22:26 greatest among you must become like the youngest   6
    22:27 But I am among you as one who serves.   7
    22:37 'And he was counted among the lawless';   13
    22:55 sat down together, Peter sat among them.   12
    24: 5 "Why do you look for the living among the dead?   13
    24:36 Jesus himself stood among them   7
Jhn 1:14 And the Word became flesh and lived among us   6
    1:26 Among you stands one whom you do not know   12
    6: 9 But what are they among so many people?"   3
    6:43 "Do not complain among yourselves.   13
    6:52 The Jews then disputed among themselves, saying   15
    6:64 among you there are some who do not believe."   5
    7:12 complaining about him among the crowds.   6
    11:54 no longer walked about openly among the Jews   6
    12:20 Now among those who went up to worship   5
    15:24 If I had not done among them the works   6
    16:19 "Are you discussing among yourselves   13
    20:19 Jesus came and stood among them and said   4
    20:26 Jesus came and stood among them and said   4

Act	1:15	In those days Peter stood up among the believers	7
	1:17	he was numbered among us	6
	1:21	the Lord Jesus went in and out among us	9
	2:22	signs that God did through him among you	7
	4:12	no other name under heaven given among mortals	6
	4:17	keep it from spreading further among the people	3
	4:34	There was not a needy person among them	6
	5:12	wonders were done among the people	6
	6: 8	did great wonders and signs among the people.	6
	9:28	So he went in and out among them in Jerusalem ·	13
	9:32	Peter went here and there among all the believers	2
	11:20	among them were some men of Cyprus and Cyrene	5
	12:18	there was no small commotion among the soldiers	6
	15: 7	in the early days God made a choice among you	6
	15:12	God had done through them among the Gentiles.	6
	15:22	leaders among the brothers	6
	18:11	teaching the word of God among them.	6
	20:18	"You yourselves know how I lived among you	13
	20:25	you, among whom I have gone about proclaiming	6
	20:29	savage wolves will come in among you	3
	20:32	among all who are sanctified.	6
	21:19	things that God had done among the Gentiles	6
	21:20	thousands of believers there are among the Jews	6
	21:21	you teach all the Jews living among the Gentiles	10
	25: 6	After he had stayed among them	6
	26: 4	spent from the beginning among my own people	6
	26:18	a place among those who are sanctified by faith	6
	27:21	Paul then stood up among them and said, "Men	7
	27:22	no loss of life among you, but only of the ship.	5
Rom	1: 5	among all the Gentiles for the sake of his name	6
	1:13	in order that I may reap some harvest among you	6
	1:13	as I have among the rest of the Gentiles.	6
	1:24	degrading of their bodies among themselves	6
	2:24	"The name of God is blasphemed among the Gentiles	6
	12: 3	I say to everyone among you not to think of yourself	6
	15: 9	"Therefore I will confess you among the Gentiles	6
	16: 6	Greet Mary, who has worked very hard among you.	3
	16: 7	they are prominent among the apostles	6
1Co	1: 6	testimony of Christ has been strengthened among you—	6
	1:10	that there be no divisions among you	6
	1:11	that there are quarrels among you, my brothers	6
	2: 2	For I decided to know nothing among you	6
	2: 6	Yet among the mature we do speak wisdom	6
	3: 3	as there is jealousy and quarreling among you	6
	5: 1	there is sexual immorality among you	6
	5: 1	of a kind that is not found even among pagans;	6
	5: 2	would have been removed from among you?	12
	6: 5	there is no one among you wise enough to decide	6
	11:18	I hear that there are divisions among you;	6
	11:19	Indeed, there have to be factions among you	6
	11:19	will it become clear who among you are genuine.	6
	14:25	declaring, "God is really among you."	6
	16:10	see that he has nothing to fear among you	15
2Co	1:19	Jesus Christ, whom we proclaimed among you	6
	2:15	among those who are being saved	6
	2:15	among those who are perishing;	6
	8: 6	also complete this generous undertaking among you.	3
	8:18	the brother who is famous among all the churches	2
	10:15	our sphere of action among you may be greatly enlarged	6
	12:12	The signs of a true apostle were performed among you	6
Gal	1:14	many among my people of the same age	6
	1:16	I might proclaim him among the Gentiles	6
	2: 2	the gospel that I proclaim among the Gentiles	6
	3: 5	work miracles among you	6
Eph	1:18	his glorious inheritance among the saints	6
	2: 2	is now at work among those who are disobedient.	6
	2: 3	All of us once lived among them	6
	5: 3	greed, must not even be mentioned among you	6
Php	1: 6	that the one who began a good work among you	6
Col	1: 6	so it has been bearing fruit among yourselves	6
	1:27	how great among the Gentiles	6
	4:16	when this letter has been read among you	14
1Th	1: 5	what kind of persons we proved to be among you	6
	1: 9	what kind of welcome we had among you	15
	2: 7	we were gentle among you	7
	5:12	respect those who labor among you	6
	5:13	Be at peace among yourselves.	6
2Th	1: 4	boast of you among the churches of God	6
	1:10	marveled at on that day among all who have believed	6
	3: 1	just as it is among you	15
1Ti	3:16	proclaimed among Gentiles, believed	6

2Ti	3: 6	For among them are those who…	5
Heb	13:21	working among us that which is pleasing in his sight	6
Jas	2: 4	have you not made distinctions among yourselves	6
	3: 6	placed among our members as a world of iniquity;	6
	3:13	Who is wise and understanding among you?	6
	4: 1	Those conflicts and disputes among you,	6
	5:13	Are any among you suffering? They should pray.	6
	5:14	Are any among you sick? They should call for the elders	6
	5:19	if anyone among you wanders from the truth	6
1Pe	2:12	Conduct yourselves honorably among the Gentiles	6
	4:12	fiery ordeal that is taking place among you to test you	6
	5: 1	as an elder myself…I exhort the elders among you	6
2Pe	2: 1	false prophets also arose among the people	6
	2: 1	just as there will be false teachers among you	6
	2: 8	living among them day after day, was tormented	6
1Jn	4: 9	God's love was revealed among us in this way:	6
	4:17	Love has been perfected among us in this:	13
Rev	2: 1	who walks among the seven golden lampstands:	7
	2:13	Antipas…who was killed among you	14
	5: 6	I saw…among the elders a Lamb standing	7
	6:15	hid…among the rocks of the mountains	3
	21: 3	"See, the home of God is among mortals.	13

Amos

   1. Ἀμώς, *Amōs, 322*

Mat	1:10	and Manasseh the father of Amos	1
	1:10	and Amos the father of Josiah	1
Lke	3:25	son of Mattathias, son of Amos	1

amount

   1. Contextual: Not in Greek

Lke	3:13	"Collect no more than the amount prescribed for you."	1

Amphipolis

   1. Ἀμφίπολις, *Amphipolis, 315*

Act	17: 1	Paul and Silas had passed through Amphipolis	1

ample

   1. πολύς, *polys, 4498*

Lke	12:19	Soul, you have ample goods laid up for many years;	1

Ampliatus

   1. Ἀμπλιᾶτος, *Ampliatos, 309*

Rom	16: 8	Greet Ampliatus, my beloved in the Lord.	1

Ananias

   1. Ἀνανίας, *Hananias, 393*

Act	5: 1	Ananias, with the consent of his wife Sapphira	1
	5: 3	"Ananias," Peter asked	1
	5: 5	when Ananias heard these words	1
	9:10	there was a disciple in Damascus named Ananias.	1
	9:10	The Lord said to him in a vision, "Ananias."	1
	9:12	he has seen in a vision a man named Ananias come	1
	9:13	Ananias answered, "Lord	1
	9:17	So Ananias went and entered the house.	1
	22:12	Ananias, who was a devout man according to the law	1
	23: 2	the high priest Ananias ordered…to strike him	1
	24: 1	the high priest Ananias came down with some elders	1

ancestor   *See also* inherit from ancestor

   1. Contextual: Not in Greek
   2. πατήρ, *patēr, 4252*
   3. πατριάρχης, *patriarchēs, 4256*
   4. πατρικός, *patrikos, 4257*
   5. πατρῷος, *patrōos, 4262*
   6. πρεσβύτερος, *presbyteros, 4565*
   7. πρόγονος, *progonos, 4591*
   8. προπάτωρ, *propatōr, 4635*

Mat	3: 9	say to yourselves, 'We have Abraham as our ancestor';	2
	23:30	'If we had lived in the days of our ancestors	2
	23:32	Fill up, then, the measure of your ancestors.	2
Mrk	11:10	the coming kingdom of our ancestor David!	2
Lke	1:32	give to him the throne of his ancestor David.	2
	1:55	according to the promise he made to our ancestors	2
	1:72	he has shown the mercy promised to our ancestors	2
	1:73	the oath that he swore to our ancestor Abraham	2
	3: 8	'We have Abraham as our ancestor';	2
	6:23	what their ancestors did to the prophets.	2
	6:26	what their ancestors did to the false prophets	2

Lke	11:47	tombs of the prophets whom your ancestors killed.	2
	11:48	approve of the deeds of your ancestors;	2
Jhn	4:12	Are you greater than our ancestor Jacob	2
	4:20	Our ancestors worshiped on this mountain	2
	6:31	Our ancestors ate the manna in the wilderness;	2
	6:49	Your ancestors ate the manna in the wilderness	2
	6:58	not like...your ancestors ate, and they died.	2
	8:56	Your ancestor Abraham rejoiced	2
Act	2:29	I may say to you confidently of our ancestor	3
	3:13	the God of our ancestors	2
	3:25	the covenant that God gave to your ancestors	2
	4:25	Holy Spirit through our ancestor David, your servant:	2
	5:30	The God of our ancestors raised up Jesus,	2
	7: 2	The God of glory appeared to our ancestor Abraham	2
	7:11	our ancestors could find no food.	2
	7:12	he sent our ancestors there on their first visit.	2
	7:15	He himself died there as well as our ancestors	2
	7:19	forced our ancestors to abandon their infants	2
	7:32	'I am the God of your ancestors	2
	7:38	spoke to him at Mount Sinai, and with our ancestors;	2
	7:39	Our ancestors were unwilling to obey him;	2
	7:44	"Our ancestors had the tent of testimony	2
	7:45	Our ancestors in turn brought it in with Joshua	2
	7:45	that God drove out before our ancestors.	2
	7:51	just as your ancestors used to do.	2
	7:52	prophets did your ancestors not persecute?	2
	13:17	The God of this people Israel chose our ancestors	2
	13:32	what God promised to our ancestors	2
	13:36	beside his ancestors, and experienced corruption;	2
	15:10	neither our ancestors nor we have been able to bear?	2
	17:26	From one ancestor he made all nations	1
	22:14	God of our ancestors has chosen you to know his will	2
	24:14	I admit to you...I worship the God of our ancestors	5
	26: 6	hope in the promise made by God to our ancestors	2
	28:17	against our people or the customs of our ancestors	5
	28:25	was right in saying to your ancestors	2
Rom	4: 1	Abraham, our ancestor according to the flesh?	8
	4:11	to make him the ancestor of all who believe	2
	4:12	likewise the ancestor of the circumcised	2
	4:12	the faith that our ancestor Abraham had	2
	9:10	conceived...by one husband, our ancestor Isaac.	2
	11:28	beloved, for the sake of their ancestors;	2
1Co	10: 1	our ancestors were all under the cloud	2
Gal	1:14	zealous for the traditions of my ancestors.	4
2Ti	1: 3	God—whom I worship...as my ancestors did	7
Heb	1: 1	God spoke to our ancestors in many and various ways	2
	3: 9	where your ancestors put me to the test	2
	7:10	for he was still in the loins of his ancestor	2
	8: 9	like the covenant that I made with their ancestors	2
	11: 2	by faith our ancestors received approval.	6
Jas	2:21	Was not our ancestor Abraham justified by works	2
2Pe	3: 4	For ever since our ancestors died	2

ancestral

1. πατρῷος, *patrōos, 4262*

Act	22: 3	educated strictly according to our ancestral law	1

ancestry

1. γενεαλογέω, *genealogeō, 1156*

Heb	7: 6	this man, who does not belong to their ancestry	1

anchor   *See also* weigh anchor

1. ἄγκυρα, *ankyra, 46*

Act	27:29	they let down four anchors from the stern	1
	27:30	on the pretext of putting out anchors	1
	27:40	cast off the anchors and left them in the sea.	1
Heb	6:19	hope, a sure and steadfast anchor of the soul	1

sea anchor

1. σκεῦος, *skeuos, 5007*

Act	27:17	they lowered the sea anchor and so were driven.	1

ancient   *See also* ancient *time*

1. ἀρχαῖος, *archaios, 792*

Lke	9: 8	that one of the ancient prophets had arisen.	1
	9:19	that one of the ancient prophets has arisen."	1
2Pe	2: 5	if he did not spare the ancient world	1
Rev	12: 9	ancient serpent, who is called the Devil	1
	20: 2	He seized the dragon, that ancient serpent	1

and   Not Indexed

Andrew

1. Ἀνδρέας, *Andreas, 436*

Mat	4:18	Simon, who is called Peter, and Andrew his brother	1
	10: 2	and his brother Andrew;	1
Mrk	1:16	saw Simon and his brother Andrew casting a net	1
	1:29	entered the house of Simon and Andrew	1
	3:18	Andrew, and Philip, and Bartholomew, and Matthew	1
	13: 3	James, John, and Andrew asked him privately	1
Lke	6:14	Simon, whom he named Peter, and his brother Andrew	1
Jhn	1:40	One...was Andrew, Simon Peter's brother.	1
	1:44	from Bethsaida, the city of Andrew and Peter.	1
	6: 8	Andrew, Simon Peter's brother, said to him	1
	12:22	Philip went and told Andrew;	1
	12:22	Andrew and Philip went and told Jesus.	1
Act	1:13	Peter, and John, and James, and Andrew	1

Andronicus

1. Ἀνδρόνικος, *Andronikos, 438*

Rom	16: 7	Greet Andronicus and Junia, my relatives	1

angel

1. Contextual: Not in Greek
2. ἄγγελος, *angelos, 34*

Mat	1:20	an angel of the Lord appeared to him in a dream	2
	1:24	he did as the angel of the Lord commanded him;	2
	2:13	an angel of the Lord appeared to Joseph in a dream	2
	2:19	Herod died, an angel of the Lord suddenly appeared	2
	4: 6	'He will command his angels concerning you,'	2
	4:11	left him, and suddenly angels came and waited	2
	13:39	and the reapers are angels.	2
	13:41	The Son of Man will send his angels	2
	13:49	The angels will come out and separate	2
	16:27	"For the Son of Man is to come with his angels	2
	18:10	in heaven their angels continually see the face	2
	22:30	but are like angels in heaven.	2
	24:31	send out his angels with a loud trumpet call	2
	24:36	neither the angels of heaven, nor the Son	2
	25:31	all the angels with him	2
	25:41	fire prepared for the devil and his angels;	2
	26:53	send me more than twelve legions of angels?	2
	28: 2	an angel of the Lord, descending from heaven	2
	28: 5	the angel said to the women, "Do not be afraid;	2
Mrk	1:13	the angels waited on him.	2
	8:38	glory of his Father with the holy angels."	2
	12:25	are like angels in heaven.	2
	13:27	Then he will send out the angels	2
	13:32	neither the angels in heaven, nor the Son	2
Lke	1:11	there appeared to him an angel of the Lord	2
	1:13	the angel said to him, "Do not be afraid	2
	1:18	Zechariah said to the angel, "How will I know	2
	1:19	The angel replied, "I am Gabriel.	2
	1:26	the angel Gabriel was sent by God	2
	1:30	The angel said to her, "Do not be afraid, Mary	2
	1:34	Mary said to the angel, "How can this be	2
	1:35	The angel said to her, "The Holy Spirit will come	2
	1:38	the angel departed from her.	2
	2: 9	an angel of the Lord stood before them	2
	2:10	the angel said to them, "Do not be afraid;	2
	2:13	suddenly there was with the angel a multitude	2
	2:15	When the angels had left them and gone into heaven	2
	2:21	he was called Jesus, the name given by the angel	2
	4:10	'He will command his angels concerning you,	2
	9:26	the glory of the Father and of the holy angels.	2
	12: 8	also will acknowledge before the angels of God;	2
	12: 9	will be denied before the angels of God.	2
	15:10	joy in the presence of the angels of God	2
	16:22	carried away by the angels to be with Abraham.	2
	22:43	[[Then an angel from heaven appeared to him]]	2
	24:23	that they had indeed seen a vision of angels	2
Jhn	1:51	the angels of God ascending and descending	2
	12:29	Others said, "An angel has spoken to him."	2
	20:12	she saw two angels in white	2
Act	5:19	an angel of the Lord opened the prison doors	2
	6:15	his face was like the face of an angel.	2
	7:30	an angel appeared to him in the wilderness	2
	7:35	the angel who appeared to him in the bush.	2
	7:38	the angel who spoke to him at Mount Sinai	2
	7:53	ones that received the law as ordained by angels	2

	8:26	an angel of the Lord said to Philip, "Get up and go	2
	10: 3	a vision in which he clearly saw an angel of God	2
	10: 7	When the angel who spoke to him had left	2
	10:22	was directed by a holy angel to send for you	2
	11:13	He told us how he had seen the angel standing	2
	12: 7	Suddenly an angel of the Lord appeared	2
	12: 8	The angel said to him, "Fasten your belt	2
	12: 9	what was happening with the angel's help was real;	2
	12:10	suddenly the angel left him.	2
	12:11	"Now I am sure that the Lord has sent his angel	2
	12:15	They said, "It is his angel."	2
	12:23	immediately...an angel of the Lord struck him down	2
	23: 8	there is no resurrection, or angel, or spirit;	2
	23: 9	What if a spirit or an angel has spoken to him?"	2
	27:23	last night there stood by me an angel	2
Rom	8:38	neither death, nor life, nor angels	2
1Co	4: 9	a spectacle to the world, to angels and to mortals.	2
	6: 3	Do you not know that we are to judge angels	2
	11:10	symbol of authority on her head, because of the angels.	2
	13: 1	If I speak in the tongues of mortals and of angels	2
2Co	11:14	Satan disguises himself as an angel of light.	2
Gal	1: 8	even if we or an angel from heaven should proclaim	2
	3:19	ordained through angels by a mediator.	2
	4:14	as an angel of God, as Christ Jesus.	2
Col	2:18	self-abasement and worship of angels	2
2Th	1: 7	revealed from heaven with his mighty angels	2
1Ti	3:16	vindicated in spirit, seen by angels	2
	5:21	of God and of Christ Jesus and of the elect angels	2
Heb	1: 4	having become as much superior to angels as	2
	1: 5	which of the angels did God ever say, "You are my Son;	2
	1: 6	he says, "Let all God's angels worship him."	2
	1: 7	Of the angels he says, "He makes his angels winds	2
	1: 7	Of the angels he says, "He makes his angels winds	2
	1:13	But to which of the angels has he ever said, "Sit	2
	1:14	Are not all angels spirits in the divine service,	1
	2: 2	For if the message declared through angels was valid	2
	2: 5	God did not subject the coming world...to angels.	2
	2: 7	made them for a little while lower than the angels;	2
	2: 9	for a little while was made lower than the angels	2
	2:16	For it is clear that he did not come to help angels	2
	12:22	innumerable angels in festal gathering	2
	13: 2	some have entertained angels without knowing it.	2
1Pe	1:12	things into which angels long to look!	2
	3:22	angels, authorities, and powers made subject to him.	2
2Pe	2: 4	if God did not spare the angels when they sinned	2
	2:11	angels, though greater in might and power	2
Jde	1: 6	the angels who did not keep their own position	2
Rev	1: 1	he made it known by sending his angel	2
	1:20	seven stars are the angels of the seven churches	2
	2: 1	"To the angel of the church in Ephesus write:	2
	2: 8	"And to the angel of the church in Smyrna write:	2
	2:12	"And to the angel of the church in Pergamum write:	2
	2:18	"And to the angel of the church in Thyatira write:	2
	3: 1	"And to the angel of the church in Sardis write:	2
	3: 5	I will confess your name...before his angels.	2
	3: 7	to the angel of the church in Philadelphia write:	2
	3:14	"And to the angel of the church in Laodicea write:	2
	5: 2	a mighty angel proclaiming with a loud voice	2
	5:11	I heard the voice of many angels	2
	7: 1	After this I saw four angels standing	2
	7: 2	I saw another angel ascending from the rising...sun	2
	7: 2	he called with a loud voice to the four angels	2
	7:11	all the angels stood around the throne	2
	8: 2	And I saw the seven angels who stand before God	2
	8: 3	Another angel with a golden censer came and stood	2
	8: 4	rose...before God from the hand of the angel.	2
	8: 5	Then the angel took the censer and filled it	2
	8: 6	Now the seven angels who had the seven trumpets	2
	8: 7	The first angel blew his trumpet	1
	8: 8	The second angel blew his trumpet	2
	8:10	The third angel blew his trumpet, and a great star	2
	8:12	The fourth angel blew his trumpet	2
	8:13	trumpets that the...angels are about to blow!"	2
	9: 1	And the fifth angel blew his trumpet, and I saw	2
	9:11	as king over them the angel of the bottomless pit;	2
	9:13	Then the sixth angel blew his trumpet, and I heard	2
	9:14	saying to the sixth angel who had the trumpet	2
	9:14	"Release the four angels who are bound	2
	9:15	So the four angels were released	2
	10: 1	another mighty angel coming down from heaven	2
	10: 5	the angel whom I saw standing on the sea and the land	2

	10: 7	the seventh angel is to blow his trumpet,	2
	10: 8	the scroll that is open in the hand of the angel	2
	10: 9	So I went to the angel and told him to give me	2
	10:10	took the little scroll from the hand of the angel	2
	11:15	Then the seventh angel blew his trumpet	2
	12: 7	Michael and his angels fought...the dragon.	2
	12: 7	The dragon and his angels fought back	2
	12: 9	and his angels were thrown down with him.	2
	14: 6	Then I saw another angel flying in midheaven	2
	14: 8	another angel, a second, followed, saying	2
	14: 9	Then another angel, a third, followed them, crying	2
	14:10	tormented...in the presence of the holy angels	2
	14:15	Another angel came out of the temple, calling	2
	14:17	another angel came out of the temple in heaven	2
	14:18	Then another angel came out from the altar	2
	14:18	the angel who has authority over fire	1
	14:19	So the angel swung his sickle over the earth	2
	15: 1	I saw...seven angels with seven plagues	2
	15: 6	out of the temple came the seven angels	2
	15: 7	the four living creatures gave the seven angels	2
	15: 8	seven plagues of the seven angels were ended.	2
	16: 1	voice from the temple telling the seven angels	2
	16: 2	first angel went and poured his bowl on the earth	1
	16: 3	The second angel poured his bowl into the sea	1
	16: 4	The third angel poured his bowl into the rivers	1
	16: 5	And I heard the angel of the waters say	2
	16: 8	The fourth angel poured his bowl on the sun	1
	16:10	The fifth angel poured his bowl on the throne	1
	16:12	sixth angel poured his bowl on the great river	1
	16:17	The seventh angel poured his bowl into the air	1
	17: 1	one of the seven angels who had the seven bowls	2
	17: 7	But the angel said to me, "Why are you so amazed?	2
	18: 1	I saw another angel coming down from heaven	2
	18:21	Then a mighty angel took up a stone	2
	19: 9	And the angel said to me, "Write this:	1
	19:17	Then I saw an angel standing in the sun	2
	20: 1	Then I saw an angel coming down from heaven	2
	21: 9	one of the seven angels who had the seven bowls	2
	21:12	and at the gates twelve angels	2
	21:15	angel who talked to me had a measuring rod of gold	1
	21:17	human measurement, which the angel was using.	2
	22: 1	angel showed me the river of the water of life	1
	22: 6	the Lord...sent his angel to show his servants	2
	22: 8	I fell down to worship at the feet of the angel	2
	22:16	I, Jesus, who sent my angel to you	2

like an angel

1. ἰσάγγελος, *isangelos, 2694*

Lke	20:36	they are like angels and are children of God	1

anger   *See also* provoke to anger

1. ἀγανακτέω, *aganakteō, 24*
2. θυμός, *thymos, 2596*
3. ὀργή, *orgē, 3973*
4. ὀργίζω, *orgizō, 3974*
5. παροργισμός, *parorgismos, 4240*

Mat	18:34	in anger his lord handed him over to be tortured	4
Mrk	3: 5	He looked around at them with anger;	3
	14: 4	some were there who said to one another in anger	1
2Co	12:20	there may perhaps be quarreling, jealousy, anger	2
Gal	5:20	idolatry, sorcery, enmities, strife, jealousy, anger	2
Eph	4:26	do not let the sun go down on your anger	5
	4:31	wrath and anger and wrangling and slander	3
Col	3: 8	get rid of...anger, wrath, malice, slander	3
1Ti	2: 8	lifting up holy hands without anger or argument;	3
Heb	3:11	As in my anger I swore, 'They will not enter	3
	4: 3	"As in my anger I swore, 'They shall not enter	3
	11:27	unafraid of the king's anger;	2
Jas	1:19	let everyone be quick to listen...slow to anger;	3
	1:20	your anger does not produce God's righteousness.	3
Rev	14:10	poured unmixed into the cup of his anger	3

angry   *See also* make angry

1. ἀγανακτέω, *aganakteō, 24*
2. θυμομαχέω, *thymomacheō, 2595*
3. ὀργίζω, *orgizō, 3974*
4. προσοχθίζω, *prosochthizō, 4696*
5. χολάω, *cholaō, 5957*

Mat	5:22	you are angry with a brother or sister, you will be	3
	20:24	they were angry with the two brothers.	1

Mat 21:15 they became angry   1
   26: 8 when the disciples saw it, they were angry   1
Mrk 10:41 they began to be angry with James and John.   1
Lke 14:21 the owner of the house became angry and said   3
   15:28 he became angry and refused to go in.   3
Jhn 7:23 are you angry with me   5
Act 12:20 Herod was angry with the people of Tyre and Sidon.   2
Eph 4:26 Be angry but do not sin;   3
Heb 3:10 Therefore I was angry with that generation   4
   3:17 But with whom was he angry forty years?   4
Rev 12:17 Then the dragon was angry with the woman   3

anguish

1. ἀγωνία, *agōnia, 75*
2. θλῖψις, *thlipsis, 2568*
3. ὀδύνη, *odynē, 3850*
4. συνοχή, *synochē, 5330*

Lke 22:44 ⟦In his anguish he prayed more earnestly,⟧   1
Jhn 16:21 she no longer remembers the anguish   2
Rom 2: 9 There will be anguish and distress   2
   9: 2 great sorrow and unceasing anguish in my heart.   3
2Co 2: 4 much distress and anguish of heart   4

animal   *See also* fight with a wild animal, four-footed animal

1. ζῷον, *zōon, 2442*
2. θηρίον, *thērion, 2563*
3. κτῆνος, *ktēnos, 3229*

Lke 10:34 Then he put him on his own animal   3
1Co 15:39 one flesh for human beings, another for animals   3
Heb 12:20 "If even an animal touches the mountain   2
   13:11 the bodies of those animals   1
2Pe 2:12 like irrational animals, mere creatures of instinct   1
Jde 1:10 like irrational animals, they know by instinct.   1

wild animal

1. θηρίον, *thērion, 2563*

Rev 6: 8 kill...pestilence, and by the wild animals   1

ankle

1. σφυδρόν, *sphydron, 5383*

Act 3: 7 his feet and ankles were made strong.   1

Anna

1. Ἅννα, *Hanna, 483*

Lke 2:36 a prophet, Anna the daughter of Phanuel   1

Annas

1. Ἅννας, *Hannas, 484*

Lke 3: 2 during the high priesthood of Annas and Caiaphas   1
Jhn 18:13 First they took him to Annas   1
   18:24 Then Annas sent him bound to Caiaphas   1
Act 4: 6 with Annas the high priest, Caiaphas, John,   1

annihilate

1. καταργέω, *katargeō, 2934*

2Th 2: 8 annihilating him by the manifestation of his coming.   1

announce

1. ἀγγέλλω, *angellō, 33*
2. ἀναγγέλλω, *anangellō, 334*
3. ἀπαγγέλλω, *apangellō, 550*
4. εὐαγγελίζω, *euangelizō, 2294*
5. κηρύσσω, *kēryssō, 3062*
6. λαλέω, *laleō, 3281*

Jhn 20:18 Mary Magdalene went and announced to the disciples   1
Act 3:21 God announced long ago through his holy prophets.   6
   5:25 Then someone arrived and announced, "Look,   3
   10:37 after the baptism that John announced: 5
   12:14 announced that Peter was standing at the gate.   3
1Pe 1:12 the things that have now been announced to you   2
Rev 10: 7 as he announced to his servants the prophets."   4

announce good news

1. εὐαγγελίζω, *euangelizō, 2294*

1Pe 1:25 That word is the good news that was announced   1

announce the gospel

1. εὐαγγελίζω, *euangelizō, 2294*

2. εὐαγγέλιον, *euangelion, 2295*

Rom 1: 9 I serve...by announcing the gospel of his Son   2
Gal 4:13 first announced the gospel to you;   1

annoy much

1. διαπονέομαι, *diaponeomai, 1387*

Act 4: 2 much annoyed because they were teaching the people   1

annoy very much

1. διαπονέομαι, *diaponeomai, 1387*

Act 16:18 Paul, very much annoyed, turned and said   1

annul

1. ἀθετέω, *atheteō, 119*
2. ἀκυρόω, *akyroō, 218*
3. λύω, *lyō, 3395*

Jhn 10:35 and the scripture cannot be annulled   3
Gal 3:15 no one adds to it or annuls it.   1
   3:17 not annul a covenant previously ratified by God   2

anoint

1. ἀλείφω, *aleiphō, 230*
2. ἐγχρίω, *enchriō, 1608*
3. μυρίζω, *myrizō, 3690*
4. χρῖσμα, *chrisma, 5984*
5. Χριστός, *Christos, 5986*
6. χρίω, *chriō, 5987*

Mrk 6:13 anointed with oil many who were sick   1
   14: 8 anointed my body beforehand for its burial.   3
   16: 1 so that they might go and anoint him.   1
Lke 4:18 he has anointed me to bring good news to the poor.   6
   7:38 anointing them with the ointment.   1
   7:46 You did not anoint my head with oil   1
   7:46 she has anointed my feet with ointment.   1
Jhn 1:41 the Messiah" (which is translated Anointed).   5
   11: 2 Mary was the one who anointed the Lord with perfume   1
   12: 3 anointed Jesus' feet, and wiped them   1
Act 4:27 against your holy servant Jesus, whom you anointed   6
   10:38 how God anointed Jesus of Nazareth   6
2Co 1:21 God who establishes us...and has anointed us   6
Heb 1: 9 God, has anointed you with the oil of gladness   6
Jas 5:14 have them pray over them, anointing them with oil   1
1Jn 2:20 you have been anointed by the Holy One   4
   2:27 the anointing that you received from him   4
   2:27 as his anointing teaches you about all things   4
Rev 3:18 salve to anoint your eyes so that you may see.   2

another   *See also* another *disciple,* another *way,* dispute with one another, go to another country, love for one another, one after another, one another

1. Contextual: Not in Greek
2. ἀδελφός, *adelphos, 81*
3. ἀλλήλων, *allēlōn, 253*
4. ἄλλος, *allos, 257*
5. ἀλλότριος, *allotrios, 259*
6. αὐτός, *autos, 899*
7. δέ, *de, 1254*
8. δόξα, *doxa, 1518*
9. εἷς, *heis, 1651*
10. ἕκαστος, *hekastos, 1667*
11. ἕτερος, *heteros, 2283*
12. ἡμέρα, *hēmera, 2465*
13. λίθος, *lithos, 3345*
14. λύπη, *lypē, 3383*
15. ὅς, *hos, 4005*
16. πάλιν, *palin, 4099*
17. πολίτης, *politēs, 4489*
18. προστίθημι, *prostithēmi, 4707*
19. τὶς, *tis, 5516*
20. τυφλός, *typhlos, 5603*

Mat 2:12 left for their own country by another road.   4
   8: 9 to one, 'Go,' and he goes, and to another, 'Come,'   4
   8:21 Another of his disciples said to him   11
   11: 3 or are we to wait for another?"   11
   13:23 yields...in another sixty, and in another thirty   7
   13:23 yields...in another sixty, and in another thirty   7
   13:24 He put before them another parable: 4
   13:31 He put before them another parable: 4

	13:33 He told them another parable:	4
	15:14 if one blind person guides another, both will fall	20
	18:15 "If another member of the church sins against you	1
	18:21 if another member of the church sins against me	1
	19: 9 and marries another commits adultery."	4
	21:33 "Listen to another parable.	4
	21:35 beat one, killed another, and stoned another.	15
	21:35 beat one, killed another, and stoned another.	15
	22: 5 went away, one to his farm, another to his business	15
	24: 2 not one stone will be left here upon another;	13
	25:15 to one he gave five talents, to another two	15
	25:15 to another two, to another one	15
	25:32 he will separate people one from another	3
	26:22 and began to say to him one after another	10
	26:71 to the porch, another servant-girl saw him	4
Mrk	10:11 "Whoever divorces his wife and marries another	4
	10:12 if she divorces her husband and marries another	4
	12: 4 again he sent another slave to them;	4
	12: 5 he sent another, and that one they killed.	4
	13: 2 Not one stone will be left here upon another;	13
	14:19 to say to him one after another, "Surely, not I?"	9
	14:58 I will build another, not made with hands.' "	4
	16:12 [[After this he appeared in another form to two]]	11
Lke	6: 6 On another sabbath he entered the synagogue	11
	7: 8 to another, 'Come,' and he comes	4
	7:19 or are we to wait for another?"	4
	7:20 or are we to wait for another?' "	4
	9:56 Then they went on to another village.	11
	9:59 To another he said, "Follow me."	11
	9:61 Another said, "I will follow you, Lord;	11
	14:19 Another said, 'I have bought five yoke of oxen	11
	14:20 Another said, 'I have just been married	11
	14:31 going out to wage war against another king	11
	16: 7 he asked another, 'And how much do you owe?'	11
	16:12 not been faithful with what belongs to another	5
	16:18 divorces his wife and marries another	11
	19:44 will not leave within you one stone upon another;	13
	20:11 he sent another slave;	11
	21: 6 not one stone will be left upon another;	13
	22:59 still another kept insisting, "Surely	4
Jhn	4:37 'One sows and another reaps.'	4
	5:32 There is another who testifies on my behalf	4
	5:43 if another comes in his own name	4
	14:16 give you another Advocate, to be with you	4
	18:15 Simon Peter and another disciple followed Jesus.	4
	19:37 again another passage of scripture says	11
Act	1:20 'Let another take his position of overseer.'	11
	2:12 were amazed and perplexed, saying to one another	4
	7:18 until another king who had not known Joseph	11
	12:17 Then he left and went to another place.	11
	13:35 Therefore he has also said in another psalm	11
	17: 7 saying that there is another king named Jesus."	11
	19:32 some were shouting one thing, some another	4
	21:34 Some in the crowd shouted one thing, some another;	4
Rom	2: 1 in passing judgment on another you condemn	11
	7: 3 an adulteress if she lives with another man	11
	7: 3 marries another man, she is not an adulteress.	11
	7: 4 so that you may belong to another	11
	7:23 another law at war with the law of my mind	11
	9:21 object for special use and another for ordinary use?	15
	13: 8 the one who loves another has fulfilled the law.	11
	14: 4 to pass judgment on servants of another?	5
	14: 5 Some judge one day to be better than another	12
	14:13 block or hindrance in the way of another.	2
1Co	3: 4 and another, "I belong to Apollos,"	11
	4: 6 puffed up in favor of one against another.	11
	6: 1 When any of you has a grievance against another	11
	6: 5 to decide between one believer and another	6
	7: 7 one having one kind and another a different	7
	11:21 one goes hungry and another becomes drunk.	15
	12: 8 to another the utterance of knowledge	4
	12: 9 to another faith by the same Spirit	11
	12: 9 to another gifts of healing by the one Spirit	4
	12:10 to another the working of miracles	4
	12:10 to another prophecy	4
	12:10 to another the discernment of spirits,	4
	12:10 to another various kinds of tongues	11
	12:10 to another the interpretation of tongues.	4
	15:39 one flesh for human beings, another for animals	4
	15:39 another for birds, and another for fish.	4
	15:39 another for birds, and another for fish.	4

	15:40 that of the earthly is another.	11
	15:41 one glory of the sun, and another glory of the moon	4
	15:41 another glory of the stars;	4
2Co	2: 1 not to make you another painful visit.	16
	3:18 from one degree of glory to another;	8
	11: 4 For if someone comes and proclaims another Jesus	4
Gal	1: 7 not that there is another gospel	4
Php	2:27 so that I would not have one sorrow after another.	14
Col	3:13 if anyone has a complaint against another	19
Heb	4: 8 God would not speak later about another day.	4
	5: 6 as he says also in another place	11
	7:11 need…to speak of another priest arising	11
	7:13 belonged to another tribe	11
	7:15 another priest arises, resembling Melchizedek,	11
	8:11 they shall not teach one another or say	17
	12:19 that not another word be spoken to them.	18
Jas	2:25 when she…sent them out by another road?	11
	4:11 Whoever speaks evil against another or judges	2
	4:11 speaks evil against another or judges another,	2
	5:19 wanders…and is brought back by another	19
1Jn	2:11 whoever hates another believer is in the darkness	1
Rev	6: 4 And out came another horse, bright red;	4
	7: 2 I saw another angel ascending from the rising…sun	4
	8: 3 Another angel with a golden censer came and stood	4
	10: 1 And I saw another mighty angel coming down	4
	12: 3 another portent appeared in heaven:	4
	13:11 I saw another beast that rose out of the earth;	4
	14: 6 Then I saw another angel flying in midheaven	4
	14: 8 another angel, a second, followed, saying	4
	14: 9 Then another angel, a third, followed them, crying	4
	14:15 Another angel came out of the temple, calling	4
	14:17 another angel came out of the temple in heaven	4
	14:18 Then another angel came out from the altar	4
	15: 1 Then I saw another portent in heaven	4
	18: 1 I saw another angel coming down from heaven	4
	18: 4 Then I heard another voice from heaven saying	4
	20:12 another book was opened, the book of life.	4

no another

1. οὐδείς, *oudeis*, 4029

Lke	20:40 they no longer dared to ask him another question.	1

answer *See also* give an answer

1. ἀποκρίνομαι, *apokrinomai*, 646
2. ἀπόκρισις, *apokrisis*, 647
3. λέγω, *legō*, 3306
4. λόγος, *logos*, 3364
5. ὅς, *hos*, 4005
6. πρός, *pros*, 4639
7. ὑπακούω, *hypakouō*, 5634
8. φημί, *phēmi*, 5774

Mat	3:15 But Jesus answered him, "Let it be so now;	1
	4: 4 But he answered, "It is written, 'One does not live	1
	8: 8 The centurion answered, "Lord, I am not worthy	1
	11: 4 Jesus answered them, "Go and tell John	1
	12:39 he answered them, "An evil and adulterous	1
	13:11 He answered, "To you it has been given to know	1
	13:28 He answered, 'An enemy has done this.'	8
	13:37 He answered, "The one who sows the good seed	1
	13:51 They answered, "Yes."	3
	14:28 Peter answered him, "Lord, if it is you	1
	15: 3 He answered them, "And why do you break	1
	15:13 He answered	1
	15:23 he did not answer her at all.	1
	15:24 He answered,	1
	15:26 He answered	1
	15:28 Then Jesus answered her	1
	16: 2 He answered them	1
	16:16 Simon Peter answered, "You are the Messiah	1
	16:17 Jesus answered him	1
	17:17 Jesus answered	1
	19: 4 He answered, "Have you not read	1
	20:22 Jesus answered, "You do not know	1
	21:21 Jesus answered them, "Truly I tell you	1
	21:24 if you tell me the answer	5
	21:27 So they answered Jesus, "We do not know."	1
	21:29 He answered, 'I will not'; but later he changed	1
	21:30 He answered, 'I go, sir'; but he did not go.	1
	22:21 They answered, "The emperor's."	3
	22:29 Jesus answered them, "You are wrong	1

Mat	22:46	No one was able to give him an answer	4
	24: 4	Jesus answered them, "Beware that no one leads	1
	25:37	Then the righteous will answer him	1
	25:40	the king will answer them, 'Truly I tell you	1
	25:44	Then they also will answer	1
	25:45	Then he will answer them, 'Truly I tell you	1
	26:23	He answered, "The one who has dipped his hand	1
	26:62	"Have you no answer?	1
	26:66	They answered, "He deserves death."	1
	27:12	he did not answer.	1
	27:25	the people as a whole answered, "His blood be	1
Mrk	1:38	He answered, "Let us go on to the neighboring	3
	6:37	he answered them, "You give them something to eat."	1
	7:28	she answered him, "Sir, even the dogs	1
	8:28	they answered him, "John the Baptist;	3
	8:29	Peter answered him, "You are the Messiah."	1
	9:17	Someone from the crowd answered him, "Teacher	1
	9:19	He answered them, "You faithless generation	1
	10: 3	He answered, "What did Moses command you?"	1
	11:22	Jesus answered them, "Have faith in God.	1
	11:29	answer me, and I will tell you by what authority	1
	11:30	from heaven, or was it of human origin? Answer me."	1
	11:33	So they answered Jesus, "We do not know."	1
	12:16	They answered, "The emperor's."	3
	12:28	seeing that he answered them well, he asked him	1
	12:29	Jesus answered, "The first is, 'Hear, O Israel:	1
	12:34	When Jesus saw that he answered wisely	1
	14:60	"Have you no answer?	1
	14:61	he was silent and did not answer.	1
	15: 2	He answered him, "You say so."	1
	15: 4	Pilate asked him again, "Have you no answer?	1
	15: 9	answered them, "Do you want me to release for you	1
Lke	2:47	amazed at his understanding and his answers.	2
	3:16	John answered all of them by saying, "I baptize	1
	4: 4	Jesus answered him, "It is written	1
	4: 8	Jesus answered him, "It is written	1
	4:12	Jesus answered him, "It is said, 'Do not put	1
	5: 5	Simon answered, "Master, we have worked all night	1
	5:22	answered them, "Why do you raise such questions	1
	5:31	Jesus answered, "Those who are well	1
	6: 3	Jesus answered, "Have you not read what David did	1
	7:22	he answered them, "Go and tell John	1
	7:43	Simon answered, "I suppose the one	1
	9:19	They answered, "John the Baptist;	1
	9:20	Peter answered, "The Messiah of God."	1
	9:41	Jesus answered, "You faithless and perverse	1
	9:49	John answered, "Master, we saw someone	1
	10:27	He answered, "You shall love the Lord your God	1
	10:41	the Lord answered her, "Martha, Martha	1
	11: 7	he answers from within, 'Do not bother me;	1
	11:45	One of the lawyers answered him, "Teacher	1
	13:15	the Lord answered him and said, "You hypocrites!	1
	15:29	he answered his father, 'Listen! For all these	1
	16: 6	He answered, 'A hundred jugs of olive oil.'	3
	17:20	he answered, "The kingdom of God is not coming	1
	19:40	He answered, "I tell you, if these were silent	1
	20: 3	He answered them, "I will also ask you a question	1
	20: 7	So they answered that they did not know	1
	20:26	amazed by his answer, they became silent.	2
	20:39	some of the scribes answered, "Teacher	1
	22:68	if I question you, you will not answer.	1
	23: 3	He answered, "You say so."	1
	24:18	one of them, whose name was Cleopas, answered	1
Jhn	1:21	"Are you the prophet?" He answered, "No."	1
	1:22	Let us have an answer for those who sent us.	2
	1:26	John answered them, "I baptize with water.	1
	1:48	Jesus answered, "I saw you under the fig tree	1
	1:50	Jesus answered, "Do you believe because	1
	2:19	Jesus answered them, "Destroy this temple	1
	3: 3	Jesus answered him, "Very truly, I tell you	1
	3: 5	Jesus answered, "Very truly, I tell you	1
	3:10	Jesus answered him, "Are you a teacher of Israel	1
	3:27	John answered, "No one can receive anything	1
	4:10	Jesus answered her, "If you knew the gift of God	1
	4:17	The woman answered him, "I have no husband."	1
	5: 7	The sick man answered him, "Sir, I have no one	1
	5:11	he answered them, "The man who made me well said	1
	5:17	Jesus answered them, "My Father is still working	1
	6: 7	Philip answered him	1
	6:26	Jesus answered them, "Very truly, I tell you	1
	6:29	Jesus answered them, "This is the work of God	1

	6:43	Jesus answered them, "Do not complain	1
	6:68	Peter answered him, "Lord, to whom can we go?	1
	6:70	Jesus answered them, "Did I not choose you	1
	7:16	Jesus answered them, "My teaching is not mine	1
	7:20	The crowd answered, "You have a demon!	1
	7:21	Jesus answered them, "I performed one work	1
	7:46	The police answered	1
	8:14	Jesus answered, "Even if I testify	1
	8:19	Jesus answered, "You know neither me nor my Father.	1
	8:33	They answered him, "We are descendants of Abraham	1
	8:34	Jesus answered them, "Very truly, I tell you	1
	8:39	They answered him, "Abraham is our father."	1
	8:48	The Jews answered him, "Are we not right	1
	8:49	Jesus answered, "I do not have a demon;	1
	8:54	Jesus answered, "If I glorify myself	1
	9: 3	Jesus answered, "Neither this man…sinned;	1
	9:11	He answered, "The man called Jesus made mud	1
	9:20	parents answered, "We know that this is our son	1
	9:25	He answered, "I do not know whether he is a sinner.	1
	9:27	He answered them, "I have told you already	1
	9:30	The man answered, "Here is an astonishing thing!	1
	9:34	They answered him, "You were born entirely in sins	1
	9:36	He answered, "And who is he, sir?	1
	10:25	Jesus answered, "I have told you	1
	10:33	The Jews answered, "It is not for a good work	1
	10:34	Jesus answered, "Is it not written in your law	1
	11: 9	Jesus answered, "Are there not twelve hours	1
	12:23	Jesus answered them, "The hour has come	1
	12:30	Jesus answered, "This voice has come for your sake	1
	12:34	The crowd answered him, "We have heard	1
	13: 7	Jesus answered, "You do not know now what	1
	13: 8	Jesus answered, "Unless I wash you	1
	13:26	Jesus answered, "It is the one to whom I give	1
	13:36	Jesus answered, "Where I am going	1
	13:38	Jesus answered, "Will you lay down your life	1
	14:23	Jesus answered him, "Those who love me	1
	16:31	Jesus answered them, "Do you now believe?	1
	18: 5	They answered, "Jesus of Nazareth."	1
	18: 8	Jesus answered, "I told you that I am he.	1
	18:20	Jesus answered him, "I have spoken openly	1
	18:22	"Is that how you answer the high priest?"	1
	18:23	Jesus answered, "If I have spoken wrongly	1
	18:30	They answered	1
	18:34	Jesus answered, "Do you ask this on your own	1
	18:36	Jesus answered, "My kingdom is not from this	1
	18:37	Jesus answered him, "You say that I am a king.	1
	19: 7	The Jews answered him, "We have a law	1
	19: 9	But Jesus gave him no answer.	2
	19:11	Jesus answered him, "You would have no power	1
	19:15	The chief priests answered, "We have no king	1
	19:22	Pilate answered, "What I have written	1
	20:28	Thomas answered him, "My Lord and my God!"	1
	21: 5	They answered him, "No."	1
Act	4:19	Peter and John answered them, "Whether it is right	1
	5:29	Peter and the apostles answered, "We must obey God	1
	8:24	Simon answered, "Pray for me to the Lord	1
	9:10	He answered, "Here I am, Lord."	3
	9:13	Ananias answered, "Lord	1
	10: 4	He answered, "Your prayers and your alms	3
	10:22	They answered, "Cornelius, a centurion	3
	11: 9	a second time the voice answered from heaven	1
	12:13	a maid named Rhoda came to answer.	7
	16:31	They answered, "Believe on the Lord Jesus	3
	19: 3	They answered, "Into John's baptism."	3
	21:13	Then Paul answered, "What are you doing	1
	22: 8	I answered, 'Who are you, Lord?'	1
	22:28	The tribune answered, "It cost me a large sum	1
	23:20	He answered, "The Jews have agreed	3
	26:15	The Lord answered, 'I am Jesus	3
2Co	5:12	so that you may be able to answer	6
Col	4: 6	you may know how you ought to answer everyone.	1

answerable

1. ἔνοχος, *enochos*, 1944

1Co	11:27	be answerable for the body and blood of the Lord.	1

antichrist

1. ἀντίχριστος, *antichristos*, 532

1Jn	2:18	As you have heard that antichrist is coming	1
	2:18	so now many antichrists have come.	1
	2:22	This is the antichrist, the one who denies	1

	4: 3	And this is the spirit of the antichrist,	1
2Jn	1: 7	such person is the deceiver and the antichrist!	1

Antioch

1. Ἀντιόχεια, *Antiocheia, 522*
2. Ἀντιοχεύς, *Antiocheus, 523*

Act	6: 5	Parmenas, and Nicolaus, a proselyte of Antioch.	2
	11:19	traveled as far as Phoenicia, Cyprus, and Antioch	1
	11:20	who, on coming to Antioch, spoke to the Hellenists	1
	11:22	they sent Barnabas to Antioch.	1
	11:26	when he had found him, he brought him to Antioch.	1
	11:26	in Antioch that the disciples were…"Christians."	1
	11:27	prophets came down from Jerusalem to Antioch.	1
	13: 1	Now in the church at Antioch there were prophets	1
	13:14	and came to Antioch in Pisidia.	1
	14:19	Jews came there from Antioch and Iconium	1
	14:21	returned to Lystra, then on to Iconium and Antioch.	1
	14:26	From there they sailed back to Antioch	1
	15:22	send them to Antioch with Paul and Barnabas.	1
	15:23	the believers of Gentile origin in Antioch	1
	15:30	they were sent off and went down to Antioch.	1
	15:35	Paul and Barnabas remained in Antioch	1
	18:22	and then went down to Antioch.	1
Gal	2:11	when Cephas came to Antioch	1
2Ti	3:11	the things that happened to me in Antioch, Iconium	1

Antipas

1. Ἀντιπᾶς, *Antipas, 525*

Rev	2:13	you did not deny…even in the days of Antipas	1

Antipatris

1. Ἀντιπατρίς, *Antipatris, 526*

Act	23:31	and brought him during the night to Antipatris.	1

anxiety   *See also* free from anxiety

1. μέριμνα, *merimna, 3533*

2Co	11:28	my anxiety for all the churches.	1
1Pe	5: 7	Cast all your anxiety on him	1

great anxiety

1. ὀδυνάω, *odynaō, 3849*

Lke	2:48	I have been searching for you in great anxiety."	1

anxious

1. μεριμνάω, *merimnaō, 3534*

1Co	7:32	The unmarried man is anxious about the affairs	1
	7:33	married man is anxious about the affairs of the world	1
	7:34	are anxious about the affairs of the Lord	1
	7:34	married woman is anxious about the affairs of the world	1

less anxious

1. ἄλυπος, *alypos, 267*

Php	2:28	I may be less anxious.	1

any   *See also* any better off [*good*], any further [*far*], any less, any longer [*long*], any *more*, any *time*, any *way*, at any *time*, in any case, no any longer [*long*], not any longer [*long*], not any *more*, without any, without any doubt

1. Contextual: Not in Greek
2. ἐκ, *ek, 1666*
3. ἐν, *en, 1877*
4. μηδείς, *mēdeis, 3594*
5. μόνος, *monos, 3668*
6. ὅς + ἐάν, *hos + ean, 4005 + 1569*
7. ὅς + ἄν, *hos + an, 4005 + 323*
8. πᾶς, *pas, 4246*
9. τίς, *tis, 5515*
10. τὶς, *tis, 5516*

Mat	6:27	can any of you by worrying add a single hour	9
	16: 5	they had forgotten to bring any bread.	1
	16:24	"If any want to become my followers	10
	18: 6	any of you put a stumbling block before one	7
	19: 3	lawful for a man to divorce his wife for any cause?"	8
Mrk	2:26	which it is not lawful for any but the priests	1
	6:11	If any place will not welcome you	7
	8:14	the disciples had forgotten to bring any bread;	1
	8:34	to them, "If any want to become my followers	10
	9:42	"If any of you put a stumbling block	7

	12:34	After that no one dared to ask him any question.	1
	16:18	[[if they drink any deadly thing, it will not hurt]]	10
Lke	4:40	all those who had any who were sick	1
	6: 4	it is not lawful for any but the priests to eat	5
	9:23	"If any want to become my followers	10
	11:24	not finding any, it says, 'I will return	1
	12:25	can any of you by worrying add a single hour	9
	23:14	guilty of any of your charges against him.	1
Jhn	7:48	Has any one of the authorities…believed in him?	10
	20:23	If you forgive the sins of any, they are forgiven	10
	20:23	if you retain the sins of any, they are retained."	10
Act	2:45	distribute the proceeds to all, as any had need.	10
	4:32	no one claimed private ownership of any possessions	10
	4:35	was distributed to each as any had need.	10
	5:29	"We must obey God rather than any human authority.	1
	7: 5	He did not give him any of it as a heritage	3
	9: 2	found any who belonged to the Way, men or women	10
	13:15	"Brothers, if you have any word of exhortation	10
	20:26	I am not responsible for the blood of any of you	8
	26: 8	Why is it thought incredible by any of you	1
Rom	8:33	Who will bring any charge against God's elect?	1
	13: 9	You shall not covet"; and any other commandment	10
1Co	1: 7	you are not lacking in any spiritual gift	4
	3:11	For no one can lay any foundation other	1
	4: 3	I should be judged by you or by any human court.	1
	6: 1	When any of you has a grievance against another	10
	7:12	if any believer has a wife who is an unbeliever	10
	7:13	if any woman has a husband who is an unbeliever	10
	7:35	not to put any restraint upon you	1
	9: 7	not eat any of its fruit?	1
	9: 7	not get any of its milk?	2
	10:25	without raising any question	1
	10:27	eat…without raising any question	1
	11: 4	Any man who prays…with something on his head	8
	11: 5	any woman who prays or prophesies with her head	8
	15:10	On the contrary, I worked harder than any of them	8
	16: 3	when I arrive, I will send any whom you approve	6
2Co	1: 4	able to console those who are in any affliction	8
	12:17	through any of those whom I sent to you?	10
	13: 1	"Any charge must be sustained	8
Gal	1:16	I did not confer with any human being	1
Eph	5: 5	has any inheritance in the kingdom of Christ	1
Php	2: 1	If then there is any encouragement in Christ	10
	2: 1	any consolation from love	10
	2: 1	any sharing in the Spirit	10
	2: 1	any compassion and sympathy	10
	4: 8	whatever is commendable, if there is any excellence	10
	4:12	In any and all circumstances	8
1Th	2: 9	worked…so that we might not burden any of you	10
2Th	2: 3	Let no one deceive you in any way;	4
	3: 8	so that we might not burden any of you.	10
1Ti	1: 3	not to teach any different doctrine	1
	5:16	If any believing woman has…really widows	10
	5:19	Never accept any accusation against an elder	1
Tit	1:16	detestable, disobedient, unfit for any good work.	8
	2: 8	then your opponent will be put to shame	2
	3: 5	not because of any works of righteousness	1
Heb	4:12	sharper than any two-edged sword	8
	8: 2	that the Lord, and not any mortal, has set up.	1
	10:18	there is no longer any offering for sin.	1
Jas	1: 5	If any of you is lacking in wisdom, ask God	10
	1:23	For if any are hearers of the word and not doers,	10
	1:26	If any think they are religious	10
	5:12	do not swear…by any other oath	10
	5:13	Are any among you suffering? They should pray.	10
	5:13	Are any cheerful? They should sing songs of praise.	10
	5:14	Are any among you sick? They should call for the elders	10
1Pe	4:16	Yet if any of you suffers as a Christian	1
2Pe	3: 9	not wanting any to perish	10
2Jn	1: 7	any such person is the deceiver and the antichrist	1
Rev	7: 1	blow on earth or sea or against any tree.	8
	7:16	sun will not strike them, nor any scorching heat;	8
	9: 4	not to damage…any green growth or any tree	8
	9: 4	not to damage…any green growth or any tree	8
	12: 8	there was no longer any place for them in heaven.	1
	18:22	an artisan of any trade will be found	8

any kind

1. πᾶς, *pas, 4246*
2. ποικίλος, *poikilos, 4476*

Eph	5: 3	fornication and impurity of any kind, or greed	1

Jas   1: 2 whenever you face trials of any kind,   2

any other

1. ἄλλος, *allos, 257*

Rev   2:24 I do not lay on you any other burden;   1

no any

1. οὐδείς, *oudeis, 4029*

Lke   9:36 told no one any of the things they had seen.   1
Act 18:17 But Gallio paid no attention to any of these things.   1
1Co   9:15 I have made no use of any of these rights   1

not any

1. μηδείς, *mēdeis, 3594*
2. οὐδείς, *oudeis, 4029*

Lke 23:14 have not found this man guilty of any…charges   2
Jhn 16:29 speaking plainly, not in any figure of speech!   2
Act   8:16 as yet the Spirit had not come upon any of them;   2
     20:24 I do not count my life of any value   2
     24:23 not to prevent any of his friends   1
     25:18 they did not charge him with any of the crimes   2
2Co   7: 9 so that you were not harmed in any way by us.   1
Php   1:20 my…hope that I will not be put to shame in any way   2
2Th   3:11 mere busybodies, not doing any work.   1

anymore

1. ἔτι, *eti, 2285*
2. οὐκέτι, *ouketi, 4033*

Lke 20:36 Indeed they cannot die anymore   1
Rev 18:11 since no one buys their cargo anymore   2

anyone   Not Indexed

not anyone

1. μηδείς, *mēdeis, 3594*
2. οὐδείς, *oudeis, 4029*

Mat 16:20 sternly ordered the disciples not to tell anyone   1
Mrk   7:24 entered a house and did not want anyone to know   2
      8:30 ordered them not to tell anyone about him.   1
Lke   3:14 "Do not extort money from anyone by threats   1
      9:21 He…commanded them not to tell anyone,   1
Act 10:28 God has shown me that I should not call anyone   1
Rom 12:17 Do not repay anyone evil for evil   1
Col   2:18 Do not let anyone disqualify you   1
1Ti   5:22 Do not ordain anyone hastily,   1

anything   *See also* see anything different

1. Contextual: Not in Greek
2. εἷς, *heis, 1651*
3. μηδείς, *mēdeis, 3594*
4. ὁ, *ho, 3836*
5. πᾶς, *pas, 4246*
6. πᾶς + πρᾶγμα, *pas + pragma, 4246 + 4547*
7. σκεῦος, *skeuos, 5007*
8. τίς, *tis, 5515*
9. τὶς, *tis, 5516*

Mat   5:37 anything more than this comes from the evil one   4
      9:33 "Never has anything like this been seen in Israel."   1
     18:19 agree on earth about anything you ask   6
     21: 3 If anyone says anything to you, just say this,   9
Mrk   2:12 saying, "We have never seen anything like this!"   1
      4:22 nor is anything secret, except to come to light.   1
      7: 4 they do not eat anything from the market unless   1
      8: 1 again a great crowd without anything to eat   8
      8:23 he asked him, "Can you see anything?"   9
      9:22 if you are able to do anything, have pity on us   9
     11:13 whether perhaps he would find anything on it.   9
     11:16 to carry anything through the temple.   7
     11:25 forgive, if you have anything against anyone;   9
     13:15 or enter the house to take anything away;   9
Lke   8:17 anything secret that will not become known   1
     11: 7 I cannot get up and give you anything.'   1
     11: 8 though he will not get up and give him anything   1
     15:16 no one gave him anything.   1
     19: 8 if I have defrauded anyone of anything   9
     19:48 they did not find anything they could do   8
     22:35 "When I sent you out…did you lack anything?"   9
     24:41 he said to them, "Have you anything here to eat?"   9
Jhn   1:46 "Can anything good come out of Nazareth?"   9

      3:27 "No one can receive anything except what   2
     14:14 you ask me for anything, I will do it.   9
     16:23 if you ask anything of the Father in my name   9
Act 10:14 never eaten anything that is profane or unclean."   5
     17:25 as though he needed anything   9
     19:39 If there is anything further you want to know   9
     20:20 I did not shrink from doing anything helpful   1
     24:19 if they have anything against me.   9
     25: 5 if there is anything wrong about the man   9
     28:21 reported or spoken anything evil about you.   9
Rom   8:39 nor depth, nor anything else in all creation   9
      9:11 or had done anything good or bad   9
     13: 8 Owe no one anything, except to love one another;   3
     14: 2 Some believe in eating anything   5
     14:21 anything that makes your brother or sister stumble.   1
     15:18 For I will not venture to speak of anything   9
1Co   3: 7 nor the one who waters is anything   9
      6:12 I will not be dominated by anything.   9
      9:12 we endure anything rather than put an obstacle   5
     10:19 That food sacrificed to idols is anything   9
     10:19 that an idol is anything?   9
     14:35 If there is anything they desire to know   9
2Co   2:10 What I have forgiven, if I have forgiven anything   9
      3: 5 competent of ourselves to claim anything   9
     13: 7 we pray to God that you may not do anything wrong   3
     13: 8 For we cannot do anything against the truth   9
Gal   5: 6 nor uncircumcision counts for anything;   9
      6:14 May I never boast of anything except the cross   1
      6:15 neither circumcision nor uncircumcision is anything;   9
Eph   5:27 without a spot or wrinkle or anything of the kind   9
Php   3:15 if you think differently about anything   9
      4: 8 if there is anything worthy of praise   9
1Th   5: 1 you do not need to have anything written to you.   1
Phm   1:18 If he…owes you anything   1
Jas   1: 7 must not expect to receive anything from the Lord.   9
1Jn   5:14 if we ask anything according to his will, he hears   9

no anything

1. οὐδείς, *oudeis, 4029*

Mat   5:13 no longer good for anything, but is thrown out   1
Mrk   7:12 then you no longer permit doing anything   1

not anything

1. μηδείς, *mēdeis, 3594*
2. οὐδείς, *oudeis, 4029*

Jhn 16:24 you have not asked for anything in my name.   2
Act 20:20 I did not shrink from doing anything helpful   2
1Co   4: 4 I am not aware of anything against myself   2
Php   4: 6 not worry about anything   1

apart   *See also* apart from the *law*, set apart, tear apart, wrench apart

1. ἄνευ, *aneu, 459*
2. ἐάν + μή, *ean + mē, 1569 + 3590*
3. μόνος, *monos, 3668*
4. χωρίς, *chōris, 6006*

Mat 10:29 fall to the ground apart from your Father.   1
Mrk   9: 2 led them up a high mountain apart, by themselves.   3
Jhn   3: 2 do these signs…apart from the presence of God."   2
     15: 5 because apart from me you can do nothing.   4
Rom   3:21 But now, apart from law, the righteousness of God   4
      3:28 a person is justified by faith apart from works   4
      4: 6 God reckons righteousness apart from works: 4
      7: 8 Apart from the law sin lies dead.   4
      7: 9 I was once alive apart from the law   4
1Co   4: 8 apart from us you have become kings!   4
Heb 11:40 they would not, apart from us, be made perfect.   4
Jas   2:18 Show me your faith apart from your works   4
      2:20 that faith apart from works is barren?   4

Apelles

1. Ἀπελλῆς, *Apellēs, 593*

Rom 16:10 Greet Apelles, who is approved in Christ.   1

Apollonia

1. Ἀπολλωνία, *Apollōnia, 662*

Act 17: 1 Paul and Silas had passed through…Apollonia   1

Apollos

1. Ἀπολλῶς, *Apollōs, 663*

Act	18:24	a Jew named Apollos, a native of Alexandria.	1
	19: 1	While Apollos was in Corinth	1
1Co	1:12	"I belong to Paul," or "I belong to Apollos,"	1
	3: 4	and another, "I belong to Apollos,"	1
	3: 5	What then is Apollos? What is Paul?	1
	3: 6	I planted, Apollos watered	1
	3:22	whether Paul or Apollos or Cephas or the world	1
	4: 6	I have applied all this to Apollos and myself	1
	16:12	Now concerning our brother Apollos	1
Tit	3:13	send Zenas the lawyer and Apollos on their way	1

Apollyon

1. Ἀπολλύων, *Apollyōn, 661*

Rev	9:11	and in Greek he is called Apollyon.	1

apologize

1. παρακαλέω, *parakaleō, 4151*

Act	16:39	so they came and apologized to them.	1

apostle

1. Contextual: Not in Greek
2. ἀποστολή, *apostolē, 692*
3. ἀπόστολος, *apostolos, 693*

Mat	10: 2	These are the names of the twelve apostles:	3
Mrk	3:14	he appointed twelve, whom he also named apostles	3
	6:30	The apostles gathered around Jesus, and told him	3
Lke	6:13	chose twelve of them, whom he also named apostles:	3
	9:10	the apostles told Jesus all they had done.	3
	11:49	'I will send them prophets and apostles	3
	17: 5	The apostles said to the Lord, "Increase our faith!"	3
	22:14	his place at the table, and the apostles with him.	3
	24:10	who told this to the apostles.	3
Act	1: 2	instructions…to the apostles whom he had chosen.	3
	1:26	he was added to the eleven apostles	3
	2:37	said to Peter and to the other apostles	3
	2:42	devoted themselves to the apostles' teaching	3
	2:43	signs were being done by the apostles.	3
	4:33	the apostles gave their testimony	3
	4:35	laid it at the apostles' feet.	3
	4:36	Joseph, to whom the apostles gave the name Barnabas	3
	4:37	laid it at the apostles' feet.	3
	5: 2	laid it at the apostles' feet.	3
	5:12	done…through the apostles.	3
	5:18	arrested the apostles	3
	5:29	Peter and the apostles answered, "We must obey God	3
	5:40	when they had called in the apostles	3
	6: 6	had these men stand before the apostles	3
	8: 1	all except the apostles were scattered	3
	8:14	Now when the apostles at Jerusalem heard	3
	8:18	through the laying on of the apostles' hands	3
	9:27	Barnabas took him, brought him to the apostles	3
	11: 1	the apostles and the believers who were in Judea	3
	14: 4	some with the apostles.	3
	14: 6	apostles learned of it and fled to Lystra and Derbe	1
	14:14	When the apostles Barnabas and Paul heard of it	3
	15: 2	to discuss this question with the apostles	3
	15: 4	were welcomed by the church and the apostles	3
	15: 6	The apostles and the elders met together	3
	15:22	the apostles and the elders…decided	3
	15:23	"The brothers, both the apostles and the elders	3
	16: 4	decisions…reached by the apostles and elders	3
Rom	1: 1	Paul…called to be an apostle	3
	11:13	Inasmuch then as I am an apostle to the Gentiles	3
	16: 7	they are prominent among the apostles	3
1Co	1: 1	an apostle of Christ Jesus by the will of God	3
	4: 9	God has exhibited us apostles as last of all	3
	9: 1	Am I not free? Am I not an apostle?	3
	9: 2	If I am not an apostle to others,	3
	9: 5	as do the other apostles and the brothers	3
	12:28	God has appointed in the church first apostles	3
	12:29	Are all apostles? Are all prophets?	3
	15: 7	he appeared to James, then to all the apostles.	3
	15: 9	the least of the apostles, unfit to be called	3
	15: 9	unfit to be called an apostle	3
2Co	1: 1	Paul, an apostle of Christ Jesus by the will of God	3
	11:13	disguising themselves as apostles of Christ.	3
	12:12	The signs of a true apostle were performed among you	3
Gal	1: 1	Paul an apostle—sent neither by human commission	3

	1:17	to those who were already apostles before me	3
	1:19	I did not see any other apostle	3
	2: 8	making him an apostle to the circumcised	2
Eph	1: 1	Paul, an apostle of Christ Jesus by the will of God	3
	2:20	the foundation of the apostles and prophets	3
	3: 5	been revealed to his holy apostles and prophets	3
	4:11	he gave were that some would be apostles	3
Col	1: 1	Paul, an apostle of Christ Jesus by the will of God	3
1Th	2: 7	might have made demands as apostles of Christ.	3
1Ti	1: 1	Paul, an apostle of Christ Jesus by the command	3
	2: 7	For this I was appointed a herald and an apostle	3
2Ti	1: 1	Paul, an apostle of Christ Jesus by the will of God	3
	1:11	appointed a herald and an apostle and a teacher	3
Tit	1: 1	a servant of God and an apostle of Jesus Christ	3
Heb	3: 1	the apostle and high priest of our confession	3
1Pe	1: 1	Peter, an apostle of Jesus Christ	3
2Pe	1: 1	Peter, a servant and apostle of Jesus Christ	3
	3: 2	commandment of the Lord…through your apostles.	3
Jde	1:17	predictions of the apostles of our Lord Jesus	3
Rev	2: 2	tested those who claim to be apostles	3
	18:20	O heaven, you saints and apostles and prophets!	3
	21:14	twelve names of the twelve apostles of the Lamb.	3

false apostle

1. ψευδαπόστολος, *pseudapostolos, 6013*

2Co	11:13	such boasters are false apostles, deceitful workers	1

apostleship

1. ἀποστολή, *apostolē, 692*

Act	1:25	this ministry and apostleship	1
Rom	1: 5	we have received grace and apostleship	1
1Co	9: 2	you are the seal of my apostleship in the Lord.	1

apparent

1. κατά, *kata, 2848*

2Th	2: 9	apparent in the working of Satan	1

appeal *See also* listen to an appeal, make an appeal

1. ἐπερώτημα, *eperōtēma, 2090*
2. ἐπικαλέω, *epikaleō, 2126*
3. ἐρωτάω, *erōtaō, 2263*
4. ἵστημι, *histēmi, 2705*
5. παρακαλέω, *parakaleō, 4151*
6. παράκλησις, *paraklēsis, 4155*

Mat	8: 5	came to him, appealing to him	5
	26:53	Do you think that I cannot appeal to my Father	5
Lke	7: 4	they appealed to him earnestly, saying,	5
Act	25: 2	They appealed to him	5
	25:10	Paul said, "I am appealing to the emperor's tribunal;	4
	25:11	I appeal to the emperor."	2
	25:12	"You have appealed to the emperor;	2
	25:21	when Paul had appealed to be kept in custody	2
	25:25	when he appealed to his Imperial Majesty	2
	26:32	if he had not appealed to the emperor."	2
	28:19	I was compelled to appeal to the emperor	2
Rom	12: 1	I appeal to you therefore, brothers and sisters	5
	15:30	I appeal to you, brothers and sisters, by our Lord	5
1Co	1:10	I appeal to you, brothers and sisters, by the name	5
	4:16	I appeal to you, then, be imitators of me.	5
2Co	8:17	For he not only accepted our appeal	6
	10: 1	I myself, Paul, appeal to you	5
	12: 8	Three times I appealed to the Lord about this	5
1Th	2: 3	our appeal does not spring from deceit	6
	5:12	we appeal to you, brothers and sisters	3
Phm	1: 9	yet I would rather appeal to you on the basis of love	5
	1:10	I am appealing to you for my child, Onesimus	5
Heb	13:22	I appeal to you, brothers and sisters	5
1Pe	3:21	but as an appeal to God for a good conscience	1
Jde	1: 3	appeal to you to contend for the faith	5

appear

1. Contextual: Not in Greek
2. ἀναφαίνω, *anaphainō, 428*
3. γίνομαι, *ginomai, 1181*
4. ἐγείρω, *egeirō, 1586*
5. ἐμφανής, *emphanēs, 1871*
6. ἐμφανίζω, *emphanizō, 1872*
7. ἐπιφαίνω, *epiphainō, 2210*
8. ἐπιφάνεια, *epiphaneia, 2211*

9. ἐφίστημι, *ephistēmi, 2392*
10. ἰδού, *idou, 2627*
11. ὀπτάνομαι, *optanomai, 3964*
12. ὁράω, *horaō, 3972*
13. παραγίνομαι, *paraginomai, 4134*
14. φαίνω, *phainō, 5743*
15. φανερόω, *phaneroō, 5746*
16. ὡς, *hōs, 6055*

Mat	1:20	an angel of the Lord appeared to him in a dream	14
	2: 7	from them the exact time when the star had appeared.	14
	2:13	an angel of the Lord appeared to Joseph in a dream	14
	2:19	Herod died, an angel of the Lord suddenly appeared	14
	3: 1	Baptist appeared in the wilderness of Judea	13
	13:26	then the weeds appeared as well.	14
	17: 3	Suddenly there appeared to them Moses and Elijah	12
	24:24	For false messiahs and false prophets will appear	4
	24:30	the sign of the Son of Man will appear in heaven	14
	27:53	entered the holy city and appeared to many.	6
Mrk	1: 4	John the baptizer appeared in the wilderness	3
	9: 4	there appeared to them Elijah with Moses	12
	13:22	False messiahs and false prophets will appear	4
	16: 9	[he appeared first to Mary Magdalene]	14
	16:12	[After this he appeared in another form to two]	15
	16:14	[Later he appeared to the eleven themselves]	15
Lke	1:11	there appeared to him an angel of the Lord	12
	9: 8	by some that Elijah had appeared	14
	9:31	They appeared in glory and were speaking	12
	13:11	just then there appeared a woman with a spirit	10
	19:11	the kingdom of God was to appear immediately.	2
	22:43	[Then an angel from heaven appeared to him]	12
	24:34	has appeared to Simon!"	12
Jhn	21:14	Jesus appeared to the disciples	15
Act	1: 3	appearing to them during forty days	11
	2: 3	Divided tongues, as of fire, appeared among them,	12
	7: 2	The God of glory appeared to our ancestor Abraham	12
	7:30	an angel appeared to him in the wilderness	12
	7:35	the angel who appeared to him in the bush.	12
	9:17	the Lord Jesus, who appeared to you on your way	12
	10:17	suddenly the men sent by Cornelius appeared	1
	10:40	allowed him to appear	5
	12: 7	Suddenly an angel of the Lord appeared	9
	13:31	he appeared to those who came up with him	12
	26:16	I have appeared to you for this purpose	12
	26:16	those in which I will appear to you.	12
	27:20	neither sun nor stars appeared for many days	7
1Co	15: 5	that he appeared to Cephas, then to the twelve.	12
	15: 6	Then he appeared to more than five hundred	12
	15: 7	he appeared to James, then to all the apostles.	12
	15: 8	he appeared also to me.	12
2Co	5:10	For all of us must appear before the judgment seat	15
	13: 7	not that we may appear to have met the test	14
2Ti	1:10	been revealed through the appearing of our Savior	8
	4: 1	in view of his appearing and his kingdom	8
	4: 8	also to all who have longed for his appearing.	8
Tit	2:11	has appeared, bringing salvation to all,	7
	3: 4	loving kindness of God our Savior appeared	7
Heb	9:24	now to appear in the presence of God on our behalf.	6
	9:26	he has appeared once for all at the end of the age	15
	9:28	will appear a second time, not to deal with sin	12
Jas	4:14	For you are a mist that appears for a little while	14
1Pe	5: 4	when the chief shepherd appears,	15
Rev	12: 1	A great portent appeared in heaven: a woman	12
	12: 3	another portent appeared in heaven:	12
	15: 2	I saw what appeared to be a sea of glass	16

appear publicly

1. ἀνάδειξις, *anadeixis, 345*

Lke	1:80	until the day he appeared publicly to Israel.	1

appearance

1. εἰδέα, *eidea, 1624*
2. εἶδος, *eidos, 1626*
3. λόγος, *logos, 3364*
4. ὁμοίωμα, *homoiōma, 3930*
5. ὄψις, *opsis, 4071*
6. πρόσωπον, *prosōpon, 4725*
7. πρόφασις, *prophasis, 4733*

Mat	16: 3	how to interpret the appearance of the sky	6
	28: 3	His appearance was like lightning	1

Mrk	12:40	for the sake of appearance say long prayers.	7
Lke	9:29	the appearance of his face changed,	2
	12:56	You know how to interpret the appearance	6
	20:47	for the sake of appearance say long prayers.	7
Jhn	7:24	Do not judge by appearances	5
Col	2:23	These have indeed an appearance of wisdom	3
Rev	9: 7	In appearance the locusts were like horses	4

outward appearance

1. πρόσωπον, *prosōpon, 4725*

2Co	5:12	those who boast in outward appearance	1

appetite

1. κοιλία, *koilia, 3120*

Rom	16:18	such people…serve…their own appetites	1

Apphia

1. Ἀπφία, *Apphia, 722*

Phm	1: 2	Apphia our sister, to Archippus our fellow soldier	1

Appius

1. Ἄππιος, *Appios, 716*

Act	28:15	as far as the Forum of Appius and Three Taverns	1

applaud

1. συνευδοκέω, *syneudokeō, 5306*

Rom	1:32	but even applaud others who practice them.	1

apply

1. γίνομαι, *ginomai, 1181*
2. λέγω, *legō, 3306*
3. μετασχηματίζω, *metaschēmatizō, 3571*

1Co	4: 6	I have applied all this to Apollos and myself	3
	9:15	so that they may be applied in my case	1
Eph	5:32	I am applying it to Christ and the church.	2

appoint   *See also* appointed *time*

1. Contextual: Not in Greek
2. ἀναδείκνυμι, *anadeiknymi, 344*
3. ἀπόκειμαι, *apokeimai, 641*
4. διαταγή, *diatagē, 1408*
5. καθίστημι, *kathistēmi, 2770*
6. ὁρίζω, *horizō, 3988*
7. ποιέω, *poieō, 4472*
8. προχειρίζω, *procheirizō, 4741*
9. τακτός, *taktos, 5414*
10. τάσσω, *tassō, 5435*
11. τίθημι, *tithēmi, 5502*
12. χειροτονέω, *cheirotoneō, 5936*

Mrk	3:14	he appointed twelve, whom he also named apostles	7
	3:16	So he appointed the twelve: Simon	7
Lke	10: 1	After this the Lord appointed seventy others	2
Jhn	15:16	I appointed you to go and bear fruit	11
Act	3:20	may send the Messiah appointed for you…Jesus	8
	6: 3	whom we may appoint to this task	5
	7:10	who appointed him ruler over Egypt	5
	12:21	On an appointed day Herod put on his royal robes	9
	14:23	had appointed elders for them in each church	12
	15: 2	appointed to go up to Jerusalem to discuss this	10
	17:31	the world judged…by a man whom he has appointed	6
	26:16	to appoint you to serve and testify	8
Rom	13: 2	resists what God has appointed	4
1Co	12:28	God has appointed in the church first apostles	11
2Co	8:19	appointed by the churches to travel with us	12
1Ti	1:12	and appointed me to his service	11
	2: 7	For this I was appointed a herald and an apostle	11
2Ti	1:11	For this gospel I was appointed a herald	11
Tit	1: 5	appoint elders in every town, as I directed you:	5
Heb	1: 2	a Son, whom he appointed heir of all things	11
	3: 2	was faithful to the one who appointed him	7
	5: 5	but was appointed by the one who said to him	1
	7:28	the law appoints as high priests those who are subject	5
	7:28	the oath…appoints a Son who has been made perfect	1
	8: 3	every high priest is appointed to offer gifts	5
	9:27	just as it is appointed for mortals to die once	3

appoint as judge

1. καθίζω, *kathizō, 2767*

1Co	6: 4	you appoint as judges those who have no standing	1

apportion

1. μερίζω, *merizō, 3532*

Heb 7: 2 to him Abraham apportioned "one-tenth of everything."   1

approach

1. ἀπαντάω, *apantaō, 560*
2. ἐγγίζω, *engizō, 1581*
3. προσέρχομαι, *proserchomai, 4665*

Mat 8:19 A scribe then approached and said   3
13:36 And his disciples approached him, saying   3
15:12 Then the disciples approached and said to him   3
Mrk 11: 1 When they were approaching Jerusalem,   2
Lke 7:12 As he approached the gate of the town   2
15:25 when he came and approached the house   2
17:12 As he entered a village, ten lepers approached him.   1
18:35 As he approached Jericho   2
19:37 As he was now approaching   2
22:47 He approached Jesus to kiss him;   2
Act 7:31 he approached to look, there came the voice of the Lord: 3
9: 3 Now as he was going along and approaching Damascus   2
10: 9 as they were…approaching the city   2
22: 6 "While I was on my way and approaching Damascus   2
Heb 4:16 therefore approach the throne of grace with boldness   3
7:19 a better hope, through which we approach God.   2
7:25 to save those who approach God through him   3
10: 1 it can never…make perfect those who approach.   3
10:22 let us approach with a true heart   3
10:25 all the more as you see the Day approaching.   2
11: 6 for whoever would approach him must believe   3

appropriate

1. συμφέρω, *sympherō, 5237*

2Co 8:10 it is appropriate for you…to do something   1

approval *See also* give approval, receive approval, seek approval

1. δόκιμος, *dokimos, 1511*
2. ἔπαινος, *epainos, 2047*
3. χάρις, *charis, 5921*

Rom 13: 3 do what is good, and you will receive its approval;   2
14:18 is acceptable to God and has human approval.   1
1Pe 2:20 you have God's approval.   3

approve

1. δοκιμάζω, *dokimazō, 1507*
2. δόκιμος, *dokimos, 1511*
3. συνευδοκέω, *syneudokeō, 5306*

Lke 11:48 approve of the deeds of your ancestors;   3
Act 8: 1 Saul approved of their killing him.   3
22:20 I myself was standing by, approving   3
Rom 14:22 condemn themselves because of what they approve.   1
16:10 Greet Apelles, who is approved in Christ.   2
1Co 16: 3 I will send any whom you approve with letters   1
2Co 10:18 not those who commend themselves that are approved   2
1Th 2: 4 just as we have been approved by God   1
2Ti 2:15 to present yourself to God as one approved   2

apron *See also* put on an apron

1. σιμικίνθιον, *simikinthion, 4980*

Act 19:12 aprons that had touched his skin were brought   1

apt *See* apt *teacher*

Aquila

1. Ἀκύλας, *Akylas, 217*

Act 18: 2 he found a Jew named Aquila, a native of Pontus   1
18:18 accompanied by Priscilla and Aquila.   1
18:26 when Priscilla and Aquila heard him   1
Rom 16: 3 Greet Prisca and Aquila, who work with me   1
1Co 16:19 Aquila and Prisca, together with the church   1
2Ti 4:19 Greet Prisca and Aquila   1

Arab

1. Ἄραψ, *Araps, 732*

Act 2:11 Cretans and Arabs   1

Arabia

1. Ἀραβία, *Arabia, 728*

Gal 1:17 I went away at once into Arabia   1
4:25 Now Hagar is Mount Sinai in Arabia   1

Aram

1. Ἀράμ, *Aram, 730*

Mat 1: 3 and Hezron the father of Aram   1
1: 4 Aram the father of Aminadab   1

arbitrator

1. μεριστής, *meristēs, 3537*

Lke 12:14 who set me to be a judge or arbitrator over you?"   1

archangel

1. ἀρχάγγελος, *archangelos, 791*

1Th 4:16 For the Lord himself…with the archangel's call   1
Jde 1: 9 when archangel Michael contended with the devil   1

Archelaus

1. Ἀρχέλαος, *Archelaos, 793*

Mat 2:22 he heard that Archelaus was ruling over Judea   1

Archippus

1. Ἄρχιππος, *Archippos, 800*

Col 4:17 say to Archippus, "See that you complete the task   1
Phm 1: 2 Apphia our sister, to Archippus our fellow soldier   1

architect

1. τεχνίτης, *technitēs, 5493*

Heb 11:10 the city…whose architect and builder is God.   1

ardent

1. ζέω, *zeō, 2417*

Rom 12:11 not lag in zeal, be ardent in spirit   1

Areopagite

1. Ἀρεοπαγίτης, *Areopagitēs, 741*

Act 17:34 believers, including Dionysius the Areopagite   1

Areopagus

1. Ἄρειος πάγος, *Areios pagos, 740*

Act 17:19 and brought him to the Areopagus   1
17:22 Paul stood in front of the Areopagus   1

Aretas

1. Ἀρέτας, *Haretas, 745*

2Co 11:32 the governor under King Aretas guarded the city   1

argue

1. ἀνταποκρίνομαι, *antapokrinomai, 503*
2. διαλέγομαι, *dialegomai, 1363*
3. διαλογίζομαι, *dialogizomai, 1368*
4. διαλογισμός, *dialogismos, 1369*
5. συζητέω, *syzēteō, 5184*

Mat 21:25 And they argued with one another   3
Mrk 8:11 The Pharisees came and began to argue with him   5
9:14 scribes arguing with them.   5
9:16 "What are you arguing about with them?"   5
9:33 "What were you arguing about on the way?"   3
9:34 on the way they had argued with one another   2
11:31 They argued with one another   3
Act 6: 9 some of those…stood up and argued with Stephen.   5
9:29 He spoke and argued with the Hellenists;   5
17: 2 on three sabbath days argued with them   2
17:17 he argued in the synagogue with the Jews   2
18: 4 Every sabbath he would argue in the synagogue   2
19: 8 argued persuasively about the kingdom of God.   2
19: 9 argued daily in the lecture hall of Tyrannus.   2
Rom 9:20 who indeed are you, a human being, to argue with God?   1
Php 2:14 Do all things without murmuring and arguing   4

argument

1. διαλογισμός, *dialogismos, 1369*
2. λογισμός, *logismos, 3361*
3. λόγος, *logos, 3364*

Lke 9:46 An argument arose among them   1
Act 2:40 he testified with many other arguments and exhorted   3
2Co 10: 4 power to destroy strongholds. We destroy arguments   2
1Ti 2: 8 lifting up holy hands without anger or argument;   1

plausible argument

1. πιθανολογία, *pithanologia, 4391*

Col 2: 4 no one may deceive you with plausible arguments.   1

Arimathea

1. Ἀριμαθαία, *Harimathaia, 751*

Mat 27:57 a rich man from Arimathea, named Joseph   1
Mrk 15:43 Joseph of Arimathea, a respected member   1
Lke 23:51 he came from the Jewish town of Arimathea   1
Jhn 19:38 Joseph of Arimathea, who was a disciple of Jesus   1

arise

1. ἀναβαίνω, *anabainō, 326*
2. ἀνίστημι, *anistēmi, 482*
3. γίνομαι, *ginomai, 1181*
4. ἐγείρω, *egeirō, 1586*
5. εἰσέρχομαι, *eiserchomai, 1656*

Mat 8:24 A windstorm arose on the sea, so great   3
    11:11 no one has arisen greater than John   4
    13:21 and when trouble or persecution arises   3
    24:11 many false prophets will arise   4
Mrk 4:17 then, when trouble or persecution arises   3
     4:37 A great windstorm arose   3
Lke 6:48 when a flood arose   3
     9: 8 that one of the ancient prophets had arisen.   2
     9:19 that one of the ancient prophets has arisen."   2
     9:46 An argument arose among them   5
    22:24 A dispute also arose among them   3
    24:38 why do doubts arise in your hearts?   1
Jhn 3:25 Now a discussion about purification arose   3
     7:52 no prophet is to arise from Galilee."   4
Act 23: 9 Then a great clamor arose   3
Heb 7:11 need...to speak of another priest arising   2
     7:15 another priest arises, resembling Melchizedek,   2
2Pe 2: 1 false prophets also arose among the people   3

Aristarchus

1. Ἀρίσταρχος, *Aristarchos, 752*

Act 19:29 dragging with them Gaius and Aristarchus   1
    20: 4 Aristarchus and Secundus from Thessalonica   1
    27: 2 Aristarchus, a Macedonian from Thessalonica.   1
Col 4:10 Aristarchus my fellow prisoner greets you   1
Phm 1:24 so do Mark, Aristarchus, Demas, and Luke   1

Aristobulus

1. Ἀριστόβουλος, *Aristoboulos, 755*

Rom 16:10 those who belong to the family of Aristobulus.   1

ark

1. κιβωτός, *kibōtos, 3066*

Mat 24:38 until the day Noah entered the ark   1
Lke 17:27 until the day Noah entered the ark   1
Heb 9: 4 the ark of the covenant   1
    11: 7 Noah...respected the warning and built an ark   1
1Pe 3:20 during the building of the ark   1
Rev 11:19 ark of his covenant was seen within his temple;   1

arm¹ *See also* put arms around, take in one's arms

1. ἀγκάλη, *ankalē, 44*
2. βραχίων, *brachiōn, 1098*

Lke 1:51 He has shown strength with his arm;   2
     2:28 Simeon took him in his arms and praised God,   1
Jhn 12:38 to whom has the arm of the Lord been revealed?"   2
Act 13:17 with uplifted arm he led them out of it.   2

arm²

1. ὁπλίζω, *hoplizō, 3959*

1Pe 4: 1 arm yourselves also with the same intention   1

arm fully

1. καθοπλίζω, *kathoplizō, 2774*

Lke 11:21 a strong man, fully armed, guards his castle   1

armor

1. ὅπλον, *hoplon, 3960*
2. πανοπλία, *panoplia, 4110*

Lke 11:22 he takes away his armor in which he trusted   2
Rom 13:12 Let us...put on the armor of light;   1

whole armor

1. πανοπλία, *panoplia, 4110*

Eph 6:11 Put on the whole armor of God   1
     6:13 Therefore take up the whole armor of God   1

army *See also* serve in the army

1. παρεμβολή, *parembolē, 4213*
2. στράτευμα, *strateuma, 5128*
3. στρατόπεδον, *stratopedon, 5136*

Lke 21:20 "When you see Jerusalem surrounded by armies   3
Heb 11:34 put foreign armies to flight.   1
Rev 19:14 And the armies of heaven...were following him   2
    19:19 kings...with their armies gathered to make war   2
    19:19 to make war against...and against his army.   2

Arni

1. Ἀρνί, *Arni, 767*

Lke 3:33 son of Arni, son of Hezron, son of Perez   1

aroma

1. εὐωδία, *euōdia, 2380*

2Co 2:15 For we are the aroma of Christ to God   1

around *See also* all around, fasten belt around, flash around, gather around, hang around, look all around, look around, prowl around, put arms around, put around, region around, shine around, tie around, walk around, wrap around

1. Contextual: Not in Greek
2. εἰς + ὁ + ὀπίσω, *eis + ho + opisō, 1650 + 3836 + 3958*
3. ἐν + μέσος, *en + mesos, 1877 + 3545*
4. ἐπί, *epi, 2093*
5. κυκλόθεν, *kyklothen, 3239*
6. κύκλῳ, *kyklō, 3241*
7. ὅριον, *horion, 3990*
8. περί, *peri, 4309*
9. πέριξ, *perix, 4339*
10. πρός, *pros, 4639*

Mat 2:16 killed all the children in and around Bethlehem   7
     3: 4 leather belt around his waist, and his food was   8
     8:18 Now when Jesus saw great crowds around him   8
    13: 2 great crowds gathered around him   10
    18: 6 a great millstone were fastened around your neck   8
    20: 6 he went out and found others standing around;   1
    27:27 they gathered the whole cohort around him.   4
Mrk 1: 6 a leather belt around his waist   8
     1:33 gathered around the door.   10
     2:13 the whole crowd gathered around him   10
     3: 8 beyond the Jordan, and the region around Tyre   8
     3:32 A crowd was sitting around him; and they said   8
     3:34 looking at those who sat around him   8
     4: 1 a very large crowd gathered around him   10
     4:10 those who were around him along with the twelve   8
     5:21 a great crowd gathered around him;   4
     6:30 The apostles gathered around Jesus, and told him   10
     7: 1 Now when the Pharisees...gathered around him   10
     9:14 they saw a great crowd around them   8
     9:42 if a great millstone were hung around your neck   8
    10: 1 crowds again gathered around him;   10
    16: S [[they told briefly to those around Peter]]   8
Lke 13: 8 until I dig around it and put manure on   8
    17: 2 if a millstone were hung around your neck   8
    19:43 when your enemies will set up ramparts around you   1
    22:49 When those who were around him saw   8
Jhn 18:18 were standing around it and warming themselves.   1
    20:14 said this, she turned around and saw Jesus   2
Act 5:16 gather from the towns around Jerusalem   9
    28: 2 a fire and welcomed all of us around it   1
Rom 15:19 from Jerusalem and as far around as Illyricum   6
Rev 4: 3 and around the throne is a rainbow   5
     4: 4 Around the throne are twenty-four thrones   5
     4: 6 Around the throne, and on each side of the throne   3
     7:11 all the angels stood around the throne   6
     7:11 around the elders and the four living creatures   1

arouse

1. διά, *dia, 1328*
2. διεγείρω, *diegeirō, 1444*

3. κινέω, *kineō, 3075*

Act	21:30	Then all the city was aroused	3
Rom	7: 5	our sinful passions, aroused by the law	1
2Pe	3: 1	in them I am trying to arouse your sincere intention	2

Arphaxad

1. Ἀρφαξάδ, *Arphaxad, 790*

Lke	3:36	son of Cainan, son of Arphaxad	1

arrange

1. συγκεράννυμι, *synkerannymi, 5166*
2. τίθημι, *tithēmi, 5502*

1Co	12:18	as it is, God arranged the members in the body	2
	12:24	God has so arranged the body	1

arrange in advance

1. προκαταρτίζω, *prokatartizō, 4616*

2Co	9: 5	and arrange in advance for this bountiful gift	1

arrangement   *See* make an arrangement

arrest

1. ἄγω, *agō, 72*
2. δέσμιος, *desmios, 1300*
3. ἐπιβάλλω + ἐπί + ὁ + χείρ, *epiballō + epi + ho + cheir, 2095 + 2093 + 3836 + 5931*
4. ἐπιβάλλω + ὁ + χείρ, *epiballō + ho + cheir, 2095 + 3836 + 5931*
5. ἐπιλαμβάνομαι, *epilambanomai, 2138*
6. κρατέω, *krateō, 3195*
7. παραδίδωμι, *paradidōmi, 4140*
8. πιάζω, *piazō, 4389*
9. συλλαμβάνω, *syllambanō, 5197*

Mat	4:12	Now when Jesus heard that John had been arrested	7
	14: 3	For Herod had arrested John, bound him	6
	21:46	They wanted to arrest him, but they feared	6
	26: 4	and they conspired to arrest Jesus	6
	26:48	"The one I will kiss is the man; arrest him."	6
	26:50	came and laid hands on Jesus and arrested him.	6
	26:55	with swords and clubs to arrest me	9
	26:55	you did not arrest me.	6
	26:57	Those who had arrested Jesus	6
Mrk	1:14	Now after John was arrested	7
	6:17	For Herod himself had sent men who arrested John	6
	12:12	they wanted to arrest him	6
	14: 1	way to arrest Jesus by stealth and kill him;	6
	14:44	arrest him and lead him away under guard."	6
	14:46	they laid hands on him and arrested him.	6
	14:48	with swords and clubs to arrest me	9
	14:49	you did not arrest me.	6
Lke	21:12	before all this occurs, they will arrest you	3
Jhn	7:30	they tried to arrest him	8
	7:32	Pharisees sent temple police to arrest him.	8
	7:44	Some of them wanted to arrest him	8
	7:45	who asked them, "Why did you not arrest him?"	1
	8:20	but no one arrested him	8
	10:39	they tried to arrest him again	8
	11:57	let them know, so that they might arrest him.	8
	18:12	Jewish police arrested Jesus and bound him.	9
Act	1:16	Judas, who became a guide for those who arrested Jesus	9
	4: 3	they arrested them	4
	5:18	arrested the apostles	4
	12: 3	he proceeded to arrest Peter also.	9
	21:33	Then the tribune came, arrested him	5
	28:17	yet I was arrested in Jerusalem	2

arrival

1. εἰσέρχομαι, *eiserchomai, 1656*
2. παραγίνομαι, *paraginomai, 4134*
3. παρουσία, *parousia, 4242*

Act	10:25	On Peter's arrival Cornelius met him	1
	18:27	On his arrival he greatly helped	2
2Co	7: 6	consoled us by the arrival of Titus	3

arrive

1. γίνομαι, *ginomai, 1181*
2. ἐγγίζω, *engizō, 1581*
3. ἐπιβαίνω, *epibainō, 2094*
4. ἔρχομαι, *erchomai, 2262*

5. ἐφίστημι, *ephistēmi, 2392*
6. καταντάω, *katantaō, 2918*
7. καταπλέω, *katapleō, 2929*
8. κατέρχομαι, *katerchomai, 2982*
9. παραγίνομαι, *paraginomai, 4134*

Mat	24:46	whom his master will find at work when he arrives.	4
	26:47	Judas, one of the twelve, arrived;	4
Mrk	14:43	Judas, one of the twelve, arrived;	9
Lke	8:26	they arrived at the country of the Gerasenes	7
	11: 6	a friend of mine has arrived	9
	12:43	his master will find at work when he arrives.	4
Jhn	11:17	When Jesus arrived	4
Act	5:21	the high priest and those with him arrived	9
	5:25	Then someone arrived and announced, "Look,	9
	9:39	when he arrived, they took him to the room upstairs.	9
	11:11	arrived at the house where we were.	5
	13: 5	When they arrived at Salamis	1
	14:27	When they arrived, they called the church	9
	17:10	to Beroea; and when they arrived,	9
	18: 5	When Silas and Timothy arrived from Macedonia	8
	20:15	the following day we arrived opposite Chios.	6
	21: 7	we arrived at Ptolemais;	6
	21:17	When we arrived in Jerusalem	1
	23:15	we are ready to do away with him before he arrives."	2
	23:35	give you a hearing when your accusers arrive."	9
	25: 1	Three days after Festus had arrived in the province	3
	25: 7	When he arrived, the Jews...surrounded him	9
	25:13	Agrippa...arrived at Caesarea to welcome Festus.	6
	27: 7	arrived with difficulty off Cnidus	1
1Co	16: 3	when I arrive, I will send any whom you approve	9
1Ti	4:13	Until I arrive, give attention to the...reading	4
2Ti	1:17	when he arrived in Rome, he eagerly searched for me	1
	3: 7	can never arrive at a knowledge of the truth.	4
3Jn	1: 3	I was overjoyed when some of the friends arrived	4

arrive ahead

1. προέρχομαι, *proerchomai, 4601*

Mrk	6:33	they hurried...and arrived ahead of them.	1

arrogance

1. ἀλαζονεία, *alazoneia, 224*

Jas	4:16	As it is, you boast in your arrogance;	1

arrogant

1. αὐθάδης, *authadēs, 881*
2. ὑπερήφανος, *hyperēphanos, 5662*
3. φυσιόω, *physioō, 5881*

1Co	4:18	some of you...have become arrogant.	3
	4:19	find out not the talk of these arrogant people	3
	5: 2	you are arrogant! Should you not rather have mourned	3
	13: 4	love is not envious or boastful or arrogant	3
2Ti	3: 2	lovers of money, boasters, arrogant, abusive,	2
Tit	1: 7	he must not be arrogant or quick-tempered	1

arrow

1. βέλος, *belos, 1018*

Eph	6:16	able to quench all the flaming arrows of the evil one.	1

art   *See also* magic art

1. τέχνη, *technē, 5492*

Act	17:29	an image formed by the art...of mortals.	1

Artemas

1. Ἀρτεμᾶς, *Artemas, 782*

Tit	3:12	When I send Artemas to you, or Tychicus	1

Artemis

1. Ἄρτεμις, *Artemis, 783*

Act	19:24	a silversmith who made silver shrines of Artemis	1
	19:27	the temple of the great goddess Artemis	1
	19:28	"Great is Artemis of the Ephesians!"	1
	19:34	"Great is Artemis of the Ephesians!"	1
	19:35	the temple keeper of the great Artemis	1

article

1. σκεῦος, *skeuos, 5007*

Rev	18:12	all kinds of scented wood, all articles of ivory	1
	18:12	articles of costly wood, bronze, iron, and marble	1

artisan

1. τεχνίτης, *technitēs*, 5493

Act 19:24 brought no little business to the artisans;   1
    19:38 Demetrius and the artisans with him   1
Rev 18:22 an artisan...will be found in you no more;   1

as

See also adoption as a child, appoint as judge, as a *body*, as a *whole*, as *equal*, as *follows*, as *precious*, as *soon* as, as yet *unseen*, clear as crystal, entertain as a guest, even as, four times as much, give as an inheritance, give as well, just as, pour out as a libation, serve as an example, serve as deacon, serve as judge, serve as priest, soon as possible, speak of as evil, take away as captive, twice as much

1. ἀπό, *apo*, 608
2. ἐάν, *ean*, 1569
3. εἰ, *ei*, 1623
4. εἰμί, *eimi*, 1639
5. εἰς, *eis*, 1650
6. ἐκ, *ek*, 1666
7. ἐν, *en*, 1877
8. ἐπί, *epi*, 2093
9. ἤδη, *ēdē*, 2453
10. καθά, *katha*, 2745
11. καθάπερ, *kathaper*, 2749
12. καθό, *katho*, 2771
13. καθότι + ἄν, *kathoti + an*, 2776 + 323
14. καθώς, *kathōs*, 2777
15. καί, *kai*, 2779
16. κατά, *kata*, 2848
17. μετά, *meta*, 3552
18. νῦν, *nyn*, 3814
19. οἷος, *hoios*, 3888
20. ὅμοιος, *homoios*, 3927
21. ὁμοιότης, *homoiotēs*, 3928
22. ὁμοίως, *homoiōs*, 3931
23. ὁποῖος, *hopoios*, 3961
24. ὅς, *hos*, 4005
25. ὅς + τρόπος, *hos + tropos*, 4005 + 5573
26. ὅσος, *hosos*, 4012
27. ὅτι, *hoti*, 4022
28. οὖν, *oun*, 4036
29. οὗτος, *houtos*, 4047
30. οὕτως, *houtōs*, 4048
31. σύν, *syn*, 5250
32. τέ, *te*, 5445
33. τοιοῦτος, *toioutos*, 5525
34. τρόπος, *tropos*, 5573
35. ὑπέρ, *hyper*, 5642
36. ὑπόδειγμα, *hypodeigma*, 5682
37. ὡς, *hōs*, 6055
38. ὡσεί, *hōsei*, 6059
39. ὥσπερ, *hōsper*, 6061
40. ὡσπερεί, *hōsperei*, 6062

Ref	Text	No.
Mat 1:24	he did as the angel of the Lord commanded him;	37
5:48	Be perfect...as your heavenly Father is perfect.	37
6: 2	not sound a trumpet before you, as the hypocrites do	39
6: 7	heap up empty phrases as the Gentiles do;	39
6:10	Your will be done, on earth as it is in heaven.	37
6:12	And forgive us our debts, as we also have forgiven	37
7:12	do to others as you would have them do to you	30
7:29	for he taught them as one having authority	37
7:29	and not as their scribes.	37
8: 4	offer the gift...as a testimony to them."	5
9:15	guests cannot mourn as long as the bridegroom	8
10:16	so be wise as serpents and innocent as doves.	37
10:16	so be wise as serpents and innocent as doves.	37
10:18	as a testimony to them and the Gentiles.	5
12:13	and it was restored, as sound as the other.	37
13: 4	as he sowed, some seeds fell on the path	7
14: 5	because they regarded him as a prophet.	37
15:28	Let it be done for you as you wish."	37
18:17	let such a one be to you as a Gentile	39
18:33	as I had mercy on you?'	37
19:19	You shall love your neighbor as yourself."	37
21: 6	The disciples went and did as Jesus had directed	14
21:26	for all regard John as a prophet."	37
21:46	because they regarded him as a prophet.	5
22:39	'You shall love your neighbor as yourself.'	37
23: 3	but do not do as they do	16
23:37	as a hen gathers her brood under her wings	25
24:14	as a testimony to all the nations;	5
24:27	For as the lightning comes from the east	39
24:37	For as the days of Noah were	39
24:38	For as in those days before the flood	37
25:32	as a shepherd separates the sheep from the goats	39
26:19	the disciples did as Jesus had directed them	37
26:24	The Son of Man goes as it is written of him	14
27: 7	the potter's field as a place to bury foreigners	5
27:10	as the Lord commanded me."	10
27:65	go, make it as secure as you can."	37
28: 3	his clothing white as snow.	37
28: 6	not here; for he has been raised, as he said.	14
28:15	took the money and did as they were directed.	37
Mrk 1: 2	As it is written in the prophet Isaiah	14
1:22	he taught them as one having authority	37
1:22	not as the scribes.	37
1:44	as a testimony to them."	5
2:19	As long as they have the bridegroom with them	26
4: 4	as he sowed, some seed fell on the path	7
4:33	as they were able to hear it;	14
6:11	as a testimony against them."	5
7: 6	as it is written, 'This people honors me	37
9: 3	such as no one on earth could bleach them.	30
9:13	as it is written about him."	14
10: 1	as was his custom, he again taught them.	37
10:15	receive the kingdom of God as a little child	37
11:32	for all regarded John as truly a prophet.	27
12:31	'You shall love your neighbor as yourself.'	37
12:33	'to love one's neighbor as oneself,'	37
12:38	As he taught, he said, "Beware of the scribes	7
13: 9	as a testimony to them.	5
14:16	found everything as he had told them;	14
14:21	For the Son of Man goes as it is written of him	14
Lke 1:70	as he spoke through the mouth of his holy prophets	14
2:20	as it had been told them.	14
2:23	(as it is written in the law of the Lord	14
2:42	they went up as usual for the festival	16
3: 4	as it is written in the book of...Isaiah	37
3:23	was the son (as was thought) of Joseph	37
4:16	synagogue on the sabbath day, as was his custom.	16
5:14	as Moses commanded, make an offering	14
6:31	Do to others as you would have them do to you.	14
7:12	As he approached the gate of the town	37
8: 5	as he sowed, some fell on the path	7
8:42	As he went, the crowds pressed in on him.	7
9: 5	dust off your feet as a testimony against them."	5
9:34	they were terrified as they entered the cloud.	7
10:27	and your neighbor as yourself."	37
10:38	Now as they went on their way, he entered	7
11: 1	teach us to pray, as John taught his disciples."	14
11:36	as when a lamp gives you light with its rays."	37
13: 3	unless you repent, you will all perish as	22
13:34	as a hen gathers her brood under her wings	25
16: 4	so that, when I am dismissed as manager,	6
17:14	as they went, they were made clean.	7
17:24	For as the lightning flashes and lights up	39
18:17	receive the kingdom of God as a little child	37
18:35	As he approached Jericho	7
19:32	departed and found it as he had told them.	14
19:41	As he came near and saw the city, he wept over it	37
22:13	they went and found everything as he had told them;	14
22:22	the Son of Man is going as it has been determined	16
22:27	But I am among you as one who serves.	37
22:39	went, as was his custom, to the Mount of Olives;	16
23:14	as one who was perverting the people;	37
23:26	As they led him away	37
24:39	not have flesh and bones as you see that I have."	14
Jhn 1: 7	He came as a witness to testify	5
1:14	glory as of a father's only son, full	37
1:23	as the prophet Isaiah said.	14
4:51	As he was going down, his slaves met him	9
5:30	As I hear, I judge; and my judgment is just	14
6:31	as it is written, 'He gave them bread from heaven	14
7:10	went, not publicly but as it were in secret.	37
7:38	As the scripture has said, 'Out of	14
8:28	speak these things as the Father instructed me.	14
9: 8	those who had seen him before as a beggar	27
12:14	as it is written:	14

	13:15	you also should do as I have done to you.	14
	13:33	as I said to the Jews so now I say to you	14
	14:27	I do not give to you as the world gives.	14
	14:31	I do as the Father has commanded me	14
	15: 9	As the Father has loved me, so I have loved you;	14
	15:12	you love one another as I have loved you.	14
	17:11	so that they may be one, as we are one.	14
	17:18	As you have sent me into the world	14
	17:21	As you, Father, are in me and I am in you	14
	17:22	so that they may be one, as we are one	14
	20:11	As she wept, she bent over to look into the tomb;	37
	20:21	As the Father has sent me, so I send you."	14
Act	2: 3	Divided tongues, as of fire, appeared among them,	38
	2: 4	as the Spirit gave them ability.	14
	2:15	Indeed, these are not drunk, as you suppose	37
	2:22	as you yourselves know—	14
	2:45	distribute the proceeds to all, as any had need.	13
	3: 4	Peter looked intently at him, as did John, and said	31
	3:17	you acted in ignorance, as did also your rulers.	39
	4:13	recognized them as companions of Jesus.	27
	4:35	was distributed to each as any had need.	13
	5:41	As they left the council	28
	7: 5	promised to give it to him as his possession	5
	7:17	as the time drew near for the fulfillment	14
	7:21	and brought him up as her own son.	5
	7:28	kill me as you killed the Egyptian yesterday?'	34
	7:37	raise up a prophet for you…as he raised me up.'	37
	7:42	as it is written in the book of the prophets:	14
	7:44	as God directed when he spoke to Moses	14
	7:48	as the prophet says	14
	7:53	ones that received the law as ordained by angels	5
	8:36	As they were going along the road	37
	9: 3	Now as he was going along and approaching Damascus	7
	10: 4	have ascended as a memorial before God.	5
	11:15	as I began to speak, the Holy Spirit fell upon them	7
	13:23	brought to Israel a Savior, Jesus, as he promised;	16
	13:25	as John was finishing his work, he said	37
	13:33	as also it is written in the second psalm	37
	15:15	the words of the prophets, as it is written,	14
	16: 4	As they went from town to town,	37
	17: 2	Paul went in, as was his custom	16
	17: 4	as did a great many of the devout Greeks	32
	17:15	join him as soon as possible	37
	17:28	as even some of your own poets have said	37
	22: 5	as the high priest and the whole council of elders	37
	25:10	done no wrong to the Jews, as you very well know.	37
	26:29	might become such as I am—except for these chains."	23
	27:25	it will be exactly as I have been told.	34
Rom	1:13	as I have among the rest of the Gentiles.	14
	1:17	as it is written, "The one who is righteous	14
	1:21	they did not honor him as God or give thanks	37
	2:24	as it is written, "The name of God is blasphemed	14
	2:26	uncircumcision be regarded as circumcision?	5
	3: 4	let God be proved true…as it is written	14
	3: 7	why am I still being condemned as a sinner?	37
	3: 8	(as some people slander us by saying that we say)	14
	3:10	as it is written: "There is no one who is righteous	14
	4: 3	and it was reckoned to him as righteousness."	5
	4: 4	wages are not reckoned as a gift but as something due.	16
	4: 4	wages are not reckoned as a gift but as something due.	16
	4: 5	such faith is reckoned as righteousness.	5
	4: 9	"Faith was reckoned to Abraham as righteousness."	5
	4:17	as it is written, "I have made you the father	14
	4:22	his faith "was reckoned to him as righteousness."	5
	6:13	as those who have been brought from death to life	38
	6:16	if you present…to anyone as obedient slaves	5
	8:26	for we do not know how to pray as we ought	12
	8:36	As it is written, "For your sake we are being killed	14
	8:36	we are accounted as sheep to be slaughtered."	37
	9: 8	of the promise are counted as descendants.	5
	9:13	As it is written, "I have loved Jacob,	14
	9:25	As indeed he says in Hosea	37
	9:29	as Isaiah predicted, "If the Lord of hosts had	14
	9:33	as it is written, "See, I am laying in Zion	14
	10:15	As it is written, "How beautiful are the feet	14
	11: 8	as it is written, "God gave them a sluggish spirit	14
	11:26	so all Israel will be saved; as it is written	14
	12: 4	For as in one body we have many members	11
	13: 9	"Love your neighbor as yourself."	37
	13:13	live honorably as in the day	37
	14:22	The faith…have as your own conviction before God.	16

	15: 3	but, as it is written, "The insults of those	14
	15: 9	As it is written, "Therefore I will confess you	14
	15:21	as it is written, "Those who have never been told	14
1Co	1:31	that, as it is written, "Let the one who boasts	14
	2: 9	But, as it is written, "What no eye has seen	14
	3: 1	I could not speak to you as spiritual people	37
	3: 1	as people of the flesh, as infants in Christ.	37
	3: 1	as people of the flesh, as infants in Christ.	37
	3: 5	as the Lord assigned to each.	37
	3:15	saved, but only as through fire.	37
	4: 1	Think of us…as servants of Christ	37
	4:14	to admonish you as my beloved children.	37
	4:17	as I teach them everywhere in every church.	14
	7: 7	I wish that all were as I myself am.	37
	7: 8	it is well for them to remain unmarried as I am.	37
	7:25	as one who by the Lord's mercy is trustworthy.	37
	7:26	it is well for you to remain as you are.	30
	7:36	let him marry as he wishes; it is no sin.	24
	7:40	she is more blessed if she remains as she is.	30
	8: 7	the food they eat as food offered to an idol;	37
	9: 5	as do the other apostles and the brothers	37
	9:20	To the Jews I became as a Jew, in order to win Jews.	37
	9:20	To those under the law I became as one under the law	37
	9:21	those outside the law I became as one outside the law	37
	10: 6	so that we might not desire evil as they did.	14
	10: 7	Do not become idolaters as some of them did;	14
	10: 7	as it is written, "The people sat down to eat	39
	10: 8	not indulge in sexual immorality as some of them	14
	10: 9	We must not put Christ to the test, as some	14
	10:10	do not complain as some of them did	11
	10:15	I speak as to sensible people; judge for yourselves	37
	11: 1	Be imitators of me, as I am of Christ.	14
	11:18	to begin with, when you come together as a church	7
	12:18	members in the body, each one of them, as he chose.	14
	14:33	(As in all the churches of the saints	37
	14:34	be subordinate, as the law also says.	14
	15: 8	Last of all, as to one untimely born	40
	15:12	if Christ is proclaimed as raised from the dead	27
	15:22	for as all die in Adam	39
	15:38	God gives it a body as he has chosen	14
	15:48	As was the man of dust	19
	15:48	as is the man of heaven	19
2Co	1: 7	we know that as you share in our sufferings	37
	1:14	as you have already understood us in part	14
	1:14	we are your boast even as you are our boast	11
	2: 3	I wrote as I did, so that when I came	29
	2:17	in Christ we speak as persons of sincerity	37
	2:17	as persons of sincerity, as persons sent from God	37
	3: 1	do not need, as some do, letters of recommendation	37
	3: 5	to claim anything as coming from us;	37
	6: 4	as servants of God we have commended ourselves	37
	6: 8	We are treated as impostors, and yet are true;	37
	6: 9	as unknown, and yet are well known;	37
	6: 9	as dying, and see—we are alive;	37
	6: 9	as punished, and yet not killed;	37
	6:10	as sorrowful, yet always rejoicing;	37
	6:10	as poor, yet making many rich;	37
	6:10	as having nothing, and yet possessing	37
	6:13	In return—I speak as to children	37
	6:16	we are the temple of the living God; as God said	14
	8: 5	this, not merely as we expected;	14
	8: 6	that, as he had already made a beginning	14
	8: 7	Now as you excel in everything	39
	8: 8	I do not say this as a command	16
	8:15	As it is written, "The one who had much did not have	14
	9: 3	so that you may be ready, as I said you would be;	14
	9: 5	ready as a voluntary gift and not as an extortion.	37
	9: 5	ready as a voluntary gift and not as an extortion.	37
	9: 7	Each of you must give as you have made up your mind	14
	9: 9	As it is written, "He scatters abroad	14
	10: 3	Indeed, we live as human beings	7
	10: 9	seem as though I am trying to frighten you	37
	11: 3	I am afraid that as the serpent deceived Eve	37
	11:13	disguising themselves as apostles of Christ.	5
	11:14	Satan disguises himself as an angel of light.	5
	11:15	as ministers of righteousness.	37
	11:16	if you do, then accept me as a fool	37
	11:17	not with the Lord's authority, but as a fool	37
	11:21	I am speaking as a fool	7
	12:20	I come, I may find you not as I wish	19
	12:20	you may find me not as you wish;	19

2Co	13: 2	as I did when present on my second visit	37
Gal	1: 9	As we have said before, so now I repeat	37
	3: 6	it was reckoned to him as righteousness,"	5
	3:16	"And to offsprings," as of many;	37
	4:12	Friends, I beg you, become as I am	37
	4:12	I also have become as you are.	37
	4:14	welcomed me as an angel of God	37
	4:14	as an angel of God, as Christ Jesus.	37
	5:13	your freedom as an opportunity for self-indulgence	5
	5:14	"You shall love your neighbor as yourself."	37
	5:21	I am warning you, as I warned you before:	14
Eph	1:10	as a plan for the fullness of time	5
	1:17	revelation as you come to know him	7
	3: 3	as I wrote above in a few words	14
	3: 5	as it has now been revealed to his holy apostles	37
	4:16	as each part is working properly	16
	4:17	you must no longer live as the Gentiles live	14
	4:21	taught in him, as truth is in Jesus.	14
	4:32	forgiving one another, as God in Christ has forgiven	14
	5: 1	be imitators of God, as beloved children	37
	5: 2	live in love, as Christ loved us	14
	5: 3	as is proper among saints.	14
	5: 8	Live as children of light	37
	5:15	live, not as unwise people but as wise	37
	5:15	live, not as unwise people but as wise	37
	5:22	Wives, be subject to your husbands as…to the Lord.	37
	5:28	should love their wives as they do their own bodies.	37
	5:33	Each of you, however, should love his wife as himself	37
	6: 5	in singleness of heart, as you obey Christ;	37
	6: 6	as slaves of Christ, doing the will of God	37
	6: 7	as to the Lord and not to men and women	37
	6:20	I may declare it boldly, as I must speak.	37
Php	1:20	Christ will be exalted now as always in my body	37
	3: 5	a Hebrew born of Hebrews; as to the law, a Pharisee;	16
	3: 6	as to zeal, a persecutor of the church;	16
	3: 6	as to righteousness under the law, blameless.	16
Col	2: 6	As you therefore have received Christ Jesus the Lord	37
	3:12	As God's chosen ones, holy and beloved	37
	3:18	be subject…as is fitting in the Lord.	37
	3:23	put yourselves into it, as done for the Lord	37
	4: 4	so that I may reveal it clearly, as I should.	37
	4:10	as does Mark the cousin of Barnabas	15
1Th	2: 2	shamefully mistreated at Philippi, as you know	14
	2: 5	As you know and as God is our witness,	14
	2: 7	might have made demands as apostles of Christ.	37
	2:11	As you know, we dealt with each one of you	11
	2:13	but as what it really is, God's word	14
	2:14	as they did from the Jews	14
	3: 4	so it turned out, as you know.	15
	4: 1	as you learned from us how you ought to live	14
	4: 1	(as, in fact, you are doing), you should do so	14
	4:11	to work with your hands, as we directed you	14
	4:13	you may not grieve as others do who have no hope.	14
	5: 3	as labor pains come upon a pregnant woman	39
	5: 6	So then let us not fall asleep as others do	37
	5:11	build up each other, as indeed you are doing.	14
2Th	1: 3	give thanks to God for you,…as is right	14
	2: 1	As to the coming of our Lord Jesus Christ	35
	3:15	Do not regard them as enemies,	37
	3:15	but warn them as believers.	37
1Ti	1: 3	I urge you, as I did when I was on my way	14
	2:10	as is proper for women who profess reverence for God.	24
	5: 1	speak to him as to a father	37
	5: 1	speak…to younger men as brothers	37
	5: 2	older women as mothers	37
	5: 2	younger women as sisters—with absolute purity.	37
	5:10	as one who has brought up children	3
2Ti	1: 3	God—whom I worship…as my ancestors did	1
	1:12	for this reason I suffer as I do.	29
	3: 8	As Jannes and Jambres opposed Moses	34
	3: 9	as in the case of those two men	37
	4:21	as do Pudens and Linus and Claudia	15
Tit	1: 5	appoint elders in every town, as I directed you:	37
	1: 7	For a bishop, as God's steward, must be blameless;	37
Phm	1: 9	I, Paul, do this as an old man, and now also as a prisoner	33
	1: 9	and now also as a prisoner of Christ Jesus.	37
	1:16	no longer as a slave but more than a slave	37
	1:17	welcome him as you would welcome me.	37
Heb	1: 4	having become as much superior to angels as	26
	3: 5	Moses was faithful…as a servant	37
	3: 6	Christ, however, was faithful over God's house as a son	37

	3: 7	Therefore, as the Holy Spirit says	14
	3: 8	do not harden your hearts as in the rebellion	37
	3:11	As in my anger I swore, 'They will not enter	37
	3:15	As it is said, "Today, if you hear his voice	7
	3:15	do not harden your hearts as in the rebellion."	37
	4: 3	"As in my anger I swore, 'They shall not enter	37
	4:10	cease from their labors as God did from his.	39
	4:11	may fall through such disobedience as theirs.	36
	4:15	who…has been tested as we are, yet without sin.	21
	5: 6	as he says also in another place	14
	6:10	in serving the saints, as you still do.	15
	6:16	an oath given as confirmation puts an end to all dispute.	5
	9:25	as the high priest enters the Holy Place year after year	39
	10:25	as is the habit of some	14
	10:25	all the more as you see the Day approaching.	26
	11: 4	he received approval as righteous	4
	11: 8	a place that he was to receive as an inheritance;	5
	11: 9	as in a foreign land, living in tents,	37
	11: 9	living in tents, as did Isaac and Jacob	17
	11:12	"as many as the stars of heaven	14
	11:12	as the innumerable grains of sand by the seashore."	37
	11:29	passed through the Red Sea as if it were dry land	37
	12: 5	the exhortation that addresses you as children	37
	12: 7	God is treating you as children;	37
	12:10	for a short time as seemed best to them	16
Jas	2: 8	"You shall love your neighbor as yourself."	37
	2: 9	are convicted by the law as transgressors.	37
	2:12	So speak and so act as those who are to be judged	37
	2:23	and it was reckoned to him as righteousness,"	5
	4:16	As it is, you boast in your arrogance;	18
1Pe	1:15	Instead, as he who called you is holy, be holy	16
	2: 8	they disobey…as they were destined to do.	5
	2:11	I urge you as aliens and exiles to abstain	37
	2:12	though they malign you as evildoers	37
	2:13	whether of the emperor as supreme	37
	2:14	or of governors, as sent by him to punish	37
	2:16	As servants of God, live as free people,	37
	2:16	live as free people, yet do not use your freedom	37
	2:16	do not use your freedom as a pretext for evil.	37
	3: 7	paying honor to the woman as the weaker sex	37
	4: 6	though they had been judged in the flesh as everyone	16
	4: 6	they might live in the spirit as God	16
	4:11	Whoever speaks must do so as…the very words of God;	37
	4:15	let none of you suffer as a murderer, a thief	37
	4:15	let none of you suffer…even as a mischief maker.	37
	4:16	Yet if any of you suffers as a Christian	37
2Pe	1:14	as indeed our Lord Jesus Christ has made clear to me.	14
	1:19	as to a lamp shining in a dark place	37
	3: 4	all things continue as they were	30
	3: 9	The Lord is not slow…as some think of slowness	37
	3:16	speaking of this as he does in all his letters.	37
	3:16	twist…as they do the other scriptures.	37
1Jn	1: 7	if we walk in the light as he himself is in the light	37
	2:18	as you have heard that antichrist is coming	14
	2:27	as his anointing teaches you about all things	37
	3: 2	for we will see him as he is.	14
	4:17	because as he is, so are we in this world.	14
Rev	1:14	His head and his hair were white as white wool	37
	1:14	His head and his hair were…white as snow;	37
	1:15	like burnished bronze, refined as in a furnace	37
	2:27	as when clay pots are shattered	37
	6: 1	creatures call out, as with a voice of thunder,	37
	6:11	who were soon to be killed as they themselves	37
	6:12	the sun became black as sackcloth	37
	6:13	as the fig tree drops its winter fruit	37
	10: 7	as he announced to his servants the prophets."	37
	10: 9	bitter…but sweet as honey in your mouth."	37
	10:10	it was sweet as honey in my mouth	37
	11: 6	with every kind of plague, as often as they desire.	2
	17:12	they are to receive authority as kings	37
	18: 6	Render to her as she herself has rendered	37
	18: 7	As she glorified herself and lived luxuriously	26
	20: 8	they are as numerous as the sands of the sea.	37
	20:12	their works, as recorded in the books.	6
	21: 2	prepared as a bride adorned for her husband.	37
	21:18	while the city is pure gold, clear as glass.	20
	21:21	street…is pure gold, transparent as glass.	37
	22: 1	river of the water of life, bright as crystal	37

as for

1. γάρ, *gar*, *1142*

2. δέ, *de, 1254*
3. εἴτε, *eite, 1664*
4. καί, *kai, 2779*
5. περί, *peri, 4309*
6. ὑπέρ, *hyper, 5642*

Mat	13:20	As for what was sown on rocky ground	2
	13:22	As for what was sown among thorns	2
	13:23	as for what was sown on good soil	2
	22:31	as for the resurrection of the dead	5
Mrk	12:26	as for the dead being raised	5
	13: 9	"As for yourselves, beware;	2
Lke	8:14	As for what fell among the thorns	2
	8:15	as for that in the good soil	2
	9:60	as for you, go and proclaim the kingdom of God."	2
Jhn	8:38	as for you, you should do what you have heard	4
Act	7:40	as for this Moses who led us out from the land	1
	21:25	as for the Gentiles who have become believers	5
1Co	13: 8	as for prophecies, they will come to an end;	3
	13: 8	as for tongues, they will cease;	3
	13: 8	as for knowledge, it will come to an end.	3
2Co	8:23	As for Titus, he is my partner and co-worker	6
	8:23	as for our brothers, they are messengers	3
Gal	6:16	As for who will follow this rule—peace	4
1Th	2:17	As for us, brothers and sisters,	2
2Ti	4: 5	As for you, always be sober, endure suffering	2
	4: 6	As for me, I am already being poured out	1
1Jn	2:27	As for you, the anointing that you received	4
Rev	17:11	As for the beast that was and is not	4

as if

1. προσποιέω, *prospoieō, 4701*
2. ὡς, *hōs, 6055*
3. ὥσπερ, *hōsper, 6061*

Mat	25:14	"For it is as if a man, going on a journey	3
Mrk	4:26	as if someone would scatter seed on the ground	2
Lke	22:52	with swords and clubs as if I were a bandit?	2
	24:28	he walked ahead as if he were going on.	1
Rom	9:32	but as if it were based on works.	2
1Co	4: 7	why do you boast as if it were not a gift?	2
	5: 3	as if present I have already pronounced judgment	2
Col	2:20	you live as if you still belonged to the world?	2
Rev	5: 6	a Lamb standing as if it had been slaughtered	2

as it is

1. νῦν, *nyn, 3814*
2. νυνί, *nyni, 3815*

Jhn	18:36	but as it is, my kingdom is not from here."	1
1Co	7:14	as it is, they are holy.	1
	12:18	as it is, God arranged the members in the body	2
	12:20	As it is, there are many members, yet one body.	1
Heb	2: 8	As it is, we do not yet see everything	1
	9:26	But as is, it he has appeared once for all	2
	11:16	as it is, they desire a better country	1

as though

1. Contextual: Not in Greek
2. ὅτι, *hoti, 4022*
3. ὡς, *hōs, 6055*

Mat	26:55	to arrest me as though I were a bandit?	3
Mrk	14:48	to arrest me as though I were a bandit?	3
Act	3:12	as though…we had made him walk	3
	17:25	as though he needed anything	1
	23:20	as though they were going to inquire	3
Rom	9: 6	It is not as though the word of God had failed.	2
1Co	4: 9	as though sentenced to death	3
	7:29	who have wives be as though they had none	3
	7:30	those who mourn as though they were not mourning	3
	7:30	who rejoice as though they were not rejoicing	3
	7:30	those who buy as though they had no possessions	3
	7:31	as though they had no dealings with it.	3
	9:26	nor do I box as though beating the air;	3
2Co	3:18	seeing the glory of the Lord as though reflected in	1
2Th	2: 2	by letter, as though from us,	3
Heb	11:27	persevered as though he saw him who is invisible.	3
	13: 3	as though you were in prison with them;	3
	13: 3	as though you yourselves were being tortured.	3
1Pe	4:12	as though something strange were happening	3
2Jn	1: 5	dear lady, I ask you, not as though I were writing	3
Rev	1:17	When I saw him, I fell at his feet as though dead.	3

as to

1. ὅτι, *hoti, 4022*
2. περί, *peri, 4309*

Act	13:34	As to his raising him from the dead	1
1Co	8: 4	Hence, as to the eating of food offered to idols	2

Asaph

1. Ἀσάφ, *Asaph, 811*

Mat	1: 7	and Abijah the father of Asaph	1
	1: 8	Asaph the father of Jehoshaphat	1

ascend

1. ἀναβαίνω, *anabainō, 326*

Jhn	1:51	the angels of God ascending and descending	1
	3:13	No one has ascended into heaven except the one	1
	6:62	if you were to see the Son of Man ascending	1
	20:17	because I have not yet ascended to the Father.	1
	20:17	'I am ascending to my Father and your Father	1
Act	2:34	David did not ascend into the heavens	1
	10: 4	have ascended as a memorial before God.	1
Rom	10: 6	say in your heart, 'Who will ascend into heaven?' "	1
Eph	4: 8	he ascended on high he made captivity…a captive	1
	4: 9	When it says, "He ascended," what does it mean	1
	4:10	He who descended is the same one who ascended	1
Rev	7: 2	I saw another angel ascending from the rising…sun	1
	17: 8	beast…is about to ascend from the bottomless pit	1

ash   See *also* turn to ashes

1. σποδός, *spodos, 5075*

Mat	11:21	repented long ago in sackcloth and ashes.	1
Lke	10:13	sitting in sackcloth and ashes.	1
Heb	9:13	with the sprinkling of the ashes of a heifer	1

ashamed   See *also* make ashamed, no *need* to be ashamed

1. αἰσχύνομαι, *aischynomai, 159*
2. ἐντρέπω, *entrepō, 1956*
3. ἐπαισχύνομαι, *epaischynomai, 2049*

Mrk	8:38	who are ashamed of me and of my words	3
	8:38	of them the Son of Man will also be ashamed	3
Lke	9:26	who are ashamed of me and of my words	3
	9:26	of them the Son of Man will be ashamed	3
	16: 3	I am ashamed to beg.	1
Rom	1:16	For I am not ashamed of the gospel;	3
	6:21	get from the things of which you now are ashamed?	3
2Co	10: 8	I will not be ashamed	1
2Th	3:14	so that they may be ashamed.	2
2Ti	1: 8	Do not be ashamed…of the testimony about our Lord	3
	1:12	I am not ashamed, for I know the one in whom	3
	1:16	often refreshed me and was not ashamed of my chain	3
Heb	2:11	Jesus is not ashamed to call them brothers and sisters	3
	11:16	God is not ashamed to be called their God;	3

Asher

1. Ἀσήρ, *Asēr, 818*

Lke	2:36	of the tribe of Asher.	1
Rev	7: 6	from the tribe of Asher twelve thousand,	1

ashore   See *also* go ashore, run ashore

1. εἰς + ὁ + γῆ, *eis + ho + gē, 1650 + 3836 + 1178*
2. ἐπί + ὁ + αἰγιαλός, *epi + ho + aigialos, 2093 + 3836 + 129*

Mat	13:48	when it was full, they drew it ashore, sat down	2
Jhn	21: 9	they had gone ashore, they saw a charcoal fire	1
	21:11	Simon Peter went aboard and hauled the net ashore	1

Asia   See *also* official of the province of Asia

1. Ἀσία, *Asia, 823*
2. Ἀσιανός, *Asianos, 824*

Act	2: 9	Judea and Cappadocia, Pontus and Asia	1
	6: 9	those from Cilicia and Asia	1
	16: 6	forbidden…to speak the word in Asia.	1
	19:10	residents of Asia…heard the word of the Lord.	1
	19:22	he himself stayed for some time longer in Asia.	1
	19:26	in almost the whole of Asia	1
	19:27	that brought all Asia and the world to worship	1
	20: 4	as well as by Tychicus and Trophimus from Asia.	2
	20:16	so that he might not have to spend time in Asia;	1
	20:18	from the first day that I set foot in Asia	1
	21:27	the Jews from Asia…stirred up the whole crowd.	1
	24:19	there were some Jews from Asia	1

Act 27: 2	set sail to the ports along the coast of Asia	1
Rom 16: 5	Epaenetus, who was the first convert in Asia	1
1Co 16:19	The churches of Asia send greetings.	1
2Co 1: 8	the affliction we experienced in Asia;	1
2Ti 1:15	all who are in Asia have turned away from me	1
1Pe 1: 1	the Dispersion in…Asia, and Bithynia	1
Rev 1: 4	John to the seven churches that are in Asia:	1

aside *See also* draw aside, lay aside, push aside, set aside, take aside, turn aside

1. ἐκ + μέσος, *ek + mesos, 1666 + 3545*
2. παρά, *para, 4123*

1Co 16: 2	put aside and save whatever extra you earn	2
Col 2:14	He set this aside, nailing it to the cross.	1

ask

1. Contextual: Not in Greek
2. αἰτέω, *aiteō, 160*
3. ἀποκρίνομαι, *apokrinomai, 646*
4. δέομαι, *deomai, 1289*
5. διερωτάω, *dierōtaō, 1452*
6. ἐξετάζω, *exetazō, 2004*
7. ἐπερωτάω, *eperōtaō, 2089*
8. ἐρωτάω, *erōtaō, 2263*
9. λέγω, *legō, 3306*
10. μετακαλέω, *metakaleō, 3559*
11. παραιτέομαι, *paraiteomai, 4148*
12. παρακαλέω, *parakaleō, 4151*
13. πυνθάνομαι, *pynthanomai, 4785*
14. συζητέω, *syzēteō, 5184*
15. φημί, *phēmi, 5774*

Mat 2: 2	asking, "Where is the child who has been born	9
6: 8	Father knows what you need before you ask him.	2
7: 7	"Ask, and it will be given you; search,	2
7: 8	For everyone who asks receives	2
7: 9	among you who, if your child asks for bread	2
7:10	Or if the child asks for a fish, will give a snake?	2
7:11	in heaven give good things to those who ask	2
9:38	therefore ask the Lord of the harvest	4
12:10	asked him, "Is it lawful to cure on the sabbath?"	7
13:10	the disciples came and asked him	9
14: 7	to grant her whatever she might ask.	2
15:34	Jesus asked them, "How many loaves have you?"	9
16: 1	to test Jesus they asked him to show them a sign	7
16:13	he asked his disciples	8
17:10	the disciples asked him	7
17:25	he came home, Jesus spoke of it first, asking	9
18: 1	At that time the disciples came to Jesus and asked	9
18:19	agree on earth about anything you ask	2
19: 3	Pharisees came to him, and to test him they asked	9
19:17	"Why do you ask me about what is good?	8
20:20	kneeling before him, she asked a favor of him.	2
20:22	"You do not know what you are asking.	2
21:10	the whole city was in turmoil, asking	9
21:24	"I will also ask you one question;	8
24: 2	he asked them, "You see all these, do you not?	3
27:11	the governor asked him	7
27:23	he asked, "Why, what evil has he done?"	15
Mrk 1:27	and they kept on asking one another	14
4:10	asked him about the parables.	8
5: 9	Jesus asked him, "What is your name?"	7
6:22	"Ask me for whatever you wish, and I will give it."	2
6:23	"Whatever you ask me, I will give you	2
6:24	said to her mother, "What should I ask for?"	2
7: 5	the Pharisees and the scribes asked him	7
7:17	his disciples asked him about the parable.	7
8: 5	He asked them, "How many loaves do you have?"	8
8:23	he asked him, "Can you see anything?"	7
8:27	on the way he asked his disciples	7
8:29	He asked them, "But who do you say that I am?"	7
9:11	they asked him, "Why do the scribes say	7
9:16	He asked them, "What are you arguing about	7
9:18	I asked your disciples to cast it out	9
9:21	Jesus asked the father, "How long has this been	7
9:28	his disciples asked him privately	7
9:32	were afraid to ask him.	7
9:33	when he was in the house he asked them	7
10: 2	Pharisees came, and to test him they asked	7
10:10	in the house the disciples asked him again	7

10:17	ran up and knelt before him, and asked him	7
10:35	we want you to do for us whatever we ask of you."	2
10:38	"You do not know what you are asking.	2
11:29	Jesus said to them, "I will ask you one question;	7
12:28	seeing that he answered them well, he asked him	7
13: 2	Jesus asked him, "Do you see	9
13: 3	James, John, and Andrew asked him privately	7
14:14	'The Teacher asks, Where is my guest room	9
14:60	stood up before them and asked Jesus	7
14:61	the high priest asked him, "Are you the Messiah	7
15: 2	Pilate asked him, "Are you the King of the Jews?"	7
15: 4	Pilate asked him again, "Have you no answer?	7
15: 6	a prisoner for them, anyone for whom they asked.	11
15: 8	the crowd came and began to ask Pilate	9
15:14	Pilate asked them, "Why, what evil has he done?"	9
15:43	to Pilate and asked for the body of Jesus.	2
15:44	asked him whether he had been dead for some time.	7
Lke 1:63	He asked for a writing tablet and wrote	2
3:10	the crowds asked him, "What then should we do?"	7
3:12	tax collectors came to be baptized, and they asked	9
3:14	Soldiers also asked him	7
4:38	they asked him about her.	8
5: 3	asked him to put out a little way from the shore.	8
6: 9	Jesus said to them, "I ask you	7
7: 3	asking him to come and heal his slave.	8
7:19	sent them to the Lord to ask, "Are you the one	9
7:20	"John the Baptist has sent us to you to ask	9
7:36	One of the Pharisees asked Jesus to eat with him	8
8: 9	his disciples asked him what this parable meant.	7
8:30	Jesus then asked him, "What is your name?"	7
8:37	all the people…asked Jesus to leave them;	8
8:45	Jesus asked, "Who touched me?"	7
9:18	he asked them, "Who do the crowds say that I am?"	7
9:45	they were afraid to ask him about this saying.	8
10: 2	therefore ask the Lord of the harvest	4
10:29	wanting to justify himself, he asked Jesus	9
10:40	came to him and asked, "Lord, do you not care	9
11: 9	I say to you, Ask, and it will be given you;	2
11:10	For everyone who asks receives	2
11:13	give the Holy Spirit to those who ask him!"	2
13: 2	He asked them, "Do you think	3
13:23	Someone asked him, "Lord	9
14: 3	Jesus asked the lawyers and Pharisees	3
14:32	a delegation and asks for the terms of peace.	8
15:26	asked what was going on.	13
16: 5	he asked the first, 'How much do you owe	9
16: 7	he asked another, 'And how much do you owe?'	9
17:17	Then Jesus asked, "Were not ten made clean?	3
17:20	Once Jesus was asked by the Pharisees	7
17:37	they asked him, "Where, Lord?"	3
18:18	A certain ruler asked him, "Good Teacher,	7
18:36	he asked what was happening.	13
18:40	when he came near, he asked him	7
19:31	If anyone asks you, 'Why are you untying it?'	8
19:33	As they were untying the colt, its owners asked	9
20: 3	"I will also ask you a question, and you tell me:	8
20:21	they asked him, "Teacher	7
21: 7	They asked him, "Teacher, when will this be	7
22: 9	They asked him, "Where do you want us to make	9
22:11	to the owner of the house, 'The teacher asks you	9
22:23	they began to ask one another	14
22:49	When those…saw what was coming, they asked	9
22:64	they also blindfolded him and kept asking him	7
22:70	All of them asked, "Are you…the Son of God?"	9
23: 3	Pilate asked him, "Are you the king of the Jews?"	8
23: 6	he asked whether the man was a Galilean.	7
24:19	He asked them, "What things?"	9
Jhn 1:19	priests and Levites from Jerusalem to ask him	8
1:21	And they asked him, "What then? Are you Elijah?"	8
1:25	They asked him, "Why then are you baptizing	8
1:48	Nathanael asked him, "Where did you get to know me?"	9
4: 9	you, a Jew, ask a drink of me, a woman of Samaria?"	2
4:10	you would have asked him, and he would have given	2
4:40	they asked him to stay with them;	8
4:52	So he asked them the hour when he began to recover	13
5:12	They asked him, "Who is the man who said to you	8
6:67	Jesus asked the twelve	9
7:41	But some said, "Surely the Messiah does not	9
7:45	who asked them, "Why did you not arrest him?"	9
7:50	Nicodemus…who was one of them, asked,	9
9: 2	His disciples asked him, "Rabbi, who sinned	8

	9: 8	had seen him before as a beggar began to ask	9
	9:10	kept asking him, "Then how were your eyes opened?"	9
	9:15	Then the Pharisees also began to ask him	8
	9:19	asked them, "Is this your son	8
	9:21	Ask him; he is of age. He will speak for himself."	8
	9:23	his parents said, "He is of age; ask him."	7
	11:22	God will give you whatever you ask of him."	2
	11:56	looking for Jesus and were asking one another	9
	13:24	to ask Jesus of whom he was speaking.	13
	13:25	reclining next to Jesus, he asked	9
	14:13	I will do whatever you ask in my name,	2
	14:14	If in my name you ask me for anything,	2
	14:16	I will ask the Father	8
	15:16	will give you whatever you ask him in my name.	2
	16: 5	yet none of you asks me, 'Where are you going?'	8
	16:19	Jesus knew that they wanted to ask him	8
	16:23	On that day you will ask nothing of me.	8
	16:23	if you ask anything of the Father in my name	2
	16:24	Ask and you will receive, so that your joy	2
	16:26	On that day you will ask in my name.	2
	16:26	I do not say to you that I will ask the Father	8
	17: 9	I am asking on their behalf;	8
	17: 9	I am not asking on behalf of the world	8
	17:15	I am not asking you to take them out	8
	17:15	I ask you to protect them from the evil one.	1
	17:20	"I ask not only on behalf of these	8
	18: 4	Jesus…came forward and asked them	9
	18: 7	Again he asked them, "Whom are you looking for?"	7
	18:21	Why do you ask me? Ask those who heard	8
	18:21	Ask those who heard what I said to them;	8
	18:25	They asked him, "You are not also one	9
	18:26	One of the slaves…asked	9
	18:33	Pilate…summoned Jesus, and asked him	9
	18:34	Jesus answered, "Do you ask this on your own	9
	18:37	Pilate asked him, "So you are a king?"	9
	18:38	Pilate asked him, "What is truth?"	9
	19: 9	He…asked Jesus, "Where are you from?"	9
	19:15	Pilate asked them, "Shall I crucify your King?"	9
	19:31	So they asked Pilate to have the legs…broken	8
	19:38	asked Pilate to let him take away the body	8
	21:12	the disciples dared to ask him, "Who are you?"	6
Act	1: 6	So when they had come together, they asked him	8
	2: 7	Amazed and astonished, they asked,	9
	3: 2	could ask for alms from those entering the temple.	2
	3: 3	he asked them for alms.	8
	3:10	the one who used to sit and ask for alms	1
	3:14	asked to have a murderer given to you	2
	4: 9	asked how this man has been healed	1
	5: 3	"Ananias," Peter asked	9
	7: 1	the high priest asked him, "Are these things so?"	9
	7:46	and asked that he might find a dwelling place	2
	8:30	asked, "Do you understand what you are reading?"	9
	8:34	The eunuch asked Philip	3
	8:34	"About whom, may I ask you, does the prophet say	4
	9: 2	asked him for letters to the synagogues	2
	9: 5	He asked, "Who are you, Lord?"	9
	10:17	were asking for Simon's house	5
	10:18	They called out to ask whether Simon	13
	10:29	Now may I ask why you sent for me?"	13
	10:32	ask for Simon, who is called Peter;	10
	12:20	they asked for a reconciliation	2
	13:21	they asked for a king; and God gave them Saul	2
	13:28	they asked Pilate to have him killed.	2
	16:39	took them out and asked them to leave the city.	8
	17:19	brought him to the Areopagus and asked	9
	18:20	When they asked him to stay longer	8
	22:10	I asked, 'What am I to do, Lord?'	9
	22:27	The tribune came and asked Paul	9
	23:18	Paul…asked me to bring this young man to you;	8
	23:19	drew him aside privately, and asked, "What is it	13
	23:20	"The Jews have agreed to ask you to bring Paul	8
	23:34	he asked what province he belonged to	7
	25: 9	Festus, wishing to do the Jews a favor, asked Paul	3
	25:15	asked for a sentence against him.	2
	25:20	I asked whether he wished to go to Jerusalem	9
	26:15	I asked, 'Who are you, Lord?'	9
	28:20	therefore I have asked to see you	12
Rom	1:10	asking that by God's will I may somehow	4
	10:18	But I ask, have they not heard? Indeed they have;	9
	10:19	Again I ask, did Israel not understand?	9
	10:20	shown myself to those who did not ask for me."	7

	11: 1	I ask, then, has God rejected his people?	9
	11:11	So I ask, have they stumbled so as to fall?	9
1Co	14:35	let them ask their husbands at home.	7
	15:35	someone will ask, "How are the dead raised?	9
2Co	10: 2	I ask that when I am present	4
Gal	2:10	They asked only one thing, that we remember the poor	1
Eph	3:20	abundantly far more than all we can ask or imagine	2
Php	4: 3	I ask you also, my loyal companion, help these women	8
Col	1: 9	asking that you may be filled with the knowledge	2
1Th	4: 1	we ask and urge you in the Lord Jesus	8
2Th	1:11	asking that our God will make you worthy	1
Jas	1: 5	If any of you is lacking in wisdom, ask God	2
	1: 6	But ask in faith, never doubting	2
	4: 2	You do not have, because you do not ask.	2
	4: 3	You ask and do not receive	2
	4: 3	You…do not receive, because you ask wrongly	2
1Jn	3:22	we receive from him whatever we ask	2
	5:14	if we ask anything according to his will, he hears	2
	5:15	if we know that he hears us in whatever we ask	2
	5:16	you will ask, and God will give life to such a one	2
2Jn	1: 5	now, dear lady, I ask you, not as though I were writing	8

ask a question

1. ἐπερωτάω, *eperōtaō, 2089*

Mat	22:23	they asked him a question	1
	22:35	one of them, a lawyer, asked him a question	1
	22:41	Jesus asked them this question:	1
	22:46	did anyone dare to ask him any more questions.	1
Mrk	12:18	asked him a question, saying	1
	12:34	After that no one dared to ask him any question.	1
Lke	2:46	listening to them and asking them questions.	1
	20:28	asked him a question, "Teacher	1
	20:40	they no longer dared to ask him another question.	1

ask again

1. ἀπαιτέω, *apaiteō, 555*

Lke	6:30	do not ask for them again.	1

ask for

1. αἰτέω, *aiteō, 160*
2. ἐπιζητέω, *epizēteō, 2118*
3. ζητέω, *zēteō, 2426*

Mat	12:39	evil and adulterous generation asks for a sign	2
	16: 4	evil and adulterous generation asks for a sign	2
	21:22	Whatever you ask for in prayer with faith,	1
	27:20	elders persuaded the crowds to ask for Barabbas	1
	27:58	went to Pilate and asked for the body of Jesus	1
Mrk	3:32	and sisters are outside, asking for you."	3
	8:11	asking him for a sign from heaven, to test him.	3
	8:12	"Why does this generation ask for a sign?	3
	11:24	So I tell you, whatever you ask for in prayer	1
Lke	11:11	who, if your child asks for a fish	1
	11:12	Or if the child asks for an egg	1
	11:29	it asks for a sign, but no sign will be given	3
	23:25	He released the man they asked for,	1
	23:52	went to Pilate and asked for the body of Jesus.	1
Jhn	15: 7	ask for whatever you wish, and it will be done	1
	16:24	you have not asked for anything in my name.	1

ask to meet

1. μετακαλέω, *metakaleō, 3559*

Act	20:17	asking the elders of the church to meet him.	1

asleep   *See also* fall asleep

1. καθεύδω, *katheudō, 2761*
2. κοιμάω, *koimaō, 3121*
3. νυστάζω, *nystazō, 3818*

Mat	8:24	swamped by the waves; but he was asleep.	1
	13:25	everybody was asleep, an enemy came and sowed	1
	28:13	stole him away while we were asleep.'	2
Mrk	4:38	he was in the stern, asleep on the cushion;	1
	13:36	he may find you asleep when he comes suddenly.	1
	14:37	"Simon, are you asleep? Could you not keep awake	1
1Th	5:10	whether we are awake or asleep we may live with him.	1
2Pe	2: 3	and their destruction is not asleep.	3

aspire

1. ὀρέγω, *oregō, 3977*
2. φιλοτιμέομαι, *philotimeomai, 5818*

1Th 4:11 to aspire to live quietly	2
1Ti .3: 1 whoever aspires to the office of bishop	1

assassin

1. σικάριος, *sikarios, 4974*

Act 21:38 and led the four thousand assassins out	1

assemble

1. συνάγω, *synagō, 5251*
2. συνέρχομαι, *synerchomai, 5302*

Mat 28:12 After the priests had assembled with the elders	1
Mrk 14:53 the elders, and the scribes were assembled.	2
Act 4: 5 their rulers...assembled in Jerusalem,	2
10:27 he went in and found that many had assembled;	2
28:17 When they had assembled, he said to them,	2
1Co 5: 4 When you are assembled, and my spirit is present	1
Rev 16:14 to assemble them for battle on the great day	1
16:16 And they assembled them at...Harmagedon.	1

assembly

1. δῆμος, *dēmos, 1322*
2. ἐκκλησία, *ekklēsia, 1711*
3. πλῆθος, *plēthos, 4436*
4. συναγωγή, *synagōgē, 5252*

Lke 1:10 the whole assembly of the people was praying	3
23: 1 Then the assembly rose as a body	3
Act 15:12 The whole assembly kept silence	3
17: 5 Paul and Silas to bring them out to the assembly	1
19:32 for the assembly was in confusion	2
19:39 it must be settled in the regular assembly.	2
19:41 When he had said this, he dismissed the assembly.	2
23: 7 the assembly was divided.	3
Heb 12:23 to the assembly of the firstborn	2
Jas 2: 2 a person...comes into your assembly	4

assembly of the elders

1. πρεσβυτέριον, *presbyterion, 4564*

Lke 22:66 the assembly of the elders of the people	1

assert

1. φάσκω, *phaskō, 5763*

Act 24: 9 asserting that all this was true.	1
25:19 who had died, but whom Paul asserted to be alive.	1

assertion   *See* make an assertion

assign

1. δίδωμι, *didōmi, 1443*
2. μερίζω, *merizō, 3532*
3. τάσσω, *tassō, 5435*

Act 22:10 everything that has been assigned to you to do.'	3
Rom 12: 3 the measure of faith that God has assigned.	2
1Co 3: 5 as the Lord assigned to each.	1
7:17 lead the life that the Lord has assigned,	2
2Co 10:13 keep within the field that God has assigned to us	2

assist

1. ἐπαρκέω, *eparkeō, 2064*
2. ὑπηρέτης, *hypēretēs, 5677*

Act 13: 5 they had John also to assist them.	2
1Ti 5:16 let her assist them;	1
5:16 it can assist those who are real widows.	1

assistance

1. ἀντίλημψις, *antilēmpsis, 516*

1Co 12:28 then gifts of healing, forms of assistance	1

associate

1. κολλάω, *kollaō, 3140*
2. συμμέτοχος, *symmetochos, 5212*
3. συναναμείγνυμι, *synanameignymi, 5264*
4. συναπάγω, *synapagō, 5270*

Act 10:28 to associate with or to visit a Gentile	1
Rom 12:16 do not be haughty, but associate with the lowly;	4
1Co 5: 9 not to associate with sexually immoral persons	3
5:11 not to associate with anyone	3
Eph 5: 7 Therefore do not be associated with them.	2

Assos

1. Ἄσσος, *Assos, 840*

Act 20:13 went ahead to the ship and set sail for Assos	1
20:14 When he met us in Assos, we took him on board	1

assume

1. εἰμί, *eimi, 1639*
2. νομίζω, *nomizō, 3787*

Lke 2:44 Assuming that he was in the group of travelers	2
2Co 12:16 Let it be assumed that I did not burden you.	1

assurance

1. πίστις, *pistis, 4411*
2. ὑπόστασις, *hypostasis, 5712*

Act 17:31 of this he has given assurance to all	1
Heb 11: 1 Now faith is the assurance of things hoped for	2

full assurance

1. πληροφορία, *plērophoria, 4443*

Heb 6:11 the full assurance of hope to the very end	1
10:22 approach...in full assurance of faith	1

assure

1. πληροφορία, *plērophoria, 4443*

Col 2: 2 may have all the riches of assured understanding	1

assure fully

1. πληροφορέω, *plērophoreō, 4442*

Col 4:12 fully assured in everything that God wills.	1

astonish

1. ἐκπλήσσω, *ekplēssō, 1742*
2. θαυμάζω, *thaumazō, 2513*

Lke 2:48 When his parents saw him they were astonished;	1
Jhn 3: 7 Do not be astonished that I said to you	2
4:27 were astonished that he was speaking with a woman	2
5:20 so that you will be astonished.	2
5:28 Do not be astonished at this;	2
7:15 The Jews were astonished at it, saying,	2
7:21 performed one work, and all of you are astonished.	2
Act 2: 7 Amazed and astonished, they asked,	2
13:12 he was astonished at the teaching about the Lord.	1
Gal 1: 6 I am astonished that you are so quickly deserting	2
1Jn 3:13 Do not be astonished...that the world hates you.	2

astonish utterly

1. ἔκθαμβος, *ekthambos, 1702*

Act 3:11 all the people ran together...utterly astonished.	1

astonishing thing

1. θαυμαστός, *thaumastos, 2515*

Jhn 9:30 The man answered, "Here is an astonishing thing!	1

astound

1. ἐκπλήσσω, *ekplēssō, 1742*
2. ἐξίστημι, *existēmi, 2014*

Mat 7:28 the crowds were astounded at his teaching	1
13:54 so that they were astounded and said	1
19:25 they were greatly astounded and said	1
22:33 they were astounded at his teaching.	1
Mrk 1:22 They were astounded at his teaching	1
6: 2 many who heard him were astounded. They said	1
6:51 they were utterly astounded	2
7:37 They were astounded beyond measure, saying	1
10:26 They were greatly astounded and said	1
Lke 4:32 They were astounded at his teaching	1
8:56 Her parents were astounded;	2
9:43 all were astounded at the greatness of God.	2
24:22 Moreover, some women of our group astounded us.	2
Act 10:45 The circumcised believers...were astounded	2

astray   *See* go astray, lead astray

Asyncritus

1. Ἀσύγκριτος, *Asynkritos, 850*

Rom 16:14 Greet Asyncritus, Phlegon, Hermes, Patrobas	1

at *See also* all at once, at any *time*, at *hand*, at *home*, at
least, at *length*, at one's *hand*, at *table*, at *table* with, at that
moment, at that *time*, at this *moment*, foam at the mouth,
lie close at hand, look at, put at the service, set at rest, sit at
dinner, sit at table, sit at table with, take one's place at
table

1. ἀπό, *apo, 608*
2. διά, *dia, 1328*
3. εἰς, *eis, 1650*
4. ἐκ, *ek, 1666*
5. ἔμπροσθεν, *emprosthen, 1869*
6. ἐν, *en, 1877*
7. ἐπί, *epi, 2093*
8. κατά, *kata, 2848*
9. μέχρι, *mechri, 3588*
10. παρά, *para, 4123*
11. περί, *peri, 4309*
12. πρό, *pro, 4574*
13. πρός, *pros, 4639*
14. ὑπό, *hypo, 5679*

Mat	2: 2	For we observed his star at its rising,	6
	2: 9	went the star that they had seen at its rising	6
	3:10	Even now the ax is lying at the root of the trees;	13
	3:13	Jesus came from Galilee to John at the Jordan	7
	5:23	So when you are offering your gift at the altar	7
	6: 5	pray in the synagogues and at the street corners	6
	6:26	Look at the birds of the air; they neither sow	3
	7:28	the crowds were astounded at his teaching	7
	8: 6	"Lord, my servant is lying at home paralyzed	6
	9: 9	a man called Matthew sitting at the tax booth;	7
	10:19	to say will be given to you at that time;	6
	11: 6	blessed is anyone who takes no offense at me."	6
	11:25	At that time Jesus said, "I thank you, Father	6
	12: 1	At that time Jesus went through the grainfields	6
	12:41	The people of Nineveh will rise up at the judgment	6
	12:41	they repented at the proclamation of Jonah	3
	12:42	The queen of the South will rise up at the judgment	6
	13:30	at harvest time I will tell the reapers	6
	13:40	so will it be at the end of the age.	6
	13:49	So it will be at the end of the age.	6
	13:57	they took offense at him.	6
	14: 1	At that time Herod the ruler heard	6
	14:34	they came to land at Gennesaret.	3
	15:30	They put them at his feet, and he cured them	10
	17:12	the Son of Man is about to suffer at their hands."	14
	18: 1	At that time the disciples came to Jesus and asked	6
	19: 4	one who made them at the beginning	1
	19:28	at the renewal of all things, when the Son of Man	6
	20:21	one at your right hand and one at your left	4
	20:21	one at your right hand and one at your left	4
	20:23	to sit at my right hand and at my left	4
	20:23	to sit at my right hand and at my left	4
	21: 1	had reached Bethphage, at the Mount of Olives	3
	21:41	who will give him the produce at the harvest time."	6
	22:33	they were astounded at his teaching.	7
	22:44	'The Lord said to my Lord, "Sit at my right hand	4
	23: 6	They love to have the place of honor at banquets	6
	24:33	you know that he is near, at the very gates.	7
	24:45	their allowance of food at the proper time?	6
	24:50	at an hour that he does not know.	6
	25:33	he will put the sheep at his right hand	4
	25:33	the goats at the left.	4
	25:34	the king will say to those at his right hand	4
	25:41	Then he will say to those at his left hand	4
	26: 6	while Jesus was at Bethany in the house of Simon	6
	26:18	I will keep the Passover at your house	13
	26:55	At that hour Jesus said to the crowds	6
	26:58	Peter was following him at a distance	1
	26:64	the Son of Man seated at the right hand of Power	4
	27:15	Now at the festival the governor was accustomed	8
Mrk	1:22	They were astounded at his teaching	7
	2: 1	it was reported that he was at home.	6
	2:14	son of Alphaeus sitting at the tax booth	7
	3: 5	grieved at their hardness of heart	7
	5:22	he saw him, fell at his feet	13
	6: 3	And they took offense at him.	6
	6: 6	he was amazed at their unbelief.	2
	6:48	he saw that they were straining at the oars	6
	6:53	they came to land at Gennesaret	3

	7:25	and she came and bowed down at his feet.	13
	10:24	the disciples were perplexed at these words.	7
	10:37	one at your right hand and one at your left	4
	10:37	one at your right hand and one at your left	4
	10:40	to sit at my right hand or at my left	4
	10:40	to sit at my right hand or at my left	4
	11: 1	approaching Jerusalem, at Bethphage and Bethany	3
	12:17	And they were utterly amazed at him.	7
	12:36	'The Lord said to my Lord, "Sit at my right hand	4
	12:39	and places of honor at banquets!	6
	13:11	say whatever is given you at that time	6
	13:29	you know that he is near, at the very gates.	7
	14: 3	at Bethany in the house of Simon the leper	6
	14:54	Peter had followed him at a distance	1
	14:54	warming himself at the fire.	13
	14:62	Son of Man seated at the right hand of the Power,'	4
	15: 6	Now at the festival he used to release a prisoner	8
	16:19	⟦Jesus…sat down at the right hand of God.⟧	4
Lke	1:11	standing at the right side of the altar	4
	1:14	many will rejoice at his birth	7
	1:21	wondered at his delay in the sanctuary.	6
	2:18	amazed at what the shepherds told them.	11
	2:33	amazed at what was being said about him.	7
	2:47	who heard him were amazed at his understanding	7
	3: 9	Even now the ax is lying at the root of the trees;	13
	4:22	amazed at the gracious words	7
	4:23	things that we have heard you did at Capernaum.' "	3
	4:26	to a widow at Zarephath in Sidon.	3
	4:32	They were astounded at his teaching	7
	5: 9	amazed at the catch of fish that they had taken;	7
	5:27	a tax collector…sitting at the tax booth;	7
	6:20	he looked up at his disciples	3
	7:23	blessed is anyone who takes no offense at me."	6
	7:38	stood behind him at his feet, weeping	10
	8:26	they arrived at the country of the Gerasenes	3
	8:35	sitting at the feet of Jesus	10
	8:41	fell at Jesus' feet and begged him to come	10
	9:31	which he was about to accomplish at Jerusalem.	6
	9:38	I beg you to look at my son; he is my only child.	7
	9:43	all were astounded at the greatness of God.	7
	9:43	everyone was amazed at all that he was doing	7
	9:61	let me first say farewell to those at my home."	3
	10:14	at the judgment it will be more tolerable for Tyre	6
	10:20	Nevertheless, do not rejoice at this	6
	10:21	At that same hour Jesus rejoiced in the Holy Spirit	6
	10:39	a sister named Mary, who sat at the Lord's feet	13
	11:31	The queen of the South will rise at the judgment	6
	11:32	people of Nineveh will rise up at the judgment	6
	11:32	they repented at the proclamation of Jonah	3
	12:12	the Holy Spirit will teach you at that very hour	6
	12:42	to give them…food at the proper time?	6
	12:46	on a day when he does not expect him	6
	13: 1	At that very time there were some present	6
	13:17	crowd was rejoicing at all the wonderful things	7
	13:31	At that very hour some Pharisees came and said	6
	14: 8	do not sit down at the place of honor	3
	14:10	go and sit down at the lowest place	3
	14:14	repaid at the resurrection of the righteous."	6
	16:20	at his gate lay a poor man named Lazarus	13
	17:16	He prostrated himself at Jesus' feet	10
	19: 5	I must stay at your house today."	6
	19:29	at the place called the Mount of Olives,	13
	20:19	wanted to lay hands on him at that very hour	6
	20:42	'The Lord said to my Lord, "Sit at my right hand	4
	20:46	and love…places of honor at banquets.	6
	21:36	Be alert at all times	6
	22:30	you may eat and drink at my table in my kingdom	7
	22:69	seated at the right hand of the power of God."	4
	23: 7	who was himself in Jerusalem at that time.	6
	23:49	stood at a distance, watching these things.	1
	24:22	They were at the tomb early this morning	7
Jhn	3:23	John also was baptizing at Aenon near Salim	6
	3:29	rejoices greatly at the bridegroom's voice.	2
	4:45	all that he had done in Jerusalem at the festival;	6
	6:59	he was teaching in the synagogue at Capernaum.	6
	7:11	The Jews were looking for him at the festival	6
	8: 7	⟦without sin be the first to throw a stone at her⟧	7
	8:59	they picked up stones to throw at him	7
	11:10	those who walk at night stumble,	6
	11:20	she went and met him, while Mary stayed at home.	6
	11:30	still at the place where Martha had met him.	6

Jhn	11:32	Mary…knelt at his feet and said to him, "Lord	13
	12:20	among those who went up to worship at the festival	6
	13:22	The disciples looked at one another	3
	18:16	but Peter was standing outside at the gate.	13
	18:39	I release someone for you at the Passover.	6
	19:13	at a place called The Stone Pavement	3
	20:12	one at the head and the other at the feet.	13
	20:12	one at the head and the other at the feet.	13
	21:20	who had reclined next to Jesus at the supper	6
Act	2:25	he is at my right hand so that I will not be shaken;	4
	2:34	'The Lord said to my Lord, "Sit at my right hand	4
	2:46	broke bread at home and ate their food with glad	8
	3: 1	going up to the temple at the hour of prayer	7
	3: 2	People would lay him daily at the gate of the temple	13
	3: 4	Peter looked intently at him, as did John, and said	3
	3: 4	"Look at us."	3
	3:10	at the Beautiful Gate of the temple;	7
	3:10	amazement at what had happened to him.	7
	3:12	"You Israelites, why do you wonder at this	7
	4:29	now, Lord, look at their threats	7
	4:35	laid it at the apostles' feet.	10
	4:37	laid it at the apostles' feet.	13
	5: 2	laid it at the apostles' feet.	10
	5: 4	sold, were not the proceeds at your disposal?	6
	5: 9	Look, the feet…are at the door	7
	5:10	Immediately she fell down at his feet and died.	13
	5:21	they entered the temple at daybreak and went on	14
	5:23	the guards standing at the doors	7
	5:37	at the time of the census	6
	5:42	every day in the temple and at home	8
	6:15	all who sat in the council looked intently at him	3
	7:20	At this time Moses was born	6
	7:36	wonders and signs in Egypt, at the Red Sea	6
	7:38	the angel who spoke to him at Mount Sinai	6
	7:41	At that time they made a calf	6
	7:54	ground their teeth at Stephen.	7
	7:55	Jesus standing at the right hand of God.	4
	7:56	the Son of Man standing at the right hand of God!"	4
	7:58	at the feet of a young man named Saul.	10
	8:14	Now when the apostles at Jerusalem heard	6
	8:40	Philip found himself at Azotus	3
	9: 2	letters to the synagogues at Damascus	3
	9:11	at the house of Judas look for a man of Tarsus	6
	9:37	At that time she became ill and died.	6
	10: 3	One afternoon at about three o'clock	11
	10:25	and falling at his feet, worshiped him.	7
	10:30	Cornelius replied, "Four days ago at this very hour	9
	11: 6	looked at it closely I saw four-footed animals	3
	11:11	arrived at the house where we were.	7
	11:15	upon them just as it had upon us at the beginning.	6
	11:27	At that time prophets came down from Jerusalem	6
	12:14	announced that Peter was standing at the gate.	12
	13: 1	Now in the church at Antioch there were prophets	6
	13: 5	When they arrived at Salamis	6
	13: 9	Saul…looked intently at him	3
	13:12	he was astonished at the teaching about the Lord.	7
	15:31	they rejoiced at the exhortation.	7
	16:15	come and stay at my home."	3
	16:33	At the same hour of the night he took them	6
	18:18	At Cenchreae he had his hair cut,	6
	18:22	When he had landed at Caesarea, he went up	3
	20:15	The next day we touched at Samos	3
	21: 3	sailed to Syria and landed at Tyre	3
	21: 7	we arrived at Ptolemais;	3
	22: 3	brought up in this city at the feet of Gamaliel	10
	25: 4	Paul was being kept at Caesarea	3
	25:13	Agrippa…arrived at Caesarea to welcome Festus.	3
	27: 3	The next day we put in at Sidon;	3
	28:11	on a ship that had wintered at the island	6
	28:12	put in at Syracuse and stayed there	3
	28:23	they came to him at his lodgings in great numbers.	3
	28:30	He lived there two whole years at his own expense	6
Rom	3:26	prove at the present time that he…is righteous	6
	5: 6	at the right time Christ died for the ungodly.	8
	8:34	Christ Jesus…who is at the right hand of God	6
	11: 5	So too at the present time there is a remnant	6
	15:26	with the poor among the saints at Jerusalem.	6
	16: 1	Phoebe, a deacon of the church at Cenchreae	6
1Co	11:34	If you are hungry, eat at home	6
	14:35	let them ask their husbands at home.	6
	15:23	then at his coming those who belong to Christ.	6

	15:32	I fought with wild animals at Ephesus	6
	15:52	at the last trumpet. For the trumpet will sound	6
	16:17	I rejoice at the coming of Stephanas	7
2Co	3: 7	people of Israel could not gaze at Moses' face	3
	3:13	gazing at the end of the glory…being set aside.	3
	7:11	At every point you have proved yourselves	6
	7:13	we rejoiced still more at the joy of Titus	7
	11:25	a night and a day I was adrift at sea;	6
	11:26	danger at sea, danger from false brothers and sisters;	6
Eph	1:20	seated at his right hand	6
	6:18	Pray in the Spirit at all times	6
Php	2:10	at the name of Jesus every knee should bend	6
Col	3: 1	where Christ is, seated at the right hand of God.	6
1Th	2: 2	we had…been shamefully mistreated at Philippi	6
	2:16	God's wrath has overtaken them at last.	3
	2:19	before our Lord Jesus at his coming?	6
	3:13	blameless…at the coming of our Lord Jesus	6
	5:23	blameless at the coming of our Lord Jesus	6
2Th	3:16	Lord of peace himself give you peace at all times	2
2Ti	3: 7	can never arrive at a knowledge of the truth.	3
	4:13	bring the cloak that I left with Carpus at Troas	6
	4:16	At my first defense no one came to my support	6
Tit	3:12	do your best to come to me at Nicopolis	3
Heb	1: 3	he sat down at the right hand of the Majesty on high	6
	1:13	of the angels has he ever said, "Sit at my right hand	4
	4: 3	were finished at the foundation of the world.	1
	8: 1	one who is seated at the right hand of the throne	6
	9:17	For a will takes effect only at death	7
	9:26	he has appeared once for all at the end of the age	7
	10:12	"he sat down at the right hand of God,"	6
	12: 2	seat at the right hand of the throne of God.	6
	12:11	seems painful rather than pleasant at the time	13
Jas	2: 3	"Stand there," or, "Sit at my feet,"	14
	5: 9	See, the Judge is standing at the doors!	12
1Pe	1:20	He…was revealed at the end of the ages	7
	3:22	who…is at the right hand of God	6
2Pe	3:14	at peace, without spot or blemish;	6
1Jn	2:28	and not be put to shame before him at his coming.	6
Rev	1:17	When I saw him, I fell at his feet as though dead.	13
	3:20	Listen! I am standing at the door, knocking;	7
	7: 1	angels standing at the four corners of the earth	7
	8: 3	angel with a golden censer…stood at the altar;	7
	8:13	woe…at the blasts of the other trumpets	4
	9:14	angels…bound at the great river Euphrates."	7
	11:13	At that moment there was a great earthquake	6
	16:16	And they assembled them at…Harmagedon.	3
	18:19	all who had ships at sea grew rich by her wealth!	6
	19:10	Then I fell down at his feet to worship him	5
	20: 8	nations…at the four corners of the earth	6
	21:12	and at the gates twelve angels	7
	22: 8	I fell down to worship at the feet of the angel	5

at all

1. ἀρχή, *archē*, 794
2. καθόλου, *katholou*, 2773
3. λόγος, *logos*, 3364
4. μόνον, *monon*, 3667
5. ὅλως, *holōs*, 3914
6. οὐ, *ou*, 4024
7. πάντως, *pantōs*, 4122

Mat	5:34	I say to you, Do not swear at all, either by heaven	5
	15:23	he did not answer her at all.	3
	21:19	found nothing at all on it but leaves.	4
Lke	4: 2	He ate nothing at all during those days	6
Jhn	8:25	"Why do I speak to you at all?	1
	11:49	"You know nothing at all!	6
Act	4:18	not to speak or teach at all in the name of Jesus.	2
Rom	3: 9	What then? Are we any better off? No, not at all;	7
1Co	6: 7	to have lawsuits at all with one another	5
	15:29	If the dead are not raised at all	5
	16:12	he was not at all willing to come now.	7

at this

1. εὐθύς[1], *euthys*[1], 2317
2. τότε, *tote*, 5538

Mrk	5:42	At this they were overcome with amazement.	1
Act	23: 3	At this Paul said to him, "God will strike you	2

no at all

1. οὐδείς, *oudeis*, 4029

1Jn   1: 5 God is light and in him there is no darkness at all.   1

not at all
1. οὐδείς, *oudeis, 4029*
2Co 12:11 for I am not at all inferior   1

Athenian
1. Ἀθηναῖος, *Athēnaios, 122*
Act 17:21 Now all the Athenians and the foreigners   1
      17:22 "Athenians, I see how…religious you are   1

Athens
1. Ἀθῆναι, *Athēnai, 121*
Act 17:15 who conducted Paul brought him as far as Athens;   1
      17:16 While Paul was waiting for them in Athens   1
      18: 1 After this Paul left Athens and went to Corinth.   1
1Th   3: 1 we decided to be left alone in Athens;   1

athlete
1. ἀγωνίζομαι, *agōnizomai, 76*
2. ἀθλέω, *athleō, 123*
1Co   9:25 Athletes exercise self-control   1
2Ti   2: 5 in the case of an athlete, no one is crowned   2

atonement *See* make a sacrifice of atonement, sacrifice of atonement

atoning *See* atoning *sacrifice*

attack *See also* make an attack
1. ἐπέρχομαι, *eperchomai, 2088*
2. ἔργον, *ergon, 2240*
3. ἐφίστημι, *ephistēmi, 2392*
4. κατά, *kata, 2848*
Lke 11:22 one stronger than he attacks him and overpowers   1
Act 16:22 The crowd joined in attacking them   4
      17: 5 to the assembly, they attacked Jason's house.   3
2Ti   4:18 The Lord will rescue me from every evil attack   2

attain
1. καταλαμβάνω, *katalambanō, 2898*
2. καταντάω, *katantaō, 2918*
3. φθάνω, *phthanō, 5777*
Act 26: 7 a promise that our twelve tribes hope to attain   2
Rom   9:30 did not strive for righteousness, have attained it   1
Php   3:11 I may attain the resurrection from the dead.   2
      3:16 Only let us hold fast to what we have attained.   3

attainable
1. Contextual: Not in Greek
Heb   7:11 Now if perfection had been attainable   1

Attalia
1. Ἀττάλεια, *Attaleia, 877*
Act 14:25 they went down to Attalia.   1

attempt
1. ἐπιχειρέω, *epicheireō, 2217*
2. ὁρμή, *hormē, 3995*
3. πεῖρα, *peira, 4278*
4. πειράζω, *peirazō, 4279*
Act   9:26 he attempted to join the disciples;   4
      9:29 they were attempting to kill him.   1
      14: 5 an attempt was made by both Gentiles and Jews   2
      16: 7 they attempted to go into Bithynia   4
Heb 11:29 when the Egyptians attempted to do so they   3

attendant
1. διάκονος, *diakonos, 1356*
2. ὑπηρέτης, *hypēretēs, 5677*
Mat 22:13 the king said to the attendants, 'Bind him   1
Lke   4:20 the scroll, gave it back to the attendant   2

attention *See* call attention, fix attention on, give attention, pay attention, pay close attention

attentive
1. προσέχω, *prosechō, 4668*

2Pe   1:19 You will do well to be attentive to this   1

attest
1. ἀποδείκνυμι, *apodeiknymi, 617*
2. βεβαιόω, *bebaioō, 1011*
3. μαρτυρέω, *martyreō, 3455*
4. μαρτύριον, *martyrion, 3457*
Act   2:22 Jesus of Nazareth, a man attested to you by God   1
Rom   3:21 attested by the law and the prophets   3
1Ti   2: 6 this was attested at the right time.   4
Heb   2: 3 it was attested to us by those who heard him   2
      7:17 For it is attested of him   3
      11: 5 it was attested…that "he had pleased God."   3

attest well
1. μαρτυρέω, *martyreō, 3455*
1Ti   5:10 she must be well attested for her good works   1

attorney
1. ῥήτωρ, *rhētōr, 4842*
Act 24: 1 some elders and an attorney, a certain Tertullus   1

audience *See* audience *hall*

Augustan
1. σεβαστός, *sebastos, 4935*
Act 27: 1 a centurion of the Augustan Cohort, named Julius.   1

Augustus
1. Αὔγουστος, *Augoustos, 880*
Lke   2: 1 a decree went out from Emperor Augustus .   1

author
1. ἀρχηγός, *archēgos, 795*
Act   3:15 you killed the Author of life   1

authority *See also* accept authority, grant authority, symbol of authority
1. Contextual: Not in Greek
2. ἄρχων, *archōn, 807*
3. δυνατός, *dynatos, 1543*
4. ἐξουσία, *exousia, 2026*
5. ἐπιταγή, *epitagē, 2198*
6. κατά, *kata, 2848*
7. κυριότης, *kyriotēs, 3262*
Mat   7:29 for he taught them as one having authority   4
      8: 9 a man under authority, with soldiers under me;   4
      9: 6 the Son of Man has authority on earth to forgive   4
      9: 8 they glorified God, who had given such authority   4
      10: 1 and gave them authority over unclean spirits   4
      21:23 "By what authority are you doing these things   4
      21:23 who gave you this authority?"   4
      21:24 by what authority I do these things.   4
      21:27 by what authority I am doing these things.   4
      28:18 "All authority in heaven and on earth   4
Mrk   1:22 he taught them as one having authority   4
      1:27 A new teaching—with authority! He commands   4
      2:10 Son of Man has authority on earth to forgive sins"   4
      3:15 and to have authority to cast out demons.   4
      6: 7 gave them authority over the unclean spirits.   4
      11:28 "By what authority are you doing these things?   4
      11:28 Who gave you this authority to do them?"   4
      11:29 tell you by what authority I do these things.   4
      11:33 by what authority I am doing these things."   4
Lke   4: 6 I will give their glory and all this authority;   4
      4:32 because he spoke with authority.   4
      4:36 For with authority and power he commands   4
      5:24 Son of Man has authority on earth to forgive   4
      7: 8 I also am a man set under authority   4
      9: 1 gave them power and authority over all demons   4
      10:19 have given you authority to tread on snakes   4
      12: 5 who…has authority to cast into hell.   4
      12:11 the rulers, and the authorities   4
      20: 2 by what authority are you doing these things?   4
      20: 2 Who is it who gave you this authority?"   4
      20: 8 by what authority I am doing these things."   4
      20:20 jurisdiction and authority of the governor.   4
Jhn   5:27 has given him authority to execute judgment   4
      7:26 Can it be that the authorities really know   2

Jhn	7:48	Has any one of the authorities...believed in him?	2
'	12:42	many, even of the authorities, believed in him.	2
	17: 2	you have given him authority over all people	4
Act	1: 7	that the Father has set by his own authority.	4
	9:14	here he has authority from the chief priests	4
	16:19	dragged them...before the authorities.	2
	25: 5	he said, "let those of you who have the authority	3
	26:10	with authority received from the chief priests	4
	26:12	authority and commission of the chief priests	4
Rom	13: 1	be subject to the governing authorities;	4
	13: 1	for there is no authority except from God	4
	13: 1	authorities that exist have been instituted by God.	1
	13: 2	Therefore whoever resists authority resists	4
	13: 3	you wish to have no fear of the authority?	4
	13: 4	for the authority does not bear the sword in vain!	1
	13: 6	for the authorities are God's servants,	1
1Co	9: 8	Do I say this on human authority?	6
	15:24	every ruler and every authority and power.	4
2Co	10: 8	even if I boast a little too much of our authority	4
	11:17	I am saying not with the Lord's authority	6
	13:10	not have to be severe in using the authority	4
Gal	1: 1	by human commission nor from human authorities,	1
Eph	1:21	far above all rule and authority and power	4
	3:10	made known to the rulers and authorities	4
	6:12	against the rulers, against the authorities	4
Col	2:10	the head of every ruler and authority.	4
	2:15	He disarmed the rulers and authorities	4
Tit	2:15	exhort and reprove with all authority.	5
	3: 1	to be subject to rulers and authorities	4
1Pe	3:22	angels, authorities, and powers made subject to him.	4
2Pe	2:10	those who indulge...and who despise authority.	7
3Jn	1: 9	Diotrephes...does not acknowledge our authority.	1
Jde	1: 8	these dreamers...reject authority, and slander	7
	1:25	be glory, majesty, power, and authority	4
Rev	2:26	I will give authority over the nations;	4
	2:28	even as I also received authority from my Father.	1
	6: 8	they were given authority over a fourth of the earth	4
	9: 3	were given authority like the authority of scorpions	4
	9: 3	were given authority like the authority of scorpions	4
	11: 6	They have authority to shut the sky, so that no rain	4
	11: 6	authority over the waters to turn them into blood	4
	12:10	kingdom of our God and the authority of his Messiah	4
	13: 2	dragon gave it his power...and great authority.	4
	13: 4	for he had given his authority to the beast	4
	13: 5	allowed to exercise authority for...months.	4
	13: 7	It was given authority over every tribe	4
	13:12	exercises all the authority of the first beast	4
	14:18	the angel who has authority over fire	4
	16: 9	God, who had authority over these plagues	4
	17:12	they are to receive authority as kings	4
	17:13	yielding their power and authority to the beast;	4
	18: 1	I saw another angel...having great authority;	4

authority over

1. αὐθεντέω, *authenteō, 883*
2. ἐξουσιάζω, *exousiazō, 2027*

Lke	22:25	those in authority over them	2
1Co	7: 4	wife does not have authority over her own body	2
	7: 4	husband does not have authority over his own body	2
1Ti	2:12	no woman...to have authority over a man;	1

authority to judge

1. κρίμα, *krima, 3210*

Rev 20: 4 those seated on them were given authority to judge.   1

city authority

1. πολιτάρχης, *politarchēs, 4485*

Act 17: 6 dragged...before the city authorities, shouting   1

human authority

1. ἄνθρωπος, *anthrōpos, 476*

Act	5:29	"We must obey God rather than any human authority.	1
1Th	4: 8	rejects not human authority but God	1

autumn

1. φθινοπωρινός, *phthinopōrinos, 5781*

Jde 1:12 autumn trees without fruit, twice dead, uprooted;   1

avarice

1. πλεονεξία, *pleonexia, 4432*

Mrk 7:22 avarice, wickedness, deceit, licentiousness   1

avenge

1. ἐκδικέω, *ekdikeō, 1688*
2. ποιέω + ἐκδίκησις, *poieō + ekdikēsis, 4472 + 1689*

Act	7:24	he defended the oppressed man and avenged him	2
Rom	12:19	Beloved, never avenge yourselves	1
Rev	6:10	how long will it be before you judge and avenge	1
	19: 2	he has avenged on her the blood of his servants."	1

avenger

1. ἔκδικος, *ekdikos, 1690*

1Th 4: 6 because the Lord is an avenger   1

avoid

1. ἀποτρέπω, *apotrepō, 706*
2. ἐκκλίνω, *ekklinō, 1712*
3. ἐκτρέπω, *ektrepō, 1762*
4. κερδαίνω, *kerdainō, 3045*
5. μή, *mē, 3590*
6. περιίστημι, *periistēmi, 4325*

Jhn	18:28	so as to avoid ritual defilement	5
Act	27:21	avoided this damage and loss.	4
Rom	16:17	those who cause dissensions...avoid them.	2
1Ti	6:20	Avoid the profane chatter and contradictions	3
2Ti	2:14	warn them...to avoid wrangling over words	5
	2:16	Avoid profane chatter	6
	3: 5	Avoid them!	1
Tit	3: 9	avoid stupid controversies, genealogies	6

avoid quarreling

1. ἄμαχος, *amachos, 285*

Tit 3: 2 to speak evil of no one, to avoid quarreling   1

awake   *See also* keep awake, stay awake

1. γρηγορέω, *grēgoreō, 1213*
2. ἐγείρω, *egeirō, 1586*
3. ἐξυπνίζω, *exypnizō, 2030*

Mat	1:24	When Joseph awoke from sleep, he did as the angel	2
Jhn	11:11	I am going there to awaken him."	3
Eph	5:14	it says, "Sleeper, awake! Rise from the dead	2
1Th	5:10	so that whether we are awake or asleep we may live	1

aware

1. γινώσκω, *ginōskō, 1182*
2. ἐπιγινώσκω, *epiginōskō, 2105*
3. οἶδα, *oida, 3857*
4. συνείδησις, *syneidēsis, 5287*
5. σύνοιδα, *synoida, 5323*

Mat	12:15	Jesus became aware of this, he departed.	1
	16: 8	aware of it, Jesus said	1
	22:18	Jesus, aware of their malice, said	1
	26:10	Jesus, aware of this, said to them	1
Mrk	5:30	that power had gone forth from him,	2
	8:17	becoming aware of it, Jesus said to them	1
Lke	9:47	Jesus, aware of their inner thoughts	3
Jhn	6:61	aware that his disciples were complaining	3
	15:18	world hates you, be aware that it hated me	1
1Co	4: 4	I am not aware of anything against myself	5
2Ti	1:15	You are aware that all who are in Asia have turned away	3
1Pe	2:19	if, being aware of God, you endure pain	4

away   *See also* carry away, come away, cut away, do away with, draw away, drift away, drive away, fall away, flee away, get away, give away, go away, keep away, lead away, never *fades* away, pass away, pull away, put away, roll away, run away, sail away, send away, snatch away, steal away, sweep away, sweep away with the flood, swim away, take away, take away as captive, throw away, turn away, wander away, wash away, waste away, wipe away, wither away

1. αἴρω, *airō, 149*
2. ἄπειμι[1], *apeimi[1], 582*
3. ἀπό, *apo, 608*
4. ἐκ, *ek, 1666*
5. ἐκδημέω, *ekdēmeō, 1685*
6. ἔξω, *exō, 2032*
7. ἔχω, *echō, 2400*

8. ὑπάγω, *hypagō, 5632*

Mat	4:10	Jesus said to him, "Away with you, Satan!	8
	5:29	and throw it away; it is better for you to lose	3
	5:30	and throw it away; it is better for you to lose	3
	18: 8	or your foot…cut it off and throw it away;	3
	18: 9	tear it out and throw it away;	3
Mrk	7:33	took him aside in private, away from the crowd	3
	13:15	or enter the house to take anything away;	4
Lke	14:35	they throw it away.	6
	23:18	all shouted out together, "Away with this fellow!	1
Jhn	6:37	anyone who comes to me I will never drive away;	6
	11:18	Bethany was near Jerusalem, some two miles away	3
	15: 6	is thrown away like a branch and withers;	6
	19:15	They cried out, "Away with him! Away with him!	1
	19:15	"Away with him! Away with him! Crucify him!"	1
Act	1:12	is near Jerusalem, a sabbath day's journey away.	7
	21:36	followed kept shouting, "Away with him!"	1
	22:22	"Away with such a fellow from the earth!	1
2Co	5: 6	in the body we are away from the Lord	5
	5: 8	we would rather be away from the body and at home	5
	5: 9	So whether we are at home or away	5
	10: 1	bold toward you when I am away!—	2
	13:10	I write these things while I am away from you	2

far away

1. ἀπό + μακρόθεν, *apo + makrothen, 608 + 3427*
2. πόρρω, *porrō, 4522*

Lke	14:32	while the other is still far away, he sends	2
	16:23	and saw Abraham far away with Lazarus by his side.	1

awe   *See also* fill with awe, overcome with awe, stand in awe

1. δέος, *deos, 1290*
2. φόβος, *phobos, 5832*

Mrk	4:41	And they were filled with great awe	2
Lke	5:26	they glorified God and were filled with awe	2
Act	2:43	Awe came upon everyone	2
Heb	12:28	acceptable worship with reverence and awe;	1

awestruck

1. ἐπιπίπτω + φόβος, *epipiptō + phobos, 2158 + 5832*

Act	19:17	this became known…everyone was awestruck;	1

ax

1. ἀξίνη, *axinē, 544*

Mat	3:10	Even now the ax is lying at the root of the trees;	1
Lke	3: 9	Even now the ax is lying at the root of the trees;	1

Azor

1. Ἀζώρ, *Azōr, 110*

Mat	1:13	and Eliakim the father of Azor	1
	1:14	Azor the father of Zadok	1

Azotus

1. Ἄζωτος, *Azōtos, 111*

Act	8:40	Philip found himself at Azotus	1

B

Baal

1. Βάαλ, *Baal, 955*

Rom	11: 4	who have not bowed the knee to Baal."	1

babbler

1. σπερμολόγος, *spermologos, 5066*

Act	17:18	Some said, "What does this babbler want to say?"	1

nursing baby

1. θηλάζω, *thēlazō, 2558*

Mat	21:16	'Out of the mouths of infants and nursing babies	1

Babylon

1. Βαβυλών, *Babylōn, 956*

Mat	1:11	at the time of the deportation to Babylon.	1
	1:12	after the deportation to Babylon: Jechoniah was	1
	1:17	and from David to the deportation to Babylon	1
	1:17	from the deportation to Babylon to the Messiah	1

Act	7:43	I will remove you beyond Babylon.'	1
1Pe	5:13	Your sister church in Babylon, chosen together	1
Rev	14: 8	"Fallen, fallen is Babylon the great!	1
	16:19	God remembered great Babylon and gave her	1
	17: 5	"Babylon the great, mother of whores	1
	18: 2	"Fallen, fallen is Babylon the great!	1
	18:10	alas, the great city, Babylon, the mighty city!	1
	18:21	"With such violence Babylon…will be thrown down	1

back   *See also* bring back, come back, draw back, fall back, fight back, get back, get back measure, give back, go back, have back, hold back, keep back, keep back by fraud, pay back, put back, receive back, roll back, rush back, sail back, send back, shrink back, start back, step back, talk back, turn back

1. Contextual: Not in Greek
2. εἰς + ὁ + ὀπίσω, *eis + ho + opisō, 1650 + 3836 + 3958*
3. ἐνθάδε, *enthade, 1924*
4. νῶτος, *nōtos, 3822*
5. ὄπισθεν, *opisthen, 3957*
6. ὀπίσω, *opisō, 3958*
7. πάλιν, *palin, 4099*

Mat	24:18	the one in the field must not turn back	6
Mrk	11: 3	will send it back here immediately.' "	7
	13:16	must not turn back to get a coat.	2
	15:13	They shouted back, "Crucify him!"	7
Lke	9:62	puts a hand to the plow and looks back is fit	2
	17:31	likewise anyone in the field must not turn back.	2
Jhn	4: 3	he left Judea and started back to Galilee.	7
	4:16	"Go, call your husband, and come back."	3
	6:66	Because of this many of his disciples turned back	2
	18: 6	they stepped back and fell to the ground.	2
Rom	11:10	and keep their backs forever bent."	4
	11:24	be grafted back into their own olive tree.	1
2Co	1:16	to come back to you from Macedonia	7
Rev	5: 1	a scroll written on the inside and on the back	5

bad

1. Contextual: Not in Greek
2. ἥσσων, *hēssōn, 2482*
3. κακός, *kakos, 2805*
4. πονηρός, *ponēros, 4505*
5. σαπρός, *sapros, 4911*
6. φαῦλος, *phaulos, 5765*
7. χείρων, *cheirōn, 5937*

Mat	7:17	but the bad tree bears bad fruit.	5
	7:17	but the bad tree bears bad fruit.	4
	7:18	A good tree cannot bear bad fruit.	4
	7:18	nor can a bad tree bear good fruit.	5
	9:16	and a worse tear is made.	7
	12:33	or make the tree bad, and its fruit bad;	5
	12:33	or make the tree bad, and its fruit bad;	5
	12:45	worse than the first.	7
	13:48	but threw out the bad.	5
	22:10	gathered all whom they found, both good and bad;	4
	27:64	the last deception would be worse than the first."	7
Mrk	2:21	the new from the old, and a worse tear is made.	7
	5:26	no better, but rather grew worse.	7
Lke	6:43	"No good tree bears bad fruit	5
	6:43	nor again does a bad tree bear good fruit;	5
	11:26	the last state…is worse than the first."	7
	13: 2	worse sinners than all other Galileans?	1
	13: 4	do you think that they were worse offenders	1
Jhn	5:14	not sin…so that nothing worse happens to you."	7
Rom	9:11	or had done anything good or bad	6
	13: 3	not a terror to good conduct, but to bad.	3
1Co	11:17	it is not for the better but for the worse.	2
	15:33	"Bad company ruins good morals."	3
1Ti	5: 8	and is worse than an unbeliever.	7
2Ti	3:13	impostors will go from bad to worse	1
	3:13	impostors will go from bad to worse	7
Heb	10:29	How much worse punishment…will be deserved	7
2Pe	2:20	last state has become worse for them than the first.	7

bad off

1. ἑσσόομαι, *hessoomai, 2273*
2. ὑστερέω, *hystereō, 5728*

1Co	8: 8	We are no worse off if we do not eat	2
2Co	12:13	worse off than the other churches	1

bag

1. πήρα, *pēra, 4385*

Mat	10:10	no bag for your journey, or two tunics	1
Mrk	6: 8	no bread, no bag, no money in their belts;	1
Lke	9: 3	no staff, nor bag, nor bread, nor money	1
	10: 4	Carry no purse, no bag, no sandals;	1
	22:35	sent you out without a purse, bag, or sandals	1
	22:36	who has a purse must take it, and likewise a bag.	1

bail

1. ἱκανός, *hikanos, 2653*

Act 17: 9 after they had taken bail from Jason   1

Balaam

1. Βαλαάμ, *Balaam, 962*

2Pe	2:15	following the road of Balaam	1
Jde	1:11	abandon themselves to Balaam's error for the sake of gain	1
Rev	2:14	some there who hold to the teaching of Balaam	1

Balak

1. Βαλάκ, *Balak, 963*

Rev 2:14 Balaam, who taught Balak to put a stumbling block   1

fair balance

1. ἰσότης, *isotēs, 2699*

2Co	8:13	but it is a question of a fair balance	1
	8:14	in order that there may be a fair balance.	1

band   *See* wrap in bands of cloth

bandage

1. καταδέω, *katadeō, 2866*

Lke 10:34 He went to him and bandaged his wounds   1

bandit

1. λῃστής, *lēstēs, 3334*

Mat	26:55	to arrest me as though I were a bandit?	1
	27:38	Then two bandits were crucified with him	1
	27:44	The bandits who were crucified with him	1
Mrk	14:48	to arrest me as though I were a bandit?	1
	15:27	with him they crucified two bandits	1
Lke	22:52	with swords and clubs as if I were a bandit?	1
Jhn	10: 1	in by another way is a thief and a bandit.	1
	10: 8	All who came before me are thieves and bandits;	1
	18:40	Now Barabbas was a bandit.	1
2Co	11:26	in danger from rivers, danger from bandits	1

banish

1. ἀποστρέφω, *apostrephō, 695*

Rom 11:26 he will banish ungodliness from Jacob."   1

bank

1. τράπεζα, *trapeza, 5544*

Lke 19:23 Why then did you not put my money into the bank?   1

steep bank

1. κρημνός, *krēmnos, 3204*

Mat	8:32	suddenly, the whole herd rushed down the steep bank	1
Mrk	5:13	rushed down the steep bank into the sea	1
Lke	8:33	herd rushed down the steep bank into the lake	1

banker

1. τραπεζίτης, *trapezitēs, 5545*

Mat 25:27 to have invested my money with the bankers   1

banquet

1. δεῖπνον, *deipnon, 1270*
2. δοχή, *dochē, 1531*

Mat	23: 6	They love to have the place of honor at banquets	1
Mrk	6:21	when Herod on his birthday gave a banquet	1
	12:39	and places of honor at banquets!	1
Lke	5:29	Levi gave a great banquet for him in his house;	2
	14:13	when you give a banquet, invite the poor,	2
	20:46	and love…places of honor at banquets.	1

wedding banquet

1. γάμος, *gamos, 1141*

Mat	22: 2	to a king who gave a wedding banquet for his son.	1
	22: 3	who had been invited to the wedding banquet	1
	22: 4	everything is ready; come to the wedding banquet.'	1
	22: 9	invite everyone you find to the wedding banquet.'	1
	25:10	went with him into the wedding banquet;	1
Lke	12:36	to return from the wedding banquet	1
	14: 8	you are invited by someone to a wedding banquet	1

baptism   *See also* receive baptism

1. βάπτισμα, *baptisma, 967*
2. βαπτισμός, *baptismos, 968*

Mat	3: 7	Pharisees and Sadducees coming for baptism	1
	21:25	Did the baptism of John come from heaven	1
Mrk	1: 4	proclaiming a baptism of repentance	1
	10:38	be baptized with the baptism	1
	10:39	with the baptism with which I am baptized	1
	11:30	Did the baptism of John come from heaven,	1
Lke	3: 3	proclaiming a baptism of repentance	1
	7:29	baptized with John's baptism.	1
	12:50	I have a baptism with which to be baptized	1
	20: 4	Did the baptism of John come from heaven,	1
Act	1:22	beginning from the baptism of John	1
	10:37	after the baptism that John announced:	1
	13:24	proclaimed a baptism of repentance to all	1
	18:25	though he knew only the baptism of John.	1
	19: 3	They answered, "Into John's baptism."	1
	19: 4	"John baptized with the baptism of repentance	1
Rom	6: 4	we have been buried with him by baptism into death	1
Eph	4: 5	one Lord, one faith, one baptism	1
Col	2:12	you were buried with him in baptism	2
Heb	6: 2	instruction about baptisms	2
	9:10	food and drink and various baptisms	2
1Pe	3:21	baptism, which this prefigured, now saves you	1

Baptist

1. βαπτιστής, *baptistēs, 969*

Mat	3: 1	In those days John the Baptist appeared	1
	11:11	no one has arisen greater than John the Baptist;	1
	11:12	From the days of John the Baptist until now	1
	14: 2	"This is John the Baptist: he has been raised	1
	14: 8	she said, "Give me the head of John the Baptist	1
	16:14	"Some say John the Baptist, but others Elijah	1
	17:13	he was speaking to them about John the Baptist.	1
Mrk	6:25	the head of John the Baptist on a platter."	1
	8:28	they answered him, "John the Baptist;	1
Lke	7:20	"John the Baptist has sent us to you to ask	1
	7:33	For John the Baptist has come eating no bread	1
	9:19	They answered, "John the Baptist;	1

baptize

1. βαπτίζω, *baptizō, 966*

Mat	3: 6	they were baptized by him in the river Jordan	1
	3:11	"I baptize you with water for repentance, but one	1
	3:11	He will baptize you with the Holy Spirit	1
	3:13	to John at the Jordan, to be baptized by him.	1
	3:14	"I need to be baptized by you, and do you come to me?"	1
	3:16	when Jesus had been baptized, just as he came up	1
	28:19	baptizing them in the name of the Father	1
Mrk	1: 5	and were baptized by him in the river Jordan	1
	1: 8	I have baptized you with water;	1
	1: 8	he will baptize you with the Holy Spirit."	1
	1: 9	baptized by John in the Jordan.	1
	10:38	be baptized with the baptism	1
	10:38	the baptism that I am baptized with?"	1
	10:39	with the baptism with which I am baptized	1
	10:39	you will be baptized;	1
	16:16	⟦one who believes and is baptized will be saved;⟧	1
Lke	3: 7	the crowds that came out to be baptized by him	1
	3:12	Even tax collectors came to be baptized,	1
	3:16	John answered…"I baptize you with water;	1
	3:16	baptize you with the Holy Spirit and fire.	1
	3:21	Now when all the people were baptized	1
	3:21	Jesus also had been baptized and was praying	1
	7:29	baptized with John's baptism.	1
	7:30	refusing to be baptized by him	1
	12:50	I have a baptism with which to be baptized	1
Jhn	1:25	They asked him, "Why then are you baptizing	1
	1:26	John answered them, "I baptize with water.	1
	1:28	across the Jordan where John was baptizing.	1
	1:31	but I came baptizing with water for this	1
	1:33	but the one who sent me to baptize with water	1
	1:33	is the one who baptizes with the Holy Spirit.'	1

3:22 he spent some time there with them and baptized. 1
3:23 John also was baptizing at Aenon near Salim 1
3:23 and people kept coming and were being baptized 1
3:26 to whom you testified, here he is baptizing 1
4: 1 "Jesus is making and baptizing more disciples 1
4: 2 not Jesus himself but his disciples who baptized 1
10:40 to the place where John had been baptizing earlier 1
Act 1: 5 for John baptized with water 1
1: 5 you will be baptized with the Holy Spirit 1
2:38 "Repent, and be baptized every one of you 1
2:41 So those who welcomed his message were baptized 1
8:12 they were baptized, both men and women. 1
8:13 being baptized, he stayed constantly with Philip 1
8:16 they had only been baptized 1
8:36 What is to prevent me from being baptized?" 1
8:38 Philip baptized him. 1
9:18 Then he got up and was baptized 1
10:47 "Can anyone withhold the water for baptizing 1
10:48 baptized in the name of Jesus Christ. 1
11:16 'John baptized with water 1
11:16 you will be baptized with the Holy Spirit.' 1
16:15 When she and her household were baptized 1
16:33 he and his entire family were baptized without delay. 1
18: 8 many…became believers and were baptized. 1
19: 3 he said, "Into what then were you baptized?" 1
19: 4 "John baptized with the baptism of repentance 1
19: 5 baptized in the name of the Lord Jesus. 1
22:16 now why do you delay? Get up, be baptized 1
Rom 6: 3 all of us who have been baptized into Christ 1
6: 3 into Christ Jesus were baptized into his death? 1
1Co 1:13 were you baptized in the name of Paul? 1
1:14 I thank God that I baptized none of you 1
1:15 say that you were baptized in my name. 1
1:16 (I did baptize also the household of Stephanas; 1
1:16 I do not know whether I baptized anyone else.) 1
1:17 not send me to baptize but to proclaim the gospel 1
10: 2 all were baptized into Moses in the cloud 1
12:13 we were all baptized into one body 1
15:29 why are people baptized on their behalf? 1
Gal 3:27 As many of you as were baptized into Christ 1

baptizer

1. βαπτίζω, *baptizō, 966*

Mrk 1: 4 John the baptizer appeared in the wilderness 1
6:14 "John the baptizer has been raised from the dead; 1
6:24 She replied, "The head of John the baptizer." 1

Bar-Jesus

1. Βαριησοῦς, *Bariēsous, 979*

Act 13: 6 a Jewish false prophet, named Bar-Jesus. 1

Barabbas

1. Βαραββᾶς, *Barabbas, 972*

Mat 27:16 a notorious prisoner, called Jesus Barabbas. 1
27:17 Jesus Barabbas or Jesus who is called the Messiah?" 1
27:20 elders persuaded the crowds to ask for Barabbas 1
27:21 they said, "Barabbas." 1
27:26 So he released Barabbas for them; 1
Mrk 15: 7 a man called Barabbas was in prison with the rebels 1
15:11 to have him release Barabbas for them instead. 1
15:15 to satisfy the crowd, released Barabbas for them; 1
Lke 23:18 Release Barabbas for us!" 1
Jhn 18:40 shouted in reply, "Not this man, but Barabbas!" 1
18:40 Now Barabbas was a bandit. 1

Barachiah

1. Βαραχίας, *Barachias, 974*

Mat 23:35 to the blood of Zechariah son of Barachiah 1

Barak

1. Βαράκ, *Barak, 973*

Heb 11:32 to tell of Gideon, Barak, Samson, Jephthah, of David 1

barbarian

1. βάρβαρος, *barbaros, 975*

Rom 1:14 debtor both to Greeks and to barbarians 1
Col 3:11 barbarian, Scythian, slave and free; 1

bare *See also* lay bare

1. γυμνός, *gymnos, 1218*

1Co 15:37 a bare seed, perhaps of wheat 1

barley

1. κριθή, *krithē, 3208*
2. κρίθινος, *krithinos, 3209*

Jhn 6: 9 a boy…who has five barley loaves and two fish. 2
6:13 from the fragments of the five barley loaves 2
Rev 6: 6 and three quarts of barley for a day's pay 1

barn

1. ἀποθήκη, *apothēkē, 630*

Mat 6:26 they neither sow nor reap nor gather into barns 1
13:30 but gather the wheat into my barn.' " 1
Lke 12:18 I will pull down my barns and build larger ones 1
12:24 they have neither storehouse nor barn 1

Barnabas

1. Contextual: Not in Greek
2. Βαρναβᾶς, *Barnabas, 982*

Act 4:36 Joseph, to whom the apostles gave the name Barnabas 2
9:27 Barnabas took him, brought him to the apostles 2
11:22 they sent Barnabas to Antioch. 2
11:25 Barnabas went to Tarsus to look for Saul 1
11:30 sending it to the elders by Barnabas and Saul. 2
12:25 Barnabas and Saul returned to Jerusalem 2
13: 1 Barnabas, Simeon who was called Niger 2
13: 2 "Set apart for me Barnabas and Saul 2
13: 7 who summoned Barnabas and Saul 2
13:42 As Paul and Barnabas were going out, 1
13:43 many Jews…followed Paul and Barnabas 2
13:46 Paul and Barnabas spoke out boldly, saying 2
13:50 persecution against Paul and Barnabas 2
14: 1 Paul and Barnabas went into the Jewish synagogue 1
14:12 Barnabas they called Zeus 2
14:14 When the apostles Barnabas and Paul heard of it 2
14:20 The next day he went on with Barnabas to Derbe. 2
15: 2 after Paul and Barnabas had no small dissension 2
15: 2 Paul and Barnabas and some of the others 2
15:12 listened to Barnabas and Paul 2
15:22 send them to Antioch with Paul and Barnabas. 2
15:25 along with our beloved Barnabas and Paul 2
15:35 Paul and Barnabas remained in Antioch 2
15:36 After some days Paul said to Barnabas, "Come 2
15:37 Barnabas wanted to take with them John 2
15:39 Barnabas took Mark with him 2
1Co 9: 6 Or is it only Barnabas and I who have no right 2
Gal 2: 1 I went up again to Jerusalem with Barnabas 2
2: 9 gave to Barnabas and me the right hand 2
2:13 so that even Barnabas was led astray 2
Col 4:10 Mark the cousin of Barnabas 2

barrack

1. παρεμβολή, *parembolē, 4213*

Act 21:34 he ordered him to be brought into the barracks. 1
21:37 Paul was about to be brought into the barracks 1
22:24 directed that he was to be brought into the barracks 1
23:10 bring him into the barracks. 1
23:16 gained entrance to the barracks and told Paul. 1
23:32 go on with him, while they returned to the barracks. 1

barren

1. ἀργός, *argos, 734*
2. στεῖρα, *steira, 5096*

Lke 1: 7 they had no children, because Elizabeth was barren 2
1:36 the sixth month for her who was said to be barren. 2
23:29 'Blessed are the barren 2
Heb 11:11 he was too old—and Sarah herself was barren— 2
Jas 2:20 that faith apart from works is barren? 1

barrenness

1. νέκρωσις, *nekrōsis, 3740*

Rom 4:19 he considered the barrenness of Sarah's womb. 1

Barsabbas

1. Βαρσαββᾶς, *Barsabbas, 984*

Act 1:23 Joseph called Barsabbas, who was also known as Justus 1
15:22 They sent Judas called Barsabbas, and Silas 1

Bartholomew

1. Βαρθολομαῖος, *Bartholomaios, 978*

Mat 10: 3 Philip and Bartholomew; Thomas and Matthew   1
Mrk 3:18 Andrew, and Philip, and Bartholomew, and Matthew   1
Lke 6:14 James, and John, and Philip, and Bartholomew   1
Act 1:13 Philip and Thomas, Bartholomew and Matthew   1

Bartimaeus

1. Βαρτιμαῖος, *Bartimaios, 985*

Mrk 10:46 Bartimaeus son of Timaeus, a blind beggar   1

base¹

1. Contextual: Not in Greek
2. ἐκ, *ek, 1666*
3. ἐπί, *epi, 2093*

Rom 9:31 the righteousness that is based on the law   1
   9:32 but as if it were based on works.   2
Php 3: 9 the righteousness from God based on faith.   3

base²

1. πονηρός, *ponēros, 4505*

1Ti 6: 4 envy, dissension, slander, base suspicions   1

basic

1. ἀρχή, *archē, 794*

Heb 5:12 teach you...the basic elements of the oracles of God.   1
   6: 1 leaving behind the basic teaching about Christ   1

basin

1. νιπτήρ, *niptēr, 3781*

Jhn 13: 5 Then he poured water into a basin   1

basis

1. διά, *dia, 1328*
2. ἐκ, *ek, 1666*
3. κατά, *kata, 2848*

Rom 9:32 they did not strive for it on the basis of faith   2
  11: 6 it is no longer on the basis of works   2
1Ti 5:21 doing nothing on the basis of partiality.   3
Phm 1: 9 yet I would rather appeal to you on the basis of love   1

basis for accusation

1. αἴτιος, *aitios, 165*

Lke 23: 4 "I find no basis for an accusation against   1

basket   *See also* bushel basket

1. ἄγγος, *angos, 35*
2. κλάσμα, *klasma, 3083*
3. κόφινος, *kophinos, 3186*
4. σαργάνη, *sarganē, 4914*
5. σπυρίς, *spyris, 5083*

Mat 13:48 sat down, and put the good into baskets   1
  14:20 of the broken pieces, twelve baskets full.   3
  15:37 the broken pieces left over, seven baskets full.   5
  16: 9 and how many baskets you gathered?   3
  16:10 and how many baskets you gathered?   5
Mrk 6:43 they took up twelve baskets   2
  8: 8 the broken pieces left over, seven baskets full.   5
  8:19 how many baskets full of broken pieces   3
  8:20 how many baskets full of broken pieces   5
Lke 9:17 twelve baskets of broken pieces.   3
Jhn 6:13 from the fragments...they filled twelve baskets.   3
Act 9:25 lowering him in a basket.   5
2Co 11:33 let down in a basket through a window in the wall   4

batch

1. φύραμα, *phyrama, 5878*

Rom 11:16 If the part...is holy, then the whole batch is   1
1Co 5: 7 so that you may be a new batch   1

batch of dough

1. φύραμα, *phyrama, 5878*

1Co 5: 6 a little yeast leavens the whole batch of dough?   1
Gal 5: 9 A little yeast leavens the whole batch of dough.   1

bathe

1. βρέχω, *brechō, 1101*
2. λούω, *louō, 3374*

Lke 7:38 and began to bathe his feet with her tears   1
  7:44 she has bathed my feet with her tears   1
Jhn 13:10 "One who has bathed does not need to wash   2

batter

1. βασανίζω, *basanizō, 989*

Mat 14:24 boat, battered by the waves, was far from the land   1

battle

1. πόλεμος, *polemos, 4483*

1Co 14: 8 who will get ready for battle?   1
Rev 9: 7 the locusts were like horses equipped for battle.   1
  9: 9 noise of many chariots...rushing into battle.   1
  16:14 to assemble them for battle on the great day   1
  20: 8 Gog and Magog, in order to gather them for battle;   1

bay

1. κόλπος, *kolpos, 3146*

Act 27:39 they noticed a bay with a beach   1

be   Not Indexed; *See also* to [be]

beach

1. αἰγιαλός, *aigialos, 129*

Mat 13: 2 while the whole crowd stood on the beach.   1
Jhn 21: 4 Just after daybreak, Jesus stood on the beach;   1
Act 21: 5 we knelt down on the beach and prayed   1
  27:39 they noticed a bay with a beach   1
  27:40 they made for the beach.   1

bear¹   *See also* hard to bear

1. Contextual: Not in Greek
2. ἀναφέρω, *anapherō, 429*
3. ἀνέχομαι, *anechomai, 462*
4. βαστάζω, *bastazō, 1002*
5. γεννάω, *gennaō, 1164*
6. γεννητός, *gennētos, 1168*
7. γίνομαι, *ginomai, 1181*
8. ἐκ, *ek, 1666*
9. ἐν, *en, 1877*
10. ἔχω, *echō, 2400*
11. κοιλία + μήτηρ, *koilia + mētēr, 3120 + 3613*
12. ποιέω, *poieō, 4472*
13. σάρξ, *sarx, 4922*
14. στέγω, *stegō, 5095*
15. τίκτω, *tiktō, 5503*
16. φέρω, *pherō, 5770*
17. φορέω, *phoreō, 5841*

Mat 1:16 Joseph the husband of Mary, of whom Jesus was born   5
  1:21 She will bear a son, and you are to name him   15
  1:23 "Look, the virgin shall conceive and bear a son   15
  1:25 no marital relations...until she had borne a son;   15
  2: 1 In the time of King Herod, after Jesus was born   5
  2: 2 "Where is the child who has been born king of the Jews?   15
  2: 4 of them where the Messiah was to be born.   5
  3: 8 Bear fruit worthy of repentance.   12
  3:10 tree therefore that does not bear good fruit   12
  7:17 In the same way, every good tree bears good fruit   12
  7:17 but the bad tree bears bad fruit.   12
  7:18 A good tree cannot bear bad fruit   12
  7:18 nor can a bad tree bear good fruit.   12
  7:19 Every tree that does not bear good fruit is cut   12
  8:17 "He took our infirmities and bore our diseases."   4
  11:11 Truly I tell you, among those born of women   6
  13:26 when the plants came up and bore grain   12
  20:12 who have borne the burden of the day   4
  26:24 better for that one not to have been born."   5
Mrk 9:41 because you bear the name of Christ   9
  14:21 better for that one not to have been born."   5
Lke 1:13 Your wife Elizabeth will bear you a son   5
  1:31 you will conceive in your womb and bear a son   15
  1:35 therefore the child to be born will be holy   5
  1:57 and she bore a son.   5
  2:11 born this day in the city of David a Savior   15
  3: 8 Bear fruits worthy of repentance.   12
  3: 9 every tree...that does not bear good fruit   12
  6:43 "No good tree bears bad fruit   12
  6:43 nor again does a bad tree bear good fruit;   12
  7:28 among those born of women no one is greater   6

	11:27 "Blessed is the womb that bore you	4
	13: 9 If it bears fruit next year, well and good;	12
	20:24 Whose head and whose title does it bear?"	10
	23:29 the wombs that never bore	5
Jhn	1:13 who were born, not of blood	5
	3: 3 see the kingdom...without being born from above."	5
	3: 4 "How can anyone be born after having grown old?	5
	3: 4 a second time into the mother's womb and be born?"	5
	3: 5 without being born of water and Spirit.	5
	3: 6 What is born of the flesh is flesh	5
	3: 6 and what is born of the Spirit is spirit.	5
	3: 7 that I said to you, 'You must be born from above.'	5
	3: 8 So it is with everyone who is born of the Spirit."	5
	9: 2 who sinned...that he was born blind?"	5
	9: 3 he was born blind so that God's works	1
	9:19 "Is this your son, who you say was born blind?	5
	9:20 this is our son, and that he was born blind;	5
	9:32 anyone opened the eyes of a person born blind.	5
	9:34 answered him, "You were born entirely in sins	5
	12:24 if it dies, it bears much fruit.	16
	15: 2 removes every branch in me that bears no fruit.	16
	15: 2 Every branch that bears fruit he prunes	16
	15: 2 he prunes to make it bear more fruit.	16
	15: 4 Just as the branch cannot bear fruit by itself	16
	15: 5 Those who abide in me...bear much fruit	16
	15: 8 that you bear much fruit	16
	15:16 I appointed you to go and bear fruit	16
	16:12 you cannot bear them now.	4
	16:21 when her child is born,	5
	18:37 For this I was born	5
Act	7:20 At this time Moses was born	5
	15:10 neither our ancestors nor we have been able to bear?	4
	22: 3 "I am a Jew, born in Tarsus in Cilicia	5
	22:28 Paul said, "But I was born a citizen."	5
Rom	9:11 Even before they had been born	5
	13: 4 for the authority does not bear the sword in vain!	17
1Co	13: 7 It bears all things, believes all things	14
	15:49 as we have borne the image of the man of dust	17
	15:49 we will also bear the image of the man of heaven.	17
Gal	1:15 when God, who had set me apart before I was born	11
	4: 4 born of a woman, born under the law	7
	4: 4 born of a woman, born under the law	7
	4:23 child of the slave, was born according to the flesh;	5
	4:23 child of the free woman, was born through the promise.	1
	4:29 who was born according to the flesh persecuted	5
	4:29 child who was born according to the Spirit	1
	6: 2 Bear one another's burdens	4
Eph	2:11 remember that at one time you Gentiles by birth	13
	4: 2 bearing with one another in love	3
Php	2: 7 being born in human likeness.	7
	3: 5 a Hebrew born of Hebrews; as to the law, a Pharisee;	8
Col	3:13 Bear with one another	3
1Th	3: 1 Therefore when we could bear it no longer	14
	3: 5 For this reason, when I could bear it no longer	14
2Ti	2:19 God's firm foundation stands, bearing this inscription:	10
Heb	9:28 Christ...offered once to bear the sins of many	2
	11:12 from one person...descendants were born	5
	11:23 Moses was hidden...for three months after his birth	5
	13:13 and bear the abuse he endured.	16
	13:22 bear with my word of exhortation	3
Jas	3:13 your works are done with gentleness born of wisdom.	1
1Pe	2:24 He himself bore our sins in his body on the cross	2
	4:16 but glorify God because you bear this name.	9
2Pe	2:12 creatures...born to be caught and killed.	5
1Jn	2:29 everyone who does right has been born of him.	5
	3: 9 Those who have been born of God do not sin	5
	3: 9 they cannot sin, because they have been born of God.	5
	4: 7 everyone who loves is born of God and knows God.	5
	5: 1 Everyone who believes...has been born of God	5
	5: 4 for whatever is born of God conquers the world.	5
	5:18 We know that those who are born of God do not sin	5
	5:18 but the one who was born of God protects them	5
Rev	12: 4 might devour her child as soon as it was born.	15

bear[2]

1. ἄρκος, *arkos, 759*

Rev	13: 2 the beast that I saw...its feet were like a bear's	1

bear a child

1. γεννάω, *gennaō, 1164*
2. τεκνογονέω, *teknogoneō, 5449*

3. τίκτω, *tiktō, 5503*

Gal	4:24 Hagar, from Mount Sinai, bearing children for slavery.	1
	4:27 you childless one, you who bear no children	3
1Ti	5:14 I would have younger widows marry, bear children	2
Rev	12: 4 the woman who was about to bear a child	3

bear anew

1. ἀναγεννάω, *anagennaō, 335*

1Pe	1:23 You have been born anew, not of perishable...seed	1

bear false witness

1. ψευδομαρτυρέω, *pseudomartyreō, 6018*

Mat	19:18 You shall not bear false witness;	1
Mrk	10:19 shall not steal; You shall not bear false witness;	1
Lke	18:20 You shall not bear false witness;	1

bear fruit

1. Contextual: Not in Greek
2. καρποφορέω, *karpophoreō, 2844*

Mat	13:23 who indeed bears fruit and yields	2
Mrk	4:20 hear the word and accept it and bear fruit	2
Lke	8:15 and bear fruit with patient endurance.	2
Rom	7: 4 in order that we may bear fruit for God.	2
	7: 5 at work in our members to bear fruit for death.	2
Col	1: 6 it is bearing fruit and growing	2
	1: 6 so it has been bearing fruit among yourselves	1
	1:10 bear fruit in every good work	2

bear the name

1. ὀνομάζω, *onomazō, 3951*

1Co	5:11 who bears the name of brother or sister	1

bear untimely

1. ἔκτρωμα, *ektrōma, 1765*

1Co	15: 8 Last of all, as to one untimely born	1

bear up

1. αἴρω, *airō, 149*
2. βαστάζω, *bastazō, 1002*

Mat	4: 6 'On their hands they will bear you up	1
Lke	4:11 'On their hands they will bear you up	1
Rev	2: 3 and bearing up for the sake of my name	2

bear with

1. ἀνέχομαι, *anechomai, 462*

Lke	9:41 must I be with you and bear with you?	1
2Co	11: 1 bear with me in a little foolishness.	1
	11: 1 Do bear with me!	1

bear witness

1. μαρτυρέω, *martyreō, 3455*

Act	23:11 so you must bear witness also in Rome."	1

bear witness also

1. συμμαρτυρέω, *symmartyreō, 5210*

Rom	2:15 to which their own conscience also bears witness;	1

bear witness with

1. συμμαρτυρέω, *symmartyreō, 5210*

Rom	8:16 very Spirit bearing witness with our spirit	1

bearer

1. βαστάζω, *bastazō, 1002*

Lke	7:14 the bearers stood still.	1

beast

1. αὐτός, *autos, 899*
2. θηρίον, *thērion, 2563*

Jas	3: 7 For every species of beast and bird, of reptile	2
Rev	11: 7 the beast that comes up from the bottomless pit	2
	13: 1 I saw a beast rising out of the sea	2
	13: 2 And the beast that I saw was like a leopard	2
	13: 3 In amazement the whole earth followed the beast.	2
	13: 4 for he had given his authority to the beast	2
	13: 4 and they worshiped the beast, saying	2
	13: 4 "Who is like the beast, and who can fight against it?"	2
	13: 5 The beast was given a mouth	1
	13:11 I saw another beast that rose out of the earth;	2

Rev 13:12 exercises all the authority of the first beast   2
     13:12 makes...inhabitants worship the first beast   2
     13:14 it is allowed to perform on behalf of the beast   2
     13:14 telling them to make an image for the beast   2
     13:15 allowed to give breath to the image of the beast   2
     13:15 so that the image of the beast could even speak   2
     13:15 those who would not worship the image of the beast   2
     13:17 the name of the beast or the number of its name.   2
     13:18 let anyone...calculate the number of the beast   2
     14: 9 "Those who worship the beast and its image   2
     14:11 those who worship the beast and its image   2
     15: 2 those who had conquered the beast and its image   2
     16: 2 those who had the mark of the beast   2
     16:10 angel poured his bowl on the throne of the beast   2
     16:13 three foul spirits...from the mouth of the beast   2
     17: 3 and I saw a woman sitting on a scarlet beast   2
     17: 7 and of the beast with seven heads and ten horns   2
     17: 8 The beast that you saw was, and is not   2
     17: 8 inhabitants...will be amazed when they see the beast   2
     17:11 the beast that was and is not, it is an eighth   2
     17:12 receive authority...together with the beast.   2
     17:13 yielding their power and authority to the beast;   2
     17:16 they and the beast will hate the whore;   2
     17:17 by agreeing to give their kingdom to the beast   2
     18: 2 a haunt of every foul and hateful beast.   2
     19:19 Then I saw the beast and the kings of the earth   2
     19:20 And the beast was captured   2
     19:20 those who had received the mark of the beast   2
     20: 4 They had not worshiped the beast or its image   2
     20:10 where the beast and the false prophet were   2

beast of prey

     1. θηρίον, *thērion, 2563*
Act 11: 6 I saw four-footed animals, beasts of prey   1

wild beast

     1. θηρίον, *thērion, 2563*
Mrk   1:13 and he was with the wild beasts;   1

beat

     1. δέρω, *derō, 1296*
     2. ἐπιβάλλω, *epiballō, 2095*
     3. κολαφίζω, *kolaphizō, 3139*
     4. κόπτω, *koptō, 3164*
     5. πληγή, *plēgē, 4435*
     6. πληγή + ἐπιτίθημι, *plēgē + epitithēmi, 4435 + 2202*
     7. ῥάπισμα, *rhapisma, 4825*
     8. τύπτω, *typtō, 5597*
Mat 21:35 the tenants seized his slaves and beat one   1
     24:49 begins to beat his fellow slaves   8
Mrk   4:37 the waves beat into the boat   2
     12: 3 they seized him, and beat him, and sent him away   1
     12: 5 some they beat, and others they killed.   1
     13: 9 you will be beaten in synagogues;   1
     14:65 The guards also took him over and beat him.   7
Lke 10:30 robbers, who stripped him, beat him   6
     12:45 to beat the other slaves, men and women   8
     12:48 did not know and did what deserved a beating   5
     18:13 beating his breast and saying, 'God, be merciful   8
     20:10 the tenants beat him   1
     20:11 that one also they beat and insulted   1
     22:63 who were holding Jesus began to mock him and beat   1
     23:27 were beating their breasts and wailing for him.   4
     23:48 they returned home, beating their breasts.   8
Act 16:37 "They have beaten us in public, uncondemned   1
     18:17 and beat him in front of the tribunal.   8
     21:32 they stopped beating Paul.   8
     22:19 I imprisoned and beat those who believed in you.   1
1Co   4:11 we are poorly clothed and beaten and homeless   3
     9:26 nor do I box as though beating the air;   1
2Co   6: 5 beatings, imprisonments, riots, labors   5
1Pe   2:20 If you endure when you are beaten for doing wrong   3

beat against

     1. προσκόπτω, *proskoptō, 4684*
Mat   7:27 and the winds blew and beat against that house   1

beat on

     1. προσπίπτω, *prospiptō, 4700*

Mat   7:25 the winds blew and beat on that house   1

beat over the head

     1. κεφαλιόω, *kephalioō, 3052*
Mrk 12: 4 this one they beat over the head and insulted   1

beat with a rod

     1. ῥαβδίζω, *rhabdizō, 4810*
Act 16:22 and ordered them to be beaten with rods.   1
2Co 11:25 Three times I was beaten with rods.   1

beating   *See* receive a beating

beautiful

     1. ἀστεῖος, *asteios, 842*
     2. καλός, *kalos, 2819*
     3. ὡραῖος, *hōraios, 6053*
Mat 23:27 which on the outside look beautiful   3
Lke 21: 5 how it was adorned with beautiful stones   2
Act   3: 2 gate of the temple called the Beautiful Gate   3
     3:10 at the Beautiful Gate of the temple;   3
     7:20 Moses...was beautiful before God.   1
Rom 10:15 "How beautiful are the feet of those who bring   3
Heb 11:23 because they saw that the child was beautiful;   1

beauty

     1. Contextual: Not in Greek
     2. εὐπρέπεια, *euprepeia, 2346*
Jas   1:11 its flower falls, and its beauty perishes.   2
1Pe   3: 4 the lasting beauty of a gentle and quiet spirit   1

because

     1. Contextual: Not in Greek
     2. ἀντί, *anti, 505*
     3. ἀντί + ὅς, *anti + hos, 505 + 4005*
     4. ἀπό, *apo, 608*
     5. γάρ, *gar, 1142*
     6. διά, *dia, 1328*
     7. διότι, *dioti, 1484*
     8. εἵνεκεν, *heineken, 1641*
     9. ἐκ, *ek, 1666*
     10. ἐν, *en, 1877*
     11. ἕνεκεν, *heneken, 1915*
     12. ἐπεί, *epei, 2075*
     13. ἐπειδή, *epeidē, 2076*
     14. ἐπί, *epi, 2093*
     15. ἐπί + ὅς, *epi + hos, 2093 + 4005*
     16. καθότι, *kathoti, 2776*
     17. κατά, *kata, 2848*
     18. ὅτι, *hoti, 4022*
     19. περί, *peri, 4309*
     20. πρός, *pros, 4639*
     21. ὑπέρ, *hyper, 5642*
     22. χάριν, *charin, 5920*
Mat   2:18 refused to be consoled, because they are no   18
     6: 7 that they will be heard because of their many words.   10
     7:25 it did not fall, because it had been founded   5
     9:36 because they were harassed and helpless   18
     10:18 before governors and kings because of me   11
     10:22 you will be hated by all because of my name.   6
     11:20 because they did not repent.   18
     11:25 because you have hidden these things from the wise   18
     12:41 because they repented at the proclamation of Jonah   18
     12:42 because she came from the ends of the earth   18
     13:58 because of their unbelief.   6
     14: 4 because John had been telling him   5
     14: 5 because they regarded him as a prophet.   18
     15:32 because they have been with me now for three days   18
     16: 7 because we have brought no bread."   18
     17:20 He said to them, "Because of your little faith.   6
     18: 7 Woe to the world because of stumbling blocks!   4
     18:32 because you pleaded with me.   12
     19: 8 because you were so hard-hearted that Moses   20
     20: 7 They said to him, 'Because no one has hired us.'   18
     20:15 Or are you envious because I am generous?'   18
     21:46 because they regarded him as a prophet.   12
     22:29 because you know neither the scriptures   1
     24: 9 hated by all nations because of my name.   6

	24:12	because of the increase of lawlessness	6
	26:31	"You will all become deserters because of me	10
	26:33	"Though all become deserters because of you	10
	27:19	suffered…because of a dream about him."	17
Mrk	1:34	because they knew him.	18
	2: 4	because of the crowd	6
	3: 9	because of the crowd, so that they would not crush	6
	4:29	because the harvest has come."	18
	6:17	because Herod had married her.	18
	6:34	because they were like sheep without a shepherd;	18
	8: 2	because they have been with me now for three days	18
	8:16	"It is because we have no bread."	18
	9:38	to stop him, because he was not following us."	18
	9:41	because you bear the name of Christ	18
	10: 5	"Because of your hardness of heart he wrote	20
	11:18	because the whole crowd was spellbound	5
	13: 9	stand before governors and kings because of me	11
	13:13	you will be hated by all because of my name.	6
	16:14	⟦because they had not believed those who saw him⟧	18
Lke	1: 7	they had no children, because Elizabeth was barren	16
	1:20	because you did not believe my words	3
	2: 4	because he was descended from…David.	6
	2: 7	because there was no place for them in the inn.	7
	3:19	who had been rebuked by him because of Herodias	19
	3:19	because of all the evil things that Herod had done	19
	4:18	because he has anointed me to bring good news	8
	4:32	because he spoke with authority.	18
	4:41	because they knew that he was the Messiah.	18
	5:19	no way to bring him in because of the crowd	6
	6:48	because it had been well built.	6
	7:29	because they had been baptized with John's baptism.	1
	8:19	they could not reach him because of the crowd.	6
	9: 7	he was perplexed, because it was said by some	6
	9:49	stop him, because he does not follow with us."	18
	9:53	because his face was set toward Jerusalem.	18
	10:21	because you have hidden these things from the wise	18
	11: 8	because he is his friend	6
	11: 8	because of his persistence he will get up	6
	11:31	because she came from the ends of the earth	18
	11:32	because they repented at the proclamation	18
	13: 2	that because these Galileans suffered in this way	18
	13:14	indignant because Jesus had cured	18
	13:33	because it is impossible for a prophet	18
	14:14	you will be blessed, because they cannot repay	18
	15:27	because he has got him back safe and sound.'	18
	15:32	because this brother of yours was dead	18
	16: 2	because you cannot be my manager any longer.'	5
	16: 8	commended…because he had acted shrewdly;	18
	18: 5	yet because this widow keeps bothering me	6
	19: 3	because he was short in stature.	18
	19: 4	because he was going to pass that way.	18
	19: 9	because he too is a son of Abraham.	16
	19:11	because he was near Jerusalem	6
	19:11	because they supposed that the kingdom of God	1
	19:17	Because you have been trustworthy in a very small	18
	19:21	I was afraid of you, because you are a harsh man;	18
	19:44	because you did not recognize the time	3
	20:36	because they are like angels	5
	21:12	before kings and governors because of my name.	11
	21:17	You will be hated by all because of my name.	6
	21:28	because your redemption is drawing near."	7
	22:45	found them sleeping because of grief	4
	23: 8	because he had heard about him	6
	24:29	because it is almost evening and the day	18
Jhn	1:15	ranks ahead of me because he was before me.' ")	18
	1:30	who ranks ahead of me because he was before me.'	18
	1:50	"Do you believe because I told you that I saw you	18
	2:23	believed in his name because they saw the signs	1
	2:24	because he knew all people	6
	3:18	because they have not believed in the name	18
	3:19	because their deeds were evil.	5
	3:23	near Salim because water was abundant there;	18
	4:39	believed in him because of the woman's testimony	6
	4:41	And many more believed because of his word.	6
	4:42	no longer because of what you said that we believe	6
	5:16	because he was doing such things on the sabbath.	18
	5:18	because he was not only breaking the sabbath	18
	5:27	because he is the Son of Man.	18
	5:30	because I seek to do not my own will	18
	5:38	because you do not believe him whom he has sent.	18
	5:39	because you think…in them you have eternal life;	18
	6: 2	because they saw the signs that he was doing	18
	6:18	sea became rough because a strong wind was blowing.	1
	6:26	looking for me, not because you saw signs	18
	6:26	because you ate your fill of the loaves.	18
	6:41	because he said, "I am the bread	18
	6:57	I live because of the Father	6
	6:57	whoever eats me will live because of me.	6
	6:66	Because of this many of his disciples turned back	9
	7: 1	because the Jews were looking…to kill him.	18
	7: 7	because I testify…that its works are evil.	18
	7:23	because I healed a man's whole body	18
	7:29	I know him, because I am from him, and he sent me."	18
	7:30	because his hour had not yet come.	18
	7:39	because Jesus was not yet glorified.	18
	7:43	there was a division in the crowd because of him.	6
	8:14	valid because I know where I have come from	18
	8:20	because his hour had not yet come.	18
	8:37	because there is no place in you for my word.	18
	8:43	It is because you cannot accept my word.	18
	8:44	because there is no truth in him.	18
	8:45	because I tell the truth, you do not believe me.	18
	9:22	because they were afraid of the Jews;	18
	10: 4	the sheep follow him because they know his voice.	18
	10: 5	because they do not know the voice of strangers."	18
	10:13	The hired hand runs away because a hired hand	18
	10:17	the Father loves me, because I lay down my life	18
	10:19	the Jews were divided…because of these words.	6
	10:26	because you do not belong to my sheep.	18
	10:33	because you…are making yourself God."	18
	10:36	blaspheming because I said, 'I am God's Son'?	18
	11: 9	because they see the light of this world.	18
	11:10	stumble, because the light is not in them."	18
	11:31	because they thought that she was going to the tomb	1
	11:39	because he has been dead four days."	5
	12: 6	(He said this not because he cared about the poor	18
	12: 6	because he was a thief;	18
	12: 9	they came not only because of Jesus	6
	12:18	because they heard that he had performed this sign	18
	12:39	because Isaiah also said	18
	12:41	Isaiah said this because he saw his glory	18
	12:42	because of the Pharisees they did not confess it	6
	13:29	because Judas had the common purse	12
	14:11	believe me because of the works themselves.	6
	14:12	because I am going to the Father.	18
	14:17	because it neither sees him nor knows him.	18
	14:17	You know him, because he abides with you	18
	14:19	because I live, you also will live.	18
	14:28	because the Father is greater than I.	18
	15: 5	because apart from me you can do nothing.	18
	15:15	because the servant does not know what the master	18
	15:15	because I have made known to you everything	18
	15:19	Because you do not belong to the world	18
	15:21	because they do not know him who sent me.	18
	15:27	because you have been with me from the beginning.	18
	16: 3	because they have not known the Father or me.	18
	16: 4	because I was with you.	18
	16: 6	because I have said these things to you	18
	16: 9	about sin, because they do not believe in me;	18
	16:10	because I am going to the Father	18
	16:11	because the ruler of this world has been condemned.	18
	16:14	glorify me, because he will take what is mine	18
	16:17	'Because I am going to the Father'?"	18
	16:21	because her hour has come.	18
	16:21	because of the joy of having brought a human	6
	16:27	because you have loved me	18
	16:32	I am not alone because the Father is with me.	18
	17: 9	those whom you gave me, because they are yours.	18
	17:14	because they do not belong to the world	18
	17:24	glory…given me because you loved me	18
	18: 2	because Jesus often met there with his disciples.	18
	18:18	made a charcoal fire because it was cold	18
	19: 7	because he has claimed to be the Son of God."	18
	19:20	because the place where Jesus was crucified	18
	19:31	because that sabbath was a day of great solemnity.	5
	19:38	a secret one because of his fear of the Jews	6
	19:42	because it was the Jewish day of Preparation	6
	20:17	because I have not yet ascended to the Father.	5
	20:29	"Have you believed because you have seen me?	18
	21: 6	to haul it in because there were so many fish.	4
	21:12	because they knew it was the Lord.	18
	21:17	because he said to him the third time	18

Act	2: 6	because each one heard them speaking	18
	2:24	because it was impossible for him to be held	16
	2:43	because many wonders and signs were being done	1
	4: 2	much annoyed because they were teaching the people	6
	4: 9	because of a good deed done to someone who was sick	14
	4:21	no way to punish them because of the people	6
	5:38	because if this plan…is of human origin	18
	6: 1	because their widows were being neglected	18
	8:11	listened eagerly to him because…he had amazed them	6
	8:20	because you thought you could obtain God's gift	18
	9: 7	because they heard the voice but saw no one	1
	11:19	who were scattered because of the persecution	4
	12:20	because their country depended…for food.	6
	12:23	because he had not given the glory to God	3
	13:27	Because the residents of Jerusalem and their leaders	5
	14:12	because he was the chief speaker.	13
	16: 3	him circumcised because of the Jews	6
	17:18	because he was telling the good news about Jesus	18
	17:31	because he has fixed a day	16
	18: 2	because Claudius had ordered all Jews to leave	6
	18: 3	because he was of the same trade	6
	20:38	grieving especially because of what he had said	14
	21: 3	because the ship was to unload its cargo there.	5
	21:34	because of the uproar	6
	22:11	not see because of the brightness of that light	4
	22:18	because they will not accept your testimony	7
	24: 2	because of you we have long enjoyed peace	6
	24: 2	reforms…because of your foresight	6
	26: 3	because you are especially familiar	1
	27: 4	because the winds were against us.	6
	27: 9	because even the Fast had already gone by	6
	28:18	because there was no reason	6
Rom	1: 8	because your faith is proclaimed	18
	1:19	plain to them, because God has shown it to them.	5
	1:25	because they exchanged the truth about God	1
	2: 1	because you, the judge, are doing the very same	5
	2:18	because you are instructed in the law	1
	2:24	blasphemed among the Gentiles because of you."	6
	3:25	because…he had passed over the sins	6
	5: 5	because God's love has been poured	18
	5:12	death spread to all because all have sinned—	14
	5:17	If, because of the one man's trespass, death	1
	6:15	Should we sin because we are not under law	18
	6:19	because of your natural limitations.	6
	8:10	though the body is dead because of sin	6
	8:10	the Spirit is life because of righteousness.	6
	8:27	because the Spirit intercedes for the saints	18
	9:32	Because they did not strive for it on the basis of faith	18
	10: 9	because if you confess with your lips that Jesus	18
	11:20	They were broken off because of their unbelief.	1
	11:30	received mercy because of their disobedience	1
	13: 5	one must be subject, not only because of wrath	6
	13: 5	but also because of conscience.	6
	14:22	condemn themselves because of what they approve.	10
	14:23	because they do not act from faith;	18
	15:15	because of the grace given me by God	6
1Co	1: 4	because of the grace of God that has been given you	14
	2:14	because they are spiritually discerned.	18
	3:13	because it will be revealed with fire	18
	4: 9	because we have become a spectacle	18
	7: 2	because of cases of sexual immorality	6
	7: 5	tempt you because of your lack of self-control.	6
	10:17	Because there is one bread, we who are many are one	18
	10:30	because of that for which I give thanks?	21
	11: 2	I commend you because you remember me	18
	11:10	symbol of authority on her head, because of the angels.	6
	11:17	because when you come together	18
	12:15	"Because I am not a hand, I do not belong to the body,"	18
	12:16	"Because I am not an eye, I do not belong to the body,"	18
	15: 9	because I persecuted the church of God.	7
	15:15	because we testified of God that he raised Christ	18
	15:58	because know that…your labor is not in vain	1
	16:17	because they have made up for your absence;	18
2Co	1:24	because you stand firm in the faith.	5
	2:13	because I did not find my brother Titus there.	1
	3: 7	because of the glory of his face	6
	3:10	because of the greater glory;	8
	4:14	because we know that the one who raised the Lord	1
	4:18	because we look not at what can be seen	1
	5: 4	because we wish not to be unclothed	15
	5:14	because we are convinced	1

	7: 9	Now I rejoice, not because you were grieved	18
	7: 9	because your grief led to repentance;	18
	7:13	because his mind has been set at rest by all of you.	18
	7:16	because I have complete confidence in you.	18
	8:22	because of his great confidence in you.	1
	9:14	because of the surpassing grace of God	6
	11: 7	because I proclaimed God's good news to you free	18
	11:11	why? Because I do not love you? God knows I do!	18
	11:28	because of my anxiety for all the churches.	1
	12:14	because I do not want what is yours but you;	5
Gal	1:24	they glorified God because of me.	10
	2: 4	because of false believers secretly brought in	6
	2:11	because he stood self-condemned;	18
	2:16	because no one will be justified by the works	18
	3:19	It was added because of transgressions	22
	4: 6	because you are children, God has sent the Spirit	18
	4:13	know that it was because of a physical infirmity	6
Eph	4:18	because of their ignorance and hardness	6
	5: 6	for because of these things the wrath of God	6
	5:16	because the days are evil.	18
	5:30	because we are members of his body.	18
Php	1: 5	because of your sharing in the gospel	14
	1: 7	because you hold me in your heart	6
	2:26	distressed because you heard that he was ill.	7
	2:30	because he came close to death for the work of Christ	18
	3: 7	I have come to regard as loss because of Christ.	6
	3: 8	because of the surpassing value of knowing	6
	3:12	because Christ Jesus has made me his own.	15
Col	1: 5	because of the hope laid up for you in heaven.	6
1Th	1: 5	because our message of the gospel came to you	18
	2: 8	because you have become very dear to us.	7
	3: 9	joy that we feel before our God because of you?	6
	4: 6	because the Lord is an avenger	7
	5:13	esteem them…because of their work.	6
2Th	1: 3	because your faith is growing abundantly	18
	1:10	because our testimony to you was believed.	18
	2:10	because they refused to love the truth	2
	2:13	because God chose you as the first fruits	18
	3: 9	This was not because we do not have that right	18
1Ti	1:12	because he judged me faithful	18
	1:13	I received mercy because I had acted ignorantly	18
	4:10	because we have our hope set on the living God	18
2Ti	1:16	because he often refreshed me	18
	3: 9	because…their folly will become plain	5
Tit	3: 5	he saved us, not because of any works	9
Phm	1: 5	because I hear of your love	1
	1: 7	because…the saints have been refreshed	18
Heb	2: 9	because of the suffering of death	6
	2:18	Because he…was tested by what he suffered	5
	3:19	they were unable to enter because of unbelief.	6
	4: 2	because they were not united by faith with those	1
	4: 6	failed to enter because of disobedience	6
	5: 3	because of this he must offer sacrifice	6
	5: 7	he was heard because of his reverent submission.	4
	6:13	because he had no one greater by whom to swear	12
	7:18	because it was weak and ineffectual	6
	7:21	a priest with an oath, because of the one who said	6
	7:23	because they were prevented by death	6
	7:24	because he continues forever.	6
	9:15	because a death has occurred that redeems them	1
	11: 5	"he was not found, because God had taken him."	7
	11:11	because he considered him faithful	12
	11:23	because they saw that the child was beautiful;	7
	11:31	because she had received the spies in peace.	1
Jas	1: 3	because you know that the testing of your faith	1
	1:10	because the rich will disappear like a flower	18
	4: 2	You do not have, because you do not ask.	6
	4: 3	You…do not receive, because you ask wrongly	7
1Pe	2: 8	They stumble because they disobey the word	1
	2:21	because Christ also suffered for you	18
	4:14	because the spirit of glory…resting on you.	18
	4:16	but glorify God because you bear this name.	1
	5: 7	Cast…anxiety on him, because he cares for you.	18
2Pe	1: 4	the corruption…in the world because of lust	10
	1:21	because no prophecy ever came by human will,	5
	2: 2	because of these teachers the way of truth…maligned.	6
	3:12	because of which the heavens will be set ablaze	6
1Jn	2: 8	because the darkness is passing away	18
	2:11	because the darkness has brought on blindness.	18
	2:12	because your sins are forgiven on account of his	18
	2:13	because you know him who is from the beginning.	18

	2:13 because you have conquered the evil one.	18
	2:14 because you know the Father.	18
	2:14 because you know him who is from the beginning.	18
	2:14 I write to you, young people, because you are strong	18
	2:21 not because you do not know the truth	18
	2:21 I write to you…because you know it	18
	3: 9 do not sin, because God's seed abides in them;	18
	3: 9 they cannot sin, because they have been born of God.	18
	3:12 Because his own deeds were evil	18
	3:14 because we love one another.	18
	3:22 we receive…because we obey his commandments	18
	4: 7 let us love one another, because love is from God;	18
	4:13 because he has given us of his Spirit.	18
	4:17 because as he is, so are we in this world.	18
	4:19 We love because he first loved us.	18
2Jn	1: 2 because of the truth that abides in us	6
Rev	1: 9 because of the word of God	6
	3:10 Because you have kept my word	18
	3:16 So, because you are lukewarm	18
	5: 4 to weep bitterly because no one was found worthy	18
	8:11 died from the water, because it was made bitter.	18
	11:10 because these two prophets had been a torment	18
	12:12 because he knows that his time is short!"	18
	14:15 because the harvest of the earth is fully ripe."	18
	16: 6 because they shed the blood of saints and prophets	18
	16:11 cursed the God of heaven because of their pains	9
	17: 8 the beast, because it was and is not and is to come.	18

become Not Indexed

bed *See also* lie in bed, make a bed

1. κλίνη, *klinē, 3109*
2. κλινίδιον, *klinidion, 3110*
3. κοίτη, *koitē, 3130*

Mat	9: 2 a paralyzed man lying on a bed.	1
	9: 6 "Stand up, take your bed and go to your home."	1
Mrk	4:21 or under the bed, and not on the lampstand?	1
	7:30 she went home, found the child lying on the bed	1
Lke	5:18 men came, carrying a paralyzed man on a bed.	1
	5:19 let him down with his bed through the tiles	2
	5:24 stand up and take your bed and go to your home."	2
	8:16 puts it under a bed	1
	11: 7 and my children are with me in bed;	3
	17:34 on that night there will be two in one bed;	1
Rev	2:22 Beware, I am throwing her on a bed	1

in bed

1. κατάκειμαι, *katakeimai, 2879*

Mrk	1:30 Simon's mother-in-law was in bed with a fever	1

marriage bed

1. κοίτη, *koitē, 3130*

Heb	13: 4 let the marriage bed be kept undefiled;	1

bedridden

1. κατάκειμαι + ἐπί + κράβαττος, *katakeimai + epi + krabattos, 2879 + 2093 + 3187*

Act	9:33 Aeneas, who had been bedridden for eight years	1

Beelzebul

1. Βεελζεβούλ, *Beelzeboul, 1015*

Mat	10:25 called the master of the house Beelzebul	1
	12:24 "It is only by Beelzebul, the ruler of the demons	1
	12:27 If I cast out demons by Beelzebul	1
Mrk	3:22 "He has Beelzebul, and by the ruler	1
Lke	11:15 "He casts out demons by Beelzebul	1
	11:18 you say that I cast out the demons by Beelzebul.	1
	11:19 if I cast out demons by Beelzebul	1

before *See also* before one is *circumcised*, bring before, day before the sabbath, fall down before, go before, hear before, lay before, openly before, put before, say before, see before, set before, stand before, warn before

1. ἀπέναντι, *apenanti, 595*
2. ἀπό, *apo, 608*
3. ἄχρι, *achri, 948*
4. εἰς, *eis, 1650*
5. εἰς + μέσος, *eis + mesos, 1650 + 3545*
6. εἰς + ὁ + μέσος, *eis + ho + mesos, 1650 + 3836 + 3545*

7. ἐκ, *ek, 1666*
8. ἔμπροσθεν, *emprosthen, 1869*
9. ἐν, *en, 1877*
10. ἐν + μέσος, *en + mesos, 1877 + 3545*
11. ἔναντι, *enanti, 1882*
12. ἐναντίον, *enantion, 1883*
13. ἐνώπιον, *enōpion, 1967*
14. ἐπί, *epi, 2093*
15. ἔτι, *eti, 2285*
16. ἕως + ἄν, *heōs + an, 2401 + 323*
17. κατά, *kata, 2848*
18. κατέναντι, *katenanti, 2978*
19. κατενώπιον, *katenōpion, 2979*
20. μέλλω, *mellō, 3516*
21. μετά, *meta, 3552*
22. μήπω, *mēpō, 3609*
23. ὅταν, *hotan, 4020*
24. ὅτε, *hote, 4021*
25. οὐ, *ou, 4024*
26. οὐ + μή, *ou + mē, 4024 + 3590*
27. παρά, *para, 4123*
28. πρίν, *prin, 4570*
29. πρίν + ἤ, *prin + ē, 4570 + 2445*
30. πρίν + ἤ + ἄν, *prin + ē + an, 4570 + 2445 + 323*
31. πρό, *pro, 4574*
32. πρό + πρόσωπον, *pro + prosōpon, 4574 + 4725*
33. πρός, *pros, 4639*
34. πρόσωπον, *prosōpon, 4725*
35. πρότερος, *proteros, 4728*
36. προϋπάρχω, *prouparchō, 4732*
37. πρῶτον, *prōton, 4754*
38. πρῶτος, *prōtos, 4755*

Mat	1:18 engaged to Joseph, but before they lived together	29
	5:12 persecuted the prophets who were before you.	31
	5:16 In the same way, let your light shine before others	8
	5:24 leave your gift there before the altar and go;	8
	6: 1 "Beware of practicing your piety before others	8
	6: 2 you give alms, do not sound a trumpet before you	8
	6: 8 Father knows what you need before you ask him.	31
	7: 6 and do not throw your pearls before swine	8
	8:29 Have you come here to torment us before the time?"	31
	10:18 you will be dragged before governors and kings	14
	10:23 before the Son of Man comes.	16
	10:32 "Everyone…who acknowledges me before others	8
	10:32 I also will acknowledge before my Father	8
	10:33 whoever denies me before others, I also will deny	8
	10:33 deny before my Father in heaven.	8
	11:10 who will prepare your way before you.'	8
	14: 6 daughter of Herodias danced before the company	9
	15: 2 For they do not wash their hands before they eat."	23
	16:28 before they see the Son of Man coming	16
	17: 2 he was transfigured before them	8
	24:38 For as in those days before the flood	31
	25:32 All the nations will be gathered before him	8
	26:34 this very night, before the cock crows	28
	26:63 "I put you under oath before the living God	17
	26:70 he denied it before all of them, saying	8
	26:75 "Before the cock crows, you will deny me	28
	27:11 Now Jesus stood before the governor;	8
	27:24 washed his hands before the crowd, saying	1
	27:29 knelt before him and mocked him, saying	8
	27:62 the Pharisees gathered before Pilate	33
Mrk	2:12 took the mat and went out before all of them;	8
	9: 2 he was transfigured before them	8
	13: 9 stand before governors and kings because of me	14
	14: 1 It was two days before the Passover	21
	14:30 this very night, before the cock crows twice	29
	14:60 stood up before them and asked Jesus	5
	14:72 "Before the cock crows twice	28
Lke	1: 6 Both of them were righteous before God	12
	1: 8 Once when he was serving as priest before God	11
	1:15 even before his birth he will be filled with	15
	1:17 spirit and power of Elijah he will go before him	13
	1:75 in holiness and righteousness before him	13
	1:76 you will go before the Lord to prepare his ways	13
	2:21 before he was conceived in the womb.	31
	2:26 before he had seen the Lord's Messiah.	30
	4:35 When the demon had thrown him down before them,	6
	5:18 trying to bring him in and lay him before Jesus;	13

Lke	5:25	Immediately he stood up before them	13
	7:27	who will prepare your way before you.'	8
	9:27	before they see the kingdom of God."	16
	11:38	he did not first wash before dinner.	31
	12: 8	everyone who acknowledges me before others	8
	12: 8	also will acknowledge before the angels of God;	8
	12: 9	whoever denies me before others	13
	12: 9	will be denied before the angels of God.	13
	12:11	When they bring you before the synagogues	14
	12:58	you go with your accuser before a magistrate	14
	12:58	or you may be dragged before the judge	33
	15:18	I have sinned against heaven and before you;	13
	15:21	I have sinned against heaven and before you;	13
	21:12	before all this occurs, they will arrest you	31
	21:12	you will be brought before kings and governors	14
	21:36	to stand before the Son of Man."	8
	22:15	to eat this Passover with you before I suffer;	31
	22:61	"Before the cock crows today, you will deny me	28
	23: 1	brought Jesus before Pilate.	14
	23:12	before this they had been enemies.	36
	24:19	a prophet mighty in deed and word before God	12
Jhn	1:15	ranks ahead of me because he was before me.' ")	38
	1:30	who ranks ahead of me because he was before me.'	38
	1:48	under the fig tree before Philip called you."	31
	4:49	"Sir, come down before my little boy dies."	28
	5:45	that I will accuse you before the Father;	33
	6:62	the Son of Man ascending to where he was before?	35
	7:50	Nicodemus, who had gone to Jesus before	35
	8: 3	[making her stand before all of them]	10
	8: 9	[left alone with the woman standing before him.]	10
	8:58	I tell you, before Abraham was, I am."	28
	9: 8	those who had seen him before as a beggar	35
	10: 8	All who came before me are thieves and bandits;	31
	11:55	many went up...before the Passover	31
	12: 1	Six days before the Passover	31
	13: 1	Now before the festival of the Passover	31
	13:19	I tell you this now, before it occurs	31
	13:38	Very truly, I tell you, before the cock crows	26
	14:29	now I have told you this before it occurs	28
	15:18	aware that it hated me before it hated you.	37
	17: 5	glory that I had...before the world existed.	31
	17:24	loved me before the foundation of the world.	31
Act	2:20	before the coming of the Lord's great and glorious day.	28
	2:25	'I saw the Lord always before me	13
	4:10	this man is standing before you in good health	13
	5:27	they had them stand before the council.	9
	6: 6	They had these men stand before the apostles	13
	6:12	seized him, and brought him before the council.	4
	7: 2	in Mesopotamia, before he lived in Haran	29
	7:10	when he stood before Pharaoh, king of Egypt	12
	7:45	nations that God drove out before our ancestors.	34
	8:21	your heart is not right before God.	11
	8:32	like a lamb silent before its shearer	12
	9:15	to bring my name before Gentiles and kings	13
	9:21	bringing them bound before the chief priests?"	14
	10: 4	have ascended as a memorial before God.	8
	10:30	suddenly a man in dazzling clothes stood before me.	13
	10:31	your alms have been remembered before God.	13
	12: 6	The very night before Herod was going to bring	24
	12:10	came before the iron gate leading into the city.	14
	13:24	before his coming John had already proclaimed	32
	16:19	dragged them...before the authorities.	14
	17: 6	dragged...before the city authorities, shouting	14
	18:12	brought him before the tribunal.	14
	19: 9	spoke evil of the Way before the congregation	13
	22: 1	listen to the defense that I now make before you."	33
	22:30	He brought Paul down and had him stand before them.	4
	23:15	we are ready to do away with him before he arrives."	31
	23:30	to state before you what they have against him."	14
	24:19	they ought to be here before you	14
	24:20	when I stood before the council	14
	24:21	that I called out while standing before them	9
	24:21	I am on trial before you today.' "	14
	25: 9	and be tried there before me on these charges?"	14
	25:16	before the accused had met the accusers face to face	29
	25:26	Therefore I have brought him before all of you	14
	25:26	especially before you, King Agrippa	14
	26: 2	"I consider myself fortunate that it is before you	14
	27:33	Just before daybreak,	20
Rom	3:18	"There is no fear of God before their eyes."	1
	4: 2	something to boast about, but not before God.	33

	5:13	sin was indeed in the world before the law	3
	9:11	Even before they had been born	22
	14:22	The faith...have as your own conviction before God.	13
	16: 7	and they were in Christ before I was.	31
1Co	2: 7	which God decreed before the ages for our glory	31
	4: 5	do not pronounce judgment before the time	31
	4: 5	before the time, before the Lord comes	16
	6: 1	you dare to take it to court before the unrighteous	14
	6: 1	instead of taking it before the saints?	14
	6: 6	before unbelievers at that?	14
2Co	5:10	For all of us must appear before the judgment seat	8
	7:12	zeal...might be made known to you before God.	13
	10: 7	Look at what is before your eyes.	17
	12:19	We are speaking in Christ before God.	18
	12:21	my God may humble me before you	33
Gal	1:15	when God, who had set me apart before I was born	7
	1:17	to those who were already apostles before me	31
	1:20	I am writing to you, before God, I do not lie!	13
	2:14	I said to Cephas before them all	8
	3: 1	It was before your eyes	17
	3:11	no one is justified before God by the law;	27
	3:23	Now before faith came	31
Eph	1: 4	chose us in Christ before the foundation of the world	31
	1: 4	to be holy and blameless before him in love	19
	3:14	For this reason I bow my knees before the Father	33
Col	1:17	He himself is before all things	31
	1:22	blameless and irreproachable before him	19
1Th	1: 3	remembering before our God and Father your work	8
	2:19	crown of boasting before our Lord Jesus	8
	3: 9	joy that we feel before our God because of you?	8
	3:13	that you may be blameless before our God and Father	8
1Ti	6:13	in his testimony before Pontius Pilate	14
2Ti	1: 9	This grace was given to us...before the ages began	31
	2:14	Remind them...and warn them before God	13
	4:21	Do your best to come before winter.	31
Tit	1: 2	that God, who never lies, promised before the ages	31
Heb	4:13	before him no creature is hidden	13
	11: 5	For it was attested before he was taken away	31
Jas	1:27	pure and undefiled before God, the Father	27
	4:10	Humble yourselves before the Lord	13
1Pe	1:20	destined before the foundation of the world	31
1Jn	2:28	and not be put to shame before him at his coming.	2
	3:19	and will reassure our hearts before him	8
	3:21	we have boldness before God;	33
3Jn	1: 6	testified to your love before the church.	13
Jde	1:25	before all time and now and forever. Amen.	31
Rev	1: 4	from the seven spirits who are before his throne	13
	2:14	put a stumbling block before the people of Israel	13
	3: 5	I will confess your name before my Father	13
	3: 5	I will confess your name...before his angels.	13
	3: 8	Look, I have set before you an open door	13
	3: 9	make them come and bow down before your feet	13
	4:10	the twenty-four elders fall before the one	13
	4:10	they cast their crowns before the throne, singing	13
	5: 8	the twenty-four elders fell before the Lamb	13
	6:10	how long will it be before you judge and avenge	25
	7: 9	standing before the throne and before the Lamb	13
	7: 9	standing before the throne and before the Lamb	13
	7:11	they fell on their faces before the throne	13
	7:15	For this reason they are before the throne of God	13
	8: 2	And I saw the seven angels who stand before God	13
	8: 3	on the golden altar that is before the throne.	13
	8: 4	rose...before God from the hand of the angel.	13
	9:13	the four horns of the golden altar before God	13
	11: 4	two lampstands that stand before the Lord	13
	11:16	the twenty-four elders who sit...before God	13
	12: 4	Then the dragon stood before the woman	13
	12:10	who accuses them day and night before our God.	13
	14: 3	and they sing a new song before the throne	13
	14: 3	and before the four living creatures	13
	15: 4	All nations will come and worship before you	13
	20:12	dead, great and small, standing before the throne	13

beforehand *See also* declare the gospel beforehand, prepare beforehand, promise beforehand, tell beforehand, worry beforehand

  1. προλαμβάνω, *prolambanō, 4624*

Mrk 14: 8 anointed my body beforehand for its burial.   1

beg

1. αἰτέω, *aiteō, 160*
2. δέομαι, *deomai, 1289*
3. ἐπαιτέω, *epaiteō, 2050*
4. ἐρωτάω, *erōtaō, 2263*
5. παραιτέομαι, *paraiteomai, 4148*
6. παρακαλέω, *parakaleō, 4151*
7. προσαιτέω, *prosaiteō, 4644*

Mat	5:42	Give to everyone who begs from you, and do not	1
	8:31	The demons begged him, "If you cast us out, send us	6
	8:34	and when they saw him, they begged him to leave	6
	14:36	begged him that they might touch even	6
Mrk	1:40	A leper came to him begging him, and kneeling	6
	5:10	He begged him earnestly	6
	5:12	spirits begged him, "Send us into the swine;	6
	5:17	they began to beg Jesus to leave	6
	5:18	begged him that he might be with him.	6
	5:23	begged him repeatedly, "My little daughter	6
	6:56	begged him that they might touch	6
	7:26	begged him to cast the demon out of her daughter.	4
	7:32	they begged him to lay his hand on him.	6
	8:22	begged him to touch him.	6
Lke	5:12	bowed with his face to the ground and begged him	2
	6:30	Give to everyone who begs from you;	1
	8:28	I beg you, do not torment me"	2
	8:31	They begged him not to order them to go back	6
	8:32	demons begged Jesus to let them enter these.	6
	8:38	The man from whom the demons had gone begged	2
	8:41	begged him to come to his house	6
	9:38	I beg you to look at my son; he is my only child.	2
	9:40	I begged your disciples to cast it out	2
	16: 3	I am ashamed to beg.	3
	16:27	He said, 'Then, father, I beg you	4
	18:35	a blind man was sitting by the roadside begging.	3
Jhn	4:47	and begged him to come down and heal his son	4
	9: 8	"Is this not the man who used to sit and beg?"	7
Act	21:39	I beg you, let me speak to the people."	2
	24: 4	I beg you to hear us briefly with your customary	6
	26: 3	therefore I beg of you to listen to me patiently.	2
2Co	8: 4	begging us earnestly for the privilege	2
Gal	4:12	Friends, I beg you, become as I am	2
Eph	4: 1	I therefore, the prisoner in the Lord, beg you	6
2Th	2: 1	we beg you, brothers and sisters	4
Heb	12:19	a voice whose words made the hearers beg	5

beget

1. γεννάω, *gennaō, 1164*

Act	13:33	'You are my Son; today I have begotten you.'	1
Heb	1: 5	"You are my Son; today I have begotten you"?	1
	5: 5	"You are my Son; today I have begotten you";	1

beggar

1. προσαίτης, *prosaitēs, 4645*

Mrk	10:46	Bartimaeus son of Timaeus, a blind beggar	1
Jhn	9: 8	those who had seen him before as a beggar began to ask	1

beggarly

1. πτωχός, *ptōchos, 4777*

Gal	4: 9	weak and beggarly elemental spirits?	1

begin

1. Contextual: Not in Greek
2. ἀνοίγω, *anoigō, 487*
3. ἄρχω, *archō, 806*
4. γίνομαι, *ginomai, 1181*
5. ἐνάρχομαι, *enarchomai, 1887*
6. ἐπιφώσκω, *epiphōskō, 2216*
7. ἐφίστημι, *ephistēmi, 2392*
8. ἔχω, *echō, 2400*
9. ποιέω, *poieō, 4472*
10. προενάρχομαι, *proenarchomai, 4599*
11. πρῶτον, *prōton, 4754*
12. χρόνος, *chronos, 5989*

Mat	4:17	From that time Jesus began to proclaim,	3
	5: 2	he began to speak, and taught them, saying:	2
	8:15	and she got up and began to serve him.	1
	11: 7	they went away, Jesus began to speak to the crowds	3
	11:20	Then he began to reproach the cities	3
	12: 1	they began to pluck heads of grain and to eat.	3
	13:54	began to teach the people in their synagogue	1
	14:30	beginning to sink, he cried out, "Lord, save me!"	3
	16:21	From that time on, Jesus began to show his disciples	3
	16:22	Peter took him aside and began to rebuke him	3
	18:24	When he began the reckoning	3
	20: 8	beginning with the last and then going	3
	24:49	begins to beat his fellow slaves	3
	26:16	began to look for an opportunity to betray	1
	26:22	and began to say to him one after another	3
	26:37	and began to be grieved and agitated.	3
	26:74	he began to curse, and he swore an oath	3
	27:24	rather that a riot was beginning	4
Mrk	1:28	At once his fame began to spread	1
	1:31	the fever left her, and she began to serve them.	1
	1:45	he went out and began to proclaim it freely	3
	2:23	his disciples began to pluck heads of grain.	3
	4: 1	Again he began to teach beside the sea.	3
	4: 2	He began to teach them many things in parables	1
	5:17	they began to beg Jesus to leave	3
	5:20	began to proclaim in the Decapolis	3
	5:42	immediately the girl got up and began to walk about	1
	6: 2	On the sabbath he began to teach in the synagogue	3
	6: 7	began to send them out two by two	3
	6:34	he began to teach them many things.	3
	6:55	began to bring the sick on mats	3
	8:11	The Pharisees came and began to argue with him	3
	8:31	he began to teach them that the Son of Man must	3
	8:32	Peter took him aside and began to rebuke him.	3
	10:28	Peter began to say to him, "Look, we have left	3
	10:32	began to tell them what was to happen to him	3
	10:41	they began to be angry with James and John.	3
	10:47	he began to shout out and say, "Jesus,	3
	11:15	began to drive out those who were selling	3
	12: 1	he began to speak to them in parables.	3
	13: 5	Jesus began to say to them, "Beware	3
	14:11	began to look for an opportunity to betray him.	1
	14:19	They began to be distressed	3
	14:33	and began to be distressed and agitated.	3
	14:65	Some began to spit on him, to blindfold him	3
	14:69	began again to say to the bystanders	3
	14:71	he began to curse, and he swore an oath	3
	15: 8	the crowd came and began to ask Pilate	3
	15:18	began saluting him, "Hail, King of the Jews!"	3
Lke	1:62	Then they began motioning to his father	1
	1:64	he began to speak, praising God.	3
	2:38	At that moment she came, and began to praise God	1
	3: 8	Do not begin to say to yourselves	3
	3:23	Jesus…thirty years old when he began his work.	3
	4:15	He began to teach in their synagogues	3
	4:21	he began to say to them, "Today this scripture	3
	4:37	report about him began to reach every place	1
	5: 6	that their nets were beginning to break.	3
	5: 7	so that they began to sink.	1
	5:21	the scribes and the Pharisees began to question	3
	7:15	The dead man sat up and began to speak	3
	7:24	Jesus began to speak to the crowds about John:	3
	7:38	and began to bathe his feet with her tears	3
	7:49	began to say among themselves	3
	11:29	When the crowds were increasing, he began to say	3
	11:53	the Pharisees began to be very hostile toward him	3
	12: 1	he began to speak first to his disciples	3
	12:45	if he begins to beat the other slaves,	3
	13:13	she stood up straight and began praising God.	1
	13:25	begin to stand outside and to knock at the door	3
	13:26	Then you will begin to say, 'We ate and drank	3
	14:18	they all alike began to make excuses.	3
	14:29	all who see it will begin to ridicule him	3
	14:30	saying, 'This fellow began to build	3
	15:14	he began to be in need.	3
	15:24	they began to celebrate.	3
	15:28	His father came out and began to plead with him.	3
	19: 7	All who saw it began to grumble and said,	1
	19:37	began to praise God joyfully with a loud voice	3
	19:45	began to drive out those who were selling	3
	20: 9	He began to tell the people this parable:	3
	21:28	Now when these things begin to take place,	3
	22: 6	began to look for an opportunity to betray him	1
	22:23	they began to ask one another	3
	22:63	the men who were holding Jesus began to mock him	1
	23: 2	They began to accuse him, saying, "We found this	1
	23: 5	from Galilee where he began even to this place."	3

Lke	23:30	Then they will begin to say to the mountains,	3
	23:54	the sabbath was beginning.	6
	24:27	beginning with Moses and all the prophets	3
	24:47	beginning from Jerusalem.	3
Jhn	4:52	So he asked them the hour when he began to recover	8
	5: 9	he took up his mat and began to walk.	1
	6:14	they began to say, "This is indeed the prophet	1
	6:41	Then the Jews began to complain about him	1
	7:14	Jesus went up into the temple and began to teach.	1
	8: 2	⟦he sat down and began to teach them.⟧	1
	8: 9	⟦went away, one by one, beginning with the elders;⟧	3
	9: 8	had seen him before as a beggar began to ask	1
	9:15	Then the Pharisees also began to ask him	1
	11:35	Jesus began to weep.	1
	13: 5	began to wash the disciples' feet	3
Act	1: 1	all that Jesus did and taught from the beginning	3
	1:22	beginning from the baptism of John	3
	2: 4	began to speak in other languages	3
	3: 8	stood and began to walk, and he entered the temple	1
	7:32	Moses began to tremble and did not dare to look.	4
	7:58	dragged him out of the city and began to stone him;	1
	8: 1	a severe persecution began against the church	4
	8:35	Then Philip began to speak	1
	9:20	he began to proclaim Jesus in the synagogues,	1
	10:34	Peter began to speak to them: "I truly understand	1
	10:37	beginning in Galilee	3
	11: 4	Peter began to explain it to them, step by step	3
	11:15	as I began to speak, the Holy Spirit fell upon them	3
	13:16	So Paul stood up and with a gesture began to speak:	1
	14:10	the man sprang up and began to walk.	1
	18:26	He began to speak boldly in the synagogue;	3
	20: 9	began to sink off into a deep sleep	1
	23: 7	a dissension began	4
	24: 2	Paul...summoned, Tertullus began to accuse him	3
	26: 1	Paul stretched out his hand and began to defend	1
	27:13	When a moderate south wind began to blow	1
	27:13	began to sail past Crete, close to the shore.	1
	27:18	next day they began to throw the cargo overboard	9
	27:35	he broke it and began to eat.	3
	28: 2	Since it had begun to rain and was cold	7
	28: 6	and began to say that he was a god.	1
1Co	11:18	to begin with, when you come together as a church	11
2Co	3: 1	Are we beginning to commend ourselves again?	3
	8:10	who began last year not only to do something	10
Php	1: 6	that the one who began a good work among you	5
2Ti	1: 9	This grace was given to us...before the ages began	12
Tit	1: 2	that God...promised before the ages began	12
1Pe	4:17	For the time has come for judgment to begin	3
	4:17	if it begins with us, what will be the end for those	11
3Jn	1: 7	for they began their journey for the sake of Christ	1
Rev	5: 4	I began to weep bitterly because no one was found	1
	11:17	have taken your great power and begun to reign.	1

world begin

1. αἰών, *aiōn*, 172

Jhn	9:32	Never since the world began has it been heard	1

beginning   *See also* make a beginning

1. ἀρχή, *archē*, 794

Mat	19: 4	one who made them at the beginning	1
	19: 8	but from the beginning it was not so.	1
	24: 8	all this is but the beginning of the birth pangs.	1
	24:21	from the beginning of the world until now	1
Mrk	1: 1	The beginning of the good news of Jesus Christ	1
	10: 6	from the beginning of creation	1
	13: 8	This is but the beginning of the birth pangs.	1
	13:19	not been from the beginning of the creation	1
Lke	1: 2	who from the beginning were eyewitnesses	1
Jhn	1: 1	In the beginning was the Word	1
	1: 2	He was in the beginning with God.	1
	8:44	He was a murderer from the beginning	1
	15:27	because you have been with me from the beginning.	1
	16: 4	"I did not say these things...from the beginning	1
Act	11:15	upon them just as it had upon us at the beginning.	1
	26: 4	spent from the beginning among my own people	1
Col	1:18	he is the beginning, the firstborn from the dead	1
Heb	1:10	"In the beginning, Lord, you founded the earth	1
	7: 3	having neither beginning of days nor end of life	1
2Pe	3: 4	as they were from the beginning of creation!"	1
1Jn	1: 1	what was from the beginning	1
	2: 7	commandment that you have had from the beginning;	1

	2:13	because you know him who is from the beginning.	1
	2:14	because you know him who is from the beginning.	1
	2:24	Let what you heard from the beginning abide	1
	2:24	what you heard from the beginning abides in you	1
	3: 8	for the devil has been sinning from the beginning.	1
	3:11	message you have heard from the beginning	1
2Jn	1: 5	but one we have had from the beginning	1
	1: 6	just as you have heard it from the beginning	1
Rev	21: 6	Alpha and the Omega, the beginning and the end.	1
	22:13	Alpha and the Omega...the beginning and the end."	1

beguile

1. πλανάω, *planaō*, 4414

Rev	2:20	Jezebel...is teaching and beguiling	1

behalf

1. ἐνώπιον, *enōpion*, 1967
2. περί, *peri*, 4309
3. ὑπέρ, *hyper*, 5642

Jhn	5:32	There is another who testifies on my behalf	2
	5:36	testify on my behalf that the Father has sent me.	2
	5:37	the Father...has himself testified on my behalf.	2
	5:39	it is they that testify on my behalf.	2
	8:13	"You are testifying on your own behalf;	2
	8:14	"Even if I testify on my own behalf	2
	8:18	I testify on my own behalf	2
	8:18	the Father who sent me testifies on my behalf."	2
	15:26	he will testify on my behalf.	2
	16:26	that I will ask the Father on your behalf;	2
	17: 9	I am asking on their behalf;	2
	17: 9	I am not asking on behalf of the world	2
	17: 9	I am not asking on behalf of the world	2
	17:20	"I ask not only on behalf of these	2
	17:20	on behalf of those who will believe in me	2
Rom	15: 8	of the circumcised on behalf of the truth of God	3
	15:30	join me in earnest prayer to God on my behalf	3
1Co	15:29	receive baptism on behalf of the dead?	3
	15:29	why are people baptized on their behalf?	3
2Co	1:11	so that many will give thanks on our behalf	3
	5:20	we entreat you on behalf of Christ	3
	12: 5	On behalf of such a one I will boast	3
	12: 5	on my own behalf I will not boast	3
Col	1: 7	He is a faithful minister of Christ on your behalf	3
	4:12	wrestling in his prayers on your behalf	3
Heb	5: 1	things pertaining to God on their behalf	3
	6:20	Jesus, a forerunner on our behalf, has entered	3
	9:24	now to appear in the presence of God on our behalf.	3
Rev	13:12	the authority of the first beast on its behalf	1
	13:14	it is allowed to perform on behalf of the beast	1

behave

1. ἀναστρέφω, *anastrephō*, 418
2. περιπατέω, *peripateō*, 4344

1Co	3: 3	of the flesh, and behaving according to human	2
2Co	1:12	we have behaved in the world	1
1Th	4:12	that you may behave properly toward outsiders	2
1Ti	3:15	how one ought to behave in the household of God	1

not behave properly

1. ἀσχημονέω, *aschēmoneō*, 858

1Co	7:36	thinks that he is not behaving properly	1

behavior

1. κατάστημα, *katastēma*, 2949

Tit	2: 3	Likewise, tell the older women to be reverent in behavior	1

behead

1. ἀποκεφαλίζω, *apokephalizō*, 642
2. πελεκίζω, *pelekizō*, 4284

Mat	14:10	he sent and had John beheaded in the prison.	1
Mrk	6:16	"John, whom I beheaded, has been raised."	1
	6:27	He went and beheaded him in the prison	1
Lke	9: 9	Herod said, "John I beheaded;	1
Rev	20: 4	beheaded for their testimony to Jesus	2

behind   *See also* behind closed *doors*, leave behind, lie behind, stay behind

1. Contextual: Not in Greek
2. ἐκεῖ, *ekei*, 1695

3. ἐν, *en, 1877*
4. μετά, *meta, 3552*
5. ὄπισθεν, *opisthen, 3957*
6. ὀπίσω, *opisō, 3958*

Mat	9:20	came up behind him and touched the fringe	5
	16:23	and said to Peter, "Get behind me, Satan!	6
Mrk	5:27	came up behind him in the crowd	5
	8:33	"Get behind me, Satan!	6
Lke	7:38	stood behind him at his feet, weeping	6
	8:44	came up behind him and touched…his clothes	5
	12: 3	what you have whispered behind closed doors	3
	23:26	the cross…and made him carry it behind Jesus.	5
Act	17:14	Silas and Timothy remained behind.	2
Heb	6:19	enters the inner shrine behind the curtain	1
	9: 3	Behind the second curtain was a tent	4
Rev	1:10	and I heard behind me a loud voice like a trumpet	6
	4: 6	creatures, full of eyes in front and behind:	5

being *See also* come into being, human being

1. ἄνθρωπος, *anthrōpos, 476*
2. ὁ, *ho, 3836*
3. ψυχή, *psychē, 6034*

1Co	15:45	"The first man, Adam, became a living being";	3
Gal	4: 8	enslaved to beings that by nature are not gods.	2
Eph	3:16	in your inner being with power through his Spirit	1

very being

1. ὑπόστασις, *hypostasis, 5712*

Heb	1: 3	and the exact imprint of God's very being	1

Beliar

1. Βελιάρ, *Beliar, 1016*

2Co	6:15	What agreement does Christ have with Beliar?	1

belief

1. πίστις, *pistis, 4411*

2Th	2:13	through belief in the truth.	1

believe *See also* refuse to believe

1. πιστεύω, *pisteuō, 4409*
2. πίστις, *pistis, 4411*
3. πίστις + ἔχω, *pistis + echō, 4411 + 2400*
4. πιστός, *pistos, 4412*

Mat	9:28	"Do you believe that I am able to do this?"	1
	18: 6	one of these little ones who believe in me	1
	21:25	'Why then did you not believe him?'	1
	21:32	you did not believe him	1
	21:32	the tax collectors and the prostitutes believed him;	1
	21:32	you did not change your minds and believe him.	1
	24:23	do not believe it.	1
	24:26	He is in the inner rooms,' do not believe it.	1
	27:42	we will believe in him.	1
Mrk	1:15	repent, and believe in the good news."	1
	5:36	"Do not fear, only believe."	1
	9:23	All things can be done for the one who believes."	1
	9:24	cried out, "I believe; help my unbelief!"	1
	9:42	one of these little ones who believe in me	1
	11:23	believe that what you say will come to pass	1
	11:24	believe that you have received it	1
	11:31	he will say, 'Why then did you not believe him?'	1
	13:21	'Look! There he is!'—do not believe it.	1
	15:32	so that we may see and believe."	1
	16:13	⟦they did not believe them.⟧	1
	16:14	⟦because they had not believed those who saw him⟧	1
	16:16	⟦one who believes and is baptized will be saved;⟧	1
	16:17	⟦these signs will accompany those who believe:⟧	1
Lke	1:20	because you did not believe my words	1
	1:45	blessed is she who believed	1
	8:12	so that they may not believe and be saved.	1
	8:13	they believe only for a while	1
	8:50	Only believe, and she will be saved."	1
	20: 5	he will say, 'Why did you not believe him?'	1
	22:67	He replied, "If I tell you, you will not believe;	1
	24:25	to believe all that the prophets have declared!	1
Jhn	1: 7	so that all might believe through him.	1
	1:12	to all who received him, who believed in his name	1
	1:50	"Do you believe because I told you that I saw you	1
	2:11	and his disciples believed in him.	1
	2:22	and they believed the scripture and the word	1

	2:23	believed in his name because they saw the signs	1
	3:12	about earthly things and you do not believe	1
	3:12	how can you believe if I tell you about heavenly	1
	3:15	whoever believes in him may have eternal life.	1
	3:16	everyone who believes in him may not perish	1
	3:18	Those who believe in him are not condemned;	1
	3:18	those who do not believe are condemned already	1
	3:18	not believed in the name of the only Son of God.	1
	3:36	Whoever believes in the Son has eternal life;	1
	4:21	"Woman, believe me, the hour is coming	1
	4:39	Many Samaritans from that city believed in him	1
	4:41	And many more believed because of his word.	1
	4:42	no longer because of what you said that we believe	1
	4:48	"Unless you see…wonders you will not believe."	1
	4:50	The man believed the word that Jesus spoke to him	1
	4:53	he himself believed, along with his whole household.	1
	5:24	who hears my word and believes him who sent me	1
	5:38	because you do not believe him whom he has sent.	1
	5:44	How can you believe when you accept glory from	1
	5:46	If you believed Moses, you would believe me	1
	5:46	If you believed Moses, you would believe me	1
	5:47	if you do not believe what he wrote	1
	5:47	how will you believe what I say?"	1
	6:29	that you believe in him whom he has sent."	1
	6:30	so that we may see it and believe you?	1
	6:35	whoever believes in me will never be thirsty.	1
	6:36	you have seen me and yet do not believe.	1
	6:40	all who see the Son and believe in him	1
	6:47	whoever believes has eternal life.	1
	6:64	among you there are some who do not believe."	1
	6:64	who were the ones that did not believe	1
	6:69	We have come to believe	1
	7: 5	(For not even his brothers believed in him.)	1
	7:31	Yet many in the crowd believed in him	1
	7:38	and let the one who believes in me drink.	1
	7:48	Has any one…of the Pharisees believed in him?	1
	8:24	unless you believe that I am he."	1
	8:30	saying these things, many believed in him.	1
	8:31	Then Jesus said to the Jews who had believed	1
	8:45	because I tell the truth, you do not believe me.	1
	8:46	If I tell the truth, why do you not believe me?	1
	9:18	The Jews did not believe that he had been blind	1
	9:35	"Do you believe in the Son of Man?"	1
	9:36	Tell me, so that I may believe in him."	1
	9:38	He said, "Lord, I believe." And he worshiped him.	1
	10:25	"I have told you, and you do not believe.	1
	10:26	you do not believe	1
	10:37	then do not believe me.	1
	10:38	if I do them, even though you do not believe me	1
	10:38	believe the works	1
	10:42	many believed in him there.	1
	11:15	so that you may believe.	1
	11:25	who believe in me, even though they die, will live	1
	11:26	everyone who lives and believes in me	1
	11:26	Do you believe this?"	1
	11:27	I believe that you are the Messiah, the Son of God	1
	11:40	if you believed, you would see the glory of God?"	1
	11:42	so that they may believe that you sent me."	1
	11:45	Many of the Jews therefore…believed in him.	1
	11:48	everyone will believe in him	1
	12:11	Jews were deserting and were believing in Jesus.	1
	12:36	While you have the light, believe in the light	1
	12:37	they did not believe in him.	1
	12:38	"Lord, who has believed our message	1
	12:39	so they could not believe	1
	12:42	many, even of the authorities, believed in him.	1
	12:44	"Whoever believes in me believes not in me	1
	12:44	believes not in me but in him who sent me.	1
	12:46	so that everyone who believes in me	1
	13:19	you may believe that I am he.	1
	14: 1	Believe in God, believe also in me.	1
	14: 1	Believe in God, believe also in me.	1
	14:10	Do you not believe that I am in the Father	1
	14:11	Believe me that I am in the Father	1
	14:11	then believe me because of the works	1
	14:12	believes in me will also do the works that I do	1
	14:29	so that when it does occur, you may believe.	1
	16: 9	about sin, because they do not believe in me;	1
	16:27	have believed that I came from God.	1
	16:30	by this we believe that you came from God."	1
	16:31	Jesus answered them, "Do you now believe?	1

Jhn	17: 8	they have believed that you sent me.	1
	17:20	those who will believe in me through their word	1
	17:21	the world may believe that you have sent me.	1
	19:35	so that you also may believe.	1
	20: 8	also went in, and he saw and believed;	1
	20:25	I will not believe."	1
	20:27	Do not doubt but believe."	4
	20:29	"Have you believed because you have seen me?	1
	20:29	who have not seen and yet have come to believe."	1
	20:31	are written so that you may come to believe	1
	20:31	believing you may have life in his name.	1
Act	2:44	All who believed were together	1
	4: 4	many of those who heard the word believed;	1
	4:32	whole group of those who believed were of one heart	1
	8:12	when they believed Philip	1
	8:13	Even Simon himself believed.	1
	9:26	for they did not believe that he was a disciple.	1
	9:42	many believed in the Lord.	1
	10:43	who believes in him receives forgiveness	1
	11:17	when we believed in the Lord Jesus Christ	1
	13:12	the proconsul saw what had happened, he believed	1
	13:39	by this Jesus everyone who believes is set free	1
	13:41	a work that you will never believe	1
	14:23	the Lord in whom they had come to believe.	1
	15:11	we believe that we will be saved	1
	16:31	"Believe on the Lord Jesus, and you will be saved	1
	17:12	Many of them therefore believed	1
	19: 4	to believe in the one who was to come after him	1
	22:19	I imprisoned and beat those who believed in you.	1
	24:14	believing everything laid down according to the law	1
	26:27	King Agrippa, do you believe the prophets?	1
	26:27	I know that you believe."	1
Rom	3:22	faith in Jesus Christ for all who believe.	1
	4: 3	"Abraham believed God, and it was reckoned to him	1
	4:11	all who believe without being circumcised	1
	4:17	in the presence of the God in whom he believed	1
	4:18	Hoping against hope, he believed	1
	4:24	It will be reckoned to us who believe in him	1
	6: 8	we believe that we will also live with him.	1
	9:33	whoever believes in him will not be put to shame."	1
	10: 4	may be righteousness for everyone who believes.	1
	10: 9	and believe in your heart that God raised him	1
	10:10	one believes with the heart and so is justified	1
	10:11	"No one who believes in him will be put to shame."	1
	10:14	to call on one in whom they have not believed?	1
	10:14	to believe in one of whom they have never heard?	1
	10:16	"Lord, who has believed our message?"	1
	14: 2	Some believe in eating anything	1
	15:13	fill you with all joy and peace in believing	1
1Co	1:21	to save those who believe.	1
	3: 5	Servants through whom you came to believe	1
	11:18	to some extent I believe it.	1
	13: 7	It bears all things, believes all things	1
	15: 2	unless you have come to believe in vain.	1
	15:11	so we proclaim and so you have come to believe.	1
2Co	4:13	with scripture—"I believed, and so I spoke"	1
	4:13	we also believe, and so we speak	1
Gal	2:16	And we have come to believe in Christ Jesus	1
	3: 2	works of the law or by believing what you heard?	2
	3: 5	the law, or by your believing what you heard?	2
	3: 6	Just as Abraham "believed God	1
	3: 7	those who believe are the descendants of Abraham.	2
	3: 9	who believe are blessed with Abraham	2
	3: 9	blessed with Abraham who believed.	4
	3:22	might be given to those who believe.	1
Eph	1:13	you also, when you...had believed in him	1
	1:19	greatness of his power for us who believe	1
Php	1:29	the privilege not only of believing in Christ	1
1Th	4:14	since we believe that Jesus died and rose again	1
2Th	1:10	marveled at on that day among all who have believed	1
	1:10	because our testimony to you was believed.	1
	2:11	leading them to believe what is false	1
	2:12	so that all who have not believed the truth	1
1Ti	1:16	an example to those who would come to believe in him	1
	3:16	believed in throughout the world, taken up in glory.	1
	4: 3	those who believe and know the truth.	4
	4:10	Savior...especially of those who believe.	4
	6: 2	Those who have believing masters	4
Tit	3: 8	those who have come to believe in God may be careful	1
Heb	4: 3	For we who have believed enter that rest	1
	11: 6	must believe that he exists	1

Jas	2: 1	do you with your acts of favoritism really believe	3
	2:19	You believe that God is one; you do well.	1
	2:19	Even the demons believe—and shudder.	1
	2:23	"Abraham believed God, and it was reckoned to him	1
1Pe	1: 8	though you do not see him now, you believe in him	1
	2: 6	whoever believes in him will not be put to shame."	1
	2: 7	To you then who believe, he is precious;	1
1Jn	3:23	we should believe in the name of his Son Jesus	1
	4: 1	Beloved, do not believe every spirit	1
	4:16	we have known and believe the love that God has for us.	1
	5: 1	Everyone who believes that Jesus is the Christ	1
	5: 5	the one who believes that Jesus is the Son of God?	1
	5:10	Those who believe in the Son of God	1
	5:10	Those who do not believe in God have made him a liar	1
	5:10	by not believing in the testimony	1
	5:13	to you who believe in the name of the Son of God	1
Jde	1: 5	afterward destroyed those who did not believe.	1

believe firmly

1. πιστόω, *pistoō, 4413*

2Ti	3:14	what you have learned and firmly believed	1

not believe

1. ἀπιστέω, *apisteō, 601*

Mrk	16:11	〚they would not believe it.〛	1
	16:16	〚one who does not believe will be condemned.〛	1
Lke	24:11	they did not believe them.	1
1Pe	2: 7	but for those who do not believe	1

believer   *See also* family of believers

1. Contextual: Not in Greek
2. ἀδελφός, *adelphos, 81*
3. αὐτός, *autos, 899*
4. πιστεύω, *pisteuō, 4409*
5. πιστός, *pistos, 4412*

Jhn	7:38	'Out of the believer's heart shall flow rivers	3
	7:39	which believers in him were to receive;	4
Act	1:15	In those days Peter stood up among the believers	2
	5:14	more than ever believers were added to the Lord	4
	9:30	When the believers learned of it	2
	9:32	Peter went here and there among all the believers	1
	10:23	some of the believers from Joppa accompanied him.	2
	10:45	The circumcised believers...were astounded	5
	11: 1	the apostles and the believers who were in Judea	2
	11: 2	the circumcised believers criticized him	1
	11:21	a great number became believers and turned to the Lord.	4
	11:29	send relief to the believers living in Judea;	2
	12:17	he added, "Tell this to James and to the believers."	2
	13:48	as many as had been destined...became believers.	4
	14: 1	both Jews and Greeks became believers	4
	15: 3	brought great joy to all the believers.	2
	15: 5	some believers...stood up and said	4
	15: 7	hear the message of the good news and become believers.	4
	15:23	the believers of Gentile origin in Antioch	2
	15:32	said much to encourage and strengthen the believers	2
	15:33	they were sent off in peace by the believers	2
	15:36	let us return and visit the believers	2
	15:40	believers commending him to the grace of the Lord.	2
	16: 1	the son of a Jewish woman who was a believer;	5
	16: 2	He was well spoken of by the believers	2
	16:34	rejoiced...that he had become a believer in God.	4
	17: 6	they dragged Jason and some believers before	2
	17:10	the believers sent Paul and Silas off	2
	17:14	Then the believers immediately sent Paul	2
	17:34	some of them joined him and became believers	4
	18: 8	Crispus...became a believer in the Lord	4
	18: 8	Corinthians who heard Paul became believers	4
	18:18	Paul said farewell to the believers	2
	18:27	the believers encouraged him	2
	18:27	helped those who through grace had become believers	4
	19: 2	receive the Holy Spirit when you became believers?"	4
	19:18	many of those who became believers confessed	4
	20: 2	and had given the believers much encouragement	3
	21: 7	we greeted the believers	2
	21:20	thousands of believers there are among the Jews	4
	21:25	as for the Gentiles who have become believers	4
	28:14	There we found believers	2
	28:15	The believers from there, when they heard of us	2
Rom	13:11	nearer to us now than when we became believers;	4
1Co	6: 5	to decide between one believer and another	2

	6: 6	believer goes to court against a believer	2
	6: 6	believer goes to court against a believer	2
	6: 8	wrong and defraud—and believers at that.	2
	7:12	if any believer has a wife who is an unbeliever	2
	8:11	So by your knowledge those weak believers	2
	14:22	a sign not for believers but for unbelievers	4
	14:22	is not for unbelievers but for believers.	4
2Co	6:15	what does a believer share with an unbeliever?	5
1Th	1: 7	example to all the believers in Macedonia	4
	2:10	blameless our conduct was toward you believers.	4
	2:13	God's word, which is also at work in you believers.	4
2Th	3: 6	believers who are living in idleness	2
	3:15	but warn them as believers.	2
1Ti	4:12	set the believers an example in speech	5
	6: 2	those who benefit…are believers and beloved.	5
Tit	1: 6	whose children are believers	5
Jas	1: 9	Let the believer who is lowly boast in being raised up	2
1Jn	2:11	whoever hates another believer is in the darkness	2

false believer

1. ψευδάδελφος, *pseudadelphos*, 6012

Gal	2: 4	because of false believers secretly brought in	1

believing woman *See also* believing *wife*

1. πιστός, *pistos*, 4412

1Ti	5:16	If any believing woman has relatives who…	1

belly

1. κοιλία, *koilia*, 3120

Mat	12:40	three nights in the belly of the sea monster	1
Php	3:19	Their end is destruction; their god is the belly;	1

belong

1. Contextual: Not in Greek
2. ἀπό, *apo*, 608
3. γίνομαι, *ginomai*, 1181
4. εἰμί, *eimi*, 1639
5. ἐκ, *ek*, 1666
6. ἐν, *en*, 1877
7. ἐπιβάλλω, *epiballō*, 2095
8. ἔχω, *echō*, 2400
9. κατά, *kata*, 2848
10. μετέχω, *metechō*, 3576
11. υἱός, *huios*, 5626
12. ὑπάρχω, *hyparchō*, 5639

Mat	19:14	to such…that the kingdom of heaven belongs."	4
	20:14	Take what belongs to you and go;	1
	20:15	to do what I choose with what belongs to me?	1
Mrk	10:14	to such as these that the kingdom of God belongs.	4
Lke	1: 5	who belonged to the priestly order of Abijah.	5
	5: 3	into one of the boats, the one belonging to Simon	4
	15:12	share of the property that will belong to me.'	7
	16:12	not been faithful with what belongs to another	1
	18:16	to such as these that the kingdom of God belongs.	4
	20:34	"Those who belong to this age marry	11
Jhn	3:31	one who is of the earth belongs to the earth	4
	10:16	other sheep that do not belong to this fold.	4
	10:26	because you do not belong to my sheep.	4
	15:19	If you belonged to the world	5
	15:19	Because you do not belong to the world	5
	17:14	because they do not belong to the world	5
	17:14	just as I do not belong to the world.	5
	17:16	They do not belong to the world, just as I	5
	17:16	just as I do not belong to the world.	5
	18:37	Everyone who belongs to the truth listens	4
Act	2:10	Egypt and the parts of Libya belonging to Cyrene	9
	4:37	sold a field that belonged to him	12
	6: 9	Then some of those who belonged to the synagogue	5
	9: 2	found any who belonged to the Way, men or women	4
	12: 1	some who belonged to the church.	2
	15: 5	who belonged to the sect of the Pharisees	2
	23:34	he asked what province he belonged to	4
	26: 5	that I have belonged to the strictest sect	9
	27:23	the God to whom I belong and whom I worship	4
	28: 7	lands belonging to the leading man of the island	12
Rom	1: 6	who are called to belong to Jesus Christ	1
	7: 4	so that you may belong to another	3
	8: 9	Anyone who does not…does not belong to him.	4
	9: 4	Israelites, and to them belong the adoption	1

	9: 5	to them belong the patriarchs	1
	9: 6	For not all Israelites truly belong to Israel	1
	16:10	those who belong to the family of Aristobulus.	5
	16:11	those…who belong to the family of Narcissus.	5
1Co	1:12	"I belong to Paul," or "I belong to Apollos,"	4
	1:12	"I belong to Paul," or "I belong to Apollos,"	1
	1:12	"I belong to Cephas," or "I belong to Christ."	1
	1:12	"I belong to Cephas," or "I belong to Christ."	1
	3: 4	For when one says, "I belong to Paul,"	4
	3: 4	and another, "I belong to Apollos,"	1
	3:22	the present or the future—all belong to you	1
	3:23	you belong to Christ, and Christ belongs to God.	1
	3:23	you belong to Christ, and Christ belongs to God.	1
	7:22	a slave is a freed person belonging to the Lord	1
	12:15	"Because I am not a hand, I do not belong to the body,"	5
	12:16	"Because I am not an eye, I do not belong to the body,"	5
	15:23	then at his coming those who belong to Christ.	1
2Co	4: 7	that this extraordinary power belongs to God	4
	10: 7	If you are confident that you belong to Christ	4
	10: 7	just as you belong to Christ, so also do we.	1
Gal	3:29	if you belong to Christ, then you are Abraham's	1
	5:24	those who belong to Christ Jesus	1
Col	2:17	the substance belongs to Christ.	1
	2:20	you live as if you still belonged to the world?	6
1Th	5: 8	since we belong to the day, let us be sober	4
2Ti	3:17	so that everyone who belongs to God may be proficient	1
Heb	3: 6	the confidence and the pride that belong to hope.	1
	6: 9	things in your case, things that belong to salvation.	8
	7: 6	this man, who does not belong to their ancestry	5
	7:13	belonged to another tribe	10
1Pe	4:11	To him belong the glory and the power	4
1Jn	2:19	They went out from us, but they did not belong to us;	5
	2:19	for if they had belonged to us,	5
	2:19	that none of them belongs to us.	5
Rev	7:10	"Salvation belongs to our God who is seated on	1
	17:11	it is an eighth but it belongs to the seven	5

belong to others

1. ἀλλότριος, *allotrios*, 259

Act	7: 6	resident aliens in a country belonging to others	1

belonging

1. σκεῦος, *skeuos*, 5007

Lke	17:31	on the housetop who has belongings in the house	1

beloved

1. ἀγαπάω, *agapaō*, 26
2. ἀγάπη, *agapē*, 27
3. ἀγαπητός, *agapētos*, 28
4. ἀδελφός, *adelphos*, 81

Mat	3:17	my Son, the Beloved, with whom I am well pleased."	3
	12:18	my beloved, with whom my soul is well pleased.	3
	17: 5	"This is my Son, the Beloved;	3
Mrk	1:11	from heaven, "You are my Son, the Beloved;	3
	9: 7	"This is my Son, the Beloved; listen to him!"	3
	12: 6	He had still one other, a beloved son.	3
Lke	3:22	my Son, the Beloved; with you I am well pleased."	3
	20:13	I will send my beloved son;	3
Act	15:25	along with our beloved Barnabas and Paul	3
Rom	1: 7	To all God's beloved in Rome	3
	9:25	her who was not beloved I will call 'beloved.' "	1
	9:25	her who was not beloved I will call 'beloved.' "	1
	11:28	but as regards election they are beloved	3
	12:19	Beloved, never avenge yourselves	3
	16: 5	Greet my beloved Epaenetus	3
	16: 8	Greet Ampliatus, my beloved in the Lord.	3
	16: 9	Greet Urbanus…and my beloved Stachys.	3
	16:12	Greet the beloved Persis, who has worked hard	3
1Co	4:14	to admonish you as my beloved children.	3
	4:17	my beloved and faithful child in the Lord	3
	15:58	Therefore, my beloved, be steadfast	3
2Co	7: 1	Since we have these promises, beloved	3
	12:19	Everything we do, beloved, is for the sake of building	3
Eph	1: 6	he freely bestowed on us in the Beloved.	1
	5: 1	be imitators of God, as beloved children	3
Php	1:12	I want you to know, beloved	4
	2:12	my beloved, just as you have always obeyed	3
	3:13	Beloved, I do not consider that I made it	4
	4: 1	stand firm in the Lord in this way, my beloved.	3
	4: 8	Finally, beloved, whatever is true	4

Col 1: 7 Epaphras, our beloved fellow servant.   3
       1:13 transferred us into the kingdom of his beloved Son   2
       3:12 As God's chosen ones, holy and beloved   1
       4: 7 he is a beloved brother, a faithful minister   3
       4: 9 Onesimus, the faithful and beloved brother   3
       4:14 Luke, the beloved physician, and Demas greet you.   3
1Th 1: 4 For we know, brothers and sisters beloved by God   1
       4:10 we urge you, beloved, to do so more and more   4
       5: 4 you, beloved, are not in darkness   4
       5:14 we urge you, beloved, to admonish the idlers   4
       5:25 Beloved, pray for us.   4
2Th 2:13 brothers and sisters beloved by the Lord   1
       3: 6 Now we command you, beloved   4
1Ti 6: 2 those who benefit…are believers and beloved.   3
2Ti 1: 2 To Timothy, my beloved child: 3
Phm 1:16 a beloved brother—especially to me   3
Heb 6: 9 beloved, we are confident of better things in your case   3
Jas 1:16 Do not be deceived, my beloved.   3
       1:19 You must understand this, my beloved: 3
       2: 5 Listen, my beloved brothers and sisters.   3
       5: 7 Be patient, therefore, beloved, until the coming   4
       5: 9 Beloved, do not grumble against one another   4
       5:10 As an example…beloved, take the prophets   4
       5:12 Above all, my beloved, do not swear   4
1Pe 2:11 Beloved, I urge you as aliens and exiles   3
       4:12 Beloved, do not be surprised at the fiery ordeal   3
2Pe 1:17 my Son, my Beloved, with whom I am well pleased."   3
       3: 1 beloved, the second letter I am writing to you;   3
       3: 8 do not ignore this one fact, beloved   3
       3:14 Therefore, beloved, while you are waiting for these   3
       3:15 So also our beloved brother Paul wrote to you   3
       3:17 beloved, since you are forewarned, beware   3
1Jn 2: 7 Beloved, I am writing you no new commandment   3
       3: 2 Beloved, we are God's children now;   3
       3:21 Beloved, if our hearts do not condemn us   3
       4: 1 Beloved, do not believe every spirit   3
       4: 7 Beloved, let us love one another   3
       4:11 Beloved, since God loved us so much,   3
3Jn 1: 1 The elder to the beloved Gaius, whom I love   3
       1: 2 Beloved, I pray that all may go well with you   3
       1: 5 Beloved, you do faithfully   3
       1:11 Beloved, do not imitate what is evil   3
Jde 1: 1 who are called, who are beloved in God the Father   1
       1: 3 Beloved, while eagerly preparing to write to you   3
       1:17 you, beloved, must remember the predictions   3
       1:20 But you, beloved, build yourselves up   3
Rev 20: 9 and surrounded…the beloved city.   1

below

    1. κάτω, *katō, 3004*
Mrk 14:66 While Peter was below in the courtyard   1
Jhn 8:23 "You are from below, I am from above;   1
Act 2:19 signs on the earth below   1
       20: 9 he fell to the ground three floors below   1

belt *See also* fasten belt, fasten belt around

    1. ζώνη, *zōnē, 2438*
Mat 3: 4 hair with a leather belt around his waist   1
       10: 9 Take no gold, or silver, or copper in your belts   1
Mrk 1: 6 a leather belt around his waist   1
       6: 8 no bread, no bag, no money in their belts;   1
Act 21:11 came to us and took Paul's belt   1
       21:11 bind the man who owns this belt   1

judge's bench

    1. βῆμα, *bēma, 1037*
Jhn 19:13 and sat on the judge's bench   1

bend

    1. κάμπτω, *kamptō, 2828*
    2. κύπτω, *kyptō, 3252*
    3. συγκάμπτω, *synkamptō, 5159*
Jhn 8: 6 ⟦Jesus bent down and wrote with his finger⟧   2
Rom 11:10 and keep their backs forever bent."   3
Php 2:10 at the name of Jesus every knee should bend   1

bend down

    1. κατακύπτω, *katakyptō, 2893*
    2. παρακύπτω, *parakyptō, 4160*
Jhn 8: 8 ⟦once again he bent down and wrote⟧   1

       20: 5 bent down to look in and saw the linen wrappings   2

bend over

    1. ἐπιπίπτω, *epipiptō, 2158*
    2. παρακύπτω, *parakyptō, 4160*
    3. συγκύπτω, *synkyptō, 5174*
Lke 13:11 She was bent over   3
Jhn 20:11 she bent over to look into the tomb;   2
Act 20:10 Paul went down, and bending over him   1

benefactor

    1. εὐεργέτης, *euergetēs, 2309*
    2. προστάτις, *prostatis, 4706*
Lke 22:25 those in authority…are called benefactors.   1
Rom 16: 2 she has been a benefactor of many and of myself   2

beneficial

    1. συμφέρω, *sympherō, 5237*
1Co 6:12 not all things are beneficial.   1
       10:23 not all things are beneficial.   1

benefit

    1. ἀντιλαμβάνω, *antilambanō, 514*
    2. διά, *dia, 1328*
    3. ὀνίνημι, *oninēmi, 3949*
    4. σύμφορος, *symphoros, 5239*
    5. ὠφελέω, *ōpheleō, 6067*
1Co 4: 6 for your benefit, brothers and sisters   2
       7:35 I say this for your own benefit   4
       14: 6 how will I benefit you unless I speak to you   5
Gal 5: 2 Christ will be of no benefit to you.   5
1Ti 6: 2 since those who benefit…are believers   1
Phm 1:20 brother, let me have this benefit from you in the Lord!   3
Heb 4: 2 the message they heard did not benefit them   5
       13: 9 which have not benefited those who observe them.   5

material benefit

    1. σαρκικός, *sarkikos, 4920*
1Co 9:11 is it too much if we reap your material benefits?   1

Benjamin

    1. Βενιαμίν, *Beniamin, 1021*
Act 13:21 Saul son of Kish, a man of the tribe of Benjamin   1
Rom 11: 1 I myself am…a member of the tribe of Benjamin.   1
Php 3: 5 of the people of Israel, of the tribe of Benjamin   1
Rev 7: 8 from the tribe of Benjamin twelve thousand sealed.   1

bereft

    1. ἀποστερέω, *apostereō, 691*
1Ti 6: 5 who are depraved in mind and bereft of the truth   1

Bernice

    1. Βερνίκη, *Bernikē, 1022*
Act 25:13 King Agrippa and Bernice arrived   1
       25:23 So on the next day Agrippa and Bernice came   1
       26:30 king got up, and with him the governor and Bernice   1

Beroea

    1. Βέροια, *Beroia, 1023*
    2. Βεροιαῖος, *Beroiaios, 1024*
Act 17:10 the believers sent Paul and Silas off to Beroea;   1
       17:13 the word…had been proclaimed by Paul in Beroea   1
       20: 4 Sopater son of Pyrrhus from Beroea,   2

beryl

    1. βήρυλλος, *bēryllos, 1039*
Rev 21:20 the seventh chrysolite, the eighth beryl   1

beside *See also* stand beside, struggle beside

    1. ἐξίστημι, *existēmi, 2014*
    2. ἐπί, *epi, 2093*
    3. παρά, *para, 4123*
    4. πρός, *pros, 4639*
    5. σύν, *syn, 5250*
Mat 13: 1 went out of the house and sat beside the sea.   3
Mrk 2:13 Jesus went out again beside the sea;   3
       4: 1 Again he began to teach beside the sea.   3
       4: 1 the whole crowd was beside the sea on the land.   4

Lke	5: 1	Jesus was standing beside the lake of Gennesaret	3
Act	4:14	saw the man…standing beside them	5
	5:10	buried her beside her husband.	4
	8:31	he invited Philip to get in and sit beside him.	5
	13:36	David…died, was laid beside his ancestors	4
2Co	5:13	For if we are beside ourselves, it is for God;	1
Rev	15: 2	standing beside the sea of glass	2

besides

1. ἅμα, *hama, 275*
2. ἐν, *en, 1877*
3. καί, *kai, 2779*
4. πλήν, *plēn, 4440*
5. σύν, *syn, 5250*
6. χωρίς, *chōris, 6006*

Mat	14:21	five thousand men, besides women and children	6
	15:38	four thousand men, besides women and children	6
Mrk	12:32	besides him there is no other';	4
Lke	16:26	Besides all this, between you and us a great chasm	2
	24:21	Yes, and besides all this, it is now the third day	5
Rom	13:11	Besides this, you know what time it is	3
2Co	11:28	And, besides other things	6
1Ti	5:13	Besides that, they learn to be idle	1

best   *See* do one's best, good

bestow

1. τιμάω, *timaō, 5506*

Act	28:10	They bestowed many honors on us	1

bestow freely

1. χαριτόω, *charitoō, 5923*

Eph	1: 6	that he freely bestowed on us in the Beloved.	1

bestowed gift

1. χαρίζομαι, *charizomai, 5919*

1Co	2:12	understand the gifts bestowed on us by God.	1

Beth-zatha

1. Βηθζαθά, *Bēthzatha, 1032*

Jhn	5: 2	a pool, called in Hebrew Beth-zatha	1

Bethany

1. Βηθανία, *Bēthania, 1029*

Mat	21:17	to Bethany, and spent the night there.	1
	26: 6	while Jesus was at Bethany in the house of Simon	1
Mrk	11: 1	approaching Jerusalem, at Bethphage and Bethany	1
	11:11	he went out to Bethany with the twelve.	1
	11:12	On the following day, when they came from Bethany	1
	14: 3	at Bethany in the house of Simon the leper	1
Lke	19:29	When he had come near Bethphage and Bethany	1
	24:50	Then he led them out as far as Bethany	1
Jhn	1:28	This took place in Bethany across the Jordan	1
	11: 1	Now a certain man was ill, Lazarus of Bethany	1
	11:18	Bethany was near Jerusalem, some two miles away	1
	12: 1	Jesus came to Bethany, the home of Lazarus	1

Bethlehem

1. Βηθλέεμ, *Bēthleem, 1033*

Mat	2: 1	after Jesus was born in Bethlehem of Judea	1
	2: 5	They told him, "In Bethlehem of Judea;	1
	2: 6	you, Bethlehem, in the land of Judah, are by no	1
	2: 8	he sent them to Bethlehem, saying, "Go and search	1
	2:16	killed all the children in and around Bethlehem	1
Lke	2: 4	to the city of David called Bethlehem	1
	2:15	"Let us go now to Bethlehem and see this thing	1
Jhn	7:42	from Bethlehem, the village where David lived?"	1

Bethphage

1. Βηθφαγή, *Bēthphagē, 1036*

Mat	21: 1	had reached Bethphage, at the Mount of Olives	1
Mrk	11: 1	approaching Jerusalem, at Bethphage and Bethany	1
Lke	19:29	When he had come near Bethphage and Bethany	1

Bethsaida

1. Βηθσαϊδά, *Bēthsaida, 1034*

Mat	11:21	"Woe to you, Chorazin! Woe to you, Bethsaida!	1
Mrk	6:45	go on ahead to the other side, to Bethsaida	1
	8:22	They came to Bethsaida.	1

Lke	9:10	withdrew privately to a city called Bethsaida.	1
	10:13	"Woe to you, Chorazin! Woe to you, Bethsaida!	1
Jhn	1:44	Now Philip was from Bethsaida, the city of Andrew	1
	12:21	Philip, who was from Bethsaida in Galilee	1

betray

1. δῆλος + ποιέω, *dēlos + poieō, 1316 + 4472*
2. παραδίδωμι, *paradidōmi, 4140*

Mat	10: 4	and Judas Iscariot, the one who betrayed him.	2
	10:21	Brother will betray brother to death	2
	17:22	Son of Man is going to be betrayed into human hands	2
	24:10	will fall away, and they will betray one another	2
	26:15	"What will you give me if I betray him to you?"	2
	26:16	to look for an opportunity to betray him.	2
	26:21	I tell you, one of you will betray me."	2
	26:23	who has dipped his hand…will betray me.	2
	26:24	woe to that one by whom the Son of Man is betrayed!	. 2
	26:25	Judas, who betrayed him, said, "Surely not I,	2
	26:45	Son of Man is betrayed into the hands of sinners.	2
	26:73	for your accent betrays you."	1
	27: 4	"I have sinned by betraying innocent blood."	2
Mrk	3:19	Judas Iscariot, who betrayed him.	2
	9:31	"The Son of Man is to be betrayed	2
	13:12	Brother will betray brother to death	2
	14:10	went to the chief priests in order to betray him	2
	14:11	began to look for an opportunity to betray him.	2
	14:18	"Truly I tell you, one of you will betray me	2
	14:21	woe to that one by whom the Son of Man is betrayed!	2
	14:41	Son of Man is betrayed into the hands of sinners.	2
Lke	9:44	The Son of Man is going to be betrayed	2
	21:16	You will be betrayed even by parents	2
	22: 4	how he might betray him to them.	2
	22: 6	look for an opportunity to betray him to them	2
	22:21	the one who betrays me is with me, and his hand	2
	22:22	woe to that one by whom he is betrayed!"	2
	22:48	with a kiss that you are betraying the Son of Man?"	2
Jhn	6:64	who was the one that would betray him.	2
	6:71	though one of the twelve, was going to betray him.	2
	12: 4	(the one who was about to betray him), said	2
	13: 2	put it into the heart…to betray him.	2
	13:11	For he knew who was to betray him;	2
	13:21	I tell you, one of you will betray me."	2
	18: 2	Now Judas, who betrayed him, also knew the place	2
	18: 5	Judas, who betrayed him, was standing with them.	2
	21:20	"Lord, who is it that is going to betray you?"	2
1Co	11:23	the night when he was betrayed took a loaf of bread	2

betrayer

1. παραδίδωμι, *paradidōmi, 4140*
2. προδότης, *prodotēs, 4595*

Mat	26:46	let us be going. See, my betrayer is at hand."	1
	26:48	Now the betrayer had given them a sign, saying	1
	27: 3	Judas, his betrayer, saw that Jesus was condemned	1
Mrk	14:42	let us be going. See, my betrayer is at hand."	1
	14:44	Now the betrayer had given them a sign, saying	1
Act	7:52	now you have become his betrayers and murderers.	2

better   *See* any better off [*good*], good

better than

1. παρά, *para, 4123*

Rom	14: 5	Some judge one day to be better than another	1

between

1. Contextual: Not in Greek
2. ἀνά + μέσος, *ana + mesos, 324 + 3545*
3. ἐκ, *ek, 1666*
4. ἐν + μέσος, *en + mesos, 1877 + 3545*
5. μέσος, *mesos, 3545*
6. μετά, *meta, 3552*
7. μεταξύ, *metaxy, 3568*

Mat	23:35	murdered between the sanctuary and the altar.	7
Lke	11:51	perished between the altar and the sanctuary.	7
	15:12	he divided his property between them.	1
	16:26	between you and us a great chasm has been fixed	7
	17:11	through the region between Samaria and Galilee.	5
Jhn	3:25	discussion…between John's disciples and a Jew.	6
	19:18	one on either side, with Jesus between them.	5
Act	11:12	and not to make a distinction between them	1

Act	12: 6	Peter...was sleeping between two soldiers	7
	15: 9	he has made no distinction between them and us.	7
	23: 7	between the Pharisees and the Sadducees	1
Rom	10:12	there is no distinction between Jew and Greek;	1
1Co	6: 5	to decide between one believer and another	2
2Co	6:14	between righteousness and lawlessness?	1
	6:14	what fellowship is there between light and darkness?	1
	8:13	fair balance between your present abundance	1
Eph	2:14	the dividing wall, that is, the hostility between	1
Php	1:23	I am hard pressed between the two:	3
1Ti	2: 5	also one mediator between God and humankind	1
Rev	5: 6	I saw between the throne and the four living creatures	4

beware

1. βλέπω, *blepō, 1063*
2. ἰδού, *idou, 2627*
3. προσέχω, *prosechō, 4668*
4. φυλάσσω, *phylassō, 5875*

Mat	6: 1	"Beware of practicing your piety before others	3
	7:15	"Beware of false prophets	3
	10:17	Beware of them, for they will hand you over	3
	16: 6	"Watch out, and beware of the yeast	3
	16:11	Beware of the yeast of the Pharisees	3
	16:12	he had not told them to beware of the yeast	3
	24: 4	"Beware that no one leads you astray	1
Mrk	8:15	"Watch out—beware of the yeast of the Pharisees	1
	12:38	As he taught, he said, "Beware of the scribes	1
	13: 5	"Beware that no one leads you astray.	1
	13: 9	"As for yourselves, beware;	1
	13:33	Beware, keep alert; for you do not know	1
Lke	12: 1	"Beware of the yeast of the Pharisees	3
	20:46	"Beware of the scribes	3
	21: 8	he said, "Beware that you are not led astray;	1
Act	13:40	Beware, therefore, that what the prophets said	1
Php	3: 2	Beware of the dogs	1
	3: 2	beware of the evil workers	1
	3: 2	beware of those who mutilate the flesh!	1
2Ti	4:15	You also must beware of him	4
2Pe	3:17	beware that you are not carried away with the error	4
Rev	2:10	Beware, the devil is about to throw some of you	2
	2:22	Beware, I am throwing her on a bed	2

bewilder

1. συγχέω, *syncheō, 5177*

Act	2: 6	the crowd gathered and was bewildered	1

bewitch

1. βασκαίνω, *baskainō, 1001*

Gal	3: 1	You foolish Galatians! Who has bewitched you?	1

beyond *See also* beyond all *measure,* beyond *limit,* beyond *measure,* go beyond, land beyond

1. ἐπέκεινα, *epekeina, 2084*
2. λοιπός, *loipos, 3370*
3. παρά, *para, 4123*
4. πέραν, *peran, 4305*
5. ὑπέρ, *hyper, 5642*
6. χωρίς, *chōris, 6006*

Mat	4:25	Judea, and from beyond the Jordan.	4
	19: 1	went to the region of Judea beyond the Jordan.	4
Mrk	3: 8	Jerusalem, Idumea, beyond the Jordan	4
	10: 1	went to the region of Judea and beyond the Jordan.	4
Act	7:43	I will remove you beyond Babylon.'	1
1Co	1:16	beyond that, I do not know	2
	4: 6	the saying, "Nothing beyond what is written,"	5
	10:13	not let you be tested beyond your strength	5
2Co	8: 3	voluntarily gave...even beyond their means	3
Gal	1:14	I advanced in Judaism beyond many among my people	5
Heb	1: 9	the oil of gladness beyond your companions."	3
	7: 7	It is beyond dispute	6

bier

1. σορός, *soros, 5049*

Lke	7:14	he came forward and touched the bier	1

bill

1. γράμμα, *gramma, 1207*

Lke	16: 6	He said to him, 'Take your bill	1
	16: 7	to him, 'Take you bill and make it eighty.'	1

bind

1. ἀνάγκη, *anankē, 340*
2. ἀνένδεκτος, *anendektos, 450*
3. δεσμεύω, *desmeuō, 1297*
4. δέω, *deō, 1313*
5. δουλόω, *douloō, 1530*
6. εἰμί, *eimi, 1639*
7. κυριεύω, *kyrieuō, 3259*
8. περίκειμαι, *perikeimai, 4329*

Mat	13:30	Collect the weeds first and bind them in bundles	4
	14: 3	For Herod had arrested John, bound him	4
	16:19	whatever you bind on earth will be bound	4
	16:19	will be bound in heaven	4
	18: 7	Occasions for stumbling are bound to come	1
	18:18	Truly I tell you, whatever you bind on earth	4
	18:18	will be bound in heaven	4
	22:13	'Bind him hand and foot, and throw him into	4
	23:16	swears by the sanctuary is bound by nothing	6
	23:18	'Whoever swears by the altar is bound by nothing	6
	27: 2	They bound him, led him away, and handed him over	4
Mrk	6:17	bound him, and put him in prison	4
	15: 1	They bound Jesus, led him away	4
Lke	8:29	bound with chains and shackles	3
	13:16	a daughter of Abraham whom Satan bound	4
	17: 1	"Occasions for stumbling are bound to come	2
Jhn	11:44	his hands and feet bound with strips of cloth	4
	18:12	Jewish police arrested Jesus and bound him.	4
	18:24	Then Annas sent him bound to Caiaphas	4
Act	9: 2	he might bring them bound to Jerusalem.	4
	9:14	to bind all who invoke your name."	4
	9:21	bringing them bound before the chief priests?"	4
	12: 6	Peter, bound with two chains, was sleeping	4
	21:11	bound his own feet and hands with it, and said	4
	21:11	the Jews in Jerusalem will bind the man	4
	21:13	ready not only to be bound but even to die	4
	21:33	ordered him to be bound with two chains;	4
	22: 4	binding both men and women and putting them in prison	3
	22: 5	bind those who were there and to bring them back	4
	22:29	and that he had bound him.	4
	28:20	I am bound with this chain."	8
Rom	7: 1	the law is binding on a person only during...lifetime?	7
	7: 2	a married woman is bound by the law to her husband	4
1Co	7:15	in such a case the brother or sister is not bound.	5
	7:27	Are you bound to a wife? Do not seek to be free.	4
	7:39	A wife is bound as long as her husband lives.	4
Rev	9:14	"Release the four angels who are bound	4
	20: 2	the dragon...and bound him for a thousand years.	4

bind by oath

1. ἀναθεματίζω, *anathematizō, 354*
2. ὀφείλω, *opheilō, 4053*

Mat	23:16	is bound by the oath.'	2
	23:18	is bound by the oath.'	2
Act	23:12	the Jews...bound themselves by an oath	1
	23:14	"We have strictly bound ourselves by an oath	1
	23:21	have bound themselves by an oath	1

bind together

1. σύνδεσμος, *syndesmos, 5278*

Col	3:14	which binds everything together in perfect harmony.	1

bird

1. ὄρνεον, *orneon, 3997*
2. πετεινόν, *peteinon, 4374*
3. πτηνός, *ptēnos, 4764*

Mat	6:26	Look at the birds of the air; they neither sow	2
	8:20	"Foxes have holes, and birds of the air have nests;	2
	13: 4	and the birds came and ate them up.	2
	13:32	so that the birds of the air come and make nests	2
Mrk	4: 4	the birds came and ate it up.	2
	4:32	birds of the air can make nests in its shade."	2
Lke	8: 5	the birds of the air ate it up.	2
	9:58	"Foxes have holes, and birds of the air have nests;	2
	12:24	Of how much more value are you than the birds?	2
	13:19	the birds of the air made nests in its branches."	2
Act	10:12	creatures and reptiles and birds of the air.	2
	11: 6	beasts of prey, reptiles, and birds of the air.	2
Rom	1:23	for images resembling a mortal human being or birds	2
1Co	15:39	another for birds, and another for fish.	3

Jas 3: 7 For every species of beast and bird, of reptile 2
Rev 18: 2 a haunt of every foul bird, 1
    19:17 he called to all the birds that fly in midheaven 1
    19:21 and all the birds were gorged with their flesh. 1

birth See also birth *pang*, endure birth pangs, give a new birth, give birth
1. γένεσις, *genesis, 1161*
2. γενετή, *genetē, 1162*
3. ἐκ + κοιλία + μήτηρ, *ek + koilia + mētēr, 1666 + 3120 + 3613*
4. κοιλία + μήτηρ, *koilia + mētēr, 3120 + 3613*
5. κοιλία + μήτηρ + γεννάω, *koilia + mētēr + gennaō, 3120 + 3613 + 1164*
6. φύσις, *physis, 5882*

Mat 1:18 birth of Jesus the Messiah took place in this way. 1
    19:12 there are eunuchs who have been so from birth 5
Lke 1:14 many will rejoice at his birth 1
    1:15 even before his birth he will be filled with 3
Jhn 9: 1 As he walked along, he saw a man blind from birth. 2
Act 3: 2 a man lame from birth was being carried in. 4
    14: 8 never walked, for he had been crippled from birth. 4
Gal 2:15 are Jews by birth and not Gentile sinners; 6

noble birth
1. εὐγενής, *eugenēs, 2302*
1Co 1:26 not many were of noble birth. 1

birthday
1. γενέσια, *genesia, 1160*
Mat 14: 6 when Herod's birthday came 1
Mrk 6:21 when Herod on his birthday gave a banquet 1

birthright
1. πρωτοτόκια, *prōtotokia, 4757*
Heb 12:16 who sold his birthright for a single meal. 1

bishop See also office of bishop
1. ἐπίσκοπος, *episkopos, 2176*
Php 1: 1 in Philippi, with the bishops and deacons: 1
1Ti 3: 2 Now a bishop must be above reproach 1
Tit 1: 7 For a bishop, as God's steward, must be blameless; 1

bit
1. χαλινός, *chalinos, 5903*
Jas 3: 3 If we put bits into the mouths of horses 1

bite
1. δάκνω, *daknō, 1231*
Gal 5:15 If, however, you bite and devour one another, 1

Bithynia
1. Βιθυνία, *Bithynia, 1049*
Act 16: 7 they attempted to go into Bithynia 1
1Pe 1: 1 the Dispersion in...Asia, and Bithynia 1

bitter See also make bitter
1. πικραίνω, *pikrainō, 4393*
2. πικρός, *pikros, 4395*
Jas 3:14 But if you have bitter envy...in your hearts 2
Rev 10: 9 "Take it, and eat; it will be bitter to your stomach 1

bitterly
1. πικρῶς, *pikrōs, 4396*
2. πολύς, *polys, 4498*
Mat 26:75 he went out and wept bitterly. 1
Lke 22:62 he went out and wept bitterly. 1
Rev 5: 4 to weep bitterly because no one was found worthy 2

bitterness
1. πικρία, *pikria, 4394*
Act 8:23 For I see that you are in the gall of bitterness 1
Rom 3:14 "Their mouths are full of cursing and bitterness." 1
Eph 4:31 Put away from you all bitterness and wrath 1
Heb 12:15 no root of bitterness springs up 1

black
1. μέλας, *melas, 3506*

Mat 5:36 head, for you cannot make one hair white or black. 1
Rev 6: 5 I looked, and there was a black horse! Its rider 1
    6:12 the sun became black as sackcloth 1

blame
1. μωμάομαι, *mōmaomai, 3699*
2Co 8:20 We intend that no one should blame us 1

without blame
1. ἀνεπίλημπτος, *anepilēmptos, 455*
1Ti 6:14 keep the commandment without spot or blame 1

blameless See also prove blameless
1. ἄκακος, *akakos, 179*
2. ἄμεμπτος, *amemptos, 289*
3. ἀμέμπτως, *amemptōs, 290*
4. ἄμωμος, *amōmos, 320*
5. ἀνέγκλητος, *anenklētos, 441*
6. ἀπρόσκοπος, *aproskopos, 718*
1Co 1: 8 blameless on the day of our Lord Jesus Christ. 5
Eph 1: 4 to be holy and blameless before him in love 4
Php 1:10 in the day of Christ you may be pure and blameless 6
    2:15 so that you may be blameless and innocent 2
    3: 6 as to righteousness under the law, blameless. 2
Col 1:22 blameless and irreproachable before him 4
1Th 2:10 blameless our conduct was toward you believers. 3
    3:13 that you may be blameless before our God and Father 2
    5:23 blameless at the coming of our Lord Jesus 3
Tit 1: 6 someone who is blameless, married only once, 5
    1: 7 For a bishop, as God's steward, must be blameless; 5
Heb 7:26 such a high priest, holy, blameless, undefiled 1
Rev 14: 5 no lie was found; they are blameless. 4

blamelessly
1. ἄμεμπτος, *amemptos, 289*
Lke 1: 6 righteous before God, living blamelessly 1

blaspheme
1. βλασφημέω, *blasphēmeō, 1059*
Mat 9: 3 "This man is blaspheming." 1
    26:65 "He has blasphemed! 1
Mrk 3:29 whoever blasphemes against the Holy Spirit 1
Lke 12:10 whoever blasphemes against the Holy Spirit 1
Jhn 10:36 blaspheming because I said, 'I am God's Son'? 1
Act 13:45 blaspheming, they contradicted...Paul 1
    26:11 I tried to force them to blaspheme; 1
Rom 2:24 "The name of God is blasphemed among the Gentiles 1
1Ti 1:20 so that they may learn not to blaspheme. 1
    6: 1 name of God and the teaching may not be blasphemed. 1
Jas 2: 7 Is it not they who blaspheme the excellent name 1
1Pe 4: 4 They are surprised...and so they blaspheme. 1
Rev 13: 6 God, blaspheming his name and his dwelling 1

blasphemer
1. βλασφημέω, *blasphēmeō, 1059*
2. βλάσφημος, *blasphēmos, 1061*
Act 19:37 blasphemers of our goddess. 1
1Ti 1:13 I was formerly a blasphemer, a persecutor, 2

blasphemous See also blasphemous *word*
1. βλασφημία, *blasphēmia, 1060*
2. βλάσφημος, *blasphēmos, 1061*
Act 6:11 blasphemous words against Moses and God." 2
Rev 13: 1 and on its heads were blasphemous names. 1
    17: 3 beast that was full of blasphemous names 1

blasphemy See also utter blasphemy
1. βλασφημέω, *blasphēmeō, 1059*
2. βλασφημία, *blasphēmia, 1060*
Mat 12:31 people will be forgiven for every sin and blasphemy 2
    12:31 blasphemy against the Spirit will not be 2
    26:65 You have now heard his blasphemy. 2
Mrk 2: 7 this fellow speak in this way? It is blasphemy! 1
    3:28 whatever blasphemies they utter; 2
    14:64 You have heard his blasphemy! 2
Lke 5:21 "Who is this who is speaking blasphemies? 2
Jhn 10:33 "It is not for a good work...but for blasphemy 2
Rev 13: 6 It opened its mouth to utter blasphemies 2

blast

1. φωνή, *phōnē, 5889*

Rev   8:13   woe...at the blasts of the other trumpets   1

Blastus

1. Βλάστος, *Blastos, 1058*

Act   12:20   winning over Blastus, the king's chamberlain   1

blaze

1. καίω, *kaiō, 2794*

Heb   12:18   a blazing fire, and darkness, and gloom   1
Rev   8:10   great star fell from heaven, blazing like a torch   1

bleach

1. λευκαίνω, *leukainō, 3326*

Mrk   9: 3   such as no one on earth could bleach them.   1

blemish   *See also* without blemish

1. μῶμος, *mōmos, 3700*
2. σπιλάς, *spilas, 5069*

2Pe   2:13   They are blots and blemishes   1
Jde   1:12   These are blemishes on your love-feasts   2

without blemish

1. ἀμώμητος, *amōmētos, 318*
2. ἄμωμος, *amōmos, 320*
3. ἄσπιλος, *aspilos, 834*

Eph   5:27   so that she may be holy and without blemish.   2
Php   2:15   children of God without blemish   2
Heb   9:14   offered himself without blemish to God   2
1Pe   1:19   like that of a lamb without defect or blemish.   3
2Pe   3:14   found by him at peace, without spot or blemish;   1
Jde   1:24   and to make you stand without blemish   2

bless   *See also* call blessed

1. Contextual: Not in Greek
2. ἐνευλογέω, *eneulogeō, 1922*
3. εὐλογέω, *eulogeō, 2328*
4. εὐλογητός, *eulogētos, 2329*
5. κατευλογέω, *kateulogeō, 2986*
6. μακάριος, *makarios, 3421*

Mat   5: 3   "Blessed are the poor in spirit, for theirs is   6
     5: 4   "Blessed are those who mourn, for they will be   6
     5: 5   "Blessed are the meek, for they will inherit   6
     5: 6   "Blessed are those who hunger and thirst   6
     5: 7   "Blessed are the merciful, for they will receive   6
     5: 8   "Blessed are the pure in heart, for they will see   6
     5: 9   "Blessed are the peacemakers, for they will be   6
     5:10   "Blessed are those who are persecuted   6
     5:11   "Blessed are you when people revile you   6
     11: 6   blessed is anyone who takes no offense at me."   6
     13:16   blessed are your eyes, for they see   6
     14:19   he looked up to heaven, and blessed and broke   3
     16:17   "Blessed are you, Simon son of Jonah!   6
     21: 9   Blessed is the one who comes in the name   3
     23:39   'Blessed is the one who comes in the name   3
     24:46   Blessed is that slave   6
     25:34   'Come, you that are blessed by my Father   3
     26:26   loaf of bread, and after blessing it he broke it   3
Mrk   6:41   blessed and broke the loaves   3
     8: 7   after blessing them, he ordered   3
     10:16   laid his hands on them, and blessed them.   5
     11: 9   Blessed is the one who comes in the name   3
     11:10   Blessed is the coming kingdom of our ancestor   3
     14:22   and after blessing it he broke it, gave it   3
Lke   1:42   "Blessed are you among women   3
     1:42   blessed is the fruit of your womb.   3
     1:45   blessed is she who believed   6
     1:68   "Blessed be the Lord God of Israel   4
     2:34   Simeon blessed them and said to his mother Mary   3
     6:20   and said: "Blessed are you who are poor   6
     6:21   "Blessed are you who are hungry now   6
     6:21   "Blessed are you who weep now,   6
     6:22   "Blessed are you when people hate you   6
     6:28   bless those who curse you   3
     7:23   blessed is anyone who takes no offense at me."   6
     9:16   he looked up to heaven, and blessed and broke them   3
     10:23   Blessed are the eyes that see what you see!   6
     11:27   "Blessed is the womb that bore you   6
     11:28   "Blessed rather are those who hear the word of God   6
     12:37   Blessed are those slaves   6
     12:38   and finds them so, blessed are those slaves.   6
     12:43   Blessed is that slave   6
     13:35   'Blessed is the one who comes in the name   3
     14:14   you will be blessed, because they cannot repay   6
     14:15   "Blessed is anyone who will eat bread in the kingdom   6
     19:38   saying, "Blessed is the king who comes   3
     23:29   'Blessed are the barren   6
     24:30   blessed and broke it, and gave it to them.   3
     24:50   and, lifting up his hands, he blessed them.   3
     24:51   While he was blessing them, he withdrew from them   3
     24:53   were continually in the temple blessing God.   3
Jhn   12:13   Blessed is the one who comes in the name   3
     13:17   you are blessed if you do them.   6
     20:29   Blessed are those who have not seen   6
Act   3:25   all the families of the earth shall be blessed.'   2
     3:26   sent him first to you, to bless you   3
     20:35   'It is more blessed to give than to receive.' "   6
Rom   1:25   the Creator, who is blessed forever! Amen.   4
     4: 7   "Blessed are those...are forgiven   6
     4: 8   blessed is the one against whom the Lord   6
     9: 5   Messiah, who is over all, God blessed forever.   4
     12:14   Bless those who persecute you;   3
     12:14   who persecute you; bless and do not curse them.   3
     14:22   Blessed are those who have no reason to condemn   6
1Co   4:12   When reviled, we bless; when persecuted, we endure;   3
     7:40   she is more blessed if she remains as she is.   6
     10:16   The cup of blessing that we bless   3
2Co   1: 3   Blessed be the God and Father of our Lord Jesus   4
     11:31   God...(blessed be he forever!)   4
Gal   3: 8   saying, "All the Gentiles shall be blessed in you."   2
     3: 9   who believe are blessed with Abraham   3
Eph   1: 3   Blessed be the God and Father of our Lord Jesus   4
     1: 3   who has blessed us in Christ   3
1Ti   1:11   glorious gospel of the blessed God   6
     6:15   the blessed and only Sovereign   6
Tit   2:13   while we wait for the blessed hope   6
Heb   6:14   saying, "I will surely bless you and multiply you."   3
     7: 1   met Abraham...and blessed him";   3
     7: 6   blessed him who had received the promises.   3
     7: 7   the inferior is blessed by the superior.   3
     11:21   Jacob...blessed each of the sons of Joseph   3
Jas   1:12   Blessed is anyone who endures temptation.   6
     1:25   they will be blessed in their doing.   6
     3: 9   With it we bless the Lord and Father   3
1Pe   1: 3   Blessed be the God and Father of our Lord Jesus   4
     3:14   if you do suffer...you are blessed.   6
     4:14   If you are reviled...you are blessed   6
Rev   1: 3   Blessed is the one who reads aloud the words   6
     1: 3   and blessed are those who hear and who keep   1
     14:13   Blessed are the dead who from now on die in the Lord."   6
     16:15   Blessed is the one who stays awake and is clothed   6
     19: 9   Blessed are those who are invited   6
     20: 6   Blessed and holy are those who share in the first   6
     22: 7   Blessed is the one who keeps the words of the prophecy   6
     22:14   Blessed are those who wash their robes   6

blessed one

1. εὐλογητός, *eulogētos, 2329*

Mrk   14:61   the Messiah, the Son of the Blessed One?"   1

blessedness

1. μακαρισμός, *makarismos, 3422*

Rom   4: 6   So also David speaks of the blessedness of those   1
     4: 9   blessedness...pronounced only on the circumcised   1

blessing   *See also* invoke a blessing, say a blessing

1. Contextual: Not in Greek
2. αὐτός, *autos, 899*
3. εὐλογέω, *eulogeō, 2328*
4. εὐλογία, *eulogia, 2330*
5. χάρις, *charis, 5921*
6. χάρισμα, *charisma, 5922*

Rom   15:29   come in the fullness of the blessing of Christ.   4
1Co   9:23   so that I may share in its blessings.   1
     10:16   The cup of blessing that we bless   4
2Co   1:11   the blessing granted us   6
     9: 8   provide you with every blessing in abundance   5
Gal   3:14   that in Christ Jesus the blessing of Abraham   4

Eph	1: 3	blessed us…with every spiritual blessing	4
Heb	6: 7	receives a blessing from God.	4
	12:17	when he wanted to inherit the blessing	4
	12:17	even though he sought the blessing with tears.	2
Jas	3:10	From the same mouth come blessing and cursing.	4
1Pe	3: 9	but, on the contrary, repay with a blessing.	3
	3: 9	that you might inherit a blessing.	4
Rev	5:12	to receive…honor and glory and blessing!"	4
	5:13	to the Lamb be blessing and honor and glory	4
	7:12	Blessing and glory and wisdom and thanksgiving	4

spiritual blessing

1. πνευματικός, *pneumatikos, 4461*

Rom 15:27	the Gentiles…share in their spiritual blessings	1

blind

1. Contextual: Not in Greek
2. τυφλός, *typhlos, 5603*
3. τυφλόω, *typhloō, 5604*

Mat	11: 5	the blind receive their sight, the lame walk	2
	12:22	Then they brought to him a demoniac who was blind	2
	15:14	they are blind guides of the blind	2
	15:14	they are blind guides of the blind	2
	15:30	the lame, the maimed, the blind, the mute	2
	15:31	the lame walking, and the blind seeing.	2
	21:14	The blind and the lame came to him in the temple	2
	23:16	"Woe to you, blind guides, who say	2
	23:17	You blind fools!	2
	23:19	How blind you are!	2
	23:24	You blind guides! You strain out a gnat	2
	23:26	You blind Pharisee!	2
Mrk	10:46	Bartimaeus son of Timaeus, a blind beggar	2
Lke	4:18	to proclaim…recovery of sight to the blind	2
	7:21	given sight to many who were blind.	2
	7:22	the blind receive their sight, the lame walk	2
	14:13	the poor, the crippled, the lame, and the blind.	2
	14:21	bring in the poor, the crippled, the blind,	2
Jhn	5: 3	many invalids—blind, lame, and paralyzed.	2
	9: 1	As he walked along, he saw a man blind from birth.	2
	9: 2	who sinned…that he was born blind?"	2
	9: 3	he was born blind so that God's works	1
	9:13	the man who had formerly been blind.	2
	9:18	The Jews did not believe that he had been blind	2
	9:19	"Is this your son, who you say was born blind?	2
	9:20	this is our son, and that he was born blind;	2
	9:24	they called the man who had been blind	2
	9:25	I do know, that though I was blind, now I see."	2
	9:39	those who do see may become blind."	2
	9:40	said to him, "Surely we are not blind	2
	9:41	"If you were blind, you would not have sin.	2
	10:21	Can a demon open the eyes of the blind?"	2
	12:40	blinded their eyes and hardened their heart	3
Act	13:11	be blind for a while, unable to see the sun."	2
Rom	2:19	if you are sure that you are a guide to the blind	2
2Co	4: 4	the god of this world has blinded the minds	3
2Pe	1: 9	who lacks these things is nearsighted and blind	2
Rev	3:17	you are wretched, pitiable, poor, blind, and naked.	2

blind man

1. τυφλός, *typhlos, 5603*

Mat	9:27	two blind men followed him, crying loudly	1
	9:28	When he entered the house, the blind men came	1
	20:30	There were two blind men sitting by the roadside.	1
Mrk	8:22	Some people brought a blind man to him	1
	8:23	He took the blind man by the hand	1
	10:49	they called the blind man, saying to him	1
	10:51	The blind man said to him, "My teacher	1
Lke	18:35	a blind man was sitting by the roadside begging.	1
Jhn	9:17	So they said again to the blind man	1
	11:37	he who opened the eyes of the blind man	1

blind person

1. τυφλός, *typhlos, 5603*

Mat	15:14	if one blind person guides another, both will fall	1
Lke	6:39	"Can a blind person guide a blind person?	1
	6:39	"Can a blind person guide a blind person?	1
Jhn	9:32	anyone opened the eyes of a person born blind.	1

blindfold

1. περικαλύπτω, *perikalyptō, 4328*

2. περικαλύπτω + ὁ + πρόσωπον, *perikalyptō + ho + prosōpon, 4328 + 3836 + 4725*

Mrk 14:65	Some began to spit on him, to blindfold him	2
Lke 22:64	they also blindfolded him and kept asking him	1

block a way

1. ἐγκόπτω, *enkoptō, 1601*

1Th 2:18	but Satan blocked our way.	1

stumbling block   *See also* put a stumbling block

1. πρόσκομμα, *proskomma, 4682*
2. σκάνδαλον, *skandalon, 4998*

Mat	16:23	You are a stumbling block to me;	2
	18: 7	Woe to the world because of stumbling blocks!	2
	18: 7	woe to the one by whom the stumbling block comes!	2
Rom	11: 9	become…a stumbling block and a retribution for them;	2
	14:13	resolve instead never to put a stumbling block	1
1Co	1:23	a stumbling block to Jews and foolishness to Gentiles	2
	8: 9	somehow become a stumbling block to the weak.	1
Rev	2:14	put a stumbling block before the people of Israel	2

blood   *See also* shedding of blood

1. Contextual: Not in Greek
2. αἷμα, *haima, 135*

Mat	16:17	For flesh and blood has not revealed this to you	2
	23:30	in shedding the blood of the prophets.'	2
	23:35	all the righteous blood shed on earth	2
	23:35	from the blood of righteous Abel	2
	23:35	to the blood of Zechariah son of Barachiah	2
	26:28	"for this is my blood of the covenant	2
	27: 4	"I have sinned by betraying innocent blood."	2
	27: 6	since they are blood money."	2
	27: 8	has been called the Field of Blood to this day.	2
	27:24	"I am innocent of this man's blood;	2
	27:25	"His blood be on us and on our children!"	2
Mrk	14:24	to them, "This is my blood of the covenant	2
Lke	11:50	the blood of all the prophets	2
	11:51	from the blood of Abel to the blood of Zechariah	2
	11:51	from the blood of Abel to the blood of Zechariah	2
	13: 1	the Galileans whose blood Pilate had mingled	2
	22:20	the new covenant in my blood.	2
	22:44	⟦his sweat became like great drops of blood⟧	2
Jhn	1:13	who were born, not of blood	2
	6:53	flesh of the Son of Man and drink his blood	2
	6:54	Those who eat my flesh and drink my blood	2
	6:55	my flesh is true food and my blood is true drink.	2
	6:56	who eat my flesh and drink my blood abide in me	2
	19:34	at once blood and water came out.	2
Act	1:19	Hakeldama, that is, Field of Blood.)	2
	2:19	blood, and fire, and smoky mist.	2
	2:20	the moon to blood	2
	5:28	you are determined to bring this man's blood on us."	2
	15:20	from whatever has been strangled and from blood.	2
	15:29	from blood and from what is strangled	2
	18: 6	"Your blood be on your own heads! I am innocent.	2
	20:26	I am not responsible for the blood of any of you	2
	20:28	that he obtained with the blood of his own Son.	2
	21:25	abstain…from blood	2
	22:20	while the blood of your witness Stephen was shed	2
Rom	3:15	"Their feet are swift to shed blood;	2
	3:25	as a sacrifice of atonement by his blood	2
	5: 9	now that we have been justified by his blood	2
1Co	10:16	is it not a sharing in the blood of Christ?	2
	11:25	"This cup is the new covenant in my blood.	2
	11:27	be answerable for the body and blood of the Lord.	2
	15:50	flesh and blood cannot inherit the kingdom	2
Eph	1: 7	In him we have redemption through his blood	2
	2:13	have been brought near by the blood of Christ.	2
	6:12	struggle is not against enemies of blood and flesh	2
Col	1:20	making peace through the blood of his cross.	2
Heb	2:14	Since…the children share flesh and blood	2
	9: 7	not without taking the blood	2
	9:12	not with the blood of goats and calves	2
	9:12	with…his own blood	2
	9:13	the blood of goats and bulls	2
	9:14	how much more will the blood of Christ	2
	9:18	not even the first covenant was inaugurated without blood	2
	9:19	he took the blood of calves and goats	2
	9:20	saying, "This is the blood of the covenant	2
	9:21	in the same way he sprinkled with the blood	2

Heb	9:22	almost everything is purified with blood	2
	9:25	enters…with blood that is not his own;	2
	10: 4	the blood of bulls and goats	2
	10:19	we have confidence…by the blood of Jesus	2
	10:29	profaned the blood of the covenant	2
	11:28	kept the Passover and the sprinkling of blood	2
	12: 4	resisted to the point of shedding your blood.	2
	12:24	the sprinkled blood that speaks a better word	2
	12:24	that speaks a better word than the blood of Abel.	1
	13:11	whose blood is brought into the sanctuary	2
	13:12	sanctify the people by his own blood.	2
	13:20	by the blood of the eternal covenant	2
1Pe	1: 2	Jesus Christ and to be sprinkled with his blood:	2
	1:19	with the precious blood of Christ	2
1Jn	1: 7	blood of Jesus his Son cleanses us from all sin.	2
	5: 6	This is the one who came by water and blood, Jesus	2
	5: 6	but with the water and the blood.	2
	5: 8	the Spirit and the water and the blood,	2
Rev	1: 5	To him who…freed us from our sins by his blood	2
	5: 9	and by your blood you ransomed for God saints	2
	6:10	judge and avenge our blood on the inhabitants	2
	6:12	the full moon became like blood	2
	7:14	made them white in the blood of the Lamb.	2
	8: 7	there came hail and fire, mixed with blood	2
	8: 9	A third of the sea became blood	2
	11: 6	authority over the waters to turn them into blood	2
	12:11	they have conquered him by the blood of the Lamb	2
	14:20	and blood flowed from the wine press	2
	16: 3	the sea, and it became like the blood of a corpse	2
	16: 4	the rivers…and they became blood.	2
	16: 6	they shed the blood of saints and prophets	2
	16: 6	you have given them blood to drink.	2
	17: 6	the woman was drunk with the blood of the saints	2
	17: 6	drunk with…the blood of the witnesses to Jesus.	2
	18:24	And in you was found the blood of prophets	2
	19: 2	he has avenged on her the blood of his servants."	2
	19:13	He is clothed in a robe dipped in blood	2

blot

1. σπίλος, *spilos, 5070*

2Pe	2:13	They are blots and blemishes	1

blot out

1. ἐξαλείφω, *exaleiphō, 1981*

Rev	3: 5	I will not blot your name out of the book of life;	1

blow

1. πνέω, *pneō, 4463*
2. σαλπίζω, *salpizō, 4895*

Mat	7:25	rain fell, the floods came, and the winds blew	1
	7:27	the floods came, and the winds blew and beat	1
Lke	12:55	when you see the south wind blowing, you say	1
Jhn	3: 8	The wind blows where it chooses	1
	6:18	sea became rough because a strong wind was blowing.	1
Rev	7: 1	so that no wind could blow on earth or sea	1
	8: 6	angels who had…trumpets made ready to blow them.	2
	8:13	trumpets that the…angels are about to blow!"	2

blow a trumpet

1. σαλπίζω, *salpizō, 4895*

Rev	8: 7	The first angel blew his trumpet	1
	8: 8	The second angel blew his trumpet	1
	8:10	The third angel blew his trumpet, and a great star	1
	8:12	The fourth angel blew his trumpet	1
	9: 1	And the fifth angel blew his trumpet, and I saw	1
	9:13	Then the sixth angel blew his trumpet, and I heard	1
	10: 7	when the seventh angel is to blow his trumpet,	1
	11:15	Then the seventh angel blew his trumpet	1

blow about

1. περιφέρω, *peripherō, 4367*

Eph	4:14	blown about by every wind of doctrine	1

blow moderately

1. ὑποπνέω, *hypopneō, 5710*

Act	27:13	When a moderate south wind began to blow	1

Boanerges

1. Βοανηργές, *Boanērges, 1065*

Mrk	3:17	the name Boanerges, that is, Sons of Thunder);	1

boast *See also* reason to boast, something to boast about

1. Contextual: Not in Greek
2. αὐχέω, *aucheō, 902*
3. ἐγκαυχάομαι, *enkauchaomai, 1595*
4. κατακαυχάομαι, *katakauchaomai, 2878*
5. καυχάομαι, *kauchaomai, 3016*
6. καύχημα, *kauchēma, 3017*
7. καύχησις, *kauchēsis, 3018*
8. ὅς, *hos, 4005*
9. παρρησία, *parrēsia, 4244*

Rom	2:17	and boast of your relation to God	5
	2:23	You that boast in the law, do you dishonor God	5
	3:27	what becomes of boasting? It is excluded.	7
	5: 2	we boast in our hope of sharing the glory of God.	5
	5: 3	not only that, but we also boast in our sufferings	5
	5:11	boast in God through our Lord Jesus Christ	5
	11:18	If you do boast, remember that it is not you	4
1Co	1:29	so that no one might boast	5
	1:31	"Let the one who boasts, boast in the Lord."	5
	1:31	"Let the one who boasts, boast in the Lord."	5
	3:21	So let no one boast about human leaders.	5
	4: 7	why do you boast as if it were not a gift?	5
	5: 6	Your boasting is not a good thing. Do you not know	6
	13: 3	if I hand over my body so that I may boast,	5
	15:31	as certain, brothers and sisters, as my boasting	7
	15:31	a boast that I make in Christ Jesus our Lord.	8
2Co	1:12	Indeed, this is our boast	7
	1:14	on the day of the Lord Jesus we are your boast	6
	1:14	we are your boast even as you are our boast	1
	5:12	giving you an opportunity to boast about us	6
	5:12	those who boast in outward appearance	5
	7: 4	I often boast about you; I have great pride	9
	7:14	so our boasting to Titus has proved true	7
	9: 2	the subject of my boasting about you	5
	9: 3	boasting about you may not prove to have been empty	6
	10: 8	even if I boast a little too much of our authority	5
	10:13	We, however, will not boast beyond limits	5
	10:15	We do not boast beyond limits,	5
	10:16	without boasting of work already done	5
	10:17	"Let the one who boasts, boast in the Lord."	5
	10:17	"Let the one who boasts, boast in the Lord."	5
	11:10	this boast of mine will not be silenced	7
	11:12	as our equals in what they boast about.	5
	11:16	so that I too may boast a little.	5
	11:18	since many boast according to human standards	5
	11:18	I will also boast.	5
	11:21	whatever anyone dares to boast	1
	11:21	I also dare to boast of that.	1
	11:30	If I must boast, I will boast of the things	5
	11:30	I will boast of the things that show my weakness.	5
	12: 1	It is necessary to boast; nothing is to be gained	5
	12: 5	On behalf of such a one I will boast	5
	12: 5	on my own behalf I will not boast	5
	12: 6	But if I wish to boast, I will not be a fool	5
	12: 9	I will boast all the more gladly of my weaknesses	5
Gal	6:13	so that they may boast about your flesh	5
	6:14	May I never boast of anything except the cross	5
Eph	2: 9	not the result of works, so that no one may boast.	5
Php	1:26	share abundantly in your boasting in Christ Jesus	6
	2:16	that I can boast on the day of Christ	6
	3: 3	worship in the Spirit of God and boast in Christ Jesus	5
1Th	2:19	For what is our hope or joy or crown of boasting	7
2Th	1: 4	Therefore we ourselves boast of you	3
Jas	1: 9	Let the believer who is lowly boast in being raised up	5
	3: 5	the tongue…boasts of great exploits.	2
	4:16	As it is, you boast in your arrogance;	5
	4:16	boast in your arrogance; all such boasting is evil.	7

boast over

1. κατακαυχάομαι, *katakauchaomai, 2878*

Rom	11:18	do not boast over the branches.	1

boaster

1. Contextual: Not in Greek
2. ἀλαζών, *alazōn, 225*

2Co	11:13	such boasters are false apostles, deceitful workers	1
2Ti	3: 2	lovers of themselves, lovers of money, boasters,	2

boastful

1. ἀλαζών, *alazōn, 225*
2. κατακαυχάομαι, *katakauchaomai, 2878*
3. καυχάομαι, *kauchaomai, 3016*
4. καύχησις, *kauchēsis, 3018*
5. περπερεύομαι, *perpereuomai, 4371*

Rom 1:30 haughty, boastful, inventors of evil   1
1Co 13: 4 love is not envious or boastful or arrogant   5
2Co 7:14 For if I have been somewhat boastful about you   3
    11:17 saying in regard to this boastful confidence   4
Jas 3:14 do not be boastful and false to the truth.   2

boat *See also* moor a boat

1. Contextual: Not in Greek
2. πλοιάριον, *ploiarion, 4449*
3. πλοῖον, *ploion, 4450*
4. σκάφη, *skaphē, 5002*

Mat 4:21 in the boat with their father Zebedee, mending   3
    4:22 Immediately they left the boat and their father   3
    8:23 he got into the boat, his disciples followed him.   3
    8:24 so great that the boat was being swamped by the waves;   3
    9: 1 And after getting into a boat he crossed   3
    13: 2 that he got into a boat and sat there   3
    14:13 withdrew from there in a boat to a deserted place   3
    14:22 he made the disciples get into the boat   3
    14:24 by this time the boat…was far from the land   3
    14:29 He said, "Come." So Peter got out of the boat   3
    14:32 When they got into the boat, the wind ceased.   3
    14:33 those in the boat worshiped him, saying   3
    15:39 sending away the crowds, he got into the boat   3
Mrk 1:19 who were in their boat mending the nets.   3
    1:20 they left their father Zebedee in the boat   3
    3: 9 He told his disciples to have a boat ready   2
    4: 1 he got into a boat on the sea and sat there   3
    4:36 took him with them in the boat, just as he was.   3
    4:36 Other boats were with him.   3
    4:37 the waves beat into the boat   3
    4:37 so that the boat was already being swamped.   3
    5: 2 when he had stepped out of the boat   3
    5:18 As he was getting into the boat   3
    5:21 Jesus had crossed again in the boat   3
    6:32 they went away in the boat to a deserted place   3
    6:45 he made his disciples get into the boat   3
    6:47 When evening came, the boat was out on the sea   3
    6:51 got into the boat with them and the wind ceased.   3
    6:54 When they got out of the boat   3
    8:10 he got into the boat with his disciples   3
    8:13 he left them, and getting into the boat again   1
    8:14 they had only one loaf with them in the boat.   3
Lke 5: 2 he saw two boats there at the shore of the lake;   3
    5: 3 into one of the boats, the one belonging to Simon   3
    5: 3 he sat down and taught the crowds from the boat.   3
    5: 7 signaled their partners in the other boat   3
    5: 7 they came and filled both boats   3
    5:11 When they had brought their boats to shore   3
    8:22 One day he got into a boat with his disciples   3
    8:23 the boat was filling with water,   1
    8:37 So he got into the boat and returned.   3
Jhn 6:17 got into a boat   3
    6:19 walking on the sea and coming near the boat   3
    6:21 they wanted to take him into the boat   3
    6:21 immediately the boat reached the land   3
    6:22 saw that there had been only one boat there.   2
    6:22 Jesus had not got into the boat with his disciples   3
    6:23 Then some boats from Tiberias came near the place   2
    6:24 they…got into the boats and went to Capernaum   2
    21: 3 They went out and got into the boat   3
    21: 6 "Cast the net to the right side of the boat   3
    21: 8 the other disciples came in the boat   2
Act 27:30 had lowered the boat into the sea   4
    27:32 Then the soldiers cut away the ropes of the boat   4

ship's boat

1. σκάφη, *skaphē, 5002*

Act 27:16 scarcely able to get the ship's boat under control.   1

Boaz

1. Βόες, *Boes, 1067*
2. Βόος, *Boos, 1078*

Mat 1: 5 Salmon the father of Boaz by Rahab   1
    1: 5 Boaz the father of Obed by Ruth   1
Lke 3:32 son of Jesse, son of Obed, son of Boaz   2

bodily

1. σῶμα, *sōma, 5393*
2. σωματικός, *sōmatikos, 5394*
3. σωματικῶς, *sōmatikōs, 5395*

Lke 3:22 Holy Spirit descended upon him in bodily form   2
2Co 10:10 his bodily presence is weak   1
Col 2: 9 in him the whole fullness of deity dwells bodily   3
Jas 2:16 not supply their bodily needs, what is the good   1

body *See also* member of the same body

1. Contextual: Not in Greek
2. αὐτός, *autos, 899*
3. κῶλον, *kōlon, 3265*
4. ὁμοθυμαδόν, *homothymadon, 3924*
5. πτῶμα, *ptōma, 4773*
6. σάρξ, *sarx, 4922*
7. σκεῦος, *skeuos, 5007*
8. σκήνωμα, *skēnōma, 5013*
9. σῶμα, *sōma, 5393*

Mat 5:29 than for your whole body to be thrown into hell.   9
    5:30 members than for your whole body to go into hell.   9
    6:22 "The eye is the lamp of the body. So, if your eye   9
    6:22 eye is healthy, your whole body will be full of light;   9
    6:23 your eye is unhealthy, your whole body will be full   9
    6:25 or about your body, what you will wear.   9
    6:25 than food, and the body more than clothing?   9
    10:28 Do not fear those who kill the body   9
    10:28 who can destroy both soul and body in hell.   9
    14:12 His disciples came and took the body   5
    26:12 By pouring this ointment on my body   9
    26:26 "Take, eat; this is my body."   9
    27:52 many bodies of the saints who had fallen asleep   9
    27:58 went to Pilate and asked for the body of Jesus   9
    27:59 Joseph took the body   9
Mrk 5:29 she felt in her body that she was healed   9
    6:29 they came and took his body, and laid it in a tomb.   5
    14: 8 anointed my body beforehand for its burial.   9
    14:22 "Take; this is my body."   9
    15:43 to Pilate and asked for the body of Jesus.   9
    15:45 he granted the body to Joseph.   5
    15:46 taking down the body, wrapped it in the linen cloth   2
    15:47 the mother of Joses saw where the body was laid.   1
Lke 11:34 Your eye is the lamp of your body.   9
    11:34 your whole body is full of light;   9
    11:34 is not healthy, your body is full of darkness.   9
    11:36 If then your whole body is full of light   9
    12: 4 my friends, do not fear those who kill the body   9
    12:22 or about your body, what you will wear.   9
    12:23 the body more than clothing.   9
    22:19 "This is my body, which is given for you.   9
    23:52 went to Pilate and asked for the body of Jesus.   9
    23:55 saw the tomb and how his body was laid.   9
    24: 3 when they went in, they did not find the body.   9
    24:23 when they did not find his body there   9
Jhn 2:21 But he was speaking of the temple of his body.   9
    7:23 I healed a man's whole body on the sabbath?   1
    19:31 Jews did not want the bodies left on the cross   9
    19:31 and the bodies removed.   1
    19:38 to let him take away the body of Jesus.   9
    19:38 so he came and removed his body.   9
    19:40 They took the body of Jesus   9
    20:12 sitting where the body of Jesus had been lying   9
Act 5: 6 The young men came and wrapped up his body   2
    7:16 their bodies were brought back to Shechem   1
    9:40 turned to the body and said, "Tabitha, get up."   9
    12:20 they came to him in a body;   4
Rom 1:24 degrading of their bodies among themselves   9
    4:19 weaken in faith when he considered his own body   9
    6: 6 so that the body of sin might be destroyed   9
    6:12 not let sin exercise dominion in your mortal bodies   9
    7: 4 have died to the law through the body of Christ   9
    7:24 Who will rescue me from this body of death?   9
    8:10 though the body is dead because of sin   9
    8:11 will give life to your mortal bodies also   9
    8:13 if…put to death the deeds of the body   9
    8:23 adoption, the redemption of our bodies.   9

Rom 12: 1	to present your bodies as a living sacrifice	9
12: 4	For as in one body we have many members	9
12: 5	so we, who are many, are one body in Christ	9
1Co 5: 3	For though absent in body, I am present in spirit;	9
6:13	The body is meant not for fornication	9
6:13	and the Lord for the body.	9
6:15	know that your bodies are members of Christ?	9
6:16	becomes one body with her?	9
6:18	Every sin…is outside the body;	9
6:18	the fornicator sins against the body	9
6:19	do you not know that your body is a temple	9
6:20	therefore glorify God in your body.	9
7: 4	wife does not have authority over her own body	9
7: 4	husband does not have authority over his own body	9
7:34	so that they may be holy in body and spirit;	9
9:27	I punish my body and enslave it	9
10:16	is it not a sharing in the body of Christ?	9
10:17	we who are many are one body	9
11:24	"This is my body that is for you.	9
11:27	be answerable for the body and blood of the Lord.	9
11:29	who eat and drink without discerning the body	9
12:12	For just as the body is one and has many members	9
12:12	all the members of the body, though many, are one	9
12:12	members of the body, though many, are one body	9
12:13	we were all baptized into one body	9
12:14	body does not consist of one member but of many.	9
12:15	"Because I am not a hand, I do not belong to the body,"	9
12:15	that would not make it any less a part of the body.	9
12:16	"Because I am not an eye, I do not belong to the body,"	9
12:16	that would not make it any less a part of the body.	9
12:17	If the whole body were an eye	9
12:17	If the whole body were hearing,	1
12:18	as it is, God arranged the members in the body	9
12:19	all were a single member, where would the body be?	9
12:20	As it is, there are many members, yet one body.	9
12:22	the members of the body that seem to be weaker	9
12:23	members of the body that we think less honorable	9
12:24	God has so arranged the body	9
12:25	that there may be no dissension within the body	9
12:27	you are the body of Christ	9
13: 3	if I hand over my body so that I may boast,	9
15:35	With what kind of body do they come?"	9
15:37	what you sow, you do not sow the body that is to be	9
15:38	God gives it a body as he has chosen	9
15:38	to each kind of seed its own body.	9
15:40	There are both heavenly bodies and earthly	9
15:40	both heavenly bodies and earthly bodies	9
15:44	It is sown a physical body	9
15:44	it is raised a spiritual body.	9
15:44	If there is a physical body	9
15:44	there is also a spiritual body.	1
15:53	perishable body must put on imperishability,	1
15:53	this mortal body must put on immortality.	1
15:54	When this perishable body puts on imperishability	1
15:54	this mortal body puts on immortality	1
2Co 4:10	always carrying in the body the death of Jesus	9
4:10	Jesus may also be made visible in our bodies.	9
5: 6	we know that while we are at home in the body	9
5: 8	be away from the body and at home with the Lord.	9
5:10	for what has been done in the body	9
7: 1	every defilement of body and of spirit	6
7: 5	our bodies had no rest	6
12: 2	whether in the body or out of the body	9
12: 2	whether in the body or out of the body	9
12: 3	whether in the body or out of the body	9
12: 3	whether in the body or out of the body	9
Gal 6:17	I carry the marks of Jesus branded on my body.	9
Eph 1:23	which is his body, the fullness of him	9
2:16	might reconcile both groups to God in one body	9
4: 4	There is one body and one Spirit	9
4:12	for building up the body of Christ	9
4:16	the whole body, joined and knit together	9
4:16	promotes the body's growth in building itself up	9
5:23	Christ is the head of the church, the body	9
5:28	should love their wives as they do their own bodies.	9
5:29	For no one ever hates his own body	6
5:30	because we are members of his body.	9
Php 1:20	Christ will be exalted now as always in my body	9
3:21	He will transform the body of our humiliation	9
3:21	may be conformed to the body of his glory	9
Col 1:18	He is the head of the body, the church;	9

1:22	now reconciled in his fleshly body through death	9
1:24	for the sake of his body, that is, the church.	9
2: 5	For though I am absent in body	6
2:11	by putting off the body of the flesh	9
2:19	the whole body, nourished and held together	9
2:23	humility, and severe treatment of the body	9
3:15	to which indeed you were called in the one body.	9
1Th 4: 4	each one of you know how to control your own body	7
5:23	may your spirit and soul and body be kept sound	9
Heb 3:17	who sinned, whose bodies fell in the wilderness?	3
9:10	regulations for the body	6
10: 5	a body you have prepared for me;	9
10:10	the offering of the body of Jesus Christ	9
10:22	our bodies washed with pure water.	9
13:11	the bodies of those animals	9
Jas 2:26	For just as the body without the spirit is dead	9
3: 2	perfect, able to keep the whole body in check	9
3: 3	we guide their whole bodies.	9
3: 6	The tongue…stains the whole body	9
1Pe 2:24	He himself bore our sins in his body on the cross	9
3:21	not as a removal of dirt from the body	6
2Pe 1:13	I think it right, as long as I am in this body	8
Jde 1: 9	Michael…disputed about the body of Moses	9
1:23	hating even the tunic defiled by their bodies.	6

as a body
1. ἅπας, *hapas, 570*

Lke 23: 1	Then the assembly rose as a body	1

dead body
1. πτῶμα, *ptōma, 4773*

Rev 11: 8	their dead bodies will lie in the street	1
11: 9	members…gaze at their dead bodies and refuse	1

whole body
1. πᾶς, *pas, 4246*

Act 5:21	the council and the whole body of the elders	1

bold
1. ἀποτολμάω, *apotolmaō, 703*
2. θαρρέω, *tharreō, 2509*
3. παρρησία, *parrēsia, 4244*
4. τολμητής, *tolmētēs, 5532*

Rom 10:20	Isaiah is so bold as to say, "I have been found	1
2Co 10: 1	bold toward you when I am away!—	2
Phm 1: 8	For this reason, though I am bold enough in Christ	3
2Pe 2:10	Bold and willful, they are not afraid to slander	4

boldly See also declare boldly, speak boldly, speak out boldly
1. τολμάω, *tolmaō, 5528*

Mrk 15:43	went boldly to Pilate	1

rather boldly
1. τολμηρός, *tolmēros, 5529*

Rom 15:15	written to you rather boldly by way of reminder	1

boldness See also show boldness
1. παρρησία, *parrēsia, 4244*
2. τολμάω, *tolmaō, 5528*

Act 4:13	Now when they saw the boldness of Peter and John	1
4:29	to speak your word with all boldness	1
4:31	spoke the word of God with boldness.	1
28:31	teaching…with all boldness and without hindrance.	1
2Co 7: 4	we have such a hope, we act with great boldness	1
Eph 3:12	access to God in boldness and confidence through faith	1
6:19	to make known with boldness the mystery of the gospel	1
Php 1:14	dare to speak the word with greater boldness	2
1:20	that by my speaking with all boldness,	1
1Ti 3:13	great boldness in the faith that is in Christ	1
Heb 4:16	therefore approach the throne of grace with boldness	1
1Jn 3:21	we have boldness before God;	1
4:17	that we may have boldness on the day of judgment	1
5:14	this is the boldness we have in him	1

bombastic
1. ὑπέρογκος, *hyperonkos, 5665*

2Pe 2:18	For they speak bombastic nonsense,	1
Jde 1:16	bombastic in speech, flattering people	1

bond

1. δεσμός, *desmos, 1301*
2. σύνδεσμος, *syndesmos, 5278*

Lke　8:29　he would break the bonds　　　　1
Eph　4: 3　the unity of the Spirit in the bond of peace.　　2

bondage

1. δεσμός, *desmos, 1301*
2. δουλεία, *douleia, 1525*

Lke　13:16　set free from this bondage on the sabbath day?"　　1
Rom　8:21　creation...set free from its bondage to decay　　2

bone

1. ὀστέον, *osteon, 4014*

Mat　23:27　inside they are full of the bones of the dead　　1
Lke　24:39　a ghost does not have flesh and bones　　1
Jhn　19:36　"None of his bones shall be broken."　　1

book

1. αὐτός, *autos, 899*
2. βιβλίον, *biblion, 1046*
3. βίβλος, *biblos, 1047*
4. λόγος, *logos, 3364*
5. ὅς, *hos, 4005*

Mrk　12:26　have you not read in the book of Moses　　3
Lke　3: 4　as it is written in the book of...Isaiah　　3
　　　20:42　For David himself says in the book of Psalms　　3
Jhn　20:30　which are not written in this book.　　2
　　　21:25　the books that would be written.　　2
Act　1: 1　In the first book, Theophilus　　4
　　　1:20　"For it is written in the book of Psalms　　3
　　　7:42　as it is written in the book of the prophets:　　3
　　　19:19　collected their books and burned them publicly　　3
　　　19:19　the value of these books was calculated　　1
Gal　3:10　obey all the things written in the book of the law."　　2
Php　4: 3　whose names are in the book of life.　　3
2Ti　4:13　also the books, and above all the parchments.　　2
Heb　10: 7　(in the scroll of the book it is written of me)."　　2
Rev　1:11　saying, "Write in a book what you see and send it　　2
　　　3: 5　I will not blot your name out of the book of life;　　3
　　　13: 8　name has not been written...in the book of life　　2
　　　17: 8　names have not been written in the book of life　　2
　　　20:12　I saw the dead...and books were opened.　　2
　　　20:12　another book was opened, the book of life.　　2
　　　20:12　another book was opened, the book of life.　　5
　　　20:12　their works, as recorded in the books.　　2
　　　20:15　name was not found written in the book of life　　3
　　　21:27　only those...written in the Lamb's book of life.　　2
　　　22: 7　keeps the words of the prophecy of this book."　　2
　　　22: 9　with those who keep the words of this book.　　2
　　　22:10　the words of the prophecy of this book　　2
　　　22:18　hears the words of the prophecy of this book:　　2
　　　22:18　add to that person the plagues described in this book;　　2
　　　22:19　if anyone takes away from the words of the book　　2
　　　22:19　the holy city, which are described in this book.　　2

booth

1. σκηνοπηγία, *skēnopēgia, 5009*

Jhn　7: 2　Now the Jewish festival of Booths was near.　　1

tax booth

1. τελώνιον, *telōnion, 5468*

Mat　9: 9　a man called Matthew sitting at the tax booth;　　1
Mrk　2:14　son of Alphaeus sitting at the tax booth　　1
Lke　5:27　a tax collector...sitting at the tax booth;　　1

borrow

1. δανίζω, *danizō, 1247*

Mat　5:42　do not refuse anyone who wants to borrow from you.　　1

Bosor

1. Βοσόρ, *Bosor, 1082*

2Pe　2:15　the road of Balaam son of Bosor　　1

both

1. ἀμφότεροι, *amphoteroi, 317*
2. καί, *kai, 2779*
3. τέ, *te, 5445*

Mat　9:17　and so both are preserved."　　1
　　　10:28　rather fear him who can destroy both soul and body　　2
　　　13:30　Let both of them grow together until the harvest;　　1
　　　15:14　both will fall into a pit."　　1
　　　22:10　gathered all whom they found, both good and bad;　　3
Lke　1: 6　Both of them were righteous before God　　1
　　　1: 7　both were getting on in years.　　1
　　　5: 7　they came and filled both boats　　1
　　　6:39　Will not both fall into a pit?　　1
　　　7:42　not pay, he canceled the debts for both of them.　　1
　　　14: 9　who invited both of you may come and say to you　　2
　　　22:66　both chief priests and scribes　　3
Jhn　2:15　out of the temple, both the sheep and the cattle.　　3
　　　11:48　destroy both our holy place and our nation."　　2
　　　15:24　they have seen and hated both me and my Father.　　2
Act　2:10　visitors from Rome, both Jews and proselytes　　3
　　　2:29　he both died and was buried　　2
　　　2:33　he has poured out this that you both see and hear.　　2
　　　2:36　God has made him both Lord and Messiah　　2
　　　4:27　both Herod and Pontius Pilate, with the Gentiles　　3
　　　5:14　great numbers of both men and women　　3
　　　7:35　God now sent as both ruler and liberator　　2
　　　8: 3　dragging off both men and women　　3
　　　8:12　they were baptized, both men and women.　　3
　　　8:38　both of them, Philip and the eunuch, went down　　1
　　　10:39　both in Judea and in Jerusalem.　　3
　　　13:46　both Paul and Barnabas spoke out boldly, saying　　3
　　　14: 1　a great number of both Jews and Greeks　　3
　　　14: 5　an attempt was made by both Gentiles and Jews　　3
　　　15: 3　they passed through both Phoenicia and Samaria　　3
　　　19:10　both Jews and Greeks, heard the word　　3
　　　19:17　all residents of Ephesus, both Jews and Greeks　　3
　　　20:21　testified to both Jews and Greeks　　3
　　　22: 4　both men and women and putting them in prison　　3
　　　24:15　resurrection of both the righteous and the unrighteous.　　3
　　　25:24　petitioned me, both in Jerusalem and here　　3
　　　26:22　I stand here, testifying to both small and great　　3
　　　26:23　both to our people and to the Gentiles."　　3
　　　28:23　both from the law of Moses and from the prophets.　　3
Rom　1:12　by each other's faith, both yours and mine.　　3
　　　1:14　debtor both to Greeks and to barbarians　　3
　　　1:14　both to the wise and to the foolish　　3
　　　3: 9　all, both Jews and Greeks, are under...sin　　3
　　　14: 9　be Lord of both the dead and the living.　　2
1Co　1:24　to those who are the called, both Jews and Greeks　　3
　　　6:13　God will destroy both one and the other.　　2
　　　15:40　There are both heavenly bodies and earthly　　2
Eph　2:14　in his flesh he has made both groups into one　　1
　　　2:16　might reconcile both groups to God in one body　　1
　　　2:18　for through him both of us have access in one Spirit　　1
Php　1: 7　both in my imprisonment and in the defense　　3
　　　2:13　both to will and to work for his good pleasure.　　2
1Th　2:15　who killed both the Lord Jesus and the prophets　　2
1Ti　4:16　you will save both yourself and your hearers.　　2
Tit　1: 9　be able both to preach with sound doctrine　　2
Phm　1:16　both in the flesh and in the Lord.　　2
Heb　9:19　sprinkled both the scroll itself and all the people　　3
　　　9:21　both the tent and all the vessels used in worship.　　2
2Pe　3:18　glory both now and to the day of eternity. Amen.　　2
2Jn　1: 9　whoever abides...has both the Father and the Son.　　2
Rev　6:11　until the number...both of their fellow servants　　2
　　　13:16　all, both small and great, both rich and poor　　2
　　　13:16　all, both small and great, both rich and poor　　2
　　　13:16　both rich and poor, both free and slave　　2
　　　19:18　flesh of all, both free and slave,　　3
　　　19:18　flesh of all...both small and great."　　2

bother

1. κόπος + παρέχω, *kopos + parechō, 3160 + 4218*

Lke　11: 7　he answers from within, 'Do not bother me;　　1
　　　18: 5　yet because this widow keeps bothering me　　1

bottom

1. κάτω, *katō, 3004*

Mat　27:51　torn in two, from top to bottom.　　1
Mrk　15:38　torn in two, from top to bottom.　　1

bottomless *See* bottomless *pit*

bound for

1. διαπεράω, *diaperaō, 1385*
2. πλέω, *pleō, 4434*

Act 21: 2 When we found a ship bound for Phoenicia   1
    27: 6 an Alexandrian ship bound for Italy   2

boundary

1. ὁροθεσία, *horothesia, 3999*

Act 17:26 the boundaries of the places where they would live   1

boundless

1. ἀνεξιχνίαστος, *anexichniastos, 453*

Eph 3: 8 the news of the boundless riches of Christ   1

bountiful gift

1. εὐλογία, *eulogia, 2330*

2Co 9: 5 and arrange in advance for this bountiful gift   1

bountifully

1. ἐπί + εὐλογία, *epi + eulogia, 2093 + 2330*

2Co 9: 6 the one who sows bountifully will also reap   1
    9: 6 sows bountifully will also reap bountifully.   1

bow[1]

1. κάμπτω, *kamptō, 2828*
2. κλίνω, *klinō, 3111*

Lke 24: 5 bowed their faces to the ground   2
Jhn 19:30 he bowed his head and gave up his spirit.   2
Rom 11: 4 who have not bowed the knee to Baal."   1
    14:11 says the Lord, every knee shall bow to me   1
Eph 3:14 For this reason I bow my knees before the Father   1

bow[2]

1. τόξον, *toxon, 5534*

Rev 6: 2 I looked...a white horse! Its rider had a bow;   1

bow[3]

1. πρῷρα, *prōra, 4749*

Act 27:30 pretext of putting out anchors from the bow   1
    27:41 the bow stuck and remained immovable   1

bow down

1. πίπτω + ἐπί + πρόσωπον, *piptō + epi + prosōpon, 4406 + 2093 + 4725*
2. προσκυνέω, *proskyneō, 4686*
3. προσπίπτω, *prospiptō, 4700*

Mrk 5: 6 saw Jesus from a distance, he ran and bowed down   2
    7:25 and she came and bowed down at his feet.   3
1Co 14:25 person will bow down before God and worship   1
Rev 3: 9 make them come and bow down before your feet   2

bow in worship

1. προσκυνέω, *proskyneō, 4686*

Heb 11:21 "bowing in worship over the top of his staff."   1

bow to the ground

1. πίπτω, *piptō, 4406*

Lke 5:12 he bowed with his face to the ground and begged   1

bowels

1. σπλάγχνον, *splanchnon, 5073*

Act 1:18 all his bowels gushed out.   1

bowl

1. τρύβλιον, *tryblion, 5581*
2. φιάλη, *phialē, 5786*

Mat 26:23 who has dipped his hand into the bowl with me   1
Mrk 14:20 one who is dipping bread into the bowl with me.   1
Rev 5: 8 and golden bowls full of incense   2
    15: 7 seven golden bowls full of the wrath of God   2
    16: 1 pour out...the seven bowls of the wrath of God."   2
    16: 2 first angel went and poured his bowl on the earth   2
    16: 3 The second angel poured his bowl into the sea   2
    16: 4 The third angel poured his bowl into the rivers   2
    16: 8 The fourth angel poured his bowl on the sun   2
    16:10 The fifth angel poured his bowl on the throne   2

16:12 sixth angel poured his bowl on the great river   2
16:17 The seventh angel poured his bowl into the air   2
17: 1 one of the seven angels who had the seven bowls   2
21: 9 the seven bowls full of the seven last plagues   2

box

1. πυκτεύω, *pykteuō, 4782*

1Co 9:26 nor do I box as though beating the air;   1

boy *See also* little boy

1. Contextual: Not in Greek
2. αὐτός, *autos, 899*
3. παιδάριον, *paidarion, 4081*
4. παῖς, *pais, 4090*

Mat 17:18 and the boy was cured instantly.   4
Mrk 9:20 they brought the boy to him.   2
    9:20 immediately it convulsed the boy   2
    9:25 "You spirit that keeps this boy from speaking   1
    9:26 it came out, and the boy was like a corpse   1
Lke 2:43 the boy Jesus stayed behind in Jerusalem   4
    9:42 healed the boy, and gave him back to his father.   4
Jhn 6: 9 a boy here who has five barley loaves   3
Act 20:12 they had taken the boy away alive   4

brackish

1. πικρός, *pikros, 4395*

Jas 3:11 from the same opening both fresh and brackish water?   1

braid *See also* braided *hair*

1. ἐμπλοκή, *emplokē, 1862*

1Pe 3: 3 adorn yourselves outwardly by braiding your hair   1

bramble bush

1. βάτος[1], *batos[1], 1003*

Lke 6:44 nor are grapes picked from a bramble bush.   1

branch *See also* leafy branch

1. Contextual: Not in Greek
2. αὐτός, *autos, 899*
3. βάϊον, *baion, 961*
4. κλάδος, *klados, 3080*
5. κλῆμα, *klēma, 3097*

Mat 13:32 make nests in its branches."   4
    21: 8 others cut branches from the trees   4
    24:32 as soon as its branch becomes tender   4
Mrk 4:32 and puts forth large branches   4
    13:28 as soon as its branch becomes tender   4
Lke 13:19 the birds of the air made nests in its branches."   4
Jhn 12:13 they took branches of palm trees   3
    15: 2 removes every branch in me that bears no fruit.   5
    15: 2 Every branch that bears fruit he prunes   1
    15: 4 Just as the branch cannot bear fruit by itself   5
    15: 5 I am the vine, you are the branches.   5
    15: 6 is thrown away like a branch and withers;   5
    15: 6 branches are gathered, thrown into the fire   2
    19:29 sponge full of the wine on a branch of hyssop   1
Rom 11:16 if the root is holy, then the branches also are   4
    11:17 But if some of the branches were broken off   4
    11:18 do not boast over the branches.   4
    11:19 "Branches were broken off so that I might be   4
    11:21 For if God did not spare the natural branches   4
    11:24 will these natural branches be grafted back   1

palm branch

1. φοῖνιξ[1], *phoinix[1], 5836*

Rev 7: 9 in white, with palm branches in their hands.   1

brand mark

1. στίγμα, *stigma, 5116*

Gal 6:17 I carry the marks of Jesus branded on my body.   1

bread *See also* festival of unleavened bread, loaf of bread, piece of bread

1. Contextual: Not in Greek
2. ἄρτος, *artos, 788*

Mat 4: 4 written, 'One does not live by bread alone   2
    6:11 Give us this day our daily bread.   2
    7: 9 among you who, if your child asks for bread   2
    12: 4 and ate the bread of the Presence   2

15:33	"Where are we to get enough bread in the desert	2
16: 5	they had forgotten to bring any bread.	2
16: 7	because we have brought no bread."	2
16: 8	why are you talking about having no bread?	2
16:11	that I was not speaking about bread?	2
16:12	to beware of the yeast of bread	2
Mrk 2:26	ate the bread of the Presence	2
6: 8	no bread, no bag, no money in their belts;	2
6:37	and buy two hundred denarii worth of bread,	2
8: 4	feed these people with bread here in the desert?"	2
8:14	the disciples had forgotten to bring any bread;	2
8:16	"It is because we have no bread."	2
8:17	"Why are you talking about having no bread?	2
14:20	one who is dipping bread into the bowl with me.	1
Lke 4: 4	"It is written, 'One does not live by bread alone.' "	2
6: 4	took and ate the bread of the Presence	2
7:33	has come eating no bread and drinking no wine	2
9: 3	no staff, nor bag, nor bread, nor money	2
11: 3	Give us each day our daily bread.	2
14:15	anyone who will eat bread in the kingdom of God!"	2
15:17	hired hands have bread enough and to spare	2
24:30	When he was at the table with them, he took bread	2
24:35	made known to them in the breaking of the bread.	2
Jhn 6: 5	to buy bread for these people to eat?"	2
6: 7	"Six months' wages would not buy enough bread	2
6:23	the place where they had eaten the bread	2
6:31	'He gave them bread from heaven to eat.' "	2
6:32	not Moses who gave you the bread from heaven	2
6:32	my Father who gives you the true bread from heaven.	2
6:33	bread of God is that which comes down from heaven	2
6:34	said to him, "Sir, give us this bread always."	2
6:35	Jesus said to them, "I am the bread of life.	2
6:41	"I am the bread that came down from heaven."	2
6:48	I am the bread of life.	2
6:50	This is the bread that comes down from heaven	2
6:51	I am the living bread that came down from heaven.	2
6:51	Whoever eats of this bread will live forever;	2
6:51	the bread that I will give…is my flesh."	2
6:58	This is the bread that came down from heaven	2
6:58	one who eats this bread will live forever."	2
13:18	'The one who ate my bread	2
21: 9	a charcoal fire…with fish on it, and bread.	2
21:13	Jesus came and took the bread and gave it	2
Act 2:42	the breaking of bread and the prayers.	2
2:46	broke bread at home and ate their food with glad	2
20: 7	when we met to break bread	2
20:11	and after he had broken bread and eaten	2
27:35	After he had said this, he took bread;	2
1Co 10:16	The bread that we break	2
10:17	Because there is one bread, we who are many are one	2
10:17	we all partake of the one bread.	2
11:26	For as often as you eat this bread	2
11:27	Whoever, therefore, eats the bread	2
11:28	eat of the bread and drink of the cup.	2
2Co 9:10	supplies seed to the sower and bread for food	2
2Th 3: 8	we did not eat anyone's bread without paying	2
Heb 9: 2	the table, and the bread of the Presence;	2

unleavened bread

1. ἄζυμος, *azymos, 109*

Mat 26:17	On the first day of Unleavened Bread	1
Mrk 14:12	On the first day of Unleavened Bread	1
Lke 22: 1	Now the festival of Unleavened Bread,	1
22: 7	Then came the day of Unleavened Bread	1
Act 12: 3	(This was during the festival of Unleavened Bread.)	1
20: 6	we sailed…after the days of Unleavened Bread	1
1Co 5: 8	with the unleavened bread of sincerity	1

breadth

1. πλάτος, *platos, 4424*

Eph 3:18	what is the breadth and length and height	1
Rev 20: 9	They marched up over the breadth of the earth	1

break

1. βεβηλόω, *bebēloō, 1014*
2. διαρρήγνυμι, *diarrēgnymi, 1396*
3. κατάγνυμι, *katagnymi, 2862*
4. κατακλάω, *kataklaō, 2880*
5. κλάσις, *klasis, 3082*
6. κλάω, *klaō, 3089*

7.	λύω, *lyō, 3395*	
8.	παραβαίνω, *parabainō, 4124*	
9.	παράβασις, *parabasis, 4126*	
10.	παραβάτης, *parabatēs, 4127*	
11.	συνθρύπτω, *synthryptō, 5316*	
12.	συντρίβω, *syntribō, 5341*	

Mat 5:19	breaks one of the least of these commandments	7
12: 5	priests in the temple break the sabbath	1
12:20	He will not break a bruised reed	3
14:19	broke the loaves, and gave them to the disciples	6
15: 2	"Why do your disciples break the tradition	8
15: 3	"And why do you break the commandment of God	8
15:36	giving thanks he broke them and gave them	6
26:26	loaf of bread, and after blessing it he broke it	6
Mrk 6:41	blessed and broke the loaves	4
8: 6	and after giving thanks he broke them	6
8:19	I broke the five loaves for the five thousand	6
14:22	and after blessing it he broke it, gave it	6
Lke 5: 6	that their nets were beginning to break.	2
8:29	he would break the bonds	2
9:16	he looked up to heaven, and blessed and broke them	4
22:19	when he had given thanks, he broke it and gave it	6
24:30	blessed and broke it, and gave it to them.	6
24:35	made known to them in the breaking of the bread.	5
Jhn 5:18	because he was not only breaking the sabbath	7
7:23	that the law of Moses may not be broken	7
19:31	to have the legs of the crucified men broken	3
19:32	the soldiers came and broke the legs of the first	3
19:33	they did not break his legs.	3
19:36	"None of his bones shall be broken."	12
Act 2:42	the breaking of bread and the prayers.	5
2:46	broke bread at home and ate their food with glad	6
20: 7	when we met to break bread	6
20:11	and after he had broken bread and eaten	6
21:13	"What are you doing, weeping and breaking my heart?	11
27:35	he broke it and began to eat.	6
Rom 2:23	do you dishonor God by breaking the law?	9
2:25	if you break the law, your circumcision has become	10
2:27	you that have…circumcision but break the law.	10
1Co 10:16	The bread that we break	6
11:24	when he had given thanks, he broke it and said	6
Rev 5: 2	to open the scroll and break its seals?"	7

break down

1. ἐπιβάλλω, *epiballō, 2095*
2. λύω, *lyō, 3395*

Mrk 14:72	he broke down and wept.	1
Eph 2:14	broken down the dividing wall, that is, the hostility	2

break in

1. διορύσσω, *dioryssō, 1482*

Mat 6:19	consume and where thieves break in and steal;	1
6:20	where thieves do not break in and steal.	1

break in pieces

1. συντρίβω, *syntribō, 5341*

Mrk 5: 4	the shackles he broke in pieces;	1

break into

1. διορύσσω, *dioryssō, 1482*

Mat 24:43	would not have let his house be broken into.	1
Lke 12:39	he would not have let his house be broken into.	1

break off

1. ἐκκλάω, *ekklaō, 1709*

Rom 11:17	But if some of the branches were broken off	1
11:19	"Branches were broken off so that I might be	1
11:20	They were broken off because of their unbelief	1

break open

1. συντρίβω, *syntribō, 5341*

Mrk 14: 3	she broke open the jar and poured the ointment	1

break out

1. γίνομαι, *ginomai, 1181*

Act 19:23	no little disturbance broke out concerning the Way.	1
Rev 12: 7	And war broke out in heaven; Michael and his angels	1

break to pieces

1. συνθλάω, *synthlaō, 5314*

Mat 21:44 will be broken to pieces   1
Lke 20:18 will be broken to pieces;   1

break up

1. λύω, *lyō, 3395*

Act 13:43 When the meeting of the synagogue broke up   1
     27:41 the stern was being broken up by...the waves.   1

break upon

1. ἐπισκέπτομαι, *episkeptomai, 2170*

Lke   1:78 the dawn from on high will break upon us   1

breakfast

1. ἀριστάω, *aristaō, 753*

Jhn 21:12 Jesus said to them, "Come and have breakfast."   1
     21:15 When they had finished breakfast   1

breast

1. Contextual: Not in Greek
2. μαστός, *mastos, 3466*
3. στῆθος, *stēthos, 5111*

Lke 11:27 the breasts that nursed you!"   2
     18:13 beating his breast and saying, 'God, be merciful   3
     23:27 were beating their breasts and wailing for him.   1
     23:29 and the breasts that never nursed.'   2
     23:48 they returned home, beating their breasts.   3

breastplate

1. θώραξ, *thōrax, 2606*

Eph   6:14 put on the breastplate of righteousness.   1
1Th   5: 8 put on the breastplate of faith and love   1
Rev   9: 9 they had scales like iron breastplates   1
     9:17 the riders wore breastplates the color of fire   1

breath

1. πνεῦμα, *pneuma, 4460*
2. πνοή, *pnoē, 4466*

Act 17:25 gives to all mortals life and breath and all things.   2
2Th   2: 8 Jesus will destroy with the breath of his mouth   1
Rev 11:11 the breath of life from God entered them   1
     13:15 allowed to give breath to the image of the beast   1

breathe

1. ἐμπνέω, *empneō, 1863*

Act   9: 1 Saul, still breathing threats and murder   1

breathe on

1. ἐμφυσάω, *emphysaō, 1874*

Jhn 20:22 he had said this, he breathed on them and said   1

breathe one's last

1. ἀφίημι + ὁ + πνεῦμα, *aphiēmi + ho + pneuma, 918 + 3836 + 4460*
2. ἐκπνέω, *ekpneō, 1743*

Mat 27:50 Jesus cried...and breathed his last.   1
Mrk 15:37 Jesus gave a loud cry and breathed his last.   2
     15:39 saw that in this way he breathed his last   2
Lke 23:46 Having said this, he breathed his last.   2

breed

1. γεννάω, *gennaō, 1164*

2Ti   2:23 you know that they breed quarrels.   1

bride

1. γυνή, *gynē, 1222*
2. νύμφη, *nymphē, 3811*

Jhn   3:29 He who has the bride is the bridegroom.   2
Rev 18:23 the voice of bridegroom and bride will be heard   2
     19: 7 and his bride has made herself ready;   1
     21: 2 prepared as a bride adorned for her husband.   2
     21: 9 I will show you the bride, the wife of the Lamb."   2
     22:17 The Spirit and the bride say, "Come."   2

bridegroom

1. νυμφίος, *nymphios, 3812*

Mat   9:15 as long as the bridegroom is with them   1

     9:15 The days will come when the bridegroom is taken   1
     25: 1 went to meet the bridegroom.   1
     25: 5 As the bridegroom was delayed   1
     25: 6 Here is the bridegroom! Come out to meet him.'   1
     25:10 while they went to buy it, the bridegroom came   1
Mrk   2:19 while the bridegroom is with them   1
     2:19 As long as they have the bridegroom with them   1
     2:20 when the bridegroom is taken away from them   1
Lke   5:34 while the bridegroom is with them   1
     5:35 when the bridegroom will be taken away from them   1
Jhn   2: 9 the steward called the bridegroom   1
     3:29 He who has the bride is the bridegroom.   1
     3:29 friend of the bridegroom...rejoices greatly   1
     3:29 rejoices greatly at the bridegroom's voice.   1
Rev 18:23 the voice of bridegroom and bride will be heard   1

bridesmaid

1. παρθένος, *parthenos, 4221*

Mat 25: 1 Ten bridesmaids took their lamps   1
     25: 7 Then all those bridesmaids got up   1
     25:11 Later the other bridesmaids came also, saying   1

bridle   *See also* keep in check with a bridle

1. χαλιναγωγέω, *chalinagōgeō, 5902*
2. χαλινός, *chalinos, 5903*

Jas   1:26 If any...do not bridle their tongues   1
Rev 14:20 blood flowed...as high as a horse's bridle   2

briefly

1. βραχύς, *brachys, 1099*
2. συντόμως, *syntomōs, 5339*
3. ὥρα, *hōra, 6052*

Mrk 16: S [[they told briefly to those around Peter]]   2
Act 24: 4 to hear us briefly with your customary graciousness.   2
2Co   7: 8 grieved you with that letter, though only briefly).   3
Heb 13:22 I have written to you briefly.   1

bright   *See also* bright red, make bright

1. λαμπρός, *lampros, 3287*
2. λαμπρότης, *lamprotēs, 3288*
3. φωτεινός, *phōteinos, 5893*

Mat 17: 5 suddenly a bright cloud overshadowed them   3
Act 26:13 a light...brighter than the sun   2
Rev 15: 6 seven angels...robed in pure bright linen   1
     19: 8 clothed with fine linen, bright and pure"   1
     22: 1 river of the water of life, bright as crystal   1
     22:16 the descendant of David, the bright morning star."   1

brightness

1. δόξα, *doxa, 1518*

Act 22:11 not see because of the brightness of that light   1

brim

1. ἄνω, *anō, 539*

Jhn   2: 7 And they filled them up to the brim.   1

bring

1. Contextual: Not in Greek
2. ἄγω, *agō, 72*
3. ἀπάγω, *apagō, 552*
4. ἀποφέρω, *apopherō, 708*
5. βάλλω, *ballō, 965*
6. βαστάζω, *bastazō, 1002*
7. γεννάω, *gennaō, 1164*
8. γίνομαι, *ginomai, 1181*
9. δίδωμι, *didōmi, 1443*
10. εἰς, *eis, 1650*
11. εἰσφέρω, *eispherō, 1662*
12. ἐκβάλλω, *ekballō, 1675*
13. ἐπιφέρω, *epipherō, 2214*
14. ἔχω, *echō, 2400*
15. κατάγω, *katagō, 2864*
16. κατεργάζομαι, *katergazomai, 2981*
17. κομίζω, *komizō, 3152*
18. λαμβάνω, *lambanō, 3284*
19. μεταπέμπω, *metapempō, 3569*
20. παραλαμβάνω, *paralambanō, 4161*
21. παρέχω, *parechō, 4218*

22. περιφέρω, *peripherō, 4367*
23. ποιέω, *poieō, 4472*
24. προάγω, *proagō, 4575*
25. προπέμπω, *propempō, 4636*
26. προσάγω, *prosagō, 4642*
27. προσφέρω, *prospherō, 4712*
28. φέρω, *pherō, 5770*

Mat	4:24	all Syria, and they brought to him all the sick	27
	6:13	do not bring us to the time of trial, but rescue us	11
	6:34	for tomorrow will bring worries of its own.	1
	8:16	That evening they brought to him many	27
	9:32	a demoniac who was mute was brought to him.	27
	10:34	"Do not think that I have come to bring peace	5
	10:34	I have not come to bring peace, but a sword.	5
	12:20	until he brings justice to victory.	12
	12:22	Then they brought to him a demoniac who was blind	27
	14:11	The head was brought on a platter	28
	14:11	who brought it to her mother.	28
	14:18	he said, "Bring them here to me."	28
	14:35	and brought all who were sick to him	27
	15:30	crowds came to him, bringing with them the lame	14
	16: 5	they had forgotten to bring any bread.	18
	16: 7	because we have brought no bread."	18
	17:16	I brought him to your disciples	27
	17:17	Bring him here to me."	28
	18:24	one who owed him ten thousand talents was brought	27
	19:13	spoke sternly to those who brought them	1
	21: 2	untie them and bring them to me.	2
	21: 7	they brought the donkey and the colt	2
	22:19	And they brought him a denarius.	27
	25:20	bringing five more talents, saying	27
Mrk	1:32	they brought to him all who were sick	28
	2: 3	people came, bringing to him a paralyzed man	28
	6:27	with orders to bring John's head.	28
	6:28	brought his head on a platter	28
	6:55	began to bring the sick on mats	22
	7:32	They brought to him a deaf man who	28
	8:14	the disciples had forgotten to bring any bread;	18
	8:22	Some people brought a blind man to him	28
	9:17	I brought you my son; he has a spirit	28
	9:19	must I put up with you? Bring him to me."	28
	9:20	they brought the boy to him.	28
	11: 2	untie it and bring it.	28
	11: 7	they brought the colt to Jesus	28
	12:15	Bring me a denarius and let me see it."	28
	12:16	they brought one.	28
	15:22	they brought Jesus to the place called Golgotha	28
Lke	4:40	brought them to him;	2
	5:11	When they had brought their boats to shore	15
	7:37	a woman...brought an alabaster jar of ointment.	17
	9:41	Bring your son here."	26
	10:34	brought him to an inn, and took care of him.	2
	11:26	Then it goes and brings seven other spirits	20
	12:11	When they bring you before the synagogues	11
	12:49	"I came to bring fire to the earth	5
	12:51	that I have come to bring peace to the earth?	9
	18:40	Jesus...ordered the man to be brought to him	2
	19:27	bring them here and slaughter them in my presence.' "	2
	19:30	Untie it and bring it here.	2
	19:35	they brought it to Jesus;	2
	21:12	you will be brought before kings and governors	3
	22:66	they brought him to their council.	3
	23: 1	brought Jesus before Pilate.	2
	23:14	said to them, "You brought me this man	27
Jhn	1:42	He brought Simon to Jesus, who looked at him	2
	4:33	no one has brought him something to eat?"	28
	8: 3	⟦The scribes and the Pharisees brought a woman⟧	2
	9:13	They brought to the Pharisees the man	2
	10:16	I must bring them also	2
	16:21	having brought a human being into the world.	7
	18: 3	So Judas brought a detachment of soldiers	18
	18:29	"What accusation do you bring against this man?"	28
	19: 4	"Look, I am bringing him out to you	2
	19:13	he brought Jesus outside	2
	19:39	came, bringing a mixture of myrrh and aloes	28
	21:10	"Bring some of the fish that you have just caught."	28
Act	4:34	brought the proceeds of what was sold.	28
	4:37	brought the money	28
	5: 2	brought only a part	28
	5:16	bringing the sick	28

	5:21	sent to the prison to have them brought.	2
	5:26	captain went with the temple police and brought them	2
	5:27	When they had brought them	2
	6:12	seized him, and brought him before the council.	2
	9: 2	he might bring them bound to Jerusalem.	2
	9:15	an instrument whom I have chosen to bring my name	6
	9:21	bringing them bound before the chief priests?"	2
	9:27	Barnabas took him, brought him to the apostles	2
	11:13	'Send to Joppa and bring Simon, who is called Peter;	19
	11:26	when he had found him, he brought him to Antioch.	2
	13:23	brought to Israel a Savior, Jesus, as he promised;	2
	13:47	bring salvation to the ends of the earth.' "	1
	14:13	brought oxen and garlands to the gates;	28
	15: 3	brought great joy to all the believers.	23
	16:16	brought her owners a great deal of money	21
	16:30	brought them outside and said	24
	17:15	who conducted Paul brought him as far as Athens;	2
	17:19	brought him to the Areopagus and asked	2
	18:12	brought him before the tribunal.	2
	19:12	had touched his skin were brought to the sick	4
	19:24	brought no little business to the artisans.	21
	19:27	that brought all Asia and the world to worship	1
	19:37	You have brought these men here	2
	20:38	they brought him to the ship.	25
	21:16	brought us to the house of Mnason of Cyprus	2
	21:34	he ordered him to be brought into the barracks.	2
	23:10	bring him into the barracks.	2
	23:18	took him, brought him to the tribune, and said	2
	23:18	Paul...asked me to bring this young man to you;	2
	23:28	I had him brought to their council.	15
	23:31	and brought him during the night to Antipatris.	2
	24:17	to bring alms to my nation and to offer sacrifices.	23
	25: 6	ordered Paul to be brought.	2
	25:17	and ordered the man to be brought.	2
	25:23	Festus gave the order and Paul was brought in.	2
Rom	4:15	For the law brings wrath;	16
	5:16	following one trespass brought condemnation	10
	5:16	but the free gift...brings justification.	10
	7:13	Did what is good, then, bring death to me?	8
Eph	2:13	have been brought near by the blood of Christ.	8
1Th	4:14	God will bring with him those who have died.	2
2Ti	4:11	Get Mark and bring him with you	2
	4:13	bring the cloak that I left with Carpus at Troas	28
Tit	2:11	has appeared, bringing salvation to all,	1
Heb	2:10	in bringing many children to glory	2
	10:35	confidence of yours; it brings a great reward.	14
Jas	4:14	you do not even know what tomorrow will bring	1
1Pe	1:13	the grace that Jesus Christ will bring you	28
	3:18	Christ also suffered...in order to bring you to God.	26
2Pe	2:11	do not bring against them a slanderous judgment	28
2Jn	1:10	comes to you and does not bring this teaching;	28
Jde	1: 9	to bring a condemnation of slander against him	13
Rev	21:24	the kings of the earth will bring their glory	28
	21:26	bring into it the glory...of the nations.	28

bring a charge

1. διαβάλλω, *diaballō, 1330*

Lke 16: 1 and charges were brought to him   1

bring a charge against

1. ἐγκαλέω, *enkaleō, 1592*
2. κατηγορέω, *katēgoreō, 2989*

Mrk	15: 4	See how many charges they bring against you."	2
Jhn	8: 6	⟦might have some charge to bring against him.⟧	2
Act	19:38	let them bring charges there against one another.	1
	24:13	the charge that they now bring against me.	2
	28:19	I had no charge to bring against my nation.	2
Rom	8:33	Who will bring any charge against God's elect?	1

bring about

1. δείκνυμι, *deiknymi, 1259*
2. εἰς, *eis, 1650*

Rom	1: 5	to bring about the obedience of faith	2
	16:26	to bring about the obedience of faith—	2
1Ti	6:15	which he will bring about at the right time	1

bring about death

1. θανατόω, *thanatoō, 2506*

Mat 27: 1 against Jesus in order to bring about his death.   1

bring against
1. καταφέρω, *katapherō, 2965*

Act 25: 7 bringing many serious charges against him 1

bring along
1. παραλαμβάνω, *paralambanō, 4161*

Mat 12:45 it goes and brings along seven other spirits 1

bring back
1. ἄγω, *agō, 72*
2. ἀνάγω, *anagō, 343*
3. ἐπιστρέφω, *epistrephō, 2188*
4. μετατίθημι, *metatithēmi, 3572*
5. στρέφω, *strephō, 5138*

Mat 27: 3 he repented and brought back the thirty pieces 5
Act 7:16 their bodies were brought back to Shechem 4
22: 5 to bring them back to Jerusalem for punishment 1
Heb 13:20 who brought back from the dead our Lord Jesus 2
Jas 5:19 wanders…and is brought back by another 3
5:20 you should know that whoever brings back a sinner 3

bring before
1. προάγω, *proagō, 4575*
2. προσάγω, *prosagō, 4642*

Act 16:20 When they had brought them before the magistrates 2
25:26 Therefore I have brought him before all of you 1

bring close
1. παρίστημι, *paristēmi, 4225*

1Co 8: 8 "Food will not bring us close to God." 1

bring down
1. καθαιρέω, *kathaireō, 2747*
2. καταβαίνω, *katabainō, 2849*
3. κατάγω, *katagō, 2864*

Mat 11:23 No, you will be brought down to Hades. 2
Lke 1:52 brought down the powerful from their thrones 1
10:15 No, you will be brought down to Hades. 2
Act 9:30 they brought him down to Caesarea 3
22:30 He brought Paul down and had him stand before them. 3
23:15 must notify the tribune to bring him down 3
23:20 to bring Paul down to the council tomorrow 3
Rom 10: 6 (that is, to bring Christ down) 3

bring forth
1. δίδωμι, *didōmi, 1443*

Mat 13: 8 and brought forth grain 1
Mrk 4: 8 seed fell into good soil and brought forth grain 1

bring good news
1. εὐαγγελίζω, *euangelizō, 2294*

Mat 11: 5 and the poor have good news brought to them. 1
Lke 1:19 and to bring you this good news. 1
2:10 see—I am bringing you good news of great joy 1
4:18 he has anointed me to bring good news to the poor. 1
7:22 the poor have good news brought to them. 1
8: 1 bringing the good news of the kingdom of God. 1
9: 6 bringing the good news and curing diseases 1
Act 13:32 we bring you the good news 1
14:15 We are mortals…and we bring you good news 1
Rom 10:15 the feet of those who bring good news!" 1
1Th 3: 6 Timothy…has brought us the good news 1
1Pe 1:12 who brought you good news by the Holy Spirit 1

bring in
1. εἰσάγω, *eisagō, 1652*
2. εἰσφέρω, *eispherō, 1662*
3. ἔρχομαι, *erchomai, 2262*

Mrk 4:21 "Is a lamp brought in to be put under the bushel 3
Lke 2:27 when the parents brought in the child Jesus 1
5:18 trying to bring him in and lay him before Jesus; 2
5:19 no way to bring him in because of the crowd 2
14:21 bring in the poor, the crippled, the blind, 1
Jhn 18:16 went out…and brought Peter in. 1
Act 7:45 Our ancestors in turn brought it in with Joshua 1

bring in secretly
1. παρεισάγω, *pareisagō, 4206*
2. παρείσακτος, *pareisaktos, 4207*

Gal 2: 4 because of false believers secretly brought in 2
2Pe 2: 1 secretly bring in destructive opinions. 1

bring into
1. εἰσάγω, *eisagō, 1652*
2. εἰσφέρω, *eispherō, 1662*

Lke 22:54 bringing him into the high priest's house. 1
Act 9: 8 brought him into Damascus. 1
21:28 he has actually brought Greeks into the temple 1
21:29 Paul had brought him into the temple. 1
21:37 Paul was about to be brought into the barracks 1
22:24 directed that he was to be brought into the barracks 1
1Ti 6: 7 for we brought nothing into the world 2
Heb 1: 6 when he brings the firstborn into the world 1
13:11 whose blood is brought into the sanctuary 2

bring into one's presence
1. παρίστημι, *paristēmi, 4225*

2Co 4:14 and will bring us with you into his presence. 1

bring low
1. ταπείνωσις, *tapeinōsis, 5428*

Jas 1:10 and the rich in being brought low 1

bring no regret
1. ἀμεταμέλητος, *ametamelētos, 294*

2Co 7:10 that leads to salvation and brings no regret 1

bring on
1. ἐπάγω, *epagō, 2042*

Act 5:28 you are determined to bring this man's blood on us." 1
2Pe 2: 1 bringing swift destruction on themselves. 1
2: 5 he brought a flood on a world of the ungodly; 1

bring on blindness
1. τυφλόω, *typhloō, 5604*

1Jn 2:11 because the darkness has brought on blindness. 1

bring out
1. ἀνάγω, *anagō, 343*
2. ἐκβάλλω, *ekballō, 1675*
3. ἐκφέρω, *ekpherō, 1766*
4. ἐξάγω, *exagō, 1974*
5. προάγω, *proagō, 4575*

Mat 12:35 brings good things out of a good treasure 2
12:35 brings evil things out of an evil treasure. 2
13:52 master of a household who brings out of his treasure 2
Lke 15:22 'Quickly, bring out a robe—the best one— 3
Jhn 10: 4 When he has brought out all his own 2
Act 5:19 an angel…brought them out, and said 4
12: 4 intending to bring him out to the people 1
12: 6 before Herod was going to bring him out 5
12:17 how the Lord had brought him out of the prison. 4
17: 5 Paul and Silas to bring them out to the assembly 5

bring safely
1. διασῴζω, *diasōzō, 1407*

Act 27:44 so it was that all were brought safely to land. 1

bring the news
1. εὐαγγελίζω, *euangelizō, 2294*

Eph 3: 8 to bring to the Gentiles the news 1

bring to
1. εἰσφέρω, *eispherō, 1662*
2. προστίθημι, *prostithēmi, 4707*
3. προσφέρω, *prospherō, 4712*

Mat 19:13 Then little children were being brought to him 3
Mrk 2: 4 when they could not bring him to Jesus 3
10:13 People were bringing little children to him 3
Lke 11: 4 do not bring us to the time of trial." 1
18:15 People were bringing even infants to him 3
Act 11:24 a great many people were brought to the Lord. 2

bring to completion
1. ἐπιτελέω, *epiteleō, 2200*
2. τελειόω, *teleioō, 5457*

Php   1: 6 will bring it to completion by the day   1
Jas   2:22 and faith was brought to completion by the works.   2

bring to life

1. ζάω, *zaō, 2409*

Rom   6:13 as those who have been brought from death to life   1

bring to light

1. φωτίζω, *phōtizō, 5894*

1Co   4: 5 who will bring to light the things now hidden   1
2Ti   1:10 brought life and immortality to light   1

bring to trial

1. ἄγω, *agō, 72*

Mrk 13:11 When they bring you to trial and hand you over   1

bring up

1. ἀνάγω, *anagō, 343*
2. ἀνατρέφω, *anatrephō, 427*
3. ἐκτρέφω, *ektrephō, 1763*
4. τρέφω, *trephō, 5555*

Lke   2:22 they brought him up to Jerusalem to present him   1
      4:16 to Nazareth, where he had been brought up   4
Act   7:20 three months he was brought up in his father's house;   2
      7:21 and brought him up as her own son.   2
     16:34 He brought them up into the house   1
      22: 3 brought up in this city at the feet of Gamaliel   2
Rom 10: 7 (that is, to bring Christ up from the dead).   1
Eph   6: 4 bring them up in the discipline...of the Lord.   3

bring up a child

1. τεκνοτροφέω, *teknotropheō, 5452*

1Ti   5:10 as one who has brought up children   1

bring with

1. συμπαραλαμβάνω, *symparalambanō, 5221*

Act 12:25 brought with them John   1

bring word

1. ἀπαγγέλλω, *apangellō, 550*

Mat   2: 8 and when you have found him, bring me word   1

broad   *See* make broad

broil

1. ὀπτός, *optos, 3966*

Lke 24:42 They gave him a piece of broiled fish   1

broken   *See* broken *piece*

bronze   *See also* bronze *kettle*

1. χαλκός, *chalkos, 5910*
2. χαλκοῦς, *chalkous, 5911*

Rev   9:20 demons and idols of gold and silver and bronze   2
     18:12 articles of costly wood, bronze, iron, and marble   1

burnished bronze

1. χαλκολίβανον, *chalkolibanon, 5909*

Rev   1:15 his feet were like burnished bronze   1
      2:18 and whose feet are like burnished bronze: 1

brood

1. γέννημα, *gennēma, 1165*
2. νοσσιά, *nossia, 3799*
3. νοσσίον, *nossion, 3800*

Mat   3: 7 "You brood of vipers! Who warned you to flee   1
     12:34 You brood of vipers! How can you speak good   1
     23:33 You snakes, you brood of vipers!   1
     23:37 as a hen gathers her brood under her wings   3
Lke   3: 7 "You brood of vipers!   1
     13:34 as a hen gathers her brood under her wings   2

brother   *See also* false brother and sister, love of the brother and sister, Twin Brothers

1. ἀδελφός, *adelphos, 81*

Mat   1: 2 Jacob the father of Judah and his brothers   1
      1:11 Josiah the father of Jechoniah and his brothers   1
      4:18 he saw two brothers, Simon, who is called Peter   1

      4:18 Simon, who is called Peter, and Andrew his brother   1
      4:21 went from there, he saw two other brothers   1
      4:21 James son of Zebedee and his brother John   1
     10: 2 and his brother Andrew;   1
     10: 2 James son of Zebedee, and his brother John;   1
     10:21 Brother will betray brother to death   1
     10:21 Brother will betray brother to death   1
     12:46 his mother and his brothers were standing   1
     12:47 "Look, your mother and your brothers are standing   1
     12:48 "Who is my mother, and who are my brothers?"   1
     12:49 he said, "Here are my mother and my brothers!   1
     12:50 is my brother and sister and mother."   1
     13:55 are not his brothers James and Joseph and Simon   1
     14: 3 Herodias, his brother Philip's wife   1
     17: 1 Peter and James and his brother John   1
     19:29 everyone who has left houses or brothers   1
     20:24 they were angry with the two brothers.   1
     22:24 his brother shall marry the widow   1
     22:24 raise up children for his brother.'   1
     22:25 Now there were seven brothers among us;   1
     22:25 childless, leaving the widow to his brother.   1
     28:10 go and tell my brothers to go to Galilee;   1
Mrk   1:16 saw Simon and his brother Andrew casting a net   1
      1:19 James son of Zebedee and his brother John   1
      3:17 John the brother of James   1
      3:31 his mother and his brothers came;   1
      3:32 "Your mother and your brothers and sisters   1
      3:33 he replied, "Who are my mother and my brothers?"   1
      3:34 he said, "Here are my mother and my brothers!   1
      3:35 Whoever does the will of God is my brother   1
      5:37 Peter, James, and John, the brother of James.   1
      6: 3 brother of James and Joses and Judas and Simon   1
      6:17 Herodias, his brother Philip's wife   1
      6:18 not lawful for you to have your brother's wife."   1
     10:29 there is no one who has left house or brothers   1
     10:30 houses, brothers and sisters, mothers   1
     12:19 if a man's brother dies, leaving a wife   1
     12:19 and raise up children for his brother.   1
     12:20 There were seven brothers; the first married   1
     13:12 Brother will betray brother to death   1
     13:12 Brother will betray brother to death   1
Lke   3: 1 brother Philip ruler of the region   1
      3:19 Herodias, his brother's wife   1
      6:14 Simon, whom he named Peter, and his brother Andrew   1
      8:19 Then his mother and his brothers came to him   1
      8:20 he was told, "Your mother and your brothers   1
      8:21 "My mother and my brothers are those who hear   1
     12:13 tell my brother to divide the family inheritance   1
     14:12 do not invite your friends or your brothers   1
     14:26 wife and children, brothers and sisters   1
     15:27 He replied, 'Your brother has come   1
     15:32 brother of yours was dead and has come to life;   1
     16:28 for I have five brothers—that he may warn them   1
     18:29 house or wife or brothers or parents or children   1
     20:28 Moses wrote for us that if a man's brother dies   1
     20:28 raise up children for his brother.   1
     20:29 Now there were seven brothers;   1
     21:16 even by parents and brothers, by relatives   1
     22:32 strengthen your brothers."   1
Jhn   1:40 One...was Andrew, Simon Peter's brother.   1
      1:41 He first found his brother Simon and said to him   1
      2:12 with his mother, his brothers   1
      6: 8 Andrew, Simon Peter's brother, said to him   1
      7: 3 his brothers said to him, "Leave here   1
      7: 5 (For not even his brothers believed in him.)   1
      7:10 after his brothers had gone to the festival   1
     11: 2 Mary was the one...her brother Lazarus was ill.   1
     11:19 to console them about their brother.   1
     11:21 my brother would not have died.   1
     11:23 Jesus said to her, "Your brother will rise again."   1
     11:32 my brother would not have died.   1
     20:17 go to my brothers and say to them   1
Act   1:14 Mary the mother of Jesus, as well as his brothers.   1
      2:37 "Brothers, what should we do?"   1
      7: 2 Stephen replied: "Brothers and fathers, listen   1
      7:13 Joseph made himself known to his brothers   1
      7:26 you are brothers; why do you wrong each other?'   1
      9:17 laid his hands on Saul and said, "Brother Saul   1
     11:12 These six brothers also accompanied me   1
     12: 2 James, the brother of John, killed with the sword.   1
     13:15 "Brothers, if you have any word of exhortation   1

Act	13:26	brothers, you descendants of Abraham's family	1
	13:38	Let it be known to you therefore, my brothers	1
	14: 2	poisoned their minds against the brothers.	1
	15: 1	were teaching the brothers	1
	15: 7	Peter stood up and said to them, "My brothers	1
	15:13	"My brothers, listen to me.	1
	15:22	leaders among the brothers	1
	15:23	"The brothers, both the apostles and the elders	1
	21:17	the brothers welcomed us warmly.	1
	21:20	they said to him, "You see, brother	1
	22: 1	"Brothers and fathers, listen to the defense	1
	22: 5	From them I also received letters to the brothers	1
	22:13	'Brother Saul, regain your sight!'	1
	23: 1	"Brothers, up to this day I have lived my life	1
	23: 5	"I did not realize, brothers, that he was high priest;	1
	23: 6	"Brothers, I am a Pharisee, a son of Pharisees.	1
	28:17	they had assembled, he said to them, "Brothers	1
	28:21	none of the brothers coming here has reported	1
Rom	16:23	Erastus…and our brother Quartus, greet you.	1
1Co	1: 1	Paul…and our brother Sosthenes	1
	7:15	in such a case the brother or sister is not bound.	1
	9: 5	other apostles and the brothers of the Lord	1
	16:11	I am expecting him with the brothers.	1
	16:12	Now concerning our brother Apollos	1
	16:12	to visit you with the other brothers	1
2Co	1: 1	Paul…and Timothy our brother	1
	2:13	because I did not find my brother Titus there.	1
	8:18	With him we are sending the brother who is famous	1
	8:22	with them we are sending our brother	1
	8:23	as for our brothers, they are messengers	1
	9: 3	I am sending the brothers	1
	9: 5	necessary to urge the brothers to go on ahead to you	1
	12:18	I urged Titus to go, and sent the brother with him.	1
Gal	1:19	except James the Lord's brother.	1
Eph	6:21	Tychicus…a dear brother and a faithful minister	1
Php	2:25	Epaphroditus—my brother and co-worker	1
Col	1: 1	Paul, an apostle…and Timothy our brother	1
	4: 7	he is a beloved brother, a faithful minister	1
	4: 9	Onesimus, the faithful and beloved brother	1
1Th	3: 2	we sent Timothy, our brother and co-worker for God	1
1Ti	5: 1	speak…to younger men as brothers	1
Phm	1: 1	Paul…and Timothy our brother	1
	1: 7	I have indeed received much joy…my brother.	1
	1:16	a beloved brother—especially to me	1
	1:20	Yes, brother, let me have this benefit from you	1
Heb	13:23	our brother Timothy has been set free;	1
Jas	2:15	If a brother or sister is naked	1
1Pe	5:12	Silvanus, whom I consider a faithful brother,	1
2Pe	3:15	So also our beloved brother Paul wrote to you	1
1Jn	3:12	not be like Cain who…murdered his brother.	1
	3:12	deeds were evil and his brother's righteous.	1
Jde	1: 1	Jude, a servant of Jesus…and brother of James	1
Rev	1: 9	I, John, your brother who share with you in Jesus	1

brother and/or sister

1. ἀδελφός, *adelphos, 81*
2. ἀδελφότης, *adelphotēs, 82*

Mat	5:22	angry with a brother or sister, you will be liable	1
	5:22	and if you insult a brother or sister	1
	5:23	that your brother or sister has something against you	1
	5:24	first be reconciled to your brother or sister	1
	5:47	And if you greet only your brothers and sisters	1
	18:35	forgive your brother or sister from your heart."	1
Act	16:40	had seen and encouraged the brothers and sisters	1
Rom	1:13	I want you to know, brothers and sisters	1
	7: 1	Do you not know, brothers and sisters	1
	8:12	So then, brothers and sisters, we are debtors	1
	10: 1	Brothers and sisters, my heart's desire and prayer	1
	11:25	brothers and sisters, I want you to understand	1
	12: 1	I appeal to you therefore, brothers and sisters	1
	14:10	Why do you pass judgment on your brother or sister?	1
	14:10	Or you, why do you despise your brother or sister?	1
	14:15	brother or sister is being injured by what you eat	1
	14:21	anything that makes your brother or sister stumble.	1
	15:14	feel confident about you, my brothers and sisters	1
	15:30	I appeal to you, brothers and sisters, by our Lord	1
	16:14	Greet…the brothers and sisters who are with them.	1
	16:17	I urge you, brothers and sisters, to keep an eye	1
1Co	1:10	I appeal to you, brothers and sisters, by the name	1
	1:11	quarrels among you, my brothers and sisters.	1
	1:26	Consider your own call, brothers and sisters:	1

	2: 1	When I came to you, brothers and sisters	1
	3: 1	brothers and sisters, I could not speak to you as spiritual	1
	4: 6	for your benefit, brothers and sisters	1
	5:11	who bears the name of brother or sister	1
	7:24	condition you were called, brothers and sisters	1
	7:29	I mean, brothers and sisters, the appointed time	1
	10: 1	not want you to be unaware, brothers and sisters	1
	11:33	my brothers and sisters, when you come together to eat	1
	12: 1	Now concerning spiritual gifts, brothers and sisters	1
	14: 6	Now, brothers and sisters, if I come to you speaking	1
	14:20	Brothers and sisters, do not be children	1
	15: 1	Now I would remind you, brothers and sisters	1
	15: 6	appeared to…five hundred brothers and sisters	1
	15:31	as certain, brothers and sisters, as my boasting	1
	15:50	I am saying, brothers and sisters, is this:	1
	16:15	Now, brothers and sisters, you know that members	1
	16:20	All the brothers and sisters send greetings.	1
2Co	1: 8	not want you to be unaware, brothers and sisters	1
	8: 1	We want you to know, brothers and sisters,	1
	13:11	Finally, brothers and sisters, farewell.	1
Gal	1:11	I want you to know, brothers and sisters	1
	3:15	Brothers and sisters, I give an example from daily life:	1
	5:13	you were called to freedom, brothers and sisters;	1
	6:18	grace…be with your spirit, brothers and sisters.	1
Php	1:14	most of the brothers and sisters…dare to speak	1
	3: 1	Finally, my brothers and sisters, rejoice in the Lord.	1
	3:17	Brothers and sisters, join in imitating me	1
	4: 1	Therefore, my brothers and sisters, whom I love	1
Col	1: 2	To the saints and faithful brothers and sisters	1
	4:15	Give my greetings to the brothers and sisters	1
1Th	1: 4	For we know, brothers and sisters beloved by God	1
	2: 1	You yourselves know, brothers and sisters	1
	2: 9	remember our labor and toil, brothers and sisters;	1
	2:14	brothers and sisters, became imitators of the churches	1
	2:17	As for us, brothers and sisters,	1
	3: 7	For this reason, brothers and sisters,	1
	4: 1	Finally, brothers and sisters, we ask and urge you	1
	4: 6	exploit a brother or sister in this matter	1
	4:10	indeed you do love all the brothers and sisters	1
	4:13	not want you to be uninformed, brothers and sisters	1
	5: 1	the times and the seasons, brothers and sisters	1
	5:12	we appeal to you, brothers and sisters	1
	5:26	Greet all the brothers and sisters with a holy kiss.	1
2Th	1: 3	give thanks…for you, brothers and sisters,	1
	2: 1	we beg you, brothers and sisters	1
	2:13	brothers and sisters beloved by the Lord	1
	2:15	brothers and sisters, stand firm and hold fast	1
	3: 1	Finally, brothers and sisters, pray for us	1
	3:13	Brothers and sisters, do not be weary in doing	1
1Ti	4: 6	put these instructions before the brothers and sisters	1
2Ti	4:21	Linus and Claudia and all the brothers and sisters.	1
Heb	2:11	Jesus is not ashamed to call them brothers and sisters	1
	2:12	"I will proclaim your name to my brothers and sisters	1
	2:17	become like his brothers and sisters in every respect	1
	3: 1	Therefore, brothers and sisters…consider that Jesus	1
	3:12	Take care, brothers and sisters, that none of you	1
	13:22	I appeal to you, brothers and sisters	1
Jas	1: 2	My brothers and sisters, whenever you face trials	1
	2: 1	My brothers and sisters, do you…really believe	1
	2: 5	Listen, my beloved brothers and sisters.	1
	2:14	What good is it, my brothers and sisters	1
	3: 1	Not many…become teachers, my brothers and sisters	1
	3:10	My brothers and sisters, this ought not to be so.	1
	3:12	Can a fig tree, my brothers and sisters, yield olives	1
	4:11	not speak evil against one another, brothers and sisters.	1
	5:19	My brothers and sisters, if anyone among you wanders	1
1Pe	5: 9	brothers and sisters…undergoing the same kinds	2
2Pe	1:10	Therefore, brothers and sisters, be all the more eager	1
1Jn	2: 9	while hating a brother or sister, is still in the darkness.	1
	2:10	Whoever loves a brother or sister lives in the light	1
	3:10	who do not love their brothers and sisters.	1
	3:13	Do not be astonished, brothers and sisters	1
	3:15	All who hate a brother or sister are murderers	1
	3:17	has the world's goods and sees a brother or sister in need	1
	4:20	say, "I love God," and hate their brothers or sisters	1
	4:20	do not love a brother or sister whom they have seen	1
	4:21	those who love God must love their brothers and sisters	1
	5:16	If you see your brother or sister committing…sin	1
Rev	6:11	fellow servants and of their brothers and sisters	1

false brother and sister

1. ψευδάδελφος, *pseudadelphos, 6012*

2Co 11:26 danger at sea, danger from false brothers and sisters;   1

brow

1. ὀφρῦς, *ophrys, 4059*

Lke 4:29 led him to the brow of the hill   1

bruise

1. κατακόπτω, *katakoptō, 2888*
2. συντρίβω, *syntribō, 5341*

Mat 12:20 He will not break a bruised reed   2
Mrk 5: 5 bruising himself with stones.   1

brushwood

1. φρύγανον, *phryganon, 5866*

Act 28: 3 Paul had gathered a bundle of brushwood   1

brute

1. ἀνήμερος, *anēmeros, 466*
2. θηρίον, *thērion, 2563*

2Ti 3: 3 profligates, brutes, haters of good   1
Tit 1:12 are always liars, vicious brutes, lazy gluttons."   2

bucket

1. ἄντλημα, *antlēma, 534*

Jhn 4:11 you have no bucket, and the well is deep.   1

bud

1. βλαστάνω, *blastanō, 1056*

Heb 9: 4 Aaron's rod that budded   1

bugle

1. σάλπιγξ, *salpinx, 4894*

1Co 14: 8 if the bugle gives an indistinct sound   1

build

1. ἐνδώμησις, *endōmēsis, 1908*
2. κατασκευάζω, *kataskeuazō, 2941*
3. κεῖμαι, *keimai, 3023*
4. οἰκοδομέω, *oikodomeō, 3868*
5. οἰκοδομή, *oikodomē, 3869*

Mat 5:14 A city built on a hill cannot be hid.   3
    7:24 like a wise man who built his house on rock.   4
    7:26 a foolish man who built his house on sand.   4
   16:18 on this rock I will build my church   4
   21:33 dug a wine press in it, and built a watchtower.   4
   23:29 you build the tombs of the prophets   4
   26:61 to build it in three days.' "   4
   27:40 destroy the temple and build it in three days   4
Mrk 12: 1 built a watchtower; then he leased it to tenants   4
   13: 1 and what large buildings!"   5
   13: 2 "Do you see these great buildings?   5
   14:58 in three days I will build another   4
   15:29 destroy the temple and build it in three days   4
Lke 4:29 brow of the hill on which their town was built   4
   6:48 like a man building a house, who dug deeply   4
   6:48 because it had been well built.   4
   6:49 like a man who built a house on the ground   4
   7: 5 it is he who built our synagogue for us."   4
  11:47 For you build the tombs of the prophets   4
  11:48 they killed them, and you build their tombs.   4
  12:18 I will pull down my barns and build larger ones   4
  14:28 For which of you, intending to build a tower   4
  14:30 saying, 'This fellow began to build   4
  17:28 selling, planting and building,   4
Act 7:47 it was Solomon who built a house for him.   4
   7:49 What kind of house will you build for me   4
Rom 15:20 so that I do not build on someone else's foundation   4
1Co 3: 9 you are God's field, God's building.   5
Heb 3: 4 (For every house is built by someone   2
  11: 7 Noah...respected the warning and built an ark   4
1Pe 2: 5 yourselves be built into a spiritual house   4
   3:20 during the building of the ark   2
Rev 21:18 The wall is built of jasper   1

build on

1. ἐποικοδομέω, *epoikodomeō, 2224*

1Co 3:10 someone else is building on it.   1
   3:10 Each builder must choose with care how to build on it.   1
   3:12 Now if anyone builds on the foundation with gold   1
   3:14 If what has been built on the foundation   1

build together

1. συνοικοδομέω, *synoikodomeō, 5325*

Eph 2:22 you also are built together   1

build up

1. ἐποικοδομέω, *epoikodomeō, 2224*
2. οἰκοδομέω, *oikodomeō, 3868*
3. οἰκοδομή, *oikodomē, 3869*

Act 9:31 the church...had peace and was built up.   2
  20:32 a message that is able to build you up   2
Rom 15: 2 for the good purpose of building up the neighbor.   3
1Co 8: 1 Knowledge puffs up, but love builds up.   2
  10:23 not all things build up.   2
  14: 4 Those who speak in a tongue build up themselves   2
  14: 4 those who prophesy build up the church.   2
  14: 5 so that the church may be built up.   3
  14:12 strive to excel in them for building up the church.   3
  14:17 the other person is not built up.   2
  14:26 Let all things be done for building up.   3
2Co 10: 8 which the Lord gave for building you up   3
  12:19 beloved, is for the sake of building you up.   3
  13:10 for building up and not for tearing down.   3
Gal 2:18 build up again the very things that I once tore down   2
Eph 4:12 for building up the body of Christ   3
   4:16 the body's growth in building itself up in love.   3
   4:29 only what is useful for building up   3
Col 2: 7 rooted and built up in him   1
1Th 5:11 encourage one another and build up each other   2
Jde 1:20 build yourselves up on your most holy faith;   1

build upon

1. ἐποικοδομέω, *epoikodomeō, 2224*

Eph 2:20 built upon the foundation of the apostles   1

builder

1. Contextual: Not in Greek
2. αὐτός, *autos, 899*
3. δημιουργός, *dēmiourgos, 1321*
4. κατασκευάζω, *kataskeuazō, 2941*
5. οἰκοδομέω, *oikodomeō, 3868*
6. οἰκοδόμος, *oikodomos, 3871*
7. τὶς, *tis, 5516*

Mat 21:42 'The stone that the builders rejected   5
Mrk 12:10 'The stone that the builders rejected   5
Lke 20:17 'The stone that the builders rejected   5
Act 4:11 'the stone that was rejected by you, the builders;   6
1Co 3:10 Each builder must choose with care how to build on it.   1
   3:13 work of each builder will become visible   1
   3:14 builder will receive a reward.   7
   3:15 work is burned up, the builder will suffer loss;   7
   3:15 builder will be saved, but only as through fire.   2
Heb 3: 3 the builder of a house has more honor than the house   4
   3: 4 but the builder of all things is God.)   4
  11:10 the city...whose architect and builder is God.   3
1Pe 2: 7 "The stone that the builders rejected has become   5

master builder

1. ἀρχιτέκτων, *architektōn, 802*

1Co 3:10 like a skilled master builder   1

building

1. οἰκοδομή, *oikodomē, 3869*

Mat 24: 1 point out to him the buildings of the temple.   1
2Co 5: 1 we have a building from God   1

bull

1. ταῦρος, *tauros, 5436*

Heb 9:13 the blood of goats and bulls   1
  10: 4 the blood of bulls and goats   1

bulwark

1. ἑδραίωμα, *hedraiōma, 1613*

1Ti 3:15 the pillar and bulwark of the truth.   1

bundle

1. δέσμη, *desmē, 1299*
2. πλῆθος, *plēthos, 4436*

Mat 13:30 Collect the weeds first and bind them in bundles   1
Act 28: 3 Paul had gathered a bundle of brushwood   2

burden   *See also* carry heavy burdens

1. ἀβαρής, *abarēs, 4*
2. βαρέω, *bareō, 976*
3. βάρος, *baros, 983*
4. ἐπιβαρέω, *epibareō, 2096*
5. καταβαρέω, *katabareō, 2851*
6. καταναρκάω, *katanarkaō, 2915*
7. φορτίον, *phortion, 5845*

Mat 11:30 For my yoke is easy, and my burden is light."   7
   20:12 who have borne the burden of the day   3
   23: 4 They tie up heavy burdens, hard to bear   7
Lke 11:46 you load people with burdens hard to bear   7
Act 15:28 no further burden than these essentials: 3
2Co   5: 4 we groan under our burden   2
   11: 9 I did not burden anyone   6
   11: 9 continue to refrain from burdening you in any way.   1
   12:13 except that I myself did not burden you?   6
   12:14 I will not be a burden   6
   12:16 Let it be assumed that I did not burden you.   5
Gal   6: 2 Bear one another's burdens   3
1Th   2: 9 worked...so that we might not burden any of you   4
2Th   3: 8 so that we might not burden any of you.   4
1Ti   5:16 let the church not be burdened   2
Rev   2:24 I do not lay on you any other burden;   3

burdensome

1. βαρύς, *barys, 987*

1Jn   5: 3 And his commandments are not burdensome   1

burial

1. ἐνταφιάζω, *entaphiazō, 1946*
2. ἐνταφιασμός, *entaphiasmos, 1947*
3. ὀστέον, *osteon, 4014*

Mat 26:12 she has prepared me for burial.   1
Mrk 14: 8 anointed my body beforehand for its burial.   2
Jhn 12: 7 she might keep it for the day of my burial.   2
   19:40 according to the burial custom of the Jews.   1
Heb 11:22 gave instructions about his burial.   3

burn

1. ἐμπίμπρημι, *empimprēmi, 1856*
2. ζέω, *zeō, 2417*
3. καίω, *kaiō, 2794*
4. κατακαίω, *katakaiō, 2876*
5. πῦρ, *pyr, 4786*
6. πύρωσις, *pyrōsis, 4796*

Mat   3:12 the chaff he will burn with unquenchable fire."   4
   13:30 bind them in bundles to be burned   4
   22: 7 destroyed...murderers, and burned their city.   1
Lke   3:17 the chaff he will burn with unquenchable fire."   4
   24:32 "Were not our hearts burning within us   3
Jhn   5:35 He was a burning and shining lamp   3
   15: 6 gathered, thrown into the fire, and burned.   3
Act   7:30 in the flame of a burning bush.   5
   18:25 spoke with burning enthusiasm and taught accurately   2
   19:19 collected their books and burned them publicly   4
Rom 12:20 you will heap burning coals on their heads."   5
Heb 13:11 are burned outside the camp.   4
Rev   4: 5 in front of the throne burn seven flaming torches   3
   8: 8 like a great mountain, burning with fire   3
   18: 8 and she will be burned with fire;   4
   18: 9 when they see the smoke of her burning;   6
   18:18 cried out as they saw the smoke of her burning   6
   19:20 the lake of fire that burns with sulfur.   3
   21: 8 in the lake that burns with fire and sulfur   3

burn over

1. καῦσις, *kausis, 3011*

Heb   6: 8 its end is to be burned over.   1

burn up

1. κατακαίω, *katakaiō, 2876*

Mat 13:40 weeds are collected and burned up with fire   1
1Co   3:15 work is burned up, the builder will suffer loss;   1
Rev   8: 7 and a third of the earth was burned up   1
   8: 7 and a third of the trees were burned up   1
   8: 7 and all green grass was burned up.   1
   17:16 will devour her flesh and burn her up with fire.   1

burnished   *See* burnished *bronze*

burnt   *See* burnt *offering*, whole burnt *offering*

burst

1. ῥήγνυμι, *rhēgnymi, 4838*

Mat   9:17 otherwise, the skins burst, and the wine is spilled   1
Mrk   2:22 otherwise, the wine will burst the skins   1
Lke   5:37 otherwise the new wine will burst the skins   1

burst against

1. προσρήγνυμι, *prosrēgnymi, 4703*

Lke   6:48 the river burst against that house   1
   6:49 a house...the river burst against it   1

burst into song

1. ῥήγνυμι, *rhēgnymi, 4838*

Gal   4:27 burst into song and shout, you who endure no birth pangs;   1

burst open

1. λακάω, *lakaō, 3279*

Act   1:18 falling headlong, he burst open in the middle   1

bury   *See also* place to bury

1. θάπτω, *thaptō, 2507*
2. συγκομίζω, *synkomizō, 5172*

Mat   8:21 "Lord, first let me go and bury my father."   1
   8:22 and let the dead bury their own dead."   1
   14:12 took the body and buried it;   1
Lke   9:59 "Lord, first let me go and bury my father."   1
   9:60 "Let the dead bury their own dead;   1
   16:22 The rich man also died and was buried.   1
Act   2:29 he both died and was buried   1
   5: 6 then carried him out and buried him.   1
   5: 9 the feet of those who have buried your husband   1
   5:10 they carried her out and buried her   1
   8: 2 Devout men buried Stephen   2
1Co 15: 4 that he was buried, and that he was raised   1

bury with

1. συνθάπτω, *synthaptō, 5313*

Rom   6: 4 Therefore we have been buried with him by baptism   1
Col   2:12 you were buried with him in baptism   1

bush   *See also* bramble bush

1. βάτος¹, *batos¹, 1003*

Mrk 12:26 in the story about the bush   1
Lke 20:37 Moses himself showed, in the story about the bush   1
Act   7:30 in the flame of a burning bush.   1
   7:35 the angel who appeared to him in the bush.   1

bushel basket

1. μόδιος, *modios, 3654*

Mat   5:15 under the bushel basket, but on the lampstand   1
Mrk   4:21 lamp brought in to be put under the bushel basket   1

business   *See also* do business

1. ἐμπορία, *emporia, 1865*
2. ἐργασία, *ergasia, 2238*

Mat 22: 5 went away, one to his farm, another to his business   1
Act 19:24 brought no little business to the artisans.   2
   19:25 "Men...we get our wealth from this business.   2

busy

1. προσκαρτερέω, *proskartereō, 4674*

Rom 13: 6 God's servants, busy with this very thing.   1

busy life

1. πορεία, *poreia, 4512*

Jas   1:11 in the midst of a busy life, they will wither away.   1

busybody

1. περιεργάζομαι, *periergazomai, 4318*
2. περίεργος, *periergos, 4319*

2Th	3:11 mere busybodies, not doing any work.	1
1Ti	5:13 not merely idle, but also gossips and busybodies	2

but   Not Indexed; *See* nothing but

buy

1. Contextual: Not in Greek
2. ἀγοράζω, *agorazō, 60*
3. ὠνέομαι, *ōneomai, 6050*

Mat	13:44 sells all that he has and buys that field.	2
	13:46 went and sold all that he had and bought it.	2
	14:15 into the villages and buy food for themselves."	2
	21:12 all who were selling and buying in the temple	2
	25: 9 go to the dealers and buy some for yourselves.'	2
	25:10 while they went to buy it, the bridegroom came	2
	27: 7 used them to buy the potter's field	2
Mrk	6:36 buy something for themselves to eat."	2
	6:37 They said to him, "Are we to go and buy	2
	11:15 who were selling and those who were buying	2
	15:46 Joseph bought a linen cloth	2
	16: 1 the mother of James, and Salome bought spices	2
Lke	9:13 go and buy food for all these people."	2
	14:18 said to him, 'I have bought a piece of land	2
	14:19 Another said, 'I have bought five yoke of oxen	2
	17:28 they were eating and drinking, buying and selling	2
	22:36 who has no sword must sell his cloak and buy one.	2
Jhn	4: 8 had gone to the city to buy food.)	2
	6: 5 "Where are we to buy bread for these people	2
	6: 7 "Six months' wages would not buy enough bread	1
	12: 7 She bought it…for the day of my burial.	1
	13:29 "Buy what we need for the festival";	2
Act	7:16 tomb that Abraham had bought for a sum of silver	3
1Co	6:20 you were bought with a price;	2
	7:23 You were bought with a price;	2
	7:30 those who buy as though they had no possessions	2
2Pe	2: 1 They will even deny the Master who bought them	2
Rev	3:18 I counsel you to buy from me gold refined by fire	2
	13:17 no one can buy or sell who does not have the mark	2
	18:11 since no one buys their cargo anymore	2

by   *See also* bind by oath, by all *means*, by no *means*, by one's *side*, by the *sea*, choose by lot, come by, day by day, driven by the wind, eaten by worms, enter by force, extort money by threat, gain by trading, go by, go by land, inspired by God, keep back by fraud, lead by the hand, make by human hands, one by one, pass by, pass by on the other side, possessed by a demon, pounded by a storm, someone to lead by the hand, stand by, step by step, strive side by side, take by force, taught by God, walk by

1. ἀπό, *apo, 608*
2. ἄχρι, *achri, 948*
3. διά, *dia, 1328*
4. διά + χείρ, *dia + cheir, 1328 + 5931*
5. εἰς, *eis, 1650*
6. ἐκ, *ek, 1666*
7. ἐν, *en, 1877*
8. ἐν + χείρ, *en + cheir, 1877 + 5931*
9. ἐπί, *epi, 2093*
10. καί, *kai, 2779*
11. κατά, *kata, 2848*
12. μετά, *meta, 3552*
13. ὅτι, *hoti, 4022*
14. παρά, *para, 4123*
15. περί, *peri, 4309*
16. πρός, *pros, 4639*
17. ὑπέρ, *hyper, 5642*
18. ὑπό, *hypo, 5679*

Mat	1: 3 Judah the father of Perez and Zerah by Tamar	6
	1: 5 Salmon the father of Boaz by Rahab	6
	1: 5 Boaz the father of Obed by Ruth	6
	1: 6 David…father of Solomon by the wife of Uriah	6
	1:22 to fulfill what had been spoken by the Lord	18
	2: 5 Judea; for so it has been written by the prophet:	3
	2:12 left for their own country by another road.	3
	2:15 to fulfill what had been spoken by the Lord	18

	2:16 been tricked by the wise men, he was infuriated	18
	3: 6 they were baptized by him in the river Jordan	18
	3:13 to John at the Jordan, to be baptized by him.	18
	3:14 "I need to be baptized by you, and do you come to me?"	18
	4: 1 Then Jesus was led up by the Spirit	18
	4: 1 the wilderness to be tempted by the devil.	18
	4: 4 written, 'One does not live by bread alone	9
	4: 4 by bread alone, but by every word that comes	9
	4:18 As he walked by the Sea of Galilee, he saw two	14
	5:34 either by heaven, for it is the throne of God	7
	5:35 or by the earth, for it is his footstool	7
	5:35 or by Jerusalem, for it is the city	5
	5:36 And do not swear by your head,	7
	6: 2 so that they may be praised by others.	18
	7:16 You will know them by their fruits.	1
	7:20 Thus you will know them by their fruits.	1
	8:24 so great that the boat was being swamped by the waves;	18
	9:34 "By the ruler of the demons he casts out the demons."	7
	10:22 you will be hated by all because of my name.	18
	11: 2 he sent word by his disciples	3
	11: 7 A reed shaken by the wind?	18
	11:19 Yet wisdom is vindicated by her deeds."	1
	11:27 All things have been handed over to me by my Father;	18
	12:24 "It is only by Beelzebul, the ruler of the demons	7
	12:27 If I cast out demons by Beelzebul	7
	12:27 by whom do your own exorcists cast them out?	7
	12:28 if it is by the Spirit of God that I cast out demons	7
	12:33 for the tree is known by its fruit.	6
	12:37 for by your words you will be justified	6
	12:37 and by your words you will be condemned."	6
	14: 8 Prompted by her mother, she said	18
	14:13 to a deserted place by himself.	11
	14:23 he went up the mountain by himself to pray.	11
	14:24 boat, battered by the waves, was far from the land	18
	17: 1 and led them up a high mountain, by themselves.	11
	18: 7 woe to the one by whom the stumbling block comes!	3
	18:16 confirmed by the evidence of two or three	9
	18:19 it will be done for you by my Father in heaven.	14
	19:12 who have been made eunuchs by others	18
	20:17 he took the twelve disciples aside by themselves	11
	20:23 for whom it has been prepared by my Father."	18
	20:30 There were two blind men sitting by the roadside.	14
	21:23 "By what authority are you doing these things	7
	21:24 by what authority I do these things.	7
	21:27 by what authority I am doing these things.	7
	22:31 have you not read what was said to you by God	18
	22:43 "How is it then that David by the Spirit	7
	23:16 swears by the sanctuary is bound by nothing	7
	23:16 whoever swears by the gold of the sanctuary	7
	23:18 'Whoever swears by the altar is bound by nothing	7
	23:18 whoever swears by the gift that is on the altar	7
	23:20 So whoever swears by the altar	7
	23:20 swears by it and by everything on it;	7
	23:20 swears by it and by everything on it;	7
	23:21 whoever swears by the sanctuary	7
	23:21 swears by it and by the one who dwells in it;	7
	23:21 swears by it and by the one who dwells in it;	7
	23:22 whoever swears by heaven	7
	23:22 swears by the throne of God	7
	23:22 by the one who is seated upon it.	7
	24: 9 hated by all nations because of my name.	18
	24:15 as was spoken by the prophet Daniel	3
	26:24 woe to that one by whom the Son of Man is betrayed!	3
	26:52 all who take the sword will perish by the sword.	7
	27:12 when he was accused by the chief priests	18
Mrk	1: 5 and were baptized by him in the river Jordan	18
	1: 9 baptized by John in the Jordan.	18
	1:13 wilderness forty days, tempted by Satan;	18
	2: 3 a paralyzed man, carried by four of them.	18
	3:22 by the ruler of the demons he casts out demons."	7
	5:21 he was by the sea.	14
	6: 2 What deeds of power are being done by his hands!	3
	6:31 "Come away to a deserted place all by yourselves	11
	6:32 in the boat to a deserted place by themselves.	11
	8:31 rejected by the elders, the chief priests	18
	9: 2 led them up a high mountain apart, by themselves.	11
	10:46 Bartimaeus…was sitting by the roadside.	14
	11:18 the whole crowd was spellbound by his teaching.	9
	11:28 "By what authority are you doing these things?	7
	11:29 tell you by what authority I do these things.	7
	11:33 "Neither will I tell you by what authority	7

Mrk	12:36	David himself, by the Holy Spirit, declared	7
	13:13	you will be hated by all because of my name.	18
	14: 1	way to arrest Jesus by stealth and kill him;	7
	14:21	woe to that one by whom the Son of Man is betrayed!	3
	16:11	[heard that he was alive and had been seen by her]	18
	16:20	[confirmed the message by the signs]	3
Lke	1:26	the angel Gabriel was sent by God	1
	1:29	she was much perplexed by his words	9
	1:45	what was spoken to her by the Lord."	14
	1:77	by the forgiveness of their sins.	7
	1:78	By the tender mercy of our God	3
	2:21	he was called Jesus, the name given by the angel	18
	2:26	It had been revealed to him by the Holy Spirit	18
	3: 7	the crowds that came out to be baptized by him	18
	3:19	Herod the ruler, who had been rebuked by him	18
	4: 1	Jesus…was led by the Spirit in the wilderness	7
	4: 2	for forty days he was tempted by the devil.	18
	4: 4	"It is written, 'One does not live by bread alone.' "	9
	4:15	was praised by everyone.	18
	6:44	for each tree is known by its own fruit.	6
	7:24	A reed shaken by the wind?	18
	7:30	refusing to be baptized by him	18
	7:35	wisdom is vindicated by all her children."	1
	8:14	they are choked by the cares and riches	18
	8:29	be driven by the demon into the wilds.)	18
	9: 7	it was said by some that John had been raised	18
	9: 8	by some that Elijah had appeared	18
	9:22	rejected by the elders, chief priests	1
	10:22	All things have been handed over to me by my Father;	18
	10:31	Now by chance a priest was going down that road;	11
	10:40	Martha was distracted by her many tasks;	15
	10:41	you are worried and distracted by many things;	15
	11:15	"He casts out demons by Beelzebul	7
	11:18	you say that I cast out the demons by Beelzebul.	7
	11:19	if I cast out the demons by Beelzebul	7
	11:19	by whom do your exorcists cast them out?	7
	11:20	by the finger of God that I cast out the demons	7
	14: 8	you are invited by someone to a wedding banquet	18
	14: 8	has been invited by your host;	18
	16:15	what is prized by human beings	7
	16:22	carried away by the angels to be with Abraham.	18
	16:23	saw Abraham far away with Lazarus by his side.	7
	17: 1	woe to anyone by whom they come!	3
	17:20	Once Jesus was asked by the Pharisees	18
	17:25	be rejected by this generation.	1
	18:11	The Pharisee, standing by himself, was praying thus	16
	18:31	written about the Son of Man by the prophets	3
	18:35	a blind man was sitting by the roadside begging.	14
	19:22	'I will judge you by your own words	6
	20: 2	by what authority are you doing these things?	7
	20: 8	by what authority I am doing these things."	7
	20:26	amazed by his answer, they became silent.	9
	21:16	You will be betrayed even by parents	18
	21:17	You will be hated by all because of my name.	18
	21:19	By your endurance you will gain your souls.	7
	21:20	"When you see Jerusalem surrounded by armies	18
	21:24	Jerusalem will be trampled on by the Gentiles	18
	22:22	woe to that one by whom he is betrayed!"	3
	22:28	those who have stood by me in my trials;	12
Jhn	4: 6	Jesus, tired out by his journey, was sitting	6
	4: 6	Jesus…was sitting by the well.	9
	5: 2	in Jerusalem by the Sheep Gate there is a pool	9
	6:65	unless it is granted by the Father."	6
	7:24	Do not judge by appearances	11
	8: 9	[went away, one by one, beginning with the elders;]	11
	8:15	You judge by human standards; I judge no one.	11
	8:22	by saying, 'Where I am going, you cannot come'?"	13
	10: 1	who does not enter the sheepfold by the gate	3
	10: 2	The one who enters by the gate	3
	10: 3	calls his own sheep by name and leads them out.	11
	10: 9	Whoever enters by me will be saved	3
	13:35	By this everyone will know that you are my disciples	7
	14:21	those who love me will be loved by my Father	18
	15: 3	cleansed by the word that I have spoken to you.	3
	15: 4	Just as the branch cannot bear fruit by itself	1
	15: 8	My Father is glorified by this	7
	16:30	by this we believe that you came from God."	7
	21: 1	showed himself again to the disciples	9
Act	1: 3	presented himself alive…by many convincing proofs	7
	1: 7	that the Father has set by his own authority.	7
	2:22	Jesus of Nazareth, a man attested to you by God	1

	2:23	and killed by the hands of those outside the law.	3
	2:43	signs were being done by the apostles.	3
	3:16	by faith in his name	9
	3:26	by turning each of you from your wicked ways."	7
	4: 7	"By what power or by what name did you do this?"	7
	4: 7	"By what power or by what name did you do this?"	7
	4:10	by the name of Jesus Christ of Nazareth	7
	4:11	'the stone that was rejected by you, the builders;	18
	4:12	no other name…by which we must be saved."	7
	4:25	said by the Holy Spirit through our ancestor David	3
	5:16	those tormented by unclean spirits	18
	8: 6	listened eagerly to what was said by Philip	18
	10: 6	Simon, a tanner, whose house is by the seaside."	14
	10:17	suddenly the men sent by Cornelius	18
	10:17	standing by the gate.	9
	10:22	who is well spoken of by the whole Jewish nation	18
	10:22	was directed by a holy angel to send for you	18
	10:32	in the home of Simon, a tanner, by the sea.'	14
	10:36	preaching peace by Jesus Christ	3
	10:38	healing all who were oppressed by the devil	18
	10:41	to us who were chosen by God as witnesses	18
	10:42	the one ordained by God as judge of the living	18
	11:14	by which you and your entire household will be saved.'	7
	11:28	Agabus stood up and predicted by the Spirit	3
	11:30	sending it to the elders by Barnabas and Saul.	4
	13: 4	being sent out by the Holy Spirit	18
	13:39	by this Jesus everyone who believes is set free	7
	13:39	you could not be freed by the law of Moses.	7
	13:45	contradicted what was spoken by Paul.	18
	15: 3	So they were sent on their way by the church	18
	15: 4	were welcomed by the church and the apostles	1
	15:27	will tell you the same things by word of mouth.	3
	15:33	they were sent off in peace by the believers	1
	16: 2	He was well spoken of by the believers	18
	16: 4	decisions…reached by the apostles and elders	18
	16: 6	forbidden by the Holy Spirit to speak the word	18
	16:13	we went outside the gate by the river	14
	16:14	to listen eagerly to what was said by Paul.	18
	17:13	the word…had been proclaimed by Paul in Beroea	18
	17:25	nor is he served by human hands	18
	17:31	the world judged…by a man whom he has appointed	7
	18:28	showing by the scriptures that the Messiah	3
	20: 3	when a plot was made against him by the Jews	18
	20: 9	Overcome by sleep, he fell to the ground	1
	21:19	he related one by one the things that God had done	11
	21:35	he had to be carried by the soldiers.	18
	22:12	well spoken of by all the Jews living there	18
	22:30	what Paul was being accused of by the Jews,	18
	23:23	to leave by nine o'clock tonight for Caesarea	1
	23:27	This man was seized by the Jews	18
	23:27	and was about to be killed by them	18
	24:26	he hoped that money would be given him by Paul	18
	25:14	a man here who was left in prison by Felix	18
	26: 6	hope in the promise made by God to our ancestors	18
	26: 7	for this hope…that I am accused by Jews!	18
	26: 8	Why is it thought incredible by any of you	14
	27:41	the stern…broken up by the force of the waves.	18
	28: 3	when a viper, driven out by the heat	1
	28:16	Paul was allowed to live by himself	11
Rom	1: 4	by resurrection from the dead, Jesus Christ	6
	1: 9	I serve…by announcing the gospel of his Son	7
	1:10	by God's will I may somehow at last succeed	7
	1:12	mutually encouraged by each other's faith	3
	1:17	"The one who is righteous will live by faith."	6
	1:18	those who by their wickedness suppress the truth.	7
	2: 7	who by patiently doing good seek for glory	11
	2:12	all who have sinned…will be judged by the law.	3
	2:23	do you dishonor God by breaking the law?	3
	3:20	"no human being will be justified…by deeds	6
	3:21	attested by the law and the prophets	18
	3:25	as a sacrifice of atonement by his blood	7
	3:27	By what law? By that of works?	3
	3:27	No, but by the law of faith.	3
	3:31	Do we then overthrow the law by this faith?	3
	4: 2	For if Abraham was justified by works	6
	5: 1	since we are justified by faith, we have peace	6
	5: 9	now that we have been justified by his blood	7
	5:10	much more…will we be saved by his life.	7
	5:19	For just as by the one man's disobedience	3
	5:19	so by the one man's obedience the many	3
	6: 4	Therefore we have been buried with him by baptism	3

6: 4	raised from the dead by the glory of the Father	3
8: 3	what the law, weakened by the flesh, could not do:	3
8:20	by the will of the one who subjected it, in hope	3
9: 1	my conscience confirms it by the Holy Spirit	7
9:10	Rebecca when she had conceived children by one husband	6
9:12	not by works but by his call)	6
9:12	not by works but by his call)	6
10: 5	"the person who does these things will live by them."	7
10:20	"I have been found by those who did not seek me;	7
11: 5	there is a remnant, chosen by grace.	11
11:24	cut from what is by nature a wild olive tree	11
12: 1	I appeal to you…by the mercies of God	3
12: 3	For by the grace given to me I say to everyone	3
12:21	Do not be overcome by evil	18
13: 1	authorities that exist have been instituted by God.	18
14:15	brother or sister is being injured by what you eat	3
14:20	to make others fall by what you eat;	3
15: 4	so that by steadfastness and by the encouragement	3
15: 4	by the encouragement of the scriptures	3
15:13	may abound in hope by the power of the Holy Spirit.	7
15:15	because of the grace given me by God	18
15:16	be acceptable, sanctified by the Holy Spirit.	7
15:19	by the power of signs and wonders	7
15:19	by the power of the Spirit of God	7
15:24	and to be sent on by you	18
15:30	I appeal to you…by our Lord Jesus Christ	3
15:30	I appeal to you…by the love of the Spirit	3
15:32	that by God's will I may come to you with joy	3
16:18	and by smooth talk and flattery they deceive	3
1Co 1: 1	an apostle of Christ Jesus by the will of God	3
1: 9	God is faithful; by him you were called	3
1:10	by the name of our Lord Jesus Christ	3
1:11	For it has been reported to me by Chloe's people	18
1:26	not many of you were wise by human standards	11
2:12	understand the gifts bestowed on us by God.	18
2:13	in words not taught by human wisdom	7
2:13	taught by the Spirit	7
4: 3	I should be judged by you or by any human court.	18
4: 3	I should be judged by you or by any human court.	18
6: 2	if the world is to be judged by you	7
6:12	I will not be dominated by anything.	18
6:14	will also raise us by his power.	3
7: 5	except perhaps by agreement for a set time	6
7:25	as one who by the Lord's mercy is trustworthy.	18
8: 3	anyone who loves God is known by him.	18
8:11	So by your knowledge those weak believers	7
9:14	get their living by the gospel.	6
10: 9	and were destroyed by serpents.	18
10:10	and were destroyed by the destroyer.	18
11:32	when we are judged by the Lord, we are disciplined	18
12: 3	no one speaking by the Spirit of God ever says	7
12: 3	except by the Holy Spirit.	7
12: 9	to another faith by the same Spirit	7
12: 9	to another gifts of healing by the one Spirit	7
14:21	it is written, "By people of strange tongues	7
14:21	by the lips of foreigners	7
14:24	outsider who enters is reproved by all	18
14:24	called to account by all.	18
2Co 1: 1	Paul, an apostle of Christ Jesus by the will of God	3
1: 4	with which we ourselves are consoled by God.	18
1:11	you also join in helping us by your prayers	17
1:12	not by earthly wisdom but by the grace of God	7
1:12	not by earthly wisdom but by the grace of God	7
2: 6	This punishment by the majority is enough	18
2:11	so that we may not be outwitted by Satan;	18
3: 2	to be known and read by all;	18
3: 3	that you are a letter of Christ, prepared by us	18
4:16	our inner nature is being renewed day by day.	10
5: 4	what is mortal may be swallowed up by life.	18
5: 7	for we walk by faith, not by sight.	3
5: 7	for we walk by faith, not by sight.	3
6: 6	by purity, knowledge, patience, kindness	7
7: 6	consoled us by the arrival of Titus	7
7: 7	not only by his coming, but also by the consolation	7
7: 7	also by the consolation with which he was consoled	7
7: 9	so that you were not harmed in any way by us.	6
7:13	his mind has been set at rest by all of you.	1
8: 5	to the Lord and, by the will of God, to us	3
8:19	appointed by the churches to travel with us	18
9:13	glorify God by your obedience	9
10: 1	by the meekness and gentleness of Christ	3

10:11	what we say by letter when absent	3
10:12	But when they measure themselves by one another	7
11: 3	as the serpent deceived Eve by its cunning	7
13: 1	by the evidence of two or three witnesses."	9
13: 4	lives by the power of God.	6
13: 4	we will live with him by the power of God.	6
Gal 1: 1	Paul an apostle—sent neither by human commission	3
1:11	the gospel that was proclaimed by me is not of human	18
2:16	a person is not justified by the works of the law	6
2:16	so that we might be justified by faith in Christ	6
2:16	not by doing the works of the law	6
2:16	no one will be justified by the works of the law.	6
2:20	the life I now live in the flesh I live by faith	7
3: 2	Did you receive the Spirit by doing the works of the law	6
3: 2	works of the law or by believing what you heard?	6
3: 5	by your doing the works of the law	6
3: 5	the law, or by your believing what you heard?	6
3: 8	God would justify the Gentiles by faith	6
3:11	no one is justified before God by the law;	7
3:11	"The one who is righteous will live by faith."	6
3:12	"Whoever does the works of the law will live by them."	7
3:17	not annul a covenant previously ratified by God	18
3:19	ordained through angels by a mediator.	8
3:24	so that we might be justified by faith.	6
4: 9	or rather to be known by God	18
4:22	one by a slave woman and the other by a free woman.	6
4:22	one by a slave woman and the other by a free woman.	6
5: 4	You who want to be justified by the law	7
5: 5	For through the Spirit, by faith, we eagerly wait	6
5:15	you are not consumed by one another.	18
6:14	by which the world has been crucified to me	3
Eph 1: 1	Paul, an apostle of Christ Jesus by the will of God	3
2:11	remember that at one time you Gentiles by birth	7
2:11	by those who are called "the circumcision"	18
2:13	have been brought near by the blood of Christ.	7
3: 3	the mystery was made known to me by revelation	11
3: 5	has now been revealed…by the Spirit:	7
3: 7	that was given me by the working of his power.	11
3:20	by the power at work within us	11
4:14	blown about by every wind of doctrine	7
4:14	by their craftiness in deceitful scheming.	7
4:16	by every ligament with which it is equipped	3
4:22	corrupt and deluded by its lusts	11
5:13	everything exposed by the light	18
5:26	cleansing her with the washing of water by the word	7
Php 1: 6	to completion by the day of Jesus Christ.	2
1:20	whether by life or by death.	3
1:20	whether by life or by death.	3
1:28	in no way intimidated by your opponents.	18
3:21	by the power that also enables him	11
Col 1: 1	Paul, an apostle of Christ Jesus by the will of God	3
2:11	by putting off the body of the flesh	7
2:18	puffed up without cause by a human way of thinking	18
2:19	nourished and held together by its ligaments	3
1Th 1: 4	For we know, brothers and sisters beloved by God	18
2: 4	just as we have been approved by God	18
3: 3	that no one would be shaken by these persecutions.	7
4:15	this we declare to you by the word of the Lord	7
2Th 1:10	when he comes to be glorified by his saints	7
1:11	fulfill by his power every good resolve and work	7
2: 2	either by spirit or by word or by letter	3
2: 2	either by spirit or by word or by letter	3
2: 2	either by spirit or by word or by letter	3
2:13	brothers and sisters beloved by the Lord	18
2:15	taught…either by word of mouth or by our letter.	3
2:15	taught…either by word of mouth or by our letter.	3
1Ti 1: 1	an apostle…by the command of God our Savior	11
1: 4	rather than the divine training that is known by faith.	7
3: 7	Moreover, he must be well thought of by outsiders	1
4: 5	for it is sanctified by God's word	3
2Ti 1: 1	Paul, an apostle of Christ Jesus by the will of God	3
2:26	having been held captive by him to do his will.	18
Tit 1: 3	entrusted by the command of God our Savior	11
Heb 1: 1	God spoke to our ancestors…by the prophets	7
1: 2	in these last days he has spoken to us by a Son	7
2: 3	it was attested to us by those who heard him	18
2:18	Because he…was tested by what he suffered	7
3: 4	(For every house is built by someone	18
5: 4	only when called by God, just as Aaron was.	18
5:10	having been designated by God a high priest	18
5:12	For though by this time you ought to be teachers	3

Heb	5:14	faculties have been trained by practice	3
	6:13	because he had no one greater by whom to swear	11
	6:13	he swore by himself	11
	6:16	Human beings...swear by someone greater than	11
	7: 7	the inferior is blessed by the superior.	18
	9:19	had been told to all the people by Moses	18
	9:26	to remove sin by the sacrifice of himself.	3
	10:10	by God's will that we have been sanctified through	7
	10:19	we have confidence...by the blood of Jesus	7
	10:29	the blood...by which they were sanctified	7
	10:38	my righteous one will live by faith.	6
	11: 2	by faith our ancestors received approval.	7
	11: 7	by this he condemned the world	3
	11:12	the innumerable grains of sand by the seashore."	14
	11:23	By faith Moses was hidden by his parents	18
	11:35	Women received their dead by resurrection.	6
	11:37	they were killed by the sword;	7
	12: 5	or lose heart when you are punished by him;	18
	12:11	those who have been trained by it.	3
	12:28	by which we offer to God an acceptable worship	3
	13: 2	by doing that some have entertained angels	3
	13: 4	Let marriage be held in honor by all	7
	13:11	is brought into the sanctuary by the high priest	3
	13:12	sanctify the people by his own blood.	3
	13:20	by the blood of the eternal covenant	7
Jas	1:13	No one...should say, "I am being tempted by God";	1
	1:14	one is tempted by one's own desire, being lured	18
	1:27	to keep oneself unstained by the world.	1
	2: 9	are convicted by the law as transgressors.	18
	2:12	who are to be judged by the law of liberty.	3
	2:17	So faith by itself, if it has no works, is dead.	11
	2:18	and I by my works will show you my faith.	6
	2:21	Was not our ancestor Abraham justified by works	6
	2:22	and faith was brought to completion by the works.	6
	2:24	You see that a person is justified by works	6
	2:24	justified by works and not by faith alone.	6
	2:25	was not Rahab the prostitute also justified by works	6
	3: 4	they are guided by a very small rudder	18
	3: 6	and is itself set on fire by hell.	18
	3:13	Show by your good life that your works are done	6
1Pe	1: 2	chosen and destined by God the Father	11
	1: 2	sanctified by the Spirit to be obedient	7
	1: 3	By his great mercy he has given us a new birth	11
	1: 5	being protected by the power of God through faith	7
	1: 7	gold that, though perishable, is tested by fire	3
	1:12	who brought you good news by the Holy Spirit	7
	1:22	have purified your souls by your obedience	7
	2: 2	so that by it you may grow into salvation	7
	2: 4	though rejected by mortals yet chosen and precious	18
	2:14	or of governors, as sent by him to punish	3
	3: 1	won over without a word by their wives' conduct	3
2Pe	1:17	that voice was conveyed to him by the Majestic Glory	18
	1:21	and women moved by the Holy Spirit spoke from God.	18
	2: 7	greatly distressed by...the lawless	18
	2:17	waterless springs and mists driven by a storm;	18
	3: 1	arouse your sincere intention by reminding	7
	3: 2	the words spoken in the past by the holy prophets	18
1Jn	2: 3	by this we may be sure that we know him	7
	2: 5	By this we may be sure that we are in him:	7
	2:20	you have been anointed by the Holy One	1
	3:16	We know love by this, that he laid down his life	7
	3:19	by this we will know that we are from the truth	7
	3:24	And by this we know that he abides in us	7
	3:24	by the Spirit that he has given us.	6
	4: 2	By this you know the Spirit of God:	7
	4:13	By this we know that we abide in him and he in us	7
	5: 2	By this we know that we love the children of God	7
	5: 6	This is the one who came by water and blood, Jesus	3
	5:10	by not believing in the testimony	13
2Jn	1: 4	just as we have been commanded by the Father.	14
Jde	1:10	they are destroyed by those things	7
	1:12	waterless clouds carried along by the winds;	18
	1:23	hating even the tunic defiled by their bodies.	1
Rev	1: 1	he made it known by sending his angel	3
	1: 5	To him who...freed us from our sins by his blood	7
	2:11	conquers will not be harmed by the second death.	6
	3:18	I counsel you to buy from me gold refined by fire	6
	4:11	and by your will they existed and were created."	3
	5: 9	and by your blood you ransomed for God saints	7
	6: 8	kill...pestilence, and by the wild animals	18
	6:13	drops its winter fruit when shaken by a gale.	18

	9:18	By...three plagues a third of humankind was killed	1
	9:18	killed, by the fire and smoke and sulfur	6
	9:20	rest of humankind, who were not killed by...plagues	7
	10: 6	swore by him who lives forever and ever	7
	12: 6	wilderness, where she has a place prepared by God	1
	12:11	they have conquered him by the blood of the Lamb	3
	12:11	conquered him...by the word of their testimony	3
	13:14	and by the signs that it is allowed to perform	3
	18:19	all who had ships at sea grew rich by her wealth!	6
	18:23	and all nations were deceived by your sorcery.	7
	19:20	in its presence the signs by which he deceived	7
	19:21	And the rest were killed by the sword	7
	21:24	The nations will walk by its light	3

bystander

1. ἐκεῖ, *ekei, 1695*
2. ἵστημι, *histēmi, 2705*
3. παρίστημι, *paristēmi, 4225*

Mat	26:71	she said to the bystanders	1
	26:73	After a little while the bystanders came up	2
	27:47	some of the bystanders heard it, they said	2
Mrk	11: 5	some of the bystanders said to them	2
	14:69	began again to say to the bystanders	3
	14:70	after a little while the bystanders again said	3
	15:35	the bystanders heard it, they said, "Listen	3
Lke	19:24	He said to the bystanders, 'Take the pound	3

C

Caesarea

1. Καισάρεια, *Kaisareia, 2791*

Mat	16:13	into the district of Caesarea Philippi	1
Mrk	8:27	to the villages of Caesarea Philippi;	1
Act	8:40	until he came to Caesarea	1
	9:30	they brought him down to Caesarea	1
	10: 1	In Caesarea there was a man named Cornelius	1
	10:24	The following day they came to Caesarea.	1
	11:11	three men, sent to me from Caesarea, arrived	1
	12:19	Then he went down from Judea to Caesarea	1
	18:22	When he had landed at Caesarea, he went up	1
	21: 8	The next day we left and came to Caesarea;	1
	21:16	disciples from Caesarea also came along	1
	23:23	to leave by nine o'clock tonight for Caesarea	1
	23:33	When they came to Caesarea	1
	25: 1	he went up from Caesarea to Jerusalem	1
	25: 4	Paul was being kept at Caesarea	1
	25: 6	he went down to Caesarea;	1
	25:13	Agrippa...arrived at Caesarea to welcome Festus.	1

Caiaphas

1. Καϊάφας, *Kaiaphas, 2780*

Mat	26: 3	the high priest, who was called Caiaphas	1
	26:57	took him to Caiaphas the high priest	1
Lke	3: 2	during the high priesthood of Annas and Caiaphas	1
Jhn	11:49	Caiaphas, who was high priest that year, said	1
	18:13	Annas, who was the father-in-law of Caiaphas	1
	18:14	Caiaphas was the one who had advised the Jews	1
	18:24	Then Annas sent him bound to Caiaphas	1
	18:28	they took Jesus from Caiaphas	1
Act	4: 6	with Annas the high priest, Caiaphas, John,	1

Cain

1. Κάϊν, *Kain, 2782*

Heb	11: 4	a more acceptable sacrifice than Cain's.	1
1Jn	3:12	not be like Cain who...murdered his brother.	1
Jde	1:11	Woe to them! For they go the way of Cain	1

Cainan

1. Καϊνάμ, *Kainam, 2783*

| Lke | 3:36 | son of Cainan, son of Arphaxad | |
| | 3:37 | son of Jared, son of Mahalaleel, son of Cainan, | 1 |

calamity

1. στενοχωρία, *stenochōria, 5103*

| 2Co | 6: 4 | in afflictions, hardships, calamities | 1 |
| | 12:10 | hardships, persecutions, and calamities | 1 |

calculate
1. συμψηφίζω, *sympsēphizō, 5248*
2. ψηφίζω, *psēphizō, 6028*

Act 19:19 the value of these books was calculated   1
Rev 13:18 let anyone...calculate the number of the beast   2

calf   *See also* make a calf
1. μόσχος, *moschos, 3675*

Lke 15:23 get the fatted calf and kill it   1
    15:27 your father has killed the fatted calf   1
    15:30 you killed the fatted calf for him!'   1
Heb 9:12 not with the blood of goats and calves   1
    9:19 he took the blood of calves and goats   1

fat calf
1. σιτιστός, *sitistos, 4990*

Mat 22: 4 my oxen and my fat calves have been slaughtered   1

call
1. Contextual: Not in Greek
2. αἰτέω, *aiteō, 160*
3. ἐπικαλέω, *epikaleō, 2126*
4. ἐπιλέγω, *epilegō, 2141*
5. ἐπονομάζω, *eponomazō, 2226*
6. καλέω, *kaleō, 2813*
7. κλῆσις, *klēsis, 3104*
8. κλητός, *klētos, 3105*
9. κράζω, *krazō, 3189*
10. λέγω, *legō, 3306*
11. ὄνομα, *onoma, 3950*
12. ὄνομα + ἔχω, *onoma + echō, 3950 + 2400*
13. προσκαλέω, *proskaleō, 4673*
14. προσφωνέω, *prosphōneō, 4715*
15. φωνέω, *phōneō, 5888*
16. φωνή, *phōnē, 5889*
17. χρηματίζω, *chrēmatizō, 5976*
18. ὧδε, *hōde, 6045*

Mat 1:16 Jesus was born, who is called the Messiah.   10
   2: 7 Then Herod secretly called for the wise men   6
   2:15 "Out of Egypt I have called my son."   6
   2:23 he made his home in a town called Nazareth   10
   2:23 fulfilled, "He will be called a Nazorean."   6
   4:18 brothers, Simon, who is called Peter, and Andrew   10
   4:21 mending their nets, and he called them.   6
   5: 9 for they will be called children of God.   6
   5:19 teaches others to do the same, will be called least   6
   5:19 and teaches them will be called great   6
   9: 9 he saw a man called Matthew   10
   9:13 come to call not the righteous but sinners."   6
   10:25 If they have called the master of the house   3
   11:16 and calling to one another   14
   13:55 Is not his mother called Mary?   10
   18: 2 called a child, whom he put among them   13
   20: 8 'Call the laborers and give them their pay   6
   20:32 Jesus stood still and called them, saying   15
   21:13 'My house shall be called a house of prayer';   6
   22: 3 sent his slaves to call those who had been invited   6
   22:14 For many are called, but few are chosen."   8
   22:43 by the Spirit calls him Lord, saying   6
   22:45 If David thus calls him Lord, how can he be his son?"   6
   23: 7 to have people call them rabbi.   6
   23: 8 But you are not to be called rabbi.   6
   23: 9 call no one your father on earth   6
   23:10 Nor are you to be called instructors   6
   26: 3 the high priest, who was called Caiaphas   10
   26:14 one of the twelve, who was called Judas Iscariot   10
   26:36 to a place called Gethsemane;   10
   27: 8 that field has been called the Field of Blood   6
   27:16 a notorious prisoner, called Jesus Barabbas.   10
   27:17 Jesus Barabbas or Jesus who is called the Messiah?"   10
   27:22 I do with Jesus who is called the Messiah?"   10
   27:33 when they came to a place called Golgotha   10
   27:47 "This man is calling for Elijah."   15
Mrk 1:20 Immediately he called them;   6
   2:17 I have come to call not the righteous but sinners."   6
   3:31 standing outside, they sent to him and called   6
   6: 7 He called the twelve   13
   7:14 he called the crowd again and said   13
   8: 1 he called his disciples and said to them   13

   8:34 He called the crowd with his disciples   13
   9:35 He sat down, called the twelve   15
   10:18 "Why do you call me good? No one is good but God   10
   10:42 Jesus called them and said to them   13
   10:49 Jesus stood still and said, "Call him   15
   10:49 they called the blind man, saying to him   15
   10:49 "Take heart; get up, he is calling you."   15
   11:17 'My house shall be called a house of prayer   6
   12:37 calls him Lord; so how can he be his son?"   10
   12:43 he called his disciples and said to them   13
   14:32 They went to a place called Gethsemane;   11
   15: 7 a man called Barabbas was in prison with the rebels   10
   15:12 do with the man you call the King of the Jews?"   10
   15:22 they brought Jesus to the place called Golgotha   1
   15:35 "Listen, he is calling for Elijah."   15
Lke 1:26 to a town in Galilee called Nazareth   11
   1:32 will be called the Son of the Most High   6
   1:35 will be holy; he will be called Son of God.   6
   1:60 his mother said, "No; he is to be called John."   6
   1:76 you...will be called the prophet of the Most High;   6
   2: 4 to the city of David called Bethlehem   6
   2:21 he was called Jesus, the name given by the angel   6
   5:32 I have come to call not the righteous but sinners   6
   6:13 when day came, he called his disciples   14
   6:15 Simon, who was called the Zealot   6
   6:46 "Why do you call me 'Lord, Lord,' and do not   6
   7:11 Soon afterwards he went to a town called Nain   6
   8: 2 Mary, called Magdalene   6
   9:10 withdrew privately to a city called Bethsaida.   6
   15:19 I am no longer worthy to be called your son;   6
   15:21 I am no longer worthy to be called your son.'   6
   15:26 He called one of the slaves   13
   18:19 "Why do you call me good? No one is good but God   10
   19:29 at the place called the Mount of Olives,   6
   20:44 David thus calls him Lord; so how can he be his son?"   6
   21:37 on the Mount of Olives, as it was called.   6
   22: 1 which is called the Passover   10
   22: 3 Then Satan entered into Judas called Iscariot   6
   22:25 those in authority...are called benefactors.   6
   22:47 one called Judas, one of the twelve, was leading   10
   23:33 they came to the place that is called The Skull   6
   24:13 two of them were going to a village called Emmaus   11
Jhn 1:42 You are to be called Cephas"   6
   1:48 under the fig tree before Philip called you."   15
   2: 9 the steward called the bridegroom   15
   4: 5 So he came to a Samaritan city called Sychar   10
   4:16 "Go, call your husband, and come back."   15
   4:25 Messiah is coming" (who is called Christ).   10
   5: 2 a pool, called in Hebrew Beth-zatha   4
   5:18 also calling God his own Father   10
   6: 1 Sea of Galilee, also called the Sea of Tiberias.   1
   9:11 He answered, "The man called Jesus made mud   10
   9:18 until they called the parents of the man   15
   9:24 they called the man who had been blind   15
   10: 3 calls his own sheep by name and leads them out.   15
   10:35 to whom the word of God came were called 'gods'   10
   11:16 Thomas, who was called the Twin   10
   11:28 she went back and called her sister Mary,   15
   11:28 "The Teacher is here and is calling for you."   15
   11:54 went from there to a town called Ephraim   10
   12:17 when he called Lazarus out of the tomb   15
   13:13 You call me Teacher and Lord—and you are right   15
   15:15 I do not call you servants any longer   10
   15:15 I have called you friends   10
   19:13 at a place called The Stone Pavement   10
   19:17 to what is called The Place of the Skull   10
   19:17 which in Hebrew is called Golgotha.   10
   20:24 But Thomas (who was called the Twin),   10
   21: 2 Simon Peter, Thomas called the Twin   10
Act 1:12 from the mount called Olivet   6
   1:19 the field was called in their language Hakeldama   6
   1:23 they proposed two, Joseph called Barsabbas   6
   2:39 everyone whom the Lord our God calls to him."   13
   3: 2 gate of the temple called the Beautiful Gate   10
   3:11 in the portico called Solomon's Portico   6
   4:18 So they called them and ordered them not to speak   6
   6: 9 the synagogue of the Freedmen (as it was called),   10
   8:10 the power of God that is called Great."   6
   9:11 "Get up and go to the street called Straight   6
   9:41 Then calling the saints and widows   15
   10: 1 the Italian Cohort, as it was called.   6

Act	10: 5	send...for a certain Simon who is called Peter;	3
	10: 7	called two of his slaves and a devout soldier	15
	10:18	Simon, who was called Peter, was staying there.	3
	10:28	I should not call anyone profane or unclean.	10
	10:32	ask for Simon, who is called Peter;	3
	11:13	'Send to Joppa and bring Simon, who is called Peter;	3
	11:26	the disciples were first called "Christians."	17
	13: 1	Barnabas, Simeon who was called Niger	6
	13: 2	the work to which I have called them."	13
	14:12	Barnabas they called Zeus	6
	14:12	Paul they called Hermes	1
	15:22	They sent Judas called Barsabbas, and Silas	6
	15:37	wanted to take with them John called Mark.	6
	16:10	convinced that God had called us	13
	16:29	The jailer called for lights, and rushing in	2
	22:16	have your sins washed away, calling on his name.'	3
	23:17	Paul called one of the centurions and said	13
	23:18	"The prisoner Paul called me	13
	24:14	according to the Way, which they call a sect	10
	27: 8	we came to a place called Fair Havens	6
	27:14	soon a violent wind, called the northeaster	6
	27:16	a small island called Cauda	6
	28: 1	then learned that the island was called Malta.	6
Rom	1: 1	Paul...called to be an apostle	8
	1: 6	who are called to belong to Jesus Christ	8
	1: 7	God's beloved in Rome, who are called to be saints:	8
	2:17	if you call yourself a Jew and rely on the law	5
	4:17	calls into existence the things that do not exist.	6
	7: 3	Accordingly, she will be called an adulteress	17
	8:28	who are called according to his purpose.	8
	8:30	And those whom he predestined he also called;	6
	8:30	and those whom he called he also justified;	6
	9:12	not by works but by his call)	6
	9:24	us whom he has called, not from the Jews only	6
	9:25	"Those who were not my people I will call 'my people,'	6
	9:25	her who was not beloved I will call 'beloved.' "	1
	9:26	they shall be called children of the living God."	6
	11:29	the gifts and the calling of God are irrevocable.	7
1Co	1: 1	Paul, called to be an apostle of Christ Jesus	8
	1: 2	called to be saints	8
	1: 9	God is faithful; by him you were called	6
	1:24	to those who are the called, both Jews and Greeks	8
	1:26	Consider your own call, brothers and sisters:	7
	7:15	It is to peace that God has called you.	6
	7:17	to which God called you.	6
	7:18	Was anyone at the time of his call...circumcised?	6
	7:18	Was anyone at the time of his call uncircumcised?	6
	7:20	remain in the condition in which you were called.	6
	7:21	Were you a slave when called? Do not be concerned	6
	7:22	called in the Lord as a slave is a freed person	6
	7:22	whoever was free when called is a slave of Christ.	6
	7:24	In whatever condition you were called	6
	15: 9	unfit to be called an apostle	6
2Co	1:23	I call on God as witness against me:	3
Gal	1: 6	who called you in the grace of Christ	6
	1:15	called me through his grace	6
	5: 8	Such persuasion does not come from the one who calls	6
	5:13	you were called to freedom, brothers and sisters;	6
Eph	1:18	know what is the hope to which he has called you	7
	2:11	Gentiles by birth, called "the uncircumcision"	10
	2:11	by those who are called "the circumcision"	10
	4: 1	to lead a life worthy of the calling	7
	4: 1	the calling to which you have been called	6
	4: 4	just as you were called to the one hope	6
	4: 4	the one hope of your calling	7
Php	3:14	prize of the heavenly call of God in Christ Jesus.	7
Col	3:15	to which indeed you were called in the one body.	6
	4:11	Jesus who is called Justus greets you	10
1Th	2:12	who calls you into his own kingdom and glory.	6
	4: 7	God did not call us to impurity	6
	4:16	For the Lord himself...with the archangel's call	16
	5:24	who calls you is faithful, and he will do this.	6
2Th	1:11	that our God will make you worthy of his call	7
	2:14	For this purpose he called you	6
1Ti	6:12	the eternal life, to which you were called	6
2Ti	1: 9	who saved us and called us with a holy calling	6
	1: 9	who saved us and called us with a holy calling	7
Heb	2:11	Jesus is not ashamed to call them brothers and sisters	6
	3: 1	brothers and sisters, holy partners in a heavenly calling	7
	3:13	as long as it is called "today,"	6
	5: 4	only when called by God, just as Aaron was.	6

	9: 2	this is called the Holy Place.	10
	9: 3	a tent called the Holy of Holies.	10
	9:15	so that those who are called may receive	6
	11: 8	obeyed when he was called to set out	6
	11:16	God is not ashamed to be called their God;	3
	11:24	refused to be called a son of Pharaoh's daughter	10
Jas	2:23	and he was called the friend of God.	6
	5:14	They should call for the elders of the church	13
1Pe	1:15	as he who called you is holy, be holy yourselves	6
	2: 9	called you out of darkness into...light.	6
	2:21	For to this you have been called	6
	3: 6	Thus Sarah obeyed Abraham and called him lord.	6
	3: 9	It is for this that you were called	6
	5:10	who has called you to his eternal glory in Christ	6
2Pe	1: 3	through the knowledge of him who called us	6
	1:10	more eager to confirm your call and election	7
1Jn	3: 1	should be called children of God; and that is what we are.	6
Jde	1: 1	who are called, who are beloved in God the Father	8
Rev	1: 9	I, John...was on the island called Patmos	6
	2:20	Jezebel, who calls herself a prophet	10
	2:24	learned what some call 'the deep things of Satan,'	10
	6:16	calling to the mountains and rocks, "Fall on us	10
	7: 2	he called with a loud voice to the four angels	9
	9:11	and in Greek he is called Apollyon.	12
	11: 8	city that is prophetically called Sodom	6
	12: 9	serpent, who is called the Devil and Satan	6
	13:10	you must be killed. Here is a call for the endurance	18
	13:18	This calls for wisdom:	18
	14:12	Here is a call for the endurance of the saints	18
	14:15	Another angel...calling with a loud voice	9
	14:18	another angel...called with a loud voice	15
	16:16	the place that in Hebrew is called Harmagedon.	6
	17: 9	"This calls for a mind that has wisdom:	18
	17:14	those with him are called and chosen and faithful."	8
	19:11	Its rider is called Faithful and True	6
	19:13	his name is called The Word of God.	6
	19:17	with a loud voice he called to all the birds	9

call a meeting

1. συνάγω, *synagō, 5251*

Jhn	11:47	the Pharisees called a meeting of the council,	1

call attention

1. ὑπομιμνήσκω, *hypomimnēskō, 5703*

3Jn	1:10	So if I come, I will call attention to what he is doing	1

call blessed

1. μακαρίζω, *makarizō, 3420*

Lke	1:48	all generations will call me blessed;	1
Jas	5:11	Indeed we call blessed those who showed endurance.	1

call falsely

1. ψευδώνυμος, *pseudōnymos, 6024*

1Ti	6:20	what is falsely called knowledge;	1

call for

1. προσκαλέω, *proskaleō, 4673*

Lke	18:16	Jesus called for them and said,	1

call in

1. προσκαλέω, *proskaleō, 4673*

Act	5:40	when they had called in the apostles	1

call on

1. ἐπικαλέω, *epikaleō, 2126*

Act	2:21	everyone who calls on the name of the Lord	1
Rom	10:12	and is generous to all who call on him.	1
	10:13	For, "Everyone who calls on the name of the Lord	1
	10:14	to call on one in whom they have not believed?	1
1Co	1: 2	call on the name of our Lord Jesus Christ	1
2Ti	2:22	those who call on the Lord from a pure heart.	1

call on a name

1. ὀνομάζω, *onomazō, 3951*

2Ti	2:19	everyone who calls on the name of the Lord turn away	1

call out

1. αἴρω + φωνή, *airō + phōnē, 149 + 5889*
2. κράζω, *krazō, 3189*

3. λέγω, *legō, 3306*
4. φωνέω, *phōneō, 5888*

Lke	8: 8 As he said this, he called out, "Let anyone	4
	8:54 took her by the hand and called out, "Child	4
	16:24 He called out, 'Father Abraham, have mercy	4
	17:13 called out, saying, "Jesus, Master	1
Act	10:18 They called out to ask whether Simon	4
	23: 6 he called out in the council	2
	24:21 unless it was this one sentence that I called out	2
Rev	6: 1 I heard one of the four living creatures call out	3
	6: 3 the second living creature call out, "Come!"	3
	6: 5 I heard the third living creature call out, "Come!"	3
	6: 7 the fourth living creature call out, "Come!"	3
	18: 2 He called out with a mighty voice	2

call over

1. ἐπικαλέω, *epikaleō, 2126*
2. προσφωνέω, *prosphōneō, 4715*

Lke	13:12 Jesus saw her, he called her over and said	2
Act	15:17 all the Gentiles over whom my name has been called.	1

call profane

1. κοινόω, *koinoō, 3124*

Act	10:15 "What God has made clean, you must not call profane."	1
	11: 9 'What God has made clean, you must not call profane.'	1

call to

1. προσκαλέω, *proskaleō, 4673*
2. προσφωνέω, *prosphōneō, 4715*

Mat	15:10 he called the crowd to him and said to them	1
	15:32 Jesus called his disciples to him and said	1
	20:25 Jesus called them to him and said	1
Mrk	3:13 called to him those whom he wanted	1
	3:23 he called them to him	1
Lke	7:32 like children…calling to one another	2

call to account

1. ἀνακρίνω, *anakrinō, 373*

1Co	14:24 called to account by all.	1

call together

1. προσκαλέω, *proskaleō, 4673*
2. συγκαλέω, *synkaleō, 5157*
3. συνάγω, *synagō, 5251*

Mat	2: 4 calling together all the chief priests and scribes	3
Mrk	15:16 they called together the whole cohort.	2
Lke	9: 1 Then Jesus called the twelve together	2
	15: 6 he comes home, he calls together his friends	2
	15: 9 she calls together her friends and neighbors	2
	23:13 Pilate then called together the chief priests	2
Act	5:21 they called together the council	2
	6: 2 the twelve called together the whole community	1
	10:24 Cornelius…had called together his relatives	2
	14:27 they called the church together	3
	28:17 he called together the local leaders of the Jews.	2

trumpet call

1. σάλπιγξ, *salpinx, 4894*

Mat	24:31 send out his angels with a loud trumpet call	1

calm

1. γαλήνη, *galēnē, 1132*

Mat	8:26 and there was a dead calm.	1
Mrk	4:39 the wind ceased, and there was a dead calm.	1
Lke	8:24 they ceased, and there was a calm.	1

camel

1. κάμηλος, *kamēlos, 2823*

Mat	3: 4 clothing of camel's hair with a leather belt	1
	19:24 Again I tell you, it is easier for a camel	1
	23:24 You strain out a gnat but swallow a camel!	1
Mrk	1: 6 Now John was clothed with camel's hair	1
	10:25 easier for a camel to go through the eye	1
Lke	18:25 Indeed, it is easier for a camel to go	1

camp

1. παρεμβολή, *parembolē, 4213*

Heb	13:11 are burned outside the camp.	1
	13:13 Let us then go to him outside the camp	1

Rev	20: 9 and surrounded the camp of the saints	1

can

1. Contextual: Not in Greek
2. δύναμαι, *dynamai, 1538*
3. δυνατός, *dynatos, 1543*
4. ἔχω, *echō, 2400*
5. ἰσχύω, *ischyō, 2710*
6. οἶδα, *oida, 3857*
7. παράκειμαι, *parakeimai, 4154*

Mat	6:24 "No one can serve two masters; for a slave	2
	6:27 can any of you by worrying add a single hour	2
	8: 2 "Lord, if you choose, you can make me clean."	2
	8:28 so fierce that no one could pass that way.	5
	10:28 rather fear him who can destroy both soul and body	2
	12:29 Or how can one enter a strong man's house	2
	12:34 You brood of vipers! How can you speak good	2
	17:16 but they could not cure him."	2
	17:19 "Why could we not cast it out?"	2
	18:25 could not pay, his lord ordered him to be sold	4
	19:12 Let anyone accept this who can."	2
	19:25 "Then who can be saved?"	2
	26: 9 For this ointment could have been sold	2
	26:40 "So, could you not stay awake with me one hour?	5
	27:65 go, make it as secure as you can."	6
Mrk	1:40 "If you choose, you can make me clean."	2
	1:45 Jesus could no longer go into a town openly	2
	2: 4 when they could not bring him to Jesus	2
	2: 7 Who can forgive sins but God alone?"	2
	3:20 so that they could not even eat.	2
	3:23 "How can Satan cast out Satan?	2
	3:27 no one can enter a strong man's house	2
	4:32 birds of the air can make nests in its shade."	2
	5: 3 no one could restrain him any more	2
	6: 5 he could do no deed of power there	2
	6:19 wanted to kill him. But she could not	2
	7:15 that by going in can defile	2
	7:24 Yet he could not escape notice	2
	8: 4 "How can one feed these people with bread here	2
	9: 3 such as no one on earth could bleach them.	2
	9:18 they could not do so."	5
	9:23 All things can be done for the one who believes."	3
	9:28 "Why could we not cast it out?"	2
	9:29 "This kind can come out only through	2
	10:26 "Then who can be saved?"	2
	14: 5 For this ointment could have been sold	2
	14: 7 you can show kindness to them whenever you wish;	2
	14: 8 She has done what she could;	4
	14:37 you asleep? Could you not keep awake one hour?	5
Lke	1:22 When he did come out, he could not speak to them	2
	5:12 "Lord, if you choose, you can make me clean."	2
	5:21 Who can forgive sins but God alone?"	2
	6:39 "Can a blind person guide a blind person?	2
	6:42 how can you say to your neighbor, 'Friend	2
	6:48 burst against that house but could not shake it	5
	7:42 When they could not pay, he canceled the debts	4
	8:19 they could not reach him because of the crowd.	2
	8:43 on physicians, no one could cure her.	5
	9:40 they could not."	2
	12: 4 after that can do nothing more.	4
	12:25 can any of you by worrying add a single hour	2
	14: 6 they could not reply to this.	5
	14:33 none of you can become my disciple if	2
	16:13 No slave can serve two masters;	2
	18:26 who heard it said, "Then who can be saved?"	2
	19: 3 but on account of the crowd he could not	2
Jhn	1:46 "Can anything good come out of Nazareth?"	2
	3: 2 for no one can do these signs that you do	2
	3: 3 no one can see the kingdom of God without	2
	3: 4 "How can anyone be born after having grown old?	2
	3: 4 Can one enter a second time into the mother's womb	2
	3: 5 no one can enter the kingdom of God without	2
	3: 9 Nicodemus said to him, "How can these things be?"	2
	3:27 John answered, "No one can receive anything	2
	5:19 the Son can do nothing on his own	2
	5:30 "I can do nothing on my own.	2
	5:44 How can you believe when you accept glory from	2
	6:44 No one can come to me unless drawn	2
	6:52 "How can this man give us his flesh to eat?"	2
	6:60 "This teaching is difficult; who can accept it?"	2

Jhn	6:65	I have told you that no one can come to me	2
	9: 4	night is coming when no one can work.	2
	9:16	"How can a man who is a sinner perform such signs?"	2
	9:33	If this man were not from God, he could do nothing."	2
	10:21	Can a demon open the eyes of the blind?"	2
	10:29	can snatch it out of the Father's hand.	2
	11:37	"Could not he who opened the eyes of the blind	2
	12:39	so they could not believe	2
	13:37	"Lord, why can I not follow you now?	2
	14: 5	How can we know the way?"	2
	15: 4	neither can you unless you abide in me.	1
	15: 5	because apart from me you can do nothing.	2
Act	6:10	could not withstand the wisdom and the Spirit	5
	8:31	He replied, "How can I, unless someone guides me?"	2
	10:47	"Can anyone withhold the water for baptizing	2
	11:17	who was I that I could hinder God?"	3
	13:39	you could not be freed by the law of Moses.	2
	19:40	no cause that we can give to justify this	2
	21:34	as he could not learn the facts	2
	24:11	As you can find out	2
	24:13	Neither can they prove to you	2
	25: 7	charges against him, which they could not prove.	5
	25:11	no one can turn me over to them.	2
	26:32	"This man could have been set free	2
	27:12	somehow they could reach Phoenix	2
	27:15	could not be turned head-on into the wind	2
	27:39	planned to run the ship ashore, if they could.	2
	27:43	He ordered those who could swim	2
Rom	7:18	I can will what is right, but I cannot do it.	7
1Co	3: 1	I could not speak to you as spiritual people	2
	3:11	For no one can lay any foundation other	2
	7:21	Even if you can gain your freedom	2
	12: 3	no one can say "Jesus is Lord"	2
	14:31	For you can all prophesy one by one	2
2Co	3: 7	people of Israel could not gaze at Moses' face	2
Gal	3:21	if a law had been given that could make alive	2
1Th	3: 9	How can we thank God enough for you	2
1Ti	6: 7	so that we can take nothing out of it;	2
	6:16	whom no one has ever seen or can see;	2
2Ti	3: 7	can never arrive at a knowledge of the truth.	2
Heb	10: 1	it can never...make perfect those who approach.	2
	10:11	sacrifices that can never take away sins.	2
Jas	2:14	but do not have works? Can faith save you?	2
	3: 8	no one can tame the tongue—a restless evil	2
	3:12	Can a fig tree, my brothers and sisters, yield olives	2
Rev	7: 9	a great multitude that no one could count	2
	13: 4	"Who is like the beast, and who can fight against it?"	2
	13:17	no one can buy or sell who does not have the mark	2
	14: 3	No one could learn that song except	2
	15: 8	and no one could enter the temple	2

can not

   1. ἀδύνατος, *adynatos, 105*

Act	14: 8	a man sitting who could not use his feet	1
Rom	8: 3	what the law, weakened by the flesh, could not do:	1

can not speak

   1. ἄφωνος, *aphōnos, 936*

1Co	12: 2	and led astray to idols that could not speak	1

Cana

   1. Κανά, *Kana, 2830*

Jhn	2: 1	there was a wedding in Cana of Galilee	1
	2:11	the first of his signs, in Cana of Galilee	1
	4:46	Then he came again to Cana in Galilee	1
	21: 2	Nathanael of Cana in Galilee, the sons of Zebedee	1

Canaan

   1. Χανάαν, *Chanaan, 5913*

Act	7:11	came a famine throughout Egypt and Canaan	1
	13:19	destroyed seven nations in the land of Canaan	1

Canaanite

   1. Χαναναῖος, *Chananaios, 5914*

Mat	15:22	Just then a Canaanite woman from that region	1

Cananaean

   1. Καναναῖος, *Kananaios, 2831*

Mat	10: 4	Simon the Cananaean, and Judas Iscariot	1
Mrk	3:18	Thaddaeus, and Simon the Cananaean	1

cancel a debt

   1. χαρίζομαι, *charizomai, 5919*

Lke	7:42	When they could not pay, he canceled the debts	1
	7:43	one for whom he canceled the greater debt."	1

Candace

   1. Κανδάκη, *Kandakē, 2833*

Act	8:27	the Candace, queen of the Ethiopians	1

cannot

   1. μή, *mē, 3590*
   2. μή + δύναμαι, *mē + dynamai, 3590 + 1538*
   3. μήτι, *mēti, 3614*
   4. οὐ, *ou, 4024*
   5. οὐ + δύναμαι, *ou + dynamai, 4024 + 1538*
   6. οὐ + ἔχω, *ou + echō, 4024 + 2400*
   7. οὐδέ + δύναμαι, *oude + dynamai, 4028 + 1538*
   8. οὔτε + δύναμαι, *oute + dynamai, 4046 + 1538*

Mat	5:14	A city built on a hill cannot be hid.	5
	5:36	head, for you cannot make one hair white or black.	5
	6:24	the other. You cannot serve God and wealth.	5
	7:18	A good tree cannot bear bad fruit	5
	9:15	wedding guests cannot mourn as long as the bridegroom	2
	10:28	kill the body but cannot kill the soul;	2
	16: 3	but you cannot interpret the signs of the times.	5
	26:42	if this cannot pass unless I drink it	5
	26:53	Do you think that I cannot appeal to my Father	5
	27:42	"He saved others; he cannot save himself.	5
Mrk	2:19	wedding guests cannot fast while the bridegroom	5
	2:19	bridegroom with them, they cannot fast.	5
	3:24	that kingdom cannot stand.	5
	3:26	he cannot stand, but his end has come.	5
	7:18	goes into a person from outside cannot defile	5
	15:31	saying, "He saved others; he cannot save himself.	5
Lke	5:34	"You cannot make wedding guests fast	2
	11: 7	I cannot get up and give you anything.'	5
	14:14	you will be blessed, because they cannot repay	6
	14:20	just been married, and therefore I cannot come.'	5
	14:26	even life itself, cannot be my disciple.	5
	14:27	cannot be my disciple.	5
	14:32	If he cannot, then, while the other is still	1
	16: 2	you cannot be my manager any longer.'	5
	16:13	You cannot serve God and wealth."	5
	16:26	who might want to pass from here to you cannot	2
	20:36	Indeed they cannot die anymore	7
Jhn	4:29	He cannot be the Messiah, can he?"	3
	7: 7	The world cannot hate you, but it hates me	5
	7:34	where I am, you cannot come."	5
	7:36	'Where I am, you cannot come'?"	5
	8:21	Where I am going, you cannot come."	5
	8:22	by saying, 'Where I am going, you cannot come'?"	5
	8:43	It is because you cannot accept my word.	5
	10:35	and the scripture cannot be annulled	5
	13:33	'Where I am going, you cannot come.'	5
	13:36	"Where I am going, you cannot follow me now;	5
	14:17	whom the world cannot receive	5
	15: 4	Just as the branch cannot bear fruit by itself	5
	16:12	you cannot bear them now.	5
Act	4:16	we cannot deny it.	5
	4:20	for we cannot keep from speaking about what	5
	15: 1	circumcised...you cannot be saved."	5
	27:31	stay in the ship, you cannot be saved."	5
Rom	7:18	I can will what is right, but I cannot do it.	4
	8: 7	it does not submit to God's law—indeed it cannot	7
	8: 8	those who are in the flesh cannot please God.	5
	11:10	their eyes be darkened so that they cannot see	1
1Co	10:21	You cannot drink the cup of the Lord	5
	10:21	You cannot partake of the table of the Lord	5
	12:21	The eye cannot say to the hand, "I have no need	5
	15:50	flesh and blood cannot inherit the kingdom	5
2Co	4:18	what can be seen but at what cannot be seen	1
	4:18	what cannot be seen is eternal.	1
	13: 8	For we cannot do anything against the truth	5
1Ti	5:25	when they are not, they cannot remain hidden.	5
2Ti	2:13	for he cannot deny himself.	5
Heb	9: 5	Of these things we cannot speak now in detail.	4
	9: 9	cannot perfect the conscience of the worshiper	2
	12:27	so that what cannot be shaken may remain.	1
Jas	4: 2	you covet something and cannot obtain it;	5
1Jn	3: 9	they cannot sin, because they have been born of God.	5

4:20 cannot love God whom they have not seen. 5
Rev   2: 2 I know that you cannot tolerate evildoers 5
9:20 idols…which cannot see or hear or walk. 8

cannot be censured
1. ἀκατάγνωστος, *akatagnōstos, 183*
Tit   2: 8 sound speech that cannot be censured; 1

cannot be denied
1. ἀναντίρρητος, *anantirrētos, 394*
Act 19:36 Since these things cannot be denied 1

cannot be shaken
1. ἀσάλευτος, *asaleutos, 810*
Heb 12:28 since we are receiving a kingdom that cannot be shaken 1

cannot be tempted
1. ἀπείραστος, *apeirastos, 585*
Jas   1:13 for God cannot be tempted by evil 1

Capernaum
1. Καφαρναούμ, *Kapharnaoum, 3019*
Mat   4:13 left Nazareth and made his home in Capernaum 1
8: 5 When he entered Capernaum, a centurion came 1
11:23 you, Capernaum, will you be exalted to heaven? 1
17:24 When they reached Capernaum 1
Mrk 1:21 They went to Capernaum; 1
2: 1 When he returned to Capernaum after some days 1
9:33 they came to Capernaum; 1
Lke 4:23 things that we have heard you did at Capernaum.' " 1
4:31 He went down to Capernaum, a city in Galilee 1
7: 1 he entered Capernaum. 1
10:15 you, Capernaum, will you be exalted to heaven? 1
Jhn   2:12 After this he went down to Capernaum 1
4:46 there was a royal official whose son lay ill 1
6:17 started across the sea to Capernaum. 1
6:24 they…got into the boats and went to Capernaum 1
6:59 he was teaching in the synagogue at Capernaum. 1

Cappadocia
1. Καππαδοκία, *Kappadokia, 2838*
Act   2: 9 residents of Mesopotamia, Judea and Cappadocia 1
1Pe   1: 1 the Dispersion in Pontus, Galatia, Cappadocia 1

captain
1. στρατηγός, *stratēgos, 5130*
2. χιλίαρχος, *chiliarchos, 5941*
Act   4: 1 the priests, the captain of the temple 1
5:24 the captain of the temple and the chief priests 1
5:26 captain went with the temple police and brought 1
Rev 19:18 to eat the flesh of kings, the flesh of captains 2

captivate
1. αἰχμαλωτίζω, *aichmalōtizō, 170*
2Ti   3: 6 captivate silly women, overwhelmed by their sins 1

captive *See also* hold captive, make a captive, make captive, take away as captive, take captive
1. αἰχμάλωτος, *aichmalōtos, 171*
2. δέω, *deō, 1313*
Lke   4:18 has sent me to proclaim release to the captives 1
Act 20:22 captive to the Spirit, I am on my way to Jerusalem 2

captivity
1. αἰχμαλωσία, *aichmalōsia, 168*
Eph   4: 8 on high he made captivity itself a captive 1
Rev 13:10 If…to be taken captive, into captivity you go; 1

capture
1. πιάζω, *piazō, 4389*
Rev 19:20 And the beast was captured 1

care[1] *See also* choose with care, take care, take care of needs
1. μέλει, *melei, 3508*
2. μέριμνα, *merimna, 3533*
3. μεριμνάω, *merimnaō, 3534*
Mat 13:22 but the cares of the world…choke the word 2

Mrk   4:19 the cares of the world, and the lure of wealth 2
4:38 "Teacher, do you not care that we are perishing?" 1
Lke   8:14 they are choked by the cares and riches 2
10:40 do you not care that my sister has left me 1
Jhn 10:13 a hired hand does not care for the sheep. 1
12: 6 (He said this not because he cared about the poor 1
1Co 12:25 members may have the same care for one another. 3
1Pe   5: 7 Cast…anxiety on him, because he cares for you. 1

care[2]
1. ἐπιμέλεια, *epimeleia, 2149*
2. ἐπισκέπτομαι, *episkeptomai, 2170*
Act 27: 3 allowed him to go to his friends to be cared for. 1
Heb   2: 6 "What are…mortals, that you care for them? 2
Jas   1:27 to care for orphans and widows in their distress 2

care for deeply
1. ὁμείρομαι, *homeiromai, 3916*
1Th   2: 8 So deeply do we care for you 1

care for tenderly
1. θάλπω, *thalpō, 2499*
Eph   5:29 he nourishes and tenderly cares for it 1
1Th   2: 7 like a nurse tenderly caring for her own children. 1

careful *See also* make careful search
1. βλέπω + ἀκριβῶς, *blepō + akribōs, 1063 + 209*
2. φροντίζω, *phrontizō, 5863*
Eph   5:15 Be careful then how you live 1
Tit   3: 8 may be careful to devote themselves to good works; 2

carefully *See also* consider carefully, look carefully
1. ἀκριβῶς, *akribōs, 209*
2. ἐπιμελῶς, *epimelōs, 2151*
Lke   1: 3 after investigating everything carefully 1
15: 8 search carefully until she finds it? 2

careless
1. ἀργός, *argos, 734*
Mat 12:36 have to give an account for every careless word 1

cargo *See also* throw overboard cargo
1. γόμος, *gomos, 1203*
2. φορτίον, *phortion, 5845*
Act 21: 3 the ship was to unload its cargo there. 1
27:10 not only of the cargo and the ship 2
Rev 18:11 since no one buys their cargo anymore 1
18:12 cargo of gold, silver, jewels and pearls 1

carnelian
1. σάρδιον, *sardion, 4917*
Rev   4: 3 the one…looks like jasper and carnelian 1
21:20 the fifth onyx, the sixth carnelian 1

carouse
1. κῶμος, *kōmos, 3269*
2. πότος, *potos, 4542*
Gal   5:21 envy, drunkenness, carousing, and things like 1
1Pe   4: 3 living in…drunkenness, revels, carousing 2

carpenter
1. τέκτων, *tektōn, 5454*
Mat 13:55 Is not this the carpenter's son? 1
Mrk   6: 3 Is not this the carpenter, the son of Mary 1

Carpus
1. Κάρπος, *Karpos, 2842*
2Ti   4:13 bring the cloak that I left with Carpus at Troas 1

carry
1. αἴρω, *airō, 149*
2. ἀποφέρω, *apopherō, 708*
3. βαστάζω, *bastazō, 1002*
4. περιφέρω, *peripherō, 4367*
5. προσφέρω, *prospherō, 4712*
6. φέρω, *pherō, 5770*
Mat   3:11 I am not worthy to carry his sandals. 3
9: 2 just then some people were carrying a paralyzed 5

Mat 27:32 they compelled this man to carry his cross. 1
Mrk 2: 3 a paralyzed man, carried by four of them. 1
14:13 a man carrying a jar of water will meet you; 3
15:21 to carry his cross; it was Simon of Cyrene 1
Lke 5:18 men came, carrying a paralyzed man on a bed. 6
10: 4 Carry no purse, no bag, no sandals; 3
14:27 Whoever does not carry the cross 3
16:22 carried away by the angels to be with Abraham. 2
22:10 a man carrying a jar of water will meet you; 3
23:26 the cross…and made him carry it behind Jesus. 6
Jhn 5:10 it is not lawful for you to carry your mat." 1
19:17 carrying the cross by himself, he went out 3
Act 3: 2 a man lame from birth was being carried in. 3
21:35 he had to be carried by the soldiers. 3
2Co 4:10 always carrying in the body the death of Jesus 4
Gal 6: 5 For all must carry their own loads. 3
6:17 I carry the marks of Jesus branded on my body. 3
Rev 17: 7 and of the beast…that carries her. 3

carry along

1. παραφέρω, *parapherō, 4195*
Jde 1:12 waterless clouds carried along by the winds; 1

carry away

1. ἀποφέρω, *apopherō, 708*
2. βαστάζω, *bastazō, 1002*
3. παραφέρω, *parapherō, 4195*
4. συναπάγω, *synapagō, 5270*
Jhn 20:15 to him, "Sir, if you have carried him away 2
Heb 13: 9 carried away by all kinds of strange teachings; 3
2Pe 3:17 carried away with the error of the lawless 4
Rev 17: 3 So he carried me away…into a wilderness 1
21:10 And in the spirit he carried me away 1

carry heavy burdens

1. φορτίζω, *phortizō, 5844*
Mat 11:28 all you that are weary and are carrying heavy burdens 1

carry out

1. Contextual: Not in Greek
2. ἀποδίδωμι, *apodidōmi, 625*
3. ἐκκομίζω, *ekkomizō, 1714*
4. ἐκφέρω, *ekpherō, 1766*
5. ἐπιτελέω, *epiteleō, 2200*
6. ποιέω, *poieō, 4472*
7. τελέω, *teleō, 5464*
Mat 5:33 carry out the vows you have made to the Lord.' 2
Lke 7:12 a man who had died was being carried out. 3
Act 5: 6 then carried him out and buried him. 4
5: 9 they will carry you out." 4
5:10 they carried her out and buried her 4
5:15 they even carried out the sick into the streets 4
13:22 a man after my heart, who will carry out all my wishes.' 6
13:29 they had carried out everything that was written 7
27:43 kept them from carrying out their plan. 1
Eph 3:11 that he has carried out in Christ Jesus our Lord 6
Heb 9: 6 priests…carry out their ritual duties; 5
Rev 17:17 to carry out his purpose by agreeing to give 6

carry out fully

1. πληροφορέω, *plērophoreō, 4442*
2Ti 4: 5 carry out your ministry fully. 1

carry through

1. διαφέρω, *diapherō, 1422*
Mrk 11:16 to carry anything through the temple. 1

carry up

1. ἀναφέρω, *anapherō, 429*
Lke 24:51 and was carried up into heaven. 1

case *See also* report a case, settle a case, such a case

1. Contextual: Not in Greek
2. αἰτία, *aitia, 162*
3. ἄρα, *ara, 726*
4. γίνομαι, *ginomai, 1181*
5. ἐάν, *ean, 1569*
6. ἐν, *en, 1877*
7. κατά, *kata, 2848*

8. κριτήριον, *kritērion, 3215*
9. μέρος, *meros, 3538*
10. περί, *peri, 4309*
11. ὧδε, *hōde, 6045*
Mat 19:10 "If such is the case of a man with his wife 2
Jhn 18:38 "I find no case against him. 2
19: 4 to let you know that I find no case against him." 2
19: 6 I find no case against him." 2
Act 23:15 to make a more thorough examination of his case. 10
23:20 to inquire more thoroughly into his case 10
24:22 I will decide your case." 7
25:14 Festus laid Paul's case before the king, saying 7
28:18 no reason for the death penalty in my case. 6
1Co 6: 2 are you incompetent to try trivial cases? 8
6: 4 If you have ordinary cases, then, 8
7: 2 because of cases of sexual immorality 1
9:15 so that they may be applied in my case 6
2Co 4: 4 In their case the god of this world has blinded 1
9: 3 may not prove to have been empty in this case 9
Gal 5:11 In that case the offense of the cross 3
2Ti 2: 5 in the case of an athlete, no one is crowned 5
3: 9 as in the case of those two men 4
Heb 6: 9 beloved, we are confident of better things in your case 10
7: 8 In the one case, tithes are received by those 11

in any case

1. πλήν, *plēn, 4440*
Php 4:14 In any case, it was kind of you to share my distress. 1

in case

1. μήποτε, *mēpote, 3607*
Lke 14: 8 in case someone more distinguished than you 1
14:12 in case they may invite you in return 1
Act 5:39 in that case you may even be found fighting against God! 1

one case

1. μέν, *men, 3525*
Mat 13:23 yields, in one case a hundredfold, 1

present case

1. νῦν, *nyn, 3814*
Act 5:38 So in the present case, I tell you 1

cast

1. βάλλω, *ballō, 965*
2. δίδωμι, *didōmi, 1443*
3. ἐπιρίπτω, *epiriptō, 2166*
Mat 4:18 Andrew his brother, casting a net into the sea 1
17:27 go to the sea and cast a hook; 1
27:35 divided his clothes…by casting lots; 1
Mrk 9:22 often cast him into the fire and into the water 1
15:24 casting lots to decide what each should take. 1
Lke 23:34 they cast lots to divide his clothing. 1
Jhn 19:24 for my clothing they cast lots." 1
21: 6 "Cast the net to the right side of the boat 1
21: 6 So they cast it 1
Act 1:26 they cast lots for them 2
1Pe 5: 7 Cast all your anxiety on him 3
1Jn 4:18 but perfect love casts out fear; 1
Rev 4:10 they cast their crowns before the throne, singing 1

cast a net

1. ἀμφιβάλλω, *amphiballō, 311*
Mrk 1:16 Simon and…Andrew casting a net into the sea 1

cast against

1. καταφέρω, *katapherō, 2965*
Act 26:10 I also cast my vote against them 1

cast into

1. ἐμβάλλω, *emballō, 1833*
Lke 12: 5 who…has authority to cast into hell. 1

cast into hell

1. ταρταρόω, *tartaroō, 5434*
2Pe 2: 4 For if God…cast them into hell 1

cast lots

1. λαγχάνω, *lanchanō, 3275*

Jhn 19:24 but cast lots for it to see who will get it."   1

cast off
1. περιαιρέω, *periaireō, 4311*
Act 27:40 cast off the anchors and left them in the sea.   1

cast out
1. ἐκβάλλω, *ekballō, 1675*
Mat 7:22 and cast out demons in your name   1
   8:16 and he cast out the spirits with a word   1
   8:31 The demons begged him, "If you cast us out, send us   1
   9:33 when the demon had been cast out   1
   9:34 "By the ruler of the demons he casts out the demons."   1
   10: 1 authority over unclean spirits, to cast them out   1
   10: 8 cleanse the lepers, cast out demons.   1
   12:24 that this fellow casts out the demons."   1
   12:26 If Satan casts out Satan, he is divided   1
   12:27 If I cast out demons by Beelzebul   1
   12:27 by whom do your own exorcists cast them out?   1
   12:28 if it is by the Spirit of God that I cast out demons   1
   17:19 "Why could we not cast it out?"   1
Mrk 1:34 and cast out many demons;   1
   1:39 proclaiming the message…and casting out demons.   1
   3:15 and to have authority to cast out demons.   1
   3:22 by the ruler of the demons he casts out demons."   1
   3:23 "How can Satan cast out Satan?   1
   6:13 They cast out many demons, and anointed with oil   1
   7:26 begged him to cast the demon out of her daughter.   1
   9:18 I asked your disciples to cast it out   1
   9:28 "Why could we not cast it out?"   1
   9:38 we saw someone casting out demons in your name   1
   16: 9 ⟦from whom he had cast out seven demons.⟧   1
   16:17 ⟦by using my name they will cast out demons;⟧   1
Lke 9:40 I begged your disciples to cast it out   1
   9:49 we saw someone casting out demons in your name   1
   11:14 Now he was casting out a demon that was mute;   1
   11:15 "He casts out demons by Beelzebul   1
   11:18 you say that I cast out the demons by Beelzebul.   1
   11:19 if I cast out the demons by Beelzebul   1
   11:19 by whom do your exorcists cast them out?   1
   11:20 by the finger of God that I cast out the demons   1
   13:32 I am casting out demons and performing cures today   1

cast up foam
1. ἐπαφρίζω, *epaphrizō, 2072*
Jde 1:13 casting up the foam of their own shame;   1

castle
1. αὐλή, *aulē, 885*
Lke 11:21 a strong man, fully armed, guards his castle   1

castrate
1. ἀποκόπτω, *apokoptō, 644*
Gal 5:12 who unsettle you would castrate themselves!   1

catch
1. ἄγρα, *agra, 62*
2. ἅλωσις, *halōsis, 274*
3. δράσσομαι, *drassomai, 1533*
4. ἐπιλαμβάνομαι, *epilambanomai, 2138*
5. ἐφίστημι, *ephistēmi, 2392*
6. ζωγρέω, *zōgreō, 2436*
7. θηρεύω, *thēreuō, 2561*
8. καταλαμβάνω, *katalambanō, 2898*
9. λαμβάνω, *lambanō, 3284*
10. πιάζω, *piazō, 4389*
11. συγκλείω, *synkleiō, 5168*
12. συνάγω, *synagō, 5251*
13. συναρπάζω, *synarpazō, 5275*
Mat 13:47 and caught fish of every kind;   12
   14:31 reached out his hand and caught him, saying to him   4
Lke 5: 4 and let down your nets for a catch."   1
   5: 5 worked all night long but have caught nothing.   9
   5: 6 they caught so many fish   11
   5: 9 amazed at the catch of fish that they had taken;   1
   5:10 from now on you will be catching people."   6
   11:54 to catch him in something he might say.   7
   21:34 and that day does not catch you unexpectedly   5
Jhn 8: 3 ⟦a woman who had been caught in adultery;⟧   8

   8: 4 ⟦this woman was caught in the very act⟧   8
   21: 3 that night they caught nothing.   10
   21:10 "Bring some of the fish that you have just caught."   10
Act 27:15 the ship was caught and could not be turned   13
1Co 3:19 it is written, "He catches the wise   3
2Pe 2:12 creatures…born to be caught and killed.   2

catch hold
1. κρατέω, *krateō, 3195*
Mrk 14:51 They caught hold of him   1

catch up
1. ἁρπάζω, *harpazō, 773*
2Co 12: 2 a person in Christ…caught up to the third heaven   1
   12: 4 was caught up into Paradise and heard things   1
1Th 4:17 will be caught up in the clouds together with them   1

cattle
1. βοῦς, *bous, 1091*
2. κτῆνος, *ktēnos, 3229*
Jhn 2:14 he found people selling cattle, sheep,   1
   2:15 out of the temple, both the sheep and the cattle.   1
Rev 18:13 cattle and sheep, horses and chariots, slaves   2

Cauda
1. Καῦδα, *Kauda, 3007*
Act 27:16 a small island called Cauda   1

cause See also cause to *fall,* cause to *sin,* cause to *stumble*
1. αἰτία, *aitia, 162*
2. αἴτιος, *aitios, 165*
3. εἰς, *eis, 1650*
4. ποιέω, *poieō, 4472*
Mat 5:32 who divorces…causes her to commit adultery.   4
   19: 3 lawful for a man to divorce his wife for any cause?"   1
Act 19:40 no cause that we can give to justify this   2
Rom 16:17 keep an eye on those who cause dissensions   4
Gal 6: 4 that work…will become a cause for pride.   3
Rev 13:15 and cause those who would not worship   4
   13:16 Also it causes all…to be marked   4

cause division
1. αἱρετικός, *hairetikos, 148*
2. ἀποδιορίζω, *apodiorizō, 626*
Tit 3:10 have nothing more to do with anyone who causes divisions   1
Jde 1:19 these worldly people…who are causing divisions.   2

cause for a sentence
1. αἰτία, *aitia, 162*
Act 13:28 they found no cause for a sentence of death   1

cause for stumbling
1. σκάνδαλον, *skandalon, 4998*
1Jn 2:10 in such a person there is no cause for stumbling.   1

cause of sin
1. σκάνδαλον, *skandalon, 4998*
Mat 13:41 collect out of his kingdom all causes of sin   1

cause pain
1. λυπέω, *lypeō, 3382*
2Co 2: 2 if I cause you pain, who is there to make me glad   1
   2: 4 not to cause you pain, but to let you know   1
   2: 5 if anyone has caused pain, he has caused it not   1
   2: 5 he has caused it not to me   1

cause ruin
1. ἀπόλλυμι, *apollymi, 660*
Rom 14:15 Do not let what you eat cause the ruin of one   1

cause trouble
1. ἐνοχλέω, *enochleō, 1943*
Heb 12:15 root of bitterness springs up and causes trouble   1

without cause
1. δωρεάν, *dōrean, 1562*
2. εἰκῇ, *eikē, 1632*
Jhn 15:25 'They hated me without a cause.'   1

Col   2:18 puffed up without cause by a human way of thinking   2

caution

1. διαστέλλω, *diastellō, 1403*

Mrk   8:15 he cautioned them, saying, "Watch out   1

cavalry

1. ἱππικός, *hippikos, 2690*

Rev   9:16 of the troops of cavalry was two hundred million;   1

cave

1. σπήλαιον, *spēlaion, 5068*

Jhn 11:38 It was a cave, and a stone was lying against it.   1
Heb 11:38 in caves and holes in the ground.   1
Rev   6:15 everyone, slave and free, hid in the caves   1

cease

1. ἀνάπαυσις, *anapausis, 398*
2. καταπαύω, *katapauō, 2924*
3. κοπάζω, *kopazō, 3156*
4. παύω, *pauō, 4264*

Mat 14:32 When they got into the boat, the wind ceased.   3
Mrk   4:39 the wind ceased, and there was a dead calm.   3
         6:51 got into the boat with them and the wind ceased.   3
Lke   8:24 they ceased, and there was a calm.   4
Act   5:42 they did not cease to teach   4
       20: 1 After the uproar had ceased   4
       20:31 I did not cease night or day to warn everyone   4
1Co 13: 8 as for tongues, they will cease;   4
Eph   1:16 I do not cease to give thanks for you   4
Col   1: 9 we have not ceased praying for you   4
Heb   4:10 cease from their labors as God did from his.   2
       10: 2 would they not have ceased being offered   4
Rev   4: 8 Day and night without ceasing they sing   1

without ceasing

1. ἀδιαλείπτως, *adialeiptōs, 90*

Rom   1: 9 without ceasing I remember you always   1
1Th   5:17 pray without ceasing   1

celebrate

1. εὐφραίνω, *euphrainō, 2370*

Lke 15:23 let us eat and celebrate;   1
       15:24 they began to celebrate.   1
       15:29 so that I might celebrate with my friends.   1
       15:32 we had to celebrate and rejoice,   1
Rev 11:10 gloat over them and celebrate and exchange   1

celebrate the festival

1. ἑορτάζω, *heortazō, 2037*

1Co   5: 8 Therefore, let us celebrate the festival   1

cell

1. οἴκημα, *oikēma, 3862*
2. φυλακή, *phylakē, 5871*

Act 12: 7 a light shone in the cell.   1
       16:24 he put them in the innermost cell   2

cellar

1. κρύπτη, *kryptē, 3219*

Lke 11:33 after lighting a lamp puts it in a cellar   1

Cenchreae

1. Κεγχρεαί, *Kenchreai, 3020*

Act 18:18 At Cenchreae he had his hair čut,   1
Rom 16: 1 Phoebe, a deacon of the church at Cenchreae   1

censer

1. λιβανωτός, *libanōtos, 3338*

Rev   8: 3 Another angel with a golden censer came and stood   1
         8: 5 Then the angel took the censer and filled it   1

censure *See* cannot be censured

census

1. ἀπογραφή, *apographē, 615*

Act   5:37 at the time of the census   1

center

1. ἀνά + μέσος, *ana + mesos, 324 + 3545*

Rev   7:17 for the Lamb at the center of the throne will be   1

centurion

1. ἑκατοντάρχης, *hekatontarchēs, 1672*
2. κεντυρίων, *kentyriōn, 3035*

Mat   8: 5 he entered Capernaum, a centurion came to him   1
         8: 8 The centurion answered, "Lord, I am not worthy   1
         8:13 to the centurion Jesus said, "Go; let it be done   1
       27:54 Now when the centurion and those with him   1
Mrk 15:39 when the centurion, who stood facing him, saw   2
       15:44 summoning the centurion   2
       15:45 he learned from the centurion that he was dead   2
Lke   7: 2 A centurion there had a slave whom he valued   1
         7: 6 the centurion sent friends to say to him   1
       23:47 When the centurion saw what had taken place   1
Act 10: 1 Cornelius, a centurion   1
       10:22 They answered, "Cornelius, a centurion   1
       21:32 Immediately he took soldiers and centurions   1
       22:25 Paul said to the centurion who was standing by   1
       22:26 When the centurion heard that   1
       23:17 Paul called one of the centurions and said   1
       23:23 he summoned two of the centurions and said   1
       24:23 he ordered the centurion   1
       27: 1 a centurion of the Augustan Cohort, named Julius.   1
       27: 6 There the centurion found an Alexandrian ship   1
       27:11 centurion paid more attention to the pilot   1
       27:31 Paul said to the centurion and the soldiers   1
       27:43 the centurion, wishing to save Paul   1

Cephas

1. Κηφᾶς, *Kēphas, 3064*

Jhn   1:42 be called Cephas" (which is translated Peter).   1
1Co   1:12 "I belong to Cephas," or "I belong to Christ."   1
         3:22 whether Paul or Apollos or Cephas or the world   1
         9: 5 the brothers of the Lord and Cephas?   1
       15: 5 that he appeared to Cephas, then to the twelve.   1
Gal   1:18 I did go up to Jerusalem to visit Cephas   1
         2: 9 James and Cephas and John   1
         2:11 when Cephas came to Antioch   1
         2:14 I said to Cephas before them all   1

certain

1. Contextual: Not in Greek
2. νή, *nē, 3755*
3. πείθω, *peithō, 4275*
4. τὶς, *tis, 5516*

Mrk 14:51 A certain young man was following him   4
Lke   7:41 "A certain creditor had two debtors;   4
       10:38 on their way, he entered a certain village   4
       11: 1 He was praying in a certain place   4
       18: 2 He said, "In a certain city there was a judge   4
       18:18 A certain ruler asked him, "Good Teacher,   4
Act   1:14 certain women, including Mary the mother of Jesus   1
         8: 9 Now a certain man named Simon   4
         9:43 in Joppa for some time with a certain Simon, a tanner.   4
       10: 5 send…for a certain Simon who is called Peter;   4
       13: 6 they met a certain magician   4
       16:14 A certain woman named Lydia, a worshiper of God   4
       22:12 "A certain Ananias, who was a devout man   4
       23: 9 certain scribes of the Pharisees' group   4
       24: 1 some elders and an attorney, a certain Tertullus   4
       25:19 they had certain points of disagreement with him   4
       25:19 disagreement…about a certain Jesus, who had died   4
       26:26 for I am certain that none of these things   3
1Co 15:31 This is as certain…as my boasting of you   2
Heb   4: 7 again he sets a certain day—"today"   4
Jde   1: 4 For certain intruders have stolen in among you   4

certain individual

1. τὶς, *tis, 5516*

Act 15: 1 certain individuals came down from Judea   1

certain man

1. δεῖνα, *deina, 1265*
2. τὶς, *tis, 5516*

Mat 26:18 "Go into the city to a certain man, and say   1
Jhn 11: 1 Now a certain man was ill, Lazarus of Bethany   2

certain person

1. τὶς, *tis, 5516*

Act	15:24	that certain persons who have gone out from us	1
Gal	2:12	for until certain people came from James	1
1Ti	1: 3	so that you may instruct certain people	1
	1:19	certain persons…suffered shipwreck in…faith	1

certainly

1. ἀληθῶς, *alēthōs, 242*
2. ἀλλά, *alla, 247*
3. γάρ, *gar, 1142*
4. γίνομαι, *ginomai, 1181*
5. καί, *kai, 2779*
6. μέν, *men, 3525*
7. ὄντως, *ontōs, 3953*
8. πάντως, *pantōs, 4122*

Mat	26:73	"Certainly you are also one of them	1
Mrk	14:70	"Certainly you are one of them;	1
Lke	23:47	"Certainly this man was innocent."	7
Act	16:37	Certainly not! Let them come and take us out	3
	21:22	They will certainly hear that you have come.	8
Rom	6: 5	we will certainly be united with him	5
2Co	11: 6	certainly…we have made this evident to you.	2
Gal	2:17	is Christ then a servant of sin? Certainly not!	4
	3:21	opposed to the promises of God? Certainly not!	4
1Th	2:18	certainly I, Paul, wanted to again and again	6

certainty

1. ἀσφαλῶς, *asphalōs, 857*

Act	2:36	know with certainty that God has made him…Lord	1

certificate

1. βιβλίον, *biblion, 1046*

Mat	19: 7	to give a certificate of dismissal	1
Mrk	10: 4	allowed a man to write a certificate of dismissal	1

certificate of divorce

1. ἀποστάσιον, *apostasion, 687*

Mat	5:31	let him give her a certificate of divorce.'	1

certify

1. σφραγίζω, *sphragizō, 5381*

Jhn	3:33	Whoever has accepted his testimony has certified	1

chaff

1. ἄχυρον, *achyron, 949*

Mat	3:12	the granary; but the chaff he will burn	1
Lke	3:17	the chaff he will burn with unquenchable fire."	1

chain

1. ἄλυσις, *halysis, 268*
2. δεσμός, *desmos, 1301*
3. δέω, *deō, 1313*
4. σειρά, *seira, 4937*
5. σύνδεσμος, *syndesmos, 5278*

Mrk	5: 3	no one could restrain…even with a chain;	1
	5: 4	often been restrained with shackles and chains	1
	5: 4	but the chains he wrenched apart	1
Lke	8:29	bound with chains and shackles	1
Act	8:23	you are in…the chains of wickedness."	5
	12: 6	Peter, bound with two chains, was sleeping	1
	12: 7	the chains fell off his wrists.	1
	16:26	everyone's chains were unfastened.	2
	21:33	ordered him to be bound with two chains;	1
	26:29	might become such as I am—except for these chains."	2
	28:20	I am bound with this chain."	1
Eph	6:20	for which I am an ambassador in chains.	1
Col	4:18	Remember my chains. Grace be with you.	1
2Ti	1:16	often refreshed me and was not ashamed of my chain	1
	2: 9	even to the point of being chained like a criminal	1
	2: 9	But the word of God is not chained.	3
Heb	11:36	even chains and imprisonment.	2
2Pe	2: 4	God…committed them to chains of deepest darkness	4
Jde	1: 6	he has kept in eternal chains in deepest darkness	2
Rev	20: 1	the key to the bottomless pit and a great chain.	1

Chaldean

1. Χαλδαῖος, *Chaldaios, 5900*

Act	7: 4	Then he left the country of the Chaldeans	1

chamberlain

1. ἐπί + ὁ + κοιτών, *epi + ho + koitōn, 2093 + 3836 + 3131*

Act	12:20	winning over Blastus, the king's chamberlain	1

chance

1. εἰ, *ei, 1623*
2. συγκυρία, *synkyria, 5175*
3. τόπος, *topos, 5536*

Lke	10:31	Now by chance a priest was going down that road;	2
Act	27:12	on the chance that…they could reach Phoenix	1
Heb	12:17	he was rejected, for he found no chance to repent	3

change

1. ἀλλάσσω, *allassō, 248*
2. ἕτερος, *heteros, 2283*
3. μετάθεσις, *metathesis, 3557*
4. μετατίθημι, *metatithēmi, 3572*
5. ποιέω, *poieō, 4472*
6. στρέφω, *strephō, 5138*
7. τροπή, *tropē, 5572*

Mat	18: 3	unless you change and become like children	6
Lke	9:29	the appearance of his face changed,	2
Jhn	4:46	Cana…where he had changed the water into wine.	5
Act	6:14	change the customs that Moses handed on to us."	1
1Co	15:51	but we will all be changed	1
	15:52	we will be changed.	1
Gal	4:20	present with you now and could change my tone	1
Heb	1:12	and like clothing they will be changed.	1
	7:12	when there is a change in the priesthood	4
	7:12	necessarily a change in the law as well.	3
Jas	1:17	there is no variation or shadow due to change.	7

change one's mind

1. μεταβάλλω, *metaballō, 3554*
2. μεταμέλομαι, *metamelomai, 3564*

Mat	21:29	but later he changed his mind and went.	2
	21:32	you did not change your minds and believe him.	2
Act	28: 6	they changed their minds	1
Heb	7:21	"The Lord has sworn and will not change his mind	2

changer   *See* money changer

character

1. Contextual: Not in Greek
2. δοκιμή, *dokimē, 1509*

Rom	5: 4	and endurance produces character	2
	5: 4	and character produces hope	2
2Co	12: 7	the exceptional character of the revelations.	1
Heb	6:17	the unchangeable character of his purpose	1

charcoal   *See* charcoal *fire*

charge¹   *See also* bring a charge, bring a charge against, free of charge, join in a charge, put in charge

1. ἐν, *en, 1877*
2. ἐξουσία, *exousia, 2026*
3. ἐπί, *epi, 2093*
4. κλῆρος, *klēros, 3102*
5. προΐστημι, *proistēmi, 4613*

Mrk	13:34	he leaves home and puts his slaves in charge	2
Lke	19:17	take charge of ten cities.'	2
Act	8:27	a court official…in charge of her entire treasury.	3
1Th	5:12	have charge of you in the Lord and admonish you;	5
1Pe	5: 2	tend the flock of God that is in your charge	1
	5: 3	not lord it over those in your charge	4

charge²

1. παραγγέλλω, *parangellō, 4133*

1Ti	6:13	In the presence of God…I charge you	1

charge³

1. Contextual: Not in Greek
2. αἰτία, *aitia, 162*
3. αἰτία + φέρω, *aitia + pherō, 162 + 5770*
4. αἰτίωμα, *aitiōma, 166*
5. ἐγκαλέω, *enkaleō, 1592*

6. ἔγκλημα, *enklēma, 1598*
7. ἐκζητέω, *ekzēteō, 1699*
8. κατηγορέω, *katēgoreō, 2989*
9. λόγος, *logos, 3364*
10. περί, *peri, 4309*
11. ῥῆμα, *rhēma, 4839*

Mat	27:14	gave him no answer, not even to a single charge	11
	27:37	Over his head they put the charge against him	2
Mrk	15:26	The inscription of the charge against him read	2
Lke	11:50	so that this generation may be charged with	7
	11:51	it will be charged against this generation.	7
	23:14	guilty of any of your charges against him.	8
Act	19:40	we are in danger of being charged with rioting	5
	23:28	the charge for which they accused him	2
	23:29	charged with nothing deserving death	6
	24:13	the charge that they now bring against me.	10
	25: 7	bringing many serious charges against him	4
	25: 9	and be tried there before me on these charges?"	1
	25:16	to make a defense against the charge	6
	25:18	they did not charge him with any of the crimes	3
	25:20	be tried there on these charges.	1
	25:27	without indicating the charges against him."	2
2Co	13: 1	"Any charge must be sustained	11
3Jn	1:10	he is…spreading false charges against us.	9
	1:10	And not content with those charges, he refuses	1

charge against
1. κατηγορέω, *katēgoreō, 2989*

Act 25:11 if there is nothing to their charges against me   1

charge already
1. προαιτιάομαι, *proaitiaomai, 4577*

Rom 3: 9 for we have already charged that all   1

charge to an account
1. ἐλλογάω, *ellogaō, 1823*

Phm 1:18 charge that to my account.   1

chariot
1. ἅρμα, *harma, 761*
2. ῥέδη, *rhedē, 4832*

Act	8:28	was returning home; seated in his chariot,	1
	8:29	"Go over to this chariot and join it."	1
	8:38	He commanded the chariot to stop	1
Rev	9: 9	like the noise of many chariots with horses	1
	18:13	cattle and sheep, horses and chariots, slaves	2

charity *See* act of charity

chasm
1. χάσμα, *chasma, 5926*

Lke 16:26 between us and you a great chasm has been fixed   1

chaste
1. ἁγνός, *hagnos, 54*

2Co 11: 2 to present you as a chaste virgin to Christ.   1
Tit   2: 5 self-controlled, chaste, good managers of the household,   1

chastise
1. μαστιγόω, *mastigoō, 3463*

Heb 12: 6 chastises every child whom he accepts."   1

chatter
1. κενοφωνία, *kenophōnia, 3032*

1Ti   6:20 Avoid the profane chatter and contradictions   1
2Ti   2:16 Avoid profane chatter   1

check *See also* keep in check with a bridle
1. πρός, *pros, 4639*

Col   2:23 of no value in checking self-indulgence.   1

cheek
1. σιαγών, *siagōn, 4965*

Mat 5:39 anyone strikes you on the right cheek, turn   1
Lke 6:29 anyone strikes you on the cheek   1

cheer
1. εὐψυχέω, *eupsycheō, 2379*

Php 2:19 so that I may be cheered by news of you.   1

cheerful
1. εὐθυμέω, *euthymeō, 2313*
2. ἱλαρός, *hilaros, 2659*

2Co   9: 7 God loves a cheerful giver.   2
Jas   5:13 Are any cheerful? They should sing songs of praise.   1

cheerfully
1. εὐθύμως, *euthymōs, 2315*
2. μετά + χαρά, *meta + chara, 3552 + 5915*

Act 24:10 Paul replied: "I cheerfully make my defense   1
Heb 10:34 you cheerfully accepted the plundering   2

cheerfulness
1. ἱλαρότης, *hilarotēs, 2660*

Rom 12: 8 the compassionate, in cheerfulness.   1

cherub
1. Χερούβ, *Cheroub, 5938*

Heb 9: 5 above it were the cherubim of glory   1

chest
1. μαστός, *mastos, 3466*
2. στῆθος, *stēthos, 5111*

Rev   1:13 and with a golden sash across his chest.   1
    15: 6 with golden sashes across their chests.   2

treasure chest
1. θησαυρός, *thēsauros, 2565*

Mat 2:11 opening their treasure chests, they offered him   1

chief
1. ἡγέομαι, *hēgeomai, 2451*

Act 14:12 because he was the chief speaker.   1

chief priest
1. ἀρχιερεύς, *archiereus, 797*

Mat	2: 4	calling together all the chief priests and scribes	1
	16:21	at the hands of the elders and chief priests	1
	20:18	handed over to the chief priests and scribes	1
	21:15	when the chief priests and the scribes saw	1
	21:23	the chief priests and the elders of the people	1
	21:45	When the chief priests and the Pharisees heard	1
	26: 3	the chief priests and the elders…gathered	1
	26:14	Judas Iscariot, went to the chief priests	1
	26:47	the chief priests and the elders of the people.	1
	26:59	the chief priests and the whole council	1
	27: 1	all the chief priests and the elders	1
	27: 3	to the chief priests and the elders.	1
	27: 6	the chief priests, taking the pieces of silver,	1
	27:12	accused by the chief priests and elders	1
	27:20	Now the chief priests and the elders persuaded	1
	27:41	the chief priests also, along with the scribes	1
	27:62	the chief priests and the Pharisees gathered	1
	28:11	told the chief priests everything that had happened.	1
Mrk	8:31	rejected by the elders, the chief priests	1
	10:33	Son of Man will be handed over to the chief priests	1
	11:18	the chief priests and the scribes heard it	1
	11:27	the chief priests, the scribes	1
	14: 1	The chief priests and the scribes were looking for	1
	14:10	went to the chief priests in order to betray him	1
	14:43	the chief priests, the scribes, and the elders.	1
	14:53	the chief priests, the elders, and the scribes	1
	14:55	Now the chief priests and the whole council	1
	15: 1	the chief priests held a consultation with the elders	1
	15: 3	the chief priests accused him of many things.	1
	15:10	the chief priests had handed him over.	1
	15:11	the chief priests stirred up the crowd	1
	15:31	the chief priests, along with the scribes,	1
Lke	9:22	the elders, chief priests, and scribes	1
	19:47	The chief priests…looking for a way to kill him;	1
	20: 1	the chief priests and the scribes came with	1
	20:19	chief priests realized that he had told this parable	1
	22: 2	The chief priests and the scribes were looking for	1
	22: 4	conferred with the chief priests and officers	1
	22:52	the chief priests, the officers of the temple police	1
	22:66	both chief priests and scribes	1
	23: 4	Pilate said to the chief priests	1

	23:10	The chief priests and the scribes stood by	1
	23:13	Pilate then called together the chief priests	1
	24:20	our chief priests and leaders handed him over	1
Jhn	7:32	the chief priests and Pharisees sent temple police	1
	7:45	the temple police went back to the chief priests	1
	11:47	the chief priests…called a meeting of the council	1
	11:57	Now the chief priests…had given orders	1
	12:10	the chief priests planned	1
	18: 3	together with police from the chief priests	1
	18:35	the chief priests have handed you over to me.	1
	19: 6	When the chief priests and the police saw him	1
	19:15	The chief priests answered, "We have no king	1
	19:21	the chief priests of the Jews said to Pilate	1
Act	4:23	reported what the chief priests…had said	1
	5:24	when…the chief priests heard these words	1
	9:14	here he has authority from the chief priests	1
	9:21	bringing them bound before the chief priests?"	1
	22:30	and ordered the chief priests…to meet.	1
	23:14	They went to the chief priests and elders and said	1
	25: 2	the chief priests and the leaders of the Jews	1
	25:15	the chief priests and the elders of the Jews	1
	26:10	with authority received from the chief priests	1
	26:12	authority and commission of the chief priests	1

chief shepherd

1. ἀρχιποίμην, *archipoimēn, 799*

1Pe	5: 4	when the chief shepherd appears,	1

chief steward

1. ἀρχιτρίκλινος, *architriklinos, 804*

Jhn	2: 8	draw some out, and take it to the chief steward."	1

chief tax collector

1. ἀρχιτελώνης, *architelōnēs, 803*

Lke	19: 2	he was a chief tax collector and was rich.	1

child *See also* adoption as a child, bear a child, bring up a child, conceive children, deliver a child, expect a child, little child, love a child

1. Contextual: Not in Greek
2. αὐτός, *autos, 899*
3. βρέφος, *brephos, 1100*
4. γεννάω, *gennaō, 1164*
5. ἐκ, *ek, 1666*
6. νήπιος, *nēpios, 3758*
7. παιδίον, *paidion, 4086*
8. παῖς, *pais, 4090*
9. σπέρμα, *sperma, 5065*
10. τέκνον, *teknon, 5451*
11. υἱός, *huios, 5626*

Mat	1:20	for the child conceived in her is from the Holy	1
	2: 2	"Where is the child who has been born king of the Jews?	1
	2: 8	saying, "Go and search diligently for the child;	7
	2: 9	stopped over the place where the child was.	7
	2:11	entering the house, they saw the child with Mary	7
	2:13	"Get up, take the child and his mother, and flee	7
	2:13	Herod is about to search for the child, to destroy	7
	2:14	Joseph got up, took the child and his mother	7
	2:16	he sent and killed all the children	8
	2:18	Rachel weeping for her children; she refused	10
	2:20	"Get up, take the child and his mother, and go	7
	2:20	those who were seeking the child's life are dead."	7
	2:21	Joseph got up, took the child and his mother	7
	3: 9	from these stones to raise up children to Abraham.	10
	5: 9	for they will be called children of God.	11
	5:45	so that you may be children of your Father	11
	7: 9	among you who, if your child asks for bread	11
	7:10	Or if the child asks for a fish, will give a snake?	1
	7:11	know how to give good gifts to your children	10
	10:21	and a father his child	10
	10:21	children will rise against parents	10
	11:16	It is like children sitting in the marketplaces	7
	13:38	the good seed are the children of the kingdom;	11
	13:38	the weeds are the children of the evil one	11
	14:21	five thousand men, besides women and children	7
	15:26	"It is not fair to take the children's food	10
	15:38	four thousand men, besides women and children	7
	17:25	From their children or from others?"	11
	17:26	Jesus said to him, "Then the children are free.	11

	18: 2	called a child, whom he put among them	7
	18: 3	unless you change and become like children	7
	18: 4	Whoever becomes humble like this child	7
	18: 5	Whoever welcomes one such child in my name	7
	18:25	his wife and children and all his possessions	10
	19:29	sisters or father or mother or children or fields	10
	21:15	heard the children crying out in the temple	8
	22:24	raise up children for his brother.'	9
	23:15	twice as much a child of hell as yourselves.	11
	23:37	I desired to gather your children together	10
	27:25	"His blood be on us and on our children!"	10
Mrk	5:39	The child is not dead but sleeping."	7
	5:40	and took the child's father and mother	7
	5:40	and went in where the child was.	7
	7:27	He said to her, "Let the children be fed first	10
	7:27	for it is not fair to take the children's food	10
	7:28	dogs under the table eat the children's crumbs."	7
	7:30	she went home, found the child lying on the bed	7
	9:24	Immediately the father of the child cried out	7
	9:37	"Whoever welcomes one such child in my name	7
	10:24	"Children, how hard it is to enter	10
	10:29	mother or father or children or fields	10
	10:30	brothers and sisters, mothers and children	10
	12:19	leaving a wife but no child	10
	12:19	and raise up children for his brother.	9
	12:20	when he died, left no children;	9
	12:21	married the widow and died, leaving no children;	9
	12:22	none of the seven left children.	9
	13:12	a father his child	10
	13:12	children will rise against parents	10
Lke	1: 7	they had no children, because Elizabeth was barren	10
	1:17	to turn the hearts of parents to their children	10
	1:35	therefore the child to be born will be holy	1
	1:41	the child leaped in her womb.	3
	1:44	the child in my womb leaped for joy.	3
	1:59	they came to circumcise the child	7
	1:66	said, "What then will this child become?"	7
	1:76	you, child, will be called the prophet	7
	1:80	The child grew and became strong in spirit	7
	2:12	you will find a child wrapped in bands of cloth	3
	2:16	the child lying in the manger.	3
	2:17	what had been told them about this child;	7
	2:21	it was time to circumcise the child;	2
	2:27	when the parents brought in the child Jesus	7
	2:33	the child's father and mother were amazed	2
	2:34	"This child is destined for the falling and	1
	2:38	speak about the child to all	2
	2:40	The child grew and became strong	7
	2:48	"Child, why have you treated us like this?	10
	3: 8	is able from these stones to raise up children	10
	6:35	you will be children of the Most High;	11
	7:32	They are like children sitting in the marketplace	7
	7:35	wisdom is vindicated by all her children."	10
	8:51	the child's father and mother.	8
	8:54	and called out, "Child, get up!"	8
	9:48	"Whoever welcomes this child in my name	7
	11: 7	and my children are with me in bed;	7
	11:11	who, if your child asks for a fish	11
	11:12	Or if the child asks for an egg	1
	11:13	know how to give good gifts to your children	10
	13:34	I desired to gather your children together	10
	14: 5	a child or an ox that has fallen into a well	11
	14:26	father and mother, wife and children	10
	16: 8	the children of this age are more shrewd	11
	16: 8	more shrewd…than are the children of light.	11
	16:25	Abraham said, 'Child, remember	10
	18:29	house or wife or brothers or parents or children	10
	19:44	you and your children within you	10
	20:28	man shall marry the widow and raise up children	9
	20:36	they are like angels and are children of God	11
	20:36	children of God, being children of the resurrection.	11
	23:28	weep for yourselves and for your children.	10
Jhn	1:12	he gave power to become children of God	10
	4:51	his slaves…told him that his child was alive.	8
	8:39	said to them, "If you were Abraham's children	10
	8:41	said to him, "We are not illegitimate children;	4
	11:52	to gather into one the dispersed children of God.	10
	12:36	so that you may become children of light."	11
	16:21	when her child is born,	7
	21: 5	Jesus said to them, "Children, you have no fish	7
Act	2:39	For the promise is for you, for your children,	10

Act	7: 5	even though he had no child.	10
	13:33	he has fulfilled for us, their children	10
	21: 5	all of them, with wives and children	10
	21:21	tell them not to circumcise their children	10
Rom	2:20	a corrector of the foolish, a teacher of children	6
	8:14	all…led by the Spirit of God are children of God.	11
	8:16	bearing witness…that we are children of God	10
	8:17	if children, then heirs, heirs of God	10
	8:19	waits…for the revealing of the children of God;	11
	8:21	the freedom of the glory of the children of God.	10
	9: 7	and not all of Abraham's children	10
	9: 8	children of the flesh who are the children of God	10
	9: 8	children of the flesh who are the children of God	10
	9: 8	but the children of the promise are counted	10
	9:26	they shall be called children of the living God."	11
	9:27	"Though the number of the children of Israel were	11
1Co	4:14	to admonish you as my beloved children.	10
	4:17	my beloved and faithful child in the Lord	10
	7:14	Otherwise, your children would be unclean	10
	13:11	When I was a child, I spoke like a child	6
	13:11	When I was a child, I spoke like a child	6
	13:11	I thought like a child, I reasoned like a child;	6
	13:11	I thought like a child, I reasoned like a child;	6
	14:20	do not be children in your thinking.	7
2Co	6:13	In return—I speak as to children	10
	12:14	children ought not to lay up for their parents	10
	12:14	parents for their children.	10
Gal	3:26	for in Christ Jesus you are all children of God	11
	4: 6	because you are children, God has sent the Spirit	11
	4: 7	So you are no longer a slave but a child,	11
	4: 7	if a child then also an heir through God	11
	4:23	One, the child of the slave,	1
	4:23	the other, the child of the free woman,	1
	4:25	for she is in slavery with her children.	10
	4:27	children of the desolate woman are more numerous	10
	4:27	numerous than the children of the one who is married."	1
	4:28	friends, are children of the promise, like Isaac.	10
	4:29	just as at that time the child who was born	1
	4:29	child who was born according to the Spirit	1
	4:30	"Drive out the slave and her child;	11
	4:30	child of the slave will not share the inheritance	11
	4:30	not share the inheritance with the child of the free	11
	4:31	So then, friends, we are children, not of the slave	10
Eph	2: 3	we were by nature children of wrath	10
	4:14	We must no longer be children	6
	5: 1	be imitators of God, as beloved children	10
	5: 8	Live as children of light	10
	6: 1	Children, obey your parents in the Lord	10
	6: 4	fathers, do not provoke your children to anger	10
Php	2:15	be blameless and innocent, children of God	10
Col	3:20	Children, obey your parents in everything	10
	3:21	Fathers, do not provoke your children	10
1Th	2: 7	like a nurse tenderly caring for her own children.	10
	2:11	we dealt…like a father with his children	10
	5: 5	for you are all children of light	11
	5: 5	children of light and children of the day;	11
1Ti	1: 2	To Timothy, my loyal child in the faith:	10
	1:18	giving you these instructions, Timothy, my child	10
	3: 4	keeping his children submissive	10
	3:12	let them manage their children…well;	10
	5: 4	If a widow has children or grandchildren	10
2Ti	1: 2	To Timothy, my beloved child:	10
	2: 1	You then, my child, be strong in the grace	10
Tit	1: 4	To Titus, my loyal child in the faith we share:	10
	1: 6	whose children are believers	10
Phm	1:10	I am appealing to you for my child, Onesimus	10
Heb	2:10	in bringing many children to glory	11
	2:13	"Here am I and the children whom God has given me."	7
	2:14	Since…the children share flesh and blood	7
	11:23	because they saw that the child was beautiful;	7
	12: 5	the exhortation that addresses you as children	11
	12: 5	the exhortation that addresses you as children	11
	12: 6	chastises every child whom he accepts."	11
	12: 7	God is treating you as children;	11
	12: 7	for what child…a parent does not discipline?	11
	12: 8	discipline in which all children share	1
	12: 8	then you are illegitimate and not his children.	11
1Pe	1:14	Like obedient children, do not be conformed	10
2Pe	2:14	hearts trained in greed. Accursed children!	10
1Jn	2:14	I write to you, children	7
	2:18	Children, it is the last hour!	7

	3: 1	be called children of God; and that is what we are.	10
	3: 2	Beloved, we are God's children now;	10
	3: 8	Everyone who commits sin is a child of the devil;	5
	3:10	The children of God and the children of the devil	10
	3:10	The children of God and the children of the devil	10
	5: 1	everyone who loves the parent loves the child.	4
	5: 2	By this we know that we love the children of God	10
	5:19	We know that we are God's children	5
2Jn	1: 1	The elder to the elect lady and her children	10
	1: 4	to find some of your children walking in the truth	10
	1:13	The children of your elect sister send you their greetings	10
3Jn	1: 4	to hear that my children are walking in the truth.	10
Rev	2:23	and I will strike her children dead.	10
	12: 4	might devour her child as soon as it was born.	10
	12: 5	she gave birth to a son, a male child, who is to rule	1
	12: 5	her child was snatched away and taken to God	10
	12:13	pursued the woman who had given birth to the male child	1
	12:17	went off to make war on the rest of her children	9
	21: 7	I will be their God and they will be my children.	11

no child

1. ἄτεκνος, *ateknos, 866*

Lke 20:28 brother dies, leaving a wife but no children   1

only child

1. μονογενής, *monogenēs, 3666*

Lke 9:38 I beg you to look at my son; he is my only child.   1

with child

1. ἐν + γαστήρ + ἔχω, *en + gastēr + echō, 1877 + 1143 + 2400*

Mat 1:18 found to be with child from the Holy Spirit.   1

childbearing

1. τεκνογονία, *teknogonia, 5450*

1Ti 2:15 she will be saved through childbearing   1

childbirth *See* pain of childbirth

childhood

1. βρέφος, *brephos, 1100*
2. παιδιόθεν, *paidiothen, 4085*

Mrk 9:21 he said, "From childhood.   2
2Ti 3:15 from childhood you have known the sacred writings   1

childish

1. νήπιος, *nēpios, 3758*

1Co 13:11 I became an adult, I put an end to childish ways.   1

childless

1. ἄτεκνος, *ateknos, 866*
2. μή + ἔχω + σπέρμα, *mē + echō + sperma, 3590 + 2400 + 5065*
3. μή + ἔχω + τέκνον, *mē + echō + teknon, 3590 + 2400 + 5451*
4. οὐ + καταλείπω + τέκνον, *ou + kataleipō + teknon, 4024 + 2901 + 5451*
5. στεῖρα, *steira, 5096*

Mat 22:24 'If a man dies childless,   3
     22:25 childless, leaving the widow to his brother.   2
Lke 20:29 the first married, and died childless;   1
     20:31 in the same way all seven died childless.   4
Gal 4:27 "Rejoice, you childless one, you who bear no   5

Chios

1. Χίος, *Chios, 5944*

Act 20:15 the following day we arrived opposite Chios.   1

chisel

1. ἐντυπόω, *entypoō, 1963*

2Co 3: 7 chiseled in letters on stone tablets   1

Chloe

1. Χλόη, *Chloē, 5951*

1Co 1:11 For it has been reported to me by Chloe's people   1

choice *See* make a choice

choice flour

1. σεμίδαλις, *semidalis, 4947*

Rev 18:13 wine, olive oil, choice flour and wheat, cattle   1

choke

1. ἀποπνίγω, *apopnigō, 678*
2. πνίγω, *pnigō, 4464*
3. συμπνίγω, *sympnigō, 5231*

Mat	13: 7	and the thorns grew up and choked them.	2
	13:22	and the lure of wealth choke the word	3
Mrk	4: 7	the thorns grew up and choked it	3
	4:19	come in and choke the word	3
Lke	8: 7	and the thorns grew with it and choked it.	1
	8:14	they are choked by the cares and riches	3

choose

1. αἱρέομαι, *haireomai, 145*
2. αἱρετίζω, *hairetizō, 147*
3. βούλομαι, *boulomai, 1089*
4. ἐκλέγομαι, *eklegomai, 1721*
5. ἐκλεκτός, *eklektos, 1723*
6. ἐκλογή, *eklogē, 1724*
7. ἐπιλέγω, *epilegō, 2141*
8. θέλω, *thelō, 2527*
9. λαμβάνω, *lambanō, 3284*
10. προχειρίζω, *procheirizō, 4741*
11. προχειροτονέω, *procheirotoneō, 4742*

Mat	8: 2	"Lord, if you choose, you can make me clean."	8
	8: 3	saying, "I do choose. Be made clean!"	8
	11:27	anyone to whom the Son chooses to reveal him.	3
	12:18	"Here is my servant, whom I have chosen,	2
	20:14	I choose to give to this last the same as	8
	20:15	to do what I choose with what belongs to me?	8
	22:14	For many are called, but few are chosen."	5
Mrk	1:40	"If you choose, you can make me clean."	8
	1:41	"I do choose. Be made clean!"	8
	13:20	for the sake of the elect, whom he chose	4
Lke	5:12	"Lord, if you choose, you can make me clean."	8
	5:13	"I do choose. Be made clean."	8
	6:13	called his disciples and chose twelve of them	4
	9:35	"This is my Son, my Chosen; listen to him!"	4
	10:22	to whom the Son chooses to reveal him."	3
	10:42	Mary has chosen the better part	4
	14: 7	he noticed how the guests chose the places of honor	4
Jhn	3: 8	The wind blows where it chooses	8
	6:70	"Did I not choose you, the twelve?	4
	8:44	you choose to do your father's desires.	8
	13:18	I know whom I have chosen.	4
	15:16	You did not choose me but I chose you.	4
	15:16	You did not choose me but I chose you.	4
	15:19	I have chosen you out of the world	4
Act	1: 2	instructions...to the apostles whom he had chosen.	4
	1:24	Show us which one of these two you have chosen	4
	6: 5	they chose Stephen	4
	9:15	an instrument whom I have chosen to bring my name	6
	10:41	to us who were chosen by God as witnesses	11
	13:17	The God of this people Israel chose our ancestors	4
	15:22	decided to choose men from among their members	4
	15:25	to choose representatives and send them to you	4
	15:40	Paul chose Silas and set out	7
	22:14	God of our ancestors has chosen you to know his will	10
Rom	9:18	So then he has mercy on whomever he chooses	8
	9:18	and he hardens the heart of whomever he chooses.	8
	11: 5	there is a remnant, chosen by grace.	6
	16:13	Greet Rufus, chosen in the Lord;	5
1Co	1:27	God chose what is foolish in the world	4
	1:27	God chose what is weak in the world	4
	1:28	God chose what is low and despised in the world	4
	12:11	to each one individually just as the Spirit chooses.	3
	12:18	members in the body, each one of them, as he chose.	8
	15:38	God gives it a body as he has chosen	8
Eph	1: 4	just as he chose us in Christ	4
Col	1:27	To them God chose to make known	8
1Th	1: 4	For we know...that he has chosen you	6
2Th	2:13	God chose you as the first fruits for salvation	1
Heb	5: 1	Every high priest chosen from among mortals	9
	11:25	choosing rather to share ill-treatment	1

Jas	2: 5	Has not God chosen the poor in the world	4
1Pe	1: 2	chosen and destined by God the Father	5
	2: 4	chosen and precious in God's sight	5
	2: 6	in Zion...a cornerstone chosen and precious;	5
	2: 9	you are a chosen race, a royal priesthood	5
Rev	17:14	those with him are called and chosen and faithful."	5

choose by lot

1. λαγχάνω, *lanchanō, 3275*

Lke 1: 9 he was chosen by lot...to enter the sanctuary   1

choose together

1. συνεκλεκτός, *syneklektos, 5293*

1Pe 5:13 Your sister church in Babylon, chosen together   1

choose with care

1. βλέπω, *blepō, 1063*

1Co 3:10 Each builder must choose with care how to build on it.   1

Chorazin

1. Χοραζίν, *Chorazin, 5960*

Mat	11:21	"Woe to you, Chorazin! Woe to you, Bethsaida!	1
Lke	10:13	"Woe to you, Chorazin! Woe to you, Bethsaida!	1

chosen one

1. ἐκλεκτός, *eklektos, 1723*

Lke	18: 7	will not God grant justice to his chosen ones	1
	23:35	if he is the Messiah of God, his chosen one!"	1
Col	3:12	As God's chosen ones, holy and beloved	1

Christ *See also* Messiah

1. Contextual: Not in Greek
2. αὐτός, *autos, 899*
3. ὄνομα, *onoma, 3950*
4. ὅς, *hos, 4005*
5. οὗτος, *houtos, 4047*
6. Χριστός, *Christos, 5986*

Mrk	1: 1	The beginning of the good news of Jesus Christ	6
	9:41	because you bear the name of Christ	6
Jhn	1:17	grace and truth came through Jesus Christ.	6
	4:25	Messiah is coming" (who is called Christ).	6
	17: 3	Jesus Christ whom you have sent.	6
Act	2:38	be baptized...in the name of Jesus Christ	6
	3: 6	in the name of Jesus Christ of Nazareth, stand up	6
	4:10	by the name of Jesus Christ of Nazareth	6
	8:12	proclaiming...the name of Jesus Christ	6
	9:34	Peter said to him, "Aeneas, Jesus Christ heals you;	6
	10:36	preaching peace by Jesus Christ	6
	10:48	baptized in the name of Jesus Christ.	6
	11:17	when we believed in the Lord Jesus Christ	6
	15:26	for the sake of our Lord Jesus Christ.	6
	16:18	"I order you in the name of Jesus Christ	6
	24:24	heard him speak concerning faith in Christ Jesus.	6
	28:31	teaching about the Lord Jesus Christ	6
Rom	1: 1	Paul, a servant of Jesus Christ	6
	1: 4	Jesus Christ our Lord	6
	1: 6	who are called to belong to Jesus Christ	6
	1: 7	from God our Father and the Lord Jesus Christ.	6
	1: 8	I thank my God through Jesus Christ for all of you	6
	2:16	God, through Jesus Christ, will judge the secret	6
	3:22	through faith in Jesus Christ for all	6
	3:24	through the redemption that is in Christ Jesus	6
	5: 1	peace with God through our Lord Jesus Christ	6
	5: 6	at the right time Christ died for the ungodly.	6
	5: 8	while we still were sinners Christ died for us.	6
	5:11	boast in God through our Lord Jesus Christ	6
	5:15	in the grace of the one man, Jesus Christ	6
	5:17	dominion in life through the one man, Jesus Christ.	6
	5:21	leading to eternal life through Jesus Christ our Lord.	6
	6: 3	who have been baptized into Christ Jesus	6
	6: 4	so that, just as Christ was raised from the dead	6
	6: 8	But if we have died with Christ, we believe	6
	6: 9	We know that Christ...will never die again;	6
	6:11	dead to sin and alive to God in Christ Jesus.	6
	6:23	is eternal life in Christ Jesus our Lord.	6
	7: 4	have died to the law through the body of Christ	6
	7:25	Thanks be to God through Jesus Christ our Lord!	6
	8: 1	for those who are in Christ Jesus.	6
	8: 2	For the law of the Spirit of life in Christ Jesus	6

Rom	8: 9	Anyone who does not have the Spirit of Christ	6
	8:10	if Christ is in you...the Spirit is life	6
	8:11	he who raised Christ from the dead	6
	8:17	heirs of God and joint heirs with Christ	6
	8:34	Who is to condemn? It is Christ Jesus, who died	6
	8:35	Who will separate us from the love of Christ?	6
	8:39	from the love of God in Christ Jesus our Lord.	6
	9: 1	I am speaking the truth in Christ—I am not lying;	6
	9: 3	that I myself were accursed and cut off from Christ	6
	10: 4	For Christ is the end of the law	6
	10: 6	(that is, to bring Christ down)	6
	10: 7	(that is, to bring Christ up from the dead).	6
	10:17	what is heard comes through the word of Christ.	6
	12: 5	so we, who are many, are one body in Christ	6
	13:14	Instead, put on the Lord Jesus Christ	6
	14: 9	For to this end Christ died and lived again	6
	14:15	cause the ruin of one for whom Christ died.	6
	14:18	one who thus serves Christ is acceptable to God	6
	15: 3	For Christ did not please himself;	6
	15: 5	in harmony...in accordance with Christ Jesus	6
	15: 6	the God and Father of our Lord Jesus Christ.	6
	15: 7	therefore, just as Christ has welcomed you	6
	15: 8	Christ has become a servant of the circumcised	6
	15:16	to be a minister of Christ Jesus to the Gentiles	6
	15:17	In Christ Jesus, then, I have reason to boast	6
	15:18	except what Christ has accomplished through me	6
	15:19	I have fully proclaimed the good news of Christ.	6
	15:20	not where Christ has already been named	6
	15:29	come in the fullness of the blessing of Christ.	6
	15:30	I appeal to you...by our Lord Jesus Christ	6
	16: 3	who work with me in Christ Jesus	6
	16: 5	Epaenetus...first convert in Asia for Christ.	6
	16: 7	and they were in Christ before I was.	6
	16: 9	Greet Urbanus, our co-worker in Christ	6
	16:10	Greet Apelles, who is approved in Christ.	6
	16:16	All the churches of Christ greet you.	6
	16:18	For such people do not serve our Lord Christ	6
	16:20	The grace of our Lord Jesus Christ be with you.	1
	16:25	my gospel and the proclamation of Jesus Christ	6
	16:27	through Jesus Christ, to whom be the glory forever!	6
1Co	1: 1	an apostle of Christ Jesus by the will of God	6
	1: 2	to those who are sanctified in Christ Jesus	6
	1: 2	call on the name of our Lord Jesus Christ	6
	1: 3	God our Father and the Lord Jesus Christ.	6
	1: 4	grace...given you in Christ Jesus	6
	1: 6	just as the testimony of Christ has been strengthened	6
	1: 7	for the revealing of our Lord Jesus Christ.	6
	1: 8	blameless on the day of our Lord Jesus Christ.	6
	1: 9	the fellowship of his Son, Jesus Christ our Lord.	6
	1:10	by the name of our Lord Jesus Christ	6
	1:12	"I belong to Cephas," or "I belong to Christ."	6
	1:13	Has Christ been divided? Was Paul crucified for you?	6
	1:17	For Christ did not send me to baptize	6
	1:17	the cross of Christ might not be emptied of its power.	6
	1:23	we proclaim Christ crucified	6
	1:24	Christ the power of God and the wisdom of God.	6
	1:30	He is the source of your life in Christ Jesus	6
	2: 2	except Jesus Christ, and him crucified.	6
	2:16	we have the mind of Christ.	6
	3: 1	as people of the flesh, as infants in Christ.	6
	3:11	has been laid; that foundation is Jesus Christ.	6
	3:23	you belong to Christ, and Christ belongs to God.	6
	3:23	you belong to Christ, and Christ belongs to God.	6
	4: 1	Think of us...as servants of Christ	6
	4:10	We are fools for the sake of Christ, but you are wise	6
	4:10	you are wise in Christ.	6
	4:15	you might have ten thousand guardians in Christ	6
	4:15	Indeed, in Christ Jesus I became your father	6
	4:17	to remind you of my ways in Christ Jesus	6
	5: 7	our paschal lamb, Christ, has been sacrificed.	6
	6:11	justified in the name of the Lord Jesus Christ	6
	6:15	know that your bodies are members of Christ?	6
	6:15	Should I therefore take the members of Christ	6
	7:22	whoever was free when called is a slave of Christ.	6
	8: 6	one Lord, Jesus Christ	6
	8:11	weak believers for whom Christ died are destroyed.	6
	8:12	you sin against Christ.	6
	9:12	an obstacle in the way of the gospel of Christ.	6
	9:21	but am under Christ's law)	6
	10: 4	the rock was Christ.	6
	10: 9	We must not put Christ to the test, as some	6

	10:16	is it not a sharing in the blood of Christ?	6
	10:16	is it not a sharing in the body of Christ?	6
	11: 1	Be imitators of me, as I am of Christ.	6
	11: 3	understand that Christ is the head of every man	6
	11: 3	God is the head of Christ.	6
	12:12	so it is with Christ.	6
	12:27	you are the body of Christ	6
	15: 3	Christ died for our sins	6
	15:12	if Christ is proclaimed as raised from the dead	6
	15:13	then Christ has not been raised;	6
	15:14	if Christ has not been raised	6
	15:15	we testified of God that he raised Christ	6
	15:16	then Christ has not been raised.	6
	15:17	If Christ has not been raised	6
	15:18	who have died in Christ have perished.	6
	15:19	If for this life only we have hoped in Christ	6
	15:20	in fact Christ has been raised from the dead	6
	15:22	so all will be made alive in Christ.	6
	15:23	each in his own order: Christ the first fruits	6
	15:23	then at his coming those who belong to Christ.	6
	15:31	a boast that I make in Christ Jesus our Lord.	6
	15:57	victory through our Lord Jesus Christ.	6
	16:24	My love be with all of you in Christ Jesus.	6
2Co	1: 1	Paul, an apostle of Christ Jesus by the will of God	6
	1: 2	God our Father and the Lord Jesus Christ.	6
	1: 3	Father of our Lord Jesus Christ	6
	1: 5	just as the sufferings of Christ are abundant for us	6
	1: 5	our consolation is abundant through Christ	6
	1:19	the Son of God, Jesus Christ, whom we proclaimed	6
	1:21	it is God who establishes us with you in Christ	6
	2:10	has been for your sake in the presence of Christ.	6
	2:12	to proclaim the good news of Christ	6
	2:14	who in Christ always leads us in triumphal procession	6
	2:15	For we are the aroma of Christ to God	6
	2:17	in Christ we speak as persons of sincerity	6
	3: 3	that you are a letter of Christ, prepared by us	6
	3: 4	that we have through Christ toward God.	6
	3:14	since only in Christ is it set aside.	6
	4: 4	the light of the gospel of the glory of Christ	6
	4: 5	not proclaim ourselves; we proclaim Jesus as Lord	6
	4: 6	the glory of God in the face of Jesus Christ.	6
	5:10	appear before the judgment seat of Christ	6
	5:14	For the love of Christ urges us on	6
	5:16	even though we once knew Christ	6
	5:17	if anyone is in Christ, there is a new creation:	6
	5:18	who reconciled us to himself through Christ	6
	5:19	in Christ God was reconciling the world	6
	5:20	So we are ambassadors for Christ	6
	5:20	we entreat you on behalf of Christ	6
	6:15	What agreement does Christ have with Beliar?	6
	8: 9	you know the generous act of our Lord Jesus Christ	6
	8:23	messengers of the churches, the glory of Christ.	6
	9:13	confession of the gospel of Christ	6
	10: 1	by the meekness and gentleness of Christ	6
	10: 5	take every thought captive to obey Christ.	6
	10: 7	If you are confident that you belong to Christ	6
	10: 7	just as you belong to Christ, so also do we.	6
	10:14	all the way to you with the good news of Christ.	6
	11: 2	to present you as a chaste virgin to Christ.	6
	11: 3	from a sincere and pure devotion to Christ.	6
	11:10	As the truth of Christ is in me	6
	11:13	disguising themselves as apostles of Christ.	6
	11:23	Are they ministers of Christ?...I am a better one:	6
	12: 2	I know a person in Christ	6
	12: 9	so that the power of Christ may dwell in me.	6
	12:10	persecutions, and calamities for the sake of Christ;	6
	12:19	We are speaking in Christ before God.	6
	13: 3	you desire proof that Christ is speaking in me.	6
	13: 5	you not realize that Jesus Christ is in you?	6
	13:13	The grace of the Lord Jesus Christ	6
Gal	1: 1	through Jesus Christ and God the Father	6
	1: 3	God our Father and the Lord Jesus Christ	6
	1: 6	who called you in the grace of Christ	6
	1: 7	want to pervert the gospel of Christ.	6
	1:10	I would not be a servant of Christ.	6
	1:12	received it through a revelation of Jesus Christ.	6
	1:22	the churches of Judea that are in Christ;	6
	2: 4	spy on the freedom we have in Christ Jesus	6
	2:16	through faith in Jesus Christ.	6
	2:16	And we have come to believe in Christ Jesus	6
	2:16	so that we might be justified by faith in Christ	6

	2:17 if, in our effort to be justified in Christ	6	
	2:17 is Christ then a servant of sin? Certainly not!	6	
	2:19 I have been crucified with Christ;	6	
	2:20 no longer I who live, but it is Christ who lives	6	
	2:21 then Christ died for nothing.	6	
	3: 1 Jesus Christ was publicly exhibited	6	
	3:13 Christ redeemed us from the curse of the law	6	
	3:14 that in Christ Jesus the blessing of Abraham	6	
	3:16 offspring," that is, to one person, who is Christ.	6	
	3:22 what was promised through faith in Jesus Christ	6	
	3:24 the law was our disciplinarian until Christ came	6	
	3:26 for in Christ Jesus you are all children of God	6	
	3:27 As many of you as were baptized into Christ	6	
	3:27 baptized into Christ have clothed yourselves with Christ.	6	
	3:28 for all of you are one in Christ Jesus.	6	
	3:29 if you belong to Christ, then you are Abraham's	6	
	4:14 as an angel of God, as Christ Jesus.	6	
	4:19 until Christ is formed in you	6	
	5: 1 For freedom Christ has set us free.	6	
	5: 2 Christ will be of no benefit to you.	6	
	5: 4 by the law have cut yourselves off from Christ;	6	
	5: 6 in Christ Jesus neither circumcision	6	
	5:24 those who belong to Christ Jesus	6	
	6: 2 in this way you will fulfill the law of Christ.	6	
	6:12 not be persecuted for the cross of Christ.	6	
	6:14 except the cross of our Lord Jesus Christ	6	
	6:18 the grace of our Lord Jesus Christ	6	
Eph	1: 1 Paul, an apostle of Christ Jesus by the will of God	6	
	1: 1 the saints who are…faithful in Christ Jesus:	6	
	1: 2 God our Father and the Lord Jesus Christ.	6	
	1: 3 the God and Father of our Lord Jesus Christ	6	
	1: 3 who has blessed us in Christ	6	
	1: 4 just as he chose us in Christ	2	
	1: 5 adoption as his children through Jesus Christ	6	
	1: 9 his good pleasure that he set forth in Christ	2	
	1:11 In Christ we have also obtained an inheritance	4	
	1:12 we, who were the first to set our hope on Christ	6	
	1:17 God of our Lord Jesus Christ, the Father of glory	6	
	1:20 God put this power to work in Christ	6	
	2: 5 made us alive together with Christ	6	
	2: 6 in the heavenly places in Christ Jesus	6	
	2: 7 in kindness toward us in Christ Jesus.	6	
	2:10 we are what he has made us, created in Christ Jesus	6	
	2:12 you were at that time without Christ	6	
	2:13 in Christ Jesus you…have been brought near	6	
	2:13 have been brought near by the blood of Christ.	6	
	2:20 Christ Jesus himself as the cornerstone.	6	
	3: 1 Paul am a prisoner for Christ Jesus for the sake of you	6	
	3: 4 perceive my understanding of the mystery of Christ.	6	
	3: 6 sharers in the promise in Christ Jesus	6	
	3: 8 the news of the boundless riches of Christ	6	
	3:11 that he has carried out in Christ Jesus our Lord	6	
	3:17 Christ may dwell in your hearts through faith	6	
	3:19 to know the love of Christ	6	
	3:21 to him be glory in the church and in Christ Jesus	6	
	4: 7 grace according to the measure of Christ's gift.	6	
	4:12 for building up the body of Christ	6	
	4:13 to the measure of the full stature of Christ.	6	
	4:15 into him who is the head, into Christ	6	
	4:20 That is not the way you learned Christ!	6	
	4:32 forgiving one another, as God in Christ has forgiven	6	
	5: 2 live in love, as Christ loved us	6	
	5: 5 has any inheritance in the kingdom of Christ	6	
	5:14 Christ will shine on you."	6	
	5:20 in the name of our Lord Jesus Christ.	6	
	5:21 out of reverence for Christ.	6	
	5:23 just as Christ is the head of the church	6	
	5:24 Just as the church is subject to Christ	6	
	5:25 just as Christ loved the church	6	
	5:29 cares for it, just as Christ does for the church	6	
	5:32 I am applying it to Christ and the church.	6	
	6: 5 in singleness of heart, as you obey Christ;	6	
	6: 6 as slaves of Christ, doing the will of God	6	
	6:23 God the Father and the Lord Jesus Christ.	6	
	6:24 an undying love for our Lord Jesus Christ.	6	
Php	1: 1 Paul and Timothy, servants of Christ Jesus	6	
	1: 1 To all the saints in Christ Jesus	6	
	1: 2 God our Father and the Lord Jesus Christ.	6	
	1: 6 to completion by the day of Jesus Christ.	6	
	1: 8 I long…with the compassion of Christ Jesus.	6	
	1:10 in the day of Christ you may be pure and blameless	6	

	1:11 that comes through Jesus Christ	6	
	1:13 my imprisonment is for Christ;	6	
	1:15 Some proclaim Christ from envy and rivalry	6	
	1:16 These proclaim Christ out of love	1	
	1:17 the others proclaim Christ out of selfish ambition	6	
	1:18 Just this, that Christ is proclaimed in every way	6	
	1:19 the help of the Spirit of Jesus Christ	6	
	1:20 Christ will be exalted now as always in my body	6	
	1:21 For to me, living is Christ and dying is gain.	6	
	1:23 my desire is to depart and be with Christ	6	
	1:26 share abundantly in your boasting in Christ Jesus	6	
	1:27 life in a manner worthy of the gospel of Christ	6	
	1:29 the privilege not only of believing in Christ	6	
	2: 1 If then there is any encouragement in Christ	6	
	2: 5 the same mind be in you that was in Christ Jesus	6	
	2:11 every tongue should confess that Jesus Christ is Lord	6	
	2:16 that I can boast on the day of Christ	6	
	2:21 their own interests, not those of Jesus Christ.	6	
	2:30 he came close to death for the work of Christ	6	
	3: 3 worship in the Spirit of God and boast in Christ Jesus	6	
	3: 7 I have come to regard as loss because of Christ.	6	
	3: 8 the surpassing value of knowing Christ Jesus	6	
	3: 8 in order that I may gain Christ	6	
	3: 9 righteousness…that comes through faith in Christ	6	
	3:10 know Christ and the power of his resurrection	2	
	3:12 because Christ Jesus has made me his own.	6	
	3:14 prize of the heavenly call of God in Christ Jesus.	6	
	3:18 For many live as enemies of the cross of Christ;	6	
	3:20 we are expecting a Savior, the Lord Jesus Christ.	6	
	4: 7 guard your hearts and your minds in Christ Jesus.	6	
	4:19 his riches in glory in Christ Jesus.	6	
	4:21 Greet every saint in Christ Jesus.	6	
	4:23 The grace of the Lord Jesus Christ be with	6	
Col	1: 1 Paul, an apostle of Christ Jesus by the will of God	6	
	1: 2 faithful brothers and sisters in Christ in Colossae:	6	
	1: 3 God, the Father of our Lord Jesus Christ	6	
	1: 4 we have heard of your faith in Christ Jesus	6	
	1: 7 He is a faithful minister of Christ on your behalf	6	
	1:24 what is lacking in Christ's afflictions	6	
	1:27 which is Christ in you, the hope of glory.	6	
	1:28 so that we may present everyone mature in Christ.	6	
	2: 2 the knowledge of God's mystery, that is, Christ	6	
	2: 5 the firmness of your faith in Christ.	6	
	2: 6 you therefore have received Christ Jesus the Lord	6	
	2: 8 not according to Christ.	6	
	2:11 in the circumcision of Christ;	6	
	2:17 the substance belongs to Christ.	6	
	2:20 If with Christ you died to the elemental spirits	6	
	3: 1 So if you have been raised with Christ	6	
	3: 1 seek the things that are above, where Christ is	6	
	3: 3 your life is hidden with Christ in God.	6	
	3: 4 When Christ who is your life is revealed	6	
	3:11 Christ is all and in all!	6	
	3:15 let the peace of Christ rule in your hearts	6	
	3:16 Let the word of Christ dwell in you richly;	6	
	3:24 you serve the Lord Christ.	6	
	4: 3 that we may declare the mystery of Christ	6	
	4:12 Epaphras…a servant of Christ Jesus	6	
1Th	1: 1 in God the Father and the Lord Jesus Christ:	6	
	1: 3 steadfastness of hope in our Lord Jesus Christ.	6	
	2: 7 might have made demands as apostles of Christ.	6	
	2:14 imitators of the churches of God in Christ Jesus	6	
	3: 2 in proclaiming the gospel of Christ	6	
	4:16 the dead in Christ will rise first.	6	
	5: 9 salvation through our Lord Jesus Christ	6	
	5:18 is the will of God in Christ Jesus for you.	6	
	5:23 at the coming of our Lord Jesus Christ.	6	
	5:28 The grace of our Lord Jesus Christ be with you.	6	
2Th	1: 1 God our Father and the Lord Jesus Christ:	6	
	1: 2 God our Father and the Lord Jesus Christ.	6	
	1:12 the grace of our God and the Lord Jesus Christ.	6	
	2: 1 As to the coming of our Lord Jesus Christ	6	
	2:14 may obtain the glory of our Lord Jesus Christ.	6	
	2:16 Now may our Lord Jesus Christ himself	6	
	3: 5 love of God and to the steadfastness of Christ.	6	
	3: 6 in the name of our Lord Jesus Christ	6	
	3:12 exhort in the Lord Jesus Christ to do their work	6	
	3:18 The grace of our Lord Jesus Christ be with all of you.	6	
1Ti	1: 1 Paul, an apostle of Christ Jesus by the command	6	
	1: 1 God our Savior and of Christ Jesus our hope	6	
	1: 2 God the Father and Christ Jesus our Lord.	6	

1Ti	1:12	I am grateful to Christ Jesus our Lord,	6
	1:14	the faith and love that are in Christ Jesus.	6
	1:15	that Christ Jesus came into the world to save	6
	1:16	Jesus Christ might display…patience	6
	2: 5	one mediator…Christ Jesus, himself human	6
	3:13	the faith that is in Christ Jesus.	6
	4: 6	you will be a good servant of Christ Jesus	6
	5:11	their sensual desires alienate them from Christ	6
	5:21	In the presence of God and of Christ Jesus	6
	6: 3	sound words of our Lord Jesus Christ	6
	6:13	In the presence…of Christ Jesus	6
	6:14	until the manifestation of our Lord Jesus Christ	6
2Ti	1: 1	Paul, an apostle of Christ Jesus by the will of God	6
	1: 1	the promise of life that is in Christ Jesus	6
	1: 2	God the Father and Christ Jesus our Lord.	6
	1: 9	This grace was given to us in Christ Jesus	6
	1:10	the appearing of our Savior Christ Jesus	6
	1:13	in the faith and love that are in Christ Jesus.	6
	2: 1	be strong in the grace that is in Christ Jesus;	6
	2: 3	like a good soldier of Christ Jesus.	6
	2: 8	Remember Jesus Christ, raised from the dead	6
	2:10	may also obtain the salvation that is in Christ Jesus	6
	3:12	all who want to live a godly life in Christ	6
	3:15	salvation through faith in Christ Jesus.	6
	4: 1	In the presence of God and of Christ Jesus	6
Tit	1: 1	a servant of God and an apostle of Jesus Christ	6
	1: 4	God the Father and Christ Jesus our Savior.	6
	2:13	glory of our great God and Savior, Jesus Christ.	6
	3: 6	through Jesus Christ our Savior	6
Phm	1: 1	Paul, a prisoner of Christ Jesus	6
	1: 3	God our Father and the Lord Jesus Christ.	6
	1: 6	perceive all the good that we may do for Christ.	6
	1: 8	though I am bold enough in Christ to command you	6
	1: 9	now also as a prisoner of Christ Jesus.	6
	1:20	Refresh my heart in Christ.	6
	1:23	Epaphras, my fellow prisoner in Christ Jesus	6
	1:25	The grace of the Lord Jesus Christ	6
Heb	3: 6	Christ, however, was faithful over God's house as a son	6
	3:14	For we have become partners of Christ	6
	5: 5	So also Christ did not glorify himself	6
	6: 1	leaving behind the basic teaching about Christ	6
	9:11	when Christ came as a high priest	6
	9:14	how much more will the blood of Christ	6
	9:24	For Christ did not enter a sanctuary made by	6
	9:28	Christ…offered once to bear the sins of many	6
	10: 5	when Christ came into the world, he said	1
	10:10	the offering of the body of Jesus Christ	6
	10:12	when Christ had offered…a single sacrifice	5
	11:26	He considered abuse suffered for the Christ	6
	13: 8	Jesus Christ is the same yesterday and today	6
	13:21	through Jesus Christ, to whom be the glory forever	6
Jas	1: 1	servant of God and of the Lord Jesus Christ	6
	2: 1	really believe our glorious Lord Jesus Christ?	6
1Pe	1: 1	Peter, an apostle of Jesus Christ	6
	1: 2	sanctified…to be obedient to Jesus Christ	6
	1: 3	the God and Father of our Lord Jesus Christ!	6
	1: 3	the resurrection of Jesus Christ from the dead	6
	1: 7	and honor when Jesus Christ is revealed.	6
	1:11	that the Spirit of Christ within them indicated	6
	1:11	sufferings destined for Christ and the subsequent glory.	6
	1:13	Jesus Christ will bring you when he is revealed.	6
	1:19	with the precious blood of Christ	6
	2: 5	acceptable to God through Jesus Christ.	6
	2:21	because Christ also suffered for you	6
	3:15	in your hearts sanctify Christ as Lord.	6
	3:16	those who abuse you for your good conduct in Christ	6
	3:18	For Christ also suffered for sins once for all	6
	3:21	through the resurrection of Jesus Christ	6
	4: 1	Since therefore Christ suffered in the flesh	6
	4:11	God may be glorified in all things through Jesus Christ.	6
	4:13	insofar as you are sharing Christ's sufferings	6
	4:14	If you are reviled for the name of Christ	6
	5: 1	an elder myself and a witness of the sufferings of Christ	6
	5:10	who has called you to his eternal glory in Christ	6
	5:14	Peace to all of you who are in Christ.	6
2Pe	1: 1	Peter, a servant and apostle of Jesus Christ	6
	1: 1	righteousness of our…Savior Jesus Christ:	6
	1: 8	in the knowledge of our Lord Jesus Christ.	6
	1:11	kingdom of our Lord and Savior Jesus Christ	6
	1:14	as indeed our Lord Jesus Christ has made clear to me.	6
	1:16	the power and coming of our Lord Jesus Christ	6

	2:20	knowledge of our Lord and Savior Jesus Christ	6
	3:18	knowledge of our Lord and Savior Jesus Christ.	6
1Jn	1: 3	with the Father and with his Son Jesus Christ.	6
	2: 1	an advocate…Jesus Christ the righteous;	6
	2:22	the one who denies that Jesus is the Christ?	6
	3:23	believe in the name of his Son Jesus Christ	6
	4: 2	every spirit that confesses that Jesus Christ	6
	5: 1	Everyone who believes that Jesus is the Christ	6
	5: 6	the one who came by water and blood, Jesus Christ	6
	5:20	we are in him who is true, in his Son Jesus Christ.	6
2Jn	1: 3	and from Jesus Christ, the Father's Son	6
	1: 7	Jesus Christ has come in the flesh;	6
	1: 9	does not abide in the teaching of Christ,	6
3Jn	1: 7	for they began their journey for the sake of Christ	3
Jde	1: 1	Jude, a servant of Jesus Christ	6
	1: 1	To those who are…and kept safe for Jesus Christ:	6
	1: 4	and deny our only Master and Lord, Jesus Christ.	6
	1:17	of the apostles of our Lord Jesus Christ:	6
	1:21	look forward to the mercy of our Lord Jesus Christ	6
	1:25	God our Savior, through Jesus Christ our Lord	6
Rev	1: 1	The revelation of Jesus Christ, which God gave	6
	1: 2	testified…to the testimony of Jesus Christ	6
	1: 5	and from Jesus Christ, the faithful witness	6
	20: 4	and reigned with Christ a thousand years.	6
	20: 6	but they will be priests of God and of Christ	6

Christian

   1. Χριστιανός, *Christianos, 5985*

Act	11:26	the disciples were first called "Christians."	1
	26:28	so quickly persuading me to become a Christian?"	1
1Pe	4:16	Yet if any of you suffers as a Christian	1

chrysolite

   1. χρυσόλιθος, *chrysolithos, 5994*

Rev	21:20	the sixth carnelian, the seventh chrysolite	1

chrysoprase

   1. χρυσόπρασος, *chrysoprasos, 5995*

Rev	21:20	the ninth topaz, the tenth chrysoprase	1

church   *See also* member of the church

   1. Contextual: Not in Greek
   2. ἐκκλησία, *ekklēsia, 1711*

Mat	16:18	on this rock I will build my church	2
	18:17	tell it to the church;	2
	18:17	offender refuses to listen even to the church	2
Act	5:11	great fear seized the whole church	2
	8: 1	a severe persecution began against the church	2
	8: 3	Saul was ravaging the church	2
	9:31	Meanwhile the church throughout Judea, Galilee,	2
	11:22	News…came to the ears of the church in Jerusalem	2
	11:26	for an entire year they met with the church	2
	12: 1	some who belonged to the church.	2
	12: 5	the church prayed fervently to God for him.	2
	13: 1	Now in the church at Antioch there were prophets	2
	14:23	had appointed elders for them in each church	2
	14:27	they called the church together	2
	15: 3	So they were sent on their way by the church	2
	15: 4	were welcomed by the church and the apostles	2
	15:22	with the consent of the whole church, decided	2
	15:41	strengthening the churches.	2
	16: 5	So the churches were strengthened in the faith	2
	18:22	he went up to Jerusalem and greeted the church	2
	20:17	asking the elders of the church to meet him.	2
	20:28	to shepherd the church of God	2
Rom	16: 1	Phoebe, a deacon of the church at Cenchreae	2
	16: 4	give thanks, but also all the churches of the Gentiles.	2
	16: 5	Greet also the church in their house.	2
	16:16	All the churches of Christ greet you.	2
	16:23	Gaius, who is host to me and to the whole church	2
1Co	1: 2	To the church of God that is in Corinth	2
	4:17	as I teach them everywhere in every church.	2
	6: 4	who have no standing in the church?	2
	7:17	This is my rule in all the churches.	2
	10:32	to Jews or to Greeks or to the church of God	2
	11:16	no such custom, nor do the churches of God.	2
	11:18	to begin with, when you come together as a church	2
	11:22	do you show contempt for the church of God	2
	12:28	God has appointed in the church first apostles	2
	14: 4	those who prophesy build up the church.	2

	14: 5	so that the church may be built up.	2
	14:12	strive to excel in them for building up the church.	2
	14:19	nevertheless, in church I would rather speak	2
	14:23	If, therefore, the whole church comes together	2
	14:28	let them be silent in church	2
	14:33	(As in all the churches of the saints	2
	14:34	women should be silent in the churches.	2
	14:35	it is shameful for a woman to speak in church.	2
	15: 9	because I persecuted the church of God.	2
	16: 1	the directions I gave to the churches of Galatia.	2
	16:19	The churches of Asia send greetings.	2
	16:19	together with the church in their house	2
2Co	1: 1	To the church of God that is in Corinth	2
	8: 1	grace…granted to the churches of Macedonia;	2
	8:18	the brother who is famous among all the churches	2
	8:19	appointed by the churches to travel with us	2
	8:23	messengers of the churches, the glory of Christ.	2
	8:24	Therefore openly before the churches,	2
	11: 8	I robbed other churches by accepting support	2
	11:28	my anxiety for all the churches.	2
	12:13	worse off than the other churches	2
Gal	1: 2	To the churches of Galatia:	2
	1:13	I was violently persecuting the church of God	2
	1:22	the churches of Judea that are in Christ;	2
Eph	1:22	the head over all things for the church	2
	3:10	so that through the church the wisdom of God	2
	3:21	to him be glory in the church and in Christ Jesus	2
	5:23	just as Christ is the head of the church	2
	5:24	Just as the church is subject to Christ	2
	5:25	just as Christ loved the church	2
	5:27	to present the church to himself in splendor	2
	5:29	cares for it, just as Christ does for the church	2
	5:32	I am applying it to Christ and the church.	2
Php	3: 6	as to zeal, a persecutor of the church;	2
	4:15	no church shared with me	2
Col	1:18	He is the head of the body, the church;	2
	1:24	for the sake of his body, that is, the church.	2
	4:15	to Nympha and the church in her house.	2
	4:16	have it read also in the church of the Laodiceans;	2
1Th	1: 1	To the church of the Thessalonians	2
	2:14	imitators of the churches of God in Christ Jesus	2
2Th	1: 1	To the church of the Thessalonians	2
	1: 4	boast of you among the churches of God	2
1Ti	3: 5	how can he take care of God's church?	2
	3:15	which is the church of the living God	2
	5:16	let the church not be burdened	2
Phm	1: 2	the church in your house:	2
Jas	5:14	They should call for the elders of the church	2
1Pe	5:13	Your sister church in Babylon, chosen together	1
3Jn	1: 6	testified to your love before the church.	2
	1: 9	I have written something to the church;	2
	1:10	prevents those…and expels them from the church.	2
Rev	1: 4	John to the seven churches that are in Asia:	2
	1:11	in a book what you see and send it to the seven churches	2
	1:20	seven stars are the angels of the seven churches	2
	1:20	the seven lampstands are the seven churches.	2
	2: 1	"To the angel of the church in Ephesus write:	2
	2: 7	listen to what the Spirit is saying to the churches.	2
	2: 8	"And to the angel of the church in Smyrna write:	2
	2:11	listen to what the Spirit is saying to the churches.	2
	2:12	"And to the angel of the church in Pergamum write:	2
	2:17	listen to what the Spirit is saying to the churches.	2
	2:18	"And to the angel of the church in Thyatira write:	2
	2:23	And all the churches will know that I am the one	2
	2:29	listen to what the Spirit is saying to the churches.	2
	3: 1	"And to the angel of the church in Sardis write:	2
	3: 6	listen to what the Spirit is saying to the churches.	2
	3: 7	to the angel of the church in Philadelphia write:	2
	3:13	listen to what the Spirit is saying to the churches.	2
	3:14	"And to the angel of the church in Laodicea write:	2
	3:22	listen to what the Spirit is saying to the churches."	2
	22:16	to you with this testimony for the churches.	2

Chuza

1. Χουζᾶς, *Chouzas, 5966*

Lke	8: 3	Joanna, the wife of Herod's steward Chuza	1

Cilicia

1. Κιλικία, *Kilikia, 3070*

Act	6: 9	of those from Cilicia and Asia	1
	15:23	the believers…in Antioch and Syria and Cilicia	1
	15:41	He went through Syria and Cilicia	1
	21:39	Tarsus in Cilicia, a citizen of an important city;	1
	22: 3	"I am a Jew, born in Tarsus in Cilicia	1
	23:34	when he learned that he was from Cilicia	1
	27: 5	the sea that is off Cilicia and Pamphylia	1
Gal	1:21	I went into the regions of Syria and Cilicia	1

cinnamon

1. κιννάμωμον, *kinnamōmon, 3077*

Rev	18:13	cinnamon, spice, incense, myrrh, frankincense	1

circumcise *See also* without being circumcised

1. περιτέμνω, *peritemnō, 4362*
2. περιτομή, *peritomē, 4364*

Lke	1:59	they came to circumcise the child	1
	2:21	it was time to circumcise the child;	1
Jhn	7:22	you circumcise a man on the sabbath.	1
Act	7: 8	circumcised him on the eighth day;	1
	10:45	The circumcised believers…were astounded	2
	11: 2	the circumcised believers criticized him	2
	15: 1	circumcised according to the custom of Moses	1
	15: 5	"It is necessary for them to be circumcised	1
	16: 3	he took him and had him circumcised	1
	21:21	tell them not to circumcise their children	1
Rom	3:30	and he will justify the circumcised	2
	4: 9	blessedness…pronounced only on the circumcised	2
	4:10	Was it before or after he had been circumcised?	2
	4:10	It was not after, but before he was circumcised.	2
	4:12	likewise the ancestor of the circumcised	2
	4:12	circumcised who are not only circumcised	2
	15: 8	Christ has become a servant of the circumcised	2
1Co	7:18	at time of his call already circumcised?	1
Gal	2: 3	not compelled to be circumcised	1
	2: 7	entrusted with the gospel for the circumcised	2
	2: 8	making him an apostle to the circumcised	2
	2: 9	go to the Gentiles and they to the circumcised.	2
	5: 2	if you let yourselves be circumcised	1
	5: 3	to every man who lets himself be circumcised	1
	6:12	try to compel you to be circumcised	1
	6:13	Even the circumcised do not…obey the law	1
	6:13	they want you to be circumcised	1
Php	3: 5	circumcised on the eighth day	2
Col	2:11	you were circumcised with a spiritual circumcision	1
	3:11	circumcised and uncircumcised, barbarian	2

before one is circumcised

1. ἀκροβυστία, *akrobystia, 213*

Rom	4:10	Was it before or after he had been circumcised?	1
	4:10	It was not after, but before he was circumcised.	1
	4:12	faith that…Abraham had before he was circumcised	1

without being circumcised

1. ἀκροβυστία, *akrobystia, 213*

Rom	4:11	all who believe without being circumcised	1

circumcision *See also* circumcision *faction*, remove mark of circumcision

1. Contextual: Not in Greek
2. περιτέμνω, *peritemnō, 4362*
3. περιτομή, *peritomē, 4364*

Jhn	7:22	Moses gave you circumcision	3
	7:23	If a man receives circumcision on the sabbath	3
Act	7: 8	he gave him the covenant of circumcision.	3
Rom	2:25	Circumcision…is of value if you obey the law;	3
	2:25	your circumcision has become uncircumcision.	3
	2:26	uncircumcision be regarded as circumcision?	3
	2:27	you that have…circumcision but break the law.	3
	2:28	nor is true circumcision something external	3
	2:29	and real circumcision is a matter of the heart	3
	3: 1	Or what is the value of circumcision?	3
	4:11	He received the sign of circumcision as a seal	3
1Co	7:18	Let him not seek circumcision.	2
	7:19	Circumcision is nothing, and uncircumcision	3
Gal	5: 6	neither circumcision nor uncircumcision	3
	5:11	persecuted if I am still preaching circumcision?	3
	6:15	neither circumcision nor uncircumcision is anything;	3
Eph	2:11	by those who are called "the circumcision"	3
	2:11	circumcision made in the flesh by human hands	1
Php	3: 3	For it is we who are the circumcision	3
Col	2:11	you were circumcised with a spiritual circumcision	3

Col 2:11 in the circumcision of Christ;   3
    4:11 ones of the circumcision among my co-workers   3
Tit   1:10 especially those of the circumcision;   3

circumstance

  1. Contextual: Not in Greek

Php   4:12 In any and all circumstances   1
1Th   5:18 give thanks in all circumstances;   1

citizen

  1. Contextual: Not in Greek
  2. ἀνήρ, *anēr*, 467
  3. πολίτης, *politēs*, 4489

Lke 15:15 hired himself out to one of the citizens   3
    19:14 citizens of his country hated him   3
Act 19:35 "Citizens of Ephesus, who is there that does not   2
    21:39 Tarsus in Cilicia, a citizen of an important city;   3
    22:28 Paul said, "But I was born a citizen."   1

citizen with

  1. συμπολίτης, *sympolitēs*, 5232

Eph   2:19 you are citizens with the saints   1

Roman citizen

  1. Ῥωμαῖος, *Rhōmaios*, 4871

Act 16:37 uncondemned, men who are Roman citizens   1
    16:38 when they heard that they were Roman citizens;   1
    22:25 legal...to flog a Roman citizen who is   1
    22:26 This man is a Roman citizen."   1
    22:27 "Tell me, are you a Roman citizen?"   1
    22:29 he realized that Paul was a Roman citizen   1
    23:27 had learned that he was a Roman citizen   1

citizenship

  1. πολιτεία, *politeia*, 4486
  2. πολίτευμα, *politeuma*, 4487

Act 22:28 cost me a large sum of money to get my citizenship."   1
Php   3:20 our citizenship is in heaven   2

city *See also* city *authority*, city *gate*, city *official*

  1. Contextual: Not in Greek
  2. αὐτός, *autos*, 899
  3. πόλις, *polis*, 4484

Mat   4: 5 Then the devil took him to the holy city   3
    5:14 A city built on a hill cannot be hid.   3
    5:35 for it is the city of the great King.   3
    9:35 Jesus went about all the cities and villages   3
    11: 1 to teach and proclaim his message in their cities.   3
    11:20 Then he began to reproach the cities   3
    12:25 no city or house divided against itself   3
    21:10 the whole city was in turmoil, asking   3
    21:17 He left them, went out of the city to Bethany   3
    21:18 In the morning, when he returned to the city   3
    22: 7 destroyed...murderers, and burned their city.   3
    23:37 Jerusalem, the city that kills the prophets   1
    26:18 "Go into the city to a certain man, and say   3
    27:53 entered the holy city and appeared to many.   3
    28:11 some of the guard went into the city   3
Mrk   1:33 the whole city was gathered   3
    5:14 told it in the city and in the country.   3
    6:56 he went, into villages or cities or farms   3
    11:19 Jesus and his disciples went out of the city.   3
    14:13 "Go into the city   3
    14:16 the disciples set out and went to the city   3
Lke   2: 4 to the city of David called Bethlehem   3
    2:11 born this day in the city of David a Savior   3
    4:31 He went down to Capernaum, a city in Galilee   3
    4:43 proclaim the good news...to the other cities also;   3
    5:12 when he was in one of the cities   3
    7:37 a woman in the city, who was a sinner   3
    8: 1 he went on through cities and villages   3
    8:27 a man of the city who had demons met him.   3
    8:34 told it in the city and in the country.   3
    8:39 proclaiming throughout the city   3
    9:10 withdrew privately to a city called Bethsaida.   3
    13:34 Jerusalem, the city that kills the prophets   1
    18: 2 He said, "In a certain city there was a judge   3
    18: 3 In that city there was a widow who kept   3
    19:17 take charge of ten cities.'   3

    19:19 'And you, rule over five cities.'   3
    19:41 As he came near and saw the city, he wept over it   3
    21:21 those inside the city must leave   2
    22:10 "when you have entered the city   3
    23:19 an insurrection that had taken place in the city   3
    24:49 so stay here in the city until   3
Jhn   1:44 from Bethsaida, the city of Andrew and Peter.   3
    4: 5 So he came to a Samaritan city called Sychar   3
    4: 8 (His disciples had gone to the city   3
    4:28 left her water jar and went back to the city.   3
    4:30 They left the city and were on their way to him.   3
    4:39 Many Samaritans from that city believed in him   3
    19:20 the place...was near the city;   3
Act   1:13 When they had entered the city,   1
    4:27 in this city, in fact, both Herod and Pontius Pilate   3
    7:58 Then they dragged him out of the city   3
    8: 5 Philip went down to the city of Samaria   3
    8: 8 there was great joy in that city.   3
    8: 9 Simon had previously practiced magic in the city   3
    9: 6 get up and enter the city   3
    10: 9 on their journey and approaching the city   3
    11: 5 "I was in the city of Joppa praying   3
    12:10 came before the iron gate leading into the city.   3
    13:44 The next sabbath almost the whole city gathered   3
    13:50 the Jews incited...the leading men of the city   3
    14: 4 the residents of the city were divided;   3
    14: 6 fled to Lystra and Derbe, cities of Lycaonia   3
    14:13 whose temple was just outside the city   3
    14:19 they stoned Paul and dragged him out of the city   3
    14:20 he got up and went into the city.   3
    14:21 they had proclaimed the good news to that city   3
    15:21 For in every city, for generations past,   3
    15:36 in every city where we proclaimed the word   3
    16:12 a leading city of the district of Macedonia   3
    16:12 We remained in this city for some days.   3
    16:14 Lydia...was from the city of Thyatira   3
    16:20 they said, "These men are disturbing our city;   3
    16:39 took them out and asked them to leave the city.   3
    17: 5 they formed a mob and set the city in an uproar.   3
    17:16 to see that the city was full of idols.   3
    17:23 as I went through the city   1
    18:10 there are many in this city who are my people."   3
    19:29 The city was filled with the confusion;   3
    19:35 the city of the Ephesians is the temple keeper   3
    20:23 the Holy Spirit testifies to me in every city   3
    21: 5 escorted us outside the city.   3
    21:29 Trophimus the Ephesian with him in the city   3
    21:30 Then all the city was aroused   3
    21:39 Tarsus in Cilicia, a citizen of an important city;   3
    22: 3 brought up in this city at the feet of Gamaliel.   3
    24:12 stirring up a crowd...throughout the city.   3
    25:23 the prominent men of the city.   3
    26:11 I pursued them even to foreign cities.   3
    27: 8 Fair Havens, near the city of Lasea.   3
Rom 16:23 Erastus, the city treasurer, and...greet you.   3
2Co 11:26 danger from Gentiles, danger in the city   3
    11:32 the governor under King Aretas guarded the city   3
Heb 11:10 the city that has foundations   3
    11:16 indeed, he has prepared a city for them.   3
    12:22 the city of the living God   3
    13:14 For here we have no lasting city   3
    13:14 we are looking for the city that is to come.   1
2Pe   2: 6 turning the cities of Sodom and Gomorrah to ashes   3
Jde   1: 7 Sodom and Gomorrah and the surrounding cities   3
Rev   3:12 and the name of the city of my God   3
    11: 2 they will trample over the holy city   3
    11: 8 city that is prophetically called Sodom   3
    11:13 great earthquake, and a tenth of the city fell;   3
    14:20 the wine press was trodden outside the city   3
    16:19 The great city was split into three parts   3
    16:19 and the cities of the nations fell.   3
    17:18 The woman you saw is the great city   3
    18:10 alas, the great city, Babylon, the mighty city!   3
    18:10 alas, the great city, Babylon, the mighty city!   3
    18:16 "Alas, alas, the great city   3
    18:18 "What city was like the great city?"   1
    18:18 "What city was like the great city?"   3
    18:19 "Alas, alas, the great city, where all...grew rich   3
    18:21 such violence Babylon the great city will be thrown down   3
    20: 9 and surrounded...the beloved city.   3
    21: 2 I saw the holy city, the new Jerusalem, coming down   3

21:10	and showed me the holy city Jerusalem	3
21:14	And the wall of the city has twelve foundations	3
21:15	to measure the city and its gates and walls.	3
21:16	The city lies foursquare, its length the same	3
21:16	and he measured the city with his rod	3
21:18	while the city is pure gold, clear as glass.	3
21:19	The foundations of the wall of the city	3
21:21	and the street of the city is pure gold	3
21:22	I saw no temple in the city	2
21:23	the city has no need of sun or moon to shine on it	3
22: 2	through the middle of the street of the city.	2
22:14	and may enter the city by the gates.	3
22:19	take away that person's share...in the holy city	3

claim

1. Contextual: Not in Greek
2. δοκέω, *dokeō, 1506*
3. λέγω, *legō, 3306*
4. λογίζομαι, *logizomai, 3357*
5. ποιέω, *poieō, 4472*
6. φάσκω, *phaskō, 5763*

Jhn	8:53	The prophets also died. Who do you claim to be?"	5
	19: 7	because he has claimed to be the Son of God."	5
	19:12	Everyone who claims to be a king	5
Act	4:32	no one claimed private ownership of any possessions	3
	5:36	Theudas rose up, claiming to be somebody	3
Rom	1:22	Claiming to be wise, they became fools;	6
	11:25	So that you may not claim to be wiser than you are	1
	12:16	do not claim to be wiser than you are	1
1Co	8: 2	Anyone who claims to know something	2
	14:37	Anyone who claims to be a prophet,	2
2Co	3: 5	competent of ourselves to claim anything	4
2Ti	2:18	claiming that the resurrection has already taken place.	3
Rev	2: 2	tested those who claim to be apostles	3

rightful claim

1. ἐξουσία, *exousia, 2026*

1Co	9:12	If others share this rightful claim on you	1

clamor

1. κραυγή, *kraugē, 3199*

Act	23: 9	Then a great clamor arose	1

clang

1. ἀλαλάζω, *alalazo, 226*

1Co	13: 1	I am a noisy gong or a clanging cymbal.	1

classify

1. ἐγκρίνω, *enkrinō, 1605*

2Co	10:12	dare to classify or compare ourselves with some	1

Claudia

1. Κλαυδία, *Klaudia, 3086*

2Ti	4:21	as do Pudens and Linus and Claudia	1

Claudius

1. Κλαύδιος, *Klaudios, 3087*

Act	11:28	this took place during the reign of Claudius.	1
	18: 2	Claudius had ordered all Jews to leave Rome	1
	23:26	"Claudius Lysias to his Excellency the governor	1

clay

1. κεραμικός, *keramikos, 3039*
2. ὀστράκινος, *ostrakinos, 4017*
3. πηλός, *pēlos, 4384*

Rom	9:21	Has the potter no right over the clay	3
2Co	4: 7	we have this treasure in clay jars	2
2Ti	2:20	utensils...also of wood and clay	2
Rev	2:27	as when clay pots are shattered	1

clean   *See also* declare clean, make clean

1. Contextual: Not in Greek
2. καθαρίζω, *katharizō, 2751*
3. καθαρός, *katharos, 2754*

Mat	23:25	For you clean the outside of the cup	2
	23:26	First clean the inside of the cup	2
	23:26	so that the outside also may become clean.	3
	27:59	and wrapped it in a clean linen cloth	3
Lke	11:39	"Now you Pharisees clean the outside of the cup	2

	11:41	see, everything will be clean for you.	3
Jhn	13:10	is entirely clean. And you are clean	3
	13:10	you are clean, though not all of you."	3
	13:11	this reason he said, "Not all of you are clean."	3
Rom	14:20	Everything is indeed clean	3
Heb	10:22	with our hearts sprinkled clean	1

clean out

1. ἐκκαθαίρω, *ekkathairō, 1705*

1Co	5: 7	Clean out the old yeast	1

cleanse

1. ἐκκαθαίρω, *ekkathairō, 1705*
2. καθαρίζω, *katharizō, 2751*
3. καθαρισμός, *katharismos, 2752*
4. καθαρός, *katharos, 2754*

Mat	8: 3	Immediately his leprosy was cleansed.	2
	10: 8	Cure the sick, raise the dead, cleanse the lepers	2
	11: 5	lame walk, the lepers are cleansed, the deaf hear	2
Mrk	1:44	offer for your cleansing what Moses commanded	3
Lke	4:27	none of them was cleansed	2
	5:14	make an offering for your cleansing	3
	7:22	lepers are cleansed, the deaf hear	2
Jhn	15: 3	You have already been cleansed by the word	4
Act	15: 9	cleansing their hearts by faith	2
2Co	7: 1	let us cleanse ourselves from every defilement	2
Eph	5:26	cleansing her with the washing of water by the word	2
2Ti	2:21	All who cleanse themselves of the things	1
Heb	10: 2	since the worshipers, cleansed once for all	2
Jas	4: 8	Cleanse your hands, you sinners	2
2Pe	1: 9	forgetful of the cleansing of past sins.	3
1Jn	1: 7	blood of Jesus his Son cleanses us from all sin.	2
	1: 9	and cleanse us from all unrighteousness.	2

clear   *See also* eagerness to clear, make clear

1. ἀγαθός, *agathos, 19*
2. ἀπρόσκοπος, *aproskopos, 718*
3. δήπου, *dēpou, 1327*
4. διακαθαίρω, *diakathairō, 1350*
5. διακαθαρίζω, *diakatharizō, 1351*
6. καθαρός, *katharos, 2754*
7. καλός, *kalos, 2819*
8. φανερός, *phaneros, 5745*

Mat	3:12	he will clear his threshing floor and will gather	5
Lke	3:17	to clear his threshing floor	4
Act	23: 1	I have lived my life with a clear conscience	1
	24:16	I do my best always to have a clear conscience	2
1Co	11:19	will it become clear who among you are genuine.	8
1Ti	3: 9	must hold fast...the faith with a clear conscience.	6
2Ti	1: 3	God—whom I worship with a clear conscience	6
Heb	2:16	For it is clear that he did not come to help angels	3
	13:18	we are sure that we have a clear conscience	7
1Pe	3:16	Keep your conscience clear	1
Rev	21:18	while the city is pure gold, clear as glass.	6

clear as crystal

1. κρυσταλλίζω, *krystallizō, 3222*

Rev	21:11	a radiance...like jasper, clear as crystal.	1

clearly   *See also* reveal clearly, see clearly

1. τηλαυγῶς, *tēlaugōs, 5495*
2. φανερῶς, *phanerōs, 5747*

Mrk	8:25	was restored, and he saw everything clearly.	1
Act	10: 3	a vision in which he clearly saw an angel of God	2

more clearly

1. περισσότερος, *perissoteros, 4358*

Heb	6:17	when God desired to show even more clearly	1

Clement

1. Κλήμης, *Klēmēs, 3098*

Php	4: 3	together with Clement	1

Cleopas

1. Κλεοπᾶς, *Kleopas, 3093*

Lke	24:18	one of them, whose name was Cleopas, answered	1

cliff *See* hurl off a cliff

climb in
1. ἀναβαίνω, *anabainō, 326*
Jhn 10: 1 but climbs in by another way   1

climb up
1. ἀναβαίνω, *anabainō, 326*
Lke 19: 4 and climbed a sycamore tree   1

cling
1. ἀγαπάω, *agapaō, 26*
2. κολλάω, *kollaō, 3140*
3. κρατέω, *krateō, 3195*
Lke 10:11 'Even the dust of your town that clings to our feet   2
Act   3:11 While he clung to Peter and John   3
Rev 12:11 they did not cling to life even in the face of death.   1

cling so closely
1. εὐπερίστατος, *euperistatos, 2342*
Heb 12: 1 every weight and the sin that clings so closely   1

cloak
1. Contextual: Not in Greek
2. ἱμάτιον, *himation, 2668*
3. περιβόλαιον, *peribolaion, 4316*
4. φαιλόνης, *phailonēs, 5742*
Mat   5:40 your coat, give your cloak as well;   2
     9:16 a piece of unshrunk cloth on an old cloak   2
     9:16 for the patch pulls away from the cloak   2
     9:20 touched the fringe of his cloak   2
     9:21 she said to herself, "If I only touch his cloak   2
   14:36 they might touch even the fringe of his cloak;   2
   21: 7 and put their cloaks on them   2
   21: 8 large crowd spread their cloaks on the road   2
Mrk   2:21 sews a piece of unshrunk cloth on an old cloak;   2
     5:27 touched his cloak   2
     6:56 touch even the fringe of his cloak;   2
   10:50 throwing off his cloak, he sprang up   2
   11: 7 and threw their cloaks on it;   2
   11: 8 Many people spread their cloaks on the road   2
   15:17 they clothed him in a purple cloak;   1
   15:20 they stripped him of the purple cloak   1
Lke 19:35 throwing their cloaks on the colt   2
   19:36 people kept spreading their cloaks on the road.   2
   22:36 who has no sword must sell his cloak and buy one.   2
Act 12: 8 "Wrap your cloak around you and follow me."   2
   22:23 they were shouting, throwing off their cloaks,   2
2Ti   4:13 bring the cloak that I left with Carpus at Troas   4
Heb   1:12 like a cloak you will roll them up   3

Clopas
1. Κλωπᾶς, *Klōpas, 3116*
Jhn 19:25 his mother's sister, Mary the wife of Clopas   1

close *See also* behind closed *doors*, bring close, close to *shore*, come close, draw to a close, lie close at hand, pay close attention
1. ἀναγκαῖος, *anankaios, 338*
2. ἄχρι, *achri, 948*
3. εἰς, *eis, 1650*
4. μέλλω, *mellō, 3516*
Lke   7: 2 who was ill and close to death.   4
Jhn   1:18 the only Son, who is close to the Father's heart,   3
Act 10:24 called together his relatives and close friends.   1
   11: 5 it came close to me.   2

closely *See also* cling so closely, watch closely
1. ἀτενίζω, *atenizō, 867*
Act 11: 6 looked at it closely I saw four-footed animals   1

cloth *See also* dealer in purple cloth, piece of cloth, strip of cloth, wrap in bands of cloth
1. ῥάκος, *rhakos, 4820*
2. σουδάριον, *soudarion, 5051*
Mat   9:16 No one sews a piece of unshrunk cloth on   1
Mrk   2:21 sews a piece of unshrunk cloth on an old cloak;   1
Jhn 11:44 his face wrapped in a cloth.   2

   20: 7 the cloth that had been on Jesus' head   2

linen cloth
1. ὀθόνιον, *othonion, 3856*
2. σινδών, *sindōn, 4984*
Mat 27:59 and wrapped it in a clean linen cloth.   2
Mrk 14:51 wearing nothing but a linen cloth.   2
   14:52 he left the linen cloth and ran off naked.   2
   15:46 Joseph bought a linen cloth   2
   15:46 taking down the body, wrapped it in the linen cloth   2
Lke 23:53 he took it down, wrapped it in a linen cloth   2
   24:12 he saw the linen cloths by themselves   1
Jhn 19:40 and wrapped it with the spices in linen cloths   1

clothe
1. Contextual: Not in Greek
2. ἀμφιέζω, *amphiezō, 313*
3. ἀμφιέννυμι, *amphiennymi, 314*
4. ἐγκομβόομαι, *enkomboomai, 1599*
5. ἐνδιδύσκω, *endidyskō, 1898*
6. ἐνδύω, *endyō, 1907*
7. ἐπενδύομαι, *ependyomai, 2086*
8. ἱματίζω, *himatizō, 2667*
9. ἱμάτιον, *himation, 2668*
10. περιβάλλω, *periballō, 4314*
11. περιτίθημι, *peritithēmi, 4363*
Mat   6:29 his glory was not clothed like one of these.   10
     6:30 But if God so clothes the grass of the field   3
     6:30 will he not...clothe you—you of little faith?   1
Mrk   1: 6 Now John was clothed with camel's hair   6
     5:15 sitting there, clothed and in his right mind   8
   15:17 they clothed him in a purple cloak;   5
Lke   8:35 found the man...clothed and in his right mind.   8
   12:27 even Solomon in all his glory was not clothed   10
   12:28 if God so clothes the grass of the field   2
   12:28 how much more will he clothe you   1
   24:49 stay...until you have been clothed with power   6
1Co 12:23 we clothe with greater honor   11
2Co   5: 2 longing to be clothed with our heavenly dwelling   7
Gal   3:27 baptized into Christ have clothed yourselves with Christ.   6
Eph   4:24 clothe yourselves with the new self   6
Col   3:10 and have clothed yourselves with the new self   6
     3:12 clothe yourselves with compassion, kindness,   6
     3:14 Above all, clothe yourselves with love   1
1Pe   5: 5 all of you must clothe yourselves with humility   4
Rev   1:13 clothed with a long robe and with a golden sash   6
     3: 5 you conquer, you will be clothed like them in white   10
     3:18 and white robes to clothe you   10
   12: 1 a woman clothed with the sun   10
   16:15 is clothed, not going about naked   9
   17: 4 The woman was clothed in purple and scarlet   10
   18:16 the great city, clothed in fine linen   10
   19: 8 her it has been granted to be clothed with fine linen   10
   19:13 He is clothed in a robe dipped in blood   10

clothe further
1. ἐπενδύομαι, *ependyomai, 2086*
2Co   5: 4 we wish not to be unclothed but to be further clothed   1

clothe poorly
1. γυμνιτεύω, *gymniteuō, 1217*
1Co   4:11 we are poorly clothed and beaten and homeless   1

clothes
1. ἐπενδύτης, *ependytēs, 2087*
2. ἐσθής, *esthēs, 2264*
3. ἱμάτιον, *himation, 2668*
4. ἱματισμός, *himatismos, 2669*
5. χιτών, *chitōn, 5945*
Mat 17: 2 and his clothes became dazzling white.   3
   26:65 the high priest tore his clothes and said   3
   27:31 put his own clothes on him.   3
   27:35 they divided his clothes among themselves   3
Mrk   5:28 "If I but touch his clothes, I will be made well."   3
     5:30 "Who touched my clothes?"   3
     9: 3 clothes became dazzling white   3
   14:63 the high priest tore his clothes and said   5
   15:20 and put his own clothes on him.   3
   15:24 and divided his clothes among them   3

Lke	8:27	For a long time he had worn no clothes	3
	8:44	touched the fringe of his clothes	3
	9:29	his clothes became dazzling white.	4
	24: 4	two men in dazzling clothes stood beside them.	2
Jhn	19:23	they took his clothes and divided them	3
	19:24	"They divided my clothes among themselves	3
	21: 7	he put on some clothes, for he was naked	1
Act	10:30	suddenly a man in dazzling clothes stood before me.	3
	14:14	they tore their clothes	3
	18: 6	in protest he shook the dust from his clothes	3
1Ti	2: 9	gold, pearls, or expensive clothes	4
Jas	2: 2	For if a person with gold rings and in fine clothes	2
	2: 2	a poor person in dirty clothes also comes in	2
	2: 3	you take notice of the one wearing the fine clothes	2
	5: 2	and your clothes are moth-eaten.	3
Rev	3: 4	who have not soiled their clothes;	3

clothing *See also* give clothing

1. ἔνδυμα, *endyma, 1903*
2. ἱμάτιον, *himation, 2668*
3. ἱματισμός, *himatismos, 2669*
4. καταστολή, *katastolē, 2950*
5. σκέπασμα, *skepasma, 5004*

Mat	3: 4	Now John wore clothing of camel's hair	1
	6:25	than food, and the body more than clothing?	1
	6:28	And why do you worry about clothing? Consider	1
	7:15	who come to you in sheep's clothing	1
	28: 3	his clothing white as snow.	1
Lke	7:25	Look, those who put on fine clothing	3
	12:23	the body more than clothing.	1
	23:34	they cast lots to divide his clothing.	2
Jhn	19:24	for my clothing they cast lots."	3
Act	9:39	tunics and other clothing that Dorcas had made	2
	16:22	magistrates had them stripped of their clothing	2
	20:33	I coveted no one's silver or gold or clothing.	3
1Ti	2: 9	modestly and decently in suitable clothing	4
	6: 8	if we have food and clothing	5
Heb	1:11	they will all wear out like clothing;	2
	1:12	and like clothing they will be changed.	2
1Pe	3: 3	by wearing gold ornaments or fine clothing;	2

cloud

1. νεφέλη, *nephelē, 3749*
2. νέφος, *nephos, 3751*

Mat	17: 5	suddenly a bright cloud overshadowed them	1
	17: 5	and from the cloud a voice said	1
	24:30	'the Son of Man coming on the clouds of heaven'	1
	26:64	coming on the clouds of heaven."	1
Mrk	9: 7	a cloud overshadowed them	1
	9: 7	from the cloud there came a voice	1
	13:26	they will see 'the Son of Man coming in clouds'	1
	14:62	'coming with the clouds of heaven.'"	1
Lke	9:34	a cloud came and overshadowed them;	1
	9:34	they were terrified as they entered the cloud.	1
	9:35	from the cloud came a voice that said,	1
	12:54	"When you see a cloud rising in the west	1
	21:27	will see 'the Son of Man coming in a cloud'	1
Act	1: 9	a cloud took him out of their sight.	1
1Co	10: 1	our ancestors were all under the cloud	1
	10: 2	all were baptized into Moses in the cloud	1
1Th	4:17	caught up in the clouds together with them	1
Heb	12: 1	surrounded by so great a cloud of witnesses	2
Jde	1:12	waterless clouds carried along by the winds;	1
Rev	1: 7	Look! He is coming with the clouds;	1
	10: 1	coming down from heaven, wrapped in a cloud	1
	11:12	they went up to heaven in a cloud	1
	14:14	Then I looked, and there was a white cloud	1
	14:14	seated on the cloud was one like the Son of Man	1
	14:15	calling…to the one who sat on the cloud,	1
	14:16	the one who sat on the cloud swung his sickle	1

club

1. ξύλον, *xylon, 3833*

Mat	26:47	with him was a large crowd with swords and clubs	1
	26:55	with swords and clubs to arrest me	
Mrk	14:43	with him there was a crowd with swords and clubs	1
	14:48	with swords and clubs to arrest me	
Lke	22:52	with swords and clubs as if I were a bandit?	1

cluster

1. βότρυς, *botrys, 1084*

| Rev | 14:18 | and gather the clusters of the vine of the earth | 1 |

Cnidus

1. Κνίδος, *Knidos, 3118*

| Act | 27: 7 | arrived with difficulty off Cnidus | 1 |

co-worker

1. συνεργός, *synergos, 5301*

Rom	16: 9	Greet Urbanus, our co-worker in Christ	1
	16:21	Timothy, my co-worker, greets you;	1
2Co	8:23	my partner and co-worker in your service;	1
Php	2:25	my brother and co-worker and fellow soldier	1
	4: 3	with Clement and the rest of my co-workers	1
Col	4:11	ones of the circumcision among my co-workers	1
1Th	3: 2	we sent Timothy, our brother and co-worker for God	1
Phm	1: 1	To Philemon our dear friend and co-worker	1
3Jn	1: 8	so that we may become co-workers with the truth.	1

coal

1. ἄνθραξ, *anthrax, 472*

| Rom | 12:20 | you will heap burning coals on their heads." | 1 |

coast

1. ἐπί + ὁ + θάλασσα, *epi + ho + thalassa, 2093 + 3836 + 2498*
2. παράλιος, *paralios, 4163*

| Lke | 6:17 | Jerusalem, and the coast of Tyre and Sidon. | 2 |
| Act | 17:14 | the believers…sent Paul away to the coast | 1 |

along the coast

1. κατά, *kata, 2848*

| Act | 27: 2 | set sail to the ports along the coast of Asia | 1 |

coat

1. ἱμάτιον, *himation, 2668*
2. χιτών, *chitōn, 5945*

Mat	5:40	and if anyone wants to sue you and take your coat	2
	24:18	must not turn back to get a coat.	1
Mrk	13:16	not turn back to get a coat.	1
Lke	3:11	"Whoever has two coats must share	2
	6:29	from anyone who takes away your coat	1
Act	7:58	the witnesses laid their coats at the feet	1
	22:20	keeping the coats of those who killed him.'	1

cock

1. ἀλέκτωρ, *alektōr, 232*

Mat	26:34	this very night, before the cock crows	1
	26:74	At that moment the cock crowed.	1
	26:75	"Before the cock crows, you will deny me	1
Mrk	14:30	this very night, before the cock crows twice	1
	14:68	Then the cock crowed.	1
	14:72	At that moment the cock crowed for the second time.	1
	14:72	"Before the cock crows twice	1
Lke	22:34	Peter, the cock will not crow this day	1
	22:60	while he was still speaking, the cock crowed.	1
	22:61	"Before the cock crows today, you will deny me	1
Jhn	13:38	Very truly, I tell you, before the cock crows	1
	18:27	at that moment the cock crowed.	1

cockcrow

1. ἀλεκτοροφωνία, *alektorophōnia, 231*

| Mrk | 13:35 | at midnight, or at cockcrow, or at dawn, | 1 |

code *See* written code

cohort

1. σπεῖρα, *speira, 5061*

Mat	27:27	they gathered the whole cohort around him.	1
Mrk	15:16	they called together the whole cohort.	1
Act	10: 1	the Italian Cohort, as it was called.	1
	21:31	word came to the tribune of the cohort	1
	27: 1	a centurion of the Augustan Cohort, named Julius.	1

coin

1. δραχμή, *drachmē, 1534*
2. κέρμα, *kerma, 3047*
3. νόμισμα, *nomisma, 3790*

4. στατήρ, *statēr, 5088*

Mat 17:27	when you open its mouth, you will find a coin;	4
22:19	Show me the coin used for the tax."	3
Lke 15: 9	I have found the coin that I had lost.'	1
Jhn 2:15	also poured out the coins of the money changers	2

silver coin

1. ἀργύριον, *argyrion, 736*
2. δραχμή, *drachmē, 1534*

Lke 15: 8	what woman having ten silver coins	2
Act 19:19	it was found to come to fifty thousand silver coins.	1

small copper coin

1. λεπτός, *leptos, 3321*

Mrk 12:42	A poor widow came and put in two small copper coins	1
Lke 21: 2	saw a poor widow put in two small copper coins.	1

cold

1. ψῦχος, *psychos, 6036*
2. ψυχρός, *psychros, 6037*

Mat 10:42	whoever gives even a cup of cold water to one	2
Jhn 18:18	made a charcoal fire because it was cold	1
Act 28: 2	Since it had begun to rain and was cold	1
2Co 11:27	often without food, cold and naked.	1
Rev 3:15	"I know your works; you are neither cold nor hot.	2
3:15	I wish that you were either cold or hot.	2
3:16	you are lukewarm, and neither cold nor hot	2

grow cold

1. ψύχω, *psychō, 6038*

Mat 24:12	the love of many will grow cold.	1

collect

1. αἴρω, *airō, 149*
2. καρπός, *karpos, 2843*
3. λαμβάνω, *lambanō, 3284*
4. πράσσω, *prassō, 4556*
5. συλλέγω, *syllegō, 5198*
6. συμφέρω, *sympherō, 5237*

Mat 13:30	Collect the weeds first and bind them in bundles	5
13:40	as the weeds are collected and burned up	5
13:41	and they will collect out of his kingdom	5
21:34	to collect his produce.	3
Mrk 8:19	how many…broken pieces did you collect?"	1
8:20	how many…broken pieces did you collect?"	1
12: 2	to collect from them his share of the produce	3
Lke 3:13	"Collect no more than the amount prescribed	4
19:23	I could have collected it with interest.'	4
Act 19:19	collected their books and burned them publicly	6
Rom 15:28	and have delivered to them what has been collected	2

collect tithes

1. ἀποδεκατόω, *apodekatoō, 620*
2. δεκατόω, *dekatoō, 1282*

Heb 7: 5	to collect tithes from the people	1
7: 6	collected tithes from Abraham	2

collection

1. λογεία, *logeia, 3356*

1Co 16: 1	Now concerning the collection for the saints:	1
16: 2	so that collections need not be taken when I come.	1

collector   *See also* chief tax collector

1. λαμβάνω, *lambanō, 3284*

Mat 17:24	the collectors of the temple tax	1

tax collector

1. τελώνης, *telōnēs, 5467*

Mat 5:46	Do not even the tax collectors do the same?	1
9:10	many tax collectors and sinners came	1
9:11	"Why…eat with tax collectors and sinners?"	1
10: 3	Thomas and Matthew the tax collector;	1
11:19	a friend of tax collectors and sinners!'	1
18:17	be to you as a Gentile and a tax collector.	1
21:31	the tax collectors and the prostitutes	1
21:32	the tax collectors and the prostitutes believed him;	1
Mrk 2:15	many tax collectors and sinners were also sitting	1
2:16	he was eating with sinners and tax collectors	1

2:16	"Why does he eat with tax collectors and sinners?"	1
Lke 3:12	Even tax collectors came to be baptized,	1
5:27	he went out and saw a tax collector named Levi	1
5:29	was a large crowd of tax collectors and others	1
5:30	drink with tax collectors and sinners?"	1
7:29	who heard this, including the tax collectors,	1
7:34	a friend of tax collectors and sinners!'	1
15: 1	Now all the tax collectors and sinners	1
18:10	one a Pharisee and the other a tax collector.	1
18:11	or even like this tax collector.	1
18:13	the tax collector…beating his breast	1

Roman colony

1. κολωνία, *kolōnia, 3149*

Act 16:12	Philippi…a Roman colony.	1

color of fire

1. πύρινος, *pyrinos, 4791*

Rev 9:17	the riders wore breastplates the color of fire	1

Colossae

1. Κολοσσαί, *Kolossai, 3145*

Col 1: 2	faithful brothers and sisters in Christ in Colossae:	1

colt

1. πῶλος, *pōlos, 4798*

Mat 21: 2	a donkey tied, and a colt with her;	1
21: 5	and on a colt, the foal of a donkey."	1
21: 7	they brought the donkey and the colt	1
Mrk 11: 2	as you enter it, you will find tied there a colt	1
11: 4	They went away and found a colt tied near a door	1
11: 5	"What are you doing, untying the colt?"	1
11: 7	they brought the colt to Jesus	1
Lke 19:30	as you enter it you will find tied there a colt	1
19:33	As they were untying the colt, its owners asked	1
19:33	"Why are you untying the colt?"	1
19:35	throwing their cloaks on the colt	1
Jhn 12:15	your king is coming, sitting on a donkey's colt!"	1

combine   *See* combine *with*

come   *See also* our Lord come, still to come, thing to come

1. Contextual: Not in Greek
2. ἄγω, *agō, 72*
3. ἀκούω, *akouō, 201*
4. ἀναβαίνω, *anabainō, 326*
5. ἀνίστημι, *anistēmi, 482*
6. ἀπέρχομαι, *aperchomai, 599*
7. γίνομαι, *ginomai, 1181*
8. δεῦρο, *deuro, 1306*
9. δεῦτε, *deute, 1307*
10. δή, *dē, 1314*
11. διέρχομαι, *dierchomai, 1451*
12. ἐγγίζω, *engizō, 1581*
13. ἐγείρω, *egeirō, 1586*
14. εἰμί, *eimi, 1639*
15. εἰς, *eis, 1650*
16. εἰσέρχομαι, *eiserchomai, 1656*
17. εἴσοδος, *eisodos, 1658*
18. ἐκ, *ek, 1666*
19. ἐκπορεύομαι, *ekporeuomai, 1744*
20. ἔλευσις, *eleusis, 1803*
21. ἐνίστημι, *enistēmi, 1931*
22. ἐξέρχομαι, *exerchomai, 2002*
23. ἐπέρχομαι, *eperchomai, 2088*
24. ἔρχομαι, *erchomai, 2262*
25. ἐφίστημι, *ephistēmi, 2392*
26. ἔχω, *echō, 2400*
27. ἥκω, *hēkō, 2457*
28. κατά, *kata, 2848*
29. καταντάω, *katantaō, 2918*
30. κατέρχομαι, *katerchomai, 2982*
31. μέλλω, *mellō, 3516*
32. ὁράω, *horaō, 3972*
33. παραγίνομαι, *paraginomai, 4134*
34. πάρειμι, *pareimi, 4205*
35. παρέρχομαι, *parerchomai, 4216*
36. παρίστημι, *paristēmi, 4225*

37. παρουσία, *parousia, 4242*
38. πίμπλημι, *pimplēmi, 4398*
39. πίπτω, *piptō, 4406*
40. προσέρχομαι, *proserchomai, 4665*
41. συμπληρόω, *symplēroō, 5230*
42. φέρω, *pherō, 5770*
43. φθάνω, *phthanō, 5777*
44. χωρέω, *chōreō, 6003*

Mat	2: 1	wise men from the East came to Jerusalem	33
	2: 2	at its rising, and have come to pay him homage."	24
	2: 6	from you shall come a ruler who is to shepherd my	22
	3: 7	Pharisees and Sadducees coming for baptism	24
	3: 7	Who warned you to flee from the wrath to come?	31
	3:11	one who is more powerful than I is coming after me;	24
	3:13	Jesus came from Galilee to John at the Jordan	33
	3:14	"I need to be baptized by you, and do you come to me?"	24
	4: 3	The tempter came and said to him, "If you are	40
	4:11	left him, and suddenly angels came and waited	40
	5: 1	after he sat down, his disciples came to him.	40
	5:17	not think that I have come to abolish the law	24
	5:17	the prophets; I have come not to abolish	24
	5:24	reconciled…and then come and offer your gift.	24
	5:37	anything more than this comes from the evil one	14
	6:10	Your kingdom come. Your will be done, on earth as	24
	7:15	false prophets, who come to you	24
	7:25	rain fell, the floods came, and the winds blew	24
	7:27	rain fell, and the floods came, and the winds	24
	8: 7	he said to him, "I will come and cure him."	24
	8: 8	I am not worthy to have you come under my roof;	16
	8: 9	to one, 'Go,' and he goes, and to another, 'Come,'	24
	8: 9	'Come,' and he comes, and to my slave, 'Do this,'	24
	8:11	I tell you, many will come from east and west	27
	8:28	When he came to the other side	24
	8:29	Have you come here to torment us before the time?"	24
	9: 1	he crossed the sea and came to his own town.	24
	9:10	many tax collectors and sinners came	24
	9:13	come to call not the righteous but sinners."	24
	9:14	Then the disciples of John came to him, saying	40
	9:15	The days will come when the bridegroom is taken	24
	9:18	suddenly a leader of the synagogue came in	24
	9:18	but come and lay your hand on her	24
	9:23	When Jesus came to the leader's house	24
	9:28	the blind men came to him; and Jesus said to them	40
	10:13	If the house is worthy, let your peace come upon it;	24
	10:23	before the Son of Man comes.	24
	10:34	"Do not think that I have come to bring peace	24
	10:34	I have not come to bring peace, but a sword.	24
	10:35	For I have come to set a man against his father	24
	11: 3	said to him, "Are you the one who is to come	24
	11:13	prophets and the law prophesied until John came	1
	11:14	he is Elijah who is to come.	24
	11:18	For John came neither eating nor drinking	24
	11:19	the Son of Man came eating and drinking	24
	11:28	"Come to me, all you that are weary and are carrying	9
	12:28	then the kingdom of God has come to you.	43
	12:32	either in this age or in the age to come.	31
	12:42	she came from the ends of the earth	24
	12:44	'I will return to my house from which I came.'	22
	12:44	When it comes, it finds it empty, swept	24
	13: 4	and the birds came and ate them up.	24
	13:10	the disciples came and asked him	40
	13:19	the evil one comes and snatches away what is sown	24
	13:25	an enemy came and sowed weeds among the wheat	24
	13:27	the slaves of the householder came and said	40
	13:32	so that the birds of the air come and make nests	24
	13:54	came to his hometown and began to teach the people	24
	14: 6	when Herod's birthday came	7
	14:12	His disciples came and took the body	40
	14:23	When evening came, he was there alone	7
	14:25	early in the morning he came walking toward them	24
	14:28	command me to come to you on the water."	24
	14:29	He said, "Come." So Peter got out of the boat	24
	14:29	walking on the water, and came toward Jesus.	24
	14:34	they came to land at Gennesaret.	24
	15:23	And his disciples came and urged him, saying	40
	15:25	she came and knelt before him, saying	24
	16: 1	The Pharisees and Sadducees came	40
	16:13	Now when Jesus came into the district	24
	16:27	"For the Son of Man is to come with his angels	24
	16:28	see the Son of Man coming in his kingdom."	24

	17: 7	Jesus came and touched them, saying	40
	17:10	the scribes say that Elijah must come first?"	24
	17:11	He replied, "Elijah is indeed coming	24
	17:12	I tell you that Elijah has already come	24
	17:14	When they came to the crowd	24
	17:25	when he came home, Jesus spoke of it first	24
	18: 7	Occasions for stumbling are bound to come	24
	18: 7	woe to the one by whom the stumbling block comes!	24
	18:21	Then Peter came and said to him	40
	19:14	Jesus said, "Let the little children come to me	24
	19:16	someone came to him and said,	40
	19:21	then come, follow me."	8
	20: 8	evening came, the owner of the vineyard said	7
	20: 9	When those hired about five o'clock came	24
	20:10	Now when the first came	24
	20:28	the Son of Man came not to be served but to serve	24
	21: 5	Look, your king is coming to you	24
	21: 9	the one who comes in the name of the Lord!	24
	21:19	"May no fruit ever come from you again!"	7
	21:25	Did the baptism of John come from heaven	14
	21:32	For John came to you in the way of righteousness	24
	21:34	When the harvest time had come	12
	21:38	come, let us kill him	9
	21:40	Now when the owner of the vineyard comes	24
	22: 3	but they would not come.	24
	22: 4	everything is ready; come to the wedding banquet.'	9
	23:35	so that upon you may come all the righteous blood	24
	23:36	all this will come upon this generation.	27
	23:39	the one who comes in the name of the Lord.' "	24
	24: 1	his disciples came to point out to him	40
	24: 3	what will be the sign of your coming	37
	24: 5	For many will come in my name, saying	24
	24:14	then the end will come.	27
	24:27	For as the lightning comes from the east	22
	24:27	so will be the coming of the Son of Man.	37
	24:30	'the Son of Man coming on the clouds of heaven'	24
	24:37	so will be the coming of the Son of Man.	37
	24:39	they knew nothing until the flood came	24
	24:39	so too will be the coming of the Son of Man.	37
	24:42	you do not know on what day your Lord is coming.	24
	24:43	in what part of the night the thief was coming	24
	24:44	Son of Man is coming at an unexpected hour.	24
	24:50	the master of that slave will come on a day	27
	25:10	while they went to buy it, the bridegroom came	24
	25:11	Later the other bridesmaids came also, saying	24
	25:19	the master of those slaves came	24
	25:31	"When the Son of Man comes in his glory	24
	25:34	'Come, you that are blessed by my Father	9
	26: 2	after two days the Passover is coming	7
	26:40	he came to the disciples and found them sleeping;	24
	26:43	Again he came and found them sleeping	24
	26:45	Then he came to the disciples and said to them	24
	26:64	coming on the clouds of heaven."	24
	27: 1	When morning came	7
	27:33	when they came to a place called Golgotha	24
	27:45	darkness came over the whole land	7
	27:49	let us see whether Elijah will come to save him."	24
	27:57	there came a rich man from Arimathea	24
	28: 2	came and rolled back the stone and sat on it.	40
	28: 6	Come, see the place where he lay.	9
	28:13	"You must say, 'His disciples came by night	24
	28:18	Jesus came and said to them	40
Mrk	1: 7	who is more powerful than I is coming after me;	24
	1: 9	In those days Jesus came from Nazareth of Galilee	24
	1:11	a voice came from heaven, "You are my Son,	7
	1:14	after John was arrested, Jesus came to Galilee	24
	1:21	and when the sabbath came	1
	1:24	Have you come to destroy us?	24
	1:31	He came and took her by the hand and lifted her up.	40
	1:40	A leper came to him begging him, and kneeling	24
	1:45	people came to him from every quarter.	24
	2: 3	people came, bringing to him a paralyzed man	24
	2:17	I have come to call not the righteous but sinners."	24
	2:18	people came and said to him	24
	2:20	days will come when the bridegroom is taken away	24
	3: 3	"Come forward."	13
	3: 8	hearing all that he was doing, they came to him	24
	3:13	they came to him.	6
	3:26	he cannot stand, but his end has come.	26
	3:31	his mother and his brothers came;	24
	4: 4	the birds came and ate it up.	24

Ref		Text	
Mrk	4:11	for those outside, everything comes in parables;	7
	4:15	when they hear, Satan immediately comes	24
	4:22	nor is anything secret, except to come to light.	24
	4:29	because the harvest has come."	36
	4:35	On that day, when evening had come, he said	7
	5: 1	They came to the other side of the sea	24
	5:14	people came to see what it was that had happened.	24
	5:15	They came to Jesus and saw the demoniac sitting	24
	5:22	one of the leaders…named Jairus came	24
	5:23	Come and lay your hands on her	24
	5:33	came in fear and trembling	24
	5:35	some people came from the leader's house	24
	5:38	When they came to the house	24
	6: 1	left that place and came to his hometown	24
	6:21	an opportunity came	7
	6:29	they came and took his body, and laid it in a tomb.	24
	6:31	For many were coming and going	24
	6:47	When evening came, the boat was out on the sea	7
	6:48	he came towards them early in the morning	24
	6:53	they came to land at Gennesaret	24
	7: 1	some of the scribes who had come from Jerusalem	24
	7:21	from the human heart, that evil intentions come:	19
	7:23	All these evil things come from within	19
	7:25	and she came and bowed down at his feet.	24
	8: 3	some of them have come from a great distance."	27
	8:11	The Pharisees came and began to argue with him	22
	8:22	They came to Bethsaida.	24
	8:38	when he comes in the glory of his Father	24
	9: 1	the kingdom of God has come with power."	24
	9: 7	from the cloud there came a voice	7
	9:11	the scribes say that Elijah must come first?"	24
	9:12	"Elijah is indeed coming first to restore all things.	24
	9:13	I tell you that Elijah has come	24
	9:14	When they came to the disciples	24
	9:33	they came to Capernaum;	24
	10:14	"Let the little children come to me	24
	10:21	come, follow me."	8
	10:30	in the age to come eternal life.	24
	10:45	Son of Man came not to be served but to serve	24
	10:46	They came to Jericho.	24
	10:50	he sprang up and came to Jesus.	24
	11: 9	the one who comes in the name of the Lord!	24
	11:10	the coming kingdom of our ancestor David!	24
	11:12	On the following day, when they came from Bethany	22
	11:13	When he came to it, he found nothing but leaves	24
	11:15	they came to Jerusalem.	24
	11:19	when evening came, Jesus and his disciples went out	7
	11:27	Again they came to Jerusalem.	24
	11:27	the scribes, and the elders came to him	24
	11:30	Did the baptism of John come from heaven,	14
	12: 2	When the season came	1
	12: 7	'This is the heir; come, let us kill him	9
	12: 9	He will come and destroy the tenants	24
	12:14	they came and said to him, "Teacher	24
	12:18	Sadducees…came to him and asked him a question	24
	12:42	A poor widow came and put in two small copper coins	24
	13: 6	Many will come in my name and say, 'I am he!'	24
	13:26	they will see 'the Son of Man coming in clouds'	24
	13:33	for you do not know when the time will come.	14
	13:35	when the master of the house will come	24
	13:36	he may find you asleep when he comes suddenly.	24
	14: 3	a woman came with an alabaster jar of…ointment	24
	14:17	When it was evening, he came with the twelve.	24
	14:37	He came and found them sleeping;	24
	14:38	pray that you may not come into the time of trial;	24
	14:40	once more he came and found them sleeping	24
	14:41	He came a third time and said to them	24
	14:41	Enough! The hour has come;	24
	14:45	when he came, he went up to him at once and said	24
	14:62	'coming with the clouds of heaven.'"	24
	15: 8	the crowd came and began to ask Pilate	4
	15:33	darkness came over the whole land	7
	15:36	see whether Elijah will come to take him down."	24
	15:42	When evening had come	7
Lke	1:28	he came to her and said, "Greetings, favored one!	16
	1:43	that the mother of my Lord comes to me?	24
	1:57	Now the time came for Elizabeth to give birth	38
	1:59	they came to circumcise the child	24
	1:65	Fear came over all their neighbors	7
	2: 6	the time came for her to deliver her child.	38
	2:22	When the time came for their purification	38

Ref	Text	
2:27	Guided by the Spirit, Simeon came into the temple;	24
2:38	At that moment she came, and began to praise	25
2:51	he went down with them and came to Nazareth	24
3: 2	the word of God came to John son of Zechariah	7
3: 7	Who warned you to flee from the wrath to come?	31
3:12	Even tax collectors came to be baptized,	24
3:16	one who is more powerful than I is coming;	24
3:22	a voice came from heaven	7
4:16	he came to Nazareth, where he had been brought up	24
4:34	Have you come to destroy us?	24
5: 7	signaled…to come and help them.	24
5: 7	they came and filled both boats	24
5:17	(they had come from every village of Galilee	24
5:18	men came, carrying a paralyzed man on a bed.	1
5:32	I have come to call not the righteous but sinners	24
5:35	The days will come when the bridegroom	24
6: 8	"Come and stand here." He got up and stood there.	13
6:13	when day came, he called his disciples	7
6:18	They had come to hear him	24
6:47	someone is like who comes to me, hears my words	24
7: 3	asking him to come and heal his slave.	24
7: 4	When they came to Jesus	33
7: 6	am not worthy to have you come under my roof;	16
7: 7	therefore I did not presume to come to you.	24
7: 8	to another, 'Come,' and he comes	24
7: 8	to another, 'Come,' and he comes	24
7:19	"Are you the one who is to come	24
7:20	When the men had come to him, they said	33
7:20	'Are you the one who is to come	24
7:33	For John the Baptist has come eating no bread	24
7:34	the Son of Man has come eating and drinking	24
8:12	then the devil comes and takes away the word	24
8:17	that will not become known and come to light.	24
8:19	Then his mother and his brothers came to him	33
8:35	they came to Jesus	24
8:41	Just then there came a man named Jairus	24
8:47	she came trembling;	24
8:49	someone came from the leader's house to say,	24
8:51	When he came to the house	24
9:26	when he comes in his glory	24
9:34	a cloud came and overshadowed them;	7
9:35	from the cloud came a voice that said,	7
9:42	While he was coming, the demon dashed him	40
10:32	a Levite, when he came to the place and saw him	24
10:33	a Samaritan while traveling came near him;	24
11: 2	hallowed be your name. Your kingdom come.	24
11:20	then the kingdom of God has come to you.	43
11:25	When it comes, it finds it swept	24
11:31	she came from the ends of the earth	24
12:36	open…for him as soon as he comes and knocks.	24
12:37	whom the master finds alert when he comes;	24
12:37	he will come and serve them.	35
12:38	If he comes during the middle of the night,	24
12:39	at what hour the thief was coming	24
12:40	the Son of Man is coming at an unexpected hour."	24
12:45	'My master is delayed in coming,'	24
12:46	the master of that slave will come	27
12:49	"I came to bring fire to the earth	24
12:51	Do you think that I have come to bring peace	33
13: 6	he came looking for fruit on it and found none.	24
13: 7	For three years I have come looking for fruit	24
13:14	come on those days and be cured	24
13:25	'I do not know where you come from.'	14
13:27	'I do not know where you come from; go away	14
13:29	people will come from east and west	27
13:31	At that very hour some Pharisees came and said	40
13:35	not see me until the time comes when you say	27
13:35	the one who comes in the name of the Lord.'"	24
14: 9	who invited both of you may come and say to you	24
14:10	so that when your host comes, he may say to you	24
14:17	'Come; for everything is ready now.'	24
14:20	just been married, and therefore I cannot come.'	24
14:23	compel people to come in	16
14:26	"Whoever comes to me	24
14:31	to oppose the one who comes against him with	24
15: 6	he comes home, he calls together his friends	24
15:17	when he came to himself he said	24
15:25	when he came and approached the house	24
15:27	He replied, 'Your brother has come	27
16:16	and the prophets were in effect until John came	1
16:21	even the dogs would come and lick his sores.	24

16:28	will not also come into this place of torment.'	24
17: 1	"Occasions for stumbling are bound to come	24
17: 1	woe to anyone by whom they come!	24
17:20	asked…when the kingdom of God was coming	24
17:20	is not coming with things that can be observed;	24
17:22	"The days are coming when you will long to see	24
17:27	the flood came and destroyed all of them.	24
18: 3	there was a widow who kept coming to him	24
18: 5	she may not wear me out by continually coming.' "	24
18: 8	yet, when the Son of Man comes	24
18:16	"Let the little children come to me, and do not	24
18:22	then come, follow me."	8
18:30	in the age to come eternal life."	24
19: 5	When Jesus came to the place, he looked up	24
19: 9	"Today salvation has come to this house	7
19:10	Son of Man came to seek out and to save the lost."	24
19:18	the second came, saying, 'Lord	24
19:20	Then the other came, saying	24
19:38	the king who comes in the name of the Lord!	24
19:43	Indeed, the days will come upon you	27
20: 1	priests and the scribes came with the elders	25
20: 4	Did the baptism of John come from heaven,	14
20: 7	they did not know where it came from.	1
20:10	When the season came	1
20:16	He will come and destroy those tenants	24
21: 6	the days will come when not one stone will be left	24
21: 8	many will come in my name and say, 'I am he!'	24
21:27	will see 'the Son of Man coming in a cloud'	24
22: 7	Then came the day of Unleavened Bread	24
22:14	When the hour came, he took his place at the table	7
22:18	until the kingdom of God comes."	24
22:45	he got up from prayer, he came to the disciples	24
22:47	he was still speaking, suddenly a crowd came	1
22:49	When those…saw what was coming, they asked	14
22:52	who had come for him	33
22:66	When day came	7
23:26	who was coming from the country	24
23:29	For the days are surely coming when they will say	24
23:33	they came to the place that is called The Skull	24
23:42	remember me when you come into your kingdom."	24
23:44	darkness came over the whole land until three	7
24: 1	at early dawn, they came to the tomb	24
Jhn 1: 7	He came as a witness to testify	24
1: 8	but he came to testify to the light.	1
1: 9	The true light…was coming into the world.	24
1:11	He came to what was his own	24
1:15	'He who comes after me ranks ahead of me	24
1:17	grace and truth came through Jesus Christ.	7
1:27	one who is coming after me;	24
1:29	The next day he saw Jesus coming toward him	24
1:30	'After me comes a man who ranks ahead of me	24
1:31	but I came baptizing with water for this	24
1:39	He said to them, "Come and see."	24
1:39	They came and saw where he was staying	24
1:46	"Can anything good come out of Nazareth?"	14
1:46	Philip said to him, "Come and see."	24
1:47	Jesus saw Nathanael coming toward him, he said	24
2: 4	Jesus said to her…My hour has not yet come."	27
2: 9	and did not know where it came from	14
3: 2	He came to Jesus by night and said to him	24
3: 2	that you are a teacher who has come from God;	24
3: 8	do not know where it comes from or where it goes.	24
3:19	that the light has come into the world	24
3:20	hate the light and do not come to the light	24
3:21	But those who do what is true come to the light	24
3:23	and people kept coming and were being baptized	33
3:26	They came to John and said to him, "Rabbi	24
3:31	one who comes from above is above all;	24
3:31	one who comes from heaven is above all.	24
4: 5	So he came to a Samaritan city called Sychar	24
4: 7	A Samaritan woman came to draw water	24
4:15	or have to keep coming here to draw water."	11
4:16	"Go, call your husband, and come back."	24
4:21	the hour is coming when you will worship the Father	24
4:23	But the hour is coming, and is now	24
4:25	"I know that Messiah is coming	24
4:25	"When he comes, he will proclaim all things to us."	24
4:27	Just then his disciples came.	24
4:29	"Come and see a man who told me everything	9
4:35	'Four months more, then comes the harvest'?	24
4:40	So when the Samaritans came to him, they asked him	24

4:45	he came to Galilee, the Galileans welcomed him	24
4:46	Then he came again to Cana in Galilee	24
4:47	heard that Jesus had come from Judea to Galilee	27
4:54	after coming from Judea to Galilee.	24
5:24	and does not come under judgment	24
5:25	"Very truly, I tell you, the hour is coming	24
5:28	the hour is coming when all…will hear	24
5:40	you refuse to come to me to have life.	24
5:43	I have come in my Father's name	24
5:43	if another comes in his own name	24
6: 5	saw a large crowd coming toward him	24
6:14	the prophet who is to come into the world."	24
6:15	they were about to come and take him by force	24
6:16	When evening came	7
6:17	and Jesus had not yet come to them.	24
6:19	walking on the sea and coming near the boat	7
6:23	Then some boats from Tiberias came near the place	24
6:25	"Rabbi, when did you come here?"	7
6:35	Whoever comes to me will never be hungry	24
6:37	that the Father gives me will come to me	27
6:37	anyone who comes to me I will never drive away;	24
6:44	No one can come to me unless drawn	24
6:45	Everyone who has heard…comes to me.	24
6:65	I have told you that no one can come to me	24
6:69	We have come to believe	1
7: 6	Jesus said to them, "My time has not yet come	34
7:27	when the Messiah comes	24
7:28	I have not come on my own.	24
7:30	because his hour had not yet come.	24
7:31	"When the Messiah comes	24
7:34	where I am, you cannot come."	24
7:36	'Where I am, you cannot come'?"	24
7:37	"Let anyone who is thirsty come to me	24
7:41	"Surely the Messiah does not come from Galilee	24
7:42	comes from Bethlehem, the village where David lived?"	24
8: 2	⟦Early in the morning he came again to the temple.⟧	33
8: 2	⟦All the people came to him⟧	24
8:14	I know where I have come from and where I am going	24
8:14	do not know where I come from or where I am going.	24
8:20	because his hour had not yet come.	24
8:21	Where I am going, you cannot come."	24
8:22	by saying, 'Where I am going, you cannot come'?"	24
8:42	I did not come on my own, but he sent me.	24
9: 4	night is coming when no one can work.	24
9:29	we do not know where he comes from."	14
9:30	You do not know where he comes	14
9:39	Jesus said, "I came into this world for judgment	24
10: 8	All who came before me are thieves and bandits;	24
10:10	The thief comes only to steal and kill	24
10:10	I came that they may have life	24
10:12	sees the wolf coming and leaves the sheep	24
10:35	to whom the word of God came were called 'gods'	7
10:41	Many came to him, and they were saying,	24
11:19	many of the Jews had come to Martha and Mary	24
11:20	When Martha heard that Jesus was coming	24
11:27	the Son of God, the one coming into the world."	24
11:30	Now Jesus had not yet come to the village	24
11:32	When Mary came where Jesus was and saw him	24
11:34	They said to him, "Lord, come and see."	24
11:38	Jesus, again greatly disturbed, came to the tomb.	24
11:43	"Lazarus, come out!"	8
11:45	the Jews therefore, who had come with Mary	24
11:48	the Romans will come and destroy	24
11:56	Surely he will not come to the festival	24
12: 1	Jesus came to Bethany, the home of Lazarus	24
12: 9	they came not only because of Jesus	24
12:12	great crowd that had come to the festival heard	24
12:12	heard that Jesus was coming to Jerusalem.	24
12:13	the one who comes in the name of the Lord	24
12:15	your king is coming, sitting on a donkey's colt!"	24
12:23	Jesus answered them, "The hour has come	24
12:27	for this reason that I have come to this hour.	24
12:28	Then a voice came from heaven	24
12:30	Jesus answered, "This voice has come for your sake	7
12:43	more than the glory that comes from God.	1
12:46	I have come as light into the world	24
12:47	for I came not to judge the world	24
13: 1	Jesus knew that his hour had come to depart	24
13: 6	He came to Simon Peter, who said to him, "Lord	24
13:33	'Where I am going, you cannot come.'	24
14: 3	I will come again and will take you to myself	24

Jhn	14: 6	No one comes to the Father except through me.	24
	14:18	not leave you orphaned; I am coming to you.	24
	14:23	we will come to them and make our home with them.	24
	14:28	'I am going away, and I am coming to you.'	24
	14:30	the ruler of this world is coming.	24
	15:22	If I had not come and spoken to them	24
	15:26	"When the Advocate comes, whom I will send to you	24
	16: 2	Indeed, an hour is coming	24
	16: 4	so that when their hour comes you may remember	24
	16: 7	if I do not go away, the Advocate will not come	24
	16: 8	when he comes, he will prove the world wrong	24
	16:13	When the Spirit of truth comes	24
	16:13	will declare to you the things that are to come.	24
	16:21	because her hour has come.	24
	16:25	The hour is coming	24
	16:28	I came from the Father	22
	16:28	have come into the world;	24
	16:32	The hour is coming, indeed it has come	24
	16:32	The hour is coming, indeed it has come	24
	17: 1	"Father, the hour has come; glorify your Son	24
	17:11	they are in the world, and I am coming to you.	24
	17:13	now I am coming to you	24
	18: 3	came there with lanterns and torches	24
	18:37	for this I came into the world	24
	19:32	the soldiers came and broke the legs of the first	24
	19:33	when they came to Jesus	24
	19:38	so he came and removed his body.	24
	19:39	Nicodemus, who had at first come to Jesus by night	24
	19:39	came, bringing a mixture of myrrh and aloes	24
	20: 1	still dark, Mary Magdalene came to the tomb	24
	20: 6	Simon Peter came, following him	24
	20:19	Jesus came and stood among them and said	24
	20:24	Thomas…was not with them when Jesus came.	24
	20:26	Jesus came and stood among them and said	24
	20:29	who have not seen and yet have come to believe."	1
	20:31	are written so that you may come to believe	1
	21: 8	the other disciples came in the boat	24
	21:12	Jesus said to them, "Come and have breakfast."	9
	21:13	Jesus came and took the bread and gave it	24
	21:22	"If it is my will that he remain until I come	24
	21:23	"If it is my will that he remain until I come	24
Act	1:11	Jesus…will come in the same way as you saw him go	24
	2: 1	When the day of Pentecost had come	41
	2: 2	suddenly from heaven there came a sound	7
	2:20	before the coming of the Lord's great and glorious day.	24
	2:43	Awe came upon everyone	7
	3:20	so that times of refreshing may come	24
	4: 1	the Sadducees came to them	25
	5: 6	The young men came and wrapped up his body	5
	5: 7	his wife came in, not knowing what had happened.	16
	5:15	shadow might fall on some of them as he came by.	24
	7:11	came a famine throughout Egypt and Canaan	24
	7:14	all his relatives to come to him, seventy-five in all;	1
	7:23	it came into his heart to visit his relatives	4
	7:26	he came to some of them as they were quarreling	32
	7:31	to look, there came the voice of the Lord:	7
	7:34	Come now, I will send you to Egypt.'	8
	7:52	the coming of the Righteous One	20
	8:27	had come to Jerusalem to worship	24
	8:36	they came to some water;	24
	8:40	until he came to Caesarea.	24
	9: 5	reply came, "I am Jesus, whom you are persecuting.	1
	9:21	has he not come here for the purpose	24
	9:26	When he had come to Jerusalem	33
	9:38	"Please come to us without delay."	11
	10:21	what is the reason for your coming?"	34
	10:22	to send for you to come to his house	15
	10:29	So when I was sent for, I came without objection.	24
	10:33	you have been kind enough to come.	33
	11: 5	it came close to me.	24
	11:20	who, on coming to Antioch, spoke to the Hellenists	24
	11:22	News…came to the ears of the church in Jerusalem	3
	11:23	When he came and saw the grace of God, he rejoiced	33
	12:10	came before the iron gate leading into the city.	24
	12:11	Peter came to himself and said	7
	12:13	a maid named Rhoda came to answer.	40
	12:18	When morning came, there was no small commotion	7
	12:20	they came to him in a body;	34
	13:11	Immediately mist and darkness came over him	39
	13:13	and came to Perga in Pamphylia.	24
	13:14	and came to Antioch in Pisidia.	33

	13:24	before his coming John had already proclaimed	17
	13:25	No, but one is coming after me;	24
	14:23	the Lord in whom they had come to believe.	1
	14:24	passed through Pisidia and came to Pamphylia.	24
	15: 4	When they came to Jerusalem	33
	15:36	After some days Paul said to Barnabas, "Come	10
	16: 7	When they had come opposite Mysia	24
	16:15	come and stay at my home."	16
	16:35	When morning came, the magistrates sent the police	7
	16:37	Let them come and take us out themselves."	24
	16:39	so they came and apologized to them.	24
	17: 1	they came to Thessalonica	24
	17: 6	"These people…have come here also	34
	17:13	they came there too	24
	18: 2	recently come from Italy with his wife Priscilla	24
	18:24	Now there came to Ephesus a Jew named Apollos	29
	19: 1	through the interior regions and came to Ephesus	30
	19: 4	to believe in the one who was to come after him	24
	19: 6	the Holy Spirit came upon them	24
	19:19	found to come to fifty thousand silver coins.	1
	19:27	this trade of ours may come into disrepute	24
	20: 2	he came to Greece	24
	20:15	the day after that we came to Miletus.	24
	20:18	When they came to him, he said to them:	33
	20:30	Some…will come distorting the truth	5
	21: 1	we came by a straight course to Cos	24
	21: 8	The next day we left and came to Caesarea;	24
	21:11	came to us and took Paul's belt	24
	21:22	They will certainly hear that you have come.	24
	21:31	word came to the tribune of the cohort	4
	21:33	Then the tribune came, arrested him	12
	21:35	When Paul came to the steps	7
	22:13	came to me; and standing beside me, he said	24
	22:27	The tribune came and asked Paul	40
	23:27	I came with the guard and rescued him.	25
	23:33	When they came to Caesarea	16
	24:17	after some years I came to bring alms to my nation	33
	24:24	Felix came with his wife Drusilla	33
	24:25	self-control, and the coming judgment	31
	25:23	Agrippa and Bernice came with great pomp	24
	27: 5	we came to Myra in Lycia.	30
	27: 8	we came to a place called Fair Havens	24
	27:27	When the fourteenth night had come	7
	27:29	prayed for day to come.	7
	28: 9	rest of the people…also came and were cured.	40
	28:13	we weighed anchor and came to Rhegium.	29
	28:13	on the second day we came to Puteoli.	24
	28:14	so we came to Rome.	24
	28:15	came as far as the Forum of Appius…to meet us.	24
	28:23	they came to him at his lodgings in great numbers.	24
Rom	1:10	I may somehow at last succeed in coming to you.	24
	1:13	that I have often intended to come to you	24
	3: 8	"Let us do evil so that good may come"?	24
	5:14	Adam, who is a type of the one who was to come.	31
	7: 9	but when the commandment came, sin revived	24
	11:11	salvation has come to the Gentiles	1
	11:25	a hardening has come upon part of Israel	7
	11:26	it is written, "Out of Zion will come the Deliverer;	27
	15:12	Isaiah says, "The root of Jesse shall come	14
	15:22	I have so often been hindered from coming to you.	24
	15:23	I desire, as I have for many years, to come to you	24
	15:27	if the Gentiles have come to share in their	1
	15:29	I know that when I come to you	24
	15:29	come in the fullness of the blessing of Christ.	24
	15:32	that by God's will I may come to you with joy	24
1Co	2: 1	When I came to you, brothers and sisters	24
	2: 1	I did not come proclaiming the mystery of God to you	24
	2: 3	And I came to you in weakness and in fear	7
	3: 5	Servants through whom you came to believe	1
	4: 5	before the time, before the Lord comes	24
	4:18	some of you, thinking that I am not coming to you,	24
	4:19	I will come to you soon, if the Lord wills	24
	4:21	you prefer? Am I to come to you with a stick	24
	7: 5	come together again, so that Satan may not tempt	14
	10:11	on whom the ends of the ages have come.	29
	11:12	just as woman came from man	18
	11:21	For when the time comes to eat,	1
	11:26	you proclaim the Lord's death until he comes.	24
	11:34	I will give instructions when I come.	24
	13:10	when the complete comes, the partial will…end	24
	14: 6	if I come to you speaking in tongues	24

	15: 2	unless you have come to believe in vain.	1
	15:11	so we proclaim and so you have come to believe.	1
	15:23	then at his coming those who belong to Christ.	37
	15:24	Then comes the end, when he hands over the kingdom	1
	15:35	With what kind of body do they come?"	24
	16: 2	so that collections need not be taken when I come.	24
	16:10	If Timothy comes, see that he has nothing to fear	24
	16:11	so that he may come to me;	24
	16:12	he was not at all willing to come now.	24
	16:12	He will come when he has the opportunity.	24
	16:17	I rejoice at the coming of Stephanas	37
2Co	1:15	I wanted to come to you first	24
	1:16	to come back to you from Macedonia	24
	1:23	I did not come again to Corinth.	24
	2: 3	so that when I came, I might not suffer pain	24
	2:12	When I came to Troas	24
	2:14	the fragrance that comes from knowing him.	1
	3: 7	if the ministry of death…came in glory	7
	3: 8	will the ministry of the Spirit come in glory?	14
	7: 5	For even when we came into Macedonia	24
	7: 7	not only by his coming, but also by the consolation	37
	9: 4	if some Macedonians come with me and find	24
	10:14	we were the first to come all the way to you	43
	11: 4	For if someone comes and proclaims another Jesus	24
	11: 9	the friends who came from Macedonia.	24
	12:14	Here I am, ready to come to you this third time.	24
	12:20	I fear that when I come, I may find you	24
	12:21	I fear that when I come again, my God may humble me	24
	13: 1	This is the third time I am coming to you.	24
	13: 2	if I come again, I will not be lenient—	24
	13:10	so that when I come	34
Gal	2:11	when Cephas came to Antioch	24
	2:12	for until certain people came from James	24
	2:12	but after they came, he drew back	24
	2:16	And we have come to believe in Christ Jesus	1
	3:14	blessing of Abraham might come to the Gentiles	7
	3:17	law, which came four hundred thirty years later	7
	3:19	until the offspring would come	24
	3:21	righteousness would indeed come through the law.	14
	3:23	Now before faith came	24
	3:24	the law was our disciplinarian until Christ came	1
	3:25	now that faith has come	24
	4: 4	when the fullness of time had come	24
Eph	1:17	revelation as you come to know him	1
	1:21	but also in the age to come.	31
	2: 7	so that in the ages to come	23
	2:17	he came and proclaimed peace to you who were far off	24
	4:13	until all of us come to the unity of the faith	29
	5: 6	the wrath of God comes on those…disobedient	24
Php	1:26	when I come to you again.	37
	1:27	so that, whether I come and see you or am absent	24
	2:24	I trust…that I will also come soon.	24
	3: 7	I have come to regard as loss because of Christ.	1
Col	1: 6	that has come to you.	34
	1:11	all the strength that comes from his glorious power	28
	1:18	he might come to have first place in everything.	1
	2:17	These are only a shadow of what is to come.	31
	3: 6	On account of these the wrath of God is coming	24
	4: 9	he is coming with Onesimus, the faithful	1
	4:10	if he comes to you, welcome him.	24
1Th	1: 5	message of the gospel came to you not in word only	7
	1:10	Jesus, who rescues us from the wrath that is coming.	24
	2: 1	our coming to you was not in vain	17
	2: 5	we never came with words of flattery	7
	2:18	For we wanted to come to you	24
	2:19	before our Lord Jesus at his coming?	37
	3: 6	Timothy has just now come to us from you	24
	3:13	blameless…at the coming of our Lord Jesus	37
	4:15	who are left until the coming of the Lord	37
	5: 2	the day of the Lord will come like a thief	24
	5:23	blameless at the coming of our Lord Jesus	37
2Th	1:10	when he comes to be glorified by his saints	24
	2: 1	As to the coming of our Lord Jesus Christ	37
	2: 3	for that day will not come unless the rebellion	1
	2: 3	unless the rebellion comes first	24
	2: 6	that he may be revealed when his time comes.	1
	2: 8	annihilating him by the manifestation of his coming.	37
	2: 9	The coming of the lawless one	37
1Ti	1:15	Jesus came into the world to save sinners	24
	1:16	an example to those who would come to believe in him	31
	2: 4	to come to the knowledge of the truth.	24

	3:14	I hope to come to you soon	24
	4: 8	both the present life and the life to come.	31
	6: 4	disputes about words. From these come envy	7
2Ti	2:25	they will repent and come to know the truth	15
	3: 1	in the last days distressing times will come.	21
	4: 3	For the time is coming	14
	4: 6	the time of my departure has come.	25
	4: 9	Do your best to come to me soon	24
	4:13	When you come, bring the cloak that I left	24
	4:21	Do your best to come before winter.	24
Tit	3: 8	those who have come to believe in God may be careful	1
	3:12	do your best to come to me at Nicopolis	24
Heb	2: 5	Now God did not subject the coming world	31
	6: 5	the powers of the age to come	31
	7:28	the word of the oath, which came later than the law	1
	8: 8	"The days are surely coming, says the Lord	24
	9:10	imposed until the time comes to set things right.	1
	9:11	when Christ came as a high priest	33
	9:11	a high priest of the good things that have come	7
	10: 1	a shadow of the good things to come	31
	10: 7	I said, 'See, God, I have come to do your will, O God'	27
	10: 9	he added, "See, I have come to do your will."	27
	10:37	the one who is coming will come and will not delay;	27
	12:18	You have not come to something that can be touched	40
	12:22	you have come to Mount Zion	40
	13:14	we are looking for the city that is to come.	31
	13:23	if he comes in time, he will be with me when I see you.	24
Jas	3:10	From the same mouth come blessing and cursing.	22
	4: 1	and disputes among you, where do they come from?	1
	4:13	Come now, you who say, "Today or tomorrow	2
	5: 1	Come now, you rich people, weep and wail	2
	5: 7	Be patient…until the coming of the Lord.	37
	5: 8	for the coming of the Lord is near.	37
1Pe	1:21	Through him you have come to trust in God	1
	2: 4	Come to him, a living stone, though rejected	40
	4:17	For the time has come for judgment to begin	1
2Pe	1:12	established in the truth that has come to you.	34
	1:14	since I know that my death will come soon	14
	1:16	made known to you the power and coming of our Lord	37
	1:18	We ourselves heard this voice come from heaven	42
	1:21	because no prophecy ever came by human will,	42
	2: 6	an example of what is coming to the ungodly;	31
	3: 3	that in the last days scoffers will come	24
	3: 4	and saying, "Where is the promise of his coming?	37
	3: 9	but all to come to repentance.	44
	3:10	But the day of the Lord will come like a thief	27
	3:12	and hastening the coming of the day of God	37
1Jn	2: 4	says, "I have come to know him," but does not obey	1
	2:16	comes not from the Father but from the world.	14
	2:18	As you have heard that antichrist is coming	24
	2:18	so now many antichrists have come.	7
	2:21	and you know that no lie comes from the truth.	14
	2:28	and not be put to shame before him at his coming.	37
	4: 2	that Jesus Christ has come in the flesh is from God	24
	4: 3	antichrist, of which you have heard that it is coming;	24
	5: 6	This is the one who came by water and blood, Jesus	24
	5:20	we know that the Son of God has come	27
2Jn	1: 7	Jesus Christ has come in the flesh;	24
	1:10	welcome anyone who comes to you and does not bring	24
	1:12	I hope to come to you and talk with you	7
3Jn	1:10	So if I come, I will call attention to what he is doing	24
Jde	1:14	"See, the Lord is coming with ten thousands of his holy	24
Rev	1: 4	from him who is and who was and who is to come	24
	1: 7	Look! He is coming with the clouds;	24
	1: 8	Lord God, who is and who was and who is to come	24
	1:16	from his mouth came a sharp, two-edged sword	19
	2: 5	I will come to you and remove your lampstand	24
	2:16	If not, I will come to you soon and make war	24
	2:25	only hold fast to what you have until I come.	27
	3: 3	If you do not wake up, I will come like a thief	27
	3: 3	you will not know at what hour I will come to you.	27
	3: 9	make them come and bow down before your feet	27
	3:10	hour of trial that is coming on the whole world	24
	3:11	I am coming soon; hold fast to what you have	24
	4: 8	Lord God the Almighty, who was and is and is to come."	24
	6: 1	call out, as with a voice of thunder, "Come!"	24
	6: 3	the second living creature call out, "Come!"	24
	6: 5	I heard the third living creature call out, "Come!"	24
	6: 7	the fourth living creature call out, "Come!"	24
	6:12	I looked, and there came a great earthquake;	7
	6:17	for the great day of their wrath has come	24

Rev	7:13	"Who are these...and where have they come from?"	24
	8: 3	Another angel with a golden censer came and stood	24
	8: 7	there came hail and fire, mixed with blood	7
	9: 3	Then from the smoke came locusts on the earth	22
	9:12	There are still two woes to come.	24
	11: 1	"Come and measure the temple of God and the altar	13
	11:14	The third woe is coming very soon.	24
	11:18	The nations raged, but your wrath has come	24
	12:10	"Now have come the salvation and the power	7
	14: 7	"Fear God...for the hour of his judgment has come;	24
	14:15	reap, for the hour to reap has come	24
	15: 4	All nations will come and worship before you	27
	16: 2	and a foul and painful sore came on those	7
	16:13	foul spirits...coming from the mouth of the dragon	1
	16:15	("See, I am coming like a thief!	24
	16:18	there came flashes of lightning, rumblings, peals	7
	17: 1	one of the seven angels...came and said to me	24
	17: 1	"Come, I will show you the judgment	8
	17: 8	the beast, because it was and is not and is to come.	34
	17:10	one is living, and the other has not yet come;	24
	17:10	when he comes, he must remain only a little while.	24
	18: 8	therefore her plagues will come in a single day	27
	18:10	For in one hour your judgment has come."	24
	19: 5	And from the throne came a voice saying	22
	19: 7	for the marriage of the Lamb has come	24
	19:15	From his mouth comes a sharp sword	19
	19:17	"Come, gather for the great supper of God	9
	19:21	the sword that came from his mouth;	22
	21: 9	Then one of the seven angels...came and said	24
	21: 9	"Come, I will show you the bride, the wife of the Lamb."	8
	22: 7	"See, I am coming soon!	24
	22:12	"See, I am coming soon; my reward is with	24
	22:17	The Spirit and the bride say, "Come."	24
	22:17	And let everyone who hears say, "Come."	24
	22:17	And let everyone who is thirsty come.	24
	22:20	"Surely I am coming soon." Amen. Come, Lord Jesus!	24
	22:20	I am coming soon." Amen. Come, Lord Jesus!	24

come along

1. συνέρχομαι, *synerchomai*, 5302

| Act | 21:16 | disciples from Caesarea also came along | 1 |

come away

1. δεῦτε, *deute*, 1307

| Mrk | 6:31 | "Come away to a deserted place all by yourselves | 1 |

come back

1. ἐπανέρχομαι, *epanerchomai*, 2059
2. ἔρχομαι, *erchomai*, 2262

Lke	10:35	when I come back, I will repay you	1
	15:30	when this son of yours came back	2
	19:13	'Do business with these until I come back.'	2
	24:23	they came back and told us that they had...seen	2
Jhn	9: 7	Then he went and washed and came back able to see.	2

come by

1. ἔρχομαι, *erchomai*, 2262

| Mrk | 14:66 | the servant-girls of the high priest came by. | 1 |

come close

1. ἐγγίζω, *engizō*, 1581

| Php | 2:30 | he came close to death for the work of Christ | 1 |

come down

1. καταβαίνω, *katabainō*, 2849
2. κατέρχομαι, *katerchomai*, 2982

Mat	8: 1	When Jesus had come down from the mountain	1
	17: 9	As they were coming down the mountain	1
	27:40	the Son of God, come down from the cross."	1
	27:42	let him come down from the cross now	1
Mrk	3:22	the scribes who came down from Jerusalem said	1
	9: 9	As they were coming down the mountain	1
	15:30	save yourself, and come down from the cross!"	1
	15:32	King of Israel, come down from the cross now	1
Lke	6:17	He came down with them and stood on a level place	1
	9:37	when they had come down from the mountain	2
	9:54	to command fire to come down from heaven	1
	17:31	must not come down to take them away;	1
	19: 5	"Zacchaeus, hurry and come down;	1
Jhn	4:47	and begged him to come down and heal his son	1

	4:49	"Sir, come down before my little boy dies."	1
	6:33	bread of God is that which comes down from heaven	1
	6:38	I have come down from heaven, not to do my own	1
	6:41	"I am the bread that came down from heaven."	1
	6:42	can he now say, 'I have come down from heaven'?"	1
	6:50	This is the bread that comes down from heaven	1
	6:51	I am the living bread that came down from heaven.	1
	6:58	This is the bread that came down from heaven	1
Act	7:34	I have come down to rescue them.	1
	9:32	he came down also to the saints living in Lydda.	2
	10:11	something like a large sheet coming down	1
	11: 5	There was something like a large sheet coming down	1
	11:27	At that time prophets came down from Jerusalem	2
	14:11	"The gods have come down to us in human form!"	1
	15: 1	certain individuals came down from Judea	2
	21:10	a prophet named Agabus came down from Judea.	2
	24: 1	the high priest Ananias came down with some elders	1
	24:22	"When Lysias the tribune comes down	1
Jas	1:17	coming down from the Father of lights	1
	3:15	Such wisdom does not come down from above	2
Rev	3:12	the new Jerusalem that comes down from my God	1
	10: 1	another mighty angel coming down from heaven	1
	12:12	for the devil has come down to you with great wrath	1
	13:13	even making fire come down from heaven to earth	1
	18: 1	I saw another angel coming down from heaven	1
	20: 1	Then I saw an angel coming down from heaven	1
	20: 9	And fire came down from heaven and consumed them.	1
	21: 2	new Jerusalem, coming down out of heaven from God	1
	21:10	Jerusalem coming down out of heaven from God.	1

come down with

1. συγκαταβαίνω, *synkatabainō*, 5160

| Act | 25: 5 | you who have the authority come down with me | 1 |

come forward

1. ἐξέρχομαι, *exerchomai*, 2002
2. παραγίνομαι, *paraginomai*, 4134
3. προσέρχομαι, *proserchomai*, 4665
4. προσπορεύομαι, *prosporeuomai*, 4702

Mat	25:20	who had received the five talents came forward	3
	25:22	the one with the two talents also came forward	3
	25:24	had received the one talent also came forward	3
	26:60	though many false witnesses came forward.	3
	26:60	At last two came forward	3
Mrk	10:35	James and John, the sons of Zebedee, came forward	4
Lke	7:14	he came forward and touched the bier	3
	19:16	The first came forward and said, 'Lord	2
Jhn	18: 4	Jesus...came forward and asked them	1

come from

1. Contextual: Not in Greek
2. ἀπό, *apo*, 608
3. ἐκ, *ek*, 1666
4. ἐκπορεύομαι, *ekporeuomai*, 1744
5. ἐξέρχομαι, *exerchomai*, 2002
6. ἔχω, *echō*, 2400
7. παρά, *para*, 4123

Mat	4: 4	every word that comes from the mouth of God.' "	4
	13:27	Where, then, did these weeds come from?'	6
Lke	4:22	the gracious words that came from his mouth.	4
	11:24	'I will return to my house from which I came.'	5
	23:51	he came from the Jewish town of Arimathea	2
Jhn	5:44	glory that comes from the one who alone is God?	7
	8:42	I came from God and now I am here.	5
	13: 3	he had come from God and was going to God	5
	15:26	the Spirit of truth who comes from the Father	4
	16:27	have believed that I came from God.	5
	16:30	by this we believe that you came from God."	5
	17: 8	and know in truth that I came from you;	5
Rom	9: 5	from them, according to the flesh, comes the Messiah	3
	10: 3	the righteousness that comes from God	1
	10: 5	righteousness that comes from the law	3
	10: 6	But the righteousness that comes from faith says	3
	10:17	So faith comes from what is heard	3
1Co	11:12	but all things come from God.	3
2Co	3: 5	to claim anything as coming from us;	3
	3:18	for this comes from the Lord, the Spirit.	2
	4: 7	power belongs to God and does not come from us.	3
Gal	3:18	For if the inheritance comes from the law	3
	3:18	it no longer comes from the promise;	3

	5: 8	Such persuasion does not come from the one who calls	3
Php	3: 9	righteousness of my own that comes from the law	3
1Ti	1: 5	that comes from a pure heart, a good conscience	3
Jas	4: 1	Do they not come from your cravings	3
Rev	4: 5	Coming from the throne are flashes of lightning	4

come fully

1. πληρόω, *plēroō, 4444*

Jhn 7: 8 for my time has not yet fully come."   1

come here

1. παραγίνομαι, *paraginomai, 4134*
2. παρέρχομαι, *parerchomai, 4216*

Lke 17: 7 'Come here at once and take your place at the table'?   2
Act 28:21 none of the brothers coming here has reported   1

come in

1. εἰσέρχομαι, *eiserchomai, 1656*
2. εἰσπορεύομαι, *eisporeuomai, 1660*
3. ἐν, *en, 1877*
4. ἔρχομαι, *erchomai, 2262*
5. παρεισέρχομαι, *pareiserchomai, 4209*

Mat	22:11	"But when the king came in to see the guests	1
Mrk	4:19	come in and choke the word	2
	6:22	When his daughter Herodias came in and danced	1
	15:21	who was coming in from the country	4
Lke	7:45	from the time I came in she has not stopped	1
	17: 7	your slave who has just come in from plowing	1
Jhn	10: 9	and will come in and go out and find pasture.	1
Act	5:10	When the young men came in they found her dead	1
	9:12	Ananias come in and lay his hands on him	1
	10: 3	an angel of God coming in and saying to him	1
	20:29	savage wolves will come in among you	1
Rom	5:20	law came in...result that the trespass multiplied;	5
	11:25	until the full number of the Gentiles has come in.	1
2Co	3:11	much more has the permanent come in glory!	3
Jas	2: 2	a poor person in dirty clothes also comes in	1
Rev	3:20	I will come in to you and eat with you	1

come in sight

1. ἀναφαίνω, *anaphainō, 428*

Act 21: 3 We came in sight of Cyprus;   1

come into

1. εἰσέρχομαι, *eiserchomai, 1656*

Mat	26:41	that you may not come into the time of trial;	1
Lke	22:40	"Pray that you may not come into the time of trial."	1
	22:46	pray that you may not come into the time of trial."	1
Act	28:16	When we came into Rome	1
Rom	5:12	just as sin came into the world through one man	1
Heb	10: 5	when Christ came into the world, he said	1
Jas	2: 2	a person...comes into your assembly	1

come into being

1. γίνομαι, *ginomai, 1181*

Jhn	1: 3	All things came into being through him	1
	1: 3	without him not one thing came into being.	1
	1: 3	What has come into being	1
	1:10	and the world came into being through him;	1

come near

1. ἐγγίζω, *engizō, 1581*
2. προσέρχομαι, *proserchomai, 4665*

Mat	3: 2	"Repent, for the kingdom of heaven has come near."	1
	4:17	"Repent, for the kingdom of heaven has come near."	1
	10: 7	'The kingdom of heaven has come near.'	1
	21: 1	When they had come near Jerusalem	1
Mrk	1:15	the kingdom of God has come near;	1
	12:28	One of the scribes came near and heard	2
Lke	10: 9	'The kingdom of God has come near to you.'	1
	10:11	the kingdom of God has come near.'	1
	12:33	where no thief comes near and no moth destroys.	1
	15: 1	and sinners were coming near to listen to him.	1
	18:40	when he came near, he asked him	1
	19:29	When he had come near Bethphage and Bethany	1
	19:41	As he came near and saw the city, he wept over it	1
	21:20	then know that its desolation has come near.	1
	24:15	Jesus himself came near and went with them	1
	24:28	they came near the village	1

come one

1. ἔρχομαι, *erchomai, 2262*

Heb 10:37 very little while, the one who is coming will come   1

come out

1. ἐκπορεύομαι, *ekporeuomai, 1744*
2. ἐξέρχομαι, *exerchomai, 2002*
3. ἔρχομαι, *erchomai, 2262*

Mat	8:28	two demoniacs coming out of the tombs met him.	2
	8:32	"Go!" So they came out and entered the swine;	2
	8:34	Then the whole town came out to meet Jesus;	2
	13:49	The angels will come out and separate	2
	15:11	what comes out of the mouth that defiles."	1
	15:18	what comes out of the mouth	1
	15:19	For out of the heart come evil intentions, murder	2
	15:22	a Canaanite woman from that region came out	2
	17:18	Jesus rebuked the demon, and it came out of him	2
	24: 1	Jesus came out of the temple and was going away	2
	25: 6	Here is the bridegroom! Come out to meet him.'	2
	26:55	"Have you come out with swords and clubs to arrest	2
	27:53	After his resurrection they came out of the tombs	2
Mrk	1:25	"Be silent, and come out of him!"	2
	1:26	the unclean spirit...came out of him.	2
	1:38	for that is what I came out	2
	5: 8	"Come out of the man, you unclean spirit!"	2
	5:13	unclean spirits came out and entered the swine;	2
	7:15	the things that come out are what defile."	1
	7:20	what comes out of a person that defiles.	1
	9:25	come out of him, and never enter him again!"	2
	9:26	it came out, and the boy was like a corpse	2
	9:29	"This kind can come out only through	2
	13: 1	As he came out of the temple	1
	14:48	"Have you come out with swords and clubs to arrest	2
Lke	1:22	When he did come out, he could not speak to them	2
	3: 7	the crowds that came out to be baptized by him	1
	4:35	"Be silent, and come out of him!"	2
	4:35	he came out of him without having done him any harm.	2
	4:36	commands the unclean spirits, and out they come!"	2
	4:41	Demons also came out of many	2
	6:19	power came out from him and healed all of them.	2
	8:29	commanded the unclean spirit to come out	2
	8:33	Then the demons came out of the man	2
	8:35	Then people came out to see what had happened	2
	15:28	His father came out and began to plead with him.	2
	22:39	He came out and went...to the Mount of Olives;	2
	22:52	"Have you come out with swords and clubs	2
Jhn	5:29	and will come out	1
	11:44	The dead man came out	2
	19: 5	Jesus came out, wearing the crown of thorns	2
	19:34	at once blood and water came out.	2
Act	7: 7	they shall come out and worship me in this place.'	2
	8: 7	unclean spirits...came out of many	2
	16:18	"I order you...to come out of her."	2
	16:18	it came out that very hour.	2
	16:36	therefore come out now and go in peace."	2
	19:12	diseases left them, and the evil spirits came out	1
2Co	6:17	come out from them, and be separate from them	2
Eph	4:29	Let no evil talk come out of your mouths	1
Rev	6: 2	and he came out conquering and to conquer.	2
	6: 4	And out came another horse, bright red;	2
	7:14	they who have come out of the great ordeal;	3
	9:17	and smoke and sulfur came out of their mouths.	2
	9:18	smoke and sulfur coming out of their mouths.	1
	14:15	Another angel came out of the temple, calling	2
	14:17	another angel came out of the temple in heaven	2
	14:18	Then another angel came out from the altar	2
	15: 6	out of the temple came the seven angels	2
	16:17	and a loud voice came out of the temple	2
	18: 4	"Come out of her, my people	2
	20: 8	and will come out to deceive the nations	2

come over

1. διαβαίνω, *diabainō, 1329*

Act 16: 9 "Come over to Macedonia and help us."   1

come running together

1. ἐπισυντρέχω, *episyntrechō, 2192*

Mrk 9:25 Jesus saw that a crowd came running together   1

come there

1. ἐπέρχομαι, *eperchomai, 2088*

Act 14:19 Jews came there from Antioch and Iconium   1

come through

1. διά, *dia, 1328*

Rom 3:20 for through the law comes the knowledge of sin.   1
    4:13 the promise…did not come…through the law   1
    5:12 sin came into the world…death came through sin   1
    10:17 what is heard comes through the word of Christ.   1
1Co 11:12 so man comes through woman;   1
    15:21 For since death came through a human being   1
    15:21 resurrection…has also come through a human being;   1
2Co 3:11 for if what was set aside came through glory   1
Gal 2:21 if justification comes through the law   1
Php 1:11 that comes through Jesus Christ   1
    3: 9 righteousness…that comes through faith in Christ   1

come to

1. εἰσέρχομαι, *eiserchomai, 1656*
2. εἰσπορεύομαι, *eisporeuomai, 1660*
3. ἐπέρχομαι, *eperchomai, 2088*
4. ἐπιπορεύομαι, *epiporeuomai, 2164*
5. ἐφίστημι, *ephistēmi, 2392*
6. προσέρχομαι, *proserchomai, 4665*
7. συμβαίνω, *symbainō, 5201*

Mat 8: 2 a leper who came to him and knelt before him   6
    8: 5 he entered Capernaum, a centurion came to him   6
    14:15 When it was evening, the disciples came to him   6
    15: 1 Then Pharisees and scribes came to Jesus   6
    15:30 Great crowds came to him   6
    17:14 a man came to him, knelt before him   6
    17:19 Then the disciples came to Jesus privately   6
    17:24 the collectors…came to Peter and said   6
    18: 1 At that time the disciples came to Jesus and asked   6
    19: 3 Pharisees came to him, and to test him they asked   6
    20:20 the mother of the sons of Zebedee came to him   6
    21:14 The blind and the lame came to him in the temple   6
    21:23 came to him as he was teaching, and said   6
    22:23 The same day some Sadducees came to him   6
    24: 3 the disciples came to him privately, saying   6
    26: 7 a woman came to him   6
    26:17 the disciples came to Jesus, saying   6
    26:69 A servant-girl came to him and said   6
    28: 9 they came to him, took hold of his feet,   6
Mrk 6:35 grew late, his disciples came to him and said   6
Lke 8: 4 people from town after town came to him   4
    8:41 begged him to come to his house   1
    9:12 the twelve came to him and said   6
    10:40 came to him and asked, "Lord, do you not care   5
    20:27 Some Sadducees…came to him   6
Jhn 12:21 They came to Philip, who was from Bethsaida   6
Act 10:24 the following day they came to Caesarea.   1
    20:19 that came to me through the plots of the Jews.   7
    28:30 welcomed all who came to him   2
Jas 5: 1 wail for the miseries that are coming to you.   3

come to a sober mind

1. ἐκνήφω, *eknēphō, 1729*

1Co 15:34 Come to a sober and right mind, and sin no more;   1

come to an end

1. καταργέω, *katargeō, 2934*

1Co 13: 8 as for prophecies, they will come to an end;   1
    13: 8 as for knowledge, it will come to an end.   1
    13:10 the complete comes, the partial will come to an end.   1

come to ear

1. ἀκούω, *akouō, 201*

Mat 28:14 If this comes to the governor's ears   1

come to fullness

1. πληρόω, *plēroō, 4444*

Col 2:10 you have come to fullness in him   1

come to help

1. βοηθέω, *boētheō, 1070*
2. ἐπιλαμβάνομαι, *epilambanomai, 2138*

Heb 2:16 For it is clear that he did not come to help angels   2

Rev 12:16 But the earth came to the help of the woman;   1

come to judge

1. ἐπισκοπή, *episkopē, 2175*

1Pe 2:12 and glorify God when he comes to judge.   1

come to life

1. ζάω, *zaō, 2409*
2. ζωοποιέω, *zōopoieō, 2443*

Lke 15:32 brother of yours was dead and has come to life;   1
1Co 15:36 What you sow does not come to life unless it dies.   2
Rev 2: 8 the first and the last, who was dead and came to life: 1
    20: 4 They came to life and reigned with Christ   1
    20: 5 (The rest of the dead did not come to life   1

come to pass

1. γίνομαι, *ginomai, 1181*

Mrk 11:23 believe that what you say will come to pass   1

come to support

1. παραγίνομαι, *paraginomai, 4134*

2Ti 4:16 At my first defense no one came to my support   1

come to terms

1. εὐνοέω, *eunoeō, 2333*

Mat 5:25 Come to terms quickly with your accuser   1

come together

1. συνέρχομαι, *synerchomai, 5302*

Mrk 3:20 and the crowd came together again   1
Jhn 18:20 where all the Jews come together.   1
Act 1: 6 So when they had come together, they asked him   1
    19:32 did not know why they had come together   1
1Co 11:17 because when you come together   1
    11:18 to begin with, when you come together as a church   1
    11:20 When you come together, it is not really to eat   1
    11:33 brothers and sisters, when you come together to eat   1
    11:34 so that when you come together, it will not   1
    14:23 If, therefore, the whole church comes together   1
    14:26 When you come together, each one has a hymn   1

come up

1. ἀναβαίνω, *anabainō, 326*
2. βλαστάνω, *blastanō, 1056*
3. ἔρχομαι, *erchomai, 2262*
4. προσέρχομαι, *proserchomai, 4665*

Mat 3:16 just as he came up from the water, suddenly   1
    9:20 came up behind him and touched the fringe   4
    13:26 when the plants came up and bore grain   2
    17:27 take the first fish that comes up   1
    26:49 he came up to Jesus and said, "Greetings, Rabbi!"   4
    26:50 Then they came and laid hands on Jesus   4
    26:73 After a little while the bystanders came up   4
Mrk 1:10 just as he was coming up out of the water   1
    5:27 came up behind him in the crowd   3
    10: 2 Pharisees came, and to test him they asked   4
Lke 8:44 came up behind him and touched…his clothes   4
    23:36 coming up and offering him sour wine   4
Jhn 19: 3 They kept coming up to him, saying, "Hail, King   3
Act 8:39 When they came up out of the water   1
Rev 4: 1 the first voice…said, "Come up here   1
    11: 7 the beast that comes up from the bottomless pit   1
    11:12 voice from heaven saying to them, "Come up here!"   1

come up with

1. συναναβαίνω, *synanabainō, 5262*

Mrk 15:41 women who had come up with him to Jerusalem.   1
Act 13:31 he appeared to those who came up with him   1

come upon

1. Contextual: Not in Greek
2. ἐπεισέρχομαι, *epeiserchomai, 2082*
3. ἐπέρχομαι, *eperchomai, 2088*
4. ἐπιπίπτω, *epipiptō, 2158*
5. εὑρίσκω, *heuriskō, 2351*
6. ἐφίστημι, *ephistēmi, 2392*

Mat 18:28 came upon one of his fellow slaves   5
    27:32 As they went out, they came upon a man from Cyrene   5
Lke 1:35 "The Holy Spirit will come upon you   3

	21:26	foreboding of what is coming upon the world	3
	21:35	For it will come upon all	2
Act	1: 8	when the Holy Spirit has come upon you;	3
	8:16	as yet the Spirit had not come upon any of them;	4
1Th	5: 3	then sudden destruction will come upon them	6
	5: 3	as labor pains come upon a pregnant woman	1

come with

1. συνέρχομαι, *synerchomai*, 5302

Lke	23:55	The women who had come with him from Galilee	1
Jhn	11:33	and the Jews who came with her also weeping	1
Act	10:45	circumcised believers who had come with Peter	1

good news come

1. εὐαγγελίζω, *euangelizō*, 2294

Heb	4: 2	For indeed the good news came to us just as to them;	1

comfort *See also* find comfort

1. παρακαλέω, *parakaleō*, 4151
2. παράκλησις, *paraklēsis*, 4155
3. παρηγορία, *parēgoria*, 4219

Mat	5: 4	who mourn, for they will be comforted.	1
Lke	16:25	now he is comforted here, and you are in agony.	1
Act	9:31	in the comfort of the Holy Spirit	2
	20:12	were not a little comforted.	1
Col	4:11	they have been a comfort to me.	3
2Th	2:16	gave us eternal comfort and good hope	2
	2:17	comfort your hearts and strengthen them	1

command *See also* cry of command, give a command

1. διατάσσω, *diatassō*, 1411
2. ἔνταλμα, *entalma*, 1945
3. ἐντέλλω, *entellō*, 1948
4. ἐντολή, *entolē*, 1953
5. ἐντολή + δίδωμι, *entolē + didōmi*, 1953 + 1443
6. ἐντολή + λαμβάνω, *entolē + lambanō*, 1953 + 3284
7. ἐπιταγή, *epitagē*, 2198
8. ἐπιτάσσω, *epitassō*, 2199
9. κελεύω, *keleuō*, 3027
10. λέγω, *legō*, 3306
11. παραγγέλλω, *parangellō*, 4133
12. προστάσσω, *prostassō*, 4705
13. συντάσσω, *syntassō*, 5332

Mat	1:24	he did as the angel of the Lord commanded him;	12
	4: 3	"If you are the Son of God, command these stones	10
	4: 6	'He will command his angels concerning you,'	3
	8: 4	and offer the gift that Moses commanded	12
	14: 9	he commanded it to be given;	9
	14:28	command me to come to you on the water."	9
	19: 7	"Why then did Moses command	3
	27:10	as the Lord commanded me."	13
	27:64	Therefore command the tomb to be made secure	9
	28:20	everything that I have commanded you.	3
Mrk	1:27	He commands even the unclean spirits	8
	1:44	offer for your cleansing what Moses commanded	12
	9:25	I command you, come out of him, and never enter	8
	10: 3	He answered them, "What did Moses command you?"	3
	13:34	commands the doorkeeper to be on the watch	2
	16: S	⟦all that had been commanded them they told briefly⟧	11
Lke	4: 3	command this stone to become a loaf of bread."	10
	4:10	'He will command his angels concerning you,	3
	4:36	commands the unclean spirits, and out they come!"	8
	5:14	as Moses commanded, make an offering	12
	8:25	that he commands even the winds	8
	8:29	commanded the unclean spirit to come out	11
	9:21	He…commanded them not to tell anyone,	11
	9:54	do you want us to command fire to come down	10
	15:29	I have never disobeyed your command;	4
	17: 9	for doing what was commanded?	1
Jhn	8: 5	⟦Now in the law Moses commanded us to stone such⟧	3
	10:18	I have received this command from my Father."	4
	14:31	I do as the Father has commanded me	3
	15:14	You are my friends if you do what I command you.	3
Act	8:38	He commanded the chariot to stop	9
	10:33	listen to all that the Lord has commanded you to say	12
	10:42	He commanded us to preach to the people	11
	13:47	For so the Lord has commanded us, saying	3
	17:30	now he commands all people everywhere to repent	11
Rom	16:26	according to the command of the eternal God	7

1Co	7: 6	This I say by way of concession, not of command.	7
	7:25	virgins, I have no command of the Lord	7
	9:14	In the same way, the Lord commanded	1
	14:37	writing to you is a command of the Lord.	4
2Co	8: 8	I do not say this as a command	7
Col	2:22	simply human commands and teachings.	2
2Th	3: 4	and will go on doing the things that we command.	11
	3: 6	Now we command you, beloved	11
	3:12	Now such persons we command and exhort	11
1Ti	1: 1	an apostle…by the command of God our Savior	7
	6:17	command them not to be haughty	11
Tit	1: 3	by the command of God our Savior	7
Phm	1: 8	to command you to do your duty	8
1Jn	3:23	love one another, just as he has commanded us.	5
2Jn	1: 4	just as we have been commanded by the Father.	6

command solemnly

1. ἐνορκίζω, *enorkizō*, 1941

1Th	5:27	I solemnly command you by the Lord that this letter	1

commandment

1. Contextual: Not in Greek
2. ἐντολή, *entolē*, 1953
3. λόγος, *logos*, 3364

Mat	5:19	breaks one of the least of these commandments	2
	15: 3	"And why do you break the commandment of God	2
	19:17	to enter into life, keep the commandments."	2
	22:36	which commandment in the law is the greatest?"	2
	22:38	This is the greatest and first commandment.	2
	22:40	On these two commandments hang all the law	2
Mrk	7: 8	You abandon the commandment of God	2
	7: 9	a fine way of rejecting the commandment of God	2
	10: 5	he wrote this commandment for you.	2
	10:19	You know the commandments:	2
	12:28	"Which commandment is the first of all?"	2
	12:31	no other commandment greater than these."	2
Lke	1: 6	according to all the commandments and regulations	2
	18:20	You know the commandments:	2
	23:56	they rested according to the commandment.	2
Jhn	12:49	has…given me a commandment about what to say	2
	12:50	I know that his commandment is eternal life.	2
	13:34	I give you a new commandment, that	2
	14:15	"If you love me, you will keep my commandments.	2
	14:21	They who have my commandments and keep them	2
	15:10	If you keep my commandments	2
	15:10	just as I have kept my Father's commandments	2
	15:12	my commandment, that you love one another	2
Rom	7: 8	But sin, seizing an opportunity in the commandment	2
	7: 9	but when the commandment came, sin revived	2
	7:10	the very commandment that promised life	2
	7:11	For sin, seizing an opportunity in the commandment	2
	7:12	and the commandment is holy and just and good.	2
	7:13	through the commandment might become sinful	2
	13: 9	The commandments, "You shall not commit adultery;	1
	13: 9	You shall not covet"; and any other commandment	2
1Co	7:19	obeying the commandments of God is everything	2
Gal	5:14	the whole law is summed up in a single commandment	3
Eph	2:15	the law with its commandments and ordinances	2
	6: 2	this is the first commandment with a promise:	2
1Ti	6:14	keep the commandment without spot or blame	2
Tit	1:14	commandments of those who reject the truth.	2
Heb	7: 5	have a commandment in the law to collect tithes	2
	7:18	There is…the abrogation of an earlier commandment	2
	9:19	For when every commandment had been told	2
2Pe	2:21	the holy commandment that was passed on to them.	2
	3: 2	commandment of the Lord…through your apostles.	2
1Jn	2: 3	we know him, if we obey his commandments.	2
	2: 4	but does not obey his commandments, is a liar	2
	2: 7	Beloved, I am writing you no new commandment	2
	2: 7	I am writing you…an old commandment	2
	2: 7	old commandment is the word that you have heard.	2
	2: 8	Yet I am writing you a new commandment	2
	3:22	we receive…because we obey his commandments	2
	3:23	this is his commandment, that we should believe	2
	3:24	All who obey his commandments abide in him	2
	4:21	The commandment we have from him is this:	2
	5: 2	when we love God and obey his commandments	2
	5: 3	the love of God is this, that we obey his commandments.	2
	5: 3	And his commandments are not burdensome	2
2Jn	1: 5	as though I were writing you a new commandment	2

2Jn　1: 6　this is love, that we walk according to his commandments; 2
　　　1: 6　this is the commandment just as you have heard· 2
Rev　12:17　those who keep the commandments of God 2
　　　14:12　saints, those who keep the commandments of God 2

commend

1. ἐπαινέω, *epaineō, 2046*
2. μαρτυρέω, *martyreō, 3455*
3. παραδίδωμι, *paradidōmi, 4140*
4. παρατίθημι, *paratithēmi, 4192*
5. συνίστημι, *synistēmi, 5319*

Lke　16: 8　his master commended the dishonest manager 1
　　　23:46　"Father, into your hands I commend my spirit." 4
Act　14:26　where they had been commended to the grace of God 3
　　　15:40　commending him to the grace of the Lord. 3
　　　20:32　now I commend you to God 4
Rom 16: 1　I commend to you our sister Phoebe 5
1Co　11: 2　I commend you because you remember me 1
　　　11:17　in the following instructions I do not commend 1
　　　11:22　Should I commend you? In this matter I do not 1
　　　11:22　In this matter I do not commend you! 1
2Co　3: 1　Are we beginning to commend ourselves again? 5
　　　4: 2　commend ourselves to the conscience of everyone 5
　　　5:12　We are not commending ourselves to you again 5
　　　6: 4　we have commended ourselves in every way: 5
　　　10:12　with some of those who commend themselves. 5
　　　10:18　not those who commend themselves that are approved 5
　　　10:18　those whom the Lord commends. 5
　　　12:11　you should have been the ones commending me 5
Heb 11:39　though they were commended for their faith 2

commendable

1. εὔφημος, *euphēmos, 2368*
Php　4: 8　whatever is commendable, if there is any excellence 1

commendation

1. ἔπαινος, *epainos, 2047*
1Co　4: 5　Then each one will receive commendation 1

comment

1. λέγω, *legō, 3306*
Act　24:22　Felix...adjourned the hearing with the comment 1

commission

1. Contextual: Not in Greek
2. ἐπιτροπή, *epitropē, 2207*
3. οἰκονομία, *oikonomia, 3873*
Act　26:12　authority and commission of the chief priests 2
1Co　9:17　I am entrusted with a commission. 3
Gal　1: 1　by human commission nor from human authorities, 1
Eph　3: 2　the commission of God's grace that was given me 3
Col　1:25　God's commission that was given to me 3

commit　*See also* sin committed unintentionally

1. εἰμί, *eimi, 1639*
2. ἐργάζομαι, *ergazomai, 2237*
3. κατεργάζομαι, *katergazomai, 2981*
4. παραδίδωμι, *paradidōmi, 4140*
5. ποιέω, *poieō, 4472*
6. πράσσω, *prassō, 4556*

Mrk 15: 7　who had committed murder during the insurrection. 5
Jhn　8:34　everyone who commits sin is a slave to sin. 5
Act　8: 3　committed them to prison. 4
　　　25:11　committed something for which I deserve to die 6
Rom　1:27　Men committed shameless acts with men 3
1Co　6:18　Every sin that a person commits 5
2Co　11: 7　Did I commit a sin by humbling myself 5
Jas　2: 9　But if you show partiality, you commit sin 2
　　　4:17　Anyone...fails to do it, commits sin. 1
　　　5:15　and anyone who has committed sins will be forgiven. 5
1Pe　2:22　"He committed no sin 5
2Pe　2: 4　God...committed them to chains of deepest darkness 4
1Jn　3: 4　Everyone who commits sin is guilty 5
　　　3: 8　Everyone who commits sin is a child of the devil; 5

commit adultery

1. μοιχάω, *moichaō, 3656*
2. μοιχεύω, *moicheuō, 3658*
Mat　5:27　'You shall not commit adultery.' 2

5:28　who looks...with lust has already committed adultery 2
5:32　who divorces...causes her to commit adultery. 2
5:32　whoever marries a divorced woman commits adultery. 1
19: 9　and marries another commits adultery." 1
19:18　You shall not commit adultery; 2
Mrk 10:11　and marries another commits adultery against her; 1
10:12　she commits adultery." 1
10:19　shall not murder; You shall not commit adultery; 2
Lke 16:18　"Anyone who...marries another commits adultery 2
16:18　marries a woman divorced...commits adultery 2
18:20　'You shall not commit adultery; 2
Jhn　8: 4　⟦caught in the very act of committing adultery.⟧ 2
Rom　2:22　You that forbid...do you commit adultery? 2
　　　13: 9　The commandments, "You shall not commit adultery; 2
Jas　2:11　For the one who said, "You shall not commit adultery," 2
　　　2:11　if you do not commit adultery but if you murder 2
Rev　2:22　those who commit adultery with her I am throwing 2

commit an offense

1. ἁμαρτάνω, *hamartanō, 279*
Act　25: 8　in no way committed an offense against the law 1

commit fornication

1. πορνεύω, *porneuō, 4519*
Rev　17: 2　kings of the earth have committed fornication 1
　　　18: 3　kings of the earth have committed fornication 1
　　　18: 9　committed fornication and lived in luxury 1

commit in an ungodly way

1. ἀσεβέω, *asebeō, 814*
Jde　1:15　deeds...committed in such an ungodly way 1

commit murder

1. φονεύω, *phoneuō, 5839*
Jas　4: 2　You want...and do not have it; so you commit murder. 1

commit previously

1. προγίνομαι, *proginomai, 4588*
Rom　3:25　he had passed over the sins previously committed; 1

commit sin

1. ἁμαρτάνω, *hamartanō, 279*
1Jn　5:16　your brother or sister committing what is not a mortal sin 1

common　*See also* common *good*, common *purpose*, common *purse*, share in common

1. κοινός, *koinos, 3123*
Act　2:44　and had all things in common; 1
　　　4:32　everything they owned was held in common. 1

common to everyone

1. ἀνθρώπινος, *anthrōpinos, 474*
1Co　10:13　No testing...that is not common to everyone. 1

commonwealth

1. πολιτεία, *politeia, 4486*
Eph　2:12　aliens from the commonwealth of Israel 1

commotion　*See also* make a commotion

1. θόρυβος, *thorybos, 2573*
2. συστροφή, *systrophē, 5371*
3. τάραχος, *tarachos, 5431*
Mrk　5:38　he saw a commotion 1
Act　12:18　there was no small commotion among the soldiers 3
　　　19:40　to justify this commotion." 2

communion

1. κοινωνία, *koinōnia, 3126*
2Co　13:13　communion of the Holy Spirit be with all of you. 1

community

1. ἀδελφός, *adelphos, 81*
2. πλῆθος, *plēthos, 4436*
Jhn　21:23　So the rumor spread in the community 1
Act　6: 5　What they said pleased the whole community 2
　　　25:24　about whom the whole Jewish community petitioned 2

whole community

1. ἀδελφός, *adelphos, 81*
2. πλῆθος, *plēthos, 4436*

Act 6: 2 called together the whole community of the disciples   2
Eph 6:23 Peace be to the whole community, and love with faith   1

companion

1. μετά, *meta, 3552*
2. μέτοχος, *metochos, 3581*
3. περί, *peri, 4309*
4. σύζυγος, *syzygos, 5187*
5. σύν, *syn, 5250*

Mat 12: 3 David did when he and his companions were hungry?   1
   12: 4 not lawful for him or his companions to eat   1
Mrk 1:36 Simon and his companions hunted for him.   1
   2:25 he and his companions were hungry and in need   1
   2:26 he gave some to his companions."   5
Lke 6: 3 David did when he and his companions were hungry?   1
   6: 4 gave some to his companions?"   1
   9:32 Now Peter and his companions were weighed down   5
  24:33 they found the eleven and their companions   5
Act 4:13 recognized them as companions of Jesus.   5
  13:13 Paul and his companions set sail from Paphos   3
  20:34 to support myself and my companions   1
  26:13 a light…shining around me and my companions   5
Php 4: 3 you also, my loyal companion, help these women   4
Heb 1: 9 the oil of gladness beyond your companions."   2

travel companion

1. συνέκδημος, *synekdēmos, 5292*

Act 19:29 who were Paul's travel companions.   1

company *See also* enjoy company, refresh in company

1. ἀλλήλων, *allēlōn, 253*
2. μέσος, *mesos, 3545*
3. ὁμιλία, *homilia, 3918*

Mat 14: 6 daughter of Herodias danced before the company   2
Act 15:39 became so sharp that they parted company;   1
1Co 15:33 "Bad company ruins good morals."   3

compare

1. ὁμοιόω, *homoioō, 3929*
2. συγκρίνω, *synkrinō, 5173*

Mat 11:16 to what will I compare this generation?   1
  13:24 "The kingdom of heaven may be compared to someone   1
  18:23 the kingdom of heaven may be compared to   1
  22: 2 "The kingdom of heaven may be compared to a king   1
Mrk 4:30 "With what can we compare the kingdom of God   1
Lke 7:31 "To what then will I compare the people   1
  13:18 to what should I compare it?   1
  13:20 "To what should I compare the kingdom of God?   1
2Co 10:12 dare to classify or compare ourselves with some   2
  10:12 and compare themselves with one another   2

compare with

1. πρός, *pros, 4639*

Rom 8:18 the sufferings…are not worth comparing with   1

compassion *See also* fill with compassion, have compassion, move with compassion

1. σπλάγχνον, *splanchnon, 5073*
2. σπλάγχνον + οἰκτιρμός, *splanchnon + oiktirmos, 5073 + 3880*

Php 1: 8 I long…with the compassion of Christ Jesus.   1
  2: 1 any compassion and sympathy   1
Col 3:12 compassion, kindness, humility, meekness   2

compassionate

1. ἐλεέω, *eleeō, 1796*
2. πολύσπλαγχνος, *polysplanchnos, 4499*

Rom 12: 8 the compassionate, in cheerfulness.   1
Jas 5:11 how the Lord is compassionate and merciful.   2

compatriot

1. συμφυλέτης, *symphyletēs, 5241*

1Th 2:14 you suffered…from your own compatriots   1

compel

1. ἀγγαρεύω, *angareuō, 30*
2. ἀναγκάζω, *anankazō, 337*

Mat 27:32 they compelled this man to carry his cross.   1
Mrk 15:21 They compelled a passer-by, who was coming in   1
Lke 14:23 compel people to come in   2
Act 28:19 I was compelled to appeal to the emperor   2
Gal 2: 3 not compelled to be circumcised   2
  2:14 how can you compel the Gentiles to live like Jews?"   2
  6:12 try to compel you to be circumcised   2

compete

1. ἀθλέω, *athleō, 123*
2. προκαλέω, *prokaleō, 4614*
3. τρέχω, *trechō, 5556*

1Co 9:24 in a race the runners all compete   3
Gal 5:26 not become conceited, competing against one another   2
2Ti 2: 5 without competing according to the rules.   1

competence

1. ἱκανότης, *hikanotēs, 2654*

2Co 3: 5 our competence is from God   1

competent *See also* make competent

1. ἱκανός, *hikanos, 2653*

2Co 3: 5 Not that we are competent of ourselves to claim   1

complain

1. γογγύζω, *gongyzō, 1197*
2. γογγυσμός, *gongysmos, 1198*

Lke 5:30 The Pharisees and their scribes were complaining   1
Jhn 6:41 Then the Jews began to complain about him   1
  6:43 "Do not complain among yourselves.   1
  6:61 aware that his disciples were complaining   1
  7:12 there was considerable complaining about him   2
Act 6: 1 the Hellenists complained against the Hebrews   2
1Co 10:10 And do not complain as some of them did   1
1Pe 4: 9 Be hospitable to one another without complaining.   2

complaint *See also* accept a complaint

1. λόγος, *logos, 3364*
2. μομφή, *momphē, 3664*

Act 19:38 the artisans…have a complaint against anyone   1
Col 3:13 if anyone has a complaint against another   2

complete *See also* make complete

1. ἀνταναπληρόω, *antanaplēroō, 499*
2. ἀπαρτισμός, *apartismos, 568*
3. ἐπιτελέω, *epiteleō, 2200*
4. ὁλόκληρος, *holoklēros, 3908*
5. πᾶς, *pas, 4246*
6. πληρόω, *plēroō, 4444*
7. συντελέω, *synteleō, 5334*
8. τέλειος, *teleios, 5455*
9. τελειόω, *teleioō, 5457*
10. τελέω, *teleō, 5464*

Lke 12:50 what stress I am under until it is completed!   10
  14:28 to see whether he has enough to complete it?   2
Jhn 4:34 and to complete his work.   9
  5:36 works that the Father has given me to complete   9
  15:11 that your joy may be complete.   6
  16:24 will receive, so that your joy may be complete.   6
Act 12:25 after completing their mission Barnabas and Saul   6
  14:26 for the work that they had completed.   6
  21:27 When the seven days were almost completed   7
Rom 15:28 So, when I have completed this   3
1Co 13:10 when the complete comes, the partial will…end   8
2Co 7:16 because I have complete confidence in you.   5
  8: 6 also complete this generous undertaking among you.   3
  8:11 your eagerness may be matched by completing it   3
  10: 6 when your obedience is complete.   6
Col 1:24 in my flesh I am completing what is lacking   1
  4:17 say to Archippus, "See that you complete the task   6
Tit 2:10 not to pilfer, but to show complete and perfect fidelity   5
Jas 1: 4 so that you may be mature and complete   4
1Jn 1: 4 writing these things so that our joy may be complete.   6
2Jn 1:12 so that our joy may be complete.   6
Rev 6:11 rest…until the number would be complete   6

complete the rite of purification

1. ἁγνίζω, *hagnizō, 49*

Act 24:18 in the temple, completing the rite of purification 1

completely

1. τελειόω, *teleioō, 5457*

Jhn 17:23 that they may become completely one 1

completion *See also* bring to completion

1. ἐκπλήρωσις, *ekplērōsis, 1741*

Act 21:26 the completion of the days of purification 1

comprehend

1. γινώσκω, *ginōskō, 1182*
2. ἐπιγινώσκω, *epiginōskō, 2105*
3. καταλαμβάνω, *katalambanō, 2898*

1Co 2:11 So also no one comprehends what is truly God's 1
Eph 3:18 the power to comprehend, with all the saints 3
Col 1: 6 heard it and truly comprehended the grace of God. 2

compulsion

1. ἀναγκαστῶς, *anankastōs, 339*
2. ἀνάγκη, *anankē, 340*

2Co 9: 7 not reluctantly or under compulsion 2
1Pe 5: 2 tend...not under compulsion but willingly 1

comrade

1. ἀδελφός, *adelphos, 81*

Rev 12:10 the accuser of our comrades has been thrown down 1
19:10 I am a fellow servant with you and your comrades 1
22: 9 I am a fellow servant with you and your comrades 1

conceal

1. παρακαλύπτω, *parakalyptō, 4152*

Lke 9:45 its meaning was concealed from them 1

conceit *See also* puff up with conceit, swell with conceit

1. κενοδοξία, *kenodoxia, 3029*
2. φυσίωσις, *physiōsis, 5883*

2Co 12:20 anger, selfishness, slander, gossip, conceit 2
Php 2: 3 Do nothing from selfish ambition or conceit 1

conceited

1. κενόδοξος, *kenodoxos, 3030*
2. τυφόομαι, *typhoomai, 5605*

Gal 5:26 Let us not become conceited 1
1Ti 6: 4 is conceited, understanding nothing 2

conceive

1. ἀναβαίνω, *anabainō, 326*
2. γεννάω, *gennaō, 1164*
3. ἐν + γαστήρ + ἔχω, *en + gastēr + echō, 1877 + 1143 + 2400*
4. συλλαμβάνω, *syllambanō, 5197*

Mat 1:20 for the child conceived in her is from the Holy 2
1:23 "Look, the virgin shall conceive and bear a son 3
Lke 1:24 After those days his wife Elizabeth conceived 4
1:31 you will conceive in your womb and bear a son 4
1:36 Elizabeth in her old age has also conceived a son; 4
2:21 before he was conceived in the womb. 4
1Co 2: 9 nor the human heart conceived 1
Jas 1:15 when that desire has conceived, it gives birth to sin 4

conceive children

1. κοίτη + ἔχω, *koitē + echō, 3130 + 2400*

Rom 9:10 Rebecca when she had conceived children by one husband 1

concern *See also* have no concern

1. Contextual: Not in Greek
2. μέλει, *melei, 3508*
3. μεριμνάω, *merimnaō, 3534*
4. φρονέω, *phroneō, 5858*

Jhn 2: 4 "Woman, what concern is that to you and to me? 1
1Co 7:21 a slave when called? Do not be concerned about it. 2
9: 9 Is it for oxen that God is concerned? 2
Php 2:20 who will be genuinely concerned for your welfare. 3
4:10 now at last you have revived your concern 4
4:10 indeed, you were concerned for me 4

concerning

1. Contextual: Not in Greek
2. εἰς, *eis, 1650*
3. ἐπί, *epi, 2093*
4. περί, *peri, 4309*
5. ὑπέρ, *hyper, 5642*

Mat 4: 6 'He will command his angels concerning you,' 4
Lke 1: 4 the truth concerning the things 4
3:15 questioning in their hearts concerning John 4
4:10 'He will command his angels concerning you, 4
Act 1:16 concerning Judas, who became a guide 4
2:25 David says concerning him, 'I saw the Lord 2
18:25 and taught accurately the things concerning Jesus 4
19:23 no little disturbance broke out concerning the Way. 4
23: 6 concerning...the resurrection of the dead." 4
23:29 he was accused concerning questions of their law 4
24: 8 be able to learn from him concerning everything 4
24:24 heard him speak concerning faith in Christ Jesus. 4
Rom 1: 3 the gospel concerning his Son 4
4:20 made him waver concerning the promise of God 2
7: 2 discharged from the law concerning the husband 1
9:27 And Isaiah cries out concerning Israel 5
10: 5 Moses writes concerning the righteousness 1
1Co 7: 1 concerning the matters about which you wrote: 4
7:25 Now concerning virgins, I have no command 4
8: 1 Now concerning food sacrificed to idols: 4
12: 1 Now concerning spiritual gifts, brothers and sisters 4
16: 1 Now concerning the collection for the saints: 4
16:12 Now concerning our brother Apollos 4
Col 4:10 concerning whom you have...instructions 4
1Th 4: 9 Now concerning love of the brothers and sisters 4
5: 1 Now concerning the times and the seasons, 4
2Th 3: 4 we have confidence in the Lord concerning you 3
Heb 7:16 a legal requirement concerning physical descent 1
1Pe 1:10 Concerning this salvation, the prophets 4
1Jn 1: 1 concerning the word of life 4
2:26 I write...concerning those who would deceive you. 4
5:10 the testimony that God has given concerning his Son. 4

concession

1. συγγνώμη, *syngnōmē, 5152*

1Co 7: 6 This I say by way of concession, not of command. 1

condemn

1. Contextual: Not in Greek
2. καταγινώσκω, *kataginōskō, 2861*
3. καταδικάζω, *katadikazō, 2868*
4. κατακρίνω, *katakrinō, 2891*
5. κατάκρισις, *katakrisis, 2892*
6. κρίμα, *krima, 3210*
7. κρίνω, *krinō, 3212*

Mat 12: 7 you would not have condemned the guiltless. 3
12:37 and by your words you will be condemned." 3
12:41 judgment with this generation and condemn it 4
12:42 judgment with this generation and condemn it 4
20:18 and they will condemn him to death; 4
27: 3 Judas, his betrayer, saw that Jesus was condemned 4
Mrk 10:33 they will condemn him to death; 4
14:64 All of them condemned him as deserving death. 4
16:16 ⟦one who does not believe will be condemned.⟧ 4
Lke 6:37 not condemn, and you will not be condemned. 3
6:37 not condemn, and you will not be condemned. 3
11:31 rise...and condemn them 4
11:32 rise up...and condemn it 4
23:41 we indeed have been condemned justly 1
24:20 condemned to death and crucified him. 6
Jhn 3:17 God did not send the Son...to condemn the world 7
3:18 Those who believe in him are not condemned; 7
3:18 those who do not believe are condemned already 7
8:10 ⟦"Woman, where are they? Has no one condemned you?"⟧ 4
8:11 ⟦Jesus said, "Neither do I condemn you.⟧ 4
8:26 I have much to say about you and much to condemn; 7
16:11 the ruler of this world has been condemned. 7
Act 13:27 fulfilled those words by condemning him. 7
Rom 2: 1 in passing judgment...you condemn yourself 4
2:27 will condemn you that have the written code 7
3: 7 why am I still being condemned as a sinner? 7
8: 3 to deal with sin, he condemned sin in the flesh 4
8:34 Who is to condemn? It is Christ Jesus, who died 4

	14:22 Blessed...who have no reason to condemn themselves	7
	14:23 those who have doubts are condemned if they eat	4
1Co	11:32 disciplined so that we may not be condemned	4
2Co	7: 3 I do not say this to condemn you	5
Col	2:16 Therefore do not let anyone condemn you	7
2Th	2:12 all who have not believed...will be condemned.	7
Heb	11: 7 by this he condemned the world	4
Jas	5: 6 You have condemned...the righteous one	3
2Pe	2: 6 he condemned them to extinction	4
1Jn	3:20 whenever our hearts condemn us;	2
	3:21 Beloved, if our hearts do not condemn us	2

condemn to death

1. ἀναιρέω, *anaireō*, 359

Act	26:10 when they were being condemned to death.	1

condemnation *See also* sentence of condemnation

1. κατάκριμα, *katakrima*, 2890
2. κατάκρισις, *katakrisis*, 2892
3. κρίμα, *krima*, 3210
4. κρίσις, *krisis*, 3213

Mrk	12:40 They will receive the greater condemnation."	3
Lke	20:47 They will receive the greater condemnation."	3
Jhn	5:29 done evil, to the resurrection of condemnation.	4
Rom	3: 8 Their condemnation is deserved!	3
	5:16 following one trespass brought condemnation	1
	5:18 one man's trespass led to condemnation for all	1
	8: 1 no condemnation for those who are in Christ	1
1Co	11:34 come together, it will not be for your condemnation.	3
2Co	3: 9 glory in the ministry of condemnation	2
1Ti	3: 6 fall into the condemnation of the devil.	3
	5:12 so they incur condemnation	3
Jas	5:12 so that you may not fall under condemnation.	4
2Pe	2: 3 Their condemnation, pronounced against them long ago	3
Jde	1: 4 who long ago were designated for this condemnation	3
	1: 9 to bring a condemnation of slander against him	4

condition

1. Contextual: Not in Greek
2. κλῆσις, *klēsis*, 3104
3. σάρξ, *sarx*, 4922

1Co	7:20 Let each of you remain in the condition	2
	7:21 make use of your present condition	1
	7:24 In whatever condition you were called	1
Gal	4:14 though my condition put you to the test	3

conduct

1. ἀγωγή, *agōgē*, 73
2. ἀναστροφή, *anastrophē*, 419
3. γίνομαι, *ginomai*, 1181
4. ἔργον, *ergon*, 2240
5. καθίστημι, *kathistēmi*, 2770
6. περιπατέω, *peripateō*, 4344

Act	17:15 who conducted Paul brought him as far as Athens;	5
Rom	13: 3 For rulers are not a terror to good conduct	4
2Co	12:18 Did we not conduct ourselves with the same spirit?	6
Col	4: 5 Conduct yourselves wisely toward outsiders	6
1Th	2:10 blameless our conduct was toward you believers.	3
1Ti	4:12 an example in speech and conduct, in love, in faith	2
2Ti	3:10 Now you have observed my teaching, my conduct	1
1Pe	1:15 be holy yourselves in all your conduct;	2
	2:12 Conduct yourselves honorably among the Gentiles	2
	3: 1 won over without a word by their wives' conduct	2
	3:16 those who abuse you for your good conduct in Christ	2

confer

1. διατίθημι, *diatithēmi*, 1416
2. προσανατίθημι, *prosanatithēmi*, 4651
3. συλλαλέω, *syllaleō*, 5196

Lke	22: 4 conferred with the chief priests and officers	3
	22:29 I confer on you, just as my Father has conferred	1
	22:29 on you, just as my Father has conferred on me	1
Act	25:12 after he had conferred with his council	3
Gal	1:16 I did not confer with any human being	2

confer together

1. συμβούλιον + λαμβάνω, *symboulion + lambanō*, 5206 + 3284

Mat	27: 1 elders of the people conferred together against Jesus	1
	27: 7 After conferring together, they used them	1

confess

1. ἐξομολογέω, *exomologeō*, 2018
2. ὁμολογέω, *homologeō*, 3933

Mat	3: 6 in the river Jordan, confessing their sins.	1
Mrk	1: 5 confessing their sins.	1
Jhn	1:20 He confessed and did not deny it, but confessed	2
	1:20 He confessed and did not deny it, but confessed	2
	9:22 anyone who confessed Jesus to be the Messiah	2
	12:42 because of the Pharisees they did not confess it	2
Act	19:18 confessed and disclosed their practices.	1
Rom	10: 9 if you confess with your lips that Jesus is Lord	2
	10:10 one confesses with the mouth and so is saved.	2
	15: 9 "Therefore I will confess you among the Gentiles	1
Php	2:11 every tongue should confess that Jesus Christ is Lord	1
Heb	11:13 They confessed that they were strangers	2
	13:15 the fruit of lips that confess his name.	2
Jas	5:16 Therefore confess your sins to one another	1
1Jn	1: 9 If we confess our sins, he who is faithful and just	2
	2:23 everyone who confesses the Son has the Father also.	2
	4: 2 every spirit that confesses that Jesus Christ	2
	4: 3 every spirit that does not confess Jesus	2
	4:15 who confess that Jesus is the Son of God	2
2Jn	1: 7 those who do not confess that Jesus Christ has come	2
Rev	3: 5 I will confess your name before my Father	2

confession *See also* make a confession

1. ὁμολογία, *homologia*, 3934

2Co	9:13 obedience to the confession of the gospel	1
1Ti	6:12 you made the good confession in the presence	1
	6:13 who...before Pontius Pilate made the good confession	1
Heb	3: 1 the apostle and high priest of our confession	1
	4:14 let us hold fast to our confession.	1
	10:23 Let us hold fast to the confession of our hope	1

confidence *See also* have confidence, reason for confidence

1. θαρρέω, *tharreō*, 2509
2. παρρησία, *parrēsia*, 4244
3. πείθω, *peithō*, 4275
4. πεποίθησις, *pepoithēsis*, 4301
5. ὑπόστασις, *hypostasis*, 5712

2Co	3: 4 Such is the confidence that we have	4
	8:22 because of his great confidence in you.	4
	11:17 saying in regard to this boastful confidence	5
Eph	3:12 access to God in boldness and confidence through faith	4
2Th	3: 4 we have confidence in the Lord concerning you	3
Heb	3: 6 we are his house if we hold firm the confidence	2
	3:14 if only we hold our first confidence firm	5
	10:19 Therefore, my friends, since we have confidence	2
	10:35 Do not, therefore, abandon that confidence of yours;	2
	13: 6 So we can say with confidence	1
1Jn	2:28 so that when he is revealed we may have confidence	2

confident *See also* feel confident, make confident

1. θαρρέω, *tharreō*, 2509
2. πείθω, *peithō*, 4275

2Co	2: 3 I am confident about all of you	2
	5: 6 So we are always confident;	1
	10: 7 If you are confident that you belong to Christ	2
Gal	5:10 I am confident about you in the Lord	2
Php	1: 6 I am confident of this, that the one who began	2
Phm	1:21 Confident of your obedience, I am writing to you	2
Heb	6: 9 beloved, we are confident of better things in your case	2

confidently

1. παρρησία, *parrēsia*, 4244

Act	2:29 I may say to you confidently of our ancestor	1

confirm *See also* serve to confirm

1. Contextual: Not in Greek
2. βέβαιος + ποιέω, *bebaios + poieō*, 1010 + 4472
3. βεβαιόω, *bebaioō*, 1011
4. ἵστημι, *histēmi*, 2705
5. συμμαρτυρέω, *symmartyreō*, 5210

Mat	18:16 so that every word may be confirmed	4
Mrk	16:20 〚confirmed the message by the signs〛	3
Rom	9: 1 my conscience confirms it by the Holy Spirit	5

Rom 15: 8	might confirm the promises given to the patriarchs	3
Heb 7:20	This was confirmed with an oath;	1
2Pe 1:10	more eager to confirm your call and election	2

confirm fully

1. βέβαιος, *bebaios, 1010*

2Pe 1:19	we have the prophetic message more fully confirmed.	1

confirmation

1. βεβαίωσις, *bebaiōsis, 1012*

Php 1: 7	in the defense and confirmation of the gospel.	1
Heb 6:16	an oath given as confirmation puts an end to all dispute.	1

conflict

1. μεταξύ, *metaxy, 3568*
2. πολεμέω, *polemeō, 4482*
3. πόλεμος, *polemos, 4483*

Rom 2:15	their conflicting thoughts will accuse…them	1
Jas 4: 1	Those conflicts and disputes among you,	3
4: 2	you covet…so you engage in disputes and conflicts.	2

conform

1. κατά, *kata, 2848*
2. σύμμορφος, *symmorphos, 5215*
3. συσχηματίζω, *syschēmatizō, 5372*

Rom 8:29	to be conformed to the image of his Son	2
12: 2	Do not be conformed to this world	3
Php 3:21	may be conformed to the body of his glory	2
1Ti 1:11	that conforms to the glorious gospel	1
1Pe 1:14	do not be conformed to the desires	3

confound

1. συγχέω, *syncheō, 5177*

Act 9:22	confounded the Jews who lived in Damascus	1

confront suddenly

1. ἐφίστημι, *ephistēmi, 2392*

Act 6:12	they suddenly confronted him, seized him	1

confuse

1. ἀπορία, *aporia, 680*
2. ταράσσω, *tarassō, 5429*

Lke 21:25	confused by the roaring of the sea	1
Gal 1: 7	there are some who are confusing you	2
5:10	whoever…is confusing you will pay the penalty.	2

confusion

1. συγχέω, *syncheō, 5177*
2. σύγχυσις, *synchysis, 5180*

Act 19:29	The city was filled with the confusion;	2
19:32	for the assembly was in confusion	1

congregation

1. ἐκκλησία, *ekklēsia, 1711*
2. πλῆθος, *plēthos, 4436*

Act 7:38	who was in the congregation in the wilderness	1
15:30	When they gathered the congregation together	2
19: 9	spoke evil of the Way before the congregation	2
Heb 2:12	in the midst of the congregation I will praise	1

conjugal

1. Contextual: Not in Greek

1Co 7: 3	husband should give to his wife her conjugal rights	1

connection

1. εἰς, *eis, 1650*

Heb 7:14	in connection with that tribe Moses said	1

conquer

1. Contextual: Not in Greek
2. καταγωνίζομαι, *katagōnizomai, 2865*
3. νικάω, *nikaō, 3771*

Jhn 16:33	take courage; I have conquered the world!"	3
Heb 11:33	who through faith conquered kingdoms	2
1Jn 2:13	because you have conquered the evil one.	3
4: 4	you are from God, and have conquered them;	3
5: 4	for whatever is born of God conquers the world.	3
5: 4	this is the victory that conquers the world	3

5: 5	Who is it that conquers the world	3
Rev 2: 7	To everyone who conquers, I will give permission	3
2:11	Whoever conquers will not be harmed	3
2:17	To everyone who conquers I will give some…manna	3
2:26	everyone who conquers and continues to do my works	3
2:28	who conquers I will also give the morning star.	1
3: 5	you conquer, you will be clothed like them in white	3
3:12	If you conquer, I will make you a pillar	3
3:21	the one who conquers I will give a place with me	3
3:21	just as I myself conquered and sat down with my Father	3
5: 5	the Lion…the Root of David, has conquered	3
6: 2	and he came out conquering and to conquer.	3
6: 2	and he came out conquering and to conquer.	3
11: 7	the beast…will make war on them and conquer	3
12:11	they have conquered him by the blood of the Lamb	3
13: 7	to make war on the saints and to conquer them.	3
15: 2	those who had conquered the beast and its image	3
17:14	and the Lamb will conquer them	3
21: 7	Those who conquer will inherit these things	3

more than conqueror

1. ὑπερνικάω, *hypernikaō, 5664*

Rom 8:37	in all these things we are more than conquerors	1

conscience

1. ὅς, *hos, 4005*
2. συνείδησις, *syneidēsis, 5287*

Act 23: 1	lived my life with a clear conscience before God."	2
24:16	I do my best always to have a clear conscience	2
Rom 2:15	to which their own conscience also bears witness;	2
9: 1	my conscience confirms it by the Holy Spirit	2
13: 5	but also because of conscience.	2
1Co 8: 7	their conscience, being weak, is defiled.	2
8:10	might they not, since their conscience is weak	2
8:12	wound their conscience when it is weak	2
10:25	without…question on the ground of conscience	2
10:27	without…question on the ground of conscience.	2
10:28	for the sake of conscience—	2
10:29	I mean the other's conscience, not your own.	2
10:29	subject to the judgment of someone else's conscience?	2
2Co 1:12	the testimony of our conscience:	2
4: 2	commend ourselves to the conscience of everyone	2
5:11	that we are also well known to your consciences.	2
1Ti 1: 5	that comes from a pure heart, a good conscience	2
1:19	having faith and a good conscience.	2
1:19	By rejecting conscience, certain persons have	1
3: 9	must hold fast…the faith with a clear conscience.	2
4: 2	liars whose consciences are seared with a hot iron.	2
2Ti 1: 3	God—whom I worship with a clear conscience	2
Tit 1:15	Their very minds and consciences are corrupted.	2
Heb 9: 9	cannot perfect the conscience of the worshiper	2
9:14	purify our conscience from dead works	2
10:22	our hearts sprinkled clean from an evil conscience	2
13:18	we are sure that we have a clear conscience	2
1Pe 3:16	Keep your conscience clear	2
3:21	but as an appeal to God for a good conscience	2

consciousness

1. συνείδησις, *syneidēsis, 5287*

Heb 10: 2	would no longer have any consciousness of sin?	1

consent

1. ἀφίημι, *aphiēmi, 918*
2. γνώμη, *gnōmē, 1191*
3. ἐξομολογέω, *exomologeō, 2018*
4. ἐπαγγελία, *epangelia, 2039*
5. συνευδοκέω, *syneudokeō, 5306*

Mat 3:15	fulfill all righteousness." Then he consented.	1
Lke 22: 6	So he consented	3
Act 23:21	They are ready now and are waiting for your consent	4
1Co 7:12	she consents to live with him	5
7:13	he consents to live with her	5
Phm 1:14	I preferred to do nothing without your consent	2

with consent

1. σύν, *syn, 5250*

Act 5: 1	Ananias, with the consent of his wife Sapphira	1
15:22	with the consent of the whole church, decided	1

consequently
1. διό, *dio, 1475*
2. ὅθεν, *hothen, 3854*

Heb	7:25 Consequently he is able for all time to save	2
	10: 5 Consequently, when Christ came…he said	1

consider
1. Contextual: Not in Greek
2. ἀναθεωρέω, *anatheōreō, 355*
3. ἀναλογίζομαι, *analogizomai, 382*
4. βλέπω, *blepō, 1063*
5. βουλεύω, *bouleuō, 1086*
6. ἔχω, *echō, 2400*
7. ἡγέομαι, *hēgeomai, 2451*
8. καταμανθάνω, *katamanthanō, 2908*
9. κατανοέω, *katanoeō, 2917*
10. λογίζομαι, *logizomai, 3357*
11. ὁράω, *horaō, 3972*
12. σκοπέω, *skopeō, 5023*

Mat	6:28 about clothing? Consider the lilies of the field	8
Lke	11:35 consider whether the light in you is not darkness.	12
	12:24 Consider the ravens: they neither sow nor reap	9
	12:27 Consider the lilies, how they grow:	9
	14:31 what king…will not sit down first and consider	5
Act	15: 6 met together to consider this matter.	11
	26: 2 "I consider myself fortunate that it is before you	7
Rom	4:19 weaken in faith when he considered his own body	9
	4:19 he considered the barrenness of Sarah's womb.	1
	6:11 you also must consider yourselves dead to sin	10
	8:18 I consider that the sufferings of this present	10
1Co	1:26 Consider your own call, brothers and sisters:	4
	10:18 Consider the people of Israel;	4
2Co	12: 7 even considering the exceptional character	1
Php	3:13 I do not consider that I have made it my own;	10
Phm	1:17 if you consider me your partner	6
Heb	3: 1 Therefore, brothers and sisters…consider that Jesus	9
	10:24 let us consider how to provoke one another to love	9
	11:11 he considered him faithful who had promised	7
	11:19 He considered the fact that God is able even to raise	10
	11:26 He considered abuse suffered for the Christ	7
	12: 3 Consider him who endured…such hostility	3
	13: 7 consider the outcome of their way of life	2
Jas	1: 2 whenever you face trials…consider it nothing but joy	7
1Pe	4:16 as a Christian, do not consider it a disgrace	1
	5:12 Silvanus, whom I consider a faithful brother,	10

consider carefully
1. προσέχω, *prosechō, 4668*

Act	5:35 consider carefully what you propose to do to these men.	1

consider worthy
1. ἀξιόω, *axioō, 546*
2. καταξιόω, *kataxioō, 2921*

Lke	20:35 who are considered worthy of a place in that age	2
Act	5:41 rejoiced that they were considered worthy	2
1Ti	5:17 elders…be considered worthy of double honor	1

considerable   *See also* considerable *number*
1. ἱκανός, *hikanos, 2653*
2. πολύς, *polys, 4498*

Jhn	7:12 there was considerable complaining about him	2
Act	18:18 After staying there for a considerable time,	1

consideration
1. γνῶσις, *gnōsis, 1194*

1Pe	3: 7 Husbands…show consideration for your wives	1

out of consideration
1. διά, *dia, 1328*

1Co	10:28 do not eat it, out of consideration for the one	1

consist
1. εἰμί, *eimi, 1639*

Lke	12:15 one's life does not consist in the abundance	1
1Co	12:14 body does not consist of one member but of many.	1

consistent
1. ἄξιος, *axios, 545*

2. πρέπω, *prepō, 4560*

Act	26:20 and do deeds consistent with repentance.	1
Tit	2: 1 as for you, teach what is consistent with sound doctrine.	2

act consistently
1. ὀρθοποδέω, *orthopodeō, 3980*

Gal	2:14 when I saw that they were not acting consistently	1

consolation
1. παράκλησις, *paraklēsis, 4155*
2. παραμυθία, *paramythia, 4171*
3. παραμύθιον, *paramythion, 4172*

Lke	2:25 looking forward to the consolation of Israel	1
	6:24 for you have received your consolation.	1
1Co	14: 3 upbuilding and encouragement and consolation	2
2Co	1: 3 Father of mercies and the God of all consolation	1
	1: 4 with the consolation…by God	1
	1: 5 our consolation is abundant through Christ	1
	1: 6 it is for your consolation and salvation;	1
	1: 6 if we are being consoled, it is for your consolation	1
	1: 7 so also you share in our consolation.	1
	7: 4 great pride in you; I am filled with consolation;	1
	7: 7 also by the consolation with which he was consoled	1
	7:13 In addition to our own consolation	1
Php	2: 1 any consolation from love	3

console
1. παρακαλέω, *parakaleō, 4151*
2. παραμυθέομαι, *paramytheomai, 4170*

Mat	2:18 refused to be consoled, because they are no	1
Jhn	11:19 to console them about their brother.	2
	11:31 were with her in the house, consoling her	2
2Co	1: 4 who consoles us in all our affliction	1
	1: 4 so that we may be able to console	1
	1: 4 with which we ourselves are consoled by God.	1
	1: 6 if we are being consoled, it is for your consolation	1
	2: 7 so now instead you should forgive and console	1
	7: 6 God, who consoles the downcast	1
	7: 6 consoled us by the arrival of Titus	1
	7: 7 consolation with which he was consoled about you	1

conspicuous
1. πρόδηλος, *prodēlos, 4593*

1Ti	5:24 The sins of some people are conspicuous	1
	5:25 So also good works are conspicuous;	1

conspiracy
1. συνωμοσία, *synōmosia, 5350*
2. συστροφή, *systrophē, 5371*

Act	23:12 In the morning the Jews joined in a conspiracy	2
	23:13 more than forty who joined in this conspiracy.	1

conspire
1. συμβουλεύω, *symbouleuō, 5205*
2. συμβούλιον + δίδωμι, *symboulion + didōmi, 5206 + 1443*
3. συμβούλιον + λαμβάνω, *symboulion + lambanō, 5206 + 3284*

Mat	12:14 and conspired against him, how to destroy him.	3
	26: 4 and they conspired to arrest Jesus	1
Mrk	3: 6 immediately conspired with the Herodians	2

constant
1. ἐκτενής, *ektenēs, 1756*

1Pe	4: 8 maintain constant love for one another	1

constantly   *See also* stay constantly
1. ἀδιάλειπτος, *adialeiptos, 89*
2. ἀδιαλείπτως, *adialeiptōs, 90*
3. διά + πᾶς, *dia + pas, 1328 + 4246*
4. ὁμοθυμαδόν, *homothymadon, 3924*
5. πάντοτε, *pantote, 4121*

Act	1:14 were constantly devoting themselves to prayer	4
	10: 2 prayed constantly to God.	3
Php	1: 4 constantly praying with joy in…my prayers	5
1Th	1: 2 mention you in our prayers, constantly	2
	2:13 We also constantly give thanks to God for this	2
	2:16 constantly been filling up the measure of their sins;	5
2Ti	1: 3 when I remember you constantly in my prayers	1

construct

   1. κατασκευάζω, *kataskeuazō, 2941*

Heb 9: 2 a tent was constructed, the first one   1

under construction

   1. οἰκοδομέω, *oikodomeō, 3868*

Jhn 2:20 "This temple has been under construction for   1

consultation

   1. συμβούλιον, *symboulion, 5206*

Mrk 15: 1 held a consultation with the elders and scribes   1

consume

   1. ἀναλόω, *analoō, 384*
   2. ἀφανίζω, *aphanizō, 906*
   3. ἐκκαίω, *ekkaiō, 1706*
   4. ἐσθίω, *esthiō, 2266*
   5. καταναλίσκω, *katanaliskō, 2914*
   6. κατεσθίω, *katesthiō, 2983*

Mat 6:19 where moth and rust consume and where thieves   2
        6:20 in heaven, where neither moth nor rust consumes   2
Lke 9:54 fire to come down from heaven and consume them?"   1
Jhn 2:17 "Zeal for your house will consume me."   6
Rom 1:27 men…consumed with passion for one another.   3
Gal 5:15 you are not consumed by one another.   1
Heb 10:27 fire that will consume the adversaries.   4
      12:29 for indeed our God is a consuming fire.   5
Rev 11: 5 fire pours…and consumes their foes;   6
      20: 9 And fire came down from heaven and consumed them.   6

contain

   1. χωρέω, *chōreō, 6003*

Jhn 21:25 the world itself could not contain the books   1

container

   1. κόρος, *koros, 3174*

Lke 16: 7 He replied, 'A hundred containers of wheat.'   1

contempt *See* hold up to contempt, regard with contempt, show contempt, treat with contempt

contemptible

   1. ἐξουθενέω, *exoutheneō, 2024*

2Co 10:10 "His letters are weighty…his speech contemptible."   1

contend

   1. διακρίνω, *diakrinō, 1359*
   2. διαμάχομαι, *diamachomai, 1372*
   3. ἐπαγωνίζομαι, *epagōnizomai, 2043*

Act 23: 9 certain scribes…stood up and contended   2
Jde 1: 3 appeal to you to contend for the faith   3
      1: 9 when archangel Michael contended with the devil   1

content

   1. ἀρκέω, *arkeō, 758*
   2. αὐτάρκης, *autarkēs, 895*
   3. εὐδοκέω, *eudokeō, 2305*

2Co 12:10 I am content with weaknesses, insults, hardships   3
Php 4:11 I have learned to be content with whatever I have.   2
1Ti 6: 8 we will be content with these.   1
Heb 13: 5 be content with what you have;   1
3Jn 1:10 And not content with those charges, he refuses   1

contentious

   1. φιλόνεικος, *philoneikos, 5809*

1Co 11:16 if anyone is disposed to be contentious   1

contentment

   1. αὐτάρκεια, *autarkeia, 894*

1Ti 6: 6 great gain in godliness combined with contentment;   1

continually

   1. διά + πᾶς, *dia + pas, 1328 + 4246*
   2. εἰς + ὁ + διηνεκής, *eis + ho + diēnekēs, 1650 + 3836 + 1457*
   3. εἰς + τέλος, *eis + telos, 1650 + 5465*

Mat 18:10 in heaven their angels continually see the face   1
Lke 18: 5 she may not wear me out by continually coming.' "   3

      24:53 were continually in the temple blessing God.   1
Heb 9: 6 the priests go continually into the first tent   1
     10: 1 same sacrifices that are continually offered   2
     13:15 let us continually offer a sacrifice   1

continue

   1. Contextual: Not in Greek
   2. γίνομαι, *ginomai, 1181*
   3. διαμένω, *diamenō, 1373*
   4. εἰμί, *eimi, 1639*
   5. ἐμμένω, *emmenō, 1844*
   6. ἐπιμένω, *epimenō, 2152*
   7. ἱκανός, *hikanos, 2653*
   8. μένω, *menō, 3531*
   9. παραμένω, *paramenō, 4169*
   10. παρατείνω, *parateinō, 4189*
   11. προσμένω, *prosmenō, 4693*

Lke 4:44 he continued proclaiming the message   4
      7:38 continued kissing his feet and anointing   1
Jhn 8:31 "If you continue in my word   8
     12:17 the crowd…continued to testify.   1
Act 6: 7 The word of God continued to spread;   1
     12:16 Meanwhile Peter continued knocking;   6
     12:24 the word of God continued to advance and gain adherents.   1
     13:43 urged them to continue in the grace of God.   11
     14: 7 there they continued proclaiming the good news.   4
     14:22 encouraged them to continue in the faith   5
     19:10 This continued for two years   2
     20: 7 he continued speaking until midnight.   10
     20:11 he continued to converse with them   7
Rom 6: 1 continue in sin in order that grace may abound?   6
     9:11 (so that God's purpose of election might continue   8
     11:22 provided you continue in his kindness;   6
2Co 1:10 He who rescued us…will continue to rescue us   1
     11: 9 will continue to refrain from burdening you   1
Php 1:18 Yes, and I will continue to rejoice   1
     1:25 I will remain and continue with all of you   9
Col 1:23 provided that you continue securely established   6
     2: 6 continue to live your lives in him   1
1Th 3: 8 if you continue to stand firm in the Lord.   1
1Ti 2:15 they continue in faith and love and holiness   8
     4:16 attention to…teaching; continue in these things   6
     5: 5 continues in supplications and prayers   11
2Ti 3:14 as for you, continue in what you have learned   8
Heb 7:23 were prevented by death from continuing in office;   9
     7:24 because he continues forever.   8
     8: 9 for they did not continue in my covenant   5
     13: 1 Let mutual love continue.   8
1Pe 4:19 while continuing to do good.   1
2Pe 3: 4 all things continue as they were   3
Rev 2:26 everyone who conquers and continues to do my works   1

contradict

   1. ἀντιλέγω, *antilegō, 515*

Lke 21:15 will be able to withstand or contradict.   1
Act 13:45 contradicted what was spoken by Paul.   1
Tit 1: 9 to refute those who contradict it.   1

contradiction

   1. ἀντίθεσις, *antithesis, 509*

1Ti 6:20 Avoid the profane chatter and contradictions   1

contrary

   1. ἀλλά, *alla, 247*
   2. ἀλλά + πολύς + μᾶλλον, *alla + polys + mallon, 247 + 4498 + 3437*
   3. ἀντίκειμαι, *antikeimai, 512*
   4. ἀντιλέγω, *antilegō, 515*
   5. ἀπέναντι, *apenanti, 595*
   6. παρά, *para, 4123*
   7. τοὐναντίον, *tounantion, 5539*

Act 15:11 On the contrary, we believe that we will be saved   1
     17: 7 all acting contrary to the decrees of the emperor   5
     18:13 worship God in ways that are contrary to the law."   6
Rom 3:31 By no means! On the contrary, we uphold the law.   1
     10:21 my hands to a disobedient and contrary people."   4
     11:24 grafted, contrary to nature, into a cultivated   6
1Co 12:22 On the contrary, the members of the body   2
     15:10 On the contrary, I worked harder than any of them   1

Gal 1: 8 a gospel contrary to what we proclaimed 6
       1: 9 a gospel contrary to what you received 6
       2: 7 On the contrary, when they saw 7
       3:12 on the contrary, "Whoever does the works 1
1Ti 1:10 whatever else is contrary to the sound teaching 3
1Pe 3: 9 but, on the contrary, repay with a blessing. 7

contrast
    1. δέ, *de, 1254*
Gal 5:22 By contrast, the fruit of the Spirit is love, 1

contribute
    1. βάλλω, *ballō, 965*
    2. βάλλω + εἰς + ὁ + δῶρον, *ballō + eis + ho + dōron, 965 + 1650 + 3836 + 1565*
    3. κοινωνέω, *koinōneō, 3125*
    4. προσανατίθημι, *prosanatithēmi, 4651*
Mrk 12:43 all those who are contributing to the treasury. 1
     12:44 have contributed out of their abundance; 1
Lke 21: 4 have contributed out of their abundance 2
Rom 12:13 Contribute to the needs of the saints; 3
Gal 2: 6 those leaders contributed nothing to me. 4

contrive
    1. τίθημι, *tithēmi, 5502*
Act 5: 4 How is it that you have contrived this deed 1

control
    1. ἐξουσία, *exousia, 2026*
    2. κτάομαι, *ktaomai, 3227*
1Co 7:37 having his own desire under control 1
1Th 4: 4 each one of you know how to control your own body 2

outside one's control
    1. ἀνυπότακτος, *anypotaktos, 538*
Heb 2: 8 God left nothing outside their control. 1

under control
    1. περικρατής, *perikratēs, 4331*
Act 27:16 scarcely able to get the ship's boat under control. 1

controversy
    1. ζήτημα, *zētēma, 2427*
    2. ζήτησις, *zētēsis, 2428*
Act 26: 3 all the customs and controversies of the Jews; 1
1Ti 6: 4 and has a morbid craving for controversy 2
2Ti 2:23 stupid and senseless controversies; 2
Tit 3: 9 avoid stupid controversies, genealogies 2

converse
    1. ὁμιλέω, *homileō, 3917*
Act 20:11 he continued to converse with them 1
     24:26 to send for him very often and converse with him. 1

conversion
    1. ἐπιστροφή, *epistrophē, 2189*
Act 15: 3 reported the conversion of the Gentiles 1

convert
    1. αὐτός, *autos, 899*
    2. προσήλυτος, *prosēlytos, 4670*
Mat 23:15 to make a single convert 2
     23:15 you make the new convert twice as much 1

convert to Judaism
    1. προσήλυτος, *prosēlytos, 4670*
Act 13:43 many Jews and devout converts to Judaism 1

first convert
    1. ἀπαρχή, *aparchē, 569*
Rom 16: 5 Epaenetus, who was the first convert in Asia 1
1Co 16:15 were the first converts in Achaia 1

recent convert
    1. νεόφυτος, *neophytos, 3745*
1Ti 3: 6 He must not be a recent convert 1

convey
    1. φέρω, *pherō, 5770*
2Pe 1:17 that voice was conveyed to him by the Majestic Glory 1

convict
    1. ἐλέγχω, *elenchō, 1794*
Jhn 8:46 Which of you convicts me of sin? 1
Jas 2: 9 are convicted by the law as transgressors. 1
Jde 1:15 to convict everyone of all the deeds 1

conviction
    1. ἔλεγχος, *elenchos, 1793*
    2. πληροφορία, *plērophoria, 4443*
1Th 1: 5 in the Holy Spirit and with full conviction; 2
Heb 11: 1 faith is…the conviction of things not seen. 1

convince *See also* convincing *proof*
    1. δοκέω, *dokeō, 1506*
    2. ἐλέγχω, *elenchō, 1794*
    3. κρίνω, *krinō, 3212*
    4. πείθω, *peithō, 4275*
    5. συμβιβάζω, *symbibazō, 5204*
Lke 16:31 neither will they be convinced 4
     20: 6 they are convinced that John was a prophet." 4
Act 5:39 They were convinced by him 4
     16:10 convinced that God had called us 5
     18: 4 to convince Jews and Greeks. 4
     26: 9 I…was convinced that I ought to do many things 1
     28:23 trying to convince them about Jesus 4
     28:24 Some were convinced by what he had said 4
Rom 8:38 For I am convinced that neither death, nor life 4
2Co 5:14 because we are convinced 3
Php 1:25 convinced of this, I know that I will remain 4
2Ti 4: 2 whether the time is favorable or unfavorable; convince 2

convince fully
    1. πληροφορέω, *plērophoreō, 4442*
Rom 4:21 fully convinced that God was able to do 1
     14: 5 Let all be fully convinced in their own minds. 1

convulse
    1. σπαράσσω, *sparassō, 5057*
    2. συσπαράσσω, *sysparassō, 5360*
Mrk 1:26 the unclean spirit, convulsing him and crying 1
     9:20 immediately it convulsed the boy 2
     9:26 After crying out and convulsing him terribly 1
Lke 9:39 It convulses him until he foams at the mouth 1

convulsion
    1. συσπαράσσω, *sysparassō, 5360*
Lke 9:42 the demon dashed him to the ground in convulsions. 1

cool
    1. καταψύχω, *katapsychō, 2976*
Lke 16:24 cool my tongue; 1

copper *See also* small copper *coin*
    1. χαλκός, *chalkos, 5910*
Mat 10: 9 Take no gold, or silver, or copper in your belts 1

coppersmith
    1. χαλκεύς, *chalkeus, 5906*
2Ti 4:14 Alexander the coppersmith did me great harm; 1

copy
    1. ἀντίτυπος, *antitypos, 531*
Heb 9:24 a mere copy of the true one 1

corban
    1. κορβᾶν, *korban, 3167*
Mrk 7:11 Corban' (that is, an offering to God)— 1

cord
    1. σχοινίον, *schoinion, 5389*
Jhn 2:15 Making a whip of cords, he drove all of them 1

Corinth
    1. Κόρινθος, *Korinthos, 3172*

Act 18: 1 After this Paul left Athens and went to Corinth.   1
    19: 1 While Apollos was in Corinth   1
1Co 1: 2 To the church of God that is in Corinth   1
2Co 1: 1 To the church of God that is in Corinth   1
    1:23 I did not come again to Corinth.   1
2Ti 4:20 Erastus remained in Corinth;   1

Corinthian

1. Κορίνθιος, *Korinthios, 3171*

Act 18: 8 many of the Corinthians…became believers   1
2Co 6:11 We have spoken frankly to you Corinthians;   1

Cornelius

1. Κορνήλιος, *Kornēlios, 3173*

Act 10: 1 In Caesarea there was a man named Cornelius   1
    10: 3 an angel…saying to him, "Cornelius."   1
    10:17 suddenly the men sent by Cornelius   1
    10:22 They answered, "Cornelius, a centurion   1
    10:24 Cornelius was expecting them   1
    10:25 On Peter's arrival Cornelius met him   1
    10:30 Cornelius replied, "Four days ago at this very hour   1
    10:31 said, 'Cornelius, your prayer has been heard   1

corner

1. ἀρχή, *archē, 794*
2. γωνία, *gōnia, 1224*

Mat 6: 5 pray in the synagogues and at the street corners   2
Act 10:11 being lowered to the ground by its four corners.   1
    11: 5 being lowered by its four corners;   1
    26:26 this was not done in a corner.   2
1Pe 2: 7 stone…has become the very head of the corner,"   2
Rev 7: 1 angels standing at the four corners of the earth   2
    20: 8 nations…at the four corners of the earth   2

cornerstone

1. ἀκρογωνιαῖος, *akrogōniaios, 214*
2. κεφαλή + γωνία, *kephalē + gōnia, 3051 + 1224*

Mat 21:42 has become the cornerstone;   2
Mrk 12:10 has become the cornerstone;   2
Lke 20:17 has become the cornerstone'?   2
Act 4:11 it has become the cornerstone.'   2
Eph 2:20 Christ Jesus himself as the cornerstone.   1
1Pe 2: 6 in Zion…a cornerstone chosen and precious;   1

corpse

1. νεκρός, *nekros, 3738*
2. πτῶμα, *ptōma, 4773*
3. σῶμα, *sōma, 5393*

Mat 24:28 Wherever the corpse is, there the vultures   2
Mrk 9:26 it came out, and the boy was like a corpse   1
Lke 17:37 "Where the corpse is, there the vultures will gather."   3
Rev 16: 3 the sea, and it became like the blood of a corpse   1

correct

1. παιδεύω, *paideuō, 4084*

2Ti 2:25 correcting opponents with gentleness.   1

correction

1. ἐπανόρθωσις, *epanorthōsis, 2061*

2Ti 3:16 useful…for reproof, for correction   1

corrector

1. παιδευτής, *paideutēs, 4083*

Rom 2:20 a corrector of the foolish, a teacher of children   1

correspond

1. Contextual: Not in Greek
2. συστοιχέω, *systoicheō, 5368*

Gal 4:25 and corresponds to the present Jerusalem   2
    4:26 other woman corresponds to the Jerusalem above   1

corrupt

1. καταφθείρω, *kataphtheirō, 2967*
2. μιαίνω, *miainō, 3620*
3. σκολιός, *skolios, 5021*
4. φθείρω, *phtheirō, 5780*

Act 2:40 "Save yourselves from this corrupt generation."   3
2Co 7: 2 we have wronged no one, we have corrupted no one   4

Eph 4:22 corrupt and deluded by its lusts   4
2Ti 3: 8 people, of corrupt mind and counterfeit faith   1
Tit 1:15 to the corrupt and unbelieving nothing is pure.   2
    1:15 Their very minds and consciences are corrupted.   2
Rev 19: 2 judged the great whore who corrupted the earth   4

corruption

1. διαφθορά, *diaphthora, 1426*
2. φθορά, *phthora, 5785*

Act 2:27 or let your Holy One experience corruption.   1
    2:31 nor did his flesh experience corruption.'   1
    13:34 no more to return to corruption   1
    13:35 'You will not let your Holy One experience corruption.'   1
    13:36 beside his ancestors, and experienced corruption;   1
    13:37 he whom God raised up experienced no corruption.   1
Gal 6: 8 will reap corruption from the flesh;   2
2Pe 1: 4 escape from the corruption that is in the world   2
    2:19 they themselves are slaves of corruption;   2

Cos

1. Κῶς, *Kōs, 3271*

Act 21: 1 we came by a straight course to Cos   1

Cosam

1. Κωσάμ, *Kōsam, 3272*

Lke 3:28 son of Melchi, son of Addi, son of Cosam   1

cosmic   *See* cosmic *power*

cost

1. δαπάνη, *dapanē, 1252*
2. κτάομαι, *ktaomai, 3227*

Lke 14:28 does not first sit down and estimate the cost   1
Act 22:28 cost me a large sum of money to get my citizenship."   2

costly

1. πολύτιμος, *polytimos, 4501*
2. τίμιος, *timios, 5508*

Jhn 12: 3 a pound of costly perfume made of pure nard   1
Rev 18:12 articles of costly wood, bronze, iron, and marble   2

very costly

1. βαρύτιμος, *barytimos, 988*
2. πολυτελής, *polytelēs, 4500*

Mat 26: 7 alabaster jar of very costly ointment   1
Mrk 14: 3 very costly ointment of nard   2

cot

1. κλινάριον, *klinarion, 3108*

Act 5:15 laid them on cots and mats   1

council   *See also* member of the council

1. συμβούλιον, *symboulion, 5206*
2. συνέδριον, *synedrion, 5284*

Mat 5:22 insult…you will be liable to the council;   2
    10:17 they will hand you over to councils   2
    26:59 the chief priests and the whole council   2
Mrk 13: 9 they will hand you over to councils;   2
    14:55 Now the chief priests and the whole council   2
    15: 1 with the elders and scribes and the whole council.   2
Lke 22:66 they brought him to their council.   2
Jhn 11:47 the Pharisees called a meeting of the council,   2
Act 4:15 So they ordered them to leave the council   2
    5:21 the council and the whole body of the elders   2
    5:27 they had them stand before the council.   2
    5:34 a Pharisee in the council named Gamaliel   2
    5:41 As they left the council   2
    6:12 seized him, and brought him before the council.   2
    6:15 all who sat in the council looked intently at him   2
    22:30 the chief priests and the entire council to meet.   2
    23: 1 Paul was looking intently at the council he said   2
    23: 6 he called out in the council   2
    23:15 Now then, you and the council must notify   2
    23:20 to ask you to bring Paul down to the council   2
    23:28 I had him brought to their council.   2
    24:20 when I stood before the council   2
    25:12 after he had conferred with his council   1

council of elders
1. πρεσβυτέριον, *presbyterion, 4564*

Act 22: 5 the high priest and the whole council of elders   1
1Ti 4:14 laying on of hands by the council of elders.   1

counsel
1. βουλή, *boulē, 1087*
2. συμβουλεύω, *symbouleuō, 5205*

Eph 1:11 according to his counsel and will   1
Rev 3:18 I counsel you to buy from me gold refined by fire   2

counselor
1. σύμβουλος, *symboulos, 5207*

Rom 11:34 Or who has been his counselor?"   1

count
1. Contextual: Not in Greek
2. ἀριθμέω, *arithmeō, 749*
3. ἡγέομαι, *hēgeomai, 2451*
4. ἰσχύω, *ischyō, 2710*
5. λογίζομαι, *logizomai, 3357*
6. ποιέω + λόγος, *poieō + logos, 4472 + 3364*

Mat 10:30 even the hairs of your head are all counted.   2
Lke 12: 7 But even the hairs of your head are all counted.   2
    22:37 'And he was counted among the lawless';   5
Act 20:24 I do not count my life of any value   6
Rom 9: 8 of the promise are counted as descendants.   5
2Co 5:19 not counting their trespasses against them   5
Gal 5: 6 nor uncircumcision counts for anything;   4
    5: 6 that counts is faith working through love.   1
2Pe 2:13 They count it a pleasure to revel in the daytime.   3
Rev 7: 9 a great multitude that no one could count   2

count against
1. λογίζομαι, *logizomai, 3357*

2Ti 4:16 May it not be counted against them!   1

counterfeit
1. ἀδόκιμος, *adokimos, 99*

2Ti 3: 8 people, of corrupt mind and counterfeit faith   1

countless
1. ὑπερβαλλόντως, *hyperballontōs, 5649*

2Co 11:23 with countless floggings, and often near death.   1

country   *See also* go to another country, hill country
1. Contextual: Not in Greek
2. ἀγρός, *agros, 69*
3. γῆ, *gē, 1178*
4. ἔρημος + τόπος, *erēmos + topos, 2245 + 5536*
5. πατρίς, *patris, 4258*
6. χώρα, *chōra, 6001*

Mat 2:12 left for their own country by another road.   6
    8:28 to the country of the Gadarenes   6
Mrk 1:45 but stayed out in the country;   4
    5: 1 to the country of the Gerasenes.   6
    5:10 not to send them out of the country.   6
    5:14 told it in the city and in the country.   2
    6:36 may go into the surrounding country and villages   2
    15:21 who was coming in from the country   2
    16:12 [[as they were walking into the country.]]   2
Lke 8:26 they arrived at the country of the Gerasenes   6
    8:34 told it in the city and in the country.   2
    15:13 and traveled to a distant country   6
    15:14 a severe famine took place throughout that country   6
    15:15 one of the citizens of that country   6
    19:12 "A nobleman went to a distant country   6
    19:14 citizens of his country hated him   1
    21:21 those out in the country must not enter it;   6
    23:26 who was coming from the country   2
Jhn 4:44 a prophet has no honor in the prophet's own country).   5
    11:55 many went up from the country to Jerusalem   6
Act 7: 3 'Leave your country and your relatives   3
    7: 4 Then he left the country of the Chaldeans   3
    7: 4 God had him move from there to this country   3
    7: 6 resident aliens in a country belonging to others   3
    12:20 because their country depended...for food.   6
    12:20 depended on the king's country for food.   1

Heb 11:16 as it is, they desire a better country   1

own country
1. πατρίς, *patris, 4258*

Mat 13:57 are not without honor except in their own country   1

surrounding country
1. περίχωρος, *perichōros, 4369*

Lke 4:14 spread through all the surrounding country.   1
    7:17 throughout Judea and all the surrounding country   1
    8:37 all the people of the surrounding country   1
Act 14: 6 and to the surrounding country;   1

countryside
1. ἀγρός, *agros, 69*
2. γῆ, *gē, 1178*
3. χώρα, *chōra, 6001*

Mrk 1: 5 people from the whole Judean countryside   3
Lke 9:12 into the surrounding villages and countryside   1
Jhn 3:22 Jesus...went into the Judean countryside,   2
Act 8: 1 scattered throughout the countryside of Judea   3
    26:20 throughout the countryside of Judea   3

courage   *See also* keep up courage, take courage
1. θάρσος, *tharsos, 2511*
2. παρρησιάζομαι, *parrēsiazomai, 4245*

Act 28:15 Paul thanked God and took courage.   1
1Th 2: 2 courage in our God to declare to you the gospel   2

courageous
1. ἀνδρίζομαι, *andrizomai, 437*

1Co 16:13 be courageous, be strong.   1

course   *See also* of course, straight course, take a straight course
1. αἰών, *aiōn, 172*
2. δρόμος, *dromos, 1536*

Act 20:24 if only I may finish my course   2
Eph 2: 2 following the course of this world   1

court¹   *See also* court *official*, go to court, member of the court, take to court
1. αὐλή, *aulē, 885*

Rev 11: 2 do not measure the court outside the temple;   1

court²
1. Contextual: Not in Greek
2. ἀγοραῖος, *agoraios, 61*
3. ἡμέρα, *hēmera, 2465*
4. κριτήριον, *kritērion, 3215*

Mat 5:25 accuser while you are on the way to court with him   1
Act 19:38 the courts are open   2
1Co 4: 3 I should be judged by you or by any human court.   3
Jas 2: 6 Is it not they who drag you into court?   4

courtesy
1. πραΰτης, *prautēs, 4559*

Tit 3: 2 to show every courtesy to everyone.   1

courtier
1. μεγιστάν, *megistan, 3491*

Mrk 6:21 a banquet for his courtiers and officers   1

courtyard
1. αὐλή, *aulē, 885*

Mat 26:58 as far as the courtyard of the high priest;   1
    26:69 Now Peter was sitting outside in the courtyard.   1
Mrk 14:54 right into the courtyard of the high priest;   1
    14:66 While Peter was below in the courtyard   1
Lke 22:55 kindled a fire in the middle of the courtyard   1
Jhn 18:15 with Jesus into the courtyard of the high priest   1

courtyard of palace
1. αὐλή, *aulē, 885*

Mrk 15:16 soldiers led him into the courtyard of the palace   1

cousin
1. ἀνεψιός, *anepsios, 463*

Col   4:10   Mark the cousin of Barnabas   1

covenant   *See also* make a covenant
1. Contextual: Not in Greek
2. διαθήκη, *diathēkē, 1347*

Mat 26:28   for this is my blood of the covenant   2
Mrk 14:24   to them, "This is my blood of the covenant   2
Lke   1:72   remembered his holy covenant   2
    22:20   the new covenant in my blood.   2
Act   3:25   the descendants of the prophets and of the covenant   2
    7: 8   he gave him the covenant of circumcision   2
Rom   9: 4   the covenants, the giving of the law, the worship   2
    11:27   my covenant with them, when I take away their sins."   2
1Co 11:25   "This cup is the new covenant in my blood.   2
2Co   3: 6   competent to be ministers of a new covenant   2
    3:14   when they hear the reading of the old covenant   2
Gal   3:17   not annul a covenant previously ratified by God   2
    4:24   these women are two covenants.   2
Eph   2:12   strangers to the covenants of promise   2
Heb   7:22   Jesus has also become the guarantee of a better covenant.   2
    8: 6   he is the mediator of a better covenant,   2
    8: 7   For if that first covenant had been faultless   1
    8: 8   when I will establish a new covenant   2
    8: 9   like the covenant that I made with their ancestors   2
    8: 9   for they did not continue in my covenant   2
    8:10   This is the covenant that I will make   2
    8:13   In speaking of "a new covenant,"   1
    9: 1   the first covenant had regulations for worship   1
    9: 4   the ark of the covenant   2
    9: 4   the tablets of the covenant;   2
    9:15   For this reason he is the mediator of a new covenant   2
    9:15   the transgressions under the first covenant.   2
    9:18   Hence not even the first covenant was inaugurated   1
    9:20   saying, "This is the blood of the covenant   2
    10:16   "This is the covenant that I will make with them   2
    10:29   profaned the blood of the covenant   2
    12:24   to Jesus, the mediator of a new covenant   2
    13:20   by the blood of the eternal covenant   2
Rev 11:19   ark of his covenant was seen within his temple;   2

cover
1. ἐπικαλύπτω, *epikalyptō, 2128*
2. καλύπτω, *kalyptō, 2821*
3. περιβόλαιον, *peribolaion, 4316*
4. πλήρης, *plērēs, 4441*
5. συνέχω, *synechō, 5309*

Lke   5:12   there was a man covered with leprosy.   4
    23:30   to the hills, 'Cover us.'   2
Act   7:57   they covered their ears, and with a loud shout   5
Rom   4: 7   and whose sins are covered;   1
1Co 11:15   her hair is given to her for a covering.   3
Jas   5:20   and will cover a multitude of sins.   2
1Pe   4: 8   for love covers a multitude of sins.   2

cover up
1. καλύπτω, *kalyptō, 2821*
2. συγκαλύπτω, *synkalyptō, 5158*

Mat 10:26   nothing is covered up that will not be uncovered   1
Lke 12: 2   Nothing is covered up that will not be uncovered   2

covered with sores
1. ἑλκόω, *helkoō, 1815*

Lke 16:20   a poor man named Lazarus, covered with sores   1

covet
1. ἐπιθυμέω, *epithymeō, 2121*
2. ἐπιθυμία, *epithymia, 2123*
3. ζηλόω; *zēloō, 2420*

Act 20:33   I coveted no one's silver or gold or clothing.   1
Rom   7: 7   I would not have known what it is to covet   2
    7: 7   if the law had not said, "You shall not covet."   1
    13: 9   You shall not covet"; and any other commandment   1
Jas   4: 2   you covet something and cannot obtain it;   3

covetousness
1. ἐπιθυμία, *epithymia, 2123*
2. πλεονεξία, *pleonexia, 4432*

Rom 1:29   every...wickedness, evil, covetousness, malice.   2
    7: 8   sin...produced in me all kinds of covetousness.   1

cowardice
1. δειλία, *deilia, 1261*

2Ti   1: 7   for God did not give us a spirit of cowardice   1

cowardly
1. δειλός, *deilos, 1264*

Rev 21: 8   as for the cowardly, the faithless, the polluted   1

craftily   *See* deal craftily

craftiness
1. κακοήθεια, *kakoētheia, 2799*
2. πανουργία, *panourgia, 4111*

Lke 20:23   he perceived their craftiness and said to them   2
Rom 1:29   Full of envy, murder, strife, deceit, craftiness   1
1Co   3:19   "He catches the wise in their craftiness,"   2
Eph   4:14   by their craftiness in deceitful scheming.   2

crafty
1. πανοῦργος, *panourgos, 4112*

2Co 12:16   Nevertheless (you say) since I was crafty   1

crave
1. ἡδονή, *hēdonē, 2454*

Jas   4: 1   Do they not come from your cravings...at war within you?   1

morbid craving
1. νοσέω, *noseō, 3796*

1Ti   6: 4   and has a morbid craving for controversy   1

create
1. κτίζω, *ktizō, 3231*
2. κτίσμα, *ktisma, 3233*
3. ποιέω, *poieō, 4472*

Mrk 13:19   the creation that God created until now   1
1Co 11: 9   Neither was man created for the sake of woman   1
Eph   2:10   we are what he has made us, created in Christ Jesus   1
    2:15   create in himself one new humanity in place of the two   1
    3: 9   hidden for ages in God who created all things;   1
    4:24   created according to the likeness of God   1
Col   1:16   in him all things in heaven and on earth were created   1
    1:16   all things have been created through him   1
1Ti   4: 3   demand abstinence from foods, which God created   1
    4: 4   For everything created by God is good   2
Heb   1: 2   through whom he also created the worlds.   3
    12:27   what is shaken—that is, created things   3
Rev   4:11   for you created all things   1
    4:11   and by your will they existed and were created."   1
    10: 6   who created heaven and what is in it   1

creation
1. Contextual: Not in Greek
2. κτίσις, *ktisis, 3232*

Mrk 10: 6   from the beginning of creation   2
    13:19   not been from the beginning of the creation   2
    16:15   ⟦proclaim the good news to the whole creation.⟧   2
Rom   1:20   Ever since the creation of the world   2
    8:19   For the creation waits with eager longing   2
    8:20   for the creation was subjected to futility   2
    8:21   that the creation itself will be set free   2
    8:22   the whole creation has been groaning in labor pains   2
    8:23   not only the creation, but we ourselves   1
    8:39   nor depth, nor anything else in all creation   2
2Co   5:17   if anyone is in Christ, there is a new creation: 2
Gal   6:15   nor uncircumcision is anything; but a new creation   2
Col   1:15   the firstborn of all creation;   2
Heb   9:11   that is, not of this creation)   2
2Pe   3: 4   as they were from the beginning of creation!"   2
Rev   3:14   the Amen...the origin of God's creation: 2

creator
1. κτίζω, *ktizō, 3231*
2. κτίστης, *ktistēs, 3234*

Rom 1:25   served the creature rather than the Creator   1
Col   3:10   according to the image of its creator.   1
1Pe   4:19   entrust themselves to a faithful Creator   2

creature *See also* four-footed creature, living creature

1. Contextual: Not in Greek
2. θηρίον, *thērion, 2563*
3. κτίσις, *ktisis, 3232*
4. κτίσμα, *ktisma, 3233*

Act	28: 4 saw the creature hanging from his hand	2
	28: 5 He, however, shook off the creature into the fire	2
Rom	1:25 served the creature rather than the Creator	3
Col	1:23 been proclaimed to every creature under heaven.	3
Heb	4:13 before him no creature is hidden	3
Jas	1:18 become a kind of first fruits of his creatures.	4
2Pe	2:12 like irrational animals, mere creatures of instinct	1
	2:12 when those creatures are destroyed,	1
Rev	5:13 I heard every creature in heaven and on earth	4
	8: 9 a third of the living creatures in the sea died	4

sea creature

1. ἐνάλιος, *enalios, 1879*

Jas	3: 7 every species...of reptile and sea creature	1

credit

1. ἔχω, *echō, 2400*
2. κλέος, *kleos, 3094*
3. χάρις, *charis, 5921*

Lke	6:32 love those who love you, what credit is that	3
	6:33 do good to you, what credit is that to you?	3
	6:34 what credit is that to you?	3
1Pe	2:19 For it is a credit to you if...you endure pain	3
	2:20 beaten for doing wrong, what credit is that?	2
Rev	2: 6 this is to your credit: you hate...the Nicolaitans	1

creditor

1. δανιστής, *danistēs, 1250*

Lke	7:41 "A certain creditor had two debtors;	1

Crescens

1. Κρήσκης, *Krēskēs, 3206*

2Ti	4:10 Crescens has gone to Galatia, Titus to Dalmatia.	1

Cretan

1. Κρής, *Krēs, 3205*

Act	2:11 Cretans and Arabs	1
Tit	1:12 "Cretans are always liars, vicious brutes	1

Crete

1. αὐτός, *autos, 899*
2. Κρήτη, *Krētē, 3207*

Act	27: 7 sailed under the lee of Crete off Salmone.	2
	27:12 a harbor of Crete, facing southwest and northwest.	2
	27:13 sail past Crete, close to the shore.	2
	27:14 a violent wind...rushed down from Crete.	1
	27:21 not have set sail from Crete	2
Tit	1: 5 I left you behind in Crete for this reason	2

crime

1. ἀδίκημα, *adikēma, 93*
2. πονηρός, *ponēros, 4505*

Act	18:14 a matter of crime or serious villainy	1
	24:20 tell what crime they had found	1
	25:18 any of the crimes that I was expecting.	2

criminal

1. κακοποιός, *kakopoios, 2804*
2. κακός + ποιέω, *kakos + poieō, 2805 + 4472*
3. κακοῦργος, *kakourgos, 2806*

Lke	23:32 Two others also, who were criminals, were led away	3
	23:33 they crucified Jesus there with the criminals	3
	23:39 criminals who were hanged there kept deriding him	3
Jhn	18:30 "If this man were not a criminal	2
2Ti	2: 9 even to the point of being chained like a criminal	3
1Pe	4:15 let none of you suffer as...a criminal	1

cripple

1. ἀνάπειρος, *anapeiros, 401*
2. ἀσθένεια, *astheneia, 819*
3. χωλός, *chōlos, 6000*

Lke	13:11 spirit that had crippled her for eighteen years.	2
	14:13 invite the poor, the crippled, the lame,	1
	14:21 bring in the poor, the crippled, the blind,	1
Act	14: 8 never walked, for he had been crippled from birth.	3

crisis

1. ἀνάγκη, *anankē, 340*

1Co	7:26 I think that, in view of the impending crisis	1

Crispus

1. Κρίσπος, *Krispos, 3214*

Act	18: 8 Crispus, the official of the synagogue	1
1Co	1:14 baptized none of you except Crispus and Gaius	1

criticize

1. διακρίνω, *diakrinō, 1359*

Act	11: 2 the circumcised believers criticized him	1

crooked *See also* make crooked

1. σκολιός, *skolios, 5021*

Lke	3: 5 the crooked shall be made straight	1
Php	2:15 a crooked and perverse generation	1

crop

1. Contextual: Not in Greek
2. βοτάνη, *botanē, 1083*
3. καρπός, *karpos, 2843*

Lke	12:17 I have no place to store my crops?'	3
1Co	9:10 should thresh in hope of a share in the crop.	1
2Ti	2: 6 ought to have the first share of the crops.	3
Heb	6: 7 Ground that...produces a crop useful to those	2
Jas	5: 7 farmer waits for the precious crop from the earth	3

cross

1. διαπεράω, *diaperaō, 1385*
2. ξύλον, *xylon, 3833*
3. περιάγω, *periagō, 4310*
4. σταυρός, *stauros, 5089*

Mat	9: 1 And after getting into a boat he crossed	1
	10:38 whoever does not take up the cross and follow me	4
	16:24 let them deny themselves and take up their cross	4
	23:15 you cross sea and land	3
	27:32 they compelled this man to carry his cross.	4
	27:40 the Son of God, come down from the cross."	4
	27:42 let him come down from the cross now	4
Mrk	5:21 Jesus had crossed again in the boat	1
	8:34 let them deny themselves and take up their cross	4
	15:21 to carry his cross; it was Simon of Cyrene	4
	15:30 save yourself, and come down from the cross!"	4
	15:32 King of Israel, come down from the cross now	4
Lke	9:23 take up their cross daily and follow me.	4
	14:27 does not carry the cross and follow me	4
	16:26 and no one can cross from there to us.'	1
	23:26 and they laid the cross on him,	4
Jhn	19:17 carrying the cross by himself, he went out	4
	19:19 an inscription written and put on the cross.	4
	19:25 standing near the cross of Jesus were his mother	4
	19:31 Jews did not want the bodies left on the cross	4
1Co	1:17 the cross of Christ might not be emptied of its power.	4
	1:18 For the message about the cross is foolishness	4
Gal	5:11 offense of the cross has been removed.	4
	6:12 not be persecuted for the cross of Christ.	4
	6:14 except the cross of our Lord Jesus Christ	4
Eph	2:16 reconcile both...through the cross	4
Php	2: 8 obedient to the point of death—even death on a cross.	4
	3:18 For many live as enemies of the cross of Christ;	4
Col	1:20 making peace through the blood of his cross.	4
	2:14 He set this aside, nailing it to the cross.	4
Heb	12: 2 endured the cross, disregarding its shame	4
1Pe	2:24 He himself bore our sins in his body on the cross	2

cross over

1. διαπεράω, *diaperaō, 1385*
2. διέρχομαι, *dierchomai, 1451*
3. ἐξέρχομαι, *exerchomai, 2002*

Mat	14:34 When they had crossed over, they came to land	1
Mrk	6:53 When they had crossed over	1
Act	16:10 we immediately tried to cross over to Macedonia	3
	18:27 when he wished to cross over to Achaia	2

cross-examine

1. ἀποστοματίζω, *apostomatizō, 694*

Lke 11:53 and to cross-examine him about many things   1

crow

1. φωνέω, *phōneō, 5888*

Mat	26:34	this very night, before the cock crows	1
	26:74	At that moment the cock crowed.	1
	26:75	"Before the cock crows, you will deny me	1
Mrk	14:30	this very night, before the cock crows twice	1
	14:68	Then the cock crowed.	1
	14:72	At that moment the cock crowed for the second time.	1
	14:72	"Before the cock crows twice	1
Lke	22:34	Peter, the cock will not crow this day	1
	22:60	while he was still speaking, the cock crowed.	1
	22:61	"Before the cock crows today, you will deny me	1
Jhn	13:38	Very truly, I tell you, before the cock crows	1
	18:27	at that moment the cock crowed.	1

crowd

1. Contextual: Not in Greek
2. δῆμος, *dēmos, 1322*
3. ὄχλος, *ochlos, 4063*
4. πλῆθος, *plēthos, 4436*

Mat	4:25	And great crowds followed him from Galilee	3
	5: 1	Jesus saw the crowds, he went up the mountain;	3
	7:28	the crowds were astounded at his teaching	3
	8: 1	great crowds followed him;	3
	8:18	Now when Jesus saw great crowds around him	3
	9: 8	When the crowds saw it, they were filled with awe	3
	9:23	flute players and the crowd making a commotion	3
	9:25	But when the crowd had been put outside, he went	3
	9:33	who had been mute spoke; and the crowds were amazed	3
	9:36	When he saw the crowds, he had compassion for them	3
	11: 7	they went away, Jesus began to speak to the crowds	3
	12:15	Many crowds followed him, and he cured all	3
	12:23	All the crowds were amazed and said	3
	12:46	While he was still speaking to the crowds	3
	13: 2	great crowds gathered around him	3
	13: 2	while the whole crowd stood on the beach.	3
	13:34	Jesus told the crowds all these things in parables;	3
	13:36	Then he left the crowds and went into the house.	3
	14: 5	he feared the crowd	3
	14:13	But when the crowds heard it	3
	14:14	When he went ashore, he saw a great crowd;	3
	14:15	send the crowds away so that they may go	3
	14:19	he ordered the crowds to sit down on the grass.	3
	14:19	and the disciples gave them to the crowds.	3
	14:22	while he dismissed the crowds.	3
	14:23	after he had dismissed the crowds	3
	15:10	he called the crowd to him and said to them	3
	15:30	Great crowds came to him	3
	15:31	so that the crowd was amazed	3
	15:32	"I have compassion for the crowd	3
	15:33	enough bread…to feed so great a crowd?"	3
	15:35	ordering the crowd to sit down on the ground	3
	15:36	and the disciples gave them to the crowds.	3
	15:39	sending away the crowds, he got into the boat	3
	17:14	When they came to the crowd	3
	19: 2	Large crowds followed him, and he cured them	3
	20:29	a large crowd followed him.	3
	20:31	The crowd sternly ordered them to be quiet;	3
	21: 8	very large crowd spread their cloaks	3
	21: 9	The crowds that went ahead of him	3
	21:11	crowds were saying, "This is the prophet Jesus	3
	21:26	'Of human origin,' we are afraid of the crowd;	3
	21:46	they feared the crowds	3
	22:33	when the crowd heard it	3
	23: 1	to the crowds and to his disciples	3
	26:47	with him was a large crowd with swords and clubs	3
	26:55	At that hour Jesus said to the crowds	3
	27:15	to release a prisoner for the crowd,	3
	27:20	elders persuaded the crowds to ask for Barabbas	3
	27:24	washed his hands before the crowd, saying	3
Mrk	2: 4	because of the crowd	3
	2:13	the whole crowd gathered around him	3
	3: 9	because of the crowd, so that they would not crush	3
	3:20	and the crowd came together again	3
	3:32	A crowd was sitting around him; and they said	3
	4: 1	a very large crowd gathered around him	3

	4: 1	the whole crowd was beside the sea on the land.	3
	4:36	leaving the crowd behind, they took him with them	3
	5:21	a great crowd gathered around him;	3
	5:24	a large crowd followed him and pressed in on	3
	5:27	came up behind him in the crowd	3
	5:30	Jesus turned about in the crowd and said	3
	5:31	"You see the crowd pressing in on you;	3
	6:34	As he went ashore, he saw a great crowd;	3
	6:45	while he dismissed the crowd.	3
	7:14	he called the crowd again and said	3
	7:17	When he had left the crowd and entered the house	3
	7:33	took him aside in private, away from the crowd	3
	8: 1	again a great crowd without anything to eat	3
	8: 2	"I have compassion for the crowd	3
	8: 6	he ordered the crowd to sit down on the ground;	3
	8: 6	and they distributed them to the crowd.	3
	8:34	He called the crowd with his disciples	3
	9:14	they saw a great crowd around them	3
	9:15	When the whole crowd saw him,	3
	9:17	Someone from the crowd answered him, "Teacher	3
	9:25	Jesus saw that a crowd came running together	3
	10: 1	crowds again gathered around him;	3
	10:46	As he and his disciples and a large crowd	3
	11:18	because the whole crowd was spellbound	3
	11:32	they were afraid of the crowd	3
	12:12	feared the crowd.	3
	12:37	the large crowd was listening to him with delight.	3
	12:41	watched the crowd	3
	14:43	with him there was a crowd with swords and clubs	3
	15: 8	the crowd came and began to ask Pilate	3
	15:11	the chief priests stirred up the crowd	3
	15:15	So Pilate, wishing to satisfy the crowd	3
Lke	3: 7	the crowds that came out to be baptized by him	3
	3:10	the crowds asked him, "What then should we do?"	3
	4:42	the crowds were looking for him	3
	5: 1	and the crowd was pressing in on him	3
	5: 3	he sat down and taught the crowds from the boat.	3
	5:15	many crowds would gather to hear	3
	5:19	no way to bring him in because of the crowd	3
	5:19	into the middle of the crowd in front of Jesus.	1
	5:29	was a large crowd of tax collectors and others	3
	6:17	with a great crowd of his disciples	3
	6:19	all in the crowd were trying to touch him	3
	7: 9	turning to the crowd that followed him, he said	3
	7:11	his disciples and a large crowd went with him.	3
	7:12	with her was a large crowd from the town.	3
	7:24	Jesus began to speak to the crowds about John:	3
	8: 4	When a great crowd gathered	3
	8:19	they could not reach him because of the crowd.	3
	8:40	Now when Jesus returned, the crowd welcomed him	3
	8:42	As he went, the crowds pressed in on him.	3
	8:45	the crowds surround you and press in on you."	3
	9:11	When the crowds found out about it,	3
	9:12	"Send the crowd away, so that they may go	3
	9:16	and gave them…to set before the crowd.	3
	9:18	them, "Who do the crowds say that I am?"	3
	9:37	a great crowd met him.	3
	9:38	Just then a man from the crowd shouted, "Teacher	3
	11:14	mute spoke, and the crowds were amazed.	3
	11:27	a woman in the crowd raised her voice and said	3
	11:29	When the crowds were increasing, he began to say	3
	12: 1	when the crowd gathered by the thousands,	3
	12:13	Someone in the crowd said to him, "Teacher	3
	12:54	He also said to the crowds	3
	13:14	leader of the synagogue…saying to the crowd	3
	13:17	crowd was rejoicing at all the wonderful things	3
	14:25	Now large crowds were traveling with him;	3
	18:36	heard a crowd going by	3
	19: 3	but on account of the crowd he could not	3
	19:39	Some of the Pharisees in the crowd said	3
	22: 6	an opportunity…when no crowd was present.	3
	22:47	he was still speaking, suddenly a crowd came	3
	23: 4	the chief priests and the crowds	3
	23:48	when all the crowds who had gathered there	3
Jhn	5:13	for Jesus had disappeared in the crowd	3
	6: 2	A large crowd kept following him	3
	6: 5	saw a large crowd coming toward him	3
	6:22	the crowd that had stayed on the other side	3
	6:24	the crowd saw that neither Jesus nor his disciples	3
	7:12	considerable complaining about him among the crowds.	3
	7:12	were saying, "No, he is deceiving the crowd."	3

7:20	The crowd answered, "You have a demon!	3
7:31	Yet many in the crowd believed in him	3
7:32	The Pharisees heard the crowd muttering such things	3
7:40	some in the crowd said	3
7:43	there was a division in the crowd because of him.	3
7:49	this crowd, which does not know the law	3
11:42	said this for the sake of the crowd standing here	3
12: 9	When the great crowd of the Jews learned	3
12:12	great crowd that had come to the festival heard	3
12:17	So the crowd that had been with him	3
12:18	that the crowd went to meet him.	3
12:29	The crowd standing there heard it and said	3
12:34	crowd answered him, "We have heard from the law	3

Act	1:15	the crowd numbered about one hundred twenty persons)	3
	2: 6	at this sound the crowd gathered	4
	8: 6	The crowds with one accord listened eagerly	3
	13:45	when the Jews saw the crowds	3
	14:11	When the crowds saw what Paul had done	3
	14:13	he and the crowds wanted to offer sacrifice.	3
	14:14	and rushed out into the crowd, shouting	3
	14:18	they scarcely restrained the crowds	3
	14:19	won over the crowds.	3
	16:22	The crowd joined in attacking them	3
	17:13	stir up and incite the crowds.	3
	19:30	Paul wished to go into the crowd	2
	19:33	Some of the crowd gave instructions to Alexander	3
	19:35	when the town clerk had quieted the crowd	3
	21:27	stirred up the whole crowd. They seized him	3
	21:34	Some in the crowd shouted one thing, some another;	3
	21:36	The crowd that followed kept shouting	4
	24:12	They did not find me…stirring up a crowd	3
	24:18	without any crowd or disturbance.	3

crown

1. στέφανος², *stephanos²*, 5109
2. στεφανόω, *stephanoō*, 5110

Mat	27:29	twisting some thorns into a crown, they put it	1
Mrk	15:17	twisting some thorns into a crown, they put it on him.	1
Jhn	19: 2	the soldiers wove a crown of thorns	1
	19: 5	Jesus came out, wearing the crown of thorns	1
Php	4: 1	my joy and crown	1
1Th	2:19	For what is our hope or joy or crown of boasting	1
2Ti	2: 5	no one is crowned without competing according	2
	4: 8	is reserved for me the crown of righteousness	1
Heb	2: 7	you have crowned them with glory and honor	2
	2: 9	now crowned with glory and honor	2
Jas	1:12	the crown of life that the Lord has promised	1
1Pe	5: 4	you will win the crown of glory that never fades away.	1
Rev	2:10	and I will give you the crown of life.	1
	3:11	hold fast…so that no one may seize your crown.	1
	4: 4	elders…with golden crowns on their heads.	1
	4:10	they cast their crowns before the throne, singing	1
	6: 2	Its rider had a bow; a crown was given to him	1
	9: 7	On their heads…what looked like crowns of gold;	1
	12: 1	and on her head a crown of twelve stars.	1
	14:14	the Son of Man, with a golden crown on his head	1

crucify

1. Contextual: Not in Greek
2. προσπήγνυμι, *prospēgnymi*, 4699
3. σταυρόω, *stauroō*, 5090

Mat	20:19	to be mocked and flogged and crucified;	3
	23:34	some of whom you will kill and crucify	3
	26: 2	Son of Man will be handed over to be crucified."	3
	27:22	All of them said, "Let him be crucified!"	3
	27:23	"Let him be crucified!"	3
	27:26	handed him over to be crucified.	3
	27:31	Then they led him away to crucify him.	3
	27:35	when they had crucified him	3
	27:38	Then two bandits were crucified with him	3
	28: 5	you are looking for Jesus who was crucified.	3
Mrk	15:13	They shouted back, "Crucify him!"	3
	15:14	they shouted all the more, "Crucify him!"	3
	15:15	he handed him over to be crucified.	3
	15:20	they led him out to crucify him.	3
	15:24	they crucified him, and divided his clothes	3
	15:25	in the morning when they crucified him.	3
	15:27	with him they crucified two bandits	3
	16: 6	looking for Jesus of Nazareth, who was crucified.	3
Lke	23:21	they kept shouting, "Crucify, crucify him!"	3

	23:21	they kept shouting, "Crucify, crucify him!"	3
	23:23	that he should be crucified;	3
	23:33	they crucified Jesus there with the criminals	3
	24: 7	crucified, and on the third day rise again."	3
	24:20	condemned to death and crucified him.	3
Jhn	19: 6	they shouted, "Crucify him! Crucify him!"	3
	19: 6	they shouted, "Crucify him! Crucify him!"	3
	19: 6	"Take him yourselves and crucify him;	3
	19:10	I have…power to crucify you?"	3
	19:15	"Away with him! Away with him! Crucify him!"	3
	19:15	Pilate asked them, "Shall I crucify your King?"	3
	19:16	he handed him over to them to be crucified.	3
	19:18	they crucified him, and with him two others	3
	19:20	the place where Jesus was crucified	3
	19:23	When the soldiers had crucified Jesus	3
	19:31	to have the legs of the crucified men broken	1
	19:41	a garden in the place where he was crucified	3
Act	2:23	this man…you crucified and killed	2
	2:36	Lord and Messiah, this Jesus whom you crucified."	3
	4:10	Jesus Christ of Nazareth, whom you crucified	3
1Co	1:13	Has Christ been divided? Was Paul crucified for you?	3
	1:23	we proclaim Christ crucified	3
	2: 2	except Jesus Christ, and him crucified.	3
	2: 8	they would not have crucified the Lord of glory.	3
2Co	13: 4	For he was crucified in weakness	3
Gal	3: 1	Christ was publicly exhibited as crucified!	3
	5:24	crucified the flesh with its passions	3
	6:14	by which the world has been crucified to me	3
Rev	11: 8	great city…where also their Lord was crucified.	3

crucify again

1. ἀνασταυρόω, *anastauroō, 416*

Heb	6: 6	on their own they are crucifying again the Son of God	1

crucify with

1. συσταυρόω, *systauroō, 5365*

Mat	27:44	The bandits who were crucified with him	1
Mrk	15:32	Those who were crucified with him also taunted	1
Jhn	19:32	the other who had been crucified with him.	1
Rom	6: 6	We know that our old self was crucified with him	1
Gal	2:19	I have been crucified with Christ;	1

crumb

1. ψιχίον, *psichion, 6033*

Mat	15:27	"Yes, Lord, yet even the dogs eat the crumbs	1
Mrk	7:28	dogs under the table eat the children's crumbs."	1

crush

1. βαρέω, *bareō, 976*
2. θλίβω, *thlibō, 2567*
3. λικμάω, *likmaō, 3347*
4. στενοχωρέω, *stenochōreō, 5102*
5. συντρίβω, *syntribō, 5341*

Mat	21:44	it will crush anyone on whom it falls	3
Mrk	3: 9	the crowd, so that they would not crush him;	2
Lke	20:18	it will crush anyone on whom it falls."	3
Rom	16:20	God…will shortly crush Satan under your feet.	5
2Co	1: 8	we were so utterly, unbearably crushed	1
	4: 8	afflicted in every way, but not crushed;	4

crush to the ground

1. ἐδαφίζω, *edaphizō, 1610*

Lke	19:44	will crush you to the ground	1

cry

1. ἀναβοάω, *anaboaō, 331*
2. βοάω, *boaō, 1066*
3. βοή, *boē, 1068*
4. κράζω, *krazō, 3189*
5. κραυγάζω, *kraugazō, 3198*
6. κραυγή, *kraugē, 3199*
7. λέγω, *legō, 3306*
8. φωνέω, *phōneō, 5888*
9. φωνή, *phōnē, 5889*

Mat	9:27	two blind men followed him, crying loudly	4
	27:46	Jesus cried with a loud voice	1
	27:50	Jesus cried again with a loud voice	4
Mrk	1:26	convulsing him and crying with a loud voice	8
	15:37	Jesus gave a loud cry and breathed his last.	9

Lke	1:42	exclaimed with a loud cry, "Blessed are you	6
	18: 7	who cry to him day and night?	2
	23:46	Jesus, crying with a loud voice, said, "Father	8
Jhn	11:43	When he had said this, he cried with a loud voice	5
Act	8: 7	unclean spirits...crying with loud shrieks	2
Rom	8:15	a spirit of adoption. When we cry, "Abba! Father!"	4
Gal	4: 6	Spirit...into our hearts, crying, "Abba! Father!"	4
Heb	5: 7	supplications, with loud cries and tears	6
Jas	5: 4	cries of the harvesters have reached the ears	3
Rev	8:13	I heard an eagle crying with a loud voice	7
	14: 9	Then another angel, a third, followed them, crying	7
	21: 4	mourning and crying and pain will be no more	6

cry aloud

1. κράζω, *krazō, 3189*
2. κραυγάζω, *kraugazō, 3198*

Mat	12:19	He will not wrangle or cry aloud	2
Jhn	12:44	Jesus cried aloud: "Whoever believes in me	1

cry of command

1. κέλευσμα, *keleusma, 3026*

1Th	4:16	For the Lord himself, with a cry of command,	1

cry out

1. ἀνακράζω, *anakrazō, 371*
2. βοάω, *boaō, 1066*
3. κράζω, *krazō, 3189*
4. κραυγάζω, *kraugazō, 3198*
5. λέγω, *legō, 3306*

Mat	3: 3	"The voice of one crying out in the wilderness:	2
	14:26	And they cried out in fear.	3
	14:30	beginning to sink, he cried out, "Lord, save me!"	3
	21:15	heard the children crying out in the temple	3
Mrk	1: 3	the voice of one crying out in the wilderness:	2
	1:24	he cried out, "What have you to do with us	1
	6:49	they thought it was a ghost and cried out;	1
	9:24	Immediately the father of the child cried out	3
	9:26	After crying out and convulsing him terribly	3
	10:48	he cried out even more loudly, "Son of David	3
	15:34	At three o'clock Jesus cried out with a loud voice	2
Lke	3: 4	"The voice of one crying out in the wilderness:	2
	4:33	and he cried out with a loud voice	1
Jhn	1:15	(John testified to him and cried out	3
	1:23	"I am the voice of one crying out in the wilderness	2
	7:28	Jesus cried out as he was teaching in the temple	3
	7:37	Jesus was standing there, he cried out,	3
	19:12	the Jews cried out, "If you release this man	4
	19:15	They cried out, "Away with him! Away with him!	4
Act	7:60	he knelt down and cried out in a loud voice	3
	16:17	she followed Paul and us, she would cry out	3
Rom	9:27	And Isaiah cries out concerning Israel	3
Jas	5: 4	The wages...which you kept back by fraud, cry out	3
Rev	6:10	they cried out with a loud voice, "Sovereign Lord	3
	7:10	cried out in a loud voice, saying, "Salvation	3
	12: 2	and was crying out in birth pangs	3
	18:18	cried out as they saw the smoke of her burning	3
	18:19	as they wept and mourned, crying out, "Alas, alas	3
	19: 6	like the sound of mighty thunderpeals, crying out	5

crystal *See also* clear as crystal

1. κρύσταλλος, *krystallos, 3223*

Rev	4: 6	there is something like a sea of glass, like crystal.	1
	22: 1	river of the water of life, bright as crystal	1

cubit

1. πῆχυς, *pēchys, 4388*

Rev	21:17	measured its wall, one hundred forty-four cubits	1

cultivate *See also* cultivated *olive tree*

1. γεωργέω, *geōrgeō, 1175*

Heb	6: 7	useful to those for whom it is cultivated	1

cum

1. κοῦμ, *koum, 3182*

Mrk	5:41	and said to her, "Talitha cum,"	1

cummin

1. κύμινον, *kyminon, 3248*

Mat	23:23	you tithe mint, dill, and cummin	1

cunning

1. πανουργία, *panourgia, 4111*

2Co	4: 2	we refuse to practice cunning	1
	11: 3	as the serpent deceived Eve by its cunning	1

cup

1. ποτήριον, *potērion, 4539*

Mat	10:42	whoever gives even a cup of cold water to one	1
	20:22	Are you able to drink the cup that I am	1
	20:23	He said to them, "You will indeed drink my cup	1
	23:25	you clean the outside of the cup	1
	23:26	First clean the inside of the cup	1
	26:27	he took a cup	1
	26:39	if it is possible, let this cup pass from me	1
Mrk	7: 4	washing of cups, pots, and bronze kettles.)	1
	9:41	whoever gives you a cup of water to drink	1
	10:38	Are you able to drink the cup that I drink	1
	10:39	"The cup that I drink you will drink;	1
	14:23	he took a cup	1
	14:36	remove this cup from me;	1
Lke	11:39	"Now you Pharisees clean the outside of the cup	1
	22:17	he took a cup, and after giving thanks he said	1
	22:20	did the same with the cup after supper, saying,	1
	22:20	"This cup that is poured out for you	1
	22:42	if you are willing, remove this cup from me;	1
Jhn	18:11	to drink the cup that the Father has given me?"	1
1Co	10:16	The cup of blessing that we bless	1
	10:21	You cannot drink the cup of the Lord	1
	10:21	the cup of the Lord and the cup of demons.	1
	11:25	In the same way he took the cup also, after supper,	1
	11:25	"This cup is the new covenant in my blood.	1
	11:26	eat this bread and drink the cup	1
	11:27	drinks the cup of the Lord in an unworthy manner	1
	11:28	eat of the bread and drink of the cup.	1
Rev	14:10	poured unmixed into the cup of his anger	1
	17: 4	holding...a golden cup full of abominations	1
	18: 6	mix a double draught for her in the cup she mixed.	1

cure

1. θεραπεία, *therapeia, 2542*
2. θεραπεύω, *therapeuō, 2543*
3. ἰάομαι, *iaomai, 2615*
4. ἴασις, *iasis, 2617*

Mat	4:23	proclaiming the good news of the kingdom and curing	2
	4:24	paralytics, and he cured them.	2
	8: 7	he said to him, "I will come and cure him."	2
	8:16	and cured all who were sick.	2
	9:35	and curing every disease and every sickness.	2
	10: 1	and to cure every disease and every sickness.	2
	10: 8	Cure the sick, raise the dead, cleanse the lepers	2
	12:10	asked him, "Is it lawful to cure on the sabbath?"	2
	12:15	Many crowds followed him, and he cured all	2
	12:22	he cured him, so that the one who had been mute	2
	14:14	and cured their sick.	2
	15:30	They put them at his feet, and he cured them	2
	17:16	but they could not cure him."	2
	17:18	and the boy was cured instantly.	2
	19: 2	and he cured them there.	2
	21:14	came to him in the temple, and he cured them.	2
Mrk	1:34	cured many who were sick with various diseases	2
	3: 2	whether he would cure him on the sabbath	2
	3:10	he had cured many	2
	6: 5	and cured them.	2
	6:13	and cured them.	2
Lke	4:23	'Doctor, cure yourself!'	2
	4:40	and cured them.	2
	5:15	to be cured of their diseases.	2
	6: 7	to see whether he would cure on the sabbath	2
	6:18	troubled with unclean spirits were cured.	2
	7:21	Jesus had just then cured many people of diseases	2
	8: 2	some women who had been cured of evil spirits	2
	8:43	on physicians, no one could cure her.	2
	9: 1	gave them power...to cure diseases	2
	9: 6	the good news and curing diseases everywhere.	2
	9:11	healed those who needed to be cured.	1
	10: 9	cure the sick who are there, and say to them	2
	13:14	Jesus had cured on the sabbath	2
	13:14	come on those days and be cured	2
	13:32	I am casting out demons and performing cures today	4
	14: 3	"Is it lawful to cure people on the sabbath,	2

Jhn 5:10 the Jews said to the man who had been cured 2
Act 4:14 saw the man who had been cured 2
     5:16 they were all cured. 2
     8: 7 many others who were paralyzed or lame were cured. 2
     28: 8 cured him by praying and putting his hands on him. 3
     28: 9 rest of the people...also came and were cured. 2

curse

1. ἀνάθεμα, *anathema, 353*
2. ἀναθεματίζω, *anathematizō, 354*
3. ἀρά, *ara, 725*
4. βλασφημέω, *blasphēmeō, 1059*
5. ἐπικατάρατος, *epikataratos, 2129*
6. καταθεματίζω, *katathematizō, 2874*
7. κατάρα, *katara, 2932*
8. καταράομαι, *kataraomai, 2933*

Mat 26:74 he began to curse, and he swore an oath 6
Mrk 11:21 The fig tree that you cursed has withered." 8
     14:71 he began to curse, and he swore an oath 2
Lke 6:28 bless those who curse you 8
Rom 3:14 "Their mouths are full of cursing and bitterness." 3
     12:14 who persecute you; bless and do not curse them. 8
1Co 12: 3 "Let Jesus be cursed!" 1
Gal 3:10 rely on the works of the law are under a curse; 7
     3:10 for it is written, "Cursed is everyone 5
     3:13 Christ redeemed us from the curse of the law 7
     3:13 Christ redeemed us...by becoming a curse for us 7
     3:13 "Cursed is everyone who hangs on a tree"— 5
Heb 6: 8 it is worthless and on the verge of being cursed; 7
Jas 3: 9 with it we curse those...in the likeness of God. 8
     3:10 From the same mouth come blessing and cursing. 7
Rev 16: 9 but they cursed the name of God 4
     16:11 cursed the God of heaven because of their pains 4
     16:21 until they cursed God for the plague of the hail 4

curtain

1. καταπέτασμα, *katapetasma, 2925*

Mat 27:51 the curtain of the temple was torn in two 1
Mrk 15:38 the curtain of the temple was torn in two 1
Lke 23:45 the curtain of the temple was torn in two. 1
Heb 6:19 enters the inner shrine behind the curtain 1
     9: 3 Behind the second curtain was a tent 1
     10:20 through the curtain (that is, through his flesh) 1

cushion

1. προσκεφάλαιον, *proskephalaion, 4676*

Mrk 4:38 he was in the stern, asleep on the cushion; 1

custody *See also* keep in custody

1. τήρησις, *tērēsis, 5499*

Act 4: 3 put them in custody until the next day 1

custom

1. ἔθος, *ethos, 1621*
2. εἴωθα, *eiōtha, 1665*
3. καθώς, *kathōs, 2777*
4. συνήθεια, *synētheia, 5311*

Mrk 10: 1 as was his custom, he again taught them. 2
     15: 8 Pilate to do for them according to his custom. 3
Lke 1: 9 according to the custom of the priesthood 1
     4:16 synagogue on the sabbath day, as was his custom. 2
     22:39 went, as was his custom, to the Mount of Olives; 1
Jhn 18:39 you have a custom that I release someone 4
     19:40 according to the burial custom of the Jews. 1
Act 6:14 change the customs that Moses handed on to us." 1
     15: 1 circumcised according to the custom of Moses 1
     16:21 advocating customs that are not lawful for us 1
     17: 2 Paul went in, as was his custom 2
     21:21 not to circumcise...or observe the customs. 1
     25:16 not the custom of the Romans to hand over anyone 1
     26: 3 you are especially familiar with all the customs 1
     28:17 against our people or the customs of our ancestors 1
1Co 11:16 we have no such custom, nor do the churches 4

customary

1. Contextual: Not in Greek
2. ἐθίζω, *ethizō, 1616*

Lke 2:27 to do for him what was customary under the law 2
Act 24: 4 to hear us briefly with your customary graciousness. 1

cut

1. ἐκκόπτω, *ekkoptō, 1716*
2. κατανύσσομαι, *katanyssomai, 2920*
3. κείρω, *keirō, 3025*
4. κόπτω, *koptō, 3164*

Mat 21: 8 others cut branches from the trees 4
Mrk 11: 8 others spread leafy branches that they had cut 4
Act 2:37 when they heard this, they were cut to the heart 2
     18:18 At Cenchreae he had his hair cut, 3
Rom 11:24 cut from what is by nature a wild olive tree 1

cut away

1. ἀποκόπτω, *apokoptō, 644*

Act 27:32 Then the soldiers cut away the ropes of the boat 1

cut down

1. ἐκκόπτω, *ekkoptō, 1716*

Mat 3:10 good fruit is cut down and thrown into the fire. 1
     7:19 tree...is cut down and thrown into the fire. 1
Lke 3: 9 tree...is cut down and thrown into the fire." 1
     13: 7 Cut it down! Why should it be wasting the soil?' 1
     13: 9 but if not, you can cut it down.' " 1

cut in pieces

1. διχοτομέω, *dichotomeō, 1497*

Mat 24:51 He will cut him in pieces and put him with 1
Lke 12:46 will cut him in pieces, and put him with 1

cut off

1. ἀπό, *apo, 608*
2. ἀποκόπτω, *apokoptō, 644*
3. ἀφαιρέω, *aphaireō, 904*
4. ἐκκόπτω, *ekkoptō, 1716*
5. καταργέω, *katargeō, 2934*

Mat 5:30 if your right hand causes you to sin, cut it off 4
     18: 8 or your foot...cut it off and throw it away; 4
     26:51 cutting off his ear. 3
Mrk 9:43 If your hand causes you to stumble, cut it off; 2
     9:45 if your foot causes you to stumble, cut it off; 2
     14:47 struck the slave...cutting off his ear. 3
Lke 22:50 and cut off his right ear. 3
Jhn 18:10 and cut off his right ear. 2
     18:26 relative of the man whose ear Peter had cut off 2
Rom 9: 3 that I myself were accursed and cut off from Christ 1
     11:22 otherwise you also will be cut off. 4
Gal 5: 4 by the law have cut yourselves off from Christ; 5

cut off hair

1. κείρω, *keirō, 3025*

1Co 11: 6 then she should cut off her hair; 1
     11: 6 disgraceful for a woman to have her hair cut off 1

cut short

1. κολοβόω, *koloboō, 3143*

Mat 24:22 if those days had not been cut short 1
     24:22 those days will be cut short. 1
Mrk 13:20 if the Lord had not cut short those days 1
     13:20 he has cut short those days. 1

cycle

1. τροχός, *trochos, 5580*

Jas 3: 6 sets on fire the cycle of nature 1

cymbal

1. κύμβαλον, *kymbalon, 3247*

1Co 13: 1 I am a noisy gong or a clanging cymbal. 1

Cyprus

1. Κύπριος, *Kyprios, 3250*
2. Κύπρος, *Kypros, 3251*

Act 4:36 a Levite, a native of Cyprus, Joseph, 1
     11:19 traveled as far as Phoenicia, Cyprus, and Antioch 2
     11:20 among them were some men of Cyprus and Cyrene 1
     13: 4 from there they sailed to Cyprus. 2
     15:39 Barnabas...sailed away to Cyprus. 2
     21: 3 We came in sight of Cyprus; 2
     21:16 brought us to the house of Mnason of Cyprus 1
     27: 4 we sailed under the lee of Cyprus 2

Cyrene

1. Κυρηναῖος, *Kyrēnaios, 3254*
2. Κυρήνη, *Kyrēnē, 3255*

Mat 27:32 they came upon a man from Cyrene named Simon; 1
Mrk 15:21 to carry his cross; it was Simon of Cyrene 1
Lke 23:26 they seized a man, Simon of Cyrene 1
Act 2:10 Egypt and the parts of Libya belonging to Cyrene 2
    11:20 among them were some men of Cyprus and Cyrene 1
    13: 1 Lucius of Cyrene 1

Cyrenian

1. Κυρηναῖος, *Kyrēnaios, 3254*

Act 6: 9 Cyrenians, Alexandrians, and others 1

D

daily *See also* daily *life,* usual daily wage

1. ἐπιούσιος, *epiousios, 2157*
2. ἐφήμερος, *ephēmeros, 2390*
3. ἡμέρα, *hēmera, 2465*
4. καθημερινός, *kathēmerinos, 2766*
5. κατά + ἡμέρα, *kata + hēmera, 2848 + 2465*

Mat 6:11 Give us this day our daily bread. 1
    20: 2 for the usual daily wage 3
Lke 9:23 take up their cross daily and follow me. 5
    11: 3 Give us each day our daily bread. 1
Act 3: 2 People would lay him daily at the gate of the temple 5
    6: 1 neglected in the daily distribution of food 4
    16: 5 increased in numbers daily. 5
    19: 9 argued daily in the lecture hall of Tyrannus. 5
2Co 11:28 I am under daily pressure 5
Jas 2:15 If a brother or sister…lacks daily food 2

dainty

1. λιπαρός, *liparos, 3353*

Rev 18:14 your dainties and your splendor are lost to you 1

Dalmanutha

1. Δαλμανουθά, *Dalmanoutha, 1236*

Mrk 8:10 went to the district of Dalmanutha. 1

Dalmatia

1. Δαλματία, *Dalmatia, 1237*

2Ti 4:10 Crescens has gone to Galatia, Titus to Dalmatia. 1

damage

1. ἀδικέω, *adikeō, 92*
2. ὕβρις, *hybris, 5615*

Act 27:21 avoided this damage and loss. 2
Rev 6: 6 but do not damage the olive oil and the wine!" 1
    7: 2 angels who had been given power to damage earth 1
    7: 3 "Do not damage the earth or the sea or the trees 1
    9: 4 They were told not to damage the grass of the earth 1

Damaris

1. Δάμαρις, *Damaris, 1240*

Act 17:34 a woman named Damaris, and others with them. 1

Damascus

1. Δαμασκηνός, *Damaskēnos, 1241*
2. Δαμασκός, *Damaskos, 1242*

Act 9: 2 letters to the synagogues at Damascus 2
    9: 3 Now as he was going along and approaching Damascus 2
    9: 8 brought him into Damascus. 2
    9:10 there was a disciple in Damascus named Ananias. 2
    9:19 he was with the disciples in Damascus 2
    9:22 confounded the Jews who lived in Damascus 2
    9:27 how in Damascus he had spoken boldly 2
    22: 5 letters to the brothers in Damascus 2
    22: 6 "While I was on my way and approaching Damascus 2
    22:10 The Lord said to me, 'Get up and go to Damascus; 2
    22:11 took my hand and led me to Damascus. 2
    26:12 "With this in mind, I was traveling to Damascus 2
    26:20 declared first to those in Damascus 2
2Co 11:32 In Damascus, the governor under King Aretas 2
    11:32 guarded the city of Damascus in order to seize me 1
Gal 1:17 afterwards I returned to Damascus. 2

dance

1. ὀρχέομαι, *orcheomai, 4004*
2. χορός, *choros, 5962*

Mat 11:17 'We played the flute for you, and you did not dance; 1
    14: 6 the daughter of Herodias danced 1
Mrk 6:22 When his daughter Herodias came in and danced 1
Lke 7:32 played the flute for you, and you did not dance; 1
    15:25 he heard music and dancing. 2

danger

1. κινδυνεύω, *kindyneuō, 3073*
2. κίνδυνος, *kindynos, 3074*
3. ὕβρις, *hybris, 5615*

Lke 8:23 filling with water, and they were in danger. 1
Act 19:27 danger not only that this trade of ours 1
    19:40 we are in danger of being charged with rioting 1
    27:10 the voyage will be with danger and much heavy loss 3
1Co 15:30 why are we putting ourselves in danger every hour? 1
2Co 11:26 on frequent journeys, in danger from rivers 2
    11:26 in danger from rivers, danger from bandits 2
    11:26 danger from bandits, danger from my own people 2
    11:26 danger from Gentiles, danger in the city 2
    11:26 danger from Gentiles, danger in the city 2
    11:26 danger in the city, danger in the wilderness 2
    11:26 danger at sea, danger from false brothers and sisters; 2
    11:26 danger at sea, danger from false brothers and sisters; 2

dangerous

1. ἐπισφαλής, *episphalēs, 2195*

Act 27: 9 sailing was now dangerous 1

Daniel

1. Δανιήλ, *Daniēl, 1248*

Mat 24:15 as was spoken of by the prophet Daniel 1

dare

1. Contextual: Not in Greek
2. τολμάω, *tolmaō, 5528*

Mat 22:46 did anyone dare to ask him any more questions. 2
Mrk 12:34 After that no one dared to ask him any question. 2
Lke 20:40 they no longer dared to ask him another question. 2
Jhn 21:12 the disciples dared to ask him, "Who are you?" 2
Act 5:13 None of the rest dared to join them 2
    7:32 Moses began to tremble and did not dare to look. 2
    23: 4 "Do you dare to insult God's high priest?" 1
Rom 5: 7 for a good person someone might actually dare to die. 2
1Co 6: 1 you dare to take it to court before the unrighteous 2
2Co 10: 2 need not show boldness by daring to oppose 2
    10:12 We do not dare to classify or compare ourselves 2
    11:21 whatever anyone dares to boast 2
    11:21 I also dare to boast of that. 2
Php 1:14 dare to speak the word with greater boldness 1
Jde 1: 9 did not dare to bring a condemnation of slander 2

dark

1. αὐχμηρός, *auchmēros, 903*
2. σκοτία, *skotia, 5028*

Mat 10:27 What I say to you in the dark, tell in the light; 2
Lke 12: 3 Therefore whatever you have said in the dark 2
Jhn 6:17 It was now dark 2
    20: 1 first day of the week, while it was still dark 2
2Pe 1:19 as to a lamp shining in a dark place 1

while still dark

1. ἔννυχος, *ennychos, 1939*

Mrk 1:35 In the morning, while it was still very dark 1

darken

1. σκοτίζομαι, *skotizomai, 5029*
2. σκοτόω, *skotoō, 5031*

Mat 24:29 the sun will be darkened 1
Mrk 13:24 after that suffering, the sun will be darkened 1
Rom 1:21 and their senseless minds were darkened. 1
    11:10 their eyes be darkened so that they cannot see 1
Eph 4:18 They are darkened in their understanding 2
Rev 8:12 so that a third of their light was darkened; 1
    9: 2 the sun and the air were darkened with the smoke 2

darkness   *See also* full of darkness

1. γνόφος, *gnophos, 1190*
2. σκοτεινός, *skoteinos, 5027*
3. σκοτία, *skotia, 5028*
4. σκότος, *skotos, 5030*
5. σκοτόω, *skotoō, 5031*

Mat	4:16	people who sat in darkness have seen a great light	4
	6:23	your whole body will be full of darkness.	2
	6:23	If then the light in you is darkness	4
	6:23	you is darkness, how great is the darkness!	4
	8:12	heirs…will be thrown into the outer darkness	4
	22:13	and throw him into the outer darkness	4
	25:30	throw him into the outer darkness	4
	27:45	darkness came over the whole land	4
Mrk	15:33	darkness came over the whole land	4
Lke	1:79	to give light to those who sit in darkness	4
	11:35	consider whether the light in you is not darkness.	4
	11:36	full of light, with no part of it in darkness	2
	22:53	this is your hour, and the power of darkness!"	4
	23:44	darkness came over the whole land until three	4
Jhn	1: 5	The light shines in the darkness	3
	1: 5	and the darkness did not overcome it.	3
	3:19	and people loved darkness rather than light	4
	8:12	Whoever follows me will never walk in darkness	3
	12:35	so that the darkness may not overtake you.	3
	12:35	If you walk in the darkness	3
	12:46	should not remain in the darkness.	3
Act	2:20	The sun shall be turned to darkness	4
	13:11	Immediately mist and darkness came over him	4
	26:18	they may turn from darkness to light	4
Rom	2:19	a light to those who are in darkness	4
	13:12	Let us then lay aside the works of darkness	4
1Co	4: 5	the things now hidden in darkness	4
2Co	4: 6	the God who said, "Let light shine out of darkness,"	4
	6:14	what fellowship is there between light and darkness?	4
Eph	5: 8	For once you were darkness, but now in the Lord	4
	5:11	Take no part in the unfruitful works of darkness	4
	6:12	against the cosmic powers of this present darkness	4
Col	1:13	has rescued us from the power of darkness	4
1Th	5: 4	you, beloved, are not in darkness	4
	5: 5	we are not of the night or of darkness.	4
Heb	12:18	a blazing fire, and darkness, and gloom	1
1Pe	2: 9	called you out of darkness into…light.	4
2Pe	2:17	the deepest darkness has been reserved.	4
1Jn	1: 5	God is light and in him there is no darkness at all.	3
	1: 6	while we are walking in darkness	4
	2: 8	because the darkness is passing away	3
	2: 9	while hating a brother or sister, is still in the darkness.	3
	2:11	whoever hates another believer is in the darkness	3
	2:11	is in the darkness, walks in the darkness	3
	2:11	because the darkness has brought on blindness.	3
Jde	1:13	the deepest darkness has been reserved forever.	4
Rev	16:10	the beast, and its kingdom was plunged into darkness;	5

deep darkness

1. ζόφος, *zophos, 2432*

2Pe	2: 4	God…committed them to chains of deepest darkness	1
	2:17	the deepest darkness has been reserved.	1
Jde	1: 6	he has kept in eternal chains in deepest darkness	1
	1:13	the deepest darkness has been reserved forever.	1

dash

1. προσκόπτω, *proskoptō, 4684*

Mat	4: 6	so that you will not dash your foot against a stone.' "	1
Lke	4:11	you will not dash your foot against a stone.' "	1

dash down

1. ῥήγνυμι, *rhēgnymi, 4838*

Mrk	9:18	whenever it seizes him, it dashes him down;	1

dash to the ground

1. ῥήγνυμι, *rhēgnymi, 4838*

Lke	9:42	the demon dashed him to the ground in convulsions.	1

date   *See* set date

daughter

1. θυγάτηρ, *thygatēr, 2588*
2. τέκνον, *teknon, 5451*

Mat	9:18	saying, "My daughter has just died;	1
	9:22	"Take heart, daughter; your faith has made you	1
	10:35	and a daughter against her mother	1
	10:37	and whoever loves son or daughter more than me	1
	14: 6	the daughter of Herodias danced	1
	15:22	my daughter is tormented by a demon."	1
	15:28	And her daughter was healed instantly.	1
	21: 5	"Tell the daughter of Zion.	1
Mrk	5:34	"Daughter, your faith has made you well;	1
	5:35	"Your daughter is dead."	1
	6:22	When his daughter Herodias came in and danced	1
	7:26	begged him to cast the demon out of her daughter.	1
	7:29	the demon has left your daughter."	1
Lke	2:36	a prophet, Anna the daughter of Phanuel	1
	8:42	for he had an only daughter…who was dying	1
	8:48	"Daughter, your faith has made you well;	1
	8:49	"Your daughter is dead; do not trouble the teacher	1
	12:53	mother against daughter	1
	12:53	daughter against mother	1
	13:16	a daughter of Abraham whom Satan bound	1
	23:28	"Daughters of Jerusalem, do not weep for me	1
Jhn	12:15	"Do not be afraid, daughter of Zion.	1
Act	2:17	your sons and your daughters shall prophesy	1
	7:21	Pharaoh's daughter adopted him	1
	21: 9	four unmarried daughters who had the gift of prophecy.	1
2Co	6:18	be my sons and daughters, says the Lord Almighty."	1
Heb	11:24	refused to be called a son of Pharaoh's daughter	1
1Pe	3: 6	You have become her daughters as long as you do	2

little daughter

1. θυγάτριον, *thygatrion, 2589*

Mrk	5:23	"My little daughter is at the point of death.	1
	7:25	woman whose little daughter had an unclean spirit	1

daughter-in-law

1. νύμφη, *nymphē, 3811*

Mat	10:35	a daughter-in-law against her mother-in-law;	1
Lke	12:53	mother-in-law against her daughter-in-law	1
	12:53	daughter-in-law against mother-in-law."	1

David

1. Contextual: Not in Greek
2. Δαυίδ, *Dauid, 1253*

Mat	1: 1	Jesus the Messiah, the son of David, the son of Abraham.	2
	1: 6	Jesse the father of King David.	2
	1: 6	David was the father of Solomon by the wife	2
	1:17	So all the generations from Abraham to David	2
	1:17	and from David to the deportation to Babylon	2
	1:20	said, "Joseph, son of David, do not be afraid	2
	9:27	"Have mercy on us, Son of David!"	2
	12: 3	He said to them, "Have you not read what David did	2
	12:23	"Can this be the Son of David?"	2
	15:22	"Have mercy on me, Lord, Son of David;	2
	20:30	"Lord, have mercy on us, Son of David!"	2
	20:31	"Have mercy on us, Lord, Son of David!"	2
	21: 9	shouting, "Hosanna to the Son of David!	2
	21:15	"Hosanna to the Son of David,"	2
	22:42	They said to him, "The son of David."	2
	22:43	"How is it then that David by the Spirit	2
	22:45	If David thus calls him Lord, how can he be his son?"	2
Mrk	2:25	"Have you never read what David did	2
	10:47	"Jesus, Son of David, have mercy on me!"	2
	10:48	"Son of David, have mercy on me!"	2
	11:10	the coming kingdom of our ancestor David!	2
	12:35	say that the Messiah is the son of David?	2
	12:36	David himself, by the Holy Spirit, declared	2
	12:37	David himself calls him Lord; so how can he be	2
Lke	1:27	Joseph, of the house of David.	2
	1:32	give to him the throne of his ancestor David.	2
	1:69	in the house of his servant David	2
	2: 4	to the city of David called Bethlehem	2
	2: 4	descended from the house and family of David.	2
	2:11	born this day in the city of David a Savior	2
	3:31	son of Nathan, son of David	2
	6: 3	Jesus answered, "Have you not read what David did	2
	18:38	"Jesus, Son of David, have mercy on me!"	2
	18:39	"Son of David, have mercy on me!"	2
	20:41	"How can they say that the Messiah is David's son?	2
	20:42	For David himself says in the book of Psalms	2
	20:44	David thus calls him Lord; so how can he be his son?"	2

Jhn	7:42	the Messiah is descended from David	2
	7:42	from Bethlehem, the village where David lived?"	2
Act	1:16	which the Holy Spirit through David foretold	2
	2:25	David says concerning him, 'I saw the Lord	2
	2:29	say to you confidently of our ancestor David	2
	2:31	Foreseeing this, David spoke of the resurrection	1
	2:34	David did not ascend into the heavens	2
	4:25	Holy Spirit through our ancestor David, your servant:	2
	7:45	And it was there until the time of David	2
	13:22	he made David their king.	2
	13:22	'I have found David, son of Jesse, to be a man	2
	13:34	give you the holy promises made to David.'	2
	13:36	David...died, was laid beside his ancestors	2
	15:16	rebuild the dwelling of David, which has fallen;	2
Rom	1: 3	descended from David according to the flesh	2
	4: 6	So also David speaks of the blessedness of those	2
	11: 9	And David says, "Let their table become a snare	2
2Ti	2: 8	descendant of David—that is my gospel	2
Heb	4: 7	saying through David much later	2
	11:32	to tell of Gideon, Barak, Samson, Jephthah, of David	2
Rev	3: 7	holy one, the true one, who has the key of David	2
	5: 5	the Lion...the Root of David, has conquered	2
	22:16	I am the root and the descendant of David	2

dawn *See also* near dawn

1. ἀνατέλλω, *anatellō*, 422
2. ἀνατολή, *anatolē*, 424
3. αὐγή, *augē*, 879
4. διαυγάζω, *diaugazō*, 1419
5. ἐπιφώσκω, *epiphōskō*, 2216
6. πρωΐ, *prōi*, 4745

Mat	4:16	region and shadow of death light has dawned."	1
	28: 1	as the first day of the week was dawning	5
Mrk	13:35	at midnight, or at cockcrow, or at dawn,	6
Lke	1:78	the dawn from on high will break upon us	2
Act	20:11	continued to converse with them until dawn;	3
2Pe	1:19	until the day dawns and the morning star rises	4

early dawn

1. ὄρθρος, *orthros*, 3986

Lke	24: 1	on the first day of the week, at early dawn	1

day *See also* day's *pay*, four days, night and a day, pass days, write in former days

1. Contextual: Not in Greek
2. ἡμέρα, *hēmera*, 2465

Mat	3: 1	In those days John the Baptist appeared	2
	4: 2	He fasted forty days and forty nights	2
	7:22	On that day many will say to me, 'Lord, Lord	2
	9:15	The days will come when the bridegroom is taken	2
	10:15	land of Sodom and Gomorrah on the day of judgment	2
	11:12	From the days of John the Baptist until now	2
	11:22	on the day of judgment it will be more tolerable	2
	11:24	on the day of judgment it will be more tolerable	2
	12:36	the day of judgment you will have to give an account	2
	12:40	For just as Jonah was three days and three nights	2
	12:40	so for three days and three nights the Son	2
	13: 1	That same day Jesus went out of the house and sat	2
	15:32	because they have been with me now for three days	2
	16:21	and be killed, and on the third day be raised.	2
	17: 1	Six days later, Jesus took with him Peter	2
	17:23	on the third day he will be raised."	2
	20: 6	'Why are you standing here idle all day?'	2
	20:12	the burden of the day and the scorching heat.'	2
	20:19	on the third day he will be raised."	2
	22:23	The same day some Sadducees came to him	2
	22:46	nor from that day did anyone dare to ask him	2
	23:30	'If we had lived in the days of our ancestors	2
	24:19	those who are nursing infants in those days!	2
	24:22	if those days had not been cut short	2
	24:22	those days will be cut short.	2
	24:29	after the suffering of those days	2
	24:36	about that day and hour no one knows	2
	24:37	For as the days of Noah were	2
	24:38	For as in those days before the flood	2
	24:38	until the day Noah entered the ark	2
	24:42	you do not know on what day your Lord is coming.	2
	24:50	the master of that slave will come on a day	2
	25:13	you know neither the day nor the hour.	2
	26: 2	after two days the Passover is coming	2

	26:17	On the first day of Unleavened Bread	1
	26:29	until that day when I drink it new with you	2
	26:61	to build it in three days.' "	2
	27:40	destroy the temple and build it in three days	2
	27:62	next day, that is, after the day of Preparation	1
	27:63	'After three days I will rise again.'	2
	27:64	to be made secure until the third day;	2
	28: 1	as the first day of the week was dawning	1
	28:15	story is still told among the Jews to this day.	2
Mrk	1: 9	In those days Jesus came from Nazareth of Galilee	2
	1:13	He was in the wilderness forty days	2
	2: 1	When he returned to Capernaum after some days	2
	2:20	The days will come when the bridegroom is taken	2
	2:20	then they will fast on that day.	2
	4:27	sleep and rise night and day	2
	4:35	On that day, when evening had come, he said	2
	5: 5	Night and day among the tombs	2
	8: 1	In those days when there was again a great crowd	2
	8: 2	because they have been with me now for three days	2
	8:31	be killed, and after three days rise again.	2
	9: 2	Six days later, Jesus took with him Peter	2
	9:31	three days after being killed, he will rise again."	2
	10:34	after three days he will rise again."	2
	13:17	those who are nursing infants in those days!	2
	13:19	For in those days there will be suffering	2
	13:20	if the Lord had not cut short those days	2
	13:20	he has cut short those days.	2
	13:24	in those days, after that suffering	2
	13:32	about that day or hour no one knows	2
	14: 1	It was two days before the Passover	2
	14:12	On the first day of Unleavened Bread	2
	14:25	until that day when I drink it new in the kingdom	2
	14:58	in three days I will build another	2
	15:29	destroy the temple and build it in three days	2
	16: 2	very early on the first day of the week	1
	16: 9	⟦after he rose early on the first day of the week⟧	1
Lke	1: 5	In the days of King Herod of Judea	2
	1:20	unable to speak, until the day these things occur	2
	1:24	After those days his wife Elizabeth conceived	2
	1:39	In those days Mary set out	2
	1:59	On the eighth day they came to circumcise	2
	1:75	before him all our days.	2
	1:80	until the day he appeared publicly to Israel.	2
	2: 1	In those days a decree went out	2
	2:21	After eight days had passed, it was time	2
	2:37	with fasting and prayer night and day.	2
	2:44	they went a day's journey.	2
	2:46	After three days they found him in the temple	2
	4: 2	for forty days he was tempted by the devil.	2
	4: 2	He ate nothing at all during those days	2
	4:16	on the sabbath day, as was his custom.	2
	5:17	One day, while he was teaching	2
	5:35	The days will come when the bridegroom	2
	5:35	then they will fast in those days."	2
	6:12	Now during those days he went out...to pray;	2
	6:13	when day came, he called his disciples	2
	6:23	Rejoice in that day and leap for joy	2
	8:22	One day he got into a boat with his disciples	2
	9:12	The day was drawing to a close	2
	9:22	be killed, and on the third day be raised."	2
	9:28	Now about eight days after these sayings	2
	9:36	they kept silent and in those days told no one	2
	9:37	On the next day	2
	9:51	When the days drew near for him to be taken up	2
	10:12	on that day it will be more tolerable for Sodom	2
	11: 3	Give us each day our daily bread	2
	12:46	on a day when he does not expect him	2
	13:14	"There are six days on which work ought to	2
	13:14	come on those days and be cured	1
	13:14	not on the sabbath day."	2
	13:16	set free from this bondage on the sabbath day?"	1
	13:32	the third day I finish my work.	2
	13:33	tomorrow, and the next day I must be on my way	1
	14: 5	not immediately pull it out on a sabbath day?"	2
	15:13	few days later the younger son gathered all	2
	17: 4	same person sins against you seven times a day	2
	17:22	he said to the disciples, "The days are coming	2
	17:22	will long to see one of the days of the Son of Man	2
	17:24	so will the Son of Man be in his day.	2
	17:26	Just as it was in the days of Noah	2
	17:26	so too it will be in the days of the Son of Man.	2

17:27	until the day Noah entered the ark	2
17:28	Likewise, just as it was in the days of Lot:	2
17:29	on the day that Lot left Sodom	2
17:30	on the day that the Son of Man is revealed.	2
17:31	On that day, anyone on the housetop	2
18: 7	who cry to him day and night?	2
18:33	on the third day he will rise again."	2
19:42	on this day the things that make for peace!	2
19:43	Indeed, the days will come upon you	2
20: 1	One day, as he was teaching the people	2
21: 6	the days will come when not one stone will be left	2
21:22	these are days of vengeance	2
21:23	those who are nursing infants in those days!	2
21:34	and that day does not catch you unexpectedly	2
21:37	Every day he was teaching in the temple	2
22: 7	day…on which the Passover lamb had to be sacrificed.	2
22:66	When day came	2
23:12	That same day Herod and Pilate became friends	2
23:29	For the days are surely coming when they will say	2
23:54	It was the day of Preparation	2
24: 1	on the first day of the week, at early dawn	1
24: 7	crucified, and on the third day rise again."	2
24:13	that same day two of them were going to a village	2
24:18	things that have taken place there in these days?"	2
24:21	now the third day since these things took place.	2
24:29	almost evening and the day is now nearly over."	2
24:46	rise from the dead on the third day	2
Jhn 1:39	and they remained with him that day.	2
2: 1	On the third day there was a wedding in Cana	2
2:12	and they remained there a few days.	2
2:19	this temple, and in three days I will raise it up."	2
2:20	and will you raise it up in three days?"	2
4:40	and he stayed there two days.	2
4:43	the two days were over, he went from that place	2
5: 9	Now that day was a sabbath.	2
6:39	but raise it up on the last day.	2
6:40	I will raise them up on the last day."	2
6:44	I will raise that person up on the last day.	2
6:54	I will raise them up on the last day;	2
7:37	On the last day of the festival, the great day	2
7:37	On the last day of the festival, the great day	1
8:56	Abraham rejoiced that he would see my day;	2
9: 4	work the works of him who sent me while it is day;	2
9:14	it was a sabbath day when Jesus made the mud	2
11: 6	he stayed two days longer in the place	2
11: 9	Those who walk during the day do not stumble	2
11:17	Lazarus had already been in the tomb four days.	2
11:24	rise again in the resurrection on the last day."	2
11:53	So from that day on they planned	2
12: 1	Six days before the Passover	2
12: 7	she might keep it for the day of my burial.	2
12:48	on the last day the word…will serve as judge	2
14:20	On that day you will know that I am in my Father	2
16:23	On that day you will ask nothing of me.	2
16:26	On that day you will ask in my name.	2
19:31	because that sabbath was a day of great solemnity.	2
20: 1	Early on the first day of the week	1
20:19	When it was evening on that day,	2
20:19	the first day of the week	1
Act 1: 2	until the day when he was taken up to heaven	2
1: 3	appearing to them during forty days	2
1: 5	baptized with the Holy Spirit not many days from now."	2
1:12	is near Jerusalem, a sabbath day's journey away.	1
1:15	In those days Peter stood up among the believers	2
1:22	until the day when he was taken up from us	2
2: 1	When the day of Pentecost had come	2
2:17	'In the last days it will be, God declares	2
2:18	in those days I will pour out my Spirit;	2
2:20	before the coming of the Lord's great and glorious day.	2
2:29	his tomb is with us to this day.	2
2:41	that day about three thousand persons were added.	2
3:24	also predicted these days.	2
5:42	every day in the temple and at home	2
6: 1	Now during those days	2
7: 8	circumcised him on the eighth day;	2
7:26	The next day he came to some of them	2
8: 1	That day a severe persecution began	2
9: 9	For three days he was without sight	2
9:19	For several days he was with the disciples	2
9:24	They were watching the gates day and night	2
10:30	Cornelius replied, "Four days ago at this very hour	2

10:40	God raised him on the third day	2
10:48	Then they invited him to stay for several days.	2
12:21	On an appointed day Herod put on his royal robes	2
13:14	on the sabbath day they went into the synagogue	2
13:31	for many days he appeared	2
13:41	for in your days I am doing a work	2
15: 7	in the early days God made a choice among you	2
15:36	After some days Paul said to Barnabas, "Come	2
16:11	the following day to Neapolis	1
16:12	We remained in this city for some days.	2
16:13	On the sabbath day we went outside the gate	2
16:18	She kept doing this for many days.	2
17: 2	on three sabbath days argued with them	1
17:17	he argued…in the marketplace every day	2
17:31	fixed a day on which he will have the world judged	2
20: 6	we sailed…after the days of Unleavened Bread	2
20: 6	in five days we joined them in Troas	2
20: 6	Troas, where we stayed for seven days.	2
20: 7	On the first day of the week	1
20:15	the following day we arrived opposite Chios.	1
20:15	The next day we touched at Samos	1
20:15	the day after that we came to Miletus.	1
20:16	in Jerusalem, if possible, on the day of Pentecost.	2
20:18	from the first day that I set foot in Asia	2
20:26	Therefore I declare to you this day	2
20:31	I did not cease night or day to warn everyone	2
21: 1	the next day to Rhodes…from there to Patara.	1
21: 4	and stayed there for seven days.	2
21: 5	When our days there were ended	2
21: 7	stayed with them for one day.	2
21:10	While we were staying there for several days	2
21:15	After these days we got ready	2
21:18	The next day Paul went with us to visit James;	1
21:26	the next day, having purified himself, he entered	2
21:26	the completion of the days of purification	2
21:27	When the seven days were almost completed	2
23: 1	"Brothers, up to this day I have lived my life	2
24: 1	Five days later the high priest…came down	2
24:11	it is not more than twelve days since I went up	2
24:24	Some days later when Felix came with his wife	2
25: 1	Three days after Festus had arrived in the province	2
25: 6	stayed among them not more than eight or ten days	2
25:13	After several days had passed	2
25:14	Since they were staying there several days	2
26: 7	as they earnestly worship day and night.	2
26:22	To this day I have had help from God	2
27: 3	The next day we put in at Sidon;	1
27: 7	We sailed slowly for a number of days	2
27:18	next day they began to throw the cargo overboard	1
27:19	the third day…they threw the ship's tackle	1
27:20	neither sun nor stars appeared for many days	2
27:29	prayed for day to come.	2
27:33	"Today is the fourteenth day	2
28: 7	entertained us hospitably for three days.	2
28:12	Syracuse and stayed there for three days;	2
28:13	After one day there a south wind sprang up	2
28:13	on the second day we came to Puteoli.	1
28:14	were invited to stay with them for seven days.	2
28:17	Three days later he called together…leaders	2
28:23	After they had set a day to meet with him	2
Rom 2: 5	storing up wrath for yourself on the day of wrath	2
2:16	on the day when…God…will judge	2
8:36	we are being killed all day long;	2
10:21	"All day long I have held out my hands	2
11: 8	ears that would not hear, down to this very day."	2
13:12	the night is far gone, the day is near.	2
13:13	live honorably as in the day	2
14: 5	Some judge one day to be better than another	2
14: 5	while others judge all days to be alike.	2
14: 6	Those who observe the day, observe it in honor	2
1Co 1: 8	blameless on the day of our Lord Jesus Christ.	2
3:13	the Day will disclose it	2
5: 5	may be saved in the day of the Lord.	2
10: 8	twenty-three thousand fell in a single day.	2
15: 4	that he was raised on the third day	2
15:31	I die every day!	2
16: 2	On the first day of every week	1
2Co 1:14	on the day of the Lord Jesus we are your boast	2
3:14	Indeed, to this very day, when they hear	2
4:16	our inner nature is being renewed day by day.	2
4:16	our inner nature is being renewed day by day.	2

2Co	6: 2	on a day of salvation I have helped you."	2
	6: 2	see, now is the day of salvation!	2
Gal	1:18	stayed with him fifteen days;	2
	4:10	observing special days, and months, and seasons	2
Eph	4:30	marked with a seal for the day of redemption.	2
	5:16	because the days are evil.	2
	6:13	that you may be able to withstand on that evil day	2
Php	1: 5	from the first day until now.	2
	1: 6	to completion by the day of Jesus Christ.	2
	1:10	in the day of Christ you may be pure and blameless	2
	2:16	that I can boast on the day of Christ	2
Col	1: 6	from the day you heard it and truly comprehended	2
	1: 9	For this reason, since the day we heard it	2
1Th	2: 9	worked night and day, so that we might not burden	2
	3:10	Night and day we pray most earnestly that we may see	2
	5: 2	you...know very well that the day of the Lord	2
	5: 4	for that day to surprise you like a thief;	2
	5: 5	children of light and children of the day;	2
	5: 8	since we belong to the day, let us be sober	2
2Th	1:10	marveled at on that day among all who have believed	2
	2: 2	that the day of the Lord is already here.	2
	2: 3	for that day will not come unless the rebellion	1
	3: 8	with toil and labor we worked night and day	2
1Ti	5: 5	in supplications and prayers night and day;	2
2Ti	1: 3	constantly in my prayers night and day.	2
	1:12	to guard until that day what I have entrusted	2
	1:18	that he will find mercy from the Lord on that day!	2
	3: 1	in the last days distressing times will come.	2
	4: 8	the righteous judge, will give me on that day	2
Heb	1: 2	in these last days he has spoken to us by a Son	2
	3: 8	on the day of testing in the wilderness	2
	3:13	exhort one another every day	2
	4: 4	it speaks about the seventh day as follows	2
	4: 4	God rested on the seventh day from all his works."	2
	4: 7	again he sets a certain day—"today"	2
	4: 8	God would not speak later about another day.	2
	5: 7	In the days of his flesh, Jesus offered up prayers	2
	7: 3	having neither beginning of days nor end of life	2
	7:27	he has no need...to offer sacrifices day after day	1
	7:27	he has no need...to offer sacrifices day after day	2
	8: 8	"The days are surely coming, says the Lord	2
	8: 9	on the day when I took them by the hand	2
	8:10	with the house of Israel after those days	2
	10:11	every priest stands day after day at his service	2
	10:16	after those days, says the Lord:	2
	10:25	all the more as you see the Day approaching.	2
	10:32	recall those earlier days...when you endured	2
	11:30	after they had been encircled for seven days.	2
Jas	5: 3	You have laid up treasure for the last days.	2
	5: 5	have fattened your hearts in a day of slaughter.	2
1Pe	3:10	"Those who desire life and desire to see good days	2
	3:20	when God waited patiently in the days of Noah	2
2Pe	1:19	until the day dawns and the morning star rises	2
	2: 8	day after day, was tormented in his righteous soul	2
	2: 8	day after day, was tormented in his righteous soul	2
	2: 9	under punishment until the day of judgment	2
	3: 3	that in the last days scoffers will come	2
	3: 7	kept until the day of judgment and destruction	2
	3: 8	with the Lord one day is like a thousand years	2
	3: 8	and a thousand years are like one day.	2
	3:10	But the day of the Lord will come like a thief	2
	3:12	and hastening the coming of the day of God	2
	3:18	glory both now and to the day of eternity. Amen.	2
1Jn	4:17	that we may have boldness on the day of judgment	2
Jde	1: 6	kept...for the judgment of the great day.	2
Rev	1:10	I was in the spirit on the Lord's day,	1
	2:10	and for ten days you will have affliction.	2
	2:13	you did not deny...even in the days of Antipas	2
	4: 8	Day and night without ceasing they sing	2
	6:17	for the great day of their wrath has come	2
	7:15	and worship him day and night within his temple	2
	8:12	a third of the day was kept from shining	2
	9: 6	in those days people will seek death but will not find it;	2
	9:15	ready for the hour, the day, the month, and the year	2
	10: 7	in the days when the seventh angel is to blow his trumpet	2
	11: 3	prophesy for one thousand two hundred sixty days	2
	11: 6	no rain...during the days of their prophesying	2
	11: 9	For three and a half days members of the peoples	2
	11:11	after the three and a half days, the breath of life	2
	12: 6	nourished for one thousand two hundred sixty days	2
	12:10	who accuses them day and night before our God.	2

	14:11	There is no rest day or night for those	2
	16:14	for battle on the great day of God the Almighty.	2
	18: 8	therefore her plagues will come in a single day	2
	20:10	they will be tormented day and night forever	2
	21:25	Its gates will never be shut by day	2

day after day
1. κατά + ἡμέρα, *kata + hēmera, 2848 + 2465*

Mat	26:55	Day after day I sat in the temple teaching	1
Mrk	14:49	Day after day I was with you in the temple	1
Lke	22:53	I was with you day after day in the temple	1

day before the sabbath
1. προσάββατον, *prosabbaton, 4640*

Mrk	15:42	that is, the day before the sabbath	1

day by day
1. κατά + ἡμέρα, *kata + hēmera, 2848 + 2465*

Act	2:46	Day by day, as they spent much time together	1
	2:47	day by day the Lord added to their number	1

day of Preparation
1. παρασκευή, *paraskeuē, 4187*

Mrk	15:42	since it was the day of Preparation	1
Jhn	19:14	it was the day of Preparation for the Passover;	1
	19:31	Since it was the day of Preparation	1
	19:42	because it was the Jewish day of Preparation	1

early days
1. ἀρχή, *archē, 794*

Php	4:15	know that in the early days of the gospel	1

eighth day
1. ὀκταήμερος, *oktaēmeros, 3892*

Php	3: 5	circumcised on the eighth day	1

every day
1. κατά + ἡμέρα, *kata + hēmera, 2848 + 2465*

Lke	16:19	and who feasted sumptuously every day.	1
	19:47	Every day he was teaching in the temple.	1
Act	17:11	examined the scriptures every day	1

following day
1. ἐπαύριον, *epaurion, 2069*

Mrk	11:12	On the following day, when they came from Bethany	1
Act	10:24	The following day they came to Caesarea.	1

next day
1. αὔριον, *aurion, 892*
2. ἐπαύριον, *epaurion, 2069*

Mat	27:62	next day, that is, after the day of Preparation	2
Lke	10:35	The next day he took out two denarii	1
Jhn	1:29	The next day he saw Jesus coming toward him	2
	1:35	The next day John again was standing	2
	1:43	The next day Jesus decided to go to Galilee.	2
	6:22	The next day the crowd that had stayed	2
	12:12	The next day the great crowd...heard	2
Act	4: 3	put them in custody until the next day	1
	4: 5	The next day their rulers, elders,	1
	10: 9	the next day, as they were on their journey	2
	10:23	The next day he got up and went with them	2
	14:20	The next day he went on with Barnabas to Derbe.	2
	20: 7	intended to leave the next day	2
	21: 8	The next day we left and came to Caesarea;	2
	22:30	the next day he released him	2
	23:32	The next day they let the horsemen go on with him	2
	25: 6	the next day he took his seat on the tribunal	2
	25:23	So on the next day Agrippa and Bernice came	2

one day
1. γίνομαι, *ginomai, 1181*
2. δέ, *de, 1254*

Act	3: 1	One day Peter and John were going up to the temple	2
	16:16	One day, as we were going to the place of prayer	1

this day
1. σήμερον, *sēmeron, 4958*

Mat	6:11	Give us this day our daily bread.	1
	11:23	it would have remained until this day.	1

27: 8 has been called the Field of Blood to this day. 1
28:15 story is still told among the Jews to this day. 1
Mrk 14:30 this day, this very night, before the cock crows 1
Lke 2:11 born this day in the city of David a Savior 1
22:34 Peter, the cock will not crow this day 1
Act 20:26 Therefore I declare to you this day 1

this very day

1. ἄρτι, *arti, 785*
2. σήμερον, *sēmeron, 4958*

Rom 11: 8 ears that would not hear, down to this very day." 2
1Co 4:13 the dregs of all things, to this very day. 1
2Co 3:14 Indeed, to this very day, when they hear 2
3:15 Indeed, to this very day whenever Moses is read 2

daybreak

1. ἡμέρα, *hēmera, 2465*
2. ὄρθρος, *orthros, 3986*
3. πρωΐα, *prōia, 4746*

Lke 4:42 At daybreak he departed 1
Jhn 21: 4 Just after daybreak, Jesus stood on the beach; 3
Act 5:21 they entered the temple at daybreak and went on 2
27:33 Just before daybreak, 1

daylight

1. ἡμέρα, *hēmera, 2465*

Jhn 11: 9 "Are there not twelve hours of daylight? 1

daytime

1. ἡμέρα, *hēmera, 2465*

2Pe 2:13 They count it a pleasure to revel in the daytime. 1

dazzle

1. ἀστράπτω, *astraptō, 848*
2. ἐξαστράπτω, *exastraptō, 1993*
3. λαμπρός, *lampros, 3287*
4. στίλβω + λίαν, *stilbō + lian, 5118 + 3336*
5. φῶς, *phōs, 5890*

Mat 17: 2 and his clothes became dazzling white. 5
Mrk 9: 3 clothes became dazzling white 4
Lke 9:29 his clothes became dazzling white. 2
24: 4 two men in dazzling clothes stood beside them. 1
Act 10:30 suddenly a man in dazzling clothes stood before me. 3

deacon *See also* serve as deacon

1. διάκονος, *diakonos, 1356*

Rom 16: 1 Phoebe, a deacon of the church at Cenchreae 1
Php 1: 1 in Philippi, with the bishops and deacons: 1
1Ti 3: 8 Deacons likewise must be serious 1
3:12 Let deacons be married only once 1

dead *See also* dead *body*

1. Contextual: Not in Greek
2. ἀποθνῄσκω, *apothnēskō, 633*
3. θάνατος, *thanatos, 2505*
4. θνῄσκω, *thnēskō, 2569*
5. μέγας, *megas, 3489*
6. νεκρός, *nekros, 3738*
7. νεκρόω, *nekroō, 3739*

Mat 2:20 those who were seeking the child's life are dead." 4
8:22 and let the dead bury their own dead." 6
8:22 and let the dead bury their own dead." 6
8:26 and there was a dead calm. 5
9:24 the girl is not dead but sleeping." 2
10: 8 Cure the sick, raise the dead, cleanse the lepers 6
11: 5 the dead are raised, and the poor have good news 6
14: 2 he has been raised from the dead 6
17: 9 the Son of Man has been raised from the dead." 6
22:31 as for the resurrection of the dead 6
22:32 He is God not of the dead, but of the living." 6
23:27 inside they are full of the bones of the dead 6
27:64 'He has been raised from the dead,' 6
28: 7 'He has been raised from the dead 6
Mrk 4:39 the wind ceased, and there was a dead calm. 5
5:35 "Your daughter is dead. 2
5:39 The child is not dead but sleeping." 2
6:14 "John the baptizer has been raised from the dead; 6
9: 9 the Son of Man had risen from the dead. 6
9:10 what this rising from the dead could mean. 6

9:26 so that most of them said, "He is dead." 2
12:25 For when they rise from the dead 6
12:26 as for the dead being raised 6
12:27 He is God not of the dead, but of the living; 6
15:44 Pilate wondered if he were already dead; 4
15:44 whether he had been dead for some time. 2
15:45 he learned from the centurion that he was dead 1
Lke 7:22 the deaf hear, the dead are raised 6
8:49 "Your daughter is dead; do not trouble the teacher 4
8:52 "Do not weep; for she is not dead but sleeping." 2
8:53 they laughed at him, knowing that she was dead. 2
9: 7 John had been raised from the dead 6
9:60 "Let the dead bury their own dead; 6
9:60 "Let the dead bury their own dead; 6
15:24 this son of mine was dead and is alive again; 6
15:32 brother of yours was dead and has come to life; 6
16:30 if someone goes to them from the dead 6
16:31 if someone rises from the dead.' " 6
20:35 in the resurrection from the dead 6
20:37 that the dead are raised Moses himself showed 6
20:38 Now he is God not of the dead, but of the living; 6
24: 5 "Why do you look for the living among the dead? 6
24:46 rise from the dead on the third day 6
Jhn 2:22 After he was raised from the dead 6
5:21 the Father raises the dead and gives them life 6
5:25 the dead will hear the voice of the Son of God 6
11:14 Jesus told them plainly, "Lazarus is dead. 2
11:39 because he has been dead four days." 1
12: 1 whom he had raised from the dead. 6
12: 9 to see Lazarus, whom he had raised from the dead. 6
12:17 raised him from the dead 6
19:33 came to Jesus and saw that he was already dead 4
20: 9 the scripture, that he must rise from the dead. 6
21: 4 after he was raised from the dead 6
Act 3:15 the Author of life, whom God raised from the dead. 6
4: 2 in Jesus there is the resurrection of the dead. 6
4:10 whom you crucified, whom God raised from the dead. 6
5:10 When the young men came in they found her dead 6
10:41 after he rose from the dead. 6
10:42 judge of the living and the dead. 6
13:30 God raised him from the dead; 6
13:34 As to his raising him from the dead 6
14:19 supposing that he was dead. 4
17: 3 Messiah to suffer and to rise from the dead 6
17:31 given assurance…by raising him from the dead." 6
17:32 When they heard of the resurrection of the dead 6
20: 9 he fell to the ground…and was picked up dead. 6
23: 6 the hope of the resurrection of the dead." 6
24:21 about the resurrection of the dead 6
26: 8 thought incredible…that God raises the dead? 6
26:23 by being the first to rise from the dead 6
28: 6 expecting him to swell up or drop dead 6
Rom 1: 4 by resurrection from the dead, Jesus Christ 6
4:17 God…who gives life to the dead 6
4:19 his own body, which was already as good as dead 7
4:24 him who raised Jesus our Lord from the dead 6
6: 4 so that, just as Christ was raised from the dead 6
6: 9 Christ, being raised from the dead, will never die 6
6:11 you also must consider yourselves dead to sin 6
7: 4 belong…to him who has been raised from the dead 6
7: 6 dead to that which held us captive 2
7: 8 Apart from the law sin lies dead. 6
8:10 though the body is dead because of sin 7
8:11 the Spirit of him who raised Jesus from the dead 6
8:11 he who raised Christ from the dead 6
10: 7 (that is, to bring Christ up from the dead). 6
10: 9 and believe…that God raised him from the dead 6
11:15 their acceptance be but life from the dead! 6
14: 9 be Lord of both the dead and the living. 6
1Co 15:12 if Christ is proclaimed as raised from the dead 6
15:12 there is no resurrection of the dead? 6
15:13 If there is no resurrection of the dead 6
15:15 if it is true that the dead are not raised. 6
15:16 For if the dead are not raised 6
15:20 in fact Christ has been raised from the dead 6
15:21 the resurrection of the dead has also come 6
15:29 receive baptism on behalf of the dead? 6
15:29 If the dead are not raised at all 6
15:32 If the dead are not raised, "Let us eat and drink 6
15:35 someone will ask, "How are the dead raised? 6
15:42 So it is with the resurrection of the dead. 6

1Co 15:52	the dead will be raised imperishable	6
2Co 1: 9	not on ourselves but on God who raises the dead.	6
Gal 1: 1	God the Father, who raised him from the dead—	6
Eph 1:20	when he raised him from the dead	6
2: 1	You were dead through the trespasses	6
2: 5	even when we were dead through our trespasses	6
5:14	it says, "Sleeper, awake! Rise from the dead	6
Php 3:11	I may attain the resurrection from the dead.	6
Col 1:18	he is the beginning, the firstborn from the dead	6
2:12	God, who raised him from the dead.	6
2:13	when you were dead in trespasses	6
1Th 1:10	his Son from heaven, whom he raised from the dead	6
4:16	the dead in Christ will rise first.	6
1Ti 5: 6	the widow…is dead even while she lives.	4
2Ti 2: 8	Remember Jesus Christ, raised from the dead	6
4: 1	who is to judge the living and the dead	6
Heb 6: 1	the foundation: repentance from dead works	6
6: 2	resurrection of the dead, and eternal judgment.	6
9:14	purify our conscience from dead works	6
11:12	from one person, and this one as good as dead	7
11:19	God is able even to raise someone from the dead	6
11:35	Women received their dead by resurrection.	6
13:20	who brought back from the dead our Lord Jesus	6
Jas 2:17	So faith by itself, if it has no works, is dead.	6
2:26	For just as the body without the spirit is dead	6
2:26	so faith without works is also dead.	6
1Pe 1: 3	the resurrection of Jesus Christ from the dead	6
1:21	who raised him from the dead and gave him glory	6
4: 5	who stands ready to judge the living and the dead.	6
4: 6	the gospel was proclaimed even to the dead	6
Jde 1:12	autumn trees without fruit, twice dead, uprooted;	2
Rev 1: 5	Jesus Christ…the firstborn of the dead	6
1:17	When I saw him, I fell at his feet as though dead.	6
1:18	I was dead, and see, I am alive forever and ever;	6
2: 8	the first and the last, who was dead and came to life:	6
2:23	and I will strike her children dead.	3
3: 1	you have a name of being alive, but you are dead.	6
11:18	and the time for judging the dead	6
14:13	Blessed are the dead who from now on die in the Lord."	6
20: 5	(The rest of the dead did not come to life	6
20:12	dead, great and small, standing before the throne	6
20:12	dead were judged according to their works,	6
20:13	And the sea gave up the dead that were in it	6
20:13	Death and Hades gave up the dead that were in them	6

dead man

1. θνήσκω, *thnēskō, 2569*
2. νεκρός, *nekros, 3738*
3. τελευτάω, *teleutaō, 5462*

Mat 28: 4	the guards shook and became like dead men.	2
Lke 7:15	The dead man sat up and began to speak	2
Jhn 11:39	Martha, the sister of the dead man, said to him,	3
11:44	The dead man came out	1

half dead

1. ἡμιθανής, *hēmithanēs, 2467*

| Lke 10:30 | and went away, leaving him half dead. | 1 |

deadly

1. θανατηφόρος, *thanatēphoros, 2504*
2. τηλικοῦτος, *tēlikoutos, 5496*

| 2Co 1:10 | He who rescued us from so deadly a peril | 2 |
| Jas 3: 8 | the tongue…full of deadly poison. | 1 |

deadly thing

1. θανάσιμος, *thanasimos, 2503*

| Mrk 16:18 | ⟦if they drink any deadly thing, it will not hurt⟧ | 1 |

deaf

1. κωφός, *kōphos, 3273*

Mat 11: 5	lame walk, the lepers are cleansed, the deaf hear	1
Mrk 7:37	makes the deaf to hear and the mute to speak."	1
Lke 7:22	lepers are cleansed, the deaf hear	1

deaf man

1. κωφός, *kōphos, 3273*

| Mrk 7:32 | They brought to him a deaf man who | 1 |

deal *See also* great deal

1. Contextual: Not in Greek
2. εἰς, *eis, 1650*
3. ἐπί, *epi, 2093*
4. καταχράομαι, *katachraomai, 2974*
5. περί, *peri, 4309*
6. χράομαι, *chraomai, 5968*

Lke 16: 8	more shrewd in dealing with their own generation	2
Rom 8: 3	to deal with sin, he condemned sin in the flesh	5
1Co 7:31	those who deal with the world	6
7:31	as though they had no dealings with it.	4
2Co 13: 3	He is not weak in dealing with you	2
13: 4	in dealing with you we will live with him	2
1Th 2:11	we dealt with each one of you like a father	1
Heb 9:10	deal only with food and drink	3
1Pe 5: 5	with humility in your dealings with one another	1

deal craftily

1. κατασοφίζομαι, *katasophizomai, 2947*

| Act 7:19 | He dealt craftily with our race | 1 |

deal gently

1. μετριοπαθέω, *metriopatheō, 3584*

| Heb 5: 2 | able to deal gently with the ignorant and wayward | 1 |

dealer

1. πωλέω, *pōleō, 4797*

| Mat 25: 9 | go to the dealers and buy some for yourselves.' | 1 |

dealer in purple cloth

1. πορφυρόπωλις, *porphyropōlis, 4527*

| Act 16:14 | Lydia…a dealer in purple cloth. | 1 |

dear *See also* dear *friend*, dear *lady*

1. ἀγαπητός, *agapētos, 28*

| Eph 6:21 | Tychicus…a dear brother and a faithful minister | 1 |

very dear

1. ἀγαπητός, *agapētos, 28*

| 1Th 2: 8 | because you have become very dear to us. | 1 |

death *See also* bring about death, condemn to death, death *penalty*, point of death, put to death, sentence to death, stone to death

1. Contextual: Not in Greek
2. ἀπόθεσις + ὁ + σκήνωμα, *apothesis + ho + skēnōma, 629 + 3836 + 5013*
3. ἀποθνήσκω, *apothnēskō, 633*
4. θάνατος, *thanatos, 2505*
5. νεκρός, *nekros, 3738*
6. νέκρωσις, *nekrōsis, 3740*
7. ὅς, *hos, 4005*
8. τελευτάω, *teleutaō, 5462*
9. τελευτή, *teleutē, 5463*

Mat 2:15	remained there until the death of Herod.	9
4:16	region and shadow of death light has dawned."	4
10:21	Brother will betray brother to death	4
16:28	some standing here who will not taste death	4
20:18	and they will condemn him to death;	4
26:38	"I am deeply grieved, even to death;	4
26:66	They answered, "He deserves death."	4
Mrk 9: 1	some standing here who will not taste death	4
10:33	they will condemn him to death;	4
13:12	Brother will betray brother to death	4
14:34	"I am deeply grieved, even to death;	4
14:64	All of them condemned him as deserving death.	4
Lke 1:79	who sit in darkness and in the shadow of death	4
2:26	that he would not see death before	4
7: 2	who was ill and close to death.	8
9:27	some standing here who will not taste death	4
22:33	I am ready to go with you to prison and to death!"	4
23:15	he has done nothing to deserve death.	4
23:22	in him no ground for the sentence of death;	4
24:20	condemned to death and crucified him.	4
Jhn 4:47	his son, for he was at the point of death.	3
5:24	has passed from death to life	4
8:51	whoever keeps my word will never see death."	4
8:52	will never taste death.'	4

	11: 4	"This illness does not lead to death;	4
	11:13	Jesus, however, had been speaking about his death	4
	12:33	to indicate the kind of death he was to die.	4
	18:32	he indicated the kind of death he was to die.)	4
	21:19	the kind of death by which he would glorify God.)	4
Act	2:24	having freed him from death	4
	13:28	they found no cause for a sentence of death	4
	22: 4	I persecuted this Way up to the point of death	4
	23:29	charged with nothing deserving death	4
	25:11	I am not trying to escape death;	3
	25:25	I found that he had done nothing deserving death;	4
	26:31	"This man is doing nothing to deserve death	4
Rom	4:25	who was handed over to death for our trespasses	1
	5:10	reconciled to God through the death of his Son	4
	5:12	sin came into the world…death came through sin	4
	5:12	death spread to all because all have sinned—	4
	5:14	Yet death exercised dominion from Adam to Moses	4
	5:17	death exercised dominion through that one	4
	5:21	so that, just as sin exercised dominion in death	4
	6: 3	into Christ Jesus were baptized into his death?	4
	6: 4	we have been buried with him by baptism into death	4
	6: 5	if we have been united with him in a death like his	4
	6: 9	death no longer has dominion over him.	4
	6:10	The death he died, he died to sin, once for all;	7
	6:13	as those who have been brought from death to life	5
	6:16	slaves…either of sin, which leads to death	4
	6:21	The end of those things is death.	4
	6:23	For the wages of sin is death	4
	7: 5	at work in our members to bear fruit for death.	4
	7:10	the very commandment…proved to be death to me.	4
	7:13	Did what is good, then, bring death to me?	4
	7:13	sin, working death in me through what is good	4
	7:24	Who will rescue me from this body of death?	4
	8: 2	has set you free from the law of sin and of death.	4
	8: 6	To set the mind on the flesh is death	4
	8:38	neither death, nor life, nor angels	4
1Co	3:22	the world or life or death or the present	4
	11:26	you proclaim the Lord's death until he comes.	4
	15:21	For since death came through a human being	4
	15:26	The last enemy to be destroyed is death.	4
	15:54	"Death has been swallowed up in victory."	4
	15:55	"Where, O death, is your victory?	4
	15:55	Where, O death, is your sting?"	4
	15:56	The sting of death is sin	4
2Co	1: 9	felt that we had received the sentence of death	4
	2:16	to the one a fragrance from death to death	4
	2:16	to the one a fragrance from death to death	4
	3: 7	Now if the ministry of death	4
	4:10	always carrying in the body the death of Jesus	6
	4:11	always being given up to death for Jesus' sake	4
	4:12	death is at work in us, but life in you.	4
	7:10	worldly grief produces death.	4
	11:23	with countless floggings, and often near death.	4
Php	1:20	whether by life or by death.	4
	2: 8	obedient to the point of death—even death on a cross.	4
	2: 8	obedient to the point of death—even death on a cross.	4
	2:30	he came close to death for the work of Christ	4
	3:10	becoming like him in his death	4
Col	1:22	now reconciled in his fleshly body through death	4
2Ti	1:10	who abolished death and brought life	4
Heb	2: 9	because of the suffering of death	4
	2: 9	so that by the grace of God he might taste death	4
	2:14	so that through death he might destroy the one	4
	2:14	one who has the power of death, that is, the devil	4
	2:15	held in slavery by the fear of death.	4
	5: 7	to the one who was able to save him from death	4
	7:23	because they were prevented by death	4
	9:15	because a death has occurred that redeems them	4
	9:16	a will is involved, the death of the one who made it	4
	9:17	For a will takes effect only at death	5
	11: 5	he did not experience death;	4
Jas	1:15	sin, when it is fully grown, gives birth to death.	4
	5:20	will save the sinner's soul from death	4
2Pe	1:14	since I know that my death will come soon	2
1Jn	3:14	We know that we have passed from death to life	4
	3:14	Whoever does not love abides in death.	4
Rev	1:18	and I have the keys of Death and of Hades.	4
	2:10	Be faithful until death	4
	2:11	conquers will not be harmed by the second death.	4
	3: 2	strengthen what…is on the point of death	3
	6: 8	a pale green horse! Its rider's name was Death	4

	9: 6	in those days people will seek death but will not find it;	4
	9: 6	they will long to die, but death will flee from them.	4
	12:11	they did not cling to life even in the face of death.	4
	20: 6	Over these the second death has no power	4
	20:13	Death and Hades gave up the dead that were in them	4
	20:14	Death and Hades were thrown into the lake of fire.	4
	20:14	This is the second death, the lake of fire;	4
	21: 4	Death will be no more;	4
	21: 8	the lake that burns…which is the second death."	4

death-blow *See* receive a death-blow

debased

    1. ἀδόκιμος, *adokimos, 99*

Rom 1:28 God gave them up to a debased mind   1

debate

    1. ζήτησις, *zētēsis, 2428*
    2. συμβάλλω, *symballō, 5202*

Act	15: 2	had no small dissension and debate with them	1
	15: 7	After there had been much debate, Peter stood up	1
	17:18	Epicurean and Stoic philosophers debated with him.	2

debater

    1. συζητητής, *syzētētēs, 5186*

1Co 1:20 Where is the debater of this age?   1

debauchery

    1. ἀσωτία, *asōtia, 861*
    2. κοίτη, *koitē, 3130*

Rom	13:13	not in debauchery and licentiousness	2
Eph	5:18	Do not get drunk with wine, for that is debauchery;	1
Tit	1: 6	not accused of debauchery and not rebellious.	1

debt *See also* cancel a debt

    1. δάνειον, *daneion, 1245*
    2. ὀφειλή, *opheilē, 4051*
    3. ὀφείλημα, *opheilēma, 4052*
    4. ὀφείλω, *opheilō, 4053*

Mat	6:12	And forgive us our debts, as we also have forgiven	3
	18:27	released him and forgave him the debt.	1
	18:30	into prison until he would pay the debt.	4
	18:32	'You wicked slave! I forgave you all that debt	2
	18:34	until he would pay his entire debt.	4

debtor

    1. ὀφειλέτης, *opheiletēs, 4050*
    2. χρεοφειλέτης, *chreopheiletēs, 5971*

Mat	6:12	debts, as we also have forgiven our debtors.	1
Lke	7:41	"A certain creditor had two debtors;	2
	16: 5	summoning his master's debtors one by one	2
Rom	1:14	debtor both to Greeks and to barbarians	1
	8:12	we are debtors, not to the flesh	1

Decapolis

    1. Δεκάπολις, *Dekapolis, 1279*

Mat	4:25	from Galilee, the Decapolis, Jerusalem	1
Mrk	5:20	began to proclaim in the Decapolis	1
	7:31	in the region of the Decapolis.	1

decay

    1. φθορά, *phthora, 5785*

Rom 8:21 creation…set free from its bondage to decay   1

deceit

    1. ἀπάτη, *apatē, 573*
    2. δόλος, *dolos, 1515*
    3. πλάνη, *planē, 4415*

Mrk	7:22	avarice, wickedness, deceit, licentiousness	2
Jhn	1:47	an Israelite in whom there is no deceit!"	2
Act	13:10	full of all deceit and villainy	2
Rom	1:29	Full of envy, murder, strife, deceit, craftiness	2
2Co	12:16	I was crafty…I took you in by deceit.	2
Col	2: 8	captive through philosophy and empty deceit	1
1Th	2: 3	does not spring from deceit or impure motives	3
1Pe	2:22	no deceit was found in his mouth."	2
	3:10	let them keep…their lips from speaking deceit;	2

deceitful

1. δόλιος, *dolios, 1513*
2. πλάνη, *planē, 4415*
3. πλάνος, *planos, 4418*

2Co 11:13 such boasters are false apostles, deceitful workers   1
Eph   4:14 by their craftiness in deceitful scheming.   2
1Ti   4: 1 paying attention to deceitful spirits   3

deceitfulness

1. ἀπάτη, *apatē, 573*

Heb   3:13 hardened by the deceitfulness of sin.   1

deceive

1. ἀπατάω, *apataō, 572*
2. δολιόω, *dolioō, 1514*
3. ἐξαπατάω, *exapataō, 1987*
4. παραλογίζομαι, *paralogizomai, 4165*
5. πλανάω, *planaō, 4414*
6. φρεναπατάω, *phrenapataō, 5854*

Jhn   7:12 were saying, "No, he is deceiving the crowd."   5
     7:47 replied, "Surely you have not been deceived   5
Rom   3:13 they use their tongues to deceive."   2
     7:11 sin...deceived me and through it killed me.   3
    16:18 and by smooth talk and flattery they deceive   3
1Co   3:18 Do not deceive yourselves.   3
     6: 9 Do not be deceived! Fornicators, idolaters   5
    15:33 Do not be deceived: 5
2Co 11: 3 as the serpent deceived Eve by its cunning   3
Gal   6: 3 they deceive themselves.   6
     6: 7 Do not be deceived; God is not mocked   5
Eph   5: 6 Let no one deceive you with empty words   1
Col   2: 4 I am saying this so that no one may deceive you   4
2Th   2: 3 Let no one deceive you in any way;   3
1Ti   2:14 Adam was not deceived, but the woman was deceived   1
     2:14 Adam was not deceived, but the woman was deceived   3
2Ti   3:13 bad to worse, deceiving others and being deceived.   5
     3:13 bad to worse, deceiving others and being deceived.   5
Jas   1:16 Do not be deceived, my beloved.   5
     1:22 not merely hearers who deceive themselves.   4
     1:26 deceive their hearts, their religion is worthless.   1
1Jn   1: 8 If we say that we have no sin, we deceive ourselves   5
     2:26 I write...concerning those who would deceive you.   5
     3: 7 Little children, let no one deceive you.   5
Rev 13:14 it deceives the inhabitants of earth   5
    18:23 and all nations were deceived by your sorcery.   5
    19:20 he deceived those who had received the mark   5
    20: 3 so that he would deceive the nations no more   5
    20: 8 and will come out to deceive the nations   5
    20:10 the devil who had deceived them was thrown   5

deceiver

1. πλανάω, *planaō, 4414*
2. πλάνος, *planos, 4418*
3. φρεναπάτης, *phrenapatēs, 5855*

Tit   1:10 idle talkers and deceivers   3
2Jn   1: 7 Many deceivers have gone out into the world   2
     1: 7 such person is the deceiver and the antichrist!   2
Rev 12: 9 deceiver of the whole world—he was thrown down   1

decently

1. εὐσχημόνως, *euschēmonōs, 2361*
2. σωφροσύνη, *sōphrosynē, 5408*

1Co 14:40 all things should be done decently and in order.   1
1Ti   2: 9 dress themselves modestly and decently   2

deception

1. ἀπάτη, *apatē, 573*
2. πλάνη, *planē, 4415*

Mat 27:64 the last deception would be worse than the first."   2
2Th   2:10 every kind of wicked deception   1

deceptive

1. πλαστός, *plastos, 4422*

2Pe   2: 3 they will exploit you with deceptive words.   1

decide

1. Contextual: Not in Greek
2. ἀξιόω, *axioō, 546*

3. γινώσκω, *ginōskō, 1182*
4. γνώμη, *gnōmē, 1191*
5. διαγινώσκω, *diaginōskō, 1336*
6. διακρίνω, *diakrinō, 1359*
7. δοκέω, *dokeō, 1506*
8. εὐδοκέω, *eudokeō, 2305*
9. θέλω, *thelō, 2527*
10. κρίνω, *krinō, 3212*

Mrk 15:24 casting lots to decide what each should take.   1
Lke   1: 3 I too decided, after investigating everything   7
    16: 4 I have decided what to do   3
Jhn   1:43 The next day Jesus decided to go to Galilee.   9
Act   3:13 though he had decided to release him.   10
    15:22 decided to choose men from among their members   7
    15:25 we have decided unanimously to choose   7
    15:38 Paul decided not to take with them one   2
    20: 3 he decided to return through Macedonia.   4
    20:16 Paul had decided to sail past Ephesus   10
    24:22 I will decide your case."   5
    25:25 I decided to send him.   10
    27: 1 it was decided that we were to sail for Italy   10
1Co   1:21 God decided, through the foolishness   8
     2: 2 For I decided to know nothing among you   10
     6: 5 there is no one among you wise enough to decide   6
1Th   3: 1 we decided to be left alone in Athens;   8
Tit   3:12 I have decided to spend the winter there.   10

decision   *See also* reach a decision

1. διάγνωσις, *diagnōsis, 1338*
2. δόγμα, *dogma, 1504*
3. φαίνω, *phainō, 5743*

Mrk 14:64 What is your decision?"   3
Act 16: 4 delivered to them for observance the decisions   2
    25:21 in custody for the decision of his Imperial Majesty   1

decisively

1. συντέμνω, *syntemnō, 5335*

Rom   9:28 Lord will execute...quickly and decisively."   1

declare

1. Contextual: Not in Greek
2. ἀναγγέλλω, *anangellō, 334*
3. ἀπαγγέλλω, *apangellō, 550*
4. ἀποδείκνυμι, *apodeiknymi, 617*
5. διηγέομαι, *diēgeomai, 1455*
6. λαλέω, *laleō, 3281*
7. λέγω, *legō, 3306*
8. μαρτυρέω, *martyreō, 3455*
9. μαρτύρομαι, *martyromai, 3458*
10. ὁμολογέω, *homologeō, 3933*
11. ὁρίζω, *horizō, 3988*

Mat   7:23 Then I will declare to them, 'I never knew you;   10
    20:21 "Declare that these two sons of mine will sit   7
Mrk 12:36 David himself, by the Holy Spirit, declared   7
Lke   8:39 and declare how much God has done for you."   5
     8:47 declare in the presence of all the people   3
    24:25 to believe all that the prophets have declared!   6
Jhn   1:29 and declared, "Here is the Lamb of God   7
     8:26 I declare to the world what I have heard from him."   6
     8:38 I declare what I have seen in the Father's presence;   6
    13:21 Jesus was troubled in spirit, and declared   8
    16:13 will declare to you the things that are to come.   2
    16:14 will take what is mine and declare it to you.   2
    16:15 will take what is mine and declare it to you.   2
Act   2:17 'In the last days it will be, God declares   7
    20:26 Therefore I declare to you this day   9
    20:27 declaring to you the whole purpose of God.   2
    26:20 declared first to those in Damascus   3
Rom   1: 4 declared to be Son of God with power   11
1Co 14:25 declaring, "God is really among you."   3
Col   4: 3 that we may declare the mystery of Christ   6
1Th   2: 2 courage in our God to declare to you the gospel   6
     4:15 we declare to you by the word of the Lord   7
2Th   2: 4 declaring himself to be God.   4
Tit   2:15 Declare these things;   6
Heb   2: 2 For if the message declared through angels was valid   6
     2: 3 It was declared at first through the Lord   6
1Jn   1: 1 We declare to you what was from the beginning   1
     1: 2 and declare to you the eternal life   3

1: 3   we declare to you what we have seen and heard   3

declare boldly
1. παρρησιάζομαι, *parrēsiazomai, 4245*
Eph   6:20   I may declare it boldly, as I must speak.   1

declare clean
1. καθαρίζω, *katharizō, 2751*
Mrk   7:19   (Thus he declared all foods clean.)   1

declare the gospel beforehand
1. προευαγγελίζομαι, *proeuangelizomai, 4603*
Gal   3: 8   declared the gospel beforehand to Abraham   1

decline
1. οὐ + ἐπινεύω, *ou + epineuō, 4024 + 2153*
Act   18:20   When they asked him to stay…he declined;   1

decorate
1. κοσμέω, *kosmeō, 3175*
Mat   23:29   decorate the graves of the righteous   1

decrease
1. ἐλαττόω, *elattoō, 1783*
Jhn   3:30   He must increase, but I must decrease."   1

decree
1. δικαίωμα, *dikaiōma, 1468*
2. δόγμα, *dogma, 1504*
3. προορίζω, *proorizō, 4633*
Lke   2: 1   a decree went out from Emperor Augustus   2
Act   17: 7   all acting contrary to the decrees of the emperor   2
Rom   1:32   They know God's decree   1
1Co   2: 7   which God decreed before the ages for our glory   3

dedicate   *See also* gift dedicated to God
1. ἁγιάζω, *hagiazō, 39*
2Ti   2:21   dedicated and useful to the owner of the house   1

deed   *See also* do a good deed, good deed, lawless deed, righteous deed
1. ἔργον, *ergon, 2240*
2. πρᾶγμα, *pragma, 4547*
3. πρᾶξις, *praxis, 4552*
4. πράσσω, *prassō, 4556*
Mat   11:19   Yet wisdom is vindicated by her deeds."   1
    23: 5   They do all their deeds to be seen by others;   1
Lke   11:48   approve of the deeds of your ancestors;   1
    23:41   we are getting what we deserve for our deeds   4
    24:19   a prophet mighty in deed and word before God   1
Jhn   3:19   because their deeds were evil.   1
    3:20   so that their deeds may not be exposed.   1
    3:21   seen that their deeds have been done in God."   1
Act   5: 4   you have contrived this deed in your heart?   2
    7:22   was powerful in his words and deeds.   1
    26:20   and do deeds consistent with repentance.   1
Rom   2: 6   he will repay according to each one's deeds: 1
    3:20   justified…by deeds prescribed by the law   1
    8:13   if…put to death the deeds of the body   3
    15:18   obedience from the Gentiles, by word and deed   1
2Co   11:15   Their end will match their deeds.   1
Col   1:21   hostile in mind, doing evil deeds   1
    3:17   whatever you do, in word or deed   1
2Ti   4:14   the Lord will pay him back for his deeds.   1
Tit   2:14   who are zealous for good deeds.   1
Heb   10:24   to provoke one another to love and good deeds   1
1Pe   1:17   judges all people…according to their deeds   1
    2:12   they may see your honorable deeds and glorify God   1
2Pe   2: 8   day after day, was tormented…by their lawless deeds   1
    3:10   everything that is done on it will be disclosed.   1
1Jn   3:12   Because his own deeds were evil   1
2Jn   1:11   for to welcome is to participate in the evil   1
Jde   1:15   to convict everyone of all the deeds   1
Rev   14:13   "they will rest…for their deeds follow them."   1
    15: 3   "Great and amazing are your deeds, Lord God   1
    16:11   and they did not repent of their deeds.   1
    18: 6   and repay her double for her deeds;   1

deed of power
1. δύναμις, *dynamis, 1539*
2. μεγαλεῖος, *megaleios, 3483*
Mat   7:22   and do many deeds of power in your name?'   1
    11:20   in which most of his deeds of power had been done   1
    11:21   For if the deeds of power done in you had been done   1
    11:23   For if the deeds of power done in you had been done   1
    13:54   this wisdom and these deeds of power?   1
    13:58   he did not do many deeds of power there   1
Mrk   6: 2   What deeds of power are being done by his hands!   1
    6: 5   he could do no deed of power there   1
    9:39   no one who does a deed of power in my name   1
Lke   10:13   if the deeds of power done in you   1
    19:37   for all the deeds of power that they had seen   1
Act   2:11   speaking about God's deeds of power."   2
    2:22   a man attested…with deeds of power, wonders,   1
1Co   12:28   then deeds of power, then gifts of healing,   1

deep   *See also* deep darkness
1. βάθος, *bathos, 958*
2. βαθύς, *bathys, 960*
Lke   5: 4   he said to Simon, "Put out into the deep water   1
Jhn   4:11   you have no bucket, and the well is deep.   2
Act   20: 9   began to sink off into a deep sleep   2

deep thing
1. βαθύς, *bathys, 960*
Rev   2:24   learned what some call 'the deep things of Satan,'   1

too deep for a word
1. ἀλάλητος, *alalētos, 227*
Rom   8:26   intercedes with sighs too deep for words.   1

deeply   *See also* care for deeply, distress deeply, grieve deeply, move deeply, sigh deeply
1. βαθύνω, *bathynō, 959*
2. ἐκτενῶς, *ektenōs, 1757*
Lke   6:48   like a man building a house, who dug deeply   1
1Pe   1:22   love one another deeply from the heart.   2

defame
1. ἐκβάλλω + ὁ + ὄνομα + ὡς + πονηρός, *ekballō + ho + onoma + hōs + ponēros, 1675 + 3836 + 3950 + 6055 + 4505*
Lke   6:22   and defame you   1

defeat
1. ἥττημα, *hēttēma, 2488*
2. κοπή, *kopē, 3158*
3. οὐ + ἰσχύω, *ou + ischyō, 4024 + 2710*
Rom   11:12   if their defeat means riches for Gentiles   1
1Co   6: 7   to have lawsuits…is already a defeat for you.   1
Heb   7: 1   Abraham…was returning from defeating the kings   2
Rev   12: 8   but they were defeated   3

without defect
1. ἄμωμος, *amōmos, 320*
1Pe   1:19   like that of a lamb without defect or blemish.   1

defend
1. ἀμύνομαι, *amynomai, 310*
2. ἀπολογέομαι, *apologeomai, 664*
Lke   12:11   to defend yourselves or what you are to say;   2
Act   7:24   he defended the oppressed man and avenged him   1
    26: 1   Paul stretched out his hand and began to defend   2
2Co   12:19   we have been defending ourselves before you?   2

defense   *See also* make a defense, say in defense
1. ἀπολογέομαι, *apologeomai, 664*
2. ἀπολογία, *apologia, 665*
Lke   21:14   not to prepare your defense in advance;   1
Act   22: 1   listen to the defense that I now make before you."   2
1Co   9: 3   This is my defense to those who would examine me.   2
Php   1: 7   in the defense and confirmation of the gospel.   2
    1:16   put here for the defense of the gospel;   2
2Ti   4:16   At my first defense no one came to my support   2
1Pe   3:15   Always be ready to make your defense to anyone   2

deference *See also* show deference
1. πρόσωπον, *prosōpon, 4725*
2. φόβος, *phobos, 5832*

Lke 20:21 and you show deference to no 1
1Pe 2:18 Slaves, accept the authority...with all deference 2

defile
1. κοινός, *koinos, 3123*
2. κοινόω, *koinoō, 3124*
3. μιαίνω, *miainō, 3620*
4. μολύνω, *molynō, 3662*
5. σπιλόω, *spiloō, 5071*

Mat 15:11 not what goes into the mouth that defiles a person 2
15:11 what comes out of the mouth that defiles." 2
15:18 and this is what defiles. 2
15:20 These are what defile a person 2
15:20 to eat with unwashed hands does not defile." 2
Mrk 7: 2 eating with defiled hands, that is, without washing 1
7: 5 but eat with defiled hands?" 1
7:15 that by going in can defile 2
7:15 the things that come out are what defile." 2
7:18 goes into a person from outside cannot defile 2
7:20 what comes out of a person that defiles. 2
7:23 they defile a person." 2
Act 21:28 has defiled this holy place." 2
1Co 8: 7 their conscience, being weak, is defiled. 4
Heb 9:13 sanctifies those who have been defiled 2
12:15 through it many become defiled. 3
Jde 1: 8 these dreamers also defile the flesh 3
1:23 hating even the tunic defiled by their bodies. 5
Rev 14: 4 who have not defiled themselves with women 4

defilement
1. μίασμα, *miasma, 3621*
2. μολυσμός, *molysmos, 3663*

2Co 7: 1 let us cleanse ourselves from every defilement 2
2Pe 2:20 they have escaped the defilements of the world 1

ritual defilement
1. μιαίνω, *miainō, 3620*

Jhn 18:28 so as to avoid ritual defilement 1

definite
1. ἀσφαλής, *asphalēs, 855*
2. ὁρίζω, *horizō, 3988*

Act 2:23 the definite plan and foreknowledge of God 2
25:26 nothing definite to write to our sovereign about him. 1

defraud
1. ἀποστερέω, *apostereō, 691*
2. συκοφαντέω, *sykophanteō, 5193*

Mrk 10:19 shall not defraud; Honor your father and mother.' " 1
Lke 19: 8 if I have defrauded anyone of anything 2
1Co 6: 7 Why not rather be defrauded? 1
6: 8 you yourselves wrong and defraud 1

degrade
1. ἀτιμάζω, *atimazō, 869*
2. ἀτιμία, *atimia, 871*

Rom 1:24 degrading of their bodies among themselves 1
1:26 God gave them up to degrading passions. 2
1Co 11:14 if a man wears long hair, it is degrading to him 2

degree
1. Contextual: Not in Greek
2. ὅσος, *hosos, 4012*

2Co 3:18 from one degree of glory to another; 1
Heb 8: 6 a more excellent ministry, and to that degree 2

deity
1. θεῖος, *theios, 2521*
2. θεότης, *theotēs, 2540*

Act 17:29 ought not to think that the deity is like gold 1
Col 2: 9 in him the whole fullness of deity dwells bodily 2

dejection
1. κατήφεια, *katēpheia, 2993*

Jas 4: 9 be turned into mourning and your joy into dejection. 1

delay
1. βραδύνω, *bradynō, 1094*
2. μέλλω, *mellō, 3516*
3. ὀκνέω, *okneō, 3890*
4. χρονίζω, *chronizō, 5988*
5. χρόνος, *chronos, 5989*

Mat 24:48 'My master is delayed,' 4
25: 5 As the bridegroom was delayed 4
Lke 1:21 wondered at his delay in the sanctuary. 4
12:45 'My master is delayed in coming,' 4
Act 9:38 "Please come to us without delay." 3
22:16 now why do you delay? Get up, be baptized 2
1Ti 3:15 if I am delayed, you may know how 1
Heb 10:37 the one who is coming will come and will not delay; 4
Rev 10: 6 "There will be no more delay 5

delay long
1. μακροθυμέω, *makrothymeō, 3428*

Lke 18: 7 Will he delay long in helping them? 1

without delay
1. παραχρῆμα, *parachrēma, 4202*

Act 16:33 he and his entire family were baptized without delay. 1

delegation
1. πρεσβεία, *presbeia, 4561*

Lke 14:32 he sends a delegation and asks for...peace. 1
19:14 sent a delegation after him, saying, 'We do not 1

deliberately
1. θέλω, *thelō, 2527*

2Pe 3: 5 They deliberately ignore this fact 1

delight
1. ἡδέως, *hēdeōs, 2452*
2. συνήδομαι, *synēdomai, 5310*

Mrk 12:37 the large crowd was listening to him with delight. 1
Rom 7:22 For I delight in the law of God in my inmost self 2

deliver
1. ἀναδίδωμι, *anadidōmi, 347*
2. ἐπιδίδωμι, *epididōmi, 2113*
3. παραδίδωμι, *paradidōmi, 4140*
4. ῥύομαι, *rhyomai, 4861*
5. σφραγίζω, *sphragizō, 5381*

Mat 27:43 He trusts in God; let God deliver him now 4
Act 15:30 they delivered the letter. 2
16: 4 delivered to them for observance the decisions 3
23:33 delivered the letter to the governor 1
Rom 15:28 and have delivered to them what has been collected 5

deliver a child
1. τίκτω, *tiktō, 5503*

Lke 2: 6 the time came for her to deliver her child. 1

deliver a public address
1. δημηγορέω, *dēmēgoreō, 1319*

Act 12:21 Herod...delivered a public address to them 1

deliverance
1. σωτηρία, *sōtēria, 5401*

Php 1:19 this will turn out for my deliverance. 1

deliverer
1. ῥύομαι, *rhyomai, 4861*

Rom 11:26 it is written, "Out of Zion will come the Deliverer; 1

delude
1. ἀπάτη, *apatē, 573*

Eph 4:22 corrupt and deluded by its lusts 1

deluge
1. κατακλύζω, *kataklyzō, 2885*

2Pe 3: 6 world...was deluged with water and perished. 1

delusion
1. πλάνη, *planē, 4415*

2Th　2:11　For this reason God sends them a powerful delusion　　1

demand

1. Contextual: Not in Greek
2. αἰτέω, *aiteō, 160*
3. αἴτημα, *aitēma, 161*
4. ἀπαιτέω, *apaiteō, 555*
5. βάρος, *baros, 983*
6. ἐξαιτέω, *exaiteō, 1977*
7. ζητέω, *zēteō, 2426*

Lke　11:16　to test him, kept demanding from him a sign　　7
　　　12:20　your life is being demanded of you.　　4
　　　12:48　been entrusted, even more will be demanded　　2
　　　22:31　Satan has demanded to sift all of you like wheat　　6
　　　23:23　they kept urgently demanding with loud shouts　　2
　　　23:24　their demand should be granted.　　3
1Co　1:22　For Jews demand signs and Greeks desire wisdom　　2
1Th　2: 7　might have made demands as apostles of Christ.　　5
1Ti　4: ·3　demand abstinence from foods, which God created　　1
1Pe　3:15　defense to anyone who demands from you an accounting　　2

legal demand

1. δόγμα, *dogma, 1504*

Col　2:14　the record...with its legal demands.　　1

Demas

1. Δημᾶς, *Dēmas, 1318*

Col　4:14　Luke, the beloved physician, and Demas greet you.　　1
2Ti　4:10　Demas, in love with this present world　　1
Phm　1:24　so do Mark, Aristarchus, Demas, and Luke　　1

Demetrius

1. Δημήτριος, *Dēmētrios, 1320*

Act　19:24　A man named Demetrius, a silversmith　　1
　　　19:38　Demetrius and the artisans with him　　1
3Jn　1:12　Everyone has testified favorably about Demetrius　　1

demolish

1. κατασκάπτω, *kataskaptō, 2940*

Rom　11: 3　"Lord...they have demolished your altars;　　1

demon　See also possessed by a demon, possessed with a demon

1. Contextual: Not in Greek
2. δαιμονίζομαι, *daimonizomai, 1227*
3. δαιμόνιον, *daimonion, 1228*
4. δαίμων, *daimōn, 1230*

Mat　7:22　and cast out demons in your name　　3
　　　8:31　The demons begged him, "If you cast us out, send us　　4
　　　9:33　when the demon had been cast out　　3
　　　9:34　"By the ruler of the demons he casts out the demons."　　3
　　　9:34　"By the ruler of the demons he casts out the demons."　　3
　　　10: 8　cleanse the lepers, cast out demons.　　3
　　　11:18　and they say, 'He has a demon';　　3
　　　12:24　"It is only by Beelzebul, the ruler of the demons　　3
　　　12:24　that this fellow casts out the demons."　　3
　　　12:27　If I cast out demons by Beelzebul　　3
　　　12:28　if it is by the Spirit of God that I cast out demons　　3
　　　15:22　my daughter is tormented by a demon."　　2
　　　17:18　Jesus rebuked the demon, and it came out of him　　3
Mrk　1:34　and cast out many demons;　　3
　　　1:34　he would not permit the demons to speak　　3
　　　1:39　proclaiming the message...and casting out demons.　　3
　　　3:15　and to have authority to cast out demons.　　3
　　　3:22　by the ruler of the demons he casts out demons."　　3
　　　3:22　by the ruler of the demons he casts out demons."　　3
　　　6:13　They cast out many demons, and anointed with oil　　3
　　　7:26　begged him to cast the demon out of her daughter.　　3
　　　7:29　the demon has left your daughter."　　3
　　　7:30　the child lying on the bed, and the demon gone.　　3
　　　9:38　we saw someone casting out demons in your name　　3
　　　16: 9　⟦from whom he had cast out seven demons.⟧　　3
　　　16:17　⟦by using my name they will cast out demons;⟧　　3
Lke　4:33　a man who had the spirit of an unclean demon　　3
　　　4:35　When the demon had thrown him down before them,　　3
　　　4:41　Demons also came out of many, shouting　　3
　　　7:33　and you say, 'He has a demon';　　3
　　　8: 2　Mary...from whom seven demons had gone out　　3
　　　8:27　a man of the city who had demons met him.　　3

　　　8:29　be driven by the demon into the wilds.)　　3
　　　8:30　"Legion"; for many demons had entered him.　　3
　　　8:32　demons begged Jesus to let them enter these.　　1
　　　8:33　Then the demons came out of the man　　3
　　　8:35　found the man from whom the demons had gone　　3
　　　8:38　The man from whom the demons had gone begged　　3
　　　9: 1　gave them power and authority over all demons　　3
　　　9:42　the demon dashed him to the ground in convulsions.　　3
　　　9:49　we saw someone casting out demons in your name　　3
　　　10:17　in your name even the demons submit to us!"　　3
　　　11:14　Now he was casting out a demon that was mute;　　3
　　　11:14　when the demon had gone out,　　3
　　　11:15　"He casts out demons by Beelzebul　　3
　　　11:15　by Beelzebul, the ruler of the demons."　　3
　　　11:18　you say that I cast out the demons by Beelzebul.　　3
　　　11:19　if I cast out the demons by Beelzebul　　3
　　　11:20　by the finger of God that I cast out the demons　　3
　　　13:32　I am casting out demons and performing cures today ·　　3
Jhn　7:20　The crowd answered, "You have a demon!　　3
　　　8:48　you are a Samaritan and have a demon?"　　3
　　　8:49　Jesus answered, "I do not have a demon;　　3
　　　8:52　"Now we know that you have a demon.　　3
　　　10:20　saying, "He has a demon and is out of his mind.　　3
　　　10:21　"These are not the words of one who has a demon.　　2
　　　10:21　Can a demon open the eyes of the blind?"　　3
1Co　10:20　they sacrifice to demons and not to God.　　3
　　　10:20　I do not want you to be partners with demons.　　3
　　　10:21　the cup of the Lord and the cup of demons.　　3
　　　10:21　table of the Lord and the table of demons.　　3
1Ti　4: 1　deceitful spirits and teachings of demons　　3
Jas　2:19　Even the demons believe—and shudder.　　3
Rev　9:20　or give up worshiping demons and idols of gold　　3
　　　18: 2　It has become a dwelling place of demons　　3

demoniac

1. δαιμονίζομαι, *daimonizomai, 1227*

Mat　4:24　with various diseases and pains, demoniacs　　1
　　　8:28　two demoniacs coming out of the tombs met him.　　1
　　　8:33　what had happened to the demoniacs.　　1
　　　9:32　a demoniac who was mute was brought to him.　　1
　　　12:22　Then they brought to him a demoniac who was blind　　1
Mrk　5:15　came to Jesus and saw the demoniac sitting there　　1
　　　5:16　who had seen what had happened to the demoniac　　1

demonic

1. δαιμόνιον, *daimonion, 1228*

Rev　16:14　These are demonic spirits, performing signs　　1

demonstrate

1. συνίστημι, *synistēmi, 5319*

Gal　2:18　then I demonstrate that I am a transgressor.　　1

demonstration

1. ἀπόδειξις, *apodeixis, 618*

1Co　2: 4　with a demonstration of the Spirit and of power　　1

den

1. σπήλαιον, *spēlaion, 5068*

Mat　21:13　but you are making it a den of robbers."　　1
Mrk　11:17　you have made it a den of robbers."　　1
Lke　19:46　you have made it a den of robbers."　　1

denarius

1. δηνάριον, *dēnarion, 1324*

Mat　18:28　slaves who owed him a hundred denarii　　1
　　　22:19　And they brought him a denarius.　　1
Mrk　6:37　"Are we to go and buy two hundred denarii worth　　1
　　　12:15　Bring me a denarius and let me see it."　　1
　　　14: 5　sold for more than three hundred denarii　　1
Lke　7:41　owed five hundred denarii, and the other fifty　　1
　　　10:35　The next day he took out two denarii　　1
　　　20:24　"Show me a denarius.　　1
Jhn　12: 5　perfume...sold for three hundred denarii　　1

denounce

1. βλασφημέω, *blasphēmeō, 1059*

1Co　10:30　why should I be denounced　　1

deny   *See also* cannot be denied

1. αἴρω, *airō*, 149
2. ἀπαρνέομαι, *aparneomai*, 565
3. ἀρνέομαι, *arneomai*, 766
4. ἐκκόπτω, *ekkoptō*, 1716

Mat	10:33	whoever denies me before others, I also will deny	3
	10:33	whoever denies me before others, I also will deny	3
	16:24	let them deny themselves and take up their cross	2
	26:34	you will deny me three times."	2
	26:35	though I must die with you, I will not deny you."	2
	26:70	he denied it before all of them, saying	3
	26:72	Again he denied it with an oath	3
	26:75	you will deny me three times."	2
Mrk	8:34	let them deny themselves and take up their cross	2
	14:30	you will deny me three times."	2
	14:31	though I must die with you, I will not deny you."	2
	14:68	he denied it, saying, "I do not know	3
	14:70	again he denied it.	3
	14:72	you will deny me three times."	2
Lke	8:45	When all denied it, Peter said, "Master	3
	9:23	let them deny themselves and take up their cross	3
	12: 9	whoever denies me before others	3
	12: 9	will be denied before the angels of God.	2
	22:34	until you have denied three times that you know me."	2
	22:57	he denied it, saying, "Woman, I do not know him."	3
	22:61	you will deny me three times."	2
Jhn	1:20	He confessed and did not deny it, but confessed	3
	13:38	you will have denied me three times.	3
	18:25	He denied it and said, "I am not."	3
	18:27	Again Peter denied it	3
Act	4:16	we cannot deny it.	3
	8:33	In his humiliation justice was denied him.	1
2Co	11:12	to do, in order to deny an opportunity	4
1Ti	5: 8	has denied the faith and is worse than	3
2Ti	2:12	if we deny him, he will also deny us;	3
	2:12	if we deny him, he will also deny us;	3
	2:13	for he cannot deny himself.	3
	3: 5	outward form of godliness but denying its power.	3
Tit	1:16	they deny him by their actions.	3
2Pe	2: 1	They will even deny the Master who bought them	3
1Jn	2:22	the one who denies that Jesus is the Christ?	3
	2:22	the one who denies the Father and the Son.	3
	2:23	No one who denies the Son has the Father;	3
Jde	1: 4	and deny our only Master and Lord, Jesus Christ.	3
Rev	2:13	and you did not deny your faith in me	3
	3: 8	you have kept my word and have not denied my name.	3

depart

1. ἀναλύω, *analyō*, 386
2. ἀναχωρέω, *anachōreō*, 432
3. ἀπέρχομαι, *aperchomai*, 599
4. ἀφίστημι, *aphistēmi*, 923
5. ἐξέρχομαι, *exerchomai*, 2002
6. μεταβαίνω, *metabainō*, 3553
7. πορεύομαι, *poreuomai*, 4513

Mat	12:15	Jesus became aware of this, he departed.	2
	25:41	accursed, depart from me into the eternal fire	7
	27: 5	he departed; and he went and hanged himself.	2
Mrk	3: 7	Jesus departed with his disciples to the sea	2
Lke	1:38	the angel departed from her.	3
	4:13	he departed from him until an opportune time.	4
	4:42	At daybreak he departed	5
	9: 6	They departed and went through the villages	5
	19:32	So those who were sent departed	3
Jhn	12:36	he departed and hid from them.	3
	13: 1	to depart from this world and go to the Father.	6
Act	16:40	when they had seen and encouraged…they departed.	5
	18:23	After spending some time there he departed	5
Php	1:23	my desire is to depart and be with Christ	1

departure

1. ἀνάλυσις, *analysis*, 385
2. ἔξοδος, *exodos*, 2016

Lke	9:31	in glory and were speaking of his departure	2
2Ti	4: 6	the time of my departure has come.	1
2Pe	1:15	after my departure you may be able…to recall	2

depend

1. Contextual: Not in Greek

Rom	9:16	So it depends not on human will or exertion	1
1Co	4:20	For the kingdom of God depends not on talk	1

depend on

1. ἐκ, *ek*, 1666

Rom	4:16	For this reason it depends on faith	1
	12:18	so far as it depends on you, live peaceably	1

depend on for food

1. τρέφω, *trephō*, 5555

Act	12:20	country depended on the king's country for food.	1

dependent

1. χρεία, *chreia*, 5970

1Th	4:12	be dependent on no one.	1

deportation

1. μετοικεσία, *metoikesia*, 3578

Mat	1:11	at the time of the deportation to Babylon.	1
	1:12	after the deportation to Babylon: Jechoniah was	1
	1:17	and from David to the deportation to Babylon	1
	1:17	from the deportation to Babylon to the Messiah	1

deposit

1. τίθημι, *tithēmi*, 5502

Lke	19:21	you take what you did not deposit	1
	19:22	a harsh man, taking what I did not deposit	1

deprave

1. διαφθείρω, *diaphtheirō*, 1425
2. μιασμός, *miasmos*, 3622

1Ti	6: 5	wrangling among those who are depraved in mind	1
2Pe	2:10	who indulge their flesh in depraved lust,	2

deprive

1. ἀποστερέω, *apostereō*, 691
2. καθαιρέω, *kathaireō*, 2747
3. κενόω, *kenoō*, 3033

Act	19:27	she will be deprived of her majesty	2
1Co	7: 5	Do not deprive one another	1
	9:15	no one will deprive me of my ground for boasting	3

depth

1. βάθος, *bathos*, 958
2. πέλαγος, *pelagos*, 4283

Mat	13: 5	since they had no depth of soil.	1
	18: 6	and you were drowned in the depth of the sea.	2
Mrk	4: 5	since it had no depth of soil.	1
Rom	8:39	nor height, nor depth, nor anything else	1
	11:33	O the depth of the riches and wisdom	1
1Co	2:10	even the depths of God.	1
Eph	3:18	the breadth and length and height and depth	1

Derbe

1. Δερβαῖος, *Derbaios*, 1291
2. Δέρβη, *Derbē*, 1292

Act	14: 6	fled to Lystra and Derbe, cities of Lycaonia	2
	14:20	The next day he went on with Barnabas to Derbe.	2
	16: 1	Paul went on also to Derbe and to Lystra	2
	20: 4	by Gaius from Derbe, and by Timothy	1

deride

1. βλασφημέω, *blasphēmeō*, 1059

Mat	27:39	Those who passed by derided him	1
Mrk	15:29	Those who passed by derided him	1
Lke	23:39	criminals who were hanged there kept deriding him	1

descend

1. ἀνατέλλω, *anatellō*, 422
2. ἐκ, *ek*, 1666
3. ἐξέρχομαι + ὁ + ὀσφῦς, *exerchomai + ho + osphys*, 2002 + 3836 + 4019
4. καταβαίνω, *katabainō*, 2849
5. σπέρμα, *sperma*, 5065

Mat	3:16	saw the Spirit of God descending like a dove	4
	28: 2	an angel of the Lord, descending from heaven	4
Mrk	1:10	the Spirit descending like a dove on him.	4
Lke	2: 4	descended from the house and family of David.	2

	3:22	Holy Spirit descended upon him in bodily form	4
Jhn	1:32	the Spirit descending from heaven like a dove	4
	1:33	'He on whom you see the Spirit descend and remain	4
	1:51	the angels of God ascending and descending	4
	3:13	one who descended from heaven, the Son of Man.	4
	7:42	the Messiah is descended from David	5
Rom	10: 7	"or 'Who will descend into the abyss?' "	4
Eph	4: 9	descended into the lower parts of the earth?	4
	4:10	He who descended is the same one who ascended	4
1Th	4:16	the Lord himself…will descend from heaven	4
Heb	7: 5	though these also are descended from Abraham.	3
	7:14	evident that our Lord was descended from Judah	1

descend from

1. ἐκ + σπέρμα, *ek + sperma, 1666 + 5065*

| Rom | 1: 3 | descended from David according to the flesh | 1 |

descendant

1. Contextual: Not in Greek
2. γένος, *genos, 1169*
3. θυγάτηρ, *thygatēr, 2588*
4. καρπός + ὁ + ὀσφῦς, *karpos + ho + osphys, 2843 + 3836 + 4019*
5. σπέρμα, *sperma, 5065*
6. υἱός, *huios, 5626*

Mat	23:31	descendants of those who murdered the prophets.	6
Lke	1: 5	His wife was a descendant of Aaron	3
	1:55	to Abraham and to his descendants forever."	5
Jhn	8:33	They answered him, "We are descendants of Abraham	5
	8:37	I know that you are descendants of Abraham;	5
Act	2:30	put one of his descendants on his throne.	4
	3:25	the descendants of the prophets and of the covenant	6
	3:25	saying to Abraham, 'And in your descendants	5
	7: 5	to him…and to his descendants after him	5
	7: 6	his descendants would be resident aliens	5
	13:26	brothers, you descendants of Abraham's family	6
Rom	4:13	to Abraham or to his descendants through the law	5
	4:16	and be guaranteed to all his descendants	5
	4:18	"So numerous shall your descendants be."	5
	9: 7	of Abraham's children are his true descendants;	5
	9: 7	through Isaac that descendants shall be named for you."	5
	9: 8	of the promise are counted as descendants.	5
	11: 1	I myself am an Israelite, a descendant of Abraham	5
2Co	11:22	Are they descendants of Abraham? So am I.	5
Gal	3: 7	those who believe are the descendants of Abraham.	6
2Ti	2: 8	descendant of David—that is my gospel	5
Heb	2:16	come to help…the descendants of Abraham.	5
	7: 5	descendants of Levi who receive the priestly office	6
	11:12	from one person…descendants were born	1
	11:18	through Isaac that descendants shall be named	5
Rev	22:16	I am the root and the descendant of David	2

physical descent

1. σάρκινος, *sarkinos, 4921*

| Heb | 7:16 | a legal requirement concerning physical descent | 1 |

describe

1. γράφω, *graphō, 1211*
2. διηγέομαι, *diēgeomai, 1455*

Act	8:33	Who can describe his generation?	2
	9:27	described for them how…he had seen the Lord	2
	12:17	described for them how the Lord had brought him out	2
Rev	22:18	add to that person the plagues described in this book;	1
	22:19	the holy city, which are described in this book.	1

desert[1]

1. ἀφίημι, *aphiēmi, 918*
2. ἀφίστημι, *aphistēmi, 923*
3. ἐγκαταλείπω, *enkataleipō, 1593*
4. ἔρημος, *erēmos, 2245*
5. μετατίθημι, *metatithēmi, 3572*
6. σκανδαλίζω, *skandalizō, 4997*
7. ὑπάγω, *hypagō, 5632*

Mat	14:13	withdrew from there in a boat to a deserted place	4
	14:15	"This is a deserted place, and the hour is now late;	4
	26:31	"You will all become deserters because of me	6
	26:33	"Though all become deserters because of you	6
	26:33	I will never desert you."	6
	26:56	Then all the disciples deserted him and fled.	1

Mrk	1:35	he got up and went out to a deserted place	4
	6:31	"Come away to a deserted place all by yourselves.	4
	6:32	in the boat to a deserted place by themselves.	4
	6:35	"This is a deserted place, and the hour is now	4
	14:27	Jesus said to them, "You will all become deserters;	6
	14:29	"Even though all become deserters, I will not."	6
	14:50	All of them deserted him and fled.	1
Lke	4:42	he departed and went into a deserted place.	4
	5:16	he would withdraw to deserted places and pray.	4
	9:12	we are here in a deserted place."	4
Jhn	12:11	that many of the Jews were deserting	7
Act	15:38	one who had deserted them in Pamphylia	2
Gal	1: 6	I am astonished that you are so quickly deserting	5
2Ti	4:10	has deserted me and gone to Thessalonica;	3
	4:16	but all deserted me.	3

desert[2]

1. ἐρημία, *erēmia, 2244*
2. ἐρημόω, *erēmoō, 2246*

Mat	15:33	"Where are we to get enough bread in the desert	1
Mrk	8: 4	feed these people with bread here in the desert?"	1
Lke	11:17	kingdom divided against itself becomes a desert	2
Heb	11:38	wandered in deserts and mountains	1

deserve

1. ἄξιος, *axios, 545*
2. ἀξιόω, *axioō, 546*
3. ἔνδικος, *endikos, 1899*
4. ἔνοχος, *enochos, 1944*
5. κατά, *kata, 2848*

Mat	10:10	for laborers deserve their food.	1
	26:66	They answered, "He deserves death."	4
Mrk	14:64	All of them condemned him as deserving death.	4
Lke	10: 7	the laborer deserves to be paid.	1
	12:48	did not know and did what deserved a beating	1
	23:15	he has done nothing to deserve death.	1
	23:41	we are getting what we deserve for our deeds	1
Act	23:29	charged with nothing deserving death	1
	25:11	committed something for which I deserve to die	1
	25:25	I found that he had done nothing deserving death;	1
	26:31	"This man is doing nothing to deserve death	1
Rom	1:32	that those who practice such things deserve to die	1
	3: 8	Their condemnation is deserved!	3
1Ti	5:18	"The laborer deserves to be paid."	1
Heb	10:29	How much worse…do you think will be deserved	2
Rev	2:23	I will give to each of you as your works deserve.	5
	16: 6	given them blood to drink. It is what they deserve!"	1

design

1. νόημα, *noēma, 3784*

| 2Co | 2:11 | for we are not ignorant of his designs. | 1 |

designate

1. καλέω, *kaleō, 2813*
2. προγράφω, *prographō, 4592*
3. προσαγορεύω, *prosagoreuō, 4641*

Lke	2:23	shall be designated as holy to the Lord")	1
Heb	5:10	having been designated by God a high priest	3
Jde	1: 4	who long ago were designated for this condemnation	2

desire *See also* sensual desires *alienate*

1. Contextual: Not in Greek
2. ἀγαπάω, *agapaō, 26*
3. βούλομαι, *boulomai, 1089*
4. ἐπιθυμέω, *epithymeō, 2121*
5. ἐπιθυμητής, *epithymētēs, 2122*
6. ἐπιθυμία, *epithymia, 2123*
7. ἐπιποθία + ἔχω, *epipothia + echō, 2163 + 2400*
8. εὐδοκία, *eudokia, 2306*
9. ζητέω, *zēteō, 2426*
10. θέλημα, *thelēma, 2525*
11. θέλω, *thelō, 2527*
12. ὀρέγω, *oregō, 3977*

Mat	9:13	Go and learn what this means, 'I desire mercy	11
	12: 7	'I desire mercy and not sacrifice,'	11
	23:37	How often have I desired to gather your children	11
Mrk	4:19	and the desire for other things	6
Lke	5:39	no one after drinking old wine desires new	11
	10:24	many prophets and kings desired to see	11

Lke	13:34	I desired to gather your children together	11
	22:15	"I have eagerly desired to eat this Passover	4
Jhn	8:44	you choose to do your father's desires.	6
	17:24	Father, I desire that those also…may be with me	11
Rom	9:22	What if God, desiring to show his wrath	11
	10: 1	Brothers and sisters, my heart's desire and prayer	8
	13:14	no provision for the flesh, to gratify its desires.	6
	15:23	I desire, as I have for many years, to come to you	7
1Co	1:22	For Jews demand signs and Greeks desire wisdom	9
	7:37	having his own desire under control	10
	10: 6	so that we might not desire evil as they did.	5
	14:35	If there is anything they desire to know	11
2Co	8:10	to do something but even to desire to do something	11
	13: 3	since you desire proof that Christ is speaking	9
Gal	4:21	Tell me, you who desire to be subject to the law	11
	5:16	do not gratify the desires of the flesh.	6
	5:17	what the flesh desires is opposed to the Spirit	4
	5:17	the Spirit desires is opposed to the flesh;	1
	5:24	the flesh with its passions and desires.	6
Eph	2: 3	following the desires of flesh and senses	10
Php	1:23	my desire is to depart and be with Christ	6
Col	3: 5	fornication, impurity, passion, evil desire	6
1Ti	1: 7	desiring to be teachers of the law	11
	2: 4	who desires everyone to be saved	11
	2: 8	I desire, then, that…the men should pray	3
	3: 1	to the office of bishop desires a noble task.	4
	6: 9	trapped by many senseless and harmful desires	6
2Ti	3: 6	swayed by all kinds of desires	6
	4: 3	teachers to suit their own desires	6
Tit	3: 8	I desire that you insist on these things	3
Heb	6:17	when God desired to show even more clearly	3
	10: 5	"Sacrifices and offerings you have not desired	11
	10: 8	"You have neither desired nor taken pleasure in	11
	11:16	as it is, they desire a better country	12
	13:18	desiring to act honorably in all things.	11
Jas	1:14	one is tempted by one's own desire, being lured	6
	1:15	when that desire has conceived, it gives birth to sin	6
1Pe	1:14	the desires that you formerly had in ignorance.	6
	2:11	to abstain from the desires of the flesh	6
	3:10	"Those who desire life and desire to see good days	11
	3:10	"Those who desire life and desire to see good days	2
	4: 2	no longer by human desires but by the will of God.	6
2Pe	2:18	with licentious desires of the flesh they entice	6
1Jn	2:16	the desire of the flesh, the desire of the eyes	6
	2:16	the desire of the flesh, the desire of the eyes	6
	2:17	the world and its desire are passing away,	6
Jde	1: 5	Now I desire to remind you	3
Rev	11: 6	with every kind of plague, as often as they desire.	11

desolate

1. ἔρημος, *erēmos, 2245*
2. ἐρημόω, *erēmoō, 2246*
3. ἐρήμωσις, *erēmōsis, 2247*

Mat	23:38	See, your house is left to you, desolate.	1
	24:15	"So when you see the desolating sacrilege	3
Mrk	13:14	when you see the desolating sacrilege set up	3
Act	1:20	'Let his homestead become desolate	1
Rev	17:16	they will make her desolate and naked;	2

desolate woman

1. ἔρημος, *erēmos, 2245*

Gal	4:27	children of the desolate woman are more numerous	1

desolation

1. ἐρήμωσις, *erēmōsis, 2247*

Lke	21:20	then know that its desolation has come near.	1

despair *See also* drive to despair

1. ἐξαπορέω, *exaporeō, 1989*

2Co	1: 8	we despaired of life itself.	1

despicable

1. στυγητός, *stygētos, 5144*

Tit	3: 3	despicable, hating one another.	1

despise

1. ἐκπτύω, *ekptyō, 1746*
2. ἐξουθενέω, *exoutheneō, 2024*
3. καταφρονέω, *kataphroneō, 2969*

Mat	6:24	or be devoted to the one and despise the other	3

	18:10	that you do not despise one of these little ones;	3
Lke	16:13	be devoted to the one and despise the other.	3
Rom	2: 4	Or do you despise the riches of his kindness	3
	14: 3	Those who eat must not despise those who abstain	2
	14:10	Or you, why do you despise your brother or sister?	2
1Co	1:28	God chose what is low and despised in the world	2
	16:11	therefore let no one despise him.	2
Gal	4:14	you did not scorn or despise me	1
1Th	5:20	Do not despise the words of prophets	2
1Ti	4:12	Let no one despise your youth	3
2Pe	2:10	those who indulge…and who despise authority.	3

destine

1. κεῖμαι, *keimai, 3023*
2. προγινώσκω, *proginōskō, 4589*
3. πρόγνωσις, *prognōsis, 4590*
4. προορίζω, *proorizō, 4633*
5. τάσσω, *tassō, 5435*
6. τίθημι, *tithēmi, 5502*
7. υἱός, *huios, 5626*

Lke	2:34	destined for the falling and the rising of many	1
Jhn	17:12	not…lost except the one destined to be lost	7
Act	13:48	as many as had been destined for eternal life	5
Eph	1: 5	He destined us for adoption as his children	4
	1:11	destined according to the purpose of him	4
1Th	3: 3	know that this is what we are destined for.	1
	5: 9	For God has destined us not for wrath	6
1Pe	1: 2	chosen and destined by God the Father	3
	1:20	destined before the foundation of the world	2
	2: 8	they disobey…as they were destined to do.	6

destine for

1. εἰς, *eis, 1650*

1Pe	1:11	sufferings destined for Christ and the subsequent glory.	1

destine one

1. υἱός, *huios, 5626*

2Th	2: 3	the one destined for destruction.	1

destitute

1. ὑστερέω, *hystereō, 5728*

Heb	11:37	destitute, persecuted, tormented—	1

destroy

1. αἴρω, *airō, 149*
2. ἀναιρέω, *anaireō, 359*
3. ἀπόλλυμι, *apollymi, 660*
4. διαφθείρω, *diaphtheirō, 1425*
5. καθαίρεσις, *kathairesis, 2746*
6. καθαιρέω, *kathaireō, 2747*
7. καταλύω, *katalyō, 2907*
8. καταργέω, *katargeō, 2934*
9. λύω, *lyō, 3395*
10. πορθέω, *portheō, 4514*
11. φθείρω, *phtheirō, 5780*
12. φθορά, *phthora, 5785*

Mat	2:13	Herod…to search for the child, to destroy him."	3
	9:17	the wine is spilled, and the skins are destroyed;	3
	10:28	rather fear him who can destroy both soul and body	3
	12:14	and conspired against him, how to destroy him.	3
	22: 7	sent his troops, destroyed those murderers	3
	26:61	'I am able to destroy the temple of God	7
	27:40	saying, "You who would destroy the temple	7
Mrk	1:24	Have you come to destroy us?	3
	3: 6	how to destroy him.	3
	9:22	into the water, to destroy him;	3
	12: 9	He will come and destroy the tenants	3
	14:58	will destroy this temple that is made with hands	7
	15:29	You who would destroy the temple	7
Lke	4:34	Have you come to destroy us?	3
	5:37	the skins will be destroyed.	3
	6: 9	to save life or to destroy it?"	3
	12:33	where no thief comes near and no moth destroys	4
	17:27	the flood came and destroyed all of them.	3
	17:29	destroyed all of them	3
	20:16	He will come and destroy those tenants	3
Jhn	2:19	"Destroy this temple, and in three days I	9
	10:10	thief comes only to steal and kill and destroy.	3
	11:48	destroy both our holy place and our nation."	1

	11:50	than to have the whole nation destroyed."	3
Act	6:14	Jesus of Nazareth will destroy this place	7
	13:19	After he had destroyed seven nations in the land	6
Rom	6: 6	so that the body of sin might be destroyed	8
	14:20	Do not, for the sake of food, destroy the work	7
1Co	1:19	"I will destroy the wisdom of the wise	3
	3:17	If anyone destroys God's temple	11
	3:17	God will destroy that person.	11
	6:13	God will destroy both one and the other.	8
	8:11	weak believers for whom Christ died are destroyed.	3
	10: 9	and were destroyed by serpents.	3
	10:10	and were destroyed by the destroyer.	3
	15:24	after he has destroyed every ruler	8
	15:26	The last enemy to be destroyed is death.	8
2Co	4: 9	struck down, but not destroyed;	3
	5: 1	if the earthly tent we live in is destroyed	7
	10: 4	they have divine power to destroy strongholds.	5
	10: 4	power to destroy strongholds. We destroy arguments	6
Gal	1:13	and was trying to destroy it.	10
	1:23	proclaiming the faith he once tried to destroy."	10
2Th	2: 8	whom the Lord Jesus will destroy	2
Heb	2:14	destroy the one who has the power of death	8
Jas	4:12	who is able to save and to destroy.	3
2Pe	2:12	when those creatures are destroyed,	12
	2:12	creatures are destroyed, they also will be destroyed,	11
1Jn	3: 8	to destroy the works of the devil.	9
Jde	1: 5	afterward destroyed those who did not believe.	3
	1:10	they are destroyed by those things	11
Rev	8: 9	and a third of the ships were destroyed.	4
	11:18	and for destroying those who destroy the earth."	4
	11:18	and for destroying those who destroy the earth."	4

destroyer

    1. ὀλοθρευτής, *olothreutēs, 3904*
    2. ὀλοθρεύω, *olothreuō, 3905*

| 1Co | 10:10 | and were destroyed by the destroyer. | 1 |
| Heb | 11:28 | the destroyer of the firstborn | 2 |

destruction

    1. ἀπώλεια, *apōleia, 724*
    2. ὄλεθρος, *olethros, 3897*

Mat	7:13	the road is easy that leads to destruction	1
Rom	9:22	the objects of wrath that are made for destruction;	1
1Co	5: 5	for the destruction of the flesh	2
Php	1:28	For them this is evidence of their destruction	1
	3:19	Their end is destruction; their god is the belly;	1
1Th	5: 3	then sudden destruction will come upon them	2
2Th	1: 9	suffer the punishment of eternal destruction	2
	2: 3	the one destined for destruction.	1
1Ti	6: 9	plunge people into ruin and destruction.	1
2Pe	2: 1	bringing swift destruction on themselves.	1
	2: 3	and their destruction is not asleep.	1
	3: 7	day of judgment and destruction of the godless.	1
	3:16	the ignorant…twist to their own destruction	1
Rev	17: 8	beast…is about to ascend…and go to destruction.	1
	17:11	As for the beast…it goes to destruction.	1

destructive

    1. ἀπώλεια, *apōleia, 724*

| 2Pe | 2: 1 | secretly bring in destructive opinions. | 1 |

detachment of soldiers

    1. σπεῖρα, *speira, 5061*

| Jhn | 18: 3 | So Judas brought a detachment of soldiers | 1 |

detail

    1. μέρος, *meros, 3538*

| Heb | 9: 5 | Of these things we cannot speak now in detail. | 1 |

detain

    1. ἐγκόπτω, *enkoptō, 1601*

| Act | 24: 4 | to detain you no further | 1 |

detect

    1. προλαμβάνω, *prolambanō, 4624*

| Gal | 6: 1 | friends, if anyone is detected in a transgression | 1 |

determine

    1. βούλομαι, *boulomai, 1089*

---

    2. δοκιμάζω, *dokimazō, 1507*
    3. εὐδοκέω, *eudokeō, 2305*
    4. κρίνω, *krinō, 3212*
    5. ὁρίζω, *horizō, 3988*

Lke	22:22	the Son of Man is going as it has been determined	5
Act	5:28	you are determined to bring this man's blood on us."	1
	11:29	The disciples determined…each would send relief	5
Rom	2:18	know his will and determine what is best	2
1Co	7:37	determined in his own mind to keep her	4
Php	1:10	to help you to determine what is best	2
1Th	2: 8	determined to share with you not only the gospel of God	3

detestable

    1. βδελυκτός, *bdelyktos, 1008*

| Tit | 1:16 | detestable, disobedient, unfit for any good work. | 1 |

deviate

    1. ἀστοχέω, *astocheō, 846*

| 1Ti | 1: 6 | Some people have deviated from these | 1 |

devil

    1. Contextual: Not in Greek
    2. διάβολος, *diabolos, 1333*

Mat	4: 1	the wilderness to be tempted by the devil.	2
	4: 5	Then the devil took him to the holy city	2
	4: 8	Again, the devil took him to a very high mountain	2
	4:11	Then the devil left him, and suddenly angels came	2
	13:39	the enemy who sowed them is the devil;	2
	25:41	into the eternal fire prepared for the devil	2
Lke	4: 2	for forty days he was tempted by the devil.	2
	4: 3	The devil said to him, "If you are the Son of God	2
	4: 5	Then the devil led him up	1
	4: 6	the devil said to him, "To you I will give	2
	4: 9	the devil took him to Jerusalem	1
	4:13	When the devil had finished every test	2
	8:12	then the devil comes and takes away the word	2
Jhn	6:70	Yet one of you is a devil."	2
	8:44	You are from your father the devil	2
	13: 2	The devil had already put it into the heart	2
Act	10:38	healing all who were oppressed by the devil	2
	13:10	said, "You son of the devil	2
Eph	4:27	do not make room for the devil.	2
	6:11	able to stand against the wiles of the devil.	2
1Ti	3: 6	fall into the condemnation of the devil.	2
	3: 7	fall into disgrace and the snare of the devil.	2
2Ti	2:26	they may escape from the snare of the devil	2
Heb	2:14	one who has the power of death, that is, the devil	2
Jas	4: 7	Resist the devil, and he will flee from you.	2
1Pe	5: 8	Like a roaring lion your adversary the devil prowls	2
1Jn	3: 8	Everyone who commits sin is a child of the devil;	2
	3: 8	for the devil has been sinning from the beginning.	2
	3: 8	to destroy the works of the devil.	2
	3:10	The children of God and the children of the devil	2
Jde	1: 9	when archangel Michael contended with the devil	2
Rev	2:10	devil is about to throw some of you into prison	2
	12: 9	serpent, who is called the Devil and Satan	2
	12:12	for the devil has come down to you with great wrath	2
	20: 2	that ancient serpent, who is the Devil and Satan	2
	20:10	the devil who had deceived them was thrown	2

devilish

    1. δαιμονιώδης, *daimoniōdēs, 1229*

| Jas | 3:15 | wisdom…is earthly, unspiritual, devilish. | 1 |

devise

    1. λαμβάνω, *lambanō, 3284*

| Mat | 28:12 | assembled with the elders, they devised a plan | 1 |

devise cleverly

    1. σοφίζω, *sophizō, 5054*

| 2Pe | 1:16 | For we did not follow cleverly devised myths | 1 |

devoid

    1. μή + ἔχω, *mē + echō, 3590 + 2400*

| Jde | 1:19 | worldly people, devoid of the Spirit | 1 |

devote

    1. ἀντέχω, *antechō, 504*
    2. εἰμί, *eimi, 1639*

3. ἐπακολουθέω, *epakoloutheō, 2051*
4. πλήρης, *plērēs, 4441*
5. προΐστημι, *proistēmi, 4613*
6. προσκαρτερέω, *proskartereō, 4674*
7. σχολάζω, *scholazō, 5390*
8. τάσσω, *tassō, 5435*

Mat	6:24	or be devoted to the one and despise the other	1
Lke	16:13	be devoted to the one and despise the other.	1
Act	1:14	were constantly devoting themselves to prayer	6
	2:42	They devoted themselves to the apostles' teaching	6
	6: 4	we, for our part, will devote ourselves to prayer	6
	9:36	She was devoted to good works and acts of charity.	4
1Co	7: 5	to devote yourselves to prayer	7
	16:15	devoted themselves to the service of the saints;	8
Col	4: 2	Devote yourselves to prayer	6
1Ti	4:15	Put these things into practice, devote yourself	2
	5:10	devoted herself to doing good in every way.	3
Tit	3: 8	may be careful to devote themselves to good works;	5
	3:14	learn to devote themselves to good works	5

devotion

1. Contextual: Not in Greek
2. εὐπάρεδρος, *euparedros, 2339*
3. καρδία, *kardia, 2840*

Act	11:23	remain faithful…with steadfast devotion;	3
1Co	7:35	unhindered devotion to the Lord.	2
2Co	11: 3	from a sincere and pure devotion to Christ.	1

devour

1. ἐσθίω, *esthiō, 2266*
2. καταπίνω, *katapinō, 2927*
3. κατεσθίω, *katesthiō, 2983*

Mrk	12:40	They devour widows' houses	3
Lke	15:30	who has devoured your property with prostitutes	3
	20:47	They devour widows' houses	3
Gal	5:15	If, however, you bite and devour one another,	3
1Pe	5: 8	the devil prowls…looking for someone to devour.	2
Rev	12: 4	might devour her child as soon as it was born.	3
	17:16	will devour her flesh and burn her up with fire.	1

devout

1. εὐλαβής, *eulabēs, 2327*
2. εὐσεβής, *eusebēs, 2356*
3. ὅσιος, *hosios, 4008*
4. σέβω, *sebō, 4936*

Lke	2:25	this man was righteous and devout	1
Act	2: 5	devout Jews from every nation under heaven	1
	8: 2	Devout men buried Stephen	1
	10: 7	called two of his slaves and a devout soldier	2
	13:43	many Jews and devout converts to Judaism	4
	13:50	the Jews incited the devout women of high standing	4
	17: 4	as did a great many of the devout Greeks	4
	22:12	Ananias, who was a devout man according to the law	1
Tit	1: 8	upright, devout, and self-controlled.	3

devout man

1. εὐσεβής, *eusebēs, 2356*

Act	10: 2	devout man who feared God with all his household;	1

devout person

1. σέβω, *sebō, 4936*

Act	17:17	he argued…with the Jews and the devout persons	1

diadem

1. διάδημα, *diadēma, 1343*

Rev	12: 3	and ten horns, and seven diadems on his heads.	1
	13: 1	a beast…and on its horns were ten diadems	1
	19:12	and on his head are many diadems;	1

die

1. ἀποθνήσκω, *apothnēskō, 633*
2. ἀπόλλυμι, *apollymi, 660*
3. ἐκψύχω, *ekpsychō, 1775*
4. θάνατος, *thanatos, 2505*
5. θανατόω, *thanatoō, 2506*
6. θνήσκω, *thnēskō, 2569*
7. κοιμάω, *koimaō, 3121*
8. μή + ζῳογονέω, *mē + zōogoneō, 3590 + 2441*
9. τελευτάω, *teleutaō, 5462*

Mat	2:19	When Herod died, an angel of the Lord suddenly	9
	9:18	saying, "My daughter has just died;	9
	22:24	'If a man dies childless,	1
	22:25	the first married, and died	9
	22:27	Last of all, the woman herself died.	1
	26:35	"Even though I must die with you, I will not deny	1
Mrk	9:48	where their worm never dies	9
	12:19	if a man's brother dies, leaving a wife	1
	12:20	when he died, left no children;	1
	12:21	the second married the widow and died	1
	12:22	Last of all the woman herself died.	1
Lke	7:12	a man who had died was being carried out.	6
	8:42	daughter, about twelve years old, who was dying	1
	15:17	here I am dying of hunger!	2
	16:22	The poor man died	1
	16:22	The rich man also died and was buried.	1
	20:28	Moses wrote for us that if a man's brother dies	1
	20:29	the first married, and died childless;	1
	20:31	in the same way all seven died childless.	1
	20:32	Finally the woman also died.	1
	20:36	Indeed they cannot die anymore	1
Jhn	4:49	"Sir, come down before my little boy dies."	1
	6:49	ate the manna in the wilderness, and they died	1
	6:50	so that one may eat of it and not die.	1
	6:58	not like…your ancestors ate, and they died.	1
	8:21	search for me, but you will die in your sin.	1
	8:24	I told you that you would die in your sins	1
	8:24	for you will die in your sins	1
	8:52	Abraham died, and so did the prophets;	1
	8:53	Are you greater than our father Abraham, who died?	1
	8:53	The prophets also died. Who do you claim to be?"	1
	11:16	"Let us also go, that we may die with him."	1
	11:21	my brother would not have died.	1
	11:25	who believe in me, even though they die, will live	1
	11:26	lives and believes in me will never die.	1
	11:32	my brother would not have died.	1
	11:37	"Could not he…have kept this man from dying?"	1
	11:50	to have one man die for the people	1
	11:51	Jesus was about to die for the nation	1
	12:24	a grain of wheat falls into the earth and dies	1
	12:24	if it dies, it bears much fruit.	1
	12:33	to indicate the kind of death he was to die.	1
	18:14	better to have one person die for the people.	1
	18:32	he indicated the kind of death he was to die.)	1
	19: 7	according to that law he ought to die	1
	21:23	the rumor…that this disciple would not die.	1
	21:23	Jesus did not say to him that he would not die	1
Act	2:29	he both died and was buried	9
	5: 5	he fell down and died.	3
	5:10	Immediately she fell down at his feet and died.	3
	7: 4	After his father died, God had him move from there	1
	7:15	He himself died there as well as our ancestors	9
	7:19	abandon their infants so that they would die	8
	7:60	When he had said this, he died.	7
	9:37	At that time she became ill and died.	1
	12:23	he was eaten by worms and died.	3
	13:36	David…died, was laid beside his ancestors	7
	21:13	ready not only to be bound but even to die	1
	25:11	committed something for which I deserve to die	4
	25:19	who had died, but whom Paul asserted to be alive.	6
Rom	1:32	that those who practice such things deserve to die	4
	5: 6	at the right time Christ died for the ungodly.	1
	5: 7	rarely will anyone die for a righteous person	1
	5: 7	for a good person someone might actually dare to die.	1
	5: 8	while we still were sinners Christ died for us.	1
	5:15	if the many died through the one man's trespass	1
	6: 2	How can we who died to sin go on living in it?	1
	6: 7	For whoever has died is freed from sin.	1
	6: 8	But if we have died with Christ, we believe	1
	6: 9	We know that Christ…will never die again;	1
	6:10	The death he died, he died to sin, once for all;	1
	6:10	The death he died, he died to sin, once for all;	1
	7: 2	but if her husband dies, she is discharged	1
	7: 3	But if her husband dies, she is free from that law	1
	7: 4	you have died to the law through the body	5
	7:10	I died, and the very commandment that promised life	1
	8:13	if you live according to the flesh, you will die;	1
	8:34	Who is to condemn? It is Christ Jesus, who died	1
	14: 7	and we do not die to ourselves.	1
	14: 8	and if we die, we die to the Lord;	1
	14: 8	and if we die, we die to the Lord;	1

14: 8 whether we live or whether we die, we are the Lord's.   1
14: 9 For to this end Christ died and lived again   1
14:15 cause the ruin of one for whom Christ died.   1
1Co 7:39 if the husband dies, she is free to marry   7
8:11 weak believers for whom Christ died are destroyed.   1
9:15 I would rather die than that—no one will deprive me   1
11:30 many of you are weak and ill, and some have died.   7
15: 3 Christ died for our sins   1
15: 6 though some have died.   7
15:18 Then those also who have died in Christ   7
15:20 first fruits of those who have died.   7
15:22 for as all die in Adam   1
15:31 I die every day!   1
15:32 "Let us eat and drink, for tomorrow we die."   1
15:36 What you sow does not come to life unless it dies.   1
15:51 We will not all die   7
2Co 5:14 we are convinced that one has died for all;   1
5:14 therefore all have died.   1
5:15 he died for all, so that those who live   1
5:15 but for who died and was raised for them.   1
6: 9 as dying, and see—we are alive;   1
Gal 2:19 For through the law I died to the law   1
2:21 then Christ died for nothing.   1
Php 1:21 For to me, living is Christ and dying is gain.   1
2:27 He was indeed so ill that he nearly died.   4
Col 2:20 If with Christ you died to the elemental spirits   1
3: 3 for you have died, and your life is hidden   1
1Th 4:13 uninformed…about those who have died   7
4:14 since we believe that Jesus died and rose again   1
4:14 bring with him those who have died.   7
4:15 will by no means precede those who have died.   7
5:10 who died for us, so that…we may live with him   1
Heb 9:27 just as it is appointed for mortals to die once   1
10:28 Anyone who has violated the law of Moses dies   1
11: 4 he died, but through his faith he still speaks.   1
11:13 All of these died in faith   1
11:21 Jacob, when dying, blessed…the sons of Joseph   7
2Pe 3: 4 For ever since our ancestors died   7
Rev 8: 9 a third of the living creatures in the sea died   1
8:11 the waters became wormwood, and many died   1
9: 6 they will long to die, but death will flee from them.   1
14:13 Blessed are the dead who from now on die in the Lord."   1
16: 3 and every living thing in the sea died.   1

die surely
1. τελευτάω + θάνατος, *teleutaō + thanatos, 5462 + 2505*
Mat 15: 4 speaks evil of father or mother must surely die.'   1
Mrk 7:10 'Whoever speaks evil of father…must surely die.'   1

die together
1. συναποθνήσκω, *synapothnēskō, 5271*
2Co 7: 3 to die together and to live together.   1

die with
1. συναποθνήσκω, *synapothnēskō, 5271*
Mrk 14:31 though I must die with you, I will not deny you."   1
2Ti 2:11 If we have died with him, we will also live with him;   1

differ
1. διαφέρω, *diapherō, 1422*
2. διάφορος, *diaphoros, 1427*
Rom 12: 6 gifts that differ according to the grace given   2
1Co 15:41 star differs from star in glory.   1

different *See also* see anything different, teach different doctrine
1. ἕτερος, *heteros, 2283*
2Co 11: 4 if you receive a different spirit   1
11: 4 a different gospel from the one you accepted   1
Gal 1: 6 turning to a different gospel—   1

different kind
1. γένος, *genos, 1169*
2. οὕτως, *houtōs, 4048*
1Co 7: 7 having one kind and another a different kind   2
14:10 There are doubtless many different kinds of sounds   1

differently
1. ἑτέρως, *heterōs, 2284*

Php 3:15 if you think differently about anything   1

difficult
1. σκληρός, *sklēros, 5017*
Jhn 6:60 "This teaching is difficult; who can accept it?"   1

difficulty
1. μόλις, *molis, 3660*
Act 27: 7 arrived with difficulty off Cnidus   1
27: 8 Sailing past it with difficulty   1

dig
1. ὀρύσσω, *oryssō, 4002*
2. σκάπτω, *skaptō, 4999*
Mat 21:33 dug a wine press in it, and built a watchtower.   1
Mrk 12: 1 dug a pit for the wine press   1
Lke 6:48 like a man building a house, who dug deeply   2
13: 8 until I dig around it and put manure on   2
16: 3 I am not strong enough to dig   2

dig a hole
1. ὀρύσσω, *oryssō, 4002*
Mat 25:18 dug a hole in the ground and hid his master's money.   1

dig through
1. ἐξορύσσω, *exoryssō, 2021*
Mrk 2: 4 and after having dug through it   1

dignity
1. σεμνότης, *semnotēs, 4949*
1Ti 2: 2 peaceable life in all godliness and dignity.   1

diligence
1. σπουδή, *spoudē, 5082*
Rom 12: 8 the leader, in diligence;   1
Heb 6:11 each one of you to show the same diligence   1

diligently
1. ἀκριβῶς, *akribōs, 209*
Mat 2: 8 saying, "Go and search diligently for the child;   1

dill
1. ἄνηθον, *anēthon, 464*
Mat 23:23 you tithe mint, dill, and cummin   1

dimly
1. ἐν + αἴνιγμα, *en + ainigma, 1877 + 141*
1Co 13:12 For now we see in a mirror, dimly,   1

dine
1. ἀριστάω, *aristaō, 753*
Lke 11:37 a Pharisee invited him to dine with him;   1

dinner *See also* dinner guest, sit at dinner
1. ἄριστον, *ariston, 756*
2. δεῖπνον, *deipnon, 1270*
Mat 22: 4 Look, I have prepared my dinner   1
Lke 11:38 he did not first wash before dinner.   1
14:12 "When you give a luncheon or a dinner   2
14:16 "Someone gave a great dinner and invited many.   2
14:17 At the time for the dinner he sent his slave   2
14:24 who were invited will taste my dinner.' "   2
Jhn 12: 2 There they gave a dinner for him. Martha served   2

Dionysius
1. Διονύσιος, *Dionysios, 1477*
Act 17:34 believers, including Dionysius the Areopagite   1

Diotrephes
1. Διοτρέφης, *Diotrephēs, 1485*
3Jn 1: 9 Diotrephes, who likes to put himself first   1

dip
1. βάπτω, *baptō, 970*
2. ἐμβάπτω, *embaptō, 1835*
Mat 26:23 "The one who has dipped his hand into the bowl   2
Mrk 14:20 one who is dipping bread into the bowl with me.   2
Lke 16:24 send Lazarus to dip the tip of his finger in water   1

Jhn 13:26 I give this piece of bread when I have dipped it   1
     13:26 had dipped the piece of bread, he gave it to Judas   1
Rev 19:13 He is clothed in a robe dipped in blood   1

direct

1. Contextual: Not in Greek
2. βούλομαι, *boulomai, 1089*
3. διατάσσω, *diatassō, 1411*
4. διδάσκω, *didaskō, 1438*
5. κατευθύνω, *kateuthynō, 2985*
6. κελεύω, *keleuō, 3027*
7. παραγγέλλω, *parangellō, 4133*
8. συντάσσω, *syntassō, 5332*
9. τάσσω, *tassō, 5435*
10. χρηματίζω, *chrēmatizō, 5976*

Mat 21: 6 The disciples went and did as Jesus had directed   8
     26:19 the disciples did as Jesus had directed them   8
     28:15 took the money and did as they were directed.   4
     28:16 to the mountain to which Jesus had directed   9
Lke 8:55 he directed them to give her something   3
Act 7:44 as God directed when he spoke to Moses   1
     10:22 was directed by a holy angel to send for you   10
     22:24 directed that he was to be brought into the barracks   6
1Th 3:11 our Lord Jesus direct our way to you.   5
      4:11 to work with your hands, as we directed you   7
2Th 3: 5 May the Lord direct your hearts to the love of God   5
Tit 1: 5 appoint elders in every town, as I directed you: 3
Jas 3: 4 wherever the will of the pilot directs.   2

direction   *See* give directions

dirt

1. ῥύπος, *rhypos, 4866*

1Pe 3:21 not as a removal of dirt from the body   1

dirty

1. ῥυπαρός, *rhyparos, 4865*

Jas 2: 2 a poor person in dirty clothes also comes in   1

disagree

1. ἀσύμφωνος, *asymphōnos, 851*

Act 28:25 they disagreed with each other;   1

disagreement   *See also* point of disagreement, sharp disagreement

1. Contextual: Not in Greek

Act 15:39 disagreement became so sharp that they parted   1

disappear

1. ἀφανισμός, *aphanismos, 907*
2. γίνομαι + εἰς + οὐδείς, *ginomai + eis + oudeis, 1181 + 1650 + 4029*
3. ἐκνεύω, *ekneuō, 1728*
4. παρέρχομαι, *parerchomai, 4216*

Jhn 5:13 for Jesus had disappeared in the crowd   3
Act 5:36 were dispersed and disappeared.   2
Heb 8:13 what is obsolete...will soon disappear.   1
Jas 1:10 the rich will disappear like a flower in the field.   4

disappoint

1. καταισχύνω, *kataischynō, 2875*

Rom 5: 5 and hope does not disappoint us   1

disarm

1. ἀπεκδύομαι, *apekdyomai, 588*

Col 2:15 He disarmed the rulers and authorities   1

disbelieve

1. ἀπιστέω, *apisteō, 601*

Lke 24:41 While in their joy they were disbelieving   1

discern

1. ἀνακρίνω, *anakrinō, 373*
2. διακρίνω, *diakrinō, 1359*
3. δοκιμάζω, *dokimazō, 1507*
4. συνετός, *synetos, 5305*

Rom 12: 2 so that you may discern what is the will of God   3
1Co 1:19 the discernment of the discerning I will thwart."   4

2:14 because they are spiritually discerned.   1
2:15 Those who are spiritual discern all things   1
11:29 who eat and drink without discerning the body   2

discernment

1. διάκρισις, *diakrisis, 1360*
2. σύνεσις, *synesis, 5304*

1Co 1:19 the discernment of the discerning I will thwart."   2
     12:10 to another the discernment of spirits,   1

discharge

1. ἐκβάλλω, *ekballō, 1675*
2. καταργέω, *katargeō, 2934*

Act 16:37 now are they going to discharge us in secret?   1
Rom 7: 2 discharged from the law concerning the husband   2
      7: 6 But now we are discharged from the law   2

disciple   *See also* make disciples

1. Contextual: Not in Greek
2. μαθητεύω, *mathēteuō, 3411*
3. μαθητής, *mathētēs, 3412*
4. μαθήτρια, *mathētria, 3413*

Mat 5: 1 after he sat down, his disciples came to him.   3
      8:21 Another of his disciples said to him   3
      8:23 he got into the boat, his disciples followed him.   3
      9:10 sitting with him and his disciples.   3
      9:11 Pharisees saw this, they said to his disciples   3
      9:14 Then the disciples of John came to him, saying   3
      9:14 Pharisees fast often, but your disciples do not fast?"   3
      9:19 Jesus got up and followed him, with his disciples.   3
      9:37 Then he said to his disciples   3
     10: 1 Jesus summoned his twelve disciples and gave them   3
     10:24 "A disciple is not above the teacher   3
     10:25 it is enough for the disciple   3
     10:42 a cup of cold water...in the name of a disciple   3
     11: 1 instructing his twelve disciples   3
     11: 2 he sent word by his disciples   3
     12: 1 his disciples were hungry   3
     12: 2 your disciples are doing what is not lawful to do   3
     12:49 pointing to his disciples, he said,   3
     13:10 the disciples came and asked him   3
     13:36 And his disciples approached him, saying   3
     14:12 His disciples came and took the body   3
     14:15 When it was evening, the disciples came to him   3
     14:19 broke the loaves, and gave them to the disciples   3
     14:19 and the disciples gave them to the crowds.   3
     14:22 he made the disciples get into the boat   3
     14:26 when the disciples saw him walking on the sea   3
     15: 2 "Why do your disciples break the tradition   3
     15:12 Then the disciples approached and said to him   3
     15:23 And his disciples came and urged him, saying   3
     15:32 Jesus called his disciples to him and said   3
     15:33 The disciples said to him   3
     15:36 he broke them and gave them to the disciples   3
     15:36 and the disciples gave them to the crowds.   3
     16: 5 When the disciples reached the other side   3
     16:13 he asked his disciples   3
     16:20 Then he sternly ordered the disciples   3
     16:21 From that time on, Jesus began to show his disciples   3
     16:24 Then Jesus told his disciples   3
     17: 6 When the disciples heard this   3
     17:10 the disciples asked him   3
     17:13 Then the disciples understood   3
     17:16 I brought him to your disciples   3
     17:19 Then the disciples came to Jesus privately   3
     18: 1 At that time the disciples came to Jesus and asked   3
     19:10 His disciples said to him, "If such is the case   3
     19:13 The disciples spoke sternly to those   3
     19:23 Jesus said to his disciples, "Truly I tell you   3
     19:25 When the disciples heard this   3
     20:17 he took the twelve disciples aside by themselves   3
     21: 1 Jesus sent two disciples   3
     21: 6 The disciples went and did as Jesus had directed   3
     21:20 When the disciples saw it, they were amazed,   3
     22:16 So they sent their disciples to him   3
     23: 1 to the crowds and to his disciples   3
     24: 1 his disciples came to point out to him   3
     24: 3 the disciples came to him privately, saying   3
     26: 1 he said to his disciples   3
     26: 8 when the disciples saw it, they were angry   3

	26:17 the disciples came to Jesus, saying	3
	26:18 Passover at your house with my disciples.' "	3
	26:19 the disciples did as Jesus had directed them	3
	26:26 broke it, gave it to the disciples, and said	3
	26:35 And so said all the disciples.	3
	26:36 he said to his disciples	3
	26:40 he came to the disciples and found them sleeping;	3
	26:45 Then he came to the disciples and said to them	3
	26:56 Then all the disciples deserted him and fled.	3
	27:57 who was also a disciple of Jesus.	2
	27:64 otherwise his disciples may go and steal him away	3
	28: 7 Then go quickly and tell his disciples	3
	28: 8 ran to tell his disciples.	3
	28:13 "You must say, 'His disciples came by night	3
	28:16 Now the eleven disciples went to Galilee	3
Mrk	2:15 sitting with Jesus and his disciples	3
	2:16 said to his disciples	3
	2:18 John's disciples and the Pharisees were fasting;	3
	2:18 "Why do John's disciples…fast	3
	2:18 the disciples of the Pharisees fast	3
	2:18 your disciples do not fast?"	3
	2:23 his disciples began to pluck heads of grain.	3
	3: 7 Jesus departed with his disciples to the sea	3
	3: 9 He told his disciples to have a boat ready	3
	4:34 he explained everything in private to his disciples.	3
	5:31 his disciples said to him, "You see the crowd	3
	6: 1 his disciples followed him.	3
	6:29 When his disciples heard about it	3
	6:35 grew late, his disciples came to him and said	3
	6:41 broke the loaves, and gave them to his disciples	3
	6:45 he made his disciples get into the boat	3
	7: 2 noticed that some of his disciples were eating	3
	7: 5 "Why do your disciples not live according	3
	7:17 his disciples asked him about the parable.	3
	8: 1 he called his disciples and said to them	3
	8: 4 His disciples replied, "How can one feed	3
	8: 6 he broke them and gave them to his disciples	3
	8:10 he got into the boat with his disciples	3
	8:14 the disciples had forgotten to bring any bread;	1
	8:27 Jesus went on with his disciples	3
	8:27 on the way he asked his disciples	3
	8:33 turning and looking at his disciples	3
	8:34 He called the crowd with his disciples	3
	9:14 When they came to the disciples	3
	9:18 I asked your disciples to cast it out	3
	9:28 his disciples asked him privately	3
	9:31 for he was teaching his disciples, saying	3
	10:10 in the house the disciples asked him again	3
	10:13 the disciples spoke sternly to them.	3
	10:23 Jesus looked around and said to his disciples	3
	10:24 the disciples were perplexed at these words.	3
	10:46 As he and his disciples and a large crowd	3
	11: 1 he sent two of his disciples	3
	11:14 his disciples heard it.	3
	11:19 Jesus and his disciples went out of the city.	1
	12:43 he called his disciples and said to them	3
	13: 1 one of his disciples said to him, "Look, Teacher	3
	14:12 his disciples said to him, "Where do you want us	3
	14:13 he sent two of his disciples, saying to them,	3
	14:14 where I may eat the Passover with my disciples?'	3
	14:16 the disciples set out and went to the city	3
	14:32 he said to his disciples, "Sit here while I pray."	3
	16: 7 tell his disciples and Peter that he is going	3
Lke	5:30 their scribes were complaining to his disciples	3
	5:33 "John's disciples…frequently fast and pray,	3
	5:33 like the disciples of the Pharisees	1
	5:33 but your disciples eat and drink."	1
	6: 1 his disciples plucked some heads of grain	3
	6:13 when day came, he called his disciples	3
	6:17 with a great crowd of his disciples	3
	6:20 he looked up at his disciples	3
	6:40 A disciple is not above the teacher	3
	7:11 his disciples and a large crowd went with him.	3
	7:18 disciples of John reported all these things	3
	7:18 John summoned two of his disciples	3
	8: 9 his disciples asked him what this parable meant.	3
	8:22 One day he got into a boat with his disciples	3
	9:14 he said to his disciples, "Make them sit down	3
	9:16 gave them to the disciples	3
	9:18 with only the disciples near him	3
	9:40 I begged your disciples to cast it out	3

	9:43 he said to his disciples	3
	9:54 When his disciples James and John saw it	3
	10:23 Then turning to the disciples, Jesus said	3
	11: 1 after he had finished, one of his disciples said	3
	11: 1 teach us to pray, as John taught his disciples."	3
	12: 1 he began to speak first to his disciples	3
	12:22 He said to his disciples, "Therefore I tell you	3
	14:26 even life itself, cannot be my disciple.	3
	14:27 cannot be my disciple.	3
	14:33 none of you can become my disciple if	3
	16: 1 Then Jesus said to the disciples,	3
	17: 1 Jesus said to his disciples,	3
	17:22 he said to the disciples, "The days are coming	3
	18:15 when the disciples saw it, they sternly ordered	3
	19:29 he sent two of the disciples	3
	19:37 the whole multitude of the disciples	3
	19:39 "Teacher, order your disciples to stop."	3
	20:45 he said to the disciples	3
	22:11 where I may eat the Passover with my disciples?" '	3
	22:39 the disciples followed him.	3
	22:45 he got up from prayer, he came to the disciples	3
Jhn	1:35 John again was standing with two of his disciples	3
	1:37 The two disciples heard him say this	3
	2: 2 Jesus and his disciples had also been invited	3
	2:11 and his disciples believed in him.	3
	2:12 with his mother…and his disciples;	3
	2:17 His disciples remembered that it was written	3
	2:22 his disciples remembered that he had said this;	3
	3:22 Jesus and his disciples went into the Judean	3
	3:25 discussion…between John's disciples and a Jew.	3
	4: 1 making and baptizing more disciples than John"	3
	4: 2 not Jesus himself but his disciples who baptized	3
	4: 8 (His disciples had gone to the city	3
	4:27 Just then his disciples came.	3
	4:31 the disciples were urging him, "Rabbi, eat	3
	4:33 So the disciples said to one another	3
	6: 3 and sat down there with his disciples.	3
	6: 8 One of his disciples, Andrew	3
	6:12 he told his disciples, "Gather up the fragments	3
	6:16 his disciples went down to the sea	3
	6:22 Jesus had not got into the boat with his disciples	3
	6:22 his disciples had gone away alone.	3
	6:24 neither Jesus nor his disciples were there	3
	6:60 When many of his disciples heard it, they said	3
	6:61 aware that his disciples were complaining	3
	6:66 Because of this many of his disciples turned back	3
	7: 3 disciples also may see the works you are doing;	3
	8:31 you are truly my disciples;	3
	9: 2 His disciples asked him, "Rabbi, who sinned	3
	9:27 Do you also want to become his disciples?"	3
	9:28 they reviled him, saying, "You are his disciple	3
	9:28 we are disciples of Moses.	3
	11: 7 Then after this he said to the disciples	3
	11: 8 The disciples said to him, "Rabbi	3
	11:12 The disciples said to him, "Lord	3
	11:54 and he remained there with the disciples.	3
	12: 4 Judas Iscariot, one of his disciples	3
	12:16 disciples did not understand these things at first;	3
	13: 5 began to wash the disciples' feet	3
	13:22 The disciples looked at one another	3
	13:23 One of his disciples—the one whom Jesus loved	3
	13:35 everyone will know that you are my disciples	3
	15: 8 and become my disciples.	3
	16:17 some of his disciples said to one another	3
	16:29 His disciples said, "Yes	3
	18: 1 he went out with his disciples	3
	18: 1 a garden, which he and his disciples entered.	3
	18: 2 Jesus often met there with his disciples.	3
	18:15 Simon Peter and another disciple followed Jesus.	3
	18:15 that disciple was known to the high priest	3
	18:16 So the other disciple, who was known	3
	18:17 "You are not also one of this man's disciples	3
	18:19 about his disciples and about his teaching.	3
	18:25 "You are not also one of his disciples	3
	19:26 and the disciple whom he loved standing beside	3
	19:27 he said to the disciple, "Here is your mother."	3
	19:27 the disciple took her into his own home.	3
	19:38 Joseph of Arimathea, who was a disciple of Jesus	3
	20: 2 went to Simon Peter and the other disciple	3
	20: 3 Then Peter and the other disciple set out	3
	20: 4 the other disciple outran Peter	3

Jhn 20: 8 the other disciple, who reached the tomb first   3
     20:10 the disciples returned to their homes.   3
     20:18 Mary Magdalene went and announced to the disciples   3
     20:19 the house where the disciples had met   3
     20:20 the disciples rejoiced when they saw the Lord.   3
     20:25 the other disciples told him   3
     20:26 later his disciples were again in the house   3
     20:30 many other signs in the presence of his disciples   3
     21: 1 showed himself again to the disciples   3
     21: 2 sons of Zebedee, and two others of his disciples.   3
     21: 4 the disciples did not know that it was Jesus.   3
     21: 7 That disciple whom Jesus loved said to Peter   3
     21: 8 the other disciples came in the boat   3
     21:12 the disciples dared to ask him, "Who are you?"   3
     21:14 Jesus appeared to the disciples   3
     21:20 saw the disciple whom Jesus loved following   3
     21:23 the rumor...that this disciple would not die.   3
     21:24 the disciple who is testifying to these   3
Act   6: 1 when the disciples were increasing in number   3
     6: 2 called together the whole community of the disciples   3
     6: 7 the number of the disciples increased greatly   3
     9: 1 murder against the disciples of the Lord   3
     9:10 there was a disciple in Damascus named Ananias.   3
     9:19 he was with the disciples in Damascus   3
     9:25 his disciples took him by night   3
     9:26 he attempted to join the disciples;   3
     9:26 for they did not believe that he was a disciple.   3
     9:36 in Joppa there was a disciple whose name was Tabitha   4
     9:38 disciples...sent two men to him with the request   3
     11:26 the disciples were first called "Christians."   3
     11:29 The disciples determined...each would send relief   3
     13:52 the disciples were filled with joy   3
     14:20 when the disciples surrounded him, he got up   3
     14:22 strengthened the souls of the disciples   3
     14:28 stayed there with the disciples for some time.   3
     15:10 by placing on the neck of the disciples a yoke   3
     16: 1 where there was a disciple named Timothy   3
     18:23 strengthening all the disciples.   3
     18:27 wrote to the disciples to welcome him.   3
     19: 1 Ephesus, where he found some disciples.   3
     19: 9 he left them, taking the disciples with him   3
     19:30 the disciples would not let him;   3
     20: 1 Paul sent for the disciples;   3
     20:30 in order to entice the disciples to follow them.   3
     21: 4 looked up the disciples and stayed there   3
     21:16 Some of the disciples from Caesarea also came   3
     21:16 Mnason of Cyprus, an early disciple   3

another disciple
   1. ἀδελφός, *adelphos, 81*
Lke 17: 3 If another disciple sins, you must rebuke   1

fellow disciple
   1. συμμαθητής, *symmathētēs, 5209*
Jhn 11:16 Thomas...said to his fellow disciples   1

disciplinarian
   1. παιδαγωγός, *paidagōgos, 4080*
Gal   3:24 the law was our disciplinarian until Christ came   1
     3:25 we are no longer subject to a disciplinarian   1

discipline
   1. Contextual: Not in Greek
   2. νήφω, *nēphō, 3768*
   3. παιδεία, *paideia, 4082*
   4. παιδευτής, *paideutēs, 4083*
   5. παιδεύω, *paideuō, 4084*
1Co 11:32 when we are judged by the Lord, we are disciplined   5
Eph   6: 4 bring them up in the discipline...of the Lord.   3
Heb 12: 5 do not regard lightly the discipline of the Lord   3
     12: 6 for the Lord disciplines those whom he loves   5
     12: 7 Endure trials for the sake of discipline.   3
     12: 7 whom a parent does not discipline?   5
     12: 8 If you do not have that discipline   3
     12: 9 we had human parents to discipline us   4
     12:10 they disciplined us for a short time   5
     12:10 he disciplines us for our good   1
     12:11 discipline always seems painful rather than pleasant   3
1Pe   1:13 Therefore prepare your minds for action; discipline   2
     4: 7 therefore be serious and discipline yourselves   2

     5: 8 Discipline yourselves, keep alert.   2
Rev   3:19 I reprove and discipline those whom I love.   5

disclose
   1. ἀναγγέλλω, *anangellō, 334*
   2. δηλόω, *dēloō, 1317*
   3. εὑρίσκω, *heuriskō, 2351*
   4. φανερός, *phaneros, 5745*
   5. φανερόω, *phaneroō, 5746*
Mrk   4:22 there is nothing hidden, except to be disclosed;   5
Lke   8:17 nothing is hidden that will not be disclosed   4
Act 19:18 confessed and disclosed their practices.   1
Rom   3:21 the righteousness of God has been disclosed   5
     16:26 but is now disclosed   5
1Co   3:13 the Day will disclose it   2
     4: 5 who...will disclose the purposes of the heart.   5
     14:25 the secrets of the unbeliever's heart are disclosed   4
Heb   9: 8 the way into the sanctuary has not yet been disclosed   5
2Pe   3:10 and everything that is done on it will be disclosed.   3

discredit
   1. βλασφημέω, *blasphēmeō, 1059*
Tit   2: 5 the word of God may not be discredited.   1

discuss
   1. ἀντιβάλλω, *antiballō, 506*
   2. διαλαλέω, *dialaleō, 1362*
   3. διαλέγομαι, *dialegomai, 1363*
   4. διαλογίζομαι, *dialogizomai, 1368*
   5. ζητέω, *zēteō, 2426*
   6. περί, *peri, 4309*
   7. συζητέω, *syzēteō, 5184*
   8. συλλογίζομαι, *syllogizomai, 5199*
   9. συμβάλλω, *symballō, 5202*
Mrk   2: 8 that they were discussing these questions   4
Lke   6:11 filled with fury and discussed with one another   2
     20: 5 They discussed it with one another, saying   8
     20:14 saw him, they discussed it among themselves   4
     24:15 they were talking and discussing   7
     24:17 he said to them, "What are you discussing   1
Jhn 16:19 he said to them, "Are you discussing   5
Act   4:15 they discussed the matter with one another.   9
     15: 2 to go up to Jerusalem to discuss this question   6
     24:25 as he discussed justice, self-control,   3

discussion   *See also* have a discussion, hold a discussion
   1. ζήτησις, *zētēsis, 2428*
Jhn   3:25 Now a discussion about purification arose   1

disease
   1. Contextual: Not in Greek
   2. ἀσθένεια, *astheneia, 819*
   3. μάστιξ, *mastix, 3465*
   4. νόσος, *nosos, 3798*
Mat   4:23 curing every disease and every sickness   4
     4:24 those who were afflicted with various diseases   4
     8:17 "He took our infirmities and bore our diseases."   4
     9:35 and curing every disease and every sickness.   4
     10: 1 and to cure every disease and every sickness.   4
Mrk   1:34 cured many who were sick with various diseases   4
     3:10 so that all who had diseases pressed upon him   3
     5:29 she was healed of her disease.   3
     5:34 go in peace, and be healed of your disease."   3
Lke   4:40 any who were sick with various kinds of diseases   4
     5:15 to be cured of their diseases.   4
     6:18 to be healed of their diseases;   4
     7:21 cured many people of diseases, plagues,   4
     9: 1 gave them power...to cure diseases   4
     9: 6 the good news and curing diseases everywhere.   1
Act 19:12 diseases left them, and the evil spirits came out   4
     28: 9 the people on the island who had diseases   2

disfigure
   1. ἀφανίζω, *aphanizo, 906*
Mat   6:16 the hypocrites, for they disfigure their faces   1

disgrace   *See also* expose to public disgrace
   1. αἰσχύνη, *aischynē, 158*
   2. αἰσχύνομαι, *aischynomai, 159*

3. καταισχύνω, *kataischynō, 2875*
4. ὀνειδισμός, *oneidismos, 3944*
5. ὄνειδος, *oneidos, 3945*

Lke   1:25 the disgrace I have endured among my people."   5
      14: 9 then in disgrace you would…take the lowest place.   1
1Co 11: 4 with something on his head disgraces his head   3
      11: 5 with her head unveiled disgraces her head   3
2Co 7:14 I was not disgraced;   3
1Ti   3: 7 fall into disgrace and the snare of the devil.   4
1Pe 4:16 as a Christian, do not consider it a disgrace   2

disgraceful

1. αἰσχρός, *aischros, 156*

1Co 11: 6 disgraceful for a woman to have her hair cut off   1

disguise

1. μετασχηματίζω, *metaschēmatizō, 3571*

2Co 11:13 disguising themselves as apostles of Christ.   1
      11:14 Satan disguises himself as an angel of light.   1
      11:15 if his ministers also disguise themselves   1

dish

1. Contextual: Not in Greek
2. πίναξ, *pinax, 4402*

Lke 11:39 the outside of the cup and of the dish   2
Jhn 13:26 piece of bread when I have dipped it in the dish   1

dishonest

1. ἀδικία, *adikia, 94*
2. ἄδικος, *adikos, 96*

Lke 16: 8 his master commended the dishonest manager   1
      16: 9 make friends…by means of dishonest wealth   1
      16:10 whoever is dishonest in a very little   2
      16:10 is dishonest also in much.   2
      16:11 not been faithful with the dishonest wealth   2

dishonor   *See also* suffer dishonor

1. ἀτιμάζω, *atimazō, 869*
2. ἀτιμία, *atimia, 871*

Jhn 8:49 I honor my Father, and you dishonor me.   1
Rom 2:23 do you dishonor God by breaking the law?   1
1Co 15:43 It is sown in dishonor, it is raised in glory.   2
2Co 6: 8 in honor and dishonor   2
Jas   2: 6 But you have dishonored the poor.   1

dismal

1. σκυθρωπός, *skythrōpos, 5034*

Mat 6:16 you fast, do not look dismal, like the hypocrites   1

dismiss

1. ἀπελαύνω, *apelaunō, 590*
2. ἀπολύω, *apolyō, 668*
3. μεθίστημι, *methistēmi, 3496*

Mat 1:19 to public disgrace, planned to dismiss her quietly.   2
      14:22 while he dismissed the crowds.   2
      14:23 after he had dismissed the crowds   2
Mrk 6:45 while he dismissed the crowd.   2
Lke 2:29 now you are dismissing your servant in peace   2
      16: 4 so that, when I am dismissed as manager,   3
Act 18:16 he dismissed them from the tribunal.   1
      19:41 When he had said this, he dismissed the assembly.   2
      23:22 So the tribune dismissed the young man   2

dismissal

1. ἀποστάσιον, *apostasion, 687*

Mat 19: 7 to give a certificate of dismissal   1
Mrk 10: 4 allowed a man to write a certificate of dismissal   1

disobedience

1. ἀπείθεια, *apeitheia, 577*
2. παρακοή, *parakoē, 4157*

Rom 5:19 For just as by the one man's disobedience   2
      11:30 received mercy because of their disobedience   1
      11:32 For God has imprisoned all in disobedience   1
2Co 10: 6 We are ready to punish every disobedience   2
Heb 2: 2 every…disobedience received a just penalty.   2
      4: 6 failed to enter because of disobedience   1
      4:11 no one may fall through such disobedience   1

disobedient

1. ἀνυπότακτος, *anypotaktos, 538*
2. ἀπείθεια, *apeitheia, 577*
3. ἀπειθέω, *apeitheō, 578*
4. ἀπειθής, *apeithēs, 579*

Lke   1:17 the disobedient to the wisdom of the righteous   4
Act 26:19 I was not disobedient to the heavenly vision   4
Rom 10:21 my hands to a disobedient and contrary people."   3
      11:30 Just as you were once disobedient to God   3
      11:31 so they have now been disobedient in order that   3
Eph 2: 2 is now at work among those who are disobedient.   2
      5: 6 wrath…comes on those who are disobedient.   2
Col 3: 6 wrath of God is coming on those who are disobedient   2
1Ti 1: 9 law is laid down…for the lawless and disobedient   1
2Ti 3: 2 disobedient to their parents, ungrateful, unholy   4
Tit 1:16 detestable, disobedient, unfit for any good work.   4
      3: 3 For we ourselves were once foolish, disobedient   4
Heb 3:18 if not to those who were disobedient?   3
      11:31 did not perish with those who were disobedient   3

disobey

1. ἀπειθέω, *apeitheō, 578*
2. παρέρχομαι, *parerchomai, 4216*

Lke 15:29 I have never disobeyed your command;   2
Jhn 3:36 whoever disobeys the Son will not see life   1
1Pe 2: 8 They stumble because they disobey the word   1

disorder

1. ἀκαταστασία, *akatastasia, 189*

1Co 14:33 for God is a God not of disorder but of peace.   1
2Co 12:20 slander, gossip, conceit, and disorder.   1
Jas 3:16 there will also be disorder and wickedness of every kind. 1

disperse

1. διαλύω, *dialyō, 1370*
2. διασκορπίζω, *diaskorpizō, 1399*

Jhn 11:52 to gather into one the dispersed children of God.   2
Act 5:36 all who followed him were dispersed   1

dispersion

1. διασπορά, *diaspora, 1402*

Jhn 7:35 Does he intend to go to the Dispersion   1
Jas 1: 1 To the twelve tribes in the Dispersion: 1
1Pe 1: 1 To the exiles of the Dispersion   1

display

1. ἐνδείκνυμι, *endeiknymi, 1892*

1Ti 1:16 Christ might display the utmost patience   1

displease

1. μή + ἀρέσκω, *mē + areskō, 3590 + 743*

1Th 2:15 drove us out; they displease God and oppose everyone   1

disposal

1. ἐξουσία, *exousia, 2026*

Act 5: 4 sold, were not the proceeds at your disposal?   1

dispose

1. δοκέω, *dokeō, 1506*
2. θέλω, *thelō, 2527*

1Co 10:27 you are disposed to go   2
      11:16 if anyone is disposed to be contentious   1

dispossess

1. κατάσχεσις, *kataschesis, 2959*

Act 7:45 when they dispossessed the nations   1

dispute   *See also* engage in dispute

1. ἀντιλογία, *antilogia, 517*
2. διαλέγομαι, *dialegomai, 1363*
3. μάχη, *machē, 3480*
4. μάχομαι, *machomai, 3481*
5. φιλονεικία, *philoneikia, 5808*

Lke 22:24 A dispute also arose among them   5
Jhn 6:52 The Jews then disputed among themselves, saying   4
Act 24:12 They did not find me disputing with anyone   2
2Co 7: 5 disputes without and fears within.   3
Heb 6:16 an oath given as confirmation puts an end to all dispute. 1

Heb 7: 7 It is beyond dispute   1
Jas   4: 1 Those conflicts and disputes among you,   3
Jde   1: 9 Michael...disputed about the body of Moses   2

dispute about words
1. λογομαχία, *logomachia, 3363*

1Ti   6: 4 has a morbid craving...for disputes about words   1

dispute with one another
1. συζητέω, *syzēteō, 5184*

Mrk 12:28 heard them disputing with one another   1

disqualify
1. ἀδόκιμος, *adokimos, 99*
2. καταβραβεύω, *katabrabeuō, 2857*

1Co   9:27 I myself should not be disqualified.   1
Col   2:18 Do not let anyone disqualify you   2

disregard
1. καταφρονέω, *kataphroneō, 2969*

Heb 12: 2 endured the cross, disregarding its shame   1

disrepute
1. ἀπελεγμός, *apelegmos, 591*
2. ἄτιμος, *atimos, 872*

Act 19:27 this trade of ours may come into disrepute   1
1Co   4:10 You are held in honor, but we in disrepute.   2

disrespectful
1. καταφρονέω, *kataphroneō, 2969*

1Ti   6: 2 Those...must not be disrespectful   1

dissension
1. διχοστασία, *dichostasia, 1496*
2. ἔρις, *eris, 2251*
3. στάσις, *stasis, 5087*
4. σχίσμα, *schisma, 5388*

Act 15: 2 had no small dissension and debate with them   3
       23: 7 a dissension began   3
       23:10 When the dissension became violent   3
Rom 16:17 those who cause dissensions and offenses   1
1Co 12:25 that there may be no dissension within the body   4
Gal   5:20 strife, jealousy, anger, quarrels, dissensions   1
1Ti   6: 4 envy, dissension, slander, base suspicions   2
Tit   3: 9 dissensions, and quarrels about the law   2

dissipation
1. ἀπάτη, *apatē, 573*
2. ἀσωτία, *asōtia, 861*
3. κραιπάλη, *kraipalē, 3190*

Lke 21:34 weighed down with dissipation and drunkenness   3
1Pe   4: 4 no longer join them in the same excesses of dissipation   2
2Pe   2:13 They are...reveling in their dissipation   1

dissolute
1. ἀσώτως, *asōtōs, 862*

Lke 15:13 he squandered his property in dissolute living.   1

dissolve
1. λύω, *lyō, 3395*

2Pe   3:10 and the elements will be dissolved with fire   1
       3:11 Since all these things are to be dissolved in this way   1
       3:12 the heavens will be set ablaze and dissolved   1

distance
1. ἀπό, *apo, 608*
2. μακράν, *makran, 3426*
3. μακρόθεν, *makrothen, 3427*
4. πόρρωθεν, *porrōthen, 4523*

Mat   8:30 was feeding at some distance from them.   2
       26:58 Peter was following him at a distance   3
       27:55 Many women...looking on from a distance;   3
Mrk   5: 6 When he saw Jesus from a distance, he ran   3
       11:13 Seeing in the distance a fig tree in leaf   3
       14:54 Peter had followed him at a distance   3
       15:40 There were also women looking on from a distance;   3
Lke 17:12 ten lepers approached him. Keeping their distance   4
       22:54 Peter was following at a distance.   3

       23:49 the women...stood at a distance   3
Heb 11:13 from a distance they saw and greeted them.   4
Rev 14:20 for a distance of about two hundred miles.   1

great distance
1. μακρόθεν, *makrothen, 3427*

Mrk   8: 3 some of them have come from a great distance."   1

distant
1. μακρός, *makros, 3431*

Lke 15:13 and traveled to a distant country   1
       19:12 "A nobleman went to a distant country   1

distinct
1. διαστολή, *diastolē, 1405*

1Co 14: 7 If they do not give distinct notes   1

distinction *See also* make a distinction
1. διαστολή, *diastolē, 1405*

Rom 3:22 all who believe. For there is no distinction   1
       10:12 there is no distinction between Jew and Greek;   1

distinguish
1. διάκρισις, *diakrisis, 1360*

Heb 5:14 to distinguish good from evil.   1

more distinguished
1. ἔντιμος, *entimos, 1952*

Lke 14: 8 more distinguished than you has been invited   1

distort truth
1. διαστρέφω, *diastrephō, 1406*

Act 20:30 Some...will come distorting the truth   1

distract
1. θορυβάζω, *thorybazō, 2571*
2. περισπάω, *perispaō, 4352*

Lke 10:40 Martha was distracted by her many tasks;   2
       10:41 you are worried and distracted by many things;   1

distress
1. ἀδημονέω, *adēmoneō, 86*
2. ἀνάγκη, *anankē, 340*
3. βασανίζω, *basanizō, 989*
4. ἐκθαμβέω, *ekthambeō, 1701*
5. θλῖψις, *thlipsis, 2568*
6. λυπέω, *lypeō, 3382*
7. στενοχωρία, *stenochōria, 5103*
8. συνοχή, *synochē, 5330*
9. χαλεπός, *chalepos, 5901*

Mat   8: 6 at home paralyzed, in terrible distress."   3
       17:23 And they were greatly distressed.   6
       18:31 they were greatly distressed   6
       26:22 they became greatly distressed and began to say   6
Mrk 14:19 They began to be distressed   6
       14:33 and began to be distressed and agitated.   4
Lke 21:23 will be great distress on the earth   2
       21:25 on the earth distress among nations   8
Rom 2: 9 There will be anguish and distress   7
       8:35 Will hardship, or distress, or persecution   7
1Co   7:28 who marry will experience distress in this life   5
2Co   2: 4 I wrote you out of much distress and anguish   5
Php   2:26 distressed because you heard that he was ill.   1
       4:14 it was kind of you to share my distress.   5
1Th   3: 7 during all our distress and persecution   2
2Ti   3: 1 in the last days distressing times will come.   9
Jas   1:27 to care for orphans and widows in their distress   5
Rev   2:22 I am throwing into great distress   5

distress deeply
1. παροξύνω, *paroxynō, 4236*

Act 17:16 he was deeply distressed to see...idols   1

distress greatly
1. καταπονέω, *kataponeō, 2930*

2Pe   2: 7 greatly distressed by...the lawless   1

distribute

1. διαδίδωμι, *diadidōmi, 1344*
2. διαμερίζω, *diamerizō, 1374*
3. μερισμός, *merismos, 3536*
4. παρατίθημι, *paratithēmi, 4192*

Mrk 8: 6 to his disciples to distribute; 4
   8: 6 and they distributed them to the crowd. 4
   8: 7 ordered that these too should be distributed. 4
Lke 18:22 Sell...and distribute the money to the poor 1
Jhn 6:11 he distributed them to those who were seated; 1
Act 2:45 distribute the proceeds to all, as any had need. 2
   4:35 was distributed to each as any had need. 1
Heb 2: 4 distributed according to his will. 3

distribution

1. διακονία, *diakonia, 1355*

Act 6: 1 neglected in the daily distribution of food 1

district

1. γῆ, *gē, 1178*
2. μερίς, *meris, 3535*
3. μέρος, *meros, 3538*

Mat 2:22 he went away to the district of Galilee. 3
   9:26 report of this spread throughout that district. 1
   9:31 spread the news about him throughout that district. 1
  15:21 and went away to the district of Tyre and Sidon. 3
  16:13 into the district of Caesarea Philippi 3
Mrk 8:10 went to the district of Dalmanutha. 3
Act 16:12 a leading city of the district of Macedonia 2

distrust

1. ἀπιστία, *apistia, 602*

Rom 4:20 No distrust made him waver 1

disturb

1. ἐκταράσσω, *ektarassō, 1752*
2. ταράσσω, *tarassō, 5429*

Act 15:24 certain persons...have said things to disturb you 2
  16:20 they said, "These men are disturbing our city; 1
  17: 8 were disturbed when they heard this 2

disturb greatly

1. ἐμβριμάομαι, *embrimaomai, 1839*

Jhn 11:33 he was greatly disturbed in spirit and deeply moved. 1
  11:38 Jesus, again greatly disturbed, came to the tomb. 1

disturbance

1. θόρυβος, *thorybos, 2573*
2. τάραχος, *tarachos, 5431*

Act 19:23 no little disturbance broke out concerning the Way. 2
  24:18 without any crowd or disturbance. 1

divide

1. διαδίδωμι, *diadidōmi, 1344*
2. διαιρέω, *diaireō, 1349*
3. διαμερίζω, *diamerizō, 1374*
4. μερίζω, *merizō, 3532*
5. μερισμός, *merismos, 3536*
6. μεσότοιχον, *mesotoichon, 3546*
7. ποιέω, *poieō, 4472*
8. σχίζω, *schizō, 5387*
9. σχίσμα, *schisma, 5388*

Mat 12:25 "Every kingdom divided against itself 4
  12:25 no city or house divided against itself 4
  12:26 he is divided against himself; 4
  27:35 they divided his clothes among themselves 3
Mrk 3:24 If a kingdom is divided against itself 4
  3:25 if a house is divided against itself 4
  3:26 risen up against himself and is divided 4
  6:41 he divided the two fish among them all. 4
  15:24 they crucified him, and divided his clothes 3
Lke 11:17 "Every kingdom divided against itself 4
  11:18 If Satan also is divided against himself 4
  11:22 divides his plunder. 3
  12:13 tell my brother to divide the family inheritance 4
  12:52 five in one household will be divided 3
  12:53 they will be divided: 3
  15:12 he divided his property between them. 2

22:17 "Take this and divide it among yourselves; 3
  23:34 they cast lots to divide his clothing. 3
Jhn 9:16 And they were divided. 9
  10:19 Again the Jews were divided 9
  19:23 his clothes and divided them into four parts 7
  19:24 "They divided my clothes among themselves 3
Act 2: 3 Divided tongues, as of fire, appeared among them, 3
  14: 4 the residents of the city were divided; 8
  23: 7 the assembly was divided. 8
1Co 1:13 Has Christ been divided? Was Paul crucified for you? 4
  7:34 his interests are divided. 4
Eph 2:14 broken down the dividing wall, that is, the hostility 6
Heb 4:12 piercing until it divides soul from spirit 5

divination

1. πύθων, *pythōn, 4780*

Act 16:16 met a slave-girl who had a spirit of divination 1

divine *See also* divine *nature*, divine *reply*, divine *service*

1. θεῖος, *theios, 2521*
2. θεός, *theos, 2536*

Mat 16:23 setting your mind not on divine things but on human 2
Mrk 8:33 you are setting your mind not on divine things 2
Lke 2:52 Jesus increased...in divine and human favor. 2
Rom 3:25 in his divine forbearance he had passed over 2
2Co 10: 4 they have divine power to destroy strongholds. 2
  11: 2 I feel a divine jealousy for you 2
1Ti 1: 4 rather than the divine training that is known by faith. 2
2Pe 1: 3 His divine power has given us everything 1
  1: 4 may become participants of the divine nature. 1

divinity

1. δαιμόνιον, *daimonion, 1228*

Act 17:18 "He seems to be a proclaimer of foreign divinities." 1

division *See also* cause division

1. διαμερισμός, *diamerismos, 1375*
2. σχίσμα, *schisma, 5388*

Lke 12:51 No, I tell you, but rather division! 1
Jhn 7:43 there was a division in the crowd because of him. 2
1Co 1:10 that there be no divisions among you 2
  11:18 I hear that there are divisions among you; 2

divorce *See also* certificate of divorce

1. ἀπολύω, *apolyō, 668*
2. ἀφίημι, *aphiēmi, 918*

Mat 5:31 "It was also said, 'Whoever divorces his wife 1
  5:32 I say to you that anyone who divorces his wife 1
  19: 3 lawful for a man to divorce his wife for any cause?" 1
  19: 7 a certificate of dismissal and to divorce her?" 1
  19: 8 Moses allowed you to divorce your wives 1
  19: 9 I say to you, whoever divorces his wife 1
Mrk 10: 2 "Is it lawful for a man to divorce his wife?" 1
  10: 4 a certificate of dismissal and to divorce her." 1
  10:11 "Whoever divorces his wife and marries another 1
  10:12 if she divorces her husband and marries another 1
Lke 16:18 "Anyone who divorces his wife 1
  16:18 whoever marries a woman divorced from her husband 1
1Co 7:11 the husband should not divorce his wife. 2
  7:12 he should not divorce her. 2
  7:13 she should not divorce him. 2

divorce woman

1. ἀπολύω, *apolyō, 668*

Mat 5:32 whoever marries a divorced woman commits adultery. 1

do *See also* nothing more to do, nothing to do

1. Contextual: Not in Greek
2. ἀπό, *apo, 608*
3. γίνομαι, *ginomai, 1181*
4. γογγύζω, *gongyzō, 1197*
5. διακονέω, *diakoneō, 1354*
6. εἰμί, *eimi, 1639*
7. ἐκ, *ek, 1666*
8. ἐν, *en, 1877*
9. ἐνδείκνυμι, *endeiknymi, 1892*
10. ἐπιθυμέω, *epithymeō, 2121*
11. ἐργάζομαι, *ergazomai, 2237*
12. ἔργον, *ergon, 2240*

13.	ἐσθίω, *esthiō*, 2266	
14.	ἔχω, *echō*, 2400	
15.	ἰσχύω, *ischyō*, 2710	
16.	κατατίθημι, *katatithēmi*, 2960	
17.	κατεργάζομαι, *katergazomai*, 2981	
18.	λαμβάνω, *lambanō*, 3284	
19.	μή + γέ, *mē + ge*, 3590 + 1145	
20.	παρά, *para*, 4123	
21.	παρέχω, *parechō*, 4218	
22.	πειράζω, *peirazō*, 4279	
23.	περιπατέω, *peripateō*, 4344	
24.	ποιέω, *poieō*, 4472	
25.	ποίησις, *poiēsis*, 4474	
26.	πορνεύω, *porneuō*, 4519	
27.	πρᾶξις, *praxis*, 4552	
28.	πράσσω, *prassō*, 4556	
29.	συναναμείγνυμι, *synanameignymi*, 5264	
30.	τηρέω, *tēreō*, 5498	
31.	ὠφελέω, *ōpheleō*, 6067	

Mat	1:24 he did as the angel of the Lord commanded him;	24
	5:19 teaches others to do the same, will be called least	1
	5:19 whoever does them and teaches them will be called	24
	5:46 Do not even the tax collectors do the same?	24
	5:47 what more are you doing than others?	24
	5:47 than others? Do not even the Gentiles do the same?	24
	6: 2 as the hypocrites do in the synagogues	24
	6: 3 your left hand know what your right hand is doing	24
	6: 4 so that your alms may be done in secret	6
	6: 7 heap up empty phrases as the Gentiles do;	1
	6:10 Your will be done, on earth as it is in heaven.	3
	7:12 do to others as you would have them do to you	24
	7:12 do to others as you would have them do to you	24
	7:21 the one who does the will of my Father in heaven.	24
	7:22 and do many deeds of power in your name?'	24
	8: 9 to my slave, 'Do this,' and the slave does it."	24
	8: 9 to my slave, 'Do this,' and the slave does it."	24
	8:13 let it be done for you according to your faith.	3
	8:29 "What have you to do with us, Son of God?	1
	9:28 "Do you believe that I am able to do this?"	24
	9:29 "According to your faith let it be done to you."	3
	11: 2 John heard in prison what the Messiah was doing	12
	11:20 in which most of his deeds of power had been done	3
	11:21 For if the deeds of power done in you had been done	3
	11:21 For if the deeds of power done in you had been done	3
	11:23 For if the deeds of power done in you had been done	3
	11:23 For if the deeds of power done in you had been done	3
	12: 2 your disciples are doing what is not lawful to do	24
	12: 2 what is not lawful to do on the sabbath."	24
	12: 3 David did when he and his companions were hungry?	24
	12:12 So it is lawful to do good on the sabbath."	24
	12:50 For whoever does the will of my Father in heaven	24
	13:28 He answered, 'An enemy has done this.'	24
	13:58 he did not do many deeds of power there	3
	15:28 Let it be done for you as you wish."	3
	16:27 he will repay everyone for what has been done.	27
	17:12 but they did to him whatever they pleased.	24
	18:19 it will be done for you by my Father in heaven.	3
	18:35 So my heavenly Father will also do	24
	19:16 "Teacher, what good deed must I do	24
	20: 5 he did the same.	24
	20:15 Am I not allowed to do what I choose	24
	20:32 "What do you want me to do for you?"	24
	21: 6 The disciples went and did as Jesus had directed	24
	21:15 the amazing things that he did	24
	21:21 will you do what has been done to the fig tree	24
	21:21 will you do what has been done to the fig tree	1
	21:21 it will be done.	3
	21:23 "By what authority are you doing these things	24
	21:24 by what authority I do these things.	24
	21:27 by what authority I am doing these things.	24
	21:31 Which of the two did the will of his father?"	24
	21:40 what will he do to those tenants?"	24
	21:42 this was the Lord's doing	20
	22:26 The second did the same, so also the third	1
	23: 3 therefore, do whatever they teach you and follow	24
	23: 3 but do not do as they do	24
	23: 3 but do not do as they do	12
	23: 5 They do all their deeds to be seen by others;	24
	25:40 just as you did it to one of the least of these	24
	25:40 to one of the least…you did it to me.'	24

	25:45 you did not do it to one of the least of these	24
	25:45 you did not do it to me.'	24
	26:13 what she has done will be told in remembrance	24
	26:19 the disciples did as Jesus had directed them	24
	26:42 if this cannot pass…your will be done."	3
	26:50 "Friend, do what you are here to do."	1
	26:50 "Friend, do what you are here to do."	1
	27:19 "Have nothing to do with that innocent man	1
	27:22 "Then what should I do with Jesus	24
	27:23 he asked, "Why, what evil has he done?"	24
	27:24 So when Pilate saw that he could do nothing	31
	28:15 took the money and did as they were directed.	24
Mrk	1:24 "What have you to do with us, Jesus of Nazareth?	1
	1:38 for that is what I came out to do."	1
	2:24 "Look, why are they doing what is not lawful	24
	2:25 "Have you never read what David did	24
	3: 4 lawful to do good or to do harm on the sabbath	24
	3: 8 hearing all that he was doing, they came to him	24
	3:35 Whoever does the will of God is my brother	24
	5: 7 "What have you to do with me, Jesus	1
	5:19 tell them how much the Lord has done for you	24
	5:20 how much Jesus had done for him;	24
	5:32 He looked all around to see who had done it.	24
	6: 2 What deeds of power are being done by his hands!	3
	6: 5 he could do no deed of power there	24
	6:30 told him all that they had done and taught.	24
	7:12 then you no longer permit doing anything	24
	7:13 you do many things like this."	24
	7:37 "He has done everything well	24
	9:13 they did to him whatever they pleased	24
	9:18 they could not do so."	1
	9:22 if you are able to do anything, have pity on us	1
	9:39 no one who does a deed of power in my name	24
	10:17 what must I do to inherit eternal life?"	24
	10:35 we want you to do for us whatever we ask of you."	24
	10:36 "What is it you want me to do for you?"	24
	10:51 "What do you want me to do for you?"	24
	11: 3 If anyone says to you, 'Why are you doing this?'	24
	11: 5 "What are you doing, untying the colt?"	24
	11:23 it will be done for you.	6
	11:28 "By what authority are you doing these things?	24
	11:28 Who gave you this authority to do them?"	24
	11:29 tell you by what authority I do these things.	24
	11:33 by what authority I am doing these things."	24
	12: 9 What then will the owner of the vineyard do?	24
	12:11 this was the Lord's doing	20
	14: 8 She has done what she could;	24
	14: 9 what she has done will be told in remembrance	24
	15: 8 Pilate to do for them according to his custom.	24
	15:12 "Then what do you wish me to do with the man	24
	15:14 Pilate asked him, "Why, what evil has he done?"	24
Lke	1:25 "This is what the Lord has done for me	24
	1:49 for the Mighty One has done great things for me	24
	2:27 to do for him what was customary under the law	24
	3:10 the crowds asked him, "What then should we do?"	24
	3:11 whoever has food must do likewise."	24
	3:12 "Teacher, what should we do?"	24
	3:14 "And we, what should we do?"	24
	3:19 because of all the evil things that Herod had done	24
	4:23 'Do here also in your hometown	24
	4:23 things that we have heard you did at Capernaum.' "	3
	4:34 What have you to do with us, Jesus of Nazareth?	1
	5: 6 When they had done this	24
	6: 2 "Why are you doing what is not lawful	24
	6: 3 David did when he and his companions were hungry?	24
	6:10 He did so, and his hand was restored.	24
	6:11 what they might do to Jesus.	24
	6:23 what their ancestors did to the prophets.	24
	6:26 what their ancestors did to the false prophets	24
	6:27 Love your enemies, do good to those who hate you	24
	6:31 Do to others as you would have them do to you.	24
	6:31 Do to others as you would have them do to you.	24
	6:33 even sinners do the same.	24
	6:46 call me 'Lord, Lord,' and do not do what I tell	24
	7: 4 "He is worthy of having you do this for him	21
	7: 8 to my slave, 'Do this,' and the slave does it."	24
	7: 8 to my slave, 'Do this,' and the slave does it."	24
	8:21 those who hear the word of God and do it."	24
	8:28 "What have you to do with me	1
	8:39 and declare how much God has done for you."	24
	8:39 proclaiming…how much Jesus had done for him.	24

9:10	the apostles told Jesus all they had done.	24
9:15	They did so and made them all sit down.	24
9:43	everyone was amazed at all that he was doing	24
10:13	if the deeds of power done in you	3
10:13	if the deeds of power…had been done in Tyre	3
10:25	"what must I do to inherit eternal life?"	24
10:28	the right answer; do this, and you will live."	24
10:37	Jesus said to him, "Go and do likewise."	24
12: 4	after that can do nothing more.	24
12:17	he thought to himself, 'What should I do	24
12:18	'I will do this: I will pull down my barns	24
12:26	you are not able to do so small a thing as that	1
12:47	did not prepare himself or do what was wanted	24
12:48	did not know and did what deserved a beating	24
13:17	the wonderful things that he was doing.	3
14:22	'Sir, what you ordered has been done	3
16: 3	the manager said to himself, 'What will I do	24
16: 4	I have decided what to do	24
16:26	might want to pass from here to you cannot do so	1
17: 9	for doing what was commanded?	24
17:10	when you have done all that you were ordered	24
17:10	we have done only what we ought	24
17:10	we have done only what we ought to have done!' "	24
18:15	they sternly ordered them not to do it	1
18:18	what must I do to inherit eternal life?"	24
18:41	"What do you want me to do for you?"	24
19:48	they did not find anything they could do	24
20: 2	by what authority you are doing these things?	24
20: 8	by what authority I am doing these things."	24
20:13	the owner of the vineyard said, 'What shall I do?	24
20:15	will the owner of the vineyard do to them?	24
22:19	Do this in remembrance of me."	24
22:23	which one of them it could be who would do this.	28
22:42	yet, not my will but yours be done."	3
23:15	he has done nothing to deserve death.	28
23:22	"Why, what evil has he done?	24
23:31	if they do this when the wood is green	24
23:34	[[for they do not know what they are doing."]]	24
23:41	this man has done nothing wrong."	28
Jhn 2: 5	said to the servants, "Do whatever he tells you."	24
2:11	Jesus did this, the first of his signs, in Cana	24
2:18	"What sign can you show us for doing this?"	24
2:23	because they saw the signs that he was doing.	24
3: 2	for no one can do these signs that you do	24
3: 2	for no one can do these signs that you do	24
3:20	For all who do evil hate the light	28
3:21	But those who do what is true come to the light	24
3:21	seen that their deeds have been done in God."	11
4:29	man who told me everything I have ever done!	24
4:34	"My food is to do the will of him who sent me	24
4:39	"He told me everything I have ever done."	24
4:45	all that he had done in Jerusalem at the festival;	24
4:54	Now this was the second sign that Jesus did	24
5:16	because he was doing such things on the sabbath.	24
5:19	the Son can do nothing on his own	24
5:19	only what he sees the Father doing;	24
5:19	whatever the Father does, the Son does likewise.	24
5:19	whatever the Father does, the Son does likewise.	24
5:20	shows him all that he himself is doing;	24
5:29	who have done good, to the resurrection of life	24
5:29	those who have done evil, to…condemnation	28
5:30	"I can do nothing on my own.	24
5:30	because I seek to do not my own will	1
5:36	the very works that I am doing	24
6: 2	signs that he was doing for the sick.	24
6: 6	he himself knew what he was going to do.	24
6:14	When the people saw the sign that he had done	24
6:28	"What must we do to perform the works of God?"	24
6:38	come down from heaven, not to do my own will	24
7: 3	disciples also may see the works you are doing;	24
7: 4	If you do these things, show yourself to the world	24
7:17	Anyone who resolves to do the will of God	24
7:31	will he do more signs than this man has done?"	24
7:31	will he do more signs than this man has done?"	24
7:51	a hearing to find out what they are doing	24
8:28	I do nothing on my own	24
8:29	I always do what is pleasing to him."	24
8:38	you should do what you have heard from the Father."	24
8:39	you would be doing what Abraham did	24
8:39	you would be doing what Abraham did	12
8:40	This is not what Abraham did.	24

8:41	You are indeed doing what your father does."	24
8:41	You are indeed doing what your father does."	12
8:44	you choose to do your father's desires.	24
8:52	Abraham died, and so did the prophets;	1
9:26	They said to him, "What did he do to you?	24
9:33	If this man were not from God, he could do nothing."	24
10:25	The works that I do in my Father's name	24
10:37	If I am not doing the works of my Father	24
10:38	if I do them, even though you do not believe me	24
11:45	had come with Mary and had seen what Jesus did	24
11:46	told them what he had done.	24
11:47	"What are we to do? This man is performing…signs.	24
12:16	written of him and had been done to him.	24
12:19	"You see, you can do nothing.	31
13: 7	"You do not know now what I am doing	24
13:12	"Do you know what I have done to you?	24
13:15	you also should do as I have done to you.	24
13:15	you also should do as I have done to you.	24
13:17	you are blessed if you do them.	24
13:27	"Do quickly what you are going to do."	24
13:27	"Do quickly what you are going to do."	24
14:10	the Father who dwells in me does his works.	24
14:12	believes in me will also do the works that I do	24
14:12	believes in me will also do the works that I do	24
14:12	will do greater works than these	24
14:13	I will do whatever you ask in my name,	24
14:14	you ask me for anything, I will do it.	24
14:31	I do as the Father has commanded me	24
15: 5	because apart from me you can do nothing.	24
15: 7	whatever you wish, and it will be done for you.	3
15:14	You are my friends if you do what I command you.	24
15:15	servant does not know what the master is doing;	24
15:21	they will do all these things to you	24
15:24	If I had not done among them the works	24
15:24	done among them the works that no one else did	24
16: 2	think that by doing so they are offering worship	1
16: 3	they will do this	24
17: 4	the work that you gave me to do.	24
18:35	What have you done?"	24
19:25	And that is what the soldiers did.	24
20:30	Now Jesus did many other signs	24
21:25	there are also many other things that Jesus did;	24
Act 1: 1	I wrote about all that Jesus did and taught	24
2:22	signs that God did through him among you	24
2:37	"Brothers, what should we do?"	24
2:43	signs were being done by the apostles.	3
3:17	you acted in ignorance, as did also your rulers.	1
4: 7	"By what power or by what name did you do this?"	24
4:16	said, "What will we do with them?	24
4:16	a notable sign has been done through them;	3
4:28	to do whatever your hand…had predestined	24
5:12	Now many signs and wonders were done	3
5:35	consider carefully what you propose to do to these	28
6: 8	did great wonders and signs among the people.	24
7:51	just as your ancestors used to do.	1
8: 6	hearing and seeing the signs that he did	24
9: 6	you will be told what you are to do."	24
9:13	how much evil he has done to your saints	24
10:35	anyone who fears him and does what is right	11
10:39	We are witnesses to all that he did	24
11:30	this they did, sending it to the elders	24
12: 8	He did so. Then he said to him	24
13:41	for in your days I am doing a work	11
14: 3	granting…wonders to be done through them.	3
14:11	When the crowds saw what Paul had done	24
14:15	"Friends, why are you doing this?	24
14:27	related all that God had done with them	24
15: 4	they reported all that God had done with them.	24
15:12	signs and wonders that God had done through them	24
15:29	you will do well. Farewell."	28
15:36	see how they are doing."	14
16:18	She kept doing this for many days.	24
16:30	"Sirs, what must I do to be saved?"	24
17: 4	as did a great many of the devout Greeks	1
19:11	God did extraordinary miracles through Paul	24
19:14	Seven sons of…Sceva were doing this.	24
19:36	you ought to be quiet and do nothing rash.	28
20:20	I did not shrink from doing anything helpful	1
21:13	"What are you doing, weeping and breaking my heart?	24
21:14	except to say, "The Lord's will be done."	3
21:19	things that God had done among the Gentiles	24

Act	21:22	What then is to be done?	6
	21:23	So do what we tell you.	24
	21:33	he inquired who he was and what he had done.	24
	22:10	I asked, 'What am I to do, Lord?'	24
	22:10	everything that has been assigned to you to do.'	24
	22:26	"What are you about to do?	24
	24:18	While I was doing this	1
	25: 9	Festus, wishing to do the Jews a favor, asked Paul	16
	25:25	I found that he had done nothing deserving death;	28
	26: 9	I…was convinced that I ought to do many things	28
	26:10	that is what I did in Jerusalem;	24
	26:20	and do deeds consistent with repentance.	28
	26:26	this was not done in a corner.	28
	26:31	"This man is doing nothing to deserve death	28
	28:17	though I had done nothing against our people	24
Rom	1:28	and to things that should not be done.	24
	1:32	they not only do them but even applaud	24
	2: 1	you, the judge, are doing the very same things.	28
	2: 2	God's judgment on those who do such things	28
	2: 3	when you judge those who do such things	28
	2: 3	and yet do them yourself	24
	2: 7	who by patiently doing good seek for glory	12
	2: 9	and distress for everyone who does evil	17
	2:10	and honor and peace for everyone who does good	11
	2:14	Gentiles…do instinctively what the law requires	24
	3: 8	"Let us do evil so that good may come"?	24
	4:21	that God was able to do what he had promised.	24
	7:15	I do not do what I want	28
	7:15	but I do the very thing I hate.	24
	7:16	Now if I do what I do not want, I agree	24
	7:17	But in fact it is no longer I that do it, but sin	17
	7:18	I can will what is right, but I cannot do it.	17
	7:19	For I do not do the good I want, but the evil	24
	7:19	but the evil I do not want is what I do.	28
	7:20	Now if I do what I do not want, it is no longer I	24
	7:20	it is no longer I that do it, but sin	17
	7:21	when I want to do what is good, evil lies close	24
	8: 3	For God has done what the law…could not do:	1
	8: 3	what the law, weakened by the flesh, could not do:	1
	9:11	or had done anything good or bad	28
	9:23	he has done so in order to make known the riches	1
	10: 5	"the person who does these things will live by them."	24
	12:20	by doing this you will heap burning coals	24
	13: 3	Then do what is good	24
	13: 4	if you do what is wrong, you should be afraid	24
	13:10	Love does no wrong to a neighbor;	11
	14:21	or do anything that makes your brother…stumble.	1
	15:27	They were pleased to do this	1
	16:21	so do Lucius and Jason and Sosipater, my relatives.	1
1Co	3:13	test what sort of work each has done.	6
	5: 2	that he who has done this would have been removed	28
	5: 4	on the man who has done such a thing.	17
	5:12	For what have I to do with judging those outside?	1
	7:37	to keep her as his fianc,e, he will do well.	24
	7:38	So then, he who marries his fianc,e does well;	24
	7:38	he who refrains from marriage will do better.	24
	8: 8	and no better off if we do.	13
	9:17	For if I do this of my own will, I have a reward;	28
	9:23	I do it all for the sake of the gospel	24
	9:25	they do it to receive a perishable wreath	1
	10: 6	so that we might not desire evil as they did.	10
	10: 7	Do not become idolaters as some of them did;	1
	10: 8	not indulge in sexual immorality as some of them did	26
	10: 9	not put Christ to the test, as some of them did	22
	10:10	not complain as some of them did	4
	10:31	So, whether you eat or drink, or whatever you do	24
	10:31	do everything for the glory of God.	24
	10:33	as I try to please everyone in everything I do	1
	11:16	no such custom, nor do the churches of God.	1
	11:24	Do this in remembrance of me."	24
	11:25	Do this, as often as you drink it	24
	14:15	What should I do then? I will pray with the spirit	6
	14:26	What should be done then, my friends?	6
	14:26	Let all things be done for building up.	3
	14:40	all things should be done decently and in order.	3
	15:29	Otherwise, what will those people do	24
	16:10	he is doing the work of the Lord just as I am;	11
	16:14	Let all that you do be done in love.	1
	16:14	Let all that you do be done in love.	3
2Co	1:17	Was I vacillating when I wanted to do this?	1
	2: 3	I wrote as I did, so that when I came	1

	2:11	we do this so that we may not be outwitted	1
	3: 1	I do not need, as some do, letters of recommendation	1
	5:10	for what has been done in the body	28
	8:10	who began last year not only to do something	24
	8:10	to do something but even to desire to do something	1
	8:11	now finish doing it, so that your eagerness	24
	8:21	for we intend to do what is right	1
	10: 7	just as you belong to Christ, so also do we.	1
	10:11	we will also do when present.	12
	11:11	why? Because I do not love you? God knows I do!	1
	11:12	what I do I will also continue to do	24
	11:12	what I do I will also continue to do	24
	11:16	if you do, then accept me as a fool	19
	12:19	Everything we do…is for the sake of building you up.	1
	13: 7	we pray to God that you may not do anything wrong	24
	13: 7	that you may do what is right	24
	13: 8	For we cannot do anything against the truth	1
Gal	2:10	which was actually what I was eager to do.	24
	2:16	not by doing the works of the law	1
	3: 2	Did you receive the Spirit by doing the works of the law	1
	3: 5	by your doing the works of the law	1
	3:12	"Whoever does the works of the law will live by them."	24
	5:17	to prevent you from doing what you want.	24
	5:21	those who do such things	28
	6: 9	let us not grow weary in doing what is right	24
Eph	2: 8	this is not your own doing; it is the gift of God	7
	5:12	to mention what such people do secretly;	3
	5:29	cares for it, just as Christ does for the church	1
	6: 6	as slaves of Christ, doing the will of God	24
	6: 8	knowing that whatever good we do	24
	6: 9	masters, do the same to them.	24
	6:13	and having done everything, to stand firm.	17
	6:21	you also may know how I am and what I am doing	28
Php	1:28	of your salvation. And this is God's doing.	2
	2: 3	Do nothing from selfish ambition or conceit	1
	2:14	Do all things without murmuring and arguing	24
	3:13	one thing I do: forgetting what lies behind	1
	4: 9	doing the things that you have learned and received	28
	4:13	I can do all things through him who strengthens me.	15
Col	1:21	hostile in mind, doing evil deeds	8
	3:17	whatever you do, in word or deed	24
	3:17	do everything in the name of the Lord Jesus	1
	3:23	put yourselves into it, as done for the Lord	1
1Th	4: 1	(as, in fact, you are doing), you should do so	23
	4:10	indeed you do love all the brothers and sisters	24
	4:13	you may not grieve as others do who have no hope.	1
	5: 6	So then let us not fall asleep as others do	1
	5:11	build up each other, as indeed you are doing.	24
	5:15	always seek to do good to one another and to all.	1
	5:24	who calls you is faithful, and he will do this.	24
2Th	3: 4	you are doing and will go on doing	24
	3: 4	you are doing and will go on doing	24
	3:14	who do not obey…have nothing to do with them	29
1Ti	4:16	in doing this you will save…yourself	24
	5:10	devoted herself to doing good in every way.	12
	5:21	doing nothing on the basis of partiality.	24
2Ti	1:12	for this reason I suffer as I do.	1
	2:26	having been held captive by him to do his will.	1
	4: 5	do the work of an evangelist	24
	4:14	Alexander the coppersmith did me great harm;	9
	4:21	as do Pudens and Linus and Claudia	1
Tit	1: 5	you should put in order what remained to be done	1
	3: 5	any works of righteousness that we had done	24
Phm	1: 8	to command you to do your duty	1
	1:14	I preferred to do nothing without your consent	24
	1:21	knowing that you will do even more than I say.	24
	1:24	so do Mark, Aristarchus, Demas, and Luke	1
Heb	6: 3	we will do this, if God permits.	24
	6:10	in serving the saints, as you still do.	5
	7:27	this he did once for all when he offered himself.	24
	10: 7	I said, 'See, God, I have come to do your will, O God'	24
	10: 9	he added, "See, I have come to do your will."	24
	10:36	so that when you have done the will of God	24
	11:29	when the Egyptians attempted to do so they	18
	13: 6	I will not be afraid. What can anyone do to me?"	24
	13:17	Let them do this with joy and not with sighing	24
	13:19	I urge you all the more to do this	24
	13:21	so that you may do his will	24
Jas	1:25	they will be blessed in their doing.	25
	2: 8	You do well if you really fulfull the royal law	24
	2:19	You believe that God is one; you do well.	24

	3:13 that your works are done with gentleness born of wisdom.	1
	3:15 Such wisdom does not come down from above	6
	4:15 "If the Lord wishes, we will live and do this	24
	4:17 knows the right thing to do and fails to do it	24
	4:17 knows the right thing to do and fails to do it	24
1Pe	3:11 let them turn away from evil and do good;	24
	3:12 the face of the Lord is against those who do evil."	24
	3:16 yet do it with gentleness and reverence.	1
	4: 3 in doing what the Gentiles like to do	17
	4: 3 in doing what the Gentiles like to do	1
	4:11 Whoever speaks must do so as...the very words of God;	1
	4:11 whoever serves must do so with the strength	1
2Pe	1:10 for if you do this, you will never stumble.	24
	1:19 You will do well to be attentive to this	24
1Jn	1: 6 we lie and do not do what is true;	24
	2:17 but those who do the will of God live forever.	24
	2:29 everyone who does right has been born of him.	24
	3: 7 Everyone who does what is right is righteous	24
	3: 9 Those who have been born of God do not sin	24
	3:10 all who do not do what is right are not from God	24
	3:22 obey his commandments and do what pleases him.	24
3Jn	1: 5 Beloved, you do faithfully	24
	1: 5 whatever you do for the friends	11
	1: 6 You will do well to send them on	24
	1:10 So if I come, I will call attention to what he is doing	24
	1:10 and even prevents those who want to do so	1
Rev	2: 5 repent, and do the works you did at first.	24
	2: 5 repent, and do the works you did at first.	1
	2:22 unless they repent of their doings;	12
	2:26 everyone who conquers and continues to do my works	30
	16:17 voice came...from the throne, saying, "It is done!"	3
	19:10 but he said to me, "You must not do that!	1
	21: 6 Then he said to me, "It is done!	3
	22:11 Let...the righteous still do right	24

do a good deed

    1. εὐεργεσία, *euergesia, 2307*

Act	4: 9 because of a good deed done to someone who was sick	1

do away with

    1. ἀναιρέω, *anaireō, 359*

Act	23:15 we are ready to do away with him before he arrives."	1

do business

    1. ἐμπορεύομαι, *emporeuomai, 1864*
    2. πραγματεύομαι, *pragmateuomai, 4549*

Lke	19:13 'Do business with these until I come back.'	2
Jas	4:13 spend a year there, doing business and making money."	1

do evil

    1. ἀδικέω, *adikeō, 92*
    2. κακοποιέω, *kakopoieō, 2803*

1Pe	3:17 suffer for doing good...than to suffer for doing evil.	2
3Jn	1:11 whoever does evil has not seen God.	2
Rev	22:11 Let the evildoer still do evil	1

do good

    1. ἀγαθοεργέω, *agathoergeō, 14*
    2. ἀγαθοποιέω, *agathopoieō, 16*
    3. ἀγαθοποιία, *agathopoiia, 17*
    4. εὐεργετέω, *euergeteō, 2308*
    5. εὐποιία, *eupoiia, 2343*
    6. χρήσιμος, *chrēsimos, 5978*

Lke	6: 9 lawful to do good or to do harm on the sabbath	2
	6:33 If you do good to those who do good to you	2
	6:33 If you do good to those who do good to you	2
	6:35 love your enemies, do good, and lend	2
Act	10:38 how he went about doing good	4
	14:17 doing good—giving you rains from heaven	2
1Ti	6:18 They are to do good, to be rich in good works	1
2Ti	2:14 avoid wrangling over words, which does no good	6
Heb	13:16 Do not neglect to do good	5
1Pe	3: 6 become her daughters as long as you do what is good	2
	3:17 For it is better to suffer for doing good	2
	4:19 while continuing to do good.	3
3Jn	1:11 Whoever does good is from God;	2

do harm

    1. βλάπτω, *blaptō, 1055*

	2. κακοποιέω, *kakopoieō, 2803*	
Mrk	3: 4 lawful to do good or to do harm on the sabbath	2
Lke	4:35 he came out of him without having done him any harm.	1
	6: 9 lawful to do good or to do harm on the sabbath	2

do military service

    1. στρατεύομαι, *strateuomai, 5129*

1Co	9: 7 pays the expenses for doing military service?	1

do much

    1. περισσεύω, *perisseuō, 4355*

1Th	4: 1 you are doing), you should do so more and more.	1
	4:10 we urge you, beloved, to do so more and more	1

do one's best

    1. ἀσκέω, *askeō, 828*
    2. σπουδάζω, *spoudazō, 5079*

Act	24:16 I do my best always to have a clear conscience	1
2Ti	2:15 Do your best to present yourself to God as...	2
	4: 9 Do your best to come to me soon	2
	4:21 Do your best to come before winter.	2
Tit	3:12 do your best to come to me at Nicopolis	2

do right

    1. ἀγαθοποιέω, *agathopoieō, 16*
    2. ἀγαθοποιός, *agathopoios, 18*
    3. καλοποιέω, *kalopoieō, 2818*

2Th	3:13 and sisters, do not be weary in doing what is right.	3
1Pe	2:14 sent by him...to praise those who do right.	2
	2:15 that by doing right you should silence	1
	2:20 if you endure when you do right and suffer for it	1

do well

    1. εὖ, *eu, 2292*
    2. εὖγε, *euge, 2301*

Mat	25:21 'Well done, good and trustworthy slave;	1
	25:23 'Well done, good and trustworthy slave;	1
Lke	19:17 He said to him, 'Well done, good slave!	2

do work

    1. διακονέω, *diakoneō, 1354*
    2. ἐργάζομαι, *ergazomai, 2237*

Lke	10:40 sister has left me to do all the work by myself?	1
	13:14 six days on which work ought to be done;	2
2Th	3:11 mere busybodies, not doing any work.	2
	3:12 to do their work quietly	2

do wrong

    1. ἀδικέω, *adikeō, 92*
    2. ἀδικία, *adikia, 94*
    3. ἁμαρτάνω, *hamartanō, 279*
    4. κακοποιός, *kakopoios, 2804*

Mat	20:13 'Friend, I am doing you no wrong;	1
Act	25:10 I have done no wrong to the Jews	1
2Co	7:12 not on account of the one who did the wrong	1
Gal	4:12 You have done me no wrong.	1
Col	3:25 will be paid back for whatever wrong has been done	1
1Pe	2:14 sent by him to punish those who do wrong	4
	2:20 If you endure when you are beaten for doing wrong	3
2Pe	2:13 suffering the penalty for doing wrong.	2
	2:15 Balaam...who loved the wages of doing wrong	2

doctor

    1. ἰατρός, *iatros, 2620*

Lke	4:23 'Doctor, cure yourself!'	1

doctrine   *See also* teach different doctrine

    1. διδασκαλία, *didaskalia, 1436*

Mat	15: 9 in vain...teaching human precepts as doctrines.' "	1
Mrk	7: 7 teaching human precepts as doctrines.'	1
Eph	4:14 blown about by every wind of doctrine	1
2Ti	4: 3 when people will not put up with sound doctrine	1
Tit	1: 9 be able both to preach with sound doctrine	1
	2: 1 as for you, teach what is consistent with sound doctrine.	1
	2:10 may be an ornament to the doctrine of God our Savior.	1

doer

    1. ποιητής, *poiētēs, 4475*

Rom 2:13 but the doers of the law who will be justified. 1
Jas 1:22 But be doers of the word, and not merely hearers 1
1:23 For if any are hearers of the word and not doers, 1
1:25 being not hearers who forget but doers who act 1
4:11 if you judge the law, you are not a doer of the law 1

dog

1. κυνάριον, *kynarion, 3249*
2. κύων, *kyōn, 3264*

Mat 7: 6 "Do not give what is holy to dogs; and do not throw 2
15:26 and throw it to the dogs." 1
15:27 "Yes, Lord, yet even the dogs eat the crumbs 1
Mrk 7:27 throw it to the dogs." 1
7:28 "Sir, even the dogs under the table eat 1
Lke 16:21 even the dogs would come and lick his sores. 2
Php 3: 2 Beware of the dogs 2
2Pe 2:22 "The dog turns back to its own vomit," 2
Rev 22:15 Outside are the dogs and sorcerers 2

dominate

1. ἐξουσιάζω, *exousiazo, 2027*
1Co 6:12 I will not be dominated by anything. 1

dominion *See also* exercise dominion

1. κράτος, *kratos, 3197*
2. κυριότης, *kyriotēs, 3262*
Eph 1:21 rule and authority and power and dominion 2
Col 1:16 thrones or dominions or rulers 2
1Ti 6:16 to him be honor and eternal dominion. Amen. 1
Rev 1: 6 to him be glory and dominion forever and ever. 1

dominion over

1. κυριεύω, *kyrieuō, 3259*
Rom 6: 9 death no longer has dominion over him. 1
6:14 For sin will have no dominion over you 1

donkey

1. ὄνος, *onos, 3952*
2. ὑποζύγιον, *hypozygion, 5689*
Mat 21: 2 immediately you will find a donkey tied 1
21: 5 humble, and mounted on a donkey 1
21: 5 and on a colt, the foal of a donkey." 2
21: 7 they brought the donkey and the colt 1
Lke 13:15 untie his ox or his donkey from the manger 1
Jhn 12:15 your king is coming, sitting on a donkey's colt!" 1
2Pe 2:16 a speechless donkey spoke with a human voice 2

young donkey

1. ὀνάριον, *onarion, 3942*
Jhn 12:14 Jesus found a young donkey and sat on it; 1

doom to perish

1. καταργέω, *katargeō, 2934*
1Co 2: 6 rulers of this age, who are doomed to perish. 1

door *See also* next door

1. Contextual: Not in Greek
2. θύρα, *thyra, 2598*
Mat 6: 6 whenever you pray, go into your room and shut the door 2
7: 7 knock, and the door will be opened for you. 1
7: 8 for everyone who knocks, the door will be opened. 1
25:10 the door was shut. 2
27:60 rolled a great stone to the door of the tomb 2
Mrk 1:33 gathered around the door. 2
2: 2 not even in front of the door; 2
11: 4 They went away and found a colt tied near a door 2
15:46 rolled a stone against the door of the tomb. 2
Lke 11: 7 door has already been locked, and my children 2
11: 9 knock, and the door will be opened for you 1
11:10 for everyone who knocks, the door will be opened. 1
12:36 so that they may open the door for him 1
13:24 "Strive to enter through the narrow door; 2
13:25 owner of the house has got up and shut the door 2
13:25 to knock at the door, saying, 'Lord, open to us,' 2
Jhn 20:19 the doors of the house…were locked 2
20:26 Although the doors were shut 2
Act 5: 9 Look, the feet…are at the door 2
5:19 an angel of the Lord opened the prison doors 2
5:23 the guards standing at the doors 2

12: 6 guards in front of the door 2
14:27 how he had opened a door of faith for the Gentiles. 2
16:26 immediately all the doors were opened 2
16:27 woke up and saw the prison doors wide open 2
21:30 immediately the doors were shut. 2
1Co 16: 9 for a wide door for effective work has opened 2
2Co 2:12 a door was opened for me in the Lord; 2
Col 4: 3 God will open to us a door for the word 2
Jas 5: 9 See, the Judge is standing at the doors! 2
Rev 3: 8 Look, I have set before you an open door 2
3:20 Listen! I am standing at the door, knocking; 2
3:20 if you hear my voice and open the door 2
4: 1 I looked, and there in heaven a door stood open! 2

behind closed doors

1. ταμεῖον, *tameion, 5421*
Lke 12: 3 what you have whispered behind closed doors 1

doorkeeper

1. θυρωρός, *thyrōros, 2601*
Mrk 13:34 commands the doorkeeper to be on the watch 1

Dorcas

1. Δορκάς, *Dorkas, 1520*
Act 9:36 whose name was Tabitha, which in Greek is Dorcas. 1
9:39 tunics and other clothing that Dorcas had made 1

double

1. δεύτερος, *deuteros, 1311*
2. διπλοῦς, *diplous, 1487*
2Co 1:15 so that you might have a double favor; 1
1Ti 5:17 elders…be considered worthy of double honor 2
Rev 18: 6 and repay her double for her deeds; 2
18: 6 mix a double draught for her in the cup she mixed. 2

double-minded

1. δίψυχος, *dipsychos, 1500*
Jas 1: 7 being double-minded and unstable in every way, 1
4: 8 purify your hearts, you double-minded. 1

double-tongued

1. δίλογος, *dilogos, 1474*
1Ti 3: 8 not double-tongued, not indulging in much wine 1

doubt

1. ἄπιστος, *apistos, 603*
2. διακρίνω, *diakrinō, 1359*
3. διαλογισμός, *dialogismos, 1369*
4. διστάζω, *distazō, 1491*
Mat 14:31 "You of little faith, why did you doubt?" 4
21:21 if you have faith and do not doubt 2
28:17 they worshiped him; but some doubted. 4
Mrk 11:23 do not doubt in your heart 2
Lke 24:38 why do doubts arise in your hearts? 3
Jhn 20:27 Do not doubt but believe." 1
Rom 14:23 those who have doubts are condemned if they eat 2
Jas 1: 6 But ask in faith, never doubting 2
1: 6 the one who doubts is like a wave of the sea 2

no doubt

1. γάρ, *gar, 1142*
Gal 1:13 heard, no doubt, of my earlier life in Judaism. 1

without any doubt

1. ὁμολογουμένως, *homologoumenōs, 3935*
1Ti 3:16 Without any doubt, the mystery of our religion is great: 1

doubter

1. ἄνθρωπος, *anthrōpos, 476*
Jas 1: 7 for the doubter, being double-minded and unstable 1

doubtless

1. εἰ + τυγχάνω, *ei + tynchanō, 1623 + 5593*
2. πάντως, *pantōs, 4122*
Lke 4:23 "Doubtless you will quote to me this proverb 2
1Co 14:10 There are doubtless many different kinds of sounds 1

dough　*See also* batch of dough
　1. Contextual: Not in Greek
Rom 11:16　If the part of the dough offered as first fruits　　1

dove
　1. περιστερά, *peristera, 4361*
Mat　3:16　saw the Spirit of God descending like a dove　　1
　　10:16　so be wise as serpents and innocent as doves.　　1
　　21:12　and the seats of those who sold doves.　　1
Mrk　1:10　the Spirit descending like a dove on him.　　1
　　11:15　the seats of those who sold doves;　　1
Lke　3:22　in bodily form like a dove.　　1
Jhn　1:32　the Spirit descending from heaven like a dove　　1
　　2:14　he found people selling cattle, sheep, and doves　　1
　　2:16　He told those who were selling the doves　　1

down　*See also* bend down, bow down, break down, bring down, come down, come down with, cut down, dash down, fall down, fall down before, go down, kneel down, lay down, let down, look down, make *sit* down, path down, press down, pull down, run down, rush down, set down, sit down, sit down to eat, sit down together, step down, stoop down, strike down, sweep down, take down, tear down, throw down, turn upside down, weigh down, write down
　1. ἕως, *heōs, 2401*
　2. κατά, *kata, 2848*
　3. καταβαίνω, *katabainō, 2849*
　4. κάτω, *katō, 3004*
Mat　4:　6　"If you are the Son of God, throw yourself down;　　4
　　8:32　suddenly, the whole herd rushed down the steep bank　　2
　　22:26　so also the third, down to the seventh.　　1
Mrk　5:13　rushed down the steep bank into the sea　　2
Lke　4:　9　throw yourself down from here　　4
　　8:33　herd rushed down the steep bank into the lake　　2
　　19:　6　he hurried down　　3
Jhn　8:　6　⟦Jesus bent down and wrote with his finger⟧　　4

down to
　1. ἕως, *heōs, 2401*
Rom 11:　8　ears that would not hear, down to this very day."　　1

downcast
　1. ταπεινός, *tapeinos, 5424*
2Co　7:　6　God, who consoles the downcast　　1

drag
　1. ἄγω, *agō, 72*
　2. ἑλκύω, *helkyō, 1816*
　3. κατασύρω, *katasyrō, 2955*
　4. σύρω, *syrō, 5359*
Mat　10:18　you will be dragged before governors and kings　　1
Lke　12:58　or you may be dragged before the judge　　3
Jhn　21:　8　dragging the net full of fish　　4
Act　14:19　they stoned Paul and dragged him out of the city　　4
　　16:19　and dragged them into the marketplace　　2
　　17:　6　they dragged Jason and some believers before　　4
　　21:30　seized Paul and dragged him out of the temple　　2
Jas　2:　6　Is it not they who drag you into court?　　2

drag off
　1. σύρω, *syrō, 5359*
Act　8:　3　dragging off both men and women　　1

drag out
　1. ἐκβάλλω, *ekballō, 1675*
Act　7:58　Then they dragged him out of the city　　1

drag with
　1. συναρπάζω, *synarpazō, 5275*
Act　19:29　dragging with them Gaius and Aristarchus　　1

dragon
　1. Contextual: Not in Greek
　2. δράκων, *drakōn, 1532*
Rev　12:　3　great red dragon, with seven heads and ten horns　　2
　　12:　4　Then the dragon stood before the woman　　2

　　12:　7　Michael…angels fought against the dragon.　　2
　　12:　7　The dragon and his angels fought back　　2
　　12:　9　The great dragon was thrown down　　2
　　12:13　when the dragon saw that he had been thrown down　　2
　　12:16　river that the dragon had poured from his mouth.　　2
　　12:17　Then the dragon was angry with the woman　　2
　　12:18　the dragon took his stand on the sand of the seashore.　　1
　　13:　2　the dragon gave it his power and his throne　　2
　　13:　4　They worshiped the dragon　　2
　　13:11　and it spoke like a dragon.　　2
　　16:13　foul spirits…coming from the mouth of the dragon　　2
　　20:　2　He seized the dragon, that ancient serpent　　2

draught
　1. Contextual: Not in Greek
Rev　18:　6　mix a double draught for her in the cup she mixed.　　1

draw¹
　1. ἀποσπάω, *apospaō, 685*
　2. ἑλκύω, *helkyō, 1816*
　3. σπάω, *spaō, 5060*
Mat　26:51　put his hand on his sword, drew it,　　1
Mrk　14:47　one of those who stood near drew his sword　　3
Jhn　18:10　Simon Peter, who had a sword, drew it　　2
Act　16:27　he drew his sword and was about to kill himself　　3

draw²
　1. ἀναβιβάζω, *anabibazō, 328*
　2. ἀντλέω, *antleō, 533*
　3. ἑλκύω, *helkyō, 1816*
Mat　13:48　when it was full, they drew it ashore, sat down　　1
Jhn　2:　9　the servants who had drawn the water knew)　　2
　　4:　7　A Samaritan woman came to draw water　　2
　　4:15　or have to keep coming here to draw water."　　2
　　6:44　unless drawn by the Father who sent me;　　3
　　12:32　I…will draw all people to myself."　　3

draw aside
　1. ἀναχωρέω, *anachōreō, 432*
Act　23:19　The tribune…drew him aside privately, and asked　　1

draw away
　1. μεθίστημι, *methistēmi, 3496*
Act　19:26　drawn away a considerable number of people　　1

draw back
　1. ἀφίστημι, *aphistēmi, 923*
　2. ὑποστέλλω, *hypostellō, 5713*
Act　22:29　those who were about to examine him drew back　　1
Gal　2:12　he drew back and kept himself separate　　2

draw near
　1. ἐγγίζω, *engizō, 1581*
　2. συμπληρόω, *symplēroō, 5230*
Lke　9:51　When the days drew near for him to be taken up　　2
　　21:28　because your redemption is drawing near."　　1
Act　7:17　time drew near for the fulfillment of the promise　　1
Jas　4:　8　Draw near to God, and he will draw near to you.　　1
　　4:　8　Draw near to God, and he will draw near to you.　　1

draw out
　1. ἀντλέω, *antleō, 533*
Jhn　2:　8　draw some out, and take it to the chief steward."　　1

draw to a close
　1. κλίνω, *klinō, 3111*
Lke　9:12　The day was drawing to a close　　1

dreadful　*See* dreadful *portent*

dream
　1. ἐνυπνιάζομαι, *enypniazomai, 1965*
　2. ἐνύπνιον, *enypnion, 1966*
　3. ὄναρ, *onar, 3941*
Mat　1:20　an angel of the Lord appeared to him in a dream　　3
　　2:12　having been warned in a dream not to return to Herod　　3
　　2:13　an angel of the Lord appeared to Joseph in a dream　　3
　　2:19　an angel…appeared in a dream to Joseph in Egypt　　3

Mat	2:22	And after being warned in a dream, he went away	3
	27:19	suffered…because of a dream about him."	3
Act	2:17	your old men shall dream dreams.	1
	2:17	your old men shall dream dreams.	2

dreamer

1. ἐνυπνιάζομαι, *enypniazomai, 1965*

Jde   1: 8   these dreamers also defile the flesh   1

dregs

1. περίψημα, *peripsēma, 4370*

1Co   4:13   the dregs of all things, to this very day.   1

dress

1. Contextual: Not in Greek
2. ἀμφιέννυμι, *amphiennymi, 314*
3. ἐνδιδύσκω, *endidyskō, 1898*
4. κοσμέω, *kosmeō, 3175*
5. περιβάλλω, *periballō, 4314*

Mat	11: 8	to see? Someone dressed in soft robes?	2
Mrk	16: 5	they saw a young man, dressed in a white robe	5
Lke	7:25	Someone dressed in soft robes?	2
	16:19	who was dressed in purple and fine linen	3
Jhn	19: 2	and they dressed him in a purple robe.	5
1Ti	2: 9	women should dress themselves modestly	4
Rev	3: 4	with me, dressed in white, for they are worthy.	1
	4: 4	elders, dressed in white robes, with golden	5

dress for action

1. περιζώννυμι + ὁ + ὀσφῦς, *perizōnnymi + ho + osphys, 4322 + 3836 + 4019*

Lke   12:35   "Be dressed for action and have your lamps lit;   1

drift across

1. διαφέρω, *diapherō, 1422*

Act   27:27   as we were drifting across the sea of Adria   1

drift away

1. παραρρέω, *pararreō, 4184*

Heb   2: 1   so that we do not drift away from it.   1

drink   *See also* give drink, give to drink

1. οἶνος + πολύς, *oinos + polys, 3885 + 4498*
2. πίνω, *pinō, 4403*
3. πόμα, *poma, 4503*
4. πόσις, *posis, 4530*

Mat	6:25	life, what you will eat or what you will drink	2
	6:31	'What will we eat?' or 'What will we drink?'	2
	11:18	For John came neither eating nor drinking	2
	11:19	the Son of Man came eating and drinking	2
	20:22	Are you able to drink the cup that I am	2
	20:22	to drink the cup that I am about to drink?"	2
	20:23	He said to them, "You will indeed drink my cup	2
	24:38	before the flood they were eating and drinking	2
	24:49	eats and drinks with drunkards	2
	26:27	"Drink from it, all of you;	2
	26:29	never again drink of this fruit of the vine	2
	26:29	until that day when I drink it new with you	2
	26:42	if this cannot pass unless I drink it	2
	27:34	they offered him wine to drink, mixed with gall;	2
	27:34	when he tasted it, he would not drink it.	2
Mrk	10:38	Are you able to drink the cup that I drink	2
	10:38	Are you able to drink the cup that I drink	2
	10:39	"The cup that I drink you will drink;	2
	10:39	"The cup that I drink you will drink;	2
	14:23	and all of them drank from it.	2
	14:25	I will never again drink of the fruit of the vine	2
	14:25	when I drink it new in the kingdom of God."	2
	16:18	⟦if they drink any deadly thing, it will not hurt⟧	2
Lke	1:15	He must never drink wine or strong drink;	2
	5:30	"Why do you eat and drink with tax collectors	2
	5:33	but your disciples eat and drink."	2
	5:39	no one after drinking old wine desires new	2
	7:33	has come eating no bread and drinking no wine	2
	7:34	the Son of Man has come eating and drinking	2
	10: 7	eating and drinking whatever they provide	2
	12:19	relax, eat, drink, be merry.'	2
	12:29	what you are to eat and what you are to drink	2
	12:45	to eat and drink and get drunk	2

	13:26	'We ate and drank with you	2
	17: 8	while I eat and drink;	2
	17: 8	later you may eat and drink'?	2
	17:27	They were eating and drinking, and marrying	2
	17:28	they were eating and drinking, buying and selling	2
	22:18	I will not drink of the fruit of the vine	2
	22:30	you may eat and drink at my table in my kingdom	2
Jhn	4: 7	Jesus said to her, "Give me a drink."	2
	4: 9	you, a Jew, ask a drink of me, a woman of Samaria?"	2
	4:10	who it is that is saying to you, 'Give me a drink,'	2
	4:12	with his sons and his flocks drank from it?"	2
	4:13	who drinks of this water will be thirsty again	2
	4:14	who drink of the water that I will give them	2
	6:53	flesh of the Son of Man and drink his blood	2
	6:54	Those who eat my flesh and drink my blood	2
	6:55	my flesh is true food and my blood is true drink.	4
	6:56	who eat my flesh and drink my blood abide in me	2
	7:38	and let the one who believes in me drink.	2
	18:11	to drink the cup that the Father has given me?"	2
Act	9: 9	neither ate nor drank.	2
	23:12	an oath neither to eat nor drink	2
	23:21	an oath neither to eat nor drink	2
Rom	14:17	For the kingdom of God is not food and drink	4
	14:21	it is good not to eat meat or drink wine	2
1Co	9: 4	Do we not have the right to our food and drink?	2
	10: 4	all drank the same spiritual drink.	2
	10: 4	all drank the same spiritual drink.	3
	10: 4	they drank from the spiritual rock	2
	10: 7	sat down to eat and drink, and they rose up to play."	2
	10:21	You cannot drink the cup of the Lord	2
	10:31	So, whether you eat or drink, or whatever you do	2
	11:22	What! Do you not have homes to eat and drink in?	2
	11:25	Do this, as often as you drink it	2
	11:26	eat this bread and drink the cup	2
	11:27	drinks the cup of the Lord in an unworthy manner	2
	11:28	eat of the bread and drink of the cup.	2
	11:29	all who eat and drink without discerning	2
	11:29	eat and drink judgment against themselves.	2
	15:32	"Let us eat and drink, for tomorrow we die."	2
Col	2:16	condemn you in matters of food and drink	4
Tit	2: 3	not to be slanderers or slaves to drink;	1
Heb	6: 7	Ground that drinks up the rain…falling	2
	9:10	food and drink and various baptisms	3
Rev	14:10	they will also drink the wine of God's wrath	2
	16: 6	you have given them blood to drink.	2
	18: 3	drunk of the wine of the wrath of her fornication	2

drink only water

1. ὑδροποτέω, *hydropoteō, 5621*

1Ti   5:23   No longer drink only water, but take a little wine   1

drink with

1. συμπίνω, *sympinō, 5228*

Act   10:41   who ate and drank with him   1

make drink

1. ποτίζω, *potizō, 4540*

1Co   12:13   were all made to drink of one Spirit.   1
Rev   14: 8   She has made all nations drink of the wine   1

strong drink

1. σίκερα, *sikera, 4975*

Lke   1:15   He must never drink wine or strong drink;   1

drive

1. ἐλαύνω, *elaunō, 1785*
2. περιτρέπω, *peritrepō, 4365*
3. φέρω, *pherō, 5770*

Lke	8:29	be driven by the demon into the wilds.)	1
Act	26:24	Paul! Too much learning is driving you insane!"	2
	27:15	we gave way to it and were driven.	3
	27:17	they lowered the sea anchor and so were driven.	3
Jas	3: 4	it takes strong winds to drive them,	1
2Pe	2:17	waterless springs and mists driven by a storm;	1

drive away

1. ἐκβάλλω, *ekballō, 1675*

Jhn   6:37   anyone who comes to me I will never drive away;   1

drive out

1. ἐκβάλλω, *ekballō, 1675*
2. ἐκδιώκω, *ekdiōkō, 1691*
3. ἐξαίρω, *exairō, 1976*
4. ἐξέρχομαι, *exerchomai, 2002*
5. ἐξωθέω, *exōtheō, 2034*

Mat	21:12	drove out all who were selling and buying	1
Mrk	1:12	the Spirit immediately drove him out	1
	11:15	began to drive out those who were selling	1
Lke	4:29	They got up, drove him out of the town	1
	19:45	began to drive out those who were selling	1
Jhn	2:15	he drove all of them out of the temple	1
	9:34	And they drove him out.	1
	9:35	Jesus heard that they had driven him out	1
	12:31	now the ruler of this world will be driven out.	1
Act	7:45	nations that God drove out before our ancestors.	5
	13:50	and drove them out of their region.	1
	28: 3	when a viper, driven out by the heat	4
1Co	5:13	"Drive out the wicked person from among you."	3
Gal	4:30	"Drive out the slave and her child;	1
1Th	2:15	drove us out; they displease God and oppose everyone	2

drive to despair

1. ἐξαπορέω, *exaporeō, 1989*

2Co	4: 8	perplexed, but not driven to despair;	1

driven by the wind

1. ἀνεμίζω, *anemizō, 448*

Jas	1: 6	wave of the sea...driven and tossed by the wind;	1

droop

1. παρίημι, *pariēmi, 4223*

Heb	12:12	Therefore lift your drooping hands	1

drop

1. βάλλω, *ballō, 965*
2. καταβαίνω, *katabainō, 2849*
3. καταπίπτω, *katapiptō, 2928*
4. πίπτω, *piptō, 4406*

Lke	16:17	one stroke of a letter in the law to be dropped.	4
Act	28: 6	expecting him to swell up or drop dead	3
Rev	6:13	as the fig tree drops its winter fruit	1
	16:21	huge hailstones...dropped from heaven on people	2

great drop

1. θρόμβος, *thrombos, 2584*

Lke	22:44	⟦his sweat became like great drops of blood⟧	1

dropsy

1. ὑδρωπικός, *hydrōpikos, 5622*

Lke	14: 2	in front of him, there was a man who had dropsy.	1

drown

1. ἀποπνίγω, *apopnigō, 678*
2. καταπίνω, *katapinō, 2927*
3. καταποντίζω, *katapontizō, 2931*
4. πνίγω, *pnigō, 4464*

Mat	18: 6	and you were drowned in the depth of the sea.	3
Mrk	5:13	drowned in the sea.	4
Lke	8:33	and the herd...was drowned.	1
Heb	11:29	the Egyptians...were drowned.	2

drowsy

1. νυστάζω, *nystazō, 3818*

Mat	25: 5	all of them became drowsy and slept.	1

drunk

1. μεθύσκω, *methyskō, 3499*
2. μεθύω, *methyō, 3501*

Jhn	2:10	inferior wine after the guests have become drunk.	1
Act	2:15	Indeed, these are not drunk, as you suppose	2
1Co	11:21	one goes hungry and another becomes drunk.	2
1Th	5: 7	those who are drunk get drunk at night.	2
Rev	17: 2	the inhabitants of the earth have become drunk."	1
	17: 6	the woman was drunk with the blood of the saints	2

get drunk

1. μεθύσκω, *methyskō, 3499*

Lke	12:45	to eat and drink and get drunk	1
Eph	5:18	Do not get drunk with wine, for that is debauchery;	1
1Th	5: 7	those who are drunk get drunk at night.	1

drunkard

1. μέθυσος, *methysos, 3500*
2. μεθύω, *methyō, 3501*
3. οἰνοπότης, *oinopotēs, 3884*
4. πάροινος, *paroinos, 4232*

Mat	11:19	and they say, 'Look, a glutton and a drunkard	3
	24:49	eats and drinks with drunkards	2
Lke	7:34	and you say, 'Look, a glutton and a drunkard	3
1Co	5:11	is an idolater, reviler, drunkard, or robber	1
	6:10	thieves, the greedy, drunkards	1
1Ti	3: 3	not a drunkard, not violent but gentle	4

drunkenness

1. μέθη, *methē, 3494*
2. οἰνοφλυγία, *oinophlygia, 3886*

Lke	21:34	weighed down with dissipation and drunkenness	1
Rom	13:13	not in reveling and drunkenness	1
Gal	5:21	envy, drunkenness, carousing, and things like	1
1Pe	4: 3	living in...drunkenness, revels, carousing	2

Drusilla

1. Δρούσιλλα, *Drousilla, 1537*

Act	24:24	Felix came with his wife Drusilla	1

dry

1. ἐκμάσσω, *ekmassō, 1726*
2. ξηρός, *xēros, 3831*

Lke	7:38	dry them with her hair. Then she continued	1
	7:44	dried them with her hair.	1
	23:31	what will happen when it is dry?"	2
Heb	11:29	passed through the Red Sea as if it were dry land	2

dry up

1. ξηραίνω, *xērainō, 3830*

Rev	16:12	its water was dried up in order to prepare the way	1

due[1] *See also due time*

1. Contextual: Not in Greek
2. δεῖ, *dei, 1256*
3. ὀφειλή, *opheilē, 4051*
4. ὀφείλημα, *opheilēma, 4052*

Rom	1:27	received in their own persons the due penalty	2
	4: 4	wages are not reckoned as a gift but as something due.	4
	13: 7	Pay to all what is due them	3
	13: 7	Pay...taxes to whom taxes are due	1
	13: 7	Pay...revenue to whom revenue is due	1
	13: 7	Pay...respect to whom respect is due	1
	13: 7	Pay...honor to whom honor is due.	1

due[2]

1. ἴδιος, *idios, 2625*

Tit	1: 3	in due time he revealed his word	1

due[3]

1. Contextual: Not in Greek

Jas	1:17	there is no variation or shadow due to change.	1

dull

1. νωθρός, *nōthros, 3821*

Heb	5:11	since you have become dull in understanding.	1

grow dull

1. παχύνω, *pachynō, 4266*

Mat	13:15	For this people's heart has grown dull	1
Act	28:27	For this people's heart has grown dull	1

during

1. Contextual: Not in Greek
2. γίνομαι, *ginomai, 1181*
3. διά, *dia, 1328*
4. ἐν, *en, 1877*
5. ἐπί, *epi, 2093*
6. κατά, *kata, 2848*
7. χρόνος, *chronos, 5989*

Mat 26: 5 "Not during the festival, or there may be a riot   4
Mrk 14: 2 "Not during the festival, or there may be a riot   4
    15: 7 who had committed murder during the insurrection.   4
Lke 3: 2 during the high priesthood of Annas and Caiaphas   5
    4: 2 He ate nothing at all during those days   4
    6:12 Now during those days he went out...to pray;   4
    12:38 If he comes during the middle of the night,   4
    16:25 during your lifetime you received your good things   4
Jhn 2:23 he was in Jerusalem during the Passover festival   4
    11: 9 Those who walk during the day do not stumble   4
    13: 2 And during supper   2
    19:31 Jews did not want the bodies left on the cross   4
Act 1: 3 appearing to them during forty days   3
    1:21 during all the time that the Lord Jesus went   4
    5:19 during the night an angel of the Lord opened   3
    6: 1 Now during those days   4
    7: 6 and mistreat them during four hundred years.   1
    11:28 this took place during the reign of Claudius.   5
    12: 3 (This was during the festival of Unleavened Bread.)   1
    13:17 during their stay in the land of Egypt   4
    16: 9 During the night Paul had a vision: there stood   3
    23:31 and brought him during the night to Antipatris.   3
Rom 7: 1 the law is binding on a person only during...lifetime?   7
2Co 8: 2 for during a severe ordeal of affliction   4
1Th 3: 7 during all our distress and persecution   5
2Th 1: 4 and faith during all your persecutions   4
Phm 1:10 whose father I have become during my imprisonment.   4
    1:13 during my imprisonment for the gospel;   4
Heb 9: 9 during which gifts and sacrifices are offered   6
1Pe 1:17 during the time of your exile.   1
    3:20 during the building of the ark   1
Rev 11: 6 no rain...during the days of their prophesying   1

dust

1. Contextual: Not in Greek
2. κονιορτός, *koniortos, 3155*
3. χοϊκός, *choikos, 5954*
4. χοῦς, *chous, 5967*

Mat 10:14 shake off the dust from your feet as you leave   2
Mrk 6:11 shake off the dust that is on your feet   4
Lke 9: 5 shake the dust off your feet   2
    10:11 'Even the dust of your town that clings to our feet   2
Act 13:51 they shook the dust off their feet in protest   2
    18: 6 in protest he shook the dust from his clothes   1
    22:23 their cloaks, and tossing dust into the air   2
1Co 15:47 The first man was from the earth, a man of dust;   3
    15:48 As was the man of dust   3
    15:48 so are those who are of the dust;   3
    15:49 as we have borne the image of the man of dust   3
Rev 18:19 And they threw dust on their heads, as they wept   4

duty

1. Contextual: Not in Greek
2. ἀνήκω, *anēkō, 465*
3. τάξις, *taxis, 5423*

Lke 1: 8 and his section was on duty   3
1Ti 6: 2 Teach and urge these duties.   1
Phm 1: 8 to command you to do your duty   2

acceptable duty

1. εὐάρεστος, *euarestos, 2298*

Col 3:20 this is your acceptable duty in the Lord.   1

religious duty

1. εὐσεβέω, *eusebeō, 2355*

1Ti 5: 4 learn their religious duty to their own family   1

ritual duty

1. λατρεία, *latreia, 3301*

Heb 9: 6 priests...carry out their ritual duties;   1

dwell

1. εἰμί, *eimi, 1639*
2. ἐμβατεύω, *embateuō, 1836*
3. ἐνοικέω, *enoikeō, 1940*
4. κατοικέω, *katoikeō, 2997*
5. μένω, *menō, 3531*
6. οἰκέω, *oikeō, 3861*
7. σκηνόω, *skēnoō, 5012*

Mat 23:21 swears by it and by the one who dwells in it;   4
Jhn 14:10 the Father who dwells in me does his works.   5
Act 7:48 Yet the Most High does not dwell in houses   4
Rom 7:17 no longer I...but sin that dwells within me.   6
    7:18 For I know that nothing good dwells within me   6
    7:20 no longer I...but sin that dwells within me.   6
    7:23 to the law of sin that dwells in my members.   1
    8: 9 since the Spirit of God dwells in you.   6
    8:11 If the Spirit...dwells in you   6
1Co 3:16 God's Spirit dwells in you?   6
Eph 3:17 Christ may dwell in your hearts through faith   4
Col 1:19 in him all the fullness of God was pleased to dwell   4
    2: 9 in him the whole fullness of deity dwells bodily   4
    2:18 dwelling on visions, puffed up without cause   2
    3:16 Let the word of Christ dwell in you richly;   3
1Ti 6:16 dwells in unapproachable light   4
Rev 12:12 Rejoice then, you heavens and those who dwell in them!   7
    13: 6 his dwelling, that is, those who dwell in heaven.   7
    21: 3 He will dwell with them;   7

dwell in

1. ἐνοικέω, *enoikeō, 1940*
2. ἐπισκηνόω, *episkēnoō, 2172*

Rom 8:11 through his Spirit that dwells in you.   1
2Co 12: 9 so that the power of Christ may dwell in me.   2

make dwell

1. κατοικίζω, *katoikizō, 3001*

Jas 4: 5 the spirit that he has made to dwell in us"?   1

dwelling

1. οἰκητήριον, *oikētērion, 3863*
2. σκηνή, *skēnē, 5008*

Mat 17: 4 if you wish, I will make three dwellings here   2
Mrk 9: 5 let us make three dwellings   2
Lke 9:33 let us make three dwellings   2
Act 15:16 rebuild the dwelling of David, which has fallen;   2
2Co 5: 2 longing to be clothed with our heavenly dwelling   1
Jde 1: 6 the angels who...left their proper dwelling   1
Rev 13: 6 God, blaspheming his name and his dwelling   2

dwelling place

1. κατοικητήριον, *katoikētērion, 2999*
2. μονή, *monē, 3665*
3. σκήνωμα, *skēnōma, 5013*

Jhn 14: 2 in my Father's house there are many dwelling places.   2
Act 7:46 find a dwelling place for the house of Jacob.   3
Eph 2:22 built...spiritually into a dwelling place for God.   1
Rev 18: 2 It has become a dwelling place of demons   1

dysentery

1. δυσεντέριον, *dysenterion, 1548*

Act 28: 8 lay sick in bed with fever and dysentery.   1

E

each   *See also* on each *side*

1. Contextual: Not in Greek
2. ἀνά, *ana, 324*
3. εἷς, *heis, 1651*
4. εἷς + κατά + εἷς, *heis + kata + heis, 1651 + 2848 + 1651*
5. ἕκαστος, *hekastos, 1667*
6. ἴδιος, *idios, 2625*
7. κατά, *kata, 2848*
8. τίς, *tis, 5515*

Mat 20: 9 each of them received the usual daily wage.   2
    20:10 each of them also received the usual daily wage.   2
    25:15 to each according to his ability.   5
Mrk 13:34 puts his slaves in charge, each with his work   5
    15:24 casting lots to decide what each should take.   8
Lke 4:40 he laid his hands on each of them   5
    6:44 for each tree is known by its own fruit.   5
    9:14 sit down in groups of about fifty each."   2
    11: 3 Give us each day our daily bread.   7
    13:15 Does not each of you on the sabbath untie his ox   5
Jhn 2: 6 jars...each holding twenty or thirty gallons.   2
    6: 7 enough bread for each of them to get a little."   5
    7:53 ⟦each of them went home⟧   5

	19:23	into four parts, one for each soldier.	5
Act	2: 3	and a tongue rested on each of them.	5
	2: 6	each one heard them speaking in the native language	5
	2: 6	heard them speaking in the native language of each	6
	2: 8	each of us, in our own native language?	5
	3:26	by turning each of you from your wicked ways."	5
	4:35	was distributed to each as any had need.	5
	11:29	The disciples determined…each would send relief	5
	14:23	had appointed elders for them in each church	7
	17:27	though indeed he is not far from each one of us.	5
	21:26	the sacrifice would be made for each of them.	5
Rom	12: 3	each according to the measure of faith	5
	14:12	So then, each of us will be accountable to God.	5
	15: 2	Each of us must please our neighbor for the good	5
1Co	1:12	each of you says, "I belong to Paul,"	5
	3: 5	as the Lord assigned to each.	5
	3: 8	each will receive wages according to the labor	5
	3: 8	will receive wages according to the labor of each.	6
	3:10	Each builder must choose with care how to build on it.	5
	3:13	work of each builder will become visible	5
	3:13	test what sort of work each has done.	5
	7: 7	each has a particular gift from God	5
	7:17	let each of you lead the life that the Lord	5
	7:20	Let each of you remain in the condition	5
	11:21	each of you goes ahead with your own supper	5
	12: 7	To each is given the manifestation of the Spirit	5
	12:18	members in the body, each one of them, as he chose.	5
	14:27	each in turn; and let one interpret.	1
	15:23	each in his own order: Christ the first fruits	5
	15:38	to each kind of seed its own body.	5
	16: 2	each of you is to put aside	5
2Co	5:10	so that each may receive recompense	5
	9: 7	Each of you must give as you have made up your mind	5
Eph	4: 7	each of us was given grace according	5
	4:16	as each part is working properly	5
	5:33	Each of you, however, should love his wife	5
Php	2: 4	Let each of you look not to your own interests	5
1Th	2:11	we dealt with each one of you like a father	5
	5:11	encourage one another and build up each other	3
Heb	8:11	shall not teach…say to each other	5
	11:21	Jacob…blessed each of the sons of Joseph	5
1Pe	4:10	serve one another with whatever gift each…received.	5
3Jn	1:15	Greet the friends there, each by name.	7
Rev	2:23	I will give to each of you as your works deserve.	5
	4: 8	four living creatures, each…with six wings	4
	5: 8	fell before the Lamb, each holding a harp	5
	6:11	They were each given a white robe and told	5
	16:21	hailstones, each weighing about a hundred pounds	1
	21:21	each of the gates is a single pearl	5
	22: 2	tree of life…producing its fruit each month;	5

each man

1. ἕκαστος, *hekastos, 1667*

1Co 7: 2 each man should have his own wife   1

each one

1. ἕκαστος, *hekastos, 1667*

Jhn	16:32	when you will be scattered, each one to his home	1
Rom	2: 6	he will repay according to each one's deeds:	1
1Co	4: 5	Then each one will receive commendation	1
	12:11	who allots to each one individually	1
	14:26	When you come together, each one has a hymn	1
1Th	4: 4	each one of you know how to control your own body	1
Heb	6:11	we want each one of you to show…diligence	1

each other

1. ἀλλήλων, *allēlōn, 253*
2. ἑαυτοῦ, *heautou, 1571*

Lke	23:12	Herod and Pilate became friends with each other;	1
	24:14	talking with each other about all these things	1
	24:17	discussing with each other while you walk along?"	1
	24:32	said to each other, "Were not our hearts burning	1
Act	7:26	'Men, you are brothers; why do you wrong each other?'	1
	28:25	they disagreed with each other;	1
Rom	1:12	mutually encouraged by each other's faith	1
Gal	5:17	these are opposed to each other	1
Col	3:13	if anyone has a complaint…forgive each other;	2

each woman

1. ἕκαστος, *hekastos, 1667*

1Co 7: 2 and each woman her own husband.   1

eager *See also* eager *expectation*, eager *longing*

1. ζηλόω, *zēloō, 2420*
2. ζηλωτής, *zēlōtēs, 2421*
3. σπεύδω, *speudō, 5067*
4. σπουδάζω, *spoudazō, 5079*
5. σπουδαῖος, *spoudaios, 5080*

Act	20:16	he was eager to be in Jerusalem	3
1Co	14:12	since you are eager for spiritual gifts	2
	14:39	So, my friends, be eager to prophesy	1
2Co	8:22	and found eager in many matters	5
Gal	2:10	which was actually what I was eager to do.	4
1Pe	3:13	if you are eager to do what is good?	2
2Pe	1:10	more eager to confirm your call and election	4

more eager

1. σπουδαῖος, *spoudaios, 5080*
2. σπουδαίως, *spoudaiōs, 5081*

2Co	8:17	but since he is more eager than ever,	1
	8:22	who is now more eager than ever	1
Php	2:28	I am the more eager to send him, therefore	2

eagerly *See also* listen eagerly, wait eagerly

1. ἐπιθυμία, *epithymia, 2123*
2. προθυμία, *prothymia, 4608*
3. προθύμως, *prothymōs, 4610*
4. σπουδαίως, *spoudaiōs, 5081*
5. σπουδή + πᾶς, *spoudē + pas, 5082 + 4246*

Lke	22:15	"I have eagerly desired to eat this Passover	1
Act	17:11	they welcomed the message very eagerly	2
2Ti	1:17	he eagerly searched for me and found me	4
1Pe	5: 2	tend…not for sordid gain but eagerly.	3
Jde	1: 3	Beloved, while eagerly preparing to write to you	5

eagerness

1. ὀρέγω, *oregō, 3977*
2. προθυμία, *prothymia, 4608*
3. πρόθυμος, *prothymos, 4609*
4. σπουδάζω, *spoudazō, 5079*
5. σπουδή, *spoudē, 5082*

Rom	1:15	my eagerness to proclaim the gospel to you	3
2Co	8: 7	in utmost eagerness, and in our love for you	5
	8:11	so that your eagerness may be matched by completing	2
	8:12	if the eagerness is there, the gift is acceptable	2
	8:16	in the heart of Titus the same eagerness for you	5
	9: 2	for I know your eagerness	2
1Th	2:17	we longed with great eagerness to see you	4
1Ti	6:10	in their eagerness to be rich some have wandered	1

eagerness to clear

1. ἀπολογία, *apologia, 665*

2Co 7:11 what eagerness to clear yourselves   1

eagle

1. ἀετός, *aetos, 108*

Rev	4: 7	the fourth living creature like a flying eagle.	1
	8:13	I heard an eagle crying with a loud voice	1
	12:14	woman was given the two wings of the great eagle	1

ear *See also* come to ear

1. ἀκοή, *akoē, 198*
2. οὖς, *ous, 4044*
3. ὠτάριον, *ōtarion, 6064*
4. ὠτίον, *ōtion, 6065*

Mat	11:15	Let anyone with ears listen!	2
	13: 9	Let anyone with ears listen!"	2
	13:15	and their ears are hard of hearing	2
	13:15	and listen with their ears	2
	13:16	and your ears, for they hear.	2
	13:43	Let anyone with ears listen!	2
	26:51	cutting off his ear.	4
Mrk	4: 9	he said, "Let anyone with ears to hear listen!"	2
	4:23	Let anyone with ears to hear listen!"	2
	7:33	put his fingers into his ears, and he spat	2
	7:35	his ears were opened, his tongue was released	1
	8:18	Do you have ears, and fail to hear?	2
	14:47	struck the slave…cutting off his ear.	3
Lke	8: 8	"Let anyone with ears to hear listen!"	2

Lke	9:44	"Let these words sink into your ears:	2
	14:35	Let anyone with ears to hear listen!"	2
	22:50	and cut off his right ear.	2
	22:51	he touched his ear and healed him.	4
Jhn	18:10	and cut off his right ear.	3
	18:26	relative of the man whose ear Peter had cut off	4
Act	7:51	uncircumcised in heart and ears	2
	7:57	they covered their ears, and with a loud shout	2
	11:22	News…came to the ears of the church in Jerusalem	2
	28:27	their ears are hard of hearing	2
	28:27	listen with their ears	2
Rom	11: 8	eyes…not see and ears that would not hear	2
1Co	2: 9	"What no eye has seen, nor ear heard	2
	12:16	if the ear would say, "Because I am not an eye	2
2Ti	4: 3	having itching ears, they will accumulate	1
Jas	5: 4	cries…reached the ears of the Lord of hosts.	2
1Pe	3:12	and his ears are open to their prayer.	2
Rev	2: 7	Let anyone who has an ear listen	2
	2:11	who has an ear listen to what the Spirit is saying	2
	2:17	who has an ear listen to what the Spirit is saying	2
	2:29	Let anyone who has an ear listen	2
	3: 6	Let anyone who has an ear listen	2
	3:13	Let anyone who has an ear listen	2
	3:22	Let anyone who has an ear listen	2
	13: 9	Let anyone who has an ear listen:	2

earlier   *See* make earlier

early   *See also* early *dawn*, early *days*

1. ἀρχαῖος, *archaios, 792*
2. βαθύς, *bathys, 960*
3. ποτέ, *pote, 4537*
4. προάγω, *proagō, 4575*
5. πρόϊμος, *proimos, 4611*
6. πρότερος, *proteros, 4728*
7. πρωΐ, *prōi, 4745*
8. πρῶτον, *prōton, 4754*

Mrk	16: 2	very early on the first day of the week	7
	16: 9	⟦after he rose early on the first day of the week⟧	7
Lke	24: 1	on the first day of the week, at early dawn	2
Jhn	10:40	to the place where John had been baptizing earlier	8
	20: 1	Early on the first day of the week,	7
Act	15: 7	in the early days God made a choice among you	1
	21:16	Mnason of Cyprus, an early disciple	1
Gal	1:13	heard, no doubt, of my earlier life in Judaism.	3
Heb	7:18	There is…the abrogation of an earlier commandment	4
	10:32	recall those earlier days…when you endured	6
Jas	5: 7	until it receives the early and the late rains.	5

early in the morning

1. ὀρθρίζω, *orthrizō, 3983*
2. ὀρθρινός, *orthrinos, 3984*
3. ὄρθρος, *orthros, 3986*
4. πρωΐ, *prōi, 4745*
5. τέταρτος + φυλακή + ὁ + νύξ, *tetartos + phylakē + ho + nyx, 5480 + 5871 + 3836 + 3816*

Mat	14:25	early in the morning he came walking toward them	5
	20: 1	a landowner who went out early in the morning	4
Mrk	6:48	he came towards them early in the morning	5
Lke	21:38	all the people would get up early in the morning	1
	24:22	They were at the tomb early this morning	2
Jhn	8: 2	⟦Early in the morning he came again to the temple.⟧	3
	18:28	It was early in the morning.	4

earn

1. ἐσθίω, *esthiō, 2266*

2Th	3:12	to earn their own living.	1

earn extra

1. εὐοδόω, *euodoō, 2338*

1Co	16: 2	put aside and save whatever extra you earn	1

earnest

1. Contextual: Not in Greek
2. ζηλεύω, *zēleuō, 2418*

Rom	15:30	join me in earnest prayer to God on my behalf	1
Rev	3:19	Be earnest, therefore, and repent.	2

earnestly

1. ἐκτένεια, *ekteneia, 1755*
2. μετά + πολύς + παράκλησις, *meta + polys + paraklēsis, 3552 + 4498 + 4155*
3. πολύς, *polys, 4498*
4. σπουδαίως, *spoudaiōs, 5081*
5. ὑπερεκπερισσοῦ, *hyperekperissou, 5655*

Mrk	5:10	He begged him earnestly	3
Lke	7: 4	they appealed to him earnestly, saying,	4
Act	26: 7	as they earnestly worship day and night.	1
2Co	8: 4	begging us earnestly for the privilege	2
1Th	3:10	Night and day we pray most earnestly that we may see	5

more earnestly

1. ἐκτενῶς, *ektenōs, 1757*

Lke	22:44	⟦In his anguish he prayed more earnestly,⟧	1

earnestness

1. σπουδή, *spoudē, 5082*

2Co	7:11	what earnestness this godly grief has produced	1
	8: 8	your love against the earnestness of others.	1

earth

1. γῆ, *gē, 1178*
2. ἐπίγειος, *epigeios, 2103*

Mat	5: 5	the meek, for they will inherit the earth.	1
	5:13	"You are the salt of the earth; but if salt has lost	1
	5:18	For truly I tell you, until heaven and earth pass	1
	5:35	or by the earth, for it is his footstool	1
	6:10	Your will be done, on earth as it is in heaven.	1
	6:19	"Do not store up for yourselves treasures on earth	1
	9: 6	the Son of Man has authority on earth to forgive	1
	10:34	to bring peace to the earth;	1
	11:25	"I thank you, Father, Lord of heaven and earth	1
	12:40	the Son of Man will be in the heart of the earth.	1
	12:42	she came from the ends of the earth	1
	16:19	whatever you bind on earth will be bound	1
	16:19	whatever you loose on earth	1
	17:25	From whom do kings of the earth take toll	1
	18:18	Truly I tell you, whatever you bind on earth	1
	18:18	whatever you loose on earth	1
	18:19	truly I tell you, if two of you agree on earth	1
	23: 9	call no one your father on earth	1
	23:35	all the righteous blood shed on earth	1
	24:30	then all the tribes of the earth will mourn	1
	24:35	Heaven and earth will pass away	1
	27:51	The earth shook, and the rocks were split.	1
	28:18	"All authority in heaven and on earth	1
Mrk	2:10	Son of Man has authority on earth to forgive sins"	1
	4:28	The earth produces of itself, first the stalk	1
	4:31	the smallest of all the seeds on earth;	1
	9: 3	such as no one on earth could bleach them.	1
	13:27	from the ends of the earth to the ends of heaven.	1
	13:31	Heaven and earth will pass away	1
Lke	2:14	on earth peace among those whom he favors!"	1
	5:24	authority on earth to forgive sins"	1
	10:21	"I thank you, Father, Lord of heaven and earth	1
	11:31	she came from the ends of the earth	1
	12:49	"I came to bring fire to the earth	1
	12:51	that I have come to bring peace to the earth?	1
	12:56	to interpret the appearance of earth and sky	1
	16:17	it is easier for heaven and earth to pass away	1
	18: 8	will he find faith on earth?"	1
	21:23	will be great distress on the earth	1
	21:25	on the earth distress among nations	1
	21:33	Heaven and earth will pass away	1
	21:35	all who live on the face of the whole earth.	1
Jhn	3:31	one who is of the earth belongs to the earth	1
	3:31	one who is of the earth belongs to the earth	1
	12:24	a grain of wheat falls into the earth and dies	1
	12:32	when I am lifted up from the earth	1
	17: 4	I glorified you on earth	1
Act	1: 8	Judea and Samaria, and to the ends of the earth."	1
	2:19	signs on the earth below	1
	3:25	all the families of the earth shall be blessed.'	1
	4:24	the heaven and the earth, the sea	1
	4:26	The kings of the earth took their stand	1
	7:49	'Heaven is my throne, and the earth is my footstool.	1
	8:33	For his life is taken away from the earth."	1
	13:47	bring salvation to the ends of the earth.' "	1

	14:15	the living God, who made the heaven and the earth	1
	17:24	he who is Lord of heaven and earth	1
	17:26	to inhabit the whole earth	1
	22:22	"Away with such a fellow from the earth!	1
Rom	9:17	so that my name may be proclaimed in all the earth."	1
	9:28	Lord will execute his sentence on the earth	1
	10:18	"Their voice has gone out to all the earth	1
1Co	8: 5	may be so-called gods in heaven or on earth	1
	10:26	for "the earth and its fullness are the Lord's."	1
	15:47	The first man was from the earth, a man of dust;	1
Eph	1:10	things in heaven and things on earth.	1
	3:15	every family in heaven and on earth takes its name.	1
	4: 9	descended into the lower parts of the earth?	1
	6: 3	you may live long on the earth."	1
Php	2:10	in heaven and on earth and under the earth	2
Col	1:16	in him all things in heaven and on earth were created	1
	1:20	all things, whether on earth or in heaven	1
	3: 2	not on things that are on earth	1
Heb	1:10	"In the beginning, Lord, you founded the earth	1
	8: 4	Now if he were on earth, he would not be a priest	1
	11:13	they were strangers and foreigners on the earth	1
	12:25	they refused the one who warned them on earth	1
	12:26	At that time his voice shook the earth;	1
	12:26	shake not only the earth but also the heaven."	1
Jas	5: 5	You have lived on the earth in luxury	1
	5: 7	farmer waits for the precious crop from the earth	1
	5:12	do not swear, either by heaven or by earth	1
	5:17	it did not rain on the earth.	1
	5:18	and the earth yielded its harvest.	1
2Pe	3: 5	an earth was formed out of water and by means of water	1
	3: 7	by the same word the present heavens and earth	1
	3:10	and the earth…will be disclosed.	1
	3:13	we wait for new heavens and a new earth	1
Rev	1: 5	Jesus Christ…the ruler of the kings of the earth.	1
	1: 7	on his account all the tribes of the earth will wail.	1
	3:10	to test the inhabitants of the earth.	1
	5: 3	no one in heaven or on earth or under the earth	1
	5: 3	no one in heaven or on earth or under the earth	1
	5: 6	seven spirits of God sent out into all the earth.	1
	5:10	and they will reign on earth."	1
	5:13	I heard every creature in heaven and on earth	1
	5:13	every creature…under the earth and in the sea	1
	6: 4	rider was permitted to take peace from the earth	1
	6: 8	they were given authority over a fourth of the earth	1
	6: 8	kill…by the wild animals of the earth.	1
	6:10	avenge our blood on the inhabitants of the earth?"	1
	6:13	the stars of the sky fell to the earth	1
	6:15	Then the kings of the earth and the magnates	1
	7: 1	angels standing at the four corners of the earth	1
	7: 1	holding back the four winds of the earth	1
	7: 1	so that no wind could blow on earth or sea	1
	7: 2	angels who had been given power to damage earth	1
	7: 3	"Do not damage the earth or the sea or the trees	1
	8: 5	filled it with fire…and threw it on the earth;	1
	8: 7	with blood, and they were hurled to the earth;	1
	8: 7	and a third of the earth was burned up	1
	8:13	"Woe, woe, woe to the inhabitants of the earth	1
	9: 1	I saw a star that had fallen from heaven to earth	1
	9: 3	Then from the smoke came locusts on the earth	1
	9: 3	like the authority of scorpions of the earth.	1
	9: 4	They were told not to damage the grass of the earth	1
	10: 6	who created…the earth and what is in it	1
	11: 4	that stand before the Lord of the earth.	1
	11: 6	and to strike the earth with every kind of plague	1
	11:10	the inhabitants of the earth will gloat	1
	11:10	a torment to the inhabitants of the earth.	1
	11:18	and for destroying those who destroy the earth."	1
	12: 4	the stars of heaven and threw them to the earth.	1
	12: 9	the deceiver…—he was thrown down to the earth	1
	12:12	woe to the earth and the sea, for the devil has come	1
	12:13	saw that he had been thrown down to the earth	1
	12:16	But the earth came to the help of the woman;	1
	13: 3	In amazement the whole earth followed the beast.	1
	13: 8	all the inhabitants of the earth will worship it	1
	13:11	I saw another beast that rose out of the earth;	1
	13:12	it makes the earth and its inhabitants worship	1
	13:13	even making fire come down from heaven to earth	1
	13:14	it deceives the inhabitants of earth	1
	14: 3	who have been redeemed from the earth.	1
	14: 6	gospel to proclaim to those who live on the earth	1
	14: 7	and worship him who made heaven and earth	1

	14:15	because the harvest of the earth is fully ripe."	1
	14:16	the one…on the cloud swung his sickle over the earth	1
	14:16	swung his sickle…and the earth was reaped.	1
	14:18	and gather the clusters of the vine of the earth	1
	14:19	So the angel swung his sickle over the earth	1
	14:19	the angel…gathered the vintage of the earth	1
	16: 1	pour out on the earth the seven bowls of the wrath	1
	16: 2	first angel went and poured his bowl on the earth	1
	16:18	as had not occurred since people were upon the earth	1
	17: 2	kings of the earth have committed fornication	1
	17: 2	the inhabitants of the earth have become drunk."	1
	17: 5	mother of whores and of earth's abominations."	1
	17: 8	And the inhabitants of the earth…will be amazed	1
	17:18	that rules over the kings of the earth."	1
	18: 1	and the earth was made bright with his splendor.	1
	18: 3	kings of the earth have committed fornication	1
	18: 3	the merchants of the earth have grown rich	1
	18: 9	the kings of the earth…will weep and wail	1
	18:11	the merchants of the earth weep and mourn for her	1
	18:23	your merchants were the magnates of the earth	1
	18:24	blood…of all who have been slaughtered on earth."	1
	19: 2	judged the great whore who corrupted the earth	1
	19:19	Then I saw the beast and the kings of the earth	1
	20: 8	nations…at the four corners of the earth	1
	20: 9	They marched up over the breadth of the earth	1
	20:11	earth and the heaven fled from his presence	1
	21: 1	Then I saw a new heaven and a new earth;	1
	21: 1	first heaven and the first earth had passed away	1
	21:24	the kings of the earth will bring their glory	1

under the earth

1. καταχθόνιος, *katachthonios, 2973*

Php	2:10	in heaven and on earth and under the earth	1

earthly

1. ἐπί + ὁ + γῆ, *epi + ho + gē, 2093 + 3836 + 1178*
2. ἐπίγειος, *epigeios, 2103*
3. κατά + σάρξ, *kata + sarx, 2848 + 4922*
4. κοσμικός, *kosmikos, 3176*
5. σαρκικός, *sarkikos, 4920*
6. σάρξ, *sarx, 4922*

1Co	15:40	both heavenly bodies and earthly bodies	2
	15:40	that of the earthly is another.	2
2Co	1:12	not by earthly wisdom but by the grace of God	5
	5: 1	For we know that if the earthly tent we live	2
Eph	6: 5	Slaves, obey your earthly masters with fear	3
Col	3: 5	Put to death, therefore, whatever in you is earthly:	1
	3:22	Slaves, obey your earthly masters in everything	3
Heb	9: 1	worship and an earthly sanctuary.	4
Jas	3:15	wisdom…is earthly, unspiritual, devilish.	2
1Pe	4: 2	so as to live for the rest of your earthly life	6

earthly thing

1. γῆ, *gē, 1178*
2. ἐπίγειος, *epigeios, 2103*

Jhn	3:12	If I have told you about earthly things	2
	3:31	to the earth and speaks about earthly things.	1
Php	3:19	their minds are set on earthly things.	2

earthquake

1. σεισμός, *seismos, 4939*

Mat	24: 7	famines and earthquakes in various places:	1
	27:54	saw the earthquake and what took place	1
	28: 2	suddenly there was a great earthquake;	1
Mrk	13: 8	there will be earthquakes in various places;	1
Lke	21:11	there will be great earthquakes	1
Act	16:26	Suddenly there was an earthquake, so violent	1
Rev	6:12	I looked, and there came a great earthquake;	1
	8: 5	flashes of lightning, and an earthquake.	1
	11:13	At that moment there was a great earthquake	1
	11:13	seven thousand people were killed in the earthquake	1
	11:19	peals of thunder, an earthquake, and heavy hail.	1
	16:18	a violent earthquake, such as had not occurred	1
	16:18	so violent was that earthquake.	1

ease

1. προσψαύω, *prospsauō, 4718*

Lke	11:46	do not lift a finger to ease them.	1

east

1. ἀνατολή, *anatolē*, 424
2. ἀνατολή + ἥλιος, *anatolē + hēlios*, 424 + 2463

Mat	2: 1	wise men from the East came to Jerusalem	1
	8:11	I tell you, many will come from east and west	1
	24:27	For as the lightning comes from the east	1
Mrk	16: S	⟦sent out through them, from east to west,⟧	1
Lke	13:29	people will come from east and west	1
Rev	16:12	to prepare the way for the kings from the east.	2
	21:13	on the east three gates, on the north three gates	1

easy

1. εὔκοπος, *eukopos*, 2324
2. εὐρύχωρος, *eurychōros*, 2353
3. χρηστός, *chrēstos*, 5982

Mat	7:13	for the gate is wide and the road is easy	2
	9: 5	For which is easier, to say, 'Your sins are forgiven,'	1
	11:30	For my yoke is easy, and my burden is light."	3
	19:24	Again I tell you, it is easier for a camel	1
Mrk	2: 9	Which is easier, to say to the paralytic	1
	10:25	easier for a camel to go through the eye	1
Lke	5:23	Which is easier, to say, 'Your sins are forgiven	1
	16:17	it is easier for heaven and earth to pass away	1
	18:25	Indeed, it is easier for a camel to go	1

eat *See also* sit down to eat

1. ἀνακλίνω, *anaklinō*, 369
2. βιβρώσκω, *bibrōskō*, 1048
3. βρῶμα, *brōma*, 1109
4. βρώσιμος, *brōsimos*, 1110
5. βρῶσις, *brōsis*, 1111
6. γεύομαι, *geuomai*, 1174
7. δειπνέω, *deipneō*, 1268
8. ἐσθίω, *esthiō*, 2266
9. κατάκειμαι, *katakeimai*, 2879
10. κατεσθίω, *katesthiō*, 2983
11. μεταλαμβάνω, *metalambanō*, 3561
12. προσλαμβάνω, *proslambanō*, 4689
13. τρώγω, *trōgō*, 5592

Mat	6:25	life, what you will eat or what you will drink	8
	6:31	'What will we eat?' or 'What will we drink?'	8
	8:11	and will eat with Abraham	1
	9:11	"Why does your teacher eat with tax collectors	8
	11:18	For John came neither eating nor drinking	8
	11:19	the Son of Man came eating and drinking	8
	12: 1	they began to pluck heads of grain and to eat.	8
	12: 4	He entered the house of God and ate the bread	8
	12: 4	not lawful for him or his companions to eat	8
	14:16	you give them something to eat."	8
	14:20	all ate and were filled;	8
	14:21	who ate were about five thousand men, besides	8
	15: 2	For they do not wash their hands before they eat."	8
	15:20	to eat with unwashed hands does not defile."	8
	15:27	"Yes, Lord, yet even the dogs eat the crumbs	8
	15:32	and have nothing to eat;	8
	15:37	all of them ate and were filled;	8
	15:38	who had eaten were four thousand men, besides	8
	24:38	eating and drinking, marrying	13
	24:49	eats and drinks with drunkards	8
	26:17	make the preparations for you to eat the Passover?"	8
	26:21	they were eating, he said, "Truly I tell you	8
	26:26	While they were eating, Jesus took a loaf of bread	8
	26:26	"Take, eat; this is my body."	8
Mrk	1: 6	ate locusts and wild honey.	8
	2:16	Pharisees saw that he was eating with sinners	8
	2:16	"Why does he eat with tax collectors and sinners?"	8
	2:26	ate the bread of the Presence	8
	2:26	it is not lawful for any but the priests to eat	8
	3:20	so that they could not even eat.	8
	5:43	and told them to give her something to eat.	8
	6:31	they had no leisure even to eat.	8
	6:36	buy something for themselves to eat."	8
	6:37	he answered them, "You give them something to eat."	8
	6:37	give it to them to eat?"	8
	6:42	all ate and were filled;	8
	6:44	had eaten the loaves numbered five thousand men	8
	7: 2	eating with defiled hands, that is, without washing	8
	7: 3	(For the Pharisees, and all the Jews, do not eat	8
	7: 4	they do not eat anything from the market unless	8

	7: 5	but eat with defiled hands?"	8
	7:28	dogs under the table eat the children's crumbs."	8
	8: 1	again a great crowd without anything to eat	. 8
	8: 2	have nothing to eat.	8
	8: 8	They ate and were filled;	8
	11:14	"May no one ever eat fruit from you again."	8
	14:12	the preparations for you to eat the Passover?"	8
	14:14	where I may eat the Passover with my disciples?'	8
	14:18	when they had taken their places and were eating	8
	14:18	one who is eating with me."	8
	14:22	While they were eating, he took a loaf of bread	8
Lke	4: 2	He ate nothing at all during those days	8
	5:30	"Why do you eat and drink with tax collectors	8
	5:33	but your disciples eat and drink."	8
	6: 1	heads of grain…and ate them	8
	6: 4	took and ate the bread of the Presence	8
	6: 4	it is not lawful for any but the priests to eat	8
	7:33	For John the Baptist has come eating no bread	8
	7:34	the Son of Man has come eating and drinking	8
	7:36	One of the Pharisees asked Jesus to eat with him	8
	7:37	he was eating in the Pharisee's house	9
	8:55	give her something to eat.	8
	9:13	he said to them, "You give them something to eat."	8
	9:17	all ate and were filled;	8
	10: 7	eating and drinking whatever they provide	8
	10: 8	eat what is set before you;	8
	12:19	relax, eat, drink, be merry."	8
	12:22	worry about your life, what you will eat	8
	12:29	what you are to eat and what you are to drink	8
	12:45	to eat and drink and get drunk	8
	13:26	'We ate and drank with you	8
	13:29	and will eat in the kingdom of God.	1
	14: 1	house of a leader of the Pharisees to eat a meal	8
	14:15	"Blessed is anyone who will eat bread in the kingdom	8
	15:16	the pods that the pigs were eating;	8
	15:23	let us eat and celebrate;	8
	17: 8	while I eat and drink;	8
	17: 8	later you may eat and drink'?	8
	17:27	They were eating and drinking, and marrying	8
	17:28	they were eating and drinking, buying and selling	8
	22: 8	the Passover meal for us that we may eat it."	8
	22:11	where I may eat the Passover with my disciples?" '	8
	22:15	"I have eagerly desired to eat this Passover	8
	22:16	I tell you, I will not eat it until it is fulfilled	8
	22:30	you may eat and drink at my table in my kingdom	8
	24:41	he said to them, "Have you anything here to eat?"	4
	24:43	he took it and ate in their presence.	8
Jhn	4:31	the disciples were urging him, "Rabbi, eat	8
	4:32	"I have food to eat that you do not know	8
	4:33	no one has brought him something to eat?"	8
	6: 5	to buy bread for these people to eat?"	8
	6:13	fragments…left by those who had eaten	2
	6:23	the place where they had eaten the bread	8
	6:26	because you ate your fill of the loaves.	8
	6:31	Our ancestors ate the manna in the wilderness;	8
	6:31	'He gave them bread from heaven to eat.' "	8
	6:49	Your ancestors ate the manna in the wilderness	8
	6:50	so that one may eat of it and not die.	8
	6:51	Whoever eats of this bread will live forever;	8
	6:52	"How can this man give us his flesh to eat?"	8
	6:53	unless you eat the flesh of the Son of Man	8
	6:54	Those who eat my flesh and drink my blood	13
	6:56	who eat my flesh and drink my blood abide in me	13
	6:57	whoever eats me will live because of me.	13
	6:58	not like…your ancestors ate, and they died.	8
	6:58	one who eats this bread will live forever."	13
	13:18	'The one who ate my bread	13
	18:28	and to be able to eat the Passover.	8
Act	2:46	ate their food with glad and generous hearts	11
	9: 9	neither ate nor drank.	8
	10:10	He became hungry and wanted something to eat;	6
	10:13	he heard a voice saying, "Get up, Peter; kill and eat."	8
	10:14	never eaten anything that is profane or unclean."	8
	11: 7	'Get up, Peter; kill and eat.'	8
	20:11	and after he had broken bread and eaten	6
	23:12	an oath neither to eat nor drink	8
	23:21	an oath neither to eat nor drink	8
	27:33	without food, having eaten nothing.	12
	27:35	he broke it and began to eat.	8
Rom	14: 2	Some believe in eating anything	8
	14: 2	while the weak eat only vegetables.	8

14: 3	Those who eat must not despise those who abstain	8
14: 3	who abstain must not pass judgment on those who eat;	8
14: 6	Also those who eat, eat in honor of the Lord	8
14: 6	Also those who eat, eat in honor of the Lord	8
14:15	brother or sister is being injured by what you eat	3
14:15	Do not let what you eat cause the ruin of one	3
14:20	to make others fall by what you eat;	8
14:21	it is good not to eat meat or drink wine	8
14:23	those who have doubts are condemned if they eat	8

1Co 8: 4 Hence, as to the eating of food offered to idols — 5
8: 7 the food they eat as food offered to an idol; — 8
8: 8 We are no worse off if we do not eat — 8
8:10 see you...eating in the temple of an idol — 9
8:10 to the point of eating food sacrificed to idols? — 8
8:13 I will never eat meat, so that I may not — 8
9: 7 not eat any of its fruit? — 8
10: 3 all ate the same spiritual food — 8
10: 7 "The people sat down to eat and drink — 8
10:18 who eat the sacrifices partners in the altar? — 8
10:25 Eat whatever is sold in the meat market — 8
10:27 eat whatever is set before you — 8
10:28 do not eat it, out of consideration for the one — 8
10:31 So, whether you eat or drink, or whatever you do — 8
11:20 it is not really to eat the Lord's supper. — 8
11:21 For when the time comes to eat, — 8
11:22 What! Do you not have homes to eat and drink in? — 8
11:26 For as often as you eat this bread — 8
11:27 Whoever, therefore, eats the bread — 8
11:28 Examine yourselves, and only then eat of the bread — 8
11:29 For all who eat and drink — 8
11:29 eat and drink judgment against themselves. — 8
11:33 brothers and sisters, when you come together to eat — 8
11:34 If you are hungry, eat at home — 8
15:32 "Let us eat and drink, for tomorrow we die." — 8
2Th 3: 8 we did not eat anyone's bread without paying — 8
3:10 Anyone unwilling to work should not eat. — 8
Heb 13:10 who officiate in the tent have no right to eat. — 8
Jas 5: 3 their rust...will eat your flesh like fire. — 8
Rev 2: 7 I will give permission to eat from the tree of life — 8
2:14 that they would eat food sacrificed to idols — 8
2:20 and to eat food sacrificed to idols. — 8
3:20 I will come in to you and eat with you — 7
10: 9 "Take it, and eat; it will be bitter to your stomach — 10
10:10 I took the little scroll...and ate it; — 10
10:10 when I had eaten it, my stomach was made bitter. — 8
19:18 to eat the flesh of kings, the flesh of captains — 8

eat one's fill
1. χορτάζω, *chortazō, 5963*
Jas 2:16 "Go in peace; keep warm and eat your fill," — 1

eat up
1. κατεσθίω, *katesthiō, 2983*
Mat 13: 4 and the birds came and ate them up. — 1
Mrk 4: 4 the birds came and ate it up. — 1
Lke 8: 5 the birds of the air ate it up. — 1

eat with
1. συνεσθίω, *synesthiō, 5303*
Lke 15: 2 "This fellow welcomes sinners and eats with them." — 1
Act 10:41 who ate and drank with him — 1
11: 3 "Why did you...eat with them?" — 1
1Co 5:11 Do not even eat with such a one. — 1
Gal 2:12 he used to eat with the Gentiles. — 1

eaten by worms
1. σκωληκόβρωτος, *skōlēkobrōtos, 5037*
Act 12:23 he was eaten by worms and died. — 1

Eber
1. Ἔβερ, *Eber, 1576*
Lke 3:35 son of Peleg, son of Eber, son of Shelah — 1

edge
1. στόμα, *stoma, 5125*
Lke 21:24 they will fall by the edge of the sword — 1
Heb 11:34 escaped the edge of the sword — 1

edict
1. διάταγμα, *diatagma, 1409*

Heb 11:23 they were not afraid of the king's edict. — 1

educate
1. παιδεύω, *paideuō, 4084*
Act 22: 3 educated strictly according to our ancestral law — 1

effect *See also* take effect
1. Contextual: Not in Greek
2. διά, *dia, 1328*
3. ἔργον, *ergon, 2240*
4. τύπος, *typos, 5596*
5. ὡς, *hōs, 6055*
Lke 16:16 "The law and the prophets were in effect until — 1
Act 23:25 He wrote a letter to this effect: — 4
Rom 5:16 is not like the effect of the one man's sin. — 2
2Th 2: 2 to the effect that the day of the Lord is already here. — 5
Jas 1: 4 let endurance have its full effect — 3

effective *See also* effective *work*
1. ἐνεργέω, *energeō, 1919*
2. ἐνεργής, *energēs, 1921*
Phm 1: 6 may become effective when you perceive all the good — 2
Jas 5:16 prayer of the righteous is powerful and effective. — 1

effective through
1. διά, *dia, 1328*
Rom 3:25 atonement by his blood, effective through faith. — 1

effort *See also* make every effort
1. ἐργασία, *ergasia, 2238*
2. ζητέω, *zēteō, 2426*
3. σπουδή, *spoudē, 5082*
Lke 12:58 on the way make an effort to settle the case — 1
Gal 2:17 if, in our effort to be justified in Christ — 2
2Pe 1: 5 make every effort to support your faith — 3

egg
1. ᾠόν, *ōon, 6051*
Lke 11:12 Or if the child asks for an egg — 1

Egypt
1. Αἴγυπτος, *Aigyptos, 131*
Mat 2:13 take the child and his mother, and flee to Egypt — 1
2:14 his mother by night, and went to Egypt — 1
2:15 "Out of Egypt I have called my son." — 1
2:19 an angel...appeared in a dream to Joseph in Egypt — 1
Act 2:10 Egypt and the parts of Libya belonging to Cyrene — 1
7: 9 "The patriarchs...sold him into Egypt; — 1
7:10 when he stood before Pharaoh, king of Egypt — 1
7:10 who appointed him ruler over Egypt — 1
7:11 came a famine throughout Egypt and Canaan — 1
7:12 when Jacob heard that there was grain in Egypt — 1
7:15 Jacob went down to Egypt. — 1
7:17 our people in Egypt increased and multiplied — 1
7:18 king who had not known Joseph ruled over Egypt. — 1
7:34 mistreatment of my people who are in Egypt — 1
7:34 Come now, I will send you to Egypt.' — 1
7:36 wonders and signs in Egypt, at the Red Sea — 1
7:39 in their hearts they turned back to Egypt — 1
7:40 this Moses who led us out from the land of Egypt — 1
13:17 during their stay in the land of Egypt — 1
Heb 3:16 left Egypt under the leadership of Moses? — 1
8: 9 to lead them out of the land of Egypt; — 1
11:26 greater wealth than the treasures of Egypt — 1
11:27 By faith he left Egypt — 1
Jde 1: 5 once for all saved a people out of the land of Egypt — 1
Rev 11: 8 city...prophetically called Sodom and Egypt — 1

Egyptian
1. Αἰγύπτιος, *Aigyptios, 130*
Act 7:22 instructed in all the wisdom of the Egyptians — 1
7:24 avenged him by striking down the Egyptian. — 1
7:28 kill me as you killed the Egyptian yesterday?' — 1
21:38 Then you are not the Egyptian who... — 1
Heb 11:29 when the Egyptians attempted to do so — 1

eight
1. ὀκτώ, *oktō, 3893*
Lke 2:21 After eight days had passed, it was time —

Lke 9:28 Now about eight days after these sayings 1
Act 9:33 Aeneas, who had been bedridden for eight years 1
25: 6 stayed among them not more than eight or ten days 1
1Pe 3:20 in which a few, that is, eight persons, were saved 1

eighteen

1. δέκα + καί + ὀκτώ, *deka + kai + oktō, 1274 + 2779 + 3893*
2. δεκαοκτώ, *dekaoktō, 1277*

Lke 13: 4 eighteen who were killed when the tower of Siloam 2
13:11 spirit that had crippled her for eighteen years. 2
13:16 whom Satan bound for eighteen long years 1

eighth *See also* eighth *day*

1. ὄγδοος, *ogdoos, 3838*

Lke 1:59 On the eighth day they came to circumcise 1
Act 7: 8 circumcised him on the eighth day; 1
Rev 17:11 the beast that was and is not, it is an eighth 1
21:20 the seventh chrysolite, the eighth beryl 1

eighty

1. ὀγδοήκοντα, *ogdoēkonta, 3837*

Lke 16: 7 to him, 'Take you bill and make it eighty.' 1

eighty-four

1. ὀγδοήκοντα + τέσσαρες, *ogdoēkonta + tessares, 3837 + 5475*

Lke 2:37 then as a widow to the age of eighty-four 1

either *See also* either *side*

1. Contextual: Not in Greek
2. εἴτε, *eite, 1664*
3. ἤ, *ē, 2445*
4. ἤτοι, *ētoi, 2486*
5. μήτε, *mēte, 3612*
6. οὔτε, *oute, 4046*

Mat 5:34 either by heaven, for it is the throne of God 5
6:24 slave will either hate the one and love the other 3
12:32 either in this age or in the age to come. 6
12:33 "Either make the tree good, and its fruit good; 3
Lke 16:13 slave will either hate the one and love the other 3
Act 24:12 stirring up a crowd either in the synagogues 6
Rom 6:16 slaves...either of sin, which leads to death 4
2Th 2: 2 either by spirit or by word or by letter 5
2:15 taught...either by word of mouth or by our letter. 2
1Ti 1: 7 understanding either what they are saying or... 5
Jas 5:12 do not swear, either by heaven or by earth 5
1Jn 3: 6 no one who sins has either seen him or known him. 1
Rev 3:15 I wish that you were either cold or hot. 1

Elamite

1. Ἐλαμίτης, *Elamitēs, 1780*

Act 2: 9 Parthians, Medes, Elamites, 1

too elated

1. ὑπεραίρομαι, *hyperairomai, 5643*

2Co 12: 7 Therefore, to keep me from being too elated. 1
12: 7 to torment me, to keep me from being too elated. 1

elder *See also* assembly of the elders, council of elders

1. γερουσία, *gerousia, 1172*
2. μείζων, *meizōn, 3505*
3. πρεσβύτερος, *presbyteros, 4565*

Mat 15: 2 break the tradition of the elders? 3
16:21 at the hands of the elders and chief priests 3
21:23 the chief priests and the elders of the people 3
26: 3 Then the chief priests and the elders 3
26:47 the chief priests and the elders of the people. 3
26:57 the scribes and the elders had gathered. 3
27: 1 chief priests and the elders of the people 3
27: 3 to the chief priests and the elders. 3
27:12 accused by the chief priests and elders 3
27:20 Now the chief priests and the elders persuaded 3
27:41 chief priests...with the scribes and elders 3
28:12 After the priests had assembled with the elders 3
Mrk 7: 3 observing the tradition of the elders; 3
7: 5 according to the tradition of the elders 3
8:31 rejected by the elders, the chief priests 3
11:27 the scribes, and the elders came to him 3
14:43 the chief priests, the scribes, and the elders. 3

14:53 the chief priests, the elders, and the scribes 3
15: 1 held a consultation with the elders and scribes 3
Lke 7: 3 he sent some Jewish elders to him 3
9:22 rejected by the elders, chief priests 3
15:25 "Now his elder son was in the field; 3
20: 1 priests and the scribes came with the elders 3
22:52 officers of the temple police, and the elders 3
Jhn 8: 9 [[went away, one by one, beginning with the elders;]] 3
Act 4: 5 their rulers, elders, and scribes 3
4: 8 "Rulers of the people and elders 3
4:23 what the chief priests and the elders had said 3
5:21 and the whole body of the elders of Israel 1
6:12 They stirred up the people as well as the elders 3
11:30 this they did, sending it to the elders 3
14:23 had appointed elders for them in each church 3
15: 2 to discuss this question with...the elders. 3
15: 4 welcomed by...the apostles and the elders 3
15: 6 The apostles and the elders met together 3
15:22 the apostles and the elders...decided 3
15:23 "The brothers, both the apostles and the elders 3
16: 4 decisions...reached by the apostles and elders 3
20:17 asking the elders of the church to meet him. 3
21:18 all the elders were present. 3
23:14 They went to the chief priests and elders and said 3
24: 1 the high priest Ananias came down with some elders 3
25:15 the chief priests and the elders of the Jews 3
Rom 9:12 she was told, "The elder shall serve the younger." 2
1Ti 5:17 the elders who rule well 3
5:19 Never accept any accusation against an elder 3
Tit 1: 5 appoint elders in every town, as I directed you: 3
Jas 5:14 They should call for the elders of the church 3
1Pe 5: 1 as an elder myself...I exhort the elders among you 3
5: 5 who are younger must accept the authority of the elders. 3
2Jn 1: 1 The elder to the elect lady and her children 3
3Jn 1: 1 The elder to the beloved Gaius, whom I love 3
Rev 4: 4 seated on the thrones are twenty-four elders 3
4:10 the twenty-four elders fall...and worship 3
5: 5 Then one of the elders said to me, "Do not weep. 3
5: 6 I saw...among the elders a Lamb standing 3
5: 8 the twenty-four elders fell before the Lamb 3
5:11 throne and the living creatures and the elders; 3
5:14 And the elders fell down and worshiped. 3
7:11 around the elders and the four living creatures 3
7:13 Then one of the elders addressed me, saying 3
11:16 the twenty-four elders who sit...before God 3
14: 3 before the throne...and before the elders. 3
19: 4 the twenty-four elders...fell down and worshiped 3

elder oneself

1. συμπρεσβύτερος, *sympresbyteros, 5236*

1Pe 5: 1 an elder myself and a witness of the sufferings of Christ 1

Eleazar

1. Ἐλεάζαρ, *Eleazar, 1789*

Mat 1:15 Eliud the father of Eleazar 1
1:15 and Eleazar the father of Matthan 1

elect

1. ἐκλεκτός, *eklektos, 1723*
2. ἐκλογή, *eklogē, 1724*

Mat 24:22 for the sake of the elect 1
24:24 to lead astray, if possible, even the elect. 1
24:31 they will gather his elect from the four winds 1
Mrk 13:20 for the sake of the elect, whom he chose 1
13:22 to lead astray, if possible, the elect. 1
13:27 gather his elect from the four winds 1
Rom 8:33 Who will bring any charge against God's elect? 1
11: 7 The elect obtained it, but the rest were hardened 2
1Ti 5:21 of God and of Christ Jesus and of the elect angels 1
2Ti 2:10 everything for the sake of the elect 1
Tit 1: 1 for the sake of the faith of God's elect 1
2Jn 1: 1 The elder to the elect lady and her children 1
1:13 The children of your elect sister send you their greetings. 1

election

1. ἐκλογή, *eklogē, 1724*

Rom 9:11 (so that God's purpose of election might continue 1
11:28 but as regards election they are beloved 1
2Pe 1:10 more eager to confirm your call and election 1

elegant

1. λαμπρός, *lampros, 3287*

Lke 23:11 then he put an elegant robe on him   1

element

1. στοιχεῖον, *stoicheion, 5122*

Heb 5:12 teach you...the basic elements of the oracles of God.   1
2Pe 3:10 and the elements will be dissolved with fire   1
     3:12 and the elements will melt with fire?   1

elemental *See* elemental *spirit*

eleven

1. ἕνδεκα, *hendeka, 1894*

Mat 28:16 Now the eleven disciples went to Galilee   1
Mrk 16:14 ⟦Later he appeared to the eleven themselves⟧   1
Lke 24: 9 told all this to the eleven and to all the rest.   1
     24:33 they found the eleven and their companions   1
Act   1:26 he was added to the eleven apostles.   1
      2:14 Peter, standing with the eleven   1

eleventh

1. ἑνδέκατος, *hendekatos, 1895*

Rev 21:20 the tenth chrysoprase, the eleventh jacinth   1

Eli

1. ἠλί¹, *ēli¹, 2458*

Mat 27:46 "Eli, Eli, lema sabachthani?"   1
     27:46 "Eli, Eli, lema sabachthani?"   1

Eliakim

1. Ἐλιακίμ, *Eliakim, 1806*

Mat   1:13 and Abiud the father of Eliakim   1
      1:13 and Eliakim the father of Azor   1
Lke   3:30 son of Jonam, son of Eliakim   1

Eliezer

1. Ἐλιέζερ, *Eliezer, 1808*

Lke   3:29 son of Joshua, son of Eliezer   1

Elijah

1. Ἠλίας, *Ēlias, 2460*

Mat 11:14 he is Elijah who is to come.   1
     16:14 "Some say John the Baptist, but others Elijah   1
     17: 3 Suddenly there appeared to them Moses and Elijah   1
     17: 4 one for you, one for Moses, and one for Elijah."   1
     17:10 the scribes say that Elijah must come first?"   1
     17:11 He replied, "Elijah is indeed coming   1
     17:12 I tell you that Elijah has already come   1
     27:47 "This man is calling for Elijah."   1
     27:49 let us see whether Elijah will come to save him."   1
Mrk   6:15 others said, "It is Elijah."   1
      8:28 others, Elijah; and still others, one of the prophets."   1
      9: 4 there appeared to them Elijah with Moses   1
      9: 5 one for you, one for Moses, and one for Elijah."   1
      9:11 the scribes say that Elijah must come first?"   1
      9:12 "Elijah is indeed coming first to restore all things.   1
      9:13 I tell you that Elijah has come   1
     15:35 "Listen, he is calling for Elijah."   1
     15:36 let us see whether Elijah will come   1
Lke   1:17 With the spirit and power of Elijah he will go   1
      4:25 were many widows in Israel in the time of Elijah   1
      4:26 yet Elijah was sent to none of them   1
      9: 8 by some that Elijah had appeared   1
      9:19 but others, Elijah;   1
      9:30 two men, Moses and Elijah, talking to him.   1
      9:33 one for you, one for Moses, and one for Elijah"   1
Jhn   1:21 And they asked him, "What then? Are you Elijah?"   1
      1:25 if you are neither the Messiah, nor Elijah   1
Rom 11: 2 Do you not know what the scripture says of Elijah   1
Jas   5:17 Elijah was a human being like us,   1

Elisha

1. Ἐλισαῖος, *Elisaios, 1811*

Lke   4:27 lepers in Israel in the time of the prophet Elisha   1

Eliud

1. Ἐλιούδ, *Elioud, 1809*

Mat   1:14 and Achim the father of Eliud   1

1:15 Eliud the father of Eleazar   1

Elizabeth

1. Ἐλισάβετ, *Elisabet, 1810*

Lke   1: 5 her name was Elizabeth.   1
      1: 7 they had no children, because Elizabeth was barren   1
      1:13 Your wife Elizabeth will bear you a son   1
      1:24 After those days his wife Elizabeth conceived   1
      1:36 now, your relative Elizabeth in her old age   1
      1:40 entered the house...and greeted Elizabeth.   1
      1:41 When Elizabeth heard Mary's greeting, the child   1
      1:41 Elizabeth was filled with the Holy Spirit   1
      1:57 Now the time came for Elizabeth to give birth   1

Elmadam

1. Ἐλμαδάμ, *Elmadam, 1825*

Lke   3:28 son of Cosam, son of Elmadam, son of Er   1

eloi

1. ἐλωί, *elōi, 1830*

Mrk 15:34 "Eloi, Eloi, lema sabachthani?"   1
     15:34 "Eloi, Eloi, lema sabachthani?"   1

eloquent

1. λόγιος, *logios, 3360*
2. λόγος, *logos, 3364*

Act 18:24 an eloquent man, well-versed in the scriptures.   1
1Co   1:17 proclaim the gospel, not with eloquent wisdom   2

else *See also* everyone else, or else, someone else

1. Contextual: Not in Greek
2. ἄλλος, *allos, 257*
3. ἕτερος, *heteros, 2283*
4. λοιπός, *loipos, 3370*

Jhn 10:29 Father has given me is greater than all else   1
     15:24 done among them the works that no one else did   2
Act   4:12 There is salvation in no one else   2
      8:34 does the prophet say this...about someone else?"   3
Rom   8:32 not with him also give us everything else?   1
      8:39 nor depth, nor anything else in all creation   3
1Co   1:16 I do not know whether I baptized anyone else.)   2
      2:15 are themselves subject to no one else's scrutiny.   1
Php   1:13 the whole imperial guard and to everyone else   4
      3: 4 If anyone else has reason to be confident   2
1Ti   1:10 whatever else is contrary to the sound teaching   3

Elymas

1. Ἐλύμας, *Elymas, 1829*

Act 13: 8 the magician Elymas...opposed them   1

embark

1. ἐπιβαίνω, *epibainō, 2094*

Act 27: 2 Embarking on a ship of Adramyttium   1

embodiment

1. μόρφωσις, *morphōsis, 3673*

Rom   2:20 in the law the embodiment of knowledge and truth   1

embrace

1. ἐπιπίπτω + ἐπί + ὁ + τράχηλος, *epipiptō + epi + ho + trachēlos, 2158 + 2093 + 3836 + 5549*

Act 20:37 they embraced Paul and kissed him   1

emerald

1. σμαράγδινος, *smaragdinos, 5039*
2. σμάραγδος, *smaragdos, 5040*

Rev   4: 3 a rainbow that looks like an emerald.   1
     21:19 every jewel;...the fourth emerald   2

Emmanuel

1. Ἐμμανουήλ, *Emmanouēl, 1842*

Mat   1:23 a son, and they shall name him Emmanuel,"   1

Emmaus

1. Ἐμμαοῦς, *Emmaous, 1843*

Lke 24:13 two of them were going to a village called Emmaus   1

emperor

1. βασιλεύς, *basileus, 995*
2. Καῖσαρ, *Kaisar, 2790*

Mat	22:17	Is it lawful to pay taxes to the emperor, or not?"	2
	22:21	They answered, "The emperor's."	2
	22:21	"Give therefore to the emperor	2
	22:21	the things that are the emperor's	2
Mrk	12:14	Is it lawful to pay taxes to the emperor, or not?	2
	12:16	They answered, "The emperor's."	2
	12:17	"Give to the emperor the things that are	2
	12:17	to the emperor the things that are the emperor's	2
Lke	2: 1	a decree went out from Emperor Augustus	2
	3: 1	fifteenth year of the reign of Emperor Tiberius	2
	20:22	Is it lawful for us to pay taxes to the emperor	2
	20:24	They said, "The emperor's."	2
	20:25	to the emperor the things that are the emperor's	2
	20:25	to the emperor the things that are the emperor's	2
	23: 2	forbidding us to pay taxes to the emperor	2
Jhn	19:12	you are no friend of the emperor.	2
	19:12	Everyone…sets himself against the emperor."	2
	19:15	"We have no king but the emperor."	2
Act	17: 7	all acting contrary to the decrees of the emperor	2
	25: 8	or against the temple, or against the emperor."	2
	25:10	Paul said, "I am appealing to the emperor's tribunal;	2
	25:11	I appeal to the emperor."	2
	25:12	"You have appealed to the emperor;	2
	25:12	to the emperor you will go."	2
	25:21	until I could send him to the emperor."	2
	26:32	if he had not appealed to the emperor."	2
	27:24	you must stand before the emperor;	2
	28:19	I was compelled to appeal to the emperor	2
Php	4:22	especially those of the emperor's household.	2
1Pe	2:13	whether of the emperor as supreme	1
	2:17	Fear God. Honor the emperor.	1

employ

1. ἐργάζομαι, *ergazomai, 2237*

1Co	9:13	who are employed in the temple service	1

empty　*See also* heap up empty phrases, prove empty

1. κενός, *kenos, 3031*
2. κενόω, *kenoō, 3033*
3. σχολάζω, *scholazō, 5390*

Mat	12:44	When it comes, it finds it empty, swept	3
Lke	1:53	sent the rich away empty.	1
Eph	5: 6	Let no one deceive you with empty words	1
Php	2: 7	emptied himself, taking the form of a slave	2
Col	2: 8	captive through philosophy and empty deceit	1

empty of power

1. κενόω, *kenoō, 3033*

1Co	1:17	the cross of Christ might not be emptied of its power.	1

empty-handed

1. κενός, *kenos, 3031*

Mrk	12: 3	beat him, and sent him away empty-handed.	1
Lke	20:10	the tenants…sent him away empty-handed.	1
	20:11	and sent away empty-handed.	1

enable

1. Contextual: Not in Greek
2. δίδωμι, *didōmi, 1443*
3. δύναμαι, *dynamai, 1538*
4. ἱκανόω, *hikanoō, 2655*

Act	7:10	enabled him to win favor and to show wisdom	2
Eph	3: 4	a reading of which will enable you to perceive	3
Php	2:13	for it is God who is at work in you, enabling you	1
	3:21	by the power that also enables him	3
Col	1:12	has enabled you to share in the inheritance	4

enact

1. νομοθετέω, *nomotheteō, 3793*

Heb	8: 6	which has been enacted through better promises.	1

encircle

1. κυκλόω, *kykloō, 3240*

Heb	11:30	after they had been encircled for seven days.	1

encourage

1. εὔθυμος, *euthymos, 2314*
2. οἰκοδομέω, *oikodomeō, 3868*
3. παρακαλέω, *parakaleō, 4151*
4. παράκλησις, *paraklēsis, 4155*
5. παραμυθέομαι, *paramytheomai, 4170*
6. προτρέπω, *protrepō, 4730*
7. σωφρονίζω, *sōphronizō, 5405*

Act	14:22	encouraged them to continue in the faith	3
	15:32	said much to encourage and strengthen the believers	3
	16:40	had seen and encouraged the brothers and sisters	3
	18:27	the believers encouraged him	6
	20: 1	after encouraging them and saying farewell	3
	27:36	Then all of them were encouraged	1
1Co	8:10	might they not…be encouraged to the point of eating	2
	14:31	so that all may learn and all be encouraged.	3
Eph	6:22	to encourage your hearts.	3
Col	2: 2	I want their hearts to be encouraged	3
	4: 8	that he may encourage your hearts;	3
1Th	2:12	urging and encouraging you and pleading	5
	3: 2	and encourage you for the sake of your faith	3
	3: 7	encouraged about you through your faith.	3
	4:18	encourage one another with these words.	3
	5:11	Therefore encourage one another	3
	5:14	encourage the fainthearted, help the weak	5
2Ti	4: 2	convince, rebuke, and encourage	3
Tit	2: 4	may encourage the young women to love their husbands	7
Heb	6:18	might be strongly encouraged to seize the hope	4
	10:25	but encouraging one another	3
1Pe	5:12	I have written this short letter to encourage you	3

encourage mutually

1. συμπαρακαλέω, *symparakaleō, 5220*

Rom	1:12	so that we may be mutually encouraged	1

encouragement　*See also* give encouragement

1. λόγος, *logos, 3364*
2. παράκλησις, *paraklēsis, 4155*

Act	4:36	Barnabas (which means "son of encouragement").	2
	20: 2	and had given the believers much encouragement	1
Rom	15: 4	by the encouragement of the scriptures	2
	15: 5	May the God of steadfastness and encouragement	2
1Co	14: 3	upbuilding and encouragement and consolation	2
Php	2: 1	If then there is any encouragement in Christ	2
Phm	1: 7	received much joy and encouragement from your love	2

end　*See also* come to an end, put an end

1. Contextual: Not in Greek
2. ἄκρον, *akron, 216*
3. ἐκλείπω, *ekleipō, 1722*
4. ἐξαρτίζω, *exartizō, 1992*
5. ἐπιτελέω, *epiteleō, 2200*
6. ἔσχατος, *eschatos, 2274*
7. πέρας, *peras, 4306*
8. πίμπλημι, *pimplēmi, 4398*
9. πίπτω, *piptō, 4406*
10. συντέλεια, *synteleia, 5333*
11. τελειόω, *teleioō, 5457*
12. τελέω, *teleō, 5464*
13. τέλος, *telos, 5465*

Mat	10:22	But the one who endures to the end will be saved.	13
	12:42	she came from the ends of the earth	7
	13:39	the harvest is the end of the age.	10
	13:40	so will it be at the end of the age.	10
	13:49	So it will be at the end of the age.	10
	24: 3	the end of the age?"	10
	24: 6	this must take place, but the end is not yet.	13
	24:13	the one who endures to the end will be saved.	13
	24:14	then the end will come.	13
	24:31	from one end of heaven to the other.	2
	26:58	in order to see how this would end.	13
	28:20	I am with you always, to the end of the age."	10
Mrk	3:26	he cannot stand, but his end has come.	13
	13: 7	must take place, but the end is still to come.	13
	13:13	one who endures to the end will be saved.	13
	13:27	from the ends of the earth to the ends of heaven.	2
	13:27	from the ends of the earth to the ends of heaven.	2
Lke	1:23	When his time of service was ended	8
	1:33	of his kingdom there will be no end."	13

	2:43 the festival was ended and they started to return	11
	11:31 she came from the ends of the earth	7
	21: 9 the end will not follow immediately."	13
Jhn	13: 1 he loved them to the end.	13
Act	1: 8 Judea and Samaria, and to the ends of the earth."	6
	13:47 bring salvation to the ends of the earth.' "	6
	21: 5 When our days there were ended	4
Rom	6:21 The end of those things is death.	13
	6:22 The end is eternal life.	13
	10: 4 For Christ is the end of the law	13
	10:18 and their words to the ends of the world."	7
1Co	1: 8 He will also strengthen you to the end	13
	10:11 on whom the ends of the ages have come.	13
	13: 8 Love never ends.	9
	15:24 Then comes the end, when he hands over the kingdom	13
2Co	1:13 I hope you will understand until the end	13
	3:13 gazing at the end of the glory...being set aside.	13
	11:15 Their end will match their deeds.	13
Gal	3: 3 are you now ending with the flesh?	5
Php	3:19 Their end is destruction; their god is the belly;	13
2Th	1:11 To this end we always pray for you	1
1Ti	4:10 For to this end we toil and struggle	1
Heb	1:12 you are the same, and your years will never end."	3
	3:14 if only we hold...firm to the end.	13
	6: 8 its end is to be burned over.	13
	6:11 the full assurance of hope to the very end	13
	6:16 an oath given as confirmation puts an end to all dispute.	7
	7: 3 having neither beginning of days nor end of life	13
	9:26 he has appeared once for all at the end of the age	10
1Pe	1:20 He...was revealed at the end of the ages	6
	4: 7 The end of all things is near;	13
	4:17 what will be the end for those who do not obey	13
Rev	2:26 continues to do my works to the end,	13
	15: 1 for with them the wrath of God is ended.	12
	15: 8 seven plagues of the seven angels were ended.	12
	20: 3 until the thousand years were ended.	12
	20: 5 until the thousand years were ended.)	12
	20: 7 When the thousand years are ended,	12
	21: 6 Alpha and the Omega, the beginning and the end.	13
	22:13 Alpha and the Omega...the beginning and the end."	13

end of life

1. τελευτάω, *teleutaō, 5462*

Heb	11:22 Joseph, at the end of his life	1

to an end

1. εἰς, *eis, 1650*

Rom	14: 9 For to this end Christ died and lived again	1
Eph	6:18 To that end keep alert and always persevere	1

endless

1. ἀπέραντος, *aperantos, 596*

1Ti	1: 4 with myths and endless genealogies	1

endurance   *See also* show endurance

1. ὑπομονή, *hypomonē, 5705*

Lke	21:19 By your endurance you will gain your souls.	1
Rom	5: 3 knowing that suffering produces endurance	1
	5: 4 and endurance produces character	1
2Co	6: 4 through great endurance, in afflictions	1
1Ti	6:11 faith, love, endurance, gentleness.	1
Tit	2: 2 sound in faith, in love, and in endurance.	1
Heb	10:36 For you need endurance	1
Jas	1: 3 testing of your faith produces endurance;	1
	1: 4 let endurance have its full effect	1
	5:11 You have heard of the endurance of Job	1
2Pe	1: 6 and self-control with endurance	1
	1: 6 and endurance with godliness	1
Rev	13:10 a call for the endurance and faith of the saints.	1
	14:12 Here is a call for the endurance of the saints	1

patient endurance

1. ὑπομονή, *hypomonē, 5705*

Lke	8:15 and bear fruit with patient endurance.	1
Rev	1: 9 share with you...the patient endurance	1
	2: 2 "I know your works...and your patient endurance.	1
	2:19 "I know your works—your...patient endurance.	1
	3:10 you have kept my word of patient endurance	1

endure

1. Contextual: Not in Greek
2. ἀνέχομαι, *anechomai, 462*
3. εἰμί, *eimi, 1639*
4. μένω, *menō, 3531*
5. πάσχω, *paschō, 4248*
6. στέγω, *stegō, 5095*
7. ὑπομένω, *hypomenō, 5702*
8. ὑπομονή, *hypomonē, 5705*
9. ὑποφέρω, *hypopherō, 5722*
10. φέρω, *pherō, 5770*

Mat	10:22 But the one who endures to the end will be saved.	7
	13:21 but endures only for a while	3
	24:13 the one who endures to the end will be saved.	7
Mrk	4:17 endure only for a while;	3
	5:26 She had endured much under many physicians	5
	13:13 one who endures to the end will be saved.	7
Lke	1:25 the disgrace I have endured among my people."	1
Jhn	3:36 but must endure God's wrath.	4
	6:27 the food that endures for eternal life	4
Act	20:19 humility and with tears, enduring the trials	1
Rom	9:22 endured with much patience the objects of wrath	10
1Co	4:12 When reviled, we bless; when persecuted, we endure;	2
	9:12 we endure anything rather than put an obstacle	6
	10:13 so that you may be able to endure it.	9
	13: 7 hopes all things, endures all things.	7
2Co	9: 9 his righteousness endures forever."	4
Col	1:11 to endure everything with patience, while joyfully	8
2Th	1: 4 the afflictions that you are enduring.	2
2Ti	2:10 Therefore I endure everything	7
	2:12 if we endure, we will also reign with him;	7
	3:11 What persecutions I endured!	9
Heb	10:32 you endured a hard struggle with sufferings	7
	12: 2 endured the cross, disregarding its shame	7
	12: 3 Consider him who endured...such hostility	7
	12: 7 Endure trials for the sake of discipline.	7
	12:20 they could not endure the order that was given	10
	13:13 and bear the abuse he endured.	1
Jas	1:12 Blessed is anyone who endures temptation.	7
1Pe	1:23 through the living and enduring word of God.	4
	1:25 but the word of the Lord endures forever."	4
	2:19 you endure pain while suffering unjustly.	9
	2:20 If you endure when you are beaten for doing wrong	7
	2:20 if you endure when you do right and suffer	7

endure birth pangs

1. ὠδίνω, *ōdinō, 6048*

Gal	4:27 and shout, you who endure no birth pangs;	1

endure patiently

1. μακροθυμέω, *makrothymeō, 3428*
2. ὑπομονή, *hypomonē, 5705*

2Co	1: 6 when you patiently endure the same sufferings	2
Heb	6:15 having patiently endured, obtained the promise.	1
Rev	2: 3 I also know that you are enduring patiently	2

endure suffering

1. κακοπαθέω, *kakopatheō, 2802*
2. πάσχω, *paschō, 4248*

Lke	17:25 he must endure much suffering and be rejected	2
2Ti	4: 5 As for you, always be sober, endure suffering	1

enemy

1. Contextual: Not in Greek
2. ἔχθρα, *echthra, 2397*
3. ἐχθρός, *echthros, 2398*

Mat	5:43 love your neighbor and hate your enemy.'	3
	5:44 I say to you, Love your enemies and pray for those	3
	13:25 an enemy came and sowed weeds among the wheat	3
	13:28 He answered, 'An enemy has done this.'	3
	13:39 the enemy who sowed them is the devil;	3
	22:44 until I put your enemies under your feet" '?	3
Mrk	12:36 until I put your enemies under your feet." '	3
Lke	1:71 that we would be saved from our enemies	3
	1:74 rescued from the hands of our enemies	3
	6:27 Love your enemies, do good to those who hate you	3
	6:35 love your enemies, do good, and lend	3
	10:19 authority...over all the power of the enemy;	3
	19:27 as for these enemies of mine	3

Lke	19:43	when your enemies will set up ramparts around you	3
	20:43	until I make your enemies your footstool." '	3
	23:12	before this they had been enemies.	2
Act	2:35	until I make your enemies your footstool." '	3
	13:10	you enemy of all righteousness	3
Rom	5:10	while we were enemies, we were reconciled to God	3
	11:28	As regards the gospel they are enemies of God	3
	12:20	No, "if your enemies are hungry, feed them;	3
1Co	15:25	until he has put all his enemies under his feet.	3
	15:26	The last enemy to be destroyed is death.	3
Gal	4:16	become your enemy by telling you the truth?	3
Eph	6:12	struggle is not against enemies of blood and flesh	1
Php	3:18	For many live as enemies of the cross of Christ;	3
2Th	3:15	Do not regard them as enemies,	3
Heb	1:13	until I make your enemies a footstool for your feet"?	3
	10:13	"until his enemies would be made a footstool	3
Jas	4:4	a friend of the world becomes an enemy of God.	3
Rev	11:12	went up to heaven…while their enemies watched	3

energy

1. ἐνέργεια, *energeia, 1918*

Col	1:29	the energy that he powerfully inspires within me.	1

engage

1. ἔχω, *echō, 2400*
2. μνηστεύω, *mnēsteuō, 3650*

Mat	1:18	his mother Mary had been engaged to Joseph	2
Lke	1:27	a virgin engaged to a man whose name was Joseph	2
	2:5	registered with Mary, to whom he was engaged	2
2Co	4:1	by God's mercy that we are engaged in this ministry	1

engage in dispute

1. μάχομαι, *machomai, 3481*

Jas	4:2	you covet…so you engage in disputes and conflicts.	1

enjoy

1. ἔχω, *echō, 2400*
2. τυγχάνω, *tynchanō, 5593*

Act	24:2	because of you we have long enjoyed peace	2
Heb	11:25	to enjoy the fleeting pleasures of sin.	1

enjoy company

1. ἐμπίμπλημι, *empimplēmi, 1855*

Rom	15:24	once I have enjoyed your company for a little	1

enjoyment

1. ἀπόλαυσις, *apolausis, 656*

1Ti	6:17	richly provides us with everything for our enjoyment.	1

enlarge

1. μεγαλύνω, *megalynō, 3486*

2Co	10:15	our sphere of action among you may be greatly enlarged	1

enlighten

1. ἐπίγνωσις, *epignōsis, 2106*
2. φωτίζω, *phōtizō, 5894*

Jhn	1:9	The true light, which enlightens everyone	2
Rom	10:2	a zeal for God, but it is not enlightened.	1
Eph	1:18	so that, with the eyes of your heart enlightened	2
Heb	6:4	those who have once been enlightened	2
	10:32	after you had been enlightened	2

enlist

1. στρατολογέω, *stratologeō, 5133*

2Ti	2:4	the soldier's aim is to please the enlisting officer.	1

enmity

1. ἔχθρα, *echthra, 2397*

Gal	5:20	idolatry, sorcery, enmities, strife, jealousy, anger	1
Jas	4:4	friendship with the world is enmity with God?	1

Enoch

1. Ἐνώχ, *Henōch, 1970*

Lke	3:37	son of Methuselah, son of Enoch	1
Heb	11:5	By faith Enoch was taken	1
Jde	1:14	It was also about these that Enoch…prophesied	1

Enos

1. Ἐνώς, *Enōs, 1968*

Lke	3:38	son of Enos, son of Seth, son of Adam	1

enough

See also have more than enough, kind enough, readily enough

1. Contextual: Not in Greek
2. ἀπέχω, *apechō, 600*
3. ἀρκετός, *arketos, 757*
4. ἀρκέω, *arkeō, 758*
5. αὐτάρκεια, *autarkeia, 894*
6. ἱκανός, *hikanos, 2653*
7. οὕτως, *houtōs, 4048*
8. πολύς, *polys, 4498*
9. τοσοῦτος, *tosoutos, 5537*

Mat	6:34	Today's trouble is enough for today.	3
	10:25	it is enough for the disciple	3
	15:33	"Where are we to get enough bread in the desert	9
	25:9	'No! there will not be enough for you and for us;	4
Mrk	14:41	Enough! The hour has come;	2
Lke	14:28	to see whether he has enough to complete it?	1
	16:3	I am not strong enough to dig	1
	22:38	He replied, "It is enough."	6
Jhn	6:7	"Six months' wages would not buy enough bread	4
1Co	6:5	there is no one among you wise enough to decide	7
2Co	2:6	This punishment by the majority is enough	6
	9:8	so that by always having enough of everything	5
1Th	3:9	How can we thank God enough for you	1
Phm	1:8	though I am bold enough in Christ to command you	8
1Pe	4:3	You have already spent enough time in doing	3

enough and to spare

1. περισσεύω, *perisseuō, 4355*

Lke	15:17	my father's hired hands have bread enough and to spare	1

enrage

1. διαπρίω, *diapriō, 1391*
2. ἐμμαίνομαι, *emmainomai, 1841*
3. θυμός + πλήρης, *thymos + plērēs, 2596 + 4441*
4. ὀργίζω, *orgizō, 3974*

Mat	22:7	The king was enraged. He sent his troops	4
Act	5:33	When they heard this, they were enraged	1
	7:54	When they heard these things, they became enraged	1
	19:28	When they heard this, they were enraged	3
	26:11	since I was so furiously enraged at them	2

enrich

1. πλουτίζω, *ploutizō, 4457*

1Co	1:5	for in every way you have been enriched in him	1
2Co	9:11	You will be enriched in every way	1

enroll

1. ἀπογράφω, *apographō, 616*

Heb	12:23	who are enrolled in heaven	1

enslave

1. δουλαγωγέω, *doulagōgeō, 1524*
2. δουλεύω, *douleuō, 1526*
3. δουλόω, *douloō, 1530*
4. καταδουλόω, *katadouloō, 2871*

Act	7:6	who would enslave them and mistreat them	3
Rom	6:6	and we might no longer be enslaved to sin.	2
	6:22	freed from sin and enslaved to God	3
1Co	9:27	I punish my body and enslave it	1
Gal	2:4	so that they might enslave us—	4
	4:3	enslaved to the elemental spirits of the world.	3
	4:8	enslaved to beings that by nature are not gods.	2
	4:9	you want to be enslaved to them again?	2

entangle

1. ἐμπλέκω, *emplekō, 1861*

2Pe	2:20	again entangled in them and overpowered	1

get entangled

1. ἐμπλέκω, *emplekō, 1861*

2Ti	2:4	gets entangled in everyday affairs;	1

enter

1. Contextual: Not in Greek
2. ἀπέρχομαι, *aperchomai, 599*

3. εἴσειμι, *eiseimi, 1655*
4. εἰσέρχομαι, *eiserchomai, 1656*
5. εἴσοδος, *eisodos, 1658*
6. εἰσπορεύομαι, *eisporeuomai, 1660*
7. ἔρχομαι + εἰς, *erchomai + eis, 2262 + 1650*
8. χωρέω, *chōreō, 6003*

Mat	2:11	entering the house, they saw the child with Mary	7
	5:20	Pharisees, you will never enter the kingdom	4
	7:13	"Enter through the narrow gate; for the gate is wide	4
	7:21	"Not everyone...will enter the kingdom of heaven	4
	8: 5	When he entered Capernaum, a centurion came	4
	8:14	When Jesus entered Peter's house	7
	8:32	"Go!" So they came out and entered the swine;	2
	9:28	When he entered the house, the blind men came	7
	10: 5	and enter no town of the Samaritans	4
	10:11	Whatever town or village you enter	4
	10:12	As you enter the house, greet it.	4
	12: 4	He entered the house of God and ate the bread	4
	12: 9	and entered their synagogue;	7
	12:29	Or how can one enter a strong man's house	4
	12:45	and they enter and live there;	4
	15:17	goes into the mouth enters the stomach	8
	18: 3	you will never enter the kingdom of heaven.	4
	18: 8	it is better for you to enter life maimed or lame	4
	18: 9	it is better for you to enter life with one eye	4
	19:17	to enter into life, keep the commandments."	4
	19:23	to enter the kingdom of heaven.	4
	19:24	someone who is rich to enter the kingdom of God."	4
	21:10	When he entered Jerusalem	4
	21:12	Jesus entered the temple	4
	21:23	When he entered the temple	7
	24:38	until the day Noah entered the ark	4
	25:21	enter into the joy of your master.'	4
	25:23	enter into the joy of your master.'	4
	27:53	entered the holy city and appeared to many.	4
Mrk	1:21	he entered the synagogue and taught.	4
	1:29	entered the house of Simon and Andrew	7
	2:26	He entered the house of God	4
	3: 1	Again he entered the synagogue	4
	3:27	no one can enter a strong man's house	4
	5:12	"Send us into the swine; let us enter them."	4
	5:13	unclean spirits came out and entered the swine;	4
	5:39	When he had entered, he said to them	4
	6:10	He said to them, "Wherever you enter a house,	4
	7:17	When he had left the crowd and entered the house	4
	7:19	since it enters, not the heart but the stomach	6
	7:24	entered a house and did not want anyone to know	4
	9:25	come out of him, and never enter him again!"	4
	9:28	When he had entered the house	4
	9:43	it is better for you to enter life maimed	4
	9:45	it is better for you to enter life lame	4
	9:47	to enter the kingdom of God with one eye	4
	10:15	as a little child will never enter it."	4
	10:23	to enter the kingdom of God!"	4
	10:24	how hard it is to enter the kingdom of God!	4
	10:25	who is rich to enter the kingdom of God."	4
	11: 2	as you enter it, you will find tied there a colt	6
	11:11	he entered Jerusalem and went into the temple;	4
	11:15	he entered the temple	4
	13:15	must not go down or enter the house	4
	14:14	he enters, say to the owner of the house	4
	16: 5	As they entered the tomb, they saw a young man	4
Lke	1: 9	he was chosen by lot...to enter the sanctuary	4
	1:40	she entered the house of Zechariah	4
	4:38	leaving the synagogue he entered Simon's house.	4
	6: 4	He entered the house of God	4
	6: 6	he entered the synagogue and taught	4
	7: 1	he entered Capernaum.	4
	7:44	I entered your house;	4
	8:16	so that those who enter may see the light.	6
	8:30	"Legion"; for many demons had entered him.	4
	8:32	demons begged Jesus to let them enter these.	4
	8:33	the demons...entered the swine	4
	8:51	he did not allow anyone to enter with him	4
	9: 4	Whatever house you enter, stay there	4
	9:34	they were terrified as they entered the cloud.	4
	9:52	they entered a village of the Samaritans	4
	10: 5	Whatever house you enter, first say, 'Peace	4
	10: 8	Whenever you enter a town and its people welcome	4
	10:10	whenever you enter a town	4

	10:38	on their way, he entered a certain village	4
	11:26	they enter and live there;	4
	11:33	so that those who enter may see the light.	6
	11:52	you did not enter yourselves	4
	11:52	you hindered those who were entering."	4
	13:24	"Strive to enter through the narrow door;	4
	13:24	many...will try to enter and will not be able.	4
	17:12	As he entered a village, ten lepers approached him.	4
	17:27	until the day Noah entered the ark	4
	18:17	will never enter it."	4
	18:24	"How hard it is...to enter the kingdom of God!	6
	18:25	someone who is rich to enter the kingdom of God."	4
	19: 1	He entered Jericho and was passing through	4
	19:30	as you enter it you will find tied there a colt	6
	19:45	he entered the temple	4
	21:21	those out in the country must not enter it;	4
	22: 3	Then Satan entered into Judas called Iscariot	4
	22:10	"when you have entered the city	4
	22:10	follow him into the house he enters	6
	24:26	suffer these things and then enter into his glory?"	4
Jhn	3: 4	Can one enter a second time into the mother's womb	4
	3: 5	no one can enter the kingdom of God without	4
	4:38	and you have entered into their labor."	4
	10: 1	who does not enter the sheepfold by the gate	4
	10: 2	The one who enters by the gate	4
	10: 9	Whoever enters by me will be saved	4
	13:27	the piece of bread, Satan entered into him.	4
	18: 1	a garden, which he and his disciples entered.	4
	18:28	They themselves did not enter the headquarters	4
	18:33	Pilate entered the headquarters again	4
	19: 9	He entered his headquarters again and asked	4
Act	1:13	When they had entered the city,	4
	3: 2	could ask for alms from those entering the temple.	6
	3: 8	stood and began to walk, and he entered the temple	4
	5:21	they entered the temple at daybreak and went on	4
	8: 3	by entering house after house;	6
	9: 6	get up and enter the city	4
	9:17	So Ananias went and entered the house.	4
	11: 8	nothing...unclean has ever entered my mouth.'	4
	11:12	we entered the man's house.	4
	14:22	that we must enter the kingdom of God."	4
	19: 8	He entered the synagogue	4
	21:26	entered the temple with them, making public	3
	25:23	and they entered the audience hall	4
1Co	14:23	outsiders or unbelievers enter	4
	14:24	an unbeliever or outsider who enters	4
Heb	3:11	'They will not enter my rest.' "	4
	3:18	swear that they would not enter his rest	4
	3:19	they were unable to enter because of unbelief.	4
	4: 1	while the promise of entering his rest is still open	4
	4: 3	For we who have believed enter that rest	4
	4: 3	'They shall not enter my rest,' "	4
	4: 5	"They shall not enter my rest."	4
	4: 6	Since therefore it remains open for some to enter it	4
	4: 6	failed to enter because of disobedience	4
	4:10	for those who enter God's rest	4
	4:11	Let us therefore make every effort to enter that rest	4
	6:19	a hope that enters the inner shrine	4
	6:20	Jesus, a forerunner on our behalf, has entered	4
	9:12	he entered once for all into the Holy Place	4
	9:24	For Christ did not enter a sanctuary made by	4
	9:24	but he entered into heaven itself	1
	9:25	as the high priest enters the Holy Place year after year	4
	10:19	we have confidence to enter the sanctuary	5
Rev	11:11	the breath of life from God entered them	4
	15: 8	and no one could enter the temple	4
	21:27	But nothing unclean will enter it	4
	22:14	and may enter the city by the gates.	4

enter by force

1. βιάζω, *biazō, 1041*
Lke 16:16 everyone tries to enter it by force.   1

entertain

1. ξενίζω, *xenizō, 3826*
Act 28: 7 who received us and entertained us hospitably   1
Heb 13: 2 some have entertained angels without knowing it.   1

entertain as a guest

1. ὑποδέχομαι, *hypodechomai, 5685*

Act 17: 7 Jason has entertained them as guests. 1

enthusiasm
1. εὔνοια, *eunoia, 2334*
2. πνεῦμα, *pneuma, 4460*

Act 18:25 spoke with burning enthusiasm and taught accurately 2
Eph 6: 7 Render service with enthusiasm, 1

entice
1. ἄγω, *agō, 72*
2. ἀποσπάω, *apospaō, 685*
3. δελεάζω, *deleazō, 1284*

Act 20:30 in order to entice the disciples to follow them. 2
1Co 12: 2 enticed and led astray to idols that could not speak 1
Jas 1:14 by one's own desire, being lured and enticed 3
2Pe 2:14 They entice unsteady souls. 3
  2:18 with licentious desires of the flesh they entice 3

entire *See also* entire *household*
1. ὅλος, *holos, 3910*
2. πᾶς, *pas, 4246*

Mat 18:34 until he would pay his entire debt. 2
Lke 1:65 throughout the entire hill country of Judea. 1
  13:17 the entire crowd was rejoicing at all 2
Act 2: 2 it filled the entire house where they were sitting. 1
  2:36 Therefore let the entire house of Israel know 2
  8:27 a court official…in charge of her entire treasury. 2
  11:14 you and your entire household will be saved.' 2
  11:26 for an entire year they met with the church 1
  16:33 he and his entire family were baptized without delay. 2
  20:18 how I lived among you the entire time 2
  22:30 the chief priests and the entire council to meet. 2
Gal 5: 3 he is obliged to obey the entire law. 1

entirely
1. ὅλος, *holos, 3910*
2. ὁλοτελής, *holotelēs, 3911*
3. πάντως, *pantōs, 4122*

Jhn 9:34 answered him, "You were born entirely in sins 1
  13:10 but is entirely clean. 1
1Co 9:10 does he not speak entirely for our sake? 3
1Th 5:23 May the God of peace himself sanctify you entirely; 2

entrance *See also* gain entrance
1. θύρα, *thyra, 2598*

Mrk 16: 3 the stone for us from the entrance to the tomb?" 1

entrap
1. παγιδεύω, *pagideuō, 4074*

Mat 22:15 and plotted to entrap him in what he said. 1

entreat
1. δέομαι, *deomai, 1289*

2Co 5:20 we entreat you on behalf of Christ 1

entrust *See also* treasure entrusted
1. Contextual: Not in Greek
2. παραδίδωμι, *paradidōmi, 4140*
3. παραθήκη, *parathēkē, 4146*
4. παρατίθημι, *paratithēmi, 4192*
5. πιστεύω, *pisteuō, 4409*
6. τίθημι, *tithēmi, 5502*

Mat 25:14 entrusted his property to them; 2
Lke 12:48 to whom much has been entrusted 4
  16:11 who will entrust to you the true riches? 5
Jhn 2:24 Jesus on his part would not entrust himself to them 5
Act 14:23 they entrusted them to the Lord 4
Rom 3: 2 the Jews were entrusted with the oracles of God. 5
  6:17 form of teaching to which you were entrusted 2
1Co 9:17 I am entrusted with a commission. 5
2Co 5:19 entrusting the message of reconciliation to us. 6
Gal 2: 7 entrusted with the gospel for the uncircumcised 5
  2: 7 entrusted with the gospel for the circumcised 1
1Th 2: 4 entrusted with the message of the gospel, 5
1Ti 1:11 glorious gospel…which he entrusted to me. 5
  6:20 Timothy, guard what has been entrusted to you. 3
2Ti 1:12 to guard until that day what I have entrusted 3
  2: 2 what you have heard…entrust to faithful people 4
Tit 1: 3 the proclamation with which I have been entrusted 5

1Pe 2:23 he entrusted himself to the one who judges justly. 2
  4:19 entrust themselves to a faithful Creator 4
Jde 1: 3 faith…once for all entrusted to the saints. 2

entry
1. εἴσοδος, *eisodos, 1658*

2Pe 1:11 entry into the eternal kingdom of our Lord 1

envious
1. ζηλόω, *zēloō, 2420*
2. ὀφθαλμός + πονηρός, *ophthalmos + ponēros, 4057 + 4505*

Mat 20:15 Or are you envious because I am generous?' 2
1Co 13: 4 love is not envious or boastful or arrogant 1

envy
1. ζῆλος, *zēlos, 2419*
2. ὀφθαλμός + πονηρός, *ophthalmos + ponēros, 4057 + 4505*
3. φθονέω, *phthoneō, 5783*
4. φθόνος, *phthonos, 5784*

Mrk 7:22 envy, slander, pride, folly. 2
Rom 1:29 Full of envy, murder, strife, deceit, craftiness 4
Gal 5:21 envy, drunkenness, carousing, and things like 4
  5:26 envying one another. 3
Php 1:15 Some proclaim Christ from envy and rivalry 4
1Ti 6: 4 disputes about words. From these come envy 4
Tit 3: 3 passing our days in malice and envy 4
Jas 3:14 But if you have bitter envy…in your hearts 1
  3:16 For where there is envy and selfish ambition 1
1Pe 2: 1 Rid yourselves, therefore, of all…envy, 4

Epaenetus
1. Ἐπαίνετος, *Epainetos, 2045*

Rom 16: 5 Epaenetus, who was the first convert in Asia 1

Epaphras
1. Ἐπαφρᾶς, *Epaphras, 2071*

Col 1: 7 Epaphras, our beloved fellow servant. 1
  4:12 Epaphras, who is one of you…greets you 1
Phm 1:23 Epaphras, my fellow prisoner in Christ Jesus 1

Epaphroditus
1. Ἐπαφρόδιτος, *Epaphroditos, 2073*

Php 2:25 to send to you Epaphroditus—my brother 1
  4:18 satisfied, now that I have received from Epaphroditus 1

Ephesian
1. Ἐφέσιος, *Ephesios, 2386*

Act 19:28 "Great is Artemis of the Ephesians!" 1
  19:34 "Great is Artemis of the Ephesians!" 1
  19:35 the city of the Ephesians is the temple keeper 1
  21:29 had previously seen Trophimus the Ephesian 1

Ephesus
1. Ἐφέσιος, *Ephesios, 2386*
2. Ἔφεσος, *Ephesos, 2387*

Act 18:19 they reached Ephesus, he left them there 2
  18:21 Then he set sail from Ephesus. 2
  18:24 Now there came to Ephesus a Jew named Apollos 2
  19: 1 through the interior regions and came to Ephesus 2
  19:17 this became known to all residents of Ephesus 2
  19:26 not only in Ephesus but…whole of Asia 2
  19:35 "Citizens of Ephesus, who is there that does not 1
  20:16 Paul had decided to sail past Ephesus 2
  20:17 From Miletus he sent a message to Ephesus 2
1Co 15:32 I fought with wild animals at Ephesus 2
  16: 8 I will stay in Ephesus until Pentecost 2
Eph 1: 1 the saints who are in Ephesus and are faithful 2
1Ti 1: 3 I urge you…to remain in Ephesus 2
2Ti 1:18 you know…how much service he rendered in Ephesus 2
  4:12 I have sent Tychicus to Ephesus. 2
Rev 1:11 to the seven churches, to Ephesus, to Smyrna 2
  2: 1 "To the angel of the church in Ephesus write: 2

ephphatha
1. ἐφφαθά, *ephphatha, 2395*

Mrk 7:34 "Ephphatha," that is, "Be opened." 1

Ephraim
1. Ἐφραίμ, *Ephraim, 2394*

Jhn 11:54 went from there to a town called Ephraim 1

Epicurean

1. Ἐπικούρειος, *Epikoureios, 2134*

Act 17:18 Epicurean and Stoic philosophers debated with him. 1

epileptic

1. σεληνιάζομαι, *selēniazomai, 4944*

Mat   4:24 pains, demoniacs, epileptics, and paralytics 1
      17:15 have mercy on my son, for he is an epileptic 1

equal

1. ἴσος, *isos, 2698*

Mat 20:12 you have made them equal to us 1
Jhn   5:18 making himself equal to God. 1
Rev 21:16 its length and width and height are equal. 1

as equal

1. καθώς, *kathōs, 2777*

2Co 11:12 an opportunity to be recognized as our equals 1

equality

1. ἴσος, *isos, 2698*

Php   2: 6 not regard equality with God as…to be exploited 1

equip

1. ἐξαρτίζω, *exartizō, 1992*
2. ἐπιχορηγία, *epichorēgia, 2221*
3. ἑτοιμάζω, *hetoimazō, 2286*
4. καταρτισμός, *katartismos, 2938*

Eph   4:12 to equip the saints for the work of ministry 4
      4:16 every ligament with which it is equipped 2
2Ti   3:17 equipped for every good work. 1
Rev   9: 7 the locusts were like horses equipped for battle. 3

Er

1. Ἤρ, *Ēr, 2474*

Lke   3:28 son of Cosam, son of Elmadam, son of Er 1

erase

1. ἐξαλείφω, *exaleiphō, 1981*

Col   2:14 erasing the record that stood against us 1

Erastus

1. Ἔραστος, *Erastos, 2235*

Act 19:22 sent two of his helpers, Timothy and Erastus 1
Rom 16:23 Erastus, the city treasurer, and…greet you. 1
2Ti   4:20 Erastus remained in Corinth; 1

erect

1. ἐπιτελέω, *epiteleō, 2200*

Heb   8: 5 Moses, when he was about to erect the tent 1

error

1. πλάνη, *planē, 4415*

Rom   1:27 received…the due penalty for their error. 1
2Pe   2:18 escaped from those who live in error. 1
      3:17 carried away with the error of the lawless 1
1Jn   4: 6 the spirit of truth and the spirit of error. 1
Jde   1:11 abandon themselves to Balaam's error for the sake of gain 1

Esau

1. Ἠσαῦ, *Ēsau, 2481*

Rom   9:13 "I have loved Jacob, but I have hated Esau." 1
Heb 11:20 invoked blessings for the future on Jacob and Esau. 1
      12:16 no one becomes like Esau, an immoral and godless 1

escape *See also* try to escape

1. Contextual: Not in Greek
2. ἀνανήφω, *ananēphō, 392*
3. ἀποφεύγω, *apopheugō, 709*
4. διασώζω, *diasōzō, 1407*
5. διαφεύγω, *diapheugō, 1423*
6. ἐκφεύγω, *ekpheugō, 1767*
7. ἐξέρχομαι, *exerchomai, 2002*
8. φεύγω, *pheugō, 5771*

Mat 23:33 How can you escape being sentenced to hell? 8
Lke 21:36 may have the strength to escape all these things 6

Jhn 10:39 he escaped from their hands. 7
Act 16:27 supposed that the prisoners had escaped. 6
      27:30 the sailors tried to escape from the ship 8
      27:42 so that none might swim away and escape; 5
      28: 4 though he has escaped from the sea 4
Rom   2: 3 you will escape the judgment of God? 6
2Co 11:33 escaped from his hands. 6
1Th   5: 3 there will be no escape! 6
2Ti   2:26 they may escape from the snare of the devil 2
Heb   2: 3 how can we escape if we neglect 6
      11:34 escaped the edge of the sword 8
      12:25 if they did not escape when they refused the one 6
      12:25 much less will we escape 1
2Pe   1: 4 escape from the corruption that is in the world 3
      2:18 escaped from those who live in error. 3
      2:20 they have escaped the defilements of the world 3

escape notice

1. λανθάνω, *lanthanō, 3291*

Mrk   7:24 Yet he could not escape notice 1
Act 26:26 none of these things has escaped his notice 1

escort

1. προπέμπω, *propempō, 4636*

Act 21: 5 escorted us outside the city. 1

Esli

1. Ἐσλί, *Hesli, 2268*

Lke   3:25 son of Nahum, son of Esli, son of Naggai 1

especially

1. Contextual: Not in Greek
2. μάλιστα, *malista, 3436*
3. μᾶλλον, *mallon, 3437*

Jhn 19:31 especially because that sabbath was a day of great 1
Act 20:38 grieving especially because of what he had said 2
      25:26 especially before you, King Agrippa 2
      26: 3 you are especially familiar with all the customs 2
1Co 14: 1 especially that you may prophesy. 3
Gal   6:10 especially for those of the family 2
Php   4:22 especially those of the emperor's household. 2
1Ti   4:10 Savior…especially of those who believe. 2
      5: 8 not provide…especially for family members 2
      5:17 especially those who labor in preaching 2
Tit   1:10 especially those of the circumcision; 2
Phm   1:16 especially to me but how much more to you 2
2Pe   2:10 especially those who indulge their flesh in 2

essential

1. ἐπάναγκες, *epanankes, 2055*

Act 15:28 no further burden than these essentials: 1

establish

1. βεβαιόω, *bebaioō, 1011*
2. θεμελιόω, *themelioō, 2530*
3. ἵστημι, *histēmi, 2705*
4. στηρίζω, *stērizō, 5114*
5. συντελέω, *synteleō, 5334*
6. φέρω, *pherō, 5770*

Rom 10: 3 and seeking to establish their own 3
2Co   1:21 it is God who establishes us with you in Christ 1
Col   2: 7 built up in him and established in the faith 1
Heb   8: 8 when I will establish a new covenant 5
      9:16 the death…must be established. 6
      10: 9 in order to establish the second. 3
1Pe   5:10 will…restore, support, strengthen, and establish you. 2
2Pe   1:12 you know them already and are established in the truth 4

establish securely

1. θεμελιόω, *themelioō, 2530*

Col   1:23 provided that you continue securely established 1

esteem *See also* hold in high esteem

1. ἡγέομαι, *hēgeomai, 2451*

1Th   5:13 esteem them very highly in love 1

estimate

1. ψηφίζω, *psēphizō, 6028*

Lke 14:28 does not first sit down and estimate the cost 1

estrange

1. ἀπαλλοτρίόω, *apallotrioō, 558*

Col   1:21   you who were once estranged and hostile in mind   1

eternal

1. ἀΐδιος, *aidios, 132*
2. αἰών, *aiōn, 172*
3. αἰώνιος, *aiōnios, 173*

Mat   18: 8   to be thrown into the eternal fire.   3
     19:16   to have eternal life?"   3
     19:29   and will inherit eternal life.   3
     25:41   accursed, depart from me into the eternal fire   3
     25:46   these will go away into eternal punishment   3
     25:46   but the righteous into eternal life."   3
Mrk   3:29   but is guilty of an eternal sin"   3
     10:17   what must I do to inherit eternal life?"   3
     10:30   in the age to come eternal life.   3
     16: S   ⟦imperishable proclamation of eternal salvation⟧   3
Lke   10:25   "what must I do to inherit eternal life?"   3
     16: 9   welcome you into the eternal homes.   3
     18:18   what must I do to inherit eternal life?"   3
     18:30   in the age to come eternal life."   3
Jhn   3:15   whoever believes in him may have eternal life.   3
     3:16   may not perish but may have eternal life.   3
     3:36   Whoever believes in the Son has eternal life;   3
     4:14   a spring of water gushing up to eternal life."   3
     4:36   and is gathering fruit for eternal life   3
     5:24   who hears...and believes...has eternal life   3
     5:39   you think that in them you have eternal life;   3
     6:27   the food that endures for eternal life   3
     6:40   all who...believe...may have eternal life;   3
     6:47   whoever believes has eternal life.   3
     6:54   Those who...drink my blood have eternal life   3
     6:68   You have the words of eternal life.   3
     10:28   I give them eternal life   3
     12:25   will keep it for eternal life.   3
     12:50   I know that his commandment is eternal life.   3
     17: 2   to give eternal life to all   3
     17: 3   this is eternal life, that they may know you   3
Act   13:46   judge yourselves to be unworthy of eternal life   3
     13:48   as many as had been destined for eternal life   3
Rom   1:20   eternal power and divine nature   1
     2: 7   he will give eternal life;   3
     5:21   leading to eternal life through Jesus Christ our Lord.   3
     6:22   The end is eternal life.   3
     6:23   the free gift of God is eternal life in Christ   3
     16:26   according to the command of the eternal God   3
2Co   4:17   preparing us for an eternal weight of glory   3
     4:18   what cannot be seen is eternal.   3
     5: 1   not made with hands, eternal in the heavens.   3
Gal   6: 8   will reap eternal life from the Spirit.   3
Eph   3:11   This was in accordance with the eternal purpose   2
2Th   1: 9   suffer the punishment of eternal destruction   3
     2:16   gave us eternal comfort and good hope   3
1Ti   1:16   who would come to believe in him for eternal life.   3
     6:12   the eternal life, to which you were called   3
     6:16   to him be honor and eternal dominion. Amen.   3
2Ti   2:10   salvation...with eternal glory.   3
Tit   1: 2   in the hope of eternal life   3
     3: 7   become heirs according to the hope of eternal life.   3
Heb   5: 9   he became the source of eternal salvation   3
     6: 2   resurrection of the dead, and eternal judgment.   3
     9:12   thus obtaining eternal redemption.   3
     9:14   who through the eternal Spirit offered himself   3
     9:15   may receive the promised eternal inheritance   3
     13:20   by the blood of the eternal covenant   3
1Pe   5:10   who has called you to his eternal glory in Christ   3
2Pe   1:11   entry into the eternal kingdom of our Lord   3
1Jn   1: 2   and declare to you the eternal life   3
     2:25   this is what he has promised us, eternal life.   3
     3:15   murderers do not have eternal life abiding in them.   3
     5:11   the testimony: God gave us eternal life   3
     5:13   so that you may know that you have eternal life.   3
     5:20   He is the true God and eternal life.   3
Jde   1: 6   he has kept in eternal chains in deepest darkness   1
     1: 7   by undergoing a punishment of eternal fire.   3
     1:21   the mercy of our Lord...leads to eternal life.   3
Rev   14: 6   another angel...with an eternal gospel to proclaim   3

eternity

1. αἰών, *aiōn, 172*

2Pe   3:18   glory both now and to the day of eternity. Amen.   1

Ethiopian

1. Αἰθίοψ, *Aithiops, 134*

Act   8:27   an Ethiopian eunuch, a court official   1
     8:27   the Candace, queen of the Ethiopians   1

Eubulus

1. Εὔβουλος, *Euboulos, 2300*

2Ti   4:21   Eubulus sends greetings to you   1

Eunice

1. Εὐνίκη, *Eunikē, 2332*

2Ti   1: 5   your grandmother Lois and your mother Eunice   1

eunuch   *See also* make a eunuch

1. εὐνοῦχος, *eunouchos, 2336*

Mat   19:12   there are eunuchs who have been so from birth   1
     19:12   there are eunuchs who have been made eunuchs   1
     19:12   eunuchs who have made themselves eunuchs   1
Act   8:27   an Ethiopian eunuch, a court official   1
     8:34   The eunuch asked Philip   1
     8:36   the eunuch said, "Look, here is water!   1
     8:38   both of them, Philip and the eunuch, went down   1
     8:39   the eunuch saw him no more   1

Euodia

1. Εὐοδία, *Euodia, 2337*

Php   4: 2   I urge Euodia and...Syntyche to be of the same mind   1

Euphrates

1. Εὐφράτης, *Euphratēs, 2371*

Rev   9:14   angels...bound at the great river Euphrates."   1
     16:12   angel poured his bowl on the great river Euphrates   1

Eutychus

1. Εὔτυχος, *Eutychos, 2366*

Act   20: 9   Eutychus, who was sitting in the window   1

evangelist

1. εὐαγγελιστής, *euangelistēs, 2296*

Act   21: 8   we went into the house of Philip the evangelist   1
Eph   4:11   some prophets, some evangelists   1
2Ti   4: 5   do the work of an evangelist   1

Eve

1. Εὔα, *Heua, 2293*

2Co   11: 3   as the serpent deceived Eve by its cunning   1
1Ti   2:13   For Adam was formed first, then Eve;   1

even   *See also* if even, never even

1. ἀλλά, *alla, 247*
2. γάρ, *gar, 1142*
3. γέ, *ge, 1145*
4. δέ, *de, 1254*
5. ἔτι, *eti, 2285*
6. ἕως, *heōs, 2401*
7. καί, *kai, 2779*
8. κἄν, *kan, 2829*
9. μόνον, *monon, 3667*
10. πολύς, *polys, 4498*
11. τέ, *te, 5445*

Mat   3:10   Even now the ax is lying at the root of the trees;   4
     5:46   Do not even the tax collectors do the same?   7
     5:47   than others? Do not even the Gentiles do the same?   7
     8:27   that even the winds and the sea obey him?"   7
     10:30   even the hairs of your head are all counted.   7
     10:42   whoever gives even a cup of cold water to one   9
     13:12   even what they have will be taken away.   7
     14:36   they might touch even the fringe of his cloak;   9
     15:27   "Yes, Lord, yet even the dogs eat the crumbs   7
     18:17   offender refuses to listen even to the church   7
     24:24   to lead astray, if possible, even the elect.   7
     25:29   even what they have will be taken away.   7
Mrk   1:27   He commands even the unclean spirits   7
     2:28   the Son of Man is lord even of the sabbath."   7

4:25	have nothing, even what they have will be taken	7
4:41	that even the wind and the sea obey him?"	7
6:23	I will give you, even half of my kingdom."	6
6:56	touch even the fringe of his cloak;	8
7:28	"Sir, even the dogs under the table eat	7
7:37	even makes the deaf to hear and the mute to speak."	7
10:48	he cried out even more loudly, "Son of David	10

Lke	1:15	even before his birth he will be filled with	7
	3: 9	Even now the ax is lying at the root of the trees;	7
	3:12	Even tax collectors came to be baptized,	7
	6:29	do not withhold even your shirt.	7
	6:32	even sinners love those who love them.	7
	6:33	even sinners do the same.	7
	6:34	Even sinners lend to sinners	7
	7:49	"Who is this who even forgives sins?"	7
	8:18	even what they seem to have will be taken	7
	8:25	that he commands even the winds	7
	10:11	'Even the dust of your town that clings to our feet	7
	10:17	"Lord, in your name even the demons submit	7
	11: 8	even though he will not get up and give him	7
	12: 7	But even the hairs of your head are all counted.	7
	14:26	yes, and even life itself,	7
	16:21	even the dogs would come and lick his sores.	7
	18:11	or even like this tax collector.	7
	18:15	People were bringing even infants to him	7
	18:39	he shouted even more loudly,	10
	19:26	even what they have will be taken away.	7
	19:42	saying, "If you, even you, had only recognized	7
	21:16	You will be betrayed even by parents	7
	23:11	Even Herod with his soldiers treated him	7
Jhn	11:22	even now I know that God will give you whatever	7
	12:42	many, even of the authorities, believed in him.	7
Act	2:18	Even upon my slaves, both men and women,	3
	5:15	they even carried out the sick into the streets	7
	5:39	you may even be found fighting against God!"	7
	8:13	Even Simon himself believed.	7
	10:45	had been poured out even on the Gentiles	7
	11:18	God has given even to the Gentiles the repentance	7
	14:18	Even with these words, they scarcely restrained	7
	15:17	even all the Gentiles over whom my name has been called.	7
	17:28	as even some of your own poets have said	7
	19:31	even some officials of the province of Asia,	7
	20:30	Some even from your own group will come	7
	21:13	ready not only to be bound but even to die	7
	24: 6	He even tried to profane the temple	7
	26:11	I pursued them even to foreign cities.	7
	27: 9	because even the Fast had already gone by	7
Rom	1:32	but even applaud others who practice them.	7
	3:12	no one who shows kindness, there is not even one."	6
	5:11	But more than that, we even boast in God	7
	5:14	even over those whose sins were not like	7
	9:11	Even before they had been born	2
1Co	2:10	even the depths of God.	7
	3: 2	Even now you are still not ready	1
	7:21	Even if you can gain your freedom	7
	7:29	even those who have wives be as though they had none	7
	8: 5	even though there may be so-called gods in heaven	7
	15:15	We are even found to be misrepresenting God	7
	16: 6	stay with you or even spend the winter	7
2Co	1:14	we are your boast even as you are our boast	7
	4: 3	even if our gospel is veiled	7
	5:16	even though we once knew Christ	7
	7: 5	For even when we came into Macedonia	7
	7: 8	For even if I made you sorry with my letter	7
	8:10	to do something but even to desire to do something	7
	10: 8	even if I boast a little too much of our authority	11
	10:13	to reach out even as far as you.	7
	11:14	Even Satan disguises himself as an angel	2
	12: 7	even considering the exceptional character	7
	12:11	even though I am nothing.	7
Gal	1: 8	even if we or an angel from heaven should proclaim	7
	2:13	so that even Barnabas was led astray	7
Eph	2: 5	even when we were dead through our trespasses	7
	5:12	shameful even to mention what such people do	7
Php	2: 8	obedient to the point of death—even death on a cross.	4
	2:17	even if I am being poured out as a libation	7
	3:18	and now I tell you even with tears	7
	4:16	even when I was in Thessalonica, you sent me help	7
2Th	3:10	For even when we were with you	7
1Ti	5:25	even when they are not, they cannot remain hidden.	7
Phm	1:19	say nothing about your owing me even your own self.	7

	1:21	knowing that you will do even more than I say.	7
Heb	6: 9	Even though we speak in this way	7
	7: 4	Even Abraham…gave him a tenth of the spoils.	7
	7: 9	One might even say	7
	7:15	It is even more obvious	5
	9: 1	Now even the first covenant had regulations	7
	11:19	God is able even to raise someone from the dead	7
	11:36	even chains and imprisonment.	5
	12: 9	Should we not be even more willing to be subject	10
Jas	2:19	Even the demons believe—and shudder.	7
1Pe	3: 1	even if some of them do not obey the word,	7
	3:14	even if you do suffer for doing what is right	7
	4: 6	the gospel was proclaimed even to the dead	7
2Pe	2: 1	They will even deny the Master who bought them	7
Jde	1:23	hating even the tunic defiled by their bodies.	7
Rev	1: 7	even those who pierced him;	7
	2:13	you did not deny…even in the days of Antipas	7
	13:13	even making fire come down from heaven to earth	7
	13:15	so that the image of the beast could even speak	7

even as

1. καθώς, *kathōs, 2777*
2. ὡς, *hōs, 6055*

Jhn	17:23	and have loved them even as you have loved me.	1
1Co	13:12	even as I have been fully known.	1
Rev	2:28	even as I also received authority from my Father.	2

even if

1. ἐάν, *ean, 1569*
2. εἰ, *ei, 1623*
3. κἄν, *kan, 2829*

Mat	21:21	but even if you say to this mountain	3
Lke	16:31	if someone rises from the dead.' "	1
Jhn	8:14	"Even if I testify on my own behalf	3
	8:16	Yet even if I do judge, my judgment is valid;	1
Act	13:41	never believe, even if someone tells you.' "	1
1Pe	1: 6	even if now for a little while you have had to suffer	2

even in the face of

1. ἄχρι, *achri, 948*

Rev	12:11	they did not cling to life even in the face of death.	1

even more

1. μᾶλλον, *mallon, 3437*
2. περισσότερος, *perissoteros, 4358*

Lke	12:48	been entrusted, even more will be demanded	2
Act	22: 2	they became even more quiet. Then he said:	1
1Co	14: 5	to speak in tongues, but even more to prophesy.	1

even so

1. καί, *kai, 2779*
2. οὕτως, *houtōs, 4048*

1Th	2: 4	entrusted with…the gospel, even so we speak	2
	4:14	even so, through Jesus, God will bring	2
2Pe	2: 2	Even so, many will follow their licentious ways	1

even that

1. κἀκεῖνος, *kakeinos, 2797*

Rom	11:23	And even those of Israel, if they do not persist	1

even then

1. οὕτως, *houtōs, 4048*

1Co	14:21	yet even then they will not listen to me,"	1

even though

1. Contextual: Not in Greek
2. ἀλλά, *alla, 247*
3. δέ, *de, 1254*
4. ἐάν, *ean, 1569*
5. εἰ, *ei, 1623*
6. καί, *kai, 2779*
7. καίπερ, *kaiper, 2788*
8. κἄν, *kan, 2829*
9. ὡς, *hōs, 6055*

Mat	26:35	"Even though I must die with you, I will not deny	8
Mrk	14:29	"Even though all become deserters, I will not."	6
	14:31	"Even though I must die with you, I will not deny	4
Lke	6: 8	Even though he knew what they were thinking	3
Jhn	10:38	if I do them, even though you do not believe me	8

Jhn	11:25	who believe in me, even though they die, will live	8
Act	7: 5	even though he had no child.	1
	13:28	Even though they found no cause for…death	6
	28:19	even though I had no charge to bring against my nation.	9
2Co	4:16	Even though our outer nature is wasting away	5
	5: 6	even though we know that while we are at home	6
Php	3: 4	even though I, too, have reason for confidence	7
1Ti	1:13	even though I was formerly a blasphemer,	1
Heb	11:11	even though he was too old	6
	12:17	even though he sought the blessing with tears.	7
1Pe	1: 8	even though you do not see him now, you believe	1
2Pe	2: 5	even though he saved Noah	2
3Jn	1: 5	even though they are strangers to you;	6
Rev	2: 9	"I know…your poverty, even though you are rich.	2

even to all

1. ὅσος, *hosos, 4012*

Rev	1: 2	testified…even to all that he saw.	1

no even

4. οὐδέ, *oude, 4028*

Mrk	6:31	they had no leisure even to eat.	4

not even

1. μηδέ, *mēde, 3593*
2. μήτε, *mēte, 3612*
3. οὐ, *ou, 4024*
4. οὐδέ, *oude, 4028*

Mat	6:29	even Solomon in all his glory was not clothed	4
	21:32	even after you saw it, you did not change your minds	4
	27:14	gave him no answer, not even to a single charge	4
Mrk	2: 2	not even in front of the door;	1
	3:20	so that they could not even eat.	1
	5: 3	no one could restrain…even with a chain;	4
	8:26	"Do not even go into the village."	1
	14:59	even on this point their testimony did not agree.	4
Lke	7: 9	not even in Israel have I found such faith."	4
	9: 3	not even an extra tunic.	2
	12:27	even Solomon in all his glory was not clothed	4
	18:13	would not even look up to heaven	4
Jhn	7: 5	(For not even his brothers believed in him.)	4
Act	7: 5	not even a foot's length	4
	19: 2	not even heard that there is a Holy Spirit."	4
Rom	3:10	"There is no one who is righteous, not even one;	4
1Co	4: 3	I do not even judge myself.	4
	5: 1	of a kind that is not found even among pagans;	4
	5:11	Do not even eat with such a one.	1
Gal	2: 3	even Titus, who was with me, was not compelled	4
	6:13	Even the circumcised do not…obey the law	4
Eph	5: 3	greed, must not even be mentioned among you	1
Heb	9:18	Hence not even the first covenant was inaugurated	4
Jas	4:14	Yet you do not even know what tomorrow	3

evening

1. ἑσπέρα, *hespera, 2270*
2. ὀψέ, *opse, 4067*
3. ὀψία, *opsia, 4068*

Mat	8:16	That evening they brought to him many	3
	14:15	When it was evening, the disciples came to him	3
	14:23	When evening came, he was there alone	3
	16: 2	"When it is evening, you say, 'It will be fair	3
	20: 8	evening came, the owner of the vineyard said	3
	26:20	When it was evening	3
	27:57	When it was evening, there came a rich man	3
Mrk	1:32	That evening, at sundown	3
	4:35	On that day, when evening had come, he said	3
	6:47	When evening came, the boat was out on the sea	3
	11:19	when evening came, Jesus and his disciples went out	2
	13:35	in the evening, or at midnight, or at cockcrow	3
	14:17	When it was evening, he came with the twelve.	3
	15:42	When evening had come	3
Lke	24:29	almost evening and the day is now nearly over."	1
Jhn	6:16	When evening came	3
	20:19	When it was evening on that day,	3
Act	4: 3	it was already evening.	1
	28:23	From morning until evening	1

event

1. Contextual: Not in Greek
2. πρᾶγμα, *pragma, 4547*

Lke	1: 1	an orderly account of the events	2
Heb	11: 7	warned by God about events as yet unseen	1

ever   *See also* more than ever, nothing ever

1. Contextual: Not in Greek
2. αἰών, *aiōn, 172*
3. ποτέ, *pote, 4537*
4. πώποτε, *pōpote, 4799*

Jhn	1:18	No one has ever seen God.	4
1Co	12: 3	no one speaking by the Spirit of God ever says	1
2Co	8:17	but since he is more eager than ever,	1
Gal	1: 5	to whom be the glory forever and ever. Amen.	2
Eph	3:21	to all generations, forever and ever. Amen.	2
	5:29	For no one ever hates his own body	3
Php	4:20	To our God and Father be glory forever and ever.	2
1Ti	1:17	be honor and glory forever and ever. Amen.	2
	6:16	whom no one has ever seen or can see;	1
2Ti	4:18	To him be the glory forever and ever. Amen.	2
Heb	1: 5	which of the angels did God ever say, "You are my Son;	3
	1: 8	"Your throne, O God, is forever and ever	2
	1:13	But to which of the angels has he ever said, "Sit	3
	7:13	from which no one has ever served at the altar.	1
	13:21	to whom be the glory forever and ever. Amen.	2
1Pe	4:11	glory and the power forever and ever. Amen.	2
	5:11	To him be the power forever and ever. Amen.	1
2Pe	1:21	because no prophecy ever came by human will,	3
1Jn	4:12	No one has ever seen God;	4
Rev	1: 6	to him be glory and dominion forever and ever.	2
	1:18	I was dead, and see, I am alive forever and ever;	2
	4: 9	thanks to the one…who lives forever and ever	2
	4:10	worship the one who lives forever and ever;	2
	5:13	honor and glory and might forever and ever!"	2
	7:12	might be to our God forever and ever! Amen."	2
	10: 6	swore by him who lives forever and ever	2
	11:15	Messiah, and he will reign forever and ever."	2
	14:11	smoke of their torment goes up forever and ever.	2
	15: 7	the wrath of God, who lives forever and ever;	2
	19: 3	The smoke goes up from her forever and ever."	2
	20:10	be tormented day and night forever and ever.	2
	22: 5	and they will reign forever and ever.	2

ever since

1. ἀπό, *apo, 608*
2. ἀπό + ὅς, *apo + hos, 608 + 4005*

Rom	1:20	Ever since the creation of the world	1
2Pe	3: 4	For ever since our ancestors died	2

no ever

1. μηκέτι, *mēketi, 3600*
2. οὐδέπω, *oudepō, 4031*
3. οὔπω, *oupō, 4037*

Mat	21:19	"May no fruit ever come from you again!"	1
Mrk	11:14	"May no one ever eat fruit from you again."	1
Lke	23:53	where no one had ever been laid.	3
Jhn	19:41	a new tomb in which no one had ever been laid.	2

none ever

1. οὐκέτι + πᾶς, *ouketi + pas, 4033 + 4246*

Act	20:25	now I know that none of you…will ever see	1

every   *See also* every *day*, every *quarter*, every *side*, every *time*, every *way*, make every effort

1. Contextual: Not in Greek
2. ἕκαστος, *hekastos, 1667*
3. κατά, *kata, 2848*
4. πᾶς, *pas, 4246*

Mat	3:10	every tree therefore that does not bear good	4
	4: 4	by bread alone, but by every word that comes	4
	4:23	curing every disease and every sickness	4
	4:23	curing every disease and every sickness	4
	7:17	In the same way, every good tree bears good fruit	4
	7:19	Every tree that does not bear good fruit is cut	4
	9:35	and curing every disease and every sickness.	4
	9:35	and curing every disease and every sickness.	4
	10: 1	and to cure every disease and every sickness.	4
	10: 1	and to cure every disease and every sickness.	4
	12:25	"Every kingdom divided against itself	4
	12:31	people will be forgiven for every sin and blasphemy	4
	12:36	have to give an account for every careless word	4

	13:52	"Therefore every scribe who has been trained	4
	15:13	"Every plant that my heavenly Father has	4
	18:16	so that every word may be confirmed	4
Lke	2:23	"Every firstborn male shall be designated as holy	4
	2:41	Now every year his parents went to Jerusalem	3
	3: 5	Every valley shall be filled	4
	3: 5	every mountain and hill shall be made low	4
	3: 9	every tree…that does not bear good fruit	4
	4:13	When the devil had finished every test	4
	4:37	report about him began to reach every place	4
	5:17	(they had come from every village of Galilee	4
	10: 1	to every town and place	4
	11:17	"Every kingdom divided against itself	4
	21:37	Every day he was teaching in the temple	1
Jhn	15: 2	removes every branch in me that bears no fruit.	4
	15: 2	Every branch that bears fruit he prunes	4
Act	2: 5	devout Jews from every nation under heaven	4
	5:42	every day in the temple and at home	4
	10:35	in every nation anyone who fears him	4
	13:27	the prophets that are read every sabbath	4
	15:21	For in every city, for generations past,	3
	15:21	read aloud every sabbath in the synagogues."	4
	15:36	in every city where we proclaimed the word	4
	17:17	he argued…in the marketplace every day	4
	17:22	extremely religious you are in every way.	4
	18: 4	Every sabbath he would argue in the synagogue	4
	20:23	the Holy Spirit testifies to me in every city	3
	22:19	in every synagogue I imprisoned and beat	3
Rom	3: 2	Much, in every way.	4
	3:19	so that every mouth may be silenced	4
	13: 1	Let every person be subject to the governing	4
	14:11	says the Lord, every knee shall bow to me	4
	14:11	and every tongue shall give praise to God."	4
1Co	1: 2	all those who in every place call on the name	4
	4:17	as I teach them everywhere in every church.	4
	6:18	Every sin that a person commits	4
	11: 3	understand that Christ is the head of every man	4
	15:24	after he has destroyed every ruler	4
	15:24	destroyed every ruler and every authority	4
	15:30	why are we putting ourselves in danger every hour?	4
	15:31	I die every day!	3
	16: 2	On the first day of every week	1
2Co	2:14	spreads in every place the fragrance	4
	7: 1	let us cleanse ourselves from every defilement	4
	7:11	At every point you have proved yourselves	4
	9: 8	provide you with every blessing in abundance	4
	9: 8	share abundantly in every good work.	4
	10: 5	every proud obstacle raised up against the knowledge	4
	10: 5	take every thought captive to obey Christ.	4
	10: 6	We are ready to punish every disobedience	4
Gal	5: 3	to every man who lets himself be circumcised	4
Eph	1: 3	blessed us…with every spiritual blessing	4
	1:21	and above every name that is named	4
	3:15	every family in heaven and on earth takes its name.	4
	4:14	blown about by every wind of doctrine	4
	4:16	every ligament with which it is equipped	4
	6:18	Pray in the Spirit…in every prayer	4
Php	1: 4	praying with joy in every one of my prayers	4
	1:18	Just this, that Christ is proclaimed in every way	4
	2: 9	the name that is above every name	4
	2:10	at the name of Jesus every knee should bend	4
	2:11	every tongue should confess that Jesus Christ is Lord	4
	4:19	my God will fully satisfy every need of yours	4
	4:21	Greet every saint in Christ Jesus.	4
Col	1:10	bear fruit in every good work	4
	1:23	been proclaimed to every creature under heaven.	4
	2:10	the head of every ruler and authority.	4
1Th	1: 8	in every place your faith in God has become known	4
	5:22	abstain from every form of evil.	4
2Th	1:11	fulfill…every good resolve and work of faith	4
	2: 4	exalts himself above every so-called god	4
	2:17	strengthen them in every good work and word.	4
	3:17	This is the mark in every letter of mine;	4
1Ti	2: 8	in every place the men should pray	4
2Ti	2:21	ready for every good work.	4
	3:17	equipped for every good work.	4
	4:18	The Lord will rescue me from every evil attack	4
Tit	1: 5	appoint elders in every town, as I directed you:	3
	2: 9	to give satisfaction in every respect;	4
	3: 1	to be obedient, to be ready for every good work	4
	3: 2	to show every courtesy to everyone.	4

Heb	2: 2	every transgression…received a just penalty.	4
	2:17	become like his brothers and sisters in every respect	4
	3: 4	(For every house is built by someone	4
	3:13	exhort one another every day	2
	4:15	one who in every respect has been tested	4
	5: 1	Every high priest chosen from among mortals	4
	8: 3	every high priest is appointed to offer gifts	4
	9:19	For when every commandment had been told	4
	10:11	every priest stands day after day at his service	4
	12: 1	Therefore…let us also lay aside every weight	4
	12: 6	chastises every child whom he accepts."	4
Jas	1: 7	being double-minded and unstable in every way,	4
	1:17	Every generous act of giving…is from above	4
	1:17	with every perfect gift, is from above	4
	3: 7	For every species of beast and bird, of reptile	4
	3:16	there will also be disorder and wickedness of every kind.	4
1Pe	2:13	accept the authority of every human institution	4
2Pe	1: 5	make every effort to support your faith	4
1Jn	4: 1	Beloved, do not believe every spirit	4
	4: 2	every spirit that confesses that Jesus Christ	4
	4: 3	every spirit that does not confess Jesus	4
Rev	1: 7	He is coming…every eye will see him	4
	5: 9	ransomed for God saints from every tribe and language	4
	5:13	I heard every creature in heaven and on earth	4
	6:14	every mountain and island was removed	4
	7: 4	sealed out of every tribe of the people of Israel:	4
	7: 9	multitude…from every nation, from all tribes	4
	7:17	God will wipe away every tear from their eyes."	4
	13: 7	every tribe and people and language and nation	4
	14: 6	to every nation and tribe and language and people.	4
	16: 3	and every living thing in the sea died.	4
	16:20	And every island fled away	4
	18: 2	a haunt of every foul spirit	4
	18: 2	a haunt of every foul bird,	4
	18: 2	a haunt of every foul and hateful beast.	4
	21: 4	he will wipe every tear from their eyes.	4
	21:19	foundations…are adorned with every jewel;	4

every kind

1. πᾶς, *pas, 4246*

Mat	13:47	and caught fish of every kind;	1
Rom	1:29	They were filled with every kind of wickedness	1
1Co	1: 5	in speech and knowledge of every kind—	1
Eph	4:19	greedy to practice every kind of impurity.	1
2Th	2:10	every kind of wicked deception	1
Rev	11: 6	and to strike the earth with every kind of plague	1

every one

1. εἷς, *heis, 1651*
2. ἕκαστος, *hekastos, 1667*
3. ὅσος, *hosos, 4012*

Mat	18:35	will also do to every one of you	2
Jhn	21:25	if every one of them were written down	1
Act	2:38	"Repent, and be baptized every one of you	2
2Co	1:20	in him every one of God's promises is a "Yes."	3

everybody

1. ἄνθρωπος, *anthrōpos, 476*

Mat	13:25	everybody was asleep, an enemy came and sowed	1

everyday

1. βίος, *bios, 1050*

2Ti	2: 4	gets entangled in everyday affairs;	1

everyone *See also* common to everyone

1. Contextual: Not in Greek
2. ἄνθρωπος, *anthrōpos, 476*
3. εἷς + ἕκαστος, *heis + hekastos, 1651 + 1667*
4. εἷς + ἕκαστος + πᾶς, *heis + hekastos + pas, 1651 + 1667 + 4246*
5. ἕκαστος, *hekastos, 1667*
6. ὁ, *ho, 3836*
7. ὅσος + ἐάν, *hosos + ean, 4012 + 1569*
8. ὅσος + ἄν, *hosos + an, 4012 + 323*
9. πᾶς, *pas, 4246*
10. πᾶς + ἄνθρωπος, *pas + anthrōpos, 4246 + 476*
11. πᾶς + ψυχή, *pas + psychē, 4246 + 6034*
12. πᾶς + ψυχή + ἄνθρωπος, *pas + psychē + anthrōpos, 4246 + 6034 + 476*

Mat	5:28	I say to you that everyone who looks at a woman	9
	5:42	Give to everyone who begs from you, and do not	6
	7: 8	For everyone who asks receives	9
	7: 8	and everyone who searches finds	6
	7: 8	for everyone who knocks, the door will be opened.	6
	7:21	"Not everyone who says to me, 'Lord, Lord,'	9
	7:24	"Everyone then who hears these words of mine	9
	7:26	And everyone who hears these words of mine	9
	10:32	"Everyone therefore who acknowledges me before	9
	16:27	he will repay everyone for what has been done.	5
	19:11	"Not everyone can accept this teaching	9
	19:29	everyone who has left houses or brothers	9
	22: 9	invite everyone you find to the wedding banquet.'	7
Mrk	1:37	"Everyone is searching for you."	9
	5:20	and everyone was amazed.	9
	9:49	"For everyone will be salted with fire.	9
Lke	4:15	was praised by everyone.	9
	6:30	Give to everyone who begs from you;	9
	6:40	everyone…will be like the teacher.	9
	9:43	everyone was amazed at all that he was doing	9
	11: 4	we ourselves forgive everyone indebted	9
	11:10	For everyone who asks receives	9
	11:10	everyone who searches finds	6
	11:10	for everyone who knocks, the door will be opened.	6
	12: 8	I tell you, everyone who acknowledges me	9
	12:10	everyone who speaks a word against the Son of Man	9
	12:41	telling this parable for us or for everyone?"	9
	12:48	everyone to whom much has been given	9
	16:16	everyone tries to enter it by force.	9
	20:18	Everyone who falls on that stone	9
Jhn	1: 9	The true light, which enlightens everyone	10
	2:10	said to him, "Everyone serves the good wine first	9
	2:25	for he himself knew what was in everyone.	2
	3: 8	So it is with everyone who is born of the Spirit."	9
	3:16	everyone who believes in him may not perish	9
	4:13	"Everyone who drinks…will be thirsty again	9
	6:45	Everyone who has heard…comes to me.	9
	8:34	everyone who commits sin is a slave to sin.	9
	11:26	everyone who lives and believes in me	9
	11:48	everyone will believe in him	9
	12:46	so that everyone who believes in me	9
	13:35	everyone will know that you are my disciples	9
	18:37	Everyone who belongs to the truth listens	9
	19:12	Everyone who claims to be a king	9
Act	1:24	"Lord, you know everyone's heart.	9
	2:21	everyone who calls on the name of the Lord	9
	2:39	everyone whom the Lord our God calls to him."	8
	2:43	Awe came upon everyone	11
	3:23	everyone who does not listen to that prophet	11
	10:43	everyone who believes in him receives	9
	13:39	by this Jesus everyone who believes is set free	9
	16:26	everyone's chains were unfastened.	9
	19:17	this became known…everyone was awestruck;	9
	20:31	not cease…to warn everyone with tears.	5
	21:28	This is the man who is teaching everyone everywhere	9
Rom	1:16	it is the power of God for salvation to everyone	9
	2: 9	and distress for everyone who does evil	12
	2:10	and honor and peace for everyone who does good	9
	3: 4	Although everyone is a liar, let God be proved true	10
	10: 4	may be righteousness for everyone who believes.	9
	10:13	For, "Everyone who calls on the name of the Lord	9
	12: 3	I say to everyone among you not to think of yourself	9
1Co	8: 7	not everyone, however, who has this knowledge.	9
	10:33	as I try to please everyone in everything I do	9
	12: 6	the same God who activates all of them in everyone.	9
	16:16	of everyone who works and toils with	9
2Co	4: 2	commend ourselves to the conscience of everyone	10
Gal	3:10	for it is written, "Cursed is everyone	9
	3:13	"Cursed is everyone who hangs on a tree"—	9
Eph	3: 9	to make everyone see what is the plan of the mystery	9
Php	1:13	the whole imperial guard and to everyone else	9
	4: 5	Let your gentleness be known to everyone.	10
Col	1:28	warning everyone and teaching everyone	10
	1:28	teaching everyone in all wisdom	10
	1:28	so that we may present everyone mature in Christ.	10
	4: 6	you may know how you ought to answer everyone.	3
1Th	2:15	drove us out; they displease God and oppose everyone	10
2Th	1: 3	the love of everyone of you for one another	4
1Ti	2: 1	thanksgivings be made for everyone	10
	2: 4	who desires everyone to be saved	10
2Ti	2:19	everyone who calls on the name of the Lord turn away	9

	2:24	kindly to everyone, an apt teacher, patient	9
	3: 9	their folly will become plain to everyone.	9
	3:17	so that everyone who belongs to God may be proficient	2
Tit	3: 2	to show every courtesy to everyone.	10
	3: 8	these things are excellent and profitable to everyone.	2
Heb	2: 9	by the grace of God he might taste death for everyone.	9
	5:13	for everyone who lives on milk	9
	12:14	Pursue peace with everyone	9
Jas	1:19	let everyone be quick to listen, slow to speak	10
1Pe	2:17	Honor everyone. Love the family of believers.	9
	4: 6	though they had been judged in the flesh as everyone	2
1Jn	2:23	everyone who confesses the Son has the Father also.	6
	2:29	everyone who does right has been born of him.	9
	3: 4	Everyone who commits sin is guilty	9
	3: 7	Everyone who does what is right is righteous	6
	3: 8	Everyone who commits sin is a child of the devil;	6
	4: 7	everyone who loves is born of God and knows God.	9
	5: 1	Everyone who believes that Jesus is the Christ	9
	5: 1	Everyone who loves the parent loves the child.	9
2Jn	1: 9	Everyone who does not abide in the teaching of Christ,	9
3Jn	1:12	Everyone has testified favorably about Demetrius	9
Jde	1:15	to convict everyone of all the deeds	11
Rev	2: 7	To everyone who conquers, I will give permission	6
	2:17	To everyone who conquers I will give some…manna	6
	2:26	everyone who conquers and continues to do my works	6
	6:15	everyone, slave and free, hid in the caves	9
	13: 8	everyone whose name has not been written	1
	22:12	to repay according to everyone's work.	5
	22:15	everyone who loves and practices falsehood.	9
	22:17	And let everyone who hears say, "Come."	6
	22:17	And let everyone who is thirsty come.	6
	22:18	I warn everyone who hears the words	9

everyone else

   1. λοιπός, *loipos, 3370*

Eph	2: 3	children of wrath, like everyone else.	1

everything

   1. Contextual: Not in Greek
   2. ἄπας, *hapas, 570*
   3. ὁ, *ho, 3836*
   4. πᾶς, *pas, 4246*

Mat	7:12	"In everything do to others as you would have them	4
	18:26	and I will pay you everything.'	4
	19:27	"Look, we have left everything and followed you.	4
	22: 4	everything is ready; come to the wedding banquet.'	4
	23:20	swears by it and by everything on it;	4
	28:11	told the chief priests everything that had happened.	2
	28:20	everything that I have commanded you.	4
Mrk	4:11	for those outside, everything comes in parables;	4
	4:34	he explained everything in private to his disciples.	4
	7:37	"He has done everything well	4
	8:25	was restored, and he saw everything clearly.	2
	10:28	we have left everything and followed you."	4
	11:11	when he had looked around at everything	4
	12:44	out of her poverty has put in everything she had	4
	13:23	alert; I have already told you everything.	4
	14:16	found everything as he had told them;	1
Lke	1: 3	after investigating everything carefully	4
	2:39	When they had finished everything	4
	5:11	they left everything and followed him.	4
	5:28	he got up, left everything, and followed him.	4
	11:41	see, everything will be clean for you.	4
	14:17	'Come; for everything is ready now.'	1
	15:14	When he had spent everything	4
	18:31	everything that is written about the Son of Man	4
	22:13	they went and found everything as he had told them;	1
	24:44	everything written about me in the law of Moses	4
Jhn	4:29	man who told me everything I have ever done!	4
	4:39	"He told me everything I have ever done."	4
	6:37	Everything that the Father gives me will come	4
	10:41	everything that John said about this man was true."	4
	14:26	the Holy Spirit…will teach you everything	4
	15:15	everything that I have heard from my Father.	4
	17: 7	everything you have given me is from you;	4
	21:17	he said to him, "Lord, you know everything;	4
Act	4:24	the earth, the sea, and everything in them	4
	4:32	everything they owned was held in common.	2
	10: 8	after telling them everything	2
	11:10	everything was pulled up again to heaven.	2

13:29	they had carried out everything that was written	4
17:24	The God who made the world and everything in it	4
22:10	everything that has been assigned to you to do.'	4
24: 8	be able to learn from him concerning everything	4
24:14	believing everything laid down according to the law	4
Rom 8:32	will he not with him also give us everything	4
14:20	Everything is indeed clean	4
1Co 2:10	the Spirit searches everything, even the depths	4
7:19	obeying the commandments of God is everything	1
10:31	do everything for the glory of God.	4
10:33	as I try to please everyone in everything I do	4
11: 2	because you remember me in everything	4
2Co 2: 9	know whether you are obedient in everything.	4
4:15	Yes, everything is for your sake	4
5:17	everything old has passed away;	3
5:17	passed away; see, everything has become new!	1
6:10	having nothing, and yet possessing everything.	4
7:14	just as everything we said to you was true	4
8: 7	Now as you excel in everything	4
9: 8	so that by always having enough of everything	4
12:19	Everything we do…is for the sake of building you up.	4
Gal 6:15	but a new creation is everything!	1
Eph 5:13	everything exposed by the light	4
5:14	for everything that becomes visible is light.	4
5:20	giving thanks to God the Father…for everything	4
5:24	wives ought to be, in everything	4
6:13	and having done everything, to stand firm.	2
6:21	Tychicus will tell you everything.	4
Php 3: 8	More than that, I regard everything as loss	4
4: 6	in everything by prayer and supplication	4
Col 1:11	to endure everything with patience, while joyfully	4
1:18	he might come to have first place in everything.	4
3:14	which binds everything together in perfect harmony.	1
3:17	do everything in the name of the Lord Jesus	4
3:20	Children, obey your parents in everything	4
3:22	Slaves, obey your earthly masters in everything	4
4: 9	They will tell you about everything here	4
4:12	fully assured in everything that God wills.	4
1Th 5:21	test everything; hold fast to what is good;	4
1Ti 4: 4	For everything created by God is good	4
6:17	richly provides us with everything for our enjoyment.	4
2Ti 2:10	Therefore I endure everything	4
Tit 2:10	in everything they may be an ornament to the doctrine	4
Heb 2: 8	do not yet see everything in subjection to them	4
7: 2	to him Abraham apportioned "one-tenth of everything."	4
8: 5	"See that you make everything	4
9:22	almost everything is purified with blood	4
13:21	make you complete in everything good	4
2Pe 1: 3	His divine power has given us everything	4
3:10	everything that is done on it will be disclosed.	1
1Jn 3:20	God is greater…and he knows everything.	4

everywhere

1. Contextual: Not in Greek
2. πανταχῇ, *pantachē*, 4114
3. πανταχοῦ, *pantachou*, 4116

Mrk 16:20	⟦and proclaimed the good news everywhere⟧	3
Lke 9: 6	the good news and curing diseases everywhere.	3
Act 17:30	now he commands all people everywhere to repent	3
21:28	This is the man who is teaching everyone everywhere	2
24: 3	We welcome this in every way and everywhere	3
28:22	we know that everywhere it is spoken against."	3
1Co 4:17	as I teach them everywhere in every church.	3
2Th 3: 1	may spread rapidly and be glorified everywhere	1

evidence

1. ἔνδειγμα, *endeigma*, 1891
2. ἔνδειξις, *endeixis*, 1893
3. ἐπί, *epi*, 2093
4. μαρτύριον, *martyrion*, 3457
5. στόμα, *stoma*, 5125

Mat 18:16	confirmed by the evidence of two or three	5
2Co 13: 1	by the evidence of two or three witnesses."	5
Php 1:28	For them this is evidence of their destruction	2
2Th 1: 5	is evidence of the righteous judgment of God	1
1Ti 5:19	except on the evidence of two or three witnesses.	3
Jas 5: 3	and their rust will be evidence against you	4

evident See also make evident

1. δῆλος, *dēlos*, 1316

2.	πρόδηλος, *prodēlos*, 4593	
Gal 3:11	Now it is evident that no one is justified	1
Heb 7:14	evident that our Lord was descended from Judah	2

evil See also do evil, speak evil, speak of as evil

1. κακία, *kakia*, 2798
2. κακός, *kakos*, 2805
3. κακῶς, *kakōs*, 2809
4. πονηρία, *ponēria*, 4504
5. πονηρός, *ponēros*, 4505
6. σαπρός, *sapros*, 4911
7. φαῦλος, *phaulos*, 5765

Mat 5:11	utter all kinds of evil against you falsely	5
5:45	he makes his sun rise on the evil and on the good	5
7:11	If you then, who are evil, know how to give good gifts	5
9: 4	"Why do you think evil in your hearts?	5
12:34	How can you speak good things, when you are evil?	5
12:35	and the evil person brings evil things out of	5
12:35	brings evil things out of an evil treasure.	5
12:39	"An evil and adulterous generation asks for	5
12:45	So will it be also with this evil generation."	5
13:49	and separate the evil from the righteous	5
15:19	For out of the heart come evil intentions, murder	5
16: 4	An evil and adulterous generation	5
27:23	he asked, "Why, what evil has he done?"	2
Mrk 7:21	from the human heart, that evil intentions come:	2
15:14	Pilate asked them, "Why, what evil has he done?"	2
Lke 6:45	evil person out of evil treasure produces evil;	5
6:45	evil person out of evil treasure produces evil;	5
6:45	evil person out of evil treasure produces evil;	5
7:21	diseases, plagues, and evil spirits	5
8: 2	some women who had been cured of evil spirits	5
11:13	If you then, who are evil, know how to give	5
11:29	"This generation is an evil generation;	5
23:22	"Why, what evil has he done?	2
Jhn 3:19	because their deeds were evil.	5
3:20	For all who do evil hate the light	7
5:29	those who have done evil, to…condemnation	7
7: 7	I testify against it that its works are evil.	5
Act 9:13	how much evil he has done to your saints	2
19:12	diseases left them, and the evil spirits came out	5
19:13	use the name…over those who had evil spirits	5
19:15	the evil spirit said to them in reply,	5
19:16	the man with the evil spirit leaped on them	5
23: 5	shall not speak evil of a leader of your people.' "	3
28:21	reported or spoken anything evil about you.	5
Rom 1:29	every…wickedness, evil, covetousness, malice.	4
1:30	haughty, boastful, inventors of evil	2
2: 9	and distress for everyone who does evil	2
3: 8	"Let us do evil so that good may come"?	2
7:19	but the evil I do not want is what I do.	2
7:21	I want to do what is good, evil lies close at hand.	2
12: 9	hate what is evil, hold fast to what is good;	5
12:17	Do not repay anyone evil for evil	2
12:17	Do not repay anyone evil for evil	2
12:21	Do not be overcome by evil	2
12:21	but overcome evil with good.	2
16:19	and guileless in what is evil.	2
1Co 5: 8	the old yeast, the yeast of malice and evil	4
10: 6	so that we might not desire evil as they did.	2
14:20	be infants in evil, but in thinking be adults.	1
2Co 5:10	done in the body, whether good or evil.	7
Gal 1: 4	to set us free from the present evil age	5
Eph 4:29	Let no evil talk come out of your mouths	6
5:16	because the days are evil.	5
6:12	against the spiritual forces of evil	4
6:13	that you may be able to withstand on that evil day	5
Php 3: 2	beware of the evil workers	2
Col 1:21	hostile in mind, doing evil deeds	5
3: 5	fornication, impurity, passion, evil desire	5
1Th 5:15	See that none of you repays evil for evil	2
5:15	See that none of you repays evil for evil	2
5:22	abstain from every form of evil.	5
2Th 3: 2	that we may be rescued from wicked and evil people;	5
1Ti 6:10	the love of money is a root of all kinds of evil	2
2Ti 4:18	The Lord will rescue me from every evil attack	5
Tit 2: 8	having nothing evil to say of us.	7
Heb 3:12	none of you may have an evil, unbelieving heart	5
5:14	to distinguish good from evil.	5
10:22	our hearts sprinkled clean from an evil conscience	5

Jas 1:13 for God cannot be tempted by evil   2
     2: 4 and become judges with evil thoughts?   5
     3: 8 no one can tame the tongue—a restless evil   2
     4:16 boast in your arrogance; all such boasting is evil.   5
1Pe 2:16 do not use your freedom as a pretext for evil.   1
     3: 9 Do not repay evil for evil   2
     3: 9 Do not repay evil for evil   2
     3:10 let them keep their tongues from evil   2
     3:11 let them turn away from evil and do good;   2
     3:12 the face of the Lord is against those who do evil."   2
1Jn 3:12 Because his own deeds were evil   5
2Jn 1:11 for to welcome is to participate in the evil   5
3Jn 1:11 Beloved, do not imitate what is evil   2

evil one

   1. πονηρός, *ponēros, 4505*

Mat 5:37 anything more than this comes from the evil one   1
     6:13 time of trial, but rescue us from the evil one   1
     13:19 the evil one comes and snatches away what is sown   1
     13:38 the weeds are the children of the evil one   1
Jhn 17:15 I ask you to protect them from the evil one.   1
Eph 6:16 able to quench all the flaming arrows of the evil one.   1
2Th 3: 3 he will strengthen you and guard you from the evil   1
1Jn 2:13 because you have conquered the evil one.   1
     2:14 and you have overcome the evil one.   1
     3:12 not be like Cain who was from the evil one   1
     5:18 and the evil one does not touch them.   1
     5:19 the whole world lies under the power of the evil one.   1

evil thing

   1. κακός, *kakos, 2805*
   2. πονηρός, *ponēros, 4505*

Mat 12:35 brings evil things out of an evil treasure.   2
Mrk 7:23 All these evil things come from within   2
Lke 3:19 because of all the evil things that Herod had done   2
     16:25 Lazarus in like manner evil things;   1

more evil

   1. πονηρός, *ponēros, 4505*

Mat 12:45 seven other spirits more evil than itself   1
Lke 11:26 seven other spirits more evil than itself   1

evildoer

   1. ἀδικέω, *adikeō, 92*
   2. ἐργάζομαι + ἀνομία, *ergazomai + anomia, 2237 + 490*
   3. ἐργάτης + ἀδικία, *ergatēs + adikia, 2239 + 94*
   4. κακοποιός, *kakopoios, 2804*
   5. κακός, *kakos, 2805*
   6. ποιέω + ἀνομία, *poieō + anomia, 4472 + 490*
   7. πονηρός, *ponēros, 4505*

Mat 5:39 But I say to you, Do not resist an evildoer.   7
     7:23 'I never knew you; go away from me, you evildoers.'   2
     13:41 all causes of sin and all evildoers   6
Lke 13:27 go away from me, all you evildoers!'   3
1Pe 2:12 though they malign you as evildoers   4
Rev 2: 2 I know that you cannot tolerate evildoers   5
     22:11 Let the evildoer still do evil   1

exact *See* exact *imprint,* learn *exact*

exactly

   1. οὕτως, *houtōs, 4048*

Act 27:25 it will be exactly as I have been told.   1

exaggerate

   1. ἐπιβαρέω, *epibareō, 2096*

2Co 2: 5 not to exaggerate it—to all of you.   1

exalt

   1. μεγαλύνω, *megalynō, 3486*
   2. ὑπεραίρομαι, *hyperairomai, 5643*
   3. ὑψόω, *hypsoō, 5738*

Mat 11:23 you, Capernaum, will you be exalted to heaven?   3
     23:12 All who exalt themselves will be humbled   3
     23:12 all who humble themselves will be exalted.   3
Lke 10:15 you, Capernaum, will you be exalted to heaven?   3
     14:11 For all who exalt themselves will be humbled   3
     14:11 those who humble themselves will be exalted."   3
     18:14 all who exalt themselves will be humbled   3

     18:14 all who humble themselves will be exalted."   3
Act 2:33 Being therefore exalted at the right hand of God   3
     5:31 God exalted him at his right hand as Leader   3
2Co 11: 7 humbling myself so that you might be exalted   3
Php 1:20 Christ will be exalted now as always in my body   1
2Th 2: 4 exalts himself above every so-called god   2
Jas 4:10 Humble yourselves…and he will exalt you.   3
1Pe 5: 6 so that he may exalt you in due time.   3

exalt above

   1. ὑψηλός, *hypsēlos, 5734*

Heb 7:26 a high priest…exalted above the heavens.   1

exalt highly

   1. ὑπερυψόω, *hyperypsoō, 5671*

Php 2: 9 Therefore God also highly exalted him   1

examination *See* make an examination

examine

   1. ἀνακρίνω, *anakrinō, 373*
   2. ἀνάκρισις, *anakrisis, 374*
   3. ἀνετάζω, *anetazō, 458*
   4. δοκιμάζω, *dokimazō, 1507*
   5. πειράζω, *peirazō, 4279*

Lke 23:14 here I have examined him in your presence   1
Act 12:19 he examined the guards   1
     17:11 examined the scriptures every day   1
     22:24 ordered him to be examined by flogging   3
     22:29 those who were about to examine him drew back   3
     24: 8 By examining him yourself   1
     25:26 after we have examined him   2
     28:18 When they had examined me   1
1Co 9: 3 This is my defense to those who would examine me.   1
     11:28 Examine yourselves, and only then eat of the bread   4
2Co 13: 5 Examine yourselves to see whether you are living   5

example *See also* give an example, make an example, serve as an example

   1. δεῖγμα, *deigma, 1257*
   2. ἴχνος, *ichnos, 2717*
   3. κατά, *kata, 2848*
   4. τύπος, *typos, 5596*
   5. ὑπογραμμός, *hypogrammos, 5681*
   6. ὑπόδειγμα, *hypodeigma, 5682*
   7. ὑποτύπωσις, *hypotypōsis, 5721*

Jhn 13:15 For I have set you an example   6
Rom 4:12 but who also follow the example of the faith   2
1Co 10: 6 Now these things occurred as examples for us   4
Gal 3:15 I give an example from daily life: 3
Php 3:17 who live according to the example you have in us.   4
1Th 1: 7 you became an example to all the believers   4
2Th 3: 9 in order to give you an example to imitate.   4
1Ti 1:16 an example to those who would come to believe in him   7
     4:12 set the believers an example in speech   4
Jas 5:10 As an example of suffering and patience   6
1Pe 2:21 Christ also suffered…leaving you an example   5
     5: 3 but be examples to the flock.   4
2Pe 2: 6 an example of what is coming to the ungodly;   6
Jde 1: 7 serve as an example by undergoing a punishment   1

exceed

   1. περισσεύω, *perisseuō, 4355*

Mat 5:20 tell you, unless your righteousness exceeds   1

excel

   1. περισσεύω, *perisseuō, 4355*

1Co 14:12 strive to excel in them for building up the church.   1
     15:58 always excelling in the work of the Lord   1
2Co 8: 7 Now as you excel in everything   1
     8: 7 want you to excel also in this generous undertaking.   1

excellence

   1. ἀρετή, *aretē, 746*

Php 4: 8 whatever is commendable, if there is any excellence   1

Excellency

   1. βασιλεύς, *basileus, 995*
   2. κράτιστος, *kratistos, 3196*

Act 23:26 to his Excellency the governor Felix, greetings. 2
24: 2 Excellency, because of you we have long enjoyed peace 2
26: 7 for this hope, your Excellency, that I am accused 1
26:13 along the road, your Excellency, I saw a light 1

excellent

1. καλός, *kalos, 2819*

Tit 3: 8 these things are excellent and profitable to everyone. 1
Jas 2: 7 Is it not they who blaspheme the excellent name 1

more excellent

1. διάφορος, *diaphoros, 1427*
2. ὑπερβολή, *hyperbolē, 5651*

1Co 12:31 I will show you a still more excellent way. 2
Heb 1: 4 the name he has inherited is more excellent 1
8: 6 Jesus has now obtained a more excellent ministry 1

most excellent

1. κράτιστος, *kratistos, 3196*

Lke 1: 3 write an orderly account…most excellent Theophilus 1
Act 26:25 "I am not out of my mind, most excellent Festus 1

except

1. Contextual: Not in Greek
2. ἀλλά + μή, *alla + mē, 247 + 3590*
3. ἐάν, *ean, 1569*
4. ἐάν + μή, *ean + mē, 1569 + 3590*
5. εἰ + μή, *ei + mē, 1623 + 3590*
6. εἰ + μή + μόνον, *ei + mē + monon, 1623 + 3590 + 3667*
7. εἰ + μήτι, *ei + mēti, 1623 + 3614*
8. ἐκτός + εἰ + μή, *ektos + ei + mē, 1760 + 1623 + 3590*
9. μή, *mē, 3590*
10. οὐ, *ou, 4024*
11. παρεκτός, *parektos, 4211*
12. πλήν, *plēn, 4440*
13. χωρίς, *chōris, 6006*

Mat 5:32 his wife, except on the ground of unchastity 11
11:27 and no one knows the Son except the Father 5
11:27 and no one knows the Father except the Son 5
12:39 except the sign of the prophet Jonah. 5
13:57 are not without honor except in their own country 5
16: 4 except the sign of Jonah." 5
17: 8 they saw no one except Jesus himself alone. 5
19: 9 divorces his wife, except for unchastity 9
Mrk 4:22 there is nothing hidden, except to be disclosed; 3
4:22 nor is anything secret, except to come to light. 2
4:34 he did not speak to them except in parables 13
5:37 He allowed no one to follow him except Peter 5
6: 4 without honor, except in their hometown 5
6: 5 except that he laid his hands on a few sick 5
6: 8 nothing for their journey except a staff; 6
Lke 4:26 sent to none of them except to a widow at Zarephath 5
4:27 except Naaman the Syrian." 5
8:51 except Peter, John, and James, 5
10:22 no one knows who the Son is except the Father 5
10:22 who the Father is except the Son 5
11:29 no sign…except the sign of Jonah. 5
17:18 Was none of them found…except this foreigner?" 5
Jhn 3:13 except the one who descended from heaven 5
3:27 except what has been given from heaven. 4
6:46 except the one who is from God; 5
13:10 does not need to wash, except for the feet 5
14: 6 No one comes to the Father except through me. 5
17:12 not…lost except the one destined to be lost 5
Act 8: 1 all except the apostles were scattered 12
11:19 spoke the word to no one except Jews. 6
20:23 except that the Holy Spirit testifies to me 12
21:14 except to say, "The Lord's will be done." 1
26:29 might become such as I am—except for these chains." 11
Rom 13: 1 for there is no authority except from God 5
13: 8 Owe no one anything, except to love one another; 5
15:18 except what Christ has accomplished through me 10
1Co 1:14 baptized none of you except Crispus and Gaius 5
2: 2 except Jesus Christ, and him crucified. 5
2:11 except the human spirit that is within? 5
2:11 except the Spirit of God. 5
7: 5 except perhaps by agreement for a set time 7
12: 3 except by the Holy Spirit. 5
2Co 12: 5 I will not boast, except of my weaknesses. 5

12:13 except that I myself did not burden you? 5
Gal 1:19 except James the Lord's brother. 5
6:14 May I never boast of anything except the cross 5
Php 4:15 no church shared with me…except you alone. 5
1Ti 5:19 except on the evidence of two or three witnesses. 8
Rev 2:17 that no one knows except the one who receives it. 5
14: 3 No one could learn that song except 5

exceptional

1. ὑπερβολή, *hyperbolē, 5651*

2Co 12: 7 the exceptional character of the revelations. 1

excess

1. ἀνάχυσις, *anachysis, 431*

1Pe 4: 4 no longer join them in the same excesses of dissipation 1

excessive

1. περισσότερος, *perissoteros, 4358*

2Co 2: 7 so that he may not be overwhelmed by excessive sorrow. 1

exchange

1. ἀλλάσσω, *allassō, 248*
2. μεταλλάσσω, *metallassō, 3563*
3. πέμπω, *pempō, 4287*

Rom 1:23 exchanged the glory of the immortal God 1
1:25 they exchanged the truth about God for a lie 2
1:26 exchanged natural intercourse for unnatural 2
Rev 11:10 gloat…celebrate and exchange presents 3

exclaim

1. ἀναφωνέω, *anaphōneō, 430*
2. λέγω, *legō, 3306*
3. φημί + μέγας + ὁ + φωνή, *phēmi + megas + ho + phōnē, 5774 + 3489 + 3836 + 5889*

Lke 1:42 exclaimed with a loud cry, "Blessed are you 1
Jhn 1:36 as he watched Jesus walk by, he exclaimed, "Look, 2
Act 26:24 Festus exclaimed, "You are out of your mind, Paul! 3

exclude

1. ἀφορίζω, *aphorizō, 928*
2. ἐκκλείω, *ekkleiō, 1710*

Lke 6:22 when they exclude you, revile you 1
Rom 3:27 what becomes of boasting? It is excluded. 2
Gal 4:17 want to exclude you, so that you may make much 2

excuse   See also make an excuse

1. ἀπολογέομαι, *apologeomai, 664*
2. πρόφασις, *prophasis, 4733*

Jhn 15:22 now they have no excuse for their sin. 2
Rom 2:15 thoughts will accuse or perhaps excuse them 1

no excuse

1. ἀναπολόγητος, *anapologētos, 406*

Rom 2: 1 Therefore you have no excuse 1

without excuse

1. ἀναπολόγητος, *anapologētos, 406*

Rom 1:20 So they are without excuse; 1

execute

1. ἔκδικος, *ekdikos, 1690*
2. ποιέω, *poieō, 4472*

Jhn 5:27 has given him authority to execute judgment 2
Rom 9:28 Lord will execute his sentence on the earth 2
13: 4 to execute wrath on the wrongdoer. 1
Jde 1:15 to execute judgment on all, and to convict everyone 2

exercise

1. ποιέω, *poieō, 4472*

Rev 13: 5 allowed to exercise authority for…months. 1
13:12 exercises all the authority of the first beast 1

exercise dominion

1. βασιλεύω, *basileuō, 996*

Rom 5:14 Yet death exercised dominion from Adam to Moses 1
5:17 death exercised dominion through that one 1
5:17 exercise dominion in life through the one man 1
5:21 so that, just as sin exercised dominion in death 1

Rom 5:21 grace might...exercise dominion through justification 1
     6:12 not let sin exercise dominion in your mortal bodies 1

exercise oversight

1. ἐπισκοπέω, *episkopeō, 2174*

1Pe 5: 2 exercising the oversight, not under compulsion 1

exercise self-control

1. ἐγκρατεύομαι, *enkrateuomai, 1603*

1Co 9:25 Athletes exercise self-control 1

exertion

1. τρέχω, *trechō, 5556*

Rom 9:16 So it depends not on human will or exertion 1

exhibit

1. ἀποδείκνυμι, *apodeiknymi, 617*

1Co 4: 9 I think that God has exhibited us apostles 1

exhibit publicly

1. προγράφω, *prographō, 4592*

Gal 3: 1 Christ was publicly exhibited as crucified! 1

exhort

1. παρακαλέω, *parakaleō, 4151*
2. παράκλησις, *paraklēsis, 4155*

Act 2:40 he testified with many other arguments and exhorted 1
    11:23 he exhorted them all to remain faithful to the Lord 1
2Th 3:12 Now such persons we command and exhort 1
1Ti 4:13 reading of scripture, to exhorting, to teaching. 2
Tit 2:15 exhort and reprove with all authority. 1
Heb 3:13 exhort one another every day 1
1Pe 5: 1 as an elder myself...I exhort the elders among you 1

exhortation

1. παρακαλέω, *parakaleō, 4151*
2. παράκλησις, *paraklēsis, 4155*

Lke 3:18 So, with many other exhortations, he proclaimed 1
Act 13:15 "Brothers, if you have any word of exhortation 2
    15:31 they rejoiced at the exhortation. 2
Rom 12: 8 the exhorter, in exhortation; 2
Heb 12: 5 the exhortation that addresses you as children 2
    13:22 bear with my word of exhortation 2

exhorter

1. παρακαλέω, *parakaleō, 4151*

Rom 12: 8 the exhorter, in exhortation; 1

exile

1. παρεπίδημος, *parepidēmos, 4215*
2. παροικία, *paroikia, 4229*

1Pe 1: 1 To the exiles of the Dispersion 1
    1:17 during the time of your exile. 2
    2:11 I urge you as aliens and exiles to abstain 1

exist

1. Contextual: Not in Greek
2. εἰμί, *eimi, 1639*

Jhn 17: 5 glory that I had...before the world existed. 2
Rom 4:17 calls into existence the things that do not exist. 2
    13: 1 authorities that exist have been instituted by God. 2
1Co 8: 6 from whom are all things and for whom we exist 1
    8: 6 through whom we exist. 1
Heb 2:10 for whom and through whom all things exist 1
    11: 6 must believe that he exists 2
2Pe 3: 5 by the word of God heavens existed long ago 2
1Jn 2: 4 in such a person the truth does not exist; 2
Rev 4:11 and by your will they existed and were created." 2

existence

1. εἰμί, *eimi, 1639*
2. προστάσσω, *prostassō, 4705*

Act 17:26 he allotted the times of their existence 2
Rom 4:17 calls into existence the things that do not exist. 1

no existence

1. οὐδείς, *oudeis, 4029*

1Co 8: 4 we know that "no idol in the world really exists," 1

exodus

1. ἔξοδος, *exodos, 2016*

Heb 11:22 made mention of the exodus of the Israelites 1

exorcist

1. ἐξορκιστής, *exorkistēs, 2020*
2. υἱός, *huios, 5626*

Mat 12:27 by whom do your own exorcists cast them out? 2
Lke 11:19 by whom do your exorcists cast them out? 2
Act 19:13 Then some itinerant Jewish exorcists 1

expect

1. ἀπεκδέχομαι, *apekdechomai, 587*
2. ἐκδέχομαι, *ekdechomai, 1683*
3. ἐλπίζω, *elpizō, 1827*
4. οἴομαι, *oiomai, 3887*
5. προσδοκάω, *prosdokaō, 4659*
6. προσδοκία, *prosdokia, 4660*
7. ὑπονοέω, *hyponoeō, 5706*

Mat 24:50 on a day when he does not expect him 5
Lke 12:46 on a day when he does not expect him 5
Act 3: 5 expecting to receive something from them. 5
    10:24 Cornelius was expecting them 5
    12:11 from all that the Jewish people were expecting." 6
    25:18 any of the crimes that I was expecting. 7
    28: 6 They were expecting him to swell up 5
1Co 16:11 I am expecting him with the brothers. 2
2Co 8: 5 this, not merely as we expected; 3
Php 3:20 we are expecting a Savior, the Lord Jesus Christ. 1
Jas 1: 7 the doubter...must not expect to receive anything 4

expect a child

1. ἔγκυος, *enkyos, 1607*

Lke 2: 5 engaged and who was expecting a child. 1

expect in return

1. ἀπελπίζω, *apelpizō, 594*

Lke 6:35 do good, and lend, expecting nothing in return. 1

expectation *See* fill with expectation

eager expectation

1. ἀποκαραδοκία, *apokaradokia, 638*

Php 1:20 It is my eager expectation and hope 1

expel

1. ἐκβάλλω, *ekballō, 1675*

3Jn 1:10 prevents those...and expels them from the church. 1

expense

1. μίσθωμα, *misthōma, 3637*
2. ὀψώνιον, *opsōnion, 4072*

Act 28:30 He lived there two whole years at his own expense 1
1Co 9: 7 pays the expenses for doing military service? 2

expensive

1. πολυτελής, *polytelēs, 4500*

1Ti 2: 9 gold, pearls, or expensive clothes 1

experience

1. γίνομαι, *ginomai, 1181*
2. ἐνεργέω, *energeō, 1919*
3. ἔχω, *echō, 2400*
4. ὁράω, *horaō, 3972*
5. πάσχω, *paschō, 4248*

Act 2:27 or let your Holy One experience corruption. 4
    2:31 nor did his flesh experience corruption.' 4
    13:35 'You will not let your Holy One experience corruption.' 4
    13:36 beside his ancestors, and experienced corruption; 4
    13:37 he whom God raised up experienced no corruption. 4
1Co 7:28 who marry will experience distress in this life 3
2Co 1: 6 which you experience when you patiently endure 2
    1: 8 the affliction we experienced in Asia; 1
Gal 3: 4 Did you experience so much for nothing? 5
Heb 11: 5 he did not experience death; 4

explain

1. διανοίγω, *dianoigō, 1380*

2. διασαφέω, *diasapheō, 1397*
3. ἐκτίθημι, *ektithēmi, 1758*
4. ἐπιλύω, *epilyō, 2147*
5. λέγω, *legō, 3306*
6. φράζω, *phrazō, 5851*

Mat	13:36 "Explain to us the parable of the weeds	2
	15:15 Peter said to him, "Explain this parable to us."	6
Mrk	4:34 he explained everything in private to his disciples.	4
Act	11: 4 Peter began to explain it to them, step by step	3
	17: 3 explaining and proving that it was necessary	1
	18:26 explained the Way of God to him more accurately	3
	28:23 he explained the matter to them	3
Heb	5:11 have much to say that is hard to explain	5

explain rightly

1. ὀρθοτομέω, *orthotomeō, 3982*

2Ti 2:15 rightly explaining the word of truth.   1

exploit *See also* something to exploit

1. Contextual: Not in Greek
2. ἐμπορεύομαι, *emporeuomai, 1864*
3. πλεονεκτέω, *pleonekteō, 4430*

1Th	4: 6 that no one wrong or exploit a brother or sister	3
Jas	3: 5 the tongue...boasts of great exploits.	1
2Pe	2: 3 they will exploit you with deceptive words.	2

expose

1. βλέπω, *blepō, 1063*
2. ἐλέγχω, *elenchō, 1794*

Jhn	3:20 so that their deeds may not be exposed.	2
Eph	5:11 but instead expose them.	2
	5:13 everything exposed by the light	2
Rev	16:15 not going about naked and exposed to shame.")	1

expose publicly

1. θεατρίζω, *theatrizō, 2518*

Heb 10:33 sometimes being publicly exposed to abuse   1

expose to public disgrace

1. δειγματίζω, *deigmatizō, 1258*

Mat 1:19 Joseph...unwilling to expose her to public disgrace   1

expressly

1. ῥητῶς, *rhētōs, 4843*

1Ti 4: 1 Now the Spirit expressly says   1

extend

1. διώκω, *diōkō, 1503*
2. πλεονάζω, *pleonazō, 4429*

Rom	12:13 extend hospitality to strangers.	1
2Co	4:15 that grace, as it extends to more and more people	2

extent

1. μέρος, *meros, 3538*

1Co	11:18 to some extent I believe it.	1
2Co	2: 5 to some extent—not to exaggerate it	1

external

1. ἐν + ὁ + φανερός, *en + ho + phaneros, 1877 + 3836 + 5745*

Rom 2:28 nor is true circumcision something external   1

extinction

1. καταστροφή, *katastrophē, 2953*

2Pe 2: 6 he condemned them to extinction   1

extol

1. μεγαλύνω, *megalynō, 3486*

Act 10:46 speaking in tongues and extolling God.   1

extort money by threat

1. διασείω, *diaseiō, 1398*

Lke 3:14 "Do not extort money from anyone by threats   1

extortion

1. πλεονεξία, *pleonexia, 4432*

2Co 9: 5 ready as a voluntary gift and not as an extortion.   1

---

extra *See also* earn extra

1. δύο, *dyo, 1545*

Lke 9: 3 not even an extra tunic.   1

extraordinary

1. οὐ + ὁ + τυγχάνω, *ou + ho + tynchanō, 4024 + 3836 + 5593*
2. ὑπερβολή, *hyperbolē, 5651*

Act	19:11 God did extraordinary miracles through Paul	1
2Co	4: 7 that this extraordinary power belongs to God	2

extreme

1. κατά + βάθος, *kata + bathos, 2848 + 958*

2Co 8: 2 their abundant joy and their extreme poverty   1

extremely *See* extremely *religious*

exult

1. ἀγαλλιάω, *agalliaō, 22*

Rev 19: 7 Let us rejoice and exult and give him the glory   1

eye *See also* keep an eye on

1. ὄμμα, *omma, 3921*
2. ὀφθαλμός, *ophthalmos, 4057*
3. πρόσωπον, *prosōpon, 4725*
4. τρῆμα, *trēma, 5557*
5. τρυμαλιά, *trymalia, 5584*
6. τρύπημα, *trypēma, 5585*

Mat	5:29 If your right eye causes you to sin, tear it out	2
	5:38 heard that it was said, 'An eye for an eye and a tooth	2
	5:38 'An eye for an eye and a tooth for a tooth.'	2
	6:22 "The eye is the lamp of the body. So, if your eye	2
	6:22 So, if your eye is healthy, your whole body will be	2
	6:23 if your eye is unhealthy, your whole body will be	2
	7: 3 do you see the speck in your neighbor's eye	2
	7: 3 but do not notice the log in your own eye?	2
	7: 4 'Let me take the speck out of your eye,'	2
	7: 4 while the log is in your own eye?	2
	7: 5 hypocrite, first take the log out of your own eye	2
	7: 5 to take the speck out of your neighbor's eye.	2
	9:29 Then he touched their eyes and said	2
	9:30 their eyes were opened.	2
	13:15 and they have shut their eyes;	2
	13:15 so that they might not look with their eyes	2
	13:16 blessed are your eyes, for they see	2
	18: 9 if your eye causes you to stumble, tear it out	2
	18: 9 have two eyes and to be thrown into the hell of fire.	2
	19:24 for a camel to go through the eye of a needle	6
	20:33 They said to him, "Lord, let our eyes be opened."	2
	20:34 Moved with compassion, Jesus touched their eyes.	1
	21:42 it is amazing in our eyes'?	2
	26:43 for their eyes were heavy.	2
Mrk	8:18 Do you have eyes, and fail to see?	2
	8:23 when he had put saliva on his eyes	1
	8:25 Then Jesus laid his hands on his eyes again;	2
	9:47 if your eye causes you to stumble, tear it out;	2
	9:47 have two eyes and to be thrown into hell	2
	10:25 a camel to go through the eye of a needle	5
	12:11 it is amazing in our eyes'?"	2
	14:40 their eyes were very heavy;	2
Lke	2:30 for my eyes have seen your salvation	2
	4:20 The eyes of all in the synagogue were fixed on him.	2
	6:41 do you see the speck in your neighbor's eye	2
	6:41 do not notice the log in your own eye?	2
	6:42 let me take the speck out of your eye,'	2
	6:42 you...do not see the log in your own eye?	2
	6:42 first take the log out of your own eye	2
	6:42 take the speck out of your neighbor's eye.	2
	10:23 "Blessed are the eyes that see what you see!	2
	11:34 Your eye is the lamp of your body.	2
	11:34 If your eye is healthy	2
	18:25 to go through the eye of a needle	4
	19:42 now they are hidden from your eyes.	2
	24:16 their eyes were kept from recognizing him.	2
	24:31 their eyes were opened, and they recognized him;	2
Jhn	9: 6 and spread the mud on the man's eyes	2
	9:10 asking him, "Then how were your eyes opened?"	2
	9:11 made mud, spread it on my eyes, and said to me	2
	9:14 when Jesus made the mud and opened his eyes.	2

Jhn	9:15	He said to them, "He put mud on my eyes.	2
	9:17	It was your eyes he opened."	2
	9:21	nor do we know who opened his eyes.	2
	9:26	How did he open your eyes?"	2
	9:30	and yet he opened my eyes.	2
	9:32	anyone opened the eyes of a person born blind.	2
	10:21	Can a demon open the eyes of the blind?"	2
	11:37	he who opened the eyes of the blind man	2
	12:40	blinded their eyes and hardened their heart	2
	12:40	so that they might not look with their eyes	2
Act	9: 8	though his eyes were open, he could see nothing;	2
	9:18	something like scales fell from his eyes	2
	9:40	she opened her eyes	2
	26:18	to open their eyes	2
	28:27	they have shut their eyes;	2
	28:27	so that they might not look with their eyes	2
Rom	3:18	"There is no fear of God before their eyes."	2
	11: 8	eyes that would not see and ears that would not	2
	11:10	their eyes be darkened so that they cannot see	2
1Co	2: 9	"What no eye has seen, nor ear heard	2
	12:16	"Because I am not an eye, I do not belong to the body,"	2
	12:17	If the whole body were an eye	2
	12:21	The eye cannot say to the hand, "I have no need	2
	15:52	in a moment, in the twinkling of an eye	2
2Co	10: 7	Look at what is before your eyes.	3
Gal	3: 1	It was before your eyes	2
	4:15	torn out your eyes and given them to me.	2
Eph	1:18	so that, with the eyes of your heart enlightened	2
Heb	4:13	the eyes of the one to whom we must render an account.	2
1Pe	3:12	For the eyes of the Lord are on the righteous	2
2Pe	2:14	They have eyes full of adultery	2
1Jn	1: 1	what we have seen with our eyes	2
	2:16	the desire of the flesh, the desire of the eyes	2
Rev	1: 7	He is coming…every eye will see him	2
	1:14	his eyes were like a flame of fire	2
	2:18	the Son of God, who has eyes like a flame of fire	2
	3:18	salve to anoint your eyes so that you may see.	2
	4: 6	creatures, full of eyes in front and behind:	2
	4: 8	are full of eyes all around and inside	2
	5: 6	a Lamb…having seven horns and…seven eyes	2
	7:17	God will wipe away every tear from their eyes."	2
	19:12	His eyes are like a flame of fire	2
	21: 4	he will wipe every tear from their eyes.	2

one eye

1. μονόφθαλμος, *monophthalmos, 3669*

Mat	18: 9	it is better for you to enter life with one eye	1
Mrk	9:47	to enter the kingdom of God with one eye	1

eyewitness

1. αὐτόπτης, *autoptes, 898*
2. ἐπόπτης, *epoptēs, 2228*

Lke	1: 2	who from the beginning were eyewitnesses	1
2Pe	1:16	but we had been eyewitnesses of his majesty.	2

F

face *See also* even in the face of, face to face, strike on the face

1. Contextual: Not in Greek
2. βλέπω, *blepō, 1063*
3. ἐναντίος, *enantios, 1885*
4. ἔχω, *echō, 2400*
5. ὄψις, *opsis, 4071*
6. περιπίπτω, *peripiptō, 4346*
7. πρόσωπον, *prosōpon, 4725*
8. στόμα, *stoma, 5125*

Mat	6:16	the hypocrites, for they disfigure their faces	7
	6:17	when you fast, put oil on your head and wash your face	7
	17: 2	and his face shone like the sun	7
	18:10	the face of my Father in heaven.	7
	26:67	Then they spat in his face and struck him;	7
Mrk	15:39	when the centurion, who stood facing him, saw	3
Lke	5:12	he bowed with his face to the ground and begged	7
	9:29	the appearance of his face changed,	7
	9:51	he set his face to go to Jerusalem.	7
	9:53	because his face was set toward Jerusalem.	7
	21:35	all who live on the face of the whole earth.	7
	24: 5	bowed their faces to the ground	7

Jhn	11:44	his face wrapped in a cloth.	5
	16:33	In the world you face persecution.	4
Act	6:15	his face was like the face of an angel.	7
	6:15	his face was like the face of an angel.	7
	20:25	none of you…will ever see my face again.	7
	27:12	a harbor of Crete, facing southwest and northwest.	2
1Co	13:12	but then we will see face to face.	7
	13:12	but then we will see face to face.	7
2Co	3: 7	people of Israel could not gaze at Moses' face	7
	3: 7	the glory of his face, a glory now set aside	7
	3:13	not like Moses, who put a veil over his face	7
	3:18	all of us, with unveiled faces, seeing the glory	7
	4: 6	the glory of God in the face of Jesus Christ.	7
	11:20	or puts on airs, or gives you a slap in the face.	7
Gal	2:11	I opposed him to his face	7
Jas	1: 2	whenever you face trials of any kind,	6
1Pe	3:12	the face of the Lord is against those who do evil."	7
2Jn	1:12	I hope to…talk with you face to face	8
	1:12	I hope to…talk with you face to face	8
3Jn	1:14	and we will talk together face to face.	8
	1:14	and we will talk together face to face.	8
Rev	1:16	face was like the sun shining with full force.	5
	4: 7	the third living creature with a face like a human	7
	4: 7	third living creature with a face like a human face	1
	6:16	and hide us from the face of the one seated	7
	7:11	they fell on their faces before the throne	7
	9: 7	their faces were like human faces	7
	9: 7	their faces were like human faces	7
	10: 1	his face was like the sun, and his legs like	7
	11:16	elders…fell on their faces and worshiped God	7
	22: 4	they will see his face	7

face to face

1. κατά + πρόσωπον, *kata + prosōpon, 2848 + 4725*
2. πρόσωπον, *prosōpon, 4725*
3. πρόσωπον + ἐν + σάρξ, *prosōpon + en + sarx, 4725 + 1877 + 4922*

Act	25:16	before the accused had met the accusers face to face	1
2Co	10: 1	who am humble when face to face with you	1
Col	2: 1	for all who have not seen me face to face.	3
1Th	2:17	we longed…to see you face to face.	2
	3:10	we may see you face to face	2

fact *See also* if in fact, in fact

1. Contextual: Not in Greek
2. ἀλήθεια, *alētheia, 237*
3. ἀσφαλής, *asphalēs, 855*

Lke	20:37	the fact that the dead are raised Moses…showed	1
Act	4:27	in this city, in fact, both Herod and Pontius Pilate	2
	21:34	as he could not learn the facts	3
Heb	11:19	He considered the fact that God is able even to raise	1
2Pe	3: 5	They deliberately ignore this fact	1
	3: 8	do not ignore this one fact, beloved	1

faction

1. αἵρεσις, *hairesis, 146*

1Co	11:19	Indeed, there have to be factions among you	1
Gal	5:20	anger, quarrels, dissensions, factions	1

circumcision faction

1. περιτομή, *peritomē, 4364*

Gal	2:12	for fear of the circumcision faction.	1

faculty

1. αἰσθητήριον, *aisthētērion, 152*

Heb	5:14	faculties have been trained by practice	1

never fades away

1. ἀμαράντινος, *amarantinos, 277*

1Pe	5: 4	you will win the crown of glory that never fades away.	1

fail

1. ἀδόκιμος, *adokimos, 99*
2. ἀσθένημα, *asthenēma, 821*
3. ἐκλείπω, *ekleipō, 1722*
4. ἐκπίπτω, *ekpiptō, 1738*
5. ἐπιλείπω, *epileipō, 2142*
6. καταλύω, *katalyō, 2907*
7. μή, *mē, 3590*

8. οὐ, *ou*, 4024
9. πταίω, *ptaiō*, 4760

Mat 16:11 How could you fail to perceive   8
Mrk 8:18 Do you have eyes, and fail to see?   8
      8:18 Do you have ears, and fail to hear?   8
Lke 22:32 prayed for you that your own faith may not fail;   3
     23:45 while the sun's light failed;   3
Act 5:38 if this plan…is of human origin, it will fail;   6
Rom 9: 6 It is not as though the word of God had failed.   4
     11: 7 Israel failed to obtain what it was seeking.   8
     15: 1 ought to put up with the failings of the weak   2
2Co 13: 6 I hope you will find out that we have not failed.   1
     13: 7 though we may seem to have failed.   1
Heb 4: 6 failed to enter because of disobedience   8
     11:32 time would fail me to tell of Gideon, Barak,   5
Jas 2:10 whoever…fails in one point has become accountable   9
      4:17 knows the right thing to do and fails to do it   7

fail to meet the test

1. ἀδόκιμος, *adokimos*, 99

2Co 13: 5 unless, indeed, you fail to meet the test!   1

fail to obtain

1. ὑστερέω, *hystereō*, 5728

Heb 12:15 no one fails to obtain the grace of God;   1

fail to reach

1. ὑστερέω, *hystereō*, 5728

Heb 4: 1 that none…should seem to have failed to reach it.   1

fail to understand

1. ἀσύνετος, *asynetos*, 852

Mrk 7:18 "Then do you also fail to understand?   1

faint

1. ἀποψύχω, *apopsychō*, 715
2. ἐκλύω, *eklyō*, 1725

Mat 15:32 for they might faint on the way."   2
Mrk 8: 3 they will faint on the way   2
Lke 21:26 People will faint from fear and foreboding   1

fainthearted

1. ὀλιγόψυχος, *oligopsychos*, 3901

1Th 5:14 encourage the fainthearted, help the weak   1

fair *See also* fair *balance,* fair *weather*

1. καλός, *kalos*, 2819

Mat 15:26 "It is not fair to take the children's food   1
Mrk 7:27 for it is not fair to take the children's food   1

Fair Havens

1. Καλοὶ λιμένες, *Kaloi limenes*, 2816

Act 27: 8 we came to a place called Fair Havens   1

fairly

1. ἰσότης, *isotēs*, 2699

Col 4: 1 Masters, treat your slaves justly and fairly   1

faith

1. Contextual: Not in Greek
2. αὐτός, *autos*, 899
3. οὗτος, *houtos*, 4047
4. πιστεύω, *pisteuō*, 4409
5. πίστις, *pistis*, 4411

Mat 8:10 in no one in Israel have I found such faith.   5
      8:13 let it be done for you according to your faith."   4
      9: 2 When Jesus saw their faith, he said   5
      9:22 "Take heart…your faith has made you well."   5
      9:29 "According to your faith let it be done to you."   5
     15:28 Jesus answered her, "Woman, great is your faith!   5
     17:20 if you have faith the size of a mustard seed   5
     21:21 if you have faith and do not doubt   5
     21:22 ask for in prayer with faith, you will receive."   4
     23:23 justice and mercy and faith.   5
Mrk 2: 5 When Jesus saw their faith   5
      4:40 "Why are you afraid? Have you still no faith?"   5
      5:34 "Daughter, your faith has made you well;   5
     10:52 "Go; your faith has made you well."   5

11:22 Jesus answered them, "Have faith in God.   5
Lke 5:20 When he saw their faith, he said   5
      7: 9 not even in Israel have I found such faith."   5
      7:50 "Your faith has saved you; go in peace."   5
      8:25 He said to them, "Where is your faith?"   5
      8:48 "Daughter, your faith has made you well;   5
     17: 5 The apostles said to the Lord, "Increase our faith!"   5
     17: 6 "If you had faith the size of a mustard seed   5
     17:19 go on your way; your faith has made you well."   5
     18: 8 will he find faith on earth?"   5
     18:42 "Receive your sight; your faith has saved you."   5
     22:32 prayed for you that your own faith may not fail;   5
Act 3:16 by faith in his name   5
      3:16 the faith that is through Jesus   5
      6: 5 Stephen, a man full of faith and the Holy Spirit   5
      6: 7 the priests became obedient to the faith.   5
     11:24 a good man, full of the Holy Spirit and of faith.   5
     13: 8 to turn the proconsul away from the faith.   5
     14: 9 and seeing that he had faith to be healed   5
     14:22 encouraged them to continue in the faith   5
     14:27 how he had opened a door of faith for the Gentiles.   5
     15: 9 cleansing their hearts by faith   5
     16: 5 So the churches were strengthened in the faith   5
     20:21 faith toward our Lord Jesus   5
     24:24 heard him speak concerning faith in Christ Jesus.   5
     26:18 among those who are sanctified by faith in me.'   5
     27:25 I have faith in God   4
Rom 1: 5 to bring about the obedience of faith   5
      1: 8 your faith is proclaimed throughout the world.   5
      1:12 mutually encouraged by each other's faith   5
      1:16 for salvation to everyone who has faith   4
      1:17 revealed through faith for faith;   5
      1:17 revealed through faith for faith;   5
      1:17 "The one who is righteous will live by faith."   5
      3:22 the righteousness of God through faith in Jesus   5
      3:25 atonement by his blood, effective through faith.   5
      3:26 that he justifies the one who has faith in Jesus.   5
      3:27 No, but by the law of faith.   5
      3:28 a person is justified by faith apart from works   5
      3:30 the circumcised on the ground of faith   5
      3:30 and the uncircumcised through that same faith.   5
      3:31 Do we then overthrow the law by this faith?   5
      4: 5 such faith is reckoned as righteousness.   5
      4: 9 "Faith was reckoned to Abraham as righteousness."   5
      4:11 righteousness that he had by faith   5
      4:12 the faith that our ancestor Abraham had   5
      4:13 but through the righteousness of faith.   5
      4:14 faith is null and the promise is void.   5
      4:16 For this reason it depends on faith   5
      4:16 but also to those who share the faith of Abraham   5
      4:19 He did not weaken in faith   5
      4:20 but he grew strong in his faith as he gave glory   5
      4:22 his faith "was reckoned to him as righteousness."   1
      5: 1 since we are justified by faith, we have peace   5
      9:30 attained it…righteousness through faith;   5
      9:32 they did not strive for it on the basis of faith   5
     10: 6 But the righteousness that comes from faith says   5
     10: 8 (that is, the word of faith that we proclaim);   5
     10:17 So faith comes from what is heard   5
     11:20 but you stand only through faith.   5
     12: 3 the measure of faith that God has assigned.   5
     12: 6 prophecy, in proportion to faith;   5
     14: 1 Welcome those who are weak in faith   5
     14:22 The faith…have as your own conviction before God.   5
     14:23 because they do not act from faith;   5
     14:23 for whatever does not proceed from faith is sin.   5
     16:26 to bring about the obedience of faith—   5
1Co 2: 5 your faith might rest not on human wisdom   5
     12: 9 to another faith by the same Spirit   5
     13: 2 if I have all faith, so as to remove mountains   5
     13:13 And now faith, hope, and love abide, these three;   5
     15:14 and your faith has been in vain.   5
     15:17 your faith is futile   5
     16:13 Keep alert, stand firm in your faith   5
2Co 1:24 not mean to imply that we lord it over your faith;   5
      1:24 because you stand firm in the faith.   5
      4:13 spirit of faith that is in accordance with scripture   5
      5: 7 for we walk by faith, not by sight.   5
      8: 7 in faith, in speech, in knowledge   5
     10:15 our hope is that, as your faith increases   5
     13: 5 to see whether you are living in the faith.   5

Gal	1:23	proclaiming the faith he once tried to destroy."	5
	2:16	through faith in Jesus Christ.	5
	2:16	so that we might be justified by faith in Christ	5
	2:20	the life I now live in the flesh I live by faith	5
	3: 8	God would justify the Gentiles by faith	5
	3:11	"The one who is righteous will live by faith."	5
	3:12	the law does not rest on faith:	5
	3:14	receive the promise of the Spirit through faith.	5
	3:22	what was promised through faith in Jesus Christ	5
	3:23	Now before faith came	5
	3:23	until faith would be revealed.	5
	3:24	so that we might be justified by faith.	5
	3:25	now that faith has come	5
	3:26	you are all children of God through faith.	5
	5: 5	For through the Spirit, by faith, we eagerly wait	5
	5: 6	faith working through love.	5
	6:10	for those of the family of faith.	5
Eph	1:15	have heard of your faith in the Lord Jesus	5
	2: 8	For by grace you have been saved through faith	5
	3:12	access to God in boldness and confidence through faith	5
	3:17	Christ may dwell in your hearts through faith	5
	4: 5	one Lord, one faith, one baptism	5
	4:13	until all of us come to the unity of the faith	5
	6:16	With all of these, take the shield of faith	5
	6:23	Peace be to the whole community, and love with faith	5
Php	1:25	for your progress and joy in faith	5
	1:27	striving...with one mind for the faith of the gospel	5
	2:17	over the sacrifice and the offering of your faith	5
	3: 9	righteousness...that comes through faith in Christ	5
	3: 9	the righteousness from God based on faith.	5
Col	1: 4	we have heard of your faith in Christ Jesus	5
	1:23	securely established and steadfast in the faith	5
	2: 5	the firmness of your faith in Christ.	5
	2: 7	built up in him and established in the faith	5
	2:12	through faith in the power of God	5
1Th	1: 3	work of faith and labor of love	5
	1: 8	in every place your faith in God has become known	5
	3: 2	and encourage you for the sake of your faith	5
	3: 5	I sent to find out about your faith;	5
	3: 6	good news of your faith and love.	5
	3: 7	encouraged about you through your faith.	5
	3:10	restore whatever is lacking in your faith.	5
	5: 8	put on the breastplate of faith and love	5
2Th	1: 3	because your faith is growing abundantly	5
	1: 4	for your steadfastness and faith	5
	1:11	fulfill...every good resolve and work of faith	5
	3: 2	for not all have faith.	5
1Ti	1: 2	To Timothy, my loyal child in the faith:	5
	1: 4	rather than the divine training that is known by faith.	5
	1: 5	a good conscience, and sincere faith.	5
	1:14	the faith and love that are in Christ Jesus.	5
	1:19	having faith and a good conscience.	5
	1:19	persons have suffered shipwreck in the faith	5
	2: 7	a teacher of the Gentiles in faith and truth.	5
	2:15	they continue in faith and love and holiness	5
	3: 9	they must hold fast to the mystery of the faith	5
	3:13	great boldness in the faith that is in Christ	5
	4: 1	in later times some will renounce the faith	5
	4: 6	nourished on the words of the faith	5
	4:12	an example in speech and conduct, in love, in faith	5
	5: 8	has denied the faith and is worse than	5
	6:10	some have wandered away from the faith	5
	6:11	pursue righteousness, godliness, faith, love	5
	6:12	Fight the good fight of the faith;	5
	6:21	some have missed the mark as regards the faith.	5
2Ti	1: 5	I am reminded of your sincere faith	5
	1: 5	a faith that lived first in your grandmother	1
	1:13	in the faith and love that are in Christ Jesus.	5
	2:18	They are upsetting the faith of some.	5
	2:22	pursue righteousness, faith, love, and peace	5
	3: 8	people, of corrupt mind and counterfeit faith	5
	3:10	my aim in life, my faith, my patience, my love	5
	3:15	salvation through faith in Christ Jesus.	5
	4: 7	I have finished the race, I have kept the faith.	5
Tit	1: 1	for the sake of the faith of God's elect	5
	1: 4	To Titus, my loyal child in the faith we share:	5
	1:13	so that they may become sound in the faith	5
	2: 2	sound in faith, in love, and in endurance.	5
	3:15	Greet those who love us in the faith.	5
Phm	1: 5	your faith toward the Lord Jesus.	5
	1: 6	the sharing of your faith	5

Heb	4: 2	they were not united by faith with those who listened.	5
	6: 1	the foundation:...faith toward God	5
	6:12	through faith and patience inherit the promises	5
	10:22	approach...in full assurance of faith	5
	10:38	my righteous one will live by faith.	5
	10:39	those who have faith and so are saved.	5
	11: 1	Now faith is the assurance of things hoped for	5
	11: 2	by faith our ancestors received approval.	3
	11: 3	By faith we understand...	5
	11: 4	By faith...a more acceptable sacrifice	5
	11: 4	through his faith he still speaks.	2
	11: 5	By faith Enoch was taken	5
	11: 6	without faith it is impossible to please God	5
	11: 7	By faith Noah...respected the warning	5
	11: 7	righteousness that is in accordance with faith.	5
	11: 8	By faith Abraham obeyed	5
	11: 9	By faith he stayed for a time in the land	5
	11:11	By faith he received power of procreation	5
	11:13	All of these died in faith	5
	11:17	By faith Abraham...offered up Isaac.	5
	11:20	By faith Isaac invoked blessings for the future	5
	11:21	By faith Jacob...blessed...the sons of Joseph	5
	11:22	By faith Joseph...made mention of the exodus	5
	11:23	By faith Moses was hidden by his parents	5
	11:24	By faith Moses...refused to be called a son	5
	11:27	By faith he left Egypt	5
	11:28	By faith he kept the Passover	5
	11:29	By faith the people passed through the Red Sea	5
	11:30	By faith the walls of Jericho fell	5
	11:31	By faith Rahab the prostitute did not perish	5
	11:33	who through faith conquered kingdoms	5
	11:39	though they were commended for their faith	5
	12: 2	Jesus the pioneer and perfecter of our faith	5
	13: 7	imitate their faith.	5
Jas	1: 3	testing of your faith produces endurance;	5
	1: 6	But ask in faith, never doubting	5
	2: 5	be rich in faith and to be heirs of the kingdom	5
	2:14	if you say you have faith but do not have works?	5
	2:14	but do not have works? Can faith save you?	5
	2:17	So faith by itself, if it has no works, is dead.	5
	2:18	someone will say, "You have faith and I have works."	5
	2:18	Show me your faith apart from your works	5
	2:18	and I by my works will show you my faith.	5
	2:20	that faith apart from works is barren?	5
	2:22	You see that faith was active...with his works	5
	2:22	and faith was brought to completion by the works.	5
	2:24	justified by works and not by faith alone.	5
	2:26	so faith without works is also dead.	5
	5:15	The prayer of faith will save the sick	5
1Pe	1: 5	being protected by the power of God through faith	5
	1: 7	the genuineness of your faith...may be found	5
	1: 9	you are receiving the outcome of your faith	5
	1:21	so that your faith and hope are set on God.	5
	5: 9	Resist him, steadfast in your faith	5
2Pe	1: 1	received a faith as precious as ours	5
	1: 5	to support your faith with goodness	5
1Jn	5: 4	the victory that conquers the world, our faith.	5
Jde	1: 3	appeal to you to contend for the faith	5
	1:20	build yourselves up on your most holy faith;	5
Rev	2:13	and you did not deny your faith in me	5
	2:19	"I know your works—your love, faith, service,	5
	13:10	a call for the endurance and faith of the saints.	5
	14:12	and hold fast to the faith of Jesus.	5

lack of faith

1. ἀπιστία, *apistia, 602*

Mrk	16:14	⟦he upbraided them for their lack of faith⟧	1

little faith

1. ὀλιγοπιστία, *oligopistia, 3898*
2. ὀλιγόπιστος, *oligopistos, 3899*

Mat	6:30	not much more clothe you—you of little faith?	2
	8:26	"Why are you afraid, you of little faith?"	2
	14:31	"You of little faith, why did you doubt?"	2
	16: 8	"You of little faith, why are you talking	2
	17:20	He said to them, "Because of your little faith.	1
Lke	12:28	will he clothe you—you of little faith!	2

faithful   *See also* remain faithful

1. Contextual: Not in Greek

2. πιστός, *pistos*, 4412

Mat	24:45	"Who then is the faithful and wise slave	2
Lke	12:42	"Who then is the faithful and prudent manager	2
	16:10	"Whoever is faithful in a very little	2
	16:10	is faithful also in much;	2
	16:11	not been faithful with the dishonest wealth	2
	16:12	if you have not been faithful	2
Act	16:15	"If you have judged me to be faithful to the Lord	2
1Co	1: 9	God is faithful; by him you were called	2
	4:17	my beloved and faithful child in the Lord	2
	10:13	God is faithful, and he will not let you be tested	2
2Co	1:18	As surely as God is faithful	2
Eph	1: 1	the saints who are…faithful in Christ Jesus:	2
	6:21	Tychicus…a dear brother and a faithful minister	2
Col	1: 2	To the saints and faithful brothers and sisters	2
	1: 7	He is a faithful minister of Christ on your behalf	2
	4: 7	he is a beloved brother, a faithful minister	2
	4: 9	Onesimus, the faithful and beloved brother	2
1Th	5:24	who calls you is faithful, and he will do this.	2
2Th	3: 3	the Lord is faithful;	2
1Ti	1:12	because he judged me faithful	2
	3:11	temperate, faithful in all things.	2
2Ti	2: 2	what you have heard…entrust to faithful people	2
	2:13	if we are faithless, he remains faithful	2
Heb	2:17	might be a merciful and faithful high priest	2
	3: 2	was faithful to the one who appointed him	2
	3: 2	just as Moses also "was faithful in all God's house."	1
	3: 5	Now Moses was faithful in all God's house	2
	3: 6	Christ, however, was faithful over God's house as a son	1
	10:23	for he who has promised is faithful.	2
	11:11	he considered him faithful who had promised	2
1Pe	4:19	entrust themselves to a faithful Creator	2
	5:12	Silvanus, whom I consider a faithful brother,	2
1Jn	1: 9	he who is faithful and just will forgive us our sins	2
3Jn	1: 5	Beloved, you do faithfully	2
Rev	1: 5	and from Jesus Christ, the faithful witness	2
	2:10	Be faithful until death	2
	3:14	words of the Amen, the faithful and true witness	2
	17:14	those with him are called and chosen and faithful."	2
	19:11	Its rider is called Faithful and True	2

faithful one

1. πιστός, *pistos*, 4412

Rev	2:13	the days of Antipas my witness, my faithful one	1

faithfulness

1. Contextual: Not in Greek

2. πίστις, *pistis*, 4411

Rom	3: 3	Will their faithlessness nullify the faithfulness	2
Gal	5:22	patience, kindness, generosity, faithfulness	2
3Jn	1: 3	testified to your faithfulness to the truth	1

faithless

1. ἀπιστέω, *apisteō*, 601

2. ἄπιστος, *apistos*, 603

3. ἀσύνθετος, *asynthetos*, 853

Mat	17:17	"You faithless and perverse generation	2
Mrk	9:19	He answered them, "You faithless generation	2
Lke	9:41	"You faithless and perverse generation	2
Rom	1:31	foolish, faithless, heartless, ruthless.	3
2Ti	2:13	if we are faithless, he remains faithful	1
Rev	21: 8	as for the cowardly, the faithless, the polluted	2

faithlessness

1. ἀπιστία, *apistia*, 602

Rom	3: 3	Will their faithlessness nullify the faithfulness	1

fall

1. ἀποπίπτω, *apopiptō*, 674
2. ἄπταιστος, *aptaistos*, 720
3. βρέχω, *brechō*, 1101
4. γίνομαι, *ginomai*, 1181
5. ἐκπίπτω, *ekpiptō*, 1738
6. ἐμπίπτω, *empiptō*, 1860
7. ἐπιπίπτω, *epipiptō*, 2158
8. ἔρχομαι, *erchomai*, 2262
9. καταβαίνω, *katabainō*, 2849
10. καταπίπτω, *katapiptō*, 2928
11. πίπτω, *piptō*, 4406

12. πτῶσις, *ptōsis*, 4774
13. συμπίπτω, *sympiptō*, 5229

Mat	7:25	rain fell, the floods came, and the winds blew	9
	7:25	it did not fall, because it had been founded	11
	7:27	rain fell, and the floods came, and the winds	9
	7:27	and it fell—and great was its fall!"	11
	7:27	and it fell—and great was its fall!"	12
	10:29	Yet not one of them will fall to the ground	11
	13: 4	as he sowed, some seeds fell on the path	11
	13: 5	Other seeds fell on rocky ground	11
	13: 7	Other seeds fell among thorns	11
	13: 8	Other seeds fell on good soil	11
	15:14	both will fall into a pit."	11
	15:27	crumbs that fall from their masters' table."	11
	17: 6	they fell to the ground	11
	17:15	he often falls into the fire	11
	18:26	So the slave fell on his knees before him	11
	21:44	The one who falls on this stone	11
	21:44	it will crush anyone on whom it falls	11
	24:29	the stars will fall from heaven	11
Mrk	4: 4	as he sowed, some seed fell on the path	11
	4: 5	Other seed fell on rocky ground	11
	4: 7	Other seed fell among thorns	11
	4: 8	Other seed fell into good soil	11
	5:22	he saw him, fell at his feet	11
	9:20	he fell on the ground and rolled about	11
	13:25	the stars will be falling from heaven	11
Lke	2:34	destined for the falling and the rising of many	12
	6:49	immediately it fell	13
	8: 5	as he sowed, some fell on the path	11
	8: 6	Some fell on the rock;	10
	8: 7	Some fell among thorns	11
	8: 8	Some fell into good soil, and when it grew	11
	8:14	As for what fell among the thorns	11
	8:41	fell at Jesus' feet and begged him to come	11
	10:18	Satan fall from heaven like a flash of lightning.	11
	11:17	becomes a desert, and house falls on house.	11
	13: 4	killed when the tower of Siloam fell on them	11
	14: 5	a child or an ox that has fallen into a well	11
	16:21	with what fell from the rich man's table;	11
	20:18	Everyone who falls on that stone	11
	20:18	it will crush anyone on whom it falls."	11
	21:24	they will fall by the edge of the sword	11
	23:30	begin to say to the mountains, 'Fall on us';	11
Jhn	12:24	a grain of wheat falls into the earth and dies	11
	18: 6	they stepped back and fell to the ground.	11
Act	1:18	falling headlong, he burst open in the middle	4
	1:26	the lot fell on Matthias;	11
	9: 4	He fell to the ground and heard a voice saying	11
	9:18	something like scales fell from his eyes	1
	10:25	and falling at his feet, worshiped him.	11
	15:16	rebuild the dwelling of David, which has fallen;	11
	20: 9	he fell to the ground three floors below	11
	22: 7	I fell to the ground and heard a voice saying	11
	22:17	praying in the temple, I fell into a trance	4
	26:14	When we had all fallen to the ground	10
Rom	11:11	have they stumbled so as to fall? By no means!	11
	11:22	severity toward those who have fallen	11
	14: 4	before their own lord that they stand or fall.	11
	15: 3	"The insults…have fallen on me."	7
1Co	10: 8	twenty-three thousand fell in a single day.	11
	10:12	watch out that you do not fall.	11
1Ti	3: 6	fall into the condemnation of the devil.	6
	6: 9	those who want to be rich fall into temptation	6
Heb	3:17	who sinned, whose bodies fell in the wilderness?	11
	4:11	so that no one may fall through such disobedience	11
	6: 7	that drinks up the rain falling on it repeatedly	8
	11:30	By faith the walls of Jericho fell	11
Jas	1:11	its flower falls, and its beauty perishes.	5
	5:12	so that you may not fall under condemnation.	11
1Pe	1:24	The grass withers, and the flower falls	5
Jde	1:24	Now to him who is able to keep you from falling	2
Rev	1:17	When I saw him, I fell at his feet as though dead.	11
	2: 5	Remember then from what you have fallen;	11
	4:10	the twenty-four elders fall…and worship	11
	5: 8	the twenty-four elders fell before the Lamb	11
	6:13	the stars of the sky fell to the earth	11
	6:16	"Fall on us and hide us from the face of the one	11
	7:11	they fell on their faces before the throne	11
	8:10	great star fell from heaven, blazing like a torch	11
	8:10	star fell…and it fell on a third of the rivers	11

Rev 9: 1 I saw a star that had fallen from heaven to earth   11
     11: 6 shut the sky, so that no rain may fall during the days   3
     11:13 great earthquake, and a tenth of the city fell;   11
     11:16 elders...fell on their faces and worshiped God   11
     14: 8 "Fallen, fallen is Babylon the great!   11
     14: 8 "Fallen, fallen is Babylon the great!   11
     16:19 and the cities of the nations fell.   11
     17:10 of whom five have fallen, one is living,   11
     18: 2 "Fallen, fallen is Babylon the great!   11
     18: 2 "Fallen, fallen is Babylon the great!   11

cause to fall

1. σκανδαλίζω, *skandalizō, 4997*

1Co 8:13 Therefore, if food is a cause of their falling   1
     8:13 so that I may not cause one of them to fall.   1

fall asleep

1. ἀφυπνόω, *aphypnoō, 934*
2. καθεύδω, *katheudō, 2761*
3. κοιμάω, *koimaō, 3121*

Mat 27:52 saints who had fallen asleep were raised.   3
Lke   8:23 while they were sailing he fell asleep.   1
Jhn 11:11 "Our friend Lazarus has fallen asleep   3
     11:12 if he has fallen asleep, he will be all right."   3
1Th   5: 6 So then let us not fall asleep as others do   2

fall away

1. ἀφίστημι, *aphistēmi, 923*
2. ἐκπίπτω, *ekpiptō, 1738*
3. παραπίπτω, *parapiptō, 4178*
4. σκανδαλίζω, *skandalizō, 4997*

Mat 13:21 persecution arises...person immediately falls away.   4
     24:10 Then many will fall away, and they will betray   4
Mrk   4:17 immediately they fall away.   4
Lke   8:13 and in a time of testing fall away.   1
Gal   5: 4 you have fallen away from grace.   2
Heb   6: 6 and then have fallen away   3

fall back

1. πάλιν, *palin, 4099*

Rom 8:15 a spirit of slavery to fall back into fear   1

fall down

1. καταβαίνω, *katabainō, 2849*
2. πίπτω, *piptō, 4406*
3. προσπίπτω, *prospiptō, 4700*

Mat   4: 9 you, if you will fall down and worship me."   2
     18:29 Then his fellow slave fell down and pleaded   2
Lke   5: 8 he fell down at Jesus' knees, saying   3
     22:44 ⟦great drops of blood falling down on the ground.⟧   1
Act   5: 5 he fell down and died.   2
     5:10 Immediately she fell down at his feet and died.   2
Rev   5:14 And the elders fell down and worshiped.   2
     19: 4 living creatures fell down and worshiped God   2
     19:10 Then I fell down at his feet to worship him   2
     22: 8 I fell down to worship at the feet of the angel   2

fall down before

1. προσπίπτω, *prospiptō, 4700*

Mrk   3:11 they fell down before him and shouted   1
     5:33 But the woman...fell down before him   1
Lke   8:28 he fell down before him and shouted   1
     8:47 and falling down before him, she declared   1
Act 16:29 he fell down trembling before Paul and Silas.   1

fall from heaven

1. διοπετής, *diopetēs, 1479*

Act 19:35 and of the statue that fell from heaven?   1

fall into

1. γίνομαι, *ginomai, 1181*
2. ἐμπίπτω, *empiptō, 1860*
3. περιπίπτω, *peripiptō, 4346*

Mat 12:11 it falls into a pit on the sabbath;   2
Lke   6:39 Will not both fall into a pit?   2
     10:30 fell into the hands of robbers   3
     10:36 who fell into the hands of the robbers?"   2
Act 10:10 while it was being prepared, he fell into a trance.   1
1Ti   3: 7 fall into disgrace and the snare of the devil.   2

Heb 10:31 to fall into the hands of the living God.   2

fall off

1. ἐκπίπτω, *ekpiptō, 1738*

Act 12: 7 the chains fell off his wrists.   1

fall on

1. ἐπισκιάζω, *episkiazō, 2173*

Act   5:15 shadow might fall on some of them as he came by.   1

fall short

1. ὑστερέω, *hystereō, 5728*

Rom 3:23 all have sinned and fall short of the glory of God;   1

fall upon

1. ἐπιπίπτω, *epipiptō, 2158*

Act 10:44 the Holy Spirit fell upon all who heard the word.   1
     11:15 as I began to speak, the Holy Spirit fell upon them   1

make fall

1. πρόσκομμα, *proskomma, 4682*
2. σκάνδαλον, *skandalon, 4998*

Rom 9:33 make people stumble, a rock that will make them fall   2
     14:20 but it is wrong for you to make others fall   1
1Pe   2: 8 a rock that makes them fall."   2

false

false *See also* bear false witness, false *accusation*, false *apostle*, false *believer*, false *brother and sister*, false *messiah*, false *motive*, false *prophet*, false *teacher*, false *testimony*, false *witness*, give false testimony, prove false

1. ἀδικία, *adikia, 94*
2. πονηρός, *ponēros, 4505*
3. ψευδής, *pseudēs, 6014*
4. ψεύδομαι, *pseudomai, 6017*
5. ψεῦδος, *pseudos, 6022*

Jhn   7:18 there is nothing false in him.   1
Act   6:13 They set up false witnesses who said   3
2Th   2:11 leading them to believe what is false   5
Jas   3:14 do not be boastful and false to the truth.   4
3Jn   1:10 he is...spreading false charges against us.   2
Rev   2: 2 tested those...and have found them to be false.   3

falsehood

1. ψεῦδος, *pseudos, 6022*
2. ψεῦσμα, *pseusma, 6025*

Rom 3: 7 But if through my falsehood God's truthfulness   2
Eph   4:25 So then, putting away falsehood   1
Rev 21:27 anyone who practices abomination or falsehood   1
     22:15 everyone who loves and practices falsehood.   1

falsely

falsely *See also* call falsely, swear falsely

1. ψεύδομαι, *pseudomai, 6017*

Mat   5:11 evil against you falsely on my account.   1

falsify

1. δολόω, *doloō, 1516*

2Co   4: 2 practice cunning or to falsify God's word;   1

fame

1. ἀκοή, *akoē, 198*

Mat   4:24 So his fame spread throughout all Syria   1
Mrk   1:28 At once his fame began to spread   1

familiar

1. γνώστης, *gnōstēs, 1195*

Act 26: 3 you are especially familiar with all the customs   1

family

family *See also* family *inheritance*, family *member*, member of a family, member of God's family

1. ἀδελφός, *adelphos, 81*
2. γένος, *genos, 1169*
3. ὁ, *ho, 3836*
4. οἰκεῖος, *oikeios, 3858*
5. οἶκος, *oikos, 3875*
6. παρά, *para, 4123*
7. πατριά, *patria, 4255*

Mrk   3:21 When his family heard it   6

Lke	2: 4	descended from the house and family of David.	7
Act	3:25	all the families of the earth shall be blessed.'	7
	4: 6	and all who were of the high-priestly family.	2
	7:13	Joseph's family became known to Pharaoh.	2
	13:26	brothers, you descendants of Abraham's family	2
	16:33	he and his entire family were baptized without delay.	3
Rom	8:29	he might be the firstborn within a large family.	1
	16:10	those who belong to the family of Aristobulus.	3
	16:11	those…who belong to the family of Narcissus.	3
Gal	6:10	for those of the family of faith.	4
Eph	3:15	every family in heaven and on earth takes its name.	7
1Ti	5: 4	learn their religious duty to their own family	5
Tit	1:11	since they are upsetting whole families	5

family of believers

1. ἀδελφότης, *adelphotēs, 82*

1Pe	2:17	Honor everyone. Love the family of believers.	1

famine

1. λιμός, *limos, 3350*

Mat	24: 7	there will be famines and earthquakes	1
Mrk	13: 8	there will be famines.	1
Lke	4:25	there was a severe famine over all the land;	1
	15:14	a severe famine took place throughout that country	1
	21:11	in various places famines and plagues;	1
Act	7:11	came a famine throughout Egypt and Canaan	1
	11:28	there would be a severe famine over all the world;	1
Rom	8:35	or famine, or nakedness, or peril, or sword?	1
Rev	6: 8	authority…to kill with sword, famine, and pestilence,	1
	18: 8	plagues…pestilence and mourning and famine	1

famish

1. πεινάω, *peinaō, 4277*

Mat	4: 2	and forty nights, and afterwards he was famished.	1
Lke	4: 2	when they were over, he was famished.	1

famous

1. ἔπαινος, *epainos, 2047*

2Co	8:18	the brother who is famous among all the churches	1

far   *See also* far *above*, far *away*, go far, thus far, further

1. Contextual: Not in Greek
2. ἀπέχω, *apechō, 600*
3. ἄχρι, *achri, 948*
4. ἕως, *heōs, 2401*
5. μακράν, *makran, 3426*
6. μέχρι, *mechri, 3588*
7. πολύς + μᾶλλον, *polys + mallon, 4498 + 3437*
8. πόρρω, *porrō, 4522*
9. στάδιον + πολύς, *stadion + polys, 5084 + 4498*

Mat	14:24	the boat…was far from the land	9
	15: 8	but their hearts are far from me;	8
	24:27	lightning…flashes as far as the west	4
	26:58	as far as the courtyard of the high priest;	4
Mrk	7: 6	their hearts are far from me;	8
	12:34	"You are not far from the kingdom of God."	5
Lke	7: 6	when he was not far from the house	5
	15:20	while he was still far off,	2
	24:50	Then he led them out as far as Bethany	4
Jhn	21: 8	for they were not far from the land	5
Act	11:19	traveled as far as Phoenicia, Cyprus, and Antioch	4
	13: 6	had gone through the whole island as far as Paphos	3
	17:15	who conducted Paul brought him as far as Athens;	4
	17:27	though indeed he is not far from each one of us.	5
	22:21	I will send you far away to the Gentiles.' "	5
	28:15	as far as the Forum of Appius and Three Taverns	3
Rom	12:18	so far as it depends on you, live peaceably	1
	15:19	from Jerusalem and as far around as Illyricum	6
2Co	10:13	to reach out even as far as you.	3
Php	1:23	that is far better;	7

any further

1. ἔτι, *eti, 2285*

Mrk	5:35	Why trouble the teacher any further?"	1

far more

1. Contextual: Not in Greek
2. περισσοτέρως, *perissoterōs, 4359*

2Co	11:23	with far greater labors, far more imprisonments	2

Gal	1:14	for I was far more zealous for the traditions	2
Eph	3:20	is able to accomplish abundantly far more	1

far off

1. ἀπό + μακρόθεν, *apo + makrothen, 608 + 3427*
2. μακράν, *makran, 3426*
3. μακρόθεν, *makrothen, 3427*

Lke	15:20	while he was still far off,	2
	18:13	the tax collector, standing far off	3
Act	2:39	the promise is…for all who are far away	2
Eph	2:13	you who once were far off	2
	2:17	he came and proclaimed peace to you who were far off	2
Rev	18:10	they will stand far off, in fear of her torment	1
	18:15	merchants of these wares…will stand far off	1
	18:17	all whose trade is on the sea, stood far off	1

fare

1. γίνομαι, *ginomai, 1181*

Rom	9:29	we would have fared like Sodom	1

farewell   *See also* say farewell

1. ῥώννυμι, *rhōnnymi, 4874*
2. χαίρω, *chairō, 5897*

Act	15:29	you will do well. Farewell."	1
2Co	13:11	Finally, brothers and sisters, farewell.	2

farm

1. ἀγρός, *agros, 69*

Mat	22: 5	went away, one to his farm, another to his business	1
Mrk	6:56	he went, into villages or cities or farms	1

farmer

1. γεωργός, *geōrgos, 1177*

2Ti	2: 6	It is the farmer who does the work	1
Jas	5: 7	farmer waits for the precious crop from the earth	1

farther

1. διΐστημι, *diistēmi, 1460*

Act	27:28	a little farther on they took soundings again	1

fast   *See also* hold fast, stand fast

1. νηστεία, *nēsteia, 3763*
2. νηστεύω, *nēsteuō, 3764*

Mat	4: 2	He fasted forty days and forty nights	2
	6:16	whenever you fast, do not look dismal	2
	6:16	so as to show others that they are fasting.	2
	6:17	when you fast, put oil on your head and wash your face	2
	6:18	so that your fasting may be seen not by others	2
	9:14	"Why do we and the Pharisees fast often,	2
	9:14	Pharisees fast often, but your disciples do not fast?"	2
	9:15	and then they will fast.	2
Mrk	2:18	John's disciples and the Pharisees were fasting;	2
	2:18	the disciples of the Pharisees fast	2
	2:18	your disciples do not fast?"	2
	2:19	wedding guests cannot fast while the bridegroom	2
	2:19	bridegroom with them, they cannot fast.	2
	2:20	then they will fast on that day.	2
Lke	2:37	worshiped there with fasting and prayer	1
	5:33	"John's disciples…frequently fast and pray,	2
	5:34	"You cannot make wedding guests fast	2
	5:35	then they will fast in those days."	2
	18:12	I fast twice a week; I give a tenth of all	2
Act	13: 2	While they were worshiping the Lord and fasting	2
	13: 3	Then after fasting and praying	2
	14:23	with prayer and fasting they entrusted them	1
	27: 9	because even the Fast had already gone by	1

fasten

1. ἀσφαλίζω, *asphalizō, 856*
2. καθάπτω, *kathaptō, 2750*
3. κρεμάννυμι, *kremannymi, 3203*

Mat	18: 6	a great millstone were fastened around your neck	3
Act	16:24	fastened their feet in the stocks.	1
	28: 3	a viper…fastened itself on his hand.	2

fasten belt

1. ζώννυμι, *zōnnymi, 2439*
2. περιζώννυμι, *perizōnnymi, 4322*

Lke	12:37	he will fasten his belt and have them sit down	2

Jhn 21:18 were younger, you used to fasten your own belt   1
Act 12: 8 "Fasten your belt and put on your sandals."   1

fasten belt around

1. ζώννυμι, *zōnnymi, 2439*
2. περιζώννυμι, *perizōnnymi, 4322*

Jhn 21:18 someone else will fasten a belt around you   1
Eph 6:14 fasten the belt of truth around your waist   2

fat *See* fat *calf*

father *See also* kill one's father

1. Contextual: Not in Greek
2. γεννάω, *gennaō, 1164*
3. ἐκ, *ek, 1666*
4. ἐκεῖνος, *ekeinos, 1697*
5. ὁ, *ho, 3836*
6. πατήρ, *patēr, 4252*

Mat 1: 2 Abraham was the father of Isaac   2
     1: 2 and Isaac the father of Jacob   2
     1: 2 and Jacob the father of Judah   2
     1: 3 Judah the father of Perez and Zerah by Tamar   2
     1: 3 Perez the father of Hezron   2
     1: 3 and Hezron the father of Aram   2
     1: 4 Aram the father of Aminadab   2
     1: 4 Aminadab the father of Nahshon   2
     1: 4 and Nahshon the father of Salmon   2
     1: 5 Salmon the father of Boaz by Rahab   2
     1: 5 Boaz the father of Obed by Ruth   2
     1: 5 and Obed the father of Jesse   2
     1: 6 Jesse the father of King David.   2
     1: 6 David was the father of Solomon by the wife   2
     1: 7 Solomon the father of Rehoboam   2
     1: 7 and Rehoboam the father of Abijah   2
     1: 7 and Abijah the father of Asaph   2
     1: 8 Asaph the father of Jehoshaphat   2
     1: 8 and Jehoshaphat the father of Joram   2
     1: 8 and Joram the father of Uzziah   2
     1: 9 Uzziah the father of Jotham   2
     1: 9 and Jotham the father of Ahaz   2
     1: 9 and Ahaz the father of Hezekiah   2
     1:10 Hezekiah the father of Manasseh   2
     1:10 and Manasseh the father of Amos   2
     1:10 and Amos the father of Josiah   2
     1:11 Josiah the father of Jechoniah and his brothers   2
     1:12 Jechoniah was the father of Salathiel   2
     1:12 Salathiel the father of Zerubbabel   2
     1:13 Zerubbabel the father of Abiud   2
     1:13 and Abiud the father of Eliakim   2
     1:13 and Eliakim the father of Azor   2
     1:14 Azor the father of Zadok   2
     1:14 and Zadok the father of Achim   2
     1:14 and Achim the father of Eliud   2
     1:15 Eliud the father of Eleazar   2
     1:15 and Eleazar the father of Matthan   2
     1:15 Matthan, and Matthan the father of Jacob   2
     1:16 Jacob the father of Joseph the husband of Mary   2
     2:22 in place of his father Herod, he was afraid to go   6
     4:21 in the boat with their father Zebedee, mending   6
     4:22 the boat and their father, and followed him.   6
     5:16 give glory to your Father in heaven.   6
     5:45 be children of your Father in heaven;   6
     5:48 Be perfect...as your heavenly Father is perfect.   6
     6: 1 for then you have no reward from your Father   6
     6: 4 your Father who sees in secret will reward you.   6
     6: 6 shut the door and pray to your Father who is   6
     6: 6 your Father who sees in secret will reward you.   6
     6: 8 like them, for your Father knows what you need   6
     6: 9 "Pray then in this way: Our Father in heaven   6
     6:14 your heavenly Father will also forgive you;   6
     6:15 neither will your Father forgive your   6
     6:18 fasting may be seen not by others but by your Father   6
     6:18 Father who is in secret; and your Father who sees   6
     6:26 barns, and yet your heavenly Father feeds them.   6
     6:32 these things; and indeed your heavenly Father knows   6
     7:11 how much more will your Father in heaven   6
     7:21 the one who does the will of my Father in heaven.   6
     8:21 "Lord, first let me go and bury my father."   6
    10:20 the Spirit of your Father speaking through you.   6
    10:21 and a father his child   6

    10:29 fall to the ground apart from your Father.   6
    10:32 I also will acknowledge before my Father   6
    10:33 deny before my Father in heaven.   6
    10:35 For I have come to set a man against his father   6
    10:37 Whoever loves father or mother more than me   6
    11:25 "I thank you, Father, Lord of heaven and earth   6
    11:26 yes, Father, for such was your gracious will.   6
    11:27 All things have been handed over to me by my Father;   6
    11:27 and no one knows the Son except the Father   6
    11:27 and no one knows the Father except the Son   6
    12:50 For whoever does the will of my Father in heaven   6
    13:43 in the kingdom of their Father.   6
    15: 4 'Honor your father and your mother,'   6
    15: 4 'Whoever speaks evil of father or mother   6
    15: 5 you say that whoever tells father or mother   6
    15: 5 that person need not honor the father.   6
    15:13 that my heavenly Father has not planted   6
    16:17 but my Father in heaven.   6
    16:27 come with his angels in the glory of his Father   6
    18:10 the face of my Father in heaven.   6
    18:14 So it is not the will of your Father in heaven   6
    18:19 it will be done for you by my Father in heaven.   6
    18:35 So my heavenly Father will also do   6
    19: 5 'For this reason a man shall leave his father   6
    19:19 Honor your father and mother;   6
    19:29 brothers or sisters or father or mother   6
    20:23 for whom it has been prepared by my Father."   6
    21:30 father went to the second and said the same;   1
    21:31 Which of the two did the will of his father?"   6
    23: 9 call no one your father on earth   6
    23: 9 you have one Father—the one in heaven.   6
    24:36 but only the Father.   6
    25:34 'Come, you that are blessed by my Father   6
    26:29 new with you in my Father's kingdom."   6
    26:39 "My Father, if it is possible, let this cup   6
    26:42 "My Father, if this cannot pass unless I drink   6
    26:53 Do you think that I cannot appeal to my Father   6
    28:19 baptizing them in the name of the Father   6
Mrk 1:20 they left their father Zebedee in the boat   6
    5:40 and took the child's father and mother   6
    7:10 For Moses said, 'Honor your father and your mother';   6
    7:10 'Whoever speaks evil of father or mother   6
    7:11 you say that if anyone tells father or mother   6
    7:12 doing anything for a father or mother   6
    8:38 glory of his Father with the holy angels."   6
    9:21 Jesus asked the father, "How long has this been   6
    9:24 Immediately the father of the child cried out   6
   10: 7 a man shall leave his father and mother   6
   10:19 shall not defraud; Honor your father and mother.' "   6
   10:29 house or brothers or sisters or mother or father   6
   11:25 so that your Father in heaven may also   6
   13:12 a father his child   6
   13:32 nor the Son, but only the Father.   6
   14:36 "Abba, Father, for you all things are possible;   6
   15:21 the father of Alexander and Rufus.   6
Lke 1:59 going to name him Zechariah after his father.   6
    1:62 Then they began motioning to his father   6
    1:67 Then his father Zechariah was filled   6
    2:33 the child's father and mother were amazed   6
    2:48 Look, your father and I have been searching   6
    2:49 not know that I must be in my Father's house?"   6
    6:36 Be merciful, just as your Father is merciful.   6
    8:51 the child's father and mother.   6
    9:26 the glory of the Father and of the holy angels.   6
    9:42 healed the boy, and gave him back to his father.   6
    9:59 "Lord, first let me go and bury my father."   6
   10:21 "I thank you, Father, Lord of heaven and earth   6
   10:21 yes, Father, for such was your gracious will.   6
   10:22 no one knows who the Son is except the Father   6
   10:22 no one knows who the Son is except the Father   6
   10:22 who the Father is except the Son   6
   11: 2 He said to them, "When you pray, say: Father   6
   11:13 will the heavenly Father give the Holy Spirit   6
   12:30 your Father knows that you need them.   6
   12:32 it is your Father's good pleasure   6
   12:53 father against son and son against father   6
   12:53 father against son and son against father   6
   14:26 does not hate father and mother, wife   6
   15:12 The younger of them said to his father, 'Father   6
   15:12 The younger of them said to his father, 'Father   6
   15:17 'How many of my father's hired hands have bread   6

15:18	I will get up and go to my father	6
15:18	I will say to him, "Father, I have sinned	6
15:20	he set off and went to his father.	6
15:20	his father saw him and was filled with compassion;	6
15:21	the son said to him, 'Father, I have sinned	6
15:22	the father said to his slaves	6
15:27	your father has killed the fatted calf	6
15:28	His father came out and began to plead with him.	6
15:29	he answered his father, 'Listen! For all these	6
15:31	father said to him, 'Son, you are always with me	5
16:24	He called out, 'Father Abraham, have mercy	6
16:27	He said, 'Then, father, I beg you	6
16:27	I beg you to send him to my father's house	6
16:30	He said, 'No, father Abraham;' "	6
18:20	Honor your father and mother.' "	6
22:29	on you, just as my Father has conferred on me	6
22:42	"Father, if you are willing	6
23:34	[Jesus said, "Father, forgive them;]	6
23:46	Jesus, crying with a loud voice, said, "Father	6
24:49	I am sending upon you what my Father promised;	6
Jhn 1:14	glory as of a father's only son, full	6
1:18	the only Son, who is close to the Father's heart,	6
2:16	Stop making my Father's house a marketplace!"	6
3:35	The Father loves the Son and has placed all things	6
4:21	the hour is coming when you will worship the Father	6
4:23	will worship the Father in spirit and truth	6
4:23	the Father seeks such as these to worship him.	6
4:53	The father realized that this was the hour	6
5:17	Jesus answered them, "My Father is still working	6
5:18	also calling God his own Father	6
5:19	only what he sees the Father doing;	6
5:19	whatever the Father does, the Son does likewise.	4
5:20	The Father loves the Son	6
5:21	Indeed, just as the Father raises the dead	6
5:22	The Father judges no one	6
5:23	just as they honor the Father.	6
5:23	does not honor the Father who sent him.	6
5:26	For just as the Father has life in himself	6
5:36	works that the Father has given me to complete	6
5:36	testify on my behalf that the Father has sent me.	6
5:37	the Father who sent me has himself testified	6
5:43	I have come in my Father's name	6
5:45	that I will accuse you before the Father;	6
6:27	on him that God the Father has set his seal."	6
6:32	my Father who gives you the true bread from heaven.	6
6:37	Everything that the Father gives me will come	6
6:40	This is indeed the will of my Father	6
6:42	Jesus…whose father and mother we know?	6
6:44	unless drawn by the Father who sent me;	6
6:45	who has heard and learned from the Father	6
6:46	Not that anyone has seen the Father	6
6:46	he has seen the Father.	6
6:57	Just as the living Father sent me	6
6:57	I live because of the Father	6
6:65	unless it is granted by the Father."	6
8:16	but I and the Father who sent me.	6
8:18	the Father who sent me testifies on my behalf."	6
8:19	Then they said to him, "Where is your Father?"	6
8:19	Jesus answered, "You know neither me nor my Father.	6
8:19	If you knew me, you would know my Father also."	6
8:27	he was speaking to them about the Father.	6
8:28	speak these things as the Father instructed me.	6
8:38	I declare what I have seen in the Father's presence;	6
8:38	you should do what you have heard from the Father."	6
8:39	They answered him, "Abraham is our father."	6
8:41	You are indeed doing what your father does."	6
8:41	we have one father, God himself."	6
8:42	"If God were your Father, you would love me	6
8:44	You are from your father the devil	6
8:44	you choose to do your father's desires.	6
8:44	for he is a liar and the father of lies.	6
8:49	I honor my Father, and you dishonor me.	6
8:53	Are you greater than our father Abraham, who died?	6
8:54	It is my Father who glorifies me	6
10:15	just as the Father knows me and I know the Father.	6
10:15	just as the Father knows me and I know the Father.	6
10:17	For this reason the Father loves me	6
10:18	I have received this command from my Father."	6
10:25	The works that I do in my Father's name	6
10:29	What my Father has given me is greater than all	6
10:29	can snatch it out of the Father's hand.	6
10:30	The Father and I are one."	6
10:32	shown you many good works from the Father.	6
10:36	the one whom the Father has sanctified and sent	6
10:37	If I am not doing the works of my Father	6
10:38	the Father is in me and I am in the Father."	6
10:38	the Father is in me and I am in the Father."	6
11:41	"Father, I thank you for having heard me.	6
12:26	Whoever serves me, the Father will honor.	6
12:27	'Father, save me from this hour'?	6
12:28	Father, glorify your name."	6
12:49	the Father who sent me	6
12:50	I speak just as the Father has told me."	6
13: 1	to depart from this world and go to the Father.	6
13: 3	the Father had given all things into his hands	6
14: 2	In my Father's house there are many dwelling places.	6
14: 6	No one comes to the Father except through me.	6
14: 7	If you know me, you will know my Father also	6
14: 8	Philip said to him, "Lord, show us the Father	6
14: 9	Whoever has seen me has seen the Father.	6
14: 9	How can you say, 'Show us the Father'?	6
14:10	I am in the Father and the Father is in me?	6
14:10	I am in the Father and the Father is in me?	6
14:10	I am in the Father and the Father is in me?	6
14:11	I am in the Father and the Father is in me;	6
14:11	I am in the Father and the Father is in me;	6
14:12	because I am going to the Father.	6
14:13	so that the Father may be glorified in the Son.	6
14:16	I will ask the Father	6
14:20	On that day you will know that I am in my Father	6
14:21	those who love me will be loved by my Father	6
14:23	my Father will love them	6
14:24	not mine, but is from the Father who sent me.	6
14:26	Holy Spirit, whom the Father will send in my name	6
14:28	that I am going to the Father	6
14:28	the Father is greater than I.	6
14:31	I do as the Father has commanded me	6
14:31	so that the world may know that I love the Father.	6
15: 1	my Father is the vinegrower.	6
15: 8	My Father is glorified by this	6
15: 9	As the Father has loved me, so I have loved you;	6
15:10	just as I have kept my Father's commandments	6
15:15	everything that I have heard from my Father.	6
15:16	so that the Father will give you whatever	6
15:23	Whoever hates me hates my Father also.	6
15:24	they have seen and hated both me and my Father.	6
15:26	whom I will send to you from the Father	6
15:26	the Spirit of truth who comes from the Father	6
16: 3	because they have not known the Father or me.	6
16:10	because I am going to the Father	6
16:15	All that the Father has is mine.	6
16:17	'Because I am going to the Father'?"	6
16:23	if you ask anything of the Father in my name	6
16:25	tell you plainly of the Father.	6
16:26	I do not say to you that I will ask the Father	6
16:27	for the Father himself loves you	6
16:28	I came from the Father	6
16:28	leaving the world and am going to the Father."	6
16:32	I am not alone because the Father is with me.	6
17: 1	"Father, the hour has come; glorify your Son	6
17: 5	now, Father, glorify me in your own presence	6
17:11	Holy Father, protect them in your name	6
17:21	As you, Father, are in me and I am in you	6
17:24	Father, I desire that those also…may be with me	6
17:25	"Righteous Father, the world does not know you	6
18:11	to drink the cup that the Father has given me?"	6
20:17	because I have not yet ascended to the Father.	6
20:17	'I am ascending to my Father and your Father	6
20:17	'I am ascending to my Father and your Father	6
20:21	As the Father has sent me, so I send you."	6
Act 1: 4	to wait there for the promise of the Father.	6
1: 7	that the Father has set by his own authority.	6
2:33	having received from the Father the promise	6
7: 2	Stephen replied: "Brothers and fathers, listen	6
7: 4	After his father died, God had him move from there	6
7: 8	so Abraham became the father of Isaac	2
7: 8	Isaac became the father of Jacob	1
7:14	Joseph sent and invited his father Jacob	6
7:20	three months he was brought up in his father's house;	6
7:29	Midian. There he became the father of two sons.	2
16: 1	his father was a Greek.	6
16: 3	for they all knew that his father was a Greek.	6

Act	22: 1	"Brothers and fathers, listen to the defense	6
	28: 8	the father of Publius lay sick in bed	6
Rom	1: 7	Grace to you and peace from God our Father	6
	4:16	Abraham (for he is the father of all of us	6
	4:17	"I have made you the father of many nations")	6
	4:18	that he would become "the father of many nations,"	6
	6: 4	raised from the dead by the glory of the Father	6
	8:15	a spirit of adoption. When we cry, "Abba! Father!"	6
	15: 6	the God and Father of our Lord Jesus Christ.	6
1Co	1: 3	peace from God our Father and the Lord Jesus	6
	4:15	you do not have many fathers.	6
	4:15	Indeed, in Christ Jesus I became your father	2
	5: 1	a man is living with his father's wife.	6
	8: 6	yet for us there is one God, the Father	6
	15:24	when he hands over the kingdom to God the Father	6
2Co	1: 2	Grace to you and peace from God our Father	6
	1: 3	Blessed be the God and Father of our Lord Jesus	6
	1: 3	Father of mercies and the God of all consolation	6
	6:18	I will be your father, and you shall be my sons	6
	11:31	The God and Father of the Lord Jesus	6
Gal	1: 1	through Jesus Christ and God the Father	6
	1: 3	Grace to you and peace from God our Father	6
	1: 4	according to the will of our God and Father	6
	4: 2	until the date set by the father.	6
	4: 6	Spirit...into our hearts, crying, "Abba! Father!"	6
Eph	1: 2	Grace to you and peace from God our Father	6
	1: 3	the God and Father of our Lord Jesus Christ	6
	1:17	God of our Lord Jesus Christ, the Father of glory	6
	2:18	both of us have access in one Spirit to the Father.	6
	3:14	For this reason I bow my knees before the Father	6
	4: 6	one God and Father of all, who is above all	6
	5:20	giving thanks to God the Father at all times	6
	5:31	a man will leave his father and mother	6
	6: 2	"Honor your father and mother"	6
	6: 4	fathers, do not provoke your children to anger	6
	6:23	God the Father and the Lord Jesus Christ.	6
Php	1: 2	Grace to you and peace from God our Father	6
	2:11	to the glory of God the Father.	6
	2:22	how like a son with a father he has served with me	6
	4:20	To our God and Father be glory forever and ever.	6
Col	1: 2	Grace to you and peace from God our Father.	6
	1: 3	God, the Father of our Lord Jesus Christ	6
	1:12	giving thanks to the Father	6
	3:17	giving thanks to God the Father through him.	6
	3:21	Fathers, do not provoke your children	6
1Th	1: 1	in God the Father and the Lord Jesus Christ:	6
	1: 3	remembering before our God and Father your work	6
	2:11	we dealt...like a father with his children	6
	3:11	Now may our God and Father himself	6
	3:13	that you may be blameless before our God and Father	6
2Th	1: 1	God our Father and the Lord Jesus Christ:	6
	1: 2	Grace to you and peace from God our Father	6
	2:16	Lord Jesus Christ himself and God our Father	6
1Ti	1: 2	Grace, mercy, and peace from God the Father	6
	5: 1	speak to him as to a father	6
2Ti	1: 2	Grace, mercy, and peace from God the Father	6
Tit	1: 4	Grace and peace from God the Father	6
Phm	1: 3	Grace to you and peace from God our Father	6
	1:10	whose father I have become during my imprisonment.	2
Heb	1: 5	"I will be his Father, and he will be my Son"?	6
	2:11	those who are sanctified all have one Father.	3
	12: 9	be subject to the Father of spirits and live?	6
Jas	1:17	coming down from the Father of lights	6
	1:27	pure and undefiled before God, the Father	6
	3: 9	With it we bless the Lord and Father	6
1Pe	1: 2	chosen and destined by God the Father	6
	1: 3	Blessed be the God and Father of our Lord Jesus	6
	1:17	If you invoke as Father the one who judges all	6
2Pe	1:17	he received honor and glory from God the Father	6
1Jn	1: 2	the eternal life that was with the Father	6
	1: 3	with the Father and with his Son Jesus Christ.	6
	2: 1	we have an advocate with the Father, Jesus Christ	6
	2:13	I am writing to you, fathers, because you know him	6
	2:14	because you know the Father.	6
	2:14	I write to you, fathers, because you know him	6
	2:15	love of the Father is not in those	6
	2:16	comes not from the Father but from the world.	6
	2:22	the one who denies the Father and the Son.	6
	2:23	No one who denies the Son has the Father;	6
	2:23	everyone who confesses the Son has the Father also.	6
	2:24	then you will abide in the Son and in the Father.	6

	3: 1	See what love the Father has given us	6
	4:14	Father has sent his Son as the Savior of the world.	6
2Jn	1: 3	from God the Father and from Jesus Christ	6
	1: 3	and from Jesus Christ, the Father's Son	6
	1: 4	just as we have been commanded by the Father.	6
	1: 9	whoever abides...has both the Father and the Son.	6
Jde	1: 1	who are called, who are beloved in God the Father	6
Rev	1: 6	a kingdom, priests serving his God and Father	6
	2:28	even as I also received authority from my Father.	6
	3: 5	I will confess your name before my Father	6
	3:21	and sat down with my Father on his throne.	6
	14: 1	his Father's name written on their foreheads.	6

without father

1. ἀπάτωρ, apatōr, 574

Heb	7: 3	Without father, without mother, without genealogy	1

father-in-law

1. πενθερός, pentheros, 4290

Jhn	18:13	Annas, who was the father-in-law of Caiaphas	1

fathom

1. ὀργυιά, orgyia, 3976

Act	27:28	So they took soundings and found twenty fathoms;	1
	27:28	they took soundings again and found fifteen fathoms.	1

fatted

1. σιτευτός, siteutos, 4988

Lke	15:23	get the fatted calf and kill it	1
	15:27	your father has killed the fatted calf	1
	15:30	you killed the fatted calf for him!'	1

fatten

1. τρέφω, trephō, 5555

Jas	5: 5	you have fattened your hearts	1

fault *See* find fault, point out a fault

faultless

1. ἄμεμπτος, amemptos, 289

Heb	8: 7	For if that first covenant had been faultless	1

favor *See also* look on with favor

1. βουλή, boulē, 1087
2. δεκτός, dektos, 1283
3. εὐδοκία, eudokia, 2306
4. τὶς, tis, 5516
5. ὑπέρ, hyper, 5642
6. χάρις, charis, 5921
7. χαριτόω, charitoō, 5923

Mat	20:20	she asked a favor of him.	4
Lke	1:28	he came to her and said, "Greetings, favored one!	7
	1:30	you have found favor with God.	6
	2:14	on earth peace among those whom he favors!"	3
	2:40	the favor of God was upon him.	6
	2:52	Jesus increased...in divine and human favor.	6
	4:19	to proclaim the year of the Lord's favor."	2
Act	7:10	enabled him to win favor and to show wisdom	6
	7:46	who found favor with God	6
	24:27	wanted to grant the Jews a favor	6
	25: 3	requested, as a favor to them against Paul	6
	25: 9	Festus, wishing to do the Jews a favor, asked Paul	6
	27:12	the majority was in favor of putting to sea from there	1
1Co	4: 6	puffed up in favor of one against another.	5
2Co	1:15	so that you might have a double favor;	6

favorable *See* favorable *time*

favorably *See* look favorably, look on favorably, testify favorably

favoritism

1. προσωπολημψία, prosōpolēmpsia, 4721

Jas	2: 1	do you with your acts of favoritism really believe	1

fear *See also* nothing to fear

1. Contextual: Not in Greek
2. ἔκφοβος, ekphobos, 1769

3. μή, *mē, 3590*
4. πτόησις, *ptoēsis, 4766*
5. φοβέομαι, *phobeomai, 5828*
6. φόβος, *phobos, 5832*

Mat	10:26	"So have no fear of them; for nothing is covered	5
	10:28	Do not fear those who kill the body	5
	10:28	rather fear him who can destroy both soul and body	5
	14: 5	he feared the crowd	5
	14:26	And they cried out in fear.	6
	17: 6	fell to the ground and were overcome by fear.	5
	21:46	they feared the crowds	5
	28: 4	For fear of him the guards shook	6
	28: 8	they left the tomb quickly with fear	6
Mrk	5:33	came in fear and trembling	5
	5:36	"Do not fear, only believe."	5
	6:20	for Herod feared John…and he protected him.	5
	12:12	feared the crowd.	5
Lke	1:12	he was terrified; and fear overwhelmed him.	6
	1:50	His mercy is for those who fear him	5
	1:65	Fear came over all their neighbors	6
	7:16	Fear seized all of them; and they glorified God	6
	8:37	they were seized with great fear.	6
	8:50	Jesus heard this, he replied, "Do not fear.	5
	12: 4	my friends, do not fear those who kill the body	5
	12: 5	I will warn you whom to fear:	5
	12: 5	fear him who, after he has killed, has authority	5
	12: 5	Yes, I tell you, fear him!	5
	18: 2	a judge who neither feared God nor had respect	5
	18: 4	I have no fear of God and no respect for anyone	5
	20:19	they feared the people.	5
	21:26	People will faint from fear and foreboding	6
	23:40	rebuked him, saying, "Do you not fear God	5
Jhn	7:13	no one would speak openly…for fear of the Jews.	6
	12:42	for fear that they would be put out of the synagogue;	3
	19:38	a secret one because of his fear of the Jews	6
	20:19	the doors…were locked…for fear of the Jews	6
Act	5: 5	great fear seized all who heard of it.	6
	5:11	great fear seized the whole church	6
	9:31	Living in the fear of the Lord	6
	10: 2	devout man who feared God with all his household;	5
	10:35	anyone who fears him and does what is right	5
	13:16	"You Israelites, and others who fear God, listen.	5
	13:26	and others who fear God	5
	23:10	fearing that they would tear Paul to pieces	5
	27:17	then, fearing that they would run on the Syrtis	5
	27:29	Fearing that we might run on the rocks	5
Rom	3:18	"There is no fear of God before their eyes."	6
	8:15	a spirit of slavery to fall back into fear	6
	13: 3	you wish to have no fear of the authority?	5
1Co	2: 3	in weakness and in fear and in much trembling.	6
2Co	5:11	Therefore, knowing the fear of the Lord	6
	7: 1	making holiness perfect in the fear of God.	6
	7: 5	disputes without and fears within.	6
	7:15	you welcomed him with fear and trembling.	6
	12:20	I fear that when I come, I may find you	5
	12:20	I fear that there may perhaps be quarreling,	1
	12:21	I fear that when I come again, my God may humble me	1
Gal	2:12	for fear of the circumcision faction.	5
Eph	6: 5	obey your earthly masters with fear and trembling	6
Php	2:12	your own salvation with fear and trembling;	6
Col	3:22	wholeheartedly, fearing the Lord.	5
1Ti	5:20	so that the rest also may stand in fear.	6
Heb	2:15	held in slavery by the fear of death.	6
	12:21	Moses said, "I tremble with fear.")	2
1Pe	2:17	Love the family of believers. Fear God.	5
	3: 6	do what is good and never let fears alarm you.	4
	3:14	Do not fear what they fear, and do not be intimidated	5
	3:14	Do not fear what they fear, and do not be intimidated	6
1Jn	4:18	There is no fear in love	6
	4:18	but perfect love casts out fear;	5
	4:18	for fear has to do with punishment	6
	4:18	whoever fears has not reached perfection in love.	5
Jde	1:23	have mercy on still others with fear	6
Rev	2:10	Do not fear what you are about to suffer.	5
	11:18	all who fear your name, both small and great	5
	14: 7	"Fear God and give him glory	5
	15: 4	Lord, who will not fear and glorify your name?	5
	18:10	they will stand far off, in fear of her torment	6
	18:15	in fear of her torment, weeping and mourning	6
	19: 5	his servants, and all who fear him, small and great."	5

reverent fear

1. φόβος, *phobos, 5832*

1Pe	1:17	live in reverent fear	1

without fear

1. ἀφόβως, *aphobōs, 925*

Lke	1:74	that we…might serve him without fear	1
Php	1:14	speak the word with greater boldness and without fear.	1
Jde	1:12	love-feasts, while they feast with you without fear	1

fearful

1. μέγας, *megas, 3489*
2. φοβερός, *phoberos, 5829*

Heb	10:27	a fearful prospect of judgment, and a fury of fire	2
Rev	16:21	they cursed God…so fearful was that plague.	1

fearful thing

1. φοβερός, *phoberos, 5829*

Heb	10:31	It is a fearful thing to fall into the hands	1

feast

1. εὐφραίνω, *euphrainō, 2370*
2. συνευωχέομαι, *syneuōcheomai, 5307*

Lke	16:19	and who feasted sumptuously every day.	1
2Pe	2:13	They are…feast with you.	2

feast with

1. συνευωχέομαι, *syneuōcheomai, 5307*

Jde	1:12	love-feasts, while they feast with you without fear	1

feed

1. βόσκω, *boskō, 1081*
2. ποιμαίνω, *poimainō, 4477*
3. ποτίζω, *potizō, 4540*
4. τρέφω, *trephō, 5555*
5. χορτάζω, *chortazō, 5963*
6. ψωμίζω, *psōmizō, 6039*

Mat	6:26	barns, and yet your heavenly Father feeds them.	4
	8:30	Now a large herd of swine was feeding	1
	15:33	enough bread…to feed so great a crowd?"	5
Mrk	5:11	the hillside a great herd of swine was feeding;	1
	7:27	He said to her, "Let the children be fed first	5
	8: 4	"How can one feed these people with bread here	5
Lke	8:32	on the hillside a large herd of swine was feeding;	1
	12:24	yet God feeds them.	4
	15:15	who sent him to his fields to feed the pigs.	1
Jhn	21:15	Jesus said to him, "Feed my lambs."	1
	21:17	Jesus said to him, "Feed my sheep.	1
Rom	12:20	No, "if your enemies are hungry, feed them;	6
1Co	3: 2	I fed you with milk, not solid food	3
Jde	1:12	feast with you without fear, feeding themselves.	2

feel

1. Contextual: Not in Greek
2. γινώσκω, *ginōskō, 1182*
3. χαίρω, *chairō, 5897*

Mrk	5:29	she felt in her body that she was healed	2
2Co	1: 9	felt that we had received the sentence of death	1
	7: 9	you felt a godly grief	1
Gal	4:15	What has become of the goodwill you felt?	1
1Th	3: 9	joy that we feel before our God because of you?	3

feel confident

1. πείθω, *peithō, 4275*

Rom	15:14	I myself feel confident about you, my brothers	1

feel hurt

1. λυπέω, *lypeō, 3382*

Jhn	21:17	Peter felt hurt because he said to him	1

feel jealousy

1. ζηλόω, *zēloō, 2420*

2Co	11: 2	I feel a divine jealousy for you	1

Felix

1. Φῆλιξ, *Phēlix, 5772*

Act	23:24	and take him safely to Felix the governor."	1
	23:26	to his Excellency the governor Felix, greetings.	1

Act 24:22 Felix...adjourned the hearing with the comment 1
24:24 Felix came with his wife Drusilla 1
24:25 Felix became frightened and said 1
24:27 Felix was succeeded by Porcius Festus; 1
24:27 Felix left Paul in prison. 1
25:14 a man here who was left in prison by Felix. 1

fellow *See also* fellow *disciple*, fellow *heir*, fellow *Israelite*, fellow *prisoner*, fellow *servant*, fellow *slave*, fellow *soldier*, fellow *worker*, pestilent fellow, such a fellow, this fellow

1. ἀνήρ, *anēr, 467*
2. ἄνθρωπος, *anthrōpos, 476*

Lke 14:30 saying, 'This fellow began to build 2
Act 5:35 he said to them, "Fellow Israelites, 1
21:28 shouting, "Fellow Israelites, help! 1

fellowship

1. κοινωνία, *koinōnia, 3126*

Act 2:42 the apostles' teaching and fellowship 1
1Co 1: 9 called into the fellowship of his Son, Jesus 1
2Co 6:14 what fellowship is there between light and darkness? 1
Gal 2: 9 to Barnabas and me...the right hand of fellowship 1
1Jn 1: 3 so that you also may have fellowship with us; 1
1: 3 our fellowship is with the Father 1
1: 6 If we say that we have fellowship with him 1
1: 7 we have fellowship with one another 1

female

1. θῆλυς, *thēlys, 2559*

Mat 19: 4 'made them male and female,' 1
Mrk 10: 6 'God made them male and female.' 1
Gal 3:28 there is no longer male and female; 1

fence

1. φραγμός, *phragmos, 5850*

Mat 21:33 put a fence around it, dug a wine press in it 1
Mrk 12: 1 put a fence around it 1

fervently *See also* pray fervently

1. ἐκτενῶς, *ektenōs, 1757*

Act 12: 5 prayed fervently to God for him. 1

festal *See* festal *gathering*

festival *See also* celebrate the festival

1. ἑορτή, *heortē, 2038*
2. ἡμέρα, *hēmera, 2465*

Mat 26: 5 "Not during the festival, or there may be a riot 1
27:15 Now at the festival the governor was accustomed 1
Mrk 14: 2 "Not during the festival, or there may be a riot 1
15: 6 Now at the festival he used to release a prisoner 1
Lke 2:41 to Jerusalem for the festival of the Passover. 1
2:42 they went up as usual for the festival 1
2:43 the festival was ended and they started to return 2
22: 1 Now the festival of Unleavened Bread, 1
Jhn 2:23 he was in Jerusalem during the Passover festival 1
4:45 all that he had done in Jerusalem at the festival; 1
4:45 for they too had gone to the festival. 1
5: 1 After this there was a festival of the Jews 1
6: 4 the Passover, the festival of the Jews, was near. 1
7: 2 Now the Jewish festival of Booths was near. 1
7: 8 Go to the festival yourselves. 1
7: 8 I am not going to this festival 1
7:10 after his brothers had gone to the festival 1
7:11 The Jews were looking for him at the festival 1
7:14 About the middle of the festival 1
7:37 On the last day of the festival, the great day 1
11:56 Surely he will not come to the festival 1
12:12 great crowd that had come to the festival heard 1
12:20 among those who went up to worship at the festival 1
13: 1 Now before the festival of the Passover 1
13:29 "Buy what we need for the festival"; 1
Act 12: 3 (This was during the festival of Unleavened Bread.) 2
Col 2:16 observing festivals, new moons, or sabbaths. 1

festival of the Dedication

1. ἐγκαίνια, *enkainia, 1589*

Jhn 10:22 the festival of the Dedication took place in Jerusalem. 1

festival of unleavened bread

1. ἄζυμος, *azymos, 109*

Mrk 14: 1 Passover and the festival of Unleavened Bread. 1

Festus

1. Φῆστος, *Phēstos, 5776*

Act 24:27 Felix was succeeded by Porcius Festus; 1
25: 1 Three days after Festus had arrived in the province 1
25: 4 Festus replied that Paul was being kept 1
25: 9 Festus, wishing to do the Jews a favor, asked Paul 1
25:12 Then Festus...replied 1
25:13 Agrippa...arrived at Caesarea to welcome Festus. 1
25:14 Festus laid Paul's case before the king, saying 1
25:22 Agrippa said to Festus, "I would like to hear 1
25:23 Festus gave the order and Paul was brought in. 1
25:24 Festus said, "King Agrippa 1
26:24 Festus exclaimed, "You are out of your mind, Paul! 1
26:25 "I am not out of my mind, most excellent Festus 1
26:32 Agrippa said to Festus 1

fever

1. πυρέσσω, *pyressō, 4789*
2. πυρετός, *pyretos, 4790*

Mat 8:14 saw his mother-in-law lying in bed with a fever; 1
8:15 he touched her hand, and the fever left her 2
Mrk 1:30 Simon's mother-in-law was in bed with a fever 1
1:31 the fever left her, and she began to serve them. 2
Lke 4:38 mother-in-law was suffering from a high fever 2
4:39 he stood over her and rebuked the fever 2
Jhn 4:52 at one in the afternoon the fever left him." 2
Act 28: 8 lay sick in bed with fever and dysentery. 2

few

1. ὀλίγος, *oligos, 3900*
2. οὐ + πολύς, *ou + polys, 4024 + 4498*

Mat 7:14 and there are few who find it. 1
9:37 but the laborers are few; 1
15:34 They said, "Seven, and a few small fish." 1
22:14 For many are called, but few are chosen." 1
Mrk 6: 5 he laid his hands on a few sick people 1
8: 7 They had also a few small fish; 1
Lke 10: 2 harvest is plentiful, but the laborers are few; 1
13:23 "Lord, will only a few be saved?" 1
15:13 few days later the younger son gathered all 2
Jhn 2:12 and they remained there a few days. 2
Act 17: 4 not a few of the leading women. 1
17:12 not a few Greek women and men of high standing. 1
Eph 3: 3 as I wrote above in a few words 1
1Pe 3:20 ark, in which a few...were saved through water. 1
Rev 3: 4 Yet you have still a few persons in Sardis 1

few things

1. ὀλίγος, *oligos, 3900*

Mat 25:21 you have been trustworthy in a few things 1
25:23 you have been trustworthy in a few things 1
Rev 2:14 But I have a few things against you: 1

fiancée

1. παρθένος, *parthenos, 4221*

1Co 7:36 is not behaving properly toward his fiancée 1
7:37 to keep her as his fiancée, he will do well. 1
7:38 So then, he who marries his fiancée does well; 1

fidelity

1. πίστις, *pistis, 4411*

Tit 2:10 not to pilfer, but to show complete and perfect fidelity 1

field *See also* live in a field

1. ἀγρός, *agros, 69*
2. γεώργιον, *geōrgion, 1176*
3. μέτρον, *metron, 3586*
4. χόρτος, *chortos, 5965*
5. χώρα, *chōra, 6001*
6. χωρίον, *chōrion, 6005*

Mat 6:28 about clothing? Consider the lilies of the field 1
6:30 the grass of the field, which is alive today 1
13:24 someone who sowed good seed in his field; 1
13:27 'Master, did you not sow good seed in your field? 1
13:31 that someone took and sowed in his field; 1

13:36	the parable of the weeds of the field."	1	
13:38	the field is the world	1	
13:44	like treasure hidden in a field	1	
13:44	sells all that he has and buys that field.	1	
19:29	sisters or father or mother or children or fields	1	
24:18	the one in the field must not turn back	1	
24:40	Then two will be in the field;	1	
27: 7	used them to buy the potter's field	1	
27: 8	that field has been called the Field of Blood	1	
27: 8	has been called the Field of Blood to this day.	1	
27:10	and they gave them for the potter's field	1	

Mrk 10:29 mother or father or children or fields   1
    10:30 mothers and children, and fields   1
    11: 8 branches that they had cut in the fields.   1
    13:16 one in the field must not turn back   1
Lke 12:28 the grass of the field, which is alive today   1
    15:15 who sent him to his fields to feed the pigs.   1
    15:25 "Now his elder son was in the field;   1
    17: 7 from plowing or tending sheep in the field   1
    17:31 likewise anyone in the field must not turn back.   1
Jhn 4:35 see how the fields are ripe for harvesting.   5
Act 1:18 acquired a field with the reward of his wickedness;   6
    1:19 so that the field was called…Hakeldama   6
    1:19 Hakeldama, that is, Field of Blood.)   6
    4:37 sold a field that belonged to him   6
1Co 3: 9 you are God's field, God's building.   2
2Co 10:13 keep within the field that God has assigned to us   3
Jas 1:10 the rich will disappear like a flower in the field.   4
    1:11 the sun rises…and withers the field;   4
    5: 4 The wages of the laborers who mowed your fields   5

fierce

  1. μέγας, *megas, 3489*
  2. χαλεπός, *chalepos, 5901*
Mat 8:28 so fierce that no one could pass that way.   2
Rev 16: 9 they were scorched by the fierce heat   1

fiery   *See* fiery *ordeal*

fifteen

  1. δεκαπέντε, *dekapente, 1278*
Act 27:28 they took soundings again and found fifteen fathoms.   1
Gal 1:18 stayed with him fifteen days;   1

fifteen hundred miles

  1. στάδιον + δώδεκα + χιλιάς, *stadion + dōdeka + chilias,*
    5084 + 1557 + 5942
Rev 21:16 he measured the city…fifteen hundred miles   1

fifteenth

  1. πεντεκαιδέκατος, *pentekaidekatos, 4298*
Lke 3: 1 In the fifteenth year of the reign of…Tiberius   1

fifth

  1. πέμπτος, *pemptos, 4286*
Rev 6: 9 When he opened the fifth seal, I saw   1
    9: 1 And the fifth angel blew his trumpet, and I saw   1
   16:10 The fifth angel poured his bowl on the throne   1
   21:20 the fifth onyx, the sixth carnelian   1

fifty

  1. πεντήκοντα, *pentēkonta, 4299*
Mrk 6:40 sat down in groups of hundreds and of fifties.   1
Lke 7:41 owed five hundred denarii, and the other fifty   1
    9:14 sit down in groups of about fifty each."   1
   16: 6 bill, sit down quickly, and make it fifty.'   1
Jhn 8:57 "You are not yet fifty years old   1
Act 13:20 for about four hundred fifty years.   1

fifty thousand

  1. μυριάς + πέντε, *myrias + pente, 3689 + 4297*
Act 19:19 it was found to come to fifty thousand silver coins.   1

fifty-three

  1. πεντήκοντα + τρεῖς, *pentēkonta + treis, 4299 + 5552*
Jhn 21:11 full of large fish, a hundred fifty-three   1

fig

  1. σῦκον, *sykon, 5192*

Mat 7:16 gathered from thorns, or figs from thistles?   1
Mrk 11:13 for it was not the season for figs.   1
Lke 6:44 Figs are not gathered from thorns   1
Jas 3:12 a fig tree…yield olives, or a grapevine figs?   1

fig tree

  1. συκῆ, *sykē, 5190*
Mat 21:19 seeing a fig tree by the side of the road,   1
   21:19 And the fig tree withered at once.   1
   21:20 "How did the fig tree wither at once?"   1
   21:21 will you do what has been done to the fig tree   1
   24:32 "From the fig tree learn its lesson: 1
Mrk 11:13 Seeing in the distance a fig tree in leaf   1
   11:20 they saw the fig tree withered away to its roots.   1
   11:21 The fig tree that you cursed has withered."   1
   13:28 "From the fig tree learn its lesson: 1
Lke 13: 6 "A man had a fig tree planted in his vineyard;   1
   13: 7 I have come looking for fruit on this fig tree   1
   21:29 "Look at the fig tree and all the trees;   1
Jhn 1:48 "I saw you under the fig tree   1
    1:50 I told you that I saw you under the fig tree?   1
Jas 3:12 Can a fig tree, my brothers and sisters, yield olives   1
Rev 6:13 as the fig tree drops its winter fruit   1

fight

  1. ἀγών, *agōn, 74*
  2. ἀγωνίζομαι, *agōnizomai, 76*
  3. πολεμέω, *polemeō, 4482*
  4. στρατεία, *strateia, 5127*
  5. στρατεύομαι, *strateuomai, 5129*
Jhn 18:36 my followers would be fighting   2
1Ti 1:18 by following them you may fight the good fight   5
    1:18 by following them you may fight the good fight   4
    6:12 Fight the good fight of the faith;   2
    6:12 Fight the good fight of the faith;   1
2Ti 4: 7 I have fought the good fight   2
    4: 7 I have fought the good fight   1
Rev 12: 7 Michael…angels fought against the dragon.   3
   13: 4 "Who is like the beast, and who can fight against it?"   3

fight against God

  1. θεομάχος, *theomachos, 2534*
Act 5:39 you may even be found fighting against God!"   1

fight back

  1. πολεμέω, *polemeō, 4482*
Rev 12: 7 The dragon and his angels fought back   1

fight with a wild animal

  1. θηριομαχέω, *thēriomacheō, 2562*
1Co 15:32 I fought with wild animals at Ephesus   1

figuratively   *See* speak figuratively

figure

  1. παροιμία, *paroimia, 4231*
Jhn 16:25 when I will no longer speak to you in figures   1

figure of speech

  1. παροιμία, *paroimia, 4231*
Jhn 10: 6 Jesus used this figure of speech with them   1
   16:25 said these things to you in figures of speech.   1
   16:29 speaking plainly, not in any figure of speech!   1

figurehead

  1. παράσημος, *parasēmos, 4185*
Act 28:11 with the Twin Brothers as its figurehead.   1

fill   *See also* eat one's fill

  1. γεμίζω, *gemizō, 1153*
  2. ἐμπίμπλημι, *empimplēmi, 1855*
  3. ἐν, *en, 1877*
  4. μεστόω, *mestoō, 3551*
  5. πίμπλημι, *pimplēmi, 4398*
  6. πλήρης, *plērēs, 4441*
  7. πληρόω, *plēroō, 4444*
  8. συμπληρόω, *symplēroō, 5230*
  9. χορτάζω, *chortazō, 5963*

Mat	5: 6	righteousness, for they will be filled.	9
	14:20	all ate and were filled;	9
	15:37	all of them ate and were filled;	9
	22:10	so the wedding hall was filled with guests.	5
	27:48	ran and got a sponge, filled it with sour wine	5
Mrk	6:42	all ate and were filled;	9
	8: 8	They ate and were filled;	9
	15:36	filled a sponge with sour wine, put it on a stick	1
Lke	1:15	he will be filled with the Holy Spirit.	5
	1:41	Elizabeth was filled with the Holy Spirit	5
	1:53	he has filled the hungry with good things	2
	1:67	Zechariah was filled with the Holy Spirit	5
	2:40	grew and became strong, filled with wisdom;	7
	3: 5	Every valley shall be filled	7
	4:14	Jesus, filled with the power of the Spirit,	3
	4:28	all in the synagogue were filled with rage.	5
	5: 7	they came and filled both boats	5
	5:26	they glorified God and were filled with awe	5
	6:11	they were filled with fury	5
	6:21	for you will be filled.	9
	8:23	filling with water, and they were in danger.	8
	9:17	all ate and were filled.	9
	14:23	so that my house may be filled.	1
	15:16	He would gladly have filled himself with the pods	9
Jhn	2: 7	Jesus said to them, "Fill the jars with water."	1
	2: 7	And they filled them up to the brim.	1
	6:13	from the fragments…they filled twelve baskets.	1
	6:26	because you ate your fill of the loaves.	9
	12: 3	The house was filled with the fragrance	7
	16: 6	sorrow has filled your hearts.	7
Act	2: 2	it filled the entire house where they were sitting.	7
	2: 4	All of them were filled with the Holy Spirit	5
	2:13	"They are filled with new wine."	4
	3:10	they were filled with wonder and amazement	5
	4: 8	Then Peter, filled with the Holy Spirit, said	5
	4:31	they were all filled with the Holy Spirit	5
	5: 3	"why has Satan filled your heart to lie	7
	5:17	filled with jealousy	5
	5:28	you have filled Jerusalem with your teaching	7
	7:55	filled with the Holy Spirit, he gazed into heaven	6
	9:17	be filled with the Holy Spirit."	5
	13: 9	Paul, filled with the Holy Spirit	5
	13:45	they were filled with jealousy;	5
	13:52	the disciples were filled with joy	7
	14:17	filling you with food and your hearts with joy."	2
	19:29	The city was filled with the confusion;	5
Rom	1:29	They were filled with every kind of wickedness	7
	15:13	the God of hope fill you with all joy and peace	7
	15:14	filled with all knowledge, and able to instruct	7
2Co	7: 4	great pride in you; I am filled with consolation;	7
Eph	1:23	the fullness of him who fills all in all.	7
	3:19	you may be filled with all the fullness of God.	7
	4:10	so that he might fill all things.)	7
	5:18	be filled with the Spirit	7
Col	1: 9	you may be filled with the knowledge of God's will	7
2Ti	1: 4	so that I may be filled with joy.	7
Rev	8: 5	took the censer and filled it with fire	1
	15: 8	and the temple was filled with smoke	1

fill up

1. ἀναπληρόω, *anaplēroō, 405*
2. πληρόω, *plēroō, 4444*

Mat	23:32	Fill up, then, the measure of your ancestors.	2
1Th	2:16	constantly been filling up the measure of their sins;	1

fill with awe

1. φοβέομαι, *phobeomai, 5828*

Mat	9: 8	When the crowds saw it, they were filled with awe	1
Mrk	4:41	And they were filled with great awe	1

fill with compassion

1. σπλαγχνίζομαι, *splanchnizomai, 5072*

Lke	15:20	father saw him and was filled with compassion;	1

fill with expectation

1. προσδοκάω, *prosdokaō, 4659*

Lke	3:15	As the people were filled with expectation	1

filth

1. ἀκαθαρσία, *akatharsia, 174*

Mat	23:27	bones of the dead and of all kinds of filth.	1

filthy

1. ῥυπαίνω, *rhypainō, 4862*
2. ῥυπαρός, *rhyparos, 4865*

Rev	22:11	Let…the filthy still be filthy	2
	22:11	Let…the filthy still be filthy	1

finally

1. ἔσχατος, *eschatos, 2274*
2. λοιπός, *loipos, 3370*
3. τέλος, *telos, 5465*
4. ὕστερος, *hysteros, 5731*

Mat	21:37	Finally he sent his son to them, saying	4
Mrk	12: 6	Finally he sent him to them, saying	1
Lke	20:32	Finally the woman also died.	4
2Co	13:11	Finally, brothers and sisters, farewell.	2
Eph	6:10	Finally, be strong in the Lord	2
Php	3: 1	Finally, my brothers and sisters, rejoice in the Lord.	2
	4: 8	Finally, beloved, whatever is true	2
1Th	4: 1	Finally, brothers and sisters, we ask and urge you	2
2Th	3: 1	Finally, brothers and sisters, pray for us	2
1Pe	3: 1	Finally, all of you, have unity of spirit, sympathy	3

find   *See also* try to find out

1. Contextual: Not in Greek
2. ἀνευρίσκω, *aneuriskō, 461*
3. εἰμί, *eimi, 1639*
4. εὑρίσκω, *heuriskō, 2351*
5. ἔχω, *echō, 2400*
6. καταλαμβάνω, *katalambanō, 2898*

Mat	1:18	lived together, she was found to be with child	4
	2: 8	for the child; and when you have found him,	4
	7: 7	will be given you; search, and you will find;	4
	7: 8	and everyone who searches finds	4
	7:14	and there are few who find it.	4
	8:10	in no one in Israel have I found such faith.	4
	10:39	Those who find their life will lose it	4
	10:39	who lose their life for my sake will find it.	4
	11:29	and you will find rest for your souls.	4
	12:43	but it finds none.	4
	12:44	When it comes, it finds it empty, swept	4
	13:44	which someone found and hid;	4
	13:46	on finding one pearl of great value	4
	16:25	who lose their life for my sake will find it.	4
	17:27	when you open its mouth, you will find a coin;	4
	18:13	if he finds it, truly I tell you, he rejoices	4
	20: 6	he went out and found others standing around;	4
	21: 2	immediately you will find a donkey tied	4
	21:19	found nothing at all on it but leaves.	4
	22: 9	invite everyone you find to the wedding banquet.'	4
	22:10	gathered all whom they found, both good and bad;	4
	24:46	whom his master will find at work when he arrives.	4
	26:40	he came to the disciples and found them sleeping;	4
	26:43	Again he came and found them sleeping	4
	26:60	they found none	4
Mrk	1:37	they found him, they said to him	4
	7:30	she went home, found the child lying on the bed	4
	11: 2	as you enter it, you will find tied there a colt	4
	11: 4	They went away and found a colt tied near a door	4
	11:13	whether perhaps he would find anything on it.	4
	11:13	When he came to it, he found nothing but leaves	4
	13:36	he may find you asleep when he comes suddenly.	4
	14:16	found everything as he had told them;	4
	14:37	He came and found them sleeping;	4
	14:40	once more he came and found them sleeping	4
	14:55	they found none.	4
Lke	1:30	you have found favor with God.	4
	2:12	you will find a child wrapped in bands of cloth	4
	2:16	they went with haste and found Mary and Joseph	2
	2:45	When they did not find him	4
	2:46	After three days they found him in the temple	4
	4:17	found the place where it was written:	4
	5:19	finding no way to bring him	4
	6: 7	that they might find an accusation against him.	4
	7: 9	not even in Israel have I found such faith."	4
	7:10	they found the slave in good health.	4
	8:35	found the man from whom the demons had gone	4
	9:36	When the voice had spoken, Jesus was found alone.	4
	11: 9	search, and you will find; knock, and the door	4

11:10	everyone who searches finds	4
11:24	not finding any, it says, 'I will return	4
11:25	When it comes, it finds it swept	4
12:37	those slaves whom the master finds alert	4
12:38	and finds them so, blessed are those slaves.	4
12:43	his master will find at work when he arrives.	4
13: 6	he came looking for fruit on it and found none.	4
13: 7	and still I find none.	4
15: 4	go after the one that is lost until he finds it?	4
15: 5	he has found it, he lays it on his shoulders	4
15: 6	for I have found my sheep that was lost.'	4
15: 8	search carefully until she finds it?	4
15: 9	When she has found it	4
15: 9	I have found the coin that I had lost.'	4
15:24	he was lost and is found!'	4
15:32	he was lost and has been found.' "	4
17:18	Was none of them found to return and give praise	4
18: 8	will he find faith on earth?"	4
19:30	as you enter it you will find tied there a colt	4
19:32	departed and found it as he had told them.	4
19:48	they did not find anything they could do	4
22:13	they went and found everything as he had told them;	4
22:45	found them sleeping because of grief	4
23: 2	"We found this man perverting our nation	4
23: 4	"I find no basis for an accusation against	4
23:14	have not found this man guilty of any…charges	4
23:22	I have found in him no ground for the sentence	4
24: 2	They found the stone rolled away from the tomb	4
24: 3	when they went in, they did not find the body.	4
24:23	when they did not find his body there	4
24:24	and found it just as the women had said;	4
24:33	they found the eleven and their companions	4
Jhn 1:41	He first found his brother Simon and said to him	4
1:41	"We have found the Messiah"	4
1:43	He found Philip and said to him, "Follow me."	4
1:45	Philip found Nathanael and said to him	4
1:45	"We have found him about whom Moses…wrote	4
2:14	In the temple he found people selling	4
5:14	Later Jesus found him in the temple and said	4
6:25	they found him on the other side of the sea	4
7:34	You will search for me, but you will not find me;	4
7:35	that we will not find him?	4
7:36	'You will search for me and you will not find me'	4
9:35	he found him, he said, "Do you believe	4
10: 9	and will come in and go out and find pasture.	4
11:17	he found that Lazarus had…been in the tomb	4
12:14	Jesus found a young donkey and sat on it;	4
18:38	"I find no case against him.	4
19: 4	to let you know that I find no case against him."	4
19: 6	I find no case against him."	4
21: 6	you will find some."	4
Act 4:21	they let them go, finding no way to punish them	4
5:10	When the young men came in they found her dead	4
5:22	they did not find them in the prison;	4
5:23	"We found the prison securely locked	4
5:23	when we opened them, we found no one inside."	4
5:39	you may even be found fighting against God!"	4
7:11	our ancestors could find no food.	4
7:46	who found favor with God	4
7:46	find a dwelling place for the house of Jacob.	4
8:40	Philip found himself at Azotus	4
9: 2	so that if he found any who belonged to the Way	4
9:33	There he found a man named Aeneas	4
10:27	he went in and found that many had assembled;	4
11:26	when he had found him, he brought him to Antioch.	4
12:19	Herod had searched for him and could not find him	4
13:22	'I have found David, son of Jesse, to be a man	4
13:28	they found no cause for a sentence of death	4
17: 6	When they could not find them	4
17:23	I found among them an altar with the inscription	4
17:27	grope for him and find him	4
18: 2	he found a Jew named Aquila, a native of Pontus	4
19: 1	Ephesus, where he found some disciples.	4
19:19	found to come to fifty thousand silver coins.	4
21: 2	When we found a ship bound for Phoenicia	4
23: 9	"We find nothing wrong with this man.	4
23:29	I found that he was accused	4
24: 5	We have, in fact, found this man a pestilent fellow	4
24:12	They did not find me disputing with anyone	4
24:18	they found me in the temple, completing the rite	4
24:20	tell what crime they had found	4

25:25	I found that he had done nothing deserving death;	6
27: 6	There the centurion found an Alexandrian ship	4
27:28	So they took soundings and found twenty fathoms;	4
27:28	they took soundings again and found fifteen fathoms.	4
28:14	There we found believers	4
Rom 7:21	So I find it to be a law that when I want to do	4
10:20	"I have been found by those who did not seek me;	4
1Co 4: 2	that they be found trustworthy.	4
5: 1	of a kind that is not found even among pagans;	1
15:15	We are even found to be misrepresenting God	4
2Co 2:13	because I did not find my brother Titus there.	4
5: 3	we have taken it off we will not be found naked.	4
8:22	and found eager in many matters	3
9: 4	if some…find that you are not ready	4
12:20	I come, I may find you not as I wish	4
12:20	you may find me not as you wish;	4
Gal 2:17	we ourselves have been found to be sinners	4
Eph 5: 9	fruit of the light is found in all that is good	1
Php 2: 7	being found in human form	4
3: 9	and be found in him	4
2Ti 1:17	he eagerly searched for me and found me	4
1:18	the Lord grant that he will find mercy from the Lord	4
Heb 4:16	so that we may receive mercy and find grace	4
11: 5	"he was not found, because God had taken him."	4
12:17	he was rejected, for he found no chance to repent	4
1Pe 1: 7	faith…may be found to result in praise and glory	4
2:22	no deceit was found in his mouth."	4
2Pe 3:14	strive to be found by him at peace, without spot	4
2Jn 1: 4	to find some of your children walking in the truth	4
Jde 1: 3	I find it necessary to write and appeal to you	5
Rev 2: 2	tested those…and have found them to be false.	4
3: 2	for I have not found your works perfect	4
5: 4	because no one was found worthy to open the scroll	4
9: 6	in those days people will seek death but will not find it;	4
14: 5	in their mouth no lie was found;	4
16:20	and no mountains were to be found;	4
18:14	lost to you, never to be found again!"	4
18:21	Babylon…will be found no more;	4
18:22	an artisan…will be found in you no more;	4
18:24	And in you was found the blood of prophets	4
20:11	and no place was found for them.	4
20:15	name was not found written in the book of life	4
22: 3	Nothing accursed will be found there any more.	3

find comfort

1. παρακαλέω, *parakaleō*, 4151

2Co 7:13	In this we find comfort.	1

find fault

1. μέμφομαι, *memphomai*, 3522
2. μωμάομαι, *mōmaomai*, 3699

Rom 9:19	"Why then does he still find fault?	1
2Co 6: 3	so that no fault may be found with our ministry	2
Heb 8: 8	God finds fault with them when he says:	1

find out

1. Contextual: Not in Greek
2. γινώσκω, *ginōskō*, 1182
3. ἐξετάζω, *exetazō*, 2004
4. ἐπιγινώσκω, *epiginōskō*, 2105

Mat 10:11	find out who in it is worthy	3
Mrk 6:38	When they had found out, they said	2
Lke 1:62	find out what name he wanted to give him.	1
9:11	When the crowds found out about it,	2
19:15	might find out what they had gained by trading.	2
Jhn 7:51	a hearing to find out what they are doing	2
Act 22:24	to find out the reason for this outcry against him.	4
22:30	to find out what Paul was being accused of	2
24:11	As you can find out	4
1Co 4:19	find out not the talk of these arrogant people	2
2Co 13: 6	I hope you will find out that we have not failed.	2
1Th 3: 5	I sent to find out about your faith;	2

fine *See also* fine *linen*, fine *way*

1. ἔνδοξος, *endoxos*, 1902
2. ἔνδυσις, *endysis*, 1906
3. καλός, *kalos*, 2819
4. λαμπρός, *lampros*, 3287

Mat 13:45	like a merchant in search of fine pearls;	3
Lke 7:25	Look, those who put on fine clothing	1

Jas	2: 2	For if a person with gold rings and in fine clothes	4
	2: 3	you take notice of the one wearing the fine clothes	4
1Pe	3: 3	by wearing gold ornaments or fine clothing;	2

finger

1. δάκτυλος, *daktylos, 1235*
2. χείρ, *cheir, 5931*

Mat	23: 4	are unwilling to lift a finger to move them.	1
Mrk	7:33	put his fingers into his ears, and he spat	1
Lke	11:20	by the finger of God that I cast out the demons	1
	11:46	do not lift a finger to ease them.	1
	15:22	put a ring on his finger and sandals on his feet.	2
	16:24	send Lazarus to dip the tip of his finger in water	1
Jhn	8: 6	[Jesus…wrote with his finger on the ground.]	1
	20:25	put my finger in the mark of the nails	1
	20:27	Then he said to Thomas, "Put your finger here	1

finish

1. Contextual: Not in Greek
2. γίνομαι, *ginomai, 1181*
3. διανύω, *dianyō, 1382*
4. ἐκτελέω, *ekteleō, 1754*
5. ἐπιτελέω, *epiteleō, 2200*
6. παύω, *pauō, 4264*
7. πληρόω, *plēroō, 4444*
8. συντελέω, *synteleō, 5334*
9. τελειόω, *teleioō, 5457*
10. τελέω, *teleō, 5464*

Mat	7:28	Now when Jesus had finished saying these	10
	11: 1	Now when Jesus had finished instructing	10
	13:53	When Jesus had finished these parables	10
	19: 1	When Jesus had finished saying these	10
	26: 1	When Jesus had finished saying all these	10
Lke	2:39	When they had finished everything	10
	4:13	When the devil had finished every test	8
	5: 4	When he had finished speaking, he said to Simon	6
	7: 1	After Jesus had finished all his sayings	7
	11: 1	after he had finished, one of his disciples said	6
	13:32	the third day I finish my work.	9
	14:29	laid a foundation, is not able to finish	4
	14:30	began to build and was not able to finish.'	4
Jhn	17: 4	finishing the work that you gave me	9
	19:28	Jesus knew that all was now finished	10
	19:30	he said, "It is finished."	10
	21:15	When they had finished breakfast	1
Act	13:25	as John was finishing his work, he said	7
	20:24	if only I may finish my course	9
	20:36	When he had finished speaking, he knelt down	1
	21: 7	When we had finished the voyage from Tyre	3
2Co	8:11	now finish doing it, so that your eagerness	5
2Ti	4: 7	I have finished the race, I have kept the faith.	10
Heb	4: 3	though his works were finished	2
1Pe	4: 1	whoever has suffered…has finished with sin)	6
Rev	11: 7	When they have finished their testimony	10

finish speaking

1. σιγάω, *sigaō, 4967*

| Act | 15:13 | After they finished speaking, James replied | 1 |

fire *See also* color of fire, set on fire

1. καυσόω, *kausoō, 3012*
2. πῦρ, *pyr, 4786*
3. πυρά, *pyra, 4787*
4. φῶς, *phōs, 5890*

Mat	3:10	good fruit is cut down and thrown into the fire.	2
	3:11	baptize you with the Holy Spirit and fire.	2
	3:12	the chaff he will burn with unquenchable fire."	2
	5:22	'You fool,' you will be liable to the hell of fire.	2
	7:19	tree…is cut down and thrown into the fire.	2
	13:40	weeds are collected and burned up with fire	2
	13:42	throw them into the furnace of fire	2
	13:50	throw them into the furnace of fire	2
	17:15	he often falls into the fire	2
	18: 8	to be thrown into the eternal fire.	2
	18: 9	have two eyes and to be thrown into the hell of fire.	2
	25:41	accursed, depart from me into the eternal fire	2
Mrk	9:22	often cast him into the fire and into the water	2
	9:43	to go to hell, to the unquenchable fire.	2
	9:48	the fire is never quenched.	2

	9:49	"For everyone will be salted with fire.	2
	14:54	warming himself at the fire.	4
Lke	3: 9	tree…is cut down and thrown into the fire."	2
	3:16	baptize you with the Holy Spirit and fire.	2
	3:17	the chaff he will burn with unquenchable fire."	2
	9:54	to command fire to come down from heaven	2
	12:49	"I came to bring fire to the earth	2
	17:29	rained fire and sulfur from heaven	2
	22:55	When they had kindled a fire	2
Jhn	15: 6	branches are gathered, thrown into the fire	2
Act	2: 3	Divided tongues, as of fire, appeared among them,	2
	2:19	blood, and fire, and smoky mist.	2
	28: 2	they kindled a fire and welcomed all of us	3
	28: 3	putting it on the fire	3
	28: 5	He, however, shook off the creature into the fire	2
1Co	3:13	because it will be revealed with fire	2
	3:13	fire will test what sort of work	2
	3:15	saved, but only as through fire.	2
2Th	1: 8	in flaming fire, inflicting vengeance on those	2
Heb	1: 7	"He makes…his servants flames of fire."	2
	10:27	a fearful prospect of judgment, and a fury of fire	2
	11:34	quenched raging fire	2
	12:18	a blazing fire, and darkness, and gloom	2
	12:29	for indeed our God is a consuming fire.	2
Jas	3: 5	How great a forest is set ablaze by a small fire!	2
	3: 6	And the tongue is a fire.	2
	5: 3	their rust…will eat your flesh like fire.	2
1Pe	1: 7	gold that, though perishable, is tested by fire	2
2Pe	3: 7	and earth…have been reserved for fire	2
	3:10	and the elements will be dissolved with fire	1
	3:12	and the elements will melt with fire?	2
Jde	1: 7	by undergoing a punishment of eternal fire.	2
	1:23	save others by snatching them out of the fire;	2
Rev	1:14	his eyes were like a flame of fire	2
	2:18	the Son of God, who has eyes like a flame of fire	2
	3:18	I counsel you to buy from me gold refined by fire	2
	8: 5	took the censer and filled it with fire	2
	8: 7	there came hail and fire, mixed with blood	2
	8: 8	like a great mountain, burning with fire	2
	9:17	fire and smoke…came out of their mouths.	2
	9:18	killed, by the fire and smoke and sulfur	2
	10: 1	and his legs like pillars of fire.	2
	11: 5	fire pours from their mouth and consumes	2
	13:13	even making fire come down from heaven to earth	2
	14:10	they will be tormented with fire and sulfur	2
	14:18	the angel who has authority over fire	2
	15: 2	appeared to be a sea of glass mixed with fire	2
	16: 8	and it was allowed to scorch people with fire;	2
	17:16	will devour her flesh and burn her up with fire.	2
	18: 8	and she will be burned with fire;	2
	19:12	His eyes are like a flame of fire	2
	19:20	These two were thrown alive into the lake of fire	2
	20: 9	And fire came down from heaven and consumed them.	2
	20:10	thrown into the lake of fire and sulfur	2
	20:14	Death and Hades were thrown into the lake of fire.	2
	20:14	This is the second death, the lake of fire;	2
	20:15	was thrown into the lake of fire.	2
	21: 8	in the lake that burns with fire and sulfur	2

charcoal fire

1. ἀνθρακιά, *anthrakia, 471*

| Jhn | 18:18 | the slaves…had made a charcoal fire | 1 |
| | 21: 9 | they saw a charcoal fire there | 1 |

firelight

1. φῶς, *phōs, 5890*

| Lke | 22:56 | a servant-girl, seeing him in the firelight | 1 |

firm *See also* have a firm grasp, hold firm, stand firm

1. βέβαιος, *bebaios, 1010*
2. ἑδραῖος, *hedraios, 1612*
3. στερεός, *stereos, 5104*

1Co	7:37	someone stands firm in his resolve	2
2Ti	2:19	God's firm foundation stands, bearing this inscription:	3
Heb	3:14	if only we hold our first confidence firm	1

firmly *See* believe firmly, hold firmly

firmness

1. στερέωμα, *stereōma, 5106*

Col 2: 5 the firmness of your faith in Christ.   1

first *See also* first *convert,* first *fruit,* first *installment,* first *place,* like to put first, set one's hope first, speak first

1. Contextual: Not in Greek
2. ἀρχή, *archē, 794*
3. εἷς, *heis, 1651*
4. πρότερος, *proteros, 4728*
5. πρῶτον, *prōton, 4754*
6. πρῶτος, *prōtos, 4755*
7. πρώτως, *prōtōs, 4759*

Mat	5:24	first be reconciled to your brother or sister	5
	6:33	But strive first for the kingdom of God	5
	7: 5	hypocrite, first take the log out of your own eye	5
	8:21	"Lord, first let me go and bury my father."	5
	10: 2	first, Simon, also known as Peter	6
	12:29	without first tying up the strong man?	5
	12:45	worse than the first.	6
	13:30	Collect the weeds first and bind them in bundles	5
	17:10	the scribes say that Elijah must come first?"	5
	17:27	take the first fish that comes up	6
	19:30	many who are first will be last	6
	19:30	first will be last, and the last will be first.	6
	20: 8	the last and then going to the first.'	6
	20:10	Now when the first came	6
	20:16	last will be first, and the first will be last."	6
	20:16	last will be first, and the first will be last."	6
	20:27	whoever wishes to be first among you	6
	21:28	he went to the first and said	6
	21:31	They said, "The first." Jesus said to them	6
	21:36	Again he sent other slaves, more than the first;	6
	22:25	the first married, and died	6
	22:38	This is the greatest and first commandment.	6
	23:26	First clean the inside of the cup	5
	26:17	On the first day of Unleavened Bread	6
	27:64	the last deception would be worse than the first."	6
	28: 1	as the first day of the week was dawning	3
Mrk	3:27	without first tying up the strong man;	5
	4:28	The earth produces of itself, first the stalk	5
	7:27	He said to her, "Let the children be fed first	5
	9:11	the scribes say that Elijah must come first?"	5
	9:12	"Elijah is indeed coming first to restore all things.	5
	9:35	"Whoever wants to be first must be last of all	6
	10:31	many who are first will be last	6
	10:31	first will be last, and the last will be first."	6
	10:44	whoever wishes to be first among you	6
	12:20	There were seven brothers; the first married	6
	12:28	"Which commandment is the first of all?"	6
	12:29	Jesus answered, "The first is, 'Hear, O Israel:	6
	13:10	good news must first be proclaimed to all nations.	5
	14:12	On the first day of Unleavened Bread	6
	16: 2	very early on the first day of the week	3
	16: 9	[after he rose early on the first day of the week]	6
	16: 9	[he appeared first to Mary Magdalene]	5
Lke	2: 2	This was the first registration	6
	6:42	first take the log out of your own eye	5
	9:59	"Lord, first let me go and bury my father."	5
	9:61	let me first say farewell to those at my home."	5
	10: 5	Whatever house you enter, first say, 'Peace	5
	11:26	the last state…is worse than the first."	6
	11:38	he did not first wash before dinner.	5
	12: 1	he began to speak first to his disciples	5
	13:30	Indeed, some are last who will be first	6
	13:30	some are first who will be last."	6
	14:18	The first said to him, 'I have bought…land	6
	14:28	does not first sit down and estimate the cost	5
	14:31	what king…will not sit down first and consider	5
	16: 5	he asked the first, 'How much do you owe	6
	17:25	first he must endure much suffering and be rejected	5
	19:16	The first came forward and said, 'Lord	6
	20:29	the first married, and died childless;	6
	21: 9	these things must take place first	5
	24: 1	on the first day of the week, at early dawn	3
Jhn	1:41	He first found his brother Simon and said to him	5
	2:10	said to him, "Everyone serves the good wine first	5
	2:11	Jesus did this, the first of his signs, in Cana	2
	6:64	Jesus knew from the first	2
	7:51	judge people without first giving them a hearing	5
	8: 7	[who is without sin be the first to throw a stone]	6
	12:16	disciples did not understand these things at first;	5

	18:13	First they took him to Annas	5
	19:32	the soldiers came and broke the legs of the first	6
	19:39	Nicodemus, who had at first come to Jesus by night	5
	20: 1	Early on the first day of the week	3
	20: 4	outran Peter and reached the tomb first.	6
	20: 8	the other disciple, who reached the tomb first	6
	20:19	the first day of the week	3
Act	1: 1	In the first book, Theophilus	6
	3:26	sent him first to you, to bless you	5
	7:12	he sent our ancestors there on their first visit.	5
	11:26	the disciples were first called "Christians."	7
	12:10	they had passed the first and the second guard	6
	13:46	the word of God should be spoken first to you.	5
	15:14	how God first looked favorably on the Gentiles	5
	18:19	but first he himself went into the synagogue	1
	20: 7	On the first day of the week	3
	20:18	from the first day that I set foot in Asia	6
	26:20	declared first to those in Damascus	5
	26:23	by being the first to rise from the dead	6
	27:43	who could swim to jump overboard first	6
Rom	1: 8	First, I thank my God through Jesus Christ	5
	1:16	to the Jew first and also to the Greek.	5
	2: 9	the Jew first and also the Greek	5
	2:10	the Jew first and also the Greek.	5
	10:19	First Moses says, "I will make you jealous	6
1Co	12:28	God has appointed in the church first apostles	5
	14:30	let the first person be silent.	6
	15: 3	For I handed on to you as of first importance	5
	15:45	"The first man, Adam, became a living being";	6
	15:46	it is not the spiritual that is first	5
	15:47	The first man was from the earth, a man of dust;	6
	16: 2	On the first day of every week	3
2Co	1:15	I wanted to come to you first	4
	8: 5	they gave themselves first to the Lord	5
	10:14	we were the first to come all the way to you	1
Gal	4:13	I first announced the gospel to you;	4
Eph	6: 2	this is the first commandment with a promise:	6
Php	1: 5	from the first day until now.	6
1Th	4:16	the dead in Christ will rise first.	5
2Th	2: 3	unless the rebellion comes first	5
1Ti	2: 1	First of all, then, I urge that…	5
	2:13	For Adam was formed first, then Eve;	6
	3:10	let them first be tested;	5
	5: 4	they should first learn their religious duty	5
	5:12	having violated their first pledge.	6
2Ti	1: 5	a faith that lived first in your grandmother	5
	2: 6	ought to have the first share of the crops.	5
	4:16	At my first defense no one came to my support	6
Tit	3:10	After a first and second admonition,	3
Heb	2: 3	It was declared at first through the Lord	2
	3:14	if only we hold our first confidence firm	2
	7:27	to offer sacrifices day after day, first for his own sins	4
	8: 7	For if that first covenant had been faultless	6
	8:13	he has made the first one obsolete.	6
	9: 1	the first covenant had regulations for worship	6
	9: 2	a tent was constructed, the first one	6
	9: 6	the priests go continually into the first tent	6
	9: 8	as long as the first tent is still standing.	6
	9:15	the transgressions under the first covenant.	6
	9:18	Hence not even the first covenant was inaugurated	6
	10: 9	He abolishes the first	6
Jas	3:17	wisdom from above is first pure, then peaceable	5
2Pe	1:20	First of all you must understand this	5
	2:20	last state has become worse for them than the first.	6
1Jn	4:19	We love because he first loved us.	6
Rev	1:17	"Do not be afraid; I am the first and the last	6
	2: 4	you have abandoned the love you had at first.	6
	2: 5	repent, and do the works you did at first.	6
	2: 8	the words of the first and the last	6
	2:19	that your last works are greater than the first.	6
	4: 1	the first voice, which I had heard speaking to me	6
	4: 7	the first living creature like a lion	6
	8: 7	The first angel blew his trumpet	6
	9:12	The first woe has passed.	3
	13:12	exercises all the authority of the first beast	6
	13:12	makes…inhabitants worship the first beast	6
	16: 2	first angel went and poured his bowl on the earth	6
	20: 5	This is the first resurrection.	6
	20: 6	holy are those who share in the first resurrection.	6
	21: 1	first heaven and the first earth had passed away	6
	21: 1	first heaven and the first earth had passed away	6

Rev 21:19 adorned with every jewel; the first was jasper   6
     22:13 I am the Alpha and the Omega, the first and the last   6

first of all

1. πρῶτον, *prōton, 4754*

2Pe 3: 3 First of all you must understand this   1

first thing

1. πρῶτος, *prōtos, 4755*

Rev 21: 4 for the first things have passed away."   1

from the very first

1. ἄνωθεν, *anōthen, 540*

Lke 1: 3 investigating…carefully from the very first   1

firstborn

1. αὐτός, *autos, 899*
2. διανοίγω + μήτρα, *dianoigō + mētra, 1380 + 3616*
3. πρωτότοκος, *prōtotokos, 4758*

Lke 2: 7 she gave birth to her firstborn son   3
     2:23 "Every firstborn male shall be designated as holy   2
Rom 8:29 he might be the firstborn within a large family.   3
Col 1:15 the firstborn of all creation;   3
     1:18 he is the beginning, the firstborn from the dead   3
Heb 1: 6 when he brings the firstborn into the world   3
     11:28 the destroyer of the firstborn   3
     11:28 the destroyer…would not touch the firstborn   1
     12:23 to the assembly of the firstborn   3
Rev 1: 5 Jesus Christ…the firstborn of the dead   3

fish

1. Contextual: Not in Greek
2. ἁλιεύς, *halieus, 243*
3. ἁλιεύω, *halieuō, 244*
4. ἰχθύς, *ichthys, 2716*
5. ὀψάριον, *opsarion, 4066*
6. προσφάγιον, *prosphagion, 4709*

Mat 4:19 me, and I will make you fish for people."   2
     7:10 Or if the child asks for a fish, will give a snake?   4
     13:47 and caught fish of every kind;   1
     14:17 "We have nothing here but five loaves and two fish."   4
     14:19 Taking the five loaves and the two fish   4
     15:36 he took the seven loaves and the fish;   4
     17:27 take the first fish that comes up   4
Mrk 1:17 "Follow me and I will make you fish for people."   2
     6:38 they said, "Five, and two fish."   4
     6:41 Taking the five loaves and the two fish   4
     6:41 he divided the two fish among them all.   4
     6:43 full of broken pieces and of the fish.   4
Lke 5: 6 they caught so many fish   4
     5: 9 amazed at the catch of fish that they had taken;   4
     9:13 "We have no more than five loaves and two fish   4
     9:16 taking the five loaves and the two fish   4
     11:11 who, if your child asks for a fish   4
     11:11 will give a snake instead of a fish?   4
     24:42 They gave him a piece of broiled fish   4
Jhn 6: 9 a boy…who has five barley loaves and two fish.   5
     6:11 so also the fish, as much as they wanted.   5
     21: 3 Simon Peter said to them, "I am going fishing."   3
     21: 5 Jesus said to them, "Children, you have no fish   6
     21: 6 to haul it in because there were so many fish.   4
     21: 8 dragging the net full of fish   4
     21: 9 a charcoal fire…with fish on it, and bread.   5
     21:10 "Bring some of the fish that you have just caught."   5
     21:11 full of large fish, a hundred fifty-three   4
     21:13 and did the same with the fish.   5
1Co 15:39 another for birds, and another for fish.   4

small fish

1. ἰχθύδιον, *ichthydion, 2715*

Mat 15:34 They said, "Seven, and a few small fish."   1
Mrk 8: 7 They had also a few small fish;   1

fisherman

1. ἁλιεύς, *halieus, 243*

Mat 4:18 a net into the sea—for they were fishermen.   1
Mrk 1:16 for they were fishermen.   1
Lke 5: 2 the fishermen had gone out of them   1

fit *See also* see fit

1. εὔθετος, *euthetos, 2310*

Lke 9:62 is fit for the kingdom of God."   1
     14:35 fit neither for the soil nor for the manure pile;   1

fitting

1. ἀνήκω, *anēkō, 465*
2. ἀξίως, *axiōs, 547*
3. πρέπω, *prepō, 4560*

Rom 16: 2 welcome her in the Lord as is fitting for the saints   2
Col 3:18 be subject…as is fitting in the Lord.   1
Heb 2:10 was fitting that God…should make…perfect   3
     7:26 fitting that we should have such a high priest   3

five

1. πέντε, *pente, 4297*

Mat 14:17 "We have nothing here but five loaves and two fish."   1
     14:19 Taking the five loaves and the two fish   1
     16: 9 Do you not remember the five loaves   1
     25: 2 Five of them were foolish, and five were wise.   1
     25: 2 Five of them were foolish, and five were wise.   1
     25:15 to one he gave five talents, to another two   1
     25:16 had received the five talents went off at once   1
     25:16 made five more talents.   1
     25:20 who had received the five talents came forward   1
     25:20 bringing five more talents, saying   1
     25:20 'Master, you handed over to me five talents;   1
     25:20 see, I have made five more talents.'   1
Mrk 6:38 they said, "Five, and two fish."   1
     6:41 Taking the five loaves and the two fish   1
     8:19 I broke the five loaves for the five thousand   1
Lke 1:24 for five months she remained in seclusion.   1
     9:13 "We have no more than five loaves and two fish   1
     9:16 taking the five loaves and the two fish   1
     12: 6 Are not five sparrows sold for two pennies?   1
     12:52 five in one household will be divided   1
     14:19 Another said, 'I have bought five yoke of oxen   1
     16:28 for I have five brothers—that he may warn them   1
     19:18 'Lord, your pound has made five pounds.'   1
     19:19 'And you, rule over five cities.'   1
Jhn 4:18 for you have had five husbands   1
     5: 2 a pool…which has five porticoes.   1
     6: 9 a boy…who has five barley loaves and two fish.   1
     6:13 from the fragments of the five barley loaves   1
Act 4: 4 they numbered about five thousand.   1
     20: 6 in five days we joined them in Troas   1
     24: 1 Five days later the high priest…came down   1
1Co 14:19 I would rather speak five words with my mind…than   1
Rev 9: 5 were allowed to torture them for five months   1
     9:10 their power to harm people for five months.   1
     17:10 of whom five have fallen, one is living,   1

five hundred

1. πεντακόσιοι, *pentakosioi, 4296*

Lke 7:41 owed five hundred denarii, and the other fifty   1
1Co 15: 6 Then he appeared to more than five hundred   1

five o'clock

1. ἑνδέκατος, *hendekatos, 1895*
2. ἑνδέκατος + ὥρα, *hendekatos + hōra, 1895 + 6052*

Mat 20: 6 about five o'clock he went out   1
     20: 9 When those hired about five o'clock came   2

five thousand

1. πεντακισχίλιοι, *pentakischilioi, 4295*

Mat 14:21 who ate were about five thousand men, besides   1
     16: 9 remember the five loaves for the five thousand   1
Mrk 6:44 had eaten the loaves numbered five thousand men   1
     8:19 I broke the five loaves for the five thousand   1
Lke 9:14 For there were about five thousand men.   1
Jhn 6:10 so they sat down, about five thousand in all   1

five times

1. πεντάκις, *pentakis, 4294*

2Co 11:24 Five times I have received from the Jews   1

fix

1. ἀτενίζω, *atenizō, 867*
2. ἵστημι, *histēmi, 2705*

3. στηρίζω, *stērizō, 5114*

Lke   4:20 The eyes of all in the synagogue were fixed on him.   1
   16:26 between you and us a great chasm has been fixed   3
Act 17:31 fixed a day on which he will have the world judged   2

fix attention on
1. ἐπέχω, *epechō, 2091*

Act   3: 5 he fixed his attention on them   1

flame
1. πῦρ, *pyr, 4786*
2. πυρόω, *pyroō, 4792*
3. φλόξ, *phlox, 5825*

Lke 16:24 for I am in agony in these flames.'   3
Act   7:30 in the flame of a burning bush.   3
Eph   6:16 able to quench all the flaming arrows of the evil one.   2
2Th   1: 8 in flaming fire, inflicting vengeance on those   3
Heb   1: 7 "He makes…his servants flames of fire."   3
Rev   1:14 his eyes were like a flame of fire   3
   2:18 the Son of God, who has eyes like a flame of fire   3
   4: 5 in front of the throne burn seven flaming torches   1
  19:12 His eyes are like a flame of fire   3

flash
1. ἀστράπτω, *astraptō, 848*
2. φαίνω, *phainō, 5743*

Mat 24:27 lightning…flashes as far as the west   2
Lke 17:24 For as the lightning flashes and lights up   1

flash around
1. περιαστράπτω, *periastraptō, 4313*

Act   9: 3 suddenly a light from heaven flashed around him.   1

flash of lightning
1. ἀστραπή, *astrapē, 847*

Lke 10:18 "I watched Satan fall from heaven like a flash of lightning.   1
Rev   4: 5 Coming from the throne are flashes of lightning   1
   8: 5 flashes of lightning, and an earthquake.   1
  11:19 flashes of lightning, rumblings, peals of thunder   1
  16:18 flashes of lightning, rumblings, peals of thunder   1

flask
1. ἀγγεῖον, *angeion, 31*

Mat 25: 4 the wise took flasks of oil with their lamps.   1

flatter
1. θαυμάζω, *thaumazō, 2513*

Jde   1:16 speech, flattering people to their own advantage.   1

flattery
1. εὐλογία, *eulogia, 2330*
2. κολακεία, *kolakeia, 3135*

Rom 16:18 and by smooth talk and flattery they deceive   1
1Th   2: 5 we never came with words of flattery   2

flee
1. καταφεύγω, *katapheugō, 2966*
2. φεύγω, *pheugō, 5771*

Mat   2:13 take the child and his mother, and flee to Egypt   2
   3: 7 Who warned you to flee from the wrath to come?   2
  10:23 flee to the next;   2
  24:16 those in Judea must flee to the mountains;   2
  26:56 Then all the disciples deserted him and fled.   2
Mrk 13:14 those in Judea must flee to the mountains;   2
  14:50 All of them deserted him and fled.   2
  16: 8 So they went out and fled from the tomb   2
Lke   3: 7 Who warned you to flee from the wrath to come?   2
  21:21 those in Judea must flee to the mountains   2
Act   7:29 When he heard this, Moses fled   2
  14: 6 apostles learned of it and fled to Lystra and Derbe   1
1Co 10:14 my dear friends, flee from the worship of idols.   2
Jas   4: 7 Resist the devil, and he will flee from you.   2
Rev   9: 6 they will long to die, but death will flee from them.   2
  12: 6 and the woman fled into the wilderness   2
  20:11 earth and the heaven fled from his presence   2

flee away
1. φεύγω, *pheugō, 5771*

Rev 16:20 And every island fled away   1

flee out
1. ἐκφεύγω, *ekpheugō, 1767*

Act 19:16 they fled out of the house naked and wounded.   1

fleeting
1. πρόσκαιρος, *proskairos, 4672*

Heb 11:25 to enjoy the fleeting pleasures of sin.   1

flesh   *See also* mutilate the flesh, person of the flesh
1. σαρκικός, *sarkikos, 4920*
2. σάρκινος, *sarkinos, 4921*
3. σάρξ, *sarx, 4922*

Mat 16:17 For flesh and blood has not revealed this to you   3
  19: 5 and the two shall become one flesh'?   3
  19: 6 So they are no longer two, but one flesh.   3
  26:41 but the flesh is weak."   3
Mrk 10: 8 the two shall become one flesh.'   3
  10: 8 So they are no longer two, but one flesh.   3
  14:38 the flesh is weak."   3
Lke   3: 6 all flesh shall see the salvation of God.' "   3
  24:39 a ghost does not have flesh and bones   3
Jhn   1:13 born, not of blood or of the will of the flesh   3
   1:14 And the Word became flesh and lived among us   3
   3: 6 What is born of the flesh is flesh   3
   3: 6 What is born of the flesh is flesh   3
   6:51 the bread that I will give…is my flesh."   3
   6:52 "How can this man give us his flesh to eat?"   3
   6:53 unless you eat the flesh of the Son of Man   3
   6:54 Those who eat my flesh and drink my blood   3
   6:55 my flesh is true food and my blood is true drink.   3
   6:56 who eat my flesh and drink my blood abide in me   3
   6:63 the flesh is useless.   3
Act   2:17 I will pour out my Spirit upon all flesh   3
   2:26 moreover my flesh will live in hope.   3
   2:31 nor did his flesh experience corruption.'   3
Rom   1: 3 descended from David according to the flesh   3
   4: 1 Abraham, our ancestor according to the flesh?   3
   7: 5 While we were living in the flesh   3
   7:14 that the law is spiritual; but I am of the flesh   2
   7:18 nothing good dwells within me, that is, in my flesh.   3
   7:25 but with my flesh I am a slave to the law of sin.   3
   8: 3 what the law, weakened by the flesh, could not do: 3
   8: 3 his own Son in the likeness of sinful flesh   3
   8: 3 to deal with sin, he condemned sin in the flesh   3
   8: 4 in us, who walk not according to the flesh   3
   8: 5 For those who live according to the flesh   3
   8: 5 set their minds on the things of the flesh   3
   8: 6 To set the mind on the flesh is death   3
   8: 7 the mind that is set on the flesh is hostile to God;   3
   8: 8 those who are in the flesh cannot please God.   3
   8: 9 you are not in the flesh; you are in the Spirit   3
   8:12 we are debtors, not to the flesh   3
   8:12 not to the flesh, to live according to the flesh—   3
   8:13 if you live according to the flesh, you will die;   3
   9: 3 my own people, my kindred according to the flesh.   3
   9: 5 and from them, according to the flesh   3
   9: 8 children of the flesh who are the children of God   3
  13:14 and make no provision for the flesh   3
1Co   3: 3 for you are still of the flesh.   1
   3: 3 of the flesh, and behaving according to human   1
   5: 5 for the destruction of the flesh   3
   6:16 it is said, "The two shall be one flesh."   3
  15:39 Not all flesh is alike   3
  15:39 one flesh for human beings, another for animals   3
  15:50 flesh and blood cannot inherit the kingdom   3
2Co   4:11 Jesus may be made visible in our mortal flesh.   3
  12: 7 a thorn was given me in the flesh   3
Gal   2:20 the life I now live in the flesh I live by faith   3
   3: 3 are you now ending with the flesh?   3
   4:23 child of the slave, was born according to the flesh;   3
   4:29 who was born according to the flesh persecuted   3
   5:16 do not gratify the desires of the flesh.   3
   5:17 what the flesh desires is opposed to the Spirit   3
   5:17 the Spirit desires is opposed to the flesh;   3
   5:19 Now the works of the flesh are obvious: 3
   5:24 crucified the flesh with its passions   3
   6: 8 If you sow to your own flesh,   3
   6: 8 will reap corruption from the flesh;   3

Gal	6:12	who want to make a good showing in the flesh	3
	6:13	so that they may boast about your flesh.	3
Eph	2: 3	lived among them in the passions of our flesh	3
	2: 3	following the desires of flesh and senses	3
	2:11	circumcision made in the flesh by human hands	3
	2:14	in his flesh he has made both groups into one	3
	5:31	the two will become one flesh."	3
	6:12	struggle is not against enemies of blood and flesh	3
Php	1:22	If I am to live in the flesh	3
	1:24	to remain in the flesh is more necessary	3
	3: 3	have no confidence in the flesh	3
	3: 4	I...have reason for confidence in the flesh.	3
	3: 4	else has reason to be confident in the flesh	3
Col	1:24	in my flesh I am completing what is lacking	3
	2:11	by putting off the body of the flesh	3
	2:13	the uncircumcision of your flesh	3
1Ti	3:16	He was revealed in flesh	3
Phm	1:16	both in the flesh and in the Lord.	3
Heb	2:14	Since...the children share flesh and blood	3
	5: 7	In the days of his flesh, Jesus offered up prayers	3
	9:13	sanctifies...so that their flesh is purified	3
	10:20	through the curtain (that is, through his flesh)	3
Jas	5: 3	their rust...will eat your flesh like fire.	3
1Pe	1:24	For "All flesh is like grass	3
	2:11	to abstain from the desires of the flesh	1
	3:18	Christ...was put to death in the flesh	3
	4: 1	Since therefore Christ suffered in the flesh	3
	4: 1	(for whoever has suffered in the flesh	3
	4: 6	so that, though they had been judged in the flesh	3
2Pe	2:10	who indulge their flesh in depraved lust,	3
	2:18	with licentious desires of the flesh they entice	3
1Jn	2:16	the desire of the flesh, the desire of the eyes	3
	4: 2	that Jesus Christ has come in the flesh is from God	3
2Jn	1: 7	Jesus Christ has come in the flesh;	3
Jde	1: 8	these dreamers also defile the flesh	3
Rev	17:16	will devour her flesh and burn her up with fire.	3
	19:18	to eat the flesh of kings, the flesh of captains	3
	19:18	to eat the flesh of kings, the flesh of captains	3
	19:18	to eat...the flesh of the mighty	3
	19:18	to eat...the flesh of horses and their riders	3
	19:18	flesh of all, both free and slave,	3
	19:21	and all the birds were gorged with their flesh.	3

fleshly

1. σάρξ, *sarx, 4922*

Col	1:22	now reconciled in his fleshly body through death	1

flight *See also* put to flight

1. φυγή, *phygē, 5870*

Mat	24:20	Pray that your flight may not be in winter	1

flock

1. θρέμμα, *thremma, 2576*
2. ποίμνη, *poimnē, 4479*
3. ποίμνιον, *poimnion, 4480*

Mat	26:31	the sheep of the flock will be scattered.'	2
Lke	2: 8	keeping watch over their flock by night.	2
	12:32	"Do not be afraid, little flock	3
Jhn	4:12	with his sons and his flocks drank from it?"	1
	10:16	there will be one flock, one shepherd.	2
Act	20:28	Keep watch over yourselves and over all the flock	3
	20:29	savage wolves...not sparing the flock.	3
1Co	9: 7	who tends a flock and does not get any...milk?	2
1Pe	5: 2	tend the flock of God that is in your charge	3
	5: 3	but be examples to the flock.	3

flog

1. δέρω, *derō, 1296*
2. μαστιγόω, *mastigoō, 3463*
3. μαστίζω, *mastizō, 3464*
4. μάστιξ, *mastix, 3465*
5. παιδεύω, *paideuō, 4084*
6. πληγή, *plēgē, 4435*
7. φραγελλόω, *phragelloō, 5849*

Mat	10:17	and flog you in their synagogues;	2
	20:19	to be mocked and flogged and crucified;	2
	23:34	some you will flog in your synagogues	2
	27:26	after flogging Jesus, he handed him over	7
Mrk	10:34	mock him, and spit upon him, and flog him	2
	15:15	after flogging Jesus, he handed him over	7

Lke	18:33	they have flogged him, they will kill him,	2
	23:16	I will therefore have him flogged and release him."	5
	23:22	therefore have him flogged and then release him."	5
Jhn	19: 1	Pilate took Jesus and had him flogged.	2
Act	5:40	the apostles, they had them flogged.	1
	16:23	After they had given him a severe flogging	6
	22:24	ordered him to be examined by flogging	4
	22:25	legal...to flog a Roman citizen who is	3
2Co	11:23	with countless floggings, and often near death.	6
Heb	11:36	Others suffered mocking and flogging	4

flood *See also* sweep away with the flood

1. κατακλυσμός, *kataklysmos, 2886*
2. πλήμμυρα, *plēmmyra, 4439*
3. ποταμός, *potamos, 4532*

Mat	7:25	rain fell, the floods came, and the winds blew	3
	7:27	rain fell, and the floods came, and the winds	3
	24:38	For as in those days before the flood	1
	24:39	they knew nothing until the flood came	1
Lke	6:48	when a flood arose	2
	17:27	the flood came and destroyed all of them.	1
2Pe	2: 5	he brought a flood on a world of the ungodly;	1

three floors

1. τρίστεγον, *tristegon, 5566*

Act	20: 9	he fell to the ground three floors below	1

threshing floor

1. ἅλων, *halōn, 272*

Mat	3:12	clear his threshing floor and will gather his wheat	1
Lke	3:17	to clear his threshing floor	1

flour *See also* choice flour

1. ἄλευρον, *aleuron, 236*

Mat	13:33	mixed in with three measures of flour	1
Lke	13:21	took and mixed in with three measures of flour	1

flow

1. ἐκπορεύομαι, *ekporeuomai, 1744*
2. ἐξέρχομαι, *exerchomai, 2002*
3. ῥέω, *rheō, 4835*

Jhn	7:38	shall flow rivers of living water.' "	3
Rev	14:20	and blood flowed from the wine press	2
	22: 1	flowing from the throne of God and of the Lamb	1

flower

1. ἄνθος, *anthos, 470*

Jas	1:10	the rich will disappear like a flower in the field.	1
	1:11	its flower falls, and its beauty perishes.	1
1Pe	1:24	and all its glory like the flower of grass.	1
	1:24	The grass withers, and the flower falls	1

flute *See also* play the flute

1. αὐλός, *aulos, 888*

1Co	14: 7	produce sound, such as the flute or the harp.	1

flute player

1. αὐλητής, *aulētēs, 886*

Mat	9:23	and saw the flute players and the crowd	1

flutist

1. αὐλητής, *aulētēs, 886*

Rev	18:22	the sound...of flutists and trumpeters	1

fly

1. πέτομαι, *petomai, 4375*

Rev	4: 7	the fourth living creature like a flying eagle.	1
	8:13	heard an eagle crying...as it flew in midheaven	1
	12:14	could fly from the serpent into the wilderness	1
	14: 6	Then I saw another angel flying in midheaven	1
	19:17	he called to all the birds that fly in midheaven	1

foal

1. υἱός, *huios, 5626*

Mat	21: 5	and on a colt, the foal of a donkey."	1

foam *See also* cast up foam

1. ἀφρίζω, *aphrizō, 930*

Mrk   9:18 he foams and grinds his teeth and becomes rigid;   1

foam at the mouth

1. ἀφρίζω, *aphrizō, 930*
2. ἀφρός, *aphros, 931*

Mrk   9:20 rolled about, foaming at the mouth.   1
Lke   9:39 It convulses him until he foams at the mouth   2

foe

1. ἐχθρός, *echthros, 2398*

Mat 10:36 one's foes will be members of one's own household.   1
Rev 11: 5 fire pours…and consumes their foes;   1

fold

1. αὐλή, *aulē, 885*

Jhn 10:16 other sheep that do not belong to this fold.   1

follow *See also* following *day*

1. Contextual: Not in Greek
2. ἀκολουθέω, *akoloutheō, 199*
3. ἀπέρχομαι + ὀπίσω, *aperchomai + opisō, 599 + 3958*
4. δεῦτε + ὀπίσω, *deute + opisō, 1307 + 3958*
5. ἐκ, *ek, 1666*
6. ἐν, *en, 1877*
7. ἐξακολουθέω, *exakoloutheō, 1979*
8. ἐπακολουθέω, *epakoloutheō, 2051*
9. ἔπειμι, *epeimi, 2079*
10. ἔρχομαι + ὀπίσω, *erchomai + opisō, 2262 + 3958*
11. κατά, *kata, 2848*
12. κατακολουθέω, *katakoloutheō, 2887*
13. λαμβάνω, *lambanō, 3284*
14. ὀπίσω, *opisō, 3958*
15. οὗτος, *houtos, 4047*
16. παρακολουθέω, *parakoloutheō, 4158*
17. πείθω, *peithō, 4275*
18. περιπατέω, *peripateō, 4344*
19. ποιέω, *poieō, 4472*
20. πορεύομαι, *poreuomai, 4513*
21. στοιχέω, *stoicheō, 5123*
22. συνακολουθέω, *synakoloutheō, 5258*
23. τηρέω, *tēreō, 5498*

Mat   4:19 he said to them, "Follow me, and I will make you   4
       4:20 Immediately they left their nets and followed   2
       4:22 the boat and their father, and followed him.   2
       4:25 And great crowds followed him from Galilee   2
       8: 1 great crowds followed him;   2
       8:10 he was amazed and said to those who followed him   2
       8:19 "Teacher, I will follow you wherever you go."   2
       8:22 Jesus said to him, "Follow me, and let the dead   2
       8:23 he got into the boat, his disciples followed him.   2
       9: 9 and he said to him, "Follow me."   2
       9: 9 "Follow me." And he got up and followed him.   2
       9:19 Jesus got up and followed him, with his disciples.   2
       9:27 two blind men followed him, crying loudly   2
      10: 5 Jesus sent out with the following instructions   1
      10:38 whoever does not take up the cross and follow me   2
      12:15 Many crowds followed him, and he cured all   2
      14:13 they followed him on foot from the towns.   2
      16:24 take up their cross and follow me.   2
      19: 2 Large crowds followed him, and he cured them   2
      19:21 then come, follow me."   2
      19:27 "Look, we have left everything and followed you.   2
      19:28 you who have followed me   2
      20:29 a large crowd followed him.   2
      20:34 they regained their sight and followed him.   2
      21: 9 that followed were shouting, "Hosanna   2
      23: 3 therefore, do whatever they teach you and follow   23
      26:58 Peter was following him at a distance   2
      27:55 they had followed Jesus from Galilee   2
Mrk   1:17 "Follow me and I will make you fish for people."   4
       1:18 immediately they left their nets and followed   2
       1:20 and followed him.   3
       2:14 he said to him, "Follow me."   2
       2:14 he got up and followed him.   2
       2:15 there were many who followed him.   2
       3: 7 a great multitude from Galilee followed   2
       5:24 a large crowd followed him and pressed in on   2
       5:37 He allowed no one to follow him except Peter   22
       6: 1 his disciples followed him.   2

       8:34 take up their cross and follow me.   2
       9:38 to stop him, because he was not following us."   2
      10:21 come, follow me."   2
      10:28 we have left everything and followed you."   2
      10:32 those who followed were afraid.   2
      10:52 regained his sight and followed him on the way.   2
      11: 9 went ahead and those who followed were shouting   2
      14:13 a jar of water will meet you; follow him   2
      14:51 A certain young man was following him   22
      14:54 Peter had followed him at a distance   2
      15:41 These used to follow him and provided for him   2
Lke   5:11 they left everything and followed him.   2
       5:27 he said to him, "Follow me."   2
       5:28 he got up, left everything, and followed him.   2
       7: 9 turning to the crowd that followed him, he said   2
       9:11 crowds found out about it, they followed him;   2
       9:23 take up their cross daily and follow me.   2
       9:49 stop him, because he does not follow with us."   2
       9:57 "I will follow you wherever you go."   2
       9:59 To another he said, "Follow me."   2
       9:61 Another said, "I will follow you, Lord;   2
      14:27 does not carry the cross and follow me   10
      18:22 then come, follow me."   2
      18:28 "Look, we have left our homes and followed you."   2
      18:43 Immediately he regained his sight and followed   2
      21: 9 the end will not follow immediately."   1
      22:10 follow him into the house he enters   2
      22:39 the disciples followed him.   2
      22:54 Peter was following at a distance.   2
      23:27 A great number of the people followed him   2
      23:49 the women who had followed him from Galilee   22
      23:55 The women…followed, and they saw the tomb   12
Jhn   1:37 heard him say this, and they followed Jesus.   2
       1:38 Jesus turned and saw them following, he said   2
       1:40 two who heard John speak and followed him   2
       1:43 He found Philip and said to him, "Follow me."   2
       6: 2 A large crowd kept following him   2
       8:12 Whoever follows me will never walk in darkness   2
      10: 4 he goes ahead of them, and the sheep follow him   2
      10: 5 They will not follow a stranger   2
      10:27 I know them, and they follow me.   2
      11:31 They followed her   2
      12:26 Whoever serves me must follow me   2
      13:36 "Where I am going, you cannot follow me now;   2
      13:36 you will follow afterward."   2
      13:37 "Lord, why can I not follow you now?   2
      18:15 Simon Peter and another disciple followed Jesus.   2
      20: 6 Simon Peter came, following him   2
      21:19 After this he said to him, "Follow me."   2
      21:20 the disciple whom Jesus loved following them;   2
      21:22 what is that to you? Follow me!"   2
Act   5:36 all who followed him were dispersed   17
       5:37 and got people to follow him;   14
       5:37 all who followed him were scattered.   17
      12: 8 "Wrap your cloak around you and follow me."   2
      12: 9 Peter went out and followed him;   2
      13:43 many Jews…followed Paul and Barnabas   2
      14:16 allowed all the nations to follow their own ways;   20
      15:23 with the following letter: 1
      16:11 the following day to Neapolis   9
      16:17 she followed Paul and us, she would cry out   12
      16:24 Following these instructions   13
      20:15 the following day we arrived opposite Chios.   9
      20:30 in order to entice the disciples to follow them.   14
      21:36 The crowd that followed kept shouting   2
      27:44 the rest to follow, some on planks and others   1
Rom   4:12 but who also follow the example of the faith   21
       5:16 For the judgment following one trespass   5
       5:16 the free gift following many trespasses brings   5
1Co 10: 4 from the spiritual rock that followed them   2
      11:17 in the following instructions I do not commend   15
      16: 1 follow the directions I gave to the churches   19
Gal   6:16 who will follow this rule—peace be upon them   21
Eph   2: 2 following the course of this world   11
       2: 2 following the ruler of the power of the air   11
       2: 3 following the desires of flesh and senses   19
Col   3: 7 These are the ways you also once followed   18
1Ti   1:18 by following them you may fight the good fight   6
       4: 6 the sound teaching that you have followed.   16
       5:15 For some have already turned away to follow Satan.   14
       5:24 the sins of others follow them there.   8

1Pe	2:21	an example, so that you should follow in his steps.	8
2Pe	1:16	For we did not follow cleverly devised myths	7
	2: 2	Even so, many will follow their licentious ways	7
	2:15	following the road of Balaam	7
Rev	6: 8	Its rider's name was Death, and Hades followed	2
	13: 3	In amazement the whole earth followed the beast.	14
	14: 4	these follow the Lamb wherever he goes.	2
	14: 8	another angel, a second, followed, saying	2
	14: 9	Then another angel, a third, followed them, crying	2
	14:13	"they will rest...for their deeds follow them."	2
	19:14	armies of heaven...following him on white horses.	2

as follows

1. οὕτως, *houtōs, 4048*

Heb	4: 4	it speaks about the seventh day as follows	1

get to follow

1. ἀφίστημι, *aphistēmi, 923*

Act	5:37	and got people to follow him;	1

follower

1. ἀκολουθέω, *akoloutheō, 199*
2. ὀπίσω, *opisō, 3958*
3. ὑπηρέτης, *hypēretēs, 5677*

Mat	16:24	"If any want to become my followers	2
Mrk	8:34	to them, "If any want to become my followers	1
Lke	9:23	"If any want to become my followers	2
Jhn	18:36	my followers would be fighting	3

folly

1. ἄνοια, *anoia, 486*
2. ἀφροσύνη, *aphrosynē, 932*

Mrk	7:22	envy, slander, pride, folly.	2
2Ti	3: 9	their folly will become plain to everyone.	1

food *See also* allowance of food, depend on for food, get food, give food, solid food

1. Contextual: Not in Greek
2. ἄρτος, *artos, 788*
3. βρῶμα, *brōma, 1109*
4. βρῶσις, *brōsis, 1111*
5. διατροφή, *diatrophē, 1418*
6. ἐσθίω, *esthiō, 2266*
7. τράπεζα, *trapeza, 5544*
8. τροφή, *trophē, 5575*
9. χόρτασμα, *chortasma, 5964*

Mat	3: 4	waist, and his food was locusts and wild honey.	8
	6:25	Is not life more than food, and the body	8
	10:10	for laborers deserve their food.	8
	14:15	into the villages and buy food for themselves."	3
	15:26	"It is not fair to take the children's food	2
	25:35	for I was hungry and you gave me food	6
	25:42	for I was hungry and you gave me no food	6
Mrk	2:25	were hungry and in need of food	1
	7:19	(Thus he declared all foods clean.)	3
	7:27	for it is not fair to take the children's food	2
Lke	3:11	whoever has food must do likewise."	3
	9:13	go and buy food for all these people."	3
	12:23	For life is more than food	8
Jhn	4: 8	had gone to the city to buy food.)	8
	4:32	"I have food to eat that you do not know	4
	4:34	"My food is to do the will of him who sent me	3
	6:27	Do not work for the food that perishes	4
	6:27	the food that endures for eternal life	4
	6:55	my flesh is true food and my blood is true drink.	4
Act	2:46	ate their food with glad and generous hearts	8
	6: 1	neglected in the daily distribution of food	1
	7:11	our ancestors could find no food.	9
	9:19	taking some food, he regained his strength.	8
	14:17	filling you with food and your hearts with joy."	8
	16:34	and set food before them;	7
	23:14	an oath to taste no food until we have killed Paul.	1
	27:33	Paul urged all of them to take some food, saying	8
	27:34	Therefore I urge you to take some food	8
	27:36	were encouraged and took food for themselves.	8
Rom	14:17	For the kingdom of God is not food and drink	4
	14:20	Do not, for the sake of food, destroy the work	3
1Co	6:13	"Food is meant for the stomach	3
	6:13	the stomach for food,"	3

	8: 7	the food they eat as food offered to an idol;	1
	8: 8	"Food will not bring us close to God."	3
	8:13	Therefore, if food is a cause of their falling	3
	9: 4	Do we not have the right to our food and drink?	6
	10: 3	all ate the same spiritual food	3
2Co	9:10	supplies seed to the sower and bread for food	4
Col	2:16	condemn you in matters of food and drink	4
1Ti	4: 3	demand abstinence from foods, which God created	3
	6: 8	if we have food and clothing	5
Heb	5:12	You need milk, not solid food;	8
	5:14	solid food is for the mature	8
	9:10	deal only with food and drink	3
	13: 9	strengthened...not by regulations about food	3
Jas	2:15	If a brother or sister...lacks daily food	8

food offered to an idol

1. εἰδωλόθυτος, *eidōlothytos, 1628*

1Co	8: 4	Hence, as to the eating of food offered to idols	1
	8: 7	the food they eat as food offered to an idol;	1

food sacrificed to an idol

1. εἰδωλόθυτος, *eidōlothytos, 1628*

1Co	8: 1	Now concerning food sacrificed to idols:	1
	8:10	to the point of eating food sacrificed to idols?	1
	10:19	That food sacrificed to idols is anything	1
Rev	2:14	that they would eat food sacrificed to idols	1
	2:20	and to eat food sacrificed to idols.	1

without food

1. ἀσιτία, *asitia, 826*
2. ἄσιτος, *asitos, 827*
3. νηστεία, *nēsteia, 3763*

Act	27:21	they had been without food for a long time	1
	27:33	have been in suspense and remaining without food	2
2Co	11:27	hungry and thirsty, often without food	3

fool

1. ἀφροσύνη, *aphrosynē, 932*
2. ἄφρων, *aphrōn, 933*
3. μωραίνω, *mōrainō, 3701*
4. μωρός, *mōros, 3704*

Mat	5:22	you say, 'You fool,' you will be liable to the hell	4
	23:17	You blind fools!	4
Lke	11:40	You fools! Did not the one who made the outside	2
	12:20	God said to him, 'You fool!	2
Rom	1:22	Claiming to be wise, they became fools;	3
1Co	3:18	you should become fools so that you may become wise.	4
	4:10	We are fools for the sake of Christ, but you are wise	4
	15:36	Fool! What you sow does not come to life	2
2Co	11:16	I repeat, let no one think that I am a fool;	2
	11:16	if you do, then accept me as a fool	2
	11:17	not with the Lord's authority, but as a fool	1
	11:19	For you gladly put up with fools, being wise	2
	11:21	I am speaking as a fool	1
	12: 6	But if I wish to boast, I will not be a fool	2
	12:11	I have been a fool! You forced me to it.	2

foolish *See also* make foolish

1. ἀνόητος, *anoētos, 485*
2. ἀσύνετος, *asynetos, 852*
3. ἄφρων, *aphrōn, 933*
4. μωρός, *mōros, 3704*

Mat	7:26	will be like a foolish man who built his house	4
	25: 2	Five of them were foolish, and five were wise.	4
	25: 3	When the foolish took their lamps	4
	25: 8	The foolish said to the wise	4
Lke	24:25	he said to them, "Oh, how foolish you are,	1
Rom	1:14	both to the wise and to the foolish	1
	1:31	foolish, faithless, heartless, ruthless.	2
	2:20	a corrector of the foolish, a teacher of children	3
	10:19	with a foolish nation I will make you angry."	2
1Co	1:27	God chose what is foolish in the world	4
Gal	3: 1	You foolish Galatians! Who has bewitched you?	1
	3: 3	Are you so foolish?	1
Eph	5:17	So do not be foolish	3
Tit	3: 3	For we ourselves were once foolish, disobedient	1
1Pe	2:15	silence the ignorance of the foolish.	3

foolishness

1. ἀφροσύνη, *aphrosynē, 932*
2. μωρία, *mōria, 3702*
3. μωρός, *mōros, 3704*

1Co	1:18	foolishness to those who are perishing	2
	1:21	through the foolishness of our proclamation, to save	2
	1:23	a stumbling block to Jews and foolishness to Gentiles	2
	1:25	For God's foolishness is wiser than human wisdom	3
	2:14	for they are foolishness to them	2
	3:19	For the wisdom of this world is foolishness with God.	2
2Co	11: 1	bear with me in a little foolishness.	1

foot *See also* set foot, trample under foot

1. Contextual: Not in Greek
2. βάσις, *basis, 1000*
3. πούς, *pous, 4546*
4. ὑποπόδιον, *hypopodion, 5711*

Mat	4: 6	so that you will not dash your foot against a stone.' "	3
	7: 6	or they will trample them under foot and turn	3
	10:14	shake off the dust from your feet as you leave	3
	15:30	They put them at his feet, and he cured them	3
	18: 8	"If your hand or your foot causes you to stumble	3
	18: 8	than to have two hands or two feet	3
	22:13	'Bind him hand and foot, and throw him into	3
	22:44	until I put your enemies under your feet" '?	3
	28: 9	took hold of his feet, and worshiped him.	3
Mrk	5:22	he saw him, fell at his feet	3
	6:11	shake off the dust that is on your feet	3
	7:25	and she came and bowed down at his feet.	3
	9:45	if your foot causes you to stumble, cut it off;	3
	9:45	have two feet and to be thrown into hell.	3
	12:36	until I put your enemies under your feet." '	3
Lke	1:79	to guide our feet into the way of peace."	3
	4:11	you will not dash your foot against a stone.' "	3
	7:38	stood behind him at his feet, weeping	3
	7:38	and began to bathe his feet with her tears	3
	7:38	kissing his feet and anointing them	3
	7:44	you gave me no water for my feet	3
	7:44	she has bathed my feet with her tears	3
	7:45	she has not stopped kissing my feet.	3
	7:46	she has anointed my feet with ointment.	3
	8:35	sitting at the feet of Jesus	3
	8:41	fell at Jesus' feet and begged him to come	3
	9: 5	shake the dust off your feet	3
	10:11	'Even the dust of your town that clings to our feet	3
	10:39	a sister named Mary, who sat at the Lord's feet	3
	15:22	put a ring on his finger and sandals on his feet.	3
	17:16	He prostrated himself at Jesus' feet	3
	24:39	Look at my hands and my feet; see that it is I	3
	24:40	he showed them his hands and his feet	3
Jhn	11: 2	wiped his feet with her hair;	3
	11:32	Mary...knelt at his feet and said to him, "Lord	3
	11:44	his hands and feet bound with strips of cloth	3
	12: 3	anointed Jesus' feet, and wiped them	3
	13: 5	began to wash the disciples' feet	3
	13: 6	to him, "Lord, are you going to wash my feet?"	3
	13: 8	Peter said to him, "You will never wash my feet."	3
	13: 9	Simon Peter said to him, "Lord, not my feet only	3
	13:10	does not need to wash, except for the feet	3
	13:12	After he had washed their feet	3
	13:14	I, your Lord and Teacher, have washed your feet	3
	13:14	you also ought to wash one another's feet.	3
	20:12	one at the head and the other at the feet.	3
Act	3: 7	his feet and ankles were made strong.	2
	4:35	laid it at the apostles' feet.	3
	4:37	laid it at the apostles' feet.	3
	5: 2	laid it at the apostles' feet.	3
	5: 9	the feet of those who have buried your husband	3
	5:10	Immediately she fell down at his feet and died.	3
	7: 5	not even a foot's length	3
	7:33	'Take off the sandals from your feet	3
	7:58	at the feet of a young man named Saul.	3
	10:25	and falling at his feet, worshiped him.	3
	13:25	to untie the thong of the sandals on his feet.'	3
	13:51	they shook the dust off their feet in protest	3
	14: 8	a man sitting who could not use his feet	3
	14:10	said in a loud voice, "Stand upright on your feet."	3
	16:24	fastened their feet in the stocks.	3
	21:11	bound his own feet and hands with it, and said	3
	22: 3	brought up in this city at the feet of Gamaliel	3

	26:16	get up and stand on your feet;	3
Rom	3:15	"Their feet are swift to shed blood;	3
	10:15	"How beautiful are the feet of those who bring	3
	16:20	God...will shortly crush Satan under your feet.	3
1Co	12:15	If the foot would say, "Because I am not a hand	3
	12:21	the head to the feet, "I have no need of you."	3
	15:25	until he has put all his enemies under his feet.	3
	15:27	all things in subjection under his feet."	3
Eph	1:22	he has put all things under his feet	3
	6:15	As shoes for your feet put on	3
1Ti	5:10	washed the saints' feet, helped the afflicted	3
Heb	1:13	until I make your enemies a footstool for your feet"?	3
	2: 8	subjecting all things under their feet."	3
	10:13	his enemies would be made a footstool for his feet."	3
	12:13	make straight paths for your feet	3
Jas	2: 3	"Stand there," or, "Sit at my feet,"	4
Rev	1:15	his feet were like burnished bronze	3
	1:17	When I saw him, I fell at his feet as though dead.	3
	2:18	and whose feet are like burnished bronze:	3
	3: 9	make them come and bow down before your feet	3
	10: 2	Setting his right foot on the sea	3
	10: 2	right foot on the sea and his left foot on the land	1
	11:11	they stood on their feet, and those who saw them	3
	12: 1	clothed with the sun, with the moon under her feet	3
	13: 2	the beast that I saw...its feet were like a bear's	3
	19:10	Then I fell down at his feet to worship him	3
	22: 8	I fell down to worship at the feet of the angel	3

on foot

1. πεζῇ, *pezē, 4270*

Mat	14:13	they followed him on foot from the towns.	1
Mrk	6:33	they hurried there on foot from all the towns	1

footstool

1. ὑποπόδιον, *hypopodion, 5711*

Mat	5:35	or by the earth, for it is his footstool	1
Lke	20:43	until I make your enemies your footstool." '	1
Act	2:35	until I make your enemies your footstool." '	1
	7:49	'Heaven is my throne, and the earth is my footstool.	1
Heb	1:13	until I make your enemies a footstool for your feet"?	1
	10:13	his enemies would be made a footstool for his feet."	1

for *See also* as for, ask for, basis for accusation, bound for, call for, care for deeply, care for tenderly, cause for a sentence, cause for stumbling, depend on for food, destine for, dress for action, greedy for gain, greedy for money, grope for, ground for boasting, ground for sentence, leap for joy, live for pleasure, look for, love for one another, make for, motion for silence, occasion for stumbling, once for all, pit for the wine press, prepare for action, reason for confidence, reverence for God, send for, shout for joy, stay for a time, too deep for a word

1. ἀντί, *anti, 505*
2. ἀπό, *apo, 608*
3. ἄχρι, *achri, 948*
4. γάρ, *gar, 1142*
5. δέ, *de, 1254*
6. διά, *dia, 1328*
7. διότι, *dioti, 1484*
8. εἰ, *ei, 1623*
9. εἰς, *eis, 1650*
10. ἐκ, *ek, 1666*
11. ἐν, *en, 1877*
12. ἐπειδή, *epeidē, 2076*
13. ἐπί, *epi, 2093*
14. ἔτι, *eti, 2285*
15. ἕως, *heōs, 2401*
16. ἵνα, *hina, 2671*
17. καθάπερ, *kathaper, 2749*
18. καθώς, *kathōs, 2777*
19. καί, *kai, 2779*
20. κατά, *kata, 2848*
21. μήποτε, *mēpote, 3607*
22. ὅτι, *hoti, 4022*
23. παρά, *para, 4123*
24. περί, *peri, 4309*
25. πρός, *pros, 4639*
26. ὑπέρ, *hyper, 5642*

27. χάριν, *charin,* 5920
28. ὥστε, *hōste,* 6063

Mat	1:20 for the child conceived in her is from the Holy	4
	1:21 Jesus, for he will save his people from their	4
	2: 2 For we observed his star at its rising,	4
	2: 5 Judea; for so it has been written by the prophet:	4
	2: 6 for from you shall come a ruler who is to shepherd	4
	2: 8 saying, "Go and search diligently for the child;	24
	2:12 they left for their own country by another	9
	2:13 for Herod is about to search for the child	4
	2:20 for those who were seeking the child's life	4
	3: 2 "Repent, for the kingdom of heaven has come near."	4
	3: 7 Pharisees and Sadducees coming for baptism	13
	3: 9 for I tell you, God is able from these stones	4
	3:11 "I baptize you with water for repentance, but one	9
	3:15 for it is proper for us in this way	4
	4: 6 for it is written, 'He will command his angels	4
	4:10 "Away with you, Satan! for it is written,	4
	4:17 "Repent, for the kingdom of heaven has come near."	4
	4:18 a net into the sea—for they were fishermen.	4
	5: 3 spirit, for theirs is the kingdom of heaven.	22
	5: 4 who mourn, for they will be comforted.	22
	5: 5 the meek, for they will inherit the earth.	22
	5: 6 righteousness, for they will be filled.	22
	5: 7 the merciful, for they will receive mercy.	22
	5: 8 are the pure in heart, for they will see God.	22
	5: 9 for they will be called children of God.	22
	5:10 for theirs is the kingdom of heaven.	22
	5:12 Rejoice and be glad, for your reward is great	22
	5:12 for in the same way they persecuted the prophets	4
	5:13 no longer good for anything, but is thrown out	9
	5:18 For truly I tell you, until heaven and earth pass	4
	5:20 For I tell you, unless your righteousness	4
	5:34 either by heaven, for it is the throne of God	22
	5:35 or by the earth, for it is his footstool	22
	5:35 for it is the city of the great King.	22
	5:36 head, for you cannot make one hair white or black.	22
	5:38 heard that it was said, 'An eye for an eye and a tooth	1
	5:38 'An eye for an eye and a tooth for a tooth.'	1
	5:44 enemies and pray for those who persecute you	26
	5:45 for he makes his sun rise on the evil and on	22
	5:46 For if you love those who love you, what reward	4
	6: 5 not be like the hypocrites; for they love to stand	22
	6: 7 for they think that they will be heard because	4
	6: 8 like them, for your Father knows what you need	4
	6:14 For if you forgive others their trespasses	4
	6:16 the hypocrites, for they disfigure their faces	4
	6:21 For where your treasure is, there your heart will	4
	6:24 for a slave will either hate the one and love	4
	6:32 For it is the Gentiles who strive for all these	4
	6:34 for tomorrow will bring worries of its own.	4
	7: 2 For with the judgment you make	4
	7: 8 For everyone who asks receives	4
	7:12 do to you; for this is the law and the prophets.	4
	7:13 for the gate is wide and the road is easy	22
	7:29 for he taught them as one having authority	4
	8: 9 For I also am a man under authority, with soldiers	4
	9: 5 For which is easier, to say, 'Your sins are forgiven,'	4
	9:13 For I have come to call not the righteous	4
	9:16 for the patch pulls away from the cloak	4
	9:21 for she said to herself, "If I only touch	4
	9:24 he said, "Go away; for the girl is not dead	4
	9:36 When he saw the crowds, he had compassion for them	24
	10:10 no bag for your journey, or two tunics	9
	10:10 for laborers deserve their food.	4
	10:17 Beware of them, for they will hand you over	4
	10:19 for what you are to say will be given to you	4
	10:20 for it is not you who speak, but the Spirit	4
	10:23 for truly I tell you, you will not have gone	4
	10:26 for nothing is covered up that will not be uncovered	4
	10:35 For I have come to set a man against his father	4
	11:13 For all the prophets and the law prophesied	4
	11:18 For John came neither eating nor drinking	4
	11:21 For if the deeds of power done in you had been done	22
	11:23 For if the deeds of power done in you had been done	22
	11:26 yes, Father, for such was your gracious will.	22
	11:29 for I am gentle and humble in heart	22
	11:30 For my yoke is easy, and my burden is light."	4
	12: 8 For the Son of Man is lord of the sabbath."	4
	12:33 for the tree is known by its fruit.	4
	12:34 For out of the abundance of the heart	4
	12:36 have to give an account for every careless word	24
	12:37 for by your words you will be justified	4
	12:40 For just as Jonah was three days and three nights	4
	12:50 For whoever does the will of my Father in heaven	4
	13:12 For to those who have, more will be given	4
	13:15 For this people's heart has grown dull	4
	13:16 blessed are your eyes, for they see	22
	13:16 and your ears, for they hear.	22
	13:29 'No; for in gathering the weeds you would uproot	21
	14: 3 For Herod had arrested John, bound him	4
	14:14 and he had compassion for them	13
	14:24 for the wind was against them.	4
	15: 2 For they do not wash their hands before they eat."	4
	15: 4 For God said, 'Honor your father	4
	15:19 For out of the heart come evil intentions, murder	4
	15:23 "Send her away, for she keeps shouting after us."	22
	15:32 "I have compassion for the crowd	13
	15:32 for they might faint on the way."	21
	16: 2 'It will be fair weather, for the sky is red.'	4
	16: 3 for the sky is red and threatening.'	4
	16:17 For flesh and blood has not revealed this to you	22
	16:23 for you are setting your mind not on divine things	22
	16:25 For those who want to save their life will lose it	4
	16:26 For what will it profit them if they gain	4
	16:27 "For the Son of Man is to come with his angels	4
	16:27 he will repay everyone for what has been done.	20
	17:15 have mercy on my son, for he is an epileptic	22
	17:20 For truly I tell you, if you have faith	4
	17:27 take that and give it to them for you and me."	1
	18:10 for, I tell you, in heaven	4
	18:20 For where two or three are gathered in my name	4
	19: 3 lawful for a man to divorce his wife for any cause?"	20
	19: 9 divorces his wife, except for unchastity	13
	19:12 For there are eunuchs who have been so from birth	4
	19:14 for it is to such as these that the kingdom	4
	19:22 for he had many possessions.	4
	19:26 "For mortals it is impossible	23
	19:26 but for God all things are possible."	23
	20: 1 "For the kingdom of heaven is like a landowner	4
	20: 1 to hire laborers for his vineyard.	9
	20: 2 for the usual daily wage	10
	20:28 to give his life a ransom for many."	1
	21:26 for all regard John as a prophet."	4
	21:32 For John came to you in the way of righteousness	4
	22:14 For many are called, but few are chosen."	4
	22:16 for you do not regard people with partiality	4
	22:28 For all of them had married her."	4
	22:30 For in the resurrection they neither marry	4
	23: 3 for they do not practice what they teach.	4
	23: 5 for they make their phylacteries broad	4
	23: 8 for you have one teacher	4
	23: 9 for you have one Father—the one in heaven.	4
	23:10 for you have one instructor, the Messiah.	22
	23:13 For you lock people out of the kingdom of heaven.	22
	23:13 For you do not go in yourselves	4
	23:15 For you cross sea and land	22
	23:17 For which is greater, the gold or the sanctuary	4
	23:19 For which is greater, the gift or the altar	4
	23:23 For you tithe mint, dill, and cummin	22
	23:25 For you clean the outside of the cup	22
	23:27 For you are like whitewashed tombs	22
	23:29 For you build the tombs of the prophets	22
	23:39 For I tell you, you will not see me again until	4
	24: 5 For many will come in my name, saying	4
	24: 6 for this must take place, but the end is not yet.	4
	24: 7 For nation will rise against nation	4
	24:21 For at that time there will be great suffering	4
	24:24 For false messiahs and false prophets will appear	4
	24:27 For as the lightning comes from the east	4
	24:37 For as the days of Noah were	4
	24:38 For as in those days before the flood	4
	24:42 Keep awake therefore, for you do not know	22
	24:44 for the Son of Man is coming at an unexpected hour.	22
	25: 8 for our lamps are going out.'	22
	25:13 for you know neither the day nor the hour.	22
	25:14 "For it is as if a man, going on a journey	4
	25:29 For to all those who have, more will be given	4
	25:35 for I was hungry and you gave me food	4
	25:42 for I was hungry and you gave me no food	4
	26: 9 For this ointment could have been sold	4
	26:10 She has performed a good service for me.	9

	26:11	For you always have the poor with you	4
	26:12	she has prepared me for burial.	25
	26:28	for this is my blood of the covenant	4
	26:28	my blood…which is poured out for many	24
	26:28	for many for the forgiveness of sins.	9
	26:31	for it is written, 'I will strike the shepherd	4
	26:42	Again he went away for the second time and prayed	10
	26:43	for their eyes were heavy.	4
	26:44	he went away and prayed for the third time	10
	26:52	for all who take the sword will perish	4
	26:73	for your accent betrays you."	4
	27:10	and they gave them for the potter's field	9
	27:18	For he realized that it was out of jealousy	4
	27:19	for today I have suffered a great deal	4
	27:43	for he said, 'I am God's Son.' "	4
	28: 2	for an angel of the Lord, descending from heaven	4
	28: 4	For fear of him the guards shook	2
	28: 6	He is not here; for he has been raised,	4
Mrk	1: 4	repentance for the forgiveness of sins.	9
	1:16	for they were fishermen.	4
	1:22	for he taught them as one having authority	4
	1:38	for that is what I came out	4
	1:44	offer for your cleansing what Moses commanded	24
	2:15	for there were many who followed him.	4
	2:27	"The sabbath was made for humankind	6
	2:27	for humankind, and not humankind for the sabbath;	6
	3:10	for he had cured many	4
	3:21	for people were saying, "He has gone out	4
	3:30	for they had said, "He has an unclean spirit."	22
	4:19	and the desire for other things	24
	4:22	For there is nothing hidden, except to be	4
	4:25	For to those who have, more will be given;	4
	5: 4	for he had often been restrained with shackles	6
	5: 8	For he had said to him, "Come out of the man	4
	5: 9	He replied, "My name is Legion; for we are many."	22
	5:28	for she said, "If I but touch his clothes	4
	6: 8	ordered them to take nothing for their journey	9
	6:14	for Jesus' name had become known.	4
	6:17	For Herod himself had sent men who arrested John	4
	6:18	For John had been telling Herod, "It is not lawful	4
	6:20	for Herod feared John…and he protected him.	4
	6:31	For many were coming and going	4
	6:34	he had compassion for them	13
	6:50	for they all saw him and were terrified.	4
	6:52	for they did not understand about the loaves	4
	7: 3	(For the Pharisees, and all the Jews, do not eat	4
	7:10	For Moses said, 'Honor your father and your mother';	4
	7:21	For it is from within, from the human heart	4
	7:27	for it is not fair to take the children's food	4
	7:29	"For saying that, you may go—the demon has left	6
	8: 2	"I have compassion for the crowd	13
	8:19	I broke the five loaves for the five thousand	9
	8:20	"And the seven for the four thousand,	9
	8:33	for you are setting your mind not on divine things	22
	8:35	For those who want to save their life will lose	4
	8:36	For what will it profit them to gain	4
	9: 6	for they were terrified.	4
	9:31	for he was teaching his disciples, saying	4
	9:34	for on the way they had argued with one another	4
	9:39	for no one who does a deed of power in my name	4
	9:40	Whoever is not against us is for us.	26
	9:41	For truly I tell you, whoever gives you a cup	4
	9:49	"For everyone will be salted with fire.	4
	10:14	for it is to such…the kingdom of God belongs.	4
	10:22	for he had many possessions.	4
	10:27	"For mortals it is impossible, but not for God;	23
	10:27	"For mortals it is impossible, but not for God;	23
	10:27	for God all things are possible."	23
	10:45	For the Son of Man came not to be served but	4
	10:45	to give his life a ransom for many."	1
	11:13	for it was not the season for figs.	4
	11:18	for they were afraid of him	4
	11:32	for all regarded John as truly a prophet.	4
	12:14	for you do not regard people with partiality	4
	12:23	For the seven had married her."	4
	12:25	For when they rise from the dead	4
	12:44	For all of them have contributed…abundance;	4
	13: 8	For nation will rise against nation	4
	13:11	for it is not you who speak, but the Holy Spirit.	4
	13:19	For in those days there will be suffering	4
	13:33	Beware, keep alert; for you do not know	4

	13:35	Therefore, keep awake—for you do not know	4
	14: 2	for they said, "Not during the festival	4
	14: 5	For this ointment could have been sold	4
	14: 6	She has performed a good service for me.	11
	14: 7	For you always have the poor with you	4
	14: 8	anointed my body beforehand for its burial.	9
	14:21	For the Son of Man goes as it is written of him	22
	14:24	my blood…which is poured out for many.	26
	14:27	for it is written, 'I will strike the shepherd	22
	14:40	for their eyes were very heavy;	4
	14:56	For many gave false testimony against him	4
	14:70	you are one of them; for you are a Galilean."	4
	14:72	At that moment the cock crowed for the second time.	10
	15:10	For he realized that it was out of jealousy	4
	16: 8	for terror and amazement had seized them;	4
	16: 8	they said nothing to anyone, for they were afraid.	4
Lke	1:13	for your prayer has been heard.	7
	1:15	for he will be great in the sight of the Lord.	4
	1:18	For I am an old man, and my wife is getting on	4
	1:30	for you have found favor with God.	4
	1:37	For nothing will be impossible with God."	22
	1:44	For as soon as I heard the sound of your greeting	4
	1:44	the child in my womb leaped for joy.	11
	1:48	for he has looked with favor on…his servant.	22
	1:49	for the Mighty One has done great things for me	22
	1:66	For, indeed, the hand of the Lord was with him.	4
	1:68	for he has looked favorably on his people	22
	1:76	for you will go before the Lord to prepare	4
	2:10	for see—I am bringing you good news	4
	2:20	for all they had heard and seen	13
	2:27	to do for him what was customary under the law	24
	2:30	for my eyes have seen your salvation	22
	2:32	a light for revelation to the Gentiles	9
	2:34	destined for the falling and the rising of many	9
	3: 3	repentance for the forgiveness of sins	9
	3: 8	for I tell you, God is able from these stones	4
	4: 6	authority; for it has been given over to me	22
	4:10	for it is written, 'He will command his angels	4
	4:36	For with authority and power he commands	22
	4:43	for I was sent for this purpose."	22
	5: 4	and let down your nets for a catch."	9
	5: 8	"Go away from me, Lord, for I am a sinful man!"	22
	5: 9	For he and all who were with him were amazed	4
	5:14	make an offering for your cleansing	24
	5:14	your cleansing, for a testimony to them."	9
	6:19	for power came out from him and healed all	22
	6:20	for yours is the kingdom of God.	22
	6:21	for you will be filled.	22
	6:21	who weep now, for you will laugh.	22
	6:23	for surely your reward is great in heaven;	4
	6:23	for that is what their ancestors did to the prophets.	4
	6:24	for you have received your consolation.	22
	6:25	full now, for you will be hungry.	22
	6:25	for you will mourn and weep.	22
	6:26	for that is what their ancestors did	4
	6:28	pray for those who abuse you.	24
	6:32	For even sinners love those who love them.	4
	6:35	for he is kind to the ungrateful and the wicked.	22
	6:38	for the measure you give will be the measure	4
	6:44	for each tree is known by its own fruit.	4
	6:45	for out of the abundance of the heart	4
	7: 5	for he loves our people,	4
	7: 6	for I am not worthy to have you come	4
	7: 8	I also am a man set under authority	4
	7:13	he had compassion for her and said to her	13
	7:30	lawyers rejected God's purpose for themselves	9
	7:33	For John the Baptist has come eating no bread	4
	7:44	you gave me no water for my feet	13
	8: 6	it withered for lack of moisture.	6
	8:13	they believe only for a while	25
	8:17	For nothing is hidden that will not be disclosed	4
	8:18	for to those who have, more will be given;	4
	8:29	for Jesus had commanded the unclean spirit	4
	8:29	(For many times it had seized him;	4
	8:30	"Legion"; for many demons had entered him.	22
	8:37	for they were seized with great fear.	22
	8:40	for they were all waiting for him.	4
	8:42	for he had an only daughter…who was dying	22
	8:43	suffering from hemorrhages for twelve years;	2
	8:46	for I noticed that power had gone out from me."	4
	8:52	"Do not weep; for she is not dead but sleeping."	4

Lke	9: 3	He said to them, "Take nothing for your journey	9
	9:12	for we are here in a deserted place."	22
	9:13	go and buy food for all these people."	9
	9:14	For there were about five thousand men.	4
	9:24	For those who want to save their life will lose	4
	9:48	for the least among all of you is the greatest."	4
	9:50	for whoever is not against you is for you."	4
	9:50	for whoever is not against you is for you."	26
	10: 7	for the laborer deserves to be paid.	4
	10:13	For if the deeds of power done in you	22
	10:21	yes, Father, for such was your gracious will.	22
	10:24	For I tell you that many prophets and kings	4
	11: 4	for we ourselves forgive everyone indebted	4
	11: 6	for a friend of mine has arrived	12
	11:10	For everyone who asks receives	4
	11:18	for you say that I cast out the demons by Beelzebul.	22
	11:30	For just as Jonah became a sign to the people	4
	11:42	For you tithe mint and rue and herbs	22
	11:43	For you love to have the seat of honor	22
	11:44	Woe to you! For you are like unmarked graves	22
	11:46	For you load people with burdens hard to bear	22
	11:47	For you build the tombs of the prophets	22
	11:48	for they killed them, and you build their tombs.	22
	11:52	For you have taken away the key of knowledge;	22
	12:12	for the Holy Spirit will teach you at that very	4
	12:15	for one's life does not consist in…possessions."	22
	12:17	for I have no place to store my crops?'	22
	12:19	Soul, you have ample goods laid up for many years;	9
	12:23	For life is more than food	4
	12:30	For it is the nations of the world that strive	4
	12:32	for it is your Father's good pleasure	22
	12:34	for where your treasure is, there your heart	4
	12:40	for the Son of Man is coming at an unexpected	22
	12:41	telling this parable for us or for everyone?"	25
	12:41	telling this parable for us or for everyone?"	25
	12:57	you not judge for yourselves what is right?	2
	13:24	for many, I tell you, will try to enter	22
	13:31	"Get away from here, for Herod wants to kill you."	22
	14:11	For all who exalt themselves will be humbled	22
	14:14	for you will be repaid at the resurrection	4
	14:17	'Come; for everything is ready now.'	22
	14:24	For I tell you, none of those who were invited	4
	14:28	For which of you, intending to build a tower	4
	14:32	a delegation and asks for the terms of peace.	25
	14:35	fit neither for the soil nor for the manure pile;	9
	14:35	fit neither for the soil nor for the manure pile;	9
	15: 6	for I have found my sheep that was lost.'	22
	15: 9	for I have found the coin that I had lost.'	22
	15:24	for this son of mine was dead and is alive again;	22
	16: 8	for the children of this age are more shrewd	22
	16:13	for slave will either hate the one and love	4
	16:15	for what is prized by human beings	22
	16:24	for I am in agony in these flames.'	22
	16:28	for I have five brothers—that he may warn them	4
	17: 2	for you to cause…little ones to stumble.	16
	17: 9	for doing what was commanded?	22
	17:21	For, in fact, the kingdom of God is among you."	4
	17:24	For as the lightning flashes and lights up	4
	18: 4	For a while he refused;	13
	18:14	for all who exalt themselves will be humbled	22
	18:16	for it is to such as these that the kingdom of God	4
	18:23	he became sad; for he was very rich.	4
	18:27	impossible for mortals is possible for God."	23
	18:27	impossible for mortals is possible for God."	23
	18:32	For he will be handed over to the Gentiles;	4
	19: 5	for I must stay at your house today."	4
	19:10	For the Son of Man came to seek out and to save	4
	19:21	for I was afraid of you, because you are a harsh	4
	19:37	for all the deeds of power that they had seen	24
	19:48	for all the people were spellbound	4
	20: 6	for they are convinced that John was a prophet."	4
	20:33	For the seven had married her."	4
	20:38	for to him all of them are alive."	4
	20:40	For they no longer dared to ask him another question.	4
	20:42	For David himself says in the book of Psalms	4
	21: 4	for all of them have contributed…abundance	4
	21: 8	for many will come in my name and say, 'I am he!'	4
	21: 9	for these things must take place first	4
	21:15	for I will give you words and a wisdom	4
	21:22	for these are days of vengeance	22
	21:23	For there will be great distress on the earth	4
	21:26	for the powers of the heavens will be shaken.	4
	21:30	you can see for yourselves	2
	21:35	For it will come upon all	4
	22: 2	for they were afraid of the people.	4
	22:16	for I tell you, I will not eat it until	4
	22:18	for I tell you that from now on I will not drink	4
	22:19	"This is my body, which is given for you.	26
	22:20	"This cup that is poured out for you	26
	22:22	For the Son of Man is going as it has been determined	22
	22:27	For who is greater,	4
	22:32	prayed for you that your own faith may not fail;	24
	22:37	For I tell you, this scripture must be fulfilled	4
	22:52	who had come for him	13
	22:59	for he is a Galilean."	4
	23: 8	for he had been wanting to see him for a long	4
	23: 8	he had been wanting to see him for a long time	10
	23:15	Neither has Herod, for he sent him back to us.	4
	23:19	for an insurrection that had taken place	6
	23:25	put in prison for insurrection and murder	6
	23:28	"Daughters of Jerusalem, do not weep for me	13
	23:28	weep for yourselves and for your children.	13
	23:28	weep for yourselves and for your children.	13
	23:29	For the days are surely coming when they will say	22
	23:31	For if they do this when the wood is green	22
	23:34	[[for they do not know what they are doing."]]	4
	23:41	for we are getting what we deserve for our deeds	4
	23:48	crowds who had gathered there for this spectacle	13
	24:39	for a ghost does not have flesh and bones	22
Jhn	2: 6	water jars…for the Jewish rites of purification	20
	2:18	"What sign can you show us for doing this?"	22
	2:25	for he himself knew what was in everyone.	4
	3: 2	for no one can do these signs that you do	4
	3:16	"For God so loved the world that he gave	4
	3:20	For all who do evil hate the light	4
	3:34	for he gives the Spirit without measure.	4
	4:18	for you have had five husbands	4
	4:22	for salvation is from the Jews.	22
	4:23	for the Father seeks such as these to worship him.	4
	4:35	see how the fields are ripe for harvesting.	25
	4:36	and is gathering fruit for eternal life	9
	4:37	For here the saying holds true, 'One sows	4
	4:42	for we have heard for ourselves	4
	4:44	(for Jesus himself had testified that a prophet	4
	4:45	for they too had gone to the festival.	4
	4:47	his son, for he was at the point of death.	4
	5:13	for Jesus had disappeared in the crowd	4
	5:19	for whatever the Father does, the Son does likewise.	4
	5:26	For just as the Father has life in himself	4
	5:28	for the hour is coming when all…will hear	22
	5:35	you were willing to rejoice for a while	25
	5:46	you would believe me, for he wrote about me.	4
	6: 2	signs that he was doing for the sick.	13
	6: 5	to buy bread for these people to eat?"	16
	6: 6	for he himself knew what he was going to do.	4
	6: 7	enough bread for each of them to get a little."	16
	6:27	the food that endures for eternal life	9
	6:27	For it is on him that God…has set his seal."	4
	6:33	For the bread of God is that which comes down	4
	6:38	for I have come down from heaven, not to do	22
	6:51	bread that I will give for the life of the world	26
	6:55	for my flesh is true food and my blood is true	4
	6:64	for Jesus knew from the first	4
	6:71	for he…was going to betray him.	4
	7: 4	for no one who wants to be widely known acts	4
	7: 5	(For not even his brothers believed in him.)	4
	7: 8	for my time has not yet fully come."	22
	7:13	no one would speak openly…for fear of the Jews.	6
	7:39	as yet there was no Spirit,	4
	8:16	for it is not I alone who judge	22
	8:24	for you will die in your sins	4
	8:29	for I always do what is pleasing to him."	22
	8:42	for I came from God and now I am here.	4
	8:44	for he is a liar and the father of lies.	22
	9:16	for he does not observe the sabbath."	22
	9:21	he is of age. He will speak for himself."	24
	9:22	for the Jews had already agreed	4
	9:24	So for the second time they called the man	10
	9:39	Jesus said, "I came into this world for judgment	9
	10:11	lays down his life for the sheep.	26
	10:13	a hired hand does not care for the sheep.	24
	10:15	I lay down my life for the sheep.	26

10:32	For which of these are you going to stone me?"	6
10:33	"It is not for a good work that we…stone you	24
10:33	"It is not for a good work…but for blasphemy	24
11: 4	rather it is for God's glory	26
11:41	"Father, I thank you for having heard me.	22
11:50	to have one man die for the people	26
11:51	Jesus was about to die for the nation	26
11:52	not for the nation only	26
12: 7	she might keep it for the day of my burial.	9
12:23	"The hour…for the Son of Man to be glorified.	16
12:25	will keep it for eternal life.	9
12:35	"The light is with you for a little longer.	14
12:43	for they loved human glory more than the glory	4
12:47	for I came not to judge the world	4
12:49	for I have not spoken on my own	22
13:11	For he knew who was to betray him;	4
13:13	you are right, for that is what I am.	4
13:15	For I have set you an example	4
13:29	"Buy what we need for the festival";	9
13:35	if you have love for one another."	11
13:37	I will lay down my life for you."	26
13:38	answered, "Will you lay down your life for me?	26
14:30	for the ruler of this world is coming.	4
15:13	to lay down one's life for one's friends.	26
15:22	now they have no excuse for their sin.	24
16: 7	for if I do not go away, the Advocate will not	4
16:13	for he will not speak on his own	4
16:27	for the Father himself loves you	4
17: 8	for the words that you gave to me I have given	22
18:14	better to have one person die for the people.	26
18:37	For this I was born	9
18:37	for this I came into the world	9
19:24	but cast lots for it to see who will get it."	24
19:24	for my clothing they cast lots."	13
20: 9	for as yet they did not understand the scripture	4
20:19	the doors…were locked…for fear of the Jews	6
21: 7	he put on some clothes, for he was naked	4
21: 8	for they were not far from the land	4
Act 1: 5	for John baptized with water	22
1:17	for he was numbered among us	22
1:20	"For it is written in the book of Psalms	4
2:15	for it is only nine o'clock in the morning.	4
2:25	For David says concerning him, 'I saw the Lord	4
2:25	for he is at my right hand so that I will not be shaken;	22
2:27	For you will not abandon my soul to Hades	22
2:34	For David did not ascend into the heavens	4
2:39	For the promise is for you, for your children,	4
3:10	the one who used to sit and ask for alms	25
4: 3	for it was already evening.	4
4:12	for there is no other name under heaven given	4
4:16	For it is obvious to all who live in Jerusalem	4
4:20	for we cannot keep from speaking about what	4
4:21	for all of them praised God for what had happened.	22
4:21	all of them praised God for what had happened.	13
4:22	For the man on whom this sign of healing	4
4:27	For in this city, in fact, both Herod	4
4:34	for as many as owned lands or houses	4
5:26	for they were afraid of being stoned by the people.	4
5:36	For some time ago Theudas rose up	4
6:14	for we have heard him say	4
7:33	for the place where you are standing is holy ground.	4
8: 7	for unclean spirits…came out of many	4
8:15	The two went down and prayed for them	24
8:16	(for as yet the Spirit had not come upon any of them;	4
8:21	for your heart is not right before God.	4
8:23	For I see that you are in the gall of bitterness	4
8:24	Simon answered, "Pray for me to the Lord	26
8:33	For his life is taken away from the earth."	22
9:15	for he is an instrument whom I have chosen	22
9:33	Aeneas, who had been bedridden for eight years	10
10:14	for I have never eaten anything that is profane	22
10:20	for I have sent them."	22
10:21	what is the reason for your coming?"	6
10:33	Therefore I sent for you immediately	25
10:38	doing good and healing…for God was with him.	22
10:46	for they heard them speaking in tongues	4
11: 8	for nothing profane or unclean has ever entered	22
11:24	for he was a good man, full of the Holy Spirit	22
12: 5	the church prayed fervently to God for him.	24
13: 2	for the work to which I have called them."	9
13: 8	(for that is the translation of his name)	4

13:11	be blind for a while, unable to see the sun."	3
13:15	word of exhortation for the people, give it."	25
13:31	for many days he appeared	13
13:36	For David…died, was laid beside his ancestors	4
13:41	for in your days I am doing a work	22
13:47	For so the Lord has commanded us, saying	4
13:48	as many as had been destined for eternal life	9
14: 3	speaking boldly for the Lord	13
14:26	for the work that they had completed.	9
15:21	For…Moses has had those who proclaim him	4
15:21	For in every city, for generations past,	10
15:28	For it has seemed good to the Holy Spirit and to us	4
16: 3	for they all knew that his father was a Greek.	4
16:18	She kept doing this for many days.	13
16:28	"Do not harm yourself, for we are all here."	4
17:23	For as I went through the city	4
17:28	For 'In him we live and move and have our being';	4
17:28	'For we too are his offspring.'	4
18:10	for I am with you, and no one will lay a hand	7
18:10	for there are many in this city who are my people."	7
18:18	After staying there for a considerable time,	14
18:18	farewell to the believers and sailed for Syria	9
18:18	he had his hair cut, for he was under a vow.	4
18:28	for he powerfully refuted the Jews in public	4
19: 8	and for three months spoke out boldly	13
19:10	This continued for two years	13
19:32	for the assembly was in confusion	4
19:34	for about two hours all of them shouted	13
19:40	For we are in danger of being charged with rioting	4
20: 1	and saying farewell, he left for Macedonia.	9
20: 3	He was about to set sail for Syria	9
20:10	"Do not be alarmed, for his life is in him."	4
20:13	went ahead to the ship and set sail for Assos	13
20:13	for he had made this arrangement	4
20:16	For Paul had decided to sail past Ephesus	4
20:26	I am not responsible for the blood of any of you	2
20:27	for I did not shrink from declaring to you	4
20:35	the words of the Lord Jesus, for he himself said	22
21: 2	When we found a ship bound for Phoenicia	9
21:13	For I am ready not only to be bound	4
21:13	die in Jerusalem for the name of the Lord Jesus."	26
21:24	pay for the shaving of their heads	13
21:26	the sacrifice would be made for each of them.	26
21:29	For they had previously seen Trophimus	4
22: 5	to bring them back to Jerusalem for punishment	16
22:15	for you will be his witness to all the world	22
22:21	he said to me, 'Go, for I will send you	22
22:22	For he should not be allowed to live."	4
23: 5	for it is written, 'You shall not speak evil of	4
23:11	For just as you have testified for me in Jerusalem	4
23:11	just as you have testified for me in Jerusalem	24
23:17	for he has something to report to him."	4
23:21	for more than forty of their men are	4
23:21	They are ready now and are waiting for your consent	2
23:23	to leave by nine o'clock tonight for Caesarea	15
23:28	the charge for which they accused him	6
24:10	for many years you have been a judge	10
25:21	in custody for the decision of his Imperial Majesty	9
25:27	for it seems to me unreasonable	4
26: 1	"You have permission to speak for yourself."	24
26: 7	for this hope, your Excellency, that I am accused	24
26:16	for I have appeared to you for this purpose	4
26:26	for I am certain that none of these things	4
26:26	for this was not done in a corner.	4
27: 1	it was decided that we were to sail for Italy	9
27: 6	an Alexandrian ship bound for Italy	9
27: 7	We sailed slowly for a number of days	11
27:12	harbor was not suitable for spending the winter	25
27:20	neither sun nor stars appeared for many days	13
27:22	for there will be no loss of life among you	4
27:23	For last night there stood by me an angel	4
27:25	for I have faith in God	4
27:34	for it will help you survive;	4
27:34	for none of you will lose a hair from your heads	4
27:40	they made for the beach.	9
27:43	jump overboard…and make for the land	13
28:20	For this reason therefore I have asked to see	6
28:22	for with regard to this sect	4
28:27	For this people's heart has grown dull	4
Rom 1: 1	Paul…set apart for the gospel of God	9
1: 8	I thank my God through Jesus Christ for all of you	24

Rom	1: 9	For God...is my witness	4
	1:11	For I am longing to see you	4
	1:16	For I am not ashamed of the gospel;	4
	1:16	it is the power of God for salvation to everyone	9
	1:17	For in it the righteousness of God is revealed	4
	1:17	revealed through faith for faith;	9
	1:18	For the wrath of God is revealed from heaven	4
	1:19	For what can be known about God is plain to them	7
	1:21	for though they knew God, they did not honor him	7
	1:23	for images resembling a mortal human being or birds	11
	1:25	they exchanged the truth about God for a lie	11
	1:26	exchanged natural intercourse for unnatural	9
	1:27	men...consumed with passion for one another.	9
	2: 1	for in passing judgment on another you condemn	4
	2: 9	and distress for everyone who does evil	13
	2:11	For God shows no partiality.	4
	2:13	For it is not the hearers of the law who are righteous	4
	2:24	For, as it is written, "The name of God is blasphemed	4
	2:28	For a person is not a Jew who is one outwardly	4
	3: 2	For in the first place the Jews were entrusted	4
	3: 9	for we have already charged that all	4
	3:20	For "no human being will be justified in his sight"	7
	3:20	through the law comes the knowledge of sin.	4
	3:22	faith in Jesus Christ for all who believe.	9
	3:22	all who believe. For there is no distinction	4
	3:28	For we hold that a person is justified by faith	4
	4: 2	For if Abraham was justified by works	4
	4: 3	For what does the scripture say?	4
	4:13	For the promise that he would inherit the world	4
	4:15	For the law brings wrath;	4
	4:24	but for ours also.	6
	4:25	who was handed over to death for our trespasses	6
	4:25	and was raised for our justification.	6
	5: 6	For while we were still weak...Christ died	4
	5: 6	at the right time Christ died for the ungodly.	26
	5: 7	rarely will anyone die for a righteous person	26
	5: 7	perhaps for a good person someone might...die.	26
	5: 8	But God proves his love for us	9
	5: 8	while we still were sinners Christ died for us.	26
	5:10	For if while we were enemies, we were reconciled	4
	5:15	For if the many died through the one man's trespass	4
	5:15	the grace of God...abounded for the many.	9
	5:16	For the judgment following one trespass	4
	5:18	one man's trespass led to condemnation for all	9
	5:18	leads to justification and life for all.	9
	5:19	For just as by the one man's disobedience	4
	6: 5	For if we have been united with him in a death	4
	6: 7	For whoever has died is freed from sin.	4
	6:14	For sin will have no dominion over you	4
	6:19	For just as you once presented your members	4
	6:19	as slaves to righteousness for sanctification.	9
	6:23	For the wages of sin is death	4
	7: 1	for I am speaking to those who know the law	4
	7: 7	Yet, if it had not been for the law	6
	7:11	For sin, seizing an opportunity in the commandment	4
	7:14	For we know that the law is spiritual	4
	7:15	I do not do what I want	4
	7:18	For I know that nothing good dwells within me	4
	7:19	For I do not do the good I want, but the evil	4
	7:22	For I delight in the law of God in my inmost self	4
	8: 2	For the law of the Spirit of life in Christ Jesus	4
	8: 3	For God has done what the law...could not do:	4
	8: 5	For those who live according to the flesh	4
	8:13	for if you live according to the flesh, you will die;	4
	8:14	For all who are led by the Spirit of God	4
	8:15	For you did not receive a spirit of slavery	4
	8:19	For the creation waits with eager longing	4
	8:20	for the creation was subjected to futility	4
	8:24	For in hope we were saved.	4
	8:24	For who hopes for what is seen?	4
	8:26	for we do not know how to pray as we ought	4
	8:27	because the Spirit intercedes for the saints	26
	8:28	work together for good for those who love God	9
	8:29	For those whom he foreknew he also predestined	22
	8:31	If God is for us, who is against us?	26
	8:32	not withhold his own Son, but gave him up for all	26
	8:34	Christ Jesus...who indeed intercedes for us.	26
	8:38	For I am convinced that neither death, nor life	4
	9: 3	For I could wish that I myself were accursed	4
	9: 6	For not all Israelites truly belong to Israel	4
	9: 9	For this is what the promise said, "About this time	4

	9:15	For he says to Moses, "I will have mercy	4
	9:17	For the scripture says to Pharaoh	4
	9:17	for the very purpose of showing my power in you	9
	9:19	For who can resist his will?"	4
	9:21	out of the same lump one object for special use	9
	9:21	object for special use and another for ordinary use?	9
	9:22	the objects of wrath that are made for destruction;	9
	9:23	the riches of his glory for the objects of mercy	13
	9:23	which he has prepared beforehand for glory	9
	9:28	for Lord will execute his sentence on the earth	4
	10: 1	my heart's desire and prayer to God for them	26
	10: 3	For, being ignorant of the righteousness	4
	10: 4	For Christ is the end of the law	4
	10:10	For one believes with the heart and so is justified	4
	10:12	For there is no distinction between Jew and Greek;	4
	10:13	For, "Everyone who calls on the name of the Lord	4
	10:16	for Isaiah says, "Lord, who has believed	4
	11:15	For if their rejection is the reconciliation	4
	11:21	For if God did not spare the natural branches	4
	11:23	for God has the power to graft them in again.	4
	11:24	For if you have been cut from	4
	11:29	for the gifts and the calling of God are	4
	11:32	For God has imprisoned all in disobedience	4
	11:34	"For who has known the mind of the Lord?	4
	11:36	For from him and through him and to him are all	22
	12: 3	For by the grace given to me I say to everyone	4
	12: 4	For as in one body we have many members	4
	12:17	Do not repay anyone evil for evil	1
	12:19	for it is written, "Vengeance is mine, I will repay	4
	12:20	for by doing this you will heap burning coals	4
	13: 1	for there is no authority except from God	4
	13: 3	For rulers are not a terror to good conduct	4
	13: 4	for it is God's servant for your good.	4
	13: 4	for it is God's servant for your good.	9
	13: 4	for the authority does not bear the sword in vain!	4
	13: 6	for the authorities are God's servants,	4
	13: 8	for the one who loves...has fulfilled the law.	4
	13:11	For salvation is nearer to us now	4
	14: 3	for God has welcomed them.	4
	14: 4	for the Lord is able to make them stand.	4
	14: 9	For to this end Christ died and lived again	4
	14:10	For we will all stand before the judgment seat	4
	14:11	For it is written, "As I live, says the Lord	4
	14:15	cause the ruin of one for whom Christ died.	26
	14:17	For the kingdom of God is not food and drink	4
	14:23	for whatever does not proceed from faith is sin.	5
	15: 3	For Christ did not please himself;	4
	15: 4	For whatever was written in former days	4
	15: 4	was written for our instruction	9
	15: 7	Welcome one another...for the glory of God.	9
	15: 8	For I tell you that Christ has become a servant	4
	15: 9	the Gentiles might glorify God for his mercy.	26
	15:17	I have reason to boast of my work for God.	25
	15:18	For I will not venture to speak of anything	4
	15:23	I desire, as I have for many years, to come to you	2
	15:24	For I do hope to see you on my journey	4
	15:24	I have enjoyed your company for a little while	2
	15:26	for Macedonia and Achaia have been pleased	4
	15:27	for if the Gentiles have come to share in	4
	16: 2	for she has been a benefactor of many and of myself	4
	16: 4	who risked their necks for my life	26
	16: 5	Epaenetus...first convert in Asia for Christ.	9
	16:18	For such people do not serve our Lord Christ	4
	16:19	For while your obedience is known to all	4
1Co	1: 4	I give thanks to my God always for you	24
	1: 5	for in every way you have been enriched in him	22
	1:11	For it has been reported to me by Chloe's people	4
	1:13	Has Christ been divided? Was Paul crucified for you?	26
	1:17	For Christ did not send me to baptize	4
	1:18	For the message about the cross is foolishness	4
	1:19	For it is written, "I will destroy the wisdom	4
	1:21	For since...the world did not know God	4
	1:22	For Jews demand signs and Greeks desire wisdom	12
	1:25	For God's foolishness is wiser than human wisdom	22
	2: 2	For I decided to know nothing among you	4
	2: 7	which God decreed before the ages for our glory	9
	2: 8	for if they had, they would not have crucified	4
	2:10	for the Spirit searches everything, even the depths	4
	2:11	For what human being knows what is truly human	4
	2:14	for they are foolishness to them	4
	2:16	"For who has known the mind of the Lord	4

3: 2	for you were not ready for solid food.	4
3: 3	for you are still of the flesh.	4
3: 3	For as long as there is jealousy and quarreling	4
3: 4	For when one says, "I belong to Paul,"	4
3: 9	For we are God's servants, working together	4
3:11	For no one can lay any foundation other	4
3:13	for the Day will disclose it	4
3:17	For God's temple is holy, and you are that temple.	4
3:19	For the wisdom of this world is foolishness with God.	4
3:19	For it is written, "He catches the wise	4
3:21	For all things are yours	4
4: 7	For who sees anything different in you?	4
4: 9	For I think that God has exhibited us apostles	4
4:15	For though you might have ten thousand guardians	4
4:20	For the kingdom of God depends not on talk	4
5: 1	for a man is living with his father's wife.	28
5: 3	For though absent in body, I am present in spirit;	4
5: 5	for the destruction of the flesh	9
5: 7	For our paschal lamb, Christ, has been sacrificed.	4
5:12	For what have I to do with judging those outside?	4
6:16	For it is said, "The two shall be one flesh."	4
6:20	For you were bought with a price;	4
7: 5	except perhaps by agreement for a set time	25
7: 9	For it is better to marry than to be aflame	4
7:14	For the unbelieving husband is made holy	4
7:16	Wife, for all you know	4
7:22	For whoever was called in the Lord as a slave	4
7:31	For the present form of this world is passing away.	4
7:35	I say this for your own benefit	25
8: 6	from whom are all things and for whom we exist	9
8:10	For if others see you, who possess knowledge, eating	4
8:11	weak believers for whom Christ died are destroyed.	6
9: 2	for you are the seal of my apostleship in the Lord.	4
9: 9	For it is written in the law of Moses	4
9:10	for whoever plows should plow in hope	22
9:16	for an obligation is laid on me	4
9:17	For if I do this of my own will, I have a reward;	4
9:19	For though I am free with respect to all	4
10: 4	For they drank from the spiritual rock	4
10:17	for we all partake of the one bread.	4
10:26	for "the earth and its fullness are the Lord's."	4
10:29	For why should my liberty be subject	4
10:31	do everything for the glory of God.	9
11: 6	For if a woman will not veil herself	4
11: 7	For a man ought not to have his head veiled	4
11:12	For just as woman came from man	4
11:13	Judge for yourselves: is it proper	11
11:15	For her hair is given to her for a covering.	22
11:15	her hair is given to her for a covering.	1
11:17	it is not for the better but for the worse.	9
11:17	it is not for the better but for the worse.	9
11:18	For, to begin with, when you come together	4
11:19	for only so will it become clear who among you	16
11:21	For when the time comes to eat,	4
11:23	For I received from the Lord	4
11:24	"This is my body that is for you.	26
11:26	For as often as you eat this bread	4
11:29	For all who eat and drink	4
11:34	come together, it will not be for your condemnation.	9
12: 7	To each is given…the Spirit for the common good.	25
12:12	For just as the body is one and has many members	4
12:13	For in the one Spirit we were all baptized	4
12:25	members may have the same care for one another.	26
13: 9	For we know only in part	4
13:12	For now we see in a mirror, dimly,	4
14: 2	For those who speak in a tongue do not speak	4
14: 2	for nobody understands them,	4
14: 8	who will get ready for battle?	9
14: 9	For you will be speaking into the air.	4
14:12	strive to excel in them for building up the church.	25
14:14	For if I pray in a tongue, my spirit prays	4
14:17	For you may give thanks well enough	4
14:26	Let all things be done for building up.	25
14:31	For you can all prophesy one by one	4
14:33	for God is a God not of disorder but of peace.	4
14:34	For they are not permitted to speak	4
14:35	For it is shameful for a woman to speak in church.	4
15: 3	For I handed on to you as of first importance	4
15: 3	Christ died for our sins	26
15: 9	For I am the least of the apostles	4
15:16	For if the dead are not raised	4

15:19	If for this life only we have hoped in Christ	11
15:21	For since death came through a human being	4
15:22	for as all die in Adam	4
15:25	For he must reign until he has put all	4
15:27	For "God has put all things in subjection	4
15:32	"Let us eat and drink, for tomorrow we die."	4
15:34	for some people have no knowledge of God.	4
15:52	at the last trumpet. For the trumpet will sound	4
15:53	For this perishable body must put on imperishability,	4
16: 1	Now concerning the collection for the saints:	9
16: 5	for I intend to pass through Macedonia	4
16: 7	for I hope to spend some time with you	4
16: 9	for a wide door for effective work has opened	4
16:10	for he is doing the work of the Lord just as I am;	4
16:11	for I am expecting him with the brothers.	4
16:18	for they refreshed my spirit as well as yours.	4
2Co 1: 5	For just as the sufferings of Christ are abundant	22
1: 5	just as the sufferings of Christ are abundant for us	9
1: 6	it is for your consolation and salvation;	26
1: 6	if we are being consoled, it is for your consolation	26
1: 7	Our hope for you is unshaken;	26
1: 8	for we were so utterly, unbearably crushed	22
1:13	For we write you nothing other than what you can read	4
1:19	For the Son of God, Jesus Christ, whom we proclaimed	4
1:20	For in him every one of God's promises is a "Yes."	4
2: 2	For if I cause you pain, who is there to make me glad	4
2: 4	For I wrote you out of much distress	4
2: 4	know the abundant love that I have for you	9
2: 8	I urge you to reaffirm your love for him.	9
2:11	for we are not ignorant of his designs.	4
2:15	For we are the aroma of Christ to God	22
2:16	Who is sufficient for these things?	25
2:17	For we are not peddlers of God's word like so many;	4
3: 6	for the letter kills, but the Spirit gives life.	4
3: 9	For if there was glory in the ministry	4
3:11	for if what was set aside came through glory	4
3:18	for this comes from the Lord, the Spirit.	17
4: 5	For we do not proclaim ourselves; we proclaim Jesus	4
4: 6	For it is the God who said, "Let light shine	22
4:11	For while we live, we are always being given up	4
4:17	For this slight momentary affliction	4
4:18	for what can be seen is temporary	4
5: 1	For we know that if the earthly tent we live	4
5: 2	For in this tent we groan	4
5: 4	For while we are still in this tent	4
5: 5	He who has prepared us for this very thing is God	9
5: 7	for we walk by faith, not by sight.	4
5:10	For all of us must appear before the judgment seat	4
5:10	for what has been done in the body	25
5:13	For if we are beside ourselves, it is for God;	4
5:14	For the love of Christ urges us on	4
5:14	we are convinced that one has died for all;	26
5:15	he died for all, so that those who live	26
5:15	who died and was raised for them.	26
5:20	So we are ambassadors for Christ	26
6: 2	For he says, "At an acceptable time	4
6:14	For what partnership is there between righteousness	4
6:16	For we are the temple of the living God	4
7: 3	for I said before that you are in our hearts	4
7: 5	For even when we came into Macedonia	4
7: 7	your zeal for me	26
7: 8	For even if I made you sorry with my letter	22
7: 8	for I see that I grieved you with that letter	4
7: 9	for you felt a godly grief	4
7:10	For godly grief produces a repentance	4
7:11	For see what earnestness this godly grief	4
7:12	in order that your zeal for us might be made known	26
7:14	For if I have been somewhat boastful about you	22
8: 2	for during a severe ordeal of affliction	22
8: 3	For…they voluntarily gave according to their means	22
8: 7	in utmost eagerness, and in our love for you	11
8: 9	For you know the generous act of our Lord Jesus Christ	4
8:12	For if the eagerness is there, the gift is acceptable	4
8:14	so that their abundance may be for your need	9
8:16	in the heart of Titus the same eagerness for you	26
8:17	For he not only accepted our appeal	22
8:18	famous…for his proclaiming the good news;	11
8:19	for the glory of the Lord himself	25
8:21	for we intend to do what is right	4
9: 2	for I know your eagerness	4
9: 7	for God loves a cheerful giver.	4

2Co	9:10	supplies seed to the sower and bread for food	9
	9:11	enriched in every way for your great generosity	9
	9:12	for the rendering of this ministry	22
	9:14	while they long for you and pray for you	26
	9:15	Thanks be to God for his indescribable gift!	13
	10: 4	for the weapons of our warfare are not merely human	4
	10: 8	which the Lord gave for building you up	9
	10: 8	building you up and not for tearing you down	9
	10:10	For they say, "His letters are weighty and strong	22
	10:14	For we were not overstepping our limits	4
	10:18	For it is not those who commend themselves	4
	11: 2	for I promised you in marriage to one husband	4
	11: 4	For if someone comes and proclaims another Jesus	4
	11: 9	for my needs were supplied by the friends	4
	11:13	For such boasters are false apostles,	4
	11:19	For you gladly put up with fools, being wise	4
	11:20	For you put up with it when someone makes slaves	4
	12: 6	for I will be speaking the truth.	4
	12: 9	for power is made perfect in weakness."	4
	12:10	for whenever I am weak, then I am strong.	4
	12:11	for I am not at all inferior	4
	12:14	for children ought not to lay up for their parents	4
	12:15	most gladly spend and be spent for you.	26
	12:20	For I fear that when I come, I may find you	4
	13: 4	For he was crucified in weakness	4
	13: 4	For we are weak in him	4
	13: 8	For we cannot do anything against the truth	4
	13: 8	but only for the truth.	26
	13: 9	For we rejoice when we are weak and you are strong.	4
	13:10	for building up and not for tearing down.	9
	13:10	for building up and not for tearing down.	9
Gal	1: 4	who gave himself for our sins	26
	1:11	For I want you to know, brothers and sisters	4
	1:12	for I did not receive it from a human source	4
	2: 5	we did not submit to them even for a moment	25
	2: 8	(for he who worked through Peter	4
	2:12	for until certain people came from James	4
	2:19	For through the law I died to the law	4
	2:20	Son of God, who loved me and gave himself for me.	26
	2:21	for if justification comes through the law	4
	3:10	For all who rely on the works of the law	4
	3:10	for it is written, "Cursed is everyone	4
	3:11	for "The one who is righteous will live by faith."	22
	3:13	Christ redeemed us…by becoming a curse for us	26
	3:13	for it is written, "Cursed is everyone who hangs	22
	3:18	For if the inheritance comes from the law	4
	3:21	For if a law had been given that could make alive	4
	3:26	for in Christ Jesus you are all children of God	4
	3:28	for all of you are one in Christ Jesus.	4
	4:11	afraid that my work for you may have been wasted.	9
	4:12	for I also have become as you are.	22
	4:15	For I testify that, had it been possible	4
	4:18	It is good to be made much of for a good purpose	11
	4:20	for I am perplexed about you.	22
	4:22	For it is written that Abraham had two sons	4
	4:24	Hagar, from Mount Sinai, bearing children for slavery.	9
	4:25	for she is in slavery with her children.	4
	4:27	For it is written, "Rejoice, you childless one	4
	4:27	for the children of the desolate woman are more	22
	4:30	for the child of the slave will not share	4
	5: 5	For through the Spirit, by faith, we eagerly wait	4
	5: 6	For in Christ Jesus neither circumcision	4
	5:13	For you were called to freedom, brothers and sisters;	4
	5:14	For the whole law is summed up in a single commandment	4
	5:17	For what the flesh desires is opposed to the Spirit	4
	5:17	for these are opposed to each other	4
	6: 3	For if those who are nothing think they are	4
	6: 5	For all must carry their own loads.	4
	6: 7	for you reap whatever you sow.	4
	6: 9	for we will reap at harvest time	4
	6:10	opportunity, let us work for the good of all	25
	6:10	especially for those of the family	25
	6:15	For neither circumcision nor uncircumcision is anything;	4
	6:17	for I carry the marks of Jesus branded on my body.	4
Eph	1: 5	He destined us for adoption as his children	9
	1:12	might live for the praise of his glory.	9
	1:16	I do not cease to give thanks for you	26
	1:19	greatness of his power for us who believe	9
	2: 8	For by grace you have been saved through faith	4
	2:10	For we are what he has made us, created in Christ	4
	2:10	created in Christ Jesus for good works	13
	2:14	For he is our peace; in his flesh he has made	4
	2:18	for through him both of us have access in one Spirit	22
	3: 2	for surely you have already heard of the commission	8
	3: 2	commission of God's grace that was given me for you	9
	3: 9	plan of the mystery hidden for ages in God	2
	3:13	not lose heart over my sufferings for you;	26
	4:12	to equip the saints for the work of ministry	9
	4:12	for building up the body of Christ	9
	4:21	For surely you have heard about him	8
	4:25	for we are members of one another.	22
	4:29	only what is useful for building up	25
	4:30	marked with a seal for the day of redemption.	9
	5: 2	Christ…gave himself up for us	26
	5: 6	for because of these things the wrath of God	4
	5: 8	For once you were darkness, but now in the Lord	4
	5: 9	for the fruit of the light is found in all…good	4
	5:12	For it is shameful even to mention	4
	5:14	for everything that becomes visible is light.	4
	5:18	Do not get drunk with wine, for that is debauchery;	11
	5:20	giving thanks to God the Father…for everything	26
	5:23	For the husband is the head of the wife	22
	5:25	loved the church and gave himself up for her	26
	5:29	For no one ever hates his own body	4
	6: 1	obey your parents in the Lord, for this is right.	4
	6:12	For our struggle is not against enemies of blood	22
	6:18	in supplication for all the saints.	24
	6:19	Pray also for me, so that when I speak,	26
	6:20	for which I am an ambassador in chains.	26
Php	1: 4	in every one of my prayers for all of you	26
	1: 8	For God is my witness, how I long for all of you	4
	1:11	for the glory and praise of God.	9
	1:13	my imprisonment is for Christ;	11
	1:16	put here for the defense of the gospel;	9
	1:19	for I know that through your prayers	4
	1:19	this will turn out for my deliverance.	9
	1:21	For to me, living is Christ and dying is gain.	4
	1:23	for that is far better;	4
	1:24	is more necessary for you.	6
	1:25	for your progress and joy in faith	9
	1:29	For he has graciously granted you the privilege	22
	1:29	suffering for him as well	26
	2:13	for it is God who is at work in you, enabling you	4
	2:13	both to will and to work for his good pleasure.	26
	2:26	for he has been longing for all of you	12
	2:30	he came close to death for the work of Christ	6
	3: 3	For it is we who are the circumcision	4
	3:14	I press on toward the goal for the prize	9
	3:18	For many live as enemies of the cross of Christ;	4
	4:10	now at last you have revived your concern	26
	4:11	for I have learned to be content with whatever	4
	4:16	For even when I was in Thessalonica, you sent me help	22
	4:16	you sent me help for my needs more than once.	9
Col	1: 3	In our prayers for you	24
	1: 4	the love that you have for all the saints	9
	1: 9	we have not ceased praying for you	26
	1:16	for in him all things in heaven and on earth	22
	1:16	all things have been created through him and for him	9
	1:19	For in him all the fullness of God was pleased	22
	1:25	God's commission that was given to me for you	9
	1:29	For this I toil and struggle with all the energy	9
	2: 1	For I want you to know…I am struggling for you	4
	2: 1	want you to know how much I am struggling for you	26
	2: 5	For though I am absent in body	4
	2: 9	For in him the whole fullness of deity dwells bodily	22
	3: 3	for you have died, and your life is hidden	4
	3:20	for this is your acceptable duty in the Lord.	4
	3:25	For the wrongdoer will be paid back	4
	4: 3	At the same time pray for us as well	24
	4: 3	mystery of Christ, for which I am in prison	6
	4:11	among my co-workers for the kingdom of God	9
	4:13	For I testify for him that he has worked hard for you	4
	4:13	I testify for him that he has worked hard for you	26
1Th	1: 2	We always give thanks to God for all of you	24
	1: 8	for the word of the Lord has sounded forth from you	4
	1: 9	For the people of those regions report about us	4
	2: 3	For our appeal does not spring from deceit	4
	2:13	We also constantly give thanks to God for this	6
	2:14	For you…became imitators of the churches	4
	2:14	for you suffered the same things	22
	2:17	for a short time, we were made orphans	25
	2:18	For we wanted to come to you	7

	2:19	For what is our hope or joy or crown of boasting	4
	3: 3	know that this is what we are destined for.	9
	3: 8	For we now live, if you continue to stand firm	22
	3: 9	How can we thank God enough for you	24
	3: 9	for all the joy that we feel before our God	13
	3:12	increase and abound in love for one another	9
	3:12	abound in love for one another and for all,	9
	3:12	just as we abound in love for you.	9
	4: 2	For you know what instructions we gave you	4
	4: 3	For this is the will of God, your sanctification:	4
	4: 7	For God did not call us to impurity	4
	4: 9	for you…have been taught by God to love	4
	4:14	For since we believe that Jesus died and rose again	4
	4:15	For this we declare to you by the word of the Lord	4
	4:16	For the Lord himself, with a cry of command,	22
	5: 2	For you yourselves know very well	4
	5: 4	for that day to surprise you like a thief;	16
	5: 5	for you are all children of light	4
	5: 7	for those who sleep sleep at night	4
	5: 9	For God has destined us not for wrath	22
	5: 9	For God has destined us not for wrath	9
	5: 9	for obtaining salvation through our Lord Jesus	9
	5:10	who died for us, so that…we may live with him	26
	5:15	See that none of you repays evil for evil	1
	5:18	for this is the will of God in Christ Jesus	4
	5:18	the will of God in Christ Jesus for you.	9
	5:25	Beloved, pray for us.	24
2Th	1: 3	We must always give thanks to God for you	24
	1: 3	the love of everyone of you for one another	9
	1: 4	for your steadfastness and faith	26
	1: 5	kingdom of God, for which you are also suffering.	26
	1:11	To this end we always pray for you	24
	2: 3	for that day will not come unless the rebellion	22
	2: 7	For the mystery of lawlessness is already at work	4
	2:13	we must always give thanks to God for you	24
	2:13	God chose you as the first fruits for salvation	9
	3: 1	Finally, brothers and sisters, pray for us	24
	3: 2	for not all have faith.	4
	3: 7	for you yourselves know how you ought to imitate us;	4
	3:10	For even when we were with you	4
	3:11	For we hear that some of you are living in idleness	4
1Ti	1:16	who would come to believe in him for eternal life.	9
	2: 1	thanksgivings be made for everyone	26
	2: 2	for kings and all who are in high positions	26
	2: 5	For there is one God;	4
	2: 6	who gave himself a ransom for all	26
	2: 7	For this I was appointed a herald and an apostle	9
	2:13	For Adam was formed first, then Eve;	4
	3: 5	for if someone does not know how to manage	5
	3:13	for those who serve well as deacons	4
	4: 4	For everything created by God is good	22
	4: 5	for it is sanctified by God's word	4
	4: 8	for, while physical training is of some value	4
	4:10	For to this end we toil and struggle	4
	4:16	for in doing this you will save…yourself	4
	5: 4	for this is pleasing in God's sight.	4
	5:10	she must be well attested for her good works	11
	5:11	for when their sensual desires alienate them	4
	5:12	for having violated their first pledge.	22
	5:15	For some have already turned away to follow Satan.	4
	5:18	for the scripture says, "You shall not muzzle an ox	4
	6: 4	and has a morbid craving for controversy	24
	6: 7	for we brought nothing into the world	4
	6:10	For the love of money is a root of all kinds of evil	4
	6:17	richly provides us with everything for our enjoyment.	9
	6:19	the treasure of a good foundation for the future	9
2Ti	1: 6	For this reason I remind you to rekindle the gift	6
	1: 7	for God did not give us a spirit of cowardice	4
	1:11	For this gospel I was appointed a herald	9
	1:12	for this reason I suffer as I do.	6
	1:12	for I know the one in whom I have put my trust	4
	2: 7	for the Lord will give you understanding	4
	2: 9	for which I suffer hardship, even…being chained	11
	2:13	for he cannot deny himself.	4
	2:16	for it will lead people into more and more impiety	4
	2:20	some for special use, some for ordinary.	9
	2:20	some for special use, some for ordinary.	9
	2:21	ready for every good work.	4
	3: 2	For people will be lovers of themselves,	4
	3: 6	For among them are those who…	4
	3:15	that are able to instruct you for salvation	9

	3:16	inspired by God and is useful for teaching	25
	3:16	useful…for reproof, for correction	25
	3:16	useful…for reproof, for correction	25
	3:16	useful…for training in righteousness	25
	3:17	equipped for every good work.	25
	4: 3	For the time is coming	4
	4:10	for Demas, in love with this present world	4
	4:11	for he is useful in my ministry.	4
	4:14	the Lord will pay him back for his deeds.	20
	4:15	for he strongly opposed our message.	4
	4:18	save me for his heavenly kingdom.	9
Tit	1: 7	For a bishop, as God's steward, must be blameless;	4
	1:11	teaching for sordid gain	27
	1:13	For this reason rebuke them sharply	6
	1:16	detestable, disobedient, unfit for any good work.	25
	2:11	For the grace of God has appeared	4
	2:14	who gave himself for us that he might redeem us	26
	3: 1	to be obedient, to be ready for every good work	25
	3: 3	For we ourselves were once foolish, disobedient	4
	3: 9	for they are unprofitable and worthless.	4
	3:12	for I have decided to spend the winter there.	4
Phm	1: 5	I hear of your love for all the saints	9
	1: 6	perceive all the good that we may do for Christ.	9
	1:10	I am appealing to you for my child, Onesimus	24
	1:15	was separated from you for a while	25
	1:22	for I am hoping…to be restored to you.	4
Heb	1: 5	For to which of the angels did God ever say,	4
	2: 2	For if the message declared through angels was valid	4
	2: 9	by the grace of God he might taste death for everyone.	26
	2:10	for whom and through whom all things exist	6
	2:11	For the one who sanctifies and those who are sanctified	4
	2:11	For this reason Jesus is not ashamed to call them brothers	6
	2:16	For it is clear that he did not come to help angels	4
	3: 4	(For every house is built by someone	4
	3:14	For we have become partners of Christ	4
	4: 2	For indeed the good news came to us just as to them;	4
	4: 3	For we who have believed enter that rest	4
	4: 4	For in one place it speaks about the seventh day	4
	4: 8	For if Joshua had given them rest	4
	4:10	for those who enter God's rest	4
	4:15	For we do not have a high priest who is unable	4
	5: 1	to offer gifts and sacrifices for sins.	26
	5: 3	he must offer sacrifice for his own sins	24
	5: 3	as well as for those of the people.	24
	5:12	For though by this time you ought to be teachers	4
	5:13	for everyone who lives on milk	4
	6: 4	For it is impossible to restore again to repentance	4
	6: 7	useful to those for whom it is cultivated	6
	6:10	For God is not unjust; he will not overlook your work	4
	6:10	the love that you showed for his sake	9
	7:10	for he was still in the loins of his ancestor	4
	7:11	for the people received the law under this priesthood	4
	7:12	For when there is a change in the priesthood	4
	7:14	For it is evident…our Lord…descended from Judah	4
	7:17	For it is attested of him	4
	7:19	(for the law made nothing perfect);	4
	7:20	for others who became priests took their office	4
	7:25	Consequently he is able for all time to save	9
	7:25	he always lives to make intercession for them.	26
	7:26	For it was fitting that we should have such a high priest	4
	7:27	to offer sacrifices day after day, first for his own sins	26
	7:28	For the law appoints as high priests	4
	8: 3	For every high priest is appointed to offer gifts	4
	8: 5	for Moses, when he was about to erect the tent	18
	8: 7	For if that first covenant had been faultless	4
	8: 9	for they did not continue in my covenant	22
	8:11	'Know the Lord,' for they shall all know me	22
	8:12	For I will be merciful toward their iniquities	22
	9: 2	For a tent was constructed, the first one	4
	9: 7	taking the blood that he offers for himself	26
	9:13	For if the blood of goats and bulls	4
	9:17	For a will takes effect only at death	4
	9:19	For when every commandment had been told	4
	9:20	the covenant that God has ordained for you."	25
	9:24	For Christ did not enter a sanctuary made by	4
	10: 4	For it is impossible for the blood of bulls	4
	10:12	offered for all time a single sacrifice for sins	9
	10:12	offered for all time a single sacrifice for sins	26
	10:14	For by a single offering he has perfected	4
	10:14	perfected for all time those who are sanctified.	9
	10:15	also testifies to us, for after saying	4

Heb	10:18	there is no longer any offering for sin.	24
	10:23	for he who has promised is faithful.	4
	10:26	For if we willfully persist in sin	4
	10:26	there no longer remains a sacrifice for sins	24
	10:30	For we know the one who said, "Vengeance is mine	4
	10:34	For you had compassion for those who were in prison	4
	10:36	For you need endurance	4
	10:37	For yet "in a very little while,	4
	11: 5	For it was attested before he was taken away	4
	11: 6	for whoever would approach him must believe	4
	11: 8	when he was called to set out for a place	9
	11:10	For he looked forward to the city	4
	11:14	for people who speak in this way make it clear	4
	11:20	invoked blessings for the future on Jacob and Esau.	24
	11:26	for he was looking ahead to the reward.	4
	11:27	for he persevered as though he saw him	4
	11:30	after they had been encircled for seven days.	13
	11:32	For time would fail me to tell of Gideon,	4
	11:39	though they were commended for their faith	6
	12: 6	for the Lord disciplines those whom he loves	4
	12: 7	for what child…a parent does not discipline?	4
	12:10	For they disciplined us for a short time	4
	12:10	they disciplined us for a short time	25
	12:10	he disciplines us for our good	13
	12:16	who sold his birthright for a single meal.	1
	12:17	he was rejected, for he found no chance to repent	4
	12:20	(For they could not endure the order	4
	12:25	for if they did not escape when they refused	4
	12:29	for indeed our God is a consuming fire.	4
	13: 2	for by doing that some have entertained angels	4
	13: 4	for God will judge fornicators and adulterers.	4
	13: 5	for he has said, "I will never leave you	4
	13: 9	for it is well for the heart to be strengthened	4
	13:11	For the bodies of those animals	4
	13:11	as a sacrifice for sin	24
	13:14	For here we have no lasting city	4
	13:16	for such sacrifices are pleasing to God.	4
	13:17	for they are keeping watch over your souls	4
	13:17	for that would be harmful to you.	4
	13:18	Pray for us;	24
	13:22	for I have written to you briefly.	4
Jas	1: 6	for the one who doubts is like a wave of the sea	4
	1: 7	for the doubter, being double-minded and unstable	4
	1:11	For the sun rises with its scorching heat	4
	1:13	for God cannot be tempted by evil	4
	1:20	for your anger does not produce God's righteousness.	4
	1:23	For if any are hearers of the word and not doers,	22
	1:24	for they look at themselves and, on going away	4
	2: 2	For if a person with gold rings and in fine clothes	4
	2:10	For whoever keeps the whole law but fails	4
	2:11	For the one who said, "You shall not commit adultery,"	4
	2:13	For judgment will be without mercy	4
	2:26	For just as the body without the spirit is dead	4
	3: 2	For all of us make many mistakes.	4
	3: 7	For every species of beast and bird, of reptile	4
	3:16	For where there is envy and selfish ambition	4
	4:14	For you are a mist that appears for a little while	4
	4:14	For you are a mist that appears for a little while	25
	5: 1	weep and wail for the miseries that are coming	13
	5: 3	You have laid up treasure for the last days.	11
	5: 8	for the coming of the Lord is near.	22
	5:16	pray for one another, so that you may be healed.	26
1Pe	1: 4	inheritance that is…kept in heaven for you	9
	1: 5	for a salvation ready to be revealed	9
	1:16	for it is written, "You shall be holy, for I am	7
	1:16	it is written, "You shall be holy, for I am holy."	22
	1:24	For "All flesh is like grass	7
	2: 6	For it stands in scripture:	7
	2:15	For it is God's will that by doing right	22
	2:19	For it is a credit to you if…you endure pain	4
	2:21	For to this you have been called	4
	2:21	because Christ also suffered for you	26
	2:25	For you were going astray like sheep	4
	3: 9	Do not repay evil for evil	1
	3: 9	Do not repay…abuse for abuse;	1
	3: 9	It is for this that you were called	9
	3:10	For "Those who desire life and desire to see good	4
	3:12	For the eyes of the Lord are on the righteous	22
	3:14	even if you do suffer for doing what is right	6
	3:15	an accounting for the hope that is in you;	24
	3:17	For it is better to suffer for doing good	4

	3:18	For Christ also suffered for sins once for all	22
	3:18	Christ also suffered for sins once for all	24
	3:18	the righteous for the unrighteous	26
	4: 1	(for whoever has suffered in the flesh	22
	4: 6	For this is the reason the gospel was proclaimed	4
	4: 8	maintain constant love for one another	9
	4: 8	for love covers a multitude of sins.	22
	4:14	If you are reviled for the name of Christ	11
	4:17	For the time has come for judgment to begin	22
	5: 5	for "God opposes the proud, but gives grace	22
	5: 7	Cast…anxiety on him, because he cares for you.	24
2Pe	1: 8	For if these things are yours and are increasing	4
	1: 9	For anyone who lacks these things is nearsighted	4
	1:10	for if you do this, you will never stumble.	4
	1:11	For in this way, entry into the eternal kingdom	4
	1:16	We did not follow cleverly devised myths	4
	1:17	For he received honor and glory from God	4
	2: 4	For if God did not spare the angels	4
	2: 8	(for that righteous man…was tormented	4
	2:18	For they speak bombastic nonsense,	4
	2:19	for people are slaves to whatever masters them.	4
	2:20	For if, after they have escaped the defilements	4
	2:21	For it would have been better for them	4
	3: 4	For ever since our ancestors died	4
1Jn	2: 2	he is the atoning sacrifice for our sins	24
	2: 2	the atoning sacrifice for our sins, and not for ours only	24
	2: 2	but also for the sins of the whole world.	24
	2:16	for all that is in the world	22
	2:19	for if they had belonged to us,	4
	3: 2	for we will see him as he is.	22
	3: 8	for the devil has been sinning from the beginning.	22
	3:11	For this is message you have heard	22
	3:16	We know love…that he laid down his life for us	26
	3:16	we ought to lay down our lives for one another.	26
	3:20	for God is greater than our hearts	22
	4: 1	for many false prophets have gone out	22
	4: 4	for the one who is in you is greater	22
	4: 8	for God is love.	22
	4:10	sent his Son to be the atoning sacrifice for our sins.	24
	4:16	we have known and believe the love that God has for us.	11
	4:18	for fear has to do with punishment	22
	4:20	for those who do not love a brother or sister	4
	5: 3	For the love of God is this, that we obey	4
	5: 4	for whatever is born of God conquers the world.	22
	5: 6	for the Spirit is the truth.	22
	5: 9	for this is the testimony of God	22
2Jn	1:11	for to welcome is to participate in the evil	4
3Jn	1: 5	whatever you do for the friends	9
	1: 7	for they began their journey for the sake of Christ	4
Jde	1: 4	For certain intruders have stolen in among you	4
	1: 4	who long ago were designated for this condemnation	9
	1: 6	kept…for the judgment of the great day.	9
	1:11	Woe to them! For they go the way of Cain	22
	1:18	for they said to you, "In the last time	22
Rev	1: 3	for the time is near.	4
	3: 2	for I have not found your works perfect	4
	3: 4	with me, dressed in white, for they are worthy.	22
	3:17	For you say, 'I am rich, I have prospered	22
	4:11	for you created all things	22
	5: 9	for you were slaughtered and by your blood you	22
	6: 9	those who had been slaughtered for the word	6
	6: 9	slaughtered…for the testimony they had given;	6
	6:17	for the great day of their wrath has come	22
	7:17	for the Lamb…will be their shepherd,	22
	9: 7	the locusts were like horses equipped for battle.	9
	9:15	angels…who had been held ready for the hour	9
	9:19	For the power of the horses is in their mouths	4
	11: 2	for it is given over to the nations	22
	11:17	for have taken your great power and begun to reign.	22
	12:10	for the accuser of our comrades has been thrown down	22
	12:11	for they did not cling to life	19
	12:12	for the devil has come down to you with great wrath	22
	13: 4	for he had given his authority to the beast	22
	13:18	number of the beast, for it is the number of a person.	4
	14: 4	not defiled themselves…for they are virgins;	4
	14: 7	"Fear God…for the hour of his judgment has come;	22
	14:13	"they will rest…for their deeds follow them."	4
	14:15	reap, for the hour to reap has come	22
	14:18	gather the clusters…for its grapes are ripe."	22
	15: 1	for with them the wrath of God is ended.	22
	15: 4	who will not fear…For you alone are holy.	22

15: 4 for your judgments have been revealed."	22
16: 5 "You are just…for you have judged these things;	22
16:14 to assemble them for battle on the great day	9
16:21 until they cursed God for the plague of the hail	10
17:14 Lamb…for he is Lord of lords and King of kings	22
17:17 For God has put it into their hearts	4
18: 3 For all the nations have drunk of the wine	22
18: 5 for her sins are heaped high as heaven	22
18: 6 and repay her double for her deeds;	20
18: 8 for mighty is the Lord God who judges her."	22
18:10 For in one hour your judgment has come."	22
18:11 the merchants of the earth weep and mourn for her	13
18:17 For in one hour all this wealth has been laid waste!"	22
18:19 For in one hour she has been laid waste."	22
18:20 For God has given judgment for you against her.	22
18:23 for your merchants were the magnates of the earth	22
19: 2 for his judgments are true and just;	22
19: 6 For the Lord our God the Almighty reigns.	22
19: 7 for the marriage of the Lamb has come	22
19: 8 for the fine linen is the righteous deeds	4
19:10 For the testimony of Jesus is the spirit of prophecy."	4
19:17 "Come, gather for the great supper of God	9
20: 4 beheaded for their testimony to Jesus	6
20: 4 who had been beheaded…for the word of God.	6
20: 8 Gog and Magog, in order to gather them for battle;	9
21: 1 for the first heaven…had passed away	4
21: 4 for the first things have passed away."	22
21: 5 "Write this, for these words are trustworthy	22
21:22 for its temple is the Lord God the Almighty	4
21:23 for the glory of God is its light	4
22: 2 leaves…are for the healing of the nations.	9
22: 5 for the Lord God will be their light	22
22: 6 for the Lord…has sent his angel to show	19
22:10 for the time is near.	4
22:16 to you with this testimony for the churches.	13

for indeed

1. εἴπερ, *eiper, 1642*

2Th 1: 6 For it is indeed just of God	1

for then

1. εἰ + δέ + μή + γέ, *ei + de + mē + ge, 1623 + 1254 + 3590 + 1145*

Mat 6: 1 for then you have no reward from your Father	1

forbearance

1. ἀνοχή, *anochē, 496*

Rom 2: 4 despise…his…forbearance and patience?	1
3:25 in his divine forbearance he had passed over	1

forbid   *See also* God forbid, heaven forbid

1. κωλύω, *kōlyō, 3266*
2. λέγω + μή, *legō + mē, 3306 + 3590*

Lke 23: 2 forbidding us to pay taxes to the emperor	1
Act 16: 6 forbidden by the Holy Spirit to speak the word	1
Rom 2:22 You that forbid adultery	2
1Co 14:39 do not forbid speaking in tongues;	1
1Ti 4: 3 They forbid marriage and demand abstinence	1

force   *See also* enter by force, take by force

1. ἀγγαρεύω, *angareuō, 30*
2. ἀναγκάζω, *anankazō, 337*
3. ἀνάγκη, *anankē, 340*
4. βία, *bia, 1040*
5. ἰσχύω, *ischyō, 2710*
6. κακόω, *kakoō, 2808*

Mat 5:41 if anyone forces you to go one mile, go also	1
Act 7:19 forced our ancestors to abandon their infants	6
26:11 I tried to force them to blaspheme;	2
27:41 the stern…broken up by the force of the waves.	4
2Co 12:11 I have been a fool! You forced me to it.	2
Phm 1:14 good deed might be voluntary and not something forced.	3
Heb 9:17 since it is not in force as long as	5

full force

1. δύναμις, *dynamis, 1539*

Rev 1:16 face was like the sun shining with full force.	1

spiritual force

1. πνευματικός, *pneumatikos, 4461*

Eph 6:12 against the spiritual forces of evil	1

forebode

1. προσδοκία, *prosdokia, 4660*

Lke 21:26 foreboding of what is coming upon the world	1

forecourt

1. προαύλιον, *proaulion, 4580*

Mrk 14:68 he went out into the forecourt.	1

forehead

1. μέτωπον, *metōpon, 3587*

Rev 7: 3 marked…with a seal on their foreheads."	1
9: 4 who do not have the seal of God on their foreheads.	1
13:16 to be marked on the right hand or the forehead	1
14: 1 his Father's name written on their foreheads.	1
14: 9 receive a mark on their foreheads or on their hands	1
17: 5 on her forehead was written a name, a mystery:	1
20: 4 and had not received its mark on their foreheads	1
22: 4 and his name will be on their foreheads.	1

foreign

1. ἀλλότριος, *allotrios, 259*
2. ἔξω, *exō, 2032*
3. ξένος, *xenos, 3828*

Act 17:18 "He seems to be a proclaimer of foreign divinities."	3
26:11 I pursued them even to foreign cities.	2
Heb 11: 9 as in a foreign land, living in tents,	1
11:34 put foreign armies to flight.	1

foreigner

1. ἀλλογενής, *allogenēs, 254*
2. βάρβαρος, *barbaros, 975*
3. ἕτερος, *heteros, 2283*
4. ξένος, *xenos, 3828*
5. παρεπίδημος, *parepidēmos, 4215*

Mat 27: 7 the potter's field as a place to bury foreigners	4
Lke 17:18 Was none of them found…except this foreigner?"	1
Act 17:21 Now all the Athenians and the foreigners	4
1Co 14:11 I will be a foreigner to the speaker	2
14:11 the speaker a foreigner to me.	2
14:21 by the lips of foreigners	3
Heb 11:13 they were strangers and foreigners on the earth	5

foreknow

1. προγινώσκω, *proginōskō, 4589*

Rom 8:29 For those whom he foreknew he also predestined	1
11: 2 not rejected his people whom he foreknew.	1

foreknowledge

1. πρόγνωσις, *prognōsis, 4590*

Act 2:23 the definite plan and foreknowledge of God	1

foremost

1. πρῶτος, *prōtos, 4755*

1Ti 1:15 sinners—of whom I am the foremost.	1
1:16 so that in me, as the foremost	1

forerunner

1. πρόδρομος, *prodromos, 4596*

Heb 6:20 Jesus, a forerunner on our behalf, has entered	1

foresail

1. ἀρτέμων, *artemōn, 784*

Act 27:40 then hoisting the foresail to the wind	1

foresee

1. προοράω, *prooraō, 4632*

Act 2:31 Foreseeing this, David spoke of the resurrection	1
Gal 3: 8 the scripture, foreseeing that God would justify	1

foresight

1. πρόνοια, *pronoia, 4630*

Act 24: 2 reforms…because of your foresight	1

forest

1. ὕλη, *hylē, 5627*

Jas 3: 5 How great a forest is set ablaze by a small fire!	1

foretell

1. προκαταγγέλλω, *prokatangellō, 4615*
2. προλέγω, *prolegō, 4625*

Act 1:16 which the Holy Spirit through David foretold 2
3:18 In this way God fulfilled what he had foretold 1
7:52 They killed those who foretold 1

forever

1. ἀεί, *aei, 107*
2. αἰών, *aiōn, 172*
3. αἰώνιος, *aiōnios, 173*
4. διά + πᾶς, *dia + pas, 1328 + 4246*
5. εἰς + αἰών, *eis + aiōn, 1650 + 172*
6. εἰς + ὁ + αἰών, *eis + ho + aiōn, 1650 + 3836 + 172*
7. εἰς + ὁ + διηνεκής, *eis + ho + diēnekēs, 1650 + 3836 + 1457*
8. εἰς + πᾶς + ὁ + αἰών, *eis + pas + ho + aiōn, 1650 + 4246 + 3836 + 172*
9. πάντοτε, *pantote, 4121*

Lke 1:33 He will reign over the house of Jacob forever 6
1:55 to Abraham and to his descendants forever." 6
Jhn 6:51 Whoever eats of this bread will live forever; 6
6:58 one who eats this bread will live forever." 6
8:35 the son has a place there forever. 6
12:34 that the Messiah remains forever. 6
14:16 another Advocate, to be with you forever. 6
Act 7:51 you are forever opposing the Holy Spirit 1
Rom 1:25 the Creator, who is blessed forever! Amen. 6
9: 5 who is over all, God blessed forever. Amen. 6
11:10 and keep their backs forever bent." 4
11:36 To him be the glory forever. Amen. 6
16:27 through Jesus Christ, to whom be the glory forever! 6
2Co 9: 9 his righteousness endures forever." 6
11:31 God…(blessed be he forever!) 6
Gal 1: 5 to whom be the glory forever and ever. Amen. 6
Eph 3:21 to all generations, forever and ever. Amen. 2
Php 4:20 To our God and Father be glory forever and ever. 6
1Th 4:17 so we will be with the Lord forever. 9
1Ti 1:17 be honor and glory forever and ever. Amen. 6
2Ti 4:18 To him be the glory forever and ever. Amen. 6
Phm 1:15 you might have him back forever 3
Heb 1: 8 "Your throne, O God, is forever and ever 6
5: 6 a priest forever, according to the order of Melchizedek." 6
6:20 having become a high priest forever 6
7: 3 he remains a priest forever. 7
7:17 a priest forever, according to the order of Melchizedek." 6
7:21 'You are a priest forever' " 6
7:24 because he continues forever. 6
7:28 appoints a Son who has been made perfect forever. 6
13: 8 Jesus Christ is the same yesterday…and forever. 6
13:21 to whom be the glory forever and ever. Amen. 6
1Pe 1:25 but the word of the Lord endures forever." 6
4:11 glory and the power forever and ever. Amen. 6
5:11 To him be the power forever and ever. Amen. 6
1Jn 2:17 but those who do the will of God live forever. 6
2Jn 1: 2 the truth that…will be with us forever: 6
Jde 1:13 deepest darkness has been reserved forever. 5
1:25 before all time and now and forever. Amen. 8
Rev 1: 6 to him be glory and dominion forever and ever. 6
1:18 I was dead, and see, I am alive forever and ever; 6
4: 9 thanks to the one…who lives forever and ever 6
4:10 worship the one who lives forever and ever; 6
5:13 honor and glory and might forever and ever!" 6
7:12 might be to our God forever and ever! Amen." 6
10: 6 swore by him who lives forever and ever 6
11:15 Messiah, and he will reign forever and ever." 6
14:11 smoke of their torment goes up forever and ever. 5
15: 7 the wrath of God, who lives forever and ever; 6
19: 3 The smoke goes up from her forever and ever." 6
20:10 be tormented day and night forever and ever. 6
22: 5 and they will reign forever and ever. 6

forewarn

1. προγινώσκω, *proginōskō, 4589*

2Pe 3:17 beloved, since you are forewarned, beware 1

forfeit

1. ζημιόω, *zēmioō, 2423*

Mat 16:26 gain the whole world but forfeit their life? 1
Mrk 8:36 to gain the whole world and forfeit their life? 1

Lke 9:25 but lose or forfeit themselves? 1

forget

1. ἐκλανθάνομαι, *eklanthanomai, 1720*
2. ἐπιλανθάνομαι, *epilanthanomai, 2140*
3. ἐπιλησμονή, *epilēsmonē, 2144*

Mat 16: 5 they had forgotten to bring any bread. 2
Mrk 8:14 the disciples had forgotten to bring any bread; 2
Lke 12: 6 not one of them is forgotten in God's sight. 2
Php 3:13 one thing I do: forgetting what lies behind 2
Heb 12: 5 you have forgotten the exhortation 1
Jas 1:24 immediately forget what they were like. 2
1:25 being not hearers who forget but doers who act 3

forgetful

1. λήθη + λαμβάνω, *lēthē + lambanō, 3330 + 3284*

2Pe 1: 9 forgetful of the cleansing of past sins. 1

forgive

1. Contextual: Not in Greek
2. ἀπολύω, *apolyō, 668*
3. ἄφεσις, *aphesis, 912*
4. ἀφίημι, *aphiēmi, 918*
5. χαρίζομαι, *charizomai, 5919*

Mat 6:12 And forgive us our debts, as we also have forgiven 4
6:12 debts, as we also have forgiven our debtors. 4
6:14 For if you forgive others their trespasses 4
6:14 your heavenly Father will also forgive you; 4
6:15 if you do not forgive others, neither will 4
6:15 neither will your Father forgive your 4
9: 2 "Take heart, son; your sins are forgiven." 4
9: 5 For which is easier, to say, 'Your sins are forgiven,' 4
9: 6 Man has authority on earth to forgive sins" 4
12:31 people will be forgiven for every sin and blasphemy 4
12:31 blasphemy against the Spirit will not be forgiven 4
12:32 a word against the Son of Man will be forgiven 4
12:32 against the Holy Spirit will not be forgiven. 4
18:21 sins against me, how often should I forgive? 4
18:27 released him and forgave him the debt. 4
18:32 'You wicked slave! I forgave you all that debt 4
18:35 if you do not forgive your brother or sister 4
Mrk 2: 5 "Son, your sins are forgiven." 4
2: 7 Who can forgive sins but God alone?" 4
2: 9 'Your sins are forgiven,' 4
2:10 Son of Man has authority on earth to forgive sins" 4
3:28 people will be forgiven for their sins 4
4:12 so that they may not turn again and be forgiven.' " 4
11:25 "Whenever you stand praying, forgive 4
11:25 may also forgive you your trespasses." 4
Lke 5:20 "Friend, your sins are forgiven you." 4
5:21 Who can forgive sins but God alone?" 4
5:23 easier, to say, 'Your sins are forgiven you,' 4
5:24 authority on earth to forgive sins" 4
6:37 Forgive, and you will be forgiven; 2
6:37 Forgive, and you will be forgiven; 2
7:47 her sins, which were many, have been forgiven; 4
7:47 one to whom little is forgiven, loves little." 4
7:48 he said to her, "Your sins are forgiven." 4
7:49 "Who is this who even forgives sins?" 4
11: 4 forgive us our sins 4
11: 4 we ourselves forgive everyone indebted 4
12:10 everyone…will be forgiven; 4
12:10 against the Holy Spirit will not be forgiven. 4
17: 3 if there is repentance, you must forgive. 4
17: 4 you must forgive." 4
23:34 ⟦Jesus said, "Father, forgive them;⟧ 4
Jhn 20:23 If you forgive the sins of any, they are forgiven 4
20:23 If you forgive the sins of any, they are forgiven 4
Act 2:38 so that your sins may be forgiven; 3
8:22 the intent of your heart may be forgiven you. 4
Rom 4: 7 those whose iniquities are forgiven 4
2Co 2: 7 so now instead you should forgive and console 5
2:10 Anyone whom you forgive, I also forgive. 5
2:10 Anyone whom you forgive, I also forgive. 1
2:10 What I have forgiven, if I have forgiven anything 5
2:10 What I have forgiven, if I have forgiven anything 5
12:13 Forgive me this wrong! 5
Eph 4:32 forgiving one another, as God in Christ has forgiven 5
4:32 forgiving one another, as God in Christ has forgiven 5
Col 2:13 when he forgave us all our trespasses 5

3:13 if anyone has a complaint…forgive each other; 5
3:13 just as the Lord has forgiven you 5
3:13 so you also must forgive. 1
Jas 5:15 and anyone who has committed sins will be forgiven. 4
1Jn 1: 9 he who is faithful and just will forgive us our sins 4
2:12 because your sins are forgiven on account of his 4

forgiveness

1. ἄφεσις, *aphesis, 912*
Mat 26:28 for many for the forgiveness of sins. 1
Mrk 1: 4 repentance for the forgiveness of sins. 1
3:29 can never have forgiveness 1
Lke 1:77 by the forgiveness of their sins. 1
3: 3 repentance for the forgiveness of sins 1
24:47 repentance and forgiveness of sins 1
Act 5:31 repentance to Israel and forgiveness of sins. 1
10:43 receives forgiveness of sins through his name." 1
13:38 forgiveness of sins is proclaimed to you; 1
26:18 they may receive forgiveness of sins 1
Eph 1: 7 the forgiveness of our trespasses 1
Col 1:14 we have redemption, the forgiveness of sins. 1
Heb 9:22 there is no forgiveness of sins. 1
10:18 Where there is forgiveness of these 1

winnowing fork

1. πτύον, *ptyon, 4768*
Mat 3:12 His winnowing fork is in his hand 1
Lke 3:17 His winnowing fork is in his hand 1

form

1. Contextual: Not in Greek
2. εἶδος, *eidos, 1626*
3. εἰκών, *eikōn, 1635*
4. μορφή, *morphē, 3671*
5. μορφόω, *morphoō, 3672*
6. ὁμοιόω, *homoioō, 3929*
7. πλάσσω, *plassō, 4421*
8. συνίστημι, *synistēmi, 5319*
9. σχῆμα, *schēma, 5386*
10. τύπος, *typos, 5596*
Mrk 16:12 ⟦After this he appeared in another form to two⟧ 4
Lke 3:22 Holy Spirit descended upon him in bodily form 2
Jhn 5:37 never heard his voice or seen his form 2
Act 14:11 "The gods have come down to us in human form!" 6
17:29 an image formed by the art…of mortals. 1
Rom 6:17 form of teaching to which you were entrusted 10
1Co 7:31 the present form of this world is passing away. 9
12:28 then deeds of power, then gifts of healing, 1
12:28 forms of assistance, forms of leadership 1
Gal 4:19 until Christ is formed in you 5
Php 2: 6 who, though he was in the form of God, 4
2: 7 emptied himself, taking the form of a slave 4
2: 7 being found in human form 9
1Th 5:22 abstain from every form of evil. 2
1Ti 2:13 For Adam was formed first, then Eve; 7
Heb 10: 1 not the true form of these realities 3
2Pe 3: 5 an earth was formed out of water and by means of water 8

form a mob

1. ὀχλοποιέω, *ochlopoieō, 4062*
Act 17: 5 they formed a mob and set the city in an uproar. 1

outward form

1. μόρφωσις, *morphōsis, 3673*
2Ti 3: 5 holding to the outward form of godliness 1

former See also former *time*, write in former days

1. γίνομαι, *ginomai, 1181*
2. ἕτερος, *heteros, 2283*
3. πρότερος, *proteros, 4728*
Eph 3: 5 In former generations this mystery was not made known 2
4:22 put away your former way of life, your old self 3
Heb 7:23 the former priests were many in number 1

formerly

1. ποτέ, *pote, 4537*
2. πρότερος, *proteros, 4728*
3. τότε, *tote, 5538*
Jhn 9:13 the man who had formerly been blind. 1

Gal 1:23 "The one who formerly was persecuting us 1
4: 8 Formerly, when you did not know God 3
1Ti 1:13 even though I was formerly a blasphemer, 2
Phm 1:11 Formerly he was useless to you 1
Heb 4: 6 those who formerly received the good news 2
1Pe 1:14 the desires that you formerly had in ignorance. 2

fornication See also commit fornication, practice fornication

1. πορνεία, *porneia, 4518*
Mat 15:19 evil intentions, murder, adultery, fornication 1
Mrk 7:21 fornication, theft, murder 1
Act 15:20 from fornication and from whatever has been strangled 1
15:29 from what is strangled and from fornication. 1
21:25 from what is strangled and from fornication." 1
1Co 6:13 is meant not for fornication but for the Lord 1
6:18 Shun fornication! 1
Gal 5:19 fornication, impurity, licentiousness 1
Eph 5: 3 fornication and impurity of any kind, or greed 1
Col 3: 5 fornication, impurity, passion, evil desire 1
1Th 4: 3 that you abstain from fornication; 1
Rev 2:21 but she refuses to repent of her fornication. 1
9:21 And they did not repent of…their fornication 1
14: 8 drink of the wine of the wrath of her fornication." 1
17: 2 and with the wine of whose fornication 1
17: 4 and the impurities of her fornication; 1
18: 3 drunk of the wine of the wrath of her fornication 1
19: 2 who corrupted the earth with her fornication 1

fornicator

1. πορνεύω, *porneuō, 4519*
2. πόρνος, *pornos, 4521*
1Co 6: 9 Do not be deceived! Fornicators, idolaters 2
6:18 the fornicator sins against the body 1
Eph 5: 5 no fornicator or impure person 2
1Ti 1:10 fornicators, sodomites, slave traders, liars 2
Heb 13: 4 God will judge fornicators and adulterers. 2
Rev 21: 8 the murderers, the fornicators, the sorcerers 2
22:15 Outside are the…fornicators and murderers 2

forsake

1. ἀποστασία, *apostasia, 686*
2. ἐγκαταλείπω, *enkataleipō, 1593*
Mat 27:46 "My God, my God, why have you forsaken me?" 2
Mrk 15:34 "My God, my God, why have you forsaken me?" 2
Act 21:21 you teach all the Jews…to forsake Moses 1
2Co 4: 9 persecuted, but not forsaken; 2
Heb 13: 5 he has said, "I will never leave you or forsake you." 2

forth See bring forth, go forth, pour forth, put forth, set forth, sound forth

fortunate

1. μακάριος, *makarios, 3421*
Act 26: 2 "I consider myself fortunate that it is before you 1

Fortunatus

1. Φορτουνᾶτος, *Phortounatos, 5847*
1Co 16:17 at the coming of Stephanas and Fortunatus 1

fortune-telling

1. μαντεύομαι, *manteuomai, 3446*
Act 16:16 brought…a great deal of money by fortune-telling. 1

forty

1. τεσσεράκοντα, *tesserakonta, 5477*
Mat 4: 2 He fasted forty days and forty nights 1
4: 2 He fasted forty days and forty nights 1
Mrk 1:13 He was in the wilderness forty days 1
Lke 4: 2 for forty days he was tempted by the devil. 1
Act 1: 3 appearing to them during forty days 1
4:22 the man…was more than forty years old. 1
7:30 "Now when forty years had passed 1
7:36 and in the wilderness for forty years. 1
7:42 forty years in the wilderness, O house of Israel? 1
13:21 God gave them Saul…who reigned for forty years. 1
23:13 more than forty who joined in this conspiracy. 1
23:21 more than forty of their men are lying in ambush 1
2Co 11:24 from the Jews the forty lashes minus one. 1
Heb 3:10 for forty years. Therefore I was angry 1

Heb 3:17 But with whom was he angry forty years?   1

forty years

1. τεσσερακονταετής, *tesserakontaetēs, 5478*

Act 7:23 "When he was forty years old   1
    13:18 For about forty years he put up with them   1

forty-four

1. τεσσεράκοντα + τέσσαρες, *tesserakonta + tessares, 5477 + 5475*

Rev 7: 4 one hundred forty-four thousand, sealed   1
    14: 1 one hundred forty-four thousand who had his name   1
    14: 3 except the one hundred forty-four thousand   1
    21:17 measured its wall, one hundred forty-four cubits   1

forty-six

1. τεσσεράκοντα + καί + ἕξ, *tesserakonta + kai + hex, 5477 + 2779 + 1971*

Jhn 2:20 temple...under construction for forty-six years,   1

forty-two

1. τεσσεράκοντα + καί + δύο, *tesserakonta + kai + dyo, 5477 + 2779 + 1545*

Rev 11: 2 trample over the holy city for forty-two months.   1
    13: 5 to exercise authority for forty-two months.   1

forum

1. φόρον, *phoron, 5842*

Act 28:15 as far as the Forum of Appius and Three Taverns   1

forward *See also* come forward, look forward, push forward, put forward, run forward, strain forward

1. εἰς + ὁ + μέσος, *eis + ho + mesos, 1650 + 3836 + 3545*

Mrk 3: 3 "Come forward."   1

foul

1. ἀκάθαρτος, *akathartos, 176*
2. κακός, *kakos, 2805*

Rev 16: 2 and a foul and painful sore came on those   2
    16:13 I saw three foul spirits like frogs coming from   1
    18: 2 a haunt of every foul spirit   1
    18: 2 a haunt of every foul bird,   1
    18: 2 a haunt of every foul and hateful beast.   1

found

1. θεμελιόω, *themelioō, 2530*

Mat 7:25 because it had been founded on rock.   1
Heb 1:10 "In the beginning, Lord, you founded the earth   1

foundation

1. Contextual: Not in Greek
2. θεμέλιον, *themelion, 2528*
3. θεμέλιος, *themelios, 2529*
4. καταβολή, *katabolē, 2856*
5. ὅς, *hos, 4005*

Mat 13:35 hidden from the foundation of the world."   4
    25:34 from the foundation of the world;   4
Lke 6:48 who dug deeply and laid the foundation on rock;   3
    6:49 a house on the ground without a foundation.   3
    11:50 blood...shed since the foundation of the world   4
    14:29 Otherwise, when he has laid a foundation   3
Jhn 17:24 loved me before the foundation of the world.   4
Act 16:26 the foundations of the prison were shaken;   2
Rom 15:20 so that I do not build on someone else's foundation   3
1Co 3:10 I laid a foundation   3
    3:11 For no one can lay any foundation other   3
    3:11 has been laid; that foundation is Jesus Christ.   5
    3:12 Now if anyone builds on the foundation with gold   3
    3:14 If what has been built on the foundation   1
Eph 1: 4 chose us in Christ before the foundation of the world   4
    2:20 built upon the foundation of the apostles   3
1Ti 6:19 storing up...the treasure of a good foundation   3
2Ti 2:19 God's firm foundation stands, bearing this inscription: 3
Heb 4: 3 were finished at the foundation of the world.   4
    6: 1 not laying again the foundation: repentance   3
    9:26 since the foundation of the world.   4
    11:10 the city that has foundations   3
1Pe 1:20 destined before the foundation of the world   4
Rev 13: 8 written from the foundation of the world   4

    17: 8 written...from the foundation of the world   4
    21:14 And the wall of the city has twelve foundations   3
    21:19 The foundations of the wall of the city   3

four

1. τέσσαρες, *tessares, 5475*
2. τέταρτος, *tetartos, 5480*

Mat 24:31 they will gather his elect from the four winds   1
Mrk 2: 3 a paralyzed man, carried by four of them.   1
    13:27 gather his elect from the four winds   1
Jhn 11:17 Lazarus had already been in the tomb four days.   1
    19:23 his clothes and divided them into four parts   1
Act 10:11 being lowered to the ground by its four corners.   1
    10:30 Cornelius replied, "Four days ago at this very hour   2
    11: 5 being lowered by its four corners;   1
    12: 4 handed him over to four squads of soldiers   1
    21: 9 four unmarried daughters who had the gift of prophecy.   1
    21:23 We have four men who are under a vow.   1
    27:29 they let down four anchors from the stern   1
Rev 4: 6 Around the throne...are four living creatures   1
    4: 8 four living creatures, each...with six wings   1
    5: 6 the throne and the four living creatures   1
    5: 8 the four living creatures...fell before the Lamb   1
    5:14 the four living creatures said, "Amen!"   1
    6: 1 I heard one of the four living creatures call out   1
    6: 6 a voice in the midst of the four living creatures   1
    7: 1 After this I saw four angels standing   1
    7: 1 angels standing at the four corners of the earth   1
    7: 1 angels...holding back the four winds   1
    7: 2 he called with a loud voice to the four angels   1
    7:11 around the elders and the four living creatures   1
    9:13 a voice from the four horns of the golden altar   1
    9:14 "Release the four angels who are bound   1
    9:15 So the four angels were released   1
    14: 3 and before the four living creatures   1
    15: 7 Then one of the four living creatures gave   1
    19: 4 four living creatures fell down and worshiped   1
    20: 8 nations...at the four corners of the earth   1

four days

1. τεταρταῖος, *tetartaios, 5479*

Jhn 11:39 because he has been dead four days."   1

four hundred

1. τετρακόσιοι, *tetrakosioi, 5484*

Act 5:36 a number of men, about four hundred, joined him;   1
    7: 6 and mistreat them during four hundred years.   1
    13:20 for about four hundred fifty years.   1
Gal 3:17 law, which came four hundred thirty years later   1

four miles

1. τριάκοντα + στάδιον, *triakonta + stadion, 5558 + 5084*

Jhn 6:19 When they had rowed about three or four miles   1

four months

1. τετράμηνος, *tetramēnos, 5485*

Jhn 4:35 'Four months more, then comes the harvest'?   1

four o'clock in the afternoon

1. δέκατος + ὥρα, *dekatos + hōra, 1281 + 6052*

Jhn 1:39 It was about four o'clock in the afternoon.   1

four thousand

1. τετρακισχίλιοι, *tetrakischilioi, 5483*

Mat 15:38 who had eaten were four thousand men, besides   1
    16:10 Or the seven loaves for the four thousand   1
Mrk 8: 9 Now there were about four thousand people   1
    8:20 "And the seven for the four thousand,   1
Act 21:38 and led the four thousand assassins out   1

four times as much

1. τετραπλοῦς, *tetraplous, 5487*

Lke 19: 8 I will pay back four times as much."   1

four-footed animal

1. τετράπους, *tetrapous, 5488*

Act 11: 6 I saw four-footed animals, beasts of prey   1
Rom 1:23 or birds or four-footed animals or reptiles.   1

four-footed creature

1. τετράπους, *tetrapous, 5488*

Act 10:12 four-footed creatures and reptiles and birds   1

foursquare

1. τετράγωνος, *tetragōnos, 5481*

Rev 21:16 The city lies foursquare, its length the same   1

fourteen

1. δεκατέσσαρες, *dekatessares, 1280*

Mat 1:17 Abraham to David are fourteen generations;   1
     1:17 deportation to Babylon, fourteen generations;   1
     1:17 to Babylon to the Messiah, fourteen generations.   1
2Co 12: 2 who fourteen years ago was caught up   1
Gal 2: 1 Then after fourteen years I went up again   1

fourteenth

1. τεσσαρεσκαιδέκατος, *tessareskaidekatos, 5476*

Act 27:27 When the fourteenth night had come   1
     27:33 "Today is the fourteenth day   1

fourth

1. τέταρτος, *tetartos, 5480*

Rev 4: 7 the fourth living creature like a flying eagle.   1
     6: 7 When he opened the fourth seal, I heard the voice   1
     6: 7 I heard the voice of the fourth living creature   1
     6: 8 they were given authority over a fourth of the earth   1
     8:12 The fourth angel blew his trumpet   1
     16: 8 The fourth angel poured his bowl on the sun   1
     21:19 every jewel;…the fourth emerald   1

fox

1. ἀλώπηξ, *alōpēx, 273*

Mat 8:20 Jesus said to him, "Foxes have holes   1
Lke 9:58 Jesus said to him, "Foxes have holes   1
     13:32 He said to them, "Go and tell that fox for me,   1

fragment

1. κλάσμα, *klasma, 3083*

Jhn 6:12 "Gather up the fragments left over   1
     6:13 from the fragments of the five barley loaves   1

fragrance

1. ὀσμή, *osmē, 4011*

Jhn 12: 3 was filled with the fragrance of the perfume.   1
2Co 2:14 the fragrance that comes from knowing him.   1
     2:16 to the one a fragrance from death to death   1
     2:16 to the other a fragrance from life to life.   1

fragrant

1. εὐωδία, *euōdia, 2380*
2. ὀσμή + εὐωδία, *osmē + euōdia, 4011 + 2380*

Eph 5: 2 a fragrant offering and sacrifice to God.   2
Php 4:18 a fragrant offering, a sacrifice acceptable   1

frankincense

1. λίβανος, *libanos, 3337*

Mat 2:11 they offered him gifts of gold, frankincense,   1
Rev 18:13 cinnamon, spice, incense, myrrh, frankincense   1

frankly

1. ἀνοίγω, *anoigō, 487*

2Co 6:11 We have spoken frankly to you Corinthians;   1

frankness

1. ἁπλότης, *haplotēs, 605*

2Co 1:12 with frankness and godly sincerity   1

free   *See also* free *gift,* make free, set free

1. Contextual: Not in Greek
2. ἀπαλλάσσω, *apallassō, 557*
3. ἀπογίνομαι, *apoginomai, 614*
4. ἄφεσις, *aphesis, 912*
5. δικαιόω, *dikaioō, 1467*
6. ἐλεύθερος, *eleutheros, 1801*
7. ἐλευθερόω, *eleutheroō, 1802*
8. λύσις, *lysis, 3386*
9. λύω, *lyō, 3395*

Mat 17:26 Jesus said to him, "Then the children are free.   6
Lke 1:64 his mouth was opened and his tongue freed   1
     4:18 to let the oppressed go free   4
Jhn 8:33 you mean by saying, 'You will be made free'?"   6
     8:36 Son makes you free, you will be free indeed.   6
Act 2:24 having freed him from death   9
     13:39 you could not be freed by the law of Moses.   5
Rom 6: 7 For whoever has died is freed from sin.   5
     6:20 you were free in regard to righteousness.   6
     6:22 But now that you have been freed from sin   7
     7: 3 But if her husband dies, she is free from that law   6
1Co 7:22 whoever was free when called is a slave of Christ.   6
     7:27 Are you bound to a wife? Do not seek to be free.   8
     7:27 Are you free from a wife? Do not seek a wife.   9
     7:39 she is free to marry anyone she wishes   6
     9: 1 Am I not free? Am I not an apostle?   6
     9:19 For though I am free with respect to all   6
     12:13 Jews or Greeks, slaves or free   6
Gal 3:28 there is no longer slave or free   6
     4:26 Jerusalem above; she is free, and she is our mother.   6
Eph 6: 8 whether we are slaves or free.   6
Col 3:11 barbarian, Scythian, slave and free;   6
Heb 2:15 free those who all their lives were held in slavery   2
1Pe 2:24 free from sins, we might live for righteousness;   3
Rev 1: 5 To him who…freed us from our sins by his blood   9
     6:15 everyone, slave and free, hid in the caves   6
     13:16 both rich and poor, both free and slave   6
     19:18 flesh of all, both free and slave,   6

free from anxiety

1. ἀμέριμνος, *amerimnos, 291*

1Co 7:32 I want you to be free from anxieties.   1

free from law

1. ἄνομος, *anomos, 491*

1Co 9:21 (though I am not free from God's law   1

free from love of money

1. ἀφιλάργυρος, *aphilargyros, 921*

Heb 13: 5 Keep your lives free from the love of money   1

free of charge

1. ἀδάπανος, *adapanos, 78*
2. δωρεάν, *dōrean, 1562*

1Co 9:18 I may make the gospel free of charge   1
2Co 11: 7 I proclaimed God's good news to you free of charge?   2

free person

1. ἀπελεύθερος, *apeleutheros, 592*
2. ἐλεύθερος, *eleutheros, 1801*

1Co 7:22 a slave is a freed person belonging to the Lord   1
1Pe 2:16 live as free people, yet do not use your freedom   2

free woman

1. ἐλεύθερος, *eleutheros, 1801*

Gal 4:22 one by a slave woman and the other by a free woman.   1
     4:23 child of the free woman, was born through the promise.   1
     4:30 not share the inheritance with the child of the free woman   1
     4:31 not of the slave but of the free woman.   1

freedman

1. Λιβερτῖνος, *Libertinos, 3339*

Act 6: 9 who belonged to the synagogue of the Freedmen   1

freedom

1. ἐλευθερία, *eleutheria, 1800*
2. ἐλεύθερος, *eleutheros, 1801*

Rom 8:21 the freedom of the glory of the children of God.   1
1Co 7:21 Even if you can gain your freedom   2
2Co 3:17 where the Spirit of the Lord is, there is freedom.   1
Gal 2: 4 who slipped in to spy on the freedom   1
     5: 1 For freedom Christ has set us free.   1
     5:13 you were called to freedom, brothers and sisters;   1
     5:13 only do not use your freedom as an opportunity   1
1Pe 2:16 do not use your freedom as a pretext for evil.   1
2Pe 2:19 They promise them freedom   1

freely   *See also* bestow freely

1. παρρησιάζομαι, *parrēsiazomai, 4245*

2. πολύς, *polys, 4498*

Mrk	1:45	he went out and began to proclaim it freely	2
Act	26:26	to him I speak freely;	1

frequent

1. πολλάκις, *pollakis, 4490*
2. πυκνός, *pyknos, 4781*

2Co	11:26	on frequent journeys, in danger from rivers	1
1Ti	5:23	your stomach and your frequent ailments.	2

frequently

1. πυκνός, *pyknos, 4781*

Lke	5:33	"John's disciples…frequently fast and pray,	1

fresh

1. γλυκύς, *glykys, 1184*
2. καινός, *kainos, 2785*

Mat	9:17	but new wine is put into fresh wineskins	2
Mrk	2:22	one puts new wine into fresh wineskins."	2
Lke	5:38	new wine must be put into fresh wineskins.	2
Jas	3:11	from the same opening both fresh and brackish water?	1
	3:12	No more can salt water yield fresh.	1

friend

1. ἀδελφός, *adelphos, 81*
2. ἀνήρ, *anēr, 467*
3. ἀνήρ + ἀδελφός, *anēr + adelphos, 467 + 81*
4. ἄνθρωπος, *anthrōpos, 476*
5. γνωστός, *gnōstos, 1196*
6. ἑταῖρος, *hetairos, 2279*
7. ἴδιος, *idios, 2625*
8. ὁ, *ho, 3836*
9. φίλος, *philos, 5813*

Mat	11:19	a friend of tax collectors and sinners!'	9
	20:13	'Friend, I am doing you no wrong;	6
	22:12	said to him, 'Friend, how did you get in here	6
	26:50	"Friend, do what you are here to do."	6
Mrk	5:19	"Go home to your friends	8
Lke	2:44	among their relatives and friends.	5
	5:20	"Friend, your sins are forgiven you."	4
	6:42	how can you say to your neighbor, 'Friend	1
	7: 6	the centurion sent friends to say to him	9
	7:34	a friend of tax collectors and sinners!'	9
	11: 5	one of you has a friend, and you go to him	9
	11: 5	'Friend, lend me three loaves of bread;	9
	11: 6	a friend of mine has arrived	9
	11: 8	because he is his friend	9
	12: 4	my friends, do not fear those who kill	9
	12:14	"Friend, who set me to be a judge or arbitrator	4
	14:10	'Friend, move up higher';	9
	14:12	do not invite your friends or your brothers	9
	15: 6	he calls together his friends and neighbors	9
	15: 9	she calls together her friends and neighbors	9
	15:29	so that I might celebrate with my friends.	9
	16: 9	make friends…by means of dishonest wealth	9
	21:16	parents and brothers, by relatives and friends;	9
	23:12	Herod and Pilate became friends with each other;	9
Jhn	3:29	friend of the bridegroom…rejoices greatly	9
	11:11	"Our friend Lazarus has fallen asleep	9
	15:13	to lay down one's life for one's friends.	9
	15:14	You are my friends if you do what I command you.	9
	15:15	I have called you friends	9
	19:12	you are no friend of the emperor.	9
Act	1:16	"Friends, the scripture had to be fulfilled	3
	3:17	now, friends, I know that you acted in ignorance	1
	4:23	they went to their friends	7
	6: 3	Therefore, friends, select…seven men	1
	10:24	called together his relatives and close friends.	9
	14:15	"Friends, why are you doing this?	2
	24:23	not to prevent any of his friends	7
	27: 3	allowed him to go to his friends to be cared for.	9
Rom	7: 4	my friends, you have died to the law	1
1Co	14:26	What should be done then, my friends?	1
	14:39	So, my friends, be eager to prophesy	1
2Co	11: 9	my needs were supplied by the friends	1
Gal	4:12	Friends, I beg you, become as I am	1
	4:28	you, my friends, are children of the promise	1
	4:31	So then, friends, we are children, not of the slave	1
	5:11	my friends, why am I still being persecuted	1

	6: 1	friends, if anyone is detected in a transgression	1
Php	4:21	The friends who are with me greet you.	1
Heb	10:19	Therefore, my friends, since we have confidence	1
Jas	2:23	and he was called the friend of God.	9
	4: 4	whoever wishes to be a friend of the world	9
3Jn	1: 3	I was overjoyed when some of the friends arrived	1
	1: 5	whatever you do for the friends	1
	1:10	he refuses to welcome the friends	1
	1:15	The friends send you their greetings.	9
	1:15	Greet the friends there, each by name.	9

dear friend

1. ἀγαπητός, *agapētos, 28*

1Co	10:14	my dear friends, flee from the worship of idols.	1
Phm	1: 1	To Philemon our dear friend and co-worker	1

friendly

1. φίλος, *philos, 5813*

Act	19:31	some officials…who were friendly to him	1

friendship

1. φιλία, *philia, 5802*

Jas	4: 4	friendship with the world is enmity with God?	1

frighten

1. ἐκφοβέω, *ekphobeō, 1768*
2. ἔμφοβος, *emphobos, 1873*
3. ταράσσω, *tarassō, 5429*
4. φοβέομαι, *phobeomai, 5828*

Mat	2: 3	When King Herod heard this, he was frightened	3
	14:30	he noticed the strong wind, he became frightened	4
Lke	24:38	He said to them, "Why are you frightened	3
Act	24:25	Felix became frightened and said	2
2Co	10: 9	as though I am trying to frighten you with my letters.	1

fringe

1. κράσπεδον, *kraspedon, 3192*

Mat	9:20	touched the fringe of his cloak	1
	14:36	they might touch even the fringe of his cloak;	1
	23: 5	and their fringes long.	1
Mrk	6:56	touch even the fringe of his cloak;	1
Lke	8:44	touched the fringe of his clothes	1

fro *See* toss to and fro

frog

1. βάτραχος, *batrachos, 1005*

Rev	16:13	I saw three foul spirits like frogs coming from	1

from *See also* apart from the law, come from, descend from, fall from heaven, free from anxiety, free from law, free from love of money, from *heaven*, from the very *first*, go from, go from place to place, go from town to town, inherit from ancestor, keep from, keep from hearing, keep from speaking, man from Nazareth, pour from, proceed from, send from, separated from, spring from, suffer from a hemorrhage, vanish from sight, where from

1. ἀπό, *apo, 608*
2. διά, *dia, 1328*
3. ἐκ, *ek, 1666*
4. ἐκ + μέσος, *ek + mesos, 1666 + 3545*
5. ἐν, *en, 1877*
6. ἐπί, *epi, 2093*
7. καί, *kai, 2779*
8. κατά, *kata, 2848*
9. μή, *mē, 3590*
10. οὐ, *ou, 4024*
11. παρά, *para, 4123*
12. περί, *peri, 4309*
13. τέ, *te, 5445*
14. ὑπό, *hypo, 5679*

Mat	1:17	So all the generations from Abraham to David	1
	1:17	and from David to the deportation to Babylon	1
	1:17	from the deportation to Babylon to the Messiah	1
	1:18	found to be with child from the Holy Spirit.	3
	1:20	for the child conceived in her is from the Holy	3
	1:21	he will save his people from their sins."	1
	1:24	When Joseph awoke from sleep, he did as the angel	1

2: 1	wise men from the East came to Jerusalem	1
2: 6	for from you shall come a ruler who is to shepherd	3
2: 7	learned from them the exact time when the star	11
2:16	time that he had learned from the wise men.	11
3: 7	Who warned you to flee from the wrath to come?	1
3: 9	I tell you, God is able from these stones to raise	3
3:13	Jesus came from Galilee to John at the Jordan	1
3:16	just as he came up from the water, suddenly	1
3:17	a voice from heaven said, "This is my Son	3
4: 4	every word that comes from the mouth of God.' "	2
4:17	From that time Jesus began to proclaim,	1
4:25	And great crowds followed him from Galilee	1
5:18	will pass from the law until all is accomplished	1
5:37	anything more than this comes from the evil one	3
5:42	do not refuse anyone who wants to borrow from you.	1
6: 1	for then you have no reward from your Father	11
6:13	time of trial, but rescue us from the evil one	1
7:16	Are grapes gathered from thorns	1
7:16	gathered from thorns, or figs from thistles?	1
7:23	'I never knew you; go away from me, you evildoers.'	1
8: 1	When Jesus had come down from the mountain	1
8:11	I tell you, many will come from east and west	1
8:30	was feeding at some distance from them.	1
9:15	the bridegroom is taken away from them	1
9:16	for the patch pulls away from the cloak	1
10:27	proclaim from the housetops.	6
11:12	From the days of John the Baptist until now	1
11:25	these things from the wise and the intelligent	1
11:29	Take my yoke upon you, and learn from me;	1
12:38	"Teacher, we wish to see a sign from you."	1
12:42	she came from the ends of the earth	3
13:12	but from those who have nothing,	1
13:35	hidden from the foundation of the world."	1
13:49	and separate the evil from the righteous	4
14: 2	he has been raised from the dead	1
14:13	they followed him on foot from the towns.	1
14:24	the boat…was far from the land	1
15: 1	scribes came to Jesus from Jerusalem and said	1
15: 5	'Whatever support you might have had from me	3
15: 8	but their hearts are far from me;	1
15:18	comes out of the mouth proceeds from the heart	3
15:22	Just then a Canaanite woman from that region	1
15:27	crumbs that fall from their masters' table."	1
16: 1	they asked him to show them a sign from heaven.	3
16:21	From that time on, Jesus began to show his disciples	1
17: 5	and from the cloud a voice said	3
17: 9	the Son of Man has been raised from the dead."	3
17:25	From whom do kings of the earth take toll	1
17:25	From their children or from others?"	1
17:25	From their children or from others?"	1
17:26	When Peter said, "From others,"	1
18:35	forgive your brother or sister from your heart."	1
19: 8	but from the beginning it was not so.	1
19:12	there are eunuchs who have been so from birth	3
21: 8	others cut branches from the trees	1
21:11	"This is the prophet Jesus from Nazareth	1
21:19	"May no fruit ever come from you again!"	3
21:25	Did the baptism of John come from heaven	3
21:25	"If we say, 'From heaven,' he will say to us	3
21:43	the kingdom of God will be taken away from you	1
22:46	nor from that day did anyone dare to ask him	1
23:34	pursue from town to town	1
23:35	from the blood of righteous Abel	1
24:21	from the beginning of the world until now	1
24:27	For as the lightning comes from the east	1
24:29	the stars will fall from heaven	1
24:31	they will gather his elect from the four winds	3
24:31	from one end of heaven to the other.	1
24:32	"From the fig tree learn its lesson:	1
25:28	So take the talent from him	1
25:29	but from those who have nothing,	1
25:32	he will separate people one from another	1
25:32	as a shepherd separates the sheep from the goats	1
25:34	from the foundation of the world;	1
25:41	accursed, depart from me into the eternal fire	1
26:16	from that moment he began to look for an opportunity	1
26:27	"Drink from it, all of you;	3
26:39	if it is possible, let this cup pass from me	1
26:47	from the chief priests and the elders	1
26:64	From now on you will see the Son of Man	1
27:40	the Son of God, come down from the cross."	1

	27:42	let him come down from the cross now	1
	27:45	From noon on, darkness came over the whole land	1
	27:51	torn in two, from top to bottom.	1
	27:55	Many women…looking on from a distance;	1
	27:55	they had followed Jesus from Galilee	1
	27:57	there came a rich man from Arimathea	1
	27:64	'He has been raised from the dead,'	1
	28: 2	an angel of the Lord, descending from heaven	3
	28: 7	'He has been raised from the dead	1
Mrk	1: 9	In those days Jesus came from Nazareth of Galilee	1
	1:11	a voice came from heaven, "You are my Son,	3
	2:20	when the bridegroom is taken away from them	1
	2:21	otherwise, the patch pulls away from it	1
	3: 7	a great multitude from Galilee followed	1
	3: 8	great numbers from Judea, Jerusalem, Idumea,	1
	3:22	the scribes who came down from Jerusalem said	1
	4:25	from those who have nothing, even what they have	1
	5: 6	When he saw Jesus from a distance, he ran	1
	5:30	aware that power had gone forth from him,	3
	5:35	some people came from the leader's house	1
	6:14	"John the baptizer has been raised from the dead;	3
	6:33	they hurried there on foot from all the towns	1
	7: 1	some of the scribes who had come from Jerusalem	1
	7: 4	they do not eat anything from the market unless	1
	7: 6	their hearts are far from me;	1
	7:11	support you might have had from me is Corban'	3
	7:21	from the human heart, that evil intentions come:	3
	7:31	Then he returned from the region of Tyre	3
	8: 3	some of them have come from a great distance."	1
	8:11	asking him for a sign from heaven, to test him.	1
	9: 7	from the cloud there came a voice	3
	9: 9	the Son of Man had risen from the dead.	3
	9:10	what this rising from the dead could mean.	3
	9:17	Someone from the crowd answered him, "Teacher	3
	9:21	he said, "From childhood.	3
	10: 6	from the beginning of creation	1
	11:12	On the following day, when they came from Bethany	1
	11:14	"May no one ever eat fruit from you again."	3
	11:30	Did the baptism of John come from heaven,	3
	11:31	"If we say, 'From heaven,' he will say	3
	12: 2	to collect from them his share of the produce	11
	12:25	For when they rise from the dead	3
	12:34	"You are not far from the kingdom of God."	1
	13:19	not been from the beginning of the creation	1
	13:25	the stars will be falling from heaven	3
	13:27	gather his elect from the four winds	3
	13:27	from the ends of the earth to the ends of heaven.	1
	13:28	"From the fig tree learn its lesson:	1
	14:23	and all of them drank from it.	3
	14:35	if it were possible, the hour might pass from him.	1
	14:36	remove this cup from me;	1
	14:43	from the chief priests, the scribes, and the elders.	11
	15:21	who was coming in from the country	1
	15:30	save yourself, and come down from the cross!"	1
	15:32	King of Israel, come down from the cross now	1
	15:38	torn in two, from top to bottom.	1
	15:40	There were also women looking on from a distance;	1
	15:45	he learned from the centurion that he was dead	1
	16: 3	the stone for us from the entrance to the tomb?"	3
	16: 8	So they went out and fled from the tomb	1
	16: 9	⟦from whom he had cast out seven demons.⟧	11
	16: S	⟦sent out through them, from east to west,⟧	1
Lke	1: 2	who from the beginning were eyewitnesses	1
	1:38	the angel departed from her.	1
	1:48	Surely, from now on all generations will call me	1
	1:52	brought down the powerful from their thrones	1
	1:70	the mouth of his holy prophets from of old	1
	1:71	that we would be saved from our enemies	3
	1:71	saved…from the hand of all who hate us.	3
	1:74	rescued from the hands of our enemies	3
	1:78	the dawn from on high will break upon us	3
	2: 1	a decree went out from Emperor Augustus	11
	2: 4	Joseph also went from the town of Nazareth	3
	3: 7	Who warned you to flee from the wrath to come?	1
	3: 8	God is able from these stones to raise up children	3
	3:22	a voice came from heaven	3
	4: 1	Jesus…returned from the Jordan	1
	4:13	he departed from him until an opportune time.	1
	4:22	the gracious words that came from his mouth.	3
	4:42	wanted to prevent him from leaving them.	9
	5: 3	asked him to put out a little way from the shore.	1

Lke	5: 3	he sat down and taught the crowds from the boat.	3
	5: 8	"Go away from me, Lord, for I am a sinful man!"	1
	5:10	from now on you will be catching people."	1
	5:17	(they had come from every village of Galilee	3
	5:35	when the bridegroom will be taken away from them	1
	5:36	"No one tears a piece from a new garment	1
	5:36	the piece from the new will not match the old.	1
	6:17	a great multitude of people from all Judea	1
	6:19	power came out from him and healed all of them.	11
	6:29	from anyone who takes away your coat	1
	6:34	lend to those from whom you hope to receive	11
	6:44	Figs are not gathered from thorns	3
	6:44	nor are grapes picked from a bramble bush.	3
	7: 6	when he was not far from the house	1
	7:45	from the time I came in she has not stopped	1
	8: 2	Mary…from whom seven demons had gone out	1
	8:12	takes away the word from their hearts	1
	8:18	and from those who do not have,	1
	8:35	found the man from whom the demons had gone	1
	8:38	The man from whom the demons had gone begged	1
	8:46	I noticed that power had gone out from me."	1
	8:49	someone came from the leader's house to say,	11
	9: 7	John had been raised from the dead	3
	9:35	from the cloud came a voice that said,	3
	9:37	when they had come down from the mountain	1
	9:38	Just then a man from the crowd shouted, "Teacher	1
	9:45	its meaning was concealed from them	1
	9:54	to command fire to come down from heaven	1
	10: 7	Do not move about from house to house.	3
	10:18	Satan fall from heaven like a flash of lightning.	3
	10:21	hidden these things from the wise	1
	10:30	"A man was going down from Jerusalem to Jericho	1
	11:16	to test him, kept demanding from him a sign	11
	11:16	kept demanding from him a sign from heaven	3
	11:31	she came from the ends of the earth	3
	11:51	from the blood of Abel to the blood of Zechariah	1
	12: 3	will be proclaimed from the housetops.	6
	12:36	to return from the wedding banquet	3
	12:48	From everyone to whom much has been given	11
	12:52	From now on five in one household will be	1
	13:15	untie his ox or his donkey from the manger	1
	13:16	set free from this bondage on the sabbath day?"	1
	13:27	go away from me, all you evildoers!'	1
	13:29	people will come from east and west	1
	13:29	come from east and west, from north and south	1
	16: 3	my master is taking the position away from me?	1
	16:18	whoever marries a woman divorced from her husband	1
	16:21	with what fell from the rich man's table;	1
	16:30	if someone goes to them from the dead	1
	16:31	if someone rises from the dead.' "	3
	17:24	lights up the sky from one side to the other	3
	17:29	rained fire and sulfur from heaven	1
	18:34	in fact, what he said was hidden from them	1
	19:24	'Take the pound from him	1
	19:26	but from those who have nothing,	1
	19:42	now they are hidden from your eyes.	1
	20: 4	Did the baptism of John come from heaven,	3
	20: 5	"If we say, 'From heaven,' he will say	3
	20:35	in the resurrection from the dead	3
	21:11	dreadful portents and great signs from heaven.	1
	21:26	People will faint from fear and foreboding	1
	22:18	from now on I will not drink of the fruit	1
	22:41	he withdrew from them about a stone's throw	1
	22:42	if you are willing, remove this cup from me;	1
	22:43	[[Then an angel from heaven appeared to him]]	1
	22:45	he got up from prayer, he came to the disciples	1
	22:69	from now on the Son of Man will be seated	1
	22:71	We have heard it ourselves from his own lips!"	1
	23: 5	from Galilee where he began even to this place."	1
	23:26	who was coming from the country	1
	23:49	the women who had followed him from Galilee	1
	23:55	The women who had come with him from Galilee	3
	24: 2	They found the stone rolled away from the tomb	1
	24: 9	returning from the tomb, they told all this	1
	24:13	Emmaus, about seven miles from Jerusalem	1
	24:16	their eyes were kept from recognizing him.	9
	24:31	he vanished from their sight.	1
	24:46	rise from the dead on the third day	3
	24:47	beginning from Jerusalem.	1
	24:49	you have been clothed with power from on high."	3
	24:51	While he was blessing them, he withdrew from them	1

Jhn	1: 6	was a man sent from God, whose name was John.	11
	1:16	From his fullness we have all received, grace	3
	1:19	Jews sent priests and Levites from Jerusalem	3
	1:24	Now they had been sent from the Pharisees.	3
	1:32	the Spirit descending from heaven like a dove	3
	1:44	Now Philip was from Bethsaida, the city of Andrew	1
	1:45	found him…Jesus son of Joseph from Nazareth."	1
	2:22	After he was raised from the dead	3
	3: 2	that you are a teacher who has come from God;	1
	3:13	one who descended from heaven, the Son of Man.	3
	3:27	except what has been given from heaven.	3
	3:31	one who comes from heaven is above all.	3
	4:12	with his sons and his flocks drank from it?"	3
	4:22	for salvation is from the Jews.	3
	4:39	Many Samaritans from that city believed in him	3
	4:47	heard that Jesus had come from Judea to Galilee	3
	4:54	after coming from Judea to Galilee.	3
	5:24	has passed from death to life.	3
	5:41	I do not accept glory from human beings.	11
	5:44	you accept glory from one another	11
	6:23	Then some boats from Tiberias came near the place	3
	6:31	'He gave them bread from heaven to eat.' "	3
	6:32	not Moses who gave you the bread from heaven	3
	6:32	my Father who gives you the true bread from heaven.	3
	6:33	bread of God is that which comes down from heaven	3
	6:38	I have come down from heaven, not to do my own	1
	6:41	"I am the bread that came down from heaven."	3
	6:42	can he now say, 'I have come down from heaven'?"	3
	6:45	who has heard and learned from the Father	11
	6:46	except the one who is from God;	11
	6:50	This is the bread that comes down from heaven	3
	6:51	I am the living bread that came down from heaven.	3
	6:58	This is the bread that came down from heaven	3
	6:64	Jesus knew from the first	3
	7:17	will know whether the teaching is from God	3
	7:22	not from Moses, but from the patriarchs)	3
	7:22	not from Moses, but from the patriarchs)	3
	7:29	I know him, because I am from him, and he sent me."	11
	7:41	"Surely the Messiah does not come from Galilee	3
	7:42	the Messiah is descended from David	3
	7:42	from Bethlehem, the village where David lived?"	1
	7:52	replied, "Surely you are not also from Galilee	3
	7:52	no prophet is to arise from Galilee."	3
	8:11	[[Go your way, and from now on do not sin again."]]	1
	8:23	"You are from below, I am from above;	3
	8:23	"You are from below, I am from above;	3
	8:26	I declare to the world what I have heard from him."	11
	8:38	you should do what you have heard from the Father."	11
	8:40	has told you the truth that I heard from God.	11
	8:42	I came from God and now I am here.	3
	8:44	You are from your father the devil	3
	8:44	He was a murderer from the beginning	1
	8:47	Whoever is from God hears the words of God.	3
	8:47	that you are not from God."	3
	9: 1	As he walked along, he saw a man blind from birth.	3
	9:16	"This man is not from God	11
	9:33	If this man were not from God, he could do nothing."	11
	10: 5	they will run from him	1
	10:18	No one takes it from me	1
	10:18	I have received this command from my Father."	11
	10:32	shown you many good works from the Father.	3
	10:39	he escaped from their hands.	3
	11:37	"Could not he…have kept this man from dying?"	9
	11:53	So from that day on they planned	1
	11:55	many went up from the country to Jerusalem	3
	12: 1	whom he had raised from the dead.	3
	12: 9	to see Lazarus, whom he had raised from the dead.	3
	12:17	raised him from the dead	3
	12:21	They came to Philip, who was from Bethsaida	1
	12:27	'Father, save me from this hour'?	3
	12:28	Then a voice came from heaven	3
	12:32	when I am lifted up from the earth	3
	12:34	answered him, "We have heard from the law	3
	12:36	he departed and hid from them.	1
	13: 1	to depart from this world and go to the Father.	3
	13: 3	he had come from God and was going to God	1
	13: 4	got up from the table, took off his outer robe	3
	14: 7	From now on you do know him and have seen him."	1
	15:15	everything that I have heard from my Father.	11
	15:26	whom I will send to you from the Father	11
	15:26	the Spirit of truth who comes from the Father	11

15:27	because you have been with me from the beginning.	1
16: 4	"I did not say these things…from the beginning	3
16:22	no one will take your joy from you.	1
16:27	have believed that I came from God.	11
16:28	I came from the Father	11
16:30	by this we believe that you came from God."	1
17: 6	those whom you gave me from the world.	3
17: 7	everything you have given me is from you;	11
17: 8	and know in truth that I came from you;	11
17:15	I ask you to protect them from the evil one.	3
18: 3	together with police from the chief priests	3
18:28	they took Jesus from Caiaphas	3
18:36	answered, "My kingdom is not from this world.	3
18:36	If my kingdom were from this world	3
19:12	From then on Pilate tried to release him	3
19:23	seamless, woven in one piece from the top.	3
19:27	from that hour the disciple took her	1
20: 1	the stone had been removed from the tomb.	3
20: 9	the scripture, that he must rise from the dead.	3
21: 8	for they were not far from the land	1
21:14	after he was raised from the dead.	3

Act

1:11	who has been taken up from you into heaven	1
1:12	Then they returned to Jerusalem from the mount	1
1:22	beginning from the baptism of John	1
1:22	until the day when he was taken up from us	1
1:25	the place…from which Judas turned aside	1
2: 2	suddenly from heaven there came a sound	3
2: 5	devout Jews from every nation under heaven	1
2:33	having received from the Father the promise	11
2:40	"Save yourselves from this corrupt generation."	1
3: 2	a man lame from birth was being carried in.	3
3: 2	could ask for alms from those entering the temple.	11
3: 5	expecting to receive something from them.	11
3:15	the Author of life, whom God raised from the dead.	3
3:20	may come from the presence of the Lord	1
3:22	from your own people a prophet like me.	3
3:24	from Samuel and those after him,	1
3:26	by turning each of you from your wicked ways."	1
4:10	whom you crucified, whom God raised from the dead.	3
5:38	keep away from these men and let them alone;	1
6: 9	of those from Cilicia and Asia	1
7:10	rescued him from all his afflictions	3
7:16	bought…from the sons of Hamor in Shechem	11
7:37	a prophet for you from your own people	3
7:40	this Moses who led us out from the land of Egypt	3
8:10	All of them, from the least to the greatest,	1
8:26	the road that goes down from Jerusalem to Gaza."	1
8:33	For his life is taken away from the earth."	1
9: 3	suddenly a light from heaven flashed around him.	3
9: 8	Saul got up from the ground	1
9:13	I have heard from many about this man	1
9:14	here he has authority from the chief priests	11
9:18	something like scales fell from his eyes	1
10:23	some of the believers from Joppa accompanied him.	1
10:41	after he rose from the dead.	3
11: 5	a large sheet coming down from heaven	3
11: 9	a second time the voice answered from heaven	3
11:11	three men, sent to me from Caesarea, arrived	1
11:27	At that time prophets came down from Jerusalem	1
12:11	and rescued me from the hands of Herod	3
12:19	Then he went down from Judea to Caesarea	1
13: 8	to turn the proconsul away from the faith.	1
13:13	Paul and his companions set sail from Paphos	1
13:14	they went on from Perga	1
13:29	took him down from the tree and laid him in a tomb.	1
13:30	God raised him from the dead;	3
13:31	came up with him from Galilee to Jerusalem	1
13:34	As to his raising him from the dead	3
13:39	set free from all those sins	1
14: 8	never walked, for he had been crippled from birth.	3
14:15	turn from these worthless things to the living God	1
14:18	restrained the crowds from offering sacrifice	9
14:19	Jews came there from Antioch and Iconium	1
15: 1	certain individuals came down from Judea	1
15:18	known from long ago.'	1
15:24	that certain persons who have gone out from us	3
15:29	If you keep yourselves from these	3
16:11	We set sail from Troas	1
17: 2	argued with them from the scriptures	1
17: 3	Messiah to suffer and to rise from the dead	3
17: 9	after they had taken bail from Jason	11

17:26	From one ancestor he made all nations	3
17:27	though indeed he is not far from each one of us.	1
17:31	given assurance…by raising him from the dead."	3
18: 2	recently come from Italy with his wife Priscilla	1
18: 5	When Silas and Timothy arrived from Macedonia	1
18: 6	From now on I will go to the Gentiles."	1
18:16	he dismissed them from the tribunal.	1
18:21	Then he set sail from Ephesus.	1
19:25	"Men…we get our wealth from this business.	3
20: 6	we sailed from Philippi	1
20:17	From Miletus he sent a message to Ephesus	1
20:18	from the first day that I set foot in Asia	1
20:24	the ministry that I received from the Lord	11
20:30	Some even from your own group will come	3
21: 1	When we had parted from them and set sail	1
21: 7	When we had finished the voyage from Tyre	1
21:10	a prophet named Agabus came down from Judea.	1
21:16	Some of the disciples from Caesarea also came	1
21:27	the Jews from Asia…stirred up the whole crowd.	1
22: 5	From them I also received letters to the brothers	11
22: 6	a great light from heaven suddenly shone about me.	3
22:22	"Away with such a fellow from the earth!	1
22:29	who were about to examine him drew back from him	1
23:34	when he learned that he was from Cilicia	1
24: 8	be able to learn from him concerning everything	11
24:19	there were some Jews from Asia	1
25: 1	he went up from Caesarea to Jerusalem	1
25: 7	the Jews who had gone down from Jerusalem	1
26: 4	"All the Jews know my way of life from my youth	3
26: 4	spent from the beginning among my own people	1
26:10	with authority received from the chief priests	11
26:17	I will rescue you from your people	3
26:17	I will rescue you…from the Gentiles	3
26:18	they may turn from darkness to light	1
26:22	To this day I have had help from God	1
26:23	by being the first to rise from the dead	3
27:14	a violent wind…rushed down from Crete.	8
27:21	not have set sail from Crete	1
27:29	they let down four anchors from the stern	3
27:30	the sailors tried to escape from the ship	3
27:30	pretext of putting out anchors from the bow	3
27:34	for none of you will lose a hair from your heads	1
28: 4	saw the creature hanging from his hand	3
28: 4	though he has escaped from the sea	3
28:21	"We have received no letters from Judea about you	1
28:22	we would like to hear from you what you think,	11
28:23	From morning until evening	1
28:23	both from the law of Moses and from the prophets.	1

Rom

1: 7	Grace to you and peace from God our Father	1
1:18	For the wrath of God is revealed from heaven	1
2:29	person receives praise not from others but from God.	3
2:29	person receives praise not from others but from God.	3
4:24	him who raised Jesus our Lord from the dead	3
5: 9	will we be saved through him from the wrath of God	1
5:14	Yet death exercised dominion from Adam to Moses	1
6: 4	so that, just as Christ was raised from the dead	3
6: 7	For whoever has died is freed from sin.	1
6: 9	Christ, being raised from the dead, will never die	3
6:13	as those who have been brought from death to life	3
6:17	you…have become obedient from the heart	3
6:18	and that you, having been set free from sin	1
6:21	get from the things of which you now are ashamed?	6
6:22	But now that you have been freed from sin	1
7: 2	discharged from the law concerning the husband	1
7: 3	But if her husband dies, she is free from that law	1
7: 4	belong…to him who has been raised from the dead	3
7: 6	But now we are discharged from the law	1
7:24	Who will rescue me from this body of death?	3
8: 2	has set you free from the law of sin and of death.	1
8:11	the Spirit of him who raised Jesus from the dead	3
8:11	he who raised Christ from the dead	3
8:21	creation…set free from its bondage to decay	1
8:35	Who will separate us from the love of Christ?	1
8:39	will be able to separate us from the love of God	1
9:24	not from the Jews only but also from the Gentiles?	3
9:24	not from the Jews only but also from the Gentiles?	3
10: 7	(that is, to bring Christ up from the dead).	3
10: 9	and believe…that God raised him from the dead	3
11:15	their acceptance be but life from the dead!	3
11:24	cut from what is by nature a wild olive tree	3
11:26	he will banish ungodliness from Jacob."	1

Rom	11:36	For from him and through him and to him are all	3
	13: 1	for there is no authority except from God	14
	13:11	it is now the moment for you to wake from sleep.	3
	14:23	because they do not act from faith;	3
	15:19	from Jerusalem and as far around as Illyricum	1
	15:31	I may be rescued from the unbelievers in Judea	1
1Co	1: 3	Grace to you and peace from God our Father	1
	1:30	who became for us wisdom from God, and righteousness	1
	2:12	the Spirit that is from God	3
	4: 5	will receive commendation from God.	1
	5: 2	would have been removed from among you?	3
	6:19	Holy Spirit within you, which you have from God	1
	7: 7	each has a particular gift from God	3
	7:10	the wife should not separate from her husband	1
	7:27	Are you free from a wife? Do not seek a wife.	1
	8: 6	from whom are all things and for whom we exist	3
	9:13	get their food from the temple	3
	10: 4	they drank from the spiritual rock	3
	10:14	my dear friends, flee from the worship of idols.	1
	11: 8	man was not made from woman, but woman from man.	3
	11: 8	man was not made from woman, but woman from man.	3
	11:23	For I received from the Lord	1
	15:12	if Christ is proclaimed as raised from the dead	3
	15:20	in fact Christ has been raised from the dead	3
	15:47	The first man was from the earth, a man of dust;	3
	15:47	the second man is from heaven.	3
2Co	1: 2	Grace to you and peace from God our Father	1
	1:10	He who rescued us from so deadly a peril	3
	1:16	to come back to you from Macedonia	1
	2: 3	from those who should have made me rejoice;	1
	2:16	to the one a fragrance from death to death	3
	2:16	to the other a fragrance from life to life.	3
	3: 1	letters of recommendation to you or from you	3
	3: 5	our competence is from God	3
	3:18	from one degree of glory to another;	1
	5: 1	we have a building from God	3
	5: 6	in the body we are away from the Lord	1
	5: 8	we would rather be away from the body and at home	3
	5:16	From now on, therefore, we regard	1
	5:18	All this is from God, who reconciled us	3
	6:17	come out from them, and be separate from them	4
	7: 1	let us cleanse ourselves from every defilement	1
	11: 3	from a sincere and pure devotion to Christ.	1
	11: 4	a different spirit from the one you received	10
	11: 4	a different gospel from the one you accepted	10
	11: 9	the friends who came from Macedonia.	1
	11:24	received from the Jews the forty lashes	14
	11:26	danger from bandits, danger from my own people	3
	11:26	danger from Gentiles, danger in the city	3
	11:26	danger at sea, danger from false brothers and sisters;	5
	12: 6	what is seen in me or heard from me	3
Gal	1: 1	by human commission nor from human authorities,	1
	1: 1	God the Father, who raised him from the dead—	3
	1: 3	Grace to you and peace from God our Father	1
	1: 4	to set us free from the present evil age	3
	1: 8	even if we or an angel from heaven should proclaim	3
	1:12	for I did not receive it from a human source	11
	2: 6	from those who were…acknowledged leaders	1
	2:12	for until certain people came from James	1
	3: 2	The only thing I want to learn from you is this:	1
	3:13	Christ redeemed us from the curse of the law	3
	4:24	Hagar, from Mount Sinai, bearing children for slavery.	1
	5: 4	by the law have cut yourselves off from Christ;	1
	5: 7	who prevented you from obeying the truth?	9
	6: 8	will reap corruption from the flesh;	3
	6: 8	will reap eternal life from the Spirit.	3
Eph	1: 2	Grace to you and peace from God our Father	1
	1:20	when he raised him from the dead	3
	3:15	from whom every family…takes its name.	3
	4:16	from whom the whole body, joined and knit together	3
	4:31	Put away from you all bitterness and wrath	1
	5:14	it says, "Sleeper, awake! Rise from the dead	3
	6: 6	doing the will of God from the heart.	3
	6: 8	we will receive the same again from the Lord	11
	6:23	from God the Father and the Lord Jesus Christ.	1
Php	1: 2	Grace to you and peace from God our Father	1
	1: 5	from the first day until now.	1
	1:15	Some proclaim Christ from envy and rivalry	2
	1:15	but others from goodwill.	2
	2: 3	Do nothing from selfish ambition or conceit	8
	3: 9	the righteousness from God based on faith.	3

	3:11	I may attain the resurrection from the dead.	3
	3:20	from there that we are expecting a Savior, the Lord	3
	4:18	satisfied, now that I have received from Epaphroditus	11
Col	1: 2	Grace to you and peace from God our Father.	1
	1: 6	from the day you heard it and truly comprehended	1
	1: 7	This you learned from Epaphras	1
	1:13	has rescued us from the power of darkness	3
	1:18	he is the beginning, the firstborn from the dead	3
	1:23	without shifting from the hope promised by the gospel	1
	2:12	God, who raised him from the dead.	3
	2:19	from whom the whole body, nourished	3
	3: 8	malice, slander, and abusive language from your mouth.	3
	3:24	from the Lord you will receive the inheritance	1
	4:16	see that you read also the letter from Laodicea.	3
1Th	1: 8	the word of the Lord has sounded forth from you	1
	1: 9	how you turned to God from idols	1
	1:10	to wait for his Son from heaven	3
	1:10	his Son from heaven, whom he raised from the dead	3
	1:10	Jesus, who rescues us from the wrath that is coming.	3
	2: 6	nor did we seek praise from mortals	3
	2: 6	whether from you or from others	1
	2: 6	whether from you or from others	1
	2:13	the word of God that you heard from us	11
	2:14	you suffered…from your own compatriots	14
	2:14	as they did from the Jews	14
	3: 6	Timothy has just now come to us from you	1
	4: 1	as you learned from us how you ought to live	11
	4: 3	that you abstain from fornication;	1
	4:16	the Lord himself…will descend from heaven	1
	5:22	abstain from every form of evil.	1
2Th	1: 2	Grace to you and peace from God our Father	1
	1: 7	when the Lord Jesus is revealed from heaven	1
	1: 9	separated…from the glory of his might	1
	2: 2	by letter, as though from us,	2
	3: 2	that we may be rescued from wicked and evil people;	1
	3: 3	he will strengthen you and guard you from the evil	1
	3: 6	keep away from believers who…	1
	3: 6	the tradition that they received from us.	11
1Ti	1: 2	Grace, mercy, and peace from God the Father	1
	6: 4	disputes about words. From these come envy	3
	6:10	some have wandered away from the faith	1
2Ti	1: 2	Grace, mercy, and peace from God the Father	1
	1:13	sound teaching that you have heard from me	11
	1:18	the Lord grant that he will find mercy from the Lord	11
	2: 2	have heard from me through many witnesses	11
	2: 8	Remember Jesus Christ, raised from the dead	3
	2:18	who have swerved from the truth by claiming	12
	2:19	"Let everyone…turn away from wickedness."	1
	2:22	those who call on the Lord from a pure heart.	3
	2:26	they may escape from the snare of the devil	3
	3:11	Yet the Lord rescued me from all of them.	3
	3:14	knowing from whom you learned it	11
	3:15	from childhood you have known the sacred writings	1
	4: 4	will turn away from listening to the truth	1
	4:17	So I was rescued from the lion's mouth.	3
	4:18	The Lord will rescue me from every evil attack	1
Tit	1: 4	Grace and peace from God the Father	1
	2:14	that he might redeem us from all iniquity	1
Phm	1: 3	Grace to you and peace from God our Father	1
	1: 7	received much joy and encouragement from your love	6
Heb	3:12	evil…heart that turns away from the living God.	1
	4: 4	God rested on the seventh day from all his works."	1
	4:10	cease from their labors as God did from his.	1
	4:10	cease from their labors as God did from his.	1
	4:12	piercing until it divides soul from spirit	7
	4:12	until it divides…joints from marrow;	7
	5: 7	to the one who was able to save him from death	3
	5:14	to distinguish good from evil.	13
	6: 1	the foundation: repentance from dead works	1
	6: 7	receives a blessing from God.	1
	7: 1	Abraham…was returning from defeating the kings	1
	7: 5	though these also are descended from Abraham.	3
	7:13	from which no one has ever served at the altar.	1
	7:14	evident that our Lord was descended from Judah	3
	7:26	blameless, undefiled, separated from sinners	1
	8:11	from the least of them to the greatest.	1
	9:14	purify our conscience from dead works	1
	10:22	our hearts sprinkled clean from an evil conscience	1
	11: 3	was made from things that are not visible.	3
	11:12	Therefore from one person, and this one as good as dead	1
	11:19	God is able even to raise someone from the dead	3

	12: 3	endured such hostility against himself from sinners	14
	12:25	if we reject the one who warns from heaven!	1
	13:10	We have an altar from which those who officiate	3
	13:20	who brought back the dead our Lord Jesus	3
	13:24	Those from Italy send you greetings.	1
Jas	1: 7	must not expect to receive anything from the Lord.	11
	1:17	coming down from the Father of lights	1
	3:10	From the same mouth come blessing and cursing.	3
	3:11	Does a spring pour forth...fresh and brackish water?	3
	4: 7	Resist the devil, and he will flee from you.	1
	5:19	if anyone among you wanders from the truth	1
	5:20	brings back a sinner from wandering will save	3
	5:20	will save the sinner's soul from death	3
1Pe	1: 3	the resurrection of Jesus Christ from the dead	3
	1:12	by the Holy Spirit sent from heaven	1
	1:18	you were ransomed from the futile ways	3
	1:21	who raised him from the dead and gave him glory	3
	1:22	love one another deeply from the heart.	3
	3:10	let them keep their tongues from evil	1
	3:10	let them keep...their lips from speaking deceit;	9
	3:11	let them turn away from evil and do good;	1
2Pe	1:17	he received honor and glory from God the Father	11
	1:18	We ourselves heard this voice come from heaven	3
	1:21	and women moved by the Holy Spirit spoke from God.	1
	2: 9	the Lord knows how to rescue the godly from trial	3
	2:11	against them a slanderous judgment from the Lord.	11
	2:21	to turn back from the holy commandment	3
	3: 4	as they were from the beginning of creation!"	1
1Jn	1: 1	what was from the beginning	1
	1: 5	the message we have heard from him and proclaim	1
	1: 7	blood of Jesus his Son cleanses us from all sin.	1
	1: 9	and cleanse us from all unrighteousness.	1
	2: 7	commandment that you have had from the beginning;	1
	2:13	because you know him who is from the beginning.	1
	2:14	because you know him who is from the beginning.	1
	2:16	comes not from the Father but from the world.	3
	2:16	comes not from the Father but from the world.	3
	2:19	They went out from us, but they did not belong to us;	3
	2:21	and you know that no lie comes from the truth.	3
	2:24	Let what you heard from the beginning abide	1
	2:24	what you heard from the beginning abides in you	1
	2:27	the anointing that you received from him	1
	3: 8	for the devil has been sinning from the beginning.	1
	3:10	all who do not do what is right are not from God	3
	3:11	message you have heard from the beginning	1
	3:12	not be like Cain who was from the evil one	3
	3:14	We know that we have passed from death to life	3
	3:19	by this we will know that we are from the truth	3
	3:22	we receive from him whatever we ask	1
	4: 1	test the spirits to see whether they are from God;	3
	4: 2	that Jesus Christ has come in the flesh is from God	3
	4: 3	spirit that does not confess Jesus is not from God.	3
	4: 4	Little children, you are from God	3
	4: 5	They are from the world;	3
	4: 5	therefore what they say is from the world	3
	4: 6	We are from God. Whoever knows God listens to us	3
	4: 6	whoever is not from God does not listen to us.	3
	4: 6	From this we know the spirit of truth	3
	4: 7	let us love one another, because love is from God;	3
	4:21	The commandment we have from him is this:	1
	5:21	Little children, keep yourselves from idols.	1
2Jn	1: 3	Grace, mercy, and peace will be with us from God	11
	1: 3	and from Jesus Christ, the Father's Son	11
	1: 5	but one we have had from the beginning	1
	1: 6	just as you have heard it from the beginning	1
3Jn	1: 7	accepting no support from non-believers.	1
	1:10	prevents those...and expels them from the church.	3
	1:11	Whoever does good is from God;	3
Jde	1:14	Enoch, in the seventh generation from Adam	1
Rev	1: 4	Grace to you and peace from him who is and who was	1
	1: 4	from the seven spirits who are before his throne	1
	1: 5	and from Jesus Christ, the faithful witness	1
	1: 5	To him who...freed us from our sins by his blood	3
	1:16	from his mouth came a sharp, two-edged sword	3
	2: 5	and remove your lampstand from its place	3
	2: 7	I will give permission to eat from the tree of life	3
	2:28	even as I also received authority from my Father.	11
	3:10	I will keep you from the hour of trial	3
	3:12	the new Jerusalem that comes down from my God	1
	3:18	I counsel you to buy from me gold refined by fire	11
	4: 5	Coming from the throne are flashes of lightning	3

	5: 7	He went and took the scroll from the right hand	3
	5: 9	ransomed for God saints from every tribe and language	3
	6: 4	rider was permitted to take peace from the earth	3
	6:14	mountain and island was removed from its place.	3
	6:16	hide us from...the one seated on the throne	1
	6:16	hide us...from the wrath of the Lamb;	1
	7: 2	I saw another angel ascending from the rising...sun	1
	7: 5	From the tribe of Judah twelve thousand sealed,	3
	7: 5	from the tribe of Reuben twelve thousand,	3
	7: 5	from the tribe of Gad twelve thousand,	3
	7: 6	from the tribe of Asher twelve thousand,	3
	7: 6	from the tribe of Naphtali twelve thousand,	3
	7: 6	from the tribe of Manasseh twelve thousand,	3
	7: 7	from the tribe of Simeon twelve thousand,	3
	7: 7	from the tribe of Levi twelve thousand,	3
	7: 7	from the tribe of Issachar twelve thousand,	3
	7: 8	from the tribe of Zebulun twelve thousand,	3
	7: 8	from the tribe of Joseph twelve thousand,	3
	7: 8	from the tribe of Benjamin twelve thousand sealed.	3
	7: 9	multitude...from every nation, from all tribes	3
	7:17	God will wipe away every tear from their eyes."	3
	8: 4	rose...before God from the hand of the angel.	3
	8:10	great star fell from heaven, blazing like a torch	3
	8:11	died from the water, because it was made bitter.	3
	9: 1	I saw a star that had fallen from heaven to earth	3
	9: 2	and from the shaft rose smoke like the smoke	3
	9: 3	Then from the smoke came locusts on the earth	3
	9: 6	they will long to die, but death will flee from them.	1
	9:13	a voice from the four horns of the golden altar	3
	10: 1	another mighty angel coming down from heaven	3
	10: 4	but I heard a voice from heaven saying	3
	10: 8	voice that I had heard from heaven spoke to me	3
	10:10	took the little scroll from the hand of the angel	3
	11: 5	fire pours from their mouth and consumes	3
	11: 7	the beast that comes up from the bottomless pit	3
	11:11	the breath of life from God entered them	3
	11:12	Then they heard a loud voice from heaven saying	3
	12:14	could fly from the serpent into the wilderness	1
	12:15	Then from his mouth the serpent poured water	3
	12:16	river that the dragon had poured from his mouth.	3
	13: 8	written from the foundation of the world	1
	13:13	even making fire come down from heaven to earth	3
	14: 2	I heard a voice from heaven	3
	14: 3	who have been redeemed from the earth.	1
	14: 4	redeemed from humankind as first fruits for God	1
	14:13	I heard a voice from heaven saying, "Write this:	3
	14:13	the dead who from now on die in the Lord."	1
	14:13	"they will rest from their labors	3
	14:18	Then another angel came out from the altar	3
	14:20	and blood flowed from the wine press	3
	15: 8	smoke from the glory of God and from his power	3
	15: 8	smoke from the glory of God and from his power	3
	16: 1	Then I heard a loud voice from the temple	3
	16:12	to prepare the way for the kings from the east.	1
	16:13	foul spirits...coming from the mouth of the dragon	3
	16:13	three foul spirits...from the mouth of the beast	3
	16:13	spirits...from the mouth of the false prophet.	3
	16:17	voice came...from the throne, saying, "It is done!"	1
	16:21	huge hailstones...dropped from heaven on people	3
	17: 8	beast...is about to ascend from the bottomless pit	3
	17: 8	written...from the foundation of the world	1
	18: 1	I saw another angel coming down from heaven	3
	18: 3	grown rich from the power of her luxury."	3
	18: 4	Then I heard another voice from heaven saying	3
	18:14	"The fruit...your soul longed has gone from you,	1
	18:15	The merchants...who gained wealth from her,	1
	19: 5	And from the throne came a voice saying	1
	19:15	From his mouth comes a sharp sword	3
	19:21	the sword that came from his mouth;	3
	20: 1	Then I saw an angel coming down from heaven	3
	20: 7	Satan will be released from his prison	3
	20: 9	And fire came down from heaven and consumed them.	3
	20:11	earth and the heaven fled from his presence	1
	21: 2	new Jerusalem, coming down out of heaven from God	1
	21: 3	I heard a loud voice from the throne saying	3
	21: 4	he will wipe every tear from their eyes.	1
	21: 6	as a gift from the spring of the water of life.	3
	21:10	Jerusalem coming down out of heaven from God.	1
	22: 1	flowing from the throne of God and of the Lamb	3
	22:19	if anyone takes away from the words of the book	1

from above

   1. ἄνωθεν, *anōthen, 540*

Jhn	3: 3	see the kingdom…without being born from above."	1
	3: 7	that I said to you, 'You must be born from above.'	1
	3:31	one who comes from above is above all;	1
	19:11	unless it had been given you from above;	1
Jas	1:17	with every perfect gift, is from above	1
	3:15	Such wisdom does not come down from above	1
	3:17	wisdom from above is first pure, then peaceable	1

from among

   1. ἐκ, *ek, 1666*

Act	6: 3	select from among yourselves seven men of good standing	1
	15:14	to take from among them a people for his name.	1
	15:22	decided to choose men from among their members	1
1Co	5:13	"Drive out the wicked person from among you."	1
Heb	5: 1	Every high priest chosen from among mortals	1

from here

   1. ἔνθεν, *enthen, 1925*

   2. ἐντεῦθεν, *enteuthen, 1949*

Lke	13:31	"Get away from here, for Herod wants to kill you."	2
	16:26	so that those who might want to pass from here	1
Jhn	18:36	but as it is, my kingdom is not from here."	2

from now

   1. μετά, *meta, 3552*

Act	1: 5	baptized with the Holy Spirit not many days from now."	1

from now on

   1. λοιπός, *loipos, 3370*

1Co	7:29	from now on, let even those who have wives be	1
Gal	6:17	From now on, let no one make trouble for me;	1
2Ti	4: 8	From now on there is reserved for me the crown	1

from there

   1. ἐκεῖθεν, *ekeithen, 1696*

   2. κἀκεῖθεν, *kakeithen, 2796*

Mat	4:21	went from there, he saw two other brothers	1
	9:27	As Jesus went on from there	1
	11: 1	from there to teach and proclaim his message	1
	14:13	withdrew from there in a boat to a deserted place	1
Mrk	7:24	From there he set out	1
	9:30	They went on from there	2
Lke	9: 4	stay there, and leave from there.	1
	16:26	and no one can cross from there to us.'	1
Jhn	11:54	went from there to a town called Ephraim	1
Act	7: 4	After his father died, God had him move from there	2
	13: 4	from there they sailed to Cyprus.	1
	14:26	From there they sailed back to Antioch	2
	16:12	and from there to Philippi	2
	20:15	We sailed from there, and on the following day	2
	21: 1	the next day to Rhodes…from there to Patara.	2
	27: 4	Putting out to sea from there	2
	27:12	the majority was in favor of putting to sea from there	1
	28:15	The believers from there, when they heard of us	2

from this

   1. ὅθεν, *hothen, 3854*

1Jn	2:18	From this we know that it is the last hour.	1

from what

   1. πόθεν, *pothen, 4470*

Rev	2: 5	Remember then from what you have fallen;	1

from which

   1. ὅθεν, *hothen, 3854*

Mat	12:44	'I will return to my house from which I came.'	1
Lke	11:24	'I will return to my house from which I came.'	1

front

   1. ἔμπροσθεν, *emprosthen, 1869*

   2. ἐνώπιον, *enōpion, 1967*

   3. μέσος, *mesos, 3545*

   4. πρό, *pro, 4574*

   5. προάγω, *proagō, 4575*

   6. πρός, *pros, 4639*

Mrk	2: 2	not even in front of the door;	6
Lke	5:19	into the middle of the crowd in front of Jesus.	1

	14: 2	Just then, in front of him, there was a man	1
	18:39	Those who were in front sternly ordered him	5
Act	12: 6	guards in front of the door	4
	17:22	Paul stood in front of the Areopagus	3
	18:17	and beat him in front of the tribunal.	1
Rev	4: 5	in front of the throne burn seven flaming torches	2
	4: 6	in front of the throne there is something like a sea	2
	4: 6	creatures, full of eyes in front and behind:	1

fruit   *See also* bear fruit

   1. Contextual: Not in Greek

   2. γένημα, *genēma, 1163*

   3. καρπός, *karpos, 2843*

   4. ὀπώρα, *opōra, 3967*

Mat	3: 8	Bear fruit worthy of repentance.	3
	3:10	tree therefore that does not bear good fruit	3
	7:16	You will know them by their fruits.	3
	7:17	In the same way, every good tree bears good fruit	3
	7:17	but the bad tree bears bad fruit.	3
	7:18	A good tree cannot bear bad fruit	3
	7:18	nor can a bad tree bear good fruit.	3
	7:19	Every tree that does not bear good fruit is cut	3
	7:20	Thus you will know them by their fruits.	3
	12:33	"Either make the tree good, and its fruit good;	3
	12:33	or make the tree bad, and its fruit bad;	3
	12:33	for the tree is known by its fruit.	3
	21:19	"May no fruit ever come from you again!"	3
	21:43	a people that produces the fruits of the kingdom.	3
	26:29	never again drink of this fruit of the vine	2
Mrk	11:14	"May no one ever eat fruit from you again."	3
	14:25	I will never again drink of the fruit of the vine	2
Lke	1:42	blessed is the fruit of your womb.	3
	3: 8	Bear fruits worthy of repentance.	3
	3: 9	every tree…that does not bear good fruit	3
	6:43	"No good tree bears bad fruit	3
	6:43	nor again does a bad tree bear good fruit;	3
	6:44	for each tree is known by its own fruit.	3
	8:14	their fruit does not mature.	1
	13: 6	he came looking for fruit on it and found none.	3
	13: 7	I have come looking for fruit on this fig tree	3
	13: 9	If it bears fruit next year, well and good;	3
	22:18	I will not drink of the fruit of the vine	2
Jhn	4:36	and is gathering fruit for eternal life	3
	12:24	if it dies, it bears much fruit.	3
	15: 2	removes every branch in me that bears no fruit.	3
	15: 2	Every branch that bears fruit he prunes	3
	15: 2	he prunes to make it bear more fruit.	3
	15: 4	Just as the branch cannot bear fruit by itself	3
	15: 5	Those who abide in me…bear much fruit	3
	15: 8	that you bear much fruit	3
	15:16	I appointed you to go and bear fruit	3
	15:16	fruit that will last	3
1Co	9: 7	not eat any of its fruit?	3
Gal	5:22	the fruit of the Spirit is love, joy, peace	3
Eph	5: 9	fruit of the light is found in all that is good	3
Heb	12:11	it yields the peaceful fruit of righteousness	3
	13:15	the fruit of lips that confess his name.	3
Jas	3:17	wisdom…is…full of mercy and good fruits	3
Rev	18:14	"The fruit for which your soul longed has gone	4
	22: 2	the tree of life with its twelve kinds of fruit	3
	22: 2	tree of life…producing its fruit each month;	3

first fruit

   1. ἀπαρχή, *aparchē, 569*

Rom	8:23	we…who have the first fruits of the Spirit	1
	11:16	If the part of the dough offered as first fruits	1
1Co	15:20	first fruits of those who have died.	1
	15:23	each in his own order: Christ the first fruits	1
2Th	2:13	God chose you as the first fruits for salvation	1
Jas	1:18	so that we would become a kind of first fruits	1
Rev	14: 4	redeemed from humankind as first fruits for God	1

winter fruit

   1. ὄλυνθος, *olynthos, 3913*

Rev	6:13	as the fig tree drops its winter fruit	1

without fruit

   1. ἄκαρπος, *akarpos, 182*

Jde	1:12	autumn trees without fruit, twice dead, uprooted;	1

fruitful

1. καρπός, *karpos, 2843*
2. καρποφόρος, *karpophoros, 2845*

Act 14:17 giving you rains from heaven and fruitful seasons   2
Php   1:22 that means fruitful labor for me;   1

fulfill

1. ἀναπληρόω, *anaplēroō, 405*
2. γίνομαι, *ginomai, 1181*
3. ἐκπληρόω, *ekplēroō, 1740*
4. πληροφορέω, *plērophoreō, 4442*
5. πληρόω, *plēroō, 4444*
6. πλήρωμα, *plērōma, 4445*
7. τελειόω, *teleioō, 5457*
8. τελέω, *teleō, 5464*
9. τέλος, *telos, 5465*

Mat   1:22 All this took place to fulfill what had been spoken   5
       2:15 This was to fulfill what had been spoken   5
       2:17 Then was fulfilled what had been spoken   5
       2:23 spoken through the prophets might be fulfilled   5
       3:15 proper for us in this way to fulfill all righteousness."   5
       4:14 spoken through the prophet Isaiah might be fulfilled: 5
       5:17 I have come not to abolish but to fulfill.   5
       8:17 to fulfill what had been spoken through the prophet   5
      12:17 to fulfill what had been spoken through the prophet   5
      13:14 With them indeed is fulfilled the prophecy   1
      13:35 to fulfill what had been spoken through the prophet: 5
      21: 4 This took place to fulfill what had been spoken   5
      26:54 how then would the scriptures be fulfilled   5
      26:56 scriptures of the prophets may be fulfilled."   5
      27: 9 Then was fulfilled what had been spoken   5
Mrk   1:15 saying, "The time is fulfilled   5
      14:49 let the scriptures be fulfilled."   5
Lke   1: 1 that have been fulfilled among us   4
       1:20 which will be fulfilled in their time   5
       4:21 scripture has been fulfilled in your hearing."   5
      21:24 until the times of the Gentiles are fulfilled.   5
      22:16 I tell you, I will not eat it until it is fulfilled   5
      22:37 this scripture must be fulfilled in me   8
      22:37 what is written about me is being fulfilled."   9
      24:44 everything…must be fulfilled."   5
Jhn   3:29 For this reason my joy has been fulfilled.   5
      12:38 to fulfill the word spoken by the prophet Isaiah: 5
      13:18 to fulfill the scripture, 'The one   5
      15:25 to fulfill the word that is written in their law   5
      17:12 so that the scripture might be fulfilled.   5
      18: 9 This was to fulfill the word that he had spoken   5
      18:32 to fulfill what Jesus had said   5
      19:24 This was to fulfill what the scripture says,   5
      19:28 he said (in order to fulfill the scripture),   7
      19:36 so that the scripture might be fulfilled   5
Act   1:16 "Friends, the scripture had to be fulfilled   5
       3:18 In this way God fulfilled what he had foretold   5
      13:27 fulfilled those words by condemning him.   5
      13:33 he has fulfilled for us, their children   3
Rom   8: 4 requirement of the law might be fulfilled in us   5
      13: 8 the one who loves another has fulfilled the law.   5
      13:10 therefore, love is the fulfilling of the law.   6
1Co 15:54 then the saying that is written will be fulfilled: 2
Gal   6: 2 in this way you will fulfill the law of Christ.   1
2Th   1:11 fulfill by his power every good resolve and work   5
Jas   2: 8 You do well if you really fulfill the royal law   8
       2:23 Thus the scripture was fulfilled that says   5
Rev 10: 7 the mystery of God will be fulfilled, as he announced   8
      17:17 until the words of God will be fulfilled.   8

fulfilling   *See* succeed in fulfilling

fulfillment

1. Contextual: Not in Greek
2. πίμπλημι, *pimplēmi, 4398*
3. τελείωσις, *teleiōsis, 5459*

Lke   1:45 fulfillment of what was spoken to her   3
      21:22 as a fulfillment of all that is written.   2
Act   7:17 time drew near for the fulfillment of the promise   1
Jas   1:18 In fulfillment of his own purpose he gave us birth   1

full   *See also* full *accord,* full *assurance,* full *force,* full *inclusion,* full *number,* make full, make full use

1. Contextual: Not in Greek
2. γέμω, *gemō, 1154*
3. ἐμπίμπλημι, *empimplēmi, 1855*
4. μέγας, *megas, 3489*
5. μεστός, *mestos, 3550*
6. ὅλος, *holos, 3910*
7. πᾶς, *pas, 4246*
8. πλήρης, *plērēs, 4441*
9. πληρόω, *plēroō, 4444*
10. πλήρωμα, *plērōma, 4445*
11. πολύς, *polys, 4498*
12. τέλειος, *teleios, 5455*

Mat   6:22 eye is healthy, your whole body will be full of light;   1
       6:23 your whole body will be full of darkness.   1
      13:48 when it was full, they drew it ashore, sat down   9
      14:20 of the broken pieces, twelve baskets full.   8
      15:37 the broken pieces left over, seven baskets full.   8
      23:25 inside they are full of greed and self-indulgence.   2
      23:27 inside they are full of the bones of the dead   2
      23:28 inside you are full of hypocrisy and lawlessness.   5
Mrk   4:28 then the head, then the full grain in the head.   8
       6:43 took up twelve baskets full of broken pieces   10
       8: 8 the broken pieces left over, seven baskets full.   1
       8:19 how many baskets full of broken pieces   8
       8:20 how many baskets full of broken pieces   10
Lke   4: 1 Jesus, full of the Holy Spirit, returned   8
       6:25 "Woe to you who are full now,   3
      11:36 it will be as full of light   6
      11:39 inside you are full of greed and wickedness.   2
Jhn   1:14 of a father's only son, full of grace and truth.   8
      19:29 A jar full of sour wine was standing there.   5
      19:29 they put a sponge full of the wine on a branch   5
      21: 8 dragging the net full of fish   1
      21:11 full of large fish, a hundred fifty-three   5
Act   6: 3 full of the Spirit and of wisdom   8
       6: 5 Stephen, a man full of faith and the Holy Spirit   8
       6: 8 Stephen, full of grace and power   8
      11:24 a good man, full of the Holy Spirit and of faith.   8
      13:10 full of all deceit and villainy   8
Rom   1:29 Full of envy, murder, strife, deceit, craftiness   5
       3:14 "Their mouths are full of cursing and bitterness."   2
      15:14 that you yourselves are full of goodness   5
Eph   4:13 to the measure of the full stature of Christ.   10
Php   1: 9 with knowledge and full insight   7
       4:18 I have been paid in full and have more than enough;   7
1Th   1: 5 in the Holy Spirit and with full conviction;   11
1Ti   1:15 The saying is sure and worthy of full acceptance   7
       2:11 woman learn in silence with full submission   7
       4: 9 is sure and worthy of full acceptance.   7
Jas   1: 4 let endurance have its full effect   12
       3: 8 the tongue…full of deadly poison.   5
       3:17 wisdom…is…full of mercy and good fruits   5
2Pe   2:14 They have eyes full of adultery   5
2Jn   1: 8 so that you do not lose…but may receive a full reward.   8
Rev   4: 6 creatures, full of eyes in front and behind: 2
       4: 8 are full of eyes all around and inside   2
       5: 8 and golden bowls full of incense   2
       5:12 singing with full voice, "Worthy is the Lamb   4
       6:12 the full moon became like blood   6
      15: 7 seven golden bowls full of the wrath of God   2
      17: 3 beast that was full of blasphemous names   2
      17: 4 holding…a golden cup full of abominations   2
      21: 9 the seven bowls full of the seven last plagues   2

full of darkness

1. σκοτεινός, *skoteinos, 5027*

Lke 11:34 is not healthy, your body is full of darkness.   1

full of idols

1. κατείδωλος, *kateidōlos, 2977*

Act 17:16 to see that the city was full of idols.   1

full of light

1. φωτεινός, *phōteinos, 5893*

Lke 11:34 your whole body is full of light;   1
      11:36 If then your whole body is full of light   1

fullness   *See also* come to fullness

1. πλήρωμα, *plērōma, 4445*

Jhn	1:16	From his fullness we have all received, grace	1
Rom	15:29	come in the fullness of the blessing of Christ.	1
1Co	10:26	for "the earth and its fullness are the Lord's."	1
Gal	4: 4	when the fullness of time had come	1
Eph	1:10	as a plan for the fullness of time	1
	1:23	the fullness of him who fills all in all.	1
	3:19	you may be filled with all the fullness of God.	1
Col	2: 9	in him the whole fullness of deity dwells bodily	1

fullness of God

1. πλήρωμα, *plērōma, 4445*

Col	1:19	in him all the fullness of God was pleased to dwell	1

fully   *See also* arm fully, assure fully, carry out fully, come fully, confirm fully, convince fully, fully *ripe*, grow fully, know fully, make fully known, proclaim fully, qualify fully, satisfy fully

1. πᾶς, *pas, 4246*

Col	1:10	worthy of the Lord, fully pleasing to him	1
Jde	1: 5	to remind you, though you are fully informed,	1

function

1. πρᾶξις, *praxis, 4552*

Rom	12: 4	and not all the members have the same function	1

furiously

1. Contextual: Not in Greek

Act	26:11	since I was so furiously enraged at them	1

furnace

1. κάμινος, *kaminos, 2825*

Mat	13:42	throw them into the furnace of fire	1
	13:50	throw them into the furnace of fire	1
Rev	1:15	like burnished bronze, refined as in a furnace	1
	9: 2	rose smoke like the smoke of a great furnace	1

furnish

1. στρωννύω, *strōnnyō, 5143*

Mrk	14:15	a large room upstairs, furnished and ready.	
Lke	22:12	show you a large room upstairs, already furnished.	1

further   *See also* clothe further, far

1. Contextual: Not in Greek
2. ἔτι, *eti, 2285*
3. περαιτέρω, *peraiterō, 4304*
4. πολύς, *polys, 4498*

Lke	22:71	they said, "What further testimony do we need?	2
Act	4:17	keep it from spreading further among the people	4
	15:28	no further burden than these essentials:	4
	19:39	If there is anything further you want to know	3
	24: 4	to detain you no further	4
	28:25	they were leaving, Paul made one further statement:	1
Heb	7:11	what further need would there have been	2

no further

1. μηκέτι, *mēketi, 3600*
2. οὐκέτι, *ouketi, 4033*

Mrk	15: 5	Jesus made no further reply	2
Rom	15:23	But now, with no further place for me	1

furthermore

1. καί, *kai, 2779*

Heb	7:23	Furthermore, the former priests were many in number	1

fury

1. ἄνοια, *anoia, 486*
2. ζῆλος, *zēlos, 2419*
3. θυμός, *thymos, 2596*

Lke	6:11	they were filled with fury	1
Rom	2: 8	for those...there will be wrath and fury.	3
Heb	10:27	a fearful prospect of judgment, and a fury of fire	2
Rev	16:19	gave her the wine-cup of the fury of his wrath.	3
	19:15	of the fury of the wrath of God the Almighty.	3

futile

1. μάταιος, *mataios, 3469*

2. ματαιόω, *mataioō, 3471*

Rom	1:21	but they became futile in their thinking	2
1Co	3:20	the thoughts of the wise, that they are futile."	1
	15:17	your faith is futile	1
1Pe	1:18	you were ransomed from the futile ways	1

futility

1. ματαιότης, *mataiotēs, 3470*

Rom	8:20	for the creation was subjected to futility	1
Eph	4:17	in the futility of their minds.	1

future

1. μέλλω, *mellō, 3516*

1Co	3:22	the present or the future—all belong to you	1
1Ti	6:19	the treasure of a good foundation for the future	1
Heb	11:20	invoked blessings for the future on Jacob and Esau.	1

G

Gabbatha

1. Γαββαθᾶ, *Gabbatha, 1119*

Jhn	19:13	or in Hebrew Gabbatha.	1

Gabriel

1. Γαβριήλ, *Gabriēl, 1120*

Lke	1:19	"I am Gabriel. I stand in the presence of God	1
	1:26	the angel Gabriel was sent by God	1

Gad

1. Γάδ, *Gad, 1122*

Rev	7: 5	from the tribe of Gad twelve thousand,	1

gad about

1. περιέρχομαι, *perierchomai, 4320*

1Ti	5:13	gadding about from house to house;	1

Gadarene

1. Γαδαρηνός, *Gadarēnos, 1123*

Mat	8:28	to the country of the Gadarenes	1

gain   *See also* greedy for gain, means of gain

1. γίνομαι, *ginomai, 1181*
2. εὑρίσκω, *heuriskō, 2351*
3. κερδαίνω, *kerdainō, 3045*
4. κέρδος, *kerdos, 3046*
5. κτάομαι, *ktaomai, 3227*
6. μισθός, *misthos, 3635*
7. ὄφελος, *ophelos, 4055*
8. περιποιέω, *peripoieō, 4347*
9. πορισμός, *porismos, 4516*
10. συμφέρω, *sympherō, 5237*
11. ὠφελέω, *ōpheleō, 6067*

Mat	16:26	gain the whole world but forfeit their life?	3
Mrk	8:36	what will it profit them to gain the whole world	3
Lke	9:25	does it profit them if they gain the whole world	3
	21:19	By your endurance you will gain your souls.	5
Rom	4: 1	What then are we to say was gained by Abraham	2
1Co	7:21	Even if you can gain your freedom	1
	13: 3	but do not have love, I gain nothing.	11
	15:32	what would I have gained by it?	7
2Co	12: 1	It is necessary to boast; nothing is to be gained	10
Php	1:21	For to me, living is Christ and dying is gain.	4
	3: 7	whatever gains I had	4
	3: 8	in order that I may gain Christ	3
1Ti	3:13	gain a good standing for themselves	8
	6: 6	great gain in godliness combined with contentment;	9
Tit	1:11	teaching for sordid gain	4
Jde	1:11	abandon themselves to Balaam's error for the sake of gain	6

gain adherent

1. πληθύνω, *plēthynō, 4437*

Act	12:24	the word of God continued to advance and gain adherents	1

gain by trading

1. διαπραγματεύομαι, *diapragmateuomai, 1390*

Lke	19:15	might find out what they had gained by trading.	1

gain entrance
1. εἰσέρχομαι, *eiserchomai, 1656*
Act 23:16 gained entrance to the barracks and told Paul.   1

gain wealth
1. πλουτέω, *plouteō, 4456*
Rev 18:15 The merchants of these wares, who gained wealth   1

sordid gain
1. αἰσχροκερδῶς, *aischrokerdōs, 154*
1Pe 5: 2 tend…not for sordid gain but eagerly.   1

Gaius
1. Γάϊος, *Gaios, 1127*
Act 19:29 dragging with them Gaius and Aristarchus   1
    20: 4 by Gaius from Derbe, and by Timothy   1
Rom 16:23 Gaius, who is host to me and to the whole church   1
1Co 1:14 baptized none of you except Crispus and Gaius   1
3Jn 1: 1 The elder to the beloved Gaius, whom I love   1

Galatia
1. Γαλατία, *Galatia, 1130*
2. Γαλατικός, *Galatikos, 1131*
Act 16: 6 They went through the region of Phrygia and Galatia   2
   18:23 the region of Galatia and Phrygia   2
1Co 16: 1 the directions I gave to the churches of Galatia.   1
Gal 1: 2 To the churches of Galatia: 1
2Ti 4:10 Crescens has gone to Galatia, Titus to Dalmatia.   1
1Pe 1: 1 the Dispersion in Pontus, Galatia, Cappadocia   1

Galatian
1. Γαλάτης, *Galatēs, 1129*
Gal 3: 1 You foolish Galatians! Who has bewitched you?   1

gale
1. ἄνεμος + μέγας, *anemos + megas, 449 + 3489*
Rev 6:13 drops its winter fruit when shaken by a gale.   1

Galilean
1. Γαλιλαῖος, *Galilaios, 1134*
Mat 26:69 "You also were with Jesus the Galilean."   1
Mrk 14:70 you are one of them; for you are a Galilean."   1
Lke 13: 1 the Galileans whose blood Pilate had mingled   1
   13: 2 that because these Galileans suffered in this way   1
   13: 2 worse sinners than all other Galileans?   1
   22:59 for he is a Galilean."   1
   23: 6 he asked whether the man was a Galilean.   1
Jhn 4:45 he came to Galilee, the Galileans welcomed him   1
Act 2: 7 "Are not all these who are speaking Galileans?   1
   5:37 After him Judas the Galilean rose up   1

Galilee
1. Γαλιλαία, *Galilaia, 1133*
2. Γαλιλαῖος, *Galilaios, 1134*
Mat 2:22 he went away to the district of Galilee.   1
   3:13 Jesus came from Galilee to John at the Jordan   1
   4:12 John had been arrested, he withdrew to Galilee.   1
   4:15 sea, across the Jordan, Galilee of the Gentiles—   1
   4:18 As he walked by the Sea of Galilee, he saw two   1
   4:23 Jesus went throughout Galilee, teaching   1
   4:25 And great crowds followed him from Galilee   1
   15:29 he passed along the Sea of Galilee   1
   17:22 As they were gathering in Galilee   1
   19: 1 left Galilee and went to teh region of Judea   1
   21:11 the prophet Jesus from Nazareth in Galilee."   1
   26:32 I will go ahead of you to Galilee."   1
   27:55 they had followed Jesus from Galilee   1
   28: 7 indeed he is going ahead of you to Galilee;   1
   28:10 go and tell my brothers to go to Galilee;   1
   28:16 Now the eleven disciples went to Galilee   1
Mrk 1: 9 In those days Jesus came from Nazareth of Galilee   1
   1:14 after John was arrested, Jesus came to Galilee   1
   1:16 Jesus passed along the Sea of Galilee   1
   1:28 the surrounding region of Galilee.   1
   1:39 he went throughout Galilee   1
   3: 7 a great multitude from Galilee followed   1
   6:21 and for the leaders of Galilee.   1
   7:31 went by way of Sidon towards the Sea of Galilee   1
   9:30 They went on…and passed through Galilee.   1

   14:28 I will go before you to Galilee."   1
   15:41 and provided for him when he was in Galilee;   1
   16: 7 he is going ahead of you to Galilee;   1
Lke 1:26 to a town in Galilee called Nazareth   1
   2: 4 from the town of Nazareth in Galilee to Judea   1
   2:39 they returned to Galilee, to their own town   1
   3: 1 Herod was ruler of Galilee   1
   4:14 Jesus…returned to Galilee   1
   4:31 He went down to Capernaum, a city in Galilee   1
   5:17 had come from every village of Galilee and Judea   1
   8:26 which is opposite Galilee.   1
   17:11 through the region between Samaria and Galilee.   1
   23: 5 from Galilee where he began even to this place."   1
   23:49 the women who had followed him from Galilee   1
   23:55 The women who had come with him from Galilee   1
   24: 6 while he was still in Galilee   1
Jhn 1:43 The next day Jesus decided to go to Galilee.   1
   2: 1 there was a wedding in Cana of Galilee   1
   2:11 the first of his signs, in Cana of Galilee   1
   4: 3 he left Judea and started back to Galilee.   1
   4:43 he went from that place to Galilee   1
   4:45 he came to Galilee, the Galileans welcomed him   1
   4:46 Then he came again to Cana in Galilee   1
   4:47 heard that Jesus had come from Judea to Galilee   1
   4:54 after coming from Judea to Galilee.   1
   6: 1 Jesus went to the other side of the Sea of Galilee   1
   7: 1 After this Jesus went about in Galilee.   1
   7: 9 saying this, he remained in Galilee.   1
   7:41 "Surely the Messiah does not come from Galilee   1
   7:52 replied, "Surely you are not also from Galilee   1
   7:52 no prophet is to arise from Galilee."   1
   12:21 Philip, who was from Bethsaida in Galilee   1
   21: 2 Nathanael of Cana in Galilee, the sons of Zebedee   1
Act 1:11 said, "Men of Galilee, why do you stand looking up   2
   9:31 the church throughout Judea, Galilee, and   1
   10:37 beginning in Galilee   1
   13:31 came up with him from Galilee to Jerusalem   1

gall
1. χολή, *cholē, 5958*
Mat 27:34 they offered him wine to drink, mixed with gall;   1
Act 8:23 For I see that you are in the gall of bitterness   1

Gallio
1. Γαλλίων, *Galliōn, 1136*
Act 18:12 when Gallio was proconsul of Achaia   1
   18:14 Gallio said to the Jews   1
   18:17 But Gallio paid no attention to any of these things.   1

gallon *See* thirty gallons, twenty gallons

Gamaliel
1. Γαμαλιήλ, *Gamaliēl, 1137*
Act 5:34 a Pharisee in the council named Gamaliel   1
   22: 3 brought up in this city at the feet of Gamaliel   1

gangrene
1. γάγγραινα, *gangraina, 1121*
2Ti 2:17 their talk will spread like gangrene.   1

garden
1. κῆπος, *kēpos, 3057*
Lke 13:19 that someone took and sowed in the garden;   1
Jhn 18: 1 to a place where there was a garden   1
   18:26 "Did I not see you in the garden with him?"   1
   19:41 Now there was a garden in the place   1
   19:41 and in the garden there was a new tomb   1

gardener
1. ἀμπελουργός, *ampelourgos, 307*
2. κηπουρός, *kēpouros, 3058*
Lke 13: 7 he said to the gardener, 'See here!   1
Jhn 20:15 Supposing him to be the gardener, she said   2

garland
1. στέμμα, *stemma, 5098*
Act 14:13 brought oxen and garlands to the gates;   1

garment

1. ἱμάτιον, *himation, 2668*

Lke	5:36	"No one tears a piece from a new garment	1
	5:36	and sews it on an old garment;	1

gate   *See also* woman who guards the gate

1. Contextual: Not in Greek
2. θύρα, *thyra, 2598*
3. πύλη, *pylē, 4783*
4. πυλών, *pylōn, 4784*

Mat	7:13	"Enter through the narrow gate; for the gate is wide	3
	7:13	for the gate is wide and the road is easy	3
	7:14	For the gate is narrow and the road is hard	3
	16:18	gates of Hades will not prevail against it.	3
	24:33	you know that he is near, at the very gates.	2
Mrk	13:29	you know that he is near, at the very gates.	2
Lke	7:12	As he approached the gate of the town	3
	16:20	at his gate lay a poor man named Lazarus	4
Jhn	10: 1	who does not enter the sheepfold by the gate	2
	10: 2	The one who enters by the gate	2
	10: 3	The gatekeeper opens the gate for him	1
	10: 7	I am the gate for the sheep.	2
	10: 9	I am the gate.	2
	18:16	but Peter was standing outside at the gate.	2
Act	3: 2	People would lay him daily at the gate of the temple	2
	3: 2	gate of the temple called the Beautiful Gate	1
	3:10	at the Beautiful Gate of the temple;	3
	9:24	They were watching the gates day and night	3
	10:17	standing by the gate.	4
	12:10	came before the iron gate leading into the city.	3
	12:13	When he knocked at the outer gate,	2
	12:14	instead of opening the gate, she ran in	4
	12:14	announced that Peter was standing at the gate.	4
	12:16	when they opened the gate, they saw him	1
	14:13	brought oxen and garlands to the gates;	4
	16:13	we went outside the gate by the river	3
Rev	21:12	It has a great, high wall with twelve gates	4
	21:12	and at the gates twelve angels	4
	21:12	gates are inscribed the names of the twelve tribes	1
	21:13	on the east three gates, on the north three gates	4
	21:13	on the east three gates, on the north three gates	4
	21:13	on the south three gates, and on the west	4
	21:13	and on the west three gates.	4
	21:15	to measure the city and its gates and walls.	4
	21:21	And the twelve gates are twelve pearls	4
	21:21	each of the gates is a single pearl	4
	21:25	Its gates will never be shut by day	4
	22:14	may enter the city by the gates.	4

city gate

1. πύλη, *pylē, 4783*

Heb	13:12	Jesus also suffered outside the city gate	1

gatekeeper

1. θυρωρός, *thyrōros, 2601*

Jhn	10: 3	The gatekeeper opens the gate for him	1

gather   *See also* festal gathering

1. Contextual: Not in Greek
2. ἐπισυνάγω, *episynagō, 2190*
3. ἔρχομαι, *erchomai, 2262*
4. λαμβάνω, *lambanō, 3284*
5. συλλέγω, *syllegō, 5198*
6. συμπαραγίνομαι, *symparaginomai, 5219*
7. συμπορεύομαι, *symporeuomai, 5233*
8. συνάγω, *synagō, 5251*
9. συναθροίζω, *synathroizō, 5255*
10. σύνειμι², *syneimi², 5290*
11. συνέρχομαι, *synerchomai, 5302*
12. συστρέφω, *systrephō, 5370*
13. τρυγάω, *trygaō, 5582*

Mat	3:12	clear his threshing floor and will gather his wheat	8
	6:26	they neither sow nor reap nor gather into barns	8
	7:16	Are grapes gathered from thorns	5
	12:30	and whoever does not gather with me scatters.	8
	13: 2	great crowds gathered around him	8
	13:28	'Then do you want us to go and gather them?'	5
	13:29	in gathering the weeds you would uproot the wheat	5
	13:30	but gather the wheat into my barn.' "	8

	16: 9	and how many baskets you gathered?	4
	16:10	and how many baskets you gathered?	4
	17:22	As they were gathering in Galilee	12
	18:20	For where two or three are gathered in my name	8
	22:10	gathered all whom they found, both good and bad;	8
	22:34	they gathered together	8
	23:37	as a hen gathers her brood under her wings	2
	24:28	there the vultures will gather.	8
	24:31	they will gather his elect from the four winds	2
	25:24	gathering where you did not scatter seed;	8
	25:26	gather where I did not scatter?	8
	25:32	All the nations will be gathered before him	8
	26: 3	the elders of the people gathered in the palace	8
	26:57	the scribes and the elders had gathered.	8
	27:17	So after they had gathered, Pilate said to them	8
	27:62	the chief priests and the Pharisees gathered	8
Mrk	1:33	the whole city was gathered	2
	2:13	the whole crowd gathered around him	3
	4: 1	a very large crowd gathered around him	8
	5:21	a great crowd gathered around him;	8
	6:30	The apostles gathered around Jesus, and told him	8
	10: 1	crowds again gathered around him;	7
	13:27	gather his elect from the four winds	2
Lke	3:17	to gather the wheat into his granary;	8
	5:15	many crowds would gather to hear	11
	6:44	Figs are not gathered from thorns	5
	8: 4	When a great crowd gathered	10
	11:23	whoever does not gather with me scatters.	8
	12: 1	when the crowd gathered by the thousands,	2
	13:34	as a hen gathers her brood under her wings	1
	15:13	the younger son gathered all he had	8
	17:37	there the vultures will gather."	2
	23:48	crowds who had gathered there for this spectacle	6
Jhn	4:36	and is gathering fruit for eternal life	8
	11:52	to gather into one the dispersed children of God.	8
	15: 6	branches are gathered, thrown into the fire	8
Act	2: 6	at this sound the crowd gathered	11
	5:16	gather from the towns around Jerusalem	11
	12:12	many had gathered and were praying,	9
	13:44	The next sabbath almost the whole city gathered	8
	16:13	and spoke to the women who had gathered	11
	28: 3	Paul had gathered a bundle of brushwood	12
Rev	14:18	and gather the clusters of the vine of the earth	13
	14:19	the angel...gathered the vintage of the earth	13
	19:17	"Come, gather for the great supper of God	8
	19:19	kings...with their armies gathered to make war	8
	20: 8	Gog and Magog, in order to gather them for battle;	8

gather around

1. κυκλόω, *kykloō, 3240*
2. συνάγω, *synagō, 5251*

Mat	27:27	they gathered the whole cohort around him.	2
Mrk	2: 2	So many gathered around	2
	7: 1	Now when the Pharisees...gathered around him	2
Jhn	10:24	the Jews gathered around him and said to him	1

gather together

1. ἀθροίζω, *athroizō, 125*
2. ἐπισυνάγω, *episynagō, 2190*
3. ἐπισυναγωγή, *episynagōgē, 2191*
4. ὁμοῦ, *homou, 3938*
5. συνάγω, *synagō, 5251*
6. συναθροίζω, *synathroizō, 5255*

Mat	22:41	Now while the Pharisees were gathered together	5
	23:37	I desired to gather your children together	2
Lke	13:34	I desired to gather your children together	2
	22:66	the assembly of the elders...gathered together	5
	24:33	the eleven and their companions gathered together.	1
Jhn	21: 2	Gathered there together were Simon Peter,	4
Act	4:26	the rulers have gathered together	5
	4:27	Gentiles and the peoples of Israel, gathered together	5
	4:31	the place in which they were gathered together	5
	15:30	When they gathered the congregation together	5
	19:25	These he gathered together	6
2Th	2: 1	our being gathered together to him	3

gather up

1. αἴρω, *airō, 149*
2. ἀνακεφαλαιόω, *anakephalaioō, 368*
3. συνάγω, *synagō, 5251*

Lke	9:17	What was left over was gathered up	1
Jhn	6:12	"Gather up the fragments left over	3
	6:13	So they gathered them up	3
Eph	1:10	to gather up all things in him	2

festal gathering

1. πανήγυρις, *panēgyris, 4108*

Heb	12:22	innumerable angels in festal gathering	1

Gaza

1. Γάζα¹, *Gaza¹, 1124*

Act	8:26	the road that goes down from Jerusalem to Gaza."	1

gaze

1. ἀτενίζω, *atenizō, 867*
2. βλέπω, *blepō, 1063*

Act	1:10	While he was going and they were gazing up	1
	7:55	filled with the Holy Spirit, he gazed into heaven	1
2Co	3: 7	people of Israel could not gaze at Moses' face	1
	3:13	gazing at the end of the glory…being set aside.	1
Rev	11: 9	members…gaze at their dead bodies and refuse	2

genealogy

1. γενεαλογία, *genealogia, 1157*
2. γένεσις, *genesis, 1161*

Mat	1: 1	An account of the genealogy of Jesus the Messiah	2
1Ti	1: 4	with myths and endless genealogies	1
Tit	3: 9	avoid stupid controversies, genealogies	1

without genealogy

1. ἀγενεαλόγητος, *agenealogētos, 37*

Heb	7: 3	Without father, without mother, without genealogy	1

general

1. χιλίαρχος, *chiliarchos, 5941*

Rev	6:15	and the generals and the rich and the powerful	1

generation

1. Contextual: Not in Greek
2. γενεά, *genea, 1155*

Mat	1:17	So all the generations from Abraham to David	2
	1:17	Abraham to David are fourteen generations;	2
	1:17	deportation to Babylon, fourteen generations;	2
	1:17	to Babylon to the Messiah, fourteen generations.	2
	11:16	to what will I compare this generation?	2
	12:39	"An evil and adulterous generation asks for	2
	12:41	rise up at the judgment with this generation	2
	12:42	at the judgment with this generation	2
	12:45	So will it be also with this evil generation."	2
	16: 4	An evil and adulterous generation	2
	17:17	"You faithless and perverse generation	2
	23:36	all this will come upon this generation.	2
	24:34	this generation will not pass away	2
Mrk	8:12	"Why does this generation ask for a sign?	2
	8:12	no sign will be given to this generation."	2
	8:38	in this adulterous and sinful generation	2
	9:19	He answered them, "You faithless generation	2
	13:30	this generation will not pass away	2
Lke	1:48	all generations will call me blessed;	2
	1:50	who fear him from generation to generation.	2
	1:50	who fear him from generation to generation.	2
	7:31	will I compare the people of this generation	2
	9:41	"You faithless and perverse generation	2
	11:29	"This generation is an evil generation;	2
	11:29	"This generation is an evil generation;	2
	11:30	so the Son of Man will be to this generation.	2
	11:31	rise…with the people of this generation	2
	11:32	rise up at the judgment with this generation	2
	11:50	so that this generation may be charged with	2
	11:51	it will be charged against this generation.	2
	16: 8	more shrewd in dealing with their own generation	2
	17:25	be rejected by this generation.	2
	21:32	this generation will not pass away	2
Act	2:40	"Save yourselves from this corrupt generation."	2
	8:33	Who can describe his generation?	2
	13:36	served the purpose of God in his own generation	2
	14:16	In past generations he allowed all the nations	2
	15:21	For in every city, for generations past,	2
Eph	3: 5	In former generations this mystery was not made known	2

	3:21	to him be glory…to all generations	2
Php	2:15	a crooked and perverse generation	2
Col	1:26	mystery…hidden throughout the ages and generations	2
Heb	3:10	Therefore I was angry with that generation	2
Jde	1:14	Enoch, in the seventh generation from Adam	1

generosity

1. ἀγαθωσύνη, *agathōsynē, 20*
2. ἁπλότης, *haplotēs, 605*

Rom	12: 8	the giver, in generosity;	2
2Co	8: 2	in a wealth of generosity on their part.	2
	9:11	enriched in every way for your great generosity	2
	9:13	the generosity of your sharing with them	2
Gal	5:22	love, joy, peace, patience, kindness, generosity	1

generous *See also* generous *act,* generous *gift,* generous *undertaking*

1. ἀγαθός, *agathos, 19*
2. ἀφελότης, *aphelotēs, 911*
3. εὐμετάδοτος, *eumetadotos, 2331*
4. πλουτέω, *plouteō, 4456*

Mat	20:15	Or are you envious because I am generous?'	1
Act	2:46	ate their food with glad and generous hearts	2
Rom	10:12	and is generous to all who call on him	4
1Ti	6:18	rich in good works, generous, and ready to share	3
Jas	1:17	Every generous act of giving…is from above	1

generously

1. ἁπλῶς, *haplōs, 607*
2. πολύς, *polys, 4498*

Act	10: 2	gave alms generously to the people	2
Jas	1: 5	ask God, who gives to all generously	1

Gennesaret

1. Γεννησαρέτ, *Gennēsaret, 1166*

Mat	14:34	they came to land at Gennesaret.	1
Mrk	6:53	they came to land at Gennesaret	1
Lke	5: 1	Jesus was standing beside the lake of Gennesaret	1

Gentile

1. ἀλλόφυλος, *allophylos, 260*
2. ἐθνικός, *ethnikos, 1618*
3. ἔθνος, *ethnos, 1620*
4. Ἑλληνίς, *Hellēnis, 1820*

Mat	4:15	sea, across the Jordan, Galilee of the Gentiles—	3
	5:47	than others? Do not even the Gentiles do the same?	2
	6: 7	heap up empty phrases as the Gentiles do;	2
	6:32	the Gentiles who strive for all these things;	3
	10: 5	"Go nowhere among the Gentiles	3
	10:18	as a testimony to them and the Gentiles.	3
	12:18	he will proclaim justice to the Gentiles.	3
	12:21	in his name the Gentiles will hope."	3
	18:17	let such a one be to you as a Gentile	2
	20:19	hand him over to the Gentiles to be mocked	3
	20:25	the rulers of the Gentiles lord it over them	3
Mrk	7:26	the woman was a Gentile, of Syrophoenician origin.	4
	10:33	hand him over to the Gentiles;	3
	10:42	"You know that among the Gentiles	3
Lke	2:32	a light for revelation to the Gentiles	3
	18:32	For he will be handed over to the Gentiles;	3
	21:24	Jerusalem will be trampled on by the Gentiles	3
	21:24	until the times of the Gentiles are fulfilled.	3
	22:25	he said to them, "The kings of the Gentiles	3
Act	4:25	'Why did the Gentiles rage	3
	4:27	with the Gentiles and the peoples of Israel	3
	9:15	to bring my name before Gentiles and kings	3
	10:28	to associate with or to visit a Gentile	1
	10:45	had been poured out even on the Gentiles	3
	11: 1	heard that the Gentiles had also accepted	3
	11:18	God has given even to the Gentiles the repentance	3
	13:46	we are now turning to the Gentiles.	3
	13:47	'I have set you to be a light for the Gentiles	3
	13:48	When the Gentiles heard this, they were glad	3
	14: 2	the unbelieving Jews stirred up the Gentiles	3
	14: 5	an attempt was made by both Gentiles and Jews	3
	14:27	how he had opened a door of faith for the Gentiles.	3
	15: 3	reported the conversion of the Gentiles	3
	15: 7	through whom the Gentiles would hear the message	3
	15:12	God had done through them among the Gentiles.	3

Act	15:14	how God first looked favorably on the Gentiles	3
	15:17	all the Gentiles over whom my name has been called.	3
	15:19	not trouble those Gentiles who are turning to God	3
	15:23	the believers of Gentile origin in Antioch	3
	18: 6	From now on I will go to the Gentiles."	3
	21:11	will hand him over to the Gentiles.' "	3
	21:19	things that God had done among the Gentiles	3
	21:21	you teach all the Jews living among the Gentiles	3
	21:25	as for the Gentiles who have become believers	3
	22:21	I will send you far away to the Gentiles.' "	3
	26:17	I will rescue you...from the Gentiles	3
	26:20	also to the Gentiles	3
	26:23	both to our people and to the Gentiles."	3
	28:28	salvation of God has been sent to the Gentiles;	3
Rom	1: 5	among all the Gentiles for the sake of his name	3
	1:13	as I have among the rest of the Gentiles.	3
	2:14	When Gentiles, who do not possess the law	3
	2:24	"The name of God is blasphemed among the Gentiles	3
	3:29	Is he not the God of Gentiles also?	3
	3:29	God of Gentiles also? Yes, of Gentiles also	3
	9:24	not from the Jews only but also from the Gentiles?	3
	9:30	Gentiles, who did not strive for righteousness	3
	11:11	salvation has come to the Gentiles	3
	11:12	if their defeat means riches for Gentiles	3
	11:13	Now I am speaking to you Gentiles.	3
	11:13	Inasmuch then as I am an apostle to the Gentiles	3
	11:25	until the full number of the Gentiles has come in.	3
	15: 9	the Gentiles might glorify God for his mercy.	3
	15: 9	"Therefore I will confess you among the Gentiles	3
	15:10	"Rejoice, O Gentiles, with his people";	3
	15:11	and again, "Praise the Lord, all you Gentiles	3
	15:12	the one who rises to rule the Gentiles;	3
	15:12	in him the Gentiles shall hope."	3
	15:16	to be a minister of Christ Jesus to the Gentiles	3
	15:16	the offering of the Gentiles may be acceptable	3
	15:18	to win obedience from the Gentiles	3
	15:27	for if the Gentiles have come to share in	3
	16: 4	give thanks, but also all the churches of the Gentiles.	3
	16:26	is made known to all the Gentiles	3
1Co	1:23	a stumbling block to Jews and foolishness to Gentiles	3
2Co	11:26	danger from Gentiles, danger in the city	3
Gal	1:16	I might proclaim him among the Gentiles	3
	2: 2	the gospel that I proclaim among the Gentiles	3
	2: 8	worked through me in sending me to the Gentiles)	3
	2: 9	go to the Gentiles and they to the circumcised.	3
	2:12	he used to eat with the Gentiles.	3
	2:14	how can you compel the Gentiles to live like Jews?"	3
	2:15	are Jews by birth and not Gentile sinners;	3
	3: 8	God would justify the Gentiles by faith	3
	3: 8	saying, "All the Gentiles shall be blessed in you."	3
	3:14	blessing of Abraham might come to the Gentiles	3
Eph	2:11	remember that at one time you Gentiles by birth	3
	3: 1	prisoner for Christ Jesus for the sake of you Gentiles	3
	3: 6	that is, the Gentiles have become fellow heirs	3
	3: 8	to bring to the Gentiles the news	3
	4:17	you must no longer live as the Gentiles live	3
Col	1:27	how great among the Gentiles	3
1Th	2:16	by hindering us from speaking to the Gentiles	3
	4: 5	like the Gentiles who do not know God;	3
1Ti	2: 7	a teacher of the Gentiles in faith and truth.	3
	3:16	proclaimed among Gentiles, believed	3
2Ti	4:17	all the Gentiles might hear it.	3
1Pe	2:12	Conduct yourselves honorably among the Gentiles	3
	4: 3	in doing what the Gentiles like to do	3

like a Gentile

1. ἐθνικῶς, *ethnikōs, 1619*

Gal	2:14	"If you, though a Jew, live like a Gentile	1

gentle

1. ἐπιεικής, *epieikēs, 2117*
2. νήπιος, *nēpios, 3758*
3. πραΰς, *praus, 4558*

Mat	11:29	for I am gentle and humble in heart	3
1Th	2: 7	we were gentle among you	2
1Ti	3: 3	not a drunkard, not violent but gentle	1
Tit	3: 2	to be gentle, and to show every courtesy	1
Jas	3:17	wisdom from above is...gentle, willing to yield	1
1Pe	2:18	not only those who are kind and gentle	1
	3: 4	the lasting beauty of a gentle and quiet spirit	3

gentleness

1. ἐπιείκεια, *epieikeia, 2116*
2. ἐπιεικής, *epieikēs, 2117*
3. πραϋπαθία, *praupathia, 4557*
4. πραΰτης, *prautēs, 4559*

1Co	4:21	with love in a spirit of gentleness?	4
2Co	10: 1	by the meekness and gentleness of Christ	1
Gal	5:23	gentleness, and self-control.	4
	6: 1	restore such a one in a spirit of gentleness.	4
Eph	4: 2	with all humility and gentleness	4
Php	4: 5	Let your gentleness be known to everyone.	2
1Ti	6:11	faith, love, endurance, gentleness.	3
2Ti	2:25	correcting opponents with gentleness.	4
Jas	3:13	that your works are done with gentleness born of wisdom.	4
1Pe	3:16	yet do it with gentleness and reverence.	4

gently   *See* deal gently

genuine

1. ἀνυπόκριτος, *anypokritos, 537*
2. δόκιμος, *dokimos, 1511*

Rom	12: 9	Let love be genuine; hate what is evil	1
1Co	11:19	will it become clear who among you are genuine.	2
2Co	6: 6	kindness, holiness of spirit, genuine love	1
1Pe	1:22	so that you have genuine mutual love	1

genuinely

1. γνησίως, *gnēsiōs, 1189*

Php	2:20	who will be genuinely concerned for your welfare.	1

genuineness

1. γνήσιος, *gnēsios, 1188*
2. δόκιμον, *dokimion, 1510*

2Co	8: 8	I am testing the genuineness of your love	1
1Pe	1: 7	the genuineness of your faith...may be found	2

Gerasene

1. Γερασηνός, *Gerasēnos, 1170*

Mrk	5: 1	to the country of the Gerasenes.	1
Lke	8:26	they arrived at the country of the Gerasenes	1
	8:37	the surrounding country of the Gerasenes	1

gesture

1. κατασείω + ὁ + χείρ, *kataseiō + ho + cheir, 2939 + 3836 + 5931*

Act	13:16	So Paul stood up and with a gesture began to speak:	1

get   *See also* get *drunk,* get *entagled,* get *ready,* get *to* follow

1. Contextual: Not in Greek
2. αἴρω, *airō, 149*
3. ἀναλαμβάνω, *analambanō, 377*
4. ἀπολαμβάνω, *apolambanō, 655*
5. γίνομαι, *ginomai, 1181*
6. εἰμί, *eimi, 1639*
7. ἐσθίω, *esthiō, 2266*
8. εὑρίσκω, *heuriskō, 2351*
9. ἔχω, *echō, 2400*
10. λαμβάνω, *lambanō, 3284*
11. ὑπάγω, *hypagō, 5632*
12. φέρω, *pherō, 5770*

Mat	13:54	"Where did this man get this wisdom	1
	13:56	Where then did this man get all this?"	1
	15:33	"Where are we to get enough bread in the desert	1
	16:23	and said to Peter, "Get behind me, Satan!	11
	21:38	let us kill him and get his inheritance.'	9
	24:18	must not turn back to get a coat.	2
	27:48	At once one of them ran and got a sponge	10
Mrk	6: 2	"Where did this man get all this?	1
	6:39	he ordered them to get all the people to sit	1
	8:33	"Get behind me, Satan!	11
	13:16	must not turn back to get a coat.	2
Lke	9:12	to lodge and get provisions;	8
	15:23	get the fatted calf and kill it	12
	19:12	to get royal power for himself and then return.	10
	23:41	we are getting what we deserve for our deeds	4
Jhn	1:48	Nathanael asked him, "Where did you get to know me?"	1
	4:11	Where do you get that living water?	9
	6: 7	enough bread for each of them to get a little."	10
	19:24	but cast lots for it to see who will get it."	6

Act	19:25	"Men, you know that we get our wealth	6
	22:28	cost me a large sum of money to get my citizenship."	1
	27:16	scarcely able to get the ship's boat under control.	5
Rom	6:21	what advantage did you then get from the things	9
	6:22	the advantage you get is sanctification.	9
1Co	9: 7	not get any of its milk?	7
2Ti	4:11	Get Mark and bring him with you	3
Jas	4: 3	in order to spend what you get on your pleasures.	1

get a living

1. ζάω, *zaō, 2409*

1Co	9:14	get their living by the gospel.	1

get a measure

1. μετρέω, *metreō, 3582*

Mrk	4:24	the measure you give will be the measure you get	1

get away

1. ἐξέρχομαι, *exerchomai, 2002*

Lke	13:31	"Get away from here, for Herod wants to kill you."	1

get back

1. ἀπολαμβάνω, *apolambanō, 655*

Lke	15:27	because he has got him back safe and sound.'	1
	18:30	who will not get back very much more in this age	1

get back measure

1. ἀντιμετρέω, *antimetreō, 520*

Lke	6:38	measure you give will be the measure you get back."	1

get food

1. ἐσθίω, *esthiō, 2266*

1Co	9:13	get their food from the temple	1

get in

1. ἀναβαίνω, *anabainō, 326*
2. εἰσέρχομαι, *eiserchomai, 1656*

Mat	22:12	how did you get in here without a wedding robe?'	2
Act	8:31	he invited Philip to get in and sit beside him.	1

get into

1. ἀναβαίνω, *anabainō, 326*
2. ἐμβαίνω, *embainō, 1832*

Mat	8:23	when he got into the boat, his disciples followed	2
	9: 1	And after getting into a boat he crossed	2
	13: 2	that he got into a boat and sat there	2
	14:22	he made the disciples get into the boat	2
	14:32	When they got into the boat, the wind ceased.	1
	15:39	sending away the crowds, he got into the boat	2
Mrk	4: 1	he got into a boat on the sea and sat there	2
	5:18	As he was getting into the boat	2
	6:45	he made his disciples get into the boat	2
	6:51	got into the boat with them and the wind ceased.	1
	8:10	he got into the boat with his disciples	2
	8:13	he left them, and getting into the boat again	2
Lke	5: 3	got into one of the boats, the one belonging to Simon	2
	8:22	One day he got into a boat with his disciples	2
	8:37	So he got into the boat and returned.	2
Jhn	6:17	got into a boat	2
	6:24	they…got into the boats and went to Capernaum	2
	21: 3	They went out and got into the boat	2

get into with

1. συνεισέρχομαι, *syneiserchomai, 5291*

Jhn	6:22	Jesus had not got into the boat with his disciples	1

get on

1. προβαίνω, *probainō, 4581*

Lke	1: 7	both were getting on in years.	1
	1:18	old man, and my wife is getting on in years."	1

get out

1. ἐξέρχομαι, *exerchomai, 2002*
2. καταβαίνω, *katabainō, 2849*

Mat	5:26	you will never get out until you have paid the last	1
	14:29	He said, "Come." So Peter got out of the boat	2
Mrk	6:54	When they got out of the boat	1
Lke	12:59	I tell you, you will never get out	1
Act	22:18	'Hurry and get out of Jerusalem quickly	1

get up

1. Contextual: Not in Greek
2. ἀνίστημι, *anistēmi, 482*
3. ἐγείρω, *egeirō, 1586*

Mat	2:13	"Get up, take the child and his mother, and flee	3
	2:14	Joseph got up, took the child and his mother	3
	2:20	"Get up, take the child and his mother, and go	3
	2:21	Joseph got up, took the child and his mother	3
	8:15	and she got up and began to serve him.	3
	8:26	Then he got up and rebuked the winds and the sea;	3
	9: 9	"Follow me." And he got up and followed him.	2
	9:19	Jesus got up and followed him, with his disciples.	3
	9:25	took her by the hand, and the girl got up.	3
	17: 7	"Get up and do not be afraid."	3
	25: 7	Then all those bridesmaids got up	3
	26:46	Get up, let us be going. See, my betrayer	3
Mrk	1:35	he got up and went out to a deserted place	2
	2:14	he got up and followed him.	2
	5:41	which means, "Little girl, get up!"	3
	5:42	immediately the girl got up and began to walk about	2
	10:49	"Take heart; get up, he is calling you."	3
	14:42	Get up, let us be going. See, my betrayer	3
Lke	4:29	They got up, drove him out of the town	2
	4:39	Immediately she got up and began to serve them.	2
	5:28	he got up, left everything, and followed him.	2
	6: 8	"Come and stand here." He got up and stood there.	2
	8:54	and called out, "Child, get up!"	3
	8:55	Her spirit returned, and she got up at once.	2
	11: 7	I cannot get up and give you anything.'	2
	11: 8	though he will not get up and give him anything	2
	11: 8	because of his persistence he will get up	3
	13:25	owner of the house has got up and shut the door	3
	15:18	I will get up and go to my father	2
	17:19	"Get up and go on your way; your faith	2
	21:38	all the people would get up early in the morning	1
	22:45	he got up from prayer, he came to the disciples	2
	22:46	Get up and pray	2
	24:12	Peter got up and ran to the tomb	2
	24:33	That same hour they got up and returned to Jerusalem;	2
Jhn	11:29	when she heard it, she got up quickly and went	3
	11:31	The Jews…saw Mary get up quickly and go out.	2
	13: 4	got up from the table, took off his outer robe	3
Act	8:26	"Get up and go toward the south	2
	8:27	he got up and went.	2
	9: 6	get up and enter the city	2
	9: 8	Saul got up from the ground	3
	9:11	"Get up and go to the street called Straight	2
	9:18	Then he got up and was baptized	2
	9:34	Jesus Christ heals you; get up and make your bed!"	2
	9:34	immediately he got up.	2
	9:39	So Peter got up and went with them;	2
	9:40	turned to the body and said, "Tabitha, get up."	2
	10:13	he heard a voice saying, "Get up, Peter; kill and eat."	2
	10:20	Now get up, go down	2
	10:23	The next day he got up and went with them	2
	10:26	Peter made him get up, saying, "Stand up;	3
	11: 7	'Get up, Peter; kill and eat.'	2
	12: 7	woke him, saying, "Get up quickly."	2
	14:20	he got up and went into the city.	2
	22:10	The Lord said to me, 'Get up and go to Damascus;	2
	22:16	now why do you delay? Get up, be baptized	2
	26:16	get up and stand on your feet;	2
	26:30	Then the king got up, and with him the governor	2

Gethsemane

1. Γεθσημανί, *Gethsēmani, 1149*

Mat	26:36	to a place called Gethsemane;	1
Mrk	14:32	They went to a place called Gethsemane;	1

ghost

1. πνεῦμα, *pneuma, 4460*
2. φάντασμα, *phantasma, 5753*

Mat	14:26	they were terrified, saying, "It is a ghost!"	2
Mrk	6:49	they thought it was a ghost and cried out;	2
Lke	24:37	thought that they were seeing a ghost.	1
	24:39	a ghost does not have flesh and bones	1

Gideon

1. Γεδεών, *Gedeōn, 1146*

Heb	11:32	time would fail me to tell of Gideon, Barak,	1

gift *See also* bestowed gift, bountiful gift, give a gift, have the gift of prophecy, receive a gift in return

1. Contextual: Not in Greek
2. δόμα, *doma, 1517*
3. δωρεά, *dōrea, 1561*
4. δωρεάν, *dōrean, 1562*
5. δώρημα, *dōrēma, 1564*
6. δῶρον, *dōron, 1565*
7. λαμβάνω, *lambanō, 3284*
8. ὁ, *ho, 3836*
9. χάρις, *charis, 5921*
10. χάρισμα, *charisma, 5922*

Mat	2:11	opening their treasure chests, they offered him gifts	6
	5:23	So when you are offering your gift at the altar	6
	5:24	leave your gift there before the altar and go;	6
	5:24	reconciled…and then come and offer your gift.	6
	7:11	know how to give good gifts to your children	2
	8: 4	and offer the gift that Moses commanded	6
	23:18	whoever swears by the gift that is on the altar	6
	23:19	which is greater, the gift or the altar	6
	23:19	or the altar that makes the gift sacred?	6
Lke	11:13	know how to give good gifts to your children	2
	21: 1	rich people putting their gifts into the treasury;	6
Jhn	4:10	Jesus answered her, "If you knew the gift of God	3
Act	2:38	you will receive the gift of the Holy Spirit	3
	8:20	thought you could obtain God's gift with money!	3
	10:45	the gift of the Holy Spirit had been poured out	3
	11:17	God gave them the same gift that he gave us	3
Rom	1:11	so that I may share with you some spiritual gift	10
	3:24	they are now justified by his grace as a gift	4
	4: 4	wages are not reckoned as a gift but as something due.	9
	11:29	the gifts and the calling of God are irrevocable.	10
	12: 6	have gifts that differ according to the grace	10
1Co	2:14	do not receive the gifts of God's Spirit	8
	4: 7	why do you boast as if it were not a gift?	7
	7: 7	each has a particular gift from God	10
	12: 4	are varieties of gifts, but the same Spirit;	10
	12: 9	to another gifts of healing by the one Spirit	10
	12:28	then deeds of power, then gifts of healing,	10
	12:30	Do all possess gifts of healing?	10
	12:31	strive for the greater gifts.	10
	16: 3	to take your gift to Jerusalem.	9
2Co	8:12	if the eagerness is there, the gift is acceptable	1
	9:15	Thanks be to God for his indescribable gift!	3
Eph	2: 8	this is not your own doing; it is the gift of God	6
	3: 7	according to the gift of God's grace	3
	4: 7	grace according to the measure of Christ's gift.	3
	4: 8	he gave gifts to his people."	2
	4:11	the gifts he gave were that some would be apostles	1
Php	4:17	Not that I seek the gift	2
	4:18	have received from Epaphroditus the gifts you sent	8
1Ti	4:14	Do not neglect the gift that is in you	10
2Ti	1: 6	I remind you to rekindle the gift of God	10
Heb	2: 4	by gifts of the Holy Spirit, distributed	1
	5: 1	to offer gifts and sacrifices for sins.	6
	6: 4	and have tasted the heavenly gift	3
	8: 3	is appointed to offer gifts and sacrifices;	6
	8: 4	since there are priests who offer gifts	6
	9: 9	gifts and sacrifices are offered	6
	11: 4	God himself giving approval to his gifts;	6
Jas	1:17	with every perfect gift, is from above	5
1Pe	4:10	serve one another with whatever gift each…received.	10
Rev	21: 6	as a gift from the spring of the water of life.	4
	22:17	who wishes take the water of life as a gift.	4

free gift

1. δωρεά, *dōrea, 1561*
2. δώρημα, *dōrēma, 1564*
3. χάρισμα, *charisma, 5922*

Rom	5:15	But the free gift is not like the trespass.	3
	5:15	the free gift in the grace of the one man, Jesus	1
	5:16	the free gift is not like…the one man's sin.	2
	5:16	the free gift following many trespasses brings	3
	5:17	who receive…the free gift of righteousness	1
	6:23	the free gift of God is eternal life in Christ	3

generous gift

1. ἁδρότης, *hadrotēs, 103*

2Co	8:20	no one should blame us about this generous gift	1

gift dedicated to God

1. ἀνάθημα, *anathēma, 356*

Lke	21: 5	it was adorned with…gifts dedicated to God	1

gracious gift

1. χάρις, *charis, 5921*

1Pe	3: 7	they too are also heirs of the gracious gift of life	1

spiritual gift

1. πνεῦμα, *pneuma, 4460*
2. πνευματικός, *pneumatikos, 4461*
3. χάρισμα, *charisma, 5922*

1Co	1: 7	you are not lacking in any spiritual gift	3
	12: 1	Now concerning spiritual gifts, brothers and sisters	2
	14: 1	Pursue love and strive for the spiritual gifts	2
	14:12	since you are eager for spiritual gifts	1

voluntary gift

1. εὐλογία, *eulogia, 2330*

2Co	9: 5	ready as a voluntary gift and not as an extortion.	1

girl *See also* little girl

1. κοράσιον, *korasion, 3166*

Mat	9:24	he said, "Go away; for the girl is not dead	1
	9:25	took her by the hand, and the girl got up.	1
	14:11	and given to the girl	1
Mrk	5:42	immediately the girl got up and began to walk about	1
	6:22	and the king said to the girl	1
	6:28	gave it to the girl.	1
	6:28	the girl gave it to her mother.	1

give

1. Contextual: Not in Greek
2. ἀποδίδωμι, *apodidōmi, 625*
3. ἀφίημι, *aphiēmi, 918*
4. γίνομαι, *ginomai, 1181*
5. διατίθημι, *diatithēmi, 1416*
6. δίδωμι, *didōmi, 1443*
7. δόσις, *dosis, 1521*
8. δωρέομαι, *dōreomai, 1563*
9. εἰμί, *eimi, 1639*
10. ἐπί, *epi, 2093*
11. ἐπιδίδωμι, *epididōmi, 2113*
12. ἐπιτίθημι, *epitithēmi, 2202*
13. ἔχω, *echō, 2400*
14. καλέω, *kaleō, 2813*
15. λαμβάνω, *lambanō, 3284*
16. λέγω, *legō, 3306*
17. μαρτυρέω, *martyreō, 3455*
18. παραδίδωμι, *paradidōmi, 4140*
19. παρατίθημι, *paratithēmi, 4192*
20. παρέχω, *parechō, 4218*
21. ποιέω, *poieō, 4472*
22. ποτίζω, *potizō, 4540*
23. πρός, *pros, 4639*
24. χαρίζομαι, *charizomai, 5919*

Mat	4: 9	"All these I will give you, if you will fall down	6
	5:31	let him give her a certificate of divorce.'	6
	5:40	your coat, give your cloak as well;	3
	5:42	Give to everyone who begs from you, and do not	6
	6: 2	"So whenever you give alms, do not sound a trumpet	21
	6: 3	when you give alms, do not let your left hand know	21
	6:11	Give us this day our daily bread.	6
	7: 6	"Do not give what is holy to dogs; and do not throw	6
	7: 7	"Ask, and it will be given you; search,	6
	7: 9	asks for bread, will give a stone?	11
	7:10	Or if the child asks for a fish, will give a snake?	11
	7:11	If you then, who are evil, know how to give good gifts	6
	7:11	in heaven give good things to those who ask	6
	9: 8	they glorified God, who had given such authority	6
	10: 1	and gave them authority over unclean spirits	6
	10: 8	You received without payment; give without payment.	6
	10:19	for what you are to say will be given to you	6
	10:42	whoever gives even a cup of cold water to one	22
	12:39	but no sign will be given to it	6
	13:11	"To you it has been given to know the secrets	6
	13:11	but to them it has not been given.	6
	13:12	For to those who have, more will be given	6

14: 8	she said, "Give me the head of John the Baptist	6
14: 9	he commanded it to be given;	6
14:11	and given to the girl	6
14:16	you give them something to eat."	6
14:19	broke the loaves, and gave them to the disciples	6
14:19	and the disciples gave them to the crowds.	1
15:36	he broke them and gave them to the disciples	6
15:36	and the disciples gave them to the crowds.	1
16: 4	but no sign will be given to it	6
16:19	I will give you the keys of the kingdom of heaven	6
16:26	what will they give in return for their life?	6
17:27	take that and give it to them for you and me."	6
19: 7	did Moses command us to give a certificate	6
19:11	but only those to whom it is given.	6
19:21	sell…and give the money to the poor	6
20: 8	'Call the laborers and give them their pay	2
20:14	I choose to give to this last the same as	6
20:14	give to this last the same as I give to you.	1
20:28	to give his life a ransom for many."	6
21:23	who gave you this authority?"	6
21:41	who will give him the produce at the harvest time."	2
21:43	given to a people that produces the fruits	6
22: 2	to a king who gave a wedding banquet for his son.	21
22:21	"Give therefore to the emperor	2
24:29	the moon will not give its light;	6
24:45	to give the other slaves their allowance of food	6
25: 8	'Give us some of your oil	6
25:15	to one he gave five talents, to another two	6
25:28	give it to the one with the ten talents.	6
25:29	For to all those who have, more will be given	6
25:35	for I was hungry and you gave me food	6
25:42	for I was hungry and you gave me no food	6
26: 9	and the money given to the poor."	6
26:15	said, "What will you give me if I betray him	6
26:26	broke it, gave it to the disciples, and said	6
26:27	after giving thanks he gave it to them, saying	6
26:48	Now the betrayer had given them a sign, saying	6
27:10	and they gave them for the potter's field	6
27:58	then Pilate ordered it to be given to him.	2
28:12	to give a large sum of money to the soldiers	6
28:18	in heaven and on earth has been given to me.	6
Mrk 2:26	he gave some to his companions."	6
3:16	Simon (to whom he gave the name Peter);	12
3:17	whom he gave the name Boanerges	12
4:11	given the secret of the kingdom of God	6
4:25	For to those who have, more will be given;	6
5:43	and told them to give her something to eat.	6
6: 2	What is this wisdom that has been given to him?	6
6: 7	gave them authority over the unclean spirits.	6
6:21	when Herod on his birthday gave a banquet	21
6:22	"Ask me for whatever you wish, and I will give it."	6
6:23	"Whatever you ask me, I will give you	6
6:25	"I want you to give me at once the head of John	6
6:28	gave it to the girl.	6
6:28	the girl gave it to her mother.	6
6:37	he answered them, "You give them something to eat."	6
6:37	give it to them to eat?"	6
6:41	broke the loaves, and gave them to his disciples	6
8: 6	he broke them and gave them to his disciples	6
8:12	no sign will be given to this generation."	6
8:37	what can they give in return for their life?	6
10:21	sell what you own, and give the money to the poor	6
10:45	to give his life a ransom for many."	6
11:28	Who gave you this authority to do them?"	6
12: 9	give the vineyard to others.	6
12:17	"Give to the emperor the things that are	2
13:11	say whatever is given you at that time	6
13:24	the moon will not give its light	6
14: 5	and the money given to the poor."	6
14:11	greatly pleased, and promised to give him money.	6
14:22	broke it, gave it to them, and said, "Take;	6
14:23	after giving thanks he gave it to them	6
14:44	Now the betrayer had given them a sign, saying	6
15:37	Jesus gave a loud cry and breathed his last.	3
Lke 1:32	the Lord God will give to him the throne	6
1:77	to give knowledge of salvation to his people	6
2:21	he was called Jesus, the name given by the angel	14
4: 6	I will give their glory and all this authority;	6
4: 6	I give it to anyone I please.	6
4:17	the scroll of the prophet Isaiah was given to him.	11
5:29	Levi gave a great banquet for him in his house;	21

6: 4	gave some to his companions?"	6
6:30	Give to everyone who begs from you;	6
6:38	give, and it will be given to you.	6
6:38	give, and it will be given to you.	6
7:15	Jesus gave him to his mother.	6
7:21	given sight to many who were blind.	24
7:44	you gave me no water for my feet	6
7:45	You gave me no kiss	6
8:10	"To you it has been given to know the secrets	6
8:18	to those who have, more will be given;	6
8:55	give her something to eat.	6
9: 1	gave them power and authority over all demons	6
9:13	he said to them, "You give them something to eat."	6
9:16	gave them to the disciples	6
10:19	have given you authority to tread on snakes	6
10:35	gave them to the innkeeper, and said	6
11: 3	Give us each day our daily bread.	6
11: 7	I cannot get up and give you anything.'	6
11: 8	though he will not get up and give him anything	6
11: 8	he will get up and give him whatever he needs.	6
11: 9	I say to you, Ask, and it will be given you;	6
11:11	will give a snake instead of a fish?	11
11:12	asks for an egg, will give a scorpion?	11
11:13	know how to give good gifts to your children	6
11:13	will the heavenly Father give the Holy Spirit	6
11:29	it asks for a sign, but no sign will be given	6
11:41	give for alms those things that are within;	6
12:32	Father's good pleasure to give you the kingdom.	6
12:33	Sell your possessions, and give alms.	6
12:42	to give them their allowance of food	6
12:48	everyone to whom much has been given	6
14: 9	'Give this person your place,'	6
14:12	"When you give a luncheon or a dinner	21
14:13	when you give a banquet, invite the poor,	21
14:16	"Someone gave a great dinner and invited many.	21
15:12	give me the share of the property	6
15:16	no one gave him anything.	6
15:29	yet you have never given me even a young goat	6
16: 2	Give me an accounting of your management	2
16:12	who will give you what is your own?	6
17:18	Was none of them found to return and give praise	6
19: 8	half of my possessions…I will give to the poor;	6
19:13	ten of his slaves, and gave them ten pounds	6
19:15	these slaves, to whom he had given the money	6
19:24	give it to the one who has ten pounds.'	6
19:26	to all those who have, more will be given;	6
20: 2	Who is it who gave you this authority?"	6
20:10	give him his share of the produce of the vineyard;	6
20:16	give the vineyard to others."	6
20:25	give to the emperor the things that are the emperor's	2
21:15	For I will give you words and a wisdom	6
22: 5	greatly pleased and agreed to give him money.	6
22:19	gave it to them, saying, "This is my body	6
22:19	"This is my body, which is given for you.	6
24:42	They gave him a piece of broiled fish	11
Jhn 1:12	he gave power to become children of God	6
1:17	The law indeed was given through Moses;	6
1:19	This is the testimony given by John	1
3:16	God so loved the world that he gave his only Son	6
3:27	except what has been given from heaven.	6
3:34	for he gives the Spirit without measure.	6
4: 5	ground that Jacob had given to his son Joseph.	6
4: 7	Jesus said to her, "Give me a drink."	6
4:10	who it is that is saying to you, 'Give me a drink,'	6
4:10	and he would have given you living water."	6
4:12	Jacob, who gave us the well, and with his sons	6
4:14	who drink of the water that I will give them	6
4:14	The water that I will give will become in them	6
4:15	give me this water, so that I may never be thirsty	6
5:22	has given all judgment to the Son	6
5:27	has given him authority to execute judgment	6
5:36	works that the Father has given me to complete	6
6:27	which the Son of Man will give you.	6
6:30	"What sign are you going to give us then,	21
6:31	'He gave them bread from heaven to eat.' "	6
6:32	not Moses who gave you the bread from heaven	6
6:32	my Father who gives you the true bread from heaven.	6
6:33	gives life to the world."	6
6:34	said to him, "Sir, give us this bread always."	6
6:37	Everything that the Father gives me will come	6
6:39	lose nothing of all that he has given me	6

Jhn	6:51 bread that I will give for the life of the world	6
	6:52 "How can this man give us his flesh to eat?"	6
	7:19 "Did not Moses give you the law?	6
	7:22 Moses gave you circumcision	6
	9:24 "Give glory to God!	6
	10:28 I give them eternal life	6
	10:29 What my Father has given me is greater than all	6
	11:22 God will give you whatever you ask of him."	6
	11:57 the Pharisees had given orders	6
	12: 2 There they gave a dinner for him. Martha served	21
	12: 5 the money given to the poor?"	6
	12:49 has...given me a commandment about what to say	6
	13: 3 the Father had given all things into his hands	6
	13:26 I give this piece of bread when I have dipped it	6
	13:26 dipped the piece of bread, he gave it to Judas	6
	13:29 that he should give something to the poor.	6
	13:34 I give you a new commandment, that	6
	14:16 he will give you another Advocate,	6
	14:27 Peace I leave with you; my peace I give to you.	6
	14:27 I do not give to you as the world gives.	6
	14:27 I do not give to you as the world gives.	6
	15:16 so that the Father will give you whatever	6
	16:23 ask...in my name, he will give it to you.	6
	17: 2 you have given him authority over all people	6
	17: 2 to give eternal life to all	6
	17: 2 to all whom you have given him.	6
	17: 4 the work that you gave me to do.	6
	17: 6 those whom you gave me from the world.	6
	17: 6 gave them to me, and they have kept your word.	6
	17: 7 everything you have given me is from you;	6
	17: 8 words that you gave to me I have given to them	6
	17: 8 words that you gave to me I have given to them	6
	17: 9 those whom you gave me, because they are yours.	6
	17:11 protect them in your name that you have given me	6
	17:12 your name that you have given me.	6
	17:14 I have given them your word	6
	17:22 The glory that you have given me	6
	17:22 glory...I have given them	6
	17:24 those also, whom you have given me	6
	17:24 to see my glory, which you have given me	6
	18: 9 not lose a single one of those whom you gave me."	6
	18:11 to drink the cup that the Father has given me?"	6
	19: 9 But Jesus gave him no answer.	6
	19:11 unless it had been given you from above;	6
	21:13 came and took the bread and gave it to them	6
Act	2: 4 as the Spirit gave them ability.	6
	3: 6 no silver or gold, but what I have I give you;	6
	3:14 asked to have a murderer given to you	24
	3:16 the faith...has given him this perfect health	6
	3:25 the covenant that God gave to your ancestors	5
	4:12 no other name under heaven given among mortals	6
	4:33 the apostles gave their testimony	2
	5:31 that he might give repentance to Israel	6
	5:32 whom God has given to those who obey him."	6
	7: 5 He did not give him any of it as a heritage	6
	7: 5 promised to give it to him as his possession	6
	7: 8 he gave him the covenant of circumcision.	6
	7:38 he received living oracles to give to us.	6
	8:18 the Spirit was given through the laying on	6
	8:19 saying, "Give me also this power	6
	9:41 He gave her his hand and helped her up.	6
	10: 2 gave alms generously to the people	21
	11:17 If then God gave them the same gift	6
	11:17 God gave them the same gift that he gave us	1
	11:18 God has given even to the Gentiles the repentance	6
	12:23 because he had not given the glory to God	6
	13:15 word of exhortation for the people, give it."	16
	13:20 he gave them judges until the time of...Samuel.	6
	13:21 they asked for a king; and God gave them Saul	6
	13:34 give you the holy promises made to David.'	6
	14:17 giving you rains from heaven and fruitful seasons	6
	15: 8 giving them the Holy Spirit, just as he did to us;	6
	16:23 After they had given them a severe flogging	12
	17:25 he himself gives to all mortals life and breath	6
	17:31 of this he has given assurance to all	20
	19:40 no cause that we can give to justify this	2
	20:32 give you the inheritance	6
	20:35 'It is more blessed to give than to receive.' "	6
	24:26 he hoped that money would be given him by Paul	6
	25:16 had been given an opportunity to make a defense	15
Rom	2: 7 he will give eternal life;	1

	4:20 grew strong in his faith as he gave glory to God	6
	5: 5 the Holy Spirit that has been given to us.	6
	8:32 will he not with him also give us everything	24
	11: 8 as it is written, "God gave them a sluggish spirit	6
	12: 3 by the grace given to me I say to everyone	6
	12: 6 that differ according to the grace given to us:	6
	15: 8 might confirm the promises given to the patriarchs	1
	15:15 because of the grace given me by God	6
1Co	1: 4 because of the grace of God that has been given you	6
	3:10 According to the grace of God given to me	6
	7: 3 husband should give to his wife her conjugal rights	2
	7:25 I give my opinion as one who by the Lord's mercy	6
	9:16 this gives me no ground for boasting	9
	10:32 Give no offense to Jews or to Greeks	4
	11:15 her hair is given to her for a covering.	6
	12: 7 To each is given the manifestation of the Spirit	6
	12: 8 To one is given through the Spirit the utterance	6
	12:24 giving the greater honor to the inferior member	6
	14: 7 If they do not give distinct notes	6
	14: 8 if the bugle gives an indistinct sound	6
	15:38 God gives it a body as he has chosen	6
	15:57 thanks be to God, who gives us the victory	6
2Co	1:22 giving us his Spirit in our hearts as a first installment.	6
	4: 6 to give the light of the knowledge of the glory	23
	5: 5 who has given us the Spirit as a guarantee.	6
	5:12 giving you an opportunity to boast about us	6
	5:18 given us the ministry of reconciliation;	6
	8: 3 they voluntarily gave according to their means	1
	8: 5 they gave themselves first to the Lord	6
	8:10 in this matter I am giving my advice:	6
	9: 7 Each of you must give as you have made up your mind	1
	9: 9 "He scatters abroad, he gives to the poor;	6
	9:14 the surpassing grace of God that he has given you.	10
	10: 8 which the Lord gave for building you up	6
	12: 7 a thorn was given me in the flesh	6
	13:10 that the Lord has given me for building up	6
Gal	1: 4 who gave himself for our sins	6
	2: 9 recognized the grace that had been given to me	6
	2: 9 gave to Barnabas and me the right hand	6
	2:20 Son of God, who loved me and gave himself for me.	18
	3:15 I give an example from daily life:	16
	3:21 if a law had been given that could make alive	6
	3:22 might be given to those who believe.	6
	4:15 tear out your eyes and given them to me.	6
Eph	1:17 may give you a spirit of wisdom and revelation	6
	3: 2 the commission of God's grace that was given me	6
	3: 7 that was given me by the working of his power.	6
	3: 8 this grace was given to me	6
	4: 7 each of us was given grace according	6
	4: 8 he gave gifts to his people."	6
	4:11 he gave were that some would be apostles	6
	4:29 that your words may give grace to those who hear.	6
	6:19 so that when I speak, a message may be given to me	6
Php	2: 9 highly exalted him and gave him the name	24
	2:30 for those services that you could not give me.	1
	4:15 in the matter of giving and receiving,	7
Col	1:25 God's commission that was given to me	6
1Th	4: 2 For you know what instructions we gave you	6
	4: 8 who also gives his Holy Spirit to you.	6
2Th	1: 7 give relief to the afflicted as well as to us	1
	2:16 loved us and through grace gave us eternal comfort	6
	3: 9 in order to give you an example to imitate.	6
	3:16 Lord of peace himself give you peace at all times	6
1Ti	1:18 I am giving you these instructions, Timothy,	19
	2: 6 who gave himself a ransom for all	6
	4:14 which was given to you through prophecy	6
	5:14 give the adversary no occasion to revile us.	6
2Ti	1: 7 for God did not give us a spirit of cowardice	6
	1: 9 This grace was given to us in Christ Jesus	6
	2: 7 the Lord will give you understanding	6
	4: 8 which the Lord, the righteous judge, will give	2
Tit	2:14 who gave himself for us that he might redeem us	6
Heb	2:13 "Here am I and the children whom God has given me."	6
	6:16 an oath given as confirmation puts an end to all dispute.	1
	7: 4 Abraham...gave him a tenth of the spoils.	6
	12:28 Therefore...let us give thanks	13
	13:17 and will give an account.	2
Jas	1: 5 ask God, who gives to all generously	6
	1: 5 and it will be given you.	6
	4: 6 But he gives all the more grace; therefore it says	6
	4: 6 "God...gives grace to the humble."	6

5:18	Then he prayed again, and the heaven gave rain	6

1Pe	1:21	who raised him from the dead and gave him glory	6
	4: 5	give an accounting to him who stands ready to judge	2
	5: 5	"God...gives grace to the humble."	6
2Pe	1: 3	His divine power has given us everything	8
	1: 4	he has given us, through these things, his...promises	8
	3:15	Paul wrote...according to the wisdom given him	6
1Jn	3: 1	See what love the Father has given us	6
	3:24	by the Spirit that he has given us.	6
	4:13	because he has given us of his Spirit.	6
	5:10	the testimony that God has given concerning his Son.	17
	5:11	the testimony: God gave us eternal life	6
	5:16	you will ask, and God will give life to such a one	6
	5:20	the Son of God...has given us understanding	6
Rev	1: 1	The revelation of Jesus Christ, which God gave	6
	2:10	and I will give you the crown of life.	6
	2:17	To everyone who conquers I will give some...manna	6
	2:17	and I will give a white stone	6
	2:21	I gave her time to repent, but she refuses	6
	2:23	I will give to each of you as your works deserve.	6
	2:26	I will give authority over the nations;	6
	2:28	who conquers I will also give the morning star.	6
	3:21	I will give a place with me on my throne	6
	4: 9	whenever the living creatures give glory	6
	6: 2	Its rider had a bow; a crown was given to him	6
	6: 4	and he was given a great sword.	6
	6: 8	they were given authority over a fourth of the earth	6
	6: 9	slaughtered...for the testimony they had given;	13
	6:11	They were each given a white robe and told	6
	7: 2	angels who had been given power to damage earth	6
	8: 2	and seven trumpets were given to them.	6
	8: 3	he was given a great quantity of incense to offer	6
	9: 1	given the key to the shaft of the bottomless pit;	6
	9: 3	were given authority like the authority of scorpions	6
	10: 9	angel and told me to give me the little scroll;	6
	11: 1	Then I was given a measuring rod like a staff	6
	11:13	terrified and gave glory to the God of heaven.	6
	12:14	woman was given the two wings of the great eagle	6
	13: 2	the dragon gave it his power and his throne	6
	13: 4	for he had given his authority to the beast	6
	13: 5	The beast was given a mouth	6
	13: 7	It was given authority over every tribe	6
	13:15	allowed to give breath to the image of the beast	6
	14: 7	"Fear God and give him glory	6
	15: 7	the four living creatures gave the seven angels	6
	16: 6	you have given them blood to drink.	6
	16: 9	and they did not repent and give him glory.	6
	16:19	gave her the wine-cup of the fury of his wrath.	6
	17:17	by agreeing to give their kingdom to the beast	6
	18: 7	give her a like measure of torment and grief.	6
	19: 7	Let us rejoice and exult and give him the glory	6
	20: 4	those seated on them were given authority to judge.	6
	21: 6	thirsty I will give water as a gift from the spring	6

give a command

1. ἐντέλλω, *entellō, 1948*
2. παραγγέλλω, *parangellō, 4133*

Jhn	15:17	I am giving you these commands so that you	1
1Co	7:10	married I give this command—not I but the Lord	2
2Th	3:10	we gave you this command:	2
1Ti	5: 7	Give these commands as well	2

give a gift

1. προδίδωμι, *prodidōmi, 4594*

Rom	11:35	given a gift to him, to receive a gift in return?"	1

give a hearing

1. ἀκούω, *akouō, 201*
2. διακούω, *diakouō, 1358*

Jhn	7:51	judge people without first giving them a hearing	1
Act	23:35	give you a hearing when your accusers arrive."	2

give a measure

1. μετρέω, *metreō, 3582*

Mat	7: 2	you will be judged, and the measure you give	1
Mrk	4:24	the measure you give will be the measure you get	1
Lke	6:38	measure you give will be the measure you get back."	1

give a message

1. λαλέω, *laleō, 3281*

Act	11:14	he will give you a message	1

give a name

1. ἐπικαλέω, *epikaleō, 2126*
2. καλέω, *kaleō, 2813*

Lke	1:62	find out what name he wanted to give him.	2
Act	4:36	Joseph, to whom the apostles gave the name Barnabas	1

give a new birth

1. ἀναγεννάω, *anagennaō, 335*

1Pe	1: 3	By his great mercy he has given us a new birth	1

give a report

1. ἐμφανίζω, *emphanizō, 1872*

Act	25: 2	gave him a report against Paul.	1

give a shout

1. κράζω, *krazō, 3189*

Rev	10: 3	gave a great shout, like a lion roaring.	1

give a slap

1. δέρω, *derō, 1296*

2Co	11:20	or puts on airs, or gives you a slap in the face.	1

give a tenth

1. ἀποδεκατόω, *apodekatoō, 620*

Lke	18:12	I give a tenth of all my income.'	1

give a verdict

1. ἐπικρίνω, *epikrinō, 2137*

Lke	23:24	So Pilate gave his verdict	1

give an account

1. ἀποδίδωμι, *apodidōmi, 625*

Mat	12:36	on the day of judgment you will have to give an account	1

give an answer

1. ἀποκρίνομαι, *apokrinomai, 646*

Mat	22:46	No one was able to give him an answer	1
	27:14	he gave him no answer, not even to a single charge	1
Lke	10:28	"You have given the right answer; do this,	1
	23: 9	but Jesus gave him no answer.	1

give an example

1. ὑποδείκνυμι, *hypodeiknymi, 5683*

Act	20:35	In all this I have given you an example	1

give an opportunity

1. ἀποβαίνω, *apobainō, 609*

Lke	21:13	This will give you an opportunity to testify.	1

give an order

1. διαστέλλω, *diastellō, 1403*
2. κελεύω, *keleuō, 3027*
3. παραγγέλλω, *parangellō, 4133*

Mat	8:18	he gave orders to go over to the other side.	2
Act	5:28	saying, "We gave you strict orders not to teach	3
	25:23	Festus gave the order and Paul was brought in.	2
Heb	12:20	they could not endure the order that was given	1

give approval

1. μαρτυρέω, *martyreō, 3455*

Heb	11: 4	God himself giving approval to his gifts;	1

give as an inheritance

1. κατακληρονομέω, *kataklēronomeō, 2883*

Act	13:19	he gave them their land as an inheritance	1

give as well

1. προστίθημι, *prostithēmi, 4707*

Mat	6:33	all these things will be given to you as well.	1
Lke	12:31	these things will be given to you as well.	1

give attention

1. προσέχω, *prosechō, 4668*

1Ti	4:13	give attention to the public reading of scripture	1

give away

1. ψωμίζω, *psōmizō, 6039*

1Co 13: 3 If I give away all my possessions 1

give back
1. ἀποδίδωμι, *apodidōmi, 625*

Lke 4:20 the scroll, gave it back to the attendant 1
    9:42 healed the boy, and gave him back to his father. 1

give birth
1. ἀποκυέω, *apokyeō, 652*
2. τίκτω, *tiktō, 5503*

Lke 1:57 Now the time came for Elizabeth to give birth 2
    2: 7 she gave birth to her firstborn son 2
Jas 1:15 when that desire has conceived, it gives birth to sin 2
    1:15 sin, when it is fully grown, gives birth to death. 1
    1:18 of his own purpose he gave us birth 1
Rev 12: 2 in birth pangs, in the agony of giving birth. 2
    12: 5 she gave birth to a son, a male child, who is to rule 2
    12:13 pursued the woman who had given birth to the male child. 2

give clothing
1. περιβάλλω, *periballō, 4314*

Mat 25:36 I was naked and you gave me clothing 1
    25:38 or naked and gave you clothing? 1
    25:43 naked and you did not give me clothing 1

give directions
1. διατάσσω, *diatassō, 1411*

1Co 16: 1 follow the directions I gave to the churches 1

give drink
1. ποτίζω, *potizō, 4540*

Mat 25:35 I was thirsty and you gave me something to drink 1
    25:37 or thirsty and gave you something to drink? 1
    25:42 I was thirsty and you gave me nothing to drink 1
Rom 12:20 if they are thirsty, give them something to drink; 1

give encouragement
1. παρακαλέω, *parakaleō, 4151*

Act 20: 2 and had given the believers much encouragement 1

give false testimony
1. ψευδομαρτυρέω, *pseudomartyreō, 6018*

Mrk 14:56 For many gave false testimony against him 1
    14:57 Some stood up and gave false testimony against him 1

give food
1. τρέφω, *trephō, 5555*

Mat 25:37 that we saw you hungry and gave you food 1

give glory
1. δοξάζω, *doxazō, 1519*

Mat 5:16 give glory to your Father in heaven. 1

give greetings
1. ἀσπάζομαι, *aspazomai, 832*

Col 4:15 Give my greetings to the brothers and sisters 1

give growth
1. αὐξάνω, *auxanō, 889*

1Co 3: 6 Apollos watered, but God gave the growth. 1
    3: 7 but only God who gives the growth. 1

give in marriage
1. γαμίζω, *gamizō, 1139*
2. γαμίσκω, *gamiskō, 1140*

Mat 22:30 they neither marry nor are given in marriage 1
    24:38 marrying and giving in marriage 1
Mrk 12:25 they neither marry nor are given in marriage 1
Lke 17:27 and marrying and being given in marriage 1
    20:34 who belong to this age…are given in marriage; 2
    20:35 neither marry nor are given in marriage. 1

give instruction
1. διατάσσω, *diatassō, 1411*
2. ἐντέλλω, *entellō, 1948*
3. συμβιβάζω, *symbibazō, 5204*

Act 1: 2 after giving instructions…to the apostles 2
    19:33 Some of the crowd gave instructions to Alexander 3
1Co 11:34 I will give instructions when I come. 1

Heb 11:22 gave instructions about his burial. 2

give judgment
1. κρίνω, *krinō, 3212*

Rev 18:20 For God has given judgment for you against her. 1

give life
1. ζῳογονέω, *zōogoneō, 2441*
2. ζῳοποιέω, *zōopoieō, 2443*

Jhn 5:21 the Father raises the dead and gives them life 2
    5:21 so also the Son gives life to whomever he wishes. 2
    6:63 It is the spirit that gives life; 2
Rom 4:17 God…who gives life to the dead 2
    8:11 will give life to your mortal bodies also 2
2Co 3: 6 the letter kills, but the Spirit gives life. 2
1Ti 6:13 God, who gives life to all things 1

give light
1. ἐπιφαίνω, *epiphainō, 2210*
2. λάμπω, *lampō, 3290*
3. φωτίζω, *phōtizō, 5894*

Mat 5:15 and it gives light to all in the house. 2
Lke 1:79 to give light to those who sit in darkness 1
    11:36 as when a lamp gives you light with its rays." 3

give lodging
1. ξενίζω, *xenizō, 3826*

Act 10:23 So Peter invited them in and gave them lodging. 1

give offense
1. σκανδαλίζω, *skandalizō, 4997*

Mat 17:27 However, so that we do not give offense to them 1

give out
1. ὑστερέω, *hystereō, 5728*

Jhn 2: 3 When the wine gave out, the mother of Jesus said 1

give over
1. δίδωμι, *didōmi, 1443*
2. παραδίδωμι, *paradidōmi, 4140*

Lke 4: 6 authority; for it has been given over to me 2
Rev 11: 2 for it is given over to the nations 1

give permission
1. δίδωμι, *didōmi, 1443*
2. ἐπιτρέπω, *epitrepō, 2205*

Mrk 5:13 So he gave them permission. 2
Lke 8:32 So he gave them permission. 2
Jhn 19:38 Pilate gave him permission; 2
Act 21:40 When he had given him permission 2
Rev 2: 7 To everyone who conquers, I will give permission 1

give praise
1. ἐξομολογέω, *exomologeō, 2018*

Rom 14:11 and every tongue shall give praise to God." 1

give recognition
1. ἐπιγινώσκω, *epiginōskō, 2105*

1Co 16:18 So give recognition to such persons. 1

give rest
1. ἀναπαύω, *anapauō, 399*
2. καταπαύω, *katapauō, 2924*

Mat 11:28 and I will give you rest. 1
Heb 4: 8 For if Joshua had given them rest 2

give satisfaction
1. εὐάρεστος, *euarestos, 2298*

Tit 2: 9 to give satisfaction in every respect; 1

give still more
1. προστίθημι, *prostithēmi, 4707*

Mrk 4:24 still more will be given you. 1

give strength
1. ἐνδυναμόω, *endynamoō, 1904*
2. ἐνισχύω, *enischyō, 1932*

Lke 22:43 ⟦Then an angel from heaven…gave him strength.⟧ 2

2Ti   4:17 the Lord stood by me and gave me strength   1

give thanks

   1. εὐχαριστέω, *eucharisteō, 2373*

Mat 15:36 giving thanks he broke them and gave them   1
  26:27 after giving thanks he gave it to them, saying   1
Mrk   8: 6 and after giving thanks he broke them   1
  14:23 after giving thanks he gave it to them   1
Lke 22:17 he took a cup, and after giving thanks he said   1
  22:19 when he had given thanks, he broke it and gave it   1
Jhn   6:11 when he had given thanks   1
  6:23 after the Lord had given thanks.   1
Act 27:35 giving thanks to God in the presence of all   1
Rom   1:21 did not honor him as God or give thanks to him   1
  14: 6 in honor of the Lord, since they give thanks to God;   1
  14: 6 abstain in honor of the Lord and give thanks to God.   1
  16: 4 give thanks, but also all the churches of the Gentiles.   1
1Co   1: 4 I give thanks to my God always for you   1
  10:30 because of that for which I give thanks?   1
  11:24 when he had given thanks, he broke it and said   1
  14:17 For you may give thanks well enough   1
2Co   1:11 so that many will give thanks on our behalf   1
Eph   1:16 I do not cease to give thanks for you   1
  5:20 giving thanks to God the Father at all times   1
Col   1:12 giving thanks to the Father   1
  3:17 giving thanks to God the Father through him.   1
1Th   1: 2 We always give thanks to God for all of you   1
  2:13 We also constantly give thanks to God for this   1
  5:18 give thanks in all circumstances;   1
2Th   1: 3 We must always give thanks to God for you   1
  2:13 we must always give thanks to God for you   1
Rev 11:17 singing, "We give you thanks, Lord God Almighty   1

give to

   1. ἐπιδίδωμι, *epididōmi, 2113*

Lke 24:30 blessed and broke it, and gave it to them.   1

give to drink

   1. ποτίζω, *potizō, 4540*

Mat 27:48 put it on a stick, and gave it to him to drink.   1
Mrk   9:41 whoever gives you a cup of water to drink   1
  15:36 gave it to him to drink, saying, "Wait   1

give to God

   1. δῶρον, *dōron, 1565*

Mat 15: 5 support you might have had from me is given to God,'   1

give up

   1. ἀποτάσσω, *apotassō, 698*
   2. ἀφίημι, *aphiēmi, 918*
   3. δίδωμι, *didōmi, 1443*
   4. ἐκλύω, *eklyō, 1725*
   5. μή, *mē, 3590*
   6. μηκέτι, *mēketi, 3600*
   7. παραδίδωμι, *paradidōmi, 4140*

Lke 14:33 if you do not give up all your possessions.   1
Jhn 19:30 he bowed his head and gave up his spirit.   7
Rom   1:24 God gave them up in the lusts of their hearts   7
  1:26 God gave them up to degrading passions.   7
  1:27 the men...giving up natural intercourse with women   2
  1:28 God gave them up to a debased mind   7
  8:32 not withhold his own Son, but gave him up for all   7
2Co   4:11 always being given up to death for Jesus' sake   7
Gal   6: 9 if we do not give up.   4
Eph   4:28 Thieves must give up stealing;   6
  5: 2 Christ...gave himself up for us   7
  5:25 loved the church and gave himself up for her   7
Rev   9:20 or give up worshiping demons and idols of gold   5
  20:13 And the sea gave up the dead that were in it   3
  20:13 Death and Hades gave up the dead that were in them   3

give water

   1. ποτίζω, *potizō, 4540*

Lke 13:15 and lead it away to give it water?   1

give way

   1. ἐπιδίδωμι, *epididōmi, 2113*

Act 27:15 we gave way to it and were driven.   1

giver

   1. δότης, *dotēs, 1522*
   2. μεταδίδωμι, *metadidōmi, 3556*

Rom 12: 8 the giver, in generosity;   2
2Co   9: 7 God loves a cheerful giver.   1

giving   *See* act of giving

giving of the law

   1. νομοθεσία, *nomothesia, 3792*

Rom   9: 4 the covenants, the giving of the law, the worship   1

glad   *See also* make glad

   1. ἀγαλλίασις, *agalliasis, 21*
   2. ἀγαλλιάω, *agalliaō, 22*
   3. εὐφραίνω, *euphrainō, 2370*
   4. χαίρω, *chairō, 5897*

Mat   5:12 Rejoice and be glad, for your reward is great   2
Lke 23: 8 When Herod saw Jesus, he was very glad   4
Jhn   8:56 he saw it and was glad."   4
  11:15 For your sake I am glad I was not there   4
Act   2:26 my heart was glad, and my tongue rejoiced;   3
  2:46 ate their food with glad and generous hearts   1
  13:48 they were glad and praised the word of the Lord;   4
Php   2:17 I am glad and rejoice with all of you   4
  2:18 you also must be glad and rejoice with me.   4
1Pe   4:13 so that you may also be glad and shout for joy   2

gladly

   1. ἐπιθυμέω, *epithymeō, 2121*
   2. ἡδέως, *hēdeōs, 2452*

Lke 15:16 He would gladly have filled himself with the pods   1
2Co 11:19 For you gladly put up with fools, being wise   2
  12: 9 I will boast all the more gladly of my weaknesses   2

most gladly

   1. ἡδέως, *hēdeōs, 2452*

2Co 12:15 most gladly spend and be spent for you.   1

gladness

   1. ἀγαλλίασις, *agalliasis, 21*
   2. εὐφροσύνη, *euphrosynē, 2372*

Lke   1:14 You will have joy and gladness   1
Act   2:28 make me full of gladness with your presence.'   2
Heb   1: 9 God, has anointed you with the oil of gladness   1

glass

   1. ὑάλινος, *hyalinos, 5612*
   2. ὕαλος, *hyalos, 5613*

Rev   4: 6 there is something like a sea of glass, like crystal.   1
  15: 2 appeared to be a sea of glass mixed with fire   1
  15: 2 standing beside the sea of glass   1
  21:18 while the city is pure gold, clear as glass.   2
  21:21 street...is pure gold, transparent as glass.   2

gloat

   1. χαίρω, *chairō, 5897*

Rev 11:10 gloat over them and celebrate and exchange   1

gloom

   1. ζόφος, *zophos, 2432*

Heb 12:18 a blazing fire, and darkness, and gloom   1

glorify

   1. δοξάζω, *doxazō, 1519*
   2. ἐνδοξάζομαι, *endoxazomai, 1901*

Mat   9: 8 they glorified God, who had given such authority   1
Mrk   2:12 so that they were all amazed and glorified God   1
Lke   2:20 glorifying and praising God   1
  5:25 and went to his home, glorifying God.   1
  5:26 they glorified God and were filled with awe   1
  7:16 Fear seized all of them; and they glorified God   1
  18:43 and followed him, glorifying God;   1
Jhn   7:39 because Jesus was not yet glorified.   1
  8:54 "If I glorify myself, my glory is nothing.   1
  8:54 It is my Father who glorifies me   1
  11: 4 the Son of God may be glorified through it."   1
  12:16 when Jesus was glorified, then they remembered   1

Jhn	12:23	"The hour…for the Son of Man to be glorified.	1
	12:28	Father, glorify your name."	1
	12:28	"I have glorified it, and I will glorify it again."	1
	12:28	"I have glorified it, and I will glorify it again."	1
	13:31	"Now the Son of Man has been glorified	1
	13:31	God has been glorified in him.	1
	13:32	If God has been glorified in him.	1
	13:32	God will also glorify him in himself	1
	13:32	and will glorify him at once.	1
	14:13	so that the Father may be glorified in the Son.	1
	15: 8	My Father is glorified by this	1
	16:14	He will glorify me, because he will take	1
	17: 1	"Father, the hour has come; glorify your Son	1
	17: 1	glorify your Son so that the Son may glorify you	1
	17: 4	I glorified you on earth	1
	17: 5	now, Father, glorify me in your own presence	1
	17:10	I have been glorified in them.	1
	21:19	the kind of death by which he would glorify God.)	1
Act	3:13	God…has glorified his servant Jesus	1
Rom	8:30	and those whom he justified he also glorified.	1
	11:13	an apostle to the Gentiles, I glorify my ministry	1
	15: 6	together you may with one voice glorify the God	1
	15: 9	the Gentiles might glorify God for his mercy.	1
1Co	6:20	therefore glorify God in your body.	1
2Co	9:13	glorify God by your obedience	1
Gal	1:24	they glorified God because of me.	1
2Th	1:10	when he comes to be glorified by his saints	2
	1:12	that the name of our Lord Jesus may be glorified	2
	3: 1	word of the Lord may spread rapidly and be glorified	1
Heb	5: 5	did not glorify himself in becoming a high priest	1
1Pe	2:12	and glorify God when he comes to judge.	1
	4:11	God may be glorified in all things through Jesus Christ.	1
	4:16	but glorify God because you bear this name.	1
Rev	15: 4	Lord, who will not fear and glorify your name?	1
	18: 7	As she glorified herself and lived luxuriously	1

glorify with

1. συνδοξάζω, *syndoxazō, 5280*

Rom	8:17	so that we may also be glorified with him.	1

glorious

1. δόξα, *doxa, 1518*
2. δοξάζω, *doxazō, 1519*
3. ἐπιφανής, *epiphanēs, 2212*

Act	2:20	before the coming of the Lord's great and glorious day.	3
Eph	1: 6	to the praise of his glorious grace	1
	1:18	what are the riches of his glorious inheritance	1
Col	1:11	all the strength that comes from his glorious power	1
1Ti	1:11	that conforms to the glorious gospel	1
Jas	2: 1	really believe our glorious Lord Jesus Christ?	1
1Pe	1: 8	rejoice with an indescribable and glorious joy	2

glorious one

1. δόξα, *doxa, 1518*

2Pe	2:10	they are not afraid to slander the glorious ones	1
Jde	1: 8	reject authority, and slander the glorious ones.	1

glory   *See also* give glory

1. Contextual: Not in Greek
2. δόξα, *doxa, 1518*
3. δοξάζω, *doxazō, 1519*

Mat	6:29	Solomon in all his glory was not clothed like one	2
	16:27	come with his angels in the glory of his Father	2
	19:28	Son of Man is seated on the throne of his glory	2
	24:30	with power and great glory.	2
	25:31	"When the Son of Man comes in his glory	2
	25:31	then he will sit on the throne of his glory.	2
Mrk	8:38	when he comes in the glory of his Father	2
	10:37	one at your left, in your glory."	2
	13:26	coming in clouds' with great power and glory.	2
Lke	2: 9	the glory of the Lord shone around them	2
	2:14	"Glory to God in the highest heaven	2
	2:32	for glory to your people Israel."	2
	4: 6	I will give their glory and all this authority;	2
	9:26	when he comes in his glory	2
	9:26	the glory of the Father and of the holy angels.	1
	9:31	They appeared in glory and were speaking	2
	9:32	since they had stayed awake, they saw his glory	2
	12:27	even Solomon in all his glory was not clothed	2
	19:38	Peace in heaven, and glory in the highest heaven!"	2

	21:27	coming in a cloud' with power and great glory.	2
	24:26	suffer these things and then enter into his glory?"	2
Jhn	1:14	we have seen his glory, the glory as of a father's	2
	1:14	glory as of a father's only son, full	2
	2:11	Jesus did this…and revealed his glory;	2
	5:41	I do not accept glory from human beings.	2
	5:44	you accept glory from one another	2
	5:44	do not seek the glory that comes from…God?	2
	7:18	Those…seek their own glory;	2
	7:18	seeks the glory of him who sent him is true	2
	8:50	Yet I do not seek my own glory;	2
	8:54	"If I glorify myself, my glory is nothing.	2
	9:24	"Give glory to God!	2
	11: 4	rather it is for God's glory	2
	11:40	if you believed, you would see the glory of God?"	2
	12:41	because he saw his glory and spoke about him.	2
	12:43	for they loved human glory more than the glory	2
	12:43	more than the glory that comes from God.	2
	17: 5	glory that I had…before the world existed.	2
	17:22	The glory that you have given me	2
	17:24	to see my glory, which you have given me	2
Act	7: 2	The God of glory appeared to our ancestor Abraham	2
	7:55	saw the glory of God and Jesus standing	2
	12:23	because he had not given the glory to God	2
Rom	1:23	exchanged the glory of the immortal God	2
	2: 7	seek for glory and honor and immortality	2
	2:10	glory and honor and peace for everyone	2
	3: 7	if…God's truthfulness abounds to his glory	2
	3:23	all have sinned and fall short of the glory of God;	2
	4:20	grew strong in his faith as he gave glory to God	2
	5: 2	we boast in our hope of sharing the glory of God.	2
	6: 4	raised from the dead by the glory of the Father	2
	8:18	the glory about to be revealed to us.	2
	8:21	the freedom of the glory of the children of God.	2
	9: 4	to them belong the adoption, the glory	2
	9:23	in order to make known the riches of his glory	2
	9:23	which he has prepared beforehand for glory	2
	11:36	To him be the glory forever. Amen.	2
	15: 7	Welcome one another…for the glory of God.	2
	16:27	through Jesus Christ, to whom be the glory forever!	2
1Co	2: 7	which God decreed before the ages for our glory	2
	2: 8	they would not have crucified the Lord of glory.	2
	10:31	do everything for the glory of God.	2
	11:15	if a woman has long hair, it is her glory?	2
	15:40	the glory of the heavenly is one thing	2
	15:41	one glory of the sun, and another glory of the moon	2
	15:41	one glory of the sun, and another glory of the moon	2
	15:41	another glory of the stars;	2
	15:41	star differs from star in glory.	2
	15:43	It is sown in dishonor, it is raised in glory.	2
2Co	1:20	that we say the "Amen," to the glory of God.	2
	3: 7	if the ministry of death…came in glory	2
	3: 7	the glory of his face, a glory now set aside	2
	3: 7	the glory of his face, a glory now set aside	1
	3: 8	will the ministry of the Spirit come in glory?	2
	3: 9	For if there was glory in the ministry	2
	3: 9	does the ministry of justification abound in glory	2
	3:10	Indeed, what once had glory has lost its glory	3
	3:10	Indeed, what once had glory has lost its glory	3
	3:10	because of the greater glory;	2
	3:11	for if what was set aside came through glory	2
	3:11	much more has the permanent come in glory!	2
	3:13	gazing at the end of the glory…being set aside.	1
	3:18	seeing the glory of the Lord as though reflected in	2
	3:18	from one degree of glory to another;	2
	4: 4	the light of the gospel of the glory of Christ	2
	4: 6	the light of the knowledge of the glory of God	2
	4:15	increase thanksgiving, to the glory of God.	2
	4:17	preparing us for an eternal weight of glory	2
	8:19	for the glory of the Lord himself	2
	8:23	messengers of the churches, the glory of Christ.	2
Gal	1: 5	to whom be the glory forever and ever. Amen.	2
Eph	1:12	might live for the praise of his glory.	2
	1:14	to the praise of his glory.	2
	1:17	God of our Lord Jesus Christ, the Father of glory	2
	3:13	my sufferings for you; they are your glory.	2
	3:16	according to the riches of his glory	2
	3:21	to him be glory in the church and in Christ Jesus	2
Php	1:11	for the glory and praise of God.	2
	2:11	to the glory of God the Father.	2
	3:19	their glory is in their shame;	2

	3:21	may be conformed to the body of his glory	2
	4:19	his riches in glory in Christ Jesus.	2
	4:20	To our God and Father be glory forever and ever.	2
Col	1:27	the riches of the glory of this mystery	2
	1:27	which is Christ in you, the hope of glory.	2
	3: 4	you also will be revealed with him in glory.	2
1Th	2:12	who calls you into his own kingdom and glory.	2
	2:20	Yes, you are our glory and joy!	2
2Th	1: 9	separated…from the glory of his might	2
	2:14	may obtain the glory of our Lord Jesus Christ.	2
1Ti	1:17	be honor and glory forever and ever. Amen.	2
	3:16	believed in throughout the world, taken up in glory.	2
2Ti	2:10	salvation…with eternal glory.	2
	4:18	To him be the glory forever and ever. Amen.	2
Tit	2:13	the manifestation of the glory of our great God	2
Heb	1: 3	He is the reflection of God's glory	2
	2: 7	you have crowned them with glory and honor	2
	2: 9	now crowned with glory and honor	2
	2:10	in bringing many children to glory	2
	3: 3	Yet Jesus is worthy of more glory than Moses,	2
	9: 5	above it were the cherubim of glory	2
	13:21	to whom be the glory forever and ever. Amen.	2
1Pe	1: 7	faith…may be found to result in praise and glory	2
	1:11	sufferings destined for Christ and the subsequent glory.	2
	1:21	who raised him from the dead and gave him glory	2
	1:24	and all its glory like the flower of grass.	2
	4:11	To him belong the glory and the power	2
	4:13	be glad and shout for joy when his glory is revealed.	2
	4:14	the spirit of glory, which is the Spirit of God,	2
	5: 1	one who shares in the glory to be revealed	2
	5: 4	you will win the crown of glory that never fades away.	2
	5:10	who has called you to his eternal glory in Christ	2
2Pe	1: 3	called us by his own glory and goodness.	2
	1:17	he received honor and glory from God the Father	2
	1:17	that voice was conveyed to him by the Majestic Glory	2
	3:18	To him be the glory both now and to…eternity.	2
Jde	1:24	make you stand…in the presence of his glory	2
	1:25	to the only God…be glory, majesty, power	2
Rev	1: 6	to him be glory and dominion forever and ever.	2
	4: 9	creatures give glory and honor and thanks to the one	2
	4:11	Lord and God, to receive glory and honor and power	2
	5:12	to receive…honor and glory and blessing!"	2
	5:13	to the Lamb be blessing and honor and glory	2
	7:12	Blessing and glory and wisdom and thanksgiving	2
	11:13	terrified and gave glory to the God of heaven.	2
	14: 7	"Fear God and give him glory	2
	15: 8	smoke from the glory of God and from his power	2
	16: 9	and they did not repent and give him glory.	2
	19: 1	Salvation and glory and power to our God	2
	19: 7	Let us rejoice and exult and give him the glory	2
	21:11	It has the glory of God and a radiance	2
	21:23	for the glory of God is its light	2
	21:24	the kings of the earth will bring their glory	2
	21:26	the glory and the honor of the nations.	2

glutton

1. γαστήρ, *gastēr, 1143*
2. φάγος, *phagos, 5741*

Mat	11:19	and they say, 'Look, a glutton and a drunkard	2
Lke	7:34	and you say, 'Look, a glutton and a drunkard	2
Tit	1:12	are always liars, vicious brutes, lazy gluttons."	1

gnash

1. βρυγμός, *brygmos, 1106*

Mat	8:12	there will be weeping and gnashing of teeth."	1
	13:42	there will be weeping and gnashing of teeth.	1
	13:50	there will be weeping and gnashing of teeth.	1
	22:13	there will be weeping and gnashing of teeth.'	1
	24:51	there will be weeping and gnashing of teeth.	1
	25:30	there will be weeping and gnashing of teeth.'	1
Lke	13:28	There will be weeping and gnashing of teeth	1

gnat

1. κώνωψ, *kōnōps, 3270*

Mat	23:24	You strain out a gnat but swallow a camel!	1

gnaw

1. μασάομαι, *masaomai, 3460*

Rev	16:10	people gnawed their tongues in agony	1

go   *See also* let go

1. Contextual: Not in Greek
2. ἄγω, *agō, 72*
3. ἀναβαίνω, *anabainō, 326*
4. ἀναχωρέω, *anachōreō, 432*
5. ἄπειμι², *apeimi², 583*
6. ἀπέρχομαι, *aperchomai, 599*
7. ἄφιξις, *aphixis, 922*
8. γίνομαι, *ginomai, 1181*
9. δεῦρο, *deuro, 1306*
10. διέρχομαι, *dierchomai, 1451*
11. εἴσειμι, *eiseimi, 1655*
12. εἰσέρχομαι, *eiserchomai, 1656*
13. ἐκλείπω, *ekleipō, 1722*
14. ἐκπορεύομαι, *ekporeuomai, 1744*
15. ἐξέρχομαι, *exerchomai, 2002*
16. ἔρχομαι, *erchomai, 2262*
17. μέλλω, *mellō, 3516*
18. παραγίνομαι, *paraginomai, 4134*
19. περιπατέω, *peripateō, 4344*
20. πορεύομαι, *poreuomai, 4513*
21. προβαίνω, *probainō, 4581*
22. προκόπτω, *prokoptō, 4621*
23. προσέρχομαι, *proserchomai, 4665*
24. ὑπάγω, *hypagō, 5632*
25. φέρω, *pherō, 5770*

Mat	2: 8	he sent them to Bethlehem, saying, "Go and search	20
	2: 8	so that I may also go and pay him homage."	16
	2:14	his mother by night, and went to Egypt	4
	2:20	his mother, and go to the land of Israel, for those	20
	2:22	in place of his father Herod, he was afraid to go	6
	4:21	went from there, he saw two other brothers	21
	5:24	leave your gift there before the altar and go;	24
	5:30	members than for your whole body to go into hell.	6
	5:41	if anyone forces you to go one mile, go also	1
	5:41	forces you to go one mile, go also the second mile.	24
	8: 4	but go, show yourself to the priest	24
	8: 9	I say to one, 'Go,' and he goes, and to another,	20
	8: 9	I say to one, 'Go,' and he goes, and to another,	20
	8:13	Jesus said, "Go; let it be done for you	24
	8:19	"Teacher, I will follow you wherever you go."	6
	8:21	"Lord, first let me go and bury my father."	6
	8:25	they went and woke him up, saying, "Lord, save	23
	8:32	he said to them, "Go!" So they came out	24
	8:33	The swineherds ran off, and on going into the town	6
	9: 6	"Stand up, take your bed and go to your home."	24
	9: 7	he stood up and went to his home.	6
	9:13	Go and learn what this means, 'I desire mercy	20
	10: 5	"Go nowhere among the Gentiles	6
	10: 6	go rather to the lost sheep	20
	10: 7	As you go, proclaim the good news	20
	11: 4	Jesus answered them, "Go and tell John	20
	12: 1	At that time Jesus went through the grainfields	20
	12:45	it goes and brings along seven other spirits	20
	13:28	'Then do you want us to go and gather them?'	6
	13:36	Then he left the crowds and went into the house.	16
	13:44	in his joy he goes and sells all that he has	24
	13:46	went and sold all that he had and bought it.	6
	14:12	then they went and told Jesus.	16
	14:15	so that they may go into the villages	6
	15:39	and went to the region of Magadan.	16
	16:21	must go to Jerusalem and undergo great suffering	6
	17:22	Son of Man is going to be betrayed into human hands	17
	17:27	do not give offense to them, go to the sea	20
	18:12	and go in search of the one that went astray?	20
	18:15	go and point out the fault	24
	18:30	then he went and threw him into prison	6
	18:31	they went and reported to their lord	16
	19: 1	went to the region of Judea beyond the Jordan.	16
	19:15	he laid his hands on them and went on his way.	20
	19:21	to be perfect, go, sell your possessions	24
	20: 4	he said to them, 'You also go into the vineyard	24
	20: 4	So they went.	6
	20: 7	He said to them, 'You also go into the vineyard.'	24
	20:14	Take what belongs to you and go;	24
	21: 2	to them, "Go into the village ahead of you	20
	21: 6	The disciples went and did as Jesus had directed	20
	21:19	seeing a fig tree…he went to it	16
	21:28	'Son, go and work in the vineyard today.'	24

Mt	21:29	but later he changed his mind and went.	6
	21:30	he answered, 'I go, sir'; but he did not go.	1
	21:30	he answered, 'I go, sir'; but he did not go.	6
	22: 9	Go therefore into the main streets, and invite	20
	22:15	Then the Pharisees went and plotted	20
	25: 1	went to meet the bridegroom.	15
	25: 9	you had better go to the dealers and buy some	20
	25:10	while they went to buy it, the bridegroom came	6
	25:25	so I was afraid, and I went and hid your talent	6
	26:14	Judas Iscariot, went to the chief priests	20
	26:18	"Go into the city to a certain man, and say	24
	26:24	The Son of Man goes as it is written of him	24
	26:36	Then Jesus went with them to a place	16
	26:36	"Sit here while I go over there and pray."	6
	26:46	Get up, let us be going. See, my betrayer	2
	27: 5	he departed; and he went and hanged himself.	6
	27:64	otherwise his disciples may go and steal him away	16
	27:65	go, make it as secure as you can."	24
	27:66	they went with the guard and made the tomb secure	20
	28: 1	the other Mary went to see the tomb.	16
	28: 7	Then go quickly and tell his disciples	20
	28:10	go and tell my brothers to go to Galilee;	24
	28:10	go and tell my brothers to go to Galilee;	6
	28:11	While they were going	20
	28:11	some of the guard went into the city	16
	28:16	Now the eleven disciples went to Galilee	20
	28:19	Go therefore and make disciples of all nations	20
Mrk	1:39	he went throughout Galilee	16
	1:44	go, show yourself to the priest	24
	2:11	stand up, take your mat and go to your home."	24
	3:19	Then he went home;	16
	5:19	"Go home to your friends	24
	5:24	he went with him.	6
	5:34	go in peace, and be healed of your disease."	24
	6:27	He went and beheaded him in the prison	6
	6:31	For many were coming and going	24
	6:33	Now many saw them going and recognized them	24
	6:36	so that they may go into the surrounding country	6
	6:37	They said to him, "Are we to go and buy	6
	6:38	"How many loaves have you? Go and see."	24
	7:29	"For saying that, you may go—the demon has left	24
	7:30	she went home, found the child lying on the bed	6
	7:30	the child lying on the bed, and the demon gone.	15
	7:31	went by way of Sidon towards the Sea of Galilee	16
	8:10	went to the district of Dalmanutha.	16
	10: 1	He left that place and went to the region of Judea	16
	10:21	go, sell what you own, and give the money	24
	10:52	"Go; your faith has made you well."	24
	11: 2	said to them, "Go into the village ahead of you	24
	11:11	he entered Jerusalem and went into the temple;	1
	11:13	he went to see whether perhaps he would find	16
	14:10	went to the chief priests in order to betray him	6
	14:12	"Where do you want us to go	6
	14:13	"Go into the city	24
	14:16	the disciples set out and went to the city	16
	14:21	For the Son of Man goes as it is written of him	24
	14:32	They went to a place called Gethsemane;	16
	14:42	let us be going. See, my betrayer is at hand."	2
	16: 1	so that they might go and anoint him.	16
	16: 2	when the sun had risen, they went to the tomb.	16
	16: 7	But go, tell his disciples and Peter	24
	16:15	[["Go into all the world and proclaim the good news]]	20
Lke	1:23	he went to his home.	6
	1:39	went with haste to a Judean town in the hill country	20
	1:59	going to name him Zechariah after his father.	1
	2: 3	All went to their own towns to be registered.	20
	2: 4	Joseph also went from the town of Nazareth	3
	2: 5	He went to be registered with Mary	1
	2:15	When the angels had left them and gone into heaven	1
	2:15	"Let us go now to Bethlehem and see this thing	10
	2:16	they went with haste and found Mary and Joseph	16
	2:41	Now every year his parents went to Jerusalem	20
	2:44	they went a day's journey.	16
	3: 3	He went into all the region around the Jordan	16
	4:42	he departed and went into a deserted place.	20
	5:14	"Go...and show yourself to the priest	6
	5:24	stand up and take your bed and go to your home."	20
	5:25	and went to his home, glorifying God.	6
	7: 6	Jesus went with them	20
	7: 8	I say to one, 'Go,' and he goes	20
	7: 8	I say to one, 'Go,' and he goes	20

	7:11	Soon afterwards he went to a town called Nain	20
	7:22	"Go and tell John what you have seen and heard:	20
	7:24	When John's messengers had gone	6
	7:50	"Your faith has saved you; go in peace."	20
	8:35	found the man from whom the demons had gone	15
	8:38	The man from whom the demons had gone begged	15
	8:42	As he went, the crowds pressed in on him.	24
	8:48	your faith has made you well; go in peace."	20
	9:12	so that they may go into the surrounding villages	20
	9:13	go and buy food for all these people."	20
	9:44	The Son of Man is going to be betrayed	17
	9:51	he set his face to go to Jerusalem.	20
	9:57	As they were going along the road, someone said	20
	9:57	"I will follow you wherever you go."	6
	9:59	"Lord, first let me go and bury my father."	6
	9:60	as for you, go and proclaim the kingdom of God."	6
	10: 1	where he himself intended to go.	16
	10:37	Jesus said to him, "Go and do likewise."	20
	11: 5	one of you has a friend, and you go to him	20
	11:26	Then it goes and brings seven other spirits	20
	11:53	When he went outside,	15
	12:54	you immediately say, 'It is going to rain';	16
	12:58	you go with your accuser before a magistrate	24
	13:32	He said to them, "Go and tell that fox for me,	20
	14: 1	when Jesus was going to the house of a leader	16
	14:10	go and sit down at the lowest place	20
	14:19	I am going to try them out;	20
	15: 4	go after the one that is lost until he finds it?	20
	15:15	So he went and hired himself out	20
	15:18	I will get up and go to my father	20
	15:20	he set off and went to his father.	16
	15:28	he became angry and refused to go in.	12
	16: 9	so that when it is gone, they may welcome you	13
	16:30	if someone goes to them from the dead	20
	17:14	"Go and show yourselves to the priests."	20
	17:14	as they went, they were made clean.	24
	17:23	Do not go, do not set off in pursuit.	6
	19: 4	he was going to pass that way.	17
	19: 7	"He has gone to be the guest of...a sinner."	12
	19:12	"A nobleman went to a distant country	20
	19:30	saying, "Go into the village ahead	24
	21: 8	'The time is near!' Do not go after them.	20
	22: 8	So Jesus sent Peter and John, saying, "Go	20
	22:13	they went and found everything as he had told them;	6
	22:22	the Son of Man is going as it has been determined	20
	22:33	I am ready to go with you to prison and to death!"	20
	22:39	went, as was his custom, to the Mount of Olives;	20
	24:12	he went home, amazed at what had happened	6
	24:13	two of them were going to a village called Emmaus	20
	24:24	Some of those who were with us went to the tomb	6
	24:28	came near the village to which they were going	20
	24:28	he walked ahead as if he were going on.	20
Jhn	1:43	The next day Jesus decided to go to Galilee.	15
	3: 8	do not know where it comes from or where it goes.	24
	3:22	Jesus...went into the Judean countryside,	16
	3:26	here he is baptizing, and all are going to him."	16
	4: 8	(His disciples had gone to the city	6
	4:16	"Go, call your husband, and come back."	24
	4:45	for they too had gone to the festival.	16
	4:47	he went and begged him to come down and heal	6
	4:50	Jesus said to him, "Go; your son will live."	20
	6: 1	Jesus went to the other side of the Sea of Galilee	6
	6: 6	he himself knew what he was going to do.	17
	6:21	reached the land toward which they were going.	24
	6:24	they...got into the boats and went to Capernaum	16
	6:30	"What sign are you going to give us then,	1
	6:68	Peter answered him, "Lord, to whom can we go?	6
	6:71	though one of the twelve, was going to betray him.	17
	7: 3	"Leave here and go to Judea	24
	7: 8	Go to the festival yourselves.	3
	7: 8	I am not going to this festival	3
	7:10	after his brothers had gone to the festival	3
	7:10	he...went, not publicly but as it were in secret.	3
	7:33	then I am going to him who sent me.	24
	7:35	"Where does this man intend to go	20
	7:35	Does he intend to go to the Dispersion	20
	7:50	Nicodemus, who had gone to Jesus before	16
	7:53	[[each of them went home]]	20
	8: 1	[[Jesus went to the Mount of Olives.]]	20
	8:14	I know where I have come from and where I am going	24
	8:14	do not know where I come from or where I am going.	24

8:21	Where I am going, you cannot come."	24
8:22	the Jews said, "Is he going to kill himself?	1
8:22	by saying, 'Where I am going, you cannot come'?"	24
9: 7	saying to him, "Go, wash in the pool of Siloam"	24
9: 7	Then he went and washed and came back able to see.	6
9:11	'Go to Siloam and wash.' Then I went and washed	24
9:11	Then I went and washed and received my sight."	6
10: 4	he goes ahead of them, and the sheep follow him	20
10:32	For which of these are you going to stone me?"	1
10:33	not for a good work that we are going to stone you	1
11: 7	"Let us go to Judea again."	2
11: 8	are you going there again?"	24
11:11	I am going there to awaken him."	20
11:15	let us go to him."	2
11:16	"Let us also go, that we may die with him."	2
11:29	when she heard it, she got up quickly and went	16
11:31	thought that she was going to the tomb to weep	24
11:44	said to them, "Unbind him, and let him go."	24
11:46	some of them went to the Pharisees	6
11:54	went from there to a town called Ephraim	6
12:19	Look, the world has gone after him!"	6
12:22	Philip went and told Andrew;	16
12:22	Andrew and Philip went and told Jesus.	16
12:35	do not know where you are going.	24
13: 3	he had come from God and was going to God	24
13: 6	to him, "Lord, are you going to wash my feet?"	1
13:33	'Where I am going, you cannot come.'	24
13:36	Peter said to him, "Lord, where are you going?"	24
13:36	"Where I am going, you cannot follow me now;	24
14: 2	I go to prepare a place for you?	20
14: 3	if I go and prepare a place for you	20
14: 4	you know the way to the place where I am going."	24
14: 5	"Lord, we do not know where you are going.	24
14:12	because I am going to the Father.	20
14:28	that I am going to the Father	20
15:16	I appointed you to go and bear fruit	24
16: 5	now I am going to him who sent me;	24
16: 5	yet none of you asks me, 'Where are you going?'	24
16: 7	if I go, I will send him to you.	20
16:10	because I am going to the Father	24
16:17	'Because I am going to the Father'?"	24
16:28	leaving the world and am going to the Father."	20
18: 8	So if you are looking for me, let these men go."	24
20: 2	went to Simon Peter and the other disciple	16
20: 3	went toward the tomb.	16
20:17	go to my brothers and say to them	20
20:18	Mary Magdalene went and announced to the disciples	16
21: 3	Simon Peter said to them, "I am going fishing."	24
21: 3	They said to him, "We will go with you."	16
21:18	and to go wherever you wished.	19
21:18	take you where you do not wish to go."	1
Act 1:10	While he was going and they were gazing up	20
1:11	Jesus…will come in the same way as you saw him go	20
1:13	they went to the room upstairs	3
1:25	to go to his own place."	20
4:23	they went to their friends	16
5:20	"Go, stand in the temple and tell the people	20
5:22	when the temple police went	18
5:26	captain went with the temple police and brought	6
7: 3	go to the land that I will show you.'	9
8:26	"Get up and go toward the south	20
8:27	he got up and went.	20
8:36	As they were going along the road	20
8:39	went on his way rejoicing.	20
9: 1	Saul…went to the high priest	23
9:11	"Get up and go to the street called Straight	20
9:15	the Lord said to him, "Go	20
9:17	So Ananias went and entered the house.	6
10:20	go down, and go with them without hesitation;	20
10:23	The next day he got up and went with them	15
11: 3	saying, "Why did you go to uncircumcised men	12
11:25	Barnabas went to Tarsus to look for Saul	15
12: 6	before Herod was going to bring him out	17
12:12	as he realized this, he went to the house of Mary	16
12:17	Then he left and went to another place.	20
13:51	and went to Iconium.	16
16: 7	they attempted to go into Bithynia	20
16:16	as we were going to the place of prayer	20
16:19	owners saw that their hope of making money was gone	15
16:36	therefore come out now and go in peace."	20
16:37	now are they going to discharge us in secret?	1

17:10	they went to the Jewish synagogue.	5
18: 1	After this Paul left Athens and went to Corinth.	16
18: 6	From now on I will go to the Gentiles."	20
19:21	resolved…to go on to Jerusalem.	20
19:21	"After I have gone there, I must also see Rome."	8
20:14	we took him on board and went to Mitylene.	16
20:29	after I have gone, savage wolves will come	7
21:18	The next day Paul went with us to visit James;	11
22: 5	in Damascus, and I went	20
22:10	The Lord said to me, 'Get up and go to Damascus;	20
22:21	he said to me, 'Go, for I will send you	20
23:16	he went and gained entrance to the barracks	18
23:20	as though they were going to inquire	17
25: 4	he himself intended to go there shortly.	14
25:12	to the emperor you will go."	20
25:20	I asked whether he wished to go to Jerusalem	20
27: 3	allowed him to go to his friends to be cared for.	20
28:26	'Go to this people and say, You will indeed listen	20
Rom 15:24	when I go to Spain. For I do hope to see you	20
15:25	I am going to Jerusalem in a ministry to the saints;	20
1Co 10:27	you are disposed to go	20
16: 4	If it seems advisable that I should go also	20
16: 6	may send me on my way, wherever I go.	20
2Co 8:17	he is going to you of his own accord.	15
12: 1	go on to visions and revelations of the Lord.	16
12:18	I urged Titus to go, and sent the brother with him.	1
Gal 1:21	I went into the regions of Syria and Cilicia	16
2: 9	agreeing that we should go to the Gentiles	1
Php 2:23	as soon as I see how things go with me;	1
2Ti 3:13	impostors will go from bad to worse	22
4:10	has deserted me and gone to Thessalonica;	20
4:10	Crescens has gone to Galatia, Titus to Dalmatia.	1
Heb 6: 1	Therefore let us go on toward perfection,	25
9: 7	only the high priest goes into the second	1
11: 8	he set out, not knowing where he was going.	16
13:13	Let us then go to him outside the camp	15
Jas 2:16	"Go in peace; keep warm and eat your fill,"	24
4:13	tomorrow we will go to such and such a town	20
1Pe 3:19	he went and made a proclamation to the spirits in prison	20
3:22	who has gone into heaven	20
1Jn 2:11	and does not know the way to go	24
Jde 1:11	Woe to them! For they go the way of Cain	20
Rev 5: 7	He went and took the scroll from the right hand	16
10: 8	"Go, take the scroll that is open in the hand	24
10: 9	So I went to the angel and told him to give me	6
13:10	If…to be taken captive, into captivity you go;	24
14: 4	these follow the Lamb wherever he goes.	24
16: 1	"Go and pour out on the earth the seven bowls	24
16: 2	first angel went and poured his bowl on the earth	6
17: 8	beast…is about to ascend…and go to destruction.	24
17:11	As for the beast…it goes to destruction.	24
18:14	"The fruit for which your soul longed has gone	6

go aboard

    1. ἀναβαίνω, *anabainō, 326*

Jhn 21:11 Simon Peter went aboard and hauled the net ashore   1

go about

    1. διέρχομαι, *dierchomai, 1451*
    2. περιάγω, *periagō, 4310*
    3. περιέρχομαι, *perierchomai, 4320*
    4. περιπατέω, *peripateō, 4344*

Mat 9:35	Jesus went about all the cities and villages	2
Mrk 6: 6	he went about among the villages teaching.	2
Jhn 6:66	and no longer went about with him.	4
7: 1	After this Jesus went about in Galilee.	4
7: 1	He did not wish to go about in Judea	4
Act 10:38	how he went about doing good	1
13:11	he went about groping for someone to lead him	2
20:25	I have gone about proclaiming the kingdom	1
Heb 11:37	they went about in skins of sheep and goats	3
Rev 16:15	not going about naked and exposed to shame.")	4

go abroad

    1. ἐκπορεύομαι, *ekporeuomai, 1744*

Rev 16:14 who go abroad to the kings of the whole world   1

go across

    1. ἀπέρχομαι, *aperchomai, 599*
    2. διέρχομαι, *dierchomai, 1451*

Mrk 4:35 "Let us go across to the other side."   2
      8:13 he went across to the other side.   1
Lke 8:22 "Let us go across to the other side of the lake."   2

go ahead

1. προάγω, *proagō, 4575*
2. προέρχομαι, *proerchomai, 4601*
3. προλαμβάνω, *prolambanō, 4624*

Mat 2: 9 and there, ahead of them, went the star   1
    21: 9 The crowds that went ahead of him   1
    21:31 going into the kingdom of God ahead of you.   1
    26:32 I will go ahead of you to Galilee."   1
    28: 7 indeed he is going ahead of you to Galilee;   1
Mrk 11: 9 who went ahead and those who followed were shouting   1
    16: 7 he is going ahead of you to Galilee;   1
Act 20: 5 went ahead and were waiting for us in Troas;   2
    20:13 went ahead to the ship and set sail for Assos   2
1Co 11:21 each of you goes ahead with your own supper   3

go along

1. πορεύομαι, *poreuomai, 4513*

Act 9: 3 Now as he was going along and approaching Damascus   1

go and meet

1. ὑπαντάω, *hypantaō, 5636*

Jhn 11:20 she went and met him, while Mary stayed at home.   1

go ashore

1. ἀποβαίνω, *apobainō, 609*
2. ἐξέρχομαι, *exerchomai, 2002*

Mat 14:14 When he went ashore, he saw a great crowd;   2
Mrk 6:34 As he went ashore, he saw a great crowd;   2
Jhn 21: 9 they had gone ashore, they saw a charcoal fire   1

go astray

1. πλανάω, *planaō, 4414*

Mat 18:12 and one of them has gone astray   1
    18:12 and go in search of the one that went astray?   1
    18:13 the ninety-nine that never went astray   1
Heb 3:10 'They always go astray in their hearts   1
1Pe 2:25 For you were going astray like sheep   1
2Pe 2:15 They have left the straight road and have gone astray   1

go away

1. ἀναχωρέω, *anachōreō, 432*
2. ἀπέρχομαι, *aperchomai, 599*
3. ἀποδημέω, *apodēmeō, 623*
4. ἀποχωρέω, *apochōreō, 713*
5. ἀφίστημι, *aphistēmi, 923*
6. ἐξέρχομαι, *exerchomai, 2002*
7. πορεύομαι, *poreuomai, 4513*
8. ὑπάγω, *hypagō, 5632*

Mat 2:22 And after being warned in a dream, he went away   1
    7:23 'I never knew you; go away from me, you evildoers.'   4
    9:24 he said, "Go away; for the girl is not dead   1
    9:31 But they went away and spread the news about him   6
    9:32 After they had gone away, a demoniac who was mute   6
    11: 7 As they went away, Jesus began to speak   7
    13:25 sowed weeds among the wheat, and then went away.   2
    14:16 Jesus said to them, "They need not go away;   2
    15:21 and went away to the district of Tyre and Sidon.   1
    16: 4 Then he left them and went away.   2
    19:22 he went away grieving   2
    22: 5 But they made light of it and went away   2
    22:22 they left him and went away.   2
    24: 1 Jesus came out of the temple and was going away   7
    25:15 Then he went away.   3
    25:46 these will go away into eternal punishment   2
    26:42 Again he went away for the second time and prayed   2
    26:44 So leaving them again, he went away   2
    27:60 stone to the door of the tomb and went away.   2
Mrk 5:20 he went away and began to proclaim   2
    6:32 they went away in the boat to a deserted place   2
    7:24 he set out and went away to the region of Tyre.   2
    10:22 he was shocked and went away grieving   2
    11: 4 They went away and found a colt tied near a door   2
    12:12 So they left him and went away.   2
    14:39 again he went away and prayed   2
Lke 5: 8 "Go away from me, Lord, for I am a sinful man!"   6

      8:39 So he went away   2
    10:30 robbers...went away, leaving him half dead.   2
    13:27 go away from me, all you evildoers!'   5
    22: 4 he went away and conferred with the chief priests   2
Jhn 5:15 The man went away and told the Jews   2
    6:22 his disciples had gone away alone.   2
    6:67 "Do you also wish to go away?"   8
    8: 9 ⟦When they heard it, they went away, one by one⟧   6
    8:21 "I am going away, and you will search for me   8
    10:40 He went away again across the Jordan   2
    14:28 'I am going away, and I am coming to you.'   8
    16: 7 it is to your advantage that I go away   2
    16: 7 if I do not go away, the Advocate will not come   2
Act 24:25 "Go away for the present;   7
Gal 1:17 I went away at once into Arabia   2
Jas 1:24 they look at themselves and, on going away   2

go back

1. ἀπέρχομαι, *aperchomai, 599*
2. ἔρχομαι, *erchomai, 2262*

Mrk 16:13 ⟦they went back and told the rest⟧   1
Lke 8:31 not to order them to go back into the abyss.   1
Jhn 4:28 left her water jar and went back to the city.   1
    7:45 the temple police went back to the chief priests   2
    11:28 she went back and called her sister Mary,   1

go before

1. προάγω, *proagō, 4575*
2. προέρχομαι, *proerchomai, 4601*
3. προπορεύομαι, *proporeuomai, 4638*

Mrk 14:28 I will go before you to Galilee."   1
Lke 1:17 spirit and power of Elijah he will go before him   2
    1:76 you will go before the Lord to prepare his ways   3

go beyond

1. προάγω, *proagō, 4575*

2Jn 1: 9 does not abide in the teaching of Christ, but goes beyond   1

go by

1. διαπορεύομαι, *diaporeuomai, 1388*
2. παρέρχομαι, *parerchomai, 4216*

Lke 18:36 heard a crowd going by   1
Act 27: 9 because even the Fast had already gone by   2

go by land

1. πεζεύω, *pezeuō, 4269*

Act 20:13 intending to go by land himself.   1

go down

1. ἐπιδύω, *epidyō, 2115*
2. καταβαίνω, *katabainō, 2849*
3. κατέρχομαι, *katerchomai, 2982*

Mat 24:17 the one on the housetop must not go down   2
Mrk 13:15 one on the housetop must not go down   2
Lke 2:51 he went down with them and came to Nazareth   2
    4:31 He went down to Capernaum, a city in Galilee   3
    10:30 "A man was going down from Jerusalem to Jericho   2
    10:31 Now by chance a priest was going down that road;   2
    18:14 this man went down to his home justified   2
Jhn 2:12 After this he went down to Capernaum   2
    4:51 As he was going down, his slaves met him   2
    6:16 his disciples went down to the sea   2
Act 7:15 Jacob went down to Egypt.   2
    8: 5 Philip went down to the city of Samaria   3
    8:15 The two went down and prayed for them   2
    8:26 the road that goes down from Jerusalem to Gaza."   2
    8:38 Philip and the eunuch, went down into the water   2
    10:20 Now get up, go down   2
    10:21 Peter went down to the men and said, "I am the one   2
    12:19 Then he went down from Judea to Caesarea   3
    13: 4 they went down to Seleucia.   3
    14:25 they went down to Attalia.   2
    15:30 they were sent off and went down to Antioch.   3
    16: 8 so, passing by Mysia, they went down to Troas.   3
    18:22 and then went down to Antioch.   2
    20:10 Paul went down, and bending over him   2
    23:10 the tribune...ordered the soldiers to go down   2
    25: 6 he went down to Caesarea;   2
    25: 7 the Jews who had gone down from Jerusalem   2

Eph 4:26 do not let the sun go down on your anger   1

go far

1. προβαίνω, *probainō, 4581*
2. προέρχομαι, *proerchomai, 4601*
3. προκόπτω, *prokoptō, 4621*

Mat 26:39 going a little farther, he threw himself on   2
Mrk 1:19 As he went a little farther   1
       14:35 going a little farther, he threw himself on   2
Rom 13:12 the night is far gone, the day is near.   3

go forth

1. ἐξέρχομαι, *exerchomai, 2002*

Mrk 5:30 aware that power had gone forth from him,   1

go from

1. ἐξέρχομαι, *exerchomai, 2002*

Jhn 4:43 he went from that place to Galilee   1

go from place to place

1. διέρχομαι, *dierchomai, 1451*

Act 8: 4 went from place to place, proclaiming the word.   1

go from town to town

1. διαπορεύομαι, *diaporeuomai, 1388*

Act 16: 4 As they went from town to town,   1

go here and there

1. διέρχομαι, *dierchomai, 1451*

Act 9:32 Peter went here and there among all the believers   1

go hungry

1. πεινάω, *peinaō, 4277*

1Co 11:21 one goes hungry and another becomes drunk.   1
Php 4:12 I have learned the secret of…going hungry   1

go in

1. ἀποστέλλω, *apostellō, 690*
2. εἰσέρχομαι, *eiserchomai, 1656*
3. εἰσπορεύομαι, *eisporeuomai, 1660*

Mat 9:25 he went in and took her by the hand   2
       23:13 you do not go in yourselves   2
       23:13 when others are going in, you stop them.   2
Mrk 4:29 at once he goes in with his sickle   1
       5:40 and went in where the child was.   3
       7:15 that by going in can defile   3
Lke 11:37 so he went in and took his place at the table.   2
       24: 3 when they went in, they did not find the body.   2
       24:29 So he went in to stay with them.   2
Jhn 20: 5 but he did not go in.   2
       20: 8 also went in, and he saw and believed;   2
Act 1:21 the Lord Jesus went in and out among us   2
       9:28 So he went in and out among them in Jerusalem   3
       10:27 he went in and found that many had assembled;   2
       17: 2 Paul went in, as was his custom   2

go inside

1. εἰσέρχομαι, *eiserchomai, 1656*

Mat 26:58 going inside, he sat with the guards   1

go into

1. εἴσειμι, *eiseimi, 1655*
2. εἰσέρχομαι, *eiserchomai, 1656*
3. εἰσπορεύομαι, *eisporeuomai, 1660*

Mat 6: 6 whenever you pray, go into your room and shut the door   2
       15:11 not what goes into the mouth that defiles a person   2
       15:17 Do you not see that whatever goes into the mouth   3
       25:10 who were ready went with him into the wedding   2
Mrk 1:45 Jesus could no longer go into a town openly   2
       6:56 wherever he went, into villages or cities   3
       7:18 whatever goes into a person from outside   3
       8:26 "Do not even go into the village."   2
Lke 7:36 he went into the Pharisee's house   2
Jhn 20: 6 Simon Peter came…and went into the tomb.   2
Act 3: 3 saw Peter and John about to go into the temple   1
       13:14 on the sabbath day they went into the synagogue   2
       14: 1 Paul and Barnabas went into the Jewish synagogue   2
       14:20 he got up and went into the city.   2
       18:19 but first he himself went into the synagogue   2

       19:30 Paul wished to go into the crowd   2
       21: 8 we went into the house of Philip the evangelist   2
Heb 9: 6 the priests go continually into the first tent   1

go off

1. ἀπέρχομαι, *aperchomai, 599*
2. πορεύομαι, *poreuomai, 4513*

Mat 25:16 had received the five talents went off at once   2
       25:18 the one who had received the one talent went off   1
Rev 12:17 went off to make war on the rest of her children   1

go on

1. Contextual: Not in Greek
2. ἄγω, *agō, 72*
3. ἀπέρχομαι, *aperchomai, 599*
4. γίνομαι, *ginomai, 1181*
5. διέρχομαι, *dierchomai, 1451*
6. εἰμί, *eimi, 1639*
7. ἐξέρχομαι, *exerchomai, 2002*
8. ἐπιβαίνω, *epibainō, 2094*
9. ἔτι, *eti, 2285*
10. καταντάω, *katantaō, 2918*
11. μεταβαίνω, *metabainō, 3553*
12. παράγω, *paragō, 4135*
13. πορεύομαι, *poreuomai, 4513*
14. προστίθημι, *prostithēmi, 4707*

Mat 9:27 As Jesus went on from there   12
       11: 1 he went on from there to teach and proclaim   11
Mrk 1:38 "Let us go on to the neighboring towns   2
       8:27 Jesus went on with his disciples   7
       9:30 They went on from there   7
Lke 9:56 Then they went on to another village.   13
       15:26 asked what was going on.   6
       19:11 he went on to tell a parable   14
       19:28 After he had said this, he went on ahead   13
Act 5:21 at daybreak and went on with their teaching.   1
       5:24 wondering what might be going on.   4
       13:14 they went on from Perga   5
       14:20 The next day he went on with Barnabas to Derbe.   7
       16: 1 Paul went on also to Derbe and to Lystra   10
       21: 4 they told Paul not to go on to Jerusalem.   8
       23:32 The next day they let the horsemen go on with him   3
Rom 6: 2 How can we who died to sin go on living in it?   9
2Co 2:13 I said farewell to them and went on to Macedonia.   7
2Th 3: 4 you are doing and will go on doing   1

go on a journey

1. ἀποδημέω, *apodēmeō, 623*
2. ἀπόδημος, *apodēmos, 624*

Mat 25:14 "For it is as if a man, going on a journey   1
Mrk 13:34 It is like a man going on a journey   2

go on ahead

1. προάγω, *proagō, 4575*
2. προέρχομαι, *proerchomai, 4601*

Mat 14:22 and go on ahead to the other side   1
Mrk 6:45 go on ahead to the other side, to Bethsaida   1
2Co 9: 5 necessary to urge the brothers to go on ahead to you   2

go on board

1. ἀναβαίνω, *anabainō, 326*
2. ἐπιβαίνω, *epibainō, 2094*

Act 21: 2 we went on board and set sail.   2
       21: 6 we went on board the ship, and they returned home.   1

go on one's way

1. πορεύομαι, *poreuomai, 4513*
2. ὑπάγω, *hypagō, 5632*

Lke 4:30 passed through the midst of them and went on his way.   1
       8:14 as they go on their way   1
       10: 3 Go on your way. See, I am sending you out   2
       10:38 Now as they went on their way, he entered   1
       17:19 go on your way; your faith has made you well."   1
Jhn 8:11 ⟦Go your way, and from now on do not sin again."⟧   1

go on through

1. διοδεύω, *diodeuō, 1476*

Lke 8: 1 Soon afterwards he went on through cities   1

go out

1. Contextual: Not in Greek
2. ἀποβαίνω, *apobainō, 609*
3. εἰμί, *eimi, 1639*
4. ἐκβάλλω, *ekballō, 1675*
5. ἐκπορεύομαι, *ekporeuomai, 1744*
6. ἔξειμι¹, *exeimi¹, 1996*
7. ἐξέρχομαι, *exerchomai, 2002*
8. πορεύομαι, *poreuomai, 4513*
9. σβέννυμι, *sbennymi, 4931*

Mat	3: 5	of Jerusalem and all Judea were going out to him	5
	11: 7	"What did you go out into the wilderness to look at?	7
	11: 8	What then did you go out to see?	7
	11: 9	What then did you go out to see? A prophet?	7
	12:14	the Pharisees went out and conspired	7
	12:43	"When the unclean spirit has gone out of a person	7
	13: 1	That same day Jesus went out of the house and sat	7
	13: 3	"Listen! A sower went out to sow.	7
	15:17	the stomach, and goes out into the sewer?	4
	18:28	that same slave, as he went out	7
	20: 1	a landowner who went out early in the morning	7
	20: 3	went out about nine o'clock, he saw others	7
	20: 5	When he went out again about noon	7
	20: 6	about five o'clock he went out	7
	21:17	He left them, went out of the city to Bethany	7
	22:10	Those slaves went out into the streets	7
	24:26	He is in the wilderness,' do not go out.	7
	25: 8	for our lamps are going out.'	9
	26:30	they went out to the Mount of Olives.	7
	26:71	he went out to the porch, another servant-girl	7
	26:75	he went out and wept bitterly.	7
	27:32	As they went out, they came upon a man from Cyrene	7
Mrk	1: 5	the people of Jerusalem were going out to him	5
	1:35	he got up and went out to a deserted place	7
	1:45	he went out and began to proclaim it freely	7
	2:12	took the mat and went out before all of them;	7
	2:13	Jesus went out again beside the sea;	7
	3: 6	The Pharisees went out	7
	3:21	they went out to restrain him	7
	4: 3	"Listen! A sower went out to sow.	7
	6:12	So they went out and proclaimed	7
	6:24	She went out and said to her mother	7
	7:19	since it enters...the stomach, and goes out	5
	11:11	he went out to Bethany with the twelve.	7
	11:19	Jesus and his disciples went out of the city.	5
	14:26	they went out to the Mount of Olives.	7
	14:68	he went out into the forecourt.	7
	16: 8	So they went out and fled from the tomb	7
	16:10	⟦She went out and told those who had been with him⟧	8
	16:20	⟦they went out and proclaimed the good news⟧	7
Lke	2: 1	a decree went out from Emperor Augustus	7
	5: 2	the fishermen had gone out of them	2
	5:27	After this he went out and saw a tax collector	7
	6:12	he went out to the mountain to pray;	7
	7:24	did you go out into the wilderness to look at?	7
	7:25	What then did you go out to see?	7
	7:26	What then did you go out to see? A prophet?	7
	8: 2	Mary...from whom seven demons had gone out	7
	8: 5	"A sower went out to sow his seed;	7
	8:46	I noticed that power had gone out from me."	7
	10:10	go out into its streets and say	7
	11:14	when the demon had gone out,	7
	11:24	the unclean spirit has gone out of a person	7
	14:18	I must go out and see it;	7
	14:21	'Go out at once into the streets and lanes	7
	14:23	'Go out into the roads and lanes	7
	14:31	what king, going out to wage war against another	8
	21:37	at night he would go out and spend the night	7
	22:62	he went out and wept bitterly.	7
Jhn	8:59	Jesus hid himself and went out of the temple.	7
	10: 9	and will come in and go out and find pasture.	7
	11:31	The Jews...saw Mary get up quickly and go out.	7
	12:13	and went out to meet him	7
	13:30	he immediately went out. And it was night.	7
	13:31	When he had gone out, Jesus said	7
	18: 1	he went out...across the Kidron valley	7
	18:16	the other disciple...went out, spoke to the woman	7
	18:29	Pilate went out to them and said	7
	18:38	he went out to the Jews again	7
	19: 4	Pilate went out again and said to them	7

	19:17	carrying the cross by himself, he went out	7
	21: 3	They went out and got into the boat	7
Act	1:21	the Lord Jesus went in and out among us	7
	9:28	So he went in and out among them in Jerusalem	5
	12: 9	Peter went out and followed him;	7
	13:42	Paul and Barnabas were going out, the people urged	6
	15:24	that certain persons who have gone out from us	7
Rom	10:18	"Their voice has gone out to all the earth	7
1Co	5:10	since you would then need to go out of the world.	7
2Co	7:15	his heart goes out all the more to you	3
1Jn	2:19	They went out from us, but they did not belong to us;	7
	2:19	But by going out they made it plain	1
	4: 1	many false prophets have gone out into the world.	1
2Jn	1: 7	Many deceivers have gone out into the world	7
Rev	3:12	the temple of my God; you will never go out of it.	7

go out of one's mind

1. ἐξίστημι, *existēmi, 2014*

Mrk	3:21	for people were saying, "He has gone out of his mind."	1

go outside

1. ἐξέρχομαι, *exerchomai, 2002*

Act	12:10	they went outside and walked along a lane	1
	16:13	we went outside the gate by the river	1

go over

1. ἀπέρχομαι, *aperchomai, 599*
2. προσέρχομαι, *proserchomai, 4665*

Mat	8:18	he gave orders to go over to the other side.	1
Act	8:29	"Go over to this chariot and join it."	2

go through

1. διαπορεύομαι, *diaporeuomai, 1388*
2. διέρχομαι, *dierchomai, 1451*
3. εἰσέρχομαι, *eiserchomai, 1656*
4. παραπορεύομαι, *paraporeuomai, 4182*

Mat	19:24	for a camel to go through the eye of a needle	2
Mrk	2:23	he was going through the grainfields;	4
	10:25	a camel to go through the eye of a needle	2
Lke	6: 1	while Jesus was going through the grainfields	1
	9: 6	They departed and went through the villages	2
	13:22	Jesus went through one town and village	1
	17:11	Jesus going through the region between Samaria	2
	18:25	to go through the eye of a needle	3
Jhn	4: 4	he had to go through Samaria.	2
Act	13: 6	When they had gone through the whole island	2
	15:41	He went through Syria and Cilicia	2
	16: 6	They went through the region of Phrygia and Galatia	2
	17:23	as I went through...I found among them an altar	2
	18:23	went from place to place through the region	2
	19:21	Paul resolved...to go through Macedonia	2
	20: 2	When he had gone through those regions	2

go through all

1. τελέω, *teleō, 5464*

Mat	10:23	you will not have gone through all the towns	1

go through rite of purification

1. ἁγνίζω, *hagnizō, 49*

Act	21:24	go through the rite of purification with them	1

go through suffering

1. πάσχω, *paschō, 4248*

Mrk	9:12	that he is to go through many sufferings	1

go throughout

1. περιάγω, *periagō, 4310*

Mat	4:23	Jesus went throughout Galilee, teaching	1

go to

1. ἀπέρχομαι, *aperchomai, 599*
2. εἰσέρχομαι, *eiserchomai, 1656*
3. εἰσπορεύομαι, *eisporeuomai, 1660*
4. ἕως, *heōs, 2401*
5. πρός, *pros, 4639*
6. προσέρχομαι, *proserchomai, 4665*

Mat	2:21	his mother, and went to the land of Israel.	2
	20: 8	the last and then going to the first.'	4
	21:28	he went to the first and said	6

21:30	father went to the second and said the same;	6
27:58	went to Pilate and asked for the body of Jesus	6
Mrk 1:21	They went to Capernaum;	3
9:43	to have two hands and to go to hell	1
15:43	went boldly to Pilate	2
Lke 4:16	he went to the synagogue on the sabbath day,	2
8:24	They went to him and woke him up, shouting,	6
10:34	He went to him and bandaged his wounds	6
23:52	This man went to Pilate and asked for the body	6
Jhn 13: 1	to depart from this world and go to the Father.	5
Act 16:40	leaving the prison they went to Lydia's home;	2
18: 7	went to the house of a man named Titius Justus	2
22:26	he went to the tribune and said to him	6
23:14	They went to the chief priests and elders and said	6

go to another country

1. ἀποδημέω, *apodēmeō, 623*

Mat 21:33	and went to another country.	1
Mrk 12: 1	and went to another country.	1
Lke 20: 9	and went to another country	1

go to court

1. κρίνω, *krinō, 3212*

1Co 6: 6	believer goes to court against a believer	1

go to meet

1. ὑπαντάω, *hypantaō, 5636*

Jhn 12:18	that the crowd went to meet him.	1

go to see

1. προσέρχομαι, *proserchomai, 4665*

Act 18: 2	Paul went to see them	1

go up

1. ἀναβαίνω, *anabainō, 326*
2. ἀνέρχομαι, *anerchomai, 456*
3. ἀπέρχομαι, *aperchomai, 599*
4. προσέρχομαι, *proserchomai, 4665*

Mat 5: 1	Jesus saw the crowds, he went up the mountain;	1
14:23	he went up the mountain by himself to pray.	1
15:29	he went up the mountain, where he sat down.	1
20:17	While Jesus was going up to Jerusalem	1
20:18	"See, we are going up to Jerusalem	1
Mrk 3:13	He went up the mountain	1
6:46	he went up on the mountain to pray.	3
10:32	They were on the road, going up to Jerusalem	1
10:33	saying, "See, we are going up to Jerusalem	1
14:45	he went up to him at once and said, "Rabbi!"	4
Lke 2:42	they went up as usual for the festival	1
5:19	they went up on the roof	1
9:28	and went up on the mountain to pray.	1
18:10	"Two men went up to the temple to pray	1
18:31	"See, we are going up to Jerusalem	1
19:28	he went on ahead, going up to Jerusalem.	1
Jhn 2:13	and Jesus went up to Jerusalem.	1
5: 1	and Jesus went up to Jerusalem.	1
6: 3	Jesus went up the mountain	2
7:14	Jesus went up into the temple and began to teach.	1
11:55	many went up from the country to Jerusalem	1
12:20	among those who went up to worship at the festival	1
Act 3: 1	One day Peter and John were going up to the temple	1
10: 9	Peter went up on the roof to pray.	1
11: 2	when Peter went up to Jerusalem	1
15: 2	appointed to go up to Jerusalem to discuss this	1
18:22	he went up to Jerusalem and greeted the church	1
21:12	people there urged him not to go up to Jerusalem.	1
21:15	we got ready and started to go up to Jerusalem.	1
24:11	since I went up to worship in Jerusalem.	1
25: 1	he went up from Caesarea to Jerusalem	1
25: 9	"Do you wish to go up to Jerusalem	1
Gal 1:17	nor did I go up to Jerusalem	2
1:18	Then after three years I did go up to Jerusalem	2
2: 1	I went up again to Jerusalem with Barnabas	1
2: 2	I went up in response to a revelation.	1
Rev 11:12	they went up to heaven in a cloud	1
14:11	smoke of their torment goes up forever and ever.	1
19: 3	The smoke goes up from her forever and ever."	1

go upstairs

1. ἀναβαίνω, *anabainō, 326*

Act 20:11	Paul went upstairs, and after he had broken bread	1

go well

1. εὐοδόω, *euodoō, 2338*

3Jn 1: 2	Beloved, I pray that all may go well with you	1

go with

1. συμπορεύομαι, *symporeuomai, 5233*
2. συνεισέρχομαι, *syneiserchomai, 5291*
3. συνέρχομαι, *synerchomai, 5302*

Lke 7:11	his disciples and a large crowd went with him.	1
24:15	Jesus himself came near and went with them	1
Jhn 18:15	he went with Jesus into the courtyard	2
Act 9:39	So Peter got up and went with them;	3
11:12	The Spirit told me to go with them	3

goad

1. κέντρον, *kentron, 3034*

Act 26:14	It hurts you to kick against the goads.'	1

goal *See also* reach a goal

1. σκοπός, *skopos, 5024*

Php 3:14	I press on toward the goal for the prize	1

goat

1. αἴγειος, *aigeios, 128*
2. ἐρίφιον, *eriphion, 2252*
3. ἔριφος, *eriphos, 2253*
4. τράγος, *tragos, 5543*

Mat 25:32	as a shepherd separates the sheep from the goats	3
25:33	the goats at the left.	2
Heb 9:12	not with the blood of goats and calves	4
9:13	the blood of goats and bulls	4
9:19	he took the blood of calves and goats	4
10: 4	the blood of bulls and goats	4
11:37	they went about in skins of sheep and goats	1

young goat

1. ἔριφος, *eriphos, 2253*

Lke 15:29	yet you have never given me even a young goat	1

God *See also* fight against God, fullness of God, gift dedicated to God, give to God, inspired by God, lover of God, member of God's family, offering to God, reverence for God, taught by God

1. Contextual: Not in Greek
2. αὐτός, *autos, 899*
3. θεός, *theos, 2536*
4. ὁ, *ho, 3836*
5. ὅς, *hos, 4005*

Mat 1:23	Emmanuel," which means, "God is with us."	3
3: 9	for I tell you, God is able from these stones	3
3:16	heavens were opened…and he saw the Spirit of God	3
4: 3	"If you are the Son of God, command these stones	3
4: 4	every word that comes from the mouth of God.' "	3
4: 6	"If you are the Son of God, throw yourself down;	3
4: 7	written, 'Do not put the Lord your God to the test.' "	3
4:10	'Worship the Lord your God, and serve only him.' "	3
5: 8	are the pure in heart, for they will see God.	3
5: 9	for they will be called children of God.	3
5:34	either by heaven, for it is the throne of God	3
6:24	the other. You cannot serve God and wealth.	3
6:30	But if God so clothes the grass of the field	3
6:33	But strive first for the kingdom of God	3
8:29	"What have you to do with us, Son of God?	3
9: 8	they glorified God, who had given such authority	3
12: 4	He entered the house of God and ate the bread	3
12:28	if it is by the Spirit of God that I cast out demons	3
12:28	then the kingdom of God has come to you.	3
14:33	"Truly you are the Son of God."	3
15: 3	"And why do you break the commandment of God	3
15: 4	For God said, 'Honor your father	3
15: 6	you make void the word of God.	3
15:31	And they praised the God of Israel.	3
16:16	"You are the Messiah, the Son of the living God."	3
19: 6	Therefore what God has joined together	3
19:24	someone who is rich to enter the kingdom of God."	3
19:26	but for God all things are possible."	3
21:31	going into the kingdom of God ahead of you.	3

Mat	21:43	the kingdom of God will be taken away from you	3
	22:16	teach the way of God in accordance with truth	3
	22:21	and to God the things that are God's."	3
	22:21	and to God the things that are God's."	3
	22:29	neither the scriptures nor the power of God.	3
	22:31	have you not read what was said to you by God	3
	22:32	'I am the God of Abraham, the God of Isaac	3
	22:32	'I am the God of Abraham, the God of Isaac	3
	22:32	the God of Isaac, and the God of Jacob'?	3
	22:32	He is God not of the dead, but of the living."	3
	22:37	love the Lord your God with all your heart	3
	23:22	swears by the throne of God	3
	26:61	'I am able to destroy the temple of God	3
	26:63	"I put you under oath before the living God	3
	26:63	tell us if you are the Messiah, the Son of God."	3
	27:40	If you are the Son of God, come down	3
	27:43	He trusts in God; let God deliver him now	3
	27:43	He trusts in God; let God deliver him now	1
	27:43	for he said, 'I am God's Son.' "	3
	27:46	"My God, my God, why have you forsaken me?"	3
	27:46	"My God, my God, why have you forsaken me?"	3
	27:54	"Truly this man was God's Son!"	3
Mrk	1: 1	Jesus Christ, the Son of God.	3
	1:14	proclaiming the good news of God	3
	1:15	the kingdom of God has come near;	3
	1:24	I know who you are, the Holy One of God."	3
	2: 7	Who can forgive sins but God alone?"	3
	2:12	so that they were all amazed and glorified God	3
	2:26	He entered the house of God	3
	3:11	"You are the Son of God!"	3
	3:35	Whoever does the will of God is my brother	3
	4:11	given the secret of the kingdom of God	3
	4:26	"The kingdom of God is as if someone would scatter	3
	4:30	"With what can we compare the kingdom of God	3
	5: 7	Jesus, Son of the Most High God?	3
	5: 7	I adjure you by God, do not torment me."	3
	7: 8	You abandon the commandment of God	3
	7: 9	a fine way of rejecting the commandment of God	3
	7:13	thus making void the word of God	3
	9: 1	the kingdom of God has come with power."	3
	9:47	to enter the kingdom of God with one eye	3
	10: 6	'God made them male and female.'	1
	10: 9	Therefore what God has joined together	3
	10:14	to such as these that the kingdom of God belongs.	3
	10:15	receive the kingdom of God as a little child	3
	10:18	you call me good? No one is good but God alone.	3
	10:23	to enter the kingdom of God!"	3
	10:24	how hard it is to enter the kingdom of God!	3
	10:25	who is rich to enter the kingdom of God."	3
	10:27	"For mortals it is impossible, but not for God;	3
	10:27	for God all things are possible."	3
	11:22	Jesus answered them, "Have faith in God.	3
	12:14	teach the way of God in accordance with truth.	3
	12:17	and to God the things that are God's."	3
	12:17	and to God the things that are God's."	3
	12:24	know neither the scriptures nor the power of God?	3
	12:26	how God said to him, 'I am the God of Abraham	3
	12:26	'I am the God of Abraham, the God of Isaac	3
	12:26	'I am the God of Abraham, the God of Isaac	3
	12:26	the God of Isaac, and the God of Jacob'?	3
	12:27	He is God not of the dead, but of the living;	3
	12:29	the Lord our God, the Lord is one;	3
	12:30	shall love the Lord your God with all your heart	3
	12:34	"You are not far from the kingdom of God."	3
	13:19	the creation that God created until now	3
	14:25	when I drink it new in the kingdom of God."	3
	15:34	which means, "My God, my God, why have you forsaken	3
	15:34	"My God, my God, why have you forsaken me?"	3
	15:39	he said, "Truly this man was God's Son!"	3
	15:43	waiting expectantly for the kingdom of God	3
	16:19	⟦Jesus...sat down at the right hand of God.⟧	3
Lke	1: 6	Both of them were righteous before God	3
	1: 8	Once when he was serving as priest before God	3
	1:16	people of Israel to the Lord their God.	3
	1:19	"I am Gabriel. I stand in the presence of God	3
	1:26	the angel Gabriel was sent by God	3
	1:30	you have found favor with God.	3
	1:32	the Lord God will give to him the throne	3
	1:35	will be holy; he will be called Son of God.	3
	1:37	For nothing will be impossible with God."	3
	1:47	my spirit rejoices in God my Savior	3

	1:64	he began to speak, praising God.	3
	1:68	"Blessed be the Lord God of Israel	3
	1:78	By the tender mercy of our God	3
	2:13	praising God and saying	3
	2:14	"Glory to God in the highest heaven	3
	2:20	glorifying and praising God	3
	2:28	Simeon took him in his arms and praised God,	3
	2:38	At that moment she came, and began to praise God	3
	2:40	the favor of God was upon him.	3
	3: 2	the word of God came to John son of Zechariah	3
	3: 6	all flesh shall see the salvation of God.' "	3
	3: 8	God is able from these stones to raise up children	3
	3:38	son of Seth, son of Adam, son of God.	3
	4: 3	devil said to him, "If you are the Son of God	3
	4: 8	"It is written, 'Worship the Lord your God	3
	4: 9	saying to him, "If you are the Son of God	3
	4:12	'Do not put the Lord your God to the test.' "	3
	4:34	I know who you are, the Holy One of God."	3
	4:41	"You are the Son of God!"	3
	4:43	proclaim the good news of the kingdom of God	3
	5: 1	pressing in on him to hear the word of God	3
	5:21	Who can forgive sins but God alone?"	3
	5:25	and went to his home, glorifying God.	3
	5:26	they glorified God and were filled with awe	3
	6: 4	He entered the house of God	3
	6:12	and he spent the night in prayer to God.	3
	6:20	for yours is the kingdom of God.	3
	7:16	Fear seized all of them; and they glorified God	3
	7:16	"God has looked favorably on his people!"	3
	7:28	least in the kingdom of God is greater than he."	3
	7:29	the people...acknowledged the justice of God	3
	7:30	lawyers rejected God's purpose for themselves	3
	8: 1	bringing the good news of the kingdom of God.	3
	8:10	given to know the secrets of the kingdom of God;	3
	8:11	the parable is this: The seed is the word of God.	3
	8:21	those who hear the word of God and do it."	3
	8:28	Jesus, Son of the Most High God?	3
	8:39	and declare how much God has done for you."	3
	9: 2	to proclaim the kingdom of God and to heal.	3
	9:11	spoke to them about the kingdom of God	3
	9:20	Peter answered, "The Messiah of God."	3
	9:27	before they see the kingdom of God."	3
	9:43	all were astounded at the greatness of God.	3
	9:60	as for you, go and proclaim the kingdom of God."	3
	9:62	is fit for the kingdom of God."	3
	10: 9	'The kingdom of God has come near to you.'	3
	10:11	the kingdom of God has come near.'	3
	10:27	love the Lord your God with all your heart	3
	11:20	by the finger of God that I cast out the demons	3
	11:20	then the kingdom of God has come to you.	3
	11:28	those who hear the word of God and obey it!"	3
	11:42	neglect justice and the love of God;	3
	11:49	Therefore also the Wisdom of God said,	3
	12: 6	not one of them is forgotten in God's sight.	3
	12: 8	also will acknowledge before the angels of God;	3
	12: 9	will be denied before the angels of God.	3
	12:20	God said to him, 'You fool!	3
	12:21	are not rich toward God."	3
	12:24	yet God feeds them.	3
	12:28	if God so clothes the grass of the field	3
	13:13	she stood up straight and began praising God.	3
	13:18	said therefore, "What is the kingdom of God like?	3
	13:20	"To what should I compare the kingdom of God?	3
	13:28	all the prophets in the kingdom of God	3
	13:29	and will eat in the kingdom of God.	3
	14:15	anyone who will eat bread in the kingdom of God!"	3
	15:10	joy in the presence of the angels of God	3
	16:13	You cannot serve God and wealth."	3
	16:15	God knows your hearts;	3
	16:15	an abomination in the sight of God.	3
	16:16	the good news of the kingdom of God is proclaimed	3
	17:15	turned back, praising God with a loud voice.	3
	17:18	none...found to return and give praise to God	3
	17:20	asked...when the kingdom of God was coming	3
	17:20	asked...when the kingdom of God was coming	3
	17:21	in fact, the kingdom of God is among you."	3
	18: 2	a judge who neither feared God nor had respect	3
	18: 4	I have no fear of God and no respect for anyone	3
	18: 7	will not God grant justice to his chosen ones	3
	18:11	'God, I thank you that I am not like other people:	3
	18:13	and saying, 'God, be merciful to me, a sinner!'	3

18:16	to such as these that the kingdom of God belongs.	3
18:17	whoever does not receive the kingdom of God	3
18:19	you call me good? No one is good but God alone.	3
18:24	"How hard it is…to enter the kingdom of God!	3
18:25	someone who is rich to enter the kingdom of God."	3
18:27	impossible for mortals is possible for God."	3
18:29	left house…for the sake of the kingdom of God	3
18:43	and followed him, glorifying God;	3
18:43	all the people, when they saw it, praised God.	3
19:11	the kingdom of God was to appear immediately.	3
19:37	began to praise God joyfully with a loud voice	3
19:44	recognize the time of your visitation from God."	1
20:21	teach the way of God in accordance with truth.	3
20:25	to God the things that are God's."	3
20:25	to God the things that are God's."	3
20:36	they are like angels and are children of God	3
20:37	where he speaks of the Lord as the God of Abraham	3
20:37	the God of Isaac, and the God of Jacob.	3
20:37	the God of Isaac, and the God of Jacob.	3
20:38	Now he is God not of the dead, but of the living;	3
21:31	you know that the kingdom of God is near.	3
22:16	until it is fulfilled in the kingdom of God."	3
22:18	until the kingdom of God comes."	3
22:69	seated at the right hand of the power of God."	3
22:70	asked, "Are you, then, the Son of God?"	3
23:35	if he is the Messiah of God, his chosen one!"	3
23:40	rebuked him, saying, "Do you not fear God	3
23:47	he praised God and said	3
23:51	waiting expectantly for the kingdom of God.	3
24:19	a prophet mighty in deed and word before God	3
24:53	were continually in the temple blessing God.	3
Jhn 1: 1	the Word was with God, and the Word was God.	3
1: 1	the Word was with God, and the Word was God.	3
1: 2	He was in the beginning with God.	3
1: 6	was a man sent from God, whose name was John.	3
1:12	he gave power to become children of God	3
1:13	born, not…of the will of man, but of God.	3
1:18	No one has ever seen God.	3
1:18	It is God the only Son, who is close to	3
1:29	"Here is the Lamb of God who takes away the sin	3
1:34	testified that this is the Son of God."	3
1:36	exclaimed, "Look, here is the Lamb of God!"	3
1:49	"Rabbi, you are the Son of God!	3
1:51	the angels of God ascending and descending	3
3: 2	that you are a teacher who has come from God;	3
3: 2	do these signs…apart from the presence of God."	3
3: 3	no one can see the kingdom of God without	3
3: 5	no one can enter the kingdom of God without	3
3:16	God so loved the world that he gave his only Son	3
3:17	"Indeed, God did not send the Son into the world	3
3:18	not believed in the name of the only Son of God.	3
3:21	seen that their deeds have been done in God."	3
3:33	certified this, that God is true.	3
3:34	He whom God has sent speaks the words of God	3
3:34	He whom God has sent speaks the words of God	3
3:36	but must endure God's wrath.	3
4:10	Jesus answered her, "If you knew the gift of God	3
4:24	God is spirit, and those who worship him	3
5:18	also calling God his own Father	3
5:18	making himself equal to God.	3
5:25	the dead will hear the voice of the Son of God.	3
5:42	you do not have the love of God in you.	3
5:44	glory that comes from the one who alone is God?	3
6:27	on him that God the Father has set his seal."	3
6:28	"What must we do to perform the works of God?"	3
6:29	Jesus answered them, "This is the work of God	3
6:33	bread of God is that which comes down from heaven	3
6:45	'And they shall all be taught by God.'	3
6:46	except the one who is from God;	3
6:69	and know that you are the Holy One of God."	3
7:17	Anyone who resolves to do the will of God	2
7:17	will know whether the teaching is from God	3
8:40	has told you the truth that I heard from God.	3
8:41	we have one father, God himself."	3
8:42	"If God were your Father, you would love me	3
8:42	I came from God and now I am here.	3
8:47	Whoever is from God hears the words of God.	3
8:47	Whoever is from God hears the words of God.	3
8:47	that you are not from God."	3
8:54	of whom you say, 'He is our God,'	3
9: 3	so that God's works might be revealed in him.	3

9:16	"This man is not from God	3
9:24	"Give glory to God!	3
9:29	We know that God has spoken to Moses	3
9:31	We know that God does not listen to sinners	3
9:33	If this man were not from God, he could do nothing."	3
10:33	only a human being, are making yourself God."	3
10:35	to whom the word of God came were called 'gods'	3
10:36	blaspheming because I said, 'I am God's Son'?	3
11: 4	rather it is for God's glory	3
11: 4	so that the Son of God may be glorified	3
11:22	God will give you whatever you ask of him."	3
11:27	I believe that you are the Messiah, the Son of God	3
11:40	if you believed, you would see the glory of God?"	3
11:52	to gather into one the dispersed children of God.	3
12:43	more than the glory that comes from God.	3
13: 3	he had come from God and was going to God	3
13: 3	he had come from God and was going to God	3
13:31	God has been glorified in him.	3
13:32	If God has been glorified in him	3
13:32	God will also glorify him in himself	3
14: 1	Believe in God, believe also in me.	3
16: 2	by doing so they are offering worship to God.	3
16:27	have believed that I came from God.	3
16:30	by this we believe that you came from God."	3
17: 3	they may know you, the only true God	3
19: 7	because he has claimed to be the Son of God."	3
20:17	'I am ascending…to my God and your God.' "	3
20:17	'I am ascending…to my God and your God.' "	3
20:28	Thomas answered him, "My Lord and my God!"	3
20:31	Jesus is the Messiah, the Son of God	3
21:19	the kind of death by which he would glorify God.)	3
Act 1: 3	speaking about the kingdom of God	3
2:11	speaking about God's deeds of power."	3
2:17	'In the last days it will be, God declares	3
2:22	Jesus of Nazareth, a man attested to you by God	3
2:22	signs that God did through him among you	3
2:23	the definite plan and foreknowledge of God	3
2:24	But God raised him up	3
2:30	knew that God had sworn with an oath to him	3
2:32	This Jesus God raised up	3
2:33	Being therefore exalted at the right hand of God	3
2:36	know with certainty that God has made him…Lord	3
2:39	everyone whom the Lord our God calls to him."	3
2:47	praising God and having the goodwill	3
3: 8	walking and leaping and praising God.	3
3: 9	All the people saw him walking and praising God	3
3:13	The God of Abraham, the God of Isaac, and the God	3
3:13	The God of Abraham, the God of Isaac, and the God	3
3:13	of Abraham, the God of Isaac, and the God of Jacob	3
3:13	the God of our ancestors	3
3:15	the Author of life, whom God raised from the dead.	3
3:18	In this way God fulfilled what he had foretold	3
3:19	Repent therefore, and turn to God	1
3:21	God announced long ago through his holy prophets.	3
3:22	'The Lord your God will raise up…a prophet	3
3:25	the covenant that God gave to your ancestors	3
3:26	God raised up his servant	3
4:10	whom you crucified, whom God raised from the dead.	3
4:19	"Whether it is right in God's sight	3
4:19	to listen to you rather than to God	3
4:21	all of them praised God for what had happened.	3
4:24	raised their voices together to God and said	3
4:31	spoke the word of God with boldness.	3
5: 4	You did not lie to us but to God!"	3
5:29	"We must obey God rather than any human authority.	3
5:30	The God of our ancestors raised up Jesus,	3
5:31	God exalted him at his right hand as Leader	3
5:32	whom God has given to those who obey him."	3
5:39	if it is of God, you will not be able	3
6: 2	neglect the word of God in order to wait on tables.	3
6: 7	The word of God continued to spread;	3
6:11	blasphemous words against Moses and God."	3
7: 2	The God of glory appeared to our ancestor Abraham	3
7: 4	After his father died, God had him move from there	1
7: 6	God spoke in these terms	3
7: 7	I will judge the nation that they serve,' said God	3
7: 9	but God was with him	3
7:17	promise that God had made to Abraham	3
7:20	Moses…was beautiful before God.	3
7:25	God through him was rescuing them	3
7:32	'I am the God of your ancestors	3

Act	7:32 the God of Abraham, Isaac, and Jacob.'	3
	7:35 God now sent as both ruler and liberator	3
	7:37 'God will raise up a prophet for you	3
	7:42 God turned away from them and handed them over	3
	7:44 as God directed when he spoke to Moses	1
	7:45 nations that God drove out before our ancestors.	3
	7:46 who found favor with God	3
	7:55 saw the glory of God and Jesus standing	3
	7:55 Jesus standing at the right hand of God.	3
	7:56 the Son of Man standing at the right hand of God!"	3
	8:10 the power of God that is called Great."	3
	8:12 proclaiming the good news about the kingdom of God	3
	8:14 Samaria had accepted the word of God	3
	8:20 thought you could obtain God's gift with money!	3
	8:21 your heart is not right before God.	3
	9:20 "He is the Son of God."	3
	10: 2 devout man who feared God with all his household;	3
	10: 2 prayed constantly to God.	3
	10: 3 an angel of God coming in and saying to him	3
	10: 4 have ascended as a memorial before God.	3
	10:15 "What God has made clean, you must not call profane."	3
	10:28 God has shown me that I should not call anyone	3
	10:31 your alms have been remembered before God.	3
	10:33 all of us are here in the presence of God	3
	10:34 "I truly understand that God shows no partiality	3
	10:38 how God anointed Jesus of Nazareth	3
	10:38 doing good and healing…for God was with him.	3
	10:40 God raised him on the third day	3
	10:41 to us who were chosen by God as witnesses	3
	10:42 the one ordained by God as judge of the living	3
	10:46 speaking in tongues and extolling God.	3
	11: 1 the Gentiles had also accepted the word of God.	3
	11: 9 'What God has made clean, you must not call profane.'	3
	11:17 If then God gave them the same gift	3
	11:17 who was I that I could hinder God?"	3
	11:18 they praised God, saying	3
	11:18 God has given even to the Gentiles the repentance	3
	11:23 When he came and saw the grace of God, he rejoiced	3
	12: 5 the church prayed fervently to God for him.	3
	12:23 because he had not given the glory to God	3
	12:24 the word of God continued to advance and gain adherents.	3
	13: 5 proclaimed the word of God in the synagogues	3
	13: 7 wanted to hear the word of God.	3
	13:16 "You Israelites, and others who fear God, listen.	3
	13:17 The God of this people Israel chose our ancestors	3
	13:21 they asked for a king; and God gave them Saul	3
	13:23 God has brought to Israel a Savior	3
	13:26 and others who fear God	3
	13:30 God raised him from the dead;	3
	13:32 what God promised to our ancestors	1
	13:36 served the purpose of God in his own generation	3
	13:37 he whom God raised up experienced no corruption.	3
	13:43 urged them to continue in the grace of God.	3
	13:46 the word of God should be spoken first to you.	3
	14:15 the living God, who made the heaven and the earth	3
	14:22 that we must enter the kingdom of God."	3
	14:26 where they had been commended to the grace of God	3
	14:27 related all that God had done with them	3
	15: 4 they reported all that God had done with them.	3
	15: 7 in the early days God made a choice among you	3
	15: 8 God, who knows the human heart, testified to them	3
	15:10 Now therefore why are you putting God to the test	3
	15:12 signs and wonders that God had done through them	3
	15:14 how God first looked favorably on the Gentiles	3
	15:19 not trouble those Gentiles who are turning to God	3
	16:10 convincéd that God had called us	3
	16:14 A certain woman named Lydia, a worshiper of God	3
	16:17 "These men are slaves of the Most High God	3
	16:25 were praying and singing hymns to God	3
	16:34 rejoiced…that he had become a believer in God.	3
	17:13 learned that the word of God had been proclaimed	3
	17:24 The God who made the world and everything in it	3
	17:27 so that they would search for God	3
	17:29 Since we are God's offspring	3
	17:30 God has overlooked the times of human ignorance	3
	18: 7 Titius Justus, a worshiper of God;	3
	18:11 teaching the word of God among them.	3
	18:13 worship God in ways that are contrary to the law."	3
	18:21 "I will return to you, if God wills."	3
	18:26 explained the Way of God to him more accurately	3
	19: 8 argued persuasively about the kingdom of God.	3

	19:11 God did extraordinary miracles through Paul	3
	20:21 testified…about repentance toward God	3
	20:24 testify to the good news of God's grace.	3
	20:27 declaring to you the whole purpose of God.	3
	20:28 to shepherd the church of God	3
	20:32 now I commend you to God	3
	21:19 things that God had done among the Gentiles	3
	21:20 When they heard it, they praised God.	3
	22: 3 zealous for God, just as all of you are today	3
	22:14 he said, 'The God of our ancestors has chosen you	3
	23: 1 lived my life with a clear conscience before God."	3
	23: 3 "God will strike you, you whitewashed wall!	3
	23: 4 "Do you dare to insult God's high priest?"	3
	24:14 I admit to you…I worship the God of our ancestors	3
	24:15 I have a hope in God—	3
	24:16 a clear conscience toward God and all people.	3
	26: 6 hope in the promise made by God to our ancestors	3
	26: 8 thought incredible…that God raises the dead?	3
	26:18 turn…from the power of Satan to God	3
	26:20 they should repent and turn to God	3
	26:22 To this day I have had help from God	3
	26:29 "Whether quickly or not, I pray to God	3
	27:23 the God to whom I belong and whom I worship	3
	27:24 indeed, God has granted safety to all those	3
	27:25 I have faith in God	3
	27:35 giving thanks to God in the presence of all	3
	28:15 Paul thanked God and took courage.	3
	28:23 testifying to the kingdom of God	3
	28:28 salvation of God has been sent to the Gentiles;	3
	28:31 proclaiming the kingdom of God	3
Rom	1: 1 Paul…set apart for the gospel of God	3
	1: 4 declared to be Son of God with power	3
	1: 7 To all God's beloved in Rome	3
	1: 7 Grace to you and peace from God our Father	3
	1: 8 I thank my God through Jesus Christ for all of you	3
	1: 9 For God…is my witness	3
	1:10 by God's will I may somehow at last succeed	3
	1:16 it is the power of God for salvation to everyone	3
	1:17 For in it the righteousness of God is revealed	3
	1:18 For the wrath of God is revealed from heaven	3
	1:19 For what can be known about God is plain to them	3
	1:19 plain to them, because God has shown it to them.	3
	1:21 for though they knew God, they did not honor him	3
	1:21 they did not honor him as God or give thanks	3
	1:23 exchanged the glory of the immortal God	3
	1:24 God gave them up in the lusts of their hearts	3
	1:25 they exchanged the truth about God for a lie	3
	1:26 God gave them up to degrading passions.	3
	1:28 since they did not see fit to acknowledge God	3
	1:28 God gave them up to a debased mind	3
	1:32 They know God's decree	3
	2: 2 God's judgment on those who do such things	3
	2: 3 you will escape the judgment of God?	3
	2: 4 God's kindness is meant to lead you to repentance?	3
	2: 5 when God's righteous judgment will be revealed.	3
	2:11 For God shows no partiality	3
	2:13 hearers of the law who are righteous in God's sight	3
	2:16 God…will judge the secret thoughts of all.	3
	2:17 and boast of your relation to God	3
	2:23 do you dishonor God by breaking the law?	3
	2:24 "The name of God is blasphemed among the Gentiles	3
	2:29 person receives praise not from others but from God.	3
	3: 2 the Jews were entrusted with the oracles of God.	3
	3: 3 faithlessness nullify the faithfulness of God?	3
	3: 4 Although everyone is a liar, let God be proved true	3
	3: 5 our injustice serves to confirm the justice of God	3
	3: 5 That God is unjust to inflict wrath on us?	3
	3: 6 For then how could God judge the world?	3
	3: 7 if…God's truthfulness abounds to his glory	3
	3:11 there is no one who seeks God.	3
	3:18 "There is no fear of God before their eyes."	3
	3:19 the whole world may be held accountable to God.	3
	3:21 the righteousness of God has been disclosed	3
	3:22 the righteousness of God through faith in Jesus	3
	3:23 all have sinned and fall short of the glory of God;	3
	3:25 whom God put forward as a sacrifice of atonement	1
	3:29 Or is God the God of Jews only?	3
	3:29 Or is God the God of Jews only?	1
	3:29 Is he not the God of Gentiles also?	1
	3:30 since God is one; and he will justify	3
	4: 2 something to boast about, but not before God.	3

4: 3	"Abraham believed God, and it was reckoned to him	3
4: 6	those to whom God reckons righteousness	3
4:17	in the presence of the God in whom he believed	3
4:20	made him waver concerning the promise of God	3
4:20	grew strong in his faith as he gave glory to God	3
4:21	that God was able to do what he had promised.	1
5: 1	peace with God through our Lord Jesus Christ	3
5: 2	we boast in our hope of sharing the glory of God.	3
5: 5	God's love has been poured into our hearts	3
5: 8	But God proves his love for us	3
5: 9	will we be saved through him from the wrath of God.	1
5:10	while we were enemies, we were reconciled to God	3
5:11	boast in God through our Lord Jesus Christ	3
5:15	the grace of God…abounded for the many.	3
6:10	but the life he lives, he lives to God.	3
6:11	dead to sin and alive to God in Christ Jesus.	3
6:13	but present yourselves to God	3
6:13	present your members to God as instruments	3
6:17	But thanks be to God	3
6:22	freed from sin and enslaved to God	3
6:23	the free gift of God is eternal life in Christ	3
7: 4	in order that we may bear fruit for God.	3
7:22	For I delight in the law of God in my inmost self	3
7:25	Thanks be to God through Jesus Christ our Lord!	3
7:25	with my mind I am a slave to the law of God	3
8: 3	For God has done what the law…could not do:	3
8: 7	the mind that is set on the flesh is hostile to God;	3
8: 7	it does not submit to God's law—indeed it cannot	3
8: 8	those who are in the flesh cannot please God.	3
8: 9	since the Spirit of God dwells in you.	3
8:14	all…led by the Spirit of God are children of God.	3
8:14	all…led by the Spirit of God are children of God.	3
8:16	bearing witness…that we are children of God	3
8:17	heirs of God and joint heirs with Christ	3
8:19	waits…for the revealing of the children of God;	3
8:21	the freedom of the glory of the children of God.	3
8:27	God, who searches the heart, knows	1
8:27	Spirit intercedes…according to the will of God.	3
8:28	work together for good for those who love God	3
8:31	If God is for us, who is against us?	3
8:33	Who will bring any charge against God's elect?	3
8:33	It is God who justifies.	3
8:34	Christ Jesus…who is at the right hand of God	3
8:39	will be able to separate us from the love of God	3
9: 5	Messiah, who is over all, God blessed forever.	3
9: 6	It is not as though the word of God had failed.	3
9: 8	children of the flesh who are the children of God	3
9:11	(so that God's purpose of election might continue	3
9:14	Is there injustice on God's part? By no means!	3
9:16	on human will or exertion, but on God who shows mercy.	3
9:20	who indeed are you, a human being, to argue with God?	3
9:22	What if God, desiring to show his wrath	3
9:26	they shall be called children of the living God."	3
10: 1	my heart's desire and prayer to God for them	3
10: 2	I can testify that they have a zeal for God	3
10: 3	the righteousness that comes from God	3
10: 3	they have not submitted to God's righteousness.	3
10: 9	and believe…that God raised him from the dead	3
11: 1	I ask, then, has God rejected his people?	3
11: 2	God has not rejected his people	3
11: 2	of Elijah, how he pleads with God against Israel?	3
11: 8	as it is written, "God gave them a sluggish spirit	3
11:21	For if God did not spare the natural branches	3
11:22	Note then the kindness and the severity of God:	3
11:22	God's kindness toward you, provided you continue	3
11:23	for God has the power to graft them in again.	3
11:28	As regards the gospel they are enemies of God	1
11:29	the gifts and the calling of God are irrevocable.	3
11:30	Just as you were once disobedient to God	3
11:32	For God has imprisoned all in disobedience	3
11:33	the riches and wisdom and knowledge of God!	3
12: 1	I appeal to you…by the mercies of God	3
12: 1	as a living sacrifice, holy and acceptable to God	3
12: 2	so that you may discern what is the will of God	3
12: 3	the measure of faith that God has assigned.	3
12:19	but leave room for the wrath of God;	1
13: 1	for there is no authority except from God	3
13: 1	authorities that exist have been instituted by God.	3
13: 2	resists what God has appointed	3
13: 4	for it is God's servant for your good.	3
13: 4	It is the servant of God to execute wrath	3

13: 6	for the authorities are God's servants,	3
14: 3	for God has welcomed them.	3
14: 6	in honor of the Lord, since they give thanks to God;	3
14: 6	abstain in honor of the Lord and give thanks to God.	3
14:10	will all stand before the judgment seat of God.	3
14:11	and every tongue shall give praise to God."	3
14:12	So then, each of us will be accountable to God.	3
14:17	For the kingdom of God is not food and drink	3
14:18	one who thus serves Christ is acceptable to God	3
14:20	Do not…destroy the work of God.	3
14:22	The faith…have as your own conviction before God.	3
15: 5	May the God of steadfastness and encouragement	3
15: 6	the God and Father of our Lord Jesus Christ.	3
15: 7	Welcome one another…for the glory of God.	3
15: 8	of the circumcised on behalf of the truth of God	3
15: 9	the Gentiles might glorify God for his mercy.	3
15:13	the God of hope fill you with all joy and peace	3
15:15	because of the grace given me by God	3
15:16	in the priestly service of the gospel of God	3
15:17	I have reason to boast of my work for God.	3
15:19	by the power of the Spirit of God	3
15:30	join me in earnest prayer to God on my behalf	3
15:32	that by God's will I may come to you with joy	3
15:33	The God of peace be with all of you. Amen.	3
16:20	The God of peace will shortly crush Satan	3
16:25	Now to God who is able to strengthen you	4
16:26	according to the command of the eternal God	3
16:27	to the only wise God, through Jesus Christ,	3
1Co 1: 1	an apostle of Christ Jesus by the will of God	3
1: 2	To the church of God that is in Corinth	3
1: 3	Grace to you and peace from God our Father	3
1: 4	I give thanks to my God always for you	3
1: 4	because of the grace of God that has been given you	3
1: 9	God is faithful; by him you were called	3
1:14	I thank God that I baptized none of you	3
1:18	to us who are being saved it is the power of God.	3
1:20	Has not God made foolish the wisdom of the world?	3
1:21	in the wisdom of God, the world did not know God	3
1:21	the world did not know God through wisdom	3
1:21	God decided, through the foolishness	3
1:24	Christ the power of God and the wisdom of God.	3
1:24	Christ the power of God and the wisdom of God.	3
1:25	For God's foolishness is wiser than human wisdom	3
1:25	God's weakness is stronger than human strength	3
1:27	God chose what is foolish in the world	3
1:27	God chose what is weak in the world	3
1:28	God chose what is low and despised in the world	3
1:29	boast in the presence of God.	3
1:30	who became for us wisdom from God, and righteousness	3
2: 1	the mystery of God to you in lofty words or wisdom.	3
2: 5	not on human wisdom but on the power of God.	3
2: 7	we speak God's wisdom, secret and hidden,	3
2: 7	which God decreed before the ages for our glory	3
2: 9	what God has prepared for those who love him"	3
2:10	God has revealed to us through the Spirit;	3
2:10	even the depths of God.	3
2:11	So also no one comprehends what is truly God's	3
2:11	except the Spirit of God.	3
2:12	the Spirit that is from God	3
2:12	understand the gifts bestowed on us by God.	3
2:14	do not receive the gifts of God's Spirit	3
3: 6	Apollos watered, but God gave the growth.	3
3: 7	but only God who gives the growth.	3
3: 9	For we are God's servants, working together	3
3: 9	you are God's field, God's building.	3
3: 9	you are God's field, God's building.	3
3:10	According to the grace of God given to me	3
3:16	Do you not know that you are God's temple	3
3:16	God's Spirit dwells in you?	3
3:17	If anyone destroys God's temple	3
3:17	God will destroy that person.	3
3:17	God's temple is holy, and you are that temple.	3
3:19	For the wisdom of this world is foolishness with God.	3
3:23	you belong to Christ, and Christ belongs to God.	3
4: 1	stewards of God's mysteries.	3
4: 5	will receive commendation from God.	3
4: 9	I think that God has exhibited us apostles	3
4:20	For the kingdom of God depends not on talk	3
5:13	God will judge those outside.	3
6: 9	wrongdoers will not inherit the kingdom of God?	3
6:10	none of these will inherit the kingdom of God.	3

1Co	6:11	in the Spirit of our God.	3
	6:13	God will destroy both one and the other.	3
	6:14	God raised the Lord and will also raise us	3
	6:19	Holy Spirit within you, which you have from God	3
	6:20	therefore glorify God in your body.	3
	7: 7	each has a particular gift from God	3
	7:15	It is to peace that God has called you.	3
	7:17	to which God called you.	3
	7:19	obeying the commandments of God is everything	3
	7:24	there remain with God.	3
	7:40	I think that I too have the Spirit of God.	3
	8: 3	anyone who loves God is known by him.	3
	8: 4	and that "there is no God but one."	3
	8: 6	yet for us there is one God, the Father	3
	8: 8	"Food will not bring us close to God."	3
	9: 9	Is it for oxen that God is concerned?	3
	9:21	(though I am not free from God's law	3
	10: 5	God was not pleased with most of them	3
	10:13	God is faithful, and he will not let you be tested	3
	10:20	they sacrifice to demons and not to God.	3
	10:31	do everything for the glory of God.	3
	10:32	to Jews or to Greeks or to the church of God	3
	11: 3	God is the head of Christ.	3
	11: 7	since he is the image and reflection of God;	3
	11:12	but all things come from God.	3
	11:13	for a woman to pray to God with her head unveiled?	3
	11:16	no such custom, nor do the churches of God.	3
	11:22	do you show contempt for the church of God	3
	12: 3	no one speaking by the Spirit of God ever says	3
	12: 6	the same God who activates all of them in everyone.	3
	12:18	as it is, God arranged the members in the body	3
	12:24	God has so arranged the body	3
	12:28	God has appointed in the church first apostles	3
	14: 2	in a tongue do not speak to other people but to God;	3
	14:18	I thank God that I speak in tongues	3
	14:25	person will bow down before God and worship	3
	14:25	declaring, "God is really among you."	3
	14:28	speak to themselves and to God.	3
	14:33	for God is a God not of disorder but of peace.	3
	14:33	for God is a God not of disorder but of peace.	1
	14:36	Or did the word of God originate with you?	3
	15: 9	because I persecuted the church of God	3
	15:10	by the grace of God I am what I am	3
	15:10	the grace of God that is with me.	3
	15:15	We are even found to be misrepresenting God	3
	15:15	we testified of God that he raised Christ	3
	15:24	when he hands over the kingdom to God the Father	3
	15:27	For "God has put all things in subjection	1
	15:28	so that God may be all in all.	3
	15:34	for some people have no knowledge of God.	3
	15:38	God gives it a body as he has chosen	3
	15:50	cannot inherit the kingdom of God	3
	15:57	thanks be to God, who gives us the victory	3
2Co	1: 1	Paul, an apostle of Christ Jesus by the will of God	3
	1: 1	To the church of God that is in Corinth	3
	1: 2	Grace to you and peace from God our Father	3
	1: 3	Blessed be the God and Father of our Lord Jesus	3
	1: 3	Father of mercies and the God of all consolation	3
	1: 4	with which we ourselves are consoled by God	3
	1: 9	not on ourselves but on God who raises the dead.	3
	1:12	not by earthly wisdom but by the grace of God	3
	1:18	As surely as God is faithful	3
	1:19	the Son of God, Jesus Christ, whom we proclaimed	3
	1:20	in him every one of God's promises is a "Yes."	3
	1:20	that we say the "Amen," to the glory of God.	3
	1:21	it is God who establishes us with you in Christ	3
	1:23	I call on God as witness against me:	3
	2:14	thanks be to God	3
	2:15	For we are the aroma of Christ to God	3
	2:17	we are not peddlers of God's word like so many;	3
	2:17	as persons of sincerity, as persons sent from God	3
	3: 3	not with ink but with the Spirit of the living God	3
	3: 4	that we have through Christ toward God.	3
	3: 5	our competence is from God	3
	4: 1	by God's mercy that we are engaged in this ministry	1
	4: 2	practice cunning or to falsify God's word;	3
	4: 2	to the conscience of everyone in the sight of God.	3
	4: 4	the glory of Christ, who is the image of God.	3
	4: 6	the God who said, "Let light shine out of darkness,"	3
	4: 6	the glory of God in the face of Jesus Christ.	3
	4: 7	power belongs to God and does not come from us.	3

	4:15	increase thanksgiving, to the glory of God.	3
	5: 1	we have a building from God	3
	5: 5	He who has prepared us for this very thing is God	3
	5:11	we ourselves are well known to God	3
	5:13	For if we are beside ourselves, it is for God;	3
	5:18	All this is from God, who reconciled us	3
	5:19	in Christ God was reconciling the world	3
	5:20	God is making his appeal through us;	3
	5:20	on behalf of Christ, be reconciled to God.	3
	5:21	in him we might become the righteousness of God.	3
	6: 1	not to accept the grace of God in vain.	3
	6: 4	as servants of God we have commended ourselves	3
	6: 7	truthful speech, and the power of God;	3
	6:16	What agreement has the temple of God with idols?	3
	6:16	we are the temple of the living God; as God said	3
	6:16	we are the temple of the living God; as God said	3
	6:16	I will be their God, and they shall be my people.	3
	7: 1	making holiness perfect in the fear of God.	3
	7: 6	God, who consoles the downcast	3
	7:12	zeal…might be made known to you before God.	3
	8: 1	the grace of God that has been granted	3
	8: 5	to the Lord and, by the will of God, to us	3
	8:16	thanks be to God who put in the heart of Titus	3
	9: 7	God loves a cheerful giver.	3
	9: 8	God is able to provide you with every blessing	3
	9:11	will produce thanksgiving to God through us;	3
	9:12	also overflows with many thanksgivings to God.	3
	9:13	glorify God by your obedience	3
	9:14	the surpassing grace of God that he has given you.	3
	9:15	Thanks be to God for his indescribable gift!	3
	10: 5	proud obstacle raised up against the knowledge of God	3
	10:13	keep within the field that God has assigned to us	3
	11: 7	I proclaimed God's good news to you free of charge?	3
	11:11	why? Because I do not love you? God knows I do!	3
	11:31	The God and Father of the Lord Jesus	3
	12: 2	I do not know; God knows.	3
	12: 3	I do not know; God knows—	3
	12:19	We are speaking in Christ before God.	3
	12:21	my God may humble me before you	3
	13: 4	lives by the power of God.	3
	13: 4	we will live with him by the power of God.	3
	13: 7	we pray to God that you may not do anything wrong	3
	13:11	the God of love and peace will be with you.	3
	13:13	the love of God, and the communion	3
Gal	1: 1	through Jesus Christ and God the Father	3
	1: 3	Grace to you and peace from God our Father	3
	1: 4	according to the will of our God and Father	3
	1:10	seeking human approval, or God's approval?	3
	1:13	I was violently persecuting the church of God	3
	1:15	when God, who had set me apart before I was born	3
	1:20	I am writing to you, before God, I do not lie!	3
	1:24	they glorified God because of me.	3
	2: 6	God shows no partiality)	3
	2:19	so that I might live to God.	3
	2:20	I live by faith in the Son of God	3
	2:21	I do not nullify the grace of God;	3
	3: 5	does God supply you with the Spirit	1
	3: 6	Just as Abraham "believed God	3
	3: 8	God would justify the Gentiles by faith	3
	3:11	no one is justified before God by the law;	3
	3:17	not annul a covenant previously ratified by God	3
	3:18	God granted it to Abraham through the promise.	3
	3:20	but God is one.	3
	3:21	Is the law then opposed to the promises of God?	3
	3:26	you are all children of God through faith.	3
	4: 4	God sent his Son, born of a woman,	3
	4: 6	God has sent the Spirit of his Son into our hearts	3
	4: 7	if a child then also an heir through God	3
	4: 8	Formerly, when you did not know God	3
	4: 9	Now, however, that you have come to know God	3
	4: 9	or rather to be known by God	3
	4:14	as an angel of God, as Christ Jesus.	3
	5:21	will not inherit the kingdom of God.	3
	6: 7	Do not be deceived; God is not mocked	3
	6:16	upon the Israel of God.	3
Eph	1: 1	Paul, an apostle of Christ Jesus by the will of God	3
	1: 2	Grace to you and peace from God our Father	3
	1: 3	Blessed be the God and Father of our Lord Jesus	3
	1:14	toward redemption as God's own people	1
	1:17	God of our Lord Jesus Christ, the Father of glory	3
	1:20	God put this power to work in Christ	1

	2: 4	God, who is rich in mercy	3
	2: 8	this is not your own doing; it is the gift of God	3
	2:10	for good works, which God prepared beforehand	3
	2:16	might reconcile both groups to God in one body	3
	2:19	you are…members of the household of God	3
	2:22	built…spiritually into a dwelling place for God.	3
	3: 2	the commission of God's grace that was given me	3
	3: 7	according to the gift of God's grace	3
	3: 9	plan of the mystery hidden for ages in God	3
	3:10	the wisdom of God in its rich variety	3
	3:12	access to God in boldness and confidence through faith	1
	3:19	you may be filled with all the fullness of God.	3
	4: 6	one God and Father of all, who is above all	3
	4:13	the knowledge of the Son of God	3
	4:18	alienated from the life of God	3
	4:24	created according to the likeness of God	3
	4:30	do not grieve the Holy Spirit of God	3
	4:32	forgiving one another, as God in Christ has forgiven	3
	5: 1	be imitators of God, as beloved children	3
	5: 2	a fragrant offering and sacrifice to God.	3
	5: 5	in the kingdom of Christ and of God.	3
	5: 6	the wrath of God comes on those…disobedient	3
	5:20	giving thanks to God the Father at all times	3
	6: 6	doing the will of God from the heart.	3
	6:11	Put on the whole armor of God	3
	6:13	Therefore take up the whole armor of God	3
	6:17	the sword of the Spirit, which is the word of God.	3
	6:23	God the Father and the Lord Jesus Christ.	3
Php	1: 2	Grace to you and peace from God our Father	3
	1: 3	I thank my God every time I remember you	3
	1: 7	all of you share in God's grace with me	1
	1: 8	For God is my witness, how I long for all of you	3
	1:11	for the glory and praise of God.	3
	1:28	of your salvation. And this is God's doing.	3
	2: 6	who, though he was in the form of God,	3
	2: 6	not regard equality with God as…to be exploited	3
	2: 9	Therefore God also highly exalted him	3
	2:11	to the glory of God the Father.	3
	2:13	for it is God who is at work in you, enabling you	3
	2:15	be blameless and innocent, children of God	3
	2:27	God had mercy on him, and not only on him but on me	3
	3: 3	worship in the Spirit of God and boast in Christ	3
	3: 9	the righteousness from God based on faith.	3
	3:14	prize of the heavenly call of God in Christ Jesus.	3
	3:15	this too God will reveal to you.	3
	4: 6	let your requests be made known to God.	3
	4: 7	the peace of God, which surpasses all understanding	3
	4: 9	the God of peace will be with you.	3
	4:18	a sacrifice acceptable and pleasing to God.	3
	4:19	my God will fully satisfy every need of yours	3
	4:20	To our God and Father be glory forever and ever.	3
Col	1: 1	Paul, an apostle of Christ Jesus by the will of God	3
	1: 2	Grace to you and peace from God our Father.	3
	1: 3	we always thank God, the Father of our Lord Jesus	3
	1: 6	heard it and truly comprehended the grace of God.	3
	1: 9	you may be filled with the knowledge of God's will	2
	1:10	grow in the knowledge of God.	3
	1:15	He is the image of the invisible God	3
	1:20	through him God was pleased to reconcile to himself	1
	1:25	God's commission that was given to me	3
	1:25	to make the word of God fully known	3
	1:27	To them God chose to make known	3
	2: 2	the knowledge of God's mystery, that is, Christ	3
	2:12	through faith in the power of God	3
	2:13	God made you alive together with him	1
	2:19	grows with a growth that is from God.	3
	3: 1	where Christ is, seated at the right hand of God.	3
	3: 3	your life is hidden with Christ in God.	3
	3: 6	On account of these the wrath of God is coming	3
	3:12	As God's chosen ones, holy and beloved	3
	3:16	sing psalms, hymns, and spiritual songs to God	3
	3:17	giving thanks to God the Father through him.	3
	4: 3	that God will open to us a door for the word	3
	4:11	among my co-workers for the kingdom of God	3
	4:12	fully assured in everything that God wills.	3
1Th	1: 1	in God the Father and the Lord Jesus Christ:	3
	1: 2	We always give thanks to God for all of you	3
	1: 3	remembering before our God and Father your work	3
	1: 4	For we know, brothers and sisters beloved by God	3
	1: 8	every place your faith in God has become known	3
	1: 9	how you turned to God from idols	3

	1: 9	to serve a living and true God	3
	2: 2	as you know, we had courage in our God	3
	2: 2	to declare to you the gospel of God	3
	2: 4	just as we have been approved by God	3
	2: 4	not to please mortals, but to please God	3
	2: 5	As you know and as God is our witness,	3
	2: 8	determined to share with you not only the gospel of God	3
	2: 9	while we proclaimed to you the gospel of God.	3
	2:10	You are witnesses, and God also	3
	2:12	pleading that you lead a life worthy of God	3
	2:13	We also constantly give thanks to God for this	3
	2:13	when you received the word of God	3
	2:13	but as what it really is, God's word	3
	2:14	imitators of the churches of God in Christ Jesus	3
	2:15	drove us out; they displease God and oppose everyone	3
	2:16	God's wrath has overtaken them at last.	1
	3: 2	we sent Timothy, our brother and co-worker for God	3
	3: 9	How can we thank God enough for you	3
	3: 9	joy that we feel before our God because of you?	3
	3:11	Now may our God and Father himself	3
	3:13	that you may be blameless before our God and Father	3
	4: 1	how you ought to live and to please God	3
	4: 3	For this is the will of God, your sanctification:	3
	4: 5	like the Gentiles who do not know God;	3
	4: 7	God did not call us to impurity	3
	4: 8	rejects not human authority but God	3
	4:14	God will bring with him those who have died.	3
	4:16	with the sound of God's trumpet, will descend	3
	5: 9	For God has destined us not for wrath	3
	5:18	for this is the will of God in Christ Jesus	3
	5:23	May the God of peace himself sanctify you entirely;	3
2Th	1: 1	God our Father and the Lord Jesus Christ:	3
	1: 2	Grace to you and peace from God our Father	3
	1: 3	We must always give thanks to God for you	3
	1: 4	boast of you among the churches of God	3
	1: 5	is evidence of the righteous judgment of God	3
	1: 5	to make you worthy of the kingdom of God	3
	1: 6	For it is indeed just of God	3
	1: 8	vengeance on those who do not know God	3
	1:11	that our God will make you worthy of his call	3
	1:12	according to the grace of our God	3
	2: 4	he takes his seat in the temple of God	3
	2: 4	declaring himself to be God.	3
	2:11	For this reason God sends them a powerful delusion	3
	2:13	we must always give thanks to God for you	3
	2:13	God chose you as the first fruits for salvation	3
	2:16	Lord Jesus Christ himself and God our Father	3
	3: 5	May the Lord direct your hearts to the love of God	3
1Ti	1: 1	an apostle…by the command of God our Savior	3
	1: 2	Grace, mercy, and peace from God the Father	3
	1:11	glorious gospel of the blessed God	3
	1:17	the King of the ages, immortal, invisible, the only God	3
	2: 3	is acceptable in the sight of God our Savior	3
	2: 5	For there is one God;	3
	2: 5	also one mediator between God and humankind	3
	3: 5	how can he take care of God's church?	3
	3:15	how one ought to behave in the household of God	3
	3:15	which is the church of the living God	3
	4: 3	demand abstinence from foods, which God created	3
	4: 4	For everything created by God is good	3
	4: 5	is sanctified by God's word and by prayer.	3
	4:10	because we have our hope set on the living God	3
	5: 4	for this is pleasing in God's sight.	3
	5: 5	The real widow…has set her hope on God	3
	5:21	In the presence of God and of Christ Jesus	3
	6: 1	name of God and the teaching may not be blasphemed.	3
	6:11	as for you, man of God, shun all this;	3
	6:13	God, who gives life to all things	3
	6:17	to set their hopes…on God	3
2Ti	1: 1	Paul, an apostle of Christ Jesus by the will of God	3
	1: 2	Grace, mercy, and peace from God the Father	3
	1: 3	I am grateful to God—whom I worship	3
	1: 6	rekindle the gift of God that is within you	3
	1: 7	for God did not give us a spirit of cowardice	3
	1: 8	relying on the power of God	3
	2: 9	But the word of God is not chained.	3
	2:14	Remind them…and warn them before God	3
	2:15	Do your best to present yourself to God as…	3
	2:19	God's firm foundation stands, bearing this inscription:	3
	2:25	opponents with gentleness. God may perhaps	3
	3:17	so that everyone who belongs to God may be proficient	3

2Ti	4: 1	In the presence of God and of Christ Jesus,	3
Tit	1: 1	Paul, a servant of God and an apostle of Jesus	3
	1: 1	for the sake of the faith of God's elect	3
	1: 2	eternal life that God, who never lies, promised	3
	1: 3	by the command of God our Savior	3
	1: 4	Grace and peace from God the Father	3
	1: 7	For a bishop, as God's steward, must be blameless;	3
	1:16	They profess to know God	3
	2: 5	the word of God may not be discredited.	3
	2:10	may be an ornament to the doctrine of God our Savior.	3
	2:11	For the grace of God has appeared	3
	2:13	glory of our great God and Savior, Jesus Christ.	3
	3: 4	loving kindness of God our Savior appeared	3
	3: 8	those who have come to believe in God may be careful	3
Phm	1: 3	Grace to you and peace from God our Father	3
	1: 4	I always thank my God	3
Heb	1: 1	Long ago God spoke to our ancestors in many…ways	3
	1: 3	He is the reflection of God's glory	1
	1: 3	and the exact imprint of God's very being	2
	1: 5	which of the angels did God ever say, "You are my Son;	1
	1: 6	he says, "Let all God's angels worship him."	3
	1: 8	"Your throne, O God, is forever and ever	3
	1: 9	therefore God, your God, has anointed you	3
	1: 9	therefore God, your God, has anointed you	3
	2: 4	while God added his testimony by signs and wonders	3
	2: 5	Now God did not subject the coming world	1
	2: 8	God left nothing outside their control.	1
	2: 9	so that by the grace of God he might taste death	3
	2:10	was fitting that God…should make…perfect	2
	2:13	"Here am I and the children whom God has given me."	3
	2:17	faithful high priest in the service of God	3
	3: 2	just as Moses also "was faithful in all God's house."	2
	3: 4	but the builder of all things is God.)	3
	3: 5	Now Moses was faithful in all God's house	2
	3: 6	Christ, however, was faithful over God's house as a son	2
	3:12	evil…heart that turns away from the living God.	3
	4: 3	just as God has said, "As in my anger I swore	1
	4: 4	God rested on the seventh day from all his works."	3
	4: 8	God would not speak later about another day.	1
	4: 9	a sabbath rest still remains for the people of God;	3
	4:10	for those who enter God's rest	2
	4:10	cease from their labors as God did from his.	3
	4:12	Indeed, the word of God is living and active	3
	4:14	a great high priest…Jesus, the Son of God	3
	5: 1	things pertaining to God on their behalf	3
	5: 4	only when called by God, just as Aaron was.	3
	5:10	having been designated by God a high priest	3
	5:12	teach you…the basic elements of the oracles of God.	3
	6: 1	the foundation:…faith toward God	3
	6: 3	we will do this, if God permits.	3
	6: 5	have tasted the goodness of the word of God	3
	6: 6	on their own they are crucifying again the Son of God	3
	6: 7	receives a blessing from God.	3
	6:10	For God is not unjust; he will not overlook your work	3
	6:13	When God made a promise to Abraham	3
	6:17	when God desired to show even more clearly	3
	6:18	it is impossible that God would prove false	3
	7: 1	Melchizedek of Salem, priest of the Most High God	3
	7: 3	resembling the Son of God, he remains a priest	3
	7:19	a better hope, through which we approach God.	3
	7:25	to save those who approach God through him	3
	8: 8	God finds fault with them when he says:	1
	8:10	I will be their God, and they shall be my people.	3
	9:14	offered himself without blemish to God	3
	9:14	from dead works to worship the living God!	3
	9:20	the covenant that God has ordained for you."	3
	9:24	now to appear in the presence of God on our behalf.	3
	10: 7	I said, 'See, God, I have come to do your will, O God'	1
	10: 7	I said, 'See, God, I have come to do your will, O God'	3
	10:10	by God's will that we have been sanctified through	5
	10:12	"he sat down at the right hand of God,"	3
	10:21	since we have a great priest over the house of God	3
	10:29	those who have spurned the Son of God	3
	10:31	to fall into the hands of the living God.	3
	10:36	the will of God, you may receive what was promised.	3
	11: 3	the worlds were prepared by the word of God	3
	11: 4	Abel offered to God a more acceptable sacrifice	3
	11: 4	God himself giving approval to his gifts;	3
	11: 5	"he was not found, because God had taken him."	3
	11: 5	it was attested…that "he had pleased God."	3
	11: 6	without faith it is impossible to please God	1

	11: 7	warned by God about events as yet unseen	1
	11:10	the city…whose architect and builder is God.	3
	11:16	God is not ashamed to be called their God;	3
	11:16	God is not ashamed to be called their God;	3
	11:19	God is able even to raise someone from the dead	3
	11:25	share ill-treatment with the people of God	3
	11:40	since God had provided something better	3
	12: 2	seat at the right hand of the throne of God.	3
	12: 7	God is treating you as children;	3
	12:15	no one fails to obtain the grace of God;	3
	12:22	the city of the living God	3
	12:23	God the judge of all	3
	12:28	by which we offer to God an acceptable worship	3
	12:29	for indeed our God is a consuming fire.	3
	13: 4	God will judge fornicators and adulterers.	3
	13: 7	those who spoke the word of God to you;	3
	13:15	offer a sacrifice of praise to God	3
	13:16	for such sacrifices are pleasing to God.	3
	13:20	the God of peace, who brought back from the dead	3
Jas	1: 1	servant of God and of the Lord Jesus Christ	3
	1: 5	If any of you is lacking in wisdom, ask God	3
	1:13	No one…should say, "I am being tempted by God";	3
	1:13	for God cannot be tempted by evil	3
	1:20	your anger does not produce God's righteousness.	3
	1:27	pure and undefiled before God, the Father	3
	2: 5	Has not God chosen the poor in the world	3
	2:19	You believe that God is one; you do well.	3
	2:23	"Abraham believed God, and it was reckoned to him	3
	2:23	and he was called the friend of God.	3
	3: 9	we curse those who are made in the likeness of God.	3
	4: 4	friendship with the world is enmity with God?	3
	4: 4	a friend of the world becomes an enemy of God.	3
	4: 5	"God yearns jealously for the spirit	1
	4: 6	"God opposes the proud, but gives grace	3
	4: 7	Submit yourselves therefore to God.	3
	4: 8	Draw near to God, and he will draw near to you.	3
1Pe	1: 2	chosen and destined by God the Father	3
	1: 3	Blessed be the God and Father of our Lord Jesus	3
	1: 5	being protected by the power of God through faith	3
	1:21	Through him you have come to trust in God	3
	1:21	so that your faith and hope are set on God.	3
	1:23	through the living and enduring word of God.	3
	2: 4	chosen and precious in God's sight	3
	2: 5	offer spiritual sacrifices acceptable to God	3
	2: 9	you are…a holy nation, God's own people	1
	2:10	but now you are God's people;	3
	2:12	and glorify God when he comes to judge.	3
	2:15	For it is God's will that by doing right	3
	2:16	As servants of God, live as free people,	3
	2:17	Love the family of believers. Fear God.	3
	2:19	if, being aware of God, you endure pain	3
	2:20	you have God's approval.	3
	3: 4	spirit, which is very precious in God's sight.	3
	3: 5	women who hoped in God used to adorn themselves	3
	3:17	to suffer…if suffering should be God's will	3
	3:18	Christ also suffered…in order to bring you to God.	3
	3:20	when God waited patiently in the days of Noah	3
	3:21	but as an appeal to God for a good conscience	3
	3:22	who…is at the right hand of God	3
	4: 2	no longer by human desires but by the will of God.	3
	4: 6	they might live in the spirit as God	3
	4:10	Like good stewards of the manifold grace of God	3
	4:11	do so as one speaking the very words of God;	3
	4:11	do so with the strength that God supplies	3
	4:11	God may be glorified in all things through Jesus Christ.	3
	4:14	the spirit of glory, which is the Spirit of God,	3
	4:16	but glorify God because you bear this name.	3
	4:17	for judgment to begin with the household of God;	3
	4:17	the end for those who do not obey the gospel of God?	3
	4:19	let those suffering in accordance with God's will	3
	5: 2	tend the flock of God that is in your charge	3
	5: 2	tend…as God would have you do it—	3
	5: 5	"God opposes the proud, but gives grace	3
	5: 6	Humble yourselves…under the mighty hand of God	3
	5:10	the God of all grace, who has called you	3
	5:12	to testify that this is the true grace of God.	3
2Pe	1: 1	the righteousness of our God and Savior Jesus	3
	1: 2	in the knowledge of God and of Jesus our Lord.	3
	1:17	he received honor and glory from God the Father	3
	1:21	and women moved by the Holy Spirit spoke from God.	3
	2: 4	if God did not spare the angels when they sinned	3

	3: 5	by the word of God heavens existed long ago	3
	3:12	and hastening the coming of the day of God	3
1Jn	1: 5	God is light and in him there is no darkness at all.	3
	2: 5	truly in this person the love of God has reached perfection.	3
	2:14	and the word of God abides in you	3
	2:17	but those who do the will of God live forever.	3
	3: 1	should be called children of God; and that is what we are.	3
	3: 2	Beloved, we are God's children now;	3
	3: 8	The Son of God was revealed for this purpose	3
	3: 9	Those who have been born of God do not sin	3
	3: 9	do not sin, because God's seed abides in them;	2
	3: 9	they cannot sin, because they have been born of God.	3
	3:10	The children of God and the children of the devil	3
	3:10	all who do not do what is right are not from God	3
	3:17	How does God's love abide in anyone	3
	3:20	for God is greater than our hearts	3
	3:21	we have boldness before God;	3
	4: 1	test the spirits to see whether they are from God;	3
	4: 2	By this you know the Spirit of God:	3
	4: 2	that Jesus Christ has come in the flesh is from God	3
	4: 3	spirit that does not confess Jesus is not from God.	3
	4: 4	Little children, you are from God	3
	4: 6	We are from God. Whoever knows God listens to us	3
	4: 6	We are from God. Whoever knows God listens to us	3
	4: 6	whoever is not from God does not listen to us.	3
	4: 7	let us love one another, because love is from God;	3
	4: 7	everyone who loves is born of God and knows God.	3
	4: 7	everyone who loves is born of God and knows God.	3
	4: 8	Whoever does not love does not know God	3
	4: 8	for God is love.	3
	4: 9	God's love was revealed among us in this way:	3
	4: 9	God sent his only Son into the world	3
	4:10	not that we loved God but that he loved us	3
	4:11	since God loved us so much, we also ought to love	3
	4:12	No one has ever seen God;	3
	4:12	if we love one another, God lives in us	3
	4:15	God abides in those who confess that Jesus	3
	4:15	who confess that Jesus is the Son of God	3
	4:15	God abides in those…and they abide in God.	3
	4:16	we have known and believe the love that God has for us.	3
	4:16	God is love, and those who abide in love abide in God	3
	4:16	God is love, and those who abide in love abide in God	3
	4:16	and God abides in them.	3
	4:20	Those who say, "I love God," and hate	3
	4:20	cannot love God whom they have not seen.	3
	4:21	those who love God must love their brothers and sisters	3
	5: 1	Everyone who believes…has been born of God	3
	5: 2	By this we know that we love the children of God	3
	5: 2	when we love God and obey his commandments.	3
	5: 3	the love of God is this, that we obey his commandments.	3
	5: 4	for whatever is born of God conquers the world.	3
	5: 5	the one who believes that Jesus is the Son of God?	3
	5: 9	human testimony, the testimony of God is greater;	3
	5: 9	for this is the testimony of God	3
	5:10	Those who believe in the Son of God	3
	5:10	Those who do not believe in God have made him a liar	3
	5:10	the testimony that God has given concerning his Son.	3
	5:11	the testimony: God gave us eternal life	3
	5:12	whoever does not have the Son of God does not have life.	3
	5:13	to you who believe in the name of the Son of God	3
	5:16	you will ask, and God will give life to such a one	1
	5:18	We know that those who are born of God do not sin	3
	5:18	but the one who was born of God protects them	3
	5:19	We know that we are God's children	3
	5:20	we know that the Son of God has come	3
	5:20	He is the true God and eternal life.	3
2Jn	1: 3	from God the Father and from Jesus Christ	3
	1: 9	Everyone who…does not have God;	3
3Jn	1: 6	to send them on…in a manner worthy of God;	3
	1:11	Whoever does good is from God;	3
	1:11	whoever does evil has not seen God	3
Jde	1: 1	who are called, who are beloved in God the Father	3
	1: 4	ungodly, who pervert the grace of our God	3
	1:21	keep yourselves in the love of God;	3
	1:25	to the only God our Savior, through Jesus Christ	3
Rev	1: 1	The revelation of Jesus Christ, which God gave	3
	1: 2	who testified to the word of God	3
	1: 6	a kingdom, priests serving his God and Father	3
	1: 8	"I am the Alpha and the Omega," says the Lord God	3
	1: 9	because of the word of God	3
	2: 7	the tree of life that is in the paradise of God.	3

	2:18	words of the Son of God, who has eyes like a flame	3
	3: 1	the seven spirits of God and the seven stars;	3
	3: 2	not found your works perfect in the sight of my God	3
	3:12	the temple of my God; you will never go out of it.	3
	3:12	I will write on you the name of my God	3
	3:12	and the name of the city of my God	3
	3:12	the new Jerusalem that comes down from my God	3
	3:14	the Amen…the origin of God's creation:	3
	4: 5	torches…which are the seven spirits of God;	3
	4: 8	Lord God the Almighty, who was and is and is to come."	3
	4:11	"You are worthy, our Lord and God, to receive glory	3
	5: 6	seven spirits of God sent out into all the earth.	3
	5: 9	ransomed for God saints from every tribe and language	3
	5:10	to be a kingdom and priests serving our God	3
	6: 9	slaughtered for the word of God and for the testimony	3
	7: 2	another angel…having the seal of the living God	3
	7: 3	until we have marked the servants of our God with a seal	3
	7:10	"Salvation…to our God who is seated on the throne	3
	7:11	they fell on their faces…and worshiped God	3
	7:12	might be to our God forever and ever! Amen."	3
	7:15	For this reason they are before the throne of God	3
	7:17	God will wipe away every tear from their eyes."	3
	8: 2	And I saw the seven angels who stand before God	3
	8: 4	rose…before God from the hand of the angel.	3
	9: 4	who do not have the seal of God on their foreheads.	3
	9:13	the four horns of the golden altar before God	3
	10: 7	the mystery of God will be fulfilled, as he announced	3
	11: 1	the temple of God…and those who worship there	3
	11:11	the breath of life from God entered them	3
	11:13	terrified and gave glory to the God of heaven.	3
	11:16	the twenty-four elders who sit…before God	3
	11:16	elders…fell on their faces and worshiped God	3
	11:17	singing, "We give you thanks, Lord God Almighty	3
	11:19	Then God's temple in heaven was opened	3
	12: 5	her child was snatched away and taken to God	3
	12: 6	wilderness, where she has a place prepared by God	3
	12:10	salvation…power and the kingdom of our God	3
	12:10	who accuses them day and night before our God.	3
	12:17	those who keep the commandments of God	3
	13: 6	to utter blasphemies against God, blaspheming	3
	14: 4	redeemed…as first fruits for God and the Lamb	3
	14: 7	"Fear God and give him glory	3
	14:10	they will also drink the wine of God's wrath	3
	14:12	saints, those who keep the commandments of God	3
	14:19	into the great wine press of the wrath of God.	3
	15: 1	for with them the wrath of God is ended.	3
	15: 2	standing…with harps of God in their hands.	3
	15: 3	they sing the song of Moses, the servant of God	3
	15: 3	amazing are your deeds, Lord God the Almighty!	3
	15: 7	seven golden bowls full of the wrath of God	3
	15: 8	smoke from the glory of God and from his power	3
	16: 1	pour out…the seven bowls of the wrath of God."	3
	16: 7	the altar respond, "Yes, O Lord God, the Almighty	3
	16: 9	but they cursed the name of God	3
	16:11	cursed the God of heaven because of their pains	3
	16:14	for battle on the great day of God the Almighty.	3
	16:19	God remembered great Babylon and gave her	3
	16:21	until they cursed God for the plague of the hail	3
	17:17	For God has put it into their hearts	3
	17:17	until the words of God will be fulfilled.	3
	18: 5	and God has remembered her iniquities.	3
	18: 8	for mighty is the Lord God who judges her."	3
	18:20	For God has given judgment for you against her.	3
	19: 1	Salvation and glory and power to our God	3
	19: 4	living creatures fell down and worshiped God	3
	19: 5	"Praise our God, all you his servants	3
	19: 6	For the Lord our God the Almighty reigns.	3
	19: 9	And he said to me, "These are true words of God."	3
	19:10	Worship God! For the testimony of Jesus	3
	19:13	his name is called The Word of God.	3
	19:15	of the fury of the wrath of God the Almighty.	3
	19:17	"Come, gather for the great supper of God	3
	20: 4	who had been beheaded…for the word of God.	3
	20: 6	but they will be priests of God and of Christ	3
	21: 2	new Jerusalem, coming down out of heaven from God	3
	21: 3	"See, the home of God is among mortals.	3
	21: 3	and God himself will be with them;	3
	21: 7	I will be their God and they will be my children.	3
	21:10	Jerusalem coming down out of heaven from God.	3
	21:11	It has the glory of God and a radiance	3
	21:22	for its temple is the Lord God the Almighty	3

Rev	21:23	for the glory of God is its light	3
	22: 1	flowing from the throne of God and of the Lamb	3
	22: 3	the throne of God and of the Lamb will be in it	3
	22: 5	for the Lord God will be their light	3
	22: 6	the Lord, the God of the spirits of the prophets	3
	22: 9	who keep the words of this book. Worship God!"	3
	22:18	God will add to that person the plagues	3
	22:19	God will take away that person's share in the tree	3

god

1. Contextual: Not in Greek
2. θεός, *theos, 2536*

Jhn	10:34	'I said, you are gods'?	2
	10:35	to whom the word of God came were called 'gods'	2
Act	7:40	'Make gods for us who will lead the way for us;	2
	7:43	the star of your god Rephan	2
	12:22	shouting, "The voice of a god, and not of a mortal!"	2
	14:11	"The gods have come down to us in human form!"	2
	17:23	'To an unknown god.'	2
	19:26	saying that gods made with hands are not gods.	1
	19:26	saying that gods made with hands are not gods.	2
	28: 6	and began to say that he was a god.	2
1Co	8: 5	may be so-called gods in heaven or on earth	2
	8: 5	as in fact there are many gods and many lords—	2
2Co	4: 4	the god of this world has blinded the minds	2
Gal	4: 8	enslaved to beings that by nature are not gods.	2
Php	3:19	Their end is destruction; their god is the belly;	2
2Th	2: 4	every so-called god or object of worship	2

God forbid

1. ἵλεως, *hileōs, 2664*

| Mat | 16:22 | rebuke him, saying, "God forbid it, Lord! | 1 |

without God

1. ἄθεος, *atheos, 117*

| Eph | 2:12 | having no hope and without God in the world. | 1 |

God-fearing

1. φοβέομαι + ὁ + θεός, *phobeomai + ho + theos, 5828 + 3836 + 2536*

| Act | 10:22 | a centurion, an upright and God-fearing man | 1 |

God-hater

1. θεοστυγής, *theostygēs, 2539*

| Rom | 1:30 | slanderers, God-haters, insolent, haughty | 1 |

goddess

1. θεά, *thea, 2516*
2. θεός, *theos, 2536*

| Act | 19:27 | the temple of the great goddess Artemis | 1 |
| | 19:37 | blasphemers of our goddess. | 2 |

godless

1. ἀσεβής, *asebēs, 815*

| 1Ti | 1: 9 | law is laid down…for the godless and sinful | 1 |
| 2Pe | 3: 7 | day of judgment and destruction of the godless. | 1 |

godless person

1. βέβηλος, *bebēlos, 1013*

| Heb | 12:16 | becomes like Esau, an immoral and godless person | 1 |

godliness

1. εὐσέβεια, *eusebeia, 2354*

1Ti	2: 2	peaceable life in all godliness and dignity.	1
	4: 7	Train yourself in godliness	1
	4: 8	godliness is valuable in every way	1
	6: 3	the teaching that is in accordance with godliness	1
	6: 5	imagining that godliness is a means of gain.	1
	6: 6	great gain in godliness combined with contentment;	1
	6:11	pursue righteousness, godliness, faith, love	1
2Ti	3: 5	holding to the outward form of godliness	1
Tit	1: 1	the truth that is in accordance with godliness	1
2Pe	1: 3	everything needed for life and godliness	1
	1: 6	and endurance with godliness	1
	1: 7	and godliness with mutual affection	1
	3:11	in leading lives of holiness and godliness	1

godly *See also* godly *life*

1. εὐσεβής, *eusebēs, 2356*

	2.	εὐσεβῶς, *eusebōs, 2357*
	3.	θεός, *theos, 2536*
	4.	κατά + θεός, *kata + theos, 2848 + 2536*
2Co	1:12	with frankness and godly sincerity	3
	7: 9	you felt a godly grief	4
	7:10	For godly grief produces a repentance	4
	7:11	what earnestness this godly grief has produced	4
Tit	2:12	in the present age to live lives that are self-controlled,	2
2Pe	2: 9	the Lord knows how to rescue the godly from trial	1

Gog

1. Γώγ, *Gōg, 1223*

| Rev | 20: 8 | to deceive the nations…Gog and Magog | 1 |

gold *See also* gold *ring*

1. χρυσίον, *chrysion, 5992*
2. χρυσός, *chrysos, 5996*
3. χρυσοῦς, *chrysous, 5997*

Mat	2:11	they offered him gifts of gold, frankincense,	2
	10: 9	Take no gold, or silver, or copper in your belts	2
	23:16	whoever swears by the gold of the sanctuary	2
	23:17	which is greater, the gold or the sanctuary	2
	23:17	or the sanctuary that has made the gold sacred?	2
Act	3: 6	no silver or gold, but what I have I give you;	1
	17:29	ought not to think that the deity is like gold	2
	20:33	I coveted no one's silver or gold or clothing.	1
1Co	3:12	builds on the foundation with gold, silver	2
1Ti	2: 9	not with their hair braided, or with gold,	1
2Ti	2:20	there are utensils not only of gold and silver	3
Heb	9: 4	the ark…overlaid on all sides with gold	1
Jas	5: 3	Your gold and silver have rusted	2
1Pe	1: 7	faith—being more precious than gold	1
	1:18	with perishable things like silver or gold	1
	3: 3	adorn yourselves outwardly by…wearing gold ornaments	1
Rev	3:18	I counsel you to buy from me gold refined by fire	1
	9: 7	On their heads…what looked like crowns of gold;	2
	9:20	demons and idols of gold and silver and bronze	3
	17: 4	and adorned with gold and jewels and pearls	1
	18:12	cargo of gold, silver, jewels and pearls	2
	18:16	adorned with gold, with jewels, and with pearls!	1
	21:15	angel who talked to me had a measuring rod of gold	3
	21:18	while the city is pure gold, clear as glass.	1
	21:21	and the street of the city is pure gold	1

golden

1. χρυσοῦς, *chrysous, 5997*

Heb	9: 4	In it stood the golden altar of incense	1
	9: 4	in which there were a golden urn holding the manna	1
Rev	1:12	and on turning I saw seven golden lampstands	1
	1:13	and with a golden sash across his chest.	1
	1:20	seven stars…and the seven golden lampstands:	1
	2: 1	who walks among the seven golden lampstands:	1
	4: 4	elders…with golden crowns on their heads.	1
	5: 8	and golden bowls full of incense	1
	8: 3	Another angel with a golden censer came and stood	1
	8: 3	prayers of all the saints on the golden altar	1
	9:13	a voice from the four horns of the golden altar	1
	14:14	the Son of Man, with a golden crown on his head	1
	15: 6	with golden sashes across their chests.	1
	15: 7	seven golden bowls full of the wrath of God	1
	17: 4	holding…a golden cup full of abominations	1

Golgotha

1. Γολγοθᾶ, *Golgotha, 1201*

Mat	27:33	when they came to a place called Golgotha	1
Mrk	15:22	they brought Jesus to the place called Golgotha	1
Jhn	19:17	which in Hebrew is called Golgotha.	1

Gomorrah

1. Γόμορρα, *Gomorra, 1202*

Mat	10:15	for the land of Sodom and Gomorrah	1
Rom	9:29	fared like Sodom and been made like Gomorrah."	1
2Pe	2: 6	turning the cities of Sodom and Gomorrah to ashes	1
Jde	1: 7	Sodom and Gomorrah and the surrounding cities	1

gong

1. χαλκός, *chalkos, 5910*

| 1Co | 13: 1 | I am a noisy gong or a clanging cymbal. | 1 |

good *See also* announce good news, bring good news, do a good deed, do good, good *health*, good *manager* of household, good news *come*, good *order*, good *pleasure*, good *purpose*, good *repute*, good *resolve*, good *seat*, good *standing*, hater of good, make a good showing, proclaim the good news, proclamation of good news, receive the good news, seem good, show good sense, teach what is good, tell the good news

1. Contextual: Not in Greek
2. ἀγαθός, *agathos*, 19
3. ἀγαθωσύνη, *agathōsynē*, 20
4. διαφέρω, *diapherō*, 1422
5. ἰσχύω, *ischyō*, 2710
6. καλός, *kalos*, 2819
7. καλός + μᾶλλον, *kalos + mallon*, 2819 + 3437
8. καλῶς, *kalōs*, 2822
9. κρείττων, *kreittōn*, 3202
10. λυσιτελέω, *lysiteleō*, 3387
11. μᾶλλον, *mallon*, 3437
12. ὄφελος, *ophelos*, 4055
13. πρῶτος, *prōtos*, 4755
14. συμφέρω, *sympherō*, 5237
15. ὑπέρ, *hyper*, 5642
16. ὑπερέχω, *hyperechō*, 5660
17. χρηστός, *chrēstos*, 5982
18. ὠφελέω, *ōpheleō*, 6067

Mat	3:10	tree therefore that does not bear good fruit	6
	5:13	no longer good for anything, but is thrown out	5
	5:16	so that they may see your good works and give glory	6
	5:29	and throw it away; it is better for you to lose	14
	5:30	and throw it away; it is better for you to lose	14
	5:45	he makes his sun rise on the evil and on the good	2
	7:11	know how to give good gifts to your children	2
	7:17	In the same way, every good tree bears good fruit	2
	7:17	In the same way, every good tree bears good fruit	6
	7:18	A good tree cannot bear bad fruit	2
	7:18	nor can a bad tree bear good fruit.	6
	7:19	Every tree that does not bear good fruit is cut	6
	12:12	So it is lawful to do good on the sabbath."	8
	12:33	"Either make the tree good, and its fruit good;	6
	12:33	"Either make the tree good, and its fruit good;	6
	12:35	The good person brings good things out of a good	2
	12:35	brings good things out of a good treasure	2
	13: 8	Other seeds fell on good soil	6
	13:23	as for what was sown on good soil	6
	13:24	someone who sowed good seed in his field;	6
	13:27	'Master, did you not sow good seed in your field?	6
	13:37	"The one who sows the good seed is the Son of Man;	6
	13:38	the good seed are the children of the kingdom;	6
	13:48	sat down, and put the good into baskets	6
	17: 4	"Lord, it is good for us to be here;	6
	18: 6	it would be better for you	14
	18: 8	it is better for you to enter life maimed or lame	6
	18: 9	it is better for you to enter life with one eye	6
	19:10	it is better not to marry."	14
	19:17	"Why do you ask me about what is good?	2
	19:17	There is only one who is good.	2
	22:10	gathered all whom they found, both good and bad;	2
	25: 9	you had better go to the dealers and buy some	11
	25:21	'Well done, good and trustworthy slave;	2
	25:23	'Well done, good and trustworthy slave;	2
	26:10	She has performed a good service for me.	6
	26:24	It would have been better for that one	6
Mrk	3: 4	lawful to do good or to do harm on the sabbath	2
	4: 8	Other seed fell into good soil	6
	4:20	these are the ones sown on the good soil:	6
	5:26	no better, but rather grew worse.	18
	9: 5	"Rabbi, it is good for us to be here;	6
	9:42	it would be better for you	7
	9:43	it is better for you to enter life maimed	6
	9:45	it is better for you to enter life lame	6
	9:47	it is better for you to enter the kingdom of God	6
	9:50	Salt is good;	6
	10:17	"Good Teacher, what must I do	2
	10:18	"Why do you call me good? No one is good but God	2
	10:18	"Why do you call me good? No one is good but God	2
	14: 6	She has performed a good service for me.	6
	14:21	better for that one not to have been born."	6
Lke	3: 9	every tree…that does not bear good fruit	6
	5:39	but says, 'The old is good.' "	17
	6:27	Love your enemies, do good to those who hate you	8
	6:38	good measure, pressed down, shaken together	6
	6:43	"No good tree bears bad fruit	6
	6:43	nor again does a bad tree bear good fruit;	6
	6:45	The good person out of the good treasure	2
	6:45	person out of the good treasure of the heart	2
	6:45	The good person…produces good	2
	8: 8	Some fell into good soil, and when it grew	2
	8:15	as for that in the good soil	6
	8:15	hold it fast in an honest and good heart	2
	9:33	"Master, it is good for us to be here;	6
	10:42	Mary has chosen the better part	2
	11:13	know how to give good gifts to your children	2
	13: 9	If it bears fruit next year, well and good;	1
	14:34	"Salt is good;	6
	15:22	'Quickly, bring out a robe—the best one—	13
	17: 2	It would be better for you	10
	18:18	asked him, "Good Teacher, what must I do	2
	18:19	"Why do you call me good? No one is good but God	2
	18:19	"Why do you call me good? No one is good but God	2
	19:17	He said to him, 'Well done, good slave!	2
	23:50	there was a good and righteous man named Joseph	2
Jhn	1:46	"Can anything good come out of Nazareth?"	2
	2:10	said to him, "Everyone serves the good wine first	6
	2:10	But you have kept the good wine until now."	6
	5:29	who have done good, to the resurrection of life	2
	10:11	"I am the good shepherd.	6
	10:11	The good shepherd lays down his life	6
	10:14	I am the good shepherd.	6
	10:32	shown you many good works from the Father.	6
	10:33	"It is not for a good work that we…stone you	6
	11:50	You do not understand that it is better	14
	18:14	better to have one person die for the people.	14
Act	9:36	She was devoted to good works and acts of charity.	2
	11:24	a good man, full of the Holy Spirit and of faith.	2
Rom	2: 7	who by patiently doing good seek for glory	2
	2:10	and honor and peace for everyone who does good	2
	2:18	know his will and determine what is best	4
	3: 8	"Let us do evil so that good may come"?	2
	4:19	his own body, which was already as good as dead	1
	7:12	and the commandment is holy and just and good.	2
	7:13	Did what is good, then, bring death to me?	2
	7:13	sin, working death in me through what is good	2
	7:16	I agree that the law is good.	6
	7:18	For I know that nothing good dwells within me	2
	7:19	For I do not do the good I want, but the evil	2
	7:21	I want to do what is good, evil lies close at hand.	6
	8:28	work together for good for those who love God	2
	9:11	or had done anything good or bad	2
	10:15	the feet of those who bring good news!"	2
	12: 2	what is good and acceptable and perfect.	2
	12: 9	hate what is evil, hold fast to what is good;	2
	12:21	but overcome evil with good.	2
	13: 3	For rulers are not a terror to good conduct	2
	13: 3	Then do what is good	2
	13: 4	for it is God's servant for your good.	2
	14:16	So do not let your good be spoken of as evil.	2
	14:21	it is good not to eat meat or drink wine	6
	15: 2	must please our neighbor for the good purpose of	2
	16:19	I want you to be wise in what is good	2
1Co	7: 9	it is better to marry than to be aflame with passion.	9
	11:17	it is not for the better but for the worse.	9
	15:33	"Bad company ruins good morals."	17
2Co	5:10	done in the body, whether good or evil.	2
	9: 8	share abundantly in every good work.	2
	11:23	Are they ministers of Christ?…I am a better one:	15
	12: 6	no one may think better of me than what is seen	15
Gal	4: 1	heirs…are no better than slaves,	4
	4:18	It is good to be made much of for a good purpose	6
	6:10	opportunity, let us work for the good of all	2
Eph	2:10	created in Christ Jesus for good works	2
	5: 9	found in all that is good and right and true.	3
	6: 8	knowing that whatever good we do	2
Php	1: 6	that the one who began a good work among you	2
	1:10	to help you to determine what is best	4
	1:23	that is far better;	9
	2: 3	regard others as better than yourselves.	16
Col	1:10	bear fruit in every good work	2
1Th	5:15	always seek to do good to one another and to all.	2

1Th	5:21	test everything; hold fast to what is good;	6
2Th	1:11	fulfill…every good resolve and work of faith	3
	2:16	gave us eternal comfort and good hope	2
	2:17	strengthen them in every good work and word.	2
1Ti	1: 5	that comes from a pure heart, a good conscience	2
	1: 8	Now we know that the law is good	6
	1:18	by following them you may fight the good fight	6
	1:19	having faith and a good conscience.	6
	2:10	with good works, as is proper for women	2
	3:13	gain a good standing for themselves	6
	4: 4	For everything created by God is good	6
	4: 6	you will be a good servant of Christ Jesus	6
	5:10	she must be well attested for her good works	6
	5:10	devoted herself to doing good in every way.	2
	5:25	So also good works are conspicuous;	6
	6:12	Fight the good fight of the faith;	6
	6:12	you made the good confession in the presence	6
	6:13	who…before Pontius Pilate made the good confession	6
	6:18	They are to do good, to be rich in good works	6
	6:19	storing up…the treasure of a good foundation	6
2Ti	1:14	Guard the good treasure entrusted to you	6
	2: 3	like a good soldier of Christ Jesus.	6
	2:21	ready for every good work.	2
	3:17	equipped for every good work	2
	4: 7	I have fought the good fight	6
Tit	1:16	detestable, disobedient, unfit for any good work.	2
	2: 7	in all respects a model of good works	6
	2:14	who are zealous for good deeds.	6
	3: 1	to be obedient, to be ready for every good work	2
	3: 8	may be careful to devote themselves to good works;	6
	3:14	learn to devote themselves to good works	6
Phm	1: 6	perceive all the good that we may do for Christ.	2
Heb	5:14	to distinguish good from evil.	6
	7:19	on the other hand, the introduction of a better hope	9
	7:22	Jesus has also become the guarantee of a better covenant.	9
	8: 6	he is the mediator of a better covenant,	9
	8: 6	which has been enacted through better promises.	9
	9:23	heavenly things…need better sacrifices than these.	9
	10:24	to provoke one another to love and good deeds	6
	10:34	possessed something better and more lasting.	9
	11:12	from one person, and this one as good as dead	1
	11:16	as it is, they desire a better country	9
	11:35	in order to obtain a better resurrection.	9
	11:40	since God had provided something better	9
	12:10	he disciplines us for our good	14
	12:24	that speaks a better word than the blood of Abel.	9
	13:21	make you complete in everything good	2
Jas	2:14	What good is it, my brothers and sisters	12
	2:16	what is the good of that?	12
	3:13	Show by your good life that your works are done	6
	3:17	wisdom…is…full of mercy and good fruits	2
1Pe	2: 3	if indeed you have tasted that the Lord is good.	17
	3:10	"Those who desire life and desire to see good days	2
	3:11	let them turn away from evil and do good;	2
	3:13	if you are eager to do what is good?	2
	3:16	those who abuse you for your good conduct in Christ	2
	3:17	For it is better to suffer for doing good	9
	3:21	but as an appeal to God for a good conscience	2
	4:10	Like good stewards of the manifold grace of God	6
2Pe	2:21	better for them never to have known the way	9
3Jn	1:11	do not imitate what is evil but imitate what is good.	2

any better off

1. προέχω, *proechō, 4604*

Rom	3: 9	What then? Are we any better off? No, not at all;	1

common good

1. συμφέρω, *sympherō, 5237*

1Co	12: 7	To each is given…the Spirit for the common good.	1

good deed

1. ἀγαθός, *agathos, 19*

Mat	19:16	"Teacher, what good deed must I do	1
Phm	1:14	your good deed might be voluntary and not something forced.	1

good man

1. ἀγαθός, *agathos, 19*

Jhn	7:12	While some were saying, "He is a good man,"	1

good news

1. εὐαγγέλιον, *euangelion, 2295*

Mat	4:23	proclaiming the good news of the kingdom and curing	1
	9:35	proclaiming the good news of the kingdom,	1
	24:14	this good news of the kingdom will be proclaimed	1
	26:13	wherever this good news is proclaimed	1
Mrk	1: 1	The beginning of the good news of Jesus Christ	1
	1:14	proclaiming the good news of God	1
	1:15	repent, and believe in the good news."	1
	10:29	for my sake and for the sake of the good news	1
	13:10	good news must first be proclaimed to all nations.	1
	14: 9	the good news is proclaimed in the whole world	1
	16:15	[["Go into all the world and proclaim the good news]]	1
Act	15: 7	the Gentiles would hear the message of the good news	1
	20:24	testify to the good news of God's grace.	1
Rom	10:16	But not all have obeyed the good news;	1
	15:19	I have fully proclaimed the good news of Christ.	1
1Co	15: 1	the good news that I proclaimed to you	1
2Co	10:14	all the way to you with the good news of Christ.	1
	11: 7	I proclaimed God's good news to you free of charge?	1

good person

1. ἀγαθός, *agathos, 19*

Rom	5: 7	perhaps for a good person someone might…die.	1

good thing

1. ἀγαθός, *agathos, 19*
2. καλός, *kalos, 2819*
3. κρείττων, *kreittōn, 3202*

Mat	7:11	in heaven give good things to those who ask	1
	12:34	You brood of vipers! How can you speak good things	1
	12:35	brings good things out of a good treasure	1
Lke	1:53	he has filled the hungry with good things	1
	16:25	during your lifetime you received your good things	1
1Co	5: 6	Your boasting is not a good thing. Do you not know	2
Gal	6: 6	share in all good things with their teacher.	1
Heb	6: 9	beloved, we are confident of better things in your case	3
	9:11	a high priest of the good things that have come	1
	10: 1	a shadow of the good things to come	1

spiritual good

1. πνευματικός, *pneumatikos, 4461*

1Co	9:11	If we have sown spiritual good among you	1

goodness   *See also* lover of goodness

1. ἀγαθωσύνη, *agathōsynē, 20*
2. ἀρετή, *aretē, 746*
3. καλός, *kalos, 2819*
4. χρηστότης, *chrēstotēs, 5983*

Rom	15:14	that you yourselves are full of goodness	1
Tit	3: 4	the goodness and loving kindness of God	4
Heb	6: 5	have tasted the goodness of the word of God	3
2Pe	1: 3	called us by his own glory and goodness.	2
	1: 5	to support your faith with goodness	2
	1: 5	to support…goodness with knowledge	2

goods

1. ἀγαθός, *agathos, 19*
2. βίος, *bios, 1050*
3. ὁ, *ho, 3836*
4. ὕπαρξις, *hyparxis, 5638*

Lke	6:30	anyone takes away your goods	3
	12:18	there I will store all my grain and my goods.	1
	12:19	Soul, you have ample goods laid up for many years;	1
Act	2:45	they would sell their possessions and goods	4
1Jn	3:17	has the world's goods and sees a brother or sister in need	2

goodwill

1. εὐδοκία, *eudokia, 2306*
2. μακαρισμός, *makarismos, 3422*
3. προθυμία, *prothymia, 4608*
4. χάρις, *charis, 5921*

Act	2:47	having the goodwill of all the people.	4
2Co	8:19	glory of the Lord himself and to show our goodwill.	3
Gal	4:15	What has become of the goodwill you felt?	2
Php	1:15	but others from goodwill.	1

gorge

1. χορτάζω, *chortazō, 5963*

Rev 19:21 and all the birds were gorged with their flesh.   1

gospel   *See also* announce the gospel, declare the gospel beforehand, message of the gospel, proclaim the gospel, work of the gospel

1. Contextual: Not in Greek
2. εὐαγγέλιον, *euangelion, 2295*
3. ὅς, *hos, 4005*

Mrk	8:35	lose their life...for the sake of the gospel	2
Rom	1: 1	Paul...set apart for the gospel of God	2
	1: 3	the gospel concerning his Son	1
	1:16	For I am not ashamed of the gospel;	2
	2:16	according to my gospel, God...will judge	2
	11:28	As regards the gospel they are enemies of God	2
	15:16	in the priestly service of the gospel of God	2
	16:25	to strengthen you according to my gospel	2
1Co	4:15	I became your father through the gospel.	2
	9:12	an obstacle in the way of the gospel of Christ.	2
	9:14	those who proclaim the gospel	2
	9:14	get their living by the gospel.	2
	9:18	I may make the gospel free of charge	2
	9:18	make full use of my rights in the gospel.	2
	9:23	I do it all for the sake of the gospel	2
2Co	4: 3	even if our gospel is veiled	2
	4: 4	the light of the gospel of the glory of Christ	2
	9:13	confession of the gospel of Christ	2
	11: 4	a different gospel from the one you accepted	2
Gal	1: 6	turning to a different gospel—	2
	1: 7	not that there is another gospel	1
	1: 7	want to pervert the gospel of Christ.	2
	1:11	the gospel that was proclaimed by me is not of human	2
	2: 2	the gospel that I proclaim among the Gentiles	2
	2: 5	the truth of the gospel might always remain	2
	2: 7	entrusted with the gospel for the uncircumcised	2
	2: 7	entrusted with the gospel for the circumcised	1
	2:14	acting consistently with the truth of the gospel	2
Eph	1:13	the word of truth, the gospel of your salvation	2
	3: 6	sharers in the promise...through the gospel.	2
	3: 7	Of this gospel I have become a servant	3
	6:19	to make known with boldness the mystery of the gospel	2
Php	1: 5	because of your sharing in the gospel	2
	1: 7	in the defense and confirmation of the gospel.	2
	1:12	actually helped to spread the gospel	2
	1:16	put here for the defense of the gospel;	2
	1:27	life in a manner worthy of the gospel of Christ	2
	1:27	striving...with one mind for the faith of the gospel	2
	4:15	know that in the early days of the gospel	2
Col	1: 5	in the word of the truth, the gospel	2
	1:23	without shifting from the hope promised by the gospel	2
	1:23	I, Paul, became a servant of this gospel.	3
1Th	2: 2	to declare to you the gospel of God	2
	2: 8	determined to share with you not only the gospel of God	2
	2: 9	while we proclaimed to you the gospel of God.	2
2Th	1: 8	who do not obey the gospel of our Lord Jesus.	2
1Ti	1:11	that conforms to the glorious gospel	2
2Ti	1: 8	join with me in suffering for the gospel	2
	1:10	brought life...to light through the gospel.	2
	1:11	For this gospel I was appointed a herald	1
	2: 8	descendant of David—that is my gospel	2
Phm	1:13	during my imprisonment for the gospel;	2
1Pe	4:17	the end for those who do not obey the gospel of God?	2
Rev	14: 6	another angel...with an eternal gospel to proclaim	2

gossip

1. φλύαρος, *phlyaros, 5827*
2. ψιθυρισμός, *psithyrismos, 6030*
3. ψιθυριστής, *psithyristēs, 6031*

Rom	1:29	Full of envy, murder...they are gossips	3
2Co	12:20	anger, selfishness, slander, gossip, conceit	2
1Ti	5:13	not merely idle, but also gossips and busybodies	1

govern

1. ὑπερέχω, *hyperechō, 5660*

Rom 13: 1 be subject to the governing authorities;   1

governor   *See also* governor's *headquarters*

1. ἐθνάρχης, *ethnarchēs, 1617*

2. ἡγεμονεύω, *hēgemoneuō, 2448*
3. ἡγεμών, *hēgemōn, 2450*

Mat	10:18	you will be dragged before governors and kings	3
	27: 2	handed him over to Pilate the governor.	3
	27:11	Now Jesus stood before the governor;	3
	27:11	the governor asked him	3
	27:14	so that the governor was greatly amazed.	3
	27:15	the governor was accustomed to release	3
	27:21	The governor again said to them	3
	27:27	Then the soldiers of the governor took Jesus	3
	28:14	If this comes to the governor's ears	3
Mrk	13: 9	stand before governors and kings because of me	3
Lke	2: 2	while Quirinius was governor of Syria.	2
	3: 1	Pontius Pilate was governor of Judea	2
	20:20	jurisdiction and authority of the governor.	3
	21:12	you will be brought before kings and governors	3
Act	23:24	and take him safely to Felix the governor."	3
	23:26	to his Excellency the governor Felix, greetings.	3
	23:33	delivered the letter to the governor	3
	24: 1	reported their case against Paul to the governor.	3
	24:10	When the governor motioned to him to speak	3
	26:30	king got up, and with him the governor and Bernice	3
2Co	11:32	the governor under King Aretas guarded the city	1
1Pe	2:14	or of governors, as sent by him to punish	3

grace

1. Contextual: Not in Greek
2. χάρις, *charis, 5921*

Jhn	1:14	of a father's only son, full of grace and truth.	2
	1:16	we have all received, grace upon grace.	2
	1:16	we have all received, grace upon grace.	2
	1:17	grace and truth came through Jesus Christ.	2
Act	4:33	great grace was upon them all.	2
	6: 8	Stephen, full of grace and power	2
	11:23	When he came and saw the grace of God, he rejoiced	2
	13:43	urged them to continue in the grace of God.	2
	14: 3	who testified to the word of his grace	2
	14:26	where they had been commended to the grace of God	2
	15:11	saved through the grace of the Lord Jesus	2
	15:40	commending him to the grace of the Lord.	2
	18:27	helped those who through grace had become believers	2
	20:24	testify to the good news of God's grace.	2
	20:32	I commend you...to the message of his grace	2
Rom	1: 5	we have received grace and apostleship	2
	1: 7	Grace to you and peace from God our Father	2
	3:24	they are now justified by his grace as a gift	2
	4:16	in order that the promise may rest on grace	2
	5: 2	we have obtained access to this grace	2
	5:15	the grace of God...abounded for the many.	2
	5:15	the free gift in the grace of the one man, Jesus	2
	5:17	those who receive the abundance of grace	2
	5:20	where sin increased, grace abounded all the more	2
	5:21	grace might...exercise dominion through justification	2
	6: 1	continue in sin in order that grace may abound?	2
	6:14	since you are not under law but under grace.	2
	6:15	because we are not under law but under grace?	2
	11: 5	there is a remnant, chosen by grace.	2
	11: 6	if it is by grace, it is no longer on the basis	2
	11: 6	otherwise grace would no longer be grace.	2
	11: 6	otherwise grace would no longer be grace.	2
	12: 3	For by the grace given to me I say to everyone	2
	12: 6	gifts that differ according to the grace given	2
	15:15	because of the grace given me by God	2
	16:20	The grace of our Lord Jesus Christ be with you.	2
1Co	1: 3	Grace to you and peace from God our Father	2
	1: 4	because of the grace of God that has been given you	2
	3:10	According to the grace of God given to me	2
	15:10	by the grace of God I am what I am	2
	15:10	his grace toward me has not been in vain.	2
	15:10	though it was not I, but the grace of God	2
	16:23	The grace of the Lord Jesus be with you.	2
2Co	1: 2	Grace to you and peace from God our Father	2
	1:12	not by earthly wisdom but by the grace of God	2
	4:15	that grace, as it extends to more and more people	2
	6: 1	not to accept the grace of God in vain.	2
	8: 1	the grace of God that has been granted	2
	9:14	the surpassing grace of God that he has given you.	2
	12: 9	he said to me, "My grace is sufficient for you	2
	13:13	The grace of the Lord Jesus Christ	2
Gal	1: 3	Grace to you and peace from God our Father	2

Gal	1: 6	who called you in the grace of Christ	2
	1:15	called me through his grace	2
	2: 9	recognized the grace that had been given to me	2
	2:21	I do not nullify the grace of God;	2
	5: 4	you have fallen away from grace.	2
	6:18	the grace of our Lord Jesus Christ	2
Eph	1: 2	Grace to you and peace from God our Father	2
	1: 6	to the praise of his glorious grace	2
	1: 7	according to the riches of his grace	2
	2: 5	by grace you have been saved	2
	2: 7	might show the immeasurable riches of his grace	2
	2: 8	For by grace you have been saved through faith	2
	3: 2	the commission of God's grace that was given me	2
	3: 7	according to the gift of God's grace	2
	3: 8	this grace was given to me	2
	4: 7	each of us was given grace according	2
	4:29	that your words may give grace to those who hear.	2
	6:24	Grace be with all who have an undying love	2
Php	1: 2	Grace to you and peace from God our Father	2
	1: 7	all of you share in God's grace with me	2
	4:23	The grace of the Lord Jesus Christ be with	2
Col	1: 2	Grace to you and peace from God our Father.	2
	1: 6	heard it and truly comprehended the grace of God.	2
	4:18	Remember my chains. Grace be with you.	2
1Th	1: 1	Grace to you and peace.	2
	5:28	The grace of our Lord Jesus Christ be with you.	2
2Th	1: 2	Grace to you and peace from God our Father	2
	1:12	according to the grace of our God	2
	2:16	through grace gave us eternal comfort and good hope	2
	3:18	The grace of our Lord Jesus Christ be with all of you.	2
1Ti	1: 2	Grace, mercy, and peace from God the Father	2
	1:14	the grace of our Lord overflowed for me	2
	6:21	Grace be with you.	2
2Ti	1: 2	Grace, mercy, and peace from God the Father	2
	1: 9	called us...according to his own purpose and grace	2
	1: 9	This grace was given to us in Christ Jesus	1
	2: 1	be strong in the grace that is in Christ Jesus;	2
	4:22	The Lord be with your spirit. Grace be with you.	2
Tit	1: 4	Grace and peace from God the Father	2
	2:11	For the grace of God has appeared	2
	3: 7	that, having been justified by his grace, we might	2
	3:15	Grace be with all of you.	2
Phm	1: 3	Grace to you and peace from God our Father	2
	1:25	The grace of the Lord Jesus Christ	2
Heb	2: 9	so that by the grace of God he might taste death	2
	4:16	therefore approach the throne of grace with boldness	2
	4:16	so that we may receive mercy and find grace	2
	10:29	outraged the Spirit of grace?	2
	12:15	no one fails to obtain the grace of God;	2
	13: 9	is well for the heart to be strengthened by grace	2
	13:25	Grace be with all of you.	2
Jas	4: 6	But he gives all the more grace; therefore it says	2
	4: 6	"God...gives grace to the humble."	2
1Pe	1: 2	May grace and peace be yours in abundance.	2
	1:10	the prophets who prophesied of the grace	2
	1:13	set all your hope on the grace that Jesus Christ	2
	4:10	Like good stewards of the manifold grace of God	2
	5: 5	"God...gives grace to the humble."	2
	5:10	the God of all grace, who has called you	2
	5:12	to testify that this is the true grace of God.	2
2Pe	1: 2	May grace and peace be yours in abundance	2
	3:18	grow in the grace and knowledge of our Lord	2
2Jn	1: 3	Grace, mercy, and peace will be with us from God	2
Jde	1: 4	ungodly, who pervert the grace of our God	2
Rev	1: 4	Grace to you and peace from him who is and who was	2
	22:21	The grace of the Lord Jesus be with all	2

gracious   *See also* gracious *gift*, gracious *will*

    1. χάρις, *charis, 5921*

Lke	4:22	amazed at the gracious words	1
Col	4: 6	Let your speech always be gracious	1

graciously   *See* grant privilege graciously

graciousness

    1. ἐπιείκεια, *epieikeia, 2116*

Act	24: 4	to hear us briefly with your customary graciousness.	1

graft

    1. ἐγκεντρίζω, *enkentrizō, 1596*

Rom	11:17	a wild olive shoot, were grafted in their place	1

graft in

    1. ἐγκεντρίζω, *enkentrizō, 1596*

Rom	11:19	were broken off so that I might be grafted in."	1
	11:23	even those of Israel...will be grafted in	1
	11:23	for God has the power to graft them in again.	1

graft into

    1. ἐγκεντρίζω, *enkentrizō, 1596*

Rom	11:24	grafted...into a cultivated olive tree	1
	11:24	branches be grafted back into their own olive	1

grain   *See also* head of grain, tread out grain

    1. Contextual: Not in Greek
    2. καρπός, *karpos, 2843*
    3. κόκκος, *kokkos, 3133*
    4. σιτίον, *sition, 4989*
    5. σῖτος, *sitos, 4992*

Mat	13: 8	and brought forth grain	2
	13:26	when the plants came up and bore grain	2
Mrk	4: 7	it yielded no grain.	2
	4: 8	seed fell into good soil and brought forth grain	2
	4:28	then the head, then the full grain in the head.	5
	4:29	when the grain is ripe	2
Lke	12:18	there I will store all my grain and my goods.	5
Jhn	12:24	unless a grain of wheat falls into the earth	3
	12:24	it remains just a single grain;	1
Act	7:12	when Jacob heard that there was grain in Egypt	4
1Co	15:37	perhaps of wheat or of some other grain.	1

grain of sand

    1. ἄμμος, *ammos, 302*

Heb	11:12	the innumerable grains of sand by the seashore."	1

grainfield

    1. σπόριμος, *sporimos, 5077*

Mat	12: 1	At that time Jesus went through the grainfields	1
Mrk	2:23	he was going through the grainfields;	1
Lke	6: 1	while Jesus was going through the grainfields	1

granary

    1. ἀποθήκη, *apothēkē, 630*

Mat	3:12	and will gather his wheat into the granary;	1
Lke	3:17	to gather the wheat into his granary;	1

grandchildren

    1. ἔκγονος, *ekgonos, 1681*

1Ti	5: 4	If a widow has children or grandchildren	1

grandmother

    1. μάμμη, *mammē, 3439*

2Ti	1: 5	lived first in your grandmother Lois	1

grant

    1. γίνομαι, *ginomai, 1181*
    2. δίδωμι, *didōmi, 1443*
    3. δωρέομαι, *dōreomai, 1563*
    4. εἰς, *eis, 1650*
    5. κατατίθημι, *katatithēmi, 2960*
    6. ποιέω, *poieō, 4472*
    7. χαρίζομαι, *charizomai, 5919*

Mat	14: 7	to grant her whatever she might ask.	2
	20:23	this is not mine to grant	2
Mrk	10:37	"Grant us to sit, one at your right hand	2
	10:40	is not mine to grant	2
	15:45	he granted the body to Joseph.	3
Lke	1:73	swore to our ancestor Abraham, to grant us	2
	18: 7	will not God grant justice to his chosen ones	6
	18: 8	he will quickly grant justice to them.	6
	23:24	their demand should be granted.	1
Jhn	5:26	has granted the Son also to have life in himself;	2
	6:65	unless it is granted by the Father."	2
Act	4:29	grant to your servants to speak your word	2
	14: 3	granting signs...to be done through them.	2
	24:27	wanted to grant the Jews a favor	5
	27:24	God has granted safety to all those who are sailing	7
Rom	15: 5	May the God...grant you to live in harmony	2
2Co	1:11	the blessing granted us	4

8: 1 grace…granted to the churches of Macedonia; 2
Gal 3:18 God granted it to Abraham through the promise. 7
Eph 3:16 he may grant that you may be strengthened 2
2Ti 1:16 May the Lord grant mercy 2
    1:18 the Lord grant that he will find mercy from the Lord 2
    2:25 God may perhaps grant that they will repent 2
Rev 19: 8 her it has been granted to be clothed with fine linen 2

grant authority

1. δίδωμι, *didōmi*, 1443

Rev 11: 3 I will grant my two witnesses authority to prophesy 1

grant justice

1. ἐκδικέω, *ekdikeō*, 1688

Lke 18: 3 saying, 'Grant me justice against my opponent.' 1
    18: 5 I will grant her justice 1

grant privilege graciously

1. χαρίζομαι, *charizomai*, 5919

Php 1:29 he has graciously granted you the privilege 1

grape

1. σταφυλή, *staphylē*, 5091

Mat 7:16 Are grapes gathered from thorns 1
Lke 6:44 nor are grapes picked from a bramble bush. 1
Rev 14:18 gather the clusters…for its grapes are ripe." 1

grapevine

1. ἄμπελος, *ampelos*, 306

Jas 3:12 a fig tree…yield olives, or a grapevine figs? 1

grasp *See also* have a firm grasp

1. γινώσκω, *ginōskō*, 1182

Lke 18:34 they did not grasp what was said. 1

grass

1. χόρτος, *chortos*, 5965

Mat 6:30 But if God so clothes the grass of the field 1
    14:19 he ordered the crowds to sit down on the grass. 1
Mrk 6:39 to sit down in groups on the green grass. 1
Lke 12:28 if God so clothes the grass of the field 1
Jhn 6:10 Now there was a great deal of grass in the place; 1
1Pe 1:24 For "All flesh is like grass 1
    1:24 and all its glory like the flower of grass. 1
    1:24 The grass withers, and the flower falls 1
Rev 8: 7 and all green grass was burned up. 1
    9: 4 They were told not to damage the grass of the earth 1

grateful

1. χάρις, *charis*, 5921
2. χάρις + ἔχω, *charis + echō*, 5921 + 2400

1Ti 1:12 I am grateful to Christ Jesus our Lord, 1
2Ti 1: 3 I am grateful to God—whom I worship 2

gratify

1. εἰς, *eis*, 1650
2. τελέω, *teleō*, 5464

Rom 13:14 no provision for the flesh, to gratify its desires. 1
Gal 5:16 do not gratify the desires of the flesh. 2

gratitude

1. εὐχαριστία, *eucharistia*, 2374
2. χάρις, *charis*, 5921

Act 24: 3 We welcome this…with utmost gratitude. 1
Col 3:16 with gratitude in your hearts sing psalms, hymns, 2

grave

1. μνημεῖον, *mnēmeion*, 3646
2. τάφος, *taphos*, 5439

Mat 23:29 decorate the graves of the righteous 1
Lke 11:44 Woe to you! For you are like unmarked graves 1
Jhn 5:28 all who are in their graves will hear his voice 1
Rom 3:13 "Their throats are opened graves; 2

gravity

1. σεμνότης, *semnotēs*, 4949

Tit 2: 7 in your teaching show integrity, gravity 1

---

great *See also* great *anxiety*, great *distance*, great *drop*, great *many*, great *millstone*, great *number*, great *quantity*, great *solemnity*, great *value*, make great

1. Contextual: Not in Greek
2. ἡλίκος, *hēlikos*, 2462
3. ἱκανός, *hikanos*, 2653
4. κράτος, *kratos*, 3197
5. μεγαλύνω, *megalynō*, 3486
6. μέγας, *megas*, 3489
7. μείζων, *meizōn*, 3505
8. ὀνικός, *onikos*, 3948
9. πᾶς, *pas*, 4246
10. περισσότερος, *perissoteros*, 4358
11. περισσοτέρως, *perissoterōs*, 4359
12. πολύς, *polys*, 4498
13. προβαίνω, *probainō*, 4581
14. τοσοῦτος, *tosoutos*, 5537
15. ὑπερβάλλω, *hyperballō*, 5650

Mat 4:16 people who sat in darkness have seen a great light 6
    4:25 And great crowds followed him from Galilee 12
    5:12 your reward is great in heaven, for in the same way they 12
    5:19 will be called great in the kingdom of heaven. 6
    5:35 for it is the city of the great King. 6
    7:27 and it fell—and great was its fall!" 6
    8: 1 great crowds followed him; 12
    8:18 Now when Jesus saw great crowds around him 1
    8:24 A windstorm arose on the sea, so great 6
    11:11 no one has arisen greater than John the Baptist; 7
    11:11 least in the kingdom of heaven is greater than he. 7
    12: 6 something greater than the temple is here. 7
    12:41 see, something greater than Jonah is here! 12
    12:42 see, something greater than Solomon is here! 12
    13: 2 great crowds gathered around him 12
    13:32 when it has grown it is the greatest of shrubs 7
    14:14 When he went ashore, he saw a great crowd; 12
    15:28 Jesus answered her, "Woman, great is your faith! 6
    15:30 Great crowds came to him 12
    16:21 must go to Jerusalem and undergo great suffering 12
    18: 1 "Who is the greatest in the kingdom of heaven?" 7
    18: 4 is the greatest in the kingdom of heaven. 7
    18: 6 a great millstone were fastened around your neck 8
    20:26 whoever wishes to be great among you 6
    22:36 which commandment in the law is the greatest?" 6
    22:38 This is the greatest and first commandment. 6
    23:11 The greatest among you will be your servant. 7
    23:17 which is greater, the gold or the sanctuary 7
    23:19 which is greater, the gift or the altar 7
    24:21 For at that time there will be great suffering 6
    24:24 false prophets will appear and produce great signs 6
    24:30 with power and great glory. 12
    27:60 rolled a great stone to the door of the tomb 6
    28: 2 suddenly there was a great earthquake; 6
    28: 8 with fear and great joy 6
Mrk 3: 7 a great multitude from Galilee followed 12
    3: 8 great numbers from Judea, Jerusalem, Idumea, 12
    4:32 becomes the greatest of all shrubs 7
    4:37 A great windstorm arose 6
    4:41 And they were filled with great awe 6
    5:11 the hillside a great herd of swine was feeding; 6
    5:21 a great crowd gathered around him; 12
    6:34 As he went ashore, he saw a great crowd; 12
    8: 1 In those days when there was again a great crowd 12
    8:31 the Son of Man must undergo great suffering, 12
    9:14 they saw a great crowd around them 12
    9:34 who was the greatest. 7
    10:43 whoever wishes to become great among you 6
    12:31 no other commandment greater than these." 7
    12:40 They will receive the greater condemnation." 10
    13: 2 "Do you see these great buildings? 6
    13:26 coming in clouds' with great power and glory. 12
Lke 1:15 for he will be great in the sight of the Lord. 6
    1:32 He will be great 6
    1:58 the Lord had shown his great mercy to her 5
    2:10 see—I am bringing you good news of great joy 6
    2:36 She was of a great age 13
    5:29 Levi gave a great banquet for him in his house; 6
    6:17 with a great crowd of his disciples 12
    6:17 a great multitude of people from all Judea 12
    6:23 for surely your reward is great in heaven; 12

Lke	6:35	Your reward will be great	12
	6:49	great was the ruin of that house."	6
	7:16	"A great prophet has risen among us!"	6
	7:28	no one is greater than John;	7
	7:28	least in the kingdom of God is greater than he."	7
	7:43	one for whom he canceled the greater debt."	12
	7:47	hence she has shown great love.	12
	8: 4	When a great crowd gathered	12
	8:37	they were seized with great fear.	6
	9:22	"The Son of Man must undergo great suffering,	12
	9:37	a great crowd met him.	12
	9:46	which one of them was the greatest.	7
	9:48	least among all of you is the greatest."	6
	11:31	see, something greater than Solomon is here!	12
	11:32	see, something greater than Jonah is here!	12
	14:16	"Someone gave a great dinner and invited many.	6
	16:26	between you and us a great chasm has been fixed	6
	20:47	They will receive the greater condemnation."	10
	21:11	there will be great earthquakes	6
	21:11	dreadful portents and great signs from heaven.	6
	21:23	will be great distress on the earth	6
	21:27	coming in a cloud' with power and great glory.	12
	22:24	of them was to be regarded as the greatest.	7
	22:26	greatest among you must become like the youngest	7
	22:27	For who is greater,	7
	23:27	A great number of the people followed him	12
	24:52	and returned to Jerusalem with great joy;	6
Jhn	4:12	Are you greater than our ancestor Jacob	7
	5:20	he will show him greater works than these	7
	5:36	I have a testimony greater than John's.	7
	7:37	On the last day of the festival, the great day	6
	8:53	Are you greater than our father Abraham, who died?	7
	10:29	What my Father has given me is greater than all	7
	12: 9	When the great crowd of the Jews learned	12
	12:12	great crowd that had come to the festival heard	12
	13:16	servants are not greater than their master	7
	13:16	nor are messengers greater than the one who sent	7
	14:12	will do greater works than these	7
	14:28	the Father is greater than I.	7
	15:13	No one has greater love than this	7
	15:20	'Servants are not greater than their master.'	7
	19:11	handed me over to you is guilty of a greater sin."	7
Act	2:20	before the coming of the Lord's great and glorious day.	6
	4:33	With great power	6
	4:33	great grace was upon them all.	6
	5: 5	great fear seized all who heard of it.	6
	5:11	great fear seized the whole church	6
	6: 7	a great many of the priests	12
	6: 8	did great wonders and signs among the people.	6
	7:11	there came a famine…and great suffering	6
	8: 8	there was great joy in that city.	12
	8: 9	saying that he was someone great.	6
	8:10	All of them, from the least to the greatest,	6
	8:10	the power of God that is called Great."	6
	8:13	saw the signs and great miracles that took place.	6
	11:21	a great number became believers and turned to the Lord.	12
	14: 1	that a great number…became believers.	12
	15: 3	brought great joy to all the believers.	6
	17: 4	as did a great many of the devout Greeks	12
	19:27	the temple of the great goddess Artemis	6
	19:28	"Great is Artemis of the Ephesians!"	6
	19:34	"Great is Artemis of the Ephesians!"	6
	19:35	the temple keeper of the great Artemis	6
	21:35	the violence of the mob was so great that	1
	21:40	when there was a great hush	12
	22: 6	a great light from heaven suddenly shone about me.	3
	23: 9	Then a great clamor arose	6
	25:23	Agrippa and Bernice came with great pomp	12
	26:22	I stand here, testifying to both small and great	6
Rom	9: 2	great sorrow and unceasing anguish in my heart.	6
1Co	12:23	we clothe with greater honor	10
	12:23	treated with greater respect;	10
	12:24	giving the greater honor to the inferior member	10
	12:31	strive for the greater gifts.	7
	13:13	and the greatest of these is love.	7
	14: 5	One who prophesies is greater than one who speaks	7
2Co	3:10	because of the greater glory;	15
	3:12	we have such a hope, we act with great boldness	12
	6: 4	through endurance, in afflictions	12
	7: 4	boast about you; I have great pride in you;	12
	8:22	because of his great confidence in you.	12

	9:11	enriched in every way for your great generosity	9
Eph	1:19	according to the working of his great power.	4
	2: 4	out of the great love with which he loved us	12
	5:32	This is a great mystery	6
Php	1:14	dare to speak the word with greater boldness	11
1Th	2: 2	in spite of great opposition.	12
	2:17	we longed with great eagerness to see you	11
1Ti	3:13	great boldness in the faith that is in Christ	12
	3:16	the mystery of our religion is great:	6
	6: 6	great gain in godliness combined with contentment;	6
2Ti	4:14	Alexander the coppersmith did me great harm;	12
Tit	2:13	glory of our great God and Savior, Jesus Christ.	6
Heb	2: 1	Therefore we must pay greater attention	11
	4:14	Since, then, we have a great high priest	6
	6:13	because he had no one greater by whom to swear	7
	6:16	Human beings…swear by someone greater than	7
	8:11	from the least of them to the greatest.	6
	9:11	then through the greater and perfect tent	7
	10:21	since we have a great priest over the house of God	6
	10:35	confidence of yours; it brings a great reward.	6
	11:26	greater wealth than the treasures of Egypt	7
	12: 1	surrounded by so great a cloud of witnesses	14
	13:20	our Lord Jesus, the great shepherd of the sheep	6
Jas	3: 1	we…will be judged with greater strictness.	7
	3: 5	the tongue…boasts of great exploits.	6
	3: 5	How great a forest is set ablaze by a small fire!	2
1Pe	1: 3	By his great mercy he has given us a new birth	12
2Pe	2:11	angels, though greater in might and power	7
1Jn	3:20	for God is greater than our hearts	7
	4: 4	greater than the one who is in the world.	7
	5: 9	human testimony, the testimony of God is greater;	7
3Jn	1: 4	I have no greater joy than this	7
Jde	1: 6	kept…for the judgment of the great day.	6
Rev	2:19	that your last works are greater than the first.	12
	2:22	I am throwing into great distress	6
	6: 4	and he was given a great sword.	6
	6:12	I looked, and there came a great earthquake;	6
	6:17	for the great day of their wrath has come	6
	7: 9	a great multitude that no one could count	12
	7:14	they who have come out of the great ordeal;	6
	8: 8	something like a great mountain, burning	6
	8:10	great star fell from heaven, blazing like a torch	6
	9: 2	rose smoke like the smoke of a great furnace	6
	9:14	angels…bound at the great river Euphrates."	6
	10: 3	gave a great shout, like a lion roaring.	6
	11: 8	the great city that is prophetically called	6
	11:13	At that moment there was a great earthquake	6
	11:17	have taken your great power and begun to reign.	6
	11:18	all who fear your name, both small and great	6
	12: 1	A great portent appeared in heaven: a woman	6
	12: 3	great red dragon, with seven heads and ten horns	6
	12: 9	The great dragon was thrown down	6
	12:12	for the devil has come down to you with great wrath	6
	12:14	woman was given the two wings of the great eagle	6
	13: 2	dragon gave it his power…and great authority.	6
	13:13	It performs great signs, even making fire come down	6
	13:16	all, both small and great, both rich and poor	6
	14: 8	"Fallen, fallen is Babylon the great!	6
	14:19	into the great wine press of the wrath of God.	6
	15: 1	another portent in heaven, great and amazing:	6
	15: 3	"Great and amazing are your deeds, Lord God	6
	16:12	angel poured his bowl on the great river Euphrates	6
	16:14	for battle on the great day of God the Almighty.	6
	16:19	The great city was split into three parts	6
	16:19	God remembered great Babylon and gave her	6
	17: 1	I will show you the judgment of the great whore	6
	17: 5	"Babylon the great, mother of whores	6
	17:18	The woman you saw is the great city	6
	18: 1	I saw another angel…having great authority;	6
	18: 2	"Fallen, fallen is Babylon the great!	6
	18:10	alas, the great city, Babylon, the mighty city!	6
	18:16	"Alas, alas, the great city	6
	18:18	"What city was like the great city?"	6
	18:19	"Alas, alas, the great city, where all…grew rich	6
	18:21	angel took up a stone like a great millstone	6
	18:21	such violence Babylon the great city will be thrown down	6
	19: 1	what seemed to be the loud voice of a great multitude	12
	19: 2	judged the great whore who corrupted the earth	6
	19: 5	his servants, and all who fear him, small and great."	6
	19: 6	what seemed to be the voice of a great multitude	12
	19:17	"Come, gather for the great supper of God	6

19:18	flesh of all…both small and great."	6
20: 1	the key to the bottomless pit and a great chain.	6
20:11	I saw a great white throne and the one who sat on it;	6
20:12	dead, great and small, standing before the throne	6
21:10	he carried me away to a great, high mountain	6
21:12	It has a great, high wall with twelve gates	6

far greater

1. περισσοτέρως, *perissoterōs, 4359*

2Co 11:23	with far greater labors, far more imprisonments	1

great deal

1. πολύς, *polys, 4498*

Mat 27:19	for today I have suffered a great deal	1
Jhn 6:10	Now there was a great deal of grass in the place;	1
Act 16:16	brought her owners a great deal of money	1

great one

1. μέγας, *megas, 3489*

Mat 20:25	their great ones are tyrants over them.	1
Mrk 10:42	their great ones are tyrants over them.	1

great thing

1. μέγας, *megas, 3489*
2. μείζων, *meizōn, 3505*

Lke 1:49	for the Mighty One has done great things for me	1
Jhn 1:50	You will see greater things than these."	2

how great

1. πηλίκος, *pēlikos, 4383*
2. πόσος, *posos, 4531*
3. τίς, *tis, 5515*

Mat 6:23	you is darkness, how great is the darkness!	2
Col 1:27	how great…are the riches…of this mystery	3
Heb 7: 4	See how great he is!	1

so great

1. τηλικοῦτος, *tēlikoutos, 5496*
2. τοσοῦτος, *tosoutos, 5537*

Mat 15:33	enough bread…to feed so great a crowd?"	2
Heb 2: 3	if we neglect so great a salvation?	1

very great

1. μέγιστος, *megistos, 3492*

2Pe 1: 4	his precious and very great promises	1

greater and greater iniquity

1. ἀνομία + εἰς + ἀνομία, *anomia + eis + anomia, 490 + 1650 + 490*

Rom 6:19	to impurity and to greater and greater iniquity	1

greatly *See also* distress greatly, disturb greatly, please greatly, puzzle greatly, rejoice greatly

1. εἰς + περισσεία, *eis + perisseia, 1650 + 4353*
2. λίαν, *lian, 3336*
3. μεγάλως, *megalōs, 3487*
4. μέγας, *megas, 3489*
5. περισσῶς, *perissōs, 4360*
6. πολύς, *polys, 4498*
7. σφόδρα, *sphodra, 5379*

Mat 17:23	And they were greatly distressed.	7
18:31	they were greatly distressed	7
19:25	they were greatly astounded and said	7
26:22	became greatly distressed and began to say	7
27:14	so that the governor was greatly amazed.	2
Mrk 6:20	When he heard him, he was greatly perplexed;	6
10:26	They were greatly astounded and said	5
Act 6: 7	the number of the disciples increased greatly	7
18:27	greatly helped those who…had become believers	6
2Co 10:15	our sphere of action among you may be greatly enlarged	1
Php 4:10	I rejoice in the Lord greatly	3
Rev 17: 6	When I saw her, I was greatly amazed.	4

greatness

1. μεγαλειότης, *megaleiotēs, 3484*
2. μέγεθος, *megethos, 3490*

Lke 9:43	all were astounded at the greatness of God.	1
Eph 1:19	what is the immeasurable greatness of his power	2

Greece

1. Ἑλλάς, *Hellas, 1817*

Act 20: 2	he came to Greece	1

greed

1. ἁρπαγή, *harpagē, 771*
2. πλεονεξία, *pleonexia, 4432*

Mat 23:25	inside they are full of greed and self-indulgence.	1
Lke 11:39	inside you are full of greed and wickedness.	1
12:15	Be on your guard against all kinds of greed;	2
Eph 5: 3	fornication and impurity of any kind, or greed	2
Col 3: 5	evil desire, and greed (which is idolatry).	2
1Th 2: 5	we never came…with a pretext for greed;	2
2Pe 2: 3	And in their greed they will exploit you	2
2:14	They have hearts trained in greed.	2

greedy

1. πλεονέκτης, *pleonektēs, 4431*
2. πλεονεξία, *pleonexia, 4432*

1Co 5:10	the greedy and robbers, or idolaters	1
5:11	who is sexually immoral or greedy	1
6:10	thieves, the greedy, drunkards	1
Eph 4:19	greedy to practice every kind of impurity.	2
5: 5	one who is greedy (that is, an idolater)	1

greedy for gain

1. αἰσχροκερδής, *aischrokerdēs, 153*

Tit 1: 7	addicted to wine or violent or greedy for gain;	1

greedy for money

1. αἰσχροκερδής, *aischrokerdēs, 153*

1Ti 3: 8	not indulging in much wine, not greedy for money;	1

Greek

1. Ἕλλην, *Hellēn, 1818*
2. Ἑλληνικός, *Hellēnikos, 1819*
3. Ἑλληνίς, *Hellēnis, 1820*
4. Ἑλληνιστί, *Hellēnisti, 1822*

Jhn 7:35	to go to the Dispersion among the Greeks	1
7:35	Does he intend to…teach the Greeks?	1
12:20	among those who went up…were some Greeks.	1
19:20	it was written in Hebrew, in Latin, and in Greek.	4
Act 14: 1	a great number of both Jews and Greeks	1
16: 1	his father was a Greek.	1
16: 3	for they all knew that his father was a Greek.	1
17: 4	as did a great many of the devout Greeks	1
17:12	not a few Greek women and men of high standing.	3
18: 4	to convince Jews and Greeks.	1
19:10	both Jews and Greeks, heard the word	1
19:17	all residents of Ephesus, both Jews and Greeks	1
20:21	testified to both Jews and Greeks	1
21:28	he has actually brought Greeks into the temple	1
21:37	The tribune replied, "Do you know Greek?	4
Rom 1:14	debtor both to Greeks and to barbarians	1
1:16	to the Jew first and also to the Greek.	1
2: 9	the Jew first and also the Greek	1
2:10	the Jew first and also the Greek.	1
3: 9	all, both Jews and Greeks, are under…sin	1
10:12	there is no distinction between Jew and Greek;	1
1Co 1:22	For Jews demand signs and Greeks desire wisdom	1
1:24	to those who are the called, both Jews and Greeks	1
10:32	to Jews or to Greeks or to the church of God	1
12:13	Jews or Greeks, slaves or free	1
Gal 2: 3	though he was a Greek.	1
3:28	There is no longer Jew or Greek	1
Col 3:11	In that renewal there is no longer Greek and Jew	1
Rev 9:11	and in Greek he is called Apollyon.	2

in Greek

1. διερμηνεύω, *diermēneuō, 1450*

Act 9:36	whose name was Tabitha, which in Greek is Dorcas.	1

green *See also* green *growth*, pale green

1. ὑγρός, *hygros, 5619*
2. χλωρός, *chlōros, 5952*

Mrk 6:39	to sit down in groups on the green grass.	2
Lke 23:31	if they do this when the wood is green	1
Rev 8: 7	and all green grass was burned up.	2

greet

1. Contextual: Not in Greek
2. ἀσπάζομαι, *aspazomai, 832*

Mat 5:47 And if you greet only your brothers and sisters   2
     10:12 As you enter the house, greet it.   2
Mrk 9:15 with awe, and they ran forward to greet him.   2
Lke 1:40 entered the house…and greeted Elizabeth.   2
     10: 4 greet no one on the road.   2
Act 18:22 he went up to Jerusalem and greeted the church   2
     21: 7 we greeted the believers   2
     21:19 After greeting them   2
Rom 16: 3 Greet Prisca and Aquila, who work with me   2
     16: 5 Greet also the church in their house.   1
     16: 5 Greet my beloved Epaenetus   2
     16: 6 Greet Mary, who has worked very hard among you.   2
     16: 7 Greet Andronicus and Junia, my relatives   2
     16: 8 Greet Ampliatus, my beloved in the Lord.   2
     16: 9 Greet Urbanus, our co-worker in Christ   2
     16:10 Greet Apelles, who is approved in Christ.   2
     16:10 Greet those who belong to…Aristobulus.   2
     16:11 Greet my relative Herodion.   2
     16:11 Greet those in the Lord who belong to the family   2
     16:12 Greet those workers in the Lord   2
     16:12 Greet the beloved Persis, who has worked hard   2
     16:13 Greet Rufus, chosen in the Lord;   2
     16:13 Greet Rufus…and greet his mother   1
     16:14 Greet Asyncritus, Phlegon, Hermes, Patrobas   2
     16:15 Greet Philologus, Julia, Nereus and his sister   2
     16:16 Greet one another with a holy kiss.   2
     16:16 All the churches of Christ greet you.   2
     16:21 Timothy, my co-worker, greets you;   2
     16:22 I Tertius…greet you in the Lord.   2
     16:23 Gaius, who is host to me…greets you.   2
     16:23 Erastus…and our brother Quartus, greet you.   2
1Co 16:19 greet you warmly in the Lord.   2
     16:20 Greet one another with a holy kiss.   2
2Co 13:12 Greet one another with a holy kiss.   2
     13:12 All the saints greet you.   2
Php 4:21 Greet every saint in Christ Jesus.   2
     4:21 The friends who are with me greet you.   2
     4:22 All the saints greet you   2
Col 4:10 Aristarchus my fellow prisoner greets you   2
     4:11 Jesus who is called Justus greets you   1
     4:12 Epaphras, who is one of you…greets you.   2
     4:14 Luke, the beloved physician, and Demas greet you.   2
1Th 5:26 Greet all the brothers and sisters with a holy kiss.   2
2Ti 4:19 Greet Prisca and Aquila   2
Tit 3:15 Greet those who love us in the faith.   2
Heb 11:13 from a distance they saw and greeted them.   2
     13:24 Greet all your leaders and all the saints.   2
1Pe 5:14 Greet one another with a kiss of love.   2
3Jn 1:15 Greet the friends there, each by name.   2

greet with respect

1. ἀσπασμός, *aspasmos, 833*

Mat 23: 7 greeted with respect in the marketplaces   1
Mrk 12:38 to be greeted with respect in the marketplaces   1
Lke 11:43 to be greeted with respect in the marketplaces.   1
     20:46 love to be greeted with respect in the marketplaces   1

greeting   *See also* give greetings, send greetings

1. ἀσπασμός, *aspasmos, 833*
2. χαίρω, *chairō, 5897*

Mat 26:49 he came up to Jesus and said, "Greetings, Rabbi!"   2
     28: 9 Suddenly Jesus met them and said, "Greetings!"   2
Lke 1:28 he came to her and said, "Greetings, favored one!   2
     1:29 pondered what sort of greeting this might be.   1
     1:41 When Elizabeth heard Mary's greeting, the child   1
     1:44 as soon as I heard the sound of your greeting   1
Act 15:23 to the believers…greetings.   2
     23:26 to his Excellency the governor Felix, greetings.   2
1Co 16:21 I, Paul, write this greeting with my own hand.   1
Col 4:18 I, Paul, write this greeting with my own hand.   1
2Th 3:17 I, Paul, write this greeting with my own hand.   1
Jas 1: 1 To the twelve tribes…Greetings.   2

grief

1. λυπέω, *lypeō, 3382*
2. λύπη, *lypē, 3383*
3. πένθος, *penthos, 4292*

Lke 22:45 found them sleeping because of grief   2
2Co 7: 9 because your grief led to repentance;   1
     7: 9 you felt a godly grief   1
     7:10 For godly grief produces a repentance   2
     7:10 worldly grief produces death.   2
     7:11 what earnestness this godly grief has produced   1
Rev 18: 7 give her a like measure of torment and grief.   3
     18: 7 I am no widow, and I will never see grief,'   3

grievance

1. πρᾶγμα, *pragma, 4547*

1Co 6: 1 When any of you has a grievance against another   1

grieve

1. λυπέω, *lypeō, 3382*
2. ὀδυνάω, *odynaō, 3849*
3. συλλυπέω, *syllypeō, 5200*

Mat 14: 9 The king was grieved   1
     19:22 he went away grieving   1
     26:37 and began to be grieved and agitated.   1
Mrk 3: 5 grieved at their hardness of heart   3
     10:22 he was shocked and went away grieving   1
Act 20:38 grieving especially because of what he had said   2
2Co 7: 8 I see that I grieved you with that letter   1
     7: 9 Now I rejoice, not because you were grieved   1
Eph 4:30 do not grieve the Holy Spirit of God   1
1Th 4:13 so that you may not grieve as others do   1

grieve deeply

1. περίλυπος, *perilypos, 4337*

Mat 26:38 "I am deeply grieved, even to death;   1
Mrk 6:26 The king was deeply grieved;   1
     14:34 "I am deeply grieved, even to death;   1

grind

1. βρύχω, *brychō, 1107*
2. τρίζω, *trizō, 5563*

Mrk 9:18 he foams and grinds his teeth and becomes rigid;   2
Act 7:54 ground their teeth at Stephen.   1

grind meal

1. ἀλήθω, *alēthō, 241*
2. ἀλήθω + ἐν + ὁ + μύλος, *alēthō + en + ho + mylos, 241 + 1877 + 3836 + 3685*

Mat 24:41 Two women will be grinding meal together;   2
Lke 17:35 There will be two women grinding meal together;   1

groan

1. στεναγμός, *stenagmos, 5099*
2. στενάζω, *stenazō, 5100*
3. συστενάζω, *systenazō, 5367*

Act 7:34 heard their groaning   1
Rom 8:22 the whole creation has been groaning in labor pains   3
     8:23 groan inwardly while we wait for adoption   2
2Co 5: 2 For in this tent we groan   2
     5: 4 we groan under our burden   2

grope for

1. ζητέω, *zēteō, 2426*
2. ψηλαφάω, *psēlaphaō, 6027*

Act 13:11 groping for someone to lead him by the hand.   1
     17:27 and perhaps grope for him and find him   2

ground[1]   *See also* bow to the ground, crush to the ground, dash to the ground, plot of ground, throw oneself on the ground

1. Contextual: Not in Greek
2. γῆ, *gē, 1178*
3. ἔδαφος, *edaphos, 1611*
4. χαμαί, *chamai, 5912*

Mat 10:29 Yet not one of them will fall to the ground   2
     15:35 ordering the crowd to sit down on the ground   2
     25:18 dug a hole in the ground and hid his master's money.   2
     25:25 I went and hid your talent in the ground.   2
Mrk 4:26 as if someone would scatter seed on the ground   2
     4:31 when sown upon the ground, is the smallest   2
     8: 6 he ordered the crowd to sit down on the ground;   2
     9:20 he fell on the ground and rolled about   2
     14:35 a little farther, he threw himself on the ground   2

Lke   6:49 a house on the ground without a foundation.   2
      22:44 ⟦great drops of blood falling down on the ground.⟧   2
      24: 5 bowed their faces to the ground   2
Jhn   8: 6 ⟦Jesus…wrote with his finger on the ground.⟧   2
      8: 8 ⟦and wrote on the ground.⟧   2
      9: 6 When he had said this, he spat on the ground   4
      18: 6 they stepped back and fell to the ground.   4
Act   7:33 the place where you are standing is holy ground.   2
      9: 4 He fell to the ground and heard a voice saying   2
      9: 8 Saul got up from the ground   2
      10:11 being lowered to the ground by its four corners.   2
      20: 9 he fell to the ground three floors below   1
      22: 7 I fell to the ground and heard a voice saying   3
      26:14 When we had all fallen to the ground   2
Heb   6: 7 Ground that drinks up the rain…falling   2
      11:38 in caves and holes in the ground.   2

ground²

1. διά, *dia, 1328*
2. ἐκ, *ek, 1666*
3. θεμελιόω, *themelioō, 2530*
4. λόγος, *logos, 3364*
5. ὅτι, *hoti, 4022*

Mat   5:32 his wife, except on the ground of unchastity   4
Rom   3:30 the circumcised on the ground of faith   2
1Co 10:25 without…question on the ground of conscience   1
      10:27 without…question on the ground of conscience.   1
Eph   3:17 being rooted and grounded in love.   3
1Ti   6: 2 on the ground that they are members of the church;   5

ground for boasting

1. καύχημα, *kauchēma, 3017*

1Co   9:15 no one will deprive me of my ground for boasting   1
      9:16 this gives me no ground for boasting   1

ground for sentence

1. αἴτιος, *aitios, 165*

Lke 23:22 in him no ground for the sentence of death;   1

rocky ground

1. πετρώδης, *petrōdēs, 4378*

Mat 13: 5 Other seeds fell on rocky ground   1
      13:20 As for what was sown on rocky ground   1
Mrk   4: 5 Other seed fell on rocky ground   1
      4:16 the ones sown on rocky ground: 1

to the ground

1. ἐπί + πρόσωπον, *epi + prosōpon, 2093 + 4725*

Mat 17: 6 they fell to the ground   1

group

1. Contextual: Not in Greek
2. αὐτός, *autos, 899*
3. κλισία, *klisia, 3112*
4. μέρος, *meros, 3538*
5. πρασιά + πρασιά, *prasia + prasia, 4555 + 4555*
6. συμπόσιον + συμπόσιον, *symposion + symposion, 5235 + 5235*

Mrk   6:39 sit down in groups on the green grass.   6
      6:40 So they sat down in groups   5
Lke   9:14 sit down in groups of about fifty each."   3
      24:22 Moreover, some women of our group astounded us.   1
Act 20:30 Some even from your own group will come   2
      23: 9 certain scribes of the Pharisees' group   4
Eph   2:14 in his flesh he has made both groups into one   1
      2:16 might reconcile both groups to God in one body   1

group of travelers

1. συνοδία, *synodia, 5322*

Lke   2:44 Assuming that he was in the group of travelers   1

whole group

1. πλῆθος, *plēthos, 4436*

Act   4:32 whole group of those who believed were of one heart   1

grow See also grow *cold*, grow *dull*, grow *old*, grow *rich*, grow *short*, grow *strong*, grow *weary*

1. αὐξάνω, *auxanō, 889*
2. γίνομαι, *ginomai, 1181*

3. εἰμί, *eimi, 1639*
4. ἔρχομαι, *erchomai, 2262*
5. μηκύνω, *mēkynō, 3602*
6. φύω, *phyō, 5886*

Mat   6:28 how they grow; they neither toil nor spin   1
      13:32 when it has grown it is the greatest of shrubs   1
Mrk   4:27 the seed would sprout and grow   5
      5:26 no better, but rather grew worse.   4
      6:35 When it grew late, his disciples came to him   2
Lke   1:80 The child grew and became strong in spirit   1
      2:40 The child grew and became strong   1
      8: 8 Some fell into good soil, and when it grew   6
      12:27 Consider the lilies, how they grow: 1
      13:19 it grew and became a tree   1
Jhn   3: 4 "How can anyone be born after having grown old?   3
Act 19:20 word of the Lord grew mightily and prevailed.   1
Eph   2:21 grows into a holy temple in the Lord;   1
Col   1: 6 bearing fruit and growing in the whole world   1
      1:10 grow in the knowledge of God.   1
      2:19 grows with a growth that is from God.   1
Heb 11:24 Moses, when he was grown up   2
1Pe   2: 2 so that by it you may grow into salvation   1
2Pe   3:18 grow in the grace and knowledge of our Lord   1

grow abundantly

1. ὑπεραυξάνω, *hyperauxanō, 5647*

2Th   1: 3 because your faith is growing abundantly   1

grow fully

1. ἀποτελέω, *apoteleō, 699*

Jas   1:15 sin, when it is fully grown, gives birth to death.   1

grow together

1. συναυξάνω, *synauxanō, 5277*

Mat 13:30 Let both of them grow together until the harvest;   1

grow up

1. ἀναβαίνω, *anabainō, 326*
2. αὐξάνω, *auxanō, 889*
3. φύω, *phyō, 5886*

Mat 13: 7 and the thorns grew up and choked them.   1
Mrk   4: 7 the thorns grew up and choked it   1
      4: 8 brought forth grain, growing up and increasing   1
      4:32 yet when it is sown it grows up   1
Lke   8: 6 as it grew up, it withered   3
Eph   4:15 grow up in every way into him who is the head   2

grow with

1. συμφύω, *symphyō, 5243*

Lke   8: 7 and the thorns grew with it and choked it.   1

growth See also give growth

1. αὔξησις, *auxēsis, 890*

Eph   4:16 promotes the body's growth in building itself up   1
Col   2:19 grows with a growth that is from God.   1

green growth

1. χλωρός, *chlōros, 5952*

Rev   9: 4 not to damage…any green growth or any tree   1

rank growth

1. περισσεία, *perisseia, 4353*

Jas   1:21 all sordidness and rank growth of wickedness   1

grudge

1. ἐνέχω, *enechō, 1923*

Mrk   6:19 Herodias had a grudge against him   1

grumble

1. γογγύζω, *gongyzō, 1197*
2. διαγογγύζω, *diagongyzō, 1339*
3. στενάζω, *stenazō, 5100*

Mat 20:11 they grumbled against the landowner   1
Lke 15: 2 the Pharisees and the scribes were grumbling   2
      19: 7 All who saw it began to grumble and said,   2
Jas   5: 9 Beloved, do not grumble against one another   3

grumbler

1. γογγυστής, *gongystēs, 1199*

Jde 1:16 These are grumblers and malcontents;   1

guarantee

1. ἀρραβών, *arrabōn, 775*
2. βέβαιος, *bebaios, 1010*
3. ἔγγυος, *engyos, 1583*
4. μεσιτεύω, *mesiteuō, 3541*

Rom 4:16 and be guaranteed to all his descendants   2
2Co 5: 5 who has given us the Spirit as a guarantee.   1
Heb 6:17 he guaranteed it by an oath   4
   7:22 Jesus has also become the guarantee of a better covenant.   3

guard *See also* imperial guard, keep under guard, soldier of the guard, woman who guards the gate

1. κουστωδία, *koustōdia, 3184*
2. στράτευμα, *strateuma, 5128*
3. συγκλείω, *synkleiō, 5168*
4. τηρέω, *tēreō, 5498*
5. ὑπηρέτης, *hypēretēs, 5677*
6. φρουρέω, *phroureō, 5864*
7. φυλακή, *phylakē, 5871*
8. φύλαξ, *phylax, 5874*
9. φυλάσσω, *phylassō, 5875*

Mat 5:25 to the guard, and you will be thrown into prison.   5
   26:58 with the guards in order to see how this would end.   5
   27:66 they went with the guard and made the tomb secure   1
   28: 4 For fear of him the guards shook   4
   28:11 some of the guard went into the city   1
Mrk 14:54 he was sitting with the guards   5
   14:65 The guards also took him over and beat him.   5
Lke 11:21 a strong man, fully armed, guards his castle   9
Jhn 17:12 I guarded them, and not one of them was lost   9
Act 5:23 the guards standing at the doors   8
   12: 4 four squads of soldiers to guard him   9
   12: 6 guards...were keeping watch over the prison.   8
   12:10 they had passed the first and the second guard   7
   12:19 he examined the guards   8
   21:24 you yourself observe and guard the law.   9
   23:27 I came with the guard and rescued him.   2
   28:16 with the soldier who was guarding him.   9
2Co 11:32 the governor under King Aretas guarded the city   6
Gal 3:23 guarded under the law until faith   3
Php 4: 7 guard your hearts and your minds in Christ Jesus.   6
2Th 3: 3 he will strengthen you and guard you from the evil   9
1Ti 6:20 Timothy, guard what has been entrusted to you.   9
2Ti 1:12 I am sure that he is able to guard until that day   9
   1:14 Guard the good treasure entrusted to you   9

guard of soldiers

1. κουστωδία, *koustōdia, 3184*

Mat 27:65 said to them, "You have a guard of soldiers;   1

on guard

1. βλέπω, *blepō, 1063*
2. προσέχω, *prosechō, 4668*
3. φυλάσσω, *phylassō, 5875*

Lke 12:15 Be on your guard against all kinds of greed;   3
   17: 3 Be on your guard! If another disciple sins,   2
   21:34 "Be on guard   2
2Jn 1: 8 Be on your guard,   1

under guard

1. ἀσφαλῶς, *asphalōs, 857*

Mrk 14:44 arrest him and lead him away under guard."   1

guardian

1. ἐπίσκοπος, *episkopos, 2176*
2. ἐπίτροπος, *epitropos, 2208*
3. παιδαγωγός, *paidagōgos, 4080*

1Co 4:15 you might have ten thousand guardians in Christ   3
Gal 4: 2 they remain under guardians and trustees   2
1Pe 2:25 the shepherd and guardian of your souls.   1

guest *See also* entertain as a guest, guest *room*

1. Contextual: Not in Greek
2. ἀνάκειμαι, *anakeimai, 367*

3. καλέω, *kaleō, 2813*
4. καταλύω, *katalyō, 2907*
5. συνανάκειμαι, *synanakeimai, 5263*
6. υἱός, *huios, 5626*

Mat 9:15 Jesus said to them, "The wedding guests cannot mourn   6
   14: 9 out of regard for his oaths and for the guests   5
   22:10 so the wedding hall was filled with guests.   2
   22:11 "But when the king came in to see the guests   2
Mrk 2:19 wedding guests cannot fast while the bridegroom   6
   6:22 she pleased Herod and his guests;   5
   6:26 yet out of regard for his oaths and for the guests   2
Lke 5:34 "You cannot make wedding guests fast   6
   14: 7 he noticed how the guests chose the places of honor   3
   19: 7 to be the guest of one who is a sinner."   4
Jhn 2:10 inferior wine after the guests have become drunk.   1

dinner guest

1. συνανάκειμαι, *synanakeimai, 5263*

Lke 14:15 One of the dinner guests, on hearing this,   1

guide

1. ἐν, *en, 1877*
2. κατευθύνω, *kateuthynō, 2985*
3. μετάγω, *metagō, 3555*
4. ὁδηγέω, *hodēgeō, 3842*
5. ὁδηγός, *hodēgos, 3843*
6. στοιχέω, *stoicheō, 5123*

Mat 15:14 they are blind guides of the blind   5
   15:14 if one blind person guides another, both will fall   4
   23:16 "Woe to you, blind guides, who say   5
   23:24 You blind guides! You strain out a gnat   5
Lke 1:79 to guide our feet into the way of peace."   2
   2:27 Guided by the Spirit, Simeon came into the temple;   1
   6:39 "Can a blind person guide a blind person?   4
Jhn 16:13 he will guide you into all the truth;   4
Act 1:16 Judas, who became a guide for those who arrested Jesus   5
   8:31 He replied, "How can I, unless someone guides me?"   4
Rom 2:19 if you are sure that you are a guide to the blind   5
Gal 5:25 let us also be guided by the Spirit.   6
Jas 3: 3 we guide their whole bodies.   3
   3: 4 they are guided by a very small rudder   3
Rev 7:17 he will guide them to springs of the water of life   4

guile

1. δόλος, *dolos, 1515*

1Pe 2: 1 Rid yourselves...of all malice, and all guile   1

guileless

1. ἀκέραιος, *akeraios, 193*

Rom 16:19 and guileless in what is evil.   1

guiltless

1. ἁγνός, *hagnos, 54*
2. ἀναίτιος, *anaitios, 360*

Mat 12: 5 break the sabbath and yet are guiltless?   2
   12: 7 you would not have condemned the guiltless.   2
2Co 7:11 proved yourselves guiltless in the matter.   1

guilty

1. αἴτιος, *aitios, 165*
2. ἔνοχος, *enochos, 1944*
3. ἔχω, *echō, 2400*
4. ποιέω, *poieō, 4472*

Mrk 3:29 but is guilty of an eternal sin"   2
Lke 23:14 guilty of any of your charges against him.   1
Jhn 19:11 handed me over to you is guilty of a greater sin."   3
1Jn 3: 4 Everyone who commits sin is guilty of lawlessness;   4

gush out

1. ἐκχέω, *ekcheō, 1772*

Act 1:18 all his bowels gushed out.   1

gush up

1. ἅλλομαι, *hallomai, 256*

Jhn 4:14 a spring of water gushing up to eternal life."   1

H

habit
1. ἔθος, *ethos, 1621*
Heb 10:25 as is the habit of some   1

Hades
1. ᾅδης, *hadēs, 87*
Mat 11:23 No, you will be brought down to Hades.   1
   16:18 gates of Hades will not prevail against it.   1
Lke 10:15 No, you will be brought down to Hades.   1
   16:23 In Hades, where he was being tormented,   1
Act 2:27 you will not abandon my soul to Hades   1
    2:31 'He was not abandoned to Hades   1
Rev 1:18 and I have the keys of Death and of Hades.   1
    6: 8 Its rider's name was Death, and Hades followed   1
   20:13 Death and Hades gave up the dead that were in them   1
   20:14 Death and Hades were thrown into the lake of fire.   1

Hagar
1. Ἀγάρ, *Hagar, 29*
Gal 4:24 Hagar, from Mount Sinai, bearing children for slavery.   1
    4:25 Now Hagar is Mount Sinai in Arabia   1

hail[1]
1. χάλαζα, *chalaza, 5898*
Rev 8: 7 there came hail and fire, mixed with blood   1
   11:19 peals of thunder, an earthquake, and heavy hail.   1
   16:21 until they cursed God for the plague of the hail   1

hail[2]
1. χαίρω, *chairō, 5897*
Mat 27:29 mocked him, saying, "Hail, King of the Jews!"   1
Mrk 15:18 began saluting him, "Hail, King of the Jews!"   1
Jhn 19: 3 to him, saying, "Hail, King of the Jews!"   1

hailstone
1. χάλαζα, *chalaza, 5898*
Rev 16:21 huge hailstones...dropped from heaven on people   1

hair *See also* cut off hair, wear long hair
1. θρίξ, *thrix, 2582*
2. κεφαλή, *kephalē, 3051*
3. κόμη, *komē, 3151*
Mat 3: 4 clothing of camel's hair with a leather belt   1
    5:36 head, for you cannot make one hair white or black.   1
   10:30 even the hairs of your head are all counted.   1
Mrk 1: 6 Now John was clothed with camel's hair   1
Lke 7:38 dry them with her hair. Then she continued   1
    7:44 dried them with her hair.   1
   12: 7 But even the hairs of your head are all counted.   1
   21:18 not a hair of your head will perish.   1
Jhn 11: 2 wiped his feet with her hair;   1
   12: 3 wiped them with her hair.   1
Act 18:18 At Cenchreae he had his hair cut,   2
   27:34 for none of you will lose a hair from your heads   1
1Co 11:15 her hair is given to her for a covering.   3
1Pe 3: 3 adorn yourselves outwardly by braiding your hair   1
Rev 1:14 His head and his hair were white as white wool   1
    9: 8 their hair like women's hair, and their teeth like   1
    9: 8 their hair like women's hair, and their teeth like   1

braided hair
1. πλέγμα, *plegma, 4427*
1Ti 2: 9 not with their hair braided, or with gold,   1

long hair
1. κομάω, *komaō, 3150*
1Co 11:15 if a woman has long hair, it is her glory?   1

Hakeldama
1. Ἀκελδαμάχ, *Hakeldamach, 192*
Act 1:19 the field was called in their language Hakeldama   1

half *See also* half dead
1. ἥμισυς, *hēmisys, 2468*
Mrk 6:23 I will give you, even half of my kingdom."   1

Lke 19: 8 half of my possessions...I will give to the poor;   1
Rev 11: 9 For three and a half days members of the peoples   1
   11:11 after the three and a half days, the breath of life   1
   12:14 nourished for a time, and times, and half a time.   1

half an hour
1. ἡμιώριον, *hēmiōrion, 2469*
Rev 8: 1 silence in heaven for about half an hour.   1

audience hall
1. ἀκροατήριον, *akroatērion, 211*
Act 25:23 and they entered the audience hall   1

lecture hall
1. σχολή, *scholē, 5391*
Act 19: 9 argued daily in the lecture hall of Tyrannus.   1

wedding hall
1. γάμος, *gamos, 1141*
Mat 22:10 so the wedding hall was filled with guests.   1

Hallelujah
1. ἀλληλουϊά, *hallēlouia, 252*
Rev 19: 1 a great multitude in heaven, saying, "Hallelujah!   1
   19: 3 Once more they said, "Hallelujah!   1
   19: 4 worshiped God...saying, "Amen. Hallelujah!"   1
   19: 6 "Hallelujah! For the Lord our God...reigns.   1

hallow
1. ἁγιάζω, *hagiazō, 39*
Mat 6: 9 Our Father in heaven, hallowed be your name.   1
Lke 11: 2 hallowed be your name. Your kingdom come.   1

Hamor
1. Ἐμμώρ, *Hemmōr, 1846*
Act 7:16 bought...from the sons of Hamor in Shechem.   1

hand *See also* lead by the hand, lie close at hand, make by human hands, make with hands, make with human hands, not made with hands, someone to lead by the hand
1. Contextual: Not in Greek
2. χείρ, *cheir, 5931*
Mat 3:12 winnowing fork is in his hand, and he will clear   2
    4: 6 and 'On their hands they will bear you up   2
    5:30 if your right hand causes you to sin, cut it off   2
    8: 3 He stretched out his hand and touched him   2
    8:15 he touched her hand, and the fever left her   2
    9:18 but come and lay your hand on her   2
    9:25 he went in and took her by the hand   2
   12:10 a man was there with a withered hand   2
   12:13 Then he said to the man, "Stretch out your hand."   2
   14:31 Jesus immediately reached out his hand   2
   15: 2 For they do not wash their hands before they eat."   2
   15:20 to eat with unwashed hands does not defile."   2
   17:12 the Son of Man is about to suffer at their hands."   1
   17:22 Son of Man is going to be betrayed into human hands   2
   18: 8 "If your hand or your foot causes you to stumble   2
   18: 8 than to have two hands or two feet   2
   19:13 that he might lay his hands on them and pray.   2
   19:15 he laid his hands on them and went on his way.   2
   22:13 'Bind him hand and foot, and throw him into   2
   26:23 "The one who has dipped his hand into the bowl   2
   26:45 Son of Man is betrayed into the hands of sinners.   2
   26:50 came and laid hands on Jesus and arrested him.   2
   26:51 put his hand on his sword, drew it,   2
   27:24 and washed his hands before the crowd   2
Mrk 1:31 He came and took her by the hand and lifted her up.   2
    1:41 Moved with pity, Jesus stretched out his hand   2
    3: 1 a man was there who had a withered hand.   2
    3: 3 he said to the man who had the withered hand   2
    3: 5 said to the man, "Stretch out your hand."   2
    3: 5 He stretched it out, and his hand was restored.   2
    5:23 Come and lay your hands on her   2
    5:41 He took her by the hand and said to her,   2
    6: 2 What deeds of power are being done by his hands!   2
    6: 5 he laid his hands on a few sick people   2
    7: 2 eating with defiled hands, that is, without washing   2
    7: 3 do not eat unless they thoroughly wash their hands   2
    7: 5 but eat with defiled hands?"   2

Mrk	7:32	they begged him to lay his hand on him.	2
	8:23	He took the blind man by the hand	2
	8:23	and laid his hands on him	2
	8:25	Then Jesus laid his hands on his eyes again;	2
	9:27	Jesus took him by the hand and lifted him up	2
	9:31	betrayed into human hands	2
	9:43	If your hand causes you to stumble, cut it off;	2
	9:43	to have two hands and to go to hell	2
	10:16	laid his hands on them, and blessed them.	2
	14:41	Son of Man is betrayed into the hands of sinners.	2
	14:46	they laid hands on him and arrested him.	2
	16:18	[[they will pick up snakes in their hands]]	2
	16:18	[[they will lay their hands on the sick]]	2
Lke	1:66	For, indeed, the hand of the Lord was with him.	2
	1:71	saved...from the hand of all who hate us.	2
	1:74	rescued from the hands of our enemies	2
	3:17	His winnowing fork is in his hand	2
	4:11	'On their hands they will bear you up	2
	4:40	he laid his hands on each of them	2
	5:13	Jesus stretched out his hand, touched him,	2
	6: 1	rubbed them in their hands	2
	6: 6	was a man there whose right hand was withered.	2
	6: 8	he said to the man who had the withered hand	2
	6:10	said to him, "Stretch out your hand."	2
	6:10	He did so, and his hand was restored.	2
	8:54	took her by the hand and called out, "Child	2
	9:44	to be betrayed into human hands."	2
	9:62	"No one who puts a hand to the plow	2
	10:30	fell into the hands of robbers	1
	10:36	who fell into the hands of the robbers?"	1
	13:13	he laid his hands on her	2
	20:19	wanted to lay hands on him at that very hour	2
	22:21	with me, and his hand is on the table.	2
	22:53	you did not lay hands on me.	2
	23:46	"Father, into your hands I commend my spirit."	2
	24:39	Look at my hands and my feet; see that it is I	2
	24:40	he showed them his hands and his feet	2
	24:50	and, lifting up his hands, he blessed them.	2
Jhn	3:35	and has placed all things in his hands.	2
	7:30	no one laid hands on him	2
	7:44	but no one laid hands on him.	2
	10:28	No one will snatch them out of my hand.	2
	10:29	can snatch it out of the Father's hand.	2
	10:39	he escaped from their hands.	2
	11:44	his hands and feet bound with strips of cloth	2
	13: 3	the Father had given all things into his hands	2
	13: 9	not my feet only but also my hands and my head!"	2
	20:20	he showed them his hands and his side.	2
	20:25	"Unless I see the mark of the nails in his hands	2
	20:25	my hand in his side	2
	20:27	"Put your finger here and see my hands.	2
	20:27	Reach out your hand and put it in my side.	2
	21:18	you grow old, you will stretch out your hands	2
Act	2:23	and killed by the hands of those outside the law.	2
	3: 7	he took him by the right hand and raised him up;	2
	4:28	whatever your hand and your plan had predestined	2
	4:30	while you stretch out your hand to heal	2
	6: 6	who prayed and laid their hands on them.	2
	7:41	reveled in the works of their hands.	2
	7:50	Did not my hand make all these things?'	2
	8:17	Then Peter and John laid their hands on them	2
	8:18	through the laying on of the apostles' hands	2
	8:19	anyone on whom I lay my hands	2
	9:12	Ananias come in and lay his hand on him	2
	9:17	laid his hands on Saul and said, "Brother Saul	2
	9:41	He gave her his hand and helped her up.	2
	11:21	The hand of the Lord was with them	2
	12: 1	King Herod laid violent hands upon some	2
	12:11	and rescued me from the hands of Herod	2
	12:17	motioned to them with his hand to be silent	2
	13: 3	they laid their hands on them and sent them off.	2
	13:11	now listen—the hand of the Lord is against you	2
	17:25	nor is he served by human hands	2
	18:10	no one will lay a hand on you to harm you	1
	19: 6	When Paul had laid his hands on them	2
	19:26	saying that gods made with hands are not gods.	2
	20:34	worked with my own hands to support myself	2
	21:11	bound his own feet and hands with it, and said	2
	23:19	The tribune took him by the hand	2
	26: 1	Paul stretched out his hand and began to defend	2
	28: 3	a viper...fastened itself on his hand.	2

	28: 4	saw the creature hanging from his hand	2
	28: 8	cured him by praying and putting his hands on him.	2
Rom	10:21	"All day long I have held out my hands	2
1Co	4:12	we grow weary from the work of our own hands.	2
	12:15	"Because I am not a hand, I do not belong to the body,"	2
	12:21	The eye cannot say to the hand, "I have no need	2
	16:21	I, Paul, write this greeting with my own hand.	2
2Co	11:33	escaped from his hands.	2
Gal	6:11	I am writing in my own hand!	2
Eph	4:28	labor and work honestly with their own hands	2
Col	4:18	I, Paul, write this greeting with my own hand.	2
1Th	4:11	to work with your hands, as we directed you	2
2Th	3:17	I, Paul, write this greeting with my own hand.	2
1Ti	2: 8	lifting up holy hands without anger or argument;	2
	4:14	laying on of hands by the council of elders.	2
2Ti	1: 6	within you through the laying on of my hands;	2
Phm	1:19	I, Paul, am writing this with my own hand: I will repay	2
Heb	1:10	the heavens are the work of your hands;	2
	6: 2	baptisms, laying on of hands,	2
	8: 9	on the day when I took them by the hand	2
	10:31	to fall into the hands of the living God.	2
	12:12	Therefore lift your drooping hands	2
Jas	4: 8	Cleanse your hands, you sinners	2
1Pe	5: 6	Humble yourselves...under the mighty hand of God	2
1Jn	1: 1	we have looked at and touched with our hands	2
Rev	1:16	In his right hand he held seven stars	2
	6: 5	Its rider held a pair of scales in his hand	2
	7: 9	in white, with palm branches in their hands.	2
	8: 4	rose...before God from the hand of the angel.	2
	9:20	did not repent of the works of their hands	2
	10: 2	He held a little scroll open in his hand.	2
	10: 5	the angel...raised his right hand to heaven	2
	10: 8	the scroll that is open in the hand of the angel	2
	10:10	took the little scroll from the hand of the angel	2
	13:16	to be marked on the right hand or the forehead	2
	14: 9	receive a mark on their foreheads or on their hands	2
	14:14	crown on his head, and a sharp sickle in his hand!	2
	17: 4	holding in her hand a golden cup	2
	20: 1	holding in his hand the key to the bottomless pit	2
	20: 4	its mark on their foreheads or their hands.	2

at hand

1. ἐγγίζω, *engizō*, 1581

Mat	26:45	See, the hour is at hand	1
	26:46	let us be going. See, my betrayer is at hand."	1
Mrk	14:42	let us be going. See, my betrayer is at hand."	1

at one's hand

1. ἀπό, *apo*, 608

Mat	16:21	at the hands of the elders and chief priests	1

hand on

1. παραδίδωμι, *paradidōmi*, 4140

Mrk	7:13	through your tradition that you have handed on.	1
Lke	1: 2	just as they were handed on to us by those	1
Act	6:14	change the customs that Moses handed on to us."	1
1Co	11: 2	traditions just as I handed them on to you.	1
	11:23	what I also handed on to you	1
	15: 3	For I handed on to you as of first importance	1

hand over

1. ἔκδοτος, *ekdotos*, 1692
2. παραδίδωμι, *paradidōmi*, 4140
3. χαρίζομαι, *charizomai*, 5919

Mat	5:25	or your accuser may hand you over to the judge	2
	10:17	Beware of them, for they will hand you over	2
	10:19	When they hand you over, do not worry	2
	11:27	All things have been handed over to me by my Father;	2
	18:34	in anger his lord handed him over to be tortured	2
	20:18	the Son of Man will be handed over	2
	20:19	hand him over to the Gentiles to be mocked	2
	24: 9	"Then they will hand you over to be tortured	2
	25:20	'Master, you handed over to me five talents;	2
	25:22	'Master, you handed over to me two talents;	2
	26: 2	Son of Man will be handed over to be crucified."	2
	27: 2	handed him over to Pilate the governor.	2
	27:18	out of jealousy that they had handed him over.	2
	27:26	handed him over to be crucified.	2
Mrk	10:33	Son of Man will be handed over to the chief priests	2
	10:33	hand him over to the Gentiles;	2

	13: 9	they will hand you over to councils;	2
	13:11	When they bring you to trial and hand you over	2
	15: 1	led him away, and handed him over to Pilate.	2
	15:10	the chief priests had handed him over.	2
	15:15	he handed him over to be crucified.	2
Lke	10:22	All things have been handed over to me by my Father;	2
	12:58	the judge hand you over to the officer	2
	18:32	For he will be handed over to the Gentiles;	2
	20:20	so as to hand him over to…the governor	2
	21:12	hand you over to synagogues and prisons	2
	23:25	he handed Jesus over as they wished.	2
	24: 7	must be handed over to sinners	2
	24:20	our chief priests and leaders handed him over	2
Jhn	18:30	we would not have handed him over	2
	18:35	the chief priests have handed you over to me.	2
	18:36	to keep me from being handed over to the Jews.	2
	19:11	who handed me over to you is guilty of a greater sin."	2
	19:16	he handed him over to them to be crucified.	2
Act	2:23	handed over to you according to the definite plan	1
	3:13	Jesus, whom you handed over	2
	7:42	God…handed them over to worship the host of heaven	2
	12: 4	handed him over to four squads of soldiers	2
	21:11	will hand him over to the Gentiles.' "	2
	25:16	not the custom of the Romans to hand over anyone	3
	28:17	in Jerusalem and handed over to the Romans.	2
Rom	4:25	who was handed over to death for our trespasses	2
1Co	5: 5	you are to hand this man over to Satan	2
	13: 3	if I hand over my body so that I may boast,	2
	15:24	Then comes the end, when he hands over the kingdom	2

hired hand

  1. Contextual: Not in Greek
  2. μίσθιος, *misthios, 3634*
  3. μισθωτός, *misthōtos, 3638*

Lke	15:17	'How many of my father's hired hands have bread	2
	15:19	treat me like one of your hired hands." '	2
Jhn	10:12	The hired hand, who is not the shepherd	3
	10:13	The hired hand runs away because a hired hand	1
	10:13	The hired hand runs away because a hired hand	3

in hand

  1. ἔχω, *echō, 2400*

Rev	15: 2	standing…with harps of God in their hands.	1

left hand

  1. ἀριστερός, *aristeros, 754*
  2. εὐώνυμος, *euōnymos, 2381*

Mat	6: 3	when you give alms, do not let your left hand know	1
	25:41	Then he will say to those at his left hand	2

on the one hand

  1. μέν, *men, 3525*

Heb	7:18	There is, on the one hand, the abrogation	1

on the other hand

  1. δέ, *de, 1254*

1Co	14: 3	On the other hand, those who prophesy speak	1
Heb	7:19	on the other hand, the introduction of a better hope	1

own hand

  1. αὐτόχειρ, *autocheir, 901*

Act	27:19	with their own hands they threw the ship's tackle	1

right hand

  1. δεξιός, *dexios, 1288*

Mat	6: 3	your left hand know what your right hand is doing	1
	20:21	one at your right hand and one at your left	1
	20:23	to sit at my right hand and at my left	1
	22:44	'The Lord said to my Lord, "Sit at my right hand	1
	25:33	he will put the sheep at his right hand	1
	25:34	the king will say to those at his right hand	1
	26:64	the Son of Man seated at the right hand of Power	1
	27:29	They put a reed in his right hand	1
Mrk	10:37	one at your right hand and one at your left	1
	10:40	to sit at my right hand or at my left	1
	12:36	'The Lord said to my Lord, "Sit at my right hand	1
	14:62	Son of Man seated at the right hand of the Power,'	1
	16:19	[[Jesus…sat down at the right hand of God.]]	1
Lke	20:42	'The Lord said to my Lord, "Sit at my right hand	1

	22:69	seated at the right hand of the power of God."	1
Act	2:25	he is at my right hand so that I will not be shaken;	1
	2:33	Being therefore exalted at the right hand of God	1
	2:34	'The Lord said to my Lord, "Sit at my right hand	1
	5:31	God exalted him at his right hand as Leader	1
	7:55	Jesus standing at the right hand of God.	1
	7:56	the Son of Man standing at the right hand of God!"	1
Rom	8:34	Christ Jesus…who is at the right hand of God	1
2Co	6: 7	for the right hand and for the left;	1
Gal	2: 9	to Barnabas and me…the right hand of fellowship	1
Eph	1:20	seated him at his right hand	1
Col	3: 1	where Christ is, seated at the right hand of God.	1
Heb	1: 3	he sat down at the right hand of the Majesty on high	1
	1:13	of the angels has he ever said, "Sit at my right hand	1
	8: 1	one who is seated at the right hand of the throne	1
	10:12	"he sat down at the right hand of God,"	1
	12: 2	seat at the right hand of the throne of God.	1
1Pe	3:22	who…is at the right hand of God	1
Rev	1:17	But he placed his right hand on me, saying,	1
	1:20	the seven stars that you saw in my right hand	1
	2: 1	him who holds the seven stars in his right hand	1
	5: 1	Then I saw in the right hand of the one seated	1
	5: 7	He went and took the scroll from the right hand	1

handkerchief

  1. σουδάριον, *soudarion, 5051*

Act	19:12	so that when the handkerchiefs…were brought	1

handle

  1. ἅπτω, *haptō, 721*

Col	2:21	"Do not handle, Do not taste, Do not touch"?	1

hang

  1. ἀπάγχω, *apanchō, 551*
  2. κρεμάννυμι, *kremannymi, 3203*
  3. περίκειμαι, *perikeimai, 4329*

Mat	22:40	On these two commandments hang all the law	2
	27: 5	he departed; and he went and hanged himself.	1
Mrk	9:42	if a great millstone were hung around your neck	3
Lke	23:39	criminals who were hanged there kept deriding him	2
Act	5:30	whom you had killed by hanging him on a tree.	2
	10:39	They put him to death by hanging him on a tree;	2
	28: 4	saw the creature hanging from his hand	2
Gal	3:13	"Cursed is everyone who hangs on a tree"—	2

hang around

  1. περίκειμαι, *perikeimai, 4329*

Lke	17: 2	if a millstone were hung around your neck	1

happen

  1. Contextual: Not in Greek
  2. γίνομαι, *ginomai, 1181*
  3. εἰμί, *eimi, 1639*
  4. ἐπέρχομαι, *eperchomai, 2088*
  5. ἔρχομαι, *erchomai, 2262*
  6. κατά, *kata, 2848*
  7. συμβαίνω, *symbainō, 5201*
  8. συναντάω, *synantaō, 5267*

Mat	8:33	they told the whole story about what had happened	1
	16:22	This must never happen to you."	3
	18:31	his fellow slaves saw what had happened	2
	26:54	which say it must happen in this way?"	2
	28:11	told the chief priests everything that had happened.	2
Mrk	5:14	people came to see what it was that had happened.	2
	5:16	who had seen what had happened to the demoniac	2
	5:33	the woman, knowing what had happened to her, came	2
	9:21	"How long has this been happening to him?"	2
	10:32	began to tell them what was to happen to him	7
Lke	1:43	why has this happened to me	1
	8:34	When the swineherds saw what had happened	2
	8:35	Then people came out to see what had happened	2
	8:56	he ordered them to tell no one what had happened.	2
	12:54	and so it happens.	2
	12:55	'There will be scorching heat'; and it happens.	2
	18:36	he asked what was happening.	3
	23:31	what will happen when it is dry?"	2
	24:12	he went home, amazed at what had happened	2
	24:14	about all these things that had happened.	7
	24:35	Then they told what had happened on the road	1

Jhn	5:14	not sin...so that nothing worse happens to you."	2
	18: 4	Jesus, knowing all that was to happen to him	5
Act	3:10	amazement at what had happened to him.	7
	4:21	all of them praised God for what had happened.	2
	5: 7	his wife came in, not knowing what had happened.	2
	7:40	we do not know what has happened to him.'	2
	8:24	nothing of what you have said may happen to me."	4
	10:16	This happened three times	2
	11:10	This happened three times;	2
	12: 9	what was happening with the angel's help was real;	2
	13:12	the proconsul saw what had happened, he believed	2
	13:40	that what the prophets said does not happen to you:	4
	20:22	not knowing what will happen to me there	8
	28: 6	saw that nothing unusual had happened to him	2
	28: 8	It so happened that the father of Publius lay sick	2
	28: 9	After this happened, the rest of the people	2
Rom	9:10	something similar happened to Rebecca	1
1Co	10:11	things happened to them to serve as an example	7
Php	1:12	what has happened to me has actually helped	6
2Ti	3:11	the things that happened to me in Antioch, Iconium	2
1Pe	4:12	as though something strange were happening	7
2Pe	2:22	It has happened to them according to the true proverb	7

happen to be there
1. παρατυγχάνω, *paratynchanō, 4193*

Act 17:17 he argued...with those who happened to be there. 1

happy
1. χαίρω, *chairō, 5897*

Lke 19: 6 down and was happy to welcome him. 1

Haran
1. Χαρράν, *Charran, 5924*

Act 7: 2 in Mesopotamia, before he lived in Haran 1
7: 4 Then he left...and settled in Haran. 1

harass
1. σκύλλω, *skyllō, 5035*

Mat 9:36 because they were harassed and helpless 1

harbor
1. λιμήν, *limēn, 3348*

Act 27:12 Since the harbor was not suitable for...winter 1
27:12 a harbor of Crete, facing southwest and northwest. 1

hard *See also* press hard
1. βαρέως, *bareōs, 977*
2. δυσερμήνευτος, *dysermēneutos, 1549*
3. δύσκολος, *dyskolos, 1551*
4. δυσκόλως, *dyskolōs, 1552*
5. θλίβω, *thlibō, 2567*
6. μόλις, *molis, 3660*
7. περισσότερος, *perissoteros, 4358*
8. πολύς, *polys, 4498*
9. σκληρότης, *sklērotēs, 5018*

Mat	7:14	For the gate is narrow and the road is hard	5
	13:15	and their ears are hard of hearing	1
	19:23	it will be hard for a rich person to enter	4
Mrk	10:23	"How hard it will be for those who have wealth	4
	10:24	how hard it is to enter the kingdom of God!	3
Lke	18:24	"How hard it is for those who have wealth to enter	4
Act	28:27	their ears are hard of hearing	1
Rom	2: 5	by your hard and impenitent heart	9
	16:12	beloved Persis, who has worked hard in the Lord.	8
1Co	15:10	On the contrary, I worked harder than any of them	7
Col	4:13	I testify for him that he has worked hard for you	8
Heb	5:11	have much to say that is hard to explain	2
	10:32	you endured a hard struggle with sufferings	8
1Pe	4:18	"If it is hard for the righteous to be saved	6

hard to bear
1. δυσβάστακτος, *dysbastaktos, 1546*

Mat 23: 4 They tie up heavy burdens, hard to bear 1
Lke 11:46 you load people with burdens hard to bear 1

hard to understand
1. δυσνόητος, *dysnoētos, 1554*

2Pe 3:16 There are some things in them hard to understand 1

very hard
1. πολύς, *polys, 4498*

Rom 16: 6 Greet Mary, who has worked very hard among you. 1

hard-hearted
1. σκληροκαρδία, *sklērokardia, 5016*

Mat 19: 8 so hard-hearted that Moses allowed you 1

harden
1. πωρόω, *pōroō, 4800*
2. πώρωσις, *pōrōsis, 4801*
3. σκληρύνω, *sklērynō, 5020*

Mrk	6:52	their hearts were hardened.	1
	8:17	Are your hearts hardened?	1
Jhn	12:40	blinded their eyes and hardened their heart	1
Rom	11: 7	The elect obtained it, but the rest were hardened	1
	11:25	a hardening has come upon part of Israel	2
2Co	3:14	their minds were hardened.	1
Heb	3: 8	do not harden your hearts as in the rebellion	3
	3:13	hardened by the deceitfulness of sin.	3
	3:15	do not harden your hearts as in the rebellion."	3
	4: 7	do not harden your hearts."	3

harden the heart
1. σκληρύνω, *sklērynō, 5020*

Rom 9:18 and he hardens the heart of whomever he chooses. 1

hardness
1. πώρωσις, *pōrōsis, 4801*

Mrk 3: 5 grieved at their hardness of heart 1
Eph 4:18 their ignorance and hardness of heart. 1

hardness of heart
1. σκληροκαρδία, *sklērokardia, 5016*

Mrk 10: 5 "Because of your hardness of heart he wrote 1

hardship *See also* suffer hardship
1. ἀνάγκη, *anankē, 340*
2. θλῖψις, *thlipsis, 2568*
3. μόχθος, *mochthos, 3677*

Rom	8:35	Will hardship, or distress, or persecution	2
2Co	6: 4	in afflictions, hardships, calamities	1
	11:27	in toil and hardship	3
	12:10	I am content with weaknesses, insults, hardships	1

harm *See also* do harm, inflict harm
1. ἀδικέω, *adikeō, 92*
2. ζημιόω, *zēmioō, 2423*
3. κακός, *kakos, 2805*
4. κακός + πράσσω, *kakos + prassō, 2805 + 4556*
5. κακόω, *kakoō, 2808*

Act	16:28	"Do not harm yourself, for we are all here."	4
	18:10	no one will lay a hand on you to harm you	5
	28: 5	shook off the creature...and suffered no harm.	3
2Co	7: 9	so that you were not harmed in any way by us.	2
2Ti	4:14	Alexander the coppersmith did me great harm;	3
1Pe	3:13	Now who will harm you if you are eager	5
Rev	2:11	conquers will not be harmed by the second death.	1
	9:10	is their power to harm people for five months.	1
	11: 5	if anyone wants to harm them, fire pours	1
	11: 5	anyone who wants to harm them must be killed	1

Harmagedon
1. Ἀρμαγεδών, *Harmagedōn, 762*

Rev 16:16 the place that in Hebrew is called Harmagedon. 1

harmful
1. ἀλυσιτελής, *alysitelēs, 269*
2. βλαβερός, *blaberos, 1054*

1Ti 6: 9 trapped by many senseless and harmful desires 2
Heb 13:17 for that would be harmful to you. 1

harmony
1. αὐτός, *autos, 899*

Rom 12:16 Live in harmony with one another; 1
15: 5 to live in harmony with one another 1

perfect harmony

1. τελειότης, *teleiotēs, 5456*

Col 3:14 which binds everything together in perfect harmony. 1

harp

1. κιθάρα, *kithara, 3067*

1Co 14: 7 produce sound, such as the flute or the harp. 1
Rev 5: 8 fell before the Lamb, each holding a harp 1
14: 2 like the sound of harpists playing on their harps 1
15: 2 standing...with harps of God in their hands. 1

harpist

1. κιθαρῳδός, *kitharōdos, 3069*

Rev 14: 2 like the sound of harpists playing on their harps 1
18:22 and the sound of harpists and minstrels 1

harsh

1. αὐστηρός, *austēros, 893*
2. σκληρός, *sklēros, 5017*
3. σκολιός, *skolios, 5021*

Mat 25:24 'Master, I knew that you were a harsh man 2
Lke 19:21 I was afraid of you, because you are a harsh man; 1
19:22 You knew, did you, that I was a harsh man 1
1Pe 2:18 kind and gentle but also those who are harsh. 3

harsh thing

1. σκληρός, *sklēros, 5017*

Jde 1:15 harsh things that ungodly sinners have spoken 1

harshly *See* speak harshly, treat harshly

harvest *See also* harvest *time*

1. γένημα, *genēma, 1163*
2. θερισμός, *therismos, 2546*
3. ἴδιος, *idios, 2625*
4. καρπός, *karpos, 2843*

Mat 9:37 "The harvest is plentiful 2
9:38 therefore ask the Lord of the harvest 2
9:38 to send out laborers into his harvest." 2
13:30 Let both of them grow together until the harvest; 2
13:30 at harvest time I will tell the reapers 2
13:39 the harvest is the end of the age 2
21:34 When the harvest time had come 4
Mrk 4:29 because the harvest has come." 2
Lke 10: 2 harvest is plentiful, but the laborers are few; 2
10: 2 therefore ask the Lord of the harvest 2
10: 2 to send out laborers into his harvest. 2
Jhn 4:35 'Four months more, then comes the harvest'? 2
4:35 see how the fields are ripe for harvesting. 2
Rom 1:13 in order that I may reap some harvest among you 4
2Co 9:10 increase the harvest of your righteousness. 1
Gal 6: 9 we will reap at harvest time 3
Php 1:11 produced the harvest of righteousness 4
Jas 3:18 a harvest of righteousness is sown in peace 4
5:18 and the earth yielded its harvest. 4
Rev 14:15 because the harvest of the earth is fully ripe." 2

harvester

1. θερίζω, *therizō, 2545*

Jas 5: 4 cries of the harvesters have reached the ears 1

haste

1. σπεύδω, *speudō, 5067*
2. σπουδή, *spoudē, 5082*

Lke 1:39 went with haste to a Judean town in the hill country 2
2:16 they went with haste and found Mary and Joseph 1

hasten

1. σπεύδω, *speudō, 5067*

2Pe 3:12 and hastening the coming of the day of God 1

hastily

1. ταχέως, *tacheōs, 5441*

1Ti 5:22 Do not ordain anyone hastily, 1

hate

1. Contextual: Not in Greek
2. ἀποστυγέω, *apostygeō, 696*

3. μισέω, *miseō, 3631*

Mat 5:43 love your neighbor and hate your enemy.' 3
6:24 slave will either hate the one and love the other 3
10:22 you will be hated by all because of my name. 3
24: 9 hated by all nations because of my name. 3
24:10 betray one another and hate one another. 3
Mrk 13:13 you will be hated by all because of my name. 3
Lke 1:71 saved...from the hand of all who hate us. 3
6:22 "Blessed are you when people hate you 3
6:27 Love your enemies, do good to those who hate you 3
14:26 does not hate father and mother, wife 3
16:13 slave will either hate the one and love the other 3
19:14 citizens of his country hated him 3
21:17 You will be hated by all because of my name. 3
Jhn 3:20 For all who do evil hate the light 3
7: 7 The world cannot hate you, but it hates me 3
7: 7 The world cannot hate you, but it hates me 3
12:25 who hate their life in this world will keep it 3
15:18 "If the world hates you...it hated me 3
15:18 aware that it hated me before it hated you. 3
15:18 aware that it hated me before it hated you. 1
15:19 therefore the world hates you. 3
15:23 Whoever hates me hates my Father also. 3
15:23 Whoever hates me hates my Father also. 3
15:24 they have seen and hated both me and my Father. 3
15:25 'They hated me without a cause.' 3
17:14 the world has hated them 3
Rom 7:15 but I do the very thing I hate. 3
9:13 "I have loved Jacob, but I have hated Esau." 3
12: 9 hate what is evil, hold fast to what is good; 2
Eph 5:29 For no one ever hates his own body 3
Tit 3: 3 despicable, hating one another. 3
Heb 1: 9 You have loved righteousness and hated wickedness; 3
1Jn 2: 9 while hating a brother or sister, is still in the darkness. 3
2:11 whoever hates another believer is in the darkness 3
3:13 Do not be astonished...that the world hates you. 3
3:15 All who hate a brother or sister are murderers 3
4:20 say, "I love God," and hate their brothers or sisters 3
Jde 1:23 hating even the tunic defiled by their bodies. 3
Rev 2: 6 you hate the works of the Nicolaitans 3
2: 6 works of the Nicolaitans, which I also hate. 3
17:16 they and the beast will hate the whore; 3

hateful

1. μισέω, *miseō, 3631*

Rev 18: 2 a haunt of every foul and hateful beast. 1

hater of good

1. ἀφιλάγαθος, *aphilagathos, 920*

2Ti 3: 3 profligates, brutes, haters of good 1

haughty

1. μέγας, *megas, 3489*
2. ὑπερήφανος, *hyperēphanos, 5662*
3. ὑψηλός + φρονέω, *hypsēlos + phroneō, 5734 + 5858*
4. ὑψηλοφρονέω, *hypsēlophroneō, 5735*

Rom 1:30 slanderers, God-haters, insolent, haughty 2
12:16 do not be haughty, but associate with the lowly; 3
1Ti 6:17 command them not to be haughty 4
Rev 13: 5 a mouth uttering haughty and blasphemous words 1

haul

1. ἑλκύω, *helkyō, 1816*

Jhn 21: 6 now they were not able to haul it in 1
21:11 Simon Peter went aboard and hauled the net ashore 1

haunt

1. φυλακή, *phylakē, 5871*

Rev 18: 2 a haunt of every foul spirit 1
18: 2 a haunt of every foul bird, 1
18: 2 a haunt of every foul and hateful beast. 1

have

1. βίος, *bios, 1050*
2. γίνομαι, *ginomai, 1181*
3. διά, *dia, 1328*
4. δίδωμι, *didōmi, 1443*
5. δοκέω, *dokeō, 1506*
6. εἰμί, *eimi, 1639*

7. ἐκ, *ek, 1666*
8. ἐν, *en, 1877*
9. ἔχω, *echō, 2400*
10. καλέω, *kaleō, 2813*
11. μεταλαμβάνω, *metalambanō, 3561*
12. ὁράω, *horaō, 3972*
13. παρά, *para, 4123*
14. πάρειμι, *pareimi, 4205*
15. τυγχάνω, *tynchanō, 5593*
16. ὑπάρχω, *hyparchō, 5639*

Mat	3: 9	say to yourselves, 'We have Abraham as our ancestor';	9
	5:23	that your brother or sister has something against you	9
	5:46	love those who love you, what reward do you have?	9
	6: 1	for then you have no reward from your Father	9
	7:29	for he taught them as one having authority	9
	8:20	Jesus said to him, "Foxes have holes	9
	8:20	but the Son of Man has nowhere to lay his head."	9
	9: 6	you may know that the Son of Man has authority	9
	9:12	"Those who are well have no need of a physician	9
	11:18	and they say, 'He has a demon';	9
	12:11	"Suppose one of you has only one sheep	9
	13: 5	where they did not have much soil	9
	13: 5	since they had no depth of soil.	9
	13: 6	since they had no root, they withered away.	9
	13:12	For to those who have, more will be given	9
	13:12	but from those who have nothing,	9
	13:12	even what they have will be taken away.	9
	13:21	yet such a person has no root	9
	13:44	sells all that he has and buys that field.	9
	13:46	went and sold all that he had and bought it.	9
	14: 4	"It is not lawful for you to have her."	9
	14:17	"We have nothing here but five loaves and two fish."	9
	15:32	and have nothing to eat;	9
	15:34	Jesus asked them, "How many loaves have you?"	9
	16: 8	why are you talking about having no bread?	9
	17:20	if you have faith the size of a mustard seed	9
	18: 8	than to have two hands or two feet	9
	18: 9	have two eyes and to be thrown into the hell of fire.	9
	18:12	If a shepherd has a hundred sheep,	2
	19:16	to have eternal life?"	9
	19:21	you will have treasure in heaven;	9
	19:22	for he had many possessions.	9
	19:27	What then will we have?"	6
	21:21	if you have faith and do not doubt	9
	21:28	"What do you think? A man had two sons;	9
	23: 8	you have one teacher, and you are all students.	6
	23: 9	for you have one Father—the one in heaven.	6
	23:10	for you have one instructor, the Messiah.	6
	25:25	Here you have what is yours.'	9
	25:29	For to all those who have, more will be given	9
	25:29	but from those who have nothing,	9
	25:29	even what they have will be taken away.	9
	26:11	For you always have the poor with you	9
	26:11	you will not always have me.	9
	27:16	At that time they had a notorious prisoner	9
	27:65	said to them, "You have a guard of soldiers;	9
Mrk	1:22	he taught them as one having authority	9
	2:10	Son of Man has authority on earth to forgive sins"	9
	2:17	"Those who are well have no need of a physician	9
	2:19	As long as they have the bridegroom with them	9
	3: 1	a man was there who had a withered hand.	9
	3: 3	he said to the man who had the withered hand	9
	3:10	so that all who had diseases pressed upon him	9
	3:15	and to have authority to cast out demons.	9
	3:22	"He has Beelzebul, and by the ruler	9
	3:29	can never have forgiveness	9
	3:30	for they had said, "He has an unclean spirit."	9
	4: 5	where it did not have much soil	9
	4: 5	since it had no depth of soil.	9
	4: 6	since it had no root, it withered away.	9
	4:17	they have no root, and endure only	9
	4:25	For to those who have, more will be given;	9
	4:25	from those who have nothing, even what they have	9
	4:25	have nothing, even what they have will be taken	9
	4:40	"Why are you afraid? Have you still no faith?"	9
	5:15	right mind, the very man who had had the legion;	9
	5:26	spent all that she had;	13
	6:18	not lawful for you to have your brother's wife."	9
	6:38	"How many loaves have you? Go and see."	9
	7:25	woman whose little daughter had an unclean spirit	9

	8: 2	have nothing to eat.	9
	8: 5	He asked them, "How many loaves do you have?"	9
	8: 7	They had also a few small fish;	9
	8:14	they had only one loaf with them in the boat.	9
	8:16	"It is because we have no bread."	9
	8:17	"Why are you talking about having no bread?	9
	8:18	Do you have eyes, and fail to see?	9
	8:18	Do you have ears, and fail to hear?	9
	9:17	he has a spirit that makes him unable to speak;	9
	9:43	to have two hands and to go to hell	9
	9:45	to enter life lame than to have two feet	9
	9:47	have two eyes and to be thrown into hell	9
	9:50	Have salt in yourselves	9
	10:21	you will have treasure in heaven;	9
	10:22	for he had many possessions.	9
	10:23	"How hard it will be for those who have wealth	9
	11:22	Jesus answered them, "Have faith in God.	9
	11:25	forgive, if you have anything against anyone;	9
	12: 6	He had still one other, a beloved son.	9
	12:44	out of her poverty has put in everything she had	9
	14: 7	For you always have the poor with you	9
	14: 7	but you will not always have me.	9
Lke	1: 7	they had no children, because Elizabeth was barren	6
	1:14	You will have joy and gladness	6
	1:61	"None of your relatives has this name."	10
	3: 8	'We have Abraham as our ancestor';	9
	3:11	"Whoever has two coats must share	9
	3:11	must share with anyone who has none;	9
	3:11	whoever has food must do likewise."	9
	4:33	a man who had the spirit of an unclean demon	9
	4:40	all those who had any who were sick	9
	5:24	Son of Man has authority on earth to forgive	9
	5:31	"Those who are well have no need of a physician	9
	6: 8	he said to the man who had the withered hand	9
	7:33	and you say, 'He has a demon';	9
	7:40	"Simon, I have something to say to you."	9
	7:41	"A certain creditor had two debtors;	6
	8:13	But these have no root,	9
	8:18	to those who have, more will be given;	9
	8:18	and from those who do not have,	9
	8:18	what they seem to have will be taken away."	9
	8:27	a man of the city who had demons met him.	9
	8:42	for he had an only daughter…who was dying	6
	8:43	though she had spent all she had on physicians	1
	9:13	"We have no more than five loaves and two fish	6
	9:58	Jesus said to him, "Foxes have holes	9
	9:58	the Son of Man has nowhere to lay his head."	9
	10:39	She had a sister named Mary	6
	11: 5	one of you has a friend, and you go to him	9
	11: 6	I have nothing to set before him.'	9
	12: 5	who…has authority to cast into hell.	9
	12:17	for I have no place to store my crops?'	9
	12:19	Soul, you have ample goods laid up for many years;	9
	12:24	they have neither storehouse nor barn	6
	12:50	I have a baptism with which to be baptized	9
	13: 6	"A man had a fig tree planted in his vineyard;	9
	14:28	to see whether he has enough to complete it?	9
	15: 4	"Which one of you, having a hundred sheep	9
	15: 8	what woman having ten silver coins	9
	15:11	Jesus said, "There was a man who had two sons.	9
	16: 1	"There was a rich man who had a manager	9
	16:28	for I have five brothers—that he may warn them	9
	16:29	Abraham said, 'They have Moses and the prophets;	9
	17: 6	"If you had faith the size of a mustard seed	9
	18:22	you will have treasure in heaven;	9
	18:24	hard it is for those who have wealth to enter	9
	19:24	give it to the one who has ten pounds.'	9
	19:25	they said to him, 'Lord, he has ten pounds!')	9
	19:26	to all those who have, more will be given;	9
	19:26	but from those who have nothing,	9
	19:26	even what they have will be taken away.	9
	21: 4	put in all she had to live on."	9
	22:36	"But now, the one who has a purse must take it	9
	22:36	one who has no sword must sell his cloak	9
	24:39	a ghost does not have flesh and bones	9
	24:39	not have flesh and bones as you see that I have."	9
	24:41	he said to them, "Have you anything here to eat?"	9
Jhn	1:22	Let us have an answer for those who sent us.	4
	2: 3	mother of Jesus said to him, "They have no wine."	9
	3:15	whoever believes in him may have eternal life.	9
	3:16	may not perish but may have eternal life.	9

3:29	He who has the bride is the bridegroom.	9
3:36	Whoever believes in the Son has eternal life;	9
4:11	you have no bucket, and the well is deep.	9
4:17	The woman answered him, "I have no husband."	9
4:17	"You are right in saying, 'I have no husband';	9
4:18	for you have had five husbands	9
4:18	and the one you have now is not your husband.	9
4:32	"I have food to eat that you do not know	9
4:44	a prophet has no honor in the prophet's own country).	9
5: 2	a pool…which has five porticoes.	9
5: 7	I have no one to put me into the pool	9
5:24	who hears…and believes…has eternal life	9
5:26	For just as the Father has life in himself	9
5:26	has granted the Son also to have life in himself;	9
5:36	I have a testimony greater than John's.	9
5:38	you do not have his word abiding in you	9
5:39	you think that in them you have eternal life;	9
5:40	you refuse to come to me to have life.	9
5:42	I know that you do not have the love of God	9
6: 9	a boy…who has five barley loaves and two fish.	9
6:40	all who…believe…may have eternal life;	9
6:47	whoever believes has eternal life.	9
6:53	you have no life in you.	9
6:54	Those who…drink my blood have eternal life	9
6:68	You have the words of eternal life.	9
7:20	The crowd answered, "You have a demon!	9
8: 6	[might have some charge to bring against him.]	9
8:12	will have the light of life."	9
8:26	I have much to say about you and much to condemn;	9
8:41	we have one father, God himself."	9
8:48	you are a Samaritan and have a demon?"	9
8:49	Jesus answered, "I do not have a demon;	9
8:52	"Now we know that you have a demon.	9
9:41	"If you were blind, you would not have sin.	9
10:10	I came that they may have life	9
10:10	they may have life, and have it abundantly.	9
10:16	I have other sheep that do not belong to this fold.	9
10:18	I have power to lay it down	9
10:18	I have power to take it up again.	9
10:20	saying, "He has a demon and is out of his mind.	9
12: 8	You always have the poor with you	9
12: 8	but you do not always have me."	9
12:35	Walk while you have the light	9
12:36	While you have the light, believe in the light	9
12:48	one who rejects me…has a judge;	9
13: 8	"Unless I wash you, you have no share with me."	9
13:29	because Judas had the common purse	9
13:35	if you have love for one another."	9
14:21	They who have my commandments and keep them	9
14:30	He has no power over me;	9
15:13	No one has greater love than this	9
15:22	they would not have sin;	9
15:22	now they have no excuse for their sin.	9
15:24	they would not have sin.	9
16:12	"I still have many things to say to you	9
16:15	All that the Father has is mine.	9
16:21	When a woman is in labor, she has pain	9
16:22	So you have pain now; but I will see you again	9
16:33	so that in me you may have peace.	9
17: 5	glory that I had…before the world existed.	9
17:13	so that they may have my joy made complete	9
18:10	Simon Peter, who had a sword, drew it	9
18:39	you have a custom that I release someone	6
19: 7	The Jews answered him, "We have a law	9
19:10	Do you not know that I have power to release you	9
19:11	"You would have no power over me	9
19:15	"We have no king but the emperor."	9
20:31	believing you may have life in his name.	9
21: 5	Jesus said to them, "Children, you have no fish	9
Act 2:44	and had all things in common;	9
2:45	distribute the proceeds to all, as any had need.	9
2:47	praising God and having the goodwill	9
3: 6	Peter said, "I have no silver or gold	16
3: 6	no silver or gold, but what I have I give you;	9
4:14	they had nothing to say in opposition.	9
4:35	was distributed to each as any had need.	9
7: 5	even though he had no child.	6
7:44	"Our ancestors had the tent of testimony	6
8:21	You have no part or share in this	6
9:14	here he has authority from the chief priests	9
9:31	the church…had peace and was built up.	9

13: 5	they had John also to assist them.	9
13:15	"Brothers, if you have any word of exhortation	6
14: 9	and seeing that he had faith to be healed	9
15: 2	after Paul and Barnabas had no small dissension	2
15:21	Moses has had those who proclaim him	9
16: 9	During the night Paul had a vision: there stood	12
16:16	met a slave-girl who had a spirit of divination	9
19:13	use the name…over those who had evil spirits	9
19:38	the artisans…have a complaint against anyone	9
21: 9	He had four unmarried daughters	6
21:23	We have four men who are under a vow.	6
23:17	for he has something to report to him."	9
23:18	he has something to tell you."	9
23:19	"What is it that you have to report to me?"	9
24:15	I have a hope in God—	9
24:16	I do my best always to have a clear conscience	9
24:19	if they have anything against me.	9
24:23	but to let him have some liberty	9
24:25	when I have an opportunity, I will send for you."	11
25:19	they had certain points of disagreement with him	9
25:26	I have nothing definite to write	9
25:26	I may have something to write	9
26:22	To this day I have had help from God	15
28: 9	the people on the island who had diseases	9
28:19	I had no charge to bring against my nation.	9
Rom 2: 1	Therefore you have no excuse	6
2:14	though not having the law, are a law to themselves.	9
2:20	having in the law the embodiment of knowledge	9
2:27	will condemn you that have the written code	3
3:26	that he justifies the one who has faith in Jesus.	7
4: 2	he has something to boast about	9
5: 1	since we are justified by faith, we have peace	9
8: 9	Anyone who does not have the Spirit of Christ	9
8:23	we…who have the first fruits of the Spirit	9
9: 2	I have great sorrow and unceasing anguish	6
9: 9	I will return and Sarah shall have a son."	6
9:21	Has the potter no right over the clay	9
10: 2	I can testify that they have a zeal for God	9
11:23	for God has the power to graft them in again.	6
12: 4	For as in one body we have many members	9
12: 4	and not all the members have the same function	9
12: 6	We have gifts that differ according to the grace	9
14:22	The faith that you have, have as your own	9
14:22	The faith…have as your own conviction before God.	9
15: 4	by steadfastness…we might have hope.	9
15:17	In Christ Jesus, then, I have reason to boast	9
1Co 2:16	we have the mind of Christ.	9
3: 8	plants and the one who waters have a common purpose	6
4: 7	What do you have that you did not receive?	9
4:15	you might have ten thousand guardians in Christ	9
6: 1	When any of you has a grievance against another	9
6: 4	If you have ordinary cases, then,	9
6: 7	to have lawsuits at all with one another	9
6:19	Holy Spirit within you, which you have from God	9
7: 2	each man should have his own wife	9
7: 7	each has a particular gift from God	9
7:12	if any believer has a wife who is an unbeliever	9
7:13	if any woman has a husband who is an unbeliever	9
7:25	virgins, I have no command of the Lord	9
7:29	who have wives be as though they had none	9
7:29	who have wives be as though they had none	9
7:37	having his own desire under control	9
7:40	that I too have the Spirit of God.	9
8: 7	not everyone, however, who has this knowledge.	8
9: 4	Do we not have the right to our food and drink?	9
9: 5	have the right to be accompanied by a believing wife	9
9: 6	Or is it only Barnabas and I who have no right	9
9:17	For if I do this of my own will, I have a reward;	9
11:10	a woman ought to have a symbol of authority	9
11:16	we have no such custom, nor do the churches	9
11:22	What! Do you not have homes to eat and drink in?	9
11:22	humiliate those who have nothing?	9
12:12	For just as the body is one and has many members	9
12:21	eye cannot say to the hand, "I have no need of you,"	9
12:21	the head to the feet, "I have no need of you."	9
13: 1	speak in the tongues…but do not have love	9
13: 2	And if I have prophetic powers	9
13: 2	if I have all faith, so as to remove mountains	9
13: 2	but do not have love, I am nothing.	9
13: 3	but do not have love, I gain nothing.	9
14:26	When you come together, each one has a hymn	9

1Co	15:34	for some people have no knowledge of God.	9
	16:10	If Timothy comes, see that he has nothing to fear	2
2Co	1:15	so that you might have a double favor;	9
	2: 4	to let you know the abundant love that I have	9
	3: 4	Such is the confidence that we have	9
	3:12	we have such a hope, we act with great boldness	9
	4: 7	we have this treasure in clay jars	9
	4:13	just as we have the same spirit of faith	9
	5: 1	we have a building from God	9
	6:10	as having nothing, and yet possessing	9
	7: 1	Since we have these promises, beloved	9
	7: 5	our bodies had no rest	9
	8:12	gift is acceptable according to what one has	9
	8:12	not according to what one does not have.	9
	9: 8	so that by always having enough of everything	9
Gal	2: 4	spy on the freedom we have in Christ Jesus	9
	4:22	For it is written that Abraham had two sons	9
	6:10	So then, whenever we have an opportunity	9
Eph	1: 7	In him we have redemption through his blood	9
	2:12	having no hope and without God in the world.	9
	2:18	for through him both of us have access in one Spirit	9
	3:12	in whom we have access to God in boldness	9
	4:28	so as to have something to share with the needy.	9
	5: 5	has any inheritance in the kingdom of Christ	9
	6: 9	you know that both of you have the same Master	6
Php	1:30	having the same struggle that you saw	9
	1:30	the same struggle that you saw I had	8
	1:30	and now hear that I still have.	8
	2: 2	having the same love, being in full accord	9
	2:20	I have no one like him	9
	2:27	so that I would not have one sorrow after another.	9
	3: 4	even though I, too, have reason for confidence	9
	3: 4	If anyone else has reason to be confident	5
	3: 7	whatever gains I had	6
	3: 9	not having a righteousness of my own	9
	3:17	who live according to the example you have in us.	9
	4:11	I have learned to be content with whatever I have.	6
Col	1: 4	the love that you have for all the saints	9
	1:14	in whom we have redemption, the forgiveness	9
	1:18	he might come to have first place in everything.	2
	2:23	These have indeed an appearance of wisdom	9
	3:13	if anyone has a complaint against another	9
	4: 1	know that you also have a Master in heaven.	9
1Th	1: 8	so that we have no need to speak about it	9
	1: 9	what kind of welcome we had among you	9
	4:13	you may not grieve as others do who have no hope.	9
2Th	3: 9	This was not because we do not have that right	9
1Ti	1:19	having faith and a good conscience.	9
	5: 4	If a widow has children or grandchildren	9
	5:16	If any believing woman has relatives who…	9
	6: 2	Those who have believing masters	9
	6: 8	if we have food and clothing	9
	6:16	It is he alone who has immortality	9
Tit	2: 8	having nothing evil to say of us.	9
Heb	2:14	destroy the one who has the power of death	9
	3: 3	the builder of a house has more honor than the house	9
	3:12	that none of you may have an evil…heart	8
	4:14	Since, then, we have a great high priest	9
	4:15	For we do not have a high priest who is unable	9
	6:13	because he had no one greater by whom to swear	9
	6:19	We have this hope, a sure and steadfast anchor	9
	7: 3	having neither beginning of days nor end of life	9
	7: 5	have a commandment in the law	9
	7:27	he has no need…to offer sacrifices day after day	9
	8: 1	we have such a high priest	9
	8: 3	necessary…also to have something to offer.	9
	9: 1	the first covenant had regulations for worship	9
	10: 1	Since the law has only a shadow of the good things	9
	10: 2	would no longer have any consciousness of sin?	9
	10:19	Therefore, my friends, since we have confidence	9
	11:10	the city that has foundations	9
	11:15	they would have had opportunity to return.	9
	12: 8	If you do not have that discipline	6
	12: 9	Moreover, we had human parents	9
	13: 5	be content with what you have;	14
	13:10	We have an altar from which those who officiate	9
	13:10	who officiate in the tent have no right to eat.	9
	13:14	For here we have no lasting city	9
	13:18	we are sure that we have a clear conscience	9
Jas	1: 4	let endurance have its full effect	9
	2:14	if you say you have faith but do not have works?	9

	2:14	if you say you have faith but do not have works?	9
	2:17	So faith by itself, if it has no works, is dead.	9
	2:18	someone will say, "You have faith and I have works."	9
	2:18	someone will say, "You have faith and I have works."	9
	3:14	But if you have bitter envy…in your hearts	9
	4: 2	want something and do not have it; so you commit murder	9
	4: 2	You do not have, because you do not ask.	9
2Pe	1:19	we have the prophetic message more fully confirmed.	9
	2:14	They have eyes full of adultery	9
	2:14	They have hearts trained in greed.	9
1Jn	1: 3	so that you also may have fellowship with us;	9
	1: 6	If we say that we have fellowship with him	9
	1: 7	we have fellowship with one another	9
	1: 8	If we say that we have no sin, we deceive ourselves	9
	2: 1	if anyone does sin, we have an advocate	9
	2: 7	commandment that you have had from the beginning;	9
	2:23	No one who denies the Son has the Father;	9
	2:23	everyone who confesses the Son has the Father also.	9
	2:28	so that when he is revealed we may have confidence	9
	3: 3	all who have this hope in him purify themselves	9
	3:15	murderers do not have eternal life abiding in them.	9
	3:17	has the world's goods and sees a brother or sister in need	9
	3:21	we have boldness before God;	9
	4:16	we have known and believe the love that God has for us.	9
	4:17	that we may have boldness on the day of judgment	9
	4:18	for fear has to do with punishment	9
	4:21	The commandment we have from him is this:	9
	5:10	Those who believe…have the testimony in their hearts.	9
	5:12	Whoever has the Son has life;	9
	5:12	Whoever has the Son has life;	9
	5:12	whoever does not have the Son of God does not have life.	9
	5:12	whoever does not have the Son of God does not have life.	9
	5:13	so that you may know that you have eternal life.	9
	5:14	this is the boldness we have in him	9
2Jn	1: 5	but one we have had from the beginning	9
	1: 9	Everyone who…does not have God;	9
	1: 9	whoever abides in the teaching has both the Father	9
	1:12	Although I have much to write to you	9
3Jn	1: 4	I have no greater joy than this	9
	1:13	I have much to write to you	9
Rev	1:18	and I have the keys of Death and of Hades.	9
	2: 4	But I have this against you	9
	2: 7	Let anyone who has an ear listen	9
	2:10	and for ten days you will have affliction.	9
	2:11	who has an ear listen to what the Spirit is saying	9
	2:12	the words of him who has the sharp two-edged sword:	9
	2:14	But I have a few things against you:	9
	2:14	you have some there who hold to the teaching of Balaam	9
	2:15	have some who hold to the teaching of the Nicolaitans.	9
	2:17	who has an ear listen to what the Spirit is saying	9
	2:18	words of the Son of God, who has eyes like a flame	9
	2:20	But I have this against you:	9
	2:25	only hold fast to what you have until I come.	9
	2:29	Let anyone who has an ear listen	9
	3: 1	the words of him who has the seven spirits of God	9
	3: 1	"I know your works; you have a name of being alive	9
	3: 4	Yet you have still a few persons in Sardis	9
	3: 6	Let anyone who has an ear listen	9
	3: 7	holy one, the true one, who has the key of David	9
	3: 8	I know that you have but little power	9
	3:11	I am coming soon; hold fast to what you have	9
	3:13	Let anyone who has an ear listen	9
	3:22	Let anyone who has an ear listen	9
	5: 6	a Lamb…having seven horns and…seven eyes	9
	6: 2	I looked…a white horse! Its rider had a bow;	9
	7: 2	another angel…having the seal of the living God	9
	8: 6	Now the seven angels who had the seven trumpets	9
	9: 4	but only those people who do not have the seal	9
	9: 9	they had scales like iron breastplates	9
	9:10	They have tails like scorpions, with stingers	9
	9:11	They have as king…the angel of the bottomless pit;	9
	9:14	saying to the sixth angel who had the trumpet	9
	9:19	their tails are like serpents, having heads;	9
	11: 6	They have authority to shut the sky, so that no rain	9
	11: 6	and they have authority over the waters	9
	12: 6	wilderness, where she has a place prepared by God	9
	13: 1	I saw a beast…having ten horns and seven heads;	9
	13: 9	Let anyone who has an ear listen:	9
	13:11	another beast…it had two horns like a lamb	9
	13:17	no one can buy or sell who does not have the mark	9
	14: 1	one hundred forty-four thousand who had his name	9

14:17	another angel...and he too had a sharp sickle.	9
14:18	the angel who has authority over fire	9
14:18	called...to him who had the sharp sickle	9
16: 2	those who had the mark of the beast	9
16: 9	God, who had authority over these plagues	9
17: 1	one of the seven angels who had the seven bowls	9
17: 3	and it had seven heads and ten horns.	9
17: 9	"This calls for a mind that has wisdom:	9
18: 1	I saw another angel...having great authority;	9
18:19	all who had ships at sea grew rich by her wealth!	9
19:12	he has a name inscribed that no one knows	9
19:16	and on his thigh he has a name inscribed	9
20: 6	Over these the second death has no power	9
21: 9	one of the seven angels who had the seven bowls	9
21:11	It has the glory of God and a radiance	9
21:12	It has a great, high wall with twelve gates	9
21:14	And the wall of the city has twelve foundations	9
21:15	angel who talked to me had a measuring rod of gold	9
21:23	the city has no need of sun or moon to shine on it	9
22:14	they will have the right to the tree of life	6

have a discussion
1. διαλέγομαι, *dialegomai, 1363*

Act 18:19 the synagogue and had a discussion with the Jews.   1

have a firm grasp
1. ἀντέχω, *antechō, 504*

Tit 1: 9 He must have a firm grasp of the word   1

have a place
1. μένω, *menō, 3531*

Jhn 8:35 The slave does not have a permanent place   1
      8:35 the son has a place there forever.   1

have abundance
1. περισσεύω, *perisseuō, 4355*

Mat 25:29 they will have an abundance;

have all one wants
1. κορέννυμι, *korennymi, 3170*

1Co 4: 8 Already you have all you want!   1

have an abundance
1. περισσεύω, *perisseuō, 4355*

Mat 13:12 they will have an abundance;   1

have back
1. ἀπέχω, *apechō, 600*

Phm 1:15 you might have him back forever   1

have compassion
1. οἰκτίρω, *oiktirō, 3882*
2. σπλαγχνίζομαι, *splanchnizomai, 5072*
3. συμπαθέω, *sympatheō, 5217*

Mat 9:36 When he saw the crowds, he had compassion for them   2
      14:14 and he had compassion for them   2
      15:32 "I have compassion for the crowd   2
Mrk 6:34 he had compassion for them   2
      8: 2 "I have compassion for the crowd   2
Lke 7:13 he had compassion for her and said to her   2
Rom 9:15 I will have compassion on whom I have compassion."   1
      9:15 I will have compassion on whom I have compassion."   1
Heb 10:34 For you had compassion for those who were in prison   3

have confidence
1. θαρρέω, *tharreō, 2509*
2. πείθω, *peithō, 4275*

2Co 5: 8 Yes, we do have confidence   1
      7:16 because I have complete confidence in you.   1
Php 3: 3 have no confidence in the flesh   2

have knowledge
1. γινώσκω, *ginōskō, 1182*
2. οἶδα, *oida, 3857*

1Co 8: 2 does not yet have the necessary knowledge;   1
1Jn 2:20 and all of you have knowledge.   2

have little
1. ταπεινόω, *tapeinoō, 5427*

Php 4:12 I know what it is to have little,   1

have marital relations
1. γινώσκω, *ginōskō, 1182*

Mat 1:25 had no marital relations with her until she   1

have mercy
1. ἐλεάω, *eleaō, 1790*
2. ἐλεέω, *eleeō, 1796*

Mat 9:27 "Have mercy on us, Son of David!"   2
      15:22 "Have mercy on me, Lord, Son of David;   2
      17:15 have mercy on my son, for he is an epileptic   2
      18:33 you not have had mercy on your fellow slave   2
      18:33 as I had mercy on you?'   2
      20:30 "Lord, have mercy on us, Son of David!"   2
      20:31 "Have mercy on us, Lord, Son of David!"   2
Mrk 10:47 "Jesus, Son of David, have mercy on me!"   2
      10:48 "Son of David, have mercy on me!"   2
Lke 16:24 He called out, 'Father Abraham, have mercy   2
      17:13 "Jesus, Master, have mercy on us!"   2
      18:38 "Jesus, Son of David, have mercy on me!"   2
      18:39 "Son of David, have mercy on me!"   2
Rom 9:15 For he says to Moses, "I will have mercy   2
      9:15 "I will have mercy on whom I have mercy   2
      9:18 So then he has mercy on whomever he chooses   2
Php 2:27 God had mercy on him, and not only on him but on me   2
Jde 1:22 And have mercy on some who are wavering;   1
      1:23 have mercy on still others with fear   1

have more than enough
1. περισσεύω, *perisseuō, 4355*

Php 4:18 I have been paid in full and have more than enough;   1

have no concern
1. ἀμελέω, *ameleō, 288*

Heb 8: 9 so I had no concern for them, says the Lord.   1

have pain
1. λυπέω, *lypeō, 3382*

Jhn 16:20 you will have pain   1

have patience
1. μακροθυμέω, *makrothymeō, 3428*

Mat 18:26 'Have patience with me, and I will pay you   1
      18:29 'Have patience with me, and I will pay you.'   1

have pity
1. σπλαγχνίζομαι, *splanchnizomai, 5072*

Mrk 9:22 to do anything, have pity on us and help us."   1

have plenty
1. περισσεύω, *perisseuō, 4355*

Php 4:12 have little, and I know what it is to have plenty.   1
      4:12 of having plenty and of being in need.   1

have the gift of prophecy
1. προφητεύω, *prophēteuō, 4736*

Act 21: 9 four unmarried daughters who had the gift of prophecy.   1

have to
1. δεῖ, *dei, 1256*
2. ὀφείλω, *opheilō, 4053*
3. συμβαίνω, *symbainō, 5201*

Lke 15:32 we had to celebrate and rejoice,   1
      22: 7 on which the Passover lamb had to be sacrificed.   1
Jhn 4: 4 he had to go through Samaria.   1
Act 1:16 "Friends, the scripture had to be fulfilled   1
      21:35 he had to be carried by the soldiers.   3
      27:26 we will have to run aground on some island."   1
1Co 7:36 if his passions are strong, and so it has to be   2
      11:19 Indeed, there have to be factions among you   1
Heb 2:17 Therefore he had to become like his brothers and sisters   2
      9:26 he would have had to suffer again and again   1
1Pe 1: 6 now for a little while you have had to suffer   1

have too little
1. ἐλαττονέω, *elattoneō, 1782*

2Co 8:15 the one who had little did not have too little."   1

have too much

    1. πλεονάζω, *pleonazō*, 4429

2Co 8:15 "The one who had much did not have too much   1

havoc   *See* make havoc

hay

    1. χόρτος, *chortos*, 5965

1Co 3:12 gold, silver, precious stones, wood, hay, straw—   1

he   Not Indexed

head   *See also* beat over the head

    1. Contextual: Not in Greek
    2. εἰκών, *eikōn*, 1635
    3. κεφαλή, *kephalē*, 3051
    4. στάχυς¹, *stachys¹*, 5092

Mat	5:36 And do not swear by your head,	3
	6:17 when you fast, put oil on your head and wash your face	3
	8:20 but the Son of Man has nowhere to lay his head."	3
	10:30 even the hairs of your head are all counted.	3
	14: 8 she said, "Give me the head of John the Baptist	3
	14:11 The head was brought on a platter	3
	22:20 "Whose head is this, and whose title?"	2
	26: 7 poured it on his head as he sat at the table.	3
	27:29 thorns into a crown, they put it on his head.	3
	27:30 took the reed and struck him on the head.	3
	27:37 Over his head they put the charge against him	3
	27:39 who passed by derided him, shaking their heads	3
Mrk	4:28 then the head, then the full grain in the head.	4
	4:28 then the head, then the full grain in the head.	4
	6:24 She replied, "The head of John the baptizer."	3
	6:25 the head of John the Baptist on a platter."	3
	6:27 with orders to bring John's head.	3
	6:28 brought his head on a platter	3
	12:16 "Whose head is this, and whose title?"	2
	14: 3 and poured the ointment on his head.	3
	15:19 They struck his head with a reed, spat upon him	3
	15:29 shaking their heads and saying, "Aha!	3
Lke	7:46 You did not anoint my head with oil	3
	9:58 the Son of Man has nowhere to lay his head."	3
	12: 7 But even the hairs of your head are all counted.	3
	20:24 Whose head and whose title does it bear?"	2
	21:18 not a hair of your head will perish.	3
	21:28 stand up and raise your heads	3
Jhn	13: 9 not my feet only but also my hands and my head!"	3
	19: 2 crown of thorns and put it on his head	3
	19:30 he bowed his head and gave up his spirit.	3
	20: 7 the cloth that had been on Jesus' head	3
	20:12 one at the head and the other at the feet.	3
Act	18: 6 "Your blood be on your own heads! I am innocent.	3
	21:24 pay for the shaving of their heads	3
	27:34 for none of you will lose a hair from your heads	3
Rom	12:20 you will heap burning coals on their heads."	3
1Co	11: 3 understand that Christ is the head of every man	3
	11: 3 the husband is the head of his wife	3
	11: 3 God is the head of Christ.	3
	11: 4 prays or prophesies with something on his head	3
	11: 4 with something on his head disgraces his head	3
	11: 5 who prays or prophesies with her head unveiled	3
	11: 5 with her head unveiled disgraces her head	3
	11: 5 one and the same thing as having her head shaved.	1
	11: 7 For a man ought not to have his head veiled	3
	11:10 ought to have a symbol of authority on her head	3
	11:13 for a woman to pray to God with her head unveiled?	1
	12:21 the head to the feet, "I have no need of you."	3
Eph	1:22 has made him the head over all things	3
	4:15 grow up in every way into him who is the head	3
	5:23 For the husband is the head of the wife	3
	5:23 just as Christ is the head of the church	3
Col	1:18 He is the head of the body, the church;	3
	2:10 the head of every ruler and authority.	3
	2:19 not holding fast to the head	3
1Pe	2: 7 stone...has become the very head of the corner,"	3
Rev	1:14 His head and his hair were white as white wool	3
	4: 4 elders...with golden crowns on their heads.	3
	9: 7 On their heads were what looked like crowns	3
	9:17 the heads of the horses were like lions' heads	3
	9:17 the heads of the horses were like lions' heads	3
	9:19 their tails are like serpents, having heads;	3

	10: 1 mighty angel...with a rainbow over his head;	3
	12: 1 and on her head a crown of twelve stars.	3
	12: 3 great red dragon, with seven heads and ten horns	3
	12: 3 and ten horns, and seven diadems on his heads.	3
	13: 1 I saw a beast...having ten horns and seven heads;	3
	13: 1 and on its heads were blasphemous names.	3
	13: 3 One of its heads seemed to have received a death-blow	3
	14:14 the Son of Man, with a golden crown on his head	3
	17: 3 and it had seven heads and ten horns.	3
	17: 7 and of the beast with seven heads and ten horns	3
	17: 9 the seven heads are seven mountains	3
	18:19 And they threw dust on their heads, as they wept	3
	19:12 and on his head are many diadems;	3

head of grain

    1. στάχυς¹, *stachys¹*, 5092

Mat	12: 1 they began to pluck heads of grain and to eat.	1
Mrk	2:23 his disciples began to pluck heads of grain.	1
Lke	6: 1 his disciples plucked some heads of grain	1

head-on   *See* turn head-on

headlong

    1. πρηνής, *prēnēs*, 4568

Act 1:18 falling headlong, he burst open in the middle   1

headquarters

    1. πραιτώριον, *praitōrion*, 4550

Jhn	18:28 from Caiaphas to Pilate's headquarters.	1
	18:28 They themselves did not enter the headquarters	1
	18:33 Pilate entered the headquarters again	1
	19: 9 He entered his headquarters again and asked	1
Act	23:35 kept under guard in Herod's headquarters.	1

governor's headquarters

    1. πραιτώριον, *praitōrion*, 4550

Mat	27:27 the governor took Jesus into the governor's headquarters	1
Mrk	15:16 the palace (that is, the governor's headquarters);	1

heal

    1. διασῴζω, *diasōzō*, 1407
    2. θεραπεύω, *therapeuō*, 2543
    3. ἰάομαι, *iaomai*, 2615
    4. ἴασις, *iasis*, 2617
    5. σῴζω, *sōzō*, 5392
    6. ὑγιής, *hygiēs*, 5618
    7. ὑγιής + ποιέω, *hygiēs + poieō*, 5618 + 4472

Mat	8: 8 speak the word, and my servant will be healed.	3
	8:13 And the servant was healed in that hour.	3
	13:15 and turn—and I would heal them.'	3
	14:36 and all who touched it were healed.	1
	15:28 And her daughter was healed instantly.	3
Mrk	5:29 she felt in her body that she was healed	3
	5:34 go in peace, and be healed of your disease."	6
	6:56 all who touched it were healed.	5
Lke	5:17 the power of the Lord was with him to heal.	3
	6:18 to be healed of their diseases;	3
	6:19 power came out from him and healed all of them.	3
	7: 3 asking him to come and heal his slave.	1
	7: 7 speak the word, and let my servant be healed.	3
	8:36 had been possessed by demons had been healed	5
	8:47 how she had been immediately healed.	3
	9: 2 to proclaim the kingdom of God and to heal.	3
	9:11 healed those who needed to be cured.	3
	9:42 healed the boy, and gave him back to his father.	3
	14: 4 Jesus took him and healed him, and sent him away.	3
	17:15 one of them, when he saw that he was healed	3
	22:51 he touched his ear and healed him.	3
Jhn	4:47 and begged him to come down and heal his son	3
	5:13 the man who had been healed did not know	3
	7:23 I healed a man's whole body on the sabbath?	7
	12:40 turn—and I would heal them."	3
Act	4: 9 asked how this man has been healed	5
	4:30 while you stretch out your hand to heal	4
	9:34 Peter said to him, "Aeneas, Jesus Christ heals you;	3
	14: 9 and seeing that he had faith to be healed	5
	28:27 turn—and I would heal them.'	3
Heb	12:13 not be put out of joint, but rather be healed.	3
Jas	5:16 pray for one another, so that you may be healed.	3

1Pe	2:24	by his wounds you have been healed.	3
Rev	13: 3	but its mortal wound had been healed.	2
	13:12	the first beast, whose mortal wound had been healed.	2

healing

1. θεραπεία, *therapeia, 2542*
2. ἴαμα, *iama, 2611*
3. ἰάομαι, *iaomai, 2615*
4. ἴασις, *iasis, 2617*

Act	4:22	man on whom this sign of healing had been performed	4
	10:38	healing all who were oppressed by the devil	3
1Co	12: 9	to another gifts of healing by the one Spirit	2
	12:28	then deeds of power, then gifts of healing,	2
	12:30	Do all possess gifts of healing?	2
Rev	22: 2	leaves…are for the healing of the nations.	1

good health

1. ὑγιαίνω, *hygiainō, 5617*
2. ὑγιής, *hygiēs, 5618*

Lke	7:10	they found the slave in good health.	1
Act	4:10	this man is standing before you in good health	2
3Jn	1: 2	I pray…that you may be in good health	1

perfect health

1. ὁλοκληρία, *holoklēria, 3907*

Act	3:16	the faith…has given him this perfect health	1

healthy

1. ἁπλοῦς, *haplous, 606*

Mat	6:22	if your eye is healthy, your whole body will be full	1
Lke	11:34	If your eye is healthy	1

not healthy

1. πονηρός, *ponēros, 4505*

Lke	11:34	is not healthy, your body is full of darkness.	1

heap

1. κολλάω, *kollaō, 3140*
2. λέγω, *legō, 3306*
3. σωρεύω, *sōreuō, 5397*

Lke	22:65	They kept heaping many other insults on him	2
Rom	12:20	you will heap burning coals on their heads."	3
Rev	18: 5	for her sins are heaped high as heaven	1

heap up empty phrases

1. βατταλογέω, *battalogeō, 1006*

Mat	6: 7	"When you are praying, do not heap up empty phrases	1

hear

1. Contextual: Not in Greek
2. ἀκοή, *akoē, 198*
3. ἀκούω, *akouō, 201*
4. γίνομαι, *ginomai, 1181*
5. γίνομαι + εἰς + ὁ + οὖς, *ginomai + eis + ho + ous, 1181 + 1650 + 3836 + 4044*
6. εἰσακούω, *eisakouō, 1653*
7. λόγος, *logos, 3364*
8. οὖς, *ous, 4044*

Mat	2: 3	When King Herod heard this, he was frightened	3
	2: 9	When they had heard the king, they set out;	3
	2:18	"A voice was heard in Ramah, wailing and loud	3
	2:22	he heard that Archelaus was ruling over Judea	3
	4:12	Now when Jesus heard that John had been arrested	3
	5:21	"You have heard that it was said…of ancient times	3
	5:27	"You have heard that it was said, 'You shall not	3
	5:33	"Again, you have heard that it was said to those	3
	5:38	"You have heard that it was said, 'An eye for an eye	3
	5:43	"You have heard that it was said, 'You shall love	3
	6: 7	that they will be heard because of their many words.	6
	7:24	"Everyone then who hears these words of mine	3
	7:26	And everyone who hears these words of mine	3
	8:10	When Jesus heard him, he was amazed	3
	9:12	But when he heard this, he said	3
	10:27	what you hear whispered, proclaim	3
	11: 2	John heard in prison what the Messiah was doing	3
	11: 4	"Go and tell John what you hear and see:	3
	11: 5	lame walk, the lepers are cleansed, the deaf hear	3
	12:19	nor will anyone hear his voice in the streets.	3
	12:24	when the Pharisees heard it, they said	3

	13:13	hearing they do not listen, nor do they understand.'	3
	13:15	and their ears are hard of hearing	3
	13:16	and your ears, for they hear.	3
	13:17	and to hear what you hear, but did not hear it.	3
	13:17	and to hear what you hear, but did not hear it.	3
	13:17	and to hear what you hear, but did not hear it.	3
	13:18	"Hear then the parable of the sower.	3
	13:19	When anyone hears the word of the kingdom	3
	13:20	this is the one who hears the word	3
	13:22	this is the one who hears the word	3
	13:23	this is the one who hears the word	3
	14: 1	At that time Herod the ruler heard	3
	14:13	when Jesus heard this, he withdrew from there	3
	14:13	But when the crowds heard it	3
	15:12	when they heard what you said?"	3
	17: 6	When the disciples heard this	3
	19:22	the young man heard this word, he went away	3
	19:25	When the disciples heard this	3
	20:24	When the ten heard it	3
	20:30	When they heard that Jesus was passing by	3
	21:15	heard the children crying out in the temple	1
	21:16	said to him, "Do you hear what these are saying?"	3
	21:45	priests and the Pharisees heard his parables	3
	22:22	When they heard this, they were amazed;	3
	22:33	when the crowd heard it	3
	22:34	When the Pharisees heard	3
	24: 6	you will hear of wars and rumors of wars;	3
	26:65	You have now heard his blasphemy.	3
	27:13	hear how many accusations they make against you?"	3
	27:47	some of the bystanders heard it, they said	3
Mrk	2:17	When Jesus heard this, he said to them	3
	3: 8	hearing all that he was doing, they came to him	3
	3:21	When his family heard it	3
	4: 9	he said, "Let anyone with ears to hear listen!"	3
	4:15	when they hear, Satan immediately comes	3
	4:16	they hear the word, they immediately receive	3
	4:18	these are the ones who hear the word	3
	4:20	they hear the word and accept it	3
	4:23	Let anyone with ears to hear listen!"	3
	4:24	"Pay attention to what you hear;	3
	4:33	as they were able to hear it;	3
	5:27	She had heard about Jesus	3
	6: 2	many who heard him were astounded. They said	3
	6:11	they refuse to hear you	3
	6:14	King Herod heard of it	3
	6:16	when Herod heard of it, he said	3
	6:20	When he heard him, he was greatly perplexed;	3
	6:29	When his disciples heard about it	3
	6:55	to wherever they heard he was.	3
	7:25	immediately heard about him, and she came	3
	7:37	makes the deaf to hear and the mute to speak."	3
	8:18	Do you have ears, and fail to hear?	3
	10:22	When he heard this, he was shocked	7
	10:41	When the ten heard this, they began to be angry	3
	10:47	When he heard that it was Jesus of Nazareth	3
	11:14	his disciples heard it.	3
	11:18	the chief priests and the scribes heard it	3
	12:28	heard them disputing with one another	3
	12:29	Jesus answered, "The first is, 'Hear, O Israel:	3
	13: 7	When you hear of wars and rumors of wars	3
	14:11	When they heard it, they were greatly pleased	3
	14:58	"We heard him say, 'I will destroy this temple	3
	14:64	You have heard his blasphemy!	3
	15:35	the bystanders heard it, they said, "Listen	3
	16:11	[when they heard that he was alive]	3
Lke	1:13	for your prayer has been heard.	6
	1:41	When Elizabeth heard Mary's greeting, the child	3
	1:44	as soon as I heard the sound of your greeting	5
	1:58	Her neighbors and relatives heard	3
	1:66	All who heard them pondered them and said,	3
	2:18	all who heard it were amazed	3
	2:20	for all they had heard and seen	3
	2:47	all who heard him were amazed	3
	4:21	scripture has been fulfilled in your hearing."	8
	4:23	things that we have heard you did at Capernaum.' "	3
	4:28	When they heard this	3
	5: 1	pressing in on him to hear the word of God	3
	5:15	many crowds would gather to hear	3
	6:18	They had come to hear him	3
	6:47	who comes to me, hears my words, and acts on them.	3
	6:49	one who hears and does not act	3

Lke	7: 1 all his sayings in the hearing of the people	2
	7: 3 When he heard about Jesus	3
	7: 9 When Jesus heard this he was amazed at him	3
	7:22 "Go and tell John what you have seen and heard:	3
	7:22 lepers are cleansed, the deaf hear	3
	7:29 (And all the people who heard this	3
	8: 8 "Let anyone with ears to hear listen!"	3
	8:12 The ones on the path are those who have heard;	3
	8:13 when they hear the word, receive it with joy.	3
	8:14 these are the ones who hear;	3
	8:15 who, when they hear the word, hold it fast	3
	8:21 those who hear the word of God and do it."	3
	8:50 Jesus heard this, he replied, "Do not fear.	3
	9: 7 Now Herod the ruler heard about all that	3
	9: 9 who is this about whom I hear such things?"	3
	10:24 to hear what you hear, but did not hear it."	3
	10:24 to hear what you hear, but did not hear it."	3
	10:24 to hear what you hear, but did not hear it."	3
	11:28 "Blessed rather are those who hear the word of God	3
	12: 3 said in the dark will be heard in the light	3
	14:15 One of the dinner guests, on hearing this,	3
	14:35 Let anyone with ears to hear listen!"	3
	15:25 he heard music and dancing.	3
	16: 2 'What is this that I hear about you?	3
	16:14 The Pharisees, who were lovers of money, heard all	3
	18:22 When Jesus heard this, he said to him,	3
	18:23 when he heard this, he became sad;	3
	18:26 who heard it said, "Then who can be saved?"	3
	18:36 heard a crowd going by	3
	19:48 the people were spellbound by what they heard.	3
	20:16 When they heard this, they said, "Heaven forbid!"	3
	20:45 In the hearing of all the people	3
	21: 9 "When you hear of wars and insurrections	3
	22:71 We have heard it ourselves from his own lips!"	3
	23: 6 When Pilate heard this	3
	23: 8 because he had heard about him	3
Jhn	1:37 The two disciples heard him say this	3
	1:40 One of the two who heard John speak…was Andrew	3
	3: 8 The wind blows…and you hear the sound of it	3
	3:29 The friend…who stands and hears him, rejoices	3
	3:32 He testifies to what he has seen and heard	3
	4: 1 when Jesus learned that the Pharisees had heard	3
	4:42 for we have heard for ourselves	3
	4:47 heard that Jesus had come from Judea to Galilee	3
	5:24 who hears my word and believes him who sent me	3
	5:25 the dead will hear the voice of the Son of God	3
	5:25 those who hear will live.	3
	5:28 all who are in their graves will hear his voice	3
	5:30 As I hear, I judge; and my judgment is just	3
	5:37 You have never heard his voice	3
	6:45 Everyone who has heard and learned	3
	6:60 When many of his disciples heard it, they said	3
	7:32 The Pharisees heard the crowd muttering such things	3
	7:40 When they heard these words	3
	8: 9 ⟦When they heard it, they went away, one by one⟧	3
	8:26 I declare to the world what I have heard from him."	3
	8:38 you should do what you have heard from the Father."	3
	8:40 has told you the truth that I heard from God.	3
	8:47 Whoever is from God hears the words of God.	3
	8:47 The reason you do not hear them is	3
	9:27 Why do you want to hear it again?	3
	9:32 Never since the world began has it been heard	3
	9:35 Jesus heard that they had driven him out	3
	9:40 the Pharisees near him heard this and said	3
	10: 3 the sheep hear his voice.	3
	10:27 My sheep hear my voice. I know them	3
	11: 4 when Jesus heard it, he said	3
	11: 6 after having heard that Lazarus was ill	3
	11:20 When Martha heard that Jesus was coming	3
	11:29 when she heard it, she got up quickly and went	3
	11:41 "Father, I thank you for having heard me.	3
	11:42 I knew that you always hear me	3
	12:12 great crowd that had come to the festival heard	3
	12:18 they heard that he had performed this sign	3
	12:29 The crowd standing there heard it and said	3
	12:34 answered him, "We have heard from the law	3
	12:47 anyone who hears my words and does not keep them	3
	14:24 the word that you hear is not mine	3
	14:28 You heard me say to you, 'I am going away	3
	15:15 everything that I have heard from my Father.	3
	16:13 will speak whatever he hears, and	3

	18:21 Ask those who heard what I said to them;	3
	19: 8 Now when Pilate heard this,	3
	19:13 When Pilate heard these words	3
	21: 7 When Simon Peter heard that it was the Lord	3
Act	1: 4 he said, "is what you have heard from me;	3
	2: 6 each one heard them speaking in the native language	3
	2: 8 how is it that we hear	3
	2:11 in our own languages we hear them speaking	3
	2:33 he has poured out this that you both see and hear.	3
	2:37 when they heard this, they were cut to the heart	3
	4: 4 many of those who heard the word believed;	3
	4:20 speaking about what we have seen and heard."	3
	4:24 When they heard it	3
	5: 5 when Ananias heard these words	3
	5: 5 great fear seized all who heard of it.	3
	5:11 all who heard of these things.	3
	5:21 When they heard this	3
	5:24 when…the chief priests heard these words	3
	5:33 When they heard this, they were enraged	3
	6:11 "We have heard him speak blasphemous words	3
	6:14 we have heard him say	3
	7:12 when Jacob heard that there was grain in Egypt	3
	7:29 When he heard this, Moses fled	7
	7:34 heard their groaning	3
	7:54 When they heard these things, they became enraged	3
	8: 6 hearing and seeing the signs that he did	3
	8:14 Now when the apostles at Jerusalem heard	3
	8:30 Philip…heard him reading the prophet Isaiah.	3
	9: 4 He fell to the ground and heard a voice saying	3
	9: 7 heard the voice but saw no one.	3
	9:13 I have heard from many about this man	3
	9:21 All who heard him were amazed and said	3
	9:38 disciples, who heard that Peter was there	3
	10:13 he heard a voice saying, "Get up, Peter; kill and eat."	4
	10:22 to hear what you have to say."	3
	10:31 said, 'Cornelius, your prayer has been heard	6
	10:44 the Holy Spirit fell upon all who heard the word.	3
	10:46 for they heard them speaking in tongues	3
	11: 1 heard that the Gentiles had also accepted	3
	11: 7 I also heard a voice saying to me, 'Get up, Peter;	3
	11:18 When they heard this, they were silenced.	3
	13: 7 wanted to hear the word of God.	3
	13:44 gathered to hear the word of the Lord.	3
	13:48 When the Gentiles heard this, they were glad	3
	14:14 When the apostles Barnabas and Paul heard of it	3
	15: 7 the Gentiles would hear the message of the good news	3
	15:24 Since we have heard	3
	16:38 when they heard that they were Roman citizens;	3
	17: 8 were disturbed when they heard this	3
	17:21 telling or hearing something new.	3
	17:32 When they heard of the resurrection of the dead	3
	17:32 others said, "We will hear you again about this."	3
	18: 8 Corinthians who heard Paul became believers	3
	18:26 when Priscilla and Aquila heard him	3
	19: 2 not even heard that there is a Holy Spirit."	3
	19: 5 On hearing this, they were baptized	3
	19:10 residents of Asia…heard the word of the Lord.	3
	19:26 You also see and hear	3
	19:28 When they heard this, they were enraged	3
	21:12 When we heard this	3
	21:20 When they heard it, they praised God.	3
	21:22 They will certainly hear that you have come.	3
	22: 2 When they heard him addressing them	3
	22: 7 I fell to the ground and heard a voice saying	3
	22: 9 did not hear the voice of the one who was speaking	3
	22:14 see the Righteous One and to hear his own voice;	3
	22:15 his witness…of what you have seen and heard.	3
	22:26 When the centurion heard that	3
	23:16 the son of Paul's sister heard about the ambush;	3
	24: 4 to hear us briefly with your customary graciousness.	3
	24:22 Felix…adjourned the hearing with the comment	1
	24:24 heard him speak concerning faith in Christ Jesus.	3
	25:22 "I would like to hear the man myself."	3
	25:22 "Tomorrow," he said, "you will hear him."	3
	26:14 heard a voice saying to me in the Hebrew language	3
	28:15 The believers from there, when they heard of us	3
	28:22 we would like to hear from you what you think,	3
	28:27 their ears are hard of hearing	3
Rom	10:14 to believe in one of whom they have never heard?	3
	10:14 how are they to hear without someone to proclaim	3
	10:17 So faith comes from what is heard	2

	10:17	what is heard comes through the word of Christ.	2
	10:18	But I ask, have they not heard? Indeed they have;	3
	11: 8	eyes…not see and ears that would not hear	3
	15:21	who have never heard of him shall understand.”	3
1Co	2: 9	“What no eye has seen, nor ear heard	3
	11:18	I hear that there are divisions among you;	3
	12:17	whole body…an eye, where would the hearing be?	2
	12:17	If the whole body were hearing,	2
2Co	3:14	when they hear the reading of the old covenant	1
	12: 4	heard things that are not to be told	3
	12: 6	what is seen in me or heard from me	3
Gal	1:13	heard, no doubt, of my earlier life in Judaism.	3
	1:23	they only heard it said	3
	3: 2	works of the law or by believing what you heard?	2
	3: 5	the law, or by your believing what you heard?	2
Eph	1:13	you also, when you had heard the word of truth	3
	1:15	I have heard of your faith in the Lord	3
	3: 2	for surely you have already heard of the commission	3
	4:21	For surely you have heard about him	3
	4:29	that your words may give grace to those who hear.	3
Php	1:27	see you or am absent and hear about you,	3
	1:30	and now hear that I still have.	3
	2:26	distressed because you heard that he was ill.	3
	4: 9	things that you have learned and received and heard	3
Col	1: 4	we have heard of your faith in Christ Jesus	3
	1: 6	from the day you heard it and truly comprehended	3
	1: 9	For this reason, since the day we heard it	3
	1:23	the gospel that you heard	3
1Th	2:13	the word of God that you heard from us	2
2Th	3:11	we hear that some of you are living in idleness	3
2Ti	1:13	sound teaching that you have heard from me	3
	2: 2	what you have heard from me	3
	4:17	all the Gentiles might hear it.	3
Phm	1: 5	because I hear of your love	3
Heb	2: 1	pay greater attention to what we have heard	3
	2: 3	it was attested to us by those who heard him	3
	3: 7	“Today, if you hear his voice	3
	3:15	As it is said, “Today, if you hear his voice	3
	3:16	who were they who heard and yet were rebellious?	3
	4: 2	the message they heard did not benefit them	2
	4: 7	“Today, if you hear his voice	3
	5: 7	he was heard because of his reverent submission.	6
Jas	5:11	You have heard of the endurance of Job	3
2Pe	1:18	We ourselves heard this voice come from heaven	3
	2: 8	by their lawless deeds that he saw and heard)	2
1Jn	1: 1	what…from the beginning, what we have heard	3
	1: 3	we declare to you what we have seen and heard	3
	1: 5	the message we have heard from him and proclaim	3
	2: 7	old commandment is the word that you have heard.	3
	2:18	As you have heard that antichrist is coming	3
	2:24	Let what you heard from the beginning abide	3
	2:24	what you heard from the beginning abides in you	3
	3:11	message you have heard from the beginning	3
	4: 3	antichrist, of which you have heard that it is coming;	3
	5:14	if we ask anything according to his will, he hears	3
	5:15	if we know that he hears us in whatever we ask	3
2Jn	1: 6	just as you have heard it from the beginning	3
3Jn	1: 4	to hear that my children are walking in the truth.	3
Rev	1: 3	and blessed are those who hear and who keep	3
	1:10	and I heard behind me a loud voice like a trumpet	3
	3: 3	Remember then what you received and heard;	3
	3:20	if you hear my voice and open the door	3
	4: 1	the first voice, which I had heard speaking to me	3
	5:11	Then I looked, and I heard the voice of many angels	3
	5:13	I heard every creature in heaven and on earth	3
	6: 1	I heard one of the four living creatures call out	3
	6: 3	I heard the second living creature call out	3
	6: 5	I heard the third living creature call out, “Come!”	3
	6: 6	I heard what seemed to be a voice in the midst	3
	6: 7	I heard the voice of the fourth living creature	3
	7: 4	I heard the number of those who were sealed	3
	8:13	I heard an eagle crying with a loud voice	3
	9:13	I heard a voice from the four horns of the…altar	3
	9:16	number of the troops…I heard their number.	3
	9:20	idols…which cannot see or hear or walk.	3
	10: 4	I was about to write, but I heard a voice	3
	10: 8	voice that I had heard from heaven spoke to me	3
	11:12	Then they heard a loud voice from heaven saying	3
	12:10	Then I heard a loud voice in heaven, proclaiming	3
	14: 2	I heard a voice from heaven	3
	14: 2	the voice I heard was like the sound of harpists	3

	14:13	I heard a voice from heaven saying, “Write this:	3
	16: 1	Then I heard a loud voice from the temple	3
	16: 5	And I heard the angel of the waters say	3
	16: 7	I heard the altar respond, “Yes, O Lord God,	3
	18: 4	Then I heard another voice from heaven saying	3
	18:22	sound of harpists…will be heard in you no more;	3
	18:22	the millstone will be heard in you no more;	3
	18:23	the voice…will be heard in you no more;	3
	19: 1	After this I heard what seemed to be the loud voice	3
	19: 6	Then I heard what seemed to be the voice	3
	21: 3	I heard a loud voice from the throne saying	3
	22: 8	I, John, am the one who heard and saw these things.	3
	22: 8	when I heard and saw them, I fell down to worship	3
	22:17	And let everyone who hears say, “Come.”	3
	22:18	I warn everyone who hears the words	3

hear before

   1. προακούω, *proakouō, 4578*

Col	1: 5	You have heard of this hope before in the word	1

hearer

   1. ἀκούω, *akouō, 201*
   2. ἀκροατής, *akroatēs, 212*

Rom	2:13	it is not the hearers of the law who are righteous	2
1Ti	4:16	you will save both yourself and your hearers.	1
Heb	12:19	a voice whose words made the hearers beg	1
Jas	1:22	But be doers of the word, and not merely hearers	2
	1:23	For if any are hearers of the word and not doers,	2
	1:25	being not hearers who forget but doers who act	2

heart   *See also* harden the heart, hardness of heart, know the heart, know the human heart, lose heart, take heart

   1. Contextual: Not in Greek
   2. ἑαυτοῦ, *heautou, 1571*
   3. καρδία, *kardia, 2840*
   4. κοιλία, *koilia, 3120*
   5. κόλπος, *kolpos, 3146*
   6. σπλάγχνον, *splanchnon, 5073*
   7. ψυχή, *psychē, 6034*

Mat	5: 8	are the pure in heart, for they will see God.	3
	5:28	committed adultery with her in his heart.	3
	6:21	treasure is, there your heart will be also.	3
	9: 4	“Why do you think evil in your hearts?	3
	11:29	for I am gentle and humble in heart	3
	12:34	For out of the abundance of the heart	3
	12:40	the Son of Man will be in the heart of the earth.	3
	13:15	For this people's heart has grown dull	3
	13:15	and understand with their heart	3
	13:19	and snatches away what is sown in the heart;	3
	15: 8	but their hearts are far from me;	3
	15:18	comes out of the mouth proceeds from the heart	3
	15:19	For out of the heart come evil intentions, murder	3
	18:35	forgive your brother or sister from your heart.”	3
	22:37	love the Lord your God with all your heart	3
Mrk	2: 6	questioning in their hearts	3
	2: 8	“Why do you raise such questions in your hearts?	3
	3: 5	grieved at their hardness of heart	3
	6:52	their hearts were hardened.	3
	7: 6	their hearts are far from me;	3
	7:19	since it enters, not the heart but the stomach	3
	7:21	from the human heart, that evil intentions come:	3
	8:17	Are your hearts hardened?	3
	11:23	do not doubt in your heart	3
	12:30	shall love the Lord your God with all your heart	3
	12:33	'to love him with all the heart	3
Lke	1:17	to turn the hearts of parents to their children	3
	1:51	in the thoughts of their hearts.	3
	2:19	pondered them in her heart.	3
	2:51	His mother treasured all these things in her heart.	3
	3:15	questioning in their hearts concerning John	3
	5:22	“Why do you raise such questions in your hearts?	3
	6:45	person out of the good treasure of the heart	3
	6:45	out of the abundance of the heart	3
	8:12	takes away the word from their hearts	3
	8:15	hold it fast in an honest and good heart	3
	10:27	love the Lord your God with all your heart	3
	12:34	there your heart will be also.	3
	16:15	God knows your hearts;	3
	21:34	so that your hearts are not weighed down	3
	24:25	slow of heart to believe	3

Lke	24:32	"Were not our hearts burning within us	3
	24:38	why do doubts arise in your hearts?	3
Jhn	1:18	the only Son, who is close to the Father's heart,	5
	7:38	'Out of the believer's heart shall flow rivers	4
	12:40	blinded their eyes and hardened their heart	3
	12:40	understand with their heart	3
	13: 2	the heart of Judas son of Simon Iscariot	3
	14: 1	not let your hearts be troubled. Believe in God	3
	14:27	Do not let your hearts be troubled	3
	16: 6	sorrow has filled your hearts.	3
	16:22	and your hearts will rejoice	3
Act	2:26	my heart was glad, and my tongue rejoiced;	3
	2:37	when they heard this, they were cut to the heart	3
	2:46	ate their food with glad and generous hearts	3
	4:32	who believed were of one heart and soul	3
	5: 3	"why has Satan filled your heart to lie	3
	5: 4	you have contrived this deed in your heart?	3
	7:23	it came into his heart to visit his relatives	3
	7:39	in their hearts they turned back to Egypt	3
	7:51	uncircumcised in heart and ears	3
	8:21	your heart is not right before God.	3
	8:22	the intent of your heart may be forgiven you.	3
	13:22	a man after my heart, who will carry out all my wishes.'	3
	14:17	filling you with food and your hearts with joy."	3
	15: 9	cleansing their hearts by faith	3
	16:14	opened her heart to listen eagerly to what was said	3
	21:13	"What are you doing, weeping and breaking my heart?	3
	28:27	For this people's heart has grown dull	3
	28:27	understand with their heart	3
Rom	1:24	God gave them up in the lusts of their hearts	3
	2: 5	by your hard and impenitent heart	3
	2:15	what the law requires is written on their hearts	3
	2:29	and real circumcision is a matter of the heart	3
	5: 5	God's love has been poured into our hearts	3
	6:17	you...have become obedient from the heart	3
	8:27	God, who searches the heart, knows	3
	9: 2	great sorrow and unceasing anguish in my heart.	3
	10: 1	Brothers and sisters, my heart's desire and prayer	3
	10: 6	"Do not say in your heart, 'Who will ascend	3
	10: 8	"The word is near you, on your lips and in your heart"	3
	10: 9	and believe in your heart that God raised him	3
	10:10	one believes with the heart and so is justified	3
	16:18	they deceive the hearts of the simple-minded.	3
1Co	2: 9	nor the human heart conceived	3
	4: 5	and will disclose the purposes of the heart.	3
	14:25	the secrets of the unbeliever's heart are disclosed	3
2Co	1:22	giving us his Spirit in our hearts as a first installment.	3
	2: 4	much distress and anguish of heart	3
	3: 2	written on our hearts, to be known and read by all;	3
	3: 3	but on tablets of human hearts.	3
	4: 6	who has shone in our hearts	3
	5:12	in outward appearance and not in the heart.	3
	6:11	our heart is wide open	3
	6:13	open wide your hearts also.	1
	7: 2	Make room in your hearts for us;	1
	7: 3	I said before that you are in our hearts	3
	7:15	his heart goes out all the more to you	6
	8:16	who put in the heart of Titus the same eagerness	3
Gal	4: 6	Spirit...into our hearts, crying, "Abba! Father!"	3
Eph	1:18	so that, with the eyes of your heart enlightened	3
	3:17	Christ may dwell in your hearts through faith	3
	4:18	their ignorance and hardness of heart.	3
	5:19	making melody to the Lord in your hearts	3
	6: 5	with fear and trembling, in singleness of heart	3
	6: 6	doing the will of God from the heart.	7
	6:22	to encourage your hearts.	3
Php	1: 7	because you hold me in your heart	3
	4: 7	guard your hearts and your minds in Christ Jesus.	3
Col	2: 2	I want their hearts to be encouraged	3
	3:15	let the peace of Christ rule in your hearts	3
	3:16	with gratitude in your hearts sing psalms, hymns,	3
	4: 8	that he may encourage your hearts;	3
1Th	2: 4	to please God who tests our hearts.	3
	2:17	separated from you—in person, not in heart	3
	3:13	And may he so strengthen your hearts in holiness	3
2Th	2:17	comfort your hearts and strengthen them	3
	3: 5	May the Lord direct your hearts to the love of God	3
1Ti	1: 5	love that comes from a pure heart	3
2Ti	2:22	those who call on the Lord from a pure heart.	3
Phm	1: 7	the hearts of the saints have been refreshed	6
	1:12	I am sending him, that is, my own heart, back to you.	6

	1:20	Refresh my heart in Christ.	6
Heb	3: 8	do not harden your hearts as in the rebellion	3
	3:10	'They always go astray in their hearts	3
	3:12	none of you may have an evil, unbelieving heart	3
	3:15	do not harden your hearts as in the rebellion."	3
	4: 7	do not harden your hearts."	3
	4:12	the thoughts and intentions of the heart.	3
	8:10	write them on their hearts	3
	10:16	I will put my laws in their hearts	3
	10:22	let us approach with a true heart	3
	10:22	our hearts sprinkled clean from an evil conscience	3
	13: 9	is well for the heart to be strengthened by grace	3
Jas	1:26	deceive their hearts, their religion is worthless.	3
	3:14	if you have...selfish ambition in your hearts	3
	4: 8	purify your hearts, you double-minded.	3
	5: 5	you have fattened your hearts	3
	5: 8	Strengthen your hearts, for the coming of the Lord	3
1Pe	1:22	love one another deeply from the heart.	3
	3:15	in your hearts sanctify Christ as Lord.	3
2Pe	1:19	and the morning star rises in your hearts.	3
	2:14	They have hearts trained in greed.	3
1Jn	3:19	and will reassure our hearts before him	3
	3:20	whenever our hearts condemn us;	3
	3:20	for God is greater than our hearts	3
	3:21	Beloved, if our hearts do not condemn us	3
	5:10	Those who believe...have the testimony in their hearts.	2
Rev	2:23	that I am the one who searches minds and hearts	3
	17:17	For God has put it into their hearts	3
	18: 7	Since in her heart she says, 'I rule as a queen;	3

tender heart

1. εὔσπλαγχνος, *eusplanchnos, 2359*

1Pe	3: 8	have...a tender heart, and a humble mind.	1

heartless

1. ἄστοργος, *astorgos, 845*

Rom	1:31	foolish, faithless, heartless, ruthless.	1

heat

1. θέρμη, *thermē, 2549*
2. καῦμα, *kauma, 3008*

Act	28: 3	when a viper, driven out by the heat	1
Rev	16: 9	they were scorched by the fierce heat	2

scorching heat

1. καῦμα, *kauma, 3008*
2. καύσων, *kausōn, 3014*

Mat	20:12	the burden of the day and the scorching heat.'	2
Lke	12:55	'There will be scorching heat'; and it happens.	2
Jas	1:11	For the sun rises with its scorching heat	2
Rev	7:16	sun will not strike them, nor any scorching heat;	1

heaven *See also* fall from heaven

1. Contextual: Not in Greek
2. ἐπουράνιος, *epouranios, 2230*
3. οὐράνιος, *ouranios, 4039*
4. οὐρανός, *ouranos, 4041*

Mat	3: 2	"Repent, for the kingdom of heaven has come near."	4
	3:16	suddenly the heavens were opened to him and he saw	4
	3:17	a voice from heaven said, "This is my Son	4
	4:17	"Repent, for the kingdom of heaven has come near."	4
	5: 3	spirit, for theirs is the kingdom of heaven.	4
	5:10	for theirs is the kingdom of heaven.	4
	5:12	for your reward is great in heaven.	4
	5:16	give glory to your Father in heaven.	4
	5:18	For truly I tell you, until heaven and earth pass	4
	5:19	will be called least in the kingdom of heaven;	4
	5:19	will be called great in the kingdom of heaven.	4
	5:20	you will never enter the kingdom of heaven.	4
	5:34	either by heaven, for it is the throne of God	4
	5:45	be children of your Father in heaven.	4
	6: 1	no reward from your Father in heaven.	4
	6: 9	Our Father in heaven, hallowed be your name.	4
	6:10	Your will be done, on earth as it is in heaven.	4
	6:20	store up for yourselves treasures in heaven.	4
	7:11	how much more will your Father in heaven	4
	7:21	"Not everyone...will enter the kingdom of heaven	4
	7:21	the one who does the will of my Father in heaven.	4
	8:11	and Isaac and Jacob in the kingdom of heaven	4
	10: 7	'The kingdom of heaven has come near.'	4

	10:32	acknowledge before my Father in heaven;	4
	10:33	deny before my Father in heaven.	4
	11:11	yet the least in the kingdom of heaven	4
	11:12	the kingdom of heaven has suffered violence	4
	11:23	you, Capernaum, will you be exalted to heaven?	4
	11:25	"I thank you, Father, Lord of heaven and earth	4
	12:50	For whoever does the will of my Father in heaven	4
	13:11	to know the secrets of the kingdom of heaven	4
	13:24	"The kingdom of heaven may be compared to someone	4
	13:31	"The kingdom of heaven is like a mustard	4
	13:33	"The kingdom of heaven is like yeast	4
	13:44	"The kingdom of heaven is like treasure	4
	13:45	"Again, the kingdom of heaven is like a merchant	4
	13:47	"Again, the kingdom of heaven is like a net	4
	13:52	scribe…trained for the kingdom of heaven	4
	14:19	he looked up to heaven, and blessed and broke	4
	16: 1	they asked him to show them a sign from heaven.	4
	16:17	but my Father in heaven.	4
	16:19	I will give you the keys of the kingdom of heaven	4
	16:19	will be bound in heaven	4
	16:19	will be loosed in heaven."	4
	18: 1	"Who is the greatest in the kingdom of heaven?"	4
	18: 3	you will never enter the kingdom of heaven.	4
	18: 4	is the greatest in the kingdom of heaven.	4
	18:10	in heaven their angels continually see the face	4
	18:10	the face of my Father in heaven.	4
	18:14	So it is not the will of your Father in heaven	4
	18:18	will be bound in heaven	4
	18:18	loose on earth will be loosed in heaven.	4
	18:19	it will be done for you by my Father in heaven.	4
	18:23	the kingdom of heaven may be compared to	4
	19:12	for the sake of the kingdom of heaven.	4
	19:14	to such…that the kingdom of heaven belongs."	4
	19:21	you will have treasure in heaven;	4
	19:23	to enter the kingdom of heaven.	4
	20: 1	"For the kingdom of heaven is like a landowner	4
	21:25	Did the baptism of John come from heaven	4
	21:25	"If we say, 'From heaven,' he will say to us	4
	22: 2	"The kingdom of heaven may be compared to a king	4
	22:30	but are like angels in heaven.	4
	23: 9	you have one Father—the one in heaven.	3
	23:13	you lock people out of the kingdom of heaven.	4
	23:22	whoever swears by heaven	4
	24:29	the stars will fall from heaven	4
	24:29	the powers of heaven will be shaken.	4
	24:30	the sign of the Son of Man will appear in heaven	4
	24:30	'the Son of Man coming on the clouds of heaven'	4
	24:31	from one end of heaven to the other.	4
	24:35	Heaven and earth will pass away	4
	24:36	neither the angels of heaven, nor the Son	4
	25: 1	"Then the kingdom of heaven will be like	4
	26:64	coming on the clouds of heaven."	4
	28: 2	an angel of the Lord, descending from heaven	4
	28:18	"All authority in heaven and on earth	4
Mrk	1:10	the heavens torn apart and the Spirit descending	4
	1:11	a voice came from heaven, "You are my Son,	4
	6:41	he looked up to heaven	4
	7:34	looking up to heaven, he sighed and said	4
	8:11	asking him for a sign from heaven, to test him.	4
	10:21	you will have treasure in heaven;	4
	11:10	Hosanna in the highest heaven!"	1
	11:25	so that your Father in heaven may also	4
	11:30	Did the baptism of John come from heaven,	4
	11:31	"If we say, 'From heaven,' he will say	4
	12:25	are like angels in heaven.	4
	13:25	the stars will be falling from heaven	4
	13:25	the powers in the heavens will be shaken.	4
	13:27	from the ends of the earth to the ends of heaven.	4
	13:31	Heaven and earth will pass away	4
	13:32	neither the angels in heaven, nor the Son	4
	14:62	'coming with the clouds of heaven.' "	4
	16:19	⟦Jesus…was taken up into heaven⟧	4
Lke	2:15	When the angels had left them and gone into heaven	4
	3:21	the heaven was opened	4
	3:22	a voice came from heaven	4
	4:25	the heaven was shut up three years and six months	4
	6:23	for surely your reward is great in heaven;	4
	9:16	he looked up to heaven, and blessed and broke them	4
	9:54	to command fire to come down from heaven	4
	10:15	you, Capernaum, will you be exalted to heaven?	4
	10:18	Satan fall from heaven like a flash of lightning.	4

	10:20	rejoice that your names are written in heaven."	4
	10:21	"I thank you, Father, Lord of heaven and earth	4
	11:16	kept demanding from him a sign from heaven	4
	12:33	an unfailing treasure in heaven	4
	15: 7	more joy in heaven over one sinner who repents	4
	15:18	I have sinned against heaven and before you;	4
	15:21	I have sinned against heaven and before you;	4
	16:17	it is easier for heaven and earth to pass away	4
	17:29	rained fire and sulfur from heaven	4
	18:13	would not even look up to heaven	4
	18:22	you will have treasure in heaven;	4
	19:38	Peace in heaven, and glory in the highest heaven!"	4
	20: 4	Did the baptism of John come from heaven,	4
	20: 5	"If we say, 'From heaven,' he will say	4
	21:11	dreadful portents and great signs from heaven.	4
	21:26	the powers of the heavens will be shaken.	4
	21:33	Heaven and earth will pass away	4
	22:43	⟦Then an angel from heaven appeared to him⟧	4
	24:51	and was carried up into heaven.	4
Jhn	1:32	the Spirit descending from heaven like a dove	4
	1:51	truly, I tell you, you will see heaven opened	4
	3:13	No one has ascended into heaven except the one	4
	3:13	one who descended from heaven, the Son of Man.	4
	3:27	except what has been given from heaven.	4
	3:31	one who comes from heaven is above all.	4
	6:31	'He gave them bread from heaven to eat.' "	4
	6:32	not Moses who gave you the bread from heaven	4
	6:32	my Father who gives you the true bread from heaven.	4
	6:33	bread of God is that which comes down from heaven	4
	6:38	come down from heaven, not to do my own will	4
	6:41	"I am the bread that came down from heaven."	4
	6:42	can he now say, 'I have come down from heaven'?"	4
	6:50	This is the bread that comes down from heaven	4
	6:51	I am the living bread that came down from heaven.	4
	6:58	This is the bread that came down from heaven	4
	12:28	Then a voice came from heaven	4
	17: 1	he looked up to heaven and said	4
Act	1: 2	until the day when he was taken up to heaven	1
	1:10	he was going and they were gazing up toward heaven	4
	1:11	why do you stand looking up toward heaven?	4
	1:11	who has been taken up from you into heaven	4
	1:11	in the same way as you saw him go into heaven."	4
	2: 2	suddenly from heaven there came a sound	4
	2: 5	devout Jews from every nation under heaven	4
	2:19	I will show portents in the heaven above	4
	2:34	David did not ascend into the heavens	4
	3:21	who must remain in heaven until the time	4
	4:12	no other name under heaven given among mortals	4
	4:24	the heaven and the earth, the sea	4
	7:42	God…handed them over to worship the host of heaven	4
	7:49	'Heaven is my throne, and the earth is my footstool.	4
	7:55	filled with the Holy Spirit, he gazed into heaven	4
	7:56	"Look," he said, "I see the heavens opened	4
	9: 3	suddenly a light from heaven flashed around him.	4
	10:11	He saw the heaven opened	4
	10:16	the thing was suddenly taken up to heaven.	4
	11: 5	a large sheet coming down from heaven	4
	11: 9	a second time the voice answered from heaven	4
	11:10	everything was pulled up again to heaven.	4
	14:15	the living God, who made the heaven and the earth	4
	17:24	he who is Lord of heaven and earth	4
	22: 6	a great light from heaven suddenly shone about me.	4
Rom	1:18	For the wrath of God is revealed from heaven	4
	10: 6	say in your heart, 'Who will ascend into heaven?' "	4
1Co	8: 5	may be so-called gods in heaven or on earth	4
	15:47	the second man is from heaven.	4
	15:48	as is the man of heaven	2
	15:48	so are those who are of heaven.	2
	15:49	we will also bear the image of the man of heaven.	2
2Co	5: 1	not made with hands, eternal in the heavens.	4
	12: 2	a person in Christ…caught up to the third heaven	4
Gal	1: 8	even if we or an angel from heaven should proclaim	4
Eph	1:10	things in heaven and things on earth.	4
	3:15	every family in heaven and on earth takes its name.	4
	4:10	who ascended far above all the heavens	4
	6: 9	both of you have the same Master in heaven,	4
Php	2:10	in heaven and on earth and under the earth	2
	3:20	our citizenship is in heaven	4
Col	1: 5	because of the hope laid up for you in heaven.	4
	1:16	in him all things in heaven and on earth were created	4
	1:20	all things, whether on earth or in heaven	4

Col	1:23	been proclaimed to every creature under heaven.	4
	4: 1	know that you also have a Master in heaven.	4
1Th	1:10	to wait for his Son from heaven	4
	4:16	the Lord himself…will descend from heaven	4
2Th	1: 7	when the Lord Jesus is revealed from heaven	4
Heb	1:10	the heavens are the work of your hands;	4
	4:14	high priest who has passed through the heavens	4
	7:26	a high priest…exalted above the heavens.	4
	8: 1	right hand of the throne of the Majesty in the heavens	4
	9:24	but he entered into heaven itself	4
	11:12	"as many as the stars of heaven	4
	12:23	who are enrolled in heaven	4
	12:25	if we reject the one who warns from heaven!	4
	12:26	shake not only the earth but also the heaven."	4
Jas	5:12	do not swear, either by heaven or by earth	4
	5:18	Then he prayed again, and the heaven gave rain	4
1Pe	1: 4	inheritance that is…kept in heaven for you	4
	1:12	by the Holy Spirit sent from heaven	4
	3:22	who has gone into heaven	4
2Pe	1:18	We ourselves heard this voice come from heaven	4
	3: 5	by the word of God heavens existed long ago	4
	3: 7	by the same word the present heavens and earth	4
	3:10	then the heavens will pass away with a loud noise	4
	3:12	the heavens will be set ablaze and dissolved	4
	3:13	we wait for new heavens and a new earth	4
Rev	3:12	city…that comes down from my God out of heaven	4
	4: 1	I looked, and there in heaven a door stood open!	4
	4: 2	I was in the spirit, and there in heaven stood a throne	4
	5: 3	no one in heaven or on earth or under the earth	4
	5:13	I heard every creature in heaven and on earth	4
	8: 1	silence in heaven for about half an hour.	4
	8:10	great star fell from heaven, blazing like a torch	4
	9: 1	I saw a star that had fallen from heaven to earth	4
	10: 1	coming down from heaven, wrapped in a cloud	4
	10: 4	but I heard a voice from heaven saying	4
	10: 5	the angel…raised his right hand to heaven	4
	10: 6	who created heaven and what is in it	4
	10: 8	Then the voice that I had heard from heaven	4
	11:12	Then they heard a loud voice from heaven saying	4
	11:12	they went up to heaven in a cloud	4
	11:13	terrified and gave glory to the God of heaven.	4
	11:15	and there were loud voices in heaven, saying	4
	11:19	Then God's temple in heaven was opened	4
	12: 1	A great portent appeared in heaven: a woman	4
	12: 3	another portent appeared in heaven:	4
	12: 4	His tail swept down a third of the stars of heaven	4
	12: 7	And war broke out in heaven; Michael and his angels	4
	12: 8	there was no longer any place for them in heaven.	4
	12:10	Then I heard a loud voice in heaven, proclaiming	4
	12:12	Rejoice then, you heavens and those who dwell in them!	4
	13: 6	his dwelling, that is, those who dwell in heaven.	4
	13:13	even making fire come down from heaven to earth	4
	14: 2	I heard a voice from heaven	4
	14: 7	and worship him who made heaven and earth	4
	14:13	I heard a voice from heaven saying, "Write this:	4
	14:17	another angel came out of the temple in heaven	4
	15: 1	Then I saw another portent in heaven	4
	15: 5	temple of the tent of witness in heaven was opened	4
	16:11	cursed the God of heaven because of their pains	4
	16:21	huge hailstones…dropped from heaven on people	4
	18: 1	I saw another angel coming down from heaven	4
	18: 4	Then I heard another voice from heaven saying	4
	18: 5	for her sins are heaped high as heaven	4
	18:20	O heaven, you saints and apostles and prophets!	4
	19: 1	a great multitude in heaven, saying, "Hallelujah!	4
	19:11	I saw heaven opened, and there was a white horse!	4
	19:14	And the armies of heaven…were following him	4
	20: 1	Then I saw an angel coming down from heaven	4
	20: 9	And fire came down from heaven and consumed them.	4
	20:11	earth and the heaven fled from his presence	4
	21: 1	Then I saw a new heaven and a new earth;	4
	21: 1	first heaven and the first earth had passed away	4
	21: 2	new Jerusalem, coming down out of heaven from God	4
	21:10	Jerusalem coming down out of heaven from God.	4

from heaven

1. οὐρανόθεν, *ouranothen, 4040*

Act	14:17	giving you rains from heaven and fruitful seasons	1
	26:13	a light from heaven, brighter than the sun	1

high heaven

1. ὕψιστος, *hypsistos, 5736*

Mat	21: 9	Hosanna in the highest heaven!"	1
Mrk	11:10	Hosanna in the highest heaven!"	1
Lke	2:14	"Glory to God in the highest heaven	1
	19:38	Peace in heaven, and glory in the highest heaven!"	1

heaven forbid

1. μή + γίνομαι, *mē + ginomai, 3590 + 1181*

Lke	20:16	When they heard this, they said, "Heaven forbid!"	1

heavenly

1. ἄνω, *anō, 539*
2. ἐκ + οὐρανός, *ek + ouranos, 1666 + 4041*
3. ἐπουράνιος, *epouranios, 2230*
4. οὐράνιος, *ouranios, 4039*
5. οὐρανός, *ouranos, 4041*

Mat	5:48	Be perfect…as your heavenly Father is perfect.	4
	6:14	your heavenly Father will also forgive you;	4
	6:26	barns, and yet your heavenly Father feeds them.	4
	6:32	these things; and indeed your heavenly Father knows	4
	15:13	"Every plant that my heavenly Father has	4
	18:35	So my heavenly Father will also do	4
Lke	2:13	with the angel a multitude of the heavenly host	4
	11:13	will the heavenly Father give the Holy Spirit	5
Act	26:19	I was not disobedient to the heavenly vision	4
1Co	15:40	There are both heavenly bodies and earthly	3
	15:40	the glory of the heavenly is one thing	3
2Co	5: 2	longing to be clothed with our heavenly dwelling	2
Php	3:14	the prize of the heavenly call of God in Christ	1
2Ti	4:18	save me for his heavenly kingdom.	3
Heb	3: 1	brothers and sisters, holy partners in a heavenly calling	3
	6: 4	and have tasted the heavenly gift	3
	8: 5	a sanctuary that is a sketch and shadow of the heavenly	3
	11:16	a better country, that is, a heavenly one.	3
	12:22	the heavenly Jerusalem	3

heavenly place

1. ἐπουράνιος, *epouranios, 2230*

Eph	1: 3	who has blessed us…in the heavenly places	1
	1:20	seated him at his right hand in the heavenly places	1
	2: 6	seated us with him in the heavenly places	1
	3:10	authorities in the heavenly places.	1
	6:12	the spiritual forces…in the heavenly places.	1

heavenly thing

1. ἐπουράνιος, *epouranios, 2230*
2. οὐρανός, *ouranos, 4041*

Jhn	3:12	believe if I tell you about heavenly things?	1
Heb	9:23	the sketches of the heavenly things	2
	9:23	but the heavenly things themselves	1

heavy   *See also* carry heavy burdens

1. βαρέω, *bareō, 976*
2. βαρύς, *barys, 987*
3. μέγας, *megas, 3489*

Mat	23: 4	They tie up heavy burdens, hard to bear	2
	26:43	for their eyes were heavy.	1
Rev	11:19	peals of thunder, an earthquake, and heavy hail.	3

much heavy

1. πολύς, *polys, 4498*

Act	27:10	the voyage will be with danger and much heavy loss	1

very heavy

1. καταβαρύνω, *katabarynō, 2852*

Mrk	14:40	their eyes were very heavy;	1

Hebrew

1. Ἑβραῖος, *Hebraios, 1578*
2. Ἑβραΐς, *Hebrais, 1579*
3. Ἑβραϊστί, *Hebraisti, 1580*

Jhn	5: 2	a pool, called in Hebrew Beth-zatha	3
	19:13	or in Hebrew Gabbatha.	3
	19:17	which in Hebrew is called Golgotha.	3
	19:20	it was written in Hebrew, in Latin, and in Greek.	3
	20:16	She turned and said to him in Hebrew, "Rabbouni!"	3
Act	6: 1	the Hellenists complained against the Hebrews	1

21:40	he addressed them in the Hebrew language, saying:	2
22: 2	him addressing them in Hebrew	2
26:14	heard a voice saying to me in the Hebrew language	2
2Co 11:22	Are they Hebrews? So am I.	1
Php 3: 5	a Hebrew born of Hebrews; as to the law, a Pharisee;	1
3: 5	a Hebrew born of Hebrews; as to the law, a Pharisee;	1
Rev 9:11	his name in Hebrew is Abaddon	3
16:16	the place that in Hebrew is called Harmagedon.	3

heel

1. πτέρνα, *pterna, 4761*

Jhn 13:18 who ate my bread has lifted his heel against me.'   1

heifer

1. δάμαλις, *damalis, 1239*

Heb 9:13 with the sprinkling of the ashes of a heifer   1

height

1. ὕψος, *hypsos, 5737*
2. ὕψωμα, *hypsōma, 5739*

Rom 8:39	nor height, nor depth, nor anything else	2
Eph 3:18	the breadth and length and height and depth	1
Rev 21:16	its length and width and height are equal.	1

heir

1. κληρονόμος, *klēronomos, 3101*
2. υἱός, *huios, 5626*

Mat 8:12	while the heirs of the kingdom will be thrown	2
21:38	'This is the heir;	1
Mrk 12: 7	'This is the heir; come, let us kill him	1
Lke 20:14	and said, 'This is the heir; let us kill him	1
Rom 4:14	If it is the adherents of the law who are…heirs	1
8:17	if children, then heirs, heirs of God	1
8:17	heirs of God and joint heirs with Christ	1
Gal 3:29	Abraham's offspring, heirs according to the promise.	1
4: 1	heirs, as long as they are minors, are no better	1
4: 7	if a child then also an heir through God	1
Tit 3: 7	become heirs according to the hope of eternal life.	1
Heb 1: 2	a Son, whom he appointed heir of all things	1
6:17	to show…to the heirs of the promise	1
11: 7	became an heir to the righteousness	1
Jas 2: 5	heirs of the kingdom that he has promised	1

fellow heir

1. συγκληρονόμος, *synklēronomos, 5169*

Eph 3: 6 that is, the Gentiles have become fellow heirs   1

heir also

1. συγκληρονόμος, *synklēronomos, 5169*

1Pe 3: 7 they too are also heirs of the gracious gift of life   1

heir with

1. συγκληρονόμος, *synklēronomos, 5169*

Heb 11: 9 heirs with him of the same promise.   1

joint heir

1. συγκληρονόμος, *synklēronomos, 5169*

Rom 8:17 heirs of God and joint heirs with Christ   1

Heli

1. Ἠλί², *Ēli², 2459*

Lke 3:23 Joseph son of Heli   1

hell   *See also* cast into hell

1. γέεννα, *geenna, 1147*

Mat 5:22	'You fool,' you will be liable to the hell of fire.	1
5:29	than for your whole body to be thrown into hell.	1
5:30	members than for your whole body to go into hell.	1
10:28	who can destroy both soul and body in hell.	1
18: 9	have two eyes and to be thrown into the hell of fire.	1
23:15	twice as much a child of hell as yourselves.	1
23:33	How can you escape being sentenced to hell?	1
Mrk 9:43	to have two hands and to go to hell	1
9:45	have two feet and to be thrown into hell.	1
9:47	have two eyes and to be thrown into hell	1
Lke 12: 5	who…has authority to cast into hell.	1
Jas 3: 6	and is itself set on fire by hell.	1

Hellenist

1. Ἑλληνιστής, *Hellēnistēs, 1821*

Act 6: 1	the Hellenists complained against the Hebrews	1
9:29	He spoke and argued with the Hellenists;	1
11:20	who, on coming to Antioch, spoke to the Hellenists	1

helmet

1. περικεφαλαία, *perikephalaia, 4330*

Eph 6:17	Take the helmet of salvation	1
1Th 5: 8	for a helmet the hope of salvation.	1

help   *See also* come to help, refuse help

1. Contextual: Not in Greek
2. ἀντέχω, *antechō, 504*
3. ἀντιλαμβάνω, *antilambanō, 514*
4. βοήθεια, *boētheia, 1069*
5. βοηθέω, *boētheō, 1070*
6. διά, *dia, 1328*
7. εἰς, *eis, 1650*
8. ἐπαρκέω, *eparkeō, 2064*
9. ἐπί, *epi, 2093*
10. ἐπικουρία, *epikouria, 2135*
11. ἐπιχορηγία, *epichorēgia, 2221*
12. ἔρχομαι, *erchomai, 2262*
13. παρίστημι, *paristēmi, 4225*
14. προσλαμβάνω, *proslambanō, 4689*
15. συλλαμβάνω, *syllambanō, 5197*
16. συμβάλλω, *symballō, 5202*
17. συναντιλαμβάνομαι, *synantilambanomai, 5269*
18. ὑπάρχω, *hyparchō, 5639*

Mat 15:25	"Lord, help me."	5
Mrk 9:22	to do anything, have pity on us and help us."	5
9:24	cried out, "I believe; help my unbelief!"	5
Lke 1:54	He has helped his servant Israel	3
5: 7	signaled…to come and help them.	15
10:40	Tell her then to help me."	17
18: 7	Will he delay long in helping them?	9
Act 16: 9	"Come over to Macedonia and help us."	5
17: 5	help of some ruffians in the marketplaces	14
18:27	greatly helped those who…had become believers	16
21:28	shouting, "Fellow Israelites, help!	5
26:22	To this day I have had help from God	10
27:34	it will help you survive;	18
Rom 8:26	Likewise the Spirit helps us in our weakness;	17
16: 2	help her in whatever she may require from you	13
2Co 6: 2	on a day of salvation I have helped you."	5
Php 1:10	to help you to determine what is best	7
1:12	actually helped to spread the gospel	12
1:19	the help of the Spirit of Jesus Christ	11
4: 3	you also, my loyal companion, help these women	15
4:16	you sent me help for my needs more than once.	1
1Th 5:14	encourage the fainthearted, help the weak	2
1Ti 5:10	washed the saints' feet, helped the afflicted	8
2Ti 1:14	with the help of the Holy Spirit living in us.	6
Heb 2:18	he is able to help those who are being tested.	5
4:16	find grace to help in time of need.	4

help up

1. ἀνίστημι, *anistēmi, 482*

Act 9:41 He gave her his hand and helped her up.   1

with help

1. διά, *dia, 1328*

Act 12: 9 what was happening with the angel's help was real;   1

helper

1. βοηθός, *boēthos, 1071*
2. διακονέω, *diakoneō, 1354*

Act 19:22	he sent two of his helpers, Timothy and Erastus,	2
Heb 13: 6	"The Lord is my helper; I will not be afraid.	1

helpful

1. συμφέρω, *sympherō, 5237*

Act 20:20 I did not shrink from doing anything helpful   1

helping   *See* join in helping

helpless

1. ῥίπτω, *rhiptō, 4849*

Mat   9:36 because they were harassed and helpless   1

hem in

1. συνέχω, *synechō, 5309*

Lke 19:43 surround you, and hem you in on every side.   1

hemorrhage *See also* suffer from a hemorrhage

1. πηγή + αἷμα, *pēgē + haima, 4380 + 135*
2. ῥύσις + αἷμα, *rhysis + haima, 4868 + 135*

Mrk 5:25 woman who had been suffering from hemorrhages   2
       5:29 Immediately her hemorrhage stopped;   1
Lke   8:43 suffering from hemorrhages for twelve years;   2
       8:44 immediately her hemorrhage stopped.   2

hen

1. ὄρνις, *ornis, 3998*

Mat 23:37 as a hen gathers her brood under her wings   1
Lke 13:34 as a hen gathers her brood under her wings   1

hence

1. ὅθεν, *hothen, 3854*
2. ὅτι, *hoti, 4022*
3. οὖν, *oun, 4036*
4. οὕτως, *houtōs, 4048*

Lke   7:47 hence she has shown great love.   2
Rom 1:15 hence my eagerness to proclaim the gospel to you   4
1Co 8: 4 Hence, as to the eating of food offered to idols   3
Heb 8: 3 hence it is necessary for this priest also...   1
       9:18 Hence not even the first covenant was inaugurated   1

herald

1. κῆρυξ, *kēryx, 3061*

1Ti 2: 7 For this I was appointed a herald and an apostle   1
2Ti 1:11 For this gospel I was appointed a herald   1
2Pe 2: 5 saved Noah, a herald of righteousness   1

herb

1. λάχανον, *lachanon, 3303*

Lke 11:42 you tithe mint and rue and herbs of all kinds   1

herd

1. ἀγέλη, *agelē, 36*

Mat 8:30 Now a large herd of swine was feeding   1
       8:31 cast us out, send us into the herd of swine."   1
       8:32 suddenly, the whole herd rushed down the steep bank   1
Mrk 5:11 the hillside a great herd of swine was feeding   1
       5:13 herd, numbering about two thousand, rushed down   1
Lke 8:32 on the hillside a large herd of swine was feeding;   1
       8:33 herd rushed down the steep bank into the lake   1

here *See also* come here, from here, go here and there, see here

1. Contextual: Not in Greek
2. αὐτός, *autos, 899*
3. εἰς + ὁ + μέσος, *eis + ho + mesos, 1650 + 3836 + 3545*
4. ἐν + οὗτος, *en + houtos, 1877 + 4047*
5. ἐνθάδε, *enthade, 1924*
6. ἔνθεν, *enthen, 1925*
7. ἐντεῦθεν, *enteuthen, 1949*
8. ἕτοιμος, *hetoimos, 2289*
9. ἥκω, *hēkō, 2457*
10. ἴδε, *ide, 2623*
11. ἰδού, *idou, 2627*
12. πάρειμι, *pareimi, 4205*
13. ὧδε, *hōde, 6045*

Mat 8:29 Have you come here to torment us   13
     12: 6 something greater than the temple is here.   13
     12:18 "Here is my servant, whom I have chosen,   11
     12:41 something greater than Jonah is here!   13
     12:42 something greater than Solomon is here!   13
     12:49 he said, "Here are my mother and my brothers!   11
     14: 8 the head of John the Baptist here on a platter   13
     14:17 "We have nothing here but five loaves and two fish."   13
     14:18 And he said, "Bring them here to me."   13
     16:28 some standing here who will not taste death   13
     17: 4 "Lord, it is good for us to be here;   13

     17: 4 if you wish, I will make three dwellings here   13
     17:17 Bring him here to me."   13
     17:20 'Move from here to there,' and it will   6
     20: 6 'Why are you standing here idle all day?'   13
     22:12 how did you get in here without a wedding robe?'   13
     24: 2 not one stone will be left here upon another;   13
     24:23 if anyone says to you, 'Look! Here is the Messiah!'   13
     25: 6 'Look! Here is the bridegroom! Come out to meet   1
     25:25 Here you have what is yours.'   10
     26:36 "Sit here while I go over there and pray."   2
     26:38 remain here, and stay awake with me."   13
     26:50 "Friend, do what you are here to do."   12
     28: 6 He is not here; for he has been raised,   13
Mrk 3:34 he said, "Here are my mother and my brothers!   10
     6: 3 are not his sisters here with us?"   13
     8: 4 feed these people with bread here in the desert?"   13
     9: 1 some standing here who will not taste death   13
     9: 5 "Rabbi, it is good for us to be here;   13
    10:49 Jesus stood still and said, "Call him here."   1
    11: 3 and will send it back here immediately.' "   13
    13: 2 Not one stone will be left here upon another;   13
    13:21 at that time, 'Look! Here is the Messiah!'   13
    14:32 to his disciples, "Sit here while I pray."   13
    14:34 remain here, and keep awake."   13
    16: 6 He has been raised; he is not here.   13
Lke 1:38 Mary said, "Here am I, the servant of the Lord;   11
     4: 9 throw yourself down from here   7
     4:23 'Do here also in your hometown   13
     6: 8 "Come and stand here." He got up and stood there.   3
     9:12 for we are here in a deserted place."   13
     9:27 some standing here who will not taste death   2
     9:33 "Master, it is good for us to be here;   13
     9:41 Bring your son here."   13
    11:31 see, something greater than Solomon is here!   13
    11:32 see, something greater than Jonah is here!   13
    15:17 have bread...but here I am dying of hunger!   13
    16:25 now he is comforted here, and you are in agony.   13
    17:21 nor will they say, 'Look, here it is!'   13
    17:23 will say to you, 'Look there!' or 'Look here!'   13
    19:20 'Lord, here is your pound.   11
    19:27 bring them here and slaughter them in my presence.' "   13
    19:30 Untie it and bring it here.   1
    22:38 They said, "Lord, look, here are two swords."   13
    23:14 here I have examined him in your presence   11
    24: 5 He is not here, but has risen.   13
    24:41 "Have you anything here to eat?"   5
    24:49 so stay here in the city until   1
Jhn 1:29 "Here is the Lamb of God who takes away the sin   10
     1:36 exclaimed, "Look, here is the Lamb of God!"   1
     1:47 "Here is truly an Israelite in whom...no deceit!"   10
     3:26 to whom you testified, here he is baptizing   10
     4:15 or have to keep coming here to draw water."   5
     4:23 But the hour is coming, and is now here   1
     4:37 For here the saying holds true, 'One sows   4
     5:25 the hour is coming, and is now here,   1
     6: 9 a boy here who has five barley loaves   13
     6:25 "Rabbi, when did you come here?"   13
     7: 3 "Leave here and go to Judea   7
     7: 6 your time is always here.   8
     7:26 here he is, speaking openly, but they say nothing   10
     8:42 I came from God and now I am here.   9
     9:30 The man answered, "Here is an astonishing thing!   4
    11:21 Martha said to Jesus, "Lord, if you had been here   13
    11:28 "The Teacher is here and is calling for you."   12
    11:32 "Lord, if you had been here   13
    11:42 said this for the sake of the crowd standing here   1
    19: 5 Pilate said to them, "Here is the man!"   11
    19:14 He said to the Jews, "Here is your King!"   10
    19:26 he said to his mother, "Woman, here is your son."   10
    19:27 he said to the disciple, "Here is your mother."   10
    20:27 "Put your finger here and see my hands.   13
Act 5:28 yet here you have filled Jerusalem   11
     9:10 He answered, "Here I am, Lord."   11
     9:14 here he has authority from the chief priests   13
     9:17 Jesus, who appeared to you on your way here   1
     9:21 And has he not come here for the purpose   13
    16:28 "Do not harm yourself, for we are all here."   5
    17: 6 "These people...have come here also   5
    19:37 You have brought these men here   1
    24:19 they ought to be here before you   12
    24:20 Or let these men here tell   1

25:14	a man here who was left in prison by Felix.	1
25:17	So when they met here	5
25:24	"King Agrippa and all here present with us	1
25:24	petitioned me, both in Jerusalem and here	5
26: 6	now I stand here on trial on account of my hope	1
26:22	I stand here, testifying to both small and great	1
2Co 12:14	Here I am, ready to come to you this third time.	11
Php 1:16	put here for the defense of the gospel;	1
Col 4: 9	They will tell you about everything here	13
Heb 2:13	"Here am I and the children whom God has given me."	11
13:14	For here we have no lasting city	13
Jas 2: 3	and say, "Have a seat here, please,"	13
Rev 4: 1	the first voice…said, "Come up here	13
11:12	voice from heaven saying to them, "Come up here!"	13
13:10	Here is a call for the endurance and faith	1
14:12	Here is a call for the endurance of the saints	1

here already

1. ἐνίστημι, *enistēmi, 1931*

2Th 2: 2	to the effect that the day of the Lord is already here.	1

here in presence

1. πάρειμι, *pareimi, 4205*

Act 10:33	all of us are here in the presence of God	1

out of here

1. ἐντεῦθεν, *enteuthen, 1949*

Jhn 2:16	"Take these things out of here!	1

heritage

1. κληρονομία, *klēronomia, 3100*

Act 7: 5	He did not give him any of it as a heritage	1

Hermas

1. Ἑρμᾶς, *Hermas, 2254*

Rom 16:14	Greet…Hermes, Patrobas, Hermas	1

Hermes

1. Ἑρμῆς, *Hermēs, 2258*

Act 14:12	Paul they called Hermes	1
Rom 16:14	Greet Asyncritus, Phlegon, Hermes, Patrobas	1

Hermogenes

1. Ἑρμογένης, *Hermogenēs, 2259*

2Ti 1:15	including Phygelus and Hermogenes.	1

Herod

1. Contextual: Not in Greek
2. Ἡρῴδης, *Hērōdēs, 2476*

Mat 2: 1	In the time of King Herod, after Jesus was born	2
2: 3	When King Herod heard this, he was frightened	2
2: 7	Then Herod secretly called for the wise men	2
2:12	having been warned in a dream not to return to Herod	2
2:13	Herod is about to search for the child, to destroy	2
2:15	remained there until the death of Herod.	2
2:16	When Herod saw that he had been tricked	2
2:19	When Herod died, an angel of the Lord suddenly	2
2:22	in place of his father Herod, he was afraid to go	2
14: 1	At that time Herod the ruler heard	2
14: 3	For Herod had arrested John, bound him	2
14: 5	Though Herod wanted to put him to death	1
14: 6	when Herod's birthday came	2
14: 6	Herodias danced…and she pleased Herod	2
Mrk 6:14	King Herod heard of it	2
6:16	when Herod heard of it, he said	2
6:17	For Herod himself had sent men who arrested John	2
6:17	because Herod had married her.	1
6:18	John had been telling Herod, "It is not lawful	2
6:20	for Herod feared John…and he protected him.	2
6:21	when Herod on his birthday gave a banquet	2
6:22	she pleased Herod and his guests;	2
8:15	the yeast of Herod."	2
Lke 1: 5	In the days of King Herod of Judea	2
3: 1	Herod was ruler of Galilee	2
3:19	Herod the ruler, who had been rebuked by him	2
3:19	because of all the evil things that Herod had done	2
8: 3	Joanna, the wife of Herod's steward Chuza	2
9: 7	Now Herod the ruler heard about all that	2
9: 9	Herod said, "John I beheaded;	2

13:31	"Get away from here, for Herod wants to kill you."	2
23: 7	that he was under Herod's jurisdiction	2
23: 7	he sent him off to Herod	2
23: 8	When Herod saw Jesus, he was very glad	2
23:11	Herod with his soldiers	2
23:12	Herod and Pilate became friends with each other;	2
23:15	Neither has Herod, for he sent him back to us.	2
Act 4:27	both Herod and Pontius Pilate, with the Gentiles	2
12: 1	King Herod laid violent hands upon some	2
12: 6	before Herod was going to bring him out	2
12:11	and rescued me from the hands of Herod	2
12:19	Herod had searched for him and could not find him	2
12:20	Herod was angry with the people of Tyre and Sidon.	1
12:21	On an appointed day Herod put on his royal robes	2
13: 1	a member of the court of Herod the ruler	2
23:35	kept under guard in Herod's headquarters.	2

Herodian

1. Ἡρῳδιανοί, *Hērōdianoi, 2477*

Mat 22:16	disciples to him, along with the Herodians	1
Mrk 3: 6	conspired with the Herodians against him	1
12:13	some Pharisees and some Herodians	1

Herodias

1. Ἡρῳδιάς, *Hērōdias, 2478*

Mat 14: 3	put him in prison on account of Herodias	1
14: 6	the daughter of Herodias danced	1
Mrk 6:17	and put him in prison on account of Herodias	1
6:19	Herodias had a grudge against him	1
6:22	When his daughter Herodias came in and danced	1
Lke 3:19	who had been rebuked by him because of Herodias	1

Herodion

1. Ἡρῳδίων, *Hērōdiōn, 2479*

Rom 16:11	Greet my relative Herodion.	1

herself Not Indexed

hesitation

1. διακρίνω, *diakrinō, 1359*

Act 10:20	go down, and go with them without hesitation;	1

hew

1. λατομέω, *latomeō, 3300*

Mat 27:60	his own new tomb, which he had hewn in the rock.	1
Mrk 15:46	a tomb that had been hewn out of the rock.	1

Hezekiah

1. Ἑζεκίας, *Hezekias, 1614*

Mat 1: 9	and Ahaz the father of Hezekiah	1
1:10	Hezekiah the father of Manasseh	1

Hezron

1. Ἑσρώμ, *Hesrōm, 2272*

Mat 1: 3	Perez the father of Hezron	1
1: 3	and Hezron the father of Aram	1
Lke 3:33	son of Arni, son of Hezron, son of Perez	1

hidden thing

1. κρυπτός, *kryptos, 3220*

1Co 4: 5	who will bring to light the things now hidden	1

hide *See also* remain hidden

1. ἀποκρύπτω, *apokryptō, 648*
2. ἀπόκρυφος, *apokryphos, 649*
3. ἀφανής, *aphanēs, 905*
4. καλύπτω, *kalyptō, 2821*
5. κρυπτός, *kryptos, 3220*
6. κρύπτω, *kryptō, 3221*
7. λανθάνω, *lanthanō, 3291*

Mat 5:14	A city built on a hill cannot be hid.	6
11:25	because you have hidden these things from the wise	6
13:35	I will proclaim what has been hidden	6
13:44	like treasure hidden in a field	6
13:44	which someone found and hid;	6
25:18	dug a hole in the ground and hid his master's money.	6
25:25	I went and hid your talent in the ground.	6
Mrk 4:22	there is nothing hidden, except to be disclosed;	5
Lke 8:16	"No one after lighting a lamp hides it	4

Lke 8:17 nothing is hidden that will not be disclosed 5
8:47 the woman saw that she could not remain hidden 7
10:21 hidden these things from the wise 1
18:34 in fact, what he said was hidden from them 6
19:42 now they are hidden from your eyes. 6
Jhn 8:59 Jesus hid himself and went out of the temple. 6
12:36 he departed and hid from them. 6
1Co 2: 7 we speak God's wisdom, secret and hidden, 1
2Co 4: 2 renounced the shameful things that one hides; 5
Eph 3: 9 plan of the mystery hidden for ages in God 1
Col 1:26 mystery that has been hidden throughout the ages 1
2: 3 in whom are hidden all the treasures of wisdom 2
3: 3 your life is hidden with Christ in God. 6
Heb 4:13 before him no creature is hidden 3
11:23 By faith Moses was hidden by his parents 6
Rev 2:17 I will give some of the hidden manna 6
6:15 everyone, slave and free, hid in the caves 6
6:16 hide us from…the one seated on the throne 6

Hierapolis

1. Ἱεράπολις, *Hierapolis, 2631*
Col 4:13 for those in Laodicea and in Hierapolis. 1

high *See also* high *heaven,* high *position,* high *standing,* hold in high esteem

1. ἀνώτερος, *anōteros, 542*
2. ἄχρι, *achri, 948*
3. μέγας, *megas, 3489*
4. ὑψηλός, *hypsēlos, 5734*
5. ὕψος, *hypsos, 5737*

Mat 4: 8 Again, the devil took him to a very high mountain 4
17: 1 and led them up a high mountain, by themselves. 4
Mrk 9: 2 led them up a high mountain apart, by themselves. 4
Lke 1:78 the dawn from on high will break upon us 5
4:38 mother-in-law was suffering from a high fever 3
14:10 'Friend, move up higher'; 1
24:49 you have been clothed with power from on high." 5
Eph 4: 8 he ascended on high he made captivity…a captive 5
Heb 1: 3 he sat down at the right hand of the Majesty on high 4
Rev 14:20 blood flowed…as high as a horse's bridle 2
18: 5 for her sins are heaped high as heaven 2
21:10 he carried me away to a great, high mountain 4
21:12 It has a great, high wall with twelve gates 4

high priest

1. ἀρχιερεύς, *archiereus, 797*

Mat 26: 3 people gathered in the palace of the high priest 1
26:51 and struck the slave of the high priest 1
26:57 took him to Caiaphas the high priest 1
26:58 as far as the courtyard of the high priest; 1
26:62 The high priest stood up and said 1
26:63 Then the high priest said to him 1
26:65 the high priest tore his clothes and said 1
Mrk 2:26 when Abiathar was high priest 1
14:47 struck the slave of the high priest 1
14:53 They took Jesus to the high priest; 1
14:54 right into the courtyard of the high priest; 1
14:60 the high priest stood up before 1
14:61 the high priest asked him, "Are you the Messiah 1
14:63 the high priest tore his clothes and said 1
14:66 the servant-girls of the high priest came by. 1
Lke 22:50 one of them struck the slave of the high priest 1
22:54 bringing him into the high priest's house. 1
Jhn 11:49 Caiaphas, who was high priest that year, said 1
11:51 being high priest that year he prophesied 1
18:10 Simon Peter…struck the high priest's slave 1
18:13 Caiaphas, the high priest that year. 1
18:15 that disciple was known to the high priest 1
18:15 with Jesus into the courtyard of the high priest 1
18:16 disciple, who was known to the high priest 1
18:19 Then the high priest questioned Jesus 1
18:22 "Is that how you answer the high priest?" 1
18:24 sent him bound to Caiaphas the high priest. 1
18:26 One of the slaves of the high priest…asked 1
Act 4: 6 with Annas the high priest, Caiaphas, John, 1
5:17 the high priest took action; 1
5:21 the high priest and those with him arrived 1
5:27 The high priest questioned them 1
7: 1 the high priest asked him, "Are these things so?" 1
9: 1 Saul…went to the high priest 1

19:14 Seven sons of a Jewish high priest named Sceva 1
22: 5 the high priest and the whole council of elders 1
23: 2 the high priest Ananias ordered…to strike him 1
23: 4 "Do you dare to insult God's high priest?" 1
23: 5 "I did not realize, brothers, that he was high priest; 1
24: 1 the high priest Ananias came down with some elders 1
Heb 2:17 might be a merciful and faithful high priest 1
3: 1 the apostle and high priest of our confession 1
4:14 Since, then, we have a great high priest 1
4:15 For we do not have a high priest who is unable 1
5: 1 Every high priest chosen from among mortals 1
5: 5 did not glorify himself in becoming a high priest 1
5:10 having been designated by God a high priest 1
6:20 having become a high priest forever 1
7:26 fitting that we should have such a high priest 1
7:27 Unlike the other high priests, he has no need 1
7:28 appoints as high priests those who are subject to weakness 1
8: 1 we have such a high priest 1
8: 3 every high priest is appointed to offer gifts 1
9: 7 only the high priest goes into the second 1
9:11 a high priest of the good things that have come 1
9:25 as the high priest enters the Holy Place year after year 1
13:11 is brought into the sanctuary by the high priest 1

high priesthood

1. ἀρχιερεύς, *archiereus, 797*
Lke 3: 2 during the high priesthood of Annas and Caiaphas 1

most high

1. ὕψιστος, *hypsistos, 5736*
Mrk 5: 7 Jesus, Son of the Most High God? 1
Lke 1:32 will be called the Son of the Most High 1
1:35 the power of the Most High will overshadow you; 1
1:76 you…will be called the prophet of the Most High; 1
6:35 you will be children of the Most High; 1
8:28 Jesus, Son of the Most High God? 1
Act 7:48 Yet the Most High does not dwell in houses 1
16:17 "These men are slaves of the Most High God 1
Heb 7: 1 King Melchizedek of Salem, priest of the Most High God 1

high-priestly

1. ἀρχιερατικός, *archieratikos, 796*
Act 4: 6 and all who were of the high-priestly family. 1

highly *See also* exalt highly, think highly, value highly

very highly

1. ὑπερεκπερισσοῦ, *hyperekperissou, 5655*
1Th 5:13 esteem them very highly in love 1

hill

1. βουνός, *bounos, 1090*
2. ὄρος, *oros, 4001*
Mat 5:14 A city built on a hill cannot be hid. 2
Lke 3: 5 every mountain and hill shall be made low 1
4:29 led him to the brow of the hill 2
23:30 to the hills, 'Cover us.' 1

hill country

1. ὀρεινός, *oreinos, 3978*
Lke 1:39 to a Judean town in the hill country 1
1:65 throughout the entire hill country of Judea. 1

hillside

1. ὄρος, *oros, 4001*
Mrk 5:11 Now there on the hillside a great herd of swine 1
Lke 8:32 on the hillside a large herd of swine was feeding; 1

himself *Not Indexed*

hinder

1. ἐγκόπτω, *enkoptō, 1601*
2. κωλύω, *kōlyō, 3266*
Lke 11:52 you hindered those who were entering." 2
Act 11:17 who was I that I could hinder God?" 2
Rom 15:22 I have so often been hindered from coming to you. 1
1Th 2:16 by hindering us from speaking to the Gentiles 2
1Pe 3: 7 so that nothing may hinder your prayers. 1

hindrance in the way

1. σκάνδαλον, *skandalon, 4998*

Rom 14:13   block or hindrance in the way of another.   1

without hindrance

1. ἀκωλύτως, *akōlytōs, 219*

Act 28:31   teaching...with all boldness and without hindrance.   1

hire

1. Contextual: Not in Greek
2. μισθόω, *misthoō, 3636*

Mat 20: 1   to hire laborers for his vineyard.   2
     20: 7   They said to him, 'Because no one has hired us.'   2
     20: 9   When those hired about five o'clock came   1

hire out

1. κολλάω, *kollaō, 3140*

Lke 15:15   hired himself out to one of the citizens   1

hired man   *See also* hired *hand*

1. μισθωτός, *misthōtos, 3638*

Mrk 1:20   Zebedee in the boat with the hired men   1

hoist

1. ἐπαίρω, *epairō, 2048*

Act 27:40   then hoisting the foresail to the wind   1

hoist up

1. αἴρω, *airō, 149*

Act 27:17   After hoisting it up   1

hold   *See also* catch hold, lay hold, take hold

1. Contextual: Not in Greek
2. γίνομαι, *ginomai, 1181*
3. εἰμί, *eimi, 1639*
4. ἔνοχος, *enochos, 1944*
5. ἔχω, *echō, 2400*
6. κρατέω, *krateō, 3195*
7. λογίζομαι, *logizomai, 3357*
8. ποιέω, *poieō, 4472*
9. συνέχω, *synechō, 5309*
10. τηρέω, *tēreō, 5498*
11. χωρέω, *chōreō, 6003*

Mrk 7: 8   and hold to human tradition."   6
     15: 1   held a consultation with the elders and scribes   8
Lke 22:63   the men who were holding Jesus began to mock him   9
Jhn 2: 6   jars...each holding twenty or thirty gallons.   11
     4:37   For here the saying holds true, 'One sows   3
Act 2:24   it was impossible for him to be held in its power.   6
     4:32   everything they owned was held in common.   1
     25:21   I ordered him to be held   10
Rom 3:19   the whole world may be held accountable to God.   2
     3:28   For we hold that a person is justified by faith   7
Php 1: 7   because you hold me in your heart   5
1Ti 4: 8   holding promise for both the present life   5
2Ti 1:13   Hold to the standard of sound teaching   5
     3: 5   holding to the outward form of godliness   5
Heb 2:15   free those who all their lives were held in slavery   4
     7:24   he holds his priesthood permanently   5
     9: 4   in which there were a golden urn holding the manna   5
Rev 1:16   In his right hand he held seven stars   5
     2: 1   him who holds the seven stars in his right hand   6
     2:14   some there who hold to the teaching of Balaam   6
     2:15   some who hold to the teaching of the Nicolaitans.   6
     2:24   you in Thyatira, who do not hold this teaching   5
     5: 8   fell before the Lamb, each holding a harp   5
     6: 5   Its rider held a pair of scales in his hand   5
     10: 2   He held a little scroll open in his hand.   5
     12:17   and hold the testimony of Jesus.   5
     17: 4   holding in her hand a golden cup   5
     19:10   your comrades who hold the testimony of Jesus.   5
     20: 1   holding in his hand the key to the bottomless pit   5

hold a discussion

1. διαλέγομαι, *dialegomai, 1363*

Act 20: 7   Paul was holding a discussion with them;   1

hold against

1. ἵστημι, *histēmi, 2705*

Act 7:60   "Lord, do not hold this sin against them."   1

hold back

1. κρατέω, *krateō, 3195*

Rev 7: 1   angels...holding back the four winds   1

hold captive

1. ζωγρέω, *zōgreō, 2436*
2. κατέχω, *katechō, 2988*

Rom 7: 6   dead to that which held us captive   2
2Ti 2:26   having been held captive by him to do his will.   1

hold fast

1. Contextual: Not in Greek
2. ἐπέχω, *epechō, 2091*
3. ἔχω, *echō, 2400*
4. κατέχω, *katechō, 2988*
5. κολλάω, *kollaō, 3140*
6. κρατέω, *krateō, 3195*
7. στοιχέω, *stoicheō, 5123*

Lke 8:15   hold it fast in an honest and good heart   4
Rom 12: 9   hate what is evil, hold fast to what is good;   5
Php 2:16   holding fast to the word of life   2
     3:16   Only let us hold fast to what we have attained.   7
Col 2:19   not holding fast to the head   6
1Th 5:21   test everything; hold fast to what is good;   4
2Th 2:15   hold fast to the traditions that you were taught   6
1Ti 3: 9   they must hold fast to the mystery of the faith   3
Heb 4:14   let us hold fast to our confession.   6
     10:23   Let us hold fast to the confession of our hope   4
Rev 2:13   you are holding fast to my name   6
     2:25   only hold fast to what you have until I come.   6
     3:11   I am coming soon; hold fast to what you have   6
     14:12   and hold fast to the faith of Jesus.   1

hold firm

1. κατέχω, *katechō, 2988*

Heb 3: 6   we are his house if we hold firm the confidence   1
     3:14   if only we hold our first confidence firm   1

hold firmly

1. κατέχω, *katechō, 2988*

1Co 15: 2   saved, if you hold firmly to the message   1

hold in high esteem

1. μεγαλύνω, *megalynō, 3486*

Act 5:13   the people held them in high esteem.   1

hold in honor

1. ἔνδοξος, *endoxos, 1902*
2. τίμιος, *timios, 5508*

1Co 4:10   You are held in honor, but we in disrepute.   1
Heb 13: 4   Let marriage be held in honor by all   2

hold on

1. ἅπτω, *haptō, 721*

Jhn 20:17   Jesus said to her, "Do not hold on to me   1

hold out

1. ἐκπετάννυμι, *ekpetannymi, 1736*

Rom 10:21   "All day long I have held out my hands   1

hold ready

1. ἑτοιμάζω, *hetoimazō, 2286*

Rev 9:15   angels...who had been held ready for the hour   1

hold to

1. προσφέρω, *prospherō, 4712*

Jhn 19:29   on a branch of hyssop and held it to his mouth.   1

hold together

1. συμβιβάζω, *symbibazō, 5204*
2. συνίστημι, *synistēmi, 5319*

Col 1:17   in him all things hold together.   2
     2:19   nourished and held together by its ligaments   1

hold up to contempt

1. παραδειγματίζω, *paradeigmatizō, 4136*

Heb 6: 6 crucifying again…and are holding him up to contempt. 1

hole *See also* dig a hole

1. ὀπή, *opē, 3956*
2. φωλεός, *phōleos, 5887*

Mat 8:20 Jesus said to him, "Foxes have holes 2
Lke 9:58 Jesus said to him, "Foxes have holes 2
Heb 11:38 in caves and holes in the ground. 1

holiness

1. ἁγιασμός, *hagiasmos, 40*
2. ἅγιος, *hagios, 41*
3. ἁγιότης, *hagiotēs, 42*
4. ἁγιωσύνη, *hagiōsynē, 43*
5. ὁσιότης, *hosiotēs, 4009*

Lke 1:75 in holiness and righteousness before him 5
Rom 1: 4 with power according to the spirit of holiness 4
2Co 6: 6 kindness, holiness of spirit, genuine love 2
    7: 1 making holiness perfect in the fear of God. 4
Eph 4:24 in true righteousness and holiness. 5
1Th 3:13 And may he so strengthen your hearts in holiness 4
    4: 4 control your own body in holiness and honor 1
    4: 7 God did not call us to impurity but in holiness 1
1Ti 2:15 in faith and love and holiness, with modesty. 1
Heb 12:10 in order that we may share his holiness. 3
    12:14 holiness without which no one will see the Lord. 1
2Pe 3:11 in leading lives of holiness and godliness 2

holy *See also* make holy

1. Contextual: Not in Greek
2. ἁγιάζω, *hagiazō, 39*
3. ἅγιος, *hagios, 41*
4. ὅσιος, *hosios, 4008*

Mat 1:18 found to be with child from the Holy Spirit. 3
    1:20 child conceived in her is from the Holy Spirit 3
    3:11 baptize you with the Holy Spirit and fire. 3
    4: 5 Then the devil took him to the holy city 3
    7: 6 "Do not give what is holy to dogs; and do not throw 3
    12:32 but whoever speaks against the Holy Spirit 3
    24:15 standing in the holy place, as was spoken of 3
    27:53 entered the holy city and appeared to many. 3
    28:19 Father and of the Son and of the Holy Spirit 3
Mrk 1: 8 he will baptize you with the Holy Spirit." 3
    3:29 whoever blasphemes against the Holy Spirit 3
    6:20 knowing that he was a righteous and holy man 3
    8:38 glory of his Father with the holy angels." 3
    12:36 David himself, by the Holy Spirit, declared 3
    13:11 it is not you who speak, but the Holy Spirit. 3
Lke 1:15 he will be filled with the Holy Spirit. 3
    1:35 "The Holy Spirit will come upon you 3
    1:35 therefore the child to be born will be holy 3
    1:41 Elizabeth was filled with the Holy Spirit 3
    1:49 holy is his name. 3
    1:67 Zechariah was filled with the Holy Spirit 3
    1:70 the mouth of his holy prophets from of old 3
    1:72 remembered his holy covenant 3
    2:23 shall be designated as holy to the Lord") 3
    2:25 the Holy Spirit rested on him. 3
    2:26 It had been revealed to him by the Holy Spirit 3
    3:16 baptize you with the Holy Spirit and fire. 3
    3:22 Holy Spirit descended upon him in bodily form 3
    4: 1 Jesus, full of the Holy Spirit, returned 3
    9:26 the glory of the Father and of the holy angels. 3
    10:21 Jesus rejoiced in the Holy Spirit and said 3
    11:13 will the heavenly Father give the Holy Spirit 3
    12:10 whoever blasphemes against the Holy Spirit 3
    12:12 the Holy Spirit will teach you at that very hour 3
Jhn 1:33 is the one who baptizes with the Holy Spirit.' 3
    11:48 destroy both our holy place and our nation." 1
    14:26 the Advocate, the Holy Spirit 3
    17:11 Holy Father, protect them in your name 3
    20:22 "Receive the Holy Spirit. 3
Act 1: 2 giving instructions through the Holy Spirit 3
    1: 5 you will be baptized with the Holy Spirit 3
    1: 8 when the Holy Spirit has come upon you; 3
    1:16 which the Holy Spirit through David foretold 3
    2: 4 All of them were filled with the Holy Spirit 3

2:33 the promise of the Holy Spirit 3
2:38 you will receive the gift of the Holy Spirit. 3
3:14 you rejected the Holy and Righteous One 3
3:21 long ago through his holy prophets. 3
4: 8 Then Peter, filled with the Holy Spirit, said 3
4:25 said by the Holy Spirit through our ancestor David 3
4:27 gathered together against your holy servant 3
4:30 through the name of your holy servant Jesus." 3
4:31 they were all filled with the Holy Spirit 3
5: 3 filled your heart to lie to the Holy Spirit 3
5:32 so is the Holy Spirit 3
6: 5 Stephen, a man full of faith and the Holy Spirit 3
6:13 saying things against this holy place and the law; 3
7:33 the place where you are standing is holy ground. 3
7:51 you are forever opposing the Holy Spirit 3
7:55 filled with the Holy Spirit, he gazed into heaven 3
8:15 that they might receive the Holy Spirit 3
8:17 they received the Holy Spirit. 3
8:19 may receive the Holy Spirit." 3
9:17 be filled with the Holy Spirit." 3
9:31 in the comfort of the Holy Spirit 3
10:22 was directed by a holy angel to send for you 3
10:38 anointed Jesus of Nazareth with the Holy Spirit 3
10:44 the Holy Spirit fell upon all who heard the word. 3
10:45 the gift of the Holy Spirit had been poured out 3
10:47 who have received the Holy Spirit just as we have?" 3
11:15 as I began to speak, the Holy Spirit fell upon them 3
11:16 you will be baptized with the Holy Spirit.' 3
11:24 a good man, full of the Holy Spirit and of faith. 3
13: 2 the Holy Spirit said, "Set apart for me Barnabas 3
13: 4 being sent out by the Holy Spirit 3
13: 9 Paul, filled with the Holy Spirit 3
13:34 give you the holy promises made to David.' 4
13:52 filled with joy and with the Holy Spirit. 3
15: 8 giving them the Holy Spirit, just as he did to us; 3
15:28 For it has seemed good to the Holy Spirit and to us 3
16: 6 forbidden by the Holy Spirit to speak the word 3
19: 2 He said to them, "Did you receive the Holy Spirit 3
19: 2 not even heard that there is a Holy Spirit." 3
19: 6 the Holy Spirit came upon them 3
20:23 except that the Holy Spirit testifies to me 3
20:28 of which the Holy Spirit has made you overseers 3
21:11 "Thus says the Holy Spirit 3
21:28 has defiled this holy place." 3
28:25 "The Holy Spirit was right in saying 3
Rom 1: 2 through his prophets in the holy scriptures 3
    5: 5 poured into our hearts through the Holy Spirit 3
    7:12 So the law is holy, and the commandment is holy 3
    7:12 and the commandment is holy and just and good. 3
    9: 1 my conscience confirms it by the Holy Spirit 3
    11:16 If the part of the dough…is holy, 3
    11:16 part…is holy, then the whole batch is holy 1
    11:16 if the root is holy, then the branches also are 3
    11:16 root is holy, then the branches also are holy 1
    12: 1 as a living sacrifice, holy and acceptable to God 3
    14:17 and peace and joy in the Holy Spirit. 3
    15:13 may abound in hope by the power of the Holy Spirit. 3
    15:16 be acceptable, sanctified by the Holy Spirit. 3
    16:16 Greet one another with a holy kiss. 3
1Co 3:17 God's temple is holy, and you are that temple. 3
    6:19 a temple of the Holy Spirit within you 3
    7:14 as it is, they are holy. 3
    7:34 so that they may be holy in body and spirit; 3
    12: 3 except by the Holy Spirit. 3
    16:20 Greet one another with a holy kiss. 3
2Co 13:12 Greet one another with a holy kiss. 3
    13:13 communion of the Holy Spirit be with all of you. 3
Eph 1: 4 to be holy and blameless before him in love 3
    1:13 marked with the seal of the promised Holy Spirit; 3
    2:21 grows into a holy temple in the Lord; 3
    3: 5 been revealed to his holy apostles and prophets 3
    4:30 do not grieve the Holy Spirit of God 3
    5:27 so that she may be holy and without blemish. 3
Col 1:22 so as to present you holy…before him 3
    3:12 As God's chosen ones, holy and beloved 3
1Th 1: 5 also in power and in the Holy Spirit 3
    1: 6 with joy inspired by the Holy Spirit 3
    4: 8 who also gives his Holy Spirit to you. 3
    5:26 Greet all the brothers and sisters with a holy kiss. 3
1Ti 2: 8 lifting up holy hands without anger or argument; 4
2Ti 1: 9 who saved us and called us with a holy calling 3

	1:14	with the help of the Holy Spirit living in us.	3
Tit	3: 5	renewal by the Holy Spirit.	3
Heb	2: 4	by gifts of the Holy Spirit, distributed	3
	3: 1	brothers and sisters, holy partners in a heavenly calling	3
	3: 7	Therefore, as the Holy Spirit says	3
	6: 4	have shared in the Holy Spirit	3
	7:26	such a high priest, holy, blameless, undefiled	4
	9: 3	a tent called the Holy of Holies.	3
	9: 3	a tent called the Holy of Holies.	3
	9: 8	By this the Holy Spirit indicates	3
	10:15	the Holy Spirit also testifies to us	3
1Pe	1:12	by the Holy Spirit sent from heaven	3
	1:15	as he who called you is holy, be holy yourselves	3
	1:15	be holy yourselves in all your conduct;	3
	1:16	it is written, "You shall be holy, for I am holy."	3
	1:16	it is written, "You shall be holy, for I am holy."	3
	2: 5	like living stones…be a holy priesthood	3
	2: 9	you are…a holy nation, God's own people	3
	3: 5	the holy women who hoped in God used to adorn	3
2Pe	1:18	while we were with him on the holy mountain.	3
	1:21	and women moved by the Holy Spirit spoke from God.	3
	2:21	the holy commandment that was passed on to them.	3
	3: 2	the words spoken in the past by the holy prophets	3
Jde	1:14	"See, the Lord is coming with ten thousands of his holy	3
	1:20	pray in the Holy Spirit;	3
Rev	4: 8	sing, "Holy, holy, holy, the Lord God the Almighty	3
	4: 8	sing, "Holy, holy, holy, the Lord God the Almighty	3
	4: 8	sing, "Holy, holy, holy, the Lord God the Almighty	3
	6:10	"Sovereign Lord, holy and true, how long	3
	11: 2	they will trample over the holy city	3
	14:10	tormented…in the presence of the holy angels	3
	15: 4	who will not fear…For you alone are holy.	4
	20: 6	holy are those who share in the first resurrection.	3
	21: 2	I saw the holy city, the new Jerusalem, coming down	3
	21:10	and showed me the holy city Jerusalem	3
	22:11	Let…the holy still be holy."	3
	22:11	Let…the holy still be holy."	2
	22:19	take away that person's share…in the holy city	3

holy one

1. ἅγιος, *hagios, 41*
2. ὅσιος, *hosios, 4008*

Mrk	1:24	I know who you are, the Holy One of God."	1
Lke	4:34	I know who you are, the Holy One of God."	1
Jhn	6:69	and know that you are the Holy One of God."	1
Act	2:27	or let your Holy One experience corruption.	2
	13:35	'You will not let your Holy One experience corruption.'	2
1Jn	2:20	you have been anointed by the Holy One	1
Rev	3: 7	the words of the holy one, the true one	1
	16: 5	"You are just, O Holy One, who are and were,	2

holy place

1. ἅγιος, *hagios, 41*

Heb	9: 2	this is called the Holy Place.	1
	9:12	he entered once for all into the Holy Place	1
	9:25	as the high priest enters the Holy Place year after year	1

most holy

1. ἅγιος, *hagios, 41*

Jde	1:20	build yourselves up on your most holy faith;	1

homage   *See also* pay homage

1. προσκυνέω, *proskyneō, 4686*

Mrk	15:19	knelt down in homage to him.	1

home   *See also* make one's home, welcome into a home

1. Contextual: Not in Greek
2. αὐτό", *autos, 899*
3. ἑαυτου', *heautou, 1571*
4. ἐνδημέω, *endēmeō, 1897*
5. ἴδιο", *idios, 2625*
6. μονή, *monē, 3665*
7. οἰκία, *oikia, 3864*
8. οἶκο", *oikos, 3875*
9. ὅπου, *hopou, 3963*
10. σκηνή, *skēnē, 5008*

Mat	8: 6	"Lord, my servant is lying at home paralyzed	7
	9: 6	"Stand up, take your bed and go to your home."	8
	9: 7	he stood up and went to his home.	8
	17:25	when he came home, Jesus spoke of it first	7

Mrk	2: 1	it was reported that he was at home.	8
	2:11	stand up, take your mat and go to your home."	8
	3:19	Then he went home;	8
	5:19	"Go home to your friends	8
	7:30	she went home, found the child lying on the bed	8
	8: 3	If I send them away hungry to their homes	8
	8:26	he sent him away to his home, saying	8
	13:34	when he leaves home	7
Lke	1:23	he went to his home.	8
	1:56	returned to her home.	8
	5:24	stand up and take your bed and go to your home."	8
	5:25	and went to his home, glorifying God.	8
	8:39	"Return to your home	8
	9:61	let me first say farewell to those at my home."	8
	15: 6	he comes home, he calls together his friends	8
	16: 4	people may welcome me into their homes.'	8
	16: 9	welcome you into the eternal homes.	10
	18:14	this man went down to his home justified	8
	18:28	"Look, we have left our homes and followed you."	5
	23:48	they returned home, beating their breasts.	1
	24:12	he went home, amazed at what had happened	3
Jhn	7:53	[[each of them went home]]	8
	11:20	she went and met him, while Mary stayed at home.	8
	12: 1	Jesus came to Bethany, the home of Lazarus	9
	14:23	we will come to them and make our home with them.	6
	16:32	when you will be scattered, each one to his home	5
	19:27	the disciple took her into his own home.	5
	20:10	the disciples returned to their homes.	2
Act	2:46	broke bread at home and ate their food with glad	8
	5:42	every day in the temple and at home	8
	8:28	was returning home; seated in his chariot,	1
	10:32	he is staying in the home of Simon	7
	16:15	come and stay at my home."	8
	16:40	leaving the prison they went to Lydia's home;	1
	21: 6	we went on board the ship, and they returned home.	5
1Co	11:22	What! Do you not have homes to eat and drink in?	7
	11:34	If you are hungry, eat at home	8
	14:35	let them ask their husbands at home.	8
2Co	5: 6	we know that while we are at home in the body	4
	5: 8	be away from the body and at home with the Lord.	4
	5: 9	So whether we are at home or away	4
Rev	21: 3	"See, the home of God is among mortals.	10

at home

1. κατοικέω, *katoikeō, 2997*

2Pe	3:13	and a new earth, where righteousness is at home.	1

homeland

1. πατρίς, *patris, 4258*

Heb	11:14	they are seeking a homeland.	1

homeless

1. ἀστατέω, *astateō, 841*

1Co	4:11	we are poorly clothed and beaten and homeless	1

homestead

1. ἔπαυλις, *epaulis, 2068*

Act	1:20	'Let his homestead become desolate	1

hometown

1. πατρίς, *patris, 4258*

Mat	13:54	came to his hometown and began to teach the people	1
Mrk	6: 1	left that place and came to his hometown	1
	6: 4	without honor, except in their hometown	1
Lke	4:23	'Do here also in your hometown	1
	4:24	no prophet is accepted in the prophet's hometown.	1

honest

1. δίκαιος, *dikaios, 1465*
2. καλός, *kalos, 2819*

Lke	8:15	hold it fast in an honest and good heart	2
	20:20	sent spies who pretended to be honest	1

honestly

1. ἀγαθός, *agathos, 19*

Eph	4:28	labor and work honestly with their own hands	1

honey

1. μέλι, *meli, 3510*

Mat	3: 4	waist, and his food was locusts and wild honey.	1

Mrk 1: 6 ate locusts and wild honey. 1
Rev 10: 9 bitter...but sweet as honey in your mouth." 1
10:10 it was sweet as honey in my mouth 1

honor *See also* hold in honor, place of honor, seat of honor
1. Contextual: Not in Greek
2. δόξα, *doxa, 1518*
3. δοξάζω, *doxazō, 1519*
4. ἔντιμος + ἔχω, *entimos + echō, 1952 + 2400*
5. τιμάω, *timaō, 5506*
6. τιμή, *timē, 5507*

Mat 15: 4 'Honor your father and your mother,' 5
15: 5 that person need not honor the father. 5
15: 8 'This people honors me with their lips 5
19:19 Honor your father and mother; 5
Mrk 7: 6 'This people honors me with their lips 5
7:10 For Moses said, 'Honor your father and your mother'; 5
10:19 shall not defraud; Honor your father and mother.' " 5
Lke 14:10 then you will be honored in the presence of all 2
18:20 Honor your father and mother.' " 5
Jhn 4:44 a prophet has no honor in the prophet's own country). 6
5:23 so that all may honor the Son 5
5:23 just as they honor the Father. 5
5:23 Anyone who does not honor the Son 5
5:23 does not honor the Father who sent him. 5
8:49 I honor my Father, and you dishonor me. 5
12:26 Whoever serves me, the Father will honor. 5
Act 28:10 They bestowed many honors on us 6
Rom 1:21 they did not honor him as God or give thanks 3
2: 7 seek for glory and honor and immortality 6
2:10 and honor and peace for everyone who does good 6
12:10 outdo one another in showing honor. 6
13: 7 Pay...honor to whom honor is due. 6
13: 7 Pay...honor to whom honor is due. 6
14: 6 Those...observe it in honor of the Lord. 1
14: 6 Also those who eat, eat in honor of the Lord 1
14: 6 those who abstain, abstain in honor of the Lord 1
1Co 12:23 we clothe with greater honor 6
12:24 giving the greater honor to the inferior member 6
12:26 if one member is honored, all rejoice together 3
2Co 6: 8 in honor and dishonor 2
Eph 6: 2 "Honor your father and mother" 5
Php 2:29 Welcome him then in the Lord...and honor such people 4
1Th 4: 4 control your own body in holiness and honor 6
1Ti 1:17 be honor and glory forever and ever. Amen. 6
5: 3 Honor widows who are really widows. 5
5:17 elders...be considered worthy of double honor 6
6: 1 regard their masters as worthy of all honor 6
6:16 to him be honor and eternal dominion. Amen. 6
Heb 2: 7 you have crowned them with glory and honor 6
2: 9 now crowned with glory and honor 6
3: 3 the builder of a house has more honor than the house 6
5: 4 one does not presume to take this honor 6
1Pe 1: 7 and honor when Jesus Christ is revealed. 6
2:17 Honor everyone. Love the family of believers. 5
2:17 Fear God. Honor the emperor. 5
3: 7 paying honor to the woman as the weaker sex 6
2Pe 1:17 he received honor and glory from God the Father 6
Rev 4: 9 creatures give glory and honor and thanks to the one 6
4:11 Lord and God, to receive glory and honor and power 6
5:12 to receive...honor and glory and blessing!" 6
5:13 to the Lamb be blessing and honor and glory 6
7:12 honor and power and might be to our God forever 6
21:26 the glory and the honor of the nations. 6

without honor
1. ἄτιμος, *atimos, 872*

Mat 13:57 "Prophets are not without honor except 1
Mrk 6: 4 Jesus said to them, "Prophets are not without honor 1

honorable
1. καλός, *kalos, 2819*
2. σεμνός, *semnos, 4948*

Php 4: 8 whatever is honorable, whatever is just 2
1Pe 2:12 they may see your honorable deeds and glorify God 1

less honorable
1. ἄτιμος, *atimos, 872*

1Co 12:23 members of the body that we think less honorable 1

honorably
1. εὐσχημόνως, *euschēmonōs, 2361*
2. καλός, *kalos, 2819*
3. καλῶς, *kalōs, 2822*

Rom 13:13 live honorably as in the day 1
Heb 13:18 desiring to act honorably in all things. 3
1Pe 2:12 Conduct yourselves honorably among the Gentiles 2

hook
1. ἄγκιστρον, *ankistron, 45*

Mat 17:27 go to the sea and cast a hook; 1

hope *See also* set one's hope, set one's hope first
1. Contextual: Not in Greek
2. ἐλπίζω, *elpizō, 1827*
3. ἐλπίς, *elpis, 1828*
4. ὅς, *hos, 4005*

Mat 12:21 in his name the Gentiles will hope." 2
Lke 6:34 lend to those from whom you hope to receive 2
23: 8 was hoping to see him perform some sign. 2
24:21 we had hoped that he was the one to redeem Israel. 2
Act 2:26 moreover my flesh will live in hope. 3
16:19 owners saw that their hope of making money was gone 3
23: 6 the hope of the resurrection of the dead." 3
24:15 I have a hope in God— 3
24:15 a hope that they themselves also accept— 1
24:26 he hoped that money would be given him by Paul 2
26: 6 on account of my hope in the promise made by God 3
26: 7 a promise that our twelve tribes hope to attain 3
26: 7 for this hope, your Excellency, that I am accused 3
27:20 all hope of our being saved was...abandoned. 3
28:20 since it is for the sake of the hope of Israel 3
Rom 4:18 Hoping against hope, he believed 3
4:18 Hoping against hope, he believed 3
5: 2 we boast in our hope of sharing the glory of God. 3
5: 4 and character produces hope 3
5: 5 and hope does not disappoint us 3
8:20 by the will of the one who subjected it, in hope 3
8:24 For in hope we were saved. 3
8:24 Now hope that is seen is not hope. 3
8:24 Now hope that is seen is not hope. 3
8:24 For who hopes for what is seen? 2
8:25 if we hope for what we do not see, we wait for it 2
12:12 Rejoice in hope, be patient in suffering 3
15: 4 by steadfastness...we might have hope. 3
15:12 in him the Gentiles shall hope." 3
15:13 the God of hope fill you with all joy and peace 3
15:13 may abound in hope by the power of the Holy Spirit. 3
15:24 For I do hope to see you on my journey 2
1Co 9:10 for whoever plows should plow in hope 3
9:10 should thresh in hope of a share in the crop. 3
13: 7 hopes all things, endures all things. 2
13:13 And now faith, hope, and love abide, these three; 3
15:19 If for this life only we have hoped in Christ 2
15:32 If with merely human hopes I fought with wild animals 1
16: 7 I hope to spend some time with you 2
2Co 1: 7 Our hope for you is unshaken; 3
1:13 I hope you will understand until the end 2
3:12 we have such a hope, we act with great boldness 3
5:11 I hope that we are also well known to your consciences. 2
10:15 our hope is that, as your faith increases 3
13: 6 I hope you will find out that we have not failed. 2
Gal 5: 5 we eagerly wait for the hope of righteousness. 3
Eph 1:18 know what is the hope to which he has called you 3
2:12 having no hope and without God in the world. 3
4: 4 just as you were called to the one hope 3
Php 1:20 It is my eager expectation and hope 3
2:19 I hope in the Lord Jesus to send Timothy to you 2
2:23 I hope therefore to send him 2
Col 1: 5 because of the hope laid up for you in heaven. 3
1: 5 You have heard of this hope before in the word 4
1:23 without shifting from the hope promised by the gospel 3
1:27 which is Christ in you, the hope of glory. 3
1Th 1: 3 steadfastness of hope in our Lord Jesus Christ. 3
2:19 For what is our hope or joy or crown of boasting 3
4:13 you may not grieve as others do who have no hope. 3
5: 8 for a helmet the hope of salvation. 3
2Th 2:16 through grace gave us eternal comfort and good hope 3
1Ti 1: 1 God our Savior and of Christ Jesus our hope 3
3:14 I hope to come to you soon 2

Tit	1: 2	in the hope of eternal life	3
	2:13	while we wait for the blessed hope	3
	3: 7	become heirs according to the hope of eternal life.	3
Phm	1:22	I am hoping...to be restored to you.	2
Heb	3: 6	firm the confidence and the pride that belong to hope.	3
	6:11	the full assurance of hope to the very end	3
	6:18	to seize the hope set before us.	3
	6:19	We have this hope, a sure and steadfast anchor	4
	6:19	a hope that enters the inner shrine	1
	7:19	on the other hand, the introduction of a better hope	3
	10:23	Let us hold fast to the confession of our hope	3
	11: 1	Now faith is the assurance of things hoped for	2
1Pe	1: 3	given us a new birth into a living hope	3
	1:21	so that your faith and hope are set on God.	3
	3: 5	women who hoped in God used to adorn themselves	2
	3:15	an accounting for the hope that is in you;	3
1Jn	3: 3	all who have this hope in him purify themselves	3
2Jn	1:12	I hope to come to you and talk with you	2
3Jn	1:14	I hope to see you soon	2

horn

1. κέρας, *keras, 3043*

Rev	5: 6	a Lamb...having seven horns and...seven eyes	1
	9:13	a voice from the four horns of the golden altar	1
	12: 3	great red dragon, with seven heads and ten horns	1
	13: 1	I saw a beast...having ten horns and seven heads;	1
	13: 1	a beast...and on its horns were ten diadems	1
	13:11	another beast...it had two horns like a lamb	1
	17: 3	and it had seven heads and ten horns.	1
	17: 7	and of the beast with seven heads and ten horns	1
	17:12	And the ten horns that you saw are ten kings	1
	17:16	the ten horns that you saw, they and the beast	1

horse

1. ἵππος, *hippos, 2691*

Jas	3: 3	If we put bits into the mouths of horses	1
Rev	6: 2	I looked...a white horse! Its rider had a bow;	1
	6: 4	And out came another horse, bright red;	1
	6: 5	I looked, and there was a black horse! Its rider	1
	6: 8	a pale green horse! Its rider's name was Death	1
	9: 7	the locusts were like horses equipped for battle.	1
	9: 9	like the noise of many chariots with horses	1
	9:17	this was how I saw the horses in my vision:	1
	9:17	the heads of the horses were like lions' heads	1
	9:19	For the power of the horses is in their mouths	1
	14:20	blood flowed...as high as a horse's bridle	1
	18:13	cattle and sheep, horses and chariots, slaves	1
	19:11	I saw heaven opened, and there was a white horse!	1
	19:14	armies of heaven...following him on white horses.	1
	19:18	to eat...the flesh of horses and their riders	1
	19:19	to make war against the rider on the horse	1
	19:21	the sword of the rider on the horse	1

horseman

1. ἱππεύς, *hippeus, 2689*

Act	23:23	two hundred soldiers, seventy horsemen	1
	23:32	The next day they let the horsemen go on with him	1

Hosanna

1. ὡσαννά, *hōsanna, 6057*

Mat	21: 9	shouting, "Hosanna to the Son of David!	1
	21: 9	Hosanna in the highest heaven!"	1
	21:15	"Hosanna to the Son of David,"	1
Mrk	11: 9	"Hosanna! Blessed is the one who comes	1
	11:10	Hosanna in the highest heaven!"	1
Jhn	12:13	went out to meet him, shouting, "Hosanna!	1

Hosea

1. Ὡσηέ, *Hōsēe, 6060*

Rom	9:25	As indeed he says in Hosea	1

hospitable

1. φιλόξενος, *philoxenos, 5811*

1Ti	3: 2	respectable, hospitable, an apt teacher	1
Tit	1: 8	but he must be hospitable, a lover of goodness	1
1Pe	4: 9	Be hospitable to one another without complaining.	1

hospitably

1. φιλοφρόνως, *philophronōs, 5819*

Act	28: 7	who received us and entertained us hospitably	1

hospitality See show hospitality, show hospitality to a stranger

hospitality to a stranger

1. φιλοξενία, *philoxenia, 5810*

Rom	12:13	extend hospitality to strangers.	1

host[1]

1. Σαβαώθ, *Sabaōth, 4877*
2. στρατιά, *stratia, 5131*

Lke	2:13	with the angel a multitude of the heavenly host	2
Act	7:42	God...handed them over to worship the host of heaven	2
Rom	9:29	"If the Lord of hosts had not left survivors to us	1
Jas	5: 4	cries...reached the ears of the Lord of hosts.	1

host[2]

1. Contextual: Not in Greek
2. αὐτός, *autos, 899*
3. καλέω, *kaleō, 2813*
4. ξένος, *xenos, 3828*

Lke	14: 8	has been invited by your host;	2
	14: 9	the host who invited both of you may come and say	1
	14:10	so that when your host comes, he may say to you	3
Rom	16:23	Gaius, who is host to me and to the whole church	4

hostile

1. ἐνέχω, *enechō, 1923*
2. ἔχθρα, *echthra, 2397*
3. ἐχθρός, *echthros, 2398*

Lke	11:53	the Pharisees began to be very hostile toward him	1
Rom	8: 7	the mind that is set on the flesh is hostile to God;	2
Col	1:21	you who were once estranged and hostile in mind	3

hostility

1. ἀντιλογία, *antilogia, 517*
2. ἔχθρα, *echthra, 2397*

Eph	2:14	broken down the dividing wall, that is, the hostility	2
	2:16	thus putting to death that hostility through it	2
Heb	12: 3	who endured...such hostility against himself	1

hot See also sear with a hot iron

1. ζεστός, *zestos, 2412*

Rev	3:15	"I know your works; you are neither cold nor hot.	1
	3:15	I wish that you were either cold or hot.	1
	3:16	you are lukewarm, and neither cold nor hot	1

hour See also half an hour

1. πῆχυς, *pēchys, 4388*
2. ὥρα, *hōra, 6052*

Mat	6:27	by worrying add a single hour to your span of life?	1
	8:13	And the servant was healed in that hour.	2
	14:15	"This is a deserted place, and the hour is now late;	2
	20:12	saying, 'These last worked only one hour	2
	24:36	about that day and hour no one knows	2
	24:44	Son of Man is coming at an unexpected hour.	2
	24:50	at an hour that he does not know.	2
	25:13	you know neither the day nor the hour.	2
	26:40	"So, could you not stay awake with me one hour?	2
	26:45	See, the hour is at hand	2
	26:55	At that hour Jesus said to the crowds	2
Mrk	6:35	a deserted place, and the hour is now very late;	2
	13:32	about that day or hour no one knows	2
	14:35	if it were possible, the hour might pass from him.	2
	14:37	you asleep? Could you not keep awake one hour?	2
	14:41	Enough! The hour has come;	2
Lke	10:21	At that same hour Jesus rejoiced in the Holy Spirit	2
	12:12	the Holy Spirit will teach you at that very hour	2
	12:25	add a single hour to your span of life?	1
	12:39	at what hour the thief was coming	2
	12:40	the Son of Man is coming at an unexpected hour."	2
	12:46	at an hour that he does not know	2
	13:31	that very hour some Pharisees came and said	2
	20:19	wanted to lay hands on him at that very hour	2
	22:14	When the hour came, he took his place at the table	2
	22:53	this is your hour, and the power of darkness!"	2
	22:59	about an hour later	2
	24:33	That same hour they got up and returned to Jerusalem;	2
Jhn	2: 4	Jesus said to her...My hour has not yet come."	2

Jhn	4:21	the hour is coming when you will worship the Father	2
	4:23	But the hour is coming, and is now	2
	4:52	So he asked them the hour when he began to recover	2
	4:53	that this was the hour when Jesus had said	2
	5:25	"Very truly, I tell you, the hour is coming	2
	5:28	the hour is coming when all…will hear	2
	7:30	because his hour had not yet come.	2
	8:20	because his hour had not yet come.	2
	11: 9	"Are there not twelve hours of daylight?	2
	12:23	Jesus answered them, "The hour has come	2
	12:27	'Father, save me from this hour'?	2
	12:27	for this reason that I have come to this hour.	2
	13: 1	Jesus knew that his hour had come to depart	2
	16: 2	Indeed, an hour is coming	2
	16: 4	so that when their hour comes you may remember	2
	16:21	because her hour has come.	2
	16:25	The hour is coming	2
	16:32	The hour is coming, indeed it has come	2
	17: 1	"Father, the hour has come; glorify your Son	2
	19:27	from that hour the disciple took her	2
Act	3: 1	the hour of prayer, at three o'clock in the afternoon.	2
	5: 7	After an interval of about three hours	2
	10:30	Cornelius replied, "Four days ago at this very hour	2
	16:18	it came out that very hour.	2
	16:33	At the same hour of the night he took them	2
	19:34	for about two hours all of them shouted	2
	22:13	In that very hour I regained my sight and saw him.	2
1Co	4:11	To the present hour we are hungry and thirsty	2
	15:30	why are we putting ourselves in danger every hour?	2
1Jn	2:18	Children, it is the last hour!	2
	2:18	From this we know that it is the last hour.	2
Rev	3: 3	you will not know at what hour I will come to you.	2
	3:10	I will keep you from the hour of trial	2
	9:15	angels…who had been held ready for the hour	2
	14: 7	"Fear God…for the hour of his judgment has come;	2
	14:15	reap, for the hour to reap has come	2
	17:12	receive authority as kings for one hour	2
	18:10	For in one hour your judgment has come."	2
	18:17	in one hour all this wealth has been laid waste!"	2
	18:19	For in one hour she has been laid waste."	2

house *See also* master of the house, owner of the house

1. Contextual: Not in Greek
2. ἔσω, *esō*, 2276
3. ὁ, *ho*, 3836
4. οἰκία, *oikia*, 3864
5. οἶκος, *oikos*, 3875
6. ὅπου, *hopou*, 3963

Mat	2:11	entering the house, they saw the child with Mary	4
	5:15	and it gives light to all in the house.	4
	7:24	like a wise man who built his house on rock.	4
	7:25	the winds blew and beat on that house	4
	7:26	a foolish man who built his house on sand.	4
	7:27	and the winds blew and beat against that house	4
	8:14	When Jesus entered Peter's house	4
	9:10	And as he sat at dinner in the house	4
	9:23	When Jesus came to the leader's house	4
	9:28	When he entered the house, the blind men came	4
	10: 6	to the lost sheep of the house of Israel.	5
	10:12	As you enter the house, greet it.	4
	10:13	If the house is worthy, let your peace come upon it;	4
	10:14	as you leave that house or town.	4
	12: 4	He entered the house of God and ate the bread	5
	12:25	no city or house divided against itself	4
	12:29	Or how can one enter a strong man's house	4
	12:29	Then indeed the house can be plundered.	4
	12:44	'I will return to my house from which I came.'	5
	13: 1	went out of the house and sat beside the sea.	4
	13:36	Then he left the crowds and went into the house.	4
	13:57	in their own country and in their own house."	4
	15:24	only to the lost sheep of the house of Israel."	5
	19:29	everyone who has left houses or brothers	4
	21:13	'My house shall be called a house of prayer';	5
	21:13	'My house shall be called a house of prayer';	5
	23:38	See, your house is left to you, desolate.	5
	24:17	to take what is in the house;	4
	24:43	would not have let his house be broken into.	4
	26: 6	at Bethany in the house of Simon the leper	4
	26:18	Passover at your house with my disciples.' "	1
	26:57	in whose house the scribes…had gathered.	6

Mrk	1:29	entered the house of Simon and Andrew	4
	2:15	as he sat at dinner in Levi's house	4
	2:26	He entered the house of God	5
	3:25	if a house is divided against itself	4
	3:25	that house will not be able to stand.	4
	3:27	no one can enter a strong man's house	4
	3:27	then indeed the house can be plundered.	4
	5:35	some people came from the leader's house	1
	5:38	When they came to the house	5
	6: 4	among their own kin, and in their own house."	4
	6:10	He said to them, "Wherever you enter a house,	4
	7:17	When he had left the crowd and entered the house	5
	7:24	entered a house and did not want anyone to know	4
	9:28	When he had entered the house	5
	9:33	when he was in the house he asked them	4
	10:10	in the house the disciples asked him again	4
	10:29	there is no one who has left house or brothers	4
	10:30	houses, brothers and sisters, mothers	4
	11:17	'My house shall be called a house of prayer	5
	11:17	'My house shall be called a house of prayer	5
	12:40	They devour widows' houses	4
	13:15	must not go down or enter the house	4
	13:35	when the master of the house will come	4
	14: 3	at Bethany in the house of Simon the leper	4
Lke	1:27	Joseph, of the house of David.	5
	1:33	He will reign over the house of Jacob forever	5
	1:40	she entered the house of Zechariah	5
	1:69	in the house of his servant David	5
	2: 4	descended from the house and family of David.	5
	2:49	not know that I must be in my Father's house?"	3
	4:38	leaving the synagogue he entered Simon's house.	4
	5:29	Levi gave a great banquet for him in his house;	4
	6: 4	He entered the house of God	5
	6:48	like a man building a house, who dug deeply	4
	6:48	the river burst against that house	4
	6:49	like a man who built a house on the ground	4
	6:49	great was the ruin of that house."	4
	7: 6	when he was not far from the house	4
	7:10	those who had been sent returned to the house	5
	7:36	he went into the Pharisee's house	4
	7:37	he was eating in the Pharisee's house	4
	7:44	I entered your house;	4
	8:27	he did not live in a house but in the tombs.	4
	8:41	begged him to come to his house	5
	8:49	someone came from the leader's house to say,	1
	8:51	When he came to the house	4
	9: 4	Whatever house you enter, stay there	4
	10: 5	Whatever house you enter, first say, 'Peace	4
	10: 5	'Peace to this house!'	5
	10: 7	Remain in the same house, eating and drinking	4
	10: 7	Do not move about from house to house.	4
	10: 7	Do not move about from house to house.	4
	11:17	becomes a desert, and house falls on house.	5
	11:17	becomes a desert, and house falls on house.	5
	11:24	'I will return to my house from which I came.'	5
	12:39	he would not have let his house be broken into.	5
	13:35	See, your house is left to you.	5
	14: 1	when Jesus was going to the house of a leader	5
	14:23	so that my house may be filled.	5
	15: 8	light a lamp, sweep the house, and search	4
	15:25	when he came and approached the house	4
	16:27	I beg you to send him to my father's house	5
	17:31	on the housetop who has belongings in the house	4
	18:29	there is no one who has left house or wife	4
	19: 5	I must stay at your house today."	5
	19: 9	"Today salvation has come to this house	5
	19:46	'My house shall be a house of prayer';	5
	19:46	'My house shall be a house of prayer';	5
	20:47	They devour widows' houses	4
	22:10	follow him into the house he enters	4
	22:11	say to the owner of the house, 'The teacher asks	4
	22:54	bringing him into the high priest's house.	4
Jhn	2:16	Stop making my Father's house a marketplace!"	5
	2:17	"Zeal for your house will consume me."	5
	11:31	The Jews who were with her in the house	4
	12: 3	The house was filled with the fragrance	4
	14: 2	In my Father's house there are many dwelling places.	4
	20:19	the doors of the house…were locked	1
	20:26	his disciples were again in the house	2
Act	2: 2	it filled the entire house where they were sitting	5
	2:36	Therefore let the entire house of Israel know	5

4:34	as many as owned lands or houses	4
7:20	three months he was brought up in his father's house;	5
7:42	forty years in the wilderness, O house of Israel?	5
7:46	find a dwelling place for the house of Jacob.	5
7:47	it was Solomon who built a house for him.	5
7:48	does not dwell in houses made with human hands;	1
7:49	What kind of house will you build for me	5
9:11	at the house of Judas look for a man of Tarsus	4
9:17	So Ananias went and entered the house.	4
10: 6	Simon, a tanner, whose house is by the seaside."	4
10:17	were asking for Simon's house	4
10:22	to send for you to come to his house	5
10:30	at three o'clock, I was praying in my house	5
11:11	arrived at the house where we were.	4
11:12	we entered the man's house.	5
11:13	the angel standing in his house and saying	5
12:12	as he realized this, he went to the house of Mary	4
16:32	to him and to all who were in his house.	4
16:34	He brought them up into the house	5
17: 5	to the assembly, they attacked Jason's house.	4
18: 7	went to the house of a man named Titius Justus	4
18: 7	his house was next door to the synagogue.	4
19:16	they fled out of the house naked and wounded.	5
21: 8	we went into the house of Philip the evangelist	5
21:16	brought us to the house of Mnason of Cyprus	1
Rom 16: 5	Greet also the church in their house.	5
1Co 16:19	together with the church in their house	5
2Co 5: 1	a house not made with hands	4
Col 4:15	to Nympha and the church in her house.	5
2Ti 2:20	In a large house there are utensils	4
Phm 1: 2	the church in your house:	5
Heb 3: 2	just as Moses also "was faithful in all God's house."	5
3: 3	the builder of a house has more honor than the house	5
3: 3	builder of a house has more honor than the house	1
3: 4	(For every house is built by someone	5
3: 5	Now Moses was faithful in all God's house	5
3: 6	Christ, however, was faithful over God's house as a son	5
3: 6	we are his house if we hold firm the confidence	5
8: 8	a new covenant with the house of Israel	5
8: 8	a new covenant...with the house of Judah	5
8:10	with the house of Israel after those days	5
10:21	since we have a great priest over the house of God	5
1Pe 2: 5	yourselves be built into a spiritual house	5
2Jn 1:10	Do not receive into the house or welcome	4

house after house

　　1. κατά + ὁ + οἶκος, *kata + ho + oikos, 2848 + 3836 + 3875*

Act 8: 3	ravaging the church by entering house after house;	1

house to house

　　1. κατά + οἶκος, *kata + oikos, 2848 + 3875*
　　2. οἰκία, *oikia, 3864*

Act 20:20	teaching you publicly and from house to house	1
1Ti 5:13	gadding about from house to house;	2

household *See also* good *manager* of household, manage a household, master of a household, member of the household

　　1. οἰκετεία, *oiketeia, 3859*
　　2. οἰκία, *oikia, 3864*
　　3. οἰκιακός, *oikiakos, 3865*
　　4. οἶκος, *oikos, 3875*

Mat 10:25	will they malign those of his household!	3
24:45	whom his master has put in charge of his household	1
Lke 12:52	five in one household will be divided	4
Jhn 4:53	he himself believed, along with his whole household.	2
8:35	does not have a permanent place in the household;	2
Act 7:10	ruler over Egypt and over all his household.	4
10: 2	devout man who feared God with all his household;	4
11:14	you and your entire household will be saved.'	4
16:15	When she and her household were baptized	4
16:31	you will be saved, you and your household."	4
18: 8	Crispus...together with all his household;	4
1Co 1:16	(I did baptize also the household of Stephanas;	4
16:15	household of Stephanas were the first converts	2
Php 4:22	especially those of the emperor's household.	2
1Ti 3: 4	He must manage his own household well	4
3: 5	does not know how to manage his own household	4
3:12	let them manage...their households well;	4
3:15	how one ought to behave in the household of God	4

2Ti 1:16	grant mercy to the household of Onesiphorus	4
3: 6	those who make their way into households	2
4:19	Greet...the household of Onesiphorus.	4
Heb 11: 7	built an ark to save his household;	4
1Pe 4:17	for judgment to begin with the household of God;	4

entire household

　　1. πανοικεί, *panoikei, 4109*

Act 16:34	he and his entire household rejoiced	1

householder

　　1. οἰκοδεσπότης, *oikodespotēs, 3867*

Mat 13:27	the slaves of the householder came and said	1

housetop

　　1. δῶμα, *dōma, 1560*

Mat 10:27	proclaim from the housetops.	1
24:17	the one on the housetop must not go down	1
Mrk 13:15	one on the housetop must not go down	1
Lke 12: 3	will be proclaimed from the housetops.	1
17:31	anyone on the housetop who has belongings	1

how *See also* how great, how *long*, how *many*, how *much*, how *often*, know how

　　1. ἐν + τίς, *en + tis, 1877 + 5515*
　　2. ἰδού, *idou, 2627*
　　3. καθώς, *kathōs, 2777*
　　4. κατά, *kata, 2848*
　　5. κατά + τίς, *kata + tis, 2848 + 5515*
　　6. ὅπως, *hopōs, 3968*
　　7. ὅτι, *hoti, 4022*
　　8. οὕτως, *houtōs, 4048*
　　9. περί, *peri, 4309*
　　10. πόθεν, *pothen, 4470*
　　11. πόσος, *posos, 4531*
　　12. πῶς, *pōs, 4802*
　　13. τίς, *tis, 5515*
　　14. ὡς, *hōs, 6055*

Mat 5:13	if salt has lost its taste, how can its saltiness	1
6:28	lilies of the field, how they grow; they neither	12
7: 4	Or how can you say to your neighbor	12
10:19	do not worry about how you are to speak	12
12:14	and conspired against him, how to destroy him.	6
12:26	how then will his kingdom stand?	12
12:29	Or how can one enter a strong man's house	12
12:34	You brood of vipers! How can you speak good	12
16:11	How could you fail to perceive	12
21:20	"How did the fig tree wither at once?"	12
22:12	said to him, 'Friend, how did you get in here	12
22:43	"How is it then that David by the Spirit	12
22:45	If David thus calls him Lord, how can he be his son?"	12
23:33	How can you escape being sentenced to hell?	12
26:54	how then would the scriptures be fulfilled	12
Mrk 3: 6	how to destroy him.	6
3:23	"How can Satan cast out Satan?	12
4:13	Then how will you understand all the parables?	12
4:27	he does not know how.	14
8: 4	"How can one feed these people with bread here	10
9:12	How then is it written about the Son of Man	12
9:21	Jesus asked the father, "How long has this been	11
9:50	how can you season it?	1
10:23	"How hard it will be for those who have wealth	12
10:24	how hard it is to enter the kingdom of God!	12
12:26	how God said to him, 'I am the God of Abraham	12
12:35	"How can the scribes say that the Messiah is	12
12:37	calls him Lord; so how can he be his son?"	10
Lke 1:18	Zechariah said to the angel, "How will I know	5
1:34	"How can this be, since I am a virgin?"	12
6:42	how can you say to your neighbor, 'Friend	12
8:18	Then pay attention to how you listen;	12
8:36	told them how the one...had been healed.	12
8:47	how she had been immediately healed.	14
11:18	how will his kingdom stand?	12
12:11	do not worry about how you are to defend	12
12:27	Consider the lilies, how they grow:	12
12:49	how I wish it were already kindled!	13
14: 7	he noticed how the guests chose the places of honor	12
14:34	how can its saltiness be restored?	1
18:24	"How hard it is for those who have wealth to enter	12

Lke	20:41	"How can they say that the Messiah is David's son?	12
	20:44	David thus calls him Lord; so how can he be his son?"	12
	21: 5	how it was adorned with beautiful stones	7
	22: 4	how he might betray him to them.	12
	22:61	how he had said to him, "Before the cock crows	14
	23:55	saw the tomb and how his body was laid.	14
	24: 6	Remember how he told you	14
	24:20	how our chief priests…handed him over	6
	24:35	how he had been made known to them	14
Jhn	3: 4	"How can anyone be born after having grown old?	12
	3: 9	Nicodemus said to him, "How can these things be?"	12
	3:12	how can you believe if I tell you about heavenly	12
	4: 9	"How is it that you, a Jew, ask a drink of me	12
	4:35	see how the fields are ripe for harvesting.	7
	5:44	How can you believe when you accept glory from	12
	5:47	how will you believe what I say?"	12
	6:42	How can he…say, 'I have come down from heaven'?"	12
	6:52	"How can this man give us his flesh to eat?"	12
	7:15	"How does this man have such learning	12
	9:10	asking him, "Then how were your eyes opened?"	12
	9:15	began to ask him how he had received his sight.	12
	9:16	"How can a man who is a sinner perform such signs?"	12
	9:19	How then does he now see?"	12
	9:21	we do not know how it is that now he sees	12
	9:26	How did he open your eyes?"	12
	11:36	the Jews said, "See how he loved him!"	12
	12:34	How can you say that the Son of Man must be	12
	14: 5	How can we know the way?"	12
	14: 9	How can you say, 'Show us the Father'?	12
	14:22	"Lord, how is it that you will reveal yourself	13
	18:22	"Is that how you answer the high priest?"	8
Act	2: 8	how is it that we hear	12
	4: 9	asked how this man has been healed	1
	5: 4	How is it that you have contrived this deed	13
	5: 9	"How is it that you have agreed together	13
	8:31	He replied, "How can I, unless someone guides me?"	12
	9:27	described…how on the road he had seen the Lord	12
	9:27	how in Damascus he had spoken boldly	12
	10:38	how God anointed Jesus of Nazareth	14
	11:13	He told us how he had seen the angel standing	12
	11:16	I remembered the word of the Lord, how he had said	14
	12:17	how the Lord had brought him out of the prison.	12
	14:27	how he had opened a door of faith for the Gentiles.	7
	15:14	how God first looked favorably on the Gentiles	3
	15:36	see how they are doing."	12
	17:22	how extremely religious you are in every way.	14
	20:18	"You yourselves know how I lived among you	12
	25:20	was at a loss how to investigate these questions	9
Rom	3: 6	For then how could God judge the world?	12
	4:10	How then was it reckoned to him?	12
	6: 2	How can we who died to sin go on living in it?	12
	8:26	for we do not know how to pray as we ought	13
	10:14	how are they to call on one	12
	10:14	And how are they to believe in one	12
	10:14	how are they to hear without someone to proclaim	12
	10:15	how are they to proclaim him unless they are sent?	12
	10:15	"How beautiful are the feet of those who bring	14
	11: 2	of Elijah, how he pleads with God against Israel?	14
	11:33	How unsearchable are his judgments	14
	13:11	how it is now the moment for you to wake from sleep.	7
1Co	3:10	Each builder must choose with care how to build on it.	12
	7:32	how to please the Lord;	12
	7:33	how to please his wife	12
	7:34	how to please her husband.	12
	14: 6	how will I benefit you unless I speak to you	13
	14: 7	how will anyone know what is being played?	12
	14: 9	how will anyone know what is being said?	12
	14:16	how can anyone in the position of an outsider say	12
	15:12	how can some of you say there is no resurrection	12
	15:35	someone will ask, "How are the dead raised?	12
2Co	7:15	how you welcomed him with fear and trembling.	14
	12:13	How have you been worse off than the other churches	13
Gal	2:14	how can you compel the Gentiles to live like Jews?"	12
	4: 9	how can you turn back again to the weak	12
Eph	3: 3	how the mystery was made known to me	7
	5:15	Be careful then how you live	12
	6:21	you also may know how I am and what I am doing	4
	6:22	to let you know how we are	9
Php	1: 8	For God is my witness, how I long for all of you	14
	2:22	how like a son with a father he has served with me	7
Col	4: 6	you may know how you ought to answer everyone.	12

	4: 8	so that you may know how we are	9
1Th	1: 9	how you turned to God from idols	12
	2:10	how pure, upright, and blameless	14
	3: 9	How can we thank God enough for you	13
	4: 1	as you learned from us how you ought to live	12
2Th	3: 7	you yourselves know how you ought to imitate us;	12
1Ti	3: 5	how can he take care of God's church?	12
	3:15	you may know how one ought to behave	12
2Ti	3:15	how…you have known the sacred writings	7
Heb	2: 3	how can we escape if we neglect	12
Jas	3: 5	How great a forest is set ablaze by a small fire!	2
	5:11	how the Lord is compassionate and merciful.	7
1Jn	3:17	How does God's love abide in anyone	12
3Jn	1: 3	namely how you walk in the truth.	3
Rev	9:17	this was how I saw the horses in my vision:	8

however

1. ἀλλά, *alla*, 247
2. δέ, *de*, 1254
3. εἰ + μή, *ei + mē*, 1623 + 3590
4. οὖν, *oun*, 4036
5. πλήν, *plēn*, 4440

Mat	17:27	However, so that we do not give offense to them	2
Jhn	11:13	Jesus, however, had been speaking about his death	2
Act	13:13	John, however, left them and returned to Jerusalem;	2
	28: 5	He, however, shook off the creature into the fire	4
Rom	15:25	At present, however, I am going to Jerusalem	2
1Co	7:17	However that may be, let each of you lead the life	3
	8: 7	not everyone, however, who has this knowledge.	1
2Co	10:13	We, however, will not boast beyond limits	2
Gal	4: 9	Now, however, that you have come to know God	2
	5:15	If, however, you bite and devour one another,	2
Eph	5:33	Each of you, however, should love his wife	5
Heb	3: 6	Christ, however, was faithful over God's house as a son	2
2Pe	2:12	These people, however, are like irrational animals	2

howl

1. κράζω, *krazo*, 3189

Mrk	5: 5	on the mountains he was always howling	1

huge

1. μέγας, *megas*, 3489

Rev	16:21	huge hailstones…dropped from heaven on people	1

human   *See also* human *authority*, human *inclination*, human *standard*, human *term*, know the human heart, make by human hands, make with human hands

1. Contextual: Not in Greek
2. ἀνθρώπινος, *anthrōpinos*, 474
3. ἄνθρωπος, *anthrōpos*, 476
4. σάρκινος, *sarkinos*, 4921
5. σάρξ, *sarx*, 4922

Mat	15: 9	in vain…teaching human precepts as doctrines.' "	3
	16:23	setting your mind not on divine things but on human	3
	17:22	Son of Man is going to be betrayed into human hands	3
	21:25	from heaven, or was it of human origin?"	3
	21:26	'Of human origin,' we are afraid of the crowd;	3
Mrk	7: 7	teaching human precepts as doctrines.'	3
	7: 8	and hold to human tradition.	3
	7:21	from the human heart, that evil intentions come:	3
	8:33	mind not on divine things but on human things	3
	9:31	betrayed into human hands	3
	11:30	come from heaven, or was it of human origin?	3
	11:32	But shall we say, 'Of human origin'?"	3
Lke	2:52	Jesus increased…in divine and human favor.	3
	9:44	to be betrayed into human hands."	3
	20: 4	the baptism of John…was it of human origin?"	3
	20: 6	if we say, 'Of human origin,' all the people	3
Jhn	5:34	Not that I accept such human testimony	3
	12:43	for they loved human glory more than the glory	3
Act	5:38	if this plan or this undertaking is of human origin	3
	14:11	"The gods have come down to us in human form!"	3
	17:25	nor is he served by human hands	2
	17:30	God has overlooked the times of human ignorance	1
Rom	3: 5	(I speak in a human way.)	3
	9:16	So it depends not on human will or exertion	1
	14:18	is acceptable to God and has human approval.	3
1Co	1:25	For God's foolishness is wiser than human wisdom	3
	1:25	God's weakness is stronger than human strength	3
	2: 5	your faith might rest not on human wisdom	3

2: 9	nor the human heart conceived	3
2:11	what human being knows what is truly human	3
2:11	except the human spirit that is within?	3
2:13	in words not taught by human wisdom	2
3:21	So let no one boast about human leaders.	3
4: 3	I should be judged by you or by any human court.	2
7:23	do not become slaves of human masters.	3
9: 8	Do I say this on human authority?	3
2Co 3: 3	but on tablets of human hearts.	4
5:16	we regard no one from a human point of view;	5
5:16	once knew Christ from a human point of view	5
Gal 1: 1	by human commission nor from human authorities,	3
1: 1	by human commission nor from human authorities,	3
1:10	seeking human approval, or God's approval?	3
1:11	the gospel...is not of human origin;	3
1:12	for I did not receive it from a human source	3
Php 2: 7	being born in human likeness.	3
2: 7	being found in human form	3
Col 2: 8	according to human tradition	3
2:18	puffed up without cause by a human way of thinking	5
2:22	simply human commands and teachings.	3
1Th 2:13	you accepted it not as a human word	3
1Ti 2: 5	one mediator...Christ Jesus, himself human	3
Heb 12: 9	we had human parents to discipline us	5
Jas 3: 7	every species...has been tamed by the human species	2
1Pe 2:13	accept the authority of every human institution	2
4: 2	no longer by human desires but by the will of God.	3
2Pe 1:21	because no prophecy ever came by human will,	3
2:16	a speechless donkey spoke with a human voice	3
1Jn 5: 9	If we receive human testimony, the testimony of God	3
Rev 4: 7	the third living creature with a face like a human	3
9: 7	their faces were like human faces	3
18:13	and chariots, slaves—and human lives.	3
21:17	one hundred forty-four cubits by human measurement	3

human being

1. ἄνθρωπος, *anthrōpos, 476*
2. σάρξ, *sarx, 4922*
3. σάρξ + καί + αἷμα, *sarx + kai + haima, 4922 + 2779 + 135*

Mat 9: 8	God, who had given such authority to human beings.	1
12:12	more valuable is a human being than a sheep!	1
Lke 16:15	what is prized by human beings.	1
Jhn 5:41	I do not accept glory from human beings.	1
10:33	only a human being, are making yourself God."	1
16:21	having brought a human being into the world.	1
Rom 1:23	for images resembling a mortal human being or birds	1
3:20	For "no human being will be justified in his sight"	2
9:20	who indeed are you, a human being, to argue with God?	1
1Co 2:11	what human being knows what is truly human	1
15:21	For since death came through a human being	1
15:21	resurrection...has also come through a human being;	1
15:39	one flesh for human beings, another for animals	1
2Co 10: 3	Indeed, we live as human beings	2
Gal 1:16	I did not confer with any human being	3
Heb 2: 6	"What are human beings that you are mindful of them	1
6:16	Human beings...swear by someone greater than	1
Jas 5:17	Elijah was a human being like us,	1

merely human

1. ἄνθρωπος, *anthrōpos, 476*
2. σαρκικός, *sarkikos, 4920*

1Co 3: 4	are you not merely human?	1
15:32	If with merely human hopes I fought with wild animals	1
2Co 10: 4	for the weapons of our warfare are not merely human	2

humanity

1. ἄνθρωπος, *anthrōpos, 476*

Eph 2:15	create in himself one new humanity in place of the two	1

humankind

1. ἄνθρωπος, *anthrōpos, 476*
2. υἱός + ἄνθρωπος, *huios + anthrōpos, 5626 + 476*

Mrk 2:27	"The sabbath was made for humankind	1
2:27	for humankind, and not humankind for the sabbath;	1
Eph 3: 5	this mystery was not made known to humankind,	2
1Ti 2: 5	also one mediator between God and humankind	1
Rev 9:15	angels...ready...to kill a third of humankind.	1
9:18	By...three plagues a third of humankind was killed	1
9:20	rest of humankind, who were not killed by...plagues	1
14: 4	redeemed from humankind as first fruits for God	1

humble *See also* humble *mind*

1. πραΰς, *praus, 4558*
2. ταπεινός, *tapeinos, 5424*
3. ταπεινόω, *tapeinoō, 5427*

Mat 11:29	for I am gentle and humble in heart	2
18: 4	Whoever becomes humble like this child	3
21: 5	humble, and mounted on a donkey	1
23:12	All who exalt themselves will be humbled	3
23:12	all who humble themselves will be exalted.	3
Lke 14:11	For all who exalt themselves will be humbled	3
14:11	those who humble themselves will be exalted."	3
18:14	all who exalt themselves will be humbled	3
18:14	all who humble themselves will be exalted."	3
2Co 10: 1	who am humble when face to face with you	2
11: 7	Did I commit a sin by humbling myself	3
12:21	my God may humble me before you	3
Php 2: 8	he humbled himself and became obedient to...death	3
Jas 4: 6	"God...gives grace to the humble."	2
4:10	Humble yourselves before the Lord	3
1Pe 5: 5	"God...gives grace to the humble."	2
5: 6	Humble yourselves therefore under...God	3

humiliate

1. καταισχύνω, *kataischynō, 2875*

1Co 11:22	humiliate those who have nothing?	1
2Co 9: 4	we would be humiliated—to say nothing of you	1

humiliation

1. ταπείνωσις, *tapeinōsis, 5428*

Act 8:33	In his humiliation justice was denied him.	1
Php 3:21	He will transform the body of our humiliation	1

humility

1. ταπεινοφροσύνη, *tapeinophrosynē, 5425*

Act 20:19	serving the Lord with all humility	1
Eph 4: 2	with all humility and gentleness	1
Php 2: 3	in humility regard others as better	1
Col 2:23	in promoting self-imposed piety, humility,	1
3:12	compassion, kindness, humility, meekness	1
1Pe 5: 5	all of you must clothe yourselves with humility	1

hundred *See also* fifteen hundred miles, five hundred, four hundred, six hundred, three hundred, two hundred, two hundred miles, two hundred million

1. ἑκατόν, *hekaton, 1669*

Mat 18:12	If a shepherd has a hundred sheep,	1
18:28	slaves who owed him a hundred denarii	1
Mrk 6:40	sat down in groups of hundreds and of fifties.	1
Lke 15: 4	"Which one of you, having a hundred sheep	1
16: 6	He answered, 'A hundred jugs of olive oil.'	1
16: 7	He replied, 'A hundred containers of wheat.'	1
Jhn 19:39	myrrh and aloes, weighing about a hundred pounds	1
21:11	full of large fish, a hundred fifty-three	1
Act 1:15	the crowd numbered about one hundred twenty persons)	1
Rev 7: 4	one hundred forty-four thousand, sealed	1
14: 1	one hundred forty-four thousand who had his name	1
14: 3	except the one hundred forty-four thousand	1
21:17	measured its wall, one hundred forty-four cubits	1

hundred pounds

1. ταλαντιαῖος, *talantiaios, 5418*

Rev 16:21	hailstones, each weighing about a hundred pounds	1

hundred yards

1. διακόσιοι + πῆχυς, *diakosioi + pēchys, 1357 + 4388*

Jhn 21: 8	not far...only about a hundred yards off	1

hundred years

1. ἑκατονταετής, *hekatontaetēs, 1670*

Rom 4:19	(for he was about a hundred years old)	1

hundredfold

1. ἑκατόν, *hekaton, 1669*
2. ἑκατονταπλασίων, *hekatontaplasiōn, 1671*

Mat 13: 8	some a hundredfold, some sixty, some thirty	1
13:23	yields, in one case a hundredfold,	1
19:29	for my name's sake, will receive a hundredfold	2
Mrk 4: 8	thirty and sixty and a hundredfold."	1

Mrk 4:20 thirty and sixty and a hundredfold."   1
      10:30 who will not receive a hundredfold now   2
Lke   8: 8 when it grew, it produced a hundredfold."   2

hunger *See also* satisfy hunger

   1. λιμός, *limos, 3350*
   2. νηστεία, *nēsteia, 3763*
   3. πεινάω, *peinaō, 4277*
Mat 5: 6 "Blessed are those who hunger and thirst   3
Lke 15:17 here I am dying of hunger!   1
2Co 6: 5 riots, labors, sleepless nights, hunger;   2
Rev 7:16 They will hunger no more, and thirst no   3

hungry *See also* go hungry

   1. λιμός, *limos, 3350*
   2. νῆστις, *nēstis, 3765*
   3. πεινάω, *peinaō, 4277*
   4. πρόσπεινος, *prospeinos, 4698*
Mat 12: 1 his disciples were hungry   3
     12: 3 David did when he and his companions were hungry?   3
     15:32 I do not want to send them away hungry   2
     21:18 he was hungry.   3
     25:35 for I was hungry and you gave me food   3
     25:37 that we saw you hungry and gave you food   3
     25:42 for I was hungry and you gave me no food   3
     25:44 that we saw you hungry or thirsty   3
Mrk 2:25 he and his companions were hungry and in need   3
      8: 3 If I send them away hungry to their homes   2
     11:12 when they came from Bethany, he was hungry.   3
Lke 1:53 he has filled the hungry with good things   3
      6: 3 David did when he and his companions were hungry?   3
      6:21 "Blessed are you who are hungry now   3
      6:25 full now, for you will be hungry.   3
Jhn 6:35 Whoever comes to me will never be hungry   3
Act 10:10 He became hungry and wanted something to eat;   4
Rom 12:20 No, "if your enemies are hungry, feed them;   3
1Co 4:11 To the present hour we are hungry and thirsty   3
     11:34 If you are hungry, eat at home   3
2Co 11:27 hungry and thirsty, often without food   1

hunt

   1. καταδιώκω, *katadiōkō, 2870*
Mrk 1:36 Simon and his companions hunted for him.   1

hurl

   1. βάλλω, *ballō, 965*
Rev 8: 7 with blood, and they were hurled to the earth;   1

hurl off a cliff

   1. κατακρημνίζω, *katakrēmnizō, 2889*
Lke 4:29 so that they might hurl him off the cliff   1

hurry

   1. σπεύδω, *speudō, 5067*
   2. συντρέχω, *syntrechō, 5340*
Mrk 6:33 they hurried there on foot from all the towns   2
Lke 19: 5 "Zacchaeus, hurry and come down;   1
     19: 6 he hurried down   1
Act 22:18 'Hurry and get out of Jerusalem quickly   1

hurt *See also* feel hurt

   1. ἀδικέω, *adikeō, 92*
   2. βλάπτω, *blaptō, 1055*
   3. σκληρός, *sklēros, 5017*
Mrk 16:18 ⟦if they drink any deadly thing, it will not hurt⟧   2
Lke 10:19 nothing will hurt you.   1
Act 26:14 It hurts you to kick against the goads.'   3

husband *See also* love a husband

   1. Contextual: Not in Greek
   2. ἀδελφός, *adelphos, 81*
   3. ἀνήρ, *anēr, 467*
Mat 1:16 Joseph the husband of Mary, of whom Jesus was born   3
      1:19 Her husband Joseph, being a righteous man   3
Mrk 10:12 if she divorces her husband and marries another   3
Lke 2:36 lived with her husband seven years   3
     16:18 whoever marries a woman divorced from her husband   3
Jhn 4:16 "Go, call your husband, and come back."   3
      4:17 The woman answered him, "I have no husband."   3

      4:17 "You are right in saying, 'I have no husband';   3
      4:18 for you have had five husbands   3
      4:18 and the one you have now is not your husband.   3
Act 5: 8 "Tell me whether you and your husband sold the land   1
      5: 9 the feet of those who have buried your husband   3
      5:10 buried her beside her husband.   3
Rom 7: 2 a married woman is bound by the law to her husband   3
      7: 2 but if her husband dies, she is discharged   3
      7: 2 discharged from the law concerning the husband   3
      7: 3 with another man while her husband is alive.   3
      7: 3 But if her husband dies, she is free from that law   3
      9:10 Rebecca when she had conceived children by one husband   1
1Co 7: 2 and each woman her own husband.   3
      7: 3 husband should give to his wife her conjugal rights   3
      7: 3 likewise the wife to her husband.   3
      7: 4 but the husband does;   3
      7: 4 husband does not have authority over his own body   3
      7:10 the wife should not separate from her husband   3
      7:11 or else be reconciled to her husband)   3
      7:11 the husband should not divorce his wife.   3
      7:13 if any woman has a husband who is an unbeliever   3
      7:14 For the unbelieving husband is made holy   3
      7:14 made holy through her husband.   2
      7:16 you might save your husband.   3
      7:16 Husband, for all you know   3
      7:34 how to please her husband.   3
      7:39 A wife is bound as long as her husband lives.   3
      7:39 if the husband dies, she is free to marry   3
     11: 3 the husband is the head of his wife   3
     14:35 let them ask their husbands at home.   3
2Co 11: 2 for I promised you in marriage to one husband   3
Eph 5:22 Wives, be subject to your husbands as you are to the Lord.   3
      5:23 For the husband is the head of the wife   3
      5:24 ought to be, in everything, to their husbands.   3
      5:25 Husbands, love your wives   3
      5:28 In the same way, husbands should love their wives   3
      5:33 a wife should respect her husband.   3
Col 3:18 Wives, be subject to your husbands   3
      3:19 Husbands, love your wives   3
Tit 2: 5 submissive to their husbands   3
1Pe 3: 1 Wives…accept the authority of your husbands   3
      3: 5 women…accepting the authority of their husbands.   3
      3: 7 Husbands…show consideration for your wives in your life   3
Rev 21: 2 prepared as a bride adorned for her husband.   3

hush

   1. σιγή, *sigē, 4968*
Act 21:40 when there was a great hush   1

Hymenaeus

   1. Ὑμέναιος, *Hymenaios, 5628*
1Ti 1:20 among them are Hymenaeus and Alexander   1
2Ti 2:17 Among them are Hymenaeus and Philetus   1

hymn *See also* sing a hymn

   1. ὕμνος, *hymnos, 5631*
   2. ψαλμός, *psalmos, 6011*
1Co 14:26 When you come together, each one has a hymn   2
Eph 5:19 as you sing psalms and hymns and spiritual songs   1
Col 3:16 sing psalms, hymns, and spiritual songs to God   1

hypocrisy *See also* join in hypocrisy

   1. ὑπόκρισις, *hypokrisis, 5694*
Mat 23:28 inside you are full of hypocrisy and lawlessness.   1
Mrk 12:15 knowing their hypocrisy, he said to them   1
Lke 12: 1 yeast of the Pharisees, that is, their hypocrisy.   1
Gal 2:13 led astray by their hypocrisy.   1
1Ti 4: 2 through the hypocrisy of liars   1

without hypocrisy

   1. ἀνυπόκριτος, *anypokritos, 537*
Jas 3:17 without a trace of partiality or hypocrisy.   1

hypocrite

   1. ὑποκριτής, *hypokritēs, 5695*
Mat 6: 2 not sound a trumpet before you, as the hypocrites do   1
      6: 5 whenever you pray, do not be like the hypocrites;   1
      6:16 you fast, do not look dismal, like the hypocrites   1
      7: 5 hypocrite, first take the log out of your own eye   1
     15: 7 You hypocrites! Isaiah prophesied rightly about you   1

	22:18	you putting me to the test, you hypocrites?	1
	23:13	woe to you, scribes and Pharisees, hypocrites!	1
	23:15	Woe to you, scribes and Pharisees, hypocrites!	1
	23:23	"Woe to you, scribes and Pharisees, hypocrites!	1
	23:25	"Woe to you, scribes and Pharisees, hypocrites!	1
	23:27	"Woe to you, scribes and Pharisees, hypocrites!	1
	23:29	"Woe to you, scribes and Pharisees, hypocrites!	1
	24:51	and put him with the hypocrites	1
Mrk	7: 6	"Isaiah prophesied rightly about you hypocrites	1
Lke	6:42	hypocrite, first take the log out of your own eye	1
	12:56	You hypocrites! You know how to interpret	1
	13:15	the Lord answered him and said, "You hypocrites!	1

hyssop

1. ὕσσωπος, *hyssōpos, 5727*

Jhn	19:29	sponge full of the wine on a branch of hyssop	1
Heb	9:19	with water and scarlet wool and hyssop	1

I

I Not Indexed; *See* I am

I am

1. ἐγώ, *egō, 1609*
2. ἐγώ + εἰμί, *egō + eimi, 1609 + 1639*
3. εἰμί, *eimi, 1639*

Mat	18:20	I am there among them."	3
	22:32	'I am the God of Abraham, the God of Isaac	2
	28:20	I am with you always, to the end of the age."	2
Mrk	12:26	'I am the God of Abraham, the God of Isaac	1
	14:62	Jesus said, "I am; and 'you will see	2
Lke	22:70	He said to them, "You say that I am."	2
Jhn	4:26	Jesus said to her, "I am he, the one…speaking	2
	6:35	Jesus said to them, "I am the bread of life.	2
	6:41	"I am the bread that came down from heaven."	2
	6:48	I am the bread of life.	2
	6:51	I am the living bread that came down from heaven.	2
	8:12	"I am the light of the world.	2
	8:24	unless you believe that I am he."	2
	8:28	then you will realize that I am he	2
	8:58	I tell you, before Abraham was, I am."	2
	9: 5	I am the light of the world."	3
	10: 7	I am the gate for the sheep.	2
	10: 9	I am the gate.	2
	10:11	"I am the good shepherd.	2
	10:14	I am the good shepherd.	2
	11:25	Jesus said to her, "I am the resurrection	2
	13:13	you are right, for that is what I am.	3
	13:19	you may believe that I am he.	2
	13:33	Little children, I am with you only a little longer.	3
	14: 6	"I am the way, and the truth, and the life.	2
	15: 1	"I am the true vine	2
	15: 5	I am the vine, you are the branches.	2
	18: 5	Jesus replied, "I am he."	2
	18: 6	When Jesus said to them, "I am he,"	2
	18: 8	Jesus answered, "I told you that I am he.	2
Act	9: 5	reply came, "I am Jesus, whom you are persecuting.	3
Rev	1: 8	"I am the Alpha and the Omega," says the Lord God	2
	1:17	"Do not be afraid; I am the first and the last	2
	2:23	I am the one who searches minds and hearts	2
	21: 6	I am Alpha and the Omega, the beginning and the end.	2
	22:13	I am the Alpha and the Omega, the first and the last	1
	22:16	I am the root and the descendant of David	2

Iconium

1. Ἰκόνιον, *Ikonion, 2658*

Act	13:51	and went to Iconium.	1
	14: 1	The same thing occurred in Iconium,	1
	14:19	Jews came there from Antioch and Iconium	1
	14:21	returned to Lystra, then on to Iconium and Antioch.	1
	16: 2	He was well spoken of…in Lystra and Iconium.	1
2Ti	3:11	in Antioch, Iconium, and Lystra.	1

idle *See also* idle *tale*, idle *talker*

1. ἀργέω, *argeō, 733*
2. ἀργός, *argos, 734*
3. ἀτακτέω, *atakteō, 863*

Mat	20: 3	he saw others standing idle in the marketplace;	2
	20: 6	'Why are you standing here idle all day?'	2

2Th	3: 7	we were not idle when we were with you	3
1Ti	5:13	Besides that, they learn to be idle	2
	5:13	not merely idle, but also gossips and busybodies	2
2Pe	2: 3	Their condemnation…has not been idle	1

idleness

1. ἀτάκτως, *ataktōs, 865*

2Th	3: 6	believers who are living in idleness	1
	3:11	we hear that some of you are living in idleness	1

idler

1. ἄτακτος, *ataktos, 864*

1Th	5:14	we urge you, beloved, to admonish the idlers	1

idol *See also* food offered to an idol, food sacrificed to an idol, full of idols, sacrifice to idol, temple of an idol, worship of an idol

1. εἴδωλον, *eidōlon, 1631*

Act	7:41	offered a sacrifice to the idol	1
	15:20	abstain only from things polluted by idols	1
Rom	2:22	You that abhor idols, do you rob temples?	1
1Co	8: 4	we know that "no idol in the world really exists,"	1
	8: 7	have become so accustomed to idols until now	1
	10:19	that an idol is anything?	1
	12: 2	and led astray to idols that could not speak	1
2Co	6:16	What agreement has the temple of God with idols?	1
1Th	1: 9	how you turned to God from idols	1
1Jn	5:21	Little children, keep yourselves from idols.	1
Rev	9:20	or give up worshiping demons and idols of gold	1

idolater

1. εἰδωλολάτρης, *eidōlolatrēs, 1629*

1Co	5:10	the greedy and robbers, or idolaters	1
	5:11	is an idolater, reviler, drunkard, or robber	1
	6: 9	Do not be deceived! Fornicators, idolaters	1
	10: 7	Do not become idolaters as some of them did;	1
Eph	5: 5	one who is greedy (that is, an idolater)	1
Rev	21: 8	as for…sorcerers, the idolaters, and all liars	1
	22:15	Outside are the…murderers and idolaters	1

idolatry

1. εἰδωλολατρία, *eidōlolatria, 1630*

Gal	5:20	idolatry, sorcery, enmities, strife, jealousy, anger	1
Col	3: 5	evil desire, and greed (which is idolatry).	1
1Pe	4: 3	living in…carousing, and lawless idolatry.	1

Idumea

1. Ἰδουμαία, *Idoumaia, 2628*

Mrk	3: 8	Jerusalem, Idumea, beyond the Jordan	1

if *See also* as if, even if

1. Contextual: Not in Greek
2. ἄν, *an, 323*
3. ἐάν, *ean, 1569*
4. ἐάνπερ, *eanper, 1570*
5. εἰ, *ei, 1623*
6. εἴπερ, *eiper, 1642*
7. εἴτε, *eite, 1664*
8. ἐπάν, *epan, 2054*
9. ἵνα, *hina, 2671*
10. κἄν, *kan, 2829*
11. ὅταν, *hotan, 4020*
12. ὅτι, *hoti, 4022*

Mat	4: 3	"If you are the Son of God, command these stones	5
	4: 6	"If you are the Son of God, throw yourself down;	5
	4: 9	"All these I will give you, if you will fall down	3
	5:13	the earth; but if salt has lost its taste, how can	3
	5:22	But I say to you that if you are angry	1
	5:22	and if you insult a brother or sister	1
	5:22	if you say, 'You fool,' you will be liable	1
	5:23	the altar, if you remember that your brother or sister	1
	5:29	If your right eye causes you to sin, tear it out	5
	5:30	if your right hand causes you to sin, cut it off	5
	5:39	But if anyone strikes you on the right cheek	1
	5:40	and if anyone wants to sue you and take your coat	1
	5:41	if anyone forces you to go one mile, go also	1
	5:46	For if you love those who love you, what reward	3
	5:47	And if you greet only your brothers and sisters	3
	6:14	For if you forgive others their trespasses	3

Mat	6:15	if you do not forgive others, neither will	3
	6:22	So, if your eye is healthy, your whole body will be	3
	6:23	if your eye is unhealthy, your whole body will be	3
	6:23	If then the light in you is darkness	5
	6:30	But if God so clothes the grass of the field	5
	7: 9	among you who, if your child asks for bread	1
	7:10	Or if the child asks for a fish, will give a snake?	1
	7:11	If you then, who are evil, know how to give good gifts	5
	8: 2	"Lord, if you choose, you can make me clean."	3
	8:31	The demons begged him, "If you cast us out, send us	5
	9:21	she said to herself, "If I only touch his cloak	3
	10:13	If the house is worthy, let your peace come upon it;	3
	10:13	if it is not worthy, let your peace return to you.	3
	10:14	If anyone will not welcome you or listen	2
	10:25	If they have called the master of the house	5
	11:14	if you are willing to accept it, he is Elijah	5
	11:21	For if the deeds of power done in you had been done	5
	11:23	For if the deeds of power done in you had been done	5
	12: 7	if you had known what this means, 'I desire mercy	5
	12:26	If Satan casts out Satan, he is divided	5
	12:27	If I cast out demons by Beelzebul	5
	12:28	if it is by the Spirit of God that I cast out demons	5
	14:28	"Lord, if it is you, command me to come to you	5
	15:14	if one blind person guides another, both will fall	3
	16:24	"If any want to become my followers	5
	16:26	if they gain the whole world but forfeit their life?	3
	17: 4	if you wish, I will make three dwellings here	5
	17:20	if you have faith the size of a mustard seed	3
	18: 6	"If any of you put a stumbling block before one	1
	18: 6	if a great millstone were fastened around your neck	9
	18: 8	"If your hand or your foot causes you to stumble	5
	18: 9	if your eye causes you to stumble, tear it out	5
	18:12	If a shepherd has a hundred sheep,	5
	18:13	if he finds it, truly I tell you, he rejoices	3
	18:15	"If another member of the church sins against you	3
	18:15	If the member listens to you, you have regained	3
	18:16	if you are not listened to, take one or two	3
	18:17	If the member refuses to listen to them	3
	18:17	if the offender refuses to listen even to the church	3
	18:19	truly I tell you, if two of you agree on earth	3
	18:21	if another member of the church sins against me	1
	18:35	if you do not forgive your brother or sister	3
	19:10	"If such is the case of a man with his wife	5
	19:17	If you wish to enter into life, keep	5
	19:21	"If you wish to be perfect, go, sell	5
	21: 3	If anyone says anything to you, just say this,	3
	21:21	if you have faith and do not doubt	3
	21:24	if you tell me the answer	3
	21:25	"If we say, 'From heaven,' he will say to us	3
	21:26	if we say, 'Of human origin,' we are afraid	3
	22:24	'If a man dies childless,	3
	22:45	If David thus calls him Lord, how can he be his son?"	5
	23:30	'If we had lived in the days of our ancestors	5
	24:22	if those days had not been cut short	5
	24:23	Then if anyone says to you, 'Look!	3
	24:24	to lead astray, if possible, even the elect.	5
	24:26	So, if they say to you, 'Look!	3
	24:26	If they say, 'Look! He is in the inner rooms,'	1
	24:43	if the owner of the house had known	5
	24:48	if that wicked slave says to himself	3
	26:15	"What will you give me if I betray him to you?"	1
	26:39	"My Father, if it is possible, let this cup	5
	26:42	if this cannot pass unless I drink it	5
	26:63	tell us if you are the Messiah, the Son of God."	5
	27:40	If you are the Son of God, come down	5
	27:43	let God deliver him now, if he wants to;	5
	28:14	If this comes to the governor's ears	3
Mrk	1:40	"If you choose, you can make me clean."	3
	3:24	If a kingdom is divided against itself	3
	3:25	if a house is divided against itself	3
	3:26	if Satan has risen up against himself	5
	5:28	"If I but touch his clothes, I will be made well."	3
	6:11	If any place will not welcome you	1
	7:11	you say that if anyone tells father or mother	3
	8: 3	If I send them away hungry to their homes	3
	8:34	to them, "If any want to become my followers	5
	9:22	if you are able to do anything, have pity on us	5
	9:23	Jesus said to him, "If you are able!	5
	9:42	"If any of you put a stumbling block	1
	9:42	if a great millstone were hung around your neck	5
	9:43	If your hand causes you to stumble, cut it off;	3

	9:45	if your foot causes you to stumble, cut it off;	3
	9:47	if your eye causes you to stumble, tear it out;	3
	9:50	if salt has lost its saltiness	3
	10:12	if she divorces her husband and marries another	3
	11: 3	If anyone says to you, 'Why are you doing this?'	3
	11:23	Truly I tell you, if you say to this mountain	1
	11:23	if you do not doubt in your heart	1
	11:25	forgive, if you have anything against anyone;	5
	11:31	"If we say, 'From heaven,' he will say	3
	12:19	if a man's brother dies, leaving a wife	3
	13:20	if the Lord had not cut short those days	5
	13:21	if anyone says to you at that time, 'Look!	3
	13:22	to lead astray, if possible, the elect.	5
	14:35	if it were possible, the hour might pass from him.	5
	15:44	Pilate wondered if he were already dead;	5
	16:18	[[if they drink any deadly thing, it will not hurt]]	10
Lke	4: 3	devil said to him, "If you are the Son of God	5
	4: 7	If you…will worship me, it will all be yours."	3
	4: 9	saying to him, "If you are the Son of God	5
	5: 5	Yet if you say so, I will let down the nets."	1
	5:12	"Lord, if you choose, you can make me clean."	3
	6:29	If anyone strikes you on the cheek	1
	6:30	if anyone takes away your goods	1
	6:32	"If you love those who love you, what credit	5
	6:33	If you do good to those who do good to you	3
	6:34	If you lend to those from whom you…receive	3
	7:39	he said to himself, "If this man were a prophet	5
	9:23	"If any want to become my followers	5
	9:25	does it profit them if they gain the whole world	1
	10: 6	if anyone is there who shares in peace	3
	10: 6	if not, it will return to you.	5
	10:13	if the deeds of power done in you	5
	11:11	who, if your child asks for a fish	1
	11:12	Or if the child asks for an egg	1
	11:13	If you then, who are evil, know how to give	5
	11:18	If Satan also is divided against himself	5
	11:19	Now if I cast out the demons by Beelzebul	5
	11:20	if it is by the finger of God that I cast out	5
	11:34	If your eye is healthy	11
	11:34	if it is not healthy, your body is full of darkness.	8
	11:36	If then your whole body is full of light	5
	12:26	If then you are not able to do so small	5
	12:28	if God so clothes the grass of the field	5
	12:38	If he comes during the middle of the night,	10
	12:39	if the owner of the house had known at what hour	5
	12:45	if that slave says to himself	3
	12:45	if he begins to beat the other slaves,	1
	13: 9	If it bears fruit next year, well and good;	10
	13: 9	but if not, you can cut it down.' "	5
	14: 5	he said to them, "If one of you has a child	1
	14:32	If he cannot, then, while the other is still	5
	14:33	if you do not give up all your possessions.	1
	14:34	if salt has lost its taste	3
	15: 8	having ten silver coins, if she loses one	3
	16:11	If then you have not been faithful with	5
	16:12	if you have not been faithful	5
	16:30	if someone goes to them from the dead	3
	16:31	'If they do not listen to Moses and the prophets	5
	17: 2	if a millstone were hung around your neck	5
	17: 3	If another disciple sins, you must rebuke	3
	17: 3	if there is repentance, you must forgive.	3
	17: 4	if the same person sins against you seven times	3
	17: 6	"If you had faith the size of a mustard seed	5
	19: 8	if I have defrauded anyone of anything	5
	19:31	If anyone asks you, 'Why are you untying it?'	3
	19:40	He answered, "I tell you, if these were silent	3
	20: 5	"If we say, 'From heaven,' he will say	3
	20: 6	if we say, 'Of human origin,' all the people	3
	20:28	Moses wrote for us that if a man's brother dies	3
	22:42	if you are willing, remove this cup from me;	5
	22:67	"If you are the Messiah, tell us."	5
	22:67	He replied, "If I tell you, you will not believe;	5
	22:68	if I question you, you will not answer.	3
	23:31	For if they do this when the wood is green	5
	23:35	if he is the Messiah of God, his chosen one!"	5
	23:37	"If you are the King of the Jews, save yourself!"	5
Jhn	1:25	if you are neither the Messiah, nor Elijah	5
	3:12	If I have told you about earthly things	5
	3:12	believe if I tell you about heavenly things?	3
	4:10	Jesus answered her, "If you knew the gift of God	5
	5:31	"If I testify about myself	3

5:43	if another comes in his own name	3
5:46	If you believed Moses, you would believe me	5
5:47	if you do not believe what he wrote	5
6:62	if you were to see the Son of Man ascending	3
7: 4	If you do these things, show yourself to the world	5
7:23	If a man receives circumcision on the sabbath	5
8:19	If you knew me, you would know my Father also."	5
8:31	"If you continue in my word	3
8:36	So if the Son makes you free, you will be free	3
8:39	said to them, "If you were Abraham's children	5
8:42	"If God were your Father, you would love me	5
8:46	If I tell the truth, why do you not believe me?	5
8:54	"If I glorify myself, my glory is nothing.	3
8:55	if I would say that I do not know him,	10
9:33	If this man were not from God, he could do nothing."	5
9:41	"If you were blind, you would not have sin.	5
10:24	If you are the Messiah, tell us plainly."	5
10:35	If those to whom the word of God came were called	5
10:37	If I am not doing the works of my Father	5
10:38	if I do them, even though you do not believe me	5
11:12	if he has fallen asleep, he will be all right."	5
11:21	Martha said to Jesus, "Lord, if you had been here	5
11:32	"Lord, if you had been here	5
11:40	if you believed, you would see the glory of God?"	3
11:48	If we let him go on like this	3
12:24	if it dies, it bears much fruit.	3
12:35	If you walk in the darkness	1
13:14	So if I, your Lord and Teacher, have washed	5
13:17	If you know these things	5
13:17	you are blessed if you do them.	3
13:32	If God has been glorified in him	5
13:35	if you have love for one another."	3
14: 2	If it were not so, would I have told you	5
14: 3	if I go and prepare a place for you	3
14: 7	If you know me, you will know my Father also	5
14:11	but if you do not, then believe me because	5
14:14	if in my name you ask me for anything,	3
14:15	"If you love me, you will keep my commandments.	3
14:28	If you loved me, you would rejoice	5
15: 7	If you abide in me, and my words abide in you	3
15:10	If you keep my commandments	3
15:14	You are my friends if you do what I command you.	3
15:18	"If the world hates you…it hated me	5
15:19	If you belonged to the world	5
15:20	If they persecuted me, they will persecute you;	5
15:20	if they kept my word, they will keep yours also.	5
15:22	If I had not come and spoken to them	5
15:24	If I had not done among them the works	5
16: 7	if I do not go away, the Advocate will not come	3
16: 7	if I go, I will send him to you.	3
16:23	if you ask anything of the Father in my name	2
18: 8	So if you are looking for me, let these men go."	5
18:23	Jesus answered, "If I have spoken wrongly	5
18:23	If I have spoken rightly, why do you strike me?"	5
18:30	"If this man were not a criminal	5
18:36	If my kingdom were from this world	5
19:12	the Jews cried out, "If you release this man	3
20:15	to him, "Sir, if you have carried him away	5
20:23	If you forgive the sins of any, they are forgiven	2
20:23	if you retain the sins of any, they are retained."	2
21:22	"If it is my will that he remain until I come	3
21:23	"If it is my will that he remain until I come	3
21:25	if every one of them were written down	3

Act	4: 9	if we are questioned today	5
	5:38	if this plan or this undertaking is of human origin	3
	5:39	if it is of God, you will not be able	5
	8:22	if possible, the intent…may be forgiven you.	5
	9: 2	so that if he found any who belonged to the Way	3
	11:17	If then God gave them the same gift	5
	13:15	"Brothers, if you have any word of exhortation	5
	15:29	If you keep yourselves from these	1
	16:15	"If you have judged me to be faithful to the Lord	5
	18:14	"If it were a matter of crime or serious villainy	5
	18:21	"I will return to you, if God wills."	1
	19:38	If therefore Demetrius and the artisans with him	5
	19:39	If there is anything further you want to know	5
	20:16	in Jerusalem, if possible, on the day of Pentecost.	5
	23: 9	What if a spirit or an angel has spoken to him?"	5
	24:19	if they have anything against me.	5
	25: 5	if there is anything wrong about the man	5
	25:11	Now if I am in the wrong	5

25:11	if there is nothing to their charges against me	5
26: 5	if they are willing to testify	3
26:32	if he had not appealed to the emperor."	5
27:39	planned to run the ship ashore, if they could.	5

Rom	2:17	if you call yourself a Jew and rely on the law	5
	2:19	if you are sure that you are a guide to the blind	1
	2:25	Circumcision…is of value if you obey the law;	3
	2:25	if you break the law, your circumcision has become	3
	2:26	if those who are uncircumcised keep the…law	3
	3: 3	What if some were unfaithful?	5
	3: 5	if our injustice serves to confirm the justice of God	5
	3: 7	But if through my falsehood God's truthfulness	5
	4: 2	For if Abraham was justified by works	5
	4:14	If it is the adherents of the law who are…heirs	5
	5:10	For if while we were enemies, we were reconciled	5
	5:15	if the many died through the one man's trespass	5
	5:17	If, because of the one man's trespass, death	5
	6: 5	For if we have been united with him in a death	5
	6: 8	But if we have died with Christ, we believe	5
	6:16	if you present…to anyone as obedient slaves	1
	7: 2	but if her husband dies, she is discharged	3
	7: 3	an adulteress if she lives with another man	3
	7: 3	But if her husband dies, she is free from that law	3
	7: 3	and if she marries another man	1
	7: 7	Yet, if it had not been for the law	5
	7: 7	if the law had not said, "You shall not covet."	5
	7:16	Now if I do what I do not want, I agree	5
	7:20	Now if I do what I do not want, it is no longer I	5
	8:10	if Christ is in you…the Spirit is life	5
	8:11	If the Spirit of him who raised Jesus from the dead	5
	8:13	for if you live according to the flesh, you will die;	5
	8:13	but if by the Spirit you put to death the deeds	5
	8:17	if children, then heirs, heirs of God	5
	8:25	if we hope for what we do not see, we wait for it	5
	8:31	If God is for us, who is against us?	5
	9:22	What if God, desiring to show his wrath	5
	9:23	what if he has done so in order to make known	1
	9:29	"If the Lord of hosts had not left survivors to us	5
	10: 9	if you confess with your lips that Jesus is Lord	3
	11: 6	if it is by grace, it is no longer on the basis	5
	11:12	Now if their stumbling means riches for the world	5
	11:12	if their defeat means riches for Gentiles	1
	11:15	For if their rejection is the reconciliation	5
	11:16	If the part of the dough offered as first fruits	5
	11:16	if the root is holy, then the branches also are	5
	11:17	But if some of the branches were broken off	5
	11:18	If you do boast, remember that it is not you	5
	11:21	For if God did not spare the natural branches	5
	11:23	if they do not persist in unbelief	3
	11:24	For if you have been cut from	5
	12:18	If it is possible…live peaceably with all.	5
	12:20	No, "if your enemies are hungry, feed them;	3
	12:20	if they are thirsty, give them something to drink;	3
	13: 4	if you do what is wrong, you should be afraid	3
	14: 8	If we live, we live to the Lord	3
	14: 8	and if we die, we die to the Lord;	3
	14:15	If your brother or sister is being injured by	5
	14:23	those who have doubts are condemned if they eat	3
	15:27	for if the Gentiles have come to share in	5

1Co	2: 8	for if they had, they would not have crucified	5
	3:12	Now if anyone builds on the foundation with gold	5
	3:14	If what has been built on the foundation	5
	3:15	If the work is burned up, the builder will suffer loss;	5
	3:17	If anyone destroys God's temple	5
	3:18	If you think that you are wise in this age	5
	4: 7	And if you received it, why do you boast	5
	4:19	I will come to you soon, if the Lord wills	3
	6: 2	if the world is to be judged by you	5
	6: 4	If you have ordinary cases, then,	3
	7: 9	if they are not practicing self-control	5
	7:11	if she does separate, let her remain unmarried	3
	7:12	if any believer has a wife who is an unbeliever	5
	7:13	if any woman has a husband who is an unbeliever	5
	7:15	if the unbelieving partner separates,	5
	7:21	Even if you can gain your freedom	5
	7:28	if you marry, you do not sin	3
	7:28	if a virgin marries, she does not sin.	3
	7:36	If anyone thinks that he is not behaving	5
	7:36	if his passions are strong, and so it has to be	3
	7:37	if someone stands firm in his resolve	1
	7:39	if the husband dies, she is free to marry	3

1Co	7:40	she is more blessed if she remains as she is.	3
	8: 8	We are no worse off if we do not eat	3
	8: 8	and no better off if we do.	3
	8:10	if others see you, who possess knowledge, eating	3
	8:13	Therefore, if food is a cause of their falling	5
	9: 2	If I am not an apostle to others,	5
	9:11	If we have sown spiritual good among you	5
	9:11	is it too much if we reap your material benefits?	5
	9:12	If others share this rightful claim on you	5
	9:16	If I proclaim the gospel	5
	9:16	woe to me if I do not proclaim the gospel!	3
	9:17	For if I do this of my own will, I have a reward;	5
	9:17	if not of my own will, I am entrusted with	5
	10:12	So if you think you are standing, watch out	1
	10:27	If an unbeliever invites you to a meal	5
	10:28	if someone says to you	3
	10:30	If I partake with thankfulness	5
	11: 6	For if a woman will not veil herself	5
	11: 6	if it is disgraceful…to have her hair cut off	5
	11:14	if a man wears long hair, it is degrading to him	3
	11:15	if a woman has long hair, it is her glory?	3
	11:16	if anyone is disposed to be contentious	5
	11:31	if we judged ourselves, we would not be judged	5
	11:34	If you are hungry, eat at home	5
	12:15	If the foot would say, "Because I am not a hand	3
	12:16	if the ear would say, "Because I am not an eye	3
	12:17	If the whole body were an eye	5
	12:17	If the whole body were hearing,	5
	12:19	If all were a single member, where would the body be?	5
	12:26	If one member suffers, all suffer together	7
	12:26	if one member is honored, all rejoice together	7
	13: 1	If I speak in the tongues of mortals and of angels	3
	13: 2	And if I have prophetic powers	3
	13: 2	if I have all faith, so as to remove mountains	3
	13: 3	If I give away all my possessions	10
	13: 3	if I hand over my body so that I may boast,	3
	14: 6	if I come to you speaking in tongues	3
	14: 7	If they do not give distinct notes	3
	14: 8	if the bugle gives an indistinct sound	3
	14: 9	if in a tongue you utter speech	3
	14:11	If then I do not know the meaning of a sound	3
	14:14	For if I pray in a tongue, my spirit prays	3
	14:16	Otherwise, if you say a blessing with the spirit	3
	14:23	If, therefore, the whole church comes together	3
	14:24	if all prophesy	3
	14:27	If anyone speaks in a tongue	7
	14:28	if there is no one to interpret	3
	14:30	If a revelation is made to someone else sitting	3
	14:35	If there is anything they desire to know	5
	15: 2	saved, if you hold firmly to the message	5
	15:12	if Christ is proclaimed as raised from the dead	5
	15:13	If there is no resurrection of the dead	5
	15:14	if Christ has not been raised	5
	15:15	whom he did not raise if it is true	6
	15:16	For if the dead are not raised	5
	15:17	If Christ has not been raised	5
	15:19	If for this life only we have hoped in Christ	5
	15:29	If the dead are not raised at all	5
	15:32	If with merely human hopes I fought with wild animals	5
	15:32	If the dead are not raised, "Let us eat and drink	5
	15:44	If there is a physical body	5
	16: 4	If it seems advisable that I should go also	3
	16: 7	some time with you, if the Lord permits.	3
	16:10	If Timothy comes, see that he has nothing to fear	3
2Co	1: 6	If we are being afflicted, it is for your consolation	7
	1: 6	if we are being consoled, it is for your consolation	7
	2: 2	if I cause you pain, who is there to make me glad	5
	2: 5	if anyone has caused pain, he has caused it not	5
	2:10	What I have forgiven, if I have forgiven anything	5
	3: 7	Now if the ministry of death	5
	3: 9	For if there was glory in the ministry	5
	3:11	for if what was set aside came through glory	5
	4: 3	even if our gospel is veiled	5
	5: 1	For we know that if the earthly tent we live	3
	5: 3	if indeed, when we have taken it off	5
	5:13	For if we are beside ourselves, it is for God;	7
	5:13	if we are in our right mind, it is for you.	7
	5:17	So if anyone is in Christ	5
	7: 8	For even if I made you sorry with my letter	5
	7:14	For if I have been somewhat boastful about you	5
	8:12	if the eagerness is there, the gift is acceptable	5

	9: 4	if some Macedonians come with me and find	3
	10: 7	If you are confident that you belong to Christ	5
	10: 8	even if I boast a little too much of our authority	5
	11: 4	For if someone comes and proclaims another Jesus	5
	11: 4	if you receive a different spirit	1
	11:15	if his ministers also disguise themselves	5
	11:16	if you do, then accept me as a fool	5
	11:30	If I must boast, I will boast of the things	5
	12: 6	But if I wish to boast, I will not be a fool	3
	12:15	If I love you more, am I to be loved less?	5
	13: 2	if I come again, I will not be lenient—	3
Gal	1: 8	even if we or an angel from heaven should proclaim	3
	1: 9	if anyone proclaims to you a gospel	5
	1:10	If I were still pleasing people	5
	2:14	"If you, though a Jew, live like a Gentile	5
	2:17	if, in our effort to be justified in Christ	5
	2:18	if I build up again the very things	5
	2:21	for if justification comes through the law	5
	3: 4	if it really was for nothing.	5
	3:18	For if the inheritance comes from the law	5
	3:21	if a law had been given that could make alive	5
	3:29	if you belong to Christ, then you are Abraham's	5
	4: 7	if a child then also an heir through God	5
	5: 2	if you let yourselves be circumcised	3
	5:11	persecuted if I am still preaching circumcision?	5
	5:15	If, however, you bite and devour one another,	5
	5:18	if you are led by the Spirit	5
	5:25	If we live by the Spirit	5
	6: 1	friends, if anyone is detected in a transgression	3
	6: 3	if those who are nothing think they are something	5
	6: 8	If you sow to your own flesh,	12
	6: 8	if you sow to the Spirit	1
	6: 9	if we do not give up.	1
Php	1:22	If I am to live in the flesh	5
	2: 1	If then there is any encouragement in Christ	5
	2:17	even if I am being poured out as a libation	5
	3: 4	If anyone else has reason to be confident	5
	3:11	if somehow I may attain the resurrection	5
	3:15	if you think differently about anything	5
	4: 8	whatever is commendable, if there is any excellence	5
	4: 8	if there is anything worthy of praise	5
Col	2:20	If with Christ you died to the elemental spirits	5
	3: 1	So if you have been raised with Christ	5
	3:13	if anyone has a complaint against another	3
	4:10	if he comes to you, welcome him.	3
1Th	3: 8	if you continue to stand firm in the Lord.	3
1Ti	1: 8	law is good, if one uses it legitimately.	3
	3: 5	if someone does not know how to manage his own	5
	3:10	then, if they prove themselves blameless	1
	3:15	if I am delayed, you may know how	3
	4: 6	If you put these…before the brothers and sisters	1
	5: 4	If a widow has children or grandchildren	5
	5:16	If any believing woman has…really widows	5
	6: 8	if we have food and clothing	1
2Ti	2:11	If we have died with him, we will also live with him;	5
	2:12	if we endure, we will also reign with him;	5
	2:12	if we deny him, he will also deny us;	5
	2:13	if we are faithless, he remains faithful	5
Phm	1:17	So if you consider me your partner	5
	1:18	If he has wronged you in any way, or owes you	5
Heb	2: 2	For if the message declared through angels was valid	5
	2: 3	if we neglect so great a salvation?	1
	3: 6	we are his house if we hold firm the confidence	4
	3: 7	"Today, if you hear his voice	3
	3:15	As it is said, "Today, if you hear his voice	3
	3:18	if not to those who were disobedient?	5
	4: 7	"Today, if you hear his voice	3
	4: 8	For if Joshua had given them rest	5
	6: 3	we will do this, if God permits.	4
	6: 8	if it produces thorns and thistles	1
	7:11	Now if perfection had been attainable	5
	8: 4	Now if he were on earth, he would not be a priest	5
	8: 7	For if that first covenant had been faultless	5
	9:13	For if the blood of goats and bulls	5
	10:26	For if we willfully persist in sin	1
	11:15	If they had been thinking of the land	5
	12: 8	If you do not have that discipline	5
	12:25	for if they did not escape when they refused	5
	12:25	if we reject the one who warns from heaven!	1
	13:23	if he comes in time, he will be with me when I see you.	3
Jas	1: 5	If any of you is lacking in wisdom, ask God	5

	1:23 For if any are hearers of the word and not doers,	5
	1:26 If any think they are religious	5
	2: 2 For if a person with gold rings and in fine clothes	3
	2: 8 You do well if you really fulfull the royal law	5
	2: 9 But if you show partiality, you commit sin	5
	2:11 if you do not commit adultery but if you murder	5
	2:14 if you say you have faith but do not have works?	5
	2:15 If a brother or sister is naked	3
	2:17 So faith by itself, if it has no works, is dead.	3
	3: 3 If we put bits into the mouths of horses	5
	3:14 But if you have bitter envy…in your hearts	5
	4:11 if you judge the law, you are not a doer of the law	5
	4:15 "If the Lord wishes, we will live and do this	3
	5:19 if anyone among you wanders from the truth	3
1Pe	1:17 If you invoke as Father the one who judges all	5
	2: 3 if indeed you have tasted that the Lord is good.	5
	2:19 if, being aware of God, you endure pain	5
	2:20 If you endure when you are beaten for doing wrong	5
	2:20 if you endure when you do right and suffer	5
	3: 1 even if some of them do not obey the word,	5
	3:13 if you are eager to do what is good?	3
	3:14 even if you do suffer for doing what is right	5
	3:17 to suffer…if suffering should be God's will	5
	4:14 If you are reviled for the name of Christ	5
	4:16 Yet if any of you suffers as a Christian	5
	4:17 if it begins with us, what will be the end for those	5
	4:18 "If it is hard for the righteous to be saved	5
2Pe	1: 8 For if these things are yours and are increasing	1
	1:10 for if you do this, you will never stumble.	1
	2: 4 For if God did not spare the angels	5
	2: 5 if he did not spare the ancient world	1
	2: 6 if by turning the cities…to ashes	1
	2: 7 and if he recused Lot, a righteous man	1
	2:20 For if, after they have escaped the defilements	5
1Jn	1: 6 If we say that we have fellowship with him	3
	1: 7 if we walk in the light as he himself is in the light	3
	1: 8 If we say that we have no sin, we deceive ourselves	3
	1: 9 If we confess our sins, he who is faithful and just	3
	1:10 If we say that we have not sinned, we make him a liar	3
	2: 1 if anyone does sin, we have an advocate	3
	2: 3 we know him, if we obey his commandments.	3
	2:19 for if they had belonged to us,	5
	2:24 If what you heard from the beginning abides	3
	2:29 If you know that he is righteous, you may be sure	3
	3:21 Beloved, if our hearts do not condemn us	3
	4:12 if we love one another, God lives in us	3
	5: 9 If we receive human testimony, the testimony of God	5
	5:14 if we ask anything according to his will, he hears	3
	5:15 if we know that he hears us in whatever we ask	3
	5:16 If you see your brother or sister committing…sin	3
3Jn	1:10 So if I come, I will call attention to what he is doing	3
Rev	2: 5 If not, I will come to you and remove your lampstand	5
	2:16 Repent then. If not, I will come…and make war	5
	3: 3 If you do not wake up, I will come like a thief	3
	3: 5 If you conquer, you will be clothed like them in white	1
	3:12 If you conquer, I will make you a pillar	1
	3:20 if you hear my voice and open the door	3
	11: 5 if anyone wants to harm them, fire pours	5
	13:10 If you are to be taken captive	5
	13:10 if you kill with the sword	5
	22:18 if anyone adds to them, God will add to that person	3
	22:19 if anyone takes away from the words of the book	3

if even

1. κἄν, *kan, 2829*

Heb	12:20 "If even an animal touches the mountain	1

if in fact

1. εἴπερ, *eiper, 1642*

Rom	8:17 heirs with Christ—if, in fact, we suffer with him	1

if only

1. ἐάνπερ, *eanper, 1570*
2. εἰ, *ei, 1623*
3. ὡς, *hōs, 6055*

Lke	19:42 saying, "If you, even you, had only recognized	2
Act	20:24 if only I may finish my course	3
Heb	3:14 if only we hold our first confidence firm	1

ignorance

1. ἄγνοια, *agnoia, 53*
2. ἀγνωσία, *agnōsia, 57*

Act	3:17 now, friends, I know that you acted in ignorance	1
	17:30 God has overlooked the times of human ignorance	1
Eph	4:18 their ignorance and hardness of heart.	1
1Pe	1:14 the desires that you formerly had in ignorance.	1
	2:15 silence the ignorance of the foolish.	2

ignorant

1. ἀγνοέω, *agnoeō, 51*
2. ἀμαθής, *amathēs, 276*

Rom	10: 3 For, being ignorant of the righteousness	1
2Co	2:11 for we are not ignorant of his designs.	1
Heb	5: 2 able to deal gently with the ignorant and wayward	1
2Pe	3:16 which the ignorant and unstable twist	2

ignorantly

1. ἀγνοέω, *agnoeō, 51*

1Ti	1:13 because I had acted ignorantly in unbelief	1

ignore

1. λανθάνω, *lanthanō, 3291*

2Pe	3: 5 They deliberately ignore this fact	1
	3: 8 do not ignore this one fact, beloved	1

ill   *See also* ill repute

1. ἄρρωστος, *arrōstos, 779*
2. ἀσθένεια, *astheneia, 819*
3. ἀσθενέω, *astheneō, 820*
4. κακῶς, *kakōs, 2809*

Lke	7: 2 who was ill and close to death.	4
Jhn	4:46 there was a royal official whose son lay ill	3
	5: 5 who had been ill for thirty-eight years.	2
	11: 1 Now a certain man was ill, Lazarus of Bethany	3
	11: 2 Mary was the one…her brother Lazarus was ill.	3
	11: 3 "Lord, he whom you love is ill."	3
	11: 6 after having heard that Lazarus was ill	3
Act	9:37 At that time she became ill and died.	3
1Co	11:30 many of you are weak and ill, and some have died.	1
Php	2:26 distressed because you heard that he was ill.	3
	2:27 He was indeed so ill that he nearly died.	3
2Ti	4:20 Trophimus I left ill in Miletus.	3

ill-treatment   *See* share ill-treatment

illegitimate

1. νόθος, *nothos, 3785*
2. πορνεία, *porneia, 4518*

Jhn	8:41 said to him, "We are not illegitimate children;	2
Heb	12: 8 then you are illegitimate and not his children.	1

illness

1. ἀσθένεια, *astheneia, 819*

Jhn	11: 4 "This illness does not lead to death;	1

Illyricum

1. Ἰλλυρικόν, *Illyrikon, 2665*

Rom	15:19 from Jerusalem and as far around as Illyricum	1

image

1. εἰκών, *eikōn, 1635*
2. τύπος, *typos, 5596*
3. χάραγμα, *charagma, 5916*

Act	7:43 the images that you made to worship;	2
	17:29 an image formed by the art…of mortals.	3
Rom	1:23 for images resembling a mortal human being or birds	1
	8:29 to be conformed to the image of his Son	1
1Co	11: 7 since he is the image and reflection of God;	1
	15:49 as we have borne the image of the man of dust	1
	15:49 we will also bear the image of the man of heaven.	1
2Co	3:18 transformed into the same image	1
	4: 4 the glory of Christ, who is the image of God.	1
Col	1:15 He is the image of the invisible God	1
	3:10 according to the image of its creator.	1
Rev	13:14 telling them to make an image for the beast	1
	13:15 allowed to give breath to the image of the beast	1
	13:15 so that the image of the beast could even speak	1

Rev 13:15 those who would not worship the image of the beast 1
    14: 9 "Those who worship the beast and its image 1
    14:11 those who worship the beast and its image 1
    15: 2 those who had conquered the beast and its image 1
    16: 2 the mark of the beast and who worshiped its image. 1
    19:20 and those who worshiped its image. 1
    20: 4 They had not worshiped the beast or its image 1

imagination

    1. ἐνθύμησις, *enthymēsis, 1927*

Act 17:29 by the art and imagination of mortals. 1

imagine

    1. λογίζομαι, *logizomai, 3357*
    2. μελετάω, *meletaō, 3509*
    3. νοέω, *noeō, 3783*
    4. νομίζω, *nomizō, 3787*

Act 4:25 the peoples imagine vain things? 2
Rom 2: 3 Do you imagine, whoever you are, that when you judge 1
Eph 3:20 abundantly far more than all we can ask or imagine 3
1Ti 6: 5 imagining that godliness is a means of gain. 4

imitate

    1. Contextual: Not in Greek
    2. μιμέομαι, *mimeomai, 3628*
    3. συμμιμητής, *symmimētēs, 5213*

Php 3:17 Brothers and sisters, join in imitating me 3
2Th 3: 7 you yourselves know how you ought to imitate us; 2
    3: 9 in order to give you an example to imitate. 2
Heb 13: 7 imitate their faith. 2
3Jn 1:11 Beloved, do not imitate what is evil 2
    1:11 do not imitate what is evil but imitate what is good. 1

imitator

    1. μιμητής, *mimētēs, 3629*

1Co 4:16 I appeal to you, then, be imitators of me. 1
    11: 1 Be imitators of me, as I am of Christ. 1
Eph 5: 1 be imitators of God, as beloved children 1
1Th 1: 6 you became imitators of us and of the Lord 1
    2:14 imitators of the churches of God in Christ Jesus 1
Heb 6:12 imitators of those who…inherit the promises. 1

immeasurable

    1. ὑπερβάλλω, *hyperballō, 5650*

Eph 1:19 what is the immeasurable greatness of his power 1
    2: 7 might show the immeasurable riches of his grace 1

immediately

    1. ἐξαυτῆς, *exautēs, 1994*
    2. εὐθέως, *eutheōs, 2311*
    3. εὐθύς¹, *euthys¹, 2317*
    4. παραχρῆμα, *parachrēma, 4202*

Mat 4:20 Immediately they left their nets and followed 2
    4:22 Immediately they left the boat and their father 2
    8: 3 Immediately his leprosy was cleansed. 2
    13:20 and immediately receives it with joy; 3
    13:21 persecution arises…person immediately falls away. 3
    14:22 Immediately he made the disciples get into the boat 2
    14:27 immediately Jesus spoke to them and said 3
    14:31 Jesus immediately reached out his hand 2
    20:34 Immediately they regained their sight 2
    21: 2 immediately you will find a donkey tied 2
    21: 3 he will send them immediately." 2
    24:29 "Immediately after the suffering 2
Mrk 1:12 the Spirit immediately drove him out 3
    1:18 immediately they left their nets and followed 3
    1:20 Immediately he called them; 3
    1:42 Immediately the leprosy left him 3
    2:12 he stood up, and immediately took the mat 3
    3: 6 immediately conspired with the Herodians 3
    4:15 when they hear, Satan immediately comes 3
    4:16 immediately receive it with joy. 3
    4:17 immediately they fall away. 3
    5: 2 immediately a man out of the tombs…met him 3
    5:29 Immediately her hemorrhage stopped; 3
    5:30 Immediately aware that power had gone forth 3
    5:42 immediately the girl got up and began to walk about 3
    6:25 Immediately she rushed back to the king 3
    6:27 Immediately the king sent a soldier of the guard 3

    6:45 Immediately he made his disciples 3
    6:50 But immediately he spoke to them and said 3
    7:25 immediately heard about him, and she came 3
    7:35 immediately his ears were opened, his tongue 2
    8:10 immediately he got into the boat 3
    9:15 they were immediately overcome with awe 3
    9:20 immediately it convulsed the boy 3
    9:24 Immediately the father of the child cried out 3
    10:52 Immediately he regained his sight 3
    11: 2 immediately as you enter it, you will find 3
    11: 3 will send it back here immediately.' " 3
    14:43 Immediately, while he was still speaking 3
Lke 1:64 Immediately his mouth was opened 4
    4:39 Immediately she got up and began to serve them. 4
    5:13 Immediately the leprosy left him. 2
    5:25 Immediately he stood up before them 4
    6:49 immediately it fell 3
    8:44 immediately her hemorrhage stopped. 4
    8:47 how she had been immediately healed. 4
    12:54 you immediately say, 'It is going to rain'; 2
    13:13 immediately she stood up straight 4
    14: 5 not immediately pull it out on a sabbath day?" 2
    18:43 Immediately he regained his sight and followed 4
    19:11 the kingdom of God was to appear immediately. 4
    21: 9 the end will not follow immediately." 2
Jhn 6:21 immediately the boat reached the land 2
    13:30 he immediately went out. And it was night. 3
Act 3: 7 immediately his feet…were made strong. 4
    5:10 Immediately she fell down at his feet and died. 4
    9:18 immediately something like scales fell 2
    9:20 immediately he began to proclaim Jesus 2
    9:34 immediately he got up. 2
    10:33 Therefore I sent for you immediately 1
    12:23 immediately…an angel of the Lord struck him down 4
    13:11 Immediately mist and darkness came over him 4
    16:10 we immediately tried to cross over to Macedonia 2
    16:26 immediately all the doors were opened 4
    17:14 Then the believers immediately sent Paul 2
    21:30 immediately the doors were shut. 2
    21:32 Immediately he took soldiers and centurions 1
    22:29 Immediately those who were about to examine him 2
Jas 1:24 immediately forget what they were like. 2

immoral

    1. πόρνος, *pornos, 4521*

1Co 5:10 not at all meaning the immoral of this world 1

immoral person

    1. πόρνος, *pornos, 4521*

Heb 12:16 becomes like Esau, an immoral and godless person, 1

sexually immoral

    1. πόρνος, *pornos, 4521*

1Co 5:11 who is sexually immoral or greedy 1

sexually immoral person

    1. πόρνος, *pornos, 4521*

1Co 5: 9 not to associate with sexually immoral persons 1

sexual immorality *See also* indulge in sexual immorality

    1. πορνεία, *porneia, 4518*

1Co 5: 1 there is sexual immorality among you 1
    7: 2 because of cases of sexual immorality 1
2Co 12:21 impurity, sexual immorality, and licentiousness 1

immortal

    1. ἄφθαρτος, *aphthartos, 915*

Rom 1:23 exchanged the glory of the immortal God 1
1Ti 1:17 the King of the ages, immortal, invisible, the only God 1

immortality

    1. ἀθανασία, *athanasia, 114*
    2. ἀφθαρσία, *aphtharsia, 914*

Rom 2: 7 seek for glory and honor and immortality 2
1Co 15:53 this mortal body must put on immortality. 1
    15:54 this mortal body puts on immortality 1
1Ti 6:16 It is he alone who has immortality 1
2Ti 1:10 brought life and immortality to light 2

immovable

1. ἀμετακίνητος, *ametakinētos, 293*
2. ἀσάλευτος, *asaleutos, 810*

Act 27:41 the bow stuck and remained immovable   2
1Co 15:58 my beloved, be steadfast, immovable   1

impartially

1. ἀπροσωπολήμπτως, *aprosōpolēmptōs, 719*

1Pe   1:17 invoke…the one who judges all people impartially   1

impediment in speech

1. μογιλάλος, *mogilalos, 3652*

Mrk   7:32 deaf man who had an impediment in his speech;   1

impending

1. ἐνίστημι, *enistēmi, 1931*

1Co   7:26 I think that, in view of the impending crisis   1

impenitent

1. ἀμετανόητος, *ametanoētos, 295*

Rom   2: 5 by your hard and impenitent heart   1

imperial guard

1. πραιτώριον, *praitōrion, 4550*

Php   1:13 throughout the whole imperial guard   1

imperial majesty

1. σεβαστός, *sebastos, 4935*

Act 25:21 in custody for the decision of his Imperial Majesty   1
    25:25 when he appealed to his Imperial Majesty   1

imperishability

1. ἀφθαρσία, *aphtharsia, 914*

1Co 15:53 perishable body must put on imperishability,   1
    15:54 When this perishable body puts on imperishability   1

imperishable

1. ἀφθαρσία, *aphtharsia, 914*
2. ἄφθαρτος, *aphthartos, 915*

Mrk 16: S ⟦imperishable proclamation of eternal salvation⟧   2
1Co   9:25 but we an imperishable one.   2
    15:42 what is raised is imperishable.   1
    15:50 the perishable inherit the imperishable.   1
    15:52 the dead will be raised imperishable   2
1Pe   1: 4 into an inheritance that is imperishable   2
    1:23 not of perishable but of imperishable seed   2

impiety

1. ἀσέβεια, *asebeia, 813*

2Ti   2:16 it will lead people into more and more impiety   1
Tit   2:12 training us to renounce impiety   1

implacable

1. ἄσπονδος, *aspondos, 836*

2Ti   3: 3 inhuman, implacable, slanderers, profligates   1

implant

1. ἔμφυτος, *emphytos, 1875*

Jas   1:21 welcome with meekness the implanted word   1

imply

1. Contextual: Not in Greek
2. φημί, *phēmi, 5774*

1Co 10:19 What do I imply then?   2
    10:20 No, I imply that what pagans sacrifice   1
2Co   1:24 not mean to imply that we lord it over your faith;   1

importance

1. Contextual: Not in Greek

1Co 15: 3 For I handed on to you as of first importance   1

important

1. Contextual: Not in Greek
2. οὐ + ἄσημος, *ou + asēmos, 4024 + 817*

Mrk 12:33 much more important than all whole burnt offerings   1
Act 21:39 Tarsus in Cilicia, a citizen of an important city;   2

impose

1. ἐπίκειμαι, *epikeimai, 2130*

Heb   9:10 imposed until the time comes to set things right.   1

impose on

1. ἐπιτίθημι, *epitithēmi, 2202*

Act 15:28 to impose on you no further burden than these   1

impossible

1. ἀδυνατέω, *adynateō, 104*
2. ἀδύνατος, *adynatos, 105*
3. οὐ + δυνατός, *ou + dynatos, 4024 + 1543*
4. οὐ + ἐνδέχομαι, *ou + endechomai, 4024 + 1896*

Mat 17:20 and nothing will be impossible for you."   1
    19:26 "For mortals it is impossible   2
Mrk 10:27 "For mortals it is impossible, but not for God;   2
Lke   1:37 For nothing will be impossible with God."   1
    13:33 because it is impossible for a prophet   4
    18:27 impossible for mortals is possible for God."   2
Act   2:24 it was impossible for him to be held in its power.   3
Heb   6: 4 For it is impossible to restore again to repentance   2
    6:18 it is impossible that God would prove false   2
    10: 4 For it is impossible for the blood of bulls   2
    11: 6 without faith it is impossible to please God   2

impostor

1. γόης, *goēs, 1200*
2. πλάνος, *planos, 4418*

Mat 27:63 "Sir, we remember what that impostor said   2
2Co   6: 8 We are treated as impostors, and yet are true;   2
2Ti   3:13 impostors will go from bad to worse   1

exact imprint

1. χαρακτήρ, *charaktēr, 5917*

Heb   1: 3 and the exact imprint of God's very being   1

imprison

1. συγκλείω, *synkleiō, 5168*
2. φρουρέω, *phroureō, 5864*
3. φυλακίζω, *phylakizō, 5872*

Act 22:19 I imprisoned and beat those who believed in you.   3
Rom 11:32 For God has imprisoned all in disobedience   1
Gal   3:22 scripture has imprisoned all things under the power   1
    3:23 we were imprisoned and guarded under the law   2

imprisonment

1. δεσμός, *desmos, 1301*
2. φυλακή, *phylakē, 5871*

Act 20:23 imprisonment and persecutions are waiting for me.   1
    23:29 nothing deserving death or imprisonment.   1
    26:31 nothing to deserve death or imprisonment."   1
2Co   6: 5 beatings, imprisonments, riots, labors   2
    11:23 with far greater labors, far more imprisonments   2
Php   1: 7 both in my imprisonment and in the defense   1
    1:13 my imprisonment is for Christ;   1
    1:14 made confident in the Lord by my imprisonment   1
    1:17 intending to increase my suffering in my imprisonment.   1
Phm   1:10 whose father I have become during my imprisonment.   1
    1:13 during my imprisonment for the gospel;   1
Heb 11:36 even chains and imprisonment.   2

impure person   *See also* impure *motive*

1. ἀκάθαρτος, *akathartos, 176*

Eph   5: 5 no fornicator or impure person   1

impurity

1. ἀκαθαρσία, *akatharsia, 174*
2. ἀκάθαρτος, *akathartos, 176*

Rom   1:24 God gave them up…to impurity   1
    6:19 once presented your members as slaves to impurity   1
2Co 12:21 impurity, sexual immorality, and licentiousness   1
Gal   5:19 fornication, impurity, licentiousness   1
Eph   4:19 greedy to practice every kind of impurity.   1
    5: 3 fornication and impurity of any kind, or greed   1
Col   3: 5 fornication, impurity, passion, evil desire   1
1Th   4: 7 God did not call us to impurity   1
Rev 17: 4 and the impurities of her fornication;   2

in *See also* aim in life, arrange in advance, bow in worship, break in, break in pieces, bring in, bring in secretly, call in, climb in, come in, come in sight, commit in an ungodly way, cut in pieces, dealer in purple cloth, dwell in, early in the morning, engage in dispute, even in the face of, expect in return, four o'clock in the afternoon, get in, give in marriage, go in, graft in, hem in, hindrance in the way, hold in high esteem, hold in honor, if in fact, impediment in speech, in *addition*, in *an uproar*, in *any case*, in *bed*, in *case*, in *Greek*, in *hand*, in *mind*, in one's *place*, in *power*, in *prison*, in *prison* with, in this *term*, in *time*, in *turn*, in *way*, increase in number, indulge in sexual immorality, invite in return, join in a charge, join in helping, join in hypocrisy, join in suffering, keep in check with a bridle, keep in custody, keep in suspense, lead in triumphal procession, lie in ambush, lie in bed, lie in wait, live in, live in a field, live in luxury, live in peace, live in pleasure, look in, many in number, mix in, nine o'clock in the morning, not in the least, obstacle in the way, offer in sacrifice, one in the afternoon, persist in sin, prepare in advance, press in on, promise in marriage, provide in abundance, put in, put in charge, put in order, put in subjection, receive a gift in return, refresh in company, remain in seclusion, run in, rush in, saw in two, say in defense, say in opposition, see reflected in a mirror, serve in the army, set in an uproar, set off in pursuit, share in common, share in suffering, slip in, speak in the past, stand in awe, steal in, succeed in fulfilling, take in one's arms, testify in advance, three in the afternoon, three o'clock in the afternoon, wrap in bands of cloth, write in former days

1. ἀνά, *ana*, 324
2. ἀνά + μέσος, *ana + mesos*, 324 + 3545
3. ἀναπληρόω, *anaplēroō*, 405
4. ἀπό, *apo*, 608
5. ἄχρι, *achri*, 948
6. διά, *dia*, 1328
7. εἰς, *eis*, 1650
8. ἐκ, *ek*, 1666
9. ἐκεῖ, *ekei*, 1695
10. ἐν, *en*, 1877
11. ἐπί, *epi*, 2093
12. καθώς, *kathōs*, 2777
13. κατά, *kata*, 2848
14. μετά, *meta*, 3552
15. ὅπου, *hopou*, 3963
16. παρά, *para*, 4123
17. περί, *peri*, 4309
18. πρός, *pros*, 4639
19. ὑπέρ, *hyper*, 5642
20. ὑπό, *hypo*, 5679
21. ὡς, *hōs*, 6055

Mat	1:20 an angel of the Lord appeared to him in a dream	13
	1:20 for the child conceived in her is from the Holy	10
	2: 1 In the time of King Herod, after Jesus was born	10
	2: 1 after Jesus was born in Bethlehem of Judea	10
	2: 5 They told him, "In Bethlehem of Judea;	10
	2:12 having been warned in a dream not to return to Herod	13
	2:13 an angel of the Lord appeared to Joseph in a dream	13
	2:16 killed all the children in and around Bethlehem	10
	2:18 "A voice was heard in Ramah, wailing and loud	10
	2:19 an angel...appeared in a dream to Joseph in Egypt	13
	2:19 an angel...appeared in a dream to Joseph in Egypt	10
	2:22 And after being warned in a dream, he went away	13
	2:23 he made his home in a town called Nazareth	7
	3: 1 In those days John the Baptist appeared	10
	3: 1 Baptist appeared in the wilderness of Judea	10
	3: 3 "The voice of one crying out in the wilderness:	10
	3: 6 they were baptized by him in the river Jordan	10
	3:12 His winnowing fork is in his hand	10
	4:13 left Nazareth and made his home in Capernaum	7
	4:13 Capernaum by the sea, in the territory of Zebulun	10
	4:16 people who sat in darkness have seen a great light	10
	4:16 those who sat in the region and shadow of death	10
	4:21 in the boat with their father Zebedee, mending	10

4:23 throughout Galilee, teaching in their synagogues	10
5:12 for your reward is great in heaven	10
5:15 and it gives light to all in the house.	10
5:16 give glory to your Father in heaven.	10
5:19 will be called least in the kingdom of heaven;	10
5:19 will be called great in the kingdom of heaven.	10
5:28 committed adultery with her in his heart.	10
5:45 be children of your Father in heaven;	10
6: 1 no reward from your Father in heaven.	10
6: 2 as the hypocrites do in the synagogues	10
6: 2 in the synagogues and in the streets	10
6: 4 so that your alms may be done in secret	10
6: 4 your Father who sees in secret will reward you.	10
6: 5 for they love to stand and pray in the synagogues	10
6: 6 Father who is in secret; and your Father who sees	10
6: 6 your Father who sees in secret will reward you.	10
6: 9 "Pray then in this way: Our Father in heaven	10
6:10 Your will be done, on earth as it is in heaven.	10
6:18 Father who is in secret; and your Father who sees	10
6:18 your Father who sees in secret will reward you.	10
6:20 store up for yourselves treasures in heaven	10
6:23 If then the light in you is darkness	10
6:29 even Solomon in all his glory was not clothed	10
7: 3 do you see the speck in your neighbor's eye	10
7: 3 but do not notice the log in your own eye?	10
7: 4 while the log is in your own eye?	10
7:11 how much more will your Father in heaven	10
7:15 who come to you in sheep's clothing	10
7:21 the one who does the will of my Father in heaven.	10
8:10 in no one in Israel have I found such faith.	16
8:10 in no one in Israel have I found such faith.	10
8:11 and Isaac and Jacob in the kingdom of heaven	10
8:13 And the servant was healed in that hour.	10
8:32 into the sea and perished in the water.	10
9: 4 "Why do you think evil in your hearts?	10
9:10 And as he sat at dinner in the house	10
9:33 "Never has anything like this been seen in Israel."	10
9:35 teaching in their synagogues, and proclaiming	10
10: 9 Take no gold, or silver, or copper in your belts	7
10:11 find out who in it is worthy	10
10:17 and flog you in their synagogues;	10
10:23 When they persecute you in one town	10
10:27 What I say to you in the dark, tell in the light;	10
10:27 What I say to you in the dark, tell in the light;	10
10:28 who can destroy both soul and body in hell.	10
10:32 acknowledge before my Father in heaven;	10
10:33 deny before my Father in heaven.	10
10:41 Whoever welcomes a prophet in the name of a prophet	7
10:41 in the name of a righteous person	7
10:42 a cup of cold water...in the name of a disciple	7
11: 1 to teach and proclaim his message in their cities.	10
11: 2 John heard in prison what the Messiah was doing	10
11: 8 to see? Someone dressed in soft robes?	10
11: 8 those who wear soft robes are in royal palaces.	10
11:11 yet the least in the kingdom of heaven	10
11:16 It is like children sitting in the marketplaces	10
11:20 in which most of his deeds of power had been done	10
11:21 For if the deeds of power done in you had been done	10
11:21 had been done in Tyre and Sidon	10
11:21 they would have repented long ago in sackcloth	10
11:23 For if the deeds of power done in you had been done	10
11:23 For if the deeds of power done in you had been done	10
12: 5 Or have you not read in the law	10
12: 5 on the sabbath the priests in the temple break	10
12:19 nor will anyone hear his voice in the streets.	10
12:32 either in this age or in the age to come.	10
12:32 either in this age or in the age to come.	10
12:40 three nights in the belly of the sea monster	10
12:40 the Son of Man will be in the heart of the earth.	10
12:50 For whoever does the will of my Father in heaven	10
13: 3 he told them many things in parables, saying:	10
13:10 "Why do you speak to them in parables?"	10
13:13 The reason I speak to them in parables	10
13:19 and snatches away what is sown in the heart;	10
13:24 someone who sowed good seed in his field;	10
13:27 'Master, did you not sow good seed in your field?	10
13:30 Collect the weeds first and bind them in bundles	7
13:31 that someone took and sowed in his field;	10
13:32 make nests in its branches."	10
13:33 mixed in with three measures of flour	7
13:34 Jesus told the crowds all these things in parables;	10

13:35	"I will open my mouth to speak in parables;	10
13:43	Then the righteous will shine like the sun	10
13:44	like treasure hidden in a field	10
13:44	in his joy he goes and sells all that he has	4
13:54	began to teach the people in their synagogue	10
13:57	are not without honor except in their own country	10
13:57	in their own country and in their own house."	10
14: 2	for this reason these powers are at work in him."	10
14: 3	bound him, and put him in prison	10
14:10	he sent and had John beheaded in the prison.	10
14:13	withdrew from there in a boat to a deserted place	10
14:26	And they cried out in fear.	4
14:33	those in the boat worshiped him, saying	10
15:33	"Where are we to get enough bread in the desert	10
16:17	but my Father in heaven.	10
16:19	will be bound in heaven	10
16:19	will be loosed in heaven."	10
16:27	come with his angels in the glory of his Father	10
16:28	see the Son of Man coming in his kingdom."	10
17:22	As they were gathering in Galilee	10
18: 1	"Who is the greatest in the kingdom of heaven?"	10
18: 4	is the greatest in the kingdom of heaven.	10
18: 5	Whoever welcomes one such child in my name	11
18: 6	one of these little ones who believe in me	7
18: 6	and you were drowned in the depth of the sea.	10
18:10	in heaven their angels continually see the face	10
18:10	the face of my Father in heaven.	10
18:14	So it is not the will of your Father in heaven	10
18:18	will be bound in heaven	10
18:18	loose on earth will be loosed in heaven.	10
18:19	it will be done for you by my Father in heaven.	10
18:20	For where two or three are gathered in my name	7
19:21	you will have treasure in heaven;	10
20: 3	he saw others standing idle in the marketplace;	10
20:21	and one at your left, in your kingdom."	10
21: 9	the one who comes in the name of the Lord!	10
21: 9	Hosanna in the highest heaven!"	10
21:12	all who were selling and buying in the temple	10
21:14	The blind and the lame came to him in the temple	10
21:15	heard the children crying out in the temple	10
21:22	Whatever you ask for in prayer with faith,	10
21:28	'Son, go and work in the vineyard today.'	10
21:32	For John came to you in the way of righteousness	10
21:33	dug a wine press in it, and built a watchtower.	10
21:42	"Have you never read in the scriptures:	10
21:42	it is amazing in our eyes'?	10
22: 1	Once more Jesus spoke to them in parables, saying:	10
22:15	and plotted to entrap him in what he said.	10
22:28	In the resurrection, then, whose wife	10
22:30	For in the resurrection they neither marry	10
22:30	but are like angels in heaven.	10
22:36	which commandment in the law is the greatest?"	10
23: 6	They love…the best seats in the synagogue	10
23: 7	greeted with respect in the marketplaces	10
23:30	'If we had lived in the days of our ancestors	10
23:30	in shedding the blood of the prophets.'	10
23:34	some you will flog in your synagogues	10
23:39	the one who comes in the name of the Lord.' " ·	10
24: 5	For many will come in my name, saying	11
24:15	standing in the holy place, as was spoken of	10
24:16	those in Judea must flee to the mountains;	10
24:17	to take what is in the house;	8
24:18	the one in the field must not turn back	10
24:19	those who are nursing infants in those days!	10
24:26	they say to you, 'Look! He is in the wilderness,'	10
24:26	If they say, 'Look! He is in the inner rooms,'	10
24:30	the sign of the Son of Man will appear in heaven	10
24:38	For as in those days before the flood	10
24:40	Then two will be in the field;	10
25:21	you have been trustworthy in a few things	11
25:23	you have been trustworthy in a few things	11
25:25	I went and hid your talent in the ground.	10
25:31	"When the Son of Man comes in his glory	10
25:36	I was in prison and you visited me.'	10
25:39	that we saw you sick or in prison and visited	10
25:43	sick and in prison and you did not visit me.'	10
25:44	a stranger or naked or sick or in prison	10
26: 3	the elders of the people gathered in the palace	7
26: 6	while Jesus was at Bethany in the house of Simon	10
26:13	this good news is proclaimed in the whole world	10
26:13	has done will be told in remembrance of her."	7

26:29	new with you in my Father's kingdom."	10
26:55	Day after day I sat in the temple teaching	10
26:61	to build it in three days.' "	6
26:67	Then they spat in his face and struck him;	7
26:69	Now Peter was sitting outside in the courtyard.	10
27: 5	Throwing down the pieces of silver in the temple	7
27:29	They put a reed in his right hand	10
27:40	destroy the temple and build it in three days	10
27:42	we will believe in him.	11
27:43	He trusts in God; let God deliver him now	11
27:51	the curtain of the temple was torn in two	7
27:59	and wrapped it in a clean linen cloth	10
27:60	laid it in his own new tomb	10
27:60	his own new tomb, which he had hewn in the rock.	10
28:18	"All authority in heaven and on earth	10
28:19	baptizing them in the name of the Father	7
Mrk 1: 2	As it is written in the prophet Isaiah	10
1: 3	the voice of one crying out in the wilderness:	10
1: 4	John the baptizer appeared in the wilderness	10
1: 5	and were baptized by him in the river Jordan	10
1: 9	In those days Jesus came from Nazareth of Galilee	10
1: 9	baptized by John in the Jordan.	7
1:13	He was in the wilderness forty days	10
1:15	repent, and believe in the good news."	10
1:19	who were in their boat mending the nets.	10
1:20	they left their father Zebedee in the boat	10
1:23	Just then there was in their synagogue a man	10
1:39	proclaiming the message in their synagogues	7
1:45	but stayed out in the country;	11
2: 6	questioning in their hearts	10
2: 8	"Why do you raise such questions in your hearts?	10
2:15	as he sat at dinner in Levi's house	10
3:23	spoke to them in parables	10
4: 2	He began to teach them many things in parables	10
4: 2	He began to teach them many things in parables	10
4:11	for those outside, everything comes in parables;	10
4:15	takes away the word that is sown in them.	7
4:28	then the head, then the full grain in the head.	10
4:32	birds of the air can make nests in its shade."	20
4:34	he explained everything in private to his disciples.	13
4:36	took him with them in the boat, just as he was.	10
4:38	he was in the stern, asleep on the cushion;	10
5:13	drowned in the sea.	10
5:14	told it in the city and in the country.	7
5:14	told it in the city and in the country.	7
5:20	began to proclaim in the Decapolis	10
5:21	Jesus had crossed again in the boat	10
5:27	came up behind him in the crowd	10
5:30	Jesus turned about in the crowd and said	10
5:34	go in peace, and be healed of your disease."	7
6: 2	On the sabbath he began to teach in the synagogue	10
6: 4	without honor, except in their hometown	10
6: 4	among their own kin, and in their own house."	10
6: 8	no bread, no bag, no money in their belts;	7
6:14	for this reason these powers are at work in him."	10
6:17	and put him in prison on account of Herodias	10
6:27	He went and beheaded him in the prison	10
6:29	they came and took his body, and laid it in a tomb.	10
6:32	they went away in the boat to a deserted place	10
6:56	they laid the sick in the marketplaces	10
7:15	that by going in can defile	7
7:31	in the region of the Decapolis.	2
7:33	took him aside in private, away from the crowd	13
8: 1	In those days when there was again a great crowd	10
8: 4	feed these people with bread here in the desert?"	11
8:14	they had only one loaf with them in the boat.	10
8:38	in this adulterous and sinful generation	10
8:38	when he comes in the glory of his Father	10
9:33	when he was in the house he asked them	10
9:37	"Whoever welcomes one such child in my name	11
9:38	we saw someone casting out demons in your name	10
9:39	no one who does a deed of power in my name	11
9:42	one of these little ones who believe in me	7
9:50	Have salt in yourselves	10
10:10	in the house the disciples asked him again	7
10:21	you will have treasure in heaven;	10
10:30	receive a hundredfold now in this age	10
10:30	in the age to come eternal life.	10
10:37	one at your left, in your glory."	10
11: 4	near a door, outside in the street.	11
11: 8	branches that they had cut in the fields.	8

Mrk 11: 9	the one who comes in the name of the Lord!	10
11:10	Hosanna in the highest heaven!"	10
11:13	Seeing in the distance a fig tree in leaf	4
11:15	those who were buying in the temple	10
11:23	do not doubt in your heart	10
11:25	so that your Father in heaven may also	10
11:27	As he was walking in the temple	10
12: 1	he began to speak to them in parables.	10
12:11	it is amazing in our eyes'?"	10
12:23	In the resurrection whose wife will she be?	10
12:25	are like angels in heaven.	10
12:26	have you not read in the book of Moses	10
12:35	While Jesus was teaching in the temple, he said	10
12:38	who like to walk around in long robes	10
12:38	to be greeted with respect in the marketplaces	10
12:39	and to have the best seats in the synagogues	10
13: 6	Many will come in my name and say, 'I am he!'	11
13: 9	you will be beaten in synagogues;	7
13:14	then those in Judea must flee to the mountains;	10
13:16	one in the field must not turn back	7
13:17	those who are nursing infants in those days!	10
13:24	in those days, after that suffering	10
13:25	the powers in the heavens will be shaken.	10
13:26	they will see 'the Son of Man coming in clouds'	10
13:32	neither the angels in heaven, nor the Son	10
14: 3	at Bethany in the house of Simon the leper	10
14: 9	the good news is proclaimed in the whole world	7
14: 9	what she has done will be told in remembrance	7
14:25	when I drink it new in the kingdom of God."	10
14:49	Day after day I was with you in the temple	10
14:58	in three days I will build another	6
14:66	While Peter was below in the courtyard	10
15:29	destroy the temple and build it in three days	10
15:38	the curtain of the temple was torn in two	7
15:41	and provided for him when he was in Galilee;	10
15:46	laid it in a tomb	10
16:12	[[After this he appeared in another form to two]]	10
16:18	[[they will pick up snakes in their hands]]	10
Lke 1: 5	In the days of King Herod of Judea	10
1: 7	both were getting on in years	10
1:18	old man, and my wife is getting on in years."	10
1:20	which will be fulfilled in their time	7
1:21	wondered at his delay in the sanctuary.	10
1:22	realized that he had seen a vision in the sanctuary.	10
1:26	In the sixth month the angel Gabriel was sent	10
1:31	you will conceive in your womb and bear a son	10
1:36	Elizabeth in her old age has also conceived a son;	10
1:39	In those days Mary set out	10
1:39	to a Judean town in the hill country	7
1:41	the child leaped in her womb.	10
1:44	the child in my womb leaped for joy.	10
1:47	my spirit rejoices in God my Savior	11
1:69	in the house of his servant David	10
1:75	in holiness and righteousness before him	10
1:79	to give light to those who sit in darkness	10
1:80	he was in the wilderness	10
2: 1	In those days a decree went out	10
2: 4	from the town of Nazareth in Galilee to Judea	4
2: 7	laid him in a manger	10
2: 7	because there was no place for them in the inn.	10
2: 8	In that region there were shepherds	10
2:11	born this day in the city of David a Savior	10
2:12	lying in a manger."	10
2:14	"Glory to God in the highest heaven	10
2:16	the child lying in the manger.	10
2:19	pondered them in her heart.	10
2:21	before he was conceived in the womb.	10
2:23	(as it is written in the law of the Lord	10
2:24	what is stated in the law of the Lord	10
2:25	Now there was a man in Jerusalem	10
2:28	Simeon took him in his arms and praised God,	7
2:29	now you are dismissing your servant in peace	10
2:31	which you have prepared in the presence of all	13
2:34	the falling and the rising of many in Israel	10
2:43	the boy Jesus stayed behind in Jerusalem	10
2:44	Assuming that he was in the group of travelers	10
2:46	After three days they found him in the temple	10
2:49	not know that I must be in my Father's house?"	10
2:51	His mother treasured all these things in her heart.	10
2:52	Jesus increased in wisdom and in years	10
2:52	Jesus increased...in divine and human favor.	16

3: 1	In the fifteenth year of the reign of...Tiberius	10
3: 2	John son of Zechariah in the wilderness.	10
3: 4	as it is written in the book of...Isaiah	10
3: 4	"The voice of one crying out in the wilderness:	10
3:15	questioning in their hearts concerning John	10
3:17	His winnowing fork is in his hand	10
3:20	added to them all by shutting up John in prison	10
4: 1	Jesus...was led by the Spirit in the wilderness	10
4: 5	showed him in an instant all the kingdoms	10
4:15	He began to teach in their synagogues	10
4:20	The eyes of all in the synagogue were fixed on him.	10
4:21	scripture has been fulfilled in your hearing."	10
4:23	'Do here also in your hometown	10
4:24	no prophet is accepted in the prophet's hometown.	10
4:25	were many widows in Israel in the time of Elijah	10
4:25	were many widows in Israel in the time of Elijah	10
4:27	There were also many lepers in Israel	10
4:28	all in the synagogue were filled with rage.	10
4:33	In the synagogue there was a man	10
4:44	the message in the synagogues of Judea.	7
5: 7	signaled their partners in the other boat	10
5:12	when he was in one of the cities	10
5:22	"Why do you raise such questions in your hearts?	10
5:29	Levi gave a great banquet for him in his house;	10
5:35	then they will fast in those days."	10
6:12	and he spent the night in prayer to God.	10
6:23	Rejoice in that day and leap for joy	10
6:23	for surely your reward is great in heaven;	10
6:41	do you see the speck in your neighbor's eye	10
6:41	do not notice the log in your own eye?	10
6:42	let me take out the speck in your eye,'	10
6:42	you...do not see the log in your own eye?	10
7: 1	all his sayings in the hearing of the people	7
7: 9	not even in Israel have I found such faith."	10
7:25	Someone dressed in soft robes?	10
7:25	live in luxury are in royal palaces.	10
7:28	yet the least in the kingdom of God	10
7:32	They are like children sitting in the marketplace	10
7:37	a woman in the city, who was a sinner	10
7:37	he was eating in the Pharisee's house	10
7:50	"Your faith has saved you; go in peace."	7
8: 4	he said in a parable:	6
8:10	to others I speak in parables	10
8:13	and in a time of testing fall away.	10
8:15	as for that in the good soil	10
8:15	hold it fast in an honest and good heart	10
8:27	he did not live in a house but in the tombs.	10
8:27	he did not live in a house but in the tombs.	10
8:34	told it in the city and in the country.	7
8:34	told it in the city and in the country.	7
8:48	your faith has made you well; go in peace."	7
9:12	for we are here in a deserted place."	10
9:26	when he comes in his glory	10
9:31	They appeared in glory and were speaking	10
9:36	they kept silent and in those days told no one	10
9:48	"Whoever welcomes this child in my name	11
9:49	we saw someone casting out demons in your name	10
10: 1	sent them on ahead of him in pairs	1
10: 7	Remain in the same house, eating and drinking	10
10:13	if the deeds of power done in you	10
10:13	if the deeds of power...had been done in Tyre	10
10:13	sitting in sackcloth and ashes.	10
10:17	"Lord, in your name even the demons submit	10
10:20	rejoice that your names are written in heaven."	10
10:21	Jesus rejoiced in the Holy Spirit and said	10
10:26	"What is written in the law? What do you read	10
11: 1	He was praying in a certain place	10
11: 7	and my children are with me in bed;	7
11:22	he takes away his armor in which he trusted	11
11:27	a woman in the crowd raised her voice and said	8
11:33	after lighting a lamp puts it in a cellar	7
11:35	consider whether the light in you is not darkness.	10
11:43	love to have the seat of honor in the synagogues	10
11:43	to be greeted with respect in the marketplaces.	10
12: 3	Therefore whatever you have said in the dark	10
12: 3	said in the dark will be heard in the light	10
12:13	Someone in the crowd said to him, "Teacher	8
12:15	one's life does not consist in the abundance	10
12:27	even Solomon in all his glory was not clothed	10
12:33	an unfailing treasure in heaven	10
12:52	five in one household will be divided	10

12:54	"When you see a cloud rising in the west	11
12:58	the officer throw you in prison.	7
13: 6	"A man had a fig tree planted in his vineyard;	10
13:10	Now he was teaching in one of the synagogues	10
13:19	that someone took and sowed in the garden;	7
13:19	the birds of the air made nests in its branches."	10
13:26	you taught in our streets.'	10
13:28	all the prophets in the kingdom of God	10
13:29	and will eat in the kingdom of God.	10
13:35	the one who comes in the name of the Lord.' "	10
14: 9	then in disgrace you would…take the lowest place.	14
14:15	anyone who will eat bread in the kingdom of God!"	10
15: 4	does not leave the ninety-nine in the wilderness	10
15: 7	more joy in heaven over one sinner who repents	10
15:25	"Now his elder son was in the field;	10
16:10	"Whoever is faithful in a very little	10
16:10	is faithful also in much;	10
16:10	whoever is dishonest in a very little	10
16:10	is dishonest also in much.	10
16:23	In Hades, where he was being tormented,	10
16:24	for I am in agony in these flames.'	10
17: 6	'Be uprooted and planted in the sea,'	10
17: 7	from plowing or tending sheep in the field	8
17:24	so will the Son of Man be in his day.	10
17:26	Just as it was in the days of Noah	10
17:26	so too it will be in the days of the Son of Man.	10
17:28	Likewise, just as it was in the days of Lot:	10
17:31	on the housetop who has belongings in the house	10
17:31	likewise anyone in the field must not turn back.	10
17:34	on that night there will be two in one bed;	11
18: 2	He said, "In a certain city there was a judge	10
18: 3	In that city there was a widow who kept	10
18: 9	to some who trusted in themselves	11
18:22	you will have treasure in heaven;	10
18:30	who will not get back very much more in this age	10
18:30	in the age to come eternal life."	10
19:17	you have been trustworthy in a very small thing	10
19:20	I wrapped it up in a piece of cloth	10
19:38	the king who comes in the name of the Lord!	10
19:38	Peace in heaven, and glory in the highest heaven!"	10
19:38	Peace in heaven, and glory in the highest heaven!"	10
19:39	Some of the Pharisees in the crowd said	4
19:47	Every day he was teaching in the temple.	10
20: 1	as he was teaching the people in the temple	10
20:33	In the resurrection, therefore, whose wife	10
20:42	For David himself says in the book of Psalms	10
20:46	the scribes, who like to walk around in long robes	10
20:46	love to be greeted with respect in the marketplaces	10
20:46	and love…the best seats in the synagogues	10
21: 2	saw a poor widow put in two small copper coins.	9
21: 8	many will come in my name and say, 'I am he!'	11
21:21	Then those in Judea must flee to the mountains	10
21:21	those out in the country must not enter it;	10
21:23	those who are nursing infants in those days!	10
21:25	"There will be signs in the sun, the moon,	10
21:27	will see 'the Son of Man coming in a cloud'	10
21:37	Every day he was teaching in the temple	10
21:38	in the morning to listen to him in the temple.	10
22:16	until it is fulfilled in the kingdom of God."	10
22:19	Do this in remembrance of me."	7
22:20	the new covenant in my blood.	10
22:28	those who have stood by me in my trials;	10
22:30	you may eat and drink at my table in my kingdom	10
22:37	this scripture must be fulfilled in me	10
22:44	⟦In his anguish he prayed more earnestly,⟧	10
22:53	I was with you day after day in the temple	10
22:55	kindled a fire in the middle of the courtyard	10
22:56	a servant-girl, seeing him in the firelight	18
23: 7	who was himself in Jerusalem at that time.	10
23:19	a man who had been put in prison	10
23:19	an insurrection that had taken place in the city	10
23:22	I have found in him no ground for the sentence	10
23:25	the one who had been put in prison	7
23:43	today you will be with me in Paradise."	10
23:53	and laid it in a rock-hewn tomb	10
24: 4	two men in dazzling clothes stood beside them.	10
24: 6	while he was still in Galilee	10
24:18	things that have taken place there in these days?"	10
24:19	a prophet mighty in deed and word before God	10
24:27	the things about himself in all the scriptures.	10
24:35	made known to them in the breaking of the bread.	10

	24:38	why do doubts arise in your hearts?	10
	24:41	While in their joy they were disbelieving	4
	24:44	everything written about me in the law of Moses	10
	24:47	proclaimed in his name to all nations	11
	24:49	so stay here in the city until	10
	24:53	were continually in the temple blessing God.	10
Jhn	1: 1	In the beginning was the Word	10
	1: 2	He was in the beginning with God.	10
	1: 4	in him was life, and the life was the light of all	10
	1: 5	The light shines in the darkness	10
	1:10	He was in the world	10
	1:12	to all who received him, who believed in his name	7
	1:23	"I am the voice of one crying out in the wilderness	10
	1:28	This took place in Bethany across the Jordan	10
	1:45	found him about whom Moses in the law…wrote	10
	1:47	an Israelite in whom there is no deceit!"	10
	2: 1	there was a wedding in Cana of Galilee	10
	2:11	the first of his signs, in Cana of Galilee	10
	2:11	and his disciples believed in him.	7
	2:14	In the temple he found people selling	10
	2:19	this temple, and in three days I will raise it up."	10
	2:20	and will you raise it up in three days?"	10
	2:23	When he was in Jerusalem during the Passover	10
	2:23	believed in his name because they saw the signs	7
	2:25	for he himself knew what was in everyone.	10
	3:14	as Moses lifted up the serpent in the wilderness	10
	3:15	whoever believes in him may have eternal life.	10
	3:16	everyone who believes in him may not perish	7
	3:18	Those who believe in him are not condemned;	7
	3:18	not believed in the name of the only Son of God.	7
	3:21	seen that their deeds have been done in God."	10
	3:35	and has placed all things in his hands.	10
	3:36	Whoever believes in the Son has eternal life;	7
	4:14	will become in them a spring of water gushing up	10
	4:20	place where people must worship is in Jerusalem	10
	4:21	neither on this mountain nor in Jerusalem.	10
	4:23	will worship the Father in spirit and truth	10
	4:24	must worship in spirit and truth."	10
	4:39	Many Samaritans from that city believed in him	7
	4:44	a prophet has no honor in the prophet's own country).	10
	4:45	all that he had done in Jerusalem at the festival;	10
	4:46	there was a royal official whose son lay ill	10
	5: 2	in Jerusalem by the Sheep Gate there is a pool	10
	5: 3	In these lay many invalids—blind, lame	10
	5:14	Later Jesus found him in the temple and said	10
	5:26	For just as the Father has life in himself	10
	5:26	has granted the Son also to have life in himself;	10
	5:28	all who are in their graves will hear his voice	10
	5:35	willing to rejoice for a while in his light.	10
	5:38	you do not have his word abiding in you	10
	5:39	you think that in them you have eternal life;	10
	5:42	you do not have the love of God in you.	10
	5:43	I have come in my Father's name	10
	5:43	if another comes in his own name	10
	6:10	Now there was a great deal of grass in the place;	10
	6:29	that you believe in him whom he has sent."	7
	6:31	Our ancestors ate the manna in the wilderness;	10
	6:35	whoever believes in me will never be thirsty.	7
	6:40	all who see the Son and believe in him	7
	6:45	It is written in the prophets	10
	6:49	Your ancestors ate the manna in the wilderness	10
	6:53	you have no life in you.	10
	6:56	who eat my flesh and drink my blood abide in me	10
	6:56	who…drink my blood abide in me, and I in them	10
	6:59	he was teaching in the synagogue at Capernaum.	10
	7: 1	After this Jesus went about in Galilee.	10
	7: 1	He did not wish to go about in Judea	10
	7: 4	who wants to be widely known acts in secret.	10
	7: 5	(For not even his brothers believed in him.)	7
	7: 9	saying this, he remained in Galilee.	10
	7:10	went, not publicly but as it were in secret.	10
	7:18	there is nothing false in him.	10
	7:28	Jesus cried out as he was teaching in the temple	10
	7:31	Yet many in the crowd believed in him	8
	7:31	Yet many in the crowd believed in him	7
	7:38	and let the one who believes in me drink.	7
	7:39	which believers in him were to receive;	7
	7:43	there was a division in the crowd because of him.	10
	7:48	Has any one…of the Pharisees believed in him?	7
	8: 3	⟦a woman who had been caught in adultery;⟧	11
	8: 4	⟦caught in the very act of committing adultery.⟧	11

Jhn	8: 5	[[Now in the law Moses commanded us to stone such]]	10
	8:12	Whoever follows me will never walk in darkness	10
	8:17	In your law it is written	10
	8:20	he was teaching in the treasury of the temple	10
	8:21	search for me, but you will die in your sin.	10
	8:24	I told you that you would die in your sins	10
	8:24	for you will die in your sins	10
	8:30	saying these things, many believed in him.	7
	8:31	"If you continue in my word	10
	8:35	does not have a permanent place in the household;	10
	8:37	because there is no place in you for my word.	10
	8:44	and does not stand in the truth	10
	8:44	because there is no truth in him.	10
	9: 3	so that God's works might be revealed in him.	10
	9: 5	As long as I am in the world	10
	9: 7	saying to him, "Go, wash in the pool of Siloam"	7
	9:34	answered him, "You were born entirely in sins	10
	9:35	"Do you believe in the Son of Man?"	7
	9:36	Tell me, so that I may believe in him."	7
	10:22	festival of the Dedication took place in Jerusalem.	10
	10:23	and Jesus was walking in the temple	10
	10:23	in the temple, in the portico of Solomon.	10
	10:25	The works that I do in my Father's name	10
	10:34	Jesus answered, "Is it not written in your law	10
	10:38	the Father is in me and I am in the Father."	10
	10:38	the Father is in me and I am in the Father."	10
	10:42	many believed in him there.	7
	11: 6	two days longer in the place where he was.	10
	11:10	stumble, because the light is not in them."	10
	11:17	Lazarus had already been in the tomb four days.	10
	11:24	rise again in the resurrection on the last day."	10
	11:25	who believe in me, even though they die, will live	7
	11:26	everyone who lives and believes in me	7
	11:31	The Jews who were with her in the house	10
	11:45	Many of the Jews therefore…believed in him.	7
	11:48	everyone will believe in him	7
	11:54	Ephraim in the region near the wilderness;	7
	11:56	as they stood in the temple	10
	12:11	Jews were deserting and were believing in Jesus.	7
	12:13	the one who comes in the name of the Lord	10
	12:25	who hate their life in this world will keep it	10
	12:35	If you walk in the darkness	10
	12:36	While you have the light, believe in the light	7
	12:37	they did not believe in him.	7
	12:42	many, even of the authorities, believed in him.	7
	12:44	"Whoever believes in me believes not in me	7
	12:44	believes not in me but in him who sent me.	7
	12:44	believes not in me but in him who sent me.	7
	12:46	so that everyone who believes in me	7
	12:46	should not remain in the darkness.	10
	13: 1	Having loved his own who were in the world	10
	13:31	God has been glorified in him.	10
	13:32	If God has been glorified in him	10
	13:32	God will also glorify him in himself	10
	14: 1	Believe in God, believe also in me.	7
	14: 1	Believe in God, believe also in me.	7
	14: 2	In my Father's house there are many dwelling places.	10
	14:10	Do you not believe that I am in the Father	10
	14:10	I am in the Father and the Father is in me?	10
	14:10	the Father who dwells in me does his works.	10
	14:11	Believe me that I am in the Father	10
	14:11	I am in the Father and the Father is in me;	10
	14:12	believes in me will also do the works that I do	7
	14:13	I will do whatever you ask in my name,	10
	14:13	so that the Father may be glorified in the Son.	10
	14:14	If in my name you ask me for anything,	10
	14:17	he abides with you, and he will be in you.	10
	14:20	On that day you will know that I am in my Father	10
	14:20	I am in my Father, and you in me, and I in you	10
	14:20	I am in my Father, and you in me, and I in you	10
	14:26	Holy Spirit, whom the Father will send in my name	10
	15: 2	removes every branch in me that bears no fruit.	10
	15: 4	Abide in me as I abide in you.	10
	15: 4	Abide in me as I abide in you.	10
	15: 4	unless it abides in the vine	10
	15: 4	neither can you unless you abide in me.	10
	15: 5	Those who abide in me and I in them	10
	15: 5	Those who abide in me and I in them	10
	15: 6	Whoever does not abide in me	10
	15: 7	If you abide in me, and my words abide in you	10
	15: 7	If you abide in me, and my words abide in you	10

	15: 9	so I have loved you; abide in my love.	10
	15:10	you will abide in my love	10
	15:10	just as I…abide in his love.	10
	15:11	so that my joy may be in you	10
	15:16	will give you whatever you ask him in my name.	10
	15:25	to fulfill the word that is written in their law	10
	16: 9	about sin, because they do not believe in me;	7
	16:23	if you ask anything of the Father in my name	10
	16:24	you have not asked for anything in my name.	10
	16:25	said these things to you in figures of speech.	10
	16:25	when I will no longer speak to you in figures	10
	16:26	On that day you will ask in my name.	10
	16:33	so that in me you may have peace.	10
	16:33	In the world you face persecution.	10
	17:10	I have been glorified in them.	10
	17:11	now I am no longer in the world	10
	17:11	they are in the world, and I am coming to you.	10
	17:11	Holy Father, protect them in your name	10
	17:12	with them, I protected them in your name	10
	17:13	I speak these things in the world	10
	17:13	they may have my joy made complete in themselves.	10
	17:17	Sanctify them in the truth; your word is truth.	10
	17:19	so that they also may be sanctified in truth.	10
	17:20	those who will believe in me through their word	7
	17:21	As you, Father, are in me and I am in you	10
	17:21	As you, Father, are in me and I am in you	10
	17:21	may they also be in us, so that the world	10
	17:23	I in them and you in me	10
	17:23	I in them and you in me	10
	17:26	love…may be in them, and I in them."	10
	17:26	love…may be in them, and I in them."	10
	18:20	always taught in synagogues and in the temple	10
	18:20	always taught in synagogues and in the temple	10
	18:20	I have said nothing in secret.	10
	18:26	"Did I not see you in the garden with him?"	10
	19:23	seamless, woven in one piece from the top.	6
	19:41	a garden in the place where he was crucified	10
	19:41	and in the garden there was a new tomb	10
	19:41	a new tomb in which no one had ever been laid.	10
	20: 7	and the cloth…rolled up in a place by itself.	7
	20:12	she saw two angels in white	10
	20:25	"Unless I see the mark of the nails in his hands	10
	20:25	put my finger in the mark of the nails	7
	20:25	my hand in his side	7
	20:27	Reach out your hand and put it in my side.	7
	20:30	which are not written in this book.	10
	20:31	believing you may have life in his name.	10
	21:23	So the rumor spread in the community	7
Act	1: 8	you will be my witnesses in Jerusalem	10
	1: 8	in Jerusalem, in all Judea and Samaria	10
	1:10	suddenly two men in white robes stood by them.	10
	1:15	In those days Peter stood up among the believers	10
	1:20	"For it is written in the book of Psalms	10
	1:20	let there be no one to live in it';	10
	2: 1	they were all together in one place.	11
	2: 5	from every nation under heaven living in Jerusalem.	7
	2:17	'In the last days it will be, God declares	10
	2:18	in those days I will pour out my Spirit;	10
	2:19	I will show portents in the heaven above	10
	2:26	moreover my flesh will live in hope.	11
	2:38	be baptized…in the name of Jesus Christ	11
	2:46	as they spent much time together in the temple	10
	3: 6	in the name of Jesus Christ of Nazareth, stand up	10
	3:11	in the portico called Solomon's Portico	11
	3:13	rejected in the presence of Pilate	13
	3:17	now, friends, I know that you acted in ignorance	13
	3:25	saying to Abraham, 'And in your descendants	10
	4: 2	proclaiming that in Jesus there is the resurrection	10
	4: 3	put them in custody until the next day	7
	4: 5	their rulers…assembled in Jerusalem,	10
	4: 7	they had made the prisoners stand in their midst,	10
	4:12	There is salvation in no one else	10
	4:17	to speak no more to anyone in this name."	11
	4:18	not to speak or teach at all in the name of Jesus.	11
	4:24	the earth, the sea, and everything in them	10
	4:27	For in this city, in fact, both Herod	10
	4:27	in this city, in fact, both Herod and Pontius Pilate	11
	4:31	the place in which they were gathered together	10
	5: 4	you have contrived this deed in your heart?	10
	5:12	they were all together in Solomon's Portico.	10
	5:18	put them in the public prison.	10

Ref	Text	Num
5:20	"Go, stand in the temple and tell the people	10
5:22	they did not find them in the prison;	10
5:25	the men whom you put in prison	10
5:25	standing in the temple and teaching the people!"	10
5:28	strict orders not to teach in this name	11
5:34	a Pharisee in the council named Gamaliel	10
5:40	ordered them not to speak in the name of Jesus	11
5:42	every day in the temple and at home	10
6: 1	neglected in the daily distribution of food	10
6: 7	the disciples increased greatly in Jerusalem	10
6:15	all who sat in the council looked intently at him	10
7: 2	our ancestor Abraham when he was in Mesopotamia	10
7: 2	in Mesopotamia, before he lived in Haran	10
7: 4	Then he left…and settled in Haran.	10
7: 4	this country in which you are now living.	7
7: 6	resident aliens in a country belonging to others	10
7: 7	they shall come out and worship me in this place.'	10
7:12	when Jacob heard that there was grain in Egypt ·	7
7:14	all his relatives to come to him, seventy-five in all;	10
7:16	laid in the tomb that Abraham had bought	10
7:16	bought…from the sons of Hamor in Shechem.	10
7:17	our people in Egypt increased and multiplied	10
7:20	three months he was brought up in his father's house;	10
7:22	instructed in all the wisdom of the Egyptians	10
7:22	was powerful in his words and deeds.	10
7:29	became a resident alien in the land of Midian.	10
7:30	an angel appeared to him in the wilderness	10
7:30	in the flame of a burning bush.	10
7:34	mistreatment of my people who are in Egypt	10
7:35	the angel who appeared to him in the bush.	10
7:36	having performed wonders and signs in Egypt	10
7:36	and in the wilderness for forty years.	10
7:38	who was in the congregation in the wilderness	10
7:38	who was in the congregation in the wilderness	10
7:39	in their hearts they turned back to Egypt	10
7:41	reveled in the works of their hands.	10
7:42	as it is written in the book of the prophets:	10
7:42	forty years in the wilderness, O house of Israel?	10
7:44	the tent of testimony in the wilderness	10
7:48	Yet the Most High does not dwell in houses	10
8: 1	persecution…against the church in Jerusalem	10
8: 8	there was great joy in that city.	10
8: 9	Simon had previously practiced magic in the city	10
8:16	baptized in the name of the Lord Jesus).	7
8:21	You have no part or share in this	10
8:23	For I see that you are in the gall of bitterness	7
8:28	was returning home; seated in his chariot,	11
8:33	In his humiliation justice was denied him.	10
9:10	there was a disciple in Damascus named Ananias.	10
9:10	The Lord said to him in a vision, "Ananias."	10
9:12	he has seen in a vision a man named Ananias come	10
9:13	evil he has done to your saints in Jerusalem;	10
9:19	he was with the disciples in Damascus	10
9:20	he began to proclaim Jesus in the synagogues,	10
9:21	"Is not this the man who made havoc in Jerusalem	7
9:22	confounded the Jews who lived in Damascus	10
9:25	lowering him in a basket.	10
9:27	how in Damascus he had spoken boldly	10
9:27	he had spoken boldly in the name of Jesus.	10
9:28	So he went in and out among them in Jerusalem	7
9:28	speaking boldly in the name of the Lord.	10
9:36	in Joppa there was a disciple whose name was Tabitha	10
9:37	they laid her in a room upstairs.	10
9:42	many believed in the Lord.	11
9:43	in Joppa for some time with a certain Simon, a tanner.	10
10: 1	In Caesarea there was a man named Cornelius	10
10: 3	a vision in which he clearly saw an angel of God	10
10: 3	an angel of God coming in and saying to him	18
10:12	In it were all kinds of four-footed creatures	10
10:30	at three o'clock, I was praying in my house	10
10:30	suddenly a man in dazzling clothes stood before me.	10
10:32	he is staying in the home of Simon	10
10:35	in every nation anyone who fears him	10
10:37	beginning in Galilee	4
10:39	both in Judea and in Jerusalem.	10
10:39	both in Judea and in Jerusalem.	10
10:43	who believes in him receives forgiveness	7
10:48	baptized in the name of Jesus Christ.	10
11: 1	the apostles and the believers who were in Judea	13
11: 5	"I was in the city of Joppa praying	10
11: 5	in a trance I saw a vision.	10
11:13	the angel standing in his house and saying	10
11:17	when we believed in the Lord Jesus Christ	11
11:22	News…came to the ears of the church in Jerusalem	10
11:26	in Antioch that the disciples were…"Christians."	10
11:29	send relief to the believers living in Judea;	10
12: 4	When he had seized him, he put him in prison	7
12: 5	While Peter was kept in prison	10
12: 7	a light shone in the cell.	10
13: 1	Now in the church at Antioch there were prophets	13
13: 5	proclaimed the word of God in the synagogues	10
13:17	during their stay in the land of Egypt	10
13:18	he put up with them in the wilderness.	10
13:19	After he had destroyed seven nations in the land	10
13:29	took him down from the tree and laid him in a tomb.	7
13:33	as also it is written in the second psalm	10
13:35	Therefore he has also said in another psalm	10
13:41	for in your days I am doing a work	10
14: 1	The same thing occurred in Iconium,	10
14: 8	In Lystra there was a man sitting	10
14:15	the earth and the sea and all that is in them.	10
14:16	In past generations he allowed all the nations	10
14:23	the Lord in whom they had come to believe.	7
14:25	When they had spoken the word in Perga	10
15: 7	you know that in the early days God made a choice	4
15:21	read aloud every sabbath in the synagogues."	10
15:23	the believers of Gentile origin in Antioch	13
15:33	they were sent off in peace by the believers	14
15:35	Paul and Barnabas remained in Antioch	10
15:36	in every city where we proclaimed the word	13
15:38	one who had deserted them in Pamphylia	4
15:38	and had not accompanied them in the work.	7
16: 2	He was well spoken of…in Lystra and Iconium.	10
16: 3	because of the Jews who were in those places	10
16: 4	the apostles and elders who were in Jerusalem.	10
16: 6	forbidden…to speak the word in Asia.	10
16:12	We remained in this city for some days.	10
16:18	"I order you in the name of Jesus Christ	10
16:24	he put them in the innermost cell	7
16:24	fastened their feet in the stocks.	7
16:32	to him and to all who were in his house.	10
16:36	therefore come out now and go in peace."	10
17: 2	Paul went in, as was his custom	18
17:11	were more receptive than those in Thessalonica	10
17:13	the word…had been proclaimed by Paul in Beroea	10
17:16	While Paul was waiting for them in Athens	10
17:17	he argued in the synagogue with the Jews	10
17:17	he argued…in the marketplace every day	10
17:21	the Athenians…spend their time in nothing	7
17:22	Paul stood in front of the Areopagus	10
17:24	The God who made the world and everything in it	10
17:24	God…does not live in shrines made by human hands	10
17:28	For 'In him we live and move and have our being';	10
17:31	will have the world judged in righteousness	10
18: 4	Every sabbath he would argue in the synagogue	10
18: 9	One night the Lord said to Paul in a vision	6
18:10	there are many in this city who are my people."	10
18:24	an eloquent man, well-versed in the scriptures.	10
18:26	He began to speak boldly in the synagogue;	10
19: 1	While Apollos was in Corinth	10
19: 4	to believe in the one who was to come after him	7
19: 4	who was to come after him, that is, in Jesus."	7
19: 5	baptized in the name of the Lord Jesus.	7
19: 9	argued daily in the lecture hall of Tyrannus.	10
19:21	Paul resolved in the Spirit to go	10
19:22	he himself stayed for some time longer in Asia.	7
19:39	it must be settled in the regular assembly.	10
20: 5	went ahead and were waiting for us in Troas;	10
20: 6	in five days we joined them in Troas	5
20: 6	in five days we joined them in Troas	7
20: 8	There were many lamps in the room upstairs	10
20: 9	Eutychus, who was sitting in the window	11
20:10	"Do not be alarmed, for his life is in him."	10
20:14	When he met us in Assos, we took him on board	7
20:16	so that he might not have to spend time in Asia;	10
20:16	he was eager to be in Jerusalem	7
20:18	from the first day that I set foot in Asia	7
21:11	the Jews in Jerusalem will bind the man	10
21:13	die in Jerusalem for the name of the Lord Jesus."	7
21:17	When we arrived in Jerusalem	7
21:27	who had seen him in the temple	10
21:29	Trophimus the Ephesian with him in the city	10

Act 21:34	Some in the crowd shouted one thing, some another;	10	
22: 3	"I am a Jew, born in Tarsus in Cilicia	10	
22: 3	brought up in this city at the feet of Gamaliel	10	
22: 4	both men and women and putting them in prison	7	
22: 5	letters to the brothers in Damascus	7	
22:17	was praying in the temple	10	
22:19	I imprisoned and beat those who believed in you.	11	
23: 6	he called out in the council	10	
23:11	just as you have testified for me in Jerusalem	7	
23:11	so you must bear witness also in Rome."	7	
23:35	kept under guard in Herod's headquarters.	10	
24:11	since I went up to worship in Jerusalem.	7	
24:12	disputing with anyone in the temple	10	
24:12	stirring up a crowd either in the synagogues	10	
24:14	written in the prophets.	10	
24:15	I have a hope in God—	7	
24:18	in the temple, completing the rite of purification	10	
24:24	heard him speak concerning faith in Christ Jesus.	7	
25:15	When I was in Jerusalem	7	
25:24	petitioned me, both in Jerusalem and here	10	
26: 4	among my own people and in Jerusalem.	10	
26:10	that is what I did in Jerusalem;	10	
26:10	I not only locked up many of the saints in prison	10	
26:11	punishing them often in all the synagogues	13	
26:18	among those who are sanctified by faith in me.'	7	
26:20	declared first to those in Damascus	10	
26:21	Jews seized me in the temple and tried to kill me.	10	
26:26	this was not done in a corner.	10	
27:31	"Unless these men stay in the ship	10	
27:37	two hundred seventy-six persons in the ship.)	10	
27:40	cast off the anchors and left them in the sea.	7	
28: 7	Now in the neighborhood of that place were lands	10	
28:17	yet I was arrested in Jerusalem	8	
Rom 1: 2	through his prophets in the holy scriptures	10	
1: 7	To all God's beloved in Rome	10	
1: 9	I remember you always in my prayers	11	
1:15	proclaim the gospel to you also who are in Rome.	10	
1:17	For in it the righteousness of God is revealed	10	
1:21	but they became futile in their thinking	10	
1:24	God gave them up in the lusts of their hearts	10	
1:27	received in their own persons the due penalty	10	
2: 1	for in passing judgment on another you condemn	10	
2:18	because you are instructed in the law	8	
2:19	a light to those who are in darkness	10	
2:20	having in the law the embodiment of knowledge	10	
2:23	You that boast in the law, do you dishonor God	10	
3: 2	Much, in every way.	13	
3: 4	"So that you may be justified in your words	10	
3: 4	and prevail in your judging."	10	
3:16	ruin and misery are in their paths	10	
3:24	through the redemption that is in Christ Jesus	10	
3:25	in his divine forbearance he had passed over	10	
4:24	It will be reckoned to us who believe in him	11	
5: 2	access to this grace in which we stand;	10	
5: 2	we boast in our hope of sharing the glory of God.	11	
5: 3	not only that, but we also boast in our sufferings	10	
5:11	boast in God through our Lord Jesus Christ	10	
5:13	sin was indeed in the world before the law	10	
5:15	the free gift in the grace of the one man, Jesus	10	
5:17	exercise dominion in life through the one man	10	
5:21	so that, just as sin exercised dominion in death	10	
6: 2	How can we who died to sin go on living in it?	10	
6: 4	so we too might walk in newness of life.	10	
6:11	dead to sin and alive to God in Christ Jesus.	10	
6:12	not let sin exercise dominion in your mortal bodies	10	
6:23	the free gift of God is eternal life in Christ	10	
7: 5	While we were living in the flesh	10	
7: 5	sinful passions…were at work in our members	10	
7: 6	we are slaves…in the new life of the Spirit.	10	
7: 8	But sin, seizing an opportunity in the commandment	6	
7: 8	sin…produced in me all kinds of covetousness.	10	
7:11	For sin, seizing an opportunity in the commandment	6	
7:18	nothing good dwells within me, that is, in my flesh.	10	
7:22	For I delight in the law of God in my inmost self	13	
7:23	but I see in my members another law	10	
7:23	to the law of sin that dwells in my members.	10	
8: 1	no condemnation for those who are in Christ	10	
8: 2	For the law of the Spirit of life in Christ Jesus	10	
8: 3	his own Son in the likeness of sinful flesh	10	
8: 3	to deal with sin, he condemned sin in the flesh	10	
8: 4	requirement of the law might be fulfilled in us	10	

8: 8	those who are in the flesh cannot please God.	10	
8: 9	you are not in the flesh; you are in the Spirit	10	
8: 9	you are not in the flesh; you are in the Spirit	10	
8: 9	since the Spirit of God dwells in you.	10	
8:10	if Christ is in you…the Spirit is life	10	
8:11	If the Spirit…dwells in you	10	
8:11	through his Spirit that dwells in you.	10	
8:20	by the will of the one who subjected it, in hope	11	
8:37	No, in all these things we are more	10	
8:39	from the love of God in Christ Jesus our Lord.	10	
9: 1	I am speaking the truth in Christ—I am not lying;	10	
9:17	for the very purpose of showing my power in you	10	
9:17	so that my name may be proclaimed in all the earth."	10	
9:25	As indeed he says in Hosea	10	
9:26	"And in the very place where it was said to them	10	
9:33	"See, I am laying in Zion a stone	10	
9:33	whoever believes in him will not be put to shame."	11	
10: 6	"Do not say in your heart, 'Who will ascend	10	
10: 8	"The word is near you, on your lips and in your heart"	10	
10: 9	and believe in your heart that God raised him	10	
10:11	"No one who believes in him will be put to shame."	11	
10:14	to call on one in whom they have not believed?	7	
11:32	For God has imprisoned all in disobedience	7	
12: 4	For as in one body we have many members	10	
12: 5	so we, who are many, are one body in Christ	10	
12: 6	prophecy, in proportion to faith;	13	
12: 7	ministry, in ministering;	10	
12: 7	the teacher, in teaching;	10	
12: 8	the exhorter, in exhortation;	10	
12: 8	the giver, in generosity;	10	
12: 8	the leader, in diligence;	10	
12: 8	the compassionate, in cheerfulness.	10	
13: 9	commandments…are summed up in this word	10	
13:13	live honorably as in the day	10	
14: 5	Let all be fully convinced in their own minds.	10	
14:14	I know and am persuaded in the Lord Jesus	10	
14:14	persuaded…that nothing is unclean in itself;	6	
14:15	you are no longer walking in love.	13	
14:17	and peace and joy in the Holy Spirit.	10	
15:12	in him the Gentiles shall hope."	11	
15:13	fill you with all joy and peace in believing	10	
15:13	may abound in hope by the power of the Holy Spirit.	10	
15:17	In Christ Jesus, then, I have reason to boast	10	
15:23	with no further place for me in these regions	10	
15:27	to be of service to them in material things.	10	
15:29	come in the fullness of the blessing of Christ.	10	
15:30	join me in earnest prayer to God on my behalf	10	
15:31	I may be rescued from the unbelievers in Judea	10	
16: 2	welcome her in the Lord as is fitting for the saints	10	
16: 2	help her in whatever she may require from you	10	
16: 3	who work with me in Christ Jesus	10	
16: 5	Greet also the church in their house.	13	
16: 7	and they were in Christ before I was.	10	
16: 8	Greet Ampliatus, my beloved in the Lord.	10	
16: 9	Greet Urbanus, our co-worker in Christ	10	
16:10	Greet Apelles, who is approved in Christ.	10	
16:11	Greet those in the Lord who belong to the family	10	
16:12	Greet those workers in the Lord	10	
16:12	beloved Persis, who has worked hard in the Lord.	10	
16:13	Greet Rufus, chosen in the Lord;	10	
16:19	I want you to be wise in what is good	7	
16:19	and guileless in what is evil.	7	
16:22	I Tertius…greet you in the Lord.	10	
1Co 1: 2	To the church of God that is in Corinth	10	
1: 2	to those who are sanctified in Christ Jesus	10	
1: 2	together with all those who in every place	10	
1: 4	grace…given you in Christ Jesus	10	
1: 5	for in every way you have been enriched in him	10	
1: 5	for in every way you have been enriched in him	10	
1: 5	in speech and knowledge of every kind—	10	
1: 7	you are not lacking in any spiritual gift	10	
1:10	be united in the same mind and the same purpose.	10	
1:13	were you baptized in the name of Paul?	7	
1:15	say that you were baptized in my name.	7	
1:21	in the wisdom of God, the world did not know God	10	
1:30	He is the source of your life in Christ Jesus	10	
1:31	"Let the one who boasts, boast in the Lord."	10	
2: 1	the mystery of God to you in lofty words or wisdom.	13	
2: 3	And I came to you in weakness and in fear	10	
2: 3	And I came to you in weakness and in fear	10	
2: 3	in weakness and in fear and in much trembling.	10	

3: 1	as people of the flesh, as infants in Christ.	10
3:16	God's Spirit dwells in you?	10
3:18	If you think that you are wise in this age	10
3:19	"He catches the wise in their craftiness,"	10
4:10	you are wise in Christ.	10
4:15	you might have ten thousand guardians in Christ	10
4:15	Indeed, in Christ Jesus I became your father	10
4:17	my beloved and faithful child in the Lord	10
4:17	to remind you of my ways in Christ Jesus	10
4:17	as I teach them everywhere in every church.	10
5: 4	in the name of the Lord Jesus	10
5: 5	his spirit may be saved in the day of the Lord.	10
5: 9	I wrote to you in my letter	10
6: 4	who have no standing in the church?	10
6:11	justified in the name of the Lord Jesus Christ	10
6:11	in the Spirit of our God.	10
6:20	therefore glorify God in your body.	10
7:15	in such a case the brother or sister is not bound.	10
7:17	This is my rule in all the churches.	10
7:20	Let each of you remain in the condition	10
7:20	remain in the condition in which you were called	10
7:22	called in the Lord as a slave is a freed person	10
7:24	In whatever condition you were called	10
7:37	someone stands firm in his resolve	10
7:37	determined in his own mind to keep her	10
7:39	marry anyone she wishes, only in the Lord.	10
7:40	in my judgment she is more blessed	13
8: 4	we know that "no idol in the world really exists,"	10
8: 5	may be so-called gods in heaven or on earth	10
8:10	see you…eating in the temple of an idol	10
9: 1	Are you not my work in the Lord?	10
9: 2	you are the seal of my apostleship in the Lord.	10
9: 9	For it is written in the law of Moses	10
9:10	for whoever plows should plow in hope	11
9:10	should thresh in hope of a share in the crop.	11
9:18	make full use of my rights in the gospel.	10
9:24	Do you not know that in a race	10
10: 2	all were baptized into Moses in the cloud	10
10: 2	baptized…in the cloud and in the sea	10
10: 5	and they were struck down in the wilderness.	10
10:25	Eat whatever is sold in the meat market	10
11:11	in the Lord woman is not independent of man	10
11:22	Should I commend you? In this matter I do not	10
11:24	Do this in remembrance of me."	7
11:25	"This cup is the new covenant in my blood.	10
11:25	as often as you drink it, in remembrance of me."	7
12: 6	the same God who activates all of them in everyone.	10
12:13	For in the one Spirit we were all baptized	10
12:18	as it is, God arranged the members in the body	10
12:28	God has appointed in the church first apostles	10
13: 6	it does not rejoice in wrongdoing	11
13: 9	For we know only in part	8
13: 9	we prophesy only in part;	8
13:12	For now we see in a mirror, dimly,	6
13:12	Now I know only in part; then I will know fully	8
14: 6	I speak to you in some revelation or knowledge	10
14: 9	if in a tongue you utter speech	6
14:10	many different kinds of sounds in the world	10
14:16	how can anyone in the position of an outsider say	3
14:19	nevertheless, in church I would rather speak	10
14:19	than ten thousand words in a tongue	10
14:21	In the law it is written, "By people of strange tongues	10
14:27	each in turn; and let one interpret.	1
14:28	let them be silent in church	10
14:33	(As in all the churches of the saints	10
14:34	women should be silent in the churches.	10
14:35	it is shameful for a woman to speak in church.	10
14:40	all things should be done decently and in order.	13
15: 1	which you in turn received, in which also you stand	10
15:17	you are still in your sins.	10
15:18	Then those also who have died in Christ	10
15:19	If for this life only we have hoped in Christ	10
15:22	for as all die in Adam	10
15:22	so all will be made alive in Christ.	10
15:23	each in his own order: Christ the first fruits	10
15:28	so that God may be all in all.	10
15:31	a boast that I make in Christ Jesus our Lord.	10
15:41	star differs from star in glory.	10
15:43	It is sown in dishonor, it is raised in glory.	10
15:43	It is sown in dishonor, it is raised in glory.	10
15:43	It is sown in weakness, it is raised in power.	10

15:43	It is sown in weakness, it is raised in power.	10
15:52	in a moment, in the twinkling of an eye	10
15:52	in a moment, in the twinkling of an eye	10
15:54	"Death has been swallowed up in victory."	7
15:58	always excelling in the work of the Lord	10
15:58	know that in the Lord your labor is not in vain	10
16: 7	I do not want to see you now just in passing	10
16: 8	I will stay in Ephesus until Pentecost	10
16:11	Send him on his way in peace	10
16:13	Keep alert, stand firm in your faith	10
16:14	Let all that you do be done in love.	10
16:19	together with the church in their house	13
16:19	greet you warmly in the Lord.	10
16:24	My love be with all of you in Christ Jesus.	10

2Co

1: 1	To the church of God that is in Corinth	10
1: 4	who consoles us in all our affliction	11
1: 4	able to console those who are in any affliction	10
1: 8	the affliction we experienced in Asia;	10
1:12	we have behaved in the world	10
1:14	as you have already understood us in part	4
1:19	not "Yes and No"; but in him it is always "Yes."	10
1:20	in him every one of God's promises is a "Yes."	10
1:21	it is God who establishes us with you in Christ	7
1:22	giving us his Spirit in our hearts as a first installment.	10
2: 9	know whether you are obedient in everything.	7
2:10	has been for your sake in the presence of Christ.	10
2:12	a door was opened for me in the Lord;	10
2:14	who in Christ always leads us in triumphal procession	10
2:14	spreads in every place the fragrance	10
2:17	in Christ we speak as persons of sincerity	10
3: 7	chiseled in letters on stone tablets	10
3: 7	if the ministry of death…came in glory	10
3: 8	will the ministry of the Spirit come in glory?	10
3:14	since only in Christ is it set aside.	10
4: 4	In their case the god of this world has blinded	10
4: 6	who has shone in our hearts	10
4: 6	the glory of God in the face of Jesus Christ.	10
4: 7	we have this treasure in clay jars	10
4: 8	afflicted in every way, but not crushed;	10
4:10	always carrying in the body the death of Jesus	10
4:10	Jesus may also be made visible in our bodies.	10
4:11	Jesus may be made visible in our mortal flesh.	10
4:12	death is at work in us, but life in you.	10
4:12	death is at work in us, but life in you.	10
5: 1	not made with hands, eternal in the heavens.	10
5: 2	For in this tent we groan	10
5: 4	while we are still in this tent	10
5: 6	we know that while we are at home in the body	10
5:10	for what has been done in the body	6
5:12	those who boast in outward appearance	10
5:12	in outward appearance and not in the heart.	10
5:17	if anyone is in Christ, there is a new creation:	10
5:19	in Christ God was reconciling the world	10
5:21	in him we might become the righteousness of God.	10
6: 1	not to accept the grace of God in vain.	7
6: 3	We are putting no obstacle in anyone's way	10
6: 4	we have commended ourselves in every way:	10
6: 4	through great endurance, in afflictions	10
6: 8	in honor and dishonor	6
6: 8	in ill repute and good repute.	6
6:12	There is no restriction in our affections	10
6:12	no restriction in our affections, but only in yours	10
6:16	"I will live in them and walk among them	10
7: 1	making holiness perfect in the fear of God.	10
7: 3	I said before that you are in our hearts	10
7: 4	boast about you; I have great pride in you;	19
7: 4	I am overjoyed in all our affliction.	11
7: 5	we were afflicted in every way	10
7: 9	so that you were not harmed in any way by us.	10
7:13	In this we find comfort.	6
7:16	because I have complete confidence in you.	10
8: 2	overflowed in a wealth of generosity	7
8: 7	Now as you excel in everything	10
8: 7	want you to excel also in this generous undertaking.	10
8:10	in this matter I am giving my advice:	10
8:16	who put in the heart of Titus the same eagerness	10
8:22	and found eager in many matters	10
8:22	because of his great confidence in you.	7
9: 3	may not prove to have been empty in this case	10
9: 4	we would be humiliated…in this undertaking	10
9: 8	share abundantly in every good work.	7

2Co	9:11	You will be enriched in every way	10
	10:15	We do not boast…in the labors of others;	10
	10:16	we may proclaim the good news in lands beyond you	7
	10:16	work already done in someone else's sphere of action.	10
	10:17	"Let the one who boasts, boast in the Lord."	10
	11: 6	in every way…we have made this evident to you.	10
	11: 6	in all things we have made this evident to you.	10
	11: 9	continue to refrain from burdening you in any way.	10
	11:10	As the truth of Christ is in me	10
	11:10	will not be silenced in the regions of Achaia.	10
	11:12	as our equals in what they boast about.	10
	11:20	or puts on airs, or gives you a slap in the face.	7
	11:26	danger from Gentiles, danger in the city	10
	11:26	danger in the city, danger in the wilderness	10
	11:32	In Damascus, the governor under King Aretas	10
	11:33	let down in a basket through a window in the wall	10
	11:33	let down in a basket through a window in the wall	6
	12: 2	I know a person in Christ	10
	12: 2	whether in the body or out of the body	10
	12: 3	whether in the body or out of the body	10
	12: 9	for power is made perfect in weakness."	10
	12: 9	so that the power of Christ may dwell in me.	11
	12:19	We are speaking in Christ before God.	10
	13: 3	you desire proof that Christ is speaking in me.	10
	13: 3	is powerful in you.	10
	13: 4	For he was crucified in weakness	8
	13: 4	we are weak in him	10
	13: 5	to see whether you are living in the faith.	10
	13: 5	you not realize that Jesus Christ is in you?	10
Gal	1: 6	who called you in the grace of Christ	10
	1:13	heard, no doubt, of my earlier life in Judaism.	10
	1:14	I advanced in Judaism beyond many among my people	10
	1:22	the churches of Judea that are in Christ;	10
	2: 2	that I was not running, or had not run, in vain.	7
	2: 4	spy on the freedom we have in Christ Jesus	10
	2:16	And we have come to believe in Christ Jesus	7
	2:17	if, in our effort to be justified in Christ	10
	2:20	but it is Christ who lives in me	10
	2:20	the life I now live in the flesh I live by faith	10
	3: 8	saying, "All the Gentiles shall be blessed in you."	10
	3:10	obey all the things written in the book of the law."	10
	3:14	that in Christ Jesus the blessing of Abraham	10
	3:26	for in Christ Jesus you are all children of God	10
	3:28	for all of you are one in Christ Jesus.	10
	4:19	until Christ is formed in you	10
	4:25	Now Hagar is Mount Sinai in Arabia	10
	5: 6	For in Christ Jesus neither circumcision	10
	5:10	I am confident about you in the Lord	10
	5:14	the whole law is summed up in a single commandment	10
	6: 1	friends, if anyone is detected in a transgression	10
	6: 1	restore such a one in a spirit of gentleness.	10
	6: 6	share in all good things with their teacher.	10
	6:12	who want to make a good showing in the flesh	10
Eph	1: 1	the saints who are in Ephesus and are faithful	10
	1: 1	the saints who are…faithful in Christ Jesus:	10
	1: 3	who has blessed us in Christ	10
	1: 3	who has blessed us…in the heavenly places	10
	1: 4	just as he chose us in Christ	10
	1: 4	to be holy and blameless before him in love	10
	1: 6	that he freely bestowed on us in the Beloved.	10
	1: 7	In him we have redemption through his blood	10
	1: 9	his good pleasure that he set forth in Christ	10
	1:10	to gather up all things in him	10
	1:10	things in heaven and things on earth.	11
	1:11	In Christ we have also obtained an inheritance	10
	1:13	In him you also, when you had heard the word	10
	1:13	you also, when you…had believed in him	10
	1:15	have heard of your faith in the Lord Jesus	10
	1:16	as I remember you in my prayers.	11
	1:20	God put this power to work in Christ	10
	1:20	seated him at his right hand in the heavenly places	10
	1:21	not only in this age	10
	1:21	but also in the age to come.	10
	1:23	the fullness of him who fills all in all.	10
	2: 2	in which you once lived	10
	2: 3	lived among them in the passions of our flesh	10
	2: 4	God, who is rich in mercy	10
	2: 6	seated us with him in the heavenly places	10
	2: 6	in the heavenly places in Christ Jesus	10
	2: 7	so that in the ages to come	10
	2: 7	in kindness toward us in Christ Jesus.	10

	2: 7	in kindness toward us in Christ Jesus.	10
	2:10	we are what he has made us, created in Christ Jesus	10
	2:11	circumcision made in the flesh by human hands	10
	2:12	having no hope and without God in the world.	10
	2:13	now in Christ Jesus you…have been brought	10
	2:14	in his flesh he has made both groups into one	10
	2:15	create in himself one new humanity in place of the two	10
	2:16	might reconcile both groups to God in one body	10
	2:18	for through him both of us have access in one Spirit	10
	2:21	In him the whole structure is joined together	10
	2:21	grows into a holy temple in the Lord;	10
	2:22	in whom you also are built together	10
	3: 3	as I wrote above in a few words	10
	3: 6	sharers in the promise in Christ Jesus	10
	3: 9	plan of the mystery hidden for ages in God	10
	3:10	authorities in the heavenly places.	10
	3:11	that he has carried out in Christ Jesus our Lord	10
	3:12	in whom we have access to God in boldness	10
	3:12	access to God in boldness and confidence through faith	10
	3:15	every family in heaven and on earth takes its name.	10
	3:16	in your inner being with power through his Spirit	7
	3:17	Christ may dwell in your hearts through faith	10
	3:17	being rooted and grounded in love.	10
	3:21	to him be glory in the church and in Christ Jesus	10
	3:21	to him be glory in the church and in Christ Jesus	10
	4: 1	I therefore, the prisoner in the Lord, beg you	10
	4: 2	bearing with one another in love	10
	4: 3	the unity of the Spirit in the bond of peace.	10
	4: 6	who is above all and through all and in all.	10
	4:14	by their craftiness in deceitful scheming.	18
	4:15	But speaking the truth in love	10
	4:16	the body's growth in building itself up in love.	7
	4:16	the body's growth in building itself up in love.	10
	4:17	Now this I affirm and insist on in the Lord:	10
	4:17	in the futility of their minds.	10
	4:21	have heard about him and were taught in him	10
	4:21	taught in him, as truth is in Jesus.	10
	4:24	in true righteousness and holiness.	10
	4:32	forgiving one another, as God in Christ has forgiven	10
	5: 2	live in love, as Christ loved us	10
	5: 5	has any inheritance in the kingdom of Christ	10
	5: 8	now in the Lord you are light.	10
	5: 9	fruit of the light is found in all that is good	10
	5:20	in the name of our Lord Jesus Christ.	10
	5:24	so also wives ought to be, in everything	10
	6: 1	Children, obey your parents in the Lord	10
	6: 4	bring them up in the discipline…of the Lord.	10
	6: 5	with fear and trembling, in singleness of heart	10
	6: 9	both of you have the same Master in heaven,	10
	6:10	Finally, be strong in the Lord	10
	6:10	be strong…in the strength of his power.	10
	6:12	the spiritual forces…in the heavenly places.	10
	6:18	Pray in the Spirit at all times	10
	6:18	Pray in the Spirit…in every prayer	6
	6:20	for which I am an ambassador in chains.	10
	6:21	a faithful minister in the Lord.	10
Php	1: 1	To all the saints in Christ Jesus	10
	1: 1	saints in Christ Jesus who are in Philippi	10
	1: 4	praying with joy in every one of my prayers	10
	1: 5	because of your sharing in the gospel	7
	1: 7	because you hold me in your heart	10
	1: 7	both in my imprisonment and in the defense	10
	1: 7	both in my imprisonment and in the defense	10
	1:10	in the day of Christ you may be pure and blameless	7
	1:14	made confident in the Lord by my imprisonment	10
	1:18	Christ is proclaimed…and in that I rejoice.	10
	1:20	my…hope that I will not be put to shame in any way	10
	1:20	Christ will be exalted now as always in my body	10
	1:22	If I am to live in the flesh	10
	1:24	to remain in the flesh is more necessary	10
	1:26	share abundantly in your boasting in Christ Jesus	10
	1:27	that you are standing firm in one spirit,	10
	1:28	in no way intimidated by your opponents.	10
	1:29	the privilege not only of believing in Christ	7
	2: 1	If then there is any encouragement in Christ	10
	2: 5	Let the same mind be in you	10
	2: 5	the same mind be in you that was in Christ Jesus	10
	2: 6	who, though he was in the form of God,	10
	2: 7	being born in human likeness.	10
	2: 7	being found in human form	21
	2:12	have always obeyed me, not only in my presence	10

	2:12	in my presence, but much more now in my absence	10
	2:13	for it is God who is at work in you, enabling you	10
	2:15	in which you shine like stars in the world.	10
	2:15	in which you shine like stars in the world.	10
	2:16	I did not run in vain or labor in vain.	7
	2:16	I did not run in vain or labor in vain.	7
	2:19	I hope in the Lord Jesus to send Timothy to you	10
	2:22	he has served with me in the work of the gospel.	7
	2:24	I trust in the Lord	10
	2:29	Welcome him then in the Lord with all joy	10
	3: 1	Finally, my brothers and sisters, rejoice in the Lord.	10
	3: 3	worship in the Spirit of God and boast in Christ Jesus	10
	3: 3	have no confidence in the flesh	10
	3: 4	I…have reason for confidence in the flesh.	10
	3: 4	else has reason to be confident in the flesh	10
	3: 9	and be found in him	10
	3:14	prize of the heavenly call of God in Christ Jesus.	10
	3:19	their glory is in their shame;	10
	3:20	our citizenship is in heaven	10
	4: 1	stand firm in the Lord in this way, my beloved.	10
	4: 2	I urge Syntyche to be of the same mind in the Lord.	10
	4: 3	struggled beside me in the work of the gospel	10
	4: 3	whose names are in the book of life.	10
	4: 4	Rejoice in the Lord always;	10
	4: 6	in everything by prayer and supplication	10
	4: 7	guard your hearts and your minds in Christ Jesus.	10
	4: 9	have learned and received and heard and seen in me	10
	4:10	I rejoice in the Lord greatly	10
	4:12	In any and all circumstances	10
	4:15	know that in the early days of the gospel	10
	4:15	in the matter of giving and receiving,	7
	4:16	even when I was in Thessalonica, you sent me help	10
	4:19	according to his riches in glory in Christ	10
	4:19	his riches in glory in Christ Jesus.	10
	4:21	Greet every saint in Christ Jesus.	10
Col	1: 2	faithful brothers and sisters in Christ in Colossae:	10
	1: 2	faithful brothers and sisters in Christ in Colossae:	10
	1: 4	we have heard of your faith in Christ Jesus	10
	1: 5	because of the hope laid up for you in heaven.	10
	1: 5	heard of this hope…in the word of the truth	10
	1: 6	bearing fruit and growing in the whole world	10
	1: 8	has made known to us your love in the Spirit.	10
	1: 9	knowledge of God's will in all spiritual wisdom	10
	1:10	bear fruit in every good work	10
	1:12	the inheritance of the saints in the light.	10
	1:14	in whom we have redemption, the forgiveness	10
	1:16	in him all things in heaven and on earth were created	10
	1:16	in him all things in heaven and on earth were created	10
	1:17	in him all things hold together.	10
	1:18	he might come to have first place in everything.	10
	1:19	in him all the fullness of God was pleased to dwell	10
	1:20	all things, whether on earth or in heaven	10
	1:22	now reconciled in his fleshly body through death	10
	1:24	I am now rejoicing in my sufferings for your sake	10
	1:24	in my flesh I am completing what is lacking	10
	1:27	which is Christ in you, the hope of glory.	10
	1:28	teaching everyone in all wisdom	10
	1:28	so that we may present everyone mature in Christ.	10
	2: 1	struggling for you and for those in Laodicea	10
	2: 2	hearts to be encouraged and united in love,	10
	2: 3	in whom are hidden all the treasures of wisdom	10
	2: 5	the firmness of your faith in Christ.	7
	2: 6	continue to live your lives in him	10
	2: 7	rooted and built up in him	10
	2: 7	abounding in thanksgiving.	10
	2: 9	in him the whole fullness of deity dwells bodily	10
	2:10	you have come to fullness in him	10
	2:11	In him also you were circumcised with a spiritual	10
	2:11	in the circumcision of Christ;	10
	2:12	you were buried with him in baptism	10
	2:13	when you were dead in trespasses	10
	2:15	triumphing over them in it.	10
	2:16	condemn you in matters of food and drink	10
	3: 3	your life is hidden with Christ in God.	10
	3: 4	you also will be revealed with him in glory.	10
	3:10	which is being renewed in knowledge	7
	3:11	In that renewal there is no longer Greek and Jew	15
	3:11	Christ is all and in all!	10
	3:15	let the peace of Christ rule in your hearts	10
	3:15	to which indeed you were called in the one body.	10
	3:16	Let the word of Christ dwell in you richly;	10

	3:16	teach and admonish one another in all wisdom;	10
	3:16	with gratitude in your hearts sing psalms, hymns,	10
	3:17	whatever you do, in word or deed	10
	3:17	do everything in the name of the Lord Jesus	10
	3:18	be subject…as is fitting in the Lord.	10
	3:20	Children, obey your parents in everything	13
	3:20	this is your acceptable duty in the Lord.	10
	3:22	Slaves, obey your earthly masters in everything	13
	4: 1	know that you also have a Master in heaven.	10
	4: 2	keeping alert in it with thanksgiving.	10
	4: 7	Tychicus…fellow servant in the Lord.	10
	4:12	wrestling in his prayers on your behalf	10
	4:12	fully assured in everything that God wills.	10
	4:13	for those in Laodicea and in Hierapolis.	10
	4:13	for those in Laodicea and in Hierapolis.	10
	4:15	greetings to the brothers and sisters in Laodicea	10
	4:15	to Nympha and the church in her house.	13
	4:16	have it read also in the church of the Laodiceans;	10
	4:17	the task that you have received in the Lord."	10
1Th	1: 1	in God the Father and the Lord Jesus Christ:	10
	1: 2	mention you in our prayers, constantly	11
	1: 5	message of the gospel came to you not in word only	10
	1: 5	also in power and in the Holy Spirit	10
	1: 5	also in power and in the Holy Spirit	10
	1: 7	example to all the believers in Macedonia	10
	1: 7	an example to all the believers…in Achaia	10
	1: 8	sounded forth from you not only in Macedonia	10
	1: 8	in every place your faith in God has become known	10
	1: 8	in every place your faith in God has become known	18
	2: 2	courage in our God to declare to you the gospel	10
	2:13	God's word, which is also at work in you believers.	10
	2:14	imitators of the churches of God in Christ Jesus	10
	2:14	churches…that are in Judea	10
	3: 1	we decided to be left alone in Athens;	10
	3: 2	co-worker for God in proclaiming the gospel	10
	3: 5	our labor had been in vain.	7
	3: 8	if you continue to stand firm in the Lord.	10
	3:13	And may he so strengthen your hearts in holiness	10
	4: 1	we ask and urge you in the Lord Jesus	10
	4: 4	control your own body in holiness and honor	10
	4: 6	exploit a brother or sister in this matter	10
	4: 6	the Lord is an avenger in all these things	17
	4: 7	God did not call us to impurity but in holiness	10
	4:16	the dead in Christ will rise first.	10
	4:17	will be caught up in the clouds together with them	10
	4:17	together with them to meet the Lord in the air;	7
	5: 2	day of the Lord will come like a thief in the night.	10
	5: 4	you, beloved, are not in darkness	10
	5:12	have charge of you in the Lord and admonish you;	10
	5:13	esteem them very highly in love	10
	5:18	give thanks in all circumstances;	10
	5:18	for this is the will of God in Christ Jesus	10
2Th	1: 1	in God our Father and the Lord Jesus Christ:	10
	1: 8	in flaming fire, inflicting vengeance on those	10
	1:12	name of our Lord Jesus may be glorified in you	10
	1:12	Jesus may be glorified in you, and you in him,	10
	2: 2	not to be quickly shaken in mind or alarmed	4
	2: 3	Let no one deceive you in any way;	13
	2: 4	he takes his seat in the temple of God	7
	2:17	strengthen them in every good work and word.	10
	3: 4	we have confidence in the Lord concerning you	10
	3: 6	in the name of our Lord Jesus Christ	10
	3:12	exhort in the Lord Jesus Christ to do their work	10
	3:14	those who do not obey what we say in this letter;	6
	3:16	Lord of peace himself give you peace…in all ways	10
	3:17	This is the mark in every letter of mine;	10
1Ti	1: 2	To Timothy, my loyal child in the faith:	10
	1: 3	I urge you…to remain in Ephesus	10
	1:13	because I had acted ignorantly in unbelief	10
	1:14	the faith and love that are in Christ Jesus.	10
	1:16	so that in me, as the foremost	10
	1:16	an example to those who would come to believe in him	11
	1:19	persons have suffered shipwreck in the faith	17
	2: 2	for kings and all who are in high positions	10
	2: 2	peaceable life in all godliness and dignity.	10
	2: 7	a teacher of the Gentiles in faith and truth.	10
	2: 8	in every place the men should pray	10
	2: 9	modestly and decently in suitable clothing	10
	2:11	Let a woman learn in silence	10
	2:15	they continue in faith and love and holiness	10
	3: 4	submissive and respectful in every way	14

1Ti	3:11	temperate, faithful in all things.	10
	3:13	great boldness in the faith that is in Christ	10
	3:13	great boldness in the faith that is in Christ	10
	3:15	how one ought to behave in the household of God	10
	3:16	He was revealed in flesh	10
	3:16	vindicated in spirit, seen by angels	10
	3:16	believed in throughout the world, taken up in glory.	10
	4: 1	in later times some will renounce the faith	10
	4: 7	Train yourself in godliness	18
	4: 8	godliness is valuable in every way	18
	4:12	set the believers an example in speech	10
	4:12	an example in speech and conduct, in love, in faith	10
	4:12	an example in speech and conduct, in love, in faith	10
	4:12	conduct, in love, in faith, in purity.	10
	4:14	Do not neglect the gift that is in you	10
	5:17	especially those who labor in preaching	10
	6:17	As for those who in the present age are rich	10
	6:18	They are to do good, to be rich in good works	10
2Ti	1: 1	the promise of life that is in Christ Jesus	10
	1: 3	when I remember you constantly in my prayers	10
	1: 5	a faith that lived first in your grandmother	10
	1: 5	a faith that…now, I am sure, lives in you.	10
	1: 9	This grace was given to us in Christ Jesus	10
	1:13	in the faith and love that are in Christ Jesus.	10
	1:13	in the faith and love that are in Christ Jesus.	10
	1:14	with the help of the Holy Spirit living in us.	10
	1:15	all who are in Asia have turned away from me	10
	1:17	when he arrived in Rome, he eagerly searched for me	10
	1:18	you know…how much service he rendered in Ephesus	10
	2: 1	You then, my child, be strong in the grace	10
	2: 1	be strong in the grace that is in Christ Jesus;	10
	2: 7	will give you understanding in all things.	10
	2:10	may also obtain the salvation that is in Christ Jesus	10
	2:20	In a large house there are utensils	10
	3: 1	You must understand this, that in the last days	10
	3:11	things that happened to me in Antioch, Iconium	10
	3:12	all who want to live a godly life in Christ	10
	3:14	as for you, continue in what you have learned	10
	3:15	salvation through faith in Christ Jesus.	10
	3:16	useful…for training in righteousness	10
	4:11	for he is useful in my ministry.	7
	4:20	Erastus remained in Corinth;	10
	4:20	Trophimus I left ill in Miletus.	10
Tit	1: 2	in the hope of eternal life	11
	1: 4	To Titus, my loyal child in the faith we share:	13
	1: 5	I left you behind in Crete for this reason	10
	1:13	so that they may become sound in the faith	10
	2: 3	Likewise, tell the older women to be reverent in behavior	10
	2: 7	in your teaching show integrity, gravity	10
	2: 9	to give satisfaction in every respect;	10
	2:10	so that in everything they may be an ornament	10
	2:12	in the present age to live lives that are self-controlled,	10
	3: 3	passing our days in malice and envy	10
	3:15	Greet those who love us in the faith.	10
Phm	1: 2	the church in your house:	13
	1: 4	When I remember you in my prayers	11
	1: 8	though I am bold enough in Christ to command you	10
	1:16	both in the flesh and in the Lord.	10
	1:16	both in the flesh and in the Lord.	10
	1:20	brother, let me have this benefit from you in the Lord!	10
	1:20	Refresh my heart in Christ.	10
	1:23	Epaphras, my fellow prisoner in Christ Jesus	10
Heb	1: 2	in these last days he has spoken to us by a Son	11
	1:10	"In the beginning, Lord, you founded the earth	13
	2: 8	Now in subjecting all things to them	10
	2:12	in the midst of the congregation I will praise	10
	2:13	And again, "I will put my trust in him."	11
	3: 2	just as Moses also "was faithful in all God's house."	10
	3: 5	Now Moses was faithful in all God's house	10
	3: 8	do not harden your hearts as in the rebellion	10
	3: 8	on the day of testing in the wilderness	10
	3:11	As in my anger I swore, 'They will not enter	10
	3:15	do not harden your hearts as in the rebellion."	10
	3:17	who sinned, whose bodies fell in the wilderness?	10
	4: 3	"As in my anger I swore, 'They shall not enter	10
	4: 5	And again in this place it says	10
	4: 7	saying…in the words already quoted	12
	4:16	find grace to help in time of need.	7
	5: 6	as he says also in another place	10
	5: 7	In the days of his flesh, Jesus offered up prayers	10
	6:17	In the same way, when God desired to show	10
	6:18	in which it is impossible that God would prove false	10
	7: 5	have a commandment in the law to collect tithes	13
	7:10	for he was still in the loins of his ancestor	10
	8: 1	Now the main point in what we are saying is this:	11
	8: 1	right hand of the throne of the Majesty in the heavens	10
	8: 9	for they did not continue in my covenant	10
	8:10	I will put my laws in their minds	7
	8:13	In speaking of "a new covenant,"	10
	9: 2	in which were the lampstand, the table	10
	9: 4	in which there were a golden urn holding the manna	10
	9: 5	Of these things we cannot speak now in detail.	13
	10: 3	in these sacrifices there is a reminder of sin	10
	10: 7	(in the scroll of the book it is written of me)."	10
	10:16	I will put my laws in their hearts	11
	10:22	approach…in full assurance of faith	10
	10:38	My soul takes no pleasure in anyone who shrinks back."	10
	11: 9	By faith he stayed for a time in the land	7
	11: 9	living in tents, as did Isaac and Jacob	10
	11:13	All of these died in faith	13
	11:31	she had received the spies in peace.	14
	11:34	became mighty in war	10
	11:37	they went about in skins of sheep and goats	10
	11:38	wandered in deserts and mountains	11
	12:23	who are enrolled in heaven	10
	13:18	desiring to act honorably in all things.	10
	13:21	make you complete in everything good	10
Jas	1: 1	To the twelve tribes in the Dispersion:	10
	1: 4	be mature and complete, lacking in nothing.	10
	1: 6	But ask in faith, never doubting	10
	1: 7	being double-minded and unstable in every way,	10
	1: 9	Let the believer who is lowly boast in being raised up	10
	1:10	and the rich in being brought low	10
	1:23	those who look at themselves in a mirror;	10
	1:25	they will be blessed in their doing.	10
	1:27	to care for orphans and widows in their distress	10
	2: 2	For if a person with gold rings and in fine clothes	10
	2: 2	a poor person in dirty clothes also comes in	10
	2: 5	be rich in faith and to be heirs of the kingdom	10
	2:10	whoever…fails in one point has become accountable	10
	2:16	"Go in peace; keep warm and eat your fill,"	10
	3: 2	who makes no mistakes in speaking is perfect.	10
	3: 9	we curse those who are made in the likeness of God.	13
	3:14	if you have…selfish ambition in your hearts	10
	3:18	a harvest of righteousness is sown in peace	10
	4: 5	the spirit that he has made to dwell in us"?	10
	4:16	As it is, you boast in your arrogance;	10
	5: 5	have fattened your hearts in a day of slaughter.	10
	5:10	the prophets who spoke in the name of the Lord.	10
	5:14	anointing them with oil in the name of the Lord.	10
1Pe	1: 4	inheritance that is…kept in heaven for you	10
	1: 5	salvation ready to be revealed in the last time.	10
	1: 6	In this you rejoice	10
	1: 8	though you do not see him now, you believe in him	7
	1:14	the desires that you formerly had in ignorance.	10
	1:15	be holy yourselves in all your conduct;	10
	1:17	live in reverent fear	10
	1:21	Through him you have come to trust in God	7
	2: 6	For it stands in scripture:	10
	2: 6	"See, I am laying in Zion a stone, a cornerstone	10
	2: 6	whoever believes in him will not be put to shame."	11
	2:22	no deceit was found in his mouth."	10
	2:24	He himself bore our sins in his body on the cross	10
	3: 5	women who hoped in God used to adorn themselves	7
	3:15	in your hearts sanctify Christ as Lord.	10
	3:15	an accounting for the hope that is in you;	10
	3:16	those who abuse you for your good conduct in Christ	10
	3:19	in which also he went and made a proclamation	10
	3:19	he went and made a proclamation to the spirits in prison	10
	3:20	when God waited patiently in the days of Noah	10
	3:20	ark, in which a few…were saved through water.	7
	4: 3	living in licentiousness, passions	10
	4: 4	no longer join them in the same excesses of dissipation	7
	4:11	God may be glorified in all things through Jesus Christ.	10
	5: 6	so that he may exalt you in due time.	10
	5: 9	your brothers and sisters in all the world	10
	5:10	who has called you to his eternal glory in Christ	10
	5:12	this is the true grace of God. Stand fast in it.	7
	5:13	Your sister church in Babylon, chosen together	10
	5:14	Peace to all of you who are in Christ.	10
2Pe	1: 2	in the knowledge of God and of Jesus our Lord.	10
	1: 4	escape from the corruption that is in the world	10

	1: 8	in the knowledge of our Lord Jesus Christ.	7
	1:12	you know them already and are established in the truth	10
	1:13	I think it right, as long as I am in this body	10
	1:19	as to a lamp shining in a dark place	10
	1:19	and the morning star rises in your hearts.	10
	2: 3	And in their greed they will exploit you	10
	2:10	who indulge their flesh in depraved lust,	10
	2:13	They count it a pleasure to revel in the daytime.	10
	2:13	They are…reveling in their dissipation	10
	2:18	escaped from those who live in error.	10
	3: 1	in them I am trying to arouse your sincere intention	10
	3: 3	that in the last days scoffers will come	11
	3:11	in leading lives of holiness and godliness	10
	3:16	speaking of this as he does in all his letters.	10
	3:16	There are some things in them hard to understand	10
	3:18	grow in the grace and knowledge of our Lord	10
1Jn	1: 5	God is light and in him there is no darkness at all.	10
	1: 6	while we are walking in darkness	10
	1: 7	if we walk in the light as he himself is in the light	10
	1: 7	if we walk in the light as he himself is in the light	10
	1: 8	we deceive ourselves, and the truth is not in us.	10
	1:10	we make him a liar, and his word is not in us.	10
	2: 4	in such a person the truth does not exist;	10
	2: 5	truly in this person the love of God has…perfection.	10
	2: 5	By this we may be sure that we are in him:	10
	2: 6	whoever says, "I abide in him," ought to walk	10
	2: 8	a new commandment that is true in him and in you	10
	2: 8	a new commandment that is true in him and in you	10
	2: 9	Whoever says, "I am in the light,"	10
	2: 9	while hating a brother or sister, is still in the darkness.	10
	2:10	Whoever loves a brother or sister lives in the light	10
	2:10	in such a person there is no cause for stumbling.	10
	2:11	whoever hates another believer is in the darkness	10
	2:11	is in the darkness, walks in the darkness	10
	2:14	and the word of God abides in you	10
	2:15	Do not love the world or the things in the world.	10
	2:15	love…is not in those who love the world	10
	2:16	for all that is in the world	10
	2:24	what you heard from the beginning abide in you.	10
	2:24	what you heard from the beginning abides in you	10
	2:24	then you will abide in the Son and in the Father.	10
	2:24	then you will abide in the Son and in the Father.	10
	2:27	the anointing…abides in you	10
	2:27	just as it has taught you, abide in him.	10
	2:28	now, little children, abide in him	10
	3: 3	all who have this hope in him purify themselves	11
	3: 5	and in him there is no sin.	10
	3: 6	No one who abides in him sins;	10
	3: 9	do not sin, because God's seed abides in them;	10
	3:10	children of the devil are revealed in this way:	10
	3:14	Whoever does not love abides in death.	10
	3:15	murderers do not have eternal life abiding in them.	10
	3:17	How does God's love abide in anyone	10
	3:18	let us love, not in word…but in truth and action.	10
	3:24	All who obey his commandments abide in him	10
	3:24	and he abides in them.	10
	3:24	And by this we know that he abides in us	10
	4: 2	that Jesus Christ has come in the flesh is from God	10
	4: 3	coming; and now it is already in the world.	10
	4: 4	for the one who is in you is greater	10
	4: 4	greater than the one who is in the world.	10
	4: 9	God's love was revealed among us in this way:	10
	4:10	In this is love, not that we loved God	10
	4:12	if we love one another, God lives in us	10
	4:12	God lives in us, and his love is perfected in us.	10
	4:13	By this we know that we abide in him and he in us	10
	4:13	By this we know that we abide in him and he in us	10
	4:15	God abides in those who confess that Jesus	10
	4:15	God abides in those…and they abide in God.	10
	4:16	God is love, and those who abide in love abide in God	10
	4:16	God is love, and those who abide in love abide in God	10
	4:16	and God abides in them.	10
	4:17	Love has been perfected among us in this:	10
	4:17	because as he is, so are we in this world.	10
	4:18	There is no fear in love	10
	4:18	whoever fears has not reached perfection in love.	10
	5:10	Those who believe in the Son of God	7
	5:10	Those who believe…have the testimony in their hearts.	10
	5:10	by not believing in the testimony	7
	5:11	eternal life, and this life is in his Son.	10
	5:13	to you who believe in the name of the Son of God	7

	5:14	this is the boldness we have in him	18
	5:20	we are in him who is true, in his Son Jesus Christ.	10
	5:20	we are in him who is true, in his Son Jesus Christ.	10
2Jn	1: 1	lady and her children, whom I love in the truth	10
	1: 2	because of the truth that abides in us	10
	1: 3	from Jesus Christ…in truth and love.	10
	1: 4	to find some of your children walking in the truth	10
	1: 6	this is the commandment…—you must walk in it.	10
	1: 7	Jesus Christ has come in the flesh;	10
	1: 9	does not abide in the teaching of Christ,	10
	1: 9	whoever abides in the teaching has both the Father	10
3Jn	1: 1	the beloved Gaius, whom I love in truth.	10
	1: 3	namely how you walk in the truth.	10
	1: 4	to hear that my children are walking in the truth.	10
Jde	1: 1	who are called, who are beloved in God the Father	10
	1: 6	he has kept in eternal chains in deepest darkness	20
	1:18	they said to you, "In the last time there will be	11
	1:20	pray in the Holy Spirit;	10
	1:21	keep yourselves in the love of God;	10
Rev	1: 3	who hear and who keep what is written in it;	10
	1: 4	John to the seven churches that are in Asia:	10
	1: 9	I, John, your brother who share with you in Jesus	10
	1:10	I was in the spirit on the Lord's day,	10
	1:11	saying, "Write in a book what you see and send it	7
	1:13	in the midst of the lampstands I saw one like the Son	10
	1:15	like burnished bronze, refined as in a furnace	10
	1:16	In his right hand he held seven stars	10
	1:20	the seven stars that you saw in my right hand	11
	2: 1	"To the angel of the church in Ephesus write:	10
	2: 1	him who holds the seven stars in his right hand	10
	2: 7	the tree of life that is in the paradise of God.	10
	2: 8	"And to the angel of the church in Smyrna write:	10
	2:12	"And to the angel of the church in Pergamum write:	10
	2:13	you did not deny…even in the days of Antipas	10
	2:18	"And to the angel of the church in Thyatira write:	10
	2:24	But to the rest of you in Thyatira	10
	3: 1	"And to the angel of the church in Sardis write:	10
	3: 4	Yet you have still a few persons in Sardis	10
	3: 4	with me, dressed in white, for they are worthy.	10
	3: 5	you conquer, you will be clothed like them in white	10
	3: 7	to the angel of the church in Philadelphia write:	10
	3:12	I will make you a pillar in the temple of my God;	10
	3:14	"And to the angel of the church in Laodicea write:	10
	4: 1	I looked, and there in heaven a door stood open!	10
	4: 2	At once I was in the spirit, and there in heaven	10
	4: 2	I was in the spirit, and there in heaven stood a throne	10
	4: 4	elders, dressed in white robes, with golden	10
	5: 1	Then I saw in the right hand of the one seated	11
	5: 3	no one in heaven or on earth or under the earth	10
	5:13	I heard every creature in heaven and on earth	10
	5:13	every creature…under the earth and in the sea	11
	5:13	every creature…and all that is in them, singing	10
	6: 5	Its rider held a pair of scales in his hand	10
	6: 6	I heard what seemed to be a voice in the midst	10
	6:15	everyone, slave and free, hid in the caves	7
	7: 9	in white, with palm branches in their hands.	10
	7:14	made them white in the blood of the Lamb.	10
	8: 1	silence in heaven for about half an hour.	10
	8: 9	a third of the living creatures in the sea died	10
	8:13	heard an eagle crying…as it flew in midheaven	10
	9: 6	in those days people will seek death but will not find it;	10
	9:10	in their tails is their power to harm people	10
	9:11	and in Greek he is called Apollyon.	10
	9:17	this was how I saw the horses in my vision:	10
	9:19	For the power of the horses is in their mouths	10
	9:19	power…is in their mouths and in their tails;	10
	10: 2	He held a little scroll open in his hand.	10
	10: 6	who created heaven and what is in it	10
	10: 6	who created…the earth and what is in it	10
	10: 6	who created…the sea and what is in it:	10
	10: 7	in the days when the seventh angel is to blow his trumpet	10
	10: 8	the scroll that is open in the hand of the angel	10
	10: 9	bitter…but sweet as honey in your mouth."	10
	10:10	it was sweet as honey in my mouth	10
	11: 8	their dead bodies will lie in the street	11
	11: 9	and refuse to let them be placed in a tomb;	7
	11:12	they went up to heaven in a cloud	10
	11:13	seven thousand people were killed in the earthquake	10
	11:15	and there were loud voices in heaven, saying	10
	11:19	Then God's temple in heaven was opened	10
	12: 1	A great portent appeared in heaven: a woman	10

Rev 12: 3	another portent appeared in heaven:	10
12: 7	And war broke out in heaven; Michael and his angels	10
12: 8	there was no longer any place for them in heaven.	10
12:10	Then I heard a loud voice in heaven, proclaiming	10
12:12	Rejoice then, you heavens and those who dwell in them!	10
13: 6	his dwelling, that is, those who dwell in heaven.	10
13: 8	name has not been written...in the book of life	10
14: 5	in their mouth no lie was found;	10
14: 6	Then I saw another angel flying in midheaven	10
14: 7	He said in a loud voice, "Fear God	10
14:13	Blessed are the dead who from now on die in the Lord."	10
14:14	crown on his head, and a sharp sickle in his hand!	10
14:17	another angel came out of the temple in heaven	10
15: 1	Then I saw another portent in heaven	10
15: 5	temple of the tent of witness in heaven was opened	10
16: 3	and every living thing in the sea died.	10
16:10	people gnawed their tongues in agony	8
17: 3	So he carried me away in the spirit	10
17: 4	holding in her hand a golden cup	10
17: 8	names have not been written in the book of life	11
18: 4	"Come out...so that you do not share in her plagues;	8
18: 6	mix a double draught for her in the cup she mixed.	10
18: 7	Since in her heart she says, 'I rule as a queen;	10
18: 8	therefore her plagues will come in a single day	10
18:10	they will stand far off, in fear of her torment	6
18:15	in fear of her torment, weeping and mourning	6
18:22	sound of harpists...will be heard in you no more;	10
18:22	an artisan...will be found in you no more;	10
18:22	the millstone will be heard in you no more;	10
18:23	and the light of a lamp will shine in you no more;	10
18:23	the voice...will be heard in you no more;	10
18:24	And in you was found the blood of prophets	10
19: 1	a great multitude in heaven, saying, "Hallelujah!	10
19:11	and in righteousness he judges and makes war.	10
19:17	Then I saw an angel standing in the sun	10
19:17	he called to all the birds that fly in midheaven	10
20: 1	holding in his hand the key to the bottomless pit	11
20: 6	holy are those who share in the first resurrection.	10
20:12	their works, as recorded in the books.	10
20:13	And the sea gave up the dead that were in it	10
20:13	Death and Hades gave up the dead that were in them	10
20:15	name was not found written in the book of life	10
21: 8	their place will be in the lake that burns	10
21:10	And in the spirit he carried me away	10
21:22	I saw no temple in the city	10
21:27	only those...written in the Lamb's book of life.	10
22: 3	the throne of God and of the Lamb will be in it	10
22:18	add to that person the plagues described in this book;	10
22:19	take away that person's share in the tree of life	4
22:19	take away that person's share...in the holy city	8
22:19	the holy city, which are described in this book.	10

in fact

1. Contextual: Not in Greek
2. γάρ, *gar*, 1142
3. ἰδού, *idou*, 2627
4. καί, *kai*, 2779
5. μέν, *men*, 3525
6. νυνί, *nyni*, 3815
7. οὖν, *oun*, 4036
8. ὥσπερ, *hōsper*, 6061

Lke 17:21	in fact, the kingdom of God is among you."	3
18:34	in fact, what he said was hidden from them	4
Jhn 14:12	in fact will do greater works than these	1
Act 24: 5	We have, in fact, found this man a pestilent fellow	2
25: 3	They were, in fact, planning an ambush to kill him	1
Rom 7:17	But in fact it is no longer I that do it, but sin	6
1Co 6: 7	In fact, to have lawsuits at all with one another	7
8: 5	as in fact there are many gods and many lords—	8
15:20	in fact Christ has been raised from the dead	6
Gal 4:24	One woman, in fact, is Hagar, from Mount Sinai	5
1Th 3: 4	In fact, when we were with you, we told you	2
4: 1	(as, in fact, you are doing), you should do so	4

inasmuch

1. ἐπί + ὅσος, *epi + hosos*, 2093 + 4012

Rom 11:13	Inasmuch then as I am an apostle to the Gentiles	1

inaugurate

1. ἐγκαινίζω, *enkainizō*, 1590

Heb 9:18	not even the first covenant was inaugurated without blood.	1

incense   *See also* altar of incense, offer incense

1. θυμίαμα, *thymiama*, 2592

Lke 1:11	at the right side of the altar of incense.	1
Rev 5: 8	and golden bowls full of incense	1
8: 3	a great quantity of incense to offer with the prayers	1
8: 4	the smoke of the incense...rose before God	1
18:13	cinnamon, spice, incense, myrrh, frankincense	1

incense offering

1. θυμίαμα, *thymiama*, 2592

Lke 1:10	Now at the time of the incense offering	1

incite

1. παροτρύνω, *parotrynō*, 4241
2. ταράσσω, *tarassō*, 5429

Act 13:50	the Jews incited the devout women of high standing	1
17:13	stir up and incite the crowds.	2

human inclination

1. ἄνθρωπος, *anthrōpos*, 476

1Co 3: 3	flesh, and behaving according to human inclinations?	1

include

1. ἐν, *en*, 1877
2. καί, *kai*, 2779
3. ὅς, *hos*, 4005
4. σύν, *syn*, 5250

Lke 7:29	who heard this, including the tax collectors,	2
23:49	all his acquaintances, including the women	2
Act 1:14	certain women, including Mary the mother of Jesus	2
17:12	including not a few Greek women and men	2
17:34	believers, including Dionysius the Areopagite	1
Rom 1: 6	including yourselves who are called to belong	1
9:24	including us whom he has called	2
2Co 1: 1	including all the saints throughout Achaia:	4
2Ti 1:15	including Phygelus and Hermogenes.	3

not include

1. ἐκτός, *ektos*, 1760

1Co 15:27	it is plain that this does not include the one	1

full inclusion

1. πλήρωμα, *plērōma*, 4445

Rom 11:12	how much more will their full inclusion mean!	1

income

1. κτάομαι, *ktaomai*, 3227

Lke 18:12	I give a tenth of all my income.'	1

incompetent

1. ἀνάξιος, *anaxios*, 396

1Co 6: 2	are you incompetent to try trivial cases?	1

increase

1. αὐξάνω, *auxanō*, 889
2. ἐγείρω, *egeirō*, 1586
3. ἐπαθροίζω, *epathroizō*, 2044
4. περισσεύω, *perisseuō*, 4355
5. πλεονάζω, *pleonazō*, 4429
6. πληθύνω, *plēthynō*, 4437
7. προκόπτω, *prokoptō*, 4621
8. προστίθημι, *prostithēmi*, 4707

Mat 24:12	because of the increase of lawlessness	6
Mrk 4: 8	brought forth grain, growing up and increasing	1
Lke 2:52	Jesus increased in wisdom and in years	7
11:29	When the crowds were increasing, he began to say	3
17: 5	The apostles said to the Lord, "Increase our faith!"	8
Jhn 3:30	He must increase, but I must decrease."	1
Act 6: 7	the number of the disciples increased greatly	6
7:17	our people in Egypt increased and multiplied	4
16: 5	increased in numbers daily.	4
Rom 5:20	where sin increased, grace abounded all the more	5
2Co 4:15	increase thanksgiving, to the glory of God.	1
9:10	increase the harvest of your righteousness.	1
10:15	our hope is that, as your faith increases	1
Php 1:17	not sincerely but intending to increase my suffering	2
1Th 3:12	may the Lord make you increase and abound in love	5

2Th	1: 3 the love of everyone…is increasing.	5
2Pe	1: 8 For if these things are yours and are increasing	5

increase in number

1. πληθύνω, *plēthynō, 4437*

Act	6: 1 when the disciples were increasing in number	1
	9:31 it increased in numbers.	1

more increasingly

1. μᾶλλον, *mallon, 3437*

Act	9:22 Saul became increasingly more powerful	1

incredible

1. ἄπιστος, *apistos, 603*

Act	26: 8 Why is it thought incredible by any of you	1

incur

1. ἔχω, *echō, 2400*
2. λαμβάνω, *lambanō, 3284*

Rom	13: 2 and those who resist will incur judgment.	2
1Ti	5:12 so they incur condemnation	1

indebted

1. ὀφείλω, *opheilō, 4053*

Lke	11: 4 we ourselves forgive everyone indebted	1

indeed   *See also* for indeed, listen indeed, look indeed, unless indeed

1. Contextual: Not in Greek
2. ἀληθῶς, *alēthōs, 242*
3. ἀλλά, *alla, 247*
4. γάρ, *gar, 1142*
5. γέ, *ge, 1145*
6. δέ, *de, 1254*
7. δή, *dē, 1314*
8. ἰδού, *idou, 2627*
9. καί, *kai, 2779*
10. μέν, *men, 3525*
11. μενοῦνγε, *menounge, 3529*
12. ὄντως, *ontōs, 3953*
13. ὅτι, *hoti, 4022*
14. οὖν, *oun, 4036*

Mat	6:32 these things; and indeed your heavenly Father knows	4
	12:29 Then indeed the house can be plundered.	9
	13:14 With them indeed is fulfilled the prophecy	9
	13:23 who indeed bears fruit and yields	7
	17:11 He replied, "Elijah is indeed coming	10
	20:23 He said to them, "You will indeed drink my cup	10
	26:41 the spirit indeed is willing	10
	28: 7 indeed he is going ahead of you to Galilee;	8
Mrk	3:27 then indeed the house can be plundered.	9
	8:37 Indeed, what can they give in return for their life?	4
	9:12 "Elijah is indeed coming first to restore all things.	10
	14:38 the spirit indeed is willing	10
Lke	1:66 For, indeed, the hand of the Lord was with him.	9
	13:30 Indeed, some are last who will be first	8
	18:25 Indeed, it is easier for a camel to go	4
	19:43 Indeed, the days will come upon you	13
	20:36 Indeed they cannot die anymore	4
	22:37 indeed what is written about me is being fulfilled."	4
	23:15 Indeed, he has done nothing to deserve death.	8
	23:41 we indeed have been condemned justly	10
	24:23 that they had indeed seen a vision of angels	9
	24:34 They were saying, "The Lord has risen indeed	12
Jhn	1:17 The law indeed was given through Moses;	13
	3:17 "Indeed, God did not send the Son into the world	4
	5:21 Indeed, just as the Father raises the dead	4
	6:14 they began to say, "This is indeed the prophet	2
	6:40 This is indeed the will of my Father	4
	8:36 Son makes you free, you will be free indeed.	12
	8:41 You are indeed doing what your father does."	1
	16: 2 Indeed, an hour is coming	3
	16:32 The hour is coming, indeed it has come	9
Act	2:15 Indeed, these are not drunk, as you suppose	4
	17:27 though indeed he is not far from each one of us.	5
	26: 9 Indeed, I…was convinced that I ought to do	14
	26:26 Indeed the king knows about these things	4
	27:24 indeed, God has granted safety to all those	8
Rom	2:25 Circumcision indeed is of value if you obey	10

	5: 7 Indeed, rarely will anyone die for a righteous	4
	5:13 sin was indeed in the world before the law	4
	8: 7 it does not submit to God's law—indeed it cannot	4
	8:34 Christ Jesus…who indeed intercedes for us.	9
	9:20 who indeed are you, a human being, to argue with God?	11
	9:25 As indeed he says in Hosea	9
	10:18 But I ask, have they not heard? Indeed they have;	11
	14:20 Everything is indeed clean	10
	15:27 and indeed they owe it to them;	9
1Co	4: 8 Indeed, wish that you had become kings,	5
	4:15 Indeed, in Christ Jesus I became your father	4
	8: 5 Indeed, even though there may be so-called gods	4
	9:10 It was indeed written for our sake	4
	9:15 Indeed, I would rather die than that	4
	11: 8 Indeed, man was not made from woman	4
	11:19 Indeed, there have to be factions among you	4
	12:14 Indeed, the body does not consist of one member	4
	15:41 indeed, star differs from star in glory.	4
2Co	1: 9 Indeed, we felt that we had received	3
	1:12 Indeed, this is our boast	4
	3:10 Indeed, what once had glory has lost its glory	4
	3:14 Indeed, to this very day, when they hear	4
	3:15 Indeed, to this very day whenever Moses is read	3
	5: 3 if indeed, when we have taken it off	5
	10: 3 Indeed, we live as human beings	4
	12:11 Indeed you should have been the ones commending me	4
Gal	3:21 righteousness would indeed come through the law.	12
Php	2:27 He was indeed so ill that he nearly died.	9
	4:10 indeed, you were concerned for me	9
	4:15 You Philippians indeed know	6
Col	2:23 These have indeed an appearance of wisdom	10
	3:15 to which indeed you were called in the one body.	9
1Th	3: 3 Indeed, you yourselves know that this	4
	4:10 indeed you do love all the brothers and sisters	4
	5:11 build up each other, as indeed you are doing.	9
2Ti	3:12 Indeed, all…will be persecuted.	6
Phm	1: 7 I have indeed received much joy and encouragement	4
	1:11 now he is indeed useful both to you and to me.	9
Heb	4: 2 For indeed the good news came to us just as to them;	9
	4:12 Indeed, the word of God is living and active	4
	9:22 Indeed…everything is purified with blood	9
	11: 2 Indeed, by faith our ancestors received approval.	4
	11:16 indeed, he has prepared a city for them.	4
	12:21 Indeed, so terrifying was the sight	9
	12:29 for indeed our God is a consuming fire.	9
Jas	5:11 Indeed we call blessed those who showed endurance.	8
1Pe	2: 3 if indeed you have tasted that the Lord is good.	1
2Pe	1:14 as indeed our Lord Jesus Christ has made clear to me.	9

independent

1. χωρίς, *chōris, 6006*

1Co	11:11 woman is not independent of man or man independent	1
	11:11 not independent of man or man independent of woman.	1

indescribable

1. ἀνεκδιήγητος, *anekdiēgētos, 442*
2. ἀνεκλάλητος, *aneklalētos, 443*

2Co	9:15 Thanks be to God for his indescribable gift!	1
1Pe	1: 8 rejoice with an indescribable and glorious joy	2

indestructible

1. ἀκατάλυτος, *akatalytos, 186*

Heb	7:16 through the power of an indestructible life.	1

indicate

1. δηλόω, *dēloō, 1317*
2. σημαίνω, *sēmainō, 4955*

Jhn	12:33 to indicate the kind of death he was to die.	2
	18:32 he indicated the kind of death he was to die.)	2
	21:19 to indicate the kind of death by which	2
Act	25:27 without indicating the charges against him."	2
Heb	9: 8 By this the Holy Spirit indicates	1
	12:27 indicates the removal of what is shaken	1
1Pe	1:11 that the Spirit of Christ within them indicated	1

indignant

1. ἀγανακτέω, *aganakteō, 24*
2. πυρόω, *pyroō, 4792*

Mrk	10:14 he was indignant and said to them	1
Lke	13:14 indignant because Jesus had cured	1

2Co 11:29 Who is made to stumble, and I am not indignant? 2

indignation
1. ἀγανάκτησις, *aganaktēsis, 25*
2Co 7:11 what indignation, what alarm, what longing 1

indispensable
1. ἀναγκαῖος, *anankaios, 338*
1Co 12:22 that seem to be weaker are indispensable 1

indistinct
1. ἄδηλος, *adēlos, 83*
1Co 14: 8 if the bugle gives an indistinct sound 1

individual *See* certain individual

individually
1. ἐκ + μέρος, *ek + meros, 1666 + 3538*
2. ἴδιος, *idios, 2625*
3. κατά + εἷς, *kata + heis, 2848 + 1651*
Rom 12: 5 and individually we are members one of another. 3
1Co 12:11 who allots to each one individually 2
    12:27 individually members of it. 1

indulge
1. πορεύομαι, *poreuomai, 4513*
2. πορεύομαι + κατά, *poreuomai + kata, 4513 + 2848*
3. πορεύομαι + ὀπίσω, *poreuomai + opisō, 4513 + 3958*
4. προσέχω, *prosechō, 4668*
1Ti 3: 8 not double-tongued, not indulging in much wine 4
2Pe 2:10 who indulge their flesh in depraved lust, 3
     3: 3 scoffing and indulging their own lusts 2
Jde 1:16 malcontents; they indulge their own lusts; 1
     1:18 scoffers, indulging their own ungodly lusts." 1

indulge in sexual immorality
1. ἐκπορνεύω, *ekporneuō, 1745*
2. πορνεύω, *porneuō, 4519*
1Co 10: 8 We must not indulge in sexual immorality as some 2
Jde 1: 7 indulged in sexual immorality and pursued unnatural lust 1

ineffective
1. οὐ + ἀργός, *ou + argos, 4024 + 734*
2Pe 1: 8 keep you from being ineffective and unfruitful 1

ineffectual
1. ἀνωφελής, *anōphelēs, 543*
Heb 7:18 because it was weak and ineffectual 1

infant *See also* nurse an infant
1. βρέφος, *brephos, 1100*
2. νηπιάζω, *nēpiazō, 3757*
3. νήπιος, *nēpios, 3758*
Mat 11:25 and have revealed them to infants; 3
    21:16 'Out of the mouths of infants and nursing babies 3
Lke 10:21 revealed them to infants; 3
    18:15 People were bringing even infants to him 1
Act 7:19 forced our ancestors to abandon their infants 1
1Co 3: 1 as people of the flesh, as infants in Christ. 3
    14:20 be infants in evil, but in thinking be adults. 2
Heb 5:13 being still an infant, is unskilled in the word 3
1Pe 2: 2 Like newborn infants, long for...spiritual milk 1

inferior
1. ἐλάσσων, *elassōn, 1781*
2. ὑστερέω, *hystereō, 5728*
Jhn 2:10 inferior wine after the guests have become drunk. 1
1Co 12:24 giving the greater honor to the inferior member 2
2Co 11: 5 I am not...inferior to these super-apostles. 2
    12:11 not at all inferior to these super-apostles 2
Heb 7: 7 the inferior is blessed by the superior. 1

infirmity
1. ἀσθένεια, *astheneia, 819*
Mat 8:17 "He took our infirmities and bore our diseases." 1
Lke 8: 2 been cured of evil spirits and infirmities: 1
Gal 4:13 You know that it was because of a physical infirmity 1

inflict
1. δίδωμι, *didōmi, 1443*
2. ἐπιφέρω, *epipherō, 2214*
Rom 3: 5 That God is unjust to inflict wrath on us? 2
2Th 1: 8 inflicting vengeance on those who do not know 1

inflict harm
1. ἀδικέω, *adikeō, 92*
Rev 9:19 their tails;...and with them they inflict harm. 1

inform
1. ἐμφανίζω, *emphanizō, 1872*
2. μηνύω, *mēnyō, 3606*
3. οἶδα, *oida, 3857*
Act 23:22 "Tell no one that you have informed me of this." 1
    23:30 When I was informed that...a plot 2
    24:22 was rather well informed about the Way 3
    25:15 the chief priests...informed me about him 1
1Co 10:28 out of consideration for the one who informed 2
Jde 1: 5 to remind you, though you are fully informed, 3

infuriate
1. θυμόω + λίαν, *thymoō + lian, 2597 + 3336*
Mat 2:16 been tricked by the wise men, he was infuriated 1

inhabit
1. κατοικέω, *katoikeō, 2997*
Act 17:26 to inhabit the whole earth 1

inhabitant
1. κατοικέω, *katoikeō, 2997*
Rev 3:10 to test the inhabitants of the earth. 1
     6:10 judge and avenge our blood on the inhabitants 1
     8:13 "Woe, woe, woe to the inhabitants of the earth 1
    11:10 the inhabitants of the earth will gloat 1
    11:10 a torment to the inhabitants of the earth. 1
    13: 8 all the inhabitants of the earth will worship it 1
    13:12 it makes the earth and its inhabitants worship 1
    13:14 it deceives the inhabitants of earth 1
    17: 2 the inhabitants of the earth have become drunk." 1
    17: 8 And the inhabitants of the earth...will be amazed 1

inherit
1. κληρονομέω, *klēronomeō, 3099*
2. κληρονόμος, *klēronomos, 3101*
Mat 5: 5 the meek, for they will inherit the earth. 1
    19:29 and will inherit eternal life. 1
    25:34 inherit the kingdom prepared for you 1
Mrk 10:17 what must I do to inherit eternal life?" 1
Lke 10:25 "what must I do to inherit eternal life?" 1
    18:18 what must I do to inherit eternal life?" 1
Rom 4:13 promise...that he would inherit the world 2
1Co 6: 9 wrongdoers will not inherit the kingdom of God? 1
     6:10 none of these will inherit the kingdom of God. 1
    15:50 flesh and blood cannot inherit the kingdom 1
    15:50 the perishable inherit the imperishable. 1
Gal 5:21 will not inherit the kingdom of God. 1
Heb 1: 4 the name he has inherited is more excellent 1
     1:14 for the sake of those who are to inherit salvation? 1
     6:12 imitators of those who...inherit the promises. 1
    12:17 when he wanted to inherit the blessing 1
1Pe 3: 9 that you might inherit a blessing. 1
Rev 21: 7 Those who conquer will inherit these things 1

inherit from ancestor
1. πατροπαράδοτος, *patroparadotos, 4261*
1Pe 1:18 futile ways inherited from your ancestors 1

inheritance *See also* give as an inheritance, obtain an inheritance
1. κληρονομία, *klēronomia, 3100*
2. κλῆρος, *klēros, 3102*
Mat 21:38 let us kill him and get his inheritance.' 1
Mrk 12: 7 the inheritance will be ours.' 1
Lke 20:14 so that the inheritance may be ours.' 1
Act 20:32 give you the inheritance 1
Gal 3:18 For if the inheritance comes from the law 1
Eph 1:14 this is the pledge of our inheritance 1

1:18 what are the riches of his glorious inheritance   1
5: 5 has any inheritance in the kingdom of Christ   1
Col   1:12 the inheritance of the saints in the light.   2
3:24 you will receive the inheritance as your reward;   1
Heb   9:15 may receive the promised eternal inheritance   1
11: 8 a place that he was to receive as an inheritance;   1
1Pe   1: 4 into an inheritance that is imperishable   1

family inheritance
1. κληρονομία, *klēronomia, 3100*
Lke 12:13 to divide the family inheritance with me."   1

share inheritance
1. κληρονομέω, *klēronomeō, 3099*
Gal   4:30 child of the slave will not share the inheritance   1

inhuman
1. ἄστοργος, *astorgos, 845*
2Ti   3: 3 inhuman, implacable, slanderers, profligates   1

iniquity *See also* greater and greater iniquity
1. ἀδίκημα, *adikēma, 93*
2. ἀδικία, *adikia, 94*
3. ἀνομία, *anomia, 490*
Rom   4: 7 those whose iniquities are forgiven   3
Tit   2:14 that he might redeem us from all iniquity   3
Heb   8:12 For I will be merciful toward their iniquities   2
Jas   3: 6 The tongue…among our members as a world of iniquity;   2
Rev 18: 5 and God has remembered her iniquities.   1

injure
1. λυπέω, *lypeō, 3382*
Rom 14:15 brother or sister is being injured by what you eat   1

injustice
1. ἀδικία, *adikia, 94*
Rom   3: 5 our injustice serves to confirm the justice of God   1
9:14 Is there injustice on God's part? By no means!   1

ink
1. μέλας, *melas, 3506*
2Co   3: 3 written not with ink but with the Spirit   1
2Jn   1:12 I would rather not use paper and ink;   1
3Jn   1:13 but I would rather not write with pen and ink;   1

inmost
1. ἔσω, *esō, 2276*
Rom   7:22 For I delight in the law of God in my inmost self   1

inn
1. κατάλυμα, *katalyma, 2906*
2. πανδοχεῖον, *pandocheion, 4106*
Lke   2: 7 because there was no place for them in the inn.   1
10:34 brought him to an inn, and took care of him.   2

inner *See also* inner *room*
1. ἔσω, *esō, 2276*
2. ἐσώτερος, *esōteros, 2278*
3. καρδία, *kardia, 2840*
4. κρυπτός, *kryptos, 3220*
Lke   2:35 inner thoughts of many will be revealed   3
9:47 Jesus, aware of their inner thoughts   3
2Co   4:16 our inner nature is being renewed day by day.   1
Eph   3:16 in your inner being with power through his Spirit   1
Heb   6:19 enters the inner shrine behind the curtain   2
1Pe   3: 4 let your adornment be the inner self   4

innermost
1. ἐσώτερος, *esōteros, 2278*
Act 16:24 he put them in the innermost cell   1

innkeeper
1. πανδοχεύς, *pandocheus, 4107*
Lke 10:35 gave them to the innkeeper, and said   1

innocent
1. ἀθῷος, *athōos, 127*
2. ἀκέραιος, *akeraios, 193*

3. δίκαιος, *dikaios, 1465*
4. καθαρός, *katharos, 2754*
Mat 10:16 so be wise as serpents and innocent as doves.   2
27: 4 "I have sinned by betraying innocent blood."   1
27:24 "I am innocent of this man's blood;   1
Lke 23:47 "Certainly this man was innocent."   3
Act 18: 6 "Your blood be on your own heads! I am innocent.   4
Php   2:15 so that you may be blameless and innocent   2
1Ti   1: 9 the law is laid down not for the innocent   3

innocent man
1. δίκαιος, *dikaios, 1465*
Mat 27:19 "Have nothing to do with that innocent man   1

innumerable
1. ἀναρίθμητος, *anarithmētos, 410*
2. μυριάς, *myrias, 3689*
Heb 11:12 the innumerable grains of sand by the seashore."   1
12:22 innumerable angels in festal gathering   2

inquire
1. ἐραυνάω, *eraunaō, 2236*
2. πυνθάνομαι, *pynthanomai, 4785*
Mat   2: 4 he inquired of them where the Messiah was to be   2
Act   4: 7 they inquired, "By what power   2
21:33 he inquired who he was and what he had done.   2
23:20 to inquire more thoroughly into his case   2
1Pe   1:11 inquiring about the person or time   1

inquiry *See* make inquiry

insane
1. μανία, *mania, 3444*
Act 26:24 Paul! Too much learning is driving you insane!"   1

insatiable
1. ἀκατάπαυστος, *akatapaustos, 188*
2Pe   2:14 eyes full of adultery, insatiable for sin.   1

inscribe
1. γράφω, *graphō, 1211*
2. ἐπιγράφω, *epigraphō, 2108*
Rev 19:12 he has a name inscribed that no one knows   1
19:16 and on his thigh he has a name inscribed   1
21:12 gates are inscribed the names of the twelve tribes   2

inscription
1. ἐπιγραφή, *epigraphē, 2107*
2. ἐπιγράφω, *epigraphō, 2108*
3. σφραγίς, *sphragis, 5382*
4. τίτλος, *titlos, 5518*
Mrk 15:26 The inscription of the charge against him read   1
Lke 23:38 There was also an inscription over him   1
Jhn 19:19 Pilate also had an inscription written   4
19:20 Many of the Jews read this inscription   4
Act 17:23 I found among them an altar with the inscription   2
2Ti   2:19 God's firm foundation stands, bearing this inscription: 3

inscrutable
1. ἀνεξιχνίαστος, *anexichniastos, 453*
Rom 11:33 and how inscrutable his ways!   1

inside *See also* go inside
1. ἐν + μέσος, *en + mesos, 1877 + 3545*
2. ἐντός, *entos, 1955*
3. ἔσω, *esō, 2276*
4. ἔσωθεν, *esōthen, 2277*
Mat 23:25 inside they are full of greed and self-indulgence.   4
23:26 First clean the inside of the cup   2
23:27 inside they are full of the bones of the dead   4
23:28 inside you are full of hypocrisy and lawlessness.   4
26:58 going inside, he sat with the guards   3
Lke 11:39 inside you are full of greed and wickedness.   4
11:40 one who made the outside make the inside also?   4
21:21 those inside the city must leave   1
Act   5:23 when we opened them, we found no one inside."   3
1Co   5:12 those who are inside that you are to judge?   3
Rev   4: 8 are full of eyes all around and inside   4

Rev 5: 1 a scroll written on the inside and on the back 4

insight

  1. αἴσθησις, *aisthēsis, 151*
  2. φρόνησις, *phronēsis, 5860*
Eph 1: 8 With all wisdom and insight 2
Php 1: 9 with knowledge and full insight 1

insincerity

  1. ὑπόκρισις, *hypokrisis, 5694*
1Pe 2: 1 Rid yourselves, therefore, of all…insincerity, 1

insist

  1. διαβεβαιόομαι, *diabebaioomai, 1331*
  2. διισχυρίζομαι, *diischyrizomai, 1462*
  3. ζητέω, *zēteō, 2426*
  4. θέλω, *thelō, 2527*
  5. μαρτύρομαι, *martyromai, 3458*
  6. παραγγέλλω, *parangellō, 4133*
Lke 22:59 still another kept insisting, "Surely 2
Act 12:15 she insisted that it was so 2
1Co 13: 5 It does not insist on its own way; 3
Eph 4:17 Now this I affirm and insist on in the Lord: 5
Col 2:18 insisting on self-abasement 4
1Ti 4:11 These are the things you must insist on and teach. 6
Tit 3: 8 I desire that you insist on these things 1

insistent

  1. ἐπισχύω, *epischyō, 2196*
Lke 23: 5 they were insistent and said, "He stirs up 1

insofar

  1. καθό, *katho, 2771*
1Pe 4:13 insofar as you are sharing Christ's sufferings 1

insolent

  1. ὑβριστής, *hybristēs, 5616*
Rom 1:30 slanderers, God-haters, insolent, haughty 1

inspire

  1. Contextual: Not in Greek
  2. ἐνεργέω, *energeō, 1919*
Col 1:29 the energy that he powerfully inspires within me. 2
1Th 1: 6 with joy inspired by the Holy Spirit 1

inspired by God

  1. θεόπνευστος, *theopneustos, 2535*
2Ti 3:16 All scripture is inspired by God 1

first installment

  1. ἀρραβών, *arrabōn, 775*
2Co 1:22 giving us his Spirit in our hearts as a first installment. 1

instant

  1. στιγμή + χρόνος, *stigmē + chronos, 5117 + 5989*
Lke 4: 5 in an instant all the kingdoms of the world. 1

instantly

  1. ἀπό + ὁ + ὥρα + ἐκεῖνος, *apo + ho + hōra + ekeinos, 608 + 3836 + 6052 + 1697*
Mat 9:22 And instantly the woman was made well. 1
 15:28 And her daughter was healed instantly. 1
 17:18 and the boy was cured instantly. 1

instead

  1. ἀλλά, *alla, 247*
  2. ἀντί, *anti, 505*
  3. δέ, *de, 1254*
  4. μᾶλλον, *mallon, 3437*
  5. οὐ, *ou, 4024*
  6. οὐχί, *ouchi, 4049*
  7. πλήν, *plēn, 4440*
  8. τοὐναντίον + μᾶλλον, *tounantion + mallon, 5539 + 3437*
Mrk 15:11 to have him release Barabbas for them instead. 4
Lke 11:11 will give a snake instead of a fish? 2
 12:31 Instead, strive for his kingdom 7
Jhn 19:34 Instead, one of the soldiers pierced his side 1
Act 7:39 instead, they pushed him aside 1

 12:14 instead of opening the gate, she ran in 5
 25:19 Instead they had certain points of disagreement 3
Rom 13:14 Instead, put on the Lord Jesus Christ 1
 14:13 resolve instead never to put a stumbling block 4
1Co 6: 1 instead of taking it before the saints? 6
2Co 2: 7 so now instead you should forgive and console 8
Eph 5: 4 instead, let there be thanksgiving. 4
 5:11 but instead expose them. 4
Jas 4:15 Instead you ought to say, "If the Lord wishes 2
1Pe 1:15 Instead, as he who called you is holy, be holy 1
2Jn 1:12 instead I hope to come to you and talk 1
3Jn 1:14 instead I hope to see you soon 3

instigate secretly

  1. ὑποβάλλω, *hypoballō, 5680*
Act 6:11 Then they secretly instigated some men to say 1

instinct

  1. φυσικός, *physikos, 5879*
  2. φυσικῶς, *physikōs, 5880*
2Pe 2:12 like irrational animals, mere creatures of instinct 1
Jde 1:10 like irrational animals, they know by instinct. 2

instinctively

  1. φύσις, *physis, 5882*
Rom 2:14 Gentiles…do instinctively what the law requires 1

institute

  1. τάσσω, *tassō, 5435*
Rom 13: 1 authorities that exist have been instituted by God. 1

institution

  1. κτίσις, *ktisis, 3232*
1Pe 2:13 accept the authority of every human institution 1

instruct

  1. διατάσσω, *diatassō, 1411*
  2. διδάσκω, *didaskō, 1438*
  3. κατηχέω, *katēcheō, 2994*
  4. μανθάνω, *manthanō, 3443*
  5. νουθεσία, *nouthesia, 3804*
  6. νουθετέω, *noutheteō, 3805*
  7. παιδεύω, *paideuō, 4084*
  8. παραγγέλλω, *parangellō, 4133*
  9. σοφίζω, *sophizō, 5054*
  10. συμβιβάζω, *symbibazō, 5204*
Mat 11: 1 Now when Jesus had finished instructing 1
Lke 1: 4 the things about which you have been instructed. 3
Jhn 8:28 speak these things as the Father instructed me. 2
Act 7:22 instructed in all the wisdom of the Egyptians 7
 18:25 He had been instructed in the Way of the Lord; 3
Rom 2:18 because you are instructed in the law 3
 15:14 and able to instruct one another. 6
1Co 2:16 so as to instruct him?" 10
 10:11 they were written down to instruct us 5
 14:19 in order to instruct others 3
1Ti 1: 3 so that you may instruct certain people 8
2Ti 3: 7 who are always being instructed 4
 3:15 that are able to instruct you for salvation 9

instruction *See also* give instruction

  1. Contextual: Not in Greek
  2. διαστέλλω, *diastellō, 1403*
  3. διατάσσω, *diatassō, 1411*
  4. διδασκαλία, *didaskalia, 1436*
  5. διδαχή, *didachē, 1439*
  6. ἐντολή, *entolē, 1953*
  7. νουθεσία, *nouthesia, 3804*
  8. παραγγελία, *parangelia, 4132*
  9. παραγγέλλω, *parangellō, 4133*
Mat 10: 5 Jesus sent out with the following instructions 9
Act 15:24 though with no instructions from us 2
 16:24 Following these instructions 8
 17:15 instructions to have Silas and Timothy join him 6
 23:31 according to their instructions, took Paul 3
Rom 15: 4 was written for our instruction 4
1Co 11:17 in the following instructions I do not commend 9
Eph 6: 4 in the discipline and instruction of the Lord. 7

Col	4:10	you have received instructions	6
1Th	4: 2	For you know what instructions we gave you	8
1Ti	1: 5	But the aim of such instruction is love	8
	1:18	I am giving you these instructions, Timothy,	8
	3:14	I am writing these instructions to you	1
	4: 6	put these instructions before the brothers and sisters	1
	5:21	I warn you to keep these instructions without prejudice	1
Heb	6: 2	instruction about baptisms	5

instructor
1. καθηγητής, *kathēgētēs, 2762*

Mat 23:10 Nor are you to be called instructors 1
  23:10 you have one instructor, the Messiah. 1

instrument
1. Contextual: Not in Greek
2. ὅπλον, *hoplon, 3960*
3. σκεῦος, *skeuos, 5007*

Act 9:15 he is an instrument whom I have chosen to bring my name 3
Rom 6:13 your members...as instruments of wickedness 2
  6:13 members to God as instruments of righteousness. 2
1Co 14: 7 with lifeless instruments that produce sound, 1

insult
1. ἀτιμάζω, *atimazō, 869*
2. βλασφημέω, *blasphēmeō, 1059*
3. λέγω + ῥακά, *legō + rhaka, 3306 + 4819*
4. λοιδορέω, *loidoreō, 3366*
5. ὀνειδίζω, *oneidizō, 3943*
6. ὀνειδισμός, *oneidismos, 3944*
7. ὑβρίζω, *hybrizō, 5614*
8. ὕβρις, *hybris, 5615*

Mat 5:22 and if you insult a brother or sister 3
Mrk 12: 4 this one they beat over the head and insulted 1
Lke 11:45 when you say these things, you insult us too." 7
  18:32 will be mocked and insulted and spat upon. 7
  20:11 that one also they beat and insulted 1
  22:65 They kept heaping many other insults on him 2
Act 23: 4 "Do you dare to insult God's high priest?" 4
Rom15: 3 "The insults of those who insult you 6
  15: 3 "The insults of those who insult you 5
2Co 12:10 I am content with weaknesses, insults, hardships 8

insurrection
1. ἀκαταστασία, *akatastasia, 189*
2. στάσις, *stasis, 5087*

Mrk 15: 7 who had committed murder during the insurrection. 2
Lke 21: 9 "When you hear of wars and insurrections 1
  23:19 for an insurrection that had taken place 2
  23:25 put in prison for insurrection and murder 2

integrity
1. ἀφθορία, *aphthoria, 917*

Tit 2: 7 in your teaching show integrity, gravity 1

intelligent
1. συνετός, *synetos, 5305*

Mat 11:25 these things from the wise and the intelligent 1
Lke 10:21 hidden...from the wise and the intelligent 1
Act 13: 7 proconsul, Sergius Paulus, an intelligent man, 1

intelligible
1. εὔσημος, *eusēmos, 2358*

1Co 14: 9 you utter speech that is not intelligible 1

intend
1. Contextual: Not in Greek
2. βούλομαι, *boulomai, 1089*
3. εἰς, *eis, 1650*
4. θέλω, *thelō, 2527*
5. μέλλω, *mellō, 3516*
6. οἴομαι, *oiomai, 3887*
7. προνοέω, *pronoeō, 4629*
8. προτίθημι, *protithēmi, 4729*
9. στέλλω, *stellō, 5097*

Mrk 6:48 He intended to pass them by. 4
Lke 10: 1 where he himself intended to go. 5
  14:28 For which of you, intending to build a tower 4

Jhn	7:35	"Where does this man intend to go	5
	7:35	Does he intend to go to the Dispersion	5
Act	12: 4	intending to bring him out to the people	2
	20: 7	intended to leave the next day	5
	20:13	intending to take Paul on board there;	5
	20:13	intending to go by land himself.	5
	25: 4	he himself intended to go there shortly.	5
Rom	1:13	that I have often intended to come to you	8
1Co	16: 5	for I intend to pass through Macedonia	1
2Co	8:20	We intend that no one should blame us	9
	8:21	for we intend to do what is right	7
Php	1:17	not sincerely but intending to increase my suffering	6
2Th	1: 5	intended to make you worthy of the kingdom	3
2Pe	1:12	I intend to keep on reminding you of these things	5

intent
1. ἐπίνοια, *epinoia, 2154*

Act 8:22 the intent of your heart may be forgiven you. 1

intention
1. διαλογισμός, *dialogismos, 1369*
2. διάνοια, *dianoia, 1379*
3. ἔννοια, *ennoia, 1936*

Mat 15:19 For out of the heart come evil intentions, murder 1
Mrk 7:21 from the human heart, that evil intentions come: 1
Heb 4:12 the thoughts and intentions of the heart. 3
1Pe 4: 1 arm yourselves also with the same intention 3
2Pe 3: 1 arouse your sincere intention by reminding 2

intently *See* look intently

intercede
1. ἐντυγχάνω, *entynchanō, 1961*
2. ὑπερεντυγχάνω, *hyperentynchanō, 5659*

Rom 8:26 that very Spirit intercedes with sighs 2
  8:27 because the Spirit intercedes for the saints 1
  8:34 Christ Jesus...who indeed intercedes for us. 1

intercession *See also* make intercession
1. ἔντευξις, *enteuxis, 1950*

1Ti 2: 1 supplications, prayers, intercessions 1

intercourse
1. χρῆσις, *chrēsis, 5979*

Rom 1:26 exchanged natural intercourse for unnatural 1
  1:27 the men...giving up natural intercourse with women 1

interest[1]
1. Contextual: Not in Greek
2. ὁ, *ho, 3836*

1Co 7:34 his interests are divided. 1
Php 2: 4 Let each of you look not to your own interests 2
  2: 4 but to the interests of others. 2
  2:21 All of them are seeking their own interests 2

interest[2]
1. τόκος, *tokos, 5527*

Mat 25:27 what was my own with interest. 1
Lke 19:23 I could have collected it with interest.' 1

interior
1. ἀνωτερικός, *anōterikos, 541*

Act 19: 1 Paul passed through the interior regions 1

interpret
1. Contextual: Not in Greek
2. διακρίνω, *diakrinō, 1359*
3. διερμηνευτής, *diermēneutēs, 1449*
4. διερμηνεύω, *diermēneuō, 1450*
5. δοκιμάζω, *dokimazō, 1507*
6. συγκρίνω, *synkrinō, 5173*

Mat 16: 3 You know how to interpret 2
  16: 3 but you cannot interpret the signs of the times. 1
Lke 12:56 You know how to interpret the appearance 5
  12:56 not know how to interpret the present time? 5
  24:27 he interpreted to them the things about himself 4
1Co 2:13 interpreting spiritual things to those 6
  12:30 Do all speak in tongues? Do all interpret? 4

1Co 14: 5 unless someone interprets, so that the church 4
14:13 should pray for the power to interpret. 4
14:27 each in turn; and let one interpret. 4
14:28 if there is no one to interpret 3

interpretation

1. ἐπίλυσις, *epilysis, 2146*
2. ἑρμηνεία, *hermēneia, 2255*

1Co 12:10 to another the interpretation of tongues. 2
14:26 a tongue, or an interpretation. 2
2Pe 1:20 a matter of one's own interpretation 1

interval

1. διάστημα, *diastēma, 1404*

Act 5: 7 After an interval of about three hours 1

intimidate

1. πτύρω, *ptyrō, 4769*
2. ταράσσω, *tarassō, 5429*

Php 1:28 in no way intimidated by your opponents. 1
1Pe 3:14 Do not fear what they fear, and do not be intimidated 2

into *See also* break into, bring into, bring into one's presence, burst into song, cast into, cast into hell, come into, come into being, fall into, get into, get into with, go into, graft into, put into, put into practice, sell into slavery, welcome into a home

1. εἰς, *eis, 1650*
2. ἐν, *en, 1877*
3. ἐπί, *epi, 2093*
4. ἔσω, *esō, 2276*

Mat 3:10 good fruit is cut down and thrown into the fire. 1
3:12 and will gather his wheat into the granary; 1
4: 1 led up by the Spirit into the wilderness 1
4:18 Andrew his brother, casting a net into the sea 1
5:25 to the guard, and you will be thrown into prison. 1
5:29 than for your whole body to be thrown into hell. 1
5:30 members than for your whole body to go into hell. 1
6: 6 whenever you pray, go into your room and shut the door 1
6:26 they neither sow nor reap nor gather into barns 1
6:30 alive today and tomorrow is thrown into the oven 1
7:19 tree…is cut down and thrown into the fire. 1
8:12 heirs…will be thrown into the outer darkness 1
8:23 when he got into the boat, his disciples followed 1
8:31 cast us out, send us into the herd of swine." 1
8:32 down the steep bank into the sea and perished 1
8:33 The swineherds ran off, and on going into the town 1
9: 1 And after getting into a boat he crossed 1
9:17 Neither is new wine put into old wineskins; 1
9:17 but new wine is put into fresh wineskins 1
9:38 to send out laborers into his harvest." 1
10:16 sending you out like sheep into the midst of wolves; 2
11: 7 "What did you go out into the wilderness to look at? 1
12:11 it falls into a pit on the sabbath; 1
13: 2 that he got into a boat and sat there 1
13:30 but gather the wheat into my barn.' " 1
13:36 Then he left the crowds and went into the house. 1
13:42 throw them into the furnace of fire 1
13:47 like a net that was thrown into the sea 1
13:48 sat down, and put the good into baskets 1
13:50 throw them into the furnace of fire 1
14:15 so that they may go into the villages 1
14:22 he made the disciples get into the boat 1
14:32 When they got into the boat, the wind ceased. 1
15:11 not what goes into the mouth that defiles a person 1
15:14 both will fall into a pit." 1
15:17 Do you not see that whatever goes into the mouth 1
15:17 the stomach, and goes out into the sewer? 1
15:39 sending away the crowds, he got into the boat 1
16:13 Now when Jesus came into the district 1
17:15 he often falls into the fire 1
17:15 and often into the water. 1
17:22 Son of Man is going to be betrayed into human hands 1
18: 8 to be thrown into the eternal fire. 1
18: 9 have two eyes and to be thrown into the hell of fire. 1
18:30 then he went and threw him into prison 1
19:17 to enter into life, keep the commandments." 1
20: 2 he sent them into his vineyard. 1
20: 4 he said to them, 'You also go into the vineyard 1

20: 7 He said to them, 'You also go into the vineyard.' 1
21: 2 to them, "Go into the village ahead of you 1
21:21 'Be lifted up and thrown into the sea,' 1
21:31 going into the kingdom of God ahead of you. 1
22: 9 Go therefore into the main streets, and invite 3
22:10 Those slaves went out into the streets 1
22:13 and throw him into the outer darkness 1
25:10 went with him into the wedding banquet; 1
25:21 enter into the joy of your master.' 1
25:23 enter into the joy of your master.' 1
25:30 throw him into the outer darkness 1
25:41 accursed, depart from me into the eternal fire 1
25:46 these will go away into eternal punishment 1
25:46 but the righteous into eternal life." 1
26:18 "Go into the city to a certain man, and say 1
26:23 who has dipped his hand into the bowl with me 2
26:41 that you may not come into the time of trial; 1
26:45 Son of Man is betrayed into the hands of sinners. 1
26:52 "Put your sword back into its place; 1
27: 6 "It is not lawful to put them into the treasury 1
27:27 Then the soldiers of the governor took Jesus 1
28:11 some of the guard went into the city 1
Mrk 1:12 immediately drove him out into the wilderness. 1
1:16 Simon and…Andrew casting a net into the sea 2
1:45 Jesus could no longer go into a town openly 1
2:22 no one puts new wine into old wineskins; 1
2:22 one puts new wine into fresh wineskins." 1
4: 1 he got into a boat on the sea and sat there 1
4: 8 Other seed fell into good soil 1
4:37 the waves beat into the boat 1
5:12 "Send us into the swine; let us enter them." 1
5:13 rushed down the steep bank into the sea 1
5:18 As he was getting into the boat 1
6:36 so that they may go into the surrounding country 1
6:45 he made his disciples get into the boat 1
6:51 got into the boat with them and the wind ceased. 1
6:56 wherever he went, into villages or cities 1
7:18 whatever goes into a person from outside 1
7:19 the stomach, and goes out into the sewer?" 1
7:33 put his fingers into his ears, and he spat 1
8:10 he got into the boat with his disciples 1
8:13 he left them, and getting into the boat again 1
8:26 "Do not even go into the village." 1
9:22 often cast him into the fire and into the water 1
9:22 often cast him into the fire and into the water 1
9:31 betrayed into human hands 1
9:42 you were thrown into the sea. 1
9:45 have two feet and to be thrown into hell. 1
9:47 have two eyes and to be thrown into hell 1
11: 2 said to them, "Go into the village ahead of you 1
11:11 he entered Jerusalem and went into the temple; 1
11:23 'Be taken up and thrown into the sea,' 1
12:41 the crowd putting money into the treasury. 1
14:13 "Go into the city 1
14:20 one who is dipping bread into the bowl with me. 1
14:38 pray that you may not come into the time of trial; 1
14:41 Son of Man is betrayed into the hands of sinners. 1
14:54 right into the courtyard of the high priest; 1
14:68 he went out into the forecourt. 1
15:16 soldiers led him into the courtyard of the palace 4
16:12 ⟦as they were walking into the country.⟧ 1
16:15 ⟦"Go into all the world and proclaim the good news⟧ 1
16:19 ⟦Jesus…was taken up into heaven⟧ 1
Lke 1:79 to guide our feet into the way of peace." 1
2:15 When the angels had left them and gone into heaven 1
2:27 Guided by the Spirit, Simeon came into the temple; 1
3: 3 He went into all the region around the Jordan 1
3: 9 tree…is cut down and thrown into the fire." 1
3:17 to gather the wheat into his granary; 1
4:42 he departed and went into a deserted place. 1
5: 3 into one of the boats, the one belonging to Simon 1
5: 4 he said to Simon, "Put out into the deep water 1
5:19 into the middle of the crowd in front of Jesus. 1
5:37 no one puts new wine into old wineskins; 1
5:38 new wine must be put into fresh wineskins. 1
6:38 good measure…will be put into your lap; 1
6:39 Will not both fall into a pit? 1
7:24 did you go out into the wilderness to look at? 1
7:36 he went into the Pharisee's house 1
8: 8 Some fell into good soil, and when it grew 1
8:22 One day he got into a boat with his disciples 1

	8:29	be driven by the demon into the wilds.)	1
	8:31	not to order them to go back into the abyss.	1
	8:33	herd rushed down the steep bank into the lake	1
	8:37	So he got into the boat and returned.	1
	9:12	so that they may go into the surrounding villages	1
	9:44	"Let these words sink into your ears:	1
	9:44	to be betrayed into human hands."	1
	10: 2	to send out laborers into his harvest.	1
	10: 3	like lambs into the midst of wolves.	2
	10:10	go out into its streets and say	1
	10:36	who fell into the hands of the robbers?"	1
	12: 5	who…has authority to cast into hell.	1
	12:28	tomorrow is thrown into the oven	1
	14: 5	a child or an ox that has fallen into a well	1
	14:21	'Go out at once into the streets and lanes	1
	14:23	'Go out into the roads and lanes	1
	16: 4	people may welcome me into their homes.'	1
	16: 9	welcome you into the eternal homes.	1
	16:28	will not also come into this place of torment.'	1
	17: 2	if…you were thrown into the sea	1
	19:23	Why then did you not put my money into the bank?	3
	19:30	saying, "Go into the village ahead	1
	21: 1	rich people putting their gifts into the treasury;	1
	22: 3	Then Satan entered into Judas called Iscariot	1
	22:10	follow him into the house he enters	1
	22:40	"Pray that you may not come into the time of trial."	1
	22:46	pray that you may not come into the time of trial."	1
	22:54	bringing him into the high priest's house.	1
	23:42	remember me when you come into your kingdom."	1
	23:46	"Father, into your hands I commend my spirit."	1
	24:26	suffer these things and then enter into his glory?"	1
	24:51	and was carried up into heaven.	1
Jhn	1: 9	The true light…was coming into the world.	1
	3: 4	Can one enter a second time into the mother's womb	1
	3:13	No one has ascended into heaven except the one	1
	3:17	"Indeed, God did not send the Son into the world	1
	3:19	that the light has come into the world	1
	3:22	Jesus…went into the Judean countryside,	1
	3:24	John…had not yet been thrown into prison.	1
	4:38	and you have entered into their labor."	1
	5: 7	I have no one to put me into the pool	1
	6:14	the prophet who is to come into the world."	1
	6:17	got into a boat	1
	6:21	they wanted to take him into the boat	1
	6:22	Jesus had not got into the boat with his disciples	1
	6:24	they…got into the boats and went to Capernaum	1
	7:14	Jesus went up into the temple and began to teach.	1
	9:39	Jesus said, "I came into this world for judgment	1
	10:36	the Father has sanctified and sent into the world	1
	11:27	the Son of God, the one coming into the world."	1
	11:52	to gather into one the dispersed children of God.	1
	12:24	a grain of wheat falls into the earth and dies	1
	12:46	I have come as light into the world	1
	13: 2	The devil had already put it into the heart	1
	13: 3	the Father had given all things into his hands	1
	13: 5	Then he poured water into a basin	1
	13:27	the piece of bread, Satan entered into him.	1
	15: 6	branches are gathered, thrown into the fire	1
	16:13	he will guide you into all the truth;	2
	16:20	your pain will turn into joy.	1
	16:21	having brought a human being into the world.	1
	16:28	have come into the world;	1
	17:18	As you have sent me into the world	1
	17:18	so I have sent them into the world.	1
	18:11	"Put your sword back into its sheath.	1
	18:15	he went with Jesus into the courtyard	1
	18:37	for this I came into the world	1
	19:27	the disciple took her into his own home.	1
	20: 6	Simon Peter came…and went into the tomb.	1
	20:11	she bent over to look into the tomb;	1
	21: 3	They went out and got into the boat	1
	21: 7	and jumped into the sea.	1
Act	1:11	who has been taken up from you into heaven	1
	1:11	in the same way as you saw him go into heaven."	1
	2:34	David did not ascend into the heavens	1
	3: 3	saw Peter and John about to go into the temple	1
	5:15	they even carried out the sick into the streets	1
	7: 9	"The patriarchs…sold him into Egypt;	1
	7:23	it came into his heart to visit his relatives	3
	7:55	filled with the Holy Spirit, he gazed into heaven	1
	8:38	Philip and the eunuch, went down into the water	1

	9: 8	brought him into Damascus.	1
	10:10	while it was being prepared, he fell into a trance.	3
	12:10	came before the iron gate leading into the city.	1
	13:14	on the sabbath day they went into the synagogue	1
	14: 1	Paul and Barnabas went into the Jewish synagogue	1
	14:14	and rushed out into the crowd, shouting	1
	14:20	he got up and went into the city.	1
	16: 7	they attempted to go into Bithynia	1
	16:19	and dragged them into the marketplace	1
	16:23	they threw them into prison	1
	16:34	He brought them up into the house	1
	16:37	have thrown us into prison;	1
	18:19	but first he himself went into the synagogue	1
	19: 3	he said, "Into what then were you baptized?"	1
	19: 3	They answered, "Into John's baptism."	1
	19:27	this trade of ours may come into disrepute	1
	19:30	Paul wished to go into the crowd	1
	19:31	urging him not to venture into the theater.	1
	21: 8	we went into the house of Philip the evangelist	1
	21:28	he has actually brought Greeks into the temple	1
	21:29	Paul had brought him into the temple.	1
	21:34	he ordered him to be brought into the barracks.	1
	21:37	Paul was about to be brought into the barracks	1
	21:38	led…out into the wilderness?"	1
	22:17	praying in the temple, I fell into a trance	2
	22:23	their cloaks, and tossing dust into the air	1
	22:24	directed that he was to be brought into the barracks	1
	23:10	bring him into the barracks.	1
	27:30	had lowered the boat into the sea	1
	27:38	throwing the wheat into the sea.	1
	28: 5	He, however, shook off the creature into the fire	1
	28:16	When we came into Rome	1
Rom	5: 5	God's love has been poured into our hearts	2
	5:12	just as sin came into the world through one man	1
	6: 3	who have been baptized into Christ Jesus	1
	6: 3	into Christ Jesus were baptized into his death?	1
	6: 4	we have been buried with him by baptism into death	1
	8:15	a spirit of slavery to fall back into fear	1
	10: 6	say in your heart, 'Who will ascend into heaven?' "	1
	10: 7	"or 'Who will descend into the abyss?' "	1
	11:24	grafted…into a cultivated olive tree	1
1Co	1: 9	called into the fellowship of his Son, Jesus	1
	10: 2	all were baptized into Moses in the cloud	1
	12:13	we were all baptized into one body	1
	14: 9	For you will be speaking into the air.	1
2Co	7: 5	For even when we came into Macedonia	1
	12: 4	was caught up into Paradise and heard things	1
Gal	1:17	I went away at once into Arabia	1
	1:21	I went into the regions of Syria and Cilicia	1
	3:27	As many of you as were baptized into Christ	1
	4: 6	Spirit…into our hearts, crying, "Abba! Father!"	1
Eph	2:21	grows into a holy temple in the Lord;	1
	2:22	built…spiritually into a dwelling place for God.	1
	4: 9	descended into the lower parts of the earth?	1
	4:15	grow up in every way into him who is the head	1
Col	1:13	transferred us into the kingdom of his beloved Son	1
1Th	2:12	who calls you into his own kingdom and glory.	1
1Ti	1:15	Jesus came into the world to save sinners	1
	3: 6	fall into the condemnation of the devil.	1
	3: 7	fall into disgrace and the snare of the devil.	1
	6: 7	for we brought nothing into the world	1
	6: 9	those who want to be rich fall into temptation	1
	6: 9	plunge people into ruin and destruction.	1
2Ti	2:16	it will lead people into more and more impiety	3
	3: 6	those who make their way into households	1
Heb	1: 6	when he brings the firstborn into the world	1
	9: 6	the priests go continually into the first tent	1
	9: 7	only the high priest goes into the second	1
	9:12	he entered once for all into the Holy Place	1
	9:24	but he entered into heaven itself	1
	10: 5	when Christ came into the world, he said	1
	10:31	to fall into the hands of the living God.	1
	13:11	whose blood is brought into the sanctuary	1
Jas	1:25	those who look into the perfect law	1
	2: 2	a person…comes into your assembly	1
	2: 6	Is it not they who drag you into court?	1
	3: 3	If we put bits into the mouths of horses	1
	4: 9	Let your laughter be turned into mourning	1
	4: 9	be turned into mourning and your joy into dejection.	1
1Pe	1: 3	given us a new birth into a living hope	1
	1: 4	into an inheritance that is imperishable	1

1Pe 1:12 things into which angels long to look!   1
       2: 2 so that by it you may grow into salvation   1
       2: 9 called…out of darkness into his marvelous light.   1
       3:22 who has gone into heaven   1
2Pe 1:11 entry into the eternal kingdom of our Lord   1
1Jn 4: 1 many false prophets have gone out into the world.   1
       4: 9 God sent his only Son into the world   1
2Jn 1: 7 Many deceivers have gone out into the world   1
       1:10 Do not receive into the house or welcome   1
Jde 1: 4 pervert the grace of our God into licentiousness   1
Rev 2:10 devil is about to throw some of you into prison   1
       2:22 I am throwing into great distress   1
       5: 6 seven spirits of God sent out into all the earth.   1
       8: 8 something like…was thrown into the sea.   1
       9: 9 noise of many chariots…rushing into battle.   1
       11: 6 authority over the waters to turn them into blood   1
       12: 6 and the woman fled into the wilderness   1
       12:14 could fly from the serpent into the wilderness   1
       13:10 If…to be taken captive, into captivity you go;   1
       14:10 poured unmixed into the cup of his anger   2
       14:19 the angel…threw it into the great wine press   1
       16: 3 The second angel poured his bowl into the sea   1
       16: 4 The third angel poured his bowl into the rivers   1
       16:17 The seventh angel poured his bowl into the air   3
       16:19 The great city was split into three parts   1
       17: 3 So he carried me away…into a wilderness   1
       17:17 For God has put it into their hearts   1
       18:21 took up a stone…and threw it into the sea   1
       19:20 These two were thrown alive into the lake of fire   1
       20: 3 and threw him into the pit, and locked   1
       20:10 the devil…was thrown into the lake of fire   1
       20:14 Death and Hades were thrown into the lake of fire.   1
       20:15 was thrown into the lake of fire.   1
       21:24 kings of the earth will bring their glory into it   1
       21:26 bring into it the glory…of the nations.   1

introduction
    1. ἐπεισαγωγή, *epeisagōgē, 2081*
Heb 7:19 on the other hand, the introduction of a better hope   1

intruder
    1. ἄνθρωπος, *anthrōpos, 476*
Jde   1: 4 For certain intruders have stolen in among you   1

invalid
    1. ἀσθενέω, *astheneō, 820*
Jhn   5: 3 In these lay many invalids—blind, lame   1

inventor
    1. ἐφευρετής, *epheuretēs, 2388*
Rom 1:30 haughty, boastful, inventors of evil   1

invest
    1. βάλλω, *ballō, 965*
Mat 25:27 Then you ought to have invested my money   1

investigate
    1. ζήτησις, *zētēsis, 2428*
    2. παρακολουθέω, *parakoloutheō, 4158*
Lke   1: 3 after investigating everything carefully   2
Act 25:20 was at a loss how to investigate these questions   1

invisible
    1. ἀόρατος, *aoratos, 548*
Rom 1:20 his eternal power and divine nature, invisible   1
Col   1:15 He is the image of the invisible God   1
       1:16 were created, things visible and invisible   1
1Ti   1:17 the King of the ages, immortal, invisible, the only God   1
Heb 11:27 persevered as though he saw him who is invisible.   1

invite
    1. εἰσκαλέομαι, *eiskaleomai, 1657*
    2. ἐρωτάω, *erōtaō, 2263*
    3. καλέω, *kaleō, 2813*
    4. μετακαλέω, *metakaleō, 3559*
    5. παρακαλέω, *parakaleō, 4151*
    6. φωνέω, *phōneō, 5888*
Mat 22: 3 sent his slaves to call those who had been invited   3
       22: 4 'Tell those who have been invited: 3
       22: 8 but those invited were not worthy.   3

       22: 9 invite everyone you find to the wedding banquet.'   3
Lke 7:39 Now when the Pharisee who had invited him saw it   3
       11:37 a Pharisee invited him to dine with him;   2
       14: 8 you are invited by someone to a wedding banquet   3
       14: 8 more distinguished than you has been invited   3
       14: 9 who invited both of you may come and say to you   3
       14:10 when you are invited   3
       14:12 He said also to the one who had invited him   3
       14:12 do not invite your friends or your brothers   6
       14:13 when you give a banquet, invite the poor,   3
       14:16 "Someone gave a great dinner and invited many.   3
       14:17 to say to those who had been invited, 'Come;   3
       14:24 none of those who were invited will taste   3
Jhn   2: 2 Jesus…had also been invited to the wedding.   3
Act   7:14 Joseph sent and invited his father Jacob   4
       8:31 he invited Philip to get in and sit beside him.   5
       10:23 So Peter invited them in and gave them lodging.   1
       10:48 Then they invited him to stay for several days.   2
       28:14 were invited to stay with them for seven days.   5
1Co 10:27 If an unbeliever invites you to a meal   3
Rev 19: 9 those who are invited to the marriage supper   3

invite in return
    1. ἀντικαλέω, *antikaleō, 511*
Lke 14:12 in case they may invite you in return   1

invoke
    1. ἐπικαλέω, *epikaleō, 2126*
Act   9:14 to bind all who invoke your name."   1
       9:21 among those who invoked this name?   1
Jas   2: 7 the excellent name that was invoked over you?   1
1Pe   1:17 If you invoke as Father the one who judges all   1

invoke a blessing
    1. εὐλογέω, *eulogeō, 2328*
Heb 11:20 invoked blessings for the future on Jacob and Esau.   1

involve
    1. Contextual: Not in Greek
    2. εἰμί, *eimi, 1639*
Gal   3:20 Now a mediator involves more than one   2
Heb   9:16 Where a will is involved   1

inwardly
    1. ἐν, *en, 1877*
    2. ἐν + ὁ + κρυπτός, *en + ho + kryptos, 1877 + 3836 + 3220*
    3. ἔσωθεν, *esōthen, 2277*
Mat   7:15 in sheep's clothing but inwardly are ravenous   3
Rom   2:29 person is a Jew who is one inwardly   2
       8:23 groan inwardly while we wait for adoption   1

iron *See also* sear with a hot iron
    1. σίδηρος, *sidēros, 4970*
    2. σιδηροῦς, *sidērous, 4971*
Act 12:10 came before the iron gate leading into the city.   2
Rev   2:27 to rule them with an iron rod   2
       9: 9 they had scales like iron breastplates   2
       12: 5 who is to rule all the nations with a rod of iron   2
       18:12 articles of costly wood, bronze, iron, and marble   1
       19:15 and he will rule them with a rod of iron;   2

irrational
    1. ἄλογος, *alogos, 263*
2Pe   2:12 like irrational animals, mere creatures of instinct   1
Jde   1:10 like irrational animals, they know by instinct.   1

irreproachable
    1. ἀνέγκλητος, *anenklētos, 441*
Col   1:22 blameless and irreproachable before him   1

irrevocable
    1. ἀμεταμέλητος, *ametamelētos, 294*
Rom 11:29 the gifts and the calling of God are irrevocable.   1

irritable
    1. παροξύνω, *paroxynō, 4236*
1Co 13: 5 it is not irritable or resentful;   1

Isaac

1. Ἰσαάκ, *Isaak, 2693*

Mat	1: 2	Abraham was the father of Isaac	1
	1: 2	and Isaac the father of Jacob	1
	8:11	eat with Abraham and Isaac and Jacob	1
	22:32	'I am the God of Abraham, the God of Isaac	1
Mrk	12:26	the God of Isaac, and the God of Jacob'?	1
Lke	3:34	son of Jacob, son of Isaac	1
	13:28	when you see Abraham and Isaac and Jacob	1
	20:37	the God of Isaac, and the God of Jacob.	1
Act	3:13	The God of Abraham, the God of Isaac, and the God	1
	7: 8	so Abraham became the father of Isaac	1
	7: 8	Isaac became the father of Jacob	1
	7:32	the God of Abraham, Isaac, and Jacob.'	1
Rom	9: 7	through Isaac that descendants shall be named for you."	1
	9:10	conceived...by one husband, our ancestor Isaac.	1
Gal	4:28	friends, are children of the promise, like Isaac.	1
Heb	11: 9	living in tents, as did Isaac and Jacob	1
	11:17	Abraham, when put to the test, offered up Isaac.	1
	11:18	through Isaac that descendants shall be named	1
	11:20	By faith Isaac invoked blessings for the future	1
Jas	2:21	when he offered his son Isaac on the altar?	1

Isaiah

1. Ἠσαΐας, *Ēsaias, 2480*

Mat	3: 3	of whom the prophet Isaiah spoke when he said	1
	4:14	spoken through the prophet Isaiah might be fulfilled:	1
	8:17	what had been spoken through the prophet Isaiah	1
	12:17	what had been spoken through the prophet Isaiah:	1
	13:14	indeed is fulfilled the prophecy of Isaiah	1
	15: 7	You hypocrites! Isaiah prophesied rightly about you	1
Mrk	1: 2	As it is written in the prophet Isaiah	1
	7: 6	"Isaiah prophesied rightly about you hypocrites	1
Lke	3: 4	the book of the words of the prophet Isaiah	1
	4:17	the scroll of the prophet Isaiah was given to him.	1
Jhn	1:23	as the prophet Isaiah said.	1
	12:38	to fulfill the word spoken by the prophet Isaiah:	1
	12:39	because Isaiah also said	1
	12:41	Isaiah said this because he saw his glory	1
Act	8:28	he was reading the prophet Isaiah.	1
	8:30	Philip...heard him reading the prophet Isaiah.	1
	28:25	saying...through the prophet Isaiah	1
Rom	9:27	And Isaiah cries out concerning Israel	1
	9:29	as Isaiah predicted, "If the Lord of hosts had	1
	10:16	for Isaiah says, "Lord, who has believed	1
	10:20	Isaiah is so bold as to say, "I have been found	1
	15:12	again Isaiah says, "The root of Jesse shall come	1

Iscariot

1. Ἰσκαριώτης, *Iskariōtēs, 2697*

Mat	10: 4	Simon the Cananaean, and Judas Iscariot	1
	26:14	one of the twelve, who was called Judas Iscariot	1
Mrk	3:19	Judas Iscariot, who betrayed him.	1
	14:10	Then Judas Iscariot, who was one of the twelve	1
Lke	6:16	Judas Iscariot, who became a traitor.	1
	22: 3	Then Satan entered into Judas called Iscariot	1
Jhn	6:71	He was speaking of Judas son of Simon Iscariot	1
	12: 4	Judas Iscariot, one of his disciples	1
	13: 2	the heart of Judas son of Simon Iscariot	1
	13:26	he gave it to Judas son of Simon Iscariot.	1
	14:22	Judas (not Iscariot) said to him, "Lord,	1

island

1. νῆσος, *nēsos, 3762*

Act	13: 6	had gone through the whole island as far as Paphos	1
	27:26	we will have to run aground on some island."	1
	28: 1	then learned that the island was called Malta.	1
	28: 7	lands belonging to the leading man of the island	1
	28: 9	the people on the island who had diseases	1
	28:11	on a ship that had wintered at the island	1
Rev	1: 9	I, John...was on the island called Patmos	1
	6:14	every mountain and island was removed	1
	16:20	And every island fled away	1

small island

1. νησίον, *nēsion, 3761*

| Act | 27:16 | a small island called Cauda | 1 |

Israel

1. Contextual: Not in Greek

2. αὐτός, *autos, 899*

3. Ἰσραήλ, *Israēl, 2702*

Mat	2: 6	a ruler who is to shepherd my people Israel.' "	3
	2:20	his mother, and go to the land of Israel, for those	3
	2:21	his mother, and went to the land of Israel.	3
	8:10	in no one in Israel have I found such faith.	3
	9:33	"Never has anything like this been seen in Israel."	3
	10: 6	to the lost sheep of the house of Israel	3
	10:23	gone through all the towns of Israel	3
	15:24	only to the lost sheep of the house of Israel."	3
	15:31	And they praised the God of Israel.	3
	19:28	judging the twelve tribes of Israel.	3
	27: 9	some of the people of Israel had set a price	3
	27:42	He is the King of Israel;	3
Mrk	12:29	Jesus answered, "The first is, 'Hear, O Israel:	3
	15:32	Let the Messiah, the King of Israel, come down	3
Lke	1:16	turn many of the people of Israel to the Lord	3
	1:54	He has helped his servant Israel	3
	1:68	"Blessed be the Lord God of Israel	3
	1:80	until the day he appeared publicly to Israel.	3
	2:25	looking forward to the consolation of Israel	3
	2:32	for glory to your people Israel."	3
	2:34	the falling and the rising of many in Israel	3
	4:25	were many widows in Israel in the time of Elijah	3
	4:27	There were also many lepers in Israel	3
	7: 9	not even in Israel have I found such faith."	3
	22:30	judging the twelve tribes of Israel.	3
	24:21	had hoped that he was the one to redeem Israel.	3
Jhn	1:31	that he might be revealed to Israel."	3
	1:49	the Son of God! You are the King of Israel!"	3
	3:10	Jesus answered him, "Are you a teacher of Israel	3
	12:13	the King of Israel!"	3
Act	1: 6	the time when you will restore the kingdom to Israel?"	3
	2:36	Therefore let the entire house of Israel know	3
	4:10	known...to all the people of Israel	3
	4:27	with the Gentiles and the peoples of Israel	3
	5:21	and the whole body of the elders of Israel	3
	5:31	that he might give repentance to Israel	3
	7:42	forty years in the wilderness, O house of Israel?	3
	9:15	Gentiles and kings and before the people of Israel;	3
	10:36	You know the message he sent to the people of Israel	3
	13:17	The God of this people Israel chose our ancestors	3
	13:23	brought to Israel a Savior, Jesus, as he promised;	3
	13:24	already proclaimed...to all the people of Israel.	3
	28:20	since it is for the sake of the hope of Israel	3
Rom	9: 6	Israelites truly belong to Israel	3
	9:27	And Isaiah cries out concerning Israel	3
	9:27	"Though the number of the children of Israel were	3
	9:31	but Israel, who did strive for the righteousness	3
	10:19	Again I ask, did Israel not understand?	3
	10:21	of Israel he says, "All day long I have held out	3
	11: 2	of Elijah, how he pleads with God against Israel?	3
	11: 7	Israel failed to obtain what it was seeking.	3
	11:11	so as to make Israel jealous.	2
	11:23	And even those of Israel, if they do not persist	1
	11:25	a hardening has come upon part of Israel	3
	11:26	so all Israel will be saved; as it is written	3
1Co	10:18	Consider the people of Israel;	3
2Co	3: 7	people of Israel could not gaze at Moses' face	3
	3:13	to keep the people of Israel from gazing	3
Gal	6:16	upon the Israel of God.	3
Eph	2:12	aliens from the commonwealth of Israel	3
Php	3: 5	a member of the people of Israel,	3
Heb	8: 8	a new covenant with the house of Israel	3
	8:10	with the house of Israel after those days	3
	11:28	the destroyer...would not touch the firstborn	1
Rev	2:14	put a stumbling block before the people of Israel	3
	7: 4	sealed out of every tribe of the people of Israel:	3

Israelite

1. ἐκ + Ἰσραήλ, *ek + Israēl, 1666 + 2702*

2. Ἰσραηλίτης, *Israēlitēs, 2703*

3. υἱός + Ἰσραήλ, *huios + Israēl, 5626 + 2702*

Jhn	1:47	an Israelite in whom there is no deceit!"	2
Act	2:22	"You that are Israelites, listen to what I have	2
	3:12	"You Israelites, why do you wonder at this	2
	5:35	he said to them, "Fellow Israelites,	2
	7:23	to visit his relatives, the Israelites.	3
	7:37	This is the Moses who said to the Israelites	3
	13:16	"You Israelites, and others who fear God, listen.	2

Act 21:28 shouting, "Fellow Israelites, help!   2
Rom 9: 4 They are Israelites, and to them belong   2
    9: 6 For not all Israelites truly belong to Israel   1
   11: 1 I myself am an Israelite, a descendant of Abraham   2
2Co 11:22 Are they Israelites? So am I.   2
Heb 11:22 made mention of the exodus of the Israelites   3
Rev 21:12 names of the twelve tribes of the Israelites;   3

fellow Israelite

  1. ἀδελφός, *adelphos, 81*

Act 2:29 "Fellow Israelites, I may say to you confidently   1

Issachar

  1. Ἰσσαχάρ, *Issachar, 2704*

Rev 7: 7 from the tribe of Issachar twelve thousand,   1

it, itself Not Indexed

Italian

  1. Ἰταλικός, *Italikos, 2713*

Act 10: 1 the Italian Cohort, as it was called.   1

Italy

  1. Ἰταλία, *Italia, 2712*

Act 18: 2 recently come from Italy with his wife Priscilla   1
   27: 1 it was decided that we were to sail for Italy   1
   27: 6 an Alexandrian ship bound for Italy   1
Heb 13:24 Those from Italy send you greetings.   1

itch

  1. κνήθω, *knēthō, 3117*

2Ti 4: 3 having itching ears, they will accumulate   1

itinerant

  1. περιέρχομαι, *perierchomai, 4320*

Act 19:13 Then some itinerant Jewish exorcists   1

Ituraea

  1. Ἰτουραῖος, *Itouraios, 2714*

Lke 3: 1 the region of Ituraea and Trachonitis   1

ivory

  1. ἐλεφάντινος, *elephantinos, 1804*

Rev 18:12 all kinds of scented wood, all articles of ivory   1

J

jacinth

  1. ὑάκινθος, *hyakinthos, 5611*

Rev 21:20 the tenth chrysoprase, the eleventh jacinth   1

Jacob

  1. Ἰακώβ, *Iakōb, 2609*

Mat 1: 2 and Isaac the father of Jacob   1
   1: 2 and Jacob the father of Judah   1
   1:15 Matthan, and Matthan the father of Jacob   1
   1:16 Jacob the father of Joseph the husband of Mary   1
   8:11 eat with Abraham and Isaac and Jacob   1
  22:32 the God of Isaac, and the God of Jacob'?   1
Mrk 12:26 the God of Isaac, and the God of Jacob'?   1
Lke 1:33 He will reign over the house of Jacob forever   1
   3:34 son of Jacob, son of Isaac   1
  13:28 Abraham and Isaac and Jacob and all the prophets   1
  20:37 the God of Isaac, and the God of Jacob.   1
Jhn 4: 5 ground that Jacob had given to his son Joseph.   1
   4: 6 Jacob's well was there, and Jesus...sitting   1
   4:12 Are you greater than our ancestor Jacob   1
Act 3:13 of Abraham, the God of Isaac, and the God of Jacob   1
   7: 8 Isaac became the father of Jacob   1
   7: 8 Jacob of the twelve patriarchs.   1
   7:12 when Jacob heard that there was grain in Egypt   1
   7:14 Joseph sent and invited his father Jacob   1
   7:15 Jacob went down to Egypt.   1
   7:32 the God of Abraham, Isaac, and Jacob.'   1
   7:46 find a dwelling place for the house of Jacob.   1
Rom 9:13 "I have loved Jacob, but I have hated Esau."   1
  11:26 he will banish ungodliness from Jacob."   1
Heb 11: 9 living in tents, as did Isaac and Jacob   1

  11:20 invoked blessings for the future on Jacob and Esau.   1
  11:21 Jacob, when dying, blessed...the sons of Joseph   1

jailer

  1. Contextual: Not in Greek
  2. δεσμοφύλαξ, *desmophylax, 1302*

Act 16:23 ordered the jailer to keep them securely.   2
  16:27 When the jailer woke up   2
  16:29 The jailer called for lights, and rushing in   1
  16:36 the jailer reported the message to Paul, saying   2

Jairus

  1. Ἰάϊρος, *Iairos, 2608*

Mrk 5:22 one of the leaders of the synagogue named Jairus   1
Lke 8:41 Just then there came a man named Jairus   1

Jambres

  1. Ἰαμβρῆς, *Iambrēs, 2612*

2Ti 3: 8 As Jannes and Jambres opposed Moses   1

James

  1. Ἰάκωβος, *Iakōbos, 2610*

Mat 4:21 saw two other brothers, James son of Zebedee   1
  10: 2 James son of Zebedee, and his brother John;   1
  10: 3 James son of Alphaeus, and Thaddaeus;   1
  13:55 are not his brothers James and Joseph and Simon   1
  17: 1 Jesus took with him Peter and James and...John   1
  27:56 Mary the mother of James and Joseph   1
Mrk 1:19 he saw James son of Zebedee   1
   1:29 entered the house...with James and John.   1
   3:17 James son of Zebedee   1
   3:17 John the brother of James   1
   3:18 and Thomas, and James son of Alphaeus   1
   5:37 Peter, James, and John, the brother of James.   1
   5:37 Peter, James, and John, the brother of James.   1
   6: 3 brother of James and Joses and Judas and Simon   1
   9: 2 Jesus took with him Peter and James and John   1
  10:35 James and John, the sons of Zebedee, came forward   1
  10:41 they began to be angry with James and John.   1
  13: 3 Peter, James, John, and Andrew asked him   1
  14:33 He took with him Peter and James and John   1
  15:40 Mary the mother of James the younger and of Joses   1
  16: 1 Mary Magdalene, and Mary the mother of James   1
Lke 5:10 so also were James and John, sons of Zebedee   1
   6:14 Andrew, and James, and John, and Philip   1
   6:15 and Thomas, and James son of Alphaeus   1
   6:16 Judas son of James, and Judas Iscariot   1
   8:51 except Peter, John, and James,   1
   9:28 Jesus took with him Peter and John and James   1
   9:54 When his disciples James and John saw it   1
  24:10 Mary the mother of James, and the other women   1
Act 1:13 Peter, and John, and James, and Andrew   1
   1:13 James son of Alphaeus, and Simon the Zealot   1
   1:13 Simon the Zealot, and Judas son of James.   1
  12: 2 James, the brother of John, killed with the sword.   1
  12:17 he added, "Tell this to James and to the believers."   1
  15:13 After they finished speaking, James replied   1
  21:18 The next day Paul went with us to visit James;   1
1Co 15: 7 he appeared to James, then to all the apostles.   1
Gal 1:19 except James the Lord's brother.   1
   2: 9 James and Cephas and John   1
   2:12 for until certain people came from James   1
Jas 1: 1 James, a servant of God and of the Lord Jesus   1
Jde 1: 1 Jude, a servant of Jesus...and brother of James   1

Jannai

  1. Ἰανναί, *Iannai, 2613*

Lke 3:24 son of Melchi, son of Jannai, son of Joseph   1

Jannes

  1. Ἰάννης, *Iannēs, 2614*

2Ti 3: 8 As Jannes and Jambres opposed Moses   1

jar

  1. ἀλάβαστρος, *alabastros, 223*
  2. κεράμιον, *keramion, 3040*
  3. σκεῦος, *skeuos, 5007*
  4. ὑδρία, *hydria, 5620*

Mrk 14: 3 she broke open the jar and poured the ointment   1

14:13 a man carrying a jar of water will meet you; 2
Lke   8:16 hides it under a jar 3
22:10 a man carrying a jar of water will meet you; 2
Jhn   2: 7 Jesus said to them, "Fill the jars with water." 4
19:29 A jar full of sour wine was standing there. 3
2Co   4: 7 we have this treasure in clay jars 3

alabaster jar
1. ἀλάβαστρος, *alabastros, 223*
Mat 26: 7 with an alabaster jar 1
Mrk 14: 3 with an alabaster jar of very costly ointment 1
Lke   7:37 a woman…brought an alabaster jar of ointment. 1

water jar
1. ὑδρία, *hydria, 5620*
Jhn   2: 6 Now standing there were six stone water jars 1
4:28 the woman left her water jar and went back 1

Jared
1. Ἰάρετ, *Iaret, 2616*
Lke   3:37 son of Jared, son of Mahalaleel, son of Cainan, 1

Jason
1. Ἰάσων, *Iasōn, 2619*
Act 17: 5 to the assembly, they attacked Jason's house. 1
17: 6 they dragged Jason and some believers before 1
17: 7 Jason has entertained them as guests. 1
17: 9 they had taken bail from Jason and the others 1
Rom 16:21 so do Lucius and Jason and Sosipater, my relatives. 1

jasper
1. ἴασπις, *iaspis, 2618*
Rev   4: 3 the one…looks like jasper and carnelian 1
21:11 a radiance…like jasper, clear as crystal. 1
21:18 The wall is built of jasper 1
21:19 adorned with every jewel; the first was jasper 1

jealous *See also* make jealous
1. ζηλόω, *zēloō, 2420*
Act   7: 9 "The patriarchs, jealous of Joseph 1
17: 5 the Jews became jealous 1

jealously
1. φθόνος, *phthonos, 5784*
Jas   4: 5 "God yearns jealously for the spirit 1

jealousy *See also* feel jealousy, provoke to jealousy
1. ζῆλος, *zēlos, 2419*
2. φθόνος, *phthonos, 5784*
Mat 27:18 out of jealousy that they had handed him over. 2
Mrk 15:10 For he realized that it was out of jealousy 2
Act   5:17 filled with jealousy 1
13:45 they were filled with jealousy; 1
Rom 13:13 not in quarreling and jealousy. 1
1Co   3: 3 as there is jealousy and quarreling among you 1
2Co 11: 2 I feel a divine jealousy for you 1
12:20 there may perhaps be quarreling, jealousy, anger 1
Gal   5:20 idolatry, sorcery, enmities, strife, jealousy, anger 1

Jechoniah
1. Ἰεχονίας, *Iechonias, 2651*
Mat   1:11 Josiah the father of Jechoniah and his brothers 1
1:12 Jechoniah was the father of Salathiel 1

Jehoshaphat
1. Ἰωσαφάτ, *Iōsaphat, 2734*
Mat   1: 8 Asaph the father of Jehoshaphat 1
1: 8 and Jehoshaphat the father of Joram 1

Jephthah
1. Ἰεφθάε, *Iephthae, 2650*
Heb 11:32 to tell of Gideon, Barak, Samson, Jephthah, of David 1

Jeremiah
1. Ἰερεμίας, *Ieremias, 2635*
Mat   2:17 what had been spoken through the prophet Jeremiah: 1
16:14 others Elijah, and still others Jeremiah 1
27: 9 what had been spoken through the prophet Jeremiah 1

Jericho
1. Ἰεριχώ, *Ierichō, 2637*
Mat 20:29 As they were leaving Jericho 1
Mrk 10:46 They came to Jericho. 1
10:46 As he…and a large crowd were leaving Jericho 1
Lke 10:30 "A man was going down from Jerusalem to Jericho 1
18:35 As he approached Jericho 1
19: 1 He entered Jericho and was passing through 1
Heb 11:30 By faith the walls of Jericho fell 1

Jerusalem *See also* person of Jerusalem
1. Contextual: Not in Greek
2. Ἰερουσαλήμ, *Ierousalēm, 2647*
Mat   2: 1 wise men from the East came to Jerusalem 2
2: 3 he was frightened, and all Jerusalem with him; 2
3: 5 Then the people of Jerusalem and all Judea 2
4:25 from Galilee, the Decapolis, Jerusalem 2
5:35 or by Jerusalem, for it is the city 2
15: 1 scribes came to Jesus from Jerusalem and said 2
16:21 must go to Jerusalem and undergo great suffering 2
20:17 While Jesus was going up to Jerusalem 2
20:18 "See, we are going up to Jerusalem 2
21: 1 When they had come near Jerusalem 2
21:10 When he entered Jerusalem 2
23:37 "Jerusalem, Jerusalem,…that kills the prophets 2
23:37 "Jerusalem, Jerusalem,…that kills the prophets 2
Mrk   3: 8 Jerusalem, Idumea, beyond the Jordan 2
3:22 the scribes who came down from Jerusalem said 2
7: 1 some of the scribes who had come from Jerusalem 2
10:32 They were on the road, going up to Jerusalem 2
10:33 saying, "See, we are going up to Jerusalem 2
11: 1 When they were approaching Jerusalem, 2
11:11 he entered Jerusalem and went into the temple; 2
11:15 they came to Jerusalem. 2
11:27 Again they came to Jerusalem. 2
15:41 women who had come up with him to Jerusalem. 2
Lke   2:22 they brought him up to Jerusalem to present him 2
2:25 was a man in Jerusalem whose name was Simeon; 2
2:38 who were looking for the redemption of Jerusalem. 2
2:41 Now every year his parents went to Jerusalem 2
2:43 the boy Jesus stayed behind in Jerusalem 2
2:45 they returned to Jerusalem to search for him. 2
4: 9 the devil took him to Jerusalem 2
5:17 (they had come…from Jerusalem); 2
6:17 Judea, Jerusalem, and the coast of Tyre 2
9:31 which he was about to accomplish at Jerusalem. 2
9:51 he set his face to go to Jerusalem. 2
9:53 because his face was set toward Jerusalem. 2
10:30 "A man was going down from Jerusalem to Jericho 2
13: 4 than all the others living in Jerusalem? 2
13:22 teaching as he made his way to Jerusalem. 2
13:33 for a prophet to be killed outside of Jerusalem.' 2
13:34 Jerusalem, Jerusalem, the city that kills 2
13:34 Jerusalem, the city that kills the prophets 2
17:11 On the way to Jerusalem 2
18:31 "See, we are going up to Jerusalem 2
19:11 because he was near Jerusalem 2
19:28 he went on ahead, going up to Jerusalem. 2
21:20 "When you see Jerusalem surrounded by armies 2
21:24 Jerusalem will be trampled on by the Gentiles 2
23: 7 who was himself in Jerusalem at that time. 2
23:28 "Daughters of Jerusalem, do not weep for me 2
24:13 Emmaus, about seven miles from Jerusalem 2
24:18 the only stranger in Jerusalem who does not know 2
24:33 That same hour they got up and returned to Jerusalem; 2
24:47 beginning from Jerusalem. 2
24:52 and returned to Jerusalem with great joy; 2
Jhn   1:19 Jews sent priests and Levites from Jerusalem 2
2:13 and Jesus went up to Jerusalem. 2
2:23 When he was in Jerusalem during the Passover 2
4:20 place where people must worship is in Jerusalem 2
4:21 neither on this mountain nor in Jerusalem. 2
4:45 all that he had done in Jerusalem at the festival; 2
5: 1 and Jesus went up to Jerusalem. 2
5: 2 in Jerusalem by the Sheep Gate there is a pool 2
10:22 festival of the Dedication took place in Jerusalem. 2
11:18 Bethany was near Jerusalem, some two miles away 2
11:55 many went up from the country to Jerusalem 2
12:12 heard that Jesus was coming to Jerusalem. 2
Act   1: 4 he ordered them not to leave Jerusalem 2

Act	1: 8	you will be my witnesses in Jerusalem	2
	1:12	Then they returned to Jerusalem from the mount	2
	1:12	the mount called Olivet, which is near Jerusalem	2
	1:19	known to all the residents of Jerusalem	2
	2: 5	from every nation under heaven living in Jerusalem.	2
	2:14	"Men of Judea and all who live in Jerusalem	2
	4: 5	their rulers…assembled in Jerusalem,	2
	4:16	is obvious to all who live in Jerusalem	2
	5:16	gather from the towns around Jerusalem	2
	5:28	you have filled Jerusalem with your teaching	2
	6: 7	the disciples increased greatly in Jerusalem	2
	8: 1	persecution…against the church in Jerusalem	2
	8:14	Now when the apostles at Jerusalem heard	2
	8:25	they returned to Jerusalem	2
	8:26	the road that goes down from Jerusalem to Gaza."	2
	8:27	had come to Jerusalem to worship	2
	9: 2	he might bring them bound to Jerusalem.	2
	9:13	evil he has done to your saints in Jerusalem;	2
	9:21	"Is not this the man who made havoc in Jerusalem	2
	9:26	When he had come to Jerusalem	2
	9:28	So he went in and out among them in Jerusalem	2
	10:39	both in Judea and in Jerusalem.	2
	11: 2	when Peter went up to Jerusalem	2
	11:22	News…came to the ears of the church in Jerusalem	2
	11:27	prophets came down from Jerusalem to Antioch.	2
	12:25	Barnabas and Saul returned to Jerusalem	2
	13:13	John, however, left them and returned to Jerusalem;	2
	13:27	Because the residents of Jerusalem and their leaders	2
	13:31	came up with him from Galilee to Jerusalem	2
	15: 2	appointed to go up to Jerusalem to discuss this	2
	15: 4	When they came to Jerusalem	2
	16: 4	the apostles and elders who were in Jerusalem.	2
	18:22	he went up to Jerusalem and greeted the church	1
	19:21	resolved…to go on to Jerusalem.	2
	20:16	he was eager to be in Jerusalem	2
	20:22	captive to the Spirit, I am on my way to Jerusalem	2
	21: 4	they told Paul not to go on to Jerusalem.	2
	21:11	the Jews in Jerusalem will bind the man	2
	21:12	people there urged him not to go up to Jerusalem.	2
	21:13	die in Jerusalem for the name of the Lord Jesus."	2
	21:15	we got ready and started to go up to Jerusalem.	2
	21:17	When we arrived in Jerusalem	2
	21:31	all Jerusalem was in an uproar.	2
	22: 5	to bring them back to Jerusalem for punishment	2
	22:17	"After I had returned to Jerusalem	2
	22:18	'Hurry and get out of Jerusalem quickly	2
	23:11	just as you have testified for me in Jerusalem	2
	24:11	since I went up to worship in Jerusalem.	2
	25: 1	he went up from Caesarea to Jerusalem	2
	25: 3	to have him transferred to Jerusalem.	2
	25: 7	the Jews who had gone down from Jerusalem	2
	25: 9	"Do you wish to go up to Jerusalem	2
	25:15	When I was in Jerusalem	2
	25:20	I asked whether he wished to go to Jerusalem	2
	25:24	petitioned me, both in Jerusalem and here	2
	26: 4	among my own people and in Jerusalem.	2
	26:10	that is what I did in Jerusalem;	2
	26:20	then in Jerusalem	2
	28:17	yet I was arrested in Jerusalem	2
Rom	15:19	from Jerusalem and as far around as Illyricum	2
	15:25	I am going to Jerusalem in a ministry to the saints;	2
	15:26	with the poor among the saints at Jerusalem.	2
	15:31	that my ministry to Jerusalem may be acceptable	2
1Co	16: 3	to take your gift to Jerusalem.	2
Gal	1:17	nor did I go up to Jerusalem	2
	1:18	I did go up to Jerusalem to visit Cephas	2
	2: 1	I went up again to Jerusalem with Barnabas	2
	4:25	and corresponds to the present Jerusalem	2
	4:26	Jerusalem above; she is free, and she is our mother.	2
Heb	12:22	the heavenly Jerusalem	2
Rev	3:12	the new Jerusalem that comes down from my God	2
	21: 2	new Jerusalem, coming down out of heaven from God	2
	21:10	Jerusalem coming down out of heaven from God.	2

Jesse

1. Ἰεσσαί, *Iessai, 2649*

Mat	1: 5	and Obed the father of Jesse	1
	1: 6	Jesse the father of King David.	1
Lke	3:32	son of Jesse, son of Obed, son of Boaz	1
Act	13:22	'I have found David, son of Jesse, to be a man	1
Rom	15:12	again Isaiah says, "The root of Jesse shall come	1

Jesus

1. Contextual: Not in Greek
2. αὐτός, *autos, 899*
3. Ἰησοῦς, *Iēsous, 2652*
4. ὁ, *ho, 3836*
5. ὅς, *hos, 4005*
6. οὗτος, *houtos, 4047*

Mat	1: 1	An account of the genealogy of Jesus the Messiah	3
	1:16	Joseph the husband of Mary, of whom Jesus was born	3
	1:18	birth of Jesus the Messiah took place in this way.	3
	1:21	you are to name him Jesus, for he will save his	3
	1:25	she had borne a son; and he named him Jesus.	3
	2: 1	In the time of King Herod, after Jesus was born	3
	3:13	Jesus came from Galilee to John at the Jordan	3
	3:15	But Jesus answered him, "Let it be so now;	3
	3:16	when Jesus had been baptized, just as he came up	3
	4: 1	Then Jesus was led up by the Spirit	3
	4: 7	Jesus said to him, "Again it is written, 'Do not	3
	4:10	Jesus said to him, "Away with you, Satan!	3
	4:12	Now when Jesus heard that John had been arrested	1
	4:17	From that time Jesus began to proclaim,	3
	4:23	Jesus went throughout Galilee, teaching	1
	5: 1	Jesus saw the crowds, he went up the mountain;	1
	7:28	Now when Jesus had finished saying these	3
	8: 1	When Jesus had come down from the mountain	2
	8: 4	Jesus said to him, "See that you say nothing	3
	8:10	When Jesus heard him, he was amazed	3
	8:13	to the centurion Jesus said, "Go; let it be done	3
	8:14	When Jesus entered Peter's house	3
	8:18	Now when Jesus saw great crowds around him	3
	8:20	Jesus said to him, "Foxes have holes	3
	8:22	Jesus said to him, "Follow me, and let the dead	3
	8:34	Then the whole town came out to meet Jesus;	3
	9: 2	When Jesus saw their faith, he said	3
	9: 4	Jesus, perceiving their thoughts, said	3
	9: 9	As Jesus was walking along, he saw a man	3
	9:15	Jesus said to them, "The wedding guests cannot mourn	3
	9:19	Jesus got up and followed him, with his disciples.	3
	9:22	Jesus turned, and seeing her he said, "Take heart	3
	9:23	When Jesus came to the leader's house	3
	9:27	As Jesus went on from there	3
	9:28	the blind men came to him; and Jesus said to them	3
	9:30	Then Jesus sternly ordered them	3
	9:35	Jesus went about all the cities and villages	3
	10: 1	Jesus summoned his twelve disciples and gave them	1
	10: 5	These twelve Jesus sent out with the following	3
	11: 1	Now when Jesus had finished instructing	3
	11: 4	Jesus answered them, "Go and tell John	3
	11: 7	As they went away, Jesus began to speak	3
	11:25	At that time Jesus said, "I thank you, Father	3
	12: 1	At that time Jesus went through the grainfields	3
	12:15	Jesus became aware of this, he departed.	3
	12:48	to the one who had told him this, Jesus replied	1
	13: 1	That same day Jesus went out of the house and sat	3
	13:34	Jesus told the crowds all these things in parables;	3
	13:53	When Jesus had finished these parables	3
	13:57	But Jesus said to them	3
	14: 1	the ruler heard reports about Jesus;	3
	14:12	then they went and told Jesus.	3
	14:13	when Jesus heard this, he withdrew from there	3
	14:16	Jesus said to them, "They need not go away;	3
	14:27	immediately Jesus spoke to them and said	3
	14:29	walking on the water, and came toward Jesus.	3
	14:31	Jesus immediately reached out his hand	3
	15: 1	scribes came to Jesus from Jerusalem and said	3
	15:21	Jesus left that place and went away	3
	15:28	Then Jesus answered her	3
	15:29	Jesus had left that place	3
	15:32	Jesus called his disciples to him and said	3
	15:34	Jesus asked them, "How many loaves have you?"	3
	16: 1	to test Jesus they asked him to show them a sign	1
	16: 6	Jesus said to them	3
	16: 8	aware of it, Jesus said	3
	16:13	Now when Jesus came into the district	3
	16:17	Jesus answered him	3
	16:21	From that time on, Jesus began to show his disciples	3
	16:24	Then Jesus told his disciples	3
	17: 1	Six days later, Jesus took with him Peter	3
	17: 4	Peter said to Jesus	3
	17: 7	Jesus came and touched them, saying	3

17: 8	they saw no one except Jesus himself alone.	3
17: 9	coming down the mountain, Jesus ordered them	3
17:17	Jesus answered	3
17:18	Jesus rebuked the demon, and it came out of him	3
17:19	Then the disciples came to Jesus privately	3
17:22	Jesus said to them	3
17:25	when he came home, Jesus spoke of it first	3
17:26	Jesus said to him, "Then the children are free.	3
18: 1	At that time the disciples came to Jesus and asked	3
18:22	Jesus said to him, "Not seven times, but,	3
19: 1	When Jesus had finished saying these	3
19:14	Jesus said, "Let the little children come to me	3
19:18	And Jesus said, "You shall not murder;	3
19:21	Jesus said to him, "If you wish to be perfect	3
19:23	Jesus said to his disciples, "Truly I tell you	3
19:26	Jesus looked at them and said, "For mortals	3
19:28	Jesus said to them, "Truly I tell you	3
20:17	While Jesus was going up to Jerusalem	3
20:22	Jesus answered, "You do not know	3
20:25	Jesus called them to him and said	3
20:30	When they heard that Jesus was passing by	3
20:32	Jesus stood still and called them, saying	3
20:34	Moved with compassion, Jesus touched their eyes.	3
21: 1	Jesus sent two disciples	3
21: 6	The disciples went and did as Jesus had directed	3
21:11	"This is the prophet Jesus from Nazareth	3
21:12	Jesus entered the temple	3
21:16	Jesus said to them, "Yes;	3
21:21	Jesus answered them, "Truly I tell you	3
21:24	Jesus said to them, "I will also ask you	3
21:27	So they answered Jesus, "We do not know."	3
21:31	They said, "The first." Jesus said to them	3
21:42	Jesus said to them, "Have you never read	3
22: 1	Once more Jesus spoke to them in parables, saying:	3
22:18	Jesus, aware of their malice, said	3
22:29	Jesus answered them, "You are wrong	3
22:41	Jesus asked them this question:	3
23: 1	Then Jesus said to the crowds	3
24: 1	Jesus came out of the temple and was going away	3
24: 4	Jesus answered them, "Beware that no one leads	3
26: 1	When Jesus had finished saying all these	3
26: 4	to arrest Jesus by stealth and kill him.	3
26: 6	while Jesus was at Bethany in the house of Simon	3
26:10	Jesus, aware of this, said to them	3
26:17	the disciples came to Jesus, saying	3
26:19	the disciples did as Jesus had directed them	3
26:26	While they were eating, Jesus took a loaf of bread	3
26:31	Jesus said to them, "You will all become deserters	3
26:34	Jesus said to him, "Truly I tell you	3
26:36	Then Jesus went with them to a place	3
26:49	he came up to Jesus and said, "Greetings, Rabbi!"	3
26:50	Jesus said to him, "Friend, do what you are here	3
26:50	came and laid hands on Jesus and arrested him.	3
26:51	Suddenly, one of those with Jesus	3
26:52	Then Jesus said to him, "Put your sword back	3
26:55	At that hour Jesus said to the crowds	3
26:57	Those who had arrested Jesus	3
26:59	looking for false testimony against Jesus	3
26:63	Jesus was silent. Then the high priest said	3
26:64	Jesus said to him, "You have said so.	3
26:69	"You also were with Jesus the Galilean."	3
26:71	"This man was with Jesus of Nazareth."	3
26:75	Peter remembered what Jesus had said:	3
27: 1	elders…conferred together against Jesus	3
27: 3	Judas, his betrayer, saw that Jesus was condemned	1
27:11	Now Jesus stood before the governor;	3
27:11	Jesus said, "You say so."	3
27:16	a notorious prisoner, called Jesus Barabbas.	3
27:17	Jesus Barabbas or Jesus who is called the Messiah?"	3
27:17	Jesus Barabbas or Jesus who is called the Messiah?"	3
27:20	to ask for Barabbas and to have Jesus killed.	3
27:22	I do with Jesus who is called the Messiah?"	3
27:26	after flogging Jesus, he handed him over	3
27:27	Then the soldiers of the governor took Jesus	3
27:37	"This is Jesus, the King of the Jews."	3
27:46	Jesus cried with a loud voice	3
27:50	Jesus cried again with a loud voice	3
27:54	keeping watch over Jesus, saw the earthquake	3
27:55	they had followed Jesus from Galilee	3
27:57	who was also a disciple of Jesus.	3
27:58	went to Pilate and asked for the body of Jesus	3

	28: 5	you are looking for Jesus who was crucified.	3
	28: 9	Suddenly Jesus met them and said, "Greetings!"	3
	28:10	Then Jesus said to them, "Do not be afraid;	3
	28:16	to the mountain to which Jesus had directed	3
	28:18	Jesus came and said to them	3
Mrk	1: 1	The beginning of the good news of Jesus Christ	3
	1: 9	In those days Jesus came from Nazareth of Galilee	3
	1:14	after John was arrested, Jesus came to Galilee	3
	1:16	As Jesus passed along the Sea of Galilee	1
	1:17	Jesus said to them, "Follow me	3
	1:24	"What have you to do with us, Jesus of Nazareth?	3
	1:25	Jesus rebuked him, saying, "Be silent,	3
	1:41	Moved with pity, Jesus stretched out his hand	1
	1:45	Jesus could no longer go into a town openly	2
	2: 4	when they could not bring him to Jesus	2
	2: 5	When Jesus saw their faith	3
	2: 8	At once Jesus perceived in his spirit	3
	2:13	Jesus went out again beside the sea;	1
	2:15	sitting with Jesus and his disciples	3
	2:17	When Jesus heard this, he said to them	3
	2:19	Jesus said to them, "The wedding guests cannot	3
	3: 7	Jesus departed with his disciples to the sea	3
	5: 6	When he saw Jesus from a distance, he ran	3
	5: 7	"What have you to do with me, Jesus	3
	5: 9	Jesus asked him, "What is your name?"	1
	5:15	They came to Jesus and saw the demoniac sitting	3
	5:17	they began to beg Jesus to leave	2
	5:19	Jesus refused, and said to him	1
	5:20	how much Jesus had done for him;	3
	5:21	Jesus had crossed again in the boat to the other side	3
	5:27	She had heard about Jesus	3
	5:30	Jesus turned about in the crowd and said	3
	5:36	Jesus said to the leader of the synagogue	3
	6: 4	Jesus said to them, "Prophets are not without honor	3
	6:14	Jesus' name had become known.	2
	6:30	The apostles gathered around Jesus, and told him	3
	7:36	Jesus ordered them to tell no one;	1
	8:17	becoming aware of it, Jesus said to them	1
	8:25	Then Jesus laid his hands on his eyes again;	1
	8:27	Jesus went on with his disciples	3
	9: 2	Six days later, Jesus took with him Peter	3
	9: 4	who were talking with Jesus.	3
	9: 5	Peter said to Jesus, "Rabbi, it is good	3
	9: 8	saw no one with them any more, but only Jesus.	3
	9:21	Jesus asked the father, "How long has this been	1
	9:23	Jesus said to him, "If you are able!	3
	9:25	Jesus saw that a crowd came running together	3
	9:27	Jesus took him by the hand and lifted him up	3
	9:39	Jesus said, "Do not stop him;	3
	10: 5	Jesus said to them, "Because of your hardness	3
	10:14	when Jesus saw this, he was indignant	3
	10:18	Jesus said to him, "Why do you call me good?	3
	10:21	Jesus, looking at him, loved him and said	3
	10:23	Jesus looked around and said to his disciples	3
	10:24	Jesus said to them again	3
	10:27	Jesus looked at them and said	3
	10:29	Jesus said, "Truly I tell you, there is no one	3
	10:32	Jesus was walking ahead of them;	3
	10:38	Jesus said to them, "You do not know	3
	10:39	Jesus said to them, "The cup that I drink	3
	10:42	Jesus called them and said to them	3
	10:47	When he heard that it was Jesus of Nazareth	3
	10:47	"Jesus, Son of David, have mercy on me!"	3
	10:49	Jesus stood still and said, "Call him	3
	10:50	he sprang up and came to Jesus.	3
	10:51	Jesus said…"What do you want me to do for you?"	3
	10:52	Jesus said to him, "Go; your faith has made	3
	11: 6	They told them what Jesus had said;	3
	11: 7	they brought the colt to Jesus	3
	11:19	Jesus and his disciples went out of the city.	1
	11:22	Jesus answered them, "Have faith in God.	3
	11:29	Jesus said to them, "I will ask you one question;	3
	11:33	So they answered Jesus, "We do not know."	3
	11:33	Jesus said to them, "Neither will I tell you	3
	12:17	Jesus said to them, "Give to the emperor	3
	12:24	Jesus said to them, "Is not this the reason	3
	12:29	Jesus answered, "The first is, 'Hear, O Israel:	3
	12:34	When Jesus saw that he answered wisely	3
	12:35	While Jesus was teaching in the temple, he said	3
	13: 2	Jesus asked him, "Do you see	3
	13: 5	Jesus began to say to them, "Beware	3

Mrk 14: 1	way to arrest Jesus by stealth and kill him;	2
14: 6	Jesus said, "Let her alone; why do you trouble her?	3
14:18	taken their places and were eating, Jesus said	3
14:27	Jesus said to them, "You will all become deserters;	3
14:30	Jesus said to him, "Truly I tell you	3
14:48	Jesus said to them, "Have you come out	3
14:53	They took Jesus to the high priest;	3
14:55	looking for testimony against Jesus	3
14:60	stood up before them and asked Jesus	3
14:62	Jesus said, "I am; and 'you will see	3
14:67	"You also were with Jesus, the man from Nazareth."	3
14:72	Peter remembered that Jesus had said to him	3
15: 1	They bound Jesus, led him away	3
15: 5	Jesus made no further reply	3
15:15	after flogging Jesus, he handed him over	3
15:22	they brought Jesus to the place called Golgotha	2
15:34	At three o'clock Jesus cried out with a loud voice	3
15:37	Jesus gave a loud cry and breathed his last.	3
15:43	to Pilate and asked for the body of Jesus.	3
16: 6	you are looking for Jesus of Nazareth	3
16:19	⟦the Lord Jesus, after he had spoken to them⟧	3
16: S	⟦afterward Jesus himself sent out through them,⟧	3
Lke 1:31	you will name him Jesus.	3
2:21	he was called Jesus, the name given by the angel	3
2:27	when the parents brought in the child Jesus	3
2:43	the boy Jesus stayed behind in Jerusalem	3
2:52	Jesus increased in wisdom and in years	3
3:21	Jesus also had been baptized and was praying	3
3:23	Jesus was about thirty years old when he began	3
4: 1	Jesus, full of the Holy Spirit, returned	3
4: 4	Jesus answered him, "It is written	3
4: 8	Jesus answered him, "It is written	3
4:12	Jesus answered him, "It is said, 'Do not put	3
4:14	Jesus, filled with the power of the Spirit,	3
4:34	What have you to do with us, Jesus of Nazareth?	3
4:35	Jesus rebuked him, saying, "Be silent	3
5: 1	Jesus was standing beside the lake of Gennesaret	2
5: 8	he fell down at Jesus' knees, saying	3
5:10	Jesus said to Simon, "Do not be afraid;	3
5:12	When he saw Jesus	3
5:13	Jesus stretched out his hand, touched him,	1
5:15	the word about Jesus spread abroad;	2
5:18	trying to bring him in and lay him before Jesus;	2
5:19	into the middle of the crowd in front of Jesus.	3
5:22	When Jesus perceived their questionings	3
5:31	Jesus answered, "Those who are well	3
5:34	Jesus said to them, "You cannot make wedding guests	3
6: 1	while Jesus was going through the grainfields	2
6: 3	Jesus answered, "Have you not read what David did	3
6: 9	Jesus said to them, "I ask you	3
6:11	what they might do to Jesus.	3
7: 1	After Jesus had finished all his sayings	1
7: 3	When he heard about Jesus	3
7: 4	When they came to Jesus	3
7: 6	Jesus went with them	3
7: 9	When Jesus heard this he was amazed at him	3
7:15	Jesus gave him to his mother.	1
7:21	Jesus had just then cured many people of diseases	1
7:24	Jesus began to speak to the crowds about John:	1
7:36	One of the Pharisees asked Jesus to eat with him	2
7:40	Jesus spoke up and said to him, "Simon	3
7:43	Jesus said to him, "You have judged rightly."	4
8:28	When he saw Jesus, he fell down before him	3
8:28	Jesus, Son of the Most High God?	3
8:29	for Jesus had commanded the unclean spirit	1
8:30	Jesus then asked him, "What is your name?"	3
8:32	demons begged Jesus to let them enter these.	2
8:35	they came to Jesus	3
8:35	sitting at the feet of Jesus	3
8:37	all the people…asked Jesus to leave them;	2
8:38	Jesus sent him away, saying	1
8:39	proclaiming…how much Jesus had done for him.	3
8:40	Now when Jesus returned, the crowd welcomed him	3
8:41	fell at Jesus' feet and begged him to come	3
8:45	Jesus asked, "Who touched me?"	3
8:46	Jesus said, "Someone touched me;	3
8:50	Jesus heard this, he replied, "Do not fear.	3
9: 1	Then Jesus called the twelve together	1
9:10	the apostles told Jesus all they had done.	2
9:18	Once when Jesus was praying alone	2
9:28	Jesus took with him Peter and John and James	1

9:33	Peter said to Jesus, "Master, it is good	3
9:36	When the voice had spoken, Jesus was found alone.	3
9:41	Jesus answered, "You faithless and perverse	3
9:42	But Jesus rebuked the unclean spirit	3
9:47	Jesus, aware of their inner thoughts	3
9:50	Jesus said to him, "Do not stop him;	3
9:58	Jesus said to him, "Foxes have holes	3
9:60	Jesus said to him, "Let the dead	1
9:62	Jesus said to him, "No one	3
10:21	Jesus rejoiced in the Holy Spirit and said	1
10:23	Then turning to the disciples, Jesus said	1
10:25	Just then a lawyer stood up to test Jesus.	2
10:29	wanting to justify himself, he asked Jesus	3
10:30	Jesus replied, "A man was going down	3
10:37	Jesus said to him, "Go and do likewise."	3
13:12	When Jesus saw her, he called her over and said	3
13:14	Jesus had cured on the sabbath	3
13:22	Jesus went through one town and village	1
14: 1	when Jesus was going to the house of a leader	2
14: 3	Jesus asked the lawyers and Pharisees	3
14: 4	they were silent. So Jesus took him and healed him	1
14:16	Jesus said to him, "Someone gave a great dinner	4
15:11	Jesus said, "There was a man who had two sons.	1
16: 1	Then Jesus said to the disciples,	1
17: 1	Jesus said to his disciples,	1
17:11	Jesus going through the region between Samaria	2
17:13	called out, saying, "Jesus, Master	3
17:16	He prostrated himself at Jesus' feet	2
17:17	Then Jesus asked, "Were not ten made clean?	3
17:20	Once Jesus was asked by the Pharisees	1
18: 1	Jesus told them a parable	1
18:16	Jesus called for them and said,	3
18:19	Jesus said to him, "Why do you call me good?	3
18:22	When Jesus heard this, he said to him,	3
18:24	Jesus looked at him and said, "How hard it is	3
18:37	They told him, "Jesus of Nazareth is passing by."	3
18:38	"Jesus, Son of David, have mercy on me!"	3
18:40	Jesus stood still and ordered the man to be brought	3
18:42	Jesus said to him, "Receive your sight;	3
19: 3	He was trying to see who Jesus was,	3
19: 5	When Jesus came to the place, he looked up	3
19: 9	Jesus said to him, "Today salvation has come	3
19:35	they brought it to Jesus;	3
19:35	on the colt, they set Jesus on it.	3
20: 8	Jesus said to them, "Neither will I tell you	3
20:34	Jesus said to them, "Those who belong to this age	3
22: 2	were looking for a way to put Jesus to death	2
22: 8	So Jesus sent Peter and John, saying, "Go	1
22:34	Jesus said, "I tell you, Peter,	4
22:47	He approached Jesus to kiss him;	3
22:48	Jesus said to him, "Judas	3
22:51	Jesus said, "No more of this!"	3
22:52	Then Jesus said to the chief priests	3
22:63	the men who were holding Jesus began to mock him	2
23: 1	brought Jesus before Pilate.	2
23: 8	When Herod saw Jesus, he was very glad	3
23: 9	but Jesus gave him no answer.	2
23:20	Pilate, wanting to release Jesus, addressed them	3
23:25	he handed Jesus over as they wished.	3
23:26	the cross…and made him carry it behind Jesus.	3
23:28	Jesus turned to them and said	3
23:33	they crucified Jesus there with the criminals	2
23:34	⟦Jesus said, "Father, forgive them;⟧	3
23:42	he said, "Jesus, remember me	3
23:46	Jesus, crying with a loud voice, said, "Father	3
23:52	went to Pilate and asked for the body of Jesus.	3
24:15	Jesus himself came near and went with them	3
24:19	replied, "The things about Jesus of Nazareth	3
24:36	Jesus himself stood among them	2
Jhn 1:17	grace and truth came through Jesus Christ.	3
1:29	The next day he saw Jesus coming toward him	3
1:36	as he watched Jesus walk by, he exclaimed, "Look,	3
1:37	heard him say this, and they followed Jesus.	3
1:38	Jesus turned and saw them following, he said	3
1:42	He brought Simon to Jesus, who looked at him	3
1:43	The next day Jesus decided to go to Galilee.	3
1:45	found him…Jesus son of Joseph from Nazareth."	3
1:47	Jesus saw Nathanael coming toward him, he said	3
1:48	Jesus answered, "I saw you under the fig tree	3
1:50	Jesus answered, "Do you believe because	3
2: 1	in Cana…and the mother of Jesus was there.	3

2: 2	Jesus and his disciples had also been invited	3
2: 3	When the wine gave out, the mother of Jesus said	3
2: 4	Jesus said to her, "Woman	3
2: 7	Jesus said to them, "Fill the jars with water."	3
2:11	Jesus did this, the first of his signs, in Cana	3
2:13	and Jesus went up to Jerusalem.	3
2:19	Jesus answered them, "Destroy this temple	3
2:22	believed…the word that Jesus had spoken.	3
2:24	Jesus on his part would not entrust himself to them	3
3: 2	He came to Jesus by night and said to him	2
3: 3	Jesus answered him, "Very truly, I tell you	3
3: 5	Jesus answered, "Very truly, I tell you	3
3:10	Jesus answered him, "Are you a teacher of Israel	3
3:22	Jesus and his disciples went into the Judean	3
4: 1	when Jesus learned that the Pharisees had heard	3
4: 1	"Jesus is making and baptizing more disciples	3
4: 2	although it was not Jesus himself…who baptized	3
4: 6	Jesus, tired out by his journey, was sitting	3
4: 7	Jesus said to her, "Give me a drink."	3
4:10	Jesus answered her, "If you knew the gift of God	3
4:13	Jesus said to her, "Everyone who drinks	3
4:16	Jesus said to her, "Go, call your husband	1
4:17	Jesus said to her, "You are right in saying	3
4:21	Jesus said to her, "Woman, believe me	3
4:26	Jesus said to her, "I am he, the one…speaking	3
4:34	Jesus said to them, "My food is to do the will	3
4:44	(for Jesus himself had testified that a prophet	3
4:47	heard that Jesus had come from Judea to Galilee	3
4:48	Then Jesus said to him, "Unless you see signs	3
4:50	Jesus said to him, "Go; your son will live."	3
4:50	The man believed the word that Jesus spoke to him	3
4:53	this was the hour when Jesus had said to him	3
4:54	Now this was the second sign that Jesus did	3
5: 1	and Jesus went up to Jerusalem.	3
5: 6	When Jesus saw him lying there	3
5: 8	Jesus said to him, "Stand up, take your mat	3
5:13	for Jesus had disappeared in the crowd	3
5:14	Later Jesus found him in the temple and said	3
5:15	it was Jesus who had made him well.	3
5:16	Therefore the Jews started persecuting Jesus	3
5:17	Jesus answered them, "My Father is still working	3
5:19	Jesus said to them, "Very truly, I tell you	3
6: 1	Jesus went to the other side of the Sea of Galilee	3
6: 3	Jesus went up the mountain	3
6: 5	Jesus said to Philip, "Where are we to buy bread	3
6:10	Jesus said, "Make the people sit down."	3
6:11	Then Jesus took the loaves	3
6:15	Jesus realized that they were about to come	3
6:17	and Jesus had not yet come to them.	3
6:19	they saw Jesus walking on the sea	3
6:22	Jesus had not got into the boat with his disciples	3
6:24	neither Jesus nor his disciples were there	3
6:24	went to Capernaum looking for Jesus.	3
6:26	Jesus answered them, "Very truly, I tell you	3
6:29	Jesus answered them, "This is the work of God	3
6:32	Jesus said to them, "Very truly, I tell you	3
6:35	Jesus said to them, "I am the bread of life.	3
6:42	saying, "Is not this Jesus, the son of Joseph	3
6:43	Jesus answered them, "Do not complain	3
6:53	Jesus said to them, "Very truly, I tell you	3
6:61	Jesus…said to them, "Does this offend you?	3
6:64	Jesus knew from the first	3
6:67	Jesus asked the twelve	3
6:70	Jesus answered them, "Did I not choose you	3
7: 1	After this Jesus went about in Galilee.	3
7: 6	Jesus said to them, "My time has not yet come	3
7:14	Jesus went up into the temple and began to teach.	3
7:16	Jesus answered them, "My teaching is not mine	3
7:21	Jesus answered them, "I performed one work	3
7:28	Jesus cried out as he was teaching in the temple	3
7:33	Jesus then said, "I will be with you	3
7:37	Jesus was standing there, he cried out,	3
7:39	because Jesus was not yet glorified.	3
7:50	Nicodemus, who had gone to Jesus before	2
8: 1	〚Jesus went to the Mount of Olives.〛	3
8: 6	〚Jesus bent down and wrote with his finger〛	3
8: 9	Jesus was left alone with the woman	1
8:10	〚Jesus straightened up and said to her, "Woman〛	3
8:11	〚Jesus said, "Neither do I condemn you.〛	3
8:12	Again Jesus spoke to them, saying, "I am the light	3
8:14	Jesus answered, "Even if I testify	3

8:19	Jesus answered, "You know neither me nor my Father.	3
8:25	Jesus said to them, "Why do I speak to you	3
8:28	So Jesus said, "When you have lifted up the Son	3
8:31	Then Jesus said to the Jews who had believed	3
8:34	Jesus answered them, "Very truly, I tell you	3
8:39	Jesus said to them, "If you were Abraham's	3
8:42	Jesus said to them, "If God were your Father	3
8:49	Jesus answered, "I do not have a demon;	3
8:54	Jesus answered, "If I glorify myself	3
8:58	Jesus said to them, "Very truly, I tell you	3
8:59	Jesus hid himself and went out of the temple.	3
9: 3	Jesus answered, "Neither this man…sinned;	3
9:11	He answered, "The man called Jesus made mud	3
9:14	it was a sabbath day when Jesus made the mud	3
9:22	anyone who confessed Jesus to be the Messiah	2
9:35	Jesus heard that they had driven him out	3
9:37	Jesus said to him, "You have seen him	3
9:39	Jesus said, "I came into this world for judgment	3
9:41	Jesus said to them, "If you were blind	3
10: 6	Jesus used this figure of speech with them	3
10: 7	So again Jesus said to them, "Very truly	3
10:23	and Jesus was walking in the temple	3
10:25	Jesus answered, "I have told you	3
10:32	Jesus replied, "I have shown you	3
10:34	Jesus answered, "Is it not written in your law	3
11: 3	the sisters sent a message to Jesus,	2
11: 4	when Jesus heard it, he said	3
11: 5	Jesus loved Martha and her sister and Lazarus	3
11: 9	Jesus answered, "Are there not twelve hours	3
11:13	Jesus, however, had been speaking about his death	3
11:14	Jesus told them plainly, "Lazarus is dead.	3
11:17	When Jesus arrived	3
11:20	When Martha heard that Jesus was coming	3
11:21	Martha said to Jesus, "Lord, if you had been here	3
11:23	Jesus said to her, "Your brother will rise again."	3
11:25	Jesus said to her, "I am the resurrection	3
11:30	Now Jesus had not yet come to the village	3
11:32	When Mary came where Jesus was and saw him	3
11:33	When Jesus saw her weeping	3
11:35	Jesus began to weep.	3
11:38	Jesus, again greatly disturbed, came to the tomb.	3
11:39	Jesus said, "Take away the stone."	3
11:40	Jesus said to her, "Did I not tell you	3
11:41	Jesus looked upward and said, "Father	3
11:44	Jesus said to them, "Unbind him,	3
11:45	had come with Mary and had seen what Jesus did	1
11:51	Jesus was about to die for the nation	3
11:54	Jesus therefore no longer walked about openly	3
11:56	They were looking for Jesus	3
11:57	orders that anyone who knew where Jesus was	1
12: 1	Jesus came to Bethany, the home of Lazarus	3
12: 3	anointed Jesus' feet, and wiped them	3
12: 7	Jesus said, "Leave her alone.	3
12: 9	they came not only because of Jesus	3
12:11	Jews were deserting and were believing in Jesus.	3
12:12	heard that Jesus was coming to Jerusalem.	3
12:14	Jesus found a young donkey and sat on it;	3
12:16	when Jesus was glorified, then they remembered	3
12:21	"Sir, we wish to see Jesus."	3
12:22	Andrew and Philip went and told Jesus.	3
12:23	Jesus answered them, "The hour has come	3
12:30	Jesus answered, "This voice has come for your sake	3
12:35	Jesus said to them, "The light is with you	3
12:36	After Jesus had said this	3
12:44	Jesus cried aloud: "Whoever believes in me	3
13: 1	Jesus knew that his hour had come to depart	3
13: 3	Jesus, knowing that the Father had given all things	1
13: 7	Jesus answered, "You do not know now what	3
13: 8	Jesus answered, "Unless I wash you	3
13:10	Jesus said to him, "One who has bathed	3
13:21	Jesus was troubled in spirit, and declared	3
13:23	One of his disciples—the one whom Jesus loved	3
13:24	to ask Jesus of whom he was speaking.	1
13:25	So while reclining next to Jesus, he asked	3
13:26	Jesus answered, "It is the one to whom I give	3
13:27	Jesus said to him, "Do quickly what you…do."	3
13:29	Some thought that…Jesus was telling him	3
13:31	When he had gone out, Jesus said	3
13:36	Jesus answered, "Where I am going	3
13:38	Jesus answered, "Will you lay down your life	3
14: 6	Jesus said to him, "I am the way, and the truth	3

Jhn	14: 9	Jesus said to him, "Have I been with you all	3
	14:23	Jesus answered him, "Those who love me	3
	16:19	Jesus knew that they wanted to ask him	3
	16:31	Jesus answered them, "Do you now believe?	3
	17: 1	After Jesus had spoken these words	3
	17: 3	Jesus Christ whom you have sent.	3
	18: 1	After Jesus had spoken these words	3
	18: 2	Jesus often met there with his disciples.	3
	18: 4	Jesus, knowing all that was to happen to him	3
	18: 5	They answered, "Jesus of Nazareth."	3
	18: 5	Jesus replied, "I am he."	1
	18: 6	When Jesus said to them, "I am he,"	1
	18: 7	And they said, "Jesus of Nazareth."	3
	18: 8	Jesus answered, "I told you that I am he.	3
	18:11	Jesus said to Peter	3
	18:12	Jewish police arrested Jesus and bound him.	3
	18:15	Simon Peter and another disciple followed Jesus.	3
	18:15	he went with Jesus into the courtyard	3
	18:19	Then the high priest questioned Jesus	3
	18:20	Jesus answered, "I have spoken openly	3
	18:22	one of the police…struck Jesus on the face,	3
	18:23	Jesus answered, "If I have spoken wrongly	3
	18:28	they took Jesus from Caiaphas	3
	18:32	to fulfill what Jesus had said	3
	18:33	Pilate…summoned Jesus, and asked him	3
	18:34	Jesus answered, "Do you ask this on your own	3
	18:36	Jesus answered, "My kingdom is not from this	3
	18:37	Jesus answered, "You say that I am a king.	3
	19: 1	Pilate took Jesus and had him flogged.	3
	19: 5	Jesus came out, wearing the crown of thorns	3
	19: 9	He…asked Jesus, "Where are you from?"	3
	19: 9	But Jesus gave him no answer.	3
	19:11	Jesus answered him, "You would have no power	3
	19:13	he brought Jesus outside	3
	19:16	to be crucified. So they took Jesus;	3
	19:18	one on either side, with Jesus between them.	3
	19:19	"Jesus of Nazareth, the King of the Jews."	3
	19:20	the place where Jesus was crucified	3
	19:23	When the soldiers had crucified Jesus	3
	19:25	standing near the cross of Jesus were his mother	3
	19:26	When Jesus saw his mother	3
	19:28	Jesus knew that all was now finished	3
	19:30	When Jesus had received the wine, he said	3
	19:33	when they came to Jesus	3
	19:38	was a disciple of Jesus, though a secret one	3
	19:38	to let him take away the body of Jesus.	3
	19:39	Nicodemus, who had at first come to Jesus by night	2
	19:40	They took the body of Jesus	3
	19:42	they laid Jesus there.	3
	20: 2	the other disciple, the one whom Jesus loved	3
	20: 7	the cloth that had been on Jesus' head	2
	20:12	sitting where the body of Jesus had been lying	3
	20:14	she turned around and saw Jesus standing	3
	20:14	she did not know that it was Jesus.	3
	20:15	Jesus said to her, "Woman, why are you weeping?	3
	20:16	Jesus said to her, "Mary!"	3
	20:17	Jesus said to her, "Do not hold on to me	3
	20:19	Jesus came and stood among them and said	3
	20:21	Jesus said to them again, "Peace be with you.	3
	20:24	Thomas…was not with them when Jesus came.	3
	20:26	Jesus came and stood among them and said	3
	20:29	Jesus said to him, "Have you believed	3
	20:30	Now Jesus did many other signs	3
	20:31	Jesus is the Messiah, the Son of God	3
	21: 1	After these things Jesus showed himself again	3
	21: 4	Just after daybreak, Jesus stood on the beach;	3
	21: 4	the disciples did not know that it was Jesus.	3
	21: 5	Jesus said to them, "Children, you have no fish	3
	21: 7	That disciple whom Jesus loved said to Peter	3
	21:10	Jesus said to them, "Bring some of the fish	3
	21:12	Jesus said to them, "Come and have breakfast."	3
	21:13	Jesus came and took the bread and gave it	3
	21:14	Jesus appeared to the disciples	3
	21:15	Jesus said to Simon Peter, "Simon son of John	3
	21:15	Jesus said to him, "Feed my lambs."	1
	21:16	Jesus said to him, "Tend my sheep."	1
	21:17	Jesus said to him, "Feed my sheep.	3
	21:20	saw the disciple whom Jesus loved following	3
	21:20	who had reclined next to Jesus at the supper	2
	21:21	When Peter saw him, he said to Jesus, "Lord	3
	21:22	Jesus said to him, "If it is my will	3
	21:23	Jesus did not say to him that he would not die	3
	21:25	there are also many other things that Jesus did;	3
Act	1: 1	I wrote about all that Jesus did and taught	3
	1:11	This Jesus, who has been taken up from you	3
	1:14	Mary the mother of Jesus, as well as his brothers.	3
	1:16	Judas, who became a guide for those who arrested Jesus	3
	1:21	the Lord Jesus went in and out among us	3
	2:22	Jesus of Nazareth, a man attested to you by God	3
	2:32	This Jesus God raised up	3
	2:36	Lord and Messiah, this Jesus whom you crucified."	3
	2:38	be baptized…in the name of Jesus Christ	3
	3: 6	in the name of Jesus Christ of Nazareth, stand up	3
	3:13	God…has glorified his servant Jesus	3
	3:16	the faith that is through Jesus	2
	3:20	may send the Messiah appointed for you…Jesus	3
	4: 2	in Jesus there is the resurrection of the dead.	3
	4:10	by the name of Jesus Christ of Nazareth	3
	4:11	Jesus is 'the stone that was rejected by you,	1
	4:13	recognized them as companions of Jesus.	3
	4:18	not to speak or teach at all in the name of Jesus.	3
	4:27	against your holy servant Jesus, whom you anointed	3
	4:30	through the name of your holy servant Jesus."	3
	4:33	testimony to the resurrection of the Lord Jesus	3
	5:30	God…raised up Jesus, whom you had killed	3
	5:40	ordered them not to speak in the name of Jesus	3
	5:42	proclaim Jesus as the Messiah.	3
	6:14	Jesus of Nazareth will destroy this place	3
	7:55	Jesus standing at the right hand of God.	3
	7:59	"Lord Jesus, receive my spirit."	3
	8:12	proclaiming…the name of Jesus Christ	3
	8:16	baptized in the name of the Lord Jesus).	3
	8:35	he proclaimed to him the good news about Jesus.	3
	9: 5	reply came, "I am Jesus, whom you are persecuting.	3
	9:17	the Lord Jesus, who appeared to you on your way	3
	9:20	he began to proclaim Jesus in the synagogues,	3
	9:22	by proving that Jesus was the Messiah.	6
	9:27	he had spoken boldly in the name of Jesus.	3
	9:34	Peter said to him, "Aeneas, Jesus Christ heals you;	3
	10:36	preaching peace by Jesus Christ	3
	10:38	how God anointed Jesus of Nazareth	3
	10:48	baptized in the name of Jesus Christ.	3
	11:17	when we believed in the Lord Jesus Christ	3
	11:20	proclaiming the Lord Jesus.	3
	13:23	brought to Israel a Savior, Jesus, as he promised;	3
	13:33	he has fulfilled…by raising Jesus;	3
	13:39	by this Jesus everyone who believes is set free	1
	15:11	saved through the grace of the Lord Jesus	3
	15:26	for the sake of our Lord Jesus Christ.	3
	16: 7	The Spirit of Jesus did not allow them;	3
	16:18	"I order you in the name of Jesus Christ	3
	16:31	"Believe on the Lord Jesus, and you will be saved	3
	17: 3	"This is the Messiah, Jesus whom I am proclaiming	3
	17: 7	saying that there is another king named Jesus."	3
	17:18	because he was telling the good news about Jesus	3
	18: 5	testifying to the Jews that the Messiah was Jesus.	3
	18:25	and taught accurately the things concerning Jesus	3
	18:28	showing…that the Messiah is Jesus.	3
	19: 4	who was to come after him, that is, in Jesus."	3
	19: 5	baptized in the name of the Lord Jesus.	3
	19:13	to use the name of the Lord Jesus	3
	19:13	"I adjure you by the Jesus whom Paul proclaims."	3
	19:15	"Jesus I know, and Paul I know; but who are you?"	3
	19:17	the name of the Lord Jesus was praised.	3
	20:21	faith toward our Lord Jesus.	3
	20:24	ministry that I received from the Lord Jesus	3
	20:35	the words of the Lord Jesus, for he himself said	3
	21:13	die in Jerusalem for the name of the Lord Jesus."	3
	22: 8	'I am Jesus of Nazareth whom you are persecuting.'	3
	22:18	saw Jesus saying to me, 'Hurry	2
	24:24	heard him speak concerning faith in Christ Jesus.	3
	25:19	disagreement…about a certain Jesus, who had died	3
	26: 9	against the name of Jesus of Nazareth.	3
	26:15	'I am Jesus whom you are persecuting.	3
	28:23	trying to convince them about Jesus	3
	28:31	teaching about the Lord Jesus Christ	3
Rom	1: 1	Paul, a servant of Jesus Christ	3
	1: 4	Jesus Christ our Lord	3
	1: 6	who are called to belong to Jesus Christ	3
	1: 7	from God our Father and the Lord Jesus Christ.	3
	1: 8	I thank my God through Jesus Christ for all of you	3
	2:16	God, through Jesus Christ, will judge the secret	3

	3:22 through faith in Jesus Christ for all	3
	3:24 through the redemption that is in Christ Jesus	3
	3:26 that he justifies the one who has faith in Jesus.	3
	4:24 him who raised Jesus our Lord from the dead	3
	5: 1 peace with God through our Lord Jesus Christ	3
	5:11 boast in God through our Lord Jesus Christ	3
	5:15 in the grace of the one man, Jesus Christ	3
	5:17 dominion in life through the one man, Jesus Christ.	3
	5:21 leading to eternal life through Jesus Christ our Lord.	3
	6: 3 who have been baptized into Christ Jesus	3
	6:11 dead to sin and alive to God in Christ Jesus.	3
	6:23 is eternal life in Christ Jesus our Lord.	3
	7:25 Thanks be to God through Jesus Christ our Lord!	3
	8: 1 for those who are in Christ Jesus.	3
	8: 2 For the law of the Spirit of life in Christ Jesus	3
	8:11 the Spirit of him who raised Jesus from the dead	3
	8:34 Who is to condemn? It is Christ Jesus, who died	3
	8:39 from the love of God in Christ Jesus our Lord.	3
	10: 9 if you confess with your lips that Jesus is Lord	3
	13:14 Instead, put on the Lord Jesus Christ	3
	14:14 I know and am persuaded in the Lord Jesus	3
	15: 5 in harmony...in accordance with Christ Jesus	3
	15: 6 the God and Father of our Lord Jesus Christ.	3
	15:16 to be a minister of Christ Jesus to the Gentiles	3
	15:17 In Christ Jesus, then, I have reason to boast	3
	15:30 I appeal to you...by our Lord Jesus Christ	3
	16: 3 who work with me in Christ Jesus	3
	16:20 The grace of our Lord Jesus Christ be with you.	3
	16:25 my gospel and the proclamation of Jesus Christ	3
	16:27 through Jesus Christ, to whom be the glory forever!	3
1Co	1: 1 an apostle of Christ Jesus by the will of God	3
	1: 2 to those who are sanctified in Christ Jesus	3
	1: 2 call on the name of our Lord Jesus Christ	3
	1: 3 God our Father and the Lord Jesus Christ.	3
	1: 4 grace...given you in Christ Jesus	3
	1: 7 for the revealing of our Lord Jesus Christ.	3
	1: 8 blameless on the day of our Lord Jesus Christ.	3
	1: 9 the fellowship of his Son, Jesus Christ our Lord.	3
	1:10 by the name of our Lord Jesus Christ	3
	1:30 He is the source of your life in Christ Jesus	3
	2: 2 except Jesus Christ, and him crucified.	3
	3:11 has been laid; that foundation is Jesus Christ.	3
	4:15 Indeed, in Christ Jesus I became your father	3
	4:17 to remind you of my ways in Christ Jesus	3
	5: 4 in the name of the Lord Jesus	3
	5: 4 with the power of our Lord Jesus	3
	6:11 justified in the name of the Lord Jesus Christ	3
	8: 6 one Lord, Jesus Christ	3
	9: 1 Have I not seen Jesus our Lord?	3
	11:23 the Lord Jesus on the night when he was betrayed	3
	12: 3 "Let Jesus be cursed!"	3
	12: 3 no one can say "Jesus is Lord"	3
	15:31 a boast that I make in Christ Jesus our Lord.	3
	15:57 victory through our Lord Jesus Christ.	3
	16:23 The grace of the Lord Jesus be with you.	3
	16:24 My love be with all of you in Christ Jesus.	3
2Co	1: 1 Paul, an apostle of Christ Jesus by the will of God	3
	1: 2 God our Father and the Lord Jesus Christ.	3
	1: 3 Father of our Lord Jesus Christ	3
	1:14 on the day of the Lord Jesus we are your boast	3
	1:19 the Son of God, Jesus Christ, whom we proclaimed	3
	4: 5 not proclaim ourselves; we proclaim Jesus as Lord	3
	4: 5 and ourselves as your slaves for Jesus' sake	3
	4: 6 the glory of God in the face of Jesus Christ.	3
	4:10 always carrying in the body the death of Jesus	3
	4:10 so that the life of Jesus may also be made visible	3
	4:11 always being given up to death for Jesus' sake	3
	4:11 so that the life of Jesus may be made visible	3
	4:14 know that the one who raised the Lord Jesus	3
	4:14 will raise us also with Jesus	3
	8: 9 you know the generous act of our Lord Jesus Christ	3
	11: 4 For if someone comes and proclaims another Jesus	3
	11:31 The God and Father of the Lord Jesus	3
	13: 5 you not realize that Jesus Christ is in you?	3
	13:13 The grace of the Lord Jesus Christ	3
Gal	1: 1 through Jesus Christ and God the Father	3
	1: 3 God our Father and the Lord Jesus Christ	3
	1:12 received it through a revelation of Jesus Christ	3
	2: 4 spy on the freedom we have in Christ Jesus	3
	2:16 through faith in Jesus Christ.	3
	2:16 And we have come to believe in Christ Jesus	3

	3: 1 Jesus Christ was publicly exhibited	3
	3:14 that in Christ Jesus the blessing of Abraham	3
	3:22 what was promised through faith in Jesus Christ	3
	3:26 for in Christ Jesus you are all children of God	3
	3:28 for all of you are one in Christ Jesus.	3
	4:14 as an angel of God, as Christ Jesus.	3
	5: 6 in Christ Jesus neither circumcision	3
	5:24 those who belong to Christ Jesus	3
	6:14 except the cross of our Lord Jesus Christ	3
	6:17 I carry the marks of Jesus branded on my body.	3
	6:18 the grace of our Lord Jesus Christ	3
Eph	1: 1 Paul, an apostle of Christ Jesus by the will of God	3
	1: 1 the saints who are...faithful in Christ Jesus:	3
	1: 2 God our Father and the Lord Jesus Christ.	3
	1: 3 the God and Father of our Lord Jesus Christ	3
	1: 5 adoption as his children through Jesus Christ	3
	1:15 have heard of your faith in the Lord Jesus	3
	1:17 God of our Lord Jesus Christ, the Father of glory	3
	2: 6 in the heavenly places in Christ Jesus	3
	2: 7 in kindness toward us in Christ Jesus.	3
	2:10 we are what he has made us, created in Christ Jesus	3
	2:13 in Christ Jesus you...have been brought near	3
	2:20 Christ Jesus himself as the cornerstone.	3
	3: 1 Paul am a prisoner for Christ Jesus for the sake of you	3
	3: 6 sharers in the promise in Christ Jesus	3
	3:11 that he has carried out in Christ Jesus our Lord	3
	3:21 to him be glory in the church and in Christ Jesus	3
	4:21 taught in him, as truth is in Jesus.	3
	5:20 in the name of our Lord Jesus Christ.	3
	6:23 God the Father and the Lord Jesus Christ.	3
	6:24 An undying love for our Lord Jesus Christ.	3
Php	1: 1 Paul and Timothy, servants of Christ Jesus	3
	1: 1 To all the saints in Christ Jesus	3
	1: 2 God our Father and the Lord Jesus Christ.	3
	1: 6 to completion by the day of Jesus Christ.	3
	1: 8 I long...with the compassion of Christ Jesus.	3
	1:11 that comes through Jesus Christ	3
	1:19 the help of the Spirit of Jesus Christ	3
	1:26 share abundantly in your boasting in Christ Jesus	3
	2: 5 the same mind be in you that was in Christ Jesus	3
	2:10 at the name of Jesus every knee should bend	3
	2:11 every tongue should confess that Jesus Christ is Lord	3
	2:19 hope in the Lord Jesus to send Timothy to you soon	3
	2:21 their own interests, not those of Jesus Christ.	3
	3: 3 worship in the Spirit of God and boast in Christ Jesus	3
	3: 8 the surpassing value of knowing Christ Jesus	3
	3:12 because Christ Jesus has made me his own.	3
	3:14 prize of the heavenly call of God in Christ Jesus.	3
	3:20 we are expecting a Savior, the Lord Jesus Christ.	3
	4: 7 guard your hearts and your minds in Christ Jesus.	3
	4:19 his riches in glory in Christ Jesus.	3
	4:21 Greet every saint in Christ Jesus.	3
	4:23 The grace of the Lord Jesus Christ be with	3
Col	1: 1 Paul, an apostle of Christ Jesus by the will of God	3
	1: 3 God, the Father of our Lord Jesus Christ	3
	1: 4 we have heard of your faith in Christ Jesus	3
	2: 6 you therefore have received Christ Jesus the Lord	3
	3:17 do everything in the name of the Lord Jesus	3
	4:11 Jesus who is called Justus greets you	3
	4:12 Epaphras...a servant of Christ Jesus	3
1Th	1: 1 in God the Father and the Lord Jesus Christ:	3
	1: 3 steadfastness of hope in our Lord Jesus Christ.	3
	1:10 Jesus, who rescues us from the wrath that is coming.	3
	2:14 imitators of the churches of God in Christ Jesus	3
	2:15 who killed both the Lord Jesus and the prophets	3
	2:19 crown of boasting before our Lord Jesus	3
	3:11 our Lord Jesus direct our way to you.	3
	3:13 the coming of our Lord Jesus with all his saints.	3
	4: 1 we ask and urge you in the Lord Jesus	3
	4: 2 instructions we gave you through the Lord Jesus.	3
	4:14 since we believe that Jesus died and rose again	3
	4:14 through Jesus, God will bring with him those who...	3
	5: 9 salvation through our Lord Jesus Christ	3
	5:18 is the will of God in Christ Jesus for you.	3
	5:23 at the coming of our Lord Jesus Christ.	3
	5:28 The grace of our Lord Jesus Christ be with you.	3
2Th	1: 1 God our Father and the Lord Jesus Christ:	3
	1: 2 God our Father and the Lord Jesus Christ.	3
	1: 7 when the Lord Jesus is revealed from heaven	3
	1: 8 who do not obey the gospel of our Lord Jesus.	3
	1:12 that the name of our Lord Jesus may be glorified	3

2Th	1:12	the grace of our God and the Lord Jesus Christ.	3
	2: 1	As to the coming of our Lord Jesus Christ	3
	2: 8	whom the Lord Jesus will destroy	3
	2:14	may obtain the glory of our Lord Jesus Christ.	3
	2:16	Now may our Lord Jesus Christ himself	3
	3: 6	in the name of our Lord Jesus Christ	3
	3:12	exhort in the Lord Jesus Christ to do their work	3
	3:18	The Grace of our Lord Jesus Christ be with all of you.	3
1Ti	1: 1	Paul, an apostle of Christ Jesus by the command	3
	1: 1	God our Savior and of Christ Jesus our hope	3
	1: 2	God the Father and Christ Jesus our Lord.	3
	1:12	I am grateful to Christ Jesus our Lord,	3
	1:14	the faith and love that are in Christ Jesus.	3
	1:15	Jesus came into the world to save sinners	3
	1:16	Jesus Christ might display...patience	3
	2: 5	one mediator...Christ Jesus, himself human	3
	3:13	the faith that is in Christ Jesus.	3
	4: 6	you will be a good servant of Christ Jesus	3
	5:21	of God and of Christ Jesus and of the elect angels	3
	6: 3	sound words of our Lord Jesus Christ	3
	6:13	In the presence...of Christ Jesus	3
	6:14	until the manifestation of our Lord Jesus Christ	3
2Ti	1: 1	Paul, an apostle of Christ Jesus by the will of God	3
	1: 1	the promise of life that is in Christ Jesus	3
	1: 2	God the Father and Christ Jesus our Lord.	3
	1: 9	This grace was given to us in Christ Jesus	3
	1:10	the appearing of our Savior Christ Jesus	3
	1:13	in the faith and love that are in Christ Jesus.	3
	2: 1	be strong in the grace that is in Christ Jesus;	3
	2: 3	like a good soldier of Christ Jesus.	3
	2: 8	Remember Jesus Christ, raised from the dead	3
	2:10	may also obtain the salvation that is in Christ Jesus	3
	3:12	want to live a godly life in Christ Jesus	3
	3:15	salvation through faith in Christ Jesus.	3
	4: 1	In the presence of God and of Christ Jesus	3
Tit	1: 1	a servant of God and an apostle of Jesus Christ	3
	1: 4	God the Father and Christ Jesus our Savior.	3
	2:13	glory of our great God and Savior, Jesus Christ.	3
	3: 6	through Jesus Christ our Savior	3
Phm	1: 1	Paul, a prisoner of Christ Jesus	3
	1: 3	God our Father and the Lord Jesus Christ.	3
	1: 5	your faith toward the Lord Jesus.	3
	1: 9	now also as a prisoner of Christ Jesus.	3
	1:23	Epaphras, my fellow prisoner in Christ Jesus	3
	1:25	The grace of the Lord Jesus Christ	3
Heb	2: 9	but we do see Jesus...now crowned with glory	3
	2:11	For this reason Jesus is not ashamed to call them brothers	1
	3: 1	Therefore, brothers and sisters...consider that Jesus	3
	3: 3	Yet Jesus is worthy of more glory than Moses,	6
	4:14	a great high priest...Jesus, the Son of God	3
	5: 7	In the days of his flesh, Jesus offered up prayers	5
	6:20	Jesus, a forerunner on our behalf, has entered	3
	7:22	Jesus has also become the guarantee of a better covenant.	3
	8: 6	Jesus has now obtained a more excellent ministry	1
	10:10	the offering of the body of Jesus Christ	3
	10:19	we have confidence...by the blood of Jesus	3
	12: 2	Jesus the pioneer and perfecter of our faith	3
	12:24	to Jesus, the mediator of a new covenant	3
	13: 8	Jesus Christ is the same yesterday and today	3
	13:12	Jesus also suffered outside the city gate	3
	13:20	who brought back from the dead our Lord Jesus	3
	13:21	through Jesus Christ, to whom be the glory forever	3
Jas	1: 1	servant of God and the Lord Jesus Christ	3
	2: 1	really believe our glorious Lord Jesus Christ?	3
1Pe	1: 1	Peter, an apostle of Jesus Christ	3
	1: 2	sanctified...to be obedient to Jesus Christ	3
	1: 3	the God and Father of our Lord Jesus Christ!	3
	1: 3	the resurrection of Jesus Christ from the dead	3
	1: 7	and honor when Jesus Christ is revealed.	3
	1:13	Jesus Christ will bring you when he is revealed.	3
	2: 5	acceptable to God through Jesus Christ.	3
	3:21	through the resurrection of Jesus Christ	3
	4:11	God may be glorified in all things through Jesus Christ.	3
2Pe	1: 1	Peter, a servant and apostle of Jesus Christ	3
	1: 1	righteousness of our...Savior Jesus Christ:	3
	1: 2	in the knowledge of God and of Jesus our Lord.	3
	1: 8	in the knowledge of our Lord Jesus Christ.	3
	1:11	kingdom of our Lord and Savior Jesus Christ	3
	1:14	as indeed our Lord Jesus Christ has made clear to me.	3
	1:16	the power and coming of our Lord Jesus Christ	3
	2:20	knowledge of our Lord and Savior Jesus Christ	3

	3:18	knowledge of our Lord and Savior Jesus Christ.	3
1Jn	1: 3	with the Father and with his Son Jesus Christ.	3
	1: 7	blood of Jesus his Son cleanses us from all sin.	3
	2: 1	an advocate...Jesus Christ the righteous;	3
	2:22	the one who denies that Jesus is the Christ?	3
	3:23	believe in the name of his Son Jesus Christ	3
	4: 2	every spirit that confesses that Jesus Christ	3
	4: 3	every spirit that does not confess Jesus	3
	4:15	who confess that Jesus is the Son of God	3
	5: 1	Everyone who believes that Jesus is the Christ	3
	5: 5	the one who believes that Jesus is the Son of God?	3
	5: 6	the one who came by water and blood, Jesus Christ	3
	5:20	we are in him who is true, in his Son Jesus Christ.	3
2Jn	1: 3	and from Jesus Christ, the Father's Son	3
	1: 7	Jesus Christ has come in the flesh;	3
Jde	1: 1	Jude, a servant of Jesus Christ	3
	1: 1	To those who are...and kept safe for Jesus Christ:	3
	1: 4	and deny our only Master and Lord, Jesus Christ.	3
	1:17	of the apostles of our Lord Jesus Christ;	3
	1:21	look forward to the mercy of our Lord Jesus Christ	3
	1:25	God our Savior, through Jesus Christ our Lord	3
Rev	1: 1	The revelation of Jesus Christ, which God gave	3
	1: 2	testified...to the testimony of Jesus Christ	3
	1: 5	and from Jesus Christ, the faithful witness	3
	1: 9	I, John, your brother who share with you in Jesus	3
	1: 9	because of...the testimony of Jesus.	3
	12:17	and hold the testimony of Jesus.	3
	14:12	and hold fast to the faith of Jesus.	3
	17: 6	drunk with...the blood of the witnesses to Jesus.	3
	19:10	your comrades who hold the testimony of Jesus.	3
	19:10	testimony of Jesus is the spirit of prophecy."	3
	20: 4	beheaded for their testimony to Jesus	3
	22:16	I, Jesus, who sent my angel to you	3
	22:20	I am coming soon." Amen. Come, Lord Jesus!	3
	22:21	The grace of the Lord Jesus be with all	3

Jew *See also* live like a Jew

   1. Contextual: Not in Greek

   2. Ἰουδαῖος, Ioudaios, 2681

Mat	2: 2	"Where is the child who has been born king of the Jews?	2
	27:11	"Are you the King of the Jews?"	2
	27:29	mocked him, saying, "Hail, King of the Jews!"	2
	27:37	"This is Jesus, the King of the Jews."	2
	28:15	story is still told among the Jews to this day.	2
Mrk	7: 3	(For the Pharisees, and all the Jews, do not eat	2
	15: 2	Pilate asked him, "Are you the King of the Jews?"	2
	15: 9	want me to release for you the King of the Jews?"	2
	15:12	do with the man you call the King of the Jews?"	2
	15:18	began saluting him, "Hail, King of the Jews!"	2
	15:26	"The King of the Jews."	2
Lke	23: 3	Pilate asked him, "Are you the king of the Jews?"	2
	23:37	"If you are the King of the Jews, save yourself!"	2
	23:38	"This is the King of the Jews."	2
Jhn	1:19	Jews sent priests and Levites from Jerusalem	2
	2:13	The Passover of the Jews was near	2
	2:18	The Jews then said to him, "What sign can you	2
	2:20	The Jews then said, "This temple has been	2
	3: 1	Nicodemus, a leader of the Jews.	2
	3:25	discussion...between John's disciples and a Jew.	2
	4: 9	you, a Jew, ask a drink of me, a woman of Samaria?"	2
	4: 9	(Jews do not share things in common with Samaritans.)	2
	4:22	for salvation is from the Jews.	2
	5: 1	After this there was a festival of the Jews	2
	5:10	the Jews said to the man who had been cured	2
	5:15	The man went away and told the Jews	2
	5:16	Therefore the Jews started persecuting Jesus	2
	5:18	the Jews were seeking all the more to kill him	2
	6: 4	the Passover, the festival of the Jews, was near.	2
	6:41	Then the Jews began to complain about him	2
	6:52	The Jews then disputed among themselves, saying	2
	7: 1	because the Jews were looking...to kill him.	2
	7:11	The Jews were looking for him at the festival	2
	7:13	no one would speak openly...for fear of the Jews.	2
	7:15	The Jews were astonished at it, saying,	2
	7:35	The Jews said to one another	2
	8:22	the Jews said, "Is he going to kill himself?	2
	8:31	Then Jesus said to the Jews who had believed	2
	8:48	The Jews answered him, "Are we not right	2
	8:52	The Jews said to him, "Now we know	2
	8:57	Then the Jews said to him	2
	9:18	The Jews did not believe that he had been blind	2

9:22	because they were afraid of the Jews;	2
9:22	the Jews had already agreed	2
10:19	Again the Jews were divided	2
10:24	the Jews gathered around him and said to him	2
10:31	The Jews took up stones again to stone him.	2
10:33	The Jews answered, "It is not for a good work	2
11: 8	the Jews were just now trying to stone you	2
11:19	many of the Jews had come to Martha and Mary	2
11:31	The Jews who were with her in the house	2
11:33	and the Jews who came with her also weeping	2
11:36	the Jews said, "See how he loved him!"	2
11:45	Many of the Jews therefore…believed in him	2
11:54	no longer walked about openly among the Jews	2
11:55	Now the Passover of the Jews was near	2
12: 9	great crowd of the Jews learned that he was there	2
12:11	that many of the Jews were deserting	2
13:33	as I said to the Jews so now I say to you	2
18:14	Caiaphas was the one who had advised the Jews	2
18:20	where all the Jews come together.	2
18:31	The Jews replied, "We are not permitted	2
18:33	"Are you the King of the Jews?"	2
18:35	Pilate replied, "I am not a Jew, am I?	2
18:36	to keep me from being handed over to the Jews.	2
18:38	went out to the Jews again and told them	2
18:39	release for you the King of the Jews?"	2
19: 3	to him, saying, "Hail, King of the Jews!"	2
19: 7	The Jews answered him, "We have a law	2
19:12	the Jews cried out, "If you release this man	2
19:14	He said to the Jews, "Here is your King!"	2
19:19	"Jesus of Nazareth, the King of the Jews."	2
19:20	Many of the Jews read this inscription	2
19:21	the chief priests of the Jews said to Pilate	2
19:21	"Do not write, 'The King of the Jews,'	2
19:21	but, 'This man said, I am King of the Jews.' "	2
19:31	Jews did not want the bodies left on the cross	2
19:38	a secret one because of his fear of the Jews	2
19:40	according to the burial custom of the Jews.	2
20:19	the doors…were locked…for fear of the Jews	2
Act 2: 5	devout Jews from every nation under heaven	2
2:10	visitors from Rome, both Jews and proselytes	2
9:22	confounded the Jews who lived in Damascus	2
9:23	the Jews plotted to kill him	2
10:28	"You yourselves know that it is unlawful for a Jew	2
11:19	spoke the word to no one except Jews.	2
12: 3	After he saw that it pleased the Jews	2
13: 5	in the synagogues of the Jews.	2
13:43	many Jews and devout converts to Judaism	2
13:45	when the Jews saw the crowds	2
13:50	the Jews incited the devout women of high standing	2
14: 1	a great number of both Jews and Greeks	2
14: 2	the unbelieving Jews stirred up the Gentiles	2
14: 4	some sided with the Jews	2
14: 5	an attempt was made by both Gentiles and Jews	2
14:19	Jews came there from Antioch and Iconium	2
16: 3	him circumcised because of the Jews	2
16:20	"These men are disturbing our city; they are Jews	2
17: 1	where there was a synagogue of the Jews.	2
17: 5	the Jews became jealous	2
17:11	These Jews were more receptive	1
17:13	when the Jews of Thessalonica learned	2
17:17	he argued in the synagogue with the Jews	2
18: 2	he found a Jew named Aquila, a native of Pontus	2
18: 2	Claudius had ordered all Jews to leave Rome	2
18: 4	to convince Jews and Greeks.	2
18: 5	testifying to the Jews that the Messiah was Jesus.	2
18:12	the Jews made a united attack on Paul	2
18:14	Gallio said to the Jews	2
18:14	justified in accepting the complaint of you Jews;	2
18:19	the synagogue and had a discussion with the Jews.	2
18:24	Now there came to Ephesus a Jew named Apollos	2
18:28	for he powerfully refuted the Jews in public	2
19:10	both Jews and Greeks, heard the word	2
19:17	all residents of Ephesus, both Jews and Greeks	2
19:33	Alexander, whom the Jews had pushed forward.	2
19:34	when they recognized that he was a Jew	2
20: 3	when a plot was made against him by the Jews	2
20:19	that came to me through the plots of the Jews.	2
20:21	testified to both Jews and Greeks	2
21:11	the Jews in Jerusalem will bind the man	2
21:20	thousands of believers there are among the Jews	2
21:21	you teach all the Jews living among the Gentiles	2

21:27	the Jews from Asia…stirred up the whole crowd.	2
21:39	Paul replied, "I am a Jew, from Tarsus in Cilicia	2
22: 3	"I am a Jew, born in Tarsus in Cilicia	2
22:12	well spoken of by all the Jews living there	2
22:30	what Paul was being accused of by the Jews,	2
23:12	In the morning the Jews joined in a conspiracy	2
23:20	"The Jews have agreed to ask you to bring Paul	2
23:27	This man was seized by the Jews	2
24: 5	an agitator among all the Jews	2
24: 9	The Jews also joined in the charge	2
24:19	there were some Jews from Asia	2
24:27	wanted to grant the Jews a favor	2
25: 2	the chief priests and the leaders of the Jews	2
25: 7	the Jews who had gone down from Jerusalem	2
25: 8	in no way committed an offense against the law	2
25: 9	Festus, wishing to do the Jews a favor, asked Paul	2
25:10	I have done no wrong to the Jews	2
25:15	the chief priests and the elders of the Jews	2
26: 2	against all the accusations of the Jews	2
26: 3	all the customs and controversies of the Jews;	2
26: 4	"All the Jews know my way of life from my youth	2
26: 7	for this hope…that I am accused by Jews!	2
26:21	Jews seized me in the temple and tried to kill me.	2
28:17	he called together the local leaders of the Jews.	2
28:19	when the Jews objected	2
Rom 1:16	to the Jew first and also to the Greek.	2
2: 9	the Jew first and also the Greek	2
2:10	the Jew first and also the Greek.	2
2:17	if you call yourself a Jew and rely on the law	2
2:28	For a person is not a Jew who is one outwardly	2
2:29	person is a Jew who is one inwardly	2
3: 1	Then what advantage has the Jew?	2
3: 2	the Jews were entrusted with the oracles of God.	1
3: 9	all, both Jews and Greeks, are under…sin	2
3:29	Or is God the God of Jews only?	2
9:24	not from the Jews only but also from the Gentiles?	2
10:12	there is no distinction between Jew and Greek;	2
1Co 1:22	For Jews demand signs and Greeks desire wisdom	2
1:23	a stumbling block to Jews and foolishness to Gentiles	2
1:24	to those who are the called, both Jews and Greeks	2
9:20	To the Jews I became as a Jew, in order to win Jews.	2
9:20	To the Jews I became as a Jew, in order to win Jews.	2
9:20	To the Jews I became as a Jew, in order to win Jews.	2
10:32	Give no offense to Jews or to Greeks	2
12:13	Jews or Greeks, slaves or free	2
2Co 11:24	received from the Jews the forty lashes	2
Gal 2:13	the other Jews joined him in this hypocrisy	2
2:14	"If you, though a Jew, live like a Gentile	2
2:15	are Jews by birth and not Gentile sinners;	2
3:28	There is no longer Jew or Greek	2
Col 3:11	In that renewal there is no longer Greek and Jew	2
1Th 2:14	as they did from the Jews	2
Rev 2: 9	those who say that they are Jews and are not	2
3: 9	those…who say that they are Jews and are not	2

like a Jew

1. Ἰουδαϊκῶς, *Ioudaikōs*, 2680

Gal 2:14	live like a Gentile and not like a Jew	1

jewel

1. λίθος, *lithos*, 3345
2. λίθος + τίμιος, *lithos + timios*, 3345 + 5508

Rev 17: 4	and adorned with gold and jewels and pearls	2
18:12	cargo of gold, silver, jewels and pearls	2
18:16	adorned with gold, with jewels, and with pearls!	2
21:11	a radiance like a very rare jewel, like jasper	1
21:19	foundations…are adorned with every jewel;	2

Jewish

1. Ἰουδαϊκός, *Ioudaikos*, 2679
2. Ἰουδαῖος, *Ioudaios*, 2681

Lke 7: 3	he sent some Jewish elders to him	2
23:51	he came from the Jewish town of Arimathea	2
Jhn 2: 6	water jars…for the Jewish rites of purification	2
7: 2	Now the Jewish festival of Booths was near.	2
18:12	their officer, and the Jewish police arrested	2
19:42	because it was the Jewish day of Preparation	2
Act 10:22	who is well spoken of by the whole Jewish nation	2
12:11	from all that the Jewish people were expecting."	2
13: 6	a certain magician, a Jewish false prophet	2

Act	14: 1	Paul and Barnabas went into the Jewish synagogue	2
	16: 1	the son of a Jewish woman who was a believer;	2
	17:10	they went to the Jewish synagogue.	2
	19:13	Then some itinerant Jewish exorcists	2
	19:14	Seven sons of a Jewish high priest named Sceva	2
	24:24	his wife Drusilla, who was Jewish,	2
	25:24	about whom the whole Jewish community petitioned	2
Tit	1:14	not paying attention to Jewish myths	1

Jezebel

1. Ἰεζάβελ, *Iezabel, 2630*

Rev	2:20	against you: you tolerate that woman Jezebel	1

Joanan

1. Ἰωανάν, *Iōanan, 2720*

Lke	3:27	son of Joanan, son of Rhesa	1

Joanna

1. Ἰωάννα, *Iōanna, 2721*

Lke	8: 3	Joanna, the wife of Herod's steward Chuza	1
	24:10	Now it was Mary Magdalene, Joanna	1

Job

1. Ἰώβ, *Iōb, 2724*

Jas	5:11	You have heard of the endurance of Job	1

Joda

1. Ἰωδά, *Iōda, 2726*

Lke	3:26	son of Semein, son of Josech, son of Joda	1

Joel

1. Ἰωήλ, *Iōēl, 2727*

Act	2:16	this is what was spoken through the prophet Joel:	1

John

1. Contextual: Not in Greek
2. αὐτός, *autos, 899*
3. Ἰωάννης, *Iōannēs, 2722*

Mat	3: 1	In those days John the Baptist appeared	3
	3: 4	Now John wore clothing of camel's hair	3
	3:13	Jesus came from Galilee to John at the Jordan	3
	3:14	John would have prevented him, saying, "I need	3
	4:12	Now when Jesus heard that John had been arrested	3
	4:21	James son of Zebedee and his brother John	3
	9:14	Then the disciples of John came to him, saying	3
	10: 2	James son of Zebedee, and his brother John;	3
	11: 2	John heard in prison what the Messiah was doing	3
	11: 4	"Go and tell John what you hear and see:	3
	11: 7	began to speak to the crowds about John:	3
	11:11	no one has arisen greater than John the Baptist;	3
	11:12	From the days of John the Baptist until now	3
	11:13	the prophets and the law prophesied until John	3
	11:18	For John came neither eating nor drinking	3
	14: 2	"This is John the Baptist: he has been raised	3
	14: 3	For Herod had arrested John, bound him	3
	14: 4	because John had been telling him	3
	14: 8	she said, "Give me the head of John the Baptist	3
	14:10	he sent and had John beheaded in the prison.	3
	16:14	"Some say John the Baptist, but others Elijah	3
	17: 1	Peter and James and his brother John	3
	17:13	he was speaking to them about John the Baptist.	3
	21:25	Did the baptism of John come from heaven	3
	21:26	for all regard John as a prophet."	3
	21:32	For John came to you in the way of righteousness	3
Mrk	1: 4	John the baptizer appeared in the wilderness	3
	1: 6	Now John was clothed with camel's hair	3
	1: 9	baptized by John in the Jordan.	3
	1:14	Now after John was arrested	3
	1:19	James son of Zebedee and his brother John	3
	1:29	entered the house...with James and John.	3
	2:18	John's disciples and the Pharisees were fasting;	3
	2:18	"Why do John's disciples...fast	3
	3:17	John the brother of James	3
	5:37	Peter, James, and John, the brother of James.	3
	6:14	"John the baptizer has been raised from the dead;	3
	6:16	"John, whom I beheaded, has been raised."	3
	6:17	For Herod himself had sent men who arrested John	3
	6:18	John had been telling Herod, "It is not lawful	3
	6:20	for Herod feared John...and he protected him.	3

	6:24	She replied, "The head of John the baptizer."	3
	6:25	the head of John the Baptist on a platter."	3
	6:27	with orders to bring John's head.	2
	8:28	they answered him, "John the Baptist;	3
	9: 2	Jesus took with him Peter and James and John	3
	9:38	John said to him, "Teacher, we saw someone	3
	10:35	James and John, the sons of Zebedee, came forward	3
	10:41	they began to be angry with James and John.	3
	11:30	Did the baptism of John come from heaven,	3
	11:32	for all regarded John as truly a prophet.	3
	13: 3	Peter, James, John, and Andrew asked him	3
	14:33	He took with him Peter and James and John	3
Lke	1:13	you will name him John.	3
	1:60	his mother said, "No; he is to be called John."	3
	1:63	for a writing tablet and wrote, "His name is John."	3
	3: 2	the word of God came to John son of Zechariah	3
	3: 7	John said to the crowds that came out	1
	3:15	questioning in their hearts concerning John	3
	3:16	John answered all of them by saying, "I baptize	3
	3:20	added to them all by shutting up John in prison	3
	5:10	so also were James and John, sons of Zebedee	3
	5:33	"John's disciples...frequently fast and pray,	3
	6:14	Andrew, and James, and John, and Philip	3
	7:18	disciples of John reported all these things	3
	7:18	John summoned two of his disciples	3
	7:20	"John the Baptist has sent us to you to ask	3
	7:22	"Go and tell John what you have seen and heard:	3
	7:24	When John's messengers had gone	3
	7:24	Jesus began to speak to the crowds about John:	3
	7:28	no one is greater than John;	3
	7:29	baptized with John's baptism.	3
	7:33	For John the Baptist has come eating no bread	3
	8:51	except Peter, John, and James,	3
	9: 7	John had been raised from the dead	3
	9: 9	Herod said, "John I beheaded;	3
	9:19	They answered, "John the Baptist;	3
	9:28	Jesus took with him Peter and John and James	3
	9:49	John answered, "Master, we saw someone	3
	9:54	When his disciples James and John saw it	3
	11: 1	teach us to pray, as John taught his disciples."	3
	16:16	law and the prophets were in effect until John	3
	20: 4	Did the baptism of John come from heaven,	3
	20: 6	they are convinced that John was a prophet."	3
	22: 8	So Jesus sent Peter and John, saying, "Go	3
Jhn	1: 6	was a man sent from God, whose name was John.	3
	1:15	(John testified to him and cried out	3
	1:19	This is the testimony given by John	3
	1:26	John answered them, "I baptize with water.	3
	1:28	across the Jordan where John was baptizing.	3
	1:32	And John testified, "I saw the Spirit descending	3
	1:35	John again was standing with two of his disciples	3
	1:40	One of the two who heard John speak...was Andrew	3
	1:42	"You are Simon son of John.	3
	3:23	John also was baptizing at Aenon near Salim	3
	3:24	John...had not yet been thrown into prison.	3
	3:25	discussion...between John's disciples and a Jew.	3
	3:26	They came to John and said to him, "Rabbi	3
	3:27	John answered, "No one can receive anything	3
	4: 1	making and baptizing more disciples than John"	3
	5:33	You sent messengers to John	3
	5:36	I have a testimony greater than John's.	3
	10:40	to the place where John had been baptizing earlier	3
	10:41	they were saying, "John performed no sign	3
	10:41	everything that John said about this man was true."	3
	21:15	Jesus said to Simon Peter, "Simon son of John	3
	21:16	A second time he said to him, "Simon son of John	3
	21:17	"Simon son of John, do you love me?"	3
Act	1: 5	for John baptized with water	3
	1:13	Peter, and John, and James, and Andrew	3
	1:22	beginning from the baptism of John	3
	3: 1	One day Peter and John were going up to the temple	3
	3: 3	saw Peter and John about to go into the temple	3
	3: 4	Peter looked intently at him, as did John, and said	3
	3:11	While he clung to Peter and John	3
	4: 1	While Peter and John were speaking to the people	3
	4: 6	Caiaphas, John, and Alexander	3
	4:13	Now when they saw the boldness of Peter and John	3
	4:19	Peter and John answered them, "Whether it is right	3
	8:14	they sent Peter and John to them.	3
	8:17	Then Peter and John laid their hands on them	1
	8:25	Now after Peter and John had testified and spoken	1

	10:37	after the baptism that John announced:	3
	11:16	'John baptized with water	3
	12: 2	James, the brother of John, killed with the sword.	3
	12:12	Mary the mother of John whose other name was Mark	3
	12:25	John, whose other name was Mark.	3
	13: 5	they had John also to assist them.	3
	13:13	John, however, left them and returned to Jerusalem;	3
	13:24	before his coming John had already proclaimed	3
	13:25	as John was finishing his work, he said	3
	15:37	wanted to take with them John called Mark.	3
	18:25	though he knew only the baptism of John.	3
	19: 3	They answered, "Into John's baptism."	3
	19: 4	"John baptized with the baptism of repentance	3
Gal	2: 9	James and Cephas and John	3
Rev	1: 1	by sending his angel to his servant John	3
	1: 4	John to the seven churches that are in Asia:	3
	1: 9	I, John, your brother who share with you in Jesus	3
	22: 8	I, John, am the one who heard and saw these things.	3

join

1. γίνομαι, *ginomai, 1181*
2. ἔρχομαι, *erchomai, 2262*
3. κολλάω, *kollaō, 3140*
4. παραλαμβάνω, *paralambanō, 4161*
5. ποιέω, *poieō, 4472*
6. προσκληρόω, *prosklēroō, 4677*
7. προσκλίνω, *prosklinō, 4679*
8. προσκολλάω, *proskollaō, 4681*
9. συναγωνίζομαι, *synagōnizomai, 5253*
10. συνεφίστημι, *synephistēmi, 5308*
11. συντρέχω, *syntrechō, 5340*

Mat	19: 5	and be joined to his wife	3
Mrk	10: 7	be joined to his wife	8
Act	5:13	None of the rest dared to join them	3
	5:36	a number of men, about four hundred, joined him;	7
	8:29	"Go over to this chariot and join it."	3
	9:26	he attempted to join the disciples;	3
	16:22	The crowd joined in attacking them	10
	17: 4	were persuaded and joined Paul and Silas	6
	17:15	instructions to have Silas and Timothy join him	2
	17:34	some of them joined him and became believers	3
	20: 6	in five days we joined them in Troas	2
	21:24	Join these men, go through the rite of purification	4
	23:12	In the morning the Jews joined in a conspiracy	5
	23:13	more than forty who joined in this conspiracy.	5
Rom	15:30	join me in earnest prayer to God on my behalf	9
Eph	5:31	be joined to his wife	8
Php	3:17	Brothers and sisters, join in imitating me	1
1Pe	4: 4	They are surprised that you no longer join them	11

join in a charge

1. συνεπιτίθημι, *synepitithēmi, 5298*

Act	24: 9	The Jews also joined in the charge	1

join in helping

1. συνυπουργέω, *synypourgeō, 5348*

2Co	1:11	you also join in helping us by your prayers	1

join in hypocrisy

1. συνυποκρίνομαι, *synypokrinomai, 5347*

Gal	2:13	the other Jews joined him in this hypocrisy	1

join in suffering

1. συγκακοπαθέω, *synkakopatheō, 5155*

2Ti	1: 8	join with me in suffering for the gospel	1

join together

1. συζεύγνυμι, *syzeugnymi, 5183*
2. συναρμολογέω, *synarmologeō, 5274*

Mat	19: 6	Therefore what God has joined together	1
Mrk	10: 9	Therefore what God has joined together	1
Eph	2:21	In him the whole structure is joined together	2
	4:16	the whole body, joined and knit together	2

joint *See also* joint *heir,* put out of joint

1. ἁρμός, *harmos, 765*

Heb	4:12	until it divides...joints from marrow;	1

Jonah *See also* son of Jonah

1. Ἰωνᾶς, *Iōnas, 2731*

Mat	12:39	except the sign of the prophet Jonah.	1
	12:40	For just as Jonah was three days and three nights	1
	12:41	they repented at the proclamation of Jonah	1
	12:41	see, something greater than Jonah is here!	1
	16: 4	except the sign of Jonah."	1
Lke	11:29	no sign...except the sign of Jonah.	1
	11:30	as Jonah became a sign to the people of Nineveh	1
	11:32	they repented at the proclamation of Jonah	1
	11:32	see, something greater than Jonah is here!	1

Jonam

1. Ἰωνάμ, *Iōnam, 2729*

Lke	3:30	son of Joseph, son of Jonam	1

Joppa

1. Ἰόππη, *Ioppē, 2673*

Act	9:36	in Joppa there was a disciple whose name was Tabitha	1
	9:38	Since Lydda was near Joppa	1
	9:42	This became known throughout Joppa	1
	9:43	in Joppa for some time with a certain Simon, a tanner.	1
	10: 5	Now send men to Joppa	1
	10: 8	he sent them to Joppa.	1
	10:23	some of the believers from Joppa accompanied him.	1
	10:32	Send therefore to Joppa and ask for Simon	1
	11: 5	"I was in the city of Joppa praying	1
	11:13	'Send to Joppa and bring Simon, who is called Peter;	1

Joram

1. Ἰωράμ, *Iōram, 2732*

Mat	1: 8	and Jehoshaphat the father of Joram	1
	1: 8	and Joram the father of Uzziah	1

Jordan

1. Ἰορδάνης, *Iordanēs, 2674*

Mat	3: 5	to him, and all the region along the Jordan	1
	3: 6	they were baptized by him in the river Jordan	1
	3:13	Jesus came from Galilee to John at the Jordan	1
	4:15	Naphtali, on the road by the sea, across the Jordan	1
	4:25	Judea, and from beyond the Jordan.	1
	19: 1	went to the region of Judea beyond the Jordan.	1
Mrk	1: 5	and were baptized by him in the river Jordan	1
	1: 9	baptized by John in the Jordan.	1
	3: 8	beyond the Jordan, and the region around Tyre	1
	10: 1	went to the region of Judea and beyond the Jordan.	1
Lke	3: 3	He went into all the region around the Jordan	1
	4: 1	Jesus...returned from the Jordan	1
Jhn	1:28	This took place in Bethany across the Jordan	1
	3:26	"Rabbi, the one who was with you across the Jordan	1
	10:40	He went away again across the Jordan	1

Jorim

1. Ἰωρίμ, *Iōrim, 2733*

Lke	3:29	son of Eliezer, son of Jorim, son of Matthat	1

Josech

1. Ἰωσήχ, *Iōsēch, 2738*

Lke	3:26	son of Semein, son of Josech, son of Joda	1

Joseph

1. Contextual: Not in Greek
2. Ἰωσήφ, *Iōsēph, 2737*
3. ὁ, *ho, 3836*

Mat	1:16	Jacob the father of Joseph the husband of Mary	2
	1:18	his mother Mary had been engaged to Joseph	2
	1:19	Her husband Joseph, being a righteous man	2
	1:20	said, "Joseph, son of David, do not be afraid	2
	1:24	When Joseph awoke from sleep, he did as the angel	2
	2:13	an angel of the Lord appeared to Joseph in a dream	2
	2:14	Joseph got up, took the child and his mother	3
	2:19	an angel...appeared in a dream to Joseph in Egypt	2
	2:21	Joseph got up, took the child and his mother	3
	13:55	are not his brothers James and Joseph and Simon	2
	27:56	Mary the mother of James and Joseph	2
	27:57	a rich man from Arimathea, named Joseph	2
	27:59	Joseph took the body	2
Mrk	15:43	Joseph of Arimathea, a respected member	2
	15:45	he granted the body to Joseph.	2

Mrk	15:46	Joseph bought a linen cloth	1
Lke	1:27	a virgin engaged to a man whose name was Joseph	2
	2: 4	Joseph also went from the town of Nazareth	2
	2:16	they went with haste and found Mary and Joseph	2
	3:23	was the son (as was thought) of Joseph	2
	3:24	son of Melchi, son of Jannai, son of Joseph	2
	3:30	son of Joseph, son of Jonam	2
	4:22	They said, "Is not this Joseph's son?"	2
	23:50	there was a good and righteous man named Joseph	2
Jhn	1:45	found him…Jesus son of Joseph from Nazareth."	2
	4: 5	ground that Jacob had given to his son Joseph.	2
	6:42	saying, "Is not this Jesus, the son of Joseph	2
	19:38	Joseph of Arimathea, who was a disciple of Jesus	2
Act	1:23	they proposed two, Joseph called Barsabbas	2
	4:36	a Levite, a native of Cyprus, Joseph,	2
	7: 9	"The patriarchs, jealous of Joseph	2
	7:13	Joseph made himself known to his brothers	2
	7:13	Joseph's family became known to Pharaoh.	2
	7:14	Joseph sent and invited his father Jacob	2
	7:18	another king who had not known Joseph	2
Heb	11:21	Jacob…blessed each of the sons of Joseph	2
	11:22	By faith Joseph…made mention of the exodus	2
Rev	7: 8	from the tribe of Joseph twelve thousand,	2

Joses

1. Ἰωσῆς, *Iōsēs, 2736*

Mrk	6: 3	brother of James and Joses and Judas and Simon	1
	15:40	Mary the mother of James the younger and of Joses	1
	15:47	Mary Magdalene and Mary the mother of Joses saw	1

Joshua

1. Ἰησοῦς, *Iēsous, 2652*

Lke	3:29	son of Joshua, son of Eliezer	1
Act	7:45	Our ancestors in turn brought it in with Joshua	1
Heb	4: 8	For if Joshua had given them rest	1

Josiah

1. Ἰωσίας, *Iōsias, 2739*

Mat	1:10	and Amos the father of Josiah	1
	1:11	Josiah the father of Jechoniah and his brothers	1

Jotham

1. Ἰωαθάμ, *Iōatham, 2718*

Mat	1: 9	Uzziah the father of Jotham	1
	1: 9	and Jotham the father of Ahaz	1

journey   *See also* go on a journey, proceed on a journey

1. διαπορεύομαι, *diaporeuomai, 1388*
2. ἐξέρχομαι, *exerchomai, 2002*
3. ὁδοιπορέω, *hodoiporeō, 3844*
4. ὁδοιπορία, *hodoiporia, 3845*
5. ὁδός, *hodos, 3847*

Mat	10:10	no bag for your journey, or two tunics	5
Mrk	6: 8	ordered them to take nothing for their journey	5
	10:17	As he was setting out on a journey	5
Lke	2:44	they went a day's journey.	5
	9: 3	He said to them, "Take nothing for your journey	5
Jhn	4: 6	Jesus, tired out by his journey, was sitting	4
Act	1:12	is near Jerusalem, a sabbath day's journey away.	5
	10: 9	the next day, as they were on their journey	3
Rom	15:24	For I do hope to see you on my journey	1
2Co	11:26	on frequent journeys, in danger from rivers	4
3Jn	1: 7	for they began their journey for the sake of Christ	2

joy   *See also* leap for joy, shout for joy

1. Contextual: Not in Greek
2. ἀγαλλίασις, *agalliasis, 21*
3. εὐφροσύνη, *euphrosynē, 2372*
4. χαρά, *chara, 5915*

Mat	2:10	star had stopped, they were overwhelmed with joy.	4
	13:20	and immediately receives it with joy;	4
	13:44	in his joy he goes and sells all that he has	4
	25:21	enter into the joy of your master.'	4
	25:23	enter into the joy of your master.'	4
	28: 8	with fear and great joy	4
Mrk	4:16	immediately receive it with joy.	4
Lke	1:14	You will have joy and gladness	4
	1:44	the child in my womb leaped for joy.	2
	2:10	see—I am bringing you good news of great joy	4

	8:13	when they hear the word, receive it with joy.	4
	10:17	The seventy returned with joy, saying,	4
	15: 7	more joy in heaven over one sinner who repents	4
	15:10	joy in the presence of the angels of God	4
	24:41	While in their joy they were disbelieving	4
	24:52	and returned to Jerusalem with great joy;	4
Jhn	3:29	For this reason my joy has been fulfilled.	4
	15:11	so that my joy may be in you	4
	15:11	that your joy may be complete.	4
	16:20	your pain will turn into joy.	4
	16:21	the joy of having brought a human being into	4
	16:22	no one will take your joy from you.	4
	16:24	will receive, so that your joy may be complete.	4
	17:13	they may have my joy made complete in themselves.	4
Act	8: 8	there was great joy in that city.	4
	13:52	the disciples were filled with joy	4
	14:17	filling you with food and your hearts with joy."	3
	15: 3	brought great joy to all the believers.	4
Rom	14:17	and peace and joy in the Holy Spirit.	4
	15:13	the God of hope fill you with all joy and peace	4
	15:32	that by God's will I may come to you with joy	4
2Co	1:24	we are workers with you for your joy	4
	2: 3	that my joy would be the joy of all of you.	4
	2: 3	that my joy would be the joy of all of you.	1
	7:13	we rejoiced still more at the joy of Titus	4
	8: 2	their abundant joy and their extreme poverty	4
Gal	5:22	love, joy, peace, patience, kindness, generosity	4
Php	1: 4	constantly praying with joy in…my prayers	4
	1:25	for your progress and joy in faith	4
	2: 2	make my joy complete: be of the same mind	4
	2:29	Welcome him then in the Lord with all joy	4
	4: 1	my joy and crown	4
1Th	1: 6	with joy inspired by the Holy Spirit	4
	2:19	For what is our hope or joy or crown of boasting	4
	2:20	Yes, you are our glory and joy!	4
	3: 9	for all the joy that we feel before our God	4
2Ti	1: 4	so that I may be filled with joy.	4
Phm	1: 7	received much joy and encouragement from your love	4
Heb	12: 2	for the sake of the joy that was set before him	4
	13:17	Let them do this with joy and not with sighing	4
Jas	1: 2	whenever you face trials…consider it nothing but joy	4
	4: 9	be turned into mourning and your joy into dejection.	4
1Pe	1: 8	rejoice with an indescribable and glorious joy	4
1Jn	1: 4	writing these things so that our joy may be complete.	4
2Jn	1:12	so that our joy may be complete.	4
3Jn	1: 4	I have no greater joy than this	4

joyfully

1. χαίρω, *chairō, 5897*
2. χαρά, *chara, 5915*

Lke	19:37	began to praise God joyfully with a loud voice	1
Col	1:11	to endure everything with patience, while joyfully	2

Judah

1. Ἰούδας, *Ioudas, 2683*

Mat	1: 2	Jacob the father of Judah and his brothers	1
	1: 3	Judah the father of Perez and Zerah by Tamar	1
	2: 6	you, Bethlehem, in the land of Judah, are by no	1
	2: 6	are by no means least among the rulers of Judah;	1
Lke	3:30	son of Simeon, son of Judah	1
	3:33	son of Hezron, son of Perez, son of Judah	1
Heb	7:14	evident that our Lord was descended from Judah	1
	8: 8	a new covenant…with the house of Judah	1
Rev	5: 5	See, the Lion of the tribe of Judah…has conquered	1
	7: 5	From the tribe of Judah twelve thousand sealed,	1

Judaism   *See also* convert to Judaism

1. Ἰουδαϊσμός, *Ioudaismos, 2682*

Gal	1:13	heard, no doubt, of my earlier life in Judaism.	1
	1:14	I advanced in Judaism beyond many among my people	1

Judas

1. Ἰούδας, *Ioudas, 2683*

Mat	10: 4	Simon the Cananaean, and Judas Iscariot	1
	13:55	James and Joseph and Simon and Judas?	1
	26:14	one of the twelve, who was called Judas Iscariot	1
	26:25	Judas, who betrayed him, said, "Surely not I,	1
	26:47	Judas, one of the twelve, arrived;	1
	27: 3	Judas, his betrayer, saw that Jesus was condemned	1
Mrk	3:19	Judas Iscariot, who betrayed him.	

	6: 3	brother of James and Joses and Judas and Simon	1
	14:10	Then Judas Iscariot, who was one of the twelve	1
	14:43	while he was still speaking, Judas…arrived;	1
Lke	6:16	Judas son of James, and Judas Iscariot	1
	6:16	Judas Iscariot, who became a traitor.	1
	22: 3	Then Satan entered into Judas called Iscariot	1
	22:47	one called Judas, one of the twelve, was leading	1
	22:48	Jesus said to him, "Judas	1
Jhn	6:71	He was speaking of Judas son of Simon Iscariot	1
	12: 4	Judas Iscariot, one of his disciples	1
	13: 2	the heart of Judas son of Simon Iscariot	1
	13:26	he gave it to Judas son of Simon Iscariot.	1
	13:29	because Judas had the common purse	1
	14:22	Judas (not Iscariot) said to him, "Lord,	1
	18: 2	Now Judas, who betrayed him, also knew the place	1
	18: 3	So Judas brought a detachment of soldiers	1
	18: 5	Judas, who betrayed him, was standing with them.	1
Act	1:13	Simon the Zealot, and Judas son of James.	1
	1:16	Judas, who became a guide for those who arrested Jesus	1
	1:25	the place…from which Judas turned aside	1
	5:37	After him Judas the Galilean rose up	1
	9:11	at the house of Judas look for a man of Tarsus	1
	15:22	They sent Judas called Barsabbas, and Silas	1
	15:27	We have therefore sent Judas and Silas	1
	15:32	Judas and Silas, who were themselves prophets	1

Jude

1. Ἰούδας, *Ioudas, 2683*

Jde	1: 1	Jude, a servant of Jesus…and brother of James	1

Judea

1. Ἰουδαία, *Ioudaia, 2677*
2. Ἰουδαῖος, *Ioudaios, 2681*
3. Ἰούδας, *Ioudas, 2683*

Mat	2: 1	after Jesus was born in Bethlehem of Judea	1
	2: 5	They told him, "In Bethlehem of Judea;	1
	2:22	he heard that Archelaus was ruling over Judea	1
	3: 1	Baptist appeared in the wilderness of Judea	1
	3: 5	Then the people of Jerusalem and all Judea	1
	4:25	Judea, and from beyond the Jordan.	1
	19: 1	went to the region of Judea beyond the Jordan.	1
	24:16	those in Judea must flee to the mountains;	1
Mrk	1: 5	people from the whole Judean countryside	2
	3: 8	great numbers from Judea, Jerusalem, Idumea,	1
	10: 1	went to the region of Judea and beyond the Jordan.	1
	13:14	those in Judea must flee to the mountains;	1
Lke	1: 5	In the days of King Herod of Judea	1
	1:39	to a Judean town in the hill country	3
	1:65	throughout the entire hill country of Judea.	1
	2: 4	from the town of Nazareth in Galilee to Judea	1
	3: 1	Pontius Pilate was governor of Judea	1
	4:44	the message in the synagogues of Judea.	1
	5:17	had come from every village of Galilee and Judea	1
	6:17	Judea, Jerusalem, and the coast of Tyre	1
	7:17	throughout Judea and all the surrounding country	1
	21:21	those in Judea must flee to the mountains	1
	23: 5	teaching throughout all Judea	1
Jhn	3:22	Jesus…went into the Judean countryside,	2
	4: 3	he left Judea and started back to Galilee.	1
	4:47	heard that Jesus had come from Judea to Galilee	1
	4:54	after coming from Judea to Galilee.	1
	7: 1	He did not wish to go about in Judea	1
	7: 3	"Leave here and go to Judea	1
	11: 7	"Let us go to Judea again."	1
Act	1: 8	in Jerusalem, in all Judea and Samaria	1
	2: 9	residents of Mesopotamia, Judea and Cappadocia	1
	2:14	"Men of Judea and all who live in Jerusalem	2
	8: 1	scattered throughout the countryside of Judea	1
	9:31	the church throughout Judea, Galilee, and	1
	10:37	That message spread throughout Judea	1
	10:39	both in Judea and in Jerusalem.	2
	11: 1	the apostles and the believers who were in Judea	1
	11:29	send relief to the believers living in Judea;	1
	12:19	Then he went down from Judea to Caesarea	1
	15: 1	certain individuals came down from Judea	1
	21:10	a prophet named Agabus came down from Judea.	1
	26:20	throughout the countryside of Judea	1
	28:21	"We have received no letters from Judea about you	1
Rom	15:31	I may be rescued from the unbelievers in Judea	1
2Co	1:16	and have you send me on to Judea.	1

Gal	1:22	the churches of Judea that are in Christ;	1
1Th	2:14	churches…that are in Judea	1

judge *See also* appoint as judge, authority to judge, come to judge, judge's *bench*, serve as judge

1. Contextual: Not in Greek
2. ἀνακρίνω, *anakrinō, 373*
3. δικαστής, *dikastēs, 1471*
4. ἡγέομαι, *hēgeomai, 2451*
5. κρίμα + λαμβάνω, *krima + lambanō, 3210 + 3284*
6. κρίνω, *krinō, 3212*
7. κριτής, *kritēs, 3216*
8. κριτικός, *kritikos, 3217*

Mat	5:25	you over to the judge, and the judge to the guard	7
	5:25	you over to the judge, and the judge to the guard	7
	7: 1	"Do not judge, so that you may not be judged.	6
	7: 1	"Do not judge, so that you may not be judged.	6
	7: 2	you will be judged, and the measure you give	6
	12:27	Therefore they will be your judges.	7
	19:28	judging the twelve tribes of Israel.	6
Lke	6:37	"Do not judge, and you will not be judged;	6
	6:37	"Do not judge, and you will not be judged;	6
	7:43	Jesus said to him, "You have judged rightly."	6
	11:19	Therefore they will be your judges.	7
	12:14	who set me to be a judge or arbitrator over you?"	7
	12:57	you not judge for yourselves what is right?	6
	12:58	or you may be dragged before the judge	7
	12:58	the judge hand you over to the officer	7
	18: 2	He said, "In a certain city there was a judge	7
	18: 6	"Listen to what the unjust judge says.	7
	19:22	'I will judge you by your own words	6
	22:30	judging the twelve tribes of Israel.	6
Jhn	5:22	The Father judges no one	6
	5:30	As I hear, I judge; and my judgment is just	6
	7:24	Do not judge by appearances	6
	7:24	judge with right judgment."	6
	7:51	"Our law does not judge people	6
	8:15	You judge by human standards; I judge no one.	6
	8:15	You judge by human standards; I judge no one.	6
	8:16	Yet even if I do judge, my judgment is valid;	6
	8:16	for it is not I alone who judge	1
	8:50	there is one who seeks it and he is the judge.	6
	12:47	I do not judge anyone who hears my words	6
	12:47	for I came not to judge the world	6
	12:48	one who rejects me…has a judge.	6
	18:31	judge him according to your law."	6
Act	4:19	you must judge;	6
	7: 7	I will judge the nation that they serve,' said God	6
	7:27	'Who made you a ruler and a judge over us?	3
	7:35	'Who made you a ruler and a judge?'	3
	10:42	judge of the living and the dead.	7
	13:20	he gave them judges until the time of…Samuel.	7
	13:46	judge yourselves to be unworthy of eternal life	6
	16:15	"If you have judged me to be faithful to the Lord	6
	17:31	fixed a day on which he will have the world judged	6
	18:15	I do not wish to be a judge of these matters."	7
	23: 3	sitting there to judge me according to the law	6
	24:10	many years you have been a judge over this nation.	7
Rom	2: 1	you have no excuse…when you judge others;	6
	2: 1	you, the judge, are doing the very same things.	6
	2: 3	when you judge those who do such things	6
	2:12	all who have sinned…will be judged by the law.	6
	2:16	God…will judge the secret thoughts of all.	6
	3: 4	and prevail in your judging."	6
	3: 6	For then how could God judge the world?	6
	14: 5	Some judge one day to be better than another	6
	14: 5	while others judge all days to be alike.	6
1Co	4: 3	I should be judged by you or by any human court.	2
	4: 3	I do not even judge myself.	2
	4: 4	It is the Lord who judges me.	2
	5:12	For what have I to do with judging those outside?	6
	5:12	those who are inside that you are to judge?	6
	5:13	God will judge those outside.	6
	6: 2	know that the saints will judge the world?	6
	6: 2	if the world is to be judged by you	6
	6: 3	Do you not know that we are to judge angels	6
	10:15	I speak as to sensible people; judge for yourselves	6
	11:13	Judge for yourselves: is it proper	6
	11:31	if we judged ourselves, we would not be judged	6
	11:32	when we are judged by the Lord, we are disciplined	6

1Ti	1:12	because he judged me faithful	4
2Ti	4: 1	who is to judge the living and the dead	6
	4: 8	which the Lord, the righteous judge, will give	7
Heb	4:12	able to judge the thoughts...of the heart.	8
	10:30	And again, "The Lord will judge his people."	6
	12:23	God the judge of all	7
	13: 4	God will judge fornicators and adulterers.	6
Jas	2: 4	and become judges with evil thoughts?	7
	2:12	who are to be judged by the law of liberty.	6
	3: 1	we...will be judged with greater strictness.	5
	4:11	speaks evil against another or judges another,	6
	4:11	speaks evil against the law and judges the law;	6
	4:11	if you judge the law, you are not a doer of the law	6
	4:11	you are not a doer of the law but a judge.	7
	4:12	There is one lawgiver and judge	7
	4:12	So who, then, are you to judge your neighbor?	6
	5: 9	do not grumble...so that you may not be judged.	6
	5: 9	See, the Judge is standing at the doors!	7
1Pe	1:17	If you invoke as Father the one who judges all	6
	2:23	he entrusted himself to the one who judges justly.	6
	4: 5	who stands ready to judge the living and the dead.	6
	4: 6	so that, though they had been judged in the flesh	6
	4: 6	judged in the flesh as everyone is judged,	1
Rev	6:10	how long will it be before you judge and avenge	6
	11:18	and the time for judging the dead	6
	16: 5	"You are just...for you have judged these things;	6
	18: 8	for mighty is the Lord God who judges her."	6
	19: 2	he has judged the great whore	6
	19:11	and in righteousness he judges and makes war.	6
	20:12	dead were judged according to their works,	6
	20:13	all were judged according to what they had done.	6

judge oneself

1. διακρίνω, *diakrinō*, *1359*

1Co	11:31	if we judged ourselves, we would not be judged	1

judgment

See also give judgment, judgment *seat*, make judgment, pass judgment, pronounce judgment, subject to judgment

1. γνώμη, *gnōmē*, *1191*
2. δικαίωμα, *dikaiōma*, *1468*
3. κρίμα, *krima*, *3210*
4. κρίνω, *krinō*, *3212*
5. κρίσις, *krisis*, *3213*

Mat	5:21	'whoever murders shall be liable to judgment.'	5
	5:22	angry...you will be liable to judgment;	5
	7: 2	For with the judgment you make	3
	10:15	land of Sodom and Gomorrah on the day of judgment	5
	11:22	on the day of judgment it will be more tolerable	5
	11:24	on the day of judgment it will be more tolerable	5
	12:36	the day of judgment you will have to give an account	5
	12:41	The people of Nineveh will rise up at the judgment	5
	12:42	The queen of the South will rise up at the judgment	5
Lke	10:14	at the judgment it will be more tolerable for Tyre	5
	11:31	The queen of the South will rise at the judgment	5
	11:32	people of Nineveh will rise up at the judgment	5
Jhn	3:19	this is the judgment, that the light has come	5
	5:22	has given all judgment to the Son	5
	5:24	and does not come under judgment	5
	5:27	has given him authority to execute judgment	5
	5:30	As I hear, I judge; and my judgment is just	5
	7:24	judge with right judgment."	5
	8:16	Yet even if I do judge, my judgment is valid;	5
	9:39	Jesus said, "I came into this world for judgment	3
	12:31	Now is the judgment of this world;	5
	16: 8	about sin and righteousness and judgment:	5
	16:11	about judgment, because the ruler of this world	5
Act	21:25	we have sent a letter with our judgment	4
	24:25	self-control, and the coming judgment	3
Rom	2: 2	God's judgment on those who do such things	3
	2: 3	you will escape the judgment of God?	3
	5:16	For the judgment following one trespass	3
	11:33	How unsearchable are his judgments	3
	13: 2	and those who resist incur judgment.	3
1Co	7:40	in my judgment she is more blessed	1
	11:29	eat and drink judgment against themselves.	3
2Th	1: 5	is evidence of the righteous judgment of God	5
1Ti	5:24	are conspicuous and precede them to judgment	5
Heb	6: 2	resurrection of the dead, and eternal judgment.	3
	9:27	to die once, and after that the judgment	5

	10:27	a fearful prospect of judgment, and a fury of fire	5
Jas	2:13	For judgment will be without mercy	5
	2:13	mercy triumphs over judgment.	5
1Pe	4:17	For the time has come for judgment to begin	3
2Pe	2: 4	into hell...to be kept until the judgment;	5
	2: 9	under punishment until the day of judgment	5
	2:11	do not bring against them a slanderous judgment	5
	3: 7	kept until the day of judgment and destruction	5
1Jn	4:17	that we may have boldness on the day of judgment	5
Jde	1: 6	kept...for the judgment of the great day.	5
	1:15	to execute judgment on all, and to convict everyone	5
Rev	14: 7	"Fear God...for the hour of his judgment has come;	5
	15: 4	for your judgments have been revealed."	2
	16: 7	Lord God...your judgments are true and just!"	5
	17: 1	I will show you the judgment of the great whore	3
	18:10	For in one hour your judgment has come."	5
	18:20	For God has given judgment for you against her.	3
	19: 2	for his judgments are true and just;	5

righteous judgment

1. δικαιοκρισία, *dikaiokrisia*, *1464*

Rom	2: 5	when God's righteous judgment will be revealed.	1

sober judgment

1. σωφρονέω, *sōphroneō*, *5404*

Rom	12: 3	but to think with sober judgment	1

jug

1. βάτος², *batos²*, *1004*

Lke	16: 6	He answered, 'A hundred jugs of olive oil.'	1

Julia

1. Ἰουλία, *Ioulia*, *2684*

Rom	16:15	Greet Philologus, Julia, Nereus and his sister	1

Julius

1. Ἰούλιος, *Ioulios*, *2685*

Act	27: 1	a centurion of the Augustan Cohort, named Julius.	1
	27: 3	Julius treated Paul kindly	1

jump

1. βάλλω, *ballō*, *965*

Jhn	21: 7	and jumped into the sea.	1

jump overboard

1. ἀπορίπτω, *aporiptō*, *681*

Act	27:43	who could swim to jump overboard first	1

jump up

1. ἐξάλλομαι, *exallomai*, *1982*

Act	3: 8	Jumping up, he stood and began to walk	1

Junia

1. Ἰουνιᾶς, *Iounias*, *2687*

Rom	16: 7	Greet Andronicus and Junia, my relatives	1

jurisdiction

1. ἀρχή, *archē*, *794*
2. ἐξουσία, *exousia*, *2026*

Lke	20:20	jurisdiction and authority of the governor.	1
	23: 7	that he was under Herod's jurisdiction	2

just¹

See also just *requirement*

1. Contextual: Not in Greek
2. ἄρτι, *arti*, *785*
3. ἄχρι, *achri*, *948*
4. ἤδη, *ēdē*, *2453*
5. νῦν, *nyn*, *3814*
6. ὀλίγως, *oligōs*, *3903*
7. πλήν, *plēn*, *4440*

Mat	9:18	saying, "My daughter has just died;	2
	21: 3	If anyone says anything to you, just say this,	1
Mrk	11: 3	just say this, 'The Lord needs it	1
Lke	14:20	Another said, 'I have just been married	1
	17: 7	your slave who has just come in from plowing	1
	19:31	just say this, 'The Lord needs it.' "	1
Jhn	12:24	it remains just a single grain;	1
	21: 4	Just after daybreak, Jesus stood on the beach;	4

	21:10 "Bring some of the fish that you have just caught."	5
Act	27:33 Just before daybreak,	3
1Co	16: 7 I do not want to see you now just in passing	1
Php	1:18 Just this, that Christ is proclaimed in every way	7
2Pe	2:18 they entice…people who have just escaped	6

just[2]

1. δίκαιος, *dikaios, 1465*
2. ἔνδικος, *endikos, 1899*

Jhn	5:30 As I hear, I judge; and my judgment is just	1
Rom	7:12 and the commandment is holy and just and good.	1
Php	4: 8 whatever is honorable, whatever is just	1
2Th	1: 6 For it is indeed just of God	1
Heb	2: 2 every…disobedience received a just penalty.	2
1Jn	1: 9 he who is faithful and just will forgive us our sins	1
Rev	15: 3 Just and true are your ways, King of the nations!	1
	16: 5 "You are just, O Holy One, who are and were,	1
	16: 7 Lord God…your judgments are true and just!"	1
	19: 2 for his judgments are true and just;	1

just as

1. Contextual: Not in Greek
2. ἐν, *en, 1877*
3. ἐπί + ὅσος, *epi + hosos, 2093 + 4012*
4. εὐθύς[1], *euthys[1], 2317*
5. καθάπερ, *kathaper, 2749*
6. καθώς, *kathōs, 2777*
7. καθώσπερ, *kathōsper, 2778*
8. κατά + ὅς + τρόπος, *kata + hos + tropos, 2848 + 4005 + 5573*
9. κατά + ὅσος, *kata + hosos, 2848 + 4012*
10. ὁμοίως, *homoiōs, 3931*
11. ὡς, *hōs, 6055*
12. ὡσαύτως, *hōsautōs, 6058*
13. ὥσπερ, *hōsper, 6061*

Mat	3:16 just as he came up from the water, suddenly	4
	12:40 For just as Jonah was three days and three nights	13
	13:40 Just as the weeds are collected	13
	20:28 just as the Son of Man came not to be served	13
	25:40 just as you did it to one of the least of these	3
	25:45 just as you did not do it to one of the least	3
Mrk	1:10 just as he was coming up out of the water	4
	4:36 took him with them in the boat, just as he was.	11
	16: 7 there you will see him, just as he told you."	6
Lke	1: 2 just as they were handed on to us by those	6
	6:36 Be merciful, just as your Father is merciful.	6
	9:33 Just as they were leaving him	2
	11:30 For just as Jonah became a sign to the people	6
	13: 5 unless you repent, you will all perish just as	12
	17:26 Just as it was in the days of Noah	6
	17:28 Likewise, just as it was in the days of Lot:	6
	22:29 on you, just as my Father has conferred on me	6
	24:24 and found it just as the women had said;	6
Jhn	3:14 just as Moses lifted up the serpent	6
	5:21 Indeed, just as the Father raises the dead	13
	5:23 just as they honor the Father.	6
	5:26 For just as the Father has life in himself	13
	6:57 Just as the living Father sent me	6
	10:15 just as the Father knows me and I know the Father.	6
	12:50 I speak just as the Father has told me."	6
	13:34 Just as I have loved you	6
	15: 4 Just as the branch cannot bear fruit by itself	6
	15:10 just as I have kept my Father's commandments	6
	17:14 just as I do not belong to the world.	6
	17:16 just as I do not belong to the world.	6
Act	7:51 just as your ancestors used to do.	11
	10:47 who have received the Holy Spirit just as we have?"	11
	11:15 fell upon them just as it had upon us	13
	15: 8 giving them the Holy Spirit, just as he did to us;	6
	15:11 we will be saved…just as they will."	8
	22: 3 zealous for God, just as all of you are today	6
	23:11 just as you have testified for me in Jerusalem	11
Rom	5:12 just as sin came into the world through one man	13
	5:18 just as one man's trespass led to condemnation	11
	5:19 For just as by the one man's disobedience	13
	5:21 so that, just as sin exercised dominion in death	13
	6: 4 so that, just as Christ was raised from the dead	13
	6:19 just as you once presented your members as slaves	13
	11:30 Just as you were once disobedient to God	13
	15: 7 therefore, just as Christ has welcomed you	6

1Co	1: 6 just as the testimony of Christ has been strengthened	6
	7:22 just as whoever was free when called	10
	10:33 just as I try to please everyone in everything I do	6
	11: 2 traditions just as I handed them on to you.	6
	11:12 just as woman came from man	13
	12:11 to each one individually just as the Spirit chooses.	6
	12:12 For just as the body is one and has many members	5
	15:49 Just as we have borne the image of the man of dust	6
	16:10 he is doing the work of the Lord just as I am;	11
2Co	1: 5 just as the sufferings of Christ are abundant for us	6
	4:13 just as we have the same spirit of faith	1
	7:14 just as everything we said to you was true	11
	10: 7 just as you belong to Christ, so also do we.	6
Gal	2: 7 just as Peter had been entrusted	6
	3: 6 Just as Abraham "believed God	6
	4:29 just as at that time the child who was born	13
Eph	1: 4 just as he chose us in Christ	6
	4: 4 just as you were called to the one hope	6
	5:23 just as Christ is the head of the church	11
	5:24 Just as the church is subject to Christ	11
	5:25 just as Christ loved the church	6
	5:29 cares for it, just as Christ does for the church	6
Php	2:12 my beloved, just as you have always obeyed	6
Col	1: 6 Just as it is bearing fruit and growing	6
	2: 7 just as you were taught	6
	3:13 just as the Lord has forgiven you	6
1Th	1: 5 just as you know what kind of persons we proved to be	6
	2: 4 just as we have been approved by God	6
	3: 6 and long to see us—just as we long to see you.	5
	3:12 just as we abound in love for you.	5
	4: 6 just as we have already told you beforehand	6
2Th	3: 1 just as it is among you	6
Heb	3: 2 just as Moses also "was faithful in all God's house."	11
	3: 3 just as the builder of a house has more honor than	9
	4: 2 For indeed the good news came to us just as to them;	5
	4: 3 just as God has said, "As in my anger I swore	6
	5: 4 only when called by God, just as Aaron was.	7
	9:27 just as it is appointed for mortals to die once	9
Jas	2:26 For just as the body without the spirit is dead	13
2Pe	2: 1 just as there will be false teachers among you	11
1Jn	2: 6 ought to walk just as he walked.	6
	2:27 just as it has taught you, abide in him.	6
	3: 3 all…purify themselves, just as he is pure.	6
	3: 7 who does what is right is righteous, just as he is righteous.	6
	3:23 love one another, just as he has commanded us.	6
2Jn	1: 4 just as we have been commanded by the Father.	6
	1: 6 this is the commandment just as you have heard	6
3Jn	1: 2 just as it is well with your soul.	6
Rev	3:21 just as I myself conquered and sat down with my Father	11

just like

1. ὁμοιοπαθής, *homoiopathēs, 3926*

Act	14:15 We are mortals just like you	1

just now

1. ἄρτι, *arti, 785*
2. νῦν, *nyn, 3814*

Jhn	11: 8 the Jews were just now trying to stone you	2
1Th	3: 6 Timothy has just now come to us from you	1

just outside

1. πρό, *pro, 4574*

Act	14:13 whose temple was just outside the city	1

just so

1. οὕτως, *houtōs, 4048*

Lke	15: 7 Just so, I tell you, there will be more joy	1
	15:10 Just so, I tell you, there is joy	1

just then

1. ἐν + ἐκεῖνος + ὁ + ὥρα, *en + ekeinos + ho + hōra, 1877 + 1697 + 3836 + 6052*
2. ἐπί + οὗτος, *epi + houtos, 2093 + 4047*
3. εὐθύς[1], *euthys[1], 2317*
4. ἰδού, *idou, 2627*

Mat	9: 2 just then some people were carrying a paralyzed	4
	15:22 Just then a Canaanite woman from that region	4
Mrk	1:23 Just then there was in their synagogue a man	3
Lke	5:18 Just then some men came, carrying a paralyzed man	4
	7:21 Jesus had just then cured many people of diseases	1

Lke	8:41	Just then there came a man named Jairus	4
	9:38	Just then a man from the crowd shouted, "Teacher	4
	10:25	Just then a lawyer stood up to test Jesus.	4
	14: 2	Just then, in front of him, there was a man	4
Jhn	4:27	Just then his disciples came.	2

justice　*See also* acknowledge justice, grant justice

1. δικαιοσύνη, *dikaiosynē, 1466*
2. δίκη, *dikē, 1472*
3. ἐκδίκησις, *ekdikēsis, 1689*
4. κρίσις, *krisis, 3213*

Mat	12:18	he will proclaim justice to the Gentiles.	4
	12:20	until he brings justice to victory.	4
	23:23	justice and mercy and faith.	4
Lke	11:42	neglect justice and the love of God;	4
	18: 7	will not God grant justice to his chosen ones	3
	18: 8	he will quickly grant justice to them.	3
Act	8:33	In his humiliation justice was denied him.	4
	24:25	as he discussed justice, self-control,	1
	28: 4	justice has not allowed him to live."	2
Rom	3: 5	our injustice serves to confirm the justice of God	1
Heb	11:33	administered justice, obtained promises	1

justification

1. δικαιοσύνη, *dikaiosynē, 1466*
2. δικαίωμα, *dikaiōma, 1468*
3. δικαίωσις, *dikaiōsis, 1470*

Rom	4:25	and was raised for our justification.	3
	5:16	but the free gift...brings justification.	2
	5:18	leads to justification and life for all.	3
	5:21	grace might...exercise dominion through justification	1
2Co	3: 9	does the ministry of justification abound in glory	1
Gal	2:21	if justification comes through the law	1

justify

1. δικαιοσύνη, *dikaiosynē, 1466*
2. δικαιόω, *dikaioō, 1467*
3. κατά + λόγος, *kata + logos, 2848 + 3364*
4. λόγος, *logos, 3364*

Mat	12:37	for by your words you will be justified	2
Lke	10:29	wanting to justify himself, he asked Jesus	2
	16:15	"You are those who justify yourselves	2
	18:14	this man went down to his home justified	2
Act	18:14	I would be justified in accepting the complaint	3
	19:40	to justify this commotion."	4
Rom	2:13	but the doers of the law who will be justified.	2
	3: 4	"So that you may be justified in your words	2
	3:20	For "no human being will be justified in his sight"	2
	3:24	they are now justified by his grace as a gift	2
	3:26	that he justifies the one who has faith in Jesus.	2
	3:28	a person is justified by faith apart from works	2
	3:30	and he will justify the circumcised	2
	4: 2	For if Abraham was justified by works	2
	4: 5	trusts him who justifies the ungodly	2
	5: 1	since we are justified by faith, we have peace	2
	5: 9	now that we have been justified by his blood	2
	8:30	and those whom he called he also justified;	2
	8:30	and those whom he justified he also glorified.	2
	8:33	It is God who justifies.	2
	10:10	one believes with the heart and so is justified	1
1Co	6:11	justified in the name of the Lord Jesus Christ	2
Gal	2:16	a person is not justified by the works of the law	2
	2:16	so that we might be justified by faith in Christ	2
	2:16	no one will be justified by the works of the law.	2
	2:17	if, in our effort to be justified in Christ	2
	3: 8	God would justify the Gentiles by faith	2
	3:11	no one is justified before God by the law;	2
	3:24	so that we might be justified by faith.	2
	5: 4	You who want to be justified by the law	2
Tit	3: 7	that, having been justified by his grace, we might	2
Jas	2:21	Was not our ancestor Abraham justified by works	2
	2:24	You see that a person is justified by works	2
	2:25	was not Rahab the prostitute also justified by works	2

justly

1. δίκαιος, *dikaios, 1465*
2. δικαίως, *dikaiōs, 1469*

Lke	23:41	we indeed have been condemned justly	2
Col	4: 1	Masters, treat your slaves justly and fairly	1
1Pe	2:23	he entrusted himself to the one who judges justly.	2

Justus

1. Ἰοῦστος, *Ioustos, 2688*

Act	1:23	Joseph called Barsabbas, who was also known as Justus	1
	18: 7	went to the house of a man named Titius Justus	1
Col	4:11	Jesus who is called Justus greets you	1

K

keep

1. Contextual: Not in Greek
2. διατηρέω, *diatēreō, 1413*
3. εἰμί, *eimi, 1639*
4. ἔχω, *echō, 2400*
5. ἵστημι, *histēmi, 2705*
6. καθίστημι, *kathistēmi, 2770*
7. καταλείπω, *kataleipō, 2901*
8. κατέχω, *katechō, 2988*
9. κρατέω, *krateō, 3195*
10. μή, *mē, 3590*
11. παύω, *pauō, 4264*
12. ποιέω, *poieō, 4472*
13. τελέω, *teleō, 5464*
14. τηρέω, *tēreō, 5498*
15. φυλάσσω, *phylassō, 5875*

Mat	15:23	"Send her away, for she keeps shouting after us."	1
	19:17	to enter into life, keep the commandments."	14
	19:20	"I have kept all these;	15
	26:18	I will keep the Passover at your house	12
	28:14	we will satisfy him and keep you out of trouble."	12
Mrk	1:27	and they kept on asking one another	1
	7: 9	in order to keep your tradition!	5
	9:10	So they kept the matter to themselves	9
	10:20	"Teacher, I have kept all these since my youth."	15
	11:18	they kept looking for a way to kill him;	1
Lke	1:22	He kept motioning to them and remained	3
	11:16	to test him, kept demanding from him a sign	1
	12:29	do not keep striving for what you are to eat	1
	12:29	and do not keep worrying.	1
	13:14	leader of the synagogue...kept saying to the crowd	1
	17:12	ten lepers approached him. Keeping their distance	5
	18: 5	yet because this widow keeps bothering me	1
	18:21	He replied, "I have kept all these since my youth."	15
	19:36	people kept spreading their cloaks on the road.	1
	19:47	leaders...kept looking for a way to kill him	1
	22:59	still another kept insisting, "Surely	1
	22:64	they also blindfolded him and kept asking him	1
	22:65	They kept heaping many other insults on him	1
	23:21	they kept shouting, "Crucify, crucify him!"	1
	23:23	they kept urgently demanding with loud shouts	1
	24:16	their eyes were kept from recognizing him.	9
Jhn	2:10	But you have kept the good wine until now."	14
	3:23	and people kept coming and were being baptized	1
	6: 2	A large crowd kept following him	1
	7:19	Yet none of you keeps the law.	12
	8:51	whoever keeps my word will never see death."	14
	8:52	yet you say, 'Whoever keeps my word	14
	8:55	I do know him and I keep his word.	14
	9: 9	He kept saying, "I am the man."	1
	9:10	kept asking him, "Then how were your eyes opened?"	1
	11:37	"Could not he...have kept this man from dying?"	12
	12: 6	he kept the common purse	4
	12: 7	she might keep it for the day of my burial.	14
	12:25	will keep it for eternal life.	15
	12:47	anyone who hears my words and does not keep them	15
	14:15	"If you love me, you will keep my commandments.	14
	14:21	They who have my commandments and keep them	14
	14:23	"Those who love me will keep my word	14
	14:24	Whoever does not love me does not keep my words;	14
	15:10	If you keep my commandments	14
	15:10	just as I have kept my Father's commandments	14
	15:20	if they kept my word, they will keep yours also.	14
	15:20	if they kept my word, they will keep yours also.	14
	17: 6	gave them to me, and they have kept your word.	14
	19: 3	They kept coming up to him, saying, "Hail, King	1
Act	7:53	received the law...and yet you have not kept it."	15
	12: 5	While Peter was kept in prison	14
	12:22	The people kept shouting, "The voice of a god,	1
	15: 5	ordered to keep the law of Moses."	14

15:29	If you keep yourselves from these	2
16:18	She kept doing this for many days.	1
16:23	ordered the jailer to keep them securely.	14
21:36	The crowd that followed kept shouting	1
22:20	keeping the coats of those who killed him.'	15
25: 4	Paul was being kept at Caesarea	14
Rom 2:26	if those who are uncircumcised keep the…law	15
2:27	physically uncircumcised but keep the law	13
11: 4	"I have kept for myself seven thousand who have not	7
11:10	and keep their backs forever bent."	1
1Co 7:37	to keep her as his fianc,e, he will do well.	14
2Co 10:13	keep within the field that God has assigned to us	1
Col 4: 2	keeping alert in it with thanksgiving.	1
1Th 5:23	may your spirit and soul and body be kept sound	14
1Ti 2:12	she is to keep silent.	3
3: 4	keeping his children submissive	4
5:21	I warn you to keep these instructions without prejudice	15
5:22	keep yourself pure.	14
6:14	keep the commandment without spot or blame	14
2Ti 4: 7	I have finished the race, I have kept the faith.	14
Phm 1:13	I wanted to keep him with me	8
Heb 11:28	By faith he kept the Passover	12
13: 4	let the marriage bed be kept undefiled;	1
13: 5	Keep your lives free from the love of money	1
Jas 1:27	to keep oneself unstained by the world.	14
2:10	For whoever keeps the whole law but fails	14
2:16	"Go in peace; keep warm and eat your fill,"	1
1Pe 1: 4	inheritance that is…kept in heaven for you	14
3:10	let them keep their tongues from evil	11
3:16	Keep your conscience clear	4
5: 8	Discipline yourselves, keep alert.	1
2Pe 1: 8	keep you from being ineffective and unfruitful	6
2: 4	into hell…to be kept until the judgment;	14
2: 9	and to keep the unrighteous under punishment	14
3: 7	kept until the day of judgment and destruction	14
1Jn 5:21	Little children, keep yourselves from idols.	15
Jde 1: 6	the angels who did not keep their own position	14
1: 6	he has kept in eternal chains in deepest darkness	14
1:21	keep yourselves in the love of God;	14
1:24	Now to him who is able to keep you from falling	15
Rev 1: 3	who hear and who keep what is written in it;	14
3: 8	you have kept my word and have not denied my name.	14
3:10	you have kept my word of patient endurance	14
3:10	I will keep you from the hour of trial	14
3:18	keep the shame of your nakedness from being seen;	10
12:17	those who keep the commandments of God	14
14:12	saints, those who keep the commandments of God	14
22: 7	Blessed is the one who keeps the words of the prophecy	14
22: 9	with those who keep the words of this book.	14

keep alert
1. ἀγρυπνέω, *agrypneō, 70*
2. γρηγορέω, *grēgoreō, 1213*

Mrk 13:33	Beware, keep alert; for you do not know	1
1Co 16:13	Keep alert, stand firm in your faith	2
Eph 6:18	To that end keep alert and always persevere	1

keep an eye on
1. σκοπέω, *skopeō, 5023*

Rom 16:17	keep an eye on those who cause dissensions	1

keep awake
1. γρηγορέω, *grēgoreō, 1213*

Mat 24:42	Keep awake therefore, for you do not know	1
25:13	Keep awake therefore, for you know neither	1
Mrk 13:35	Therefore, keep awake—for you do not know	1
13:37	what I say to you I say to all: Keep awake."	1
14:34	remain here, and keep awake."	1
14:37	you asleep? Could you not keep awake one hour?	1
14:38	Keep awake and pray that you may not come	1
1Th 5: 6	let us keep awake and be sober;	1

keep away
1. ἀφίστημι, *aphistēmi, 923*
2. στέλλω, *stellō, 5097*

Act 5:38	keep away from these men and let them alone;	1
2Th 3: 6	keep away from believers who…	2

keep back
1. νοσφίζω, *nosphizō, 3802*

Act 5: 2	he kept back some of the proceeds	1
5: 3	to keep back part of the proceeds of the land?	1

keep back by fraud
1. ἀποστερέω, *apostereō, 691*

Jas 5: 4	The wages…which you kept back by fraud, cry out	1

keep from
1. κωλύω, *kōlyō, 3266*
2. μή, *mē, 3590*

Jhn 16: 1	to keep you from stumbling.	2
18:36	to keep me from being handed over to the Jews.	2
Act 4:17	keep it from spreading further among the people	2
4:20	for we cannot keep from speaking about what	2
27:43	kept them from carrying out their plan.	1
2Co 3:13	to keep the people of Israel from gazing	2
4: 4	to keep them from seeing the light of the gospel	2
12: 7	Therefore, to keep me from being too elated.	2
12: 7	to torment me, to keep me from being too elated.	2
Rev 8:12	a third of the day was kept from shining	2

keep from hearing
1. κωφός, *kōphos, 3273*

Mrk 9:25	spirit that keeps this boy from speaking and hearing	1

keep from speaking
1. ἄλαλος, *alalos, 228*

Mrk 9:25	"You spirit that keeps this boy from speaking	1

keep in check with a bridle
1. χαλιναγωγέω, *chalinagōgeō, 5902*

Jas 3: 2	able to keep the whole body in check with a bridle.	1

keep in custody
1. τηρέω, *tēreō, 5498*

Act 24:23	keep him in custody	1
25:21	when Paul had appealed to be kept in custody	1

keep in suspense
1. αἴρω + ὁ + ψυχή, *airō + ho + psychē, 149 + 3836 + 6034*

Jhn 10:24	"How long will you keep us in suspense?	1

keep on
1. ἀεί, *aei, 107*
2. ἐπιμένω, *epimenō, 2152*

Jhn 8: 7	⟦When they kept on questioning him⟧	2
2Pe 1:12	I intend to keep on reminding you of these things	1

keep one's life
1. ζῳογονέω, *zōogoneō, 2441*

Lke 17:33	who lose their life will keep it.	1

keep safe
1. τηρέω, *tēreō, 5498*

Jde 1: 1	To those who are…and kept safe for Jesus Christ:	1

keep secret
1. σιγάω, *sigaō, 4967*

Rom 16:25	the mystery that was kept secret for long ages	1

keep separate
1. ἀφορίζω, *aphorizō, 928*

Gal 2:12	he drew back and kept himself separate	1

keep silence
1. σιγάω, *sigaō, 4967*

Act 15:12	The whole assembly kept silence	1

keep silent
1. σιγάω, *sigaō, 4967*

Lke 9:36	they kept silent and in those days told no one	1

keep under guard
1. φυλάσσω, *phylassō, 5875*

Lke 8:29	he was kept under guard and bound with chains	1
Act 23:35	he ordered that he be kept under guard	1

keep up courage

1. εὐθυμέω, euthymeō, 2313
2. θαρσέω, tharseō, 2510

Act	23:11	stood near him and said, "Keep up your courage!	2
	27:22	I urge you now to keep up your courage	1
	27:25	So keep up your courage, men	1

keep watch over

1. ἀγρυπνέω, agrypneō, 70
2. προσέχω, prosechō, 4668
3. τηρέω, tēreō, 5498
4. φυλάσσω, phylassō, 5875

Mat	27:36	they sat down there and kept watch over him.	3
	27:54	keeping watch over Jesus, saw the earthquake	3
Lke	2: 8	keeping watch over their flock by night.	4
Act	12: 6	guards…were keeping watch over the prison.	3
	20:28	Keep watch over yourselves and over all the flock	2
Heb	13:17	for they are keeping watch over your souls	1

temple keeper

1. νεωκόρος, neōkoros, 3753

Act	19:35	the temple keeper of the great Artemis	1

bronze kettle

1. χαλκίον, chalkion, 5908

Mrk	7: 4	washing of cups, pots, and bronze kettles.)	1

key

1. κλείς, kleis, 3090

Mat	16:19	I will give you the keys of the kingdom of heaven	1
Lke	11:52	you have taken away the key of knowledge;	1
Rev	1:18	and I have the keys of Death and of Hades.	1
	3: 7	holy one, the true one, who has the key of David	1
	9: 1	given the key to the shaft of the bottomless pit;	1
	20: 1	holding in his hand the key to the bottomless pit	1

kick

1. λακτίζω, laktizō, 3280

Act	26:14	It hurts you to kick against the goads.'	1

Kidron

1. Κεδρών, Kedrōn, 3022

Jhn	18: 1	he went out…across the Kidron valley	1

kill

1. Contextual: Not in Greek
2. ἀναίρεσις, anairesis, 358
3. ἀναιρέω, anaireō, 359
4. ἀποθνήσκω, apothnēskō, 633
5. ἀποκτείνω, apokteinō, 650
6. ἀπόλλυμι, apollymi, 660
7. διαχειρίζω, diacheirizō, 1429
8. θανατόω, thanatoō, 2506
9. θύω, thyō, 2604
10. φθορά, phthora, 5785

Mat	2:16	he sent and killed all the children	3
	10:28	Do not fear those who kill the body	5
	10:28	kill the body but cannot kill the soul;	5
	16:21	and be killed, and on the third day be raised.	5
	17:23	they will kill him, and on the third day	5
	21:35	beat one, killed another, and stoned another.	5
	21:38	let us kill him and get his inheritance.'	5
	21:39	and killed him.	5
	22: 6	mistreated them, and killed them.	5
	23:34	some of whom you will kill and crucify	5
	23:37	Jerusalem, the city that kills the prophets	5
	26: 4	to arrest Jesus by stealth and kill him.	5
	27:20	to ask for Barabbas and to have Jesus killed.	6
Mrk	3: 4	to save life or to kill?"	5
	6:19	wanted to kill him. But she could not	5
	8:31	be killed, and after three days rise again.	5
	9:31	they will kill him	5
	9:31	three days after being killed, he will rise again."	5
	10:34	flog him, and kill him;	5
	11:18	they kept looking for a way to kill him;	6
	12: 5	he sent another, and that one they killed.	5
	12: 5	some they beat, and others they killed.	5
	12: 7	'This is the heir; come, let us kill him	5

	12: 8	they seized him, killed him	5
	14: 1	way to arrest Jesus by stealth and kill him;	5
Lke	9:22	be killed, and on the third day be raised."	5
	11:47	tombs of the prophets whom your ancestors killed.	5
	11:48	they killed them, and you build their tombs.	5
	11:49	some of whom they will kill and persecute,'	5
	12: 4	my friends, do not fear those who kill the body	5
	12: 5	fear him who, after he has killed, has authority	5
	13: 4	killed when the tower of Siloam fell on them	5
	13:31	"Get away from here, for Herod wants to kill you."	5
	13:33	for a prophet to be killed outside of Jerusalem.'	6
	13:34	Jerusalem, the city that kills the prophets	5
	15:23	get the fatted calf and kill it	9
	15:27	your father has killed the fatted calf	9
	15:30	you killed the fatted calf for him!'	9
	18:33	they have flogged him, they will kill him,	5
	19:47	leaders…kept looking for a way to kill him	6
	20:14	'This is the heir; let us kill him	5
	20:15	they threw him out of the vineyard and killed him.	5
Jhn	5:18	the Jews were seeking all the more to kill him	5
	7: 1	were looking for an opportunity to kill him.	5
	7:19	you looking for an opportunity to kill me?"	5
	7:20	Who is trying to kill you?"	5
	7:25	this the man whom they are trying to kill?	5
	8:22	the Jews said, "Is he going to kill himself?	5
	8:37	yet you look for an opportunity to kill me	5
	8:40	now you are trying to kill me	5
	10:10	thief comes only to steal and kill and destroy.	9
	16: 2	when those who kill you will think that	5
Act	2:23	this man…you crucified and killed	3
	3:15	you killed the Author of life	5
	5:30	whom you had killed by hanging him on a tree.	7
	5:33	they were enraged and wanted to kill them.	3
	5:36	but he was killed	3
	7:28	Do you want to kill me as you killed the Egyptian	3
	7:28	kill me as you killed the Egyptian yesterday?'	3
	7:52	They killed those who foretold	5
	8: 1	Saul approved of their killing him.	2
	9:23	the Jews plotted to kill him	3
	9:24	watching the gates…so that they might kill him;	3
	9:29	they were attempting to kill him.	3
	10:13	he heard a voice saying, "Get up, Peter; kill and eat."	9
	11: 7	'Get up, Peter; kill and eat.'	9
	12: 2	He had James, the brother of John, killed	3
	13:28	they asked Pilate to have him killed.	3
	16:27	he drew his sword and was about to kill himself	3
	21:31	While they were trying to kill him	5
	22:20	keeping the coats of those who killed him.'	3
	23:12	until they had killed Paul.	5
	23:14	an oath to taste no food until we have killed Paul.	5
	23:21	until they kill him.	3
	23:27	and was about to be killed by them	3
	25: 3	planning an ambush to kill him along the way.	3
	26:21	Jews seized me in the temple and tried to kill me.	7
	27:42	The soldiers' plan was to kill the prisoners	5
Rom	7:11	sin…deceived me and through it killed me.	5
	8:36	"For your sake we are being killed all day	8
	11: 3	"Lord, they have killed your prophets	5
2Co	3: 6	the letter kills, but the Spirit gives life.	5
	6: 9	as punished, and yet not killed;	8
1Th	2:15	who killed both the Lord Jesus and the prophets	5
Heb	11:37	they were killed by the sword;	4
2Pe	2:12	creatures…born to be caught and killed.	10
Rev	2:13	Antipas…who was killed among you	5
	6: 8	authority…to kill with sword, famine, and pestilence,	5
	6:11	who were soon to be killed as they themselves	5
	6:11	to be killed as they themselves had been killed.	1
	9: 5	allowed to torture…but not to kill them	5
	9:15	angels…ready…to kill a third of humankind.	5
	9:18	By…three plagues a third of humankind was killed	5
	9:20	rest of humankind, who were not killed by…plagues	5
	11: 5	must be killed in this manner.	5
	11: 7	make war on them and conquer them and kill them	5
	11:13	seven thousand people were killed in the earthquake	5
	13:10	if you kill with the sword	5
	13:10	if you kill…with the sword you must be killed.	5
	13:15	those who would not worship…to be killed.	5
	19:21	And the rest were killed by the sword	5

kill one's father

1. πατρολῴας, patrolōas, 4260

1Ti 1: 9 for those who kill their father or mother | 1

kill one's mother

   1. μητρολῴας, *mētrolōas, 3618*

1Ti 1: 9 for those who kill their father or mother | 1

kin

   1. συγγενής, *syngenēs, 5150*

Mrk 6: 4 among their own kin, and in their own house." | 1

kind[1] *See also* all kinds, any kind, different kind, every kind, same kind, various kinds, what kind

   1. Contextual: Not in Greek
   2. γένος, *genos, 1169*
   3. οὕτως, *houtōs, 4048*
   4. ποῖος, *poios, 4481*
   5. πρᾶγμα, *pragma, 4547*
   6. τὶς, *tis, 5516*
   7. τοιοῦτος, *toioutos, 5525*

Mat 13:47 and caught fish of every kind; | 2
Mrk 9:29 "This kind can come out only through | 2
Jhn 12:33 to indicate the kind of death he was to die. | 4
    18:32 he indicated the kind of death he was to die.) | 4
    21:19 the kind of death by which he would glorify God.) | 4
1Co 5: 1 of a kind that is not found even among pagans; | 7
    7: 7 one having one kind and another a different | 3
    12:10 to another various kinds of tongues | 2
    12:28 forms of leadership, various kinds of tongues. | 2
    15:38 to each kind of seed its own body. | 1
Eph 5:27 without a spot or wrinkle or anything of the kind | 7
Jas 1:18 so that we would become a kind of first fruits | 6
    3:16 there will also be disorder and wickedness of every kind. | 5
Rev 22: 2 the tree of life with its twelve kinds of fruit | 1

kind[2]

   1. ἀγαθός, *agathos, 19*
   2. καλῶς, *kalōs, 2822*
   3. χρηστεύομαι, *chrēsteuomai, 5980*
   4. χρηστός, *chrēstos, 5982*

Lke 6:35 he is kind to the ungrateful and the wicked. | 4
1Co 13: 4 Love is patient; love is kind; | 3
Eph 4:32 be kind to one another, tenderhearted | 4
Php 4:14 it was kind of you to share my distress. | 2
Tit 2: 5 chaste, good managers of the household, kind | 1
1Pe 2:18 not only those who are kind and gentle | 1

kind enough

   1. καλῶς, *kalōs, 2822*

Act 10:33 you have been kind enough to come. | 1

kindle

   1. ἀνάπτω, *anaptō, 409*
   2. ἅπτω, *haptō, 721*
   3. περιάπτω, *periaptō, 4312*

Lke 12:49 how I wish it were already kindled! | 1
    22:55 When they had kindled a fire | 3
Act 28: 2 they kindled a fire and welcomed all of us | 2

kindly *See also* speak kindly

   1. ἀγαθός, *agathos, 19*
   2. ἤπιος, *ēpios, 2473*
   3. φιλανθρώπως, *philanthrōpōs, 5793*

Act 27: 3 Julius treated Paul kindly | 3
1Th 3: 6 told us also that you always remember us kindly | 1
2Ti 2:24 kindly to everyone, an apt teacher, patient | 2

kindness *See also* loving kindness

   1. εὖ, *eu, 2292*
   2. φιλανθρωπία, *philanthrōpia, 5792*
   3. χρηστός, *chrēstos, 5982*
   4. χρηστότης, *chrēstotēs, 5983*

Mrk 14: 7 you can show kindness to them whenever you wish; | 1
Act 28: 2 The natives showed us unusual kindness. | 2
Rom 2: 4 Or do you despise the riches of his kindness | 4
    2: 4 God's kindness is meant to lead you to repentance? | 3
    3:12 no one who shows kindness, there is not even one." | 4
    11:22 Note then the kindness and the severity of God: | 4
    11:22 God's kindness toward you, provided you continue | 4

    11:22 provided you continue in his kindness; | 4
2Co 6: 6 by purity, knowledge, patience, kindness | 4
Gal 5:22 love, joy, peace, patience, kindness, generosity | 4
Eph 2: 7 in kindness toward us in Christ Jesus. | 4
Col 3:12 compassion, kindness, humility, meekness | 4

kindred

   1. ἀδελφός, *adelphos, 81*
   2. συγγενής, *syngenēs, 5150*

Rom 9: 3 my own people, my kindred according to the flesh. | 2
Heb 7: 5 the people, that is, from their kindred | 1

king

   1. βασιλεύς, *basileus, 995*
   2. βασιλεύω, *basileuō, 996*
   3. βασιλικός, *basilikos, 997*

Mat 1: 6 Jesse the father of King David. | 1
    2: 1 In the time of King Herod, after Jesus was born | 1
    2: 2 "Where is the child who has been born king of the Jews? | 1
    2: 3 When King Herod heard this, he was frightened | 1
    2: 9 When they had heard the king, they set out; | 1
    5:35 for it is the city of the great King. | 1
    10:18 you will be dragged before governors and kings | 1
    14: 9 The king was grieved | 1
    17:25 From whom do kings of the earth take toll | 1
    18:23 a king who wished to settle accounts | 1
    21: 5 Look, your king is coming to you | 1
    22: 2 "The kingdom of heaven may be compared to a king | 1
    22: 7 The king was enraged. He sent his troops | 1
    22:11 "But when the king came in to see the guests | 1
    22:13 the king said to the attendants, 'Bind him | 1
    25:34 the king will say to those at his right hand | 1
    25:40 the king will answer them, 'Truly I tell you | 1
    27:11 "Are you the King of the Jews?" | 1
    27:29 mocked him, saying, "Hail, King of the Jews!" | 1
    27:37 "This is Jesus, the King of the Jews." | 1
    27:42 He is the King of Israel; | 1
Mrk 6:14 King Herod heard of it | 1
    6:22 and the king said to the girl | 1
    6:25 Immediately she rushed back to the king | 1
    6:26 The king was deeply grieved; | 1
    6:27 Immediately the king sent a soldier of the guard | 1
    13: 9 stand before governors and kings because of me | 1
    15: 2 Pilate asked him, "Are you the King of the Jews?" | 1
    15: 9 want me to release for you the King of the Jews?" | 1
    15:12 do with the man you call the King of the Jews?" | 1
    15:18 began saluting him, "Hail, King of the Jews!" | 1
    15:26 "The King of the Jews." | 1
    15:32 Let the Messiah, the King of Israel, come down | 1
Lke 1: 5 In the days of King Herod of Judea | 1
    10:24 many prophets and kings desired to see | 1
    14:31 what king, going out to wage war against another | 1
    14:31 going out to wage war against another king | 1
    19:27 who did not want me to be king over them | 2
    19:38 the king who comes in the name of the Lord! | 1
    21:12 you will be brought before kings and governors | 1
    22:25 "The kings…lord it over them; | 1
    23: 2 saying that he himself is the Messiah, a king." | 1
    23: 3 Pilate asked him, "Are you the king of the Jews?" | 1
    23:37 "If you are the King of the Jews, save yourself!" | 1
    23:38 "This is the King of the Jews." | 1
Jhn 1:49 the Son of God! You are the King of Israel!" | 1
    6:15 and take him by force to make him king | 1
    12:13 the King of Israel!" | 1
    12:15 your king is coming, sitting on a donkey's colt!" | 1
    18:33 "Are you the King of the Jews?" | 1
    18:37 Pilate asked him, "So you are a king?" | 1
    18:37 Jesus answered, "You say that I am a king. | 1
    18:39 release for you the King of the Jews?" | 1
    19: 3 to him, saying, "Hail, King of the Jews!" | 1
    19:12 Everyone who claims to be a king | 1
    19:14 He said to the Jews, "Here is your King!" | 1
    19:15 Pilate asked them, "Shall I crucify your King?" | 1
    19:15 "We have no king but the emperor." | 1
    19:19 "Jesus of Nazareth, the King of the Jews." | 1
    19:21 "Do not write, 'The King of the Jews,' | 1
    19:21 but, 'This man said, I am King of the Jews.' " | 1
Act 4:26 The kings of the earth took their stand | 1
    7:10 when he stood before Pharaoh, king of Egypt | 1
    7:18 until another king who had not known Joseph | 1

Act	9:15	to bring my name before Gentiles and kings	1
	12: 1	King Herod laid violent hands upon some	1
	12:20	winning over Blastus, the king's chamberlain	1
	12:20	country depended on the king's country for food.	3
	13:21	they asked for a king; and God gave them Saul	1
	13:22	he made David their king.	1
	17: 7	saying that there is another king named Jesus."	1
	25:13	King Agrippa and Bernice arrived	1
	25:14	Festus laid Paul's case before the king, saying	1
	25:24	"King Agrippa and all here present with us	1
	25:26	especially before you, King Agrippa	1
	26: 2	"I consider myself fortunate...King Agrippa	1
	26:19	"After that, King Agrippa, I was not disobedient	1
	26:26	the king knows about these things	1
	26:27	King Agrippa, do you believe the prophets?	1
	26:30	Then the king got up, and with him the governor	1
1Co	4: 8	apart from us you have become kings!	2
	4: 8	Indeed, wish that you had become kings,	2
2Co	11:32	the governor under King Aretas guarded the city	1
1Ti	1:17	the King of the ages, immortal, invisible, the only God	1
	2: 2	for kings and all who are in high positions	1
	6:15	the King of kings and Lord of lords.	1
	6:15	the King of kings and Lord of lords.	2
Heb	7: 1	King Melchizedek of Salem, priest of the Most High God	1
	7: 1	Abraham...was returning from defeating the kings	1
	7: 2	His name...means "king of righteousness"	1
	7: 2	he is also king of Salem, that is, "king of peace."	1
	7: 2	he is also king of Salem, that is, "king of peace."	1
	11:23	they were not afraid of the king's edict.	1
	11:27	unafraid of the king's anger;	1
Rev	1: 5	Jesus Christ...the ruler of the kings of the earth.	1
	6:15	Then the kings of the earth and the magnates	1
	9:11	as king over them the angel of the bottomless pit;	1
	10:11	many peoples and nations and languages and kings."	1
	15: 3	Just and true are your ways, King of the nations!	1
	16:12	to prepare the way for the kings from the east.	1
	16:14	who go abroad to the kings of the whole world	1
	17: 2	kings of the earth have committed fornication	1
	17: 9	seven mountains...also, they are seven kings	1
	17:12	And the ten horns that you saw are ten kings	1
	17:12	they are to receive authority as kings	1
	17:14	Lamb...for he is Lord of lords and King of kings	1
	17:14	Lamb...for he is Lord of lords and King of kings	1
	17:18	that rules over the kings of the earth."	1
	18: 3	kings of the earth have committed fornication	1
	18: 9	the kings of the earth...will weep and wail	1
	19:16	a name inscribed, "King of kings and Lord of lords."	1
	19:16	a name inscribed, "King of kings and Lord of lords."	1
	19:18	to eat the flesh of kings, the flesh of captains	1
	19:19	Then I saw the beast and the kings of the earth	1
	21:24	the kings of the earth will bring their glory	1

king with

1. συμβασιλεύω, *symbasileuō*, 5203

1Co	4: 8	so that we might be kings with you!	1

kingdom

1. Contextual: Not in Greek
2. αὐτός, *autos*, 899
3. βασιλεία, *basileia*, 993

Mat	3: 2	"Repent, for the kingdom of heaven has come near."	3
	4: 8	showed him all the kingdoms of the world	3
	4:17	"Repent, for the kingdom of heaven has come near."	3
	4:23	proclaiming the good news of the kingdom and curing	3
	5: 3	spirit, for theirs is the kingdom of heaven.	3
	5:10	for theirs is the kingdom of heaven.	3
	5:19	will be called least in the kingdom of heaven;	3
	5:19	will be called great in the kingdom of heaven.	3
	5:20	you will never enter the kingdom of heaven.	3
	6:10	Your kingdom come. Your will be done, on earth as	3
	6:33	But strive first for the kingdom of God	3
	7:21	"Not everyone...will enter the kingdom of heaven	3
	8:11	and Isaac and Jacob in the kingdom of heaven	3
	8:12	while the heirs of the kingdom will be thrown	3
	9:35	proclaiming the good news of the kingdom,	3
	10: 7	'The kingdom of heaven has come near.'	3
	11:11	yet the least in the kingdom of heaven	3
	11:12	the kingdom of heaven has suffered violence	3
	12:25	"Every kingdom divided against itself	3
	12:26	how then will his kingdom stand?	3

	12:28	then the kingdom of God has come to you.	3
	13:11	to know the secrets of the kingdom of heaven	3
	13:19	When anyone hears the word of the kingdom	3
	13:24	"The kingdom of heaven may be compared to someone	3
	13:31	"The kingdom of heaven is like a mustard	3
	13:33	"The kingdom of heaven is like yeast	3
	13:38	the good seed are the children of the kingdom;	3
	13:41	and they will collect out of his kingdom	3
	13:43	in the kingdom of their Father.	3
	13:44	"The kingdom of heaven is like treasure	3
	13:45	"Again, the kingdom of heaven is like a merchant	3
	13:47	"Again, the kingdom of heaven is like a net	3
	13:52	scribe...trained for the kingdom of heaven	3
	16:19	I will give you the keys of the kingdom of heaven	3
	16:28	see the Son of Man coming in his kingdom."	3
	18: 1	"Who is the greatest in the kingdom of heaven?"	3
	18: 3	you will never enter the kingdom of heaven.	3
	18: 4	is the greatest in the kingdom of heaven.	3
	18:23	the kingdom of heaven may be compared to	3
	19:12	for the sake of the kingdom of heaven.	3
	19:14	to such...that the kingdom of heaven belongs."	3
	19:23	to enter the kingdom of heaven.	3
	19:24	someone who is rich to enter the kingdom of God."	3
	20: 1	"For the kingdom of heaven is like a landowner	3
	20:21	and one at your left, in your kingdom."	3
	21:31	going into the kingdom of God ahead of you.	3
	21:43	the kingdom of God will be taken away from you	3
	21:43	a people that produces the fruits of the kingdom.	2
	22: 2	"The kingdom of heaven may be compared to a king	3
	23:13	you lock people out of the kingdom of heaven.	3
	24: 7	kingdom against kingdom	3
	24: 7	kingdom against kingdom	3
	24:14	this good news of the kingdom will be proclaimed	3
	25: 1	"Then the kingdom of heaven will be like	3
	25:34	inherit the kingdom prepared for you	3
	26:29	new with you in my Father's kingdom."	3
Mrk	1:15	the kingdom of God has come near;	3
	3:24	If a kingdom is divided against itself	3
	3:24	that kingdom cannot stand.	3
	4:11	given the secret of the kingdom of God	3
	4:26	"The kingdom of God is as if someone would scatter	3
	4:30	"With what can we compare the kingdom of God	3
	6:23	I will give you, even half of my kingdom."	3
	9: 1	the kingdom of God has come with power."	3
	9:47	to enter the kingdom of God with one eye	3
	10:14	to such as these that the kingdom of God belongs.	3
	10:15	receive the kingdom of God as a little child	3
	10:23	to enter the kingdom of God!"	3
	10:24	how hard it is to enter the kingdom of God!	3
	10:25	who is rich to enter the kingdom of God."	3
	11:10	the coming kingdom of our ancestor David!	3
	12:34	"You are not far from the kingdom of God."	3
	13: 8	kingdom against kingdom;	3
	13: 8	kingdom against kingdom;	3
	14:25	when I drink it new in the kingdom of God."	3
	15:43	waiting expectantly for the kingdom of God	3
Lke	1:33	of his kingdom there will be no end."	3
	4: 5	in an instant all the kingdoms of the world.	3
	4:43	proclaim the good news of the kingdom of God	3
	6:20	for yours is the kingdom of God.	3
	7:28	least in the kingdom of God is greater	3
	8: 1	bringing the good news of the kingdom of God.	3
	8:10	given to know the secrets of the kingdom of God;	3
	9: 2	he sent them out to proclaim the kingdom of God	3
	9:11	spoke to them about the kingdom of God	3
	9:27	before they see the kingdom of God."	3
	9:60	as for you, go and proclaim the kingdom of God."	3
	9:62	is fit for the kingdom of God."	3
	10: 9	'The kingdom of God has come near to you.'	3
	10:11	the kingdom of God has come near.'	3
	11: 2	hallowed be your name. Your kingdom come.	3
	11:17	"Every kingdom divided against itself	3
	11:18	how will his kingdom stand?	3
	11:20	then the kingdom of God has come to you.	3
	12:31	Instead, strive for his kingdom	3
	12:32	Father's good pleasure to give you the kingdom.	3
	13:18	said therefore, "What is the kingdom of God like?	3
	13:20	"To what should I compare the kingdom of God?	3
	13:28	all the prophets in the kingdom of God	3
	13:29	and will eat in the kingdom of God.	3
	14:15	anyone who will eat bread in the kingdom of God!"	3

16:16	the good news of the kingdom of God is proclaimed	3
17:20	asked…when the kingdom of God was coming	3
17:20	he answered, "The kingdom of God is not coming	3
17:21	in fact, the kingdom of God is among you."	3
18:16	to such as these that the kingdom of God belongs.	3
18:17	whoever does not receive the kingdom of God	3
18:24	"How hard it is…to enter the kingdom of God!	3
18:25	someone who is rich to enter the kingdom of God."	3
18:29	left house…for the sake of the kingdom of God	3
19:11	the kingdom of God was to appear immediately.	3
21:10	kingdom against kingdom;	3
21:10	kingdom against kingdom;	3
21:31	you know that the kingdom of God is near.	3
22:16	until it is fulfilled in the kingdom of God."	3
22:18	until the kingdom of God comes."	3
22:29	I confer on you…a kingdom	3
22:30	you may eat and drink at my table in my kingdom	3
23:42	remember me when you come into your kingdom."	3
23:51	waiting expectantly for the kingdom of God.	3
Jhn 3: 3	no one can see the kingdom of God without	3
3: 5	no one can enter the kingdom of God without	3
18:36	answered, "My kingdom is not from this world.	3
18:36	If my kingdom were from this world	3
18:36	but as it is, my kingdom is not from here."	3
Act 1: 3	speaking about the kingdom of God.	3
1: 6	the time when you will restore the kingdom to Israel?"	3
8:12	proclaiming the good news about the kingdom of God	3
14:22	that we must enter the kingdom of God."	3
19: 8	argued persuasively about the kingdom of God.	3
20:25	I have gone about proclaiming the kingdom	3
28:23	testifying to the kingdom of God	3
28:31	proclaiming the kingdom of God	3
Rom 14:17	For the kingdom of God is not food and drink	3
1Co 4:20	For the kingdom of God depends not on talk	3
6: 9	wrongdoers will not inherit the kingdom of God?	3
6:10	none of these will inherit the kingdom of God.	3
15:24	when he hands over the kingdom to God the Father	3
15:50	cannot inherit the kingdom of God	3
Gal 5:21	will not inherit the kingdom of God.	3
Eph 5: 5	has any inheritance in the kingdom of Christ	3
Col 1:13	transferred us into the kingdom of his beloved Son	3
4:11	among my co-workers for the kingdom of God	3
1Th 2:12	who calls you into his own kingdom and glory.	3
2Th 1: 5	to make you worthy of the kingdom of God	3
2Ti 4: 1	in view of his appearing and his kingdom	3
4:18	save me for his heavenly kingdom.	3
Heb 1: 8	the righteous scepter is the scepter of your kingdom.	3
11:33	who through faith conquered kingdoms	3
12:28	since we are receiving a kingdom that cannot be shaken	3
Jas 2: 5	heirs of the kingdom that he has promised	3
2Pe 1:11	entry into the eternal kingdom of our Lord	3
Rev 1: 6	made us to be a kingdom, priests serving his God	3
1: 9	share with you in Jesus…the kingdom	3
5:10	you have made them to be a kingdom and priests	3
11:15	"The kingdom of the world has become the kingdom	3
11:15	become the kingdom of our Lord and of his Messiah	1
12:10	salvation…power and the kingdom of our God	3
16:10	the beast, and its kingdom was plunged into darkness;	3
17:12	ten kings who have not yet received a kingdom	3
17:17	by agreeing to give their kingdom to the beast	3

kinsfolk

1. ἀδελφός, *adelphos, 81*

Act 7:25	He supposed that his kinsfolk would understand	1

Kish

1. Κίς, *Kis, 3078*

Act 13:21	Saul son of Kish, a man of the tribe of Benjamin	1

kiss

1. καταφιλέω, *kataphileō, 2968*
2. φιλέω, *phileō, 5797*
3. φίλημα, *philēma, 5799*

Mat 26:48	"The one I will kiss is the man; arrest him."	2
26:49	and kissed him.	1
Mrk 14:44	"The one I will kiss is the man;	2
14:45	said, "Rabbi!" and kissed him.	1
Lke 7:38	kissing his feet and anointing them	1
7:45	You gave me no kiss	3
7:45	she has not stopped kissing my feet.	1

15:20	ran and put his arms around him and kissed him.	1
22:47	He approached Jesus to kiss him;	2
22:48	with a kiss that you are betraying the Son of Man?"	3
Act 20:37	they embraced Paul and kissed him	1
Rom 16:16	Greet one another with a holy kiss.	3
1Co 16:20	Greet one another with a holy kiss.	3
2Co 13:12	Greet one another with a holy kiss.	3
1Th 5:26	Greet all the brothers and sisters with a holy kiss.	3
1Pe 5:14	Greet one another with a kiss of love.	3

knee

1. γόνυ, *gony, 1205*
2. προσκυνέω, *proskyneō, 4686*

Mat 18:26	So the slave fell on his knees before him	2
Lke 5: 8	he fell down at Jesus' knees, saying	1
Rom 11: 4	who have not bowed the knee to Baal."	1
14:11	says the Lord, every knee shall bow to me	1
Eph 3:14	For this reason I bow my knees before the Father	1
Php 2:10	at the name of Jesus every knee should bend	1
Heb 12:12	and strengthen your weak knees	1

kneel

1. γονυπετέω, *gonypeteō, 1206*
2. πίπτω, *piptō, 4406*
3. προσκυνέω, *proskyneō, 4686*

Mat 8: 2	a leper who came to him and knelt before him	3
9:18	a leader…came in and knelt before him	3
15:25	she came and knelt before him, saying	3
17:14	a man came to him, knelt before him	1
20:20	kneeling before him, she asked a favor of him.	3
27:29	knelt before him and mocked him, saying	1
Mrk 1:40	kneeling he said to him	1
10:17	a man ran up and knelt before him, and asked	1
Jhn 11:32	Mary…knelt at his feet and said to him, "Lord	2

kneel down

1. πίπτω, *piptō, 4406*
2. τίθημι + ὁ + γόνυ, *tithēmi + ho + gony, 5502 + 3836 + 1205*

Mat 2:11	his mother; and they knelt down and paid him homage.	1
Mrk 15:19	knelt down in homage to him.	2
Lke 22:41	knelt down, and prayed	2
Act 7:60	he knelt down and cried out in a loud voice	2
9:40	Peter…knelt down and prayed.	2
20:36	he knelt down with them all and prayed.	2
21: 5	we knelt down on the beach and prayed	2

knit together

1. συμβιβάζω, *symbibazō, 5204*

Eph 4:16	the whole body, joined and knit together	1

knock

1. κρούω, *krouō, 3218*

Mat 7: 7	knock, and the door will be opened for you.	1
7: 8	for everyone who knocks, the door will be opened.	1
Lke 11: 9	knock, and the door will be opened for you	1
11:10	for everyone who knocks, the door will be opened.	1
12:36	open…for him as soon as he comes and knocks.	1
13:25	begin to stand outside and to knock at the door	1
Act 12:13	When he knocked at the outer gate,	1
12:16	Meanwhile Peter continued knocking;	1
Rev 3:20	Listen! I am standing at the door, knocking;	1

know   *See also* want to know

1. Contextual: Not in Greek
2. ἀφικνέομαι, *aphikneomai, 919*
3. γινώσκω, *ginōskō, 1182*
4. γνωρίζω, *gnōrizō, 1192*
5. γνῶσις, *gnōsis, 1194*
6. γνωστός, *gnōstos, 1196*
7. ἐξέρχομαι, *exerchomai, 2002*
8. ἐπιγινώσκω, *epiginōskō, 2105*
9. ἐπίγνωσις, *epignōsis, 2106*
10. ἐπικαλέω, *epikaleō, 2126*
11. ἐπίσταμαι, *epistamai, 2179*
12. λέγω, *legō, 3306*
13. μανθάνω, *manthanō, 3443*
14. μηνύω, *mēnyō, 3606*
15. οἶδα, *oida, 3857*
16. οὐ + ἀγνοέω, *ou + agnoeō, 4024 + 51*

17. φανερός, *phaneros, 5745*

Mat	6: 3	your left hand know what your right hand is doing	3
	6: 8	like them, for your Father knows what you need	15
	6:32	your heavenly Father knows that you need all these	15
	7:16	You will know them by their fruits.	8
	7:20	Thus you will know them by their fruits.	8
	7:23	Then I will declare to them, 'I never knew you;	3
	9: 6	But so that you may know that the Son of Man	15
	9:30	"See that no one knows of this."	3
	10: 2	first, Simon, also known as Peter	12
	10:26	and nothing secret that will not become known.	3
	11:27	and no one knows the Son except the Father	8
	11:27	and no one knows the Father except the Son	8
	12: 7	if you had known what this means, 'I desire mercy	3
	12:16	ordered them not to make him known.	17
	12:25	He knew what they were thinking and said to them	15
	12:33	for the tree is known by its fruit.	3
	13:11	"To you it has been given to know the secrets	3
	15:12	"Do you know that the Pharisees took offense	15
	20:22	"You do not know what you are asking.	15
	20:25	"You know that the rulers of the Gentiles	15
	21:27	So they answered Jesus, "We do not know."	15
	22:16	"Teacher, we know that you are sincere	15
	22:29	because you know neither the scriptures	15
	24:32	you know that summer is near.	3
	24:33	you know that he is near, at the very gates.	3
	24:36	about that day and hour no one knows	15
	24:39	they knew nothing until the flood came	3
	24:42	Keep awake therefore, for you do not know	15
	24:43	if the owner of the house had known	15
	24:50	at an hour that he does not know.	3
	25:12	'Truly I tell you, I do not know you.'	15
	25:13	you know neither the day nor the hour.	15
	25:24	'Master, I knew that you were a harsh man	3
	25:26	You knew…that I reap where I did not sow	15
	26: 2	"You know that after two days	15
	26:70	"I do not know what you are talking about."	15
	26:72	"I do not know the man."	15
	26:74	"I do not know the man!"	15
	28: 5	I know that you are looking for Jesus	15
Mrk	1:24	I know who you are, the Holy One of God."	15
	1:34	because they knew him.	15
	2:10	so that you may know	15
	3:12	he sternly ordered them not to make him known.	17
	4:27	he does not know how.	15
	5:33	the woman, knowing what had happened to her, came	15
	5:43	He strictly ordered them that no one should know	3
	6:14	Jesus' name had become known.	17
	6:20	knowing that he was a righteous and holy man	15
	7:24	entered a house and did not want anyone to know	3
	9: 6	He did not know what to say	15
	9:30	He did not want anyone to know it;	3
	10:19	You know the commandments:	15
	10:38	"You do not know what you are asking.	15
	10:42	"You know that among the Gentiles	15
	11:33	So they answered Jesus, "We do not know."	15
	12:14	we know that you are sincere, and show deference	15
	12:15	knowing their hypocrisy, he said to them	15
	12:24	know neither the scriptures nor the power of God?	15
	13:28	you know that summer is near.	3
	13:29	you know that he is near, at the very gates.	3
	13:32	about that day or hour no one knows	15
	13:33	Beware, keep alert; for you do not know	15
	13:35	Therefore, keep awake—for you do not know	15
	14:40	they did not know what to say to him.	15
	14:68	"I do not know or understand what you are talking	15
	14:71	"I do not know this man you are talking about."	15
Lke	1: 4	so that you may know the truth	8
	1:18	said to the angel, "How will I know that this	3
	2:43	his parents did not know it.	3
	2:49	not know that I must be in my Father's house?"	15
	4:34	I know who you are, the Holy One of God."	15
	4:41	because they knew that he was the Messiah.	15
	5:24	you may know that the Son of Man has authority	15
	6: 8	he knew what they were thinking	15
	6:44	for each tree is known by its own fruit.	3
	7:39	known who and what kind of woman this is	3
	8:10	"To you it has been given to know the secrets	3
	8:17	that will not become known and come to light.	3
	8:53	they laughed at him, knowing that she was dead.	15
	9:33	not knowing what he said.	15

	10:11	Yet know this:	3
	10:22	no one knows who the Son is except the Father	3
	11:17	he knew what they were thinking and said	15
	12: 2	and nothing secret that will not become known.	3
	12:30	your Father knows that you need them.	15
	12:39	know this: if the owner of the house had known	3
	12:39	if the owner of the house had known at what hour	15
	12:46	at an hour that he does not know	3
	12:47	That slave who knew what his master wanted	3
	12:48	did not know and did what deserved a beating	3
	13:25	'I do not know where you come from.'	15
	13:27	he will say, 'I do not know	15
	16:15	God knows your hearts;	3
	18:20	You know the commandments:	15
	19:22	You knew, did you, that I was a harsh man	15
	20: 7	they did not know where it came from.	15
	20:21	we know that you are right in what you say	15
	21:20	then know that its desolation has come near.	3
	21:30	know that summer is already near.	3
	21:31	you know that the kingdom of God is near.	3
	22:34	until you have denied three times that you know me."	15
	22:57	he denied it, saying, "Woman, I do not know him."	15
	22:60	"Man, I do not know what you are talking about!"	15
	23:34	[[for they do not know what they are doing."]]	15
	24:18	does not know the things that have taken place	3
Jhn	1:10	yet the world did not know him.	3
	1:26	Among you stands one whom you do not know	15
	1:31	I myself did not know him;	15
	1:33	I myself did not know him	15
	1:48	Nathanael asked him, "Where did you get to know me?"	3
	2: 9	and did not know where it came from	15
	2: 9	(though the servants who had drawn the water knew)	15
	2:24	because he knew all people	3
	2:25	for he himself knew what was in everyone.	3
	3: 2	"Rabbi, we know that you are a teacher	15
	3: 8	do not know where it comes from or where it goes.	15
	3:11	"Very truly, I tell you, we speak of what we know	15
	4:10	Jesus answered her, "If you knew the gift of God	15
	4:22	You worship what you do not know;	15
	4:22	we worship what we know	15
	4:25	"I know that Messiah is coming"	15
	4:32	"I have food to eat that you do not know	15
	4:42	we know that this is truly the Savior	15
	5: 6	and knew that he had been there a long time	3
	5:13	man who had been healed did not know who it was	15
	5:32	I know that his testimony to me is true.	15
	5:42	I know that you do not have the love of God	3
	6: 6	he himself knew what he was going to do.	15
	6:42	Jesus…whose father and mother we know?	15
	6:64	Jesus knew from the first	15
	6:69	and know that you are the Holy One of God."	3
	7:17	will know whether the teaching is from God	3
	7:26	Can it be that the authorities really know	3
	7:27	Yet we know where this man is from;	15
	7:27	no one will know where he is from."	3
	7:28	"You know me, and you know where I am from.	15
	7:28	"You know me, and you know where I am from.	15
	7:28	who sent me is true, and you do not know him.	15
	7:29	I know him, because I am from him, and he sent me."	15
	7:49	this crowd, which does not know the law	3
	8:14	valid because I know where I have come from	15
	8:14	do not know where I come from or where I am going.	15
	8:19	Jesus answered, "You know neither me nor my Father.	15
	8:19	If you knew me, you would know my Father also."	15
	8:19	If you knew me, you would know my Father also."	15
	8:32	you will know the truth	3
	8:37	I know that you are descendants of Abraham;	15
	8:52	"Now we know that you have a demon.	3
	8:55	you do not know him. But I know him;	3
	8:55	you do not know him. But I know him;	15
	8:55	if I would say that I do not know him,	15
	8:55	I do know him and I keep his word.	15
	9:12	"Where is he?" He said, "I do not know."	15
	9:20	parents answered, "We know that this is our son	15
	9:21	we do not know how it is that now he sees	15
	9:21	nor do we know who opened his eyes.	15
	9:24	We know that this man is a sinner."	15
	9:25	"I do not know whether he is a sinner.	15
	9:25	One thing I do know, that though I was blind,	15
	9:29	We know that God has spoken to Moses	15
	9:29	we do not know where he comes from."	15

9:30	You do not know where he comes	15
9:31	We know that God does not listen to sinners	15
10: 4	the sheep follow him because they know his voice.	15
10: 5	because they do not know the voice of strangers."	15
10:14	I know my own and my own know me	3
10:14	I know my own and my own know me	3
10:15	just as the Father knows me and I know the Father.	3
10:15	just as the Father knows me and I know the Father.	3
10:27	I know them, and they follow me.	3
10:38	so that you may know and understand	3
11:22	even now I know that God will give you whatever	15
11:24	said to him, "I know that he will rise again	15
11:42	I knew that you always hear me	15
11:49	"You know nothing at all!	15
11:57	orders that anyone who knew where Jesus was	3
11:57	let them know, so that they might arrest him.	14
12:35	do not know where you are going.	15
12:50	I know that his commandment is eternal life.	15
13: 1	Jesus knew that his hour had come to depart	15
13: 3	knowing that the Father had given all things	15
13: 7	"You do not know now what I am doing	15
13:11	For he knew who was to betray him;	15
13:12	"Do you know what I have done to you?	3
13:17	If you know these things	15
13:18	I know whom I have chosen.	15
13:28	no one at the table knew why he said this to him.	3
13:35	everyone will know that you are my disciples	3
14: 4	you know the way to the place where I am going."	15
14: 5	"Lord, we do not know where you are going.	15
14: 5	How can we know the way?"	15
14: 7	If you know me, you will know my Father also	3
14: 7	If you know me, you will know my Father also	3
14: 7	From now on you do know him and have seen him."	3
14: 9	Philip, and you still do not know me?	3
14:17	because it neither sees him nor knows him.	3
14:17	You know him, because he abides with you	3
14:20	On that day you will know that I am in my Father	3
14:31	so that the world may know that I love the Father.	3
15:15	servant does not know what the master is doing;	15
15:21	because they do not know him who sent me.	15
16: 3	because they have not known the Father or me.	3
16:18	We do not know what he is talking about."	15
16:19	Jesus knew that they wanted to ask him	3
16:30	Now we know that you know all things	15
16:30	Now we know that you know all things	15
17: 3	this is eternal life, that they may know you	3
17: 7	Now they know that everything...is from you;	3
17: 8	and know in truth that I came from you;	3
17:23	the world may know that you have sent me	3
17:25	"Righteous Father, the world does not know you	3
17:25	but I know you;	3
17:25	these know that you have sent me.	3
18: 2	Now Judas, who betrayed him, also knew the place	15
18: 4	Jesus, knowing all that was to happen to him	15
18:15	that disciple was known to the high priest	6
18:16	disciple, who was known to the high priest	6
18:21	what I said to them; they know what I said."	15
19: 4	to let you know that I find no case against him."	3
19:10	Do you not know that I have power to release you	15
19:28	Jesus knew that all was now finished	15
19:35	he knows that he tells the truth.)	15
20: 2	we do not know where they have laid him."	15
20:13	I do not know where they have laid him."	15
20:14	she did not know that it was Jesus.	15
21: 4	the disciples did not know that it was Jesus.	15
21:12	because they knew it was the Lord.	15
21:15	to him, "Yes, Lord; you know that I love you."	15
21:16	to him, "Yes, Lord; you know that I love you."	15
21:17	he said to him, "Lord, you know everything;	15
21:17	you know everything; you know that I love you."	3
21:24	we know that his testimony is true.	15

Act	1: 7	"It is not for you to know the times or periods	3
	1:19	This became known to all the residents	6
	1:23	Joseph called Barsabbas, who was also known as Justus	10
	2:14	let this be known to you, and listen to what I say.	6
	2:22	as you yourselves know—	15
	2:30	knew that God had sworn with an oath to him	15
	2:36	Therefore let the entire house of Israel know	3
	3:16	this man...whom you see and know;	15
	3:17	now, friends, I know that you acted in ignorance	15
	4:10	let it be known to all of you	6

5: 7	his wife came in, not knowing what had happened.	15
7:13	Joseph's family became known to Pharaoh.	17
7:18	another king who had not known Joseph	15
7:40	we do not know what has happened to him.'	15
9:24	their plot became known to Saul.	3
9:42	This became known throughout Joppa	6
10:28	"You yourselves know that it is unlawful for a Jew	11
10:36	You know the message he sent to the people of Israel	15
13: 9	Saul, also known as Paul	1
13:38	Let it be known to you therefore, my brothers	6
15: 7	you know that in the early days God made a choice	11
15:18	known from long ago.'	6
16: 3	for they all knew that his father was a Greek.	15
17:19	"May we know what this new teaching is	3
17:20	so we would like to know what it means."	3
18:25	though he knew only the baptism of John.	11
19:15	"Jesus I know, and Paul I know; but who are you?"	3
19:15	"Jesus I know, and Paul I know; but who are you?"	11
19:17	this became known to all residents of Ephesus	6
19:25	and said, "Men, you know	11
19:32	most of them did not know why they had come	15
19:35	who is there that does not know that the city	3
20:18	"You yourselves know how I lived among you	11
20:22	not knowing what will happen to me there	15
20:25	now I know that none of you...will ever see	15
20:29	I know that...savage wolves will come	15
20:34	You know for yourselves	3
21:24	Thus all will know	3
21:37	The tribune replied, "Do you know Greek?	3
22:14	God of our ancestors has chosen you to know his will	3
22:19	I said, 'Lord, they themselves know	11
23:28	Since I wanted to know the charge	8
24:10	knowing that...you have been a judge	11
25:10	done no wrong to the Jews, as you very well know.	8
26: 4	"All the Jews know my way of life from my youth	15
26:26	the king knows about these things	11
26:27	I know that you believe."	15
28:22	we know that everywhere it is spoken against."	6
28:28	Let it be known to you then that this salvation	6

Rom	1:13	I want you to know, brothers and sisters	16
	1:19	For what can be known about God is plain to them	6
	1:21	for though they knew God, they did not honor him	3
	1:32	They know God's decree	8
	2: 2	"We know that God's judgment on those who do such	15
	2:18	know his will and determine what is best	3
	3:17	the way of peace they have not known."	3
	3:19	Now we know that whatever the law says	15
	5: 3	knowing that suffering produces endurance	15
	6: 6	We know that our old self was crucified with him	3
	6: 9	We know that Christ...will never die again;	15
	6:16	Do you not know that if you present yourselves	15
	7: 1	for I am speaking to those who know the law	3
	7: 7	not been for the law, I would not have known sin.	3
	7: 7	I would not have known what it is to covet	15
	7:14	For we know that the law is spiritual	15
	7:18	For I know that nothing good dwells within me	15
	8:22	We know that...creation has been groaning	15
	8:26	for we do not know how to pray as we ought	15
	8:27	knows what is the mind of the Spirit	15
	8:28	We know that all things work together for good	15
	11: 2	Do you not know what the scripture says of Elijah	15
	11:34	"For who has known the mind of the Lord?	3
	13:11	Besides this, you know what time it is	15
	14:14	I know and am persuaded in the Lord Jesus	15
	15:29	I know that when I come to you	15
	16:19	For while your obedience is known to all	2

1Co	1:16	I do not know whether I baptized anyone else.)	15
	1:21	the world did not know God through wisdom	3
	2: 2	For I decided to know nothing among you	15
	2:11	what human being knows what is truly human	15
	2:16	"For who has known the mind of the Lord	3
	3:16	Do you not know that you are God's temple	15
	3:20	"The Lord knows the thoughts of the wise, that	3
	5: 6	Your boasting is not a good thing. Do you not know	15
	6: 2	know that the saints will judge the world?	15
	6: 3	Do you not know that we are to judge angels	15
	6: 9	Do you not know that wrongdoers will not inherit	15
	6:15	know that your bodies are members of Christ?	15
	6:16	know that whoever is united to a prostitute	15
	6:19	do you not know that your body is a temple	15
	7:16	Wife, for all you know	15

1Co	7:16	Husband, for all you know	15
	8: 1	we know that "all of us possess knowledge."	15
	8: 2	Anyone who claims to know something	3
	8: 3	anyone who loves God is known by him.	3
	8: 4	we know that "no idol in the world really exists,"	15
	9:13	Do you not know that those who are employed	15
	9:24	Do you not know that in a race	15
	12: 2	You know that when you were pagans	15
	13: 9	For we know only in part	3
	13:12	Now I know only in part; then I will know fully	3
	14: 7	how will anyone know what is being played?	3
	14: 9	how will anyone know what is being said?	3
	14:11	If then I do not know the meaning of a sound	15
	14:16	since the outsider does not know what you are saying?	15
	14:35	If there is anything they desire to know	13
	15:58	know that in the Lord your labor is not in vain	15
	16:15	know that members of the household of Stephanas	15
2Co	1: 7	we know that as you share in our sufferings	15
	2: 4	to let you know the abundant love that I have	3
	2: 9	know whether you are obedient in everything.	3
	2:14	the fragrance that comes from knowing him.	5
	3: 2	to be known and read by all;	3
	4:14	know that the one who raised the Lord Jesus	15
	5: 1	For we know that if the earthly tent we live	15
	5: 6	we know that while we are at home in the body	15
	5:11	Therefore, knowing the fear of the Lord	15
	5:16	even though we once knew Christ	3
	5:16	we know him no longer in that way.	3
	5:21	For our sake he made him to be sin who knew no sin	3
	8: 9	you know the generous act of our Lord Jesus Christ	3
	9: 2	for I know your eagerness	15
	11:11	why? Because I do not love you? God knows I do!	15
	11:31	God…knows that I do not lie.	15
	12: 2	I know a person in Christ	15
	12: 2	I do not know; God knows.	15
	12: 2	I do not know; God knows.	15
	12: 3	I know that such a person	15
	12: 3	I do not know; God knows—	15
	12: 3	I do not know; God knows—	15
Gal	2:16	know that a person is not justified by the works	15
	4: 8	Formerly, when you did not know God	15
	4: 9	Now, however, that you have come to know God	3
	4: 9	or rather to be known by God	3
	4:13	You know that it was because of a physical infirmity	15
Eph	1:17	revelation as you come to know him	9
	1:18	know what is the hope to which he has called you	15
	3:19	to know the love of Christ	3
	6: 8	knowing that whatever good we do	15
	6: 9	you know that both of you have the same Master	15
	6:21	you also may know how I am and what I am doing	15
	6:22	to let you know how we are	3
Php	1:12	I want you to know, beloved	3
	1:13	so that it has become known	17
	1:16	knowing that I have been put here	15
	1:19	for I know that through your prayers	15
	1:22	and I do not know which I prefer.	4
	1:25	convinced of this, I know that I will remain	15
	1:27	will know that you are standing firm	1
	2:22	Timothy's worth you know	3
	3: 8	the surpassing value of knowing Christ Jesus	5
	3:10	I want to know Christ and the power of his resurrection	3
	4: 5	Let your gentleness be known to everyone.	3
	4:12	I know what it is to have little,	15
	4:12	have little, and I know what it is to have plenty.	15
	4:15	You Philippians indeed know	15
Col	2: 1	want you to know how much I am struggling for you	15
	3:24	know that…you will receive the inheritance	15
	4: 1	know that you also have a Master in heaven.	15
	4: 6	you may know how you ought to answer everyone.	15
	4: 8	so that you may know how we are	3
1Th	1: 4	For we know, brothers and sisters beloved by God	15
	1: 5	you know what kind of persons we proved to be	15
	1: 8	every place your faith in God has become known	7
	2: 1	You yourselves know, brothers and sisters	15
	2: 2	shamefully mistreated at Philippi, as you know	15
	2: 5	As you know and as God is our witness,	15
	2:11	As you know, we dealt with each one of you	15
	3: 3	know that this is what we are destined for.	15
	3: 4	so it turned out, as you know.	15
	4: 2	For you know what instructions we gave you	15
	4: 5	like the Gentiles who do not know God;	15
	5: 2	you…know very well that the day of the Lord	15
2Th	1: 8	vengeance on those who do not know God	15
	2: 6	you know what is now restraining him	15
	3: 7	you yourselves know how you ought to imitate us;	15
1Ti	1: 4	rather than the divine training that is known by faith.	1
	1: 8	Now we know that the law is good	15
	3:15	you may know how one ought to behave	15
	4: 3	those who believe and know the truth.	8
2Ti	1:12	for I know the one in whom I have put my trust	15
	1:18	you know very well how much service he rendered	3
	2:19	"The Lord knows those who are his,"	3
	2:23	you know that they breed quarrels.	15
	2:25	they will repent and come to know the truth	9
	3:14	knowing from whom you learned it	15
	3:15	from childhood you have known the sacred writings	15
Tit	1:16	They profess to know God	15
	3:11	since you know that such a person is perverted	15
Phm	1:21	knowing that you will do even more than I say.	15
Heb	3:10	and they have not known my ways.'	3
	8:11	say to each other, 'Know the Lord,'	3
	8:11	'Know the Lord,' for they shall all know me	15
	10:30	we know the one who said, "Vengeance is mine	15
	10:34	knowing that you…possessed something better	3
	11: 8	he set out, not knowing where he was going.	11
	12:17	You know that later…he was rejected	15
	13:23	I want you to know…	3
Jas	1: 3	because you know that the testing of your faith	3
	3: 1	for you know that we who teach will be judged	15
	4: 4	Do you not know that friendship with the world	15
	4:14	Yet you do not even know what tomorrow	11
	4:17	knows the right thing to do and fails to do it	15
	5:20	you should know that whoever brings back a sinner	3
1Pe	1:18	You know that you were ransomed	15
	5: 9	know that your brothers and sisters in all the world	15
2Pe	1:12	you know them already and are established in the truth	15
	1:14	know that my death will come soon	15
	2:21	better for them never to have known the way	8
	2:21	than, after knowing it, to turn back	8
1Jn	2: 3	by this we may be sure that we know him	3
	2: 4	says, "I have come to know him," but does not obey	3
	2:11	and does not know the way to go	15
	2:13	because you know him who is from the beginning.	3
	2:14	because you know the Father.	3
	2:14	because you know him who is from the beginning.	3
	2:18	From this we know that it is the last hour.	3
	2:21	not because you do not know the truth	15
	2:21	I write to you…because you know it	15
	2:21	and you know that no lie comes from the truth.	1
	2:29	If you know that he is righteous, you may be sure	15
	3: 1	The reason the world does not know us	3
	3: 1	is that it did not know him.	3
	3: 2	What we do know is this: when he is revealed,	15
	3: 5	You know that he was revealed to take away sins	15
	3: 6	no one who sins has either seen him or known him.	3
	3:14	We know that we have passed from death to life	15
	3:15	you know that murderers do not have eternal life.	15
	3:16	We know love by this, that he laid down his life	3
	3:19	by this we will know that we are from the truth	3
	3:20	God is greater…and he knows everything.	3
	3:24	And by this we know that he abides in us	3
	4: 2	By this you know the Spirit of God:	3
	4: 6	We are from God. Whoever knows God listens to us	3
	4: 6	From this we know the spirit of truth	3
	4: 7	everyone who loves is born of God and knows God.	3
	4: 8	Whoever does not love does not know God	3
	4:13	By this we know that we abide in him and he in us	3
	4:16	we have known and believe the love that God has for us.	3
	5: 2	By this we know that we love the children of God	3
	5:13	so that you may know that you have eternal life.	15
	5:15	if we know that he hears us in whatever we ask	15
	5:15	we know that we have obtained the requests	15
	5:18	We know that those who are born of God do not sin	15
	5:19	We know that we are God's children	15
	5:20	we know that the Son of God has come	15
	5:20	understanding so that we may know him who is true;	3
2Jn	1: 1	and not only I but also all who know the truth	3
3Jn	1:12	and you know that our testimony is true.	15
Jde	1:10	destroyed by those things…they know by instinct.	11
Rev	2: 2	"I know your works, your toil and your patient	15
	2: 2	I know that you cannot tolerate evildoers	1
	2: 3	I also know that you are enduring patiently	1

2: 9	"I know your affliction and your poverty	15
2:13	"I know where you are living, where Satan's throne is.	15
2:17	a new name…that no one knows except the one	15
2:19	"I know your works—your love, faith, service,	15
2:19	I know that your last works are greater	1
2:23	And all the churches will know that I am the one	3
3: 1	"I know your works; you have a name of being alive	15
3: 3	you will not know at what hour I will come to you.	3
3: 8	"I know your works.	15
3: 8	I know that you have but little power	1
3:15	"I know your works; you are neither cold nor hot.	15
7:14	I said to him, "Sir, you are the one that knows."	15
12:12	because he knows that his time is short!"	15
19:12	he has a name inscribed that no one knows	15

know a long time

1. προγινώσκω, *proginōskō, 4589*

Act 26: 5 They have known for a long time 1

know fully

1. ἐπιγινώσκω, *epiginōskō, 2105*

1Co 13:12 Now I know only in part; then I will know fully 1
13:12 even as I have been fully known. 1

know how

1. γινώσκω, *ginōskō, 1182*
2. οἶδα, *oida, 3857*

Mat 7:11	If you then, who are evil, know how to give good gifts	2
16: 3	You know how to interpret	1
Lke 11:13	you…know how to give good gifts	2
12:56	You know how to interpret the appearance	2
12:56	do you not know how to interpret the present	2
1Th 4: 4	each one of you know how to control your own body	2
1Ti 3: 5	does not know how to manage his own household	2
2Pe 2: 9	the Lord knows how to rescue the godly from trial	2

know the heart

1. καρδιογνώστης, *kardiognōstēs, 2841*

Act 1:24 "Lord, you know everyone's heart. 1

know the human heart

1. καρδιογνώστης, *kardiognōstēs, 2841*

Act 15: 8 God, who knows the human heart, testified to them 1

know well

1. ἐπιγινώσκω, *epiginōskō, 2105*
2. φανερόω, *phaneroō, 5746*

2Co 5:11	we ourselves are well known to God	2
5:11	that we are also well known to your consciences.	2
6: 9	as unknown, and yet are well known;	1

know widely

1. παρρησία, *parrēsia, 4244*

Jhn 7: 4 who wants to be widely known acts in secret. 1

not know

1. ἀγνοέω, *agnoeō, 51*

Rom 6: 3 Do you not know that all of us 1
7: 1 Do you not know, brothers and sisters 1

without knowing

1. λανθάνω, *lanthanō, 3291*

Heb 13: 2 some have entertained angels without knowing it. 1

knowledge *See also* have knowledge

1. γινώσκω, *ginōskō, 1182*
2. γνῶσις, *gnōsis, 1194*
3. ἐπίγνωσις, *epignōsis, 2106*
4. σύνοιδα, *synoida, 5323*

Lke 1:77	to give knowledge of salvation to his people	2
11:52	you have taken away the key of knowledge;	2
Act 5: 2	with his wife's knowledge	4
Rom 2:20	in the law the embodiment of knowledge and truth	2
3:20	for through the law comes the knowledge of sin.	3
11:33	the riches and wisdom and knowledge of God!	2
15:14	filled with all knowledge, and able to instruct	2
1Co 1: 5	in speech and knowledge of every kind—	2
8: 1	we know that "all of us possess knowledge."	2
8: 1	Knowledge puffs up, but love builds up.	2

8: 2	does not yet have the necessary knowledge;	1
8: 7	not everyone, however, who has this knowledge.	2
8:10	For if others see you, who possess knowledge, eating	2
8:11	So by your knowledge those weak believers	2
12: 8	to another the utterance of knowledge	2
13: 2	and understand all mysteries and all knowledge	2
13: 8	as for knowledge, it will come to an end.	2
14: 6	I speak to you in some revelation or knowledge	2
2Co 4: 6	the light of the knowledge of the glory of God	2
6: 6	by purity, knowledge, patience, kindness	2
8: 7	in faith, in speech, in knowledge	2
10: 5	proud obstacle raised up against the knowledge of God	2
11: 6	untrained in speech, not in knowledge	2
Eph 3:19	the love of Christ that surpasses knowledge	2
4:13	the knowledge of the Son of God	3
Php 1: 9	with knowledge and full insight	3
Col 1: 9	you may be filled with the knowledge of God's will	3
1:10	grow in the knowledge of God.	3
2: 2	the knowledge of God's mystery, that is, Christ	3
2: 3	all the treasures of wisdom and knowledge.	2
3:10	which is being renewed in knowledge	3
1Ti 2: 4	to come to the knowledge of the truth.	3
6:20	what is falsely called knowledge;	2
2Ti 3: 7	can never arrive at a knowledge of the truth.	3
Tit 1: 1	and the knowledge of the truth	3
Heb 10:26	after having received the knowledge of the truth	3
2Pe 1: 2	in the knowledge of God and of Jesus our Lord.	3
1: 3	through the knowledge of him who called us	3
1: 5	to support…goodness with knowledge	2
1: 6	and knowledge with self-control	2
1: 8	in the knowledge of our Lord Jesus Christ.	3
2:20	knowledge of our Lord and Savior Jesus Christ	3
3:18	grow in the grace and knowledge of our Lord	2

no knowledge

1. ἀγνωσία, *agnōsia, 57*

1Co 15:34 for some people have no knowledge of God. 1

known *See* make fully known, make known, well known, widely known

Korah

1. Κόρε, *Kore, 3169*

Jde 1:11 and perish in Korah's rebellion. 1

L

labor *See also* labor *pains*

1. ἔργον, *ergon, 2240*
2. κοπιάω, *kopiaō, 3159*
3. κόπος, *kopos, 3160*
4. μόχθος, *mochthos, 3677*
5. τίκτω, *tiktō, 5503*

Jhn 4:38	I sent you to reap that for which you did not labor.	2
4:38	Others have labored, and you have entered	2
4:38	and you have entered into their labor."	3
16:21	When a woman is in labor, she has pain	5
1Co 3: 8	will receive wages according to the labor of each.	3
15:58	in the Lord your labor is not in vain.	3
2Co 6: 5	beatings, imprisonments, riots, labors	3
10:15	We do not boast…in the labors of others;	3
11:23	with far greater labors, far more imprisonments	3
Eph 4:28	rather let them labor and work honestly	2
Php 1:22	that means fruitful labor for me;	1
2:16	I did not run in vain or labor in vain.	2
1Th 1: 3	work of faith and labor of love	3
2: 9	remember our labor and toil, brothers and sisters;	3
3: 5	our labor had been in vain.	3
5:12	respect those who labor among you	2
2Th 3: 8	with toil and labor we worked night and day	4
1Ti 5:17	especially those who labor in preaching	2
Heb 4:10	cease from their labors as God did from his.	1
Rev 14:13	"they will rest from their labors	3

laborer

1. ἐργάτης, *ergatēs, 2239*

Mat 9:37 but the laborers are few; 1
9:38 to send out laborers into his harvest." 1

Mat 10:10	for laborers deserve their food.	1
20: 1	to hire laborers for his vineyard.	1
20: 2	After agreeing with the laborers	1
20: 8	'Call the laborers and give them their pay	1
Lke 10: 2	harvest is plentiful, but the laborers are few;	1
10: 2	to send out laborers into his harvest.	1
10: 7	the laborer deserves to be paid.	1
1Ti 5:18	"The laborer deserves to be paid."	1
Jas 5: 4	The wages of the laborers who mowed your fields	1

lack *See also* lack of *faith,* lack of *self-control*

1. λείπω, *leipō, 3309*
2. μή + ἔχω, *mē + echō, 3590 + 2400*
3. μή + πάρειμι, *mē + pareimi, 3590 + 4205*
4. ὑστερέω, *hystereō, 5728*
5. ὑστέρημα, *hysterēma, 5729*

Mat 19:20	what do I still lack?"	4
Mrk 10:21	"You lack one thing;	4
Lke 8: 6	it withered for lack of moisture.	2
18:22	still one thing lacking. Sell all that	1
22:35	"When I sent you out…did you lack anything?"	4
1Co 1: 7	you are not lacking in any spiritual gift	4
Col 1:24	what is lacking in Christ's afflictions	5
1Th 3:10	restore whatever is lacking in your faith.	5
Tit 3:13	see that they lack nothing.	1
Jas 1: 4	be mature and complete, lacking in nothing.	1
1: 5	If any of you is lacking in wisdom, ask God	1
2:15	If a brother or sister…lacks daily food	1
2Pe 1: 9	For anyone who lacks these things is nearsighted	3

lady

1. κυρία, *kyria, 3257*

2Jn 1: 1	The elder to the elect lady and her children	1

dear lady

1. κυρία, *kyria, 3257*

2Jn 1: 5	now, dear lady, I ask you, not as though I were writing	1

lag

1. ὀκνηρός, *oknēros, 3891*

Rom 12:11	not lag in zeal, be ardent in spirit	1

lake

1. λίμνη, *limnē, 3349*

Lke 5: 1	Jesus was standing beside the lake of Gennesaret	1
5: 2	he saw two boats there at the shore of the lake;	1
8:22	"Let us go across to the other side of the lake."	1
8:23	A windstorm swept down on the lake	1
8:33	herd rushed down the steep bank into the lake	1
Rev 19:20	These two were thrown alive into the lake of fire	1
20:10	thrown into the lake of fire and sulfur	1
20:14	Death and Hades were thrown into the lake of fire.	1
20:14	This is the second death, the lake of fire;	1
20:15	was thrown into the lake of fire.	1
21: 8	in the lake that burns with fire and sulfur	1

lamb

1. Contextual: Not in Greek
2. ἀμνός, *amnos, 303*
3. ἀρήν, *arēn, 748*
4. ἀρνίον, *arnion, 768*

Lke 10: 3	like lambs into the midst of wolves.	3
Jhn 1:29	"Here is the Lamb of God who takes away the sin	2
1:36	exclaimed, "Look, here is the Lamb of God!"	2
21:15	Jesus said to him, "Feed my lambs."	4
Act 8:32	like a lamb silent before its shearer	2
1Pe 1:19	like that of a lamb without defect or blemish.	2
Rev 5: 6	I saw…among the elders a Lamb standing	4
5: 8	the twenty-four elders fell before the Lamb	4
5:12	"Worthy is the Lamb that was slaughtered to receive	4
5:13	"To the one seated on the throne and to the Lamb	4
6: 1	I saw the Lamb open one of the seven seals	4
6:16	hide us…from the wrath of the Lamb;	4
7: 9	standing before the throne and before the Lamb	4
7:10	"Salvation belongs…to the Lamb!"	4
7:14	made them white in the blood of the Lamb.	4
7:17	for the Lamb…will be their shepherd,	4
8: 1	When the Lamb opened the seventh seal	4
12:11	they have conquered him by the blood of the Lamb	4

13: 8	the book of life of the Lamb that was slaughtered.	4
13:11	another beast…it had two horns like a lamb	4
14: 1	and there was the Lamb, standing on Mount Zion!	4
14: 4	these follow the Lamb wherever he goes.	4
14: 4	redeemed…as first fruits for God and the Lamb	4
14:10	tormented…in the presence of the Lamb.	4
15: 3	the song of Moses…and the song of the Lamb:	4
17:14	they will make war on the Lamb	4
17:14	and the Lamb will conquer them	4
19: 7	for the marriage of the Lamb has come	4
19: 9	invited to the marriage supper of the Lamb."	4
21: 9	I will show you the bride, the wife of the Lamb."	4
21:14	twelve names of the twelve apostles of the Lamb.	4
21:22	its temple is the Lord God…and the Lamb.	4
21:23	God is its light, and its lamp is the Lamb.	4
21:27	only those…written in the Lamb's book of life.	4
22: 1	flowing from the throne of God and of the Lamb	4
22: 3	the throne of God and of the Lamb will be in it	4

paschal lamb

1. πάσχα, *pascha, 4247*

1Co 5: 7	our paschal lamb, Christ, has been sacrificed.	1

passover lamb

1. πάσχα, *pascha, 4247*

Mrk 14:12	when the Passover lamb is sacrificed	1
Lke 22: 7	on which the Passover lamb had to be sacrificed.	1

lame

1. χωλός, *chōlos, 6000*

Mat 11: 5	the blind receive their sight, the lame walk	1
15:30	crowds came to him, bringing with them the lame	1
15:31	the maimed whole, the lame walking	1
18: 8	it is better for you to enter life maimed or lame	1
21:14	The blind and the lame came to him in the temple	1
Mrk 9:45	it is better for you to enter life lame	1
Lke 7:22	the blind receive their sight, the lame walk	1
14:13	the poor, the crippled, the lame, and the blind.	1
14:21	the poor, the crippled, the blind, and the lame.'	1
Jhn 5: 3	many invalids—blind, lame, and paralyzed	1
Act 3: 2	a man lame from birth was being carried in.	1
8: 7	many others who were paralyzed or lame were cured.	1
Heb 12:13	so that what is lame may not be put out of joint	1

Lamech

1. Λάμεχ, *Lamech, 3285*

Lke 3:36	son of Shem, son of Noah, son of Lamech	1

lament

1. ταλαιπωρέω, *talaipōreō, 5415*

Jas 4: 9	Lament and mourn and weep.	1

lamentation

1. κοπετός, *kopetos, 3157*
2. ὀδυρμός, *odyrmos, 3851*

Mat 2:18	wailing and loud lamentation, Rachel weeping	2
Act 8: 2	made loud lamentation over him.	1

lamp

1. λαμπάς, *lampas, 3286*
2. λύχνος, *lychnos, 3394*

Mat 5:15	No one after lighting a lamp puts it under	2
6:22	"The eye is the lamp of the body. So, if your eye	2
25: 1	Ten bridesmaids took their lamps	1
25: 3	When the foolish took their lamps	1
25: 4	the wise took flasks of oil with their lamps.	1
25: 7	trimmed their lamps.	1
25: 8	for our lamps are going out.'	1
Mrk 4:21	"Is a lamp brought in to be put under the bushel	2
Lke 8:16	"No one after lighting a lamp hides it	2
11:33	after lighting a lamp puts it in a cellar	2
11:34	Your eye is the lamp of your body.	2
11:36	as when a lamp gives you light with its rays."	2
12:35	"Be dressed for action and have your lamps lit;	2
15: 8	does not light a lamp, sweep the house,	2
Jhn 5:35	He was a burning and shining lamp	2
Act 20: 8	There were many lamps in the room upstairs	1
2Pe 1:19	as to a lamp shining in a dark place	2
Rev 18:23	and the light of a lamp will shine in you no more;	2

21:23 God is its light, and its lamp is the Lamb.   2
22: 5 they need no light of lamp or sun   2

lampstand

1. λυχνία, *lychnia, 3393*

Mat 5:15 under the bushel basket, but on the lampstand   1
Mrk 4:21 or under the bed, and not on the lampstand?   1
Lke 8:16 puts it on a lampstand   1
11:33 puts it in a cellar, but on the lampstand   1
Heb 9: 2 in which were the lampstand, the table   1
Rev 1:12 and on turning I saw seven golden lampstands   1
1:13 the midst of the lampstands I saw one like the Son   1
1:20 seven stars…and the seven golden lampstands: 1
1:20 the seven lampstands are the seven churches.   1
2: 1 who walks among the seven golden lampstands: 1
2: 5 and remove your lampstand from its place   1
11: 4 two lampstands that stand before the Lord   1

land¹   *See also* go by land, piece of land

1. Contextual: Not in Greek
2. γῆ, *gē, 1178*
3. ἐκεῖνος, *ekeinos, 1697*
4. ξηρός, *xēros, 3831*
5. χώρα, *chōra, 6001*
6. χωρίον, *chōrion, 6005*

Mat 2: 6 you, Bethlehem, in the land of Judah, are by no   2
2:20 his mother, and go to the land of Israel, for those   2
2:21 his mother, and went to the land of Israel.   2
4:15 "Land of Zebulun, land of Naphtali   2
4:15 "Land of Zebulun, land of Naphtali   2
10:15 for the land of Sodom and Gomorrah   2
11:24 it will be more tolerable for the land of Sodom   2
14:24 the boat…was far from the land   2
14:34 they came to land at Gennesaret.   2
23:15 you cross sea and land   4
27:45 darkness came over the whole land   2
Mrk 4: 1 the whole crowd was beside the sea on the land.   2
6:47 he was alone on the land.   2
6:53 they came to land at Gennesaret   2
15:33 darkness came over the whole land   2
Lke 4:25 there was a severe famine over all the land;   2
8:27 As he stepped out on land   2
12:16 "The land of a rich man produced abundantly.   5
23:44 darkness came over the whole land until three   2
Jhn 6:21 immediately the boat reached the land   2
21: 8 for they were not far from the land   2
Act 4:34 as many as owned lands or houses   6
5: 3 to keep back part of the proceeds of the land?   6
5: 8 "Tell me whether you and your husband sold the land   6
7: 3 go to the land that I will show you.'   2
7:29 became a resident alien in the land of Midian.   2
7:40 this Moses who led us out from the land of Egypt   2
13:17 during their stay in the land of Egypt   2
13:19 destroyed seven nations in the land of Canaan   2
13:19 he gave them their land as an inheritance   2
27:27 sailors suspected that they were nearing land.   5
27:39 In the morning they did not recognize the land   2
27:43 jump overboard…and make for the land   2
27:44 so it was that all were brought safely to land.   2
28: 7 lands belonging to the leading man of the island   6
Heb 8: 9 to lead them out of the land of Egypt;   2
11: 9 By faith he stayed for a time in the land   2
11: 9 as in a foreign land, living in tents,   1
11:15 If they had been thinking of the land   3
11:29 passed through the Red Sea as if it were dry land   2
Jde 1: 5 once for all saved a people out of the land of Egypt   2
Rev 10: 2 right foot on the sea and his left foot on the land   2
10: 5 the angel whom I saw standing on the sea and the land   2
10: 8 angel who is standing on the sea and on the land."   2

land²

1. κατέρχομαι, *katerchomai, 2982*

Act 18:22 When he had landed at Caesarea, he went up   1
21: 3 sailed to Syria and landed at Tyre   1

land beyond

1. ὑπερέκεινα, *hyperekeina, 5654*

2Co 10:16 we may proclaim the good news in lands beyond you   1

landowner

1. οἰκοδεσπότης, *oikodespotēs, 3867*

Mat 20: 1 "For the kingdom of heaven is like a landowner   1
20:11 they grumbled against the landowner   1
21:33 There was a landowner who planted a vineyard   1

lane

1. ῥύμη, *rhymē, 4860*
2. φραγμός, *phragmos, 5850*

Lke 14:21 'Go out at once into the streets and lanes   1
14:23 'Go out into the roads and lanes   2
Act 12:10 they went outside and walked along a lane   1

language   *See also* Lycaonian language

1. γλῶσσα, *glōssa, 1185*
2. διάλεκτος, *dialektos, 1365*

Act 1:19 the field was called in their language Hakeldama   2
2: 4 began to speak in other languages   1
2:11 in our own languages we hear them speaking   1
21:40 he addressed them in the Hebrew language, saying: 2
26:14 heard a voice saying to me in the Hebrew language   2
Rev 5: 9 ransomed for God saints from every tribe and language   1
7: 9 from all tribes and peoples and languages   1
10:11 many peoples and nations and languages and kings."   1
11: 9 the peoples and tribes and languages and nations   1
13: 7 every tribe and people and language and nation   1
14: 6 to every nation and tribe and language and people.   1
17:15 peoples and multitudes and nations and languages.   1

abusive language

1. αἰσχρολογία, *aischrologia, 155*

Col 3: 8 malice, slander, and abusive language from your mouth.   1

native language

1. διάλεκτος, *dialektos, 1365*

Act 2: 6 each one heard them speaking in the native language   1
2: 8 each of us, in our own native language?   1

lantern

1. φανός, *phanos, 5749*

Jhn 18: 3 came there with lanterns and torches   1

Laodicea

1. Λαοδίκεια, *Laodikeia, 3293*

Col 2: 1 struggling for you and for those in Laodicea   1
4:13 for those in Laodicea and in Hierapolis.   1
4:15 greetings to the brothers and sisters in Laodicea   1
4:16 see that you read also the letter from Laodicea.   1
Rev 1:11 seven churches, to Ephesus…and to Laodicea."   1
3:14 "And to the angel of the church in Laodicea write: 1

Laodicean

1. Λαοδικεύς, *Laodikeus, 3294*

Col 4:16 have it read also in the church of the Laodiceans;   1

lap

1. κόλπος, *kolpos, 3146*

Lke 6:38 good measure…will be put into your lap;   1

large   *See also* large *sum*

1. ἱκανός, *hikanos, 2653*
2. μέγας, *megas, 3489*
3. μείζων, *meizōn, 3505*
4. πηλίκος, *pēlikos, 4383*
5. πολύς, *polys, 4498*
6. ποταπός, *potapos, 4534*
7. τηλικοῦτος, *tēlikoutos, 5496*

Mat 8:30 Now a large herd of swine was feeding   5
19: 2 Large crowds followed him, and he cured them   5
20:29 a large crowd followed him.   5
26:47 with him was a large crowd with swords and clubs   5
Mrk 4:32 and puts forth large branches   2
5:24 a large crowd followed him and pressed in on   5
10:46 As he and his disciples and a large crowd   1
12:37 the large crowd was listening to him with delight.   5
13: 1 "Look, Teacher, what large stones   6
13: 1 and what large buildings!"   6
14:15 He will show you a large room upstairs   2

Mrk	16: 4	the stone, which was very large,...rolled back.	2
Lke	5:29	was a large crowd of tax collectors and others	5
	7:11	his disciples and a large crowd went with him.	5
	7:12	with her was a large crowd from the town.	1
	8:32	on the hillside a large herd of swine was feeding;	1
	12:18	I will pull down my barns and build larger ones	3
	14:25	Now large crowds were traveling with him;	5
	22:12	He will show you a large room upstairs,	2
Jhn	6: 2	A large crowd kept following him	5
	6: 5	he looked up and saw a large crowd coming	5
	21:11	full of large fish, a hundred fifty-three	2
Act	10:11	and something like a large sheet coming down	2
	11: 5	There was something like a large sheet coming down	2
	22:28	cost me a large sum of money to get my citizenship."	5
Rom	8:29	he might be the firstborn within a large family.	5
Gal	6:11	See what large letters I make when I am writing	4
2Ti	2:20	In a large house there are utensils	2
Jas	3: 4	Or look at ships: though they are so large	7

very large

1. πολύς, *polys*, 4498

Mat	21: 8	very large crowd spread their cloaks	1
Mrk	4: 1	a very large crowd gathered around him	1

Lasea

1. Λασαία, *Lasaia*, 3297

Act	27: 8	Fair Havens, near the city of Lasea.	1

lash

1. Contextual: Not in Greek

2Co	11:24	from the Jews the forty lashes minus one.	1

last[1] *See also* breathe one's last, last *state*, last *year*

1. ἔσχατος, *eschatos*, 2274
2. ἤδη + ποτέ, *ēdē + pote*, 2453 + 4537
3. λοιπός, *loipos*, 3370
4. οὗτος, *houtos*, 4047
5. ποτέ, *pote*, 4537
6. τέλος, *telos*, 5465
7. ὕστερος, *hysteros*, 5731

Mat	5:26	get out until you have paid the last penny.	1
	19:30	many who are first will be last	1
	19:30	first will be last, and the last will be first.	1
	20: 8	beginning with the last and then going	1
	20:12	saying, 'These last worked only one hour	1
	20:14	give to this last the same as I give to you.	1
	20:16	So the last will be first, and the first	1
	20:16	last will be first, and the first will be last."	1
	22:27	Last of all, the woman herself died.	7
	26:60	At last two came forward	7
	27:64	the last deception would be worse than the first."	1
Mrk	9:35	"Whoever wants to be first must be last of all	1
	10:31	many who are first will be last	1
	10:31	first will be last, and the last will be first."	1
	12:22	Last of all the woman herself died.	1
Lke	12:59	until you have paid the very last penny."	1
	13:30	Indeed, some are last who will be first	1
	13:30	some are first who will be last."	1
Jhn	6:39	but raise it up on the last day.	1
	6:40	I will raise them up on the last day."	1
	6:44	I will raise that person up on the last day.	1
	6:54	I will raise them up on the last day;	1
	7:37	On the last day of the festival, the great day	1
	11:24	rise again in the resurrection on the last day."	1
	12:48	on the last day the word...will serve as judge	1
Act	2:17	'In the last days it will be, God declares	1
	27:20	hope of our being saved was at last abandoned.	3
	27:23	last night there stood by me an angel	4
Rom	1:10	I may somehow at last succeed in coming to you.	2
1Co	15: 8	Last of all, as to one untimely born	1
	15:26	The last enemy to be destroyed is death.	1
	15:45	the last Adam became a life-giving spirit.	1
	15:52	at the last trumpet. For the trumpet will sound	1
Php	4:10	now at last you have revived your concern	5
1Th	2:16	God's wrath has overtaken them at last.	6
2Ti	3: 1	in the last days distressing times will come.	1
Heb	1: 2	in these last days he has spoken to us by a Son	1
Jas	5: 3	You have laid up treasure for the last days.	1
1Pe	1: 5	salvation ready to be revealed in the last time.	1
2Pe	3: 3	that in the last days scoffers will come	1

1Jn	2:18	Children, it is the last hour!	1
	2:18	From this we know that it is the last hour.	1
Jde	1:18	"In the last time there will be scoffers	1
Rev	1:17	"Do not be afraid; I am the first and the last	1
	2: 8	the words of the first and the last	1
	2:19	that your last works are greater than the first.	1
	15: 1	angels with seven plagues, which are the last	1
	21: 9	the seven bowls full of the seven last plagues	1
	22:13	I am the Alpha and the Omega, the first and the last	1

last[2]

1. ἄφθαρτος, *aphthartos*, 915
2. μένω, *menō*, 3531

Jhn	15:16	fruit that will last	2
Heb	10:34	possessed something better and more lasting.	2
	13:14	For here we have no lasting city	2
1Pe	3: 4	the lasting beauty of a gentle and quiet spirit	1

last of all

1. ἔσχατος, *eschatos*, 2274

1Co	4: 9	God has exhibited us apostles as last of all	1

late

1. Contextual: Not in Greek
2. διίστημι, *diistēmi*, 1460
3. μετά, *meta*, 3552
4. μετά + οὗτος, *meta + houtos*, 3552 + 4047
5. μετέπειτα, *metepeita*, 3575
6. ὄψιμος, *opsimos*, 4069
7. ὄψιος, *opsios*, 4070
8. παρέρχομαι, *parerchomai*, 4216
9. πολύς, *polys*, 4498
10. ὕστερος, *hysteros*, 5731
11. χρόνος, *chronos*, 5989
12. ὥρα + πολύς, *hōra + polys*, 6052 + 4498

Mat	14:15	"This is a deserted place, and the hour is now late;	8
	17: 1	Six days later, Jesus took with him Peter	3
	21:29	but later he changed his mind and went.	10
	25:11	Later the other bridesmaids came also, saying	10
Mrk	6:35	When it grew late, his disciples came to him	12
	6:35	a deserted place, and the hour is now very late;	9
	9: 2	Six days later, Jesus took with him Peter	3
	11:11	as it was already late	7
	16:14	⟦Later he appeared to the eleven themselves⟧	10
Lke	15:13	few days later the younger son gathered all	3
	17: 8	later you may eat and drink'?	3
	18: 4	later he said to himself	3
	22:58	A little later someone else, on seeing him, said	3
	22:59	about an hour later	2
Jhn	5:14	Later Jesus found him in the temple and said	4
	13: 7	later you will understand."	3
	20:26	A week later his disciples were...in the house	3
Act	24: 1	Five days later the high priest...came down	3
	24:24	Some days later when Felix came with his wife	3
	28:11	Three months later we set sail	3
	28:17	Three days later he called together...leaders	3
Gal	3:17	law, which came four hundred thirty years later	3
1Ti	4: 1	in later times some will renounce the faith	10
Heb	3: 5	to testify to the things...spoken later.	1
	4: 7	saying through David much later	11
	4: 8	God would not speak later about another day.	3
	7:28	the word of the oath, which came later than the law	3
	12:11	later it yields the...fruit of righteousness	10
	12:17	You know that later...he was rejected	5
Jas	5: 7	until it receives the early and the late rains.	6

Latin

1. Ῥωμαϊστί, *Rhōmaisti*, 4872

Jhn	19:20	it was written in Hebrew, in Latin, and in Greek.	1

laugh

1. γελάω, *gelaō*, 1151
2. καταγελάω, *katagelaō*, 2860

Mat	9:24	And they laughed at him.	2
Mrk	5:40	And they laughed at him.	2
Lke	6:21	who weep now, for you will laugh.	1
	6:25	"Woe to you who are laughing now,	1
	8:53	they laughed at him, knowing that she was dead.	2

laughter

1. γέλως, *gelōs*, *1152*

Jas	4: 9	Let your laughter be turned into mourning	1

lavish

1. περισσεύω, *perisseuō*, *4355*

Eph	1: 8	that he lavished on us.	1

law *See also* free from law, giving of the law, receive the law, teacher of the law, violation of the law

1. Contextual: Not in Greek
2. νομικός, *nomikos*, *3788*
3. νόμος, *nomos*, *3795*

Mat	5:17	come to abolish the law or the prophets;	3
	5:18	will pass from the law until all is accomplished	3
	7:12	do to you; for this is the law and the prophets.	3
	11:13	the prophets and the law prophesied until John	3
	12: 5	Or have you not read in the law	3
	22:36	which commandment in the law is the greatest?"	3
	22:40	On these two commandments hang all the law	3
	23:23	have neglected the weightier matters of the law:	3
Lke	2:22	purification according to the law of Moses	3
	2:23	(as it is written in the law of the Lord	3
	2:24	what is stated in the law of the Lord	3
	2:27	to do for him what was customary under the law	3
	2:39	required by the law of the Lord	3
	10:26	"What is written in the law? What do you read	3
	16:16	"The law and the prophets were in effect until	3
	16:17	one stroke of a letter in the law to be dropped.	3
	24:44	everything written about me in the law of Moses	3
Jhn	1:17	The law indeed was given through Moses;	3
	1:45	found him about whom Moses in the law...wrote	3
	7:19	"Did not Moses give you the law?	3
	7:19	Yet none of you keeps the law.	3
	7:23	that the law of Moses may not be broken	3
	7:49	this crowd, which does not know the law	3
	7:51	"Our law does not judge people	3
	8: 5	[Now in the law Moses commanded us to stone such]	3
	8:17	In your law it is written	3
	10:34	Jesus answered, "Is it not written in your law	3
	12:34	answered him, "We have heard from the law	3
	15:25	to fulfill the word that is written in their law	3
	18:31	judge him according to your law."	3
	19: 7	The Jews answered him, "We have a law	3
	19: 7	according to that law he ought to die	3
Act	6:13	saying things against this holy place and the law;	3
	7:53	ones that received the law as ordained by angels	3
	13:15	After the reading of the law and the prophets	3
	13:39	you could not be freed by the law of Moses.	3
	15: 5	ordered to keep the law of Moses."	3
	18:13	worship God in ways that are contrary to the law."	3
	18:15	questions about words and names and your own law	3
	21:20	they are all zealous for the law.	3
	21:24	you yourself observe and guard the law.	3
	21:28	against our people, our law, and this place;	3
	22: 3	educated strictly according to our ancestral law	3
	22:12	Ananias, who was a devout man according to the law	3
	23: 3	sitting there to judge me according to the law	3
	23:29	he was accused concerning questions of their law	3
	24:14	believing everything laid down according to the law	3
	25: 8	in no way committed an offense against the law	3
	28:23	both from the law of Moses and from the prophets.	3
Rom	2:12	and all who have sinned under the law	3
	2:12	all who have sinned...will be judged by the law.	3
	2:13	it is not the hearers of the law who are righteous	3
	2:13	but the doers of the law who will be justified.	3
	2:14	When Gentiles, who do not possess the law	3
	2:14	Gentiles...do instinctively what the law requires	3
	2:14	though not having the law, are a law to themselves.	3
	2:15	what the law requires is written on their hearts	3
	2:17	if you call yourself a Jew and rely on the law	3
	2:18	because you are instructed in the law	3
	2:20	having in the law the embodiment of knowledge	3
	2:23	You that boast in the law, do you dishonor God	3
	2:23	do you dishonor God by breaking the law?	3
	2:25	Circumcision...is of value if you obey the law;	3
	2:25	if you break the law, your circumcision has become	3
	2:26	uncircumcised keep the requirements of the law	3
	2:27	physically uncircumcised but keep the law	3

	2:27	you that have...circumcision but break the law.	3
	3:19	Now we know that whatever the law says	3
	3:19	the law...speaks to those who are under the law	3
	3:20	justified...by deeds prescribed by the law	3
	3:20	for through the law comes the knowledge of sin.	3
	3:21	But now, apart from law, the righteousness of God	3
	3:21	attested by the law and the prophets	3
	3:27	By what law? By that of works?	3
	3:27	No, but by the law of faith.	3
	3:28	by faith apart from works prescribed by the law.	3
	3:31	Do we then overthrow the law by this faith?	3
	3:31	By no means! On the contrary, we uphold the law.	3
	4:13	the promise...did not come...through the law	3
	4:14	If it is the adherents of the law who are...heirs	3
	4:15	For the law brings wrath;	3
	4:15	but where there is no law, neither is there violation.	3
	4:16	not only to the adherents of the law	3
	5:13	sin was indeed in the world before the law	3
	5:13	but sin is not reckoned when there is no law.	3
	5:20	law came in...result that the trespass multiplied;	3
	6:14	since you are not under law but under grace.	3
	6:15	Should we sin because we are not under law	3
	7: 1	for I am speaking to those who know the law	3
	7: 1	the law is binding on a person only during...lifetime?	3
	7: 2	a married woman is bound by the law to her husband	3
	7: 2	discharged from the law concerning the husband	3
	7: 3	But if her husband dies, she is free from that law	3
	7: 4	have died to the law through the body of Christ	3
	7: 5	our sinful passions, aroused by the law	3
	7: 6	But now we are discharged from the law	3
	7: 7	What then should we say? That the law is sin?	3
	7: 7	Yet, if it had not been for the law	3
	7: 7	if the law had not said, "You shall not covet."	3
	7: 8	Apart from the law sin lies dead.	3
	7: 9	I was once alive apart from the law	3
	7:12	So the law is holy, and the commandment is holy	3
	7:14	that the law is spiritual; but I am of the flesh	3
	7:16	I agree that the law is good.	3
	7:21	a law that when I want to do what is good,	3
	7:22	For I delight in the law of God in my inmost self	3
	7:23	another law at war with the law of my mind	3
	7:23	another law at war with the law of my mind	3
	7:23	to the law of sin that dwells in my members.	3
	7:25	with my mind I am a slave to the law of God	3
	7:25	but with my flesh I am a slave to the law of sin.	3
	8: 2	For the law of the Spirit of life in Christ Jesus	3
	8: 2	has set you free from the law of sin and of death.	3
	8: 3	For God has done what the law...could not do:	3
	8: 4	the just requirement of the law might be fulfilled	3
	8: 7	it does not submit to God's law—indeed it cannot	3
	9:31	the righteousness that is based on the law	3
	9:31	Israel...did not succeed in fulfilling that law.	3
	10: 4	For Christ is the end of the law	3
	10: 5	righteousness that comes from the law	3
	13: 8	the one who loves another has fulfilled the law.	3
	13:10	therefore, love is the fulfilling of the law.	3
1Co	9: 8	Does not the law also say the same?	3
	9: 9	For it is written in the law of Moses	3
	9:20	To those under the law I became as one under the law	3
	9:20	To those under the law I became as one under the law	3
	9:20	(though I myself am not under the law)	3
	9:20	so that I might win those under the law.	3
	14:21	In the law it is written, "By people of strange tongues	3
	14:34	be subordinate, as the law also says.	3
	15:56	the power of sin is the law.	3
Gal	2:16	a person is not justified by the works of the law	3
	2:16	not by doing the works of the law	3
	2:16	no one will be justified by the works of the law.	3
	2:19	For through the law I died to the law	3
	2:19	For through the law I died to the law	3
	2:21	if justification comes through the law	3
	3: 2	Did you receive the Spirit by doing the works of the law	3
	3: 5	by your doing the works of the law	3
	3:10	rely on the works of law are under a curse;	3
	3:10	obey all the things written in the book of the law."	3
	3:11	no one is justified before God by the law;	3
	3:12	the law does not rest on faith;	3
	3:12	"Whoever does the works of the law will live by them."	1
	3:13	Christ redeemed us from the curse of the law	3
	3:17	the law, which came four hundred thirty years later	3
	3:18	For if the inheritance comes from the law	3

Gal	3:19	Why then the law?	3
	3:21	Is the law then opposed to the promises of God?	3
	3:21	if a law had been given that could make alive	3
	3:21	righteousness would indeed come through the law.	3
	3:23	we were imprisoned and guarded under the law	3
	3:24	the law was our disciplinarian until Christ came	3
	4: 4	born of a woman, born under the law	3
	4: 5	in order to redeem those who were under the law	3
	4:21	Tell me, you who desire to be subject to the law	3
	4:21	will you not listen to the law?	3
	5: 3	he is obliged to obey the entire law.	3
	5: 4	You who want to be justified by the law	3
	5:14	the whole law is summed up in a single commandment	3
	5:18	led by the Spirit, you are not subject to the law.	3
	5:23	There is no law against such things.	3
	6: 2	in this way you will fulfill the law of Christ.	3
	6:13	Even the circumcised do not…obey the law	3
Eph	2:15	the law with its commandments and ordinances	3
Php	3: 5	a Hebrew born of Hebrews; as to the law, a Pharisee;	3
	3: 6	as to righteousness under the law, blameless.	3
	3: 9	righteousness of my own that comes from the law	3
1Ti	1: 8	Now we know that the law is good	3
	1: 9	the law is laid down not for the innocent	3
Tit	3: 9	dissensions, and quarrels about the law	2
Heb	7: 5	have a commandment in the law to collect tithes	3
	7:12	necessarily a change in the law as well.	3
	7:19	(for the law made nothing perfect);	3
	7:28	the law appoints as high priests those who are subject	3
	7:28	the word of the oath, which came later than the law	3
	8: 4	priests who offer gifts according to the law.	3
	8:10	I will put my laws in their minds	3
	9:19	told to all the people…in accordance with the law	3
	9:22	under the law almost everything is purified	3
	10: 1	Since the law has only a shadow of the good things	3
	10: 8	(these are offered according to the law)	3
	10:16	I will put my laws in their hearts	3
	10:28	Anyone who has violated the law of Moses dies	3
Jas	1:25	those who look into the perfect law	3
	1:25	the perfect law, the law of liberty	1
	2: 8	You do well if you really fulfill the royal law	3
	2: 9	are convicted by the law as transgressors.	3
	2:10	For whoever keeps the whole law but fails	3
	2:11	you have become a transgressor of the law.	3
	2:12	who are to be judged by the law of liberty.	3
	4:11	speaks evil against the law and judges the law;	3
	4:11	speaks evil against the law and judges the law	3
	4:11	if you judge the law, you are not a doer of the law	3
	4:11	if you judge the law, you are not a doer of the law	3

apart from the law

1. ἀνόμως, *anomōs, 492*

Rom	2:12	All who have sinned apart from the law	1
	2:12	will also perish apart from the law	1

outside the law

1. ἄνομος, *anomos, 491*

Act	2:23	and killed by the hands of those outside the law.	1
1Co	9:21	To those outside the law I became as one outside	1
	9:21	those outside the law I became as one outside the law	1
	9:21	so that I might win those outside the law.	1

under law

1. ἔννομος, *ennomos, 1937*

1Co	9:21	but am under Christ's law)	1

lawful

1. ἔξεστι, *exesti, 2003*

Mat	12: 2	your disciples are doing what is not lawful to do	1
	12: 4	which it was not lawful for him…to eat	1
	12:10	asked him, "Is it lawful to cure on the sabbath?"	1
	12:12	So it is lawful to do good on the sabbath."	1
	14: 4	"It is not lawful for you to have her."	1
	19: 3	"Is it lawful for a man to divorce his wife	1
	22:17	Is it lawful to pay taxes to the emperor, or not?"	1
	27: 6	"It is not lawful to put them into the treasury	1
Mrk	2:24	"Look, why are they doing what is not lawful	1
	2:26	which it is not lawful for any but the priests	1
	3: 4	he said to them, "Is it lawful to do good	1
	6:18	not lawful for you to have your brother's wife."	1
	10: 2	"Is it lawful for a man to divorce his wife?"	1

	12:14	Is it lawful to pay taxes to the emperor, or not?	1
Lke	6: 2	doing what is not lawful on the sabbath?"	1
	6: 4	it is not lawful for any but the priests to eat	1
	6: 9	lawful to do good or to do harm on the sabbath	1
	14: 3	"Is it lawful to cure people on the sabbath,	1
	20:22	Is it lawful for us to pay taxes to the emperor	1
Jhn	5:10	it is not lawful for you to carry your mat."	1
Act	16:21	advocating customs that are not lawful for us	1
1Co	6:12	"All things are lawful for me,"	1
	6:12	"All things are lawful for me,"	1
	10:23	"All things are lawful,"	1
	10:23	"All things are lawful,"	1

lawgiver

1. νομοθέτης, *nomothetēs, 3794*

Jas	4:12	There is one lawgiver and judge	1

lawless

1. ἀθέμιτος, *athemitos, 116*
2. ἄθεσμος, *athesmos, 118*
3. ἄνομος, *anomos, 491*

Lke	22:37	'And he was counted among the lawless';	3
1Ti	1: 9	law is laid down…for the lawless and disobedient	3
1Pe	4: 3	living in…carousing, and lawless idolatry.	1
2Pe	2: 7	distressed by the licentiousness of the lawless	2
	2: 8	day after day, was tormented…by their lawless deeds	3
	3:17	carried away with the error of the lawless	2

lawless deed

1. ἀνομία, *anomia, 490*

Heb	10:17	remember their sins and their lawless deeds no more."	1

lawless one

1. ἀνομία, *anomia, 490*
2. ἄνομος, *anomos, 491*
3. ὅς, *hos, 4005*

2Th	2: 3	the lawless one is revealed	1
	2: 8	then the lawless one will be revealed	2
	2: 9	The coming of the lawless one	3

lawlessness

1. ἀνομία, *anomia, 490*

Mat	23:28	inside you are full of hypocrisy and lawlessness.	1
	24:12	because of the increase of lawlessness	1
2Co	6:14	between righteousness and lawlessness?	1
2Th	2: 7	the mystery of lawlessness is already at work	1
1Jn	3: 4	Everyone who commits sin is guilty of lawlessness;	1
	3: 4	sin is lawlessness.	1

lawsuit

1. κρίμα, *krima, 3210*

1Co	6: 7	to have lawsuits at all with one another	1

lawyer

1. νομικός, *nomikos, 3788*

Mat	22:35	one of them, a lawyer, asked him a question	1
Lke	7:30	the Pharisees and the lawyers rejected	1
	10:25	Just then a lawyer stood up to test Jesus.	1
	11:45	One of the lawyers answered him, "Teacher	1
	11:46	he said, "Woe also to you lawyers!	1
	11:52	Woe to you lawyers!	1
	14: 3	Jesus asked the lawyers and Pharisees	1
Tit	3:13	send Zenas the lawyer and Apollos on their way	1

lay

1. ἀνακλίνω, *anaklinō, 369*
2. ἀποτίθημι, *apotithēmi, 700*
3. βάλλω, *ballō, 965*
4. καταβάλλω, *kataballō, 2850*
5. κεῖμαι, *keimai, 3023*
6. κλίνω, *klinō, 3111*
7. προστίθημι, *prostithēmi, 4707*
8. τίθημι, *tithēmi, 5502*

Mat	8:20	but the Son of Man has nowhere to lay his head."	6
	27:60	laid it in his own new tomb	8
Mrk	6:29	they came and took his body, and laid it in a tomb.	8
	6:56	they laid the sick in the marketplaces	8
	10:16	laid his hands on them, and blessed them.	8
	15:46	laid it in a tomb	8

	15:47	the mother of Joses saw where the body was laid.	8
	16: 6	Look, there is the place they laid him.	8
Lke	2: 7	laid him in a manger	1
	5:18	trying to bring him in and lay him before Jesus;	8
	6:48	who dug deeply and laid the foundation on rock;	8
	9:58	the Son of Man has nowhere to lay his head."	6
	14:29	Otherwise, when he has laid a foundation	8
	23:53	and laid it in a rock-hewn tomb	8
	23:53	where no one had ever been laid.	5
	23:55	saw the tomb and how his body was laid.	8
Jhn	11:34	He said, "Where have you laid him?"	8
	19:41	a new tomb in which no one had ever been laid.	8
	19:42	they laid Jesus there.	8
	20: 2	we do not know where they have laid him."	8
	20:13	I do not know where they have laid him."	8
	20:15	tell me where you have laid him,	8
Act	3: 2	People would lay him daily at the gate of the temple	8
	4:35	laid it at the apostles' feet.	8
	4:37	laid it at the apostles' feet.	8
	5: 2	laid it at the apostles' feet.	8
	5:15	laid them on cots and mats	8
	7:16	laid in the tomb that Abraham had bought	8
	7:58	the witnesses laid their coats at the feet	2
	9:37	they laid her in a room upstairs.	8
	13:29	took him down from the tree and laid him in a tomb.	8
	13:36	David...died, was laid beside his ancestors	7
Rom	9:33	"See, I am laying in Zion a stone	8
1Co	3:10	I laid a foundation	8
	3:11	For no one can lay any foundation other	8
	3:11	has been laid; that foundation is Jesus Christ.	5
Heb	6: 1	not laying again the foundation: repentance	4
1Pe	2: 6	"See, I am laying in Zion a stone, a cornerstone	8
Rev	2:24	I do not lay on you any other burden;	3

lay aside

1. ἀποτίθημι, *apotithēmi, 700*

Rom	13:12	Let us then lay aside the works of darkness	1
Heb	12: 1	Therefore...let us also lay aside every weight	1

lay bare

1. τραχηλίζω, *trachēlizō, 5548*

Heb	4:13	all are naked and laid bare to the eyes of the one	1

lay before

1. ἀνατίθημι, *anatithēmi, 423*

Act	25:14	Festus laid Paul's case before the king, saying	1
Gal	2: 2	I laid before them...the gospel	1

lay down

1. Contextual: Not in Greek
2. κεῖμαι, *keimai, 3023*
3. τίθημι, *tithēmi, 5502*

Jhn	10:11	The good shepherd lays down his life	3
	10:15	I lay down my life for the sheep.	3
	10:17	the Father loves me, because I lay down my life	3
	10:18	I lay it down of my own accord.	3
	10:18	I have power to lay it down	3
	13:37	I will lay down my life for you."	3
	13:38	answered, "Will you lay down your life for me?	3
	15:13	to lay down one's life for one's friends.	3
Act	24:14	believing everything laid down according to the law	1
1Ti	1: 9	the law is laid down not for the innocent	2
1Jn	3:16	We know love by this, that he laid down his life	3
	3:16	we ought to lay down our lives for one another.	3

lay hold

1. κρατέω, *krateō, 3195*

Mat	12:11	will you not lay hold of it and lift it out?	1

lay on

1. ἐκτείνω, *ekteinō, 1753*
2. ἐπιβάλλω, *epiballō, 2095*
3. ἐπίθεσις, *epithesis, 2120*
4. ἐπίκειμαι, *epikeimai, 2130*
5. ἐπιτίθημι, *epitithēmi, 2202*

Mat	9:18	but come and lay your hand on her	5
	19:13	that he might lay his hands on them and pray.	5
	19:15	he laid his hands on them and went on his way.	5
	23: 4	and lay them on the shoulders of others;	5

	26:50	Then they came and laid hands on Jesus	2
Mrk	5:23	Come and lay your hands on her	5
	6: 5	he laid his hands on a few sick people	5
	7:32	they begged him to lay his hand on him.	5
	8:23	and laid his hands on him	5
	8:25	Then Jesus laid his hands on his eyes again;	5
	14:46	they laid hands on him and arrested him.	2
	16:18	[[they will lay their hands on the sick]]	5
Lke	4:40	he laid his hands on each of them	5
	13:13	he laid his hands on her	5
	15: 5	he has found it, he lays it on his shoulders	5
	20:19	wanted to lay hands on him at that very hour	2
	22:53	you did not lay hands on me.	1
	23:26	and they laid the cross on him,	5
Jhn	7:30	no one laid hands on him	2
	7:44	but no one laid hands on him.	2
Act	6: 6	who prayed and laid their hands on them.	5
	8:17	Then Peter and John laid their hands on them	5
	8:18	through the laying on of the apostles' hands	3
	8:19	anyone on whom I lay my hands	5
	9:12	Ananias come in and lay his hands on him	5
	9:17	laid his hands on Saul and said, "Brother Saul	5
	13: 3	they laid their hands on them and sent them off.	5
	18:10	no one will lay a hand on you to harm you	5
	19: 6	When Paul had laid his hands on them	5
1Co	9:16	for an obligation is laid on me	4
1Ti	4:14	laying on of hands by the council of elders.	3
2Ti	1: 6	within you through the laying on of my hands;	3
Heb	6: 2	baptisms, laying on of hands,	3

lay up

1. ἀπόκειμαι, *apokeimai, 641*
2. θησαυρίζω, *thēsaurizō, 2564*
3. κεῖμαι, *keimai, 3023*

Lke	12:19	Soul, you have ample goods laid up for many years;	3
2Co	12:14	children ought not to lay up for their parents	2
Col	1: 5	because of the hope laid up for you in heaven.	1

lay up treasure

1. θησαυρίζω, *thēsaurizō, 2564*

Jas	5: 3	You have laid up treasure for the last days.	1

lay upon

1. ἐπιβάλλω, *epiballō, 2095*

Act	12: 1	King Herod laid violent hands upon some	1

lay waste

1. ἐρημόω, *erēmoō, 2246*

Mat	12:25	divided against itself is laid waste	1
Rev	18:17	in one hour all this wealth has been laid waste!"	1
	18:19	For in one hour she has been laid waste."	1

Lazarus

1. Contextual: Not in Greek
2. αὐτός, *autos, 899*
3. Λάζαρος, *Lazaros, 3276*

Lke	16:20	at his gate lay a poor man named Lazarus	3
	16:23	saw Abraham far away with Lazarus by his side.	3
	16:24	send Lazarus to dip the tip of his finger in water	3
	16:25	Lazarus in like manner evil things;	3
Jhn	11: 1	Now a certain man was ill, Lazarus of Bethany	3
	11: 2	Mary was the one,...her brother Lazarus was ill.	3
	11: 5	Jesus loved Martha and her sister and Lazarus	3
	11: 6	after having heard that Lazarus was ill	1
	11:11	"Our friend Lazarus has fallen asleep	3
	11:14	Jesus told them plainly, "Lazarus is dead.	3
	11:17	Lazarus had already been in the tomb four days.	2
	11:43	"Lazarus, come out!"	3
	12: 1	Jesus came to Bethany, the home of Lazarus	3
	12: 2	Lazarus was one of those at the table with him.	3
	12: 9	to see Lazarus, whom he had raised from the dead.	3
	12:10	planned to put Lazarus to death as well	3
	12:17	when he called Lazarus out of the tomb	3

lazy

1. ἀργός, *argos, 734*
2. ὀκνηρός, *oknēros, 3891*

Mat	25:26	his master replied, 'You wicked and lazy slave!	2
Tit	1:12	are always liars, vicious brutes, lazy gluttons."	1

lead · *See also* someone to lead by the hand

1. ἄγω, *agō, 72*
2. ἀπάγω, *apagō, 552*
3. διάγω, *diagō, 1341*
4. εἰς, *eis, 1650*
5. προέρχομαι, *proerchomai, 4601*
6. προκόπτω, *prokoptō, 4621*
7. πρός, *pros, 4639*
8. πρῶτος, *prōtos, 4755*
9. φέρω, *pherō, 5770*

Mat	7:13	the road is easy that leads to destruction	2
	7:14	the road is hard that leads to life	2
Mrk	15:16	soldiers led him into the courtyard of the palace	2
Lke	4: 1	Jesus…was led by the Spirit in the wilderness	1
	4:29	led him to the brow of the hill	1
	22:47	one called Judas, one of the twelve, was leading	5
Jhn	11: 4	"This illness does not lead to death;	7
Act	8:32	"Like a sheep he was led to the slaughter	1
	12:10	came before the iron gate leading into the city.	9
	16:12	a leading city of the district of Macedonia	8
	17: 4	not a few of the leading women.	8
Rom	2: 4	God's kindness is meant to lead you to repentance?	1
	8:14	all…led by the Spirit of God are children of God.	1
Gal	5:18	if you are led by the Spirit	1
2Th	2:11	leading them to believe what is false	4
1Ti	2: 2	we may lead a quiet and peaceable life	3
2Ti	2:16	it will lead people into more and more impiety	6

lead a life

1. ἀναστροφή, *anastrophē, 419*
2. περιπατέω, *peripateō, 4344*

1Co	7:17	However that may be, let each of you lead the life	2
Eph	4: 1	to lead a life worthy of the calling	2
Col	1:10	so that you may lead lives worthy of the Lord	2
1Th	2:12	pleading that you lead a life worthy of God	2
2Pe	3:11	in leading lives of holiness and godliness	1

lead astray

1. ἀπάγω, *apagō, 552*
2. ἀποπλανάω, *apoplanaō, 675*
3. πλανάω, *planaō, 4414*
4. συναπάγω, *synapagō, 5270*
5. φθείρω, *phtheirō, 5780*

Mat	24: 4	"Beware that no one leads you astray.	3
	24: 5	'I am the Messiah!' and they will lead many astray.	3
	24:11	false prophets will arise and lead many astray.	3
	24:24	produce great signs and omens, to lead astray	3
Mrk	13: 5	"Beware that no one leads you astray.	3
	13: 6	and they will lead many astray.	3
	13:22	to lead astray, if possible, the elect.	2
Lke	21: 8	he said, "Beware that you are not led astray;	3
1Co	12: 2	enticed and led astray to idols that could not speak	1
2Co	11: 3	your thoughts will be led astray	5
Gal	2:13	led astray by their hypocrisy.	4
Tit	3: 3	once foolish, disobedient, led astray	3

lead away

1. ἄγω, *agō, 72*
2. ἀπάγω, *apagō, 552*
3. ἀποφέρω, *apopherō, 708*

Mat	27: 2	led him away, and handed him over to Pilate	2
	27:31	Then they led him away to crucify him.	2
Mrk	14:44	arrest him and lead him away under guard."	2
	15: 1	They bound Jesus, led him away	3
Lke	13:15	and lead it away to give it water?	2
	22:54	Then they seized him and led him away	1
	23:26	As they led him away	2
	23:32	Two others also, who were criminals, were led away	1

lead by the hand

1. χειραγωγέω, *cheiragōgeō, 5932*

Act	9: 8	so they led him by the hand	1
	22:11	took my hand and led me to Damascus.	1

lead in triumphal procession

1. θριαμβεύω, *thriambeuō, 2581*

2Co	2:14	who in Christ always leads us in triumphal procession	1

lead out

1. ἐκφέρω, *ekpherō, 1766*
2. ἐξάγω, *exagō, 1974*

Mrk	8:23	led him out of the village;	1
	15:20	they led him out to crucify him.	2
Lke	24:50	Then he led them out as far as Bethany	2
Jhn	10: 3	calls his own sheep by name and leads them out.	2
Act	7:36	He led them out	2
	7:40	this Moses who led us out from the land of Egypt	2
	13:17	with uplifted arm he led them out of it.	2
	21:38	and led the four thousand assassins out	2
Heb	8: 9	to lead them out of the land of Egypt;	2

lead the way

1. προπορεύομαι, *proporeuomai, 4638*

Act	7:40	'Make gods for us who will lead the way for us;	1

lead to

1. εἰς, *eis, 1650*

Act	11:18	to the Gentiles the repentance that leads to life."	1
Rom	5:18	one man's trespass led to condemnation for all	1
	5:18	leads to justification and life for all.	1
	5:21	leading to eternal life through Jesus Christ our Lord.	1
	6:16	slaves…either of sin, which leads to death	1
	6:16	or of obedience, which leads to righteousness?	1
2Co	7: 9	because your grief led to repentance;	1
	7:10	that leads to salvation and brings no regret	1
Jde	1:21	the mercy of our Lord…leads to eternal life.	1

lead up

1. ἀνάγω, *anagō, 343*
2. ἀναφέρω, *anapherō, 429*

Mat	4: 1	Then Jesus was led up by the Spirit	1
	17: 1	and led them up a high mountain, by themselves.	2
Mrk	9: 2	led them up a high mountain apart, by themselves.	2
Lke	4: 5	Then the devil led him up	1

leader

1. Contextual: Not in Greek
2. ἀρχηγός, *archēgos, 795*
3. ἀρχισυνάγωγος, *archisynagōgos, 801*
4. ἄρχων, *archōn, 807*
5. δοκέω, *dokeō, 1506*
6. ἡγέομαι, *hēgeomai, 2451*
7. προΐστημι, *proistēmi, 4613*
8. πρῶτος, *prōtos, 4755*

Mat	9:18	suddenly a leader of the synagogue came in	4
	9:23	When Jesus came to the leader's house	4
Mrk	5:35	some people came from the leader's house	3
	6:21	and for the leaders of Galilee.	8
Lke	8:41	Jairus, a leader of the synagogue.	4
	8:49	someone came from the leader's house to say,	3
	14: 1	to the house of a leader of the Pharisees	4
	19:47	scribes, and the leaders of the people	8
	22:26	the leader like one who serves.	6
	23:13	chief priests, the leaders, and the people	4
	23:35	leaders scoffed at him, saying, "He saved others;	4
	24:20	our chief priests and leaders handed him over	4
Jhn	3: 1	Nicodemus, a leader of the Jews.	4
Act	5:31	God exalted him…as Leader and Savior	2
	13:27	Because the residents of Jerusalem and their leaders	4
	15:22	leaders among the brothers	6
	23: 5	shall not speak evil of a leader of your people.' "	4
	25: 2	the chief priests and the leaders of the Jews	8
	28:17	he called together the local leaders of the Jews.	8
Rom	12: 8	the leader, in diligence;	7
1Co	3:21	So let no one boast about human leaders.	1
Gal	2: 2	in a private meeting with the acknowledged leaders)	1
	2: 6	those leaders contributed nothing to me.	5
Heb	13: 7	Remember your leaders	6
	13:17	Obey your leaders and submit to them	6
	13:24	Greet all your leaders and all the saints.	6

acknowledged leader

1. τὶς, *tis, 5516*

Gal	2: 6	those who were supposed to be acknowledged leaders	1

leader of the synagogue

1. ἀρχισυνάγωγος, *archisynagōgos, 801*

Mrk 5:22 one of the leaders of the synagogue named Jairus came 1
       5:36 Jesus said to the leader of the synagogue 1
       5:38 came to the house of the leader of the synagogue 1
Lke 13:14 the leader of the synagogue, indignant 1

leadership
1. κυβέρνησις, *kybernēsis, 3236*
1Co 12:28 forms of assistance, forms of leadership 1

under the leadership
1. διά, *dia, 1328*
Heb 3:16 left Egypt under the leadership of Moses? 1

leading man
1. πρῶτος, *prōtos, 4755*
Act 13:50 the Jews incited…the leading men of the city 1
      28: 7 lands belonging to the leading man of the island 1

leaf *See also* sprout leaves
1. φύλλον, *phyllon, 5877*
Mat 21:19 found nothing at all on it but leaves. 1
       24:32 becomes tender and puts forth its leaves 1
Mrk 11:13 Seeing in the distance a fig tree in leaf 1
       11:13 When he came to it, he found nothing but leaves 1
       13:28 becomes tender and puts forth its leaves 1
Rev 22: 2 the leaves…are for the healing of the nations. 1

leafy branch
1. στιβάς, *stibas, 5115*
Mrk 11: 8 and others spread leafy branches 1

leap
1. ἅλλομαι, *hallomai, 256*
2. ἐφάλλομαι, *ephallomai, 2383*
3. σκιρτάω, *skirtaō, 5015*
Lke 1:41 the child leaped in her womb. 3
       1:44 the child in my womb leaped for joy. 3
Act 3: 8 walking and leaping and praising God. 1
       19:16 the man with the evil spirit leaped on them 2

leap for joy
1. σκιρτάω, *skirtaō, 5015*
Lke 6:23 Rejoice in that day and leap for joy 1

learn
1. ἀκριβόω, *akriboō, 208*
2. γινώσκω, *ginōskō, 1182*
3. ἐπιγινώσκω, *epiginōskō, 2105*
4. μανθάνω, *manthanō, 3443*
5. παιδεύω, *paideuō, 4084*
6. παραλαμβάνω, *paralambanō, 4161*
7. πυνθάνομαι, *pynthanomai, 4785*
8. συνοράω, *synoraō, 5328*
Mat 2:16 time that he had learned from the wise men. 1
       9:13 Go and learn what this means, 'I desire mercy 4
       11:29 Take my yoke upon you, and learn from me; 4
       24:32 "From the fig tree learn its lesson: 4
Mrk 13:28 "From the fig tree learn its lesson: 4
       15:45 he learned from the centurion that he was dead 2
Lke 7:37 learned that he was eating 3
       23: 7 when he learned that he was under Herod's 3
Jhn 4: 1 when Jesus learned that the Pharisees had heard 4
       6:45 who has heard and learned from the Father 4
       12: 9 great crowd of the Jews learned that he was there 2
Act 9:30 When the believers learned of it 3
       14: 6 apostles learned of it and fled to Lystra and Derbe 8
       17:13 when the Jews of Thessalonica learned 2
       21:34 as he could not learn the facts 2
       23:27 had learned that he was a Roman citizen 4
       23:34 when he learned that he was from Cilicia 7
       24: 8 be able to learn from him concerning everything 3
       28: 1 then learned that the island was called Malta. 3
Rom 16:17 oposition to the teaching that you have learned 4
1Co 4: 6 so that you may learn through us the meaning 4
       14:31 so that all may learn and all be encouraged. 4
Gal 3: 2 The only thing I want to learn from you is this: 4
Eph 4:20 That is not the way you learned Christ! 4
Php 4: 9 things that you have learned and received and heard 4
       4:11 I have learned to be content with whatever I have. 4

Col 1: 7 This you learned from Epaphras 4
1Th 4: 1 as you learned from us how you ought to live 6
1Ti 1:20 so that they may learn not to blaspheme. 5
       2:11 Let a woman learn in silence 4
       5: 4 they should first learn their religious duty 4
       5:13 Besides that, they learn to be idle 4
2Ti 3:14 as for you, continue in what you have learned 4
       3:14 knowing from whom you learned it 4
Tit 3:14 learn to devote themselves to good works 4
Heb 5: 8 he learned obedience through what he suffered; 4
Rev 2:24 you in Thyatira…who have not learned 2
       3: 9 and they will learn that I have loved you. 2
       14: 3 No one could learn that song except 4

learn exact
1. ἀκριβόω, *akriboō, 208*
Mat 2: 7 learned from them the exact time when the star 1

learn the secret
1. μυέω, *myeō, 3679*
Php 4:12 I have learned the secret of being well-fed 1

learning
1. γράμμα, *gramma, 1207*
2. οἶδα + γράμμα, *oida + gramma, 3857 + 1207*
Jhn 7:15 "How does this man have such learning 2
Act 26:24 Paul! Too much learning is driving you insane!" 1

lease
1. ἐκδίδωμι, *ekdidōmi, 1686*
Mat 21:33 Then he leased it to tenants 1
       21:41 and lease the vineyard to other tenants 1
Mrk 12: 1 built a watchtower; then he leased it to tenants 1
Lke 20: 9 planted a vineyard, and leased it to tenants 1

least *See also* not in the least
1. ἐλάχιστος, *elachistos, 1788*
2. μικρός, *mikros, 3625*
Mat 2: 6 are by no means least among the rulers of Judah; 1
       5:19 breaks one of the least of these commandments 1
       5:19 will be called least in the kingdom of heaven; 1
       11:11 yet the least in the kingdom of heaven 2
       25:40 just as you did it to one of the least of these 1
       25:45 you did not do it to one of the least of these 1
Lke 7:28 yet the least in the kingdom of God 2
       9:48 least among all of you is the greatest." 2
Act 8:10 All of them, from the least to the greatest, 2
1Co 15: 9 For I am the least of the apostles 1
Heb 8:11 from the least of them to the greatest. 2

at least
1. γέ, *ge, 1145*
Lke 11: 8 at least because of his persistence 1
1Co 9: 2 not an apostle to others, at least I am to you; 1

very least
1. ἐλάχιστος, *elachistos, 1788*
Eph 3: 8 Although I am the very least of all the saints, 1

leather
1. δερμάτινος, *dermatinos, 1294*
Mat 3: 4 clothing of camel's hair with a leather belt 1
Mrk 1: 6 a leather belt around his waist 1

leave *See also* take leave
1. ἀναχωρέω, *anachōreō, 432*
2. ἀνίημι, *aniēmi, 479*
3. ἀνίστημι, *anistēmi, 482*
4. ἀπαλλάσσω, *apallassō, 557*
5. ἀπέρχομαι, *aperchomai, 599*
6. ἀπό, *apo, 608*
7. ἀπολείπω, *apoleipō, 657*
8. ἀπολύω, *apolyō, 668*
9. ἀποχωρέω, *apochōreō, 713*
10. ἀφίημι, *aphiēmi, 918*
11. ἀφίστημι, *aphistēmi, 923*
12. διαχωρίζω, *diachōrizō, 1431*
13. δίδωμι, *didōmi, 1443*

14. ἐάω, *eaō, 1572*
15. ἐγκαταλείπω, *enkataleipō, 1593*
16. ἐκπορεύομαι, *ekporeuomai, 1744*
17. ἐκχωρέω, *ekchōreō, 1774*
18. ἔξειμι¹, *exeimi¹, 1996*
19. ἐξέρχομαι, *exerchomai, 2002*
20. ἔχω, *echō, 2400*
21. καταλείπω, *kataleipō, 2901*
22. μένω, *menō, 3531*
23. μεταβαίνω, *metabainō, 3553*
24. μεταίρω, *metairō, 3558*
25. περιλείπομαι, *perileipomai, 4335*
26. περισσεύω, *perisseuō, 4355*
27. πορεύομαι, *poreuomai, 4513*
28. πορεύομαι + ἀπό, *poreuomai + apo, 4513 + 608*
29. ὑπολείπω, *hypoleipō, 5699*
30. ὑπολιμπάνω, *hypolimpanō, 5701*
31. χωρίζω, *chōrizō, 6004*

Mat	2:12	they left for their own country by another	1
	2:13	Now after they had left, an angel	1
	4:11	Then the devil left him, and suddenly angels came	10
	4:13	left Nazareth and made his home in Capernaum	21
	4:20	Immediately they left their nets and followed	10
	4:22	Immediately they left the boat and their father	10
	5:24	leave your gift there before the altar and go;	10
	8:15	he touched her hand, and the fever left her	10
	8:34	they begged him to leave their neighborhood.	23
	10:11	and stay there until you leave.	19
	10:14	as you leave that house or town.	19
	12: 9	He left that place and entered	23
	13:36	Then he left the crowds and went into the house.	10
	13:53	When Jesus had finished…he left that place	24
	15:21	Jesus left that place and went away	19
	15:29	Jesus had left that place	23
	16: 4	Then he left them and went away.	21
	18:12	not leave the ninety-nine on the mountains	10
	19: 1	left Galilee and went to teh region of Judea	24
	19: 5	'For this reason a man shall leave his father	21
	19:27	"Look, we have left everything and followed you.	10
	19:29	everyone who has left houses or brothers	10
	20:29	As they were leaving Jericho	16
	21:17	He left them, went out of the city to Bethany	21
	22:22	they left him and went away.	10
	22:25	childless, leaving the widow to his brother.	10
	23:38	See, your house is left to you, desolate.	10
	24: 2	not one stone will be left here upon another;	10
	24:40	one will be taken and one will be left.	10
	24:41	one will be taken and one will be left.	10
	26:44	So leaving them again, he went away	10
	28: 8	they left the tomb quickly with fear	5
Mrk	1:18	immediately they left their nets and followed	10
	1:20	they left their father Zebedee in the boat	10
	1:29	As soon as they left the synagogue	19
	1:31	the fever left her, and she began to serve them.	10
	1:42	Immediately the leprosy left him	5
	5:17	to beg Jesus to leave their neighborhood.	5
	6: 1	He left that place and came to	19
	6:10	stay there until you leave the place.	19
	6:11	as you leave, shake off the dust	16
	7:17	When he had left the crowd and entered the house	6
	7:29	the demon has left your daughter."	19
	8:13	he left them, and getting into the boat again	10
	10: 1	He left that place and went to the region of Judea	3
	10: 7	a man shall leave his father and mother	21
	10:28	we have left everything and followed you."	10
	10:29	there is no one who has left house or brothers	10
	10:46	As he…and a large crowd were leaving Jericho	16
	12:12	So they left him and went away.	10
	12:19	if a man's brother dies, leaving a wife	21
	12:20	when he died, left no children;	10
	12:21	married the widow and died, leaving no children;	21
	12:22	none of the seven left children.	10
	13: 2	Not one stone will be left here upon another;	10
	13:34	when he leaves home	10
	14:52	he left the linen cloth and ran off naked.	21
Lke	2:15	When the angels had left them and gone into heaven	5
	2:37	She never left the temple	11
	4:38	leaving the synagogue	6
	4:39	rebuked the fever, and it left her.	10
	4:42	wanted to prevent him from leaving them.	28

	5:11	they left everything and followed him.	10
	5:13	Immediately the leprosy left him.	5
	5:28	he got up, left everything, and followed him.	21
	8:37	all the people…asked Jesus to leave them;	5
	9: 4	stay there, and leave from there.	19
	9: 5	as you are leaving that town shake the dust off	19
	9:33	Just as they were leaving him	12
	9:39	mauls him and will scarcely leave him.	9
	10:30	robbers…went away, leaving him half dead.	10
	10:40	sister has left me to do all the work by myself?	21
	13:35	See, your house is left to you.	10
	15: 4	does not leave the ninety-nine in the wilderness	21
	17:29	on the day that Lot left Sodom	19
	17:34	one will be taken and the other left.	10
	17:35	one will be taken and the other left."	10
	18:28	"Look, we have left our homes and followed you."	10
	18:29	there is no one who has left house or wife	10
	19:44	will not leave within you one stone upon another;	10
	20:28	brother dies, leaving a wife but no children	20
	21: 6	not one stone will be left upon another;	10
	21:21	those inside the city must leave	17
Jhn	4: 3	he left Judea and started back to Galilee.	10
	4:28	the woman left her water jar and went back	10
	4:30	They left the city and were on their way to him.	19
	4:52	at one in the afternoon the fever left him."	10
	6:13	fragments…left by those who had eaten	26
	7: 3	"Leave here and go to Judea	23
	8: 9	[[Jesus was left alone with the woman]]	21
	8:29	sent me is with me; he has not left me alone	10
	10:12	leaves the sheep and runs away	10
	14:18	"I will not leave you orphaned; I am coming	10
	14:27	Peace I leave with you; my peace I give to you.	10
	16:28	I am leaving the world and am going to the Father."	10
	16:32	and you will leave me alone.	10
	19:31	Jews did not want the bodies left on the cross	22
Act	1: 4	he ordered them not to leave Jerusalem	31
	4:15	So they ordered them to leave the council	5
	5:41	As they left the council	27
	7: 3	'Leave your country and your relatives	19
	7: 4	Then he left the country of the Chaldeans	19
	10: 7	When the angel who spoke to him had left	5
	12:10	suddenly the angel left him.	11
	12:17	Then he left and went to another place.	19
	13:13	John, however, left them and returned to Jerusalem;	9
	14:17	yet he has not left himself without a witness	10
	16:39	took them out and asked them to leave the city.	5
	16:40	leaving the prison they went to Lydia's home;	19
	17:15	receiving instructions…they left him	18
	17:33	At that point Paul left them.	19
	18: 1	After this Paul left Athens and went to Corinth.	31
	18: 2	Claudius had ordered all Jews to leave Rome	31
	18: 7	he left the synagogue and went to the house	23
	18:19	they reached Ephesus, he left them there	21
	19: 9	he left them, taking the disciples with him	11
	19:12	diseases left them, and the evil spirits came out	4
	20: 1	and saying farewell, he left for Macedonia.	19
	20: 7	intended to leave the next day	18
	20:11	continued to converse with them…then he left.	19
	21: 3	leaving it on our left, we sailed to Syria	21
	21: 5	we left and proceeded on our journey;	19
	21: 8	The next day we left and came to Caesarea;	19
	23:23	to leave by nine o'clock tonight for Caesarea	27
	24:27	Felix left Paul in prison.	21
	25:14	a man here who was left in prison by Felix.	21
	26:31	as they were leaving, they said to one another	1
	27:40	cast off the anchors and left them in the sea.	14
	28:25	they were leaving, Paul made one further statement:	8
Rom	9:29	"If the Lord of hosts had not left survivors to us	15
	11: 3	I alone am left, and they are seeking my life."	29
	12:19	but leave room for the wrath of God;	13
2Co	12: 8	I appealed…that it would leave me	11
Eph	5:31	"For this reason a man will leave his father	21
Php	4:15	when I left Macedonia	19
1Th	3: 1	we decided to be left alone in Athens;	21
	4:15	who are left until the coming of the Lord	25
	4:17	Then we who are alive, who are left	25
2Ti	4:13	bring the cloak that I left with Carpus at Troas	7
	4:20	Trophimus I left ill in Miletus.	7
Heb	2: 8	God left nothing outside their control.	10
	3:16	left Egypt under the leadership of Moses?	19
	11:27	By faith he left Egypt	21

13: 5 he has said, "I will never leave you or forsake you." 2
1Pe 2:21 Christ also suffered...leaving you an example 30
2Pe 2:15 They have left the straight road and have gone astray 21
Jde 1: 6 the angels who...left their proper dwelling 7

leave alone
1. ἀφίημι, *aphiēmi, 918*
2. μονόω, *monoō, 3670*

Jhn 12: 7 Jesus said, "Leave her alone. 1
1Ti 5: 5 The real widow, left alone, has set her hope 2

leave behind
1. ἀπολείπω, *apoleipō, 657*
2. ἀφίημι, *aphiēmi, 918*
3. ἐκβαίνω, *ekbainō, 1674*

Mrk 4:36 leaving the crowd behind, they took him with them 2
Tit 1: 5 I left you behind in Crete for this reason 1
Heb 6: 1 leaving behind the basic teaching about Christ 2
       11:15 the land that they had left behind 3

leave out
1. ἐκβάλλω, *ekballō, 1675*

Rev 11: 2 court outside the temple; leave that out 1

leave over
1. περίσσευμα, *perisseuma, 4354*
2. περισσεύω, *perisseuō, 4355*

Mat 14:20 left over of the broken pieces, twelve baskets full. 2
       15:37 the broken pieces left over, seven baskets full. 2
Mrk 8: 8 they took up the broken pieces left over 1
Lke 9:17 What was left over was gathered up 2
Jhn 6:12 "Gather up the fragments left over 2

leaven
1. ζυμόω, *zymoō, 2435*

Mat 13:33 until all of it was leavened." 1
Lke 13:21 until all of it was leavened." 1
1Co 5: 6 a little yeast leavens the whole batch of dough? 1
Gal 5: 9 A little yeast leavens the whole batch of dough. 1

lecture *See* lecture *hall*

lee *See* run under the lee, sail under the lee

left *See also* left hand
1. ἀριστερός, *aristeros, 754*
2. εὐώνυμος, *euōnymos, 2381*

Mat 20:21 one at your right hand and one at your left 2
       20:23 to sit at my right hand and at my left 2
       25:33 the goats at the left. 2
       27:38 one on his right and one on his left. 2
Mrk 10:37 one at your left, in your glory." 1
       10:40 to sit at my right hand or at my left 2
       15:27 one on his right and one on his left. 2
Lke 23:33 one on his right and one on his left. 1
Act 21: 3 leaving it on our left, we sailed to Syria 2
2Co 6: 7 for the right hand and for the left; 1
Rev 10: 2 right foot on the sea and his left foot on the land 2

leg
1. πούς, *pous, 4546*
2. σκέλος, *skelos, 5003*

Jhn 19:31 to have the legs of the crucified men broken 2
       19:32 the soldiers came and broke the legs of the first 2
       19:33 they did not break his legs. 2
Rev 10: 1 and his legs like pillars of fire. 1

legal *See also* legal demand
1. ἔξεστι, *exesti, 2003*
2. νόμος, *nomos, 3795*

Act 22:25 legal...to flog a Roman citizen who is 1
Heb 7:16 a legal requirement concerning physical descent 2

legion
1. λεγιών, *legiōn, 3305*

Mat 26:53 send me more than twelve legions of angels? 1
Mrk 5: 9 He replied, "My name is Legion; for we are many." 1
       5:15 right mind, the very man who had had the legion; 1

Lke 8:30 He said, "Legion"; 1

legitimately
1. νομίμως, *nomimōs, 3789*

1Ti 1: 8 law is good, if one uses it legitimately. 1

leisure
1. εὐκαιρέω, *eukaireō, 2320*

Mrk 6:31 they had no leisure even to eat. 1

lema
1. λεμά, *lema, 3316*

Mat 27:46 "Eli, Eli, lema sabachthani?" 1
Mrk 15:34 "Eloi, Eloi, lema sabachthani?" 1

lend
1. δανίζω, *danizō, 1247*
2. κίχρημι, *kichrēmi, 3079*

Lke 6:34 If you lend to those from whom you...receive 1
       6:34 Even sinners lend to sinners 1
       6:35 do good, and lend, expecting nothing in return. 1
       11: 5 'Friend, lend me three loaves of bread; 2

length
1. βῆμα, *bēma, 1037*
2. μῆκος, *mēkos, 3601*

Act 7: 5 not even a foot's length 1
Eph 3:18 what is the breadth and length and height 2
Rev 21:16 its length the same as its width; 2
       21:16 its length and width and height are equal. 2

at length
1. ἐν + λόγος, *en + logos, 1877 + 3364*

Lke 23: 9 He questioned him at some length 1

lenient
1. φείδομαι, *pheidomai, 5767*

2Co 13: 2 if I come again, I will not be lenient— 1

leopard
1. πάρδαλις, *pardalis, 4203*

Rev 13: 2 And the beast that I saw was like a leopard 1

leper
1. λεπρός, *lepros, 3320*

Mat 8: 2 a leper who came to him and knelt before him 1
       10: 8 Cure the sick, raise the dead, cleanse the lepers 1
       11: 5 the lame walk, the lepers are cleansed 1
       26: 6 at Bethany in the house of Simon the leper 1
Mrk 1:40 A leper came to him begging him, and kneeling 1
       14: 3 at Bethany in the house of Simon the leper 1
Lke 4:27 There were also many lepers in Israel 1
       7:22 lepers are cleansed, the deaf hear 1
       17:12 As he entered a village, ten lepers approached him. 1

leprosy
1. λέπρα, *lepra, 3319*

Mat 8: 3 Immediately his leprosy was cleansed. 1
Mrk 1:42 Immediately the leprosy left him. 1
Lke 5:12 there was a man covered with leprosy. 1
       5:13 Immediately the leprosy left him. 1

less *See also* less anxious, less honorable, less respectable
1. ἐλάσσων, *elassōn, 1781*
2. ἥσσων, *hēssōn, 2482*
3. μᾶλλον, *mallon, 3437*

2Co 12:15 If I love you more, am I to be loved less? 2
1Ti 5: 9 put on the list if she is not less than sixty 1
Heb 12:25 much less will we escape if we reject 3

any less
1. παρά, *para, 4123*

1Co 12:15 that would not make it any less a part of the body. 1
       12:16 that would not make it any less a part of the body. 1

lesson
1. διδαχή, *didachē, 1439*
2. παραβολή, *parabolē, 4130*

Mat 24:32 "From the fig tree learn its lesson: 2
Mrk 13:28 "From the fig tree learn its lesson: 2
1Co 14:26 a hymn, a lesson, a revelation, a tongue   1

let

1. ἀφίημι, *aphiēmi, 918*
2. δίδωμι, *didōmi, 1443*
3. ἐάω, *eaō, 1572*
4. ἐπιτρέπω, *epitrepō, 2205*
5. ἵνα, *hina, 2671*

Mat 3:15 But Jesus answered him, "Let it be so now;   1
     7: 4 'Let me take the speck out of your eye,'   1
     8:21 "Lord, first let me go and bury my father."   4
     8:22 Jesus said to him, "Follow me, and let the dead   1
     13:30 Let both of them grow together until the harvest;   1
     19:14 Jesus said, "Let the little children come to me   1
     24:43 would not have let his house be broken into.   3
Mrk 7:27 He said to her, "Let the children be fed first   1
     10:14 "Let the little children come to me   1
     14:49 let the scriptures be fulfilled."   5
Lke 6:42 let me take out the speck in your eye,'   1
     8:32 demons begged Jesus to let them enter these.   4
     9:59 "Lord, first let me go and bury my father."   4
     9:60 "Let the dead bury their own dead;   1·
     9:61 let me first say farewell to those at my home."   4
     12:39 he would not have let his house be broken into.   1
     18:16 "Let the little children come to me, and do not   1
     18:41 He said, "Lord, let me see again."   5
Jhn 11:44 said to them, "Unbind him, and let him go."   1
     18: 8 So if you are looking for me, let these men go."   1
Act 2:27 or let your Holy One experience corruption.   2
     13:35 'You will not let your Holy One experience corruption.'   2
     19:30 the disciples would not let him;   3
     21:39 I beg you, let me speak to the people."   4
     23:32 The next day they let the horsemen go on with him   3
1Co 10:13 not let you be tested beyond your strength   3
Rev 11: 9 and refuse to let them be placed in a tomb;   1

let alone

1. ἀφίημι, *aphiēmi, 918*
2. ἔα, *ea, 1568*

Mat 15:14 Let them alone; they are blind guides   1
Mrk 14: 6 "Let her alone; why do you trouble her?   1
Lke 4:34 "Let us alone! What have you to do with us,   2
     13: 8 He replied, 'Sir, let it alone for one more year   1
Act 5:38 keep away from these men and let them alone;   1

let down

1. καθίημι, *kathiēmi, 2768*
2. ῥίπτω, *rhiptō, 4849*
3. χαλάω, *chalaō, 5899*

Mrk 2: 4 let down the mat on which the paralytic lay.   3
Lke 5: 4 and let down your nets for a catch."   3
     5: 5 Yet if you say so, I will let down the nets."   3
     5:19 let him down with his bed through the tiles   1
Act 9:25 and let him down through an opening in the wall   1
     27:29 they let down four anchors from the stern   2
2Co 11:33 let down in a basket through a window in the wall   3

let go

1. ἀπολύω, *apolyō, 668*
2. ἀποστέλλω, *apostellō, 690*
3. ἀφίημι, *aphiēmi, 918*

Lke 4:18 to let the oppressed go free   2
Jhn 11:48 If we let him go on like this   3
Act 4:21 they let them go, finding no way to punish them   1
     5:40 and let them go.   1
     16:35 sent the police, saying, "Let those men go."   1
     16:36 "The magistrates sent word to let you go;   1
     17: 9 they let them go.   1

let out

1. λύω, *lyō, 3395*

Rev 20: 3 After that he must be let out for a little while.   1

letter   *See also* send a letter, stroke of a letter

1. Contextual: Not in Greek
2. γράμμα, *gramma, 1207*
3. γράφω, *graphō, 1211*

4. ἐπιστολή, *epistolē, 2186*
5. ἰῶτα, *iōta, 2740*

Mat 5:18 not one letter, not one stroke of a letter   5
Act 9: 2 asked him for letters to the synagogues   4
     15:23 with the following letter: 3
     15:30 they delivered the letter.   4
     22: 5 From them I also received letters to the brothers   4
     23:25 He wrote a letter to this effect: 4
     23:33 delivered the letter to the governor   4
     23:34 On reading the letter   1
     28:21 "We have received no letters from Judea about you   2
Rom 16:22 I Tertius, the writer of this letter, greet you   4
1Co 5: 9 I wrote to you in my letter   4
     16: 3 I will send any whom you approve with letters   4
2Co 3: 1 do not need, as some do, letters of recommendation   4
     3: 2 You yourselves are our letter   4
     3: 3 that you are a letter of Christ, prepared by us   4
     3: 6 new covenant, not of letter but of spirit;   2
     3: 6 the letter kills, but the Spirit gives life.   2
     3: 7 chiseled in letters on stone tablets   2
     7: 8 For even if I made you sorry with my letter   4
     7: 8 I see that I grieved you with that letter   4
     10: 9 as though I am trying to frighten you with my letters.   4
     10:10 For they say, "His letters are weighty and strong   4
     10:11 what we say by letter when absent   4
Gal 6:11 See what large letters I make when I am writing   4
Col 4:16 when this letter has been read among you   4
     4:16 see that you read also the letter from Laodicea.   1
1Th 5:27 command you by the Lord that this letter be read   4
2Th 2: 2 by letter, as though from us,   4
     2:15 taught...either by word of mouth or by our letter.   4
     3:14 those who do not obey what we say in this letter;   4
     3:17 This is the mark in every letter of mine;   4
1Pe 5:12 I have written this short letter to encourage you   1
2Pe 3: 1 This is now, beloved, the second letter I am writing   4
     3:16 speaking of this as he does in all his letters.   4

level

1. πεδινός, *pedinos, 4268*

Lke 6:17 came down with them and stood on a level place   1

Levi

1. αὐτός, *autos, 899*
2. Λευί, *Leui, 3322*

Mrk 2:14 walking along, he saw Levi son of Alphaeus   2
     2:15 as he sat at dinner in Levi's house   1
Lke 3:24 son of Matthat, son of Levi   2
     3:29 son of Matthat, son of Levi   2
     5:27 he went out and saw a tax collector named Levi   2
     5:29 Levi gave a great banquet for him in his house;   2
Heb 7: 5 descendants of Levi who receive the priestly office   2
     7: 9 Levi himself...paid tithes through Abraham   2
Rev 7: 7 from the tribe of Levi twelve thousand,   2

Levite

1. Λευίτης, *Leuitēs, 3324*

Lke 10:32 So likewise a Levite, when he came to the place   1
Jhn 1:19 Jews sent priests and Levites from Jerusalem   1
Act 4:36 a Levite, a native of Cyprus, Joseph,   1

Levitical

1. Λευιτικός, *Leuitikos, 3325*

Heb 7:11 attainable through the levitical priesthood   1

liable

1. ἔνοχος, *enochos, 1944*

Mat 5:21 'whoever murders shall be liable to judgment.'   1
     5:22 angry...you will be liable to judgment;   1
     5:22 insult...you will be liable to the council;   1
     5:22 'You fool,' you will be liable to the hell of fire.   1

liar

1. ψευδής, *pseudēs, 6014*
2. ψευδολόγος, *pseudologos, 6016*
3. ψεύστης, *pseustēs, 6026*

Jhn 8:44 for he is a liar and the father of lies.   3
     8:55 I would be a liar like you.   3
Rom 3: 4 Although everyone is a liar, let God be proved true   3
1Ti 1:10 fornicators, sodomites, slave traders, liars   3

4: 2 through the hypocrisy of liars 2
Tit 1:12 "Cretans are always liars, vicious brutes 3
1Jn 1:10 If we say that we have not sinned, we make him a liar 3
2: 4 but does not obey his commandments, is a liar 3
2:22 Who is the liar but the one who denies 3
4:20 and hate their brothers or sisters, are liars; 3
5:10 Those who do not believe in God have made him a liar 3
Rev 21: 8 as for...sorcerers, the idolaters, and all liars 1

libation *See* pour out as a libation

liberator
1. λυτρωτής, *lytrōtēs, 3392*
Act 7:35 God now sent as both ruler and liberator 1

liberty
1. ἄνεσις, *anesis, 457*
2. ἐλευθερία, *eleutheria, 1800*
3. ἐξουσία, *exousia, 2026*
Act 24:23 but to let him have some liberty 1
1Co 8: 9 But take care that this liberty of yours does not 3
10:29 why should my liberty be subject to the judgment 2
Jas 1:25 the perfect law, the law of liberty 2
2:12 who are to be judged by the law of liberty. 2

Libya
1. Λιβύη, *Libyē, 3340*
Act 2:10 Egypt and the parts of Libya belonging to Cyrene 1

licentious *See also* licentious *way*
1. ἀσέλγεια, *aselgeia, 816*
2Pe 2:18 with licentious desires of the flesh they entice 1

licentiousness
1. ἀσέλγεια, *aselgeia, 816*
Mrk 7:22 avarice, wickedness, deceit, licentiousness 1
Rom 13:13 not in debauchery and licentiousness 1
2Co 12:21 impurity, sexual immorality, and licentiousness 1
Gal 5:19 fornication, impurity, licentiousness 1
Eph 4:19 have abandoned themselves to licentiousness 1
1Pe 4: 3 living in licentiousness, passions 1
2Pe 2: 7 distressed by the licentiousness of the lawless 1
Jde 1: 4 pervert the grace of our God into licentiousness 1

lick
1. ἐπιλείχω, *epileichō, 2143*
Lke 16:21 even the dogs would come and lick his sores. 1

lie¹ *See also* never lie
1. Contextual: Not in Greek
2. βάλλω, *ballō, 965*
3. κατάκειμαι, *katakeimai, 2879*
4. κεῖμαι, *keimai, 3023*
Mat 3:10 Even now the ax is lying at the root of the trees; 4
8: 6 "Lord, my servant is lying at home paralyzed 2
9: 2 a paralyzed man lying on a bed. 2
28: 6 Come, see the place where he lay. 4
Mrk 2: 4 let down the mat on which the paralytic lay. 3
7:30 she went home, found the child lying on the bed 2
Lke 2:12 lying in a manger." 4
2:16 the child lying in the manger. 4
3: 9 Even now the ax is lying at the root of the trees; 4
16:20 at his gate lay a poor man named Lazarus 2
Jhn 4:46 there was a royal official whose son lay ill 1
5: 3 In these lay many invalids—blind, lame 3
5: 6 When Jesus saw him lying there 3
20: 5 and saw the linen wrappings lying there 4
20: 6 He saw the linen wrappings lying there 4
20: 7 the cloth...not lying with the linen wrappings 4
20:12 sitting where the body of Jesus had been lying 4
Rom 7: 8 Apart from the law sin lies dead. 1
2Co 3:15 a veil lies over their minds; 4
1Jn 5:19 the whole world lies under the power of the evil one. 4
Rev 11: 8 their dead bodies will lie in the street 1
21:16 The city lies foursquare, its length the same 4

lie²
1. αὐτός, *autos, 899*
2. ψεύδομαι, *pseudomai, 6017*

3. ψεῦδος, *pseudos, 6022*
4. ψεῦδος + λαλέω, *pseudos + laleō, 6022 + 3281*
Jhn 8:44 When he lies, he speaks according to his own nature 4
8:44 for he is a liar and the father of lies. 1
Act 5: 3 filled your heart to lie to the Holy Spirit 2
5: 4 You did not lie to us but to God!" 2
Rom 1:25 they exchanged the truth about God for a lie 3
9: 1 I am speaking the truth in Christ—I am not lying; 2
2Co 11:31 God...knows that I do not lie. 2
Gal 1:20 I am writing to you, before God, I do not lie! 2
Col 3: 9 Do not lie to one another 2
2Th 2: 9 Satan, who uses all power, signs, lying wonders 3
1Ti 2: 7 (I am telling the truth, I am not lying) 2
1Jn 1: 6 we lie and do not do what is true; 2
2:21 and you know that no lie comes from the truth. 3
2:27 anointing teaches...and is true and is not a lie 3
Rev 3: 9 say that they are Jews and are not, but are lying 2
14: 5 in their mouth no lie was found; 3

lie against
1. ἐπίκειμαι, *epikeimai, 2130*
Jhn 11:38 It was a cave, and a stone was lying against it. 1

lie ahead
1. ἔμπροσθεν, *emprosthen, 1869*
Php 3:13 straining forward to what lies ahead 1

lie behind
1. ὀπίσω, *opisō, 3958*
Php 3:13 one thing I do: forgetting what lies behind 1

lie close at hand
1. παράκειμαι, *parakeimai, 4154*
Rom 7:21 I want to do what is good, evil lies close at hand. 1

lie in ambush
1. ἐνεδρεύω, *enedreuō, 1910*
Act 23:21 more than forty of their men are lying in ambush 1

lie in bed
1. βάλλω, *ballō, 965*
2. κατάκειμαι, *katakeimai, 2879*
Mat 8:14 saw his mother-in-law lying in bed with a fever; 1
Act 28: 8 the father of Publius lay sick in bed 2

lie in wait
1. ἐνεδρεύω, *enedreuō, 1910*
Lke 11:54 lying in wait for him 1

lie on
1. κατάκειμαι, *katakeimai, 2879*
Lke 5:25 took what he had been lying on, and went 1

life *See also* aim in life, bring to life, busy life, come to life, end of life, give life, keep one's life, lead a life, live a life, span of life, way of life
1. Contextual: Not in Greek
2. ἀναστροφή, *anastrophē, 419*
3. βίος, *bios, 1050*
4. βιωτικός, *biōtikos, 1053*
5. εἰμί, *eimi, 1639*
6. ζάω, *zaō, 2409*
7. ζωή, *zōē, 2437*
8. ὅς, *hos, 4005*
9. οὗτος, *houtos, 4047*
10. σάρξ, *sarx, 4922*
11. τρόπος, *tropos, 5573*
12. χρόνος, *chronos, 5989*
13. ψυχή, *psychē, 6034*
Mat 2:20 those who were seeking the child's life are dead." 13
6:25 I tell you, do not worry about your life 13
6:25 Is not life more than food, and the body 13
7:14 the road is hard that leads to life 7
10:39 Those who find their life will lose it 13
10:39 who lose their life for my sake will find it. 13
16:25 those who want to save their life will lose it 13
16:25 who lose their life for my sake will find it. 13
16:26 gain the whole world but forfeit their life? 13

Mat	16:26	what will they give in return for their life?	13
	18: 8	it is better for you to enter life maimed or lame	7
	18: 9	it is better for you to enter life with one eye	7
	19:16	to have eternal life?"	7
	19:17	to enter into life, keep the commandments."	7
	19:29	and will inherit eternal life.	7
	20:28	to give his life a ransom for many."	13
	25:46	but the righteous into eternal life."	7
Mrk	3: 4	to save life or to kill?"	13
	8:35	those who want to save their life will lose it	13
	8:35	who lose their life for my sake	13
	8:36	to gain the whole world and forfeit their life?	13
	8:37	what can they give in return for their life?	13
	9:43	it is better for you to enter life maimed	7
	9:45	it is better for you to enter life lame	7
	10:17	what must I do to inherit eternal life?"	7
	10:30	in the age to come eternal life.	7
	10:45	to give his life a ransom for many."	13
Lke	6: 9	to save life or to destroy it?"	13
	8:14	the cares and riches and pleasures of life	3
	9:24	who want to save their life will lose it	13
	9:24	who lose their life for my sake will save it.	13
	10:25	"what must I do to inherit eternal life?"	7
	12:15	one's life does not consist in the abundance	7
	12:20	This very night your life is being demanded	13
	12:22	do not worry about your life	13
	12:23	For life is more than food	13
	14:26	yes, and even life itself,	13
	17:33	who try to make their life secure will lose it	13
	18:18	what must I do to inherit eternal life?"	7
	18:30	in the age to come eternal life."	7
	21:34	drunkenness and the worries of this life	4
Jhn	1: 4	in him was life, and the life was the light of all	7
	1: 4	and the life was the light of all people.	7
	3:15	whoever believes in him may have eternal life.	7
	3:16	may not perish but may have eternal life.	7
	3:36	Whoever believes in the Son has eternal life;	7
	3:36	whoever disobeys the Son will not see life	7
	4:14	a spring of water gushing up to eternal life."	7
	4:36	and is gathering fruit for eternal life	7
	5:24	who hears…and believes…has eternal life	7
	5:24	has passed from death to life.	7
	5:26	For just as the Father has life in himself	7
	5:26	has granted the Son also to have life in himself;	7
	5:29	who have done good, to the resurrection of life	7
	5:39	you think that in them you have eternal life;	7
	5:40	you refuse to come to me to have life.	7
	6:27	the food that endures for eternal life	7
	6:33	gives life to the world."	7
	6:35	Jesus said to them, "I am the bread of life.	7
	6:40	all who…believe…may have eternal life;	7
	6:47	whoever believes has eternal life.	7
	6:48	I am the bread of life.	7
	6:51	bread that I will give for the life of the world	7
	6:53	you have no life in you.	7
	6:54	Those who…drink my blood have eternal life	7
	6:63	The words…are spirit and life.	7
	6:68	You have the words of eternal life.	7
	8:12	will have the light of life."	7
	10:10	I came that they may have life	7
	10:11	The good shepherd lays down his life	13
	10:15	I lay down my life for the sheep.	13
	10:17	the Father loves me, because I lay down my life	13
	10:28	I give them eternal life	7
	11:25	"I am the resurrection and the life.	7
	12:25	Those who love their life lose it	13
	12:25	who hate their life in this world will keep it	13
	12:25	will keep it for eternal life.	13
	12:50	I know that his commandment is eternal life.	7
	13:37	I will lay down my life for you."	13
	13:38	answered, "Will you lay down your life for me?	13
	14: 6	"I am the way, and the truth, and the life.	7
	15:13	to lay down one's life for one's friends.	13
	17: 2	to give eternal life to all	7
	17: 3	this is eternal life, that they may know you	7
	20:31	believing you may have life in his name.	7
Act	2:28	You have made known to me the ways of life;	7
	3:15	you killed the Author of life	7
	5:20	tell the people the whole message about this life."	7
	8:33	For his life is taken away from the earth."	7
	11:18	to the Gentiles the repentance that leads to life."	7

	13:46	judge yourselves to be unworthy of eternal life	7
	13:48	as many as had been destined for eternal life	7
	15:26	who have risked their lives	13
	17:25	gives to all mortals life and breath and all things.	7
	20:10	"Do not be alarmed, for his life is in him."	13
	20:24	I do not count my life of any value	13
	26: 4	a life spent from the beginning among my own people	1
	27:10	not only of…the ship, but also of our lives."	13
	27:22	no loss of life among you, but only of the ship.	13
Rom	2: 7	he will give eternal life;	7
	5:10	much more…will we be saved by his life.	7
	5:17	exercise dominion in life through the one man	7
	5:18	leads to justification and life for all.	7
	5:21	leading to eternal life through Jesus Christ our Lord.	7
	6: 4	so we too might walk in newness of life	7
	6:10	but the life he lives, he lives to God.	8
	6:22	The end is eternal life.	7
	6:23	the free gift of God is eternal life in Christ	7
	7: 6	we are slaves…in the new life of the Spirit.	1
	7:10	the very commandment that promised life	7
	8: 2	For the law of the Spirit of life in Christ Jesus	7
	8: 6	to set the mind on the Spirit is life and peace.	7
	8:10	the Spirit is life because of righteousness.	7
	8:38	neither death, nor life, nor angels	7
	11: 3	I alone am left, and they are seeking my life."	13
	11:15	their acceptance be but life from the dead!	7
	16: 4	who risked their necks for my life	13
1Co	1:30	He is the source of your life in Christ Jesus	5
	3:22	the world or life or death or the present	7
	7:28	who marry will experience distress in this life	10
	15:19	If for this life only we have hoped in Christ	7
2Co	1: 8	we despaired of life itself.	6
	2:16	to the other a fragrance from life to life.	7
	2:16	to the other a fragrance from life to life.	7
	4:10	so that the life of Jesus may also be made visible	7
	4:11	so that the life of Jesus may be made visible	7
	4:12	death is at work in us, but life in you.	7
	5: 4	what is mortal may be swallowed up by life.	7
Gal	1:13	heard, no doubt, of my earlier life in Judaism.	2
	2:20	the life I now live in the flesh I live by faith	8
	6: 8	will reap eternal life from the Spirit.	7
Eph	4:18	alienated from the life of God	7
Php	1:20	whether by life or by death.	7
	2:16	holding fast to the word of life	7
	2:30	risking his life to make up for those services	13
	4: 3	whose names are in the book of life.	7
Col	3: 3	your life is hidden with Christ in God.	7
	3: 4	When Christ who is your life is revealed	7
	3: 7	once followed, when you were living that life.	9
1Ti	1:16	who would come to believe in him for eternal life.	7
	2: 2	we may lead a quiet and peaceable life	3
	4: 8	holding promise for both the present life	7
	4: 8	both the present life and the life to come.	1
	6:12	the eternal life, to which you were called	7
	6:19	take hold of the life that really is life.	7
	6:19	take hold of the life that really is life.	1
2Ti	1: 1	the promise of life that is in Christ Jesus	7
	1:10	brought life and immortality to light	7
Tit	1: 2	eternal life that God, who never lies, promised	7
	2:12	in the present age to live lives that are self-controlled,	1
	3: 7	become heirs according to the hope of eternal life.	7
Heb	2:15	free those who all their lives were held in slavery	6
	7: 3	having neither beginning of days nor end of life	7
	7:16	through the power of an indestructible life.	7
	13: 5	Keep your lives free from the love of money	11
Jas	1:12	the crown of life that the Lord has promised	7
	3:13	Show by your good life that your works are done	2
	4:14	What is your life? For you are a mist	7
1Pe	3: 2	when they see the purity and reverence of your lives.	2
	3: 7	they too are also heirs of the gracious gift of life	7
	3:10	"Those who desire life and desire to see good days	7
	4: 2	so as to live for the rest of your earthly life	12
2Pe	1: 3	everything needed for life and godliness	7
1Jn	1: 1	concerning the word of life	7
	1: 2	this life was revealed, and we have seen it	7
	1: 2	and declare to you the eternal life	7
	2:25	this is what he has promised us, eternal life.	7
	3:14	We know that we have passed from death to life	7
	3:15	murderers do not have eternal life abiding in them.	7
	3:16	We know love by this, that he laid down his life	13
	3:16	we ought to lay down our lives for one another.	13

5:11 the testimony: God gave us eternal life 7
5:11 eternal life, and this life is in his Son. 7
5:12 Whoever has the Son has life; 7
5:12 whoever does not have the Son of God does not have life. 7
5:13 so that you may know that you have eternal life. 7
5:16 you will ask, and God will give life to such a one 7
5:20 He is the true God and eternal life. 7
Jde 1:21 the mercy of our Lord…leads to eternal life. 7
Rev 2: 7 I will give permission to eat from the tree of life 7
2:10 and I will give you the crown of life. 7
3: 5 I will not blot your name out of the book of life; 7
7:17 he will guide them to springs of the water of life 7
11:11 the breath of life from God entered them 7
12:11 they did not cling to life even in the face of death. 13
13: 8 name has not been written…in the book of life 7
17: 8 names have not been written in the book of life 7
18:13 and chariots, slaves—and human lives. 13
20:12 another book was opened, the book of life. 7
20:15 name was not found written in the book of life 7
21: 6 as a gift from the spring of the water of life. 7
21:27 only those…written in the Lamb's book of life. 7
22: 1 angel showed me the river of the water of life 7
22: 2 the tree of life with its twelve kinds of fruit 7
22:14 they will have the right to the tree of life 7
22:17 Let anyone who wishes take the water of life 7
22:19 take away that person's share in the tree of life 7

daily life

1. ἄνθρωπος, *anthrōpos, 476*

Gal 3:15 I give an example from daily life: 1

godly life

1. εὐσεβῶς, *eusebōs, 2357*

2Ti 3:12 all who want to live a godly life in Christ 1

life together

1. συνοικέω, *synoikeō, 5324*

1Pe 3: 7 show consideration for your wives in your life together 1

life-giving

1. ζωοποιέω, *zōopoieō, 2443*

1Co 15:45 the last Adam became a life-giving spirit. 1

lifeless

1. ἄψυχος, *apsychos, 953*

1Co 14: 7 with lifeless instruments that produce sound, 1

lifetime

1. ζάω, *zaō, 2409*
2. ζωή, *zōē, 2437*

Lke 16:25 during your lifetime you received your good things 2
Rom 7: 1 the law is binding on a person only during…lifetime? 1

lift

1. Contextual: Not in Greek
2. ἀνορθόω, *anorthoō, 494*

Mat 23: 4 are unwilling to lift a finger to move them. 1
Lke 11:46 do not lift a finger to ease them. 1
Heb 12:12 Therefore lift your drooping hands 2

lift against

1. ἐπαίρω, *epairō, 2048*

Jhn 13:18 who ate my bread has lifted his heel against me.' 1

lift out

1. ἐγείρω, *egeirō, 1586*

Mat 12:11 will you not lay hold of it and lift it out? 1

lift up

1. αἴρω, *airō, 149*
2. ἐγείρω, *egeirō, 1586*
3. ἐπαίρω, *epairō, 2048*
4. ὑψόω, *hypsoō, 5738*

Mat 21:21 'Be lifted up and thrown into the sea,' 1
Mrk 1:31 He came and took her by the hand and lifted her up. 2
9:27 Jesus took him by the hand and lifted him up 2
Lke 1:52 and lifted up the lowly; 4
24:50 and, lifting up his hands, he blessed them. 3
Jhn 3:14 as Moses lifted up the serpent in the wilderness 4

3:14 so must the Son of Man be lifted up 4
8:28 "When you have lifted up the Son of Man 4
12:32 when I am lifted up from the earth 4
12:34 you say that the Son of Man must be lifted up? 4
Act 1: 9 he was lifted up, and a cloud took him 3
1Ti 2: 8 lifting up holy hands without anger or argument; 3

ligament

1. ἀφή, *haphē, 913*

Eph 4:16 every ligament with which it is equipped 1
Col 2:19 held together by its ligaments and sinews 1

light¹ *See also* bring to light, full of light, give light, make light

1. Contextual: Not in Greek
2. ἅπτω, *haptō, 721*
3. καίω, *kaiō, 2794*
4. φανερός, *phaneros, 5745*
5. φέγγος, *phengos, 5766*
6. φῶς, *phōs, 5890*
7. φωτεινός, *phōteinos, 5893*
8. φωτίζω, *phōtizō, 5894*
9. φωτισμός, *phōtismos, 5895*

Mat 4:16 people who sat in darkness have seen a great light 6
4:16 region and shadow of death light has dawned." 6
5:14 "You are the light of the world. 6
5:15 No one after lighting a lamp puts it under 3
5:16 In the same way, let your light shine before others 6
6:22 eye is healthy, your whole body will be full of light; 7
6:23 If then the light in you is darkness 6
10:27 What I say to you in the dark, tell in the light; 6
24:29 the moon will not give its light; 5
Mrk 4:22 nor is anything secret, except to come to light. 4
13:24 the moon will not give its light 5
Lke 2:32 a light for revelation to the Gentiles 6
8:16 "No one after lighting a lamp hides it 2
8:16 so that those who enter may see the light. 6
8:17 that will not become known and come to light. 4
11:33 after lighting a lamp puts it in a cellar 2
11:33 so that those who enter may see the light. 6
11:35 consider whether the light in you is not darkness. 6
11:36 it will be as full of light 7
12: 3 said in the dark will be heard in the light 6
12:35 "Be dressed for action and have your lamps lit; 3
15: 8 does not light a lamp, sweep the house, 2
16: 8 more shrewd…than are the children of light. 6
23:45 while the sun's light failed; 1
Jhn 1: 4 and the life was the light of all people. 6
1: 5 The light shines in the darkness 6
1: 7 He came…to testify to the light 6
1: 8 He himself was not the light, but he came to 6
1: 8 but he came to testify to the light. 6
1: 9 The true light, which enlightens everyone 6
3:19 that the light has come into the world 6
3:19 and people loved darkness rather than light 6
3:20 For all who do evil hate the light 6
3:20 hate the light and do not come to the light 6
3:21 But those who do what is true come to the light 6
5:35 willing to rejoice for a while in his light. 6
8:12 "I am the light of the world. 6
8:12 will have the light of life." 6
9: 5 I am the light of the world." 6
11: 9 because they see the light of this world. 6
11:10 stumble, because the light is not in them." 6
12:35 "The light is with you for a little longer. 6
12:35 Walk while you have the light 6
12:36 While you have the light, believe in the light 6
12:36 While you have the light, believe in the light 6
12:36 so that you may become children of light." 6
12:46 I have come as light into the world 6
Act 9: 3 suddenly a light from heaven flashed around him. 6
12: 7 a light shone in the cell. 6
13:47 'I have set you to be a light for the Gentiles 6
16:29 The jailer called for lights, and rushing in 6
22: 6 a great light from heaven suddenly shone about me. 6
22: 9 Now those who were with me saw the light 6
22:11 not see because of the brightness of that light 6
26:13 your Excellency, I saw a light from heaven 6
26:18 they may turn from darkness to light 6
26:23 he would proclaim light…to our people 6

Rom	2:19	a light to those who are in darkness	6
	13:12	Let us...put on the armor of light;	6
2Co	4: 4	to keep them from seeing the light of the gospel	9
	4: 6	the God who said, "Let light shine out of darkness,"	6
	4: 6	to give the light of the knowledge of the glory	9
	6:14	what fellowship is there between light and darkness?	6
	11:14	Satan disguises himself as an angel of light.	6
Eph	5: 8	now in the Lord you are light.	6
	5: 8	Live as children of light	6
	5: 9	fruit of the light is found in all that is good	6
	5:13	everything exposed by the light	6
	5:14	for everything that becomes visible is light.	6
Col	1:12	the inheritance of the saints in the light.	6
1Th	5: 5	for you are all children of light	6
1Ti	6:16	dwells in unapproachable light	6
Jas	1:17	coming down from the Father of lights	6
1Pe	2: 9	called...out of darkness into his marvelous light.	6
1Jn	1: 5	God is light and in him there is no darkness at all.	6
	1: 7	if we walk in the light as he himself is in the light	6
	1: 7	if we walk in the light as he himself is in the light	6
	2: 8	and the true light is already shining.	6
	2: 9	Whoever says, "I am in the light,"	6
	2:10	Whoever loves a brother or sister lives in the light	6
Rev	8:12	so that a third of their light was darkened;	1
	18:23	and the light of a lamp will shine in you no more;	6
	21:23	for the glory of God is its light	8
	21:24	The nations will walk by its light	6
	22: 5	they need no light of lamp or sun	6
	22: 5	for the Lord God will be their light	8

light²

1. ἐλαφρός, *elaphros*, 1787
2. ὀλίγος, *oligos*, 3900

Mat	11:30	For my yoke is easy, and my burden is light."	1
Lke	12:48	one...will receive a light beating.	2

light up

1. λάμπω, *lampō*, 3290

Lke	17:24	lights up the sky from one side to the other	1

lighten

1. κουφίζω, *kouphizō*, 3185

Act	27:38	they lightened the ship	1

lightning *See also* flash of lightning

1. ἀστραπή, *astrapē*, 847

Mat	24:27	For as the lightning comes from the east	1
	28: 3	His appearance was like lightning	1
Lke	17:24	For as the lightning flashes and lights up	1

like¹ *See also* just like, like a *Gentile*, like a *Jew*, like an *angel*, like *manner*, like *measure*, live like a Jew, look like, make like, work like a slave

1. ἔοικα, *eoika*, 2036
2. ἰσόψυχος, *isopsychos*, 2701
3. καθάπερ, *kathaper*, 2749
4. καθώς, *kathōs*, 2777
5. κατά, *kata*, 2848
6. ὁμοιοπαθής, *homoiopathēs*, 3926
7. ὅμοιος, *homoios*, 3927
8. ὁμοιόω, *homoioō*, 3929
9. ὁμοίωμα, *homoiōma*, 3930
10. ὁμοίως, *homoiōs*, 3931
11. οὕτως, *houtōs*, 4048
12. παρομοιάζω, *paromoiazō*, 4234
13. παρόμοιος, *paromoios*, 4235
14. συμμορφίζω, *symmorphizō*, 5214
15. ὡς, *hōs*, 6055
16. ὡς + ἐάν, *hōs + ean*, 6055 + 1569
17. ὡσεί, *hōsei*, 6059
18. ὥσπερ, *hōsper*, 6061

Mat	3:16	saw the Spirit of God descending like a dove	17
	6: 5	whenever you pray, do not be like the hypocrites;	15
	6: 8	Do not be like them, for your Father knows	8
	6:16	you fast, do not look dismal, like the hypocrites	15
	6:29	his glory was not clothed like one of these.	15
	7:24	will be like a wise man who built his house	8
	7:26	does not act on them will be like a foolish man	8
	9:36	helpless, like sheep without a shepherd.	17

	10:16	"See, I am sending you out like sheep	15
	10:25	the disciple to be like the teacher	15
	10:25	and the slave like the master.	15
	11:16	It is like children sitting in the marketplaces	7
	13:31	"The kingdom of heaven is like a mustard	7
	13:33	"The kingdom of heaven is like yeast	7
	13:43	Then the righteous will shine like the sun	15
	13:44	"The kingdom of heaven is like treasure	7
	13:45	"Again, the kingdom of heaven is like a merchant	7
	13:47	"Again, the kingdom of heaven is like a net	7
	13:52	is like the master of a household who brings out	7
	17: 2	and his face shone like the sun	15
	18: 3	unless you change and become like children	15
	18: 4	Whoever becomes humble like this child	15
	20: 1	"For the kingdom of heaven is like a landowner	7
	22:30	but are like angels in heaven.	15
	22:39	a second is like it: 'You shall love your neighbor	7
	23:27	you are like whitewashed tombs	12
	25: 1	"Then the kingdom of heaven will be like	8
	28: 3	His appearance was like lightning	15
	28: 4	the guards shook and became like dead men.	15
Mrk	1:10	the Spirit descending like a dove on him.	15
	4:31	It is like a mustard seed	15
	6:15	"It is a prophet, like one of the prophets of old."	15
	6:34	because they were like sheep without a shepherd;	15
	7:13	you do many things like this."	13
	8:24	see people, but they look like trees, walking."	15
	9:26	it came out, and the boy was like a corpse	17
	12:25	are like angels in heaven.	15
	13:34	It is like a man going on a journey	15
Lke	3:22	in bodily form like a dove.	15
	5:33	like the disciples of the Pharisees	10
	6:40	everyone...will be like the teacher.	15
	6:47	someone is like who comes to me, hears my words	7
	6:48	That one is like a man building a house	7
	6:49	like a man who built a house on the ground	7
	7:31	what are they like?	7
	7:32	They are like children sitting in the marketplace	7
	10: 3	See, I am sending you out like lambs	15
	10:18	Satan fall from heaven like a flash of lightning.	15
	11:44	Woe to you! For you are like unmarked graves	15
	12:27	was not clothed like one of these.	15
	12:36	be like those who are waiting for their master	7
	13:18	"What is the kingdom of God like?	7
	13:19	It is like a mustard seed that someone took	7
	13:21	It is like yeast that a woman took and mixed	7
	15:19	treat me like one of your hired hands." '	15
	17:30	it will be like that on the day	5
	18:11	I thank you that I am not like other people:	18
	18:11	or even like this tax collector.	15
	21:35	like a trap. For it will come upon all	15
	22:26	greatest among you must become like the youngest	15
	22:26	the leader like one who serves.	15
	22:31	Satan has demanded to sift all of you like wheat	15
	22:44	[[his sweat became like great drops of blood]]	17
Jhn	1:32	the Spirit descending from heaven like a dove	15
	6:58	not like...your ancestors ate, and they died.	4
	8:55	I would be a liar like you.	7
	9: 9	were saying, "No, but it is someone like him."	7
	15: 6	is thrown away like a branch and withers;	15
Act	2: 2	a sound like the rush of a violent wind	18
	3:22	from your own people a prophet like me.	15
	6:15	his face was like the face of an angel	17
	8:32	"Like a sheep he was led to the slaughter	15
	8:32	like a lamb silent before its shearer	15
	9:18	something like scales fell from his eyes	15
	10:11	and something like a large sheet coming down	15
	11: 5	There was something like a large sheet coming down	15
	17:29	ought not to think that the deity is like gold	7
Rom	5:14	sins were not like the transgression of Adam	9
	5:15	But the free gift is not like the trespass.	15
	5:16	the free gift is not like...the one man's sin.	15
	6: 5	if we have been united with him in a death like his	9
	9:27	the children of Israel were like the sand of the sea	15
	9:29	we would have fared like Sodom	15
	9:29	fared like Sodom and been made like Gomorrah."	15
1Co	3:10	like a skilled master builder	15
	4:13	We have become like the rubbish of the world,	15
	13:11	When I was a child, I spoke like a child	15
	13:11	I thought like a child, I reasoned like a child;	15
	13:11	I thought like a child, I reasoned like a child;	15

2Co	2:17	we are not peddlers of God's word like so many;	15
	3:13	not like Moses, who put a veil over his face	3
Gal	4:28	friends, are children of the promise, like Isaac.	5
	5:21	drunkenness, carousing, and things like these	7
Eph	2: 3	children of wrath, like everyone else.	15
Php	2:15	in which you shine like stars in the world.	15
	2:20	I have no one like him	2
	2:22	how like a son with a father he has served with me	15
	3:10	becoming like him in his death	14
1Th	2: 7	like a nurse tenderly caring for her own children.	16
	2:11	we dealt with each one of you like a father	15
	4: 5	like the Gentiles who do not know God;	3
	5: 2	the day of the Lord will come like a thief	15
	5: 4	for that day to surprise you like a thief;	15
2Ti	2: 3	Share in suffering like a good soldier	15
	2: 9	even to the point of being chained like a criminal	15
	2:17	their talk will spread like gangrene.	15
Heb	1:11	they will all wear out like clothing;	15
	1:12	like a cloak you will roll them up	17
	1:12	and like clothing they will be changed.	15
	2:17	become like his brothers and sisters in every respect	8
	8: 9	like the covenant that I made with their ancestors	5
	12:16	no one becomes like Esau, an immoral and godless	15
Jas	1: 6	the one who doubts is like a wave of the sea	1
	1:10	the rich will disappear like a flower in the field.	15
	1:23	they are like those who look at themselves	1
	5: 3	their rust…will eat your flesh like fire.	15
	5:17	Elijah was a human being like us,	6
1Pe	1:14	Like obedient children, do not be conformed	15
	1:19	like that of a lamb without defect or blemish.	15
	1:24	For "All flesh is like grass	15
	1:24	and all its glory like the flower of grass.	15
	2: 2	Like newborn infants, long for…spiritual milk	15
	2: 5	like living stones, let yourselves be built	15
	2:25	For you were going astray like sheep	15
	4:10	Like good stewards of the manifold grace of God	15
	5: 8	Like a roaring lion your adversary the devil prowls	15
2Pe	2:12	like irrational animals, mere creatures of instinct	15
	3: 8	with the Lord one day is like a thousand years	15
	3: 8	and a thousand years are like one day.	15
	3:10	But the day of the Lord will come like a thief	15
1Jn	3: 2	when he is revealed, we will be like him	7
	3:12	not be like Cain who…murdered his brother.	4
Jde	1:10	like irrational animals, they know by instinct.	15
Rev	1:10	and I heard behind me a loud voice like a trumpet	15
	1:13	midst of the lampstands I saw one like the Son of Man	7
	1:14	his eyes were like a flame of fire	15
	1:15	his feet were like burnished bronze	7
	1:15	his voice was like the sound of many waters.	15
	1:16	face was like the sun shining with full force.	15
	2:18	the Son of God, who has eyes like a flame of fire	15
	2:18	and whose feet are like burnished bronze:	7
	3: 3	If you do not wake up, I will come like a thief	15
	3: 5	you conquer, you will be clothed like them in white	11
	4: 1	which I had heard speaking to me like a trumpet	15
	4: 3	the one…looks like jasper and carnelian	7
	4: 3	a rainbow that looks like an emerald.	7
	4: 6	in front of the throne there is something like a sea	15
	4: 6	there is something like a sea of glass, like crystal.	7
	4: 7	the first living creature like a lion	7
	4: 7	the second living creature like an ox	7
	4: 7	the third living creature with a face like a human	15
	4: 7	the fourth living creature like a flying eagle.	7
	6:12	the full moon became like blood	15
	6:14	The sky vanished like a scroll rolling itself up	15
	8: 8	something like a great mountain, burning	15
	8:10	great star fell from heaven, blazing like a torch	15
	9: 2	rose smoke like the smoke of a great furnace	15
	9: 3	were given authority like the authority of scorpions	15
	9: 5	their torture was like the torture of a scorpion	15
	9: 7	the locusts were like horses equipped for battle.	7
	9: 7	On their heads were what looked like crowns	15
	9: 7	their faces were like human faces	15
	9: 8	their hair like women's hair, and their teeth like	15
	9: 8	and their teeth like lions' teeth;	15
	9: 9	they had scales like iron breastplates	15
	9: 9	the noise of their wings was like the noise	15
	9:10	They have tails like scorpions, with stingers	7
	9:17	the heads of the horses were like lions' heads	15
	9:19	their tails are like serpents, having heads;	7
	10: 1	his face was like the sun, and his legs like	15

	10: 1	and his legs like pillars of fire.	15
	10: 3	gave a great shout, like a lion roaring.	18
	11: 1	Then I was given a measuring rod like a staff	7
	12:15	the serpent poured water like a river	15
	13: 2	And the beast that I saw was like a leopard	7
	13: 2	the beast that I saw…its feet were like a bear's	15
	13: 2	the beast…its mouth was like a lion's mouth.	15
	13: 4	"Who is like the beast, and who can fight against it?"	7
	13:11	another beast…it had two horns like a lamb	7
	13:11	and it spoke like a dragon.	15
	14: 2	a voice from heaven like the sound of many waters	15
	14: 2	a voice…like the sound of loud thunder;	15
	14: 2	like the sound of harpists playing on their harps	15
	14:14	seated on the cloud was one like the Son of Man	7
	16: 3	the sea, and it became like the blood of a corpse	15
	16:13	I saw three foul spirits like frogs coming from	15
	16:15	("See, I am coming like a thief!	15
	18:18	"What city was like the great city?"	7
	18:21	angel took up a stone like a great millstone	15
	19: 6	like the sound of many waters	15
	19: 6	like the sound of mighty thunderpeals, crying out	15
	19:12	His eyes are like a flame of fire	15
	21:11	a radiance like a very rare jewel, like jasper	7
	21:11	a radiance like a very rare jewel, like jasper	15

like²

1. ἀξιόω, *axioō*, 546
2. βούλημα, *boulēma*, 1088
3. βούλομαι, *boulomai*, 1089
4. ἡδέως, *hēdeōs*, 2452
5. θέλω, *thelō*, 2527

Mrk	6:20	yet he liked to listen to him.	4
	12:38	who like to walk around in long robes	5
Lke	20:46	the scribes, who like to walk around in long robes	5
Act	17:20	so we would like to know what it means."	3
	25:22	"I would like to hear the man myself."	3
	28:22	we would like to hear from you what you think,	1
1Co	14: 5	Now I would like all of you to speak in tongues	5
1Pe	4: 3	in doing what the Gentiles like to do	2

like this

1. οὕτως, *houtōs*, 4048

Mat	9:33	"Never has anything like this been seen in Israel."	1
Mrk	2:12	saying, "We have never seen anything like this!"	1
Lke	2:48	"Child, why have you treated us like this?	1
Jhn	7:46	"Never has anyone spoken like this!"	1
	11:48	If we let him go on like this	1
Rom	9:20	"Why have you made me like this?"	1

like to put first

1. φιλοπρωτεύω, *philoprōteuō*, 5812

3Jn	1: 9	Diotrephes, who likes to put himself first	1

likeness

1. ὁμοίωμα, *homoiōma*, 3930
2. ὁμοίωσις, *homoiōsis*, 3932

Rom	8: 3	his own Son in the likeness of sinful flesh	1
Php	2: 7	being born in human likeness.	1
Jas	3: 9	we curse those who are made in the likeness of God.	2

according to the likeness

1. κατά, *kata*, 2848

Eph	4:24	created according to the likeness of God	1

likewise

1. καί, *kai*, 2779
2. ὁμοίως, *homoiōs*, 3931
3. παραπλησίως, *paraplēsiōs*, 4181
4. ὡς, *hōs*, 6055
5. ὡσαύτως, *hōsautōs*, 6058

Mrk	12:21	the third likewise;	5
Lke	3:11	whoever has food must do likewise."	2
	10:32	So likewise a Levite, when he came to the place	2
	10:37	Jesus said to him, "Go and do likewise."	2
	17:28	Likewise, just as it was in the days of Lot:	2
	17:31	likewise anyone in the field must not turn back.	2
	22:36	who has a purse must take it, and likewise a bag.	2
Jhn	5:19	whatever the Father does, the Son does likewise.	2
Rom	4:12	likewise the ancestor of the circumcised	1

Rom	8:26	Likewise the Spirit helps us in our weakness;	5
1Co	7: 3	likewise the wife to her husband.	2
	7: 4	likewise the husband does not have authority	2
1Ti	3: 8	Deacons likewise must be serious	5
	3:11	Women likewise must be serious	5
Tit	2: 3	Likewise, tell the older women to be reverent	5
	2: 6	Likewise, urge the younger men	5
Heb	2:14	he himself likewise shared the same things	3
Jas	2:25	Likewise, was not Rahab the prostitute also…justified	2
Jde	1: 7	Likewise, Sodom and Gomorrah and the surrounding	4
Rev	8:12	from shining, and likewise the night.	2

lily

1. κρίνον, *krinon*, 3211

Mat	6:28	about clothing? Consider the lilies of the field	1
Lke	12:27	Consider the lilies, how they grow:	1

limit

1. Contextual: Not in Greek

2Co	10:14	For we were not overstepping our limits	1

beyond limit

1. ἄμετρος, *ametros*, 296

2Co	10:13	We, however, will not boast beyond limits	1
	10:15	We do not boast beyond limits,	1

limitation

1. ἀσθένεια, *astheneia*, 819

Rom	6:19	because of your natural limitations.	1

linen   *See also* linen *cloth*, linen *wrapping*

1. λίνον, *linon*, 3351

Rev	15: 6	seven angels…robed in pure bright linen	1

fine linen

1. βύσσινος, *byssinos*, 1115
2. βύσσος, *byssos*, 1116

Lke	16:19	who was dressed in purple and fine linen	2
Rev	18:12	cargo of…fine linen, purple, silk and scarlet	1
	18:16	the great city, clothed in fine linen	1
	19: 8	her it has been granted to be clothed with fine linen	1
	19: 8	fine linen is the righteous deeds of the saints.	1
	19:14	wearing fine linen, white and pure	1

Linus

1. Λίνος, *Linos*, 3352

2Ti	4:21	as do Pudens and Linus and Claudia	1

lion

1. λέων, *leōn*, 3329

2Ti	4:17	So I was rescued from the lion's mouth.	1
Heb	11:33	obtained promises, shut the mouths of lions	1
1Pe	5: 8	Like a roaring lion your adversary the devil prowls	1
Rev	4: 7	the first living creature like a lion	1
	5: 5	See, the Lion of the tribe of Judah…has conquered	1
	9: 8	and their teeth like lions' teeth;	1
	9:17	the heads of the horses were like lions' heads	1
	10: 3	gave a great shout, like a lion roaring.	1
	13: 2	the beast…its mouth was like a lion's mouth.	1

lip

1. στόμα, *stoma*, 5125
2. χεῖλος, *cheilos*, 5927

Mat	15: 8	'This people honors me with their lips	2
Mrk	7: 6	'This people honors me with their lips	2
Lke	22:71	We have heard it ourselves from his own lips!"	1
Rom	3:13	"The venom of vipers is under their lips."	2
	10: 8	"The word is near you, on your lips and in your heart"	1
	10: 9	if you confess with your lips that Jesus is Lord	1
1Co	14:21	by the lips of foreigners	2
Heb	13:15	the fruit of lips that confess his name.	2
1Pe	3:10	let them keep…their lips from speaking deceit;	2

listen   *See also* refuse to listen

1. ἀκοή, *akoē*, 198
2. ἀκούω, *akouō*, 201
3. εἰσακούω, *eisakouō*, 1653
4. ἐνωτίζομαι, *enōtizomai*, 1969
5. ἐπακούω, *epakouō*, 2052

6. ἐπακροάομαι, *epakroaomai*, 2053
7. ἴδε, *ide*, 2623
8. ἰδού, *idou*, 2627
9. πειθαρχέω, *peitharcheō*, 4272

Mat	10:14	If anyone will not welcome you or listen	2
	11:15	Let anyone with ears listen!	2
	12:42	to listen to the wisdom of Solomon	2
	13: 3	"Listen! A sower went out to sow.	8
	13: 9	Let anyone with ears listen!"	2
	13:13	hearing they do not listen, nor do they understand.'	2
	13:15	and listen with their ears	2
	13:43	Let anyone with ears listen!	2
	15:10	"Listen and understand:	2
	17: 5	listen to him!"	2
	18:15	If the member listens to you, you have regained	2
	18:16	if you are not listened to, take one or two	2
	21:33	"Listen to another parable.	2
Mrk	4: 3	"Listen! A sower went out to sow.	2
	4: 9	he said, "Let anyone with ears to hear listen!"	2
	4:23	Let anyone with ears to hear listen!"	2
	6:20	yet he liked to listen to him.	2
	7:14	"Listen to me, all of you, and understand:	2
	9: 7	"This is my Son, the Beloved; listen to him!"	2
	12:37	the large crowd was listening to him with delight.	7
	15:35	"Listen, he is calling for Elijah."	2
Lke	2:46	listening to them and asking them questions.	2
	6:27	I say to you that listen, Love your enemies	2
	8: 8	"Let anyone with ears to hear listen!"	2
	8:10	listening they may not understand.'	2
	8:18	Then pay attention to how you listen;	2
	9:35	"This is my Son, my Chosen; listen to him!"	2
	10:16	"Whoever listens to you listens to me	2
	10:16	"Whoever listens to you listens to me	2
	10:39	listened to what he was saying.	2
	11:31	to listen to the wisdom of Solomon	2
	13:32	'Listen, I am casting out demons and	8
	14:35	Let anyone with ears to hear listen!"	2
	15: 1	and sinners were coming near to listen to him.	2
	15:29	'Listen! For all these years I have been working	8
	16:29	they should listen to them.'	2
	16:31	"If they do not listen to Moses and the prophets	2
	18: 6	"Listen to what the unjust judge says."	2
	19:11	As they were listening to this	2
	21:38	in the morning to listen to him in the temple.	2
	22:10	"Listen," he said to them	8
	22:31	"Simon, Simon, listen! Satan has demanded to sift	8
Jhn	9:27	you would not listen.	2
	9:31	We know that God does not listen to sinners	2
	9:31	he does listen to one who worships him	2
	10: 8	the sheep did not listen to them.	2
	10:16	they will listen to my voice.	2
	10:20	is out of his mind. Why listen to him?"	2
	18:37	who belongs to the truth listens to my voice."	2
Act	2:14	let this be known to you, and listen to what I say.	4
	2:22	Israelites, listen to what I have to say: Jesus	2
	3:22	You must listen to whatever he tells you.	2
	3:23	everyone who does not listen to that prophet	2
	4:19	to listen to you rather than to God	2
	7: 2	Stephen replied: "Brothers and fathers, listen	2
	10:33	listen to all that the Lord has commanded you to say	2
	13:11	now listen—the hand of the Lord is against you	8
	13:16	"You Israelites, and others who fear God, listen.	2
	14: 9	He listened to Paul as he was speaking.	2
	15:12	listened to Barnabas and Paul	2
	15:13	"My brothers, listen to me.	2
	16:14	Lydia, a worshiper of God, was listening to us;	2
	16:25	the prisoners were listening to them.	6
	22: 1	listen to the defense that I now make before you."	2
	22:22	Up to this point they listened to him	2
	26: 3	therefore I beg of you to listen to me patiently.	2
	26:29	but also all who are listening to me today	9
	27:21	you should have listened to me	9
	28:27	listen with their ears	2
	28:28	sent to the Gentiles; they will listen."	2
1Co	14:21	they will not listen to me," says the Lord.	3
	15:51	Listen, I will tell you a mystery!	8
2Co	6: 2	"At an acceptable time I have listened to you	5
Gal	4:21	will you not listen to the law?	2
	5: 2	Listen! I, Paul, am telling you	7
2Ti	2:14	does no good but only ruins those who are listening.	1
	4: 4	will turn away from listening to the truth	1

Heb	4: 2	they were not united by faith with those who listened.	2
Jas	1:19	let everyone be quick to listen, slow to speak	2
	2: 5	Listen, my beloved brothers and sisters.	2
	5: 4	Listen! The wages of the laborers	8
1Jn	4: 5	and the world listens to them.	2
	4: 6	We are from God. Whoever knows God listens to us	2
	4: 6	whoever is not from God does not listen to us.	2
Rev	2: 7	Let anyone who has an ear listen	2
	2:11	who has an ear listen to what the Spirit is saying	2
	2:17	listen to what the Spirit is saying to the churches.	2
	2:29	listen to what the Spirit is saying to the churches.	2
	3: 6	listen to what the Spirit is saying	2
	3:13	listen to what the Spirit is saying to the churches.	2
	3:20	Listen! I am standing at the door, knocking;	8
	3:22	listen to what the Spirit is saying to the churches."	2
	13: 9	Let anyone who has an ear listen:	2

listen eagerly

1. προσέχω, *prosechō, 4668*

Act	8: 6	The crowds with one accord listened eagerly	1
	8:10	All of them...listened to him eagerly	1
	8:11	they listened eagerly to him	1
	16:14	to listen eagerly to what was said by Paul.	1

listen indeed

1. ἀκούω + ἀκοή, *akouō + akoē, 201 + 198*
2. ἀκούω + ἀκούω, *akouō + akouō, 201 + 201*

Mat	13:14	'You will indeed listen, but never understand	1
Mrk	4:12	and may indeed listen, but not understand;	2
Act	28:26	You will indeed listen, but never understand	1

listen to an appeal

1. παρακαλέω, *parakaleō, 4151*

| 2Co | 13:11 | Put things in order, listen to my appeal | 1 |

literal

1. γράμμα, *gramma, 1207*

| Rom | 2:29 | a matter of the heart—it is spiritual and not literal. | 1 |

little   *See also* have little, have too little, little *daughter*, little *faith*, little *scroll*

1. βραχύς, *brachys, 1099*
2. μέρος, *meros, 3538*
3. μετρίως, *metriōs, 3585*
4. μικρός, *mikros, 3625*
5. ὀλίγος, *oligos, 3900*
6. τὶς, *tis, 5516*

Mat	10:42	a cup of cold water to one of these little ones	4
	26:39	going a little farther, he threw himself on	4
	26:73	After a little while the bystanders came up	4
Mrk	1:19	As he went a little farther	5
	14:35	a little farther, he threw himself on the ground	4
Lke	5: 3	asked him to put out a little way from the shore.	5
	7:47	one to whom little is forgiven, loves little."	5
	7:47	one to whom little is forgiven, loves little."	5
	12:32	"Do not be afraid, little flock	4
	22:58	A little later someone else, on seeing him, said	1
Jhn	6: 7	enough bread for each of them to get a little."	1
	7:33	"I will be with you a little while longer	4
	12:35	"The light is with you for a little longer.	4
	13:33	Little children, I am with you only a little longer.	4
	14:19	In a little while the world will no longer see	4
	16:16	"A little while, and you will no longer see me	4
	16:16	again a little while, and you will see me."	4
	16:17	'A little while, and you will no longer see me	4
	16:17	again a little while, and you will see me';	4
	16:18	"What does he mean by this 'a little while'?	4
	16:19	'A little while, and you will no longer see me	4
	16:19	again a little while, and you will see me'?	4
Act	19:23	no little disturbance broke out concerning the Way.	5
	19:24	brought no little business to the artisans.	5
	20:12	were not a little comforted.	3
	27:28	a little farther on they took soundings again	1
Rom	15:24	I have enjoyed your company for a little while	2
1Co	5: 6	a little yeast leavens the whole batch of dough?	4
2Co	8:15	the one who had little did not have too little."	5
	10: 8	even if I boast a little too much of our authority	6
	11: 1	bear with me in a little foolishness.	4
	11:16	so that I too may boast a little.	4

Gal	5: 9	A little yeast leavens the whole batch of dough.	4
1Ti	5:23	No longer drink only water, but take a little wine	5
Heb	10:37	For yet "in a very little while,	4
Rev	3: 8	I know that you have but little power	4
	6:11	They were each...told to rest a little longer	4
	17:10	when he comes, he must remain only a little while.	5
	20: 3	After that he must be let out for a little while.	4

little boy

1. παιδίον, *paidion, 4086*

| Jhn | 4:49 | "Sir, come down before my little boy dies." | 1 |

little child

1. παιδίον, *paidion, 4086*
2. τεκνίον, *teknion, 5448*
3. τέκνον, *teknon, 5451*

Mat	19:13	Then little children were being brought to him	1
	19:14	Jesus said, "Let the little children come to me	1
Mrk	9:36	he took a little child and put it among them	1
	10:13	People were bringing little children to him	1
	10:14	"Let the little children come to me	1
	10:15	receive the kingdom of God as a little child	1
Lke	9:47	took a little child and put it by his side	1
	18:16	"Let the little children come to me, and do not	1
	18:17	receive the kingdom of God as a little child	1
Jhn	13:33	Little children, I am with you only a little longer.	2
Gal	4:19	little children, for whom I am again in the pain	3
1Jn	2: 1	My little children, I am writing these things to you	2
	2:12	I am writing to you, little children	2
	2:28	now, little children, abide in him	2
	3: 7	Little children, let no one deceive you.	2
	3:18	Little children, let us love, not in word or speech	2
	4: 4	Little children, you are from God	2
	5:21	Little children, keep yourselves from idols.	2

little girl

1. κοράσιον, *korasion, 3166*

| Mrk | 5:41 | which means, "Little girl, get up!" | 1 |

little one

1. μικρός, *mikros, 3625*

Mat	18: 6	one of these little ones who believe in me	1
	18:10	that you do not despise one of these little ones;	1
	18:14	that one of these little ones should be lost.	1
Mrk	9:42	one of these little ones who believe in me	1
Lke	17: 2	to cause one of these little ones to stumble.	1

little while

1. βραχύς + τὶς, *brachys + tis, 1099 + 5516*
2. μικρός, *mikros, 3625*
3. ὀλίγος, *oligos, 3900*

Mrk	14:70	after a little while the bystanders again said	2
Heb	2: 7	made them for a little while lower than the angels;	1
	2: 9	for a little while was made lower than the angels	1
Jas	4:14	For you are a mist that appears for a little while	3
1Pe	1: 6	now for a little while you have had to suffer	3
	5:10	after you have suffered for a little while	3

very little

1. ἐλάχιστος, *elachistos, 1788*

Lke	16:10	"Whoever is faithful in a very little	1
	16:10	whoever is dishonest in a very little	1

live   *See also* place one lives

1. Contextual: Not in Greek
2. ἀναστρέφω, *anastrephō, 418*
3. ἄρτος, *artos, 788*
4. βίος, *bios, 1050*
5. βιόω, *bioō, 1051*
6. γίνομαι, *ginomai, 1181*
7. ἐγκατοικέω, *enkatoikeō, 1594*
8. εἰμί, *eimi, 1639*
9. ἐμμένω, *emmenō, 1844*
10. ἐνοικέω, *enoikeō, 1940*
11. ἐπιδημέω, *epidēmeō, 2111*
12. ἔχω + ψυχή, *echō + psychē, 2400 + 6034*
13. ζάω, *zaō, 2409*
14. κάθημαι, *kathēmai, 2764*
15. κατασκηνόω, *kataskēnoō, 2942*

16. κατοικέω, *katoikeō, 2997*
17. κατοίκησις + ἔχω, *katoikēsis + echō, 2998 + 2400*
18. μένω, *menō, 3531*
19. μετέχω, *metechō, 3576*
20. οἰκέω, *oikeō, 3861*
21. οἰκία, *oikia, 3864*
22. περιπατέω, *peripateō, 4344*
23. πορεύομαι, *poreuomai, 4513*
24. σκηνόω, *skēnoō, 5012*
25. ὑπάρχω, *hyparchō, 5639*
26. φρονέω, *phroneō, 5858*

Mat	4: 4	written, 'One does not live by bread alone	13
	9:18	lay your hand on her, and she will live."	13
	12:45	and they enter and live there;	16
	16:16	"You are the Messiah, the Son of the living God."	13
	22:32	He is God not of the dead, but of the living."	13
	23:30	'If we had lived in the days of our ancestors	8
	26:63	"I put you under oath before the living God	13
Mrk	5: 3	He lived among the tombs;	17
	5:23	so that she may be made well, and live."	13
	7: 5	"Why do your disciples not live	22
	12:27	He is God not of the dead, but of the living;	13
	12:44	everything she had, all she had to live on."	4
Lke	1: 6	righteous before God, living blamelessly	23
	2:36	lived with her husband seven years	13
	4: 4	"It is written, 'One does not live by bread alone.' "	13
	7:25	live in luxury are in royal palaces.	25
	8:27	he did not live in a house but in the tombs.	18
	10:28	the right answer; do this, and you will live."	13
	11:26	they enter and live there;	16
	13: 4	than all the others living in Jerusalem?	16
	15:13	he squandered his property in dissolute living.	13
	20:38	Now he is God not of the dead, but of the living;	13
	21: 4	put in all she had to live on."	4
	21:35	all who live on the face of the whole earth.	14
	24: 5	"Why do you look for the living among the dead?	13
Jhn	1:14	And the Word became flesh and lived among us	24
	4:10	and he would have given you living water."	13
	4:11	Where do you get that living water?	13
	4:50	Jesus said to him, "Go; your son will live."	13
	4:53	Jesus had said to him, "Your son will live."	13
	5:25	those who hear will live.	13
	6:51	I am the living bread that came down from heaven.	13
	6:51	Whoever eats of this bread will live forever;	13
	6:57	Just as the living Father sent me	13
	6:57	I live because of the Father	13
	6:57	whoever eats me will live because of me.	13
	6:58	one who eats this bread will live forever."	13
	7:38	shall flow rivers of living water.' "	13
	7:42	from Bethlehem, the village where David lived?"	8
	11:25	who believe in me, even though they die, will live	13
	11:26	everyone who lives and believes in me	13
	14:19	because I live, you also will live.	13
	14:19	because I live, you also will live.	13
Act	1:20	let there be no one to live in it';	16
	2: 5	from every nation under heaven living in Jerusalem.	16
	2:14	"Men of Judea and all who live in Jerusalem	16
	2:26	moreover my flesh will live in hope.	15
	4:16	is obvious to all who live in Jerusalem	16
	7: 2	in Mesopotamia, before he lived in Haran	16
	7: 4	this country in which you are now living.	16
	7:38	he received living oracles to give to us.	13
	9:22	confounded the Jews who lived in Damascus	16
	9:31	Living in the fear of the Lord	23
	9:32	he came down also to the saints living in Lydda.	16
	10:42	judge of the living and the dead.	13
	11:29	send relief to the believers living in Judea;	16
	14:15	turn from these worthless things to the living God	13
	17:21	the foreigners living there	11
	17:24	God...does not live in shrines made by human hands	16
	17:28	'In him we live and move and have our being';	13
	20:18	"You yourselves know how I lived among you	6
	21:21	you teach all the Jews living among the Gentiles	1
	22:12	well spoken of by all the Jews living there	16
	22:22	he should not be allowed to live."	13
	25:24	shouting that he ought not to live any longer.	13
	26: 5	and lived as a Pharisee.	13
	28: 4	justice has not allowed him to live."	13
	28:16	Paul was allowed to live by himself	18
	28:30	He lived there two whole years at his own expense	9

Rom	1:17	"The one who is righteous will live by faith."	13
	6: 2	How can we who died to sin go on living in it?	13
	6:10	but the life he lives, he lives to God.	13
	6:10	but the life he lives, he lives to God.	13
	7: 2	woman is bound...to her husband as long as he lives;	13
	7: 3	an adulteress if she lives with another man	6
	7: 5	While we were living in the flesh	8
	8: 5	For those who live according to the flesh	8
	8: 5	but those who live according to the Spirit	1
	8:12	not to the flesh, to live according to the flesh—	13
	8:13	if you live according to the flesh, you will die;	13
	8:13	put to death the deeds of the body, you will live.	13
	9:26	they shall be called children of the living God."	13
	10: 5	"the person who does these things will live by them."	13
	12: 1	to present your bodies as a living sacrifice	13
	12:16	Live in harmony with one another;	26
	13:13	live honorably as in the day	22
	14: 7	We do not live to ourselves	13
	14: 8	If we live, we live to the Lord	13
	14: 8	If we live, we live to the Lord	13
	14: 8	whether we live or whether we die, we are the Lord's.	13
	14: 9	For to this end Christ died and lived again	13
	14: 9	be Lord of both the dead and the living.	13
	14:11	"As I live, says the Lord, every knee shall bow	13
	15: 5	to live in harmony with one another	26
1Co	7:12	she consents to live with him	20
	7:13	he consents to live with her	20
	7:39	A wife is bound as long as her husband lives.	13
	9: 6	have no right to refrain from working for a living?	1
	15:45	"The first man, Adam, became a living being";	13
2Co	3: 3	not with ink but with the Spirit of the living God	13
	4:11	while we live, we are always being given up	13
	5: 1	if the earthly tent we live in is destroyed	21
	5:15	so that those who live might live no longer	13
	5:15	so that those who live might live no longer	13
	6:16	we are the temple of the living God; as God said	13
	6:16	"I will live in them and walk among them	10
	10: 3	Indeed, we live as human beings	22
	13: 4	lives by the power of God.	13
	13: 4	in dealing with you we will live with him	13
	13: 5	to see whether you are living in the faith.	8
Gal	2:14	"If you, though a Jew, live like a Gentile	13
	2:19	so that I might live to God.	13
	2:20	no longer I who live, but it is Christ who lives	13
	2:20	but it is Christ who lives in me	13
	2:20	the life I now live in the flesh I live by faith	13
	2:20	the life I now live in the flesh I live by faith	13
	3:11	"The one who is righteous will live by faith."	13
	3:12	"Whoever does the works of the law will live by them."	13
	5:16	Live by the Spirit, I say	22
	5:25	If we live by the Spirit	13
Eph	1:12	might live for the praise of his glory.	8
	2: 2	in which you once lived	22
	2: 3	All of us once lived among them	2
	4:17	you must no longer live as the Gentiles live	22
	4:17	you must no longer live as the Gentiles live	22
	5: 2	live in love, as Christ loved us	22
	5: 8	Live as children of light	22
	5:15	Be careful then how you live	22
Php	1:21	For to me, living is Christ and dying is gain.	13
	1:22	If I am to live in the flesh	13
	3:17	observe those who live according to the example	22
	3:18	For many live as enemies of the cross of Christ;	22
Col	2:20	you live as if you still belonged to the world?	13
	3: 7	once followed, when you were living that life.	13
1Th	1: 9	to serve a living and true God	13
	3: 8	For now we live, if you continue to stand firm	13
	4: 1	how you ought to live and to please God	22
	5:10	whether we are awake or asleep we may live with him.	13
2Th	3: 6	believers who are living in idleness	22
	3:11	we hear that some of you are living in idleness	22
	3:12	to earn their own living.	3
1Ti	3:15	which is the church of the living God	13
	4:10	because we have our hope set on the living God	13
	5: 6	the widow...is dead even while she lives.	13
2Ti	1: 5	a faith that lived first in your grandmother	10
	1: 5	a faith that...now, I am sure, lives in you.	1
	3:12	all who want to live a godly life in Christ	13
	4: 1	who is to judge the living and the dead	13
Tit	2:12	in the present age to live lives that are self-controlled,	13
Heb	3:12	evil...heart that turns away from the living God.	13

	4:12 Indeed, the word of God is living and active	13
	5:13 for everyone who lives on milk	19
	7: 8 one of whom it is testified that he lives.	13
	7:25 since he always lives to make intercession	13
	9:14 from dead works to worship the living God!	13
	10:20 by the new and living way that he opened for us	13
	10:31 to fall into the hands of the living God.	13
	10:38 my righteous one will live by faith.	13
	11: 9 living in tents, as did Isaac and Jacob	16
	12: 9 be subject to the Father of spirits and live?	13
	12:22 the city of the living God	13
Jas	4:15 "If the Lord wishes, we will live and do this	13
1Pe	1: 3 given us a new birth into a living hope	13
	1:17 live in reverent fear	2
	1:23 through the living and enduring word of God.	13
	2: 4 Come to him, a living stone, though rejected	13
	2: 5 like living stones, let yourselves be built	13
	2:16 live as free people, yet do not use your freedom	1
	2:24 free from sins, we might live for righteousness;	13
	4: 2 so as to live for the rest of your earthly life	5
	4: 3 living in licentiousness, passions	23
	4: 5 who stands ready to judge the living and the dead.	13
	4: 6 they might live in the spirit as God	13
2Pe	2: 8 living among them day after day, was tormented	7
	2:18 escaped from those who live in error.	2
1Jn	2:10 Whoever loves a brother or sister lives in the light	18
	2:17 but those who do the will of God live forever.	18
	4: 9 so that we might live through him.	13
	4:12 if we love one another, God lives in us.	18
Rev	2:13 "I know where you are living, where Satan's throne is.	16
	2:13 who was killed among you, where Satan lives.	16
	4: 9 thanks to the one…who lives forever and ever	13
	4:10 worship the one who lives forever and ever;	13
	7: 2 another angel…having the seal of the living God	13
	8: 9 a third of the living creatures in the sea died	12
	10: 6 swore by him who lives forever and ever	13
	13:14 that had been wounded by the sword and yet lived;	13
	14: 6 gospel to proclaim to those who live on the earth	14
	15: 7 the wrath of God, who lives forever and ever;	13
	17:10 one is living, and the other has not yet come;	8

live a life
1. περιπατέω, *peripateō*, 4344
2. πολιτεύομαι, *politeuomai*, 4488

Act	23: 1 I have lived my life with a clear conscience	2
Php	1:27 Only, live your life in a manner worthy	2
Col	2: 6 continue to live your lives in him	1

live for pleasure
1. σπαταλάω, *spatalaō*, 5059

1Ti	5: 6 but the widow who lives for pleasure is dead	1

live in
1. ἐνοικέω, *enoikeō*, 1940

2Ti	1:14 with the help of the Holy Spirit living in us.	1

live in a field
1. ἀγραυλέω, *agrauleō*, 64

Lke	2: 8 there were shepherds living in the fields	1

live in luxury
1. στρηνιάω, *strēniaō*, 5139
2. τρυφάω, *tryphaō*, 5587

Jas	5: 5 You have lived on the earth in luxury	2
Rev	18: 9 committed fornication and lived in luxury	1

live in peace
1. εἰρηνεύω, *eirēneuō*, 1644

2Co	13:11 agree with one another, live in peace;	1

live in pleasure
1. σπαταλάω, *spatalaō*, 5059

Jas	5: 5 You have lived on the earth…in pleasure;	1

live like a Jew
1. ἰουδαΐζω, *ioudaizō*, 2678

Gal	2:14 how can you compel the Gentiles to live like Jews?"	1

live long
1. μακροχρόνιος, *makrochronios*, 3432

Eph	6: 3 you may live long on the earth."	1

live luxuriously
1. στρηνιάω, *strēniaō*, 5139

Rev	18: 7 As she glorified herself and lived luxuriously	1

live peaceably
1. εἰρηνεύω, *eirēneuō*, 1644

Rom	12:18 If it is possible…live peaceably with all.	1

live quietly
1. ἡσυχάζω, *hēsychazō*, 2483

1Th	4:11 to aspire to live quietly	1

live together
1. συζάω, *syzaō*, 5182
2. συνέρχομαι, *synerchomai*, 5302

Mat	1:18 engaged to Joseph, but before they lived together	2
2Co	7: 3 to die together and to live together.	1

live with
1. ἔχω, *echō*, 2400
2. συζάω, *syzaō*, 5182

Rom	6: 8 we believe that we will also live with him.	2
1Co	5: 1 a man is living with his father's wife.	1
2Ti	2:11 If we have died with him, we will also live with him;	2

living   *See* get a living

living creature
1. ζῷον, *zōon*, 2442

Rev	4: 6 Around the throne…are four living creatures	1
	4: 7 the first living creature like a lion	1
	4: 7 the second living creature like an ox	1
	4: 7 the third living creature with a face like a human	1
	4: 7 the fourth living creature like a flying eagle.	1
	4: 8 four living creatures, each…with six wings	1
	4: 9 whenever the living creatures give glory	1
	5: 6 the throne and the four living creatures	1
	5: 8 the four living creatures…fell before the Lamb	1
	5:11 throne and the living creatures and the elders;	1
	5:14 the four living creatures said, "Amen!"	1
	6: 1 I heard one of the four living creatures call out	1
	6: 3 the second living creature call out, "Come!"	1
	6: 5 I heard the third living creature call out, "Come!"	1
	6: 6 a voice in the midst of the four living creatures	1
	6: 7 I heard the voice of the fourth living creature	1
	7:11 around the elders and the four living creatures	1
	14: 3 and before the four living creatures	1
	15: 7 Then one of the four living creatures gave	1
	19: 4 four living creatures fell down and worshiped	1

living one
1. ζάω, *zaō*, 2409

Rev	1:18 and the living one. I was dead, and see, I am alive	1

living thing
1. ζωή, *zōē*, 2437

Rev	16: 3 and every living thing in the sea died.	1

load
1. φορτίζω, *phortizō*, 5844
2. φορτίον, *phortion*, 5845

Lke	11:46 you load people with burdens hard to bear	1
Gal	6: 5 For all must carry their own loads.	2

loaf
1. ἄρτος, *artos*, 788

Mat	14:17 "We have nothing here but five loaves and two fish."	1
	14:19 Taking the five loaves and the two fish	1
	14:19 broke the loaves, and gave them to the disciples	1
	15:34 Jesus asked them, "How many loaves have you?"	1
	15:36 he took the seven loaves and the fish;	1
	16: 9 Do you not remember the five loaves	1
	16:10 Or the seven loaves for the four thousand	1
Mrk	6:38 "How many loaves have you? Go and see."	1

Mrk	6:41	Taking the five loaves and the two fish	1
	6:41	blessed and broke the loaves	1
	6:44	had eaten the loaves numbered five thousand men	1
	6:52	for they did not understand about the loaves	1
	8: 5	He asked them, "How many loaves do you have?"	1
	8: 6	he took the seven loaves	1
	8:14	they had only one loaf with them in the boat.	1
	8:19	I broke the five loaves for the five thousand	1
Lke	9:13	"We have no more than five loaves and two fish	1
	9:16	taking the five loaves and the two fish	1
Jhn	6: 9	a boy…who has five barley loaves and two fish.	1
	6:11	Then Jesus took the loaves	1
	6:13	from the fragments of the five barley loaves	1
	6:26	because you ate your fill of the loaves.	1

loaf of bread

    1. ἄρτος, *artos, 788*

Mat	4: 3	command these stones to become loaves of bread."	1
	26:26	While they were eating, Jesus took a loaf of bread	1
Mrk	14:22	he took a loaf of bread, and after blessing it	1
Lke	4: 3	command this stone to become a loaf of bread."	1
	11: 5	'Friend, lend me three loaves of bread;	1
	22:19	he took a loaf of bread	1
1Co	11:23	the night when he was betrayed took a loaf of bread	1

local

    1. Contextual: Not in Greek

Act	28:17	he called together the local leaders of the Jews.	1

lock

    1. κλείω, *kleiō, 3091*

Mat	23:13	you lock people out of the kingdom of heaven.	1
Lke	11: 7	door has already been locked, and my children	1
Jhn	20:19	the doors of the house…were locked	1
Act	5:23	"We found the prison securely locked	1
Rev	20: 3	into the pit, and locked and sealed it over him	1

lock up

    1. κατακλείω, *katakleiō, 2881*

Act	26:10	I not only locked up many of the saints in prison	1

locust

    1. ἀκρίς, *akris, 210*

Mat	3: 4	waist, and his food was locusts and wild honey.	1
Mrk	1: 6	ate locusts and wild honey.	1
Rev	9: 3	Then from the smoke came locusts on the earth	1
	9: 7	the locusts were like horses equipped for battle.	1

lodge

    1. καταλύω, *katalyō, 2907*
    2. ξενίζω, *xenizō, 3826*

Lke	9:12	to lodge and get provisions;	1
Act	10: 6	he is lodging with Simon, a tanner	2

lodging   *See also* give lodging

    1. ξενία, *xenia, 3825*

Act	28:23	they came to him at his lodgings in great numbers.	1

lofty

    1. ὑπεροχή, *hyperochē, 5667*

1Co	2: 1	the mystery of God to you in lofty words or wisdom.	1

log

    1. δοκός, *dokos, 1512*

Mat	7: 3	but do not notice the log in your own eye?	1
	7: 4	while the log is in your own eye?	1
	7: 5	hypocrite, first take the log out of your own eye	1
Lke	6:41	do not notice the log in your own eye?	1
	6:42	you…do not see the log in your own eye?	1
	6:42	first take the log out of your own eye	1

loin

    1. ὀσφῦς, *osphys, 4019*

Heb	7:10	for he was still in the loins of his ancestor	1

Lois

    1. Λωΐς, *Lōis, 3396*

2Ti	1: 5	lived first in your grandmother Lois	1

long[1]   *See also* delay long, know a long time, live long, long *hair*, long *robe*, long *time*, wear long hair

    1. Contextual: Not in Greek
    2. αἰώνιος, *aiōnios, 173*
    3. ἄχρι, *achri, 948*
    4. ἐπί + ὅσος, *epi + hosos, 2093 + 4012*
    5. ἐπί + ὅσος + χρόνος, *epi + hosos + chronos, 2093 + 4012 + 5989*
    6. ἔτι, *eti, 2285*
    7. ἱκανός, *hikanos, 2653*
    8. μακρός, *makros, 3431*
    9. μεγαλύνω, *megalynō, 3486*
    10. ὅπου, *hopou, 3963*
    11. ὅσος, *hosos, 4012*
    12. ὅταν, *hotan, 4020*
    13. ὅτε, *hote, 4021*
    14. πολύς, *polys, 4498*
    15. πολύς + χρόνος, *polys + chronos, 4498 + 5989*
    16. χρόνος, *chronos, 5989*

Mat	5:13	It is no longer good for anything, but is	6
	9:15	guests cannot mourn as long as the bridegroom	11
	23: 5	and their fringes long.	9
	25:19	After a long time the master…came	14
Mrk	2:19	As long as they have the bridegroom with them	16
	9:21	Jesus asked the father, "How long has this been	16
	12:40	for the sake of appearance say long prayers.	8
Lke	5: 5	"Master, we have worked all night long but	1
	8:27	For a long time he had worn no clothes	7
	13:16	whom Satan bound for eighteen long years	1
	20: 9	went to another country for a long time	7
	20:47	for the sake of appearance say long prayers.	8
	23: 8	he had been wanting to see him for a long time	7
Jhn	5: 6	and knew that he had been there a long time	14
	7:33	"I will be with you a little while longer	6
	9: 5	As long as I am in the world	12
	11: 6	he stayed two days longer in the place	1
	12:35	"The light is with you for a little longer.	16
	13:33	Little children, I am with you only a little longer.	1
Act	8:11	for a long time he had amazed them with his magic.	7
	14: 3	So they remained for a long time	7
	18:20	When they asked him to stay longer	15
	19:22	he himself stayed for some time longer in Asia.	1
	20: 9	while Paul talked still longer.	14
	24: 2	because of you we have long enjoyed peace	14
	27:21	they had been without food for a long time	14
	28: 6	after they had waited a long time	14
Rom	7: 2	woman is bound…to her husband as long as he lives;	1
	8:36	we are being killed all day long;	1
	10:21	"All day long I have held out my hands	1
	16:25	the mystery that was kept secret for long ages	2
1Co	3: 3	For as long as there is jealousy and quarreling	10
	7:39	A wife is bound as long as her husband lives.	5
Gal	4: 1	heirs, as long as they are minors, are no better	5
1Th	3: 6	and long to see us—just as we long to see you.	1
Heb	3:13	as long as it is called "today,"	3
	9: 8	as long as the first tent is still standing.	1
	9:17	as long as the one who made it is alive.	13
	10: 2	would no longer have any consciousness of sin?	6
1Pe	3: 6	become her daughters as long as you do what is good	1
2Pe	1:13	I think it right, as long as I am in this body	4
Rev	6:11	They were each…told to rest a little longer	16
	12: 8	there was no longer any place for them in heaven.	6

long[2]

    1. ἀγαπάω, *agapaō, 26*
    2. ἐπιθυμέω, *epithymeō, 2121*
    3. ἐπιθυμία, *epithymia, 2123*
    4. ἐπιποθέω, *epipotheō, 2160*
    5. ἐπιπόθησις, *epipothēsis, 2161*
    6. ἐπιπόθητος, *epipothētos, 2162*

Mat	13:17	prophets and righteous people longed to see	2
Lke	16:21	who longed to satisfy his hunger	2
	17:22	will long to see one of the days of the Son of Man	2
Rom	1:11	For I am longing to see you	4
2Co	5: 2	longing to be clothed with our heavenly dwelling	4
	7: 7	as he told us of your longing, your mourning	5
	7:11	what indignation, what alarm, what longing	5
	9:14	while they long for you and pray for you	4
Php	1: 8	For God is my witness, how I long for all of you	4

2:26 for he has been longing for all of you   4
4: 1 my brothers and sisters, whom I love and long for   6
1Th 2:17 we longed with great eagerness to see you   3
3: 6 and long to see us—just as we long to see you.   4
2Ti 1: 4 Recalling your tears, I long to see you   4
4: 8 also to all who have longed for his appearing.   1
1Pe 1:12 things into which angels long to look!   2
2: 2 long for the pure, spiritual milk   4
Rev 9: 6 they will long to die, but death will flee from them.   2
18:14 "The fruit for which your soul longed has gone   3

how long

1. ἕως + πότε, *heōs + pote, 2401 + 4536*

Mat 17:17 how much longer must I be with you?   1
17:17 How much longer must I put up with you?   1
Mrk 9:19 how much longer must I be among you?   1
9:19 How much longer must I put up with you?   1
Lke 9:41 how much longer must I be with you and bear   1
Jhn 10:24 "How long will you keep us in suspense?   1
Rev 6:10 how long will it be before you judge and avenge   1

long ago

1. αἰών, *aiōn, 172*
2. ἀπό + αἰών, *apo + aiōn, 608 + 172*
3. ἔκπαλαι, *ekpalai, 1732*
4. πάλαι, *palai, 4093*
5. ποτέ, *pote, 4537*

Mat 11:21 they would have repented long ago in sackcloth   4
Lke 10:13 they would have repented long ago   4
Act 3:21 long ago through his holy prophets.   2
15:18 known from long ago.'   1
Heb 1: 1 Long ago God spoke to our ancestors in many…ways   4
1Pe 3: 5 in this way long ago that the holy women   5
2Pe 2: 3 Their condemnation, pronounced against them long ago   3
3: 5 by the word of God heavens existed long ago   3
Jde 1: 4 who long ago were designated for this condemnation   4

any longer

1. ἔτι, *eti, 2285*
2. μηκέτι, *mēketi, 3600*

Lke 16: 2 you cannot be my manager any longer.'   1
Act 25:24 shouting that he ought not to live any longer.   2

no longer

1. μή, *mē, 3590*
2. μηδέ, *mēde, 3593*
3. μηκέτι, *mēketi, 3600*
4. οὐ, *ou, 4024*
5. οὐκέτι, *ouketi, 4033*

Mat 19: 6 So they are no longer two, but one flesh.   5
Mrk 1:45 Jesus could no longer go into a town openly   3
2: 2 that there was no longer room for them   3
7:12 then you no longer permit doing anything   5
10: 8 So they are no longer two, but one flesh.   5
Lke 15:19 I am no longer worthy to be called your son;   5
15:21 I am no longer worthy to be called your son.'   5
20:40 they no longer dared to ask him another question.   5
Jhn 4:42 "It is no longer because of what you said   5
6:66 and no longer went about with him.   5
11:54 Jesus therefore no longer walked about openly   5
14:19 the world will no longer see me   5
14:30 I will no longer talk much with you   5
16:10 you will see me no longer;   5
16:16 "A little while, and you will no longer see me   5
16:17 'A little while, and you will no longer see me   4
16:19 'A little while, and you will no longer see me   4
16:21 she no longer remembers the anguish   5
16:25 when I will no longer speak to you in figures   5
17:11 now I am no longer in the world   5
Rom 6: 6 and we might no longer be enslaved to sin.   3
6: 9 death no longer has dominion over him.   5
6:13 No longer present your members to sin   2
7:17 But in fact it is no longer I that do it, but sin   5
7:20 it is no longer I that do it, but sin   5
11: 6 it is no longer on the basis of works   5
11: 6 otherwise grace would no longer be grace.   5
14:13 therefore no longer pass judgment on one another   3
14:15 you are no longer walking in love.   5
2Co 5:15 so that those who live might live no longer   3
5:16 we know him no longer in that way.   5

Gal 2:20 no longer I who live, but it is Christ who lives   5
3:18 it no longer comes from the promise;   5
3:25 we are no longer subject to a disciplinarian   5
3:28 There is no longer Jew or Greek   4
3:28 there is no longer slave or free   4
3:28 there is no longer male and female;   4
4: 7 So you are no longer a slave but a child,   5
Eph 2:19 you are no longer strangers and aliens   5
4:14 We must no longer be children   3
4:17 you must no longer live as the Gentiles live   3
Col 3:11 In that renewal there is no longer Greek and Jew   4
1Th 3: 1 Therefore when we could bear it no longer   3
3: 5 For this reason, when I could bear it no longer   3
1Ti 5:23 No longer drink only water, but take a little wine   3
Phm 1:16 no longer as a slave but more than a slave   5
Heb 10:18 there is no longer any offering for sin   5
10:26 there no longer remains a sacrifice for sins   5
1Pe 4: 2 no longer by human desires but by the will of God.   3
4: 4 They are surprised that you no longer join them   1

not any longer

1. μηκέτι, *mēketi, 3600*
2. οὐκέτι, *ouketi, 4033*

Lke 8:49 do not trouble the teacher any longer."   1
Jhn 15:15 I do not call you servants any longer   2

eager longing

1. ἀποκαραδοκία, *apokaradokia, 638*

Rom 8:19 For the creation waits with eager longing   1

look

1. Contextual: Not in Greek
2. αἴρω + ὁ + ὀφθαλμός, *airō + ho + ophthalmos, 149 + 3836 + 4057*
3. ἀφοράω, *aphoraō, 927*
4. βλέπω, *blepō, 1063*
5. γίνομαι, *ginomai, 1181*
6. ἐμβλέπω, *emblepō, 1838*
7. ἐπεῖδον, *epeidon, 2078*
8. ζητέω, *zēteō, 2426*
9. θεωρέω, *theōreō, 2555*
10. ἴδε, *ide, 2623*
11. ἰδού, *idou, 2627*
12. κατανοέω, *katanoeō, 2917*
13. ὅρασις, *horasis, 3970*
14. ὁράω, *horaō, 3972*
15. παρακύπτω, *parakyptō, 4160*
16. περιβλέπω, *periblepō, 4315*
17. σκοπέω, *skopeō, 5023*
18. φαίνω, *phainō, 5743*

Mat 1:23 "Look, the virgin shall conceive and bear a son   11
5:28 I say to you that everyone who looks at a woman   4
6:16 you fast, do not look dismal, like the hypocrites   5
11: 8 Look, those who wear soft robes   11
11:19 and they say, 'Look, a glutton and a drunkard   11
12: 2 "Look, your disciples are doing what is not lawful   11
12:47 "Look, your mother and your brothers are standing   11
13:15 so that they might not look with their eyes   14
19:27 "Look, we have left everything and followed you.   11
21: 5 Look, your king is coming to you   11
22: 4 Look, I have prepared my dinner   11
23:27 which on the outside look beautiful   18
23:28 you also on the outside look righteous to others   18
24:23 if anyone says to you, 'Look! Here is the Messiah!'   11
24:26 they say to you, 'Look! He is in the wilderness,'   11
24:26 If they say, 'Look! He is in the inner rooms,'   11
25: 6 'Look! Here is the bridegroom! Come out to meet   11
26:16 to look for an opportunity to betray him.   8
Mrk 2:24 "Look, why are they doing what is not lawful   10
3:34 looking at those who sat around him   16
8:24 see people, but they look like trees, walking."   14
8:33 turning and looking at his disciples   14
10:21 Jesus, looking at him, loved him and said   6
10:27 Jesus looked at them and said   6
10:28 "Look, we have left everything and followed you."   11
11:21 Peter remembered and said to him, "Rabbi, look!   10
13: 1 one of his disciples said to him, "Look, Teacher   10
13:21 at that time, 'Look! Here is the Messiah!'   10
13:21 'Look! There he is!'—do not believe it.   10

Mrk 15:40	There were also women looking on from a distance;	9
16: 6	Look, there is the place they laid him.	10
Lke 2:48	Look, your father and I have been searching	11
7:25	Look, those who put on fine clothing	11
7:34	and you say, 'Look, a glutton and a drunkard	11
8:10	so that 'looking they may not perceive	4
9:62	puts a hand to the plow and looks back is fit	4
17:21	nor will they say, 'Look, here it is!'	11
17:23	They will say to you, 'Look there!' or 'Look here!'	11
17:23	will say to you, 'Look there!' or 'Look here!'	11
18:24	Jesus looked at him and said, "How hard it is	14
18:28	"Look, we have left our homes and followed you."	11
19: 8	Zacchaeus…said to the Lord, "Look	11
21:29	"Look at the fig tree and all the trees;	14
22:38	They said, "Lord, look, here are two swords."	11
24:39	Look at my hands and my feet; see that it is I	14
Jhn 1:36	exclaimed, "Look, here is the Lamb of God!"	10
11:41	Jesus looked upward and said, "Father	2
12:15	Look, your king is coming, sitting on a donkey's	11
12:19	Look, the world has gone after him!"	10
12:40	so that they might not look with their eyes	14
13:22	The disciples looked at one another	4
19: 4	"Look, I am bringing him out to you	10
19:37	will look on the one whom they have pierced."	14
20:11	she bent over to look into the tomb;	1
Act 1:11	why do you stand looking up toward heaven?	6
3: 4	"Look at us."	4
4:29	now, Lord, look at their threats	7
5: 9	Look, the feet…are at the door	11
5:25	Then someone arrived and announced, "Look,	11
7:31	as he approached to look, there came the voice	12
7:32	Moses began to tremble and did not dare to look.	12
7:56	"Look," he said, "I see the heavens opened	11
8:36	the eunuch said, "Look, here is water!	11
10:19	the Spirit said to him, "Look	11
13:41	'Look, you scoffers! Be amazed and perish	14
28:27	so that they might not look with their eyes	14
2Co 4:18	because we look not at what can be seen	17
10: 7	Look at what is before your eyes.	4
Php 2: 4	Let each of you look not to your own interests	17
Heb 12: 2	looking to Jesus the pioneer…of our faith	3
Jas 1:25	those who look into the perfect law	15
3: 4	Or look at ships: though they are so large	11
1Pe 1:12	things into which angels long to look!	15
Rev 1: 7	Look! He is coming with the clouds;	11
3: 8	Look, I have set before you an open door	11
4: 1	I looked, and there in heaven a door stood open!	14
4: 3	the one…looks like jasper and carnelian	13
4: 3	a rainbow that looks like an emerald.	13
5: 3	no one…was able to open the scroll or to look	4
5: 4	no one was found worthy…to look into it	4
5:11	Then I looked, and I heard the voice of many angels	14
6: 2	I looked, and there was a white horse! Its rider	14
6: 5	I looked, and there was a black horse! Its rider	14
6: 8	I looked and there was a pale green horse!	14
6:12	When he opened the sixth seal, I looked,	14
7: 9	After this I looked, and there was a great multitude	14
8:13	Then I looked, and I heard an eagle crying	14
14: 1	I looked, and there was the Lamb…on Mount Zion!	14
14:14	Then I looked, and there was a white cloud	14
15: 5	After this I looked, and the temple…was opened	14

look ahead

1. ἀποβλέπω, *apoblepō*, 611

Heb 11:26 he was looking ahead to the reward.　1

look all around

1. περιβλέπω, *periblepō*, 4315

Mrk 5:32 He looked all around to see who had done it.　1

look around

1. ἐπαίρω + ὁ + ὀφθαλμός, *epairō + ho + ophthalmos*, 2048 + 3836 + 4057

2. περιβλέπω, *periblepō*, 4315

Mrk 3: 5	He looked around at them with anger;	2
9: 8	Suddenly when they looked around, they saw no one	2
10:23	Jesus looked around and said to his disciples	2
11:11	when he had looked around at everything	2
Lke 6:10	looking around at all of them	2
Jhn 4:35	I tell you, look around you, and see how the fields	1

look at

1. ἐμβλέπω, *emblepō*, 1838
2. ἐπιβλέπω, *epiblepō*, 2098
3. θεάομαι, *theaomai*, 2517
4. κατανοέω, *katanoeō*, 2917

Mat 6:26	Look at the birds of the air; they neither sow	1
11: 7	"What did you go out into the wilderness to look at?	3
19:26	Jesus looked at them and said, "For mortals	1
Lke 7:24	did you go out into the wilderness to look at?	3
9:38	I beg you to look at my son; he is my only child.	2
20:17	he looked at them and said, "What then does	1
22:61	The Lord turned and looked at Peter.	1
Jhn 1:42	who looked at him and said, "You are Simon	1
Act 11: 6	looked at it closely I saw four-footed animals	4
Jas 1:23	those who look at themselves in a mirror;	4
1:24	they look at themselves and, on going away	4
1Jn 1: 1	what we have looked at and touched	3

look carefully

1. ἀναθεωρέω, *anatheōreō*, 355

Act 17:23 and looked carefully at the objects of your worship　1

look down

1. περιφρονέω, *periphroneō*, 4368

Tit 2:15 Let no one look down on you.　1

look favorably

1. ἐπισκέπτομαι, *episkeptomai*, 2170

Lke 7:16	"God has looked favorably on his people!"	1
Act 15:14	how God first looked favorably on the Gentiles	1

look for

1. ἀναζητέω, *anazēteō*, 349
2. ἐπιζητέω, *epizēteō*, 2118
3. ζητέω, *zēteō*, 2426
4. προσδέχομαι, *prosdechomai*, 4657

Mat 12:43	through waterless regions looking for a resting place	3
26:59	whole council were looking for false testimony	3
28: 5	you are looking for Jesus who was crucified.	3
Mrk 11:18	they kept looking for a way to kill him;	3
14: 1	The chief priests and the scribes were looking for	3
14:11	began to look for an opportunity to betray him.	3
14:55	looking for testimony against Jesus	3
16: 6	you are looking for Jesus of Nazareth	3
Lke 2:38	who were looking for the redemption of Jerusalem.	4
2:44	they started to look for him among their relatives	1
4:42	the crowds were looking for him	2
11:24	waterless regions looking for a resting place	3
13: 6	he came looking for fruit on it and found none.	3
13: 7	For three years I have come looking for fruit	3
19:47	leaders…kept looking for a way to kill him	3
22: 2	were looking for a way to put Jesus to death	3
22: 6	look for an opportunity to betray him to them	3
24: 5	"Why do you look for the living among the dead?	3
Jhn 1:38	he said to them, "What are you looking for?"	3
6:24	went to Capernaum looking for Jesus.	3
6:26	looking for me, not because you saw signs	3
7: 1	were looking for an opportunity to kill him.	3
7:11	The Jews were looking for him at the festival	3
7:19	you looking for an opportunity to kill me?"	3
8:37	yet you look for an opportunity to kill me	3
11:56	They were looking for Jesus	3
13:33	You will look for me;	3
18: 4	"Whom are you looking for?"	3
18: 7	Again he asked them, "Whom are you looking for?"	3
18: 8	So if you are looking for me, let these men go."	3
20:15	why are you weeping? Whom are you looking for?"	3
Act 9:11	at the house of Judas look for a man of Tarsus	3
10:21	"I am the one you are looking for;	3
11:25	Barnabas went to Tarsus to look for Saul	1
Heb 8: 7	there would have been no need to look for a second	3
13:14	we are looking for the city that is to come.	2
1Pe 5: 8	the devil prowls…looking for someone to devour.	3

look forward

1. ἐκδέχομαι, *ekdechomai*, 1683
2. προσδέχομαι, *prosdechomai*, 4657

Lke 2:25	looking forward to the consolation of Israel	2
Heb 11:10	For he looked forward to the city	1

Jde 1:21 look forward to the mercy of our Lord Jesus Christ   2

look in

1. Contextual: Not in Greek

Lke 24:12 stooping and looking in, he saw the linen   1
Jhn 20: 5 bent down to look in and saw the linen wrappings   1

look indeed

1. βλέπω + βλέπω, *blepō + blepō, 1063 + 1063*

Mat 13:14 and you will indeed look, but never perceive.   1
Mrk   4:12 that 'they may indeed look, but not perceive   1
Act 28:26 you will indeed look, but never perceive.   1

look intently

1. ἀτενίζω, *atenizō, 867*
2. διαβλέπω, *diablepō, 1332*

Mrk   8:25 he looked intently and his sight was restored   2
Act   3: 4 Peter looked intently at him, as did John, and said   1
      6:15 all who sat in the council looked intently at him   1
     13: 9 Saul…looked intently at him   1
     14: 9 Paul, looking at him intently   1
     23: 1 Paul was looking intently at the council he said   1

look like

1. ὅμοιος, *homoios, 3927*

Rev   9: 7 On their heads were what looked like crowns   1

look on

1. θεωρέω, *theōreō, 2555*

Mat 27:55 Many women…looking on from a distance;   1

look on favorably

1. ἐπεῖδον, *epeidon, 2078*
2. ἐπισκέπτομαι, *episkeptomai, 2170*

Lke   1:25 done for me when he looked favorably on me   1
      1:68 for he has looked favorably on his people   2

look on with favor

1. ἐπιβλέπω, *epiblepō, 2098*

Lke   1:48 for he has looked with favor on…his servant.   1

look sad

1. σκυθρωπός, *skythrōpos, 5034*

Lke 24:17 They stood still, looking sad.   1

look up

1. ἀναβλέπω, *anablepō, 329*
2. ἀνευρίσκω, *aneuriskō, 461*
3. ἐπαίρω + ὁ + ὀφθαλμός, *epairō + ho + ophthalmos, 2048 + 3836 + 4057*

Mat 14:19 he looked up to heaven, and blessed and broke   1
     17: 8 when they looked up, they saw no one   3
Mrk   6:41 he looked up to heaven   1
      7:34 looking up to heaven, he sighed and said   1
      8:24 man looked up and said, "I can see people   1
     16: 4 they looked up, they saw that the stone   1
Lke   6:20 he looked up at his disciples   3
      9:16 he looked up to heaven, and blessed and broke them   1
     16:23 In Hades…he looked up and saw Abraham   3
     18:13 would not even look up to heaven   3
     19: 5 he looked up and said to him   1
     21: 1 He looked up and saw rich people   1
Jhn   6: 5 he looked up and saw a large crowd coming   3
     17: 1 he looked up to heaven and said   3
Act 21: 4 looked up the disciples and stayed there   2

loose

1. λύω, *lyō, 3395*

Mat 16:19 whatever you loose on earth   1
     16:19 will be loosed in heaven."   1
     18:18 whatever you loose on earth   1
     18:18 loose on earth will be loosed in heaven.   1

loosen

1. ἀνίημι, *aniēmi, 479*

Act 27:40 loosened the ropes that tied the steering-oars;   1

Lord *See also* our Lord come

1. Contextual: Not in Greek

2. κυριακός, *kyriakos, 3258*
3. κυριεύω, *kyrieuō, 3259*
4. κύριος, *kyrios, 3261*

Mat   1:20 an angel of the Lord appeared to him in a dream   4
      1:22 to fulfill what had been spoken by the Lord   4
      1:24 he did as the angel of the Lord commanded him;   4
      2:13 an angel of the Lord appeared to Joseph in a dream   4
      2:15 to fulfill what had been spoken by the Lord   4
      2:19 Herod died, an angel of the Lord suddenly appeared   4
      3: 3 'Prepare the way of the Lord, make his paths   4
      4: 7 written, 'Do not put the Lord your God to the test.' "   4
      4:10 'Worship the Lord your God, and serve only him.' "   4
      5:33 carry out the vows you have made to the Lord.'   4
      7:21 "Not everyone who says to me, 'Lord, Lord,'   4
      7:21 "Not everyone who says to me, 'Lord, Lord,'   4
      7:22 On that day many will say to me, 'Lord, Lord   4
      7:22 On that day many will say to me, 'Lord, Lord   4
      8: 2 "Lord, if you choose, you can make me clean."   4
      8: 6 "Lord, my servant is lying at home paralyzed   4
      8: 8 The centurion answered, "Lord, I am not worthy   4
      8:21 "Lord, first let me go and bury my father."   4
      8:25 they went and woke him up, saying, "Lord, save   4
      9:28 They said to him, "Yes, Lord."   4
      9:38 therefore ask the Lord of the harvest   4
     11:25 "I thank you, Father, Lord of heaven and earth   4
     14:28 "Lord, if it is you, command me to come to you   4
     14:30 beginning to sink, he cried out, "Lord, save me!"   4
     15:22 "Have mercy on me, Lord, Son of David;   4
     15:25 "Lord, help me."   4
     15:27 "Yes, Lord, yet even the dogs eat the crumbs   4
     16:22 rebuke him, saying, "God forbid it, Lord!   4
     17: 4 "Lord, it is good for us to be here;   4
     17:15 said, "Lord, have mercy on my son   4
     18:21 "Lord, if another member of the church sins   4
     20:30 "Lord, have mercy on us, Son of David!"   4
     20:31 "Have mercy on us, Lord, Son of David!"   4
     20:33 They said to him, "Lord, let our eyes be opened."   4
     21: 3 'The Lord needs them.'   4
     21: 9 the one who comes in the name of the Lord!   4
     21:42 this was the Lord's doing   4
     22:37 love the Lord your God with all your heart   4
     22:43 by the Spirit calls him Lord, saying   4
     22:44 'The Lord said to my Lord, "Sit at my right hand   4
     22:44 'The Lord said to my Lord, "Sit at my right hand   4
     22:45 If David thus calls him Lord, how can he be his son?"   4
     23:39 the one who comes in the name of the Lord.' "   4
     24:42 you do not know on what day your Lord is coming.   4
     25:11 'Lord, lord, open to us.'   4
     25:37 'Lord, when was it that we saw you hungry   4
     25:44 'Lord, when was it that we saw you hungry   4
     26:22 "Surely not I, Lord?"   4
     27:10 as the Lord commanded me."   4
     28: 2 an angel of the Lord, descending from heaven   4
Mrk   1: 3 'Prepare the way of the Lord   4
      5:19 tell them how much the Lord has done for you   4
     11: 3 say this, 'The Lord needs it   4
     11: 9 the one who comes in the name of the Lord!   4
     12:11 this was the Lord's doing   4
     12:29 the Lord our God, the Lord is one;   4
     12:29 the Lord our God, the Lord is one;   4
     12:30 shall love the Lord your God with all your heart   4
     12:36 'The Lord said to my Lord, "Sit at my right hand   4
     12:36 'The Lord said to my Lord, "Sit at my right hand   4
     12:37 calls him Lord; so how can he be his son?"   4
     13:20 if the Lord had not cut short those days   4
     16:19 ⟦the Lord Jesus, after he had spoken to them⟧   4
     16:20 ⟦while the Lord worked with them⟧   4
Lke   1: 6 commandments and regulations of the Lord.   4
      1: 9 enter the sanctuary of the Lord and offer incense.   4
      1:11 there appeared to him an angel of the Lord   4
      1:15 for he will be great in the sight of the Lord.   4
      1:16 turn many of the people of Israel to the Lord   4
      1:17 to make ready a people prepared for the Lord."   4
      1:25 "This is what the Lord has done for me   4
      1:28 "Greetings, favored one! The Lord is with you."   4
      1:32 the Lord God will give to him the throne   4
      1:38 Mary said, "Here am I, the servant of the Lord;   4
      1:43 that the mother of my Lord comes to me?   4
      1:45 what was spoken to her by the Lord."   4
      1:46 Mary said, "My soul magnifies the Lord   4
      1:58 the Lord had shown his great mercy to her   4

Lke	1:66	For, indeed, the hand of the Lord was with him.	4
	1:68	"Blessed be the Lord God of Israel	4
	1:76	you will go before the Lord to prepare his ways	4
	2: 9	an angel of the Lord stood before them	4
	2: 9	the glory of the Lord shone around them	4
	2:11	a Savior, who is the Messiah, the Lord.	4
	2:15	which the Lord has made known to us."	4
	2:22	to present him to the Lord	4
	2:23	(as it is written in the law of the Lord	4
	2:23	shall be designated as holy to the Lord")	4
	2:24	what is stated in the law of the Lord	4
	2:26	before he had seen the Lord's Messiah.	4
	2:39	required by the law of the Lord	4
	3: 4	'Prepare the way of the Lord	4
	4: 8	"It is written, 'Worship the Lord your God	4
	4:12	'Do not put the Lord your God to the test.' "	4
	4:18	"The Spirit of the Lord is upon me	4
	4:19	to proclaim the year of the Lord's favor."	4
	5: 8	"Go away from me, Lord, for I am a sinful man!"	4
	5:12	"Lord, if you choose, you can make me clean."	4
	5:17	the power of the Lord was with him to heal.	4
	6:46	"Why do you call me 'Lord, Lord,' and do not	4
	6:46	"Why do you call me 'Lord, Lord,' and do not	4
	7: 6	"Lord, do not trouble yourself, for I am not	4
	7:13	When the Lord saw her	4
	7:19	sent them to the Lord to ask, "Are you the one	4
	9:54	"Lord, do you want us to command fire to come down	4
	9:59	"Lord, first let me go and bury my father."	4
	9:61	Another said, "I will follow you, Lord;	4
	10: 1	After this the Lord appointed seventy others	4
	10: 2	therefore ask the Lord of the harvest	4
	10:17	"Lord, in your name even the demons submit	4
	10:21	"I thank you, Father, Lord of heaven and earth	4
	10:27	love the Lord your God with all your heart	4
	10:39	a sister named Mary, who sat at the Lord's feet	4
	10:40	came to him and asked, "Lord, do you not care	4
	10:41	the Lord answered her, "Martha, Martha	4
	11: 1	"Lord, teach us to pray	4
	11:39	the Lord said to him, "Now you Pharisees clean	4
	12:41	Peter said, "Lord, are you telling this parable	4
	12:42	the Lord said, "Who then is the faithful	4
	13:15	the Lord answered him and said, "You hypocrites!	4
	13:23	Someone asked him, "Lord	4
	13:25	to knock at the door, saying, 'Lord, open to us,'	4
	13:35	the one who comes in the name of the Lord.' "	4
	17: 5	The apostles said to the Lord, "Increase our faith!"	4
	17: 6	The Lord replied, "If you had faith	4
	17:37	they asked him, "Where, Lord?"	4
	18: 6	the Lord said, "Listen	4
	18:41	He said, "Lord, let me see again."	4
	19: 8	Zacchaeus stood there and said to the Lord,	4
	19: 8	possessions, Lord, I will give to the poor;	4
	19:16	The first came forward and said, 'Lord	4
	19:18	'Lord, your pound has made five pounds.'	4
	19:20	'Lord, here is your pound.	4
	19:25	they said to him, 'Lord, he has ten pounds!')	4
	19:31	say this, 'The Lord needs it.' "	4
	19:34	They said, "The Lord needs it."	4
	19:38	the king who comes in the name of the Lord!	4
	20:37	where he speaks of the Lord as the God of Abraham	4
	20:42	'The Lord said to my Lord, "Sit at my right hand	4
	20:42	'The Lord said to my Lord, "Sit at my right hand	4
	20:44	David thus calls him Lord; so how can he be his son?"	4
	22:33	he said to him, "Lord, I am ready to go with you	4
	22:38	They said, "Lord, look, here are two swords."	4
	22:49	"Lord, should we strike with the sword?"	4
	22:61	The Lord turned and looked at Peter.	4
	22:61	Peter remembered the word of the Lord	4
	24:34	They were saying, "The Lord has risen indeed	4
Jhn	1:23	'Make straight the way of the Lord,' "	4
	6:23	after the Lord had given thanks.	4
	6:68	Peter answered him, "Lord, to whom can we go?	4
	9:38	He said, "Lord, I believe." And he worshiped him.	4
	11: 2	Mary was the one who anointed the Lord with perfume	4
	11: 3	"Lord, he whom you love is ill."	4
	11:12	The disciples said to him, "Lord	4
	11:21	Martha said to Jesus, "Lord, if you had been here	4
	11:27	She said to him, "Yes, Lord, I believe	4
	11:32	Mary...knelt at his feet and said to him, "Lord	4
	11:34	They said to him, "Lord, come and see."	4
	11:39	"Lord, already there is a stench	4

	12:13	the one who comes in the name of the Lord	4
	12:38	"Lord, who has believed our message	4
	12:38	to whom has the arm of the Lord been revealed?"	4
	13: 6	to him, "Lord, are you going to wash my feet?"	4
	13: 9	Simon Peter said to him, "Lord, not my feet only	4
	13:13	You call me Teacher and Lord—and you are right	4
	13:14	So if I, your Lord and Teacher, have washed	4
	13:25	he asked him, "Lord, who is it?"	4
	13:36	Peter said to him, "Lord, where are you going?"	4
	13:37	"Lord, why can I not follow you now?	4
	14: 5	Thomas said to him, "Lord, we do not know	4
	14: 8	Philip said to him, "Lord, show us the Father	4
	14:22	"Lord, how is it that you will reveal yourself	4
	20: 2	"They have taken the Lord out of the tomb	4
	20:13	"They have taken away my Lord	4
	20:18	"I have seen the Lord";	4
	20:20	the disciples rejoiced when they saw the Lord.	4
	20:25	"We have seen the Lord."	4
	20:28	Thomas answered him, "My Lord and my God!"	4
	21: 7	"It is the Lord!"	4
	21: 7	When Simon Peter heard that it was the Lord	4
	21:12	because they knew it was the Lord.	4
	21:15	to him, "Yes, Lord; you know that I love you."	4
	21:16	to him, "Yes, Lord; you know that I love you."	4
	21:17	he said to him, "Lord, you know everything;	4
	21:20	"Lord, who is it that is going to betray you?"	4
	21:21	he said to Jesus, "Lord, what about him?"	4
Act	1: 6	"Lord, is this the time when you will restore	4
	1:21	the Lord Jesus went in and out among us	4
	1:24	"Lord, you know everyone's heart.	4
	2:20	before the coming of the Lord's great and glorious day.	4
	2:21	everyone who calls on the name of the Lord	4
	2:25	'I saw the Lord always before me	4
	2:34	'The Lord said to my Lord, "Sit at my right hand	4
	2:34	'The Lord said to my Lord, "Sit at my right hand	4
	2:36	God has made him both Lord and Messiah	4
	2:39	everyone whom the Lord our God calls to him."	4
	2:47	day by day the Lord added to their number	4
	3:20	may come from the presence of the Lord	4
	3:22	'The Lord your God will raise up...a prophet	4
	4:26	against the Lord and against his Messiah.'	4
	4:29	now, Lord, look at their threats	4
	4:33	testimony to the resurrection of the Lord Jesus	4
	5: 9	to put the Spirit of the Lord to the test?	4
	5:14	more than ever believers were added to the Lord	4
	5:19	an angel of the Lord opened the prison doors	4
	7:31	to look, there came the voice of the Lord:	4
	7:33	the Lord said to him, 'Take off the sandals	4
	7:49	house will you build for me, says the Lord	4
	7:59	"Lord Jesus, receive my spirit."	4
	7:60	"Lord, do not hold this sin against them."	4
	8:16	baptized in the name of the Lord Jesus).	4
	8:22	Repent...and pray to the Lord	4
	8:24	Simon answered, "Pray for me to the Lord	4
	8:25	had testified and spoken the word of the Lord	4
	8:26	an angel of the Lord said to Philip, "Get up and go	4
	8:39	the Spirit of the Lord snatched Philip away;	4
	9: 1	murder against the disciples of the Lord	4
	9: 5	He asked, "Who are you, Lord?"	4
	9:10	The Lord said to him in a vision, "Ananias."	4
	9:10	He answered, "Here I am, Lord."	4
	9:11	The Lord said to him, "Get up and go	4
	9:13	Ananias answered, "Lord	4
	9:15	the Lord said to him, "Go	4
	9:17	the Lord Jesus, who appeared to you on your way	4
	9:27	he had seen the Lord, who had spoken to him	4
	9:28	speaking boldly in the name of the Lord.	4
	9:31	Living in the fear of the Lord	4
	9:35	saw him and turned to the Lord.	4
	9:42	many believed in the Lord.	4
	10: 4	stared at him...and said, "What is it, Lord?"	4
	10:14	Peter said, "By no means, Lord;	4
	10:33	listen to all that the Lord has commanded you to say	4
	10:36	peace by Jesus Christ—he is Lord of all.	4
	11: 8	I replied, 'By no means, Lord;	4
	11:16	I remembered the word of the Lord, how he had said	4
	11:17	when we believed in the Lord Jesus Christ	4
	11:20	proclaiming the Lord Jesus.	4
	11:21	The hand of the Lord was with them	4
	11:21	a great number became believers and turned to the Lord.	4
	11:23	he exhorted them all to remain faithful to the Lord	4

11:24	a great many people were brought to the Lord.	4
12: 7	Suddenly an angel of the Lord appeared	4
12:11	"Now I am sure that the Lord has sent his angel	4
12:17	how the Lord had brought him out of the prison.	4
12:23	immediately…an angel of the Lord struck him down	4
13: 2	While they were worshiping the Lord and fasting	4
13:10	making crooked the straight paths of the Lord?	4
13:11	now listen—the hand of the Lord is against you	4
13:12	he was astonished at the teaching about the Lord.	4
13:44	gathered to hear the word of the Lord.	4
13:47	For so the Lord has commanded us, saying	4
13:48	they were glad and praised the word of the Lord;	4
13:49	Thus the word of the Lord spread	4
14: 3	speaking boldly for the Lord	4
14:23	the Lord in whom they had come to believe.	4
15:11	saved through the grace of the Lord Jesus	4
15:17	so that all other peoples may seek the Lord	4
15:17	says the Lord, who has been making these things	4
15:26	for the sake of our Lord Jesus Christ.	4
15:35	taught and proclaimed the word of the Lord.	4
15:36	where we proclaimed the word of the Lord	4
15:40	commending him to the grace of the Lord.	4
16:14	The Lord opened her heart to listen eagerly	4
16:15	"If you have judged me to be faithful to the Lord	4
16:31	"Believe on the Lord Jesus, and you will be saved	4
16:32	They spoke the word of the Lord to him	4
17:24	he who is Lord of heaven and earth	4
18: 8	Crispus…became a believer in the Lord	4
18: 9	One night the Lord said to Paul in a vision	4
18:25	He had been instructed in the Way of the Lord;	4
19: 5	baptized in the name of the Lord Jesus.	4
19:10	residents of Asia…heard the word of the Lord.	4
19:13	to use the name of the Lord Jesus	4
19:17	the name of the Lord Jesus was praised.	4
19:20	word of the Lord grew mightily and prevailed.	4
20:19	serving the Lord with all humility	4
20:21	faith toward our Lord Jesus.	4
20:24	ministry that I received from the Lord Jesus	4
20:35	the words of the Lord Jesus, for he himself said	4
21:13	die in Jerusalem for the name of the Lord Jesus."	4
21:14	except to say, "The Lord's will be done."	4
22: 8	I answered, 'Who are you, Lord?'	4
22:10	I asked, 'What am I to do, Lord?'	4
22:10	The Lord said to me, 'Get up and go to Damascus;	4
22:19	I said, 'Lord, they themselves know	4
23:11	the Lord stood near him and said	4
26:15	I asked, 'Who are you, Lord?'	4
26:15	The Lord answered, 'I am Jesus	4
28:31	teaching about the Lord Jesus Christ	4
Rom 1: 4	Jesus Christ our Lord	4
1: 7	from God our Father and the Lord Jesus Christ.	4
4: 8	the one…whom the Lord will not reckon sin."	4
4:24	him who raised Jesus our Lord from the dead	4
5: 1	peace with God through our Lord Jesus Christ	4
5:11	boast in God through our Lord Jesus Christ	4
5:21	leading to eternal life through Jesus Christ our Lord.	4
6:23	is eternal life in Christ Jesus our Lord.	4
7:25	Thanks be to God through Jesus Christ our Lord!	4
8:39	from the love of God in Christ Jesus our Lord.	4
9:28	Lord will execute his sentence on the earth	4
9:29	"If the Lord of hosts had not left survivors to us	4
10: 9	if you confess with your lips that Jesus is Lord	4
10:12	the same Lord is Lord of all	4
10:12	the same Lord is Lord of all	1
10:13	For, "Everyone who calls on the name of the Lord	4
10:16	"Lord, who has believed our message?"	4
11: 3	"Lord, they have killed your prophets	4
11:34	"For who has known the mind of the Lord?	4
12:11	be ardent in spirit, serve the Lord.	4
12:19	"Vengeance is mine, I will repay, says the Lord."	4
13:14	Instead, put on the Lord Jesus Christ	4
14: 4	for the Lord is able to make them stand.	4
14: 6	the day, observe it in honor of the Lord.	4
14: 6	Also those who eat, eat in honor of the Lord	4
14: 6	those who abstain, abstain in honor of the Lord	4
14: 8	If we live, we live to the Lord	4
14: 8	and if we die, we die to the Lord;	4
14: 8	whether we live or whether we die, we are the Lord's.	4
14: 9	be Lord of both the dead and the living.	3
14:11	"As I live, says the Lord, every knee shall bow	4
14:14	I know and am persuaded in the Lord Jesus	4

15: 6	the God and Father of our Lord Jesus Christ.	4
15:11	and again, "Praise the Lord, all you Gentiles	4
15:30	I appeal to you…by our Lord Jesus Christ	4
16: 2	welcome her in the Lord as is fitting for the saints	4
16: 8	Greet Ampliatus, my beloved in the Lord.	4
16:11	Greet those in the Lord who belong to the family	4
16:12	Greet those workers in the Lord	4
16:12	beloved Persis, who has worked hard in the Lord.	4
16:13	Greet Rufus, chosen in the Lord;	4
16:18	For such people do not serve our Lord Christ	4
16:20	The grace of our Lord Jesus Christ be with you.	4
16:22	I Tertius…greet you in the Lord.	4
1Co 1: 2	call on the name of our Lord Jesus Christ	4
1: 2	Lord Jesus Christ, both their Lord and ours:	1
1: 3	God our Father and the Lord Jesus Christ.	4
1: 7	as you wait for the revealing of our Lord Jesus	4
1: 8	blameless on the day of our Lord Jesus Christ.	4
1: 9	the fellowship of his Son, Jesus Christ our Lord.	4
1:10	by the name of our Lord Jesus Christ	4
1:31	"Let the one who boasts, boast in the Lord."	4
2: 8	they would not have crucified the Lord of glory.	4
2:16	"For who has known the mind of the Lord	4
3: 5	as the Lord assigned to each.	4
3:20	"The Lord knows the thoughts of the wise, that	4
4: 4	It is the Lord who judges me.	4
4: 5	before the time, before the Lord comes	4
4:17	my beloved and faithful child in the Lord	4
4:19	I will come to you soon, if the Lord wills	4
5: 4	in the name of the Lord Jesus	4
5: 4	with the power of our Lord Jesus	4
5: 5	may be saved in the day of the Lord.	4
6:11	justified in the name of the Lord Jesus Christ	4
6:13	is meant not for fornication but for the Lord	4
6:13	and the Lord for the body.	4
6:14	God raised the Lord and will also raise us	4
6:17	anyone united to the Lord becomes one spirit	4
7:10	married I give this command—not I but the Lord	4
7:12	To the rest I say—I and not the Lord	4
7:17	lead the life that the Lord has assigned,	4
7:22	called in the Lord as a slave is a freed person	4
7:22	a slave is a freed person belonging to the Lord	4
7:25	virgins, I have no command of the Lord	4
7:25	one who by the Lord's mercy is trustworthy.	4
7:32	is anxious about the affairs of the Lord	4
7:32	how to please the Lord;	4
7:34	are anxious about the affairs of the Lord	4
7:35	unhindered devotion to the Lord.	4
7:39	marry anyone she wishes, only in the Lord.	4
8: 6	one Lord, Jesus Christ	4
9: 1	Have I not seen Jesus our Lord?	4
9: 1	Are you not my work in the Lord?	4
9: 2	you are the seal of my apostleship in the Lord.	4
9: 5	the brothers of the Lord and Cephas?	4
9:14	In the same way, the Lord commanded	4
10:21	the cup of the Lord and the cup of demons.	4
10:21	You cannot partake of the table of the Lord	4
10:22	are we provoking the Lord to jealousy?	4
10:26	for "the earth and its fullness are the Lord's."	4
11:11	in the Lord woman is not independent of man	4
11:20	it is not really to eat the Lord's supper.	2
11:23	For I received from the Lord	4
11:23	the Lord Jesus on the night when he was betrayed	4
11:26	you proclaim the Lord's death until he comes.	4
11:27	drinks the cup of the Lord in an unworthy manner	4
11:27	be answerable for the body and blood of the Lord.	4
11:32	when we are judged by the Lord, we are disciplined	4
12: 3	no one can say "Jesus is Lord"	4
12: 5	are varieties of services, but the same Lord;	4
14:21	they will not listen to me," says the Lord.	4
14:37	writing to you is a command of the Lord.	4
15:31	a boast that I make in Christ Jesus our Lord.	4
15:57	victory through our Lord Jesus Christ.	4
15:58	always excelling in the work of the Lord	4
15:58	in the Lord your labor is not in vain.	4
16: 7	some time with you, if the Lord permits.	4
16:10	he is doing the work of the Lord just as I am;	4
16:19	greet you warmly in the Lord.	4
16:22	anyone be accursed who has no love for the Lord.	4
16:23	The grace of the Lord Jesus be with you.	4
2Co 1: 2	God our Father and the Lord Jesus Christ.	4
1: 3	Father of our Lord Jesus Christ	4

2Co	1:14	on the day of the Lord Jesus we are your boast	4
	2:12	a door was opened for me in the Lord;	4
	3:16	when one turns to the Lord, the veil is removed.	4
	3:17	Now the Lord is the Spirit	4
	3:17	where the Spirit of the Lord is, there is freedom.	4
	3:18	seeing the glory of the Lord as though reflected in	4
	3:18	for this comes from the Lord, the Spirit.	4
	4: 5	not proclaim ourselves; we proclaim Jesus as Lord	4
	4:14	know that the one who raised the Lord Jesus	4
	5: 6	in the body we are away from the Lord	4
	5: 8	be away from the body and at home with the Lord.	4
	5:11	Therefore, knowing the fear of the Lord	4
	6:17	be separate from them, says the Lord	4
	6:18	be my sons and daughters, says the Lord Almighty."	4
	8: 5	they gave themselves first to the Lord	4
	8: 9	you know the generous act of our Lord Jesus Christ	4
	8:19	for the glory of the Lord himself	4
	8:21	what is right not only in the Lord's sight	4
	10: 8	which the Lord gave for building you up	4
	10:17	"Let the one who boasts, boast in the Lord."	4
	10:18	those whom the Lord commends.	4
	11:17	I am saying not with the Lord's authority	4
	11:31	The God and Father of the Lord Jesus	4
	12: 1	go on to visions and revelations of the Lord.	4
	12: 8	Three times I appealed to the Lord about this	4
	13:10	that the Lord has given me for building up	4
	13:13	The grace of the Lord Jesus Christ	4
Gal	1: 3	God our Father and the Lord Jesus Christ	4
	1:19	except James the Lord's brother.	4
	5:10	I am confident about you in the Lord	4
	6:14	except the cross of our Lord Jesus Christ	4
	6:18	the grace of our Lord Jesus Christ	4
Eph	1: 2	God our Father and the Lord Jesus Christ.	4
	1: 3	the God and Father of our Lord Jesus Christ	4
	1:15	have heard of your faith in the Lord Jesus	4
	1:17	God of our Lord Jesus Christ, the Father of glory	4
	2:21	grows into a holy temple in the Lord;	4
	3:11	that he has carried out in Christ Jesus our Lord	4
	4: 1	I therefore, the prisoner in the Lord, beg you	4
	4: 5	one Lord, one faith, one baptism	4
	4:17	Now this I affirm and insist on in the Lord:	4
	5: 8	now in the Lord you are light.	4
	5:10	Try to find out what is pleasing to the Lord.	4
	5:17	but understand what the will of the Lord is.	4
	5:19	singing and making melody to the Lord	4
	5:20	in the name of our Lord Jesus Christ.	4
	5:22	Wives, be subject to your husbands as you are to the Lord	4
	6: 1	Children, obey your parents in the Lord	4
	6: 4	in the discipline and instruction of the Lord.	4
	6: 7	as to the Lord and not to men and women	4
	6: 8	we will receive the same again from the Lord	4
	6:10	Finally, be strong in the Lord	4
	6:21	a faithful minister in the Lord.	4
	6:23	God the Father and the Lord Jesus Christ.	4
	6:24	an undying love for our Lord Jesus Christ.	4
Php	1: 2	God our Father and the Lord Jesus Christ.	4
	1:14	made confident in the Lord by my imprisonment	4
	2:11	every tongue should confess that Jesus Christ is Lord	4
	2:19	I hope in the Lord Jesus to send Timothy to you	4
	2:24	I trust in the Lord	4
	2:29	Welcome him then in the Lord with all joy	4
	3: 1	Finally, my brothers and sisters, rejoice in the Lord.	4
	3: 8	knowing Christ Jesus my Lord.	4
	3:20	we are expecting a Savior, the Lord Jesus Christ.	4
	4: 1	stand firm in the Lord in this way, my beloved.	4
	4: 2	I urge Syntyche to be of the same mind in the Lord.	4
	4: 4	Rejoice in the Lord always;	4
	4: 5	The Lord is near.	4
	4:10	I rejoice in the Lord greatly	4
	4:23	The grace of the Lord Jesus Christ be with	4
Col	1: 3	God, the Father of our Lord Jesus Christ	4
	1:10	so that you may lead lives worthy of the Lord	4
	2: 6	you therefore have received Christ Jesus the Lord	4
	3:13	just as the Lord has forgiven you	4
	3:17	do everything in the name of the Lord Jesus	4
	3:18	be subject…as is fitting in the Lord.	4
	3:20	this is your acceptable duty in the Lord.	4
	3:22	wholeheartedly, fearing the Lord.	4
	3:23	put yourselves into it, as done for the Lord	4
	3:24	from the Lord you will receive the inheritance	4
	3:24	you serve the Lord Christ.	4

	4: 7	Tychicus…fellow servant in the Lord.	4
	4:17	the task that you have received in the Lord."	4
1Th	1: 1	in God the Father and the Lord Jesus Christ:	4
	1: 3	steadfastness of hope in our Lord Jesus Christ.	4
	1: 6	you became imitators of us and of the Lord	4
	1: 8	the word of the Lord has sounded forth from you	4
	2:15	who killed both the Lord Jesus and the prophets	4
	2:19	crown of boasting before our Lord Jesus	4
	3: 8	if you continue to stand firm in the Lord.	4
	3:11	our Lord Jesus direct our way to you.	4
	3:12	may the Lord make you increase and abound in love	4
	3:13	the coming of our Lord Jesus with all his saints.	4
	4: 1	we ask and urge you in the Lord Jesus	4
	4: 2	instructions we gave you through the Lord Jesus.	4
	4: 6	because the Lord is an avenger	4
	4:15	this we declare to you by the word of the Lord	4
	4:15	who are left until the coming of the Lord	4
	4:16	For the Lord himself, with a cry of command,	4
	4:17	together with them to meet the Lord in the air;	4
	4:17	so we will be with the Lord forever.	4
	5: 2	the day of the Lord will come like a thief	4
	5: 9	for obtaining salvation through our Lord Jesus	4
	5:12	have charge of you in the Lord and admonish you;	4
	5:23	blameless at the coming of our Lord Jesus	4
	5:27	command you by the Lord that this letter be read	4
	5:28	The grace of our Lord Jesus Christ be with you.	4
2Th	1: 1	God our Father and the Lord Jesus Christ:	4
	1: 2	God our Father and the Lord Jesus Christ.	4
	1: 7	when the Lord Jesus is revealed from heaven	4
	1: 8	who do not obey the gospel of our Lord Jesus.	4
	1: 9	separated from the presence of the Lord	4
	1:12	that the name of our Lord Jesus may be glorified	4
	1:12	the grace of our God and the Lord Jesus Christ.	4
	2: 1	As to the coming of our Lord Jesus Christ	4
	2: 2	that the day of the Lord is already here.	4
	2: 8	whom the Lord Jesus will destroy	4
	2:13	brothers and sisters beloved by the Lord	4
	2:14	may obtain the glory of our Lord Jesus Christ.	4
	2:16	Now may our Lord Jesus Christ himself	4
	3: 1	so that the word of the Lord may spread rapidly	4
	3: 3	the Lord is faithful;	4
	3: 4	we have confidence in the Lord concerning you	4
	3: 5	May the Lord direct your hearts to the love of God	4
	3: 6	in the name of our Lord Jesus Christ	4
	3:12	exhort in the Lord Jesus Christ to do their work	4
	3:16	Now may the Lord of peace himself give you peace	4
	3:16	The Lord be with all of you.	4
	3:18	The grace of our Lord Jesus Christ be with all of you.	4
1Ti	1: 2	God the Father and Christ Jesus our Lord.	4
	1:12	I am grateful to Christ Jesus our Lord,	4
	1:14	the grace of our Lord overflowed for me	4
	6: 3	sound words of our Lord Jesus Christ	4
	6:14	until the manifestation of our Lord Jesus Christ	4
	6:15	the King of kings and Lord of lords.	4
2Ti	1: 2	God the Father and Christ Jesus our Lord.	4
	1: 8	Do not be ashamed…of the testimony about our Lord	4
	1:16	May the Lord grant mercy	4
	1:18	the Lord grant that he will find mercy from the Lord	4
	1:18	that he will find mercy from the Lord on that day!	4
	2: 7	the Lord will give you understanding	4
	2:19	"The Lord knows those who are his,"	4
	2:19	everyone who calls on the name of the Lord turn away	4
	2:22	those who call on the Lord from a pure heart.	4
	2:24	the Lord's servant must not be quarrelsome	4
	3:11	Yet the Lord rescued me from all of them.	4
	4: 8	which the Lord, the righteous judge, will give	4
	4:14	the Lord will pay him back for his deeds.	4
	4:17	the Lord stood by me and gave me strength	4
	4:18	The Lord will rescue me from every evil attack	4
	4:22	The Lord be with your spirit. Grace be with you.	4
Phm	1: 3	God our Father and the Lord Jesus Christ.	4
	1: 5	your faith toward the Lord Jesus.	4
	1:16	both in the flesh and in the Lord.	4
	1:20	brother, let me have this benefit from you in the Lord!	4
	1:25	The grace of the Lord Jesus Christ	4
Heb	1:10	"In the beginning, Lord, you founded the earth	4
	2: 3	It was declared at first through the Lord	4
	7:14	evident that our Lord was descended from Judah	4
	7:21	"The Lord has sworn and will not change his mind	4
	8: 2	that the Lord, and not any mortal, has set up.	4
	8: 8	"The days are surely coming, says the Lord	4

	8: 9	so I had no concern for them, says the Lord.	4
	8:10	This is the covenant…says the Lord:	4
	8:11	say to each other, 'Know the Lord,'	4
	10:16	after those days, says the Lord:	4
	10:30	And again, "The Lord will judge his people."	4
	12: 5	do not regard lightly the discipline of the Lord	4
	12: 6	for the Lord disciplines those whom he loves	4
	12:14	holiness without which no one will see the Lord.	4
	13: 6	"The Lord is my helper; I will not be afraid.	4
	13:20	who brought back from the dead our Lord Jesus	4
Jas	1: 1	servant of God and of the Lord Jesus Christ	4
	1: 7	must not expect to receive anything from the Lord.	4
	1:12	the crown of life that the Lord has promised	1
	2: 1	really believe our glorious Lord Jesus Christ?	4
	3: 9	With it we bless the Lord and Father	4
	4:10	Humble yourselves before the Lord	4
	4:15	"If the Lord wishes, we will live and do this	4
	5: 4	cries…reached the ears of the Lord of hosts.	4
	5: 7	Be patient…until the coming of the Lord.	4
	5: 8	for the coming of the Lord is near.	4
	5:10	the prophets who spoke in the name of the Lord.	4
	5:11	and you have seen the purpose of the Lord	4
	5:11	how the Lord is compassionate and merciful.	4
	5:14	anointing them with oil in the name of the Lord.	4
	5:15	and the Lord will raise them up;	4
1Pe	1: 3	the God and Father of our Lord Jesus Christ!	4
	1:25	but the word of the Lord endures forever."	4
	2: 3	if indeed you have tasted that the Lord is good.	4
	2:13	For the Lord's sake accept the authority	4
	3:12	For the eyes of the Lord are on the righteous	4
	3:12	the face of the Lord is against those who do evil."	4
	3:15	in your hearts sanctify Christ as Lord.	4
2Pe	1: 2	in the knowledge of God and of Jesus our Lord.	4
	1: 8	in the knowledge of our Lord Jesus Christ.	4
	1:11	kingdom of our Lord and Savior Jesus Christ	4
	1:14	as indeed our Lord Jesus Christ has made clear to me.	4
	1:16	the power and coming of our Lord Jesus Christ	4
	2: 9	the Lord knows how to rescue the godly from trial	4
	2:11	against them a slanderous judgment from the Lord.	4
	2:20	knowledge of our Lord and Savior Jesus Christ	4
	3: 2	the commandment of the Lord and Savior spoken	4
	3: 8	with the Lord one day is like a thousand years	4
	3: 9	The Lord is not slow about his promise	4
	3:10	But the day of the Lord will come like a thief	4
	3:15	regard the patience of our Lord as salvation.	4
	3:18	knowledge of our Lord and Savior Jesus Christ.	4
Jde	1: 4	and deny our only Master and Lord, Jesus Christ.	4
	1: 5	that the Lord, who once for all saved a people	4
	1: 9	but said, "The Lord rebuke you!"	4
	1:14	"See, the Lord is coming with ten thousands of his holy	4
	1:17	predictions of the apostles of our Lord Jesus	4
	1:21	look forward to the mercy of our Lord Jesus Christ	4
	1:25	God our Savior, through Jesus Christ our Lord	4
Rev	1: 8	"I am the Alpha and the Omega," says the Lord God	4
	1:10	I was in the spirit on the Lord's day,	2
	4: 8	Lord God the Almighty, who was and is and is to come."	4
	4:11	"You are worthy, our Lord and God, to receive glory	4
	11: 4	two olive trees…that stand before the Lord	4
	11: 8	great city…where also their Lord was crucified.	4
	11:15	become the kingdom of our Lord and of his Messiah	4
	11:17	singing, "We give you thanks, Lord God Almighty	4
	14:13	Blessed are the dead who from now on die in the Lord."	4
	15: 3	amazing are your deeds, Lord God the Almighty!	4
	15: 4	Lord, who will not fear and glorify your name?	4
	16: 7	the altar respond, "Yes, O Lord God, the Almighty	4
	17:14	Lamb…for he is Lord of lords and King of kings	4
	18: 8	for mighty is the Lord God who judges her."	4
	19: 6	For the Lord our God the Almighty reigns.	4
	19:16	a name inscribed, "King of kings and Lord of lords."	4
	21:22	for its temple is the Lord God the Almighty	4
	22: 5	for the Lord God will be their light	4
	22: 6	the Lord, the God of the spirits of the prophets	4
	22:20	I am coming soon." Amen. Come, Lord Jesus!	4
	22:21	The grace of the Lord Jesus be with all	4

lord

1. κυριεύω, *kyrieuō, 3259*
2. κύριος, *kyrios, 3261*

Mat	12: 8	For the Son of Man is lord of the sabbath."	2
	18:25	could not pay, his lord ordered him to be sold	2
	18:27	the lord of that slave released him	2

	18:31	they went and reported to their lord	2
	18:32	Then his lord summoned him and said to him	2
	18:34	in anger his lord handed him over to be tortured	2
	25:11	'Lord, lord, open to us.'	2
Mrk	2:28	the Son of Man is lord even of the sabbath."	2
Lke	6: 5	"The Son of Man is lord of the sabbath."	2
Rom	14: 4	It is before their own lord that they stand	2
1Co	8: 5	as in fact there are many gods and many lords—	2
1Ti	6:15	the King of kings and Lord of lords.	1
1Pe	3: 6	Thus Sarah obeyed Abraham and called him lord.	2
Rev	17:14	Lamb…for he is Lord of lords and King of kings	2
	19:16	a name inscribed, "King of kings and Lord of lords."	2

lord it over

1. κατακυριεύω, *katakyrieuō, 2894*
2. κυριεύω, *kyrieuō, 3259*

Mat	20:25	the rulers of the Gentiles lord it over them	1
Mrk	10:42	recognize as their rulers lord it over them	1
Lke	22:25	"The kings…lord it over them;	2
2Co	1:24	not mean to imply that we lord it over your faith;	2
1Pe	5: 3	not lord it over those in your charge	1

sovereign Lord

1. δεσπότης, *despotēs, 1305*

Act	4:24	"Sovereign Lord, who made the heaven	1
Rev	6:10	"Sovereign Lord, holy and true, how long	1

lose

1. ἀπόλλυμι, *apollymi, 660*
2. ἀπώλεια, *apōleia, 724*
3. διαγίνομαι, *diaginomai, 1335*
4. ἐκπίπτω, *ekpiptō, 1738*
5. οὐ, *ou, 4024*

Mat	5:29	is better for you to lose one of your members	1
	5:30	is better for you to lose one of your members	1
	10: 6	go rather to the lost sheep	1
	10:39	Those who find their life will lose it	1
	10:39	who lose their life for my sake will find it.	1
	10:42	none of these will lose their reward."	1
	15:24	"I was sent only to the lost sheep	1
	16:25	those who want to save their life will lose it	1
	16:25	who lose their life for my sake will find it.	1
	18:14	that one of these little ones should be lost.	1
Mrk	2:22	the wine is lost, and so are the skins;	1
	8:35	those who want to save their life will lose it	1
	8:35	who lose their life for my sake	1
	9:41	will by no means lose the reward.	1
Lke	9:24	who want to save their life will lose it	1
	9:24	who lose their life for my sake will save it.	1
	9:25	but lose or forfeit themselves?	1
	15: 4	a hundred sheep and losing one of them	1
	15: 4	go after the one that is lost until he finds it?	1
	15: 6	I have found my sheep that was lost.'	1
	15: 8	having ten silver coins, if she loses one	1
	15: 9	I have found the coin that I had lost.'	1
	15:24	he was lost and is found!'	1
	15:32	he was lost and has been found.' "	1
	17:33	who try to make their life secure will lose it	1
	17:33	who lose their life will keep it.	1
	19:10	Son of Man came to seek out and to save the lost."	1
Jhn	6:12	so that nothing may be lost."	1
	6:39	I should lose nothing of all that he has given	1
	12:25	Those who love their life lose it	1
	17:12	I guarded them, and not one of them was lost	1
	17:12	not…lost except the one destined to be lost	1
	18: 9	"I did not lose a single one of those	1
Act	27: 9	Since much time had been lost	3
	27:34	for none of you will lose a hair from your heads	1
2Co	3:10	Indeed, what once had glory has lost its glory	5
Heb	10:39	those who shrink back and so are lost	2
2Pe	3:17	not carried away…and lose your own stability.	4
2Jn	1: 8	so that you do not lose what we have worked for	1
Rev	18:14	your dainties and your splendor are lost to you	1

lose all sensitivity

1. ἀπαλγέω, *apalgeō, 556*

Eph	4:19	They have lost all sensitivity	1

lose heart

1. ἀθυμέω, *athymeō, 126*

2. ἐγκακέω, *enkakeō, 1591*
3. ἐκλύω, *eklyō, 1725*
4. ἐκλύω + ὁ + ψυχή, *eklyō + ho + psychē, 1725 + 3836 + 6034*

Lke	18: 1	their need to pray always and not to lose heart.	2
2Co	4: 1	engaged in this ministry, we do not lose heart.	2
	4:16	So we do not lose heart.	2
Eph	3:13	I pray therefore that you may not lose heart	2
Col	3:21	not provoke your children, or they may lose heart	1
Heb	12: 3	you may not grow weary or lose heart.	4
	12: 5	or lose heart when you are punished by him;	3

lose saltiness

1. ἄναλος, *analos, 383*

Mrk	9:50	if salt has lost its saltiness	1

lose taste

1. μωραίνω, *mōrainō, 3701*

Mat	5:13	if salt has lost its taste, how can its saltiness	1
Lke	14:34	if salt has lost its taste	1

lose time

1. ἀναβολή, *anabolē, 332*

Act	25:17	I lost no time, but on the next day took my seat	1

loss   *See also* suffer loss

1. ἀποβολή, *apobolē, 613*
2. ἀπορέω, *aporeō, 679*
3. ζημία, *zēmia, 2422*

Act	25:20	was at a loss how to investigate these questions	2
	27:10	the voyage will be with danger and much heavy loss	3
	27:21	avoided this damage and loss.	3
	27:22	no loss of life among you, but only of the ship.	1
Php	3: 7	I have come to regard as loss because of Christ.	3
	3: 8	More than that, I regard everything as loss	3

lost   *See* lose

Lot

1. Λώτ, *Lōt, 3397*

Lke	17:28	Likewise, just as it was in the days of Lot:	1
	17:29	on the day that Lot left Sodom	1
	17:32	Remember Lot's wife.	1
2Pe	2: 7	and if he recused Lot, a righteous man	1

lot   *See also* cast lots, choose by lot

1. κλῆρος, *klēros, 3102*

Mat	27:35	divided his clothes...by casting lots;	1
Mrk	15:24	casting lots to decide what each should take.	1
Lke	23:34	they cast lots to divide his clothing.	1
Jhn	19:24	for my clothing they cast lots."	1
Act	1:26	they cast lots for them	1
	1:26	the lot fell on Matthias;	1

loud

1. Contextual: Not in Greek
2. ἰσχυρός, *ischyros, 2708*
3. μέγας, *megas, 3489*
4. πολύς, *polys, 4498*

Mat	2:18	wailing and loud lamentation, Rachel weeping	4
	20:31	but they shouted even more loudly	1
	24:31	send out his angels with a loud trumpet call	3
	27:46	Jesus cried with a loud voice	3
	27:50	Jesus cried again with a loud voice	3
Mrk	1:26	convulsing him and crying with a loud voice	3
	10:48	he cried out even more loudly, "Son of David	1
	15:34	At three o'clock Jesus cried out with a loud voice	3
	15:37	Jesus gave a loud cry and breathed his last.	3
Lke	1:42	exclaimed with a loud cry, "Blessed are you	3
	4:33	and he cried out with a loud voice	3
	17:15	turned back, praising God with a loud voice.	3
	18:39	he shouted even more loudly,	1
	19:37	began to praise God joyfully with a loud voice	3
	23:23	they kept urgently demanding with loud shouts	3
	23:46	Jesus, crying with a loud voice, said, "Father	3
Jhn	11:43	When he had said this, he cried with a loud voice	3
Act	7:57	they covered their ears, and with a loud shout	3
	7:60	he knelt down and cried out in a loud voice	3
	8: 2	made loud lamentation over him.	3
	8: 7	unclean spirits...crying with loud shrieks	3

	14:10	said in a loud voice, "Stand upright on your feet."	3
	16:28	Paul shouted in a loud voice, "Do not harm yourself	3
Heb	5: 7	supplications, with loud cries and tears	2
Rev	1:10	and I heard behind me a loud voice like a trumpet	3
	5: 2	a mighty angel proclaiming with a loud voice	3
	6:10	they cried out with a loud voice, "Sovereign Lord	3
	7: 2	he called with a loud voice to the four angels	3
	7:10	cried out in a loud voice, saying, "Salvation	3
	8:13	I heard an eagle crying with a loud voice	3
	11:12	Then they heard a loud voice from heaven saying	3
	11:15	and there were loud voices in heaven, saying	3
	12:10	Then I heard a loud voice in heaven, proclaiming	3
	14: 2	a voice...like the sound of loud thunder;	3
	14: 7	He said in a loud voice, "Fear God	3
	14: 9	another angel...crying with a loud voice	3
	14:15	Another angel...calling with a loud voice	3
	14:18	another angel...called with a loud voice	3
	16: 1	Then I heard a loud voice from the temple	3
	16:17	and a loud voice came out of the temple	3
	19: 1	what seemed to be the loud voice of a great multitude	3
	19:17	with a loud voice he called to all the birds	3
	21: 3	I heard a loud voice from the throne saying	3

loud noise

1. ῥοιζηδόν, *rhoizēdon, 4853*

2Pe	3:10	then the heavens will pass away with a loud noise	1

loudly   *See also* shout loudly

1. λέγω, *legō, 3306*
2. πολύς, *polys, 4498*

Mat	9:27	two blind men followed him, crying loudly	1
Mrk	5:38	people weeping and wailing loudly.	2

love   *See also* free from love of money, show love

1. Contextual: Not in Greek
2. ἀγαπάω, *agapaō, 26*
3. ἀγάπη, *agapē, 27*
4. ἀγαπητός, *agapētos, 28*
5. αὐτός, *autos, 899*
6. φιλέω, *phileō, 5797*
7. φιλόστοργος, *philostorgos, 5816*

Mat	5:43	love your neighbor and hate your enemy.'	2
	5:44	I say to you, Love your enemies and pray for those	2
	5:46	For if you love those who love you, what reward	2
	5:46	For if you love those who love you, what reward	2
	6: 5	not be like the hypocrites; for they love to stand	6
	6:24	slave will either hate the one and love the other	2
	10:37	Whoever loves father or mother more than me	6
	10:37	and whoever loves son or daughter more than me	6
	19:19	You shall love your neighbor as yourself."	2
	22:37	love the Lord your God with all your heart	2
	22:39	'You shall love your neighbor as yourself.'	2
	23: 6	They love to have the place of honor at banquets	6
	24:12	the love of many will grow cold.	3
Mrk	10:21	Jesus, looking at him, loved him and said	2
	12:30	shall love the Lord your God with all your heart	2
	12:31	'You shall love your neighbor as yourself.'	2
	12:33	'to love him with all the heart	2
	12:33	'to love one's neighbor as oneself,'	2
Lke	6:27	Love your enemies, do good to those who hate you	2
	6:32	"If you love those who love you, what credit	2
	6:32	"If you love those who love you, what credit	2
	6:32	even sinners love those who love them.	2
	6:32	even sinners love those who love them.	2
	6:35	love your enemies, do good, and lend	2
	7: 5	for he loves our people,	2
	7:42	Now which of them will love him more?"	2
	7:47	one to whom little is forgiven, loves little."	2
	10:27	love the Lord your God with all your heart	2
	11:42	neglect justice and the love of God;	3
	11:43	For you love to have the seat of honor	2
	16:13	slave will either hate the one and love the other	2
	20:46	love to be greeted with respect in the marketplaces	6
Jhn	3:16	God so loved the world that he gave his only Son	2
	3:19	and people loved darkness rather than light	2
	3:35	The Father loves the Son and has placed all things	2
	5:20	The Father loves the Son	6
	5:42	I know that you do not have the love of God	3
	8:42	"If God were your Father, you would love me	2
	10:17	For this reason the Father loves me	2

	11: 3	"Lord, he whom you love is ill."	6
	11: 5	Jesus loved Martha and her sister and Lazarus	2
	11:36	the Jews said, "See how he loved him!"	6
	12:25	Those who love their life lose it	6
	12:43	for they loved human glory more than the glory	2
	13: 1	Having loved his own who were in the world	2
	13: 1	he loved them to the end.	2
	13:23	One of his disciples—the one whom Jesus loved	2
	13:34	that you love one another.	2
	13:34	Just as I have loved you	2
	13:34	you also should love one another.	2
	13:35	if you have love for one another."	3
	14:15	"If you love me, you will keep my commandments.	2
	14:21	and keep them are those who love me;	2
	14:21	those who love me will be loved by my Father	2
	14:21	those who love me will be loved by my Father	2
	14:21	I will love them and reveal myself to them."	2
	14:23	"Those who love me will keep my word	2
	14:23	my Father will love them	2
	14:24	Whoever does not love me does not keep my words;	2
	14:28	If you loved me, you would rejoice	2
	14:31	so that the world may know that I love the Father.	2
	15: 9	As the Father has loved me, so I have loved you;	2
	15: 9	As the Father has loved me, so I have loved you;	2
	15: 9	so I have loved you; abide in my love.	3
	15:10	you will abide in my love	3
	15:10	just as I…abide in his love.	3
	15:12	my commandment, that you love one another	2
	15:12	you love one another as I have loved you.	2
	15:13	No one has greater love than this	3
	15:17	these commands so that you may love one another.	2
	15:19	the world would love you as its own.	6
	16:27	for the Father himself loves you	6
	16:27	because you have loved me	6
	17:23	and have loved them even as you have loved me.	2
	17:23	and have loved them even as you have loved me.	2
	17:24	loved me before the foundation of the world.	2
	17:26	the love with which you have loved me	3
	17:26	the love with which you have loved me	2
	19:26	and the disciple whom he loved standing beside	2
	20: 2	the other disciple, the one whom Jesus loved	6
	21: 7	That disciple whom Jesus loved said to Peter	2
	21:15	"Simon son of John, do you love me more than these?"	2
	21:15	to him, "Yes, Lord; you know that I love you."	6
	21:16	"Simon son of John, do you love me?"	2
	21:16	to him, "Yes, Lord; you know that I love you."	6
	21:17	"Simon son of John, do you love me?"	6
	21:17	he said to him the third time, "Do you love me?"	6
	21:17	you know everything; you know that I love you."	6
	21:20	saw the disciple whom Jesus loved following	2
Rom	5: 5	God's love has been poured into our hearts	3
	5: 8	But God proves his love for us	3
	8:28	work together for good for those who love God	2
	8:35	Who will separate us from the love of Christ?	3
	8:37	more than conquerors through him who loved us.	2
	8:39	will be able to separate us from the love of God	3
	9:13	"I have loved Jacob, but I have hated Esau."	2
	12: 9	Let love be genuine; hate what is evil	3
	12:10	love one another with mutual affection;	7
	13: 8	Owe no one anything, except to love one another;	2
	13: 8	the one who loves another has fulfilled the law.	2
	13: 9	"Love your neighbor as yourself."	2
	13:10	Love does no wrong to a neighbor;	3
	13:10	therefore, love is the fulfilling of the law.	3
	14:15	you are no longer walking in love.	3
	15:30	I appeal to you…by the love of the Spirit	3
1Co	2: 9	what God has prepared for those who love him"	2
	4:21	with love in a spirit of gentleness?	3
	8: 1	Knowledge puffs up, but love builds up.	3
	8: 3	anyone who loves God is known by him.	2
	13: 1	speak in the tongues…but do not have love	3
	13: 2	but do not have love, I am nothing.	3
	13: 3	but do not have love, I gain nothing.	3
	13: 4	Love is patient; love is kind;	3
	13: 4	Love is patient; love is kind;	3
	13: 4	love is not envious or boastful or arrogant	3
	13: 8	Love never ends.	3
	13:13	And now faith, hope, and love abide, these three;	3
	13:13	and the greatest of these is love.	3
	14: 1	Pursue love and strive for the spiritual gifts	3
	16:14	Let all that you do be done in love.	3

	16:22	anyone be accursed who has no love for the Lord.	6
	16:24	My love be with all of you in Christ Jesus.	3
2Co	2: 4	to let you know the abundant love that I have	3
	2: 8	I urge you to reaffirm your love for him.	3
	5:14	For the love of Christ urges us on	3
	6: 6	kindness, holiness of spirit, genuine love	3
	8: 7	in utmost eagerness, and in our love for you	3
	8: 8	I am testing the genuineness of your love	3
	8:24	before the churches, show them the proof of your love	3
	9: 7	God loves a cheerful giver.	2
	11:11	why? Because I do not love you? God knows I do!	2
	12:15	If I love you more, am I to be loved less?	2
	12:15	If I love you more, am I to be loved less?	2
	13:11	the God of love and peace will be with you.	3
	13:13	the love of God, and the communion	3
Gal	2:20	Son of God, who loved me and gave himself for me.	3
	5: 6	faith working through love.	3
	5:13	through love become slaves to one another.	3
	5:14	"You shall love your neighbor as yourself."	2
	5:22	love, joy, peace, patience, kindness, generosity	3
Eph	1: 4	to be holy and blameless before him in love	3
	1:15	your love toward all the saints	3
	2: 4	out of the great love with which he loved us	3
	2: 4	out of the great love with which he loved us	3
	3:17	being rooted and grounded in love.	3
	3:19	to know the love of Christ	3
	4: 2	bearing with one another in love	3
	4:15	But speaking the truth in love	3
	4:16	the body's growth in building itself up in love.	3
	5: 2	live in love, as Christ loved us	3
	5: 2	live in love, as Christ loved us	2
	5:25	Husbands, love your wives	2
	5:25	just as Christ loved the church	2
	5:28	In the same way, husbands should love their wives	2
	5:28	He who loves his wife loves himself.	2
	5:28	He who loves his wife loves himself.	2
	5:33	Each of you, however, should love his wife as himself	2
	6:23	Peace be to the whole community, and love with faith	3
	6:24	an undying love for our Lord Jesus Christ.	2
Php	1: 9	prayer, that your love may overflow more and more	3
	1:16	These proclaim Christ out of love	3
	2: 1	any consolation from love	3
	2: 2	having the same love, being in full accord	3
	4: 1	my brothers and sisters, whom I love and long for	4
Col	1: 4	the love that you have for all the saints	3
	1: 8	has made known to us your love in the Spirit.	3
	2: 2	hearts to be encouraged and united in love,	3
	3:14	Above all, clothe yourselves with love	3
	3:19	Husbands, love your wives	2
1Th	1: 3	work of faith and labor of love	3
	3: 6	good news of your faith and love.	3
	3:12	may the Lord make you increase and abound in love	3
	3:12	just as we abound in love for you.	1
	4: 9	taught by God to love one another;	2
	4:10	indeed you do love all the brothers and sisters	5
	5: 8	put on the breastplate of faith and love	3
	5:13	esteem them very highly in love	3
2Th	1: 3	the love of everyone of you for one another	3
	2:10	because they refused to love the truth	3
	2:16	who loved us and through grace gave us eternal comfort	2
	3: 5	May the Lord direct your hearts to the love of God	3
1Ti	1: 5	But the aim of such instruction is love	3
	1:14	the faith and love that are in Christ Jesus.	3
	2:15	they continue in faith and love and holiness	3
	4:12	an example in speech and conduct, in love, in faith	3
	6:11	pursue righteousness, godliness, faith, love,	3
2Ti	1: 7	a spirit of power and of love and of self-discipline.	3
	1:13	in the faith and love that are in Christ Jesus.	3
	2:22	pursue righteousness, faith, love, and peace	3
	3:10	my patience, my love, my steadfastness	3
	4:10	Demas, in love with this present world	2
Tit	2: 2	sound in faith, in love, and in endurance.	3
	3:15	Greet those who love us in the faith.	6
Phm	1: 5	because I hear of your love	3
	1: 7	received much joy and encouragement from your love	3
	1: 9	yet I would rather appeal to you on the basis of love	3
Heb	1: 9	You have loved righteousness and hated wickedness;	2
	6:10	the love that you showed for his sake	3
	10:24	to provoke one another to love and good deeds	3
	12: 6	for the Lord disciplines those whom he loves	3
Jas	1:12	crown…Lord has promised to those who love him.	2

Jas	2: 5	that he has promised to those who love him?	2
	2: 8	"You shall love your neighbor as yourself."	2
1Pe	1: 8	have not seen him, you love him;	2
	1:22	love one another deeply from the heart.	2
	2:17	Honor everyone. Love the family of believers.	2
	4: 8	maintain constant love for one another	3
	4: 8	for love covers a multitude of sins.	3
	5:14	Greet one another with a kiss of love.	3
2Pe	1: 7	and mutual affection with love.	3
	2:15	Balaam…who loved the wages of doing wrong	2
1Jn	2: 5	in this person the love of God has reached perfection.	3
	2:10	Whoever loves a brother or sister lives in the light	2
	2:15	Do not love the world or the things in the world.	3
	2:15	love of the Father is not in those	3
	2:15	love…is not in those who love the world	2
	3: 1	See what love the Father has given us	3
	3:10	who do not love their brothers and sisters.	3
	3:11	that we should love one another.	2
	3:14	because we love one another.	2
	3:14	Whoever does not love abides in death.	2
	3:16	We know love by this, that he laid down his life	3
	3:17	How does God's love abide in anyone	3
	3:18	let us love, not in word or speech, but in truth	3
	3:23	we should believe…and love one another	2
	4: 7	Beloved, let us love one another	2
	4: 7	let us love one another, because love is from God;	3
	4: 7	everyone who loves is born of God and knows God.	2
	4: 8	Whoever does not love does not know God	2
	4: 8	for God is love.	3
	4: 9	God's love was revealed among us in this way:	3
	4:10	In this is love, not that we loved God	2
	4:10	not that we loved God but that he loved us	2
	4:10	not that we loved God but that he loved us	2
	4:11	since God loved us so much, we also ought to love	2
	4:11	we also ought to love one another.	2
	4:12	if we love one another, God lives in us	2
	4:12	God lives in us, and his love is perfected in us.	3
	4:16	we have known and believe the love that God has for us.	3
	4:16	God is love, and those who abide in love abide in God	3
	4:16	God is love, and those who abide in love abide in God	3
	4:17	Love has been perfected among us in this:	3
	4:18	There is no fear in love	3
	4:18	but perfect love casts out fear;	3
	4:18	whoever fears has not reached perfection in love.	3
	4:19	We love because he first loved us.	2
	4:19	We love because he first loved us.	2
	4:20	Those who say, "I love God," and hate	2
	4:20	do not love a brother or sister whom they have seen	2
	4:20	cannot love God whom they have not seen.	2
	4:21	those who love God must love their brothers and sisters	2
	4:21	those who love God must love their brothers and sisters	2
	5: 1	everyone who loves the parent loves the child.	2
	5: 1	everyone who loves the parent loves the child.	2
	5: 2	By this we know that we love the children of God	2
	5: 2	when we love God and obey his commandments.	2
	5: 3	the love of God is this, that we obey his commandments.	3
2Jn	1: 1	lady and her children, whom I love in the truth	2
	1: 3	from Jesus Christ…in truth and love.	3
	1: 5	new commandment…let us love one another.	2
	1: 6	this is love, that we walk according to his commandments;	3
3Jn	1: 1	the beloved Gaius, whom I love in truth.	2
	1: 6	testified to your love before the church.	3
Jde	1: 2	May mercy, peace, and love be yours in abundance.	3
	1:21	keep yourselves in the love of God;	3
Rev	1: 5	To him who loves us and freed us from our sins	2
	2: 4	you have abandoned the love you had at first.	3
	2:19	"I know your works—your love, faith, service,	3
	3: 9	and they will learn that I have loved you.	2
	3:19	I reprove and discipline those whom I love.	6
	22:15	everyone who loves and practices falsehood.	6

love a child

1. φιλότεκνος, *philoteknos, 5817*

Tit	2: 4	to love their husbands, to love their children	1

love a husband

1. φίλανδρος, *philandros, 5791*

Tit	2: 4	may encourage the young women to love their husbands	1

love for one another

1. φιλάδελφος, *philadelphos, 5790*

1Pe	3: 8	all of you, have…love for one another	1

love of money

1. φιλαργυρία, *philargyria, 5794*

1Ti	6:10	the love of money is a root of all kinds of evil	1

love of the brother and sister

1. φιλαδελφία, *philadelphia, 5789*

1Th	4: 9	Now concerning love of the brothers and sisters	1

mutual love

1. φιλαδελφία, *philadelphia, 5789*

Heb	13: 1	Let mutual love continue.	1
1Pe	1:22	so that you have genuine mutual love	1

love-feast

1. ἀγάπη, *agapē, 27*

Jde	1:12	These are blemishes on your love-feasts	1

lover of God

1. φιλόθεος, *philotheos, 5806*

2Ti	3: 4	lovers of pleasure rather than lovers of God	1

lover of goodness

1. φιλάγαθος, *philagathos, 5787*

Tit	1: 8	but he must be hospitable, a lover of goodness	1

lover of money

1. φιλάργυρος, *philargyros, 5795*

Lke	16:14	The Pharisees, who were lovers of money, heard all	1
2Ti	3: 2	people will be lovers of themselves, lovers of money	1

lover of pleasure

1. φιλήδονος, *philēdonos, 5798*

2Ti	3: 4	lovers of pleasure rather than lovers of God	1

lover of self

1. φίλαυτος, *philautos, 5796*

2Ti	3: 2	For people will be lovers of themselves,	1

not a lover of money

1. ἀφιλάργυρος, *aphilargyros, 921*

1Ti	3: 3	not quarrelsome, and not a lover of money.	1

loving kindness

1. φιλανθρωπία, *philanthrōpia, 5792*

Tit	3: 4	the goodness and loving kindness of God	1

low   *See also* bring low, make low

1. ἀγενής, *agenēs, 38*
2. ἔσχατος, *eschatos, 2274*
3. κατώτερος, *katōteros, 3005*

Lke	14: 9	you would start to take the lowest place.	2
	14:10	go and sit down at the lowest place	2
1Co	1:28	God chose what is low and despised in the world	1
Eph	4: 9	descended into the lower parts of the earth?	3

lower

1. καθίημι, *kathiēmi, 2768*
2. χαλάω, *chalaō, 5899*

Act	9:25	lowering him in a basket.	2
	10:11	being lowered to the ground by its four corners.	1
	11: 5	being lowered by its four corners;	1
	27:17	they lowered the sea anchor and so were driven.	2
	27:30	had lowered the boat into the sea	2

lowliness

1. ταπείνωσις, *tapeinōsis, 5428*

Lke	1:48	looked with favor on the lowliness of his servant.	1

lowly

1. ταπεινός, *tapeinos, 5424*

Lke	1:52	and lifted up the lowly;	1
Rom	12:16	do not be haughty, but associate with the lowly;	1
Jas	1: 9	Let the believer who is lowly boast in being raised up	1

loyal
1. γνήσιος, *gnēsios, 1188*

Php 4: 3 you also, my loyal companion, help these women   1
1Ti 1: 2 To Timothy, my loyal child in the faith: 1
Tit   1: 4 To Titus, my loyal child in the faith we share: 1

Lucius
1. Λούκιος, *Loukios, 3372*

Act 13: 1 Lucius of Cyrene   1
Rom 16:21 so do Lucius and Jason and Sosipater, my relatives.   1

Luke
1. Λουκᾶς, *Loukas, 3371*

Col 4:14 Luke, the beloved physician, and Demas greet you.   1
2Ti 4:11 Only Luke is with me.   1
Phm 1:24 Aristarchus, Demas, and Luke, my fellow workers.   1

lukewarm
1. χλιαρός, *chliaros, 5950*

Rev 3:16 you are lukewarm, and neither cold nor hot   1

lump
1. φύραμα, *phyrama, 5878*

Rom 9:21 out of the same lump one object for special use   1

luncheon
1. ἄριστον, *ariston, 756*

Lke 14:12 "When you give a luncheon or a dinner   1

lure
1. ἀπάτη, *apatē, 573*
2. ἐξέλκω, *exelkō, 1999*

Mat 13:22 and the lure of wealth choke the word   1
Mrk 4:19 the cares of the world, and the lure of wealth   1
Jas   1:14 by one's own desire, being lured and enticed   2

lust
1. ἐπιθυμέω, *epithymeō, 2121*
2. ἐπιθυμία, *epithymia, 2123*
3. σάρξ, *sarx, 4922*

Mat 5:28 who looks at a woman with lust has already   1
Rom 1:24 God gave them up in the lusts of their hearts   2
Eph 4:22 corrupt and deluded by its lusts   2
2Pe 1: 4 the corruption...in the world because of lust   2
     2:10 who indulge their flesh in depraved lust,   2
     3: 3 scoffing and indulging their own lusts   2
Jde   1: 7 indulged in sexual immorality and pursued unnatural lust   3
     1:16 malcontents; they indulge their own lusts;   2
     1:18 scoffers, indulging their own ungodly lusts."   2

lustful
1. ἐπιθυμία, *epithymia, 2123*

1Th 4: 5 not with lustful passion   1

luxury *See also* live in luxury
1. στρῆνος, *strēnos, 5140*
2. τρυφή, *tryphē, 5588*

Lke 7:25 live in luxury are in royal palaces.   2
Rev 18: 3 grown rich from the power of her luxury."   1

Lycaonia
1. Λυκαονία, *Lykaonia, 3377*

Act 14: 6 fled to Lystra and Derbe, cities of Lycaonia   1

Lycaonian language
1. Λυκαονιστί, *Lykaonisti, 3378*

Act 14:11 they shouted in the Lycaonian language   1

Lycia
1. Λυκία, *Lykia, 3379*

Act 27: 5 we came to Myra in Lycia.   1

Lydda
1. Λύδδα, *Lydda, 3375*

Act 9:32 he came down also to the saints living in Lydda.   1
     9:35 all the residents of Lydda and Sharon saw him   1
     9:38 Since Lydda was near Joppa   1

Lydia
1. Λυδία, *Lydia, 3376*

Act 16:14 A certain woman named Lydia, a worshiper of God   1
     16:40 leaving the prison they went to Lydia's home;   1

Lysanias
1. Λυσανίας, *Lysanias, 3384*

Lke 3: 1 Lysanias ruler of Abilene   1

Lysias
1. Λυσίας, *Lysias, 3385*

Act 23:26 "Claudius Lysias to his Excellency the governor   1
     24:22 "When Lysias the tribune comes down   1

Lystra
1. Λύστρα, *Lystra, 3388*

Act 14: 6 apostles learned of it and fled to Lystra and Derbe   1
     14: 8 In Lystra there was a man sitting   1
     14:21 returned to Lystra, then on to Iconium and Antioch.   1
     16: 1 Paul went on also to Derbe and to Lystra   1
     16: 2 He was well spoken of...in Lystra and Iconium.   1
2Ti 3:11 in Antioch, Iconium, and Lystra.   1

M

Maath
1. Μάαθ, *Maath, 3399*

Lke 3:26 son of Maath, son of Mattathias   1

Macedonia *See also* person of Macedonia
1. Μακεδονία, *Makedonia, 3423*
2. Μακεδών, *Makedōn, 3424*

Act 16: 9 there stood a man of Macedonia pleading with him   2
     16: 9 "Come over to Macedonia and help us."   1
     16:10 we immediately tried to cross over to Macedonia   1
     16:12 a leading city of the district of Macedonia   1
     18: 5 When Silas and Timothy arrived from Macedonia   1
     19:21 to go through Macedonia and Achaia   1
     19:22 he sent two of his helpers...to Macedonia   1
     20: 1 and saying farewell, he left for Macedonia.   1
     20: 3 he decided to return through Macedonia.   1
Rom 15:26 for Macedonia and Achaia have been pleased   1
1Co 16: 5 visit you after passing through Macedonia   1
     16: 5 for I intend to pass through Macedonia   1
2Co 1:16 I wanted to visit you on my way to Macedonia   1
     1:16 to come back to you from Macedonia   1
     2:13 I said farewell to them and went on to Macedonia.   1
     7: 5 For even when we came into Macedonia   1
     8: 1 grace...granted to the churches of Macedonia;   1
     11: 9 the friends who came from Macedonia.   1
Php 4:15 when I left Macedonia   1
1Th 1: 7 an example to all the believers in Macedonia   1
     1: 8 sounded forth from you not only in Macedonia   1
     4:10 love all the brothers and sisters throughout Macedonia.   1
1Ti 1: 3 I urge you, as I did when I was on my way to Macedonia   1

Macedonian
1. Μακεδών, *Makedōn, 3424*

Act 19:29 Macedonians who were Paul's travel companions.   1
     27: 2 Aristarchus, a Macedonian from Thessalonica.   1
2Co 9: 4 if some Macedonians come with me and find   1

madman
1. παραφρονέω, *paraphroneō, 4196*

2Co 11:23 I am talking like a madman   1

madness
1. παραφρονία, *paraphronia, 4197*

2Pe 2:16 a speechless donkey...restrained the prophet's madness.   1

Magadan
1. Μαγαδάν, *Magadan, 3400*

Mat 15:39 and went to the region of Magadan.   1

Magdalene
1. Μαγδαληνή, *Magdalēnē, 3402*

Mat 27:56 Among them were Mary Magdalene   1

Mat 27:61 Mary Magdalene and the other Mary were there 1
28: 1 Mary Magdalene and the other Mary 1
Mrk 15:40 among them were Mary Magdalene...and Salome. 1
15:47 Mary Magdalene and Mary the mother of Joses saw 1
16: 1 Mary Magdalene, and Mary the mother of James 1
16: 9 [he appeared first to Mary Magdalene] 1
Lke 8: 2 Mary, called Magdalene 1
24:10 Now it was Mary Magdalene, Joanna 1
Jhn 19:25 Mary the wife of Clopas, and Mary Magdalene. 1
20: 1 still dark, Mary Magdalene came to the tomb 1
20:18 Mary Magdalene went and announced to the disciples 1

magic *See also* practice magic
1. μαγεία, *mageia, 3404*

Act 8:11 for a long time he had amazed them with his magic. 1

magic art
1. περίεργος, *periergos, 4319*

Act 19:19 A number of those who practiced magic 1

magician
1. μάγος, *magos, 3407*

Act 13: 6 they met a certain magician 1
13: 8 the magician Elymas...opposed them 1

magistrate
1. ἄρχων, *archōn, 807*
2. στρατηγός, *stratēgos, 5130*

Lke 12:58 you go with your accuser before a magistrate 1
Act 16:20 When they had brought them before the magistrates 2
16:22 magistrates had them stripped of their clothing 2
16:35 When morning came, the magistrates sent the police 2
16:36 "The magistrates sent word to let you go; 2
16:38 police reported these words to the magistrates 2

magnate
1. μεγιστάν, *megistan, 3491*

Rev 6:15 Then the kings of the earth and the magnates 1
18:23 your merchants were the magnates of the earth 1

magnify
1. μεγαλύνω, *megalynō, 3486*

Lke 1:46 Mary said, "My soul magnifies the Lord 1

Magog
1. Μαγώγ, *Magōg, 3408*

Rev 20: 8 to deceive the nations...Gog and Magog 1

Mahaleleel
1. Μαλελεήλ, *Maleleēl, 3435*

Lke 3:37 son of Jared, son of Mahalaleel, son of Cainan, 1

maid
1. παιδίσκη, *paidiskē, 4087*

Act 12:13 a maid named Rhoda came to answer. 1

maim
1. κυλλός, *kyllos, 3245*

Mat 15:30 the lame, the maimed, the blind, the mute 1
15:31 the mute speaking, the maimed whole 1
18: 8 it is better for you to enter life maimed or lame 1
Mrk 9:43 it is better for you to enter life maimed 1

main *See* main *point*, main *street*

maintain
1. ἔχω, *echō, 2400*
2. κατέχω, *katechō, 2988*
3. τηρέω, *tēreō, 5498*

1Co 11: 2 maintain the traditions just as I handed them on 2
Eph 4: 3 every effort to maintain the unity of the Spirit 3
1Pe 4: 8 maintain constant love for one another 1

majestic
1. μεγαλοπρεπής, *megaloprepēs, 3485*

2Pe 1:17 that voice was conveyed to him by the Majestic Glory 1

majesty *See also* imperial majesty
1. μεγαλειότης, *megaleiotēs, 3484*
2. μεγαλωσύνη, *megalōsynē, 3488*

Act 19:27 she will be deprived of her majesty 1
Heb 1: 3 he sat down at the right hand of the Majesty on high 2
8: 1 right hand of the throne of the Majesty in the heavens 2
2Pe 1:16 but we had been eyewitnesses of his majesty. 1
Jde 1:25 to the only God...be glory, majesty, power 2

majority
1. πολύς, *polys, 4498*

Act 27:12 the majority was in favor of putting to sea from there 1
2Co 2: 6 This punishment by the majority is enough 1

make *See also* make *drink*, make *dwell*, make *fall*, make *rise*, make *see*, make *sit* down, make *stand*, make *waver*
1. Contextual: Not in Greek
2. αἰτέω, *aiteō, 160*
3. ἀναγκάζω, *anankazō, 337*
4. γίνομαι, *ginomai, 1181*
5. γράφω, *graphō, 1211*
6. διδῶ, *didō, 1442*
7. δίδωμι, *didōmi, 1443*
8. ἐγείρω, *egeirō, 1586*
9. εἰμί, *eimi, 1639*
10. εἰς, *eis, 1650*
11. ἔχω, *echō, 2400*
12. καθίστημι, *kathistēmi, 2770*
13. καταρτίζω, *katartizō, 2936*
14. κερδαίνω, *kerdainō, 3045*
15. κτίζω, *ktizō, 3231*
16. λέγω, *legō, 3306*
17. παρεισφέρω, *pareispherō, 4210*
18. παρέχω, *parechō, 4218*
19. ποιέω, *poieō, 4472*
20. ποίημα, *poiēma, 4473*
21. πρός, *pros, 4639*
22. τίθημι, *tithēmi, 5502*

Mat 3: 3 way of the Lord, make his paths straight.' " 19
4:19 me, and I will make you fish for people." 19
5:33 carry out the vows you have made to the Lord.' 1
5:36 head, for you cannot make one hair white or black. 19
9:16 and a worse tear is made. 4
12:16 ordered them not to make him known. 19
12:33 "Either make the tree good, and its fruit good; 19
12:33 or make the tree bad, and its fruit bad; 19
14:22 he made the disciples get into the boat 3
17: 4 if you wish, I will make three dwellings here 19
19: 4 one who made them at the beginning 15
19: 4 'made them male and female,' 19
20:12 you have made them equal to us 19
21:13 but you are making it a den of robbers." 19
23:15 to make a single convert 19
23:15 you make the new convert twice as much a child of hell 19
25:16 made five more talents. 14
25:17 who had the two talents made two more talents. 14
25:20 see, I have made five more talents.' 14
25:22 see, I have made two more talents.' 14
Mrk 1: 3 make his paths straight.' " 19
1:17 "Follow me and I will make you fish for people." 19
2:21 the new from the old, and a worse tear is made. 4
2:23 as they made their way 19
2:27 "The sabbath was made for humankind 4
3:12 he sternly ordered them not to make him known. 19
6:45 he made his disciples get into the boat 3
7:37 makes the deaf to hear and the mute to speak." 19
9: 5 let us make three dwellings 19
9:17 he has a spirit that makes him unable to speak; 1
10: 6 'God made them male and female.' 19
11:17 you have made it a den of robbers." 19
Lke 3: 4 make his paths straight. 19
3: 5 the crooked shall be made straight 10
3: 5 the rough ways made smooth; 10
5:34 "You cannot make wedding guests fast 19
9:33 let us make three dwellings 19
11:40 Did not the one who made the outside 19
11:40 one who made the outside make the inside also? 19
12:33 Make purses for yourselves 19

12:58	on the way make an effort to settle the case	7
13:22	teaching as he made his way to Jerusalem.	19
16: 6	bill, sit down quickly, and make it fifty.'	5
16: 7	to him, 'Take you bill and make it eighty.'	5
16: 9	make friends...by means of dishonest wealth	19
19:18	'Lord, your pound has made five pounds.'	19
19:46	you have made it a den of robbers."	19
20:43	until I make your enemies your footstool." '	22
23:26	the cross...and made him carry it behind Jesus.	1

Jhn
2:15	Making a whip of cords, he drove all of them	19
2:16	Stop making my Father's house a marketplace!"	19
4: 1	"Jesus is making and baptizing more disciples	19
5: 6	he said to him, "Do you want to be made well?"	4
5: 9	At once the man was made well	4
5:11	he answered them, "The man who made me well said	19
5:14	"See, you have been made well!	4
5:15	it was Jesus who had made him well.	19
5:18	making himself equal to God.	19
6:10	Jesus said, "Make the people sit down."	19
6:15	and take him by force to make him king	19
8:33	you mean by saying, 'You will be made free'?"	4
9: 6	made mud with the saliva	19
9:11	He answered, "The man called Jesus made mud	19
9:14	it was a sabbath day when Jesus made the mud	19
10:33	only a human being, are making yourself God."	19
12: 3	a pound of costly perfume made of pure nard	1
14:23	we will come to them and make our home with them.	19
15: 2	he prunes to make it bear more fruit.	1
18:18	police had made a charcoal fire	19

Act
2:35	until I make your enemies your footstool." '	22
2:36	God has made him both Lord and Messiah	19
3:12	by our own power or piety we had made him walk?	19
4:24	"Sovereign Lord, who made the heaven	19
7:27	'Who made you a ruler and a judge over us?	12
7:35	'Who made you a ruler and a judge?'	12
7:40	'Make gods for us who will lead the way for us;	19
7:43	the images that you made to worship;	19
7:44	he spoke to Moses, ordering him to make it	19
7:50	Did not my hand make all these things?'	19
8: 2	made loud lamentation over him.	19
9:39	tunics and other clothing that Dorcas had made	19
10:17	what to make of the vision that he had seen,	9
10:26	Peter made him get up, saying, "Stand up;	1
13:22	he made David their king.	8
13:34	give you the holy promises made to David.'	1
14: 5	an attempt was made by both Gentiles and Jews	4
14:15	the living God, who made the heaven and the earth	19
15:17	who has been making these things	19
17:24	The God who made the world and everything in it	19
17:26	From one ancestor he made all nations	19
19:24	a silversmith who made silver shrines of Artemis	19
19:26	saying that gods made with hands are not gods.	4
20: 3	when a plot was made against him by the Jews	4
20:28	of which the Holy Spirit has made you overseers	22
22: 1	listen to the defense that I now make before you."	1
24: 2	reforms have been made for this people	4
26: 6	hope in the promise made by God to our ancestors	4

Rom
4:11	to make him the ancestor of all who believe	9
4:17	"I have made you the father of many nations")	22
5:19	by...disobedience the many were made sinners	12
5:19	by the one man's...many will be made righteous.	12
6:12	to make you obey their passions.	10
9:20	"Why have you made me like this?"	19
9:21	to make out of the same lump one object for special	19
9:22	the objects of wrath that are made for destruction;	13
13:14	and make no provision for the flesh	19
14:19	Let us then pursue what makes for peace	1

1Co
6:15	make members of a prostitute? Never!	19
9:18	I may make the gospel free of charge	22
11: 8	man was not made from woman, but woman from man.	9
12:15	that would not make it any less a part of the body.	9
12:16	that would not make it any less a part of the body.	9
15:31	a boast that I make in Christ Jesus our Lord.	11

2Co
5:21	For our sake he made him to be sin who knew no sin	19

Gal
2: 8	making him an apostle to the circumcised	10
3:16	Now the promises were made to Abraham	16
6:11	See what large letters I make when I am writing	1
6:17	From now on, let no one make trouble for me;	18

Eph
1:22	has made him the head over all things	7
2:10	we are what he has made us, created in Christ Jesus	20
2:14	in his flesh he has made both groups into one	19

2:15	one new humanity in place of the two, thus making peace	19
4:27	do not make room for the devil.	7

1Th
2: 7	might have made demands as apostles of Christ.	9

1Ti
1:16	making me an example to those who would...believe	21
2: 1	thanksgivings be made for everyone	19
6:13	who...before Pontius Pilate made the good confession	1

Heb
1: 3	When he had made purification for sins	19
1: 7	Of the angels he says, "He makes his angels winds	19
1:13	until I make your enemies a footstool for your feet"?	22
8: 5	"See that you make everything	19
8: 9	like the covenant that I made with their ancestors	19
10:13	his enemies would be made a footstool for his feet."	22
11: 3	was made from things that are not visible.	4
12:13	make straight paths for your feet	19
12:19	a voice whose words made the hearers beg	1

Jas
3: 3	to make them obey us	1
3: 9	we curse those who are made in the likeness of God.	4
3:18	sown in peace for those who make peace.	19

1Pe
3:15	Always be ready to make your defense to anyone	21

2Pe
1: 5	make every effort to support your faith	17
2: 6	he condemned them...and made them an example	22

1Jn
1:10	If we say that we have not sinned, we make him a liar	19
2:19	But by going out they made it plain	1
5:10	Those who do not believe in God have made him a liar	19
5:15	we have obtained the requests made of him.	2

Rev
1: 6	made us to be a kingdom, priests serving his God	19
3: 9	I will make those of the synagogue of Satan	6
3: 9	make them come and bow down before your feet	19
3:12	I will make you a pillar in the temple of my God;	19
5:10	you have made them to be a kingdom and priests	19
11: 7	the beast...will make war on them and conquer	19
12:17	went off to make war on the rest of her children	19
13: 7	Also it was allowed to make war on the saints	19
13:12	it makes the earth and its inhabitants worship	19
13:13	even making fire come down from heaven to earth	19
13:14	telling them to make an image for the beast	19
14: 7	and worship him who made heaven and earth	19
17:16	they will make her desolate and naked;	19
19:19	kings...with their armies gathered to make war	19
21: 5	"See, I am making all things new."	19

make a bed
1. στρωννύω, *strōnnyō*, 5143

Act 9:34 Jesus Christ heals you; get up and make your bed!" 1

make a beginning
1. προενάρχομαι, *proenarchomai*, 4599

2Co 8: 6 as he had already made a beginning 1

make a calf
1. μοσχοποιέω, *moschopoieō*, 3674

Act 7:41 At that time they made a calf 1

make a captive
1. αἰχμαλωτεύω, *aichmalōteuō*, 169

Eph 4: 8 on high he made captivity itself a captive 1

make a choice
1. ἐκλέγομαι, *eklegomai*, 1721

Act 15: 7 in the early days God made a choice among you 1

make a commotion
1. θορυβέω, *thorybeō*, 2572

Mat 9:23 flute players and the crowd making a commotion 1
Mrk 5:39 "Why do you make a commotion and weep? 1

make a confession
1. ὁμολογέω, *homologeō*, 3933

1Ti 6:12 you made the good confession in the presence 1

make a covenant
1. διατίθημι, *diatithēmi*, 1416

Heb 8:10 This is the covenant that I will make 1
10:16 "This is the covenant that I will make with them 1

make a defense
1. ἀπολογέομαι, *apologeomai*, 664
2. ἀπολογία, *apologia*, 665

Act 19:33 tried to make a defense before the people. 1

Act 24:10 Paul replied: "I cheerfully make my defense   1
   25:16 had been given an opportunity to make a defense   2
   26: 2 I am to make my defense today   1
   26:24 While he was making this defense   1

make a difference
1. διαφέρω, *diapherō, 1422*

Gal   2: 6 (what they actually were makes no difference to me;   1

make a distinction
1. διακρίνω, *diakrinō, 1359*

Act 11:12 to go with them and not to make a distinction   1
   15: 9 he has made no distinction between them and us.   1
Jas   2: 4 have you not made distinctions among yourselves   1

make a eunuch
1. εὐνουχίζω, *eunouchizō, 2335*

Mat 19:12 who have been made eunuchs by others   1
   19:12 eunuchs who have made themselves eunuchs   1

make a good showing
1. εὐπροσωπέω, *euprosōpeō, 2349*

Gal   6:12 who want to make a good showing in the flesh   1

make a mistake
1. πταίω, *ptaiō, 4760*

Jas   3: 2 For all of us make many mistakes.   1
   3: 2 who makes no mistakes in speaking is perfect.   1

make a nest
1. κατασκηνόω, *kataskēnoō, 2942*

Mat 13:32 so that the birds of the air come and make nests   1
Mrk   4:32 birds of the air can make nests in its shade."   1
Lke 13:19 the birds of the air made nests in its branches."   1

make a payment
1. ἀποδίδωμι, *apodidōmi, 625*

Mat 18:25 ordered him to be sold…and payment to be made.   1

make a plan
1. βουλεύω, *bouleuō, 1086*

2Co   1:17 make my plans according to ordinary human standards   1

make a proclamation
1. κηρύσσω, *kēryssō, 3062*

1Pe   3:19 he went and made a proclamation to the spirits in prison   1

make a promise
1. ἐπαγγέλλομαι, *epangellomai, 2040*
2. λαλέω, *laleō, 3281*
3. ὁμολογέω, *homologeō, 3933*

Lke   1:55 according to the promise he made to our ancestors   2
Act   7:17 promise that God had made to Abraham   3
Gal   3:19 to whom the promise had been made;   1
Heb   6:13 When God made a promise to Abraham   1

make a revelation
1. ἀποκαλύπτω, *apokalyptō, 636*

1Co 14:30 If a revelation is made to someone else sitting   1

make a sacrifice
1. προσφέρω, *prospherō, 4712*

Act 21:26 the sacrifice would be made for each of them.   1

make a sacrifice of atonement
1. ἱλάσκομαι, *hilaskomai, 2661*

Heb   2:17 to make a sacrifice of atonement for the sins   1

make a slave
1. δουλόω, *douloō, 1530*
2. καταδουλόω, *katadouloō, 2871*

1Co   9:19 I have made myself a slave to all   1
2Co 11:20 put up with it when someone makes slaves of you   2

make a statement
1. λέγω, *legō, 3306*

Act 28:25 they were leaving, Paul made one further statement: 1

make a thing
1. ποίημα, *poiēma, 4473*

Rom   1:20 the things he has made.   1

make a visit
1. ἔρχομαι, *erchomai, 2262*

2Co   2: 1 not to make you another painful visit.   1

make [a will]
1. διατίθημι, *diatithēmi, 1416*

Heb   9:16 a will is involved, the death of the one who made it   1
   9:17 a will…not in force as long as the one who made it is alive   1

make alive
1. ζωοποιέω, *zōopoieō, 2443*

1Co 15:22 so all will be made alive in Christ.   1
Gal   3:21 if a law had been given that could make alive   1
1Pe   3:18 death in the flesh, but made alive in the spirit   1

make alive together
1. συζωοποιέω, *syzōopoieō, 5188*

Eph   2: 5 made us alive together with Christ   1
Col   2:13 God made you alive together with him   1

make an accusation
1. κατηγορέω, *katēgoreō, 2989*

Act 24:19 they ought…to make an accusation   1

make an accusation against
1. καταμαρτυρέω, *katamartyreō, 2909*

Mat 27:13 how many accusations they make against you?"   1

make an appeal
1. παρακαλέω, *parakaleō, 4151*

2Co   5:20 God is making his appeal through us;   1

make an arrangement
1. διατάσσω, *diatassō, 1411*

Act 20:13 he had made this arrangement   1

make an assertion
1. διαβεβαιόομαι, *diabebaioomai, 1331*

1Ti   1: 7 the things about which they make assertions.   1

make an attack
1. κατεφίσταμαι, *katephistamai, 2987*

Act 18:12 the Jews made a united attack on Paul   1

make an examination
1. διαγινώσκω, *diaginōskō, 1336*

Act 23:15 you want to make a more thorough examination   1

make an example
1. δειγματίζω, *deigmatizō, 1258*

Col   2:15 made a public example of them   1

make an excuse
1. παραιτέομαι, *paraiteomai, 4148*

Lke 14:18 they all alike began to make excuses.   1

make an offering
1. προσφέρω, *prospherō, 4712*

Lke   5:14 make an offering for your cleansing   1

make an orphan
1. ἀπορφανίζω, *aporphanizō, 682*

1Th   2:17 we were made orphans by being separated from you   1

make angry
1. παροργίζω, *parorgizō, 4239*

Rom 10:19 with a foolish nation I will make you angry."   1

make ashamed
1. ἐντρέπω, *entrepō, 1956*

1Co   4:14 I am not writing this to make you ashamed   1

make bitter
1. πικραίνω, *pikrainō, 4393*

Rev	8:11 died from the water, because it was made bitter.	1
	10:10 when I had eaten it, my stomach was made bitter.	1

make bright
1. φωτίζω, *phōtizō, 5894*

Rev	18: 1 and the earth was made bright with his splendor.	1

make broad
1. πλατύνω, *platynō, 4425*

Mat	23: 5 they make their phylacteries broad	1

make by human hands
1. χειροποίητος, *cheiropoiētos, 5935*

Act	17:24 God…does not live in shrines made by human hands	1
Eph	2:11 circumcision made in the flesh by human hands	1
Heb	9:24 not enter a sanctuary made by human hands	1

make captive
1. αἰχμαλωτίζω, *aichmalōtizō, 170*

Rom	7:23 making me captive to the law of sin	1

make careful search
1. ἐκζητέω, *ekzēteō, 1699*

1Pe	1:10 the prophets…made careful search and inquiry	1

make clean
1. καθαρίζω, *katharizō, 2751*

Mat	8: 2 "Lord, if you choose, you can make me clean."	1
	8: 3 saying, "I do choose. Be made clean!"	1
Mrk	1:40 "If you choose, you can make me clean."	1
	1:41 "I do choose. Be made clean!"	1
	1:42 the leprosy left him, and he was made clean.	1
Lke	5:12 "Lord, if you choose, you can make me clean."	1
	5:13 "I do choose. Be made clean."	1
	17:14 as they went, they were made clean.	1
	17:17 "Were not ten made clean? But the other nine	1
Act	10:15 "What God has made clean, you must not call profane."	1
	11: 9 'What God has made clean, you must not call profane.'	1

make clear
1. Contextual: Not in Greek
2. δηλόω, *dēloō, 1317*
3. ἐμφανίζω, *emphanizō, 1872*

2Co	4: 7 may be made clear that this extraordinary power	1
Heb	11:14 for people who speak in this way make it clear	3
2Pe	1:14 as indeed our Lord Jesus Christ has made clear to me.	2

make competent
1. ἱκανόω, *hikanoō, 2655*

2Co	3: 6 who has made us competent to be ministers	1

make complete
1. καταρτίζω, *katartizō, 2936*
2. πληρόω, *plēroō, 4444*

Jhn	17:13 they may have my joy made complete in themselves.	2
Php	2: 2 make my joy complete: be of the same mind	2
Heb	13:21 make you complete in everything good	1

make confident
1. πείθω, *peithō, 4275*

Php	1:14 made confident in the Lord by my imprisonment	1

make crooked
1. διαστρέφω, *diastrephō, 1406*

Act	13:10 stop making crooked the straight paths of the Lord?	1

make disciples
1. μαθητεύω, *mathēteuō, 3411*

Mat	28:19 Go therefore and make disciples of all nations	1
Act	14:21 After they…had made many disciples	1

make earlier
1. προάγω, *proagō, 4575*

1Ti	1:18 the prophecies made earlier about you	1

make every effort
1. σπουδάζω, *spoudazō, 5079*
2. σπουδαίως, *spoudaiōs, 5081*

Eph	4: 3 making every effort to maintain the unity of the Spirit	1
Tit	3:13 Make every effort to send Zenas…on their way	2
Heb	4:11 Let us therefore make every effort to enter that rest	1
2Pe	1:15 I will make every effort so that after my departure	1

make evident
1. φανερόω, *phaneroō, 5746*

2Co	11: 6 in all things we have made this evident to you.	1

make foolish
1. μωραίνω, *mōrainō, 3701*

1Co	1:20 Has not God made foolish the wisdom of the world?	1

make for
1. ἔξειμι[1], *exeimi[1], 1996*
2. κατέχω, *katechō, 2988*
3. πρός, *pros, 4639*

Lke	19:42 on this day the things that make for peace!	3
Act	27:40 they made for the beach.	2
	27:43 jump overboard…and make for the land	1

make free
1. ἐλευθερόω, *eleutheroō, 1802*

Jhn	8:32 the truth will make you free."	1
	8:36 So if the Son makes you free, you will be free	1

make full
1. πληρόω, *plēroō, 4444*

Act	2:28 you will make me full of gladness	1

make full use
1. καταχράομαι, *katachraomai, 2974*

1Co	9:18 so as not to make full use of my rights	1

make fully known
1. πληρόω, *plēroō, 4444*

Col	1:25 to make the word of God fully known	1

make glad
1. εὐφραίνω, *euphrainō, 2370*

2Co	2: 2 if I cause you pain, who is there to make me glad	1

make great
1. ὑψόω, *hypsoō, 5738*

Act	13:17 The God of this people…made the people great	1

make havoc
1. πορθέω, *portheō, 4514*

Act	9:21 "Is not this the man who made havoc in Jerusalem	1

make holy
1. ἁγιάζω, *hagiazō, 39*

1Co	7:14 For the unbelieving husband is made holy	1
	7:14 the unbelieving wife is made holy	1
Eph	5:26 in order to make her holy by cleansing her	1

make inquiry
1. ἐξεραυνάω, *exeraunaō, 2001*

1Pe	1:10 the prophets…made careful search and inquiry	1

make intercession
1. ἐντυγχάνω, *entynchanō, 1961*

Heb	7:25 since he always lives to make intercession	1

make it   *See* make [a will]

make jealous
1. παραζηλόω, *parazēloō, 4143*

Rom	10:19 make you jealous of those who are not a nation;	1
	11:11 so as to make Israel jealous.	1
	11:14 in order to make my own people jealous, and thus	1

make judgment
1. κρίνω, *krinō, 3212*

Mat   7: 2 For with the judgment you make   1

make known

1. ἀναγνωρίζω, *anagnōrizō, 341*
2. γινώσκω, *ginōskō, 1182*
3. γνωρίζω, *gnōrizō, 1192*
4. δηλόω, *dēloō, 1317*
5. ἐξηγέομαι, *exēgeomai, 2007*
6. σημαίνω, *sēmainō, 4955*
7. φανερόω, *phaneroō, 5746*

Lke   2:15 which the Lord has made known to us."   3
        2:17 they made known what had been told   3
       24:35 how he had been made known to them   2
Jhn   1:18 who has made him known.   5
       15:15 because I have made known to you everything   3
       17: 6 "I have made your name known to those   7
       17:26 I made your name known to them   3
       17:26 and I will make it known   3
Act   2:28 You have made known to me the ways of life;   3
        7:13 Joseph made himself known to his brothers   1
Rom   9:22 What if God, desiring...to make known his power 3
        9:23 in order to make known the riches of his glory 3
       16:26 is made known to all the Gentiles   3
2Co   7:12 in order that your zeal for us might be made known 7
Eph   1: 9 he has made known to us   3
        3: 3 the mystery was made known to me by revelation 3
        3: 5 In former generations this mystery was not made known 3
        3:10 might now be made known to the rulers   3
        6:19 to make known with boldness the mystery of the gospel 3
Php   4: 6 let your requests be made known to God.   3
Col   1: 8 has made known to us your love in the Spirit.   4
        1:27 To them God chose to make known   3
2Pe   1:16 made known to you the power and coming of our Lord 3
Rev   1: 1 he made it known by sending his angel   6

make light

1. ἀμελέω, *ameleō, 288*

Mat 22: 5 But they made light of it and went away   1

make like

1. ὁμοιόω, *homoioō, 3929*

Rom   9:29 fared like Sodom and been made like Gomorrah."   1

make low

1. ἐλαττόω, *elattoō, 1783*
2. ταπεινόω, *tapeinoō, 5427*

Lke   3: 5 every mountain and hill shall be made low   2
Heb   2: 7 You have made them...lower than the angels;   1
        2: 9 for a little while was made lower than the angels 1

make melody

1. ψάλλω, *psallō, 6010*

Eph   5:19 singing and making melody to the Lord   1

make mention

1. μνημονεύω, *mnēmoneuō, 3648*

Heb 11:22 made mention of the exodus of the Israelites   1

make money

1. ἐργασία, *ergasia, 2238*
2. κερδαίνω, *kerdainō, 3045*

Act 16:19 owners saw that their hope of making money was gone 1
Jas   4:13 spend a year there, doing business and making money." 2

make more

1. προσεργάζομαι, *prosergazomai, 4664*

Lke 19:16 'Lord, your pound has made ten more pounds.'   1

make much

1. ζηλόω, *zēloō, 2420*

Gal   4:17 They make much of you, but for no good purpose;   1
        4:17 to exclude you, so that you may make much of them. 1
        4:18 It is good to be made much of for a good purpose 1

make obsolete

1. παλαιόω, *palaioō, 4096*

Heb   8:13 he has made the first one obsolete.   1

make one's aim

1. φιλοτιμέομαι, *philotimeomai, 5818*

2Co   5: 9 we make it our aim to please him.   1

make one's ambition

1. φιλοτιμέομαι, *philotimeomai, 5818*

Rom 15:20 I make it my ambition to proclaim the good news   1

make one's home

1. κατοικέω, *katoikeō, 2997*

Mat   2:23 he made his home in a town called Nazareth   1
        4:13 left Nazareth and made his home in Capernaum   1

make one's own

1. καταλαμβάνω, *katalambanō, 2898*

Php   3:12 I press on to make it my own   1
        3:12 because Christ Jesus has made me his own.   1
        3:13 I do not consider that I have made it my own;   1

make one's way

1. ἐνδύνω, *endynō, 1905*
2. ἔρχομαι, *erchomai, 2262*

Jhn   5: 7 while I am making my way, someone else steps down 2
2Ti   3: 6 those who make their way into households   1

make peace

1. εἰρηνοποιέω, *eirēnopoieō, 1647*

Col   1:20 making peace through the blood of his cross.   1

make perfect

1. ἐπιτελέω, *epiteleō, 2200*
2. τελειόω, *teleioō, 5457*
3. τελέω, *teleō, 5464*

2Co   7: 1 making holiness perfect in the fear of God.   1
       12: 9 for power is made perfect in weakness."   3
Heb   2:10 make the pioneer of their salvation perfect   2
        5: 9 having been made perfect, he became the source   2
        7:19 (for the law made nothing perfect);   2
        7:28 the oath...appoints a Son who has been made perfect 2
       10: 1 it can never...make perfect those who approach. 2
       11:40 they would not, apart from us, be made perfect. 2
       12:23 to the spirits of the righteous made perfect   2

make preparation

1. ἑτοιμάζω, *hetoimazō, 2286*
2. κατασκευάζω, *kataskeuazō, 2941*

Mat 26:17 "Where do you want us to make the preparations   1
Mrk 14:12 make the preparations for you to eat the Passover?" 1
       14:15 Make preparations for us there."   1
Lke 22: 9 "Where do you want us to make preparations for it?" 1
       22:12 Make preparations for us there."   1
Heb   9: 6 Such preparations having been made   2

make progress

1. προκόπτω, *prokoptō, 4621*

2Ti   3: 9 But they will not make much progress   1

make public

1. διαγγέλλω, *diangellō, 1334*

Act 21:26 making public the completion of the...purification 1

make ready

1. ἑτοιμάζω, *hetoimazō, 2286*
2. ἑτοιμασία, *hetoimasia, 2288*

Lke   1:17 to make ready a people prepared for the Lord."   1
        9:52 he sent messengers...to make ready for him;   1
Eph   6:15 make you ready to proclaim the gospel of peace   2
Rev   8: 6 angels who had...trumpets made ready to blow them. 1
       19: 7 and his bride has made herself ready;   1

make repayment

1. ἀποδίδωμι, *apodidōmi, 625*

1Ti   5: 4 and make some repayment to their parents;   1

make rich

1. πλουτίζω, *ploutizō, 4457*

2Co   6:10 as poor, yet making many rich;   1

make room

1. χωρέω, *chōreō, 6003*

2Co 7: 2 Make room in your hearts for us;   1

make sacred

1. ἁγιάζω, *hagiazō, 39*

Mat 23:17 or the sanctuary that has made the gold sacred?   1
    23:19 or the altar that makes the gift sacred?   1

make secure

1. ἀσφαλίζω, *asphalizō, 856*
2. περιποιέω, *peripoieō, 4347*

Mat 27:64 Therefore command the tomb to be made secure   1
    27:65 go, make it as secure as you can."   1
    27:66 they went with the guard and made the tomb secure   1
Lke 17:33 who try to make their life secure will lose it   2

make sorry

1. λυπέω, *lypeō, 3382*

2Co 7: 8 For even if I made you sorry with my letter   1

make straight

1. εὐθύνω, *euthynō, 2316*

Jhn 1:23 'Make straight the way of the Lord,' "   1

make strong

1. δυναμόω, *dynamoō, 1540*
2. στερεόω, *stereoō, 5105*

Act 3: 7 his feet and ankles were made strong.   2
    3:16 his name itself has made this man strong   2
Col 1:11 May you be made strong with all the strength   1

make stumble

1. πρόσκομμα, *proskomma, 4682*
2. προσκόπτω, *proskoptō, 4684*
3. σκανδαλίζω, *skandalizō, 4997*

Rom 9:33 in Zion a stone that will make people stumble   1
    14:21 anything that makes your brother or sister stumble.   2
2Co 11:29 Who is made to stumble, and I am not indignant?   3
1Pe 2: 8 "A stone that makes them stumble   1

make subject

1. ὑποτάσσω, *hypotassō, 5718*

Php 3:21 to make all things subject to himself.   1
1Pe 3:22 angels, authorities, and powers made subject to him.   1

make the most

1. ἐξαγοράζω, *exagorazō, 1973*

Eph 5:16 making the most of the time   1
Col 4: 5 making the most of the time.   1

make up

1. ἀναπληρόω, *anaplēroō, 405*
2. προαιρέω, *proaireō, 4576*
3. τίθημι, *tithēmi, 5502*

Lke 21:14 So make up your minds   3
1Co 16:17 because they have made up for your absence;   1
2Co 9: 7 Each of you must give as you have made up your mind   2
Php 2:30 risking his life to make up for those services   1

make up one's mind

1. κρίνω, *krinō, 3212*

2Co 2: 1 I made up my mind not to make you another…visit.   1

make use

1. χράομαι, *chraomai, 5968*

1Co 7:21 make use of your present condition   1
    9:12 Nevertheless, we have not made use of this right   1
    9:15 I have made no use of any of these rights   1

make visible

1. φανερόω, *phaneroō, 5746*

2Co 4:10 Jesus may also be made visible in our bodies.   1
    4:11 so that the life of Jesus may be made visible   1

make void

1. ἀκυρόω, *akyroō, 218*

Mat 15: 6 you make void the word of God.   1

Mrk 7:13 thus making void the word of God   1

make war

1. πολεμέω, *polemeō, 4482*

Rev 2:16 make war against them with the sword of my mouth.   1
    17:14 they will make war on the Lamb   1
    19:11 and in righteousness he judges and makes war.   1

make well

1. σῴζω, *sōzō, 5392*

Mat 9:21 touch his cloak, I will be made well."   1
    9:22 "Take heart…your faith has made you well."   1
    9:22 And instantly the woman was made well.   1
Mrk 5:23 so that she may be made well, and live."   1
    5:28 "If I but touch his clothes, I will be made well."   1
    5:34 "Daughter, your faith has made you well;   1
    10:52 "Go; your faith has made you well."   1
Lke 8:48 "Daughter, your faith has made you well;   1
    17:19 go on your way; your faith has made you well."   1

make white

1. λευκαίνω, *leukainō, 3326*

Rev 7:14 they have washed their robes and made them white   1

make with hands

1. χειροποίητος, *cheiropoiētos, 5935*

Mrk 14:58 will destroy this temple that is made with hands   1
Heb 9:11 perfect tent (not made with hands   1

make with human hands

1. χειροποίητος, *cheiropoiētos, 5935*

Act 7:48 does not dwell in houses made with human hands;   1

make worthy

1. ἀξιόω, *axioō, 546*
2. καταξιόω, *kataxioō, 2921*

2Th 1: 5 to make you worthy of the kingdom of God   2
    1:11 that our God will make you worthy of his call   1

not make with hands

1. ἀχειροποίητος, *acheiropoiētos, 942*

Mrk 14:58 I will build another, not made with hands.' "   1
2Co 5: 1 a house not made with hands   1

maker *See* mischief maker

Malchus

1. Μάλχος, *Malchos, 3438*

Jhn 18:10 The slave's name was Malchus.   1

malcontent

1. μεμψίμοιρος, *mempsimoiros, 3523*

Jde 1:16 These are grumblers and malcontents;   1

male

1. ἄρσην, *arsēn, 781*

Mat 19: 4 'made them male and female,'   1
Mrk 10: 6 'God made them male and female.'   1
Lke 2:23 "Every firstborn male shall be designated as holy   1
Gal 3:28 there is no longer male and female;   1
Rev 12: 5 she gave birth to a son, a male child, who is to rule   1
    12:13 pursued the woman who had given birth to the male child.   1

male prostitute

1. μαλακός, *malakos, 3434*

1Co 6: 9 adulterers, male prostitutes, sodomites,   1

malice

1. κακία, *kakia, 2798*
2. πονηρία, *ponēria, 4504*

Mat 22:18 Jesus, aware of their malice, said   2
Rom 1:29 every…wickedness, evil, covetousness, malice.   1
1Co 5: 8 the old yeast, the yeast of malice and evil   1
Eph 4:31 wrangling and slander, together with all malice   1
Col 3: 8 wrath, malice, slander, and abusive language   1
Tit 3: 3 passing our days in malice and envy   1
1Pe 2: 1 Rid yourselves…of all malice, and all guile   1

malign

1. Contextual: Not in Greek
2. βλασφημέω, *blasphēmeō, 1059*
3. καταλαλέω, *katalaleō, 2895*

Mat	10:25	how much more will they malign	1
1Pe	2:12	though they malign you as evildoers	3
	3:16	so that, when you are maligned	3
2Pe	2: 2	these teachers the way of truth will be maligned.	2

Malta

1. Μελίτη, *Melitē, 3514*

Act	28: 1	then learned that the island was called Malta.	1

man

See also blind man, certain man, dead man, deaf man, devout man, each man, good man, hired man, innocent man, leading man, married man, mighty man, old man, one man, oppressed man, paralyzed man, poor man, rich man, righteous man, sick man, slave man, strong man, this man, unmarried man, wise man, young man

1. Contextual: Not in Greek
2. ἀδελφός, *adelphos, 81*
3. ἀνήρ, *anēr, 467*
4. ἄνθρωπος, *anthrōpos, 476*
5. ἄρσην, *arsēn, 781*
6. αὐτός, *autos, 899*
7. εἷς, *heis, 1651*
8. ὅς, *hos, 4005*
9. ὅστις, *hostis, 4015*
10. οὗτος, *houtos, 4047*
11. τὶς, *tis, 5516*
12. τοιοῦτος, *toioutos, 5525*

Mat	7:24	will be like a wise man who built his house	3
	7:26	will be like a foolish man who built his house	3
	8: 9	For I also am a man under authority, with soldiers	4
	8:20	but the Son of Man has nowhere to lay his head."	4
	8:27	amazed, saying, "What sort of man is this	1
	9: 6	you may know that the Son of Man has authority	4
	9: 9	he saw a man called Matthew	4
	10:23	before the Son of Man comes.	4
	10:35	For I have come to set a man against his father	4
	11:19	the Son of Man came eating and drinking	4
	12: 8	For the Son of Man is lord of the sabbath."	4
	12:10	a man was there with a withered hand	4
	12:13	Then he said to the man, "Stretch out your hand."	4
	12:32	Whoever speaks a word against the Son of Man	4
	12:40	the Son of Man will be in the heart of the earth.	4
	13:37	"The one who sows the good seed is the Son of Man;	4
	13:41	The Son of Man will send his angels	4
	14:21	who ate were about five thousand men, besides	3
	15:38	who had eaten were four thousand men, besides	3
	16:13	"Who do people say that the Son of Man is?"	4
	16:27	"For the Son of Man is to come with his angels	4
	16:28	before they see the Son of Man coming	4
	17: 9	until after the Son of Man has been raised	4
	17:12	the Son of Man is about to suffer at their hands."	4
	17:14	a man came to him, knelt before him	4
	17:22	Son of Man is going to be betrayed into human hands	4
	19: 3	"Is it lawful for a man to divorce his wife	4
	19: 5	'For this reason a man shall leave his father	4
	19:10	"If such is the case of a man with his wife	4
	19:28	when the Son of Man is seated on the throne	4
	20:18	the Son of Man will be handed over	4
	20:28	the Son of Man came not to be served but to serve	4
	21:28	"What do you think? A man had two sons;	4
	22:11	a man there who was not wearing a wedding robe	4
	22:24	'If a man dies childless,	11
	24:27	so will be the coming of the Son of Man.	4
	24:30	the sign of the Son of Man will appear in heaven	4
	24:30	'the Son of Man coming on the clouds of heaven'	4
	24:37	so will be the coming of the Son of Man.	4
	24:39	so too will be the coming of the Son of Man.	4
	24:44	the Son of Man is coming at an unexpected hour.	4
	25:14	"For it is as if a man, going on a journey	4
	25:24	'Master, I knew that you were a harsh man	4
	25:31	"When the Son of Man comes in his glory	4
	26: 2	the Son of Man will be handed over	4
	26:24	The Son of Man goes as it is written of him	4
	26:24	woe to that one by whom the Son of Man is betrayed!	4
	26:45	Son of Man is betrayed into the hands of sinners.	4
	26:48	"The one I will kiss is the man; arrest him."	6
	26:64	From now on you will see the Son of Man	4
	26:72	"I do not know the man."	4
	26:74	"I do not know the man!"	4
	27:32	As they went out, they came upon a man from Cyrene	4
	27:57	there came a rich man from Arimathea	4
Mrk	1:23	in their synagogue a man with an unclean spirit	4
	2:10	Son of Man has authority on earth to forgive sins"	4
	2:28	the Son of Man is lord even of the sabbath."	4
	3: 1	a man was there who had a withered hand.	4
	3: 3	he said to the man who had the withered hand	4
	3: 5	said to the man, "Stretch out your hand."	4
	5: 2	a man out of the tombs with an unclean spirit	4
	5: 8	"Come out of the man, you unclean spirit!"	4
	5:15	right mind, the very man who had had the legion;	1
	5:18	the man who had been possessed by demons	1
	6: 2	"Where did this man get all this?	1
	6:17	For Herod himself had sent men who arrested John	1
	6:20	knowing that he was a righteous and holy man	3
	6:44	had eaten the loaves numbered five thousand men	3
	8:24	man looked up and said, "I can see people	1
	8:31	the Son of Man must undergo great suffering,	4
	8:38	of them the Son of Man will also be ashamed	4
	9: 9	until after the Son of Man had risen	4
	9:12	How then is it written about the Son of Man	4
	9:31	"The Son of Man is to be betrayed	4
	10: 2	"Is it lawful for a man to divorce his wife?"	3
	10: 4	"Moses allowed a man to write a certificate	1
	10: 7	'For this reason a man shall leave his father	4
	10:17	a man ran up and knelt before him, and asked	7
	10:33	Son of Man will be handed over to the chief priests	4
	10:45	Son of Man came not to be served but to serve	4
	12: 1	"A man planted a vineyard	4
	12:19	if a man's brother dies, leaving a wife	11
	12:19	the man shall marry the widow and raise up children	2
	13:26	they will see 'the Son of Man coming in clouds'	4
	13:34	It is like a man going on a journey	4
	14:13	a man carrying a jar of water will meet you;	4
	14:21	For the Son of Man goes as it is written of him	4
	14:21	woe to that one by whom the Son of Man is betrayed!	4
	14:41	Son of Man is betrayed into the hands of sinners.	4
	14:44	"The one I will kiss is the man;	6
	14:62	Son of Man seated at the right hand of the Power,'	4
	14:71	"I do not know this man you are talking about."	4
	15: 7	a man called Barabbas was in prison with the rebels	1
	15:12	"Then what do you wish me to do with the man	8
	15:39	he said, "Truly this man was God's Son!"	4
Lke	1:27	a virgin engaged to a man whose name was Joseph	3
	2:25	Now there was a man in Jerusalem	4
	2:25	this man was righteous and devout	4
	4:33	a man who had the spirit of an unclean demon	4
	5: 8	"Go away from me, Lord, for I am a sinful man!"	3
	5:12	there was a man covered with leprosy.	3
	5:18	men came, carrying a paralyzed man on a bed.	3
	5:18	men came, carrying a paralyzed man on a bed.	4
	5:24	Son of Man has authority on earth to forgive	4
	6: 5	"The Son of Man is lord of the sabbath."	4
	6: 6	was a man there whose right hand was withered.	4
	6: 8	he said to the man who had the withered hand	3
	6:22	revile you…on account of the Son of Man.	4
	6:48	like a man building a house, who dug deeply	4
	6:49	like a man who built a house on the ground	4
	7: 8	I also am a man set under authority	4
	7:12	a man who had died was being carried out.	1
	7:20	When the men had come to him, they said	3
	7:34	the Son of Man has come eating and drinking	4
	8:27	a man of the city who had demons met him.	3
	8:29	the unclean spirit to come out of the man.	4
	8:33	Then the demons came out of the man	4
	8:35	found the man from whom the demons had gone	4
	8:38	The man from whom the demons had gone begged	3
	8:41	Just then there came a man named Jairus	3
	9:14	For there were about five thousand men.	3
	9:22	"The Son of Man must undergo great suffering,	4
	9:26	of them the Son of Man will be ashamed	4
	9:30	Suddenly they saw two men, Moses and Elijah,	3
	9:32	his glory and the two men who stood with him.	3
	9:38	Just then a man from the crowd shouted, "Teacher	3
	9:44	The Son of Man is going to be betrayed	4
	9:58	the Son of Man has nowhere to lay his head."	4
	10:30	"A man was going down from Jerusalem to Jericho	4

10:36	the man who fell into the hands of the robbers?"	1
11:30	so the Son of Man will be to this generation.	4
12: 8	the Son of Man also will acknowledge	4
12:10	who speaks a word against the Son of Man	4
12:16	"The land of a rich man produced abundantly.	4
12:40	the Son of Man is coming at an unexpected hour."	4
13: 6	"A man had a fig tree planted in his vineyard;	11
14: 2	in front of him, there was a man who had dropsy.	4
15:11	Jesus said, "There was a man who had two sons.	4
16: 1	"There was a rich man who had a manager	4
16:19	"There was a rich man	4
17:22	will long to see one of the days of the Son of Man	4
17:24	so will the Son of Man be in his day.	4
17:26	so too it will be in the days of the Son of Man.	4
17:30	on the day that the Son of Man is revealed.	4
18: 8	yet, when the Son of Man comes	4
18:10	"Two men went up to the temple to pray	4
18:31	everything that is written about the Son of Man	4
18:40	Jesus stood still and ordered the man to be brought	6
19: 2	A man was there named Zacchaeus;	3
19:10	For the Son of Man came to seek out and to save	4
19:21	I was afraid of you, because you are a harsh man;	4
19:22	You knew, did you, that I was a harsh man	4
20: 9	"A man planted a vineyard, and leased it	4
20:28	Moses wrote for us that if a man's brother dies	11
20:28	man shall marry the widow and raise up children	2
21:27	will see 'the Son of Man coming in a cloud'	4
21:36	to stand before the Son of Man."	4
22:10	a man carrying a jar of water will meet you;	4
22:22	the Son of Man is going as it has been determined	4
22:48	with a kiss that you are betraying the Son of Man?"	4
22:58	Peter said, "Man, I am not!"	4
22:60	Peter said, "Man, I do not know what you	4
22:63	the men who were holding Jesus began to mock him	3
22:69	from now on the Son of Man will be seated	4
23: 4	no basis for an accusation against this man."	4
23: 6	he asked whether the man was a Galilean.	4
23:14	said to them, "You brought me this man	4
23:14	have not found this man guilty of any…charges	4
23:19	a man who had been put in prison	9
23:25	He released the man they asked for,	8
23:26	they seized a man, Simon of Cyrene	11
23:47	"Certainly this man was innocent."	4
23:50	there was a good and righteous man named Joseph	3
24: 4	suddenly two men in dazzling clothes stood beside	3
24: 5	the men said to them, "Why do you look for	1
24: 7	the Son of Man must be handed over	4
Jhn 1: 6	was a man sent from God, whose name was John.	4
1:13	born, not of blood…or of the will of man	3
1:30	'After me comes a man who ranks ahead of me	3
1:51	ascending and descending upon the Son of Man."	4
3:13	one who descended from heaven, the Son of Man.	4
3:14	so must the Son of Man be lifted up	4
4:29	"Come and see a man who told me everything	4
4:50	The man believed the word that Jesus spoke to him	4
5: 5	One man was there who had been ill	4
5: 9	At once the man was made well	4
5:10	the Jews said to the man who had been cured	1
5:11	answered them, "The man who made me well said to me	1
5:12	They asked him, "Who is the man who said to you	4
5:13	the man who had been healed did not know who	1
5:15	The man went away and told the Jews	4
5:27	because he is the Son of Man.	4
6:27	which the Son of Man will give you.	4
6:53	unless you eat the flesh of the Son of Man	4
6:62	if you were to see the Son of Man ascending	4
7:22	you circumcise a man on the sabbath.	4
7:23	If a man receives circumcision on the sabbath	4
7:23	I healed a man's whole body on the sabbath?	4
7:35	"Where does this man intend to go	1
8:28	"When you have lifted up the Son of Man	4
8:40	a man who has told you the truth	4
9: 1	As he walked along, he saw a man blind from birth.	4
9: 6	and spread the mud on the man's eyes	6
9: 8	"Is this not the man who used to sit and beg?"	1
9: 9	He kept saying, "I am the man."	1
9:11	He answered, "The man called Jesus made mud	4
9:13	the man who had formerly been blind.	6
9:16	"This man is not from God	4
9:16	"How can a man who is a sinner perform such signs?"	4
9:18	the parents of the man who had received his sight	6

9:24	they called the man who had been blind	4
9:24	We know that this man is a sinner."	4
9:30	The man answered, "Here is an astonishing thing!	4
9:35	"Do you believe in the Son of Man?"	4
11:47	we to do? This man is performing many signs.	4
11:50	to have one man die for the people	4
12:23	"The hour…for the Son of Man to be glorified.	4
12:34	you say that the Son of Man must be lifted up?	4
12:34	Who is this Son of Man?"	4
13:31	"Now the Son of Man has been glorified	4
18:17	"You are not also one of this man's disciples	4
18:26	relative of the man whose ear Peter had cut off	8
18:29	"What accusation do you bring against this man?"	4
19: 5	Pilate said to them, "Here is the man!"	4
19:31	to have the legs of the crucified men broken	6
Act 1:10	suddenly two men in white robes stood by them.	3
1:11	said, "Men of Galilee, why do you stand looking up	3
1:21	one of the men who have accompanied us	3
2:14	"Men of Judea and all who live in Jerusalem	3
2:22	Jesus of Nazareth, a man attested to you by God	3
2:23	this man…you crucified and killed	1
3: 2	a man lame from birth was being carried in.	3
3:16	his name itself has made this man strong	10
4: 9	asked how this man has been healed	4
4:13	realized that they were uneducated and ordinary men	4
4:14	saw the man who had been cured	4
4:22	man on whom this sign of healing had been performed	4
5: 1	a man named Ananias, with the consent of his wife	3
5:14	great numbers of both men and women	3
5:25	the men whom you put in prison	3
5:28	you are determined to bring this man's blood on us."	4
5:34	ordered the men to be put outside for a short time.	4
5:35	consider…what you propose to do to these men.	4
5:36	a number of men, about four hundred, joined him;	3
5:38	keep away from these men and let them alone;	4
6: 3	select from among yourselves seven men of good standing	3
6: 5	Stephen, a man full of faith and the Holy Spirit	3
6: 6	They had these men stand before the apostles	8
6:11	Then they secretly instigated some men to say	3
6:13	"This man never stops saying things	4
7:26	'Men, you are brothers; why do you wrong each other?'	3
7:27	the man who was wronging his neighbor	1
7:56	the Son of Man standing at the right hand of God!"	4
8: 2	Devout men buried Stephen	3
8: 3	dragging off both men and women	3
8: 9	Now a certain man named Simon	3
8:12	they were baptized, both men and women.	3
9: 2	found any who belonged to the Way, men or women	3
9: 7	The men who were traveling with him	3
9:12	he has seen in a vision a man named Ananias come	3
9:13	I have heard from many about this man	3
9:21	"Is not this the man who made havoc in Jerusalem	1
9:33	There he found a man named Aeneas	4
9:38	disciples…sent two men to him with the request	3
10: 1	In Caesarea there was a man named Cornelius	3
10: 5	Now send men to Joppa	3
10:17	suddenly the men sent by Cornelius	3
10:19	three men are searching for you.	3
10:21	Peter went down to the men and said, "I am the one	3
10:22	a centurion, an upright and God-fearing man	3
10:30	suddenly a man in dazzling clothes stood before me.	3
11: 3	saying, "Why did you go to uncircumcised men	3
11:11	three men, sent to me from Caesarea, arrived	3
11:12	we entered the man's house.	3
11:20	among them were some men of Cyprus and Cyrene	3
11:24	a good man, full of the Holy Spirit and of faith.	3
13: 7	proconsul, Sergius Paulus, an intelligent man,	3
13:21	Saul son of Kish, a man of the tribe of Benjamin	3
13:22	a man after my heart, who will carry out all my wishes.'	3
14: 8	In Lystra there was a man sitting	3
14:10	the man sprang up and began to walk.	1
15:22	decided to choose men from among their members	3
16: 9	there stood a man of Macedonia pleading with him	3
16:17	"These men are slaves of the Most High God	4
16:20	they said, "These men are disturbing our city;	4
16:35	sent the police, saying, "Let those men go."	4
16:37	uncondemned, men who are Roman citizens	4
17:12	not a few Greek women and men of high standing.	3
17:31	the world judged…by a man whom he has appointed	3
18: 7	went to the house of a man named Titius Justus	11
18:13	"This man is persuading people to worship God	4

Act	18:24	an eloquent man, well-versed in the scriptures.	3
	19:16	the man with the evil spirit leaped on them	4
	19:24	A man named Demetrius, a silversmith	11
	19:25	"Men…we get our wealth from this business.	3
	19:37	You have brought these men here	3
	21:11	bind the man who owns this belt	3
	21:23	We have four men who are under a vow.	3
	21:26	Then Paul took the men	3
	21:28	This is the man who is teaching everyone everywhere	4
	22: 4	both men and women and putting them in prison	3
	22:12	Ananias, who was a devout man according to the law	3
	22:26	This man is a Roman citizen."	4
	23: 9	"We find nothing wrong with this man.	3
	23:21	more than forty of their men are lying in ambush	3
	23:27	This man was seized by the Jews	3
	23:30	there would be a plot against the man	3
	24: 5	We have, in fact, found this man a pestilent fellow	3
	24:20	Or let these men here tell	6
	25: 5	if there is anything wrong about the man	3
	25:14	a man here who was left in prison by Felix.	3
	25:17	and ordered the man to be brought.	3
	25:22	"I would like to hear the man myself."	4
	25:23	the prominent men of the city.	3
	26:31	"This man is doing nothing to deserve death	4
	26:32	"This man could have been set free	4
	27:21	"Men, you should have listened to me	3
	27:25	So keep up your courage, men	4
	28: 4	"This man must be a murderer;	4
Rom	1:27	the men…giving up natural intercourse with women	5
	1:27	Men committed shameless acts with men	5
	1:27	Men committed shameless acts with men	5
	5:12	just as sin came into the world through one man	4
	5:15	the free gift in the grace of the one man, Jesus	4
	5:19	For just as by the one man's disobedience	4
	7: 3	an adulteress if she lives with another man	3
	7: 3	marries another man, she is not an adulteress.	3
	7:24	Wretched man that I am! Who will rescue me	4
1Co	5: 1	a man is living with his father's wife.	11
	5: 4	on the man who has done such a thing.	1
	5: 5	you are to hand this man over to Satan	12
	7: 1	"It is well for a man not to touch a woman."	4
	11: 3	understand that Christ is the head of every man	3
	11: 4	Any man who prays…with something on his head	3
	11: 7	For a man ought not to have his head veiled	3
	11: 7	woman is the reflection of man.	3
	11: 8	man was not made from woman, but woman from man.	3
	11: 8	man was not made from woman, but woman from man.	3
	11: 9	Neither was man created for the sake of woman	3
	11: 9	the sake of woman, but woman for the sake of man.	3
	11:11	woman is not independent of man or man independent	3
	11:11	not independent of man or man independent of woman.	3
	11:12	just as woman came from man	3
	11:12	so man comes through woman;	3
	11:14	if a man wears long hair, it is degrading to him	3
	15:45	"The first man, Adam, became a living being";	4
	15:47	The first man was from the earth, a man of dust;	4
	15:47	The first man was from the earth, a man of dust;	1
	15:47	the second man is from heaven.	4
	15:48	As was the man of dust	1
	15:48	as is the man of heaven	1
	15:49	as we have borne the image of the man of dust	1
	15:49	we will also bear the image of the man of heaven.	1
Gal	5: 3	to every man who lets himself be circumcised	4
Eph	5:31	"For this reason a man will leave his father	4
1Ti	2: 8	in every place the men should pray	3
	2:12	no woman…to have authority over a man;	3
	6:11	as for you, man of God, shun all this;	4
2Ti	3: 9	as in the case of those two men	1
Heb	7: 6	this man, who does not belong to their ancestry	1
Rev	1:13	midst of the lampstands I saw one like the Son of Man	4
	14:14	seated on the cloud was one like the Son of Man	4

man and woman

    1. ἄνθρωπος, *anthrōpos, 476*

Eph	6: 7	as to the Lord and not to men and women	1
2Pe	1:21	men and women moved by the Holy Spirit spoke	1

man from Nazareth

    1. Ναζαρηνός, *Nazarēnos, 3716*

Mrk	14:67	"You also were with Jesus, the man from Nazareth."	1

man of Tarsus

    1. Ταρσεύς, *Tarseus, 5432*

Act	9:11	a man of Tarsus named Saul.	1

man of violence

    1. ὑβριστής, *hybristēs, 5616*

1Ti	1:13	blasphemer, a persecutor, and a man of violence.	1

Manaen

    1. Μαναήν, *Manaēn, 3441*

Act	13: 1	Manaen a member of the court of Herod	1

manage

    1. προΐστημι, *proistēmi, 4613*

1Ti	3: 4	He must manage his own household well	1
	3: 5	does not know how to manage his own household	1
	3:12	let them manage their children…well;	1

manage a household

    1. οἰκοδεσποτέω, *oikodespoteō, 3866*

1Ti	5:14	bear children, and manage their households	1

management

    1. οἰκονομία, *oikonomia, 3873*

Lke	16: 2	Give me an accounting of your management	1

manager

    1. ἐπίτροπος, *epitropos, 2208*
    2. οἰκονομέω, *oikonomeō, 3872*
    3. οἰκονομία, *oikonomia, 3873*
    4. οἰκονόμος, *oikonomos, 3874*

Mat	20: 8	the owner of the vineyard said to his manager	1
Lke	12:42	"Who then is the faithful and prudent manager	4
	16: 1	"There was a rich man who had a manager	4
	16: 2	you cannot be my manager any longer.'	2
	16: 3	the manager said to himself, 'What will I do	4
	16: 4	so that, when I am dismissed as manager,	3
	16: 8	his master commended the dishonest manager	4

good manager of household

    1. οἰκουργός, *oikourgos, 3877*

Tit	2: 5	chaste, good managers of the household, kind	1

Manasseh

    1. Μανασσῆς, *Manassēs, 3442*

Mat	1:10	Hezekiah the father of Manasseh	1
	1:10	and Manasseh the father of Amos	1
Rev	7: 6	from the tribe of Manasseh twelve thousand,	1

manger

    1. φάτνη, *phatnē, 5764*

Lke	2: 7	laid him in a manger	1
	2:12	lying in a manger."	1
	2:16	the child lying in the manger.	1
	13:15	untie his ox or his donkey from the manger	1

manifestation

    1. ἐπιφάνεια, *epiphaneia, 2211*
    2. φανέρωσις, *phanerōsis, 5748*

1Co	12: 7	To each is given the manifestation of the Spirit	2
2Th	2: 8	annihilating him by the manifestation of his coming.	1
1Ti	6:14	until the manifestation of our Lord Jesus Christ	1
Tit	2:13	the manifestation of the glory of our great God	1

manifold

    1. ποικίλος, *poikilos, 4476*

1Pe	4:10	Like good stewards of the manifold grace of God	1

manna

    1. μάννα, *manna, 3445*

Jhn	6:31	Our ancestors ate the manna in the wilderness;	1
	6:49	Your ancestors ate the manna in the wilderness	1
Heb	9: 4	in which there were a golden urn holding the manna	1
Rev	2:17	To everyone who conquers I will give some…manna	1

manner *See also* unworthy manner, worthy manner

    1. οὕτως, *houtōs, 4048*
    2. τρόπος, *tropos, 5573*

Jde 1: 7 in the same manner as they, indulged   2
Rev 11: 5 must be killed in this manner.   1

like manner

1. ὁμοίως, *homoiōs*, 3931

Lke 16:25 Lazarus in like manner evil things;   1

manure

1. κόπριον, *koprion*, 3162

Lke 13: 8 until I dig around it and put manure on   1

manure pile

1. κοπρία, *kopria*, 3161

Lke 14:35 fit neither for the soil nor for the manure pile;   1

many *See also* many *ways,* many *words*

1. ἕως, *heōs*, 2401
2. ἱκανός, *hikanos*, 2653
3. ὅσος, *hosos*, 4012
4. ὄχλος, *ochlos*, 4063
5. πλῆθος, *plēthos*, 4436
6. πολλάκις, *pollakis*, 4490
7. πολύς, *polys*, 4498
8. τοσοῦτος, *tosoutos*, 5537

Mat 3: 7 when he saw many Pharisees and Sadducees   7
     7:13 and there are many who take it.   7
     7:22 On that day many will say to me, 'Lord, Lord   7
     7:22 and do many deeds of power in your name?'   7
     8:11 I tell you, many will come from east and west   7
     8:16 That evening they brought to him many   7
     9:10 many tax collectors and sinners came   7
    10:31 you are of more value than many sparrows.   7
    12:15 Many crowds followed him, and he cured all   7
    13:17 I tell you, many prophets and righteous people   7
    13:58 he did not do many deeds of power there   7
    15:30 the blind, the mute, and many others.   7
    18:21 As many as seven times?"   1
    19:22 for he had many possessions.   7
    19:30 many who are first will be last   7
    20:28 to give his life a ransom for many."   7
    22:14 For many are called, but few are chosen."   7
    24: 5 For many will come in my name, saying   7
    24: 5 'I am the Messiah!' and they will lead many astray.   7
    24:10 Then many will fall away, and they will betray   7
    24:11 many false prophets will arise   7
    24:11 false prophets will arise and lead many astray.   7
    24:12 the love of many will grow cold.   7
    26:28 my blood…which is poured out for many   7
    26:60 though many false witnesses came forward.   7
    27:52 many bodies of the saints who had fallen asleep   7
    27:53 entered the holy city and appeared to many.   7
    27:55 Many women were also there   7
Mrk 1:34 cured many who were sick with various diseases   7
     1:34 and cast out many demons;   7
     2: 2 So many gathered around   7
     2:15 many tax collectors and sinners were also sitting   7
     2:15 there were many who followed him.   7
     3:10 he had cured many   7
     4:33 With many such parables he spoke the word   7
     5: 9 He replied, "My name is Legion; for we are many."   7
     5:26 She had endured much under many physicians   7
     6: 2 many who heard him were astounded. They said   7
     6:13 They cast out many demons, and anointed with oil   7
     6:13 anointed with oil many who were sick   7
     6:31 For many were coming and going   7
     6:33 Now many saw them going and recognized them   7
     7: 4 many other traditions that they observe   7
    10:22 for he had many possessions.   7
    10:31 many who are first will be last   7
    10:45 to give his life a ransom for many."   7
    10:48 Many sternly ordered him to be quiet   7
    11: 8 Many people spread their cloaks on the road   7
    12: 5 so it was with many others;   7
    12:41 Many rich people put in large sums.   7
    13: 6 Many will come in my name and say, 'I am he!'   7
    13: 6 and they will lead many astray.   7
    14:24 my blood…which is poured out for many.   7
    14:56 For many gave false testimony against him   7
    15:41 many other women who had come up with him   7
Lke 1: 1 many have undertaken to set down an orderly account   7

      1:14 many will rejoice at his birth   7
      1:16 turn many of the people of Israel to the Lord   7
      2:34 the falling and the rising of many in Israel   7
      2:35 inner thoughts of many will be revealed   7
      3:18 So, with many other exhortations, he proclaimed   7
      4:25 were many widows in Israel in the time of Elijah   7
      4:27 There were also many lepers in Israel   7
      4:41 Demons also came out of many, shouting   7
      5: 6 they caught so many fish   7
      5:15 many crowds would gather to hear   7
      7:21 Jesus had just then cured many people of diseases   7
      7:21 given sight to many who were blind.   7
      7:47 her sins, which were many, have been forgiven;   7
      8: 3 Joanna…and Susanna, and many others   7
      8:29 (For many times it had seized him;   7
      8:30 "Legion"; for many demons had entered him.   7
     10:24 many prophets and kings desired to see   7
     10:40 Martha was distracted by her many tasks;   7
     12: 7 you are of more value than many sparrows.   7
     12:19 Soul, you have ample goods laid up for many years;   7
     13:24 many, I tell you, will try to enter   7
     14:16 "Someone gave a great dinner and invited many.   7
     21: 8 many will come in my name and say, 'I am he!'   7
     22:65 They kept heaping many other insults on him   7
Jhn 2:23 many believed in his name because they saw the signs   7
     4:39 Many Samaritans from that city believed in him   7
     4:41 And many more believed because of his word.   7
     5: 3 In these lay many invalids—blind, lame   5
     6: 9 But what are they among so many people?"   8
     6:60 When many of his disciples heard it, they said   7
     6:66 Because of this many of his disciples turned back   7
     7:31 Yet many in the crowd believed in him   7
     8:30 saying these things, many believed in him.   7
    10:20 Many of them were saying, "He has a demon   7
    10:32 shown you many good works from the Father.   7
    10:41 Many came to him, and they were saying,   7
    10:42 many believed in him there.   7
    11:19 many of the Jews had come to Martha and Mary   7
    11:45 Many of the Jews therefore…believed in him   7
    11:47 we to do? This man is performing many signs.   7
    11:55 many went up from the country to Jerusalem   7
    12:11 that many of the Jews were deserting   7
    12:37 he had performed so many signs in their presence   8
    12:42 many, even of the authorities, believed in him.   7
    14: 2 In my Father's house there are many dwelling places.   7
    19:20 Many of the Jews read this inscription   7
    20:30 Now Jesus did many other signs   7
    21: 6 to haul it in because there were so many fish.   5
    21:11 though there were so many, the net was not torn.   8
    21:25 there are also many other things that Jesus did;   7
Act 1: 3 presented himself alive…by many convincing proofs   7
     1: 5 baptized with the Holy Spirit not many days from now."   7
     2:40 he testified with many other arguments and exhorted   7
     2:43 many wonders and signs were being done   7
     3:24 all the prophets, as many as have spoken   3
     4: 4 many of those who heard the word believed;   7
     4:34 as many as owned lands or houses   3
     5:12 Now many signs and wonders were done   7
     6: 7 a great many of the priests   4
     8: 7 spirits…came out of many who were possessed;   7
     8: 7 many others who were paralyzed or lame were cured.   7
     8:25 many villages of the Samaritans.   7
     9:13 I have heard from many about this man   7
     9:42 many believed in the Lord.   7
    10:27 he went in and found that many had assembled;   7
    12:12 many had gathered and were praying.   2
    13:31 for many days he appeared   7
    13:43 many Jews and devout converts to Judaism   7
    13:48 as many as had been destined for eternal life   3
    14:21 After they…had made many disciples   2
    14:22 saying, "It is through many persecutions   7
    15:35 and there, with many others, they taught   7
    16:18 She kept doing this for many days.   7
    17: 4 as did a great many of the devout Greeks   5
    17:12 Many of them therefore believed   7
    18: 8 many of the Corinthians…became believers   7
    18:10 there are many in this city who are my people."   7
    19:18 many of those who became believers confessed   7
    20: 8 There were many lamps in the room upstairs   2
    24:10 many years you have been a judge over this nation.   7
    25: 7 bringing many serious charges against him   7

Act	26: 9	I...was convinced that I ought to do many things	7
	26:10	I not only locked up many of the saints in prison	7
	27:20	neither sun nor stars appeared for many days	7
	28:10	They bestowed many honors on us	7
Rom	4:17	"I have made you the father of many nations")	7
	4:18	that he would become "the father of many nations,"	7
	5:15	if the many died through the one man's trespass	7
	5:15	the grace of God...abounded for the many.	7
	5:16	the free gift following many trespasses brings	7
	5:19	by...disobedience the many were made sinners	7
	5:19	by the one man's...many will be made righteous.	7
	12: 4	For as in one body we have many members	7
	12: 5	so we, who are many, are one body in Christ	7
	15:23	I desire, as I have for many years, to come to you	7
	16: 2	a benefactor of many and of myself as well.	7
1Co	1:26	not many of you were wise by human standards	7
	1:26	not many were powerful	7
	1:26	not many were of noble birth.	7
	4:15	you do not have many fathers.	7
	8: 5	as in fact there are many gods and many lords—	7
	8: 5	as in fact there are many gods and many lords—	7
	10:17	we who are many are one body	7
	10:33	not seeking my own advantage, but that of many	7
	11:30	For this reason many of you are weak and ill	7
	12:12	For just as the body is one and has many members	7
	12:12	all the members of the body, though many, are one	7
	12:14	body does not consist of one member but of many.	7
	12:20	As it is, there are many members, yet one body.	7
	14:10	There are doubtless many different kinds of sounds	8
	16: 9	there are many adversaries.	7
2Co	1:11	so that many will give thanks on our behalf	7
	1:11	granted us through the prayers of many.	7
	2: 4	anguish of heart and with many tears	7
	2:17	we are not peddlers of God's word like so many;	7
	6:10	as poor, yet making many rich;	7
	8:22	and found eager in many matters	7
	9:12	also overflows with many thanksgivings to God.	7
	11:18	since many boast according to human standards	7
	11:27	in toil...through many a sleepless night	6
	12:21	I may have to mourn over many who previously sinned	7
Gal	1:14	I advanced in Judaism beyond many among my people	7
	3:16	"And to offsprings," as of many;	7
	3:27	As many of you as were baptized into Christ	3
Php	3:18	For many live as enemies of the cross of Christ;	7
1Ti	6: 9	trapped by many senseless and harmful desires	7
	6:10	pierced themselves with many pains.	7
	6:12	confession in the presence of many witnesses.	7
2Ti	2: 2	have heard from me through many witnesses	7
Tit	1:10	There are also many rebellious people	7
Heb	2:10	in bringing many children to glory	7
	9:28	Christ...offered once to bear the sins of many	7
	11:12	"as many as the stars of heaven	5
	12:15	through it many become defiled.	7
Jas	3: 1	Not many of you should become teachers,	7
	3: 2	For all of us make many mistakes.	7
2Pe	2: 2	Even so, many will follow their licentious ways	7
1Jn	2:18	so now many antichrists have come.	7
	4: 1	many false prophets have gone out into the world.	7
2Jn	1: 7	Many deceivers have gone out into the world	7
Rev	1:15	his voice was like the sound of many waters.	7
	5:11	I heard the voice of many angels	7
	8:11	the waters became wormwood, and many died	7
	9: 9	like the noise of many chariots with horses	7
	10:11	prophesy again about many peoples and nations	7
	14: 2	a voice from heaven like the sound of many waters	7
	17: 1	the great whore who is seated on many waters	7
	19: 6	like the sound of many waters	7
	19:12	and on his head are many diadems;	7

great many

1. ἱκανός, *hikanos, 2653*

Act	11:24	a great many people were brought to the Lord.	1
	11:26	and taught a great many people	1

how many

1. πόσος, *posos, 4531*

Mat	15:34	Jesus asked them, "How many loaves have you?"	1
	16: 9	and how many baskets you gathered?	1
	16:10	and how many baskets you gathered?	1
	27:13	how many accusations they make against you?"	1
Mrk	6:38	"How many loaves have you? Go and see."	1

	8: 5	He asked them, "How many loaves do you have?"	1
	8:19	how many baskets full of broken pieces	1
	8:20	how many baskets full of broken pieces	1
	15: 4	See how many charges they bring against you."	1
Lke	15:17	'How many of my father's hired hands have bread	1
Act	21:20	how many thousands of believers there are among	1

many in number

1. πολύς, *polys, 4498*

Heb	7:23	the former priests were many in number	1

many things

1. πολύς, *polys, 4498*

Mat	13: 3	he told them many things in parables, saying:	1
	25:21	I will put you in charge of many things;	1
	25:23	I will put you in charge of many things;	1
Mrk	4: 2	He began to teach them many things in parables	1
	6:34	he began to teach them many things.	1
	7:13	you do many things like this."	1
	9:12	that he is to go through many sufferings	1
	15: 3	the chief priests accused him of many things.	1
Lke	10:41	you are worried and distracted by many things;	1
	11:53	and to cross-examine him about many things	1
Jhn	16:12	"I still have many things to say to you	1

marble

1. μάρμαρος, *marmaros, 3454*

Rev	18:12	articles of costly wood, bronze, iron, and marble	1

march up

1. ἀναβαίνω, *anabainō, 326*

Rev	20: 9	They marched up over the breadth of the earth	1

marital　*See* have marital relations

Mark

1. Μᾶρκος, *Markos, 3453*

Act	12:12	the mother of John whose other name was Mark	1
	12:25	John, whose other name was Mark.	1
	15:37	wanted to take with them John called Mark.	1
	15:39	Barnabas took Mark with him	1
Col	4:10	Mark the cousin of Barnabas	1
2Ti	4:11	Get Mark and bring him with you	1
Phm	1:24	so do Mark, Aristarchus, Demas, and Luke	1
1Pe	5:13	sends you greetings; and so does my son Mark.	1

mark　*See also* brand mark, miss the mark, remove mark of circumcision

1. σημεῖον, *sēmeion, 4956*
2. τύπος, *typos, 5596*
3. χάραγμα, *charagma, 5916*

Jhn	20:25	"Unless I see the mark of the nails in his hands	2
	20:25	put my finger in the mark of the nails	2
2Th	3:17	This is the mark in every letter of mine;	1
Rev	13:16	to be marked on the right hand or the forehead	3
	13:17	that no one can buy or sell who does not have the mark	3
	14: 9	receive a mark on their foreheads or on their hands	3
	14:11	and for anyone who receives the mark of its name."	3
	16: 2	those who had the mark of the beast	3
	19:20	those who had received the mark of the beast	3
	20: 4	had not received its mark on their foreheads	3

mark with a seal

1. σφραγίζω, *sphragizō, 5381*

Eph	1:13	marked with the seal of the promised Holy Spirit;	1
	4:30	marked with a seal for the day of redemption.	1
Rev	7: 3	until we have marked the servants of our God with a seal	1

market

1. ἀγορά, *agora, 59*

Mrk	7: 4	they do not eat anything from the market unless	1

meat market

1. μάκελλον, *makellon, 3425*

1Co	10:25	Eat whatever is sold in the meat market	1

marketplace

1. ἀγορά, *agora, 59*
2. ἀγοραῖος, *agoraios, 61*

3. ἐμπόριον, *emporion, 1866*

Mat 11:16	It is like children sitting in the marketplaces	1
20: 3	he saw others standing idle in the marketplace;	1
23: 7	greeted with respect in the marketplaces	1
Mrk 6:56	they laid the sick in the marketplaces	1
12:38	to be greeted with respect in the marketplaces	1
Lke 7:32	They are like children sitting in the marketplace	1
11:43	to be greeted with respect in the marketplaces.	1
20:46	love to be greeted with respect in the marketplaces	1
Jhn 2:16	Stop making my Father's house a marketplace!"	3
Act 16:19	and dragged them into the marketplace	1
17: 5	help of some ruffians in the marketplaces	2
17:17	he argued…in the marketplace every day	1

marriage   *See also* give in marriage, marriage *bed*, promise in marriage

1. γαμέω, *gameō, 1138*
2. γαμίζω, *gamizō, 1139*
3. γάμος, *gamos, 1141*
4. παρθενία, *parthenia, 4220*

Lke 2:36	seven years after her marriage	4
1Co 7:38	he who refrains from marriage will do better.	2
1Ti 4: 3	They forbid marriage and demand abstinence	1
Heb 13: 4	Let marriage be held in honor by all	3
Rev 19: 7	for the marriage of the Lamb has come	3
19: 9	those who are invited to the marriage supper	3

married man

1. γαμέω, *gameō, 1138*

1Co 7:33	married man is anxious about the affairs of the world	1

married woman

1. γαμέω, *gameō, 1138*

1Co 7:34	married woman is anxious about the affairs of the world	1

marrow

1. μυελός, *myelos, 3678*

Heb 4:12	until it divides…joints from marrow;	1

marry

1. Contextual: Not in Greek
2. ἀνήρ + γυνή, *anēr + gynē, 467 + 1222*
3. ἀνήρ + γυνή + ἔχω, *anēr + gynē + echō, 467 + 1222 + 2400*
4. γαμέω, *gameō, 1138*
5. γαμέω + γυνή, *gameō + gynē, 1138 + 1222*
6. γαμίζω, *gamizō, 1139*
7. γίνομαι, *ginomai, 1181*
8. γυνή + ἀνήρ, *gynē + anēr, 1222 + 467*
9. ἐπιγαμβρεύω, *epigambreuō, 2102*
10. ἔχω, *echō, 2400*
11. ἔχω + γυνή, *echō + gynē, 2400 + 1222*
12. ἔχω + ὁ + ἀνήρ, *echō + ho + anēr, 2400 + 3836 + 467*
13. λαμβάνω, *lambanō, 3284*
14. λαμβάνω + γυνή, *lambanō + gynē, 3284 + 1222*
15. ποιέω, *poieō, 4472*
16. ὕπανδρος, *hypandros, 5635*

Mat 5:32	whoever marries a divorced woman commits adultery.	4
19: 9	and marries another commits adultery."	4
19:10	it is better not to marry."	4
22:24	his brother shall marry the widow	9
22:25	the first married, and died	4
22:28	For all of them had married her."	10
22:30	they neither marry nor are given in marriage	4
24:38	marrying and giving in marriage	4
Mrk 6:17	because Herod had married her.	4
10:11	"Whoever divorces his wife and marries another	4
10:12	if she divorces her husband and marries another	4
12:19	the man shall marry the widow and raise up children	13
12:20	There were seven brothers; the first married	14
12:21	the second married the widow and died	13
12:23	For the seven had married her."	11
12:25	they neither marry nor are given in marriage	4
Lke 14:20	Another said, 'I have just been married	5
16:18	divorces his wife and marries another	4
16:18	whoever marries a woman divorced from her husband	4
17:27	They were eating and drinking, and marrying	4
20:28	man shall marry the widow and raise up children	13
20:29	the first married, and died childless;	14

20:31	the third married her	13
20:33	For the seven had married her."	11
20:34	"Those who belong to this age marry	4
20:35	neither marry nor are given in marriage.	4
Rom 7: 2	a married woman is bound by the law to her husband	16
7: 3	marries another man, she is not an adulteress.	7
1Co 7: 9	not practicing self-control, they should marry.	4
7: 9	it is better to marry than to be aflame with passion.	4
7:10	married I give this command—not I but the Lord	4
7:28	if you marry, you do not sin	4
7:28	if a virgin marries, she does not sin.	4
7:28	Yet those who marry will experience distress	1
7:36	let him marry as he wishes; it is no sin.	15
7:36	as he wishes; it is no sin. Let them marry.	4
7:38	So then, he who marries his fiancé does well;	6
7:39	she is free to marry anyone she wishes	4
Gal 4:27	numerous than the children of the one who is married."	12
1Ti 3: 2	married only once, temperate, sensible	2
3:12	Let deacons be married only once	2
5: 9	has been married only once;	8
5:11	they want to marry	4
5:14	I would have younger widows marry, bear children	4
Tit 1: 6	someone who is blameless, married only once,	3

Martha

1. Μάρθα, *Martha, 3450*

Lke 10:38	a woman named Martha welcomed him	1
10:40	Martha was distracted by her many tasks;	1
10:41	the Lord answered her, "Martha, Martha	1
10:41	the Lord answered her, "Martha, Martha	1
Jhn 11: 1	the village of Mary and her sister Martha.	1
11: 5	Jesus loved Martha and her sister and Lazarus	1
11:19	many of the Jews had come to Martha and Mary	1
11:20	When Martha heard that Jesus was coming	1
11:21	Martha said to Jesus, "Lord, if you had been here	1
11:24	Martha said to him, "I know that he will rise	1
11:30	still at the place where Martha had met him.	1
11:39	Martha, the sister of the dead man, said to him,	1
12: 2	There they gave a dinner for him. Martha served	1

marvel

1. θαυμάζω, *thaumazō, 2513*

2Th 1:10	marveled at on that day among all who have believed	1

marvelous

1. θαυμαστός, *thaumastos, 2515*

1Pe 2: 9	called…out of darkness into his marvelous light.	1

Mary

1. Μαρία, *Maria, 3451*

Mat 1:16	Joseph the husband of Mary, of whom Jesus was born	1
1:18	When his mother Mary had been engaged	1
1:20	do not be afraid to take Mary as your wife	1
2:11	saw the child with Mary his mother; and they knelt	1
13:55	Is not his mother called Mary?	1
27:56	Among them were Mary Magdalene	1
27:56	Mary the mother of James and Joseph	1
27:61	Mary Magdalene and the other Mary were there	1
27:61	Mary Magdalene and the other Mary were there	1
28: 1	Mary Magdalene and the other Mary	1
28: 1	Mary Magdalene and the other Mary	1
Mrk 6: 3	Is not this the carpenter, the son of Mary	1
15:40	among them were Mary Magdalene…and Salome.	1
15:40	Mary the mother of James the younger and of Joses	1
15:47	Mary Magdalene and Mary the mother of Joses saw	1
15:47	Mary Magdalene and Mary the mother of Joses saw	1
16: 1	Mary Magdalene, and Mary the mother of James	1
16: 1	Mary Magdalene, and Mary the mother of James	1
16: 9	⟦he appeared first to Mary Magdalene⟧	1
Lke 1:27	The virgin's name was Mary.	1
1:30	The angel said to her, "Do not be afraid, Mary	1
1:34	Mary said to the angel, "How can this be	1
1:38	Mary said, "Here am I, the servant of the Lord;	1
1:39	In those days Mary set out	1
1:41	When Elizabeth heard Mary's greeting, the child	1
1:46	Mary said, "My soul magnifies the Lord	1
1:56	Mary remained with her about three months	1
2: 5	registered with Mary, to whom he was engaged	1
2:16	they went with haste and found Mary and Joseph	1
2:19	Mary treasured all these words	1

Lke	2:34	Simeon blessed them and said to his mother Mary	1
	8: 2	Mary, called Magdalene	1
	10:39	She had a sister named Mary	1
	10:42	Mary has chosen the better part	1
	24:10	Now it was Mary Magdalene, Joanna	1
	24:10	Mary the mother of James, and the other women	1
Jhn	11: 1	the village of Mary and her sister Martha.	1
	11: 2	Mary was the one who anointed the Lord with perfume	1
	11:19	many of the Jews had come to Martha and Mary	1
	11:20	she went and met him, while Mary stayed at home.	1
	11:28	she went back and called her sister Mary,	1
	11:31	The Jews…saw Mary get up quickly and go out.	1
	11:32	When Mary came where Jesus was and saw him	1
	11:45	the Jews therefore, who had come with Mary	1
	12: 3	Mary took a pound of costly perfume	1
	19:25	his mother's sister, Mary the wife of Clopas	1
	19:25	Mary the wife of Clopas, and Mary Magdalene.	1
	20: 1	still dark, Mary Magdalene came to the tomb	1
	20:11	Mary stood weeping outside the tomb.	1
	20:16	Jesus said to her, "Mary!"	1
	20:18	Mary Magdalene went and announced to the disciples	1
Act	1:14	certain women, including Mary the mother of Jesus	1
	12:12	as he realized this, he went to the house of Mary	1
Rom	16: 6	Greet Mary, who has worked very hard among you.	1

master   *See also* master *builder*

1. Contextual: Not in Greek
2. ἄνθρωπος, *anthrōpos, 476*
3. δεσπότης, *despotēs, 1305*
4. ἐπιστάτης, *epistatēs, 2181*
5. ἡττάομαι, *hēttaomai, 2487*
6. κατακυριεύω, *katakyrieuō, 2894*
7. κύριος, *kyrios, 3261*

Mat	6:24	"No one can serve two masters; for a slave	7
	10:24	nor a slave above the master;	7
	10:25	and the slave like the master.	7
	13:27	'Master, did you not sow good seed in your field?	7
	15:27	crumbs that fall from their masters' table."	7
	24:45	whom his master has put in charge of his household	7
	24:46	whom his master will find at work when he arrives.	7
	24:48	'My master is delayed,'	7
	24:50	the master of that slave will come on a day	7
	25:18	dug a hole in the ground and hid his master's money.	7
	25:19	the master of those slaves came	7
	25:20	'Master, you handed over to me five talents;	7
	25:21	His master said to him	7
	25:21	enter into the joy of your master.'	7
	25:22	'Master, you handed over to me two talents;	7
	25:23	His master said to him	7
	25:23	enter into the joy of your master.'	7
	25:24	'Master, I knew that you were a harsh man	7
	25:26	his master replied, 'You wicked and lazy slave!	7
Mrk	13:35	when the master of the house will come	7
Lke	2:29	"Master, now you are dismissing your servant	3
	5: 5	"Master, we have worked all night long but	4
	8:24	and woke him up, shouting, "Master, Master	4
	8:24	and woke him up, shouting, "Master, Master	4
	8:45	When all denied it, Peter said, "Master	4
	9:33	"Master, it is good for us to be here;	4
	9:49	John answered, "Master, we saw someone	4
	12:36	be like those who are waiting for their master	7
	12:37	those slaves whom the master finds alert	7
	12:42	whom his master will put in charge of his slaves	7
	12:43	his master will find at work when he arrives.	7
	12:45	'My master is delayed in coming,'	7
	12:46	the master of that slave will come	7
	12:47	That slave who knew what his master wanted	7
	14:21	returned and reported this to his master.	7
	14:23	the master said to the slave, 'Go out	7
	16: 3	now that my master is taking the position away	7
	16: 5	summoning his master's debtors one by one	7
	16: 5	the first, 'How much do you owe my master?'	7
	16: 8	his master commended the dishonest manager	7
	16:13	No slave can serve two masters;	7
	17:13	called out, saying, "Jesus, Master	4
Jhn	13:16	servants are not greater than their master	7
	15:15	servant does not know what the master is doing;	7
	15:20	'Servants are not greater than their master.'	7
Act	19:16	mastered them all, and so overpowered them	6
1Co	7:23	do not become slaves of human masters.	1

Eph	6: 5	obey your earthly masters with fear and trembling	7
	6: 9	masters, do the same to them.	7
	6: 9	both of you have the same Master in heaven,	7
Col	3:22	Slaves, obey your earthly masters in everything	7
	3:23	as done for the Lord and not for your masters	2
	4: 1	Masters, treat your slaves justly and fairly	7
	4: 1	know that you also have a Master in heaven.	7
1Ti	6: 1	regard their masters as worthy of all honor	3
	6: 2	Those who have believing masters	3
Tit	2: 9	Tell slaves to be submissive to their masters	3
1Pe	2:18	Slaves, accept the authority of your masters	3
2Pe	2: 1	They will even deny the Master who bought them	3
	2:19	for people are slaves to whatever masters them.	5
Jde	1: 4	and deny our only Master and Lord, Jesus Christ.	3

master of a household

1. οἰκοδεσπότης, *oikodespotēs, 3867*

Mat	13:52	the master of a household who brings out of his treasure	1

master of the house

1. οἰκοδεσπότης, *oikodespotēs, 3867*

Mat	10:25	called the master of the house Beelzebul	1

mat

1. κράβαττος, *krabattos, 3187*

Mrk	2: 4	let down the mat on which the paralytic lay.	1
	2: 9	or to say, 'Stand up and take your mat and walk'?	1
	2:11	stand up, take your mat and go to your home."	1
	2:12	immediately took the mat and went out	1
	6:55	began to bring the sick on mats	1
Jhn	5: 8	"Stand up, take your mat and walk."	1
	5: 9	he took up his mat and began to walk.	1
	5:10	it is not lawful for you to carry your mat."	1
	5:11	'Take up your mat and walk.' "	1
Act	5:15	laid them on cots and mats	1

match

1. κατά, *kata, 2848*
2. οὕτως, *houtōs, 4048*
3. συμφωνέω, *symphōneō, 5244*

Lke	5:36	the piece from the new will not match the old.	3
2Co	8:11	your eagerness may be matched by completing it	2
	11:15	Their end will match their deeds.	1

material   *See also* material *benefit*

1. σαρκικός, *sarkikos, 4920*

Rom	15:27	to be of service to them in material things.	1

Mattatha

1. Ματταθά, *Mattatha, 3477*

Lke	3:31	son of Menna, son of Mattatha, son of Nathan	1

Mattathias

1. Ματταθίας, *Mattathias, 3478*

Lke	3:25	son of Mattathias, son of Amos	1
	3:26	son of Maath, son of Mattathias	1

matter   *See also* ordinary matter, weighty matter

1. Contextual: Not in Greek
2. γάρ, *gar, 1142*
3. λόγος, *logos, 3364*
4. οὗτος, *houtos, 4047*
5. πρᾶγμα, *pragma, 4547*
6. τίς, *tis, 5516*

Mrk	9:10	So they kept the matter to themselves	3
	10:10	the disciples asked him again about this matter.	4
Act	4:15	they discussed the matter with one another.	1
	15: 6	met together to consider this matter.	3
	18:14	a matter of crime or serious villainy	6
	18:15	a matter of questions about words and names	1
	18:15	I do not wish to be a judge of these matters."	1
	28:23	he explained the matter to them	1
Rom	2:29	and real circumcision is a matter of the heart	1
1Co	7: 1	concerning the matters about which you wrote:	1
	11:22	Should I commend you? In this matter I do not	4
2Co	7:11	proved yourselves guiltless in the matter.	5
	8:10	in this matter I am giving my advice:	1
	8:22	and found eager in many matters	1
Php	1:18	What does it matter?	2

	4:15 in the matter of giving and receiving,	3
Col	2:16 condemn you in matters of food and drink	1
1Th	4: 6 exploit a brother or sister in this matter	5
2Pe	1:20 a matter of one's own interpretation	1

Matthan

1. Ματθάν, *Matthan, 3474*

Mat	1:15 and Eleazar the father of Matthan	1
	1:15 father of Matthan, and Matthan the father	1

Matthat

1. Μαθθάτ, *Maththat, 3415*

Lke	3:24 son of Matthat, son of Levi	1
	3:29 son of Eliezer, son of Jorim, son of Matthat	1

Matthew

1. Μαθθαῖος, *Maththaios, 3414*

Mat	9: 9 he saw a man called Matthew	1
	10: 3 Thomas and Matthew the tax collector;	1
Mrk	3:18 Philip, and Bartholomew, and Matthew, and Thomas	1
Lke	6:15 Matthew, and Thomas, and James son of Alphaeus	1
Act	1:13 Philip and Thomas, Bartholomew and Matthew	1

Matthias

1. Μαθθίας, *Maththias, 3416*

Act	1:23 Joseph called Barsabbas…and Matthias.	1
	1:26 the lot fell on Matthias;	1

mature

1. τέλειος, *teleios, 5455*
2. τελεσφορέω, *telesphoreō, 5461*

Lke	8:14 their fruit does not mature.	2
1Co	2: 6 Yet among the mature we do speak wisdom	1
Php	3:15 those of us then who are mature be of the same mind;	1
Col	1:28 so that we may present everyone mature in Christ.	1
	4:12 so that you may stand mature and fully assured	1
Heb	5:14 solid food is for the mature	1
Jas	1: 4 so that you may be mature and complete	1

maturity

1. τέλειος, *teleios, 5455*

Eph	4:13 to maturity, to the measure of the full stature	1

maul

1. ῥήγνυμι, *rhēgnymi, 4838*
2. συντρίβω, *syntribō, 5341*

Mat	7: 6 and turn and maul you.	1
Lke	9:39 mauls him and will scarcely leave him.	2

may

1. δύναμαι, *dynamai, 1538*
2. ἔξεστι, *exesti, 2003*

Act	2:29 "Fellow Israelites, I may say to you confidently	2
	17:19 "May we know what this new teaching is	1
	21:37 "May I say something to you?"	2

meal   *See also* grind meal

1. Contextual: Not in Greek
2. ἄρτος, *artos, 788*
3. βρῶσις, *brōsis, 1111*

Lke	14: 1 house of a leader of the Pharisees to eat a meal	2
1Co	10:27 If an unbeliever invites you to a meal	1
Heb	12:16 who sold his birthright for a single meal.	3

passover meal

1. πάσχα, *pascha, 4247*

Mat	26:19 they prepared the Passover meal.	1
Mrk	14:16 they prepared the Passover meal.	1
Lke	22: 8 prepare the Passover meal for us that we may eat it."	1
	22:13 they prepared the Passover meal.	1

mean[1]

1. Contextual: Not in Greek
2. εἰμί, *eimi, 1639*
3. ἑρμηνεύω, *hermēneuō, 2257*
4. λέγω, *legō, 3306*
5. λόγος, *logos, 3364*
6. μεθερμηνεύω, *methermēneuō, 3493*

7. φημί, *phēmi, 5774*

Mat	1:23 Emmanuel," which means, "God is with us."	6
	9:13 Go and learn what this means, 'I desire mercy	2
	12: 7 if you had known what this means, 'I desire mercy	2
	27:33 (which means Place of a Skull)	2
Mrk	5:41 which means, "Little girl, get up!"	6
	9:10 what this rising from the dead could mean.	2
	15:22 Golgotha (which means the place of a skull).	6
	15:34 which means, "My God, my God, why have you	6
Lke	8: 9 his disciples asked him what this parable meant.	2
	20:17 "What then does this text mean: 'The stone	2
Jhn	1:38 "Rabbi" (which translated means Teacher)	4
	7:36 What does he mean by saying, 'You will search	5
	8:22 Is that what he means by saying, 'Where I am going,	1
	8:33 What do you mean by saying, 'You will be made free'?"	1
	9: 7 wash in the pool of Siloam" (which means Sent).	3
	16:17 "What does he mean by saying to us	2
	16:18 "What does he mean by this 'a little while'?	2
	16:19 what I meant when I said, 'A little while	1
	20:16 "Rabbouni!" (which means Teacher).	4
Act	2:12 "What does this mean?"	2
	4:36 Barnabas (which means "son of encouragement").	6
	17:20 so we would like to know what it means."	2
Rom	9: 8 This means that it is not the children	2
1Co	1:12 What I mean is that each of you says	4
	5:10 not at all meaning the immoral of this world	1
	7:29 I mean, brothers and sisters, the appointed time	7
	10:29 I mean the other's conscience, not your own.	4
Eph	4: 9 When it says, "He ascended," what does it mean	2
1Ti	1: 9 This means understanding that the law	1
Heb	7: 2 His name…means "king of righteousness"	3

mean[2]

1. Contextual: Not in Greek

Rom	2: 4 God's kindness is meant to lead you to repentance?	1
	11:12 Now if their stumbling means riches for the world	1
	11:12 if their defeat means riches for Gentiles	1
	11:12 how much more will their full inclusion mean!	1
1Co	6:13 "Food is meant for the stomach	1
	6:13 The body is meant not for fornication	1
2Co	1:24 not mean to imply that we lord it over your faith;	1
	8:13 I do not mean that there should be relief for others	1
Php	1:22 that means fruitful labor for me;	1

meaning

1. Contextual: Not in Greek
2. δύναμις, *dynamis, 1539*

Lke	9:45 its meaning was concealed from them	1
1Co	4: 6 learn through us the meaning of the saying,	1
	14:11 If then I do not know the meaning of a sound	2

meaningless   *See* meaningless *talk*

means[1]

1. διά, *dia, 1328*
2. ἐκ, *ek, 1666*

Lke	16: 9 make friends…by means of dishonest wealth	2
2Pe	3: 5 earth was formed out of water and by means of water	1

means[2]

1. δύναμις, *dynamis, 1539*
2. ἔχω, *echō, 2400*

2Co	8: 3 they voluntarily gave according to their means	1
	8: 3 according to their means, and even beyond their means	1
	8:11 completing it according to your means.	2

by all means

1. πάντως, *pantōs, 4122*

1Co	9:22 that I might by all means save some.	1

by no means

1. μή + γίνομαι, *mē + ginomai, 3590 + 1181*
2. μηδαμῶς, *mēdamōs, 3592*
3. οὐ + μή, *ou + mē, 4024 + 3590*
4. οὐδαμῶς, *oudamōs, 4027*

Mat	2: 6 are by no means least among the rulers of Judah;	4
Mrk	9:41 will by no means lose the reward.	3
Act	10:14 Peter said, "By no means, Lord;	2
	11: 8 I replied, 'By no means, Lord;	2

Rom 3: 4 By no means! Although everyone is a liar   1
    3: 6 By no means! For then how could God judge the world?   1
    3:31 By no means! On the contrary, we uphold the law.   1
    6: 2 By no means! How can we who died to sin go on living   1
    6:15 Should we sin…By no means!   1
    7: 7 That the law is sin? By no means!   1
    7:13 good…bring death to me? By no means!   1
    9:14 Is there injustice on God's part? By no means!   1
    11: 1 has God rejected his people? By no means!   1
    11:11 I ask, have they stumbled so as to fall? By no means!   1
1Th   4:15 will by no means precede those who have died.   3

means of gain

    1. πορισμός, *porismos, 4516*
1Ti   6: 5 imagining that godliness is a means of gain.   1

meanwhile

    1. δέ, *de, 1254*
    2. ἐν + ὁ + μεταξύ, *en + ho + metaxy, 1877 + 3836 + 3568*
    3. ἐν + ὅς, *en + hos, 1877 + 4005*
    4. καί, *kai, 2779*
    5. οὖν, *oun, 4036*
Lke   1:21 Meanwhile the people were waiting for Zechariah   4
    12: 1 Meanwhile, when the crowd gathered   3
Jhn   4:31 Meanwhile the disciples were urging him, "Rabbi,   2
    19:25 Meanwhile, standing near the cross of Jesus   1
Act   9: 1 Meanwhile Saul, still breathing threats and murder   1
    9:31 Meanwhile the church throughout Judea, Galilee,   5
    9:43 Meanwhile he stayed in Joppa for some time   1
    12:16 Meanwhile Peter continued knocking;   1
    19:32 Meanwhile, some were shouting one thing,   5
    20:12 Meanwhile they had taken the boy away alive   1

measure   *See also* get a measure, get back measure, give a measure

    1. Contextual: Not in Greek
    2. βοήθεια, *boētheia, 1069*
    3. μετρέω, *metreō, 3582*
    4. μέτρον, *metron, 3586*
    5. σάτον, *saton, 4929*
Mat   7: 2 you will be judged, and the measure you give   4
    7: 2 you give will be the measure you get.   3
    13:33 mixed in with three measures of flour   5
    23:32 Fill up, then, the measure of your ancestors.   4
Mrk   4:24 the measure you give will be the measure you get   4
Lke   6:38 good measure, pressed down, shaken together   4
    6:38 the measure you give will be the measure you get   4
    13:21 took and mixed in with three measures of flour   5
Jhn   3:34 for he gives the Spirit without measure.   4
Act   27:17 they took measures to undergird the ship;   2
Rom   12: 3 the measure of faith that God has assigned.   4
2Co   10:12 But when they measure themselves by one another   3
Eph   4: 7 grace according to the measure of Christ's gift.   4
    4:13 to the measure of the full stature of Christ.   4
1Th   2:16 constantly been filling up the measure of their sins;   1
Rev   11: 1 "Come and measure the temple of God and the altar   3
    11: 2 do not measure the court outside the temple;   3
    21:15 angel who talked to me had a measuring rod of gold   4
    21:15 to measure the city and its gates and walls.   3
    21:16 and he measured the city with his rod   3
    21:17 He also measured its wall   3

beyond all measure

    1. κατά + ὑπερβολή + εἰς + ὑπερβολή, *kata + hyperbolē + eis + hyperbolē, 2848 + 5651 + 1650 + 5651*
2Co   4:17 weight of glory beyond all measure   1

beyond measure

    1. ὑπερβολή, *hyperbolē, 5651*
    2. ὑπερπερισσῶς, *hyperperissōs, 5669*
Mrk   7:37 They were astounded beyond measure, saying   2
Rom   7:13 might become sinful beyond measure.   1

like measure

    1. τοσοῦτος, *tosoutos, 5537*
Rev   18: 7 give her a like measure of torment and grief.   1

measurement

    1. μέτρον, *metron, 3586*

Rev   21:17 one hundred forty-four cubits by human measurement   1

measuring   *See* measuring *rod*

meat   *See also* meat *market*

    1. κρέας, *kreas, 3200*
Rom   14:21 it is good not to eat meat or drink wine   1
1Co   8:13 I will never eat meat, so that I may not   1

Mede

    1. Μῆδος, *Mēdos, 3597*
Act   2: 9 Parthians, Medes, Elamites,   1

mediator

    1. μεσίτης, *mesitēs, 3542*
Gal   3:19 ordained through angels by a mediator.   1
    3:20 Now a mediator involves more than one   1
1Ti   2: 5 also one mediator between God and humankind   1
Heb   8: 6 he is the mediator of a better covenant,   1
    9:15 For this reason he is the mediator of a new covenant   1
    12:24 to Jesus, the mediator of a new covenant   1

meek

    1. πραΰς, *praus, 4558*
Mat   5: 5 "Blessed are the meek, for they will inherit   1

meekness

    1. πραΰτης, *prautēs, 4559*
2Co   10: 1 by the meekness and gentleness of Christ   1
Col   3:12 compassion, kindness, humility, meekness   1
Jas   1:21 welcome with meekness the implanted word   1

meet   *See also* ask to meet, fail to meet the test, go and meet, go to meet

    1. Contextual: Not in Greek
    2. ἀπαντάω, *apantaō, 560*
    3. ἀπάντησις, *apantēsis, 561*
    4. εἰμί, *eimi, 1639*
    5. ἐπισυναγωγή, *episynagōgē, 2191*
    6. εὑρίσκω, *heuriskō, 2351*
    7. ἔχω, *echō, 2400*
    8. συμβάλλω, *symballō, 5202*
    9. συνάγω, *synagō, 5251*
    10. συναντάω, *synantaō, 5267*
    11. συνέρχομαι, *synerchomai, 5302*
    12. ὑπαντάω, *hypantaō, 5636*
    13. ὑπάντησις, *hypantēsis, 5637*
Mat   8:28 two demoniacs coming out of the tombs met him.   12
    8:34 Then the whole town came out to meet Jesus;   13
    25: 1 went to meet the bridegroom.   13
    25: 6 Here is the bridegroom! Come out to meet him.'   3
    28: 9 Suddenly Jesus met them and said, "Greetings!"   12
Mrk   5: 2 a man…with an unclean spirit met him   12
    14:13 a man carrying a jar of water will meet you;   2
Lke   8:27 a man of the city who had demons met him.   12
    9:37 a great crowd met him.   10
    22:10 a man carrying a jar of water will meet you;   10
Jhn   4:51 As he was going down, his slaves met him   12
    11:30 still at the place where Martha had met him.   12
    12:13 went out to meet him, shouting, "Hosanna!   13
    18: 2 Jesus often met there with his disciples.   9
    20:19 the house where the disciples had met   4
Act   10:25 On Peter's arrival Cornelius met him   10
    13: 6 they met a certain magician   6
    13:43 When the meeting of the synagogue broke up   1
    16:16 met a slave-girl who had a spirit of divination   12
    20: 7 when we met to break bread   9
    20: 8 in the room upstairs where we were meeting.   9
    20:14 When he met us in Assos, we took him on board   8
    22:30 the chief priests and the entire council to meet.   11
    25:16 before the accused had met the accusers face to face   7
    25:17 So when they met here   11
    28:15 came as far as the Forum of Appius…to meet us.   3
    28:23 After they had set a day to meet with him   1
1Th   4:17 together with them to meet the Lord in the air;   3
Tit   3:14 in order to meet urgent needs   1
Heb   7: 1 met Abraham as he was returning from defeating   10
    7:10 when Melchizedek met him.   10
    10:25 not neglecting to meet together   5

meet the test
   1. δόκιμος, *dokimos, 1511*
2Co 13: 7 not that we may appear to have met the test   1

meet together
   1. συνάγω, *synagō, 5251*
Act 15: 6 The apostles and the elders met together   1

meet with
   1. συνάγω, *synagō, 5251*
Act 11:26 for an entire year they met with the church   1

meeting *See also* call a meeting

private meeting
   1. κατά + ἴδιος, *kata + idios, 2848 + 2625*
Gal 2: 2 in a private meeting with the acknowledged leaders)   1

Melchi
   1. Μελχί, *Melchi, 3518*
Lke 3:24 son of Levi, son of Melchi   1
     3:28 son of Melchi, son of Addi, son of Cosam   1

Melchizedek
   1. Μελχισέδεκ, *Melchisedek, 3519*
Heb 5: 6 a priest forever, according to the order of Melchizedek."   1
     5:10 a high priest according to the order of Melchizedek.   1
     6:20 according to the order of Melchizedek.   1
     7: 1 King Melchizedek of Salem, priest of the Most High God   1
     7:10 when Melchizedek met him.   1
     7:11 priest arising according to the order of Melchizedek   1
     7:15 another priest arises, resembling Melchizedek,   1
     7:17 a priest forever, according to the order of Melchizedek."   1

Melea
   1. Μελεά, *Melea, 3507*
Lke 3:31 son of Melea, son of Menna   1

melody *See* make melody

melt
   1. τήκομαι, *tēkomai, 5494*
2Pe 3:12 and the elements will melt with fire?   1

member
   1. Contextual: Not in Greek
   2. ἀδελφός, *adelphos, 81*
   3. αὐτός, *autos, 899*
   4. ἐκ, *ek, 1666*
   5. μέλος, *melos, 3517*
Mat 5:29 is better for you to lose one of your members   5
     5:30 is better for you to lose one of your members   5
    18:15 If the member listens to you, you have regained   2
    18:17 If the member refuses to listen to them   1
Act 15:22 decided to choose men from among their members   3
    15:31 When its members read it, they rejoiced   1
Rom 6:13 No longer present your members to sin   5
     6:13 present your members to God as instruments   5
     6:19 once presented your members as slaves to impurity   5
     6:19 present your members as slaves to righteousness   5
     7: 5 sinful passions…were at work in our members   5
     7:23 but I see in my members another law   5
     7:23 to the law of sin that dwells in my members.   5
    11: 1 I myself am…a member of the tribe of Benjamin.   1
    12: 4 For as in one body we have many members   5
    12: 4 and not all the members have the same function   5
    12: 5 and individually we are members one of another.   5
1Co 6:15 know that your bodies are members of Christ?   5
     6:15 Should I therefore take the members of Christ   5
     6:15 make them members of a prostitute? Never!   5
    12:12 For just as the body is one and has many members   5
    12:12 all the members of the body, though many, are one   5
    12:14 body does not consist of one member but of many.   5
    12:18 as it is, God arranged the members in the body   5
    12:19 all were a single member, where would the body be?   5
    12:20 As it is, there are many members, yet one body.   5
    12:22 the members of the body that seem to be weaker   5
    12:23 members of the body that we think less honorable   1

    12:23 less respectable members are treated with…respect;   1
    12:24 whereas our more respectable members do not need   1
    12:24 giving the greater honor to the inferior member   1
    12:25 members may have the same care for one another.   5
    12:26 If one member suffers, all suffer together   5
    12:26 if one member is honored, all rejoice together   5
    12:27 individually members of it.   5
    16:15 know that members of the household of Stephanas   1
Eph 4:25 we are members of one another.   5
     5:30 because we are members of his body.   5
Php 3: 5 a member of the people of Israel,   4
Jas 3: 5 So also the tongue is a small member, yet it boasts   5
    3: 6 placed among our members as a world of iniquity;   5
Rev 11: 9 members of the peoples and tribes and languages   4

family member
   1. οἰκεῖος, *oikeios, 3858*
1Ti 5: 8 not provide…especially for family members   1

member of a family
   1. ἀδελφός, *adelphos, 81*
Mat 25:40 one of the least…who are members of my family   1
1Co 8:12 thus sin against members of your family   1

member of God's family
   1. ἀδελφός, *adelphos, 81*
Gal 1: 2 all the members of God's family who are with me   1

member of the church
   1. ἀδελφός, *adelphos, 81*
Mat 18:15 "If another member of the church sins against you   1
    18:21 if another member of the church sins against me   1
1Ti 6: 2 on the ground that they are members of the church;   1

member of the council
   1. βουλευτής, *bouleutēs, 1085*
Mrk 15:43 a respected member of the council   1
Lke 23:50 who, though a member of the council   1

member of the court
   1. σύντροφος, *syntrophos, 5343*
Act 13: 1 Manaen a member of the court of Herod   1

member of the household
   1. οἰκεῖος, *oikeios, 3858*
   2. οἰκιακός, *oikiakos, 3865*
Mat 10:36 one's foes will be members of one's own household.   2
Eph 2:19 you are…members of the household of God   1

member of the same body
   1. σύσσωμος, *syssōmos, 5362*
Eph 3: 6 Gentiles have become…members of the same body   1

memorial
   1. μνημόσυνον, *mnēmosynon, 3649*
Act 10: 4 have ascended as a memorial before God.   1

memory
   1. ὑπόμνησις, *hypomnēsis, 5704*
2Pe 1:13 I think it right…to refresh your memory,   1

mend
   1. καταρτίζω, *katartizō, 2936*
Mat 4:21 with their father Zebedee, mending their nets   1
Mrk 1:19 who were in their boat mending the nets.   1

Menna
   1. Μεννά, *Menna, 3527*
Lke 3:31 son of Melea, son of Menna   1

mention *See also* make mention
   1. Contextual: Not in Greek
   2. λέγω, *legō, 3306*
   3. μνεία + ποιέω, *mneia + poieō, 3644 + 4472*
   4. ὀνομάζω, *onomazō, 3951*
Eph 5: 3 greed, must not even be mentioned among you   4
    5:12 shameful even to mention what such people do   2
1Th 1: 2 mention you in our prayers, constantly   3

2Ti   2:21   cleanse themselves of the things I have mentioned   1

merchant

    1. ἔμπορος, *emporos, 1867*

Mat 13:45   like a merchant in search of fine pearls;   1
Rev 18: 3   the merchants of the earth have grown rich   1
       18:11   the merchants of the earth weep and mourn for her   1
       18:15   The merchants of these wares, who gained wealth   1
       18:23   your merchants were the magnates of the earth   1

merciful

    1. ἐλεέω, *eleeō, 1796*
    2. ἐλεήμων, *eleēmōn, 1798*
    3. ἱλάσκομαι, *hilaskomai, 2661*
    4. ἵλεως, *hileōs, 2664*
    5. οἰκτίρμων, *oiktirmōn, 3881*

Mat   5: 7   "Blessed are the merciful, for they will receive   2
Lke   6:36   Be merciful, just as your Father is merciful.   5
       6:36   Be merciful, just as your Father is merciful.   5
       18:13   and saying, 'God, be merciful to me, a sinner!'   3
Rom 11:32   so that he may be merciful to all.   1
Heb   2:17   might be a merciful and faithful high priest   2
       8:12   For I will be merciful toward their iniquities   4
Jas   5:11   how the Lord is compassionate and merciful.   5

mercy   *See also* have mercy, receive mercy, show mercy

    1. ἐλεέω, *eleeō, 1796*
    2. ἔλεος, *eleos, 1799*
    3. οἰκτιρμός, *oiktirmos, 3880*

Mat   9:13   Go and learn what this means, 'I desire mercy   2
       12: 7   'I desire mercy and not sacrifice,'   2
       23:23   justice and mercy and faith.   2
Lke   1:50   His mercy is for those who fear him   2
       1:54   in remembrance of his mercy   2
       1:58   the Lord had shown his great mercy to her   2
       1:72   he has shown the mercy promised to our ancestors   2
       1:78   By the tender mercy of our God   2
       10:37   He said, "The one who showed him mercy."   2
Rom   9:23   the riches of his glory for the objects of mercy   2
       12: 1   I appeal to you…by the mercies of God   3
       15: 9   the Gentiles might glorify God for his mercy.   2
1Co   7:25   one who by the Lord's mercy is trustworthy.   1
2Co   1: 3   Father of mercies and the God of all consolation   3
       4: 1   by God's mercy that we are engaged in this ministry   1
Gal   6:16   follow this rule—peace be upon them, and mercy   2
Eph   2: 4   God, who is rich in mercy   2
1Ti   1: 2   Grace, mercy, and peace from God the Father   2
2Ti   1: 2   Grace, mercy, and peace from God the Father   2
       1:16   May the Lord grant mercy   2
       1:18   the Lord grant that he will find mercy from the Lord   2
Tit   3: 5   but according to his mercy   2
Heb   4:16   so that we may receive mercy and find grace   2
       10:28   violated the law of Moses dies without mercy   3
Jas   2:13   without mercy to anyone who has shown no mercy;   2
       2:13   mercy triumphs over judgment.   2
       3:17   wisdom…is…full of mercy and good fruits   2
1Pe   1: 3   By his great mercy he has given us a new birth   2
2Jn   1: 3   Grace, mercy, and peace will be with us from God   2
Jde   1: 2   May mercy, peace, and love be yours in abundance.   2
       1:21   look forward to the mercy of our Lord Jesus Christ   2

mercy seat

    1. ἱλαστήριον, *hilastērion, 2663*

Heb   9: 5   cherubim of glory overshadowing the mercy seat.   1

without mercy

    1. ἀνέλεος, *aneleos, 447*

Jas   2:13   For judgment will be without mercy   1

mere

    1. Contextual: Not in Greek
    2. ἀλλά, *alla, 247*

2Th   3:11   mere busybodies, not doing any work.   2
Heb   9:24   a mere copy of the true one   1
2Pe   2:12   like irrational animals, mere creatures of instinct   1

merely   *See also* merely *human*, merely *sleep*

    1. Contextual: Not in Greek
    2. μόνον, *monon, 3667*

2Co   8: 5   this, not merely as we expected;   1
1Ti   5:13   not merely idle, but also gossips and busybodies   2
Jas   1:22   But be doers of the word, and not merely hearers   2

merry

    1. εὐφραίνω, *euphrainō, 2370*

Lke 12:19   relax, eat, drink, be merry.'   1

Mesopotamia

    1. Μεσοποταμία, *Mesopotamia, 3544*

Act   2: 9   Elamites, and residents of Mesopotamia   1
       7: 2   our ancestor Abraham when he was in Mesopotamia   1

message   *See also* give a message, proclaim the message, send a message

    1. Contextual: Not in Greek
    2. ἀγγελία, *angelia, 32*
    3. ἀκοή, *akoē, 198*
    4. κήρυγμα, *kērygma, 3060*
    5. λέγω, *legō, 3306*
    6. λόγος, *logos, 3364*
    7. ῥῆμα, *rhēma, 4839*

Mat 28: 7   This is my message for you."   5
Mrk 16:20   [confirmed the message by the signs]   6
Jhn 11: 3   the sisters sent a message to Jesus,   5
       12:38   "Lord, who has believed our message   3
Act   2:41   So those who welcomed his message were baptized   6
       5:20   tell the people the whole message about this life."   7
       10:36   You know the message he sent to the people of Israel   6
       10:37   That message spread throughout Judea   7
       11:14   he will give you a message   7
       13:26   the message of this salvation has been sent.   6
       15: 7   the Gentiles would hear the message of the good news   6
       16:36   the jailer reported the message to Paul, saying   6
       17:11   they welcomed the message very eagerly   6
       19:31   sent him a message urging him not to venture   1
       20:17   From Miletus he sent a message to Ephesus   1
       20:32   I commend you…to the message of his grace   6
       20:32   a message that is able to build you up   1
Rom 10:16   "Lord, who has believed our message?"   3
1Co   1:18   For the message about the cross is foolishness   6
       15: 2   saved, if you hold firmly to the message   6
2Co   5:19   entrusting the message of reconciliation to us.   6
Eph   6:19   so that when I speak, a message may be given to me   6
2Ti   4: 2   proclaim the message; be persistent   6
       4:15   he strongly opposed our message.   6
       4:17   through me the message might be fully proclaimed   4
Heb   2: 2   For if the message declared through angels was valid   6
       4: 2   the message they heard did not benefit them   6
2Pe   1:19   we have the prophetic message more fully confirmed.   6
1Jn   1: 5   the message we have heard from him and proclaim   2
       3:11   message you have heard from the beginning   2

message of the gospel

    1. εὐαγγέλιον, *euangelion, 2295*

1Th   1: 5   message of the gospel came to you not in word only   1
       2: 4   entrusted with the message of the gospel, even so we speak   1

messenger   *See also* send a messenger

    1. ἄγγελος, *angelos, 34*
    2. ἀπόστολος, *apostolos, 693*

Mat 11:10   'See, I am sending my messenger ahead of you,   1
Mrk   1: 2   "See, I am sending my messenger ahead of you,   1
Lke   7:24   When John's messengers had gone   1
       7:27   'See, I am sending my messenger ahead of you,   1
       9:52   he sent messengers ahead of him.   1
Jhn 13:16   nor are messengers greater than the one who sent   2
2Co   8:23   messengers of the churches, the glory of Christ.   2
       12: 7   a messenger of Satan to torment me   1
Php   2:25   your messenger and minister to my need;   2
Jas   2:25   justified…when she welcomed the messengers   1

Messiah   *See also* Christ

    1. Μεσσίας, *Messias, 3549*
    2. Χριστός, *Christos, 5986*

Mat   1: 1   An account of the genealogy of Jesus the Messiah   2
       1:16   Jesus was born, who is called the Messiah.   2
       1:17   to Babylon to the Messiah, fourteen generations.   2
       1:18   birth of Jesus the Messiah took place in this way.   2

<table>
<tr><td>2: 4</td><td>of them where the Messiah was to be born.</td><td>2</td></tr>
<tr><td>11: 2</td><td>John heard in prison what the Messiah was doing</td><td>2</td></tr>
<tr><td>16:16</td><td>"You are the Messiah, the Son of the living God."</td><td>2</td></tr>
<tr><td>16:20</td><td>not to tell anyone that he was the Messiah.</td><td>2</td></tr>
<tr><td>22:42</td><td>"What do you think of the Messiah? Whose son</td><td>2</td></tr>
<tr><td>23:10</td><td>you have one instructor, the Messiah.</td><td>2</td></tr>
<tr><td>24: 5</td><td>'I am the Messiah!' and they will lead many astray.</td><td>2</td></tr>
<tr><td>24:23</td><td>if anyone says to you, 'Look! Here is the Messiah!'</td><td>2</td></tr>
<tr><td>26:63</td><td>tell us if you are the Messiah, the Son of God."</td><td>2</td></tr>
<tr><td>26:68</td><td>saying, "Prophesy to us, you Messiah!</td><td>2</td></tr>
<tr><td>27:17</td><td>Jesus Barabbas or Jesus who is called the Messiah?"</td><td>2</td></tr>
<tr><td>27:22</td><td>I do with Jesus who is called the Messiah?"</td><td>2</td></tr>
</table>

Mrk 8:29 Peter answered him, "You are the Messiah." 2
12:35 say that the Messiah is the son of David? 2
13:21 at that time, 'Look! Here is the Messiah!' 2
14:61 "Are you the Messiah, the Son of the Blessed 2
15:32 Let the Messiah, the King of Israel, come down 2
Lke 2:11 a Savior, who is the Messiah, the Lord. 2
2:26 before he had seen the Lord's Messiah. 2
3:15 questioning…whether he might be the Messiah 2
4:41 because they knew that he was the Messiah. 2
9:20 Peter answered, "The Messiah of God." 2
20:41 "How can they say that the Messiah is David's son? 2
22:67 "If you are the Messiah, tell us." 2
23: 2 saying that he himself is the Messiah, a king." 2
23:35 if he is the Messiah of God, his chosen one!" 2
23:39 "Are you not the Messiah? Save yourself and us!" 2
24:26 it not necessary that the Messiah should suffer 2
24:46 the Messiah is to suffer 2
Jhn 1:20 He confessed…"I am not the Messiah." 2
1:25 if you are neither the Messiah, nor Elijah 2
1:41 the Messiah" (which is translated Anointed). 1
3:28 'I am not the Messiah, but I have been sent 2
4:25 "I know that Messiah is coming" 1
4:29 He cannot be the Messiah, can he?" 2
7:26 know that this is the Messiah? 2
7:27 when the Messiah comes 2
7:31 "When the Messiah comes 2
7:41 Others said, "This is the Messiah." 2
7:41 "Surely the Messiah does not come from Galilee 2
7:42 the Messiah is descended from David 2
9:22 anyone who confessed Jesus to be the Messiah 2
10:24 If you are the Messiah, tell us plainly." 2
11:27 I believe that you are the Messiah, the Son of God 2
12:34 that the Messiah remains forever. 2
20:31 Jesus is the Messiah, the Son of God 2
Act 2:31 spoke of the resurrection of the Messiah 2
2:36 God has made him both Lord and Messiah 2
3:18 he had foretold…that his Messiah would suffer. 2
3:20 may send the Messiah appointed for you…Jesus 2
4:26 against the Lord and against his Messiah.' 2
5:42 proclaim Jesus as the Messiah. 2
8: 5 proclaimed the Messiah to them. 2
9:22 by proving that Jesus was the Messiah. 2
17: 3 necessary for the Messiah to suffer and to rise 2
17: 3 "This is the Messiah, Jesus whom I am proclaiming 2
18: 5 testifying to the Jews that the Messiah was Jesus. 2
18:28 showing…that the Messiah is Jesus. 2
26:23 that the Messiah must suffer 2
Rom 9: 5 from them, according to the flesh, comes the Messiah 2
Rev 11:15 become the kingdom of our Lord and of his Messiah 2
12:10 kingdom of our God and the authority of his Messiah 2

false messiah

1. ψευδόχριστος, *pseudochristos, 6023*

Mat 24:24 For false messiahs and false prophets will appear 1
Mrk 13:22 False messiahs and false prophets will appear 1

Methuselah

1. Μαθουσαλά, *Mathousala, 3417*

Lke 3:37 son of Methuselah, son of Enoch 1

Michael

1. Μιχαήλ, *Michaēl, 3640*

Jde 1: 9 when archangel Michael contended with the devil 1
Rev 12: 7 Michael and his angels fought…the dragon. 1

midday

1. μέσος + ἡμέρα, *mesos + hēmera, 3545 + 2465*

Act 26:13 at midday along the road…I saw a light 1

middle

1. μέσος, *mesos, 3545*
2. μεσόω, *mesoō, 3548*

Lke 5:19 into the middle of the crowd in front of Jesus. 1
22:55 kindled a fire in the middle of the courtyard 1
Jhn 7:14 About the middle of the festival 2
Act 1:18 falling headlong, he burst open in the middle 1
Rev 22: 2 through the middle of the street of the city. 1

middle of the night

1. δεύτερος + φυλακή, *deuteros + phylakē, 1311 + 5871*

Lke 12:38 If he comes during the middle of the night, 1

midheaven

1. μεσουράνημα, *mesouranēma, 3547*

Rev 8:13 heard an eagle crying…as it flew in midheaven 1
14: 6 Then I saw another angel flying in midheaven 1
19:17 he called to all the birds that fly in midheaven 1

Midian

1. Μαδιάμ, *Madiam, 3409*

Act 7:29 became a resident alien in the land of Midian. 1

midnight

1. μεσονύκτιον, *mesonyktion, 3543*
2. μέσος + νύξ, *mesos + nyx, 3545 + 3816*
3. μέσος + ὁ + νύξ, *mesos + ho + nyx, 3545 + 3836 + 3816*

Mat 25: 6 at midnight there was a shout 2
Mrk 13:35 in the evening, or at midnight, or at cockcrow 1
Lke 11: 5 go to him at midnight and say to him, 'Friend 1
Act 16:25 About midnight Paul and Silas were praying 1
20: 7 he continued speaking until midnight. 1
27:27 about midnight the sailors suspected 3

midst

1. ἐν, *en, 1877*
2. μέσος, *mesos, 3545*

Mat 10:16 sending you out like sheep into the midst of wolves; 2
Lke 4:30 passed through the midst of them and went on his way. 2
10: 3 like lambs into the midst of wolves. 2
Act 4: 7 they had made the prisoners stand in their midst, 2
Php 2:15 in the midst of a…perverse generation 2
Heb 2:12 in the midst of the congregation I will praise 2
Jas 1:11 in the midst of a busy life, they will wither away. 1
Rev 1:13 in the midst of the lampstands I saw one like the Son 2
6: 6 a voice in the midst of the four living creatures 2

might

1. γίνομαι, *ginomai, 1181*
2. δύναμαι, *dynamai, 1538*
3. ἰσχύς, *ischys, 2709*
4. κράτος, *kratos, 3197*
5. ὡς, *hōs, 6055*

Act 20:16 so that he might not have to spend time in Asia; 1
1Th 2: 7 might have made demands as apostles of Christ. 2
2Th 1: 9 separated…from the glory of his might 3
Heb 7: 9 One might even say 5
2Pe 2:11 angels, though greater in might and power 3
Rev 5:12 to receive…might and honor and glory 3
5:13 honor and glory and might forever and ever!" 4
7:12 honor and power and might be to our God forever 3

mightily

1. κράτος, *kratos, 3197*

Act 19:20 word of the Lord grew mightily and prevailed. 1

mighty

1. δύναμις, *dynamis, 1539*
2. δυνατός, *dynatos, 1543*
3. ἰσχυρός, *ischyros, 2708*
4. κέρας, *keras, 3043*
5. κραταιός, *krataios, 3193*

Lke 1:49 for the Mighty One has done great things for me 2
1:69 He has raised up a mighty savior for us 4
24:19 a prophet mighty in deed and word before God 2
2Th 1: 7 revealed from heaven with his mighty angels 1
Heb 11:34 became mighty in war 3
1Pe 5: 6 Humble yourselves…under the mighty hand of God 5

Rev 5: 2 a mighty angel proclaiming with a loud voice 3
  10: 1 another mighty angel coming down from heaven 3
  18: 2 He called out with a mighty voice 3
  18: 8 for mighty is the Lord God who judges her." 3
  18:10 alas, the great city, Babylon, the mighty city! 3
  18:21 Then a mighty angel took up a stone 3
  19: 6 like the sound of mighty thunderpeals, crying out 3

mighty act

    1. ἀρετή, *aretē, 746*

1Pe 2: 9 you may proclaim the mighty acts of him 1

mighty man

    1. ἰσχυρός, *ischyros, 2708*

Rev 19:18 to eat...the flesh of the mighty 1

mighty work

    1. δύναμις, *dynamis, 1539*

2Co 12:12 patience, signs and wonders and mighty works. 1

mile *See also* fifteen hundred miles, four miles, seven miles, three miles, two hundred miles, two miles
    1. Contextual: Not in Greek
    2. μίλιον, *milion, 3627*

Mat 5:41 forces you to go one mile, go also the second mile. 2
     5:41 forces you to go one mile, go also the second mile. 1

Miletus

    1. Μίλητος, *Milētos, 3626*

Act 20:15 the day after that we came to Miletus. 1
    20:17 From Miletus he sent a message to Ephesus 1
2Ti 4:20 Trophimus I left ill in Miletus. 1

military *See* do military service, military *tribune*

milk

    1. γάλα, *gala, 1128*

1Co 3: 2 I fed you with milk, not solid food 1
    9: 7 not get any of its milk? 1
Heb 5:12 You need milk, not solid food; 1
    5:13 for everyone who lives on milk 1
1Pe 2: 2 long for the pure, spiritual milk 1

millstone

    1. λίθος + μυλικός, *lithos + mylikos, 3345 + 3683*
    2. μύλινος, *mylinos, 3684*
    3. μύλος, *mylos, 3685*

Mat 18: 6 a great millstone were fastened around your neck 3
Lke 17: 2 if a millstone were hung around your neck 1
Rev 18:21 angel took up a stone like a great millstone 2
    18:22 the millstone will be heard in you no more; 3

great millstone

    1. μύλος + ὀνικός, *mylos + onikos, 3685 + 3948*

Mrk 9:42 if a great millstone were hung around your neck 1

mind¹ *See also* change one's mind, come to a sober mind, go out of one's mind, make up one's mind, set one's mind
    1. διάνοια, *dianoia, 1379*
    2. καρδία, *kardia, 2840*
    3. νεφρός, *nephros, 3752*
    4. νόημα, *noēma, 3784*
    5. νοῦς, *nous, 3808*
    6. πνεῦμα, *pneuma, 4460*
    7. φρονέω, *phroneō, 5858*
    8. φρόνημα, *phronēma, 5859*
    9. ψυχή, *psychē, 6034*

Mat 22:37 with all your soul, and with all your mind.' 1
Mrk 12:30 with all your soul, and with all your mind 1
Lke 10:27 with all your strength, and with all your mind; 1
    21:14 So make up your minds 2
    24:45 Then he opened their minds 5
Act 14: 2 poisoned their minds against the brothers. 9
    15:24 to disturb you and have unsettled your minds 9
Rom 1:21 and their senseless minds were darkened. 2
    1:28 God gave them up to a debased mind 5
    7:23 another law at war with the law of my mind 5
    7:25 with my mind I am a slave to the law of God 5

    8: 6 To set the mind on the flesh is death 8
    8: 6 to set the mind on the Spirit is life and peace. 8
    8: 7 the mind that is set on the flesh is hostile to God; 8
    8:27 knows what is the mind of the Spirit 8
   11:34 "For who has known the mind of the Lord? 5
   12: 2 but be transformed by the renewing of your minds. 5
   14: 5 Let all be fully convinced in their own minds. 5
1Co 1:10 be united in the same mind and the same purpose. 5
    2:16 "For who has known the mind of the Lord 5
    2:16 we have the mind of Christ. 5
    7:37 determined in his own mind to keep her 2
   14:14 my spirit prays but my mind is unproductive. 5
   14:15 I will pray with the mind also; 5
   14:15 I will sing praise with the mind also. 5
   14:19 I would rather speak five words with my mind...than 5
2Co 2:13 my mind could not rest 6
    3:14 their minds were hardened. 4
    3:15 a veil lies over their minds; 2
    4: 4 blinded the minds of the unbelievers 4
    7:13 his mind has been set at rest by all of you. 6
    9: 7 Each of you must give as you have made up your mind 2
Eph 4:17 in the futility of their minds. 5
    4:23 be renewed in the spirit of your minds 5
Php 1:27 striving side by side with one mind for the faith 9
    2: 2 make my joy complete: be of the same mind 7
    2: 2 being in full accord and of one mind. 7
    2: 5 Let the same mind be in you 7
    3:15 those of us then who are mature be of the same mind; 7
    4: 2 I urge Syntyche to be of the same mind in the Lord. 7
    4: 7 guard your hearts and your minds in Christ Jesus. 4
Col 1:21 you who were once estranged and hostile in mind 1
2Th 2: 2 not to be quickly shaken in mind or alarmed 5
1Ti 6: 5 who are depraved in mind and bereft of the truth 5
2Ti 3: 8 people, of corrupt mind and counterfeit faith 5
Tit 1:15 Their very minds and consciences are corrupted. 5
Heb 8:10 I will put my laws in their minds 1
   10:16 and I will write them on their minds," 1
1Pe 1:13 Therefore prepare your minds for action; discipline 1
Rev 2:23 that I am the one who searches minds and hearts 3
   17: 9 "This calls for a mind that has wisdom: 5

mind²

    1. πράσσω, *prassō, 4556*

1Th 4:11 to mind your own affairs 1

humble mind

    1. ταπεινόφρων, *tapeinophrōn, 5426*

1Pe 3: 8 have...a tender heart, and a humble mind. 1

in mind

    1. ἐν + ὅς, *en + hos, 1877 + 4005*

Act 26:12 "With this in mind, I was traveling to Damascus 1

out of one's mind

    1. μαίνομαι, *mainomai, 3419*

Jhn 10:20 saying, "He has a demon and is out of his mind. 1
Act 12:15 They said to her, "You are out of your mind!" 1
   26:24 Festus exclaimed, "You are out of your mind, Paul! 1
   26:25 Paul said, "I am not out of my mind 1
1Co 14:23 will they not say that you are out of your mind? 1

right mind

    1. σωφρονέω, *sōphroneō, 5404*

Mrk 5:15 sitting there, clothed and in his right mind 1
Lke 8:35 found the man...clothed and in his right mind. 1
2Co 5:13 if we are in our right mind, it is for you. 1

mindful

    1. μιμνήσκομαι, *mimnēskomai, 3630*

Heb 2: 6 "What are human beings that you are mindful of them 1

mingle

    1. μείγνυμι, *meignymi, 3502*

Lke 13: 1 the Galileans whose blood Pilate had mingled 1

minister

    1. διακονία, *diakonia, 1355*
    2. διάκονος, *diakonos, 1356*
    3. λειτουργός, *leitourgos, 3313*

Rom 12: 7 ministry, in ministering;   1
    15:16 to be a minister of Christ Jesus to the Gentiles   3
2Co 3: 6 competent to be ministers of a new covenant   2
    11:15 if his ministers also disguise themselves   2
    11:15 as ministers of righteousness.   2
    11:23 Are they ministers of Christ?…I am a better one: 2
Eph 6:21 Tychicus…a dear brother and a faithful minister   2
Php 2:25 your messenger and minister to my need;   3
Col 1: 7 He is a faithful minister of Christ on your behalf   2
    4: 7 he is a beloved brother, a faithful minister   2
Heb 8: 2 a minister in the sanctuary and the true tent   3

ministry
1. διακονέω, *diakoneō, 1354*
2. διακονία, *diakonia, 1355*
3. λειτουργία, *leitourgia, 3311*

Act 1:17 allotted his share in this ministry."   2
    1:25 this ministry and apostleship   2
   20:24 the ministry that I received from the Lord   2
  · 21:19 done among the Gentiles through his ministry.   2
Rom 11:13 an apostle to the Gentiles, I glorify my ministry   2
   12: 7 ministry, in ministering;   2
   15:25 I am going to Jerusalem in a ministry to the saints;   1
   15:31 that my ministry to Jerusalem may be acceptable   2
2Co 3: 7 Now if the ministry of death   2
   3: 8 will the ministry of the Spirit come in glory?   2
   3: 9 glory in the ministry of condemnation   2
   3: 9 does the ministry of justification abound in glory   2
   4: 1 by God's mercy that we are engaged in this ministry   2
   5:18 given us the ministry of reconciliation;   2
   6: 3 so that no fault may be found with our ministry   2
   8: 4 sharing in this ministry to the saints—   2
   9: 1 to write you about the ministry to the saints   2
   9:12 the rendering of this ministry   3
   9:13 Through the testing of this ministry   2
Eph 4:12 to equip the saints for the work of ministry   2
2Ti 4: 5 carry out your ministry fully.   2
   4:11 for he is useful in my ministry.   2
Heb 8: 6 Jesus has now obtained a more excellent ministry   3

minor
1. νήπιος, *nēpios, 3758*

Gal 4: 1 heirs, as long as they are minors, are no better   1
   4: 3 So with us; while we were minors   1

minstrel
1. μουσικός, *mousikos, 3676*

Rev 18:22 and the sound of harpists and minstrels   1

mint
1. ἡδύοσμον, *hēdyosmon, 2455*

Mat 23:23 you tithe mint, dill, and cummin   1
Lke 11:42 you tithe mint and rue and herbs of all kinds   1

minus
1. παρά, *para, 4123*

2Co 11:24 from the Jews the forty lashes minus one.   1

miracle *See also* work a miracle
1. δύναμις, *dynamis, 1539*

Act 8:13 saw the signs and great miracles that took place.   1
  19:11 God did extraordinary miracles through Paul   1
1Co 12:10 to another the working of miracles   1
Gal 3: 5 work miracles among you   1
Heb 2: 4 by signs and wonders and various miracles   1

mirror *See also* see reflected in a mirror
1. ἔσοπτρον, *esoptron, 2269*

1Co 13:12 For now we see in a mirror, dimly,   1
Jas 1:23 those who look at themselves in a mirror;   1

mischief maker
1. ἀλλοτριεπίσκοπος, *allotriepiskopos, 258*

1Pe 4:15 let none of you suffer…even as a mischief maker.   1

miserable
1. κακῶς, *kakōs, 2809*

Mat 21:41 put those wretches to a miserable death   1

misery
1. ταλαιπωρία, *talaipōria, 5416*

Rom 3:16 ruin and misery are in their paths   1
Jas 5: 1 wail for the miseries that are coming to you.   1

mismatch
1. ἑτεροζυγέω, *heterozygeō, 2282*

2Co 6:14 Do not be mismatched with unbelievers.   1

misrepresent
1. ψευδόμαρτυς, *pseudomartys, 6020*

1Co 15:15 We are even found to be misrepresenting God   1

miss the mark
1. ἀστοχέω, *astocheō, 846*

1Ti 6:21 some have missed the mark as regards the faith.   1

mission
1. διακονία, *diakonia, 1355*

Act 12:25 after completing their mission Barnabas and Saul   1

mist
1. ἀτμίς, *atmis, 874*
2. ἀχλύς, *achlys, 944*
3. ὁμίχλη, *homichlē, 3920*

Act 2:19 blood, and fire, and smoky mist.   1
  13:11 Immediately mist and darkness came over him   2
Jas 4:14 For you are a mist that appears for a little while   1
2Pe 2:17 waterless springs and mists driven by a storm;   3

mistake *See* make a mistake

mistreat
1. κακόω, *kakoō, 2808*
2. ὑβρίζω, *hybrizō, 5614*

Mat 22: 6 mistreated them, and killed them.   2
Act 7: 6 who would enslave them and mistreat them   1
  14: 5 to mistreat them and to stone them   2

mistreat shamefully
1. ὑβρίζω, *hybrizō, 5614*

1Th 2: 2 we had…been shamefully mistreated at Philippi   1

mistreatment
1. κάκωσις, *kakōsis, 2810*

Act 7:34 I have surely seen the mistreatment of my people   1

Mitylene
1. Μιτυλήνη, *Mitylēnē, 3639*

Act 20:14 we took him on board and went to Mitylene.   1

mix
1. ἐγκρύπτω, *enkryptō, 1606*
2. κεράννυμι, *kerannymi, 3042*
3. μείγνυμι, *meignymi, 3502*

Mat 13:33 yeast that a woman took and mixed   1
  27:34 they offered him wine to drink, mixed with gall;   3
Rev 8: 7 there came hail and fire, mixed with blood   3
  15: 2 appeared to be a sea of glass mixed with fire   3
  18: 6 mix a double draught for her in the cup she mixed.   2
  18: 6 mix a double draught for her in the cup she mixed.   2

mix in
1. ἐγκρύπτω, *enkryptō, 1606*

Lke 13:21 took and mixed in with three measures of flour   1

mix with myrrh
1. σμυρνίζω, *smyrnizō, 5046*

Mrk 15:23 they offered him wine mixed with myrrh;   1

mixture
1. μίγμα, *migma, 3623*

Jhn 19:39 came, bringing a mixture of myrrh and aloes   1

Mnason
1. Μνάσων, *Mnasōn, 3643*

Act 21:16 brought us to the house of Mnason of Cyprus   1

mob *See also* form a mob
1. ὄχλος, *ochlos, 4063*
Act 21:35 the violence of the mob was so great   1

mock
1. ἐμπαιγμός, *empaigmos, 1849*
2. ἐμπαίζω, *empaizō, 1850*
3. μυκτηρίζω, *myktērizō, 3682*
Mat 20:19 to be mocked and flogged and crucified;   2
      27:29 knelt before him and mocked him, saying   2
      27:31 After mocking him, they stripped him of   2
      27:41 scribes and elders, were mocking him, saying   2
Mrk 10:34 they will mock him, and spit upon him, and flog   2
      15:20 After mocking him, they stripped him of   2
      15:31 the scribes, were also mocking him among themselves   2
Lke 18:32 will be mocked and insulted and spat upon.   2
      22:63 the men who were holding Jesus began to mock him   2
      23:11 Herod...mocked him;   2
      23:36 The soldiers also mocked him   2
Gal   6: 7 Do not be deceived; God is not mocked   3
Heb 11:36 Others suffered mocking and flogging   1

model
1. τύπος, *typos, 5596*
Tit   2: 7 in all respects a model of good works   1

moderately *See* blow moderately

modestly
1. αἰδώς, *aidōs, 133*
1Ti   2: 9 women should dress themselves modestly   1

modesty
1. σωφροσύνη, *sōphrosynē, 5408*
1Ti   2:15 in faith and love and holiness, with modesty.   1

moisture
1. ἰκμάς, *ikmas, 2657*
Lke   8: 6 it withered for lack of moisture.   1

mold
1. πλάσμα, *plasma, 4420*
2. πλάσσω, *plassō, 4421*
Rom 9:20 Will what is molded say to the one who molds it   1
       9:20 Will what is molded say to the one who molds it   2

Moloch
1. Μολόχ, *Moloch, 3661*
Act   7:43 No; you took along the tent of Moloch   1

moment
1. ἄτομος, *atomos, 875*
2. ὥρα, *hōra, 6052*
Lke   2:38 At that moment she came, and began to praise God   2
Rom 13:11 it is now the moment for you to wake from sleep.   2
1Co 15:52 in a moment, in the twinkling of an eye   1
Gal   2: 5 we did not submit to them even for a moment   2
Rev 11:13 At that moment there was a great earthquake   2

at that moment
1. εὐθέως, *eutheōs, 2311*
2. εὐθύς¹, *euthys¹, 2317*
3. ἰδού, *idou, 2627*
4. παραχρῆμα, *parachrēma, 4202*
Mat 26:74 At that moment the cock crowed.   1
      27:51 At that moment the curtain of the temple was torn   3
Mrk 14:72 At that moment the cock crowed for the second time.   2
Lke 22:60 At that moment, while he was still speaking   4
Jhn 18:27 at that moment the cock crowed.   1

at this moment
1. ἰδού, *idou, 2627*
Act   9:11 At this moment he is praying   1

that moment
1. τότε, *tote, 5538*
Mat 26:16 from that moment he began to look for an opportunity   1

very moment
1. ἐξαυτῆς, *exautēs, 1994*
Act 11:11 At that very moment three men...arrived   1

momentary
1. παραυτίκα, *parautika, 4194*
2Co   4:17 this slight momentary affliction   1

money *See also* extort money by threat, free from love of money, greedy for money, love of money, lover of money, make money, not a *lover* of money, sum of money
1. Contextual: Not in Greek
2. ἀργύριον, *argyrion, 736*
3. ἐργασία, *ergasia, 2238*
4. τιμή, *timē, 5507*
5. χαλκός, *chalkos, 5910*
6. χρῆμα, *chrēma, 5975*
Mat 19:21 sell...and give the money to the poor   1
      25:18 dug a hole in the ground and hid his master's money.   2
      25:27 to have invested my money with the bankers   2
      26: 9 and the money given to the poor."   1
      27: 6 since they are blood money."   4
      28:12 to give a large sum of money to the soldiers   2
      28:15 took the money and did as they were directed.   2
Mrk   6: 8 no bread, no bag, no money in their belts;   5
      10:21 sell what you own, and give the money to the poor   1
      12:41 the crowd putting money into the treasury.   5
      14: 5 and the money given to the poor."   1
      14:11 greatly pleased, and promised to give him money.   2
Lke   9: 3 no staff, nor bag, nor bread, nor money   2
      18:22 Sell...and distribute the money to the poor   1
      19:15 these slaves, to whom he had given the money   2
      19:23 Why then did you not put my money into the bank?   2
      22: 5 greatly pleased and agreed to give him money.   2
Jhn 12: 5 the money given to the poor?"   1
Act   4:37 brought the money   6
       8:18 he offered them money   6
       8:20 thought you could obtain God's gift with money!   6
      16:16 brought...a great deal of money by fortune-telling.   3
      24:26 he hoped that money would be given him by Paul   6

money changer
1. κερματιστής, *kermatistēs, 3048*
2. κολλυβιστής, *kollybistēs, 3142*
Mat 21:12 he overturned the tables of the money changers   2
Mrk 11:15 he overturned the tables of the money changers   2
Jhn   2:14 and the money changers seated at their tables.   1
       2:15 also poured out the coins of the money changers   2

sea monster
1. κῆτος, *kētos, 3063*
Mat 12:40 three nights in the belly of the sea monster   1

month *See also* four months, three months
1. μήν¹, *mēn¹, 3604*
Lke   1:24 for five months she remained in seclusion.   1
       1:26 In the sixth month the angel Gabriel was sent   1
       1:36 the sixth month for her who was said to be barren.   1
       1:56 Mary remained with her about three months   1
       4:25 the heaven was shut up three years and six months   1
Act   7:20 three months he was brought up in his father's house;   1
      18:11 He stayed there a year and six months   1
      19: 8 and for three months spoke out boldly   1
      20: 3 where he stayed for three months.   1
      28:11 Three months later we set sail   1
Gal   4:10 observing special days, and months, and seasons   1
Jas   5:17 for three years and six months it did not rain   1
Rev   9: 5 were allowed to torture them for five months   1
       9:10 their power to harm people for five months   1
       9:15 ready for the hour, the day, the month, and the year   1
      11: 2 trample over the holy city for forty-two months.   1
      13: 5 to exercise authority for forty-two months.   1
      22: 2 tree of life...producing its fruit each month;   1

moon *See also* new moon
1. σελήνη, *selēnē, 4943*
Mat 24:29 the moon will not give its light;   1
Mrk 13:24 the moon will not give its light   1
Lke 21:25 "There will be signs in the sun, the moon,   1

Act	2:20	the moon to blood	1
1Co	15:41	one glory of the sun, and another glory of the moon	1
Rev	6:12	the full moon became like blood	1
	8:12	third of the sun was struck, and a third of the moon	1
	12: 1	clothed with the sun, with the moon under her feet	1
	21:23	the city has no need of sun or moon to shine on it	1

moor a boat

1. προσορμίζω, *prosormizō, 4694*

Mrk	6:53	they came to land…and moored the boat	1

moral

1. ἦθος, *ēthos, 2456*

1Co	15:33	"Bad company ruins good morals."	1

morale

1. τάξις, *taxis, 5423*

Col	2: 5	rejoice to see your morale	1

morbid   *See* morbid *craving*

more   *See also* abound all the more, all the more, even more, far more, give still more, have more than enough, make more, more *acceptable*, more *accurately*, more and more *people*, more *clearly*, more *distinguished*, more *eager*, more *earnestly*, more *evil*, more *excellent*, more *increasingly*, more *necessary*, more *powerful*, more *precious*, more *receptive*, more *respectable*, more *shrewd*, more *surely*, more than *conqueror*, more *thorough*, more *thoroughly*, more *tolerable*, more *valuable*, more *value*, nothing more to do, once more, one thing more, spend more

1. Contextual: Not in Greek
2. ἄλλος, *allos, 257*
3. δίς, *dis, 1489*
4. ἔτι, *eti, 2285*
5. καί, *kai, 2779*
6. μᾶλλον, *mallon, 3437*
7. μείζων, *meizōn, 3505*
8. ὅσος, *hosos, 4012*
9. περισσός, *perissos, 4356*
10. περισσότερος, *perissoteros, 4358*
11. περισσοτέρως, *perissoterōs, 4359*
12. πολύς, *polys, 4498*
13. ὑπέρ, *hyper, 5642*

Mat	5:37	anything more than this comes from the evil one	9
	5:47	what more are you doing than others?	9
	6:25	Is not life more than food, and the body	12
	6:25	than food, and the body more than clothing?	1
	6:26	them. Are you not of more value than they?	6
	6:30	will he not much more clothe you—	6
	7:11	how much more will your Father in heaven	6
	10:25	how much more will they malign	6
	11: 9	Yes, I tell you, and more than a prophet.	10
	13:12	For to those who have, more will be given	1
	18:13	he rejoices…more than over the ninety-nine	6
	20:10	they thought they would receive more;	12
	20:31	but they shouted even more loudly	7
	21:36	Again he sent other slaves, more than the first;	12
	25:16	made five more talents.	2
	25:17	who had the two talents made two more talents.	2
	25:20	bringing five more talents, saying	2
	25:20	see, I have made five more talents.'	2
	25:22	see, I have made two more talents.'	2
	25:29	For to all those who have, more will be given	1
	26:53	he will at once send me more than twelve legions	12
Mrk	4:25	For to those who have, more will be given;	1
	7:36	the more he ordered them	8
	7:36	the more zealously they proclaimed it.	6
	10:48	he cried out even more loudly, "Son of David	6
	12:43	this poor widow has put in more than all	12
Lke	3:13	"Collect no more than the amount prescribed	12
	7:26	Yes, I tell you, and more than a prophet.	10
	7:42	Now which of them will love him more?"	12
	8:18	to those who have, more will be given;	1
	9:13	"We have no more than five loaves and two fish	12
	11:13	how much more will…Father give the Holy Spirit	6
	12: 4	after that can do nothing more.	10

	12:23	For life is more than food	12
	12:23	the body more than clothing.	1
	12:24	Of how much more value are you than the birds!	6
	12:28	how much more will he clothe you	6
	13: 8	He replied, 'Sir, let it alone for one more year	5
	15: 7	more joy in heaven over one sinner who repents	1
	18:39	he shouted even more loudly,	6
	19:26	to all those who have, more will be given;	1
	21: 3	this poor widow has put in more than all of them;	12
Jhn	4: 1	making and baptizing more disciples than John"	12
	4:35	'Four months more, then comes the harvest'?	4
	4:41	And many more believed because of his word.	12
	7:31	will he do more signs than this man has done?"	12
	12:43	more than the glory that comes from God.	6
	15: 2	he prunes to make it bear more fruit.	12
	21:15	"Simon son of John, do you love me more than these?"	12
Act	4:22	the man…was more than forty years old.	12
	20:35	'It is more blessed to give than to receive.' "	6
	23:13	more than forty who joined in this conspiracy.	12
	23:21	more than forty of their men are lying in ambush	12
	24:11	it is not more than twelve days since I went up	12
	25: 6	stayed among them not more than eight or ten days	12
	27:11	centurion paid more attention to the pilot	6
Rom	11:12	how much more will their full inclusion mean!	6
	11:24	how much more will these natural branches	6
1Co	7:40	she is more blessed if she remains as she is.	1
	9:12	If others share…do not we still more?	6
	9:19	a slave to all, so that I might win more	12
	14:18	I speak in tongues more than all of you;	6
2Co	3: 8	how much more will the ministry of the Spirit come	6
	3: 9	much more does the ministry of justification	6
	3:11	much more has the permanent come in glory!	6
	7: 7	so that I rejoiced still more.	6
	7:13	we rejoiced still more at the joy of Titus	11
	12:15	If I love you more, am I to be loved less?	11
Gal	4:27	children of the desolate woman are more numerous	6
Eph	3:20	abundantly far more than all we can ask or imagine	13
Php	1: 9	prayer, that your love may overflow more and more	6
	1: 9	prayer, that your love may overflow more and more	6
	2:12	in my presence, but much more now in my absence	6
	3: 4	If anyone else has reason…I have more:	6
	4:16	you sent me help for my needs more than once.	3
1Th	4: 1	you are doing), you should do so more and more.	6
	4:10	we urge you, beloved, to do so more and more	6
2Ti	2:16	it will lead people into more and more impiety	12
	2:16	it will lead people into more and more impiety	1
Phm	1:16	especially to me but how much more to you	6
Heb	3: 3	Yet Jesus is worthy of more glory than Moses,	12
	3: 3	the builder of a house has more honor than the house	12
	7:15	It is even more obvious	10
	8:12	I will remember their sins no more."	4
	9:14	how much more will the blood of Christ	6
	10:17	remember their sins and their lawless deeds no more."	4
	10:25	all the more as you see the Day approaching.	6
	10:34	possessed something better and more lasting.	1
	11:32	And what more should I say?	4
	12: 9	Should we not be even more willing to be subject	6
	12:26	"Yet once more I will shake not only the earth	1
	12:27	This phrase, "Yet once more," indicates…	1
2Pe	1:19	we have the prophetic message more fully confirmed.	1
Rev	7:16	They will hunger no more, and thirst no	4
	7:16	will hunger no more, and thirst no more;	4
	18:21	Babylon…will be found no more;	4
	18:22	sound of harpists…will be heard in you no more;	4
	18:22	an artisan…will be found in you no more;	4
	18:22	the millstone will be heard in you no more;	4
	18:23	and the light of a lamp will shine in you no more;	4
	18:23	the voice…will be heard in you no more;	4
	20: 3	so that he would deceive the nations no more	4
	21: 1	earth had passed away, and the sea was no more.	4
	21: 4	Death will be no more;	4
	21: 4	mourning and crying and pain will be no more	4
	22: 5	And there will be no more night;	4

any more

1. ἔτι, *eti, 2285*

Rev	22: 3	Nothing accursed will be found there any more.	1

more than

1. ἐπάνω, *epanō, 2062*
2. οὐ, *ou, 4024*

  3. παρά, *para, 4123*
  4. ὑπέρ, *hyper, 5642*

Mat 10:37	Whoever loves father or mother more than me	4
10:37	and whoever loves son or daughter more than me	4
Mrk 14: 5	sold for more than three hundred denarii	1
Rom 12: 3	not to think of yourself more highly than you ought	3
1Co 15: 6	Then he appeared to more than five hundred	1
Gal 3:20	Now a mediator involves more than one	2
Phm 1:16	no longer as a slave but more than a slave	4
1:21	knowing that you will do even more than I say.	4

more than ever

  1. μᾶλλον, *mallon, 3437*
  2. πολύς, *polys, 4498*

Lke 5:15	more than ever the word about Jesus spread abroad;	1
Jhn 19: 8	he was more afraid than ever.	1
Act 5:14	more than ever believers were added to the Lord	1
1Co 7:21	make use of your…condition now more than ever	1
2Co 8:22	who is now more eager than ever	2

more than that

  1. ἔτι, *eti, 2285*
  2. μενοῦνγε, *menounge, 3529*
  3. οὐ + μόνον, *ou + monon, 4024 + 3667*

Act 21:28	more than that, he has actually brought Greeks	1
Rom 5:11	But more than that, we even boast in God	3
Php 3: 8	More than that, I regard everything as loss	2

much more

  1. περισσότερος, *perissoteros, 4358*

Mrk 12:33	much more important than all whole burnt offerings	1

no any more

  1. οὐκέτι, *ouketi, 4033*

Mrk 5: 3	no one could restrain him any more	2
9: 8	saw no one with them any more, but only Jesus.	2

no more

  1. ἐάω, *eaō, 1572*
  2. μή, *mē, 3590*
  3. μηκέτι, *mēketi, 3600*
  4. οὐ, *ou, 4024*
  5. οὐκέτι, *ouketi, 4033*
  6. οὔτε, *oute, 4046*

Mat 2:18	to be consoled, because they are no more."	4
Lke 22:51	Jesus said, "No more of this!"	1
Act 4:17	let us warn them to speak no more to anyone	3
8:39	the eunuch saw him no more	5
13:34	no more to return to corruption	3
1Co 15:34	Come to a sober and right mind, and sin no more;	2
Jas 3:12	No more can salt water yield fresh.	6
Rev 10: 6	"There will be no more delay	5

nor any more

  1. οὐκέτι, *ouketi, 4033*

Mat 22:46	nor did anyone dare to ask him any more questions.	1

not any more

  1. μηκέτι, *mēketi, 3600*

Jhn 5:14	Do not sin any more, so that nothing worse happens	1

very much more

  1. πολλαπλασίων, *pollaplasiōn, 4491*

Lke 18:30	who will not get back very much more in this age	1

moreover

  1. ἀλλά, *alla, 247*
  2. δέ, *de, 1254*
  3. εἶτα, *eita, 1663*
  4. ἔτι, *eti, 2285*
  5. ὧδε + λοιπός, *hōde + loipos, 6045 + 3370*

Lke 24:22	Moreover, some women of our group astounded us.	1
Act 2:26	moreover my flesh will live in hope.	4
1Co 4: 2	Moreover, it is required of stewards	5
1Ti 3: 7	Moreover, he must be well thought of by outsiders	2
Heb 12: 9	Moreover, we had human parents	3

morning

See also early in the morning, morning *star*, nine o'clock in the morning

  1. ἡμέρα, *hēmera, 2465*
  2. πρωΐ, *prōi, 4745*
  3. πρωΐα, *prōia, 4746*
  4. πρωϊνός, *prōinos, 4748*

Mat 16: 3	in the morning, 'It will be stormy today,	2
21:18	In the morning, when he returned to the city	2
27: 1	When morning came	3
Mrk 1:35	In the morning, while it was still very dark	2
11:20	In the morning as they passed by	2
15: 1	As soon as it was morning	2
Act 12:18	When morning came, there was no small commotion	1
16:35	When morning came, the magistrates sent the police	1
23:12	In the morning the Jews joined in a conspiracy	1
27:39	In the morning they did not recognize the land	1
28:23	From morning until evening	2
Rev 2:28	who conquers I will also give the morning star.	4
22:16	the descendant of David, the bright morning star."	4

mortal

See also all mortals

  1. ἄνθρωπος, *anthrōpos, 476*
  2. ἀποθνήσκω, *apothnēskō, 633*
  3. θάνατος, *thanatos, 2505*
  4. θνητός, *thnētos, 2570*
  5. πρός + θάνατος, *pros + thanatos, 4639 + 2505*
  6. υἱός + ἄνθρωπος, *huios + anthrōpos, 5626 + 476*
  7. φθαρτός, *phthartos, 5778*

Mat 19:26	"For mortals it is impossible	1
Mrk 10:27	"For mortals it is impossible, but not for God;	1
Lke 18:27	impossible for mortals is possible for God."	1
Act 4:12	no other name under heaven given among mortals	1
10:26	saying, "Stand up; I am only a mortal."	1
12:22	shouting, "The voice of a god, and not of a mortal!"	1
14:15	We are mortals just like you	1
17:29	by the art and imagination of mortals.	1
Rom 1:23	for images resembling a mortal human being or birds	7
6:12	not let sin exercise dominion in your mortal bodies	4
8:11	will give life to your mortal bodies also	4
1Co 4: 9	a spectacle to the world, to angels and to mortals.	1
13: 1	If I speak in the tongues of mortals and of angels	1
15:53	this mortal body must put on immortality.	4
15:54	this mortal body puts on immortality	4
2Co 4:11	Jesus may be made visible in our mortal flesh.	4
5: 4	what is mortal may be swallowed up by life.	4
12: 4	that no mortal is permitted to repeat.	1
1Th 2: 4	not to please mortals, but to please God	1
2: 6	nor did we seek praise from mortals	1
Heb 2: 6	"What are…mortals, that you care for them?	6
5: 1	Every high priest chosen from among mortals	1
7: 8	tithes are received by those who are mortal;	2
8: 2	the Lord, and not any mortal, has set up.	1
9:27	just as it is appointed for mortals to die once	1
1Pe 2: 4	though rejected by mortals yet chosen and precious	1
1Jn 5:16	your brother or sister committing what is not a mortal sin	5
5:16	give life to such a one—to those whose sin is not mortal.	5
5:16	There is sin that is mortal;	5
5:17	but there is sin that is not mortal.	5
Rev 13: 3	but its mortal wound had been healed.	3
13:12	the first beast, whose mortal wound had been healed.	3
21: 3	"See, the home of God is among mortals.	1

Moses

  1. αὐτός, *autos, 899*
  2. Μωυσῆς, *Mōysēs, 3707*

Mat 8: 4	and offer the gift that Moses commanded	2
17: 3	Suddenly there appeared to them Moses and Elijah	2
17: 4	one for you, one for Moses, and one for Elijah."	2
19: 7	"Why then did Moses command	2
19: 8	Moses allowed you to divorce your wives	2
22:24	"Teacher, Moses said	2
23: 2	"The scribes and the Pharisees sit on Moses' seat;	2
Mrk 1:44	offer for your cleansing what Moses commanded	2
7:10	For Moses said, 'Honor your father and your mother';	2
9: 4	there appeared to them Elijah with Moses	2
9: 5	one for you, one for Moses, and one for Elijah."	2
10: 3	He answered them, "What did Moses command you?"	2
10: 4	"Moses allowed a man to write a certificate	2
12:19	"Teacher, Moses wrote for us	2

	12:26	have you not read in the book of Moses	2
Lke	2:22	purification according to the law of Moses	2
	5:14	as Moses commanded, make an offering	2
	9:30	two men, Moses and Elijah, talking to him.	2
	9:33	one for you, one for Moses, and one for Elijah"	2
	16:29	Abraham replied, 'They have Moses and the prophets;	2
	16:31	'If they do not listen to Moses and the prophets	2
	20:28	Moses wrote for us that if a man's brother dies	2
	20:37	that the dead are raised Moses himself showed	2
	24:27	beginning with Moses and all the prophets	2
	24:44	everything written about me in the law of Moses	2
Jhn	1:17	The law indeed was given through Moses;	2
	1:45	"We have found him about whom Moses…wrote	2
	3:14	as Moses lifted up the serpent in the wilderness	2
	5:45	your accuser is Moses	2
	5:46	If you believed Moses, you would believe me	2
	6:32	not Moses who gave you the bread from heaven	2
	7:19	"Did not Moses give you the law?	2
	7:22	Moses gave you circumcision	2
	7:22	not from Moses, but from the patriarchs)	2
	7:23	that the law of Moses may not be broken	2
	8: 5	[[Now in the law Moses commanded us to stone such]]	2
	9:28	we are disciples of Moses.	2
	9:29	We know that God has spoken to Moses	2
Act	3:22	Moses said, 'The Lord your God will raise up	2
	6:11	blasphemous words against Moses and God."	2
	6:14	change the customs that Moses handed on to us."	2
	7:20	At this time Moses was born	2
	7:22	Moses was instructed in all the wisdom	2
	7:27	the man…pushed Moses aside, saying	1
	7:29	When he heard this, Moses fled	2
	7:31	When Moses saw it, he was amazed at the sight;	2
	7:32	Moses began to tremble and did not dare to look.	2
	7:35	this Moses whom they rejected when they said	2
	7:37	This is the Moses who said to the Israelites	2
	7:40	this Moses who led us out from the land of Egypt	2
	7:44	as God directed when he spoke to Moses	2
	13:39	you could not be freed by the law of Moses.	2
	15: 1	circumcised according to the custom of Moses	2
	15: 5	ordered to keep the law of Moses."	2
	15:21	Moses has had those who proclaim him	2
	21:21	you teach all the Jews…to forsake Moses	2
	26:22	what…Moses said would take place:	2
	28:23	both from the law of Moses and from the prophets.	2
Rom	5:14	Yet death exercised dominion from Adam to Moses	2
	9:15	For he says to Moses, "I will have mercy	2
	10: 5	Moses writes concerning the righteousness	2
	10:19	First Moses says, "I will make you jealous	2
1Co	9: 9	For it is written in the law of Moses	2
	10: 2	all were baptized into Moses in the cloud	2
2Co	3: 7	people of Israel could not gaze at Moses' face	2
	3:13	not like Moses, who put a veil over his face	2
	3:15	Indeed, to this very day whenever Moses is read	2
2Ti	3: 8	As Jannes and Jambres opposed Moses	2
Heb	3: 2	just as Moses also "was faithful in all God's house."	2
	3: 3	is worthy of…more glory than Moses	2
	3: 5	Now Moses was faithful in all God's house	2
	3:16	left Egypt under the leadership of Moses?	2
	7:14	Moses said nothing about priests.	2
	8: 5	Moses, when he was about to erect the tent	2
	9:19	had been told to all the people by Moses	2
	10:28	Anyone who has violated the law of Moses dies	2
	11:23	By faith Moses was hidden by his parents	2
	11:24	By faith Moses…refused to be called a son	2
	12:21	Moses said, "I tremble with fear.")	2
Jde	1: 9	Michael…disputed about the body of Moses	2
Rev	15: 3	they sing the song of Moses, the servant of God	2

most *See also* make the most, most *excellent*, most *gladly*, most *high*, most *holy*, pity most

1. Contextual: Not in Greek
2. πολύς, *polys*, 4498

Mat	11:20	in which most of his deeds of power had been done	2
Mrk	9:26	so that most of them said, "He is dead."	2
Act	19:32	most of them did not know why they had come	2
1Co	10: 5	God was not pleased with most of them	2
	14:27	let there be only two or at most three	2
	15: 6	most of whom are still alive	2
2Co	9: 2	your zeal has stirred up most of them.	2
Php	1:14	most of the brothers and sisters…dare to speak	2
1Th	3:10	Night and day we pray most earnestly that we may see	1

moth

1. σής, *sēs*, 4962

Mat	6:19	treasures on earth, where moth and rust consume	1
	6:20	in heaven, where neither moth nor rust consumes	1
Lke	12:33	where no thief comes near and no moth destroys.	1

moth-eaten

1. σητόβρωτος, *sētobrōtos*, 4963

Jas	5: 2	and your clothes are moth-eaten.	1

mother *See also* kill one's mother

1. Contextual: Not in Greek
2. μήτηρ, *mētēr*, 3613
3. ὁ, *ho*, 3836

Mat	1:18	When his mother Mary had been engaged	2
	2:11	saw the child with Mary his mother; and they knelt	2
	2:13	"Get up, take the child and his mother, and flee	2
	2:14	Joseph got up, took the child and his mother	2
	2:20	"Get up, take the child and his mother, and go	2
	2:21	Joseph got up, took the child and his mother	2
	10:35	and a daughter against her mother	2
	10:37	Whoever loves father or mother more than me	2
	12:46	his mother and his brothers were standing	2
	12:47	"Look, your mother and your brothers are standing	2
	12:48	"Who is my mother, and who are my brothers?"	2
	12:49	he said, "Here are my mother and my brothers!	2
	12:50	is my brother and sister and mother."	2
	13:55	Is not his mother called Mary?	2
	14: 8	Prompted by her mother, she said	2
	14:11	who brought it to her mother.	2
	15: 4	'Honor your father and your mother,'	2
	15: 4	'Whoever speaks evil of father or mother	2
	15: 5	you say that whoever tells father or mother	2
	19: 5	leave his father and mother	2
	19:19	Honor your father and mother;	2
	19:29	sisters or father or mother or children or fields	2
	20:20	the mother of the sons of Zebedee came to him	2
	27:56	Mary the mother of James and Joseph	2
	27:56	the mother of the sons of Zebedee.	2
Mrk	3:31	his mother and his brothers came;	2
	3:32	"Your mother and your brothers and sisters	2
	3:33	he replied, "Who are my mother and my brothers?"	2
	3:34	he said, "Here are my mother and my brothers!	2
	3:35	is my brother and sister and mother."	2
	5:40	and took the child's father and mother	2
	6:24	She went out and said to her mother	2
	6:28	the girl gave it to her mother.	2
	7:10	For Moses said, 'Honor your father and your mother';	2
	7:10	'Whoever speaks evil of father or mother	2
	7:11	you say that if anyone tells father or mother	2
	7:12	doing anything for a father or mother	2
	10: 7	a man shall leave his father and mother	2
	10:19	shall not defraud; Honor your father and mother.' "	2
	10:29	house or brothers or sisters or mother or father	2
	10:30	brothers and sisters, mothers and children	2
	15:40	Mary the mother of James the younger and of Joses	2
	15:47	Mary Magdalene and Mary the mother of Joses saw	3
	16: 1	Mary Magdalene, and Mary the mother of James	3
Lke	1:43	that the mother of my Lord comes to me?	2
	1:60	his mother said, "No; he is to be called John."	2
	2:33	the child's father and mother were amazed	2
	2:34	Simeon blessed them and said to his mother Mary	2
	2:48	his mother said to him, "Child, why have you	2
	2:51	His mother treasured all these things in her heart.	2
	7:12	was his mother's only son, and she was a widow;	2
	7:15	Jesus gave him to his mother.	2
	8:19	Then his mother and his brothers came to him	2
	8:20	he was told, "Your mother and your brothers	2
	8:21	"My mother and my brothers are those who hear	2
	8:51	the child's father and mother.	2
	12:53	mother against daughter	2
	12:53	daughter against mother	2
	14:26	father and mother, wife and children	2
	18:20	Honor your father and mother.' "	2
	24:10	Mary the mother of James, and the other women	3
Jhn	2: 1	in Cana…and the mother of Jesus was there.	2
	2: 3	When the wine gave out, the mother of Jesus said	2
	2: 5	His mother said to the servants	2
	2:12	with his mother, his brothers	2
	3: 4	Can one enter a second time into the mother's womb	2

Jhn 6:42 Jesus...whose father and mother we know? 2
19:25 standing near the cross of Jesus were his mother 2
19:25 his mother's sister, Mary the wife of Clopas 2
19:26 When Jesus saw his mother 2
19:26 he said to his mother, "Woman, here is your son." 2
19:27 he said to the disciple, "Here is your mother." 2
Act 1:14 certain women, including Mary the mother of Jesus 2
12:12 Mary the mother of John whose other name was Mark 2
Rom 16:13 and greet his mother—a mother to me also. 2
16:13 and greet his mother—a mother to me also. 1
Gal 4:26 Jerusalem above; she is free, and she is our mother. 2
Eph 5:31 a man will leave his father and mother 2
6: 2 "Honor your father and mother" 2
1Ti 5: 2 older women as mothers 2
2Ti 1: 5 your grandmother Lois and your mother Eunice 2
Rev 17: 5 "Babylon the great, mother of whores 2

without mother

1. ἀμήτωρ, *amētōr, 298*

Heb 7: 3 Without father, without mother, without genealogy 1

mother-in-law

1. πενθερά, *penthera, 4289*

Mat 8:14 saw his mother-in-law lying in bed with a fever; 1
10:35 a daughter-in-law against her mother-in-law; 1
Mrk 1:30 Simon's mother-in-law was in bed with a fever 1
Lke 4:38 mother-in-law was suffering from a high fever 1
12:53 mother-in-law against her daughter-in-law 1
12:53 daughter-in-law against mother-in-law." 1

motion

1. διανεύω, *dianeuō, 1377*
2. ἐννεύω, *enneuō, 1935*
3. κατασείω, *kataseiō, 2939*
4. νεύω, *neuō, 3748*

Lke 1:22 He kept motioning to them and remained 1
1:62 Then they began motioning to his father 2
Jhn 13:24 Simon Peter therefore motioned to him to ask Jesus 4
Act 12:17 motioned to them with his hand to be silent 3
24:10 When the governor motioned to him to speak 4

motion for silence

1. κατασείω + ὁ + χείρ, *kataseiō + ho + cheir, 2939 + 3836 + 5931*

Act 19:33 Alexander motioned for silence 1
21:40 motioned to the people for silence; 1

false motive

1. πρόφασις, *prophasis, 4733*

Php 1:18 whether out of false motives or true; 1

impure motive

1. ἀκαθαρσία, *akatharsia, 174*

1Th 2: 3 does not spring from deceit or impure motives 1

mount¹

1. ὄρος, *oros, 4001*

Mat 21: 1 had reached Bethphage, at the Mount of Olives 1
24: 3 When he was sitting on the Mount of Olives 1
26:30 they went out to the Mount of Olives. 1
Mrk 11: 1 Bethphage and Bethany, near the Mount of Olives 1
13: 3 When he was sitting on the Mount of Olives 1
14:26 they went out to the Mount of Olives. 1
Lke 19:29 at the place called the Mount of Olives, 1
19:37 the path down from the Mount of Olives 1
21:37 spend the night on the Mount of Olives, 1
22:39 went, as was his custom, to the Mount of Olives; 1
Jhn 8: 1 [Jesus went to the Mount of Olives.] 1
Act 1:12 Then they returned to Jerusalem from the mount 1
7:30 in the wilderness of Mount Sinai 1
7:38 the angel who spoke to him at Mount Sinai 1
Gal 4:24 Hagar, from Mount Sinai, bearing children for slavery. 1
4:25 Now Hagar is Mount Sinai in Arabia 1
Heb 12:22 you have come to Mount Zion 1
Rev 14: 1 and there was the Lamb, standing on Mount Zion! 1

mount²

1. ἐπιβαίνω, *epibainō, 2094*
2. κτῆνος, *ktēnos, 3229*

Mat 21: 5 humble, and mounted on a donkey 1
Act 23:24 Also provide mounts for Paul to ride 2

mountain

1. ὄρος, *oros, 4001*

Mat 4: 8 Again, the devil took him to a very high mountain 1
5: 1 Jesus saw the crowds, he went up the mountain 1
8: 1 When Jesus had come down from the mountain 1
14:23 he went up the mountain by himself to pray. 1
15:29 he went up the mountain, where he sat down. 1
17: 1 and led them up a high mountain, by themselves. 1
17: 9 As they were coming down the mountain 1
17:20 you will say to this mountain 1
18:12 not leave the ninety-nine on the mountains 1
21:21 but even if you say to this mountain 1
24:16 those in Judea must flee to the mountains; 1
28:16 to the mountain to which Jesus had directed 1
Mrk 3:13 He went up the mountain 1
5: 5 on the mountains he was always howling 1
6:46 he went up on the mountain to pray. 1
9: 2 led them up a high mountain apart, by themselves. 1
9: 9 As they were coming down the mountain 1
11:23 Truly I tell you, if you say to this mountain 1
13:14 those in Judea must flee to the mountains; 1
Lke 3: 5 every mountain and hill shall be made low 1
6:12 he went out to the mountain to pray; 1
9:28 and went up on the mountain to pray. 1
9:37 when they had come down from the mountain 1
21:21 those in Judea must flee to the mountains; 1
23:30 begin to say to the mountains, 'Fall on us'; 1
Jhn 4:20 Our ancestors worshiped on this mountain 1
4:21 neither on this mountain nor in Jerusalem. 1
6: 3 Jesus went up the mountain 1
6:15 he withdrew again to the mountain by himself. 1
1Co 13: 2 if I have all faith, so as to remove mountains 1
Heb 8: 5 the pattern that was shown you on the mountain." 1
11:38 wandered in deserts and mountains 1
12:20 "If even an animal touches the mountain 1
2Pe 1:18 while we were with him on the holy mountain. 1
Rev 6:14 every mountain and island was removed 1
6:15 hid...among the rocks of the mountains 1
6:16 calling to the mountains and rocks, "Fall on us 1
8: 8 something like a great mountain, burning 1
16:20 and no mountains were to be found; 1
17: 9 the seven heads are seven mountains 1
21:10 he carried me away to a great, high mountain 1

mourn

1. θρηνέω, *thrēneō, 2577*
2. κλαίω, *klaiō, 3081*
3. κόπτω, *koptō, 3164*
4. ὀδυρμός, *odyrmos, 3851*
5. πενθέω, *pentheō, 4291*
6. πένθος, *penthos, 4292*

Mat 5: 4 "Blessed are those who mourn, for they will be 5
9:15 wedding guests cannot mourn as long as the bridegroom 5
11:17 we wailed, and you did not mourn.' 3
24:30 then all the tribes of the earth will mourn 3
Mrk 16:10 [while they were mourning and weeping.] 5
Lke 6:25 for you will mourn and weep. 5
Jhn 16:20 you will weep and mourn 1
1Co 5: 2 Should you not rather have mourned 5
7:30 those who mourn as though they were not mourning 2
7:30 those who mourn as though they were not mourning 2
2Co 7: 7 as he told us of your longing, your mourning 4
12:21 I may have to mourn over many who previously sinned 5
Jas 4: 9 Lament and mourn and weep. 5
4: 9 Let your laughter be turned into mourning 6
Rev 18: 8 plagues...pestilence and mourning and famine 6
18:11 the merchants of the earth weep and mourn for her 5
18:15 fear of her torment, weeping and mourning aloud 5
18:19 as they wept and mourned, crying out, "Alas, alas 5
21: 4 mourning and crying and pain will be no more 6

mouth *See also foam at the mouth, word of mouth*

1. στόμα, *stoma, 5125*

Mat 4: 4 every word that comes from the mouth of God.' " 1
12:34 the abundance of the heart the mouth speaks. 1
13:35 "I will open my mouth to speak in parables; 1
15:11 not what goes into the mouth that defiles a person 1

15:11 what comes out of the mouth that defiles." 1
15:17 Do you not see that whatever goes into the mouth 1
15:18 what comes out of the mouth 1
17:27 when you open its mouth, you will find a coin; 1
21:16 'Out of the mouths of infants and nursing babies 1
Lke 1:64 Immediately his mouth was opened 1
1:70 as he spoke through the mouth of his holy prophets 1
4:22 the gracious words that came from his mouth. 1
6:45 the mouth speaks. 1
Jhn 19:29 held it to his mouth. 1
Act 8:32 so he does not open his mouth. 1
11: 8 nothing...unclean has ever entered my mouth.' 1
23: 2 to strike him on the mouth. 1
Rom 3:14 "Their mouths are full of cursing and bitterness." 1
3:19 so that every mouth may be silenced 1
10:10 one confesses with the mouth and so is saved. 1
Eph 4:29 Let no evil talk come out of your mouths 1
Col 3: 8 malice, slander, and abusive language from your mouth. 1
2Th 2: 8 Jesus will destroy with the breath of his mouth 1
2Ti 4:17 So I was rescued from the lion's mouth. 1
Heb 11:33 obtained promises, shut the mouths of lions 1
Jas 3: 3 If we put bits into the mouths of horses 1
3:10 From the same mouth come blessing and cursing. 1
1Pe 2:22 no deceit was found in his mouth." 1
Rev 1:16 from his mouth came a sharp, two-edged sword 1
2:16 make war against them with the sword of my mouth. 1
3:16 I am about to spit you out of my mouth. 1
9:17 and smoke and sulfur came out of their mouths. 1
9:18 smoke and sulfur coming out of their mouths. 1
9:19 For the power of the horses is in their mouths 1
10: 9 bitter...but sweet as honey in your mouth." 1
10:10 it was sweet as honey in my mouth 1
11: 5 fire pours from their mouth and consumes 1
12:15 Then from his mouth the serpent poured water 1
12:16 it opened its mouth and swallowed the river 1
12:16 river that the dragon had poured from his mouth. 1
13: 2 the beast...its mouth was like a lion's mouth. 1
13: 2 the beast...its mouth was like a lion's mouth. 1
13: 5 a mouth uttering haughty and blasphemous words 1
13: 6 It opened its mouth to utter blasphemies 1
14: 5 in their mouth no lie was found; 1
16:13 foul spirits...coming from the mouth of the dragon 1
16:13 three foul spirits...from the mouth of the beast 1
16:13 spirits...from the mouth of the false prophet. 1
19:15 From his mouth comes a sharp sword 1
19:21 the sword that came from his mouth; 1

move

1. κινέω, *kineō, 3075*
2. μεταβαίνω, *metabainō, 3553*
3. μετοικίζω, *metoikizō, 3579*
4. φέρω, *pherō, 5770*

Mat 17:20 say to this mountain, 'Move from here to there,' 2
17:20 and it will move; 2
23: 4 are unwilling to lift a finger to move them. 1
Act 7: 4 After his father died, God had him move from there 3
17:28 'In him we live and move and have our being'; 1
2Pe 1:21 and women moved by the Holy Spirit spoke from God. 4

move about

1. μεταβαίνω, *metabainō, 3553*
Lke 10: 7 Do not move about from house to house. 1

move deeply

1. ταράσσω, *tarassō, 5429*
Jhn 11:33 he was greatly disturbed in spirit and deeply moved. 1

move up

1. προσαναβαίνω, *prosanabainō, 4646*
Lke 14:10 'Friend, move up higher'; 1

move with compassion

1. σπλαγχνίζομαι, *splanchnizomai, 5072*
Mat 20:34 Moved with compassion, Jesus touched their eyes. 1

move with pity

1. σπλαγχνίζομαι, *splanchnizomai, 5072*
Mrk 1:41 Moved with pity, Jesus stretched out his hand 1
Lke 10:33 when he saw him, he was moved with pity. 1

mow

1. ἀμάω, *amaō, 286*
Jas 5: 4 The wages of the laborers who mowed your fields 1

much *See also* annoy much, annoy very much, do much, four times as much, have too much, make much, much *heavy*, much *more*, perplex much, spend much time, twice as much, very much *more*

1. Contextual: Not in Greek
2. ἱκανός, *hikanos, 2653*
3. ἴσος, *isos, 2698*
4. ὅσος, *hosos, 4012*
5. πολύς, *polys, 4498*
6. τοσοῦτος, *tosoutos, 5537*

Mat 6:30 will he not much more clothe you— 5
13: 5 where they did not have much soil 5
14: 7 so much that he promised on oath to grant her 1
Mrk 4: 5 where it did not have much soil 5
5:26 She had endured much under many physicians 5
Lke 6:34 to receive as much again. 3
12:48 everyone to whom much has been given 5
12:48 much will be required; 5
12:48 to whom much has been entrusted 5
16:10 is faithful also in much; 5
16:10 is dishonest also in much. 5
17:25 he must endure much suffering and be rejected 5
Jhn 6:11 so also the fish, as much as they wanted. 4
8:26 I have much to say about you and much to condemn; 5
8:26 I have much to say about you and much to condemn; 1
12:24 if it dies, it bears much fruit. 5
14:30 I will no longer talk much with you 5
15: 5 Those who abide in me...bear much fruit 5
15: 8 that you bear much fruit 5
Act 15: 7 After there had been much debate, Peter stood up 5
15:32 said much to encourage and strengthen the believers 5
20: 2 and had given the believers much encouragement 5
20:37 There was much weeping among them all 2
27: 9 Since much time had been lost 2
Rom 3: 2 Much, in every way. 5
5: 9 Much more surely then...will we be saved 5
5:10 much more...will we be saved by his life. 5
5:15 much more surely have the grace of God 5
5:17 much more surely will those...exercise dominion in life 5
9:22 endured with much patience the objects of wrath 5
1Co 2: 3 in weakness and in fear and in much trembling. 5
2Co 2: 4 I wrote you out of much distress and anguish 5
3: 9 much more does the ministry of justification 5
3:11 much more has the permanent come in glory! 5
8:15 "The one who had much did not have too much 5
Php 2:12 in my presence, but much more now in my absence 5
1Ti 3: 8 not double-tongued, not indulging in much wine 5
2Ti 3: 9 But they will not make much progress 5
Phm 1: 7 received much joy and encouragement from your love 5
Heb 1: 4 having become as much superior to angels as 6
4: 7 saying through David much later 6
5:11 About this we have much to say 5
2Jn 1:12 Although I have much to write to you 5
3Jn 1:13 I have much to write to you 5

how much

1. ἡλίκος, *hēlikos, 2462*
2. ὅσος, *hosos, 4012*
3. πολύς, *polys, 4498*
4. πόσος, *posos, 4531*
5. πῶς, *pōs, 4802*

Mat 7:11 how much more will your Father in heaven 4
10:25 how much more will they malign 4
12:12 How much more valuable is a human being than a sheep! 4
Mrk 5:19 tell them how much the Lord has done for you 2
5:20 how much Jesus had done for him; 2
Lke 8:39 and declare how much God has done for you." 2
8:39 proclaiming...how much Jesus had done for him. 2
11:13 how much more will...Father give the Holy Spirit 4
12:24 Of how much more value are you than the birds! 4
12:28 how much more will he clothe you 4
16: 5 the first, 'How much do you owe my master?' 4
16: 7 he asked another, 'And how much do you owe?' 4
Act 9:13 how much evil he has done to your saints 2
9:16 how much he must suffer for the sake of my name." 2

Rom	11:12	how much more will their full inclusion mean!	4
	11:24	how much more will these natural branches	4
2Co	3: 8	how much more will the ministry of the Spirit come	5
Col	2: 1	want you to know how much I am struggling for you	1
2Ti	1:18	you know very well how much service he rendered	2
Phm	1:16	especially to me but how much more to you	4
Heb	9:14	how much more will the blood of Christ	4
	10:29	How much worse punishment…will be deserved	4
	12:25	much less will we escape if we reject	3

so much

1. οὕτως, *houtōs, 4048*
2. τοσοῦτος, *tosoutos, 5537*

Gal	3: 4	Did you experience so much for nothing?	2
1Jn	4:11	since God loved us so much, we also ought to love	1

too much

1. μέγας, *megas, 3489*
2. περισσότερος, *perissoteros, 4358*
3. πολύς, *polys, 4498*

Act	26:24	Paul! Too much learning is driving you insane!"	3
1Co	9:11	is it too much if we reap your material benefits?	1
2Co	10: 8	even if I boast a little too much of our authority	2

mud

1. βόρβορος, *borboros, 1079*
2. πηλός, *pēlos, 4384*

Jhn	9: 6	made mud with the saliva	2
	9: 6	and spread the mud on the man's eyes	2
	9:11	He answered, "The man called Jesus made mud	2
	9:14	when Jesus made the mud and opened his eyes.	2
	9:15	He said to them, "He put mud on my eyes."	2
2Pe	2:22	"The sow is washed only to wallow in the mud."	1

mulberry tree

1. συκάμινος, *sykaminos, 5189*

Lke	17: 6	you could say to this mulberry tree	1

multiply

1. πλεονάζω, *pleonazō, 4429*
2. πληθύνω, *plēthynō, 4437*

Act	7:17	our people in Egypt increased and multiplied	2
Rom	5:20	with the result that the trespass multiplied;	1
2Co	9:10	supply and multiply your seed for sowing	2
Heb	6:14	saying, "I will surely bless you and multiply you."	2

multitude

1. ὄχλος, *ochlos, 4063*
2. πλῆθος, *plēthos, 4436*

Mrk	3: 7	a great multitude from Galilee followed	2
Lke	2:13	with the angel a multitude of the heavenly host	2
	6:17	a great multitude of people from all Judea	2
	19:37	the whole multitude of the disciples	2
Jas	5:20	and will cover a multitude of sins.	2
1Pe	4: 8	for love covers a multitude of sins.	2
Rev	7: 9	a great multitude that no one could count	1
	17:15	peoples and multitudes and nations and languages.	1
	19: 1	what seemed to be the loud voice of a great multitude	1
	19: 6	what seemed to be the voice of a great multitude	1

murder   *See also* commit murder

1. σφάζω, *sphazō, 5377*
2. φονεύω, *phoneuō, 5839*
3. φόνος, *phonos, 5840*

Mat	5:21	those of ancient times, 'You shall not murder'	2
	5:21	'whoever murders shall be liable to judgment.'	2
	15:19	evil intentions, murder, adultery, fornication	3
	19:18	And Jesus said, "You shall not murder;	2
	23:31	descendants of those who murdered the prophets.	2
	23:35	murdered between the sanctuary and the altar.	2
Mrk	7:21	fornication, theft, murder	3
	10:19	shall not murder; You shall not commit adultery;	2
	15: 7	who had committed murder during the insurrection.	3
Lke	18:20	You shall not murder; You shall not steal;	2
	23:19	put in prison…for murder.)	3
	23:25	put in prison for insurrection and murder	3
Act	9: 1	Saul, still breathing threats and murder	3
Rom	1:29	Full of envy, murder, strife, deceit, craftiness	3
	13: 9	You shall not murder; You shall not steal;	2

Jas	2:11	the one…also said, "You shall not murder."	2
	2:11	if you do not commit adultery but if you murder	2
	5: 6	condemned and murdered the righteous one	2
1Jn	3:12	not be like Cain who…murdered his brother.	1
	3:12	And why did he murder him?	1
Rev	9:21	And they did not repent of their murders	3

murderer

1. ἀνδροφόνος, *androphonos, 439*
2. ἀνθρωποκτόνος, *anthrōpoktonos, 475*
3. φονεύς, *phoneus, 5838*

Mat	22: 7	sent his troops, destroyed those murderers	3
Jhn	8:44	He was a murderer from the beginning	2
Act	3:14	asked to have a murderer given to you	3
	7:52	now you have become his betrayers and murderers.	3
	28: 4	"This man must be a murderer;	3
1Ti	1: 9	law is laid down…for murderers	1
1Pe	4:15	let none of you suffer as a murderer, a thief	3
1Jn	3:15	All who hate a brother or sister are murderers	2
	3:15	murderers do not have eternal life abiding in them.	2
Rev	21: 8	the murderers, the fornicators, the sorcerers	3
	22:15	Outside are the…fornicators and murderers	3

murmur

1. γογγυσμός, *gongysmos, 1198*

Php	2:14	Do all things without murmuring and arguing	1

music

1. συμφωνία, *symphōnia, 5246*

Lke	15:25	he heard music and dancing.	1

must

1. Contextual: Not in Greek
2. ἀνάγκη, *anankē, 340*
3. ἀνάγκη + ἔχω, *anankē + echō, 340 + 2400*
4. δεῖ, *dei, 1256*
5. ὁράω, *horaō, 3972*
6. ὀφείλω, *opheilō, 4053*
7. πάντως, *pantōs, 4122*

Mat	15: 4	speaks evil of father or mother must surely die.'	1
	16:21	must go to Jerusalem and undergo great suffering	4
	16:22	This must never happen to you."	1
	17:10	the scribes say that Elijah must come first?"	4
	17:17	how much longer must I be with you?	1
	17:17	How much longer must I put up with you?	1
	19:16	"Teacher, what good deed must I do	1
	20:26	whoever wishes to be great…must be your servant	1
	20:27	whoever wishes to be first…must be your slave;	1
	24: 6	this must take place, but the end is not yet.	4
	24:16	those in Judea must flee to the mountains;	1
	24:17	the one on the housetop must not go down	1
	24:18	the one in the field must not turn back	1
	24:44	Therefore you also must be ready	1
	26:35	"Even though I must die with you, I will not deny	4
	26:54	which say it must happen in this way?"	4
	28:13	"You must say, 'His disciples came by night	1
Mrk	7:10	'Whoever speaks evil of father…must surely die.'	1
	8:31	the Son of Man must undergo great suffering,	4
	9:11	the scribes say that Elijah must come first?"	4
	9:19	how much longer must I be among you?	1
	9:19	How much longer must I put up with you?	1
	9:35	"Whoever wants to be first must be last of all	1
	10:17	what must I do to inherit eternal life?"	1
	10:43	to become great…must be your servant	1
	10:44	wishes to be first…must be slave of all.	1
	13: 7	do not be alarmed; this must take place	4
	13:10	good news must first be proclaimed to all nations.	4
	13:14	those in Judea must flee to the mountains;	1
	13:15	one on the housetop must not go down	1
	13:16	one in the field must not turn back	1
	14:31	though I must die with you, I will not deny you."	4
Lke	1:15	He must never drink wine or strong drink;	1
	2:49	not know that I must be in my Father's house?"	4
	3:11	must share with anyone who has none;	1
	3:11	whoever has food must do likewise."	1
	4:43	he said to them, "I must proclaim the good news	1
	5:38	new wine must be put into fresh wineskins.	1
	9:22	"The Son of Man must undergo great suffering,	4
	9:41	how much longer must I be with you and bear	1
	10:25	"what must I do to inherit eternal life?"	1

12:40	You also must be ready, for the Son of Man	1
13:33	tomorrow, and the next day I must be on my way	4
14:18	I must go out and see it;	3
17: 3	disciple sins, you must rebuke the offender	1
17: 3	if there is repentance, you must forgive.	1
17: 4	you must forgive."	1
17:25	he must endure much suffering and be rejected	4
17:31	must not come down to take them away;	1
17:31	likewise anyone in the field must not turn back.	1
18:18	what must I do to inherit eternal life?"	1
19: 5	I must stay at your house today."	4
21: 9	these things must take place first	4
21:21	those in Judea must flee to the mountains	1
21:21	those inside the city must leave	1
21:21	those out in the country must not enter it;	1
22:26	greatest among you must become like the youngest	1
22:36	who has a purse must take it, and likewise a bag.	1
22:36	who has no sword must sell his cloak and buy one.	1
22:37	this scripture must be fulfilled in me	4
24: 7	the Son of Man must be handed over	4
24:44	everything…must be fulfilled."	4

Jhn	3: 7	that I said to you, 'You must be born from above.'	4
	3:14	so must the Son of Man be lifted up	4
	3:30	He must increase, but I must decrease."	4
	3:30	He must increase, but I must decrease."	1
	3:36	but must endure God's wrath.	1
	4:20	place where people must worship is in Jerusalem	4
	4:24	must worship in spirit and truth."	4
	6:28	"What must we do to perform the works of God?"	1
	9: 4	We must work the works of him who sent me	4
	10:16	I must bring them also	4
	12:26	Whoever serves me must follow me	1
	12:34	you say that the Son of Man must be lifted up?	4
	20: 9	the scripture, that he must rise from the dead.	4

Act	1:22	one of these must become a witness with us	4
	3:21	who must remain in heaven until the time	4
	3:22	You must listen to whatever he tells you.	1
	4:12	no other name…by which we must be saved."	4
	4:19	you must judge;	1
	5:29	"We must obey God rather than any human authority.	4
	9:16	I myself will show him how much he must suffer	4
	10:15	"What God has made clean, you must not call profane."	1
	11: 9	'What God has made clean, you must not call profane.'	1
	14:22	that we must enter the kingdom of God."	4
	16:30	"Sirs, what must I do to be saved?"	4
	19:21	"After I have gone there, I must also see Rome."	4
	19:39	it must be settled in the regular assembly.	1
	20:35	by such work we must support the weak	4
	23:11	so you must bear witness also in Rome."	4
	23:15	must notify the tribune to bring him down	1
	26:23	that the Messiah must suffer	1
	27:24	you must stand before the emperor;	4
	28: 4	"This man must be a murderer;	7

Rom	6:11	you also must consider yourselves dead to sin	1
	13: 5	Therefore one must be subject	2
	14: 3	Those who eat must not despise those who abstain	1
	14: 3	those who abstain must not pass judgment	1
	15: 2	Each of us must please our neighbor for the good	1

1Co	3:10	Each builder must choose with care how to build on it.	1
	10: 8	We must not indulge in sexual immorality as some	1
	10: 9	We must not put Christ to the test, as some	1
	14:37	must acknowledge that what I am writing	1
	15:25	For he must reign until he has put all	4
	15:53	perishable body must put on imperishability,	4
	15:53	this mortal body must put on immortality.	1

2Co	5:10	For all of us must appear before the judgment seat	4
	9: 7	Each of you must give as you have made up your mind	1
	11:21	To my shame, I must say, we were too weak for that!	1
	11:30	If I must boast, I will boast of the things	4
	13: 1	"Any charge must be sustained	1

Gal	6: 4	All must test their own work;	1
	6: 5	For all must carry their own loads.	1
	6: 6	must share in all good things with their teacher.	1

Eph	4:14	We must no longer be children	1
	4:15	we must grow up…into him who is the head	1
	4:17	you must no longer live as the Gentiles live	1
	4:28	Thieves must give up stealing;	1
	5: 3	greed, must not even be mentioned among you	1
	6:20	I may declare it boldly, as I must speak.	4

Php	2:18	you also must be glad and rejoice with me.	1

Col	3: 8	now you must get rid of all such things—anger,	1

	3:13	so you also must forgive.	1
2Th	1: 3	We must always give thanks to God for you	6
	2:13	we must always give thanks to God for you	6
1Ti	3: 2	Now a bishop must be above reproach	4
	3: 4	He must manage his own household well	1
	3: 6	He must not be a recent convert	1
	3: 7	Moreover, he must be well thought of by outsiders	4
	3: 8	Deacons likewise must be serious	1
	3: 9	they must hold fast to the mystery of the faith	1
	3:11	Women likewise must be serious	1
	4:11	These are the things you must insist on and teach.	1
	5:10	she must be well attested for her good works	1
	6: 2	Those…must not be disrespectful	1
	6: 2	rather they must serve them all the more	1
2Ti	2:24	the Lord's servant must not be quarrelsome	4
	3: 1	You must understand this, that in the last days	1
	4:15	You also must beware of him	1
Tit	1: 7	For a bishop, as God's steward, must be blameless;	4
	1: 7	he must not be arrogant or quick-tempered	1
	1: 8	but he must be hospitable, a lover of goodness	1
	1: 9	He must have a firm grasp of the word	1
	1:11	they must be silenced	4
Heb	2: 1	Therefore we must pay greater attention	4
	4:13	the eyes of the one to whom we must render an account.	1
	5: 3	because of this he must offer sacrifice	6
	9:16	the death…must be established.	2
	11: 6	must believe that he exists	4
Jas	1: 7	the doubter…must not expect to receive anything	1
	1:19	You must understand this, my beloved:	1
	5: 8	You also must be patient. Strengthen your hearts	1
1Pe	4:11	Whoever speaks must do so as…the very words of God;	1
	4:11	whoever serves must do so with the strength	1
	5: 5	who are younger must accept the authority of the elders.	1
	5: 5	all of you must clothe yourselves with humility	1
2Pe	1: 5	must make every effort to support your faith	1
	1:20	First of all you must understand this	1
	3: 3	First of all you must understand this	1
1Jn	3:12	must not be like Cain who…murdered his brother.	1
	4:21	those who love God must love their brothers and sisters	1
2Jn	1: 6	this is the commandment…—you must walk in it.	1
Jde	1:17	you, beloved, must remember the predictions	1
Rev	1: 1	show his servants what must soon take place;	4
	4: 1	I will show you what must take place after this."	4
	10:11	"You must prophesy again about many peoples	4
	11: 5	must be killed in this manner.	4
	13:10	if you kill…with the sword you must be killed.	1
	17:10	when he comes, he must remain only a little while.	4
	19:10	but he said to me, "You must not do that!	5
	20: 3	After that he must be let out for a little while.	4
	22: 6	to show his servants what must soon take place."	4
	22: 9	he said to me, "You must not do that!	5

mustard

   1. σίναπι, *sinapi, 4983*

Mat	13:31	"The kingdom of heaven is like a mustard seed	1
	17:20	if you have faith the size of a mustard seed	1
Mrk	4:31	It is like a mustard seed	1
Lke	13:19	It is like a mustard seed that someone took	1
	17: 6	"If you had faith the size of a mustard seed	1

mute

   1. ἄλαλος, *alalos, 228*

   2. κωφός, *kōphos, 3273*

   3. σιωπάω, *siōpaō, 4995*

Mat	9:32	a demoniac who was mute was brought to him.	2
	9:33	the one who had been mute spoke;	2
	12:22	brought to him a demoniac who was blind and mute;	2
	12:22	so that the one who had been mute could speak and see.	2
	15:30	the lame, the maimed, the blind, the mute	2
	15:31	when they saw the mute speaking	2
Mrk	7:37	makes the deaf to hear and the mute to speak."	1
Lke	1:20	you will become mute, unable to speak	3
	11:14	Now he was casting out a demon that was mute;	2
	11:14	the one who had been mute spoke	2

mutilate the flesh

   1. κατατομή, *katatomē, 2961*

Php	3: 2	beware of those who mutilate the flesh!	1

mutter

1. γογγύζω, *gongyzō, 1197*

Jhn   7:32   heard the crowd muttering such things about him   1

mutual   *See also* mutual *affection,* mutual *love*

1. ἀλλήλων, *allēlōn, 253*

Rom 14:19   makes for peace and for mutual upbuilding.   1

mutually   *See* encourage mutually

muzzle

1. κημόω, *kēmoō, 3055*
2. φιμόω, *phimoō, 5821*

1Co   9: 9   not muzzle an ox while it is treading out the grain."   1
1Ti   5:18   not muzzle an ox while it is treading out the grain,"   2

Myra

1. Μύρα, *Myra, 3688*

Act   27: 5   we came to Myra in Lycia.   1

myriad

1. μυριάς, *myrias, 3689*

Rev   5:11   many angels…they numbered myriads of myriads   1
      5:11   many angels…they numbered myriads of myriads   1

myrrh   *See also* mix with myrrh

1. μύρον, *myron, 3693*
2. σμύρνα¹, *smyrna¹, 5043*

Mat   2:11   gifts of gold, frankincense, and myrrh.   2
Jhn   19:39   came, bringing a mixture of myrrh and aloes   2
Rev   18:13   cinnamon, spice, incense, myrrh, frankincense   1

myself   Not Indexed

Mysia

1. Μυσία, *Mysia, 3695*

Act   16: 7   When they had come opposite Mysia   1
      16: 8   so, passing by Mysia, they went down to Troas.   1

mystery

1. μυστήριον, *mystērion, 3696*
2. ὅς, *hos, 4005*

Rom 11:25   and sisters, I want you to understand this mystery: 1
      16:25   revelation of the mystery that was kept secret   1
1Co   2: 1   the mystery of God to you in lofty words or wisdom.   1
      4: 1   stewards of God's mysteries.   1
      13: 2   and understand all mysteries and all knowledge   1
      14: 2   they are speaking mysteries in the Spirit.   1
      15:51   Listen, I will tell you a mystery!   1
Eph   1: 9   has made known…the mystery of his will   1
      3: 3   how the mystery was made known to me   1
      3: 4   perceive my understanding of the mystery of Christ.   1
      3: 5   In former generations this mystery was not made known   2
      3: 9   to make everyone see what is the plan of the mystery   1
      5:32   This is a great mystery   1
      6:19   to make known with boldness the mystery of the gospel   1
Col   1:26   mystery that has been hidden throughout the ages   1
      1:27   the riches of the glory of this mystery   1
      2: 2   the knowledge of God's mystery, that is, Christ   1
      4: 3   that we may declare the mystery of Christ   1
2Th   2: 7   the mystery of lawlessness is already at work   1
1Ti   3: 9   they must hold fast to the mystery of the faith   1
      3:16   the mystery of our religion is great: 1
Rev   1:20   As for the mystery of the seven stars   1
      10: 7   the mystery of God will be fulfilled, as he announced   1
      17: 5   on her forehead was written a name, a mystery: 1
      17: 7   I will tell you the mystery of the woman   1

myth

1. μῦθος, *mythos, 3680*

1Ti   1: 4   and not to occupy themselves with myths   1
      4: 7   Have nothing to do with profane myths…tales.   1
2Ti   4: 4   will turn away…and wander away to myths.   1
Tit   1:14   not paying attention to Jewish myths   1
2Pe   1:16   For we did not follow cleverly devised myths   1

N

Naaman

1. Ναιμάν, *Naiman, 3722*

Lke   4:27   except Naaman the Syrian."   1

Naggai

1. Ναγγαί, *Nangai, 3710*

Lke   3:25   son of Nahum, son of Esli, son of Naggai   1

Nahor

1. Ναχώρ, *Nachōr, 3732*

Lke   3:34   son of Terah, son of Nahor   1

Nahshon

1. Ναασσών, *Naassōn, 3709*

Mat   1: 4   Aminadab the father of Nahshon   1
      1: 4   and Nahshon the father of Salmon   1
Lke   3:32   son of Boaz, son of Sala, son of Nahshon   1

Nahum

1. Ναούμ, *Naoum, 3725*

Lke   3:25   son of Nahum, son of Esli, son of Naggai   1

nail

1. ἧλος, *hēlos, 2464*
2. προσηλόω, *prosēloō, 4669*

Jhn   20:25   "Unless I see the mark of the nails in his hands   1
      20:25   put my finger in the mark of the nails   1
Col   2:14   He set this aside, nailing it to the cross.   2

Nain

1. Ναΐν, *Nain, 3723*

Lke   7:11   Soon afterwards he went to a town called Nain   1

naked

1. γυμνός, *gymnos, 1218*
2. γυμνότης, *gymnotēs, 1219*

Mat   25:36   I was naked and you gave me clothing   1
      25:38   or naked and gave you clothing?   1
      25:43   naked and you did not give me clothing   1
      25:44   thirsty or a stranger or naked or sick   1
Mrk   14:52   he left the linen cloth and ran off naked.   1
Jhn   21: 7   he put on some clothes, for he was naked   1
Act   19:16   they fled out of the house naked and wounded.   1
2Co   5: 3   we have taken it off we will not be found naked.   1
      11:27   often without food, cold and naked.   2
Heb   4:13   all are naked and laid bare to the eyes of the one   1
Jas   2:15   If a brother or sister is naked   1
Rev   3:17   you are wretched, pitiable, poor, blind, and naked.   1
      16:15   not going about naked and exposed to shame.")   1
      17:16   they will make her desolate and naked;   1

nakedness

1. γυμνότης, *gymnotēs, 1219*

Rom   8:35   or famine, or nakedness, or peril, or sword?   1
Rev   3:18   keep the shame of your nakedness from being seen;   1

name   *See also* bear the name, call on a name, give a name, take a name, use a name

1. Contextual: Not in Greek
2. καλέω, *kaleō, 2813*
3. καλέω + ὁ + ὄνομα, *kaleō + ho + onoma, 2813 + 3836 + 3950*
4. καλέω + ὄνομα, *kaleō + onoma, 2813 + 3950*
5. ὄνομα, *onoma, 3950*
6. ὀνομάζω, *onomazō, 3951*
7. τοὔνομα, *tounoma, 5540*

Mat   1:21   you are to name him Jesus, for he will save his   3
      1:23   a son, and they shall name him Emmanuel,"   3
      1:25   she had borne a son; and he named him Jesus.   3
      6: 9   Our Father in heaven, hallowed be your name.   5
      7:22   'Lord, Lord, did we not prophesy in your name   5
      7:22   and cast out demons in your name   5
      7:22   and do many deeds of power in your name?'   5
      10: 2   These are the names of the twelve apostles: 5
      10:22   you will be hated by all because of my name.   5
      10:41   Whoever welcomes a prophet in the name of a prophet   5

	10:41	in the name of a righteous person	5
	10:42	a cup of cold water…in the name of a disciple	5
	12:21	in his name the Gentiles will hope."	5
	18: 5	one such child in my name welcomes me.	5
	18:20	For where two or three are gathered in my name	5
	19:29	for my name's sake, will receive a hundredfold	5
	21: 9	the one who comes in the name of the Lord!	5
	23:39	the one who comes in the name of the Lord.' "	5
	24: 5	For many will come in my name, saying	5
	24: 9	hated by all nations because of my name.	5
	27:32	they came upon a man from Cyrene named Simon;	5
	27:57	a rich man from Arimathea, named Joseph	7
	28:19	baptizing them in the name of the Father	5
Mrk	3:14	he appointed twelve, whom he also named apostles	6
	3:16	Simon (to whom he gave the name Peter);	5
	3:17	whom he gave the name Boanerges	5
	5: 9	Jesus asked him, "What is your name?"	5
	5: 9	He replied, "My name is Legion; for we are many."	5
	5:22	one of the leaders of the synagogue named Jairus	5
	6:14	Jesus' name had become known.	5
	9:37	welcomes one such child in my name welcomes me	5
	9:38	we saw someone casting out demons in your name	5
	9:39	no one who does a deed of power in my name	5
	9:41	because you bear the name of Christ	5
	11: 9	the one who comes in the name of the Lord!	5
	13: 6	Many will come in my name and say, 'I am he!'	5
	13:13	you will be hated by all because of my name.	5
	16:17	⟦by using my name they will cast out demons;⟧	5
Lke	1: 5	there was a priest named Zechariah	5
	1: 5	her name was Elizabeth.	5
	1:13	you will name him John.	3
	1:27	a virgin engaged to a man whose name was Joseph	5
	1:27	The virgin's name was Mary.	5
	1:31	you will name him Jesus.	3
	1:49	holy is his name.	5
	1:59	going to name him Zechariah after his father.	3
	1:61	"None of your relatives has this name."	5
	1:63	for a writing tablet and wrote, "His name is John."	5
	2:21	he was called Jesus, the name given by the angel	5
	2:25	was a man in Jerusalem whose name was Simeon;	5
	5:27	he went out and saw a tax collector named Levi	5
	6:13	chose twelve of them, whom he also named apostles:	6
	6:14	Simon, whom he named Peter, and his brother Andrew	6
	8:30	Jesus then asked him, "What is your name?"	5
	8:41	Just then there came a man named Jairus	5
	9:48	"Whoever welcomes this child in my name	5
	9:49	we saw someone casting out demons in your name	5
	10:17	"Lord, in your name even the demons submit	5
	10:20	rejoice that your names are written in heaven."	5
	10:38	a woman named Martha welcomed him	5
	10:39	She had a sister named Mary	2
	11: 2	hallowed be your name. Your kingdom come.	5
	13:35	the one who comes in the name of the Lord.' "	5
	16:20	at his gate lay a poor man named Lazarus	5
	19: 2	A man was there named Zacchaeus;	4
	19:38	the king who comes in the name of the Lord!	5
	21: 8	many will come in my name and say, 'I am he!'	5
	21:12	before kings and governors because of my name.	5
	21:17	You will be hated by all because of my name.	5
	23:50	there was a good and righteous man named Joseph	5
	24:18	one of them, whose name was Cleopas, answered	5
	24:47	proclaimed in his name to all nations	5
Jhn	1: 6	was a man sent from God, whose name was John.	5
	1:12	to all who received him, who believed in his name	5
	2:23	believed in his name because they saw the signs	5
	3: 1	Now there was a Pharisee named Nicodemus	5
	3:18	not believed in the name of the only Son of God.	5
	5:43	I have come in my Father's name	5
	5:43	if another comes in his own name	5
	10: 3	calls his own sheep by name and leads them out.	5
	10:25	The works that I do in my Father's name	5
	12:13	the one who comes in the name of the Lord	5
	12:28	Father, glorify your name."	5
	14:13	I will do whatever you ask in my name,	5
	14:14	If in my name you ask me for anything,	5
	14:26	Holy Spirit, whom the Father will send in my name	5
	15:16	will give you whatever you ask him in my name.	5
	15:21	do all these things to you on account of my name	5
	16:23	ask…in my name, he will give it to you.	5
	16:24	you have not asked for anything in my name.	5
	16:26	On that day you will ask in my name.	5

	17: 6	"I have made your name known to those	5
	17:11	protect them in your name that you have given me	5
	17:12	with them, I protected them in your name	5
	17:26	I made your name known to them	5
	18:10	The slave's name was Malchus.	5
	20:31	believing you may have life in his name.	5
Act	2:21	everyone who calls on the name of the Lord	5
	2:38	be baptized…in the name of Jesus Christ	5
	3: 6	in the name of Jesus Christ of Nazareth, stand up	5
	3:16	by faith in his name	5
	3:16	his name itself has made this man strong	5
	4: 7	"By what power or by what name did you do this?"	5
	4:10	by the name of Jesus Christ of Nazareth	5
	4:12	no other name under heaven given among mortals	5
	4:17	to speak no more to anyone in this name."	5
	4:18	not to speak or teach at all in the name of Jesus.	5
	4:30	through the name of your holy servant Jesus."	5
	5: 1	a man named Ananias, with the consent of his wife	5
	5:28	strict orders not to teach in this name	5
	5:34	a Pharisee in the council named Gamaliel	5
	5:40	ordered them not to speak in the name of Jesus	5
	5:41	worthy to suffer dishonor for the sake of the name.	5
	7:58	at the feet of a young man named Saul.	2
	8: 9	Now a certain man named Simon	5
	8:12	proclaiming…the name of Jesus Christ	5
	8:16	baptized in the name of the Lord Jesus).	5
	9:10	there was a disciple in Damascus named Ananias.	5
	9:11	a man of Tarsus named Saul.	5
	9:12	he has seen in a vision a man named Ananias come	5
	9:14	to bind all who invoke your name."	5
	9:15	an instrument whom I have chosen to bring my name	5
	9:16	how much he must suffer for the sake of my name."	5
	9:21	among those who invoked this name?	5
	9:27	he had spoken boldly in the name of Jesus.	5
	9:28	speaking boldly in the name of the Lord.	5
	9:33	There he found a man named Aeneas	5
	9:36	in Joppa there was a disciple whose name was Tabitha	5
	10: 1	In Caesarea there was a man named Cornelius	5
	10:43	receives forgiveness of sins through his name."	5
	10:48	baptized in the name of Jesus Christ.	5
	11:28	One of them named Agabus stood up	5
	12:13	a maid named Rhoda came to answer.	5
	13: 6	a Jewish false prophet, named Bar-Jesus.	5
	13: 8	(for that is the translation of his name)	5
	15:14	to take from among them a people for his name.	5
	15:17	all the Gentiles over whom my name has been called.	5
	16: 1	where there was a disciple named Timothy	5
	16:14	A certain woman named Lydia, a worshiper of God	5
	16:18	"I order you in the name of Jesus Christ	5
	17: 7	saying that there is another king named Jesus."	1
	17:34	a woman named Damaris, and others with them.	5
	18: 2	he found a Jew named Aquila, a native of Pontus	5
	18: 7	went to the house of a man named Titius Justus	5
	18:15	questions about words and names and your own law	5
	18:24	a Jew named Apollos, a native of Alexandria.	5
	19: 5	baptized in the name of the Lord Jesus.	5
	19:13	tried to use the name of the Lord	5
	19:14	Seven sons of a Jewish high priest named Sceva	1
	19:17	the name of the Lord Jesus was praised.	5
	19:24	A man named Demetrius, a silversmith	5
	20: 9	A young man named Eutychus	5
	21:10	a prophet named Agabus came down from Judea.	5
	21:13	die in Jerusalem for the name of the Lord Jesus."	5
	22:16	have your sins washed away, calling on his name.'	5
	26: 9	against the name of Jesus of Nazareth.	5
	27: 1	a centurion of the Augustan Cohort, named Julius.	5
	28: 7	the leading man of the island, named Publius	5
Rom	1: 5	among all the Gentiles for the sake of his name	5
	2:24	"The name of God is blasphemed among the Gentiles	5
	9: 7	through Isaac that descendants shall be named for you."	2
	9:17	so that my name may be proclaimed in all the earth."	5
	10:13	For, "Everyone who calls on the name of the Lord	5
	15: 9	among the Gentiles, and sing praises to your name";	5
	15:20	not where Christ has already been named	6
1Co	1: 2	call on the name of our Lord Jesus Christ	5
	1:10	by the name of our Lord Jesus Christ	5
	1:13	were you baptized in the name of Paul?	5
	1:15	say that you were baptized in my name.	5
	5: 4	in the name of the Lord Jesus	5
	6:11	justified in the name of the Lord Jesus Christ	5
Eph	1:21	and above every name that is named	5

Eph 1:21 and above every name that is named 6
5:20 in the name of our Lord Jesus Christ. 5
Php 2: 9 the name that is above every name 5
2: 9 the name that is above every name 5
2:10 at the name of Jesus every knee should bend 5
4: 3 whose names are in the book of life. 5
Col 3:17 do everything in the name of the Lord Jesus 5
2Th 1:12 that the name of our Lord Jesus may be glorified 5
3: 6 in the name of our Lord Jesus Christ 5
1Ti 6: 1 name of God and the teaching may not be blasphemed. 5
2Ti 2:19 everyone who calls on the name of the Lord turn away 5
Heb 1: 4 the name he has inherited is more excellent 5
2:12 "I will proclaim your name to my brothers and sisters 5
7: 2 His name…means "king of righteousness" 1
11:18 through Isaac that descendants shall be named 2
13:15 the fruit of lips that confess his name. 5
Jas 2: 7 Is it not they who blaspheme the excellent name 5
5:10 the prophets who spoke in the name of the Lord. 5
5:14 anointing them with oil in the name of the Lord. 5
1Pe 4:14 If you are reviled for the name of Christ 5
4:16 but glorify God because you bear this name. 5
1Jn 2:12 your sins are forgiven on account of his name 5
3:23 believe in the name of his Son Jesus Christ 5
5:13 to you who believe in the name of the Son of God 5
3Jn 1:15 Greet the friends there, each by name. 5
Rev 2: 3 and bearing up for the sake of my name 5
2:13 you are holding fast to my name 5
2:17 on the white stone is written a new name 5
3: 1 you have a name of being alive, but you are dead. 5
3: 5 I will not blot your name out of the book of life; 5
3: 5 I will confess your name before my Father 5
3: 8 you have kept my word and have not denied my name. 5
3:12 I will write on you the name of my God 5
3:12 the name of my God, and the name of the city 5
3:12 the name of my God…and my own new name. 5
6: 8 a pale green horse! Its rider's name was Death 5
8:11 The name of the star is Wormwood. 5
9:11 his name in Hebrew is Abaddon 5
11:18 all who fear your name, both small and great 5
13: 1 and on its heads were blasphemous names. 5
13: 6 God, blaspheming his name and his dwelling 5
13: 8 name has not been written…in the book of life 5
13:17 the name of the beast or the number of its name. 5
13:17 the name of the beast or the number of its name. 5
14: 1 one hundred forty-four thousand who had his name 5
14: 1 his Father's name written on their foreheads. 5
14:11 and for anyone who receives the mark of its name." 5
15: 2 the beast and its image and the number of its name 5
15: 4 Lord, who will not fear and glorify your name? 5
16: 9 but they cursed the name of God 5
17: 3 beast that was full of blasphemous names 5
17: 5 on her forehead was written a name, a mystery: 5
17: 8 names have not been written in the book of life 5
19:12 he has a name inscribed that no one knows 5
19:13 his name is called The Word of God. 5
19:16 and on his thigh he has a name inscribed 5
20:15 name was not found written in the book of life 1
21:12 gates are inscribed the names of the twelve tribes 5
21:14 twelve names of the twelve apostles of the Lamb. 5
22: 4 and his name will be on their foreheads. 5

other name
1. ἐπικαλέω, *epikaleō, 2126*
Act 12:12 the mother of John whose other name was Mark 1
12:25 John, whose other name was Mark. 1

namely
1. Contextual: Not in Greek
3Jn 1: 3 namely how you walk in the truth. 1

Naphtali
1. Νεφθαλίμ, *Nephthalim, 3750*
Mat 4:13 in the territory of Zebulun and Naphtali 1
4:15 "Land of Zebulun, land of Naphtali 1
Rev 7: 6 from the tribe of Naphtali twelve thousand, 1

Narcissus
1. Νάρκισσος, *Narkissos, 3727*
Rom 16:11 those…who belong to the family of Narcissus. 1

nard
1. νάρδος, *nardos, 3726*
Mrk 14: 3 very costly ointment of nard 1
Jhn 12: 3 a pound of costly perfume made of pure nard 1

narrow
1. στενός, *stenos, 5101*
Mat 7:13 "Enter through the narrow gate; for the gate is wide 1
7:14 For the gate is narrow and the road is hard 1
Lke 13:24 "Strive to enter through the narrow door; 1

Nathan
1. Ναθάμ, *Natham, 3718*
Lke 3:31 son of Menna, son of Mattatha, son of Nathan 1

Nathanael
1. Ναθαναήλ, *Nathanaēl, 3720*
Jhn 1:45 Philip found Nathanael and said to him 1
1:46 Nathanael said to him, "Can anything good come 1
1:47 Jesus saw Nathanael coming toward him, he said 1
1:48 Nathanael asked him, "Where did you get to know me?" 1
1:49 Nathanael replied, "Rabbi 1
21: 2 Nathanael of Cana in Galilee, the sons of Zebedee 1

nation
1. ἔθνος, *ethnos, 1620*
Mat 24: 7 For nation will rise against nation 1
24: 7 For nation will rise against nation 1
24: 9 hated by all nations because of my name. 1
24:14 as a testimony to all the nations; 1
25:32 All the nations will be gathered before him 1
28:19 Go therefore and make disciples of all nations 1
Mrk 11:17 a house of prayer for all the nations'? 1
13: 8 For nation will rise against nation 1
13: 8 For nation will rise against nation 1
13:10 good news must first be proclaimed to all nations. 1
Lke 12:30 the nations of the world that strive after all 1
21:10 he said to them, "Nation will rise against nation 1
21:10 he said to them, "Nation will rise against nation 1
21:24 and be taken away as captives among all nations; 1
21:25 on the earth distress among nations 1
23: 2 "We found this man perverting our nation 1
24:47 proclaimed in his name to all nations 1
Jhn 11:48 destroy both our holy place and our nation." 1
11:50 than to have the whole nation destroyed." 1
11:51 Jesus was about to die for the nation 1
11:52 not for the nation only 1
18:35 Your own nation and the chief priests 1
Act 2: 5 devout Jews from every nation under heaven 1
7: 7 I will judge the nation that they serve,' said God 1
7:45 when they dispossessed the nations 1
10:22 who is well spoken of by the whole Jewish nation 1
10:35 in every nation anyone who fears him 1
13:19 After he had destroyed seven nations in the land 1
14:16 allowed all the nations to follow their own ways; 1
17:26 From one ancestor he made all nations 1
24:10 many years you have been a judge over this nation. 1
24:17 to bring alms to my nation and to offer sacrifices. 1
28:19 I had no charge to bring against my nation. 1
Rom 4:17 "I have made you the father of many nations") 1
4:18 that he would become "the father of many nations," 1
10:19 make you jealous of those who are not a nation; 1
10:19 with a foolish nation I will make you angry." 1
1Pe 2: 9 you are…a holy nation, God's own people 1
Rev 2:26 I will give authority over the nations; 1
5: 9 every tribe and language and people and nation; 1
7: 9 multitude…from every nation, from all tribes 1
10:11 prophesy again about many peoples and nations 1
11: 2 for it is given over to the nations 1
11: 9 the peoples and tribes and languages and nations 1
11:18 The nations raged, but your wrath has come 1
12: 5 who is to rule all the nations with a rod of iron 1
13: 7 every tribe and people and language and nation 1
14: 6 to every nation and tribe and language and people. 1
14: 8 She has made all nations drink of the wine 1
15: 3 Just and true are your ways, King of the nations! 1
15: 4 All nations will come and worship before you 1
16:19 and the cities of the nations fell. 1
17:15 peoples and multitudes and nations and languages. 1
18: 3 For all the nations have drunk of the wine 1

18:23	and all nations were deceived by your sorcery.	1
19:15	a sharp sword with which to strike down the nations	1
20: 3	so that he would deceive the nations no more	1
20: 8	and will come out to deceive the nations	1
21:24	The nations will walk by its light	1
21:26	the glory and the honor of the nations.	1
22: 2	leaves…are for the healing of the nations.	1

native   *See also* native *language*

1. βάρβαρος, *barbaros, 975*
2. γένος, *genos, 1169*

Act	4:36	a Levite, a native of Cyprus, Joseph,	2
	18: 2	he found a Jew named Aquila, a native of Pontus	2
	18:24	a Jew named Apollos, a native of Alexandria.	2
	28: 2	The natives showed us unusual kindness.	1
	28: 4	When the natives saw the creature	1

natural

1. σάρξ, *sarx, 4922*
2. φυσικός, *physikos, 5879*
3. φύσις, *physis, 5882*

Rom	1:26	exchanged natural intercourse for unnatural	2
	1:27	the men…giving up natural intercourse with women	2
	6:19	because of your natural limitations.	1
	11:21	For if God did not spare the natural branches	3
	11:24	will these natural branches be grafted back	3

nature

1. Contextual: Not in Greek
2. ἄνθρωπος, *anthrōpos, 476*
3. γένεσις, *genesis, 1161*
4. φύσις, *physis, 5882*

Jhn	8:44	When he lies, he speaks according to his own nature	1
Rom	11:24	cut from what is by nature a wild olive tree	4
	11:24	grafted, contrary to nature, into a cultivated	4
1Co	11:14	Does not nature itself teach you	4
2Co	4:16	Even though our outer nature is wasting away	2
	4:16	our inner nature is being renewed day by day.	1
Gal	4: 8	enslaved to beings that by nature are not gods.	4
Eph	2: 3	we were by nature children of wrath	4
Jas	3: 6	sets on fire the cycle of nature	3
2Pe	1: 4	may become participants of the divine nature.	4

divine nature

1. θειότης, *theiotēs, 2522*

Rom	1:20	eternal power and divine nature	1

Nazarene

1. Ναζωραῖος, *Nazōraios, 3717*

Act	24: 5	a ringleader of the sect of the Nazarenes.	1

Nazareth   *See also* man from Nazareth

1. Ναζαρέθ, *Nazareth, 3714*
2. Ναζαρηνός, *Nazarēnos, 3716*
3. Ναζωραῖος, *Nazōraios, 3717*

Mat	2:23	he made his home in a town called Nazareth	1
	4:13	left Nazareth and made his home in Capernaum	1
	21:11	the prophet Jesus from Nazareth in Galilee."	1
	26:71	"This man was with Jesus of Nazareth."	3
Mrk	1: 9	In those days Jesus came from Nazareth of Galilee	1
	1:24	"What have you to do with us, Jesus of Nazareth?	2
	10:47	When he heard that it was Jesus of Nazareth	2
	16: 6	you are looking for Jesus of Nazareth	2
Lke	1:26	to a town in Galilee called Nazareth	1
	2: 4	from the town of Nazareth in Galilee to Judea	1
	2:39	to Galilee, to their own town of Nazareth.	1
	2:51	he went down with them and came to Nazareth	1
	4:16	he came to Nazareth, where he had been brought up	1
	4:34	What have you to do with us, Jesus of Nazareth?	2
	18:37	They told him, "Jesus of Nazareth is passing by."	3
	24:19	replied, "The things about Jesus of Nazareth	2
Jhn	1:45	found him…Jesus son of Joseph from Nazareth."	1
	1:46	"Can anything good come out of Nazareth?"	1
	18: 5	They answered, "Jesus of Nazareth."	3
	18: 7	And they said, "Jesus of Nazareth."	3
	19:19	"Jesus of Nazareth, the King of the Jews."	3
Act	2:22	Jesus of Nazareth, a man attested to you by God	3
	3: 6	in the name of Jesus Christ of Nazareth, stand up	3
	4:10	Jesus Christ of Nazareth, whom you crucified	3

	6:14	Jesus of Nazareth will destroy this place	3
	10:38	how God anointed Jesus of Nazareth	1
	22: 8	'I am Jesus of Nazareth whom you are persecuting.'	3
	26: 9	against the name of Jesus of Nazareth.	3

Nazorean

1. Ναζωραῖος, *Nazōraios, 3717*

Mat	2:23	fulfilled, "He will be called a Nazorean."	1

Neapolis

1. Νεά πολις, *Nea polis, 3735*

Act	16:11	the following day to Neapolis	1

near   *See also* come near, draw near, stand near

1. Contextual: Not in Greek
2. ἐγγίζω, *engizō, 1581*
3. ἐγγύς, *engys, 1584*
4. ἐν, *en, 1877*
5. κατά, *kata, 2848*
6. μετά, *meta, 3552*
7. παρά, *para, 4123*
8. πλησίον, *plēsion, 4446*
9. πρός, *pros, 4639*
10. προσάγω, *prosagō, 4642*
11. σύνειμι¹, *syneimi¹, 5289*

Mat	24:32	you know that summer is near.	3
	24:33	you know that he is near, at the very gates.	3
	26:18	'The Teacher says, My time is near;	3
Mrk	11: 1	Bethphage and Bethany, near the Mount of Olives	9
	11: 4	They went away and found a colt tied near a door	9
	13:28	you know that summer is near.	3
	13:29	you know that he is near, at the very gates.	3
Lke	5:17	teachers of the law were sitting near by	1
	9:18	with only the disciples near him	11
	10:33	a Samaritan while traveling came near him;	5
	19:11	because he was near Jerusalem	3
	21: 8	'The time is near!' Do not go after them.	2
	21:30	know that summer is already near.	3
	21:31	you know that the kingdom of God is near.	3
	22: 1	which is called the Passover, was near	2
Jhn	2:13	The Passover of the Jews was near	3
	3:23	John also was baptizing at Aenon near Salim	3
	4: 5	near the plot of ground that Jacob had given	8
	6: 4	the Passover, the festival of the Jews, was near.	3
	6:19	walking on the sea and coming near the boat	3
	6:23	Then some boats from Tiberias came near the place	3
	7: 2	Now the Jewish festival of Booths was near.	3
	9:40	Some of the Pharisees near him heard this	6
	11:18	Bethany was near Jerusalem, some two miles away	3
	11:54	Ephraim in the region near the wilderness;	3
	11:55	Now the Passover of the Jews was near	3
	19:20	the place…was near the city;	3
	19:25	standing near the cross of Jesus were his mother	7
Act	1:12	the mount called Olivet, which is near Jerusalem	3
	9:38	Since Lydda was near Joppa	3
	27: 8	Fair Havens, near the city of Lasea.	3
	27:27	sailors suspected that they were nearing land.	10
Rom	10: 8	"The word is near you, on your lips and in your heart"	3
	13:11	For salvation is nearer to us now	3
	13:12	the night is far gone, the day is near.	2
2Co	11:23	with countless floggings, and often near death.	4
Eph	2:13	have been brought near by the blood of Christ.	3
	2:17	proclaimed…peace to those who were near;	3
Php	4: 5	The Lord is near.	3
Jas	5: 8	for the coming of the Lord is near.	2
1Pe	4: 7	The end of all things is near;	2
Rev	1: 3	for the time is near.	3
	22:10	for the time is near.	3

near dawn

1. τρίτος + φυλακή, *tritos + phylakē, 5569 + 5871*

Lke	12:38	during the middle of the night, or near dawn	1

nearby   *See also* stand nearby

1. Contextual: Not in Greek
2. ἐγγύς, *engys, 1584*

Jhn	19:42	and the tomb was nearby	2
1Co	14:30	revelation is made to someone else sitting nearby	1

nearly *See also* nearly over
   1. παραπλήσιος, *paraplēsios, 4180*
Php 2:27 He was indeed so ill that he nearly died.   1

nearsighted
   1. μυωπάζω, *myōpazō, 3697*
2Pe 1: 9 who lacks these things is nearsighted and blind   1

necessarily
   1. ἀνάγκη, *anankē, 340*
Heb 7:12 necessarily a change in the law as well.   1

necessary
   1. ἀναγκαῖος, *anankaios, 338*
   2. ἀνάγκη, *anankē, 340*
   3. δεῖ, *dei, 1256*
Lke 24:26 it not necessary that the Messiah should suffer   3
Act 13:46 necessary that the word of God should be spoken   1
   15: 5 "It is necessary for them to be circumcised   3
   17: 3 necessary for the Messiah to suffer and to rise   3
1Co 8: 2 does not yet have the necessary knowledge;   3
2Co 9: 5 So I thought it necessary to urge the brothers   1
   12: 1 It is necessary to boast; nothing is to be gained   3
Php 2:25 I think it necessary to send to you   1
Heb 8: 3 hence it is necessary for this priest also   1
   9:23 Thus it was necessary…to be purified   2
Jde 1: 3 I find it necessary to write and appeal to you   2

more necessary
   1. ἀναγκαῖος, *anankaios, 338*
Php 1:24 to remain in the flesh is more necessary   1

not necessary
   1. περισσός, *perissos, 4356*
2Co 9: 1 Now it is not necessary for me to write you   1

necessity
   1. ἀνάγκη, *anankē, 340*
1Co 7:37 stands firm…being under no necessity   1

neck
   1. τράχηλος, *trachēlos, 5549*
Mat 18: 6 a great millstone were fastened around your neck   1
Mrk 9:42 if a great millstone were hung around your neck   1
Lke 17: 2 if a millstone were hung around your neck   1
Act 15:10 by placing on the neck of the disciples a yoke   1
Rom 16: 4 who risked their necks for my life   1

need *See also* take care of needs, time of need
   1. Contextual: Not in Greek
   2. ἀνάγκη, *anankē, 340*
   3. δεῖ, *dei, 1256*
   4. ἐπιτήδειος, *epitēdeios, 2201*
   5. ὀφείλω, *opheilō, 4053*
   6. πρός, *pros, 4639*
   7. προσδέομαι, *prosdeomai, 4656*
   8. τόπος, *topos, 5536*
   9. ὑστερέω, *hystereō, 5728*
   10. ὑστέρημα, *hysterēma, 5729*
   11. ὑστέρησις, *hysterēsis, 5730*
   12. χρεία, *chreia, 5970*
   13. χρεία + ἔχω, *chreia + echō, 5970 + 2400*
   14. χρῄζω, *chrēzō, 5974*
Mat 3:14 "I need to be baptized by you, and do you come to me?" 13
   6: 8 Father knows what you need before you ask him. 13
   6:32 your heavenly Father knows that you need all these 14
   9:12 "Those who are well have no need of a physician 12
  14:16 Jesus said to them, "They need not go away; 13
  15: 5 that person need not honor the father.   1
  21: 3 'The Lord needs them.' 13
  26:65 Why do we still need witnesses? 13
Mrk 2:17 "Those who are well have no need of a physician 12
  2:25 he and his companions were hungry and in need 13
  11: 3 say this, 'The Lord needs it 13
  14:63 "Why do we still need witnesses? 13
Lke 5:31 "Those who are well have no need of a physician 12
  9:11 healed those who needed to be cured. 13
  10:42 there is need of only one thing. 12

  11: 8 he will get up and give him whatever he needs. 14
  12:30 your Father knows that you need them. 14
  15: 7 who need no repentance. 13
  15:14 he began to be in need.   9
  18: 1 about their need to pray always   3
  19:31 say this, 'The Lord needs it.' " 13
  19:34 They said, "The Lord needs it." 13
  22:71 they said, "What further testimony do we need? 13
Jhn 2:25 and needed no one to testify about anyone; 13
  13:10 "One who has bathed does not need to wash 13
  13:29 "Buy what we need for the festival"; 13
  16:30 not need to have anyone question you; 13
Act 2:45 distribute the proceeds to all, as any had need. 12
  4:35 was distributed to each as any had need. 12
  17:25 as though he needed anything   7
  28:10 they put on board all the provisions we needed. 12
Rom 12:13 Contribute to the needs of the saints; 12
1Co 5:10 since you would then need to go out of the world.   5
  12:21 eye cannot say to the hand, "I have no need of you," 12
  12:21 the head to the feet, "I have no need of you." 12
  12:24 whereas our more respectable members do not need 13
  16: 2 so that collections need not be taken when I come.   1
2Co 3: 1 Surely we do not need…letters of recommendation 14
  8:14 your present abundance and their need 10
  8:14 so that their abundance may be for your need 10
  9:12 not only supplies the needs of the saints 10
  10: 2 need not show boldness by daring to oppose   1
  11: 9 when I was with you and was in need   9
  11: 9 my needs were supplied by the friends 10
Eph 4:29 useful for building up, as there is need 12
Php 2:25 your messenger and minister to my need; 12
  4:11 Not that I am referring to being in need; 11
  4:12 of having plenty and of being in need.   9
  4:16 you sent me help for my needs more than once. 12
  4:19 my God will fully satisfy every need of yours 12
1Th 1: 8 so that we have no need to speak about it 12
  4: 9 you do not need to have anyone write to you 13
  5: 1 you do not need to have anything written to you. 13
Tit 3:14 in order to meet urgent needs 12
Heb 5:12 you need someone to teach you again 13
  5:12 You need milk, not solid food; 13
  7:11 what further need would there have been 12
  7:27 he has no need…to offer sacrifices day after day   2
  8: 7 there would have been no need to look for a second   8
  9:23 heavenly things…need better sacrifices than these.   1
  10:36 For you need endurance 12
Jas 2:16 not supply their bodily needs, what is the good   4
2Pe 1: 3 everything needed for life and godliness   6
1Jn 2:27 and so you do not need anyone to teach you. 12
  3:17 has the world's goods and sees a brother or sister in need 12
Rev 3:17 For you say, 'I am rich…and I need nothing.' 13
  21:23 the city has no need of sun or moon to shine on it 12
  22: 5 they need no light of lamp or sun 13

no need to be ashamed
   1. ἀνεπαίσχυντος, *anepaischyntos, 454*
2Ti 2:15 a worker who has no need to be ashamed   1

needle
   1. βελόνη, *belonē, 1017*
   2. ῥαφίς, *rhaphis, 4827*
Mat 19:24 for a camel to go through the eye of a needle   2
Mrk 10:25 a camel to go through the eye of a needle   2
Lke 18:25 to go through the eye of a needle   1

needy
   1. ἐνδεής, *endeēs, 1890*
   2. χρεία + ἔχω, *chreia + echō, 5970 + 2400*
Act 4:34 There was not a needy person among them   1
Eph 4:28 so as to have something to share with the needy.   2

neglect
   1. ἀμελέω, *ameleō, 288*
   2. ἀφίημι, *aphiēmi, 918*
   3. ἐγκαταλείπω, *enkataleipō, 1593*
   4. ἐπιλανθάνομαι, *epilanthanomai, 2140*
   5. καταλείπω, *kataleipō, 2901*
   6. παραθεωρέω, *paratheōreō, 4145*
   7. παρέρχομαι, *parerchomai, 4216*
   8. παρίημι, *pariēmi, 4223*

Mat	23:23	have neglected the weightier matters of the law:	2
	23:23	without neglecting the others.	2
Lke	11:42	neglect justice and the love of God;	7
	11:42	without neglecting the others.	8
Act	6: 1	neglected in the daily distribution	6
	6: 2	not right that we should neglect the word of God	5
1Ti	4:14	Do not neglect the gift that is in you	1
Heb	2: 3	if we neglect so great a salvation?	1
	10:25	not neglecting to meet together	3
	13: 2	Do not neglect to show hospitality to strangers	4
	13:16	Do not neglect to do good	4

neighbor

1. Contextual: Not in Greek
2. ἀδελφός, *adelphos, 81*
3. γείτων, *geitōn, 1150*
4. ἕτερος, *heteros, 2283*
5. ἔχω, *echō, 2400*
6. περιοικέω, *perioikeō, 4340*
7. περίοικος, *perioikos, 4341*
8. πλησίον, *plēsion, 4446*

Mat	5:43	love your neighbor and hate your enemy.'	8
	7: 3	do you see the speck in your neighbor's eye	2
	7: 4	Or how can you say to your neighbor	2
	7: 5	to take the speck out of your neighbor's eye.	2
	19:19	You shall love your neighbor as yourself."	8
	22:39	'You shall love your neighbor as yourself.'	8
Mrk	1:38	"Let us go on to the neighboring towns	5
	12:31	'You shall love your neighbor as yourself.'	8
	12:33	'to love one's neighbor as oneself,'	8
Lke	1:58	Her neighbors and relatives heard	7
	1:65	Fear came over all their neighbors	6
	6:41	do you see the speck in your neighbor's eye	2
	6:42	how can you say to your neighbor, 'Friend	2
	6:42	take the speck out of your neighbor's eye.	2
	10:27	and your neighbor as yourself."	8
	10:29	"And who is my neighbor?"	8
	10:36	was a neighbor to the man	8
	14:12	your brothers or your relatives or rich neighbors	3
	15: 6	he calls together his friends and neighbors	3
	15: 9	she calls together her friends and neighbors	3
Jhn	9: 8	The neighbors and those who had seen him before	3
Act	7:27	the man who was wronging his neighbor	8
Rom	13: 9	"Love your neighbor as yourself."	8
	13:10	Love does no wrong to a neighbor;	8
	15: 2	must please our neighbor for the good purpose of	8
	15: 2	for the good purpose of building up the neighbor.	1
Gal	5:14	"You shall love your neighbor as yourself."	8
	6: 4	then that work, rather than their neighbor's work,	4
Eph	4:25	let all of us speak the truth to our neighbors	8
Jas	2: 8	"You shall love your neighbor as yourself."	8
	4:12	So who, then, are you to judge your neighbor?	8

neighborhood

1. ὅριον, *horion, 3990*
2. περί, *peri, 4309*

Mat	8:34	they begged him to leave their neighborhood.	1
Mrk	5:17	to beg Jesus to leave their neighborhood.	1
Act	28: 7	Now in the neighborhood of that place were lands	2

neither

1. μή, *mē, 3590*
2. μήτε, *mēte, 3612*
3. οὐ, *ou, 4024*
4. οὐδέ, *oude, 4028*
5. οὔτε, *oute, 4046*

Mat	6:15	neither will your Father forgive your	4
	6:20	in heaven, where neither moth nor rust consumes	5
	6:26	of the air; they neither sow nor reap nor gather	3
	6:28	how they grow; they neither toil nor spin	3
	9:17	Neither is new wine put into old wineskins;	4
	11:18	For John came neither eating nor drinking	2
	21:27	he said to them, "Neither will I tell you	4
	22:29	neither the scriptures nor the power of God.	1
	22:30	they neither marry nor are given in marriage	5
	24:36	neither the angels of heaven, nor the Son	4
	25:13	you know neither the day nor the hour.	3
Mrk	11:33	"Neither will I tell you by what authority	4
	12:24	know neither the scriptures nor the power of God?	1
	12:25	they neither marry nor are given in marriage	5

	13:32	neither the angels in heaven, nor the Son	4
Lke	12:24	Consider the ravens: they neither sow nor reap	3
	12:24	they have neither storehouse nor barn	3
	12:27	they neither toil nor spin;	3
	14:35	fit neither for the soil nor for the manure pile;	5
	16:31	neither will they be convinced	4
	18: 2	a judge who neither feared God nor had respect	1
	20: 8	Jesus said to them, "Neither will I tell you	4
	20:35	neither marry nor are given in marriage.	5
	23:15	Neither has Herod, for he sent him back to us.	4
Jhn	1:25	if you are neither the Messiah, nor Elijah	3
	4:21	neither on this mountain nor in Jerusalem.	5
	6:24	neither Jesus nor his disciples were there	3
	8:11	[[Jesus said, "Neither do I condemn you.]]	4
	8:19	Jesus answered, "You know neither me nor my Father.	5
	9: 3	"Neither this man nor his parents sinned;	5
	14:17	because it neither sees him nor knows him.	3
	15: 4	neither can you unless you abide in me.	4
Act	9: 9	neither ate nor drank.	3
	15:10	neither our ancestors nor we have been able to bear?	5
	19:37	neither temple robbers nor blasphemers	5
	23:12	an oath neither to eat nor drink	2
	23:21	an oath neither to eat nor drink	2
	24:13	Neither can they prove to you	4
	27:20	neither sun nor stars appeared for many days	2
Rom	4:15	but where there is no law, neither is there violation.	4
	8:38	For I am convinced that neither death, nor life	5
1Co	3: 7	So neither the one who plants…is anything	5
	11: 9	Neither was man created for the sake of woman	3
Gal	1: 1	Paul an apostle—sent neither by human commission	3
	5: 6	neither circumcision nor uncircumcision	5
	6:15	neither circumcision nor uncircumcision is anything;	5
Heb	7: 3	having neither beginning of days nor end of life	2
	10: 8	"You have neither desired nor taken pleasure in	5
Rev	3:15	"I know your works; you are neither cold nor hot	5
	3:16	you are lukewarm, and neither cold nor hot	5

Nereus

1. Νηρεύς, *Nēreus, 3759*

Rom	16:15	Greet Philologus, Julia, Nereus and his sister	1

Neri

1. Νηρί, *Nēri, 3760*

Lke	3:27	son of Shealtiel, son of Neri	1

nest *See also* make a nest

1. κατασκήνωσις, *kataskēnōsis, 2943*

Mat	8:20	"Foxes have holes, and birds of the air have nests;	1
Lke	9:58	"Foxes have holes, and birds of the air have nests;	1

net *See also* cast a net

1. ἀμφίβληστρον, *amphiblēstron, 312*
2. δίκτυον, *diktyon, 1473*
3. σαγήνη, *sagēnē, 4880*

Mat	4:18	Andrew his brother, casting a net into the sea	1
	4:20	Immediately they left their nets and followed	2
	4:21	with their father Zebedee, mending their nets	2
	13:47	like a net that was thrown into the sea	3
Mrk	1:18	immediately they left their nets and followed	2
	1:19	who were in their boat mending the nets.	2
Lke	5: 2	were washing their nets.	2
	5: 4	and let down your nets for a catch."	2
	5: 5	Yet if you say so, I will let down the nets."	2
	5: 6	that their nets were beginning to break.	2
Jhn	21: 6	"Cast the net to the right side of the boat	2
	21: 8	dragging the net full of fish	2
	21:11	Simon Peter went aboard and hauled the net ashore	2
	21:11	though there were so many, the net was not torn.	2

never *See also* never *fades* away

1. μή, *mē, 3590*
2. μή + γίνομαι, *mē + ginomai, 3590 + 1181*
3. μηδείς, *mēdeis, 3594*
4. μηδέποτε, *mēdepote, 3595*
5. οὐ, *ou, 4024*
6. οὐ + εἰς + ὁ + αἰών, *ou + eis + ho + aiōn, 4024 + 1650 + 3836 + 172*
7. οὐ + μή + εἰς + ὁ + αἰών, *ou + mē + eis + ho + aiōn, 4024 + 3590 + 1650 + 3836 + 172*
8. οὐ + μή + ἔτι, *ou + mē + eti, 4024 + 3590 + 2285*

9. οὐ + μή + ποτέ, *ou + mē + pote, 4024 + 3590 + 4537*
10. οὐ + μή + πώποτε, *ou + mē + pōpote, 4024 + 3590 + 4799*
11. οὐ + μή, *ou + mē, 4024 + 3590*
12. οὐδείς + πώποτε, *oudeis + pōpote, 4029 + 4799*
13. οὐδέποτε, *oudepote, 4030*
14. οὔπω, *oupō, 4037*
15. οὔτε + ποτέ, *oute + pote, 4046 + 4537*
16. οὔτε + πώποτε, *oute + pōpote, 4046 + 4799*
17. πώποτε, *pōpote, 4799*

Mat	5:20	Pharisees, you will never enter the kingdom	11
	5:26	you will never get out until you have paid the last	11
	7:23	Then I will declare to them, 'I never knew you;	13
	9:33	"Never has anything like this been seen in Israel."	13
	13:14	'You will indeed listen, but never understand	11
	13:14	and you will indeed look, but never perceive.	11
	16:22	This must never happen to you."	11
	18: 3	you will never enter the kingdom of heaven.	11
	18:13	the ninety-nine that never went astray	1
	21:16	Yes; have you never read	13
	21:42	"Have you never read in the scriptures:	13
	24:21	until now, no, and never will be.	11
	26:29	I will never again drink of this fruit	11
	26:33	I will never desert you."	13
Mrk	2:12	saying, "We have never seen anything like this!"	13
	2:25	"Have you never read what David did	13
	3:29	can never have forgiveness	6
	9:48	where their worm never dies	5
	9:48	the fire is never quenched.	5
	10:15	as a little child will never enter it."	11
	11: 2	a colt…that has never been ridden;	14
	13:19	no, and never will be.	11
Lke	1:15	He must never drink wine or strong drink;	11
	2:37	She never left the temple	5
	12:59	I tell you, you will never get out	11
	15:29	I have never disobeyed your command;	13
	18:17	will never enter it."	11
	19:30	a colt…that has never been ridden.	12
	23:29	the wombs that never bore	5
	23:29	and the breasts that never nursed.'	5
Jhn	4:14	water that I will give them will never be thirsty.	7
	4:15	give me this water, so that I may never be thirsty	1
	5:37	You have never heard his voice	16
	6:35	Whoever comes to me will never be hungry	11
	6:35	whoever believes in me will never be thirsty.	10
	6:37	anyone who comes to me I will never drive away;	11
	7:15	such learning, when he has never been taught?"	1
	7:46	"Never has anyone spoken like this!"	13
	8:12	Whoever follows me will never walk in darkness	11
	8:33	and have never been slaves to anyone.	17
	8:51	whoever keeps my word will never see death."	7
	8:52	will never taste death.'	7
	9:32	Never since the world began has it been heard	5
	10:28	they will never perish.	7
	11:26	lives and believes in me will never die.	7
	13: 8	Peter said to him, "You will never wash my feet."	7
Act	6:13	"This man never stops saying things	5
	10:14	never eaten anything that is profane or unclean."	13
	13:41	a work that you will never believe	11
	14: 8	never walked, for he had been crippled from birth.	13
	28:26	You will indeed listen, but never understand	11
	28:26	you will indeed look, but never perceive.	11
Rom	10:14	to believe in one of whom they have never heard?	5
	12:19	Beloved, never avenge yourselves	1
	14:13	resolve instead never to put a stumbling block	1
	15:21	"Those who have never been told of him shall see	5
	15:21	who have never heard of him shall understand."	5
1Co	6:15	make them members of a prostitute? Never!	2
	8:13	I will never eat meat, so that I may not	7
	13: 8	Love never ends.	13
Gal	6:14	May I never boast of anything except the cross	2
Col	3:19	love your wives and never treat them harshly.	1
1Th	2: 5	we never came with words of flattery	15
1Ti	5:19	Never accept any accusation against an elder	1
2Ti	3: 7	can never arrive at a knowledge of the truth.	4
Heb	1:12	you are the same, and your years will never end."	5
	10: 1	it can never…make perfect those who approach.	13
	10:11	sacrifices that can never take away sins.	13
	13: 5	he has said, "I will never leave you or forsake you."	11
Jas	1: 6	But ask in faith, never doubting	3
1Pe	3: 6	do what is good and never let fears alarm you.	3

2Pe	1:10	for if you do this, you will never stumble.	9
	2:21	better for them never to have known the way	1
Rev	3:12	the temple of my God; you will never go out of it.	8
	18: 7	I am no widow, and I will never see grief,'	11
	21:25	Its gates will never be shut by day	11

never again

1. μηκέτι, *mēketi, 3600*
2. οὐκέτι, *ouketi, 4033*
3. οὐκέτι + οὐ + μή, *ouketi + ou + mē, 4033 + 4024 + 3590*

Mrk	9:25	come out of him, and never enter him again!"	1
	14:25	I will never again drink of the fruit of the vine	3
Rom	6: 9	We know that Christ…will never die again;	2
Rev	18:14	lost to you, never to be found again!"	3

never even

1. οὐδέποτε, *oudepote, 4030*

Lke	15:29	yet you have never given me even a young goat	1

never lie

1. ἀψευδής, *apseudēs, 950*

Tit	1: 2	eternal life that God, who never lies, promised	1

nevertheless

1. ἀλλά, *alla, 247*
2. δέ, *de, 1254*
3. καί, *kai, 2779*
4. ὅμως, *homōs, 3940*
5. πλήν, *plēn, 4440*

Lke	7:35	Nevertheless, wisdom is vindicated by all her	3
	10:20	Nevertheless, do not rejoice at this	5
Jhn	12:42	Nevertheless…the authorities, believed	4
	16: 7	Nevertheless I tell you the truth:	1
Rom	15:15	Nevertheless on some points I have written to you	2
1Co	9:12	Nevertheless, we have not made use of this right	1
	10: 5	Nevertheless, God was not pleased with most	1
	11:11	Nevertheless, in the Lord	5
	14:19	nevertheless, in church I would rather speak	1
2Co	12:16	Nevertheless (you say) since I was crafty	1

new   *See also* give a new birth, new *wine*

1. Contextual: Not in Greek
2. καινός, *kainos, 2785*
3. καινότης, *kainotēs, 2786*
4. νέος, *neos, 3742*
5. πρόσφατος, *prosphatos, 4710*

Mat	9:17	Neither is new wine put into old wineskins;	4
	9:17	but new wine is put into fresh wineskins	4
	13:52	what is new and what is old."	2
	23:15	you make the new convert twice as much	1
	26:29	until that day when I drink it new with you	2
	27:60	laid it in his own new tomb	2
Mrk	1:27	A new teaching—with authority! He commands	2
	2:21	the new from the old, and a worse tear is made.	2
	2:22	no one puts new wine into old wineskins;	4
	2:22	one puts new wine into fresh wineskins."	4
	14:25	when I drink it new in the kingdom of God."	2
	16:17	⟦they will speak in new tongues;⟧	2
Lke	5:36	"No one tears a piece from a new garment	2
	5:36	otherwise the new will be torn	2
	5:36	the piece from the new will not match the old.	2
	5:37	no one puts new wine into old wineskins;	4
	5:37	otherwise the new wine will burst the skins	4
	5:38	new wine must be put into fresh wineskins.	4
	5:39	no one after drinking old wine desires new	4
	22:20	the new covenant in my blood.	2
Jhn	13:34	I give you a new commandment, that	2
	19:41	and in the garden there was a new tomb	2
Act	17:19	"May we know what this new teaching is	2
	17:21	telling or hearing something new.	2
Rom	6: 4	we are slaves…in the new life of the Spirit.	3
1Co	5: 7	so that you may be a new batch	4
	11:25	"This cup is the new covenant in my blood.	2
2Co	3: 6	competent to be ministers of a new covenant	2
	5:17	if anyone is in Christ, there is a new creation:	2
	5:17	passed away; see, everything has become new!	2
Gal	6:15	nor uncircumcision is anything; but a new creation	2
Eph	2:15	create in himself one new humanity in place of the two	2
	4:24	clothe yourselves with the new self	2

Col	3:10	and have clothed yourselves with the new self	4
Heb	8: 8	when I will establish a new covenant	2
	8:13	In speaking of "a new covenant,"	2
	9:15	For this reason he is the mediator of a new covenant	2
	10:20	by the new and living way that he opened for us	5
	12:24	to Jesus, the mediator of a new covenant	4
2Pe	3:13	we wait for new heavens and a new earth	2
	3:13	we wait for new heavens and a new earth	2
1Jn	2: 7	Beloved, I am writing you no new commandment	2
	2: 8	Yet I am writing you a new commandment	2
2Jn	1: 5	as though I were writing you a new commandment	2
Rev	2:17	on the white stone is written a new name	2
	3:12	the new Jerusalem that comes down from my God	2
	3:12	the name of my God…and my own new name.	2
	5: 9	They sing a new song: "You are worthy	2
	14: 3	and they sing a new song before the throne	2
	21: 1	Then I saw a new heaven and a new earth;	2
	21: 1	Then I saw a new heaven and a new earth;	2
	21: 2	new Jerusalem, coming down out of heaven from God	2
	21: 5	"See, I am making all things new."	2

new moon

1. νεομηνία, *neomēnia, 3741*

Col	2:16	observing festivals, new moons, or sabbaths.	1

newborn

1. ἀρτιγέννητος, *artigennētos, 786*

1Pe	2: 2	Like newborn infants, long for…spiritual milk	1

newness

1. καινότης, *kainotēs, 2786*

Rom	6: 4	so we too might walk in newness of life.	1

news *See also* announce good news, bring good news, bring the news, good news, good news *come*, proclaim the good news, proclamation of good news, receive the good news, spread the news, tell the good news

1. γινώσκω, *ginōskō, 1182*
2. λόγος, *logos, 3364*
3. ὁ, *ho, 3836*

Act	11:22	News…came to the ears of the church in Jerusalem	2
Php	2:19	so that I may be cheered by news of you.	1
Col	4: 7	Tychicus will tell you all the news about me;	3

next *See also* next *day*, next *year*

1. ἐν + ὁ + κόλπος, *en + ho + kolpos, 1877 + 3836 + 3146*
2. ἑξῆς, *hexēs, 2009*
3. ἔπειμι, *epeimi, 2079*
4. ἔπειτα, *epeita, 2083*
5. ἐπί + ὁ + στῆθος, *epi + ho + stēthos, 2093 + 3836 + 5111*
6. ἔρχομαι, *erchomai, 2262*
7. ἕτερος, *heteros, 2283*
8. ἔχω, *echō, 2400*
9. καί, *kai, 2779*
10. μεταξύ, *metaxy, 3568*

Mat	10:23	flee to the next;	7
Lke	9:37	On the next day	2
	13:33	tomorrow, and the next day I must be on my way	8
	20:11	Next he sent another slave;	9
Jhn	13:23	was reclining next to him;	1
	13:25	So while reclining next to Jesus, he asked	5
	21:20	who had reclined next to Jesus at the supper	5
Act	7:26	The next day he came to some of them	3
	13:42	speak about these things again the next sabbath.	10
	13:44	The next sabbath almost the whole city gathered	6
	20:15	The next day we touched at Samos	7
	21: 1	the next day to Rhodes…from there to Patara.	2
	21:18	The next day Paul went with us to visit James;	3
	21:26	the next day, having purified himself, he entered	8
	25:17	but on the next day took my seat on the tribunal	2
	27: 3	The next day we put in at Sidon;	7
	27:18	next day they began to throw the cargo overboard	2
Heb	7: 2	next he is also king of Salem, that is, "king of peace."	4

next door

1. συνομορέω, *synomoreō, 5327*

Act	18: 7	his house was next door to the synagogue.	1

Nicanor

1. Νικάνωρ, *Nikanōr, 3770*

Act	6: 5	Philip, Prochorus, Nicanor, Timon	1

Nicodemus

1. Νικόδημος, *Nikodēmos, 3773*

Jhn	3: 1	Now there was a Pharisee named Nicodemus	1
	3: 4	Nicodemus said to him, "How can anyone be born	1
	3: 9	Nicodemus said to him, "How can these things be?"	1
	7:50	Nicodemus, who had gone to Jesus before	1
	19:39	Nicodemus, who had at first come to Jesus by night	1

Nicolaitan

1. Νικολαΐτης, *Nikolaitēs, 3774*

Rev	2: 6	you hate the works of the Nicolaitans	1
	2:15	some who hold to the teaching of the Nicolaitans.	1

Nicolaus

1. Νικόλαος, *Nikolaos, 3775*

Act	6: 5	Parmenas, and Nicolaus, a proselyte of Antioch.	1

Nicopolis

1. Νικόπολις, *Nikopolis, 3776*

Tit	3:12	do your best to come to me at Nicopolis	1

Niger

1. Νίγερ, *Niger, 3769*

Act	13: 1	Barnabas, Simeon who was called Niger	1

night *See also* middle of the night, part of the night, spend the night

1. νύξ, *nyx, 3816*

Mat	2:14	Joseph got up, took the child and his mother by night	1
	4: 2	He fasted forty days and forty nights	1
	12:40	For just as Jonah was three days and three nights	1
	12:40	so for three days and three nights the Son	1
	26:31	all become deserters because of me this night;	1
	26:34	this very night, before the cock crows	1
	28:13	"You must say, 'His disciples came by night	1
Mrk	4:27	sleep and rise night and day	1
	5: 5	Night and day among the tombs	1
	14:30	this very night, before the cock crows twice	1
Lke	2: 8	keeping watch over their flock by night.	1
	2:37	with fasting and prayer night and day.	1
	5: 5	"Master, we have worked all night long but	1
	12:20	This very night your life is being demanded	1
	17:34	on that night there will be two in one bed;	1
	18: 7	who cry to him day and night?	1
	21:37	at night he would go out and spend the night	1
Jhn	3: 2	He came to Jesus by night and said to him	1
	9: 4	night is coming when no one can work.	1
	11:10	those who walk at night stumble,	1
	13:30	he immediately went out. And it was night.	1
	19:39	Nicodemus, who had at first come to Jesus by night	1
	21: 3	that night they caught nothing.	1
Act	5:19	during the night an angel of the Lord opened	1
	9:24	They were watching the gates day and night	1
	9:25	his disciples took him by night	1
	12: 6	The very night before Herod was going to bring	1
	16: 9	During the night Paul had a vision: there stood	1
	16:33	At the same hour of the night he took them	1
	17:10	That very night the believers sent Paul and Silas	1
	18: 9	One night the Lord said to Paul in a vision	1
	20:31	I did not cease night or day to warn everyone	1
	23:11	That night the Lord stood near him	1
	23:31	and brought him during the night to Antipatris.	1
	26: 7	as they earnestly worship day and night.	1
	27:23	last night there stood by me an angel	1
	27:27	When the fourteenth night had come	1
Rom	13:12	the night is far gone, the day is near.	1
1Co	11:23	the Lord Jesus on the night when he was betrayed	1
1Th	2: 9	worked night and day, so that we might not burden	1
	3:10	Night and day we pray most earnestly that we may see	1
	5: 2	day of the Lord will come like a thief in the night.	1
	5: 5	we are not of the night or of darkness.	1
	5: 7	for those who sleep sleep at night	1
	5: 7	those who are drunk get drunk at night.	1
2Th	3: 8	with toil and labor we worked night and day	1
1Ti	5: 5	in supplications and prayers night and day;	1

2Ti	1: 3	constantly in my prayers night and day.	1
Rev	4: 8	Day and night without ceasing they sing	1
	7:15	and worship him day and night within his temple	1
	8:12	from shining, and likewise the night.	1
	12:10	who accuses them day and night before our God.	1
	14:11	There is no rest day or night for those	1
	20:10	they will be tormented day and night forever	1
	21:25	and there will be no night there.	1
	22: 5	And there will be no more night;	1

night and a day

1. νυχθήμερον, *nychthēmeron, 3819*

2Co 11:25 a night and a day I was adrift at sea;   1

sleepless night

1. ἀγρυπνία, *agrypnia, 71*

2Co   6: 5 imprisonments, riots, labors, sleepless nights,   1
     11:27 in toil…through many a sleepless night   1

nine

1. ἐννέα, *ennea, 1933*

Lke 17:17 ten made clean? But the other nine, where are   1

nine o'clock

1. τρίτος + ὥρα, *tritos + hōra, 5569 + 6052*

Mat 20: 3 went out about nine o'clock, he saw others   1
Act 23:23 to leave by nine o'clock tonight for Caesarea   1

nine o'clock in the morning

1. τρίτος + ὥρα, *tritos + hōra, 5569 + 6052*
2. τρίτος + ὥρα + ὁ + ἡμέρα, *tritos + hōra + ho + hēmera,*
    5569 + 6052 + 3836 + 2465

Mrk 15:25 It was nine o'clock in the morning   1
Act   2:15 for it is only nine o'clock in the morning.   2

ninety-nine

1. ἐνενήκοντα + ἐννέα, *enenēkonta + ennea, 1916 + 1933*

Mat 18:12 not leave the ninety-nine on the mountains   1
     18:13 he rejoices…more than over the ninety-nine   1
Lke 15: 4 does not leave the ninety-nine in the wilderness   1
     15: 7 than over ninety-nine righteous persons   1

Nineveh   *See also* person of Nineveh

1. Νινευίτης, *Nineuitēs, 3780*

Mat 12:41 The people of Nineveh will rise up at the judgment   1

ninth

1. ἔνατος, *enatos, 1888*

Rev 21:20 the eighth beryl, the ninth topaz   1

no   *See also* bring no regret, by no *means*, have no concern, no *another*, no *any*, no any *more*, no *anything*, no *at all*, no *child*, no *doubt*, no *even*, no *ever*, no *excuse*, no *existence*, no further [*far*], no *knowledge*, no *longer*, no *more*, no *need* to be ashamed, no *offense*, no *opportunity*, no *present*, no *standing*, no *way*, no *yet*, still no

1. ἀλλά, *alla, 247*
2. εἰ, *ei, 1623*
3. μή, *mē, 3590*
4. μή + πᾶς, *mē + pas, 3590 + 4246*
5. μηδείς, *mēdeis, 3594*
6. μήποτε, *mēpote, 3607*
7. μήτε, *mēte, 3612*
8. οὐ, *ou, 4024*
9. οὐ + μή, *ou + mē, 4024 + 3590*
10. οὐ + πᾶς, *ou + pas, 4024 + 4246*
11. οὐδέ, *oude, 4028*
12. οὐδείς, *oudeis, 4029*
13. οὔτε, *oute, 4046*
14. οὐχί, *ouchi, 4049*

Mat	1:25	had no marital relations with her until she	8
	5:37	Let your word be 'Yes, Yes' or 'No, No'	8
	5:37	Let your word be 'Yes, Yes' or 'No, No'	8
	6: 1	for then you have no reward from your Father	8
	8:28	so fierce that no one could pass that way.	3
	9:12	"Those who are well have no need of a physician	8
	10: 5	and enter no town of the Samaritans	3
	10: 9	Take no gold, or silver, or copper in your belts	3

	10:10	no bag for your journey, or two tunics	3
	10:26	"So have no fear of them; for nothing is covered	3
	11: 6	blessed is anyone who takes no offense at me."	3
	11:23	No, you will be brought down to Hades.	3
	12:25	no city or house divided against itself	10
	12:39	but no sign will be given to it	8
	13: 5	since they had no depth of soil.	3
	13: 6	since they had no root, they withered away.	3
	13:21	yet such a person has no root	8
	13:29	'No; for in gathering the weeds you would uproot	8
	16: 4	but no sign will be given to it	8
	16: 7	because we have brought no bread."	8
	16: 8	why are you talking about having no bread?	8
	19: 6	let no one separate."	3
	20:13	'Friend, I am doing you no wrong;	8
	22:23	saying there is no resurrection;	3
	24: 4	"Beware that no one leads you astray.	3
	24:21	until now, no, and never will be.	11
	24:22	no one would be saved;	10
	25: 3	they took no oil with them;	8
	25: 9	'No! there will not be enough for you and for us;	6
	25:42	for I was hungry and you gave me no food	8
	26:62	"Have you no answer?	12
	27:14	he gave him no answer, not even to a single charge	8
Mrk	2:17	"Those who are well have no need of a physician	8
	4: 5	since it had no depth of soil.	3
	4: 6	since it had no root, it withered away.	3
	4: 7	it yielded no grain.	8
	4:17	they have no root, and endure only	8
	5:26	no better, but rather grew worse.	5
	6: 5	he could do no deed of power there	12
	6: 8	no bread, no bag, no money in their belts;	8
	6: 8	no bread, no bag, no money in their belts;	3
	6: 8	no bread, no bag, no money in their belts;	3
	8:12	Truly I tell you, no sign will be given	2
	8:16	"It is because we have no bread."	8
	8:17	"Why are you talking about having no bread?	8
	9: 3	such as no one on earth could bleach them.	8
	10: 9	let no one separate."	3
	12:18	Sadducees, who say there is no resurrection	3
	12:19	leaving a wife but no child	3
	12:20	when he died, left no children;	3
	12:21	married the widow and died, leaving no children;	3
	12:31	no other commandment greater than these."	8
	12:32	besides him there is no other';	8
	13: 5	"Beware that no one leads you astray.	3
	13:20	no one would be saved;	10
	14:60	"Have you no answer?	12
	15: 4	Pilate asked him again, "Have you no answer?	12
	15: 5	Jesus made no further reply	12
Lke	1: 7	they had no children, because Elizabeth was barren	8
	1:33	of his kingdom there will be no end."	8
	1:60	his mother said, "No; he is to be called John."	14
	2: 7	because there was no place for them in the inn.	8
	3:13	"Collect no more than the amount prescribed	5
	4:24	no prophet is accepted in the prophet's hometown.	12
	5:19	no way to bring him in because of the crowd	3
	5:31	"Those who are well have no need of a physician	8
	6:43	"No good tree bears bad fruit	3
	7:23	blessed is anyone who takes no offense at me."	3
	7:33	For John the Baptist has come eating no bread	3
	7:44	you gave me no water for my feet	8
	7:45	You gave me no kiss	8
	8:13	But these have no root;	8
	8:27	For a long time he had worn no clothes	8
	9: 3	no staff, nor bag, nor bread, nor money	7
	9:13	"We have no more than five loaves and two fish	8
	10: 4	Carry no purse, no bag, no sandals;	3
	10: 4	Carry no purse, no bag, no sandals;	3
	10: 4	Carry no purse, no bag, no sandals;	3
	10:15	No, you will be brought down to Hades.	8
	11:29	it asks for a sign, but no sign will be given	8
	11:36	full of light, with no part of it in darkness	3
	12:17	I have no place to store my crops?'	8
	12:33	where no thief comes near and no moth destroys.	8
	12:51	No, I tell you, but rather division!	14
	13: 3	No, I tell you;	14
	13: 5	No, I tell you;	14
	15: 7	who need no repentance.	8
	16:13	No slave can serve two masters;	12
	16:30	He said, 'No, father Abraham;	14

	18: 4 I have no fear of God and no respect for anyone	8
	20:27 Sadducees, those who say there is no resurrection,	3
	22:36 one who has no sword must sell his cloak	3
	23: 4 "I find no basis for an accusation against	12
	23: 9 but Jesus gave him no answer.	12
	23:22 in him no ground for the sentence of death;	12
Jhn	1:21 "Are you the prophet?" He answered, "No."	8
	1:47 an Israelite in whom there is no deceit!"	8
	2: 3 mother of Jesus said to him, "They have no wine."	8
	2:25 and needed no one to testify about anyone;	8
	3: 3 no one can see the kingdom of God without	8
	3: 5 no one can enter the kingdom of God without	8
	3:27 John answered, "No one can receive anything	8
	4:11 you have no bucket, and the well is deep.	13
	4:17 The woman answered him, "I have no husband."	8
	4:17 "You are right in saying, 'I have no husband';	8
	4:33 no one has brought him something to eat?"	3
	4:44 a prophet has no honor in the prophet's own country).	8
	5: 7 I have no one to put me into the pool	8
	6:53 you have no life in you.	8
	7:12 were saying, "No, he is deceiving the crowd."	8
	7:52 no prophet is to arise from Galilee."	8
	8:37 because there is no place in you for my word.	8
	8:44 because there is no truth in him.	8
	9: 9 were saying, "No, but it is someone like him."	14
	10:28 No one will snatch them out of my hand.	8
	10:41 they were saying, "John performed no sign	12
	12:27 No, it is for this reason that I have come	1
	13: 8 "Unless I wash you, you have no share with me."	8
	14:30 He has no power over me;	8
	15: 2 removes every branch in me that bears no fruit.	3
	15:22 now they have no excuse for their sin.	8
	18:38 "I find no case against him.	12
	19: 4 to let you know that I find no case against him."	12
	19: 6 I find no case against him."	8
	19: 9 But Jesus gave him no answer.	8
	19:11 "You would have no power over me	12
	19:12 you are no friend of the emperor.	8
	19:15 "We have no king but the emperor."	8
	21: 5 Jesus said to them, "Children, you have no fish	3
	21: 5 They answered him, "No."	8
Act	2:16 No, this is what was spoken through the prophet Joel:	1
	3: 6 Peter said, "I have no silver or gold	8
	4:12 no other name under heaven given among mortals	11
	4:21 they let them go, finding no way to punish them	5
	4:32 no one claimed private ownership of any possessions	11
	7: 5 even though he had no child.	8
	7:11 our ancestors could find no food.	8
	8:21 You have no part or share in this	8
	10:34 "I truly understand that God shows no partiality	8
	12:18 there was no small commotion among the soldiers	8
	13:28 they found no cause for a sentence of death	5
	13:37 he whom God raised up experienced no corruption.	8
	15: 2 after Paul and Barnabas had no small dissension	8
	15: 9 he has made no distinction between them and us.	12
	15:24 though with no instructions from us	8
	15:28 no further burden than these essentials:	5
	19: 2 They replied, "No, we have not even heard	1
	19:23 no little disturbance broke out concerning the Way.	8
	19:24 brought no little business to the artisans.	8
	19:40 no cause that we can give to justify this	5
	23: 8 (The Sadducees say that there is no resurrection	3
	23:14 an oath to taste no food until we have killed Paul.	5
	24: 4 to detain you no further	3
	25:10 I have done no wrong to the Jews	12
	25:17 I lost no time, but on the next day took my seat	5
	27:20 no small tempest raged,	8
	27:22 no loss of life among you, but only of the ship.	12
	28: 5 shook off the creature…and suffered no harm.	12
	28:18 no reason for the death penalty in my case.	5
	28:19 I had no charge to bring against my nation.	8
	28:21 "We have received no letters from Judea about you	13
Rom	2:11 For God shows no partiality.	8
	3: 9 What then? Are we any better off? No, not at all;	8
	3:18 "There is no fear of God before their eyes."	8
	3:20 for "no human being will be justified in his sight"	10
	3:22 all who believe. For there is no distinction.	8
	3:27 No, but by the law of faith.	14
	4:15 but where there is no law, neither is there violation.	8
	4:20 No distrust made him waver	8
	5:13 but sin is not reckoned when there was no law.	3

	6:14 For sin will have no dominion over you	8
	8: 1 no condemnation for those who are in Christ	12
	8:37 No, in all these things we are more	1
	9:21 Has the potter no right over the clay	8
	10:11 "No one who believes in him will be put to shame."	8
	10:12 there is no distinction between Jew and Greek;	8
	12:20 No, "if your enemies are hungry, feed them;	1
	13: 1 for there is no authority except from God	8
	13: 3 you wish to have no fear of the authority?	3
	13:10 Love does no wrong to a neighbor;	8
	13:14 and make no provision for the flesh	3
	14:22 Blessed are those who have no reason to condemn	3
1Co	1:10 that there be no divisions among you	3
	1:15 so that no one can say that you were baptized	3
	1:29 so that no one might boast	4
	2: 9 "What no eye has seen, nor ear heard	8
	6: 5 Can it be that there is no one among you	12
	7:25 virgins, I have no command of the Lord	8
	7:30 those who buy as though they had no possessions	3
	7:31 as though they had no dealings with it.	3
	7:36 let him marry as he wishes; it is no sin.	8
	7:37 stands firm…being under no necessity	3
	8: 4 and that "there is no God but one."	12
	8: 8 We are no worse off if we do not eat	13
	9: 6 Or is it only Barnabas and I who have no right	8
	9:15 I have made no use of any of these rights	8
	9:16 this gives me no ground for boasting	8
	10:13 No testing has overtaken you	8
	10:20 No, I imply that what pagans sacrifice	1
	11:16 we have no such custom, nor do the churches	8
	12:21 eye cannot say to the hand, "I have no need of you,"	8
	12:21 the head to the feet, "I have no need of you."	8
	12:25 that there may be no dissension within the body	3
	15:12 there is no resurrection of the dead?	8
	15:13 If there is no resurrection of the dead	8
	16:11 therefore let no one despise him.	3
	16:22 anyone be accursed who has no love for the Lord.	8
2Co	1:17 say "Yes, yes" and "No, no" at the same time?	8
	1:17 say "Yes, yes" and "No, no" at the same time?	8
	1:18 our word to you has not been "Yes and No."	8
	1:19 not "Yes and No"; but in him it is always "Yes."	8
	5:21 For our sake he made him to be sin who knew no sin	3
	6: 3 We are putting no obstacle in anyone's way	5
	6: 3 so that no fault may be found with our ministry	3
	6:12 There is no restriction in our affections	8
	7: 5 our bodies had no rest	12
	8:20 We intend that no one should blame us	3
	11:14 no wonder! Even Satan disguises himself	8
	11:16 I repeat, let no one think that I am a fool;	3
	12: 4 that no mortal is permitted to repeat.	8
	12: 6 no one may think better of me than what is seen	3
Gal	2: 6 (what they actually were makes no difference to me;	12
	2: 6 God shows no partiality)	8
	2:16 no one will be justified by the works of the law.	8
	4: 1 heirs…are no better than slaves,	12
	4:12 You have done me no wrong.	12
	4:17 They make much of you, but for no good purpose;	8
	4:27 you childless one, you who bear no children	8
	4:27 and shout, you who endure no birth pangs;	8
	5: 2 Christ will be of no benefit to you.	12
	5:23 There is no law against such things.	8
Eph	2: 9 not the result of works, so that no one may boast.	3
	2:12 having no hope and without God in the world.	3
	4:29 Let no evil talk come out of your mouths	4
	5: 5 no fornicator or impure person	10
	5:11 Take no part in the unfruitful works of darkness	3
	6: 9 with him there is no partiality.	8
Php	3: 3 have no confidence in the flesh	8
	4:15 no church shared with me	12
Col	2: 8 See to it that no one takes you captive	3
	2:23 of no value in checking self-indulgence.	8
	3:25 there is no partiality.	8
1Th	1: 8 so that we have no need to speak about it	3
	4:13 you may not grieve as others do who have no hope.	3
	5: 3 there will be no escape!	9
2Th	2: 3 Let no one deceive you in any way;	3
1Ti	2:12 I permit no woman to teach	8
	5:14 give the adversary no occasion to revile us.	5
2Ti	2:14 avoid wrangling over words, which does no good	12
Heb	4:11 so that no one may fall through such disobedience	3
	4:13 before him no creature is hidden	8

Heb	7:27	he has no need…to offer sacrifices day after day	8
	8: 7	there would have been no need to look for a second	8
	8:12	I will remember their sins no more."	9
	9:22	there is no forgiveness of sins.	8
	10: 2	would no longer have any consciousness of sin?	5
	10: 6	you have taken no pleasure.	8
	10:17	remember their sins and their lawless deeds no more."	9
	10:38	My soul takes no pleasure in anyone who shrinks back."	8
	12:15	no one fails to obtain the grace of God;	3
	12:15	no root of bitterness springs up	3
	12:16	no one becomes like Esau, an immoral and godless	3
	12:17	he was rejected, for he found no chance to repent	8
	13:10	who officiate in the tent have no right to eat.	8
	13:14	For here we have no lasting city	8
Jas	1:17	Father of lights, with whom there is no variation	8
	2:13	without mercy to anyone who has shown no mercy;	3
	2:17	So faith by itself, if it has no works, is dead.	3
	3: 2	who makes no mistakes in speaking is perfect.	8
	5:12	let your "Yes" be yes and your "No" be no	8
	5:12	let your "Yes" be yes and your "No" be no	8
1Pe	2:22	"He committed no sin	8
	2:22	no deceit was found in his mouth."	11
2Pe	1:20	no prophecy of scripture is a matter of one's own	10
	1:21	because no prophecy ever came by human will,	8
1Jn	1: 8	If we say that we have no sin, we deceive ourselves	8
	2: 7	Beloved, I am writing you no new commandment	8
	2:10	in such a person there is no cause for stumbling.	8
	2:21	and you know that no lie comes from the truth.	10
	3: 5	and in him there is no sin.	8
	4:18	There is no fear in love	8
3Jn	1: 4	I have no greater joy than this	8
	1: 7	accepting no support from non-believers.	5
Rev	7: 1	so that no wind could blow on earth or sea	3
	7:16	They will hunger no more, and thirst no	8
	7:16	will hunger no more, and thirst no more;	11
	11: 6	shut the sky, so that no rain may fall during the days	3
	12: 8	there was no longer any place for them in heaven.	11
	13:17	no one can buy or sell who does not have the mark	3
	14: 5	in their mouth no lie was found;	8
	14:11	There is no rest day or night for those	8
	16:20	and no mountains were to be found;	8
	18: 7	I am no widow, and I will never see grief,'	8
	18:21	Babylon…will be found no more;	9
	18:22	sound of harpists…will be heard in you no more;	9
	18:22	an artisan…will be found in you no more;	9
	18:22	the millstone will be heard in you no more;	9
	18:23	and the light of a lamp will shine in you no more;	9
	18:23	the voice…will be heard in you no more;	9
	20: 3	so that he would deceive the nations no more.	3
	20: 6	Over these the second death has no power	8
	20:11	and no place was found for them.	8
	21: 1	earth had passed away, and the sea was no more.	8
	21: 4	Death will be no more;	8
	21: 4	mourning and crying and pain will be no more	8
	21:22	I saw no temple in the city	8
	21:23	the city has no need of sun or moon to shine on it	8
	21:25	and there will be no night there.	8
	22: 5	And there will be no more night;	8
	22: 5	they need no light of lamp or sun	8

no one

1. μή, *mē*, 3590
2. μηδείς, *mēdeis*, 3594
3. οὐ, *ou*, 4024
4. οὐ + πᾶς, *ou + pas*, 4024 + 4246
5. οὐδέ, *oude*, 4028
6. οὐδέ + πᾶς, *oude + pas*, 4028 + 4246
7. οὐδείς, *oudeis*, 4029

Mat	5:15	No one after lighting a lamp puts it under	5
	6:24	"No one can serve two masters; for a slave	7
	8:10	in no one in Israel have I found such faith.	7
	9:16	No one sews a piece of unshrunk cloth on	7
	9:30	"See that no one knows of this."	2
	11:11	no one has arisen greater than John the Baptist;	3
	11:27	and no one knows the Son except the Father	7
	17: 8	when they looked up, they saw no one	7
	17: 9	"Tell no one about the vision	2
	20: 7	They said to him, 'Because no one has hired us.'	7
	22:16	and show deference to no one;	7
	22:46	No one was able to give him an answer	7

	23: 9	call no one your father on earth	1
	24:36	about that day and hour no one knows	7
Mrk	2:21	"No one sews a piece of unshrunk cloth	7
	2:22	no one puts new wine into old wineskins;	7
	3:27	no one can enter a strong man's house	7
	5: 3	no one could restrain him any more	7
	5: 4	no one had the strength to subdue him.	7
	5:37	He allowed no one to follow him except Peter	7
	5:43	He strictly ordered them that no one should know	2
	7:36	Jesus ordered them to tell no one;	2
	9: 8	saw no one with them any more, but only Jesus.	7
	9: 9	to tell no one about what they had seen	2
	9:39	no one who does a deed of power in my name	7
	10:18	"Why do you call me good? No one is good but God	7
	10:29	there is no one who has left house or brothers	7
	11:14	"May no one ever eat fruit from you again."	7
	12:14	you are sincere, and show deference to no one;	7
	12:34	After that no one dared to ask him any question.	7
	13:32	about that day or hour no one knows	7
Lke	5:14	he ordered him to tell no one;	2
	5:36	"No one tears a piece from a new garment	7
	5:37	"No one puts new wine into old wineskins;	7
	5:39	no one after drinking old wine desires new	7
	7:28	no one is greater than John;	7
	8:16	"No one after lighting a lamp hides it	7
	8:43	on physicians, no one could cure her.	7
	8:56	he ordered them to tell no one what had happened.	2
	9:36	they kept silent and in those days told no one	7
	9:62	"No one who puts a hand to the plow	7
	10: 4	greet no one on the road.	2
	10:22	no one knows who the Son is except the Father	7
	11:33	"No one after lighting a lamp puts it in a cellar	7
	15:16	no one gave him anything.	7
	18:19	"Why do you call me good? No one is good but God	7
	18:29	there is no one who has left house or wife	7
	20:21	and you show deference to no	3
	23:53	where no one had ever been laid.	7
Jhn	1:18	No one has ever seen God.	7
	3: 2	for no one can do these signs that you do	7
	3:13	No one has ascended into heaven except the one	7
	3:32	yet no one accepts his testimony.	7
	4:27	but no one said, "What do you want?"	7
	5:22	The Father judges no one	7
	6:44	No one can come to me unless drawn	7
	6:65	I have told you that no one can come to me	7
	7: 4	no one who wants to be widely known acts in secret.	7
	7:13	Yet no one would speak openly about him	7
	7:27	no one will know where he is from."	7
	7:30	no one laid hands on him	7
	7:44	but no one laid hands on him.	7
	8:10	[["Woman, where are they? Has no one condemned you?"]]	7
	8:11	[[She said, "No one, sir."]]	7
	8:15	You judge by human standards; I judge no one.	7
	8:20	but no one arrested him	7
	9: 4	night is coming when no one can work.	7
	10:18	No one takes it from me	7
	10:29	no one can snatch it out of the Father's hand.	7
	13:28	no one at the table knew why he said this to him.	7
	14: 6	No one comes to the Father except through me.	7
	15:13	No one has greater love than this	7
	15:24	done among them the works that no one else did	7
	16:22	no one will take your joy from you.	7
	19:41	a new tomb in which no one had ever been laid.	7
Act	1:20	let there be no one to live in it';	1
	4:12	There is salvation in no one else	7
	5:23	when we opened them, we found no one inside."	7
	9: 7	heard the voice but saw no one.	2
	11:19	spoke the word to no one except Jews.	2
	18:10	no one will lay a hand on you to harm you	7
	20:33	I coveted no one's silver or gold or clothing.	7
	23:22	"Tell no one that you have informed me of this."	2
	25:11	no one can turn me over to them.	7
Rom	3:10	"There is no one who is righteous, not even one;	3
	3:11	there is no one who has understanding	3
	3:11	there is no one who seeks God.	3
	3:12	there is no one who shows kindness	3
	13: 8	Owe no one anything, except to love one another;	2
1Co	2:11	So also no one comprehends what is truly God's	7
	2:15	are themselves subject to no one else's scrutiny.	7
	3:11	For no one can lay any foundation other	7
	3:21	So let no one boast about human leaders.	2

	9:15	no one will deprive me of my ground for boasting	7
	12: 3	no one speaking by the Spirit of God ever says	7
	12: 3	no one can say "Jesus is Lord"	7
	14:28	if there is no one to interpret	1
2Co	5:16	we regard no one from a human point of view;	7
	7: 2	we have wronged no one, we have corrupted no one	7
	7: 2	we have wronged no one, we have corrupted no one	7
	7: 2	we have taken advantage of no one.	7
Gal	3:11	no one is justified before God by the law;	7
	3:15	no one adds to it or annuls it.	7
	6:17	From now on, let no one make trouble for me;	2
Eph	5: 6	Let no one deceive you with empty words	2
	5:29	For no one ever hates his own body	7
Php	2:20	I have no one like him	7
Col	2: 4	I am saying this so that no one may deceive you	2
1Th	3: 3	that no one would be shaken by these persecutions.	2
	4: 6	that no one wrong or exploit a brother or sister	1
	4:12	be dependent on no one.	2
1Ti	4:12	Let no one despise your youth	2
	6:16	whom no one has ever seen or can see;	7
2Ti	2: 4	No one serving in the army gets entangled	7
	2: 5	no one is crowned without competing according	3
	4:16	At my first defense no one came to my support	7
Tit	2:15	Let no one look down on you.	2
	3: 2	to speak evil of no one, to avoid quarreling	2
Heb	6:13	because he had no one greater by whom to swear	7
	7:13	from which no one has ever served at the altar.	7
	12:14	holiness without which no one will see the Lord.	7
Jas	1:13	No one…should say, "I am being tempted by God";	2
	1:13	God cannot be tempted…and…tempts no one.	7
	3: 8	no one can tame the tongue—a restless evil	7
1Jn	2:23	No one who denies the Son has the Father;	6
	3: 6	No one who abides in him sins;	4
	3: 6	no one who sins has either seen him or known him.	4
	3: 7	Little children, let no one deceive you.	2
	4:12	No one has ever seen God;	7
Rev	2:17	a new name…that no one knows except the one	7
	3: 7	the true one…who opens and no one will shut	7
	3: 7	the true one…who shuts and no one opens:	7
	3: 8	an open door, which no one is able to shut.	7
	3:11	hold fast…so that no one may seize your crown.	2
	5: 3	no one in heaven or on earth or under the earth	7
	5: 4	because no one was found worthy to open the scroll	7
	7: 9	a great multitude that no one could count	7
	14: 3	No one could learn that song except	7
	15: 8	and no one could enter the temple	7
	18:11	since no one buys their cargo anymore	7
	19:12	he has a name inscribed that no one knows	7

Noah

1. Νῶε, *Nōe, 3820*

Mat	24:37	For as the days of Noah were	1
	24:38	until the day Noah entered the ark	1
Lke	3:36	son of Shem, son of Noah, son of Lamech	1
	17:26	Just as it was in the days of Noah	1
	17:27	until the day Noah entered the ark	1
Heb	11: 7	By faith Noah…respected the warning	1
1Pe	3:20	when God waited patiently in the days of Noah	1
2Pe	2: 5	saved Noah, a herald of righteousness	1

noble *See also* noble *birth*

1. καλός, *kalos, 2819*

Rom	12:17	take thought for what is noble in the sight of all.	1
1Ti	3: 1	to the office of bishop desires a noble task.	1

nobleman

1. εὐγενής, *eugenēs, 2302*

Lke	19:12	"A nobleman went to a distant country	1

nobody

1. οὐδείς, *oudeis, 4029*

1Co	14: 2	for nobody understands them,	1

noise *See also* loud noise

1. φωνή, *phōnē, 5889*

Rev	9: 9	the noise of their wings was like the noise	
	9: 9	like the noise of many chariots with horses	1

noisy

1. ἠχέω, *ēcheō, 2490*

1Co	13: 1	I am a noisy gong or a clanging cymbal.	1

non-believer

1. ἐθνικός, *ethnikos, 1618*

3Jn	1: 7	accepting no support from non-believers.	1

none *See also* none *ever*

1. μή, *mē, 3590*
2. μή + εἷς, *mē + heis, 3590 + 1651*
8. μή + τὶς, *mē + tis, 3590 + 5516*
4. οὐ, *ou, 4024*
5. οὐ + μή, *ou + mē, 4024 + 3590*
6. οὐ + πᾶς, *ou + pas, 4024 + 4246*
7. οὐ + ἅπας, *ou + hapas, 4024 + 570*
8. οὐδείς, *oudeis, 4029*
9. οὔτε, *oute, 4046*

Mat	10:42	none of these will lose their reward."	5
	12:43	but it finds none.	4
	26:60	they found none	4
Mrk	12:22	none of the seven left children.	4
	14:55	they found none.	4
Lke	1:61	"None of your relatives has this name."	8
	3:11	must share with anyone who has none;	1
	4:26	yet Elijah was sent to none of them	8
	4:27	none of them was cleansed	8
	13: 6	he came looking for fruit on it and found none.	4
	13: 7	and still I find none.	4
	14:24	For I tell you, none of those who were invited	8
	14:33	none of you can become my disciple if	6
	17:18	Was none of them found to return and give praise	4
	21:15	none of your opponents will be able	7
Jhn	7:19	Yet none of you keeps the law.	8
	16: 5	yet none of you asks me, 'Where are you going?'	8
	19:36	"None of his bones shall be broken."	4
	21:12	Now none of the disciples dared to ask him	8
Act	5:13	None of the rest dared to join them	8
	26:26	none of these things has escaped his notice	8
	27:34	for none of you will lose a hair from your heads	8
	27:42	so that none might swim away and escape;	3
	28:21	none of the brothers coming here has reported	9
1Co	1:14	I thank God that I baptized none of you	8
	2: 8	None of the rulers of this age understood this;	8
	4: 6	that none of you will be puffed up in favor of one	2
	6:10	none of these will inherit the kingdom of God.	4
	7:29	who have wives be as though they had none	1
1Th	5:15	See that none of you repays evil for evil	1
Heb	3:13	so that none of you may be hardened	1
1Pe	4:15	let none of you suffer as a murderer, a thief	1
1Jn	2:19	they made it plain that none of them belongs	6

nonsense

1. ματαιότης, *mataiotēs, 3470*

2Pe	2:18	For they speak bombastic nonsense,	1

noon

1. ἕκτος + ὥρα, *hektos + hōra, 1761 + 6052*
2. μεσημβρία, *mesēmbria, 3540*

Mat	20: 5	When he went out again about noon	1
	27:45	From noon on, darkness came over the whole land	1
Mrk	15:33	When it was noon, darkness came over the whole	1
Lke	23:44	It was now about noon,	1
Jhn	4: 6	It was about noon.	1
	19:14	it was about noon. He said to the Jews,	1
Act	10: 9	About noon the next day	1
	22: 6	about noon a great light from heaven	2

nor *See also* nor any *more*

1. ἤ, *ē, 2445*
2. καί, *kai, 2779*
3. μή, *mē, 3590*
4. μηδέ, *mēde, 3593*
5. μήτε, *mēte, 3612*
6. οὐ, *ou, 4024*
7. οὐδέ, *oude, 4028*
8. οὔτε, *oute, 4046*

Mat	6:20	in heaven, where neither moth nor rust consumes	8
	6:26	of the air; they neither sow nor reap nor gather	7
	6:26	they neither sow nor reap nor gather into barns	7
	6:28	how they grow; they neither toil nor spin	7

Mat	7:18	nor can a bad tree bear good fruit.	7
	10:24	nor a slave above the master;	7
	11:18	For John came neither eating nor drinking	5
	12:19	nor will anyone hear his voice in the streets.	7
	13:13	hearing they do not listen, nor do they understand.'	7
	22:29	neither the scriptures nor the power of God.	4
	22:30	they neither marry nor are given in marriage	8
	22:46	nor from that day did anyone dare to ask him	7
	23:10	Nor are you to be called instructors	4
	24:36	neither the angels of heaven, nor the Son	7
	25:13	you know neither the day nor the hour.	7
Mrk	4:22	nor is anything secret, except to come to light.	7
	12:24	know neither the scriptures nor the power of God?	4
	12:25	they neither marry nor are given in marriage	8
	13:32	nor the Son, but only the Father.	7
Lke	6:43	nor again does a bad tree bear good fruit;	7
	6:44	nor are grapes picked from a bramble bush.	7
	8:17	nor is anything secret that will not become known	7
	9: 3	no staff, nor bag, nor bread, nor money	5
	9: 3	no staff, nor bag, nor bread, nor money	5
	9: 3	no staff, nor bag, nor bread, nor money	5
	12:24	Consider the ravens: they neither sow nor reap	7
	12:24	they have neither storehouse nor barn	7
	12:27	they neither toil nor spin;	7
	14:35	fit neither for the soil nor for the manure pile;	8
	17:21	nor will they say, 'Look, here it is!'	7
	18: 2	neither feared God nor had respect for people.	3
	20:35	neither marry nor are given in marriage.	8
Jhn	1:25	if you are neither the Messiah, nor Elijah	7
	1:25	the Messiah, nor Elijah, nor the prophet?"	7
	4:21	neither on this mountain nor in Jerusalem.	8
	6:24	neither Jesus nor his disciples were there	7
	8:19	Jesus answered, "You know neither me nor my Father.	8
	9: 3	"Neither this man nor his parents sinned;	8
	9:21	nor do we know who opened his eyes.	6
	13:16	nor are messengers greater than the one who sent	7
	14:17	because it neither sees him nor knows him.	8
Act	2:31	nor did his flesh experience corruption.'	8
	9: 9	neither ate nor drank.	7
	15:10	neither our ancestors nor we have been able to bear?	8
	17:25	nor is he served by human hands	7
	19:37	neither temple robbers nor blasphemers	8
	23:12	an oath neither to eat nor drink	5
	23:21	an oath neither to eat nor drink	5
	27:20	neither sun nor stars appeared for many days	5
Rom	2:28	nor is true circumcision something external	7
	8:38	neither death, nor life, nor angels	8
	8:38	neither death, nor life, nor angels	8
	8:38	nor rulers, nor things present	8
	8:38	nor things present, nor things to come, nor powers	8
	8:38	nor things present, nor things to come, nor powers	8
	8:38	nor things present, nor things to come, nor powers	8
	8:39	nor height, nor depth, nor anything else	8
	8:39	nor height, nor depth, nor anything else	8
	8:39	nor depth, nor anything else in all creation	8
	9:10	Nor is that all; something similar happened	6
1Co	2: 9	"What no eye has seen, nor ear heard	6
	2: 9	nor the human heart conceived	6
	3: 7	neither the one who plants nor the one who waters is	8
	9:15	nor am I writing this	6
	9:26	nor do I box as though beating the air;	6
	11:16	no such custom, nor do the churches of God.	7
	12:21	nor again the head to the feet	1
	15:50	nor does the perishable inherit	7
2Co	7:12	nor on account of the one who was wronged	7
Gal	1: 1	by human commission nor from human authorities,	7
	1:12	from a human source, nor was I taught it	8
	1:17	nor did I go up to Jerusalem	7
	5: 6	neither circumcision nor uncircumcision	8
	6:15	nor uncircumcision is anything; but a new creation	8
1Th	2: 6	nor did we seek praise from mortals	8
Heb	7: 3	having neither beginning of days nor end of life	5
	9:25	Nor was it to offer himself again and again	7
	10: 8	"You have neither desired nor taken pleasure in	7
1Jn	3:10	nor are those who do not love their brothers and sisters.	7
Rev	3:15	"I know your works; you are neither cold nor hot.	8
	3:16	you are lukewarm, and neither cold nor hot	8
	7:16	sun will not strike them, nor any scorching heat;	7
	21:27	nor anyone who practices abomination	2

north

1. βορρᾶς, *borras, 1080*

Lke	13:29	come from east and west, from north and south	1
Rev	21:13	on the east three gates, on the north three gates	1

northeaster

1. εὐρακύλων, *eurakylōn, 2350*

Act	27:14	soon a violent wind, called the northeaster	1

northwest

1. χῶρος, *chōros, 6008*

Act	27:12	a harbor of Crete, facing southwest and northwest.	1

not Not Indexed; *See* can not, can not speak, cannot, not a *lover* of money, not a *single* one, not a *thing*, not *after* that, not *again*, not *any*, not any *longer*, not any *more*, not *anyone*, not *anything*, not *at* all, not *behave* properly, not *believe*, not *even*, not *ever*, not *healthy*, not *include*, not *know*, not *make* with hands, not *necessary*, not *obey*, not of one's *will*, not one's *own*, not *quarrelsome*, not [*quickly*], not *ready*, not *realize*, not *recognize*, not *responsible*, not *suitable*, not *tell*, not *understand*, not *yet*, so that not, still not, surely not, that not

not in the least

1. μηδείς, *mēdeis, 3594*

2Co	11: 5	I think that I am not in the least inferior	1

not one

1. οὐδείς, *oudeis, 4029*

Jhn	17:12	I guarded them, and not one of them was lost	1

not only

1. μέν, *men, 3525*
2. τέ, *te, 5445*

Act	26:10	I not only locked up many of the saints in prison	2
2Co	8:17	For he not only accepted our appeal	1

notable

1. γνωστός, *gnōstos, 1196*

Act	4:16	a notable sign has been done through them;	1

note[1]   See also take note

1. ἴδε, *ide, 2623*

Rom	11:22	Note then the kindness and the severity of God:	1

note[2]

1. φθόγγος, *phthongos, 5782*

1Co	14: 7	If they do not give distinct notes	1

nothing   See also reduce to nothing

1. Contextual: Not in Greek
2. ἄκαρπος, *akarpos, 182*
3. γυμνός, *gymnos, 1218*
4. δωρεάν, *dōrean, 1562*
5. εἰκῆ, *eikē, 1632*
6. κενῶς, *kenōs, 3036*
7. μή, *mē, 3590*
8. μή + τίς, *mē + tis, 3590 + 5516*
9. μηδείς, *mēdeis, 3594*
10. μήτιγε, *mētige, 3615*
11. οὐ, *ou, 4024*
12. οὐ + μή + εἰς + πᾶς, *ou + mē + eis + pas, 4024 + 3590 + 1650 + 4246*
13. οὐ + πᾶς, *ou + pas, 4024 + 4246*
14. οὐ + πᾶς + ῥῆμα, *ou + pas + rhēma, 4024 + 4246 + 4839*
15. οὐ + τίς, *ou + tis, 4024 + 5515*
16. οὐ + τίς, *ou + tis, 4024 + 5516*
17. οὐδέ + τίς, *oude + tis, 4028 + 5516*
18. οὐδείς, *oudeis, 4029*

Mat	8: 4	"See that you say nothing to anyone; but go	9
	10:26	nothing is covered up that will not be uncovered	18
	10:26	and nothing secret that will not become known.	1
	13:12	but from those who have nothing,	11
	13:22	and it yields nothing.	2
	13:34	without a parable he told them nothing.	18

14:17 "We have nothing here but five loaves and two fish." 11
15:32 and have nothing to eat; 11
17:20 and nothing will be impossible for you." 18
21:19 found nothing at all on it but leaves. 18
23:16 swears by the sanctuary is bound by nothing 18
23:18 'Whoever swears by the altar is bound by nothing 18
24:39 they knew nothing until the flood came 11
25:29 but from those who have nothing, 7
25:42 I was thirsty and you gave me nothing to drink 11
27:19 "Have nothing to do with that innocent man 9
27:24 So when Pilate saw that he could do nothing 18
Mrk 1:44 "See that you say nothing to anyone; 9
4:19 choke the word, and it yields nothing. 2
4:22 there is nothing hidden, except to be disclosed; 11
4:25 have nothing, even what they have will be taken 11
6:8 ordered them to take nothing for their journey 9
7:15 there is nothing outside a person 18
8:2 have nothing to eat. 15
11:13 When he came to it, he found nothing but leaves 18
14:51 wearing nothing but a linen cloth. 3
16:8 they said nothing to anyone, for they were afraid. 18
Lke 1:37 For nothing will be impossible with God." 14
4:2 He ate nothing at all during those days 18
5:5 worked all night long but have caught nothing. 18
6:35 do good, and lend, expecting nothing in return. 9
8:17 nothing is hidden that will not be disclosed 11
9:3 He said to them, "Take nothing for your journey 9
10:19 nothing will hurt you. 18
11:6 I have nothing to set before him.' 11
12:2 Nothing is covered up that will not be uncovered 18
12:2 and nothing secret that will not become known. 1
12:4 after that can do nothing more. 8
18:34 they understood nothing about all these things; 18
19:26 but from those who have nothing, 7
23:15 he has done nothing to deserve death. 18
23:41 this man has done nothing wrong." 18
Jhn 5:14 not sin...so that nothing worse happens to you." 8
5:19 the Son can do nothing on his own 18
5:30 "I can do nothing on my own. 18
6:12 so that nothing may be lost." 8
6:39 lose nothing of all that he has given me 7
7:18 there is nothing false in him. 11
7:26 here he is, speaking openly, but they say nothing 18
8:28 I do nothing on my own 18
8:54 "If I glorify myself, my glory is nothing. 18
9:33 If this man were not from God, he could do nothing." 18
11:49 "You know nothing at all! 18
12:19 "You see, you can do nothing. 18
15:5 because apart from me you can do nothing. 18
16:23 On that day you will ask nothing of me. 18
18:20 I have said nothing in secret. 18
21:3 that night they caught nothing. 18
Act 4:14 they had nothing to say in opposition. 18
8:24 nothing of what you have said may happen to me." 9
9:8 though his eyes were open, he could see nothing; 18
17:21 nothing but telling or hearing something 18
19:36 you ought to be quiet and do nothing rash. 9
21:24 nothing in what they have been told about you 18
23:9 "We find nothing wrong with this man. 18
23:29 charged with nothing deserving death 9
25:11 if there is nothing to their charges against me 18
25:25 I found that he had done nothing deserving death; 9
25:26 nothing definite to write to our sovereign about him. 11
26:22 saying nothing but what the prophets...said 18
26:31 "This man is doing nothing to deserve death 18
27:33 without food, having eaten nothing. 9
28:6 saw that nothing unusual had happened to him 9
28:17 though I had done nothing against our people 18
Rom 7:18 For I know that nothing good dwells within me 11
14:14 persuaded...that nothing is unclean in itself; 18
1Co 2:2 For I decided to know nothing among you 16
4:6 the saying, "Nothing beyond what is written," 7
6:3 to say nothing of ordinary matters? 10
7:19 Circumcision is nothing, and uncircumcision 18
7:19 Circumcision...and uncircumcision is nothing; 18
11:22 humiliate those who have nothing? 7
13:2 but do not have love, I am nothing. 18
13:3 but do not have love, I gain nothing. 18
14:10 and nothing is without sound. 18
2Co 1:13 we write you nothing other than what you can read 11
6:10 as having nothing, and yet possessing 9

6:17 touch nothing unclean; then I will welcome you 7
9:4 we would be humiliated—to say nothing of you 7
12:1 It is necessary to boast; nothing is to be gained 11
12:11 even though I am nothing. 18
Gal 2:6 those leaders contributed nothing to me. 18
2:21 then Christ died for nothing. 4
3:4 Did you experience so much for nothing? 5
3:4 if it really was for nothing. 5
6:3 if those who are nothing think they are something 9
Php 2:3 Do nothing from selfish ambition or conceit 9
2Th 3:14 who do not obey...have nothing to do with them 7
1Ti 4:4 nothing is to be rejected, provided... 18
5:21 doing nothing on the basis of partiality. 9
6:4 is conceited, understanding nothing 9
6:7 for we brought nothing into the world 18
6:7 so that we can take nothing out of it; 17
Tit 1:15 to the corrupt and unbelieving nothing is pure. 18
2:8 having nothing evil to say of us. 9
3:13 see that they lack nothing. 9
Phm 1:14 I preferred to do nothing without your consent 18
1:19 I say nothing about your owing me 7
Heb 2:8 God left nothing outside their control. 18
7:14 Moses said nothing about priests. 18
7:19 (for the law made nothing perfect); 18
Jas 1:4 be mature and complete, lacking in nothing. 9
4:5 suppose that it is for nothing that the scripture says 6
1Pe 3:7 so that nothing may hinder your prayers. 7
Rev 3:17 For you say, 'I am rich...and I need nothing.' 18
21:27 But nothing unclean will enter it 12
22:3 Nothing accursed will be found there any more. 13

nothing but
1. πᾶς, *pas, 4246*
Jas 1:2 whenever you face trials...consider it nothing but joy 1

nothing ever
1. οὐδέποτε, *oudepote, 4030*
Act 11:8 nothing profane or unclean has ever entered 1

nothing more to do
1. παραιτέομαι, *paraiteomai, 4148*
Tit 3:10 have nothing more to do with anyone who causes divisions 1

nothing to do
1. παραιτέομαι, *paraiteomai, 4148*
1Ti 4:7 Have nothing to do with profane myths...tales. 1
2Ti 2:23 Have nothing to do with...controversies; 1

nothing to fear
1. ἀφόβως, *aphobōs, 925*
1Co 16:10 If Timothy comes, see that he has nothing to fear 1

notice *See also* escape notice, take notice
1. βλέπω, *blepō, 1063*
2. γινώσκω, *ginōskō, 1182*
3. ἐπέχω, *epechō, 2091*
4. κατανοέω, *katanoeō, 2917*
5. ὁράω, *horaō, 3972*
Mat 7:3 but do not notice the log in your own eye? 4
14:30 he noticed the strong wind, he became frightened 1
22:11 he noticed a man...not wearing a wedding robe 5
Mrk 7:2 noticed that some of his disciples were eating 5
Lke 6:41 do not notice the log in your own eye? 4
8:46 I noticed that power had gone out from me." 2
14:7 he noticed how the guests chose the places of honor 3
Act 23:6 When Paul noticed that some were Sadducees 2
27:39 they noticed a bay with a beach 4

notify
1. ἐμφανίζω, *emphanizō, 1872*
Act 23:15 must notify the tribune to bring him down 1

notorious
1. ἐπίσημος, *episēmos, 2168*
Mat 27:16 At that time they had a notorious prisoner 1

nourish
1. ἐκτρέφω, *ektrephō, 1763*
2. ἐντρέφω, *entrephō, 1957*

3. ἐπιχορηγέω, *epichorēgeō, 2220*
4. τρέφω, *trephō, 5555*

Eph	5:29	he nourishes and tenderly cares for it	1
Col	2:19	nourished and held together by its ligaments	3
1Ti	4: 6	nourished on the words of the faith	2
Rev	12: 6	prepared by God, so that there she can be nourished	4
	12:14	wilderness, to her place where she is nourished	4

now *See also* from now, from now on, just now

1. Contextual: Not in Greek
2. ἄγω, *agō, 72*
3. ἀλλά, *alla, 247*
4. ἄρτι, *arti, 785*
5. γάρ, *gar, 1142*
6. δέ, *de, 1254*
7. δή, *dē, 1314*
8. ἤδη, *ēdē, 2453*
9. ἰδού, *idou, 2627*
10. καί, *kai, 2779*
11. νῦν, *nyn, 3814*
12. νυνί, *nyni, 3815*
13. οὖν, *oun, 4036*
14. πάλιν, *palin, 4099*
15. ὥστε, *hōste, 6063*

Mat	1:18	Now the birth of Jesus the Messiah took place	6
	2:13	Now after they had left, an angel	6
	3: 4	Now John wore clothing of camel's hair	6
	3:10	Even now the ax is lying at the root of the trees;	8
	3:15	But Jesus answered him, "Let it be so now;	4
	4:12	Now when Jesus heard that John had been arrested	6
	7:28	Now when Jesus had finished saying these	10
	8:18	Now when Jesus saw great crowds around him	6
	8:30	Now a large herd of swine was feeding	6
	11: 1	Now when Jesus had finished instructing	10
	11:12	From the days of John the Baptist until now	4
	14:13	Now when Jesus heard this, he withdrew from there	6
	14:15	"This is a deserted place, and the hour is now late;	8
	15:32	because they have been with me now for three days	8
	16:13	Now when Jesus came into the district	6
	20:10	Now when the first came	10
	21:40	Now when the owner of the vineyard comes	13
	22:25	Now there were seven brothers among us;	6
	22:41	Now while the Pharisees were gathered together	6
	24:21	from the beginning of the world until now	11
	26: 6	Now while Jesus was at Bethany	6
	26:48	Now the betrayer had given them a sign, saying	6
	26:59	Now the chief priests and the whole council	6
	26:64	From now on you will see the Son of Man	4
	26:65	You have now heard his blasphemy.	11
	26:69	Now Peter was sitting outside in the courtyard.	6
	27:11	Now Jesus stood before the governor;	6
	27:15	Now at the festival the governor was accustomed	6
	27:20	Now the chief priests and the elders persuaded	6
	27:42	let him come down from the cross now	11
	27:43	let God deliver him now, if he wants to;	11
	27:54	Now when the centurion and those with him	6
	28:16	Now the eleven disciples went to Galilee	6
Mrk	1: 6	Now John was clothed with camel's hair	10
	1:14	Now after John was arrested	6
	1:30	Now Simon's mother-in-law was in bed with a fever	6
	2: 6	Now some of the scribes were sitting there	6
	2:18	Now John's disciples and the Pharisees	10
	5:11	Now there on the hillside a great herd of swine	6
	5:25	Now there was a woman who had been suffering	10
	6:33	Now many saw them going and recognized them	10
	6:35	a deserted place, and the hour is now very late;	8
	7: 1	Now when the Pharisees and some of the scribes	10
	7:26	Now the woman was a Gentile	6
	8: 2	because they have been with me now for three days	8
	8: 9	Now there were about four thousand people	6
	8:14	Now the disciples had forgotten to bring any bread;	10
	10:30	receive a hundredfold now in this age	11
	13:19	the creation that God created until now	11
	14:44	Now the betrayer had given them a sign, saying	6
	14:55	Now the chief priests and the whole council	6
	15: 6	Now at the festival he used to release a prisoner	6
	15: 7	Now a man called Barabbas was in prison	6
	15:32	King of Israel, come down from the cross now	11
	15:39	Now when the centurion, who stood facing him, saw	6
	16: 9	⟦Now after he rose early on the first day of the week⟧	6

Lke	1:10	Now at the time of the incense offering	10
	1:20	But now, because you did not believe my words,	9
	1:31	And now, you will conceive in your womb	9
	1:36	And now, your relative Elizabeth in her old age	9
	1:48	Surely, from now on all generations will call me	11
	1:57	Now the time came for Elizabeth to give birth	6
	2:15	"Let us go now to Bethlehem and see this thing	7
	2:25	Now there was a man in Jerusalem	9
	2:29	now you are dismissing your servant in peace	11
	2:41	Now every year his parents went to Jerusalem	10
	3: 9	Even now the ax is lying at the root of the trees;	8
	3:21	Now when all the people were baptized	6
	4:38	Now Simon's mother-in-law was suffering…fever	6
	5:10	from now on you will be catching people."	11
	5:15	now more than ever the word about Jesus spread	1
	6:12	Now during those days he went out…to pray;	6
	6:21	"Blessed are you who are hungry now	11
	6:21	"Blessed are you who weep now,	11
	6:25	"Woe to you who are full now,	11
	6:25	"Woe to you who are laughing now,	11
	7:39	Now when the Pharisee who had invited him saw it	6
	7:42	Now which of them will love him more?"	13
	8:11	"Now the parable is this:	6
	8:32	Now there on the hillside a large herd of swine	6
	8:40	Now when Jesus returned, the crowd welcomed him	6
	8:43	Now there was a woman who had been suffering	10
	9: 7	Now Herod the ruler heard about all that	6
	9:28	Now about eight days after these sayings	6
	9:32	Now Peter and his companions were weighed down	6
	10:31	Now by chance a priest was going down that road;	6
	10:38	Now as they went on their way, he entered	6
	11:14	Now he was casting out a demon that was mute;	10
	11:19	Now if I cast out the demons by Beelzebul	6
	11:39	"Now you Pharisees clean the outside of the cup	11
	12:52	From now on five in one household will be	11
	13:10	Now he was teaching in one of the synagogues	6
	14:17	'Come; for everything is ready now.'	8
	14:25	Now large crowds were traveling with him;	6
	15: 1	Now all the tax collectors and sinners	6
	15:25	"Now his elder son was in the field;	6
	16: 3	now that my master is taking the position away	1
	16:25	now he is comforted here, and you are in agony.	11
	19:37	As he was now approaching	8
	19:42	now they are hidden from your eyes.	11
	20:29	Now there were seven brothers;	13
	20:38	Now he is God not of the dead, but of the living;	6
	21:28	Now when these things begin to take place	6
	22: 1	Now the festival of Unleavened Bread,	6
	22:18	from now on I will not drink of the fruit	11
	22:36	"But now, the one who has a purse must take it	11
	22:63	Now the men who were holding Jesus began to mock	10
	22:69	from now on the Son of Man will be seated	11
	23:44	It was now about noon,	8
	23:50	Now there was a good and righteous man named Joseph	9
	24:10	Now it was Mary Magdalene, Joanna	6
	24:13	Now on that same day two of them were going	9
	24:21	Yes, and besides all this, it is now the third day	2
	24:29	almost evening and the day is now nearly over."	8
Jhn	1:24	Now they had been sent from the Pharisees.	10
	1:44	Now Philip was from Bethsaida, the city of Andrew	6
	2: 6	Now standing there were six stone water jars	6
	2: 8	"Now draw some out, and take it to the chief steward."	11
	2:10	But you have kept the good wine until now."	4
	3: 1	Now there was a Pharisee named Nicodemus	6
	3:25	Now a discussion about purification arose	13
	4: 1	Now when Jesus learned that the Pharisees	13
	4:18	and the one you have now is not your husband.	11
	4:23	But the hour is coming, and is now	11
	4:46	Now there was a royal official whose son lay ill	10
	4:54	Now this was the second sign that Jesus did	14
	5: 2	Now in Jerusalem by the Sheep Gate there is a pool	6
	5: 9	Now that day was a sabbath.	6
	5:13	Now the man who had been healed did not know	6
	5:25	the hour is coming, and is now here,	11
	6: 4	Now the Passover…was near.	6
	6:10	Now there was a great deal of grass in the place;	6
	6:17	It was now dark	8
	6:42	can he now say, 'I have come down from heaven'?	11
	7: 2	Now the Jewish festival of Booths was near.	6
	7:25	Now some of the people of Jerusalem were saying	13
	7:39	Now he said this about the Spirit	6

8: 5	⟦Now in the law Moses commanded us to stone such⟧	6
8: 5	⟦Now what do you say?"⟧	13
8:11	⟦"Go your way, and from now on do not sin again."⟧	11
8:40	now you are trying to kill me	11
8:42	I came from God and now I am here.	1
8:52	"Now we know that you have a demon.	11
9:14	Now it was a sabbath day when Jesus made the mud	6
9:15	I washed, and now I see."	1
9:19	How then does he now see?	4
9:21	we do not know how it is that now he sees	11
9:25	I do know, that though I was blind, now I see."	4
9:41	now that you say, 'We see,' your sin remains.	11
11: 1	Now a certain man was ill, Lazarus of Bethany	6
11:18	Now Bethany was near Jerusalem, some two miles	6
11:22	even now I know that God will give you whatever	11
11:30	Now Jesus had not yet come to the village	6
11:55	Now the Passover of the Jews was near	6
11:57	Now the chief priests…had given orders	6
12:20	Now among those who went up to worship	6
12:27	"Now my soul is troubled. And what should I say	11
12:31	Now is the judgment of this world;	11
12:31	now the ruler of this world will be driven out.	11
13: 1	Now before the festival of the Passover	6
13: 7	"You do not know now what I am doing	4
13:19	I tell you this now, before it occurs	4
13:28	Now no one at the table knew why he said this	6
13:31	"Now the Son of Man has been glorified	11
13:33	as I said to the Jews so now I say to you	4
13:36	"Where I am going, you cannot follow me now;	11
13:37	"Lord, why can I not follow you now?	4
14: 7	From now on you know him and have seen him."	4
14:29	now I have told you this before it occurs	11
15:22	now they have no excuse for their sin.	11
15:24	now they have seen and hated both me	11
16: 5	now I am going to him who sent me;	11
16:12	you cannot bear them now.	4
16:22	you have pain now; but I will see you again	11
16:24	Until now you have not asked for anything	4
16:29	"Yes, now you are speaking plainly	11
16:30	Now we know that you know all things	11
16:31	Jesus answered them, "Do you now believe?	4
17: 5	now, Father, glorify me in your own presence	11
17: 7	Now they know that everything…is from you;	11
17:11	now I am no longer in the world	1
17:13	now I am coming to you	11
18: 2	Now Judas, who betrayed him, also knew the place	6
18:18	Now the slaves and the police	6
18:25	Now Simon Peter was…warming himself.	6
18:40	Now Barabbas was a bandit.	6
19: 8	Now when Pilate heard this,	13
19:14	Now it was the day of Preparation for the Passover;	6
19:23	now the tunic was seamless	6
19:28	Jesus knew that all was now finished	8
19:41	Now there was a garden in the place	6
20:30	Now Jesus did many other signs	13
21: 6	now they were not able to haul it in	10
21:12	Now none of the disciples dared to ask him	6
21:14	This was now the third time	8
Act 1:18	(Now this man acquired a field	13
2: 5	Now there were devout Jews from every nation	6
2:37	Now when they heard this	6
3:17	now, friends, I know that you acted in ignorance	11
4:13	Now when they saw the boldness of Peter and John	6
4:29	now, Lord, look at their threats	11
4:32	Now the whole group of those who believed	6
5: 5	Now when Ananias heard these words	6
5:12	Now many signs and wonders were done	6
5:24	Now when the captain of the temple	6
6: 1	Now during those days	6
7: 4	this country in which you are now living.	11
7:11	Now there came a famine throughout Egypt	6
7:30	"Now when forty years had passed	10
7:34	Come now, I will send you to Egypt.'	11
7:35	God now sent as both ruler and liberator	1
7:52	now you have become his betrayers and murderers.	11
8: 4	Now those who were scattered went from place to place	13
8: 9	Now a certain man named Simon	6
8:14	Now when the apostles at Jerusalem heard	6
8:18	Now when Simon saw that the Spirit was given	6
8:25	Now after Peter and John had testified and spoken	13
8:27	Now there was an Ethiopian eunuch	9

8:32	Now the passage of the scripture	6
9: 3	Now as he was going along and approaching Damascus	6
9:10	Now there was a disciple in Damascus	6
9:32	Now as Peter went here and there among all	6
9:36	Now in Joppa there was a disciple…Tabitha	6
10: 5	Now send men to Joppa	11
10:17	Now while Peter was greatly puzzled	6
10:20	Now get up, go down	3
10:29	Now may I ask why you sent for me?"	13
10:33	So now all of us are here	11
11: 1	Now the apostles and the believers	6
11:19	Now those who were scattered	13
12:11	"Now I am sure that the Lord has sent his angel	11
12:20	Now Herod was angry with the people of Tyre	6
13: 1	Now in the church at Antioch there were prophets	6
13:11	now listen—the hand of the Lord is against you	11
13:31	they are now his witnesses to the people.	11
13:46	we are now turning to the Gentiles.	9
15:10	Now therefore why are you putting God to the test	11
16:36	therefore come out now and go in peace."	11
16:37	now are they going to discharge us in secret?	11
17:21	Now all the Athenians and the foreigners	6
17:30	now he commands all people everywhere to repent	11
18: 6	From now on I will go to the Gentiles."	11
18:24	Now there came to Ephesus a Jew named Apollos	6
19:21	Now after these things had been accomplished	6
20:22	now, as a captive to the Spirit,	11
20:25	now I know that none of you…will ever see	11
20:32	now I commend you to God	11
22: 1	listen to the defense that I now make before you."	12
22: 9	Now those who were with me saw the light	6
22:16	now why do you delay? Get up, be baptized	11
23:15	Now then, you and the council must notify	11
23:16	Now the son of Paul's sister heard about the ambush;	6
23:21	They are ready now and are waiting for your consent	11
24:13	the charge that they now bring against me.	12
24:17	Now after some years I came to bring alms	6
25:11	Now if I am in the wrong	13
26: 6	now I stand here on trial on account of my hope	11
27: 9	sailing was now dangerous	8
27:22	I urge you now to keep up your courage	11
28: 7	Now in the neighborhood of that place were lands	6
Rom 3:19	Now we know that whatever the law says	6
3:21	But now, apart from law, the righteousness of God	12
3:24	they are now justified by his grace as a gift	1
4: 4	Now to one who works, wages are not reckoned	6
4:23	Now the words…were written not for his sake alone	1
5: 9	now that we have been justified by his blood	11
5:11	we have now received reconciliation.	11
6:19	now present your members as slaves to righteousness	11
6:21	get from the things of which you now are ashamed?	11
6:22	But now that you have been freed from sin	12
7: 6	But now we are discharged from the law	12
7:16	Now if I do what I do not want, I agree	6
7:20	Now if I do what I do not want, it is no longer I	6
8: 1	There is therefore now no condemnation	11
8:22	whole creation has been groaning…until now;	11
8:24	Now hope that is seen is not hope.	6
11:12	Now if their stumbling means riches for the world	6
11:13	Now I am speaking to you Gentiles.	6
11:30	but have now received mercy	11
11:31	so they have now been disobedient in order that	11
11:31	they too may now receive mercy.	11
13:11	it is now the moment for you to wake from sleep.	8
13:11	For salvation is nearer to us now	11
15:23	But now, with no further place for me	12
16:25	Now to God who is able to strengthen you	6
16:26	but is now disclosed	11
1Co 1:10	Now I appeal to you, brothers and sisters,	6
2:12	Now we have received not the spirit of the world	6
3: 2	Even now you are still not ready	11
3:12	Now if anyone builds on the foundation with gold	6
4: 5	who will bring to light the things now hidden	1
5:11	But now I am writing to you	11
7: 1	Now concerning the matters	6
7:21	make use of your…condition now more than ever	1
7:25	Now concerning virgins, I have no command	6
8: 1	Now concerning food sacrificed to idols:	6
8: 7	have become so accustomed to idols until now	4
10: 6	Now these things occurred as examples for us	6
11:17	Now in the following instructions I do not commend	6

1Co	12: 1	Now concerning spiritual gifts, brothers and sisters	6
	12: 4	Now there are varieties of gifts	6
	12:27	Now you are the body of Christ	6
	13:12	For now we see in a mirror, dimly,	4
	13:12	Now I know only in part; then I will know fully	4
	13:13	And now faith, hope, and love abide, these three;	12
	14: 5	Now I would like all of you to speak in tongues	6
	14: 6	Now, brothers and sisters, if I come to you speaking	11
	15: 1	Now I would remind you, brothers and sisters	6
	15:12	Now if Christ is proclaimed as raised from the dead	6
	16: 1	Now concerning the collection for the saints:	6
	16: 7	I do not want to see you now just in passing	4
	16:12	Now concerning our brother Apollos	6
	16:12	he was not at all willing to come now.	11
	16:15	Now, brothers and sisters, you know that members	6
2Co	2: 7	so now instead you should forgive and console	1
	3: 7	Now if the ministry of death	6
	3: 7	the glory of his face, a glory now set aside	1
	3:17	Now the Lord is the Spirit	6
	5:16	From now on, therefore, we regard	11
	6: 2	See, now is the acceptable time;	11
	6: 2	see, now is the day of salvation!	11
	7: 9	Now I rejoice, not because you were grieved	11
	8: 7	Now as you excel in everything	3
	8:11	now finish doing it, so that your eagerness	12
	8:22	who is now more eager than ever	12
	9: 1	Now it is not necessary for me to write you	5
	10: 8	Now, even if I boast a little too much	5
	13: 2	I warn them now while absent	11
Gal	1: 9	As we have said before, so now I repeat	4
	1:10	Am I now seeking human approval, or God's	4
	1:23	now proclaiming the faith he once tried to destroy."	11
	2:20	the life I now live in the flesh I live by faith	11
	3: 3	are you now ending with the flesh?	11
	3:11	Now it is evident that no one is justified	6
	3:16	Now the promises were made to Abraham	6
	3:20	Now a mediator involves more than one	6
	3:23	Now before faith came	6
	3:25	now that faith has come	1
	4: 9	Now, however, that you have come to know God	11
	4:16	Have I now become your enemy	15
	4:20	I wish I were present with you now	4
	4:25	Now Hagar is Mount Sinai in Arabia	6
	4:28	Now you, my friends, are children of the promise	6
	4:29	so it is now also	11
	5:19	Now the works of the flesh are obvious:	6
Eph	2: 2	the spirit that is now at work	11
	2:13	now in Christ Jesus you...have been brought	12
	3: 5	has now been revealed to his holy apostles	11
	3:10	might now be made known to the rulers	11
	3:20	Now to him who...is able to accomplish	6
	4:17	Now this I affirm and insist on in the Lord:	13
	5: 8	now in the Lord you are light.	11
Php	1: 5	from the first day until now.	11
	1:20	Christ will be exalted now as always in my body	11
	1:30	and now hear that I still have.	11
	2:12	in my presence, but much more now in my absence	11
	3:18	and now I tell you even with tears	11
	4:10	now at last you have revived your concern	8
	4:18	satisfied, now that I have received from Epaphroditus	1
Col	1:22	now reconciled in his fleshly body through death	12
	1:24	I am now rejoicing in my sufferings for your sake	11
	1:26	now been revealed to his saints.	11
	3: 8	now you must get rid of all such things—anger,	12
1Th	3: 8	For we now live, if you continue to stand firm	11
	3:11	Now may our God and Father himself	6
	4: 9	Now concerning love of the brothers and sisters	6
	5: 1	Now concerning the times and the seasons,	6
2Th	2: 6	you know what is now restraining him	11
	2: 7	until the one who now restrains it is removed.	4
	2:16	Now may our Lord Jesus Christ himself	6
	3: 6	Now we command you, beloved	6
	3:12	Now such persons we command and exhort	6
	3:16	Now may the Lord of peace himself give you peace	6
1Ti	1: 8	Now we know that the law is good	6
	3: 2	Now a bishop must be above reproach	13
	4: 1	Now the Spirit expressly says	6
2Ti	1: 5	a faith that...now, I am sure, lives in you.	1
	1:10	has now been revealed through the appearing of...	11
	3:10	Now you have observed my teaching, my conduct	6
Phm	1: 9	I, Paul, do this as an old man, and now also as a prisoner	12

	1:11	now he is indeed useful both to you and to me.	12
Heb	2: 5	Now God did not subject the coming world	5
	2: 8	Now in subjecting all things to them	5
	2: 9	now crowned with glory and honor	1
	3: 5	Now Moses was faithful in all God's house	10
	3:16	Now who were they who heard and yet were rebellious?	5
	7:11	Now if perfection had been attainable	13
	7:13	Now the one of whom these things are spoken	5
	8: 1	Now the main point in what we are saying is this:	6
	8: 4	Now if he were on earth, he would not be a priest	13
	8: 6	Jesus has now obtained a more excellent ministry	12
	9: 1	Now even the first covenant had regulations	13
	9: 5	Of these things we cannot speak now in detail.	11
	9:24	now to appear in the presence of God on our behalf.	11
	11: 1	Now faith is the assurance of things hoped for	6
	12:11	Now, discipline always seems painful	6
	12:26	now he has promised	11
	13:20	Now may the God of peace	6
Jas	2:11	Now if you do not commit adultery but if you murder	6
	4:13	Come now, you who say, "Today or tomorrow	11
	5: 1	Come now, you rich people, weep and wail	11
1Pe	1: 6	now for a little while you have had to suffer	4
	1: 8	though you do not see him now, you believe in him	4
	1:12	the things that have now been announced to you	11
	2:10	but now you are God's people;	11
	2:10	but now you have received mercy.	11
	2:25	but now you have returned to the shepherd	11
	3:13	Now who will harm you if you are eager	10
	3:21	baptism, which this prefigured, now saves you	11
	5: 1	Now as an elder myself and a witness of the sufferings	13
2Pe	3: 1	This is now, beloved, the second letter I am writing	8
	3:18	glory both now and to the day of eternity. Amen.	11
1Jn	2: 3	Now by this we may be sure that we know him	10
	2:18	so now many antichrists have come.	11
	2:28	now, little children, abide in him	11
	3: 2	Beloved, we are God's children now;	11
	4: 3	antichrist...and now it is already in the world.	11
2Jn	1: 5	now, dear lady, I ask you, not as though I were writing	11
Jde	1: 5	Now I desire to remind you	6
	1:24	Now to him who is able to keep you from falling	6
	1:25	before all time and now and forever. Amen.	11
Rev	1:19	Now write what you have seen	13
	8: 6	Now the seven angels who had the seven trumpets	10
	12:10	"Now have come the salvation and the power	4
	14:13	Blessed are the dead who from now on die in the Lord."	4

nowhere

   1. μή, *mē, 3590*
   2. οὐ + ποῦ, *ou + pou, 4024 + 4544*

Mat	8:20	but the Son of Man has nowhere to lay his head."	2
	10: 5	"Go nowhere among the Gentiles	1
Lke	9:58	the Son of Man has nowhere to lay his head."	2

null

   1. κενόω, *kenoō, 3033*

Rom	4:14	faith is null and the promise is void.	1

nullify

   1. ἀθετέω, *atheteō, 119*
   2. καταργέω, *katargeō, 2934*

Rom	3: 3	faithlessness nullify the faithfulness of God?	2
Gal	2:21	I do not nullify the grace of God;	1
	3:17	so as to nullify the promise.	2

number   *See also* increase in number, many in number

   1. Contextual: Not in Greek
   2. ἀριθμός, *arithmos, 750*
   3. αὐτός, *autos, 899*
   4. εἰμί, *eimi, 1639*
   5. ἱκανός, *hikanos, 2653*
   6. καταριθμέω, *katarithmeō, 2935*
   7. πλῆθος, *plēthos, 4436*

Mrk	3: 8	great numbers from Judea, Jerusalem, Idumea,	7
	5:13	herd, numbering about two thousand, rushed down	1
	6:44	had eaten the loaves numbered five thousand men	4
Lke	23:27	A great number of the people followed him	7
Act	1:15	the crowd numbered about one hundred twenty persons)	4
	1:17	he was numbered among us	6
	2:47	day by day the Lord added to their number	3
	4: 4	they numbered about five thousand.	2

	5:36	a number of men, about four hundred, joined him;	2
	6: 7	the number of the disciples increased greatly	2
	11:21	a great number became believers and turned to the Lord.	2
	14: 1	that a great number…became believers.	7
	16: 5	increased in numbers daily.	2
	19:19	A number of those who practiced magic	5
	27: 7	We sailed slowly for a number of days	5
Rom	9:27	"Though the number of the children of Israel were	2
Rev	5:11	many angels…they numbered myriads of myriads	2
	6:11	rest…until the number would be complete	1
	7: 4	I heard the number of those who were sealed	2
	9:16	The number of the troops…was two hundred million;	2
	9:16	number of the troops…I heard their number.	2
	13:17	the name of the beast or the number of its name.	2
	13:18	let anyone…calculate the number of the beast	2
	13:18	number of the beast, for it is the number of a person.	2
	13:18	Its number is six hundred sixty-six.	2
	15: 2	the beast and its image and the number of its name	2

considerable number

1. ἱκανός, *hikanos, 2653*

Act	19:26	drawn away a considerable number of people	1

full number

1. πλήρωμα, *plērōma, 4445*

Rom	11:25	until the full number of the Gentiles has come in.	1

great number

1. πλῆθος, *plēthos, 4436*
2. πολύς, *polys, 4498*

Act	5:14	great numbers of both men and women	1
	5:16	A great number of people would also gather	1
	28:23	they came to him at his lodgings in great numbers.	2

numerous

1. Contextual: Not in Greek
2. ἀριθμός, *arithmos, 750*
3. πολύς, *polys, 4498*

Rom	4:18	"So numerous shall your descendants be."	1
Gal	4:27	children of the desolate woman are more numerous	3
Rev	20: 8	they are as numerous as the sands of the sea.	2

nurse

1. θηλάζω, *thēlazō, 2558*
2. τρέφω, *trephō, 5555*
3. τροφός, *trophos, 5577*

Lke	11:27	the breasts that nursed you!"	1
	23:29	and the breasts that never nursed.'	2
1Th	2: 7	like a nurse tenderly caring for her own children.	3

nurse an infant

1. θηλάζω, *thēlazō, 2558*

Mat	24:19	those who are nursing infants in those days!	1
Mrk	13:17	those who are nursing infants in those days!	1
Lke	21:23	those who are nursing infants in those days!	1

nursing *See* nursing *baby*

Nympha

1. Νύμφαν, *Nymphan, 3809*

Col	4:15	to Nympha and the church in her house.	1

O

O

1. ὦ², *ō², 6043*

Rom	11:33	O the depth of the riches and wisdom	1

o'clock *See* five o'clock, four o'clock in the afternoon, nine o'clock, nine o'clock in the morning, three o'clock, three o'clock in the afternoon

oar

1. ἐλαύνω, *elaunō, 1785*

Mrk	6:48	he saw that they were straining at the oars	1

oath *See also* bind by oath, put under oath, swear an oath

1. ὅρκος, *horkos, 3992*
2. ὁρκωμοσία, *horkōmosia, 3993*

Mat	14: 7	so much that he promised on oath to grant her	1
	14: 9	out of regard for his oaths and for the guests	1
	26:72	Again he denied it with an oath	1
Mrk	6:26	yet out of regard for his oaths and for the guests	1
Lke	1:73	the oath that he swore to our ancestor Abraham	1
Act	2:30	knew that God had sworn with an oath to him	1
Heb	6:16	an oath given as confirmation puts an end to all dispute.	1
	6:17	he guaranteed it by an oath	1
	7:20	This was confirmed with an oath;	2
	7:20	took their office without an oath	2
	7:21	but this one became a priest with an oath,	2
	7:28	the word of the oath, which came later than the law	2
Jas	5:12	do not swear…by any other oath	1

Obed

1. Ἰωβήδ, *Iōbēd, 2725*

Mat	1: 5	Boaz the father of Obed by Ruth	1
	1: 5	and Obed the father of Jesse	1
Lke	3:32	son of Jesse, son of Obed, son of Boaz	1

obedience

1. ὑπακοή, *hypakoē, 5633*
2. ὑποταγή, *hypotagē, 5717*

Rom	1: 5	to bring about the obedience of faith	1
	5:19	by the one man's obedience the many…righteous.	1
	6:16	or of obedience, which leads to righteousness?	1
	15:18	to win obedience from the Gentiles	1
	16:19	For while your obedience is known to all	1
	16:26	to bring about the obedience of faith—	1
2Co	7:15	as he remembers the obedience of all of you	1
	9:13	glorify God by your obedience	2
	10: 6	when your obedience is complete.	1
Phm	1:21	Confident of your obedience, I am writing to you	1
Heb	5: 8	he learned obedience through what he suffered;	1
1Pe	1:22	have purified your souls by your obedience	1

obedient

1. πειθαρχέω, *peitharcheō, 4272*
2. ὑπακοή, *hypakoē, 5633*
3. ὑπακούω, *hypakouō, 5634*
4. ὑπήκοος, *hypēkoos, 5675*
5. ὑποτάσσω, *hypotassō, 5718*

Lke	2:51	was obedient to them.	5
Act	6: 7	the priests became obedient to the faith.	3
Rom	6:16	if you present…to anyone as obedient slaves	2
	6:17	you…have become obedient from the heart	3
2Co	2: 9	know whether you are obedient in everything	4
Php	2: 8	obedient to the point of death—even death on a cross.	4
Tit	3: 1	to be obedient, to be ready for every good work	1
1Pe	1: 2	sanctified…to be obedient to Jesus Christ	2
	1:14	Like obedient children, do not be conformed	2

obey

1. Contextual: Not in Greek
2. πειθαρχέω, *peitharcheō, 4272*
3. πείθω, *peithō, 4275*
4. ποιέω, *poieō, 4472*
5. πράσσω, *prassō, 4556*
6. τηρέω, *tēreō, 5498*
7. τήρησις, *tērēsis, 5499*
8. ὑπακοή, *hypakoē, 5633*
9. ὑπακούω, *hypakouō, 5634*
10. ὑπήκοος, *hypēkoos, 5675*
11. φυλάσσω, *phylassō, 5875*

Mat	8:27	that even the winds and the sea obey him?"	9
	28:20	teaching them to obey everything	6
Mrk	1:27	they obey him."	9
	4:41	that even the wind and the sea obey him?"	9
Lke	8:25	the winds and the water, and they obey him?"	9
	11:28	those who hear the word of God and obey it!"	11
	17: 6	it would obey you.	9
Jhn	9:31	listen to one who worships him and obeys his will.	4
Act	5:29	"We must obey God rather than any human authority.	2
	5:32	whom God has given to those who obey him."	2
	7:39	Our ancestors were unwilling to obey him;	10
Rom	2:25	Circumcision…is of value if you obey the law;	5

Rom	6:12	to make you obey their passions.	9
	6:16	you are slaves of the one whom you obey	9
	10:16	But not all have obeyed the good news;	9
1Co	7:19	obeying the commandments of God is everything	7
2Co	10: 5	take every thought captive to obey Christ.	8
Gal	3:10	does not observe and obey all the things written	4
	5: 3	he is obliged to obey the entire law.	4
	5: 7	who prevented you from obeying the truth?	3
	6:13	Even the circumcised do not...obey the law	11
Eph	6: 1	Children, obey your parents in the Lord	9
	6: 5	Slaves, obey your earthly masters with fear	9
	6: 5	in singleness of heart, as you obey Christ;	1
Php	2:12	my beloved, just as you have always obeyed	9
Col	3:20	Children, obey your parents in everything	9
	3:22	Slaves, obey your earthly masters in everything	9
2Th	1: 8	who do not obey the gospel of our Lord Jesus.	9
	3:14	those who do not obey what we say in this letter;	9
Heb	5: 9	the source of...salvation for all who obey him	9
	11: 8	By faith Abraham obeyed	9
	13:17	Obey your leaders and submit to them	3
Jas	3: 3	to make them obey us	3
1Pe	3: 6	Thus Sarah obeyed Abraham and called him lord.	9
1Jn	2: 3	we know him, if we obey his commandments.	6
	2: 4	but does not obey his commandments, is a liar	6
	2: 5	but whoever obeys his word	6
	3:22	we receive...because we obey his commandments	6
	3:24	All who obey his commandments abide in him	6
	5: 2	when we love God and obey his commandments	4
	5: 3	the love of God is this, that we obey his commandments.	6
Rev	3: 3	what you received...obey it, and repent.	6

not obey

    1. ἀπειθέω, *apeitheō*, *578*

Rom	2: 8	who are self-seeking and who obey not the truth	1
1Pe	3: 1	even if some of them do not obey the word,	1
	3:20	who in former times did not obey	1
	4:17	what will be the end for those who do not obey	1

object[1]

    1. σκεῦος, *skeuos*, *5007*

Rom	9:21	out of the same lump one object for special use	1
	9:22	endured with much patience the objects of wrath	1
	9:23	the riches of his glory for the objects of mercy	1

object[2]

    1. ἀντιλέγω, *antilegō*, *515*

Act	28:19	when the Jews objected	1

object of worship

    1. σέβασμα, *sebasma*, *4934*

Act	17:23	looked carefully at the objects of your worship	1
2Th	2: 4	every so-called god or object of worship	1

without objection

    1. ἀναντιρρήτως, *anantirrētōs*, *395*

Act	10:29	So when I was sent for, I came without objection.	1

obligation

    1. ἀνάγκη, *anankē*, *340*

1Co	9:16	for an obligation is laid on me	1

obliged

    1. ὀφειλέτης, *opheiletēs*, *4050*

Gal	5: 3	he is obliged to obey the entire law.	1

obscene

    1. αἰσχρότης, *aischrotēs*, *157*

Eph	5: 4	out of place is obscene, silly, and vulgar talk	1

observance

    1. φυλάσσω, *phylassō*, *5875*

Act	16: 4	delivered to them for observance the decisions	1

observe[1]

    1. ὁράω, *horaō*, *3972*
    2. παρατήρησις, *paratērēsis*, *4191*
    3. σκοπέω, *skopeō*, *5023*

Mat	2: 2	For we observed his star at its rising,	1
Lke	17:20	is not coming with things that can be observed;	2

Php	3:17	observe those who live according to the example	3

observe[2]

    1. ἐμμένω, *emmenō*, *1844*
    2. κρατέω, *krateō*, *3195*
    3. μέρος, *meros*, *3538*
    4. παρακολουθέω, *parakoloutheō*, *4158*
    5. παρατηρέω, *paratēreō*, *4190*
    6. περιπατέω, *peripateō*, *4344*
    7. ποιέω, *poieō*, *4472*
    8. στοιχέω, *stoicheō*, *5123*
    9. τηρέω, *tēreō*, *5498*
    10. φρονέω, *phroneō*, *5858*

Mrk	7: 3	observing the tradition of the elders;	2
	7: 4	many other traditions that they observe	2
Jhn	9:16	for he does not observe the sabbath."	9
Act	16:21	not lawful for us as Romans to adopt or observe."	7
	21:21	not to circumcise...or observe the customs.	6
	21:24	you yourself observe and guard the law.	8
Rom	14: 6	Those who observe the day, observe it in honor	10
	14: 6	the day, observe it in honor of the Lord.	10
Gal	3:10	does not observe and obey all the things written	1
	4:10	You are observing special days, and months,	5
Col	2:16	observing festivals, new moons, or sabbaths.	3
2Ti	3:10	Now you have observed my teaching, my conduct	4
Heb	13: 9	which have not benefited those who observe them.	6

obsolete   *See also* make obsolete

    1. παλαιόω, *palaioō*, *4096*

Heb	8:13	what is obsolete and growing old	1

obstacle

    1. Contextual: Not in Greek

2Co	10: 5	proud obstacle raised up against the knowledge of God	1

obstacle in the way

    1. ἐγκοπή, *enkopē*, *1600*
    2. προσκοπή, *proskopē*, *4683*

1Co	9:12	rather than put an obstacle in the way of the gospel	1
2Co	6: 3	We are putting no obstacle in anyone's way	2

obtain   *See also* fail to obtain

    1. εἰς, *eis*, *1650*
    2. ἐπιτυγχάνω, *epitynchanō*, *2209*
    3. εὑρίσκω, *heuriskō*, *2351*
    4. ἔχω, *echō*, *2400*
    5. κτάομαι, *ktaomai*, *3227*
    6. λαμβάνω, *lambanō*, *3284*
    7. περιποιέω, *peripoieō*, *4347*
    8. περιποίησις, *peripoiēsis*, *4348*
    9. τυγχάνω, *tynchanō*, *5593*

Act	8:20	thought you could obtain God's gift with money!	5
	20:28	that he obtained with the blood of his own Son.	7
Rom	5: 2	we have obtained access to this grace	4
	8:21	and will obtain the freedom of the glory	1
	11: 7	Israel failed to obtain what it was seeking.	2
	11: 7	The elect obtained it, but the rest were hardened	2
Php	3:12	Not that I have already obtained this	6
1Th	5: 9	for obtaining salvation through our Lord Jesus	8
2Th	2:14	may obtain the glory of our Lord Jesus Christ.	8
2Ti	2:10	may also obtain the salvation that is in Christ Jesus	9
Heb	6:15	thus Abraham...obtained the promise.	2
	8: 6	Jesus has now obtained a more excellent ministry	9
	9:12	thus obtaining eternal redemption.	3
	11:33	administered justice, obtained promises	2
	11:35	in order to obtain a better resurrection.	9
Jas	4: 2	you covet something and cannot obtain it;	2
1Jn	5:15	we have obtained the requests made of him.	4

obtain an inheritance

    1. κληρόω, *klēroō*, *3103*

Eph	1:11	In Christ we have also obtained an inheritance	1

obvious

    1. κατάδηλος, *katadēlos*, *2867*
    2. φανερός, *phaneros*, *5745*

Act	4:16	is obvious to all who live in Jerusalem	2
Gal	5:19	Now the works of the flesh are obvious:	2

Heb   7:15   It is even more obvious   1

occasion

1. ἀφορμή, *aphormē, 929*
2. γίνομαι, *ginomai, 1181*

Lke 14: 1 On one occasion when Jesus was going   2
1Ti   5:14 give the adversary no occasion to revile us.   1

occasion for stumbling

1. σκάνδαλον, *skandalon, 4998*

Mat 18: 7 Occasions for stumbling are bound to come   1
Lke 17: 1 "Occasions for stumbling are bound to come   1

occupy

1. προσέχω, *prosechō, 4668*
2. συνέχω, *synechō, 5309*

Act 18: 5 Paul was occupied with proclaiming the word   2
1Ti   1: 4 and not to occupy themselves with myths   1

occur

1. Contextual: Not in Greek
2. γίνομαι, *ginomai, 1181*

Lke   1:20 until the day these things occur."   2
      21:12 before all this occurs, they will arrest you   1
Jhn 13:19 I tell you this now, before it occurs   2
      13:19 so that when it does occur   2
      14:29 now I have told you this before it occurs   2
      14:29 so that when it does occur, you may believe.   2
      19:36 These things occurred so that the scripture   2
Act 14: 1 The same thing occurred in Iconium,   2
1Co 10: 6 Now these things occurred as examples for us   2
Heb   9:15 because a death has occurred that redeems them   2
Rev 16:18 as had not occurred since people were upon the earth   2

of Not Indexed

of course

1. γάρ, *gar, 1142*
2. δέ, *de, 1254*
3. ὅτι, *hoti, 4022*

Jhn   3:24 John, of course, had not yet been thrown into prison.   1
      7:22 (it is, of course, not from Moses, but from   3
1Ti   6: 6 Of course, there is great gain in godliness   2
Heb   6:16 Human beings, of course, swear by someone greater   1

of oneself

1. αὐτόματος, *automatos, 897*

Mrk   4:28 The earth produces of itself, first the stalk   1

off *See also* any better off [*good*], bad off, break off, cast off, cut off, cut off hair, drag off, fall off, far off, go off, hurl off a cliff, put off, run off, send off, set off, set off in pursuit, shake off, shake off dust in protest, sink off, strip off, take off, throw off, well off, wipe off in protest

1. ἀπό, *apo, 608*
2. ἐκ, *ek, 1666*
3. κατά, *kata, 2848*

Lke   9: 5 shake the dust off your feet   1
Jhn 21: 8 not far...only about a hundred yards off   1
Act 12: 7 the chains fell off his wrists.   2
      27: 5 the sea that is off Cilicia and Pamphylia   3
      27: 7 arrived with difficulty off Cnidus   3
      27: 7 sailed under the lee of Crete off Salmone.   3

offend

1. σκανδαλίζω, *skandalizō, 4997*

Jhn   6:61 Jesus...said to them, "Does this offend you?   1

offender

1. Contextual: Not in Greek
2. αὐτός, *autos, 899*
3. ὀφειλέτης, *opheiletēs, 4050*

Mat 18:17 offender refuses to listen even to the church   1
Lke 13: 4 worse offenders than all the others   3
      17: 3 disciple sins, you must rebuke the offender   2

offense *See also* commit an offense, give offense, take offense

1. σκάνδαλον, *skandalon, 4998*

Rom 16:17 those who cause dissensions and offenses   1
Gal   5:11 In that case the offense of the cross   1

no offense

1. ἀπρόσκοπος, *aproskopos, 718*

1Co 10:32 Give no offense to Jews or to Greeks   1

offer *See also* food offered to an idol

1. Contextual: Not in Greek
2. ἀνάγω, *anagō, 343*
3. ἀναφέρω, *anapherō, 429*
4. δίδωμι, *didōmi, 1443*
5. παρέχω, *parechō, 4218*
6. προσφέρω, *prospherō, 4712*

Mat   2:11 opening their treasure chests, they offered him gifts   6
      5:24 reconciled...and then come and offer your gift.   6
      8: 4 and offer the gift that Moses commanded   6
      27:34 they offered him wine to drink, mixed with gall;   4
Mrk   1:44 offer for your cleansing what Moses commanded   6
      15:23 they offered him wine mixed with myrrh;   4
Lke   2:24 offered a sacrifice   4
      6:29 offer the other also;   5
Jhn 16: 2 by doing so they are offering worship to God.   6
Act   7:41 offered a sacrifice to the idol   2
      7:42 'Did you offer to me slain victims and sacrifices   6
      8:18 he offered them money   6
Rom 11:16 If the part of the dough offered as first fruits   1
Heb   5: 1 to offer gifts and sacrifices for sins.   6
      7:27 he has no need...to offer sacrifices day after day   3
      7:27 this he did once for all when he offered himself.   3
      8: 3 every high priest is appointed to offer gifts   6
      8: 3 necessary...also to have something to offer.   6
      8: 4 since there are priests who offer gifts   6
      9: 7 taking the blood that he offers for himself   6
      9: 9 gifts and sacrifices are offered   6
      9:14 who through the eternal Spirit offered himself   6
      9:25 Nor was it to offer himself again and again   6
      9:28 Christ...offered once to bear the sins of many   6
      10: 1 are continually offered year after year   6
      10: 2 would they not have ceased being offered   6
      10: 8 (these are offered according to the law)   6
      10:12 when Christ had offered...a single sacrifice   6
      11: 4 Abel offered to God a more acceptable sacrifice   6
      13:15 let us continually offer a sacrifice   3
Jas   2:21 when he offered his son Isaac on the altar?   3
1Pe   2: 5 offer spiritual sacrifices acceptable to God   3
Rev   8: 3 a great quantity of incense to offer with the prayers   4

offer in sacrifice

1. ἱερόθυτος, *hierothytos, 2638*

1Co 10:28 "This has been offered in sacrifice,"   1

offer incense

1. θυμιάω, *thymiaō, 2594*

Lke   1: 9 enter the sanctuary of the Lord and offer incense.   1

offer sacrifice

1. θύω, *thyō, 2604*
2. προσφέρω, *prospherō, 4712*
3. προσφορά, *prosphora, 4714*

Act 14:13 he and the crowds wanted to offer sacrifice.   1
      14:18 restrained the crowds from offering sacrifice   1
      24:17 to bring alms to my nation and to offer sacrifices.   3
Heb   5: 3 he must offer sacrifice for his own sins   2

offer up

1. προσφέρω, *prospherō, 4712*

Heb   5: 7 In the days of his flesh, Jesus offered up prayers   1
      11:17 Abraham, when put to the test, offered up Isaac.   1
      11:17 Abraham...was ready to offer up his only son   1

offer worship

1. λατρεύω, *latreuō, 3302*

Heb   8: 5 They offer worship in a sanctuary that is a sketch   1
      12:28 by which we offer to God an acceptable worship   1

offering   *See also* incense offering, make an offering
1. λειτουργία, *leitourgia, 3311*
2. ὀσμή, *osmē, 4011*
3. περί, *peri, 4309*
4. προσφέρω, *prospherō, 4712*
5. προσφορά, *prosphora, 4714*

Mat 5:23 So when you are offering your gift at the altar   4
Lke 23:36 coming up and offering him sour wine   4
Rom 15:16 the offering of the Gentiles may be acceptable   5
Eph 5: 2 a fragrant offering and sacrifice to God.   5
Php 2:17 over the sacrifice and the offering of your faith   1
 4:18 a fragrant offering, a sacrifice acceptable   2
Heb 10: 5 "Sacrifices and offerings you have not desired   5
 10: 6 in burnt offerings and sin offerings   3
 10: 8 in sacrifices and offerings and burnt offerings   5
 10: 8 burnt offerings and sin offerings"   3
 10:10 the offering of the body of Jesus Christ   5
 10:11 offering again and again the same sacrifices   4
 10:14 by a single offering he has perfected   5
 10:18 there is no longer any offering for sin.   5

burnt offering
1. ὁλοκαύτωμα, *holokautōma, 3906*

Heb 10: 6 in burnt offerings and sin offerings   1
 10: 8 in sacrifices and offerings and burnt offerings   1

offering to God
1. δῶρον, *dōron, 1565*

Mrk 7:11 Corban' (that is, an offering to God)—   1

whole burnt offering
1. ὁλοκαύτωμα, *holokautōma, 3906*

Mrk 12:33 much more important than all whole burnt offerings   1

office   *See also* take office
1. Contextual: Not in Greek

Heb 7:23 were prevented by death from continuing in office;   1

office of bishop
1. ἐπισκοπή, *episkopē, 2175*

1Ti 3: 1 whoever aspires to the office of bishop   1

priestly office
1. ἱερατεία, *hierateia, 2632*

Heb 7: 5 descendants of Levi who receive the priestly office   1

officer
1. Contextual: Not in Greek
2. πράκτωρ, *praktōr, 4551*
3. χιλίαρχος, *chiliarchos, 5941*

Mrk 6:21 a banquet for his courtiers and officers   3
Lke 12:58 the judge hand you over to the officer   2
 12:58 the officer throw you in prison.   2
Jhn 18:12 the soldiers, their officer   3
2Ti 2: 4 the soldier's aim is to please the enlisting officer.   1

officer of the temple police
1. στρατηγός, *stratēgos, 5130*

Lke 22: 4 conferred with...officers of the temple police   1
 22:52 the chief priests, the officers of the temple police   1

official
1. βασιλικός, *basilikos, 997*

Jhn 4:49 The official said to him, "Sir, come down   1

city official
1. πολιτάρχης, *politarchēs, 4485*

Act 17: 8 The people and the city officials   1

court official
1. δυνάστης, *dynastēs, 1541*

Act 8:27 Ethiopian eunuch, a court official of the Candace   1

official of the province of Asia
1. Ἀσιάρχης, *Asiarchēs, 825*

Act 19:31 even some officials of the province of Asia,   1

official of the synagogue
1. ἀρχισυνάγωγος, *archisynagōgos, 801*

Act 13:15 the officials of the synagogue sent them a message   1
 18: 8 Crispus, the official of the synagogue   1
 18:17 seized Sosthenes, the official of the synagogue   1

royal official
1. βασιλικός, *basilikos, 997*

Jhn 4:46 there was a royal official whose son lay ill   1

officiate
1. λατρεύω, *latreuō, 3302*

Heb 13:10 who officiate in the tent have no right to eat.   1

offspring
1. γένος, *genos, 1169*
2. σπέρμα, *sperma, 5065*

Act 17:28 'For we too are his offspring.'   1
 17:29 Since we are God's offspring   1
Gal 3:16 to Abraham and to his offspring;   2
 3:16 it does not say, "And to offsprings,"   2
 3:16 "And to your offspring," that is, to one person   2
 3:19 until the offspring would come   2
 3:29 then you are Abraham's offspring   2

often
1. ὁσάκις, *hosakis, 4006*
2. ὁσάκις + ἐάν, *hosakis + ean, 4006 + 1569*
3. πολλάκις, *pollakis, 4490*
4. πολύς, *polys, 4498*

Mat 9:14 "Why do we and the Pharisees fast often,   4
 17:15 he often falls into the fire   3
 17:15 and often into the water.   3
Mrk 5: 4 often been restrained with shackles and chains   3
 9:22 often cast him into the fire and into the water   3
Jhn 18: 2 Jesus often met there with his disciples.   3
Act 26:11 punishing them often in all the synagogues   3
Rom 1:13 that I have often intended to come to you   3
 15:22 I have so often been hindered from coming to you.   4
1Co 11:25 Do this, as often as you drink it   2
 11:26 For as often as you eat this bread   2
2Co 7: 4 I often boast about you; I have great pride   4
 8:22 whom we have often tested   3
 11:23 with countless floggings, and often near death.   3
 11:27 hungry and thirsty, often without food   3
Php 3:18 I have often told you of them, and now I tell you   3
2Ti 1:16 because he often refreshed me   3
Rev 11: 6 with every kind of plague, as often as they desire.   1

how often
1. ποσάκις, *posakis, 4529*

Mat 18:21 sins against me, how often should I forgive?   1
 23:37 How often have I desired to gather your children   1
Lke 13:34 How often have I desired to gather your children   1

very often
1. πυκνός, *pyknos, 4781*

Act 24:26 for that reason he used to send for him very often   1

oh
1. ὦ2, *ō2, 6043*

Lke 24:25 he said to them, "Oh, how foolish you are,   1

oil   *See also* put oil on
1. ἔλαιον, *elaion, 1778*

Mat 25: 3 they took no oil with them;   1
 25: 4 the wise took flasks of oil with their lamps.   1
 25: 8 'Give us some of your oil   1
Mrk 6:13 anointed with oil many who were sick   1
Lke 7:46 You did not anoint my head with oil   1
 10:34 wounds, having poured oil and wine on them   1
Heb 1: 9 God, has anointed you with the oil of gladness   1
Jas 5:14 have them pray over them, anointing them with oil   1

olive oil
1. ἔλαιον, *elaion, 1778*

Lke 16: 6 He answered, 'A hundred jugs of olive oil.'   1
Rev 6: 6 but do not damage the olive oil and the wine!"   1
 18:13 wine, olive oil, choice flour and wheat, cattle   1

ointment

1. Contextual: Not in Greek
2. μύρον, *myron, 3693*

Mat	26: 7	alabaster jar of very costly ointment	2
	26: 9	For this ointment could have been sold	1
	26:12	By pouring this ointment on my body	2
Mrk	14: 3	very costly ointment of nard	2
	14: 3	and poured the ointment on his head.	1
	14: 4	"Why was the ointment wasted in this way?	2
	14: 5	For this ointment could have been sold	2
Lke	7:37	a woman…brought an alabaster jar of ointment.	2
	7:38	anointing them with the ointment.	2
	7:46	she has anointed my feet with ointment.	2
	23:56	prepared spices and ointments.	2

old[1] *See also* old *age,* old *wife*

1. Contextual: Not in Greek
2. γέρων, *gerōn, 1173*
3. καιρός + ἡλικία, *kairos + hēlikia, 2789 + 2461*
4. χρόνος, *chronos, 5989*

Mat	2:16	around Bethlehem who were two years old or under	1
Lke	2:42	when he was twelve years old	1
	3:23	Jesus was about thirty years old when he began	1
	8:42	an only daughter, about twelve years old,	1
Jhn	3: 4	"How can anyone be born after having grown old?	2
	8:57	"You are not yet fifty years old	1
Act	4:22	the man…was more than forty years old.	1
	7:23	"When he was forty years old	4
Rom	4:19	(for he was about a hundred years old)	1
1Ti	5: 9	if she is not less than sixty years old	1
Heb	11:11	even though he was too old	3

old[2]

1. Contextual: Not in Greek
2. αἰών, *aiōn, 172*

Mrk	6:15	"It is a prophet, like one of the prophets of old."	1
Lke	1:70	the mouth of his holy prophets from of old	2

old[3]

1. ἀρχαῖος, *archaios, 792*
2. παλαιός, *palaios, 4094*
3. παλαιότης, *palaiotēs, 4095*

Mat	9:16	a piece of unshrunk cloth on an old cloak	2
	9:17	Neither is new wine put into old wineskins;	2
	13:52	what is new and what is old."	2
Mrk	2:21	sews a piece of unshrunk cloth on an old cloak;	2
	2:21	the new from the old, and a worse tear is made.	2
	2:22	no one puts new wine into old wineskins;	2
Lke	5:36	and sews it on an old garment,	2
	5:36	the piece from the new will not match the old.	2
	5:37	no one puts new wine into old wineskins;	2
	5:39	no one after drinking old wine desires new	2
	5:39	but says, 'The old is good.' "	2
Rom	6: 6	We know that our old self was crucified with him	2
	7: 6	we are slaves not under the old written code	3
1Co	5: 7	Clean out the old yeast	2
	5: 8	celebrate the festival, not with the old yeast	2
2Co	3:14	when they hear the reading of the old covenant	2
	5:17	everything old has passed away;	1
Eph	4:22	put away your former way of life, your old self	2
Col	3: 9	seeing that you have stripped off the old self	2
1Jn	2: 7	I am writing you…an old commandment	2
	2: 7	old commandment is the word that you have heard.	2

grow old

1. γηράσκω, *gēraskō, 1180*

Jhn	21:18	you grow old, you will stretch out your hands	1
Heb	8:13	what is obsolete and growing old	1

old man

1. πρεσβύτερος, *presbyteros, 4565*
2. πρεσβύτης, *presbytēs, 4566*

Lke	1:18	For I am an old man, and my wife is getting on	2
Act	2:17	your old men shall dream dreams.	1
1Ti	5: 1	Do not speak harshly to an older man	1
Tit	2: 2	Tell the older men to be temperate, serious, prudent	2
Phm	1: 9	I, Paul, do this as an old man, and now also as a prisoner	2

old woman

1. πρεσβύτερος, *presbyteros, 4565*
2. πρεσβῦτις, *presbytis, 4567*

1Ti	5: 2	older women as mothers	1
Tit	2: 3	Likewise, tell the older women to be reverent	2

olive *See also* olive *oil*

1. ἐλαία, *elaia, 1777*
2. ἐλαιών, *elaiōn, 1779*

Mat	21: 1	had reached Bethphage, at the Mount of Olives	1
	24: 3	When he was sitting on the Mount of Olives	1
	26:30	they went out to the Mount of Olives.	1
Mrk	11: 1	Bethphage and Bethany, near the Mount of Olives	1
	13: 3	on the Mount of Olives opposite the temple	1
	14:26	they went out to the Mount of Olives.	1
Lke	19:29	at the place called the Mount of Olives,	2
	19:37	the path down from the Mount of Olives	1
	21:37	spend the night on the Mount of Olives,	2
	22:39	went, as was his custom, to the Mount of Olives;	1
Jhn	8: 1	⟦Jesus went to the Mount of Olives.⟧	1
Jas	3:12	Can a fig tree, my brothers and sisters, yield olives	1

cultivated olive tree

1. καλλιέλαιος, *kallielaios, 2814*

Rom	11:24	grafted…into a cultivated olive tree	1

olive tree

1. ἐλαία, *elaia, 1777*

Rom	11:17	to share the rich root of the olive tree	1
	11:24	be grafted back into their own olive tree.	1
Rev	11: 4	two olive trees…that stand before the Lord	1

wild olive shoot

1. ἀγριέλαιος, *agrielaios, 66*

Rom	11:17	and you, a wild olive shoot, were grafted	1

wild olive tree

1. ἀγριέλαιος, *agrielaios, 66*

Rom	11:24	cut from what is by nature a wild olive tree	1

Olivet

1. ἐλαιών, *elaiōn, 1779*

Act	1:12	from the mount called Olivet	1

Olympas

1. Ὀλυμπᾶς, *Olympas, 3912*

Rom	16:15	Olympas, and all the saints who are with them.	1

Omega

1. Ὦ[1], *Ō[1], 6042*

Rev	1: 8	"I am the Alpha and the Omega," says the Lord God	1
	21: 6	I am Alpha and the Omega, the beginning and the end.	1
	22:13	I am the Alpha and the Omega, the first and the last	1

omen

1. τέρας, *teras, 5469*

Mat	24:24	produce great signs and omens, to lead astray	1
Mrk	13:22	produce signs and omens, to lead astray	1

on *See also* beat on, breathe on, bring on, bring on blindness, build on, call on, call on a name, depend on, depend on for food, fall on, fix attention on, from now on, get on, go on, go on a journey, go on ahead, go on board, go on one's way, go on through, hand on, hold on, impose on, keep an eye on, keep on, lay on, lie on, look on, look on favorably, look on with favor, on each *side,* on *foot,* on *guard,* on one's *own,* on one's *way,* on the one *hand,* on the other *hand,* on *trial,* pass by on the other side, pass on, place on, pour on, press in on, press on, proceed on a journey, put a seal on, put oil on, put on, put on a list, put on airs, put on an apron, put on board, put on shoes, rely on, relying on, rest on, sacrifice on an altar, send on, send on one's way, set on, set on fire, sew on, shine on, sit on, spit on, spread on, start on one's way, strike on the face,

take on board, throw on, throw oneself on the ground, trample on, urge on

1. ἀπό, *apo*, 608
2. εἰς, *eis*, 1650
3. ἐκ, *ek*, 1666
4. ἐν, *en*, 1877
5. ἐπάνω, *epanō*, 2062
6. ἐπί, *epi*, 2093
7. ἐπί + μέσος, *epi + mesos*, 2093 + 3545
8. ἐπίκειμαι, *epikeimai*, 2130
9. κατά, *kata*, 2848
10. μετά, *meta*, 3552
11. παρά, *para*, 4123
12. περί, *peri*, 4309
13. πόρρω, *porrō*, 4522
14. πρός, *pros*, 4639
15. ὑποκάτω, *hypokatō*, 5691
16. ὡς, *hōs*, 6055

Mat	3:16	saw the Spirit of God…alighting on him.	6
	4: 5	the holy city and placed him on the pinnacle	6
	4: 6	and 'On their hands they will bear you up	6
	5:14	A city built on a hill cannot be hid.	5
	5:15	under the bushel basket, but on the lampstand	6
	5:25	accuser while you are on the way to court with him	4
	5:39	But if anyone strikes you on the right cheek, turn	2
	5:45	he makes his sun rise on the evil and on the good	6
	5:45	sends rain on the righteous and on the unrighteous.	6
	6:10	Your will be done, on earth as it is in heaven.	6
	6:19	"Do not store up for yourselves treasures on earth	6
	7:22	On that day many will say to me, 'Lord, Lord	4
	7:24	like a wise man who built his house on rock.	6
	7:25	because it had been founded on rock.	6
	7:26	a foolish man who built his house on sand.	6
	8:24	A windstorm arose on the sea, so great	4
	9: 2	a paralyzed man lying on a bed.	6
	9: 6	the Son of Man has authority on earth to forgive	6
	9:16	a piece of unshrunk cloth on an old cloak	6
	9:18	but come and lay your hand on her	6
	10:15	land of Sodom and Gomorrah on the day of judgment	4
	11:22	on the day of judgment it will be more tolerable	4
	11:24	on the day of judgment it will be more tolerable	4
	12: 2	what is not lawful to do on the sabbath."	4
	12:36	I tell you, on the day of judgment	4
	13: 2	while the whole crowd stood on the beach.	6
	13: 4	as he sowed, some seeds fell on the path	11
	13: 5	Other seeds fell on rocky ground	6
	13: 8	Other seeds fell on good soil	6
	13:19	this is what was sown on the path.	11
	13:20	As for what was sown on rocky ground	6
	13:23	as for what was sown on good soil	6
	14: 7	so much that he promised on oath to grant her	10
	14: 8	the head of John the Baptist here on a platter	6
	14:11	The head was brought on a platter	6
	14:19	he ordered the crowds to sit down on the grass.	6
	14:25	he came walking toward them on the sea.	6
	14:26	when the disciples saw him walking on the sea	6
	14:28	command me to come to you on the water."	6
	14:29	walking on the water, and came toward Jesus.	6
	15:32	for they might faint on the way."	4
	15:35	ordering the crowd to sit down on the ground	6
	16:18	on this rock I will build my church	6
	16:19	whatever you bind on earth will be bound	6
	16:19	whatever you loose on earth	6
	18:12	not leave the ninety-nine on the mountains	6
	18:18	Truly I tell you, whatever you bind on earth	6
	18:18	whatever you loose on earth	6
	18:19	truly I tell you, if two of you agree on earth	6
	19:28	Son of Man is seated on the throne of his glory	6
	19:28	will also sit on twelve thrones	6
	20:17	and said to them on the way	4
	21: 5	humble, and mounted on a donkey	6
	21: 5	and on a colt, the foal of a donkey."	6
	21: 7	and put their cloaks on them	6
	21: 7	and he sat on them.	5
	21: 8	large crowd spread their cloaks on the road	4
	21: 8	and spread them on the road.	4
	21:19	found nothing at all on it but leaves.	4
	22:40	On these two commandments hang all the law	4
	23: 2	"The scribes and the Pharisees sit on Moses' seat;	6

	23: 4	and lay them on the shoulders of others;	6
	23: 9	call no one your father on earth	6
	23:18	whoever swears by the gift that is on the altar	5
	23:20	swears by it and by everything on it;	5
	23:35	all the righteous blood shed on earth	6
	24: 3	When he was sitting on the Mount of Olives	6
	24:17	the one on the housetop must not go down	6
	24:30	'the Son of Man coming on the clouds of heaven'	6
	24:50	the master of that slave will come on a day	4
	25:31	then he will sit on the throne of his glory.	6
	26: 7	poured it on his head as he sat at the table.	6
	26:12	By pouring this ointment on my body	6
	26:50	came and laid hands on Jesus and arrested him.	6
	26:64	coming on the clouds of heaven."	6
	27:19	While he was sitting on the judgment seat	6
	27:25	"His blood be on us and on our children!"	6
	27:25	"His blood be on us and on our children!"	6
	27:29	thorns into a crown, they put it on his head.	6
	27:30	They spat on him, and took the reed and struck	2
	27:30	took the reed and struck him on the head.	2
	27:38	one on his right and one on his left.	3
	27:38	one on his right and one on his left.	3
	28: 2	came and rolled back the stone and sat on it.	5
	28:18	"All authority in heaven and on earth	6
Mrk	1:10	the Spirit descending like a dove on him.	2
	2:10	Son of Man has authority on earth to forgive sins"	6
	2:20	then they will fast on that day.	4
	2:21	sews a piece of unshrunk cloth on an old cloak;	6
	4: 1	he got into a boat on the sea and sat there	4
	4: 1	the whole crowd was beside the sea on the land.	6
	4: 4	as he sowed, some seed fell on the path	11
	4: 5	Other seed fell on rocky ground	6
	4:15	the ones on the path where the word is sown:	11
	4:16	the ones sown on rocky ground:	6
	4:20	these are the ones sown on the good soil:	6
	4:21	or under the bed, and not on the lampstand?	6
	4:26	as if someone would scatter seed on the ground	6
	4:31	the smallest of all the seeds on earth;	6
	4:35	On that day, when evening had come, he said	4
	4:38	he was in the stern, asleep on the cushion;	6
	5: 5	on the mountains he was always howling	4
	5:11	Now there on the hillside a great herd of swine	14
	6:11	shake off the dust that is on your feet	15
	6:25	the head of John the Baptist on a platter."	6
	6:28	brought his head on a platter	6
	6:39	to sit down in groups on the green grass.	6
	6:46	he went up on the mountain to pray.	2
	6:47	When evening came, the boat was out on the sea	4
	6:47	he was alone on the land.	7
	6:48	he came towards them…walking on the sea.	6
	6:49	when they saw him walking on the sea	6
	6:55	began to bring the sick on mats	6
	7:30	she went home, found the child lying on the bed	6
	8: 3	they will faint on the way	4
	8: 6	he ordered the crowd to sit down on the ground;	6
	8:23	when he had put saliva on his eyes	2
	8:25	Then Jesus laid his hands on his eyes again;	6
	8:27	on the way he asked his disciples	4
	9: 3	such as no one on earth could bleach them.	6
	9:20	he fell on the ground and rolled about	6
	9:22	to do anything, have pity on us and help us."	6
	9:33	"What were you arguing about on the way?"	4
	9:34	for on the way they had argued with one another	4
	10:16	laid his hands on them, and blessed them.	6
	10:17	As he was setting out on a journey	2
	10:32	They were on the road, going up to Jerusalem	4
	10:52	regained his sight and followed him on the way.	4
	11: 7	he sat on it.	6
	11: 8	Many people spread their cloaks on the road	2
	11:13	whether perhaps he would find anything on it.	4
	13: 3	When he was sitting on the Mount of Olives	2
	13:15	one on the housetop must not go down	6
	14:35	a little farther, he threw himself on the ground	6
	15:27	one on his right and one on his left.	3
	15:27	one on his right and one on his left.	3
	16: 5	a young man…sitting on the right side;	4
	16:18	⟦they will lay their hands on the sick⟧	6
	21:44	The one who falls on this stone	6
	21:44	it will crush anyone on whom it falls	6
Lke	1: 8	and his section was on duty	4
	1:48	looked with favor on the lowliness of his servant.	6

1:59	On the eighth day they came to circumcise	4
2:14	on earth peace among those whom he favors!"	6
2:25	the Holy Spirit rested on him.	6
4: 9	placed him on the pinnacle of the temple	6
4:11	'On their hands they will bear you up	6
4:16	he went to the synagogue on the sabbath day,	4
4:29	brow of the hill on which their town was built	6
4:31	was teaching them on the sabbath.	4
5:18	men came, carrying a paralyzed man on a bed.	6
5:19	they went up on the roof	6
5:24	Son of Man has authority on earth to forgive	6
5:25	took what he had been lying on, and went	6
5:36	and sews it on an old garment;	6
6: 6	On another sabbath he entered the synagogue	4
6: 7	to see whether he would cure on the sabbath	4
6:17	came down with them and stood on a level place	6
6:29	anyone strikes you on the cheek	6
6:48	who dug deeply and laid the foundation on rock;	6
6:49	like a man who built a house on the ground	6
8: 5	as he sowed, some fell on the path	11
8: 6	Some fell on the rock;	6
8:12	The ones on the path are those who have heard;	11
8:13	The ones on the rock	6
8:16	puts it on a lampstand	6
8:23	A windstorm swept down on the lake	2
8:27	As he stepped out on land	6
8:32	Now there on the hillside a large herd of swine	4
9:28	and went up on the mountain to pray.	2
10: 4	greet no one on the road.	9
10: 6	your peace will rest on that person;	6
10:12	on that day it will be more tolerable for Sodom	4
10:19	have given you authority to tread on snakes	5
10:34	Then he put him on his own animal	6
11:17	becomes a desert, and house falls on house.	6
11:33	puts it in a cellar, but on the lampstand	6
12:46	on a day when he does not expect him	4
12:58	on the way make an effort to settle the case	4
13: 4	killed when the tower of Siloam fell on them	6
13: 6	he came looking for fruit on it and found none.	4
13: 7	I have come looking for fruit on this fig tree	4
13:10	in one of the synagogues on the sabbath.	4
13:14	"There are six days on which work ought to	4
13:14	come on those days and be cured	4
14: 5	not immediately pull it out on a sabbath day?"	4
15: 5	he has found it, he lays it on his shoulders	6
15:22	put a ring on his finger and sandals on his feet.	2
15:22	put a ring on his finger and sandals on his feet.	2
17:11	On the way to Jerusalem	4
17:31	On that day, anyone on the housetop	4
17:31	anyone on the housetop who has belongings	6
18: 8	will he find faith on earth?"	6
19:35	throwing their cloaks on the colt	6
19:36	people kept spreading their cloaks on the road.	4
19:42	recognized on this day the things that make for peace!	4
20:18	Everyone who falls on that stone	6
20:18	it will crush anyone on whom it falls."	6
20:19	wanted to lay hands on him at that very hour	6
21:23	will be great distress on the earth	6
21:25	on the earth distress among nations	6
21:35	all who live on the face of the whole earth.	6
21:37	spend the night on the Mount of Olives,	2
22: 7	on which the Passover lamb had to be sacrificed.	4
22:21	with me, and his hand is on the table.	6
22:30	sit on thrones judging the twelve tribes	6
22:44	⟦great drops of blood falling down on the ground.⟧	6
22:53	you did not lay hands on me.	6
22:65	They kept heaping many other insults on him	2
23:30	begin to say to the mountains, 'Fall on us';	6
23:33	one on his right and one on his left.	3
23:33	one on his right and one on his left.	3
24:13	Now on that same day two of them were going	4
24:28	he walked ahead as if he were going on.	13
24:32	while he was talking to us on the road	4
24:35	Then they told what had happened on the road	4

Jhn
1:32	The Spirit descending…and it remained on him.	6
1:33	'He on whom you see the Spirit descend and remain	6
4:20	Our ancestors worshiped on this mountain	4
4:21	neither on this mountain nor in Jerusalem.	4
5:16	because he was doing such things on the sabbath.	4
5:45	accuser is Moses…on whom you have set your hope.	2
6:19	they saw Jesus walking on the sea	6

6:39	but raise it up on the last day.	4
6:40	I will raise them up on the last day."	4
6:44	I will raise that person up on the last day.	4
7:22	you circumcise a man on the sabbath.	4
7:23	If a man receives circumcision on the sabbath	4
7:23	I healed a man's whole body on the sabbath?	4
7:30	no one laid hands on him	6
7:37	On the last day of the festival, the great day	4
7:44	but no one laid hands on him.	6
8: 6	⟦Jesus…wrote with his finger on the ground.⟧	2
8: 8	⟦and wrote on the ground.⟧	2
9: 6	and spread the mud on the man's eyes	6
9:15	He said to them, "He put mud on my eyes.	6
11:24	rise again in the resurrection on the last day."	4
12:14	Jesus found a young donkey and sat on it;	6
12:15	your king is coming, sitting on a donkey's colt!"	6
12:48	on the last day the word…will serve as judge	4
14:20	On that day you will know that I am in my Father	4
16:23	On that day you will ask nothing of me.	4
16:26	On that day you will ask in my name.	4
17: 4	I glorified you on earth	6
19:13	and sat on the judge's bench	6
19:19	an inscription written and put on the cross.	6
19:31	Jews did not want the bodies left on the cross	6
19:37	will look on the one whom they have pierced."	2
20: 7	the cloth that had been on Jesus' head	6
21: 4	Just after daybreak, Jesus stood on the beach;	2
21: 9	a charcoal fire…with fish on it, and bread.	8

Act
1:26	the lot fell on Matthias;	6
2: 3	and a tongue rested on each of them.	6
2:19	signs on the earth below	6
2:30	put one of his descendants on his throne.	6
4:22	man on whom this sign of healing had been performed	6
5:15	laid them on cots and mats	6
5:28	you are determined to bring this man's blood on us."	6
5:30	whom you had killed by hanging him on a tree.	6
7:13	On the second visit	4
8:17	Then Peter and John laid their hands on them	6
9:17	laid his hands on Saul and said, "Brother Saul	6
9:17	the Lord Jesus, who appeared to you on your way	4
9:27	described…how on the road he had seen the Lord	4
10: 9	Peter went up on the roof to pray.	6
10:25	On Peter's arrival Cornelius met him	16
10:39	They put him to death by hanging him on a tree;	6
10:40	God raised him on the third day	4
10:45	had been poured out even on the Gentiles	6
12:21	Herod…took his seat on the platform	6
14:10	said in a loud voice, "Stand upright on your feet."	6
15:10	by placing on the neck of the disciples a yoke	6
16:31	"Believe on the Lord Jesus, and you will be saved	6
17: 2	on three sabbath days argued with them	6
17:31	fixed a day on which he will have the world judged	4
18: 6	"Your blood be on your own heads! I am innocent.	6
19:16	the man with the evil spirit leaped on them	6
20: 7	On the first day of the week	4
21: 5	we knelt down on the beach and prayed	6
21:40	Paul stood on the steps	6
25: 6	the next day he took his seat on the tribunal	6
25: 9	and be tried there before me on these charges?"	12
25:17	but on the next day took my seat on the tribunal	6
25:20	be tried there on these charges.	12
26:16	get up and stand on your feet;	6
27: 6	found an Alexandrian ship…and put us on board.	2
27:17	then, fearing that they would run on the Syrtis	2
27:26	we will have to run aground on some island."	2
27:29	Fearing that we might run on the rocks	9
27:39	on which planned to run the ship ashore	2
27:44	some on planks and others on pieces of the ship.	6
27:44	some on planks and others on pieces of the ship.	6
28: 3	putting it on the fire	6
28: 9	the people on the island who had diseases	4
28:11	on a ship that had wintered at the island	4

Rom
2: 2	God's judgment on those who do such things	6
2: 5	storing up wrath for yourself on the day of wrath	4
2:15	what the law requires is written on their hearts	4
2:16	on the day when…God…will judge	4
4: 9	blessedness…pronounced only on the circumcised	6
4: 9	blessedness…also on the uncircumcised?	6
9:28	Lord will execute his sentence on the earth	6
10: 8	"The word is near you, on your lips and in your heart"	4
12:20	you will heap burning coals on their heads."	6

Rom 15: 3	"The insults...have fallen on me."	6
15:15	Nevertheless on some points I have written to you	1
15:20	so that I do not build on someone else's foundation	6
1Co 1: 8	blameless on the day of our Lord Jesus Christ.	4
2: 5	your faith might rest not on human wisdom	4
2: 5	not on human wisdom but on the power of God.	4
3:12	Now if anyone builds on the foundation with gold	6
4:20	For the kingdom of God depends not on talk	4
4:20	kingdom of God depends not on talk but on power.	4
8: 5	may be so-called gods in heaven or on earth	6
10:11	on whom the ends of the ages have come.	2
11: 4	prays or prophesies with something on his head	9
11:10	ought to have a symbol of authority on her head	6
11:23	the Lord Jesus on the night when he was betrayed	4
16: 2	On the first day of every week	9
2Co 1: 9	so that we would rely not on ourselves	6
1: 9	not on ourselves but on God who raises the dead.	6
1:10	on him we have set our hope	2
1:14	on the day of the Lord Jesus we are your boast	4
3: 2	written on our hearts, to be known and read by all;	4
3: 3	not on tablets of stone	4
3: 3	but on tablets of human hearts.	4
6: 2	on a day of salvation I have helped you."	4
Gal 3:12	the law does not rest on faith;	3
3:13	"Cursed is everyone who hangs on a tree"—	6
6:17	I carry the marks of Jesus branded on my body.	4
Eph 1: 8	that he lavished on us.	2
1:10	things in heaven and things on earth.	6
1:12	we, who were the first to set our hope on Christ	4
3:15	every family in heaven and on earth takes its name.	6
4: 8	he ascended on high he made captivity...a captive	2
4:26	do not let the sun go down on your anger	6
5: 6	the wrath of God comes on those...disobedient	6
6: 3	you may live long on the earth."	6
6:13	that you may be able to withstand on that evil day	4
Php 2:16	that I can boast on the day of Christ	2
Col 1:16	in him all things in heaven and on earth were created	6
1:20	all things, whether on earth or in heaven	6
2:18	insisting on self-abasement	4
3: 2	not on things that are on earth	6
3: 6	wrath of God is coming on those who are disobedient	6
2Th 1:10	marveled at on that day among all who have believed	4
1Ti 4:10	because we have our hope set on the living God	6
5: 5	The real widow...has set her hope on God	6
6:17	to set their hopes on the uncertainty of riches	6
6:17	to set their hopes...on God	6
2Ti 1:18	that he will find mercy from the Lord on that day!	4
4: 8	the righteous judge, will give me on that day	4
Tit 3: 6	This Spirit he poured out on us richly	6
3: 8	I desire that you insist on these things	12
Heb 1: 3	he sat down at the right hand of the Majesty on high	4
3: 8	on the day of testing in the wilderness	9
4: 4	God rested on the seventh day from all his works."	4
6: 7	that drinks up the rain falling on it repeatedly	6
8: 4	Now if he were on earth, he would not be a priest	6
8: 5	the pattern that was shown you on the mountain."	4
8: 9	on the day when I took them by the hand	4
8:10	write them on their hearts	6
10:16	and I will write them on their minds,"	6
10:28	"on the testimony of two or three witnesses."	6
11:13	they were strangers and foreigners on the earth	6
12:25	they refused the one who warned them on earth	6
Jas 2:21	when he offered his son Isaac on the altar?	6
4: 3	in order to spend what you get on your pleasures	4
5: 5	You have lived on the earth in luxury	6
5:17	it did not rain on the earth.	6
1Pe 1:13	set all your hope on the grace that Jesus Christ	6
1:21	so that your faith and hope are set on God.	2
2:24	He himself bore our sins in his body on the cross	6
3:12	For the eyes of the Lord are on the righteous	6
4:14	which is the Spirit of God, is resting on you.	6
5: 7	Cast all your anxiety on him	6
2Pe 1:18	while we were with him on the holy mountain.	4
3:10	everything that is done on it will be disclosed.	4
1Jn 4:17	that we may have boldness on the day of judgment	4
Jde 1:12	These are blemishes on your love-feasts	4
1:15	to execute judgment on all, and to convict everyone	9
Rev 1: 9	I, John...was on the island called Patmos	4
1:10	I was in the spirit on the Lord's day,	4
1:17	But he placed his right hand on me, saying,	6
2:17	on the white stone is written a new name	6

2:22	Beware, I am throwing her on a bed	2
2:24	I do not lay on you any other burden;	6
3:10	hour of trial that is coming on the whole world	6
3:12	I will write on you the name of my God	6
3:21	I will give a place with me on my throne	4
3:21	and sat down with my Father on his throne.	4
4: 2	in heaven stood a throne, with one seated on the throne!	6
4: 4	seated on the thrones are twenty-four elders	6
4: 4	elders...with golden crowns on their heads.	6
4: 9	thanks to the one who is seated on the throne	6
4:10	fall before the one who is seated on the throne	6
5: 1	the one seated on the throne	6
5: 3	no one in heaven or on earth or under the earth	6
5: 7	right hand of the one who was seated on the throne.	6
5:10	and they will reign on earth."	6
5:13	I heard every creature in heaven and on earth	6
5:13	"To the one seated on the throne and to the Lamb	6
6:10	judge and avenge our blood on the inhabitants	3
6:16	"Fall on us and hide us from the face of the one	6
6:16	hide us from...the one seated on the throne	6
7: 1	so that no wind could blow on earth or sea	6
7: 3	marked...with a seal on their foreheads."	6
7:10	"Salvation...to our God who is seated on the throne	6
7:11	they fell on their faces before the throne	6
7:15	one who is seated on the throne will shelter them.	6
8: 3	prayers of all the saints on the golden altar	6
8: 5	filled it with fire...and threw it on the earth;	2
8:10	star fell...and it fell on a third of the rivers	6
8:10	it fell...on the springs of water.	6
9: 3	Then from the smoke came locusts on the earth	2
9: 4	who do not have the seal of God on their foreheads.	6
9: 7	On their heads were what looked like crowns	6
10: 2	Setting his right foot on the sea	6
10: 2	right foot on the sea and his left foot on the land	6
10: 5	the angel whom I saw standing on the sea and the land	6
10: 8	angel who is standing on the sea and on the land."	6
10: 8	angel who is standing on the sea and on the land."	6
11: 7	the beast...will make war on them and conquer	10
11:11	they stood on their feet, and those who saw them	6
11:16	the twenty-four elders who sit on their thrones	6
11:16	elders...fell on their faces and worshiped God	6
12: 1	and on her head a crown of twelve stars.	6
12: 3	and ten horns, and seven diadems on his heads.	6
12:17	went off to make war on the rest of her children	10
12:18	the dragon took his stand on the sand of the seashore.	6
13: 1	a beast...and on its horns were ten diadems	6
13: 1	and on its heads were blasphemous names.	6
13: 7	Also it was allowed to make war on the saints	10
13:16	to be marked on the right hand or the forehead	6
14: 1	and there was the Lamb, standing on Mount Zion!	6
14: 1	his Father's name written on their foreheads.	6
14: 2	like the sound of harpists playing on their harps	4
14: 6	gospel to proclaim to those who live on the earth	6
14: 9	receive a mark on their foreheads or on their hands	6
14: 9	receive a mark on their foreheads or on their hands	6
14:14	seated on the cloud was one like the Son of Man	6
14:14	the Son of Man, with a golden crown on his head	6
14:15	calling...to the one who sat on the cloud,	6
14:16	the one who sat on the cloud swung his sickle	6
16: 1	pour out on the earth the seven bowls of the wrath	2
16: 2	first angel went and poured his bowl on the earth	2
16: 2	and a foul and painful sore came on those	6
16: 8	The fourth angel poured his bowl on the sun	6
16:10	The fifth angel poured his bowl on the throne	6
16:12	angel poured his bowl on the great river Euphrates	6
16:21	huge hailstones...dropped from heaven on people	6
17: 1	the great whore who is seated on many waters	6
17: 3	and I saw a woman sitting on a scarlet beast	6
17: 5	on her forehead was written a name, a mystery:	6
17: 9	are seven mountains on which the woman is seated;	6
17:14	they will make war on the Lamb	10
18:19	And they threw dust on their heads, as they wept	6
18:24	blood...of all who have been slaughtered on earth."	6
19: 2	he has avenged on her the blood of his servants."	3
19: 4	worshiped God who is seated on the throne, saying	6
19:12	and on his head are many diadems;	6
19:14	armies of heaven...following him on white horses.	6
19:16	On his robe and on his thigh he has a name	6
19:16	On his robe and on his thigh he has a name	6
19:19	to make war against the rider on the horse	6
19:21	the sword of the rider on the horse	6

20: 4	Then I saw thrones, and those seated on them	6
20: 4	had not received its mark on their foreheads	6
20:11	I saw a great white throne and the one who sat on it;	6
21: 5	And the one who was seated on the throne said,	6
21:13	on the east three gates, on the north three gates	1
21:13	on the east three gates, on the north three gates	1
21:13	on the south three gates, and on the west	1
21:13	and on the west three gates.	1
21:14	on them are the twelve names of the twelve apostles	6
22: 4	and his name will be on their foreheads.	6

once[1]   *See also* all at once

1. Contextual: Not in Greek
2. ἄπαξ, *hapax, 562*
3. δέ, *de, 1254*
4. εἷς, *heis, 1651*

Lke	5: 1	Once while Jesus was standing beside the lake	3
	22:32	when once you have turned back	1
2Co	11:25	Once I received a stoning.	2
Php	4:16	you sent me help for my needs more than once.	2
1Ti	3: 2	married only once, temperate, sensible	4
	3:12	Let deacons be married only once	4
	5: 9	has been married only once;	4
Tit	1: 6	someone who is blameless, married only once,	4
Heb	6: 4	those who have once been enlightened	2
	9: 7	and he but once a year	2
	9:27	just as it is appointed for mortals to die once	2
	9:28	Christ…offered once to bear the sins of many	2
	12:26	"Yet once more I will shake not only the earth	2
	12:27	This phrase, "Yet once more," indicates…	2

once[2]

1. Contextual: Not in Greek
2. ἄρτι, *arti, 785*
3. ἐξαυτῆς, *exautēs, 1994*
4. εὐθέως, *eutheōs, 2311*
5. εὐθύς[1], *euthys[1], 2317*
6. παραχρῆμα, *parachrēma, 4202*
7. ταχέως, *tacheōs, 5441*

Mat	21:19	And the fig tree withered at once.	6
	21:20	"How did the fig tree wither at once?"	6
	25:16	had received the five talents went off at once	4
	26:49	At once he came up to Jesus and said,	4
	26:53	he will at once send me more than twelve legions	2
	27:48	At once one of them ran and got a sponge	4
Mrk	1:28	At once his fame began to spread	5
	1:30	they told him about her at once.	5
	1:43	sternly warning him he sent him away at once	5
	2: 8	At once Jesus perceived in his spirit	5
	4:29	at once he goes in with his sickle	5
	6:25	"I want you to give me at once the head of John	3
	6:54	people at once recognized him	5
	14:45	he went up to him at once and said, "Rabbi!"	5
Lke	8:55	Her spirit returned, and she got up at once.	6
	13:25	When once the owner of the house has got up	1
	14:21	'Go out at once into the streets and lanes	7
	17: 7	'Come here at once and take your place at the table'?	4
Jhn	5: 9	At once the man was made well	4
	13:32	and will glorify him at once.	5
	19:34	at once blood and water came out.	5
Act	23:30	I sent him to you at once	3
Rev	4: 2	At once I was in the spirit, and there in heaven	4

once[3]

1. Contextual: Not in Greek
2. ποτέ, *pote, 4537*

Rom	6:17	that you, having once been slaves of sin	1
	6:19	once presented your members as slaves to impurity	1
	7: 9	I was once alive apart from the law	2
	11:30	Just as you were once disobedient to God	2
2Co	3:10	Indeed, what once had glory has lost its glory	1
	5:16	even though we once knew Christ	1
Gal	1:23	proclaiming the faith he once tried to destroy."	2
	2:18	build up again the very things that I once tore down	1
Eph	2: 2	in which you once lived	2
	2: 3	All of us once lived among them	2
	2:13	you who once were far off	2
	5: 8	For once you were darkness, but now in the Lord	2
Col	1:21	you who were once estranged and hostile in mind	2
	3: 7	These are the ways you also once followed	2

Tit	3: 3	For we ourselves were once foolish, disobedient	2
1Pe	2:10	Once you were not a people, but now you are God's	2
	2:10	once you had not received mercy	1

once[4]

1. δέ, *de, 1254*
2. καί, *kai, 2779*
3. ὅμως, *homōs, 3940*
4. πρῶτον, *prōton, 4754*

Lke	1: 8	Once when he was serving as priest before God	1
	5:12	Once, when he was in one of the cities	2
	9:18	Once when Jesus was praying alone	2
	17:20	Once Jesus was asked by the Pharisees	1
Rom	15:24	once I have enjoyed your company for a little	4
Gal	3:15	once a person's will has been ratified	3

once again

1. πάλιν, *palin, 4099*

Jhn	8: 8	⟦once again he bent down and wrote⟧	1

once for all

1. ἄπαξ, *hapax, 562*
2. ἐφάπαξ, *ephapax, 2384*

Rom	6:10	The death he died, he died to sin, once for all;	2
Heb	7:27	this he did once for all when he offered himself.	2
	9:12	he entered once for all into the Holy Place	2
	9:26	he has appeared once for all at the end of the age	1
	10: 2	since the worshipers, cleansed once for all	1
	10:10	the offering of…Jesus Christ once for all.	2
1Pe	3:18	For Christ also suffered for sins once for all	1
Jde	1: 3	faith…once for all entrusted to the saints.	1
	1: 5	that the Lord, who once for all saved a people	1

once more

1. δεύτερος, *deuteros, 1311*
2. πάλιν, *palin, 4099*

Mat	22: 1	Once more Jesus spoke to them in parables, saying:	2
Mrk	14:40	once more he came and found them sleeping	2
Rev	19: 3	Once more they said, "Hallelujah!	1

one   *See also* add one's testimony, at one's hand, before one is *circumcised*, blessed one, breathe one's last, bring into one's *presence*, by one's *side*, change one's mind, chosen one, come one, destine one, dispute with one another, do one's best, each one, eat one's fill, every one, evil one, faithful one, glorious one, go on one's way, go out of one's mind, great one, have all one wants, holy one, in one's *place*, keep one's life, kill one's father, kill one's mother, lawless one, little one, living one, love for one another, make one's aim, make one's ambition, make one's home, make one's own, make one's way, make up one's mind, no one, not a *single* one, not of one's *will*, not one, not one's *own*, on one's *own*, on one's *way*, on the one *hand*, one *accord*, one *case*, one *day*, one *eye*, one *party*, one *piece*, one who is *spiritual*, one's *own*, out of one's *mind*, outside one's *control*, place one lives, put one's trust, righteous one, send on one's way, set one's hope, set one's hope first, set one's mind, start on one's way, such a one, take in one's arms, take one's place, take one's place at table, true one

1. Contextual: Not in Greek
2. ἀδελφός, *adelphos, 81*
3. ἄλλος, *allos, 257*
4. ἀνήρ, *anēr, 467*
5. ἄνθρωπος, *anthrōpos, 476*
6. ἀριθμός, *arithmos, 750*
7. αὐτός, *autos, 899*
8. γναφεύς, *gnapheus, 1187*
9. εἷς, *heis, 1651*
10. ἕκαστος, *hekastos, 1667*
11. ἐκεῖνος, *ekeinos, 1697*
12. μέν, *men, 3525*
13. μέρος, *meros, 3538*
14. ὁ, *ho, 3836*
15. ὅς, *hos, 4005*
16. ὅς + ἄν, *hos + an, 4005 + 323*

17. οὗτος, *houtos*, 4047
18. πᾶς, *pas*, 4246
19. πᾶς + σάρξ, *pas + sarx*, 4246 + 4922
20. σάρξ, *sarx*, 4922
21. τίς, *tis*, 5515
22. τὶς, *tis*, 5516

Mat	4: 4	written, 'One does not live by bread alone	5
	5:18	not one letter, not one stroke of a letter	9
	5:18	not one letter, not one stroke of a letter	9
	5:19	breaks one of the least of these commandments	9
	5:29	is better for you to lose one of your members	9
	5:30	is better for you to lose one of your members	9
	5:36	head, for you cannot make one hair white or black.	9
	5:41	forces you to go one mile, go also the second mile.	9
	6:24	slave will either hate the one and love the other	9
	6:24	or be devoted to the one and despise the other	9
	6:29	his glory was not clothed like one of these.	9
	8: 9	I say to one, 'Go,' and he goes, and to another,	17
	8:28	so fierce that no one could pass that way.	22
	10:23	When they persecute you in one town	17
	10:29	Yet not one of them will fall to the ground	9
	10:36	one's foes will be members of one's own household.	5
	10:42	a cup of cold water to one of these little ones	9
	11:27	and no one knows the Father except the Son	22
	12:11	"Suppose one of you has only one sheep	5
	12:11	"Suppose one of you has only one sheep	9
	12:29	Or how can one enter a strong man's house	22
	13:46	on finding one pearl of great value	9
	16:14	others Jeremiah or one of the prophets."	9
	17: 4	one for you, one for Moses, and one for Elijah."	9
	17: 4	one for you, one for Moses, and one for Elijah."	9
	17: 4	one for you, one for Moses, and one for Elijah."	9
	18: 5	Whoever welcomes one such child in my name	9
	18: 6	a stumbling block before one of these little ones	9
	18: 7	woe to the one by whom the stumbling block comes!	5
	18:10	that you do not despise one of these little ones;	9
	18:12	and one of them has gone astray	9
	18:12	and go in search of the one that went astray?	1
	18:14	that one of these little ones should be lost.	9
	18:16	not listened to, take one or two others along	9
	18:24	one who owed him ten thousand talents was brought	9
	18:28	came upon one of his fellow slaves	9
	19: 5	and the two shall become one flesh'?	9
	19: 6	So they are no longer two, but one flesh.	9
	19: 6	let no one separate."	5
	19:17	There is only one who is good.	9
	20:12	saying, 'These last worked only one hour	9
	20:13	he replied to one of them	9
	20:21	one at your right hand and one at your left	9
	20:21	one at your right hand and one at your left	9
	21:24	"I will also ask you one question;	9
	21:35	beat one, killed another, and stoned another.	15
	22: 5	went away, one to his farm, another to his business	15
	22:35	one of them, a lawyer, asked him a question	9
	23: 8	you have one teacher, and you are all students.	9
	23: 9	you have one Father—the one in heaven.	9
	23:10	you have one instructor, the Messiah.	9
	24: 2	not one stone will be left here upon another;	1
	24: 4	"Beware that no one leads you astray.	22
	24:22	no one would be saved;	20
	24:31	from one end of heaven to the other.	1
	24:40	one will be taken and one will be left.	9
	24:40	one will be taken and one will be left.	9
	24:41	one will be taken and one will be left.	9
	24:41	one will be taken and one will be left.	9
	25:15	to one he gave five talents, to another two	15
	25:15	to another two, to another one	9
	25:18	the one who had received the one talent went off	9
	25:24	had received the one talent also came forward	9
	25:32	he will separate people one from another	7
	25:40	just as you did it to one of the least of these	9
	25:45	you did not do it to one of the least of these	9
	26:14	Then one of the twelve…Judas Iscariot	9
	26:21	I tell you, one of you will betray me."	9
	26:22	and began to say to him one after another	9
	26:24	woe to that one by whom the Son of Man is betrayed!	5
	26:24	It would have been better for that one	5
	26:40	"So, could you not stay awake with me one hour?	9
	26:47	Judas, one of the twelve, arrived;	9
	26:48	"The one I will kiss is the man; arrest him."	16

	26:51	Suddenly, one of those with Jesus	9
	26:73	"Certainly you are also one of them	1
	27:38	one on his right and one on his left.	9
	27:38	one on his right and one on his left.	9
	27:48	At once one of them ran and got a sponge	9
Mrk	2:23	One sabbath he was going through	14
	5:22	Then one of the leaders of the synagogue	9
	6:15	"It is a prophet, like one of the prophets of old."	9
	8: 4	"How can one feed these people with bread here	22
	8:14	they had only one loaf with them in the boat.	9
	8:28	and still others, one of the prophets."	9
	9: 3	such as no one on earth could bleach them.	8
	9: 5	one for you, one for Moses, and one for Elijah."	9
	9: 5	one for you, one for Moses, and one for Elijah."	9
	9: 5	one for you, one for Moses, and one for Elijah."	9
	9:37	"Whoever welcomes one such child in my name	9
	9:42	one of these little ones who believe in me	9
	10: 8	the two shall become one flesh.'	9
	10: 8	So they are no longer two, but one flesh.	9
	10: 9	let no one separate."	5
	10:37	one at your right hand and one at your left	9
	10:37	one at your right hand and one at your left	9
	11:29	Jesus said to them, "I will ask you one question;	9
	12: 6	He had still one other, a beloved son.	9
	12:16	they brought one.	1
	12:28	One of the scribes came near and heard	9
	12:29	the Lord our God, the Lord is one;	9
	12:32	you have truly said that 'he is one	9
	13: 1	one of his disciples said to him, "Look, Teacher	9
	13: 2	Not one stone will be left here upon another;	1
	13: 5	"Beware that no one leads you astray.	22
	13:20	no one would be saved;	20
	14:10	Then Judas Iscariot, who was one of the twelve	9
	14:18	"Truly I tell you, one of you will betray me	9
	14:19	to say to him one after another, "Surely, not I?"	9
	14:20	He said to them, "It is one of the twelve	9
	14:21	woe to that one by whom the Son of Man is betrayed!	5
	14:21	better for that one not to have been born."	5
	14:37	you asleep? Could you not keep awake one hour?	9
	14:43	Judas, one of the twelve, arrived;	9
	14:44	"The one I will kiss is the man;	16
	14:47	one of those who stood near drew his sword	9
	14:66	one of the servant-girls of the high priest came by.	9
	15:27	one on his right and one on his left.	9
	15:27	one on his right and one on his left.	9
Lke	4: 4	"It is written, 'One does not live by bread alone.' "	5
	5: 3	into one of the boats, the one belonging to Simon	9
	5: 3	into one of the boats, the one belonging to Simon	15
	5:12	when he was in one of the cities	9
	5:17	One day, while he was teaching	9
	6: 1	One sabbath while Jesus was going through	1
	7: 8	I say to one, 'Go,' and he goes	17
	7:36	One of the Pharisees asked Jesus to eat with him	22
	7:41	one owed five hundred denarii, and the other fifty	9
	8:12	The ones on the path are those who have heard;	14
	8:13	The ones on the rock	14
	8:22	One day he got into a boat with his disciples	9
	9: 8	that one of the ancient prophets had arisen.	22
	9:19	that one of the ancient prophets has arisen."	22
	9:33	one for you, one for Moses, and one for Elijah"	9
	9:33	one for you, one for Moses, and one for Elijah"	9
	9:33	one for you, one for Moses, and one for Elijah"	9
	11: 1	after he had finished, one of his disciples said	22
	11: 5	one of you has a friend, and you go to him	21
	11:45	One of the lawyers answered him, "Teacher	22
	12: 6	not one of them is forgotten in God's sight.	9
	12:15	one's life does not consist in…possessions."	22
	12:27	was not clothed like one of these.	9
	12:44	Truly I tell you, he will put that one in charge	7
	12:52	five in one household will be divided	9
	13: 8	He replied, 'Sir, let it alone for one more year	17
	13:10	Now he was teaching in one of the synagogues	9
	14: 1	On one occasion when Jesus was going	1
	14: 5	he said to them, "If one of you has a child	21
	14:15	One of the dinner guests, on hearing this,	22
	15: 4	"Which one of you, having a hundred sheep	5
	15: 4	a hundred sheep and losing one of them	9
	15: 7	more joy in heaven over one sinner who repents	9
	15: 8	having ten silver coins, if she loses one	9
	15:10	there is joy…over one sinner who repents."	9
	15:15	hired himself out to one of the citizens	9

15:19	treat me like one of your hired hands." '	9
15:26	He called one of the slaves	9
16:13	slave will either hate the one and love the other	9
16:13	be devoted to the one and despise the other.	9
16:17	one stroke of a letter in the law to be dropped.	9
17: 2	to cause one of these little ones to stumble.	9
17:15	one of them, when he saw that he was healed	9
17:22	will long to see one of the days of the Son of Man	9
17:24	lights up the sky from one side to the other	1
17:34	on that night there will be two in one bed;	9
17:34	one will be taken and the other left.	9
17:35	one will be taken and the other left."	9
18:10	one a Pharisee and the other a tax collector.	9
19: 7	to be the guest of one who is a sinner."	4
19:44	will not leave within you one stone upon another;	1
20: 1	One day, as he was teaching the people	9
21: 6	not one stone will be left upon another;	1
22: 3	Judas…who was one of the twelve;	6
22:22	woe to that one by whom he is betrayed!"	5
22:26	the leader like one who serves.	14
22:36	who has no sword must sell his cloak and buy one.	1
22:47	one called Judas, one of the twelve, was leading	9
22:50	one of them struck the slave of the high priest	9
22:58	seeing him, said, "You also are one of them."	1
23:33	one on his right and one on his left.	15
23:33	one on his right and one on his left.	15
23:39	One of the criminals who were hanged	9
24:18	one of them, whose name was Cleopas, answered	9
Jhn 1:40	One of the two who heard John speak…was Andrew	9
2:25	and needed no one to testify about anyone;	22
3: 3	no one can see the kingdom of God without	22
3: 5	no one can enter the kingdom of God without	22
3:27	John answered, "No one can receive anything	5
3:31	one who comes from above is above all;	1
3:31	one who is of the earth belongs to the earth	1
3:31	one who comes from heaven is above all.	1
4:18	and the one you have now is not your husband.	15
4:33	no one has brought him something to eat?"	22
4:37	'One sows and another reaps.'	3
5: 5	One man was there who had been ill	22
5: 7	I have no one to put me into the pool	5
6: 8	One of his disciples, Andrew	9
6:22	saw that there had been only one boat there.	9
6:50	so that one may eat of it and not die.	22
6:64	who were the ones that did not believe	21
6:70	Yet one of you is a devil."	9
6:71	though one of the twelve, was going to betray him.	9
7:21	Jesus answered them, "I performed one work	9
7:50	Nicodemus…who was one of them, asked,	9
8: 9	〚When they heard it, they went away, one by one〛	9
8: 9	〚went away, one by one, beginning with the elders;〛	9
8:41	we have one father, God himself."	9
10:16	there will be one flock, one shepherd.	9
10:16	there will be one flock, one shepherd.	9
10:28	No one will snatch them out of my hand.	22
10:30	The Father and I are one."	9
11:49	one of them, Caiaphas	9
11:50	to have one man die for the people	9
11:52	to gather into one the dispersed children of God.	9
12: 2	Lazarus was one of those at the table with him.	9
12: 4	Judas Iscariot, one of his disciples	9
13:20	whoever receives one whom I send receives me;	22
13:21	I tell you, one of you will betray me."	9
13:23	One of his disciples—the one whom Jesus loved	9
13:26	Jesus answered, "It is the one to whom I give	11
15:13	to lay down one's life for one's friends.	7
15:13	to lay down one's life for one's friends.	7
17:11	so that they may be one, as we are one.	9
17:11	so that they may be one, as we are one.	1
17:21	they may all be one. As you, Father, are in me	9
17:22	so that they may be one, as we are one	9
17:22	so that they may be one, as we are one	9
17:23	that they may become completely one	9
18:14	better to have one person die for the people.	9
18:22	one of the police standing nearby struck Jesus	9
18:26	One of the slaves of the high priest…asked	9
19:23	into four parts, one for each soldier.	13
19:34	Instead, one of the soldiers pierced his side	9
20:12	one at the head and the other at the feet.	9
20:24	But Thomas (who was called the Twin),	9
Act 1:21	one of the men who have accompanied us	1

1:22	one of these must become a witness with us	9
1:24	Show us which one of these two you have chosen	9
2: 6	each one heard them speaking in the native language	9
2:12	were amazed and perplexed, saying to one another	3
3:10	recognized him as the one who used to sit and ask	7
4:32	who believed were of one heart and soul	9
4:32	no one claimed private ownership of any possessions	9
7:24	saw one of them being wronged	22
10:21	Peter went down to the men and said, "I am the one	15
11:28	One of them named Agabus stood up	9
15:38	one who had deserted them in Pamphylia	17
17:26	From one ancestor he made all nations	9
17:27	though indeed he is not far from each one of us.	9
21: 7	stayed with them for one day.	9
21:19	he related one by one the things that God had done	10
21:19	he related one by one the things that God had done	9
23:17	Paul called one of the centurions and said	9
24:21	unless it was this one sentence that I called out	9
28:13	After one day there a south wind sprang up	9
28:25	they were leaving, Paul made one further statement:	9
Rom 2:28	For a person is not a Jew who is one outwardly	1
2:29	person is a Jew who is one inwardly	1
3:10	"There is no one who is righteous, not even one;	9
3:12	who shows kindness, there is not even one."	9
3:30	since God is one; and he will justify	9
4: 8	blessed is the one against whom the Lord	4
5:12	just as sin came into the world through one man	9
5:15	the free gift in the grace of the one man, Jesus	9
5:16	judgment following one trespass brought condemnation	9
5:17	death exercised dominion through that one	9
5:19	For just as by the one man's disobedience	9
9:10	Rebecca when she had conceived children by one husband	9
9:21	out of the same lump one object for special use	15
10:10	one believes with the heart and so is justified	1
10:10	one confesses with the mouth and so is saved.	1
10:11	"No one who believes in him will be put to shame."	18
12: 4	For as in one body we have many members	9
12: 5	so we, who are many, are one body in Christ	9
14:15	Do not let what you eat cause the ruin of one	11
15: 6	together you may with one voice glorify the God	9
1Co 1:15	so that no one can say that you were baptized	22
1:29	so that no one might boast	20
3: 4	For when one says, "I belong to Paul,"	22
4: 6	puffed up in favor of one against another.	9
6: 5	to decide between one believer and another	14
6:13	God will destroy both one and the other.	17
6:16	becomes one body with her?	9
6:16	it is said, "The two shall be one flesh."	9
6:17	united to the Lord becomes one spirit with him.	9
7: 7	one having one kind and another a different	12
8: 4	and that "there is no God but one."	9
8: 6	yet for us there is one God, the Father	9
8: 6	one Lord, Jesus Christ	9
8:13	so that I may not cause one of them to fall.	2
9:24	only one receives the prize?	9
10:17	Because there is one bread, we who are many are one	9
10:17	we who are many are one body	9
10:17	we all partake of the one bread.	9
10:28	out of consideration for the one who informed	11
11: 5	one and the same thing as having her head shaved.	9
11:21	one goes hungry and another becomes drunk.	15
12: 8	To one is given through the Spirit the utterance	15
12: 9	to another gifts of healing by the one Spirit	9
12:11	All these are activated by one and the same Spirit	9
12:12	For just as the body is one and has many members	9
12:12	members of the body, though many, are one body	9
12:13	in the one Spirit we were all baptized	9
12:13	we were all baptized into one body	9
12:13	were all made to drink of one Spirit.	9
12:14	body does not consist of one member but of many.	9
12:18	members in the body, each one of them, as he chose.	9
12:20	As it is, there are many members, yet one body.	9
12:26	If one member suffers, all suffer together	9
12:26	if one member is honored, all rejoice together	9
14: 5	One who prophesies is greater than one who speaks	14
14: 5	greater than one who speaks in tongues	14
14:13	Therefore, one who speaks in a tongue should pray	14
14:27	each in turn; and let one interpret.	9
15: 8	Last of all, as to one untimely born	14
15:39	one flesh for human beings, another for animals	3
15:41	one glory of the sun, and another glory of the moon	3

1Co	16:11	therefore let no one despise him.	22
2Co	2:16	to the one a fragrance from death to death	15
	5:14	we are convinced that one has died for all;	9
	8:20	We intend that no one should blame us	22
	11: 2	for I promised you in marriage to one husband	9
	11: 4	proclaims another Jesus than the one we proclaimed	15
	11: 4	a different spirit from the one you received	15
	11: 4	a different gospel from the one you accepted	15
	11:16	I repeat, let no one think that I am a fool;	22
	11:24	from the Jews the forty lashes minus one.	9
	12: 6	no one may think better of me than what is seen	22
Gal	2:16	no one will be justified by the works of the law.	19
	3:20	but God is one.	9
	3:28	for all of you are one in Christ Jesus.	9
	4:22	one by a slave woman and the other by a free woman.	9
	4:23	One, the child of the slave,	12
Eph	2: 9	not the result of works, so that no one may boast.	22
	2:14	in his flesh he has made both groups into one	9
	2:15	create in himself one new humanity in place of the two	9
	2:16	might reconcile both groups to God in one body	9
	2:18	both of us have access in one Spirit to the Father.	9
	4: 4	There is one body and one Spirit	9
	4: 4	There is one body and one Spirit	9
	4: 4	just as you were called to the one hope	9
	4: 5	one Lord, one faith, one baptism	9
	4: 5	one Lord, one faith, one baptism	9
	4: 5	one Lord, one faith, one baptism	9
	4: 6	one God and Father of all, who is above all	9
	5:31	the two will become one flesh."	9
Php	1:27	that you are standing firm in one spirit,	9
	1:27	striving side by side with one mind for the faith	9
	2: 2	being in full accord and of one mind.	9
Col	2: 8	See to it that no one takes you captive	22
	3:15	to which indeed you were called in the one body.	9
1Th	2:11	we dealt with each one of you like a father	9
2Th	2: 3	Let no one deceive you in any way;	22
	2: 3	the lawless one is revealed	5
1Ti	1: 8	law is good, if one uses it legitimately.	22
	2: 5	For there is one God;	9
	2: 5	also one mediator between God and humankind	9
	6:16	whom no one has ever seen or can see;	5
Tit	1:12	one of them, their very own prophet, who said	22
Heb	2:11	those who are sanctified all have one Father.	9
	4:11	so that no one may fall through such disobedience	22
	4:13	the eyes of the one to whom we must render an account.	7
	5: 4	one does not presume to take this honor	22
	7: 8	In the one case, tithes are received by those	1
	8:11	they shall not teach one another or say	10
	12:15	no one fails to obtain the grace of God;	22
	12:16	no one becomes like Esau, an immoral and godless	22
Jas	1:14	one is tempted by one's own desire, being lured	10
	2:10	whoever…fails in one point has become accountable	9
	2:16	one of you says to them, "Go in peace;	22
	2:19	You believe that God is one; you do well.	9
	3: 8	no one can tame the tongue—a restless evil	5
	4:12	There is one lawgiver and judge	9
1Pe	5: 1	as well as one who shares in the glory to be	14
2Pe	3: 8	do not ignore this one fact, beloved	9
	3: 8	with the Lord one day is like a thousand years	9
	3: 8	and a thousand years are like one day.	9
1Jn	4: 4	for the one who is in you is greater	14
	4: 4	greater than the one who is in the world.	14
2Jn	1: 5	but one we have had from the beginning	15
Rev	2:28	one who conquers I will also give the morning star.	7
	3:21	the one who conquers I will give a place with me	7
	5: 5	Then one of the elders said to me, "Do not weep.	9
	6: 1	I saw the Lamb open one of the seven seals	9
	6: 1	I heard one of the four living creatures call out	9
	7:13	Then one of the elders addressed me, saying	9
	13: 3	One of its heads seemed to have received a death-blow	9
	13:17	no one can buy or sell who does not have the mark	22
	15: 7	Then one of the four living creatures gave	9
	17: 1	Then one of the seven angels…said to me	9
	17:10	one is living, and the other has not yet come;	9
	17:12	receive authority as kings for one hour	9
	18:10	For in one hour your judgment has come."	9
	18:17	in one hour all this wealth has been laid waste!"	9
	18:19	For in one hour she has been laid waste."	9
	21: 9	one of the seven angels who had the seven bowls	9

one after another

1. κατά, *kata, 2848*

Lke	13:22	Jesus went through one town…after another	1

one another

1. ἀδελφός, *adelphos, 81*
2. ἀλλήλων, *allēlōn, 253*
3. αὐτός, *autos, 899*
4. ἑαυτοῦ, *heautou, 1571*
5. ἕτερος, *heteros, 2283*

Mat	11:16	and calling to one another	5
	16: 7	They said to one another, "It is because	4
	21:25	And they argued with one another	4
	24:10	will fall away, and they will betray one another	2
	24:10	betray one another and hate one another.	2
Mrk	1:27	and they kept on asking one another	4
	4:41	and said to one another, "Who then is this	2
	8:16	They said to one another, "It is because	2
	9:34	on the way they had argued with one another	2
	9:50	be at peace with one another."	2
	10:26	greatly astounded and said to one another,	4
	11:31	They argued with one another	4
	12: 7	those tenants said to one another	4
	14: 4	some were there who said to one another in anger	4
	16: 3	They had been saying to one another	4
Lke	2:15	the shepherds said to one another, "Let us go	2
	4:36	were all amazed and kept saying to one another	2
	6:11	discussed with one another what they might do	2
	7:32	like children…calling to one another	2
	8:25	amazed, and said to one another	2
	12: 1	so that they trampled on one another	2
	20: 5	They discussed it with one another, saying	4
	22:23	they began to ask one another	4
Jhn	4:33	So the disciples said to one another	2
	5:44	you accept glory from one another	2
	7:35	The Jews said to one another	4
	11:56	They were…asking one another	2
	12:19	The Pharisees then said to one another	4
	13:14	you also ought to wash one another's feet.	2
	13:22	The disciples looked at one another	2
	13:34	that you love one another.	2
	13:34	you also should love one another.	2
	13:35	if you have love for one another."	2
	15:12	my commandment, that you love one another	2
	15:17	these commands so that you may love one another.	2
	16:17	some of his disciples said to one another	2
	19:24	they said to one another, "Let us not tear it	2
Act	4:15	they discussed the matter with one another.	2
	19:38	let them bring charges there against one another.	2
	21: 6	and said farewell to one another	2
	26:31	as they were leaving, they said to one another	2
	28: 4	they said to one another	2
Rom	1:27	men…consumed with passion for one another.	2
	12: 5	and individually we are members of one another.	2
	12:10	love one another with mutual affection;	2
	12:10	outdo one another in showing honor.	2
	12:16	Live in harmony with one another;	2
	13: 8	Owe no one anything, except to love one another;	2
	14:13	therefore no longer pass judgment on one another	2
	15: 5	to live in harmony with one another	2
	15: 7	Welcome one another, therefore	2
	15:14	and able to instruct one another.	2
	16:16	Greet one another with a holy kiss.	2
1Co	6: 7	to have lawsuits at all with one another	4
	7: 5	Do not deprive one another	2
	11:33	come together to eat, wait for one another.	2
	12:25	members may have the same care for one another.	2
	16:20	Greet one another with a holy kiss.	2
2Co	10:12	But when they measure themselves by one another	4
	10:12	and compare themselves with one another	4
	13:11	agree with one another, live in peace;	3
	13:12	Greet one another with a holy kiss.	2
Gal	5:13	through love become slaves to one another.	2
	5:15	If, however, you bite and devour one another,	2
	5:15	you are not consumed by one another.	2
	5:26	not become conceited, competing against one another	2
	5:26	envying one another.	2
	6: 2	Bear one another's burdens	2
Eph	4: 2	bearing with one another in love	2
	4:25	we are members of one another.	2

	4:32 be kind to one another, tenderhearted	2
	4:32 forgiving one another, as God in Christ has forgiven	4
	5:21 Be subject to one another	2
Col	3: 9 Do not lie to one another	2
	3:13 Bear with one another	2
	3:16 teach and admonish one another in all wisdom;	4
1Th	3:12 increase and abound in love for one another	2
	4: 9 taught by God to love one another;	2
	4:18 encourage one another with these words.	2
	5:11 encourage one another and build up each other	2
	5:15 always seek to do good to one another and to all.	2
2Th	1: 3 love of everyone…for one another	2
Tit	3: 3 despicable, hating one another.	2
Heb	3:13 exhort one another every day	4
	10:24 to provoke one another to love and good deeds	2
Jas	4:11 not speak evil against one another, brothers and sisters.	2
	5: 9 Beloved, do not grumble against one another	2
	5:16 Therefore confess your sins to one another	2
	5:16 pray for one another, so that you may be healed.	2
1Pe	1:22 love one another deeply from the heart.	2
	4: 8 maintain constant love for one another	4
	4: 9 Be hospitable to one another without complaining.	2
	4:10 Like good stewards…serve one another	4
	5: 5 with humility in your dealings with one another	2
	5:14 Greet one another with a kiss of love.	2
1Jn	1: 7 we have fellowship with one another	2
	3:11 that we should love one another.	2
	3:14 because we love one another.	1
	3:16 we ought to lay down our lives for one another.	1
	3:23 we should believe…and love one another	2
	4: 7 Beloved, let us love one another	2
	4:11 we also ought to love one another.	2
	4:12 if we love one another, God lives in us	2
2Jn	1: 5 new commandment…let us love one another.	2
Rev	6: 4 so that people would slaughter one another;	2

one by one

1. εἷς + ἕκαστος, *heis + hekastos, 1651 + 1667*
2. κατά + εἷς, *kata + heis, 2848 + 1651*

Lke	16: 5 summoning his master's debtors one by one	1
1Co	14:31 For you can all prophesy one by one	2

one in the afternoon

1. ἕβδομος + ὥρα, *hebdomos + hōra, 1575 + 6052*

Jhn	4:52 "Yesterday at one in the afternoon the fever left	1

one man

1. εἷς, *heis, 1651*

Rom	5:15 if the many died through the one man's trespass	1
	5:16 the free gift is not like…the one man's sin.	1
	5:17 If, because of the one man's trespass, death	1
	5:17 dominion in life through the one man, Jesus Christ.	1
	5:18 one man's trespass led to condemnation for all	1
	5:18 one man's act of righteousness leads	1
	5:19 by the one man's obedience the many…righteous.	1

one person

1. εἷς, *heis, 1651*

Gal	3:16 "And to your offspring," that is, to one person	1
Heb	11:12 from one person, and this one as good as dead	1

one place

1. ὁ + αὐτός, *ho + autos, 3836 + 899*

Act	2: 1 they were all together in one place.	1

one thing

1. Contextual: Not in Greek
2. εἷς, *heis, 1651*
3. ἕτερος, *heteros, 2283*

Mrk	10:21 "You lack one thing;	2
Lke	10:42 there is need of only one thing.	2
	18:22 still one thing lacking. Sell all that	2
Jhn	1: 3 without him not one thing came into being.	2
	9:25 One thing I do know, that though I was blind,	2
1Co	15:40 the glory of the heavenly is one thing	3
Gal	2:10 asked only one thing, that we remember the poor	1
Php	3:13 one thing I do: forgetting what lies behind	2

one thing more

1. ἅμα, *hama, 275*

Phm	1:22 One thing more—prepare a guest room for me	1

one time

1. ἐφάπαξ, *ephapax, 2384*
2. ποτέ, *pote, 4537*

1Co	15: 6 five hundred brothers and sisters at one time	1
Eph	2:11 remember that at one time you Gentiles by birth	2

one woman

1. εἷς, *heis, 1651*

Gal	4:24 One woman, in fact, is Hagar, from Mount Sinai	1

oneself

oneself Not Indexed; *See* elder oneself, judge oneself, of oneself, throw oneself on the ground

Onesimus

1. Ὀνήσιμος, *Onēsimos, 3946*

Col	4: 9 Onesimus, the faithful and beloved brother	1
Phm	1:10 I am appealing to you for my child, Onesimus	1

Onesiphorus

1. Ὀνησίφορος, *Onēsiphoros, 3947*

2Ti	1:16 grant mercy to the household of Onesiphorus	1
	4:19 Greet…the household of Onesiphorus.	1

only

only *See also* drink only water, if only, not only, only *child*, only *son*

1. Contextual: Not in Greek
2. ἀλλά, *alla, 247*
3. εἰ, *ei, 1623*
4. εἰ + μή, *ei + mē, 1623 + 3590*
5. ἔτι, *eti, 2285*
6. καί, *kai, 2779*
7. κατά, *kata, 2848*
8. μονογενής, *monogenēs, 3666*
9. μόνον, *monon, 3667*
10. μόνος, *monos, 3668*
11. ὅσος, *hosos, 4012*
12. οὕτως, *houtōs, 4048*
13. πλήν, *plēn, 4440*

Mat	4:10 'Worship the Lord your God, and serve only him.' "	10
	5:47 And if you greet only your brothers and sisters	9
	7:21 only the one who does the will of my Father	1
	8: 8 but only speak the word	9
	9:21 she said to herself, "If I only touch his cloak	9
	12: 4 but only for the priests.	10
	12:11 "Suppose one of you has only one sheep	1
	12:24 "It is only by Beelzebul, the ruler of the demons	4
	13:21 but endures only for a while	1
	15:24 "I was sent only to the lost sheep	4
	19:11 but only those to whom it is given.	2
	19:17 There is only one who is good.	1
	20:12 saying, 'These last worked only one hour	1
	21:21 not only will you do what has been done	9
	24:36 but only the Father.	10
Mrk	4:17 endure only for a while;	1
	5:36 "Do not fear, only believe."	9
	8:14 they had only one loaf with them in the boat.	4
	9: 8 saw no one with them any more, but only Jesus.	10
	9:29 can come out only through prayer."	4
	13:32 nor the Son, but only the Father.	4
Lke	4: 8 serve only him.' "	10
	7: 7 But only speak the word	1
	7:12 was his mother's only son, and she was a widow;	8
	8:13 they believe only for a while	1
	8:42 for he had an only daughter…who was dying	8
	8:50 Only believe, and she will be saved."	9
	9:18 with only the disciples near him	1
	10:42 there is need of only one thing.	1
	13:23 "Lord, will only a few be saved?"	1
	17:10 we have done only what we ought	1
	24:18 the only stranger in Jerusalem who does not know	10
Jhn	3:16 God so loved the world that he gave his only Son	8
	3:18 not believed in the name of the only Son of God.	8
	5:18 because he was not only breaking the sabbath	9
	5:19 only what he sees the Father doing;	1

Jhn	6:22	saw that there had been only one boat there.	4
	10:10	The thief comes only to steal and kill	4
	10:33	only a human being, are making yourself God."	1
	11:52	not for the nation only	9
	12: 9	they came not only because of Jesus	9
	13: 9	not my feet only but also my hands and my head!"	9
	13:33	Little children, I am with you only a little longer.	5
	17: 3	they may know you, the only true God	10
	17:20	"I ask not only on behalf of these	9
	21: 8	not far…only about a hundred yards off	2
Act	2:15	for it is only nine o'clock in the morning.	1
	5: 2	brought only a part	1
	8:16	they had only been baptized	9
	10:26	saying, "Stand up; I am only a mortal."	1
	15:20	abstain only from things polluted by idols	1
	18:25	though he knew only the baptism of John.	9
	19:26	not only in Ephesus but…whole of Asia	9
	19:27	danger not only that this trade of ours	9
	21:13	ready not only to be bound but even to die	9
	26:29	not only you but also all who are listening	9
	27:10	not only of the cargo and the ship	9
	27:22	no loss of life among you, but only of the ship.	13
Rom	1:32	they not only do them but even applaud	9
	3:29	Or is God the God of Jews only?	9
	4: 9	blessedness…pronounced only on the circumcised	1
	4:12	circumcised who are not only circumcised	9
	4:16	not only to the adherents of the law	9
	5: 3	not only that, but we also boast in our sufferings	9
	7: 1	the law is binding on a person only during…lifetime?	11
	8:23	not only the creation, but we ourselves	9
	9:24	not from the Jews only but also from the Gentiles?	9
	9:27	only a remnant of them will be saved;	1
	11:20	but you stand only through faith.	1
	13: 5	one must be subject, not only because of wrath	9
	14: 2	while the weak eat only vegetables.	1
	16: 4	to whom not only I…give thanks	10
	16:27	to the only wise God, through Jesus Christ,	10
1Co	3: 7	but only God who gives the growth.	1
	3:15	saved, but only as through fire.	12
	7:39	marry anyone she wishes, only in the Lord.	9
	9: 6	Or is it only Barnabas and I who have no right	10
	9:24	only one receives the prize?	1
	11:19	for only so will it become clear who among you	6
	11:28	Examine yourselves, and only then eat of the bread	12
	13:12	Now I know only in part; then I will know fully	1
	14:27	let there be only two or at most three	7
	14:36	Or are you the only ones it has reached?)	10
	15:19	If for this life only we have hoped in Christ	9
2Co	3:14	since only in Christ is it set aside.	1
	6:12	no restriction in our affections, but only in yours	1
	7: 7	not only by his coming, but also by the consolation	9
	7: 8	grieved you with that letter, though only briefly).	6
	8:10	who began last year not only to do something	9
	8:19	not only that, but he has also been appointed	9
	8:21	what is right not only in the Lord's sight	9
	9:12	not only supplies the needs of the saints	9
	13: 8	but only for the truth.	1
Gal	1:23	they only heard it said	9
	2: 2	(though only in a private meeting	1
	2:10	asked only one thing, that we remember the poor	9
	4:18	not only when I am present with you.	9
	5:13	only do not use your freedom as an opportunity	9
	6:12	only that they may not be persecuted	9
Eph	1:21	not only in this age	9
	4:29	only what is useful for building up	3
	6: 6	not only while being watched, and in order to please	1
Php	1:27	Only, live your life in a manner worthy	9
	1:29	the privilege not only of believing in Christ	9
	2:12	have always obeyed me, not only in my presence	9
	2:27	God had mercy on him, and not only on him but on me	9
	3:16	Only let us hold fast to what we have attained.	13
Col	2:17	These are only a shadow of what is to come	1
	3:22	not only while being watched and in order to please	1
	4:11	the only ones of the circumcision among my co-workers	10
1Th	1: 5	message of the gospel came to you not in word only	9
	1: 8	sounded forth from you not only in Macedonia	9
	2: 8	determined to share with you not only the gospel of God	9
2Th	2: 7	only until the one who now restrains it	9
1Ti	1:17	the King of the ages, immortal, invisible, the only God	10
	3: 2	married only once, temperate, sensible	1
	3:12	Let deacons be married only once	1

	5: 9	has been married only once;	1
	6:15	the blessed and only Sovereign	10
2Ti	2:14	does no good but only ruins those who are listening.	1
	2:20	there are utensils not only of gold and silver	9
	4: 8	and not only to me but also to all	9
	4:11	Only Luke is with me.	10
Tit	1: 6	someone who is blameless, married only once,	1
Heb	5: 4	takes it only when called by God	1
	9: 7	only the high priest goes into the second	10
	9:10	deal only with food and drink	9
	9:17	a will takes effect only at death	1
	10: 1	Since the law has only a shadow of the good things	1
	12:26	"Yet once more I will shake not only the earth	9
1Pe	2:18	not only those who are kind and gentle	9
2Pe	2:22	"The sow is washed only to wallow in the mud."	1
1Jn	2: 2	the atoning sacrifice for our sins, and not for ours only	9
	4: 9	God sent his only Son into the world	8
	5: 6	the one who came…not with the water only	9
2Jn	1: 1	and not only I but also all who know the truth	10
Jde	1: 4	and deny our only Master and Lord, Jesus Christ.	10
	1:25	to the only God our Savior, through Jesus Christ	10
Rev	2:25	only hold fast to what you have until I come.	13
	17:10	when he comes, he must remain only a little while.	1

only thing

1. Contextual: Not in Greek
2. μόνον, *monon*, 3667

Gal	3: 2	The only thing I want to learn from you is this:	2
	5: 6	only thing that counts is faith working through love.	1

onyx

1. σαρδόνυξ, *sardonyx*, 4918

Rev	21:20	the fifth onyx, the sixth carnelian	1

open *See also* break open, burst open, open *statement*

1. Contextual: Not in Greek
2. ἄγω, *agō*, 72
3. ἀνοίγω, *anoigō*, 487
4. διανοίγω, *dianoigō*, 1380
5. ἐγκαινίζω, *enkainizō*, 1590
6. καταλείπω, *kataleipō*, 2901

Mat	2:11	opening their treasure chests, they offered him	3
	3:16	suddenly the heavens were opened to him and he saw	3
	7: 7	knock, and the door will be opened for you.	3
	7: 8	for everyone who knocks, the door will be opened.	3
	9:30	their eyes were opened.	3
	13:35	"I will open my mouth to speak in parables;	3
	17:27	when you open its mouth, you will find a coin;	3
	20:33	They said to him, "Lord, let our eyes be opened."	3
	25:11	'Lord, lord, open to us.'	3
	27:52	The tombs also were opened	3
Mrk	7:34	"Ephphatha," that is, "Be opened."	4
	7:35	his ears were opened, his tongue was released	3
Lke	1:64	Immediately his mouth was opened	3
	3:21	the heaven was opened	3
	11: 9	knock, and the door will be opened for you	3
	11:10	for everyone who knocks, the door will be opened.	3
	12:36	so that they may open the door for him	3
	13:25	to knock at the door, saying, 'Lord, open to us,'	3
	24:31	their eyes were opened, and they recognized him;	4
	24:32	while he was opening the scriptures to us?"	4
	24:45	Then he opened their minds	4
Jhn	1:51	truly, I tell you, you will see heaven opened	3
	9:10	asking him, "Then how were your eyes opened?"	3
	9:14	when Jesus made the mud and opened his eyes.	3
	9:17	It was your eyes he opened."	3
	9:21	nor do we know who opened his eyes.	3
	9:26	How did he open your eyes?"	3
	9:30	and yet he opened my eyes.	3
	9:32	anyone opened the eyes of a person born blind.	3
	10: 3	The gatekeeper opens the gate for him	3
	10:21	Can a demon open the eyes of the blind?"	3
	11:37	he who opened the eyes of the blind man	3
Act	5:19	an angel of the Lord opened the prison doors	3
	5:23	when we opened them, we found no one inside."	3
	7:56	"Look," he said, "I see the heavens opened	4
	8:32	so he does not open his mouth.	3
	9: 8	though his eyes were open, he could see nothing;	3
	9:40	she opened her eyes	3
	10:11	He saw the heaven opened	3

12:10	It opened for them of its own accord	3
12:14	instead of opening the gate, she ran in	3
12:16	when they opened the gate, they saw him	3
14:27	how he had opened a door of faith for the Gentiles.	3
16:14	opened her heart to listen eagerly to what was said	4
16:26	immediately all the doors were opened	3
19:38	the courts are open	2
26:18	to open their eyes	3
Rom 3:13	"Their throats are opened graves;	3
1Co 16: 9	for a wide door for effective work has opened	3
2Co 2:12	a door was opened for me in the Lord;	3
Col 4: 3	that God will open to us a door for the word	3
Heb 4: 1	while the promise of entering his rest is still open	6
4: 6	Since therefore it remains open for some to enter it	1
10:20	by the new and living way that he opened for us	5
1Pe 3:12	and his ears are open to their prayer.	1
Rev 3: 7	the true one...who opens and no one will shut	3
3: 7	the true one...who shuts and no one opens:	3
3: 8	Look, I have set before you an open door	3
3:20	if you hear my voice and open the door	3
4: 1	I looked, and there in heaven a door stood open!	3
5: 2	"Who is worthy to open the scroll and break	3
5: 3	no one...was able to open the scroll or to look	3
5: 4	because no one was found worthy to open the scroll	3
5: 5	so that he can open the scroll and its seven seals."	3
5: 9	worthy...to take the scroll and to open its seals	3
6: 1	I saw the Lamb open one of the seven seals	3
6: 3	When he opened the second seal, I heard	3
6: 5	When he opened the third seal, I heard	3
6: 7	When he opened the fourth seal, I heard the voice	3
6: 9	When he opened the fifth seal, I saw	3
6:12	When he opened the sixth seal, I looked,	3
8: 1	When the Lamb opened the seventh seal	3
9: 2	he opened the shaft of the bottomless pit	3
10: 2	He held a little scroll open in his hand.	3
10: 8	the scroll that is open in the hand of the angel	3
11:19	Then God's temple in heaven was opened	3
12:16	it opened its mouth and swallowed the river	3
13: 6	It opened its mouth to utter blasphemies	3
15: 5	temple of the tent of witness in heaven was opened	3
19:11	I saw heaven opened, and there was a white horse!	3
20:12	I saw the dead...and books were opened.	3
20:12	another book was opened, the book of life.	3

open wide

1. πλατύνω, *platynō, 4425*

2Co 6:11	our heart is wide open to you	1
6:13	open wide your hearts also.	1

wide open

1. ἀνοίγω, *anoigō, 487*

Act 16:27	woke up and saw the prison doors wide open	1

opening

1. Contextual: Not in Greek
2. ὀπή, *opē, 3956*

Act 9:25	and let him down through an opening in the wall	1
Jas 3:11	Does a spring pour forth from the same opening	2

openly   *See also* quite openly

1. παρρησία, *parrēsia, 4244*
2. φανερῶς, *phanerōs, 5747*

Mrk 1:45	Jesus could no longer go into a town openly	2
Jhn 7:13	Yet no one would speak openly about him	1
7:26	here he is, speaking openly, but they say nothing	1
11:54	no longer walked about openly among the Jews	1
18:20	"I have spoken openly to the world;	1

openly before

1. πρόσωπον, *prosōpon, 4725*

2Co 8:24	Therefore openly before the churches,	1

opinion

1. αἵρεσις, *hairesis, 146*
2. γνώμη, *gnōmē, 1191*
3. διαλογισμός, *dialogismos, 1369*

Rom 14: 1	not for the purpose of quarreling over opinions.	3
1Co 7:25	I give my opinion as one who by the Lord's mercy	2
2Pe 2: 1	secretly bring in destructive opinions.	1

opponent

1. ἀντιδιατίθημι, *antidiatithēmi, 507*
2. ἀντίδικος, *antidikos, 508*
3. ἀντίκειμαι, *antikeimai, 512*
4. ἐναντίος, *enantios, 1885*

Lke 13:17	all his opponents were put to shame;	3
18: 3	saying, 'Grant me justice against my opponent.'	2
21:15	none of your opponents will be able	3
Php 1:28	in no way intimidated by your opponents.	3
2Ti 2:25	correcting opponents with gentleness.	1
Tit 2: 8	then any opponent will be put to shame	4

opportune   *See* opportune *time*

1. καιρός, *kairos, 2789*

Lke 4:13	he departed from him until an opportune time.	1

opportunity   *See also* give an opportunity

1. Contextual: Not in Greek
2. ἀφορμή, *aphormē, 929*
3. εὐκαιρέω, *eukaireō, 2320*
4. εὐκαιρία, *eukairia, 2321*
5. εὔκαιρος, *eukairos, 2322*
6. εὐκαίρως, *eukairōs, 2323*
7. καιρός, *kairos, 2789*
8. τόπος, *topos, 5536*

Mat 26:16	to look for an opportunity to betray him.	4
Mrk 6:21	an opportunity came	5
14:11	began to look for an opportunity to betray him.	6
Lke 22: 6	look for an opportunity to betray him to them	4
Jhn 7: 1	were looking for an opportunity to kill him.	1
7:19	you looking for an opportunity to kill me?"	1
8:37	yet you look for an opportunity to kill me	1
Act 24:25	when I have an opportunity, I will send for you."	7
25:16	had been given an opportunity to make a defense	8
Rom 7: 8	But sin, seizing an opportunity in the commandment	2
7:11	For sin, seizing an opportunity in the commandment	2
1Co 16:12	He will come when he has the opportunity.	3
2Co 5:12	giving you an opportunity to boast about us	2
11:12	to do, in order to deny an opportunity	2
11:12	who want an opportunity to be recognized	2
Gal 5:13	your freedom as an opportunity for self-indulgence	2
6:10	So then, whenever we have an opportunity	7
Heb 11:15	they would have had opportunity to return.	7

no opportunity

1. ἀκαιρέομαι, *akaireomai, 177*

Php 4:10	but had no opportunity to show it	1

oppose

1. ἀνθίστημι, *anthistēmi, 468*
2. ἀντίκειμαι, *antikeimai, 512*
3. ἀντιλέγω, *antilegō, 515*
4. ἀντιπίπτω, *antipiptō, 528*
5. ἀντιτάσσω, *antitassō, 530*
6. ἐναντίος, *enantios, 1885*
7. ἐπί, *epi, 2093*
8. κατά, *kata, 2848*
9. ὑπαντάω, *hypantaō, 5636*

Lke 2:34	to be a sign that will be opposed	3
14:31	to oppose the one who comes against him with	9
Act 7:51	you are forever opposing the Holy Spirit	4
13: 8	the magician Elymas...opposed them	1
18: 6	When they opposed and reviled him	5
2Co 10: 2	oppose those who think we	7
Gal 2:11	I opposed him to his face	1
3:21	Is the law then opposed to the promises of God?	8
5:17	what the flesh desires is opposed to the Spirit	8
5:17	the Spirit desires is opposed to the flesh;	8
5:17	these are opposed to each other	2
1Th 2:15	drove us out; they displease God and oppose everyone	6
2Th 2: 4	opposes and exalts himself	2
2Ti 3: 8	As Jannes and Jambres opposed Moses	1
3: 8	these people...also oppose the truth.	1
4:15	he strongly opposed our message.	1
Jas 4: 6	"God opposes the proud, but gives grace	5
1Pe 5: 5	"God opposes the proud, but gives grace	5

opposite

1. ἄντικρυς, *antikrys, 513*
2. ἀντιπέρα, *antipera, 527*
3. ἀπέναντι, *apenanti, 595*
4. κατά, *kata, 2848*
5. κατέναντι, *katenanti, 2978*

Mat 27:61 sitting opposite the tomb. — 3
Mrk 12:41 He sat down opposite the treasury — 5
    13: 3 on the Mount of Olives opposite the temple — 5
Lke 8:26 which is opposite Galilee. — 2
Act 16: 7 When they had come opposite Mysia — 4
    20:15 the following day we arrived opposite Chios. — 1

opposition See also say in opposition

1. ἀγών, *agōn, 74*
2. παρά, *para, 4123*

Rom 16:17 offenses, in opposition to the teaching — 2
1Th 2: 2 in spite of great opposition. — 1

oppress

1. θραύω, *thrauō, 2575*
2. καταδυναστεύω, *katadynasteuō, 2872*

Lke 4:18 to let the oppressed go free — 1
Act 10:38 healing all who were oppressed by the devil — 2
Jas 2: 6 Is it not the rich who oppress you? — 2

oppressed man

1. καταπονέω, *kataponeō, 2930*

Act 7:24 he defended the oppressed man and avenged him — 1

or Not Indexed

or else

1. ἤ, *ē, 2445*
2. μή, *mē, 3590*

Mrk 13:36 or else he may find you asleep when he comes suddenly. — 2
1Co 7:11 or else be reconciled to her husband) — 1

oracle

1. λόγιον, *logion, 3359*

Act 7:38 he received living oracles to give to us. — 1
Rom 3: 2 the Jews were entrusted with the oracles of God. — 1
Heb 5:12 teach you…the basic elements of the oracles of God. — 1

ordain

1. διαταγή, *diatagē, 1408*
2. διατάσσω, *diatassō, 1411*
3. ἐντέλλω, *entellō, 1948*
4. ἐπιτίθημι + χείρ, *epitithēmi + cheir, 2202 + 5931*
5. ὁρίζω, *horizō, 3988*

Act 7:53 ones that received the law as ordained by angels — 1
    10:42 the one ordained by God as judge of the living — 5
Gal 3:19 ordained through angels by a mediator. — 2
1Ti 5:22 Do not ordain anyone hastily. — 4
Heb 9:20 the covenant that God has ordained for you." — 3

ordeal

1. δοκιμή, *dokimē, 1509*
2. θλῖψις, *thlipsis, 2568*

2Co 8: 2 for during a severe ordeal of affliction — 1
Rev 7:14 they who have come out of the great ordeal; — 2

fiery ordeal

1. πύρωσις, *pyrōsis, 4796*

1Pe 4:12 fiery ordeal that is taking place among you to test you — 1

order¹ See also give an order, put in order

1. τάγμα, *tagma, 5413*
2. τάξις, *taxis, 5423*

1Co 14:40 all things should be done decently and in order. — 2
    15:23 each in his own order: Christ the first fruits — 1
Heb 5: 6 a priest forever, according to the order of Melchizedek." — 2
    5:10 a high priest according to the order of Melchizedek. — 2
    6:20 according to the order of Melchizedek. — 2
    7:11 priest arising according to the order of Melchizedek — 2
    7:11 rather than one according to the order of Aaron? — 2
    7:17 a priest forever, according to the order of Melchizedek." — 2

order²

1. Contextual: Not in Greek
2. εἰ + πώς, *ei + pōs, 1623 + 4803*
3. εἰς, *eis, 1650*
4. ἔνεκεν, *heneken, 1915*
5. ἵνα, *hina, 2671*
6. ὅπως, *hopōs, 3968*
7. πρός, *pros, 4639*
8. πώς, *pōs, 4803*
9. ὡς, *hōs, 6055*
10. ὥστε, *hōste, 6063*

Mat 6: 1 before others in order to be seen by them; — 7
    19:13 in order that he might lay his hands on them — 5
    26:58 in order to see how this would end. — 1
    27: 1 against Jesus in order to bring about his death. — 10
Mrk 4:12 in order that 'they may indeed look, but not — 5
    7: 9 in order to keep your tradition! — 5
    10:13 in order that he might touch them; — 5
    14:10 went to the chief priests in order to betray him — 5
Lke 20:10 in order that they might give him his share — 5
    20:20 in order to trap him by what he said — 5
Jhn 3:17 but in order that the world might be saved — 5
    7:23 in order that the law of Moses may not be broken — 5
    10:17 I lay down my life in order to take it up again. — 5
    19:28 he said (in order to fulfill the scripture), — 5
Act 5:15 in order that Peter's shadow might fall on some — 5
    6: 2 neglect the word of God in order to wait on tables. — 1
    20:30 in order to entice the disciples to follow them. — 1
    22: 5 in order to bind those who were there — 1
Rom 1:13 in order that I may reap some harvest among you — 5
    4:16 in order that the promise may rest on grace — 5
    6: 1 continue in sin in order that grace may abound? — 5
    7: 4 in order that we may bear fruit for God. — 5
    7:13 in order that sin might be shown to be sin — 5
    8:29 in order that he might be the firstborn — 3
    9:23 in order to make known the riches of his glory — 5
    11:14 in order to make my own people jealous, and thus — 2
    11:31 in order that, by the mercy shown to you — 5
    15: 8 in order that he might confirm the promises — 3
    15: 9 in order that the Gentiles might glorify God — 1
1Co 1:31 in order that, as it is written, "Let the one who boasts — 5
    9:20 To the Jews I became as a Jew, in order to win Jews. — 5
    14:19 in order to instruct others — 5
2Co 7:12 in order that your zeal for us might be made known — 4
    8:14 in order that there may be a fair balance. — 6
    9: 3 in order that our boasting about you may not prove — 5
    11: 8 accepting support from them in order to serve you. — 7
    11:12 to do, in order to deny an opportunity — 5
    11:32 the governor…guarded the city…in order to seize me — 1
Gal 2: 2 in order to make sure that I was not…in vain — 8
    3:14 in order that in Christ Jesus the blessing — 5
    4: 5 in order to redeem those who were under the law — 5
Eph 5:26 in order to make her holy by cleansing her — 5
    6: 6 while being watched, and in order to please — 9
Php 2:28 in order that you may rejoice at seeing him again — 5
    3: 8 in order that I may gain Christ — 5
Col 3:22 not only while being watched and in order to please — 9
2Th 3: 9 in order to give you an example to imitate. — 5
Tit 3:14 in order to meet urgent needs — 3
Phm 1:14 in order that your good deed might be voluntary — 5
Heb 10: 9 in order to establish the second. — 5
    11:35 in order to obtain a better resurrection. — 5
    12:10 in order that we may share his holiness. — 3
    13:12 in order to sanctify the people — 5
Jas 4: 3 in order to spend what you get on your pleasures. — 5
1Pe 2: 9 in order that you may proclaim the mighty acts — 6
    3:18 Christ also suffered…in order to bring you to God. — 5
Rev 16:12 its water was dried up in order to prepare the way — 5
    20: 8 Gog and Magog, in order to gather them for battle; — 1

order³

1. διαστέλλω, *diastellō, 1403*
2. διατάσσω, *diatassō, 1411*
3. ἐντέλλω, *entellō, 1948*
4. ἐντολή, *entolē, 1953*
5. ἐπιτάσσω, *epitassō, 2199*
6. ἐπιτιμάω, *epitimaō, 2203*
7. κελεύω, *keleuō, 3027*
8. λέγω, *legō, 3306*

9. παραγγέλλω, *parangellō, 4133*
10. προστάσσω, *prostassō, 4705*

Mat	12:16 ordered them not to make him known.	6
	14:19 he ordered the crowds to sit down on the grass.	7
	15:35 ordering the crowd to sit down on the ground	9
	17: 9 coming down the mountain, Jesus ordered them	3
	18:25 could not pay, his lord ordered him to be sold	7
	27:58 then Pilate ordered it to be given to him.	7
Mrk	3:12 he sternly ordered them not to make him known.	6
	5:43 He strictly ordered them that no one should know	1
	6: 8 ordered them to take nothing for their journey	9
	6:27 with orders to bring John's head.	5
	6:39 he ordered them to get all the people to sit	5
	7:36 Jesus ordered them to tell no one;	1
	7:36 the more he ordered them	1
	8: 6 he ordered the crowd to sit down on the ground;	9
	8: 7 after blessing them, he ordered	8
	9: 9 he ordered them to tell no one about	1
Lke	5:14 he ordered him to tell no one.	9
	8:31 They begged him not to order them to go back	5
	8:56 he ordered them to tell no one what had happened.	9
	14:22 'Sir, what you ordered has been done	5
	17:10 when you have done all that you were ordered	2
	18:40 Jesus stood still and ordered the man to be brought	7
	19:15 he ordered these slaves	8
	19:39 "Teacher, order your disciples to stop."	6
Jhn	11:57 the Pharisees had given orders	4
Act	1: 4 he ordered them not to leave Jerusalem	9
	4:15 So they ordered them to leave the council	7
	4:18 So they called them and ordered them not to speak	9
	5:34 ordered the men to be put outside for a short time.	7
	5:40 ordered them not to speak in the name of Jesus	9
	7:44 he spoke to Moses, ordering him to make it	2
	10:48 he ordered them to be baptized	10
	12:19 and ordered them to be put to death.	7
	15: 5 ordered to keep the law of Moses."	9
	16:18 "I order you in the name of Jesus Christ	9
	16:22 and ordered them to be beaten with rods.	7
	16:23 ordered the jailer to keep them securely.	9
	18: 2 Claudius had ordered all Jews to leave Rome	2
	21:33 ordered him to be bound with two chains;	7
	21:34 he ordered him to be brought into the barracks.	7
	22:24 ordered him to be examined by flogging	8
	22:30 and ordered the chief priests...to meet.	7
	23: 2 the high priest Ananias ordered...to strike him	5
	23: 3 in violation of the law you order me to be struck?"	7
	23:10 the tribune...ordered the soldiers to go down	7
	23:22 the young man, ordering him, "Tell no one	9
	23:30 ordering his accusers also to state before you	9
	23:35 he ordered that he be kept under guard	7
	24:23 he ordered the centurion	2
	25: 6 ordered Paul to be brought.	7
	25:17 and ordered the man to be brought.	7
	25:21 I ordered him to be held	7
	27:43 He ordered those who could swim	7

good order

1. εὐσχήμων, *euschēmōn, 2363*
1Co 7:35 but to promote good order 1

order sternly

1. διαστέλλω, *diastellō, 1403*
2. ἐμβριμάομαι, *embrimaomai, 1839*
3. ἐπιτιμάω, *epitimaō, 2203*

Mat	9:30 Then Jesus sternly ordered them	2
	16:20 Then he sternly ordered the disciples	1
	20:31 The crowd sternly ordered them to be quiet;	3
Mrk	8:30 he sternly ordered them not to tell anyone	3
	10:48 Many sternly ordered him to be quiet	3
Lke	9:21 He sternly ordered and commanded them	3
	18:15 when the disciples saw it, they sternly ordered	3
	18:39 Those who were in front sternly ordered him	3

priestly order

1. ἐφημερία, *ephēmeria, 2389*
Lke 1: 5 who belonged to the priestly order of Abijah. 1

strict order

1. παραγγελία, *parangelia, 4132*
Act 5:28 saying, "We gave you strict orders not to teach 1

---

orderly *See* orderly *account*

ordinance

1. δόγμα, *dogma, 1504*
Eph 2:15 the law with its commandments and ordinances 1

ordinary *See also* ordinary *use*

1. Contextual: Not in Greek
2. ἀτιμία, *atimia, 871*
3. βιωτικός, *biōtikos, 1053*
4. ἰδιώτης, *idiōtēs, 2626*

Act	4:13 realized that they were uneducated and ordinary men	4
1Co	6: 4 If you have ordinary cases, then,	3
2Co	1:17 make my plans according to ordinary human standards	1
2Ti	2:20 some for special use, some for ordinary.	2

ordinary matter

1. βιωτικός, *biōtikos, 1053*
1Co 6: 3 to say nothing of ordinary matters? 1

origin

1. ἀρχή, *archē, 794*
2. γένος, *genos, 1169*
3. ἐκ, *ek, 1666*
4. κατά, *kata, 2848*

Mat	21:25 from heaven, or was it of human origin?"	3
	21:26 'Of human origin,' we are afraid of the crowd;	3
Mrk	7:26 the woman was a Gentile, of Syrophoenician origin.	2
	11:30 come from heaven, or was it of human origin?	3
	11:32 But shall we say, 'Of human origin'?"	3
Lke	20: 4 the baptism of John...was it of human origin?"	3
	20: 6 if we say, 'Of human origin,' all the people	3
Act	5:38 if this plan or this undertaking is of human origin	3
	15:23 the believers of Gentile origin in Antioch	3
Gal	1:11 the gospel...is not of human origin;	4
Rev	3:14 the Amen...the origin of God's creation:	1

originate

1. ἐξέρχομαι, *exerchomai, 2002*
1Co 14:36 Or did the word of God originate with you? 1

ornament

1. Contextual: Not in Greek
2. κοσμέω, *kosmeō, 3175*
Tit 2:10 may be an ornament to the doctrine of God our Savior. 2
1Pe 3: 3 adorn yourselves outwardly by...wearing gold ornaments 1

orphan *See also* make an orphan

1. ὀρφανός, *orphanos, 4003*
Jhn 14:18 not leave you orphaned; I am coming to you. 1
Jas 1:27 to care for orphans and widows in their distress 1

other *See also* any other, belong to others, each other, on the other *hand*, other *name*, other *side*, pass by on the other side, with *seven* others

1. Contextual: Not in Greek
2. ἀδελφός, *adelphos, 81*
3. ἄκρον, *akron, 216*
4. ἀλλήλων, *allēlōn, 253*
5. ἄλλος, *allos, 257*
6. ἀλλότριος, *allotrios, 259*
7. ἄνθρωπος, *anthrōpos, 476*
8. αὐτός, *autos, 899*
9. δέ, *de, 1254*
10. εἷς, *heis, 1651*
11. ἐκεῖ, *ekei, 1695*
12. ἐκεῖνος, *ekeinos, 1697*
13. ἕτερος, *heteros, 2283*
14. ἔτι, *eti, 2285*
15. κἀκεῖνος, *kakeinos, 2797*
16. κατάλοιπος, *kataloipos, 2905*
17. λοιπός, *loipos, 3370*
18. ὁ, *ho, 3836*
19. ὅς, *hos, 4005*
20. οὗτος, *houtos, 4047*
21. τὶς, *tis, 5516*

Mat 4:21 went from there, he saw two other brothers 5

Mat	5:16	In the same way, let your light shine before others	7
	5:19	teaches others to do the same, will be called least	7
	5:39	on the right cheek, turn the other also;	5
	5:47	what more are you doing than others?	1
	6: 1	"Beware of practicing your piety before others	7
	6: 2	so that they may be praised by others.	7
	6: 5	so that they may be seen by others	7
	6:14	For if you forgive others their trespasses	7
	6:15	if you do not forgive others, neither will	7
	6:16	so as to show others that they are fasting.	7
	6:18	fasting may be seen not by others but by your Father	7
	6:24	slave will either hate the one and love the other	13
	6:24	or be devoted to the one and despise the other	13
	7:12	do to others as you would have them do to you	7
	10:32	"Everyone…who acknowledges me before others	7
	10:33	whoever denies me before others, I also will deny	7
	12:13	and it was restored, as sound as the other.	5
	12:45	it goes and brings along seven other spirits	13
	13: 5	Other seeds fell on rocky ground	5
	13: 7	Other seeds fell among thorns	5
	13: 8	Other seeds fell on good soil	5
	15:30	the blind, the mute, and many others.	13
	16:14	"Some say John the Baptist, but others Elijah	5
	16:14	others Elijah, and still others Jeremiah	13
	17:25	From their children or from others?"	6
	17:26	When Peter said, "From others,"	6
	18:16	not listened to, take one or two others along	14
	19:12	who have been made eunuchs by others	7
	20: 3	he saw others standing idle in the marketplace;	5
	20: 6	he went out and found others standing around;	5
	21: 8	others cut branches from the trees	5
	21:36	Again he sent other slaves, more than the first;	5
	21:41	and lease the vineyard to other tenants	5
	22: 4	Again he sent other slaves, saying	5
	23: 4	and lay them on the shoulders of others;	7
	23: 5	They do all their deeds to be seen by others;	7
	23:13	when others are going in, you stop them.	18
	23:23	without neglecting the others.	15
	23:28	you also on the outside look righteous to others	7
	24:31	from one end of heaven to the other.	3
	24:45	to give the other slaves their allowance of food	1
	25:11	Later the other bridesmaids came also, saying	17
	27:42	"He saved others; he cannot save himself.	5
	27:49	the others said, "Wait, let us see	17
	27:61	Mary Magdalene and the other Mary were there	5
	28: 1	Mary Magdalene and the other Mary	5
Mrk	4: 5	Other seed fell on rocky ground	5
	4: 7	Other seed fell among thorns	5
	4: 8	Other seed fell into good soil	5
	4:18	others are those sown among the thorns:	5
	4:36	Other boats were with him.	5
	6:15	others said, "It is Elijah."	5
	6:15	others said, "It is a prophet	5
	7: 4	many other traditions that they observe	1
	8:28	others, Elijah; and still others, one of the prophets."	5
	8:28	and still others, one of the prophets."	5
	11: 8	and others spread leafy branches	5
	12: 5	so it was with many others;	5
	12: 5	some they beat, and others they killed.	19
	12: 6	He had still one other, a beloved son.	1
	12: 9	give the vineyard to others.	5
	12:31	no other commandment greater than these."	5
	12:32	besides him there is no other';	5
	15:31	saying, "He saved others; he cannot save himself.	5
	15:41	many other women who had come up with him	5
Lke	3:18	So, with many other exhortations, he proclaimed	13
	4:43	proclaim the good news…to the other cities also;	13
	5: 7	signaled their partners in the other boat	13
	5:29	was a large crowd of tax collectors and others	5
	6:29	offer the other also;	5
	6:31	Do to others as you would have them do to you.	7
	7:41	owed five hundred denarii, and the other fifty	13
	8: 3	Joanna…and Susanna, and many others	13
	8:10	to others I speak in parables	17
	9: 8	by others that one of the ancient prophets	5
	9:19	but others, Elijah;	5
	9:19	others, that one of the ancient prophets has arisen."	5
	10: 1	After this the Lord appointed seventy others	13
	11:16	Others, to test him, kept demanding from him a sign	13
	11:26	seven other spirits more evil than itself	13
	11:42	without neglecting the others.	15

	12: 8	everyone who acknowledges me before others	7
	12: 9	whoever denies me before others	7
	12:45	to beat the other slaves, men and women	1
	13: 2	worse sinners than all other Galileans?	18
	13: 4	than all the others living in Jerusalem?	7
	14:32	while the other is still far away, he sends	8
	16:13	slave will either hate the one and love the other	13
	16:13	be devoted to the one and despise the other.	13
	16:15	who justify yourselves in the sight of others;	7
	17:17	ten made clean? But the other nine, where are	1
	17:24	lights up the sky from one side to the other	1
	17:34	one will be taken and the other left.	13
	17:35	one will be taken and the other left."	13
	18: 9	to some who…regarded others with contempt:	17
	18:10	one a Pharisee and the other a tax collector.	13
	18:11	I thank you that I am not like other people:	17
	18:14	this man…rather than the other;	12
	19:20	Then the other came, saying	13
	20:16	give the vineyard to others."	5
	22:65	They kept heaping many other insults on him	13
	23:32	Two others also, who were criminals, were led away	13
	23:35	"He saved others; let him save himself	5
	23:40	the other rebuked him, saying, "Do you not fear God	13
Jhn	4:38	Others have labored, and you have entered	5
	7:12	others were saying, "No, he is deceiving	5
	7:41	Others said, "This is the Messiah."	5
	9: 9	Others were saying, "No, but it is someone like him."	5
	9:16	others said, "How can a man who is a sinner	5
	10:16	other sheep that do not belong to this fold.	5
	10:21	Others were saying, "These are not the words	5
	12:29	Others said, "An angel has spoken to him."	5
	18:16	So the other disciple, who was known	5
	18:34	did others tell you about me?"	5
	19:18	they crucified him, and with him two others	5
	19:32	the other who had been crucified with him.	5
	20: 2	went to Simon Peter and the other disciple	5
	20: 3	Then Peter and the other disciple set out	5
	20: 4	the other disciple outran Peter	5
	20: 8	the other disciple, who reached the tomb first	5
	20:12	one at the head and the other at the feet.	10
	20:25	the other disciples told him	5
	20:30	Now Jesus did many other signs	5
	21: 2	sons of Zebedee, and two others of his disciples.	5
	21: 8	the other disciples came in the boat	5
Act	2: 4	began to speak in other languages	13
	2:13	others sneered and said	13
	2:37	said to Peter and to the other apostles	17
	2:40	he testified with many other arguments and exhorted	13
	4:12	no other name under heaven given among mortals	13
	6: 9	others of those from Cilicia and Asia	1
	8: 7	many others who were paralyzed or lame were cured.	1
	9:39	showing tunics and other clothing	1
	13:16	"You Israelites, and others who fear God, listen.	18
	13:26	and others who fear God	18
	15: 2	Paul and Barnabas and some of the others	5
	15:17	so that all other peoples may seek the Lord	16
	15:35	and there, with many others, they taught	13
	17: 9	they had taken bail from Jason and the others	17
	17:18	Others said, "He seems to be a proclaimer	18
	17:32	some scoffed; but others said, "We will hear you	18
	17:34	a woman named Damaris, and others with them.	13
	23: 6	some were Sadducees and others were Pharisees	13
	27: 1	Paul and some other prisoners	13
	27:44	some on planks and others on pieces of the ship.	19
	28:24	while others refused to believe.	18
Rom	1:32	but even applaud others who practice them.	1
	2: 1	you have no excuse…when you judge others;	1
	2:21	that teach others, will you not teach yourself?	13
	2:29	person receives praise not from others but from God.	7
	13: 9	You shall not covet"; and any other commandment	13
	14: 5	while others judge all days to be alike.	19
	14:20	but it is wrong for you to make others fall	1
1Co	3:11	For no one can lay any foundation other	5
	6:13	God will destroy both one and the other.	20
	8:10	if others see you, who possess knowledge, eating	21
	9: 2	If I am not an apostle to others,	5
	9: 5	as do the other apostles and the brothers	17
	9:12	If others share this rightful claim on you	5
	9:27	so that after proclaiming to others I myself	5
	10:24	your own advantage, but that of the other.	13
	10:29	I mean the other's conscience, not your own.	13

	14: 2	speak in a tongue do not speak to other people	1
	14: 3	those who prophesy speak to other people	1
	14:19	in order to instruct others	5
	14:29	let the others weigh what is said.	5
	15:37	perhaps of wheat or of some other grain.	17
	16:12	to visit you with the other brothers	1
2Co	1:13	we write you nothing other than what you can read	5
	2:16	to the other a fragrance from life to life.	19
	5:11	we try to persuade others;	7
	8: 8	your love against the earnestness of others.	13
	8:13	should be relief for others and pressure on you	5
	8:21	also in the sight of others.	7
	9:13	your sharing with them and with all others	1
	10:15	We do not boast...in the labors of others;	6
	11: 8	I robbed other churches by accepting support	5
	12:13	worse off than the other churches	17
	13: 2	who sinned previously and all the others	17
Gal	1:19	I did not see any other apostle	13
	2:13	the other Jews joined him in this hypocrisy	17
	4:22	one by a slave woman and the other by a free woman.	10
	4:23	the other, the child of the free woman,	9
Php	1:15	but others from goodwill.	21
	1:17	the others proclaim Christ out of selfish ambition	18
	2: 3	regard others as better than yourselves.	4
	2: 4	but to the interests of others.	13
1Th	2: 6	whether from you or from others	5
	4:13	you may not grieve as others do who have no hope.	17
	5: 6	So then let us not fall asleep as others do	17
	5:11	encourage one another and build up each other	10
1Ti	5:22	and do not participate in the sins of others;	6
	5:24	the sins of others follow them there.	21
2Ti	2: 2	who will be able to teach others as well.	13
	3:13	bad to worse, deceiving others and being deceived.	1
Heb	7: 8	In the one case...in the other	11
	7:20	for others who became priests took their office	18
	7:27	Unlike the other high priests, he has no need	1
	8:11	shall not teach...say to each other	2
	11:35	Others were tortured, refusing to accept release	5
	11:36	Others suffered mocking and flogging	13
Jas	5:12	do not swear...by any other oath	5
2Pe	3:16	twist...as they do the other scriptures.	17
Jde	1:23	save others by snatching them out of the fire;	19
	1:23	have mercy on still others with fear	19
Rev	8:13	woe...at the blasts of the other trumpets	17
	17:10	one is living, and the other has not yet come;	5

other person

1. ἕτερος, *heteros, 2283*

1Co	14:17	the other person is not built up.	1

other thing

1. ἄλλος, *allos, 257*
2. λοιπός, *loipos, 3370*
3. παρεκτός, *parektos, 4211*

Mrk	4:19	and the desire for other things	2
Jhn	21:25	there are also many other things that Jesus did;	1
1Co	11:34	About the other things I will give instructions	2
2Co	11:28	And, besides other things	3

other woman

1. λοιπός, *loipos, 3370*

Lke	24:10	and the other women with them who told this	1

otherwise *See also* teach otherwise

1. ἄλλος, *allos, 257*
2. εἰ + δέ + μή, *ei + de + mē, 1623 + 1254 + 3590*
3. εἰ + δέ + μή + γέ, *ei + de + mē + ge, 1623 + 1254 + 3590 + 1145*
4. ἐπεί, *epei, 2075*
5. ἐπεί + ἄρα, *epei + ara, 2075 + 726*
6. ἵνα + μήποτε, *hina + mēpote, 2671 + 3607*
7. μή + πώς, *mē + pōs, 3590 + 4803*
8. μήποτε, *mēpote, 3607*

Mat	9:17	otherwise, the skins burst, and the wine is spilled	3
	27:64	otherwise his disciples may go and steal him away	8
Mrk	2:21	otherwise, the patch pulls away from it	2
	2:22	otherwise, the wine will burst the skins	2
Lke	5:36	otherwise the new will be torn	3
	5:37	otherwise the new wine will burst the skins	3
	14:29	Otherwise, when he has laid a foundation	6

Rom	11: 6	otherwise grace would no longer be grace.	4
	11:22	otherwise you also will be cut off.	4
1Co	7:14	Otherwise, your children would be unclean	5
	14:16	Otherwise, if you say a blessing with the spirit	4
	15:29	Otherwise, what will those people do	4
2Co	9: 4	otherwise, if some Macedonians come with me	7
Gal	5:10	confident...that you will not think otherwise.	1
Heb	10: 2	Otherwise, would they not have ceased	4

ought

1. Contextual: Not in Greek
2. δεῖ, *dei, 1256*
3. ὀφείλω, *opheilō, 4053*
4. χρή, *chrē, 5973*

Mat	23:23	these you ought to have practiced	2
	25:27	Then you ought to have invested my money	2
Mrk	13:14	set up where it ought not to be	2
Lke	11:42	these you ought to have practiced	2
	12:12	what you ought to say."	2
	13:14	six days on which work ought to be done;	2
	13:16	ought not this woman...be set free from this	2
	17:10	we have done only what we ought	3
Jhn	13:14	you also ought to wash one another's feet.	3
	19: 7	according to that law he ought to die	3
Act	17:29	ought not to think that the deity is like gold	3
	19:36	you ought to be quiet and do nothing rash.	2
	24:19	they ought to be here before you	2
	25:24	shouting that he ought not to live any longer.	2
	26: 9	I...was convinced that I ought to do many things	2
Rom	8:26	for we do not know how to pray as we ought	2
	12: 3	more highly than you ought to think	2
	15: 1	ought to put up with the failings of the weak	3
	15:27	they ought also to be of service to them	3
1Co	11: 7	For a man ought not to have his head veiled	3
	11:10	a woman ought to have a symbol of authority	3
2Co	12:14	children ought not to lay up for their parents	3
Eph	5:24	so also wives ought to be, in everything	1
Col	4: 6	you may know how you ought to answer everyone.	2
1Th	4: 1	how you ought to live and to please God	2
2Th	3: 7	you yourselves know how you ought to imitate us;	2
1Ti	3:15	you may know how one ought to behave	2
2Ti	2: 6	ought to have the first share of the crops.	2
Heb	5:12	For though by this time you ought to be teachers	3
Jas	3:10	My brothers and sisters, this ought not to be so.	4
	4:15	Instead you ought to say, "If the Lord wishes	1
2Pe	3:11	what sort of persons ought you to be	2
1Jn	2: 6	ought to walk just as he walked.	3
	3:16	we ought to lay down our lives for one another.	3
	4:11	we also ought to love one another.	3
3Jn	1: 8	Therefore we ought to support such people	3

our Lord come

1. μαράνα θά, *marana tha, 3448*

1Co	16:22	Our Lord, come!	1

ourselves Not Indexed

out *See also* blot out, break out, bring out, call out, carry out, carry out fully, cast out, clean out, come out, cry out, drag out, draw out, drive out, find out, flee out, get out, give out, go out, go out of one's mind, gush out, hire out, hold out, lead out, leave out, let out, lift out, out of *consideration*, out of *here*, out of one's *mind*, out of *pity*, out of *place*, out of the *synagogue*, out of *trouble*, point out, point out a fault, pour out, pour out as a libation, pull out, put out, put out of joint, put out of the synagogue, reach out, root out utterly, rush out, seek out, send out, set out, shout out, speak out boldly, step out, strain out, stretch out, take out, tear out, throw out, tire out, tread out grain, try out, try to find out, turn out, watch out, way out, wear out, wipe out, work out

1. ἀπό, *apo, 608*
2. διά, *dia, 1328*
3. ἐκ, *ek, 1666*
4. ἐκτός, *ektos, 1760*
5. ἔμπροσθεν, *emprosthen, 1869*
6. ἐν, *en, 1877*
7. ἔξω, *exō, 2032*

    8. ἔξωθεν, *exōthen, 2033*
    9. χωρίς, *chōris, 6006*

Mat	2:15	"Out of Egypt I have called my son."	3
	5:13	but is thrown out and trampled under foot.	7
	7: 4	'Let me take the speck out of your eye,'	3
	7: 5	hypocrite, first take the log out of your own eye	3
	7: 5	to take the speck out of your neighbor's eye.	3
	8:28	two demoniacs coming out of the tombs met him.	3
	12:34	For out of the abundance of the heart	3
	12:35	brings good things out of a good treasure	3
	12:35	brings evil things out of an evil treasure.	3
	12:43	"When the unclean spirit has gone out of a person	1
	13:41	and they will collect out of his kingdom	3
	13:48	but threw out the bad.	7
	13:52	master of a household who brings out of his treasure	3
	14:29	He said, "Come." So Peter got out of the boat	1
	15:11	what comes out of the mouth that defiles."	3
	15:18	what comes out of the mouth	3
	15:19	For out of the heart come evil intentions, murder	3
	17:18	Jesus rebuked the demon, and it came out of him	1
	21:16	'Out of the mouths of infants and nursing babies	3
	21:17	He left them, went out of the city to Bethany	7
	21:39	they seized him, threw him out of the vineyard	7
	23:13	you lock people out of the kingdom of heaven	5
	24: 1	Jesus came out of the temple and was going away	1
	26:75	he went out and wept bitterly.	7
	27:18	For he realized that it was out of jealousy	2
	27:53	After his resurrection they came out of the tombs	3
Mrk	1:10	just as he was coming up out of the water	3
	1:25	"Be silent, and come out of him!"	3
	1:26	the unclean spirit…came out of him.	3
	1:45	but stayed out in the country.	7
	5: 2	when he had stepped out of the boat	3
	5: 2	a man out of the tombs with an unclean spirit	3
	5: 8	"Come out of the man, you unclean spirit!"	3
	5:10	not to send them out of the country.	7
	6:54	When they got out of the boat	3
	7:15	the things that come out are what defile."	3
	7:20	what comes out of a person that defiles.	3
	7:26	begged him to cast the demon out of her daughter.	3
	8:23	led him out of the village;	7
	9:25	come out of him, and never enter him again!"	3
	11:19	Jesus and his disciples went out of the city.	7
	12: 8	and threw him out of the vineyard.	7
	12:44	have contributed out of their abundance;	3
	12:44	out of her poverty has put in everything she had	3
	13: 1	As he came out of the temple	3
	14:68	he went out into the forecourt.	7
	15:10	For he realized that it was out of jealousy	2
	15:46	a tomb that had been hewn out of the rock.	3
Lke	4:29	They got up, drove him out of the town	7
	4:35	"Be silent, and come out of him!"	1
	4:35	he came out of him without having done him any harm.	1
	4:41	Demons also came out of many	1
	5: 2	the fishermen had gone out of them	1
	6:42	first take the log out of your own eye	3
	6:45	person out of the good treasure of the heart	3
	6:45	evil person out of evil treasure produces evil;	3
	6:45	out of the abundance of the heart	3
	8: 3	who provided for them out of their resources.	3
	8:29	the unclean spirit to come out of the man.	1
	8:33	Then the demons came out of the man	1
	11:24	the unclean spirit has gone out of a person	1
	13:28	and you yourselves thrown out.	7
	20:15	they threw him out of the vineyard and killed him.	7
	21: 4	have contributed out of their abundance	3
	21: 4	she out of her poverty has put in all she had	3
	22:62	he went out and wept bitterly.	7
	24:50	Then he led them out as far as Bethany	7
Jhn	1:46	"Can anything good come out of Nazareth?"	3
	2:15	he drove all of them out of the temple	3
	7:38	'Out of the believer's heart shall flow rivers	3
	8:59	Jesus hid himself and went out of the temple.	3
	9:34	And they drove him out.	7
	9:35	Jesus heard that they had driven him out	7
	10:28	No one will snatch them out of my hand.	3
	10:29	no one can snatch it out of the Father's hand.	3
	11:43	"Lazarus, come out!"	7
	12:17	when he called Lazarus out of the tomb	3
	12:31	now the ruler of this world will be driven out.	7
	15:19	I have chosen you out of the world	3

	17:15	not asking you to take them out of the world	3
	18:29	Pilate went out to them and said	7
	19: 4	Pilate went out again and said to them	7
	19: 4	"Look, I am bringing him out to you"	7
	19: 5	Jesus came out, wearing the crown of thorns	7
	20: 2	"They have taken the Lord out of the tomb"	3
Act	1: 9	a cloud took him out of their sight.	1
	3:23	will be utterly rooted out of the people.'	3
	7:58	Then they dragged him out of the city	7
	8:39	When they came up out of the water	3
	12:17	how the Lord had brought him out of the prison.	3
	13:17	with uplifted arm he led them out of it.	3
	13:50	and drove them out of their region.	1
	14:19	they stoned Paul and dragged him out of the city	7
	16:18	"I order you…to come out of her."	1
	19:16	they fled out of the house naked and wounded.	3
	21:30	seized Paul and dragged him out of the temple	7
	22:18	'Hurry and get out of Jerusalem quickly	3
Rom	9:21	to make out of the same lump one object for special	3
	11:26	it is written, "Out of Zion will come the Deliverer;	3
1Co	5:10	since you would then need to go out of the world.	3
2Co	2: 4	For I wrote you out of much distress	3
	4: 6	the God who said, "Let light shine out of darkness,"	3
	12: 2	whether in the body or out of the body	4
	12: 3	whether in the body or out of the body	9
Eph	2: 4	out of the great love with which he loved us	2
	4:29	Let no evil talk come out of your mouths	3
	5:21	out of reverence for Christ.	6
Php	1:16	These proclaim Christ out of love	3
	1:17	the others proclaim Christ out of selfish ambition	3
Heb	8: 9	to lead them out of the land of Egypt;	3
	11:34	won strength out of weakness	1
1Pe	2: 9	called you out of darkness into…light.	3
2Pe	3: 5	an earth was formed out of water and by means of water	3
1Jn	4:18	but perfect love casts out fear;	7
Jde	1: 5	once for all saved a people out of the land of Egypt	3
	1:23	save others by snatching them out of the fire;	3
Rev	3: 5	I will not blot your name out of the book of life;	3
	3:12	the temple of my God; you will never go out of it.	7
	3:12	city…that comes down from my God out of heaven	3
	3:16	I am about to spit you out of my mouth.	3
	7: 4	sealed out of every tribe of the people of Israel:	3
	7:14	they who have come out of the great ordeal;	3
	9:17	and smoke and sulfur came out of their mouths.	3
	9:18	smoke and sulfur coming out of their mouths.	3
	11: 2	court outside the temple; leave that out	8
	13: 1	I saw a beast rising out of the sea	3
	13:11	I saw another beast that rose out of the earth;	3
	14:15	Another angel came out of the temple, calling	3
	14:17	another angel came out of the temple in heaven	3
	15: 6	out of the temple came the seven angels	3
	16:17	and a loud voice came out of the temple	3
	18: 4	"Come out of her, my people	3
	21: 2	new Jerusalem, coming down out of heaven from God	3
	21:10	Jerusalem coming down out of heaven from God.	3

outcome

    1. ἔκβασις, *ekbasis, 1676*
    2. τέλος, *telos, 5465*

Heb	13: 7	consider the outcome of their way of life	1
1Pe	1: 9	you are receiving the outcome of your faith	2

outcry

    1. ἐπιφωνέω, *epiphōneō, 2215*

Act 22:24 to find out the reason for this outcry against him.   1

outdo

    1. προηγέομαι, *proēgeomai, 4605*

Rom 12:10 outdo one another in showing honor.   1

outer   *See also* outer *robe*

    1. ἔξω, *exō, 2032*
    2. ἐξώτερος, *exōteros, 2035*
    3. πυλών, *pylōn, 4784*

Mat	8:12	heirs…will be thrown into the outer darkness	2
	22:13	and throw him into the outer darkness	2
	25:30	throw him into the outer darkness	2
Act	12:13	When he knocked at the outer gate,	3
2Co	4:16	Even though our outer nature is wasting away	1

outrage

1. ἐνυβρίζω, *enybrizō, 1964*

Heb 10:29 outraged the Spirit of grace?   1

outrun

1. προτρέχω, *protrechō, 4731*

Jhn 20: 4 the other disciple outran Peter   1

outside   *See also* go outside, just outside, outside one's
control, outside the *law,* put outside

1. ἐκτός, *ektos, 1760*
2. ἔξω, *exō, 2032*
3. ἔξωθεν, *exōthen, 2033*
4. κἀκεῖθεν, *kakeithen, 2796*

Mat	12:46 his mother and his brothers were standing outside	2
	12:47 are standing outside, wanting to speak to you."	2
	23:25 you clean the outside of the cup	3
	23:26 so that the outside also may become clean.	1
	23:27 which on the outside look beautiful	3
	23:28 you also on the outside look righteous to others	3
	26:69 Now Peter was sitting outside in the courtyard.	2
Mrk	3:31 standing outside, they sent to him and called	2
	3:32 mother and your brothers and sisters are outside	2
	4:11 for those outside, everything comes in parables;	2
	7:15 there is nothing outside a person	3
	7:18 goes into a person from outside cannot defile	3
	11: 4 near a door, outside in the street.	2
Lke	1:10 whole assembly of the people was praying outside.	2
	8:20 your brothers are standing outside	2
	11:39 "Now you Pharisees clean the outside of the cup	3
	11:40 Did not the one who made the outside	3
	11:53 When he went outside,	4
	13:25 begin to stand outside and to knock at the door	2
	13:33 for a prophet to be killed outside of Jerusalem.'	2
Jhn	18:16 but Peter was standing outside at the gate.	2
	19:13 he brought Jesus outside	2
	20:11 Mary stood weeping outside the tomb.	2
Act	5:34 ordered the men to be put outside for a short time.	2
	9:40 Peter put all of them outside, and then he knelt	2
	16:13 we went outside the gate by the river	2
	16:30 brought them outside and said	2
	21: 5 escorted us outside the city.	2
1Co	5:12 For what have I to do with judging those outside?	2
	5:13 God will judge those outside.	2
	6:18 Every sin...is outside the body;	1
Heb	13:11 are burned outside the camp.	2
	13:12 Jesus also suffered outside the city gate	2
	13:13 Let us then go to him outside the camp	2
Rev	11: 2 do not measure the court outside the temple;	3
	14:20 the wine press was trodden outside the city	3
	22:15 Outside are the dogs and sorcerers	2

outsider

1. Contextual: Not in Greek
2. ἔξω, *exō, 2032*
3. ἔξωθεν, *exōthen, 2033*
4. ἰδιώτης, *idiōtēs, 2626*

1Co	14:16 how can anyone in the position of an outsider say	4
	14:16 since the outsider does not know what you are saying?	1
	14:23 outsiders or unbelievers enter	4
	14:24 an unbeliever or outsider who enters	4
Col	4: 5 Conduct yourselves wisely toward outsiders	2
1Th	4:12 that you may behave properly toward outsiders	2
1Ti	3: 7 Moreover, he must be well thought of by outsiders	3

outward   *See* outward *appearance,* outward *form*

outwardly

1. ἐν + ὁ + φανερός, *en + ho + phaneros, 1877 + 3836 + 5745*
2. ἔξωθεν, *exōthen, 2033*

Rom	2:28 For a person is not a Jew who is one outwardly	1
1Pe	3: 3 Do not adorn yourselves outwardly	2

outwit

1. πλεονεκτέω, *pleonekteō, 4430*

2Co 2:11 so that we may not be outwitted by Satan;   1

oven

1. κλίβανος, *klibanos, 3106*

Mat	6:30 alive today and tomorrow is thrown into the oven	1
Lke	12:28 tomorrow is thrown into the oven	1

over[1]   *See also* authority over, beat over the head, bend
over, boast over, burn over, call over, come over, cross
over, dominion over, give over, go over, hand over, keep
watch over, leave over, lord it over, pass over, run over,
think over, triumph over, turn over, tyrant over, win over,
wrangle over words

1. εἰς, *eis, 1650*
2. ἐν, *en, 1877*
3. ἐπάνω, *epanō, 2062*
4. ἐπί, *epi, 2093*
5. κατά, *kata, 2848*
6. ὑπέρ, *hyper, 5642*

Mat	2: 9 it stopped over the place where the child	3
	18:13 if he finds it...he rejoices over it	4
	18:13 he rejoices...more than over the ninety-nine	4
	27:37 Over his head they put the charge against him	3
	27:45 darkness came over the whole land	4
Mrk	15:33 darkness came over the whole land	4
Lke	1:33 He will reign over the house of Jacob forever	4
	1:65 Fear came over all their neighbors	4
	2: 8 keeping watch over their flock by night.	4
	4:25 there was a severe famine over all the land;	4
	4:39 he stood over her and rebuked the fever	3
	9: 1 gave them power and authority over all demons	4
	10:19 authority...over all the power of the enemy;	4
	11:44 people walk over them without realizing it."	3
	12:14 who set me to be a judge or arbitrator over you?"	4
	15: 7 more joy in heaven over one sinner who repents	4
	15: 7 than over ninety-nine righteous persons	4
	15:10 there is joy...over one sinner who repents."	4
	19:14 'We do not want this man to rule over us.'	4
	19:19 'And you, rule over five cities.'	3
	19:27 who did not want me to be king over them	4
	19:41 he came near and saw the city, he wept over it	4
	23:38 There was also an inscription over him	4
	23:44 darkness came over the whole land until three	4
Jhn	14:30 He has no power over me;	2
	19:11 "You would have no power over me	5
Act	7:10 who appointed him ruler over Egypt	4
	7:10 appointed him ruler...over all his household.	4
	7:18 king who had not known Joseph ruled over Egypt.	4
	7:27 'Who made you a ruler and a judge over us?	4
	8: 2 made loud lamentation over him.	4
	11:19 the persecution that took place over Stephen	4
	11:28 there would be a severe famine over all the world;	4
	13:11 Immediately mist and darkness came over him	4
	15:17 all the Gentiles over whom my name has been called.	4
	19:13 use the name...over those who had evil spirits	4
Rom	5:14 even over those whose sins were not like	4
	9: 5 Messiah, who is over all, God blessed forever.	4
	16:19 is known to all, so that I rejoice over you	4
2Co	3:13 not like Moses, who put a veil over his face	4
	3:15 a veil lies over their minds;	4
Eph	1:22 has made him the head over all things	6
	3:13 not lose heart over my sufferings for you;	2
Php	2:17 over the sacrifice and the offering of your faith	4
Heb	3: 6 Christ, however, was faithful over God's house as a son	4
	10:21 a great priest over the house of God	4
	11:21 "bowing in worship over the top of his staff."	4
	13:17 for they are keeping watch over your souls	6
Jas	2: 7 the excellent name that was invoked over you?	4
	5:14 and have them pray over them, anointing them	4
Rev	2:26 I will give authority over the nations;	4
	6: 8 they were given authority over a fourth of the earth	4
	9:11 They have as king over them the angel	4
	10: 1 mighty angel...with a rainbow over his head;	4
	11: 6 authority over the waters to turn them into blood	4
	11:10 gloat over them and celebrate and exchange	4
	13: 7 It was given authority over every tribe	4
	14:16 the one...on the cloud swung his sickle over the earth	4
	14:18 the angel who has authority over fire	4
	14:19 So the angel swung his sickle over the earth	1
	16: 9 God, who had authority over these plagues	4
	17:18 the great city that rules over the kings	4
	18: 9 the kings...will weep and wail over her	4
	18:20 Rejoice over her, O heaven, you saints and apostles	4
	20: 3 into the pit, and locked and sealed it over him	3

Rev 20: 6 Over these the second death has no power   4
     20: 9 They marched up over the breadth of the earth   4

over²

1. διαγίνομαι, *diaginomai, 1335*
2. μετά, *meta, 3552*
3. συντελέω, *synteleō, 5334*

Mrk 16: 1 When the sabbath was over   1
Lke 4: 2 when they were over, he was famished.   3
Jhn 4:43 the two days were over, he went from that place   2

nearly over

1. κλίνω, *klinō, 3111*

Lke 24:29 almost evening and the day is now nearly over."   1

over there

1. ἐκεῖ, *ekei, 1695*

Mat 26:36 "Sit here while I go over there and pray."   1

overboard *See* jump overboard, throw overboard, throw overboard cargo

overcome

1. καταλαμβάνω, *katalambanō, 2898*
2. καταφέρω, *katapherō, 2965*
3. μέγας, *megas, 3489*
4. νικάω, *nikaō, 3771*
5. σφόδρα, *sphodra, 5379*

Mat 17: 6 fell to the ground and were overcome by fear.   5
Mrk 5:42 At this they were overcome with amazement.   3
Jhn 1: 5 and the darkness did not overcome it.   1
Act 20: 9 Overcome by sleep, he fell to the ground   2
Rom 12:21 Do not be overcome by evil   4
     12:21 but overcome evil with good.   4
1Jn 2:14 and you have overcome the evil one.   4

overcome with amazement

1. ἐξίστημι + ἔκστασις, *existēmi + ekstasis, 2014 + 1749*

Mrk 5:42 At this they were overcome with amazement.   1

overcome with awe

1. ἐκθαμβέω, *ekthambeō, 1701*

Mrk 9:15 they were immediately overcome with awe   1

overflow

1. περισσεύω, *perisseuō, 4355*
2. ὑπερπλεονάζω, *hyperpleonazō, 5670*

2Co 8: 2 overflowed in a wealth of generosity   1
     9:12 also overflows with many thanksgivings to God.   1
Php 1: 9 prayer, that your love may overflow more and more   1
1Ti 1:14 the grace of our Lord overflowed for me   2

overhear

1. παρακούω, *parakouō, 4159*

Mrk 5:36 But overhearing what they said   1

overjoyed

1. ὑπερπερισσεύω + χαρά, *hyperperisseuō + chara, 5668 + 5915*
2. χαίρω + λίαν, *chairō + lian, 5897 + 3336*
3. χαρά, *chara, 5915*

Act 12:14 she was so overjoyed that, instead of opening   3
2Co 7: 4 I am overjoyed in all our affliction.   1
2Jn 1: 4 I was overjoyed to find some of your children   2
3Jn 1: 3 I was overjoyed when some of the friends arrived   2

overlay

1. περικαλύπτω, *perikalyptō, 4328*

Heb 9: 4 the ark...overlaid on all sides with gold   1

overlook

1. ἐπιλανθάνομαι, *epilanthanomai, 2140*
2. ὑπεροράω, *hyperoraō, 5666*

Act 17:30 God has overlooked the times of human ignorance   2
Heb 6:10 For God is not unjust; he will not overlook your work   1

overpower

1. ἡττάομαι, *hēttaomai, 2487*

2. ἰσχύω, *ischyō, 2710*
3. νικάω, *nikaō, 3771*

Lke 11:22 one stronger than he attacks him and overpowers   3
Act 19:16 mastered them all, and so overpowered them   2
2Pe 2:20 again entangled in them and overpowered   1

overseer *See also* position of overseer

1. ἐπίσκοπος, *episkopos, 2176*

Act 20:28 of which the Holy Spirit has made you overseers   1

overshadow

1. ἐπισκιάζω, *episkiazō, 2173*
2. κατασκιάζω, *kataskiazō, 2944*

Mat 17: 5 suddenly a bright cloud overshadowed them   1
Mrk 9: 7 a cloud overshadowed them   1
Lke 1:35 the power of the Most High will overshadow you;   1
     9:34 a cloud came and overshadowed them;   1
Heb 9: 5 cherubim of glory overshadowing the mercy seat.   2

oversight *See* exercise oversight

overstep

1. ὑπερεκτείνω, *hyperekteinō, 5657*

2Co 10:14 For we were not overstepping our limits   1

overtake

1. καταλαμβάνω, *katalambanō, 2898*
2. λαμβάνω, *lambanō, 3284*
3. φθάνω, *phthanō, 5777*

Jhn 12:35 so that the darkness may not overtake you.   1
1Co 10:13 No testing has overtaken you   2
1Th 2:16 God's wrath has overtaken them at last.   3

overthrow

1. καταλύω, *katalyō, 2907*
2. καταργέω, *katargeō, 2934*

Act 5:39 you will not be able to overthrow them   1
Rom 3:31 Do we then overthrow the law by this faith?   2

overturn

1. ἀνατρέπω, *anatrepō, 426*
2. καταστρέφω, *katastrephō, 2951*

Mat 21:12 he overturned the tables of the money changers   2
Mrk 11:15 he overturned the tables of the money changers   2
Jhn 2:15 and overturned their tables.   1

overwhelm

1. ἐπιπίπτω, *epipiptō, 2158*
2. καταπίνω, *katapinō, 2927*
3. σωρεύω, *sōreuō, 5397*
4. χαίρω + μέγας + σφόδρα, *chairō + megas + sphodra, 5897 + 3489 + 5379*

Mat 2:10 star had stopped, they were overwhelmed with joy.   4
Lke 1:12 he was terrified; and fear overwhelmed him.   1
2Co 2: 7 so that he may not be overwhelmed by excessive sorrow.   2
2Ti 3: 6 captive silly women, overwhelmed by their sins   3

owe

1. ὀφειλέτης, *opheiletēs, 4050*
2. ὀφείλω, *opheilō, 4053*
3. προσοφείλω, *prosopheilō, 4695*

Mat 18:24 one who owed him ten thousand talents was brought   1
     18:28 slaves who owed him a hundred denarii   2
     18:28 'Pay what you owe.'   2
Lke 7:41 owed five hundred denarii, and the other fifty   2
     16: 5 the first, 'How much do you owe my master?'   2
     16: 7 he asked another, 'And how much do you owe?'   2
Rom 13: 8 Owe no one anything, except to love one another;   2
     15:27 and indeed they owe it to them;   1
Phm 1:18 If he has wronged you in any way, or owes you anything   2
     1:19 say nothing about your owing me even your own self.   3

own¹ *See also* make one's own, own *country*, own *hand*

1. Contextual: Not in Greek
2. εἰμί, *eimi, 1639*
3. ἔχω, *echō, 2400*
4. κτήτωρ, *ktētōr, 3230*

Mrk 10:21 sell what you own, and give the money to the poor   3

Lke	18:22	Sell all that you own and distribute the money	3
Act	4:32	everything they owned was held in common.	1
	4:34	as many as owned lands or houses	4
	21:11	bind the man who owns this belt	2

own[2]

1. αὐτός, *autos, 899*
2. ἴδιος, *idios, 2625*
3. περιούσιος, *periousios, 4342*
4. περιποίησις, *peripoiēsis, 4348*

1Co	7:35	I say this for your own benefit	1
Eph	1:14	toward redemption as God's own people	4
Tit	2:14	purify for himself a people of his own	3
Heb	7:27	to offer sacrifices day after day, first for his own sins	2
	9:12	with…his own blood	2
	13:12	sanctify the people by his own blood.	2
Jas	1:14	one is tempted by one's own desire, being lured	2
1Pe	2: 9	you are…a holy nation, God's own people	4
2Pe	1: 3	called us by his own glory and goodness.	2
	1:20	a matter of one's own interpretation	2
	2:16	was rebuked for his own transgression;	2
	2:22	"The dog turns back to its own vomit,"	2
	3: 3	scoffing and indulging their own lusts	2
	3:16	the ignorant…twist to their own destruction	2
	3:17	not carried away…and lose your own stability.	2

not one's own

1. ἀλλότριος, *allotrios, 259*

Heb	9:25	enters…with blood that is not his own;	1

on one's own

1. ἀπό, *apo, 608*
2. ἐκ, *ek, 1666*

Jhn	5:19	the Son can do nothing on his own	1
	5:30	"I can do nothing on my own.	1
	7:17	whether I am speaking on my own.	1
	7:18	Those who speak on their own	1
	7:28	I have not come on my own.	1
	8:28	I do nothing on my own	1
	8:42	I did not come on my own, but he sent me.	1
	11:51	He did not say this on his own	1
	12:49	for I have not spoken on my own	2
	14:10	I do not speak on my own;	1
	16:13	for he will not speak on his own	1
	18:34	Jesus answered, "Do you ask this on your own	1

one's own

1. αὐτός, *autos, 899*
2. ἑαυτοῦ, *heautou, 1571*
3. ἴδιος, *idios, 2625*
4. κατά, *kata, 2848*
5. οὗτος, *houtos, 4047*

Mat	2:12	they left for their own country by another	1
	6:34	for tomorrow will bring worries of its own.	2
	9: 1	he crossed the sea and came to his own town.	3
	10:36	one's foes will be members of one's own household.	1
	13:57	in their own country and in their own house."	1
	27:31	put his own clothes on him.	1
	27:60	laid it in his own new tomb	1
Mrk	6: 4	among their own kin, and in their own house."	1
	6: 4	among their own kin, and in their own house."	1
	15:20	and put his own clothes on him.	1
Lke	2: 3	All went to their own towns to be registered.	2
	2:35	and a sword will pierce your own soul too."	1
	2:39	they returned to Galilee, to their own town	2
	6:41	do not notice the log in your own eye?	3
	6:44	for each tree is known by its own fruit.	2
	9:60	"Let the dead bury their own dead;	3
	10:34	Then he put him on his own animal	3
	16: 8	more shrewd in dealing with their own generation	2
	22:71	We have heard it ourselves from his own lips!"	1
Jhn	1:11	He came to what was his own	3
	1:11	and his own people did not accept him.	3
	4:44	a prophet has no honor in the prophet's own country).	3
	5:18	also calling God his own Father	3
	5:43	if another comes in his own name	3
	7:18	Those…seek their own glory;	3
	8:44	When he lies, he speaks according to his own nature	3
	10: 3	calls his own sheep by name and leads them out.	3
	10: 4	When he has brought out all his own	3

	10:12	not the shepherd and does not own the sheep	3
	13: 1	Having loved his own who were in the world	3
	15:19	the world would love you as its own.	3
Act	1: 7	that the Father has set by his own authority.	3
	1:25	to go to his own place."	3
	2: 8	each of us, in our own native language?	3
	3:12	by our own power or piety we had made him walk?	3
	13:36	served the purpose of God in his own generation	3
	14:16	allowed all the nations to follow their own ways;	1
	18:15	questions about words and names and your own law	4
	20:28	that he obtained with the blood of his own Son.	3
	20:34	worked with my own hands to support myself	5
	22:14	to see the Righteous One and to hear his own voice;	1
	25:19	disagreement…about their own religion	3
	28:30	He lived there two whole years at his own expense	3
Rom	2:15	to which their own conscience also bears witness;	1
	4:19	weaken in faith when he considered his own body	2
	8: 3	sending his own Son in the likeness of sinful	2
	8:32	He who did not withhold his own Son, but gave	3
	10: 3	and seeking to establish their own	3
	11:24	be grafted back into their own olive tree.	3
	14: 4	It is before their own lord that they stand	3
	14: 5	Let all be fully convinced in their own minds.	3
	16:18	such people…serve…their own appetites	2
1Co	4:12	we grow weary from the work of our own hands.	3
	6:19	and that you are not your own?	2
	7: 2	each man should have his own wife	2
	7: 2	and each woman her own husband.	3
	7: 4	wife does not have authority over her own body	3
	7: 4	husband does not have authority over his own body	3
	7:37	having his own desire under control	3
	7:37	determined in his own mind to keep her	3
	10:24	Do not seek your own advantage	2
	10:29	I mean the other's conscience, not your own.	2
	11:21	each of you goes ahead with your own supper	3
	13: 5	It does not insist on its own way;	2
	15:23	each in his own order: Christ the first fruits	3
	15:38	to each kind of seed its own body.	3
Gal	6: 4	All must test their own work;	2
	6: 5	For all must carry their own loads.	2
	6: 8	If you sow to your own flesh,	2
Eph	4:28	labor and work honestly with their own hands	3
	5:28	should love their wives as they do their own bodies.	2
	5:29	For no one ever hates his own body	2
Php	2: 4	Let each of you look not to your own interests	2
	2:12	work out your own salvation with fear	2
	2:21	All of them are seeking their own interests	2
1Th	2: 7	like a nurse tenderly caring for her own children.	2
	2: 8	share…also our own selves	2
	2:12	who calls you into his own kingdom and glory.	2
	2:14	you suffered…from your own compatriots	3
	4: 4	each one of you know how to control your own body	2
	4:11	to mind your own affairs	3
2Th	3:12	to earn their own living.	2
1Ti	3: 4	He must manage his own household well	3
	3: 5	does not know how to manage his own household	3
	5: 4	learn their religious duty to their own family	3
2Ti	1: 9	called us…according to his own purpose and grace	3
	4: 3	teachers to suit their own desires	3
Tit	1:12	one of them, their very own prophet, who said	3
Heb	6: 6	on their own they are crucifying again the Son of God	2
1Jn	3:12	Because his own deeds were evil	1
Jde	1: 6	the angels who did not keep their own position	2
	1:13	casting up the foam of their own shame;	2
	1:16	malcontents; they indulge their own lusts;	2
	1:18	scoffers, indulging their own ungodly lusts."	2

owner

1. κύριος, *kyrios, 3261*

Mat	20: 8	evening came, the owner of the vineyard said	1
	21:40	Now when the owner of the vineyard comes	1
Mrk	12: 9	What then will the owner of the vineyard do?	1
Lke	19:33	As they were untying the colt, its owners asked	1
	20:13	the owner of the vineyard said, 'What shall I do?	1
	20:15	will the owner of the vineyard do to them?	1
Act	16:16	brought her owners a great deal of money	1
	16:19	owners saw that their hope of making money was gone	1
Gal	4: 1	though they are the owners of all the property;	1

owner of the house

1. δεσπότης, *despotēs, 1305*

2. οἰκοδεσπότης, *oikodespotēs, 3867*

Mat	24:43	if the owner of the house had known	2
Mrk	14:14	he enters, say to the owner of the house	2
Lke	12:39	if the owner of the house had known at what hour	2
	13:25	When once the owner of the house has got up	2
	14:21	Then the owner of the house became angry	2
	22:11	say to the owner of the house, 'The teacher asks	2
2Ti	2:21	dedicated and useful to the owner of the house	1

owner of the ship

1. ναύκληρος, *nauklēros, 3729*

Act 27:11 to the pilot and to the owner of the ship   1

private ownership

1. ἴδιος, *idios, 2625*

Act 4:32 no one claimed private ownership of any possessions   1

ox

1. βοῦς, *bous, 1091*
2. μόσχος, *moschos, 3675*
3. ταῦρος, *tauros, 5436*

Mat	22: 4	my oxen and my fat calves have been slaughtered	3
Lke	13:15	Does not each of you on the sabbath untie his ox	1
	14: 5	a child or an ox that has fallen into a well	1
	14:19	Another said, 'I have bought five yoke of oxen	1
Act	14:13	brought oxen and garlands to the gates;	3
1Co	9: 9	not muzzle an ox while it is treading out the grain."	1
	9: 9	Is it for oxen that God is concerned?	1
1Ti	5:18	not muzzle an ox while it is treading out the grain,"	1
Rev	4: 7	the second living creature like an ox	2

P

pagan

1. Contextual: Not in Greek
2. ἔθνος, *ethnos, 1620*

1Co	5: 1	of a kind that is not found even among pagans;	2
	10:20	No, I imply that what pagans sacrifice	1
	12: 2	You know that when you were pagans	2

pain *See also* cause pain, have pain

1. βάσανος, *basanos, 992*
2. λυπέω, *lypeō, 3382*
3. λύπη, *lypē, 3383*
4. ὀδύνη, *odynē, 3850*
5. πόνος, *ponos, 4506*

Mat	4:24	with various diseases and pains, demoniacs	1
Jhn	16:20	your pain will turn into joy.	3
	16:21	When a woman is in labor, she has pain	3
	16:22	you have pain now; but I will see you again	3
2Co	2: 2	but the one whom I have pained?	2
	2: 3	so that when I came, I might not suffer pain	3
1Ti	6:10	pierced themselves with many pains.	4
1Pe	2:19	you endure pain while suffering unjustly.	3
Rev	16:11	cursed the God…because of their pains and sores	5
	21: 4	mourning and crying and pain will be no more	5

labor pains

1. συνωδίνω, *synōdinō, 5349*
2. ὠδίν, *ōdin, 6047*

Rom	8:22	the whole creation has been groaning in labor pains	1
1Th	5: 3	as labor pains come upon a pregnant woman	2

pain of childbirth

1. ὠδίνω, *ōdinō, 6048*

Gal 4:19 for whom I am again in the pain of childbirth   1

painful

1. λύπη, *lypē, 3383*
2. πονηρός, *ponēros, 4505*

2Co	2: 1	not to make you another painful visit.	1
Heb	12:11	discipline always seems painful rather than pleasant	1
Rev	16: 2	and a foul and painful sore came on those	2

pair

1. δύο, *dyo, 1545*
2. ζεῦγος, *zeugos, 2414*

Lke	2:24	"a pair of turtledoves or two young pigeons."	2
	10: 1	sent them on ahead of him in pairs	1

pair of scales

1. ζυγός, *zygos, 2433*

Rev 6: 5 Its rider held a pair of scales in his hand   1

palace *See also* courtyard of palace

1. Contextual: Not in Greek
2. αὐλή, *aulē, 885*
3. οἶκος, *oikos, 3875*

Mat	11: 8	those who wear soft robes are in royal palaces.	3
	26: 3	people gathered in the palace of the high priest	2
Lke	7:25	live in luxury are in royal palaces.	1

pale green

1. χλωρός, *chlōros, 5952*

Rev 6: 8 a pale green horse! Its rider's name was Death   1

palm tree *See also* palm *branch*

1. φοῖνιξ¹, *phoinix¹, 5836*

Jhn 12:13 they took branches of palm trees   1

Pamphylia

1. Παμφυλία, *Pamphylia, 4103*

Act	2:10	Phrygia and Pamphylia	1
	13:13	and came to Perga in Pamphylia.	1
	14:24	passed through Pisidia and came to Pamphylia.	1
	15:38	one who had deserted them in Pamphylia	1
	27: 5	the sea that is off Cilicia and Pamphylia	1

birth pang *See also* endure birth pangs

1. ὠδίν, *ōdin, 6047*
2. ὠδίνω, *ōdinō, 6048*

Mat	24: 8	all this is but the beginning of the birth pangs.	1
Mrk	13: 8	This is but the beginning of the birth pangs.	1
Rev	12: 2	and was crying out in birth pangs	2

paper

1. χάρτης, *chartēs, 5925*

2Jn 1:12 I would rather not use paper and ink;   1

Paphos

1. Πάφος, *Paphos, 4265*

Act	13: 6	had gone through the whole island as far as Paphos	1
	13:13	Paul and his companions set sail from Paphos	1

parable

1. παραβολή, *parabolē, 4130*

Mat	13: 3	he told them many things in parables, saying:	1
	13:10	"Why do you speak to them in parables?"	1
	13:13	The reason I speak to them in parables	1
	13:18	"Hear then the parable of the sower.	1
	13:24	He put before them another parable:	1
	13:31	He put before them another parable:	1
	13:33	He told them another parable:	1
	13:34	Jesus told the crowds all these things in parables;	1
	13:34	without a parable he told them nothing.	1
	13:35	"I will open my mouth to speak in parables;	1
	13:36	"Explain to us the parable of the weeds	1
	13:53	When Jesus had finished these parables	1
	15:15	Peter said to him, "Explain this parable to us."	1
	21:33	"Listen to another parable.	1
	21:45	priests and the Pharisees heard his parables	1
	22: 1	Once more Jesus spoke to them in parables, saying:	1
Mrk	3:23	spoke to them in parables	1
	4: 2	He began to teach them many things in parables	1
	4:10	asked him about the parables.	1
	4:11	for those outside, everything comes in parables;	1
	4:13	"Do you not understand this parable?	1
	4:13	Then how will you understand all the parables?	1
	4:30	what parable will we use for it?	1
	4:33	With many such parables he spoke the word	1
	4:34	he did not speak to them except in parables	1
	7:17	his disciples asked him about the parable.	1
	12: 1	he began to speak to them in parables.	1
	12:12	he had told this parable against them	1
Lke	5:36	He also told them a parable:	1
	6:39	He also told them a parable:	1

8: 4 he said in a parable: 1
8: 9 his disciples asked him what this parable meant.   1
8:10 to others I speak in parables   1
8:11 the parable is this: The seed is the word of God.   1
12:16 he told them a parable: "The land   1
12:41 telling this parable for us or for everyone?"   1
13: 6 he told this parable: "A man had a fig tree   1
14: 7 chose the places of honor, he told them a parable.   1
15: 3 So he told them this parable: 1
18: 1 Jesus told them a parable   1
18: 9 He also told this parable to some   1
19:11 he went on to tell a parable   1
20: 9 He began to tell the people this parable: 1
20:19 he had told this parable against them   1
21:29 he told them a parable: 1

paradise

1. παράδεισος, *paradeisos, 4137*

Lke 23:43 today you will be with me in Paradise."   1
2Co 12: 4 was caught up into Paradise and heard things   1
Rev   2: 7 the tree of life that is in the paradise of God.   1

paralytic

1. παραλυτικός, *paralytikos, 4166*

Mat 4:24 pains, demoniacs, epileptics, and paralytics   1
9: 2 he said to the paralytic, "Take heart, son;   1
9: 6 he then said to the paralytic—"Stand up   1
Mrk 2: 4 let down the mat on which the paralytic lay.   1
2: 5 he said to the paralytic   1
2: 9 Which is easier, to say to the paralytic   1
2:10 he said to the paralytic—   1

paralyze

1. ξηρός, *xēros, 3831*
2. παραλυτικός, *paralytikos, 4166*
3. παραλύω, *paralyō, 4168*

Mat 8: 6 "Lord, my servant is lying at home paralyzed   2
Lke 5:18 men came, carrying a paralyzed man on a bed.   3
5:24 he said to the one who was paralyzed—   3
Jhn 5: 3 many invalids—blind, lame, and paralyzed.   1
Act 8: 7 many others who were paralyzed or lame were cured.   3
9:33 bedridden for eight years, for he was paralyzed.   3

paralyzed man

1. παραλυτικός, *paralytikos, 4166*

Mat 9: 2 just then some people were carrying a paralyzed man   1
Mrk 2: 3 a paralyzed man, carried by four of them.   1

parchment

1. μεμβράνα, *membrana, 3521*

2Ti 4:13 also the books, and above all the parchments.   1

parent

1. Contextual: Not in Greek
2. γεννάω, *gennaō, 1164*
3. γονεύς, *goneus, 1204*
4. πατήρ, *patēr, 4252*
5. πρόγονος, *progonos, 4591*

Mat 10:21 children will rise against parents   3
Mrk 13:12 children will rise against parents   3
Lke 1:17 to turn the hearts of parents to their children   4
2:27 when the parents brought in the child Jesus   3
2:41 Now every year his parents went to Jerusalem   3
2:43 his parents did not know it.   3
2:48 When his parents saw him they were astonished;   1
8:56 Her parents were astounded;   3
18:29 house or wife or brothers or parents or children   3
21:16 You will be betrayed even by parents   3
Jhn 9: 2 who sinned, this man or his parents   3
9: 3 "Neither this man nor his parents sinned;   3
9:18 until they called the parents of the man   3
9:20 parents answered, "We know that this is our son   3
9:22 His parents said this because they were afraid   3
9:23 his parents said, "He is of age; ask him."   3
Rom 1:30 inventors of evil, rebellious toward parents   3
2Co 12:14 children ought not to lay up for their parents   3
12:14 parents for their children.   3
Eph 6: 1 Children, obey your parents in the Lord   3
Col 3:20 Children, obey your parents in everything   3

1Ti 5: 4 and make some repayment to their parents;   5
2Ti 3: 2 disobedient to their parents, ungrateful, unholy   3
Heb 11:23 was hidden by his parents for three months   4
12: 7 whom a parent does not discipline?   4
12: 9 we had human parents to discipline us   4
1Jn 5: 1 everyone who loves the parent loves the child.   2

Parmenas

1. Παρμενᾶς, *Parmenas, 4226*

Act 6: 5 Parmenas, and Nicolaus, a proselyte of Antioch.   1

part[1] *See also* take part

1. Contextual: Not in Greek
2. ἀπό, *apo, 608*
3. ἐκ, *ek, 1666*
4. μερίς, *meris, 3535*
5. μέρος, *meros, 3538*
6. παρά, *para, 4123*

Lke 10:42 Mary has chosen the better part   4
11:36 full of light, with no part of it in darkness   5
Jhn 2:24 Jesus on his part would not entrust himself to them   1
19:23 his clothes and divided them into four parts   5
Act 2:10 Egypt and the parts of Libya belonging to Cyrene   5
5: 2 brought only a part   5
5: 3 to keep back part of the proceeds of the land?   2
6: 4 we, for our part, will devote ourselves to prayer   1
8:21 You have no part or share in this   4
Rom 9:14 Is there injustice on God's part? By no means!   6
11:16 If the part of the dough offered as first fruits   1
11:25 a hardening has come upon part of Israel   5
1Co 12:15 that would not make it any less a part of the body.   3
12:16 that would not make it any less a part of the body.   3
13: 9 For we know only in part   5
13: 9 we prophesy only in part;   5
13:12 Now I know only in part; then I will know fully   5
2Co 1:14 as you have already understood us in part   5
8: 2 in a wealth of generosity on their part.   1
Eph 4: 9 descended into the lower parts of the earth?   5
4:16 as each part is working properly   5
Rev 2: 9 on the part of those who say that they are Jews   3
16:19 The great city was split into three parts   5

part[2]

1. ἀποσπάω, *apospaō, 685*
2. ἀποχωρίζω, *apochōrizō, 714*

Act 15:39 became so sharp that they parted company;   2
21: 1 When we had parted from them and set sail   1

part of the night

1. φυλακή, *phylakē, 5871*

Mat 24:43 in what part of the night the thief was coming   1

partake

1. μετέχω, *metechō, 3576*

1Co 10:17 we all partake of the one bread.   1
10:21 You cannot partake of the table of the Lord   1
10:30 If I partake with thankfulness   1

Parthian

1. Πάρθοι, *Parthoi, 4222*

Act 2: 9 Parthians, Medes, Elamites,   1

partial

1. ἐκ + μέρος, *ek + meros, 1666 + 3538*

1Co 13:10 the complete comes, the partial will come to an end.   1

partiality *See also* show partiality

1. πρόσκλισις, *prosklisis, 4680*
2. προσωπολήμπτης, *prosōpolēmptēs, 4720*
3. προσωπολημψία, *prosōpolēmpsia, 4721*
4. πρόσωπον, *prosōpon, 4725*

Mat 22:16 for you do not regard people with partiality   4
Mrk 12:14 for you do not regard people with partiality   4
Act 10:34 "I truly understand that God shows no partiality   2
Rom 2:11 For God shows no partiality.   3
Eph 6: 9 with him there is no partiality.   3
Col 3:25 there is no partiality.   3
1Ti 5:21 doing nothing on the basis of partiality.   1

without partiality

1. ἀδιάκριτος, *adiakritos, 88*

Jas   3:17 wisdom…is…without a trace of partiality   1

participant

1. κοινωνός, *koinōnos, 3128*

2Pe   1: 4 may become participants of the divine nature.   1

participate

1. κοινωνέω, *koinōneō, 3125*

1Ti   5:22 and do not participate in the sins of others;   1
2Jn   1:11 for to welcome is to participate in the evil   1

particular

1. ἴδιος, *idios, 2625*

1Co   7: 7 each has a particular gift from God   1

partner

1. Contextual: Not in Greek
2. κοινωνός, *koinōnos, 3128*
3. μέτοχος, *metochos, 3581*

Lke   5: 7 they signaled their partners   3
      5:10 sons of Zebedee, who were partners with Simon.   2
1Co   7:15 if the unbelieving partner separates,   1
     10:18 who eat the sacrifices partners in the altar?   2
     10:20 I do not want you to be partners with demons.   2
2Co   8:23 As for Titus, he is my partner and co-worker   2
Phm   1:17 if you consider me your partner   2
Heb   3: 1 brothers and sisters, holy partners in a heavenly calling 3
      3:14 For we have become partners of Christ   3
     10:33 sometimes being partners with those so treated.   2

partnership

1. μετοχή, *metochē, 3580*

2Co   6:14 what partnership is there between righteousness   1

one party

1. εἷς, *heis, 1651*

Gal   3:20 Now a mediator involves more than one party   1

paschal   *See* paschal *lamb*

pass   *See also* come to pass

1. ἀπέρχομαι, *aperchomai, 599*
2. διαβαίνω, *diabainō, 1329*
3. διαγίνομαι, *diaginomai, 1335*
4. διέρχομαι, *dierchomai, 1451*
5. ἔρχομαι, *erchomai, 2262*
6. μεταβαίνω, *metabainō, 3553*
7. παρέρχομαι, *parerchomai, 4216*
8. πάροδος, *parodos, 4227*
9. πίμπλημι, *pimplēmi, 4398*
10. πληρόω, *plēroō, 4444*

Mat   5:18 will pass from the law until all is accomplished   7
      8:28 so fierce that no one could pass that way.   7
     15:29 he passed along the Sea of Galilee   5
     26:39 if it is possible, let this cup pass from me   7
     26:42 if this cannot pass unless I drink it   7
Mrk 14:35 if it were possible, the hour might pass from him.   7
Lke   2:21 After eight days had passed, it was time   9
     16:26 so that those who might want to pass from here   2
     19: 4 he was going to pass that way.   4
Jhn   5:24 has passed from death to life.   6
Act   7:30 "Now when forty years had passed   10
      9:23 After some time had passed   10
     12:10 they had passed the first and the second guard   4
     24:27 After two years had passed   10
     25:13 After several days had passed   3
1Co 10: 1 all passed through the sea   4
     16: 7 I do not want to see you now just in passing   8
1Jn   3:14 We know that we have passed from death to life   6
Rev   9:12 The first woe has passed.   1
     11:14 The second woe has passed. The third woe   1

pass along

1. παράγω, *paragō, 4135*

Mrk   1:16 Jesus passed along the Sea of Galilee   1

pass away

1. ἀπέρχομαι, *aperchomai, 599*
2. παράγω, *paragō, 4135*
3. παρέρχομαι, *parerchomai, 4216*

Mat   5:18 until heaven and earth pass away, not one letter   3
     24:34 this generation will not pass away   3
     24:35 Heaven and earth will pass away   3
     24:35 but my words will not pass away.   3
Mrk 13:30 this generation will not pass away   3
     13:31 Heaven and earth will pass away   3
     13:31 my words will not pass away.   3
Lke 16:17 it is easier for heaven and earth to pass away   3
     21:32 this generation will not pass away   3
     21:33 Heaven and earth will pass away   3
     21:33 my words will not pass away.   3
1Co   7:31 the present form of this world is passing away.   2
2Co   5:17 everything old has passed away;   3
2Pe   3:10 then the heavens will pass away with a loud noise   3
1Jn   2: 8 because the darkness is passing away   2
      2:17 the world and its desire are passing away,   2
Rev 21: 1 first heaven and the first earth had passed away   1
     21: 4 for the first things have passed away."   1

pass by

1. παράγω, *paragō, 4135*
2. παραπορεύομαι, *paraporeuomai, 4182*
3. παρέρχομαι, *parerchomai, 4216*

Mat 20:30 When they heard that Jesus was passing by   1
     27:39 Those who passed by derided him   2
Mrk   6:48 He intended to pass them by.   3
     11:20 In the morning as they passed by   2
     15:29 Those who passed by derided him   2
Lke 18:37 They told him, "Jesus of Nazareth is passing by."   3
Act 16: 8 so, passing by Mysia, they went down to Troas.   3

pass by on the other side

1. ἀντιπαρέρχομαι, *antiparerchomai, 524*

Lke 10:31 when he saw him, he passed by on the other side.   1
     10:32 a Levite…passed by on the other side.   1

pass days

1. διάγω, *diagō, 1341*

Tit   3: 3 passing our days in malice and envy   1

pass judgment

1. κρίνω, *krinō, 3212*

Rom   2: 1 in passing judgment on another you condemn   1
     14: 3 abstain must not pass judgment on those who eat;   1
     14: 4 to pass judgment on servants of another?   1
     14:10 Why do you pass judgment on your brother or sister?   1
     14:13 therefore no longer pass judgment on one another   1

pass on

1. παραδίδωμι, *paradidōmi, 4140*

2Pe   2:21 the holy commandment that was passed on to them.   1

pass over

1. πάρεσις, *paresis, 4217*

Rom   3:25 he had passed over the sins previously committed;   1

pass through

1. διαβαίνω, *diabainō, 1329*
2. διέρχομαι, *dierchomai, 1451*
3. διοδεύω, *diodeuō, 1476*
4. παραπορεύομαι, *paraporeuomai, 4182*

Mrk   9:30 They went on…and passed through Galilee.   4
Lke   4:30 passed through the midst of them and went on his way.   2
     19: 1 He entered Jericho and was passing through   2
Act   8:40 as he was passing through the region, he proclaimed   2
     14:24 passed through Pisidia and came to Pamphylia.   2
     15: 3 they passed through both Phoenicia and Samaria   2
     17: 1 Paul and Silas had passed through Amphipolis   3
     19: 1 Paul passed through the interior regions   2
1Co 16: 5 visit you after passing through Macedonia   2
     16: 5 for I intend to pass through Macedonia   2
Heb   4:14 high priest who has passed through the heavens   2
     11:29 passed through the Red Sea as if it were dry land   1

passage

1. Contextual: Not in Greek
2. περιοχή, *periochē, 4343*

Jhn 19:37 again another passage of scripture says 1
Act 8:32 passage of the scripture that he was reading 2

passer-by

1. παράγω, *paragō, 4135*

Mrk 15:21 They compelled a passer-by, who was coming in 1

passion *See also* aflame with passion

1. ἐπιθυμία, *epithymia, 2123*
2. ὄρεξις, *orexis, 3979*
3. πάθημα, *pathēma, 4077*
4. πάθος, *pathos, 4079*

Rom 1:26 God gave them up to degrading passions. 4
     1:27 men...consumed with passion for one another. 2
     6:12 to make you obey their passions. 1
     7: 5 our sinful passions, aroused by the law 3
Gal 5:24 the flesh with its passions and desires. 3
Eph 2: 3 lived among them in the passions of our flesh 1
Col 3: 5 fornication, impurity, passion, evil desire 4
1Th 4: 5 not with lustful passion 4
2Ti 2:22 Shun youthful passions 1
Tit 2:12 to renounce impiety and worldly passions 1
     3: 3 slaves to various passions and pleasures 1
1Pe 4: 3 living in licentiousness, passions 1

strong passion

1. ὑπέρακμος, *hyperakmos, 5644*

1Co 7:36 if his passions are strong, and so it has to be 1

passover *See also* passover *lamb*, passover *meal*

1. πάσχα, *pascha, 4247*

Mat 26: 2 after two days the Passover is coming 1
     26:17 make the preparations for you to eat the Passover?" 1
     26:18 I will keep the Passover at your house 1
Mrk 14: 1 It was two days before the Passover 1
     14:12 the preparations for you to eat the Passover?" 1
     14:14 where I may eat the Passover with my disciples?' 1
Lke 2:41 to Jerusalem for the festival of the Passover. 1
     22: 1 which is called the Passover 1
     22:11 where I may eat the Passover with my disciples?" ' 1
     22:15 "I have eagerly desired to eat this Passover 1
Jhn 2:13 The Passover of the Jews was near 1
     2:23 he was in Jerusalem during the Passover festival 1
     6: 4 the Passover, the festival of the Jews, was near. 1
     11:55 Now the Passover of the Jews was near 1
     11:55 many went up...before the Passover 1
     12: 1 Six days before the Passover 1
     13: 1 Now before the festival of the Passover 1
     18:28 and to be able to eat the Passover. 1
     18:39 I release someone for you at the Passover. 1
     19:14 it was the day of Preparation for the Passover; 1
Act 12: 4 to bring him out to the people after the Passover. 1
Heb 11:28 By faith he kept the Passover 1

past *See also* sail past, speak in the past

1. ἀρχαῖος, *archaios, 792*
2. πάλαι, *palai, 4093*
3. παροίχομαι, *paroichomai, 4233*

Act 14:16 In past generations he allowed all the nations 3
     15:21 For in every city, for generations past, 1
2Pe 1: 9 forgetful of the cleansing of past sins. 2

pastor

1. ποιμήν, *poimēn, 4478*

Eph 4:11 some evangelists, some pastors and teachers 1

pasture

1. νομή, *nomē, 3786*

Jhn 10: 9 and will come in and go out and find pasture. 1

Patara

1. Πάταρα, *Patara, 4249*

Act 21: 1 the next day to Rhodes...from there to Patara. 1

patch

1. πλήρωμα, *plērōma, 4445*

Mat 9:16 for the patch pulls away from the cloak 1
Mrk 2:21 otherwise, the patch pulls away from it 1

path

1. ὁδός, *hodos, 3847*
2. τρίβος, *tribos, 5561*
3. τροχιά, *trochia, 5579*

Mat 3: 3 way of the Lord, make his paths straight.' " 2
     13: 4 as he sowed, some seeds fell on the path 1
     13:19 this is what was sown on the path. 1
Mrk 1: 3 make his paths straight,' " 2
     4: 4 as he sowed, some seed fell on the path 1
     4:15 the ones on the path where the word is sown: 1
Lke 3: 4 make his paths straight. 2
     8: 5 as he sowed, some fell on the path 1
     8:12 The ones on the path are those who have heard; 1
Act 13:10 making crooked the straight paths of the Lord? 1
Rom 3:16 ruin and misery are in their paths 1
Heb 12:13 make straight paths for your feet 3

path down

1. κατάβασις, *katabasis, 2853*

Lke 19:37 the path down from the Mount of Olives 1

patience *See also* have patience

1. μακροθυμία, *makrothymia, 3429*
2. ὑπομονή, *hypomonē, 5705*

Rom 2: 4 despise...his...forbearance and patience? 1
     8:25 if we hope...we wait for it with patience. 2
     9:22 endured with much patience the objects of wrath 1
2Co 6: 6 by purity, knowledge, patience, kindness 1
     12:12 with utmost patience, signs and wonders 2
Gal 5:22 love, joy, peace, patience, kindness, generosity 1
Eph 4: 2 humility and gentleness, with patience 1
Col 1:11 to endure everything with patience, while joyfully 1
     3:12 kindness, humility, meekness, and patience. 1
1Ti 1:16 Christ might display the utmost patience 1
2Ti 3:10 my aim in life, my faith, my patience, my love 1
     4: 2 with the utmost patience in teaching. 1
Heb 6:12 through faith and patience inherit the promises 1
Jas 5:10 As an example of suffering and patience 1
2Pe 3:15 regard the patience of our Lord as salvation. 1

patient *See also* patient *endurance*

1. ἀνεξίκακος, *anexikakos, 452*
2. μακροθυμέω, *makrothymeō, 3428*
3. ὑπομένω, *hypomenō, 5702*

Rom 12:12 Rejoice in hope, be patient in suffering 3
1Co 13: 4 Love is patient; love is kind; 2
1Th 5:14 help the weak, be patient with all of them. 2
2Ti 2:24 kindly to everyone, an apt teacher, patient 1
Jas 5: 7 Be patient...until the coming of the Lord. 2
     5: 7 waits for the...crop...being patient with it 2
     5: 8 You also must be patient. Strengthen your hearts 2
2Pe 3: 9 The Lord...is patient with you 2

patiently *See also* endure patiently

1. μακροθυμία, *makrothymia, 3429*
2. μακροθύμως, *makrothymōs, 3430*
3. ὑπομονή, *hypomonē, 5705*

Act 26: 3 therefore I beg of you to listen to me patiently. 2
Rom 2: 7 who by patiently doing good seek for glory 3
1Pe 3:20 when God waited patiently in the days of Noah 1

Patmos

1. Πάτμος, *Patmos, 4253*

Rev 1: 9 I, John...was on the island called Patmos 1

patriarch

1. πατήρ, *patēr, 4252*
2. πατριάρχης, *patriarchēs, 4256*

Jhn 7:22 not from Moses, but from the patriarchs) 1
Act 7: 8 Jacob of the twelve patriarchs. 2
     7: 9 "The patriarchs...sold him into Egypt; 2
Rom 9: 5 to them belong the patriarchs 1
     15: 8 might confirm the promises given to the patriarchs 1
Heb 7: 4 Abraham the patriarch gave him a tenth 2

Patrobas

  1. Πατροβᾶς, *Patrobas, 4259*

Rom 16:14 Greet Asyncritus, Phlegon, Hermes, Patrobas   1

pattern

  1. τύπος, *typos, 5596*

Act   7:44 according to the pattern he had seen.   1
Heb   8: 5 make everything according to the pattern   1

Paul

  1. Contextual: Not in Greek
  2. αὐτός, *autos, 899*
  3. ὅς, *hos, 4005*
  4. Παῦλος, *Paulos, 4263*

Act 13: 9 Saul, also known as Paul   4
     13:13 Paul and his companions set sail from Paphos   4
     13:16 So Paul stood up and with a gesture began to speak: 4
     13:42 As Paul and Barnabas were going out,   1
     13:43 many Jews...followed Paul and Barnabas   4
     13:45 contradicted what was spoken by Paul.   4
     13:46 Paul and Barnabas spoke out boldly, saying   4
     13:50 and stirred up persecution against Paul   4
     14: 1 Paul and Barnabas went into the Jewish synagogue   1
     14: 9 He listened to Paul as he was speaking.   4
     14: 9 Paul, looking at him intently   3
     14:11 When the crowds saw what Paul had done   4
     14:12 Paul they called Hermes   4
     14:14 When the apostles Barnabas and Paul heard of it   4
     14:19 they stoned Paul and dragged him out of the city   4
     15: 2 after Paul and Barnabas had no small dissension   4
     15: 2 Paul and Barnabas and some of the others   4
     15:12 listened to Barnabas and Paul   4
     15:22 send them to Antioch with Paul and Barnabas.   4
     15:25 along with our beloved Barnabas and Paul   4
     15:35 Paul and Barnabas remained in Antioch   4
     15:36 After some days Paul said to Barnabas, "Come   4
     15:38 Paul decided not to take with them one   4
     15:40 Paul chose Silas and set out   4
     16: 1 Paul went on also to Derbe and to Lystra   1
     16: 3 Paul wanted Timothy to accompany him;   4
     16: 9 During the night Paul had a vision: there stood   4
     16:14 to listen eagerly to what was said by Paul.   4
     16:17 she followed Paul and us, she would cry out   4
     16:18 Paul, very much annoyed, turned and said   4
     16:19 they seized Paul and Silas   4
     16:25 Paul and Silas were praying and singing hymns   4
     16:28 Paul shouted in a loud voice, "Do not harm yourself   4
     16:29 he fell down trembling before Paul and Silas.   4
     16:36 the jailer reported the message to Paul, saying   4
     16:37 Paul replied, "They have beaten us in public   4
     17: 1 Paul and Silas had passed through Amphipolis   1
     17: 2 Paul went in, as was his custom   4
     17: 4 were persuaded and joined Paul and Silas   4
     17: 5 searching for Paul and Silas to bring them out   1
     17:10 the believers sent Paul and Silas off   4
     17:13 the word...had been proclaimed by Paul in Beroea   4
     17:14 the believers...sent Paul away to the coast   4
     17:15 who conducted Paul brought him as far as Athens;   4
     17:16 While Paul was waiting for them in Athens   4
     17:22 Paul stood in front of the Areopagus   4
     17:33 At that point Paul left them.   4
     18: 1 After this Paul left Athens and went to Corinth.   1
     18: 2 Paul went to see them   1
     18: 5 Paul was occupied with proclaiming the word   4
     18: 8 Corinthians who heard Paul became believers   1
     18: 9 One night the Lord said to Paul in a vision   4
     18:12 the Jews made a united attack on Paul   4
     18:14 Just as Paul was about to speak,   4
     18:18 Paul said farewell to the believers   4
     19: 1 Paul passed through the interior regions   4
     19: 4 Paul said, "John baptized   4
     19: 6 When Paul had laid his hands on them   4
     19:11 God did extraordinary miracles through Paul   4
     19:13 "I adjure you by the Jesus whom Paul proclaims."   4
     19:15 "Jesus I know, and Paul I know; but who are you?"   4
     19:21 Paul resolved in the Spirit to go   4
     19:26 this Paul has persuaded   4
     19:29 who were Paul's travel companions.   4
     19:30 Paul wished to go into the crowd   4
     20: 1 Paul sent for the disciples;   4

     20: 7 Paul was holding a discussion with them;   4
     20: 9 while Paul talked still longer.   4
     20:10 Paul went down, and bending over him   4
     20:11 Paul went upstairs, and after he had broken bread   1
     20:13 intending to take Paul on board there;   4
     20:16 Paul had decided to sail past Ephesus   4
     20:37 they embraced Paul and kissed him   4
     21: 4 they told Paul not to go on to Jerusalem.   4
     21:11 came to us and took Paul's belt   4
     21:13 Then Paul answered, "What are you doing   4
     21:18 The next day Paul went with us to visit James;   4
     21:26 Then Paul took the men   4
     21:29 Paul had brought him into the temple.   4
     21:30 seized Paul and dragged him out of the temple   4
     21:32 they stopped beating Paul.   4
     21:35 When Paul came to the steps   1
     21:37 Paul was about to be brought into the barracks   4
     21:39 Paul replied, "I am a Jew, from Tarsus in Cilicia   4
     21:40 Paul stood on the steps   4
     22:25 Paul said to the centurion who was standing by   4
     22:27 The tribune came and asked Paul   2
     22:28 Paul said, "But I was born a citizen."   4
     22:29 he realized that Paul was a Roman citizen   1
     22:30 to find out what Paul was being accused of   1
     22:30 He brought Paul down and had him stand before them.
     23: 1 Paul was looking intently at the council he said   4
     23: 3 Paul said to him, "God will strike you   4
     23: 5 Paul said, "I did not realize, brothers   4
     23: 6 When Paul noticed that some were Sadducees   4
     23:10 fearing that they would tear Paul to pieces   4
     23:12 until they had killed Paul.   4
     23:14 an oath to taste no food until we have killed Paul.   4
     23:16 the son of Paul's sister heard about the ambush;   4
     23:16 gained entrance to the barracks and told Paul.   4
     23:17 Paul called one of the centurions and said   4
     23:18 "The prisoner Paul called me   4
     23:20 to ask you to bring Paul down to the council   4
     23:24 Also provide mounts for Paul to ride   4
     23:31 according to their instructions, took Paul   4
     23:33 they presented Paul also before him.   4
     24: 1 reported their case against Paul to the governor.   4
     24: 2 When Paul had been summoned, Tertullus began   2
     24:10 Paul replied: "I cheerfully make my defense   4
     24:24 he sent for Paul and heard him   4
     24:26 he hoped that money would be given him by Paul   4
     24:27 Felix left Paul in prison.   4
     25: 2 gave him a report against Paul.   4
     25: 3 requested, as a favor to them against Paul   2
     25: 4 Paul was being kept at Caesarea   4
     25: 6 ordered Paul to be brought.   4
     25: 8 Paul said in his defense   4
     25: 9 Festus, wishing to do the Jews a favor, asked Paul   4
     25:10 Paul said, "I am appealing to the emperor's tribunal;   4
     25:14 Festus laid Paul's case before the king, saying   4
     25:19 who had died, but whom Paul asserted to be alive.   4
     25:21 when Paul had appealed to be kept in custody   4
     25:23 Festus gave the order and Paul was brought in.   4
     26: 1 Agrippa said to Paul, "You have permission   4
     26: 1 Paul stretched out his hand and began to defend   4
     26:24 Festus exclaimed, "You are out of your mind, Paul!   4
     26:25 Paul said, "I am not out of my mind   4
     26:28 Agrippa said to Paul   4
     26:29 Paul replied, "Whether quickly or not,   4
     27: 1 they transferred Paul...to a centurion   4
     27: 3 Julius treated Paul kindly   4
     27: 9 Paul advised them   4
     27:11 than to what Paul said.   4
     27:21 Paul then stood up among them and said, "Men   4
     27:24 he said, 'Do not be afraid, Paul;   4
     27:31 Paul said to the centurion and the soldiers   4
     27:33 Paul urged all of them to take some food, saying   4
     27:43 the centurion, wishing to save Paul   4
     28: 3 Paul had gathered a bundle of brushwood   4
     28: 8 Paul visited him and cured him by praying   4
     28:15 Paul thanked God and took courage.   4
     28:16 Paul was allowed to live by himself   4
     28:25 they were leaving, Paul made one further statement: 4
Rom   1: 1 Paul, a servant of Jesus Christ   4
1Co   1: 1 Paul, called to be an apostle of Christ Jesus   4
     1:12 "I belong to Paul," or "I belong to Apollos,"   4
     1:13 Has Christ been divided? Was Paul crucified for you?   4

1:13 were you baptized in the name of Paul? 4
3: 4 For when one says, "I belong to Paul," 4
3: 5 What then is Apollos? What is Paul? 4
3:22 whether Paul or Apollos or Cephas or the world 4
16:21 I, Paul, write this greeting with my own hand. 4
2Co 1: 1 Paul, an apostle of Christ Jesus by the will of God 4
10: 1 I myself, Paul, appeal to you 4
Gal 1: 1 Paul an apostle—sent neither by human commission 4
5: 2 Listen! I, Paul, am telling you 4
Eph 1: 1 Paul, an apostle of Christ Jesus by the will of God 4
3: 1 Paul am a prisoner for Christ Jesus for the sake of you 4
Php 1: 1 Paul and Timothy, servants of Christ Jesus 4
Col 1: 1 Paul, an apostle of Christ Jesus by the will of God 4
1:23 I, Paul, became a servant of this gospel. 4
4:18 I, Paul, write this greeting with my own hand. 4
1Th 1: 1 Paul, Silvanus, and Timothy 4
2:18 I, Paul, wanted to again and again 4
2Th 1: 1 Paul, Silvanus, and Timothy 4
3:17 I, Paul, write this greeting with my own hand. 4
1Ti 1: 1 Paul, an apostle of Christ Jesus by the command 4
2Ti 1: 1 Paul, an apostle of Christ Jesus by the will of God 4
Tit 1: 1 Paul, a servant of God and an apostle of Jesus 4
Phm 1: 1 Paul, a prisoner of Christ Jesus 4
1: 9 I, Paul, do this as an old man, and now also as a prisoner 4
1:19 I, Paul, am writing this with my own hand: I will repay 4
2Pe 3:15 So also our beloved brother Paul wrote to you 4

Paulus

1. Παῦλος, *Paulos, 4263*
Act 13: 7 He was with the proconsul, Sergius Paulus, 1

pay

1. Contextual: Not in Greek
2. ἀπέχω, *apechō, 600*
3. ἀποδίδωμι, *apodidōmi, 625*
4. ἀπονέμω, *aponemō, 671*
5. βαστάζω, *bastazō, 1002*
6. δαπανάω, *dapanaō, 1251*
7. δίδωμι, *didōmi, 1443*
8. ἵστημι, *histēmi, 2705*
9. μισθός, *misthos, 3635*
10. τελέω, *teleō, 5464*

Mat 5:26 get out until you have paid the last penny. 3
17:24 "Does your teacher not pay the temple tax?" 10
18:25 could not pay, his lord ordered him to be sold 3
18:26 and I will pay you everything.' 3
18:28 'Pay what you owe.' 3
18:29 'Have patience with me, and I will pay you.' 3
18:30 into prison until he would pay the debt. 3
18:34 until he would pay his entire debt. 3
20: 4 and I will pay you whatever is right.' 7
20: 8 'Call the laborers and give them their pay 9
22:17 Is it lawful to pay taxes to the emperor, or not?" 7
26:15 They paid him thirty pieces of silver. 8
Mrk 12:14 Is it lawful to pay taxes to the emperor, or not? 7
12:15 Should we pay them, or should we not?" 7
Lke 7:42 When they could not pay, he canceled the debts 3
10: 7 the laborer deserves to be paid. 9
12:59 until you have paid the very last penny." 3
20:22 Is it lawful for us to pay taxes to the emperor 7
23: 2 forbidding us to pay taxes to the emperor 7
Act 21:24 pay for the shaving of their heads 6
Rom 13: 6 For the same reason you also pay taxes 10
13: 7 Pay to all what is due them 3
1Co 9: 7 pays the expenses for doing military service? 1
Gal 5:10 whoever…is confusing you will pay the penalty. 5
Php 4:18 I have been paid in full and have more than enough; 9
1Ti 5:18 "The laborer deserves to be paid." 9
1Pe 3: 7 paying honor to the woman as the weaker sex 4

day's pay

1. δηνάριον, *dēnarion, 1324*
Rev 6: 6 "A quart of wheat for a day's pay 1
6: 6 and three quarts of barley for a day's pay 1

pay a tithe

1. δεκατόω, *dekatoō, 1282*
Heb 7: 9 Levi himself…paid tithes through Abraham 1

pay attention

1. βλέπω, *blepō, 1063*
2. μέλει, *melei, 3508*
3. πείθω, *peithō, 4275*
4. προσέχω, *prosechō, 4668*
Mrk 4:24 "Pay attention to what you hear; 1
Lke 8:18 Then pay attention to how you listen; 1
Act 18:17 But Gallio paid no attention to any of these things. 2
27:11 centurion paid more attention to the pilot 3
1Ti 4: 1 paying attention to deceitful spirits 4
Tit 1:14 not paying attention to Jewish myths 4
Heb 2: 1 Therefore we must pay greater attention 4

pay back

1. ἀποδίδωμι, *apodidōmi, 625*
2. κομίζω, *komizō, 3152*
Lke 19: 8 I will pay back four times as much." 1
Col 3:25 will be paid back for whatever wrong has been done 2
2Ti 4:14 the Lord will pay him back for his deeds. 1

pay close attention

1. ἐπέχω, *epechō, 2091*
1Ti 4:16 Pay close attention to yourself and to your teaching; 1

pay homage

1. προσκυνέω, *proskyneō, 4686*
Mat 2: 2 at its rising, and have come to pay him homage." 1
2: 8 so that I may also go and pay him homage." 1
2:11 his mother; and they knelt down and paid him homage. 1

without paying

1. δωρεάν, *dōrean, 1562*
2Th 3: 8 we did not eat anyone's bread without paying 1

without payment

1. δωρεάν, *dōrean, 1562*
Mat 10: 8 You received without payment; give without payment. 1
10: 8 You received without payment; give without payment. 1

peace *See also* live in peace, make peace

1. εἰρηνεύω, *eirēneuō, 1644*
2. εἰρήνη, *eirēnē, 1645*
3. σιωπάω, *siōpaō, 4995*
Mat 10:13 If the house is worthy, let your peace come upon it; 2
10:13 if it is not worthy, let your peace return to you. 2
10:34 "Do not think that I have come to bring peace 2
10:34 I have not come to bring peace, but a sword. 2
Mrk 4:39 said to the sea, "Peace! Be still!" 3
5:34 go in peace, and be healed of your disease." 2
9:50 be at peace with one another." 1
Lke 1:79 to guide our feet into the way of peace." 2
2:14 on earth peace among those whom he favors!" 2
2:29 now you are dismissing your servant in peace 2
7:50 "Your faith has saved you; go in peace." 2
8:48 your faith has made you well; go in peace." 2
10: 5 'Peace to this house!' 2
10: 6 if anyone is there who shares in peace 2
10: 6 your peace will rest on that person; 2
12:51 that I have come to bring peace to the earth? 2
14:32 a delegation and asks for the terms of peace. 2
19:38 Peace in heaven, and glory in the highest heaven!" 2
19:42 on this day the things that make for peace! 2
24:36 and said to them, "Peace be with you." 2
Jhn 14:27 Peace I leave with you; my peace I give to you. 2
14:27 Peace I leave with you; my peace I give to you. 2
16:33 so that in me you may have peace. 2
20:19 "Peace be with you." 2
20:21 Jesus said to them again, "Peace be with you. 2
20:26 stood among them and said, "Peace be with you." 2
Act 9:31 the church…had peace and was built up. 2
10:36 preaching peace by Jesus Christ 2
15:33 they were sent off in peace by the believers 2
16:36 therefore come out now and go in peace." 2
24: 2 because of you we have long enjoyed peace 2
Rom 1: 7 Grace to you and peace from God our Father 2
2:10 and honor and peace for everyone who does good 2
3:17 the way of peace they have not known." 2
5: 1 peace with God through our Lord Jesus Christ 2
8: 6 to set the mind on the Spirit is life and peace. 2

Rom 14:17	kingdom of God is…righteousness and peace	2
14:19	Let us then pursue what makes for peace	2
15:13	the God of hope fill you with all joy and peace	2
15:33	The God of peace be with all of you. Amen.	2
16:20	The God of peace will shortly crush Satan	2
1Co 1: 3	Grace to you and peace from God our Father	2
7:15	It is to peace that God has called you.	2
14:33	for God is a God not of disorder but of peace.	2
16:11	Send him on his way in peace	2
2Co 1: 2	Grace to you and peace from God our Father	2
13:11	the God of love and peace will be with you.	2
Gal 1: 3	Grace to you and peace from God our Father	2
5:22	love, joy, peace, patience, kindness, generosity	2
6:16	follow this rule—peace be upon them, and mercy	2
Eph 1: 2	Grace to you and peace from God our Father	2
2:14	For he is our peace; in his flesh he has made	2
2:15	one new humanity in place of the two, thus making peace	2
2:17	he came and proclaimed peace to you who were far off	2
2:17	proclaimed…peace to those who were near;	2
4: 3	the unity of the Spirit in the bond of peace.	2
6:15	make you ready to proclaim the gospel of peace.	2
6:23	Peace be to the whole community, and love with faith	2
Php 1: 2	Grace to you and peace from God our Father	2
4: 7	the peace of God, which surpasses all understanding	2
4: 9	the God of peace will be with you.	2
Col 1: 2	Grace to you and peace from God our Father.	2
3:15	let the peace of Christ rule in your hearts	2
1Th 1: 1	Grace to you and peace.	2
5: 3	When they say, "There is peace and security,"	2
5:13	Be at peace among yourselves.	1
5:23	May the God of peace himself sanctify you entirely;	2
2Th 1: 2	Grace to you and peace from God our Father	2
3:16	Now may the Lord of peace himself give you peace	2
3:16	Lord of peace himself give you peace at all times	2
1Ti 1: 2	Grace, mercy, and peace from God the Father	2
2Ti 1: 2	Grace, mercy, and peace from God the Father	2
2:22	pursue righteousness, faith, love, and peace	2
Tit 1: 4	Grace and peace from God the Father	2
Phm 1: 3	Grace to you and peace from God our Father	2
Heb 7: 2	he is also king of Salem, that is, "king of peace."	2
11:31	she had received the spies in peace.	2
12:14	Pursue peace with everyone	2
13:20	the God of peace, who brought back from the dead	2
Jas 2:16	"Go in peace; keep warm and eat your fill,"	2
3:18	a harvest of righteousness is sown in peace	2
3:18	sown in peace for those who make peace.	2
1Pe 1: 2	May grace and peace be yours in abundance.	2
3:11	let them seek peace and pursue it.	2
5:14	Peace to all of you who are in Christ.	2
2Pe 1: 2	May grace and peace be yours in abundance	2
3:14	at peace, without spot or blemish;	2
2Jn 1: 3	Grace, mercy, and peace will be with us from God	2
3Jn 1:15	Peace to you. The friends send you their greetings.	2
Jde 1: 2	May mercy, peace, and love be yours in abundance.	2
Rev 1: 4	Grace to you and peace from him who is and who was	2
6: 4	rider was permitted to take peace from the earth	2

peaceable

1. εἰρηνικός, *eirēnikos, 1646*
2. ἡσύχιος, *hēsychios, 2485*

1Ti 2: 2	we may lead a quiet and peaceable life	2
Jas 3:17	wisdom from above is first pure, then peaceable	1

peaceably *See* live peaceably

peaceful

1. εἰρηνικός, *eirēnikos, 1646*

Heb 12:11	it yields the peaceful fruit of righteousness	1

peacemaker

1. εἰρηνοποιός, *eirēnopoios, 1648*

Mat 5: 9	"Blessed are the peacemakers, for they will be	1

peal of thunder

1. βροντή, *brontē, 1103*

Rev 4: 5	Coming…rumblings and peals of thunder	1
8: 5	there were peals of thunder, rumblings, flashes	1
11:19	flashes of lightning, rumblings, peals of thunder	1
16:18	flashes of lightning, rumblings, peals of thunder	1

pearl

1. μαργαρίτης, *margaritēs, 3449*

Mat 7: 6	and do not throw your pearls before swine	1
13:45	like a merchant in search of fine pearls;	1
13:46	on finding one pearl of great value	1
1Ti 2: 9	with their hair braided, or with gold, pearls,	1
Rev 17: 4	and adorned with gold and jewels and pearls	1
18:12	cargo of gold, silver, jewels and pearls	1
18:16	adorned with gold, with jewels, and with pearls!	1
21:21	And the twelve gates are twelve pearls	1
21:21	each of the gates is a single pearl	1

peddler

1. καπηλεύω, *kapēleuō, 2836*

2Co 2:17	we are not peddlers of God's word like so many;	1

Peleg

1. Φάλεκ, *Phalek, 5744*

Lke 3:35	son of Serug, son of Reu, son of Peleg	1

pen

1. κάλαμος, *kalamos, 2812*

3Jn 1:13	but I would rather not write with pen and ink;	1

penalty

1. ἀντιμισθία, *antimisthia, 521*
2. κρίμα, *krima, 3210*
3. μισθαποδοσία, *misthapodosia, 3632*
4. μισθός, *misthos, 3635*

Rom 1:27	received in their own persons the due penalty	1
Gal 5:10	whoever…is confusing you will pay the penalty.	2
Heb 2: 2	every…disobedience received a just penalty.	3
2Pe 2:13	suffering the penalty for doing wrong.	4

death penalty

1. θάνατος, *thanatos, 2505*

Act 28:18	no reason for the death penalty in my case.	1

penny

1. ἀσσάριον, *assarion, 837*
2. κοδράντης, *kodrantēs, 3119*
3. λεπτός, *leptos, 3321*

Mat 5:26	get out until you have paid the last penny.	2
10:29	Are not two sparrows sold for a penny?	1
Mrk 12:42	two small copper coins, which are worth a penny.	2
Lke 12: 6	Are not five sparrows sold for two pennies?	1
12:59	until you have paid the very last penny."	3

Pentecost

1. πεντηκοστή, *pentēkostē, 4300*

Act 2: 1	When the day of Pentecost had come	1
20:16	in Jerusalem, if possible, on the day of Pentecost.	1
1Co 16: 8	I will stay in Ephesus until Pentecost	1

people *See also* all people

1. Contextual: Not in Greek
2. γένος, *genos, 1169*
3. δῆμος, *dēmos, 1322*
4. ἔθνος, *ethnos, 1620*
5. λαός, *laos, 3295*
6. ὄχλος, *ochlos, 4063*
7. πλῆθος, *plēthos, 4436*
8. σάρξ, *sarx, 4922*
9. υἱός, *huios, 5626*

Mat 1:21	he will save his people from their sins."	5
2: 4	scribes of the people, he inquired of them where	5
2: 6	a ruler who is to shepherd my people Israel.' "	5
4:16	the people who sat in darkness have seen a great	5
4:23	disease and every sickness among the people.	5
13:15	For this people's heart has grown dull	5
15: 8	'This people honors me with their lips	5
21:23	the chief priests and the elders of the people	5
21:43	a people that produces the fruits of the kingdom.	4
26: 3	the elders of the people gathered in the palace	5
26: 5	or there may be a riot among the people."	5
26:47	the chief priests and the elders of the people.	5
27: 1	chief priests and the elders of the people	5
27: 9	some of the people of Israel had set a price	9

	27:25 the people as a whole answered, "His blood be	5
	27:64 steal him away, and tell the people	5
Mrk	7: 6 'This people honors me with their lips	5
	14: 2 or there may be a riot among the people."	5
Lke	1:10 the whole assembly of the people was praying	5
	1:16 turn many of the people of Israel to the Lord	9
	1:17 to make ready a people prepared for the Lord."	5
	1:21 the people were waiting for Zechariah	5
	1:68 for he has looked favorably on his people	5
	1:77 to give knowledge of salvation to his people	5
	2:10 great joy for all the people:	5
	2:31 have prepared in the presence of all peoples	5
	2:32 for glory to your people Israel."	5
	3:15 As the people were filled with expectation	5
	3:18 he proclaimed the good news to the people.	5
	3:21 Now when all the people were baptized	5
	6:17 a great multitude of people from all Judea	5
	7: 1 all his sayings in the hearing of the people	5
	7: 5 for he loves our people,	4
	7:16 "God has looked favorably on his people!"	5
	7:29 (And all the people who heard this	5
	8:37 all the people of the surrounding country	7
	8:47 declared in the presence of all the people	5
	9:13 go and buy food for all these people."	5
	18:43 all the people, when they saw it, praised God.	5
	19:47 scribes, and the leaders of the people	5
	19:48 the people were spellbound by what they heard.	5
	20: 1 as he was teaching the people in the temple	5
	20: 6 all the people will stone us;	5
	20: 9 He began to tell the people this parable:	5
	20:19 they feared the people.	5
	20:26 they were not able in the presence of the people	5
	20:45 In the hearing of all the people	5
	21:23 and wrath against this people;	5
	21:38 all the people would get up early in the morning	5
	22: 2 they were afraid of the people.	5
	22:66 the assembly of the elders of the people	5
	23: 5 insistent and said, "He stirs up the people	5
	23:13 chief priests, the leaders, and the people	5
	23:14 as one who was perverting the people;	5
	23:27 A great number of the people followed him	5
	23:35 the people stood by, watching;	5
	24:19 before God and all the people	5
Jhn	1:11 and his own people did not accept him.	1
	8: 2 〚All the people came to him〛	5
	11:50 to have one man die for the people	5
	18:14 better to have one person die for the people.	5
Act	2:47 having the goodwill of all the people.	5
	3: 9 All the people saw him walking and praising God	5
	3:11 all the people ran together to them	5
	3:12 When Peter saw it, he addressed the people	5
	3:23 will be utterly rooted out of the people.'	5
	4: 1 While Peter and John were speaking to the people	5
	4: 2 much annoyed because they were teaching the people	5
	4: 8 "Rulers of the people and elders	5
	4:10 known...to all the people of Israel	5
	4:17 keep it from spreading further among the people	5
	4:21 no way to punish them because of the people	5
	4:25 the peoples imagine vain things?	5
	4:27 with the Gentiles and the peoples of Israel	5
	5:12 wonders were done among the people	5
	5:13 the people held them in high esteem.	5
	5:20 tell the people the whole message about this life."	5
	5:25 standing in the temple and teaching the people!"	5
	5:26 they were afraid of being stoned by the people.	5
	5:34 Gamaliel...respected by all the people	5
	5:37 and got people to follow him;	5
	6: 8 did great wonders and signs among the people.	5
	6:12 They stirred up the people as well as the elders	5
	7:17 our people in Egypt increased and multiplied	5
	7:34 mistreatment of my people who are in Egypt	5
	8: 9 and amazed the people of Samaria	4
	9:15 Gentiles and kings and before the people of Israel;	9
	10: 2 gave alms generously to the people	5
	10:36 You know the message he sent to the people of Israel	9
	10:41 not to all the people but to us	5
	10:42 He commanded us to preach to the people	5
	11:24 a great many people were brought to the Lord.	6
	11:26 and taught a great many people	6
	12: 4 intending to bring him out to the people	5
	12:11 from all that the Jewish people were expecting."	5

	12:22 The people kept shouting, "The voice of a god,	3
	13:15 word of exhortation for the people, give it."	5
	13:17 The God of this people Israel chose our ancestors	5
	13:17 chose our ancestors and made the people great	5
	13:24 already proclaimed...to all the people of Israel.	5
	13:31 they are now his witnesses to the people.	5
	15:14 to take from among them a people for his name.	5
	17: 8 The people and the city officials	6
	18:10 there are many in this city who are my people."	5
	19: 4 telling the people to believe	5
	19:26 drawn away a considerable number of people	6
	19:33 tried to make a defense before the people.	3
	21:28 against our people, our law, and this place;	5
	21:30 and the people rushed together.	5
	21:39 I beg you, let me speak to the people."	5
	21:40 motioned to the people for silence;	5
	23: 5 shall not speak evil of a leader of your people.' "	5
	24: 2 reforms have been made for this people	4
	26: 4 spent from the beginning among my own people	4
	26:17 I will rescue you from your people	5
	26:23 both to our people and to the Gentiles."	5
	28:17 though I had done nothing against our people	5
	28:26 'Go to this people and say, You will indeed listen	5
	28:27 For this people's heart has grown dull	5
Rom	9:25 "Those who were not my people I will call 'my people,'	5
	9:25 "Those who were not my people I will call 'my people,'	5
	9:26 where it was said to them, 'You are not my people,'	5
	10:21 my hands to a disobedient and contrary people."	5
	11: 1 I ask, then, has God rejected his people?	5
	11: 2 God has not rejected his people	5
	11:14 in order to make my own people jealous, and thus	8
	15:10 "Rejoice, O Gentiles, with his people";	5
	15:11 and let all the peoples praise him";	5
1Co	10: 7 "The people sat down to eat and drink	5
	10:18 Consider the people of Israel;	8
	14:21 I will speak to this people;	5
2Co	3: 7 people of Israel could not gaze at Moses' face	9
	3:13 to keep the people of Israel from gazing	9
	6:16 I will be their God, and they shall be my people.	5
	11:26 danger from bandits, danger from my own people	2
Gal	1:14 many among my people of the same age	2
Eph	1:14 toward redemption as God's own people	1
Php	3: 5 a member of the people of Israel,	2
Tit	2:14 purify for himself a people of his own	5
Heb	2:17 a sacrifice of atonement for the sins of the people.	5
	4: 9 a sabbath rest still remains for the people of God;	5
	5: 3 as well as for those of the people.	5
	7: 5 the people, that is, from their kindred	5
	7:11 for the people received the law under this priesthood	5
	7:27 for his own sins, and then for those of the people;	5
	8:10 I will be their God, and they shall be my people.	5
	9: 7 for the sins committed unintentionally by the people.	5
	9:19 had been told to all the people by Moses	5
	9:19 sprinkled both the scroll itself and all the people	5
	10:30 And again, "The Lord will judge his people."	5
	11:25 share ill-treatment with the people of God	5
	11:29 By faith the people passed through the Red Sea	1
	13:12 sanctify the people by his own blood.	5
1Pe	2: 9 you are...a holy nation, God's own people	5
	2:10 Once you were not a people, but now you are God's	5
	2:10 but now you are God's people;	5
2Pe	2: 1 false prophets also arose among the people	5
Jde	1: 5 that the Lord, who once for all saved a people	5
Rev	2:14 put a stumbling block before the people of Israel	9
	5: 9 every tribe and language and people and nation;	5
	7: 4 sealed out of every tribe of the people of Israel:	9
	7: 9 from all tribes and peoples and languages	5
	10:11 prophesy again about many peoples and nations	5
	11: 9 the peoples and tribes and languages and nations	5
	13: 7 every tribe and people and language and nation	5
	14: 6 to every nation and tribe and language and people.	5
	17:15 peoples and multitudes and nations and languages.	5
	18: 4 "Come out of her, my people	5
	21: 3 He will dwell with them; they will be his peoples	5

more and more people

   1. πολύς, *polys, 4498*

2Co	4:15 that grace, as it extends to more and more people	1

people there

   1. ἐντόπιος, *entopios, 1954*

Act 21:12 we and the people there urged him not to go up   1

perceive

1. αἰσθάνομαι, *aisthanomai, 150*
2. βλέπω, *blepō, 1063*
3. ἐπιγινώσκω, *epiginōskō, 2105*
4. ἐπίγνωσις, *epignōsis, 2106*
5. κατανοέω, *katanoeō, 2917*
6. νοέω, *noeō, 3783*
7. ὁράω, *horaō, 3972*

Mat 9: 4 Jesus, perceiving their thoughts, said   7
     13:13 that 'seeing they do not perceive   2
     13:14 and you will indeed look, but never perceive.   7
     16: 9 Do you still not perceive?   6
     16:11 How could you fail to perceive   6
Mrk 2: 8 At once Jesus perceived in his spirit   3
     4:12 that 'they may indeed look, but not perceive   7
     8:17 Do you still not perceive or understand?   6
Lke 5:22 When Jesus perceived their questionings   3
     8:10 so that 'looking they may not perceive   2
     9:45 so that they could not perceive it.   1
     20:23 he perceived their craftiness and said to them   5
Act 28:26 you will indeed look, but never perceive.   7
Eph 3: 4 perceive my understanding of the mystery of Christ.   6
Phm 1: 6 may become effective when you perceive all the good   4

Perez

1. Φαρές, *Phares, 5756*

Mat 1: 3 Judah the father of Perez and Zerah by Tamar   1
     1: 3 Perez the father of Hezron   1
Lke 3:33 son of Hezron, son of Perez, son of Judah   1

perfect *See also* make perfect, perfect *harmony*, perfect *health*

1. ἀγαθός, *agathos, 19*
2. κατάρτισις, *katartisis, 2937*
3. πληρόω, *plēroō, 4444*
4. τέλειος, *teleios, 5455*
5. τελειόω, *teleioō, 5457*

Mat 5:48 Be perfect, therefore, as your heavenly Father   4
     5:48 Be perfect…as your heavenly Father is perfect.   4
     19:21 to be perfect, go, sell your possessions   4
Rom 12: 2 what is good and acceptable and perfect.   4
2Co 13: 9 is what we pray for, that you may become perfect.   2
Tit 2:10 not to pilfer, but to show complete and perfect fidelity   1
Heb 9: 9 cannot perfect the conscience of the worshiper   5
     9:11 then through the greater and perfect tent   4
     10:14 perfected for all time those who are sanctified.   5
Jas 1:17 with every perfect gift, is from above   4
     1:25 those who look into the perfect law   4
     3: 2 who makes no mistakes in speaking is perfect.   4
1Jn 4:12 God lives in us, and his love is perfected in us.   5
     4:17 Love has been perfected among us in this: 5
     4:18 but perfect love casts out fear;   4
Rev 3: 2 for I have not found your works perfect   3

perfecter

1. τελειωτής, *teleiōtēs, 5460*

Heb 12: 2 Jesus the pioneer and perfecter of our faith   1

perfection *See also* reach perfection

1. τελειότης, *teleiotēs, 5456*
2. τελείωσις, *teleiōsis, 5459*

Heb 6: 1 Therefore let us go on toward perfection,   1
     7:11 Now if perfection had been attainable   2

perform

1. ἀποτελέω, *apoteleō, 699*
2. γίνομαι, *ginomai, 1181*
3. ἐργάζομαι, *ergazomai, 2237*
4. κατεργάζομαι, *katergazomai, 2981*
5. ποιέω, *poieō, 4472*

Mat 26:10 She has performed a good service for me.   3
Mrk 14: 6 She has performed a good service for me.   3
Lke 13:32 I am casting out demons and performing cures today   1
     23: 8 was hoping to see him perform some sign.   2
Jhn 6:28 "What must we do to perform the works of God?"   3
     7:21 Jesus answered them, "I performed one work   5
     9:16 "How can a man who is a sinner perform such signs?"   5

10:41 they were saying, "John performed no sign   5
11:47 we to do? This man is performing many signs.   5
12:18 they heard that he had performed this sign   5
12:37 he had performed so many signs in their presence   5
Act 4:22 man on whom this sign of healing had been performed   2
     4:30 signs and wonders are performed   2
     7:36 having performed wonders and signs in Egypt   5
2Co 12:12 The signs of a true apostle were performed among you   4
Rev 13:13 It performs great signs, even making fire come down   5
     13:14 and by the signs that it is allowed to perform   5
     16:14 These are demonic spirits, performing signs   5
     19:20 performed in its presence the signs by which he deceived   5

perform work

1. ἐργάζομαι, *ergazomai, 2237*

Jhn 6:30 What work are you performing?   1

perfume

1. μύρον, *myron, 3693*

Jhn 11: 2 Mary was the one who anointed the Lord with perfume   1
     12: 3 a pound of costly perfume made of pure nard   1
     12: 3 was filled with the fragrance of the perfume.   1
     12: 5 "Why was this perfume not sold   1

Perga

1. Πέργη, *Pergē, 4308*

Act 13:13 and came to Perga in Pamphylia.   1
     13:14 they went on from Perga   1
     14:25 When they had spoken the word in Perga   1

Pergamum

1. Πέργαμος, *Pergamos, 4307*

Rev 1:11 seven churches…to Pergamum, to Thyatira   1
     2:12 "And to the angel of the church in Pergamum write: 1

perhaps

1. Contextual: Not in Greek
2. ἄν, *an, 323*
3. ἄρα, *ara, 726*
4. εἰ + ἄρα + γέ, *ei + ara + ge, 1623 + 726 + 1145*
5. εἰ + τυγχάνω, *ei + tynchanō, 1623 + 5593*
6. ἴσως, *isōs, 2711*
7. μή + πώς, *mē + pōs, 3590 + 4803*
8. μήποτε, *mēpote, 3607*
9. τάχα, *tacha, 5440*
10. τυγχάνω, *tynchanō, 5593*

Mrk 11:13 whether perhaps he would find anything on it.   3
Lke 20:13 perhaps they will respect him.'   6
Act 17:27 and perhaps grope for him and find him   4
Rom 2:15 thoughts will accuse or perhaps excuse them   1
     5: 7 perhaps for a good person someone might…die.   9
     11:21 perhaps he will not spare you.   7
1Co 7: 5 except perhaps by agreement for a set time   2
     15:37 perhaps of wheat or of some other grain.   5
     16: 6 perhaps I will stay with you   10
2Co 12:20 there may perhaps be quarreling, jealousy, anger   7
2Ti 2:25 God may perhaps grant that they will repent   8
Phm 1:15 Perhaps this is the reason he was separated from you   9

peril

1. θάνατος, *thanatos, 2505*
2. κίνδυνος, *kindynos, 3074*

Rom 8:35 or famine, or nakedness, or peril, or sword?   2
2Co 1:10 He who rescued us from so deadly a peril   1

period

1. καιρός, *kairos, 2789*

Act 1: 7 "It is not for you to know the times or periods   1

perish *See also* doom to perish

1. ἀποθνήσκω, *apothnēskō, 633*
2. ἀπόλλυμι, *apollymi, 660*
3. ἀφανίζω, *aphanizō, 906*
4. εἰς + ἀπώλεια, *eis + apōleia, 1650 + 724*
5. συναπόλλυμι, *synapollymi, 5272*
6. φθορά, *phthora, 5785*

Mat 8:25 "Lord, save us! We are perishing!"   2
     8:32 into the sea and perished in the water.   1

	26:52 all who take the sword will perish by the sword.	2
Mrk	4:38 "Teacher, do you not care that we are perishing?"	2
Lke	8:24 "Master, Master, we are perishing!"	2
	11:51 perished between the altar and the sanctuary.	2
	13: 3 unless you repent, you will all perish as	2
	13: 5 unless you repent, you will all perish just as	2
	21:18 not a hair of your head will perish.	2
Jhn	3:16 everyone who believes in him may not perish	2
	6:27 Do not work for the food that perishes	2
	10:28 they will never perish.	2
Act	5:37 he also perished	2
	8:20 Peter said to him, "May your silver perish with you	4
	13:41 'Look, you scoffers! Be amazed and perish	3
Rom	2:12 will also perish apart from the law	2
1Co	1:18 foolishness to those who are perishing	2
	15:18 who have died in Christ have perished.	2
2Co	2:15 among those who are perishing;	2
	4: 3 it is veiled to those who are perishing.	2
Col	2:22 refer to things that perish with use;	6
2Th	2:10 wicked deception for those who are perishing,	2
Heb	1:11 they will perish, but you remain;	2
	11:31 did not perish with those who were disobedient	5
Jas	1:11 its flower falls, and its beauty perishes.	2
2Pe	3: 6 world…was deluged with water and perished.	2
	3: 9 not wanting any to perish	2
Jde	1:11 and perish in Korah's rebellion.	2

perishable

1. ἀπόλλυμι, *apollymi, 660*
2. φθαρτός, *phthartos, 5778*
3. φθορά, *phthora, 5785*

1Co	9:25 they do it to receive a perishable wreath	2
	15:42 What is sown is perishable	3
	15:50 the perishable inherit the imperishable.	3
	15:53 perishable body must put on imperishability,	2
	15:54 When this perishable body puts on imperishability	2
1Pe	1: 7 gold that, though perishable, is tested by fire	1
	1:23 not of perishable but of imperishable seed	2

perishable thing

1. φθαρτός, *phthartos, 5778*

1Pe	1:18 with perishable things like silver or gold	1

perjurer

1. ἐπίορκος, *epiorkos, 2156*

1Ti	1:10 sodomites, slave traders, liars, perjurers	1

permanent

1. εἰς + ὁ + αἰών, *eis + ho + aiōn, 1650 + 3836 + 172*
2. μένω, *menō, 3531*

Jhn	8:35 does not have a permanent place in the household;	1
2Co	3:11 much more has the permanent come in glory!	2

permanently

1. ἀπαράβατος, *aparabatos, 563*

Heb	7:24 he holds his priesthood permanently	1

permission *See also* give permission

1. ἐπιτρέπω, *epitrepō, 2205*

Act	26: 1 "You have permission to speak for yourself."	1

permit

1. ἀφίημι, *aphiēmi, 918*
2. δίδωμι, *didōmi, 1443*
3. ἔξεστι, *exesti, 2003*
4. ἐπιτρέπω, *epitrepō, 2205*

Mrk	1:34 he would not permit the demons to speak	1
	7:12 then you no longer permit doing anything	1
Jhn	18:31 "We are not permitted to put anyone to death."	3
1Co	14:34 For they are not permitted to speak	4
	16: 7 some time with you, if the Lord permits.	4
2Co	12: 4 that no mortal is permitted to repeat.	3
1Ti	2:12 I permit no woman to teach	4
Heb	6: 3 we will do this, if God permits.	4
Rev	6: 4 rider was permitted to take peace from the earth	2

perplex

1. ἀπορέω, *aporeō, 679*
2. διαπορέω, *diaporeō, 1389*

	3. θαμβέω, *thambeō, 2501*	
Mrk	6:20 When he heard him, he was greatly perplexed;	1
	10:24 the disciples were perplexed at these words.	3
Lke	9: 7 he was perplexed, because it was said by some	1
	24: 4 While they were perplexed about this	1
Act	2:12 All were amazed and perplexed	2
	5:24 they were perplexed about them	2
2Co	4: 8 perplexed, but not driven to despair;	1
Gal	4:20 I am perplexed about you.	1

perplex much

1. διαταράσσω, *diatarassō, 1410*

Lke	1:29 she was much perplexed by his words	1

persecute

1. διώκω, *diōkō, 1503*
2. θλίβω, *thlibō, 2567*

Mat	5:10 "Blessed are those who are persecuted	1
	5:11 revile you and persecute you and utter all kinds	1
	5:12 for in the same way they persecuted the prophets	1
	5:44 enemies and pray for those who persecute you	1
	10:23 When they persecute you in one town	1
Lke	11:49 some of whom they will kill and persecute,'	1
	21:12 arrest you and persecute you;	1
Jhn	5:16 Therefore the Jews started persecuting Jesus	1
	15:20 If they persecuted me, they will persecute you;	1
	15:20 If they persecuted me, they will persecute you;	1
Act	7:52 prophets did your ancestors not persecute?	1
	9: 4 "Saul, Saul, why do you persecute me?"	1
	9: 5 reply came, "I am Jesus, whom you are persecuting.	1
	22: 4 I persecuted this Way up to the point of death	1
	22: 7 'Saul, Saul, why are you persecuting me?'	1
	22: 8 'I am Jesus of Nazareth whom you are persecuting.'	1
	26:14 'Saul, Saul, why are you persecuting me?	1
	26:15 'I am Jesus whom you are persecuting.	1
Rom	12:14 Bless those who persecute you;	1
1Co	4:12 When reviled, we bless; when persecuted, we endure;	1
	15: 9 because I persecuted the church of God.	1
2Co	4: 9 persecuted, but not forsaken;	1
Gal	1:13 I was violently persecuting the church of God	1
	1:23 "The one who formerly was persecuting us	1
	4:29 who was born according to the flesh persecuted	1
	5:11 why am I still being persecuted	1
	6:12 not be persecuted for the cross of Christ.	1
2Ti	3:12 Indeed, all…will be persecuted.	1
Heb	11:37 destitute, persecuted, tormented—	2

persecution *See also* suffer persecution

1. διωγμός, *diōgmos, 1501*
2. θλῖψις, *thlipsis, 2568*

Mat	13:21 and when trouble or persecution arises	1
Mrk	4:17 then, when trouble or persecution arises	1
	10:30 children, and fields, with persecutions	1
Jhn	16:33 In the world you face persecution.	2
Act	8: 1 a severe persecution began against the church	1
	11:19 who were scattered because of the persecution	2
	13:50 and stirred up persecution against Paul	1
	14:22 saying, "It is through many persecutions	2
	20:23 imprisonment and persecutions are waiting for me.	2
Rom	8:35 Will hardship, or distress, or persecution	1
2Co	12:10 hardships, persecutions, and calamities	1
1Th	1: 6 in spite of persecution you received the word	2
	3: 3 that no one would be shaken by these persecutions.	2
	3: 7 during all our distress and persecution	2
2Th	1: 4 and faith during all your persecutions	1
2Ti	3:11 my persecutions, and my suffering	1
	3:11 What persecutions I endured!	1
Heb	10:33 being publicly exposed to abuse and persecution	2
Rev	1: 9 share with you in Jesus the persecution	2

persecutor

1. διώκτης, *diōktēs, 1502*
2. διώκω, *diōkō, 1503*

Php	3: 6 as to zeal, a persecutor of the church;	2
1Ti	1:13 I was formerly a blasphemer, a persecutor,	1

perseverance

1. ὑπομονή, *hypomonē, 5705*

Heb	12: 1 let us run with perseverance the race	1

persevere

1. καρτερέω, *kartereō, 2846*
2. παραμένω, *paramenō, 4169*
3. προσκαρτερέω, *proskartereō, 4674*
4. προσκαρτέρησις, *proskarterēsis, 4675*

Rom	12:12 persevere in prayer.	3
Eph	6:18 To that end keep alert and always persevere	4
Heb	11:27 persevered as though he saw him who is invisible.	1
Jas	1:25 look into the perfect law…and persevere	2

Persis

1. Περσίς, *Persis, 4372*

Rom 16:12 Greet the beloved Persis, who has worked hard		1

persist

1. Contextual: Not in Greek
2. ἐπιμένω, *epimenō, 2152*

Rom	11:23 if they do not persist in unbelief	2
Heb	10:26 For if we willfully persist in sin	1

persist in sin

1. ἁμαρτάνω, *hamartanō, 279*

1Ti 5:20 those who persist in sin		1

persistence

1. ἀναίδεια, *anaideia, 357*

Lke 11: 8 because of his persistence he will get up		1

persistent

1. ἐφίστημι, *ephistēmi, 2392*

2Ti 4: 2 be persistent whether the time is favorable		1

person

See also blind person, certain person, devout person, free person, godless person, good person, immoral person, impure person, one person, other person, poor person, rebellious person, rich person, righteous person, sensible person, sexually immoral person, sick person, some person, spiritual person, such a person, this person, unwise person, what sort of person, wicked person, worldly person, young person

1. Contextual: Not in Greek
2. ἀδελφός, *adelphos, 81*
3. ἀνήρ, *anēr, 467*
4. ἄνθρωπος, *anthrōpos, 476*
5. αὐτός, *autos, 899*
6. ἑαυτοῦ, *heautou, 1571*
7. ἡμέτερος, *hēmeteros, 2466*
8. ὁ, *ho, 3836*
9. ὄνομα, *onoma, 3950*
10. οὗτος, *houtos, 4047*
11. πρόσωπον, *prosōpon, 4725*
12. σάρξ, *sarx, 4922*
13. τίς, *tis, 5515*
14. τὶς, *tis, 5516*
15. υἱός + ὁ + ἄνθρωπος, *huios + ho + anthrōpos, 5626 + 3836 + 476*
16. ψυχή, *psychē, 6034*

Mat	3: 5 Then the people of Jerusalem and all Judea	1
	4:19 me, and I will make you fish for people."	4
	5:11 "Blessed are you when people revile you	1
	9: 2 just then some people were carrying a paralyzed	1
	12:31 people will be forgiven for every sin and blasphemy	4
	12:35 The good person brings good things out of a good	4
	12:35 and the evil person brings evil things out of	4
	12:41 The people of Nineveh will rise up at the judgment	3
	12:43 "When the unclean spirit has gone out of a person	4
	12:45 the last state of that person is worse	4
	13:21 persecution arises…person immediately falls away.	1
	13:54 began to teach the people in their synagogue	5
	14:35 After the people of that place recognized him	3
	15: 5 that person need not honor the father.	1
	15:11 not what goes into the mouth that defiles a person	4
	15:20 These are what defile a person	4
	16:13 "Who do people say that the Son of Man is?"	4
	22:16 for you do not regard people with partiality	4
	23: 7 to have people call them rabbi.	4
	23:13 you lock people out of the kingdom of heaven.	4

	25:32 he will separate people one from another	1
Mrk	1: 5 people from the whole Judean countryside	1
	1:17 "Follow me and I will make you fish for people."	4
	1:45 people came to him from every quarter.	1
	2: 3 some people came, bringing to him a paralyzed	1
	2:18 people came and said to him	1
	3:21 for people were saying, "He has gone out	1
	3:28 people will be forgiven for their sins	15
	5:14 people came to see what it was that had happened.	1
	5:35 some people came from the leader's house	1
	5:38 people weeping and wailing loudly.	1
	6:39 he ordered them to get all the people to sit	1
	6:41 loaves…to set before the people;	5
	6:54 people at once recognized him	1
	7:15 there is nothing outside a person	4
	7:18 whatever goes into a person from outside	4
	7:20 what comes out of a person that defiles.	4
	7:23 they defile a person."	4
	8: 4 feed these people with bread here in the desert?"	1
	8: 9 Now there were about four thousand people	1
	8:22 Some people brought a blind man to him	1
	8:24 "I can see people, but they look like trees	4
	8:27 his disciples, "Who do people say that I am?"	4
	10:13 People were bringing little children to him	1
	11: 8 Many people spread their cloaks on the road	1
	12:14 for you do not regard people with partiality	4
Lke	1:25 the disgrace I have endured among my people."	1
	5:10 from now on you will be catching people."	4
	6:22 "Blessed are you when people hate you	4
	6:45 The good person out of the good treasure	4
	6:45 evil person out of evil treasure produces evil;	1
	7:21 Jesus had just then cured many people of diseases	1
	7:31 will I compare the people of this generation	4
	8: 4 people from town after town came to him	8
	8:35 Then people came out to see what had happened	1
	10: 6 your peace will rest on that person;	5
	10: 8 you enter a town and its people welcome you	1
	11:24 the unclean spirit has gone out of a person	4
	11:26 the last state of that person is worse	4
	11:31 rise…with the people of this generation	3
	11:32 people of Nineveh will rise up at the judgment	3
	11:44 people walk over them without realizing it."	4
	11:46 you load people with burdens hard to bear	4
	13:29 people will come from east and west	1
	14: 3 lawful to cure people on the sabbath, or not?"	1
	14:23 compel people to come in	1
	16: 4 people may welcome me into their homes.'	1
	17: 4 if the same person sins against you seven times	1
	18: 2 neither feared God nor had respect for people.	4
	18:11 I thank you that I am not like other people:	4
	18:15 People were bringing even infants to him	1
	19:36 people kept spreading their cloaks on the road.	1
	21:26 People will faint from fear and foreboding	4
Jhn	1: 4 and the life was the light of all people.	4
	2:14 In the temple he found people selling	1
	3:19 and people loved darkness rather than light	4
	3:23 and people kept coming and were being baptized	1
	4:20 place where people must worship is in Jerusalem	1
	4:28 went back to the city. She said to the people	4
	6: 5 are we to buy bread for these people to eat?"	1
	6: 9 But what are they among so many people?"	1
	6:10 Jesus said, "Make the people sit down."	4
	6:14 When the people saw the sign that he had done	4
	6:44 I will raise that person up on the last day.	5
	7:51 "Our law does not judge people	4
	17: 2 you have given him authority over all people	12
	18:14 better to have one person die for the people.	4
Act	1:15 the crowd numbered about one hundred twenty persons)	9
	2:41 that day about three thousand persons were added.	16
	3: 2 People would lay him daily at the gate of the temple	1
	3:22 from your own people a prophet like me.	2
	4:34 There was not a needy person among them	14
	5:16 people would also gather from the towns	1
	7:37 a prophet for you from your own people	2
	7:51 "You stiff-necked people	1
	10:47 the water for baptizing these people	1
	13:42 Paul and Barnabas were going out, the people urged	1
	15:17 so that all other peoples may seek the Lord	4
	17: 6 "These people who have been turning the world	1
	17:30 now he commands all people everywhere to repent	4
	18:13 "This man is persuading people to worship God	1

19:29	people rushed together to the theater	1
24:16	a clear conscience toward God and all people.	4
27:37	two hundred seventy-six persons in the ship.)	16
28: 9	the people on the island who had diseases	8
Rom 1:27	received in their own persons the due penalty	6
2:28	For a person is not a Jew who is one outwardly	1
2:29	a person is a Jew who is one inwardly	1
3:28	a person is justified by faith apart from works	4
7: 1	the law is binding on a person only during…lifetime?	4
7: 1	law is binding…only during that person's lifetime?	1
9: 3	cut off from Christ for the sake of my own people	2
9:33	in Zion a stone that will make people stumble	1
10: 5	"the person who does these things will live by them."	4
13: 1	Let every person be subject to the governing	16
1Co 1:11	For it has been reported to me by Chloe's people	8
3:17	God will destroy that person.	10
4:19	find out not the talk of these arrogant people	1
6:18	Every sin that a person commits	4
14: 2	speak in a tongue do not speak to other people	4
14: 3	those who prophesy speak to other people	4
14:25	that person will bow down before God	1
14:30	let the first person be silent.	1
15:19	we are of all people most to be pitied.	4
15:29	Otherwise, what will those people do	8
15:29	why are people baptized on their behalf?	1
2Co 2:17	as persons of sincerity, as persons sent from God	1
2:17	as persons of sincerity, as persons sent from God	1
12: 2	I know a person in Christ	4
12: 3	I know that such a person	4
Gal 1:10	Or am I trying to please people?	4
1:10	If I were still pleasing people	4
2:16	a person is not justified by the works of the law	4
3:15	once a person's will has been ratified	4
Eph 4: 8	he gave gifts to his people."	4
4:14	blown about…by people's trickery,	4
1Th 1: 5	you know what kind of persons we proved to be	1
1: 9	For the people of those regions report about us	5
2:17	separated from you—in person, not in heart	11
2Th 3: 2	that we may be rescued from wicked and evil people;	4
1Ti 4:10	the living God, who is the Savior of all people	4
5:24	The sins of some people are conspicuous	4
6: 9	plunge people into ruin and destruction.	4
2Ti 2: 2	what you have heard…entrust to faithful people	4
2:16	it will lead people into more and more impiety	1
3: 2	For people will be lovers of themselves,	4
3: 8	so these people…also oppose the truth.	4
3:13	But wicked people…will go from bad to worse	4
4: 3	when people will not put up with sound doctrine	1
Tit 3:14	let people learn…to devote…to good works	7
Heb 11:14	for people who speak in this way make it clear	8
Jas 2: 2	For if a person with gold rings and in fine clothes	3
2:20	Do you want to be shown, you senseless person	4
2:24	You see that a person is justified by works	4
1Pe 1:11	inquiring about the person or time	13
3:20	in which a few, that is, eight persons, were saved	16
2Pe 2:12	These people, however, are like irrational animals	1
2:18	they entice…people who have just escaped	8
2:19	for people are slaves to whatever masters them.	14
Jde 1: 4	people who long ago were designated for this	8
1:10	these people slander…they do not understand	1
1:16	speech, flattering people to their own advantage	11
Rev 3: 4	Yet you have still a few persons in Sardis	9
6: 4	so that people would slaughter one another;	1
9: 4	but only those people who do not have the seal	4
9: 6	in those days people will seek death but will not find it;	4
9:10	is their power to harm people for five months.	4
11:13	seven thousand people were killed in the earthquake	4
13:18	number of the beast, for it is the number of a person.	4
16: 8	and it was allowed to scorch people with fire;	4
16:10	people gnawed their tongues in agony	1
16:18	as had not occurred since people were upon the earth	4
16:21	huge hailstones…dropped from heaven on people	4
21:26	People will bring into it the glory…of the nations.	1
22:18	God will add to that person the plagues	5
22:19	God will take away that person's share in the tree	5

person of Jerusalem

1. Ἱεροσολυμίτης, *Hierosolymitēs, 2643*

Mrk 1: 5	and all the people of Jerusalem	1
Jhn 7:25	Now some of the people of Jerusalem were saying	1

person of Macedonia

1. Μακεδών, *Makedōn, 3424*

2Co 9: 2	my boasting…to the people of Macedonia	1

person of Nineveh

1. Νινευίτης, *Nineuitēs, 3780*

Lke 11:30	as Jonah became a sign to the people of Nineveh	1
11:32	people of Nineveh will rise up at the judgment	1

person of Sidon

1. Σιδώνιος, *Sidōnios, 4973*

Act 12:20	Herod was angry with the people of Tyre and Sidon.	1

person of strange tongues

1. ἑτερόγλωσσος, *heteroglōssos, 2280*

1Co 14:21	it is written, "By people of strange tongues	1

person of the flesh

1. σάρκινος, *sarkinos, 4921*

1Co 3: 1	as people of the flesh, as infants in Christ.	1

person of Tyre

1. Τύριος, *Tyrios, 5601*

Act 12:20	Herod was angry with the people of Tyre and Sidon.	1

persuade

1. ἀναπείθω, *anapeithō, 400*
2. πείθω, *peithō, 4275*

Mat 27:20	elders persuaded the crowds to ask for Barabbas	2
Act 17: 4	Some of them were persuaded	2
18:13	"This man is persuading people to worship God	1
19:26	this Paul has persuaded	2
21:14	he would not be persuaded, we remained silent	2
23:21	do not be persuaded by them	2
26:28	so quickly persuading me to become a Christian?"	2
Rom 14:14	I know and am persuaded in the Lord Jesus	2
2Co 5:11	we try to persuade others;	2

persuasion

1. πεισμονή, *peismonē, 4282*

Gal 5: 8	Such persuasion does not come from the one who calls	1

persuasively

1. πείθω, *peithō, 4275*

Act 19: 8	argued persuasively about the kingdom of God.	1

pertain

1. πρός, *pros, 4639*

Heb 5: 1	things pertaining to God on their behalf	1

perverse

1. διαστρέφω, *diastrephō, 1406*

Mat 17:17	"You faithless and perverse generation	1
Lke 9:41	"You faithless and perverse generation	1
Php 2:15	a crooked and perverse generation	1

pervert

1. ἀποστρέφω, *apostrephō, 695*
2. διαστρέφω, *diastrephō, 1406*
3. ἐκστρέφω, *ekstrephō, 1750*
4. μεταστρέφω, *metastrephō, 3570*
5. μετατίθημι, *metatithēmi, 3572*

Lke 23: 2	"We found this man perverting our nation	2
23:14	as one who was perverting the people;	1
Gal 1: 7	want to pervert the gospel of Christ.	4
Tit 3:11	such a person is perverted and sinful	3
Jde 1: 4	ungodly, who pervert the grace of our God	5

pestilence

1. θάνατος, *thanatos, 2505*

Rev 6: 8	kill…pestilence, and by the wild animals	1
18: 8	plagues…pestilence and mourning and famine	1

pestilent fellow

1. λοιμός, *loimos, 3369*

Act 24: 5	We have, in fact, found this man a pestilent fellow	1

Peter

1. Contextual: Not in Greek

2. Πέτρος, *Petros, 4377*

Mat	4:18	Simon, who is called Peter, and Andrew his brother	2
	8:14	When Jesus entered Peter's house	2
	10: 2	first, Simon, also known as Peter	2
	14:28	Peter answered him, "Lord, if it is you	2
	14:29	He said, "Come." So Peter got out of the boat	2
	15:15	Peter said to him, "Explain this parable to us."	2
	16:16	Simon Peter answered, "You are the Messiah	2
	16:18	I tell you, you are Peter	2
	16:22	Peter took him aside and began to rebuke him	2
	16:23	and said to Peter, "Get behind me, Satan!	2
	17: 1	Jesus took with him Peter and James	2
	17: 4	Peter said to Jesus	2
	17:24	the collectors…came to Peter and said	2
	17:26	When Peter said, "From others,"	1
	18:21	Then Peter came and said to him	2
	19:27	Then Peter said in reply	2
	26:33	Peter said to him, "Though all become deserters	2
	26:35	Peter said to him, "Even though I must die	2
	26:37	took with him Peter and the two sons of Zebedee	2
	26:40	he said to Peter	2
	26:58	Peter was following him at a distance	2
	26:69	Now Peter was sitting outside in the courtyard.	2
	26:73	bystanders came up and said to Peter	2
	26:75	Peter remembered what Jesus had said:	2
Mrk	3:16	Simon (to whom he gave the name Peter);	2
	5:37	He allowed no one to follow him except Peter	2
	8:29	Peter answered him, "You are the Messiah."	2
	8:32	Peter took him aside and began to rebuke him.	2
	8:33	looking at his disciples, he rebuked Peter	2
	9: 2	Jesus took with him Peter and James and John	2
	9: 5	Peter said to Jesus, "Rabbi, it is good	2
	10:28	Peter began to say to him, "Look, we have left	2
	11:21	Peter remembered and said to him, "Rabbi, look!	2
	13: 3	Peter, James, John, and Andrew asked him	2
	14:29	Peter said to him, "Even though all become deserters	2
	14:33	He took with him Peter and James and John	2
	14:37	he said to Peter, "Simon, are you asleep?	2
	14:54	Peter had followed him at a distance	2
	14:66	While Peter was below in the courtyard	2
	14:67	saw Peter warming himself, she stared at him	2
	14:70	the bystanders again said to Peter	2
	14:72	Peter remembered that Jesus had said to him	2
	16: 7	tell his disciples and Peter that he is going	2
	16: S	⟦they told briefly to those around Peter⟧	2
Lke	5: 8	when Simon Peter saw it	2
	6:14	Simon, whom he named Peter, and his brother Andrew	2
	8:45	When all denied it, Peter said, "Master	2
	8:51	except Peter, John, and James,	2
	9:20	Peter answered, "The Messiah of God."	2
	9:28	Jesus took with him Peter and John and James	2
	9:32	Now Peter and his companions were weighed down	2
	9:33	Peter said to Jesus, "Master, it is good	2
	12:41	Peter said, "Lord, are you telling this parable	2
	18:28	Peter said, "Look, we have left our homes	2
	22: 8	So Jesus sent Peter and John, saying, "Go	2
	22:34	"I tell you, Peter, the cock will not crow	2
	22:54	Peter was following at a distance.	2
	22:55	sat down together, Peter sat among them.	2
	22:58	Peter said, "Man, I am not!"	2
	22:60	Peter said, "Man, I do not know what you	2
	22:61	The Lord turned and looked at Peter.	2
	22:61	Peter remembered the word of the Lord	2
	24:12	Peter got up and ran to the tomb	2
Jhn	1:40	One…was Andrew, Simon Peter's brother.	2
	1:42	be called Cephas" (which is translated Peter).	2
	1:44	from Bethsaida, the city of Andrew and Peter.	2
	6: 8	Andrew, Simon Peter's brother, said to him	2
	6:68	Simon Peter answered him, "Lord, to whom can we	2
	13: 6	He came to Simon Peter, who said to him, "Lord	2
	13: 8	Peter said to him, "You will never wash my feet."	2
	13: 9	Simon Peter said to him, "Lord, not my feet only	2
	13:24	Simon Peter therefore motioned to him to ask Jesus	2
	13:36	Simon Peter said to him, "Lord, where	2
	13:37	Peter said to him, "Lord, why can I not follow	2
	18:10	Simon Peter, who had a sword, drew it	2
	18:11	Jesus said to Peter	2
	18:15	Simon Peter and another disciple followed Jesus.	2
	18:16	but Peter was standing outside at the gate.	2
	18:16	went out…and brought Peter in.	2
	18:17	The woman said to Peter	2

	18:18	Peter also was standing with them	2
	18:25	Simon Peter was standing and warming himself.	2
	18:26	relative of the man whose ear Peter had cut off	2
	18:27	Again Peter denied it	2
	20: 2	went to Simon Peter and the other disciple	2
	20: 3	Then Peter and the other disciple set out	2
	20: 4	the other disciple outran Peter	2
	20: 6	Simon Peter came, following him	2
	21: 2	Simon Peter, Thomas called the Twin	2
	21: 3	Simon Peter said to them, "I am going fishing."	2
	21: 7	That disciple whom Jesus loved said to Peter	2
	21: 7	When Simon Peter heard that it was the Lord	2
	21:11	Simon Peter went aboard and hauled the net ashore	2
	21:15	Jesus said to Simon Peter, "Simon son of John	2
	21:17	Peter felt hurt because he said to him	2
	21:20	Peter turned and saw the disciple	2
	21:21	When Peter saw him, he said to Jesus, "Lord	2
Act	1:13	Peter, and John, and James, and Andrew	2
	1:15	In those days Peter stood up among the believers	2
	2:14	Peter, standing with the eleven	2
	2:37	said to Peter and to the other apostles	2
	2:38	Peter said to them, "Repent, and be baptized	2
	3: 1	One day Peter and John were going up to the temple	2
	3: 3	saw Peter and John about to go into the temple	2
	3: 4	Peter looked intently at him, as did John, and said	2
	3: 6	Peter said, "I have no silver or gold	2
	3:11	While he clung to Peter and John	2
	3:12	When Peter saw it, he addressed the people	2
	4: 1	While Peter and John were speaking to the people	1
	4: 8	Then Peter, filled with the Holy Spirit, said	2
	4:13	Now when they saw the boldness of Peter and John	2
	4:19	Peter and John answered them, "Whether it is right	2
	5: 3	"Ananias," Peter asked	2
	5: 8	Peter said to her, "Tell me	2
	5: 9	Peter said to her, "How is it that you have agreed	2
	5:15	Peter's shadow might fall on some of them	2
	5:29	Peter and the apostles answered, "We must obey God	2
	8:14	they sent Peter and John to them.	2
	8:17	Then Peter and John laid their hands on them	1
	8:20	Peter said to him, "May your silver perish with you	2
	8:25	Now after Peter and John had testified and spoken	1
	9:32	Peter went here and there among all the believers	2
	9:34	Peter said to him, "Aeneas, Jesus Christ heals you;	2
	9:38	disciples, who heard that Peter was there	2
	9:39	So Peter got up and went with them;	2
	9:40	Peter put all of them outside, and then he knelt	2
	9:40	seeing Peter, she sat up.	2
	10: 5	send…for a certain Simon who is called Peter;	2
	10: 9	Peter went up on the roof to pray.	2
	10:13	he heard a voice saying, "Get up, Peter; kill and eat."	2
	10:14	Peter said, "By no means, Lord;	2
	10:17	Now while Peter was greatly puzzled	2
	10:18	Simon, who was called Peter, was staying there.	2
	10:19	While Peter was still thinking about the vision	2
	10:21	Peter went down to the men and said, "I am the one	2
	10:23	So Peter invited them in and gave them lodging.	1
	10:25	On Peter's arrival Cornelius met him	2
	10:26	Peter made him get up, saying, "Stand up;	2
	10:32	ask for Simon, who is called Peter;	2
	10:34	Peter began to speak to them: "I truly understand	2
	10:44	While Peter was still speaking	2
	10:45	circumcised believers who had come with Peter	2
	10:46	Then Peter said	2
	11: 2	when Peter went up to Jerusalem	2
	11: 4	Peter began to explain it to them, step by step	2
	11: 7	'Get up, Peter; kill and eat.'	2
	11:13	'Send to Joppa and bring Simon, who is called Peter;	2
	12: 3	he proceeded to arrest Peter also.	2
	12: 5	While Peter was kept in prison	2
	12: 6	Peter, bound with two chains, was sleeping	2
	12: 7	He tapped Peter on the side and woke him, saying	2
	12: 9	Peter went out and followed him;	1
	12:11	Peter came to himself and said	2
	12:14	On recognizing Peter's voice,	2
	12:14	announced that Peter was standing at the gate.	2
	12:16	Meanwhile Peter continued knocking;	2
	12:18	no small commotion…over what had become of Peter.	2
	15: 7	Peter stood up and said to them, "My brothers	2
Gal	2: 7	just as Peter had been entrusted	2
	2: 8	(for he who worked through Peter	2
1Pe	1: 1	Peter, an apostle of Jesus Christ	2

2Pe 1: 1 Simeon Peter, a servant and apostle of Jesus   2

petition

1. ἐντυγχάνω, *entynchanō, 1961*
Act 25:24 about whom the whole Jewish community petitioned   1

Phanuel

1. Φανουήλ, *Phanouēl, 5750*
Lke 2:36 a prophet, Anna the daughter of Phanuel   1

Pharaoh

1. Φαραώ, *Pharaō, 5755*
Act 7:10 when he stood before Pharaoh, king of Egypt   1
      7:13 Joseph's family became known to Pharaoh.   1
      7:21 Pharaoh's daughter adopted him   1
Rom 9:17 For the scripture says to Pharaoh   1
Heb 11:24 refused to be called a son of Pharaoh's daughter   1

Pharisee

1. Φαρισαῖος, *Pharisaios, 5757*
Mat 3: 7 when he saw many Pharisees and Sadducees   1
      5:20 exceeds that of the scribes and Pharisees   1
      9:11 When the Pharisees saw this, they said   1
      9:14 "Why do we and the Pharisees fast often,   1
      9:34 But the Pharisees said, "By the ruler of the demons   1
    12: 2 When the Pharisees saw it, they said to him,   1
    12:14 the Pharisees went out and conspired   1
    12:24 when the Pharisees heard it, they said   1
    12:38 Then some of the scribes and Pharisees said   1
    15: 1 Then Pharisees and scribes came to Jesus   1
    15:12 "Do you know that the Pharisees took offense   1
    16: 1 The Pharisees and Sadducees came   1
    16: 6 the yeast of the Pharisees and Sadducees."   1
    16:11 the yeast of the Pharisees and Sadducees!"   1
    16:12 the teaching of the Pharisees and Sadducees.   1
    19: 3 Pharisees came to him, and to test him they asked   1
    21:45 priests and the Pharisees heard his parables   1
    22:15 Then the Pharisees went and plotted   1
    22:34 When the Pharisees heard   1
    22:41 Now while the Pharisees were gathered together   1
    23: 2 "The scribes and the Pharisees sit on Moses' seat;   1
    23:13 woe to you, scribes and Pharisees, hypocrites!   1
    23:15 Woe to you, scribes and Pharisees, hypocrites!   1
    23:23 "Woe to you, scribes and Pharisees, hypocrites!   1
    23:25 "Woe to you, scribes and Pharisees, hypocrites!   1
    23:26 You blind Pharisee!   1
    23:27 "Woe to you, scribes and Pharisees, hypocrites!   1
    23:29 "Woe to you, scribes and Pharisees, hypocrites!   1
    27:62 the chief priests and the Pharisees gathered   1
Mrk 2:16 the scribes of the Pharisees   1
      2:18 John's disciples and the Pharisees were fasting;   1
      2:18 the disciples of the Pharisees fast   1
      2:24 Pharisees said to him, "Look, why are they doing   1
      3: 6 The Pharisees went out   1
      7: 1 Now when the Pharisees…gathered around him   1
      7: 3 (For the Pharisees, and all the Jews, do not eat   1
      7: 5 the Pharisees and the scribes asked him   1
      8:11 The Pharisees came and began to argue with him   1
      8:15 "Watch out—beware of the yeast of the Pharisees   1
    10: 2 Pharisees came, and to test him they asked   1
    12:13 some Pharisees and some Herodians   1
Lke 5:17 Pharisees and teachers of the law were sitting   1
      5:21 the scribes and the Pharisees began to question   1
      5:30 The Pharisees and their scribes were complaining   1
      5:33 like the disciples of the Pharisees   1
      6: 2 some of the Pharisees said, "Why are you doing   1
      6: 7 The scribes and the Pharisees watched him   1
      7:30 the Pharisees and the lawyers rejected   1
      7:36 One of the Pharisees asked Jesus to eat with him   1
      7:36 he went into the Pharisee's house   1
      7:37 he was eating in the Pharisee's house   1
      7:39 Now when the Pharisee who had invited him saw it   1
    11:37 a Pharisee invited him to dine with him;   1
    11:38 The Pharisee was amazed to see   1
    11:39 "Now you Pharisees clean the outside of the cup   1
    11:42 woe to you Pharisees!   1
    11:43 Woe to you Pharisees!   1
    11:53 the Pharisees began to be very hostile toward him   1
    12: 1 yeast of the Pharisees, that is, their hypocrisy.   1
    13:31 At that very hour some Pharisees came and said   1

    14: 1 to the house of a leader of the Pharisees   1
    14: 3 Jesus asked the lawyers and Pharisees   1
    15: 2 the Pharisees and the scribes were grumbling   1
    16:14 The Pharisees, who were lovers of money, heard all   1
    17:20 Once Jesus was asked by the Pharisees   1
    18:10 one a Pharisee and the other a tax collector.   1
    18:11 The Pharisee, standing by himself, was praying thus   1
    19:39 Some of the Pharisees in the crowd said   1
Jhn 1:24 Now they had been sent from the Pharisees.   1
      3: 1 Now there was a Pharisee named Nicodemus   1
      4: 1 when Jesus learned that the Pharisees had heard   1
      7:32 The Pharisees heard the crowd muttering such things   1
      7:32 the chief priests and Pharisees sent temple police   1
      7:45 went back to the chief priests and Pharisees   1
      7:47 Pharisees replied, "Surely you have not been   1
      7:48 Has any one…of the Pharisees believed in him?   1
      8: 3 ⟦The scribes and the Pharisees brought a woman⟧   1
      8:13 Then the Pharisees said to him   1
      9:13 They brought to the Pharisees the man   1
      9:15 Then the Pharisees also began to ask him   1
      9:16 Some of the Pharisees said   1
      9:40 Some of the Pharisees near him heard this   1
    11:46 some of them went to the Pharisees   1
    11:47 the Pharisees called a meeting of the council,   1
    11:57 the Pharisees had given orders   1
    12:19 The Pharisees then said to one another   1
    12:42 because of the Pharisees they did not confess it   1
    18: 3 chief priests and the Pharisees   1
Act 5:34 a Pharisee in the council named Gamaliel   1
    15: 5 who belonged to the sect of the Pharisees   1
    23: 6 some were Sadducees and others were Pharisees   1
    23: 6 "Brothers, I am a Pharisee, a son of Pharisees.   1
    23: 6 "Brothers, I am a Pharisee, a son of Pharisees.   1
    23: 7 dissension…between the Pharisees and…Sadducees   1
    23: 8 the Pharisees acknowledge all three.)   1
    23: 9 certain scribes of the Pharisees' group   1
    26: 5 and lived as a Pharisee.   1
Php 3: 5 a Hebrew born of Hebrews; as to the law, a Pharisee;   1

Philadelphia

1. Φιλαδέλφεια, *Philadelpheia, 5788*
Rev 1:11 seven churches…to Sardis, to Philadelphia   1
      3: 7 to the angel of the church in Philadelphia write: 1

Philemon

1. Φιλήμων, *Philēmōn, 5800*
Phm 1: 1 To Philemon our dear friend and co-worker   1

Philetus

1. Φίλητος, *Philētos, 5801*
2Ti 2:17 Among them are Hymenaeus and Philetus   1

Philip

1. Contextual: Not in Greek
2. Φίλιππος, *Philippos, 5805*
Mat 10: 3 Philip and Bartholomew; Thomas and Matthew   2
    14: 3 Herodias, his brother Philip's wife   2
Mrk 3:18 Andrew, and Philip, and Bartholomew, and Matthew   2
      6:17 Herodias, his brother Philip's wife   2
Lke 3: 1 Philip ruler of the region of Ituraea   2
      6:14 James, and John, and Philip, and Bartholomew   2
Jhn 1:43 He found Philip and said to him, "Follow me."   2
      1:44 Now Philip was from Bethsaida, the city of Andrew   2
      1:45 Philip found Nathanael and said to him   2
      1:46 Philip said to him, "Come and see."   2
      1:48 under the fig tree before Philip called you."   2
      6: 5 Jesus said to Philip, "Where are we to buy bread   2
      6: 7 Philip answered him   2
    12:21 They came to Philip, who was from Bethsaida   2
    12:22 Philip went and told Andrew;   2
    12:22 Andrew and Philip went and told Jesus.   2
    14: 8 Philip said to him, "Lord, show us the Father   2
    14: 9 Philip, and you still do not know me?   2
Act 1:13 Philip and Thomas, Bartholomew and Matthew   2
      6: 5 Philip, Prochorus, Nicanor, Timon   2
      8: 5 Philip went down to the city of Samaria   2
      8: 6 listened eagerly to what was said by Philip   2
      8:12 when they believed Philip   2
      8:13 being baptized, he stayed constantly with Philip   2
      8:26 an angel of the Lord said to Philip, "Get up and go   2

Act 8:29 the Spirit said to Philip, "Go over   2
      8:30 Philip ran up to it and heard him reading   2
      8:31 he invited Philip to get in and sit beside him.   2
      8:34 The eunuch asked Philip   2
      8:35 Then Philip began to speak   2
      8:38 both of them, Philip and the eunuch, went down   2
      8:38 Philip baptized him.   1
      8:39 the Spirit of the Lord snatched Philip away;   2
      8:40 Philip found himself at Azotus   2
     21: 8 we went into the house of Philip the evangelist   2

Philippi

  1. Φίλιπποι, *Philippoi, 5804*
  2. Φίλιππος, *Philippos, 5805*
Mat 16:13 into the district of Caesarea Philippi   2
Mrk 8:27 to the villages of Caesarea Philippi;   2
Act 16:12 and from there to Philippi   1
     20: 6 we sailed from Philippi   1
Php   1: 1 saints in Christ Jesus who are in Philippi   1
1Th   2: 2 we had…been shamefully mistreated at Philippi   1

Philippian

  1. Φιλιππήσιος, *Philippēsios, 5803*
Php   4:15 You Philippians indeed know   1

Philologus

  1. Φιλόλογος, *Philologos, 5807*
Rom 16:15 Greet Philologus, Julia, Nereus and his sister   1

philosopher

  1. φιλόσοφος, *philosophos, 5815*
Act 17:18 Epicurean and Stoic philosophers debated with him.   1

philosophy

  1. φιλοσοφία, *philosophia, 5814*
Col   2: 8 captive through philosophy and empty deceit   1

Phlegon

  1. Φλέγων, *Phlegōn, 5823*
Rom 16:14 Greet Asyncritus, Phlegon, Hermes, Patrobas   1

Phoebe

  1. Φοίβη, *Phoibē, 5833*
Rom 16: 1 I commend to you our sister Phoebe   1

Phoenicia

  1. Φοινίκη, *Phoinikē, 5834*
Act 11:19 traveled as far as Phoenicia, Cyprus, and Antioch   1
     15: 3 they passed through both Phoenicia and Samaria   1
     21: 2 When we found a ship bound for Phoenicia   1

Phoenix

  1. Φοῖνιξ2, *Phoinix2, 5837*
Act 27:12 somehow they could reach Phoenix   1

phrase *See also* heap up empty phrases
  1. Contextual: Not in Greek
Heb 12:27 This phrase, "Yet once more," indicates…   1

Phrygia

  1. Φρυγία, *Phrygia, 5867*
Act   2:10 Phrygia and Pamphylia   1
     16: 6 They went through the region of Phrygia and Galatia   1
     18:23 the region of Galatia and Phrygia   1

Phygelus

  1. Φύγελος, *Phygelos, 5869*
2Ti   1:15 including Phygelus and Hermogenes.   1

phylactery

  1. φυλακτήριον, *phylaktērion, 5873*
Mat 23: 5 they make their phylacteries broad   1

physical *See also* physical *descent*
  1. Contextual: Not in Greek
  2. ἐν + σάρξ, *en + sarx, 1877 + 4922*
  3. σάρξ, *sarx, 4922*
  4. σωματικός, *sōmatikos, 5394*

  5. ψυχικός, *psychikos, 6035*
Rom 2:28 nor is true circumcision something…physical.   2
1Co 15:44 It is sown a physical body   5
     15:44 If there is a physical body   5
     15:46 the physical, and then the spiritual.   5
Gal   4:13 You know that it was because of a physical infirmity   3
Eph   2:11 a physical circumcision made in the flesh by human   1
1Ti   4: 8 for, while physical training is of some value   4

physically

  1. ἐκ + φύσις, *ek + physis, 1666 + 5882*
Rom 2:27 Then those who are physically uncircumcised   1

physician

  1. ἰατρός, *iatros, 2620*
Mat   9:12 "Those who are well have no need of a physician   1
Mrk   2:17 "Those who are well have no need of a physician   1
      5:26 She had endured much under many physicians   1
Lke   5:31 "Those who are well have no need of a physician   1
      8:43 though she had spent all she had on physicians   1
Col   4:14 Luke, the beloved physician, and Demas greet you.   1

pick

  1. τρυγάω, *trygaō, 5582*
Lke   6:44 nor are grapes picked from a bramble bush.   1

pick up

  1. αἴρω, *airō, 149*
Mrk 16:18 〚they will pick up snakes in their hands〛   1
Jhn   8:59 they picked up stones to throw at him   1
Act 20: 9 he fell to the ground…and was picked up dead.   1

piece *See also* break in pieces, break to pieces, cut in
pieces, tear to pieces
  1. ἐπίβλημα, *epiblēma, 2099*
  2. μέρος, *meros, 3538*
  3. τὶς, *tis, 5516*
Mat   9:16 No one sews a piece of unshrunk cloth on   1
Mrk   2:21 sews a piece of unshrunk cloth on an old cloak;   1
Lke   5:36 "No one tears a piece from a new garment   1
      5:36 the piece from the new will not match the old.   1
     24:42 They gave him a piece of broiled fish   2
Act 27:44 some on planks and others on pieces of the ship.   3

broken piece

  1. κλάσμα, *klasma, 3083*
  2. κόφινος, *kophinos, 3186*
Mat 14:20 of the broken pieces, twelve baskets full.   1
     15:37 the broken pieces left over, seven baskets full.   1
Mrk   6:43 took up twelve baskets full of broken pieces   2
      8: 8 they took up the broken pieces left over   1
      8:19 how many baskets full of broken pieces   1
      8:20 how many baskets full of broken pieces   1
Lke   9:17 twelve baskets of broken pieces.   1

one piece

  1. ὅλος, *holos, 3910*
Jhn 19:23 seamless, woven in one piece from the top.   1

piece of bread

  1. ψωμίον, *psōmion, 6040*
Jhn 13:26 I give this piece of bread when I have dipped it   1
     13:26 had dipped the piece of bread, he gave it to Judas   1
     13:27 After he received the piece of bread, Satan   1
     13:30 after receiving the piece of bread   1

piece of cloth

  1. σουδάριον, *soudarion, 5051*
Lke 19:20 I wrapped it up in a piece of cloth   1

piece of land

  1. ἀγρός, *agros, 69*
Lke 14:18 said to him, 'I have bought a piece of land   1

piece of property

  1. κτῆμα, *ktēma, 3228*
Act 5: 1 Ananias…sold a piece of property;   1

piece of silver

1. ἀργύριον, *argyrion, 736*

Mat	26:15	They paid him thirty pieces of silver.	1
	27: 3	brought back the thirty pieces of silver	1
	27: 5	Throwing down the pieces of silver in the temple	1
	27: 6	the chief priests, taking the pieces of silver,	1
	27: 9	"And they took the thirty pieces of silver	1

pierce

1. διέρχομαι, *dierchomai, 1451*
2. διϊκνέομαι, *diikneomai, 1459*
3. ἐκκεντέω, *ekkenteō, 1708*
4. νύσσω, *nyssō, 3817*
5. περιπείρω, *peripeirō, 4345*

Lke	2:35	and a sword will pierce your own soul too."	1
Jhn	19:34	one of the soldiers pierced his side with a spear	4
	19:37	will look on the one whom they have pierced."	3
1Ti	6:10	pierced themselves with many pains.	5
Heb	4:12	piercing until it divides soul from spirit	2
Rev	1: 7	even those who pierced him;	3

piety

1. δικαιοσύνη, *dikaiosynē, 1466*
2. εὐσέβεια, *eusebeia, 2354*

Mat	6: 1	"Beware of practicing your piety before others	1
Act	3:12	by our own power or piety we had made him walk?	2

self-imposed piety

1. ἐθελοθρησκία, *ethelothrēskia, 1615*

Col	2:23	in promoting self-imposed piety,	1

pig

1. χοῖρος, *choiros, 5956*

Lke	15:15	who sent him to his fields to feed the pigs.	1
	15:16	the pods that the pigs were eating;	1

pigeon

1. περιστερά, *peristera, 4361*

Lke	2:24	"a pair of turtledoves or two young pigeons."	1

Pilate

1. Contextual: Not in Greek
2. Πιλᾶτος, *Pilatos, 4397*

Mat	27: 2	handed him over to Pilate the governor.	2
	27:13	Then Pilate said to him, "Do you not hear	2
	27:17	So after they had gathered, Pilate said to them	2
	27:22	Pilate said to them, "Then what should I do	2
	27:24	So when Pilate saw that he could do nothing	2
	27:58	went to Pilate and asked for the body of Jesus	2
	27:58	then Pilate ordered it to be given to him.	2
	27:62	the Pharisees gathered before Pilate	2
	27:65	Pilate said to them, "You have a guard	2
Mrk	15: 1	led him away, and handed him over to Pilate.	2
	15: 2	Pilate asked him, "Are you the King of the Jews?"	2
	15: 4	Pilate asked him again, "Have you no answer?	2
	15: 5	so that Pilate was amazed.	2
	15: 8	the crowd came and began to ask Pilate	1
	15:12	Pilate spoke to them again, "Then what do you wish	2
	15:14	Pilate asked them, "Why, what evil has he done?"	2
	15:15	So Pilate, wishing to satisfy the crowd	2
	15:43	went boldly to Pilate	2
	15:44	Pilate wondered if he were already dead;	2
Lke	3: 1	Pontius Pilate was governor of Judea	2
	13: 1	the Galileans whose blood Pilate had mingled	2
	23: 1	brought Jesus before Pilate.	2
	23: 3	Pilate asked him, "Are you the king of the Jews?"	2
	23: 4	Pilate said to the chief priests	2
	23: 6	When Pilate heard this	2
	23:11	elegant robe on him, and sent him back to Pilate.	2
	23:12	Herod and Pilate became friends with each other;	2
	23:13	Pilate then called together the chief priests	2
	23:20	Pilate, wanting to release Jesus, addressed them	2
	23:24	So Pilate gave his verdict	2
	23:52	This man went to Pilate and asked for the body	2
Jhn	18:28	from Caiaphas to Pilate's headquarters.	1
	18:29	Pilate went out to them and said	2
	18:31	Pilate said to them, "Take him yourselves	2
	18:33	Pilate entered the headquarters again	2
	18:35	Pilate replied, "I am not a Jew, am I?	2
	18:37	Pilate asked him, "So you are a king?"	2
	18:38	Pilate asked him, "What is truth?"	2
	19: 1	Pilate took Jesus and had him flogged.	2
	19: 4	Pilate went out again and said to them	2
	19: 5	Pilate said to them, "Here is the man!"	1
	19: 6	Pilate said to them, "Take him yourselves	2
	19: 8	Now when Pilate heard this,	2
	19:10	Pilate therefore said to him, "Do you refuse	2
	19:12	From then on Pilate tried to release him	2
	19:13	When Pilate heard these words	2
	19:15	Pilate asked them, "Shall I crucify your King?"	2
	19:19	Pilate also had an inscription written	2
	19:21	the chief priests of the Jews said to Pilate	2
	19:22	Pilate answered, "What I have written	2
	19:31	So they asked Pilate to have the legs…broken	2
	19:38	asked Pilate to let him take away the body	2
	19:38	Pilate gave him permission;	2
Act	3:13	rejected in the presence of Pilate	2
	4:27	both Herod and Pontius Pilate, with the Gentiles	2
	13:28	they asked Pilate to have him killed.	2
1Ti	6:13	in his testimony before Pontius Pilate	2

pile   *See* manure pile

pilfer

1. νοσφίζω, *nosphizō, 3802*

Tit	2:10	not to pilfer, but to show complete and perfect fidelity	1

pillar

1. στῦλος, *stylos, 5146*

Gal	2: 9	Cephas and John, who were acknowledged pillars	1
1Ti	3:15	the pillar and bulwark of the truth.	1
Rev	3:12	I will make you a pillar in the temple of my God;	1
	10: 1	and his legs like pillars of fire.	1

pilot

1. εὐθύνω, *euthynō, 2316*
2. κυβερνήτης, *kybernētēs, 3237*

Act	27:11	to the pilot and to the owner of the ship	2
Jas	3: 4	wherever the will of the pilot directs.	1

pinnacle

1. πτερύγιον, *pterygion, 4762*

Mat	4: 5	placed him on the pinnacle of the temple	1
Lke	4: 9	placed him on the pinnacle of the temple	1

pioneer

1. ἀρχηγός, *archēgos, 795*

Heb	2:10	make the pioneer of their salvation perfect	1
	12: 2	Jesus the pioneer and perfecter of our faith	1

Pisidia

1. Πισιδία, *Pisidia, 4407*
2. Πισίδιος, *Pisidios, 4408*

Act	13:14	and came to Antioch in Pisidia.	2
	14:24	passed through Pisidia and came to Pamphylia.	1

pit

1. ἄβυσσος, *abyssos, 12*
2. βόθυνος, *bothynos, 1073*

Mat	12:11	it falls into a pit on the sabbath;	2
	15:14	both will fall into a pit."	2
Lke	6:39	Will not both fall into a pit?	2
Rev	20: 3	and threw him into the pit, and locked	1

bottomless pit

1. ἄβυσσος, *abyssos, 12*

Rev	9: 1	given the key to the shaft of the bottomless pit;	1
	9: 2	he opened the shaft of the bottomless pit	1
	9:11	as king over them the angel of the bottomless pit;	1
	11: 7	the beast that comes up from the bottomless pit	1
	17: 8	beast…is about to ascend from the bottomless pit	1
	20: 1	holding in his hand the key to the bottomless pit	1

pit for the wine press

1. ὑπολήνιον, *hypolēnion, 5700*

Mrk	12: 1	dug a pit for the wine press	1

pitiable

1. ἐλεεινός, *eleeinos, 1795*

Rev 3:17 not realize that you are wretched, pitiable, poor   1

pity   *See* have pity, move with pity

out of pity

1. σπλαγχνίζομαι, *splanchnizomai, 5072*

Mat 18:27 out of pity for him, the lord…released him   1

pity most

1. ἐλεεινός, *eleeinos, 1795*

1Co 15:19 we are of all people most to be pitied.   1

place   *See also* dwelling place, go from place to place, go from place to place, have a place, heavenly place, holy place, one place, place to place, take one's place, take one's place at table, take place

1. Contextual: Not in Greek
2. ἀντί, *anti, 505*
3. δίδωμι, *didōmi, 1443*
4. εἰς, *eis, 1650*
5. ἐκεῖθεν, *ekeithen, 1696*
6. ἐν, *en, 1877*
7. ἵστημι, *histēmi, 2705*
8. καθίζω, *kathizō, 2767*
9. καθίστημι, *kathistēmi, 2770*
10. κλῆρος, *klēros, 3102*
11. μέρος, *meros, 3538*
12. πού, *pou, 4543*
13. ποῦ, *pou, 4544*
14. τίθημι, *tithēmi, 5502*
15. τόπος, *topos, 5536*
16. τυγχάνω, *tynchanō, 5593*
17. χωρέω, *chōreō, 6003*
18. χωρίον, *chōrion, 6005*
19. ὧδε, *hōde, 6045*

Mat 2: 9 stopped over the place where the child was.   1
       2:22 in place of his father Herod, he was afraid to go   2
       4: 5 the holy city and placed him on the pinnacle   7
      12: 9 He left that place and entered   5
      13:53 When Jesus had finished…he left that place   5
      14:13 withdrew from there in a boat to a deserted place   15
      14:15 "This is a deserted place, and the hour is now late;   15
      14:35 After the people of that place recognized him   15
      15:21 Jesus left that place and went away   5
      15:29 Jesus had left that place   5
      24: 7 famines and earthquakes in various places: 15
      24:15 standing in the holy place, as was spoken of   15
      26:36 to a place called Gethsemane;   18
      26:52 "Put your sword back into its place;   15
      27:33 when they came to a place called Golgotha   15
      27:33 (which means Place of a Skull)   15
      28: 6 Come, see the place where he lay.   15
Mrk 1:35 he got up and went out to a deserted place   15
       6: 1 He left that place and came to   5
       6:10 stay there until you leave the place.   5
       6:11 If any place will not welcome you   15
       6:31 "Come away to a deserted place all by yourselves   15
       6:32 in the boat to a deserted place by themselves.   15
       6:35 "This is a deserted place, and the hour is now   15
      10: 1 He left that place and went to the region of Judea   5
      13: 8 there will be earthquakes in various places;   15
      14:32 They went to a place called Gethsemane;   18
      15:22 they brought Jesus to the place called Golgotha   15
      15:22 Golgotha (which means the place of a skull).   15
      16: 6 Look, there is the place they laid him.   15
Lke 2: 7 because there was no place for them in the inn.   15
       4: 9 placed him on the pinnacle of the temple   7
       4:17 found the place where it was written: 15
       4:37 report about him began to reach every place   15
       4:42 he departed and went into a deserted place.   15
       5:16 he would withdraw to deserted places and pray.   1
       6:17 came down with them and stood on a level place   15
       9:12 we are here in a deserted place."   15
      10: 1 to every town and place   15
      10:32 a Levite, when he came to the place and saw him   15
      11: 1 He was praying in a certain place   15

      12:17 I have no place to store my crops?'   13
      14: 9 'Give this person your place,'   15
      14: 9 you would start to take the lowest place.   15
      14:10 go and sit down at the lowest place   15
      16:28 will not also come into this place of torment.'   15
      19: 5 When Jesus came to the place, he looked up   15
      19:29 at the place called the Mount of Olives,   1
      20:35 who are considered worthy of a place in that age   16
      21:11 in various places famines and plagues;   15
      22:40 When he reached the place, he said to them, "Pray   15
      23: 5 from Galilee where he began even to this place."   19
      23:33 they came to the place that is called The Skull   15
Jhn 3:35 and has placed all things in his hands.   3
       4:20 the place where people must worship is in Jerusalem   15
       4:43 he went from that place to Galilee   5
       6:10 Now there was a great deal of grass in the place;   15
       6:23 Then some boats from Tiberias came near the place   15
       8:37 because there is no place in you for my word.   17
      10:40 to the place where John had been baptizing earlier   15
      11: 6 two days longer in the place where he was.   15
      11:30 still at the place where Martha had met him.   15
      11:48 destroy both our holy place and our nation."   15
      14: 2 I go to prepare a place for you?   15
      14: 3 if I go and prepare a place for you   15
      14: 4 you know the way to the place where I am going."   1
      18: 1 to a place where there was a garden   1
      18: 2 Now Judas, who betrayed him, also knew the place   15
      19:13 at a place called The Stone Pavement   15
      19:17 to what is called The Place of the Skull   15
      19:20 the place where Jesus was crucified   15
      19:41 a garden in the place where he was crucified   15
      20: 7 and the cloth…rolled up in a place by itself.   15
Act 1:25 to take the place in this ministry   15
       1:25 to go to his own place."   15
       4:31 the place in which they were gathered together   15
       6:13 saying things against this holy place and the law;   15
       6:14 Jesus of Nazareth will destroy this place   15
       7: 7 they shall come out and worship me in this place.'   15
       7:33 the place where you are standing is holy ground.   15
       7:49 what is the place of my rest?   15
      12:17 Then he left and went to another place.   15
      16: 3 because of the Jews who were in those places   15
      16:13 where we supposed there was a place of prayer;   1
      16:16 as we were going to the place of prayer   1
      21:28 against our people, our law, and this place;   15
      21:28 has defiled this holy place."   15
      26:18 a place among those who are sanctified by faith   10
      27: 8 we came to a place called Fair Havens   15
      28: 7 Now in the neighborhood of that place were lands   15
Rom 9:26 "And in the very place where it was said to them   15
      11:17 and you…were grafted in their place   6
      15:23 with no further place for me in these regions   15
1Co 1: 2 all those who in every place call on the name   15
2Co 2:14 spreads in every place the fragrance   15
Eph 2:15 create…one new humanity in place of the two   4
1Th 1: 8 in every place your faith in God has become known   15
1Ti 2: 8 in every place the men should pray   15
Heb 4: 4 For in one place it speaks about the seventh day   12
       4: 5 And again in this place it says   1
       5: 6 as he says also in another place   1
      11: 8 a place that he was to receive as an inheritance;   15
Jas 3: 6 placed among our members as a world of iniquity;   9
2Pe 1:19 as to a lamp shining in a dark place   15
Rev 1:17 But he placed his right hand on me   14
       2: 5 and remove your lampstand from its place   15
       3:21 I will give a place with me on my throne   8
       6:14 mountain and island was removed from its place.   15
      11: 9 and refuse to let them be placed in a tomb;   14
      12: 6 wilderness, where she has a place prepared by God   15
      12: 8 there was no longer any place for them in heaven.   15
      12:14 wilderness, to her place where she is nourished   15
      16:16 the place that in Hebrew is called Harmagedon.   15
      20:11 and no place was found for them.   15
      21: 8 their place will be in the lake that burns   11

first place

1. πρωτεύω, *prōteuō, 4750*
2. πρῶτον, *prōton, 4754*

Rom 3: 2 in the first place the Jews were entrusted   2
Col 1:18 he might come to have first place in everything.   1
Heb 7: 2 His name, in the first place, means "king   2

in one's place

1. ὑπέρ, *hyper, 5642*

Phm 1:13 so that he might be of service to me in your place   1

out of place

1. οὐ + ἀνήκω, *ou + anēkō, 4024 + 465*

Eph 5: 4 Entirely out of place is obscene...talk;   1

place of honor

1. πρωτοκλισία, *prōtoklisia, 4752*

Mat 23: 6 They love to have the place of honor at banquets   1
Mrk 12:39 and places of honor at banquets!   1
Lke 14: 7 he noticed how the guests chose the places of honor   1
    14: 8 do not sit down at the place of honor   1
    20:46 and love...places of honor at banquets.   1

place on

1. ἐπιτίθημι, *epitithēmi, 2202*

Act 15:10 by placing on the neck of the disciples a yoke   1

place one lives

1. κατοικία, *katoikia, 3000*

Act 17:26 the boundaries of the places where they would live   1

place to bury

1. ταφή, *taphē, 5438*

Mat 27: 7 the potter's field as a place to bury foreigners   1

place to place

1. καθεξῆς, *kathexēs, 2759*

Act 18:23 went from place to place through the region   1

resting place

1. ἀνάπαυσις, *anapausis, 398*

Mat 12:43 through waterless regions looking for a resting place   1
Lke 11:24 waterless regions looking for a resting place   1

plague

1. λοιμός, *loimos, 3369*
2. μάστιξ, *mastix, 3465*
3. πληγή, *plēgē, 4435*

Lke 7:21 cured many people of diseases, plagues,   2
    21:11 in various places famines and plagues;   1
Rev 9:18 By...three plagues a third of humankind was killed   3
    9:20 rest of humankind, who were not killed by...plagues   3
    11: 6 and to strike the earth with every kind of plague   3
    15: 1 I saw...seven angels with seven plagues   3
    15: 6 came the seven angels with the seven plagues   3
    15: 8 seven plagues of the seven angels were ended.   3
    16: 9 God, who had authority over these plagues   3
    16:21 until they cursed God for the plague of the hail   3
    16:21 they cursed God...so fearful was that plague.   3
    18: 4 "Come out...so that you do not share in her plagues;   3
    18: 8 therefore her plagues will come in a single day   3
    21: 9 the seven bowls full of the seven last plagues   3
    22:18 God will add to that person the plagues   3

plain

1. δῆλος, *dēlos, 1316*
2. ἔκδηλος, *ekdēlos, 1684*
3. φανερός, *phaneros, 5745*
4. φανερόω, *phaneroō, 5746*

Rom 1:19 For what can be known about God is plain to them   3
1Co 15:27 it is plain that this does not include the one   1
2Ti 3: 9 their folly will become plain to everyone.   2
1Jn 2:19 But by going out they made it plain   4

plainly

1. ὀρθῶς, *orthos, 3987*
2. παρρησία, *parrēsia, 4244*

Mrk 7:35 tongue was released, and he spoke plainly.   1
Jhn 10:24 If you are the Messiah, tell us plainly."   2
    11:14 Jesus told them plainly, "Lazarus is dead.   2
    16:25 tell you plainly of the Father.   2
    16:29 "Yes, now you are speaking plainly   2

plan *See also* make a plan

1. βουλεύω, *bouleuō, 1086*

2. βουλή, *boulē, 1087*
3. βούλημα, *boulēma, 1088*
4. βούλομαι, *boulomai, 1089*
5. οἰκονομία, *oikonomia, 3873*
6. ποιέω, *poieō, 4472*
7. συμβούλιον, *symboulion, 5206*

Mat 1:19 Joseph...planned to dismiss her quietly   4
    28:12 assembled with the elders, they devised a plan   7
Lke 23:51 had not agreed to their plan and action.   2
Jhn 11:53 they planned to put him to death.   1
    12:10 planned to put Lazarus to death as well   1
Act 2:23 the definite plan and foreknowledge of God   2
    4:28 whatever your hand and your plan had predestined   2
    5:38 if this plan or this undertaking is of human origin   2
    25: 3 planning an ambush to kill him along the way.   6
    27:39 planned to run the ship ashore, if they could.   1
    27:42 The soldiers' plan was to kill the prisoners   2
    27:43 kept them from carrying out their plan.   3
Eph 1:10 as a plan for the fullness of time   5
    3: 9 to make everyone see what is the plan of the mystery   5

plank

1. σανίς, *sanis, 4909*

Act 27:44 some on planks and others on pieces of the ship.   1

plant

1. φυτεία, *phyteia, 5884*
2. φυτεύω, *phyteuō, 5885*
3. χόρτος, *chortos, 5965*

Mat 13:26 when the plants came up and bore grain   3
    15:13 "Every plant that my heavenly Father has   1
    15:13 that my heavenly Father has not planted   2
    21:33 There was a landowner who planted a vineyard   2
Mrk 12: 1 "A man planted a vineyard   2
Lke 13: 6 "A man had a fig tree planted in his vineyard;   2
    17: 6 'Be uprooted and planted in the sea,'   2
    17:28 selling, planting and building,   2
    20: 9 "A man planted a vineyard, and leased it   2
1Co 3: 6 I planted, Apollos watered   2
    3: 7 neither the one who plants nor the one who waters is   2
    3: 8 one who plants and the one who waters have a common   2
    9: 7 Who plants a vineyard and does not eat   2

plate

1. παροψίς, *paropsis, 4243*

Mat 23:25 the outside of the cup and of the plate   1

platform

1. βῆμα, *bēma, 1037*

Act 12:21 Herod...took his seat on the platform   1

platter

1. πίναξ, *pinax, 4402*

Mat 14: 8 the head of John the Baptist here on a platter   1
    14:11 The head was brought on a platter   1
Mrk 6:25 the head of John the Baptist on a platter."   1
    6:28 brought his head on a platter   1

plausible *See also* plausible *argument*

1. πειθός, *peithos, 4273*

1Co 2: 4 not with plausible words of wisdom   1

play

1. αὐλέω + ἤ + κιθαρίζω, *auleō + ē + kitharizō, 884 + 2445 + 3068*
2. κιθαρίζω, *kitharizō, 3068*
3. παίζω, *paizō, 4089*

1Co 10: 7 sat down to eat and drink, and they rose up to play."   3
    14: 7 how will anyone know what is being played?   1
Rev 14: 2 like the sound of harpists playing on their harps   2

play the flute

1. αὐλέω, *auleō, 884*

Mat 11:17 'We played the flute for you, and you did not dance;   1
Lke 7:32 played the flute for you, and you did not dance;   1

player *See* flute player

plead

1. ἐντυγχάνω, *entynchanō, 1961*
2. μαρτύρομαι, *martyromai, 3458*
3. παρακαλέω, *parakaleō, 4151*

Mat	18:29	fellow slave fell down and pleaded with him	3
	18:32	because you pleaded with me.	3
Lke	15:28	His father came out and began to plead with him.	3
Act	16: 9	there stood a man of Macedonia pleading with him	3
Rom	11: 2	of Elijah, how he pleads with God against Israel?	1
1Th	2:12	and encouraging you and pleading that you	2

pleasant

1. χαρά, *chara, 5915*

Heb	12:11	discipline always seems painful rather than pleasant	1

please

1. Contextual: Not in Greek
2. ἀνθρωπάρεσκος, *anthrōpareskos, 473*
3. ἀπόδεκτος, *apodektos, 621*
4. ἀρεσκεία, *areskeia, 742*
5. ἀρέσκω, *areskō, 743*
6. ἀρεστός, *arestos, 744*
7. ἐρωτάω, *erōtaō, 2263*
8. εὐαρεστέω, *euaresteō, 2297*
9. εὐάρεστος, *euarestos, 2298*
10. εὐδοκέω, *eudokeō, 2305*
11. θέλω, *thelō, 2527*
12. καλῶς, *kalōs, 2822*
13. προσφιλής, *prosphilēs, 4713*

Mat	14: 6	Herodias danced…and she pleased Herod	5
	17:12	but they did to him whatever they pleased.	11
Mrk	6:22	she pleased Herod and his guests;	5
	9:13	they did to him whatever they pleased	11
Lke	4: 6	I give it to anyone I please.	11
	14:18	please accept my regrets.'	7
	14:19	please accept my regrets.'	7
Jhn	8:29	I always do what is pleasing to him."	6
Act	6: 5	What they said pleased the whole community	5
	9:38	"Please come to us without delay."	1
	12: 3	After he saw that it pleased the Jews	6
Rom	8: 8	those who are in the flesh cannot please God.	5
	15: 1	and not to please ourselves.	5
	15: 2	Each of us must please our neighbor for the good	5
	15: 3	For Christ did not please himself;	5
	15:26	pleased to share their resources with the poor	10
	15:27	They were pleased to do this	10
1Co	7:32	how to please the Lord;	5
	7:33	how to please his wife	5
	7:34	how to please her husband.	5
	10: 5	God was not pleased with most of them	10
	10:33	as I try to please everyone in everything I do	5
2Co	5: 9	we make it our aim to please him.	9
Gal	1:10	Or am I trying to please people?	5
	1:10	If I were still pleasing people	5
	1:15	God, who had set me apart…was pleased	10
Eph	5:10	Try to find out what is pleasing to the Lord.	9
	6: 6	while being watched, and in order to please	2
Php	4: 8	whatever is pure, whatever is pleasing	13
	4:18	a sacrifice acceptable and pleasing to God.	9
Col	1:10	worthy of the Lord, fully pleasing to him	4
	1:19	in him all the fullness of God was pleased to dwell	10
	1:20	through him God was pleased to reconcile to himself	1
	3:22	while being watched and in order to please them	2
1Th	2: 4	not to please mortals, but to please God	5
	2: 4	not to please mortals, but to please God	1
	4: 1	how you ought to live and to please God	5
1Ti	5: 4	for this is pleasing in God's sight.	3
2Ti	2: 4	the soldier's aim is to please the enlisting officer.	5
Heb	11: 5	it was attested…that "he had pleased God."	8
	11: 6	without faith it is impossible to please God	8
	13:16	for such sacrifices are pleasing to God.	8
	13:21	working…that which is pleasing in his sight	9
Jas	2: 3	and say, "Have a seat here, please,"	12
1Jn	3:22	obey his commandments and do what pleases him.	6

please greatly

1. χαίρω, *chairō, 5897*

Mrk	14:11	When they heard it, they were greatly pleased	1
Lke	22: 5	greatly pleased and agreed to give him money.	1

please well

1. εὐδοκέω, *eudokeō, 2305*

Mat	3:17	my Son, the Beloved, with whom I am well pleased."	1
	12:18	my beloved, with whom my soul is well pleased.	1
	17: 5	my Son, the Beloved; with him I am well pleased;	1
Mrk	1:11	with you I am well pleased."	1
Lke	3:22	my Son, the Beloved; with you I am well pleased."	1
2Pe	1:17	my Son, my Beloved, with whom I am well pleased."	1

pleasure   *See also* live for pleasure, live in pleasure, lover of pleasure, take pleasure

1. ἀπόλαυσις, *apolausis, 656*
2. ἡδονή, *hēdonē, 2454*

Lke	8:14	the cares and riches and pleasures of life	2
Tit	3: 3	slaves to various passions and pleasures	2
Heb	11:25	to enjoy the fleeting pleasures of sin.	1
Jas	4: 3	in order to spend what you get on your pleasures.	2
2Pe	2:13	They count it a pleasure to revel in the daytime.	2

good pleasure

1. εὐδοκέω, *eudokeō, 2305*
2. εὐδοκία, *eudokia, 2306*

Lke	12:32	it is your Father's good pleasure	1
Eph	1: 5	according to the good pleasure of his will	2
	1: 9	according to his good pleasure	2
Php	2:13	both to will and to work for his good pleasure.	2

pledge

1. ἀρραβών, *arrabōn, 775*
2. πίστις, *pistis, 4411*

Eph	1:14	this is the pledge of our inheritance	1
1Ti	5:12	having violated their first pledge.	2

plentiful

1. πολύς, *polys, 4498*

Mat	9:37	"The harvest is plentiful	1
Lke	10: 2	harvest is plentiful, but the laborers are few;	1

plenty   *See* have plenty

plot

1. ἐπιβουλή, *epiboulē, 2101*
2. συμβουλεύω, *symbouleuō, 5205*
3. συμβούλιον + λαμβάνω, *symboulion + lambanō, 5206 + 3284*

Mat	22:15	Then the Pharisees went and plotted	3
Act	9:23	the Jews plotted to kill him	2
	9:24	their plot became known to Saul.	1
	20: 3	when a plot was made against him by the Jews	1
	20:19	that came to me through the plots of the Jews.	1
	23:30	there would be a plot against the man	1

plot of ground

1. χωρίον, *chōrion, 6005*

Jhn	4: 5	near the plot of ground that Jacob had given	1

plow

1. ἀροτριάω, *arotriaō, 769*
2. ἄροτρον, *arotron, 770*

Lke	9:62	"No one who puts a hand to the plow	2
	17: 7	your slave who has just come in from plowing	1
1Co	9:10	for whoever plows should plow in hope	1
	9:10	for whoever plows should plow in hope	1

pluck

1. τίλλω, *tillō, 5504*

Mat	12: 1	they began to pluck heads of grain and to eat.	1
Mrk	2:23	his disciples began to pluck heads of grain.	1
Lke	6: 1	his disciples plucked some heads of grain	1

plunder

1. ἁρπαγή, *harpagē, 771*
2. ἁρπάζω, *harpazō, 773*
3. διαρπάζω, *diarpazō, 1395*
4. σκῦλον, *skylon, 5036*

Mat	12:29	and plunder his property	2
	12:29	Then indeed the house can be plundered.	3
Mrk	3:27	a strong man's house and plunder his property	3

3:27 then indeed the house can be plundered.   3
Lke 11:22 divides his plunder.   4
Heb 10:34 you cheerfully accepted the plundering   1

plunge

1. βυθίζω, *bythizō, 1112*
2. γίνομαι, *ginomai, 1181*

1Ti   6: 9 plunge people into ruin and destruction.   1
Rev 16:10 the beast, and its kingdom was plunged into darkness; 2

pod

1. κεράτιον, *keration, 3044*

Lke 15:16 the pods that the pigs were eating;   1

poet

1. ποιητής, *poiētēs, 4475*

Act 17:28 as even some of your own poets have said   1

point¹

1. Contextual: Not in Greek
2. ἄχρι, *achri, 948*
3. λόγος, *logos, 3364*
4. μέλλω, *mellō, 3516*
5. μέχρι, *mechri, 3588*
6. οὕτως, *houtōs, 4048*

Jhn   4:47 his son, for he was at the point of death.   4
Act 17:33 At that point Paul left them.   6
     22: 4 I persecuted this Way up to the point of death   2
     22:22 Up to this point they listened to him   3
2Co   7:11 At every point you have proved yourselves   1
Php   2: 8 obedient to the point of death—even death on a cross. 5
2Ti   2: 9 I suffer hardship, even to the point of being chained 5
Heb 12: 4 resisted to the point of shedding your blood.   5
Jas   2:10 whoever…fails in one point has become accountable   1
Rev   3: 2 strengthen what…is on the point of death   4

point²

1. ἐκτείνω + ὁ + χείρ, *ekteinō + ho + cheir, 1753 + 3836 + 5931*

Mat 12:49 pointing to his disciples, he said,   1

point³

1. Contextual: Not in Greek
2. λέγω, *legō, 3306*

2Co   9: 6 The point is this: the one who sows sparingly   1
Gal   3:17 My point is this: 2
      4: 1 My point is this: heirs, as long as they are minors 2

main point

1. κεφάλαιον, *kephalaion, 3049*

Heb   8: 1 Now the main point in what we are saying is this: 1

point of death

1. ἐσχάτως, *eschatōs, 2275*

Mrk   5:23 "My little daughter is at the point of death.   1

point of disagreement

1. ζήτημα, *zētēma, 2427*

Act 25:19 they had certain points of disagreement with him   1

point of view

1. κατά, *kata, 2848*

2Co   5:16 we regard no one from a human point of view;   1
      5:16 once knew Christ from a human point of view   1

point out

1. ἐπιδείκνυμι, *epideiknymi, 2109*

Mat 24: 1 his disciples came to point out to him   1

point out a fault

1. ἐλέγχω, *elenchō, 1794*

Mat 18:15 go and point out the fault   1

some point

1. μέρος, *meros, 3538*

Rom 15:15 Nevertheless on some points I have written to you   1

this point

1. οὕτως, *houtōs, 4048*

Mrk 14:59 even on this point their testimony did not agree.   1

to the point

1. εἰς, *eis, 1650*

1Co   8:10 might they not…be encouraged to the point of eating 1

poison

1. ἰός, *ios, 2675*
2. κακόω, *kakoō, 2808*

Act 14: 2 poisoned their minds against the brothers.   2
Jas   3: 8 the tongue…full of deadly poison.   1

police   *See also* officer of the temple police

1. ῥαβδοῦχος, *rhabdouchos, 4812*
2. ὑπηρέτης, *hypēretēs, 5677*

Jhn   7:46 The police answered   2
     18: 3 together with police from the chief priests   2
     18:12 their officer, and the Jewish police arrested   2
     18:18 police had made a charcoal fire   2
     18:22 one of the police standing nearby struck Jesus   2
     19: 6 When the chief priests and the police saw him   2
Act 16:35 When morning came, the magistrates sent the police   1
     16:38 police reported these words to the magistrates   1

temple police

1. ὑπηρέτης, *hypēretēs, 5677*

Jhn   7:32 the chief priests and Pharisees sent temple police   1
      7:45 the temple police went back to the chief priests   1
Act   5:22 when the temple police went there   1
      5:26 captain went with the temple police and brought   1

pollute

1. ἀλίσγημα, *alisgēma, 246*
2. βδελύσσομαι, *bdelyssomai, 1009*

Act 15:20 abstain only from things polluted by idols   1
Rev 21: 8 as for the cowardly, the faithless, the polluted   2

pomp

1. φαντασία, *phantasia, 5752*

Act 25:23 Agrippa and Bernice came with great pomp   1

ponder

1. διαλογίζομαι, *dialogizomai, 1368*
2. συμβάλλω, *symballō, 5202*
3. τίθημι + ἐν + ὁ + καρδία, *tithēmi + en + ho + kardia, 5502 + 1877 + 3836 + 2840*

Lke   1:29 pondered what sort of greeting this might be.   1
      1:66 All who heard them pondered them and said,   3
      2:19 pondered them in her heart.   2

Pontius

1. Πόντιος, *Pontios, 4508*

Lke   3: 1 Pontius Pilate was governor of Judea   1
Act   4:27 both Herod and Pontius Pilate, with the Gentiles   1
1Ti   6:13 in his testimony before Pontius Pilate   1

Pontus

1. Ποντικός, *Pontikos, 4507*
2. Πόντος, *Pontos, 4510*

Act   2: 9 Judea and Cappadocia, Pontus and Asia   2
     18: 2 he found a Jew named Aquila, a native of Pontus   1
1Pe   1: 1 the Dispersion in Pontus, Galatia, Cappadocia   1

pool

1. κολυμβήθρα, *kolymbēthra, 3148*

Jhn   5: 2 in Jerusalem by the Sheep Gate there is a pool   1
      5: 7 I have no one to put me into the pool   1
      9: 7 wash in the pool of Siloam" (which means Sent).   1

poor

1. πένης, *penēs, 4288*
2. πενιχρός, *penichros, 4293*
3. πτωχεύω, *ptōcheuō, 4776*
4. πτωχός, *ptōchos, 4777*

Mat   5: 3 "Blessed are the poor in spirit, for theirs is   4
     11: 5 and the poor have good news brought to them.   4

Mat	19:21	sell...and give the money to the poor	4
	26: 9	and the money given to the poor."	4
	26:11	For you always have the poor with you	4
Mrk	10:21	sell what you own, and give the money to the poor	4
	12:42	A poor widow came and put in two small copper coins	4
	12:43	this poor widow has put in more than all	4
	14: 5	and the money given to the poor."	4
	14: 7	For you always have the poor with you	4
Lke	4:18	he has anointed me to bring good news to the poor.	4
	6:20	and said: "Blessed are you who are poor	4
	7:22	the poor have good news brought to them.	4
	14:13	when you give a banquet, invite the poor,	4
	14:21	bring in the poor, the crippled, the blind,	4
	18:22	Sell...and distribute the money to the poor	4
	19: 8	half of my possessions...I will give to the poor;	4
	21: 2	saw a poor widow put in two small copper coins.	2
	21: 3	this poor widow has put in more than all of them;	4
Jhn	12: 5	the money given to the poor?"	4
	12: 6	(He said this not because he cared about the poor	4
	12: 8	You always have the poor with you	4
	13:29	that he should give something to the poor.	4
Rom	15:26	pleased to share their resources with the poor	4
2Co	6:10	as poor, yet making many rich;	4
	8: 9	yet for your sakes he became poor	3
	9: 9	"He scatters abroad, he gives to the poor;	1
Gal	2:10	asked only one thing, that we remember the poor	4
Jas	2: 3	while to the one who is poor you say, "Stand there,"	4
	2: 5	Has not God chosen the poor in the world	4
	2: 6	But you have dishonored the poor.	4
Rev	3:17	not realize that you are wretched, pitiable, poor	4
	13:16	all, both small and great, both rich and poor	4

poor man

1. πτωχός, *ptōchos, 4777*

Lke	16:20	at his gate lay a poor man named Lazarus	1
	16:22	The poor man died	1

poor person

1. πτωχός, *ptōchos, 4777*

Jas	2: 2	a poor person in dirty clothes also comes in	1

poorly   *See* clothe poorly

porch

1. πυλών, *pylōn, 4784*

Mat	26:71	he went out to the porch, another servant-girl	1

Porcius

1. Πόρκιος, *Porkios, 4517*

Act	24:27	Felix was succeeded by Porcius Festus;	1

port

1. τόπος, *topos, 5536*

Act	27: 2	set sail to the ports along the coast of Asia	1

portent

1. σημεῖον, *sēmeion, 4956*
2. τέρας, *teras, 5469*

Act	2:19	I will show portents in the heaven above	2
Rev	12: 1	A great portent appeared in heaven: a woman	1
	12: 3	another portent appeared in heaven:	1
	15: 1	Then I saw another portent in heaven	1

dreadful portent

1. φόβητρον, *phobētron, 5831*

Lke	21:11	dreadful portents and great signs from heaven.	1

portico

1. Contextual: Not in Greek
2. στοά, *stoa, 5119*

Jhn	5: 2	a pool...which has five porticoes.	2
	10:23	in the temple, in the portico of Solomon.	2
Act	3:11	in the portico called Solomon's Portico	2
	3:11	in the portico called Solomon's Portico	1
	5:12	they were all together in Solomon's Portico.	2

position

1. ἀρχή, *archē, 794*
2. οἰκονομία, *oikonomia, 3873*

	3.	τόπος, *topos, 5536*	
Lke	16: 3	my master is taking the position away from me?	2
1Co	14:16	how can anyone in the position of an outsider say	3
Jde	1: 6	the angels who did not keep their own position	1

high position

1. ὑπεροχή, *hyperochē, 5667*

1Ti	2: 2	for kings and all who are in high positions	1

position of overseer

1. ἐπισκοπή, *episkopē, 2175*

Act	1:20	'Let another take his position of overseer.'	1

possess

1. ἔχω, *echō, 2400*
2. κατέχω, *katechō, 2988*
3. ὕπαρξις, *hyparxis, 5638*

Act	8: 7	spirits...came out of many who were possessed;	1
Rom	2:14	When Gentiles, who do not possess the law	1
1Co	8: 1	we know that "all of us possess knowledge."	1
	8:10	if others see you, who possess knowledge, eating	1
	12:30	Do all possess gifts of healing?	1
2Co	6:10	having nothing, and yet possessing everything.	2
Heb	10:34	possessed something better and more lasting.	3

possessed by a demon

1. δαιμονίζομαι, *daimonizomai, 1227*

Mrk	5:18	the man who had been possessed by demons	1
Lke	8:36	one who had been possessed by demons	1

possessed with a demon

1. δαιμονίζομαι, *daimonizomai, 1227*

Mat	8:16	many who were possessed with demons;	1
Mrk	1:32	all who were sick or possessed with demons.	1

possession

1. ἔχω, *echō, 2400*
2. κατάσχεσις, *kataschesis, 2959*
3. κατέχω, *katechō, 2988*
4. κτῆμα, *ktēma, 3228*
5. ὑπάρχω, *hyparchō, 5639*

Mat	18:25	his wife and children and all his possessions	1
	19:21	to be perfect, go, sell your possessions	5
	19:22	for he had many possessions.	4
	24:47	put that one in charge of all his possessions.	5
Mrk	10:22	for he had many possessions.	4
Lke	12:15	not consist in the abundance of possessions."	5
	12:33	Sell your possessions, and give alms.	5
	12:44	put that one in charge of all his possessions.	5
	14:33	if you do not give up all your possessions.	5
	19: 8	half of my possessions...I will give to the poor;	5
Act	2:45	they would sell their possessions and goods	4
	4:32	no one claimed private ownership of any possessions	5
	7: 5	promised to give it to him as his possession	2
1Co	7:30	those who buy as though they had no possessions	3
	13: 3	If I give away all my possessions	5
Heb	10:34	the plundering of your possessions	5

possible   *See also* soon as possible

1. ἄρα, *ara, 726*
2. δυνατός, *dynatos, 1543*

Mat	19:26	but for God all things are possible."	2
	24:24	to lead astray, if possible, even the elect.	2
	26:39	"My Father, if it is possible, let this cup	2
Mrk	10:27	for God all things are possible."	2
	13:22	to lead astray, if possible, the elect.	2
	14:35	if it were possible, the hour might pass from him.	2
	14:36	"Abba, Father, for you all things are possible;	2
Lke	18:27	impossible for mortals is possible for God."	2
Act	8:22	if possible, the intent...may be forgiven you.	1
	20:16	in Jerusalem, if possible, on the day of Pentecost.	1
Rom	12:18	If it is possible...live peaceably with all.	2
Gal	4:15	I testify that, had it been possible	2

posterity

1. σπέρμα, *sperma, 5065*

Act	13:23	Of this man's posterity	1

pot

1. ξέστης, *xestēs, 3829*
2. σκεῦος, *skeuos, 5007*

Mrk   7: 4   washing of cups, pots, and bronze kettles.)   1
Rev   2:27   as when clay pots are shattered   2

potter

1. κεραμεύς, *kerameus, 3038*

Mat 27: 7   used them to buy the potter's field   1
     27:10   and they gave them for the potter's field   1
Rom   9:21   Has the potter no right over the clay   1

pound   *See also* hundred pounds

1. λίτρα, *litra, 3354*
2. μνᾶ, *mna, 3641*

Lke 19:13   ten of his slaves, and gave them ten pounds   2
     19:16   'Lord, your pound has made ten more pounds.'   2
     19:16   'Lord, your pound has made ten more pounds.'   2
     19:18   'Lord, your pound has made five pounds.'   2
     19:18   'Lord, your pound has made five pounds.'   2
     19:20   'Lord, here is your pound.   2
     19:24   'Take the pound from him   2
     19:24   give it to the one who has ten pounds.'   2
     19:25   they said to him, 'Lord, he has ten pounds!')   2
Jhn 12: 3   Mary took a pound of costly perfume   1
     19:39   myrrh and aloes, weighing about a hundred pounds   1

pounded by a storm

1. χειμάζω, *cheimazō, 5928*

Act 27:18   We were being pounded by the storm so violently   1

pour

1. βάλλω, *ballō, 965*
2. ἐκχέω, *ekcheō, 1772*
3. καταχέω, *katacheō, 2972*
4. κεράννυμι, *kerannymi, 3042*

Mat 26: 7   poured it on his head as he sat at the table.   3
     26:12   By pouring this ointment on my body   1
Jhn 13: 5   Then he poured water into a basin   1
Rom   5: 5   God's love has been poured into our hearts   2
Rev 12:15   Then from his mouth the serpent poured water   1
     12:16   river that the dragon had poured from his mouth.   1
     14:10   poured unmixed into the cup of his anger   4
     16: 2   first angel went and poured his bowl on the earth   2
     16: 3   The second angel poured his bowl into the sea   2
     16: 4   The third angel poured his bowl into the rivers   2
     16: 8   The fourth angel poured his bowl on the sun   2
     16:10   The fifth angel poured his bowl on the throne   2
     16:12   sixth angel poured his bowl on the great river   2
     16:17   The seventh angel poured his bowl into the air   2

pour forth

1. βρύω, *bryō, 1108*

Jas   3:11   Does a spring pour forth...fresh and brackish water?   1

pour from

1. ἐκπορεύομαι, *ekporeuomai, 1744*

Rev 11: 5   fire pours from their mouth and consumes   1

pour on

1. ἐπιχέω, *epicheō, 2219*
2. καταχέω, *katacheō, 2972*

Mrk 14: 3   and poured the ointment on his head.   2
Lke 10:34   wounds, having poured oil and wine on them   1

pour out

1. ἐκχέω, *ekcheō, 1772*
2. ἐκχύννομαι, *ekchynnomai, 1773*

Mat 26:28   my blood...which is poured out for many   2
Mrk 14:24   my blood...which is poured out for many.   2
Lke 22:20   "This cup that is poured out for you   2
Jhn   2:15   also poured out the coins of the money changers   1
Act   2:17   I will pour out my Spirit upon all flesh   1
     2:18   in those days I will pour out my Spirit;   1
     2:33   he has poured out this that you both see and hear.   1
     10:45   Holy Spirit had been poured out even on the Gentiles   1
Tit   3: 6   This Spirit he poured out on us richly   1
Rev 16: 1   pour out on the earth the seven bowls of the wrath   1

pour out as a libation

1. σπένδω, *spendō, 5064*

Php   2:17   even if I am being poured out as a libation   1
2Ti   4: 6   I am already being poured out as a libation   1

poverty

1. πτωχεία, *ptōcheia, 4775*
2. ὑστέρημα, *hysterēma, 5729*
3. ὑστέρησις, *hysterēsis, 5730*

Mrk 12:44   out of her poverty has put in everything she had   3
Lke 21: 4   she out of her poverty has put in all she had   2
2Co   8: 2   their abundant joy and their extreme poverty   1
     8: 9   so that by his poverty you might become rich.   1
Rev   2: 9   "I know your affliction and your poverty   1

power   *See also* deed of power, empty of power

1. Contextual: Not in Greek
2. δύναμαι, *dynamai, 1538*
3. δύναμις, *dynamis, 1539*
4. δυνατός, *dynatos, 1543*
5. ἐνέργεια, *energeia, 1918*
6. ἐξισχύω, *exischyō, 2015*
7. ἐξουσία, *exousia, 2026*
8. ἰσχύς, *ischys, 2709*
9. κράτος, *kratos, 3197*
10. ὅς, *hos, 4005*

Mat 14: 2   for this reason these powers are at work in him."   3
     22:29   neither the scriptures nor the power of God.   3
     24:29   the powers of heaven will be shaken.   3
     24:30   with power and great glory.   3
     26:64   the Son of Man seated at the right hand of Power   3
Mrk   5:30   aware that power had gone forth from him,   3
     6:14   for this reason these powers are at work in him."   3
     9: 1   the kingdom of God has come with power."   3
     12:24   know neither the scriptures nor the power of God?   3
     13:25   the powers in the heavens will be shaken.   3
     13:26   coming in clouds' with great power and glory.   3
     14:62   Son of Man seated at the right hand of the Power,'   3
Lke   1:17   With the spirit and power of Elijah he will go   3
     1:35   the power of the Most High will overshadow you;   3
     4:14   filled with the power of the Spirit   3
     4:36   For with authority and power he commands   3
     5:17   the power of the Lord was with him to heal.   3
     6:19   for power came out from him and healed all   3
     8:46   I noticed that power had gone out from me."   3
     9: 1   gave them power and authority over all demons   3
     10:19   authority...over all the power of the enemy;   3
     21:26   the powers of the heavens will be shaken.   3
     21:27   coming in a cloud' with power and great glory.   3
     22:53   this is your hour, and the power of darkness!"   7
     22:69   seated at the right hand of the power of God."   3
     24:49   you have been clothed with power from on high."   3
Jhn   1:12   he gave power to become children of God   7
     10:18   I have power to lay it down   7
     10:18   I have power to take it up again.   7
     14:30   He has no power over me;   1
     19:10   Do you not know that I have power to release you   7
     19:10   I have...power to crucify you?"   7
     19:11   "You would have no power over me   7
Act   1: 8   you will receive power when the Holy Spirit   3
     3:12   by our own power or piety we had made him walk?   3
     4: 7   "By what power or by what name did you do this?"   3
     4:33   With great power   3
     6: 8   Stephen, full of grace and power   3
     8:10   the power of God that is called Great."   3
     8:19   saying, "Give me also this power   7
     10:38   with the Holy Spirit and with power;   3
     26:18   turn...from the power of Satan to God   7
Rom   1: 4   declared to be Son of God with power   3
     1:16   it is the power of God for salvation to everyone   3
     1:20   eternal power and divine nature   3
     8:38   nor things present, nor things to come, nor powers   3
     9:17   for the very purpose of showing my power in you   3
     9:22   What if God, desiring...to make known his power   4
     11:23   for God has the power to graft them in again.   4
     15:13   may abound in hope by the power of the Holy Spirit.   3
     15:19   by the power of signs and wonders   3
     15:19   by the power of the Spirit of God   3
1Co   1:18   to us who are being saved it is the power of God.   3

1Co	1:24	Christ the power of God and the wisdom of God.	3
	2: 4	with a demonstration of the Spirit and of power	3
	2: 5	not on human wisdom but on the power of God.	3
	4:19	not the talk of these arrogant people but their power	3
	4:20	kingdom of God depends not on talk but on power.	3
	5: 4	with the power of our Lord Jesus	3
	6:14	will also raise us by his power.	3
	14:13	should pray for the power to interpret.	1
	15:24	every ruler and every authority and power.	3
	15:43	It is sown in weakness, it is raised in power.	3
	15:56	the power of sin is the law.	3
2Co	4: 7	that this extraordinary power belongs to God	3
	6: 7	truthful speech, and the power of God;	3
	10: 4	they have divine power to destroy strongholds.	4
	12: 9	for power is made perfect in weakness."	3
	12: 9	so that the power of Christ may dwell in me.	3
	13: 4	lives by the power of God.	3
	13: 4	we will live with him by the power of God.	3
Eph	1:19	what is the immeasurable greatness of his power	3
	1:19	according to the working of his great power.	8
	1:20	God put this power to work in Christ	10
	1:21	rule and authority and power and dominion	3
	2: 2	following the ruler of the power of the air	7
	3: 7	that was given me by the working of his power.	3
	3:16	in your inner being with power through his Spirit	3
	3:18	have the power to comprehend, with all the saints	6
	3:20	by the power at work within us	3
	6:10	be strong…in the strength of his power.	8
Php	3:10	know Christ and the power of his resurrection	3
	3:21	by the power that also enables him	5
Col	1:11	all the strength that comes from his glorious power	9
	1:13	has rescued us from the power of darkness	7
	1:16	dominions or rulers or powers	7
	2:12	through faith in the power of God	5
1Th	1: 5	also in power and in the Holy Spirit	3
2Th	1:11	fulfill by his power every good resolve and work	3
	2: 9	Satan, who uses all power, signs, lying wonders	3
2Ti	1: 7	a spirit of power and of love and of self-discipline.	3
	1: 8	relying on the power of God	3
	3: 5	outward form of godliness but denying its power.	3
Heb	2:14	one who has the power of death, that is, the devil	9
	6: 5	the powers of the age to come	3
	7:16	through the power of an indestructible life.	3
	11:11	By faith he received power of procreation	3
Jas	1:21	implanted word that has the power to save your souls.	2
1Pe	1: 5	being protected by the power of God through faith	3
	3:22	angels, authorities, and powers made subject to him.	3
	4:11	To him belong the glory and the power	9
	5:11	To him be the power forever and ever. Amen.	9
2Pe	1: 3	His divine power has given us everything	3
	1:16	made known to you the power and coming of our Lord	3
	2:11	angels, though greater in might and power	3
Jde	1:25	to the only God…be glory, majesty, power	9
Rev	3: 8	I know that you have but little power	3
	4:11	Lord and God, to receive glory and honor and power	3
	5:12	to receive power and wealth and wisdom and might	3
	7: 2	angels who had been given power to damage earth	1
	7:12	honor and power and might be to our God forever	3
	9:10	in their tails is their power to harm people	7
	9:19	For the power of the horses is in their mouths	7
	11:17	have taken your great power and begun to reign.	3
	12:10	salvation…power and the kingdom of our God	3
	13: 2	the dragon gave it his power and his throne	3
	15: 8	smoke from the glory of God and from his power	3
	17:13	yielding their power and authority to the beast;	3
	18: 3	grown rich from the power of her luxury."	3
	19: 1	Salvation and glory and power to our God	3
	20: 6	Over these the second death has no power	7

cosmic power
1. κοσμοκράτωρ, *kosmokratōr, 3179*

Eph	6:12	against the cosmic powers of this present darkness	1

in power
1. ὑπό, *hypo, 5679*

Act	2:24	it was impossible for him to be held in its power.	1

prophetic power
1. προφητεία, *prophēteia, 4735*

1Co	13: 2	And if I have prophetic powers	1

royal power
1. βασιλεία, *basileia, 993*

Lke	19:12	to get royal power for himself and then return.	1
	19:15	When he returned, having received royal power	1

spiritual power
1. πνευματικός, *pneumatikos, 4461*

1Co	14:37	to be a prophet, or to have spiritual powers,	1

under power
1. ἐν, *en, 1877*
2. ὑπό, *hypo, 5679*

Rom	3: 9	both Jews and Greeks, are under the power of sin	2
Gal	3:22	imprisoned all things under the power of sin	2
1Jn	5:19	the whole world lies under the power of the evil one.	1

powerful
1. δύναμις, *dynamis, 1539*
2. δυνάστης, *dynastēs, 1541*
3. δυνατέω, *dynateō, 1542*
4. δυνατός, *dynatos, 1543*
5. ἐνδυναμόω, *endynamoō, 1904*
6. ἐνέργεια, *energeia, 1918*
7. ἰσχυρός, *ischyros, 2708*
8. ἰσχύω, *ischyō, 2710*

Lke	1:52	brought down the powerful from their thrones	2
Act	7:22	was powerful in his words and deeds.	4
	9:22	Saul became increasingly more powerful	5
1Co	1:26	not many were powerful	4
2Co	13: 3	is powerful in you.	3
2Th	2:11	For this reason God sends them a powerful delusion	6
Heb	1: 3	sustains all things by his powerful word.	1
Jas	5:16	The prayer of the righteous is powerful	8
Rev	6:15	and the generals and the rich and the powerful	7

more powerful
1. ἰσχυρός, *ischyros, 2708*

Mat	3:11	one who is more powerful than I is coming after me;	1
Mrk	1: 7	who is more powerful than I is coming after me;	1
Lke	3:16	one who is more powerful than I is coming;	1

powerfully
1. δύναμις, *dynamis, 1539*
2. εὐτόνως, *eutonōs, 2364*

Act	18:28	for he powerfully refuted the Jews in public	2
Col	1:29	the energy that he powerfully inspires within me.	1

practice *See also* put into practice
1. ἕξις, *hexis, 2011*
2. ἐργασία, *ergasia, 2238*
3. περιπατέω, *peripateō, 4344*
4. ποιέω, *poieō, 4472*
5. πρᾶξις, *praxis, 4552*
6. πράσσω, *prassō, 4556*

Mat	6: 1	"Beware of practicing your piety before others	4
	23: 3	for they do not practice what they teach.	4
	23:23	these you ought to have practiced	4
Lke	11:42	these you ought to have practiced	4
Act	19:18	confessed and disclosed their practices.	5
	19:19	A number of those who practiced magic	6
Rom	1:32	that those who practice such things deserve to die	6
	1:32	but even applaud others who practice them.	6
2Co	4: 2	we refuse to practice cunning	3
	12:21	licentiousness that they have practiced.	6
Eph	4:19	greedy to practice every kind of impurity.	2
Col	3: 9	stripped off the old self with its practices	5
Heb	5:14	faculties have been trained by practice	1
Rev	21:27	nor anyone who practices abomination	4
	22:15	everyone who loves and practices falsehood.	4

practice fornication
1. πορνεύω, *porneuō, 4519*

Rev	2:14	that they would…practice fornication.	1
	2:20	beguiling my servants to practice fornication	1

practice magic
1. μαγεύω, *mageuō, 3405*

Act	8: 9	Simon had previously practiced magic in the city	1

practice self-control

1. ἐγκρατεύομαι, *enkrateuomai, 1603*

1Co	7: 9 if they are not practicing self-control	1

praise *See also* give praise, sing praise, sing songs of praise, worthy of praise

1. αἴνεσις, *ainesis, 139*
2. αἰνέω, *aineō, 140*
3. αἶνος, *ainos, 142*
4. αἶνος + δίδωμι, *ainos + didōmi, 142 + 1443*
5. ἀνθομολογέομαι, *anthomologeomai, 469*
6. δόξα, *doxa, 1518*
7. δοξάζω, *doxazō, 1519*
8. ἐπαινέω, *epaineō, 2046*
9. ἔπαινος, *epainos, 2047*
10. εὐλογέω, *eulogeō, 2328*
11. μεγαλύνω, *megalynō, 3486*
12. ὑμνέω, *hymneō, 5630*

Mat	6: 2 so that they may be praised by others.	7
	15:31 And they praised the God of Israel.	7
	21:16 you have prepared praise	3
Lke	1:64 he began to speak, praising God.	10
	2:13 praising God and saying	2
	2:20 glorifying and praising God	2
	2:28 Simeon took him in his arms and praised God,	10
	2:38 At that moment she came, and began to praise God	5
	4:15 was praised by everyone.	7
	13:13 she stood up straight and began praising God.	7
	17:15 turned back, praising God with a loud voice.	7
	17:18 none…found to return and give praise to God	6
	18:43 all the people, when they saw it, praised God.	4
	19:37 began to praise God joyfully with a loud voice	2
	23:47 he praised God and said	7
Act	2:47 praising God and having the goodwill	2
	3: 8 walking and leaping and praising God.	2
	3: 9 All the people saw him walking and praising God	2
	4:21 all of them praised God for what had happened.	7
	11:18 they praised God, saying	7
	13:48 they were glad and praised the word of the Lord;	7
	19:17 the name of the Lord Jesus was praised.	11
	21:20 When they heard it, they praised God.	7
Rom	2:29 person receives praise not from others but from God.	9
	15:11 and again, "Praise the Lord, all you Gentiles	2
	15:11 and let all the peoples praise him";	8
Eph	1: 6 to the praise of his glorious grace	9
	1:12 might live for the praise of his glory.	9
	1:14 to the praise of his glory.	9
Php	1:11 for the glory and praise of God.	9
1Th	2: 6 nor did we seek praise from mortals	6
Heb	2:12 in the midst of the congregation I will praise	12
	13:15 offer a sacrifice of praise to God	1
1Pe	1: 7 faith…may be found to result in praise and glory	9
	2:14 sent by him…to praise those who do right.	9
Rev	19: 5 "Praise our God, all you his servants	2

pray

1. Contextual: Not in Greek
2. αἰτέω, *aiteō, 160*
3. δέησις, *deēsis, 1255*
4. δέησις + ποιέω, *deēsis + poieō, 1255 + 4472*
5. δέομαι, *deomai, 1289*
6. ἐπικαλέω, *epikaleō, 2126*
7. ἐρωτάω, *erōtaō, 2263*
8. εὔχομαι, *euchomai, 2377*
9. προσευχή, *proseuchē, 4666*
10. προσεύχομαι, *proseuchomai, 4667*

Mat	5:44 enemies and pray for those who persecute you	10
	6: 5 whenever you pray, do not be like the hypocrites;	10
	6: 5 for they love to stand and pray in the synagogues	10
	6: 6 whenever you pray, go into your room and shut the door	10
	6: 6 shut the door and pray to your Father who is	10
	6: 7 "When you are praying, do not heap up empty phrases	10
	6: 9 "Pray then in this way: Our Father in heaven	10
	14:23 he went up the mountain by himself to pray.	10
	19:13 that he might lay his hands on them and pray.	10
	24:20 Pray that your flight may not be in winter.	10
	26:36 "Sit here while I go over there and pray."	10
	26:39 he threw himself on the ground and prayed	10
	26:41 Stay awake and pray that you may not come	10

	26:42 Again he went away for the second time and prayed	10
	26:44 he went away and prayed for the third time	10
Mrk	1:35 there he prayed.	10
	6:46 he went up on the mountain to pray.	10
	11:25 "Whenever you stand praying, forgive	10
	13:18 Pray that it may not be in winter.	10
	14:32 he said to his disciples, "Sit here while I pray."	10
	14:35 he threw himself on the ground and prayed	10
	14:38 pray that you may not come into the time of trial;	10
	14:39 again he went away and prayed	10
Lke	1:10 whole assembly of the people was praying outside.	10
	3:21 Jesus also had been baptized and was praying	10
	5:16 he would withdraw to deserted places and pray.	10
	5:33 "John's disciples…frequently fast and pray,	4
	6:12 he went out to the mountain to pray;	10
	6:28 pray for those who abuse you.	10
	9:18 Once when Jesus was praying alone	10
	9:28 and went up on the mountain to pray.	10
	9:29 while he was praying	10
	11: 1 He was praying in a certain place	10
	11: 1 teach us to pray, as John taught his disciples."	10
	11: 2 He said to them, "When you pray, say: Father	10
	18: 1 their need to pray always and not to lose heart.	10
	18:10 "Two men went up to the temple to pray	10
	18:11 The Pharisee, standing by himself, was praying thus	10
	21:36 praying that you may have the strength	5
	22:32 prayed for you that your own faith may not fail;	5
	22:40 "Pray that you may not come into the time of trial."	10
	22:41 knelt down, and prayed	10
	22:44 ⟦In his anguish he prayed more earnestly,⟧	10
	22:46 pray that you may not come into the time of trial."	10
Act	1:24 they prayed and said, "Lord, you know everyone's heart.	10
	4:31 When they had prayed	5
	6: 6 who prayed and laid their hands on them.	10
	7:59 While they were stoning Stephen, he prayed	6
	8:15 The two went down and prayed for them	10
	8:22 Repent…and pray to the Lord	5
	8:24 Simon answered, "Pray for me to the Lord	5
	9:11 At this moment he is praying	10
	9:40 Peter…knelt down and prayed.	10
	10: 2 prayed constantly to God.	5
	10: 9 Peter went up on the roof to pray.	10
	10:30 at three o'clock, I was praying in my house	10
	11: 5 "I was in the city of Joppa praying	10
	12: 5 prayed fervently to God for him.	9
	12:12 many had gathered and were praying.	10
	13: 3 Then after fasting and praying	10
	16:25 Paul and Silas were praying and singing hymns	10
	20:36 he knelt down with them all and prayed.	10
	21: 5 we knelt down on the beach and prayed	10
	22:17 was praying in the temple	10
	26:29 "Whether quickly or not, I pray to God	8
	27:29 prayed for day to come.	8
	28: 8 Paul visited him and cured him by praying	10
Rom	8:26 for we do not know how to pray as we ought	10
1Co	11: 4 Any man who prays…with something on his head	10
	11: 5 any woman who prays or prophesies with her head	10
	11:13 for a woman to pray to God with her head unveiled?	10
	14:13 who speaks in a tongue should pray for the power	10
	14:14 For if I pray in a tongue, my spirit prays	10
	14:14 my spirit prays but my mind is unproductive.	10
	14:15 What should I do then? I will pray with the spirit	10
	14:15 I will pray with the mind also;	10
2Co	9:14 while they long for you and pray for you	3
	13: 7 we pray to God that you may not do anything wrong	8
	13: 9 is what we pray for, that you may become perfect.	8
Eph	1:17 I pray that the God of our Lord Jesus Christ,	1
	3:13 I pray therefore that you may not lose heart	2
	3:16 I pray that, according to the riches of his glory	1
	3:18 I pray that you may have the power to comprehend	1
	6:18 Pray in the Spirit at all times	10
	6:19 Pray also for me, so that when I speak,	1
	6:20 Pray that I may declare it boldly, as I must speak.	1
Php	1: 4 constantly praying with joy in…my prayers	4
Col	1: 9 we have not ceased praying for you	10
	4: 3 At the same time pray for us as well	10
1Th	3:10 Night and day we pray most earnestly that we may see	5
	5:17 pray without ceasing	10
	5:25 Beloved, pray for us.	10
2Th	1:11 To this end we always pray for you	10
	3: 1 Finally, brothers and sisters, pray for us	10

1Ti	2: 8	in every place the men should pray	10
Phm	1: 6	I pray that…	1
Heb	13:18	Pray for us;	10
Jas	5:13	Are any among you suffering? They should pray.	10
	5:14	have them pray over them, anointing them with oil	10
	5:16	pray for one another, so that you may be healed.	8
	5:18	Then he prayed again, and the heaven gave rain	10
1Jn	5:16	I do not say that you should pray about that.	7
3Jn	1: 2	Beloved, I pray that all may go well with you	8
Jde	1:20	pray in the Holy Spirit;	10

pray fervently

1. προσεύχομαι + προσευχή, *proseuchomai + proseuchē,
4667 + 4666*

Jas   5:17   he prayed fervently that it might not rain,   1

prayer   *See also* say a prayer

1. Contextual: Not in Greek
2. δέησις, *deēsis, 1255*
3. ἔντευξις, *enteuxis, 1950*
4. εὐχή, *euchē, 2376*
5. προσευχή, *proseuchē, 4666*
6. προσεύχομαι, *proseuchomai, 4667*

Mat	21:13	'My house shall be called a house of prayer';	5
	21:22	ask for in prayer with faith, you will receive."	5
Mrk	9:29	can come out only through prayer."	5
	11:17	a house of prayer for all the nations'?	5
	11:24	So I tell you, whatever you ask for in prayer	6
Lke	1:13	for your prayer has been heard.	2
	2:37	worshiped there with fasting and prayer	2
	6:12	and he spent the night in prayer to God.	5
	19:46	'My house shall be a house of prayer';	5
	22:45	he got up from prayer, he came to the disciples	5
Act	1:14	were constantly devoting themselves to prayer	5
	2:42	the breaking of bread and the prayers.	5
	3: 1	the hour of prayer, at three o'clock in the afternoon.	5
	6: 4	we, for our part, will devote ourselves to prayer	5
	10: 4	"Your prayers and your alms have ascended	5
	10:31	said, 'Cornelius, your prayer has been heard	5
	14:23	with prayer and fasting they entrusted them	6
	16:13	where we supposed there was a place of prayer;	5
	16:16	as we were going to the place of prayer	5
Rom	1: 9	I remember you always in my prayers	5
	10: 1	Brothers and sisters, my heart's desire and prayer	2
	12:12	persevere in prayer.	5
	15:30	join me in earnest prayer to God on my behalf	5
1Co	7: 5	to devote yourselves to prayer	5
2Co	1:11	you also join in helping us by your prayers	5
	1:11	granted us through the prayers of many.	1
Eph	1:16	as I remember you in my prayers.	5
	6:18	Pray in the Spirit…in every prayer	5
Php	1: 4	praying with joy in every one of my prayers	2
	1: 9	my prayer, that your love may overflow more	6
	1:19	for I know that through your prayers	2
	4: 6	in everything by prayer and supplication	5
Col	1: 3	In our prayers for you	6
	4: 2	Devote yourselves to prayer	5
	4:12	wrestling in his prayers on your behalf	5
1Th	1: 2	mention you in our prayers, constantly	5
1Ti	2: 1	supplications, prayers, intercessions	5
	4: 5	is sanctified by God's word and by prayer.	3
	5: 5	continues in supplications and prayers	5
2Ti	1: 3	when I remember you constantly in my prayers	2
Phm	1: 4	When I remember you in my prayers	5
	1:22	through your prayers to be restored to you.	5
Heb	5: 7	In the days of his flesh, Jesus offered up prayers	2
Jas	5:15	The prayer of faith will save the sick	4
	5:16	The prayer of the righteous is powerful	5
1Pe	3: 7	so that nothing may hinder your prayers.	5
	3:12	and his ears are open to their prayer.	2
	4: 7	discipline yourselves for the sake of your prayers.	5
Rev	5: 8	bowls…which are the prayers of the saints.	5
	8: 3	a great quantity of incense to offer with the prayers	5
	8: 4	the smoke…with the prayers of the saints, rose	5

preach

1. εὐαγγελίζω, *euangelizō, 2294*
2. κηρύσσω, *kēryssō, 3062*
3. λόγος, *logos, 3364*
4. παρακαλέω, *parakaleō, 4151*

Act	10:36	preaching peace by Jesus Christ	1
	10:42	He commanded us to preach to the people	2
Rom	2:21	While you preach against stealing, do you steal?	2
Gal	5:11	persecuted if I am still preaching circumcision?	2
1Ti	5:17	those who labor in preaching and teaching;	3
Tit	1: 9	be able both to preach with sound doctrine	4

precede

1. προάγω, *proagō, 4575*
2. φθάνω, *phthanō, 5777*

1Th	4:15	will by no means precede those who have died.	2
1Ti	5:24	are conspicuous and precede them to judgment	1

precept

1. ἔνταλμα, *entalma, 1945*

Mat	15: 9	in vain…teaching human precepts as doctrines.' "	1
Mrk	7: 7	teaching human precepts as doctrines.'	1

precious

1. ἔντιμος, *entimos, 1952*
2. τιμή, *timē, 5507*
3. τίμιος, *timios, 5508*

1Co	3:12	with gold, silver, precious stones, wood, hay,	3
Jas	5: 7	farmer waits for the precious crop from the earth	3
1Pe	1:19	with the precious blood of Christ	3
	2: 4	chosen and precious in God's sight	1
	2: 6	in Zion…a cornerstone chosen and precious;	1
	2: 7	To you then who believe, he is precious;	2
2Pe	1: 4	his precious and very great promises	3

as precious

1. ἰσότιμος, *isotimos, 2700*

1Pe   1: 1   received a faith as precious as ours   1

more precious

1. πολύτιμος, *polytimos, 4501*

1Pe   1: 7   faith—being more precious than gold   1

very precious

1. πολυτελής, *polytelēs, 4500*

1Pe   3: 4   spirit, which is very precious in God's sight.   1

predestine

1. προορίζω, *proorizō, 4633*

Act	4:28	whatever your hand and your plan had predestined	1
Rom	8:29	For those whom he foreknew he also predestined	1
	8:30	And those whom he predestined he also called;	1

predict

1. καταγγέλλω, *katangellō, 2859*
2. προλέγω, *prolegō, 4625*
3. σημαίνω, *sēmainō, 4955*

Act	3:24	also predicted these days.	1
	11:28	Agabus stood up and predicted by the Spirit	3
Rom	9:29	as Isaiah predicted, "If the Lord of hosts had	2

prediction

1. προλέγω, *prolegō, 4625*

Jde   1:17   predictions of the apostles of our Lord Jesus   1

prefer

1. αἱρέομαι, *haireomai, 145*
2. θέλω, *thelō, 2527*

1Co	4:21	What would you prefer? Am I to come to you	2
Php	1:22	and I do not know which I prefer.	1
Phm	1:14	I preferred to do nothing without your consent	2

prefigure

1. ἀντίτυπος, *antitypos, 531*

1Pe   3:21   baptism, which this prefigured, now saves you   1

pregnant

1. ἐν + γαστήρ + ἔχω, *en + gastēr + echō, 1877 + 1143 + 2400*

Mat	24:19	Woe to those who are pregnant	1
Mrk	13:17	Woe to those who are pregnant	1
Lke	21:23	Woe to those who are pregnant	1
1Th	5: 3	as labor pains come upon a pregnant woman	1
Rev	12: 2	She was pregnant and was crying out in birth pangs	1

prejudice

1. πρόκριμα, *prokrima, 4622*

1Ti 5:21 I warn you to keep these instructions without prejudice   1

Preparation *See* day of Preparation

preparation

1. παρασκευή, *paraskeuē, 4187*

Mat 27:62 next day, that is, after the day of Preparation   1
Lke 23:54 It was the day of Preparation   1

prepare

1. Contextual: Not in Greek
2. διακονέω, *diakoneō, 1354*
3. ἑτοιμάζω, *hetoimazō, 2286*
4. καταρτίζω, *katartizō, 2936*
5. κατασκευάζω, *kataskeuazō, 2941*
6. κατεργάζομαι, *katergazomai, 2981*
7. παρασκευάζω, *paraskeuazō, 4186*
8. ποιέω, *poieō, 4472*

Mat 3: 3 one crying out in the wilderness: 'Prepare the way   3
     11:10 who will prepare your way before you.'   5
     20:23 for whom it has been prepared by my Father."   3
     21:16 you have prepared praise   4
     22: 4 Look, I have prepared my dinner   3
     25:34 inherit the kingdom prepared for you   3
     25:41 into the eternal fire prepared for the devil   3
     26:12 she has prepared me for burial.   8
     26:19 they prepared the Passover meal.   3
Mrk 1: 2 who will prepare your way;   5
     1: 3 'Prepare the way of the Lord   3
     10:40 is for those for whom it has been prepared."   3
     14:16 they prepared the Passover meal.   3
Lke 1:17 to make ready a people prepared for the Lord."   5
     1:76 you will go before the Lord to prepare his ways   3
     2:31 which you have prepared in the presence of all   3
     3: 4 'Prepare the way of the Lord   3
     7:27 who will prepare your way before you.'   5
     12:20 the things you have prepared, whose will they be?'   3
     12:47 did not prepare himself or do what was wanted   3
     17: 8 'Prepare supper for me   3
     22: 8 prepare the Passover meal for us that we may eat it."   3
     22:13 they prepared the Passover meal.   3
     23:56 Then they returned, and prepared spices   3
     24: 1 taking the spices that they had prepared.   3
Jhn 14: 2 I go to prepare a place for you?   3
     14: 3 if I go and prepare a place for you   3
Act 10:10 while it was being prepared, he fell into a trance.   7
1Co 2: 9 what God has prepared for those who love him"   3
2Co 3: 3 that you are a letter of Christ, prepared by us   2
     4:17 preparing us for an eternal weight of glory   6
     5: 5 He who has prepared us for this very thing is God   6
Col 1:11 prepared to endure everything with patience   1
Phm 1:22 One thing more—prepare a guest room for me   3
Heb 10: 5 a body you have prepared for me;   4
     11: 3 the worlds were prepared by the word of God   4
     11:16 indeed, he has prepared a city for them.   3
Jde 1: 3 Beloved, while eagerly preparing to write to you   8
Rev 12: 6 wilderness, where she has a place prepared by God   3
     16:12 to prepare the way for the kings from the east.   3
     21: 2 prepared as a bride adorned for her husband.   3

prepare beforehand

1. προετοιμάζω, *proetoimazō, 4602*

Rom 9:23 objects...which he has prepared beforehand   1
Eph 2:10 for good works, which God prepared beforehand   1

prepare for action

1. ἀναζώννυμι, *anazōnnymi, 350*

1Pe 1:13 Therefore prepare your minds for action; discipline   1

prepare in advance

1. προμελετάω, *promeletaō, 4627*

Lke 21:14 not to prepare your defense in advance;   1

prescribe

1. Contextual: Not in Greek
2. διατάσσω, *diatassō, 1411*

Lke 3:13 "Collect no more than the amount prescribed for you."   2

Rom 3:20 justified...by deeds prescribed by the law   1
     3:28 by faith apart from works prescribed by the law.   1

presence *See also* bring into one's presence, here in presence

1. ἀπέναντι, *apenanti, 595*
2. ἔμπροσθεν, *emprosthen, 1869*
3. ἐναντίον, *enantion, 1883*
4. ἐνώπιον, *enōpion, 1967*
5. κατέναντι, *katenanti, 2978*
6. κατενώπιον, *katenōpion, 2979*
7. μετά, *meta, 3552*
8. παρά, *para, 4123*
9. παρουσία, *parousia, 4242*
10. πρόθεσις, *prothesis, 4606*
11. πρόσωπον, *prosōpon, 4725*

Mat 12: 4 and ate the bread of the Presence   10
Mrk 2:26 ate the bread of the Presence   10
Lke 1:19 "I am Gabriel. I stand in the presence of God   4
     2:31 have prepared in the presence of all peoples   11
     6: 4 took and ate the bread of the Presence   10
     8:47 declared in the presence of all the people   4
     14:10 then you will be honored in the presence of all   4
     15:10 joy in the presence of the angels of God   4
     19:27 bring them here and slaughter them in my presence.' "   2
     20:26 they were not able in the presence of the people   3
     23:14 here I have examined him in your presence   4
     24:43 he took it and ate in their presence.   4
Jhn 3: 2 do these signs...apart from the presence of God."   7
     8:38 I declare what I have seen in the Father's presence;   8
     12:37 he had performed so many signs in their presence   2
     17: 5 now, Father, glorify me in your own presence   8
     17: 5 with the glory that I had in your presence   8
     20:30 many other signs in the presence of his disciples   4
Act 2:28 make me full of gladness with your presence.'   11
     3:13 rejected in the presence of Pilate   11
     3:16 in the presence of all of you.   1
     3:20 may come from the presence of the Lord   11
     10:33 all of us are here in the presence of God   4
     27:35 giving thanks to God in the presence of all   4
Rom 4:17 in the presence of the God in whom he believed   5
1Co 1:29 boast in the presence of God.   4
2Co 2:10 has been for your sake in the presence of Christ.   11
     2:17 sent from God and standing in his presence.   5
     10:10 his bodily presence is weak   9
Php 2:12 have always obeyed me, not only in my presence   9
2Th 1: 9 separated from the presence of the Lord   11
1Ti 5:20 rebuke them in the presence of all   4
     5:21 In the presence of God and of Christ Jesus   4
     6:12 confession in the presence of many witnesses.   4
     6:13 In the presence of God   4
2Ti 4: 1 In the presence of God and of Christ Jesus,   4
Heb 9: 2 the table, and the bread of the Presence;   10
     9:24 now to appear in the presence of God on our behalf.   11
Jde 1:24 make you stand...in the presence of his glory   6
Rev 14:10 tormented...in the presence of the holy angels   4
     14:10 tormented...in the presence of the Lamb.   4
     19:20 false prophet who had performed in its presence   4
     20:11 earth and the heaven fled from his presence   11

present¹ *See also* present case

1. δῶρον, *dōron, 1565*

Rev 11:10 gloat...celebrate and exchange presents   1

present²

1. Contextual: Not in Greek
2. λαλέω, *laleō, 3281*
3. παρίστημι, *paristēmi, 4225*

Lke 2:22 to present him to the Lord   3
Act 1: 3 After his suffering he presented himself alive   3
     17:19 what this new teaching is that you are presenting?   2
     23:33 they presented Paul also before him.   3
Rom 6:13 No longer present your members to sin   3
     6:13 but present yourselves to God   3
     6:13 present your members to God as instruments   1
     6:16 if you present...to anyone as obedient slaves   3
     6:19 once presented your members as slaves to impurity   3
     6:19 present your members as slaves to righteousness   3
     12: 1 to present your bodies as a living sacrifice   3

2Co 11: 2 to present you as a chaste virgin to Christ. 3
Eph 5:27 to present the church to himself in splendor 3
Col 1:22 so as to present you holy...before him 3
1:28 so that we may present everyone mature in Christ. 3
2Ti 2:15 Do your best to present yourself to God as... 3

present[3]

1. Contextual: Not in Greek
2. ἄρτι, *arti, 785*
3. ἐνίστημι, *enistēmi, 1931*
4. νῦν, *nyn, 3814*
5. νῦν + καιρός, *nyn + kairos, 3814 + 2789*
6. νυνί, *nyni, 3815*
7. οὗτος, *houtos, 4047*

Lke 12:56 not know how to interpret the present time? 7
Act 24:25 "Go away for the present; 4
Rom 3:26 prove at the present time that he...is righteous 4
8:18 the sufferings of this present time are not worth 4
11: 5 So too at the present time there is a remnant 4
15:25 At present, however, I am going to Jerusalem 6
1Co 3:22 the present or the future—all belong to you 3
4:11 To the present hour we are hungry and thirsty 2
7:21 make use of your present condition 1
7:31 For the present form of this world is passing away. 1
2Co 8:14 your present abundance and their need 5
Gal 1: 4 to set us free from the present evil age 3
4:25 and corresponds to the present Jerusalem 4
Eph 6:12 against the cosmic powers of this present darkness 7
1Ti 4: 8 holding promise for both the present life 4
6:17 As for those who in the present age are rich 4
2Ti 4:10 Demas, in love with this present world 4
Tit 2:12 in the present age to live lives that are self-controlled, 4
Heb 9: 9 This is a symbol of the present time 3
2Pe 3: 7 by the same word the present heavens and earth 4

present[4]

1. παραγίνομαι, *paraginomai, 4134*
2. πάρειμι, *pareimi, 4205*
3. συμπάρειμι, *sympareimi, 5223*
4. σύν, *syn, 5250*

Lke 13: 1 At that very time there were some present 2
Act 21:18 all the elders were present. 1
25:24 "King Agrippa and all here present with us 3
1Co 5: 3 For though absent in body, I am present in spirit; 2
5: 3 as if present I have already pronounced judgment 2
5: 4 When you are assembled, and my spirit is present 4
2Co 10: 2 I ask that when I am present 2
10:11 we will also do when present. 2
13: 2 as I did when present on my second visit 2
Gal 4:18 not only when I am present with you. 2
4:20 I wish I were present with you now 2

no present

1. ἄτερ, *ater, 868*

Lke 22: 6 an opportunity...when no crowd was present. 1

present thing

1. ἐνίστημι, *enistēmi, 1931*

Rom 8:38 nor things present, nor things to come, nor powers 1

preserve

1. συντηρέω, *syntēreō, 5337*

Mat 9:17 and so both are preserved." 1

press *See also pit for the wine press*

1. ληνός, *lēnos, 3332*

Rev 19:15 will tread the wine press of the fury...of God 1

press down

1. πιέζω, *piezō, 4390*

Lke 6:38 good measure, pressed down, shaken together 1

press hard

1. συνέχω, *synechō, 5309*

Php 1:23 I am hard pressed between the two: 1

press in on

1. ἀποθλίβω, *apothlibō, 632*
2. ἐπίκειμαι, *epikeimai, 2130*

3. συμπνίγω, *sympnigō, 5231*
4. συνθλίβω, *synthlibō, 5315*

Mrk 5:24 a large crowd followed him and pressed in on him 4
5:31 "You see the crowd pressing in on you; 4
Lke 5: 1 and the crowd was pressing in on him 2
8:42 As he went, the crowds pressed in on him. 3
8:45 the crowds surround you and press in on you." 1

press on

1. διώκω, *diōkō, 1503*

Php 3:12 I press on to make it my own 1
3:14 I press on toward the goal for the prize 1

press upon

1. ἐπιπίπτω, *epipiptō, 2158*

Mrk 3:10 all who had diseases pressed upon him to touch him. 1

wine press

1. ληνός, *lēnos, 3332*

Mat 21:33 dug a wine press in it, and built a watchtower. 1
Rev 14:19 into the great wine press of the wrath of God. 1
14:20 the wine press was trodden outside the city 1
14:20 and blood flowed from the wine press 1

pressure

1. ἐπίστασις, *epistasis, 2180*
2. θλῖψις, *thlipsis, 2568*

2Co 8:13 should be relief for others and pressure on you 2
11:28 I am under daily pressure 1

presume

1. Contextual: Not in Greek
2. ἀξιόω, *axioō, 546*
3. δοκέω, *dokeō, 1506*

Mat 3: 9 Do not presume to say to yourselves, 'We have 3
Lke 7: 7 therefore I did not presume to come to you. 2
Heb 5: 4 one does not presume to take this honor 1

pretend

1. ὑποκρίνομαι, *hypokrinomai, 5693*

Lke 20:20 sent spies who pretended to be honest 1

pretext

1. ἐπικάλυμμα, *epikalymma, 2127*
2. πρόφασις, *prophasis, 4733*
3. ὡς, *hōs, 6055*

Act 23:15 pretext that you want...a more thorough examination 3
27:30 on the pretext of putting out anchors 2
1Th 2: 5 we never came...with a pretext for greed; 2
1Pe 2:16 do not use your freedom as a pretext for evil. 1

prevail

1. ἰσχύω, *ischyō, 2710*
2. κατισχύω, *katischyō, 2996*
3. νικάω, *nikaō, 3771*

Mat 16:18 gates of Hades will not prevail against it. 2
Lke 23:23 their voices prevailed. 2
Act 19:20 word of the Lord grew mightily and prevailed. 1
Rom 3: 4 and prevail in your judging." 3

prevail upon

1. παραβιάζομαι, *parabiazomai, 4128*

Act 16:15 And she prevailed upon us. 1

prevent

1. διακωλύω, *diakōlyō, 1361*
2. ἐγκόπτω, *enkoptō, 1601*
3. κατέχω, *katechō, 2988*
4. κωλύω, *kōlyō, 3266*
5. μή, *mē, 3590*

Mat 3:14 John would have prevented him, saying, "I need 1
Lke 4:42 wanted to prevent him from leaving them. 3
Act 8:36 What is to prevent me from being baptized?" 4
24:23 not to prevent any of his friends 4
Rom 1:13 (but thus far have been prevented) 4
Gal 5: 7 who prevented you from obeying the truth? 2
5:17 to prevent you from doing what you want. 5
Heb 7:23 because they were prevented by death 4

3Jn 1:10 and even prevents those who want to do so   4

previously *See also* commit previously, ratify previously, see previously, sin previously

  1. προϋπάρχω, *prouparchō, 4732*

Act 8: 9 Simon had previously practiced magic in the city   1

prey *See* beast of prey

prey upon

  1. κατεσθίω, *katesthiō, 2983*

2Co 11:20 or preys upon you, or takes advantage of you   1

price *See also* set a price

  1. Contextual: Not in Greek
  2. τιμή, *timē, 5507*
  3. τοσοῦτος, *tosoutos, 5537*

Mat 27: 9 price of the one on whom a price had been set   2
Act 5: 8 sold the land for such and such a price.”   1
    5: 8 she said, “Yes, that was the price.”   3
1Co 6:20 you were bought with a price;   2
    7:23 You were bought with a price;   2

pride

  1. ἀλαζονεία, *alazoneia, 224*
  2. καύχημα, *kauchēma, 3017*
  3. καύχησις, *kauchēsis, 3018*
  4. ὑπερηφανία, *hyperēphania, 5661*

Mrk 7:22 envy, slander, pride, folly.   4
2Co 7: 4 boast about you; I have great pride in you;   3
Gal 6: 4 that work...will become a cause for pride.   2
Heb 3: 6 firm the confidence and the pride that belong to hope.   2
1Jn 2:16 the desire of the eyes, the pride in riches   1

priest *See also* chief priest, high priest, serve as priest

  1. Contextual: Not in Greek
  2. ἱερεύς, *hiereus, 2636*

Mat 8: 4 but go, show yourself to the priest   2
    12: 4 but only for the priests.   2
    12: 5 on the sabbath the priests in the temple break   2
    28:12 After the priests had assembled with the elders   1
Mrk 1:44 go, show yourself to the priest   2
    2:26 which it is not lawful for any but the priests   2
Lke 1: 5 there was a priest named Zechariah   2
    5:14 “Go...and show yourself to the priest   2
    6: 4 it is not lawful for any but the priests to eat   2
    10:31 Now by chance a priest was going down that road;   2
    17:14 “Go and show yourselves to the priests.”   2
Jhn 1:19 Jews sent priests and Levites from Jerusalem   2
Act 4: 1 the priests, the captain of the temple   2
    6: 7 the priests became obedient to the faith.   2
    14:13 The priest of Zeus...brought oxen and garlands   2
Heb 5: 6 a priest forever, according to the order of Melchizedek.”   2
    7: 1 King Melchizedek of Salem, priest of the Most High God   2
    7: 3 he remains a priest forever.   2
    7:11 need...to speak of another priest arising   2
    7:14 Moses said nothing about priests.   2
    7:15 another priest arises, resembling Melchizedek,   2
    7:16 who has become a priest, not through a legal   1
    7:17 a priest forever, according to the order of Melchizedek.”   2
    7:20 for others who became priests took their office   2
    7:21 but this one became a priest with an oath,   1
    7:21 ‘You are a priest forever’ ”   2
    7:23 the former priests were many in number   2
    8: 3 hence it is necessary for this priest also   1
    8: 4 he would not be a priest at all   2
    8: 4 since there are priests who offer gifts   1
    9: 6 the priests go continually into the first tent   2
    10:11 every priest stands day after day at his service   2
    10:21 since we have a great priest over the house of God   2
Rev 1: 6 made us to be a kingdom, priests serving his God   2
    5:10 you have made them to be a kingdom and priests   2
    20: 6 but they will be priests of God and of Christ   2

priesthood *See also* high priesthood

  1. αὐτός, *autos, 899*
  2. ἱερατεία, *hierateia, 2632*
  3. ἱεράτευμα, *hierateuma, 2633*
  4. ἱερωσύνη, *hierōsynē, 2648*

Lke 1: 9 according to the custom of the priesthood   2
Heb 7:11 attainable through the levitical priesthood   4
    7:11 for the people received the law under this priesthood   1
    7:12 when there is a change in the priesthood   4
    7:24 he holds his priesthood permanently   4
1Pe 2: 5 like living stones...be a holy priesthood   3
    2: 9 you are a chosen race, a royal priesthood   3

priestly *See* priestly *office*, priestly *order*, priestly *service*

Prisca

  1. Πρίσκα, *Priska, 4571*

Rom 16: 3 Greet Prisca and Aquila, who work with me   1
1Co 16:19 Aquila and Prisca, together with the church   1
2Ti 4:19 Greet Prisca and Aquila   1

Priscilla

  1. Πρίσκα, *Priska, 4571*

Act 18: 2 recently come from Italy with his wife Priscilla   1
    18:18 accompanied by Priscilla and Aquila.   1
    18:26 when Priscilla and Aquila heard him   1

prison

  1. δεσμωτήριον, *desmōtērion, 1303*
  2. δέω, *deō, 1313*
  3. τήρησις, *tērēsis, 5499*
  4. φυλακή, *phylakē, 5871*

Mat 5:25 to the guard, and you will be thrown into prison.   4
    11: 2 John heard in prison what the Messiah was doing   1
    14: 3 bound him, and put him in prison   4
    14:10 he sent and had John beheaded in the prison.   4
    18:30 then he went and threw him into prison   4
    25:36 I was in prison and you visited me.’   4
    25:39 we saw you sick or in prison and visited you?’   4
    25:43 sick and in prison and you did not visit me.’   4
    25:44 a stranger or naked or sick or in prison   4
Mrk 6:17 and put him in prison on account of Herodias   4
    6:27 He went and beheaded him in the prison   4
Lke 3:20 added to them all by shutting up John in prison   4
    12:58 the officer throw you in prison.   4
    21:12 hand you over to synagogues and prisons   4
    22:33 I am ready to go with you to prison and to death!”   4
    23:19 a man who had been put in prison   4
    23:25 the one who had been put in prison   4
Jhn 3:24 John...had not yet been thrown into prison.   4
Act 5:18 put them in the public prison.   3
    5:19 an angel of the Lord opened the prison doors   4
    5:21 sent to the prison to have them brought.   1
    5:22 they did not find them in the prison;   4
    5:23 “We found the prison securely locked   1
    5:25 the men whom you put in prison   4
    8: 3 committed them to prison.   4
    12: 4 When he had seized him, he put him in prison   4
    12: 5 While Peter was kept in prison   4
    12: 6 guards...were keeping watch over the prison.   4
    12:17 how the Lord had brought him out of the prison.   4
    16:23 they threw them into prison   4
    16:26 the foundations of the prison were shaken;   1
    16:27 woke up and saw the prison doors wide open   4
    16:37 have thrown us into prison;   4
    16:40 leaving the prison they went to Lydia’s home;   4
    22: 4 both men and women and putting them in prison   4
    24:27 Felix left Paul in prison.   2
    26:10 I not only locked up many of the saints in prison   4
Col 4: 3 mystery of Christ, for which I am in prison   2
1Pe 3:19 he went and made a proclamation to the spirits in prison   4
Rev 2:10 devil is about to throw some of you into prison   4
    20: 7 Satan will be released from his prison   4

in prison

  1. δέσμιος, *desmios, 1300*
  2. δέω, *deō, 1313*

Mrk 15: 7 a man called Barabbas was in prison with the rebels   2
Act 25:14 a man here who was left in prison by Felix.   1
Heb 10:34 For you had compassion for those who were in prison   1
    13: 3 Remember those who are in prison   1

in prison with

  1. συναιχμάλωτος, *synaichmalōtos, 5257*
  2. συνδέω, *syndeō, 5279*

Rom 16: 7   my relatives who were in prison with me   1
Heb 13: 3   as though you were in prison with them;   2

prisoner

1. αὐτός, *autos, 899*
2. δέσμιος, *desmios, 1300*
3. δεσμώτης, *desmōtēs, 1304*

Mat 27:15   governor was accustomed to release a prisoner   2
     27:16   At that time they had a notorious prisoner   2
Mrk 15: 6   he used to release a prisoner for them   2
Act   4: 7   they had made the prisoners stand in their midst,   1
     16:25   the prisoners were listening to them.   2
     16:27   supposed that the prisoners had escaped.   2
     23:18   "The prisoner Paul called me   2
     25:27   seems to me unreasonable to send a prisoner   2
     27: 1   Paul and some other prisoners   3
     27:42   The soldiers' plan was to kill the prisoners   3
Eph   3: 1   Paul am a prisoner for Christ Jesus for the sake of you   2
     4: 1   I therefore, the prisoner in the Lord, beg you   2
2Ti   1: 8   Do not be ashamed...of me his prisoner   2
Phm   1: 1   Paul, a prisoner of Christ Jesus   2
     1: 9   I, Paul, do this as an old man, and now also as a prisoner   2

fellow prisoner

1. συναιχμάλωτος, *synaichmalōtos, 5257*

Col   4:10   Aristarchus my fellow prisoner greets you   1
Phm   1:23   Epaphras, my fellow prisoner in Christ Jesus   1

private   *See also* private *meeting,* private *ownership*

1. ἴδιος, *idios, 2625*

Mrk   4:34   he explained everything in private to his disciples.   1
     7:33   took him aside in private, away from the crowd   1

privately

1. κατά + ἴδιος, *kata + idios, 2848 + 2625*
2. λάθρα, *lathra, 3277*

Mat 17:19   Then the disciples came to Jesus privately   1
     24: 3   the disciples came to him privately, saying   1
Mrk   9:28   his disciples asked him privately   1
     13: 3   James, John, and Andrew asked him privately   1
Lke   9:10   withdrew privately to a city called Bethsaida.   1
     10:23   the disciples, Jesus said to them privately   1
Jhn 11:28   called her sister Mary, and told her privately   2
Act 23:19   drew him aside privately, and asked, "What is it   1

privilege   *See also* grant privilege graciously

1. χάρις, *charis, 5921*

2Co   8: 4   begging us earnestly for the privilege   1

prize

1. βραβεῖον, *brabeion, 1092*
2. ὑψηλός, *hypsēlos, 5734*

Lke 16:15   what is prized by human beings   2
1Co   9:24   only one receives the prize?   1
Php   3:14   I press on toward the goal for the prize   1

proceed

1. ἐξέρχομαι, *exerchomai, 2002*
2. προστίθημι, *prostithēmi, 4707*

Mat 15:18   comes out of the mouth proceeds from the heart   1
Act 12: 3   he proceeded to arrest Peter also.   2

proceed from

1. ἐκ, *ek, 1666*

Rom 14:23   for whatever does not proceed from faith is sin.   1

proceed on a journey

1. πορεύομαι, *poreuomai, 4513*

Act 21: 5   we left and proceeded on our journey;   1

proceeds

1. Contextual: Not in Greek
2. αὐτός, *autos, 899*
3. τιμή, *timē, 5507*

Act   2:45   distribute the proceeds to all, as any had need.   2
     4:34   brought the proceeds of what was sold.   3
     5: 2   he kept back some of the proceeds   3
     5: 3   to keep back part of the proceeds of the land?   3
     5: 4   sold, were not the proceeds at your disposal?   1

procession   *See* lead in triumphal procession

Prochorus

1. Πρόχορος, *Prochoros, 4743*

Act   6: 5   Philip, Prochorus, Nicanor, Timon   1

proclaim

1. Contextual: Not in Greek
2. ἀναγγέλλω, *anangellō, 334*
3. ἀπαγγέλλω, *apangellō, 550*
4. διαγγέλλω, *diangellō, 1334*
5. ἐξαγγέλλω, *exangellō, 1972*
6. ἐρεύγομαι, *ereugomai, 2243*
7. εὐαγγελίζω, *euangelizō, 2294*
8. καταγγέλλω, *katangellō, 2859*
9. κηρύσσω, *kēryssō, 3062*
10. λέγω, *legō, 3306*

Mat   3: 1   appeared in the wilderness of Judea, proclaiming   9
     4:17   From that time Jesus began to proclaim,   9
     4:23   in their synagogues and proclaiming the good news   9
     9:35   teaching in their synagogues, and proclaiming   9
     10:27   proclaim from the housetops.   9
     12:18   he will proclaim justice to the Gentiles.   3
     13:35   I will proclaim what has been hidden   6
     24:14   this good news of the kingdom will be proclaimed   9
     26:13   wherever this good news is proclaimed   9
Mrk   1: 4   proclaiming a baptism of repentance   9
     1: 7   He proclaimed, "The one who is more powerful   9
     1:14   proclaiming the good news of God   9
     1:45   he went out and began to proclaim it freely   9
     5:20   began to proclaim in the Decapolis   9
     6:12   and proclaimed that all should repent.   9
     7:36   the more zealously they proclaimed it.   9
     13:10   good news must first be proclaimed to all nations.   9
     14: 9   the good news is proclaimed in the whole world   9
     16:15   ⟦"Go into all the world and proclaim the good news⟧   9
Lke   3: 3   proclaiming a baptism of repentance   9
     4:18   has sent me to proclaim release to the captives   9
     4:19   to proclaim the year of the Lord's favor."   9
     8: 1   proclaiming and bringing the good news   9
     8:39   proclaiming throughout the city   9
     9: 2   he sent them out to proclaim the kingdom of God   9
     9:60   as for you, go and proclaim the kingdom of God."   4
     12: 3   will be proclaimed from the housetops.   9
     24:47   proclaimed in his name to all nations   9
Jhn   4:25   "When he comes, he will proclaim all things to us."   2
Act   4: 2   proclaiming that in Jesus there is the resurrection   8
     5:42   proclaim Jesus as the Messiah.   7
     8: 4   went from place to place, proclaiming the word.   7
     8: 5   proclaimed the Messiah to them.   9
     9:20   he began to proclaim Jesus in the synagogues,   9
     11:20   proclaiming the Lord Jesus.   7
     13: 5   proclaimed the word of God in the synagogues   8
     13:38   forgiveness of sins is proclaimed to you;   8
     15:21   Moses has had those who proclaim him   9
     15:35   taught and proclaimed the word of the Lord.   7
     15:36   in every city where we proclaimed the word   8
     16:17   who proclaim to you a way of salvation."   8
     17: 3   "This is the Messiah, Jesus whom I am proclaiming   8
     17:13   the word...had been proclaimed by Paul in Beroea   8
     17:23   this I proclaim to you.   8
     18: 5   Paul was occupied with proclaiming the word   1
     19:13   "I adjure you by the Jesus whom Paul proclaims."   9
     20:25   I have gone about proclaiming the kingdom   9
     26:23   he would proclaim light...to our people   8
     28:31   proclaiming the kingdom of God   9
Rom   1: 8   your faith is proclaimed throughout the world.   8
     9:17   so that my name may be proclaimed in all the earth."   4
     10: 8   (that is, the word of faith that we proclaim);   9
     10:14   how are they to hear without someone to proclaim   9
     10:15   how are they to proclaim him unless they are sent?   9
1Co   1:23   we proclaim Christ crucified   9
     2: 1   I did not come proclaiming the mystery of God to you   8
     9:14   those who proclaim the gospel   8
     9:27   so that after proclaiming to others I myself should not   9
     11:26   you proclaim the Lord's death until he comes.   8
     15: 2   hold firmly to the message that I proclaimed   7
     15:11   so we proclaim and so you have come to believe.   9
     15:12   if Christ is proclaimed as raised from the dead   9

2Co	1:19 Jesus Christ, whom we proclaimed among you	9
	4: 5 For we do not proclaim ourselves; we proclaim Jesus	9
	4: 5 not proclaim ourselves; we proclaim Jesus as Lord	1
	11: 4 For if someone comes and proclaims another Jesus	9
	11: 4 proclaims another Jesus than the one we proclaimed	9
	11: 7 I proclaimed God's good news to you free of charge?	7
Gal	1: 8 a gospel contrary to what we proclaimed	7
	1:16 I might proclaim him among the Gentiles	7
	1:23 proclaiming the faith he once tried to destroy."	7
	2: 2 the gospel that I proclaim among the Gentiles	9
Eph	2:17 he came and proclaimed peace to you who were far off	7
Php	1:15 Some proclaim Christ from envy and rivalry	9
	1:16 These proclaim Christ out of love	1
	1:17 the others proclaim Christ out of selfish ambition	8
	1:18 Just this, that Christ is proclaimed in every way	8
Col	1:23 been proclaimed to every creature under heaven.	9
	1:28 It is he whom we proclaim	8
1Th	2: 9 while we proclaimed to you the gospel of God.	9
1Ti	3:16 proclaimed among Gentiles, believed	9
2Ti	4: 2 proclaim the message; be persistent	9
Heb	2:12 "I will proclaim your name to my brothers and sisters	3
1Pe	2: 9 you may proclaim the mighty acts of him	5
1Jn	1: 5 heard from him and proclaim to you	2
Rev	5: 2 a mighty angel proclaiming with a loud voice	9
	12:10 Then I heard a loud voice in heaven, proclaiming	10
	14: 6 another angel…with an eternal gospel to proclaim	7

proclaim already

1. προκηρύσσω, *prokēryssō, 4619*

Act	13:24 before his coming John had already proclaimed	1

proclaim fully

1. πληροφορέω, *plērophoreō, 4442*
2. πληρόω, *plēroō, 4444*

Rom	15:19 I have fully proclaimed the good news of Christ.	2
2Ti	4:17 through me the message might be fully proclaimed	1

proclaim the good news

1. εὐαγγελίζω, *euangelizō, 2294*
2. εὐαγγέλιον, *euangelion, 2295*
3. κηρύσσω, *kēryssō, 3062*

Mat	10: 7 As you go, proclaim the good news	3
Mrk	16:20 ⟦and proclaimed the good news everywhere⟧	3
Lke	3:18 he proclaimed the good news to the people.	1
	4:43 proclaim the good news of the kingdom of God	1
	16:16 the good news of the kingdom of God is proclaimed	1
Act	8:12 proclaiming the good news about the kingdom of God	1
	8:25 proclaiming the good news to many villages	1
	8:35 he proclaimed to him the good news about Jesus.	1
	8:40 he proclaimed the good news to all the towns	1
	14: 7 there they continued proclaiming the good news.	1
	14:21 they had proclaimed the good news to that city	1
	16:10 God had called us to proclaim the good news to them.	1
Rom	15:20 I make it my ambition to proclaim the good news	1
1Co	15: 1 the good news that I proclaimed to you	1
2Co	2:12 to proclaim the good news of Christ	2
	8:18 for his proclaiming the good news;	2
	10:16 we may proclaim the good news in lands beyond you	1

proclaim the gospel

1. εὐαγγελίζω, *euangelizō, 2294*
2. εὐαγγέλιον, *euangelion, 2295*

Rom	1:15 my eagerness to proclaim the gospel to you	1
1Co	1:17 not send me to baptize but to proclaim the gospel	1
	9:16 If I proclaim the gospel	1
	9:16 woe to me if I do not proclaim the gospel!	1
Gal	1: 8 proclaim to you a gospel contrary to what	1
	1: 9 if anyone proclaims to you a gospel	1
	1:11 the gospel that was proclaimed by me is not of human	1
Eph	6:15 make you ready to proclaim the gospel of peace.	2
1Th	3: 2 co-worker for God in proclaiming the gospel	1
1Pe	4: 6 the gospel was proclaimed even to the dead	1

proclaim the message

1. ἀναγγέλλω, *anangellō, 334*
2. κηρύσσω, *kēryssō, 3062*

Mat	11: 1 from there to teach and proclaim his message	2
Mrk	1:38 so that I may proclaim the message there also;	2
	1:39 proclaiming the message in their synagogues	2
	3:14 to be sent out to proclaim the message	2

Lke	4:44 he continued proclaiming the message	2
Act	20:20 anything helpful, proclaiming the message to you	1

proclaimer

1. καταγγελεύς, *katangeleus, 2858*

Act	17:18 "He seems to be a proclaimer of foreign divinities."	1

proclamation   *See also* make a proclamation

1. εὐαγγελίζω, *euangelizō, 2294*
2. κήρυγμα, *kērygma, 3060*

Mat	12:41 they repented at the proclamation of Jonah	2
Mrk	16: S ⟦imperishable proclamation of eternal salvation⟧	2
Lke	11:32 they repented at the proclamation of Jonah	2
Rom	16:25 my gospel and the proclamation of Jesus Christ	2
1Co	1:21 through the foolishness of our proclamation, to save	2
	2: 4 My speech and my proclamation	2
	9:18 Just this: that in my proclamation	1
	15:14 then our proclamation has been in vain	2
Tit	1: 3 the proclamation with which I have been entrusted	2

proclamation of good news

1. εὐαγγέλιον, *euangelion, 2295*

2Th	2:14 called…through our proclamation of the good news	1

proconsul

1. ἀνθύπατος, *anthypatos, 478*

Act	13: 7 He was with the proconsul, Sergius Paulus,	1
	13: 8 to turn the proconsul away from the faith.	1
	13:12 the proconsul saw what had happened, he believed	1
	18:12 when Gallio was proconsul of Achaia	1
	19:38 there are proconsuls;	1

procreation

1. καταβολή + σπέρμα, *katabolē + sperma, 2856 + 5065*

Heb	11:11 By faith he received power of procreation	1

produce

1. Contextual: Not in Greek
2. ἀποδίδωμι, *apodidōmi, 625*
3. δίδωμι, *didōmi, 1443*
4. ἐκφέρω, *ekpherō, 1766*
5. ἐργάζομαι, *ergazomai, 2237*
6. καρπός, *karpos, 2843*
7. καρποφορέω, *karpophoreō, 2844*
8. κατεργάζομαι, *katergazomai, 2981*
9. πληρόω, *plēroō, 4444*
10. ποιέω, *poieō, 4472*
11. προφέρω, *propherō, 4734*
12. τίκτω, *tiktō, 5503*

Mat	21:34 to collect his produce.	6
	21:41 who will give him the produce at the harvest time."	6
	21:43 a people that produces the fruits of the kingdom.	10
	24:24 false prophets will appear and produce great signs	3
Mrk	4:28 The earth produces of itself, first the stalk	7
	12: 2 share of the produce of the vineyard.	6
	13:22 produce signs and omens, to lead astray	3
Lke	6:45 The good person…produces good	11
	6:45 evil person out of evil treasure produces evil;	11
	8: 8 when it grew, it produced a hundredfold."	10
	20:10 give him his share of the produce of the vineyard;	6
Rom	5: 3 knowing that suffering produces endurance	8
	5: 4 and endurance produces character	1
	5: 4 and character produces hope	1
	7: 8 sin…produced in me all kinds of covetousness.	8
1Co	14: 7 with lifeless instruments that produce sound,	3
2Co	7:10 For godly grief produces a repentance	5
	7:10 worldly grief produces death.	8
	7:11 what earnestness this godly grief has produced	8
	9:11 which will produce thanksgiving to God through us;	8
Php	1:11 produced the harvest of righteousness	9
Heb	6: 7 Ground that…produces a crop useful to those	12
	6: 8 if it produces thorns and thistles	4
Jas	1: 3 testing of your faith produces endurance;	8
	1:20 your anger does not produce God's righteousness.	5
Rev	22: 2 tree of life…producing its fruit each month;	2

produce abundantly

1. εὐφορέω, *euphoreō, 2369*

Lke	12:16 "The land of a rich man produced abundantly.	1

profane *See also* call profane

1. βέβηλος, *bebēlos, 1013*
2. βεβηλόω, *bebēloō, 1014*
3. κοινός, *koinos, 3123*
4. κοινός + ἡγέομαι, *koinos + hēgeomai, 3123 + 2451*

Act	10:14	never eaten anything that is profane or unclean."	3
	10:28	I should not call anyone profane or unclean.	3
	11: 8	nothing profane…has ever entered my mouth.'	3
	24: 6	He even tried to profane the temple	2
1Ti	1: 9	law is laid down…for the unholy and profane	1
	4: 7	Have nothing to do with profane myths…tales.	1
	6:20	Avoid the profane chatter and contradictions	1
2Ti	2:16	Avoid profane chatter	1
Heb	10:29	profaned the blood of the covenant	4

profess

1. ἐπαγγέλλομαι, *epangellomai, 2040*
2. ὁμολογέω, *homologeō, 3933*

1Ti	2:10	as is proper for women who profess reverence for God.	1
	6:21	by professing it some have missed the mark	1
Tit	1:16	They profess to know God	2

proficient

1. ἄρτιος, *artios, 787*

2Ti	3:17	so that everyone who belongs to God may be proficient	1

profit

1. καρπός, *karpos, 2843*
2. ὠφελέω, *ōpheleō, 6067*

Mat	16:26	For what will it profit them if they gain	2
Mrk	8:36	what will it profit them to gain the whole world	2
Lke	9:25	does it profit them if they gain the whole world	2
Php	4:17	I seek the profit that accumulates to your account.	1

profitable

1. ὠφέλιμος, *ōphelimos, 6068*

Tit	3: 8	these things are excellent and profitable to everyone.	1

profligate

1. ἀκρατής, *akratēs, 203*

2Ti	3: 3	inhuman, implacable, slanderers, profligates	1

progress *See also* make progress

1. προκοπή, *prokopē, 4620*

Php	1:25	for your progress and joy in faith	1
1Ti	4:15	so that all may see your progress.	1

prominent

1. ἐξοχή, *exochē, 2029*
2. ἐπίσημος, *episēmos, 2168*

Act	25:23	the prominent men of the city.	1
Rom	16: 7	they are prominent among the apostles	2

promise *See also* make a promise

1. Contextual: Not in Greek
2. εἰς, *eis, 1650*
3. ἐπαγγελία, *epangelia, 2039*
4. ἐπαγγέλλομαι, *epangellomai, 2040*
5. ἐπάγγελμα, *epangelma, 2041*
6. μετά, *meta, 3552*
7. ὁμολογέω, *homologeō, 3933*
8. ὅς, *hos, 4005*
9. πιστός, *pistos, 4412*
10. προεπαγγέλλω, *proepangellō, 4600*

Mat	14: 7	so much that he promised on oath to grant her	7
Mrk	14:11	greatly pleased, and promised to give him money.	4
Lke	1:72	he has shown the mercy promised to our ancestors	6
	24:49	I am sending upon you what my Father promised;	3
Act	1: 4	to wait there for the promise of the Father.	3
	2:33	the promise of the Holy Spirit	3
	2:39	For the promise is for you, for your children,	3
	7: 5	promised to give it to him as his possession	4
	7:17	time drew near for the fulfillment of the promise	3
	13:23	brought to Israel a Savior, Jesus, as he promised;	3
	13:32	what God promised to our ancestors	3
	13:34	give you the holy promises made to David.'	9
	26: 6	on account of my hope in the promise made by God	3
	26: 7	a promise that our twelve tribes hope to attain	8

Rom	4:13	For the promise that he would inherit the world	3
	4:14	faith is null and the promise is void.	3
	4:16	in order that the promise may rest on grace	3
	4:20	made him waver concerning the promise of God	3
	4:21	that God was able to do what he had promised.	4
	7:10	the very commandment that promised life	2
	9: 4	giving of the law, the worship, and the promises;	3
	9: 8	but the children of the promise are counted	3
	9: 9	For this is what the promise said, "About this time	3
	15: 8	might confirm the promises given to the patriarchs	3
2Co	1:20	in him every one of God's promises is a "Yes."	3
	7: 1	Since we have these promises, beloved	3
	9: 5	this bountiful gift that you have promised	10
Gal	3:14	receive the promise of the Spirit through faith.	3
	3:16	Now the promises were made to Abraham	3
	3:17	so as to nullify the promise.	3
	3:18	it no longer comes from the promise;	3
	3:18	God granted it to Abraham through the promise.	3
	3:21	Is the law then opposed to the promises of God?	3
	3:22	what was promised through faith in Jesus Christ	3
	3:29	Abraham's offspring, heirs according to the promise.	3
	4:23	child of the free woman, was born through the promise.	3
	4:28	friends, are children of the promise, like Isaac.	3
Eph	1:13	marked with the seal of the promised Holy Spirit;	3
	2:12	strangers to the covenants of promise	3
	3: 6	sharers in the promise in Christ Jesus	3
	6: 2	this is the first commandment with a promise:	3
Col	1:23	without shifting from the hope promised by the gospel	1
1Ti	4: 8	holding promise for both the present life	3
2Ti	1: 1	God, for the sake of the promise	3
Tit	1: 2	that God, who never lies, promised before the ages	4
Heb	4: 1	while the promise of entering his rest is still open	3
	6:12	imitators of those who…inherit the promises.	3
	6:15	thus Abraham…obtained the promise.	3
	6:17	to show…to the heirs of the promise	3
	7: 6	blessed him who had received the promises.	3
	8: 6	which has been enacted through better promises.	3
	9:15	may receive the promised eternal inheritance	3
	10:23	for he who has promised is faithful.	4
	10:36	the will of God, you may receive what was promised.	3
	11: 9	stayed for a time in the land he had been promised	3
	11: 9	heirs with him of the same promise.	3
	11:11	he considered him faithful who had promised	4
	11:13	without having received the promises,	3
	11:17	He who had received the promises	3
	11:33	administered justice, obtained promises	3
	11:39	did not receive what was promised	3
	12:26	now he has promised	4
Jas	1:12	the crown of life that the Lord has promised	4
	2: 5	heirs of the kingdom that he has promised	4
2Pe	1: 4	his precious and very great promises	5
	2:19	They promise them freedom	4
	3: 4	and saying, "Where is the promise of his coming?	3
	3: 9	The Lord is not slow about his promise	3
	3:13	in accordance with his promise, we wait for new heavens	5
1Jn	2:25	this is what he has promised us, eternal life.	4

promise beforehand

1. προεπαγγέλλω, *proepangellō, 4600*

Rom	1: 2	he promised beforehand through his prophets	1

promise in marriage

1. ἁρμόζω, *harmozō, 764*

2Co	11: 2	for I promised you in marriage to one husband	1

promote

1. ἐν, *en, 1877*
2. παρέχω, *parechō, 4218*
3. ποιέω, *poieō, 4472*
4. πρός, *pros, 4639*

1Co	7:35	but to promote good order	4
Eph	4:16	promotes the body's growth in building itself up	3
Col	2:23	in promoting self-imposed piety,	1
1Ti	1: 4	endless genealogies that promote speculations	2

prompt

1. προβιβάζω, *probibazō, 4586*

Mat	14: 8	Prompted by her mother, she said	1

pronounce

1. Contextual: Not in Greek

Rom	4: 9	blessedness…pronounced only on the circumcised	1
2Pe	2: 3	Their condemnation, pronounced against them long ago	1

pronounce judgment

1. κρίνω, *krinō, 3212*

1Co	4: 5	do not pronounce judgment before the time	1
	5: 3	I have already pronounced judgment	1

proof

1. δοκιμή, *dokimē, 1509*
2. ἔνδειξις, *endeixis, 1893*

2Co	8:24	before the churches, show them the proof of your love	2
	13: 3	since you desire proof that Christ is speaking	1

convincing proof

1. τεκμήριον, *tekmērion, 5447*

Act	1: 3	presented himself alive…by many convincing proofs	1

proper   *See also* proper *time*

1. ἴδιος, *idios, 2625*
2. πρέπω, *prepō, 4560*

Mat	3:15	proper for us in this way to fulfill all righteousness."	2
1Co	11:13	is it proper for a woman to pray to God	2
Eph	5: 3	as is proper among saints.	2
1Ti	2:10	as is proper for women who profess reverence for God.	2
Jde	1: 6	the angels who…left their proper dwelling	1

properly   *See also* not behave properly

1. εὐσχημόνως, *euschēmonōs, 2361*
2. μέτρον, *metron, 3586*

Eph	4:16	as each part is working properly	2
1Th	4:12	that you may behave properly toward outsiders	1

property   *See also* piece of property

1. Contextual: Not in Greek
2. βίος, *bios, 1050*
3. οὐσία, *ousia, 4045*
4. σκεῦος, *skeuos, 5007*
5. ὑπάρχω, *hyparchō, 5639*

Mat	12:29	and plunder his property	4
	25:14	entrusted his property to them;	5
Mrk	3:27	a strong man's house and plunder his property	4
Lke	11:21	his property is safe	5
	15:12	share of the property that will belong to me.'	3
	15:12	he divided his property between them.	2
	15:13	he squandered his property in dissolute living.	3
	15:30	who has devoured your property with prostitutes	2
	16: 1	this man was squandering his property.	5
Gal	4: 1	though they are the owners of all the property;	1

prophecy   *See also* have the gift of prophecy

1. προφητεία, *prophēteia, 4735*
2. προφητεύω, *prophēteuō, 4736*

Mat	13:14	indeed is fulfilled the prophecy of Isaiah	1
Lke	1:67	with the Holy Spirit and spoke this prophecy:	2
Rom	12: 6	prophecy, in proportion to faith;	1
1Co	12:10	to another prophecy	1
	13: 8	as for prophecies, they will come to an end;	1
	14: 6	revelation or knowledge or prophecy	1
	14:22	while prophecy is not for unbelievers	1
1Ti	1:18	the prophecies made earlier about you	1
	4:14	which was given to you through prophecy	1
2Pe	1:20	no prophecy of scripture is a matter of one's own	1
	1:21	because no prophecy ever came by human will,	1
Rev	1: 3	the one who reads aloud the words of the prophecy	1
	19:10	testimony of Jesus is the spirit of prophecy."	1
	22: 7	Blessed is the one who keeps the words of the prophecy	1
	22:10	the words of the prophecy of this book	1
	22:18	hears the words of the prophecy of this book:	1
	22:19	from the words of the book of this prophecy	1

prophesy

1. προφητεία, *prophēteia, 4735*
2. προφητεύω, *prophēteuō, 4736*

Mat	7:22	'Lord, Lord, did we not prophesy in your name	2
	11:13	the prophets and the law prophesied until John	2
	15: 7	You hypocrites! Isaiah prophesied rightly about you	2
	26:68	saying, "Prophesy to us, you Messiah!	2
Mrk	7: 6	"Isaiah prophesied rightly about you hypocrites	2
	14:65	to strike him, saying to him, "Prophesy!"	2
Lke	22:64	"Prophesy! Who is it that struck you?"	2
Jhn	11:51	being high priest that year he prophesied	2
Act	2:17	your sons and your daughters shall prophesy	2
	2:18	they shall prophesy.	2
	19: 6	they spoke in tongues and prophesied	2
1Co	11: 4	prays or prophesies with something on his head	2
	11: 5	any woman who prays or prophesies with her head	2
	13: 9	we prophesy only in part;	2
	14: 1	especially that you may prophesy.	2
	14: 3	those who prophesy speak to other people	2
	14: 4	those who prophesy build up the church.	2
	14: 5	to speak in tongues, but even more to prophesy.	2
	14: 5	One who prophesies is greater than one who speaks	2
	14:24	if all prophesy	2
	14:31	For you can all prophesy one by one	2
	14:39	So, my friends, be eager to prophesy	2
1Pe	1:10	the prophets who prophesied of the grace	2
Jde	1:14	It was also about these that Enoch…prophesied	2
Rev	10:11	"You must prophesy again about many peoples	2
	11: 3	I will grant my two witnesses authority to prophesy	2
	11: 6	no rain…during the days of their prophesying	1

prophet   *See also* word of a prophet

1. Contextual: Not in Greek
2. αὐτός, *autos, 899*
3. προφήτης, *prophētēs, 4737*
4. προφῆτις, *prophētis, 4739*

Mat	1:22	spoken by the Lord through the prophet:	3
	2: 5	Judea; for so it has been written by the prophet:	3
	2:15	spoken by the Lord through the prophet, "Out of Egypt	3
	2:17	what had been spoken through the prophet Jeremiah:	3
	2:23	so that what had been spoken through the prophets	3
	3: 3	of whom the prophet Isaiah spoke when he said	3
	4:14	spoken through the prophet Isaiah might be fulfilled:	3
	5:12	they persecuted the prophets who were before	3
	5:17	come to abolish the law or the prophets;	3
	7:12	do to you; for this is the law and the prophets.	3
	8:17	what had been spoken through the prophet Isaiah	3
	10:41	Whoever welcomes a prophet in the name of a prophet	3
	10:41	Whoever welcomes a prophet in the name of a prophet	3
	10:41	will receive a prophet's reward;	3
	11: 9	What then did you go out to see? A prophet?	3
	11: 9	Yes, I tell you, and more than a prophet.	3
	11:13	For all the prophets and the law prophesied	3
	12:17	what had been spoken through the prophet Isaiah:	3
	12:39	except the sign of the prophet Jonah.	3
	13:17	I tell you, many prophets and righteous people	3
	13:35	to fulfill what had been spoken through the prophet:	3
	13:57	"Prophets are not without honor except	3
	14: 5	because they regarded him as a prophet.	3
	16:14	others Jeremiah or one of the prophets."	3
	21: 4	what had been spoken through the prophet, saying	3
	21:11	"This is the prophet Jesus from Nazareth	3
	21:26	for all regard John as a prophet."	3
	21:46	because they regarded him as a prophet.	3
	22:40	all the law and the prophets."	3
	23:29	you build the tombs of the prophets	3
	23:30	in shedding the blood of the prophets.'	3
	23:31	descendants of those who murdered the prophets.	3
	23:34	I send you prophets, sages, and scribes	3
	23:37	Jerusalem, the city that kills the prophets	3
	24:15	as was spoken of by the prophet Daniel	3
	26:56	scriptures of the prophets may be fulfilled."	3
	27: 9	what had been spoken through the prophet Jeremiah	3
Mrk	1: 2	As it is written in the prophet Isaiah	3
	6: 4	Jesus said to them, "Prophets are not without honor	3
	6:15	"It is a prophet, like one of the prophets of old."	3
	6:15	"It is a prophet, like one of the prophets of old."	3
	8:28	and still others, one of the prophets."	3
	11:32	for all regarded John as truly a prophet.	3
Lke	1:70	the mouth of his holy prophets from of old	3
	1:76	you…will be called the prophet of the Most High;	3
	2:36	a prophet, Anna the daughter of Phanuel	4
	3: 4	the book of the words of the prophet Isaiah	3
	4:17	the scroll of the prophet Isaiah was given to him.	3
	4:24	no prophet is accepted in the prophet's hometown.	3
	4:24	no prophet is accepted in the prophet's hometown.	2

Lke	4:27	lepers in Israel in the time of the prophet Elisha	3
	6:23	what their ancestors did to the prophets.	3
	7:16	"A great prophet has risen among us!"	3
	7:26	What then did you go out to see? A prophet?	3
	7:26	Yes, I tell you, and more than a prophet.	3
	7:39	he said to himself, "If this man were a prophet	3
	9: 8	that one of the ancient prophets had arisen.	3
	9:19	that one of the ancient prophets has arisen."	3
	10:24	many prophets and kings desired to see	3
	11:47	For you build the tombs of the prophets	3
	11:49	'I will send them prophets and apostles	3
	11:50	the blood of all the prophets	3
	13:28	Abraham and Isaac and Jacob and all the prophets	3
	13:33	for a prophet to be killed outside of Jerusalem.'	3
	13:34	Jerusalem, the city that kills the prophets	3
	16:16	"The law and the prophets were in effect until	3
	16:29	Abraham replied, 'They have Moses and the prophets;	3
	16:31	'If they do not listen to Moses and the prophets	3
	18:31	written about the Son of Man by the prophets	3
	20: 6	they are convinced that John was a prophet."	3
	24:19	about Jesus of Nazareth, who was a prophet	3
	24:25	to believe all that the prophets have declared!	3
	24:27	beginning with Moses and all the prophets	3
	24:44	the prophets, and the psalms	3
Jhn	1:21	"Are you the prophet?" He answered, "No."	3
	1:23	as the prophet Isaiah said.	3
	1:25	the Messiah, nor Elijah, nor the prophet?"	3
	1:45	Moses in the law and also the prophets wrote	3
	4:19	"Sir, I see that you are a prophet.	3
	4:44	a prophet has no honor in the prophet's own country).	3
	4:44	a prophet has no honor in the prophet's own country).	1
	6:14	the prophet who is to come into the world."	3
	6:45	It is written in the prophets	3
	7:40	"This is really the prophet."	3
	7:52	no prophet is to arise from Galilee."	3
	8:52	Abraham died, and so did the prophets;	3
	8:53	The prophets also died. Who do you claim to be?"	3
	9:17	He said, "He is a prophet."	3
	12:38	to fulfill the word spoken by the prophet Isaiah:	3
Act	2:16	this is what was spoken through the prophet Joel:	3
	2:30	Since he was a prophet	3
	3:18	what he had foretold through all the prophets	3
	3:21	long ago through his holy prophets.	3
	3:22	from your own people a prophet like me.	3
	3:23	everyone who does not listen to that prophet	3
	3:24	all the prophets, as many as have spoken	3
	3:25	the descendants of the prophets and of the covenant	3
	7:37	'God will raise up a prophet for you	3
	7:42	as it is written in the book of the prophets:	3
	7:48	as the prophet says	3
	7:52	prophets did your ancestors not persecute?	3
	8:28	he was reading the prophet Isaiah.	3
	8:30	Philip…heard him reading the prophet Isaiah.	3
	8:34	"About whom…does the prophet say this	3
	10:43	All the prophets testify about him	3
	11:27	At that time prophets came down from Jerusalem	3
	13: 1	at Antioch there were prophets and teachers:	3
	13:15	After the reading of the law and the prophets	3
	13:20	judges until the time of the prophet Samuel.	3
	13:27	or understand the words of the prophets	3
	13:40	what the prophets said does not happen to you	3
	15:15	This agrees with the words of the prophets	3
	15:32	Judas and Silas, who were themselves prophets	3
	21:10	a prophet named Agabus came down from Judea.	3
	24:14	written in the prophets.	3
	26:22	saying nothing but what the prophets…said	3
	26:27	King Agrippa, do you believe the prophets?	3
	28:23	both from the law of Moses and from the prophets.	3
	28:25	saying…through the prophet Isaiah	3
Rom	1: 2	he promised beforehand through his prophets	3
	3:21	attested by the law and the prophets	3
	11: 3	"Lord, they have killed your prophets	3
1Co	12:28	first apostles, second prophets, third teachers;	3
	12:29	Are all apostles? Are all prophets?	3
	14:29	Let two or three prophets speak	3
	14:32	the spirits of prophets are subject	3
	14:32	spirits of prophets are subject to the prophets	3
	14:37	Anyone who claims to be a prophet,	3
Eph	2:20	the foundation of the apostles and prophets	3
	3: 5	been revealed to his holy apostles and prophets	3
	4:11	some prophets, some evangelists	3

1Th	2:15	who killed both the Lord Jesus and the prophets	3
Tit	1:12	one of them, their very own prophet, who said	3
Heb	1: 1	God spoke to our ancestors…by the prophets	3
	11:32	David and Samuel and the prophets—	3
Jas	5:10	As an example…beloved, take the prophets	3
1Pe	1:10	the prophets who prophesied of the grace	3
2Pe	2:16	a speechless donkey…restrained the prophet's madness.	3
	3: 2	the words spoken in the past by the holy prophets	3
Rev	2:20	Jezebel, who calls herself a prophet	4
	10: 7	as he announced to his servants the prophets."	3
	11:10	because these two prophets had been a torment	3
	11:18	rewarding your servants, the prophets and saints	3
	16: 6	they shed the blood of saints and prophets	3
	18:20	O heaven, you saints and apostles and prophets!	3
	18:24	And in you was found the blood of prophets	3
	22: 6	the Lord, the God of the spirits of the prophets	3
	22: 9	you and your comrades the prophets	3

false prophet
1. ψευδοπροφήτης, *pseudoprophētēs, 6021*

Mat	7:15	"Beware of false prophets	1
	24:11	many false prophets will arise	1
	24:24	For false messiahs and false prophets will appear	1
Mrk	13:22	False messiahs and false prophets will appear	1
Lke	6:26	what their ancestors did to the false prophets	1
Act	13: 6	a certain magician, a Jewish false prophet	1
2Pe	2: 1	false prophets also arose among the people	1
1Jn	4: 1	many false prophets have gone out into the world.	1
Rev	16:13	spirits…from the mouth of the false prophet.	1
	19:20	beast was captured, and with it the false prophet	1
	20:10	where the beast and the false prophet were	1

prophetic *See also prophetic power*
1. προφητικός, *prophētikos, 4738*

Rom	16:26	through the prophetic writings is made known	1
2Pe	1:19	we have the prophetic message more fully confirmed.	1

prophetically
1. πνευματικῶς, *pneumatikōs, 4462*

Rev	11: 8	city that is prophetically called Sodom	1

proportion
1. ἀναλογία, *analogia, 381*

Rom	12: 6	prophecy, in proportion to faith;	1

propose
1. ἵστημι, *histēmi, 2705*
2. μέλλω, *mellō, 3516*

Act	1:23	they proposed two, Joseph…and Matthias.	1
	5:35	consider carefully what you propose to do to these	2

proselyte
1. προσήλυτος, *prosēlytos, 4670*

Act	2:10	visitors from Rome, both Jews and proselytes	1
	6: 5	Parmenas, and Nicolaus, a proselyte of Antioch.	1

prospect
1. ἐκδοχή, *ekdochē, 1693*

Heb	10:27	a fearful prospect of judgment, and a fury of fire	1

prosper
1. πλουτέω, *plouteō, 4456*

Rev	3:17	For you say, 'I am rich, I have prospered	1

prostitute *See also male prostitute*
1. πόρνη, *pornē, 4520*

Mat	21:31	the tax collectors and the prostitutes	1
	21:32	the tax collectors and the prostitutes believed him;	1
Lke	15:30	who has devoured your property with prostitutes	1
1Co	6:15	make them members of a prostitute? Never!	1
	6:16	whoever is united to a prostitute becomes one	1
Heb	11:31	By faith Rahab the prostitute did not perish	1
Jas	2:25	was not Rahab the prostitute also justified by works	1

prostrate
1. πίπτω + ἐπί + πρόσωπον, *piptō + epi + prosōpon, 4406 + 2093 + 4725*

Lke	17:16	He prostrated himself at Jesus' feet	1

protect

1. διαφυλάσσω, *diaphylassō, 1428*
2. συντηρέω, *syntēreō, 5337*
3. τηρέω, *tēreō, 5498*
4. φρουρέω, *phroureō, 5864*

Mrk	6:20 for Herod feared John…and he protected him.	2
Lke	4:10 command his angels concerning you, to protect you,'	1
Jhn	17:11 Holy Father, protect them in your name	3
	17:12 with them, I protected them in your name	3
	17:15 I ask you to protect them from the evil one.	3
1Pe	1: 5 being protected by the power of God through faith	4
1Jn	5:18 but the one who was born of God protects them	3

protest

1. Contextual: Not in Greek

Lke	10:11 dust…we wipe off in protest against you.	1
Act	13:51 they shook the dust off their feet in protest	1
	18: 6 in protest he shook the dust from his clothes	1

proud

1. ὑπερήφανος, *hyperēphanos, 5662*
2. ὑψηλός + φρονέω, *hypsēlos + phroneō, 5734 + 5858*
3. ὕψωμα, *hypsōma, 5739*

Lke	1:51 he has scattered the proud	1
Rom	11:20 So do not become proud, but stand in awe.	2
2Co	10: 5 proud obstacle raised up against the knowledge of God	3
Jas	4: 6 "God opposes the proud, but gives grace	1
1Pe	5: 5 "God opposes the proud, but gives grace	1

prove

1. ἀποδείκνυμι, *apodeiknymi, 617*
2. γίνομαι, *ginomai, 1181*
3. ἔνδειξις, *endeixis, 1893*
4. εὑρίσκω, *heuriskō, 2351*
5. παρατίθημι, *paratithēmi, 4192*
6. παρίστημι, *paristēmi, 4225*
7. συμβιβάζω, *symbibazō, 5204*
8. συνίστημι, *synistēmi, 5319*

Act	9:22 by proving that Jesus was the Messiah.	7
	17: 3 explaining and proving that it was necessary	5
	24:13 Neither can they prove to you	6
	25: 7 charges against him, which they could not prove.	1
Rom	3: 4 Although everyone is a liar, let God be proved true	2
	3:26 it was to prove…that he himself is righteous	3
	5: 8 But God proves his love for us	8
	7:10 the very commandment…proved to be death to me.	4
2Co	7:11 proved yourselves guiltless in the matter.	8
	7:14 so our boasting to Titus has proved true	2
1Th	1: 5 you know what kind of persons we proved to be	2

prove blameless

1. ἀνέγκλητος, *anenklētos, 441*

1Ti	3:10 then, if they prove themselves blameless	1

prove empty

1. κενόω, *kenoō, 3033*

2Co	9: 3 boasting about you may not prove to have been empty	1

prove false

1. ψεύδομαι, *pseudomai, 6017*

Heb	6:18 it is impossible that God would prove false	1

prove wrong

1. ἐλέγχω, *elenchō, 1794*

Jhn	16: 8 when he comes, he will prove the world wrong	1

proverb

1. παραβολή, *parabolē, 4130*
2. παροιμία, *paroimia, 4231*

Lke	4:23 "Doubtless you will quote to me this proverb	1
2Pe	2:22 It has happened to them according to the true proverb	2

provide

1. διακονέω, *diakoneō, 1354*
2. ἐπιχορηγέω, *epichorēgeō, 2220*
3. παρά, *para, 4123*
4. παρέχω, *parechō, 4218*
5. παρίστημι, *paristēmi, 4225*

6. ποιέω, *poieō, 4472*
7. προβλέπω, *problepō, 4587*
8. προνοέω, *pronoeō, 4629*

Mat	27:55 followed Jesus…and had provided for him.	1
Mrk	15:41 and provided for him when he was in Galilee;	1
Lke	8: 3 who provided for them out of their resources.	1
	10: 7 eating and drinking whatever they provide	3
Act	23:24 Also provide mounts for Paul to ride	5
1Co	10:13 he will also provide the way out	6
1Ti	5: 8 And whoever does not provide for relatives	8
	6:17 richly provides us with everything for our enjoyment.	4
Heb	11:40 since God had provided something better	7
2Pe	1:11 entry into the eternal kingdom…will be richly provided	2

provide in abundance

1. περισσεύω, *perisseuō, 4355*

2Co	9: 8 provide you with every blessing in abundance	1

provided

1. Contextual: Not in Greek
2. ἐάν, *ean, 1569*
3. εἰ, *ei, 1623*

Rom	11:22 provided you continue in his kindness;	2
Col	1:23 provided that you continue securely established	3
1Ti	2:15 provided they continue in faith and love	2
	4: 4 provided it is received with thanksgiving;	1

province   *See also* official of the province of Asia

1. ἐπαρχεία, *eparcheia, 2065*

Act	23:34 he asked what province he belonged to	1
	25: 1 Three days after Festus had arrived in the province	1

provision

1. ἐπισιτισμός, *episitismos, 2169*
2. πρόνοια, *pronoia, 4630*
3. πρός, *pros, 4639*

Lke	9:12 to lodge and get provisions;	1
Act	28:10 they put on board all the provisions we needed.	3
Rom	13:14 and make no provision for the flesh	2

provoke

1. ἐρεθίζω, *erethizō, 2241*
2. παροξυσμός, *paroxysmos, 4237*

Col	3:21 Fathers, do not provoke your children	1
Heb	10:24 let us consider how to provoke one another to love	2

provoke to anger

1. παροργίζω, *parorgizō, 4239*

Eph	6: 4 fathers, do not provoke your children to anger	1

provoke to jealousy

1. παραζηλόω, *parazēloō, 4143*

1Co	10:22 are we provoking the Lord to jealousy?	1

prowl around

1. περιπατέω, *peripateō, 4344*

1Pe	5: 8 your adversary the devil prowls around	1

prudent

1. σώφρων, *sōphrōn, 5409*
2. φρόνιμος, *phronimos, 5861*

Lke	12:42 "Who then is the faithful and prudent manager	2
Tit	1: 8 lover of goodness, prudent, upright	1
	2: 2 Tell the older men to be temperate, serious, prudent	1

prune

1. καθαίρω, *kathairō, 2748*

Jhn	15: 2 Every branch that bears fruit he prunes	1

psalm

1. Contextual: Not in Greek
2. ψαλμός, *psalmos, 6011*

Lke	20:42 For David himself says in the book of Psalms	2
	24:44 the prophets, and the psalms	2
Act	1:20 "For it is written in the book of Psalms	2
	13:33 as also it is written in the second psalm	2
	13:35 Therefore he has also said in another psalm	1
Eph	5:19 as you sing psalms and hymns and spiritual songs	2

Col 3:16 sing psalms, hymns, and spiritual songs to God 2

Ptolemais
1. Πτολεμαΐς, *Ptolemais, 4767*
Act 21: 7 we arrived at Ptolemais; 1

public *See also* deliver a public address, expose to public disgrace, make public
1. Contextual: Not in Greek
2. δημόσιος, *dēmosios, 1323*
3. παρρησία, *parrēsia, 4244*
Act 5:18 put them in the public prison. 2
16:37 "They have beaten us in public, uncondemned 2
18:28 for he powerfully refuted the Jews in public 2
Col 2:15 made a public example of them 3
1Ti 4:13 give attention to the public reading of scripture 1

publicly *See also* appear publicly, exhibit publicly, expose publicly
1. δημόσιος, *dēmosios, 1323*
2. ἐνώπιον + πᾶς, *enōpion + pas, 1967 + 4246*
3. φανερῶς, *phanerōs, 5747*
Jhn 7:10 went, not publicly but as it were in secret. 3
Act 19:19 collected their books and burned them publicly 2
20:20 teaching you publicly and from house to house 1

Publius
1. Πόπλιος, *Poplios, 4511*
Act 28: 7 the leading man of the island, named Publius 1
28: 8 the father of Publius lay sick in bed 1

Pudens
1. Πούδης, *Poudēs, 4545*
2Ti 4:21 as do Pudens and Linus and Claudia 1

puff up
1. φυσιόω, *physioō, 5881*
1Co 4: 6 that none of you will be puffed up in favor of one 1
8: 1 Knowledge puffs up, but love builds up. 1
Col 2:18 puffed up without cause by a human way of thinking 1

puff up with conceit
1. τυφόομαι, *typhoomai, 5605*
1Ti 3: 6 he may be puffed up with conceit 1

pull away
1. αἴρω, *airō, 149*
Mat 9:16 for the patch pulls away from the cloak 1
Mrk 2:21 otherwise, the patch pulls away from it 1

pull down
1. καθαιρέω, *kathaireō, 2747*
Lke 12:18 I will pull down my barns and build larger ones 1

pull out
1. ἀνασπάω, *anaspaō, 413*
Lke 14: 5 not immediately pull it out on a sabbath day?" 1

pull up
1. ἀνασπάω, *anaspaō, 413*
Act 11:10 everything was pulled up again to heaven. 1

punish
1. ἐκδικέω, *ekdikeō, 1688*
2. ἐκδίκησις, *ekdikēsis, 1689*
3. ἐλέγχω, *elenchō, 1794*
4. κολάζω, *kolazō, 3134*
5. παιδεύω, *paideuō, 4084*
6. τιμωρέω, *timōreō, 5512*
7. ὑπωπιάζω, *hypōpiazō, 5724*
Act 4:21 they let them go, finding no way to punish them 4
26:11 punishing them often in all the synagogues 6
1Co 9:27 I punish my body and enslave it 7
2Co 6: 9 as punished, and yet not killed; 5
10: 6 We are ready to punish every disobedience 1
Heb 12: 5 or lose heart when you are punished by him; 3
1Pe 2:14 sent by him to punish those who do wrong 2

punishment
1. δίκη, *dikē, 1472*
2. ἐκδίκησις, *ekdikēsis, 1689*
3. ἐπιτιμία, *epitimia, 2204*
4. κόλασις, *kolasis, 3136*
5. τιμωρέω, *timōreō, 5512*
6. τιμωρία, *timōria, 5513*
Mat 25:46 these will go away into eternal punishment 4
Act 22: 5 to bring them back to Jerusalem for punishment 5
2Co 2: 6 This punishment by the majority is enough 3
7:11 what longing, what zeal, what punishment! 2
2Th 1: 9 suffer the punishment of eternal destruction 1
Heb 10:29 How much worse punishment...will be deserved 6
1Jn 4:18 for fear has to do with punishment 4
Jde 1: 7 serve as an example by undergoing a punishment 1

under punishment
1. κολάζω, *kolazō, 3134*
2Pe 2: 9 and to keep the unrighteous under punishment 1

pure
1. ἁγνός, *hagnos, 54*
2. ἁγνότης, *hagnotēs, 55*
3. ἄδολος, *adolos, 100*
4. εἰλικρινής, *eilikrinēs, 1637*
5. καθαρός, *katharos, 2754*
6. ὁσίως, *hosiōs, 4010*
7. πιστικός, *pistikos, 4410*
Mat 5: 8 "Blessed are the pure in heart, for they will see 5
Jhn 12: 3 a pound of costly perfume made of pure nard 7
2Co 11: 3 from a sincere and pure devotion to Christ. 2
Php 1:10 in the day of Christ you may be pure and blameless 4
4: 8 whatever is pure, whatever is pleasing 1
1Th 2:10 how pure, upright, and blameless 6
1Ti 1: 5 love that comes from a pure heart 5
5:22 keep yourself pure. 1
2Ti 2:22 those who call on the Lord from a pure heart. 5
Tit 1:15 To the pure all things are pure 5
1:15 To the pure all things are pure 5
1:15 to the corrupt and unbelieving nothing is pure. 5
Heb 10:22 our bodies washed with pure water. 5
Jas 1:27 Religion that is pure and undefiled before God 5
3:17 wisdom from above is first pure, then peaceable 1
1Pe 2: 2 long for the pure, spiritual milk 3
1Jn 3: 3 all...purify themselves, just as he is pure. 1
Rev 15: 6 seven angels...robed in pure bright linen 5
19: 8 clothed with fine linen, bright and pure" 5
19:14 wearing fine linen, white and pure 5
21:18 while the city is pure gold, clear as glass. 5
21:21 and the street of the city is pure gold 5

purification *See also* complete the rite of purification, go through rite of purification
1. ἁγνισμός, *hagnismos, 50*
2. καθαρισμός, *katharismos, 2752*
Lke 2:22 When the time came for their purification 2
Jhn 2: 6 water jars...for the Jewish rites of purification 2
3:25 Now a discussion about purification arose 2
Act 21:26 the completion of the days of purification 1
Heb 1: 3 When he had made purification for sins 2

purify
1. ἁγνίζω, *hagnizō, 49*
2. καθαρίζω, *katharizō, 2751*
3. καθαρότης, *katharotēs, 2755*
Jhn 11:55 many went up...to purify themselves. 1
Act 21:26 the next day, having purified himself, he entered 1
Tit 2:14 purify for himself a people of his own 2
Heb 9:13 sanctifies...so that their flesh is purified 3
9:14 purify our conscience from dead works 2
9:22 almost everything is purified with blood 2
9:23 to be purified with these rites 2
Jas 4: 8 purify your hearts, you double-minded. 1
1Pe 1:22 have purified your souls by your obedience 1
1Jn 3: 3 all who have this hope in him purify themselves 1

purity
1. ἁγνεία, *hagneia, 48*

2. ἁγνός, *hagnos, 54*

3. ἁγνότης, *hagnotēs, 55*

2Co	6: 6	by purity, knowledge, patience, kindness
1Ti	4:12	conduct, in love, in faith, in purity.
	5: 2	younger women as sisters—with absolute purity.
1Pe	3: 2	when they see the purity and reverence of your lives.

2Co	6: 6	by purity, knowledge, patience, kindness	3
1Ti	4:12	conduct, in love, in faith, in purity.	1
	5: 2	younger women as sisters—with absolute purity.	1
1Pe	3: 2	when they see the purity and reverence of your lives.	2

purple   *See also* dealer in purple cloth

1. πορφύρα, *porphyra, 4525*

2. πορφυροῦς, *porphyrous, 4528*

Mrk	15:17	they clothed him in a purple cloak;	1
	15:20	they stripped him of the purple cloak	1
Lke	16:19	who was dressed in purple and fine linen	1
Jhn	19: 2	and they dressed him in a purple robe.	2
	19: 5	the crown of thorns and the purple robe.	2
Rev	17: 4	The woman was clothed in purple and scarlet	2
	18:12	cargo of…fine linen, purple, silk and scarlet	1
	18:16	clothed in fine linen, in purple and scarlet	2

purpose

1. βουλή, *boulē, 1087*

2. βούλομαι, *boulomai, 1089*

3. γνώμη, *gnōmē, 1191*

4. εἰς, *eis, 1650*

5. εἰς + ὅς, *eis + hos, 1650 + 4005*

6. εἰς + οὗτος, *eis + houtos, 1650 + 4047*

7. ἐπί + οὗτος, *epi + houtos, 2093 + 4047*

8. ὅπως, *hopōs, 3968*

9. πρόθεσις, *prothesis, 4606*

10. τέλος, *telos, 5465*

Lke	4:43	I was sent for this purpose."	7
	7:30	lawyers rejected God's purpose for themselves	1
Act	9:21	has he not come here for the purpose	6
	13:36	served the purpose of God in his own generation	1
	20:27	declaring to you the whole purpose of God.	1
	26:16	I have appeared to you for this purpose	6
	27:13	they thought they could achieve their purpose;	9
Rom	4:11	The purpose was to make him the ancestor of all	4
	8:28	who are called according to his purpose.	9
	9:11	(so that God's purpose of election might continue	9
	9:17	for the very purpose of showing my power in you	8
	14: 1	not for the purpose of quarreling over opinions.	4
	15: 2	must please our neighbor for the good purpose of	4
1Co	1:10	be united in the same mind and the same purpose.	3
	4: 5	and will disclose the purposes of the heart.	1
Eph	1:11	destined according to the purpose of him	9
	3:11	This was in accordance with the eternal purpose	9
	6:22	I am sending him to you for this very purpose	6
Col	4: 8	I have sent him to you for this very purpose	6
2Th	2:14	For this purpose he called you	5
2Ti	1: 9	called us…according to his own purpose and grace	9
Heb	6:17	the unchangeable character of his purpose	1
Jas	1:18	In fulfillment of his own purpose he gave us birth	2
	5:11	and you have seen the purpose of the Lord	10
1Jn	3: 8	The Son of God was revealed for this purpose	6
Rev	17:17	to carry out his purpose by agreeing to give	3

common purpose

1. εἷς, *heis, 1651*

1Co	3: 8	plants and the one who waters have a common purpose	1

good purpose

1. καλός, *kalos, 2819*

2. καλῶς, *kalōs, 2822*

Gal	4:17	They make much of you, but for no good purpose;	2
	4:18	It is good to be made much of for a good purpose	1

purse

1. βαλλάντιον, *ballantion, 964*

Lke	10: 4	Carry no purse, no bag, no sandals;	1
	12:33	purses for yourselves that do not wear out	1
	22:35	sent you out without a purse, bag, or sandals	1
	22:36	who has a purse must take it, and likewise a bag.	1

common purse

1. γλωσσόκομον, *glōssokomon, 1186*

Jhn	12: 6	he kept the common purse	1
	13:29	because Judas had the common purse	1

pursue

1. ἀπέρχομαι, *aperchomai, 599*

2. διώκω, *diōkō, 1503*

Mat	23:34	pursue from town to town	2
Act	26:11	I pursued them even to foreign cities.	2
Rom	14:19	Let us then pursue what makes for peace	2
1Co	14: 1	Pursue love and strive for the spiritual gifts	2
1Ti	6:11	pursue righteousness, godliness, faith, love	2
2Ti	2:22	pursue righteousness, faith, love, and peace	2
Heb	12:14	Pursue peace with everyone	2
1Pe	3:11	let them seek peace and pursue it.	2
Jde	1: 7	indulged in sexual immorality and pursued unnatural lust	1
Rev	12:13	he pursued the woman who had given birth	2

pursuit   *See* set off in pursuit

push aside

1. ἀπωθέω, *apōtheō, 723*

Act	7:27	the man…pushed Moses aside, saying	1
	7:39	Our ancestors…pushed him aside	1

push forward

1. προβάλλω, *proballō, 4582*

Act	19:33	Alexander, whom the Jews had pushed forward.	1

put   *See also* like to put first

1. Contextual: Not in Greek

2. ἀποτίθημι, *apotithēmi, 700*

3. βάλλω, *ballō, 965*

4. βλητέος, *blēteos, 1064*

5. δίδωμι, *didōmi, 1443*

6. εἰμί, *eimi, 1639*

7. ἐκτείνω, *ekteinō, 1753*

8. ἐπιτίθημι, *epitithēmi, 2202*

9. ἐργάζομαι, *ergazomai, 2237*

10. ἵστημι, *histēmi, 2705*

11. καθίζω, *kathizō, 2767*

12. κεῖμαι, *keimai, 3023*

13. παραδίδωμι, *paradidōmi, 4140*

14. ποιέω, *poieō, 4472*

15. ῥίπτω, *rhiptō, 4849*

16. συλλέγω, *syllegō, 5198*

17. τίθημι, *tithēmi, 5502*

18. φέρω, *pherō, 5770*

Mat	5:15	lighting a lamp puts it under the bushel basket	17
	9:17	Neither is new wine put into old wineskins;	3
	9:17	but new wine is put into fresh wineskins	3
	12:18	I will put my Spirit upon him	17
	13:48	sat down, and put the good into baskets	16
	14: 3	bound him, and put him in prison	2
	15:30	They put them at his feet, and he cured them	15
	18: 2	called a child, whom he put among them	10
	22:44	until I put your enemies under your feet" '?	17
	24:51	and put him with the hypocrites	17
	25:33	he will put the sheep at his right hand	10
	26:51	put his hand on his sword, drew it,	7
	27: 6	"It is not lawful to put them into the treasury	3
	27:29	They put a reed in his right hand	1
	27:37	Over his head they put the charge against him	8
Mrk	2:22	no one puts new wine into old wineskins;	3
	2:22	one puts new wine into fresh wineskins."	1
	4:21	lamp brought in to be put under the bushel basket	17
	6:17	and put him in prison on account of Herodias	1
	7:33	put his fingers into his ears, and he spat	3
	9:36	he took a little child and put it among them	10
	12:36	until I put your enemies under your feet." '	17
	12:41	the crowd putting money into the treasury.	3
	12:41	Many rich people put in large sums.	3
	12:42	A poor widow came and put in two small copper coins	3
	12:43	this poor widow has put in more than all	3
	12:44	out of her poverty has put in everything she had	3
	13:34	he leaves home and puts his slaves in charge	5
Lke	5:37	no one puts new wine into old wineskins;	3
	5:38	new wine must be put into fresh wineskins.	4
	6:38	good measure…will be put into your lap;	5
	8:16	puts it under a bed	17
	8:16	puts it on a lampstand	17
	9:47	took a little child and put it by his side	10
	11:33	after lighting a lamp puts it in a cellar	17

Lke 12:46 and put him with the unfaithful. 17
13: 8 until I dig around it and put manure on 3
15:22 put a ring on his finger and sandals on his feet. 5
19:23 Why then did you not put my money into the bank? 5
21: 1 rich people putting their gifts into the treasury; 3
21: 2 saw a poor widow put in two small copper coins. 3
21: 3 this poor widow has put in more than all of them; 3
21: 4 put in all she had to live on." 3
23:19 a man who had been put in prison 3
23:25 the one who had been put in prison 3
Jhn 5: 7 I have no one to put me into the pool 3
13: 2 The devil had already put it into the heart 3
16: 2 They will put you out of the synagogues. 14
19:19 an inscription written and put on the cross. 17
20:25 put my finger in the mark of the nails 3
20:27 Then he said to Thomas, "Put your finger here 18
20:27 Reach out your hand and put it in my side. 3
Act 2:30 put one of his descendants on his throne. 11
4: 3 put them in custody until the next day 17
5:18 put them in the public prison. 17
5:25 the men whom you put in prison 17
5:34 ordered the men to be put outside for a short time. 14
12: 4 When he had seized him, he put him in prison 17
16:24 he put them in the innermost cell 3
22: 4 both men and women and putting them in prison 13
Rom 14:13 resolve instead never to put a stumbling block 17
1Co 9:12 we endure anything rather than put an obstacle 5
15:25 until he has put all his enemies under his feet. 17
15:30 why are we putting ourselves in danger every hour? 1
16: 2 put aside and save whatever extra you earn 17
2Co 3:13 not like Moses, who put a veil over his face 17
6: 3 We are putting no obstacle in anyone's way 5
8:16 who put in the heart of Titus the same eagerness 5
Php 1:16 put here for the defense of the gospel; 12
Col 3:23 Whatever your task, put yourselves into it 9
Heb 2:13 And again, "I will put my trust in him." 6
6:16 an oath given as confirmation puts an end to all dispute. 1
8:10 I will put my laws in their minds 5
10:16 I will put my laws in their hearts 5
Jas 3: 3 If we put bits into the mouths of horses 3
Rev 2:14 put a stumbling block before the people of Israel 3
17:17 For God has put it into their hearts 5

put a seal on
1. σφραγίζω, sphragizō, 5381
2Co 1:22 by putting his seal on us 1

put a stumbling block
1. σκανδαλίζω, skandalizō, 4997
Mat 18: 6 any of you put a stumbling block before one 1
Mrk 9:42 "If any of you put a stumbling block 1

put an end
1. καταργέω, katargeō, 2934
1Co 13:11 I became an adult, I put an end to childish ways. 1

put arms around
1. ἐπιπίπτω + ἐπί + ὁ + τράχηλος, epipiptō + epi + ho + trachēlos, 2158 + 2093 + 3836 + 5549
Lke 15:20 ran and put his arms around him and kissed him. 1

put around
1. περιτίθημι, peritithēmi, 4363
Mat 21:33 put a fence around it, dug a wine press in it 1
Mrk 12: 1 put a fence around it 1

put at the service
1. ὑποτάσσω, hypotassō, 5718
1Co 16:16 I urge you to put yourselves at the service 1

put away
1. αἴρω, airō, 149
2. ἀποτίθημι, apotithēmi, 700
Eph 4:22 put away your former way of life, your old self 2
4:25 So then, putting away falsehood 2
4:31 Put away from you all bitterness and wrath 1

put back
1. ἀποστρέφω, apostrephō, 695

2. βάλλω, ballō, 965
Mat 26:52 "Put your sword back into its place; 1
Jhn 18:11 "Put your sword back into its sheath. 2

put before
1. παρατίθημι, paratithēmi, 4192
2. ὑποτίθημι, hypotithēmi, 5719
Mat 13:24 He put before them another parable: 1
13:31 He put before them another parable: 1
1Ti 4: 6 If you put these...before the brothers and sisters 2

put forth
1. ἐκφύω, ekphyō, 1770
2. ποιέω, poieō, 4472
Mat 24:32 becomes tender and puts forth its leaves 1
Mrk 4:32 and puts forth large branches 2
13:28 becomes tender and puts forth its leaves 1

put forward
1. προτίθημι, protithēmi, 4729
Rom 3:25 whom God put forward as a sacrifice of atonement 1

put in
1. κατάγω, katagō, 2864
Act 27: 3 The next day we put in at Sidon; 1
28:12 put in at Syracuse and stayed there 1

put in charge
1. καθίστημι, kathistēmi, 2770
Mat 24:45 whom his master has put in charge of his household 1
24:47 he will put that one in charge of all 1
25:21 I will put you in charge of many things; 1
25:23 I will put you in charge of many things; 1
Lke 12:42 whom his master will put in charge of his slaves 1
12:44 Truly I tell you, he will put that one in charge 1
Heb 5: 1 put in charge of things pertaining to God on their behalf 1

put in order
1. ἐπιδιορθόω, epidiorthoō, 2114
2. καταρτίζω, katartizō, 2936
3. κοσμέω, kosmeō, 3175
Mat 12:44 it finds it empty, swept, and put in order. 3
Lke 11:25 it finds it swept and put in order. 3
2Co 13:11 Put things in order, listen to my appeal 2
Tit 1: 5 you should put in order what remained to be done 1

put in subjection
1. ὑποτάσσω, hypotassō, 5718
1Co 15:27 For "God has put all things in subjection 1
15:27 "All things are put in subjection," 1
15:27 one who put all things in subjection under him. 1
15:28 one who put all things in subjection under him 1

put into
1. βάλλω, ballō, 965
Jhn 12: 6 used to steal what was put into it.) 1

put into practice
1. μελετάω, meletaō, 3509
1Ti 4:15 Put these things into practice, devote yourself to them 1

put off
1. ἀπέκδυσις, apekdysis, 589
Col 2:11 by putting off the body of the flesh 1

put oil on
1. ἀλείφω, aleiphō, 230
Mat 6:17 when you fast, put oil on your head and wash your face 1

put on
1. διαζώννυμι, diazōnnymi, 1346
2. ἐν, en, 1877
3. ἐνδύω, endyō, 1907
4. ἐπιβιβάζω, epibibazō, 2097
5. ἐπιτίθημι, epitithēmi, 2202
6. λαμβάνω, lambanō, 3284
7. περιβάλλω, periballō, 4314
8. περιτίθημι, peritithēmi, 4363

9. ὑποδέω, *hypodeō, 5686*

Mat	21: 7	and put their cloaks on them	5
	27:28	They stripped him and put a scarlet robe on him	8
	27:29	thorns into a crown, they put it on his head.	5
	27:31	put his own clothes on him.	3
	27:48	put it on a stick, and gave it to him to drink.	8
Mrk	6: 9	to wear sandals and not to put on two tunics.	3
	15:17	twisting some thorns into a crown, they put it on him.	8
	15:20	and put his own clothes on him.	3
	15:36	filled a sponge with sour wine, put it on a stick	8
Lke	7:25	Look, those who put on fine clothing	2
	10:34	Then he put him on his own animal	4
	15:22	'Quickly, bring out a robe…and put it on him;	3
	23:11	then he put an elegant robe on him	7
Jhn	9:15	He said to them, "He put mud on my eyes.	5
	13:12	After he…had put on his robe,	6
	19: 2	crown of thorns and put it on his head	5
	19:29	they put a sponge full of the wine on a branch	8
	21: 7	he put on some clothes, for he was naked	1
Act	12: 8	"Fasten your belt and put on your sandals."	9
	12:21	On an appointed day Herod put on his royal robes	3
	28: 3	putting it on the fire	5
	28: 8	cured him by praying and putting his hands on him.	5
Rom	13:12	Let us…put on the armor of light;	3
	13:14	Instead, put on the Lord Jesus Christ	3
1Co	15:53	perishable body must put on imperishability,	3
	15:53	this mortal body must put on immortality.	3
	15:54	When this perishable body puts on imperishability	3
	15:54	this mortal body puts on immortality	3
Eph	6:11	Put on the whole armor of God	3
	6:14	put on the breastplate of righteousness.	3
1Th	5: 8	put on the breastplate of faith and love	3

put on a list

1. Contextual: Not in Greek
2. καταλέγω, *katalegō, 2899*

1Ti	5: 9	Let a widow be put on the list	2
	5:11	refuse to put younger widows on the list;	1

put on airs

1. ἐπαίρω, *epairō, 2048*

2Co	11:20	or puts on airs, or gives you a slap in the face.	1

put on an apron

1. περιζώννυμι, *perizōnnymi, 4322*

Lke	17: 8	put on your apron and serve me	1

put on board

1. ἐμβιβάζω, *embibazō, 1837*
2. ἐπιτίθημι, *epitithēmi, 2202*

Act	27: 6	found an Alexandrian ship…and put us on board.	1
	28:10	they put on board all the provisions we needed.	2

put on shoes

1. ὑποδέω, *hypodeō, 5686*

Eph	6:15	As shoes for your feet put on	1

put one's trust

1. πιστεύω, *pisteuō, 4409*

2Ti	1:12	for I know the one in whom I have put my trust	1

put out

1. ἀνάγω, *anagō, 343*
2. ἐκτείνω, *ekteinō, 1753*
3. ἐπανάγω, *epanagō, 2056*

Lke	5: 3	asked him to put out a little way from the shore.	3
	5: 4	he said to Simon, "Put out into the deep water	3
	8:22	go across to the other side of the lake." So they put out	1
Act	27:30	on the pretext of putting out anchors	1

put out of joint

1. ἐκτρέπω, *ektrepō, 1762*

Heb	12:13	so that what is lame may not be put out of joint	1

put out of the synagogue

1. ἀποσυνάγωγος, *aposynagōgos, 697*

Jhn	9:22	would be put out of the synagogue.	1
	12:42	that they would be put out of the synagogue;	1

put outside

1. ἐκβάλλω, *ekballō, 1675*

Mat	9:25	But when the crowd had been put outside, he went	1
Mrk	5:40	Then he put them all outside	1
Act	9:40	Peter put all of them outside, and then he knelt	1

put saliva

1. πτύω, *ptyō, 4772*

Mrk	8:23	when he had put saliva on his eyes	1

put to

1. ἐπιβάλλω, *epiballō, 2095*

Lke	9:62	"No one who puts a hand to the plow	1

put to death

1. ἀναιρέω, *anaireō, 359*
2. ἀπάγω, *apagō, 552*
3. ἀποκτείνω, *apokteinō, 650*
4. ἀπόλλυμι, *apollymi, 660*
5. θανατόω, *thanatoō, 2506*
6. νεκρόω, *nekroō, 3739*

Mat	10:21	and have them put to death;	5
	14: 5	Though Herod wanted to put him to death	3
	21:41	put those wretches to a miserable death	4
	24: 9	hand you over…and will put you to death	3
	26:59	so that they might put him to death	5
Mrk	13:12	against parents and have them put to death;	5
	14:55	testimony against Jesus to put him to death;	5
Lke	21:16	they will put some of you to death.	5
	22: 2	were looking for a way to put Jesus to death	1
	23:32	Two others…were led away to be put to death	1
Jhn	11:53	they planned to put him to death.	3
	12:10	planned to put Lazarus to death as well	3
	18:31	"We are not permitted to put anyone to death."	3
Act	10:39	They put him to death by hanging him on a tree;	1
	12:19	and ordered them to be put to death.	2
Rom	8:13	if…you put to death the deeds of the body	5
Eph	2:16	thus putting to death that hostility through it	3
Col	3: 5	Put to death, therefore, whatever in you is earthly:	6
1Pe	3:18	Christ…was put to death in the flesh	5

put to flight

1. κλίνω, *klinō, 3111*

Heb	11:34	put foreign armies to flight.	1

put to sea

1. ἀνάγω, *anagō, 343*

Act	27: 2	we put to sea, accompanied by Aristarchus	1
	27: 4	Putting out to sea from there	1
	27:12	the majority was in favor of putting to sea from there	1

put to shame

1. αἰσχύνομαι, *aischynomai, 159*
2. ἐντρέπω, *entrepō, 1956*
3. καταισχύνω, *kataischynō, 2875*

Lke	13:17	all his opponents were put to shame;	3
Rom	9:33	whoever believes in him will not be put to shame."	3
	10:11	"No one who believes in him will be put to shame."	3
Php	1:20	my…hope that I will not be put to shame in any way	1
Tit	2: 8	then any opponent will be put to shame	2
1Pe	2: 6	whoever believes in him will not be put to shame."	3
	3:16	those who abuse…may be put to shame.	3
1Jn	2:28	and not be put to shame before him at his coming.	1

put to the test

1. ἐκπειράζω, *ekpeirazō, 1733*
2. πειράζω, *peirazō, 4279*
3. πειρασμός, *peirasmos, 4280*

Mat	4: 7	written, 'Do not put the Lord your God to the test.' "	1
	22:18	you putting me to the test, you hypocrites?	2
Mrk	12:15	"Why are you putting me to the test?	2
Lke	4:12	'Do not put the Lord your God to the test.' "	1
Act	5: 9	agreed together to put the Spirit…to the test?	2
	15:10	Now therefore why are you putting God to the test	2
1Co	10: 9	We must not put Christ to the test, as some	1
Gal	4:14	though my condition put you to the test	3
Heb	3: 9	where your ancestors put me to the test	2
	11:17	Abraham, when put to the test, offered up Isaac.	2

put to work
1. ἐνεργέω, *energeō, 1919*
Eph   1:20 God put this power to work in Christ   1

put under
1. ὑποτάσσω, *hypotassō, 5718*
Eph   1:22 he has put all things under his feet   1

put under oath
1. ἐξορκίζω, *exorkizō, 2019*
Mat 26:63 "I put you under oath before the living God   1

put up with
1. ἀνέχομαι, *anechomai, 462*
2. βαστάζω, *bastazō, 1002*
3. τροποφορέω, *tropophoreō, 5574*
Mat 17:17 How much longer must I put up with you?   1
Mrk   9:19 How much longer must I put up with you?   1
Act 13:18 he put up with them in the wilderness.   3
Rom 15: 1 ought to put up with the failings of the weak   2
2Co 11:19 For you gladly put up with fools, being wise   1
     11:20 you put up with it when someone makes slaves of you   1
2Ti   4: 3 when people will not put up with sound doctrine   1

put upon
1. ἐπιβάλλω, *epiballō, 2095*
1Co   7:35 not to put any restraint upon you   1

Puteoli
1. Ποτίολοι, *Potioloi, 4541*
Act 28:13 on the second day we came to Puteoli.   1

puzzle greatly
1. διαπορέω, *diaporeō, 1389*
Act 10:17 Now while Peter was greatly puzzled   1

Pyrrhus
1. Πύρρος, *Pyrros, 4795*
Act 20: 4 Sopater son of Pyrrhus from Beroea,   1

Q

qualify fully
1. καταρτίζω, *katartizō, 2936*
Lke   6:40 everyone who is fully qualified will be like the teacher   1

great quantity
1. πολύς, *polys, 4498*
Rev   8: 3 he was given a great quantity of incense to offer   1

quarrel
1. διάκρισις, *diakrisis, 1360*
2. ἐριθεία, *eritheia, 2249*
3. ἔρις, *eris, 2251*
4. μάχη, *machē, 3480*
5. μάχομαι, *machomai, 3481*
Act   7:26 he came to some of them as they were quarreling   5
Rom 13:13 not in quarreling and jealousy.   3
     14: 1 not for the purpose of quarreling over opinions.   1
1Co   1:11 that there are quarrels among you, my brothers   3
      3: 3 as there is jealousy and quarreling among you   3
2Co 12:20 there may perhaps be quarreling, jealousy, anger   3
Gal   5:20 anger, quarrels, dissensions, factions   2
2Ti   2:23 you know that they breed quarrels.   4
Tit   3: 9 dissensions, and quarrels about the law   4

quarrelsome
1. μάχομαι, *machomai, 3481*
2Ti   2:24 the Lord's servant must not be quarrelsome   1

not quarrelsome
1. ἄμαχος, *amachos, 285*
1Ti   3: 3 not quarrelsome, and not a lover of money.   1

quart
1. χοῖνιξ, *choinix, 5955*
Rev   6: 6 "A quart of wheat for a day's pay   1
      6: 6 and three quarts of barley for a day's pay   1

every quarter
1. πάντοθεν, *pantothen, 4119*
Mrk   1:45 people came to him from every quarter.   1

Quartus
1. Κούαρτος, *Kouartos, 3181*
Rom 16:23 Erastus…and our brother Quartus, greet you.   1

queen
1. βασίλισσα, *basilissa, 999*
Mat 12:42 The queen of the South will rise up at the judgment   1
Lke 11:31 The queen of the South will rise at the judgment   1
Act   8:27 the Candace, queen of the Ethiopians   1
Rev 18: 7 'I rule as a queen; I am no widow   1

quench
1. σβέννυμι, *sbennymi, 4931*
Mat 12:20 or quench a smoldering wick   1
Mrk   9:48 the fire is never quenched.   1
Eph   6:16 able to quench all the flaming arrows of the evil one.   1
1Th   5:19 Do not quench the Spirit.   1
Heb 11:34 quenched raging fire   1

question *See also* ask a question, raise a question
1. Contextual: Not in Greek
2. ἀνακρίνω, *anakrinō, 373*
3. διαλογίζομαι, *dialogizomai, 1368*
4. διαλογισμός, *dialogismos, 1369*
5. ἐκ, *ek, 1666*
6. ἐπερωτάω, *eperōtaō, 2089*
7. ἐρωτάω, *erōtaō, 2263*
8. ζήτημα, *zētēma, 2427*
9. λόγος, *logos, 3364*
10. συζητέω, *syzēteō, 5184*
Mat 21:24 "I will also ask you one question;   9
Mrk   2: 6 questioning in their hearts   3
      9:10 questioning what this rising from the dead could mean.   10
     11:29 Jesus said to them, "I will ask you one question;   9
Lke   3:15 questioning in their hearts concerning John   3
      5:21 the scribes and the Pharisees began to question   3
      5:22 When Jesus perceived their questionings   4
     20: 3 "I will also ask you a question, and you tell me: 9
     22:68 if I question you, you will not answer.   7
     23: 9 He questioned him at some length   6
Jhn   8: 7 〚When they kept on questioning him〛   7
     16:30 not need to have anyone question you;   7
     18:19 Then the high priest questioned Jesus   7
Act   4: 9 if we are questioned today   2
      5:27 The high priest questioned them   6
     15: 2 to go up to Jerusalem to discuss this question   8
     18:15 a matter of questions about words and names   8
     23:29 he was accused concerning questions of their law   8
     25:20 was at a loss how to investigate these questions   1
2Co   8:13 but it is a question of a fair balance   5

questions
1. Contextual: Not in Greek
Mrk   2: 8 discussing these questions among themselves;   1

quick
1. ταχύς, *tachys, 5444*
Jas   1:19 let everyone be quick to listen, slow to speak   1

quick-tempered
1. ὀργίλος, *orgilos, 3975*
Tit   1: 7 he must not be arrogant or quick-tempered   1

quickly
1. ἐν + τάχος, *en + tachos, 1877 + 5443*
2. εὐθέως, *eutheōs, 2311*
3. εὐθύς¹, *euthys¹, 2317*
4. ὀλίγος, *oligos, 3900*
5. συντελέω, *synteleō, 5334*
6. ταχέως, *tacheōs, 5441*
7. ταχύς, *tachys, 5444*

Mat	5:25	Come to terms quickly with your accuser	7
	13: 5	and they sprang up quickly	2
	28: 7	Then go quickly and tell his disciples	7
	28: 8	they left the tomb quickly with fear	7
Mrk	4: 5	and it sprang up quickly	3
Lke	15:22	'Quickly, bring out a robe—the best one—	7
	16: 6	bill, sit down quickly, and make it fifty.'	6
	18: 8	he will quickly grant justice to them.	1
Jhn	11:29	when she heard it, she got up quickly and went	7
	11:31	The Jews…saw Mary get up quickly and go out.	6
	13:27	"Do quickly what you are going to do."	6
Act	12: 7	woke him, saying, "Get up quickly."	1
	22:18	'Hurry and get out of Jerusalem quickly	1
	26:28	so quickly persuading me to become a Christian?"	4
	26:29	Paul replied, "Whether quickly or not,	4
Rom	9:28	Lord will execute…quickly and decisively."	5
Gal	1: 6	I am astonished that you are so quickly deserting	6
2Th	2: 2	not to be quickly shaken in mind or alarmed	6

not [quickly]
1. μέγας, *megas, 3489*

Act 26:29 Paul replied, "Whether quickly or not,   1

quiet
1. ἤρεμος, *ēremos, 2475*
2. ἡσυχία, *hēsychia, 2484*
3. ἡσύχιος, *hēsychios, 2485*
4. καταστέλλω, *katastellō, 2948*
5. σιγάω, *sigaō, 4967*
6. σιωπάω, *siōpaō, 4995*

Mat	20:31	The crowd sternly ordered them to be quiet;	6
Mrk	10:48	Many sternly ordered him to be quiet	6
Lke	18:39	sternly ordered him to be quiet	5
Act	19:35	when the town clerk had quieted the crowd	4
	19:36	you ought to be quiet and do nothing rash.	4
	22: 2	they became even more quiet. Then he said:	2
1Ti	2: 2	we may lead a quiet and peaceable life	1
1Pe	3: 4	the lasting beauty of a gentle and quiet spirit	3

quietly   *See also* live quietly
1. ἡσυχία, *hēsychia, 2484*
2. λάθρα, *lathra, 3277*

| Mat | 1:19 | to public disgrace, planned to dismiss her quietly. | 2 |
| 2Th | 3:12 | to do their work quietly | 1 |

Quirinius
1. Κυρήνιος, *Kyrēnios, 3256*

Lke 2: 2 while Quirinius was governor of Syria.   1

quite
1. εἰς + ὁ + παντελής, *eis + ho + pantelēs, 1650 + 3836 + 4117*
2. πολύς, *polys, 4498*

| Mrk | 12:27 | you are quite wrong." | 2 |
| Lke | 13:11 | quite unable to stand up straight. | 1 |

quite openly
1. παρρησία, *parrēsia, 4244*

Mrk 8:32 He said all this quite openly.   1

quote   *See also* word already quoted
1. λέγω, *legō, 3306*

Lke 4:23 "Doubtless you will quote to me this proverb   1

R

rabbi
1. ῥαββί, *rhabbi, 4806*

Mat	23: 7	to have people call them rabbi.	1
	23: 8	But you are not to be called rabbi	1
	26:25	Judas…said, "Surely not I, Rabbi?"	1
	26:49	he came up to Jesus and said, "Greetings, Rabbi!"	1
Mrk	9: 5	"Rabbi, it is good for us to be here;	1
	11:21	Peter remembered and said to him, "Rabbi, look!	1
	14:45	he went up to him at once and said, "Rabbi!"	1
Jhn	1:38	"Rabbi" (which translated means Teacher)	1
	1:49	"Rabbi, you are the Son of God!	1
	3: 2	"Rabbi, we know that you are a teacher	1

	3:26	They came to John and said to him, "Rabbi	1
	4:31	the disciples were urging him, "Rabbi, eat	1
	6:25	said to him, "Rabbi, when did you come here?"	1
	9: 2	His disciples asked him, "Rabbi, who sinned	1
	11: 8	The disciples said to him, "Rabbi	1

Rabbouni
1. ῥαββουνί, *rhabbouni, 4808*

Jhn 20:16 "Rabbouni!" (which means Teacher).   1

race[1]
1. γένος, *genos, 1169*

| Act | 7:19 | He dealt craftily with our race | 1 |
| 1Pe | 2: 9 | you are a chosen race, a royal priesthood | 1 |

race[2]
1. ἀγών, *agōn, 74*
2. δρόμος, *dromos, 1536*
3. στάδιον, *stadion, 5084*

1Co	9:24	in a race the runners all compete	3
2Ti	4: 7	I have finished the race, I have kept the faith.	2
Heb	12: 1	the race that is set before us	1

Rachel
1. Ῥαχήλ, *Rhachēl, 4830*

Mat 2:18 wailing and loud lamentation, Rachel weeping   1

radiance
1. φωστήρ, *phōstēr, 5891*

Rev 21:11 a radiance like a very rare jewel, like jasper   1

rage
1. δύναμις, *dynamis, 1539*
2. ἐπίκειμαι, *epikeimai, 2130*
3. θυμός, *thymos, 2596*
4. κλύδων, *klydōn, 3114*
5. ὀργίζω, *orgizō, 3974*
6. φρυάσσω, *phryassō, 5865*

Lke	4:28	all in the synagogue were filled with rage.	3
	8:24	woke up and rebuked the wind and the raging waves;	4
Act	4:25	'Why did the Gentiles rage	6
	27:20	no small tempest raged,	2
Heb	11:34	quenched raging fire	1
Rev	11:18	The nations raged, but your wrath has come	5

Rahab
1. Ῥαάβ, *Rhaab, 4805*
2. Ῥαχάβ, *Rhachab, 4829*

Mat	1: 5	Salmon the father of Boaz by Rahab	2
Heb	11:31	By faith Rahab the prostitute did not perish	1
Jas	2:25	was not Rahab the prostitute also justified by works	1

rain   *See also* send rain
1. Contextual: Not in Greek
2. βρέχω, *brechō, 1101*
3. βροχή, *brochē, 1104*
4. ὄμβρος, *ombros, 3915*
5. ὑετός, *hyetos, 5624*

Mat	7:25	rain fell, the floods came, and the winds blew	3
	7:27	rain fell, and the floods came, and the winds	3
Lke	12:54	you immediately say, 'It is going to rain';	4
	17:29	rained fire and sulfur from heaven	2
Act	14:17	giving you rains from heaven and fruitful seasons	5
	28: 2	Since it had begun to rain and was cold	5
Heb	6: 7	Ground that drinks up the rain…falling	5
Jas	5: 7	until it receives the early and the late rains.	1
	5:17	he prayed fervently that it might not rain,	2
	5:17	for three years and six months it did not rain	2
	5:18	Then he prayed again, and the heaven gave rain	5
Rev	11: 6	shut the sky, so that no rain may fall during the days	5

rainbow
1. ἶρις, *iris, 2692*

| Rev | 4: 3 | a rainbow that looks like an emerald. | |
| | 10: 1 | mighty angel…with a rainbow over his head; | 1 |

raise
1. αἴρω, *airō, 149*

2. ἀνίστημι, *anistēmi, 482*
3. ἐγείρω, *egeirō, 1586*
4. ἐξεγείρω, *exegeirō, 1995*
5. ἐπαίρω, *epairō, 2048*

Mat 10: 8	Cure the sick, raise the dead, cleanse the lepers	3
11: 5	the dead are raised, and the poor have good news	3
14: 2	he has been raised from the dead	3
16:21	and be killed, and on the third day be raised.	3
17: 9	the Son of Man has been raised from the dead."	3
17:23	on the third day he will be raised."	3
20:19	on the third day he will be raised."	3
27:52	saints who had fallen asleep were raised.	3
27:64	'He has been raised from the dead,'	3
28: 6	not here; for he has been raised, as he said.	3
28: 7	'He has been raised from the dead	3
Mrk 6:14	"John the baptizer has been raised from the dead;	3
6:16	"John, whom I beheaded, has been raised."	3
12:26	as for the dead being raised	3
16: 6	He has been raised; he is not here.	3
Lke 7:22	the deaf hear, the dead are raised	3
9: 7	John had been raised from the dead	3
9:22	be killed, and on the third day be raised."	3
11:27	a woman in the crowd raised her voice and said	5
20:37	that the dead are raised Moses himself showed	3
21:28	stand up and raise your heads	5
Jhn 2:22	After he was raised from the dead	3
5:21	the Father raises the dead and gives them life	3
12: 1	whom he had raised from the dead.	3
12: 9	to see Lazarus, whom he had raised from the dead.	3
12:17	raised him from the dead	3
21:14	after he was raised from the dead.	3
Act 2:14	Peter…raised his voice and addressed them	5
3:15	the Author of life, whom God raised from the dead.	3
4:10	whom you crucified, whom God raised from the dead.	3
4:24	raised their voices together to God and said	1
5:30	The God of our ancestors raised up Jesus,	3
10:40	God raised him on the third day	3
13:30	God raised him from the dead;	3
13:33	he has fulfilled…by raising Jesus;	2
13:34	As to his raising him from the dead	2
17:31	given assurance…by raising him from the dead."	2
26: 8	thought incredible…that God raises the dead?	3
Rom 4:24	him who raised Jesus our Lord from the dead	3
4:25	and was raised for our justification.	3
6: 4	so that, just as Christ was raised from the dead	3
6: 9	Christ, being raised from the dead, will never die	3
7: 4	belong…to him who has been raised from the dead	3
8:11	the Spirit of him who raised Jesus from the dead	3
8:11	he who raised Christ from the dead	3
8:34	Christ Jesus, who died, yes, who was raised	3
10: 9	and believe…that God raised him from the dead	3
1Co 6:14	God raised the Lord and will also raise us	3
6:14	God raised the Lord and will also raise us	4
15: 4	that he was raised on the third day	3
15:12	if Christ is proclaimed as raised from the dead	3
15:13	then Christ has not been raised;	3
15:14	if Christ has not been raised	3
15:15	we testified of God that he raised Christ	3
15:15	whom he did not raise if it is true	3
15:15	if it is true that the dead are not raised.	3
15:16	For if the dead are not raised	3
15:16	then Christ has not been raised.	3
15:17	If Christ has not been raised	3
15:20	in fact Christ has been raised from the dead	3
15:29	If the dead are not raised at all	3
15:32	If the dead are not raised, "Let us eat and drink	3
15:35	someone will ask, "How are the dead raised?	3
15:42	what is raised is imperishable.	3
15:43	It is sown in dishonor, it is raised in glory.	3
15:43	It is sown in weakness, it is raised in power.	3
15:44	it is raised a spiritual body.	3
15:52	the dead will be raised imperishable	3
2Co 1: 9	not on ourselves but on God who raises the dead.	3
4:14	know that the one who raised the Lord Jesus	3
4:14	will raise us also with Jesus	3
5:15	who died and was raised for them.	3
Gal 1: 1	God the Father, who raised him from the dead—	3
Eph 1:20	when he raised him from the dead	3
Col 2:12	God, who raised him from the dead.	3
1Th 1:10	his Son from heaven, whom he raised from the dead	3
2Ti 2: 8	Remember Jesus Christ, raised from the dead	3

Heb 11:19	God is able even to raise someone from the dead	3
1Pe 1:21	who raised him from the dead and gave him glory	3
Rev 10: 5	the angel…raised his right hand to heaven	1

raise a question

1. ἀνακρίνω, *anakrinō, 373*
2. διαλογίζομαι, *dialogizomai, 1368*

Mrk 2: 8	"Why do you raise such questions in your hearts?	2
Lke 5:22	"Why do you raise such questions in your hearts?	2
1Co 10:25	Eat…without raising any question	1
10:27	eat…without raising any question	1

raise up

1. Contextual: Not in Greek
2. ἀνίστημι, *anistēmi, 482*
3. ἐγείρω, *egeirō, 1586*
4. ἐξανίστημι, *exanistēmi, 1985*
5. ἐξεγείρω, *exegeirō, 1995*
6. ἐπαίρω, *epairō, 2048*
7. ὕψος, *hypsos, 5737*

Mat 3: 9	from these stones to raise up children to Abraham.	3
22:24	raise up children for his brother.'	2
26:32	But after I am raised up	3
Mrk 12:19	and raise up children for his brother.	4
14:28	after I am raised up, I will go before you	3
Lke 1:69	He has raised up a mighty savior for us	3
3: 8	God is able from these stones to raise up children	3
20:28	man shall marry the widow and raise up children	4
Jhn 2:19	this temple, and in three days I will raise it up."	3
2:20	and will you raise it up in three days?"	3
6:39	but raise it up on the last day.	3
6:40	I will raise them up on the last day."	2
6:44	I will raise that person up on the last day.	2
6:54	I will raise them up on the last day;	2
Act 2:24	But God raised him up	2
2:32	This Jesus God raised up	2
3: 7	he took him by the right hand and raised him up;	3
3:22	'The Lord your God will raise up…a prophet	2
3:26	God raised up his servant	2
7:37	'God will raise up a prophet for you	2
7:37	raise up a prophet for you…as he raised me up.'	1
13:37	he whom God raised up experienced no corruption.	3
Rom 9:17	"I have raised you up for the very purpose	5
2Co 10: 5	proud obstacle raised up against the knowledge of God	6
Jas 1: 9	Let the believer who is lowly boast in being raised up	7
5:15	and the Lord will raise them up;	3

raise up with

1. συνεγείρω, *synegeirō, 5283*

Eph 2: 6	raised us up with him and seated us with him	1

raise with

1. συνεγείρω, *synegeirō, 5283*

Col 2:12	you were also raised with him through faith	1
3: 1	So if you have been raised with Christ	1

Ramah

1. Ῥαμά, *Rhama, 4821*

Mat 2:18	"A voice was heard in Ramah, wailing and loud	1

rampart

1. χάραξ, *charax, 5918*

Lke 19:43	when your enemies will set up ramparts around you	1

rank See also rank *growth*

1. Contextual: Not in Greek
2. γίνομαι, *ginomai, 1181*

Jhn 1:15	'He who comes after me ranks ahead of me	2
1:30	'After me comes a man who ranks ahead of me	2
Act 10: 7	from the ranks of those who served him	1

ransom

1. ἀγοράζω, *agorazō, 60*
2. ἀντίλυτρον, *antilytron, 519*
3. λύτρον, *lytron, 3389*
4. λυτρόω, *lytroō, 3390*

Mat 20:28	to give his life a ransom for many."	3
Mrk 10:45	to give his life a ransom for many."	3
1Ti 2: 6	who gave himself a ransom for all	2

1Pe 1:18	you were ransomed from the futile ways	4
Rev 5: 9	and by your blood you ransomed for God saints	1

very rare
1. τίμιος, *timios, 5508*

Rev 21:11 a radiance like a very rare jewel, like jasper   1

rarely
1. μόλις, *molis, 3660*

Rom 5: 7 rarely will anyone die for a righteous person   1

rash
1. προπετής, *propetēs, 4637*

Act 19:36 you ought to be quiet and do nothing rash.   1

rather   *See also* rather *boldly,* rather *well*
1. Contextual: Not in Greek
2. ἀλλά, *alla, 247*
3. δέ, *de, 1254*
4. ἤ, *ē, 2445*
5. ἵνα + μή, *hina + mē, 2671 + 3590*
6. μᾶλλον, *mallon, 3437*
7. μενοῦν, *menoun, 3528*
8. οὐ, *ou, 4024*
9. παρά, *para, 4123*
10. τὶς, *tis, 5516*

Mat 10: 6	go rather to the lost sheep	6
10:28	rather fear him who can destroy both soul and body	6
27:24	rather that a riot was beginning	6
Mrk 5:26	no better, but rather grew worse.	6
Lke 11:28	"Blessed rather are those who hear the word of God	7
12:51	No, I tell you, but rather division!	4
17: 8	Would you not rather say to him, 'Prepare supper	2
18:14	this man…rather than the other;	9
22:26	rather the greatest among you must	2
Jhn 3:19	and people loved darkness rather than light	6
11: 4	rather it is for God's glory	2
Act 4:19	to listen to you rather than to God	6
5:29	"We must obey God rather than any human authority.	6
17:20	sounds rather strange to us	10
Rom 1:12	or rather so that we may be mutually encouraged	3
1:25	served the creature rather than the Creator	9
2:29	Rather, a person is a Jew who is one inwardly	2
1Co 3: 1	but rather as people of the flesh	2
5: 2	Should you not rather have mourned	6
6: 7	Why not rather be wronged?	6
6: 7	Why not rather be defrauded?	6
9:12	we endure anything rather than put an obstacle	5
9:15	I would rather die than that—no one will deprive me	6
14:19	I would rather speak five words with my mind…than	4
14:20	rather, be infants in evil, but in thinking be adults.	2
2Co 1:24	rather, we are workers with you for your joy	2
5: 8	we would rather be away from the body and at home	6
Gal 4: 9	or rather to be known by God	6
6: 4	then that work, rather than their neighbor's work,	8
Eph 4:28	rather let them labor and work honestly	6
1Ti 1: 4	rather than the divine training that is known by faith.	6
6: 2	rather they must serve them all the more	2
6:17	to set their hopes…rather on God	2
2Ti 1: 7	but rather a spirit of power and of love	2
3: 4	lovers of pleasure rather than lovers of God	6
Phm 1: 9	yet I would rather appeal to you on the basis of love	6
Heb 7:11	rather than one according to the order of Aaron?	8
11:25	choosing rather to share ill-treatment	6
12:11	discipline always seems painful rather than pleasant	2
12:13	not be put out of joint, but rather be healed.	6
1Pe 3: 4	rather, let your adornment be the inner self	2
2Jn 1:12	I would rather not use paper and ink;	1
3Jn 1:13	but I would rather not write with pen and ink;	1

ratify
1. κυρόω, *kyroō, 3263*

Gal 3:15 once a person's will has been ratified   1

ratify previously
1. προκυρόω, *prokyroō, 4623*

Gal 3:17 not annul a covenant previously ratified by God   1

ravage
1. λυμαίνω, *lymainō, 3381*

Act 8: 3 Saul was ravaging the church   1

raven
1. κόραξ, *korax, 3165*

Lke 12:24 Consider the ravens: they neither sow nor reap   1

ravenous
1. ἅρπαξ, *harpax, 774*

Mat 7:15 but inwardly are ravenous wolves.   1

ray
1. ἀστραπή, *astrapē, 847*

Lke 11:36 as when a lamp gives you light with its rays."   1

reach   *See also* fail to reach
1. γίνομαι, *ginomai, 1181*
2. εἰσέρχομαι, *eiserchomai, 1656*
3. ἐκπορεύομαι, *ekporeuomai, 1744*
4. ἔρχομαι, *erchomai, 2262*
5. ἐφικνέομαι, *ephikneomai, 2391*
6. καταντάω, *katantaō, 2918*
7. συντυγχάνω, *syntynchanō, 5344*

Mat 16: 5	When the disciples reached the other side	4
17:24	When they reached Capernaum	4
21: 1	had reached Bethphage, at the Mount of Olives	4
Lke 4:37	report about him began to reach every place	3
4:42	looking for him; and when they reached him	4
8:19	they could not reach him because of the crowd.	7
22:40	When he reached the place, he said to them, "Pray	1
Jhn 6:21	immediately the boat reached the land	1
20: 4	outran Peter and reached the tomb first.	4
20: 8	the other disciple, who reached the tomb first	4
Act 18:19	they reached Ephesus, he left them there	6
27:12	somehow they could reach Phoenix	6
1Co 14:36	Or are you the only ones it has reached?)	6
2Co 10:14	not overstepping…when we reached you;	5
Jas 5: 4	cries…have reached the ears of the Lord	2

reach a decision
1. κρίνω, *krinō, 3212*

Act 15:19	Therefore I have reached the decision	1
16: 4	decisions…reached by the apostles and elders	1

reach a goal
1. τελειόω, *teleioō, 5457*

Php 3:12 or have already reached the goal;   1

reach out
1. ἐκτείνω, *ekteinō, 1753*
2. ἐφικνέομαι, *ephikneomai, 2391*
3. φέρω, *pherō, 5770*

Mat 14:31	Jesus immediately reached out his hand	1
Jhn 20:27	Reach out your hand and put it in my side.	3
2Co 10:13	to reach out even as far as you.	2

reach perfection
1. τελειόω, *teleioō, 5457*

1Jn 2: 5	in this person the love of God has reached perfection.	1
4:18	whoever fears has not reached perfection in love.	1

reach safety
1. διασῴζω, *diasōzō, 1407*

Act 28: 1 After we had reached safety   1

read
1. ἀναγινώσκω, *anaginōskō, 336*
2. ἀνάγνωσις, *anagnōsis, 342*
3. γράφω, *graphō, 1211*
4. ἐπιγράφω, *epigraphō, 2108*

Mat 12: 3	He said to them, "Have you not read what David did	1
12: 5	Or have you not read in the law	1
19: 4	He answered, "Have you not read	1
21:16	"Yes; have you never read	1
21:42	"Have you never read in the scriptures:	1
22:31	have you not read what was said to you by God	1
27:37	they put the charge against him, which read	3

Mrk	2:25	"Have you never read what David did	1
	12:10	Have you not read this scripture: 'The stone	1
	12:26	have you not read in the book of Moses	1
	15:26	The inscription of the charge against him read	4
Lke	4:16	He stood up to read	1
	6: 3	Jesus answered, "Have you not read what David did	1
	10:26	"What is written in the law? What do you read	1
Jhn	19:19	It read, "Jesus of Nazareth, the King of the Jews."	3
	19:20	Many of the Jews read this inscription	1
Act	8:28	he was reading the prophet Isaiah.	1
	8:30	Philip…heard him reading the prophet Isaiah.	1
	8:30	asked, "Do you understand what you are reading?"	1
	8:32	passage of the scripture that he was reading	1
	13:15	After the reading of the law and the prophets	2
	13:27	the prophets that are read every sabbath	1
	15:31	When its members read it, they rejoiced	1
	23:34	On reading the letter	1
2Co	1:13	we write you nothing other than what you can read	1
	3: 2	to be known and read by all;	1
	3:14	when they hear the reading of the old covenant	2
	3:15	Indeed, to this very day whenever Moses is read	1
Eph	3: 4	a reading of which will enable you to perceive	1
Col	4:16	when this letter has been read among you	1
	4:16	have it read also in the church of the Laodiceans;	1
	4:16	see that you read also the letter from Laodicea.	1
1Th	5:27	that this letter be read to all of them.	1
1Ti	4:13	give attention to the public reading of scripture	2

read aloud

1. ἀναγινώσκω, *anaginōskō, 336*

| Act | 15:21 | read aloud every sabbath in the synagogues." | 1 |
| Rev | 1: 3 | the one who reads aloud the words of the prophecy | 1 |

reader

1. ἀναγινώσκω, *anaginōskō, 336*

| Mat | 24:15 | (let the reader understand) | 1 |
| Mrk | 13:14 | (let the reader understand) | 1 |

readily enough

1. καλῶς, *kalōs, 2822*

| 2Co | 11: 4 | you submit to it readily enough. | 1 |

ready   *See also* hold ready, make ready

1. Contextual: Not in Greek
2. δύναμαι, *dynamai, 1538*
3. ἑτοιμάζω, *hetoimazō, 2286*
4. ἕτοιμος, *hetoimos, 2289*
5. ἑτοίμως, *hetoimōs, 2290*
6. ἵνα, *hina, 2671*
7. παρασκευάζω, *paraskeuazō, 4186*
8. προσκαρτερέω, *proskartereō, 4674*

Mat	22: 4	everything is ready; come to the wedding banquet.'	4
	22: 8	Then he said to his slaves, 'The wedding is ready	4
	24:44	Therefore you also must be ready	4
	25:10	those who were ready went with him	4
Mrk	3: 9	his disciples to have a boat ready for him	8
	14:15	a large room upstairs, furnished and ready.	4
Lke	12:40	You also must be ready, for the Son of Man	4
	14:17	'Come; for everything is ready now.'	4
	22:33	I am ready to go with you to prison and to death!"	4
Act	21:13	ready not only to be bound but even to die	5
	23:15	we are ready to do away with him before he arrives."	4
	23:21	They are ready now and are waiting for your consent	4
1Co	3: 2	for you were not ready for solid food.	2
	3: 2	Even now you are still not ready	2
2Co	1:17	ready to say "Yes, yes" and "No, no"	6
	9: 2	Achaia has been ready since last year;	7
	9: 3	so that you may be ready, as I said you would be;	7
	9: 5	may be ready as a voluntary gift and not as an extortion.	4
	10: 6	We are ready to punish every disobedience	4
	12:14	Here I am, ready to come to you this third time.	5
2Ti	2:21	ready for every good work.	3
Tit	3: 1	to be obedient, to be ready for every good work	4
Heb	11:17	Abraham…was ready to offer up his only son	1
1Pe	1: 5	salvation ready to be revealed in the last time.	4
	3:15	Always be ready to make your defense to anyone	4
	4: 5	give an accounting to him who stands ready to judge	5

get ready

1. ἐπισκευάζομαι, *episkeuazomai, 2171*

2. ἑτοιμάζω, *hetoimazō, 2286*
3. παρασκευάζω, *paraskeuazō, 4186*

Act	21:15	we got ready and started to go up to Jerusalem.	1
	23:23	"Get ready to leave by nine o'clock tonight	2
1Co	14: 8	who will get ready for battle?	3

not ready

1. ἀπαρασκεύαστος, *aparaskeuastos, 564*

| 2Co | 9: 4 | if some…find that you are not ready | 1 |

ready to share

1. κοινωνικός, *koinōnikos, 3127*

| 1Ti | 6:18 | rich in good works, generous, and ready to share | 1 |

reaffirm

1. κυρόω, *kyroō, 3263*

| 2Co | 2: 8 | I urge you to reaffirm your love for him. | 1 |

real

1. Contextual: Not in Greek
2. ἀληθής, *alēthēs, 239*
3. ὄντως, *ontōs, 3953*

Act	12: 9	what was happening with the angel's help was real;	2
Rom	2:29	and real circumcision is a matter of the heart	1
1Ti	5: 5	The real widow…has set her hope on God	3
	5:16	it can assist those who are real widows.	3

reality

1. πρᾶγμα, *pragma, 4547*

| Heb | 10: 1 | not the true form of these realities | 1 |

realize

1. γινώσκω, *ginōskō, 1182*
2. ἐπιγινώσκω, *epiginōskō, 2105*
3. καταλαμβάνω, *katalambanō, 2898*
4. οἶδα, *oida, 3857*
5. πρός, *pros, 4639*
6. συνοράω, *synoraō, 5328*

Mat	21:45	they realized that he was speaking about them.	1
	27:18	For he realized that it was out of jealousy	4
Mrk	12:12	they realized that he had told this parable	1
	15:10	For he realized that it was out of jealousy	1
Lke	1:22	realized that he had seen a vision in the sanctuary.	2
	11:44	people walk over them without realizing it."	4
	20:19	chief priests realized that he had told this parable	1
Jhn	4:53	The father realized that this was the hour	1
	6:15	When Jesus realized that they were about to come	1
	8:28	then you will realize that I am he	1
Act	4:13	realized that they were uneducated and ordinary men	3
	12: 9	he not realize that what was happening	4
	12:12	As soon as he realized this, he went to the house	6
	22:29	he realized that Paul was a Roman citizen	2
	23: 5	"I did not realize, brothers, that he was high priest;	4
2Co	13: 5	you not realize that Jesus Christ is in you?	2
Heb	6:11	realize the full assurance of hope to the very end	5
Rev	3:17	not realize that you are wretched, pitiable, poor	4

not realize

1. ἀγνοέω, *agnoeō, 51*

| Rom | 2: 4 | Do you not realize that God's kindness is meant | 1 |

really

1. Contextual: Not in Greek
2. ἀληθῶς, *alēthōs, 242*
3. γέ, *ge, 1145*
4. καθώς, *kathōs, 2777*
5. μέντοι, *mentoi, 3530*
6. ὄντως, *ontōs, 3953*

Jhn	7:26	Can it be that the authorities really know	2
	7:40	"This is really the prophet."	2
1Co	5: 7	as you really are unleavened.	4
	8: 4	we know that "no idol in the world really exists,"	1
	11:20	it is not really to eat the Lord's supper.	1
	14:25	declaring, "God is really among you."	6
Gal	3: 4	if it really was for nothing.	3
1Th	2:13	but as what it really is, God's word	2
1Ti	5: 3	Honor widows who are really widows.	6
	5:16	woman has relatives who are really widows	1

	6:19 take hold of the life that really is life.	6
Jas	2: 1 do you with your acts of favoritism really believe	1
	2: 8 You do well if you really fulfill the royal law	5

reap

1. ἔχω, *echō*, 2400
2. θερίζω, *therizō*, 2545

Mat	6:26 they neither sow nor reap nor gather into barns	2
	25:24 reaping where you did not sow	2
	25:26 You knew…that I reap where I did not sow	2
Lke	12:24 Consider the ravens: they neither sow nor reap	2
	19:21 reap what you did not sow.'	2
	19:22 reaping what I did not sow?	2
Jhn	4:37 'One sows and another reaps.'	2
	4:38 I sent you to reap that for which you did not labor.	2
Rom	1:13 in order that I may reap some harvest among you	1
1Co	9:11 is it too much if we reap your material benefits?	2
2Co	9: 6 the one who sows sparingly will also reap sparingly	2
	9: 6 sows bountifully will also reap bountifully.	2
Gal	6: 7 for you reap whatever you sow.	2
	6: 8 will reap corruption from the flesh;	2
	6: 8 will reap eternal life from the Spirit.	2
	6: 9 we will reap at harvest time	2
Rev	14:15 "Use your sickle and reap	2
	14:15 reap, for the hour to reap has come	2
	14:16 swung his sickle…and the earth was reaped.	2

reaper

1. θερίζω, *therizō*, 2545
2. θεριστής, *theristēs*, 2547

Mat	13:30 at harvest time I will tell the reapers	2
	13:39 and the reapers are angels.	2
Jhn	4:36 The reaper is already receiving wages	1
	4:36 so that sower and reaper may rejoice together.	1

reason[1]

1. Contextual: Not in Greek
2. αἰτία, *aitia*, 162
3. ἀντί + οὖτος, *anti + houtos*, 505 + 4047
4. διά + οὖτος, *dia + houtos*, 1328 + 4047
5. διό, *dio*, 1475
6. διότι, *dioti*, 1484
7. εἰς + οὖτος, *eis + houtos*, 1650 + 4047
8. ἕνεκεν, *heneken*, 1915
9. οὖν, *oun*, 4036
10. οὖτος, *houtos*, 4047
11. οὖτος + χάριν, *houtos + charin*, 4047 + 5920
12. χάριν, *charin*, 5920
13. ὥστε, *hōste*, 6063

Mat	13:13 The reason I speak to them in parables	4
	14: 2 for this reason these powers are at work in him."	4
	18:23 "For this reason the kingdom of heaven	4
	19: 5 'For this reason a man shall leave his father	8
	27: 8 For this reason that field has been called	5
Mrk	6:14 for this reason these powers are at work in him."	4
	10: 7 'For this reason a man shall leave his father	8
	12:24 "Is not this the reason you are wrong	4
Jhn	1:31 I came baptizing with water for this reason	4
	3:29 For this reason my joy has been fulfilled.	9
	5:18 this reason the Jews were seeking…to kill him	4
	6:65 he said, "For this reason I have told you	4
	8:47 The reason you do not hear them is	4
	10:17 For this reason the Father loves me	4
	12:27 for this reason that I have come to this hour.	4
	13:11 this reason he said, "Not all of you are clean."	4
	16:15 For this reason I said that he will take	4
Act	10:21 what is the reason for your coming?"	2
	22:24 to find out the reason for this outcry against him.	2
	24:26 for that reason he used to send for him very often	5
	26:21 For this reason the Jews seized me in the temple	8
	28:18 no reason for the death penalty in my case.	2
	28:20 For this reason therefore I have asked to see	2
Rom	1:26 For this reason God gave them up to degrading	4
	4:16 For this reason it depends on faith	4
	8: 7 For this reason the mind that is set on the flesh	6
	13: 6 For the same reason you also pay taxes	4
	14:22 Blessed…who have no reason to condemn themselves	1
	15:22 the reason that I have so often been hindered	5
1Co	4:17 For this reason I sent you Timothy	4

	11:10 For this reason a woman ought to have a symbol	4
	11:30 For this reason many of you are weak and ill	4
2Co	1:20 For this reason it is through him that we say	5
	2: 9 I wrote for this reason: to test you	7
Gal	3: 9 For this reason, who believe are blessed	13
Eph	1:15 I have heard of your faith…and for this reason	4
	3: 1 This is the reason that I Paul am a prisoner for Christ	12
	3:14 For this reason I bow my knees before the Father	11
	5:31 "For this reason a man will leave his father	3
Col	1: 9 For this reason, since the day we heard it	4
1Th	3: 5 For this reason, when I could bear it no longer	4
	3: 7 For this reason, brothers and sisters,	4
2Th	2:11 For this reason God sends them a powerful delusion	4
1Ti	1:16 for that very reason I received mercy	4
2Ti	1: 6 For this reason I remind you to rekindle the gift	2
	1:12 for this reason I suffer as I do.	2
Tit	1: 5 I left you behind in Crete for this reason	11
	1:13 For this reason rebuke them sharply	2
Phm	1: 8 For this reason, though I am bold enough in Christ	5
	1:15 Perhaps this is the reason he was separated from you	4
Heb	2:11 For this reason Jesus is not ashamed to call them brothers	2
	9:15 For this reason he is the mediator of a new covenant	4
1Pe	4: 6 For this is the reason the gospel was proclaimed	7
2Pe	1: 5 For this very reason, you must make every effort	10
1Jn	3: 1 The reason the world does not know us	4
Rev	7:15 For this reason they are before the throne of God	4

reason[2]

1. λογίζομαι, *logizomai*, 3357

1Co	13:11 I thought like a child, I reasoned like a child;	1

reason for confidence

1. πείθω, *peithō*, 4275
2. πεποίθησις, *pepoithēsis*, 4301

Php	3: 4 even though I, too, have reason for confidence	2
	3: 4 If anyone else has reason to be confident	1

reason to boast

1. καύχησις, *kauchēsis*, 3018

Rom	15:17 I have reason to boast of my work for God.	1
2Co	8:24 and of our reason for boasting about you.	1

reassure

1. πείθω, *peithō*, 4275

1Jn	3:19 and will reassure our hearts before him	1

Rebecca

1. Ῥεβέκκα, *Rhebekka*, 4831

Rom	9:10 Rebecca when she had conceived children by one husband	1

rebel

1. στασιαστής, *stasiastēs*, 5086

Mrk	15: 7 in prison with the rebels	1

rebellion

1. ἀντιλογία, *antilogia*, 517
2. ἀποστασία, *apostasia*, 686
3. παραπικρασμός, *parapikrasmos*, 4177

2Th	2: 3 unless the rebellion comes first	2
Heb	3: 8 do not harden your hearts as in the rebellion	3
	3:15 do not harden your hearts as in the rebellion."	3
Jde	1:11 and perish in Korah's rebellion.	1

rebellious

1. ἀνυπότακτος, *anypotaktos*, 538
2. ἀπειθής, *apeithēs*, 579
3. παραπικραίνω, *parapikrainō*, 4176

Rom	1:30 inventors of evil, rebellious toward parents	2
Tit	1: 6 not accused of debauchery and not rebellious.	1
Heb	3:16 who were they who heard and yet were rebellious?	3

rebellious person

1. ἀνυπότακτος, *anypotaktos*, 538

Tit	1:10 There are also many rebellious people	1

rebirth

1. παλιγγενεσία, *palingenesia*, 4098

Tit	3: 5 through the water of rebirth	1

rebuild

1. ἀνοικοδομέω, *anoikodomeō, 488*

Act 15:16 rebuild the dwelling of David, which has fallen; 1
   15:16 its ruins I will rebuild it, and I will set it up 1

rebuke

1. ἔλεγξις + ἔχω, *elenxis + echō, 1792 + 2400*
2. ἐλέγχω, *elenchō, 1794*
3. ἐπιτιμάω, *epitimaō, 2203*

Mat 8:26 Then he got up and rebuked the winds and the sea; 3
   16:22 Peter took him aside and began to rebuke him 3
   17:18 Jesus rebuked the demon, and it came out of him 3
Mrk 1:25 Jesus rebuked him, saying, "Be silent, 3
   4:39 and rebuked the wind, and said to the sea 3
   8:32 Peter took him aside and began to rebuke him. 3
   8:33 looking at his disciples, he rebuked Peter 3
   9:25 he rebuked the unclean spirit, saying to it 3
Lke 3:19 Herod the ruler, who had been rebuked by him 2
   4:35 Jesus rebuked him, saying, "Be silent 3
   4:39 he stood over her and rebuked the fever 3
   4:41 But he rebuked them 3
   8:24 woke up and rebuked the wind and the raging waves; 3
   9:42 But Jesus rebuked the unclean spirit 3
   9:55 he turned and rebuked them. 3
   17: 3 disciple sins, you must rebuke the offender 3
   23:40 rebuked him, saying, "Do you not fear God 3
1Ti 5:20 rebuke them in the presence of all 2
2Ti 4: 2 convince, rebuke, and encourage 3
Tit 1:13 For this reason rebuke them sharply 2
2Pe 2:16 was rebuked for his own transgression; 1
Jde 1: 9 but said, "The Lord rebuke you!" 3

recall

1. ἀναμιμνήσκω, *anamimnēskō, 389*
2. μιμνήσκομαι, *mimnēskomai, 3630*
3. μνήμη + ποιέω, *mnēmē + poieō, 3647 + 4472*

2Ti 1: 4 Recalling your tears, I long to see you 2
Heb 10:32 recall those earlier days…when you endured 1
2Pe 1:15 you may be able at any time to recall these things. 3

receive

1. Contextual: Not in Greek
2. ἀναδέχομαι, *anadechomai, 346*
3. ἀπέχω, *apechō, 600*
4. ἀπολαμβάνω, *apolambanō, 655*
5. γίνομαι, *ginomai, 1181*
6. δέχομαι, *dechomai, 1312*
7. ἔχω, *echō, 2400*
8. κομίζω, *komizō, 3152*
9. λαγχάνω, *lanchanō, 3275*
10. λαμβάνω, *lambanō, 3284*
11. λῆμψις, *lēmpsis, 3331*
12. μεταλαμβάνω, *metalambanō, 3561*
13. μετάλημψις, *metalēmpsis, 3562*
14. παραλαμβάνω, *paralambanō, 4161*

Mat 6: 2 Truly I tell you, they have received their reward. 3
   6: 5 Truly I tell you, they have received their reward. 3
   6:16 Truly I tell you, they have received their reward 3
   7: 8 For everyone who asks receives 10
   10: 8 You received without payment; give without payment. 10
   10:41 will receive a prophet's reward; 10
   10:41 will receive the reward of the righteous; 10
   13:20 and immediately receives it with joy; 10
   19:29 for my name's sake, will receive a hundredfold 10
   20: 9 each of them received the usual daily wage. 10
   20:10 they thought they would receive more; 10
   20:10 each of them also received the usual daily wage. 10
   20:11 when they received it 10
   21:22 ask for in prayer with faith, you will receive." 10
   25:16 had received the five talents went off at once 10
   25:18 the one who had received the one talent went off 10
   25:20 who had received the five talents came forward 10
   25:24 had received the one talent also came forward 10
   25:27 on my return I would have received 8
Mrk 4:16 immediately receive it with joy. 10
   10:15 receive the kingdom of God as a little child 6
   10:30 who will not receive a hundredfold now 10
   11:24 believe that you have received it 10
   12:40 They will receive the greater condemnation." 10

Lke 6:24 for you have received your consolation. 3
   6:34 lend to those from whom you hope to receive 10
   8:13 when they hear the word, receive it with joy. 6
   9:53 they did not receive him 6
   11:10 For everyone who asks receives 10
   16:25 during your lifetime you received your good things 4
   18:17 whoever does not receive the kingdom of God 6
   19:15 When he returned, having received royal power 10
   20:47 They will receive the greater condemnation." 10
Jhn 1:12 to all who received him, who believed in his name 10
   1:16 From his fullness we have all received, grace 10
   3:11 yet you do not receive our testimony. 10
   3:27 "No one can receive anything except what 10
   4:36 The reaper is already receiving wages 10
   7:23 If a man receives circumcision on the sabbath 10
   7:39 which believers in him were to receive; 10
   10:18 I have received this command from my Father." 10
   12:48 one who rejects me and does not receive my word 10
   13:20 whoever receives one whom I send receives me; 10
   13:20 whoever receives one whom I send receives me; 10
   13:20 whoever receives me receives him who sent me." 10
   13:20 whoever receives me receives him who sent me." 10
   13:27 After he received the piece of bread, Satan 1
   13:30 after receiving the piece of bread 10
   14:17 whom the world cannot receive 10
   16:24 Ask and you will receive, so that your joy 10
   17: 8 they have received them 10
   19:30 When Jesus had received the wine, he said 10
   20:22 "Receive the Holy Spirit. 10
Act 1: 8 you will receive power when the Holy Spirit 10
   2:33 having received from the Father the promise 10
   2:38 you will receive the gift of the Holy Spirit. 10
   3: 5 expecting to receive something from them. 10
   7:38 he received living oracles to give to us. 6
   7:53 You are the ones that received the law 10
   7:59 "Lord Jesus, receive my spirit." 6
   8:15 that they might receive the Holy Spirit 10
   8:17 they received the Holy Spirit. 10
   8:19 may receive the Holy Spirit." 10
   10:43 receives forgiveness of sins through his name." 10
   10:47 who have received the Holy Spirit just as we have?" 10
   17:15 receiving instructions…they left him 10
   19: 2 He said to them, "Did you receive the Holy Spirit 10
   20:24 the ministry that I received from the Lord 10
   20:35 'It is more blessed to give than to receive.' " 10
   22: 5 From them I also received letters to the brothers 6
   26:10 with authority received from the chief priests 10
   26:18 they may receive forgiveness of sins 10
   28: 7 who received us and entertained us hospitably 2
   28:21 They replied, "We have received no letters 6
Rom 1: 5 through whom we have received grace 10
   1:27 received in their own persons the due penalty 4
   2:29 person receives praise not from others but from God. 1
   4:11 He received the sign of circumcision as a seal 10
   5:11 we have now received reconciliation 10
   5:17 those who receive the abundance of grace 10
   8:15 For you did not receive a spirit of slavery 10
   8:15 but you have received a spirit of adoption. 10
   13: 3 do what is good, and you will receive its approval; 7
1Co 2:12 Now we have received not the spirit of the world 10
   2:14 Those who are unspiritual do not receive the gifts 6
   3: 8 each will receive wages according to the labor 10
   3:14 builder will receive a reward. 10
   4: 5 Then each one will receive commendation 5
   4: 7 What do you have that you did not receive? 10
   4: 7 And if you received it, why do you boast 10
   9:24 only one receives the prize? 10
   9:25 they do it to receive a perishable wreath 10
   11:23 For I received from the Lord 14
   15: 1 which you in turn received, in which also you stand 14
   15: 3 what I in turn had received: 14
2Co 1: 9 felt that we had received the sentence of death 7
   11: 4 if you receive a different spirit 10
   11: 4 a different spirit from the one you received 10
   11:24 I have received from the Jews the forty lashes 10
Gal 1: 9 a gospel contrary to what you received 14
   1:12 for I did not receive it from a human source 14
   1:12 received it through a revelation of Jesus Christ. 1
   3: 2 Did you receive the Spirit by doing the works of the law 10
   3:14 receive the promise of the Spirit through faith. 10
   4: 5 so that we might receive adoption as children. 4

Php	4: 9 things that you have learned and received and heard	14
	4:15 in the matter of giving and receiving,	11
	4:18 satisfied, now that I have received from Epaphroditus	6
Col	2: 6 you therefore have received Christ Jesus the Lord	14
	3:24 from the Lord you will receive the inheritance	4
	4:10 you have received instructions	10
	4:17 the task that you have received in the Lord."	14
1Th	1: 6 in spite of persecution you received the word	6
	2:13 that when you received the word of God	14
2Th	3: 6 the tradition that they received from us.	14
1Ti	4: 3 created to be received with thanksgiving	13
	4: 4 provided it is received with thanksgiving;	10
Phm	1: 7 received much joy and encouragement from your love	7
Heb	2: 2 every…disobedience received a just penalty.	10
	4:16 so that we may receive mercy and find grace	10
	6: 7 receives a blessing from God.	12
	7: 5 descendants of Levi who receive the priestly office	10
	7: 6 blessed him who had received the promises.	7
	7: 8 tithes are received by those who are mortal;	10
	7: 9 Levi himself, who receives tithes, paid tithes	10
	9:15 may receive the promised eternal inheritance	10
	10:26 after having received the knowledge of the truth	10
	10:36 the will of God, you may receive what was promised.	8
	11: 8 a place that he was to receive as an inheritance;	10
	11:11 By faith he received power of procreation	10
	11:13 without having received the promises,	10
	11:17 He who had received the promises	2
	11:31 she had received the spies in peace.	6
	11:35 Women received their dead by resurrection.	10
	11:39 did not receive what was promised	8
	12:28 since we are receiving a kingdom that cannot be shaken	14
Jas	1: 7 must not expect to receive anything from the Lord.	10
	1:12 Such a one has stood the test and will receive	10
	4: 3 You ask and do not receive	10
	5: 7 until it receives the early and the late rains.	10
1Pe	1: 9 you are receiving the outcome of your faith	8
	4:10 serve one another with whatever gift each…received.	10
2Pe	1: 1 received a faith as precious as ours	9
	1:17 he received honor and glory from God the Father	10
1Jn	2:27 the anointing that you received from him	10
	3:22 we receive from him whatever we ask	10
	5: 9 If we receive human testimony, the testimony of God	10
2Jn	1: 8 so that you do not lose…but may receive a full reward.	4
	1:10 Do not receive into the house or welcome	10
Rev	2:17 that no one knows except the one who receives it.	10
	2:28 even as I also received authority from my Father.	10
	3: 3 Remember then what you received and heard;	10
	4:11 Lord and God, to receive glory and honor and power	10
	5:12 to receive power and wealth and wisdom and might	10
	14: 9 receive a mark on their foreheads or on their hands	10
	14:11 and for anyone who receives the mark of its name."	10
	17:12 ten kings who have not yet received a kingdom	10
	17:12 they are to receive authority as kings	10
	19:20 those who had received the mark of the beast	10
	20: 4 had not received its mark on their foreheads	10

receive a beating

1. δέρω, *derō, 1296*

Lke	12:47 That slave…will receive a severe beating.	1
	12:48 one…will receive a light beating.	1

receive a death-blow

1. σφάζω + εἰς + θάνατος, *sphazō + eis + thanatos, 5377 + 1650 + 2505*

Rev	13: 3 One of its heads seemed to have received a death-blow	1

receive a gift in return

1. ἀνταποδίδωμι, *antapodidōmi, 500*

Rom	11:35 given a gift to him, to receive a gift in return?"	1

receive a stoning

1. λιθάζω, *lithazō, 3342*

2Co	11:25 Once I received a stoning.	1

receive again

1. ἀπολαμβάνω, *apolambanō, 655*
2. κομίζω, *komizō, 3152*

Lke	6:34 to receive as much again.	1
Eph	6: 8 we will receive the same again from the Lord	2

receive approval

1. μαρτυρέω, *martyreō, 3455*

Heb	11: 2 by faith our ancestors received approval.	1
	11: 4 he received approval as righteous	1

receive back

1. κομίζω, *komizō, 3152*

Heb	11:19 figuratively speaking, he did receive him back.	1

receive baptism

1. βαπτίζω, *baptizō, 966*

1Co	15:29 receive baptism on behalf of the dead?	1

receive mercy

1. ἐλεέω, *eleeō, 1796*

Mat	5: 7 the merciful, for they will receive mercy.	1
Rom	11:30 received mercy because of their disobedience	1
	11:31 they too may now receive mercy.	1
1Ti	1:13 I received mercy because I had acted ignorantly	1
	1:16 for that very reason I received mercy	1
1Pe	2:10 once you had not received mercy	1
	2:10 but now you have received mercy.	1

receive recompense

1. κομίζω, *komizō, 3152*

2Co	5:10 so that each may receive recompense	1

receive sight

1. ἀναβλέπω, *anablepō, 329*

Mat	11: 5 the blind receive their sight, the lame walk	1
Lke	7:22 the blind receive their sight, the lame walk	1
	18:42 Jesus said to him, "Receive your sight;	1
Jhn	9:11 Then I went and washed and received my sight."	1
	9:15 began to ask him how he had received his sight.	1
	9:18 he had been blind and had received his sight	1
	9:18 the parents of the man who had received his sight	1

receive the good news

1. εὐαγγελίζω, *euangelizō, 2294*

Heb	4: 6 those who formerly received the good news	1

receive the law

1. νομοθετέω, *nomotheteō, 3793*

Heb	7:11 for the people received the law under this priesthood	1

receive the Spirit

1. πνευματικός, *pneumatikos, 4461*

Gal	6: 1 you who have received the Spirit should restore	1

recent See recent *convert*

recently

1. πρό + οὗτος + ὁ + ἡμέρα, *pro + houtos + ho + hēmera, 4574 + 4047 + 3836 + 2465*
2. προσφάτως, *prosphatōs, 4711*

Act	18: 2 recently come from Italy with his wife Priscilla	2
	21:38 who recently stirred up a revolt	1

more receptive

1. εὐγενής, *eugenēs, 2302*

Act	17:11 These Jews were more receptive	1

reckless

1. προπετής, *propetēs, 4637*

2Ti	3: 4 treacherous, reckless, swollen with conceit	1

reckon

1. ἐλλογέω, *ellogeō, 1824*
2. λογίζομαι, *logizomai, 3357*
3. συναίρω, *synairō, 5256*

Mat	18:24 When he began the reckoning	3
Rom	4: 3 and it was reckoned to him as righteousness."	2
	4: 4 wages are not reckoned as a gift but as something due.	2
	4: 5 such faith is reckoned as righteousness.	2
	4: 6 those to whom God reckons righteousness	2
	4: 8 the one…whom the Lord will not reckon sin."	2
	4: 9 "Faith was reckoned to Abraham as righteousness."	2
	4:10 How then was it reckoned to him?	2

Rom	4:11	who thus have righteousness reckoned to them	2
	4:22	his faith "was reckoned to him as righteousness."	2
	4:23	the words, "it was reckoned to him,"	2
	4:24	It will be reckoned to us who believe in him	2
	5:13	but sin is not reckoned when there is no law.	1
Gal	3: 6	it was reckoned to him as righteousness,"	2
Jas	2:23	and it was reckoned to him as righteousness,"	2

recline

1. ἀνάκειμαι, *anakeimai, 367*
2. ἀναπίπτω, *anapiptō, 404*

Jhn	13:23	was reclining next to him;	1
	13:25	So while reclining next to Jesus, he asked	2
	21:20	the disciple…who had reclined next to Jesus	2

recognize

1. γινώσκω, *ginōskō, 1182*
2. δοκέω, *dokeō, 1506*
3. ἐπιγινώσκω, *epiginōskō, 2105*
4. εὑρίσκω, *heuriskō, 2351*

Mat	14:35	After the people of that place recognized him	3
	17:12	they did not recognize him	3
Mrk	6:33	Now many saw them going and recognized them	3
	6:54	people at once recognized him	3
	10:42	recognize as their rulers lord it over them	2
Lke	19:42	saying, "If you, even you, had only recognized	1
	19:44	you did not recognize the time of your visitation	1
	24:16	their eyes were kept from recognizing him.	3
	24:31	their eyes were opened, and they recognized him;	3
Act	3:10	recognized him as the one who used to sit and ask	3
	4:13	recognized them as companions of Jesus.	3
	12:14	On recognizing Peter's voice,	3
	19:34	when they recognized that he was a Jew	3
	27:39	In the morning they did not recognize the land	3
2Co	11:12	an opportunity to be recognized as our equals	4
Gal	2: 9	recognized the grace that had been given to me	1

not recognize

1. ἀγνοέω, *agnoeō, 51*

Act	13:27	and their leaders did not recognize him	1
1Co	14:38	Anyone who does not recognize this	1
	14:38	not recognize this is not to be recognized.	1

recommendation

1. συστατικός, *systatikos, 5364*

2Co	3: 1	do not need, as some do, letters of recommendation	1

recompense *See* receive recompense

reconcile

1. ἀποκαταλλάσσω, *apokatallassō, 639*
2. διαλλάσσομαι, *diallassomai, 1367*
3. καταλλάσσω, *katallassō, 2904*
4. συναλλάσσω, *synallassō, 5261*

Mat	5:24	first be reconciled to your brother or sister	2
Act	7:26	tried to reconcile them, saying	4
Rom	5:10	while we were enemies, we were reconciled to God	3
	5:10	having been reconciled, will we be saved	3
1Co	7:11	or else be reconciled to her husband)	3
2Co	5:18	who reconciled us to himself through Christ	3
	5:19	in Christ God was reconciling the world	3
	5:20	on behalf of Christ, be reconciled to God.	3
Eph	2:16	might reconcile both groups to God in one body	1
Col	1:20	God was pleased to reconcile to himself all things	1
	1:22	now reconciled in his fleshly body through death	1

reconciliation

1. εἰρήνη, *eirēnē, 1645*
2. καταλλαγή, *katallagē, 2903*

Act	12:20	they asked for a reconciliation	1
Rom	5:11	we have now received reconciliation.	2
	11:15	if their rejection is the reconciliation	2
2Co	5:18	given us the ministry of reconciliation;	2
	5:19	entrusting the message of reconciliation to us.	2

record

1. γράφω, *graphō, 1211*
2. χειρόγραφον, *cheirographon, 5934*

Col	2:14	erasing the record that stood against us	2

Rev	20:12	their works, as recorded in the books.	1

recover

1. καλῶς + ἔχω, *kalōs + echō, 2822 + 2400*
2. κομψότερον, *kompsoteron, 3153*

Mrk	16:18	⟦and they will recover."⟧	1
Jhn	4:52	So he asked them the hour when he began to recover	2

recovery of sight

1. ἀνάβλεψις, *anablepsis, 330*

Lke	4:18	to proclaim…recovery of sight to the blind	1

red

1. ἐρυθρός, *erythros, 2261*
2. πυρράζω, *pyrrazō, 4793*
3. πυρρός, *pyrros, 4794*

Mat	16: 2	'It will be fair weather, for the sky is red.'	2
	16: 3	for the sky is red and threatening.'	2
Act	7:36	wonders and signs in Egypt, at the Red Sea	1
Heb	11:29	passed through the Red Sea as if it were dry land	1
Rev	12: 3	great red dragon, with seven heads and ten horns	3

bright red

1. πυρρός, *pyrros, 4794*

Rev	6: 4	And out came another horse, bright red;	1

redeem

1. ἀγοράζω, *agorazō, 60*
2. ἀπολύτρωσις, *apolytrōsis, 667*
3. ἐξαγοράζω, *exagorazō, 1973*
4. λυτρόω, *lytroō, 3390*
5. λύτρωσις + ποιέω, *lytrōsis + poieō, 3391 + 4472*

Lke	1:68	looked favorably on his people and redeemed	5
	24:21	had hoped that he was the one to redeem Israel.	4
Gal	3:13	Christ redeemed us from the curse of the law	3
	4: 5	in order to redeem those who were under the law	3
Tit	2:14	who gave himself for us that he might redeem us	4
Heb	9:15	because a death has occurred that redeems them	2
Rev	14: 3	who have been redeemed from the earth.	1
	14: 4	redeemed from humankind as first fruits for God	1

redemption

1. ἀπολύτρωσις, *apolytrōsis, 667*
2. λύτρωσις, *lytrōsis, 3391*

Lke	2:38	who were looking for the redemption of Jerusalem.	2
	21:28	because your redemption is drawing near."	1
Rom	3:24	through the redemption that is in Christ Jesus	1
	8:23	adoption, the redemption of our bodies.	1
1Co	1:30	sanctification and redemption	1
Eph	1: 7	In him we have redemption through his blood	1
	1:14	toward redemption as God's own people	1
	4:30	marked with a seal for the day of redemption.	1
Col	1:14	in whom we have redemption, the forgiveness	1
Heb	9:12	thus obtaining eternal redemption.	2

reduce to nothing

1. καταργέω, *katargeō, 2934*

1Co	1:28	to reduce to nothing things that are	1

reed

1. κάλαμος, *kalamos, 2812*

Mat	11: 7	A reed shaken by the wind?	1
	12:20	He will not break a bruised reed	1
	27:29	They put a reed in his right hand	1
	27:30	took the reed and struck him on the head.	1
Mrk	15:19	They struck his head with a reed, spat upon him	1
Lke	7:24	A reed shaken by the wind?	1

reef

1. τόπος + διθάλασσος, *topos + dithalassos, 5536 + 1458*

Act	27:41	striking a reef, they ran the ship aground;	1

refer

1. εἰμί, *eimi, 1639*
2. λέγω, *legō, 3306*

Jhn	11:13	they thought that he was referring merely to sleep.	2
Php	4:11	Not that I am referring to being in need;	2
Col	2:22	All these regulations refer to things that perish	1

refine

1. πυρόω, *pyroō, 4792*

Rev 1:15 like burnished bronze, refined as in a furnace 1
      3:18 I counsel you to buy from me gold refined by fire 1

reflect *See* see reflected in a mirror

reflection

1. ἀπαύγασμα, *apaugasma, 575*
2. δόξα, *doxa, 1518*

1Co 11: 7 since he is the image and reflection of God; 2
     11: 7 woman is the reflection of man. 2
Heb 1: 3 He is the reflection of God's glory 1

reform

1. διόρθωμα, *diorthōma, 1480*

Act 24: 2 reforms have been made for this people 1

refrain

1. μή, *mē, 3590*
2. τηρέω, *tēreō, 5498*
3. φείδομαι, *pheidomai, 5767*

1Co 7:38 he who refrains from marriage will do better. 1
      9: 6 have no right to refrain from working for a living? 1
2Co 11: 9 So I refrained and will continue to refrain 2
     11: 9 will continue to refrain from burdening you 2
     12: 6 I refrain from it 3

refresh

1. ἀναπαύω, *anapauō, 399*
2. ἀνάψυξις, *anapsyxis, 433*
3. ἀναψύχω, *anapsychō, 434*
4. διεγείρω, *diegeirō, 1444*

Act 3:20 so that times of refreshing may come 2
1Co 16:18 for they refreshed my spirit as well as yours. 1
2Ti 1:16 because he often refreshed me 3
Phm 1: 7 the saints have been refreshed through you 1
      1:20 Refresh my heart in Christ. 1
2Pe 1:13 I think it right...to refresh your memory, 4

refresh in company

1. συναναπαύομαι, *synanapauomai, 5265*

Rom 15:32 come...and be refreshed in your company. 1

refuge *See* take refuge

refuse

1. ἀθετέω, *atheteō, 119*
2. ἀποστρέφω, *apostrephō, 695*
3. ἀρνέομαι, *arneomai, 766*
4. μή, *mē, 3590*
5. μηδέ, *mēde, 3593*
6. οὐ, *ou, 4024*
7. οὐ + δέχομαι, *ou + dechomai, 4024 + 1312*
8. οὐ + θέλω, *ou + thelō, 4024 + 2527*
9. οὐ + ἀφίημι, *ou + aphiēmi, 4024 + 918*
10. οὔτε, *oute, 4046*
11. παραιτέομαι, *paraiteomai, 4148*

Mat 2:18 Rachel weeping...she refused to be consoled 8
      5:42 do not refuse anyone who wants to borrow 2
    18:30 he refused; then he went and threw him into prison 8
Mrk 5:19 Jesus refused, and said to him 9
      6:11 they refuse to hear you 5
      6:26 he did not want to refuse her. 1
Lke 7:30 refusing to be baptized by him 4
    15:28 he became angry and refused to go in. 8
    18: 4 For a while he refused; 8
Jhn 5:40 you refuse to come to me to have life. 8
  19:10 "Do you refuse to speak to me? 6
2Co 4: 2 we refuse to practice cunning 4
2Th 2:10 because they refused to love the truth 7
1Ti 5:11 But refuse to put younger widows on the list; 11
Heb 11:24 refused to be called a son of Pharaoh's daughter 3
    11:35 Others were tortured, refusing to accept release 6
    12:25 See that you do not refuse the one who is speaking; 11
    12:25 if they did not escape when they refused the one 11
3Jn 1:10 he refuses to welcome the friends 10
Rev 2:21 but she refuses to repent of her fornication. 8

    11: 9 and refuse to let them be placed in a tomb; 6

refuse help

1. κλείω + ὁ + σπλάγχνον, *kleiō + ho + splanchnon, 3091 + 3836 + 5073*

1Jn 3:17 sees...in need and yet refuses help? 1

refuse to believe

1. ἀπειθέω, *apeitheō, 578*
2. ἀπιστέω, *apisteō, 601*

Act 19: 9 When some stubbornly refused to believe 1
  28:24 while others refused to believe. 2

refuse to listen

1. παρακούω, *parakouō, 4159*

Mat 18:17 If the member refuses to listen to them 1
    18:17 offender refuses to listen even to the church 1

refute

1. διακατελέγχομαι, *diakatelenchomai, 1352*
2. ἐλέγχω, *elenchō, 1794*

Act 18:28 for he powerfully refuted the Jews in public 1
Tit 1: 9 to refute those who contradict it. 2

regain

1. κερδαίνω, *kerdainō, 3045*

Mat 18:15 listens to you, you have regained that one. 1

regain sight

1. ἀναβλέπω, *anablepō, 329*

Mat 20:34 Immediately they regained their sight 1
Mrk 10:52 Immediately he regained his sight 1
Lke 18:43 Immediately he regained his sight and followed 1
Act 9:12 so that he might regain his sight." 1
      9:17 so that you may regain your sight 1
    22:13 'Brother Saul, regain your sight!' 1
    22:13 In that very hour I regained my sight and saw him. 1

regain strength

1. ἐνισχύω, *enischyō, 1932*

Act 9:19 taking some food, he regained his strength. 1

regard

1. Contextual: Not in Greek
2. βλέπω, *blepō, 1063*
3. διά, *dia, 1328*
4. δοκέω, *dokeō, 1506*
5. ἐν, *en, 1877*
6. ἔχω, *echō, 2400*
7. ἡγέομαι, *hēgeomai, 2451*
8. κατά, *kata, 2848*
9. λογίζομαι, *logizomai, 3357*
10. οἶδα, *oida, 3857*
11. περί, *peri, 4309*

Mat 14: 5 because they regarded him as a prophet. 6
    14: 9 out of regard for his oaths and for the guests 3
    21:26 for all regard John as a prophet." 6
    21:46 because they regarded him as a prophet. 6
    22:16 for you do not regard people with partiality 2
Mrk 6:26 yet out of regard for his oaths and for the guests 3
    11:32 for all regarded John as truly a prophet. 6
    12:14 for you do not regard people with partiality 2
Lke 22:24 of them was to be regarded as the greatest. 4
Act 28:22 with regard to this sect 11
Rom 2:26 uncircumcision be regarded as circumcision? 9
      6:20 you were free in regard to righteousness. 1
    11:28 As regards the gospel they are enemies of God 8
    11:28 but as regards election they are beloved 8
2Co 5:16 we regard no one from a human point of view; 10
    11:17 saying in regard to this boastful confidence 5
Php 2: 3 in humility regard others as better 7
      2: 6 not regard equality with God as...to be exploited 7
      3: 7 I have come to regard as loss because of Christ. 7
      3: 8 More than that, I regard everything as loss 7
      3: 8 loss of all things, and I regard them as rubbish 7
2Th 3:15 Do not regard them as enemies, 7
1Ti 6: 1 regard their masters as worthy of all honor 7
      6:21 some have missed the mark as regards the faith. 11
1Pe 1:12 in regard to the things...now been announced 1

2Pe 3:15 regard the patience of our Lord as salvation. 7

regard lightly
1. ὀλιγωρέω, *oligōreō, 3902*
Heb 12: 5 do not regard lightly the discipline of the Lord 1

regard with contempt
1. ἐξουθενέω, *exoutheneō, 2024*
Lke 18: 9 to some who…regarded others with contempt: 1

region
1. Contextual: Not in Greek
2. κλίμα, *klima, 3107*
3. μέρος, *meros, 3538*
4. ὅριον, *horion, 3990*
5. περίχωρος, *perichōros, 4369*
6. τόπος, *topos, 5536*
7. χώρα, *chōra, 6001*
Mat 4:16 who sat in the region and shadow of death light 7
12:43 it wanders through waterless regions 6
14:35 they sent word throughout the region 5
15:22 Just then a Canaanite woman from that region 4
15:39 and went to the region of Magadan. 4
19: 1 went to the region of Judea beyond the Jordan. 4
Mrk 3: 8 beyond the Jordan, and the region around Tyre 1
6:55 and rushed about that whole region 7
7:24 he set out and went away to the region of Tyre. 4
7:31 Then he returned from the region of Tyre 4
7:31 in the region of the Decapolis. 4
10: 1 went to the region of Judea and beyond the Jordan. 4
Lke 2: 8 In that region there were shepherds 7
3: 1 Philip ruler of the region of Ituraea 7
4:37 reach every place in the region. 5
11:24 it wanders through waterless regions looking for 6
17:11 through the region between Samaria and Galilee. 1
Jhn 11:54 Ephraim in the region near the wilderness; 7
Act 8:40 as he was passing through the region, he proclaimed 1
13:49 word of the Lord spread throughout the region. 7
13:50 and drove them out of their region. 4
16: 6 They went through the region of Phrygia and Galatia 7
18:23 the region of Galatia and Phrygia 7
19: 1 Paul passed through the interior regions 3
20: 2 When he had gone through those regions 3
Rom 15:23 with no further place for me in these regions 2
2Co 11:10 will not be silenced in the regions of Achaia. 2
Gal 1:21 I went into the regions of Syria and Cilicia 2
1Th 1: 9 For the people of those regions report about us 1

region along
1. περίχωρος, *perichōros, 4369*
Mat 3: 5 to him, and all the region along the Jordan 1

region around
1. περίχωρος, *perichōros, 4369*
Lke 3: 3 He went into all the region around the Jordan 1

surrounding region
1. περίχωρος, *perichōros, 4369*
Mrk 1:28 the surrounding region of Galilee. 1

register
1. ἀπογράφω, *apographō, 616*
Lke 2: 1 all the world should be registered. 1
2: 3 All went to their own towns to be registered. 1
2: 5 registered with Mary, to whom he was engaged 1

registration
1. ἀπογραφή, *apographē, 615*
Lke 2: 2 This was the first registration 1

regret See also bring no regret
1. μεταμέλομαι, *metamelomai, 3564*
2. παραιτέομαι, *paraiteomai, 4148*
Lke 14:18 please accept my regrets.' 2
14:19 please accept my regrets.' 2
2Co 7: 8 I do not regret it (though I did regret it 1
7: 8 I do not regret it (though I did regret it 1

regular
1. ἔννομος, *ennomos, 1937*
Act 19:39 it must be settled in the regular assembly. 1

regulation See also submit to regulation
1. Contextual: Not in Greek
2. δικαίωμα, *dikaiōma, 1468*
3. ὅς, *hos, 4005*
Lke 1: 6 commandments and regulations of the Lord. 2
Col 2:22 All these regulations refer to things that perish 3
Heb 9: 1 the first covenant had regulations for worship 2
9:10 regulations for the body 2
13: 9 strengthened…not by regulations about food 1

Rehoboam
1. Ῥοβοάμ, *Rhoboam, 4850*
Mat 1: 7 Solomon the father of Rehoboam 1
1: 7 and Rehoboam the father of Abijah 1

reign
1. Contextual: Not in Greek
2. βασιλεύω, *basileuō, 996*
3. ἡγεμονία, *hēgemonia, 2449*
Lke 1:33 He will reign over the house of Jacob forever 2
3: 1 fifteenth year of the reign of Emperor Tiberius 3
Act 11:28 this took place during the reign of Claudius. 1
13:21 God gave them Saul…who reigned for forty years. 1
1Co 15:25 For he must reign until he has put all 2
Rev 5:10 and they will reign on earth." 2
11:15 Messiah, and he will reign forever and ever." 2
11:17 have taken your great power and begun to reign. 2
19: 6 For the Lord our God the Almighty reigns. 2
20: 4 and reigned with Christ a thousand years. 2
20: 6 they will reign with him a thousand years. 2
22: 5 and they will reign forever and ever. 2

reign with
1. συμβασιλεύω, *symbasileuō, 5203*
2Ti 2:12 if we endure, we will also reign with him; 1

reject
1. ἀθετέω, *atheteō, 119*
2. ἀπόβλητος, *apoblētos, 612*
3. ἀποδοκιμάζω, *apodokimazō, 627*
4. ἀποστρέφω, *apostrephō, 695*
5. ἀπωθέω, *apōtheō, 723*
6. ἀρνέομαι, *arneomai, 766*
7. ἐξουθενέω, *exoutheneō, 2024*
Mat 21:42 'The stone that the builders rejected 3
Mrk 7: 9 a fine way of rejecting the commandment of God 1
8:31 rejected by the elders, the chief priests 3
12:10 'The stone that the builders rejected 3
Lke 7:30 the lawyers rejected God's purpose 1
9:22 rejected by the elders, chief priests 3
10:16 whoever rejects you rejects me 1
10:16 whoever rejects you rejects me 1
10:16 whoever rejects me rejects the one who sent me." 1
10:16 whoever rejects me rejects the one who sent me." 1
17:25 be rejected by this generation. 3
20:17 'The stone that the builders rejected 3
Jhn 12:48 one who rejects me and does not receive my word 1
Act 3:13 rejected in the presence of Pilate 6
3:14 you rejected the Holy and Righteous One 6
4:11 'the stone that was rejected by you, the builders; 7
7:35 this Moses whom they rejected when they said 6
13:46 Since you reject it 5
Rom 11: 1 I ask, then, has God rejected his people? 5
11: 2 God has not rejected his people 5
1Th 4: 8 Therefore whoever rejects this 1
4: 8 rejects not human authority but God 1
1Ti 1:19 By rejecting conscience, certain persons have 5
4: 4 nothing is to be rejected, provided… 2
Tit 1:14 commandments of those who reject the truth. 4
Heb 12:17 he was rejected, for he found no chance to repent 3
12:25 if we reject the one who warns from heaven! 4
1Pe 2: 4 though rejected by mortals yet chosen and precious 3
2: 7 "The stone that the builders rejected has become 3
Jde 1: 8 these dreamers…reject authority, and slander 1

rejection
1. ἀποβολή, _apobolē, 613_

Rom 11:15 For if their rejection is the reconciliation   1

rejoice
1. ἀγαλλιάω, _agalliaō, 22_
2. εὐφραίνω, _euphrainō, 2370_
3. συγχαίρω, _synchairō, 5176_
4. χαίρω, _chairō, 5897_

Mat 5:12 Rejoice and be glad, for your reward is great   4
    18:13 if he finds it, truly I tell you, he rejoices   4
Lke 1:14 many will rejoice at his birth   4
    1:47 my spirit rejoices in God my Savior   1
    6:23 Rejoice in that day and leap for joy   4
    10:20 Nevertheless, do not rejoice at this   4
    10:20 rejoice that your names are written in heaven."   4
    10:21 Jesus rejoiced in the Holy Spirit and said   1
    13:17 crowd was rejoicing at all the wonderful things   4
    15: 5 he lays it on his shoulders and rejoices.   4
    15: 6 saying to them, 'Rejoice with me   3
    15:32 we had to celebrate and rejoice,   4
Jhn 4:36 so that sower and reaper may rejoice together.   4
    5:35 you were willing to rejoice for a while   1
    8:56 Abraham rejoiced that he would see my day;   1
    14:28 If you loved me, you would rejoice   4
    16:20 the world will rejoice;   4
    16:22 and your hearts will rejoice   4
    20:20 the disciples rejoiced when they saw the Lord.   4
Act 2:26 my heart was glad, and my tongue rejoiced;   1
    5:41 rejoiced that they were considered worthy   4
    8:39 went on his way rejoicing.   4
    11:23 When he came and saw the grace of God, he rejoiced   4
    15:31 they rejoiced at the exhortation.   4
    16:34 he and his entire household rejoiced   1
Rom 12:12 Rejoice in hope, be patient in suffering   4
    12:15 Rejoice with those who rejoice   4
    12:15 Rejoice with those who rejoice   4
    15:10 "Rejoice, O Gentiles, with his people";   2
    16:19 so that I rejoice over you   4
1Co 7:30 who rejoice as though they were not rejoicing   4
    7:30 who rejoice as though they were not rejoicing   4
    13: 6 it does not rejoice in wrongdoing   4
    13: 6 but rejoices in the truth.   3
    16:17 I rejoice at the coming of Stephanas   4
2Co 2: 3 from those who should have made me rejoice;   4
    6:10 as sorrowful, yet always rejoicing;   4
    7: 7 so that I rejoiced still more.   4
    7: 9 Now I rejoice, not because you were grieved   4
    7:13 we rejoiced still more at the joy of Titus   4
    7:16 I rejoice, because I have complete confidence   4
    13: 9 we rejoice when we are weak and you are strong.   4
Gal 4:27 "Rejoice, you childless one, you who bear no   2
Php 1:18 Christ is proclaimed...and in that I rejoice.   4
    1:18 Yes, and I will continue to rejoice   4
    2:28 that you may rejoice at seeing him again   4
    3: 1 Finally, my brothers and sisters, rejoice in the Lord.   4
    4: 4 Rejoice in the Lord always;   4
    4: 4 again I will say, Rejoice.   4
    4:10 I rejoice in the Lord greatly   4
Col 1:24 I am now rejoicing in my sufferings for your sake   4
    2: 5 rejoice to see your morale   4
1Th 5:16 Rejoice always   4
1Pe 1: 6 In this you rejoice   1
    1: 8 rejoice with an indescribable and glorious joy   1
    4:13 rejoice insofar as you are sharing Christ's   4
Rev 12:12 Rejoice then, you heavens and those who dwell in them!   2
    18:20 Rejoice over her, O heaven, you saints and apostles   2
    19: 7 Let us rejoice and exult and give him the glory   4

rejoice greatly
1. χαίρω + χαρά, _chairō + chara, 5897 + 5915_

Jhn 3:29 friend of the bridegroom...rejoices greatly   1

rejoice together
1. συγχαίρω, _synchairō, 5176_

1Co 12:26 if one member is honored, all rejoice together   1

rejoice with
1. συγχαίρω, _synchairō, 5176_

Lke 1:58 and they rejoiced with her.   1
    15: 9 saying, 'Rejoice with me   1
Php 2:17 I am glad and rejoice with all of you   1
    2:18 you also must be glad and rejoice with me.   1

rejoicing
1. ἀγαλλίασις, _agalliasis, 21_

Jde 1:24 in the presence of his glory with rejoicing   1

rekindle
1. ἀναζωπυρέω, _anazōpyreō, 351_

2Ti 1: 6 I remind you to rekindle the gift of God   1

relate
1. ἀναγγέλλω, _anangellō, 334_
2. ἐξηγέομαι, _exēgeomai, 2007_

Act 14:27 related all that God had done with them   1
    15:14 Simeon has related how God first looked favorably   2
    21:19 he related one by one the things that God had done   2

relation _See also_ have marital relations
1. ἐν, _en, 1877_

Rom 2:17 and boast of your relation to God   1

relative
1. Contextual: Not in Greek
2. ἀδελφός, _adelphos, 81_
3. ἴδιος, _idios, 2625_
4. συγγένεια, _syngeneia, 5149_
5. συγγενής, _syngenēs, 5150_
6. συγγενίς, _syngenis, 5151_

Lke 1:36 now, your relative Elizabeth in her old age   6
    1:58 Her neighbors and relatives heard   5
    1:61 "None of your relatives has this name."   4
    2:44 they started to look for him among their relatives   5
    14:12 your brothers or your relatives or rich neighbors   5
    21:16 parents and brothers, by relatives and friends;   5
Jhn 18:26 a relative of the man whose ear Peter had cut off   5
Act 7: 3 'Leave your country and your relatives   4
    7:14 all his relatives to come to him, seventy-five in all;   4
    7:23 it came into his heart to visit his relatives   2
    10:24 called together his relatives and close friends.   5
Rom 16: 7 Greet Andronicus and Junia, my relatives   5
    16:11 Greet my relative Herodion.   5
    16:21 so do Lucius and Jason and Sosipater, my relatives.   5
1Ti 5: 8 And whoever does not provide for relatives   3
    5:16 woman has relatives who are really widows   1

relax
1. ἀναπαύω, _anapauō, 399_

Lke 12:19 relax, eat, drink, be merry.'   1

release
1. ἀπολύτρωσις, _apolytrōsis, 667_
2. ἀπολύω, _apolyō, 668_
3. ἄφεσις, _aphesis, 912_
4. λύω, _lyō, 3395_

Mat 18:27 the lord of that slave released him   2
    27:15 governor was accustomed to release a prisoner   2
    27:17 "Whom do you want me to release for you   2
    27:21 of the two do you want me to release for you?"   2
    27:26 So he released Barabbas for them;   2
Mrk 7:35 his ears were opened, his tongue was released   4
    15: 6 he used to release a prisoner for them   2
    15: 9 want me to release for you the King of the Jews?"   2
    15:11 to have him release Barabbas for them instead.   2
    15:15 to satisfy the crowd, released Barabbas for them;   2
Lke 4:18 has sent me to proclaim release to the captives   3
    23:16 I will therefore have him flogged and release him."   2
    23:18 Release Barabbas for us!"   2
    23:20 Pilate, wanting to release Jesus, addressed them   2
    23:22 therefore have him flogged and then release him."   2
    23:25 He released the man they asked for,   2
Jhn 18:39 you have a custom that I release someone   2
    18:39 release for you the King of the Jews?"   2
    19:10 Do you not know that I have power to release you   2
    19:12 From then on Pilate tried to release him   2
    19:12 the Jews cried out, "If you release this man   2
Act 3:13 though he had decided to release him.   2

Act	4:23	After they were released	2
	22:30	the next day he released him	4
	28:18	the Romans wanted to release me	2
Heb	11:35	Others were tortured, refusing to accept release	1
Rev	9:14	"Release the four angels who are bound	4
	9:15	So the four angels were released	4
	20: 7	Satan will be released from his prison	4

relief

1. ἄνεσις, *anesis, 457*
2. διακονία, *diakonia, 1355*

Act	11:29	The disciples determined...each would send relief	2
2Co	8:13	should be relief for others and pressure on you	1
2Th	1: 7	give relief to the afflicted as well as to us	1

religion

1. δεισιδαιμονία, *deisidaimonia, 1272*
2. εὐσέβεια, *eusebeia, 2354*
3. θρησκεία, *thrēskeia, 2579*

Act	25:19	disagreement...about their own religion	1
	26: 5	the strictest sect of our religion	3
1Ti	3:16	the mystery of our religion is great:	2
Jas	1:26	deceive their hearts, their religion is worthless.	3
	1:27	Religion that is pure and undefiled before God	3

religious *See also religious duty*

1. θρῆσκος, *thrēskos, 2580*

Jas	1:26	If any think they are religious	1

extremely religious

1. δεισιδαίμων, *deisidaimōn, 1273*

Act	17:22	how extremely religious you are in every way.	1

reluctantly

1. ἐκ + λύπη, *ek + lypē, 1666 + 3383*

2Co	9: 7	not reluctantly or under compulsion	1

rely

1. ἐκ, *ek, 1666*
2. πείθω, *peithō, 4275*

2Co	1: 9	so that we would rely not on ourselves	2
Gal	3:10	rely on the works of the law are under a curse;	1

rely on

1. ἐπαναπαύομαι, *epanapauomai, 2058*

Rom	2:17	if you call yourself a Jew and rely on the law	1

relying on

1. κατά, *kata, 2848*

2Ti	1: 8	relying on the power of God	1

remain

1. Contextual: Not in Greek
2. ἀπολείπω, *apoleipō, 657*
3. δέχομαι, *dechomai, 1312*
4. διαμένω, *diamenō, 1373*
5. διατρίβω, *diatribō, 1417*
6. εἰμί, *eimi, 1639*
7. ἐπιμένω, *epimenō, 2152*
8. λείπω, *leipō, 3309*
9. λοιπός, *loipos, 3370*
10. μένω, *menō, 3531*
11. προσμένω, *prosmenō, 4693*
12. ὑπομένω, *hypomenō, 5702*

Mat	2:13	flee to Egypt, and remain there until I tell you;	6
	2:15	remained there until the death of Herod.	6
	11:23	it would have remained until this day.	10
	26:38	remain here, and stay awake with me."	10
Mrk	14:34	remain here, and keep awake."	10
Lke	1:22	motioning to them and remained unable to speak.	4
	1:56	Mary remained with her about three months	10
	8:47	the woman saw that she could not remain hidden	1
	10: 7	Remain in the same house, eating and drinking	10
Jhn	1:32	the Spirit descending...and it remained on him.	10
	1:33	'He on whom you see the Spirit descend and remain	10
	1:39	and they remained with him that day.	10
	2:12	and they remained there a few days.	10
	7: 9	saying this, he remained in Galilee.	10

	9:41	now that you say, 'We see,' your sin remains.	10
	10:40	he remained there.	10
	11:54	and he remained there with the disciples.	10
	12:24	it remains just a single grain;	10
	12:34	that the Messiah remains forever.	10
	12:46	should not remain in the darkness.	10
	21:22	"If it is my will that he remain until I come	10
	21:23	"If it is my will that he remain until I come	10
Act	3:21	who must remain in heaven until the time	3
	5: 4	While it remained unsold	10
	5: 4	did it not remain your own?	10
	14: 3	So they remained for a long time	5
	15:35	Paul and Barnabas remained in Antioch	5
	16:12	We remained in this city for some days.	5
	17:14	Silas and Timothy remained behind.	12
	21:14	he would not be persuaded, we remained silent	1
	27:33	have been in suspense and remaining without food	1
	27:41	the bow stuck and remained immovable	10
1Co	7: 8	it is well for them to remain unmarried as I am.	10
	7:11	if she does separate, let her remain unmarried	10
	7:20	Let each of you remain in the condition	10
	7:24	there remain with God.	10
	7:26	it is well for you to remain as you are.	6
	7:40	she is more blessed if she remains as she is.	10
Gal	2: 5	the truth of the gospel might always remain	4
	4: 2	they remain under guardians and trustees	6
Php	1:24	to remain in the flesh is more necessary	7
	1:25	convinced of this, I know that I will remain	10
1Ti	1: 3	I urge you...to remain in Ephesus	11
2Ti	2:13	if we are faithless, he remains faithful	10
	4:20	Erastus remained in Corinth;	10
Tit	1: 5	you should put in order what remained to be done	8
Heb	1:11	they will perish, but you remain;	4
	4: 6	Since therefore it remains open for some to enter it	2
	4: 9	a sabbath rest still remains for the people of God;	2
	7: 3	he remains a priest forever.	10
	10:26	there no longer remains a sacrifice for sins	2
	12:27	so that what cannot be shaken may remain.	10
1Jn	2:19	they would have remained with us.	10
Rev	3: 2	Wake up, and strengthen what remains	9
	17:10	when he comes, he must remain only a little while.	10

remain faithful

1. προσμένω, *prosmenō, 4693*

Act	11:23	he exhorted them all to remain faithful to the Lord	1

remain hidden

1. κρύπτω, *kryptō, 3221*

1Ti	5:25	good works...they cannot remain hidden.	1

remain in seclusion

1. περικρύβω, *perikrybō, 4332*

Lke	1:24	for five months she remained in seclusion.	1

remember

1. Contextual: Not in Greek
2. ἀναμιμνήσκω, *anamimnēskō, 389*
3. ἰδού, *idou, 2627*
4. μιμνήσκομαι, *mimnēskomai, 3630*
5. μνεία, *mneia, 3644*
6. μνεία + ἔχω, *mneia + echō, 3644 + 2400*
7. μνεία + ποιέω, *mneia + poieō, 3644 + 4472*
8. μνημονεύω, *mnēmoneuō, 3648*
9. ὑπομιμνήσκω, *hypomimnēskō, 5703*

Mat	5:23	the altar, if you remember that your brother or sister	4
	16: 9	Do you not remember the five loaves	8
	26:75	Peter remembered what Jesus had said:	4
	27:63	"Sir, we remember what that impostor said	4
	28:20	remember, I am with you always, to the end	3
Mrk	8:18	do you not remember?	8
	11:21	Peter remembered and said to him, "Rabbi, look!	2
	14:72	Peter remembered that Jesus had said to him	2
Lke	1:72	remembered his holy covenant	4
	16:25	Abraham said, 'Child, remember	4
	17:32	Remember Lot's wife.	8
	22:61	Peter remembered the word of the Lord	9
	23:42	remember me when you come into your kingdom."	4
	24: 6	Remember how he told you	4
	24: 8	they remembered his words	4
Jhn	2:17	His disciples remembered that it was written	4

	2:22 his disciples remembered that he had said this;	4
	12:16 when Jesus was glorified, then they remembered	4
	15:20 Remember the word that I said to you	8
	16: 4 you may remember that I told you about them.	8
	16:21 she no longer remembers the anguish	8
Act	10:31 your alms have been remembered before God.	4
	11:16 I remembered the word of the Lord, how he had said	4
	20:31 remembering that…I did not cease night or day	8
	20:35 remembering the words of the Lord Jesus	8
Rom	1: 9 I remember you always in my prayers	7
	11:18 remember that it is not you that support the root	1
1Co	11: 2 I commend you because you remember me	4
2Co	7:15 as he remembers the obedience of all of you	2
Gal	2:10 asked only one thing, that we remember the poor	8
Eph	1:16 remember you in my prayers.	7
	2:11 remember that at one time you Gentiles by birth	8
	2:12 remember that you were at that time without	1
Php	1: 3 I thank my God every time I remember you	5
Col	4:18 Remember my chains. Grace be with you.	8
1Th	1: 3 remembering before our God and Father your work	8
	2: 9 You remember our labor and toil, brothers	8
	3: 6 told us also that you always remember us kindly	6
2Th	2: 5 Do you not remember that I told you these things	8
2Ti	1: 3 when I remember you constantly in my prayers	6
	2: 8 Remember Jesus Christ, raised from the dead	8
Phm	1: 4 When I remember you in my prayers	7
Heb	8:12 I will remember their sins no more."	4
	10:17 remember their sins and their lawless deeds no more."	4
	13: 3 Remember those who are in prison	4
	13: 7 Remember your leaders	8
2Pe	3: 2 you should remember the words spoken in the past	4
Jde	1:17 you, beloved, must remember the predictions	4
Rev	2: 5 Remember then from what you have fallen;	8
	3: 3 Remember then what you received and heard;	8
	16:19 God remembered great Babylon and gave her	4
	18: 5 and God has remembered her iniquities.	8

remembrance

1. ἀνάμνησις, *anamnēsis, 390*
2. μιμνήσκομαι, *mimnēskomai, 3630*
3. μνημόσυνον, *mnēmosynon, 3649*

Mat	26:13 has done will be told in remembrance of her."	3
Mrk	14: 9 what she has done will be told in remembrance	3
Lke	1:54 in remembrance of his mercy	2
	22:19 Do this in remembrance of me."	1
1Co	11:24 Do this in remembrance of me."	1
	11:25 as often as you drink it, in remembrance of me."	1

remind

1. ἀναμιμνήσκω, *anamimnēskō, 389*
2. γνωρίζω, *gnōrizō, 1192*
3. λογίζομαι + πάλιν, *logizomai + palin, 3357 + 4099*
4. ὑπομιμνήσκω, *hypomimnēskō, 5703*
5. ὑπόμνησις, *hypomnēsis, 5704*
6. ὑπόμνησις + λαμβάνω, *hypomnēsis + lambanō, 5704 + 3284*

Jhn	14:26 remind you of all that I have said to you	4
1Co	4:17 to remind you of my ways in Christ Jesus	1
	15: 1 Now I would remind you, brothers and sisters	2
2Co	10: 7 remind yourself of this	3
2Ti	1: 5 I am reminded of your sincere faith	6
	1: 6 For this reason I remind you to rekindle the gift	1
	2:14 Remind them of this, and warn them	4
Tit	3: 1 Remind them to be subject to rulers	4
2Pe	1:12 I intend to keep on reminding you of these things	4
	3: 1 arouse your sincere intention by reminding	5
Jde	1: 5 Now I desire to remind you	4

reminder

1. ἀνάμνησις, *anamnēsis, 390*
2. ἐπαναμιμνήσκω, *epanamimnēskō, 2057*

Rom	15:15 written to you rather boldly by way of reminder	2
Heb	10: 3 in these sacrifices there is a reminder of sin	1

remnant

1. λεῖμμα, *leimma, 3307*
2. ὑπόλειμμα, *hypoleimma, 5698*

Rom	9:27 only a remnant of them will be saved;	2
	11: 5 So too at the present time there is a remnant	1

removal

1. ἀπόθεσις, *apothesis, 629*
2. μετάθεσις, *metathesis, 3557*

Heb	12:27 indicates the removal of what is shaken	2
1Pe	3:21 not as a removal of dirt from the body	1

remove

1. ἀθέτησις, *athetēsis, 120*
2. αἴρω, *airō, 149*
3. ἀποστεγάζω, *apostegazō, 689*
4. ἐκ + μέσος + γίνομαι, *ek + mesos + ginomai, 1666 + 3545 + 1181*
5. καταργέω, *katargeō, 2934*
6. κινέω, *kineō, 3075*
7. μεθίστημι, *methistēmi, 3496*
8. μετοικίζω, *metoikizō, 3579*
9. παραφέρω, *parapherō, 4195*
10. περιαιρέω, *periaireō, 4311*

Mrk	2: 4 they removed the roof above him;	3
	14:36 remove this cup from me;	9
Lke	22:42 if you are willing, remove this cup from me;	9
Jhn	15: 2 removes every branch in me that bears no fruit.	2
	19:31 and the bodies removed.	2
	19:38 so he came and removed his body.	2
	20: 1 the stone had been removed from the tomb.	2
Act	7:43 I will remove you beyond Babylon.'	8
	13:22 When he had removed him	7
1Co	5: 2 that he who has done this would have been removed	2
	13: 2 if I have all faith, so as to remove mountains	1
2Co	3:16 when one turns to the Lord, the veil is removed.	10
Gal	5:11 offense of the cross has been removed.	5
2Th	2: 7 until the one who now restrains it is removed.	4
Heb	9:26 to remove sin by the sacrifice of himself.	1
Rev	2: 5 and remove your lampstand from its place	6
	6:14 mountain and island was removed from its place.	6

remove mark of circumcision

1. ἐπισπάομαι, *epispaomai, 2177*

1Co	7:18 seek to remove the marks of circumcision.	1

render

1. Contextual: Not in Greek
2. ἀποδίδωμι, *apodidōmi, 625*
3. διακονία, *diakonia, 1355*

2Co	9:12 the rendering of this ministry	3
Heb	4:13 the eyes of the one to whom we must render an account.	1
Rev	18: 6 Render to her as she herself has rendered	2
	18: 6 Render to her as she herself has rendered	2

render service

1. διακονέω, *diakoneō, 1354*
2. δουλεύω, *douleuō, 1526*

Eph	6: 7 Render service with enthusiasm,	2
2Ti	1:18 you know very well how much service he rendered	1

renew

1. ἀνακαινόω, *anakainoō, 363*
2. ἀνακαίνωσις, *anakainōsis, 364*
3. ἀνανεόομαι, *ananeoomai, 391*

Rom	12: 2 but be transformed by the renewing of your minds	2
2Co	4:16 our inner nature is being renewed day by day.	1
Eph	4:23 be renewed in the spirit of your minds	3
Col	3:10 which is being renewed in knowledge	1

renewal

1. Contextual: Not in Greek
2. ἀνακαίνωσις, *anakainōsis, 364*
3. παλιγγενεσία, *palingenesia, 4098*

Mat	19:28 at the renewal of all things, when the Son of Man	3
Col	3:11 In that renewal there is no longer Greek and Jew	1
Tit	3: 5 renewal by the Holy Spirit.	2

renounce

1. ἀπεῖπον, *apeipon, 584*
2. ἀρνέομαι, *arneomai, 766*
3. ἀφίστημι, *aphistēmi, 923*

2Co	4: 2 renounced the shameful things that one hides;	1
1Ti	4: 1 in later times some will renounce the faith	3

Tit   2:12   training us to renounce impiety   2

repay

1. Contextual: Not in Greek
2. ἀνταποδίδωμι, *antapodidōmi, 500*
3. ἀνταπόδομα, *antapodoma, 501*
4. ἀποδίδωμι, *apodidōmi, 625*
5. ἀποτίνω, *apotinō, 702*
6. διπλόω, *diploō, 1488*

Mat 16:27   he will repay everyone for what has been done.   4
Lke 10:35   when I come back, I will repay you   4
     14:12   in case…you would be repaid.   3
     14:14   you will be blessed, because they cannot repay   2
     14:14   repaid at the resurrection of the righteous."   2
Rom   2: 6   he will repay according to each one's deeds: 4
     12:17   Do not repay anyone evil for evil   4
     12:19   "Vengeance is mine, I will repay, says the Lord."   2
1Th   5:15   See that none of you repays evil for evil   4
2Th   1: 6   to repay with affliction those who afflict you   2
Phm   1:19   I, Paul, am writing this with my own hand: I will repay   5
Heb 10:30   "Vengeance is mine, I will repay."   2
1Pe   3: 9   Do not repay evil for evil   4
     3: 9   but, on the contrary, repay with a blessing.   1
Rev 18: 6   and repay her double for her deeds;   6
     22:12   to repay according to everyone's work.   4

repayment   *See also* make repayment

1. ἀμοιβή, *amoibē, 304*

1Ti   5: 4   and make some repayment to their parents;   1

repeat

1. λαλέω, *laleō, 3281*
2. λέγω + πάλιν, *legō + palin, 3306 + 4099*

2Co 11:16   I repeat, let no one think that I am a fool;   2
     12: 4   that no mortal is permitted to repeat.   1
Gal   1: 9   As we have said before, so now I repeat   2

repeatedly

1. πολλάκις, *pollakis, 4490*
2. πολύς, *polys, 4498*

Mrk   5:23   begged him repeatedly, "My little daughter   2
Heb   6: 7   that drinks up the rain falling on it repeatedly   1

repent

1. μεταμέλομαι, *metamelomai, 3564*
2. μετανοέω, *metanoeō, 3566*
3. μετάνοια, *metanoia, 3567*

Mat   3: 2   "Repent, for the kingdom of heaven has come near."   2
     4:17   "Repent, for the kingdom of heaven has come near."   2
     11:20   because they did not repent.   2
     11:21   they would have repented long ago in sackcloth   2
     12:41   they repented at the proclamation of Jonah   2
     27: 3   he repented and brought back the thirty pieces   1
Mrk   1:15   repent, and believe in the good news."   2
     6:12   and proclaimed that all should repent.   2
Lke 10:13   they would have repented long ago   2
     11:32   they repented at the proclamation of Jonah   2
     13: 3   unless you repent, you will all perish as   2
     13: 5   unless you repent, you will all perish just as   2
     15: 7   more joy in heaven over one sinner who repents   2
     15:10   there is joy…over one sinner who repents."   2
     16:30   they will repent.'   2
     17: 4   turns back to you seven times and says, 'I repent,'   2
Act   2:38   "Repent, and be baptized every one of you   2
     3:19   Repent therefore, and turn to God   2
     8:22   Repent therefore of this wickedness of yours   2
     17:30   now he commands all people everywhere to repent   2
     26:20   they should repent and turn to God   2
2Co 12:21   who previously sinned and have not repented   2
2Ti   2:25   they will repent and come to know the truth   3
Heb 12:17   he was rejected, for he found no chance to repent   3
Rev   2: 5   repent, and do the works you did at first.   2
     2: 5   and remove your lampstand…unless you repent.   2
     2:16   Repent then. If not, I will come…and make war   2
     2:21   I gave her time to repent, but she refuses   2
     2:21   but she refuses to repent of her fornication.   2
     2:22   unless they repent of her doings;   2
     3: 3   what you received…obey it, and repent.   2
     3:19   Be earnest, therefore, and repent.   2

     9:20   did not repent of the works of their hands   2
     9:21   And they did not repent of their murders   2
     16: 9   and they did not repent and give him glory.   2
     16:11   and they did not repent of their deeds.   2

repentance

1. μετανοέω, *metanoeō, 3566*
2. μετάνοια, *metanoia, 3567*

Mat   3: 8   Bear fruit worthy of repentance.   2
     3:11   "I baptize you with water for repentance, but one   2
Mrk   1: 4   proclaiming a baptism of repentance   2
Lke   3: 3   proclaiming a baptism of repentance   2
     3: 8   Bear fruits worthy of repentance.   2
     5:32   I have come to call…sinners to repentance."   2
     15: 7   who need no repentance.   2
     17: 3   if there is repentance, you must forgive.   1
     24:47   repentance and forgiveness of sins   2
Act   5:31   that he might give repentance to Israel   2
     11:18   to the Gentiles the repentance that leads to life."   2
     13:24   proclaimed a baptism of repentance to all   2
     19: 4   "John baptized with the baptism of repentance   2
     20:21   testified…about repentance toward God   2
     26:20   and do deeds consistent with repentance.   2
Rom   2: 4   God's kindness is meant to lead you to repentance?   2
2Co   7: 9   because your grief led to repentance;   2
     7:10   For godly grief produces a repentance   2
Heb   6: 1   not laying again the foundation: repentance   2
     6: 4   For it is impossible to restore again to repentance   2
2Pe   3: 9   but all to come to repentance.   2

Rephan

1. Ῥαιφάν, *Rhaiphan, 4818*

Act   7:43   the star of your god Rephan   1

reply

1. Contextual: Not in Greek
2. ἀνταποκρίνομαι, *antapokrinomai, 503*
3. ἀποκρίνομαι, *apokrinomai, 646*
4. αὐτός, *autos, 899*
5. λέγω, *legō, 3306*
6. ὑπολαμβάνω, *hypolambanō, 5696*
7. φημί, *phēmi, 5774*

Mat 12:48   to the one who had told him this, Jesus replied   3
     13:29   he replied, 'No; for in gathering the weeds   7
     14:17   They replied, "We have nothing here but five loaves   5
     17:11   He replied, "Elijah is indeed coming   3
     19:27   Then Peter said in reply   3
     20:13   he replied to one of them   3
     25: 9   But the wise replied, 'No!   3
     25:12   he replied, 'Truly I tell you, I do not know you.'   3
     25:26   his master replied, 'You wicked and lazy slave!   3
     26:25   He replied, "You have said so."   5
Mrk   3:33   he replied, "Who are my mother and my brothers?"   3
     5: 9   He replied, "My name is Legion; for we are many."   5
     6:24   She replied, "The head of John the baptizer."   5
     8: 4   His disciples replied, "How can one feed   3
     10:39   They replied, "We are able."   5
     15: 5   Jesus made no further reply   3
Lke   1:19   The angel replied, "I am Gabriel.   3
     3:11   In reply he said to them, "Whoever has two coats   3
     7:40   "Teacher," he replied, "speak."   7
     8:50   Jesus heard this, he replied, "Do not fear.   3
     10:30   Jesus replied, "A man was going down   6
     13: 8   He replied, 'Sir, let it alone for one more year   3
     13:25   reply he will say to you, 'I do not know   3
     14: 6   they could not reply to this.   2
     15:27   He replied, 'Your brother has come   5
     16: 7   He replied, 'A hundred containers of wheat.'   5
     16:29   Abraham replied, 'They have Moses and the prophets;   5
     17: 6   The Lord replied, "If you had faith   5
     18:21   He replied, "I have kept all these since my youth."   5
     18:27   He replied, "What is impossible for mortals   5
     22:38   He replied, "It is enough."   5
     22:67   He replied, "If I tell you, you will not believe;   5
     23:43   He replied, "Truly I tell you   5
     24:19   replied, "The things about Jesus of Nazareth   5
Jhn   1:49   Nathanael replied, "Rabbi   3
     7:47   Pharisees replied, "Surely you have not been   3
     7:52   They replied, "Surely you are not also from Galilee   3
     10:32   Jesus replied, "I have shown you   3

	18: 5	Jesus replied, "I am he."	5
	18:31	The Jews replied, "We are not permitted	5
	18:35	Pilate replied, "I am not a Jew, am I?	3
	18:40	shouted in reply, "Not this man, but Barabbas!"	5
Act	1: 7	He replied, "It is not for you to know	5
	7: 2	Stephen replied: "Brothers and fathers, listen	7
	8:31	He replied, "How can I, unless someone guides me?"	5
	9: 5	reply came, "I am Jesus, whom you are persecuting.	1
	10:30	Cornelius replied, "Four days ago at this very hour	7
	11: 8	I replied, 'By no means, Lord;	5
	15:13	After they finished speaking, James replied	3
	16:37	Paul replied, "They have beaten us in public	7
	19: 2	They replied, "No, we have not even heard	4
	19:15	the evil spirit said to them in reply,	3
	21:37	The tribune replied, "Do you know Greek?	7
	21:39	Paul replied, "I am a Jew, from Tarsus in Cilicia	5
	24:10	Paul replied: "I cheerfully make my defense	3
	25: 4	Festus replied that Paul was being kept	3
	25:12	Then Festus...replied	3
	26:29	Paul replied, "Whether quickly or not,	1
	28:21	They replied, "We have received no letters	5

divine reply
1. χρηματισμός, *chrēmatismos, 5977*

Rom 11: 4	But what is the divine reply to him?	1

report *See also* give a report
1. ἀκοή, *akoē, 198*
2. ἀκούω, *akouō, 201*
3. ἀναγγέλλω, *anangellō, 334*
4. ἀπαγγέλλω, *apangellō, 550*
5. δηλόω, *dēloō, 1317*
6. διασαφέω, *diasapheō, 1397*
7. διηγέομαι, *diēgeomai, 1455*
8. ἐκδιηγέομαι, *ekdiēgeomai, 1687*
9. ἦχος¹, *ēchos¹, 2491*
10. φήμη, *phēmē, 5773*

Mat	9:26	the report of this spread throughout	10
	14: 1	the ruler heard reports about Jesus;	1
	18:31	they went and reported to their lord	6
Mrk	2: 1	it was reported that he was at home.	2
	5:16	Those who had seen...reported it.	7
Lke	4:14	and a report about him spread	10
	4:37	report about him began to reach every place	9
	7:18	disciples of John reported all these things	4
	14:21	So the slave returned and reported this	4
Act	4:23	reported what the chief priests...had said	4
	5:22	they returned and reported	4
	15: 3	reported the conversion of the Gentiles	8
	15: 4	they reported all that God had done with them.	3
	16:36	the jailer reported the message to Paul, saying	4
	16:38	police reported these words to the magistrates	4
	23:17	he has something to report to him."	4
	23:19	"What is it that you have to report to me?"	4
	28:21	none of the brothers coming here has reported	4
1Co	1:11	For it has been reported to me by Chloe's people	5
	5: 1	It is actually reported	2
1Th	1: 9	report about us what kind of welcome we had	4

report a case
1. ἐμφανίζω, *emphanizō, 1872*

Act 24: 1	reported their case against Paul to the governor.	1

representative
1. ἀνήρ, *anēr, 467*

Act 15:25	to choose representatives and send them to you	1

reproach
1. ὀνειδίζω, *oneidizō, 3943*

Mat 11:20	Then he began to reproach the cities	1

above reproach
1. ἀνεπίλημπτος, *anepilēmptos, 455*

1Ti	3: 2	Now a bishop must be above reproach	1
	5: 7	so that they may be above reproach.	1

reproof
1. ἐλεγμός, *elegmos, 1791*

2Ti 3:16	useful...for reproof, for correction	1

reprove
1. ἐλέγχω, *elenchō, 1794*

1Co 14:24	outsider who enters is reproved by all	1
Tit 2:15	exhort and reprove with all authority.	1
Rev 3:19	I reprove and discipline those whom I love.	1

reptile
1. ἑρπετόν, *herpeton, 2260*

Act	10:12	four-footed creatures and reptiles and birds	1
	11: 6	beasts of prey, reptiles, and birds of the air.	1
Rom	1:23	or birds or four-footed animals or reptiles.	1
Jas	3: 7	every species...of reptile and sea creature	1

good repute
1. εὐφημία, *euphēmia, 2367*

2Co 6: 8	in ill repute and good repute.	1

ill repute
1. δυσφημία, *dysphēmia, 1556*

2Co 6: 8	in ill repute and good repute.	1

request
1. αἰτέω, *aiteō, 160*
2. αἴτημα, *aitēma, 161*
3. παρακαλέω, *parakaleō, 4151*

Mrk	6:25	requested, "I want you to give me at once the head	1
Act	9:38	disciples...sent two men to him with the request	3
	25: 3	requested, as a favor to them against Paul	1
Php	4: 6	let your requests be made known to God.	2
1Jn	5:15	we have obtained the requests made of him.	2

require
1. Contextual: Not in Greek
2. ἔργον, *ergon, 2240*
3. ζητέω, *zēteō, 2426*
4. κατά, *kata, 2848*
5. χρήζω, *chrēzō, 5974*

Lke	2:39	required by the law of the Lord	4
	12:48	much will be required;	3
Rom	2:14	Gentiles...do instinctively what the law requires	1
	2:15	They show that what the law requires is written	2
	16: 2	help her in whatever she may require from you	5
1Co	4: 2	Moreover, it is required of stewards	3

requirement
1. δικαίωμα, *dikaiōma, 1468*
2. ἐντολή, *entolē, 1953*

Rom	2:26	uncircumcised keep the requirements of the law	1
Heb	7:16	a legal requirement concerning physical descent	2

just requirement
1. δικαίωμα, *dikaiōma, 1468*

Rom 8: 4	the just requirement of the law might be fulfilled	1

rescue
1. δίδωμι + σωτηρία, *didōmi + sōtēria, 1443 + 5401*
2. ἐξαιρέω, *exaireō, 1975*
3. ῥύομαι, *rhyomai, 4861*

Mat	6:13	time of trial, but rescue us from the evil one	3
Lke	1:74	rescued from the hands of our enemies	3
Act	7:10	rescued him from all his afflictions.	2
	7:25	God through him was rescuing them	1
	7:34	I have come down to rescue them.	2
	12:11	and rescued me from the hands of Herod	2
	23:27	I came with the guard and rescued him.	2
	26:17	I will rescue you from your people	2
Rom	7:24	Who will rescue me from this body of death?	3
	15:31	I may be rescued from the unbelievers in Judea	3
2Co	1:10	He who rescued us from so deadly a peril	3
	1:10	He who rescued us...will continue to rescue us	3
	1:10	set our hope that he will rescue us again	3
Col	1:13	has rescued us from the power of darkness	3
1Th	1:10	Jesus, who rescues us from the wrath that is coming.	3
2Th	3: 2	that we may be rescued from wicked and evil people;	3
2Ti	3:11	Yet the Lord rescued me from all of them.	3
	4:17	So I was rescued from the lion's mouth.	3
	4:18	The Lord will rescue me from every evil attack	3
2Pe	2: 7	and if he recused Lot, a righteous man	3

2Pe 2: 9 the Lord knows how to rescue the godly from trial 3

resemble

1. ἀφομοιόω, *aphomoioō, 926*
2. ὁμοιότης, *homoiotēs, 3928*
3. ὁμοίωμα, *homoiōma, 3930*

Rom 1:23 for images resembling a mortal human being or birds 3
Heb 7: 3 resembling the Son of God, he remains a priest 1
      7:15 another priest arises, resembling Melchizedek, 2

resentful

1. λογίζομαι + ὁ + κακός, *logizomai + ho + kakos, 3357 +
      3836 + 2805*

1Co 13: 5 it is not irritable or resentful; 1

reserve

1. ἀπόκειμαι, *apokeimai, 641*
2. θησαυρίζω, *thēsaurizō, 2564*
3. τηρέω, *tēreō, 5498*

2Ti 4: 8 is reserved for me the crown of righteousness 1
2Pe 2:17 the deepest darkness has been reserved. 3
      3: 7 and earth...have been reserved for fire 2
Jde 1:13 the deepest darkness has been reserved forever. 3

resident *See also* resident *alien*

1. κατοικέω, *katoikeō, 2997*
2. πλῆθος, *plēthos, 4436*

Act 1:19 known to all the residents of Jerusalem 1
      2: 9 Elamites, and residents of Mesopotamia 1
      9:35 all the residents of Lydda and Sharon saw him 1
      13:27 Because the residents of Jerusalem and their leaders 1
      14: 4 the residents of the city were divided; 2
      19:10 residents of Asia...heard the word of the Lord. 1
      19:17 this became known to all residents of Ephesus 1

resist

1. ἀνθίστημι, *anthistēmi, 468*
2. ἀντικαθίστημι, *antikathistēmi, 510*
3. ἀντιτάσσω, *antitassō, 530*

Mat 5:39 But I say to you, Do not resist an evildoer. 1
Rom 9:19 For who can resist his will?" 1
      13: 2 Therefore whoever resists authority resists 3
      13: 2 resists what God has appointed 1
      13: 2 and those who resist will incur judgment. 1
Heb 12: 4 not yet resisted to the point of...blood. 2
Jas 4: 7 Resist the devil, and he will flee from you. 1
      5: 6 the righteous one, who does not resist you. 3
1Pe 5: 9 Resist him, steadfast in your faith 1

resolve

1. ἐνθυμέομαι, *enthymeomai, 1926*
2. θέλω, *thelō, 2527*
3. καρδία, *kardia, 2840*
4. κρίνω, *krinō, 3212*
5. τίθημι, *tithēmi, 5502*

Mat 1:20 he had resolved to do this, an angel of the Lord 1
Jhn 7:17 Anyone who resolves to do the will of God 2
Act 19:21 Paul resolved in the Spirit to go 5
Rom 14:13 resolve instead never to put a stumbling block 4
1Co 7:37 someone stands firm in his resolve 3

good resolve

1. εὐδοκία, *eudokia, 2306*

2Th 1:11 fulfill...every good resolve and work of faith 1

resource

1. κοινωνία, *koinōnia, 3126*
2. ὑπάρχω, *hyparchō, 5639*

Lke 8: 3 who provided for them out of their resources. 2
Rom 15:26 pleased to share their resources with the poor 1

respect[1] *See also* greet with respect

1. ἐντρέπω, *entrepō, 1956*
2. εὐλαβέομαι, *eulabeomai, 2326*
3. εὐσχημοσύνη, *euschēmosynē, 2362*
4. εὐσχήμων, *euschēmōn, 2363*
5. οἶδα, *oida, 3857*
6. τίμιος, *timios, 5508*

7. φοβέομαι, *phobeomai, 5828*
8. φόβος, *phobos, 5832*

Mat 21:37 'They will respect my son.' 1
Mrk 12: 6 'They will respect my son.' 1
      15:43 a respected member of the council 4
Lke 18: 2 neither feared God nor had respect for people. 1
      18: 4 I have no fear of God and no respect for anyone 1
      20:13 perhaps they will respect him.' 1
Act 5:34 Gamaliel...respected by all the people 6
Rom 13: 7 Pay...respect to whom respect is due 8
      13: 7 Pay...respect to whom respect is due 8
1Co 12:23 treated with greater respect; 3
Eph 5:33 a wife should respect her husband. 7
1Th 5:12 respect those who labor among you 5
Heb 11: 7 Noah...respected the warning and built an ark 2
      12: 9 to discipline us, and we respected them. 1

respect[2]

1. Contextual: Not in Greek
2. ἐκ, *ek, 1666*
3. κατά, *kata, 2848*
4. περί, *peri, 4309*

1Co 9:19 For though I am free with respect to all 2
Tit 2: 7 in all respects a model of good works 4
      2: 9 to give satisfaction in every respect; 1
Heb 2:17 become like his brothers and sisters in every respect 3
      4:15 one who in every respect has been tested 3

respectable

1. κόσμιος, *kosmios, 3177*

1Ti 3: 2 respectable, hospitable, an apt teacher 1

less respectable

1. ἀσχήμων, *aschēmōn, 860*

1Co 12:23 less respectable members are treated with...respect; 1

more respectable

1. εὐσχήμων, *euschēmōn, 2363*

1Co 12:24 whereas our more respectable members do not need 1

respectful

1. σεμνότης, *semnotēs, 4949*

1Ti 3: 4 submissive and respectful in every way 1

respond

1. λέγω, *legō, 3306*

Rev 16: 7 I heard the altar respond, "Yes, O Lord God, 1

response

1. κατά, *kata, 2848*

Gal 2: 2 I went up in response to a revelation. 1

not responsible

1. καθαρός, *katharos, 2754*

Act 20:26 I am not responsible for the blood of any of you 1

rest[1] *See also* give rest, set at rest, take a rest

1. ἀνάπαυσις, *anapausis, 398*
2. ἀναπαύω, *anapauō, 399*
3. ἄνεσις, *anesis, 457*
4. ἄνεσις + ἔχω, *anesis + echō, 457 + 2400*
5. εἰμί, *eimi, 1639*
6. ἡσυχάζω, *hēsychazō, 2483*
7. καθίζω, *kathizō, 2767*
8. κατά, *kata, 2848*
9. κατάπαυσις, *katapausis, 2923*
10. καταπαύω, *katapauō, 2924*

Mat 11:29 and you will find rest for your souls. 1
Mrk 6:31 rest a while." 2
Lke 2:25 the Holy Spirit rested on him. 5
      23:56 they rested according to the commandment. 6
Act 2: 3 and a tongue rested on each of them. 7
      7:49 what is the place of my rest? 9
Rom 4:16 in order that the promise may rest on grace 8
1Co 2: 5 your faith might rest not on human wisdom 5
2Co 2:13 my mind could not rest 4
      7: 5 our bodies had no rest 3
Gal 3:12 the law does not rest on faith; 5

Heb	3:11	'They will not enter my rest.' "	9
	3:18	swear that they would not enter his rest	9
	4: 1	while the promise of entering his rest is still open	9
	4: 3	For we who have believed enter that rest	9
	4: 3	'They shall not enter my rest,' "	9
	4: 4	God rested on the seventh day from all his works."	10
	4: 5	"They shall not enter my rest."	9
	4:10	for those who enter God's rest	9
	4:11	Let us therefore make every effort to enter that rest	9
1Pe	4:14	which is the Spirit of God, is resting on you.	2
Rev	6:11	They were each…told to rest a little longer	2
	14:11	There is no rest day or night for those	1
	14:13	"they will rest from their labors	2

rest²

1. ἐπίλοιπος, *epiloipos, 2145*
2. λοιπός, *loipos, 3370*

Mat	22: 6	while the rest seized his slaves	2
Mrk	16:13	[[they went back and told the rest]]	2
Lke	12:26	why do you worry about the rest?	2
	24: 9	told all this to the eleven and to all the rest.	2
Act	5:13	None of the rest dared to join them	2
	27:44	the rest to follow, some on planks and others	2
	28: 9	the rest of the people on the island	2
Rom	1:13	as I have among the rest of the Gentiles.	2
	11: 7	The elect obtained it, but the rest were hardened	2
1Co	7:12	To the rest I say—I and not the Lord	2
Php	4: 3	with Clement and the rest of my co-workers	2
1Ti	5:20	so that the rest also may stand in fear.	2
1Pe	4: 2	so as to live for the rest of your earthly life	1
Rev	2:24	But to the rest of you in Thyatira	2
	9:20	rest of humankind, who were not killed by…plagues	2
	11:13	and the rest were terrified and gave glory	2
	12:17	went off to make war on the rest of her children	2
	19:21	And the rest were killed by the sword	2
	20: 5	(The rest of the dead did not come to life	2

rest on

1. ἐπαναπαύομαι, *epanapauomai, 2058*

Lke	10: 6	your peace will rest on that person;	1

sabbath rest

1. σαββατισμός, *sabbatismos, 4878*

Heb	4: 9	a sabbath rest still remains for the people of God;	1

resting   *See* resting *place*

restless

1. ἀκατάστατος, *akatastatos, 190*

Jas	3: 8	no one can tame the tongue—a restless evil	1

restoration

1. ἀποκατάστασις, *apokatastasis, 640*

Act	3:21	until the time of universal restoration	1

restore

1. ἀνακαινίζω, *anakainizō, 362*
2. ἀποκαθίστημι, *apokathistēmi, 635*
3. καταρτίζω, *katartizō, 2936*
4. χαρίζομαι, *charizomai, 5919*

Mat	12:13	and it was restored, as sound as the other.	2
	17:11	Elijah is…coming and will restore all things;	2
Mrk	3: 5	He stretched it out, and his hand was restored.	2
	8:25	he looked intently and his sight was restored	2
	9:12	"Elijah is indeed coming first to restore all things.	2
Lke	6:10	He did so, and his hand was restored.	2
Act	1: 6	the time when you will restore the kingdom to Israel?"	2
Gal	6: 1	restore such a one in a spirit of gentleness.	3
1Th	3:10	restore whatever is lacking in your faith.	3
Phm	1:22	through your prayers to be restored to you.	4
Heb	6: 4	For it is impossible to restore again to repentance	1
	13:19	so that I may be restored to you very soon.	2
1Pe	5:10	will…restore, support, strengthen, and establish you.	3

restore saltiness

1. ἁλίζω, *halizō, 245*
2. ἀρτύω, *artyō, 789*

Mat	5:13	how can its saltiness be restored?	1
Lke	14:34	how can its saltiness be restored?	2

restore sight

1. ἀναβλέπω, *anablepō, 329*

Act	9:18	and his sight was restored.	1

restrain

1. δέω, *deō, 1313*
2. καταπαύω, *katapauō, 2924*
3. κατέχω, *katechō, 2988*
4. κρατέω, *krateō, 3195*
5. κωλύω, *kōlyō, 3266*

Mrk	3:21	they went out to restrain him	4
	5: 3	no one could restrain him any more	1
	5: 4	often been restrained with shackles and chains	1
Act	14:18	they scarcely restrained the crowds	2
2Th	2: 6	you know what is now restraining him	3
	2: 7	until the one who now restrains it is removed.	3
2Pe	2:16	a speechless donkey…restrained the prophet's madness.	5

restraint

1. βρόχος, *brochos, 1105*

1Co	7:35	not to put any restraint upon you	1

restriction

1. στενοχωρέω, *stenochōreō, 5102*

2Co	6:12	There is no restriction in our affections	1

result

1. εἰς, *eis, 1650*
2. ἐκ, *ek, 1666*
3. ἵνα, *hina, 2671*

Rom	5:20	with the result that the trespass multiplied;	3
Eph	2: 9	not the result of works, so that no one may boast.	2
1Pe	1: 7	faith…may be found to result in praise and glory	1

resurrection

1. ἀνάστασις, *anastasis, 414*
2. ἔγερσις, *egersis, 1587*
3. ἐξανάστασις, *exanastasis, 1983*

Mat	22:23	saying there is no resurrection;	1
	22:28	In the resurrection, then, whose wife	1
	22:30	For in the resurrection they neither marry	1
	22:31	as for the resurrection of the dead	1
	27:53	After his resurrection they came out of the tombs	2
Mrk	12:18	Sadducees, who say there is no resurrection	1
	12:23	In the resurrection whose wife will she be?	1
Lke	14:14	repaid at the resurrection of the righteous."	1
	20:27	Sadducees, those who say there is no resurrection,	1
	20:33	In the resurrection, therefore, whose wife	1
	20:35	in the resurrection from the dead	1
	20:36	children of God, being children of the resurrection.	1
Jhn	5:29	who have done good, to the resurrection of life	1
	5:29	done evil, to the resurrection of condemnation.	1
	11:24	rise again in the resurrection on the last day."	1
	11:25	"I am the resurrection and the life.	1
Act	1:22	become a witness with us to his resurrection."	1
	2:31	spoke of the resurrection of the Messiah	1
	4: 2	in Jesus there is the resurrection of the dead.	1
	4:33	testimony to the resurrection of the Lord Jesus	1
	17:18	the good news about Jesus and the resurrection.)	1
	17:32	When they heard of the resurrection of the dead	1
	23: 6	the hope of the resurrection of the dead."	1
	23: 8	(The Sadducees say that there is no resurrection	1
	24:15	resurrection of both the righteous and the unrighteous.	1
	24:21	about the resurrection of the dead	1
Rom	1: 4	by resurrection from the dead, Jesus Christ	1
	6: 5	be united with him in a resurrection like his.	1
1Co	15:12	there is no resurrection of the dead?	1
	15:13	If there is no resurrection of the dead	1
	15:21	the resurrection of the dead has also come	1
	15:42	So it is with the resurrection of the dead.	1
Php	3:10	know Christ and the power of his resurrection	1
	3:11	I may attain the resurrection from the dead.	3
2Ti	2:18	claiming that the resurrection has already taken place.	1
Heb	6: 2	resurrection of the dead, and eternal judgment.	1
	11:35	Women received their dead by resurrection.	1
	11:35	in order to obtain a better resurrection.	1
1Pe	1: 3	the resurrection of Jesus Christ from the dead	1
	3:21	through the resurrection of Jesus Christ	1
Rev	20: 5	This is the first resurrection.	1

Rev 20: 6 holy are those who share in the first resurrection. 1

retain

1. κρατέω, *krateō, 3195*

Jhn 20:23 if you retain the sins of any, they are retained." 1
20:23 if you retain the sins of any, they are retained." 1

retribution

1. ἀνταπόδομα, *antapodoma, 501*

Rom 11: 9 become...a stumbling block and a retribution for them; 1

return *See also* expect in return, invite in return, receive a gift in return

1. ἀνακάμπτω, *anakamptō, 366*
2. ἀναλύω, *analyō, 386*
3. ἀναστρέφω, *anastrephō, 418*
4. ἀντάλλαγμα, *antallagma, 498*
5. ἀνταποδίδωμι, *antapodidōmi, 500*
6. ἀντιμισθία, *antimisthia, 521*
7. ἀπέρχομαι + πάλιν, *aperchomai + palin, 599 + 4099*
8. εἰσέρχομαι + πάλιν, *eiserchomai + palin, 1656 + 4099*
9. ἐξέρχομαι, *exerchomai, 2002*
10. ἐπανάγω, *epanagō, 2056*
11. ἐπανέρχομαι, *epanerchomai, 2059*
12. ἐπιστρέφω, *epistrephō, 2188*
13. ἔρχομαι, *erchomai, 2262*
14. πάλιν, *palin, 4099*
15. παραγίνομαι, *paraginomai, 4134*
16. ὑποστρέφω, *hypostrephō, 5715*

Mat 2:12 having been warned in a dream not to return to Herod 1
10:13 if it is not worthy, let your peace return to you. 12
12:44 'I will return to my house from which I came.' 12
16:26 what will they give in return for their life? 4
21:18 In the morning, when he returned to the city 10
25:27 on my return I would have received 13
Mrk 2: 1 When he returned to Capernaum after some days 8
7:31 Then he returned from the region of Tyre 9
8:37 what can they give in return for their life? 4
Lke 1:56 returned to her home. 16
2:20 The shepherds returned 16
2:39 they returned to Galilee, to their own town 12
2:43 the festival was ended and they started to return 16
2:45 they returned to Jerusalem to search for him. 16
4: 1 Jesus...returned from the Jordan 16
4:14 Jesus...returned to Galilee 16
7:10 those who had been sent returned to the house 16
8:37 So he got into the boat and returned. 16
8:39 "Return to your home 16
8:40 Now when Jesus returned, the crowd welcomed him 16
8:55 Her spirit returned, and she got up at once. 12
9:10 On their return the apostles told Jesus 16
10: 6 if not, it will return to you. 1
10:17 The seventy returned with joy, saying, 16
11:24 it says, 'I will return to my house 16
12:36 to return from the wedding banquet 2
14:21 So the slave returned and reported this 15
17:18 Was none of them found to return and give praise 16
19:12 to get royal power for himself and then return. 16
19:15 When he returned, having received royal power 11
19:23 when I returned, I could have collected it 13
23:48 they returned home, beating their breasts. 16
23:56 Then they returned, and prepared spices 16
24: 9 returning from the tomb, they told all this 16
24:33 That same hour they got up and returned to Jerusalem; 16
24:52 and returned to Jerusalem with great joy; 16
Jhn 13:12 put on his robe, and had returned to the table 14
20:10 the disciples returned to their homes. 7
Act 1:12 Then they returned to Jerusalem from the mount 16
5:22 they returned and reported 3
8:25 they returned to Jerusalem 16
8:28 was returning home; seated in his chariot, 16
12:25 Barnabas and Saul returned to Jerusalem 16
13:13 John, however, left them and returned to Jerusalem; 16
13:34 no more to return to corruption 16
14:21 returned to Lystra, then on to Iconium and Antioch. 16
15:16 'After this I will return, and I will rebuild 3
15:36 let us return and visit the believers 12
18:21 "I will return to you, if God wills." 1
20: 3 he decided to return through Macedonia. 16

21: 6 we went on board the ship, and they returned home. 16
22:17 "After I had returned to Jerusalem 16
23:32 go on with him, while they returned to the barracks. 16
Rom 9: 9 I will return and Sarah shall have a son." 13
2Co 6:13 In return—I speak as to children 6
Gal 1:17 afterwards I returned to Damascus. 16
1Th 3: 9 How can we thank God enough for you in return 5
Heb 7: 1 Abraham...was returning from defeating the kings 16
11:15 they would have had opportunity to return. 1
1Pe 2:25 but now you have returned to the shepherd 12

return abuse

1. ἀντιλοιδορέω, *antiloidoreō, 518*

1Pe 2:23 When he was abused, he did not return abuse; 1

Reu

1. Ῥαγαύ, *Rhagau, 4814*

Lke 3:35 son of Serug, son of Reu, son of Peleg 1

Reuben

1. Ῥουβήν, *Rhoubēn, 4857*

Rev 7: 5 from the tribe of Reuben twelve thousand, 1

reveal

1. ἀποκαλύπτω, *apokalyptō, 636*
2. ἀποκάλυψις, *apokalypsis, 637*
3. ἐμφανίζω, *emphanizō, 1872*
4. φανερός, *phaneros, 5745*
5. φανερόω, *phaneroō, 5746*
6. χρηματίζω, *chrēmatizō, 5976*

Mat 11:25 and have revealed them to infants; 1
11:27 anyone to whom the Son chooses to reveal him. 1
16:17 For flesh and blood has not revealed this to you 1
Lke 2:26 It had been revealed to him by the Holy Spirit 6
2:35 inner thoughts of many will be revealed 1
10:21 revealed them to infants; 1
10:22 to whom the Son chooses to reveal him." 1
17:30 on the day that the Son of Man is revealed. 1
Jhn 1:31 that he might be revealed to Israel." 5
2:11 Jesus did this...and revealed his glory; 5
9: 3 so that God's works might be revealed in him. 5
12:38 to whom has the arm of the Lord been revealed?" 1
14:21 I will love them and reveal myself to them." 3
14:22 reveal yourself to us, and not to the world?" 3
Rom 1:17 righteousness of God is revealed through faith 1
1:18 For the wrath of God is revealed from heaven 1
2: 5 when God's righteous judgment will be revealed. 2
8:18 the glory about to be revealed to us. 1
8:19 waits...for the revealing of the children of God; 2
1Co 1: 7 as you wait for the revealing of our Lord Jesus 2
2:10 God has revealed to us through the Spirit; 1
3:13 because it will be revealed with fire 1
Gal 1:16 to reveal his Son to me 1
3:23 until faith would be revealed. 1
Eph 3: 5 has now been revealed to his holy apostles 1
Php 3:15 this too God will reveal to you. 1
Col 1:26 now been revealed to his saints. 5
3: 4 When Christ who is your life is revealed 5
3: 4 you also will be revealed with him in glory. 5
2Th 1: 7 when the Lord Jesus is revealed from heaven 2
2: 3 the lawless one is revealed 1
2: 6 so that he may be revealed when his time 1
2: 8 then the lawless one will be revealed 1
1Ti 3:16 He was revealed in flesh 5
2Ti 1:10 been revealed through the appearing of our Savior 5
Tit 1: 3 in due time he revealed his word 5
1Pe 1: 5 salvation ready to be revealed in the last time. 1
1: 7 and honor when Jesus Christ is revealed. 2
1:12 It was revealed to them that they were serving 1
1:13 Jesus Christ will bring you when he is revealed. 2
1:20 He...was revealed at the end of the ages 5
4:13 be glad and shout for joy when his glory is revealed. 2
5: 1 one who shares in the glory to be revealed 1
1Jn 1: 2 this life was revealed, and we have seen it 5
1: 2 eternal life that...was revealed to us 5
2:28 so that when he is revealed we may have confidence 5
3: 2 what we will be has not yet been revealed. 5
3: 2 when he is revealed, we will be like him 5
3: 5 You know that he was revealed to take away sins 5
3: 8 The Son of God was revealed for this purpose 5

3:10 children of the devil are revealed in this way: 4
4: 9 God's love was revealed among us in this way: 5
Rev 15: 4 for your judgments have been revealed." 5

reveal clearly

1. φανερόω, *phaneroō, 5746*

Col 4: 4 so that I may reveal it clearly, as I should. 1

revel

1. ἐντρυφάω, *entryphaō, 1960*
2. εὐφραίνω, *euphrainō, 2370*
3. κῶμος, *kōmos, 3269*
4. τρυφή, *tryphē, 5588*

Act 7:41 reveled in the works of their hands. 2
Rom 13:13 not in reveling and drunkenness 3
1Pe 4: 3 living in…drunkenness, revels, carousing 3
2Pe 2:13 They count it a pleasure to revel in the daytime. 4
      2:13 They are…reveling in their dissipation 1

revelation *See also* make a revelation

1. ἀποκάλυψις, *apokalypsis, 637*

Lke 2:32 a light for revelation to the Gentiles 1
Rom 16:25 revelation of the mystery that was kept secret 1
1Co 14: 6 I speak to you in some revelation or knowledge 1
    14:26 a hymn, a lesson, a revelation, a tongue 1
2Co 12: 1 go on to visions and revelations of the Lord. 1
    12: 7 the exceptional character of the revelations. 1
Gal 1:12 received it through a revelation of Jesus Christ. 1
     2: 2 I went up in response to a revelation. 1
Eph 1:17 may give you a spirit of wisdom and revelation 1
     3: 3 the mystery was made known to me by revelation 1
Rev 1: 1 The revelation of Jesus Christ, which God gave 1

revenue

1. τέλος, *telos, 5465*

Rom 13: 7 Pay…revenue to whom revenue is due 1
    13: 7 Pay…revenue to whom revenue is due 1

reverence

1. εὐλάβεια, *eulabeia, 2325*
2. φόβος, *phobos, 5832*

Eph 5:21 out of reverence for Christ. 2
Heb 12:28 acceptable worship with reverence and awe; 1
1Pe 3: 2 when they see the purity and reverence of your lives. 2
     3:16 yet do it with gentleness and reverence. 2

reverence for God

1. θεοσέβεια, *theosebeia, 2537*

1Ti 2:10 as is proper for women who profess reverence for God. 1

reverent *See also* reverent *fear,* reverent *submission*

1. ἱεροπρεπής, *hieroprepēs, 2640*

Tit 2: 3 Likewise, tell the older women to be reverent in behavior 1

revile

1. βλασφημέω, *blasphēmeō, 1059*
2. λοιδορέω, *loidoreō, 3366*
3. λοιδορία, *loidoria, 3367*
4. ὀνειδίζω, *oneidizō, 3943*

Mat 5:11 "Blessed are you when people revile you 4
Lke 6:22 when they exclude you, revile you 4
Jhn 9:28 they reviled him, saying, "You are his disciple 2
Act 18: 6 When they opposed and reviled him 1
1Co 4:12 When reviled, we bless; when persecuted, we endure; 2
1Ti 5:14 give the adversary no occasion to revile us. 3
1Pe 4:14 If you are reviled for the name of Christ 4

reviler

1. λοίδορος, *loidoros, 3368*

1Co 5:11 is an idolater, reviler, drunkard, or robber 1
     6:10 drunkards, revilers, robbers 1

revive

1. ἀναζάω, *anazaō, 348*
2. ἀναθάλλω, *anathallō, 352*

Rom 7: 9 but when the commandment came, sin revived 1
Php 4:10 now at last you have revived your concern 2

revolt *See* stir up revolt

reward

1. ἀνταπόδοσις, *antapodosis, 502*
2. ἀποδίδωμι, *apodidōmi, 625*
3. δίδωμι + ὁ + μισθός, *didōmi + ho + misthos, 1443 + 3836 + 3635*
4. μισθαποδοσία, *misthapodosia, 3632*
5. μισθαποδότης, *misthapodotēs, 3633*
6. μισθός, *misthos, 3635*

Mat 5:12 Rejoice and be glad, for your reward is great 6
     5:46 love those who love you, what reward do you have? 6
     6: 1 for then you have no reward from your Father 6
     6: 2 Truly I tell you, they have received their reward. 6
     6: 4 your Father who sees in secret will reward you. 2
     6: 5 Truly I tell you, they have received their reward. 6
     6: 6 your Father who sees in secret will reward you. 2
     6:16 Truly I tell you, they have received their reward 6
     6:18 your Father who sees in secret will reward you. 2
    10:41 will receive a prophet's reward; 6
    10:41 will receive the reward of the righteous; 6
    10:42 none of these will lose their reward." 6
Mrk 9:41 will by no means lose the reward. 6
Lke 6:23 for surely your reward is great in heaven; 6
     6:35 Your reward will be great 6
Act 1:18 acquired a field with the reward of his wickedness; 6
1Co 3:14 builder will receive a reward. 6
     9:17 For if I do this of my own will, I have a reward; 6
     9:18 What then is my reward? 6
Col 3:24 you will receive the inheritance as your reward; 1
Heb 10:35 confidence of yours; it brings a great reward. 4
    11: 6 he rewards those who seek him. 5
    11:26 he was looking ahead to the reward. 4
2Jn 1: 8 so that you do not lose…but may receive a full reward. 6
Rev 11:18 for rewarding your servants, the prophets 3
    22:12 my reward is with me, to repay according to 6

Rhegium

1. Ῥήγιον, *Rhēgion, 4836*

Act 28:13 we weighed anchor and came to Rhegium. 1

Rhesa

1. Ῥησά, *Rhēsa, 4840*

Lke 3:27 son of Joanan, son of Rhesa 1

Rhoda

1. Ῥόδη, *Rhodē, 4851*

Act 12:13 a maid named Rhoda came to answer. 1

Rhodes

1. Ῥόδος, *Rhodos, 4852*

Act 21: 1 the next day to Rhodes…from there to Patara. 1

rich *See also* make rich

1. Contextual: Not in Greek
2. πιότης, *piotēs, 4404*
3. πλούσιος, *plousios, 4454*
4. πλουτέω, *plouteō, 4456*

Mat 19:24 someone who is rich to enter the kingdom of God." 3
    27:57 there came a rich man from Arimathea 3
Mrk 10:25 who is rich to enter the kingdom of God." 3
Lke 1:53 sent the rich away empty. 4
     6:24 woe to you who are rich 3
    12:16 "The land of a rich man produced abundantly. 3
    12:21 are not rich toward God." 4
    14:12 your brothers or your relatives or rich neighbors 3
    16: 1 "There was a rich man who had a manager 3
    16:19 "There was a rich man 3
    18:23 he became sad; for he was very rich. 3
    18:25 someone who is rich to enter the kingdom of God." 3
    19: 2 he was a chief tax collector and was rich. 3
Rom 11:17 to share the rich root of the olive tree 2
1Co 4: 8 Already you have become rich! 4
2Co 8: 9 that though he was rich, yet for your sakes 3
     8: 9 so that by his poverty you might become rich. 4
Eph 2: 4 God, who is rich in mercy 3
1Ti 6: 9 those who want to be rich fall into temptation 4
     6:10 in their eagerness to be rich some have wandered 1
     6:17 As for those who in the present age are rich 3
     6:18 They are to do good, to be rich in good works 4
Jas 1:10 and the rich in being brought low 3

Jas   1:10   because the rich will disappear like a flower   1
     1:11   the same way with the rich...they will wither away.   3
     2: 5   be rich in faith and to be heirs of the kingdom   3
     2: 6   Is it not the rich who oppress you?   3
Rev   2: 9   "I know...your poverty, even though you are rich.   3
     3:17   For you say, 'I am rich, I have prospered   3
     3:18   buy from me gold...so that you may be rich;   4
     6:15   and the generals and the rich and the powerful   3
     13:16   all, both small and great, both rich and poor   3

grow rich

1. πλουτέω, *plouteō, 4456*

Rev   18: 3   grown rich from the power of her luxury."   1
     18:19   all who had ships at sea grew rich by her wealth!   1

rich man

1. πλούσιος, *plousios, 4454*

Lke   16:21   with what fell from the rich man's table;   1
     16:22   The rich man also died and was buried.   1

rich person

1. πλούσιος, *plousios, 4454*

Mat   19:23   it will be hard for a rich person to enter   1
Mrk   12:41   Many rich people put in large sums.   1
Lke   21: 1   rich people putting their gifts into the treasury;   1
Jas   5: 1   you rich people, weep and wail for the miseries   1

rich variety

1. πολυποίκιλος, *polypoikilos, 4497*

Eph   3:10   the wisdom of God in its rich variety   1

riches

1. Contextual: Not in Greek
2. βίος, *bios, 1050*
3. πλοῦτος, *ploutos, 4458*

Lke   8:14   the cares and riches and pleasures of life   3
     16:11   who will entrust to you the true riches?   1
Rom   2: 4   Or do you despise the riches of his kindness   3
     9:23   in order to make known the riches of his glory   3
     11:12   Now if their stumbling means riches for the world   3
     11:12   if their defeat means riches for Gentiles   3
     11:33   the riches and wisdom and knowledge of God!   3
Eph   1: 7   according to the riches of his grace   3
     1:18   what are the riches of his glorious inheritance   3
     2: 7   might show the immeasurable riches of his grace   3
     3: 8   the news of the boundless riches of Christ   3
     3:16   according to the riches of his glory   3
Php   4:19   according to his riches in glory in Christ   3
Col   1:27   the riches of the glory of this mystery   3
     2: 2   may have all the riches of assured understanding   3
1Ti   6:17   to set their hopes on the uncertainty of riches   3
Jas   5: 2   Your riches have rotted   3
1Jn   2:16   the desire of the eyes, the pride in riches   2

richly

1. πλουσίως, *plousiōs, 4455*

Col   3:16   Let the word of Christ dwell in you richly;   1
1Ti   6:17   richly provides us with everything for our enjoyment.   1
Tit   3: 6   Spirit he poured out on us richly   1
2Pe   1:11   entry into the eternal kingdom...will be richly provided   1

rid

1. ἀποτίθημι, *apotithēmi, 700*

Col   3: 8   now you must get rid of all such things—anger,   1
Jas   1:21   rid yourselves of all sordidness and rank growth   1
1Pe   2: 1   Rid yourselves, therefore, of all malice,   1

ride

1. ἐπιβιβάζω, *epibibazo, 2097*
2. καθίζω, *kathizō, 2767*

Mrk   11: 2   a colt...that has never been ridden;   2
Lke   19:30   a colt...that has never been ridden.   2
Act   23:24   Also provide mounts for Paul to ride   1

ride along

1. πορεύομαι, *poreuomai, 4513*

Lke   19:36   As he rode along   1

rider

1. κάθημαι, *kathēmai, 2764*

Rev   6: 2   I looked...a white horse! Its rider had a bow;   1
     6: 4   its rider was permitted to take peace   1
     6: 5   I looked, and there was a black horse! Its rider   1
     6: 8   a pale green horse! Its rider's name was Death   1
     9:17   the riders wore breastplates the color of fire   1
     19:11   Its rider is called Faithful and True   1
     19:18   to eat...the flesh of horses and their riders   1
     19:19   to make war against the rider on the horse   1
     19:21   the sword of the rider on the horse   1

ridicule

1. ἐκμυκτηρίζω, *ekmyktērizō, 1727*
2. ἐμπαίζω, *empaizo, 1850*

Lke   14:29   all who see it will begin to ridicule him   2
     16:14   they ridiculed him.   1

right[1]   *See also* all right, do right, right *hand*, right *mind*, right *side*, right *time*, set things right

1. ἄξιος, *axios, 545*
2. ἀρεστός, *arestos, 744*
3. δίκαιος, *dikaios, 1465*
4. δικαιοσύνη, *dikaiosynē, 1466*
5. δικαίως, *dikaiōs, 1469*
6. εὐθύς2, *euthys2, 2318*
7. ἴδιος, *idios, 2625*
8. καλός, *kalos, 2819*
9. καλῶς, *kalōs, 2822*
10. ὀρθῶς, *orthōs, 3987*

Mat   20: 4   and I will pay you whatever is right.'   3
Mrk   12:32   the scribe said to him, "You are right, Teacher;   9
Lke   10:28   "You have given the right answer; do this,   10
     12:57   you not judge for yourselves what is right?   3
     20:21   that you are right in what you say and teach   10
Jhn   4:17   "You are right in saying, 'I have no husband';   9
     7:24   judge with right judgment."   3
     8:48   Jews answered him, "Are we not right in saying   9
     13:13   you are right, for that is what I am.   9
Act   4:19   "Whether it is right in God's sight   3
     6: 2   not right that we should neglect the word of God   2
     8:21   your heart is not right before God.   6
     10:35   anyone who fears him and does what is right   4
     28:25   was right in saying to your ancestors   9
Rom   7:18   I can will what is right, but I cannot do it.   8
1Co   15:34   Come to a sober and right mind, and sin no more;   5
2Co   8:21   we intend to do what is right   8
     13: 7   that you may do what is right   8
Gal   6: 9   let us not grow weary in doing what is right   8
Eph   5: 9   found in all that is good and right and true.   4
     6: 1   obey your parents in the Lord, for this is right.   3
Php   1: 7   right for me to think this way about all of you   3
2Th   1: 3   give thanks to God for you,...as is right   1
1Ti   2: 3   This is right and is acceptable   8
     2: 6   this was attested at the right time.   7
     6:15   which he will bring about at the right time   7
1Pe   3:14   even if you do suffer for doing what is right   4
2Pe   1:13   I think it right, as long as I am in this body   3
1Jn   2:29   everyone who does right has been born of him.   4
     3: 7   Everyone who does what is right is righteous   4
     3:10   all who do not do what is right are not from God   4
Rev   22:11   Let...the righteous still do right   4

right[2]

1. δεξιός, *dexios, 1288*

Mat   5:29   If your right eye causes you to sin, tear it out   1
     5:30   if your right hand causes you to sin, cut it off   1
     5:39   anyone strikes you on the right cheek, turn   1
     27:38   one on his right and one on his left.   1
Mrk   15:27   one on his right and one on his left.   1
Lke   6: 6   was a man there whose right hand was withered.   1
     22:50   and cut off his right ear.   1
     23:33   one on his right and one on his left.   1
Jhn   18:10   and cut off his right ear.   1
     21: 6   "Cast the net to the right side of the boat   1
Act   3: 7   he took him by the right hand and raised him up;   1
Rev   1:16   In his right hand he held seven stars   1
     10: 2   Setting his right foot on the sea   1
     10: 5   the angel...raised his right hand to heaven   1

13:16 to be marked on the right hand or the forehead 1

right³

1. Contextual: Not in Greek
2. δεῖ, *dei, 1256*
3. ἐξουσία, *exousia, 2026*
4. ὀφειλή, *opheilē, 4051*

Rom 9:21 Has the potter no right over the clay 3
1Co 7: 3 husband should give to his wife her conjugal rights 4
      9: 4 Do we not have the right to our food and drink? 3
      9: 5 have the right to be accompanied by a believing wife 3
      9: 6 Or is it only Barnabas and I who have no right 3
      9:12 Nevertheless, we have not made use of this right 3
      9:15 I have made no use of any of these rights 1
      9:18 make full use of my rights in the gospel. 3
2Th 3: 9 This was not because we do not have that right 3
Tit 1:11 by teaching...what it is not right to teach. 2
Heb 13:10 who officiate in the tent have no right to eat. 3
Rev 22:14 they will have the right to the tree of life 3

right⁴

1. ἕως + ἔσω, *heōs + esō, 2401 + 2276*

Mrk 14:54 right into the courtyard of the high priest; 1

right thing

1. καλός, *kalos, 2819*

Jas 4:17 knows the right thing to do and fails to do it 1

righteous   See also righteous *judgment*

1. δίκαιος, *dikaios, 1465*
2. εὐθύτης, *euthytēs, 2319*

Mat 5:45 sends rain on the righteous and on the unrighteous. 1
      9:13 come to call not the righteous but sinners." 1
   10:41 will receive the reward of the righteous; 1
   13:43 Then the righteous will shine like the sun 1
   13:49 and separate the evil from the righteous 1
   23:28 you also on the outside look righteous to others 1
   23:29 decorate the graves of the righteous 1
   23:35 all the righteous blood shed on earth 1
   23:35 from the blood of righteous Abel 1
   25:37 Then the righteous will answer him 1
   25:46 but the righteous into eternal life." 1
Mrk 2:17 I have come to call not the righteous but sinners." 1
      6:20 knowing that he was a righteous and holy man 1
Lke 1: 6 Both of them were righteous before God 1
      1:17 the disobedient to the wisdom of the righteous 1
      2:25 this man was righteous and devout 1
      5:32 I have come to call not the righteous but sinners 1
   14:14 repaid at the resurrection of the righteous." 1
   18: 9 trusted in themselves that they were righteous 1
   23:50 there was a good and righteous man named Joseph 1
Jhn 17:25 "Righteous Father, the world does not know you 1
Act 24:15 resurrection of both the righteous and the unrighteous. 1
Rom 1:17 "The one who is righteous will live by faith." 1
      2:13 it is not the hearers of the law who are righteous 1
      3:10 "There is no one who is righteous, not even one; 1
      3:26 it was to prove...that he himself is righteous 1
      5:19 by the one man's...many will be made righteous. 1
Gal 3:11 "The one who is righteous will live by faith." 1
2Th 1: 5 is evidence of the righteous judgment of God 1
2Ti 4: 8 which the Lord, the righteous judge, will give 1
Heb 1: 8 the righteous scepter is the scepter of your kingdom. 2
   11: 4 he received approval as righteous 1
  12:23 to the spirits of the righteous made perfect 1
Jas 5:16 The prayer of the righteous is powerful 1
1Pe 3:12 For the eyes of the Lord are on the righteous 1
      3:18 the righteous for the unrighteous 1
      4:18 "If it is hard for the righteous to be saved 1
2Pe 2: 8 day after day, was tormented in his righteous soul 1
1Jn 2: 1 an advocate...Jesus Christ the righteous; 1
      2:29 If you know that he is righteous, you may be sure 1
      3: 7 who does what is right is righteous, just as he is righteous. 1
      3: 7 who does what is right is righteous, just as he is righteous. 1
      3:12 deeds were evil and his brother's righteous. 1
Rev 22:11 Let...the righteous still do right 1

righteous deed

1. δικαίωμα, *dikaiōma, 1468*

Rev 19: 8 fine linen is the righteous deeds of the saints. 1

righteous man

1. δίκαιος, *dikaios, 1465*

Mat 1:19 husband Joseph, being a righteous man and unwilling 1
2Pe 2: 7 and if he recused Lot, a righteous man 1
      2: 8 (for that righteous man...was tormented 1

righteous one

1. δίκαιος, *dikaios, 1465*

Act 3:14 you rejected the Holy and Righteous One 1
      7:52 the coming of the Righteous One 1
   22:14 see the Righteous One and to hear his own voice; 1
Heb 10:38 my righteous one will live by faith. 1
Jas 5: 6 condemned and murdered the righteous one 1

righteous person

1. δίκαιος, *dikaios, 1465*

Mat 10:41 whoever welcomes a righteous person 1
   10:41 in the name of a righteous person 1
   13:17 I tell you, many prophets and righteous people 1
Lke 15: 7 than over ninety-nine righteous persons 1
Rom 5: 7 rarely will anyone die for a righteous person 1

righteousness   See also act of righteousness

1. δικαιοσύνη, *dikaiosynē, 1466*

Mat 3:15 proper for us in this way to fulfill all righteousness." 1
      5: 6 those who hunger and thirst for righteousness 1
      5:10 those who are persecuted for righteousness' sake 1
      5:20 tell you, unless your righteousness exceeds 1
      6:33 first for the kingdom of God and his righteousness 1
   21:32 For John came to you in the way of righteousness 1
Lke 1:75 in holiness and righteousness before him 1
Jhn 16: 8 about sin and righteousness and judgment: 1
   16:10 about righteousness, because I am going 1
Act 13:10 you enemy of all righteousness 1
   17:31 will have the world judged in righteousness 1
Rom 1:17 For in it the righteousness of God is revealed 1
      3:21 the righteousness of God has been disclosed 1
      3:22 the righteousness of God through faith in Jesus 1
      3:25 He did this to show his righteousness 1
      4: 3 and it was reckoned to him as righteousness." 1
      4: 5 such faith is reckoned as righteousness. 1
      4: 6 those to whom God reckons righteousness 1
      4: 9 "Faith was reckoned to Abraham as righteousness." 1
      4:11 righteousness that he had by faith 1
      4:11 who thus have righteousness reckoned to them 1
      4:13 but through the righteousness of faith. 1
      4:22 his faith "was reckoned to him as righteousness." 1
      5:17 who receive...the free gift of righteousness 1
      6:13 members to God as instruments of righteousness. 1
      6:16 or of obedience, which leads to righteousness? 1
      6:18 have become slaves of righteousness. 1
      6:19 present your members as slaves to righteousness 1
      6:20 you were free in regard to righteousness. 1
      8:10 the Spirit is life because of righteousness. 1
      9:30 Gentiles, who did not strive for righteousness 1
      9:30 attained it...righteousness through faith; 1
      9:31 but Israel, who did strive for the righteousness 1
   10: 3 the righteousness that comes from God 1
   10: 3 they have not submitted to God's righteousness. 1
   10: 4 may be righteousness for everyone who believes. 1
   10: 5 righteousness that comes from the law 1
   10: 6 But the righteousness that comes from faith says 1
   14:17 kingdom of God is...righteousness and peace 1
1Co 1:30 who became for us wisdom from God, and righteousness 1
2Co 5:21 in him we might become the righteousness of God. 1
      6: 7 with the weapons of righteousness 1
      6:14 between righteousness and lawlessness? 1
      9: 9 his righteousness endures forever." 1
      9:10 increase the harvest of your righteousness. 1
   11:15 as ministers of righteousness. 1
Gal 3: 6 it was reckoned to him as righteousness," 1
      3:21 righteousness would indeed come through the law. 1
      5: 5 we eagerly wait for the hope of righteousness. 1
Eph 4:24 in true righteousness and holiness. 1
      6:14 put on the breastplate of righteousness. 1
Php 1:11 produced the harvest of righteousness 1
      3: 6 as to righteousness under the law, blameless. 1
      3: 9 righteousness of my own that comes from the law 1
      3: 9 the righteousness from God based on faith. 1
1Ti 6:11 pursue righteousness, godliness, faith, love 1

2Ti	2:22	pursue righteousness, faith, love, and peace	1
	3:16	useful...for training in righteousness	1
	4: 8	is reserved for me the crown of righteousness	1
Tit	3: 5	not because of any works of righteousness	1
Heb	1: 9	You have loved righteousness and hated wickedness;	1
	5:13	is unskilled in the word of righteousness.	1
	7: 2	His name...means "king of righteousness"	1
	11: 7	the righteousness that is in accordance with faith.	1
	12:11	it yields the peaceful fruit of righteousness	1
Jas	1:20	your anger does not produce God's righteousness.	1
	2:23	and it was reckoned to him as righteousness,"	1
	3:18	a harvest of righteousness is sown in peace	1
1Pe	2:24	free from sins, we might live for righteousness;	1
2Pe	1: 1	the righteousness of our God and Savior Jesus	1
	2: 5	saved Noah, a herald of righteousness	1
	2:21	to have known the way of righteousness	1
	3:13	and a new earth, where righteousness is at home.	1
Rev	19:11	and in righteousness he judges and makes war.	1

rightful   *See* rightful *claim*

rightly   *See also* explain rightly

   1. καλῶς, *kalōs, 2822*
   2. ὀρθῶς, *orthōs, 3987*

Mat	15: 7	"You hypocrites! Isaiah prophesied rightly about you	1
Mrk	7: 6	"Isaiah prophesied rightly about you hypocrites	1
Lke	7:43	Jesus said to him, "You have judged rightly."	2
Jhn	18:23	if I have spoken rightly, why do you strike me?"	1

rigid

   1. ξηραίνω, *xēraiṇō, 3830*

Mrk	9:18	he foams and grinds his teeth and becomes rigid;	1

ring

   1. δακτύλιος, *daktylios, 1234*

Lke	15:22	put a ring on his finger and sandals on his feet.	1

gold ring

   1. χρυσοδακτύλιος, *chrysodaktylios, 5993*

Jas	2: 2	For if a person with gold rings and in fine clothes	1

ringleader

   1. πρωτοστάτης, *prōtostatēs, 4756*

Act	24: 5	a ringleader of the sect of the Nazarenes.	1

riot

   1. ἀκαταστασία, *akatastasia, 189*
   2. θόρυβος, *thorybos, 2573*
   3. στάσις, *stasis, 5087*

Mat	26: 5	or there may be a riot among the people."	2
	27:24	rather that a riot was beginning	2
Mrk	14: 2	or there may be a riot among the people."	2
Act	19:40	we are in danger of being charged with rioting today	3
2Co	6: 5	beatings, imprisonments, riots, labors	1

ripe

   1. ἀκμάζω, *akmazō, 196*
   2. λευκός, *leukos, 3328*
   3. παραδίδωμι, *paradidōmi, 4140*

Mrk	4:29	when the grain is ripe	3
Jhn	4:35	see how the fields are ripe for harvesting.	2
Rev	14:18	gather the clusters...for its grapes are ripe."	1

fully ripe

   1. ξηραίνω, *xēraiṇō, 3830*

Rev	14:15	because the harvest of the earth is fully ripe."	1

rise

   1. ἀναβαίνω, *anabaiṇō, 326*
   2. ἀνάστασις, *anastasis, 414*
   3. ἀνατέλλω, *anatellō, 422*
   4. ἀνατολή, *anatolē, 424*
   5. ἀνίστημι, *anistēmi, 482*
   6. ἐγείρω, *egeirō, 1586*

Mat	2: 2	For we observed his star at its rising,	4
	2: 9	went the star that they had seen at its rising	4
	13: 6	when the sun rose, they were scorched;	3
	24: 7	For nation will rise against nation	6

Mrk	4: 6	when the sun rose, it was scorched;	3
	4:27	sleep and rise night and day	6
	9: 9	until after the Son of Man had risen	5
	9:10	what this rising from the dead could mean.	5
	12:25	For when they rise from the dead	5
	13: 8	For nation will rise against nation	6
	16: 2	when the sun had risen, they went to the tomb.	3
	16: 9	⟦after he rose early on the first day of the week⟧	5
	16:14	⟦those who saw him after he had risen.⟧	6
Lke	2:34	the falling and the rising of many in Israel	2
	7:14	he said, "Young man, I say to you, rise!"	6
	7:16	"A great prophet has risen among us!"	6
	11:31	The queen of the South will rise at the judgment	6
	12:54	"When you see a cloud rising in the west	3
	16:31	if someone rises from the dead.' "	5
	21:10	he said to them, "Nation will rise against nation	6
	23: 1	Then the assembly rose as a body	5
	24: 5	He is not here, but has risen.	5
	24:34	They were saying, "The Lord has risen indeed	6
	24:46	rise from the dead on the third day	5
Jhn	14:31	Rise, let us be on our way.	6
	20: 9	the scripture, that he must rise from the dead.	5
Act	10:41	after he rose from the dead.	5
	17: 3	necessary for the Messiah to suffer and to rise	5
	26:23	by being the first to rise from the dead	2
Rom	15:12	the one who rises to rule the Gentiles;	5
Eph	5:14	it says, "Sleeper, awake! Rise from the dead	5
1Th	4:16	the dead in Christ will rise first.	5
Jas	1:11	For the sun rises with its scorching heat	3
2Pe	1:19	until the day dawns and the morning star rises	3
Rev	7: 2	I saw another angel ascending from the rising...sun	4
	8: 4	the smoke...with the prayers of the saints, rose	1
	9: 2	and from the shaft rose smoke like the smoke	1
	13: 1	I saw a beast rising out of the sea	1
	13:11	I saw another beast that rose out of the earth;	1

make rise

   1. ἀνατέλλω, *anatellō, 422*

Mat	5:45	he makes his sun rise on the evil and on the good	1

rise again

   1. ἀνίστημι, *anistēmi, 482*
   2. ἐγείρω, *egeirō, 1586*

Mat	27:63	'After three days I will rise again.'	2
Mrk	8:31	be killed, and after three days rise again.	1
	9:31	three days after being killed, he will rise again."	1
	10:34	after three days he will rise again."	1
Lke	18:33	on the third day he will rise again."	1
	24: 7	crucified, and on the third day rise again."	1
Jhn	11:23	Jesus said to her, "Your brother will rise again."	1
	11:24	said to him, "I know that he will rise again	1
1Th	4:14	since we believe that Jesus died and rose again	1

rise against

   1. ἐπανίστημι, *epanistēmi, 2060*

Mat	10:21	children will rise against parents	1
Mrk	13:12	children will rise against parents	1

rise up

   1. ἀνίστημι, *anistēmi, 482*
   2. ἐγείρω, *egeirō, 1586*

Mat	12:41	The people of Nineveh will rise up at the judgment	1
	12:42	The queen of the South will rise up at the judgment	2
Mrk	3:26	if Satan has risen up against himself	1
Lke	11:32	people of Nineveh will rise up at the judgment	1
Act	5:36	For some time ago Theudas rose up	1
	5:37	After him Judas the Galilean rose up	1
1Co	10: 7	sat down to eat and drink, and they rose up to play."	1

risk

   1. παραβολεύομαι, *paraboleuomai, 4129*
   2. παραδίδωμι, *paradidōmi, 4140*
   3. ὑποτίθημι, *hypotithēmi, 5719*

Act	15:26	who have risked their lives	2
Rom	16: 4	who risked their necks for my life	3
Php	2:30	risking his life to make up for those services	1

rite *See also* complete the rite of purification, go through rite of purification

1. Contextual: Not in Greek

Jhn	2: 6	water jars...for the Jewish rites of purification	1
Heb	9:23	to be purified with these rites	1

ritual *See* ritual *defilement*, ritual *duty*

rivalry

1. ἔρις, *eris, 2251*

Php	1:15	Some proclaim Christ from envy and rivalry	1

river

1. ποταμός, *potamos, 4532*

Mat	3: 6	they were baptized by him in the river Jordan	1
Mrk	1: 5	and were baptized by him in the river Jordan	1
Lke	6:48	the river burst against that house	1
	6:49	a house...the river burst against it	1
Jhn	7:38	shall flow rivers of living water.' "	1
Act	16:13	we went outside the gate by the river	1
2Co	11:26	on frequent journeys, in danger from rivers	1
Rev	8:10	star fell...and it fell on a third of the rivers	1
	9:14	angels...bound at the great river Euphrates."	1
	12:15	the serpent poured water like a river	1
	12:16	it opened its mouth and swallowed the river	1
	16: 4	The third angel poured his bowl into the rivers	1
	16:12	angel poured his bowl on the great river Euphrates	1
	22: 1	angel showed me the river of the water of life	1
	22: 2	On either side of the river is the tree	1

road

1. Contextual: Not in Greek
2. ὁδός, *hodos, 3847*

Mat	2:12	left for their own country by another road.	2
	4:15	land of Naphtali, on the road by the sea	2
	7:13	for the gate is wide and the road is easy	2
	7:14	For the gate is narrow and the road is hard	2
	21: 8	large crowd spread their cloaks on the road	2
	21: 8	and spread them on the road.	2
	21:19	seeing a fig tree by the side of the road,	2
Mrk	10:32	They were on the road, going up to Jerusalem	2
	11: 8	Many people spread their cloaks on the road	2
Lke	9:57	As they were going along the road, someone said	2
	10: 4	greet no one on the road.	2
	10:31	Now by chance a priest was going down that road;	2
	14:23	'Go out into the roads and lanes	2
	19:36	people kept spreading their cloaks on the road.	2
	24:32	while he was talking to us on the road	2
	24:35	Then they told what had happened on the road	2
Act	8:26	the road that goes down from Jerusalem to Gaza."	2
	8:26	(This is a wilderness road.)	1
	8:36	As they were going along the road	2
	9:27	described...how on the road he had seen the Lord	2
	26:13	at midday along the road...I saw a light	2
Jas	2:25	when she...sent them out by another road?	2
2Pe	2:15	They have left the straight road and have gone astray	2
	2:15	following the road of Balaam	2

roadside

1. ὁδός, *hodos, 3847*

Mat	20:30	There were two blind men sitting by the roadside.	1
Mrk	10:46	Bartimaeus...was sitting by the roadside.	1
Lke	18:35	a blind man was sitting by the roadside begging.	1

roar

1. ἦχος2, *ēchos2, 2492*
2. μυκάομαι, *mykaomai, 3681*
3. ὠρύομαι, *ōryomai, 6054*

Lke	21:25	confused by the roaring of the sea	1
1Pe	5: 8	Like a roaring lion your adversary the devil prowls	3
Rev	10: 3	gave a great shout, like a lion roaring.	2

rob

1. συλάω, *sylaō, 5195*

2Co	11: 8	I robbed other churches by accepting support	1

rob a temple

1. ἱεροσυλέω, *hierosyleō, 2644*

Rom	2:22	You that abhor idols, do you rob temples?	1

robber

1. ἅρπαξ, *harpax, 774*
2. λῃστής, *lēstēs, 3334*

Mat	21:13	but you are making it a den of robbers."	2
Mrk	11:17	you have made it a den of robbers."	2
Lke	10:30	fell into the hands of robbers	2
	10:36	who fell into the hands of the robbers?"	2
	19:46	you have made it a den of robbers."	2
1Co	5:10	the greedy and robbers, or idolaters	1
	5:11	is an idolater, reviler, drunkard, or robber	1
	6:10	drunkards, revilers, robbers	1

temple robber

1. ἱερόσυλος, *hierosylos, 2645*

Act	19:37	neither temple robbers nor blasphemers	1

robe *See also* soft robe

1. ἔνδυμα, *endyma, 1903*
2. ἐνδύω, *endyō, 1907*
3. ἐσθής, *esthēs, 2264*
4. ἱμάτιον, *himation, 2668*
5. περιβάλλω + στολή, *periballō + stolē, 4314 + 5124*
6. στολή, *stolē, 5124*
7. χλαμύς, *chlamys, 5948*

Mat	22:11	a man there who was not wearing a wedding robe	1
	22:12	how did you get in here without a wedding robe?'	1
	27:28	They stripped him and put a scarlet robe on him	7
	27:31	they stripped him of the robe	7
Mrk	16: 5	they saw a young man, dressed in a white robe	6
Lke	7:25	Someone dressed in soft robes?	4
	15:22	'Quickly, bring out a robe—the best one—	6
	23:11	then he put an elegant robe on him	3
Jhn	13:12	After he...had put on his robe,	4
	19: 2	and they dressed him in a purple robe.	4
	19: 5	the crown of thorns and the purple robe.	4
Act	1:10	suddenly two men in white robes stood by them.	3
	12:21	On an appointed day Herod put on his royal robes	3
Rev	3: 5	will be clothed like them in white robes	4
	3:18	and white robes to clothe you	4
	4: 4	elders, dressed in white robes, with golden	4
	6:11	They were each given a white robe and told	6
	7: 9	robed in white, with palm branches	5
	7:13	"Who are these, robed in white	5
	7:14	they have washed their robes and made them white	6
	15: 6	seven angels...robed in pure bright linen	2
	19:13	He is clothed in a robe dipped in blood	4
	19:16	On his robe and on his thigh he has a name	4
	22:14	Blessed are those who wash their robes	6

long robe

1. ποδήρης, *podērēs, 4468*
2. στολή, *stolē, 5124*

Mrk	12:38	who like to walk around in long robes	2
Lke	20:46	the scribes, who like to walk around in long robes	2
Rev	1:13	clothed with a long robe and with a golden sash	1

outer robe

1. ἱμάτιον, *himation, 2668*

Jhn	13: 4	got up from the table, took off his outer robe	1

rock

1. πέτρα, *petra, 4376*
2. τραχύς, *trachys, 5550*

Mat	7:24	like a wise man who built his house on rock.	1
	7:25	because it had been founded on rock.	1
	16:18	on this rock I will build my church	1
	27:51	The earth shook, and the rocks were split.	1
	27:60	his own new tomb, which he had hewn in the rock.	1
Mrk	15:46	a tomb that had been hewn out of the rock.	1
Lke	6:48	who dug deeply and laid the foundation on rock;	1
	8: 6	Some fell on the rock;	1
	8:13	The ones on the rock	1
Act	27:29	Fearing that we might run on the rocks	2
Rom	9:33	make people stumble, a rock that will make them fall	1
1Co	10: 4	they drank from the spiritual rock	1
	10: 4	the rock was Christ.	1
1Pe	2: 8	a rock that makes them fall."	1
Rev	6:15	hid...among the rocks of the mountains	1
	6:16	calling to the mountains and rocks, "Fall on us	1

rock-hewn
   1. λαξευτός, *laxeutos, 3292*
Lke 23:53 and laid it in a rock-hewn tomb   1

rocky   *See* rocky ground

rod   *See also* beat with a rod
   1. κάλαμος, *kalamos, 2812*
   2. ῥάβδος, *rhabdos, 4811*
Heb 9: 4 Aaron's rod that budded   2
Rev 2:27 to rule them with an iron rod   2
    12: 5 who is to rule all the nations with a rod of iron   2
    19:15 and he will rule them with a rod of iron;   2
    21:15 angel who talked to me had a measuring rod of gold   1
    21:16 and he measured the city with his rod   1

measuring rod
   1. κάλαμος, *kalamos, 2812*
Rev 11: 1 Then I was given a measuring rod like a staff   1

rogue
   1. ἄδικος, *adikos, 96*
Lke 18:11 thieves, rogues, adulterers   1

roll
   1. προσκυλίω, *proskyliō, 4685*
Mat 27:60 rolled a great stone to the door of the tomb   1
Mrk 15:46 rolled a stone against the door of the tomb.   1

roll about
   1. κυλίω, *kyliō, 3244*
Mrk 9:20 he fell on the ground and rolled about   1

roll away
   1. ἀποκυλίω, *apokyliō, 653*
Mrk 16: 3 "Who will roll away the stone for us   1
Lke 24: 2 They found the stone rolled away from the tomb   1

roll back
   1. ἀποκυλίω, *apokyliō, 653*
Mat 28: 2 came and rolled back the stone and sat on it.   1
Mrk 16: 4 that the stone…had already been rolled back.   1

roll up
   1. ἑλίσσω, *helissō, 1813*
   2. ἐντυλίσσω, *entylissō, 1962*
   3. πτύσσω, *ptyssō, 4771*
Lke 4:20 he rolled up the scroll, gave it back   3
Jhn 20: 7 and the cloth…rolled up in a place by itself.   2
Heb 1:12 like a cloak you will roll them up   1
Rev 6:14 The sky vanished like a scroll rolling itself up   1

Roman   *See also* Roman *citizen*, Roman *colony*
   1. Contextual: Not in Greek
   2. Ῥωμαῖος, *Rhōmaios, 4871*
Jhn 11:48 the Romans will come and destroy   2
Act 16:21 not lawful for us as Romans to adopt or observe."   2
    25:16 not the custom of the Romans to hand over anyone   2
    28:17 in Jerusalem and handed over to the Romans.   2
    28:18 the Romans wanted to release me   2

Rome
   1. Ῥωμαῖος, *Rhōmaios, 4871*
   2. Ῥώμη, *Rhōmē, 4873*
Act 2:10 visitors from Rome, both Jews and proselytes   1
    18: 2 Claudius had ordered all Jews to leave Rome   2
    19:21 "After I have gone there, I must also see Rome."   2
    23:11 so you must bear witness also in Rome."   2
    28:14 so we came to Rome.   2
    28:16 When we came into Rome   2
Rom 1: 7 To all God's beloved in Rome   2
    1:15 proclaim the gospel to you also who are in Rome.   2
2Ti 1:17 when he arrived in Rome, he eagerly searched for me   2

roof
   1. δῶμα, *dōma, 1560*
   2. στέγη, *stegē, 5094*
Mat 8: 8 I am not worthy to have you come under my roof;   2

Mrk 2: 4 they removed the roof above him;   2
Lke 5:19 they went up on the roof   1
    7: 6 am not worthy to have you come under my roof;   2
Act 10: 9 Peter went up on the roof to pray.   1

room[1]   *See also* make room
   1. ταμεῖον, *tameion, 5421*
Mat 6: 6 whenever you pray, go into your room and shut the door   1

room[2]
   1. τόπος, *topos, 5536*
   2. χωρέω, *chōreō, 6003*
Mrk 2: 2 that there was no longer room for them   2
Lke 14:22 there is still room.'   1
Rom 12:19 but leave room for the wrath of God;   1
Eph 4:27 do not make room for the devil.   1

guest room
   1. κατάλυμα, *katalyma, 2906*
   2. ξενία, *xenia, 3825*
Mrk 14:14 'The Teacher asks, Where is my guest room   1
Lke 22:11 "Where is the guest room   1
Phm 1:22 One thing more—prepare a guest room for me   2

inner room
   1. ταμεῖον, *tameion, 5421*
Mat 24:26 If they say, 'Look! He is in the inner rooms,'   1

room upstairs
   1. ἀνάγαιον, *anagaion, 333*
   2. ὑπερῷον, *hyperōon, 5673*
Mrk 14:15 He will show you a large room upstairs   1
Lke 22:12 show you a large room upstairs, already furnished.   1
Act 1:13 they went to the room upstairs   2
    9:37 they laid her in a room upstairs.   2
    9:39 when he arrived, they took him to the room upstairs.   2
    20: 8 There were many lamps in the room upstairs   2

root
   1. ῥίζα, *rhiza, 4844*
   2. ῥιζόω, *rhizoō, 4845*
Mat 3:10 Even now the ax is lying at the root of the trees;   1
    13: 6 since they had no root, they withered away.   1
    13:21 yet such a person has no root   1
Mrk 4: 6 since it had no root, it withered away.   1
    4:17 they have no root, and endure only   1
    11:20 they saw the fig tree withered away to its roots.   1
Lke 3: 9 Even now the ax is lying at the root of the trees;   1
    8:13 But these have no root;   1
Rom 11:16 if the root is holy, then the branches also are   1
    11:17 to share the rich root of the olive tree   1
    11:18 remember that it is not you that support the root   1
    11:18 but the root that supports you.   1
    15:12 again Isaiah says, "The root of Jesse shall come   1
Eph 3:17 being rooted and grounded in love.   2
Col 2: 7 rooted and built up in him   2
1Ti 6:10 the love of money is a root of all kinds of evil   1
Heb 12:15 no root of bitterness springs up   1
Rev 5: 5 the Lion…the Root of David, has conquered   1
    22:16 I am the root and the descendant of David   1

root out utterly
   1. ἐξολεθρεύω, *exolethreuō, 2017*
Act 3:23 will be utterly rooted out of the people.'   1

rope
   1. ζευκτηρία, *zeuktēria, 2415*
   2. σχοινίον, *schoinion, 5389*
Act 27:32 Then the soldiers cut away the ropes of the boat   2
    27:40 loosened the ropes that tied the steering-oars;   1

rot
   1. σήπω, *sēpō, 4960*
Jas 5: 2 Your riches have rotted   1

rough
   1. διεγείρω, *diegeirō, 1444*
   2. τραχύς, *trachys, 5550*
Lke 3: 5 the rough ways made smooth;   2

Jhn   6:18   The sea became rough because a strong wind was   1

row

   1. ἐλαύνω, *elaunō, 1785*

Jhn   6:19   When they had rowed about three or four miles   1

royal   *See also* royal *official,* royal *power*

   1. βασίλειος, *basileios, 994*
   2. βασιλεύς, *basileus, 995*
   3. βασιλικός, *basilikos, 997*

Mat 11: 8   those who wear soft robes are in royal palaces.   2
Lke   7:25   live in luxury are in royal palaces.   1
Act 12:21   On an appointed day Herod put on his royal robes   3
Jas   2: 8   You do well if you really fulfill the royal law   3
1Pe   2: 9   you are a chosen race, a royal priesthood   1

rub

   1. ψώχω, *psōchō, 6041*

Lke   6: 1   rubbed them in their hands   1

rubbish

   1. περικάθαρμα, *perikatharma, 4326*
   2. σκύβαλον, *skybalon, 5032*

1Co   4:13   We have become...like the rubbish of the world   1
Php   3: 8   loss of all things, and I regard them as rubbish   2

rudder

   1. πηδάλιον, *pēdalion, 4382*

Jas   3: 4   they are guided by a very small rudder   1

rude

   1. ἀσχημονέω, *aschēmoneō, 858*

1Co 13: 5   or rude. It does not insist on its own way;   1

rue

   1. πήγανον, *pēganon, 4379*

Lke 11:42   you tithe mint and rue and herbs of all kinds   1

ruffian

   1. πονηρός, *ponēros, 4505*

Act 17: 5   help of some ruffians in the marketplaces   1

Rufus

   1. Ῥοῦφος, *Rhouphos, 4859*

Mrk 15:21   the father of Alexander and Rufus.   1
Rom 16:13   Greet Rufus, chosen in the Lord;   1

ruin   *See also* cause ruin

   1. καταστροφή, *katastrophē, 2953*
   2. ὄλεθρος, *olethros, 3897*
   3. ῥῆγμα, *rhēgma, 4837*
   4. σύντριμμα, *syntrimma, 5342*
   5. φθείρω, *phtheirō, 5780*

Lke   6:49   great was the ruin of that house."   3
Rom   3:16   ruin and misery are in their paths   4
1Co 15:33   "Bad company ruins good morals."   5
1Ti   6: 9   plunge people into ruin and destruction.   2
2Ti   2:14   does no good but only ruins those who are listening.   1

ruins

   1. κατασκάπτω, *kataskaptō, 2940*

Act 15:16   its ruins I will rebuild it, and I will set it up   1

rule¹

   1. ἀνίστημι, *anistēmi, 482*
   2. ἀρχή, *archē, 794*
   3. ἄρχω, *archō, 806*
   4. βασιλεία + ἔχω, *basileia + echō, 993 + 2400*
   5. βασιλεύω, *basileuō, 996*
   6. βραβεύω, *brabeuō, 1093*
   7. γίνομαι, *ginomai, 1181*
   8. κάθημαι, *kathēmai, 2764*
   9. ποιμαίνω, *poimainō, 4477*
   10. προΐστημι, *proistēmi, 4613*

Mat   2:22   he heard that Archelaus was ruling over Judea   5
Lke 19:14   'We do not want this man to rule over us.'   5
     19:19   'And you, rule over five cities.'   7
Act   7:18   king who had not known Joseph ruled over Egypt.   1

Rom 15:12   the one who rises to rule the Gentiles;   3
Eph   1:21   far above all rule and authority and power   2
Col   3:15   let the peace of Christ rule in your hearts   6
1Ti   5:17   the elders who rule well   10
Rev   2:27   to rule them with an iron rod   9
     12: 5   who is to rule all the nations with a rod of iron   9
     17:18   that rules over the kings of the earth."   4
     18: 7   'I rule as a queen; I am no widow   8
     19:15   and he will rule them with a rod of iron;   9

rule²

   1. διατάσσω, *diatassō, 1411*
   2. κανών, *kanōn, 2834*

1Co   7:17   This is my rule in all the churches.   1
Gal   6:16   who will follow this rule—peace be upon them   2

according to the rules

   1. νομίμως, *nomimōs, 3789*

2Ti   2: 5   without competing according to the rules.   1

ruler

   1. ἀρχή, *archē, 794*
   2. ἄρχω, *archō, 806*
   3. ἄρχων, *archōn, 807*
   4. ἡγεμών, *hēgemōn, 2450*
   5. ἡγέομαι, *hēgeomai, 2451*
   6. τετραρχέω, *tetrarcheō, 5489*
   7. τετράρχης, *tetrarchēs, 5490*

Mat   2: 6   are by no means least among the rulers of Judah;   4
     2: 6   from you shall come a ruler who is to shepherd my   5
     9:34   "By the ruler of the demons he casts out demons."   3
     12:24   "It is only by Beelzebul, the ruler of the demons   3
     14: 1   At that time Herod the ruler heard   7
     20:25   the rulers of the Gentiles lord it over them   3
Mrk   3:22   by the ruler of the demons he casts out demons."   3
     10:42   recognize as their rulers lord it over them   2
Lke   3: 1   Herod was ruler of Galilee   6
     3: 1   Philip ruler of the region of Ituraea   6
     3: 1   Lysanias ruler of Abilene   6
     3:19   Herod the ruler, who had been rebuked by him   7
     9: 7   Now Herod the ruler heard about all that   7
     11:15   by Beelzebul, the ruler of the demons."   3
     12:11   bring you before the synagogues, the rulers   1
     18:18   A certain ruler asked him, "Good Teacher,   3
Jhn   12:31   now the ruler of this world will be driven out.   3
     14:30   the ruler of this world is coming.   3
     16:11   the ruler of this world has been condemned.   3
Act   3:17   you acted in ignorance, as did also your rulers.   3
     4: 5   their rulers, elders, and scribes   3
     4: 8   "Rulers of the people and elders   3
     4:26   the rulers have gathered together   3
     7:10   who appointed him ruler over Egypt   5
     7:27   'Who made you a ruler and a judge over us?   3
     7:35   'Who made you a ruler and a judge?'   3
     7:35   God now sent as both ruler and liberator   3
     13: 1   a member of the court of Herod the ruler   7
     14: 5   both Gentiles and Jews, with their rulers   3
Rom   8:38   nor rulers, nor things present   1
     13: 3   For rulers are not a terror to good conduct   3
1Co   2: 6   rulers of this age, who are doomed to perish.   3
     2: 8   None of the rulers of this age understood this;   3
     15:24   after he has destroyed every ruler   1
Eph   2: 2   following the ruler of the power of the air   3
     3:10   made known to the rulers and authorities   1
     6:12   against the rulers, against the authorities   1
Col   1:16   thrones or dominions or rulers   1
     2:10   the head of every ruler and authority.   1
     2:15   He disarmed the rulers and authorities   1
Tit   3: 1   to be subject to rulers and authorities   1
Rev   1: 5   Jesus Christ...the ruler of the kings of the earth.   3

rumbling

   1. φωνή, *phōnē, 5889*

Rev   4: 5   Coming...rumblings and peals of thunder   1
     8: 5   there were peals of thunder, rumblings, flashes   1
     11:19   flashes of lightning, rumblings, peals of thunder   1
     16:18   flashes of lightning, rumblings, peals of thunder   1

rumor

   1. ἀκοή, *akoē, 198*

2. λόγος, *logos, 3364*

Mat 24: 6 you will hear of wars and rumors of wars;   1
Mrk 13: 7 When you hear of wars and rumors of wars   1
Jhn 21:23 So the rumor spread in the community   2

run *See* come running together

1. ἐκπίπτω, *ekpiptō, 1738*
2. τρέχω, *trechō, 5556*
3. φεύγω, *pheugō, 5771*

Mat 27:48 At once one of them ran and got a sponge   2
   28: 8 ran to tell his disciples.   2
Mrk 5: 6 saw Jesus from a distance, he ran and bowed down   2
  15:36 someone ran, filled a sponge with sour wine   2
Lke 15:20 ran and put his arms around him and kissed him.   2
  24:12 Peter got up and ran to the tomb   2
Jhn 10: 5 they will run from him   3
  20: 2 she ran and went to Simon Peter   2
  20: 4 The two were running together   2
Act 27:17 then, fearing that they would run on the Syrtis   1
  27:29 Fearing that we might run on the rocks   1
1Co 9:24 Run in such a way that you may win it.   2
  9:26 So I do not run aimlessly   2
Gal 2: 2 that I was not running, or had not run, in vain.   2
  2: 2 that I was not running, or had not run, in vain.   2
  5: 7 You were running well;   2
Php 2:16 I did not run in vain or labor in vain.   2
Heb 12: 1 let us run with perseverance the race   2

run aground

1. ἐκπίπτω, *ekpiptō, 1738*
2. ἐπικέλλω, *epikellō, 2131*

Act 27:26 we will have to run aground on some island."   1
  27:41 striking a reef, they ran the ship aground;   2

run ahead

1. προτρέχω, *protrechō, 4731*

Lke 19: 4 So he ran ahead   1

run ashore

1. ἐξωθέω, *exōtheō, 2034*

Act 27:39 planned to run the ship ashore, if they could.   1

run away

1. Contextual: Not in Greek
2. φεύγω, *pheugō, 5771*

Jhn 10:12 leaves the sheep and runs away   2
  10:13 The hired hand runs away because a hired hand   1

run down

1. κατατρέχω, *katatrechō, 2963*

Act 21:32 and ran down to them.   1

run forward

1. προστρέχω, *prostrechō, 4708*

Mrk 9:15 with awe, and they ran forward to greet him.   1

run in

1. εἰστρέχω, *eistrechō, 1661*

Act 12:14 instead of opening the gate, she ran in   1

run off

1. φεύγω, *pheugō, 5771*

Mat 8:33 The swineherds ran off, and on going into the town   1
Mrk 5:14 The swineherds ran off and told it   1
  14:52 he left the linen cloth and ran off naked.   1
Lke 8:34 they ran off and told it in the city   1

run over

1. ὑπερεκχύννω, *hyperekchynnō, 5658*

Lke 6:38 pressed down, shaken together, running over   1

run together

1. συντρέχω, *syntrechō, 5340*

Act 3:11 all the people ran together to them   1

run under the lee

1. ὑποτρέχω, *hypotrechō, 5720*

Act 27:16 running under the lee of a small island   1

run up

1. προστρέχω, *prostrechō, 4708*

Mrk 10:17 a man ran up and knelt before him, and asked   1
Act 8:30 Philip ran up to it and heard him reading   1

runner

1. τρέχω, *trechō, 5556*

1Co 9:24 in a race the runners all compete   1

rush

1. ὁρμάω, *hormaō, 3994*
2. τρέχω, *trechō, 5556*
3. φέρω, *pherō, 5770*

Mat 8:32 suddenly, the whole herd rushed down the steep bank   1
Mrk 5:13 rushed down the steep bank into the sea   1
Lke 8:33 herd rushed down the steep bank into the lake   1
Act 2: 2 a sound like the rush of a violent wind   3
  7:57 with a loud shout all rushed together against him.   1
  19:29 people rushed together to the theater   1
Rev 9: 9 noise of many chariots…rushing into battle.   2

rush about

1. περιτρέχω, *peritrechō, 4366*

Mrk 6:55 and rushed about that whole region   1

rush back

1. εἰσέρχομαι + μετά + σπουδή, *eiserchomai + meta + spoudē, 1656 + 3552 + 5082*

Mrk 6:25 Immediately she rushed back to the king   1

rush down

1. βάλλω, *ballō, 965*

Act 27:14 a violent wind…rushed down from Crete.   1

rush in

1. εἰσπηδάω, *eispēdaō, 1659*

Act 16:29 The jailer called for lights, and rushing in   1

rush out

1. ἐκπηδάω, *ekpēdaō, 1737*

Act 14:14 and rushed out into the crowd, shouting   1

rush together

1. συνδρομή, *syndromē, 5282*

Act 21:30 and the people rushed together.   1

rust

1. βρῶσις, *brōsis, 1111*
2. ἰός, *ios, 2675*
3. κατιόω, *katioō, 2995*

Mat 6:19 treasures on earth, where moth and rust consume   1
  6:20 in heaven, where neither moth nor rust consumes   1
Jas 5: 3 Your gold and silver have rusted   3
  5: 3 and their rust will be evidence against you   2

Ruth

1. Ῥούθ, *Rhouth, 4858*

Mat 1: 5 Boaz the father of Obed by Ruth   1

ruthless

1. ἀνελεήμων, *aneleēmōn, 446*

Rom 1:31 foolish, faithless, heartless, ruthless.   1

S

sabachthani

1. σαβαχθάνι, *sabachthani, 4876*

Mat 27:46 "Eli, Eli, lema sabachthani?"   1
Mrk 15:34 "Eloi, Eloi, lema sabachthani?"   1

sabbath *See also* day before the sabbath, sabbath *rest*

1. σάββατον, *sabbaton, 4879*

Mat 12: 1 went through the grainfields on the sabbath;   1
  12: 2 what is not lawful to do on the sabbath."   1
  12: 5 on the sabbath the priests in the temple break   1
  12: 5 priests in the temple break the sabbath   1
  12: 8 For the Son of Man is lord of the sabbath."   1

12:10	asked him, "Is it lawful to cure on the sabbath?"	1	
12:11	it falls into a pit on the sabbath;	1	
12:12	So it is lawful to do good on the sabbath."	1	
24:20	in winter or on a sabbath.	1	
28: 1	After the sabbath	1	

Mrk	1:21	and when the sabbath came,	1
	2:23	One sabbath he was going through	1
	2:24	what is not lawful on the sabbath?"	1
	2:27	"The sabbath was made for humankind	1
	2:27	for humankind, and not humankind for the sabbath;	1
	2:28	the Son of Man is lord even of the sabbath."	1
	3: 2	whether he would cure him on the sabbath	1
	3: 4	lawful to do good or to do harm on the sabbath	1
	6: 2	On the sabbath he began to teach in the synagogue	1
	16: 1	When the sabbath was over	1

Lke	4:16	on the sabbath day, as was his custom.	1
	4:31	was teaching them on the sabbath.	1
	6: 1	One sabbath while Jesus was going through	1
	6: 2	doing what is not lawful on the sabbath?"	1
	6: 5	"The Son of Man is lord of the sabbath."	1
	6: 6	On another sabbath he entered the synagogue	1
	6: 7	to see whether he would cure on the sabbath	1
	6: 9	lawful to do good or to do harm on the sabbath	1
	13:10	in one of the synagogues on the sabbath.	1
	13:14	Jesus had cured on the sabbath	1
	13:14	not on the sabbath day."	1
	13:15	Does not each of you on the sabbath untie his ox	1
	13:16	set free from this bondage on the sabbath day?"	1
	14: 1	of the Pharisees to eat a meal on the sabbath	1
	14: 3	lawful to cure people on the sabbath, or not?"	1
	14: 5	not immediately pull it out on a sabbath day?"	1
	23:54	the sabbath was beginning.	1
	23:56	On the sabbath they rested	1

Jhn	5: 9	Now that day was a sabbath.	1
	5:10	"It is the sabbath; it is not lawful	1
	5:16	because he was doing such things on the sabbath.	1
	5:18	because he was not only breaking the sabbath	1
	7:22	you circumcise a man on the sabbath.	1
	7:23	If a man receives circumcision on the sabbath	1
	7:23	I healed a man's whole body on the sabbath?	1
	9:14	it was a sabbath day when Jesus made the mud	1
	9:16	for he does not observe the sabbath."	1
	19:31	left on the cross during the sabbath	1
	19:31	because that sabbath was a day of great solemnity.	1

Act	1:12	is near Jerusalem, a sabbath day's journey away.	1
	13:14	on the sabbath day they went into the synagogue	1
	13:27	the prophets that are read every sabbath	1
	13:42	speak about these things again the next sabbath.	1
	13:44	The next sabbath almost the whole city gathered	1
	15:21	read aloud every sabbath in the synagogues."	1
	16:13	On the sabbath day we went outside the gate	1
	17: 2	on three sabbath days argued with them	1
	18: 4	Every sabbath he would argue in the synagogue	1

Col	2:16	observing festivals, new moons, or sabbaths.	1

sackcloth

1. σάκκος, *sakkos, 4884*
2. σάκκος + τρίχινος, *sakkos + trichinos, 4884 + 5570*

Mat	11:21	repented long ago in sackcloth and ashes.	1
Lke	10:13	sitting in sackcloth and ashes.	1
Rev	6:12	the sun became black as sackcloth	2
	11: 3	authority to prophesy...wearing sackcloth."	1

sacred *See also* make sacred

1. ἱερός, *hieros, 2641*

Mrk	16: S	[sacred and imperishable proclamation of...salvation]	1
2Ti	3:15	from childhood you have known the sacred writings	1

sacrifice *See also* make a sacrifice, make a sacrifice of atonement, offer in sacrifice, offer sacrifice

1. Contextual: Not in Greek
2. θυσία, *thysia, 2602*
3. θύω, *thyō, 2604*
4. προσφορά, *prosphora, 4714*

Mat	9:13	'I desire mercy, not sacrifice.'	2
	12: 7	'I desire mercy and not sacrifice,'	2
Mrk	12:33	all whole burnt offerings and sacrifices."	2
	14:12	when the Passover lamb is sacrificed	3
Lke	2:24	offered a sacrifice	2
	13: 1	blood...had mingled with their sacrifices.	2

	22: 7	on which the Passover lamb had to be sacrificed.	3
Act	7:41	offered a sacrifice to the idol	2
	7:42	'Did you offer to me slain victims and sacrifices	2
	21:26	the sacrifice would be made for each of them.	4
Rom	12: 1	to present your bodies as a living sacrifice	2
1Co	5: 7	our paschal lamb, Christ, has been sacrificed.	3
	10:18	who eat the sacrifices partners in the altar?	2
	10:20	No, I imply that what pagans sacrifice	3
	10:20	they sacrifice to demons and not to God.	3
Eph	5: 2	a fragrant offering and sacrifice to God.	2
Php	2:17	over the sacrifice and the offering of your faith	2
	4:18	a sacrifice acceptable and pleasing to God.	2
Heb	5: 1	to offer gifts and sacrifices for sins.	2
	7:27	he has no need...to offer sacrifices day after day	2
	8: 3	is appointed to offer gifts and sacrifices;	2
	9: 9	gifts and sacrifices are offered	2
	9:23	heavenly things...need better sacrifices than these.	2
	9:26	to remove sin by the sacrifice of himself.	2
	10: 1	same sacrifices that are continually offered	2
	10: 3	in these sacrifices there is a reminder of sin	1
	10: 5	"Sacrifices and offerings you have not desired	2
	10: 8	in sacrifices and offerings and burnt offerings	2
	10:11	offering again and again the same sacrifices	2
	10:12	offered for all time a single sacrifice for sins	2
	10:26	there no longer remains a sacrifice for sins	2
	11: 4	a more acceptable sacrifice than Cain's.	2
	13:11	as a sacrifice for sin	1
	13:15	offer a sacrifice of praise to God	2
	13:16	for such sacrifices are pleasing to God.	2
1Pe	2: 5	offer spiritual sacrifices acceptable to God	2

atoning sacrifice

1. ἱλασμός, *hilasmos, 2662*

1Jn	2: 2	he is the atoning sacrifice for our sins	1
	4:10	sent his Son to be the atoning sacrifice for our sins.	1

sacrifice of atonement

1. ἱλαστήριον, *hilastērion, 2663*

Rom	3:25	as a sacrifice of atonement by his blood	1

sacrifice on an altar

1. θυσιαστήριον, *thysiastērion, 2603*

1Co	9:13	share in what is sacrificed on the altar?	1

sacrifice to idol

1. εἰδωλόθυτος, *eidōlothytos, 1628*

Act	15:29	you abstain from what has been sacrificed to idols	1
	21:25	should abstain from what has been sacrificed to idols	1

sacrilege

1. βδέλυγμα, *bdelygma, 1007*

Mat	24:15	"So when you see the desolating sacrilege	1
Mrk	13:14	when you see the desolating sacrilege set up	1

sad *See also* look sad

1. περίλυπος, *perilypos, 4337*

Lke	18:23	when he heard this, he became sad;	1

Sadducee

1. Σαδδουκαῖος, *Saddoukaios, 4881*

Mat	3: 7	when he saw many Pharisees and Sadducees	1
	16: 1	The Pharisees and Sadducees came	1
	16: 6	the yeast of the Pharisees and Sadducees."	1
	16:11	the yeast of the Pharisees and Sadducees!"	1
	16:12	the teaching of the Pharisees and Sadducees.	1
	22:23	The same day some Sadducees came to him	1
	22:34	heard that he had silenced the Sadducees	1
Mrk	12:18	Sadducees, who say there is no resurrection	1
Lke	20:27	Sadducees, those who say there is no resurrection,	1
Act	4: 1	the Sadducees came to them	1
	5:17	(that is, the sect of the Sadducees)	1
	23: 6	some were Sadducees and others were Pharisees	1
	23: 7	dissension...between the Pharisees and...Sadducees	1
	23: 8	(The Sadducees say that there is no resurrection	1

safe *See also* keep safe

1. εἰρήνη, *eirēnē, 1645*

Lke	11:21	his property is safe	1

safe and sound
  1. ὑγιαίνω, *hygiainō, 5617*

Lke 15:27 because he has got him back safe and sound.'   1

safeguard
  1. ἀσφαλής, *asphalēs, 855*

Php 3: 1 not troublesome to me, and for you it is a safeguard.   1

safety   *See also* reach safety
  1. Contextual: Not in Greek

Act 27:24 God has granted safety to all those who are sailing   1

sage
  1. σοφός, *sophos, 5055*

Mat 23:34 I send you prophets, sages, and scribes   1

sail   *See also* set sail
  1. ἀνάγω, *anagō, 343*
  2. ἀποπλέω, *apopleō, 676*
  3. ἐκπλέω, *ekpleō, 1739*
  4. πλέω, *pleō, 4434*
  5. πλόος, *ploos, 4452*

Lke 8:23 while they were sailing he fell asleep.   4
Act 13: 4 from there they sailed to Cyprus.   2
   18:18 farewell to the believers and sailed for Syria   3
   20: 6 we sailed from Philippi,   3
   20:15 We sailed from there, and on the following day   2
   21: 3 leaving it on our left, we sailed to Syria   4
   27: 1 it was decided that we were to sail for Italy   2
   27: 9 sailing was now dangerous   5
   27:24 God has granted safety to all...sailing with you.'   4
   28:10 when we were about to sail   1

sail across
  1. διαπλέω, *diapleō, 1386*

Act 27: 5 After we had sailed across the sea   1

sail away
  1. ἐκπλέω, *ekpleō, 1739*

Act 15:39 Barnabas...sailed away to Cyprus.   1

sail back
  1. ἀποπλέω, *apopleō, 676*

Act 14:26 From there they sailed back to Antioch   1

sail past
  1. παραλέγομαι, *paralegomai, 4162*
  2. παραπλέω, *parapleō, 4179*

Act 20:16 Paul had decided to sail past Ephesus   2
   27: 8 Sailing past it with difficulty   1
   27:13 sail past Crete, close to the shore.   1

sail slowly
  1. βραδυπλοέω, *bradyploeō, 1095*

Act 27: 7 We sailed slowly for a number of days   1

sail under the lee
  1. ὑποπλέω, *hypopleō, 5709*

Act 27: 4 we sailed under the lee of Cyprus   1
   27: 7 we sailed under the lee of Crete   1

sailor
  1. ναύτης, *nautēs, 3731*

Act 27:27 sailors suspected that they were nearing land.   1
   27:30 the sailors tried to escape from the ship   1
Rev 18:17 And all shipmasters and seafarers, sailors   1

saint
  1. Contextual: Not in Greek
  2. ἅγιος, *hagios, 41*

Mat 27:52 many bodies of the saints who had fallen asleep   2
Act 9:13 evil he has done to your saints in Jerusalem;   2
   9:32 he came down also to the saints living in Lydda.   2
   9:41 Then calling the saints and widows   2
   26:10 I not only locked up many of the saints in prison   2
Rom 1: 7 God's beloved in Rome, who are called to be saints: 2
   8:27 because the Spirit intercedes for the saints   2
   12:13 Contribute to the needs of the saints;   2

   15:25 I am going to Jerusalem in a ministry to the saints;   2
   15:26 with the poor among the saints at Jerusalem.   2
   15:31 my ministry...be acceptable to the saints   2
   16: 2 welcome her in the Lord as is fitting for the saints   2
   16:15 Greet...all the saints who are with them.   2
1Co 1: 2 called to be saints   2
   6: 1 instead of taking it before the saints?   2
   6: 2 know that the saints will judge the world?·   2
   14:33 (As in all the churches of the saints   2
   16: 1 Now concerning the collection for the saints: 2
   16:15 devoted themselves to the service of the saints;   2
2Co 1: 1 including all the saints throughout Achaia: 2
   8: 4 sharing in this ministry to the saints—   2
   9: 1 to write you about the ministry to the saints   2
   9:12 not only supplies the needs of the saints   2
   13:12 All the saints greet you.   2
Eph 1: 1 the saints who are in Ephesus and are faithful   2
   1:15 your love toward all the saints   2
   1:18 his glorious inheritance among the saints   2
   2:19 you are citizens with the saints   2
   3: 8 Although I am the very least of all the saints,   2
   3:18 the power to comprehend, with all the saints   2
   4:12 to equip the saints for the work of ministry   2
   5: 3 as is proper among saints.   2
   6:18 in supplication for all the saints.   2
Php 1: 1 To all the saints in Christ Jesus   2
   4:21 Greet every saint in Christ Jesus.   2
   4:22 All the saints greet you   2
Col 1: 2 To the saints and faithful brothers and sisters   2
   1: 4 the love that you have for all the saints   2
   1:12 the inheritance of the saints in the light.   2
   1:26 now been revealed to his saints.   2
1Th 3:13 the coming of our Lord Jesus with all his saints.   2
2Th 1:10 when he comes to be glorified by his saints   2
1Ti 5:10 washed the saints' feet, helped the afflicted   2
Phm 1: 5 all the saints and your faith toward the Lord Jesus.   2
   1: 7 the hearts of the saints have been refreshed   2
Heb 6:10 in serving the saints, as you still do.   2
   13:24 Greet all your leaders and all the saints.   2
Jde 1: 3 faith...once for all entrusted to the saints.   2
Rev 5: 8 bowls...which are the prayers of the saints.   2
   5: 9 and by your blood you ransomed for God saints   1
   8: 3 prayers of all the saints on the golden altar   2
   8: 4 the smoke...with the prayers of the saints, rose   2
   11:18 rewarding your servants, the prophets and saints   2
   13: 7 Also it was allowed to make war on the saints   2
   13:10 a call for the endurance and faith of the saints.   2
   14:12 Here is a call for the endurance of the saints   2
   16: 6 they shed the blood of saints and prophets   2
   17: 6 the woman was drunk with the blood of the saints   2
   18:20 O heaven, you saints and apostles and prophets!   2
   18:24 was found the blood of prophets and of saints   2
   19: 8 fine linen is the righteous deeds of the saints.   2
   20: 9 and surrounded the camp of the saints   2
   22:21 grace...be with all the saints. Amen.   2

sake
  1. Contextual: Not in Greek
  2. ἀντί, *anti, 505*
  3. διά, *dia, 1328*
  4. εἰς, *eis, 1650*
  5. ἕνεκεν, *heneken, 1915*
  6. κατά, *kata, 2848*
  7. ὄνομα, *onoma, 3950*
  8. ὑπέρ, *hyper, 5642*

Mat 5:10 those who are persecuted for righteousness' sake   5
   10:39 who lose their life for my sake will find it.   5
   15: 3 for the sake of your tradition?   3
   15: 6 for the sake of your tradition   3
   16:25 who lose their life for my sake will find it.   5
   19:12 for the sake of the kingdom of heaven.   3
   19:29 for my name's sake, will receive a hundredfold   5
   24:22 for the sake of the elect   3
Mrk 8:35 who lose their life for my sake   5
   8:35 lose their life...for the sake of the gospel   1
   10:29 for my sake and for the sake of the good news   5
   10:29 for my sake and for the sake of the good news   5
   12:40 for the sake of appearance say long prayers.   1
   13:20 for the sake of the elect, whom he chose   3
Lke 9:24 who lose their life for my sake will save it.   5

18:29	left house…for the sake of the kingdom of God	5
20:47	for the sake of appearance say long prayers.	1
Jhn 11:15	For your sake I am glad I was not there	3
11:42	I have said this for the sake of the crowd	3
12:30	Jesus answered, "This voice has come for your sake	3
17:19	for their sakes I sanctify myself	8
Act 5:41	worthy to suffer dishonor for the sake of the name.	8
9:16	how much he must suffer for the sake of my name."	8
15:26	risked their lives for the sake of our Lord	8
28:20	since it is for the sake of the hope of Israel	5
Rom 1: 5	among all the Gentiles for the sake of his name	8
4:23	the words…were written not for his sake alone	8
8:36	"For your sake we are being killed all day	5
9: 3	cut off from Christ for the sake of my own people	8
11:28	they are enemies of God for your sake;	3
11:28	beloved, for the sake of their ancestors;	3
14:20	Do not, for the sake of food, destroy the work	5
1Co 4:10	We are fools for the sake of Christ, but you are wise	3
9:10	does he not speak entirely for our sake?	3
9:10	It was indeed written for our sake	3
9:23	I do it all for the sake of the gospel	3
10:28	for the sake of conscience—	1
11: 9	Neither was man created for the sake of woman	3
11: 9	the sake of woman, but woman for the sake of man.	3
2Co 2:10	has been for your sake in the presence of Christ.	3
4: 5	and ourselves as your slaves for Jesus' sake.	3
4:11	always being given up to death for Jesus' sake	3
4:15	Yes, everything is for your sake	3
5:21	For our sake he made him to be sin who knew no sin	8
8: 9	yet for your sakes he became poor	3
12:10	persecutions, and calamities for the sake of Christ;	8
12:19	beloved, is for the sake of building you up.	8
Eph 3: 1	prisoner for Christ Jesus for the sake of you Gentiles	8
Php 3: 8	For his sake I have suffered the loss of all	3
Col 1:24	I am now rejoicing in my sufferings for your sake	8
1:24	for the sake of his body, that is, the church.	8
1Th 1: 5	among you for your sake.	3
3: 2	and encourage you for the sake of your faith	8
1Ti 5:23	take a little wine for the sake of your stomach	3
2Ti 1: 1	God, for the sake of the promise	6
2:10	everything for the sake of the elect	3
Tit 1: 1	for the sake of the faith of God's elect	6
Heb 1:14	for the sake of those who are to inherit salvation?	3
6:10	the love that you showed for his sake	7
12: 2	for the sake of the joy that was set before him	2
12: 7	Endure trials for the sake of discipline.	4
1Pe 1:20	revealed at the end…for your sake.	3
2:13	For the Lord's sake accept the authority	3
4: 7	discipline yourselves for the sake of your prayers.	4
3Jn 1: 7	for they began their journey for the sake of Christ	8
Jde 1:11	abandon themselves to Balaam's error for the sake of gain	1
Rev 2: 3	and bearing up for the sake of my name	3

Sala

1. Σαλά, *Sala, 4885*

Lke 3:32	son of Boaz, son of Sala, son of Nahshon	1

Salamis

1. Σαλαμίς, *Salamis, 4887*

Act 13: 5	When they arrived at Salamis	1

Salathiel

1. Σαλαθιήλ, *Salathiēl, 4886*

Mat 1:12	Jechoniah was the father of Salathiel	1
1:12	Salathiel the father of Zerubbabel	1

Salem

1. Σαλήμ, *Salēm, 4889*

Heb 7: 1	King Melchizedek of Salem, priest of the Most High God	1
7: 2	he is also king of Salem, that is, "king of peace."	1

Salim

1. Σαλίμ, *Salim, 4890*

Jhn 3:23	John also was baptizing at Aenon near Salim	1

saliva *See also* put saliva

1. πτύσμα, *ptysma, 4770*

Jhn 9: 6	made mud with the saliva	1

Salmon

1. Σαλμών, *Salmōn, 4891*

Mat 1: 4	and Nahshon the father of Salmon	1
1: 5	Salmon the father of Boaz by Rahab	1

Salmone

1. Σαλμώνη, *Salmōnē, 4892*

Act 27: 7	sailed under the lee of Crete off Salmone.	1

Salome

1. Σαλώμη, *Salōmē, 4897*

Mrk 15:40	among them were Mary Magdalene…and Salome.	1
16: 1	Mary the mother of James, and Salome	1

salt

1. ἅλας, *halas, 229*
2. ἁλίζω, *halizō, 245*
3. ἁλυκός, *halykos, 266*

Mat 5:13	"You are the salt of the earth; but if salt has lost	1
5:13	the earth; but if salt has lost its taste, how can	1
Mrk 9:49	"For everyone will be salted with fire.	2
9:50	Salt is good;	1
9:50	if salt has lost its saltiness	1
9:50	Have salt in yourselves	1
Lke 14:34	"Salt is good;	1
14:34	if salt has lost its taste	1
Col 4: 6	always be gracious, seasoned with salt	1
Jas 3:12	No more can salt water yield fresh.	3

saltiness *See* lose saltiness, restore saltiness

salute

1. ἀσπάζομαι, *aspazomai, 832*

Mrk 15:18	began saluting him, "Hail, King of the Jews!"	1

salvation

1. σωτηρία, *sōtēria, 5401*
2. σωτήριον, *sōtērion, 5402*
3. σωτήριος, *sōtērios, 5403*

Mrk 16: S	⟦imperishable proclamation of eternal salvation⟧	1
Lke 1:77	to give knowledge of salvation to his people	1
2:30	for my eyes have seen your salvation	2
3: 6	all flesh shall see the salvation of God.' "	2
19: 9	"Today salvation has come to this house	1
Jhn 4:22	for salvation is from the Jews.	1
Act 4:12	There is salvation in no one else	1
13:26	the message of this salvation has been sent.	1
13:47	bring salvation to the ends of the earth.' "	1
16:17	who proclaim to you a way of salvation."	1
28:28	salvation of God has been sent to the Gentiles;	2
Rom 1:16	it is the power of God for salvation to everyone	1
11:11	salvation has come to the Gentiles	1
13:11	For salvation is nearer to us now	1
2Co 1: 6	it is for your consolation and salvation;	1
6: 2	on a day of salvation I have helped you."	1
6: 2	see, now is the day of salvation!	1
7:10	that leads to salvation and brings no regret	1
Eph 1:13	the word of truth, the gospel of your salvation	1
6:17	Take the helmet of salvation	2
Php 1:28	of your salvation. And this is God's doing.	1
2:12	work out your own salvation with fear	1
1Th 5: 8	for a helmet the hope of salvation.	1
5: 9	for obtaining salvation through our Lord Jesus	1
2Th 2:13	God chose you as the first fruits for salvation	1
2Ti 2:10	may also obtain the salvation that is in Christ Jesus	1
3:15	that are able to instruct you for salvation	1
Tit 2:11	has appeared, bringing salvation to all,	3
Heb 1:14	for the sake of those who are to inherit salvation?	1
2: 3	if we neglect so great a salvation?	1
2:10	make the pioneer of their salvation perfect	1
5: 9	he became the source of eternal salvation	1
6: 9	better things in your case, things that belong to salvation.	1
1Pe 1: 5	salvation ready to be revealed in the last time.	1
1: 9	outcome of your faith, the salvation of your souls.	1
1:10	Concerning this salvation, the prophets	1
2: 2	so that by it you may grow into salvation	1
2Pe 3:15	regard the patience of our Lord as salvation.	1
Jde 1: 3	to write to you about the salvation we share	1
Rev 7:10	"Salvation belongs to our God who is seated on	1

Rev 12:10 salvation...power and the kingdom of our God   1
    19: 1 Salvation and glory and power to our God   1

salve

1. κολλούριον, *kollourion, 3141*

Rev   3:18 salve to anoint your eyes so that you may see.   1

Samaria

1. Σαμάρεια, *Samareia, 4899*
2. Σαμαρῖτις, *Samaritis, 4902*

Lke 17:11 through the region between Samaria and Galilee.   1
Jhn   4: 4 he had to go through Samaria.   1
    4: 9 you, a Jew, ask a drink of me, a woman of Samaria?"   2
Act   1: 8 Judea and Samaria, and to the ends of the earth."   1
    8: 1 throughout the countryside of Judea and Samaria.   1
    8: 5 Philip went down to the city of Samaria   1
    8: 9 and amazed the people of Samaria   1
    8:14 Samaria had accepted the word of God   1
    9:31 the church throughout Judea...and Samaria   1
  15: 3 they passed through both Phoenicia and Samaria   1

Samaritan

1. Σαμάρεια, *Samareia, 4899*
2. Σαμαρίτης, *Samaritēs, 4901*
3. Σαμαρῖτις, *Samaritis, 4902*

Mat 10: 5 and enter no town of the Samaritans   2
Lke   9:52 they entered a village of the Samaritans   2
  10:33 a Samaritan while traveling came near him;   2
  17:16 And he was a Samaritan.   2
Jhn   4: 5 So he came to a Samaritan city called Sychar   1
    4: 7 A Samaritan woman came to draw water   1
    4: 9 The Samaritan woman said to him, "How is it   3
    4: 9 (Jews do not share things in common with Samaritans.)   2
    4:39 Many Samaritans from that city believed in him   2
    4:40 So when the Samaritans came to him, they asked him   2
    8:48 that you are a Samaritan and have a demon?"   2
Act   8:25 many villages of the Samaritans.   2

same *See also* member of the same body, same *age*, same *time*, same *trade*, same *way*

1. Contextual: Not in Greek
2. αὐτός, *autos, 899*
3. ἐκεῖνος, *ekeinos, 1697*
4. ἴσος, *isos, 2698*
5. ὅμοιος, *homoios, 3927*
6. ὁμοίως, *homoiōs, 3931*
7. ὅσος, *hosos, 4012*
8. οὗτος, *houtos, 4047*
9. οὕτως, *houtōs, 4048*
10. τοιοῦτος, *toioutos, 5525*
11. ὡς, *hōs, 6055*
12. ὡσαύτως, *hōsautōs, 6058*

Mat   5:19 teaches others to do the same, will be called least   9
    5:46 Do not even the tax collectors do the same?   2
    5:47 than others? Do not even the Gentiles do the same?   2
  13: 1 That same day Jesus went out of the house and sat   3
  18:28 that same slave, as he went out   3
  20: 5 he did the same.   12
  20:14 give to this last the same as I give to you.   11
  21:30 father went to the second and said the same;   12
  22:23 The same day some Sadducees came to him   3
  22:26 The second did the same, so also the third   6
  26:44 for the third time, saying the same words.   2
Mrk 14:31 all of them said the same.   12
  14:39 went away and prayed, saying the same words.   2
Lke   6:33 even sinners do the same.   2
  10: 7 Remain in the same house, eating and drinking   2
  10:21 At that same hour Jesus rejoiced in the Holy Spirit   2
  17: 4 if the same person sins against you seven times   1
  22:20 did the same with the cup after supper, saying,   12
  23:12 That same day Herod and Pilate became friends   2
  23:40 you are under the same sentence of condemnation?   2
  24:13 Now on that same day two of them were going   2
  24:33 That same hour they got up and returned to Jerusalem;   2
Jhn 21:13 and did the same with the fish.   6
Act   1:11 Jesus...will come in the same way as you saw him go   9
  11:17 If then God gave them the same gift   4
  16:33 At the same hour of the night he took them   3
  19:25 with the workers of the same trade   10

Rom   3:30 and the uncircumcised through that same faith.   1
    9:21 out of the same lump one object for special use   2
  10:12 the same Lord is Lord of all   2
  12: 4 and not all the members have the same function   2
1Co   1:10 be united in the same mind and the same purpose.   2
    1:10 united in the same mind and the same purpose.   2
    9: 8 Does not the law also say the same?   8
  10: 3 all ate the same spiritual food   2
  10: 4 all drank the same spiritual drink.   2
  12: 4 are varieties of gifts, but the same Spirit;   2
  12: 5 are varieties of services, but the same Lord;   2
  12: 6 the same God who activates all of them in everyone.   2
  12: 8 according to the same Spirit   2
  12: 9 to another faith by the same Spirit   2
  12:11 All these are activated by one and the same Spirit   2
  12:25 members may have the same care for one another.   2
2Co   1: 6 when you patiently endure the same sufferings   2
    3:14 that same veil is still there   2
    3:18 transformed into the same image   2
    4:13 just as we have the same spirit of faith   2
    8:16 in the heart of Titus the same eagerness for you   2
  12:18 Did we not conduct ourselves with the same spirit?   2
  12:18 Did we not take the same steps?   2
Eph   4:10 He who descended is the same one who ascended   2
    6: 8 we will receive the same again from the Lord   8
    6: 9 masters, do the same to them.   2
    6: 9 both of you have the same Master in heaven,   1
Php   1:30 having the same struggle that you saw   2
    2: 2 make my joy complete: be of the same mind   2
    2: 2 having the same love, being in full accord   2
    2: 5 Let the same mind be in you   8
    3:15 those of us then who are mature be of the same mind;   8
    4: 2 I urge Syntyche to be of the same mind in the Lord.   2
Heb   1:12 you are the same, and your years will never end."   2
    6:11 each one of you to show the same diligence   2
  10: 1 same sacrifices that are continually offered   2
  10:11 offering again and again the same sacrifices   2
  11: 9 heirs with him of the same promise.   2
  13: 8 Jesus Christ is the same yesterday and today   2
Jas   3:10 From the same mouth come blessing and cursing.   2
    3:11 Does a spring pour forth from the same opening   2
1Pe   4: 1 arm yourselves also with the same intention   2
    4: 4 no longer join them in the same excesses of dissipation   2
2Pe   3: 7 by the same word the present heavens and earth   2
Jde   1: 7 in the same manner as they, indulged   5
Rev 21:16 its length the same as its width;   7

same kind

1. αὐτός, *autos, 899*

1Pe   5: 9 are undergoing the same kinds of suffering.   1

same thing

1. αὐτός, *autos, 899*

Act 14: 1 The same thing occurred in Iconium,   1
  15:27 will tell you the same things by word of mouth.   1
Rom   2: 1 you, the judge, are doing the very same things.   1
1Co 11: 5 one and the same thing as having her head shaved.   1
Php   3: 1 To write the same things to you is not troublesome   1
1Th   2:14 you suffered the same things   1
Heb   2:14 he himself likewise shared the same things   1

Samos

1. Σάμος, *Samos, 4904*

Act 20:15 The next day we touched at Samos   1

Samothrace

1. Σαμοθράκη, *Samothrakē, 4903*

Act 16:11 took a straight course to Samothrace   1

Samson

1. Σαμψών, *Sampsōn, 4907*

Heb 11:32 to tell of Gideon, Barak, Samson, Jephthah, of David   1

Samuel

1. Σαμουήλ, *Samouēl, 4905*

Act   3:24 from Samuel and those after him,   1
  13:20 judges until the time of the prophet Samuel.   1
Heb 11:32 David and Samuel and the prophets—   1

sanctification

1. ἁγιασμός, *hagiasmos, 40*

Rom	6:19	as slaves to righteousness for sanctification.	1
	6:22	the advantage you get is sanctification.	1
1Co	1:30	righteousness and sanctification	1
1Th	4: 3	For this is the will of God, your sanctification:	1
2Th	2:13	through sanctification by the Spirit	1

sanctify

1. ἁγιάζω, *hagiazō, 39*
2. ἁγιασμός, *hagiasmos, 40*

Jhn	10:36	the one whom the Father has sanctified and sent	1
	17:17	Sanctify them in the truth; your word is truth.	1
	17:19	for their sakes I sanctify myself	1
	17:19	so that they also may be sanctified in truth.	1
Act	20:32	among all who are sanctified.	1
	26:18	among those who are sanctified by faith in me.'	1
Rom	15:16	be acceptable, sanctified by the Holy Spirit.	1
1Co	1: 2	to those who are sanctified in Christ Jesus	1
	6:11	you were washed, you were sanctified	1
1Th	5:23	May the God of peace himself sanctify you entirely;	1
1Ti	4: 5	for it is sanctified by God's word	1
Heb	2:11	the one who sanctifies and those who are sanctified	1
	2:11	those who are sanctified all have one Father.	1
	9:13	sanctifies those who have been defiled	1
	10:10	by God's will that we have been sanctified through	1
	10:14	perfected for all time those who are sanctified.	1
	10:29	the blood...by which they were sanctified	1
	13:12	in order to sanctify the people	1
1Pe	1: 2	sanctified by the Spirit to be obedient	2
	3:15	in your hearts sanctify Christ as Lord.	1

sanctuary

1. Contextual: Not in Greek
2. ἅγιος, *hagios, 41*
3. ναός, *naos, 3724*
4. οἶκος, *oikos, 3875*

Mat	23:16	swears by the sanctuary is bound by nothing	3
	23:16	whoever swears by the gold of the sanctuary	3
	23:17	which is greater, the gold or the sanctuary	3
	23:21	whoever swears by the sanctuary	3
	23:35	murdered between the sanctuary and the altar.	3
Lke	1: 9	enter the sanctuary of the Lord and offer incense.	3
	1:21	wondered at his delay in the sanctuary.	3
	1:22	realized that he had seen a vision in the sanctuary.	3
	11:51	perished between the altar and the sanctuary.	4
Heb	8: 2	a minister in the sanctuary and the true tent	2
	8: 5	a sanctuary that is a sketch and shadow of the heavenly	1
	9: 1	worship and an earthly sanctuary.	2
	9: 8	the way into the sanctuary has not yet been disclosed	2
	9:24	not enter a sanctuary made by human hands	2
	10:19	we have confidence to enter the sanctuary	2
	13:11	is brought into the sanctuary by the high priest	2

sand   *See also* grain of sand

1. ἄμμος, *ammos, 302*

Mat	7:26	a foolish man who built his house on sand.	1
Rom	9:27	the children of Israel were like the sand of the sea	1
Rev	12:18	the dragon took his stand on the sand of the seashore.	1
	20: 8	they are as numerous as the sands of the sea.	1

sandal

1. σανδάλιον, *sandalion, 4908*
2. ὑπόδημα, *hypodēma, 5687*

Mat	3:11	I am not worthy to carry his sandals.	2
	10:10	or two tunics, or sandals, or a staff;	2
Mrk	1: 7	untie the thong of his sandals.	2
	6: 9	to wear sandals and not to put on two tunics.	1
Lke	3:16	I am not worthy to untie the thong of his sandals.	2
	10: 4	Carry no purse, no bag, no sandals;	2
	15:22	put a ring on his finger and sandals on his feet.	2
	22:35	sent you out without a purse, bag, or sandals	2
Jhn	1:27	I am not worthy to untie the thong of his sandal."	2
Act	7:33	'Take off the sandals from your feet	2
	12: 8	"Fasten your belt and put on your sandals."	1
	13:25	to untie the thong of the sandals on his feet.'	2

Sapphira

1. Σάπφιρα, *Sapphira, 4912*

Act	5: 1	Ananias, with the consent of his wife Sapphira	1

sapphire

1. σάπφιρος, *sapphiros, 4913*
2. ὑακίνθινος, *hyakinthinos, 5610*

Rev	9:17	the color of fire and of sapphire and of sulfur;	2
	21:19	every jewel;...the second sapphire	1

Sarah

1. Σάρρα, *Sarra, 4925*

Rom	4:19	he considered the barrenness of Sarah's womb.	1
	9: 9	I will return and Sarah shall have a son."	1
Heb	11:11	he was too old—and Sarah herself was barren—	1
1Pe	3: 6	Thus Sarah obeyed Abraham and called him lord.	1

Sardis

1. Σάρδεις, *Sardeis, 4915*

Rev	1:11	seven churches...to Sardis, to Philadelphia	1
	3: 1	"And to the angel of the church in Sardis write:	1
	3: 4	Yet you have still a few persons in Sardis	1

sash

1. ζώνη, *zōnē, 2438*

Rev	1:13	and with a golden sash across his chest.	1
	15: 6	with golden sashes across their chests.	1

Satan

1. Σατανᾶς, *Satanas, 4928*

Mat	4:10	Jesus said to him, "Away with you, Satan!	1
	12:26	If Satan casts out Satan, he is divided	1
	12:26	If Satan casts out Satan, he is divided	1
	16:23	and said to Peter, "Get behind me, Satan!	1
Mrk	1:13	wilderness forty days, tempted by Satan;	1
	3:23	"How can Satan cast out Satan?	1
	3:23	"How can Satan cast out Satan?	1
	3:26	if Satan has risen up against himself	1
	4:15	when they hear, Satan immediately comes	1
	8:33	"Get behind me, Satan!	1
Lke	10:18	Satan fall from heaven like a flash of lightning.	1
	11:18	If Satan also is divided against himself	1
	13:16	a daughter of Abraham whom Satan bound	1
	22: 3	Then Satan entered into Judas called Iscariot	1
	22:31	Satan has demanded to sift all of you like wheat	1
Jhn	13:27	the piece of bread, Satan entered into him.	1
Act	5: 3	"why has Satan filled your heart to lie	1
	26:18	turn...from the power of Satan to God	1
Rom	16:20	God...will shortly crush Satan under your feet.	1
1Co	5: 5	you are to hand this man over to Satan	1
	7: 5	come together again, so that Satan may not tempt	1
2Co	2:11	so that we may not be outwitted by Satan;	1
	11:14	Satan disguises himself as an angel of light.	1
	12: 7	a messenger of Satan to torment me	1
1Th	2:18	but Satan blocked our way.	1
2Th	2: 9	apparent in the working of Satan	1
1Ti	1:20	whom I have turned over to Satan	1
	5:15	For some have already turned away to follow Satan.	1
Rev	2: 9	but are a synagogue of Satan.	1
	2:13	"I know where you are living, where Satan's throne is.	1
	2:13	who was killed among you, where Satan lives.	1
	2:24	learned what some call 'the deep things of Satan,'	1
	3: 9	I will make those of the synagogue of Satan	1
	12: 9	serpent, who is called the Devil and Satan	1
	20: 2	that ancient serpent, who is the Devil and Satan	1
	20: 7	Satan will be released from his prison	1

satisfaction   *See* give satisfaction

satisfy

1. ἀρκέω, *arkeō, 758*
2. ἐμπίμπλημι, *empimplēmi, 1855*
3. ἱκανός + ποιέω, *hikanos + poieō, 2653 + 4472*
4. πείθω, *peithō, 4275*

Mat	28:14	we will satisfy him and keep you out of trouble."	4
Mrk	15:15	So Pilate, wishing to satisfy the crowd	3
Lke	3:14	be satisfied with your wages."	1
Jhn	6:12	When they were satisfied	2
	14: 8	we will be satisfied."	1

satisfy fully

1. πληρόω, *plēroō, 4444*

Php	4:18	I am fully satisfied, now that I have received	1

Php 4:19 my God will fully satisfy every need of yours   1

satisfy hunger

1. κορέννυμι + τροφή, *korennymi + trophē*, 3170 + 5575
2. χορτάζω, *chortazō*, 5963

Lke 16:21 satisfy his hunger with what fell from…table;   2
Act 27:38 After they had satisfied their hunger   1

Saul

1. αὐτός, *autos*, 899
2. Σαούλ, *Saoul*, 4910
3. Σαῦλος, *Saulos*, 4930

Act 7:58 at the feet of a young man named Saul.   3
     8: 1 Saul approved of their killing him.   3
     8: 3 Saul was ravaging the church   3
     9: 1 Saul, still breathing threats and murder   3
     9: 4 "Saul, Saul, why do you persecute me?"   2
     9: 4 "Saul, Saul, why do you persecute me?"   2
     9: 8 Saul got up from the ground   3
     9:11 a man of Tarsus named Saul.   3
     9:17 laid his hands on Saul and said, "Brother Saul   1
     9:17 laid his hands on Saul and said, "Brother Saul   2
     9:22 Saul became increasingly more powerful   3
     9:24 their plot became known to Saul.   3
    11:25 Barnabas went to Tarsus to look for Saul   3
    11:30 sending it to the elders by Barnabas and Saul.   3
    12:25 Barnabas and Saul returned to Jerusalem   3
    13: 1 Manaen…and Saul.   3
    13: 2 "Set apart for me Barnabas and Saul   3
    13: 7 who summoned Barnabas and Saul   3
    13: 9 Saul, also known as Paul   3
    13:21 Saul son of Kish, a man of the tribe of Benjamin   2
    22: 7 'Saul, Saul, why are you persecuting me?'   2
    22: 7 'Saul, Saul, why are you persecuting me?'   2
    22:13 'Brother Saul, regain your sight!'   2
    26:14 'Saul, Saul, why are you persecuting me?   2
    26:14 'Saul, Saul, why are you persecuting me?   2

savage

1. βαρύς, *barys*, 987

Act 20:29 savage wolves will come in among you   1

save

1. διασῴζω, *diasōzō*, 1407
2. θησαυρίζω, *thēsaurizō*, 2564
3. περιποίησις + ψυχή, *peripoiēsis + psychē*, 4348 + 6034
4. σῴζω, *sōzō*, 5392
5. σωτηρία, *sōtēria*, 5401
6. φυλάσσω, *phylassō*, 5875

Mat 1:21 Jesus, for he will save his people from their   4
     8:25 they went and woke him up, saying, "Lord, save   4
    10:22 But the one who endures to the end will be saved.   4
    14:30 beginning to sink, he cried out, "Lord, save me!"   4
    16:25 those who want to save their life will lose it   4
    19:25 "Then who can be saved?"   4
    24:13 the one who endures to the end will be saved.   4
    24:22 no one would be saved;   4
    27:40 save yourself! If you are the Son of God   4
    27:42 "He saved others; he cannot save himself.   4
    27:42 "He saved others; he cannot save himself.   4
    27:49 let us see whether Elijah will come to save him."   4
Mrk 3: 4 to save life or to kill?"   4
     8:35 those who want to save their life will lose it   4
     8:35 who lose their life…will save it.   4
    10:26 "Then who can be saved?"   4
    13:13 one who endures to the end will be saved.   4
    13:20 no one would be saved   4
    15:30 save yourself, and come down from the cross!"   4
    15:31 saying, "He saved others; he cannot save himself.   4
    15:31 saying, "He saved others; he cannot save himself.   4
    16:16 ⟦one who believes and is baptized will be saved;⟧   4
Lke 1:71 that we would be saved from our enemies   5
     6: 9 to save life or to destroy it?"   4
     7:50 "Your faith has saved you; go in peace."   4
     8:12 so that they may not believe and be saved.   4
     8:50 Only believe, and she will be saved."   4
     9:24 who want to save their life will lose it   4
     9:24 who lose their life for my sake will save it.   4
    13:23 "Lord, will only a few be saved?"   4
    18:26 who heard it said, "Then who can be saved?"   4
    18:42 "Receive your sight; your faith has saved you."   4
    19:10 Son of Man came to seek out and to save the lost."   4
    23:35 leaders scoffed at him, saying, "He saved others;   4
    23:35 "He saved others; let him save himself   4
    23:37 "If you are the King of the Jews, save yourself!"   4
    23:39 "Are you not the Messiah? Save yourself and us!"   4
Jhn 3:17 that the world might be saved through him.   4
     5:34 I say these things so that you may be saved.   4
    10: 9 Whoever enters by me will be saved   4
    12:27 'Father, save me from this hour'?   4
    12:47 not to judge the world, but to save the world.   4
Act 2:21 everyone who calls on the name…shall be saved.'   4
     2:40 "Save yourselves from this corrupt generation."   4
     2:47 those who were being saved.   4
     4:12 no other name…by which we must be saved."   4
    11:14 you and your entire household will be saved.'   4
    15: 1 circumcised…you cannot be saved."   4
    15:11 saved through the grace of the Lord Jesus   4
    16:30 "Sirs, what must I do to be saved?"   4
    16:31 you will be saved, you and your household."   4
    27:20 all hope of our being saved was…abandoned.   4
    27:31 stay in the ship, you cannot be saved."   4
    27:43 the centurion, wishing to save Paul   1
Rom 5: 9 will we be saved through him from the wrath of God   4
     5:10 much more…will we be saved by his life.   4
     8:24 For in hope we were saved.   4
     9:27 only a remnant of them will be saved;   4
    10: 1 prayer to God for them is that they may be saved.   5
    10: 9 believe in your heart…you will be saved.   4
    10:10 one confesses with the mouth and so is saved.   5
    10:13 who calls on the name of the Lord shall be saved."   4
    11:14 to make…jealous, and thus save some of them.   4
    11:26 so all Israel will be saved; as it is written   4
1Co 1:18 to us who are being saved it is the power of God.   4
     1:21 to save those who believe.   4
     3:15 builder will be saved, but only as through fire.   4
     5: 5 his spirit may be saved in the day of the Lord.   4
     7:16 you might save your husband.   4
     7:16 you might save your wife.   4
     9:22 that I might by all means save some.   4
    10:33 so that they may be saved.   4
    15: 2 through which also you are being saved   4
    16: 2 put aside and save whatever extra you earn   2
2Co 2:15 among those who are being saved   4
Eph 2: 5 by grace you have been saved   4
     2: 8 For by grace you have been saved through faith   4
1Th 2:16 so that they may be saved.   4
2Th 2:10 refused to love the truth and so be saved.   4
1Ti 1:15 Jesus came into the world to save sinners   4
     2: 4 who desires everyone to be saved   4
     2:15 she will be saved through childbearing   4
     4:16 in doing this you will save…yourself   4
2Ti 1: 9 who saved us and called us with a holy calling   4
     4:18 save me for his heavenly kingdom.   4
Tit 3: 5 he saved us, not because of any works   4
Heb 5: 7 to the one who was able to save him from death   4
     7:25 Consequently he is able for all time to save   4
     9:28 to save those who are eagerly waiting for him.   5
    10:39 those who have faith and are saved.   3
    11: 7 built an ark to save his household;   5
Jas 1:21 implanted word that has the power to save your souls.   4
     2:14 but do not have works? Can faith save you?   4
     4:12 who is able to save and to destroy.   4
     5:15 The prayer of faith will save the sick   4
     5:20 will save the sinner's soul from death   4
1Pe 3:20 in which a few, that is, eight persons, were saved   1
     3:21 baptism, which this prefigured, now saves you   4
     4:18 "If it is hard for the righteous to be saved   4
2Pe 2: 5 saved Noah, a herald of righteousness   6
Jde 1: 5 that the Lord, who once for all saved a people   4
     1:23 save others by snatching them out of the fire;   4

savior

1. σωτήρ, *sōtēr*, 5400
2. σωτηρία, *sōtēria*, 5401

Lke 1:47 my spirit rejoices in God my Savior   1
     1:69 He has raised up a mighty savior for us   2
     2:11 born this day in the city of David a Savior   1
Jhn 4:42 this is truly the Savior of the world."   1
Act 5:31 God exalted him…as Leader and Savior   1
    13:23 brought to Israel a Savior, Jesus, as he promised;   1

Eph	5:23	the church, the body of which he is the Savior.	1
Php	3:20	we are expecting a Savior, the Lord Jesus Christ.	1
1Ti	1: 1	an apostle…by the command of God our Savior	1
	2: 3	is acceptable in the sight of God our Savior	1
	4:10	the living God, who is the Savior of all people	1
2Ti	1:10	the appearing of our Savior Christ Jesus	1
Tit	1: 3	by the command of God our Savior	1
	1: 4	God the Father and Christ Jésus our Savior.	1
	2:10	may be an ornament to the doctrine of God our Savior.	1
	2:13	glory of our great God and Savior, Jesus Christ.	1
	3: 4	loving kindness of God our Savior appeared	1
	3: 6	through Jesus Christ our Savior	1
2Pe	1: 1	righteousness of our…Savior Jesus Christ:	1
	1:11	kingdom of our Lord and Savior Jesus Christ	1
	2:20	knowledge of our Lord and Savior Jesus Christ	1
	3: 2	the commandment of the Lord and Savior	1
	3:18	knowledge of our Lord and Savior Jesus Christ.	1
1Jn	4:14	Father has sent his Son as the Savior of the world.	1
Jde	1:25	to the only God our Savior, through Jesus Christ	1

saw in two

1. πρίζω, *prizō, 4569*

Heb	11:37	They were stoned to death, they were sawn in two	1

say

1. Contextual: Not in Greek
2. ἀντιλέγω, *antilegō, 515*
3. ἀπαγγέλλω, *apangellō, 550*
4. ἀποκρίνομαι, *apokrinomai, 646*
5. διά, *dia, 1328*
6. διαλογίζομαι, *dialogizomai, 1368*
7. εἰμί, *eimi, 1639*
8. ἐρωτάω, *erōtaō, 2263*
9. καλέω, *kaleō, 2813*
10. λαλέω, *laleō, 3281*
11. λαλιά, *lalia, 3282*
12. λέγω, *legō, 3306*
13. λόγος, *logos, 3364*
14. ὅτι, *hoti, 4022*
15. ῥῆμα, *rhēma, 4839*
16. στόμα, *stoma, 5125*
17. συλλαλέω, *syllaleō, 5196*
18. φημί, *phēmi, 5774*

Mat	1:20	said, "Joseph, son of David, do not be afraid	12
	2: 8	he sent them to Bethlehem, saying, "Go and search	12
	2:13	angel of the Lord appeared to Joseph…and said	12
	2:19	in a dream to Joseph in Egypt and said	12
	3: 3	prophet Isaiah spoke when he said, "The voice	12
	3: 7	coming for baptism, he said to them, "You brood	12
	3: 9	Do not presume to say to yourselves, 'We have	12
	3:14	John would have prevented him, saying, "I need	12
	3:17	from heaven said, "This is my Son, the Beloved	12
	4: 3	The tempter came and said to him, "If you are	12
	4: 6	saying to him, "If you are the Son of God, throw	12
	4: 7	Jesus said to him, "Again it is written, 'Do not	18
	4: 9	he said to him, "All these I will give you,	12
	4:10	Jesus said to him, "Away with you, Satan!	12
	4:19	he said to them, "Follow me, and I will make you	12
	5: 2	he began to speak, and taught them, saying:	12
	5:21	heard that it was said to those of ancient times	12
	5:22	But I say to you that if you are angry	12
	5:22	you say, 'You fool,' you will be liable to the hell	12
	5:27	"You have heard that it was said, 'You shall not	12
	5:28	I say to you that everyone who looks at a woman	12
	5:31	"It was also said, 'Whoever divorces his wife	12
	5:32	I say to you that anyone who divorces his wife	12
	5:33	heard that it was said to those of ancient times	12
	5:34	I say to you, Do not swear at all, either by heaven	12
	5:38	heard that it was said, 'An eye for an eye and a tooth	12
	5:39	But I say to you, Do not resist an evildoer.	12
	5:43	"You have heard that it was said, 'You shall love	12
	5:44	I say to you, Love your enemies and pray for those	12
	6:31	do not worry, saying, 'What will we eat?'	12
	7: 4	Or how can you say to your neighbor	12
	7:21	"Not everyone who says to me, 'Lord, Lord,'	12
	7:22	On that day many will say to me, 'Lord, Lord	12
	7:28	Now when Jesus had finished saying these	13
	8: 2	saying, "Lord, if you choose, you can make me clean."	12
	8: 3	saying, "I do choose. Be made clean!"	12

	8: 4	Jesus said to him, "See that you say nothing	12
	8: 4	Jesus said to him, "See that you say nothing	12
	8: 6	saying, "Lord, my servant is lying at home paralyzed	12
	8: 7	he said to him, "I will come and cure him."	12
	8: 9	I say to one, 'Go,' and he goes, and to another	12
	8:10	he was amazed and said to those who followed him	12
	8:13	to the centurion Jesus said, "Go; let it be done	12
	8:19	A scribe then approached and said	12
	8:20	Jesus said to him, "Foxes have holes	12
	8:21	Another of his disciples said to him	12
	8:22	Jesus said to him, "Follow me, and let the dead	12
	8:25	they went and woke him up, saying, "Lord, save	12
	8:26	he said to them, "Why are you afraid	12
	8:27	They were amazed, saying, "What sort of man	12
	8:32	he said to them, "Go!" So they came out	12
	9: 2	he said to the paralytic, "Take heart, son;	12
	9: 3	Then some of the scribes said to themselves	12
	9: 4	Jesus, perceiving their thoughts, said	12
	9: 5	For which is easier, to say, 'Your sins are forgiven,'	12
	9: 5	or to say, 'Stand up and walk'?	12
	9: 6	he then said to the paralytic—"Stand up	12
	9: 9	and he said to him, "Follow me."	12
	9:11	Pharisees saw this, they said to his disciples	12
	9:12	But when he heard this, he said	12
	9:14	Then the disciples of John came to him, saying	12
	9:15	Jesus said to them, "The wedding guests cannot mourn	12
	9:18	While he was saying these things to them	10
	9:18	saying, "My daughter has just died,	12
	9:21	for she said to herself, "If I only touch	12
	9:22	Jesus turned, and seeing her he said, "Take heart	12
	9:24	he said, "Go away; for the girl is not dead	12
	9:28	the blind men came to him; and Jesus said to them	12
	9:28	They said to him, "Yes, Lord."	12
	9:29	Then he touched their eyes and said	12
	9:33	the crowds were amazed and said	12
	9:34	But the Pharisees said, "By the ruler of the demons	12
	9:37	Then he said to his disciples	12
	10:19	for what you are to say will be given to you	1
	10:19	for what you are to say will be given to you	10
	10:27	What I say to you in the dark, tell in the light;	12
	11: 3	said to him, "Are you the one who is to come	12
	11:18	and they say, 'He has a demon';	12
	11:19	and they say, 'Look, a glutton and a drunkard	12
	11:25	At that time Jesus said, "I thank you, Father	4
	12: 2	the Pharisees saw it, they said to him, "Look	12
	12: 3	He said to them, "Have you not read what David did	12
	12:11	He said to them, "Suppose one of you has only one	12
	12:13	Then he said to the man, "Stretch out your hand."	12
	12:23	All the crowds were amazed and said	12
	12:24	when the Pharisees heard it, they said	12
	12:25	He knew what they were thinking and said to them	12
	12:38	Then some of the scribes and Pharisees said	4
	12:44	Then it says, 'I will return	12
	12:49	he said, "Here are my mother and my brothers!	12
	13: 3	he told them many things in parables, saying:	12
	13:14	the prophecy of Isaiah that says:	12
	13:27	the slaves of the householder came and said	12
	13:28	The slaves said to him	12
	13:36	And his disciples approached him, saying	12
	13:52	he said to them	12
	13:54	so that they were astounded and said	12
	13:57	But Jesus said to them	12
	14: 2	and he said to his servants,	12
	14: 8	she said, "Give me the head of John the Baptist	18
	14:15	the disciples came to him and said	12
	14:16	Jesus said to them, "They need not go away;	12
	14:18	he said, "Bring them here to me."	12
	14:26	they were terrified, saying, "It is a ghost!"	12
	14:27	immediately Jesus spoke to them and said	12
	14:29	He said, "Come." So Peter got out of the boat	12
	14:31	reached out his hand and caught him, saying to him	12
	14:33	those in the boat worshiped him, saying	12
	15: 1	scribes came to Jesus from Jerusalem and said	12
	15: 4	For God said, 'Honor your father	12
	15: 5	you say that whoever tells father or mother	12
	15: 7	Isaiah prophesied rightly…when he said:	12
	15:10	he called the crowd to him and said to them	12
	15:12	Then the disciples approached and said to him	12
	15:12	when they heard what you said?"	13
	15:15	Peter said to him, "Explain this parable to us."	4
	15:16	Then he said,	12

Mat 15:23 And his disciples came and urged him, saying   12
15:25 she came and knelt before him, saying   12
15:27 She said, "Yes, Lord, yet even the dogs eat   12
15:32 Jesus called his disciples to him and said   12
15:33 The disciples said to him   12
15:34 They said, "Seven, and a few small fish."   12
16: 2 "When it is evening, you say, 'It will be fair   12
16: 6 Jesus said to them   12
16: 7 They said to one another, "It is because   6
16: 8 aware of it, Jesus said   12
16:13 "Who do people say that the Son of Man is?"   12
16:14 they said, "Some say John the Baptist   12
16:14 "Some say John the Baptist, but others Elijah   1
16:15 He said to them, "But who do you say that I am?"   12
16:15 He said to them, "But who do you say that I am?"   12
16:22 rebuke him, saying, "God forbid it, Lord!   12
16:23 and said to Peter, "Get behind me, Satan!   12
17: 4 Peter said to Jesus   4
17: 5 and from the cloud a voice said   12
17: 7 Jesus came and touched them, saying   12
17:10 "Why, then, do the scribes say   12
17:15 said, "Lord, have mercy on my son   12
17:19 disciples came to Jesus privately and said   12
17:20 He said to them, "Because of your little faith.   12
17:20 you will say to this mountain   12
17:22 Jesus said to them   12
17:24 the collectors…came to Peter and said   12
17:25 He said, "Yes   12
17:26 When Peter said, "From others,"   12
17:26 Jesus said to him, "Then the children are free.   18
18: 3 said, "Truly I tell you   12
18:21 Then Peter came and said to him   12
18:22 Jesus said to him, "Not seven times, but,   12
18:26 slave fell on his knees before him, saying   12
18:28 and seizing him by the throat, he said   12
18:32 Then his lord summoned him and said to him   12
19: 1 When Jesus had finished saying these   13
19: 5 said, 'For this reason a man shall leave   12
19: 7 They said to him   12
19: 8 He said to them, "It was because you were   12
19: 9 I say to you, whoever divorces his wife   12
19:10 His disciples said to him, "If such is the case   12
19:11 he said to them, "Not everyone can accept   12
19:14 Jesus said, "Let the little children come to me   12
19:16 someone came to him and said,   12
19:17 said to him, "Why do you ask me about what is good?   12
19:18 He said to him, "Which   12
19:18 And Jesus said, "You shall not murder;   12
19:20 The young man said to him   12
19:21 Jesus said to him, "If you wish to be perfect   18
19:23 Jesus said to his disciples, "Truly I tell you   12
19:25 they were greatly astounded and said   12
19:26 Jesus looked at them and said, "For mortals   12
19:27 Then Peter said in reply   12
19:28 Jesus said to them, "Truly I tell you   12
20: 4 he said to them, 'You also go into the vineyard   12
20: 6 he said to them, 'Why are you standing here idle   12
20: 7 They said to him, 'Because no one has hired us.'   12
20: 7 He said to them, 'You also go into the vineyard.'   12
20: 8 the owner of the vineyard said to his manager   12
20:12 saying, 'These last worked only one hour   12
20:17 and said to them on the way   12
20:21 he said to her, "What do you want?"   12
20:21 She said to him   12
20:22 They said to him, "We are able."   12
20:23 He said to them, "You will indeed drink my cup   12
20:25 Jesus called them to him and said   12
20:32 Jesus stood still and called them, saying   12
20:33 They said to him, "Lord, let our eyes be opened."   12
21: 2 saying to them, "Go into the village ahead of you   12
21: 3 If anyone says anything to you, just say this,   12
21: 3 If anyone says anything to you, just say this,   12
21: 4 what had been spoken through the prophet, saying   12
21:11 crowds were saying, "This is the prophet Jesus   12
21:13 He said to them, "It is written   12
21:16 said to him, "Do you hear what these are saying?"   12
21:16 said to him, "Do you hear what these are saying?"   12
21:16 Jesus said to them, "Yes;   12
21:19 he said to it, "May no fruit ever come from you   12
21:20 the disciples saw it, they were amazed, saying   12
21:21 but even if you say to this mountain   12

21:23 came to him as he was teaching, and said   12
21:24 Jesus said to them, "I will also ask you   4
21:25 "If we say, 'From heaven,' he will say to us   12
21:25 "If we say, 'From heaven,' he will say to us   12
21:26 if we say, 'Of human origin,' we are afraid of the crowd;   12
21:27 he said to them, "Neither will I tell you   18
21:28 he went to the first and said   12
21:30 father went to the second and said the same;   12
21:31 They said, "The first." Jesus said to them   12
21:31 They said, "The first." Jesus said to them   12
21:37 Finally he sent his son to them, saying   12
21:38 the tenants saw the son, they said to themselves   12
21:41 They said to him   12
21:42 Jesus said to them, "Have you never read   12
22: 1 Once more Jesus spoke to them in parables, saying: 12
22: 4 Again he sent other slaves, saying   12
22: 8 Then he said to his slaves, 'The wedding is ready   12
22:12 and he said to him, 'Friend, how did you get in   12
22:13 the king said to the attendants, 'Bind him   12
22:15 and plotted to entrap him in what he said.   13
22:16 along with the Herodians, saying, "Teacher   12
22:18 Jesus, aware of their malice, said   12
22:20 he said to them   12
22:21 Then he said to them, "Give therefore   12
22:23 saying there is no resurrection;   12
22:23 they asked him a question, saying,   12
22:24 "Teacher, Moses said   12
22:31 have you not read what was said to you by God   12
22:37 He said to him, " 'You shall love the Lord   18
22:42 They said to him, "The son of David."   12
22:43 He said to them, "How is it   12
22:43 by the Spirit calls him Lord, saying   12
22:44 'The Lord said to my Lord, "Sit at my right hand   12
23: 1 Then Jesus said to the crowds   10
23:16 "Woe to you, blind guides, who say   12
23:18 you say, 'Whoever swears by the altar   1
23:30 say, 'If we had lived in the days of our ancestors   12
23:39 you will not see me again until you say   12
24: 3 the disciples came to him privately, saying   12
24: 5 For many will come in my name, saying   12
24:23 Then if anyone says to you, 'Look!   12
24:26 So, if they say to you, 'Look!   12
24:26 If they say, 'Look! He is in the inner rooms,'   1
24:48 if that wicked slave says to himself   12
25: 8 The foolish said to the wise   12
25:11 Later the other bridesmaids came also, saying   12
25:20 bringing five more talents, saying   12
25:21 His master said to him   18
25:22 with the two talents also came forward, saying   12
25:23 His master said to him   18
25:24 also came forward, saying   12
25:34 the king will say to those at his right hand   12
25:41 Then he will say to those at his left hand   12
26: 1 When Jesus had finished saying all these   13
26: 1 he said to his disciples   12
26: 5 they said, "Not during the festival   12
26: 8 they were angry and said, "Why this waste?   12
26:10 Jesus, aware of this, said to them   12
26:15 said, "What will you give me if I betray him   12
26:17 the disciples came to Jesus, saying   12
26:18 He said, "Go into the city to a certain man   12
26:18 into the city to a certain man, and say to him   12
26:18 'The Teacher says, My time is near;   12
26:21 they were eating, he said, "Truly I tell you   12
26:22 and began to say to him one after another   12
26:25 Judas, who betrayed him, said, "Surely not I,   4
26:25 He replied, "You have said so."   12
26:26 broke it, gave it to the disciples, and said   12
26:27 after giving thanks he gave it to them, saying   12
26:31 Jesus said to them, "You will all become deserters   12
26:33 Peter said to him, "Though all become deserters   4
26:34 Jesus said to him, "Truly I tell you   18
26:35 Peter said to him, "Even though I must die   12
26:35 And so said all the disciples.   12
26:36 he said to his disciples   12
26:38 Then he said to them, "I am deeply grieved   12
26:40 he said to Peter   12
26:44 for the third time, saying the same words.   12
26:45 Then he came to the disciples and said to them   12
26:48 Now the betrayer had given them a sign, saying   12
26:49 he came up to Jesus and said, "Greetings, Rabbi!"   12

26:50	Jesus said to him, "Friend, do what you are here	12
26:52	Then Jesus said to him, "Put your sword back	12
26:54	which say it must happen in this way?"	14
26:55	At that hour Jesus said to the crowds	12
26:61	said, "This fellow said, 'I am able to destroy	12
26:61	said, "This fellow said, 'I am able to destroy	18
26:62	The high priest stood up and said	12
26:63	Then the high priest said to him	12
26:64	Jesus said to him, "You have said so.	12
26:64	Jesus said to him, "You have said so.	12
26:65	the high priest tore his clothes and said	12
26:68	saying, "Prophesy to us, you Messiah!	12
26:69	A servant-girl came to him and said	12
26:70	he denied it before all of them, saying	12
26:71	she said to the bystanders	12
26:73	bystanders came up and said to Peter	12
26:75	Peter remembered what Jesus had said:	12
27: 4	said, "I have sinned	12
27: 4	they said, "What is that to us?	12
27: 6	chief priests, taking the pieces of silver, said	12
27:11	Jesus said, "You say so."	18
27:11	Jesus said, "You say so."	12
27:13	Then Pilate said to him, "Do you not hear	12
27:17	So after they had gathered, Pilate said to them	12
27:21	The governor again said to them	4
27:21	they said, "Barabbas."	12
27:22	Pilate said to them, "Then what should I do	12
27:22	All of them said, "Let him be crucified!"	12
27:24	washed his hands before the crowd, saying	12
27:29	knelt before him and mocked him, saying	12
27:40	saying, "You who would destroy the temple	12
27:41	scribes and elders, were mocking him, saying	12
27:43	for he said, 'I am God's Son.' "	12
27:47	some of the bystanders heard it, they said	12
27:49	the others said, "Wait, let us see	12
27:54	they were terrified and said	12
27:63	said, "Sir, we remember what that impostor said	12
27:63	said, "Sir, we remember what that impostor said	12
27:65	Pilate said to them, "You have a guard	18
28: 5	the angel said to the women, "Do not be afraid;	4
28: 6	not here; for he has been raised, as he said.	12
28: 9	Suddenly Jesus met them and said, "Greetings!"	12
28:10	Then Jesus said to them, "Do not be afraid;	12
28:13	"You must say, 'His disciples came by night	12
28:18	Jesus came and said to them	10
Mrk 1:15	saying, "The time is fulfilled	12
1:17	Jesus said to them, "Follow me	12
1:25	Jesus rebuked him, saying, "Be silent,	12
1:37	they found him, they said to him	12
1:40	kneeling he said to him	12
1:41	stretched out his hand and touched him, and said	12
1:44	saying to him, "See that you say nothing	12
1:44	"See that you say nothing to anyone;	12
2: 5	he said to the paralytic	12
2: 8	said to them, "Why do you raise such questions	12
2: 9	Which is easier, to say to the paralytic	12
2: 9	or to say, 'Stand up and take your mat and walk'?	12
2:10	he said to the paralytic—	12
2:11	"I say to you, stand up, take your mat and go	12
2:12	saying, "We have never seen anything like this!"	12
2:14	he said to him, "Follow me."	12
2:16	said to his disciples	12
2:17	When Jesus heard this, he said to them	12
2:18	people came and said to him	12
2:19	Jesus said to them, "The wedding guests cannot	12
2:24	Pharisees said to him, "Look, why are they doing	12
2:25	he said to them, "Have you never read what David	12
2:27	he said to them, "The sabbath was made for	12
3: 3	he said to the man who had the withered hand	12
3: 4	he said to them, "Is it lawful to do good	12
3: 5	said to the man, "Stretch out your hand."	12
3:21	were saying, "He has gone out of his mind."	12
3:22	the scribes who came down from Jerusalem said	12
3:30	for they had said, "He has an unclean spirit."	12
3:32	A crowd was sitting around him; and they said	12
3:34	he said, "Here are my mother and my brothers!	12
4: 2	in his teaching he said to them:	12
4: 9	he said, "Let anyone with ears to hear listen!"	12
4:11	he said to them, "To you has been given the secret	12
4:13	he said to them, "Do you not understand	12
4:21	He said to them, "Is a lamp brought	12
4:24	he said to them, "Pay attention to what you hear;	12
4:26	He also said, "The kingdom of God	12
4:30	He also said, "With what can we compare	12
4:35	when evening had come, he said to them	12
4:38	they woke him up and said to him	12
4:39	and rebuked the wind, and said to the sea	12
4:40	He said to them, "Why are you afraid?	12
4:41	and said to one another, "Who then is this	12
5: 8	For he had said to him, "Come out of the man	12
5:19	Jesus refused, and said to him	12
5:28	for she said, "If I but touch his clothes	12
5:30	Jesus turned about in the crowd and said	12
5:31	his disciples said to him, "You see the crowd	12
5:31	how can you say, 'Who touched me?' "	12
5:34	He said to her, "Daughter	12
5:35	some people came from the leader's house	12
5:36	But overhearing what they said	10
5:36	Jesus said to the leader of the synagogue	12
5:39	When he had entered, he said to them	12
5:41	He took her by the hand and said to her,	12
6: 2	many who heard him were astounded. They said	12
6: 4	Jesus said to them, "Prophets are not without honor	12
6:10	He said to them, "Wherever you enter a house,	12
6:14	Some were saying, "John the baptizer has been	12
6:15	others said, "It is Elijah."	12
6:15	others said, "It is a prophet	12
6:16	when Herod heard of it, he said	12
6:22	and the king said to the girl	12
6:24	She went out and said to her mother	12
6:31	He said to them, "Come away to a deserted place	12
6:35	grew late, his disciples came to him and said	12
6:37	They said to him, "Are we to go and buy	12
6:38	he said to them, "How many loaves have you?	12
6:38	they said, "Five, and two fish."	12
6:50	But immediately he spoke to them and said	12
7: 6	He said to them, "Isaiah prophesied rightly	12
7: 9	he said to them, "You have a fine way of rejecting	12
7:10	For Moses said, 'Honor your father and your mother';	12
7:11	you say that if anyone tells father or mother	12
7:14	he called the crowd again and said	12
7:18	He said to them, "Then do you also	12
7:20	he said, "It is what comes out of a person	12
7:27	He said to her, "Let the children be fed first	12
7:29	he said to her, "For saying that, you may go	12
7:34	looking up to heaven, he sighed and said	12
7:37	They were astounded beyond measure, saying	12
8: 1	he called his disciples and said to them	12
8: 5	They said, "Seven."	12
8:12	he sighed deeply in his spirit and said	12
8:15	he cautioned them, saying, "Watch out	12
8:16	They said to one another, "It is because	6
8:17	becoming aware of it, Jesus said to them	12
8:19	They said to him, "Twelve."	12
8:20	they said to him, "Seven."	12
8:21	he said to them, "Do you not yet understand?"	12
8:24	man looked up and said, "I can see people	12
8:26	he sent him away to his home, saying	12
8:27	his disciples, "Who do people say that I am?"	12
8:29	He asked them, "But who do you say that I am?"	12
8:32	He said all this quite openly.	10
8:33	he rebuked Peter and said	12
8:34	said to them, "If any want to become my followers	12
9: 1	he said to them, "Truly I tell you	12
9: 5	Peter said to Jesus, "Rabbi, it is good	4
9: 6	He did not know what to say	4
9:11	they asked him, "Why do the scribes say	12
9:12	He said to them, "Elijah is indeed coming first	18
9:21	he said, "From childhood.	12
9:23	Jesus said to him, "If you are able!	12
9:25	he rebuked the unclean spirit, saying to it	12
9:26	so that most of them said, "He is dead."	12
9:29	He said to them, "This kind can come out	12
9:31	he was teaching his disciples, saying to them	12
9:35	He…called the twelve, and said to them	12
9:36	taking it in his arms, he said to them	12
9:38	John said to him, "Teacher, we saw someone	18
9:39	Jesus said, "Do not stop him;	12
10: 4	They said, "Moses allowed a man	12
10: 5	Jesus said to them, "Because of your hardness	12
10:11	He said to them, "Whoever divorces his wife	12
10:14	he was indignant and said to them	12

Mrk 10:18	Jesus said to him, "Why do you call me good?	12
10:20	He said to him, "Teacher, I have kept all these	18
10:21	Jesus, looking at him, loved him and said	12
10:23	Jesus looked around and said to his disciples	12
10:24	Jesus said to them again	4
10:26	They were greatly astounded and said	12
10:27	Jesus looked at them and said	12
10:28	Peter began to say to him, "Look, we have left	12
10:29	Jesus said, "Truly I tell you, there is no one	18
10:33	saying, "See, we are going up to Jerusalem	14
10:35	came forward to him and said to him, "Teacher	12
10:36	he said to them, "What is it you want me to do	12
10:37	they said to him, "Grant us to sit	12
10:38	Jesus said to them, "You do not know	12
10:39	Jesus said to them, "The cup that I drink	12
10:42	Jesus called them and said to them	12
10:47	he began to shout out and say, "Jesus,	12
10:49	Jesus stood still and said, "Call him	12
10:49	they called the blind man, saying to him	12
10:51	Jesus said…"What do you want me to do for you?"	4
10:51	The blind man said to him, "My teacher	12
10:52	Jesus said to him, "Go; your faith has made	12
11: 2	said to them, "Go into the village ahead of you	12
11: 3	If anyone says to you, 'Why are you doing this?'	12
11: 3	say this, 'The Lord needs it	12
11: 5	some of the bystanders said to them	12
11: 6	They told them what Jesus had said;	12
11:14	He said to it, "May no one ever eat fruit from	4
11:17	He was teaching and saying, "Is it not written	12
11:21	Peter remembered and said to him, "Rabbi, look!	12
11:23	Truly I tell you, if you say to this mountain	12
11:23	believe that what you say will come to pass	10
11:28	said, "By what authority are you doing these	12
11:29	Jesus said to them, "I will ask you one question;	12
11:31	"If we say, 'From heaven,' he will say	12
11:31	he will say, 'Why then did you not believe him?'	12
11:32	But shall we say, 'Of human origin'?"	12
11:33	Jesus said to them, "Neither will I tell you	12
12: 6	Finally he sent him to them, saying	12
12: 7	those tenants said to one another	12
12:13	to trap him in what he said.	13
12:14	they came and said to him, "Teacher	12
12:15	knowing their hypocrisy, he said to them	12
12:16	he said to them, "Whose head is this,	12
12:17	Jesus said to them, "Give to the emperor	12
12:18	Sadducees, who say there is no resurrection	12
12:18	asked him a question, saying	12
12:24	Jesus said to them, "Is not this the reason	18
12:26	how God said to him, 'I am the God of Abraham	12
12:32	the scribe said to him, "You are right, Teacher;	12
12:32	you have truly said that 'he is one	12
12:34	he said to him, "You are not far from the kingdom	12
12:35	While Jesus was teaching in the temple, he said	4
12:35	can the scribes say that the Messiah is the son	12
12:36	'The Lord said to my Lord, "Sit at my right hand	12
12:38	As he taught, he said, "Beware of the scribes	12
12:43	he called his disciples and said to them	12
13: 1	one of his disciples said to him, "Look, Teacher	12
13: 5	Jesus began to say to them, "Beware	12
13: 6	Many will come in my name and say, 'I am he!'	12
13:11	not worry beforehand about what you are to say;	10
13:11	say whatever is given you at that time	10
13:21	if anyone says to you at that time, 'Look!	12
13:37	what I say to you I say to all: Keep awake."	12
13:37	what I say to you I say to all: Keep awake."	12
14: 2	for they said, "Not during the festival	12
14: 4	some were there who said to one another in anger	1
14: 6	Jesus said, "Let her alone; why do you trouble	12
14:12	his disciples said to him, "Where do you want us	12
14:13	he sent two of his disciples, saying to them, "Go	12
14:14	he enters, say to the owner of the house	12
14:18	taken their places and were eating, Jesus said	12
14:19	to say to him one after another, "Surely, not I?"	12
14:20	He said to them, "It is one of the twelve	12
14:22	broke it, gave it to them, and said, "Take;	12
14:24	said to them, "This is my blood of the covenant	12
14:27	Jesus said to them, "You will all become deserters;	12
14:29	Peter said to him, "Even though all become deserters	18
14:30	Jesus said to him, "Truly I tell you	12
14:31	he said vehemently, "Even though I must die	10
14:31	all of them said the same.	12
14:32	he said to his disciples, "Sit here while I pray."	12
14:34	he said to them, "I am deeply grieved	12
14:36	He said, "Abba, Father, for you all things are	12
14:37	he said to Peter, "Simon, are you asleep?	12
14:39	went away and prayed, saying the same words.	12
14:40	they did not know what to say to him.	4
14:41	He came a third time and said to them	12
14:44	Now the betrayer had given them a sign, saying	12
14:45	he went up to him at once and said, "Rabbi!"	12
14:48	Jesus said to them, "Have you come out	4
14:57	gave false testimony against him, saying	12
14:58	"We heard him say, 'I will destroy this temple	12
14:62	Jesus said, "I am; and 'you will see	12
14:63	the high priest tore his clothes and said	12
14:65	to strike him, saying to him, "Prophesy!"	12
14:67	and said, "You also were with Jesus,	12
14:68	he denied it, saying, "I do not know	12
14:69	began again to say to the bystanders	12
14:70	the bystanders again said to Peter	12
14:72	Peter remembered that Jesus had said to him	12
15: 2	He answered him, "You say so."	12
15:29	shaking their heads and saying, "Aha!	12
15:31	saying, "He saved others; he cannot save himself.	12
15:35	the bystanders heard it, they said, "Listen	12
15:36	gave it to him to drink, saying, "Wait	12
15:39	he said, "Truly this man was God's Son!"	12
16: 3	They had been saying to one another	12
16: 6	But he said to them, "Do not be alarmed;	12
16: 8	they said nothing to anyone, for they were afraid.	12
16:15	[[he said to them, "Go into all the world]]	12
Lke 1:13	the angel said to him, "Do not be afraid	12
1:18	Zechariah said to the angel, "How will I know	12
1:24	she remained in seclusion. She said	12
1:28	he came to her and said, "Greetings, favored one!	12
1:30	The angel said to her, "Do not be afraid, Mary	12
1:34	Mary said to the angel, "How can this be	12
1:35	The angel said to her, "The Holy Spirit will come	4
1:36	the sixth month for her who was said to be barren.	9
1:38	Mary said, "Here am I, the servant of the Lord;	12
1:46	Mary said, "My soul magnifies the Lord	12
1:60	his mother said, "No; he is to be called John."	4
1:61	They said to her, "None of your relatives	12
1:66	said, "What then will this child become?"	12
2:10	the angel said to them, "Do not be afraid;	12
2:13	praising God and saying	12
2:15	the shepherds said to one another, "Let us go	10
2:28	took him in his arms and praised God, saying,	12
2:33	amazed at what was being said about him.	10
2:34	Simeon blessed them and said to his mother Mary	12
2:48	his mother said to him, "Child, why have you	12
2:49	He said to them, "Why were you searching	12
2:50	they did not understand what he said to them	10
3: 7	John said to the crowds that came out	12
3: 8	Do not begin to say to yourselves	12
3:11	he said to them, "Whoever has two coats	12
3:13	He said to them, "Collect no more than the amount	12
3:14	He said to them, "Do not extort money from anyone	12
3:16	John answered all of them by saying, "I baptize	12
4: 3	The devil said to him, "If you are the Son of God	12
4: 6	the devil said to him, "To you I will give	12
4: 9	saying to him, "If you are the Son of God	12
4:12	Jesus answered him, "It is said, 'Do not put	12
4:21	he began to say to them, "Today this scripture	12
4:22	They said, "Is not this Joseph's son?"	12
4:23	He said to them, "Doubtless you will quote to me	12
4:23	you will say, 'Do here also in your hometown	1
4:24	he said, "Truly I tell you	12
4:35	Jesus rebuked him, saying, "Be silent	12
4:36	were all amazed and kept saying to one another	17
4:43	he said to them, "I must proclaim the good news	12
5: 4	When he had finished speaking, he said to Simon	12
5: 5	Yet if you say so, I will let down the nets."	15
5: 8	he fell down at Jesus' knees, saying	12
5:10	Jesus said to Simon, "Do not be afraid;	12
5:13	Jesus stretched out his hand, touched him,	12
5:14	"Go," he said, "and show yourself to the priest	1
5:20	When he saw their faith, he said	12
5:23	Which is easier, to say, 'Your sins are forgiven	12
5:23	or to say, 'Stand up and walk'?	12
5:24	he said to the one who was paralyzed—	12
5:24	"I say to you, stand up and take your bed	12

5:26	saying, "We have seen strange things today."	12
5:27	he said to him, "Follow me."	12
5:30	saying, "Why do you eat and drink	12
5:33	they said to him, "John's disciples,	12
5:34	Jesus said to them, "You cannot make wedding guests	12
5:39	but says, 'The old is good.' "	12
6: 2	some of the Pharisees said, "Why are you doing	12
6: 5	he said to them, "The Son of Man is lord	12
6: 8	he said to the man who had the withered hand	12
6: 9	Jesus said to them, "I ask you	12
6:10	said to him, "Stretch out your hand."	12
6:20	and said: "Blessed are you who are poor	12
6:27	I say to you that listen, Love your enemies	12
6:42	how can you say to your neighbor, 'Friend	12
7: 4	they appealed to him earnestly, saying,	12
7: 6	the centurion sent friends to say to him	12
7: 8	I say to one, 'Go,' and he goes	12
7: 9	turning to the crowd that followed him, he said	12
7:13	and said to her, "Do not weep."	12
7:14	he said, "Young man, I say to you, rise!"	12
7:14	he said, "Young man, I say to you, rise!"	12
7:16	they glorified God, saying, "A great prophet	12
7:20	When the men had come to him, they said	12
7:33	and you say, 'He has a demon';	12
7:34	and you say, 'Look, a glutton and a drunkard	12
7:39	he said to himself, "If this man were a prophet	12
7:40	Jesus spoke up and said to him, "Simon	12
7:40	"Simon, I have something to say to you."	12
7:43	Jesus said to him, "You have judged rightly."	12
7:44	Then turning toward the woman, he said to Simon	18
7:48	he said to her, "Your sins are forgiven."	12
7:49	began to say among themselves	12
7:50	he said to the woman, "Your faith has saved you;	12
8: 4	he said in a parable:	12
8: 8	As he said this, he called out, "Let anyone	12
8:10	He said, "To you it has been given to know	12
8:21	he said to them, "My mother and my brothers	4
8:22	he said to them, "Let us go across	12
8:25	He said to them, "Where is your faith?"	12
8:25	amazed, and said to one another	12
8:30	He said, "Legion";	12
8:38	Jesus sent him away, saying	12
8:45	When all denied it, Peter said, "Master	12
8:46	Jesus said, "Someone touched me;	12
8:48	He said to her, "Daughter	12
8:49	someone came from the leader's house to say,	12
8:52	he said, "Do not weep;	12
9: 3	He said to them, "Take nothing for your journey	12
9: 7	it was said by some that John had been raised	12
9: 9	Herod said, "John I beheaded;	12
9:12	the twelve came to him and said	12
9:13	he said to them, "You give them something to eat."	12
9:13	They said, "We have no more than five loaves	12
9:14	he said to his disciples, "Make them sit down	12
9:18	them, "Who do the crowds say that I am?"	12
9:20	He said to them, "But who do you say that I am?"	12
9:20	He said to them, "But who do you say that I am?"	12
9:22	saying, "The Son of Man must undergo	12
9:23	he said to them all, "If any want to become	12
9:33	Peter said to Jesus, "Master, it is good	12
9:33	not knowing what he said.	12
9:34	While he was saying this, a cloud came	12
9:35	from the cloud came a voice that said,	12
9:43	he said to his disciples	12
9:48	said to them, "Whoever welcomes this child	12
9:50	Jesus said to him, "Do not stop him;	12
9:54	they said, "Lord, do you want us to command fire	12
9:57	going along the road, someone said to him	12
9:58	Jesus said to him, "Foxes have holes	12
9:59	To another he said, "Follow me."	12
9:59	he said, "Lord, first let me go and bury my father."	12
9:60	Jesus said to him, "Let the dead	12
9:61	Another said, "I will follow you, Lord;	12
9:62	Jesus said to him, "No one	12
10: 2	He said to them, "The harvest is plentiful	12
10: 5	Whatever house you enter, first say, 'Peace	12
10: 9	cure the sick who are there, and say to them	12
10:10	go out into its streets and say	12
10:17	The seventy returned with joy, saying,	12
10:18	He said to them, "I watched Satan fall from heaven	12
10:21	rejoiced in the Holy Spirit and said, "I thank you	12

10:23	Then turning to the disciples, Jesus said	12
10:25	"Teacher," he said, "what must I do to inherit	12
10:26	He said to him, "What is written in the law?	12
10:28	he said to him, "You have given the right answer;	12
10:35	gave them to the innkeeper, and said	12
10:37	He said, "The one who showed him mercy."	12
10:37	Jesus said to him, "Go and do likewise."	12
10:39	listened to what he was saying.	13
11: 1	after he had finished, one of his disciples said	12
11: 2	He said to them, "When you pray, say: Father	12
11: 2	He said to them, "When you pray, say: Father	12
11: 5	he said to them, "Suppose one of you has a friend	12
11: 5	go to him at midnight and say to him, 'Friend	12
11: 9	I say to you, Ask, and it will be given you;	12
11:15	some of them said, "He casts out demons	12
11:17	knew what they were thinking and said to them	12
11:18	you say that I cast out the demons by Beelzebul.	12
11:24	it says, 'I will return to my house	12
11:27	While he was saying this	12
11:27	a woman in the crowd raised her voice and said	12
11:28	he said, "Blessed rather are those who hear	12
11:29	When the crowds were increasing, he began to say	12
11:39	the Lord said to him, "Now you Pharisees clean	12
11:45	"Teacher, when you say these things,	12
11:46	he said, "Woe also to you lawyers!	12
11:49	Wisdom of God said, 'I will send them prophets	12
11:54	to catch him in something he might say.	16
12: 3	Therefore whatever you have said in the dark	12
12:11	to defend yourselves or what you are to say;	12
12:12	what you ought to say."	12
12:13	Someone in the crowd said to him, "Teacher	12
12:14	he said to him, "Friend, who set me to be a judge	12
12:15	he said to them, "Take care!	12
12:18	he said, 'I will do this: I will pull down	12
12:19	I will say to my soul, Soul, you have ample goods	12
12:20	God said to him, 'You fool!	12
12:22	He said to his disciples, "Therefore I tell you	12
12:41	Peter said, "Lord, are you telling this parable	12
12:42	the Lord said, "Who then is the faithful	12
12:45	if that slave says to himself	12
12:54	He also said to the crowds	12
12:54	you immediately say, 'It is going to rain';	12
12:55	when you see the south wind blowing, you say	12
13: 7	he said to the gardener, 'See here!	12
13:12	Jesus saw her, he called her over and said	12
13:14	leader of the synagogue…saying to the crowd	4
13:15	the Lord answered him and said, "You hypocrites!	12
13:17	When he said this	12
13:18	He said therefore, "What is the kingdom of God like?	12
13:20	again he said, "To what should I compare the kingdom	12
13:23	He said to them	12
13:25	to knock at the door, saying, 'Lord, open to us,'	12
13:25	reply he will say to you, 'I do not know	12
13:26	Then you will begin to say, 'We ate and drank	12
13:27	he will say, 'I do not know	12
13:31	At that very hour some Pharisees came and said	12
13:32	He said to them, "Go and tell that fox for me,	12
13:35	not see me until the time comes when you say	12
14: 5	he said to them, "If one of you has a child	12
14: 9	who invited both of you may come and say to you	12
14:10	so that when your host comes, he may say to you	12
14:12	He said also to the one who had invited him	12
14:15	said to him, "Blessed is anyone who will eat	12
14:16	Jesus said to him, "Someone gave a great dinner	12
14:17	to say to those who had been invited, 'Come;	12
14:18	The first said to him, 'I have bought…land	12
14:19	Another said, 'I have bought five yoke of oxen	12
14:20	Another said, 'I have just been married	12
14:21	the owner of the house became angry and said	12
14:22	the slave said, 'Sir	12
14:23	the master said to the slave, 'Go out	12
14:25	he turned and said to them	12
14:30	saying, 'This fellow began to build	12
15: 2	and the scribes were grumbling and saying	12
15: 6	saying to them, 'Rejoice with me	12
15: 9	saying, 'Rejoice with me	12
15:11	Jesus said, "There was a man who had two sons.	12
15:12	The younger of them said to his father, 'Father	12
15:17	when he came to himself he said	18
15:18	I will say to him, "Father, I have sinned	12
15:21	the son said to him, 'Father, I have sinned	12

Lke	15:22	the father said to his slaves	12
	15:31	father said to him, 'Son, you are always with me	12
	16: 1	Then Jesus said to the disciples,	12
	16: 2	he summoned him and said to him, 'What is this	12
	16: 3	the manager said to himself, 'What will I do	12
	16: 6	He said to him, 'Take your bill	12
	16: 7	He said to him, 'Take you bill and make it eighty.'	12
	16:15	he said to them, "You are those who justify	12
	16:25	Abraham said, 'Child, remember	12
	16:27	He said, 'Then, father, I beg you	12
	16:30	He said, 'No, father Abraham;	12
	16:31	he said to him, 'If they do not listen to Moses	12
	17: 1	Jesus said to his disciples,	12
	17: 4	turns back to you seven times and says, 'I repent,'	12
	17: 5	The apostles said to the Lord, "Increase our faith!"	12
	17: 6	you could say to this mulberry tree	12
	17: 7	"Who among you would say to your slave	12
	17: 8	Would you not rather say to him, 'Prepare supper	12
	17:10	say, 'We are worthless slaves;	12
	17:13	called out, saying, "Jesus, Master	12
	17:14	When he saw them, he said to them, "Go	12
	17:19	he said to him, 'Get up and go on your way;	12
	17:21	nor will they say, 'Look, here it is!'	12
	17:22	he said to the disciples, "The days are coming	12
	17:23	They will say to you, 'Look there!' or 'Look here!'	12
	17:37	He said to them, "Where the corpse is,	12
	18: 2	He said, "In a certain city there was a judge	12
	18: 3	saying, 'Grant me justice against my opponent.'	12
	18: 4	later he said to himself	12
	18: 6	the Lord said, "Listen	12
	18: 6	"Listen to what the unjust judge says.	12
	18:13	beating his breast and saying, 'God, be merciful	12
	18:16	Jesus called for them and said,	12
	18:19	Jesus said to him, "Why do you call me good?	12
	18:22	When Jesus heard this, he said to him,	12
	18:24	Jesus looked at him and said, "How hard it is	12
	18:26	who heard it said, "Then who can be saved?"	12
	18:28	Peter said, "Look, we have left our homes	12
	18:29	he said to them, "Truly I tell you,	12
	18:31	took the twelve aside and said to them, "See	12
	18:34	in fact, what he said was hidden from them	15
	18:34	they did not grasp what was said.	12
	18:41	He said, "Lord, let me see again."	12
	18:42	Jesus said to him, "Receive your sight;	12
	19: 5	he looked up and said to him	12
	19: 7	All who saw it began to grumble and said,	12
	19: 8	Zacchaeus stood there and said to the Lord,	12
	19: 9	Jesus said to him, "Today salvation has come	12
	19:12	So he said, "A nobleman went	12
	19:13	said to them, 'Do business with these until	12
	19:14	a delegation after him, saying, 'We do not want	12
	19:16	The first came forward and said, 'Lord	12
	19:17	He said to him, 'Well done, good slave!	12
	19:18	the second came, saying, 'Lord	12
	19:19	He said…'And you, rule over five cities.'	12
	19:20	Then the other came, saying	12
	19:22	He said to him, 'I will judge you	12
	19:24	He said to the bystanders, 'Take the pound	12
	19:25	they said to him, 'Lord, he has ten pounds!')	12
	19:28	After he had said this, he went on ahead	12
	19:30	saying, "Go into the village ahead	12
	19:31	say this, 'The Lord needs it.' "	12
	19:34	They said, "The Lord needs it."	12
	19:38	saying, "Blessed is the king who comes	12
	19:39	Some of the Pharisees in the crowd said to him	12
	19:42	saying, "If you, even you, had only recognized	12
	19:46	said, "It is written	12
	20: 2	said to him, "Tell us	12
	20: 5	They discussed it with one another, saying	12
	20: 5	"If we say, 'From heaven,' he will say	12
	20: 5	he will say, 'Why did you not believe him?'	12
	20: 6	if we say, 'Of human origin,' all the people	12
	20: 8	Jesus said to them, "Neither will I tell you	12
	20:13	the owner of the vineyard said, 'What shall I do?	12
	20:14	and said, 'This is the heir; let us kill him	12
	20:16	When they heard this, they said, "Heaven forbid!"	12
	20:17	he looked at them and said, "What then does	12
	20:20	in order to trap him by what he said	13
	20:21	that you are right in what you say and teach	12
	20:23	he perceived their craftiness and said to them	12
	20:24	They said, "The emperor's."	12

	20:25	He said to them, "Then give to the emperor	12
	20:26	to trap him by what he said;	15
	20:27	Sadducees, those who say there is no resurrection,	2
	20:34	Jesus said to them, "Those who belong to this age	12
	20:41	he said to them, "How can they say	12
	20:41	"How can they say that the Messiah is David's son?	12
	20:42	For David himself says in the book of Psalms	12
	20:42	'The Lord said to my Lord, "Sit at my right hand	12
	20:45	he said to the disciples	12
	21: 3	He said, "Truly I tell you	12
	21: 5	some were speaking about the temple…he said	12
	21: 8	he said, "Beware that you are not led astray;	12
	21: 8	many will come in my name and say, 'I am he!'	12
	21:10	he said to them, "Nation will rise against nation	12
	22: 8	So Jesus sent Peter and John, saying, "Go	12
	22:10	"Listen," he said to them	12
	22:11	say to the owner of the house, 'The teacher asks	12
	22:15	He said to them, "I have eagerly desired to eat	12
	22:17	he took a cup, and after giving thanks he said	12
	22:19	gave it to them, saying, "This is my body	12
	22:20	did the same with the cup after supper, saying,	12
	22:25	he said to them, "The kings of the Gentiles	12
	22:33	he said to him, "Lord, I am ready to go with you	12
	22:34	Jesus said, "I tell you, Peter,	12
	22:35	He said to them, "When I sent you out without	12
	22:35	lack anything?" They said, "No, not a thing."	12
	22:36	He said to them, "But now	12
	22:38	They said, "Lord, look, here are two swords."	12
	22:40	When he reached the place, he said to them, "Pray	12
	22:46	he said to them, "Why are you sleeping?	12
	22:48	Jesus said to him, "Judas	12
	22:51	Jesus said, "No more of this!"	4
	22:52	Then Jesus said to the chief priests	12
	22:56	and said, "This man also was with him."	12
	22:57	he denied it, saying, "Woman, I do not know him."	12
	22:58	A little later someone else, on seeing him, said	18
	22:58	Peter said, "Man, I am not!"	18
	22:60	Peter said, "Man, I do not know what you	12
	22:61	how he had said to him, "Before the cock crows	12
	22:67	They said, "If you are the Messiah, tell us."	12
	22:70	He said to them, "You say that I am."	18
	22:70	He said to them, "You say that I am."	12
	22:71	they said, "What further testimony do we need?	12
	23: 2	They began to accuse him, saying, "We found this	12
	23: 2	saying that he himself is the Messiah, a king."	12
	23: 3	He answered, "You say so."	12
	23: 4	Pilate said to the chief priests	12
	23: 5	they were insistent and said, "He stirs up	12
	23:14	said to them, "You brought me this man	12
	23:22	A third time he said to them, "Why	12
	23:28	Jesus turned to them and said	12
	23:29	For the days are surely coming when they will say	12
	23:30	begin to say to the mountains, 'Fall on us';	12
	23:34	[[Jesus said, "Father, forgive them;]]	12
	23:35	leaders scoffed at him, saying, "He saved others;	12
	23:37	saying, "If you are the King of the Jews	12
	23:39	saying, "Are you not the Messiah? Save yourself	12
	23:40	rebuked him, saying, "Do you not fear God	18
	23:42	he said, "Jesus, remember me	12
	23:46	Jesus, crying with a loud voice, said, "Father	12
	23:46	Having said this, he breathed his last.	12
	23:47	he praised God and said	12
	24: 5	said to them, "Why do you look for the living	12
	24:17	he said to them, "What are you discussing	12
	24:23	a vision of angels who said that he was alive.	12
	24:24	and found it just as the women had said;	12
	24:25	he said to them, "Oh, how foolish you are,	12
	24:29	they urged him strongly, saying, "Stay with us	12
	24:32	They said to each other, "Were not our hearts	12
	24:34	They were saying, "The Lord has risen indeed	12
	24:36	and said to them, "Peace be with you."	12
	24:38	He said to them, "Why are you frightened	12
	24:40	when he had said this, he showed them	12
	24:41	he said to them, "Have you anything here to eat?"	12
	24:44	Then he said to them, "These are my words	12
	24:46	said to them, "Thus it is written	12
Jhn	1:15	"This was he of whom I said, 'He who comes after	12
	1:21	Are you Elijah?" He said, "I am not."	12
	1:22	Then they said to him, "Who are you?	12
	1:22	What do you say about yourself?"	12
	1:23	He said, "I am the voice of one crying out	18

1:23	as the prophet Isaiah said.	12
1:30	This is he of whom I said, 'After me comes a man	12
1:33	one who sent me to baptize with water said to me	12
1:37	The two disciples heard him say this	10
1:38	Jesus turned and saw them following, he said	12
1:38	They said to him, "Rabbi"	12
1:39	He said to them, "Come and see."	12
1:41	He first found his brother Simon and said to him	12
1:42	who looked at him and said, "You are Simon	12
1:43	He found Philip and said to him, "Follow me."	12
1:45	Philip found Nathanael and said to him	12
1:46	Nathanael said to him, "Can anything good come	12
1:46	Philip said to him, "Come and see."	12
1:47	Jesus saw Nathanael coming…he said of him	12
1:51	And he said to him, "Very truly, I tell you	12
2: 3	When the wine gave out, the mother of Jesus said	12
2: 4	Jesus said to her, "Woman	12
2: 5	His mother said to the servants	12
2: 7	Jesus said to them, "Fill the jars with water."	12
2: 8	He said to them, "Now draw some out	12
2:10	said to him, "Everyone serves the good wine first	12
2:18	The Jews then said to him, "What sign can you	4
2:20	The Jews then said, "This temple has been	12
2:22	his disciples remembered that he had said this;	12
3: 2	He came to Jesus by night and said to him	12
3: 4	Nicodemus said to him, "How can anyone be born	12
3: 7	Do not be astonished that I said to you	12
3: 9	Nicodemus said to him, "How can these things be?"	4
3:26	They came to John and said to him, "Rabbi	12
3:28	You yourselves are my witnesses that I said	12
4: 7	Jesus said to her, "Give me a drink."	12
4: 9	The Samaritan woman said to him, "How is it	12
4:10	who it is that is saying to you, 'Give me a drink,'	12
4:11	woman said to him, "Sir, you have no bucket,	12
4:13	Jesus said to her, "Everyone who drinks	4
4:15	The woman said to him, "Sir, give me this water	12
4:16	Jesus said to her, "Go, call your husband	12
4:17	Jesus said to her, "You are right in saying	12
4:17	"You are right in saying, 'I have no husband';	12
4:18	What you have said is true!"	12
4:19	The woman said to him, "Sir, I see	12
4:20	you say that the place where people must worship	12
4:21	Jesus said to her, "Woman, believe me	12
4:25	The woman said to him, "I know that Messiah	12
4:26	Jesus said to her, "I am he, the one…speaking	·12
4:27	but no one said, "What do you want?"	12
4:28	went back to the city. She said to the people	12
4:32	But he said to them, "I have food to eat	12
4:33	So the disciples said to one another	12
4:34	Jesus said to them, "My food is to do the will	12
4:35	Do you not say, 'Four months more	12
4:42	They said to the woman, "It is no longer	12
4:42	no longer because of what you said that we believe	11
4:48	Then Jesus said to him, "Unless you see signs	12
4:49	The official said to him, "Sir, come down	12
4:50	Jesus said to him, "Go; your son will live."	12
4:52	they said to him, "Yesterday at one in the afternoon	12
4:53	this was the hour when Jesus had said to him	12
5: 6	he said to him, "Do you want to be made well?"	12
5: 8	Jesus said to him, "Stand up, take your mat	12
5:10	the Jews said to the man who had been cured	12
5:11	answered them, "The man who made me well said to me	12
5:12	They asked him, "Who is the man who said to you	12
5:14	Later Jesus found him in the temple and said	12
5:19	Jesus said to them, "Very truly, I tell you	4
5:34	I say these things so that you may be saved.	12
5:47	how will you believe what I say?"	15
6: 5	Jesus said to Philip, "Where are we to buy bread	12
6: 6	He said this to test him	12
6: 8	Andrew, Simon Peter's brother, said to him	12
6:10	Jesus said, "Make the people sit down."	12
6:14	they began to say, "This is indeed the prophet	12
6:20	he said to them, "It is I; do not be afraid."	12
6:25	said to him, "Rabbi, when did you come here?"	12
6:28	they said to him, "What must we do	12
6:30	said to him, "What sign are you going to give	12
6:32	Jesus said to them, "Very truly, I tell you	12
6:34	said to him, "Sir, give us this bread always."	12
6:35	Jesus said to them, "I am the bread of life.	12
6:36	I said to you that you have seen me	12
6:41	because he said, "I am the bread	12

6:42	They were saying, "Is not this Jesus, the son	12
6:42	can he now say, 'I have come down from heaven'?"	12
6:52	The Jews then disputed among themselves, saying	12
6:53	Jesus said to them, "Very truly, I tell you	12
6:59	He said these things while he was teaching	12
6:60	When many of his disciples heard it, they said	12
6:61	Jesus…said to them, "Does this offend you?	12
6:65	he said, "For this reason I have told you	12
7: 3	his brothers said to him, "Leave here	12
7: 6	Jesus said to them, "My time has not yet come	12
7: 9	saying this, he remained in Galilee.	12
7:11	The Jews were…saying, "Where is he?"	12
7:12	While some were saying, "He is a good man,"	12
7:12	were saying, "No, he is deceiving the crowd."	12
7:15	The Jews were astonished at it, saying,	12
7:25	Now some of the people of Jerusalem were saying	12
7:26	here he is, speaking openly, but they say nothing	12
7:31	the crowd believed in him and were saying	12
7:33	Jesus then said, "I will be with you	12
7:35	The Jews said to one another	12
7:36	What does he mean by saying, 'You will search	12
7:38	As the scripture has said, 'Out of	12
7:39	Now he said this about the Spirit	12
7:40	some in the crowd said	12
7:41	Others said, "This is the Messiah."	12
7:42	Has not the scripture said	12
8: 4	[they said to him, "Teacher, this woman]	12
8: 5	[Now what do you say?"]	12
8: 6	[They said this to test him]	12
8: 7	[he straightened up and said to them]	12
8:10	[Jesus straightened up and said to her, "Woman]	12
8:11	[She said, "No one, sir."]	12
8:11	[Jesus said, "Neither do I condemn you.]	12
8:12	Again Jesus spoke to them, saying, "I am the light	12
8:13	Then the Pharisees said to him	12
8:19	Then they said to him, "Where is your Father?"	12
8:21	Again he said to them, "I am going away	12
8:22	the Jews said, "Is he going to kill himself?	12
8:22	by saying, 'Where I am going, you cannot come'?"	12
8:23	He said to them, "You are from below	12
8:25	They said to him, "Who are you?"	12
8:25	Jesus said to them, "Why do I speak to you	12
8:26	I have much to say about you and much to condemn;	10
8:28	So Jesus said, "When you have lifted up the Son	12
8:30	As he was saying these things, many believed	10
8:31	Then Jesus said to the Jews who had believed	12
8:33	What do you mean by saying, 'You will be made free'?"	12
8:39	Jesus said to them, "If you were Abraham's	12
8:41	said to him, "We are not illegitimate children;	12
8:42	Jesus said to them, "If God were your Father	12
8:43	Why do you not understand what I say?	11
8:48	Jews answered him, "Are we not right in saying	12
8:52	The Jews said to him, "Now we know	12
8:52	yet you say, 'Whoever keeps my word	12
8:54	of whom you say, 'He is our God,'	12
8:55	if I would say that I do not know him,	12
8:57	Then the Jews said to him	12
8:58	Jesus said to them, "Very truly, I tell you	12
9: 6	When he had said this, he spat on the ground	12
9: 7	saying to him, "Go, wash in the pool of Siloam"	12
9: 9	Some were saying, "It is he."	12
9: 9	were saying, "No, but it is someone like him."	12
9: 9	He kept saying, "I am the man."	12
9:11	made mud, spread it on my eyes, and said to me	12
9:12	They said to him, "Where is he?"	12
9:12	"Where is he?" He said, "I do not know."	12
9:15	He said to them, "He put mud on my eyes.	12
9:16	Some of the Pharisees said	12
9:16	others said, "How can a man who is a sinner	12
9:17	So they said again to the blind man	12
9:17	"What do you say about him?	12
9:17	He said, "He is a prophet."	12
9:19	"Is this your son, who you say was born blind?	12
9:22	His parents said this because they were afraid	12
9:23	his parents said, "He is of age; ask him."	12
9:24	they called the man…and they said to him	12
9:26	They said to him, "What did he do to you?	12
9:28	they reviled him, saying, "You are his disciple	12
9:35	he found him, he said, "Do you believe	12
9:37	Jesus said to him, "You have seen him	12
9:38	He said, "Lord, I believe." And he worshiped him.	18

Jhn			
9:39	Jesus said, "I came into this world for judgment	12	
9:40	the Pharisees near him heard this and said	12	
9:41	Jesus said to them, "If you were blind	12	
9:41	now that you say, 'We see,' your sin remains.	12	
10: 6	they did not understand what he was saying	10	
10: 7	So again Jesus said to them, "Very truly	12	
10:20	Many of them were saying, "He has a demon	12	
10:21	Others were saying, "These are not the words	12	
10:24	the Jews gathered around him and said to him	12	
10:34	'I said, you are gods'?	12	
10:36	you say that the one whom the Father has sanctified	12	
10:36	blaspheming because I said, 'I am God's Son'?	12	
10:41	Many came to him, and they were saying,	12	
10:41	everything that John said about this man was true."	12	
11: 4	when Jesus heard it, he said	12	
11: 7	Then after this he said to the disciples	12	
11: 8	The disciples said to him, "Rabbi	12	
11:11	After saying this, he told them	12	
11:12	The disciples said to him, "Lord	12	
11:16	Thomas…said to his fellow disciples	12	
11:21	Martha said to Jesus, "Lord, if you had been here	12	
11:23	Jesus said to her, "Your brother will rise again."	12	
11:24	Martha said to him, "I know that he will rise	12	
11:25	Jesus said to her, "I am the resurrection	12	
11:27	She said to him, "Yes, Lord, I believe	12	
11:28	When she had said this	12	
11:32	Mary…knelt at his feet and said to him, "Lord	12	
11:34	He said, "Where have you laid him?"	12	
11:34	They said to him, "Lord, come and see."	12	
11:36	the Jews said, "See how he loved him!"	12	
11:37	some of them said, "Could not he	12	
11:39	Jesus said, "Take away the stone."	12	
11:39	Martha, the sister of the dead man, said to him,	12	
11:40	Jesus said to her, "Did I not tell you	12	
11:41	Jesus looked upward and said, "Father	12	
11:42	I have said this for the sake of the crowd	12	
11:43	When he had said this, he cried with a loud voice	12	
11:44	Jesus said to them, "Unbind him,	12	
11:47	called a meeting of the council, and said	12	
11:49	Caiaphas, who was high priest that year, said	12	
11:51	He did not say this on his own	12	
12: 4	(the one who was about to betray him), said	12	
12: 6	(He said this not because he cared about the poor	12	
12: 7	Jesus said, "Leave her alone.	12	
12:19	The Pharisees then said to one another	12	
12:21	They came to Philip…and said to him	8	
12:27	"Now my soul is troubled. And what should I say	12	
12:29	heard it and said that it was thunder.	12	
12:29	Others said, "An angel has spoken to him."	12	
12:33	He said this to indicate the kind of death	12	
12:34	How can you say that the Son of Man must be	12	
12:35	Jesus said to them, "The light is with you	12	
12:36	After Jesus had said this	10	
12:39	because Isaiah also said	12	
12:41	Isaiah said this because he saw his glory	12	
12:49	has…given me a commandment about what to say	12	
13: 6	He came to Simon Peter, who said to him, "Lord	12	
13: 8	Peter said to him, "You will never wash my feet."	12	
13: 9	Simon Peter said to him, "Lord, not my feet only	12	
13:10	Jesus said to him, "One who has bathed	12	
13:11	this reason he said, "Not all of you are clean."	12	
13:12	he said to them, "Do you know what I have done	12	
13:21	After saying this Jesus	12	
13:27	Jesus said to him, "Do quickly what you…do."	12	
13:28	no one at the table knew why he said this to him.	12	
13:31	When he had gone out, Jesus said	12	
13:33	as I said to the Jews so now I say to you	12	
13:33	as I said to the Jews so now I say to you	12	
13:36	Simon Peter said to him, "Lord, where	12	
13:37	Peter said to him, "Lord, why can I not follow	12	
14: 5	Thomas said to him, "Lord, we do not know	12	
14: 6	Jesus said to him, "I am the way, and the truth	12	
14: 8	Philip said to him, "Lord, show us the Father	12	
14: 9	Jesus said to him, "Have I been with you all	12	
14: 9	How can you say, 'Show us the Father'?	12	
14:10	The words that I say to you	12	
14:22	Judas (not Iscariot) said to him, "Lord,	12	
14:25	"I have said these things to you	10	
14:26	remind you of all that I have said to you	12	
14:28	You heard me say to you, 'I am going away	12	
15:11	I have said these things to you	10	

15:20	Remember the word that I said to you	12	
16: 1	"I have said these things to you	10	
16: 4	I have said these things to you	10	
16: 4	"I did not say these things…from the beginning	12	
16: 6	because I have said these things to you	10	
16:12	"I still have many things to say to you	12	
16:15	I said that he will take what is mine	12	
16:17	some of his disciples said to one another	12	
16:17	"What does he mean by saying to us	12	
16:18	They said, "What does he mean by this	12	
16:19	he said to them, "Are you discussing	12	
16:19	what I meant when I said, 'A little while	12	
16:25	"I have said these things to you in figures	10	
16:26	I do not say to you that I will ask the Father	12	
16:29	His disciples said, "Yes	12	
16:33	I have said this to you	10	
17: 1	he looked up to heaven and said	12	
18: 6	When Jesus said to them, "I am he,"	12	
18: 7	And they said, "Jesus of Nazareth."	12	
18:11	Jesus said to Peter	12	
18:17	The woman said to Peter	12	
18:17	He said, "I am not."	12	
18:20	I have said nothing in secret.	10	
18:21	Ask those who heard what I said to them;	10	
18:21	what I said to them; they know what I said."	12	
18:22	When he had said this	12	
18:22	saying, "Is that how you answer the high priest?"	12	
18:25	He denied it and said, "I am not."	12	
18:29	Pilate went out to them and said	18	
18:31	Pilate said to them, "Take him yourselves	12	
18:32	to fulfill what Jesus had said	12	
18:37	Jesus answered, "You say that I am a king.	12	
18:38	After he had said this, he went out to the Jews	12	
19: 3	They kept coming up to him, saying, "Hail, King	12	
19: 4	Pilate went out again and said to them	12	
19: 5	Pilate said to them, "Here is the man!"	12	
19: 6	Pilate said to them, "Take him yourselves	12	
19:10	Pilate therefore said to him, "Do you refuse	12	
19:14	He said to the Jews, "Here is your King!"	12	
19:21	the chief priests of the Jews said to Pilate	12	
19:21	but, 'This man said, I am King of the Jews.' "	12	
19:24	they said to one another, "Let us not tear it	12	
19:24	This was to fulfill what the scripture says,	12	
19:26	he said to his mother, "Woman, here is your son."	12	
19:27	he said to the disciple, "Here is your mother."	12	
19:28	he said (in order to fulfill the scripture),	12	
19:30	he said, "It is finished."	12	
19:37	again another passage of scripture says	12	
20: 2	she ran…and said to them	12	
20:13	They said to her, "Woman, why are you weeping?"	12	
20:13	She said to them	12	
20:14	said this, she turned around and saw Jesus	12	
20:15	Jesus said to her, "Woman, why are you weeping?	12	
20:15	Supposing him to be the gardener, she said	12	
20:16	Jesus said to her, "Mary!"	12	
20:16	She turned and said to him in Hebrew, "Rabbouni!"	12	
20:17	Jesus said to her, "Do not hold on to me	12	
20:17	go to my brothers and say to them	12	
20:18	she told them that he had said these things	12	
20:19	Jesus came and stood among them and said	12	
20:20	After he said this, he showed them his hands	12	
20:21	Jesus said to them again, "Peace be with you.	12	
20:22	When he had said this, he breathed on them	12	
20:22	he had said this, he breathed on them and said	12	
20:25	But he said to them, "Unless I see	12	
20:26	stood among them and said, "Peace be with you."	12	
20:27	Then he said to Thomas, "Put your finger here	12	
20:29	Jesus said to him, "Have you believed	12	
21: 3	Simon Peter said to them, "I am going fishing."	12	
21: 3	They said to him, "We will go with you."	12	
21: 5	Jesus said to them, "Children, you have no fish	12	
21: 6	He said to them, "Cast the net to the right side	12	
21: 7	That disciple whom Jesus loved said to Peter	12	
21:10	Jesus said to them, "Bring some of the fish	12	
21:12	Jesus said to them, "Come and have breakfast."	12	
21:15	Jesus said to Simon Peter, "Simon son of John	12	
21:15	He said to him, "Yes, Lord; you know that I love you."	12	
21:15	Jesus said to him, "Feed my lambs."	12	
21:16	A second time he said to him, "Simon son of John	12	
21:16	He said to him, "Yes, Lord; you know that I love you."	12	
21:16	Jesus said to him, "Tend my sheep."	12	

21:17	He said to him the third time, "Simon son of John	12
21:17	because he said to him the third time	12
21:17	he said to him, "Lord, you know everything;	12
21:17	Jesus said to him, "Feed my sheep.	12
21:19	(He said this to indicate the kind of death	12
21:19	After this he said to him, "Follow me."	12
21:20	and had said, "Lord, who is it	12
21:21	When Peter saw him, he said to Jesus, "Lord	12
21:22	Jesus said to him, "If it is my will	12
21:23	Jesus did not say to him that he would not die	12

Act 1: 4	he said, "is what you have heard from me;	1
1: 9	When he had said this, as they were watching	12
1:11	said, "Men of Galilee, why do you stand looking up	12
1:15	Peter stood up…and said	12
1:24	they prayed and said, "Lord, you know everyone's heart.	12
2:12	were amazed and perplexed, saying to one another	12
2:13	others sneered and said	12
2:14	let this be known to you, and listen to what I say.	15
2:22	Israelites, listen to what I have to say: Jesus	13
2:25	David says concerning him, 'I saw the Lord	12
2:29	I may say to you confidently of our ancestor	12
2:31	saying, 'He was not abandoned to Hades	14
2:34	he himself says, 'The Lord said to my Lord	12
2:34	'The Lord said to my Lord, "Sit at my right hand	12
2:37	said to Peter and to the other apostles	12
2:38	Peter said to them, "Repent, and be baptized	18
2:40	exhorted them, saying, "Save yourselves	12
3: 4	Peter looked intently at him, as did John, and said	12
3: 6	Peter said, "I have no silver or gold	12
3:22	Moses said, 'The Lord your God will raise up	12
3:25	saying to Abraham, 'And in your descendants	12
4: 8	Then Peter, filled with the Holy Spirit, said	12
4:16	said, "What will we do with them?	12
4:23	what the chief priests and the elders had said	12
4:24	raised their voices together to God and said	12
4:25	said by the Holy Spirit through our ancestor David	12
5: 8	Peter said to her, "Tell me	4
5: 8	she said, "Yes, that was the price."	12
5: 9	Peter said to her, "How is it that you have agreed	1
5:19	an angel…brought them out, and said	12
5:28	saying, "We gave you strict orders not to teach	12
5:35	he said to them, "Fellow Israelites,	12
6: 2	said, "It is not right that we should neglect	12
6: 5	What they said pleased the whole community	13
6:11	Then they secretly instigated some men to say	12
6:13	They set up false witnesses who said	12
6:13	saying things against this holy place and the law;	10
6:14	we have heard him say	12
7: 3	said to him, 'Leave your country	12
7: 7	I will judge the nation that they serve,' said God	12
7:26	tried to reconcile them, saying	12
7:27	the man…pushed Moses aside, saying	12
7:33	the Lord said to him, 'Take off the sandals	12
7:35	this Moses whom they rejected when they said	12
7:37	This is the Moses who said to the Israelites	12
7:40	saying to Aaron, 'Make gods for us who will lead	12
7:48	as the prophet says	12
7:49	house will you build for me, says the Lord	12
7:56	"Look," he said, "I see the heavens opened	12
7:60	When he had said this, he died.	12
8: 6	listened eagerly to what was said by Philip	12
8: 9	saying that he was someone great.	12
8:10	saying, "This man is the power of God	12
8:19	saying, "Give me also this power	12
8:20	Peter said to him, "May your silver perish with you	12
8:24	nothing of what you have said may happen to me."	12
8:26	an angel of the Lord said to Philip, "Get up and go	10
8:29	the Spirit said to Philip, "Go over	12
8:34	"About whom…does the prophet say this	12
8:36	the eunuch said, "Look, here is water!	18
9: 4	He fell to the ground and heard a voice saying	12
9:10	The Lord said to him in a vision, "Ananias."	12
9:11	The Lord said to him, "Get up and go	1
9:15	the Lord said to him, "Go	12
9:17	laid his hands on Saul and said, "Brother Saul	12
9:20	began to proclaim Jesus in the synagogues, saying	14
9:21	All who heard him were amazed and said	12
9:34	Peter said to him, "Aeneas, Jesus Christ heals you;	12
9:40	turned to the body and said, "Tabitha, get up."	12
10: 3	an angel of God coming in and saying to him	12
10: 4	stared at him…and said, "What is it, Lord?"	12

10:13	he heard a voice saying, "Get up, Peter; kill and eat."	1
10:14	Peter said, "By no means, Lord;	12
10:15	The voice said to him again, a second time	1
10:19	the Spirit said to him, "Look	12
10:21	Peter went down to the men and said, "I am the one	12
10:22	to hear what you have to say."	15
10:26	Peter made him get up, saying, "Stand up;	12
10:28	he said to them, "You yourselves know	18
10:31	said, 'Cornelius, your prayer has been heard	18
10:33	listen to all that the Lord has commanded you to say	1
10:46	Then Peter said	4
11: 3	saying, "Why did you go to uncircumcised men	12
11: 4	Peter began to explain it to them…saying	12
11: 7	I also heard a voice saying to me, 'Get up, Peter;	12
11:13	the angel standing in his house and saying	12
11:16	I remembered the word of the Lord, how he had said	12
11:18	they praised God, saying	12
12: 7	He tapped Peter on the side and woke him, saying	12
12: 8	The angel said to him, "Fasten your belt	12
12: 8	He did so. Then he said to him	12
12:11	Peter came to himself and said	12
12:15	They said to her, "You are out of your mind!"	12
12:15	They said, "It is his angel."	12
13: 2	the Holy Spirit said, "Set apart for me Barnabas	12
13:10	said, "You son of the devil	12
13:15	officials of the synagogue sent them a message, saying	12
13:22	his testimony about him he said	12
13:25	as John was finishing his work, he said	12
13:35	Therefore he has also said in another psalm	12
13:40	what the prophets said does not happen to you	12
13:46	Paul and Barnabas spoke out boldly, saying	12
13:47	so the Lord has commanded us, saying	1
14:10	said in a loud voice, "Stand upright on your feet."	12
14:22	saying, "It is through many persecutions	14
15: 5	some believers…stood up and said	12
15: 7	Peter stood up and said to them, "My brothers	12
15:17	says the Lord, who has been making these things	12
15:24	certain persons…have said things to disturb you	13
15:32	said much to encourage and strengthen the believers	13
15:36	After some days Paul said to Barnabas, "Come	12
16: 9	a man of Macedonia pleading with him and saying	12
16:14	to listen eagerly to what was said by Paul.	10
16:15	she urged us, saying	12
16:18	Paul…turned and said to the spirit	12
16:20	they said, "These men are disturbing our city;	12
16:30	brought them outside and said	18
16:35	sent the police, saying, "Let those men go."	12
16:36	the jailer reported the message to Paul, saying	14
17: 3	explaining and proving…and saying	14
17: 7	saying that there is another king named Jesus."	12
17:18	Some said, "What does this babbler want to say?"	12
17:18	Some said, "What does this babbler want to say?"	12
17:18	Others said, "He seems to be a proclaimer	1
17:22	Paul stood in front of the Areopagus and said,	18
17:28	as even some of your own poets have said	12
17:32	some scoffed; but others said, "We will hear you	12
18: 6	shook the dust from his clothes and said to them	12
18: 9	One night the Lord said to Paul in a vision	12
18:13	said, "This man is persuading people to worship God	12
18:14	Gallio said to the Jews	12
18:21	but on taking leave of them, he said	12
19: 2	He said to them, "Did you receive the Holy Spirit	12
19: 3	he said, "Into what then were you baptized?"	12
19: 4	Paul said, "John baptized	12
19:13	saying, "I adjure you by the Jesus	12
19:15	the evil spirit said to them in reply,	12
19:21	He said, "After I have gone there	12
19:25	and said, "Men, you know	12
19:26	saying that gods made with hands are not gods.	12
19:35	the town clerk had quieted the crowd, he said	18
19:41	When he had said this, he dismissed the assembly.	12
20:10	in his arms, and said, "Do not be alarmed	12
20:18	When they came to him, he said to them:	12
20:35	the words of the Lord Jesus, for he himself said	12
20:38	grieving especially because of what he had said	12
21:11	bound his own feet and hands with it, and said	12
21:11	"Thus says the Holy Spirit	12
21:14	except to say, "The Lord's will be done."	12
21:20	they said to him, "You see, brother	12
21:37	brought into the barracks, he said to the tribune	12
21:37	"May I say something to you?"	12

Act	21:40	he addressed them in the Hebrew language, saying:	12
	22: 2	they became even more quiet. Then he said:	18
	22: 7	to the ground and heard a voice saying to me	12
	22: 8	he said to me, 'I am Jesus of Nazareth	12
	22:10	The Lord said to me, 'Get up and go to Damascus;	12
	22:13	came to me; and standing beside me, he said	12
	22:14	he said, 'The God of our ancestors has chosen you	12
	22:18	saw Jesus saying to me, 'Hurry	12
	22:19	I said, 'Lord, they themselves know	12
	22:21	he said to me, 'Go, for I will send you	12
	22:25	Paul said to the centurion who was standing by	12
	22:26	he went to the tribune and said to him	3
	22:27	are you a Roman citizen?" And he said, "Yes."	18
	22:28	Paul said, "But I was born a citizen."	18
	23: 1	Paul was looking intently at the council he said	12
	23: 3	Paul said to him, "God will strike you	12
	23: 4	Those standing nearby said	12
	23: 5	Paul said, "I did not realize, brothers	18
	23: 7	When he said this	12
	23: 8	(The Sadducees say that there is no resurrection	12
	23:11	the Lord stood near him and said	12
	23:14	They went to the chief priests and elders and said	12
	23:17	Paul called one of the centurions and said	18
	23:18	took him, brought him to the tribune, and said	18
	23:23	he summoned two of the centurions and said	12
	23:35	he said, "I will give you a hearing	18
	24: 2	Tertullus began to accuse him, saying:	12
	24:25	Felix became frightened and said	4
	25: 5	he said, "let those of you who have the authority	18
	25:10	Paul said, "I am appealing to the emperor's tribunal;	12
	25:14	Festus laid Paul's case before the king, saying	12
	25:22	Agrippa said to Festus, "I would like to hear	1
	25:22	"Tomorrow," he said, "you will hear him."	18
	25:24	Festus said, "King Agrippa	18
	26: 1	Agrippa said to Paul, "You have permission	18
	26:14	heard a voice saying to me in the Hebrew language	12
	26:22	saying nothing but what the prophets…said	12
	26:22	what…Moses said would take place:	10
	26:25	Paul said, "I am not out of my mind	18
	26:28	Agrippa said to Paul	1
	26:31	as they were leaving, they said to one another	10
	26:32	Agrippa said to Festus	18
	27:10	saying, "Sirs, I can see that the voyage	12
	27:11	than to what Paul said.	12
	27:21	Paul then stood up among them and said, "Men	12
	27:24	he said, 'Do not be afraid, Paul;	12
	27:31	Paul said to the centurion and the soldiers	12
	27:33	Paul urged all of them to take some food, saying	12
	27:35	After he had said this, he took bread;	12
	28: 4	they said to one another	12
	28: 6	and began to say that he was a god.	12
	28:17	When they had assembled, he said to them,	12
	28:24	Some were convinced by what he had said	12
	28:25	was right in saying to your ancestors	10
	28:26	'Go to this people and say, You will indeed listen	12
Rom	2: 2	You say, "We know that God's judgment	1
	3: 5	what should we say?	12
	3: 8	And why not say…"Let us do evil so that good	1
	3: 8	(as some people slander us by saying that we say)	18
	3: 8	(as some people slander us by saying that we say)	12
	3:19	Now we know that whatever the law says	12
	4: 1	What then are we to say was gained by Abraham	12
	4: 3	For what does the scripture say?	12
	4: 9	We say, "Faith was reckoned to Abraham	12
	4:18	according to what was said	12
	6: 1	What then are we to say? Should we continue in sin	12
	7: 7	What then should we say? That the law is sin?	12
	7: 7	if the law had not said, "You shall not covet."	12
	8:31	What then are we to say about these things?	12
	9: 9	For this is what the promise said, "About this time	13
	9:14	What then are we to say? Is there injustice on God's	12
	9:15	For he says to Moses, "I will have mercy	12
	9:17	For the scripture says to Pharaoh	12
	9:19	You will say to me then, "Why then does he…	12
	9:20	Will what is molded say to the one who molds it	12
	9:25	As indeed he says in Hosea	12
	9:26	"And in the very place where it was said to them	12
	9:30	What then are we to say? Gentiles, who did not	12
	10: 6	But the righteousness that comes from faith says	12
	10: 6	"Do not say in your heart, 'Who will ascend	12
	10: 8	But what does it say? "The word is near you	12

	10:11	The scripture says, "No one who believes in him	12
	10:16	for Isaiah says, "Lord, who has believed	12
	10:19	First Moses says, "I will make you jealous	12
	10:20	Isaiah is so bold as to say, "I have been found	12
	10:21	of Israel he says, "All day long I have held out	12
	11: 2	Do you not know what the scripture says of Elijah	12
	11: 9	And David says, "Let their table become a snare	12
	11:19	You will say, "Branches were broken off so that I	12
	12: 3	by the grace given to me I say to everyone	12
	12:19	"Vengeance is mine, I will repay, says the Lord."	12
	14:11	"As I live, says the Lord, every knee shall bow	12
	15:10	and again he says, "Rejoice, O Gentiles	12
	15:12	again Isaiah says, "The root of Jesse shall come	12
1Co	1:12	What I mean is that each of you says	12
	1:15	so that no one can say that you were baptized	12
	3: 4	For when one says, "I belong to Paul,"	12
	6: 3	to say nothing of ordinary matters?	1
	6: 5	I say this to your shame.	12
	6:16	it is said, "The two shall be one flesh."	18
	7: 6	This I say by way of concession, not of command.	12
	7: 8	To the unmarried and the widows I say	12
	7:12	To the rest I say—I and not the Lord	12
	7:35	I say this for your own benefit	12
	9: 8	Do I say this on human authority?	10
	9: 8	Does not the law also say the same?	12
	10:15	judge for yourselves what I say.	18
	10:28	if someone says to you	12
	11:22	What should I say to you?	12
	11:24	when he had given thanks, he broke it and said	12
	11:25	he took the cup also, after supper, saying	12
	12: 3	no one speaking by the Spirit of God ever says	12
	12: 3	no one can say "Jesus is Lord"	12
	12:15	If the foot would say, "Because I am not a hand	12
	12:16	if the ear would say, "Because I am not an eye	12
	12:21	The eye cannot say to the hand, "I have no need	12
	14: 9	how will anyone know what is being said?	10
	14:16	say the "Amen" to your thanksgiving	12
	14:16	since the outsider does not know what you are saying?	12
	14:21	they will not listen to me," says the Lord.	12
	14:23	will they not say that you are out of your mind?	12
	14:29	let the others weigh what is said.	1
	14:34	be subordinate, as the law also says.	12
	15:12	how can some of you say there is no resurrection	12
	15:27	when it says, "All things are put in subjection,"	12
	15:34	I say this to your shame.	10
	15:50	I am saying, brothers and sisters, is this:	18
2Co	1:17	ready to say "Yes, yes" and "No, no"	7
	1:20	it is through him that we say the "Amen,"	5
	4: 6	the God who said, "Let light shine out of darkness,"	12
	6: 2	For he says, "At an acceptable time	12
	6:16	For we are the temple of the living God; as God said	12
	6:17	be separate from them, says the Lord	12
	6:18	be my sons and daughters, says the Lord Almighty."	12
	7: 3	I do not say this to condemn you	12
	7:14	just as everything we said to you was true	10
	8: 8	I do not say this as a command	12
	9: 2	my boasting…to the people of Macedonia, saying	1
	9: 3	so that you may be ready, as I said you would be;	12
	9: 4	we would be humiliated—to say nothing of you	12
	10:10	For they say, "His letters are weighty and strong	18
	10:11	what we say by letter when absent	13
	11:17	What I am saying	10
	11:17	I am saying not with the Lord's authority	10
	11:21	To my shame, I must say, we were too weak for that!	12
	12: 9	he said to me, "My grace is sufficient for you	12
	12:16	Nevertheless (you say) since I was crafty	1
Gal	1:23	they only heard it said	14
	2:14	I said to Cephas before them all	12
	3: 8	saying, "All the Gentiles shall be blessed in you."	14
	3:16	it does not say, "And to offsprings,"	12
	3:16	but it says, "And to your offspring,"	1
	4:30	does the scripture say? "Drive out the slave	12
	5:16	Live by the Spirit, I say	12
Eph	4: 8	Therefore it is said, "When he ascended on high	12
	4: 9	When it says, "He ascended," what does it mean	1
	5:14	Therefore it says, "Sleeper, awake!	12
Php	4: 4	again I will say, Rejoice.	12
Col	2: 4	I am saying this so that no one may deceive you	12
	4:17	say to Archippus, "See that you complete the task	12
1Th	5: 3	When they say, "There is peace and security,"	12
2Th	3:14	those who do not obey what we say in this letter;	13

1Ti	1: 7	understanding either what they are saying or…	12
	4: 1	Now the Spirit expressly says	12
	5:13	saying what they should not say.	10
	5:13	saying what they should not say.	1
	5:18	for the scripture says, "You shall not muzzle an ox	12
2Ti	2: 7	Think over what I say	12
Tit	1:12	one of them, their very own prophet, who said	12
	2: 8	having nothing evil to say of us.	12
Phm	1:19	I say nothing about your owing me	12
	1:21	knowing that you will do even more than I say.	12
Heb	1: 5	which of the angels did God ever say, "You are my Son;	12
	1: 6	he says, "Let all God's angels worship him."	12
	1: 7	Of the angels he says, "He makes his angels winds	12
	1: 8	But of the Son he says, "Your throne, O God,	1
	1:13	But to which of the angels has he ever said, "Sit	12
	2:12	saying, "I will proclaim your name to my brothers	12
	3: 7	Therefore, as the Holy Spirit says	12
	3:10	I said, 'They always go astray in their hearts	12
	3:15	As it is said, "Today, if you hear his voice	12
	4: 3	just as God has said, "As in my anger I swore…	12
	4: 5	And again in this place it says	1
	4: 7	saying through David much later	12
	5: 5	but was appointed by the one who said to him	10
	5: 6	as he says also in another place	12
	5:11	About this we have much to say	13
	6:14	saying, "I will surely bless you and multiply you."	12
	7: 9	One might even say	12
	7:14	Moses said nothing about priests.	10
	7:21	a priest with an oath, because of the one who said	12
	8: 1	Now the main point in what we are saying is this:	12
	8: 8	God finds fault with them when he says:	12
	8: 8	"The days are surely coming, says the Lord	12
	8: 9	so I had no concern for them, says the Lord.	12
	8:10	This is the covenant…says the Lord:	12
	8:11	shall not teach…say to each other	12
	9:20	saying, "This is the blood of the covenant	12
	10: 5	when Christ came into the world, he said	12
	10: 7	I said, 'See, God, I have come to do your will, O God'	12
	10: 8	When he said above	12
	10:15	also testifies to us, for after saying	12
	10:16	after those days, says the Lord:	12
	10:30	we know the one who said, "Vengeance is mine	12
	11:32	And what more should I say?	12
	12:21	Moses said, "I tremble with fear.")	12
	13: 5	he has said, "I will never leave you or forsake you."	12
	13: 6	So we can say with confidence	12
Jas	1:13	No one…should say, "I am being tempted by God";	12
	2: 3	you take notice…and say	12
	2: 3	while to the one who is poor you say, "Stand there,"	12
	2:11	For the one who said, "You shall not commit adultery,"	12
	2:11	the one…also said, "You shall not murder."	12
	2:14	if you say you have faith but do not have works?	12
	2:16	one of you says to them, "Go in peace;	12
	2:18	someone will say, "You have faith and I have works."	12
	2:23	Thus the scripture was fulfilled that says	12
	4: 5	suppose that it is for nothing that the scripture says	12
	4: 6	But he gives all the more grace; therefore it says	12
	4:13	Come now, you who say, "Today or tomorrow	12
	4:15	Instead you ought to say, "If the Lord wishes	12
2Pe	1:17	conveyed to him by the Majestic Glory, saying	1
	3: 4	and saying, "Where is the promise of his coming?	12
1Jn	1: 6	If we say that we have fellowship with him	12
	1: 8	If we say that we have no sin, we deceive ourselves	12
	1:10	If we say that we have not sinned, we make him a liar	12
	2: 4	says, "I have come to know him," but does not obey	12
	2: 6	whoever says, "I abide in him," ought to walk	12
	2: 9	Whoever says, "I am in the light,"	12
	4: 5	therefore what they say is from the world	10
	4:20	Those who say, "I love God," and hate	12
	5:16	I do not say that you should pray about that.	12
Jde	1: 9	but said, "The Lord rebuke you!"	12
	1:14	Enoch…prophesied, saying	12
	1:18	they said to you, "In the last time there will be	12
Rev	1: 8	"I am the Alpha and the Omega," says the Lord God	12
	1:11	saying, "Write in a book what you see and send it	12
	1:17	saying, "Do not be afraid; I am the first and the last	12
	2: 7	listen to what the Spirit is saying to the churches.	12
	2: 9	those who say that they are Jews and are not	12
	2:11	listen to what the Spirit is saying to the churches.	12
	2:17	listen to what the Spirit is saying to the churches.	12
	2:24	to you I say, I do not lay on you any other burden;	12

	2:29	listen to what the Spirit is saying to the churches.	12
	3: 6	listen to what the Spirit is saying to the churches.	12
	3: 9	those…who say that they are Jews and are not	12
	3:13	listen to what the Spirit is saying to the churches.	12
	3:17	For you say, 'I am rich, I have prospered	12
	3:22	listen to what the Spirit is saying to the churches."	12
	4: 1	the first voice…said, "Come up here	12
	5: 5	Then one of the elders said to me, "Do not weep.	12
	5:14	the four living creatures said, "Amen!"	12
	6: 6	a voice in the midst of the…creatures saying	12
	7: 3	saying, "Do not damage the earth or the sea	12
	7:10	cried out in a loud voice, saying, "Salvation	12
	7:13	Then one of the elders addressed me, saying	12
	7:14	I said to him, "Sir, you are the one that knows."	12
	7:14	Then he said to me, "These are they	12
	9:14	saying to the sixth angel who had the trumpet	12
	10: 4	but I heard a voice from heaven saying	12
	10: 4	"Seal up what the seven thunders have said	10
	10: 8	the voice…spoke to me again, saying	12
	10: 9	and he said to me, "Take it, and eat;	12
	10:11	They said to me, "You must prophesy again	12
	11:12	Then they heard a loud voice from heaven saying	12
	11:15	and there were loud voices in heaven, saying	12
	13: 4	and they worshiped the beast, saying	12
	14: 7	He said in a loud voice, "Fear God	12
	14: 8	another angel, a second, followed, saying	12
	14:13	I heard a voice from heaven saying, "Write this:	12
	14:13	"Yes," says the Spirit	12
	16: 5	And I heard the angel of the waters say	12
	16:17	voice came…from the throne, saying, "It is done!"	12
	17: 1	one of the seven angels…came and said to me	10
	17: 7	But the angel said to me, "Why are you so amazed?	12
	17:15	And he said to me, "The waters that you saw	12
	18: 4	Then I heard another voice from heaven saying	12
	18: 7	Since in her heart she says, 'I rule as a queen;	12
	18:10	they will stand far off…and say, "Alas, alas	12
	18:21	and threw it into the sea, saying	12
	19: 1	a great multitude in heaven, saying, "Hallelujah!	12
	19: 3	Once more they said, "Hallelujah!	12
	19: 4	worshiped God…saying, "Amen. Hallelujah!"	12
	19: 5	And from the throne came a voice saying	12
	19: 9	And the angel said to me, "Write this:	12
	19: 9	And he said to me, "These are true words of God."	12
	19:10	but he said to me, "You must not do that!	12
	21: 3	I heard a loud voice from the throne saying	12
	21: 5	the one who was seated on the throne said, "See	12
	21: 5	Also he said, "Write this	12
	21: 6	Then he said to me, "It is done!	12
	21: 9	Then one of the seven angels…came and said	10
	22: 6	And he said to me, "These words are trustworthy	12
	22: 9	he said to me, "You must not do that!	12
	22:10	And he said to me, "Do not seal up the words	12
	22:17	The Spirit and the bride say, "Come."	12
	22:17	And let everyone who hears say, "Come."	12
	22:20	The one who testifies to these things says,	12

say a blessing

1. εὐλογέω, *eulogeō, 2328*

1Co	14:16	Otherwise, if you say a blessing with the spirit	1

say a prayer

1. προσεύχομαι, *proseuchomai, 4667*

Mrk	12:40	for the sake of appearance say long prayers.	1
Lke	20:47	for the sake of appearance say long prayers.	1

say before

1. προλέγω, *prolegō, 4625*

2Co	7: 3	I said before that you are in our hearts	1
Gal	1: 9	As we have said before, so now I repeat	1

say farewell

1. ἀπασπάζομαι, *apaspazomai, 571*

2. ἀποτάσσω, *apotassō, 698*

3. ἀσπάζομαι, *aspazomai, 832*

Mrk	6:46	After saying farewell to them,	2
Lke	9:61	let me first say farewell to those at my home."	2
Act	18:18	Paul said farewell to the believers	2
	20: 1	after encouraging them and saying farewell	3
	21: 6	and said farewell to one another	1
2Co	2:13	I said farewell to them and went on to Macedonia.	2

say in defense
1. ἀπολογέομαι, *apologeomai, 664*
Act 25: 8 Paul said in his defense   1

say in opposition
1. ἀντιλέγω, *antilegō, 515*
Act   4:14 they had nothing to say in opposition.   1

saying
1. Contextual: Not in Greek
2. λόγος, *logos, 3364*
3. ῥῆμα, *rhēma, 4839*
Mrk 7:29 "For saying that, you may go—the demon has left   2
      9:32 they did not understand what he was saying   3
Lke   7: 1 After Jesus had finished all his sayings   3
      9:28 Now about eight days after these sayings   2
      9:45 they did not understand this saying;   3
      9:45 they were afraid to ask him about this saying.   3
Jhn 4:37 For here the saying holds true, 'One sows   2
1Co 4: 6 learn through us the meaning of the saying,   1
   15:54 then the saying that is written will be fulfilled: 2
1Ti 1:15 The saying is sure and worthy of full acceptance   2
    3: 1 The saying is sure: 2
    4: 9 The saying is sure   2
2Ti 2:11 The saying is sure: 2
Tit   3: 8 The saying is sure.   2

scale *See also* pair of scales
1. θώραξ, *thōrax, 2606*
2. λεπίς, *lepis, 3318*
Act   9:18 something like scales fell from his eyes   2
Rev 9: 9 they had scales like iron breastplates   1

scarcely
1. μόγις, *mogis, 3653*
2. μόλις, *molis, 3660*
Lke 9:39 mauls him and will scarcely leave him.   1
Act 14:18 they scarcely restrained the crowds   2
   27:16 scarcely able to get the ship's boat under control.   2

scarlet
1. κόκκινος, *kokkinos, 3132*
Mat 27:28 They stripped him and put a scarlet robe on him   1
Heb 9:19 with water and scarlet wool and hyssop   1
Rev 17: 3 and I saw a woman sitting on a scarlet beast   1
   17: 4 The woman was clothed in purple and scarlet   1
   18:12 cargo of...fine linen, purple, silk and scarlet   1
   18:16 clothed in fine linen, in purple and scarlet   1

scatter
1. βάλλω, *ballō, 965*
2. διασκορπίζω, *diaskorpizō, 1399*
3. διασπείρω, *diaspeirō, 1401*
4. σκορπίζω, *skorpizō, 5025*
Mat 12:30 and whoever does not gather with me scatters.   4
   25:26 gather where I did not scatter?   2
   26:31 the sheep of the flock will be scattered.'   2
Mrk 4:26 as if someone would scatter seed on the ground   1
   14:27 the sheep will be scattered.'   2
Lke 1:51 he has scattered the proud   2
   11:23 whoever does not gather with me scatters.   4
Jhn 10:12 the wolf snatches them and scatters them.   4
   16:32 when you will be scattered, each one to his home   4
Act 5:37 all who followed him were scattered.   2
    8: 1 scattered throughout the countryside of Judea   3
    8: 4 those who were scattered went from place to place,   3
   11:19 who were scattered because of the persecution   3

scatter abroad
1. σκορπίζω, *skorpizō, 5025*
2Co 9: 9 "He scatters abroad, he gives to the poor;   1

scatter seed
1. διασκορπίζω, *diaskorpizō, 1399*
Mat 25:24 gathering where you did not scatter seed;   1

scent
1. θύϊνος, *thyinos, 2591*

Rev 18:12 all kinds of scented wood, all articles of ivory   1

scepter
1. ῥάβδος, *rhabdos, 4811*
Heb 1: 8 the righteous scepter is the scepter of your kingdom.   1
    1: 8 the righteous scepter is the scepter of your kingdom.   1

Sceva
1. Σκευᾶς, *Skeuas, 5005*
Act 19:14 Seven sons of a Jewish high priest named Sceva   1

scheme
1. μεθοδεία, *methodeia, 3497*
Eph 4:14 by their craftiness in deceitful scheming.   1

scoff
1. ἐκμυκτηρίζω, *ekmyktērizō, 1727*
2. ἐμπαιγμονή, *empaigmonē, 1848*
3. χλευάζω, *chleuazō, 5949*
Lke 23:35 leaders scoffed at him, saying, "He saved others;   1
Act 17:32 some scoffed; but others said, "We will hear you   3
2Pe 3: 3 scoffing and indulging their own lusts   2

scoffer
1. ἐμπαίκτης, *empaiktēs, 1851*
2. καταφρονητής, *kataphronētēs, 2970*
Act 13:41 'Look, you scoffers! Be amazed and perish   2
2Pe 3: 3 that in the last days scoffers will come   1
Jde 1:18 "In the last time there will be scoffers   1

scold
1. ἐμβριμάομαι, *embrimaomai, 1839*
Mrk 14: 5 they scolded her.   1

scorch
1. καυματίζω, *kaumatizō, 3009*
Mat 13: 6 when the sun rose, they were scorched;   1
Mrk 4: 6 when the sun rose, it was scorched;   1
Rev 16: 8 and it was allowed to scorch people with fire;   1
   16: 9 they were scorched by the fierce heat   1

scorching *See* scorching *heat*

scorn
1. ἐξουθενέω, *exoutheneō, 2024*
2. λογίζομαι + εἰς + οὐδείς, *logizomai + eis + oudeis, 3357 + 1650 + 4029*
Act 19:27 the temple of...Artemis will be scorned   2
Gal 4:14 you did not scorn or despise me   1

scorpion
1. σκορπίος, *skorpios, 5026*
Lke 10:19 authority to tread on snakes and scorpions   1
   11:12 asks for an egg, will give a scorpion?   1
Rev 9: 3 like the authority of scorpions of the earth.   1
    9: 5 their torture was like the torture of a scorpion   1
    9:10 They have tails like scorpions, with stingers   1

scribe
1. γραμματεύς, *grammateus, 1208*
Mat 2: 4 calling together all the chief priests and scribes   1
    5:20 exceeds that of the scribes and Pharisees   1
    7:29 and not as their scribes.   1
    8:19 A scribe then approached and said   1
    9: 3 Then some of the scribes said to themselves   1
   12:38 Then some of the scribes and Pharisees said   1
   13:52 "Therefore every scribe who has been trained   1
   15: 1 Then Pharisees and scribes came to Jesus   1
   16:21 of the elders and chief priests and scribes   1
   17:10 "Why, then, do the scribes say   1
   20:18 handed over to the chief priests and scribes   1
   21:15 when the chief priests and the scribes saw   1
   23: 2 "The scribes and the Pharisees sit on Moses' seat;   1
   23:13 woe to you, scribes and Pharisees, hypocrites!   1
   23:15 Woe to you, scribes and Pharisees, hypocrites!   1
   23:23 "Woe to you, scribes and Pharisees, hypocrites!   1
   23:25 "Woe to you, scribes and Pharisees, hypocrites!   1
   23:27 "Woe to you, scribes and Pharisees, hypocrites!   1
   23:29 "Woe to you, scribes and Pharisees, hypocrites!   1

	23:34	I send you prophets, sages, and scribes	1
	26:57	the scribes and the elders had gathered.	1
	27:41	chief priests...with the scribes and elders	1
Mrk	1:22	not as the scribes.	1
	2: 6	Now some of the scribes were sitting there	1
	2:16	the scribes of the Pharisees	1
	3:22	the scribes who came down from Jerusalem said	1
	7: 1	some of the scribes who had come from Jerusalem	1
	7: 5	the Pharisees and the scribes asked him	1
	8:31	chief priests, and the scribes	1
	9:11	they asked him, "Why do the scribes say	1
	9:14	scribes arguing with them.	1
	10:33	chief priests and the scribes	1
	11:18	the chief priests and the scribes heard it	1
	11:27	the chief priests, the scribes	1
	12:28	One of the scribes came near and heard	1
	12:32	the scribe said to him, "You are right, Teacher;	1
	12:35	can the scribes say that the Messiah is the son	1
	12:38	As he taught, he said, "Beware of the scribes	1
	14: 1	The chief priests and the scribes were looking for	1
	14:43	the chief priests, the scribes, and the elders.	1
	14:53	the chief priests, the elders, and the scribes	1
	15: 1	held a consultation with the elders and scribes	1
	15:31	the chief priests, along with the scribes,	1
Lke	5:21	the scribes and the Pharisees began to question	1
	5:30	The Pharisees and their scribes were complaining	1
	6: 7	The scribes and the Pharisees watched him	1
	9:22	the elders, chief priests, and scribes	1
	11:53	scribes and the Pharisees began to be very hostile	1
	15: 2	the Pharisees and the scribes were grumbling	1
	19:47	The chief priests, the scribes	1
	20: 1	priests and the scribes came with the elders	1
	20:19	the scribes and chief priests	1
	20:39	some of the scribes answered, "Teacher	1
	20:46	"Beware of the scribes	1
	22: 2	The chief priests and the scribes were looking for	1
	22:66	both chief priests and scribes	1
	23:10	The chief priests and the scribes stood by	1
Jhn	8: 3	[[The scribes and the Pharisees brought a woman]]	1
Act	4: 5	their rulers, elders, and scribes	1
	6:12	the elders and the scribes;	1
	23: 9	certain scribes of the Pharisees' group	1
1Co	1:20	Where is the one who is wise? Where is the scribe?	1

scripture

1. Contextual: Not in Greek
2. γραφή, *graphē*, 1210
3. γράφω, *graphō*, 1211

Mat	21:42	"Have you never read in the scriptures:	2
	22:29	neither the scriptures nor the power of God.	2
	26:54	how then would the scriptures be fulfilled	2
	26:56	scriptures of the prophets may be fulfilled."	2
Mrk	12:10	Have you not read this scripture: 'The stone	2
	12:24	know neither the scriptures nor the power of God?	2
	14:49	let the scriptures be fulfilled."	2
Lke	4:21	"Today this scripture has been fulfilled	2
	22:37	I tell you, this scripture must be fulfilled	3
	24:27	the things about himself in all the scriptures.	2
	24:32	while he was opening the scriptures to us?"	2
	24:45	to understand the scriptures	2
Jhn	2:22	and they believed the scripture and the word	2
	5:39	"You search the scriptures	2
	7:38	As the scripture has said, 'Out of	2
	7:42	Has not the scripture said	2
	10:35	and the scripture cannot be annulled	2
	13:18	to fulfill the scripture, 'The one	2
	17:12	so that the scripture might be fulfilled.	2
	19:24	This was to fulfill what the scripture says,	2
	19:28	he said (in order to fulfill the scripture),	2
	19:36	so that the scripture might be fulfilled	2
	19:37	again another passage of scripture says	2
	20: 9	for as yet they did not understand the scripture	2
Act	1:16	"Friends, the scripture had to be fulfilled	2
	8:32	passage of the scripture that he was reading	2
	8:35	starting with this scripture	2
	17: 2	argued with them from the scriptures	2
	17:11	examined the scriptures every day	2
	18:24	an eloquent man, well-versed in the scriptures.	2
	18:28	showing by the scriptures that the Messiah	2
Rom	1: 2	through his prophets in the holy scriptures	2
	4: 3	For what does the scripture say?	2

	9:17	For the scripture says to Pharaoh	2
	10:11	The scripture says, "No one who believes in him	2
	11: 2	Do you not know what the scripture says of Elijah	2
	15: 4	by the encouragement of the scriptures	2
1Co	15: 3	Christ died...in accordance with the scriptures	2
	15: 4	he was raised...in accordance with the scriptures	2
2Co	4:13	spirit of faith that is in accordance with scripture	3
Gal	3: 8	the scripture, foreseeing that God would justify	2
	3:22	scripture has imprisoned all things under the power	2
	4:30	does the scripture say? "Drive out the slave	2
1Ti	4:13	give attention to the public reading of scripture	1
	5:18	for the scripture says, "You shall not muzzle an ox	2
2Ti	3:16	All scripture is inspired by God	2
Jas	2: 8	fulfill the royal law according to the scripture	2
	2:23	Thus the scripture was fulfilled that says	2
	4: 5	suppose that it is for nothing that the scripture says	2
1Pe	2: 6	For it stands in scripture:	2
2Pe	1:20	no prophecy of scripture is a matter of one's own	2
	3:16	twist...as they do the other scriptures.	2

scroll

1. Contextual: Not in Greek
2. βιβλίον, *biblion*, 1046
3. κεφαλίς, *kephalis*, 3053

Lke	4:17	the scroll of the prophet Isaiah was given to him.	2
	4:17	He unrolled the scroll	2
	4:20	he rolled up the scroll, gave it back	2
Heb	9:19	sprinkled both the scroll itself and all the people	2
	10: 7	(in the scroll of the book it is written of me)."	3
Rev	5: 1	a scroll written on the inside and on the back	2
	5: 2	"Who is worthy to open the scroll and break	2
	5: 3	no one...was able to open the scroll or to look	2
	5: 4	because no one was found worthy to open the scroll	2
	5: 5	so that he can open the scroll and its seven seals."	2
	5: 7	He went and took the scroll from the right hand	1
	5: 8	When he had taken the scroll	2
	5: 9	worthy...to take the scroll and to open its seals	2
	6:14	The sky vanished like a scroll rolling itself up	2
	10: 8	the scroll that is open in the hand of the angel	2

little scroll

1. βιβλαρίδιον, *biblaridion*, 1044

Rev	10: 2	He held a little scroll open in his hand.	1
	10: 9	angel and told him to give me the little scroll;	1
	10:10	took the little scroll from the hand of the angel	1

scrutiny   *See* subject to scrutiny

Scythian

1. Σκύθης, *Skythēs*, 5033

Col	3:11	barbarian, Scythian, slave and free;	1

sea   *See also* put to sea, sea *anchor*, sea *creature*, sea *monster*

1. Contextual: Not in Greek
2. βυθός, *bythos*, 1113
3. θάλασσα, *thalassa*, 2498
4. πέλαγος, *pelagos*, 4283

Mat	4:15	land of Naphtali, on the road by the sea	3
	4:18	As he walked by the Sea of Galilee, he saw two	3
	4:18	a net into the sea—for they were fishermen.	3
	8:24	A windstorm arose on the sea, so great	3
	8:26	Then he got up and rebuked the winds and the sea;	3
	8:27	that even the winds and the sea obey him?"	3
	8:32	down the steep bank into the sea and perished	3
	9: 1	after getting into a boat he crossed the sea	1
	13: 1	went out of the house and sat beside the sea.	3
	13:47	like a net that was thrown into the sea	3
	14:25	he came walking toward them on the sea.	3
	14:26	when the disciples saw him walking on the sea	3
	15:29	he passed along the Sea of Galilee	3
	17:27	do not give offense to them, go to the sea	3
	18: 6	and you were drowned in the depth of the sea.	3
	21:21	'Be lifted up and thrown into the sea,'	3
	23:15	you cross sea and land	3
Mrk	1:16	Jesus passed along the Sea of Galilee	3
	1:16	Simon and...Andrew casting a net into the sea	3
	2:13	Jesus went out again beside the sea;	3
	3: 7	Jesus departed with his disciples to the sea	3
	4: 1	Again he began to teach beside the sea.	3

Mrk	4: 1	he got into a boat on the sea and sat there	3
	4: 1	the whole crowd was beside the sea on the land.	3
	4:39	and rebuked the wind, and said to the sea	3
	4:41	that even the wind and the sea obey him?"	3
	5: 1	They came to the other side of the sea	3
	5:13	rushed down the steep bank into the sea	3
	5:13	drowned in the sea.	3
	5:21	he was by the sea.	3
	6:47	When evening came, the boat was out on the sea	3
	6:48	he came towards them…walking on the sea.	3
	6:49	when they saw him walking on the sea	3
	7:31	went by way of Sidon towards the Sea of Galilee	3
	9:42	you were thrown into the sea.	3
	11:23	'Be taken up and thrown into the sea,'	3
Lke	17: 2	if…you were thrown into the sea	3
	17: 6	'Be uprooted and planted in the sea,'	3
	21:25	by the roaring of the sea and the waves.	3
Jhn	6: 1	Jesus went to the other side of the Sea of Galilee	3
	6: 1	Sea of Galilee, also called the Sea of Tiberias.	1
	6:16	his disciples went down to the sea	3
	6:17	started across the sea to Capernaum.	3
	6:18	The sea became rough because a strong wind was	3
	6:19	they saw Jesus walking on the sea	3
	6:22	that had stayed on the other side of the sea	3
	6:25	they found him on the other side of the sea	3
	21: 1	Jesus showed himself…by the Sea of Tiberias;	3
	21: 7	and jumped into the sea.	3
Act	4:24	the earth, the sea, and everything in them	3
	7:36	wonders and signs in Egypt, at the Red Sea	3
	10:32	in the home of Simon, a tanner, by the sea.'	3
	14:15	the earth and the sea and all that is in them.	3
	27: 5	After we had sailed across the sea	4
	27:27	as we were drifting across the sea of Adria	1
	27:30	had lowered the boat into the sea	3
	27:38	throwing the wheat into the sea.	3
	27:40	cast off the anchors and left them in the sea.	3
	28: 4	though he has escaped from the sea	3
Rom	9:27	the children of Israel were like the sand of the sea	3
1Co	10: 1	all passed through the sea	3
	10: 2	baptized…in the cloud and in the sea	3
2Co	11:25	a night and a day I was adrift at sea;	2
	11:26	danger at sea, danger from false brothers and sisters;	3
Heb	11:29	passed through the Red Sea as if it were dry land	3
Jas	1: 6	wave of the sea…driven and tossed by the wind;	3
Jde	1:13	wild waves of the sea, casting up the foam	3
Rev	4: 6	there is something like a sea of glass, like crystal.	3
	5:13	every creature…under the earth and in the sea	3
	7: 1	so that no wind could blow on earth or sea	3
	7: 2	who had been given power to damage earth and sea	3
	7: 3	"Do not damage the earth or the sea or the trees	3
	8: 8	something like…was thrown into the sea.	3
	8: 9	A third of the sea became blood	3
	8: 9	a third of the living creatures in the sea died	3
	10: 2	Setting his right foot on the sea	3
	10: 5	the angel whom I saw standing on the sea and the land	3
	10: 6	who created…the sea and what is in it:	3
	10: 8	angel who is standing on the sea and on the land."	3
	12:12	woe to the earth and the sea, for the devil has come	3
	13: 1	I saw a beast rising out of the sea	3
	14: 7	who made…the sea and the springs of water."	3
	15: 2	appeared to be a sea of glass mixed with fire	3
	15: 2	standing beside the sea of glass	3
	16: 3	The second angel poured his bowl into the sea	3
	16: 3	and every living thing in the sea died.	3
	18:17	sailors and all whose trade is on the sea	3
	18:19	all who had ships at sea grew rich by her wealth!	3
	18:21	took up a stone…and threw it into the sea	3
	20: 8	they are as numerous as the sands of the sea.	3
	20:13	And the sea gave up the dead that were in it	3
	21: 1	earth had passed away, and the sea was no more.	3

by the sea

1. παραθαλάσσιος, *parathalassios, 4144*

Mat 4:13 and made his home in Capernaum by the sea   1

seafarer

1. ἐπί + τόπος + πλέω, *epi + topos + pleō, 2093 + 5536 + 4434*

Rev 18:17 And all shipmasters and seafarers, sailors   1

seal *See also* mark with a seal, put a seal on, set seal

1. κατασφραγίζω, *katasphragizō, 2958*
2. σφραγίζω, *sphragizō, 5381*
3. σφραγίς, *sphragis, 5382*

Mat	27:66	made the tomb secure by sealing the stone.	2
Rom	4:11	He received the sign of circumcision as a seal	3
1Co	9: 2	you are the seal of my apostleship in the Lord.	3
Rev	5: 1	a scroll…sealed with seven seals;	1
	5: 1	a scroll…sealed with seven seals;	3
	5: 2	to open the scroll and break its seals?"	3
	5: 5	so that he can open the scroll and its seven seals."	3
	5: 9	worthy…to take the scroll and to open its seals	3
	6: 1	I saw the Lamb open one of the seven seals	3
	6: 3	When he opened the second seal, I heard	3
	6: 5	When he opened the third seal, I heard	3
	6: 7	When he opened the fourth seal, I heard the voice	3
	6: 9	When he opened the fifth seal, I saw	3
	6:12	When he opened the sixth seal, I looked,	3
	7: 2	another angel…having the seal of the living God	3
	7: 4	I heard the number of those who were sealed	2
	7: 4	sealed out of every tribe of the people of Israel:	2
	7: 5	From the tribe of Judah twelve thousand sealed,	2
	7: 8	from the tribe of Benjamin twelve thousand sealed.	2
	8: 1	When the Lamb opened the seventh seal	3
	9: 4	who do not have the seal of God on their foreheads.	3
	20: 3	into the pit, and locked and sealed it over him	2

seal up

1. σφραγίζω, *sphragizō, 5381*

Rev 10: 4 "Seal up what the seven thunders have said   1
      22:10 "Do not seal up the words of the prophecy   1

seamless

1. ἄραφος, *araphos, 731*

Jhn 19:23 now the tunic was seamless   1

sear with a hot iron

1. καυστηριάζω, *kaustēriazō, 3013*

1Ti 4: 2 liars whose consciences are seared with a hot iron.   1

search *See also* make careful search

1. ἀναζητέω, *anazēteō, 349*
2. ἐξετάζω, *exetazō, 2004*
3. ἐπιζητέω, *epizēteō, 2118*
4. ἐραυνάω, *eraunaō, 2236*
5. ζητέω, *zēteō, 2426*

Mat	2: 8	he sent them to Bethlehem, saying, "Go and search	2
	2:13	Herod is about to search for the child, to destroy	5
	7: 7	will be given you; search, and you will find;	5
	7: 8	and everyone who searches finds	5
	13:45	like a merchant in search of fine pearls;	5
	18:12	and go in search of the one that went astray?	5
Mrk	1:37	"Everyone is searching for you."	5
Lke	2:45	they returned to Jerusalem to search for him.	1
	2:48	I have been searching for you in great anxiety."	5
	2:49	to them, "Why were you searching for me?	5
	11: 9	search, and you will find; knock, and the door	5
	11:10	everyone who searches finds	5
	15: 8	search carefully until she finds it?	5
Jhn	5:39	"You search the scriptures	4
	7:34	You will search for me, but you will not find me;	5
	7:36	'You will search for me and you will not find me'	5
	7:52	Search and you will see	4
	8:21	"I am going away, and you will search for me	5
Act	10:19	three men are searching for you.	5
	12:19	Herod had searched for him and could not find him	3
	17: 5	searching for Paul and Silas to bring them out	5
	17:27	so that they would search for God	5
Rom	8:27	God, who searches the heart, knows	4
1Co	2:10	the Spirit searches everything, even the depths	4
2Ti	1:17	he eagerly searched for me and found me	5
Rev	2:23	that I am the one who searches minds and hearts	4

seashore

1. θάλασσα, *thalassa, 2498*
2. χεῖλος + ὁ + θάλασσα, *cheilos + ho + thalassa, 5927 + 3836 + 2498*

Heb 11:12 the innumerable grains of sand by the seashore."   2
Rev 12:18 the dragon took his stand on the sand of the seashore.   1

seaside

1. θάλασσα, *thalassa*, 2498

Act 10: 6 Simon, a tanner, whose house is by the seaside." 1

season[1]

1. καιρός, *kairos*, 2789

Mrk 11:13 for it was not the season for figs. 1
    12: 2 When the season came 1
Lke 20:10 When the season came 1
Act 14:17 giving you rains from heaven and fruitful seasons 1
Gal 4:10 days, and months, and seasons, and years. 1
1Th 5: 1 Now concerning the times and the seasons, 1

season[2]

1. ἀρτύω, *artyō*, 789

Mrk 9:50 how can you season it? 1
Col 4: 6 always be gracious, seasoned with salt 1

seat *See also* mercy seat, take a seat

1. ἀνάκειμαι, *anakeimai*, 367
2. καθέδρα, *kathedra*, 2756
3. κάθημαι, *kathēmai*, 2764
4. καθίζω, *kathizō*, 2767

Mat 19:28 when the Son of Man is seated on the throne 4
    21:12 and the seats of those who sold doves. 2
    23: 2 "The scribes and the Pharisees sit on Moses' seat; 2
    23:22 by the one who is seated upon it. 3
    26:64 the Son of Man seated at the right hand of Power 3
Mrk 11:15 the seats of those who sold doves; 2
    14:62 Son of Man seated at the right hand of the Power,' 3
Lke 22:69 seated at the right hand of the power of God." 3
Jhn 2:14 and the money changers seated at their tables. 3
    6:11 he distributed them to those who were seated; 1
Act 8:28 was returning home; seated in his chariot, 3
Eph 1:20 seated him at his right hand 4
Col 3: 1 where Christ is, seated at the right hand of God. 3
Heb 8: 1 one who is seated at the right hand of the throne 4
Jas 2: 3 and say, "Have a seat here, please," 3
Rev 4: 2 in heaven stood a throne, with one seated on the throne! 3
    4: 3 the one seated there looks like jasper 3
    4: 4 seated on the thrones are twenty-four elders 3
    4: 9 thanks to the one who is seated on the throne 3
    4:10 fall before the one who is seated on the throne 3
    5: 1 the one seated on the throne 3
    5: 7 right hand of the one who was seated on the throne. 3
    5:13 "To the one seated on the throne and to the Lamb 3
    6:16 hide us from…the one seated on the throne 3
    7:10 "Salvation…to our God who is seated on the throne 3
    7:15 one who is seated on the throne will shelter them. 3
    14:14 seated on the cloud was one like the Son of Man 3
    17: 1 the great whore who is seated on many waters 3
    17: 9 are seven mountains on which the woman is seated; 3
    17:15 waters that you saw, where the whore is seated 3
    19: 4 worshiped God who is seated on the throne, saying 3
    20: 4 Then I saw thrones, and those seated on them 4
    21: 5 And the one who was seated on the throne said, 3

good seat

1. πρωτοκαθεδρία, *prōtokathedria*, 4751

Mat 23: 6 They love…the best seats in the synagogues 1
Mrk 12:39 and to have the best seats in the synagogues 1
Lke 20:46 and love…the best seats in the synagogues 1

judgment seat

1. βῆμα, *bēma*, 1037

Mat 27:19 While he was sitting on the judgment seat 1
Rom 14:10 will all stand before the judgment seat of God. 1
2Co 5:10 appear before the judgment seat of Christ 1

seat of honor

1. πρωτοκαθεδρία, *prōtokathedria*, 4751

Lke 11:43 love to have the seat of honor in the synagogues 1

seat with

1. συγκάθημαι, *synkathēmai*, 5153
2. συγκαθίζω, *synkathizō*, 5154

Act 26:30 Bernice and those who had been seated with them; 1
Eph 2: 6 seated us with him in the heavenly places 2

seclusion *See* remain in seclusion

second

1. δευτεραῖος, *deuteraios*, 1308
2. δεύτερος, *deuteros*, 1311
3. δύο, *dyo*, 1545
4. ἕτερος, *heteros*, 2283

Mat 5:41 forces you to go one mile, go also the second mile. 3
    21:30 father went to the second and said the same; 4
    22:26 The second did the same, so also the third 2
    22:39 a second is like it: 'You shall love your neighbor 2
    26:42 Again he went away for the second time and prayed 2
Mrk 12:21 the second married the widow and died 2
    12:31 The second is this, 'You shall love your neighbor 2
    14:72 At that moment the cock crowed for the second time. 2
Lke 19:18 the second came, saying, 'Lord 2
    20:30 then the second 2
Jhn 3: 4 Can one enter a second time into the mother's womb 2
    4:54 Now this was the second sign that Jesus did 2
    9:24 for the second time they called the man 2
    21:16 A second time he said to him, "Simon son of John 2
Act 7:13 On the second visit 2
    10:15 The voice said to him again, a second time 2
    11: 9 a second time the voice answered from heaven 2
    12:10 they had passed the first and the second guard 2
    13:33 as also it is written in the second psalm 2
    28:13 on the second day we came to Puteoli. 1
1Co 12:28 first apostles, second prophets, third teachers; 2
    15:47 the second man is from heaven. 2
2Co 13: 2 as I did when present on my second visit 2
Tit 3:10 After a first and second admonition, 2
Heb 8: 7 there would have been no need to look for a second 2
    9: 3 Behind the second curtain was a tent 2
    9: 7 only the high priest goes into the second 2
    9:28 will appear a second time, not to deal with sin 2
    10: 9 in order to establish the second. 2
2Pe 3: 1 This is now, beloved, the second letter I am writing 2
Rev 2:11 conquers will not be harmed by the second death. 2
    4: 7 the second living creature like an ox 2
    6: 3 When he opened the second seal, I heard 2
    6: 3 the second living creature call out, "Come!" 2
    8: 8 The second angel blew his trumpet 2
    11:14 The second woe has passed. The third woe 2
    14: 8 another angel, a second, followed, saying 2
    16: 3 The second angel poured his bowl into the sea 2
    20: 6 Over these the second death has no power 2
    20:14 This is the second death, the lake of fire; 2
    21: 8 the lake that burns…which is the second death." 2
    21:19 every jewel;…the second sapphire 2

secret *See also* keep secret, learn the secret

1. ἀπόκρυφος, *apokryphos*, 649
2. κρυπτός, *kryptos*, 3220
3. κρύπτω, *kryptō*, 3221
4. κρυφαῖος, *kryphaios*, 3224
5. λάθρα, *lathra*, 3277
6. μυστήριον, *mystērion*, 3696

Mat 6: 4 so that your alms may be done in secret 2
    6: 4 your Father who sees in secret will reward you. 2
    6: 6 Father who is in secret; and your Father who sees 2
    6: 6 your Father who sees in secret will reward you. 2
    6:18 Father who is in secret; and your Father who sees 4
    6:18 your Father who sees in secret will reward you. 4
    10:26 and nothing secret that will not become known. 2
    13:11 to know the secrets of the kingdom of heaven 6
Mrk 4:11 given the secret of the kingdom of God 6
    4:22 nor is anything secret, except to come to light. 1
Lke 8:10 given to know the secrets of the kingdom of God; 6
    8:17 anything secret that will not become known 1
    12: 2 and nothing secret that will not become known. 2
Jhn 7: 4 who wants to be widely known acts in secret. 2
    7:10 went, not publicly but as it were in secret. 2
    18:20 I have said nothing in secret. 2
    19:38 was a disciple of Jesus, though a secret one 3
Act 16:37 now are they going to discharge us in secret? 5
Rom 2:16 God…will judge the secret thoughts of all. 2
1Co 2: 7 we speak God's wisdom, secret and hidden, 6
    14:25 the secrets of the unbeliever's heart are disclosed 2

secretly *See also* bring in secretly, instigate secretly

1. κρυφῇ, *kryphē*, 3225
2. λάθρα, *lathra*, 3277

Mat	2: 7	Then Herod secretly called for the wise men	2
Eph	5:12	to mention what such people do secretly;	1

sect

1. αἵρεσις, *hairesis, 146*

Act	5:17	(that is, the sect of the Sadducees)	1
	15: 5	who belonged to the sect of the Pharisees	1
	24: 5	a ringleader of the sect of the Nazarenes.	1
	24:14	according to the Way, which they call a sect	1
	26: 5	the strictest sect of our religion	1
	28:22	with regard to this sect	1

section

1. ἐφημερία, *ephēmeria, 2389*

Lke	1: 8	and his section was on duty	1

Secundus

1. Σεκοῦνδος, *Sekoundos, 4941*

Act	20: 4	Aristarchus and Secundus from Thessalonica	1

securely *See also* establish securely

1. ἀσφαλῶς, *asphalōs, 857*
2. ἐν + πᾶς + ἀσφάλεια, *en + pas + asphaleia, 1877 + 4246 + 854*

Act	5:23	"We found the prison securely locked	2
	16:23	ordered the jailer to keep them securely.	1

security

1. ἀσφάλεια, *asphaleia, 854*

1Th	5: 3	When they say, "There is peace and security,"	1

see *See also* go to see

1. Contextual: Not in Greek
2. αὐγάζω, *augazō, 878*
3. ἀφοράω, *aphoraō, 927*
4. βλέμμα, *blemma, 1062*
5. βλέπω, *blepō, 1063*
6. γινώσκω, *ginōskō, 1182*
7. ἐμβλέπω, *emblepō, 1838*
8. ἐπισκοπέω, *episkopeō, 2174*
9. ἐποπτεύω, *epopteuō, 2227*
10. θεάομαι, *theaomai, 2517*
11. θεωρέω, *theōreō, 2555*
12. ἴδε, *ide, 2623*
13. ἰδού, *idou, 2627*
14. καθοράω, *kathoraō, 2775*
15. νοέω, *noeō, 3783*
16. ὁράω, *horaō, 3972*
17. ποιέω, *poieō, 4472*
18. φαίνω, *phainō, 5743*
19. φανερός, *phaneros, 5745*
20. φανερόω, *phaneroō, 5746*

Mat	2: 9	went the star that they had seen at its rising	16
	2:10	When they saw that the star had stopped,	16
	2:11	entering the house, they saw the child with Mary	16
	2:16	When Herod saw that he had been tricked	16
	3: 7	when he saw many Pharisees and Sadducees	16
	3:16	heavens were opened…and he saw the Spirit of God	16
	4:16	people who sat in darkness have seen a great light	16
	4:18	he saw two brothers, Simon, who is called Peter	16
	4:21	went from there, he saw two other brothers	16
	5: 1	Jesus saw the crowds, he went up the mountain;	16
	5: 8	are the pure in heart, for they will see God.	16
	5:16	so that they may see your good works and give glory	16
	6: 1	in order to be seen by them; for then you have	10
	6: 4	your Father who sees in secret will reward you.	5
	6: 5	so that they may be seen by others	18
	6: 6	your Father who sees in secret will reward you.	5
	6:18	fasting may be seen not by others but by your Father	18
	6:18	your Father who sees in secret will reward you.	5
	7: 3	do you see the speck in your neighbor's eye	5
	8: 4	Jesus said to him, "See that you say nothing	16
	8:14	saw his mother-in-law lying in bed with a fever;	16
	8:18	Now when Jesus saw great crowds around him	16
	8:34	and when they saw him, they begged him to leave	16
	9: 2	When Jesus saw their faith, he said	16
	9: 8	When the crowds saw it, they were filled with awe	16
	9: 9	As Jesus was walking along, he saw a man	16
	9:11	When the Pharisees saw this, they said	16

	9:22	Jesus turned, and seeing her he said, "Take heart	16
	9:23	and saw the flute players and the crowd	16
	9:30	"See that no one knows of this."	16
	9:33	"Never has anything like this been seen in Israel."	18
	9:36	When he saw the crowds, he had compassion for them	16
	10:16	"See, I am sending you out like sheep	13
	11: 4	"Go and tell John what you hear and see:	5
	11: 8	What then did you go out to see?	16
	11: 9	What then did you go out to see? A prophet?	16
	11:10	'See, I am sending my messenger ahead of you,	13
	12: 2	When the Pharisees saw it, they said to him,	16
	12:22	so that the one who had been mute could speak and see.	5
	12:38	"Teacher, we wish to see a sign from you."	16
	12:41	see, something greater than Jonah is here!	13
	12:42	see, something greater than Solomon is here!	13
	13:13	that 'seeing they do not perceive	5
	13:16	blessed are your eyes, for they see	5
	13:17	righteous people longed to see what you see	16
	13:17	longed to see what you see, but did not see it	5
	13:17	longed to see what you see, but did not see it	16
	14:14	When he went ashore, he saw a great crowd;	16
	14:26	when the disciples saw him walking on the sea	16
	15:17	Do you not see that whatever goes into the mouth	15
	15:31	when they saw the mute speaking	5
	15:31	the lame walking, and the blind seeing.	5
	16:28	before they see the Son of Man coming	16
	17: 8	when they looked up, they saw no one	16
	18:10	in heaven their angels continually see the face	5
	18:31	When his fellow slaves saw	16
	20: 3	he saw others standing idle in the marketplace;	16
	20:18	"See, we are going up to Jerusalem	13
	21:15	when the chief priests and the scribes saw	16
	21:19	seeing a fig tree by the side of the road,	16
	21:20	When the disciples saw it, they were amazed,	16
	21:32	even after you saw it, you did not change your minds	16
	21:38	when the tenants saw the son	16
	22:11	"But when the king came in to see the guests	10
	23: 5	They do all their deeds to be seen by others;	10
	23:38	See, your house is left to you, desolate.	13
	23:39	you will not see me again until you say	16
	24: 2	he asked them, "You see all these, do you not?	5
	24: 6	see that you are not alarmed;	16
	24:15	"So when you see the desolating sacrilege	16
	24:30	see 'the Son of Man coming on the clouds of heaven'	16
	24:33	So also, when you see all these things	16
	25:20	see, I have made five more talents.'	12
	25:22	see, I have made two more talents.'	12
	25:37	that we saw you hungry and gave you food	16
	25:38	that we saw you a stranger and welcomed you	16
	25:39	that we saw you sick or in prison and visited	16
	25:44	that we saw you hungry or thirsty	16
	26: 8	when the disciples saw it, they were angry	16
	26:45	See, the hour is at hand	13
	26:46	let us be going. See, my betrayer is at hand."	13
	26:58	in order to see how this would end.	16
	26:64	From now on you will see the Son of Man	16
	26:71	to the porch, another servant-girl saw him	16
	27: 3	Judas, his betrayer, saw that Jesus was condemned	16
	27: 4	"What is that to us? See to it yourself."	16
	27:24	So when Pilate saw that he could do nothing	16
	27:24	see to it yourselves."	16
	27:49	let us see whether Elijah will come to save him."	16
	27:54	saw the earthquake and what took place	16
	28: 1	the other Mary went to see the tomb.	11
	28: 6	Come, see the place where he lay.	16
	28: 7	there you will see him.'	16
	28:10	there they will see me."	16
	28:17	When they saw him, they worshiped him;	16
Mrk	1: 2	"See, I am sending my messenger ahead of you,	13
	1:10	he saw the heavens torn apart	16
	1:16	saw Simon and his brother Andrew casting a net	16
	1:19	he saw James son of Zebedee	16
	1:44	"See that you say nothing to anyone;	16
	2: 5	When Jesus saw their faith	16
	2:12	saying, "We have never seen anything like this!"	16
	2:14	walking along, he saw Levi son of Alphaeus	16
	2:16	Pharisees saw that he was eating with sinners	16
	3: 2	They watched him to see whether he would cure him	1
	3:11	Whenever the unclean spirits saw him	11
	5: 6	When he saw Jesus from a distance, he ran	16
	5:14	people came to see what it was that had happened.	16

5:15	came to Jesus and saw the demoniac sitting there	11
5:16	who had seen what had happened to the demoniac	16
5:22	he saw him, fell at his feet	16
5:31	"You see the crowd pressing in on you;	5
5:32	He looked all around to see who had done it.	16
5:38	he saw a commotion	11
6:33	Now many saw them going and recognized them	16
6:34	As he went ashore, he saw a great crowd;	16
6:38	"How many loaves have you? Go and see."	16
6:48	he saw that they were straining at the oars	16
6:49	when they saw him walking on the sea	16
6:50	for they all saw him and were terrified.	16
7:18	Do you not see that whatever goes into a person	15
8:18	Do you have eyes, and fail to see?	5
8:23	he asked him, "Can you see anything?"	5
8:24	"I can see people, but they look like trees	5
8:25	was restored, and he saw everything clearly.	7
9: 1	until they see that the kingdom of God has come	16
9: 8	saw no one with them any more, but only Jesus.	16
9: 9	to tell no one about what they had seen	16
9:14	they saw a great crowd around them	16
9:15	When the whole crowd saw him,	16
9:20	When the spirit saw him	16
9:25	Jesus saw that a crowd came running together	16
9:38	we saw someone casting out demons in your name	16
10:14	when Jesus saw this, he was indignant	16
10:33	saying, "See, we are going up to Jerusalem	13
11:13	Seeing in the distance a fig tree in leaf	16
11:13	he went to see whether perhaps he would find	1
11:20	they saw the fig tree withered away to its roots.	16
12:15	Bring me a denarius and let me see it."	16
12:28	seeing that he answered them well, he asked him	16
12:34	When Jesus saw that he answered wisely	16
13: 2	"Do you see these great buildings?	5
13:14	when you see the desolating sacrilege set up	16
13:26	they will see 'the Son of Man coming in clouds'	16
13:29	So also, when you see these things taking place	16
14:42	let us be going. See, my betrayer is at hand."	13
14:62	"I am; and 'you will see the Son of Man	16
14:67	saw Peter warming himself, she stared at him	16
14:69	the servant-girl, on seeing him	16
15: 4	See how many charges they bring against you."	12
15:32	so that we may see and believe."	16
15:36	let us see whether Elijah will come	16
15:39	when the centurion, who stood facing him, saw	16
15:47	the mother of Joses saw where the body was laid.	11
16: 4	they looked up, they saw that the stone	11
16: 5	As they entered the tomb, they saw a young man	16
16: 7	there you will see him, just as he told you."	16
16:11	[heard that he was alive and had been seen by her]	10
16:14	[because they had not believed those who saw him]	10
Lke 1:12	When Zechariah saw him, he was terrified;	16
1:22	realized that he had seen a vision in the sanctuary.	16
2:10	see—I am bringing you good news of great joy	13
2:15	"Let us go now to Bethlehem and see this thing	16
2:17	When they saw this, they made known what	16
2:20	for all they had heard and seen	16
2:26	that he would not see death before	16
2:26	before he had seen the Lord's Messiah.	16
2:30	for my eyes have seen your salvation	16
2:48	When his parents saw him they were astonished;	16
3: 6	all flesh shall see the salvation of God.' "	16
5: 2	he saw two boats there at the shore of the lake;	16
5: 8	when Simon Peter saw it	16
5:12	When he saw Jesus	16
5:20	When he saw their faith, he said	16
5:26	saying, "We have seen strange things today."	16
5:27	he went out and saw a tax collector named Levi	10
6: 7	to see whether he would cure on the sabbath	1
6:41	Why do you see the speck	5
6:42	you…do not see the log in your own eye?	5
7:13	When the Lord saw her	16
7:22	"Go and tell John what you have seen and heard:	16
7:25	What then did you go out to see?	16
7:26	What then did you go out to see? A prophet?	16
7:27	'See, I am sending my messenger ahead of you,	13
7:39	Now when the Pharisee who had invited him saw it	16
7:44	"Do you see this woman?	5
8:16	so that those who enter may see the light.	5
8:20	standing outside, wanting to see you."	16
8:28	When he saw Jesus, he fell down before him	16

8:34	When the swineherds saw what had happened	16
8:35	Then people came out to see what had happened	16
8:36	Those who had seen it told them	16
8:47	the woman saw that she could not remain hidden	16
9: 9	he tried to see him.	16
9:27	before they see the kingdom of God."	16
9:30	Suddenly they saw two men, Moses and Elijah,	1
9:32	since they had stayed awake, they saw his glory	16
9:36	told no one any of the things they had seen.	16
9:49	we saw someone casting out demons in your name	16
9:54	When his disciples James and John saw it	16
10: 3	See, I am sending you out like lambs	13
10:19	See, I have given you authority	13
10:23	"Blessed are the eyes that see what you see!	5
10:23	"Blessed are the eyes that see what you see!	5
10:24	kings desired to see what you see,	16
10:24	kings desired to see what you see,	5
10:24	desired to see what you see, but did not see	16
10:31	when he saw him, he passed by on the other side.	16
10:32	a Levite, when he came to the place and saw him	16
10:33	when he saw him, he was moved with pity.	16
11:31	see, something greater than Solomon is here!	13
11:32	see, something greater than Jonah is here!	13
11:33	so that those who enter may see the light.	5
11:38	The Pharisee was amazed to see	16
11:41	see, everything will be clean for you.	13
12:54	"When you see a cloud rising in the west	16
12:55	when you see the south wind blowing, you say	1
13:12	Jesus saw her, he called her over and said	16
13:28	when you see Abraham and Isaac and Jacob	16
13:35	See, your house is left to you.	13
13:35	I tell you, you will not see me until the time	16
14:18	I must go out and see it;	16
14:28	to see whether he has enough to complete it?	1
14:29	all who see it will begin to ridicule him	11
15:20	father saw him and was filled with compassion;	16
16:23	he looked up and saw Abraham far away	16
17:14	When he saw them, he said to them, "Go	16
17:15	one of them, when he saw that he was healed	16
17:22	will long to see one of the days of the Son of Man	16
17:22	and you will not see it.	16
18:15	when the disciples saw it, they sternly ordered	16
18:31	took the twelve aside and said to them, "See	13
18:43	all the people, when they saw it, praised God.	16
19: 3	He was trying to see who Jesus was,	16
19: 4	climbed a sycamore tree to see him	16
19: 7	All who saw it began to grumble and said,	16
19:37	for all the deeds of power that they had seen	16
19:41	As he came near and saw the city, he wept over it	16
20:14	when the tenants saw him, they discussed it	16
21: 1	He looked up and saw rich people	16
21: 2	saw a poor widow put in two small copper coins.	16
21: 6	"As for these things that you see	11
21:20	"When you see Jerusalem surrounded by armies	16
21:27	will see 'the Son of Man coming in a cloud'	16
21:30	you can see for yourselves	5
21:31	So also, when you see these things taking place	16
22:21	But see, the one who betrays me is with me,	13
22:49	When those…saw what was coming, they asked	16
22:56	a servant-girl, seeing him in the firelight	16
22:58	A little later someone else, on seeing him, said	16
23: 8	When Herod saw Jesus, he was very glad	16
23: 8	he had been wanting to see him for a long time	16
23: 8	was hoping to see him perform some sign.	16
23:47	When the centurion saw what had taken place	16
23:48	all the crowds…saw what had taken place	11
23:55	The women…followed, and they saw the tomb	10
24:12	he saw the linen cloths by themselves	5
24:23	that they had indeed seen a vision of angels	16
24:24	they did not see him."	16
24:37	thought that they were seeing a ghost.	11
24:39	Look at my hands and my feet; see that it is I	1
24:39	Touch me and see;	16
24:39	not have flesh and bones as you see that I have."	11
24:49	see, I am sending upon you what my Father promised;	13
Jhn 1:14	we have seen his glory, the glory as of a father's	10
1:18	No one has ever seen God.	16
1:29	The next day he saw Jesus coming toward him	5
1:32	"I saw the Spirit descending from heaven like	10
1:33	'He on whom you see the Spirit descend and remain	16
1:34	And I myself have seen and have testified	16

Jhn	1:38	Jesus turned and saw them following, he said	10
	1:39	He said to them, "Come and see."	16
	1:39	They came and saw where he was staying	16
	1:46	Philip said to him, "Come and see."	12
	1:47	Jesus saw Nathanael coming toward him, he said	16
	1:48	"I saw you under the fig tree	16
	1:50	I told you that I saw you under the fig tree?	16
	1:50	You will see greater things than these."	16
	1:51	truly, I tell you, you will see heaven opened	16
	2:23	because they saw the signs that he was doing.	11
	3: 3	no one can see the kingdom of God without	16
	3:11	and testify to what we have seen;	16
	3:32	He testifies to what he has seen and heard	16
	3:36	whoever disobeys the Son will not see life	16
	4:19	"Sir, I see that you are a prophet.	11
	4:29	"Come and see a man who told me everything	16
	4:35	see how the fields are ripe for harvesting.	10
	4:45	had seen all that he had done in Jerusalem	16
	4:48	"Unless you see signs and wonders	16
	5: 6	When Jesus saw him lying there	16
	5:14	"See, you have been made well!	12
	5:19	only what he sees the Father doing;	5
	5:37	never heard his voice or seen his form	16
	6: 2	because they saw the signs that he was doing	11
	6: 5	he looked up and saw a large crowd coming	10
	6:14	When the people saw the sign that he had done	16
	6:19	they saw Jesus walking on the sea	11
	6:22	saw that there had been only one boat there.	16
	6:22	also saw that Jesus had not got into the boat	1
	6:24	saw that neither Jesus nor his disciples were there	16
	6:26	looking for me, not because you saw signs	16
	6:30	so that we may see it and believe you?	16
	6:36	I said to you that you have seen me	16
	6:40	all who see the Son and believe in him	11
	6:46	Not that anyone has seen the Father	16
	6:46	he has seen the Father.	16
	6:62	if you were to see the Son of Man ascending	11
	7: 3	disciples also may see the works you are doing;	11
	7:52	Search and you will see	12
	8:38	I declare what I have seen in the Father's presence;	16
	8:51	whoever keeps my word will never see death."	11
	8:56	Abraham rejoiced that he would see my day;	16
	8:56	he saw it and was glad."	16
	8:57	and have you seen Abraham?"	16
	9: 1	As he walked along, he saw a man blind from birth.	16
	9: 7	Then he went and washed and came back able to see.	5
	9: 8	those who had seen him before as a beggar	11
	9:15	I washed, and now I see."	5
	9:19	How then does he now see?"	5
	9:21	we do not know how it is that now he sees	5
	9:25	I do know, that though I was blind, now I see."	5
	9:37	Jesus said to him, "You have seen him	16
	9:39	so that those who do not see may see	5
	9:39	so that those who do not see may see	5
	9:39	those who do see may become blind."	5
	9:41	now that you say, 'We see,' your sin remains.	5
	10:12	sees the wolf coming and leaves the sheep	11
	11: 9	because they see the light of this world.	5
	11:31	The Jews…saw Mary get up quickly and go out.	16
	11:32	When Mary came where Jesus was and saw him	16
	11:33	When Jesus saw her weeping	16
	11:34	They said to him, "Lord, come and see."	12
	11:36	the Jews said, "See how he loved him!"	12
	11:40	if you believed, you would see the glory of God?"	16
	11:45	had come with Mary and had seen what Jesus did	10
	12: 9	to see Lazarus, whom he had raised from the dead.	16
	12:19	"You see, you can do nothing.	11
	12:21	"Sir, we wish to see Jesus."	16
	12:41	Isaiah said this because he saw his glory	16
	12:45	whoever sees me sees him who sent me.	11
	12:45	whoever sees me sees him who sent me.	11
	14: 7	From now on you do know him and have seen him."	16
	14: 9	Whoever has seen me has seen the Father.	16
	14: 9	Whoever has seen me has seen the Father.	16
	14:17	because it neither sees him nor knows him.	11
	14:19	the world will no longer see me	11
	14:19	but you will see me;	11
	15:24	they have seen and hated both me and my Father.	16
	16:10	you will see me no longer;	11
	16:16	"A little while, and you will no longer see me	11
	16:16	again a little while, and you will see me."	16

	16:17	'A little while, and you will no longer see me	11
	16:17	again a little while, and you will see me';	16
	16:19	'A little while, and you will no longer see me	11
	16:19	again a little while, and you will see me'?	16
	16:22	you have pain now; but I will see you again	16
	17:24	to see my glory, which you have given me	11
	18:26	"Did I not see you in the garden with him?"	16
	19: 6	When the chief priests and the police saw him	16
	19:24	but cast lots for it to see who will get it."	1
	19:26	When Jesus saw his mother	16
	19:33	came to Jesus and saw that he was already dead	16
	19:35	(He who saw this has testified	16
	20: 1	saw that the stone had been removed	5
	20: 5	bent down to look in and saw the linen wrappings	5
	20: 6	He saw the linen wrappings lying there	11
	20: 8	also went in, and he saw and believed;	16
	20:12	she saw two angels in white	11
	20:14	she turned around and saw Jesus standing	11
	20:18	"I have seen the Lord";	16
	20:20	the disciples rejoiced when they saw the Lord.	16
	20:25	"We have seen the Lord."	16
	20:25	"Unless I see the mark of the nails in his hands	16
	20:27	"Put your finger here and see my hands.	12
	20:29	"Have you believed because you have seen me?	16
	20:29	Blessed are those who have not seen	16
	21: 9	they saw a charcoal fire there	5
	21:20	saw the disciple whom Jesus loved following	5
	21:21	When Peter saw him, he said to Jesus, "Lord	16
Act	1:11	Jesus…will come in the same way as you saw him go	10
	2:17	your young men shall see visions	16
	2:33	he has poured out this that you both see and hear.	5
	3: 3	saw Peter and John about to go into the temple	16
	3: 9	All the people saw him walking and praising God	16
	3:12	When Peter saw it, he addressed the people	16
	3:16	this man…whom you see and know;	11
	4:13	Now when they saw the boldness of Peter and John	11
	4:14	saw the man who had been cured	5
	4:20	speaking about what we have seen and heard."	16
	6:15	saw that his face was like the face of an angel.	16
	7:24	saw one of them being wronged	16
	7:31	When Moses saw it, he was amazed at the sight;	16
	7:44	according to the pattern he had seen.	16
	7:55	saw the glory of God and Jesus standing	16
	7:56	"Look," he said, "I see the heavens opened	11
	8: 6	hearing and seeing the signs that he did	5
	8:13	saw the signs and great miracles that took place.	11
	8:18	Now when Simon saw that the Spirit was given	16
	8:23	For I see that you are in the gall of bitterness	16
	8:39	the eunuch saw him no more	16
	9: 7	heard the voice but saw no one.	11
	9: 8	though his eyes were open, he could see nothing;	5
	9:12	he has seen in a vision a man named Ananias come	16
	9:27	he had seen the Lord, who had spoken to him	16
	9:35	all the residents of Lydda and Sharon saw him	16
	9:40	seeing Peter, she sat up.	16
	10: 3	a vision in which he clearly saw an angel of God	16
	10:11	He saw the heaven opened	11
	10:17	what to make of the vision that he had seen,	16
	11: 5	in a trance I saw a vision.	16
	11: 6	I saw four-footed animals, beasts of prey	16
	11:13	He told us how he had seen the angel standing	16
	11:23	When he came and saw the grace of God, he rejoiced	16
	12: 3	After he saw that it pleased the Jews	16
	12: 9	he thought he was seeing a vision.	5
	12:16	opened the gate, they saw him and were amazed.	16
	13:11	be blind for a while, unable to see the sun."	5
	13:12	the proconsul saw what had happened, he believed	16
	13:45	when the Jews saw the crowds	16
	14: 9	and seeing that he had faith to be healed	16
	14:11	When the crowds saw what Paul had done	16
	15:36	see how they are doing."	1
	16:10	When he had seen the vision	16
	16:19	owners saw that their hope of making money was gone	16
	16:27	woke up and saw the prison doors wide open	16
	16:40	had seen and encouraged the brothers and sisters	16
	17:11	to see whether these things were so.	1
	17:16	to see that the city was full of idols.	11
	17:22	I see how extremely religious you are	11
	18:15	see to it yourselves;	16
	19:21	"After I have gone there, I must also see Rome."	16
	19:26	You also see and hear	11

	20:25 none of you…will ever see my face again.	16
	20:38 that they would not see him again.	11
	21:20 they said to him, "You see, brother	11
	21:27 who had seen him in the temple	10
	21:32 When they saw the tribune and the soldiers	16
	22: 9 Now those who were with me saw the light	10
	22:11 Since I could not see	7
	22:13 In that very hour I regained my sight and saw him.	1
	22:14 to see the Righteous One and to hear his own voice;	16
	22:15 his witness…of what you have seen and heard.	16
	22:18 saw Jesus saying to me, 'Hurry	16
	25:24 you see this man	11
	26:13 your Excellency, I saw a light from heaven	16
	26:16 the things in which you have seen me	16
	27:10 I can see that the voyage will be with danger	11
	28: 4 When the natives saw the creature	16
	28: 6 saw that nothing unusual had happened to him	11
	28:15 On seeing them, Paul thanked God	16
	28:20 therefore I have asked to see you	16
Rom	1:11 For I am longing to see you	16
	1:20 understood and seen through the things	14
	7:23 but I see in my members another law	5
	8:24 Now hope that is seen is not hope.	5
	8:24 For who hopes for what is seen?	5
	8:25 if we hope for what we do not see, we wait for it	5
	9:33 "See, I am laying in Zion a stone	13
	11: 8 eyes that would not see and ears that would not	5
	11:10 their eyes be darkened so that they cannot see	5
	15:21 "Those who have never been told of him shall see	16
	15:24 For I do hope to see you on my journey	10
1Co	2: 9 "What no eye has seen, nor ear heard	16
	8:10 if others see you, who possess knowledge, eating	16
	9: 1 Have I not seen Jesus our Lord?	16
	13:12 For now we see in a mirror, dimly,	5
	13:12 but then we will see face to face.	1
	16: 7 I do not want to see you now just in passing	16
	16:10 If Timothy comes, see that he has nothing to fear	5
2Co	4: 4 to keep them from seeing the light of the gospel	2
	4:18 because we look not at what can be seen	5
	4:18 what can be seen but at what cannot be seen	5
	4:18 for what can be seen is temporary	5
	4:18 what cannot be seen is eternal.	5
	5:17 passed away; see, everything has become new!	13
	6: 2 See, now is the acceptable time;	13
	6: 2 see, now is the day of salvation!	13
	6: 9 as dying, and see—we are alive;	13
	7: 8 I see that I grieved you with that letter	5
	7:11 For see what earnestness this godly grief	13
	12: 6 may think better of me than what is seen in me	5
	13: 5 to see whether you are living in the faith.	1
Gal	1:19 I did not see any other apostle	16
	2: 7 when they saw that I had been entrusted with	16
	2:14 when I saw that they were not acting consistently	16
	3: 7 so, you see, those who believe are the descendants	6
	6:11 See what large letters I make when I am writing	16
Php	1:27 so that, whether I come and see you or am absent	16
	1:30 having the same struggle that you saw	16
	2:23 as soon as I see how things go with me;	3
	2:28 that you may rejoice at seeing him again	16
	4: 9 have learned and received and heard and seen in me	16
Col	2: 1 for all who have not seen me face to face	16
	2: 5 rejoice to see your morale	5
	2: 8 See to it that no one takes you captive	5
	3: 9 seeing that you have stripped off the old self	1
	4:16 see that you read also the letter from Laodicea.	17
	4:17 say to Archippus, "See that you complete the task	5
1Th	2:17 we longed with great eagerness to see you	16
	3: 6 and long to see us—just as we long to see you.	16
	3: 6 and long to see us—just as we long to see you.	1
	3:10 that we may see you face to face	16
	5:15 See that none of you repays evil for evil	16
1Ti	3:16 vindicated in spirit, seen by angels	16
	4:15 so that all may see your progress.	19
	6:16 whom no one has ever seen or can see;	16
	6:16 whom no one has ever seen or can see;	16
2Ti	1: 4 Recalling your tears, I long to see you	16
Heb	2: 8 do not yet see everything in subjection to them	16
	2: 9 but we do see Jesus…now crowned with glory	5
	3: 9 though they had seen my works	16
	3:19 So we see that they were unable to enter	5
	7: 4 See how great he is!	11

	8: 5 "See that you make everything	16
	10: 7 I said, 'See, God, I have come to do your will, O God'	13
	10: 9 he added, "See, I have come to do your will."	13
	10:25 all the more as you see the Day approaching.	5
	11: 1 faith is…the conviction of things not seen.	5
	11: 3 so that what is seen was made	5
	11:13 from a distance they saw and greeted them.	16
	11:23 because they saw that the child was beautiful;	16
	11:27 persevered as though he saw him who is invisible.	16
	12:14 holiness without which no one will see the Lord.	16
	12:15 See to it that no one fails to obtain the grace	8
	12:16 See to it that no one becomes like Esau	1
	12:25 See that you do not refuse the one who is speaking;	5
	13:23 if he comes in time, he will be with me when I see you.	16
Jas	2:22 You see that faith was active…with his works	5
	2:24 You see that a person is justified by works	16
	5: 9 See, the Judge is standing at the doors!	13
	5:11 and you have seen the purpose of the Lord	16
1Pe	1: 8 have not seen him, you love him;	16
	1: 8 though you do not see him now, you believe in him	16
	2: 6 "See, I am laying in Zion a stone, a cornerstone	13
	2:12 they may see your honorable deeds and glorify God	9
	3: 2 when they see the purity and reverence of your lives.	9
	3:10 "Those who desire life and desire to see good days	16
2Pe	2: 8 by their lawless deeds that he saw and heard)	4
1Jn	1: 1 what we have seen with our eyes	16
	1: 2 this life was revealed, and we have seen it	16
	1: 3 we declare to you what we have seen and heard	16
	3: 1 See what love the Father has given us	16
	3: 2 for we will see him as he is.	16
	3: 6 no one who sins has either seen him or known him.	16
	3:17 has the world's goods and sees a brother or sister in need	11
	4: 1 test the spirits to see whether they are from God;	1
	4:12 No one has ever seen God;	10
	4:14 And we have seen and do testify that	10
	4:20 do not love a brother or sister whom they have seen	16
	4:20 cannot love God whom they have not seen.	16
	5:16 If you see your brother or sister committing…sin	16
3Jn	1:11 whoever does evil has not seen God.	16
	1:14 I hope to see you soon	16
Jde	1:14 "See, the Lord is coming with ten thousands of his holy	13
Rev	1: 2 testified…even to all that he saw.	16
	1: 7 He is coming…every eye will see him	16
	1:11 saying, "Write in a book what you see and send it	5
	1:12 I turned to see whose voice it was that spoke to me	5
	1:12 and on turning I saw seven golden lampstands	16
	1:13 midst of the lampstands I saw one like the Son of Man	1
	1:17 When I saw him, I fell at his feet as though dead.	16
	1:18 I was dead, and see, I am alive forever and ever;	13
	1:19 Now write what you have seen	16
	1:20 the seven stars that you saw in my right hand	16
	3:18 keep the shame of your nakedness from being seen;	20
	3:18 salve to anoint your eyes so that you may see.	5
	5: 1 Then I saw in the right hand of the one seated	16
	5: 2 I saw a mighty angel proclaiming	16
	5: 5 See, the Lion of the tribe of Judah…has conquered	13
	5: 6 I saw between the throne and the four living creatures	16
	6: 1 I saw the Lamb open one of the seven seals	16
	6: 9 I saw under the altar the souls of those	16
	7: 1 After this I saw four angels standing	16
	7: 2 I saw another angel ascending from the rising…sun	16
	8: 2 And I saw the seven angels who stand before God	16
	9: 1 I saw a star that had fallen from heaven to earth	16
	9:17 this was how I saw the horses in my vision:	16
	9:20 idols…which cannot see or hear or walk.	5
	10: 1 And I saw another mighty angel coming down	16
	10: 5 the angel whom I saw standing on the sea and the land	16
	11:11 and those who saw them were terrified.	11
	11:19 ark of his covenant was seen within his temple;	16
	12:13 when the dragon saw that he had been thrown down	16
	13: 1 I saw a beast rising out of the sea	16
	13: 2 And the beast that I saw was like a leopard	16
	13:11 I saw another beast that rose out of the earth;	16
	14: 6 Then I saw another angel flying in midheaven	16
	15: 1 Then I saw another portent in heaven	16
	15: 2 I saw what appeared to be a sea of glass	16
	16:13 I saw three foul spirits like frogs coming from	16
	16:15 ("See, I am coming like a thief!	13
	17: 3 and I saw a woman sitting on a scarlet beast	16
	17: 6 I saw that the woman was drunk with the blood	16
	17: 6 When I saw her, I was greatly amazed.	16

Rev	17: 8	The beast that you saw was, and is not	16
	17: 8	inhabitants...will be amazed when they see the beast	5
	17:12	And the ten horns that you saw are ten kings	16
	17:15	"The waters that you saw, where the whore is	16
	17:16	the ten horns that you saw, they and the beast	16
	17:18	The woman you saw is the great city	16
	18: 1	I saw another angel coming down from heaven	16
	18: 7	I am no widow, and I will never see grief,'	16
	18: 9	when they see the smoke of her burning;	5
	18:18	cried out as they saw the smoke of her burning	5
	19:11	I saw heaven opened, and there was a white horse!	16
	19:17	Then I saw an angel standing in the sun	16
	19:19	Then I saw the beast and the kings of the earth	16
	20: 1	Then I saw an angel coming down from heaven	16
	20: 4	Then I saw thrones, and those seated on them were	16
	20: 4	I also saw the souls of those who had been beheaded	1
	20:11	I saw a great white throne and the one who sat on it;	16
	20:12	And I saw the dead, great and small	16
	21: 1	Then I saw a new heaven and a new earth;	16
	21: 2	I saw the holy city, the new Jerusalem, coming down	16
	21: 3	"See, the home of God is among mortals.	13
	21: 5	"See, I am making all things new."	13
	21:22	I saw no temple in the city	16
	22: 4	they will see his face	16
	22: 7	"See, I am coming soon!	13
	22: 8	I, John, am the one who heard and saw these things.	5
	22: 8	when I heard and saw them, I fell down to worship	5
	22:12	"See, I am coming soon; my reward is with	13

make see

1. φωτίζω, *phōtizō*, 5894

Eph	3: 9	to make everyone see what is the plan of the mystery	1

see again

1. ἀναβλέπω, *anablepō*, 329

Mrk	10:51	"My teacher, let me see again."	1
Lke	18:41	He said, "Lord, let me see again."	1

see anything different

1. διακρίνω, *diakrinō*, 1359

1Co	4: 7	For who sees anything different in you?	1

see before

1. προοράω, *prooraō*, 4632

Act	2:25	'I saw the Lord always before me	1

see clearly

1. διαβλέπω, *diablepō*, 1332
2. φανερόω, *phaneroō*, 5746

Mat	7: 5	and then you will see clearly to take the speck	1
Lke	6:42	you will see clearly to take the speck out	1
Jhn	3:21	so that it may be clearly seen	2

see fit

1. δοκιμάζω, *dokimazō*, 1507

Rom	1:28	since they did not see fit to acknowledge God	1

see here

1. ἰδού, *idou*, 2627

Lke	13: 7	'See here! For three years I have come looking	1

see previously

1. προοράω, *prooraō*, 4632

Act	21:29	they had previously seen Trophimus...with him	1

see reflected in a mirror

1. κατοπτρίζω, *katoptrizō*, 3002

2Co	3:18	seeing the glory...as though reflected in a mirror	1

see surely

1. ὁράω + ὁράω, *horaō + horaō*, 3972 + 3972

Act	7:34	I have surely seen the mistreatment of my people	1

see that

1. ἵνα, *hina*, 2671

Tit	3:13	see that they lack nothing.	1

seed *See also* scatter seed

1. Contextual: Not in Greek

2. κόκκος, *kokkos*, 3133
3. σπέρμα, *sperma*, 5065
4. σπορά, *spora*, 5076
5. σπόρος, *sporos*, 5078

Mat	13: 4	as he sowed, some seeds fell on the path	1
	13: 5	Other seeds fell on rocky ground	1
	13: 7	Other seeds fell among thorns	1
	13: 8	Other seeds fell on good soil	1
	13:24	someone who sowed good seed in his field;	3
	13:27	'Master, did you not sow good seed in your field?	3
	13:31	"The kingdom of heaven is like a mustard seed	2
	13:32	it is the smallest of all the seeds	3
	13:37	"The one who sows the good seed is the Son of Man;	3
	13:38	the good seed are the children of the kingdom;	3
	17:20	if you have faith the size of a mustard seed	2
Mrk	4: 4	as he sowed, some seed fell on the path	1
	4: 5	Other seed fell on rocky ground	1
	4: 7	Other seed fell among thorns	1
	4: 8	Other seed fell into good soil	1
	4:26	as if someone would scatter seed on the ground	5
	4:27	the seed would sprout and grow	5
	4:31	It is like a mustard seed	2
	4:31	the smallest of all the seeds on earth;	3
Lke	8: 5	"A sower went out to sow his seed;	5
	8:11	the parable is this: The seed is the word of God.	5
	13:19	It is like a mustard seed that someone took	2
	17: 6	"If you had faith the size of a mustard seed	2
1Co	15:37	a bare seed, perhaps of wheat	2
	15:38	to each kind of seed its own body.	3
2Co	9:10	He who supplies seed to the sower	5
	9:10	supply and multiply your seed for sowing	5
1Pe	1:23	not of perishable but of imperishable seed	4
1Jn	3: 9	do not sin, because God's seed abides in them;	3

seek

1. Contextual: Not in Greek
2. διώκω, *diōkō*, 1503
3. ἐκζητέω, *ekzēteō*, 1699
4. ἐπιζητέω, *epizēteō*, 2118
5. ζητέω, *zēteō*, 2426

Mat	2:20	for those who were seeking the child's life	5
Jhn	4:23	the Father seeks such as these to worship him.	5
	5:18	the Jews were seeking all the more to kill him	5
	5:30	because I seek to do not my own will	5
	5:44	do not seek the glory that comes from...God?	5
	7:18	Those...seek their own glory;	5
	7:18	seeks the glory of him who sent him is true	5
	8:50	Yet I do not seek my own glory;	5
	8:50	there is one who seeks it and he is the judge.	5
Act	15:17	so that all other peoples may seek the Lord	5
Rom	2: 7	who by patiently doing good seek for glory	5
	3:11	there is no one who seeks God.	3
	10: 3	and seeking to establish their own	5
	10:20	"I have been found by those who did not seek me;	5
	11: 3	I alone am left, and they are seeking my life."	5
	11: 7	Israel failed to obtain what it was seeking.	4
1Co	7:18	seek to remove the marks of circumcision.	1
	7:18	Let him not seek circumcision.	1
	7:27	Are you bound to a wife? Do not seek to be free.	5
	7:27	Are you free from a wife? Do not seek a wife.	5
	10:24	Do not seek your own advantage	5
	10:33	not seeking my own advantage, but that of many	5
Php	2:21	All of them are seeking their own interests	5
	4:17	Not that I seek the gift	4
	4:17	I seek the profit that accumulates to your account.	4
Col	3: 1	seek the things that are above, where Christ is	5
1Th	2: 6	nor did we seek praise from mortals	5
	5:15	always seek to do good to one another and to all.	2
Heb	11: 6	he rewards those who seek him.	3
	11:14	they are seeking a homeland.	4
	12:17	even though he sought the blessing with tears.	3
1Pe	3:11	let them seek peace and pursue it.	5
Rev	9: 6	in those days people will seek death but will not find it;	5

seek approval

1. Contextual: Not in Greek
2. πείθω, *peithō*, 4275

Gal	1:10	Am I now seeking human approval, or God's	2
	1:10	seeking human approval, or God's approval?	1

seek out

1. ζητέω, *zēteō, 2426*

Lke 19:10 Son of Man came to seek out and to save the lost." 1

seem

1. δοκέω, *dokeō, 1506*
2. εἰμί, *eimi, 1639*
3. φαίνω, *phainō, 5743*
4. ὡς, *hōs, 6055*

Lke 8:18 what they seem to have will be taken away." 1
 24:11 these words seemed to them an idle tale 3
Act 17:18 "He seems to be a proclaimer of foreign divinities." 1
 25:27 seems to me unreasonable to send a prisoner 1
1Co 12:22 the members of the body that seem to be weaker 1
 16: 4 If it seems advisable that I should go also 2
2Co 10: 9 seem as though I am trying to frighten you 1
 13: 7 though we may seem to have failed. 4
Heb 4: 1 that none…should seem to have failed to reach it. 1
 12:11 discipline always seems painful rather than pleasant 1
Rev 6: 6 I heard what seemed to be a voice in the midst 4
 13: 3 One of its heads seemed to have received a death-blow 4
 19: 1 what seemed to be the loud voice of a great multitude 4
 19: 6 Then I heard what seemed to be the voice 4

seem good

1. δοκέω, *dokeō, 1506*

Act 15:28 For it has seemed good to the Holy Spirit and to us 1
Heb 12:10 for a short time as seemed best to them 1

seize

1. γίνομαι, *ginomai, 1181*
2. ἐπιβάλλω + ὁ + χείρ, *epiballō + ho + cheir, 2095 + 3836 + 5931*
3. ἐπιλαμβάνομαι, *epilambanomai, 2138*
4. ἔχω, *echō, 2400*
5. καταλαμβάνω, *katalambanō, 2898*
6. κρατέω, *krateō, 3195*
7. λαμβάνω, *lambanō, 3284*
8. πιάζω, *piazō, 4389*
9. συλλαμβάνω, *syllambanō, 5197*
10. συναρπάζω, *synarpazō, 5275*
11. συνέχω, *synechō, 5309*

Mat 18:28 and seizing him by the throat, he said 6
 21:35 the tenants seized his slaves and beat one 7
 21:39 they seized him, threw him out of the vineyard 7
 22: 6 while the rest seized his slaves 6
Mrk 9:18 whenever it seizes him, it dashes him down; 5
 12: 3 they seized him, and beat him, and sent him away 7
 12: 8 they seized him, killed him 7
 16: 8 terror and amazement had seized them; 4
Lke 5:26 Amazement seized all of them 7
 7:16 Fear seized all of them; and they glorified God 7
 8:29 (For many times it had seized him; 10
 8:37 they were seized with great fear. 11
 9:39 a spirit seizes him, and all at once he shrieks. 7
 22:54 Then they seized him and led him away 9
 23:26 they seized a man, Simon of Cyrene 3
Act 5: 5 great fear seized all who heard of it. 1
 5:11 great fear seized the whole church 1
 6:12 they suddenly confronted him, seized him 10
 12: 4 When he had seized him, he put him in prison 8
 16:19 they seized Paul and Silas 3
 18:17 seized Sosthenes, the official of the synagogue 3
 21:27 the Jews from Asia…seized him 2
 21:30 seized Paul and dragged him out of the temple 3
 23:27 This man was seized by the Jews 9
 24: 6 tried to profane the temple, and so we seized him. 6
 26:21 Jews seized me in the temple and tried to kill me. 9
Rom 7: 8 But sin, seizing an opportunity in the commandment 7
 7:11 For sin, seizing an opportunity in the commandment 7
2Co 11:32 guarded the city of Damascus in order to seize me 8
Heb 6:18 to seize the hope set before us. 6
Rev 3:11 hold fast…so that no one may seize your crown. 7
 20: 2 He seized the dragon, that ancient serpent 6

select

1. ἐπισκέπτομαι, *episkeptomai, 2170*

Act 6: 3 select from among yourselves seven men of good standing 1

Seleucia

1. Σελεύκεια, *Seleukeia, 4942*

Act 13: 4 they went down to Seleucia; 1

self *See also* lover of self

1. Contextual: Not in Greek
2. ἄνθρωπος, *anthrōpos, 476*
3. σεαυτοῦ, *seautou, 4932*
4. ψυχή, *psychē, 6034*

Rom 6: 6 We know that our old self was crucified with him 2
 7:22 For I delight in the law of God in my inmost self 2
Eph 4:22 put away your former way of life, your old self 2
 4:24 clothe yourselves with the new self 2
Col 3: 9 seeing that you have stripped off the old self 2
 3:10 and have clothed yourselves with the new self 1
1Th 2: 8 share…also our own selves 4
Phm 1:19 say nothing about your owing me even your own self. 3
1Pe 3: 4 let your adornment be the inner self 2

self-abasement

1. ταπεινοφροσύνη, *tapeinophrosynē, 5425*

Col 2:18 insisting on self-abasement 1

self-condemned

1. αὐτοκατάκριτος, *autokatakritos, 896*
2. καταγινώσκω, *kataginōskō, 2861*

Gal 2:11 because he stood self-condemned; 2
Tit 3:11 being self-condemned. 1

self-control *See also* exercise self-control, practice self-control

1. ἐγκράτεια, *enkrateia, 1602*

Act 24:25 as he discussed justice, self-control, 1
Gal 5:23 self-control. There is no law against such 1
2Pe 1: 6 and knowledge with self-control 1
 1: 6 and self-control with endurance 1

lack of self-control

1. ἀκρασία, *akrasia, 202*

1Co 7: 5 tempt you because of your lack of self-control. 1

self-controlled

1. ἐγκρατής, *enkratēs, 1604*
2. σωφρονέω, *sōphroneō, 5404*
3. σωφρόνως, *sōphronōs, 5407*
4. σώφρων, *sōphrōn, 5409*

Tit 1: 8 upright, devout, and self-controlled. 1
 2: 5 self-controlled, chaste, good managers of the household, 4
 2: 6 urge the younger men to be self-controlled. 2
 2:12 in the present age to live lives that are self-controlled, 3

self-discipline

1. σωφρονισμός, *sōphronismos, 5406*

2Ti 1: 7 a spirit of power and of love and of self-discipline. 1

self-imposed *See* self-imposed *piety*

self-indulgence

1. ἀκρασία, *akrasia, 202*
2. πλησμονή + ὁ + σάρξ, *plēsmonē + ho + sarx, 4447 + 3836 + 4922*
3. σάρξ, *sarx, 4922*

Mat 23:25 inside they are full of greed and self-indulgence. 1
Gal 5:13 your freedom as an opportunity for self-indulgence 3
Col 2:23 of no value in checking self-indulgence. 2

self-seeking

1. ἐριθεία, *eritheia, 2249*

Rom 2: 8 who are self-seeking and who obey not the truth 1

selfish *See* selfish *ambition*

selfishness

1. ἐριθεία, *eritheia, 2249*

2Co 12:20 anger, selfishness, slander, gossip, conceit 1

sell

1. ἀποδίδωμι, *apodidōmi, 625*

2. πιπράσκω, *pipraskō*, 4405
3. πωλέω, *pōleō*, 4797

Mat 10:29	Are not two sparrows sold for a penny?	3
13:44	in his joy he goes and sells all that he has	3
13:46	went and sold all that he had and bought it.	2
18:25	could not pay, his lord ordered him to be sold	2
19:21	to be perfect, go, sell your possessions	3
21:12	all who were selling and buying in the temple	3
21:12	and the seats of those who sold doves.	3
26: 9	ointment could have been sold for a large sum	2
Mrk 10:21	sell what you own, and give the money to the poor	3
11:15	who were selling and those who were buying	3
11:15	the seats of those who sold doves;	3
14: 5	For this ointment could have been sold	2
Lke 12: 6	Are not five sparrows sold for two pennies?	3
12:33	Sell your possessions, and give alms.	3
17:28	they were eating and drinking, buying and selling	3
18:22	Sell all that you own and distribute the money	3
19:45	began to drive out those who were selling	3
22:36	who has no sword must sell his cloak and buy one.	3
Jhn 2:14	he found people selling cattle, sheep,	3
2:16	He told those who were selling the doves	3
12: 5	"Why was this perfume not sold	2
Act 2:45	they would sell their possessions and goods	2
4:34	as many as owned lands…sold them	3
4:34	brought the proceeds of what was sold.	2
4:37	sold a field that belonged to him	3
5: 1	Ananias…sold a piece of property;	3
5: 4	it was sold, were not the proceeds at your disposal?	2
5: 8	"Tell me whether you and your husband sold the land	1
7: 9	"The patriarchs…sold him into Egypt;	1
1Co 10:25	Eat whatever is sold in the meat market	3
Heb 12:16	who sold his birthright for a single meal.	1
Rev 13:17	no one can buy or sell who does not have the mark	3

sell into slavery

1. πιπράσκω, *piraskō*, 4405

Rom 7:14	I am of the flesh, sold into slavery under sin.	1

Semein

1. Σεμεΐν, *Semein*, 4946

Lke 3:26	son of Semein, son of Josech, son of Joda	1

send

1. Contextual: Not in Greek
2. ἀναπέμπω, *anapempō*, 402
3. ἀποστέλλω, *apostellō*, 690
4. ἐξαποστέλλω, *exapostellō*, 1990
5. παρά, *para*, 4123
6. παρίστημι, *paristēmi*, 4225
7. πέμπω, *pempō*, 4287
8. προπέμπω, *propempō*, 4636

Mat 2: 8	he sent them to Bethlehem, saying, "Go and search	7
2:16	he sent and killed all the children	3
8:31	cast us out, send us into the herd of swine."	3
10:40	whoever welcomes me welcomes the one who sent me.	3
11: 2	he sent word by his disciples	7
11:10	'See, I am sending my messenger ahead of you,	3
13:41	The Son of Man will send his angels	3
14:10	he sent and had John beheaded in the prison.	7
15:24	"I was sent only to the lost sheep	3
20: 2	he sent them into his vineyard.	3
21: 1	Jesus sent two disciples	3
21: 3	he will send them immediately."	3
21:34	he sent his slaves to the tenants	3
21:36	Again he sent other slaves, more than the first;	3
21:37	Finally he sent his son to them, saying	3
22: 3	sent his slaves to call those who had been invited	3
22: 4	Again he sent other slaves, saying	3
22: 7	sent his troops, destroyed those murderers	7
22:16	So they sent their disciples to him	3
23:34	I send you prophets, sages, and scribes	3
23:37	stones those who are sent to it!	3
26:53	he will at once send me more than twelve legions	6
27:19	his wife sent word to him	3
Mrk 1: 2	"See, I am sending my messenger ahead of you,	3
3:31	standing outside, they sent to him and called	3
5:10	not to send them out of the country.	3
5:12	"Send us into the swine; let us enter them."	7
6:17	For Herod himself had sent men who arrested John	3

6:27	Immediately the king sent a soldier of the guard	3
9:37	welcomes not me but the one who sent me."	3
11: 1	he sent two of his disciples	3
11: 3	will send it back here immediately.' "	3
12: 2	he sent a slave to the tenants	3
12: 4	again he sent another slave to them;	3
12: 5	he sent another, and that one they killed.	3
12: 6	Finally he sent him to them, saying	3
12:13	they sent to him some Pharisees	3
14:13	he sent two of his disciples, saying to them,	3
Lke 1:19	I have been sent to speak to you	3
1:26	the angel Gabriel was sent by God	3
4:18	has sent me to proclaim release to the captives	3
4:26	yet Elijah was sent to none of them	7
4:43	I was sent for this purpose."	3
7: 3	he sent some Jewish elders to him	3
7: 6	the centurion sent friends to say to him	7
7:10	those who had been sent returned to the house	7
7:19	sent them to the Lord to ask, "Are you the one	7
7:20	"John the Baptist has sent us to you to ask	3
7:27	'See, I am sending my messenger ahead of you,	3
9:48	whoever welcomes me welcomes the one who sent me;	3
9:52	he sent messengers ahead of him.	3
10: 1	sent them on ahead of him in pairs	3
10:16	whoever rejects me rejects the one who sent me."	3
11:49	'I will send them prophets and apostles	3
13:34	stones those who are sent to it!	3
14:17	At the time for the dinner he sent his slave	3
14:32	he sends a delegation and asks for…peace.	3
15:15	who sent him to his fields to feed the pigs.	7
16:24	send Lazarus to dip the tip of his finger in water	7
16:27	I beg you to send him to my father's house	7
19:14	sent a delegation after him, saying, 'We do not	3
19:29	he sent two of the disciples	3
19:32	So those who were sent departed	3
20:10	he sent a slave to the tenants	3
20:11	he sent another slave;	7
20:12	he sent still a third;	7
20:13	I will send my beloved son;	7
20:20	So they watched him and sent spies	3
22: 8	So Jesus sent Peter and John, saying, "Go	3
24:49	I am sending upon you what my Father promised;	3
Jhn 1: 6	was a man sent from God, whose name was John.	3
1:19	Jews sent priests and Levites from Jerusalem	3
1:22	Let us have an answer for those who sent us.	7
1:24	Now they had been sent from the Pharisees.	3
1:33	but the one who sent me to baptize with water	7
3:17	"Indeed, God did not send the Son into the world	3
3:28	not the Messiah, but I have been sent ahead of him.'	3
3:34	He whom God has sent speaks the words of God	3
4:34	"My food is to do the will of him who sent me	7
4:38	I sent you to reap that for which you did not labor.	3
5:23	does not honor the Father who sent him.	7
5:24	who hears my word and believes him who sent me	7
5:30	but the will of him who sent me.	7
5:36	testify on my behalf that the Father has sent me.	3
5:37	the Father who sent me has himself testified	7
5:38	because you do not believe him whom he has sent.	3
6:29	that you believe in him whom he has sent."	3
6:38	not…own will, but the will of him who sent me.	7
6:39	this is the will of him who sent me	7
6:44	unless drawn by the Father who sent me;	7
6:57	Just as the living Father sent me	3
7:16	"My teaching is not mine but his who sent me.	7
7:18	seeks the glory of him who sent him is true	7
7:28	who sent me is true, and you do not know him.	7
7:29	I know him, because I am from him, and he sent me."	3
7:32	the chief priests and Pharisees sent temple police	3
7:33	then I am going to him who sent me.	7
8:16	but I and the Father who sent me.	7
8:18	the Father who sent me testifies on my behalf."	7
8:26	the one who sent me is true	7
8:29	the one who sent me is with me; he has not left	7
8:42	I did not come on my own, but he sent me.	7
9: 4	work the works of him who sent me while it is day;	7
9: 7	wash in the pool of Siloam" (which means Sent).	3
10:36	the one whom the Father has sanctified and sent	3
11: 3	the sisters sent a message to Jesus,	3
11:42	so that they may believe that you sent me."	3
12:44	believes not in me but in him who sent me.	7
12:45	whoever sees me sees him who sent me.	7

	12:49 the Father who sent me	7
	13:16 nor are messengers greater than the one who sent	7
	13:20 whoever receives one whom I send receives me;	7
	13:20 whoever receives me receives him who sent me."	7
	14:24 not mine, but is from the Father who sent me.	7
	14:26 Holy Spirit, whom the Father will send in my name	7
	15:21 because they do not know him who sent me.	7
	15:26 whom I will send to you from the Father	7
	16: 5 now I am going to him who sent me;	7
	16: 7 if I go, I will send him to you.	7
	17: 3 Jesus Christ whom you have sent.	3
	17: 8 they have believed that you sent me.	3
	17:18 As you have sent me into the world	3
	17:18 so I have sent them into the world.	3
	17:21 the world may believe that you have sent me.	3
	17:23 the world may know that you have sent me	3
	17:25 these know that you have sent me.	3
	18:24 Then Annas sent him bound to Caiaphas	3
	20:21 As the Father has sent me, so I send you."	3
	20:21 As the Father has sent me, so I send you."	7
Act	3:20 may send the Messiah appointed for you...Jesus	3
	3:26 sent him first to you, to bless you	3
	5:21 sent to the prison to have them brought.	3
	7:12 he sent our ancestors there on their first visit.	4
	7:14 Joseph sent and invited his father Jacob	3
	7:34 Come now, I will send you to Egypt.'	3
	7:35 God now sent as both ruler and liberator	3
	8:14 they sent Peter and John to them.	3
	9:17 the Lord Jesus...has sent me	3
	9:38 disciples...sent two men to him with the request	3
	10: 5 Now send men to Joppa	3
	10: 8 he sent them to Joppa.	3
	10:17 suddenly the men sent by Cornelius	3
	10:20 for I have sent them."	3
	10:32 Send therefore to Joppa and ask for Simon	7
	10:33 Therefore I sent for you immediately	7
	10:36 You know the message he sent to the people of Israel	3
	11:11 three men, sent to me from Caesarea, arrived	3
	11:13 'Send to Joppa and bring Simon, who is called Peter;	3
	11:22 they sent Barnabas to Antioch.	4
	11:29 The disciples determined...each would send relief	3
	11:30 this they did, sending it to the elders	3
	12:11 "Now I am sure that the Lord has sent his angel	4
	13:26 the message of this salvation has been sent.	4
	15:22 send them to Antioch with Paul and Barnabas.	7
	15:22 They sent Judas called Barsabbas, and Silas	1
	15:25 to choose representatives and send them to you	7
	15:27 We have therefore sent Judas and Silas	7
	15:33 sent off...to those who had sent them.	3
	16:35 When morning came, the magistrates sent the police	3
	19:22 he sent two of his helpers, Timothy and Erastus,	3
	19:31 sent him a message urging him not to venture	7
	20:17 From Miletus he sent a message to Ephesus	7
	23:30 I sent him to you at once	7
	25:21 until I could send him to the emperor."	7
	25:25 I decided to send him.	2
	25:27 seems to me unreasonable to send a prisoner	7
	26:17 from the Gentiles—to whom I am sending you	7
	28:28 salvation of God has been sent to the Gentiles;	3
Rom	8: 3 sending his own Son in the likeness of sinful	3
	10:15 how are they to proclaim him unless they are sent?	3
1Co	1:17 For Christ did not send me to baptize	7
	4:17 For this reason I sent you Timothy	7
	16: 3 when I arrive, I will send any whom you approve	7
2Co	1:16 and have you send me on to Judea.	8
	9: 3 I am sending the brothers	7
	12:17 through any of those whom I sent to you?	3
Gal	1: 1 Paul an apostle—sent neither by human commission	7
	2: 8 worked through me in sending me to the Gentiles)	1
	4: 4 God sent his Son, born of a woman,	4
	4: 6 God has sent the Spirit of his Son into our hearts	4
Eph	6:22 I am sending him to you for this very purpose	7
Php	2:19 hope in the Lord Jesus to send Timothy to you soon	7
	2:23 I hope therefore to send him	7
	2:25 I think it necessary to send to you	7
	2:28 the more eager to send him, therefore	7
	4:16 you sent me help for my needs more than once.	7
	4:18 have received from Epaphroditus the gifts you sent	5
Col	4: 8 I have sent him to you for this very purpose	7
1Th	3: 2 we sent Timothy, our brother and co-worker for God	7
	3: 5 I sent to find out about your faith;	7

2Th	2:11 For this reason God sends them a powerful delusion	7
2Ti	4:12 I have sent Tychicus to Ephesus.	3
Tit	3:12 When I send Artemas to you, or Tychicus	7
Heb	1:14 angels spirits in the divine service, sent to serve	3
1Pe	1:12 by the Holy Spirit sent from heaven	3
	2:14 or of governors, as sent by him to punish	7
1Jn	4: 9 God sent his only Son into the world	3
	4:10 sent his Son to be the atoning sacrifice for our sins.	3
	4:14 Father has sent his Son as the Savior of the world.	3
3Jn	1: 6 to send them on...in a manner worthy of God;	8
Rev	1: 1 he made it known by sending his angel	3
	1:11 in a book what you see and send it to the seven churches	7
	22: 6 the Lord...sent his angel to show his servants	3
	22:16 I, Jesus, who sent my angel to you	7

send a letter

1. ἐπιστέλλω, *epistellō, 2182*

Act	21:25 we have sent a letter with our judgment	1

send a message

1. ἀποστέλλω, *apostellō, 690*

Act	13:15 officials of the synagogue sent them a message,	1

send a messenger

1. ἀποστέλλω, *apostellō, 690*

Jhn	5:33 You sent messengers to John	1

send away

1. ἀπολύω, *apolyō, 668*
2. ἀποστέλλω, *apostellō, 690*
3. ἐκβάλλω, *ekballō, 1675*
4. ἐξαποστέλλω, *exapostellō, 1990*

Mat	14:15 send the crowds away so that they may go	1
	15:23 "Send her away, for she keeps shouting after us."	1
	15:32 I do not want to send them away hungry	1
	15:39 sending away the crowds, he got into the boat	1
Mrk	1:43 sternly warning him he sent him away at once	3
	6:36 send them away so that they may go into	1
	8: 3 If I send them away hungry to their homes	1
	8: 9 And he sent them away.	1
	8:26 he sent him away to his home, saying	2
	12: 3 beat him, and sent him away empty-handed.	2
Lke	1:53 sent the rich away empty.	4
	8:38 Jesus sent him away, saying	1
	9:12 "Send the crowd away, so that they may go	1
	14: 4 Jesus took him and healed him, and sent him away.	1
	20:10 the tenants...sent him away empty-handed.	4
	20:11 and sent away empty-handed.	4
Act	17:14 the believers...sent Paul away to the coast	4
	22:21 I will send you far away to the Gentiles.' "	4

send back

1. ἀναπέμπω, *anapempō, 402*

Lke	23:11 elegant robe on him, and sent him back to Pilate.	1
	23:15 Neither has Herod, for he sent him back to us.	1
Phm	1:12 I am sending him, that is, my own heart, back to you.	1

send for

1. μετακαλέω, *metakaleō, 3559*
2. μεταπέμπω, *metapempō, 3569*

Act	10: 5 send...for a certain Simon who is called Peter;	2
	10:22 "Cornelius...was directed...to send for you	2
	10:29 So when I was sent for, I came without objection.	2
	10:29 Now may I ask why you sent for me?"	2
	20: 1 Paul sent for the disciples;	2
	24:24 he sent for Paul and heard him	2
	24:25 when I have an opportunity, I will send for you."	1
	24:26 for that reason he used to send for him very often	2

send from

1. ἐκ, *ek, 1666*

2Co	2:17 as persons of sincerity, as persons sent from God	1

send greetings

1. ἀσπάζομαι, *aspazomai, 832*

1Co	16:19 The churches of Asia send greetings.	1
	16:20 All the brothers and sisters send greetings.	1
2Ti	4:21 Eubulus sends greetings to you	1
Tit	3:15 All who are with me send greetings to you.	1

Phm 1:23 Epaphras...sends greetings to you   1
Heb 13:24 Those from Italy send you greetings.   1
1Pe 5:13 sister church in Babylon...sends you greetings;   1
2Jn 1:13 The children of your elect sister send you their greetings.   1
3Jn 1:15 The friends send you their greetings.   1

send off

1. ἀναπέμπω, *anapempō, 402*
2. ἀπολύω, *apolyō, 668*
3. ἐκπέμπω, *ekpempō, 1734*
4. ἐξαποστέλλω, *exapostellō, 1990*

Lke 23: 7 he sent him off to Herod   1
Act 9:30 and sent him off to Tarsus.   4
    13: 3 they laid their hands on them and sent them off.   2
    15:30 they were sent off and went down to Antioch.   2
    15:33 they were sent off in peace by the believers   2
    17:10 the believers sent Paul and Silas off   3

send on

1. προπέμπω, *propempō, 4636*

Rom 15:24 and to be sent on by you   1

send on one's way

1. προπέμπω, *propempō, 4636*

Act 15: 3 So they were sent on their way by the church   1
1Co 16: 6 so that you may send me on my way   1
    16:11 Send him on his way in peace   1
Tit 3:13 send Zenas the lawyer and Apollos on their way   1

send out

1. ἀποστέλλω, *apostellō, 690*
2. ἐκβάλλω, *ekballō, 1675*
3. ἐκπέμπω, *ekpempō, 1734*
4. ἐξαποστέλλω, *exapostellō, 1990*

Mat 9:38 to send out laborers into his harvest."   2
    10: 5 These twelve Jesus sent out with the following   1
    10:16 "See, I am sending you out like sheep   1
    24:31 he will send out his angels with a loud trumpet   1
Mrk 3:14 to be sent out to proclaim the message   1
    6: 7 began to send them out two by two   1
    13:27 Then he will send out the angels   1
    16: S ⟦afterward Jesus himself sent out through them,⟧   4
Lke 9: 2 he sent them out to proclaim the kingdom of God   1
    10: 2 to send out laborers into his harvest.   2
    10: 3 See, I am sending you out like lambs   1
    22:35 "When I sent you out without a purse, bag,   1
Act 13: 4 being sent out by the Holy Spirit   3
Jas 2:25 when she...sent them out by another road?   2
Rev 5: 6 seven spirits of God sent out into all the earth.   1

send rain

1. βρέχω, *brechō, 1101*

Mat 5:45 sends rain on the righteous and on the unrighteous.   1

send with

1. συμπέμπω, *sympempō, 5225*
2. συναποστέλλω, *synapostellō, 5273*

2Co 8:18 With him we are sending the brother who is famous   1
    8:22 with them we are sending our brother   1
    12:18 I urged Titus to go, and sent the brother with him.   2

send word

1. ἀποστέλλω, *apostellō, 690*

Mat 14:35 they sent word throughout the region   1
Act 16:36 "The magistrates sent word to let you go;   1

sense   *See also* show good sense

1. διάνοια, *dianoia, 1379*

Eph 2: 3 following the desires of flesh and senses   1

sense of smell

1. ὄσφρησις, *osphrēsis, 4018*

1Co 12:17 where would the sense of smell be?   1

senseless

1. ἀνόητος, *anoētos, 485*
2. ἀπαίδευτος, *apaideutos, 553*
3. ἀσύνετος, *asynetos, 852*

4. κενός, *kenos, 3031*

Rom 1:21 and their senseless minds were darkened.   3
1Ti 6: 9 trapped by many senseless and harmful desires   1
2Ti 2:23 stupid and senseless controversies;   2
Jas 2:20 Do you want to be shown, you senseless person   4

sensible

1. σώφρων, *sōphrōn, 5409*

1Ti 3: 2 married only once, temperate, sensible   1

sensible person

1. φρόνιμος, *phronimos, 5861*

1Co 10:15 I speak as to sensible people; judge for yourselves   1

sensitivity   *See* lose all sensitivity

sensual   *See* sensual desires *alienate*

sentence[1]   *See also* cause for a sentence, ground for sentence

1. ἀπόκριμα, *apokrima, 645*
2. κρίσις, *krisis, 3213*
3. λόγος, *logos, 3364*

Mat 23:33 How can you escape being sentenced to hell?   2
Rom 9:28 Lord will execute his sentence on the earth   3
2Co 1: 9 felt that we had received the sentence of death   1

sentence[2]

1. φωνή, *phōnē, 5889*

Act 24:21 unless it was this one sentence that I called out   1

sentence against

1. καταδίκη, *katadikē, 2869*

Act 25:15 asked for a sentence against him.   1

sentence of condemnation

1. κρίμα, *krima, 3210*

Lke 23:40 you are under the same sentence of condemnation?   1

sentence to death

1. ἐπιθανάτιος, *epithanatios, 2119*

1Co 4: 9 as though sentenced to death   1

separate   *See also* keep separate

1. ἀφορίζω, *aphorizō, 928*
2. χωρίζω, *chōrizō, 6004*

Mat 13:49 and separate the evil from the righteous   1
    19: 6 let no one separate."   2
    25:32 he will separate people one from another   1
    25:32 as a shepherd separates the sheep from the goats   1
Mrk 10: 9 let no one separate."   2
Rom 8:35 Who will separate us from the love of Christ?   2
    8:39 will be able to separate us from the love of God   2
1Co 7:10 the wife should not separate from her husband   2
    7:11 if she does separate, let her remain unmarried   2
    7:15 if the unbelieving partner separates,   2
2Co 6:17 come out from them, and be separate from them   1
Phm 1:15 Perhaps this is the reason he was separated from you   2
Heb 7:26 blameless, undefiled, separated from sinners   2

separated from

1. ἀπό, *apo, 608*

1Th 2:17 we were made orphans by being separated from you   1
2Th 1: 9 separated from the presence of the Lord   1

Sergius

1. Σέργιος, *Sergios, 4950*

Act 13: 7 He was with the proconsul, Sergius Paulus,   1

serious

1. βαρύς, *barys, 987*
2. πονηρός, *ponēros, 4505*
3. σεμνός, *semnos, 4948*
4. σωφρονέω, *sōphroneō, 5404*

Act 18:14 a matter of crime or serious villainy   2
    25: 7 bringing many serious charges against him   1
1Ti 3: 8 Deacons likewise must be serious   3
    3:11 Women likewise must be serious   3

Tit	2: 2	Tell the older men to be temperate, serious, prudent	3
1Pe	4: 7	therefore be serious and discipline yourselves	4

serpent

1. ὄφις, *ophis, 4058*

Mat	10:16	so be wise as serpents and innocent as doves.	1
Jhn	3:14	as Moses lifted up the serpent in the wilderness	1
1Co	10: 9	and were destroyed by serpents.	1
2Co	11: 3	as the serpent deceived Eve by its cunning	1
Rev	9:19	their tails are like serpents, having heads;	1
	12: 9	ancient serpent, who is called the Devil	1
	12:14	could fly from the serpent into the wilderness	1
	12:15	Then from his mouth the serpent poured water	1
	20: 2	He seized the dragon, that ancient serpent	1

Serug

1. Σερούχ, *Serouch, 4952*

Lke	3:35	son of Serug, son of Reu, son of Peleg	1

servant

1. διάκονος, *diakonos, 1356*
2. δούλη, *doulē, 1527*
3. δοῦλος¹, *doulos¹, 1528*
4. θεράπων, *therapōn, 2544*
5. λειτουργός, *leitourgos, 3313*
6. οἰκέτης, *oiketēs, 3860*
7. παῖς, *pais, 4090*
8. ὑπηρέτης, *hypēretēs, 5677*

Mat	8: 6	"Lord, my servant is lying at home paralyzed	7
	8: 8	speak the word, and my servant will be healed.	7
	8:13	And the servant was healed in that hour.	7
	12:18	"Here is my servant, whom I have chosen,	7
	14: 2	and he said to his servants,	7
	20:26	whoever wishes to be great...must be your servant	1
	23:11	The greatest among you will be your servant.	1
Mrk	9:35	must be last of all and servant of all."	1
	10:43	to become great...must be your servant	1
Lke	1: 2	eyewitnesses and servants of the word	8
	1:38	Mary said, "Here am I, the servant of the Lord;	2
	1:48	looked with favor on the lowliness of his servant.	2
	1:54	He has helped his servant Israel	7
	1:69	in the house of his servant David	7
	2:29	now you are dismissing your servant in peace	3
	7: 7	speak the word, and let my servant be healed.	7
Jhn	2: 5	His mother said to the servants	1
	2: 9	(though the servants who had drawn the water knew)	1
	12:26	where I am, there will my servant be also.	1
	13:16	servants are not greater than their master	3
	15:15	I do not call you servants any longer	3
	15:15	servant does not know what the master is doing;	3
	15:20	'Servants are not greater than their master.'	3
Act	3:13	God...has glorified his servant Jesus	7
	3:26	God raised up his servant	7
	4:25	Holy Spirit through our ancestor David, your servant:	7
	4:27	gathered together against your holy servant	7
	4:29	grant to your servants to speak your word	3
	4:30	through the name of your holy servant Jesus."	7
Rom	1: 1	Paul, a servant of Jesus Christ	3
	13: 4	for it is God's servant for your good.	1
	13: 4	It is the servant of God to execute wrath	1
	13: 6	for the authorities are God's servants,	5
	14: 4	to pass judgment on servants of another?	6
	15: 8	Christ has become a servant of the circumcised	1
1Co	3: 5	Servants through whom you came to believe	1
	4: 1	Think of us...as servants of Christ	8
2Co	6: 4	as servants of God we have commended ourselves	1
Gal	1:10	I would not be a servant of Christ.	3
	2:17	is Christ then a servant of sin? Certainly not!	1
Eph	3: 7	Of this gospel I have become a servant	1
Php	1: 1	Paul and Timothy, servants of Christ Jesus	3
Col	1:23	I, Paul, became a servant of this gospel.	1
	1:25	I became its servant	1
	4:12	Epaphras...a servant of Christ Jesus	3
1Ti	4: 6	you will be a good servant of Christ Jesus	1
2Ti	2:24	the Lord's servant must not be quarrelsome	3
Tit	1: 1	Paul, a servant of God and an apostle of Jesus	3
Heb	1: 7	"He makes...his servants flames of fire."	5
	3: 5	Moses was faithful...as a servant	4
Jas	1: 1	James, a servant of God and of the Lord Jesus	3
1Pe	2:16	As servants of God, live as free people,	3

2Pe	1: 1	Peter, a servant and apostle of Jesus Christ	3
Jde	1: 1	Jude, a servant of Jesus...and brother of James	3
Rev	1: 1	which God gave him to show his servants	3
	1: 1	by sending his angel to his servant John	3
	2:20	beguiling my servants to practice fornication	3
	7: 3	until we have marked the servants of our God with a seal	3
	10: 7	as he announced to his servants the prophets."	3
	11:18	for rewarding your servants, the prophets	3
	15: 3	they sing the song of Moses, the servant of God	3
	19: 2	he has avenged on her the blood of his servants."	3
	19: 5	"Praise our God, all you his servants	3
	22: 3	and his servants will worship him;	3
	22: 6	the Lord...sent his angel to show his servants	3

fellow servant

1. σύνδουλος, *syndoulos, 5281*

Col	1: 7	Epaphras, our beloved fellow servant.	1
	4: 7	Tychicus...fellow servant in the Lord.	1
Rev	6:11	until the number...both of their fellow servants	1
	19:10	I am a fellow servant with you and your comrades	1
	22: 9	I am a fellow servant with you and your comrades	1

servant working together

1. συνεργός, *synergos, 5301*

1Co	3: 9	For we are God's servants, working together	1

servant-girl

1. Contextual: Not in Greek
2. παιδίσκη, *paidiskē, 4087*

Mat	26:69	A servant-girl came to him and said	2
	26:71	to the porch, another servant-girl saw him	1
Mrk	14:66	the servant-girls of the high priest came by.	2
	14:69	the servant-girl, on seeing him	2
Lke	22:56	a servant-girl, seeing him in the firelight	2

serve

1. Contextual: Not in Greek
2. διακονέω, *diakoneō, 1354*
3. διακονία, *diakonia, 1355*
4. δουλεύω, *douleuō, 1526*
5. θεραπεύω, *therapeuō, 2543*
6. λατρεύω, *latreuō, 3302*
7. παρεδρεύω, *paredreuō, 4204*
8. πρόκειμαι, *prokeimai, 4618*
9. προσέχω, *prosechō, 4668*
10. προσκαρτερέω, *proskartereō, 4674*
11. τίθημι, *tithēmi, 5502*
12. ὑπηρετέω, *hypēreteō, 5676*
13. ὑπηρέτης, *hypēretēs, 5677*

Mat	4:10	'Worship the Lord your God, and serve only him.' "	6
	6:24	"No one can serve two masters; for a slave	4
	6:24	the other. You cannot serve God and wealth.	4
	8:15	and she got up and began to serve him.	2
	20:28	the Son of Man came not to be served but to serve	2
	20:28	the Son of Man came not to be served but to serve	2
Mrk	1:31	the fever left her, and she began to serve them.	2
	10:45	Son of Man came not to be served but to serve	2
	10:45	Son of Man came not to be served but to serve	2
Lke	1:74	that we...might serve him without fear	6
	4: 8	serve only him.' "	6
	4:39	Immediately she got up and began to serve them.	2
	12:37	he will come and serve them.	2
	16:13	No slave can serve two masters;	4
	16:13	You cannot serve God and wealth."	4
	17: 8	put on your apron and serve me	2
	22:26	the leader like one who serves.	2
	22:27	one who is at the table or the one who serves?	2
	22:27	But I am among you as one who serves.	2
Jhn	2:10	said to him, "Everyone serves the good wine first	11
	12: 2	There they gave a dinner for him. Martha served	2
	12:26	Whoever serves me must follow me	2
	12:26	Whoever serves me, the Father will honor.	2
Act	6: 4	to prayer and to serving the word."	3
	7: 7	I will judge the nation that they serve,' said God	4
	10: 7	from the ranks of those who served him	10
	13:36	served the purpose of God in his own generation	12
	17:25	nor is he served by human hands	5
	20:19	serving the Lord with all humility	4
	26:16	to appoint you to serve and testify	13

Rom	1: 9	I serve with my spirit by announcing the gospel	6
	1:25	served the creature rather than the Creator	6
	9:12	she was told, "The elder shall serve the younger."	4
	12:11	be ardent in spirit, serve the Lord.	4
	14:18	one who thus serves Christ is acceptable to God	4
	16:18	For such people do not serve our Lord Christ	4
1Co	9:13	those who serve at the altar	7
2Co	11: 8	accepting support from them in order to serve you.	3
Php	2:22	he has served with me in the work of the gospel.	4
Col	3:24	you serve the Lord Christ.	4
1Th	1: 9	to serve a living and true God	4
1Ti	6: 2	rather they must serve them all the more	4
Heb	1:14	angels spirits in the divine service, sent to serve	3
	6:10	in serving the saints, as you still do.	2
	7:13	from which no one has ever served at the altar.	9
1Pe	1:12	they were serving not themselves but you	2
	4:10	Like good stewards...serve one another	2
	4:11	whoever serves must do so with the strength	2
Jde	1: 7	serve as an example by undergoing a punishment	8
Rev	1: 6	a kingdom, priests serving his God and Father	1
	5:10	to be a kingdom and priests serving our God	1

serve as an example

1. τυπικῶς, *typikōs, 5595*

1Co 10:11 things happened to them to serve as an example   1

serve as deacon

1. διακονέω, *diakoneō, 1354*

1Ti	3:10	let them serve as deacons.	1
	3:13	those who serve well as deacons	1

serve as judge

1. κρίνω, *krinō, 3212*

Jhn 12:48 the word that I have spoken will serve as judge   1

serve as priest

1. ἱερατεύω, *hierateuō, 2634*

Lke 1: 8 Once when he was serving as priest before God   1

serve in the army

1. στρατεύομαι, *strateuomai, 5129*

2Ti 2: 4 No one serving in the army gets entangled   1

serve to confirm

1. συνίστημι, *synistēmi, 5319*

Rom 3: 5 our injustice serves to confirm the justice of God   1

service *See also* do military service, put at the service, render service

1. διακονέω, *diakoneō, 1354*
2. διακονία, *diakonia, 1355*
3. εἰς, *eis, 1650*
4. ἔργον, *ergon, 2240*
5. εὐεργεσία, *euergesia, 2307*
6. λειτουργέω, *leitourgeō, 3310*
7. λειτουργία, *leitourgia, 3311*
8. πρός, *pros, 4639*

Mat	26:10	She has performed a good service for me.	4
Mrk	14: 6	She has performed a good service for me.	4
Lke	1:23	When his time of service was ended	7
Rom	15:27	they ought also to be of service to them	6
1Co	12: 5	are varieties of services, but the same Lord;	2
	16:15	devoted themselves to the service of the saints;	2
2Co	8:23	my partner and co-worker in your service;	3
Php	2:30	for those services that you could not give me.	7
1Ti	1:12	and appointed me to his service	2
	6: 2	those who benefit by their service	5
Phm	1:13	so that he might be of service to me in your place	1
Heb	2:17	faithful high priest in the service of God	8
	10:11	every priest stands day after day at his service	6
Rev	2:19	"I know your works—your love, faith, service,	2

divine service

1. λειτουργικός, *leitourgikos, 3312*

Heb 1:14 Are not all angels spirits in the divine service,   1

priestly service

1. ἱερουργέω, *hierourgeō, 2646*

Rom 15:16 in the priestly service of the gospel of God   1

temple service

1. ἱερός, *hieros, 2641*

1Co 9:13 who are employed in the temple service   1

set¹ *See also* set *time*

1. Contextual: Not in Greek
2. αἴρω, *airō, 149*
3. γίνομαι, *ginomai, 1181*
4. δίδωμι, *didōmi, 1443*
5. ἐάω, *eaō, 1572*
6. εἰμί, *eimi, 1639*
7. καθίστημι, *kathistēmi, 2770*
8. ὁρίζω, *horizō, 3988*
9. πορεύομαι, *poreuomai, 4513*
10. στηρίζω, *stērizō, 5114*
11. τάσσω, *tassō, 5435*
12. τίθημι, *tithēmi, 5502*

Lke	7: 8	I also am a man set under authority	11
	9:51	he set his face to go to Jerusalem.	10
	9:53	because his face was set toward Jerusalem.	9
	12:14	who set me to be a judge or arbitrator over you?"	7
Jhn	13:15	For I have set you an example	4
Act	1: 7	that the Father has set by his own authority.	12
	13:47	'I have set you to be a light for the Gentiles	12
	27:32	cut away the ropes of the boat and set it adrift.	5
	28:23	After they had set a day to meet with him	11
Rom	8: 6	To set the mind on the flesh is death	1
	8: 6	to set the mind on the Spirit is life and peace.	1
	8: 7	the mind that is set on the flesh is hostile to God;	1
Col	2:14	He set this aside, nailing it to the cross.	2
1Ti	4:12	set the believers an example in speech	3
Heb	4: 7	again he sets a certain day—"today"	8
1Pe	1:21	so that your faith and hope are set on God.	6
Rev	3: 8	Look, I have set before you an open door	4
	10: 2	Setting his right foot on the sea	12

set²

1. δύνω, *dynō, 1544*

Lke 4:40 As the sun was setting   1

set a price

1. τιμάω, *timaō, 5506*

Mat	27: 9	price of the one on whom a price had been set	1
	27: 9	some of the people of Israel had set a price	1

set ablaze

1. ἀνάπτω, *anaptō, 409*
2. πυρόω, *pyroō, 4792*

Jas	3: 5	How great a forest is set ablaze by a small fire!	1
2Pe	3:12	the heavens will be set ablaze and dissolved	2

set against

1. ἀντιλέγω, *antilegō, 515*
2. διχάζω, *dichazō, 1495*

Mat	10:35	For I have come to set a man against his father	2
Jhn	19:12	Everyone...sets himself against the emperor."	1

set apart

1. ἀφορίζω, *aphorizō, 928*

Act	13: 2	"Set apart for me Barnabas and Saul	1
Rom	1: 1	Paul...set apart for the gospel of God	1
Gal	1:15	when God, who had set me apart before I was born	1

set aside

1. καταργέω, *katargeō, 2934*

2Co	3: 7	the glory of his face, a glory now set aside	1
	3:11	for if what was set aside came through glory	1
	3:13	the end of the glory that was being set aside.	1
	3:14	since only in Christ is it set aside.	1

set at rest

1. ἀναπαύω, *anapauō, 399*

2Co 7:13 his mind has been set at rest by all of you.   1

set before

1. παρατίθημι, *paratithēmi, 4192*
2. πρόκειμαι, *prokeimai, 4618*

Mrk 6:41 loaves...to set before the people;   1

Lke   9:16 and gave them...to set before the crowd.   1
     10: 8 eat what is set before you;   1
     11: 6 I have nothing to set before him.'   1
Act 16:34 and set food before them;   1
1Co 10:27 eat whatever is set before you   1
Heb   6:18 to seize the hope set before us.   2
     12: 1 the race that is set before us   2
     12: 2 for the sake of the joy that was set before him   2

set date
   1. προθεσμία, *prothesmia, 4607*
Gal   4: 2 until the date set by the father.   1

set down
   1. ἀνατάσσομαι, *anatassomai, 421*
Lke   1: 1 many have undertaken to set down an orderly account   1

set foot
   1. ἐπιβαίνω, *epibainō, 2094*
Act 20:18 from the first day that I set foot in Asia   1

set forth
   1. προτίθημι, *protithēmi, 4729*
Eph   1: 9 his good pleasure that he set forth in Christ   1

set free
   1. ἀπολύω, *apolyō, 668*
   2. δικαιόω, *dikaioō, 1467*
   3. ἐλευθερόω, *eleutheroō, 1802*
   4. ἐξαιρέω, *exaireō, 1975*
   5. λύω, *lyō, 3395*
Lke 13:12 "Woman, you are set free from your ailment."   1
     13:16 set free from this bondage on the sabbath day?"   5
Act 13:39 by this Jesus everyone who believes is set free   2
     26:32 "This man could have been set free   1
Rom   6:18 and that you, having been set free from sin   3
      8: 2 has set you free from the law of sin and of death.   3
      8:21 that the creation itself will be set free   3
Gal   1: 4 to set us free from the present evil age   4
      5: 1 For freedom Christ has set us free.   3
Heb 13:23 our brother Timothy has been set free;   1

set in an uproar
   1. θορυβέω, *thorybeō, 2572*
Act 17: 5 they formed a mob and set the city in an uproar.   1

set off
   1. ἀνίστημι, *anistēmi, 482*
Lke 15:20 he set off and went to his father.   1

set off in pursuit
   1. διώκω, *diōkō, 1503*
Lke 17:23 Do not go, do not set off in pursuit.   1

set on
   1. ἐπιβιβάζω, *epibibazō, 2097*
Lke 19:35 on the colt, they set Jesus on it.   1

set on fire
   1. φλογίζω, *phlogizō, 5824*
Jas   3: 6 sets on fire the cycle of nature   1
      3: 6 and is itself set on fire by hell.   1

set one's hope
   1. ἐλπίζω, *elpizō, 1827*
Jhn   5:45 accuser is Moses...on whom you have set your hope.   1
2Co   1:10 on him we have set our hope   1
1Ti   4:10 because we have our hope set on the living God   1
      5: 5 The real widow...has set her hope on God   1
      6:17 to set their hopes on the uncertainty of riches   1
1Pe   1:13 set all your hope on the grace that Jesus Christ   1

set one's hope first
   1. προελπίζω, *proelpizō, 4598*
Eph   1:12 we, who were the first to set our hope on Christ   1

set one's mind
   1. Contextual: Not in Greek

   2. φρονέω, *phroneō, 5858*
Mat 16:23 setting your mind not on divine things but on human   2
Mrk   8:33 you are setting your mind not on divine things   2
Rom   8: 5 set their minds on the things of the flesh   2
      8: 5 set their minds on the things of the Spirit.   1
Php   3:19 their minds are set on earthly things.   2
Col   3: 2 Set your minds on things that are above   2

set out
   1. ἀνίστημι, *anistēmi, 482*
   2. ἀπέρχομαι, *aperchomai, 599*
   3. ἐκπορεύομαι, *ekporeuomai, 1744*
   4. ἐξέρχομαι, *exerchomai, 2002*
   5. πορεύομαι, *poreuomai, 4513*
Mat   2: 9 When they had heard the king, they set out;   5
Mrk   7:24 From there he set out   1
     10:17 As he was setting out on a journey   3
     14:16 the disciples set out and went to the city   4
Lke   1:39 In those days Mary set out   1
Jhn 20: 3 Then Peter and the other disciple set out   4
Act 15:40 Paul chose Silas and set out   4
Rom 15:28 I will set out by way of you to Spain;   2
Heb 11: 8 obeyed when he was called to set out   4
     11: 8 he set out, not knowing where he was going.   4

set sail
   1. ἀνάγω, *anagō, 343*
   2. πλέω, *pleō, 4434*
Act 13:13 Paul and his companions set sail from Paphos   1
     16:11 We set sail from Troas   1
     18:21 Then he set sail from Ephesus.   1
     20: 3 He was about to set sail for Syria   1
     20:13 went ahead to the ship and set sail for Assos   1
     21: 1 When we had parted from them and set sail   1
     21: 2 we went on board and set sail.   1
     27: 2 that was about to set sail to the ports   2
     27:21 not have set sail from Crete   1
     28:11 Three months later we set sail   1

set seal
   1. σφραγίζω, *sphragizō, 5381*
Jhn   6:27 on him that God the Father has set his seal."   1

set things right
   1. διόρθωσις, *diorthōsis, 1481*
Heb   9:10 imposed until the time comes to set things right.   1

set up
   1. ἀνορθόω, *anorthoō, 494*
   2. ἵστημι, *histēmi, 2705*
   3. παρεμβάλλω, *paremballō, 4212*
   4. πήγνυμι, *pēgnymi, 4381*
Mrk 13:14 when you see the desolating sacrilege set up   2
Lke 19:43 when your enemies will set up ramparts around you   3
Act   6:13 They set up false witnesses who said   2
     15:16 its ruins I will rebuild it, and I will set it up   1
Heb   8: 2 true tent that the Lord, and not any mortal, has set up.   4

Seth
   1. Σήθ, *Sēth, 4953*
Lke   3:38 son of Enos, son of Seth, son of Adam   1

settle¹
   1. κατοικέω, *katoikeō, 2997*
Act   7: 4 Then he left...and settled in Haran.   1

settle²
   1. ἐπιλύω, *epilyō, 2147*
   2. συναίρω, *synairō, 5256*
Mat 18:23 to settle accounts with his slaves.   2
     25:19 settled accounts with them.   2
Act 19:39 it must be settled in the regular assembly.   1

settle a case
   1. ἀπαλλάσσω, *apallassō, 557*
Lke 12:58 on the way make an effort to settle the case   1

seven
   1. ἑπτά, *hepta, 2231*

Mat	12:45	it goes and brings along seven other spirits	1
	15:34	They said, "Seven, and a few small fish."	1
	15:36	he took the seven loaves and the fish;	1
	15:37	the broken pieces left over, seven baskets full.	1
	16:10	Or the seven loaves for the four thousand	1
	22:25	Now there were seven brothers among us;	1
	22:28	whose wife of the seven will she be?	1
Mrk	8: 5	They said, "Seven."	1
	8: 6	he took the seven loaves	1
	8: 8	the broken pieces left over, seven baskets full.	1
	8:20	"And the seven for the four thousand,	1
	8:20	they said to him, "Seven."	1
	12:20	There were seven brothers; the first married	1
	12:22	none of the seven left children.	1
	12:23	For the seven had married her."	1
	16: 9	⟦from whom he had cast out seven demons.⟧	1
Lke	2:36	seven years after her marriage	1
	8: 2	Mary…from whom seven demons had gone out	1
	11:26	seven other spirits more evil than itself	1
	20:29	Now there were seven brothers;	1
	20:31	in the same way all seven died childless.	1
	20:33	For the seven had married her."	1
Act	6: 3	select from among yourselves seven men of good standing	1
	13:19	After he had destroyed seven nations in the land	1
	19:14	Seven sons of a Jewish high priest named Sceva	1
	20: 6	Troas, where we stayed for seven days.	1
	21: 4	and stayed there for seven days.	1
	21: 8	Philip the evangelist, one of the seven	1
	21:27	When the seven days were almost completed	1
	28:14	were invited to stay with them for seven days.	1
Heb	11:30	after they had been encircled for seven days.	1
Rev	1: 4	John to the seven churches that are in Asia:	1
	1: 4	from the seven spirits who are before his throne	1
	1:11	in a book what you see and send it to the seven churches	1
	1:12	and on turning I saw seven golden lampstands	1
	1:16	In his right hand he held seven stars	1
	1:20	the seven stars that you saw in my right hand	1
	1:20	seven stars…and the seven golden lampstands:	1
	1:20	seven stars are the angels of the seven churches	1
	1:20	seven stars are the angels of the seven churches	1
	1:20	the seven lampstands are the seven churches.	1
	1:20	the seven lampstands are the seven churches.	1
	2: 1	him who holds the seven stars in his right hand	1
	2: 1	who walks among the seven golden lampstands:	1
	3: 1	the words of him who has the seven spirits of God	1
	3: 1	the seven spirits of God and the seven stars:	1
	4: 5	in front of the throne burn seven flaming torches	1
	4: 5	torches…which are the seven spirits of God;	1
	5: 1	a scroll…sealed with seven seals;	1
	5: 5	so that he can open the scroll and its seven seals."	1
	5: 6	a Lamb…having seven horns and…seven eyes	1
	5: 6	a Lamb…having seven horns and…seven eyes	1
	5: 6	seven spirits of God sent out into all the earth.	1
	6: 1	I saw the Lamb open one of the seven seals	1
	8: 2	And I saw the seven angels who stand before God	1
	8: 2	and seven trumpets were given to them.	1
	8: 6	Now the seven angels who had the seven trumpets	1
	8: 6	Now the seven angels who had the seven trumpets	1
	10: 3	when he shouted, the seven thunders sounded.	1
	10: 4	when the seven thunders had sounded	1
	10: 4	"Seal up what the seven thunders have said	1
	11:13	seven thousand people were killed in the earthquake	1
	12: 3	great red dragon, with seven heads and ten horns	1
	12: 3	and ten horns, and seven diadems on his heads.	1
	13: 1	I saw a beast…having ten horns and seven heads;	1
	15: 1	I saw…seven angels with seven plagues	1
	15: 1	I saw…seven angels with seven plagues	1
	15: 6	out of the temple came the seven angels	1
	15: 6	came the seven angels with the seven plagues	1
	15: 7	the four living creatures gave the seven angels	1
	15: 7	seven golden bowls full of the wrath of God	1
	15: 8	seven plagues of the seven angels were ended.	1
	15: 8	seven plagues of the seven angels were ended.	1
	16: 1	voice from the temple telling the seven angels	1
	16: 1	pour out…the seven bowls of the wrath of God."	1
	17: 1	one of the seven angels who had the seven bowls	1
	17: 1	one of the seven angels who had the seven bowls	1
	17: 3	and it had seven heads and ten horns.	1
	17: 7	and of the beast with seven heads and ten horns	1
	17: 9	the seven heads are seven mountains	1
	17: 9	the seven heads are seven mountains	1

	17: 9	seven mountains…also, they are seven kings	1
	17:11	it is an eighth but it belongs to the seven	1
	21: 9	one of the seven angels who had the seven bowls	1
	21: 9	the seven bowls full of the seven last plagues	1
	21: 9	the seven bowls full of the seven last plagues	1

seven miles

1. ἑξήκοντα + στάδιον, *hexēkonta + stadion, 2008 + 5084*

Lke	24:13	Emmaus, about seven miles from Jerusalem	1

seven thousand

1. ἑπτακισχίλιοι, *heptakischilioi, 2233*

Rom	11: 4	"I have kept for myself seven thousand who have not	1

seven times

1. ἑπτάκις, *heptakis, 2232*

Mat	18:21	As many as seven times?"	1
	18:22	"Not seven times, but, I tell you, seventy-seven	1
Lke	17: 4	same person sins against you seven times a day	1
	17: 4	turns back to you seven times and says, 'I repent,'	1

with seven others

1. ὄγδοος, *ogdoos, 3838*

2Pe	2: 5	even though he saved Noah…with seven others	1

seventh

1. ἕβδομος, *hebdomos, 1575*
2. ἑπτά, *hepta, 2231*

Mat	22:26	so also the third, down to the seventh.	2
Heb	4: 4	For in one place it speaks about the seventh day	1
	4: 4	God rested on the seventh day from all his works."	1
Jde	1:14	Enoch, in the seventh generation from Adam	1
Rev	8: 1	When the Lamb opened the seventh seal	1
	10: 7	the seventh angel is to blow his trumpet,	1
	11:15	Then the seventh angel blew his trumpet	1
	16:17	The seventh angel poured his bowl into the air	1
	21:20	the sixth carnelian, the seventh chrysolite	1

seventy

1. ἑβδομήκοντα, *hebdomēkonta, 1573*

Lke	10: 1	After this the Lord appointed seventy others	1
	10:17	The seventy returned with joy, saying,	1
Act	23:23	two hundred soldiers, seventy horsemen	1

seventy-five

1. ἑβδομήκοντα + πέντε, *hebdomēkonta + pente, 1573 + 4297*

Act	7:14	all his relatives to come to him, seventy-five in all;	1

seventy-seven times

1. ἑβδομηκοντάκις + ἑπτά, *hebdomēkontakis + hepta, 1574 + 2231*

Mat	18:22	"Not seven times, but…seventy-seven times	1

seventy-six

1. ἑβδομήκοντα + ἕξ, *hebdomēkonta + hex, 1573 + 1971*

Act	27:37	(We were in all two hundred seventy-six persons	1

several

1. πολύς, *polys, 4498*
2. τὶς, *tis, 5516*

Act	9:19	For several days he was with the disciples	2
	10:48	Then they invited him to stay for several days.	2
	21:10	While we were staying there for several days	1
	25:13	After several days had passed	2
	25:14	Since they were staying there several days	1

severe   *See also* severe *treatment*

1. ἀποτόμως, *apotomōs, 705*
2. ἰσχυρός, *ischyros, 2708*
3. μέγας, *megas, 3489*
4. πολύς, *polys, 4498*

Lke	4:25	there was a severe famine over all the land;	3
	12:47	That slave…will receive a severe beating.	4
	15:14	a severe famine took place throughout that country	2
Act	8: 1	a severe persecution began against the church	3
	11:28	there would be a severe famine over all the world;	3
	16:23	After they had given them a severe flogging	4
2Co	8: 2	for during a severe ordeal of affliction	4
	13:10	not have to be severe in using the authority	1

severity

1. ἀποτομία, *apotomia, 704*

Rom	11:22	Note then the kindness and the severity of God:	1
	11:22	severity toward those who have fallen	1

sew on

1. ἐπιβάλλω, *epiballō, 2095*
2. ἐπιράπτω, *epiraptō, 2165*

Mat	9:16	No one sews a piece of unshrunk cloth on	1
Mrk	2:21	sews a piece of unshrunk cloth on an old cloak;	2
Lke	5:36	and sews it on an old garment;	1

sewer

1. ἀφεδρών, *aphedrōn, 909*

Mat	15:17	the stomach, and goes out into the sewer?	1
Mrk	7:19	the stomach, and goes out into the sewer?"	1

sex

1. σκεῦος, *skeuos, 5007*

1Pe	3: 7	paying honor to the woman as the weaker sex	1

sexual *See* indulge in sexual immorality, sexual *immorality*

sexually *See* sexually *immoral*, sexually *immoral* person

shackle

1. πέδη, *pedē, 4267*

Mrk	5: 4	often been restrained with shackles and chains	1
	5: 4	the shackles he broke in pieces;	1
Lke	8:29	bound with chains and shackles	1

shade

1. σκιά, *skia, 5014*

Mrk	4:32	birds of the air can make nests in its shade."	1

shadow

1. ἀποσκίασμα, *aposkiasma, 684*
2. σκιά, *skia, 5014*

Mat	4:16	who sat in the region and shadow of death light	2
Lke	1:79	who sit in darkness and in the shadow of death	2
Act	5:15	shadow might fall on some of them as he came by.	2
Col	2:17	These are only a shadow of what is to come	2
Heb	8: 5	worship in a sanctuary that is a sketch and shadow	2
	10: 1	Since the law has only a shadow of the good things	2
Jas	1:17	there is no variation or shadow due to change.	1

shaft

1. φρέαρ, *phrear, 5853*

Rev	9: 1	given the key to the shaft of the bottomless pit;	1
	9: 2	he opened the shaft of the bottomless pit	1
	9: 2	and from the shaft rose smoke like the smoke	1
	9: 2	were darkened with the smoke from the shaft.	1

shake

1. κινέω, *kineō, 3075*
2. σαίνω, *sainō, 4883*
3. σαλεύω, *saleuō, 4888*
4. σείω, *seiō, 4940*

Mat	11: 7	A reed shaken by the wind?	3
	24:29	the powers of heaven will be shaken.	3
	27:39	passed by derided him, shaking their heads	1
	27:51	The earth shook, and the rocks were split.	4
	28: 4	For fear of him the guards shook	4
Mrk	13:25	the powers in the heavens will be shaken.	3
	15:29	shaking their heads and saying, "Aha!	1
Lke	6:48	burst against that house but could not shake it	3
	7:24	A reed shaken by the wind?	3
	21:26	the powers of the heavens will be shaken.	3
Act	2:25	he is at my right hand so that I will not be shaken;	3
	4:31	the place...was shaken.	3
	16:26	so violent that the foundations...were shaken;	3
1Th	3: 3	that no one would be shaken by these persecutions.	2
2Th	2: 2	not to be quickly shaken in mind or alarmed	3
Heb	12:26	At that time his voice shook the earth;	3
	12:26	"Yet once more I will shake not only the earth	4
	12:27	indicates the removal of what is shaken	3
	12:27	so that what cannot be shaken may remain.	3
Rev	6:13	drops its winter fruit when shaken by a gale.	4

shake off

1. ἀποτινάσσω, *apotinassō, 701*
2. ἐκτινάσσω, *ektinassō, 1759*

Mat	10:14	shake off the dust from your feet as you leave	2
Mrk	6:11	shake off the dust that is on your feet	2
Lke	9: 5	shake the dust off your feet	1
Act	13:51	they shook the dust off their feet in protest	2
	18: 6	in protest he shook the dust from his clothes	2
	28: 5	He, however, shook off the creature into the fire	1

shake together

1. σαλεύω, *saleuō, 4888*

Lke	6:38	good measure, pressed down, shaken together	1

shame   *See also* put to shame

1. αἰσχύνη, *aischynē, 158*
2. ἀσχημοσύνη, *aschēmosynē, 859*
3. ἀτιμία, *atimia, 871*
4. ἐντροπή, *entropē, 1959*
5. καταισχύνω, *kataischynō, 2875*

1Co	1:27	to shame the wise;	5
	1:27	to shame the strong;	5
	6: 5	I say this to your shame.	4
	15:34	I say this to your shame.	4
2Co	11:21	To my shame, I must say, we were too weak for that!	3
Php	3:19	their glory is in their shame;	1
Heb	12: 2	endured the cross, disregarding its shame	1
Jde	1:13	casting up the foam of their own shame;	1
Rev	3:18	keep the shame of your nakedness from being seen;	1
	16:15	not going about naked and exposed to shame.")	2

shameful

1. αἰσχρός, *aischros, 156*

1Co	14:35	it is shameful for a woman to speak in church.	1
Eph	5:12	shameful even to mention what such people do	1

shameful thing

1. αἰσχύνη, *aischynē, 158*

2Co	4: 2	renounced the shameful things that one hides;	1

shamefully *See* mistreat shamefully

shameless act

1. ἀσχημοσύνη, *aschēmosynē, 859*

Rom	1:27	Men committed shameless acts with men	1

share   *See also* ready to share, share *inheritance*

1. Contextual: Not in Greek
2. ἀπό, *apo, 608*
3. ἐκ, *ek, 1666*
4. ἐν, *en, 1877*
5. κλῆρος, *klēros, 3102*
6. κοινός, *koinos, 3123*
7. κοινωνέω, *koinōneō, 3125*
8. κοινωνία, *koinōnia, 3126*
9. κοινωνός, *koinōnos, 3128*
10. λαμβάνω, *lambanō, 3284*
11. μερίς, *meris, 3535*
12. μέρος, *meros, 3538*
13. μέρος + ἔχω, *meros + echō, 3538 + 2400*
14. μεταδίδωμι, *metadidōmi, 3556*
15. μεταλαμβάνω, *metalambanō, 3561*
16. μετέχω, *metechō, 3576*
17. μέτοχος, *metochos, 3581*
18. ποιέω, *poieō, 4472*
19. συγκοινωνέω, *synkoinōneō, 5170*
20. συγκοινωνός, *synkoinōnos, 5171*
21. συμμερίζομαι, *symmerizomai, 5211*
22. υἱός, *huios, 5626*

Mrk	12: 2	to collect from them his share of the produce	2
Lke	3:11	must share with anyone who has none;	14
	10: 6	if anyone is there who shares in peace	22
	15:12	share of the property that will belong to me.'	12
	20:10	give him his share of the produce of the vineyard;	2
Jhn	13: 8	"Unless I wash you, you have no share with me."	12
Act	1:17	allotted his share in this ministry."	5
	8:21	You have no part or share in this	5
Rom	1:11	so that I may share with you some spiritual gift	14

Rom	4:16	but also to those who share the faith of Abraham	3
	5: 2	we boast in our hope of sharing the glory of God.	1
	11:17	to share the rich root of the olive tree	20
	15:26	pleased to share their resources with the poor	18
	15:27	the Gentiles...share in their spiritual blessings	7
1Co	9:10	should thresh in hope of a share in the crop.	16
	9:12	If others share this rightful claim on you	16
	9:13	share in what is sacrificed on the altar?	21
	9:23	so that I may share in its blessings.	20
	10:16	is it not a sharing in the blood of Christ?	8
	10:16	is it not a sharing in the body of Christ?	8
2Co	1: 7	we know that as you share in our sufferings	9
	1: 7	so also you share in our consolation.	1
	6:15	what does a believer share with an unbeliever?	11
	8: 4	sharing in this ministry to the saints—	8
	9:13	the generosity of your sharing with them	8
Gal	6: 6	share in all good things with their teacher.	7
Eph	4:28	so as to have something to share with the needy.	14
Php	1: 5	because of your sharing in the gospel	8
	1: 7	all of you share in God's grace with me	20
	1:26	share abundantly in your boasting in Christ Jesus	4
	2: 1	any sharing in the Spirit	8
	3:10	sharing of his sufferings	8
	4:14	it was kind of you to share my distress.	19
	4:15	no church shared with me	7
Col	1:12	has enabled you to share in the inheritance	11
1Th	2: 8	determined to share with you not only the gospel of God	14
2Ti	2: 6	ought to have the first share of the crops.	15
Tit	1: 4	To Titus, my loyal child in the faith we share:	6
Phm	1: 6	the sharing of your faith	8
Heb	2:14	Since...the children share flesh and blood	7
	2:14	he himself likewise shared the same things	16
	6: 4	have shared in the Holy Spirit	17
	12: 8	discipline in which all children share	17
	12:10	in order that we may share his holiness.	15
	13:16	to share what you have	8
1Pe	4:13	insofar as you are sharing Christ's sufferings	7
	5: 1	as well as one who shares in the glory to be	9
Jde	1: 3	to write to you about the salvation we share	6
Rev	1: 9	I, John, your brother who share with you in Jesus	20
	18: 4	"Come out...so that you do not share in her plagues;	10
	20: 6	holy are those who share in the first resurrection.	13
	22:19	God will take away that person's share in the tree	12

share abundantly

1. περισσεύω, *perisseuō, 4355*

| 2Co | 9: 8 | share abundantly in every good work. | 1 |

share ill-treatment

1. συγκακουχέομαι, *synkakoucheomai, 5156*

| Heb | 11:25 | share ill-treatment with the people of God | 1 |

share in common

1. συγχράομαι, *synchraomai, 5178*

| Jhn | 4: 9 | (Jews do not share things in common with Samaritans.) | 1 |

share in suffering

1. συγκακοπαθέω, *synkakopatheō, 5155*

| 2Ti | 2: 3 | Share in suffering like a good soldier | 1 |

sharer

1. συμμέτοχος, *symmetochos, 5212*

| Eph | 3: 6 | sharers in the promise in Christ Jesus | 1 |

Sharon

1. Σαρών, *Sarōn, 4926*

| Act | 9:35 | all the residents of Lydda and Sharon saw him | 1 |

sharp

1. ὀξύς, *oxys, 3955*
2. τομός, *tomos, 5533*

Heb	4:12	sharper than any two-edged sword	2
Rev	1:16	from his mouth came a sharp, two-edged sword	1
	2:12	the words of him who has the sharp two-edged sword:	1
	14:14	crown on his head, and a sharp sickle in his hand!	1
	14:17	another angel...and he too had a sharp sickle.	1
	14:18	called...to him who had the sharp sickle	1
	14:18	"Use your sharp sickle and gather the clusters	1
	19:15	From his mouth comes a sharp sword	1

sharp disagreement

1. παροξυσμός, *paroxysmos, 4237*

| Act | 15:39 | disagreement became so sharp that they parted | 1 |

sharply

1. ἀποτόμως, *apotomōs, 705*

| Tit | 1:13 | For this reason rebuke them sharply | 1 |

shatter

1. συντρίβω, *syntribō, 5341*

| Rev | 2:27 | as when clay pots are shattered | 1 |

shave

1. ξυράω, *xyraō, 3834*

Act	21:24	pay for the shaving of their heads	1
1Co	11: 5	one and the same thing as having her head shaved.	1
	11: 6	disgraceful for a woman...to be shaved	1

she   Not Indexed

Shealtiel

1. Σαλαθιήλ, *Salathiēl, 4886*

| Lke | 3:27 | son of Zerubbabel, son of Shealtiel | 1 |

shearer

1. κείρω, *keirō, 3025*

| Act | 8:32 | like a lamb silent before its shearer | 1 |

sheath

1. θήκη, *thēkē, 2557*

| Jhn | 18:11 | "Put your sword back into its sheath. | 1 |

Shechem

1. Συχέμ, *Sychem, 5374*

| Act | 7:16 | their bodies were brought back to Shechem | 1 |
| | 7:16 | bought...from the sons of Hamor in Shechem. | 1 |

shed

1. Contextual: Not in Greek
2. ἐκχέω, *echeō, 1772*
3. ἐκχύννομαι, *ekchynnomai, 1773*

Mat	23:30	in shedding the blood of the prophets.'	1
	23:35	all the righteous blood shed on earth	3
Lke	11:50	blood...shed since the foundation of the world	2
Act	22:20	while the blood of your witness Stephen was shed	3
Rom	3:15	"Their feet are swift to shed blood;	2
Heb	12: 4	resisted to the point of shedding your blood.	1
Rev	16: 6	they shed the blood of saints and prophets	2

shedding of blood

1. αἱματεκχυσία, *haimatekchysia, 136*

| Heb | 9:22 | without the shedding of blood there is no | 1 |

sheep   *See also* tend sheep

1. μηλωτή, *mēlōtē, 3603*
2. πρόβατον, *probaton, 4585*

Mat	7:15	who come to you in sheep's clothing	2
	9:36	helpless, like sheep without a shepherd.	2
	10: 6	to the lost sheep of the house of Israel.	2
	10:16	sending you out like sheep into the midst of wolves;	2
	12:11	"Suppose one of you has only one sheep	2
	12:12	more valuable is a human being than a sheep!	2
	15:24	only to the lost sheep of the house of Israel."	2
	18:12	If a shepherd has a hundred sheep,	2
	25:32	as a shepherd separates the sheep from the goats	2
	25:33	he will put the sheep at his right hand	2
	26:31	the sheep of the flock will be scattered.'	2
Mrk	6:34	because they were like sheep without a shepherd;	2
	14:27	the sheep will be scattered.'	2
Lke	15: 4	"Which one of you, having a hundred sheep	2
	15: 6	I have found my sheep that was lost.'	2
Jhn	2:14	he found people selling cattle, sheep,	2
	2:15	out of the temple, both the sheep and the cattle.	2
	10: 2	the shepherd of the sheep.	2
	10: 3	the sheep hear his voice.	2
	10: 3	calls his own sheep by name and leads them out.	2
	10: 4	he goes ahead of them, and the sheep follow him	2
	10: 7	I am the gate for the sheep.	2

10: 8 the sheep did not listen to them. 2
10:11 lays down his life for the sheep. 2
10:12 not the shepherd and does not own the sheep 2
10:12 leaves the sheep and runs away 2
10:13 a hired hand does not care for the sheep. 2
10:15 I lay down my life for the sheep. 2
10:16 other sheep that do not belong to this fold. 2
10:26 because you do not belong to my sheep. 2
10:27 My sheep hear my voice. I know them 2
21:16 Jesus said to him, "Tend my sheep." 2
21:17 Jesus said to him, "Feed my sheep. 2
Act 8:32 "Like a sheep he was led to the slaughter 2
Rom 8:36 we are accounted as sheep to be slaughtered." 2
Heb 11:37 they went about in skins of sheep and goats 1
13:20 our Lord Jesus, the great shepherd of the sheep 2
1Pe 2:25 For you were going astray like sheep 2
Rev 18:13 cattle and sheep, horses and chariots, slaves 2

Sheep Gate

1. προβατικός, *probatikos, 4583*
Jhn 5: 2 in Jerusalem by the Sheep Gate there is a pool 1

sheepfold

1. αὐλή + ὁ + πρόβατον, *aulē + ho + probaton, 885 + 3836 + 4585*
Jhn 10: 1 who does not enter the sheepfold by the gate 1

sheet

1. ὀθόνη, *othonē, 3855*
Act 10:11 something like a large sheet coming down 1
11: 5 There was something like a large sheet coming down 1

Shelah

1. Σαλά, *Sala, 4885*
Lke 3:35 son of Peleg, son of Eber, son of Shelah 1

shelter

1. σκηνόω, *skēnoō, 5012*
Rev 7:15 one who is seated on the throne will shelter them. 1

Shem

1. Σήμ, *Sēm, 4954*
Lke 3:36 son of Shem, son of Noah, son of Lamech 1

shepherd *See also* chief shepherd

1. ἄνθρωπος, *anthrōpos, 476*
2. ποιμαίνω, *poimainō, 4477*
3. ποιμήν, *poimēn, 4478*
Mat 2: 6 a ruler who is to shepherd my people Israel.' " 2
9:36 helpless, like sheep without a shepherd. 3
18:12 If a shepherd has a hundred sheep, 1
25:32 as a shepherd separates the sheep from the goats 3
26:31 it is written, 'I will strike the shepherd 3
Mrk 6:34 because they were like sheep without a shepherd; 3
14:27 it is written, 'I will strike the shepherd 3
Lke 2: 8 In that region there were shepherds 3
2:15 the shepherds said to one another, "Let us go 3
2:18 amazed at what the shepherds told them. 3
2:20 The shepherds returned 3
Jhn 10: 2 the shepherd of the sheep. 3
10:11 "I am the good shepherd. 3
10:11 The good shepherd lays down his life 3
10:12 The hired hand, who is not the shepherd 3
10:14 I am the good shepherd. 3
10:16 there will be one flock, one shepherd. 3
Act 20:28 to shepherd the church of God 2
Heb 13:20 our Lord Jesus, the great shepherd of the sheep 3
1Pe 2:25 the shepherd and guardian of your souls. 3
Rev 7:17 for the Lamb…will be their shepherd 2

shield

1. θυρεός, *thyreos, 2599*
Eph 6:16 With all of these, take the shield of faith 1

shift

1. μετακινέω, *metakineō, 3560*
Col 1:23 without shifting from the hope promised by the gospel 1

shine

1. ἐκλάμπω, *eklampō, 1719*
2. λάμπω, *lampō, 3290*
3. φαίνω, *phainō, 5743*
Mat 5:16 In the same way, let your light shine before others 2
13:43 Then the righteous will shine like the sun 1
17: 2 and his face shone like the sun 2
Jhn 1: 5 The light shines in the darkness 3
5:35 He was a burning and shining lamp 3
Act 12: 7 a light shone in the cell. 2
2Co 4: 6 the God who said, "Let light shine out of darkness," 2
4: 6 who has shone in our hearts 2
Php 2:15 in which you shine like stars in the world. 3
2Pe 1:19 as to a lamp shining in a dark place 3
1Jn 2: 8 and the true light is already shining. 3
Rev 1:16 face was like the sun shining with full force. 3
8:12 a third of the day was kept from shining 3
18:23 and the light of a lamp will shine in you no more; 3
21:23 the city has no need of sun or moon to shine on it 3

shine about

1. περιαστράπτω, *periastraptō, 4313*
Act 22: 6 a great light from heaven suddenly shone about me. 1

shine around

1. περιλάμπω, *perilampō, 4334*
Lke 2: 9 the glory of the Lord shone around them 1
Act 26:13 a light from heaven…shining around me 1

shine on

1. ἐπιφαύσκω, *epiphauskō, 2213*
Eph 5:14 Christ will shine on you." 1

ship *See also* ship's *boat*, owner of the ship

1. Contextual: Not in Greek
2. ναῦς, *naus, 3730*
3. πλοῖον, *ploion, 4450*
Act 20:13 went ahead to the ship and set sail for Assos 3
20:38 they brought him to the ship. 3
21: 2 When we found a ship bound for Phoenicia 3
21: 3 the ship was to unload its cargo there. 3
21: 6 we went on board the ship, and they returned home. 3
27: 2 Embarking on a ship of Adramyttium 3
27: 6 There the centurion found an Alexandrian ship 3
27:10 not only of…the ship, but also of our lives." 3
27:15 the ship was caught and could not be turned 3
27:17 they took measures to undergird the ship; 3
27:19 own hands they threw the ship's tackle overboard. 3
27:22 no loss of life among you, but only of the ship. 3
27:30 the sailors tried to escape from the ship 3
27:31 "Unless these men stay in the ship 3
27:37 two hundred seventy-six persons in the ship.) 3
27:38 they lightened the ship 3
27:39 planned to run the ship ashore, if they could. 3
27:41 striking a reef, they ran the ship aground; 2
27:44 some on planks and others on pieces of the ship. 3
28:11 on a ship that had wintered at the island 3
28:11 an Alexandrian ship 1
Jas 3: 4 Or look at ships: though they are so large 3
Rev 8: 9 and a third of the ships were destroyed. 3
18:19 all who had ships at sea grew rich by her wealth! 3

shipmaster

1. κυβερνήτης, *kybernētēs, 3237*
Rev 18:17 And all shipmasters and seafarers, sailors 1

shipwreck *See also* suffer shipwreck

1. ναυαγέω, *nauageō, 3728*
2Co 11:25 Three times I was shipwrecked; 1

shirt

1. χιτών, *chitōn, 5945*
Lke 6:29 do not withhold even your shirt. 1

shock

1. στυγνάζω, *stygnazō, 5145*
Mrk 10:22 When he heard this, he was shocked 1

shoot *See* wild *olive* shoot

shore

1. γῆ, *gē, 1178*
2. παρά, *para, 4123*

Lke 5: 2 he saw two boats there at the shore of the lake;   2
       5: 3 asked him to put out a little way from the shore.   1
      5:11 When they had brought their boats to shore   1

close to shore

1. ἆσσον, *asson, 839*

Act 27:13 sail past Crete, close to the shore.   1

short *See also* cut short, fall short, short *time*

1. μικρός, *mikros, 3625*
2. ὀλίγος, *oligos, 3900*
3. ὥρα, *hōra, 6052*

Lke 19: 3 because he was short in stature.   1
1Th 2:17 for a short time, we were made orphans   3
Heb 12:10 they disciplined us for a short time   2
1Pe 5:12 I have written this short letter to encourage you   2
Rev 12:12 because he knows that his time is short!"   2

grow short

1. συστέλλω, *systellō, 5366*

1Co 7:29 the appointed time has grown short;   1

shortly

1. ἐν + τάχος, *en + tachos, 1877 + 5443*

Act 25: 4 he himself intended to go there shortly.   1
Rom 16:20 God...will shortly crush Satan under your feet.   1

should

1. δεῖ, *dei, 1256*
2. καθήκω, *kathēkō, 2763*
3. ὀφείλω, *opheilō, 4053*

Mat 18:33 Should you not have had mercy on your fellow   1
Act 25:10 emperor's tribunal; this is where I should be tried.   1
     27:21 "Men, you should have listened to me   1
Rom 1:28 and to things that should not be done.   2
1Co 9:10 for whoever plows should plow in hope   3
2Co 2: 3 from those who should have made me rejoice;   1
    12:11 you should have been the ones commending me   3
Eph 5:28 In the same way, husbands should love their wives   3
Col 4: 4 so that I may reveal it clearly, as I should.   1
1Ti 5:13 saying what they should not say.   1

shoulder

1. ὦμος, *ōmos, 6049*

Mat 23: 4 and lay them on the shoulders of others;   1
Lke 15: 5 he has found it, he lays it on his shoulders   1

shout *See also* give a shout

1. ἀνακράζω, *anakrazō, 371*
2. βοάω, *boaō, 1066*
3. ἐπαίρω + ὁ + φωνή, *epairō + ho + phōnē, 2048 + 3836 + 5889*
4. ἐπιφωνέω, *epiphōneō, 2215*
5. κράζω, *krazō, 3189*
6. κραυγάζω, *kraugazō, 3198*
7. κραυγή, *kraugē, 3199*
8. λέγω, *legō, 3306*
9. φωνέω, *phōneō, 5888*
10. φωνή, *phōnē, 5889*

Mat 8:29 Suddenly they shouted, "What have you to do with us   5
    15:22 came out and started shouting   5
    15:23 "Send her away, for she keeps shouting after us."   5
    20:30 two blind men...shouted, "Lord, have mercy on us   5
    20:31 but they shouted even more loudly   5
    21: 9 shouting, "Hosanna to the Son of David!   5
    25: 6 at midnight there was a shout   7
    27:23 they shouted all the more   5
Mrk 3:11 they fell down before him and shouted   5
     5: 7 he shouted at the top of his voice   5
    11: 9 went ahead and those who followed were shouting   5
    15:13 They shouted back, "Crucify him!"   5
    15:14 they shouted all the more, "Crucify him!"   5
Lke 4:41 Demons also came out of many, shouting   6
     8:24 and woke him up, shouting, "Master, Master   8
     8:28 he fell down before him and shouted   1

     9:38 Just then a man from the crowd shouted, "Teacher   2
    18:38 he shouted, "Jesus, Son of David, have mercy   2
    23:21 they kept shouting, "Crucify, crucify him!"   4
    23:23 they kept urgently demanding with loud shouts   10
Jhn 12:13 went out to meet him, shouting, "Hosanna!   6
    18:40 shouted in reply, "Not this man, but Barabbas!"   6
    19: 6 they shouted, "Crucify him! Crucify him!"   6
Act 7:57 they covered their ears, and with a loud shout   10
    12:22 The people kept shouting, "The voice of a god,   4
    14:11 they shouted in the Lycaonian language   3
    14:14 and rushed out into the crowd, shouting   5
    16:28 Paul shouted in a loud voice, "Do not harm yourself   9
    17: 6 dragged...before the city authorities, shouting   2
    19:28 they were enraged and shouted   5
    19:32 Meanwhile, some were shouting one thing,   5
    19:34 all of them shouted in unison   5
    21:28 shouting, "Fellow Israelites, help!   5
    21:34 Some in the crowd shouted one thing, some another;   4
    21:36 The crowd that followed kept shouting   5
    22:22 then they shouted, "Away with such a fellow   3
    22:23 they were shouting, throwing off their cloaks,   6
    25:24 shouting that he ought not to live any longer.   2
Gal 4:27 and shout, you who endure no birth pangs;   2
Rev 10: 3 gave a great shout, like a lion roaring.   10
    10: 3 when he shouted, the seven thunders sounded.   5

shout for joy

1. χαίρω, *chairō, 5897*

1Pe 4:13 so that you may also be glad and shout for joy   1

shout loudly

1. κράζω, *krazō, 3189*

Lke 18:39 he shouted even more loudly,   1

shout out

1. ἀνακράζω, *anakrazō, 371*
2. κράζω, *krazō, 3189*

Mrk 10:47 he began to shout out and say, "Jesus,   2
Lke 19:40 the stones would shout out."   2
    23:18 all shouted out together, "Away with this fellow!   1

show

1. Contextual: Not in Greek
2. ἀναδείκνυμι, *anadeiknymi, 344*
3. γινώσκω, *ginōskō, 1182*
4. δείκνυμι, *deiknymi, 1259*
5. δίδωμι, *didōmi, 1443*
6. εἰμί, *eimi, 1639*
7. ἐμφανής, *emphanēs, 1871*
8. ἐνδείκνυμι, *endeiknymi, 1892*
9. ἔνδειξις, *endeixis, 1893*
10. ἐπιδείκνυμι, *epideiknymi, 2109*
11. λαμβάνω, *lambanō, 3284*
12. μηνύω, *mēnyō, 3606*
13. παρέχω, *parechō, 4218*
14. παρίστημι, *paristēmi, 4225*
15. ποιέω, *poieō, 4472*
16. ὑποδείκνυμι, *hypodeiknymi, 5683*
17. φαίνω, *phainō, 5743*
18. φανερόω, *phaneroō, 5746*

Mat 4: 8 high mountain and showed him all the kingdoms   4
     6:16 so as to show others that they are fasting,   17
     8: 4 but go, show yourself to the priest   4
    16: 1 to test Jesus they asked him to show them a sign   10
    16:21 From that time on, Jesus began to show his disciples   4
    22:19 Show me the coin used for the tax."   10
Mrk 1:44 go, show yourself to the priest   4
    14: 7 you can show kindness to them whenever you wish;   15
    14:15 He will show you a large room upstairs   4
Lke 1:51 He has shown strength with his arm;   15
     1:58 the Lord had shown his great mercy to her   1
     1:72 he has shown the mercy promised to our ancestors   15
     4: 5 showed him in an instant all the kingdoms   4
     5:14 "Go...and show yourself to the priest   4
     6:47 I will show you what someone is like   16
    10:37 He said, "The one who showed him mercy."   15
    17:14 "Go and show yourselves to the priests."   10
    20:21 and you show deference to no   11
    20:24 "Show me a denarius.   4

20:37 that the dead are raised Moses himself showed   12
22:12 He will show you a large room upstairs,   4
24:40 he showed them his hands and his feet   4
Jhn   2:18 "What sign can you show us for doing this?"   4
5:20 shows him all that he himself is doing;   4
5:20 he will show him greater works than these   4
7: 4 If you do these things, show yourself to the world   18
10:32 "I have shown you many good works from the Father.   4
14: 8 Philip said to him, "Lord, show us the Father   4
14: 9 How can you say, 'Show us the Father'?   4
20:20 After he said this, he showed them his hands   4
21: 1 After these things Jesus showed himself again   18
21: 1 and he showed himself in this way.   18
Act   1:24 Show us which one of these two you have chosen   2
2:19 I will show portents in the heaven above   5
7: 3 go to the land that I will show you.'   4
7:10 enabled him to win favor and to show wisdom   1
9:16 I myself will show him how much he must suffer   16
9:39 showing tunics and other clothing   10
9:41 he showed her to be alive.   14
10:28 God has shown me that I should not call anyone   4
10:34 "I truly understand that God shows no partiality   6
18:28 showing by the scriptures that the Messiah   10
28: 2 The natives showed us unusual kindness   13
Rom   1:19 plain to them, because God has shown it to them.   18
2:11 For God shows no partiality.   6
2:15 They show that what the law requires is written   8
3:12 no one who shows kindness, there is not even one."   15
3:25 He did this to show his righteousness   9
7:13 in order that sin might be shown to be sin   17
9:17 for the very purpose of showing my power in you   8
9:22 What if God, desiring to show his wrath   8
10:20 shown myself to those who did not ask for me."   7
12:10 outdo one another in showing honor.   1
1Co 12:31 I will show you a still more excellent way.   4
2Co   3: 3 you show that you are a letter of Christ   18
8:19 glory of the Lord himself and to show our goodwill.   8
8:24 before the churches, show them the proof of your love   8
11:30 I will boast of the things that show my weakness.   1
Eph   2: 7 might show the immeasurable riches of his grace   8
Php   4:10 but had no opportunity to show it   1
Tit   2: 7 Show yourself...a model of good works   13
2: 7 in your teaching show integrity, gravity   1
2:10 not to pilfer, but to show complete and perfect fidelity   8
3: 2 to show every courtesy to everyone.   8
Heb   6:10 the love that you showed for his sake   8
6:11 each one of you to show the same diligence   8
6:17 when God desired to show even more clearly   10
8: 5 the pattern that was shown you on the mountain."   4
Jas   2:13 without mercy to anyone who has shown no mercy;   15
2:18 Show me your faith apart from your works   4
2:18 and I by my works will show you my faith.   4
2:20 Do you want to be shown, you senseless person   3
3:13 Show by your good life that your works are done   4
1Pe   3: 7 Husbands...show consideration for your wives   1
Rev   1: 1 which God gave him to show his servants   4
4: 1 I will show you what must take place after this."   4
17: 1 "Come, I will show you the judgment   4
21: 9 I will show you the bride, the wife of the Lamb."   4
21:10 and showed me the holy city Jerusalem   4
22: 1 angel showed me the river of the water of life   4
22: 6 the Lord...sent his angel to show his servants   4
22: 8 at the feet of the angel who showed them to me;   4

show boldness
1. θαρρέω, *tharreō*, 2509
2Co 10: 2 need not show boldness by daring to oppose   1

show contempt
1. καταφρονέω, *kataphroneō*, 2969
1Co 11:22 do you show contempt for the church of God   1

show deference
1. μέλει, *melei*, 3508
Mat 22:16 and show deference to no one;   1
Mrk 12:14 you are sincere, and show deference to no one;   1

show endurance
1. ὑπομένω, *hypomenō*, 5702
Jas   5:11 Indeed we call blessed those who showed endurance.   1

show good sense
1. συνίημι, *syniēmi*, 5317
2Co 10:12 they do not show good sense.   1

show hospitality
1. ξενοδοχέω, *xenodocheō*, 3827
1Ti   5:10 has brought up children, shown hospitality   1

show hospitality to a stranger
1. φιλοξενία, *philoxenia*, 5810
Heb 13: 2 Do not neglect to show hospitality to strangers   1

show love
1. ἀγαπάω, *agapaō*, 26
Lke   7:47 hence she has shown great love.   1

show mercy
1. ἐλεάω, *eleaō*, 1790
2. ἐλεέω, *eleeō*, 1796
3. ἔλεος, *eleos*, 1799
Mrk   5:19 what mercy he has shown you."   2
Rom   9:16 on human will or exertion, but on God who shows mercy.   1
11:31 by the mercy shown to you, they...receive mercy.   3

show partiality
1. λαμβάνω + πρόσωπον + ἄνθρωπος, *lambanō + prosōpon + anthrōpos*, 3284 + 4725 + 476
2. προσωπολημπτέω, *prosōpolēmpteō*, 4719
Gal   2: 6 God shows no partiality)   1
Jas   2: 9 But if you show partiality, you commit sin   2

more shrewd
1. φρόνιμος, *phronimos*, 5861
Lke 16: 8 the children of this age are more shrewd   1

shrewdly
1. φρονίμως, *phronimōs*, 5862
Lke 16: 8 commended...because he had acted shrewdly;   1

shriek
1. κράζω, *krazō*, 3189
2. φωνή, *phōnē*, 5889
Lke   9:39 a spirit seizes him, and all at once he shrieks.   1
Act   8: 7 unclean spirits...crying with loud shrieks   2

shrine
1. Contextual: Not in Greek
2. ναός, *naos*, 3724
Act 17:24 God...does not live in shrines made by human hands   2
19:24 a silversmith who made silver shrines of Artemis   2
Heb   6:19 enters the inner shrine behind the curtain   1

shrink
1. ὑποστέλλω, *hypostellō*, 5713
Act 20:20 I did not shrink from doing anything helpful   1
20:27 I did not shrink from declaring to you   1

shrink back
1. ὑποστέλλω, *hypostellō*, 5713
2. ὑποστολή, *hypostolē*, 5714
Heb 10:38 My soul takes no pleasure in anyone who shrinks back."   1
10:39 those who shrink back and so are lost   2

shrub
1. λάχανον, *lachanon*, 3303
Mat 13:32 when it has grown it is the greatest of shrubs   1
Mrk   4:32 becomes the greatest of all shrubs   1

shudder
1. φρίσσω, *phrissō*, 5857
Jas   2:19 Even the demons believe—and shudder.   1

shun
1. φεύγω, *pheugō*, 5771
1Co   6:18 Shun fornication!   1
1Ti   6:11 as for you, man of God, shun all this;   1
2Ti   2:22 Shun youthful passions   1

shut

1. ἀποκλείω, *apokleiō, 643*
2. καμμύω, *kammyō, 2826*
3. κλείω, *kleiō, 3091*
4. φράσσω, *phrassō, 5852*

Mat	6: 6 whenever you pray, go into your room and shut the door	3
	13:15 and they have shut their eyes;	2
	25:10 the door was shut.	3
Lke	13:25 owner of the house has got up and shut the door	1
Jhn	20:26 Although the doors were shut	3
Act	21:30 immediately the doors were shut.	3
	28:27 they have shut their eyes;	2
Heb	11:33 obtained promises, shut the mouths of lions	4
Rev	3: 7 the true one…who opens and no one will shut	3
	3: 7 the true one…who shuts and no one opens:	3
	3: 8 an open door, which no one is able to shut.	3
	11: 6 They have authority to shut the sky, so that no rain	3
	21:25 Its gates will never be shut by day	3

shut up

1. κατακλείω, *katakleiō, 2881*
2. κλείω, *kleiō, 3091*

Lke	3:20 added to them all by shutting up John in prison	1
	4:25 the heaven was shut up three years and six months	2

sick

1. ἄρρωστος, *arrōstos, 779*
2. ἀσθενέω, *astheneō, 820*
3. ἀσθενής, *asthenēs, 822*
4. κακῶς, *kakōs, 2809*
5. κακῶς + ἔχω, *kakōs + echō, 2809 + 2400*
6. κάμνω, *kamnō, 2827*
7. συνέχω, *synechō, 5309*

Mat	4:24 they brought to him all the sick,	5
	8:16 and cured all who were sick.	4
	9:12 but those who are sick.	4
	10: 8 Cure the sick, raise the dead, cleanse the lepers	2
	14:14 and cured their sick.	1
	14:35 and brought all who were sick to him	4
	25:36 I was sick and you took care of me	2
	25:39 that we saw you sick or in prison and visited	2
	25:43 sick and in prison and you did not visit me.'	3
	25:44 a stranger or naked or sick or in prison	3
Mrk	1:32 they brought to him all who were sick	4
	1:34 cured many who were sick with various diseases	4
	2:17 but those who are sick;	4
	6:13 anointed with oil many who were sick	1
	6:55 began to bring the sick on mats	5
	6:56 they laid the sick in the marketplaces	2
	16:18 ⟦they will lay their hands on the sick⟧	1
Lke	4:40 all those who had any who were sick	2
	5:31 those who are sick;	4
	10: 9 cure the sick who are there, and say to them	3
Jhn	6: 2 signs that he was doing for the sick.	2
Act	4: 9 because of a good deed done to someone who was sick	3
	5:15 they even carried out the sick into the streets	3
	5:16 bringing the sick	3
	19:12 had touched his skin were brought to the sick	2
	28: 8 lay sick in bed with fever and dysentery.	7
Jas	5:14 Are any among you sick? They should call for the elders	2
	5:15 The prayer of faith will save the sick	6

sick man

1. ἀσθενέω, *astheneō, 820*

Jhn	5: 7 The sick man answered him, "Sir, I have no one	1

sick person

1. ἄρρωστος, *arrōstos, 779*

Mrk	6: 5 he laid his hands on a few sick people	1

sickle

1. δρέπανον, *drepanon, 1535*

Mrk	4:29 at once he goes in with his sickle	1
Rev	14:14 crown on his head, and a sharp sickle in his hand!	1
	14:15 "Use your sickle and reap	1
	14:16 the one who sat on the cloud swung his sickle	1
	14:17 another angel…and he too had a sharp sickle.	1
	14:18 called…to him who had the sharp sickle	1
	14:18 "Use your sharp sickle and gather the clusters	1

	14:19 So the angel swung his sickle over the earth	1

sickness

1. μαλακία, *malakia, 3433*

Mat	4:23 curing every disease and every sickness	1
	9:35 and curing every disease and every sickness.	1
	10: 1 and to cure every disease and every sickness.	1

side *See also* pass by on the other side, strive side by side

1. εἰμί, *eimi, 1639*
2. ἐπί, *epi, 2093*
3. κόλπος, *kolpos, 3146*
4. μέρος, *meros, 3538*
5. πλευρά, *pleura, 4433*
6. ὑπό, *hypo, 5679*

Mat	21:19 seeing a fig tree by the side of the road,	2
Lke	16:23 saw Abraham far away with Lazarus by his side.	3
	17:24 lights up the sky from one side to the other	6
Jhn	19:34 one of the soldiers pierced his side with a spear	5
	20:20 he showed them his hands and his side.	5
	20:25 my hand in his side	5
	20:27 Reach out your hand and put it in my side.	5
	21: 6 "Cast the net to the right side of the boat	4
Act	12: 7 He tapped Peter on the side and woke him, saying	5
	14: 4 some sided with the Jews	1

all sides

1. πάντοθεν, *pantothen, 4119*

Heb	9: 4 the ark…overlaid on all sides with gold	1

by one's side

1. παρά, *para, 4123*

Lke	9:47 took a little child and put it by his side	1

either side

1. ἐντεῦθεν + καί + ἐκεῖθεν, *enteuthen + kai + ekeithen, 1949 + 2779 + 1696*
2. ἐντεῦθεν + καί + ἐντεῦθεν, *enteuthen + kai + enteuthen, 1949 + 2779 + 1949*

Jhn	19:18 and with him two others, one on either side	2
Rev	22: 2 On either side of the river is the tree	1

every side

1. πάντοθεν, *pantothen, 4119*

Lke	19:43 surround you, and hem you in on every side.	1

on each side

1. κύκλῳ, *kyklō, 3241*

Rev	4: 6 Around the throne, and on each side of the throne	1

other side

1. πέραν, *peran, 4305*

Mat	8:18 he gave orders to go over to the other side.	1
	8:28 When he came to the other side	1
	14:22 and go on ahead to the other side	1
	16: 5 When the disciples reached the other side	1
Mrk	4:35 "Let us go across to the other side."	1
	5: 1 They came to the other side of the sea	1
	5:21 crossed again in the boat to the other side	1
	6:45 go on ahead to the other side, to Bethsaida	1
	8:13 he went across to the other side.	1
Lke	8:22 "Let us go across to the other side of the lake."	1
Jhn	6: 1 Jesus went to the other side of the Sea of Galilee	1
	6:22 that had stayed on the other side of the sea	1
	6:25 they found him on the other side of the sea	1

right side

1. δεξιός, *dexios, 1288*

Mrk	16: 5 a young man…sitting on the right side;	1
Lke	1:11 standing at the right side of the altar	1

Sidon *See also* person of Sidon

1. Σιδών, *Sidōn, 4972*
2. Σιδώνιος, *Sidōnios, 4973*

Mat	11:21 had been done in Tyre and Sidon	1
	11:22 more tolerable for Tyre and Sidon than for you.	1
	15:21 and went away to the district of Tyre and Sidon.	1
Mrk	3: 8 the Jordan, and the region around Tyre and Sidon.	1
	7:31 went by way of Sidon towards the Sea of Galilee	1

Lke	4:26 to a widow at Zarephath in Sidon.	2
	6:17 Jerusalem, and the coast of Tyre and Sidon.	1
	10:13 had been done in Tyre and Sidon	1
	10:14 more tolerable for Tyre and Sidon than for you	1
Act	27: 3 The next day we put in at Sidon;	1

sift

1. σινιάζω, *siniazō, 4985*

Lke	22:31 Satan has demanded to sift all of you like wheat	1

sigh

1. στεναγμός, *stenagmos, 5099*
2. στενάζω, *stenazō, 5100*

Mrk	7:34 looking up to heaven, he sighed and said	2
Rom	8:26 intercedes with sighs too deep for words.	1
Heb	13:17 Let them do this with joy and not with sighing	2

sigh deeply

1. ἀναστενάζω, *anastenazō, 417*

Mrk	8:12 he sighed deeply in his spirit and said	1

sight   *See also* come in sight, receive sight, recovery of sight, regain sight, restore sight, vanish from sight

1. Contextual: Not in Greek
2. βλέπω, *blepō, 1063*
3. εἶδος, *eidos, 1626*
4. ἐνώπιον, *enōpion, 1967*
5. ὅραμα, *horama, 3969*
6. ὀφθαλμός, *ophthalmos, 4057*
7. παρά, *para, 4123*
8. πρόσωπον, *prosōpon, 4725*
9. φαντάζω, *phantazō, 5751*

Mrk	8:25 he looked intently and his sight was restored	1
Lke	1:15 for he will be great in the sight of the Lord.	4
	7:21 given sight to many who were blind.	2
	12: 6 not one of them is forgotten in God's sight.	4
	16:15 who justify yourselves in the sight of others;	4
	16:15 an abomination in the sight of God.	4
Act	1: 9 a cloud took him out of their sight,	6
	4:19 "Whether it is right in God's sight	4
	7:31 When Moses saw it, he was amazed at the sight;	5
	9: 9 For three days he was without sight	2
Rom	2:13 hearers of the law who are righteous in God's sight	7
	3:20 For "no human being will be justified in his sight"	4
	12:17 take thought for what is noble in the sight of all.	4
2Co	4: 2 to the conscience of everyone in the sight of God.	4
	5: 7 for we walk by faith, not by sight.	3
	8:21 what is right not only in the Lord's sight	4
	8:21 also in the sight of others.	4
Gal	1:22 I was still unknown by sight	8
1Ti	2: 3 is acceptable in the sight of God our Savior	4
	5: 4 for this is pleasing in God's sight.	4
Heb	12:21 Indeed, so terrifying was the sight	9
	13:21 working...that which is pleasing in his sight	4
1Pe	2: 4 chosen and precious in God's sight	7
	3: 4 spirit, which is very precious in God's sight.	4
Rev	3: 2 not found your works perfect in the sight of my God	4
	13:13 making fire come down...in the sight of all;	4

sign

1. σημεῖον, *sēmeion, 4956*
2. σύσσημον, *syssēmon, 5361*

Mat	12:38 "Teacher, we wish to see a sign from you."	1
	12:39 evil and adulterous generation asks for a sign	1
	12:39 but no sign will be given to it	1
	12:39 except the sign of the prophet Jonah.	1
	16: 1 they asked him to show them a sign from heaven.	1
	16: 3 but you cannot interpret the signs of the times.	1
	16: 4 evil and adulterous generation asks for a sign	1
	16: 4 but no sign will be given to it	1
	16: 4 except the sign of Jonah."	1
	24: 3 what will be the sign of your coming	1
	24:24 false prophets will appear and produce great signs	1
	24:30 the sign of the Son of Man will appear in heaven	1
	26:48 Now the betrayer had given them a sign, saying	1
Mrk	8:11 asking him for a sign from heaven, to test him.	1
	8:12 "Why does this generation ask for a sign?	1
	8:12 Truly I tell you, no sign will be given	1
	13: 4 when will this be, and what will be the sign	1

	13:22 produce signs and omens, to lead astray	1
	14:44 Now the betrayer had given them a sign, saying	2
	16:17 ⟦these signs will accompany those who believe:⟧	1
	16:20 ⟦by the signs that accompanied it.⟧	1
Lke	2:12 This will be a sign for you:	1
	2:34 to be a sign that will be opposed	1
	11:16 kept demanding from him a sign from heaven	1
	11:29 it asks for a sign, but no sign will be given	1
	11:29 it asks for a sign, but no sign will be given	1
	11:29 no sign...except the sign of Jonah.	1
	11:30 as Jonah became a sign to the people of Nineveh	1
	21: 7 the sign that this is about to take place?"	1
	21:11 dreadful portents and great signs from heaven.	1
	21:25 "There will be signs in the sun, the moon,	1
	23: 8 was hoping to see him perform some sign.	1
Jhn	2:11 Jesus did this, the first of his signs, in Cana	1
	2:18 "What sign can you show us for doing this?"	1
	2:23 because they saw the signs that he was doing.	1
	3: 2 for no one can do these signs that you do	1
	4:48 "Unless you see signs and wonders	1
	4:54 Now this was the second sign that Jesus did	1
	6: 2 because they saw the signs that he was doing	1
	6:14 When the people saw the sign that he had done	1
	6:26 looking for me, not because you saw signs	1
	6:30 "What sign are you going to give us then,	1
	7:31 will he do more signs than this man has done?"	1
	9:16 "How can a man who is a sinner perform such signs?"	1
	10:41 they were saying, "John performed no sign	1
	11:47 we to do? This man is performing many signs.	1
	12:18 they heard that he had performed this sign	1
	12:37 he had performed so many signs in their presence	1
	20:30 Now Jesus did many other signs	1
Act	2:19 signs on the earth below	1
	2:22 with deeds of power, wonders, and signs	1
	2:43 many wonders and signs were being done	1
	4:16 a notable sign has been done through them;	1
	4:22 man on whom this sign of healing had been performed	1
	4:30 signs and wonders are performed	1
	5:12 Now many signs and wonders were done	1
	6: 8 did great wonders and signs among the people.	1
	7:36 having performed wonders and signs in Egypt	1
	8: 6 hearing and seeing the signs that he did	1
	8:13 saw the signs and great miracles that took place.	1
	14: 3 granting signs...to be done through them.	1
	15:12 signs and wonders that God had done through them	1
Rom	4:11 He received the sign of circumcision as a seal	1
	15:19 by the power of signs and wonders	1
1Co	1:22 For Jews demand signs and Greeks desire wisdom	1
	14:22 Tongues, then, are a sign not for believers	1
2Co	12:12 The signs of a true apostle were performed among you	1
	12:12 patience, signs and wonders and mighty works.	1
2Th	2: 9 Satan, who uses all power, signs, lying wonders	1
Heb	2: 4 while God added his testimony by signs and wonders	1
Rev	13:13 It performs great signs, even making fire come down	1
	13:14 and by the signs that it is allowed to perform	1
	16:14 These are demonic spirits, performing signs	1
	19:20 in its presence the signs by which he deceived	1

signal

1. κατανεύω, *kataneuō, 2916*

Lke	5: 7 they signaled their partners	1

Silas

1. Contextual: Not in Greek
2. Σίλας, *Silas, 4976*

Act	15:22 They sent Judas called Barsabbas, and Silas	2
	15:27 We have therefore sent Judas and Silas	2
	15:32 Judas and Silas, who were themselves prophets	2
	15:40 Paul chose Silas and set out	2
	16:19 they seized Paul and Silas	2
	16:25 Paul and Silas were praying and singing hymns	2
	16:29 he fell down trembling before Paul and Silas.	2
	17: 1 Paul and Silas had passed through Amphipolis	1
	17: 4 were persuaded and joined Paul and Silas	2
	17: 5 searching for Paul and Silas to bring them out	1
	17:10 the believers sent Paul and Silas off	2
	17:14 Silas and Timothy remained behind.	2
	17:15 instructions to have Silas and Timothy join him	2
	18: 5 When Silas and Timothy arrived from Macedonia	2

silence *See also* keep silence, motion for silence
1. ἐπιστομίζω, *epistomizō*, 2187
2. ἡσυχάζω, *hēsychazō*, 2483
3. ἡσυχία, *hēsychia*, 2484
4. σιγή, *sigē*, 4968
5. φιμόω, *phimoō*, 5821
6. φράσσω, *phrassō*, 5852

Mat	22:34	heard that he had silenced the Sadducees	5
Act	11:18	When they heard this, they were silenced.	2
Rom	3:19	so that every mouth may be silenced	6
2Co	11:10	this boast of mine will not be silenced	6
1Ti	2:11	Let a woman learn in silence	3
Tit	1:11	they must be silenced	1
1Pe	2:15	silence the ignorance of the foolish.	5
Rev	8: 1	silence in heaven for about half an hour.	4

silent *See also* keep silent
1. ἄφωνος, *aphōnos*, 936
2. ἡσυχάζω, *hēsychazō*, 2483
3. ἡσυχία, *hēsychia*, 2484
4. σιγάω, *sigaō*, 4967
5. σιωπάω, *siōpaō*, 4995
6. φιμόω, *phimoō*, 5821

Mat	26:63	Jesus was silent. Then the high priest said	5
Mrk	1:25	"Be silent, and come out of him!"	6
	3: 4	they were silent.	5
	9:34	they were silent	5
	14:61	he was silent and did not answer.	5
Lke	4:35	"Be silent, and come out of him!"	6
	14: 4	they were silent. So Jesus took him and healed him	2
	19:40	He answered, "I tell you, if these were silent	5
	20:26	amazed by his answer, they became silent.	4
Act	8:32	like a lamb silent before its shearer	1
	12:17	motioned to them with his hand to be silent	4
	18: 9	"Do not be afraid, but speak and do not be silent;	5
	21:14	he would not be persuaded, we remained silent	2
1Co	14:28	let them be silent in church	4
	14:30	let the first person be silent.	4
	14:34	women should be silent in the churches.	4
1Ti	2:12	she is to keep silent.	3

silk
1. σιρικός, *sirikos*, 4986

Rev	18:12	cargo of…fine linen, purple, silk and scarlet	1

silly *See also* silly *talk*

silly woman
1. γυναικάριον, *gynaikarion*, 1220

2Ti	3: 6	captivate silly women, overwhelmed by their sins	1

Siloam
1. Σιλωάμ, *Silōam*, 4978

Lke	13: 4	killed when the tower of Siloam fell on them	1
Jhn	9: 7	wash in the pool of Siloam" (which means Sent).	1
	9:11	'Go to Siloam and wash.' Then I went and washed	1

Silvanus
1. Σιλουανός, *Silouanos*, 4977

2Co	1:19	Silvanus and Timothy and I	1
1Th	1: 1	Paul, Silvanus, and Timothy	1
2Th	1: 1	Paul, Silvanus, and Timothy	1
1Pe	5:12	Through Silvanus…I have written this short letter	1

silver *See also* piece of silver, silver *coin*
1. ἀργύριον, *argyrion*, 736
2. ἄργυρος, *argyros*, 738
3. ἀργυροῦς, *argyrous*, 739

Mat	10: 9	Take no gold, or silver, or copper in your belts	2
Act	3: 6	no silver or gold, but what I have I give you;	1
	7:16	tomb that Abraham had bought for a sum of silver	1
	8:20	Peter said to him, "May your silver perish with you	1
	17:29	is like gold, or silver, or stone	2
	19:24	a silversmith who made silver shrines of Artemis	3
	20:33	I coveted no one's silver or gold or clothing.	1
1Co	3:12	builds on the foundation with gold, silver	2
2Ti	2:20	there are utensils not only of gold and silver	3
Jas	5: 3	Your gold and silver have rusted	2

1Pe	1:18	with perishable things like silver or gold	1
Rev	9:20	demons and idols of gold and silver and bronze	3
	18:12	cargo of gold, silver, jewels and pearls	2

silversmith
1. ἀργυροκόπος, *argyrokopos*, 737

Act	19:24	A man named Demetrius, a silversmith	1

Simeon
1. Contextual: Not in Greek
2. αὐτός, *autos*, 899
3. Συμεών, *Symeōn*, 5208

Lke	2:25	was a man in Jerusalem whose name was Simeon;	3
	2:27	Guided by the Spirit, Simeon came into the temple;	1
	2:28	Simeon took him in his arms and praised God,	2
	2:34	Simeon blessed them and said to his mother Mary	2
	3:30	son of Simeon, son of Judah	3
Act	13: 1	Barnabas, Simeon who was called Niger	3
	15:14	Simeon has related how God first looked favorably	3
2Pe	1: 1	Simeon Peter, a servant and apostle of Jesus	3
Rev	7: 7	from the tribe of Simeon twelve thousand,	3

similar
1. καί, *kai*, 2779

Rom	9:10	something similar happened to Rebecca	1

Simon
1. αὐτός, *autos*, 899
2. Σίμων, *Simōn*, 4981

Mat	4:18	he saw two brothers, Simon, who is called Peter	2
	10: 2	first, Simon, also known as Peter	2
	10: 4	Simon the Cananaean, and Judas Iscariot	2
	13:55	James and Joseph and Simon and Judas?	2
	16:16	Simon Peter answered, "You are the Messiah	2
	16:17	"Blessed are you, Simon son of Jonah!	2
	17:25	"What do you think, Simon?	2
	26: 6	at Bethany in the house of Simon the leper	2
	27:32	they came upon a man from Cyrene named Simon;	2
Mrk	1:16	saw Simon and his brother Andrew casting a net	2
	1:29	entered the house of Simon and Andrew	2
	1:30	Simon's mother-in-law was in bed with a fever	2
	1:36	Simon and his companions hunted for him.	2
	3:16	Simon (to whom he gave the name Peter);	2
	3:18	Thaddaeus, and Simon the Cananaean	2
	6: 3	brother of James and Joses and Judas and Simon	2
	14: 3	at Bethany in the house of Simon the leper	2
	14:37	he said to Peter, "Simon, are you asleep?	2
	15:21	to carry his cross; it was Simon of Cyrene	2
Lke	4:38	leaving the synagogue he entered Simon's house.	2
	4:38	Now Simon's mother-in-law was suffering…fever	2
	5: 3	into one of the boats, the one belonging to Simon	2
	5: 4	When he had finished speaking, he said to Simon	2
	5: 5	Simon answered, "Master, we have worked all night	2
	5: 8	when Simon Peter saw it	2
	5:10	sons of Zebedee, who were partners with Simon.	2
	5:10	Jesus said to Simon, "Do not be afraid;	2
	6:14	Simon, whom he named Peter, and his brother Andrew	2
	6:15	Simon, who was called the Zealot	2
	7:40	"Simon, I have something to say to you."	2
	7:43	Simon answered, "I suppose the one	2
	7:44	Then turning toward the woman, he said to Simon	2
	22:31	"Simon, Simon, listen! Satan has demanded to sift	2
	22:31	"Simon, Simon, listen! Satan has demanded to sift	2
	23:26	they seized a man, Simon of Cyrene	2
	24:34	has appeared to Simon!"	2
Jhn	1:40	One…was Andrew, Simon Peter's brother.	2
	1:41	He first found his brother Simon and said to him	2
	1:42	He brought Simon to Jesus, who looked at him	1
	1:42	"You are Simon son of John.	2
	6: 8	Andrew, Simon Peter's brother, said to him	2
	6:68	Simon Peter answered him, "Lord, to whom can we	2
	6:71	He was speaking of Judas son of Simon Iscariot	2
	13: 2	the heart of Judas son of Simon Iscariot	2
	13: 6	He came to Simon Peter, who said to him, "Lord	2
	13: 9	Simon Peter said to him, "Lord, not my feet only	2
	13:24	Simon Peter therefore motioned to him to ask Jesus	2
	13:26	he gave it to Judas son of Simon Iscariot.	2
	13:36	Simon Peter said to him, "Lord, where	2
	18:10	Simon Peter, who had a sword, drew it	2
	18:15	Simon Peter and another disciple followed Jesus.	2

18:25	Simon Peter was standing and warming himself.	2
20: 2	went to Simon Peter and the other disciple	2
20: 6	Simon Peter came, following him	2
21: 2	Simon Peter, Thomas called the Twin	2
21: 3	Simon Peter said to them, "I am going fishing."	2
21: 7	When Simon Peter heard that it was the Lord	2
21:11	Simon Peter went aboard and hauled the net ashore	2
21:15	Jesus said to Simon Peter, "Simon son of John	2
21:15	Jesus said to Simon Peter, "Simon son of John	2
21:16	A second time he said to him, "Simon son of John	2
21:17	He said to him the third time, "Simon son of John	2

Act	1:13	James son of Alphaeus, and Simon the Zealot	2
	8: 9	Now a certain man named Simon	2
	8:13	Even Simon himself believed.	2
	8:18	Now when Simon saw that the Spirit was given	2
	8:24	Simon answered, "Pray for me to the Lord	2
	9:43	in Joppa for some time with a certain Simon, a tanner.	2
	10: 5	send...for a certain Simon who is called Peter;	2
	10: 6	he is lodging with Simon, a tanner	2
	10:17	were asking for Simon's house	2
	10:18	ask whether Simon...was staying there.	2
	10:32	ask for Simon, who is called Peter;	2
	10:32	in the home of Simon, a tanner, by the sea.'	2
	11:13	'Send to Joppa and bring Simon, who is called Peter;	2

simple-minded

1. ἄκακος, *akakos, 179*

Rom 16:18 they deceive the hearts of the simple-minded.   1

simply

1. κατά, *kata, 2848*

Col 2:22 simply human commands and teachings.   1

sin *See also* cause of sin, commit sin, persist in sin

1. Contextual: Not in Greek
2. ἁμαρτάνω, *hamartanō, 279*
3. ἁμάρτημα, *hamartēma, 280*
4. ἁμαρτία, *hamartia, 281*

Mat	1:21	he will save his people from their sins."	4
	3: 6	in the river Jordan, confessing their sins.	4
	9: 2	"Take heart, son; your sins are forgiven."	4
	9: 5	For which is easier, to say, 'Your sins are forgiven,'	4
	9: 6	Man has authority on earth to forgive sins"	4
	12:31	people will be forgiven for every sin and blasphemy	4
	18:15	"If another member of the church sins against you	2
	18:21	if another member of the church sins against me	2
	26:28	for many for the forgiveness of sins.	4
	27: 4	"I have sinned by betraying innocent blood."	2
Mrk	1: 4	repentance for the forgiveness of sins.	4
	1: 5	confessing their sins.	4
	2: 5	"Son, your sins are forgiven."	4
	2: 7	Who can forgive sins but God alone?"	4
	2: 9	'Your sins are forgiven,'	4
	2:10	Son of Man has authority on earth to forgive sins"	4
	3:28	people will be forgiven for their sins	3
	3:29	but is guilty of an eternal sin"	3
Lke	1:77	by the forgiveness of their sins.	4
	3: 3	repentance for the forgiveness of sins	4
	5:20	"Friend, your sins are forgiven you."	4
	5:21	Who can forgive sins but God alone?"	4
	5:23	easier, to say, 'Your sins arc forgiven you,'	4
	5:24	authority on earth to forgive sins"	4
	7:47	her sins, which were many, have been forgiven;	4
	7:48	he said to her, "Your sins are forgiven."	4
	7:49	"Who is this who even forgives sins?"	4
	11: 4	forgive us our sins	4
	15:18	I have sinned against heaven and before you;	2
	15:21	I have sinned against heaven and before you;	2
	17: 3	If another disciple sins, you must rebuke	2
	17: 4	if the same person sins against you seven times	2
	24:47	repentance and forgiveness of sins	4
Jhn	1:29	who takes away the sin of the world!	4
	5:14	Do not sin any more, so that nothing worse happens	2
	8:11	⟦Go your way, and from now on do not sin again."⟧	2
	8:21	search for me, but you will die in your sin	4
	8:24	I told you that you would die in your sins	4
	8:24	for you will die in your sins	4
	8:34	everyone who commits sin is a slave to sin.	4
	8:34	everyone who commits sin is a slave to sin.	4
	8:46	Which of you convicts me of sin?	4

	9: 2	His disciples asked him, "Rabbi, who sinned	2
	9: 3	"Neither this man nor his parents sinned;	2
	9:34	answered him, "You were born entirely in sins	4
	9:41	"If you were blind, you would not have sin.	4
	9:41	now that you say, 'We see,' your sin remains.	4
	15:22	they would not have sin;	4
	15:22	now they have no excuse for their sin.	4
	15:24	they would not have sin.	4
	16: 8	about sin and righteousness and judgment:	4
	16: 9	about sin, because they do not believe in me;	4
	19:11	handed me over to you is guilty of a greater sin."	4
	20:23	If you forgive the sins of any, they are forgiven	4
	20:23	if you retain the sins of any, they are retained."	1
Act	2:38	so that your sins may be forgiven;	4
	3:19	so that your sins may be wiped out	4
	5:31	repentance to Israel and forgiveness of sins.	4
	7:60	"Lord, do not hold this sin against them."	4
	10:43	receives forgiveness of sins through his name."	4
	13:38	forgiveness of sins is proclaimed to you;	4
	13:39	set free from all those sins	1
	22:16	have your sins washed away, calling on his name.'	4
	26:18	they may receive forgiveness of sins	4
Rom	2:12	All who have sinned apart from the law	2
	2:12	and all who have sinned under the law	2
	3: 9	both Jews and Greeks, are under the power of sin	4
	3:20	for through the law comes the knowledge of sin.	4
	3:23	since all have sinned and fall short of the glory	2
	3:25	he had passed over the sins previously committed;	3
	4: 7	and whose sins are covered;	4
	4: 8	the one...whom the Lord will not reckon sin."	4
	5:12	just as sin came into the world through one man	4
	5:12	sin came into the world...death came through sin	4
	5:12	death spread to all because all have sinned—	2
	5:13	sin was indeed in the world before the law	4
	5:13	but sin is not reckoned when there is no law.	4
	5:14	sins were not like the transgression of Adam	2
	5:16	the free gift is not like...the one man's sin.	2
	5:20	where sin increased, grace abounded all the more	4
	5:21	so that, just as sin exercised dominion in death	4
	6: 1	continue in sin in order that grace may abound?	4
	6: 2	How can we who died to sin go on living in it?	4
	6: 6	so that the body of sin might be destroyed	4
	6: 6	and we might no longer be enslaved to sin.	4
	6: 7	For whoever has died is freed from sin.	4
	6:10	The death he died, he died to sin, once for all;	4
	6:11	you also must consider yourselves dead to sin	4
	6:12	not let sin exercise dominion in your mortal bodies	4
	6:13	No longer present your members to sin	4
	6:14	For sin will have no dominion over you	4
	6:15	Should we sin because we are not under law	2
	6:16	slaves...either of sin, which leads to death	4
	6:17	that you, having once been slaves of sin	4
	6:18	and that you, having been set free from sin	4
	6:20	When you were slaves of sin	4
	6:22	But now that you have been freed from sin	4
	6:23	For the wages of sin is death	4
	7: 7	What then should we say? That the law is sin?	4
	7: 7	not been for the law, I would not have known sin.	4
	7: 8	But sin, seizing an opportunity in the commandment	4
	7: 8	Apart from the law sin lies dead.	4
	7: 9	but when the commandment came, sin revived	4
	7:11	For sin, seizing an opportunity in the commandment	4
	7:13	sin, working death in me through what is good	4
	7:13	in order that sin might be shown to be sin	4
	7:13	in order that sin might be shown to be sin	4
	7:14	I am of the flesh, sold into slavery under sin.	4
	7:17	no longer I...but sin that dwells within me.	4
	7:20	no longer I...but sin that dwells within me.	4
	7:23	to the law of sin that dwells in my members.	4
	7:25	but with my flesh I am a slave to the law of sin.	4
	8: 2	has set you free from the law of sin and of death.	4
	8: 3	to deal with sin, he condemned sin in the flesh	4
	8: 3	to deal with sin, he condemned sin in the flesh	4
	8:10	though the body is dead because of sin	4
	11:27	covenant with them, when I take away their sins."	4
	14:23	for whatever does not proceed from faith is sin.	4
1Co	6:18	Every sin that a person commits	3
	6:18	the fornicator sins against the body	2
	7:28	if you marry, you do not sin	2
	7:28	if a virgin marries, she does not sin.	2
	7:36	let him marry as he wishes; it is no sin.	2

1Co	8:12	thus sin against members of your family	2
	8:12	you sin against Christ.	2
	15: 3	Christ died for our sins	4
	15:17	you are still in your sins.	4
	15:34	Come to a sober and right mind, and sin no more;	2
	15:56	The sting of death is sin	4
	15:56	the power of sin is the law.	4
2Co	5:21	For our sake he made him to be sin who knew no sin	4
	5:21	For our sake he made him to be sin who knew no sin	4
	11: 7	Did I commit a sin by humbling myself	4
Gal	1: 4	who gave himself for our sins	4
	2:17	is Christ then a servant of sin? Certainly not!	4
	3:22	scripture has imprisoned all things under the power of sin	4
Eph	2: 1	You were dead through the trespasses and sins	4
	4:26	Be angry but do not sin;	2
Col	1:14	we have redemption, the forgiveness of sins.	4
1Th	2:16	constantly been filling up the measure of their sins;	4
1Ti	5:22	and do not participate in the sins of others;	4
	5:24	The sins of some people are conspicuous	4
	5:24	the sins of others follow them there.	1
2Ti	3: 6	captivate silly women, overwhelmed by their sins	4
Heb	1: 3	When he had made purification for sins	4
	2:17	a sacrifice of atonement for the sins of the people.	4
	3:13	hardened by the deceitfulness of sin.	4
	3:17	who sinned, whose bodies fell in the wilderness?	2
	4:15	who…has been tested as we are, yet without sin.	4
	5: 1	to offer gifts and sacrifices for sins.	4
	5: 3	he must offer sacrifice for his own sins	4
	7:27	to offer sacrifices day after day, first for his own sins	4
	8:12	I will remember their sins no more."	4
	9:22	there is no forgiveness of sins.	1
	9:26	to remove sin by the sacrifice of himself.	4
	9:28	Christ…offered once to bear the sins of many	4
	9:28	will appear a second time, not to deal with sin	4
	10: 2	would no longer have any consciousness of sin?	4
	10: 3	there is a reminder of sin year after year.	4
	10: 4	the blood of…goats to take away sins.	4
	10: 6	in burnt offerings and sin offerings	4
	10: 8	burnt offerings and sin offerings"	4
	10:11	sacrifices that can never take away sins.	4
	10:12	offered for all time a single sacrifice for sins	4
	10:17	remember their sins and their lawless deeds no more."	4
	10:18	there is no longer any offering for sin.	4
	10:26	For if we willfully persist in sin	2
	10:26	there no longer remains a sacrifice for sins	4
	11:25	to enjoy the fleeting pleasures of sin.	4
	12: 1	every weight and the sin that clings so closely	4
	12: 4	In your struggle against sin	4
	13:11	as a sacrifice for sin	4
Jas	1:15	when that desire has conceived, it gives birth to sin	4
	1:15	sin, when it is fully grown, gives birth to death.	4
	2: 9	But if you show partiality, you commit sin	4
	4:17	Anyone…fails to do it, commits sin.	4
	5:15	and anyone who has committed sins will be forgiven.	4
	5:16	Therefore confess your sins to one another	4
	5:20	and will cover a multitude of sins.	4
1Pe	2:22	"He committed no sin	4
	2:24	He himself bore our sins in his body on the cross	4
	2:24	free from sins, we might live for righteousness;	4
	3:18	For Christ also suffered for sins once for all	4
	4: 1	whoever has suffered…has finished with sin)	4
	4: 8	for love covers a multitude of sins.	4
2Pe	1: 9	forgetful of the cleansing of past sins.	4
	2: 4	if God did not spare the angels when they sinned	2
	2:14	eyes full of adultery, insatiable for sin.	4
1Jn	1: 7	blood of Jesus his Son cleanses us from all sin.	4
	1: 8	If we say that we have no sin, we deceive ourselves	4
	1: 9	If we confess our sins, he who is faithful and just	4
	1: 9	he who is faithful and just will forgive us our sins	4
	1:10	If we say that we have not sinned, we make him a liar	2
	2: 1	I am writing these things to you so that you may not sin.	2
	2: 1	if anyone does sin, we have an advocate	2
	2: 2	he is the atoning sacrifice for our sins	4
	2: 2	but also for the sins of the whole world.	1
	2:12	because your sins are forgiven on account of his	4
	3: 4	Everyone who commits sin is guilty	4
	3: 4	sin is lawlessness.	4
	3: 5	You know that he was revealed to take away sins	4
	3: 5	and in him there is no sin.	4
	3: 6	No one who abides in him sins;	2
	3: 6	no one who sins has either seen him or known him.	2

	3: 8	Everyone who commits sin is a child of the devil;	4
	3: 8	for the devil has been sinning from the beginning.	2
	3: 9	Those who have been born of God do not sin	4
	3: 9	they cannot sin, because they have been born of God.	2
	4:10	sent his Son to be the atoning sacrifice for our sins	4
	5:16	your brother or sister committing what is not a mortal sin	4
	5:16	give life to such a one—to those whose sin is not mortal.	2
	5:16	There is sin that is mortal;	2
	5:17	All wrongdoing is sin	4
	5:17	but there is sin that is not mortal.	4
	5:18	We know that those who are born of God do not sin	2
Rev	1: 5	To him who…freed us from our sins by his blood	4
	18: 4	"Come out…so that you do not take part in her sins	4
	18: 5	for her sins are heaped high as heaven	4

cause to sin

1. σκανδαλίζω, *skandalizō, 4997*

Mat	5:29	If your right eye causes you to sin, tear it out	1
	5:30	if your right hand causes you to sin, cut it off	1

sin committed unintentionally

1. ἀγνόημα, *agnoēma, 52*

Heb	9: 7	for the sins committed unintentionally by the people.	1

sin previously

1. προαμαρτάνω, *proamartanō, 4579*

2Co	12:21	mourn over many who previously sinned	1
	13: 2	I warned those who sinned previously	1

without sin

1. ἀναμάρτητος, *anamartētos, 387*

Jhn	8: 7	⟦who is without sin be the first to throw a stone⟧	1

Sinai˙

1. Σινά, *Sina, 4982*

Act	7:30	in the wilderness of Mount Sinai	1
	7:38	the angel who spoke to him at Mount Sinai	1
Gal	4:24	Hagar, from Mount Sinai, bearing children for slavery.	1
	4:25	Now Hagar is Mount Sinai in Arabia	1

since   *See also* ever since

1. Contextual: Not in Greek
2. ἀπό, *apo, 608*
3. ἀπό + ὅς, *apo + hos, 608 + 4005*
4. γάρ, *gar, 1142*
5. δέ, *de, 1254*
6. διά, *dia, 1328*
7. εἰ, *ei, 1623*
8. εἴπερ, *eiper, 1642*
9. ἐκ, *ek, 1666*
10. ἐπεί, *epei, 2075*
11. ἐπειδή, *epeidē, 2076*
12. ἐπειδήπερ, *epeidēper, 2077*
13. καθώς, *kathōs, 2777*
14. ὅστις, *hostis, 4015*
15. ὅτι, *hoti, 4022*
16. οὖν, *oun, 4036*
17. τέ, *te, 5445*
18. ὡς, *hōs, 6055*

Mat	13: 5	since they had no depth of soil.	6
	13: 6	since they had no root, they withered away.	6
	27: 6	since they are blood money."	10
Mrk	4: 5	since it had no depth of soil.	6
	4: 6	since it had no root, it withered away.	6
	7:19	since it enters, not the heart but the stomach	15
	10:20	"Teacher, I have kept all these since my youth."	9
	15:42	since it was the day of Preparation	10
Lke	1: 1	Since many have undertaken to set down	12
	1:34	"How can this be, since I am a virgin?"	10
	9:32	since they had stayed awake, they saw his glory	1
	11:50	blood…shed since the foundation of the world	2
	16:16	since then the good news…is proclaimed	2
	18:21	He replied, "I have kept all these since my youth."	9
	23:40	since you are under the same sentence	15
	24:21	now the third day since these things took place.	3
Jhn	4:45	since they had seen all that he had done	1
	9:32	Never since the world began has it been heard	9
	12:11	since…many of the Jews were deserting	15
	17: 2	since you have given him authority over all people	13

	18:15	Since that disciple was known to the high priest	1
	19:31	Since it was the day of Preparation	10
Act	2:30	Since he was a prophet	16
	9:38	Since Lydda was near Joppa	5
	13:46	Since you reject it	11
	15:24	Since we have heard	11
	16:27	since he supposed that the prisoners had escaped.	1
	17:25	since he himself gives to all mortals life and breath	1
	17:29	Since we are God's offspring	16
	18:15	since it is a matter of questions about words	7
	19:36	Since these things cannot be denied	16
	19:40	since there is no cause that we can give to justify	1
	20: 7	since he intended to leave the next day	1
	21:14	Since he would not be persuaded	1
	22:11	Since I could not see	18
	22:30	Since he wanted to find out	5
	23:28	Since I wanted to know the charge	17
	24:11	since I went up to worship in Jerusalem.	2
	24:27	since he wanted to grant the Jews a favor	1
	25:14	Since they were staying there several days	18
	25:20	Since I was at a loss how to investigate	5
	26:11	since I was so furiously enraged at them	1
	27: 9	Since much time had been lost	5
	27:12	Since the harbor was not suitable for…winter	5
	27:15	Since the ship was caught	5
	27:21	Since they had been without food for a long time	17
	28: 2	Since it had begun to rain and was cold	6
	28:20	since it is for the sake of the hope of Israel	4
Rom	1:28	since they did not see fit to acknowledge God	13
	3:23	since all have sinned and fall short of the glory	4
	3:30	since God is one; and he will justify	8
	5: 1	since we are justified by faith, we have peace	1
	6:14	since you are not under law but under grace.	4
	8: 9	since the Spirit of God dwells in you.	8
	14: 6	in honor of the Lord, since they give thanks to God;	4
1Co	1:21	For since…the world did not know God	11
	5:10	since you would then need to go out of the world.	10
	8: 7	Since some have become so accustomed to idols	5
	8:10	might they not, since their conscience is weak	1
	11: 7	since he is the image and reflection of God;	1
	14: 2	since they are speaking mysteries in the Spirit.	5
	14:12	since you are eager for spiritual gifts	10
	14:16	since the outsider does not know what you are saying?	11
	15:21	For since death came through a human being	11
2Co	1:15	Since I was sure of this, I wanted to come to you	1
	3:12	Since…we have such a hope, we act with great boldness	16
	3:14	since only in Christ is it set aside.	15
	4: 1	Therefore, since it is by God's mercy	1
	5:20	since God is making his appeal through us;	18
	7: 1	Since we have these promises, beloved	16
	8:17	but since he is more eager than ever,	1
	9: 2	Achaia has been ready since last year;	2
	11:18	since many boast according to human standards	10
	12:16	Nevertheless (you say) since I was crafty	1
	13: 3	since you desire proof that Christ is speaking	10
Php	1:25	Since I am convinced of this, I know	1
	1:30	since you are having the same struggle	1
Col	1: 9	For this reason, since the day we heard it	2
	3:24	since you know…you will receive the inheritance	1
1Th	4:14	since we believe that Jesus died and rose again	7
	5: 8	But since we belong to the day, let us be sober	1
1Ti	6: 2	since those who benefit…are believers	15
Tit	1:11	since they are upsetting whole families	14
	3:11	since you know that such a person is perverted	1
Heb	2:14	Since…the children share flesh and blood	10
	4: 6	Since therefore it remains open for some to enter it	10
	4:14	Since, then, we have a great high priest	1
	5: 2	since he himself is subject to weakness;	10
	5:11	since you have become dull in understanding.	10
	7:25	since he always lives to make intercession	1
	8: 4	since there are priests who offer gifts	1
	9:17	since it is not in force as long as	10
	9:26	since the foundation of the world.	2
	10: 1	Since the law has only a shadow of the good things	4
	10: 2	since the worshipers, cleansed once for all	6
	10:19	Therefore, my friends, since we have confidence	1
	10:21	since we have a great priest over the house of God	1
	11:40	since God had provided something better	1
	12: 1	since we are surrounded by…witnesses	1
	12:28	since we are receiving a kingdom that cannot be shaken	1
1Pe	3: 7	since they too are also heirs of the gracious gift of life	18

	4: 1	Since therefore Christ suffered in the flesh	1
2Pe	1:14	since I know that my death…will come soon	1
	3:11	Since all these things are to be dissolved in this way	1
	3:17	beloved, since you are forewarned, beware	1
1Jn	4:11	since God loved us so much, we also ought to love	7
Rev	16:18	as had not occurred since people were upon the earth	3
	18: 7	Since in her heart she says, 'I rule as a queen;	15
	18:11	since no one buys their cargo anymore	15

since then

    1. λοιπός, *loipos, 3370*

Heb	10:13	and since then has been waiting	1

sincere

    1. ἀληθής, *alēthēs, 239*
    2. ἀνυπόκριτος, *anypokritos, 537*
    3. ἁπλότης, *haplotēs, 605*
    4. εἰλικρινής, *eilikrinēs, 1637*

Mat	22:16	"Teacher, we know that you are sincere	1
Mrk	12:14	you are sincere, and show deference to no one;	1
2Co	11: 3	from a sincere and pure devotion to Christ.	3
1Ti	1: 5	a good conscience, and sincere faith.	2
2Ti	1: 5	I am reminded of your sincere faith	2
2Pe	3: 1	arouse your sincere intention by reminding	4

sincerely

    1. ἁγνῶς, *hagnōs, 56*

Php	1:17	not sincerely but intending to increase my suffering	1

sincerity

    1. εἰλικρίνεια, *eilikrineia, 1636*

1Co	5: 8	the unleavened bread of sincerity and truth.	1
2Co	1:12	with frankness and godly sincerity	1
	2:17	as persons of sincerity, as persons sent from God	1

sinew

    1. σύνδεσμος, *syndesmos, 5278*

Col	2:19	held together by its ligaments and sinews	1

sinful

    1. ἁμαρτάνω, *hamartanō, 279*
    2. ἁμαρτία, *hamartia, 281*
    3. ἁμαρτωλός, *hamartōlos, 283*

Mrk	8:38	in this adulterous and sinful generation	3
Lke	5: 8	"Go away from me, Lord, for I am a sinful man!"	3
Rom	7: 5	our sinful passions, aroused by the law	2
	7:13	through the commandment might become sinful	3
	8: 3	his own Son in the likeness of sinful flesh	2
1Ti	1: 9	law is laid down…for the godless and sinful	3
Tit	3:11	such a person is perverted and sinful	1

sing

    1. ᾄδω, *adō, 106*
    2. λαλέω, *laleō, 3281*
    3. λέγω, *legō, 3306*

Eph	5:19	as you sing psalms and hymns and spiritual songs	2
	5:19	singing and making melody to the Lord	1
Col	3:16	with gratitude in your hearts sing psalms, hymns,	1
Rev	4: 8	Day and night without ceasing they sing	3
	4:10	they cast their crowns before the throne, singing	3
	5: 9	They sing a new song: "You are worthy	1
	5:12	singing with full voice, "Worthy is the Lamb	3
	5:13	every creature…and all that is in them, singing	3
	7:12	singing, "Amen! Blessing and glory and wisdom	3
	11:17	singing, "We give you thanks, Lord God Almighty	3
	14: 3	and they sing a new song before the throne	1
	15: 3	they sing the song of Moses, the servant of God	1

sing a hymn

    1. ὑμνέω, *hymneō, 5630*

Mat	26:30	When they had sung the hymn	1
Mrk	14:26	When they had sung the hymn	1
Act	16:25	Paul and Silas were praying and singing hymns	1

sing praise

    1. ψάλλω, *psallō, 6010*

Rom	15: 9	among the Gentiles, and sing praises to your name";	1
1Co	14:15	I will sing praise with the spirit	1
	14:15	I will sing praise with the mind also.	1

sing songs of praise

1. ψάλλω, *psallō*, 6010

Jas 5:13 Are any cheerful? They should sing songs of praise.   1

single

1. Contextual: Not in Greek
2. εἷς, *heis*, 1651
3. μόνος, *monos*, 3668

Mat 6:27 by worrying add a single hour to your span of life?   2
    23:15 to make a single convert   2
    27:14 gave him no answer, not even to a single charge   2
Lke 12:25 add a single hour to your span of life?   1
Jhn 12:24 it remains just a single grain;   3
1Co 10: 8 twenty-three thousand fell in a single day.   2
    12:19 all were a single member, where would the body be?   2
Gal 5:14 the whole law is summed up in a single commandment   2
Heb 10:12 offered for all time a single sacrifice for sins   2
    10:14 by a single offering he has perfected   2
    12:16 who sold his birthright for a single meal.   2
Rev 18: 8 therefore her plagues will come in a single day   2
    21:21 each of the gates is a single pearl   2

not a single one

1. οὐδείς, *oudeis*, 4029

Jhn 18: 9 "I did not lose a single one of those   1

singleness

1. ἁπλότης, *haplotēs*, 605

Eph 6: 5 with fear and trembling, in singleness of heart   1

sink

1. βυθίζω, *bythizō*, 1112
2. καταποντίζω, *katapontizō*, 2931
3. τίθημι, *tithēmi*, 5502

Mat 14:30 beginning to sink, he cried out, "Lord, save me!"   2
Lke 5: 7 so that they began to sink.   1
    9:44 "Let these words sink into your ears: 3

sink off

1. καταφέρω, *katapherō*, 2965

Act 20: 9 began to sink off into a deep sleep   1

sinner

1. ἁμαρτωλός, *hamartōlos*, 283
2. αὐτός, *autos*, 899

Mat 9:10 many tax collectors and sinners came   1
    9:11 "Why…eat with tax collectors and sinners?"   1
    9:13 come to call not the righteous but sinners."   1
    11:19 a friend of tax collectors and sinners!'   1
    26:45 Son of Man is betrayed into the hands of sinners.   1
Mrk 2:15 many tax collectors and sinners were also sitting   1
    2:16 he was eating with sinners and tax collectors   1
    2:16 "Why does he eat with tax collectors and sinners?"   1
    2:17 I have come to call not the righteous but sinners."   1
    14:41 Son of Man is betrayed into the hands of sinners.   1
Lke 5:30 drink with tax collectors and sinners?"   1
    5:32 I have come to call…sinners to repentance."   1
    6:32 even sinners love those who love them.   1
    6:33 even sinners do the same.   1
    6:34 Even sinners lend to sinners   1
    6:34 Even sinners lend to sinners   1
    7:34 a friend of tax collectors and sinners!'   1
    7:37 a woman in the city, who was a sinner   1
    7:39 who is touching him—that she is a sinner."   1
    13: 2 worse sinners than all other Galileans?   1
    15: 1 Now all the tax collectors and sinners   1
    15: 2 "This fellow welcomes sinners and eats with them."   1
    15: 7 more joy in heaven over one sinner who repents   1
    15:10 there is joy…over one sinner who repents."   1
    18:13 and saying, 'God, be merciful to me, a sinner!'   1
    19: 7 to be the guest of one who is a sinner."   1
    24: 7 must be handed over to sinners   1
Jhn 9:16 "How can a man who is a sinner perform such signs?"   1
    9:24 We know that this man is a sinner."   1
    9:25 "I do not know whether he is a sinner.   1
    9:31 We know that God does not listen to sinners   1
Rom 3: 7 why am I still being condemned as a sinner?   1
    5: 8 while we still were sinners Christ died for us.   1
    5:19 by…disobedience the many were made sinners   1

Gal 2:15 are Jews by birth and not Gentile sinners;   1
    2:17 we ourselves have been found to be sinners   1
1Ti 1:15 Jesus came into the world to save sinners   1
Heb 7:26 blameless, undefiled, separated from sinners   1
    12: 3 endured such hostility against himself from sinners   1
Jas 4: 8 Cleanse your hands, you sinners   1
    5:20 you should know that whoever brings back a sinner   1
    5:20 will save the sinner's soul from death   2
1Pe 4:18 what will become of the ungodly and the sinners?"   1
Jde 1:15 harsh things that ungodly sinners have spoken   1

sir

1. ἀνήρ, *anēr*, 467
2. κύριος, *kyrios*, 3261

Mat 21:30 he answered, 'I go, sir'; but he did not go.   2
    27:63 "Sir, we remember what that impostor said   2
Mrk 7:28 "Sir, even the dogs under the table eat   2
Lke 13: 8 He replied, 'Sir, let it alone for one more year   2
    14:22 'Sir, what you ordered has been done   2
Jhn 4:11 "Sir, you have no bucket, and the well   2
    4:15 "Sir, give me this water, so that I may never   2
    4:19 "Sir, I see that you are a prophet.   2
    4:49 "Sir, come down before my little boy dies."   2
    5: 7 The sick man answered him, "Sir, I have no one   2
    6:34 said to him, "Sir, give us this bread always."   2
    8:11 ⟦She said, "No one, sir."⟧   2
    9:36 He answered, "And who is he, sir?   2
    12:21 "Sir, we wish to see Jesus."   2
    20:15 to him, "Sir, if you have carried him away   2
Act 16:30 "Sirs, what must I do to be saved?"   2
    27:10 saying, "Sirs, I can see that the voyage   1
Rev 7:14 I said to him, "Sir, you are the one that knows."   2

sister *See also* brother and sister, false brother and sister, love of the brother and sister

1. Contextual: Not in Greek
2. ἀδελφή, *adelphē*, 80

Mat 12:50 is my brother and sister and mother."   2
    13:56 are not all his sisters with us?   2
    19:29 houses or brothers or sisters or father   2
Mrk 3:32 "Your mother and your brothers and sisters   2
    3:35 is my brother and sister and mother."   2
    6: 3 are not his sisters here with us?"   2
    10:29 house or brothers or sisters or mother or father   2
    10:30 houses, brothers and sisters, mothers   2
Lke 10:39 She had a sister named Mary   2
    10:40 do you not care that my sister has left me   2
    14:26 wife and children, brothers and sisters   2
Jhn 11: 1 the village of Mary and her sister Martha.   2
    11: 3 So the sisters sent a message to Jesus,   2
    11: 5 Jesus loved Martha and her sister and Lazarus   2
    11:28 she went back and called her sister Mary,   2
    11:39 Martha, the sister of the dead man, said to him,   2
    19:25 his mother's sister, Mary the wife of Clopas   2
Act 23:16 the son of Paul's sister heard about the ambush;   2
Rom 16: 1 I commend to you our sister Phoebe   2
    16:15 Greet Philologus, Julia, Nereus and his sister   2
1Co 7:15 in such a case the brother or sister is not bound.   2
1Ti 5: 2 younger women as sisters—with absolute purity.   2
Phm 1: 2 Apphia our sister, to Archippus our fellow soldier   2
Jas 2:15 If a brother or sister is naked   2
1Pe 5:13 Your sister church in Babylon, chosen together   1
2Jn 1:13 The children of your elect sister send you their greetings.   2

sit

1. καθέζομαι, *kathezomai*, 2757
2. κάθημαι, *kathēmai*, 2764
3. καθίζω, *kathizō*, 2767
4. παρακαθέζομαι, *parakathezomai*, 4149

Mat 4:16 people who sat in darkness have seen a great light   2
    4:16 those who sat in the region and shadow of death   2
    9: 9 a man called Matthew sitting at the tax booth;   2
    11:16 It is like children sitting in the marketplaces   2
    13: 1 went out of the house and sat beside the sea.   2
    13: 2 that he got into a boat and sat there   2
    19:28 will also sit on twelve thrones   2
    20:21 "Declare that these two sons of mine will sit   3
    20:23 to sit at my right hand and at my left   3
    20:30 There were two blind men sitting by the roadside.   2
    22:44 'The Lord said to my Lord, "Sit at my right hand   2

23: 2	"The scribes and the Pharisees sit on Moses' seat;	3
24: 3	When he was sitting on the Mount of Olives	2
25:31	then he will sit on the throne of his glory.	3
26:36	"Sit here while I go over there and pray."	3
26:55	Day after day I sat in the temple teaching	1
26:58	he sat with the guards in order to see how	2
26:69	Now Peter was sitting outside in the courtyard.	2
27:19	While he was sitting on the judgment seat	2
27:61	sitting opposite the tomb.	2
28: 2	came and rolled back the stone and sat on it.	2

Mrk 2: 6 Now some of the scribes were sitting there   2
2:14 son of Alphaeus sitting at the tax booth   2
3:32 A crowd was sitting around him; and they said   2
3:34 looking at those who sat around him   2
4: 1 he got into a boat on the sea and sat there   2
5:15 came to Jesus and saw the demoniac sitting there   2
10:37 "Grant us to sit, one at your right hand   3
10:40 to sit at my right hand or at my left   3
10:46 Bartimaeus...was sitting by the roadside.   2
11: 7 he sat on it.   3
12:36 'The Lord said to my Lord, "Sit at my right hand   2
13: 3 When he was sitting on the Mount of Olives   2
14:32 he said to his disciples, "Sit here while I pray."   3
16: 5 a young man...sitting on the right side;   2

Lke 1:79 to give light to those who sit in darkness   2
2:46 sitting among the teachers   1
5:17 Pharisees and teachers of the law were sitting   2
5:27 a tax collector...sitting at the tax booth;   2
7:32 They are like children sitting in the marketplace   2
8:35 sitting at the feet of Jesus   2
10:13 sitting in sackcloth and ashes.   2
10:39 a sister named Mary, who sat at the Lord's feet   4
18:35 a blind man was sitting by the roadside begging.   2
20:42 'The Lord said to my Lord, "Sit at my right hand   2
22:30 sit on thrones judging the twelve tribes   2
22:55 sat down together, Peter sat among them.   2

Jhn 4: 6 Jesus...was sitting by the well.   1
9: 8 "Is this not the man who used to sit and beg?"   2
12:14 Jesus found a young donkey and sat on it;   3
12:15 your king is coming, sitting on a donkey's colt!"   2
19:13 and sat on the judge's bench   3
20:12 sitting where the body of Jesus had been lying   1

Act 2: 2 it filled the entire house where they were sitting.   2
2:34 'The Lord said to my Lord, "Sit at my right hand   2
3:10 the one who used to sit and ask for alms   2
6:15 all who sat in the council looked intently at him   1
8:31 he invited Philip to get in and sit beside him.   3
14: 8 In Lystra there was a man sitting   2
20: 9 Eutychus, who was sitting in the window   1
23: 3 sitting there to judge me according to the law   2

1Co 14:30 If a revelation is made to someone else sitting   2
Heb 1:13 of the angels has he ever said, "Sit at my right hand   2
Jas 2: 3 "Stand there," or, "Sit at my feet,"   2
Rev 11:16 the twenty-four elders who sit...before God   2
14:15 calling...to the one who sat on the cloud,   2
14:16 the one who sat on the cloud swung his sickle   2
17: 3 and I saw a woman sitting on a scarlet beast   2
20:11 I saw a great white throne and the one who sat on it;   2

make sit down
1. κατακλίνω, *kataklinō, 2884*

Lke 9:14 he said to his disciples, "Make them sit down   1
9:15 They did so and made them all sit down.   1

sit at dinner
1. ἀνάκειμαι, *anakeimai, 367*
2. κατάκειμαι, *katakeimai, 2879*

Mat 9:10 And as he sat at dinner in the house   1
Mrk 2:15 as he sat at dinner in Levi's house   2

sit at table
1. ἀνάκειμαι, *anakeimai, 367*
2. κατάκειμαι, *katakeimai, 2879*

Mat 26: 7 poured it on his head as he sat at the table.   1
Mrk 14: 3 as he sat at the table, a woman came   2
16:14 [appeared...as they were sitting at the table;]   1
Lke 5:29 and others sitting at the table with them.   2

sit at table with
1. συνανάκειμαι, *synanakeimai, 5263*

Lke 14:10 presence of all who sit at the table with you.   1

sit down
1. ἀνακλίνω, *anaklinō, 369*
2. ἀναπίπτω, *anapiptō, 404*
3. κάθημαι, *kathēmai, 2764*
4. καθίζω, *kathizō, 2767*
5. κατακλίνω, *kataklinō, 2884*

Mat 5: 1 mountain; and after he sat down, his disciples came   4
13:48 when it was full, they drew it ashore, sat down   4
14:19 he ordered the crowds to sit down on the grass.   1
15:29 he went up the mountain, where he sat down.   3
15:35 ordering the crowd to sit down on the ground   2
27:36 they sat down there and kept watch over him.   3
Mrk 6:39 ordered them to get all the people to sit down   1
6:40 So they sat down in groups   2
8: 6 he ordered the crowd to sit down on the ground;   2
9:35 He sat down, called the twelve, and said   4
12:41 He sat down opposite the treasury   4
16:19 [Jesus...sat down at the right hand of God.]   4
Lke 4:20 he rolled up the scroll...and sat down.   4
5: 3 he sat down and taught the crowds from the boat.   4
14: 8 do not sit down at the place of honor   5
14:10 go and sit down at the lowest place   2
14:28 does not first sit down and estimate the cost   4
14:31 what king...will not sit down first and consider   4
16: 6 bill, sit down quickly, and make it fifty.'   4
Jhn 6: 3 and sat down there with his disciples.   3
6:10 Jesus said, "Make the people sit down."   2
6:10 so they sat down, about five thousand in all   2
8: 2 [he sat down and began to teach them.]   4
Act 13:14 they went into the synagogue and sat down.   4
16:13 we sat down and spoke to the women   4
1Co 10: 7 "The people sat down to eat and drink   4
Heb 1: 3 he sat down at the right hand of the Majesty on high   4
10:12 "he sat down at the right hand of God,"   4
Rev 3:21 and sat down with my Father on his throne.   4

sit down to eat
1. ἀνακλίνω, *anaklinō, 369*

Lke 12:37 fasten his belt and have them sit down to eat   1

sit down together
1. συγκαθίζω, *synkathizō, 5154*

Lke 22:55 sat down together, Peter sat among them.   1

sit on
1. ἐπικαθίζω, *epikathizō, 2125*

Mat 21: 7 and he sat on them.   1

sit up
1. ἀνακαθίζω, *anakathizō, 361*

Lke 7:15 The dead man sat up and began to speak   1
Act 9:40 seeing Peter, she sat up.   1

sit with
1. συγκάθημαι, *synkathēmai, 5153*
2. συνανάκειμαι, *synanakeimai, 5263*

Mat 9:10 sinners came and were sitting with him   2
Mrk 2:15 and sinners were also sitting with Jesus   2
14:54 he was sitting with the guards   1

six   *See also* six months' *wages*
1. ἕξ, *hex, 1971*

Mat 17: 1 Six days later, Jesus took with him Peter   1
Mrk 9: 2 Six days later, Jesus took with him Peter   1
Lke 4:25 the heaven was shut up three years and six months   1
13:14 "There are six days on which work ought to   1
Jhn 2: 6 Now standing there were six stone water jars   1
12: 1 Six days before the Passover   1
Act 11:12 These six brothers also accompanied me   1
18:11 He stayed there a year and six months   1
Jas 5:17 for three years and six months it did not rain   1
Rev 4: 8 four living creatures, each...with six wings   1

six hundred
1. ἑξακόσιοι, *hexakosioi, 1980*

Rev 13:18 Its number is six hundred sixty-six.   1

sixth

1. ἕκτος, *hektos, 1761*

Lke	1:26	In the sixth month the angel Gabriel was sent	1
	1:36	the sixth month for her who was said to be barren.	1
Rev	6:12	When he opened the sixth seal, I looked,	1
	9:13	Then the sixth angel blew his trumpet, and I heard	1
	9:14	saying to the sixth angel who had the trumpet	1
	16:12	sixth angel poured his bowl on the great river	1
	21:20	the fifth onyx, the sixth carnelian	1

sixty

1. ἑξήκοντα, *hexēkonta, 2008*

Mat	13: 8	some a hundredfold, some sixty, some thirty	1
	13:23	yields…in another sixty, and in another thirty	1
Mrk	4: 8	thirty and sixty and a hundredfold."	1
	4:20	thirty and sixty and a hundredfold."	1
1Ti	5: 9	if she is not less than sixty years old	1
Rev	11: 3	prophesy for one thousand two hundred sixty days	1
	12: 6	nourished for one thousand two hundred sixty days	1

sixty-six

1. ἑξήκοντα + ἕξ, *hexēkonta + hex, 2008 + 1971*

Rev	13:18	Its number is six hundred sixty-six.	1

size

1. ὡς, *hōs, 6055*

Mat	17:20	if you have faith the size of a mustard seed	1
Lke	17: 6	"If you had faith the size of a mustard seed	1

sketch

1. ὑπόδειγμα, *hypodeigma, 5682*

Heb	8: 5	worship in a sanctuary that is a sketch and shadow	1
	9:23	the sketches of the heavenly things	1

skilled

1. σοφός, *sophos, 5055*

1Co	3:10	like a skilled master builder	1

skin

1. ἀσκός, *askos, 829*
2. δέρμα, *derma, 1293*
3. χρώς, *chrōs, 5999*

Mat	9:17	otherwise, the skins burst, and the wine is spilled	1
	9:17	the wine is spilled, and the skins are destroyed;	1
Mrk	2:22	otherwise, the wine will burst the skins	1
	2:22	the wine is lost, and so are the skins;	1
Lke	5:37	otherwise the new wine will burst the skins	1
	5:37	the skins will be destroyed.	1
Act	19:12	aprons that had touched his skin were brought	3
Heb	11:37	they went about in skins of sheep and goats	2

skull

1. κρανίον, *kranion, 3191*

Mat	27:33	(which means Place of a Skull)	1
Mrk	15:22	Golgotha (which means the place of a skull).	1
Lke	23:33	they came to the place that is called The Skull	1
Jhn	19:17	to what is called The Place of the Skull	1

sky

1. οὐρανός, *ouranos, 4041*

Mat	16: 2	'It will be fair weather, for the sky is red.'	1
	16: 3	for the sky is red and threatening.'	1
	16: 3	how to interpret the appearance of the sky	1
Lke	12:56	to interpret the appearance of earth and sky	1
	17:24	lights up the sky from one side to the other	1
Rev	6:13	the stars of the sky fell to the earth	1
	6:14	The sky vanished like a scroll rolling itself up	1
	11: 6	They have authority to shut the sky, so that no rain	1

slain   *See* slain *victim*

slander

1. βλασφημέω, *blasphēmeō, 1059*
2. βλασφημία, *blasphēmia, 1060*
3. δυσφημέω, *dysphēmeō, 1555*
4. καταλαλιά, *katalalia, 2896*

Mat	15:19	fornication, theft, false witness, slander.	2
Mrk	7:22	envy, slander, pride, folly.	2

Rom	3: 8	(as some people slander us by saying that we say)	1
1Co	4:13	when slandered, we speak kindly.	3
2Co	12:20	anger, selfishness, slander, gossip, conceit	4
Eph	4:31	wrath and anger and wrangling and slander	2
Col	3: 8	wrath, malice, slander, and abusive language	2
1Ti	6: 4	envy, dissension, slander, base suspicions	2
1Pe	2: 1	Rid yourselves, therefore, of…all slander.	4
2Pe	2:10	they are not afraid to slander the glorious ones	1
	2:12	slander what they do not understand	1
Jde	1: 8	reject authority, and slander the glorious ones.	1
	1: 9	to bring a condemnation of slander against him	2
	1:10	people slander whatever they do not understand	1
Rev	2: 9	the slander…of those who say that they are Jews	2

slanderer

1. διάβολος, *diabolos, 1333*
2. κατάλαλος, *katalalos, 2897*

Rom	1:30	slanderers, God-haters, insolent, haughty	2
1Ti	3:11	not slanderers, but temperate, faithful in all	1
2Ti	3: 3	inhuman, implacable, slanderers, profligates	1
Tit	2: 3	not to be slanderers or slaves to drink;	1

slanderous

1. βλάσφημος, *blasphēmos, 1061*

2Pe	2:11	do not bring against them a slanderous judgment	1

slap   *See also* give a slap

1. ῥαπίζω, *rhapizō, 4824*

Mat	26:67	some slapped him	1

slaughter

1. θύω, *thyō, 2604*
2. κατασφάζω, *katasphazō, 2956*
3. σφαγή, *sphagē, 5375*
4. σφάζω, *sphazō, 5377*

Mat	22: 4	my oxen and my fat calves have been slaughtered	1
Lke	19:27	bring them here and slaughter them in my presence.' "	2
Act	8:32	"Like a sheep he was led to the slaughter	3
Rom	8:36	we are accounted as sheep to be slaughtered."	3
Jas	5: 5	have fattened your hearts in a day of slaughter.	3
Rev	5: 6	a Lamb standing as if it had been slaughtered	4
	5: 9	you were slaughtered and by your blood you ransomed	4
	5:12	"Worthy is the Lamb that was slaughtered to receive	4
	6: 4	so that people would slaughter one another;	4
	6: 9	those who had been slaughtered for the word	4
	13: 8	the book of life of the Lamb that was slaughtered.	4
	18:24	blood…of all who have been slaughtered on earth."	4

slave   *See also* make a slave, slave *trader*, work like a slave

1. Contextual: Not in Greek
2. αὐτός, *autos, 899*
3. δουλεύω, *douleuō, 1526*
4. δοῦλος¹, *doulos¹, 1528*
5. δοῦλος², *doulos², 1529*
6. δουλόω, *douloō, 1530*
7. θεραπεία, *therapeia, 2542*
8. οἰκέτης, *oiketēs, 3860*
9. παιδίσκη, *paidiskē, 4087*
10. παῖς, *pais, 4090*
11. σῶμα, *sōma, 5393*

Mat	6:24	for a slave will either hate the one and love	1
	8: 9	to my slave, 'Do this,' and the slave does it."	4
	8: 9	to my slave, 'Do this,' and the slave does it."	1
	10:24	nor a slave above the master;	4
	10:25	and the slave like the master.	4
	13:27	the slaves of the householder came and said	4
	13:28	The slaves said to him	4
	18:23	to settle accounts with his slaves.	4
	18:26	So the slave fell on his knees before him	4
	18:27	the lord of that slave released him	4
	18:28	that same slave, as he went out	4
	18:32	'You wicked slave! I forgave you all that debt	4
	20:27	whoever wishes to be first…must be your slave;	4
	21:34	he sent his slaves to the tenants	4
	21:35	the tenants seized his slaves and beat one	4
	21:36	Again he sent other slaves, more than the first;	4
	22: 3	sent his slaves to call those who had been invited	4
	22: 4	Again he sent other slaves, saying	4
	22: 6	while the rest seized his slaves	4

22: 8	Then he said to his slaves, 'The wedding is ready	4
22:10	Those slaves went out into the streets	4
24:45	"Who then is the faithful and wise slave	4
24:45	to give the other slaves their allowance of food	2
24:46	Blessed is that slave	4
24:48	if that wicked slave says to himself	4
24:50	the master of that slave will come on a day	4
25:14	summoned his slaves and entrusted his property	4
25:19	the master of those slaves came	4
25:21	'Well done, good and trustworthy slave;	4
25:23	'Well done, good and trustworthy slave;	4
25:26	his master replied, 'You wicked and lazy slave!	4
25:30	this worthless slave, throw	4
26:51	and struck the slave of the high priest	4
Mrk 10:44	wishes to be first…must be slave of all.	4
12: 2	he sent a slave to the tenants	4
12: 4	again he sent another slave to them;	4
13:34	he leaves home and puts his slaves in charge	4
14:47	struck the slave of the high priest	4
Lke 7: 2	A centurion there had a slave whom he valued	4
7: 3	asking him to come and heal his slave.	4
7: 8	to my slave, 'Do this,' and the slave does it."	4
7: 8	to my slave, 'Do this,' and the slave does it."	1
7:10	they found the slave in good health.	4
12:37	those slaves whom the master finds alert	4
12:38	and finds them so, blessed are those slaves.	1
12:42	whom his master will put in charge of his slaves	7
12:43	Blessed is that slave	4
12:45	if that slave says to himself	4
12:46	the master of that slave will come	4
12:47	That slave who knew what his master wanted	4
14:17	At the time for the dinner he sent his slave	4
14:21	So the slave returned and reported this	4
14:21	became angry and said to his slave	4
14:22	the slave said, 'Sir	4
14:23	the master said to the slave, 'Go out	4
15:22	the father said to his slaves	4
15:26	He called one of the slaves	10
16:13	No slave can serve two masters;	8
16:13	slave will either hate the one and love the other	1
17: 7	"Who among you would say to your slave	4
17: 9	Do you thank the slave	4
17:10	say, 'We are worthless slaves;	4
19:13	summoned ten of his slaves	4
19:15	he ordered these slaves	4
19:17	He said to him, 'Well done, good slave!	4
19:22	'I will judge you…you wicked slave!	4
20:10	he sent a slave to the tenants	4
20:11	he sent another slave;	4
22:50	one of them struck the slave of the high priest	4
Jhn 4:51	As he was going down, his slaves met him	4
8:33	and have never been slaves to anyone.	3
8:34	everyone who commits sin is a slave to sin.	4
8:35	The slave does not have a permanent place	4
18:10	Simon Peter…struck the high priest's slave	4
18:10	The slave's name was Malchus.	4
18:18	Now the slaves and the police	4
18:26	One of the slaves of the high priest…asked	4
Act 10: 7	called two of his slaves and a devout soldier	8
16:17	"These men are slaves of the Most High God	4
Rom 6:16	if you present…to anyone as obedient slaves	4
6:16	you are slaves of the one whom you obey	4
6:17	that you, having once been slaves of sin	4
6:18	have become slaves of righteousness.	6
6:19	once presented your members as slaves to impurity	5
6:19	present your members as slaves to righteousness	5
6:20	When you were slaves of sin	4
7: 6	we are slaves not under the old written code	3
7:25	with my mind I am a slave to the law of God	3
7:25	but with my flesh I am a slave to the law of sin.	1
1Co 7:21	Were you a slave when called? Do not be concerned	4
7:22	called in the Lord as a slave is a freed person	4
7:22	whoever was free when called is a slave of Christ.	4
7:23	do not become slaves of human masters.	4
12:13	Jews or Greeks, slaves or free	4
2Co 4: 5	and ourselves as your slaves for Jesus' sake.	4
Gal 3:28	there is no longer slave or free	4
4: 1	heirs…are no better than slaves,	4
4: 7	So you are no longer a slave but a child,	4
4:23	child of the slave, was born according to the flesh;	9
4:30	"Drive out the slave and her child;	9

4:30	child of the slave will not share the inheritance	9
4:31	So then, friends, we are children, not of the slave	9
5:13	through love become slaves to one another.	3
Eph 6: 5	Slaves, obey your earthly masters with fear	4
6: 6	as slaves of Christ, doing the will of God	4
6: 8	whether we are slaves or free.	4
Php 2: 7	emptied himself, taking the form of a slave	4
Col 3:11	barbarian, Scythian, slave and free;	4
3:22	Slaves, obey your earthly masters in everything	4
4: 1	Masters, treat your slaves justly and fairly	4
Tit 2: 3	not to be slanderers or slaves to drink;	6
2: 9	Tell slaves to be submissive to their masters	4
3: 3	slaves to various passions and pleasures	3
Phm 1:16	no longer as a slave but more than a slave	4
1:16	no longer as a slave but more than a slave	4
1Pe 2:18	Slaves, accept the authority of your masters	8
2Pe 2:19	they themselves are slaves of corruption;	4
2:19	for people are slaves to whatever masters them.	6
Rev 6:15	everyone, slave and free, hid in the caves	4
13:16	both rich and poor, both free and slave	4
18:13	and chariots, slaves—and human lives.	11
19:18	flesh of all, both free and slave,	4

fellow slave

   1. σύνδουλος, *syndoulos*, 5281

Mat 18:28	came upon one of his fellow slaves	1
18:29	Then his fellow slave fell down and pleaded	1
18:31	When his fellow slaves saw	1
18:33	you not have had mercy on your fellow slave	1
24:49	begins to beat his fellow slaves	1

slave man

   1. δοῦλος¹, *doulos¹*, 1528
   2. παῖς, *pais*, 4090

Lke 12:45	to beat the other slaves, men and women	2
Act 2:18	Even upon my slaves, both men and women,	1

slave woman

   1. δούλη, *doulē*, 1527
   2. παιδίσκη, *paidiskē*, 4087

Lke 12:45	to beat the other slaves, men and women	2
Act 2:18	Even upon my slaves, both men and women,	1
Gal 4:22	one by a slave woman and the other by a free woman.	2

slave-girl

   1. παιδίσκη, *paidiskē*, 4087

Act 16:16	met a slave-girl who had a spirit of divination	1

slavery   *See also* sell into slavery

   1. δουλεία, *douleia*, 1525
   2. δουλεύω, *douleuō*, 1526
   3. δοῦλος¹, *doulos¹*, 1528

Rom 8:15	For you did not receive a spirit of slavery	1
Gal 4:24	Hagar, from Mount Sinai, bearing children for slavery.	1
4:25	for she is in slavery with her children.	2
5: 1	do not submit again to a yoke of slavery.	1
1Ti 6: 1	all who are under the yoke of slavery	3
Heb 2:15	free those who all their lives were held in slavery	1

sleep

   1. καθεύδω, *katheudō*, 2761
   2. κοιμάω, *koimaō*, 3121
   3. ὕπνος, *hypnos*, 5678

Mat 1:24	When Joseph awoke from sleep, he did as the angel	3
9:24	the girl is not dead but sleeping."	1
25: 5	all of them became drowsy and slept.	1
26:40	he came to the disciples and found them sleeping;	1
26:43	Again he came and found them sleeping	1
26:45	"Are you still sleeping and taking your rest?	1
Mrk 4:27	sleep and rise night and day	1
5:39	The child is not dead but sleeping."	1
14:37	He came and found them sleeping;	1
14:40	once more he came and found them sleeping	1
14:41	"Are you still sleeping and taking your rest?	1
Lke 8:52	"Do not weep; for she is not dead but sleeping."	1
9:32	were weighed down with sleep;	3
22:45	found them sleeping because of grief	2
22:46	he said to them, "Why are you sleeping?	1
Act 12: 6	Peter…was sleeping between two soldiers	2

Act	20: 9	began to sink off into a deep sleep	3
	20: 9	Overcome by sleep, he fell to the ground	3
Rom 13:11	it is now the moment for you to wake from sleep.	3
1Th	5: 7	for those who sleep sleep at night	1
	5: 7	for those who sleep sleep at night	1

merely sleep
1. κοίμησις + ὕπνος, *koimēsis + hypnos, 3122 + 5678*

Jhn 11:13 they thought that he was referring merely to sleep.   1

sleeper
1. καθεύδω, *katheudō, 2761*

Eph 5:14 it says, "Sleeper, awake! Rise from the dead   1

sleepless *See* sleepless *night*

slight
1. ἐλαφρός, *elaphros, 1787*

2Co 4:17 this slight momentary affliction   1

slip in
1. παρεισέρχομαι, *pareiserchomai, 4209*

Gal 2: 4 who slipped in to spy on the freedom   1

slow
1. βραδύνω, *bradynō, 1094*
2. βραδύς, *bradys, 1096*

Lke 24:25	slow of heart to believe	2
Jas	1:19	let everyone be quick to listen, slow to speak	2
	1:19	let everyone be quick to listen...slow to anger;	2
2Pe	3: 9	The Lord is not slow about his promise	1

slowly *See* sail slowly

slowness
1. βραδύτης, *bradytēs, 1097*

2Pe 3: 9 The Lord is not slow...as some think of slowness   1

sluggish
1. κατάνυξις, *katanyxis, 2919*
2. νωθρός, *nōthros, 3821*

Rom 11: 8	as it is written, "God gave them a sluggish spirit	1
Heb	6:12	so that you may not become sluggish	2

small *See also* small copper *coin*, small *fish*, small *island*
1. ἡλίκος, *hēlikos, 2462*
2. μικρός, *mikros, 3625*
3. ὀλίγος, *oligos, 3900*

Mat 13:32	it is the smallest of all the seeds	2
Mrk	4:31	the smallest of all the seeds on earth;	2
Act 12:18	there was no small commotion among the soldiers	3
	15: 2	had no small dissension and debate with them	3
	26:22	I stand here, testifying to both small and great	2
	27:20	no small tempest raged,	3
Jas	3: 5	So also the tongue is a small member, yet it boasts	2
	3: 5	How great a forest is set ablaze by a small fire!	1
Rev 11:18	all who fear your name, both small and great	2
	13:16	all, both small and great, both rich and poor	2
	19: 5	his servants, and all who fear him, small and great."	2
	19:18	flesh of all...both small and great."	2
	20:12	dead, great and small, standing before the throne	2

small thing
1. ἐλάχιστος, *elachistos, 1788*

Lke 12:26 you are not able to do so small a thing as that   1

very small
1. ἐλάχιστος, *elachistos, 1788*

Jas 3: 4 they are guided by a very small rudder   1

very small thing
1. ἐλάχιστος, *elachistos, 1788*

Lke 19:17	you have been trustworthy in a very small thing	1
1Co	4: 3	with me it is a very small thing	1

smell *See* sense of smell

smoke
1. καπνός, *kapnos, 2837*

Rev	8: 4	the smoke of the incense...rose before God	1
	9: 2	and from the shaft rose smoke like the smoke	1
	9: 2	rose smoke like the smoke of a great furnace	1
	9: 2	the sun and the air were darkened with the smoke	1
	9: 3	Then from the smoke came locusts on the earth	1
	9:17	fire and smoke...came out of their mouths.	1
	9:18	killed, by the fire and smoke and sulfur	1
	14:11	smoke of their torment goes up forever and ever.	1
	15: 8	and the temple was filled with smoke	1
	18: 9	when they see the smoke of her burning;	1
	18:18	cried out as they saw the smoke of her burning	1
	19: 3	The smoke goes up from her forever and ever."	1

smoky
1. καπνός, *kapnos, 2837*

Act 2:19 blood, and fire, and smoky mist.   1

smolder
1. τύφω, *typhō, 5606*

Mat 12:20 or quench a smoldering wick   1

smooth *See also* smooth *talk*
1. λεῖος, *leios, 3308*

Lke 3: 5 the rough ways made smooth;   1

Smyrna
1. Σμύρνα², *Smyrna², 5044*

Rev	1:11	to the seven churches, to Ephesus, to Smyrna	1
	2: 8	"And to the angel of the church in Smyrna write:	1

snake
1. ὄφις, *ophis, 4058*

Mat	7:10	Or if the child asks for a fish, will give a snake?	1
	23:33	You snakes, you brood of vipers!	1
Mrk 16:18	⟦they will pick up snakes in their hands⟧	1
Lke 10:19	authority to tread on snakes and scorpions	1
	11:11	will give a snake instead of a fish?	1

snare
1. παγίς, *pagis, 4075*

Rom 11: 9	"Let their table become a snare and a trap,	1
1Ti	3: 7	fall into disgrace and the snare of the devil.	1
2Ti	2:26	they may escape from the snare of the devil	1

snatch
1. ἁρπάζω, *harpazō, 773*

Jhn 10:12	the wolf snatches them and scatters them.	1
	10:28	No one will snatch them out of my hand.	1
	10:29	can snatch it out of the Father's hand.	1
Jde	1:23	save others by snatching them out of the fire;	1

snatch away
1. ἁρπάζω, *harpazō, 773*

Mat 13:19	the evil one comes and snatches away what is sown	1
Act	8:39	the Spirit of the Lord snatched Philip away;	1
Rev 12: 5	her child was snatched away and taken to God	1

sneer
1. διαχλευάζω, *diachleuazō, 1430*

Act 2:13 others sneered and said   1

snow
1. χιών, *chiōn, 5946*

Mat 28: 3	his clothing white as snow.	1
Rev	1:14	His head and his hair were...white as snow;	1

so *See also* cling so closely, even so, just so, so *great*, so *much*, so *violent*
1. ἀλλά, *alla, 247*
2. ἄρα, *ara, 726*
3. γάρ, *gar, 1142*
4. δέ, *de, 1254*
5. διά + οὗτος, *dia + houtos, 1328 + 4047*
6. διό, *dio, 1475*

7. εἰς, *eis, 1650*
8. ἵνα, *hina, 2671*
9. καθάπερ, *kathaper, 2749*
10. καθώς, *kathōs, 2777*
11. καί, *kai, 2779*
12. λίαν, *lian, 3336*
13. ναί, *nai, 3721*
14. ὁμοίως, *homoiōs, 3931*
15. ὅπως, *hopōs, 3968*
16. ὅς, *hos, 4005*
17. οὐκοῦν, *oukoun, 4034*
18. οὖν, *oun, 4036*
19. οὕτως, *houtōs, 4048*
20. περισσῶς, *perissōs, 4360*
21. πλήν, *plēn, 4440*
22. σφόδρα, *sphodra, 5379*
23. τέ, *te, 5445*
24. τοίνυν, *toinyn, 5523*
25. τοιοῦτος, *toioutos, 5525*
26. τότε, *tote, 5538*
27. χωρίζω, *chōrizō, 6004*
28. ὡσαύτως, *hōsautōs, 6058*
29. ὥστε, *hōste, 6063*

Mat	1:17	So all the generations from Abraham to David	18
	2: 5	Judea; for so it has been written by the prophet:	19
	4:24	So his fame spread throughout all Syria	11
	5:23	So when you are offering your gift at the altar	18
	6: 2	"So whenever you give alms, do not sound a trumpet	18
	6:16	so as to show others that they are fasting.	15
	6:22	So, if your eye is healthy, your whole body will be	18
	6:30	But if God so clothes the grass of the field	19
	6:34	"So do not worry about tomorrow	18
	8:28	so fierce that no one could pass that way.	12
	8:32	"Go!" So they came out and entered the swine;	4
	10:16	so be wise as serpents and innocent as doves.	18
	10:26	"So have no fear of them; for nothing is covered	18
	10:31	So do not be afraid; you are of more value	18
	12:12	So it is lawful to do good on the sabbath."	29
	12:40	so for three days and three nights the Son	19
	12:45	So will it be also with this evil generation."	19
	13:26	So when the plants came up and bore grain	4
	13:40	so will it be at the end of the age.	19
	13:49	So it will be at the end of the age.	19
	14:29	He said, "Come." So Peter got out of the boat	11
	15: 6	So, for the sake of your tradition	11
	17:12	So also the Son of Man is about to suffer	19
	18:14	So it is not the will of your Father in heaven	19
	18:26	So the slave fell on his knees before him	18
	18:35	So my heavenly Father will also do	19
	19: 6	So they are no longer two, but one flesh.	29
	19: 8	but from the beginning it was not so.	19
	19:12	there are eunuchs who have been so from birth	19
	20: 4	So they went.	4
	20:16	So the last will be first, and the first	19
	20:26	It will not be so among you;	19
	21:27	So they answered Jesus, "We do not know."	11
	21:39	So they seized him, threw him out of the vineyard	11
	22:10	so the wedding hall was filled with guests.	11
	22:16	So they sent their disciples to him	11
	23:20	So whoever swears by the altar	18
	23:28	So you also on the outside look righteous to others	19
	24:15	"So when you see the desolating sacrilege	18
	24:26	So, if they say to you, 'Look!	18
	24:27	so will be the coming of the Son of Man.	19
	24:33	So also, when you see all these things	19
	24:37	so will be the coming of the Son of Man.	19
	24:39	so too will be the coming of the Son of Man.	19
	25:25	so I was afraid, and I went and hid your talent	11
	25:28	So take the talent from him	18
	26:19	So the disciples did as Jesus had directed them	11
	26:35	And so said all the disciples.	14
	26:40	"So, could you not stay awake with me one hour?	19
	26:44	So leaving them again, he went away	11
	27:17	So after they had gathered, Pilate said to them	18
	27:24	So when Pilate saw that he could do nothing	4
	27:26	So he released Barabbas for them;	26
	27:59	So Joseph took the body	11
	27:66	So they went with the guard and made the tomb secure	4
	28: 8	So they left the tomb quickly with fear	11

	28:15	So they took the money and did as they were directed.	4
Mrk	2:28	so the Son of Man is lord even of the sabbath."	29
	3:16	So he appointed the twelve: Simon	11
	5:13	So he gave them permission.	11
	5:24	So he went with him.	11
	6:12	So they went out and proclaimed	11
	6:40	So they sat down in groups	11
	7: 5	So the Pharisees and the scribes asked him	11
	7:30	So she went home, found the child lying on the bed	11
	9:10	So they kept the matter to themselves	11
	10: 8	So they are no longer two, but one flesh.	29
	10:42	So Jesus called them and said to them	11
	10:43	it is not so among you;	19
	10:50	So throwing off his cloak, he sprang up	4
	11:24	So I tell you, whatever you ask for in prayer	5
	11:33	So they answered Jesus, "We do not know."	11
	12: 8	So they seized him, killed him	11
	12:12	So they left him and went away.	11
	12:37	calls him Lord; so how can he be his son?"	11
	13:29	So also, when you see these things taking place	19
	14:11	So he began to look for an opportunity to betray him.	11
	14:13	So he sent two of his disciples, saying to them,	11
	14:16	So the disciples set out and went to the city	11
	14:45	So when he came, he went up to him at once	11
	15: 8	So the crowd came and began to ask Pilate	11
	15:15	So Pilate, wishing to satisfy the crowd	4
	16: 8	So they went out and fled from the tomb	11
Lke	2:16	So they went with haste and found Mary and Joseph	11
	3:18	So, with many other exhortations, he proclaimed	18
	4:44	So he continued proclaiming the message	11
	5: 7	So they signaled their partners	11
	5:10	so also were James and John, sons of Zebedee	14
	7:18	So John summoned two of his disciples	11
	8:22	So they put out	11
	8:32	So he gave them permission.	11
	8:37	So he got into the boat and returned.	4
	8:39	So he went away	11
	9:15	They did so and made them all sit down.	19
	10:32	So likewise a Levite, when he came to the place	4
	10:40	so she came to him and asked, "Lord,	4
	11:30	so the Son of Man will be to this generation.	19
	11:37	so he went in and took his place at the table.	4
	11:41	So give for alms those things that are within;	21
	11:48	So you are witnesses	2
	12:21	So it is with those who store up treasures	19
	12:28	if God so clothes the grass of the field	19
	12:38	and finds them so, blessed are those slaves.	19
	12:54	and so it happens.	19
	13: 7	So he said to the gardener, 'See here!	4
	14: 4	they were silent. So Jesus took him and healed him	11
	14:21	So the slave returned and reported this	11
	14:33	So therefore, none of you can become my disciple	19
	15: 3	So he told them this parable:	4
	15:12	So he divided his property between them.	4
	15:15	So he went and hired himself out	11
	15:20	So he set off and went to his father.	11
	16: 2	So he summoned him and said to him, 'What is this	11
	16: 5	So, summoning his master's debtors one by one	11
	16:15	So he said to them, "You are those who justify	11
	17:10	So you also, when you have done all	19
	17:24	so will the Son of Man be in his day.	19
	17:26	so too it will be in the days of the Son of Man.	19
	19: 4	So he ran ahead	11
	19: 6	So he hurried down	11
	19:12	So he said, "A nobleman went	18
	19:32	So those who were sent departed	4
	20: 7	So they answered that they did not know	11
	20:15	So they threw him out of the vineyard and killed	11
	20:20	So they watched him and sent spies	11
	20:20	so as to hand him over to…the governor	29
	20:21	So they asked him, "Teacher	11
	20:31	so in the same way all seven died childless.	11
	20:44	David thus calls him Lord; so how can he be his son?"	11
	21:14	So make up your minds	18
	21:31	So also, when you see these things taking place	19
	22: 6	So he consented	11
	22: 8	So Jesus sent Peter and John, saying, "Go	11
	22:13	So they went and found everything as he had told	4
	22:26	But not so with you; rather the greatest	19
	23:24	So Pilate gave his verdict	11
	24:29	So he went in to stay with them.	11

Lke	24:49	so stay here in the city until	4
Jhn	2: 8	to the chief steward." So they took it.	4
	3: 8	So it is with everyone who is born of the Spirit."	19
	3:14	so must the Son of Man be lifted up	19
	3:16	God so loved the world that he gave his only Son	19
	4: 5	So he came to a Samaritan city called Sychar	18
	4:33	So the disciples said to one another	18
	4:40	So when the Samaritans came to him, they asked him	18
	4:52	So he asked them the hour when he began to recover	18
	4:53	So he himself believed	11
	5:10	So the Jews said to the man who had been cured	18
	5:21	so also the Son gives life to whomever he wishes.	19
	5:26	so he has granted the Son also to have life	19
	6:10	so they sat down, about five thousand in all	18
	6:11	so also the fish, as much as they wanted.	14
	6:12	so that nothing may be lost."	8
	6:13	So they gathered them up	18
	6:24	So when the crowd saw that neither Jesus	18
	6:30	So they said to him, "What sign are you going	18
	6:53	So Jesus said to them, "Very truly, I tell you	18
	6:57	so whoever eats me will live because of me.	11
	6:67	So Jesus asked the twelve	18
	7: 3	So his brothers said to him, "Leave here	18
	7:43	So there was a division in the crowd because of him.	18
	8: 6	[so that they might have some charge to bring]	8
	8:28	So Jesus said, "When you have lifted up the Son	18
	8:36	So if the Son makes you free, you will be free	18
	8:59	So they picked up stones to throw at him	18
	9:17	So they said again to the blind man	18
	9:24	So for the second time they called the man	18
	10: 7	So again Jesus said to them, "Very truly	18
	10:16	So there will be one flock, one shepherd.	11
	10:24	So the Jews gathered around him and said to him	18
	11: 3	So the sisters sent a message to Jesus,	18
	11:36	So the Jews said, "See how he loved him!"	18
	11:41	So they took away the stone.	18
	11:47	So the chief priests...called a meeting	18
	11:53	So from that day on they planned	18
	12:10	So the chief priests planned	4
	12:17	So the crowd that had been with him	18
	12:39	so they could not believe	5
	13:14	So if I, your Lord and Teacher, have washed	18
	13:25	So while reclining next to Jesus, he asked	18
	13:26	So when he had dipped the piece of bread	18
	13:30	So, after receiving the piece of bread	18
	16:19	so he said to them, "Are you discussing	11
	16:22	So you have pain now; but I will see you again	18
	17: 5	So now, Father, glorify me in your own presence	11
	18: 3	So Judas brought a detachment of soldiers	18
	18: 8	So if you are looking for me, let these men go."	18
	18:12	So the soldiers...arrested Jesus	18
	18:16	So the other disciple, who was known	18
	18:28	so as to avoid ritual defilement	8
	18:29	So Pilate went out to them and said	18
	18:37	Pilate asked him, "So you are a king?"	17
	19: 5	So Jesus came out, wearing the crown of thorns	18
	19:16	to be crucified. So they took Jesus;	18
	19:24	So they said to one another, "Let us not tear	18
	19:29	So they put a sponge full of the wine	18
	19:31	So they asked Pilate to have the legs...broken	18
	19:38	so he came and removed his body.	18
	19:42	And so, because it was the...day of Preparation	18
	20: 2	So she ran and went to Simon Peter	18
	20:25	So the other disciples told him	18
	21: 6	So they cast it	18
	21:11	So Simon Peter went aboard and hauled the net	18
	21:23	So the rumor spread in the community	18
Act	1: 6	So when they had come together, they asked him	18
	1:21	So one of the men who have accompanied us	18
	1:23	So they proposed two, Joseph...and Matthias.	11
	2:41	So those who welcomed his message were baptized	18
	4: 3	So they arrested them	11
	4:15	So they ordered them to leave the council	4
	4:18	So they called them and ordered them not to speak	11
	5:10	so they carried her out and buried her	11
	5:22	so they returned and reported	4
	5:38	So in the present case, I tell you	11
	7: 1	high priest asked him, "Are these things so?"	19
	7: 8	And so Abraham became the father of Isaac	19
	7:15	so Jacob went down to Egypt.	11
	7:22	So Moses was instructed in all the wisdom	11

	7:43	so I will remove you beyond Babylon.'	11
	8: 8	So there was great joy in that city.	4
	8:27	So he got up and went.	11
	8:30	So Philip ran up to it and heard him reading	4
	8:32	so he does not open his mouth.	19
	9: 8	so they led him by the hand	4
	9:17	So Ananias went and entered the house.	4
	9:28	So he went in and out among them in Jerusalem	11
	9:39	So Peter got up and went with them;	4
	10:21	So Peter went down to the men and said	4
	10:23	So Peter invited them in and gave them lodging.	18
	10:29	So when I was sent for, I came without objection.	6
	10:33	So now all of us are here	18
	10:48	So he ordered them to be baptized	4
	11: 2	So when Peter went up to Jerusalem	4
	11:26	So it was that for an entire year they met	4
	12: 8	He did so. Then he said to him	19
	12:15	she insisted that it was so	19
	12:20	So they came to him in a body;	4
	13: 4	So, being sent out by the Holy Spirit	18
	13:16	So Paul stood up and with a gesture began to speak:	4
	13:47	For so the Lord has commanded us, saying	19
	13:51	so they shook the dust off their feet in protest	4
	14: 3	So they remained for a long time	18
	15: 3	So they were sent on their way by the church	18
	15:30	So they were sent off and went down to Antioch.	18
	16: 5	So the churches were strengthened in the faith	18
	16: 8	so, passing by Mysia, they went down to Troas.	4
	16:39	so they came and apologized to them.	11
	17:11	to see whether these things were so.	19
	17:17	So he argued in the synagogue with the Jews	18
	17:19	So they took him	23
	17:20	so we would like to know what it means."	18
	19:20	So the word of the Lord grew mightily	19
	19:22	So he sent two of his helpers, Timothy and Erastus,	4
	21:23	So do what we tell you.	18
	23:11	so you must bear witness also in Rome."	19
	23:18	So he took him, brought him to the tribune,	18
	23:22	So the tribune dismissed the young man	18
	23:31	So the soldiers...took Paul	18
	25: 5	"So," he said, "let those of you who have	18
	25:17	So when they met here	18
	25:23	So on the next day Agrippa and Bernice came	18
	26:11	since I was so furiously enraged at them	20
	26:22	so I stand here, testifying to both small and great	18
	27:17	they lowered the sea anchor and so were driven.	19
	27:25	So keep up your courage, men	6
	27:28	So they took soundings and found twenty fathoms;	11
	27:40	So they cast off the anchors and left them	11
	27:44	so it was that all were brought safely to land.	19
	28:14	so we came to Rome.	19
	28:25	So they disagreed with each other;	4
Rom	1:20	So they are without excuse;	7
	2:26	So, if those who are uncircumcised keep the...law	18
	4: 6	So also David speaks of the blessedness of those	9
	4:18	"So numerous shall your descendants be."	19
	5:12	and so death spread to all because all have sinned	19
	5:18	so one man's act of righteousness leads	19
	5:19	so by the one man's obedience the many	19
	5:21	so grace might also exercise dominion	19
	6: 4	so we too might walk in newness of life.	19
	6:11	So you also must consider yourselves dead to sin	19
	6:19	so now present your members as slaves to righteousness	19
	6:21	So what advantage did you then get from the things	18
	7:12	So the law is holy, and the commandment is holy	29
	7:21	So I find it to be a law that when I want to do	2
	7:25	So then with my mind I am a slave to the law of God	2
	8:12	So then, brothers and sisters, we are debtors	2
	9:16	So it depends not on human will or exertion	2
	9:18	So then he has mercy on whomever he chooses	2
	10:10	one believes with the heart and so is justified	7
	10:10	one confesses with the mouth and so is saved.	7
	10:17	So faith comes from what is heard	2
	11: 5	So too at the present time there is a remnant	19
	11:11	So I ask, have they stumbled so as to fall?	18
	11:11	have they stumbled so as to fall? By no means!	8
	11:11	so as to make Israel jealous.	7
	11:26	so all Israel will be saved; as it is written	19
	11:31	so they have now been disobedient in order that	19
	12: 5	so we, who are many, are one body in Christ	19
	14:12	So then, each of us will be accountable to God.	2

	14:16	So do not let your good be spoken of as evil.	18
	15:28	So, when I have completed this	18
	16:21	so do Lucius and Jason and Sosipater, my relatives.	11
1Co	2:11	So also no one comprehends what is truly God's	19
	3: 7	So neither the one who plants…is anything	29
	3:21	So let no one boast about human leaders.	29
	7:15	the unbelieving partner separates, let it be so;	27
	7:36	if his passions are strong, and so it has to be	19
	8:11	So by your knowledge those weak believers	3
	9:18	so as not to make full use of my rights	7
	9:26	So I do not run aimlessly	24
	10:12	So if you think you are standing, watch out	29
	10:31	So, whether you eat or drink, or whatever you do	18
	11:12	so man comes through woman;	19
	12:12	so it is with Christ.	19
	13: 2	if I have all faith, so as to remove mountains	29
	14: 9	So with yourselves; if in a tongue you utter speech	19
	14:12	So with yourselves; since you are eager	19
	14:39	So, my friends, be eager to prophesy	29
	15:11	so we proclaim and so you have come to believe.	19
	15:11	so we proclaim and so you have come to believe.	19
	15:22	so all will be made alive in Christ.	19
	15:42	So it is with the resurrection of the dead.	19
	15:48	so are those who are of the dust;	25
	15:48	so are those who are of heaven.	25
	16:18	So give recognition to such persons.	18
2Co	1: 5	so also our consolation is abundant through Christ	19
	1: 7	so also you share in our consolation.	19
	2: 1	So I made up my mind not to make you another…visit.	3
	2: 7	so now instead you should forgive and console	29
	2: 8	So I urge you to reaffirm your love for him.	6
	2:13	So I said farewell to them and went on to Macedonia.	1
	4:12	So death is at work in us, but life in you.	29
	4:13	with scripture—"I believed, and so I spoke"	6
	4:13	we also believe, and so we speak	6
	4:16	So we do not lose heart.	6
	5: 6	So we are always confident;	18
	5: 9	So whether we are at home or away	6
	5:17	So if anyone is in Christ	29
	5:20	So we are ambassadors for Christ	18
	7:12	So although I wrote to you	2
	7:14	so our boasting to Titus has proved true	19
	8: 6	so he should also complete this generous undertaking	19
	8: 7	so we want you to excel also in this	8
	9: 5	So I thought it necessary to urge the brothers	18
	10: 7	just as you belong to Christ, so also do we.	19
	11: 9	So I refrained and will continue to refrain	11
	11:15	So it is not strange if his ministers also	18
	12: 9	So, I will boast all the more gladly of my weaknesses	18
	13:10	So I write these things while I am away from you	5
Gal	1: 6	I am astonished that you are so quickly deserting	19
	1: 9	As we have said before, so now I repeat	11
	3: 3	Are you so foolish?	19
	3: 7	so, you see, those who believe are the descendants	2
	4: 3	So with us; while we were minors,	19
	4: 7	So you are no longer a slave but a child,	29
	4:29	so it is now also	19
	6: 9	So let us not grow weary in doing what is right	4
	6:10	So then, whenever we have an opportunity	18
Eph	2:17	So he came and proclaimed peace to you	11
	2:19	So then you are no longer strangers and aliens	2
	4:28	so as to have something to share with the needy.	8
	5:17	So do not be foolish	5
	5:24	so also wives ought to be, in everything	19
	5:27	so as to present the church…in splendor	8
Col	1: 6	so it has been bearing fruit among yourselves	10
	3: 1	So if you have been raised with Christ	18
	3:13	so you also must forgive.	19
1Th	2: 8	So deeply do we care for you	19
	3: 4	so it turned out, as you know.	10
	4:17	so we will be with the Lord forever.	19
	5: 6	So then let us not fall asleep as others do	18
2Th	2:10	refused to love the truth and so be saved.	7
	2:15	So then…stand firm and hold fast to the traditions	2
1Ti	5:14	So I would have younger widows marry,	18
	5:25	So also good works are conspicuous;	28
2Ti	3: 8	so these people…also oppose the truth.	19
	4:17	So I was rescued from the lion's mouth.	11
Phm	1:17	So if you consider me your partner	18
Heb	3:19	So we see that they were unable to enter	11
	5: 5	So also Christ did not glorify himself	19

	9:28	so Christ…offered once to bear the sins of many	19
	10:33	sometimes being partners with those so treated.	19
	10:39	those who shrink back and so are lost	7
	10:39	those who have faith and so are saved.	7
	11:29	when the Egyptians attempted to do so they	16
	12:21	Indeed, so terrifying was the sight	19
	13: 6	So we can say with confidence	29
Jas	2:12	So speak and so act as those who are to be judged	19
	2:12	So speak and so act as those who are to be judged	19
	2:17	So faith by itself, if it has no works, is dead.	19
	2:26	so faith without works is also dead.	19
	3: 5	So also the tongue is a small member, yet it boasts	19
	3:10	My brothers and sisters, this ought not to be so.	19
1Pe	4: 2	so as to live for the rest of your earthly life	7
2Pe	1:19	So we have the prophetic message more fully confirmed	11
	3:15	So also our beloved brother Paul wrote to you	10
1Jn	2:18	so now many antichrists have come.	11
	4:16	So we have known and believe the love that God has	11
	4:17	because as he is, so are we in this world.	11
3Jn	1:10	So if I come, I will call attention to what he is doing	5
Rev	1: 7	Look! He is coming…So it is to be. Amen.	13
	2:15	So you also have some who hold to the teaching	19
	3:16	So, because you are lukewarm	19
	9:15	So the four angels were released	11
	10: 9	So I went to the angel and told him to give me	11
	10:10	So I took the little scroll from the hand of the angel	11
	12:13	So when the dragon saw that he had been thrown down	11
	14:16	So the one who sat on the cloud swung his sickle	11
	14:19	So the angel swung his sickle over the earth	11
	16: 2	So the first angel went and poured his bowl	11
	16:18	so violent was that earthquake.	19
	16:21	they cursed God…so fearful was that plague.	22
	17: 3	So he carried me away…into a wilderness	11

so that

1. Contextual: Not in Greek
2. διά, *dia*, 1328
3. εἰς, *eis*, 1650
4. ἵνα, *hina*, 2671
5. ὅπως, *hopōs*, 3968
6. ὅπως + ἄν, *hopōs + an*, 3968 + 323
7. ὅτι, *hoti*, 4022
8. οὖν, *oun*, 4036
9. πρός, *pros*, 4639
10. πώς, *pōs*, 4803
11. ὥστε, *hōste*, 6063

Mat	2: 8	so that I may also go and pay him homage."	5
	2:23	so that what had been spoken through the prophets	5
	4:14	so that what had been spoken through the prophet	4
	5:16	so that they may see your good works and give glory	5
	5:45	so that you may be children of your Father	5
	6: 2	so that they may be praised by others.	5
	6: 4	so that your alms may be done in secret	5
	6: 5	so that they may be seen by others	5
	6:18	so that your fasting may be seen not by others	5
	7: 1	"Do not judge, so that you may not be judged.	4
	9: 6	But so that you may know that the Son of Man	4
	12:10	so that they might accuse him.	4
	12:22	so that the one who had been mute could speak and see.	11
	13:32	so that the birds of the air come and make nests	11
	13:54	so that they were astounded and said	11
	14:15	so that they may go into the villages	4
	15:31	so that the crowd was amazed	11
	17:27	However, so that we do not give offense to them	4
	18:16	so that every word may be confirmed	4
	23:26	so that the outside also may become clean.	4
	23:35	so that upon you may come all the righteous blood	5
	26:56	so that the scriptures…may be fulfilled."	4
	26:59	so that they might put him to death	5
	27:14	so that the governor was greatly amazed.	11
Mrk	1:38	so that I may proclaim the message there also;	4
	1:45	so that Jesus could no longer go into a town openly	11
	2:10	so that you may know	4
	2:12	so that they were all amazed and glorified God	11
	3: 2	so that they might accuse him.	4
	3: 9	the crowd, so that they would not crush him;	4
	3:10	so that all who had diseases pressed upon him	11
	3:20	so that they could not even eat.	11
	4:32	so that the birds of the air can make nests	11
	4:37	so that the boat was already being swamped.	11

Mrk	5:23	so that she may be made well, and live."	4
	6:36	so that they may go into the surrounding country	4
	9:26	so that most of them said, "He is dead."	11
	11:25	so that your Father in heaven may also	4
	15: 5	so that Pilate was amazed.	11
	15:32	so that we may see and believe."	4
	16: 1	so that they might go and anoint him.	4
Lke	1: 4	so that you may know the truth	4
	2:35	so that the inner thoughts of many will be revealed	6
	4:29	so that they might hurl him off the	11
	5: 7	so that they began to sink.	11
	5:24	so that you may know that the Son of Man has	4
	6: 7	so that they might find an accusation against him.	4
	8:10	so that 'looking they may not perceive	4
	8:12	so that they may not believe and be saved.	4
	8:16	so that those who enter may see the light.	4
	9:12	so that they may go into the surrounding villages	4
	9:45	so that they could not perceive it.	4
	11:33	so that those who enter may see the light.	4
	11:50	so that this generation may be charged with	4
	12: 1	so that they trampled on one another	11
	12:36	so that they may open the door for him	4
	14:10	so that when your host comes, he may say to you	4
	14:23	so that my house may be filled.	4
	15:29	so that I might celebrate with my friends.	4
	16: 4	so that, when I am dismissed as manager,	4
	16: 9	so that when it is gone, they may welcome you	4
	16:26	so that those who might want to pass from here	5
	16:28	so that they will not also come into…torment.'	4
	18: 5	so that she may not wear me out by continually	4
	19:15	so that he might find out what they had gained	4
	20:14	so that the inheritance may be ours.'	4
	22:30	so that you may eat and drink at my table	4
Jhn	1: 7	so that all might believe through him.	4
	3:16	so that everyone who believes in him may not perish	4
	3:20	so that their deeds may not be exposed.	4
	3:21	so that it may be clearly seen	4
	4:15	give me this water, so that I may never be thirsty	4
	4:36	so that sower and reaper may rejoice together.	4
	5:14	not sin…so that nothing worse happens to you."	4
	5:20	so that you will be astonished.	4
	5:23	so that all may honor the Son	4
	5:34	I say these things so that you may be saved.	4
	6:30	so that we may see it and believe you?	4
	6:50	so that one may eat of it and not die.	4
	7: 3	so that your disciples also may see the works	4
	9: 3	so that God's works might be revealed in him.	4
	9:36	Tell me, so that I may believe in him."	4
	9:39	so that those who do not see may see	4
	10:38	so that you may know and understand	4
	11: 4	so that the Son of God may be glorified	4
	11:15	so that you may believe.	4
	11:42	so that they may believe that you sent me."	4
	11:57	let them know, so that they might arrest him.	5
	12: 7	so that she might keep it for the day of my burial.	4
	12:35	so that the darkness may not overtake you.	4
	12:36	so that you may become children of light."	4
	12:40	so that they might not look with their eyes	4
	12:46	so that everyone who believes in me	4
	13:19	so that when it does occur	4
	14: 3	so that where I am, there you may be also.	4
	14:13	so that the Father may be glorified in the Son.	4
	14:29	so that when it does occur, you may believe.	4
	14:31	so that the world may know that I love the Father.	4
	15:11	so that my joy may be in you	4
	15:16	so that the Father will give you whatever	4
	15:17	these commands so that you may love one another.	4
	16: 4	so that when their hour comes you may remember	4
	16:24	will receive, so that your joy may be complete.	4
	16:33	so that in me you may have peace.	4
	17: 1	glorify your Son so that the Son may glorify you	4
	17:11	so that they may be one, as we are one.	4
	17:12	so that the scripture might be fulfilled.	4
	17:13	so that they may have my joy made complete	4
	17:19	so that they also may be sanctified in truth.	4
	17:21	so that the world may believe that you…sent me.	4
	17:22	so that they may be one, as we are one	4
	17:23	so that the world may know that you…sent me	4
	17:26	so that the love with which you have loved me	4
	19:35	so that you also may believe.	4
	19:36	so that the scripture might be fulfilled	4

	20:31	are written so that you may come to believe	4
Act	1:19	so that the field was called…Hakeldama	11
	2:25	he is at my right hand so that I will not be shaken;	4
	2:38	so that your sins may be forgiven;	3
	3: 2	so that he could ask for alms from those entering	1
	3:19	so that your sins may be wiped out	3
	3:20	so that times of refreshing may come	6
	5:15	so that they even carried out the sick into the streets	11
	7:19	abandon their infants so that they would die	3
	8:19	so that anyone…may receive the Holy Spirit."	4
	9: 2	so that if he found any who belonged to the Way	5
	9:12	so that he might regain his sight."	5
	9:17	so that you may regain your sight	5
	9:24	watching the gates…so that they might kill him;	5
	13:47	so that you may bring salvation to…the earth.' "	3
	15:17	so that all other peoples may seek the Lord	6
	17:27	so that they would search for God	1
	19:10	so that all the residents of Asia…heard	11
	19:12	so that when the handkerchiefs…were brought	11
	20:16	so that he might not have to spend time in Asia;	5
	21:35	so great that he had to be carried by the soldiers	2
	25:26	so that, after we have examined him	5
	26:18	so that they may turn from darkness to light	1
	26:18	so that they may receive forgiveness of sins	1
Rom	1:11	so that I may share with you some spiritual gift	4
	1:12	or rather so that we may be mutually encouraged	1
	3: 4	"So that you may be justified in your words	6
	3: 8	"Let us do evil so that good may come"?	4
	3:19	so that every mouth may be silenced	4
	5:21	so that, just as sin exercised dominion in death	4
	6: 4	so that, just as Christ was raised from the dead	4
	6: 6	so that the body of sin might be destroyed	4
	7: 4	so that you may belong to another	3
	7: 6	so that we are slaves not under the old written code	11
	8: 4	so that the just requirement of the law	4
	8:17	so that we may also be glorified with him.	4
	9:11	(so that God's purpose of election might	4
	9:17	so that my name may be proclaimed in all the earth."	5
	10: 4	so that there may be righteousness for everyone	3
	11:10	their eyes be darkened so that they cannot see	1
	11:19	were broken off so that I might be grafted in."	4
	11:25	So that you may not claim to be wiser than you are	4
	11:32	so that he may be merciful to all.	4
	12: 2	so that you may discern what is the will of God	3
	14: 9	so that he might be Lord of both the dead and	4
	15: 4	so that by steadfastness and by the encouragement	4
	15: 6	so that together you may with one voice glorify	4
	15:13	so that you may abound in hope by the power	3
	15:16	so that the offering of the Gentiles may be acceptable	4
	15:19	so that from Jerusalem and as far around as Illyricum	11
	15:20	so that I do not build on someone else's foundation	4
	15:32	so that by God's will I may come to you with joy	4
	16: 2	so that you may welcome her in the Lord	4
	16:19	so that I rejoice over you	8
1Co	1: 7	so that you are not lacking in any spiritual gift	11
	1: 8	so that you may be blameless on the day	1
	1:15	so that no one can say that you were baptized	4
	1:17	so that the cross of Christ might not be emptied	4
	1:29	so that no one might boast	5
	2: 5	so that your faith might rest not on human wisdom	4
	2:12	so that we may understand the gifts bestowed on us	4
	3:18	you should become fools so that you may become wise.	4
	4: 6	so that you may learn through us the meaning	4
	4: 6	so that none of you will be puffed up in favor of one	4
	4: 8	so that we might be kings with you!	4
	5: 2	so that he who has done this would have been removed	4
	5: 5	so that his spirit may be saved in the day	4
	5: 7	so that you may be a new batch	4
	7: 5	come together again, so that Satan may not tempt	4
	7:34	so that they may be holy in body and spirit;	4
	8:13	so that I may not cause one of them to fall.	4
	9:15	so that they may be applied in my case	4
	9:19	a slave to all, so that I might win more	4
	9:20	so that I might win those under the law.	4
	9:21	so that I might win those outside the law.	4
	9:22	so that I might win the weak.	4
	9:23	so that I may share in its blessings.	4
	9:27	so that after proclaiming to others I myself	10
	10: 6	so that we might not desire evil as they did.	3
	10:13	so that you may be able to endure it.	1
	10:33	so that they may be saved.	4

	11:32	disciplined so that we may not be condemned	4
	11:34	so that when you come together, it will not	4
	13: 3	if I hand over my body so that I may boast,	4
	14: 5	so that the church may be built up.	4
	14:31	so that all may learn and all be encouraged.	4
	15:28	so that God may be all in all.	4
	16: 2	so that collections need not be taken when I come.	4
	16: 6	so that you may send me on my way	4
	16:11	so that he may come to me;	4
2Co	1: 4	so that we may be able to console	3
	1: 9	so that we would rely not on ourselves	4
	1:11	so that many will give thanks on our behalf	4
	1:15	so that you might have a double favor;	4
	2: 3	so that when I came, I might not suffer pain	4
	2:11	so that we may not be outwitted by Satan;	4
	3: 7	so that the people of Israel could not gaze	11
	4: 7	so that it may be made clear that this extraordinary	4
	4:10	so that the life of Jesus may also be made visible	4
	4:11	so that the life of Jesus may be made visible	4
	4:15	so that grace, as it extends to more and more people	4
	5: 4	so that what is mortal may be swallowed up by life.	4
	5:10	so that each may receive recompense	4
	5:12	so that you may be able to answer	4
	5:15	so that those who live might live no longer	4
	5:21	so that in him we might become the righteousness	4
	6: 3	so that no fault may be found with our ministry	4
	7: 7	so that I rejoiced still more.	11
	7: 9	so that you were not harmed in any way by us.	4
	8: 6	so that we might urge Titus	3
	8: 9	so that by his poverty you might become rich.	4
	8:11	so that your eagerness may be matched by completing	5
	8:14	so that their abundance may be for your need	4
	9: 3	so that you may be ready, as I said you would be;	4
	9: 5	so that it may be ready as a voluntary gift	1
	9: 8	so that by always having enough of everything	4
	10:16	so that we may proclaim the good news in lands beyond	1
	11: 7	humbling myself so that you might be exalted	4
	11:16	so that I too may boast a little.	4
	12: 6	so that no one may think better of me than	1
	12: 9	so that the power of Christ may dwell in me.	4
	13:10	so that when I come	4
Gal	1:16	so that I might proclaim him	4
	2: 4	so that they might enslave us—	4
	2: 5	so that the truth of the gospel might always remain	4
	2:13	so that even Barnabas was led astray	11
	2:16	so that we might be justified by faith in Christ	4
	2:19	so that I might live to God.	4
	3:14	so that we might receive the promise of the Spirit	4
	3:22	so that what was promised through faith in Jesus	4
	3:24	so that we might be justified by faith.	4
	4: 5	so that we might receive adoption as children.	4
	4:17	to exclude you, so that you may make much of them.	4
	6:13	so that they may boast about your flesh.	4
Eph	1:12	so that we, who were the first to set our hope	3
	1:18	so that, with the eyes of your heart enlightened	3
	2: 7	so that in the ages to come	4
	2: 9	not the result of works, so that no one may boast.	4
	3:10	so that through the church the wisdom of God	4
	3:19	so that you may be filled with all the fullness	4
	4:10	so that he might fill all things.)	4
	4:29	so that your words may give grace	4
	5:27	so that she may be holy and without blemish.	4
	6: 3	"so that it may be well with you	4
	6:11	so that you may be able to stand against the wiles	9
	6:13	so that you may be able to withstand on that evil day	4
	6:19	so that when I speak, a message may be given to me	4
	6:21	So that you also may know how I am	4
Php	1:10	so that…you may be pure and blameless	4
	1:13	so that it has become known	11
	1:26	so that I may share abundantly in your boasting	4
	1:27	so that, whether I come and see you or am absent	4
	2:10	so that at the name of Jesus every knee should bend	4
	2:15	so that you may be blameless and innocent	4
	2:19	so that I may be cheered by news of you.	4
	2:27	so that I would not have one sorrow after another.	4
Col	1:10	so that you may lead lives worthy of the Lord	1
	1:18	so that he might come to have first place in everything.	4
	1:28	so that we may present everyone mature in Christ.	4
	2: 2	so that they may have all the riches of assured	3
	2: 4	I am saying this so that no one may deceive you	4
	4: 4	so that I may reveal it clearly, as I should.	4

	4: 6	so that you may know how you ought to answer	1
	4: 8	so that you may know how we are	4
	4:12	so that you may stand mature and fully assured	4
1Th	1: 7	so that you became an example to all the believers	11
	1: 8	so that we have no need to speak about it	11
	2: 9	worked…so that we might not burden any of you	9
	2:16	so that they may be saved.	4
	3: 3	so that no one would be shaken	1
	4:12	so that you may behave properly toward outsiders	4
	4:13	so that you may not grieve as others do	4
	5:10	who died for us, so that…we may live with him	4
2Th	1:12	so that the name of our Lord Jesus may be glorified	5
	2: 4	so that he takes his seat in the temple of God	11
	2: 6	so that he may be revealed when his time	3
	2:12	so that all who have not believed the truth	4
	2:14	so that you may obtain the glory of our Lord	3
	3: 1	so that the word of the Lord may spread rapidly	4
	3: 8	so that we might not burden any of you.	9
	3:14	so that they may be ashamed.	4
1Ti	1: 3	so that you may instruct certain people	4
	1:16	so that in me, as the foremost	4
	1:18	so that by following them you may fight the good fight	4
	1:20	so that they may learn not to blaspheme.	4
	2: 2	so that we may lead a quiet and peaceable life	4
	3: 7	so that he may not fall into disgrace	4
	3:14	I am writing these instructions to you so that	4
	4:15	so that all may see your progress.	4
	5: 7	so that they may be above reproach.	4
	5:16	so that it can assist those who are real widows.	4
	5:20	so that the rest also may stand in fear.	4
	6: 1	so that name of God…may not be blasphemed.	4
	6: 7	so that we can take nothing out of it;	7
	6:19	so that they may take hold of the life	4
2Ti	1: 4	I long to see you so that I may be filled with joy.	4
	2:10	so that they may also obtain the salvation	4
	3:17	so that everyone who belongs to God may be proficient	4
	4:17	so that…the message might be fully proclaimed	4
Tit	1: 5	so that you should put in order what remained	4
	1: 9	so that he may be able both to preach with sound doctrine	4
	1:13	so that they may become sound in the faith	4
	2: 4	so that they may encourage the young women	4
	2: 5	so that the word of God may not be discredited.	4
	2:10	so that in everything they may be an ornament	4
	3: 7	so that, having been justified by his grace,	4
	3: 8	so that those who have come to believe in God	4
	3:14	so that they may not be unproductive.	4
Phm	1:13	so that he might be of service to me in your place	4
	1:15	so that you might have him back forever	4
Heb	2: 9	so that by the grace of God he might taste death	5
	2:14	so that through death he might destroy the one	4
	2:17	so that he might be a merciful and faithful high priest	4
	3:13	so that none of you may be hardened	4
	4:11	so that no one may fall through such disobedience	4
	4:16	so that we may receive mercy and find grace	4
	6:12	so that you may not become sluggish	4
	6:18	so that through two unchangeable things	4
	9:13	sanctifies…so that their flesh is purified	9
	9:15	so that those who are called may receive	5
	10:36	so that when you have done the will of God	4
	11: 3	so that what is seen was made	3
	11: 5	so that he did not experience death;	1
	11:28	so that the destroyer…would not touch	4
	11:40	so that they would not…be made perfect.	4
	12: 3	so that you may not grow weary or lose heart.	4
	12:13	so that what is lame may not be put out of joint	4
	12:27	so that what cannot be shaken may remain.	4
	13:19	so that I may be restored to you very soon.	4
	13:21	so that you may do his will	3
Jas	1: 4	so that you may be mature and complete	4
	1:18	so that we would become a kind of first fruits	3
	5: 9	do not grumble…so that you may not be judged.	4
	5:12	so that you may not fall under condemnation.	4
	5:16	pray for one another, so that you may be healed.	5
1Pe	1: 7	so that the genuineness of your faith	4
	1:21	so that your faith and hope are set on God.	11
	1:22	so that you have genuine mutual love	3
	2: 2	so that by it you may grow into salvation	4
	2:12	so that, though they malign you as evildoers	4
	2:21	an example, so that you should follow in his steps.	4
	2:24	so that, free from sins, we might live for righteousness	4
	3: 1	so that, even if some of them do not obey the word	4

1Pe	3: 7 so that nothing may hinder your prayers.	3
	3:16 so that, when you are maligned	4
	4: 6 so that, though they had been judged in the flesh	4
	4:11 so that God may be glorified in all things	4
	4:13 so that you may also be glad and shout for joy	4
	5: 6 so that he may exalt you in due time.	4
2Pe	1: 4 promises, so that through them you may escape	4
	1:15 I will make every effort so that after my departure	1
1Jn	1: 3 so that you also may have fellowship with us;	4
	1: 4 writing these things so that our joy may be complete.	4
	2: 1 I am writing these things to you so that you may not sin.	4
	2:28 so that when he is revealed we may have confidence	4
	4: 9 so that we might live through him.	4
	5:13 so that you may know that you have eternal life.	4
	5:20 understanding so that we may know him who is true;	4
2Jn	1: 8 so that you do not lose what we have worked for	4
	1:12 so that our joy may be complete.	4
3Jn	1: 8 so that we may become co-workers with the truth.	4
Rev	2:10 throw…you into prison so that you may be tested	4
	2:14 they would eat food sacrificed to idols	1
	3:11 hold fast…so that no one may seize your crown.	4
	3:18 buy from me gold…so that you may be rich;	4
	3:18 salve to anoint your eyes so that you may see.	4
	5: 5 so that he can open the scroll and its seven seals."	1
	6: 4 so that people would slaughter one another;	4
	7: 1 so that no wind could blow on earth or sea	4
	8:12 so that a third of their light was darkened;	4
	11: 6 shut the sky, so that no rain may fall during the days	4
	12: 4 so that he might devour her child as…it was born.	4
	12: 6 prepared by God, so that there she can be nourished	4
	12:14 so that she could fly from the serpent	4
	13:15 so that the image of the beast could even speak	4
	13:17 so that no one…who does not have the mark	4
	18: 4 "Come out…so that you do not take part in her sins	4
	18: 4 "Come out…so that you do not share in her plagues;	4
	20: 3 so that he would deceive the nations no more	4
	22:14 so that they will have the right to the tree of life	4

so that not

1. μή + πώς, *mē + pōs, 3590 + 4803*
2. μήποτε, *mēpote, 3607*

Mat	4: 6 bear you up, so that you will not dash your foot	2
	13:15 so that they might not look with their eyes	2
Mrk	4:12 so that they may not turn again and be forgiven.' "	2
Lke	4:11 so that you will not dash your foot against a stone.' "	2
	21:34 so that your hearts are not weighed down	2
Act	28:27 so that they might not look with their eyes	2
2Co	2: 7 so that he may not be overwhelmed by excessive sorrow.	1
Heb	2: 1 so that we do not drift away from it.	2

so then

1. διό, *dio, 1475*
2. οὖν, *oun, 4036*
3. ὥστε, *hōste, 6063*

Rom	14: 8 so then, whether we live or whether we die,	2
1Co	7:38 So then, he who marries his fianc,e does well;	3
	11:33 So then…when you come together to eat	3
Gal	4:31 So then, friends, we are children, not of the slave	1
Eph	2:11 So then, remember that…	1
	4:25 So then, putting away falsehood	1

so-called

1. λέγω, *legō, 3306*

1Co	8: 5 even though there may be so-called gods in heaven	1
2Th	2: 4 every so-called god or object of worship	1

sober *See also* come to a sober mind, sober *judgment*

1. νήφω, *nēphō, 3768*
2. σωφροσύνη, *sōphrosynē, 5408*

Act	26:25 I am speaking the sober truth.	2
1Th	5: 6 let us keep awake and be sober;	1
	5: 8 since we belong to the day, let us be sober	1
2Ti	4: 5 As for you, always be sober, endure suffering	1

Sodom

1. Σόδομα, *Sodoma, 5047*

Mat	10:15 for the land of Sodom and Gomorrah	1
	11:23 had been done in Sodom, it would have remained	1
	11:24 it will be more tolerable for the land of Sodom	1
Lke	10:12 on that day it will be more tolerable for Sodom	1

	17:29 on the day that Lot left Sodom	1
Rom	9:29 we would have fared like Sodom	1
2Pe	2: 6 turning the cities of Sodom and Gomorrah to ashes	1
Jde	1: 7 Sodom and Gomorrah and the surrounding cities	1
Rev	11: 8 city that is prophetically called Sodom	1

sodomite

1. ἀρσενοκοίτης, *arsenokoitēs, 780*

1Co	6: 9 adulterers, male prostitutes, sodomites,	1
1Ti	1:10 fornicators, sodomites, slave traders, liars	1

soft

1. μαλακός, *malakos, 3434*

Lke	7:25 Someone dressed in soft robes?	1

soft robe

1. μαλακός, *malakos, 3434*

Mat	11: 8 to see? Someone dressed in soft robes?	1
	11: 8 those who wear soft robes are in royal palaces.	1

soil

1. γῆ, *gē, 1178*
2. μολύνω, *molynō, 3662*

Mat	13: 5 where they did not have much soil	1
	13: 5 since they had no depth of soil.	1
	13: 8 Other seeds fell on good soil	1
	13:23 as for what was sown on good soil	1
Mrk	4: 5 where it did not have much soil	1
	4: 5 since it had no depth of soil.	1
	4: 8 Other seed fell into good soil	1
	4:20 these are the ones sown on the good soil:	1
Lke	8: 8 Some fell into good soil, and when it grew	1
	8:15 as for that in the good soil	1
	13: 7 Cut it down! Why should it be wasting the soil?'	1
	14:35 fit neither for the soil nor for the manure pile;	1
Rev	3: 4 who have not soiled their clothes;	2

soldier *See also* detachment of soldiers, guard of soldiers

1. Contextual: Not in Greek
2. σπεῖρα, *speira, 5061*
3. στράτευμα, *strateuma, 5128*
4. στρατεύομαι, *strateuomai, 5129*
5. στρατιώτης, *stratiōtēs, 5132*

Mat	8: 9 a man under authority, with soldiers under me;	5
	27:27 Then the soldiers of the governor took Jesus	5
	28:12 to give a large sum of money to the soldiers	5
Mrk	15:16 soldiers led him into the courtyard of the palace	5
Lke	3:14 Soldiers also asked him	4
	7: 8 set under authority, with soldiers under me;	5
	23:11 Herod with his soldiers	3
	23:36 The soldiers also mocked him	5
Jhn	18:12 So the soldiers…arrested Jesus	2
	19: 2 the soldiers wove a crown of thorns	5
	19:23 When the soldiers had crucified Jesus	5
	19:23 into four parts, one for each soldier.	5
	19:25 And that is what the soldiers did.	5
	19:32 the soldiers came and broke the legs of the first	5
	19:34 Instead, one of the soldiers pierced his side	5
Act	10: 7 called two of his slaves and a devout soldier	5
	12: 4 four squads of soldiers to guard him	5
	12: 6 Peter…was sleeping between two soldiers	5
	12:18 there was no small commotion among the soldiers	5
	21:32 Immediately he took soldiers and centurions	5
	21:32 When they saw the tribune and the soldiers	5
	21:35 he had to be carried by the soldiers.	5
	23:10 the tribune…ordered the soldiers to go down	3
	23:23 two hundred soldiers, seventy horsemen	5
	23:31 So the soldiers…took Paul	5
	27:31 Paul said to the centurion and the soldiers	5
	27:32 Then the soldiers cut away the ropes of the boat	5
	27:42 The soldiers' plan was to kill the prisoners	5
	28:16 with the soldier who was guarding him.	5
2Ti	2: 3 like a good soldier of Christ Jesus.	5
	2: 4 the soldier's aim is to please the enlisting officer.	1

fellow soldier

1. συστρατιώτης, *systratiōtēs, 5369*

Php	2:25 my brother and co-worker and fellow soldier	1
Phm	1: 2 Apphia our sister, to Archippus our fellow soldier	1

soldier of the guard

1. σπεκουλάτωρ, *spekoulatōr, 5063*

Mrk 6:27 Immediately the king sent a soldier of the guard   1

great solemnity

1. μέγας, *megas, 3489*

Jhn 19:31 because that sabbath was a day of great solemnity.   1

solemnly *See also* command solemnly, urge solemnly, warn solemnly

1. πολύς, *polys, 4498*

Mrk 6:23 he solemnly swore to her, "Whatever you ask me   1

solid

1. στερεός, *stereos, 5104*

Heb 5:12 You need milk, not solid food;   1
 5:14 solid food is for the mature   1

solid food

1. Contextual: Not in Greek
2. βρῶμα, *brōma, 1109*

1Co 3: 2 I fed you with milk, not solid food   2
 3: 2 for you were not ready for solid food.   1

Solomon

1. Σολομών, *Solomōn, 5048*

Mat 1: 6 David was the father of Solomon by the wife   1
 1: 7 Solomon the father of Rehoboam   1
 6:29 even Solomon in all his glory was not clothed   1
 12:42 to listen to the wisdom of Solomon   1
 12:42 see, something greater than Solomon is here!   1
Lke 11:31 to listen to the wisdom of Solomon   1
 11:31 see, something greater than Solomon is here!   1
 12:27 even Solomon in all his glory was not clothed   1
Jhn 10:23 in the temple, in the portico of Solomon.   1
Act 3:11 in the portico called Solomon's Portico   1
 5:12 they were all together in Solomon's Portico.   1
 7:47 it was Solomon who built a house for him.   1

some *See also* some *point*

1. Contextual: Not in Greek
2. ἄλλος, *allos, 257*
3. ἀνήρ, *anēr, 467*
4. ἀπό, *apo, 608*
5. δέ, *de, 1254*
6. εἷς, *heis, 1651*
7. ἐκ, *ek, 1666*
8. ἕτερος, *heteros, 2283*
9. ἱκανός, *hikanos, 2653*
10. μέν, *men, 3525*
11. ὁ, *ho, 3836*
12. ὀλίγος, *oligos, 3900*
13. ὅς, *hos, 4005*
14. οὐ + ὀλίγος, *ou + oligos, 4024 + 3900*
15. πολύς, *polys, 4498*
16. τὶς, *tis, 5516*
17. ὡς, *hōs, 6055*

Mat 8:30 was feeding at some distance from them.   1
 9: 2 just then some people were carrying a paralyzed   1
 9: 3 Then some of the scribes said to themselves   16
 12:38 Then some of the scribes and Pharisees said   16
 13: 4 as he sowed, some seeds fell on the path   13
 13: 8 some a hundredfold, some sixty, some thirty   13
 13: 8 some a hundredfold, some sixty, some thirty   13
 13: 8 some a hundredfold, some sixty, some thirty   13
 16:14 "Some say John the Baptist, but others Elijah   11
 16:28 Truly I tell you, there are some standing here   16
 19: 3 Some Pharisees came to him, and to test him   1
 22:23 The same day some Sadducees came to him   1
 23:34 some of whom you will kill and crucify   7
 23:34 some you will flog in your synagogues   7
 25: 8 'Give us some of your oil   7
 25: 9 go to the dealers and buy some for yourselves.'   1
 26:67 some slapped him   11
 27: 9 some of the people of Israel had set a price   4
 27:24 took some water and washed his hands   1
 27:29 twisting some thorns into a crown, they put it   1
 27:47 some of the bystanders heard it, they said   16

 28:11 some of the guard went into the city   16
 28:17 they worshiped him; but some doubted.   11
Mrk 2: 1 When he returned to Capernaum after some days   1
 2: 3 some people came, bringing to him a paralyzed   1
 2: 6 Now some of the scribes were sitting there   16
 2:26 he gave some to his companions."   1
 4: 4 as he sowed, some seed fell on the path   13
 5:35 some people came from the leader's house   1
 6:14 Some were saying, "John the baptizer has been   1
 7: 1 some of the scribes who had come from Jerusalem   16
 7: 2 noticed that some of his disciples were eating   16
 8: 3 some of them have come from a great distance."   16
 8:22 Some people brought a blind man to him   1
 9: 1 some standing here who will not taste death   16
 9:14 some scribes arguing with them.   1
 10: 2 Some Pharisees came, and to test him they asked   1
 11: 5 some of the bystanders said to them   16
 12: 5 some they beat, and others they killed.   13
 12:13 some Pharisees and some Herodians   16
 12:13 some Pharisees and some Herodians   1
 12:18 Some Sadducees, who say there is no resurrection   1
 14: 4 some were there who said to one another in anger   16
 14:57 Some stood up and gave false testimony against him   16
 14:65 Some began to spit on him, to blindfold him   16
 15:17 twisting some thorns into a crown, they put it on him.   1
 15:35 some of the bystanders heard it, they said,   16
Lke 5:18 some men came, carrying a paralyzed man on a bed.   1
 6: 1 his disciples plucked some heads of grain   11
 6: 2 some of the Pharisees said, "Why are you doing   16
 6: 4 gave some to his companions?"   1
 7: 3 he sent some Jewish elders to him   1
 8: 2 as well as some women who had been cured   16
 8: 5 as he sowed, some fell on the path   13
 8: 6 Some fell on the rock;   8
 8: 7 Some fell among thorns   8
 8: 8 Some fell into good soil, and when it grew   8
 9: 7 it was said by some that John had been raised   16
 9: 8 by some that Elijah had appeared   16
 9:27 some standing here who will not taste death   16
 11:15 some of them said, "He casts out demons   16
 11:49 some of whom they will kill and persecute,'   7
 13: 1 At that very time there were some present   16
 13:30 Indeed, some are last who will be first   1
 13:30 some are first who will be last."   1
 13:31 At that very hour some Pharisees came and said   16
 18: 9 to some who trusted in themselves   16
 19:39 Some of the Pharisees in the crowd said   16
 20:27 Some Sadducees…came to him   16
 20:39 some of the scribes answered, "Teacher   16
 21: 5 When some were speaking about the temple   16
 21:16 they will put some of you to death.   7
 23: 8 was hoping to see him perform some sign.   16
 23: 9 He questioned him at some length   9
 24:22 Moreover, some women of our group astounded us.   16
 24:24 Some of those who were with us went to the tomb   16
Jhn 2: 8 draw some out, and take it to the chief steward."   1
 3:22 he spent some time there with them and baptized.   1
 6:23 Then some boats from Tiberias came near the place   1
 6:64 among you there are some who do not believe."   16
 7:12 While some were saying, "He is a good man,"   11
 7:25 Now some of the people of Jerusalem were saying   16
 7:40 some in the crowd said   7
 7:41 But some asked, "Surely the Messiah does not   11
 7:44 Some of them wanted to arrest him   16
 8: 6 might have some charge to bring against him.   1
 9: 9 Some were saying, "It is he."   2
 9:16 Some of the Pharisees said   16
 9:40 Some of the Pharisees near him heard this   7
 11:18 Bethany was near Jerusalem, some two miles away   17
 11:37 some of them said, "Could not he   16
 11:46 some of them went to the Pharisees   16
 12:20 among those who went up…were some Greeks.   16
 13:29 Some thought that…Jesus was telling him   16
 16:17 some of his disciples said to one another   7
 21: 6 you will find some.   1
 21: 7 he put on some clothes, for he was naked   1
 21:10 "Bring some of the fish that you have just caught."   4
Act 5: 2 he kept back some of the proceeds   4
 5:15 shadow might fall on some of them as he came by.   16
 5:36 For some time ago Theudas rose up   1
 6: 9 Then some of those who belonged to the synagogue   16

Act	6:11	Then they secretly instigated some men to say	1
	7:26	he came to some of them as they were quarreling	1
	8:36	they came to some water;	16
	9:19	taking some food, he regained his strength.	1
	9:23	After some time had passed	9
	9:43	in Joppa for some time with a certain Simon, a tanner.	9
	10:23	some of the believers from Joppa accompanied him.	16
	11:20	among them were some men of Cyprus and Cyrene	16
	12: 1	King Herod laid violent hands upon some	16
	14: 4	some sided with the Jews	11
	14: 4	some with the apostles.	11
	14:28	stayed there with the disciples for some time.	14
	15: 2	Paul and Barnabas and some of the others	16
	15: 5	some believers…stood up and said	16
	15:33	After they had been there for some time	1
	15:36	After some days Paul said to Barnabas, "Come	16
	16:12	We remained in this city for some days.	16
	17: 4	Some of them were persuaded	16
	17: 5	help of some ruffians in the marketplaces	16
	17: 6	they dragged Jason and some believers before	16
	17:18	some Epicurean and Stoic philosophers debated	16
	17:18	Some said, "What does this babbler want to say?"	16
	17:28	as even some of your own poets have said	16
	17:32	some scoffed; but others said, "We will hear you	11
	17:34	some of them joined him and became believers	16
	18:23	After spending some time there he departed	16
	19: 1	Ephesus, where he found some disciples.	16
	19: 9	When some stubbornly refused to believe	16
	19:13	Then some itinerant Jewish exorcists	16
	19:22	he himself stayed for some time longer in Asia.	1
	19:31	even some officials of the province of Asia,	16
	19:32	Meanwhile, some were shouting one thing,	2
	19:32	some were shouting one thing, some another;	1
	19:33	Some of the crowd gave instructions to Alexander	7
	20:30	Some even from your own group will come	3
	21:16	Some of the disciples from Caesarea also came	1
	21:34	Some in the crowd shouted one thing, some another;	2
	21:34	Some in the crowd shouted one thing, some another;	1
	23: 6	some were Sadducees and others were Pharisees	6
	24: 1	the high priest Ananias came down with some elders	16
	24:17	after some years I came to bring alms to my nation	15
	24:19	there were some Jews from Asia	16
	24:23	but to let him have some liberty	1
	24:24	Some days later when Felix came with his wife	16
	27: 1	Paul and some other prisoners	16
	27:26	we will have to run aground on some island."	16
	27:33	Paul urged all of them to take some food, saying	1
	27:34	Therefore I urge you to take some food	1
	27:44	some on planks and others on pieces of the ship.	13
	28:24	Some were convinced by what he had said	11
Rom	1:11	so that I may share with you some spiritual gift	16
	1:13	in order that I may reap some harvest among you	16
	3: 3	What if some were unfaithful?	16
	11:14	to make…jealous, and thus save some of them.	16
	11:17	But if some of the branches were broken off	16
	14: 2	Some believe in eating anything	13
	14: 5	Some judge one day to be better than another	13
1Co	4:18	some of you…have become arrogant.	16
	6:11	what some of you used to be.	16
	8: 7	some have become so accustomed to idols until now	16
	9:22	that I might by all means save some.	16
	10: 7	Do not become idolaters as some of them did;	16
	10: 8	not indulge in sexual immorality as some of them	16
	10: 9	We must not put Christ to the test, as some	16
	10:10	not complain as some of them did	16
	11:18	to some extent I believe it.	16
	11:30	many of you are weak and ill, and some have died.	9
	14: 6	I speak to you in some revelation or knowledge	1
	15: 6	though some have died.	16
	15:12	how can some of you say there is no resurrection	16
	15:37	perhaps of wheat or of some other grain.	16
	16: 7	I hope to spend some time with you	16
2Co	2: 5	to some extent—not to exaggerate it	4
	3: 1	do not need, as some do, letters of recommendation	16
	9: 4	if some Macedonians come with me and find	1
	10:12	classify or compare ourselves with some of those	16
Gal	1: 7	there are some who are confusing you	16
Eph	4:11	he gave were that some would be apostles	10
	4:11	some prophets, some evangelists	5
	4:11	some prophets, some evangelists	5
	4:11	some evangelists, some pastors and teachers	5

Php	1:15	Some proclaim Christ from envy and rivalry	16
2Th	3:11	we hear that some of you are living in idleness	16
1Ti	4: 1	in later times some will renounce the faith	16
	4: 8	for, while physical training is of some value	12
	5: 4	and make some repayment to their parents;	1
	5:15	For some have already turned away to follow Satan.	16
	5:24	The sins of some people are conspicuous	16
	6:10	some have wandered away from the faith	16
	6:21	some have missed the mark as regards the faith.	16
2Ti	2:18	They are upsetting the faith of some.	16
	2:20	some for special use, some for ordinary.	13
	2:20	some for special use, some for ordinary.	13
Heb	4: 6	Since therefore it remains open for some to enter it	16
	10:25	as is the habit of some	16
	13: 2	by doing that some have entertained angels	16
1Pe	3: 1	even if some of them do not obey the word,	16
2Pe	3: 9	The Lord is not slow…as some think of slowness	16
2Jn	1: 4	to find some of your children walking in the truth	7
3Jn	1: 3	I was overjoyed when some of the friends arrived	1
Jde	1:22	And have mercy on some who are wavering;	13
Rev	2:10	devil is about to throw some of you into prison	7
	2:14	some there who hold to the teaching of Balaam	1
	2:15	some who hold to the teaching of the Nicolaitans.	1
	2:17	To everyone who conquers I will give some…manna	1
	2:24	learned what some call 'the deep things of Satan,'	1

some person

1. τὶς, *tis, 5516*

Rom	3: 8	(as some people slander us by saying that we say)	1
1Co	15:34	for some people have no knowledge of God.	1
1Ti	1: 6	Some people have deviated from these	1

some things

1. τὶς, *tis, 5516*

2Pe	3:16	There are some things in them hard to understand	1

some time

1. πάλαι, *palai, 4093*

Mrk	15:44	whether he had been dead for some time.	1

somebody

1. τὶς, *tis, 5516*

Act	5:36	Theudas rose up, claiming to be somebody	1

somehow

1. εἰ + πώς, *ei + pōs, 1623 + 4803*
2. πώς, *pōs, 4803*

Act	27:12	somehow they could reach Phoenix	2
Rom	1:10	by God's will I may somehow at last succeed	1
1Co	8: 9	become a stumbling block to the weak.	2
Php	3:11	if somehow I may attain the resurrection	2
1Th	3: 5	somehow the tempter had tempted you	2

someone

1. Contextual: Not in Greek
2. ἄνθρωπος, *anthrōpos, 476*
3. εἷς, *heis, 1651*
4. ὁ, *ho, 3836*
5. ὅς, *hos, 4005*
6. πᾶς, *pas, 4246*
7. τὶς, *tis, 5516*

Mat	11: 8	to see? Someone dressed in soft robes?	2
	12:47	Someone told him, "Look, your mother	7
	13:24	someone who sowed good seed in his field;	2
	13:31	that someone took and sowed in his field;	2
	13:44	which someone found and hid;	2
	19:16	someone came to him and said,	3
	19:24	than for someone who is rich to enter the kingdom	1
Mrk	4:26	as if someone would scatter seed on the ground	2
	9:17	Someone from the crowd answered him, "Teacher	3
	9:38	we saw someone casting out demons in your name	7
	10:25	than for someone who is rich to enter the kingdom	1
	15:36	someone ran, filled a sponge with sour wine	7
Lke	6:47	someone is like who comes to me, hears my words	6
	7:25	Someone dressed in soft robes?	2
	8:46	Jesus said, "Someone touched me;	7
	8:49	someone came from the leader's house to say,	7
	9:49	we saw someone casting out demons in your name	7
	9:57	going along the road, someone said to him	7

	12:13	Someone in the crowd said to him, "Teacher	7
	13:19	It is like a mustard seed that someone took	2
	13:23	Someone asked him, "Lord	7
	14: 8	you are invited by someone to a wedding banquet	7
	14: 8	in case someone more distinguished than you	1
	14:16	"Someone gave a great dinner and invited many.	2
	16:30	if someone goes to them from the dead	7
	16:31	if someone rises from the dead.' "	7
	18:25	easier for a camel…than for someone who is rich	1
Jhn	9: 9	were saying, "No, but it is someone like him."	1
	18:39	I release someone for you at the Passover.	3
Act	4: 9	because of a good deed done to someone who was sick	1
	5:25	Then someone arrived and announced, "Look,	7
	8: 9	saying that he was someone great.	7
	8:31	He replied, "How can I, unless someone guides me?"	7
	8:34	does the prophet say this…about someone else?"	7
	13:41	never believe, even if someone tells you.' "	7
Rom	5: 7	perhaps for a good person someone might…die.	7
	10:14	how are they to hear without someone to proclaim	1
1Co	7:37	someone stands firm in his resolve	5
	10:28	if someone says to you	7
	14: 5	unless someone interprets, so that the church	1
	15:35	someone will ask, "How are the dead raised?	7
2Co	11: 4	For if someone comes and proclaims another Jesus	4
	11:20	put up with it when someone makes slaves of you	7
1Ti	3: 5	if someone does not know how to manage his own	7
Tit	1: 6	someone who is blameless, married only once,	7
Heb	2: 6	But someone has testified somewhere,	7
	3: 4	(For every house is built by someone	7
	5:12	you need someone to teach you again	7
	6:16	Human beings…swear by someone greater than themselves	4
	11:19	God is able even to raise someone from the dead	1
Jas	2:18	someone will say, "You have faith and I have works."	7
1Pe	5: 8	the devil prowls…looking for someone to devour.	7
Rev	9: 5	the torture of a scorpion when it stings someone.	2

someone else

1. ἄλλος, *allos, 257*
2. ἀλλότριος, *allotrios, 259*
3. ἕτερος, *heteros, 2283*

Lke	22:58	A little later someone else, on seeing him, said	3
Jhn	5: 7	my way, someone else steps down ahead of me."	1
	21:18	someone else will fasten a belt around you	1
Rom	15:20	so that I do not build on someone else's foundation	2
1Co	3:10	someone else is building on it.	1
	10:29	subject to the judgment of someone else's conscience?	1
	14:30	If a revelation is made to someone else sitting	1
2Co	10:16	work already done in someone else's sphere of action.	2

someone to lead by the hand

1. χειραγωγός, *cheiragōgos, 5933*

Act	13:11	groping for someone to lead him by the hand.	1

something

1. Contextual: Not in Greek
2. ὁ, *ho, 3836*
3. σκεῦος, *skeuos, 5007*
4. τίς, *tis, 5515*
5. τὶς, *tis, 5516*

Mat	5:23	that your brother or sister has something against you	5
	12: 6	something greater than the temple is here.	1
	12:41	see, something greater than Jonah is here!	1
	12:42	see, something greater than Solomon is here!	1
	14:16	you give them something to eat."	1
	25:35	I was thirsty and you gave me something to drink	1
	25:37	or thirsty and gave you something to drink?	1
Mrk	5:43	and told them to give her something to eat.	1
	6:36	buy something for themselves to eat."	4
	6:37	he answered them, "You give them something to eat."	1
Lke	7:40	"Simon, I have something to say to you."	5
	8:55	he directed them to give her something	1
	9:13	he said to them, "You give them something to eat."	1
	11:31	see, something greater than Solomon is here!	1
	11:32	see, something greater than Jonah is here!	1
	11:54	to catch him in something he might say.	5
Jhn	4:31	were urging him, "Rabbi, eat something."	1
	4:33	no one has brought him something to eat?"	1
	13:29	that he should give something to the poor.	5
Act	3: 5	expecting to receive something from them.	5
	9:18	something like scales fell from his eyes	1

	10:10	He became hungry and wanted something to eat;	1
	10:11	and something like a large sheet coming down	3
	11: 5	There was something like a large sheet coming down	3
	17:21	telling or hearing something new.	5
	21:37	"May I say something to you?"	5
	23:17	he has something to report to him."	5
	23:18	he has something to tell you."	5
	25:11	committed something for which I deserve to die	5
	25:26	I may have something to write	4
Rom	2:28	nor is true circumcision something external	2
	4: 4	wages are not reckoned as a gift but as something due.	1
	9:10	Nor is that all; something similar happened	1
	12:20	how are they to hear without someone to proclaim	1
1Co	8: 2	Anyone who claims to know something	1
	11: 4	prays or prophesies with something on his head	1
2Co	8:10	who began last year not only to do something	1
	8:10	but even to desire to do something	1
Gal	6: 3	if those who are nothing think they are something	5
Eph	4:28	so as to have something to share with the needy.	1
Heb	8: 3	necessary…also to have something to offer.	5
	10:34	possessed something better and more lasting.	1
	11:40	since God had provided something better	5
	12:18	You have not come to something that can be touched	1
Jas	4: 2	You want something and do not have it;	1
	4: 2	you covet something and cannot obtain it;	1
3Jn	1: 9	I have written something to the church;	5
Rev	4: 6	in front of the throne there is something like a sea	1
	8: 8	something like a great mountain, burning	1

something strange

1. ξένος, *xenos, 3828*

1Pe	4:12	as though something strange were happening	1

something to boast about

1. καύχημα, *kauchēma, 3017*

Rom	4: 2	he has something to boast about	1

something to exploit

1. ἁρπαγμός, *harpagmos, 772*

Php	2: 6	equality with God as something to be exploited	1

sometimes

1. οὗτος, *houtos, 4047*

Heb	10:33	sometimes being publicly exposed to abuse	1
	10:33	sometimes being partners with those so treated.	1

somewhat

1. τὶς, *tis, 5516*

2Co	7:14	For if I have been somewhat boastful about you	1

somewhere

1. πού, *pou, 4543*

Heb	2: 6	But someone has testified somewhere,	1

son

1. Contextual: Not in Greek
2. ὁ, *ho, 3836*
3. τέκνον, *teknon, 5451*
4. υἱός, *huios, 5626*

Mat	1: 1	Jesus the Messiah, the son of David, the son of Abraham.	4
	1: 1	Jesus the Messiah, the son of David, the son of Abraham.	4
	1:20	said, "Joseph, son of David, do not be afraid	4
	1:21	She will bear a son, and you are to name him	4
	1:23	"Look, the virgin shall conceive and bear a son	4
	1:25	she had borne a son; and he named him Jesus.	4
	2:15	"Out of Egypt I have called my son."	4
	3:17	my Son, the Beloved, with whom I am well pleased."	4
	4: 3	"If you are the Son of God, command these stones	4
	4: 6	"If you are the Son of God, throw yourself down;	4
	4:21	James son of Zebedee and his brother John	2
	8:20	but the Son of Man has nowhere to lay his head."	4
	8:29	"What have you to do with us, Son of God?	4
	9: 2	"Take heart, son; your sins are forgiven."	3
	9: 6	you may know that the Son of Man has authority	4
	9:27	"Have mercy on us, Son of David!"	4
	10: 2	James son of Zebedee, and his brother John;	2
	10: 3	James son of Alphaeus, and Thaddaeus;	2
	10:23	before the Son of Man comes.	4
	10:37	and whoever loves son or daughter more than me	4

Mat	11:19	the Son of Man came eating and drinking	4
	11:27	and no one knows the Son except the Father	4
	11:27	and no one knows the Father except the Son	4
	11:27	anyone to whom the Son chooses to reveal him.	4
	12: 8	For the Son of Man is lord of the sabbath."	4
	12:23	"Can this be the Son of David?"	4
	12:32	Whoever speaks a word against the Son of Man	4
	12:40	the Son of Man will be in the heart of the earth.	4
	13:37	"The one who sows the good seed is the Son of Man;	4
	13:41	The Son of Man will send his angels	4
	13:55	Is not this the carpenter's son?	4
	14:33	"Truly you are the Son of God."	4
	15:22	"Have mercy on me, Lord, Son of David;	4
	16:13	"Who do people say that the Son of Man is?"	4
	16:16	"You are the Messiah, the Son of the living God."	4
	16:27	"For the Son of Man is to come with his angels	4
	16:28	before they see the Son of Man coming	4
	17: 5	"This is my Son, the Beloved;	4
	17: 9	until after the Son of Man has been raised	4
	17:12	the Son of Man is about to suffer at their hands."	4
	17:15	have mercy on my son, for he is an epileptic	4
	17:22	Son of Man is going to be betrayed into human hands	4
	19:28	when the Son of Man is seated on the throne	4
	20:18	the Son of Man will be handed over	4
	20:20	the mother of the sons of Zebedee came to him	4
	20:20	the mother…came to him with her sons	4
	20:21	"Declare that these two sons of mine will sit	4
	20:28	the Son of Man came not to be served but to serve	4
	20:30	"Lord, have mercy on us, Son of David!"	4
	20:31	"Have mercy on us, Lord, Son of David!"	4
	21: 9	shouting, "Hosanna to the Son of David!	4
	21:15	"Hosanna to the Son of David,"	4
	21:28	"What do you think? A man had two sons;	3
	21:28	'Son, go and work in the vineyard today.'	3
	21:37	Finally he sent his son to them, saying	4
	21:37	'They will respect my son.'	4
	21:38	the tenants saw the son, they said to themselves	4
	22: 2	to a king who gave a wedding banquet for his son.	4
	22:42	you think of the Messiah? Whose son is he?"	4
	22:42	They said to him, "The son of David."	2
	22:45	If David thus calls him Lord, how can he be his son?"	4
	23:35	to the blood of Zechariah son of Barachiah	4
	24:27	so will be the coming of the Son of Man.	4
	24:30	the sign of the Son of Man will appear in heaven	4
	24:30	'the Son of Man coming on the clouds of heaven'	4
	24:36	neither the angels of heaven, nor the Son	4
	24:37	so will be the coming of the Son of Man.	4
	24:39	so too will be the coming of the Son of Man.	4
	24:44	the Son of Man is coming at an unexpected hour.	4
	25:31	"When the Son of Man comes in his glory	4
	26: 2	the Son of Man will be handed over	4
	26:24	The Son of Man goes as it is written of him	4
	26:24	woe to that one by whom the Son of Man is betrayed!	4
	26:37	took with him Peter and the two sons of Zebedee	4
	26:45	Son of Man is betrayed into the hands of sinners.	4
	26:63	tell us if you are the Messiah, the Son of God."	4
	26:64	From now on you will see the Son of Man	4
	27:40	If you are the Son of God, come down	4
	27:43	for he said, 'I am God's Son.' "	4
	27:54	"Truly this man was God's Son!"	4
	27:56	the mother of the sons of Zebedee.	4
	28:19	Father and of the Son and of the Holy Spirit	4
Mrk	1: 1	Jesus Christ, the Son of God.	4
	1:11	from heaven, "You are my Son, the Beloved;	4
	1:19	he saw James son of Zebedee	2
	2: 5	"Son, your sins are forgiven."	3
	2:10	Son of Man has authority on earth to forgive sins"	4
	2:14	walking along, he saw Levi son of Alphaeus	2
	2:28	the Son of Man is lord even of the sabbath."	4
	3:11	"You are the Son of God!"	4
	3:17	James son of Zebedee	2
	3:17	the name Boanerges, that is, Sons of Thunder);	4
	3:18	and Thomas, and James son of Alphaeus	2
	5: 7	Jesus, Son of the Most High God?	4
	6: 3	Is not this the carpenter, the son of Mary	4
	8:31	the Son of Man must undergo great suffering,	4
	8:38	of them the Son of Man will also be ashamed	4
	9: 7	"This is my Son, the Beloved; listen to him!"	4
	9: 9	until after the Son of Man had risen	4
	9:12	How then is it written about the Son of Man	4
	9:17	I brought you my son; he has a spirit	4

	9:31	"The Son of Man is to be betrayed	4
	10:33	Son of Man will be handed over to the chief priests	4
	10:35	James and John, the sons of Zebedee, came forward	4
	10:45	Son of Man came not to be served but to serve	4
	10:46	Bartimaeus son of Timaeus, a blind beggar	4
	10:47	"Jesus, Son of David, have mercy on me!"	4
	10:48	"Son of David, have mercy on me!"	4
	12: 6	He had still one other, a beloved son.	4
	12: 6	'They will respect my son.'	4
	12:35	say that the Messiah is the son of David?	4
	12:37	calls him Lord; so how can he be his son?"	4
	13:26	they will see 'the Son of Man coming in clouds'	4
	13:32	nor the Son, but only the Father.	4
	14:21	For the Son of Man goes as it is written of him	4
	14:21	woe to that one by whom the Son of Man is betrayed!	4
	14:41	Son of Man is betrayed into the hands of sinners.	4
	14:61	the Messiah, the Son of the Blessed One?"	4
	14:62	"I am; and 'you will see the Son of Man	4
	15:39	he said, "Truly this man was God's Son!"	4
Lke	1:13	Your wife Elizabeth will bear you a son	4
	1:31	you will conceive in your womb and bear a son	4
	1:32	will be called the Son of the Most High	4
	1:35	will be holy; he will be called Son of God.	4
	1:36	Elizabeth in her old age has also conceived a son;	4
	1:57	and she bore a son.	4
	2: 7	she gave birth to her firstborn son	4
	3: 2	the word of God came to John son of Zechariah	4
	3:22	"You are my Son, the Beloved;	4
	3:23	was the son (as was thought) of Joseph	4
	3:23	Joseph son of Heli	2
	3:24	son of Matthat, son of Levi	2
	3:24	son of Matthat, son of Levi	2
	3:24	son of Matthat, son of Levi	2
	3:24	son of Melchi, son of Jannai, son of Joseph	2
	3:24	son of Melchi, son of Jannai, son of Joseph	2
	3:25	son of Mattathias, son of Amos	2
	3:25	son of Mattathias, son of Amos	2
	3:25	son of Nahum, son of Esli, son of Naggai	2
	3:25	son of Nahum, son of Esli, son of Naggai	2
	3:25	son of Nahum, son of Esli, son of Naggai	2
	3:26	son of Maath, son of Mattathias	2
	3:26	son of Maath, son of Mattathias	2
	3:26	son of Semein, son of Josech, son of Joda	2
	3:26	son of Semein, son of Josech, son of Joda	2
	3:26	son of Semein, son of Josech, son of Joda	2
	3:27	son of Joanan, son of Rhesa	2
	3:27	son of Joanan, son of Rhesa	2
	3:27	son of Zerubbabel, son of Shealtiel	2
	3:27	son of Zerubbabel, son of Shealtiel	2
	3:27	son of Shealtiel, son of Neri	2
	3:28	son of Melchi, son of Addi, son of Cosam	2
	3:28	son of Melchi, son of Addi, son of Cosam	2
	3:28	son of Melchi, son of Addi, son of Cosam	2
	3:28	son of Cosam, son of Elmadam, son of Er	2
	3:28	son of Cosam, son of Elmadam, son of Er	2
	3:29	son of Joshua, son of Eliezer	2
	3:29	son of Joshua, son of Eliezer	2
	3:29	son of Eliezer, son of Jorim, son of Matthat	2
	3:29	son of Eliezer, son of Jorim, son of Matthat	2
	3:29	son of Matthat, son of Levi	2
	3:30	son of Simeon, son of Judah	2
	3:30	son of Simeon, son of Judah	2
	3:30	son of Joseph, son of Jonam	2
	3:30	son of Joseph, son of Jonam	2
	3:30	son of Jonam, son of Eliakim	2
	3:31	son of Melea, son of Menna	2
	3:31	son of Melea, son of Menna	2
	3:31	son of Menna, son of Mattatha, son of Nathan	2
	3:31	son of Menna, son of Mattatha, son of Nathan	2
	3:31	son of Nathan, son of David	2
	3:32	son of Jesse, son of Obed, son of Boaz	2
	3:32	son of Jesse, son of Obed, son of Boaz	2
	3:32	son of Jesse, son of Obed, son of Boaz	2
	3:32	son of Boaz, son of Sala, son of Nahshon	2
	3:32	son of Boaz, son of Sala, son of Nahshon	2
	3:33	son of Amminadab, son of Admin	2
	3:33	son of Amminadab, son of Admin	2
	3:33	son of Arni, son of Hezron, son of Perez	2
	3:33	son of Arni, son of Hezron, son of Perez	2
	3:33	son of Hezron, son of Perez, son of Judah	2
	3:33	son of Hezron, son of Perez, son of Judah	2

3:34	son of Jacob, son of Isaac	2
3:34	son of Jacob, son of Isaac	2
3:34	son of Isaac, son of Abraham, son of Terah	2
3:34	son of Isaac, son of Abraham, son of Terah	2
3:34	son of Isaac, son of Abraham, son of Terah	2
3:35	son of Serug, son of Reu, son of Peleg	2
3:35	son of Serug, son of Reu, son of Peleg	2
3:35	son of Serug, son of Reu, son of Peleg	2
3:35	son of Peleg, son of Eber, son of Shelah	2
3:35	son of Peleg, son of Eber, son of Shelah	2
3:36	son of Cainan, son of Arphaxad	2
3:36	son of Cainan, son of Arphaxad	2
3:36	son of Shem, son of Noah, son of Lamech	2
3:36	son of Shem, son of Noah, son of Lamech	2
3:36	son of Shem, son of Noah, son of Lamech	2
3:37	son of Methuselah, son of Enoch	2
3:37	son of Methuselah, son of Enoch	2
3:37	son of Jared, son of Mahalaleel, son of Cainan,	2
3:37	son of Jared, son of Mahalaleel, son of Cainan,	2
3:37	son of Jared, son of Mahalaleel, son of Cainan,	2
3:38	son of Enos, son of Seth, son of Adam	2
3:38	son of Enos, son of Seth, son of Adam	2
3:38	son of Seth, son of Adam, son of God.	2
3:38	son of Seth, son of Adam, son of God.	2
4: 3	devil said to him, "If you are the Son of God	4
4: 9	saying to him, "If you are the Son of God	4
4:22	They said, "Is not this Joseph's son?"	4
4:41	"You are the Son of God!"	4
5:10	so also were James and John, sons of Zebedee	4
5:24	you may know that the Son of Man has authority	4
6: 5	"The Son of Man is lord of the sabbath."	4
6:15	and Thomas, and James son of Alphaeus	1
6:16	Judas son of James, and Judas Iscariot	1
6:22	revile you...on account of the Son of Man.	4
7:12	was his mother's only son, and she was a widow;	4
7:34	the Son of Man has come eating and drinking	4
8:28	Jesus, Son of the Most High God?	4
9:22	"The Son of Man must undergo great suffering,	4
9:26	of them the Son of Man will be ashamed	4
9:35	"This is my Son, my Chosen; listen to him!"	4
9:38	I beg you to look at my son; he is my only child.	4
9:41	Bring your son here."	4
9:44	The Son of Man is going to be betrayed	4
9:58	the Son of Man has nowhere to lay his head."	4
10:22	no one knows who the Son is except the Father	4
10:22	who the Father is except the Son	4
10:22	to whom the Son chooses to reveal him."	4
11:30	so the Son of Man will be to this generation.	4
12: 8	the Son of Man also will acknowledge	4
12:10	who speaks a word against the Son of Man	4
12:40	the Son of Man is coming at an unexpected hour."	4
12:53	father against son and son against father	4
12:53	father against son and son against father	4
15:11	Jesus said, "There was a man who had two sons.	4
15:13	few days later the younger son gathered all	4
15:19	I am no longer worthy to be called your son;	4
15:21	the son said to him, 'Father, I have sinned	4
15:21	I am no longer worthy to be called your son.'	4
15:24	this son of mine was dead and is alive again;	4
15:25	"Now his elder son was in the field;	4
15:30	when this son of yours came back	4
15:31	father said to him, 'Son, you are always with me	3
17:22	will long to see one of the days of the Son of Man	4
17:24	so will the Son of Man be in his day.	4
17:26	so too it will be in the days of the Son of Man.	4
17:30	on the day that the Son of Man is revealed.	4
18: 8	yet, when the Son of Man comes	4
18:31	everything that is written about the Son of Man	4
18:38	"Jesus, Son of David, have mercy on me!"	4
18:39	"Son of David, have mercy on me!"	4
19: 9	because he too is a son of Abraham.	4
19:10	For the Son of Man came to seek out and to save	4
20:13	I will send my beloved son;	4
20:41	"How can they say that the Messiah is David's son?	4
20:44	David thus calls him Lord; so how can he be his son?"	4
21:27	will see 'the Son of Man coming in a cloud'	4
21:36	to stand before the Son of Man."	4
22:22	the Son of Man is going as it has been determined	4
22:48	with a kiss that you are betraying the Son of Man?"	4
22:69	from now on the Son of Man will be seated	4
22:70	asked, "Are you, then, the Son of God?"	4

	24: 7	the Son of Man must be handed over	4
Jhn	1:34	testified that this is the Son of God."	4
	1:42	"You are Simon son of John.	4
	1:45	found him...Jesus son of Joseph from Nazareth."	4
	1:49	"Rabbi, you are the Son of God!	4
	1:51	ascending and descending upon the Son of Man."	4
	3:13	one who descended from heaven, the Son of Man.	4
	3:14	so must the Son of Man be lifted up	4
	3:16	God so loved the world that he gave his only Son	4
	3:17	"Indeed, God did not send the Son into the world	4
	3:18	not believed in the name of the only Son of God.	4
	3:35	The Father loves the Son and has placed all things	4
	3:36	Whoever believes in the Son has eternal life;	4
	3:36	whoever disobeys the Son will not see life	4
	4: 5	ground that Jacob had given to his son Joseph.	4
	4:12	with his sons and his flocks drank from it?"	4
	4:46	there was a royal official whose son lay ill	4
	4:47	and begged him to come down and heal his son	4
	4:50	Jesus said to him, "Go; your son will live."	4
	4:53	Jesus had said to him, "Your son will live."	4
	5:19	the Son can do nothing on his own	4
	5:19	whatever the Father does, the Son does likewise.	4
	5:20	The Father loves the Son	4
	5:21	so also the Son gives life to whomever he wishes.	4
	5:22	has given all judgment to the Son	4
	5:23	so that all may honor the Son	4
	5:23	Anyone who does not honor the Son	4
	5:25	the dead will hear the voice of the Son of God	4
	5:26	has granted the Son also to have life in himself;	4
	5:27	because he is the Son of Man.	4
	6:27	which the Son of Man will give you.	4
	6:40	all who see the Son and believe in him	4
	6:42	saying, "Is not this Jesus, the son of Joseph	4
	6:53	unless you eat the flesh of the Son of Man	4
	6:62	if you were to see the Son of Man ascending	4
	6:71	He was speaking of Judas son of Simon Iscariot	1
	8:28	"When you have lifted up the Son of Man	4
	8:35	the son has a place there forever.	4
	8:36	So if the Son makes you free, you will be free	4
	9:19	"Is this your son, who you say was born blind?	4
	9:20	parents answered, "We know that this is our son	4
	9:35	"Do you believe in the Son of Man?"	4
	10:36	blaspheming because I said, 'I am God's Son'?	4
	11: 4	so that the Son of God may be glorified	4
	11:27	I believe that you are the Messiah, the Son of God	4
	12:23	"The hour...for the Son of Man to be glorified.	4
	12:34	you say that the Son of Man must be lifted up?	4
	12:34	Who is this Son of Man?"	4
	13: 2	the heart of Judas son of Simon Iscariot	1
	13:26	he gave it to Judas son of Simon Iscariot.	1
	13:31	"Now the Son of Man has been glorified	4
	14:13	so that the Father may be glorified in the Son.	4
	17: 1	"Father, the hour has come; glorify your Son	4
	17: 1	glorify your Son so that the Son may glorify you	4
	19: 7	because he has claimed to be the Son of God."	4
	19:26	he said to his mother, "Woman, here is your son."	4
	20:31	Jesus is the Messiah, the Son of God	4
	21: 2	Nathanael of Cana in Galilee, the sons of Zebedee	2
	21:15	Jesus said to Simon Peter, "Simon son of John	1
	21:16	A second time he said to him, "Simon son of John	1
	21:17	"Simon son of John, do you love me?"	1
Act	1:13	James son of Alphaeus, and Simon the Zealot	1
	1:13	Simon the Zealot, and Judas son of James.	1
	2:17	your sons and your daughters shall prophesy	4
	4:36	Barnabas (which means "son of encouragement").	4
	7:16	bought...from the sons of Hamor in Shechem.	4
	7:21	and brought him up as her own son.	4
	7:29	Midian. There he became the father of two sons.	4
	7:56	the Son of Man standing at the right hand of God!"	4
	9:20	"He is the Son of God."	4
	13:10	said, "You son of the devil	4
	13:21	Saul son of Kish, a man of the tribe of Benjamin	4
	13:22	'I have found David, son of Jesse, to be a man	2
	13:33	'You are my Son; today I have begotten you.'	4
	16: 1	the son of a Jewish woman who was a believer;	4
	19:14	Seven sons of a Jewish high priest named Sceva	4
	20: 4	Sopater son of Pyrrhus from Beroea,	1
	20:28	that he obtained with the blood of his own Son.	1
	23: 6	"Brothers, I am a Pharisee, a son of Pharisees.	4
	23:16	the son of Paul's sister heard about the ambush;	4
Rom	1: 3	the gospel concerning his Son	4

Rom	1: 4	declared to be Son of God with power	4
	1: 9	I serve…by announcing the gospel of his Son	4
	5:10	reconciled to God through the death of his Son	4
	8: 3	his own Son in the likeness of sinful flesh	4
	8:29	to be conformed to the image of his Son	4
	8:32	He who did not withhold his own Son, but gave	4
	9: 9	I will return and Sarah shall have a son.”	4
1Co	1: 9	the fellowship of his Son, Jesus Christ our Lord.	4
	15:28	then the Son himself will also be subjected	4
2Co	1:19	the Son of God, Jesus Christ, whom we proclaimed	4
	6:18	be my sons and daughters, says the Lord Almighty.”	4
Gal	1:16	to reveal his Son to me	4
	2:20	I live by faith in the Son of God	4
	4: 4	God sent his Son, born of a woman,	4
	4: 6	God has sent the Spirit of his Son into our hearts	4
	4:22	For it is written that Abraham had two sons	4
Eph	4:13	the knowledge of the Son of God	4
Php	2:22	how like a son with a father he has served with me	3
Col	1:13	transferred us into the kingdom of his beloved Son	4
1Th	1:10	to wait for his Son from heaven	4
Heb	1: 2	in these last days he has spoken to us by a Son	4
	1: 5	“You are my Son; today I have begotten you”?	4
	1: 5	“I will be his Father, and he will be my Son”?	4
	1: 8	But of the Son he says, “Your throne, O God,	4
	3: 6	Christ, however, was faithful over God’s house as a son	4
	4:14	a great high priest…Jesus, the Son of God	4
	5: 5	“You are my Son; today I have begotten you”;	4
	5: 8	Although he was a Son, he learned obedience	4
	6: 6	on their own they are crucifying again the Son of God	4
	7: 3	resembling the Son of God, he remains a priest	4
	7:28	appoints a Son who has been made perfect forever.	4
	10:29	those who have spurned the Son of God	4
	11:21	Jacob…blessed each of the sons of Joseph	4
	11:24	refused to be called a son of Pharaoh’s daughter	4
Jas	2:21	when he offered his son Isaac on the altar?	4
1Pe	5:13	sends you greetings; and so does my son Mark.	4
2Pe	1:17	my Son, my Beloved, with whom I am well pleased.”	4
	2:15	the road of Balaam son of Bosor	2
1Jn	1: 3	with the Father and with his Son Jesus Christ.	4
	1: 7	blood of Jesus his Son cleanses us from all sin.	4
	2:22	the one who denies the Father and the Son.	4
	2:23	No one who denies the Son has the Father;	4
	2:23	everyone who confesses the Son has the Father also.	4
	2:24	then you will abide in the Son and in the Father.	4
	3: 8	The Son of God was revealed for this purpose	4
	3:23	believe in the name of his Son Jesus Christ	4
	4: 9	God sent his only Son into the world	4
	4:10	sent his Son to be the atoning sacrifice for our sins.	4
	4:14	Father has sent his Son as the Savior of the world.	4
	4:15	who confess that Jesus is the Son of God	4
	5: 5	the one who believes that Jesus is the Son of God?	4
	5: 9	that he has testified to his Son.	4
	5:10	Those who believe in the Son of God	4
	5:10	Those who believe in the Son of God	4
	5:11	eternal life, and this life is in his Son.	4
	5:12	Whoever has the Son has life;	4
	5:12	whoever does not have the Son of God does not have life.	4
	5:13	to you who believe in the name of the Son of God	4
	5:20	we know that the Son of God has come	4
	5:20	we are in him who is true, in his Son Jesus Christ.	4
2Jn	1: 3	and from Jesus Christ, the Father’s Son	4
	1: 9	whoever abides…has both the Father and the Son.	4
Rev	1:13	midst of the lampstands I saw one like the Son of Man	4
	2:18	words of the Son of God, who has eyes like a flame	4
	12: 5	she gave birth to a son, a male child, who is to rule	4
	14:14	seated on the cloud was one like the Son of Man	4

only son

1. μονογενής, *monogenēs, 3666*

Jhn	1:14	glory as of a father’s only son, full	1
	1:18	It is God the only Son, who is close to	1
Heb	11:17	Abraham…was ready to offer up his only son	1

son of Jonah

1. Βαριωνᾶ, *Bariōna, 980*

Mat	16:17	“Blessed are you, Simon son of Jonah!	1

song *See also* burst into song, sing songs of praise

1. ᾠδή, *ōdē, 6046*

Eph	5:19	and hymns and spiritual songs among yourselves	1

Col	3:16	sing psalms, hymns, and spiritual songs to God	1
Rev	5: 9	They sing a new song: “You are worthy	1
	14: 3	and they sing a new song before the throne	1
	14: 3	No one could learn that song except	1
	15: 3	they sing the song of Moses, the servant of God	1
	15: 3	the song of Moses…and the song of the Lamb:	1

soon

1. ἐγγύς, *engys, 1584*
2. ἐν + τάχος, *en + tachos, 1877 + 5443*
3. ἐξαυτῆς, *exautēs, 1994*
4. εὐθέως, *eutheōs, 2311*
5. μέλλω, *mellō, 3516*
6. μετά + οὐ + πολύς, *meta + ou + polys, 3552 + 4024 + 4498*
7. ταχέως, *tacheōs, 5441*
8. ταχινός, *tachinos, 5442*
9. ταχύς, *tachys, 5444*

Act	27:14	soon a violent wind, called the northeaster	6
1Co	4:19	I will come to you soon, if the Lord wills	7
Php	2:19	hope in the Lord Jesus to send Timothy to you soon	7
	2:23	as soon as I see how things go with me;	3
	2:24	I trust…that I will also come soon.	7
1Ti	3:14	I hope to come to you soon	2
2Ti	4: 9	Do your best to come to me soon	7
Heb	8:13	what is obsolete…will soon disappear.	1
2Pe	1:14	since I know that my death will come soon	8
3Jn	1:14	I hope to see you soon	4
Rev	1: 1	show his servants what must soon take place;	2
	2:16	If not, I will come to you soon and make war	9
	3:11	I am coming soon; hold fast to what you have	9
	6:11	who were soon to be killed as they themselves	5
	22: 6	to show his servants what must soon take place.”	2
	22: 7	“See, I am coming soon!	9
	22:12	“See, I am coming soon; my reward is with	9
	22:20	“Surely I am coming soon.” Amen. Come, Lord Jesus!	9

as soon as

1. Contextual: Not in Greek
2. εὐθέως, *eutheōs, 2311*
3. εὐθύς[1], *euthys[1], 2317*
4. ὅταν, *hotan, 4020*
5. ὅταν + ἤδη, *hotan + ēdē, 4020 + 2453*
6. ὡς, *hōs, 6055*
7. ὡς + ἄν, *hōs + an, 6055 + 323*

Mat	24:32	as soon as its branch becomes tender	5
Mrk	1:29	As soon as they left the synagogue	3
	13:28	as soon as its branch becomes tender	5
	15: 1	As soon as it was morning	3
Lke	1:44	as soon as I heard the sound of your greeting	6
	12:36	that they may open the door for him as soon as he comes	2
	21:30	as soon as they sprout leaves	5
Act	12:12	As soon as he realized this, he went to the house	1
Php	2:23	as soon as I see how things go with me;	7
Rev	12: 4	might devour her child as soon as it was born.	4

soon afterward

1. ταχύς, *tachys, 5444*

Mrk	9:39	will be able soon afterward to speak evil of me.	1

soon afterwards

1. ἑξῆς, *hexēs, 2009*
2. καθεξῆς, *kathexēs, 2759*

Lke	7:11	Soon afterwards he went to a town called Nain	1
	8: 1	Soon afterwards he went on through cities	2

soon as possible

1. ταχέως, *tacheōs, 5441*

Act	17:15	join him as soon as possible	1

very soon

1. ταχέως, *tacheōs, 5441*
2. ταχύς, *tachys, 5444*

Heb	13:19	so that I may be restored to you very soon.	1
Rev	11:14	The third woe is coming very soon.	2

Sopater

1. Σώπατρος, *Sōpatros, 5396*

Act	20: 4	Sopater son of Pyrrhus from Beroea,	1

sorcerer

1. φάρμακος, *pharmakos, 5761*

Rev	21: 8	the murderers, the fornicators, the sorcerers	1
	22:15	Outside are the dogs and sorcerers	1

sorcery

1. φαρμακεία, *pharmakeia, 5758*
2. φάρμακον, *pharmakon, 5760*

Gal	5:20	idolatry, sorcery, enmities, strife, jealousy, anger	1
Rev	9:21	And they did not repent of…their sorceries	2
	18:23	and all nations were deceived by your sorcery.	1

sordid *See also* sordid *gain*

1. αἰσχρός, *aischros, 156*

Tit	1:11	teaching for sordid gain	1

sordidness

1. ῥυπαρία, *rhyparia, 4864*

Jas	1:21	rid yourselves of all sordidness and rank growth	1

sore *See also* covered with sores

1. ἕλκος, *helkos, 1814*

Lke	16:21	even the dogs would come and lick his sores.	1
Rev	16: 2	and a foul and painful sore came on those	1
	16:11	cursed the God…because of their pains and sores	1

sorrow

1. λύπη, *lypē, 3383*

Jhn	16: 6	sorrow has filled your hearts.	1
Rom	9: 2	great sorrow and unceasing anguish in my heart.	1
2Co	2: 7	so that he may not be overwhelmed by excessive sorrow.	1
Php	2:27	so that I would not have one sorrow after another.	1

sorrowful

1. λυπέω, *lypeō, 3382*

2Co	6:10	as sorrowful, yet always rejoicing;	1

sort *See* what sort, what sort of person

Sosipater

1. Σωσίπατρος, *Sōsipatros, 5399*

Rom	16:21	so do Lucius and Jason and Sosipater, my relatives.	1

Sosthenes

1. Σωσθένης, *Sōsthenēs, 5398*

Act	18:17	seized Sosthenes, the official of the synagogue	1
1Co	1: 1	Paul…and our brother Sosthenes	1

soul

1. ψυχή, *psychē, 6034*

Mat	10:28	kill the body but cannot kill the soul;	1
	10:28	who can destroy both soul and body in hell.	1
	11:29	and you will find rest for your souls.	1
	12:18	my beloved, with whom my soul is well pleased.	1
	22:37	with all your heart, and with all your soul	1
Mrk	12:30	with all your soul, and with all your mind	1
Lke	1:46	Mary said, "My soul magnifies the Lord	1
	2:35	and a sword will pierce your own soul too."	1
	10:27	with all your soul, and with all your strength	1
	12:19	I will say to my soul, Soul, you have ample goods	1
	12:19	I will say to my soul, Soul, you have ample goods	1
	21:19	By your endurance you will gain your souls.	1
Jhn	12:27	"Now my soul is troubled. And what should I say	1
Act	2:27	you will not abandon my soul to Hades	1
	4:32	who believed were of one heart and soul	1
	14:22	strengthened the souls of the disciples	1
1Th	5:23	may your spirit and soul and body be kept sound	1
Heb	4:12	piercing until it divides soul from spirit	1
	6:19	hope, a sure and steadfast anchor of the soul	1
	10:38	My soul takes no pleasure in anyone who shrinks back."	1
	13:17	for they are keeping watch over your souls	1
Jas	1:21	implanted word that has the power to save your souls.	1
	5:20	will save the sinner's soul from death	1
1Pe	1: 9	outcome of your faith, the salvation of your souls.	1
	1:22	have purified your souls by your obedience	1
	2:11	desires…that wage war against the soul.	1
	2:25	the shepherd and guardian of your souls.	1
2Pe	2: 8	day after day, was tormented in his righteous soul	1

	2:14	They entice unsteady souls.	1
3Jn	1: 2	just as it is well with your soul.	1
Rev	6: 9	I saw under the altar the souls of those	1
	18:14	"The fruit for which your soul longed has gone	1
	20: 4	I also saw the souls of those who had been beheaded	1

sound[1] *See also* safe and sound

1. Contextual: Not in Greek
2. ἀκοή, *akoē, 198*
3. ἦχος[1], *ēchos[1], 2491*
4. λαλέω, *laleō, 3281*
5. φωνή, *phōnē, 5889*

Lke	1:44	as soon as I heard the sound of your greeting	5
Jhn	3: 8	The wind blows…and you hear the sound of it	5
Act	2: 2	suddenly from heaven there came a sound	3
	2: 6	at this sound the crowd gathered	5
	17:20	sounds rather strange to us	2
1Co	14: 7	with lifeless instruments that produce sound,	5
	14: 8	if the bugle gives an indistinct sound	5
	14:10	There are doubtless many different kinds of sounds	5
	14:11	If then I do not know the meaning of a sound	5
Heb	12:19	the sound of a trumpet	3
Rev	1:15	his voice was like the sound of many waters.	5
	10: 3	when he shouted, the seven thunders sounded.	4
	10: 4	when the seven thunders had sounded	4
	14: 2	a voice from heaven like the sound of many waters	5
	14: 2	a voice…like the sound of loud thunder;	5
	14: 2	like the sound of harpists playing on their harps	1
	18:22	and the sound of harpists and minstrels	5
	18:22	and the sound of the millstone will be heard	5
	19: 6	like the sound of many waters	5
	19: 6	like the sound of mighty thunderpeals, crying out	5

sound[2]

1. καλός, *kalos, 2819*
2. ὁλόκληρος, *holoklēros, 3908*
3. ὑγιαίνω, *hygiainō, 5617*
4. ὑγιής, *hygiēs, 5618*

Mat	12:13	and it was restored, as sound as the other.	4
1Th	5:23	may your spirit and soul and body be kept sound	2
1Ti	1:10	whatever else is contrary to the sound teaching	3
	4: 6	the sound teaching that you have followed.	1
	6: 3	does not agree with the sound words of our Lord	3
2Ti	1:13	sound teaching that you have heard from me	3
	4: 3	when people will not put up with sound doctrine	3
Tit	1: 9	be able both to preach with sound doctrine	3
	1:13	so that they may become sound in the faith	3
	2: 1	as for you, teach what is consistent with sound doctrine.	3
	2: 2	sound in faith, in love, and in endurance.	3
	2: 8	sound speech that cannot be censured;	4

sound a trumpet

1. σαλπίζω, *salpizō, 4895*

Mat	6: 2	you give alms, do not sound a trumpet before you	1
1Co	15:52	at the last trumpet. For the trumpet will sound	1

sound forth

1. ἐξηχέω, *exēcheō, 2010*

1Th	1: 8	the word of the Lord has sounded forth from you	1

sound of a trumpet

1. σάλπιγξ, *salpinx, 4894*

1Th	4:16	with the sound of God's trumpet, will descend	1

without sound

1. ἄφωνος, *aphōnos, 936*

1Co	14:10	and nothing is without sound.	1

sounding *See* take a sounding

sour *See* sour *wine*

source

1. Contextual: Not in Greek
2. αἴτιος, *aitios, 165*
3. ἐκ, *ek, 1666*

1Co	1:30	He is the source of your life in Christ Jesus	3
Gal	1:12	for I did not receive it from a human source	1
Heb	5: 9	he became the source of eternal salvation	2

south   *See also* south *wind*
1. μεσημβρία, *mesēmbria, 3540*
2. νότος, *notos, 3803*

Mat 12:42 The queen of the South will rise up at the judgment   2
Lke 11:31 The queen of the South will rise at the judgment   2
     13:29 come from east and west, from north and south   2
Act   8:26 "Get up and go toward the south   1
Rev 21:13 on the south three gates, and on the west   2

southwest
1. λίψ, *lips, 3355*

Act 27:12 a harbor of Crete, facing southwest and northwest.   1

sovereign   *See also* sovereign *Lord*
1. δυνάστης, *dynastēs, 1541*
2. κύριος, *kyrios, 3261*

Act 25:26 nothing definite to write to our sovereign about him.   2
1Ti   6:15 the blessed and only Sovereign   1

sow¹
1. Contextual: Not in Greek
2. βάλλω, *ballō, 965*
3. ἐπισπείρω, *epispeirō, 2178*
4. σπείρω, *speirō, 5062*

Mat   6:26 of the air; they neither sow nor reap nor gather   4
     13: 3 "Listen! A sower went out to sow.   4
     13: 4 as he sowed, some seeds fell on the path   4
     13:19 and snatches away what is sown in the heart;   4
     13:19 this is what was sown on the path.   4
     13:20 As for what was sown on rocky ground   4
     13:22 As for what was sown among thorns   4
     13:23 as for what was sown on good soil   4
     13:24 someone who sowed good seed in his field;   4
     13:25 an enemy came and sowed weeds among the wheat   3
     13:27 'Master, did you not sow good seed in your field?   4
     13:31 that someone took and sowed in his field;   4
     13:37 "The one who sows the good seed is the Son of Man;   4
     13:39 the enemy who sowed them is the devil;   4
     25:24 reaping where you did not sow   4
     25:26 You knew…that I reap where I did not sow   4
Mrk   4: 3 "Listen! A sower went out to sow.   4
     4: 4 as he sowed, some seed fell on the path   4
     4:14 The sower sows the word.   4
     4:15 the ones on the path where the word is sown: 4
     4:15 takes away the word that is sown in them.   4
     4:16 the ones sown on rocky ground: 4
     4:18 others are those sown among the thorns: 4
     4:20 these are the ones sown on the good soil: 4
     4:31 when sown upon the ground, is the smallest   4
     4:32 yet when it is sown it grows up   4
Lke   8: 5 "A sower went out to sow his seed;   4
     8: 5 as he sowed, some fell on the path   4
     12:24 Consider the ravens: they neither sow nor reap   4
     13:19 that someone took and sowed in the garden;   2
     19:21 reap what you did not sow.'   4
     19:22 reaping what I did not sow?   4
Jhn   4:37 'One sows and another reaps.'   4
1Co   9:11 If we have sown spiritual good among you   4
     15:36 What you sow does not come to life unless it dies.   4
     15:37 what you sow, you do not sow the body that is to be   4
     15:37 what you sow, you do not sow the body that is to be   4
     15:42 What is sown is perishable   4
     15:43 It is sown in dishonor, it is raised in glory.   4
     15:43 It is sown in weakness, it is raised in power.   4
     15:44 It is sown a physical body   4
2Co   9: 6 the one who sows sparingly will also reap sparingly   4
     9: 6 the one who sows bountifully will also reap   4
     9:10 supply and multiply your seed for sowing   1
Gal   6: 7 for you reap whatever you sow.   4
     6: 8 If you sow to your own flesh,   4
     6: 8 if you sow to the Spirit   4
Jas   3:18 a harvest of righteousness is sown in peace   4

sow²
1. ὗς, *hys, 5725*

2Pe   2:22 "The sow is washed only to wallow in the mud."   1

sower
1. σπείρω, *speirō, 5062*

Mat 13: 3 "Listen! A sower went out to sow.   1
     13:18 "Hear then the parable of the sower.   1
Mrk   4: 3 "Listen! A sower went out to sow.   1
     4:14 The sower sows the word.   1
Lke   8: 5 "A sower went out to sow his seed;   1
Jhn   4:36 so that sower and reaper may rejoice together.   1
2Co   9:10 supplies seed to the sower and bread for food   1

Spain
1. Σπανία, *Spania, 5056*

Rom 15:24 when I go to Spain. For I do hope to see you   1
     15:28 I will set out by way of you to Spain;   1

span of life
1. ἡλικία, *hēlikia, 2461*

Mat   6:27 by worrying add a single hour to your span of life?   1
Lke 12:25 add a single hour to your span of life?   1

spare   *See also* enough and to spare
1. φείδομαι, *pheidomai, 5767*

Act 20:29 savage wolves…not sparing the flock.   1
Rom 11:21 For if God did not spare the natural branches   1
     11:21 perhaps he will not spare you.   1
1Co   7:28 I would spare you that.   1
2Co   1:23 it was to spare you that I did not come again   1
2Pe   2: 4 if God did not spare the angels when they sinned   1
     2: 5 if he did not spare the ancient world   1

sparingly
1. φειδομένως, *pheidomenōs, 5768*

2Co   9: 6 the one who sows sparingly will also reap sparingly   1
     9: 6 the one who sows sparingly will also reap sparingly   1

sparrow
1. στρουθίον, *strouthion, 5141*

Mat 10:29 Are not two sparrows sold for a penny?   1
     10:31 you are of more value than many sparrows.   1
Lke 12: 6 Are not five sparrows sold for two pennies?   1
     12: 7 you are of more value than many sparrows.   1

speak   *See also* can not speak, unable to speak
1. Contextual: Not in Greek
2. ἀνοίγω + ὁ + στόμα, *anoigō + ho + stoma, 487 + 3836 + 5125*
3. ἄνοιξις + ὁ + στόμα, *anoixis + ho + stoma, 489 + 3836 + 5125*
4. ἀποκρίνομαι, *apokrinomai, 646*
5. ἀποφθέγγομαι, *apophthengomai, 710*
6. γίνομαι, *ginomai, 1181*
7. λαλέω, *laleō, 3281*
8. λέγω, *legō, 3306*
9. λόγος, *logos, 3364*
10. παρά, *para, 4123*
11. παρακαλέω, *parakaleō, 4151*
12. προσλαλέω, *proslaleō, 4688*
13. στόμα, *stoma, 5125*
14. φθέγγομαι, *phthengomai, 5779*

Mat   1:22 to fulfill what had been spoken by the Lord   8
     2:15 to fulfill what had been spoken by the Lord   8
     2:17 Then was fulfilled what had been spoken   8
     2:23 so that what had been spoken through the prophets   8
     3: 3 This is the one of whom the prophet Isaiah spoke   8
     4:14 so that what had been spoken through the prophet   8
     5: 2 he began to speak, and taught them, saying: 13
     8: 8 but only speak the word   8
     8:17 to fulfill what had been spoken through the prophet   8
     9:33 the one who had been mute spoke;   7
     10:19 do not worry about how you are to speak   7
     10:20 it is not you who speak, but the Spirit   7
     10:20 the Spirit of your Father speaking through you.   7
     11: 7 they went away, Jesus began to speak to the crowds   8
     12:17 to fulfill what had been spoken through the prophet   8
     12:22 so that the one who had been mute could speak and see.   7
     12:32 Whoever speaks a word against the Son of Man   8
     12:32 but whoever speaks against the Holy Spirit   8
     12:34 You brood of vipers! How can you speak good   7
     12:34 the abundance of the heart the mouth speaks.   7
     12:46 While he was still speaking to the crowds   7
     12:46 wanting to speak to him.   7

12:47 are standing outside, wanting to speak to you."	7	
13:10 "Why do you speak to them in parables?"	7	
13:13 The reason I speak to them in parables	7	
13:35 to fulfill what had been spoken through the prophet:	8	
13:35 "I will open my mouth to speak in parables;	1	
14:27 immediately Jesus spoke to them and said	7	
15:31 when they saw the mute speaking	7	
16:11 that I was not speaking about bread?	8	
17: 5 he was still speaking, suddenly a bright cloud	7	
17:13 he was speaking to them about John the Baptist.	8	
21: 4 to fulfill what had been spoken through the prophet	8	
21:45 they realized that he was speaking about them.	8	
22: 1 Once more Jesus spoke to them in parables, saying:	8	
24:15 as was spoken of by the prophet Daniel	8	
26:47 While he was still speaking, Judas…arrived;	7	
27: 9 what had been spoken through the prophet Jeremiah	8	

Mrk 1:34 he would not permit the demons to speak	7	
2: 2 he was speaking the word to them.	7	
2: 7 "Why does this fellow speak in this way?	7	
3:23 spoke to them in parables	8	
4:33 With many such parables he spoke the word	7	
4:34 he did not speak to them except in parables	7	
5:35 While he was still speaking	7	
6:50 But immediately he spoke to them and said	7	
7:35 tongue was released, and he spoke plainly.	7	
7:37 makes the deaf to hear and the mute to speak."	7	
12: 1 he began to speak to them in parables.	7	
13:11 it is not you who speak, but the Holy Spirit.	7	
14:43 while he was still speaking, Judas…arrived;	7	
15:12 Pilate spoke to them again, "Then what do you wish	4	
16:17 [they will speak in new tongues;]	7	
16:19 [the Lord Jesus, after he had spoken to them]	7	

Lke 1:19 I have been sent to speak to you	7	
1:20 you will become mute, unable to speak	7	
1:22 When he did come out, he could not speak to them	7	
1:45 fulfillment of what was spoken to her	7	
1:64 he began to speak, praising God.	7	
1:67 with the Holy Spirit and spoke this prophecy:	8	
1:70 as he spoke through the mouth of his holy prophets	7	
2:38 speak about the child to all	7	
4:32 because he spoke with authority.	9	
4:41 would not allow them to speak	7	
5: 4 When he had finished speaking, he said to Simon	7	
5:21 "Who is this who is speaking blasphemies?	7	
6:26 "Woe to you when all speak well of you	8	
6:45 the mouth speaks.	7	
7: 7 speak the word, and let my servant be healed.	8	
7:15 The dead man sat up and began to speak	7	
7:24 Jesus began to speak to the crowds about John:	8	
7:40 "Teacher," he replied, "speak."	8	
8:10 to others I speak in parables	1	
8:49 While he was still speaking	7	
9:11 and spoke to them about the kingdom of God	7	
9:31 They appeared in glory and were speaking	8	
9:36 When the voice had spoken, Jesus was found alone.	6	
11:14 the one who had been mute spoke	7	
11:37 While he was speaking	7	
12: 1 he began to speak first to his disciples	7	
12:10 who speaks a word against the Son of Man	8	
20:37 where he speaks of the Lord as the God of Abraham	8	
20:39 "Teacher, you have spoken well."	8	
21: 5 When some were speaking about the temple	8	
22:47 he was still speaking, suddenly a crowd came	7	
22:60 At that moment, while he was still speaking	7	
24:44 "These are my words that I spoke to you	7	

Jhn 1:40 One of the two who heard John speak…was Andrew	10	
2:21 But he was speaking of the temple of his body.	8	
2:22 believed…the word that Jesus had spoken.	8	
3:11 "Very truly, I tell you, we speak of what we know	7	
3:31 to the earth and speaks about earthly things.	7	
3:34 He whom God has sent speaks the words of God	7	
4:26 "I am he, the one who is speaking to you."	7	
4:27 astonished that he was speaking with a woman	7	
4:27 or, "Why are you speaking with her?"	7	
4:50 The man believed the word that Jesus spoke to him	8	
6:63 The words that I have spoken to you	7	
6:71 He was speaking of Judas son of Simon Iscariot	8	
7:13 Yet no one would speak openly about him	7	
7:17 whether I am speaking on my own.	7	
7:18 Those who speak on their own	7	
7:26 here he is, speaking openly, but they say nothing	7	

7:46 "Never has anyone spoken like this!"	7	
8:12 Again Jesus spoke to them, saying, "I am the light	7	
8:20 He spoke these words while he was teaching	7	
8:25 "Why do I speak to you at all?	7	
8:27 he was speaking to them about the Father.	8	
8:28 speak these things as the Father instructed me.	7	
8:44 When he lies, he speaks according to his own nature	7	
9:21 he is of age. He will speak for himself."	7	
9:29 We know that God has spoken to Moses	7	
9:37 one speaking with you is he."	7	
11:13 Jesus, however, had been speaking about his death	8	
12:29 Others said, "An angel has spoken to him."	7	
12:38 to fulfill the word spoken by the prophet Isaiah:	8	
12:41 because he saw his glory and spoke about him.	7	
12:48 the word that I have spoken will serve as judge	7	
12:49 for I have not spoken on my own	7	
12:49 commandment about what to say and what to speak.	7	
12:50 What I speak, therefore	7	
12:50 I speak just as the Father has told me."	7	
13:18 I am not speaking of all of you;	8	
13:22 uncertain of whom he was speaking.	8	
13:24 to ask Jesus of whom he was speaking.	8	
14:10 I do not speak on my own;	7	
15: 3 cleansed by the word that I have spoken to you.	7	
15:22 If I had not come and spoken to them	7	
16:13 for he will not speak on his own	7	
16:13 will speak whatever he hears, and	7	
16:25 when I will no longer speak to you in figures	7	
16:29 "Yes, now you are speaking plainly	7	
17: 1 After Jesus had spoken these words	7	
17:13 I speak these things in the world	7	
18: 1 After Jesus had spoken these words	8	
18: 9 This was to fulfill the word that he had spoken	8	
18:16 spoke to the woman who guarded the gate	8	
18:20 "I have spoken openly to the world;	7	
18:23 Jesus answered, "If I have spoken wrongly	7	
18:23 if I have spoken rightly, why do you strike me?"	1	
19:10 "Do you refuse to speak to me?	7	

Act 1: 3 speaking about the kingdom of God.	8	
2: 4 began to speak in other languages	7	
2: 6 each one heard them speaking in the native language	7	
2: 7 "Are not all these who are speaking Galileans?	7	
2:11 in our own languages we hear them speaking	7	
2:16 this is what was spoken through the prophet Joel:	8	
2:31 spoke of the resurrection of the Messiah	7	
3:24 all the prophets, as many as have spoken	7	
4: 1 While Peter and John were speaking to the people	7	
4:17 let us warn them to speak no more to anyone	7	
4:18 not to speak or teach at all in the name of Jesus.	14	
4:20 speaking about what we have seen and heard."	7	
4:29 grant to your servants to speak your word	7	
4:31 spoke the word of God with boldness.	7	
5:40 ordered them not to speak in the name of Jesus	7	
6:10 the wisdom and the Spirit with which he spoke.	7	
6:11 "We have heard him speak blasphemous words	7	
7: 6 God spoke in these terms	7	
7:38 the angel who spoke to him at Mount Sinai	7	
7:44 as God directed when he spoke to Moses	7	
8:25 had testified and spoke the word of the Lord	7	
8:35 Then Philip began to speak	2	
9:27 he had seen the Lord, who had spoken to him	7	
9:29 He spoke and argued with the Hellenists;	7	
10: 7 When the angel who spoke to him had left	2	
10:34 Peter began to speak to them: "I truly understand	2	
10:44 While Peter was still speaking,	7	
10:46 for they heard them speaking in tongues	7	
11:15 as I began to speak, the Holy Spirit fell upon them	7	
11:19 spoke the word to no one except Jews.	7	
11:20 who, on coming to Antioch, spoke to the Hellenists	7	
13:16 So Paul stood up and with a gesture began to speak:	8	
13:34 he has spoken in this way	8	
13:42 urged them to speak about these things again	7	
13:43 Paul and Barnabas, who spoke to them	12	
13:45 contradicted what was spoken by Paul.	7	
13:46 the word of God should be spoken first to you.	7	
14: 1 spoke in such a way that a great number of both Jews	7	
14: 9 He listened to Paul as he was speaking.	7	
14:25 When they had spoken the word in Perga	7	
16: 6 forbidden…to speak the word in Asia.	7	
16:13 and spoke to the women who had gathered	7	
16:32 They spoke the word of the Lord to him	7	

Act	18: 9	"Do not be afraid, but speak and do not be silent;	7
	18:14	Just as Paul was about to speak,	2
	18:25	he spoke with burning enthusiasm and taught accurately	7
	19: 6	they spoke in tongues and prophesied	7
	20: 7	he continued speaking until midnight.	9
	20:36	When he had finished speaking, he knelt down	8
	21:39	I beg you, let me speak to the people."	7
	22: 9	the voice of the one who was speaking to me.	7
	23: 5	shall not speak evil of a leader of your people.' "	8
	23: 9	What if a spirit or an angel has spoken to him?"	7
	24:10	When the governor motioned to him to speak	8
	24:24	heard him speak concerning faith in Christ Jesus.	1
	26: 1	"You have permission to speak for yourself."	8
	26:25	I am speaking the sober truth.	5
	26:26	to him I speak freely;	7
	28:20	to see you and speak with you	12
	28:21	reported or spoken anything evil about you.	7
Rom	3: 5	(I speak in a human way.)	8
	3:19	the law...speaks to those who are under the law	7
	4: 6	So also David speaks of the blessedness of those	8
	6:19	I am speaking in human terms	8
	7: 1	for I am speaking to those who know the law	7
	9: 1	I am speaking the truth in Christ—I am not lying;	8
	11:13	Now I am speaking to you Gentiles.	8
	15:18	For I will not venture to speak of anything	7
1Co	2: 6	Yet among the mature we do speak wisdom	7
	2: 7	we speak God's wisdom, secret and hidden,	7
	2:13	we speak of these things in words	7
	3: 1	I could not speak to you as spiritual people	7
	9:10	does he not speak entirely for our sake?	8
	10:15	I speak as to sensible people; judge for yourselves	8
	12: 3	no one speaking by the Spirit of God ever says	7
	12:30	Do all speak in tongues? Do all interpret?	7
	13: 1	If I speak in the tongues of mortals and of angels	7
	13:11	When I was a child, I spoke like a child	7
	14: 2	For those who speak in a tongue do not speak	7
	14: 2	speak in a tongue do not speak to other people	7
	14: 2	they are speaking mysteries in the Spirit.	7
	14: 3	those who prophesy speak to other people	7
	14: 4	Those who speak in a tongue build up themselves	7
	14: 5	Now I would like all of you to speak in tongues	7
	14: 5	greater than one who speaks in tongues	7
	14: 6	if I come to you speaking in tongues	7
	14: 6	I speak to you in some revelation or knowledge	7
	14: 9	For you will be speaking into the air.	7
	14:13	Therefore, one who speaks in a tongue should pray	7
	14:18	I speak in tongues more than all of you;	7
	14:19	I would rather speak five words with my mind...than	7
	14:21	I will speak to this people;	7
	14:23	church comes together and all speak in tongues	7
	14:27	If anyone speaks in a tongue	7
	14:28	speak to themselves and to God.	7
	14:29	Let two or three prophets speak	7
	14:34	For they are not permitted to speak	7
	14:35	it is shameful for a woman to speak in church.	7
	14:39	do not forbid speaking in tongues;	7
2Co	2:17	in Christ we speak as persons of sincerity	7
	4:13	with scripture—"I believed, and so I spoke"	7
	4:13	we also believe, and so we speak	7
	6:11	We have spoken frankly to you Corinthians;	13
	6:13	In return—I speak as to children	8
	11:21	I am speaking as a fool	8
	12: 6	for I will be speaking the truth.	8
	12:19	We are speaking in Christ before God.	7
	13: 3	you desire proof that Christ is speaking in me.	7
Eph	4:25	let all of us speak the truth to our neighbors	7
	6:19	so that when I speak, a message may be given to me	3
	6:20	I may declare it boldly, as I must speak.	7
Php	1:14	dare to speak the word with greater boldness	7
	1:20	that by my speaking with all boldness,	1
1Th	1: 8	so that we have no need to speak about it	7
	2: 4	entrusted with...the gospel, even so we speak	7
	2:16	by hindering us from speaking to the Gentiles	7
1Ti	5: 1	speak to him as to a father	11
Heb	1: 1	Long ago God spoke to our ancestors in many...ways	7
	1: 2	in these last days he has spoken to us by a Son	7
	2: 5	the coming world, about which we are speaking	7
	3: 5	to testify to the things...spoken later.	7
	4: 4	For in one place it speaks about the seventh day	8
	4: 8	God would not speak later about another day.	7
	6: 9	Even though we speak in this way	7

	7:11	need...to speak of another priest arising	8
	7:13	Now the one of whom these things are spoken	8
	8:13	In speaking of "a new covenant,"	8
	9: 5	Of these things we cannot speak now in detail.	8
	11: 4	through his faith he still speaks.	7
	11:14	for people who speak in this way make it clear	8
	12:19	that not another word be spoken to them.	1
	12:24	that speaks a better word than the blood of Abel.	7
	12:25	See that you do not refuse the one who is speaking;	7
	13: 7	those who spoke the word of God to you;	7
Jas	1:19	let everyone be quick to listen, slow to speak	7
	2:12	So speak and so act as those who are to be judged	7
	3: 2	who makes no mistakes in speaking is perfect.	9
	5:10	the prophets who spoke in the name of the Lord.	7
1Pe	3:10	let them keep...their lips from speaking deceit;	7
	4:11	Whoever speaks must do so as...the very words of God;	7
	4:11	do so as one speaking the very words of God;	1
2Pe	1:21	and women moved by the Holy Spirit spoke from God.	7
	2:16	a speechless donkey spoke with a human voice	14
	2:18	For they speak bombastic nonsense,	14
	3: 2	commandment...spoken through your apostles.	1
	3:16	speaking of this as he does in all his letters.	7
Jde	1:15	harsh things that ungodly sinners have spoken	7
Rev	1:12	I turned to see whose voice it was that spoke to me	7
	4: 1	the first voice, which I had heard speaking to me	7
	10: 8	the voice...from heaven spoke to me again	7
	13:11	and it spoke like a dragon.	7
	13:15	so that the image of the beast could even speak	7

speak against

1. ἀντιλέγω, *antilegō, 515*

Act	28:22	we know that everywhere it is spoken against."	1

speak boldly

1. παρρησιάζομαι, *parrēsiazomai, 4245*

Act	9:27	he had spoken boldly in the name of Jesus.	1
	9:28	speaking boldly in the name of the Lord.	1
	14: 3	speaking boldly for the Lord	1
	18:26	He began to speak boldly in the synagogue;	1
	19: 8	and for three months spoke out boldly	1

speak evil

1. βλασφημέω, *blasphēmeō, 1059*
2. κακολογέω, *kakologeō, 2800*
3. καταλαλέω, *katalaleō, 2895*

Mat	15: 4	'Whoever speaks evil of father or mother	2
Mrk	7:10	'Whoever speaks evil of father or mother	2
	9:39	will be able soon afterward to speak evil of me.	2
Act	19: 9	spoke evil of the Way before the congregation	2
Tit	3: 2	to speak evil of no one, to avoid quarreling	1
Jas	4:11	not speak evil against one another, brothers and sisters.	3
	4:11	Whoever speaks evil against another or judges	3
	4:11	speaks evil against the law and judges the law;	3

speak figuratively

1. παραβολή, *parabolē, 4130*

Heb	11:19	and figuratively speaking, he did receive him	1

speak first

1. προφθάνω, *prophthanō, 4740*

Mat	17:25	he came home, Jesus spoke of it first, asking	1

speak harshly

1. ἐπιπλήσσω, *epiplēssō, 2159*

1Ti	5: 1	Do not speak harshly to an older man	1

speak in the past

1. προλέγω, *prolegō, 4625*

2Pe	3: 2	you should remember the words spoken in the past	1

speak kindly

1. παρακαλέω, *parakaleō, 4151*

1Co	4:13	when slandered, we speak kindly.	1

speak of as evil

1. βλασφημέω, *blasphēmeō, 1059*

Rom	14:16	So do not let your good be spoken of as evil.	1

speak out boldly
1. παρρησιάζομαι, *parrēsiazomai, 4245*

Act 13:46 Paul and Barnabas spoke out boldly, saying   1

speak sternly
1. ἐπιτιμάω, *epitimaō, 2203*

Mat 19:13 The disciples spoke sternly to those   1
Mrk 10:13 the disciples spoke sternly to them.   1

speak the truth
1. ἀληθεύω, *alētheuō, 238*

Eph 4:15 But speaking the truth in love   1

speak up
1. ἀποκρίνομαι, *apokrinomai, 646*

Lke 7:40 Jesus spoke up and said to him, "Simon   1

speak well
1. μαρτυρέω, *martyreō, 3455*

Lke 4:22 All spoke well of him   1
Act 10:22 who is well spoken of by the whole Jewish nation   1
   16: 2 He was well spoken of by the believers   1
   22:12 well spoken of by all the Jews living there   1

speaker
1. λαλέω, *laleō, 3281*
2. λόγος, *logos, 3364*

Act 14:12 because he was the chief speaker.   2
1Co 14:11 I will be a foreigner to the speaker   1
   14:11 the speaker a foreigner to me.   1

speaking *See* finish speaking, keep from speaking

spear
1. λόγχη, *lonchē, 3365*

Jhn 19:34 one of the soldiers pierced his side with a spear   1

spearman
1. δεξιολάβος, *dexiolabos, 1287*

Act 23:23 seventy horsemen, and two hundred spearmen.   1

special
1. Contextual: Not in Greek
2. τιμή, *timē, 5507*

Gal 4:10 You are observing special days, and months,   1
2Ti 2:20 some for special use, some for ordinary.   2
   2:21 will become special utensils, dedicated and useful   2

special use
1. τιμή, *timē, 5507*

Rom 9:21 out of the same lump one object for special use   1

species
1. φύσις, *physis, 5882*

Jas 3: 7 For every species of beast and bird, of reptile   1
   3: 7 every species...has been tamed by the human species   1

speck
1. κάρφος, *karphos, 2847*

Mat 7: 3 do you see the speck in your neighbor's eye   1
   7: 4 'Let me take the speck out of your eye,'   1
   7: 5 and then you will see clearly to take the speck   1
Lke 6:41 do you see the speck in your neighbor's eye   1
   6:42 let me take out the speck in your eye,'   1
   6:42 take the speck out of your neighbor's eye.   1

spectacle
1. θέατρον, *theatron, 2519*
2. θεωρία, *theōria, 2556*

Lke 23:48 crowds who had gathered there for this spectacle   2
1Co 4: 9 because we have become a spectacle   1

speculation
1. ἐκζήτησις, *ekzētēsis, 1700*

1Ti 1: 4 endless genealogies that promote speculations   1

speech *See also* figure of speech, impediment in speech
1. γλῶσσα, *glōssa, 1185*

2. λαλέω, *laleō, 3281*
3. λόγος, *logos, 3364*

1Co 1: 5 in speech and knowledge of every kind—   3
   2: 4 My speech and my proclamation   3
   14: 9 if in a tongue you utter speech   3
2Co 6: 7 truthful speech, and the power of God;   3
   8: 7 in faith, in speech, in knowledge   3
   10:10 "His letters are weighty...his speech contemptible."   3
   11: 6 I may be untrained in speech   3
Col 4: 6 Let your speech always be gracious   3
1Ti 4:12 set the believers an example in speech   3
Tit 2: 8 sound speech that cannot be censured;   3
1Jn 3:18 let us love, not in word or speech, but in truth   1
Jde 1:16 bombastic in speech, flattering people   2

speechless
1. ἄφωνος, *aphōnos, 936*
2. ἐνεός, *eneos, 1917*
3. φιμόω, *phimoō, 5821*

Mat 22:12 And he was speechless.   3
Act 9: 7 The men...stood speechless   2
2Pe 2:16 a speechless donkey spoke with a human voice   1

spellbind
1. ἐκκρεμάννυμι, *ekkremannymi, 1717*
2. ἐκπλήσσω, *ekplēssō, 1742*

Mrk 11:18 the whole crowd was spellbound by his teaching.   2
Lke 19:48 the people were spellbound by what they heard.   1

spend
1. Contextual: Not in Greek
2. γίνομαι, *ginomai, 1181*
3. δαπανάω, *dapanaō, 1251*
4. ἐκδαπανάω, *ekdapanaō, 1682*
5. ἐπιμένω, *epimenō, 2152*
6. ποιέω, *poieō, 4472*
7. προσαναλόω, *prosanaloō, 4649*

Mrk 5:26 spent all that she had;   3
Lke 8:43 though she had spent all she had on physicians   7
   15:14 When he had spent everything   3
Act 18:23 After spending some time there he departed   6
   26: 4 spent from the beginning among my own people   2
1Co 16: 7 I hope to spend some time with you   5
2Co 12:15 most gladly spend and be spent for you.   3
   12:15 most gladly spend and be spent for you.   4
Jas 4: 3 in order to spend what you get on your pleasures.   3
   4:13 spend a year there, doing business and making money."   6
1Pe 4: 3 You have already spent enough time in doing   1

spend more
1. προσδαπανάω, *prosdapanaō, 4655*

Lke 10:35 I will repay you whatever more you spend.'   1

spend much time
1. προσκαρτερέω, *proskartereō, 4674*

Act 2:46 as they spent much time together in the temple   1

spend the night
1. αὐλίζομαι, *aulizomai, 887*
2. διανυκτερεύω, *dianyktereuō, 1381*

Mat 21:17 to Bethany, and spent the night there.   1
Lke 6:12 and he spent the night in prayer to God.   2
   21:37 spend the night on the Mount of Olives,   1

spend the winter
1. παραχειμάζω, *paracheimazō, 4199*
2. παραχειμασία, *paracheimasia, 4200*

Act 27:12 harbor was not suitable for spending the winter   2
   27:12 Phoenix, where they could spend the winter   1
1Co 16: 6 stay with you or even spend the winter   1
Tit 3:12 I have decided to spend the winter there.   1

spend time
1. διατρίβω, *diatribō, 1417*
2. εὐκαιρέω, *eukaireō, 2320*
3. χρονοτριβέω, *chronotribeō, 5990*

Jhn 3:22 he spent some time there with them and baptized.   1
Act 17:21 the Athenians...spend their time in nothing   2
   20:16 so that he might not have to spend time in Asia;   3

sphere of action

1. κανών, *kanōn, 2834*

2Co 10:15 our sphere of action among you may be greatly enlarged 1
     10:16 work already done in someone else's sphere of action. 1

spice

1. ἄμωμον, *amōmon, 319*
2. ἄρωμα, *arōma, 808*

Mrk 16: 1 the mother of James, and Salome bought spices 2
Lke 23:56 Then they returned, and prepared spices 2
    24: 1 taking the spices that they had prepared. 2
Jhn 19:40 and wrapped it with the spices in linen cloths 2
Rev 18:13 cinnamon, spice, incense, myrrh, frankincense 1

spill

1. ἐκχέω, *ekcheō, 1772*

Mat 9:17 the wine is spilled, and the skins are destroyed; 1
Lke 5:37 will be spilled 1

spin

1. νήθω, *nēthō, 3756*

Mat 6:28 how they grow; they neither toil nor spin 1
Lke 12:27 they neither toil nor spin; 1

Spirit / spirit *See also* receive the Spirit

1. Contextual: Not in Greek
2. ὅς, *hos, 4005*
3. πνεῦμα, *pneuma, 4460*

Mat 1:18 found to be with child from the Holy Spirit. 3
    1:20 child conceived in her is from the Holy Spirit 3
    3:11 baptize you with the Holy Spirit and fire. 3
    3:16 heavens were opened…and he saw the Spirit of God 3
    4: 1 led up by the Spirit into the wilderness 3
    5: 3 "Blessed are the poor in spirit, for theirs is 3
    8:16 and he cast out the spirits with a word 3
    10: 1 and gave them authority over unclean spirits 3
    10:20 the Spirit of your Father speaking through you. 3
    12:18 I will put my Spirit upon him 3
    12:28 if it is by the Spirit of God that I cast out demons 3
    12:31 blasphemy against the Spirit will not be 3
    12:32 but whoever speaks against the Holy Spirit 3
    12:43 "When the unclean spirit has gone out of a person 3
    12:45 it goes and brings along seven other spirits 3
    22:43 "How is it then that David by the Spirit 3
    26:41 the spirit indeed is willing 3
    28:19 Father and of the Son and of the Holy Spirit 3
Mrk 1: 8 he will baptize you with the Holy Spirit." 3
    1:10 the Spirit descending like a dove on him. 3
    1:12 the Spirit immediately drove him out 3
    1:23 in their synagogue a man with an unclean spirit 3
    1:26 the unclean spirit, convulsing him and crying 3
    1:27 He commands even the unclean spirits 3
    2: 8 At once Jesus perceived in his spirit 3
    3:11 Whenever the unclean spirits saw him 3
    3:29 whoever blasphemes against the Holy Spirit 3
    3:30 for they had said, "He has an unclean spirit." 3
    5: 2 a man out of the tombs with an unclean spirit 3
    5: 8 "Come out of the man, you unclean spirit!" 3
    5:12 unclean spirits begged him, "Send us into the swine; 1
    5:13 unclean spirits came out and entered the swine; 3
    6: 7 gave them authority over the unclean spirits. 3
    7:25 woman whose little daughter had an unclean spirit 3
    8:12 he sighed deeply in his spirit and said 3
    9:17 he has a spirit that makes him unable to speak; 3
    9:20 When the spirit saw him 3
    9:25 he rebuked the unclean spirit, saying to it 3
    9:25 "You spirit that keeps this boy from speaking 3
    12:36 David himself, by the Holy Spirit, declared 3
    13:11 it is not you who speak, but the Holy Spirit. 3
    14:38 the spirit indeed is willing 3
Lke 1:15 he will be filled with the Holy Spirit. 3
    1:17 With the spirit and power of Elijah he will go 3
    1:35 "The Holy Spirit will come upon you 3
    1:41 Elizabeth was filled with the Holy Spirit 3
    1:47 my spirit rejoices in God my Savior 3
    1:67 with the Holy Spirit and spoke this prophecy: 3
    1:80 The child grew and became strong in spirit 3
    2:25 the Holy Spirit rested on him. 3
    2:26 It had been revealed to him by the Holy Spirit 3
    2:27 Guided by the Spirit, Simeon came into the temple; 3
    3:16 baptize you with the Holy Spirit and fire. 3
    3:22 Holy Spirit descended upon him in bodily form 3
    4: 1 Jesus, full of the Holy Spirit, returned 3
    4: 1 Jesus…was led by the Spirit in the wilderness 3
    4:14 filled with the power of the Spirit 3
    4:18 "The Spirit of the Lord is upon me 3
    4:33 a man who had the spirit of an unclean demon 3
    4:36 commands the unclean spirits, and out they come!" 3
    6:18 those who were troubled with unclean spirits 3
    7:21 diseases, plagues, and evil spirits 3
    8: 2 been cured of evil spirits and infirmities: 3
    8:29 commanded the unclean spirit to come out 3
    8:55 Her spirit returned, and she got up at once. 3
    9:39 a spirit seizes him, and all at once he shrieks. 3
    9:42 But Jesus rebuked the unclean spirit 3
    10:20 the spirits submit to you 3
    10:21 Jesus rejoiced in the Holy Spirit and said 3
    11:13 will the heavenly Father give the Holy Spirit 3
    11:24 the unclean spirit has gone out of a person 3
    11:26 seven other spirits more evil than itself 3
    12:10 whoever blasphemes against the Holy Spirit 3
    12:12 the Holy Spirit will teach you at that very hour 3
    13:11 a woman with a spirit that had crippled 3
    23:46 "Father, into your hands I commend my spirit." 3
Jhn 1:32 the Spirit descending from heaven like a dove 3
    1:33 'He on whom you see the Spirit descend and remain 3
    1:33 is the one who baptizes with the Holy Spirit.' 3
    3: 5 without being born of water and Spirit. 3
    3: 6 and what is born of the Spirit is spirit. 3
    3: 6 and what is born of the Spirit is spirit. 3
    3: 8 So it is with everyone who is born of the Spirit." 3
    3:34 for he gives the Spirit without measure. 3
    4:23 will worship the Father in spirit and truth 3
    4:24 God is spirit, and those who worship him 3
    4:24 must worship in spirit and truth." 3
    6:63 It is the spirit that gives life; 3
    6:63 The words…are spirit and life. 3
    7:39 Now he said this about the Spirit 3
    7:39 as yet there was no Spirit, 3
    11:33 he was greatly disturbed in spirit and deeply moved. 3
    13:21 Jesus was troubled in spirit, and declared 3
    14:17 This is the Spirit of truth 3
    14:26 the Advocate, the Holy Spirit 3
    15:26 the Spirit of truth who comes from the Father 3
    16:13 When the Spirit of truth comes 3
    19:30 he bowed his head and gave up his spirit. 3
    20:22 "Receive the Holy Spirit. 3
Act 1: 2 giving instructions through the Holy Spirit 3
    1: 5 you will be baptized with the Holy Spirit 3
    1: 8 when the Holy Spirit has come upon you; 3
    1:16 which the Holy Spirit through David foretold 3
    2: 4 All of them were filled with the Holy Spirit 3
    2: 4 as the Spirit gave them ability. 3
    2:17 I will pour out my Spirit upon all flesh 3
    2:18 in those days I will pour out my Spirit; 3
    2:33 the promise of the Holy Spirit 3
    2:38 you will receive the gift of the Holy Spirit. 3
    4: 8 Then Peter, filled with the Holy Spirit, said 3
    4:25 said by the Holy Spirit through our ancestor David 3
    4:31 they were all filled with the Holy Spirit 3
    5: 3 filled your heart to lie to the Holy Spirit 3
    5: 9 to put the Spirit of the Lord to the test? 3
    5:16 those tormented by unclean spirits 3
    5:32 so is the Holy Spirit 3
    6: 3 full of the Spirit and of wisdom 3
    6: 5 Stephen, a man full of faith and the Holy Spirit 3
    6:10 the wisdom and the Spirit with which he spoke. 3
    7:51 you are forever opposing the Holy Spirit 3
    7:55 filled with the Holy Spirit, he gazed into heaven 3
    7:59 "Lord Jesus, receive my spirit." 3
    8: 7 for unclean spirits…came out of many 3
    8:15 that they might receive the Holy Spirit 3
    8:16 as yet the Spirit had not come upon any of them; 1
    8:17 they received the Holy Spirit. 3
    8:18 the Spirit was given through the laying on 3
    8:19 may receive the Holy Spirit." 3
    8:29 the Spirit said to Philip, "Go over 3
    8:39 the Spirit of the Lord snatched Philip away; 3
    9:17 be filled with the Holy Spirit." 3
    9:31 in the comfort of the Holy Spirit 3

10:19	the Spirit said to him, "Look	3
10:38	anointed Jesus of Nazareth with the Holy Spirit	3
10:44	the Holy Spirit fell upon all who heard the word.	3
10:45	the gift of the Holy Spirit had been poured out	3
10:47	who have received the Holy Spirit just as we have?"	3
11:12	The Spirit told me to go with them	3
11:15	as I began to speak, the Holy Spirit fell upon them	3
11:16	you will be baptized with the Holy Spirit.'	3
11:24	a good man, full of the Holy Spirit and of faith.	3
11:28	Agabus stood up and predicted by the Spirit	3
13: 2	the Holy Spirit said, "Set apart for me Barnabas	3
13: 4	being sent out by the Holy Spirit	3
13: 9	Paul, filled with the Holy Spirit	3
13:52	filled with joy and with the Holy Spirit.	3
15: 8	giving them the Holy Spirit, just as he did to us;	3
15:28	For it has seemed good to the Holy Spirit and to us	3
16: 6	forbidden by the Holy Spirit to speak the word	3
16: 7	the Spirit of Jesus did not allow them;	3
16:16	met a slave-girl who had a spirit of divination	3
16:18	Paul…turned and said to the spirit	3
19: 2	He said to them, "Did you receive the Holy Spirit	3
19: 2	not even heard that there is a Holy Spirit."	3
19: 6	the Holy Spirit came upon them	3
19:12	diseases left them, and the evil spirits came out	3
19:13	use the name…over those who had evil spirits	3
19:15	the evil spirit said to them in reply,	3
19:16	the man with the evil spirit leaped on them	3
19:21	Paul resolved in the Spirit to go	3
20:22	captive to the Spirit, I am on my way to Jerusalem	3
20:23	except that the Holy Spirit testifies to me	3
20:28	of which the Holy Spirit has made you overseers	3
21: 4	Through the Spirit they told Paul not to go	3
21:11	"Thus says the Holy Spirit	3
23: 8	there is no resurrection, or angel, or spirit;	3
23: 9	What if a spirit or an angel has spoken to him?"	3
28:25	"The Holy Spirit was right in saying	3
Rom 1: 4	with power according to the spirit of holiness	3
1: 9	I serve with my spirit by announcing the gospel	3
5: 5	poured into our hearts through the Holy Spirit	3
7: 6	we are slaves…in the new life of the Spirit.	3
8: 2	For the law of the Spirit of life in Christ Jesus	3
8: 4	us, who walk…according to the Spirit.	3
8: 5	but those who live according to the Spirit	3
8: 5	set their minds on the things of the Spirit.	3
8: 6	to set the mind on the Spirit is life and peace.	3
8: 9	you are not in the flesh; you are in the Spirit	3
8: 9	since the Spirit of God dwells in you.	3
8: 9	Anyone who does not have the Spirit of Christ	3
8:10	the Spirit is life because of righteousness.	3
8:11	the Spirit of him who raised Jesus from the dead	3
8:11	through his Spirit that dwells in you.	3
8:13	but if by the Spirit you put to death the deeds	3
8:14	all…led by the Spirit of God are children of God.	3
8:15	For you did not receive a spirit of slavery	3
8:15	but you have received a spirit of adoption.	3
8:16	very Spirit bearing witness with our spirit	3
8:16	very Spirit bearing witness with our spirit	3
8:23	we…who have the first fruits of the Spirit	3
8:26	Likewise the Spirit helps us in our weakness;	3
8:26	that very Spirit intercedes with sighs	3
8:27	knows what is the mind of the Spirit	3
8:27	because the Spirit intercedes for the saints	1
9: 1	my conscience confirms it by the Holy Spirit	3
11: 8	as it is written, "God gave them a sluggish spirit	3
12:11	not lag in zeal, be ardent in spirit	3
14:17	and peace and joy in the Holy Spirit.	3
15:13	may abound in hope by the power of the Holy Spirit.	3
15:16	be acceptable, sanctified by the Holy Spirit.	3
15:19	by the power of the Spirit of God	3
15:30	I appeal to you…by the love of the Spirit	3
1Co 2: 4	with a demonstration of the Spirit and of power	3
2:10	God has revealed to us through the Spirit;	3
2:10	the Spirit searches everything, even the depths	3
2:11	except the human spirit that is within?	3
2:11	except the Spirit of God.	3
2:12	Now we have received not the spirit of the world	3
2:12	the Spirit that is from God	3
2:13	taught by the Spirit	3
2:14	do not receive the gifts of God's Spirit	3
3:16	God's Spirit dwells in you?	3
4:21	with love in a spirit of gentleness?	3
5: 3	For though absent in body, I am present in spirit;	3
5: 4	When you are assembled, and my spirit is present	3
5: 5	his spirit may be saved in the day of the Lord.	3
6:11	in the Spirit of our God.	3
6:17	united to the Lord becomes one spirit with him.	3
6:19	a temple of the Holy Spirit within you	3
7:34	so that they may be holy in body and spirit;	3
7:40	I think that I too have the Spirit of God.	3
12: 3	no one speaking by the Spirit of God ever says	3
12: 3	except by the Holy Spirit.	3
12: 4	are varieties of gifts, but the same Spirit;	3
12: 7	To each is given the manifestation of the Spirit	3
12: 8	To one is given through the Spirit the utterance	3
12: 8	according to the same Spirit	3
12: 9	to another faith by the same Spirit	3
12: 9	to another gifts of healing by the one Spirit	3
12:10	to another the discernment of spirits,	3
12:11	All these are activated by one and the same Spirit	3
12:11	to each one individually just as the Spirit chooses.	1
12:13	in the one Spirit we were all baptized	3
12:13	were all made to drink of one Spirit.	3
14: 2	they are speaking mysteries in the Spirit.	3
14:14	my spirit prays but my mind is unproductive.	3
14:15	What should I do then? I will pray with the spirit	3
14:15	I will sing praise with the spirit	3
14:16	Otherwise, if you say a blessing with the spirit	3
14:32	the spirits of prophets are subject	3
15:45	the last Adam became a life-giving…spirit.	3
16:18	for they refreshed my spirit as well as yours.	3
2Co 1:22	giving us his Spirit in our hearts as a first installment.	3
3: 3	not with ink but with the Spirit of the living God	3
3: 6	new covenant, not of letter but of spirit;	3
3: 6	the letter kills, but the Spirit gives life.	3
3: 8	will the ministry of the Spirit come in glory?	3
3:17	Now the Lord is the Spirit	3
3:17	where the Spirit of the Lord is, there is freedom.	3
3:18	for this comes from the Lord, the Spirit.	3
4:13	just as we have the same spirit of faith	3
5: 5	who has given us the Spirit as a guarantee.	3
6: 6	kindness, holiness of spirit, genuine love	3
7: 1	every defilement of body and of spirit	3
11: 4	if you receive a different spirit	3
12:18	Did we not conduct ourselves with the same spirit?	3
13:13	communion of the Holy Spirit be with all of you.	3
Gal 3: 2	Did you receive the Spirit by doing the works of the law	3
3: 3	Having started with the Spirit	3
3: 5	does God supply you with the Spirit	3
3:14	receive the promise of the Spirit through faith.	3
4: 6	God has sent the Spirit of his Son into our hearts	3
4:29	child who was born according to the Spirit	3
5: 5	For through the Spirit, by faith, we eagerly wait	3
5:16	Live by the Spirit, I say	3
5:17	what the flesh desires is opposed to the Spirit	3
5:17	the Spirit desires is opposed to the flesh;	3
5:18	if you are led by the Spirit	3
5:22	the fruit of the Spirit is love, joy, peace	3
5:25	If we live by the Spirit	3
5:25	let us also be guided by the Spirit.	3
6: 1	restore such a one in a spirit of gentleness.	3
6: 8	if you sow to the Spirit	3
6: 8	will reap eternal life from the Spirit.	3
6:18	grace…be with your spirit, brothers and sisters.	3
Eph 1:13	marked with the seal of the promised Holy Spirit;	3
1:17	may give you a spirit of wisdom and revelation	3
2: 2	the spirit that is now at work	3
2:18	both of us have access in one Spirit to the Father.	3
3: 5	has now been revealed…by the Spirit:	3
3:16	in your inner being with power through his Spirit	3
4: 3	the unity of the Spirit in the bond of peace.	3
4: 4	There is one body and one Spirit	3
4:23	be renewed in the spirit of your minds	3
4:30	do not grieve the Holy Spirit of God	3
5:18	be filled with the Spirit	3
6:17	the sword of the Spirit, which is the word of God.	3
6:18	Pray in the Spirit at all times	3
Php 1:19	the help of the Spirit of Jesus Christ	3
1:27	that you are standing firm in one spirit,	3
2: 1	any sharing in the Spirit	3
3: 3	worship in the Spirit of God and boast in Christ	3
4:23	The grace of the Lord…be with your spirit.	3
Col 1: 8	has made known to us your love in the Spirit.	3

Col	2: 5	yet I am with you in spirit	3
1Th	1: 5	in the Holy Spirit and with full conviction;	3
	1: 6	with joy inspired by the Holy Spirit	3
	4: 8	who also gives his Holy Spirit to you.	3
	5:19	Do not quench the Spirit.	3
	5:23	may your spirit and soul and body be kept sound	3
2Th	2: 2	either by spirit or by word or by letter	3
	2:13	through sanctification by the Spirit	3
1Ti	3:16	vindicated in spirit, seen by angels	3
	4: 1	Now the Spirit expressly says	3
	4: 1	paying attention to deceitful spirits	3
2Ti	1: 7	for God did not give us a spirit of cowardice	3
	1: 7	a spirit of power and of love and of self-discipline.	1
	1:14	with the help of the Holy Spirit living in us.	3
	4:22	The Lord be with your spirit. Grace be with you.	3
Tit	3: 5	renewal by the Holy Spirit.	3
	3: 6	This Spirit he poured out on us richly	2
Phm	1:25	the Lord Jesus Christ be with your spirit.	3
Heb	1:14	Are not all angels spirits in the divine service,	3
	2: 4	by gifts of the Holy Spirit, distributed	3
	3: 7	Therefore, as the Holy Spirit says	3
	4:12	piercing until it divides soul from spirit	3
	6: 4	have shared in the Holy Spirit	3
	9: 8	By this the Holy Spirit indicates	3
	9:14	who through the eternal Spirit offered himself	3
	10:15	the Holy Spirit also testifies to us	3
	10:29	outraged the Spirit of grace?	3
	12: 9	be subject to the Father of spirits and live?	3
	12:23	to the spirits of the righteous made perfect	3
Jas	2:26	For just as the body without the spirit is dead	3
	4: 5	"God yearns jealously for the spirit	3
1Pe	1: 2	sanctified by the Spirit to be obedient	3
	1:11	that the Spirit of Christ within them indicated	3
	1:12	by the Holy Spirit sent from heaven	3
	3: 4	the lasting beauty of a gentle and quiet spirit	3
	3:18	death in the flesh, but made alive in the spirit	3
	3:19	he went and made a proclamation to the spirits in prison	3
	4: 6	they might live in the spirit as God	3
	4:14	the spirit of glory, which is the Spirit of God,	3
	4:14	the spirit of glory, which is the Spirit of God,	1
2Pe	1:21	and women moved by the Holy Spirit spoke from God.	3
1Jn	3:24	by the Spirit that he has given us.	3
	4: 1	Beloved, do not believe every spirit	3
	4: 1	test the spirits to see whether they are from God;	3
	4: 2	By this you know the Spirit of God:	3
	4: 2	every spirit that confesses that Jesus Christ	3
	4: 3	every spirit that does not confess Jesus	3
	4: 3	And this is the spirit of the antichrist,	1
	4: 6	the spirit of truth and the spirit of error.	3
	4: 6	the spirit of truth and the spirit of error.	3
	4:13	because he has given us of his Spirit.	3
	5: 6	the Spirit is the one that testifies	3
	5: 6	for the Spirit is the truth.	3
	5: 8	the Spirit and the water and the blood,	3
Jde	1:19	worldly people, devoid of the Spirit	3
	1:20	pray in the Holy Spirit;	3
Rev	1: 4	from the seven spirits who are before his throne	3
	1:10	I was in the spirit on the Lord's day,	3
	2: 7	listen to what the Spirit is saying to the churches.	3
	2:11	listen to what the Spirit is saying to the churches.	3
	2:17	listen to what the Spirit is saying to the churches.	3
	2:29	listen to what the Spirit is saying to the churches.	3
	3: 1	the words of him who has the seven spirits of God	3
	3: 6	listen to what the Spirit is saying to the churches.	3
	3:13	listen to what the Spirit is saying to the churches.	3
	3:22	listen to what the Spirit is saying to the churches."	3
	4: 2	I was in the spirit, and there in heaven stood a throne	3
	4: 5	torches…which are the seven spirits of God;	3
	5: 6	seven spirits of God sent out into all the earth.	3
	14:13	"Yes," says the Spirit	3
	16:13	I saw three foul spirits like frogs coming from	3
	16:14	These are demonic spirits, performing signs	3
	17: 3	So he carried me away in the spirit	3
	18: 2	a haunt of every foul spirit	3
	19:10	testimony of Jesus is the spirit of prophecy."	3
	21:10	And in the spirit he carried me away	3
	22: 6	the Lord, the God of the spirits of the prophets	3
	22:17	The Spirit and the bride say, "Come."	3

elemental spirit

1. στοιχεῖον, *stoicheion, 5122*

Gal	4: 3	enslaved to the elemental spirits of the world.	1
	4: 9	weak and beggarly elemental spirits?	1
Col	2: 8	the elemental spirits of the universe	1
	2:20	died to the elemental spirits of the universe	1

spiritual *See also* spiritual *blessing,* spiritual *force,* spiritual *gift,* spiritual *good,* spiritual *power*

1. ἀχειροποίητος, *acheiropoiētos, 942*
2. λογικός, *logikos, 3358*
3. πνεῦμα, *pneuma, 4460*
4. πνευματικός, *pneumatikos, 4461*

Rom	1:11	so that I may share with you some spiritual gift	4
	2:29	a matter of the heart—it is spiritual and not literal.	3
	7:14	that the law is spiritual; but I am of the flesh	4
	12: 1	which is your spiritual worship.	2
1Co	10: 3	all ate the same spiritual food	4
	10: 4	all drank the same spiritual drink.	4
	10: 4	they drank from the spiritual rock	4
	15:44	it is raised a spiritual body.	4
	15:44	there is also a spiritual body.	4
	15:46	it is not the spiritual that is first	4
	15:46	the physical, and then the spiritual.	4
Eph	1: 3	blessed us…with every spiritual blessing	4
	5:19	and hymns and spiritual songs among yourselves	4
Col	1: 9	in all spiritual wisdom and understanding	4
	2:11	you were circumcised with a spiritual circumcision	1
	3:16	sing psalms, hymns, and spiritual songs to God	4
1Pe	2: 2	long for the pure, spiritual milk	2
	2: 5	yourselves be built into a spiritual house	4
	2: 5	offer spiritual sacrifices acceptable to God	4

one who is spiritual

1. πνευματικός, *pneumatikos, 4461*

1Co	2:13	interpreting…to those who are spiritual.	1
	2:15	Those who are spiritual discern all things	1

spiritual person

1. πνευματικός, *pneumatikos, 4461*

1Co	3: 1	could not speak to you as spiritual people	1

spiritual thing

1. πνευματικός, *pneumatikos, 4461*

1Co	2:13	interpreting spiritual things to those	1

spiritually

1. πνεῦμα, *pneuma, 4460*
2. πνευματικῶς, *pneumatikōs, 4462*

1Co	2:14	because they are spiritually discerned.	2
Eph	2:22	spiritually into a dwelling place for God.	1

spit

1. ἐμέω, *emeō, 1840*
2. ἐμπτύω, *emptyō, 1870*
3. πτύω, *ptyō, 4772*

Mat	26:67	Then they spat in his face and struck him;	2
Mrk	7:33	he spat and touched his tongue.	3
Jhn	9: 6	When he had said this, he spat on the ground	3
Rev	3:16	I am about to spit you out of my mouth.	1

spit on

1. ἐμπτύω, *emptyō, 1870*

Mat	27:30	They spat on him, and took the reed and struck	1
Mrk	14:65	Some began to spit on him, to blindfold him	1

spit upon

1. ἐμπτύω, *emptyō, 1870*

Mrk	10:34	mock him, and spit upon him, and flog him	1
	15:19	They struck his head with a reed, spat upon him	1
Lke	18:32	will be mocked and insulted and spat upon.	1

spite

1. ἐν, *en, 1877*

1Th	1: 6	in spite of persecution you received the word	1
	2: 2	in spite of great opposition.	1

splendor

1. δόξα, *doxa, 1518*
2. ἔνδοξος, *endoxos, 1902*

3. λαμπρός, *lampros, 3287*

Mat 4: 8 the kingdoms of the world and their splendor; 1
Eph 5:27 to present the church to himself in splendor 2
Rev 18: 1 and the earth was made bright with his splendor. 1
      18:14 your dainties and your splendor are lost to you 3

split

1. γίνομαι, *ginomai, 1181*
2. σχίζω, *schizō, 5387*

Mat 27:51 The earth shook, and the rocks were split. 2
Rev 16:19 The great city was split into three parts 1

spoil

1. ἀκροθίνιον, *akrothinion, 215*

Heb 7: 4 Abraham...gave him a tenth of the spoils. 1

sponge

1. σπόγγος, *spongos, 5074*

Mat 27:48 ran and got a sponge, filled it with sour wine 1
Mrk 15:36 filled a sponge with sour wine, put it on a stick 1
Jhn 19:29 they put a sponge full of the wine on a branch 1

spot

1. σπίλος, *spilos, 5070*

Eph 5:27 without a spot or wrinkle or anything of the kind 1

without spot

1. ἄσπιλος, *aspilos, 834*

1Ti 6:14 keep the commandment without spot or blame 1
2Pe 3:14 found by him at peace, without spot or blemish; 1

spread

1. Contextual: Not in Greek
2. ἀπέρχομαι, *aperchomai, 599*
3. αὐξάνω, *auxanō, 889*
4. γίνομαι, *ginomai, 1181*
5. διανέμω, *dianemō, 1376*
6. διαφέρω, *diapherō, 1422*
7. διαφημίζω, *diaphēmizō, 1424*
8. διέρχομαι, *dierchomai, 1451*
9. ἐξέρχομαι, *exerchomai, 2002*
10. νομή + ἔχω, *nomē + echō, 3786 + 2400*
11. προκοπή, *prokopē, 4620*
12. στρωννύω, *strōnnyō, 5143*
13. ὑποστρωννύω, *hypostrōnnyō, 5716*
14. φανερόω, *phaneroō, 5746*
15. φλυαρέω, *phlyareō, 5826*

Mat 4:24 So his fame spread throughout all Syria 2
      9:26 the report of this spread throughout 9
      21: 8 large crowd spread their cloaks on the road 12
      21: 8 and spread them on the road. 12
Mrk 1:28 At once his fame began to spread 9
      1:45 to spread the word 7
      11: 8 Many people spread their cloaks on the road 12
      11: 8 and others spread leafy branches 1
Lke 4:14 and a report about him spread 9
      7:17 This word about him spread 9
      19:36 people kept spreading their cloaks on the road. 13
Jhn 21:23 So the rumor spread in the community 9
Act 4:17 keep it from spreading further among the people 5
      6: 7 The word of God continued to spread; 3
      10:37 That message spread throughout Judea 4
      13:49 word of the Lord spread throughout the region. 6
Rom 5:12 death spread to all because all have sinned— 8
2Co 2:14 spreads in every place the fragrance 14
Php 1:12 actually helped to spread the gospel 11
2Ti 2:17 their talk will spread like gangrene. 10
3Jn 1:10 he is...spreading false charges against us. 15

spread abroad

1. διέρχομαι, *dierchomai, 1451*

Lke 5:15 the word about Jesus spread abroad; 1

spread on

1. ἐπιχρίω, *epichriō, 2222*

Jhn 9: 6 and spread the mud on the man's eyes 1
      9:11 made mud, spread it on my eyes, and said to me 1

spread rapidly

1. τρέχω, *trechō, 5556*

2Th 3: 1 word of the Lord may spread rapidly and be glorified 1

spread the news

1. διαφημίζω, *diaphēmizō, 1424*

Mat 9:31 But they went away and spread the news about him 1

spring

1. πηγή, *pēgē, 4380*

Jhn 4:14 a spring of water gushing up to eternal life." 1
Jas 3:11 Does a spring pour forth...fresh and brackish water? 1
2Pe 2:17 These are waterless springs and mists 1
Rev 7:17 he will guide them to springs of the water of life 1
      8:10 it fell...on the springs of water. 1
      14: 7 who made...the sea and the springs of water." 1
      16: 4 into the rivers and the springs of water 1
      21: 6 as a gift from the spring of the water of life. 1

spring from

1. ἐκ, *ek, 1666*

1Th 2: 3 our appeal does not spring from deceit 1

spring up

1. ἅλλομαι, *hallomai, 256*
2. ἀναπηδάω, *anapēdaō, 403*
3. ἐξανατέλλω, *exanatellō, 1984*
4. ἐπιγίνομαι, *epiginomai, 2104*
5. φύω, *phyō, 5886*

Mat 13: 5 and they sprang up quickly 3
Mrk 4: 5 and it sprang up quickly 3
      10:50 throwing off his cloak, he sprang up 2
Act 14:10 man sprang up and began to walk. 1
      28:13 After one day there a south wind sprang up 4
Heb 12:15 no root of bitterness springs up 5

sprinkle

1. πρόσχυσις, *proschysis, 4717*
2. ῥαντίζω, *rhantizō, 4822*
3. ῥαντισμός, *rhantismos, 4823*

Heb 9:13 with the sprinkling of the ashes of a heifer 2
      9:19 sprinkled both the scroll itself and all the people 2
      9:21 in the same way he sprinkled with the blood 2
      10:22 our hearts sprinkled clean from an evil conscience 2
      11:28 kept the Passover and the sprinkling of blood 1
      12:24 the sprinkled blood that speaks a better word 3
1Pe 1: 2 Jesus Christ and to be sprinkled with his blood: 3

sprout

1. βλαστάνω, *blastanō, 1056*

Mrk 4:27 the seed would sprout and grow 1

sprout leaves

1. προβάλλω, *proballō, 4582*

Lke 21:30 as soon as they sprout leaves 1

spurn

1. καταπατέω, *katapateō, 2922*

Heb 10:29 those who have spurned the Son of God 1

spy

1. ἐγκάθετος, *enkathetos, 1588*
2. κατασκοπέω, *kataskopeō, 2945*
3. κατάσκοπος, *kataskopos, 2946*

Lke 20:20 So they watched him and sent spies 1
Gal 2: 4 who slipped in to spy on the freedom 2
Heb 11:31 she had received the spies in peace. 3

squad

1. τετράδιον, *tetradion, 5482*

Act 12: 4 handed him over to four squads of soldiers 1

squander

1. διασκορπίζω, *diaskorpizō, 1399*

Lke 15:13 he squandered his property in dissolute living. 1
      16: 1 this man was squandering his property. 1

stability

1. στηριγμός, *stērigmos*, 5113

2Pe 3:17 not carried away...and lose your own stability. 1

Stachys

1. Στάχυς², *Stachys²*, 5093

Rom 16: 9 Greet Urbanus...and my beloved Stachys. 1

staff

1. ῥάβδος, *rhabdos*, 4811

Mat 10:10 or two tunics, or sandals, or a staff; 1
Mrk 6: 8 nothing for their journey except a staff; 1
Lke 9: 3 no staff, nor bag, nor bread, nor money 1
Heb 11:21 "bowing in worship over the top of his staff." 1
Rev 11: 1 Then I was given a measuring rod like a staff 1

stain

1. σπιλόω, *spiloō*, 5071

Jas 3: 6 The tongue...stains the whole body 1

stalk

1. χόρτος, *chortos*, 5965

Mrk 4:28 The earth produces of itself, first the stalk 1

stand[1] *See also* take a stand

1. Contextual: Not in Greek
2. ἀνίστημι, *anistēmi*, 482
3. εἰμί, *eimi*, 1639
4. ἐφίστημι, *ephistēmi*, 2392
5. ἔχω, *echō*, 2400
6. ἵστημι, *histēmi*, 2705
7. κεῖμαι, *keimai*, 3023
8. παρίστημι, *paristēmi*, 4225
9. περιέχω, *periechō*, 4321
10. περιίστημι, *periistēmi*, 4325
11. στάσις, *stasis*, 5087
12. στήκω, *stēkō*, 5112

Mat 6: 5 for they love to stand and pray in the synagogues 6
    12:25 house divided against itself will stand. 6
    12:26 how then will his kingdom stand? 6
    12:46 his mother and his brothers were standing outside 6
    12:47 are standing outside, wanting to speak to you." 6
    13: 2 while the whole crowd stood on the beach. 6
    16:28 Truly I tell you, there are some standing here 6
    20: 3 he saw others standing idle in the marketplace; 6
    20: 6 he went out and found others standing around; 6
    20: 6 'Why are you standing here idle all day?' 6
    24:15 standing in the holy place, as was spoken of 6
    27:11 Now Jesus stood before the governor; 6
Mrk 3:24 that kingdom cannot stand. 6
    3:25 that house will not be able to stand. 6
    3:26 he cannot stand, but his end has come. 6
    3:31 standing outside, they sent to him and called 12
    9: 1 some standing here who will not taste death 6
    9:27 lifted him up, and he was able to stand. 2
    11:25 "Whenever you stand praying, forgive 12
    13: 9 stand before governors and kings because of me 6
    15:39 when the centurion, who stood facing him, saw 8
Lke 1:11 standing at the right side of the altar 6
    1:19 "I am Gabriel. I stand in the presence of God 8
    4:39 he stood over her and rebuked the fever 4
    5: 1 Jesus was standing beside the lake of Gennesaret 6
    6: 8 "Come and stand here." He got up and stood there. 6
    6: 8 "Come and stand here." He got up and stood there. 6
    6:17 came down with them and stood on a level place 6
    7:38 stood behind him at his feet, weeping 6
    8:20 your brothers are standing outside 6
    9:27 some standing here who will not taste death 6
    11:18 how will his kingdom stand? 6
    13:25 begin to stand outside and to knock at the door 6
    18:11 The Pharisee, standing by himself, was praying thus 6
    18:13 the tax collector, standing far off 6
    19: 8 Zacchaeus stood there and said to the Lord, 6
    21:36 to stand before the Son of Man." 6
    23:49 stood at a distance, watching these things. 6
    24:36 Jesus himself stood among them 6
Jhn 1:26 Among you stands one whom you do not know 6
    1:35 John again was standing with two of his disciples 6
    2: 6 Now standing there were six stone water jars 7

    3:29 The friend...who stands and hears him, rejoices 6
    7:37 Jesus was standing there, he cried out, 6
    8: 9 ⟦left alone with the woman standing before him.⟧ 3
    8:44 and does not stand in the truth 6
    11:42 said this for the sake of the crowd standing here 10
    11:56 as they stood in the temple 6
    12:29 The crowd standing there heard it and said 6
    18: 5 Judas, who betrayed him, was standing with them. 6
    18:16 but Peter was standing outside at the gate. 6
    18:18 were standing around it and warming themselves. 6
    18:18 standing with them and warming himself. 6
    18:25 Simon Peter was standing and warming himself. 6
    19:25 standing near the cross of Jesus were his mother 6
    19:29 A jar full of sour wine was standing there. 7
    20:11 Mary stood weeping outside the tomb. 6
    20:14 she turned around and saw Jesus standing 6
    20:19 Jesus came and stood among them and said 6
    20:26 Jesus came and stood among them and said 6
    21: 4 Just after daybreak, Jesus stood on the beach; 6
Act 1:11 why do you stand looking up toward heaven? 6
    2:14 Peter, standing with the eleven 6
    3: 8 stood and began to walk, and he entered the temple 6
    4:14 saw the man...standing beside them 6
    5:20 "Go, stand in the temple and tell the people 6
    5:23 the guards standing at the doors 6
    5:25 standing in the temple and teaching the people!" 6
    5:27 they had them stand before the council. 6
    6: 6 They had these men stand before the apostles 6
    7:10 when he stood before Pharaoh, king of Egypt 1
    7:33 the place where you are standing is holy ground. 6
    7:55 Jesus standing at the right hand of God. 6
    7:56 the Son of Man standing at the right hand of God!" 6
    9: 7 The men...stood speechless 6
    10:30 suddenly a man in dazzling clothes stood before me. 6
    11:13 the angel standing in his house and saying 6
    12:14 announced that Peter was standing at the gate. 6
    14:10 said in a loud voice, "Stand upright on your feet." 2
    16: 9 there stood a man of Macedonia pleading with him 6
    17:22 Paul stood in front of the Areopagus 6
    21:40 Paul stood on the steps 6
    22:25 Paul said to the centurion who was standing by 6
    22:30 He brought Paul down and had him stand before them. 6
    24:20 when I stood before the council 6
    24:21 that I called out while standing before them 6
    26: 6 now I stand here on trial on account of my hope 6
    26:16 get up and stand on your feet; 6
    26:22 I stand here, testifying to both small and great 6
Rom 5: 2 access to this grace in which we stand; 6
    11:20 but you stand only through faith. 6
    14: 4 before their own lord that they stand or fall. 12
1Co 7:37 someone stands firm in his resolve 6
    10:12 So if you think you are standing, watch out 6
    15: 1 which you in turn received, in which also you stand 6
2Co 2:17 sent from God and standing in his presence. 1
Gal 2:11 because he stood self-condemned; 3
Eph 6:11 able to stand against the wiles of the devil. 6
    6:14 Stand therefore, and fasten the belt of truth 6
Col 2:14 erasing the record that stood against us 3
    4:12 so that you may stand mature and fully assured 6
1Ti 5:20 so that the rest also may stand in fear. 5
2Ti 2:19 God's firm foundation stands, bearing this inscription: 6
Heb 9: 4 In it stood the golden altar of incense 5
    9: 8 as long as the first tent is still standing. 11
    10:11 every priest stands day after day at his service 6
Jas 2: 3 while to the one who is poor you say, "Stand there," 6
    5: 9 See, the Judge is standing at the doors! 6
1Pe 2: 6 For it stands in scripture: 9
    4: 5 give an accounting to him who stands ready to judge 5
Rev 3:20 Listen! I am standing at the door, knocking; 6
    4: 1 I looked, and there in heaven a door stood open! 1
    4: 2 I was in the spirit, and there in heaven stood a throne 7
    5: 6 I saw...among the elders a Lamb standing 6
    6:17 wrath has come, and who is able to stand?" 6
    7: 1 After this I saw four angels standing 6
    7: 9 standing before the throne and before the Lamb 6
    7:11 all the angels stood around the throne 6
    8: 2 And I saw the seven angels who stand before God 6
    8: 3 Another angel with a golden censer came and stood 6
    10: 5 the angel whom I saw standing on the sea and the land 6
    10: 8 angel who is standing on the sea and on the land." 6
    11: 4 two lampstands that stand before the Lord 6

11:11 they stood on their feet, and those who saw them   6
12: 4 Then the dragon stood before the woman   6
14: 1 and there was the Lamb, standing on Mount Zion!   6
15: 2 standing beside the sea of glass   6
18:10 they will stand far off, in fear of her torment   6
18:15 merchants of these wares…will stand far off   6
18:17 all whose trade is on the sea, stood far off   6
19:17 Then I saw an angel standing in the sun   6
20:12 dead, great and small, standing before the throne   6

stand²

1. γίνομαι, *ginomai, 1181*

Jas   1:12 Such a one has stood the test and will receive   1

make stand

1. ἵστημι, *histēmi, 2705*

Jhn   8: 3 [[making her stand before all of them]]   1
Act   4: 7 they had made the prisoners stand in their midst,   1
Rom 14: 4 for the Lord is able to make them stand.   1
Jde   1:24 and to make you stand without blemish   1

stand before

1. ἐφίστημι, *ephistēmi, 2392*
2. παρίστημι, *paristēmi, 4225*

Lke   2: 9 an angel of the Lord stood before them   1
Act   4:10 this man is standing before you in good health   2
27:24 you must stand before the emperor;   2
Rom 14:10 will all stand before the judgment seat of God.   2

stand beside

1. ἐφίστημι, *ephistēmi, 2392*
2. παρίστημι, *paristēmi, 4225*

Lke 24: 4 two men in dazzling clothes stood beside them.   1
Jhn 19:26 and the disciple whom he loved standing beside   2
Act   9:39 All the widows stood beside him, weeping   2
22:13 came to me; and standing beside me, he said   1

stand by

1. διαμένω, *diamenō, 1373*
2. ἐφίστημι, *ephistēmi, 2392*
3. ἵστημι, *histēmi, 2705*
4. παρίστημι, *paristēmi, 4225*

Lke 22:28 those who have stood by me in my trials;   1
23:10 The chief priests and the scribes stood by   3
23:35 the people stood by, watching;   3
Act   1:10 suddenly two men in white robes stood by them.   4
10:17 standing by the gate.   2
22:20 I myself was standing by, approving   2
27:23 last night there stood by me an angel   4
2Ti   4:17 the Lord stood by me and gave me strength   4

stand fast

1. ἵστημι, *histēmi, 2705*

1Pe   5:12 this is the true grace of God. Stand fast in it.   1

stand firm

1. ἵστημι, *histēmi, 2705*
2. στήκω, *stēkō, 5112*

1Co 16:13 Keep alert, stand firm in your faith   2
2Co   1:24 because you stand firm in the faith.   1
Gal   5: 1 Stand firm, therefore, and do not submit   2
Eph   6:13 and having done everything, to stand firm.   1
Php   1:27 I will know that you are standing firm   2
4: 1 stand firm in the Lord in this way, my beloved.   2
1Th   3: 8 if you continue to stand firm in the Lord.   2
2Th   2:15 stand firm and hold fast to the traditions   2

stand in awe

1. φοβέομαι, *phobeomai, 5828*

Rom 11:20 So do not become proud, but stand in awe.   1

stand near

1. ἐφίστημι, *ephistēmi, 2392*
2. παρίστημι, *paristēmi, 4225*

Mrk 14:47 one of those who stood near drew his sword   2
Act 23: 2 Ananias ordered those standing near him   2
23:11 the Lord stood near him and said   1

stand nearby

1. παρίστημι, *paristēmi, 4225*

Jhn 18:22 one of the police standing nearby struck Jesus   1
Act 23: 4 Those standing nearby said   1

stand still

1. ἵστημι, *histēmi, 2705*

Mat 20:32 Jesus stood still and called them, saying   1
Mrk 10:49 Jesus stood still and said, "Call him   1
Lke   7:14 the bearers stood still.   1
18:40 Jesus stood still and ordered the man to be brought   1
24:17 They stood still, looking sad.   1

stand up

1. ἀνακύπτω, *anakyptō, 376*
2. ἀνίστημι, *anistēmi, 482*
3. ἐγείρω, *egeirō, 1586*
4. ἐξανίστημι, *exanistēmi, 1985*
5. ἵστημι, *histēmi, 2705*

Mat   9: 5 or to say, 'Stand up and walk'?   3
9: 6 "Stand up, take your bed and go to your home."   3
9: 7 he stood up and went to his home.   3
26:62 The high priest stood up and said   2
Mrk   2: 9 or to say, 'Stand up and take your mat and walk'?   3
2:11 "I say to you, stand up, take your mat and go   3
2:12 he stood up, and immediately took the mat   3
14:57 Some stood up and gave false testimony against him   2
14:60 the high priest stood up before   2
Lke   4:16 He stood up to read   2
5:23 or to say, 'Stand up and walk'?   3
5:24 "I say to you, stand up and take your bed   3
5:25 Immediately he stood up before them   2
10:25 Just then a lawyer stood up to test Jesus.   2
21:28 stand up and raise your heads   1
Jhn   5: 8 "Stand up, take your mat and walk."   3
Act   1:15 In those days Peter stood up among the believers   2
3: 6 in the name of Jesus Christ…stand up and walk."   3
5:34 Gamaliel…stood up and ordered the men   2
6: 9 some of those…stood up and argued with Stephen.   2
10:26 saying, "Stand up; I am only a mortal."   2
11:28 One of them named Agabus stood up   2
13:16 So Paul stood up and with a gesture began to speak: 2
15: 5 some believers…stood up and said   4
15: 7 Peter stood up and said to them, "My brothers   2
23: 9 certain scribes…stood up and contended   2
25:18 When the accusers stood up   5
27:21 Paul then stood up among them and said, "Men   5

stand up straight

1. ἀνακύπτω, *anakyptō, 376*
2. ἀνορθόω, *anorthoō, 494*

Lke 13:11 quite unable to stand up straight.   1
13:13 immediately she stood up straight   2

stand with

1. συνίστημι, *synistēmi, 5319*

Lke   9:32 his glory and the two men who stood with him.   1

standard

1. ὑποτύπωσις, *hypotypōsis, 5721*

2Ti   1:13 Hold to the standard of sound teaching   1

human standard

1. σάρξ, *sarx, 4922*

Jhn   8:15 You judge by human standards; I judge no one.   1
1Co   1:26 not many of you were wise by human standards   1
2Co   1:17 make my plans according to ordinary human standards   1
10: 2 who think we are acting according to human standards.   1
10: 3 we do not wage war according to human standards;   1
11:18 since many boast according to human standards   1

standing

1. βαθμός, *bathmos, 957*

1Ti   3:13 gain a good standing for themselves   1

high standing

1. εὐσχήμων, *euschēmōn, 2363*

Act 13:50 the Jews incited the devout women of high standing   1
17:12 not a few Greek women and men of high standing.   1

good standing

    1. μαρτυρέω, *martyreō, 3455*

Act 6: 3 select from among yourselves seven men of good standing 1

no standing

    1. ἐξουθενέω, *exoutheneō, 2024*

1Co 6: 4 who have no standing in the church? 1

star

    1. ἀστήρ, *astēr, 843*
    2. ἄστρον, *astron, 849*
    3. φωστήρ, *phōstēr, 5891*

Mat 2: 2 For we observed his star at its rising, 1
      2: 7 learned from them the exact time when the star 1
      2: 9 and there, ahead of them, went the star 1
      2:10 When they saw that the star had stopped, 1
    24:29 the stars will fall from heaven 1
Mrk 13:25 the stars will be falling from heaven 1
Lke 21:25 signs in the sun, the moon, and the stars 2
Act 7:43 the star of your god Rephan 2
    27:20 neither sun nor stars appeared for many days 2
1Co 15:41 another glory of the stars; 1
    15:41 star differs from star in glory. 1
    15:41 star differs from star in glory. 1
Php 2:15 in which you shine like stars in the world. 3
Heb 11:12 "as many as the stars of heaven 2
Jde 1:13 wandering stars, for whom the deepest darkness 1
Rev 1:16 In his right hand he held seven stars 1
     1:20 the seven stars that you saw in my right hand 1
     1:20 seven stars are the angels of the seven churches 1
     2: 1 him who holds the seven stars in his right hand 1
     2:28 who conquers I will also give the morning star 1
     3: 1 the seven spirits of God and the seven stars: 1
     6:13 the stars of the sky fell to the earth 1
     8:10 great star fell from heaven, blazing like a torch 1
     8:11 The name of the star is Wormwood. 1
     8:12 and a third of the moon, and a third of the stars 1
     9: 1 I saw a star that had fallen from heaven to earth 1
    12: 1 and on her head a crown of twelve stars. 1
    12: 4 His tail swept down a third of the stars of heaven 1
    22:16 the descendant of David, the bright morning star." 1

morning star

    1. φωσφόρος, *phōsphoros, 5892*

2Pe 1:19 until the day dawns and the morning star rises 1

stare

    1. ἀτενίζω, *atenizō, 867*
    2. ἐμβλέπω, *emblepō, 1838*

Mrk 14:67 saw Peter warming himself, she stared at him 2
Lke 22:56 seeing him in the firelight, stared at him and 1
Act 3:12 why do you stare at us 1
    10: 4 He stared at him in terror and said ` 1

start

    1. Contextual: Not in Greek
    2. ἄρχω, *archō, 806*
    3. ἐν, *en, 1877*
    4. ἐνάρχομαι, *enarchomai, 1887*
    5. ἔρχομαι, *erchomai, 2262*

Mat 14:29 started walking on the water 1
    15:22 came out and started shouting 1
Lke 2:43 the festival was ended and they started to return 3
     2:44 they started to look for him among their relatives 1
    14: 9 you would start to take the lowest place. 2
Jhn 5:16 Therefore the Jews started persecuting Jesus 1
     6:17 started across the sea to Capernaum. 5
Act 8:35 starting with this scripture 2
    21:15 we got ready and started to go up to Jerusalem. 1
Gal 3: 3 Having started with the Spirit 4

start back

    1. ἀπέρχομαι, *aperchomai, 599*

Jhn 4: 3 he left Judea and started back to Galilee. 1

start on one's way

    1. πορεύομαι, *poreuomai, 4513*

Jhn 4:50 The man believed…and started on his way. 1

startle

    1. πτοέω, *ptoeō, 4765*

Lke 24:37 They were startled and terrified 1

state

    1. λέγω, *legō, 3306*

Lke 2:24 what is stated in the law of the Lord 1
Act 23:30 to state before you what they have against him." 1

last state

    1. ἔσχατος, *eschatos, 2274*

Mat 12:45 the last state of that person is worse 1
Lke 11:26 the last state of that person is worse 1
2Pe 2:20 the last state has become worse for them 1

statement *See also* make a statement

    1. ῥῆμα, *rhēma, 4839*

Act 28:25 they were leaving, Paul made one further statement: 1

open statement

    1. φανέρωσις, *phanerōsis, 5748*

2Co 4: 2 by the open statement of the truth 1

statue

    1. Contextual: Not in Greek

Act 19:35 and of the statue that fell from heaven? 1

stature

    1. ἡλικία, *hēlikia, 2461*

Lke 19: 3 because he was short in stature. 1
Eph 4:13 to the measure of the full stature of Christ. 1

stay

    1. διατρίβω, *diatribō, 1417*
    2. εἰμί, *eimi, 1639*
    3. ἐπέχω, *epechō, 2091*
    4. ἐπιμένω, *epimenō, 2152*
    5. ἵστημι, *histēmi, 2705*
    6. καθέζομαι, *kathezomai, 2757*
    7. καθίζω, *kathizō, 2767*
    8. καταμένω, *katamenō, 2910*
    9. μένω, *menō, 3531*
    10. ξενίζω, *xenizō, 3826*
    11. παραμένω, *paramenō, 4169*
    12. παροικία, *paroikia, 4229*
    13. ποιέω, *poieō, 4472*
    14. προσμένω, *prosmenō, 4693*

Mat 10:11 and stay there until you leave. 9
Mrk 1:45 but stayed out in the country; 2
     6:10 stay there until you leave the place. 9
Lke 9: 4 Whatever house you enter, stay there 9
    19: 5 I must stay at your house today." 9
    24:29 they urged him strongly, saying, "Stay with us 9
    24:29 So he went in to stay with them. 9
    24:49 so stay here in the city until 7
Jhn 1:38 to him, "Rabbi"…"where are you staying?" 9
     1:39 They came and saw where he was staying 9
     4:40 they asked him to stay with them; 9
     4:40 and he stayed there two days. 9
     6:22 the crowd that had stayed on the other side 5
    11: 6 he stayed two days longer in the place 9
    11:20 she went and met him, while Mary stayed at home. 6
Act 1:13 where they were staying 8
     9:43 he stayed in Joppa for some time with a certain Simon 9
    10:18 Simon, who was called Peter, was staying there. 10
    10:32 he is staying in the home of Simon 10
    10:48 Then they invited him to stay for several days. 4
    12:19 he went down…to Caesarea and stayed there. 1
    13:17 during their stay in the land of Egypt 12
    14:28 stayed there with the disciples for some time. 1
    16:15 come and stay at my home." 9
    18: 3 he stayed with them, and they worked 9
    18:11 He stayed there a year and six months 7
    18:18 After staying there for a considerable time, 14
    18:20 When they asked him to stay longer 9
    19:22 he himself stayed for some time longer in Asia. 3
    20: 3 where he stayed for three months. 13
    20: 6 Troas, where we stayed for seven days. 1

21: 4 and stayed there for seven days. 4
21: 7 stayed with them for one day. 9
21: 8 we went into the house...and stayed with him. 9
21:10 While we were staying there for several days 4
21:16 Mnason of Cyprus...with whom we were to stay. 10
25: 6 After he had stayed among them 1
25:14 Since they were staying there several days 1
27:31 "Unless these men stay in the ship 9
28:12 Syracuse and stayed there for three days; 4
28:14 were invited to stay with them for seven days. 4
1Co 16: 6 perhaps I will stay with you 11
16: 8 I will stay in Ephesus until Pentecost 4
Gal 1:18 stayed with him fifteen days; 4

stay awake

1. γρηγορέω, *grēgoreō, 1213*
2. διαγρηγορέω, *diagrēgoreō, 1340*

Mat 24:43 he would have stayed awake 1
26:38 remain here, and stay awake with me." 1
26:40 "So, could you not stay awake with me one hour? 1
26:41 Stay awake and pray that you may not come 1
Lke 9:32 since they had stayed awake, they saw his glory 2
Rev 16:15 Blessed is the one who stays awake and is clothed 1

stay behind

1. ὑπομένω, *hypomenō, 5702*

Lke 2:43 the boy Jesus stayed behind in Jerusalem 1

stay constantly

1. προσκαρτερέω, *proskartereō, 4674*

Act 8:13 being baptized, he stayed constantly with Philip 1

stay for a time

1. παροικέω, *paroikeō, 4228*

Heb 11: 9 By faith he stayed for a time in the land 1

stay with

1. συναλίζω, *synalizō, 5259*

Act 1: 4 While staying with them, he ordered them 1

steadfast

1. βέβαιος, *bebaios, 1010*
2. ἑδραῖος, *hedraios, 1612*
3. πρόθεσις, *prothesis, 4606*
4. στερεός, *stereos, 5104*

Act 11:23 remain faithful...with steadfast devotion; 3
1Co 15:58 Therefore, my beloved, be steadfast 2
Col 1:23 securely established and steadfast in the faith 2
Heb 6:19 hope, a sure and steadfast anchor of the soul 1
1Pe 5: 9 Resist him, steadfast in your faith 4

steadfastness

1. ὑπομονή, *hypomonē, 5705*

Rom 15: 4 that by steadfastness and by the encouragement 1
15: 5 May the God of steadfastness and encouragement 1
1Th 1: 3 steadfastness of hope in our Lord Jesus Christ. 1
2Th 1: 4 for your steadfastness and faith 1
3: 5 love of God and to the steadfastness of Christ. 1
2Ti 3:10 my patience, my love, my steadfastness 1

steal

1. βαστάζω, *bastazō, 1002*
2. κλέπτω, *kleptō, 3096*

Mat 6:19 consume and where thieves break in and steal; 2
6:20 where thieves do not break in and steal. 2
19:18 You shall not steal; 2
Mrk 10:19 shall not steal; You shall not bear false witness; 2
Lke 18:20 You shall not murder; You shall not steal; 2
Jhn 10:10 thief comes only to steal and kill and destroy. 2
12: 6 used to steal what was put into it.) 1
Rom 2:21 While you preach against stealing, do you steal? 2
2:21 While you preach against stealing, do you steal? 2
13: 9 You shall not murder; You shall not steal; 2
Eph 4:28 Thieves must give up stealing; 2

steal away

1. κλέπτω, *kleptō, 3096*

Mat 27:64 otherwise his disciples may go and steal him away 1
28:13 and stole him away while we were asleep.' 1

steal in

1. παρεισδύω, *pareisdyō, 4208*

Jde 1: 4 For certain intruders have stolen in among you 1

stealth

1. δόλος, *dolos, 1515*

Mat 26: 4 to arrest Jesus by stealth and kill him. 1
Mrk 14: 1 way to arrest Jesus by stealth and kill him; 1

steep *See* steep *bank*

steering-oar

1. πηδάλιον, *pēdalion, 4382*

Act 27:40 loosened the ropes that tied the steering-oars; 1

stench

1. ὄζω, *ozō, 3853*

Jhn 11:39 "Lord, already there is a stench 1

step¹

1. ἴχνος, *ichnos, 2717*

2Co 12:18 Did we not take the same steps? 1
1Pe 2:21 an example, so that you should follow in his steps. 1

step²

1. ἀναβαθμός, *anabathmos, 325*

Act 21:35 When Paul came to the steps 1
21:40 Paul stood on the steps 1

step back

1. ἀπέρχομαι, *aperchomai, 599*

Jhn 18: 6 they stepped back and fell to the ground. 1

step by step

1. καθεξῆς, *kathexēs, 2759*

Act 11: 4 Peter began to explain it to them, step by step 1

step down

1. καταβαίνω, *katabainō, 2849*

Jhn 5: 7 my way, someone else steps down ahead of me." 1

step out

1. ἐξέρχομαι, *exerchomai, 2002*

Mrk 5: 2 when he had stepped out of the boat 1
Lke 8:27 As he stepped out on land 1

Stephanas

1. Στεφανᾶς, *Stephanas, 5107*

1Co 1:16 (I did baptize also the household of Stephanas; 1
16:15 household of Stephanas were the first converts 1
16:17 at the coming of Stephanas and Fortunatus 1

Stephen

1. Contextual: Not in Greek
2. αὐτός, *autos, 899*
3. Στέφανος¹, *Stephanos¹, 5108*

Act 6: 5 they chose Stephen 3
6: 8 Stephen, full of grace and power 3
6: 9 some of those...stood up and argued with Stephen. 3
7: 2 Stephen replied: "Brothers and fathers, listen 1
7:54 ground their teeth at Stephen. 2
7:59 While they were stoning Stephen, he prayed 3
8: 2 Devout men buried Stephen 3
11:19 the persecution that took place over Stephen 3
22:20 while the blood of your witness Stephen was shed 3

stern

1. πρύμνα, *prymna, 4744*

Mrk 4:38 he was in the stern, asleep on the cushion; 1
Act 27:29 they let down four anchors from the stern 1
27:41 the stern was being broken up by...the waves. 1

sternly *See also* order sternly, speak sternly, warn sternly

1. πολύς, *polys, 4498*

Mrk 3:12 he sternly ordered them not to make him known. 1

steward *See also* chief steward

1. ἀρχιτρίκλινος, *architriklinos, 804*

2. ἐπίτροπος, *epitropos, 2208*
3. οἰκονόμος, *oikonomos, 3874*

Lke 8: 3 Joanna, the wife of Herod's steward Chuza   2
Jhn 2: 9 When the steward tasted the water   1
      2: 9 the steward called the bridegroom   1
1Co 4: 1 stewards of God's mysteries.   3
      4: 2 Moreover, it is required of stewards   3
Tit 1: 7 For a bishop, as God's steward, must be blameless; 3
1Pe 4:10 Like good stewards of the manifold grace of God   3

stick[1]

1. κάλαμος, *kalamos, 2812*
2. ῥάβδος, *rhabdos, 4811*

Mat 27:48 put it on a stick, and gave it to him to drink.   1
Mrk 15:36 filled a sponge with sour wine, put it on a stick   1
1Co 4:21 you prefer? Am I to come to you with a stick   2

stick[2]

1. ἐρείδω, *ereidō, 2242*

Act 27:41 the bow stuck and remained immovable   1

stiff-necked

1. σκληροτράχηλος, *sklērotrachēlos, 5019*

Act 7:51 "You stiff-necked people   1

still[1] *See also* give still more, stand still, while still *dark*

1. Contextual: Not in Greek
2. ἀκμήν, *akmēn, 197*
3. ἄρτι, *arti, 785*
4. δέ, *de, 1254*
5. ἐπί, *epi, 2093*
6. ἔτι, *eti, 2285*
7. ἕως + ἄρτι, *heōs + arti, 2401 + 785*
8. λοιπός, *loipos, 3370*
9. μᾶλλον, *mallon, 3437*
10. μένω, *menō, 3531*
11. προστίθημι, *prostithēmi, 4707*

Mat 12:46 While he was still speaking to the crowds   6
     15:16 "Are you also still without understanding?   2
     16:14 others Elijah, and still others Jeremiah   1
     17: 5 he was still speaking, suddenly a bright cloud   6
     19:20 what do I still lack?"   6
     26:45 "Are you still sleeping and taking your rest?   8
     26:47 While he was still speaking, Judas…arrived;   6
     26:65 Why do we still need witnesses?   6
     27:63 what that impostor said while he was still alive   6
     28:15 this story is still told among the Jews   1
Mrk 5:35 While he was still speaking   6
      8:28 and still others, one of the prophets."   1
     12: 6 He had still one other, a beloved son.   6
     14:41 "Are you still sleeping and taking your rest?   8
     14:43 while he was still speaking, Judas…arrived;   6
     14:63 "Why do we still need witnesses?   6
Lke 8:49 While he was still speaking   6
      9:19 still others…one of the ancient prophets has arisen." 1
     13: 7 and still I find none.   1
     14:22 there is still room.'   6
     14:32 while the other is still far away, he sends   6
     15:20 while he was still far off,   6
     18:22 still one thing lacking. Sell all that   6
     20:12 he sent still a third;   11
     22:47 he was still speaking, suddenly a crowd came   6
     22:59 still another kept insisting, "Surely   1
     22:60 At that moment, while he was still speaking   6
     24: 6 while he was still in Galilee   6
     24:41 they were disbelieving and still wondering   6
     24:44 while I was still with you   6
Jhn 5:17 Jesus answered them, "My Father is still working   7
     11:30 still at the place where Martha had met him.   6
     14: 9 Philip, and you still do not know me?   1
     14:25 while I am still with you.   10
     16:12 "I still have many things to say to you   6
     20: 1 first day of the week, while it was still dark   6
Act 9: 1 Saul, still breathing threats and murder   6
     10:19 While Peter was still thinking about the vision   1
     10:44 While Peter was still speaking,   6
     20: 9 while Paul talked still longer.   5
Rom 3: 7 why am I still being condemned as a sinner?   6
      4:11 had by faith while he was still uncircumcised.   1

5: 6 For while we were still weak…Christ died   6
5: 8 while we still were sinners Christ died for us.   6
9:19 "Why then does he still find fault?   6

1Co 3: 2 Even now you are still not ready   6
      3: 3 for you are still of the flesh.   6
      8: 7 still think of the food they eat as food offered to 1
      9:12 If others share…do not we still more?   1
     12:31 I will show you a still more excellent way.   6
     15: 6 most of whom are still alive   7
     15:17 you are still in your sins.   6
2Co 3:14 that same veil is still there   10
      5: 4 while we are still in this tent   1
      7: 7 so that I rejoiced still more.   1
      7:13 we rejoiced still more at the joy of Titus   9
Gal 1:10 If I were still pleasing people   6
      1:22 I was still unknown by sight   1
      5:11 why am I still being persecuted   6
      5:11 persecuted if I am still preaching circumcision?   6
Php 1:30 and now hear that I still have.   1
      2:25 Still, I think it necessary to send to you   4
Col 2:20 you live as if you still belonged to the world?   1
2Th 2: 5 I told you these things when I was still with you? 6
Heb 4: 1 while the promise of entering his rest is still open 1
      4: 9 a sabbath rest still remains for the people of God; 1
      5:13 being still an infant, is unskilled in the word   1
      7:10 for he was still in the loins of his ancestor   6
      9: 8 as long as the first tent is still standing.   6
     11: 4 through his faith he still speaks.   6
1Jn 2: 9 while hating a brother or sister, is still in the darkness. 3
Jde 1:23 have mercy on still others with fear   1
Rev 3: 4 Yet you have still a few persons in Sardis   1
      9:12 There are still two woes to come.   6
     22:11 Let the evildoer still do evil   6
     22:11 Let…the filthy still be filthy   6
     22:11 Let…the righteous still do right   6
     22:11 Let…the holy still be holy."   6

still[2]

1. φιμόω, *phimoō, 5821*

Mrk 4:39 said to the sea, "Peace! Be still!"   1

still no

1. οὔπω, *oupō, 4037*

Mrk 4:40 "Why are you afraid? Have you still no faith?"   1

still not

1. οὔπω, *oupō, 4037*

Mat 16: 9 Do you still not perceive?   1
Mrk 8:17 Do you still not perceive or understand?   1

still to come

1. οὔπω, *oupō, 4037*

Mrk 13: 7 must take place, but the end is still to come.   1

sting

1. κέντρον, *kentron, 3034*
2. παίω, *paiō, 4091*

1Co 15:55 Where, O death, is your sting?"   1
     15:56 The sting of death is sin   1
Rev 9: 5 the torture of a scorpion when it stings someone.   2

stinger

1. κέντρον, *kentron, 3034*

Rev 9:10 They have tails like scorpions, with stingers   1

stir up

1. ἀνασείω, *anaseiō, 411*
2. ἐπεγείρω, *epegeirō, 2074*
3. ἐπίστασις + ποιέω, *epistasis + poieō, 2180 + 4472*
4. ἐρεθίζω, *erethizō, 2241*
5. σαλεύω, *saleuō, 4888*
6. συγκινέω, *synkineō, 5167*
7. συγχέω, *syncheō, 5177*
8. ταράσσω, *tarassō, 5429*

Mrk 15:11 the chief priests stirred up the crowd   1
Lke 23: 5 insistent and said, "He stirs up the people   1
Jhn 5: 7 when the water is stirred up;   8
Act 6:12 They stirred up the people as well as the elders   6
     13:50 and stirred up persecution against Paul   2

14: 2 the unbelieving Jews stirred up the Gentiles   2
17:13 stir up and incite the crowds.   5
21:27 stirred up the whole crowd. They seized him   7
24:12 They did not find me…stirring up a crowd   3
2Co 9: 2 your zeal has stirred up most of them.   4

stir up revolt
1. ἀναστατόω, *anastatoō, 415*
Act 21:38 who recently stirred up a revolt   1

stocks
1. ξύλον, *xylon, 3833*
Act 16:24 fastened their feet in the stocks.   1

Stoic
1. Στοϊκός, *Stoikos, 5121*
Act 17:18 Epicurean and Stoic philosophers debated with him.   1

stomach
1. κοιλία, *koilia, 3120*
2. στόμαχος, *stomachos, 5126*
Mat 15:17 goes into the mouth enters the stomach   1
Mrk 7:19 since it enters, not the heart but the stomach   1
1Co 6:13 "Food is meant for the stomach   1
      6:13 the stomach for food,"   1
1Ti 5:23 take a little wine for the sake of your stomach   2
Rev 10: 9 "Take it, and eat; it will be bitter to your stomach   1
      10:10 when I had eaten it, my stomach was made bitter.   1

stone
1. καταλιθάζω, *katalithazō, 2902*
2. λιθάζω, *lithazō, 3342*
3. λίθινος, *lithinos, 3343*
4. λιθοβολέω, *lithoboleō, 3344*
5. λίθος, *lithos, 3345*
6. ψῆφος, *psēphos, 6029*
Mat 3: 9 God is able from these stones to raise up   5
      4: 3 command these stones to become loaves of bread."   5
      4: 6 so that you will not dash your foot against a stone.' "   5
      7: 9 asks for bread, will give a stone?   5
      21:35 beat one, killed another, and stoned another.   4
      21:42 'The stone that the builders rejected   5
      21:44 The one who falls on this stone   5
      23:37 stones those who are sent to it!   4
      24: 2 not one stone will be left here upon another;   5
      27:60 rolled a great stone to the door of the tomb   5
      27:66 made the tomb secure by sealing the stone.   5
      28: 2 came and rolled back the stone and sat on it.   5
Mrk 5: 5 bruising himself with stones.   5
      12:10 'The stone that the builders rejected   5
      13: 1 "Look, Teacher, what large stones   5
      13: 2 Not one stone will be left here upon another;   5
      15:46 rolled a stone against the door of the tomb.   5
      16: 3 "Who will roll away the stone for us   5
      16: 4 they looked up, they saw that the stone   5
Lke 3: 8 God is able from these stones to raise up children   5
      4: 3 command this stone to become a loaf of bread."   5
      4:11 you will not dash your foot against a stone.' "   5
      13:34 stones those who are sent to it!   4
      19:40 the stones would shout out."   5
      19:44 will not leave within you one stone upon another;   5
      20: 6 all the people will stone us;   1
      20:17 'The stone that the builders rejected   5
      20:18 Everyone who falls on that stone   5
      21: 5 how it was adorned with beautiful stones   5
      21: 6 not one stone will be left upon another;   5
      22:41 he withdrew from them about a stone's throw   5
      24: 2 They found the stone rolled away from the tomb   5
Jhn 2: 6 Now standing there were six stone water jars   3
      8: 5 [[Now in the law Moses commanded us to stone such]]   2
      8: 7 [[who is without sin be the first to throw a stone]]   5
      8:59 they picked up stones to throw at him   5
      10:31 The Jews took up stones again to stone him.   5
      10:31 The Jews took up stones again to stone him.   2
      10:32 For which of these are you going to stone me?"   2
      10:33 not for a good work that we are going to stone you   2
      11: 8 the Jews were just now trying to stone you   2
      11:38 It was a cave, and a stone was lying against it.   5
      11:39 Jesus said, "Take away the stone."   2
      11:41 they took away the stone.   5

20: 1 the stone had been removed from the tomb.   5
Act 4:11 'the stone that was rejected by you, the builders;   5
      5:26 they were afraid of being stoned by the people.   2
      7:58 dragged him out of the city and began to stone him;   4
      7:59 While they were stoning Stephen, he prayed   4
      14: 5 to mistreat him and to stone them   4
      14:19 they stoned Paul and dragged him out of the city   2
      17:29 is like gold, or silver, or stone   5
Rom 9:32 They have stumbled over the stumbling stone   5
      9:33 in Zion a stone that will make people stumble   5
1Co 3:12 with gold, silver, precious stones, wood, hay,   5
2Co 3: 3 not on tablets of stone   3
      3: 7 chiseled in letters on stone tablets   5
1Pe 2: 4 Come to him, a living stone, though rejected   5
      2: 5 like living stones, let yourselves be built   5
      2: 6 "See, I am laying in Zion a stone, a cornerstone   5
      2: 7 "The stone that the builders rejected has become   5
      2: 8 "A stone that makes them stumble   5
Rev 2:17 and I will give a white stone   6
      2:17 on the white stone is written a new name   6
      9:20 idols of…silver and bronze and stone and wood   3
      18:21 angel took up a stone like a great millstone   5

stone pavement
1. λιθόστρωτος, *lithostrōtos, 3346*
Jhn 19:13 at a place called The Stone Pavement   1

stone to death
1. λιθάζω, *lithazō, 3342*
2. λιθοβολέω, *lithoboleō, 3344*
Heb 11:37 They were stoned to death, they were sawn in two   1
      12:20 it shall be stoned to death."   2

stoning *See* receive a stoning

stoop
1. παρακύπτω, *parakyptō, 4160*
Lke 24:12 stooping and looking in, he saw the linen   1

stoop down
1. κύπτω, *kyptō, 3252*
Mrk 1: 7 I am not worthy to stoop down and untie   1

stop
1. Contextual: Not in Greek
2. ἀνίημι, *aniēmi, 479*
3. διαλείπω, *dialeipō, 1364*
4. ἵστημι, *histēmi, 2705*
5. κωλύω, *kōlyō, 3266*
6. μή, *mē, 3590*
7. ξηραίνω, *xērainō, 3830*
8. οὐδέ + ἀφίημι + εἰσέρχομαι, *oude + aphiēmi + eiserchomai,*
      4028 + 918 + 1656
9. παύω, *pauō, 4264*
Mat 2: 9 it stopped over the place where the child   4
      2:10 When they saw that the star had stopped,   1
      19:14 children come to me, do not stop them;   5
      23:13 when others are going in, you stop them.   8
Mrk 5:29 Immediately her hemorrhage stopped;   7
      9:38 to stop him, because he was not following us."   5
      9:39 Jesus said, "Do not stop him;   5
      10:14 little children come to me; do not stop them;   5
Lke 7:45 she has not stopped kissing my feet.   3
      8:44 immediately her hemorrhage stopped.   4
      9:49 we tried to stop him, because he does not follow   5
      9:50 Jesus said to him, "Do not stop him;   5
      18:16 little children come to me, and do not stop them;   5
      19:39 "Teacher, order your disciples to stop."   1
Jhn 2:16 Stop making my Father's house a marketplace!"   6
Act 6:13 "This man never stops saying things   9
      8:38 He commanded the chariot to stop   4
      13:10 stop making crooked the straight paths of the Lord?   9
      21:32 they stopped beating Paul.   9
Eph 6: 9 Stop threatening them   2

store
1. συνάγω, *synagō, 5251*
Lke 12:17 I have no place to store my crops?'   1
      12:18 there I will store all my grain and my goods.   1

store up

1. θησαυρίζω, *thēsaurizō, 2564*

Mat	6:19	"Do not store up for yourselves treasures on earth	1
	6:20	store up for yourselves treasures in heaven	1
Rom	2: 5	storing up wrath for yourself on the day of wrath	1

store up treasure

1. ἀποθησαυρίζω, *apothēsaurizō, 631*
2. θησαυρίζω, *thēsaurizō, 2564*

Lke	12:21	those who store up treasures for themselves	2
1Ti	6:19	thus storing up for themselves the treasure	1

storehouse

1. ταμεῖον, *tameion, 5421*

Lke	12:24	they have neither storehouse nor barn	1

storm *See also* pounded by a storm

1. λαῖλαψ, *lailaps, 3278*

2Pe	2:17	waterless springs and mists driven by a storm;	1

stormy

1. χειμών, *cheimōn, 5930*

Mat	16: 3	'It will be stormy today, for the sky is red	1

story

1. Contextual: Not in Greek
2. λόγος, *logos, 3364*

Mat	8:33	they told the whole story about what had happened	1
	28:15	this story is still told among the Jews	2
Mrk	12:26	in the story about the bush	1
Lke	20:37	Moses himself showed, in the story about the bush	1

straight *See also* make straight, stand up straight, take a straight course

1. εὐθύς², *euthys², 2318*
2. ὀρθός, *orthos, 3981*

Mat	3: 3	way of the Lord, make his paths straight.' "	1
Mrk	1: 3	make his paths straight,' "	1
Lke	3: 4	make his paths straight.	1
	3: 5	the crooked shall be made straight	1
Act	9:11	"Get up and go to the street called Straight	1
	13:10	making crooked the straight paths of the Lord?	1
Heb	12:13	make straight paths for your feet	2
2Pe	2:15	They have left the straight road and have gone astray	1

straight course

1. εὐθυδρομέω, *euthydromeō, 2312*

Act	21: 1	we came by a straight course to Cos	1

straighten up

1. ἀνακύπτω, *anakyptō, 376*

Jhn	8: 7	⟦he straightened up and said to them⟧	1
	8:10	⟦Jesus straightened up and said to her, "Woman⟧	1

strain

1. βασανίζω, *basanizō, 989*

Mrk	6:48	he saw that they were straining at the oars	1

strain forward

1. ἐπεκτείνομαι, *epekteinomai, 2085*

Php	3:13	straining forward to what lies ahead	1

strain out

1. διϋλίζω, *diylizō, 1494*

Mat	23:24	You strain out a gnat but swallow a camel!	1

strange *See also* person of strange tongues, something strange

1. μέγας, *megas, 3489*
2. ξενίζω, *xenizō, 3826*
3. ξένος, *xenos, 3828*

Act	17:20	sounds rather strange to us	2
2Co	11:15	So it is not strange if his ministers also	1
Heb	13: 9	carried away by all kinds of strange teachings;	3

strange thing

1. παράδοξος, *paradoxos, 4141*

Lke	5:26	saying, "We have seen strange things today."	1

stranger *See also* hospitality to a stranger, show hospitality to a stranger

1. ἀλλότριος, *allotrios, 259*
2. ξένος, *xenos, 3828*
3. παροικέω, *paroikeō, 4228*

Mat	25:35	I was a stranger and you welcomed me	2
	25:38	that we saw you a stranger and welcomed you	2
	25:43	I was a stranger and you did not welcome me	2
	25:44	thirsty or a stranger or naked or sick	2
Lke	24:18	the only stranger in Jerusalem who does not know	3
Jhn	10: 5	They will not follow a stranger	1
	10: 5	because they do not know the voice of strangers."	1
Eph	2:12	strangers to the covenants of promise	2
	2:19	you are no longer strangers and aliens	2
Heb	11:13	they were strangers and foreigners on the earth	2
3Jn	1: 5	even though they are strangers to you;	2

strangle

1. πνικτός, *pniktos, 4465*

Act	15:20	from whatever has been strangled and from blood.	1
	15:29	from blood and from what is strangled	1
	21:25	from what is strangled and from fornication."	1

straw

1. καλάμη, *kalamē, 2811*

1Co	3:12	gold, silver, precious stones, wood, hay, straw—	1

street

1. ἄμφοδον, *amphodon, 316*
2. ὁδός, *hodos, 3847*
3. πλατεῖα, *plateia, 4423*
4. ῥύμη, *rhymē, 4860*

Mat	6: 2	in the synagogues and in the streets	4
	6: 5	pray in the synagogues and at the street corners	3
	12:19	nor will anyone hear his voice in the streets.	3
	22: 9	Go therefore into the main streets, and invite	2
	22:10	Those slaves went out into the streets	2
Mrk	11: 4	near a door, outside in the street.	1
Lke	10:10	go out into its streets and say	3
	13:26	you taught in our streets.'	3
	14:21	'Go out at once into the streets and lanes	3
Act	5:15	they even carried out the sick into the streets	3
	9:11	"Get up and go to the street called Straight	4
Rev	11: 8	their dead bodies will lie in the street	3
	21:21	and the street of the city is pure gold	3
	22: 2	through the middle of the street of the city.	3

main street

1. διέξοδος, *diexodos, 1447*

Mat	22: 9	Go therefore into the main streets, and invite	1

strength *See also* give strength, regain strength, win strength

1. Contextual: Not in Greek
2. δύναμαι, *dynamai, 1538*
3. δύναμις, *dynamis, 1539*
4. ἰσχύς, *ischys, 2709*
5. ἰσχύω, *ischyō, 2710*
6. κατισχύω, *katischyō, 2996*
7. κράτος, *kratos, 3197*

Mrk	5: 4	no one had the strength to subdue him.	5
	12:30	with all your mind, and with all your strength.'	4
	12:33	and 'to love him...with all the strength,'	4
Lke	1:51	He has shown strength with his arm;	7
	10:27	with all your soul, and with all your strength	4
	21:36	praying that you may have the strength	6
1Co	1:25	God's weakness is stronger than human strength	1
	10:13	not let you be tested beyond your strength	2
Eph	6:10	be strong...in the strength of his power.	7
Col	1:11	May you be made strong with all the strength	3
1Pe	4:11	do so with the strength that God supplies	4

strengthen

1. Contextual: Not in Greek
2. βεβαιόω, *bebaioō, 1011*
3. ἐνδυναμόω, *endynamoō, 1904*
4. ἐπιστηρίζω, *epistērizō, 2185*
5. κραταιόω, *krataioō, 3194*

6. σθενόω, *sthenoō, 4964*
7. στερεόω, *stereoō, 5105*
8. στηρίζω, *stērizō, 5114*

Lke 22:32 strengthen your brothers."   8
Act 14:22 strengthened the souls of the disciples   4
    15:32 said much to encourage and strengthen the believers   4
    15:41 strengthening the churches.   4
    16: 5 So the churches were strengthened in the faith   7
    18:23 strengthening all the disciples.   4
Rom 1:11 share...some spiritual gift to strengthen you   8
    16:25 Now to God who is able to strengthen you   8
1Co 1: 6 testimony of Christ has been strengthened among you—   2
    1: 8 He will also strengthen you to the end   2
Eph 3:16 he may grant that you may be strengthened   5
Php 4:13 I can do all things through him who strengthens me.   3
1Th 3: 2 to strengthen and encourage you for the sake   8
    3:13 And may he so strengthen your hearts in holiness   8
2Th 2:17 strengthen them in every good work and word.   8
    3: 3 he will strengthen you and guard you from the evil 8
1Ti 1:12 Christ Jesus our Lord, who has strengthened me   3
Heb 12:12 and strengthen your weak knees   1
    13: 9 is well for the heart to be strengthened by grace 2
Jas 5: 8 Strengthen your hearts, for the coming of the Lord   8
1Pe 5:10 will...restore, support, strengthen, and establish you.   6
Rev 3: 2 Wake up, and strengthen what remains   8

under stress

1. συνέχω, *synechō, 5309*

Lke 12:50 what stress I am under until it is completed!   1

stretch out

1. ἐκτείνω, *ekteinō, 1753*

Mat 8: 3 He stretched out his hand and touched him   1
    12:13 Then he said to the man, "Stretch out your hand." 1
    12:13 He stretched it out, and it was restored   1
Mrk 1:41 Moved with pity, Jesus stretched out his hand   1
    3: 5 said to the man, "Stretch out your hand."   1
    3: 5 He stretched it out, and his hand was restored.   1
Lke 5:13 Jesus stretched out his hand, touched him,   1
    6:10 said to him, "Stretch out your hand."   1
Jhn 21:18 you grow old, you will stretch out your hands   1
Act 4:30 while you stretch out your hand to heal   1
    26: 1 Paul stretched out his hand and began to defend   1

strict   *See also* strict *order*

1. ἀκριβής, *akribēs, 207*

Act 26: 5 the strictest sect of our religion   1

strictly

1. ἀκρίβεια, *akribeia, 205*
2. ἀνάθεμα, *anathema, 353*
3. πολύς, *polys, 4498*

Mrk 5:43 He strictly ordered them that no one should know   3
Act 22: 3 educated strictly according to our ancestral law   1
    23:14 "We have strictly bound ourselves by an oath   2

strictness

1. Contextual: Not in Greek

Jas 3: 1 we...will be judged with greater strictness.   1

strife

1. ἔρις, *eris, 2251*

Rom 1:29 Full of envy, murder, strife, deceit, craftiness   1
Gal 5:20 idolatry, sorcery, enmities, strife, jealousy, anger   1

strike

1. ἀποκτείνω, *apokteinō, 650*
2. δέρω, *derō, 1296*
3. κολαφίζω, *kolaphizō, 3139*
4. παίω, *paiō, 4091*
5. πατάσσω, *patassō, 4250*
6. περιπίπτω, *peripiptō, 4346*
7. πίπτω, *piptō, 4406*
8. πλήσσω, *plēssō, 4448*
9. ῥαπίζω, *rhapizō, 4824*
10. τύπτω, *typtō, 5597*

Mat 5:39 But if anyone strikes you on the right cheek, turn   9
    26:31 it is written, 'I will strike the shepherd   5
    26:51 and struck the slave of the high priest   5
    26:67 Then they spat in his face and struck him;   3
    26:68 Who is it that struck you?"   4
    27:30 took the reed and struck him on the head.   10
Mrk 14:27 it is written, 'I will strike the shepherd   5
    14:47 struck the slave of the high priest   4
    14:65 to blindfold him, and to strike him, saying   3
    15:19 They struck his head with a reed, spat upon him   10
Lke 6:29 anyone strikes you on the cheek   10
    22:49 should we strike with the sword?"   5
    22:50 one of them struck the slave of the high priest   5
    22:64 "Prophesy! Who is it that struck you?"   4
Jhn 18:10 Simon Peter...struck the high priest's slave   4
    18:23 if I have spoken rightly, why do you strike me?"   2
Act 23: 2 to strike him on the mouth.   10
    23: 3 "God will strike you, you whitewashed wall!   10
    23: 3 in violation of the law you order me to be struck?" 10
    27:41 striking a reef, they ran the ship aground;   6
Rev 2:23 and I will strike her children dead.   1
    7:16 sun will not strike them, nor any scorching heat;   7
    8:12 blew his trumpet, and a third of the sun was struck 8
    11: 6 and to strike the earth with every kind of plague 5

strike down

1. καταβάλλω, *kataballō, 2850*
2. καταστρώννυμι, *katastrōnnymi, 2954*
3. πατάσσω, *patassō, 4250*

Act 7:24 avenged him by striking down the Egyptian.   3
    12:23 immediately...an angel of the Lord struck him down 3
1Co 10: 5 and they were struck down in the wilderness.   2
2Co 4: 9 struck down, but not destroyed;   1
Rev 19:15 a sharp sword with which to strike down the nations   3

strike on the face

1. ῥάπισμα + δίδωμι, *rhapisma + didōmi, 4825 + 1443*

Jhn 18:22 one of the police...struck Jesus on the face,   1
    19: 3 and striking him on the face.   1

strip

1. ἐκδύω, *ekdyō, 1694*
2. περιρήγνυμι, *perirēgnymi, 4351*

Mat 27:28 They stripped him and put a scarlet robe on him   1
    27:31 they stripped him of the robe   1
Mrk 15:20 they stripped him of the purple cloak   1
Lke 10:30 robbers, who stripped him, beat him   1
Act 16:22 magistrates had them stripped of their clothing   2

strip of cloth

1. κειρία, *keiria, 3024*

Jhn 11:44 his hands and feet bound with strips of cloth   1

strip off

1. ἀπεκδύομαι, *apekdyomai, 588*

Col 3: 9 seeing that you have stripped off the old self   1

strive

1. Contextual: Not in Greek
2. ἀγωνίζομαι, *agōnizomai, 76*
3. διώκω, *diōkō, 1503*
4. ἐπιζητέω, *epizēteō, 2118*
5. ζηλόω, *zēloō, 2420*
6. ζητέω, *zēteō, 2426*
7. σπουδάζω, *spoudazō, 5079*

Mat 6:32 the Gentiles who strive for all these things;   4
    6:33 But strive first for the kingdom of God   6
Lke 12:29 do not keep striving for what you are to eat   6
    12:30 the nations of the world that strive after all   4
    12:31 Instead, strive for his kingdom   6
    13:24 "Strive to enter through the narrow door;   2
Rom 9:30 Gentiles, who did not strive for righteousness   3
    9:31 but Israel, who did strive for the righteousness   3
    9:32 they did not strive for it on the basis of faith   1
1Co 12:31 strive for the greater gifts.   5
    14: 1 Pursue love and strive for the spiritual gifts   5
    14:12 strive to excel in them for building up the church. 6
2Pe 3:14 strive to be found by him at peace, without spot   7

strive side by side

1. συναθλέω, *synathleō, 5254*

Php 1:27 striving side by side with one mind for the faith   1

stroke of a letter

1. κεραία, *keraia, 3037*

Mat 5:18 not one letter, not one stroke of a letter   1
Lke 16:17 one stroke of a letter in the law to be dropped.   1

strong *See also* make strong, strong *drink,* strong *passion*

1. δυνατός, *dynatos, 1543*
2. ἐνδυναμόω, *endynamoō, 1904*
3. ἰσχυρός, *ischyros, 2708*
4. ἰσχύω, *ischyō, 2710*
5. κραταιόω, *krataioō, 3194*
6. μέγας, *megas, 3489*
7. σκληρός, *sklēros, 5017*

Mat 14:30 he noticed the strong wind, he became frightened   3
Lke 1:80 The child grew and became strong in spirit   5
     2:40 The child grew and became strong   5
     11:22 when one stronger than he attacks him   3
     16: 3 I am not strong enough to dig   4
Jhn 6:18 sea became rough because a strong wind was blowing.   6
Rom 15: 1 We who are strong ought to put up with the failings   1
1Co 1:25 God's weakness is stronger than human strength   3
     1:27 to shame the strong;   3
     4:10 We are weak, but you are strong.   3
     10:22 Are we stronger than he?   3
     16:13 be courageous, be strong.   5
2Co 10:10 For they say, "His letters are weighty and strong   3
     12:10 whenever I am weak, then I am strong.   1
     13: 9 we rejoice when we are weak and you are strong.   1
Eph 6:10 Finally, be strong in the Lord   2
2Ti 2: 1 You then, my child, be strong in the grace   2
Heb 6:18 might be strongly encouraged to seize the hope   3
Jas 3: 4 it takes strong winds to drive them,   7
1Jn 2:14 I write to you, young people, because you are strong   3

grow strong

1. ἐνδυναμόω, *endynamoō, 1904*

Rom 4:20 but he grew strong in his faith as he gave glory   1

strong man

1. ἰσχυρός, *ischyros, 2708*

Mat 12:29 Or how can one enter a strong man's house   1
     12:29 without first tying up the strong man?   1
Mrk 3:27 no one can enter a strong man's house   1
     3:27 without first tying up the strong man;   1
Lke 11:21 a strong man, fully armed, guards his castle   1

stronghold

1. ὀχύρωμα, *ochyrōma, 4065*

2Co 10: 4 they have divine power to destroy strongholds.   1

strongly *See also* urge strongly

1. λίαν, *lian, 3336*
2. πολύς, *polys, 4498*

1Co 16:12 I strongly urged him to visit you   2
2Ti 4:15 he strongly opposed our message.   1

structure

1. οἰκοδομή, *oikodomē, 3869*

Eph 2:21 In him the whole structure is joined together   1

struggle

1. ἀγών, *agōn, 74*
2. ἀγωνίζομαι, *agōnizomai, 76*
3. ἄθλησις, *athlēsis, 124*
4. ἀνταγωνίζομαι, *antagōnizomai, 497*
5. πάλη, *palē, 4097*

Eph 6:12 struggle is not against enemies of blood and flesh   5
Php 1:30 having the same struggle that you saw   1
Col 1:29 For this I toil and struggle with all the energy   2
     2: 1 want you to know how much I am struggling for you   1
1Ti 4:10 For to this end we toil and struggle   2
Heb 10:32 you endured a hard struggle with sufferings   3
     12: 4 In your struggle against sin   4

struggle beside

1. συναθλέω, *synathleō, 5254*

Php 4: 3 they have struggled beside me   1

stubbornly

1. σκληρύνω, *sklērynō, 5020*

Act 19: 9 When some stubbornly refused to believe   1

stubbornness

1. σκληροκαρδία, *sklērokardia, 5016*

Mrk 16:14 ⟦for their lack of faith and stubbornness⟧   1

student

1. ἀδελφός, *adelphos, 81*

Mat 23: 8 you have one teacher, and you are all students.   1

stumble *See also* cause for stumbling, make stumble, occasion for stumbling, put a stumbling block

1. παράπτωμα, *paraptōma, 4183*
2. πρόσκομμα, *proskomma, 4682*
3. προσκόπτω, *proskoptō, 4684*
4. πταίω, *ptaiō, 4760*
5. σκανδαλίζω, *skandalizō, 4997*

Jhn 11: 9 Those who walk during the day do not stumble   3
     11:10 those who walk at night stumble,   3
     16: 1 to keep you from stumbling.   5
Rom 9:32 They have stumbled over the stumbling stone   3
     9:32 They have stumbled over the stumbling stone   2
     11:11 have they stumbled so as to fall? By no means!   4
     11:11 through their stumbling salvation has come   1
     11:12 Now if their stumbling means riches for the world   1
1Pe 2: 8 They stumble because they disobey the word   3
2Pe 1:10 for if you do this, you will never stumble.   4

cause to stumble

1. σκανδαλίζω, *skandalizō, 4997*

Mat 18: 8 "If your hand or your foot causes you to stumble   1
     18: 9 if your eye causes you to stumble, tear it out   1
Mrk 9:43 If your hand causes you to stumble, cut it off;   1
     9:45 if your foot causes you to stumble, cut it off;   1
     9:47 if your eye causes you to stumble, tear it out;   1
Lke 17: 2 to cause one of these little ones to stumble.   1

stumbling *See also* stumbling *block*

stupid

1. μωρός, *mōros, 3704*

2Ti 2:23 stupid and senseless controversies;   1
Tit 3: 9 avoid stupid controversies, genealogies   1

subdue

1. δαμάζω, *damazō, 1238*

Mrk 5: 4 no one had the strength to subdue him.   1

subject *See also* make subject

1. Contextual: Not in Greek
2. ἔχω, *echō, 2400*
3. περίκειμαι, *perikeimai, 4329*
4. ὑπό, *hypo, 5679*
5. ὑποτάσσω, *hypotassō, 5718*

Rom 8:20 for the creation was subjected to futility   5
     8:20 by the will of the one who subjected it, in hope   5
     13: 1 be subject to the governing authorities;   5
     13: 5 Therefore one must be subject   5
1Co 14:32 the spirits of prophets are subject   5
     15:28 When all things are subjected to him   5
     15:28 then the Son himself will also be subjected   5
2Co 9: 2 the subject of my boasting about you   1
Gal 3:25 we are no longer subject to a disciplinarian   4
     4:21 Tell me, you who desire to be subject to the law   4
     5:18 led by the Spirit, you are not subject to the law.   4
Eph 5:21 Be subject to one another   5
     5:22 Wives, be subject to your husbands as you are to the Lord.   1
     5:24 Just as the church is subject to Christ   5
Col 3:18 Wives, be subject to your husbands   5
Tit 3: 1 Remind them to be subject to rulers   5
Heb 2: 5 Now God did not subject the coming world   5
     2: 8 subjecting all things under their feet."   5
     2: 8 Now in subjecting all things to them   5
     5: 2 since he himself is subject to weakness;   3
     7:28 appoints as high priests those who are subject to weakness   2
     12: 9 be subject to the Father of spirits and live?   5

subject to judgment
1. κρίνω, *krinō, 3212*
1Co 10:29 why should my liberty be subject to the judgment   1

subject to scrutiny
1. ἀνακρίνω, *anakrinō, 373*
1Co 2:15 are themselves subject to no one else's scrutiny.   1

subjection   *See also* put in subjection
1. ὑποτάσσω, *hypotassō, 5718*
Heb 2: 8 do not yet see everything in subjection to them   1

submission
1. ὑποταγή, *hypotagē, 5717*
1Ti 2:11 woman learn in silence with full submission   1

reverent submission
1. εὐλάβεια, *eulabeia, 2325*
Heb 5: 7 he was heard because of his reverent submission.   1

submissive
1. ὑποταγή, *hypotagē, 5717*
2. ὑποτάσσω, *hypotassō, 5718*
1Ti 3: 4 submissive and respectful in every way   1
Tit 2: 5 submissive to their husbands   2
     2: 9 Tell slaves to be submissive to their masters   2

submit
1. ἀνέχομαι, *anechomai, 462*
2. εἴκω + ὁ + ὑποταγή, *eikō + ho + hypotagē, 1634 + 3836 + 5717*
3. ἐνέχω, *enechō, 1923*
4. ὑπείκω, *hypeikō, 5640*
5. ὑποτάσσω, *hypotassō, 5718*
Lke 10:17 in your name even the demons submit to us!"   5
     10:20 the spirits submit to you   5
Rom 8: 7 it does not submit to God's law—indeed it cannot   5
     10: 3 they have not submitted to God's righteousness.   5
2Co 11: 4 you submit to it readily enough.   1
Gal 2: 5 we did not submit to them even for a moment   2
     5: 1 do not submit again to a yoke of slavery.   3
Heb 13:17 Obey your leaders and submit to them   4
Jas 4: 7 Submit yourselves therefore to God.   5

submit to regulation
1. δογματίζω, *dogmatizō, 1505*
Col 2:20 Why do you submit to regulations   1

subordinate
1. ὑποτάσσω, *hypotassō, 5718*
1Co 14:34 but should be subordinate   1

subsequent
1. μετά, *meta, 3552*
1Pe 1:11 sufferings destined for Christ and the subsequent glory.   1

substance
1. σῶμα, *sōma, 5393*
Col 2:17 the substance belongs to Christ.   1

succeed[1]
1. διάδοχος, *diadochos, 1345*
Act 24:27 Felix was succeeded by Porcius Festus;   1

succeed[2]
1. εὐοδόω, *euodoō, 2338*
Rom 1:10 I may somehow at last succeed in coming to you.   1

succeed in fulfilling
1. φθάνω, *phthanō, 5777*
Rom 9:31 Israel…did not succeed in fulfilling that law.   1

such
1. Contextual: Not in Greek
2. αὐτός, *autos, 899*
3. εἴτε, *eite, 1664*
4. ὁ, *ho, 3836*
5. οἷος, *hoios, 3888*
6. οὗτος, *houtos, 4047*
7. οὕτως, *houtōs, 4048*
8. τοιοῦτος, *toioutos, 5525*
9. τοσοῦτος, *tosoutos, 5537*
Mat 8:10 in no one in Israel have I found such faith.   9
     9: 8 they glorified God, who had given such authority   8
     11:26 yes, Father, for such was your gracious will.   7
     18: 5 Whoever welcomes one such child in my name   8
     19:10 "If such is the case of a man with his wife   7
     19:14 to such as these that the kingdom of heaven   8
     24:21 such as has not been from the beginning   5
Mrk 2: 8 "Why do you raise such questions in your hearts?   6
     4:33 With many such parables he spoke the word   8
     9: 3 such as no one on earth could bleach them.   5
     9:37 "Whoever welcomes one such child in my name   8
     10:14 to such as these that the kingdom of God belongs.   8
     13:19 suffering, such as has not been   5
Lke 5:22 "Why do you raise such questions in your hearts?   1
     7: 9 not even in Israel have I found such faith."   9
     10:21 yes, Father, for such was your gracious will.   7
     18:16 to such as these that the kingdom of God belongs.   8
Jhn 4:23 the Father seeks such as these to worship him.   8
     5:34 Not that I accept such human testimony   4
     7:15 "How does this man have such learning   1
     8: 5 ⟦Now in the law Moses commanded us to stone such⟧   8
     9:16 "How can a man who is a sinner perform such signs?"   8
     15: 6 such branches are gathered, thrown into the fire   1
Act 20:35 that by such work we must support the weak   7
     26:29 might become such as I am—except for these chains."   8
Rom 4: 5 such faith is reckoned as righteousness.   2
1Co 11:16 we have no such custom, nor do the churches   8
     14: 7 produce sound, such as the flute or the harp.   3
2Co 3: 4 Such is the confidence that we have   8
     3:12 we have such a hope, we act with great boldness   8
     11:13 such boasters are false apostles, deceitful workers   8
     12: 3 I know that such a person   8
Gal 5: 8 Such persuasion does not come from the one who calls   4
Col 3: 8 now you must get rid of all such things—anger,   1
1Ti 1: 5 But the aim of such instruction is love   4
Heb 4:11 no one may fall through such disobedience   2
     7:26 fitting that we should have such a high priest   8
     8: 1 we have such a high priest   8
     9: 6 Such preparations having been made   7
     12: 3 who endured…such hostility against himself   8
     13:16 for such sacrifices are pleasing to God.   8
Jas 3:15 Such wisdom does not come down from above   6
     4:16 boast in your arrogance; all such boasting is evil.   8
Jde 1:15 that they have committed in such an ungodly way   1
Rev 16:18 such as had not occurred since people were upon the earth   5
     18:21 "With such violence Babylon…will be thrown down   7

such a case
1. τοιοῦτος, *toioutos, 5525*
1Co 7:15 in such a case the brother or sister is not bound.   1

such a fellow
1. τοιοῦτος, *toioutos, 5525*
Act 22:22 "Away with such a fellow from the earth!   1

such a one
1. Contextual: Not in Greek
2. αὐτός, *autos, 899*
3. τοιοῦτος, *toioutos, 5525*
Mat 18:17 let such a one be to you as a Gentile   1
1Co 5:11 Do not even eat with such a one.   3
2Co 12: 5 On behalf of such a one I will boast   3
Gal 6: 1 restore such a one in a spirit of gentleness.   3
1Jn 5:16 you will ask, and God will give life to such a one   2

such a person
1. αὐτός, *autos, 899*
2. ἑαυτοῦ, *heautou, 1571*
3. ὅς, *hos, 4005*
4. οὗτος, *houtos, 4047*
5. τοιοῦτος, *toioutos, 5525*
Mat 13:21 yet such a person has no root   2
Rom 2:29 Such a person receives praise…from God.   3
     16:18 For such people do not serve our Lord Christ   5

1Co	16:16	put yourselves at the service of such people	5
	16:18	So give recognition to such persons.	5
2Co	2: 6	This punishment…is enough for such a person	5
	10:11	Let such people understand	5
Eph	5:12	shameful even to mention what such people do	1
Php	2:29	Welcome him then in the Lord…and honor such people	5
2Th	3:12	Now such persons we command and exhort	5
Tit	3:11	since you know that such a person is perverted	5
1Jn	2: 4	in such a person the truth does not exist;	4
	2:10	in such a person there is no cause for stumbling.	1
2Jn	1: 7	any such person is the deceiver and the antichrist!	4
	1:11	to participate in the evil deeds of such a person.	1
3Jn	1: 8	Therefore we ought to support such people	5

such a thing

1. οὗτος, *houtos*, 4047
2. οὕτως, *houtōs*, 4048
3. τοιοῦτος, *toioutos*, 5525

Lke	9: 9	who is this about whom I hear such things?"	3
Jhn	5:16	because he was doing such things on the sabbath.	1
	7:32	The Pharisees heard the crowd muttering such things	1
Rom	1:32	that those who practice such things deserve to die	3
	2: 2	God's judgment on those who do such things	3
	2: 3	when you judge those who do such things	3
1Co	5: 4	on the man who has done such a thing.	2
Gal	5:21	those who do such things	3
	5:23	There is no law against such things.	3

such a way

1. οὕτως, *houtōs*, 4048

| Act | 14: 1 | spoke in such a way that a great number of both Jews | 1 |
| 1Co | 9:24 | Run in such a way that you may win it. | 1 |

such and such

1. ὅδε, *hode*, 3840
2. τοσοῦτος, *tosoutos*, 5537

| Act | 5: 8 | your husband sold the land for such and such | 2 |
| Jas | 4:13 | tomorrow we will go to such and such a town | 1 |

sudden

1. αἰφνίδιος, *aiphnidios*, 167

| 1Th | 5: 3 | then sudden destruction will come upon them | 1 |

suddenly *See also* confront suddenly

1. ἄφνω, *aphnō*, 924
2. ἐξαίφνης, *exaiphnēs*, 1978
3. ἐξάπινα, *exapina*, 1988
4. εὐθέως, *eutheōs*, 2311
5. εὐθύς¹, *euthys¹*, 2317
6. ἰδού, *idou*, 2627

Mat	2:19	Herod died, an angel of the Lord suddenly appeared	6
	3:16	suddenly the heavens were opened to him and he saw	6
	4:11	Then the devil left him, and suddenly angels came	6
	8:29	Suddenly they shouted, "What have you to do with us	6
	8:32	suddenly, the whole herd rushed down the steep bank	6
	9:18	suddenly a leader of the synagogue came in	6
	9:20	suddenly a woman who had been suffering	6
	17: 3	Suddenly there appeared to them Moses and Elijah	6
	17: 5	he was still speaking, suddenly a bright cloud	6
	26:51	Suddenly, one of those with Jesus	6
	28: 2	suddenly there was a great earthquake;	6
	28: 9	Suddenly Jesus met them and said, "Greetings!"	6
Mrk	9: 8	Suddenly when they looked around, they saw no one	3
	13:36	he may find you asleep when he comes suddenly.	2
Lke	2:13	suddenly there was with the angel a multitude	2
	9:30	Suddenly they saw two men, Moses and Elijah,	6
	9:39	Suddenly a spirit seizes him	6
	22:47	he was still speaking, suddenly a crowd came	6
	24: 4	suddenly two men in dazzling clothes stood beside	6
Act	1:10	suddenly two men in white robes stood by them.	6
	2: 2	suddenly from heaven there came a sound	1
	9: 3	suddenly a light from heaven flashed around him.	2
	10:16	the thing was suddenly taken up to heaven.	5
	10:17	suddenly the men sent by Cornelius	6
	10:30	suddenly a man in dazzling clothes stood before me.	6
	12: 7	Suddenly an angel of the Lord appeared	6
	12:10	suddenly the angel left him.	4
	16:26	Suddenly there was an earthquake, so violent	1
	22: 6	a great light from heaven suddenly shone about me.	2

sue

1. κρίνω, *krinō*, 3212

| Mat | 5:40 | and if anyone wants to sue you and take your coat | 1 |

suffer¹

1. Contextual: Not in Greek
2. θλῖψις, *thlipsis*, 2568
3. κακοπάθεια, *kakopatheia*, 2801
4. κακοπαθέω, *kakopatheō*, 2802
5. πάθημα, *pathēma*, 4077
6. παθητός, *pathētos*, 4078
7. πάσχω, *paschō*, 4248
8. συνέχω, *synechō*, 5309

Mat	17:12	the Son of Man is about to suffer at their hands."	7
	17:15	and he suffers terribly;	7
	24:21	For at that time there will be great suffering	2
	24:29	"Immediately after the suffering	2
	27:19	for today I have suffered a great deal	7
Mrk	13:19	For in those days there will be suffering	2
	13:24	in those days, after that suffering	2
Lke	4:38	mother-in-law was suffering from a high fever	8
	13: 2	because these Galileans suffered in this way they	7
	22:15	to eat this Passover with you before I suffer;	7
	24:26	it not necessary that the Messiah should suffer	7
	24:46	the Messiah is to suffer	7
Act	1: 3	After his suffering he presented himself alive	7
	3:18	he had foretold…that his Messiah would suffer.	7
	7:11	there came a famine…and great suffering	2
	9:16	how much he must suffer for the sake of my name."	7
	17: 3	necessary for the Messiah to suffer and to rise	7
	26:23	that the Messiah must suffer	6
	28: 5	shook off the creature…and suffered no harm.	7
Rom	5: 3	not only that, but we also boast in our sufferings	2
	5: 3	knowing that suffering produces endurance	2
	8:18	the sufferings of this present time are not worth	5
	12:12	Rejoice in hope, be patient in suffering	2
1Co	12:26	If one member suffers, all suffer together	7
2Co	1: 5	just as the sufferings of Christ are abundant for us	5
	1: 6	when you patiently endure the same sufferings	5
	1: 6	endure the same sufferings that we are also suffering.	7
	1: 7	we know that as you share in our sufferings	5
Eph	3:13	not lose heart over my sufferings for you;	2
Php	1:17	not sincerely but intending to increase my suffering	2
	1:29	suffering for him as well	7
	3:10	sharing of his sufferings	5
Col	1:24	I am now rejoicing in my sufferings for your sake	5
1Th	2:14	you suffered the same things	7
2Th	1: 5	kingdom of God, for which you are also suffering.	7
2Ti	1:12	for this reason I suffer as I do.	7
	3:11	my suffering the things that happened to me	5
Heb	2: 9	because of the suffering of death	5
	2:10	make…perfect through sufferings.	5
	2:18	Because he…was tested by what he suffered	7
	5: 8	he learned obedience through what he suffered;	7
	9:26	he would have had to suffer again and again	7
	10:32	you endured a hard struggle with sufferings	5
	13:12	Jesus also suffered outside the city gate	7
Jas	5:10	As an example of suffering and patience	3
	5:13	Are any among you suffering? They should pray.	4
1Pe	1:11	sufferings destined for Christ and the subsequent glory.	5
	2:19	you endure pain while suffering unjustly.	7
	2:20	if you endure when you do right and suffer for it	7
	2:21	because Christ also suffered for you	7
	2:23	when he suffered, he did not threaten;	7
	3:14	even if you do suffer for doing what is right	7
	3:17	For it is better to suffer for doing good	7
	3:17	to suffer…if suffering should be God's will	1
	3:17	suffer for doing good…than to suffer for doing evil.	1
	3:18	For Christ also suffered for sins once for all	7
	4: 1	Since therefore Christ suffered in the flesh	7
	4: 1	(for whoever has suffered in the flesh	7
	4:13	insofar as you are sharing Christ's sufferings	5
	4:15	let none of you suffer as a murderer, a thief	7
	4:16	Yet if any of you suffers as a Christian	1
	4:19	let those suffering in accordance with God's will	7
	5: 1	an elder myself and a witness of the sufferings of Christ	5
	5: 9	are undergoing the same kinds of suffering.	5
	5:10	after you have suffered for a little while	7
Rev	2:10	Do not fear what you are about to suffer.	7

suffer²
1. Contextual: Not in Greek
2. ἀδικέω, *adikeō, 92*
3. ἐν, *en, 1877*
4. ἔχω, *echō, 2400*
5. λυπέω, *lypeō, 3382*
6. πεῖρα + λαμβάνω, *peira + lambanō, 4278 + 3284*
7. τίνω, *tinō, 5514*

Mrk	5:25 woman who had been suffering from hemorrhages	3
Lke	8:43 suffering from hemorrhages for twelve years;	3
2Co	2: 3 so that when I came, I might not suffer pain	4
2Th	1: 9 suffer the punishment of eternal destruction	7
Heb	11:26 He considered abuse suffered for the Christ	1
	11:36 Others suffered mocking and flogging	6
1Pe	1: 6 you have had to suffer various trials	5
2Pe	2:13 suffering the penalty for doing wrong.	2

suffer already
1. προπάσχω, *propaschō, 4634*

1Th	2: 2 though we had already suffered	1

suffer dishonor
1. ἀτιμάζω, *atimazō, 869*

Act	5:41 worthy to suffer dishonor for the sake of the name.	1

suffer from a hemorrhage
1. αἱμορροέω, *haimorroeō, 137*

Mat	9:20 a woman who had been suffering from hemorrhages	1

suffer hardship
1. κακοπαθέω, *kakopatheō, 2802*

2Ti	2: 9 for which I suffer hardship, even…being chained	1

suffer loss
1. ζημιόω, *zēmioō, 2423*

1Co	3:15 work is burned up, the builder will suffer loss;	1
Php	3: 8 I have suffered the loss of all things	1

suffer persecution
1. θλίβω, *thlibō, 2567*

1Th	3: 4 that we were to suffer persecution;	1

suffer shipwreck
1. ναυαγέω, *nauageō, 3728*

1Ti	1:19 persons have suffered shipwreck in the faith	1

suffer together
1. συμπάσχω, *sympaschō, 5224*

1Co	12:26 If one member suffers, all suffer together	1

suffer violence
1. βιάζω, *biazo, 1041*

Mat	11:12 the kingdom of heaven has suffered violence	1

suffer with
1. συμπάσχω, *sympaschō, 5224*

Rom	8:17 heirs with Christ—if, in fact, we suffer with him	1

suffering See endure suffering, go through suffering, join in suffering, share in suffering, undergo suffering

sufficient
1. ἀρκέω, *arkeō, 758*
2. ἱκανός, *hikanos, 2653*

2Co	2:16 Who is sufficient for these things?	2
	12: 9 he said to me, "My grace is sufficient for you	1

suit
1. κατά, *kata, 2848*

2Ti	4: 3 teachers to suit their own desires	1

suitable
1. κόσμιος, *kosmios, 3177*

1Ti	2: 9 modestly and decently in suitable clothing	1

not suitable
1. ἀνεύθετος, *aneuthetos, 460*

Act	27:12 harbor was not suitable for spending the winter	1

sulfur
1. θεῖον, *theion, 2520*
2. θειώδης, *theiōdēs, 2523*

Lke	17:29 rained fire and sulfur from heaven	1
Rev	9:17 the color of fire and of sapphire and of sulfur;	2
	9:17 and smoke and sulfur came out of their mouths.	1
	9:18 killed, by the fire and smoke and sulfur	1
	14:10 they will be tormented with fire and sulfur	1
	19:20 the lake of fire that burns with sulfur.	1
	20:10 thrown into the lake of fire and sulfur	1
	21: 8 in the lake that burns with fire and sulfur	1

sum
1. τιμή, *time, 5507*

Act	7:16 tomb that Abraham had bought for a sum of silver	1

large sum
1. ἱκανός, *hikanos, 2653*
2. πολύς, *polys, 4498*

Mat	26: 9 ointment could have been sold for a large sum	2
	28:12 to give a large sum of money to the soldiers	1
Mrk	12:41 Many rich people put in large sums.	2

sum of money
1. κεφάλαιον, *kephalaion, 3049*

Act	22:28 cost me a large sum of money to get my citizenship."	1

sum up
1. ἀνακεφαλαιόω, *anakephalaioō, 368*
2. πληρόω, *plēroō, 4444*

Rom	13: 9 commandments…are summed up in this word	1
Gal	5:14 the whole law is summed up in a single commandment	2

summer
1. θέρος, *theros, 2550*

Mat	24:32 you know that summer is near.	1
Mrk	13:28 you know that summer is near.	1
Lke	21:30 know that summer is already near.	1

summon
1. καλέω, *kaleō, 2813*
2. προσκαλέω, *proskaleō, 4673*
3. φωνέω, *phōneō, 5888*

Mat	10: 1 Jesus summoned his twelve disciples and gave them	2
	18:32 Then his lord summoned him and said to him	2
	25:14 summoned his slaves and entrusted his property	1
Mrk	15:44 summoning the centurion	2
Lke	7:18 John summoned two of his disciples	2
	16: 2 he summoned him and said to him, 'What is this	3
	16: 5 summoning his master's debtors one by one	2
	19:13 summoned ten of his slaves	1
	19:15 to be summoned so that he might find out	3
Jhn	18:33 Pilate…summoned Jesus, and asked him	3
Act	13: 7 who summoned Barnabas and Saul	2
	23:23 he summoned two of the centurions and said	2
	24: 2 When Paul had been summoned, Tertullus began	1

sumptuously
1. λαμπρῶς, *lamprōs, 3289*

Lke	16:19 and who feasted sumptuously every day.	1

sun
1. ἥλιος, *hēlios, 2463*

Mat	5:45 he makes his sun rise on the evil and on the good	1
	13: 6 when the sun rose, they were scorched;	1
	13:43 Then the righteous will shine like the sun	1
	17: 2 and his face shone like the sun	1
	24:29 the sun will be darkened	1
Mrk	4: 6 when the sun rose, it was scorched;	1
	13:24 after that suffering, the sun will be darkened	1
	16: 2 when the sun had risen, they went to the tomb.	1
Lke	4:40 As the sun was setting	1
	21:25 "There will be signs in the sun, the moon,	1
	23:45 while the sun's light failed;	1
Act	2:20 The sun shall be turned to darkness	1
	13:11 be blind for a while, unable to see the sun."	1
	26:13 a light from heaven, brighter than the sun	1
	27:20 neither sun nor stars appeared for many days	1
1Co	15:41 one glory of the sun, and another glory of the moon	1

Eph	4:26	do not let the sun go down on your anger	1
Jas	1:11	For the sun rises with its scorching heat	1
Rev	1:16	face was like the sun shining with full force.	1
	6:12	the sun became black as sackcloth	1
	7: 2	I saw another angel ascending from the rising…sun	1
	7:16	sun will not strike them, nor any scorching heat;	1
	8:12	blew his trumpet, and a third of the sun was struck	1
	9: 2	the sun and the air were darkened with the smoke	1
	10: 1	his face was like the sun, and his legs like	1
	12: 1	a woman clothed with the sun	1
	16: 8	The fourth angel poured his bowl on the sun	1
	19:17	Then I saw an angel standing in the sun	1
	21:23	the city has no need of sun or moon to shine on it	1
	22: 5	they need no light of lamp or sun	1

sundown

1. δύνω + ὁ + ἥλιος, *dynō + ho + hēlios, 1544 + 3836 + 2463*

Mrk 1:32 That evening, at sundown   1

super-apostle

1. ὑπερλίαν + ἀπόστολος, *hyperlian + apostolos, 5663 + 693*

2Co 11: 5 I am not…inferior to these super-apostles. 1
     12:11 inferior to these super-apostles 1

superior

1. κρείττων, *kreittōn, 3202*

Heb 1: 4 having become as much superior to angels as 1
     7: 7 the inferior is blessed by the superior. 1

supper

1. δειπνέω, *deipneō, 1268*
2. δεῖπνον, *deipnon, 1270*

Lke	17: 8	'Prepare supper for me	1
	22:20	did the same with the cup after supper, saying,	1
Jhn	13: 2	And during supper	2
	21:20	who had reclined next to Jesus at the supper	2
1Co	11:20	it is not really to eat the Lord's supper.	2
	11:21	each of you goes ahead with your own supper	2
	11:25	In the same way he took the cup also, after supper,	1
Rev	19: 9	invited to the marriage supper of the Lamb."	2
	19:17	"Come, gather for the great supper of God	2

supplication

1. δέησις, *deēsis, 1255*
2. ἱκετηρία, *hiketēria, 2656*

Eph	6:18	in every prayer and supplication.	1
	6:18	in supplication for all the saints.	1
Php	4: 6	in everything by prayer and supplication	1
1Ti	2: 1	supplications, prayers, intercessions	1
	5: 5	continues in supplications and prayers	1
Heb	5: 7	Jesus offered up prayers and supplications	2

supply

1. δίδωμι, *didōmi, 1443*
2. ἐπιχορηγέω, *epichorēgeō, 2220*
3. προσαναπληρόω, *prosanaplēroō, 4650*
4. χορηγέω, *chorēgeō, 5961*

2Co	9:10	He who supplies seed to the sower	2
	9:10	supply and multiply your seed for sowing	4
	9:12	not only supplies the needs of the saints	3
	11: 9	my needs were supplied by the friends	3
Gal	3: 5	does God supply you with the Spirit	2
Jas	2:16	not supply their bodily needs, what is the good	1
1Pe	4:11	do so with the strength that God supplies	4

support *See also* come to support

1. Contextual: Not in Greek
2. ἀντιλαμβάνω, *antilambanō, 514*
3. βαστάζω, *bastazō, 1002*
4. ἐπιχορηγέω, *epichorēgeō, 2220*
5. ὀψώνιον, *opsōnion, 4072*
6. στηρίζω, *stērizō, 5114*
7. ὑπολαμβάνω, *hypolambanō, 5696*
8. χρεία, *chreia, 5970*
9. ὠφελέω, *ōpheleō, 6067*

Mat	15: 5	'Whatever support you might have had from me	9
Mrk	7:11	support you might have had from me is Corban'	9
Act	20:34	worked with my own hands to support myself	8
	20:35	by such work we must support the weak	2

Rom	11:18	remember that it is not you that support the root	3
	11:18	but the root that supports you.	1
2Co	11: 8	I robbed other churches by accepting support	5
1Pe	5:10	will…restore, support, strengthen, and establish you.	6
2Pe	1: 5	to support your faith with goodness	4
3Jn	1: 7	accepting no support from non-believers.	1
	1: 8	Therefore we ought to support such people	7

suppose

1. Contextual: Not in Greek
2. δοκέω, *dokeō, 1506*
3. ἐάν, *ean, 1569*
4. νομίζω, *nomizō, 3787*
5. οἴομαι, *oiomai, 3887*
6. ὑπολαμβάνω, *hypolambanō, 5696*
7. ὑπονοέω, *hyponoeō, 5706*

Mat	12:11	"Suppose one of you has only one sheep	3
Lke	7:43	"I suppose the one for whom he canceled	6
	11: 5	"Suppose one of you has a friend, and you go	1
	19:11	because they supposed that the kingdom of God	2
Jhn	20:15	Supposing him to be the gardener, she said	2
	21:25	I suppose that the world…could not contain	5
Act	2:15	Indeed, these are not drunk, as you suppose	6
	7:25	He supposed that his kinsfolk would understand	4
	13:25	'What do you suppose that I am? I am not he.	7
	14:19	supposing that he was dead.	4
	16:13	where we supposed there was a place of prayer;	4
	16:27	supposed that the prisoners had escaped.	4
	21:29	they supposed that Paul had brought him	4
Gal	2: 6	those who were supposed to be acknowledged leaders	2
Jas	4: 5	you suppose that it is for nothing that the scripture says	2

suppress

1. κατέχω, *katechō, 2988*

Rom 1:18 those who by their wickedness suppress the truth. 1

supreme

1. ὑπερέχω, *hyperechō, 5660*

1Pe 2:13 whether of the emperor as supreme 1

sure

1. Contextual: Not in Greek
2. ἀσφαλής, *asphalēs, 855*
3. γινώσκω, *ginōskō, 1182*
4. οἶδα + ἀληθῶς, *oida + alēthōs, 3857 + 242*
5. πείθω, *peithō, 4275*
6. πεποίθησις, *pepoithēsis, 4301*
7. πιστός, *pistos, 4412*

Act	12:11	"Now I am sure that the Lord has sent his angel	4
Rom	2:19	if you are sure that you are a guide to the blind	5
2Co	1:15	Since I was sure of this, I wanted to come to you	6
Gal	2: 2	in order to make sure that I was not…in vain	1
Eph	5: 5	Be sure of this, that no fornicator	3
1Ti	1:15	The saying is sure and worthy of full acceptance	7
	3: 1	The saying is sure:	7
	4: 9	The saying is sure	7
2Ti	1: 5	a faith that…now, I am sure, lives in you.	5
	1:12	I am sure that he is able to guard until that day	5
	2:11	The saying is sure:	7
Tit	3: 8	The saying is sure.	7
Heb	6:19	hope, a sure and steadfast anchor of the soul	2
	13:18	we are sure that we have a clear conscience	5
1Jn	2: 3	by this we may be sure that we know him	3
	2: 5	By this we may be sure that we are in him:	3
	2:29	you may be sure that everyone who does right	3

surely *See also* die surely, see surely

1. Contextual: Not in Greek
2. ἀλήθεια, *alētheia, 237*
3. γάρ, *gar, 1142*
4. γέ, *ge, 1145*
5. δέ, *de, 1254*
6. ἤ, *ē, 2445*
7. ἰδού, *idou, 2627*
8. μήν², *mēn², 3605*
9. ναί, *nai, 3721*
10. ὅτι, *hoti, 4022*

Lke	1:48	Surely, from now on all generations will call me	7
	6:23	for surely your reward is great in heaven;	7

22:59	"Surely this man also was with him;	2
23:29	For the days are surely coming when they will say	7
Jhn 7:41	"Surely the Messiah does not come from Galilee	3
7:47	replied, "Surely you have not been deceived	1
7:52	replied, "Surely you are not also from Galilee	1
9:40	said to him, "Surely we are not blind	1
11:56	Surely he will not come to the festival	10
2Co 1:18	As surely as God is faithful	5
3: 1	Surely we do not need…letters of recommendation	6
Eph 3: 2	for surely you have already heard of the commission	4
4:21	For surely you have heard about him	4
Heb 6:14	saying, "I will surely bless you and multiply you."	8
8: 8	"The days are surely coming, says the Lord	7
Rev 22:20	"Surely I am coming soon." Amen. Come, Lord Jesus!	9

more surely

1. μᾶλλον, *mallon, 3437*

Rom 5: 9	Much more surely then…will we be saved	1
5:10	much more…will we be saved by his life.	1
5:15	much more surely have the grace of God	1
5:17	much more surely will those…exercise dominion in life	1

surely not

1. μήτι, *mēti, 3614*

Mat 26:22	"Surely not I, Lord?"	1
26:25	Judas, who betrayed him, said, "Surely not I,	1
Mrk 14:19	to say to him one after another, "Surely, not I?"	1

surpass

1. ὑπερβάλλω, *hyperballō, 5650*
2. ὑπερέχω, *hyperechō, 5660*

2Co 9:14	the surpassing grace of God that he has given you.	1
Eph 3:19	the love of Christ that surpasses knowledge	1
Php 4: 7	the peace of God, which surpasses all understanding	2

surpassing *See* surpassing *value*

surprise

1. καταλαμβάνω, *katalambanō, 2898*
2. ξενίζω, *xenizō, 3826*

1Th 5: 4	for that day to surprise you like a thief;	1
1Pe 4: 4	They are surprised that you no longer join them	2
4:12	Beloved, do not be surprised at the fiery ordeal	2

surround

1. κυκλεύω, *kykleuō, 3238*
2. κυκλόω, *kykloō, 3240*
3. κύκλῳ, *kyklō, 3241*
4. περί, *peri, 4309*
5. περιΐστημι, *periistēmi, 4325*
6. περίκειμαι, *perikeimai, 4329*
7. περικυκλόω, *perikykloō, 4333*
8. συνέχω, *synechō, 5309*

Mrk 6:36	so that they may go into the surrounding country	3
Lke 8:45	the crowds surround you and press in on you."	8
9:12	so that they may go into the surrounding villages	3
19:43	surround you, and hem you in on every side.	7
21:20	"When you see Jerusalem surrounded by armies	2
Act 14:20	when the disciples surrounded him, he got up	2
25: 7	the Jews…from Jerusalem surrounded him	5
Heb 12: 1	surrounded by so great a cloud of witnesses	6
Jde 1: 7	Sodom and Gomorrah and the surrounding cities	4
Rev 5:11	the voice of many angels surrounding the throne	3
20: 9	and surrounded the camp of the saints	1

surrounding *See* surrounding *country*, surrounding *region*

survive

1. μένω, *menō, 3531*
2. σωτηρία, *sōtēria, 5401*

Act 27:34	it will help you survive;	2
1Co 3:14	built on the foundation survives	1

survivor

1. σπέρμα, *sperma, 5065*

Rom 9:29	"If the Lord of hosts had not left survivors to us	1

Susanna

1. Σουσάννα, *Sousanna, 5052*

Lke 8: 3	Joanna…and Susanna, and many others	1

suspect

1. ὑπονοέω, *hyponoeō, 5706*

Act 27:27	sailors suspected that they were nearing land.	1

suspense *See also* keep in suspense

1. προσδοκάω, *prosdokaō, 4659*

Act 27:33	have been in suspense and remaining without food	1

suspicion

1. ὑπόνοια, *hyponoia, 5707*

1Ti 6: 4	envy, dissension, slander, base suspicions	1

sustain

1. ἵστημι, *histēmi, 2705*
2. φέρω, *pherō, 5770*

2Co 13: 1	"Any charge must be sustained	1
Heb 1: 3	sustains all things by his powerful word.	2

swallow

1. καταπίνω, *katapinō, 2927*

Mat 23:24	You strain out a gnat but swallow a camel!	1
Rev 12:16	it opened its mouth and swallowed the river	1

swallow up

1. καταπίνω, *katapinō, 2927*

1Co 15:54	"Death has been swallowed up in victory."	1
2Co 5: 4	what is mortal may be swallowed up by life.	1

swamp

1. γεμίζω, *gemizō, 1153*
2. καλύπτω, *kalyptō, 2821*

Mat 8:24	so great that the boat was being swamped by the waves;	2
Mrk 4:37	so that the boat was already being swamped.	1

sway

1. ἄγω, *agō, 72*

2Ti 3: 6	swayed by all kinds of desires	1

swear

1. ὀμνύω, *omnyō, 3923*

Mat 5:34	I say to you, Do not swear at all, either by heaven	1
5:36	And do not swear by your head,	1
23:16	swears by the sanctuary is bound by nothing	1
23:16	whoever swears by the gold of the sanctuary	1
23:18	'Whoever swears by the altar is bound by nothing	1
23:18	whoever swears by the gift that is on the altar	1
23:20	So whoever swears by the altar	1
23:20	swears by it and by everything on it;	1
23:21	whoever swears by the sanctuary	1
23:21	swears by it and by the one who dwells in it;	1
23:22	whoever swears by heaven	1
23:22	swears by the throne of God	1
Mrk 6:23	he solemnly swore to her, "Whatever you ask me	1
Act 2:30	knew that God had sworn with an oath to him	1
Heb 3:11	As in my anger I swore, 'They will not enter	1
3:18	swear that they would not enter his rest	1
4: 3	"As in my anger I swore, 'They shall not enter	1
6:13	because he had no one greater by whom to swear	1
6:13	he swore by himself	1
6:16	Human beings, of course, swear by someone greater	1
7:21	"The Lord has sworn and will not change his mind	1
Jas 5:12	Above all, my beloved, do not swear	1
Rev 10: 6	swore by him who lives forever and ever	1

swear an oath

1. ὀμνύω, *omnyō, 3923*

Mat 26:74	he began to curse, and he swore an oath	1
Mrk 14:71	he began to curse, and he swore an oath	1
Lke 1:73	the oath that he swore to our ancestor Abraham	1

swear falsely

1. ἐπιορκέω, *epiorkeō, 2155*

Mat 5:33	'You shall not swear falsely, but carry out	1

sweat

1. ἱδρώς, *hidrōs, 2629*

Lke 22:44	⟦his sweat became like great drops of blood⟧	1

sweep

1. σαρόω, *saroō, 4924*

Mat	12:44	it finds it empty, swept, and put in order.	1
Lke	11:25	it finds it swept and put in order.	1
	15: 8	light a lamp, sweep the house, and search	1

sweep away

1. αἴρω, *airō, 149*

Mat 24:39 the flood came and swept them all away   1

sweep away with the flood

1. ποταμοφόρητος + ποιέω, *potamophorētos + poieō, 4533 + 4472*

Rev 12:15 to sweep her away with the flood.   1

sweep down

1. καταβαίνω, *katabainō, 2849*
2. σύρω, *syrō, 5359*

Lke 8:23 A windstorm swept down on the lake   1
Rev 12: 4 His tail swept down a third of the stars of heaven   2

sweet

1. γλυκύς, *glykys, 1184*

Rev 10: 9 bitter…but sweet as honey in your mouth."   1
    10:10 it was sweet as honey in my mouth   1

swell up

1. πίμπρημι, *pimprēmi, 4399*

Act 28: 6 They were expecting him to swell up   1

swell with conceit

1. τυφόομαι, *typhoomai, 5605*

2Ti 3: 4 treacherous, reckless, swollen with conceit   1

swerve

1. ἀστοχέω, *astocheō, 846*

2Ti 2:18 who have swerved from the truth by claiming   1

swift

1. ὀξύς, *oxys, 3955*
2. ταχινός, *tachinos, 5442*

Rom 3:15 "Their feet are swift to shed blood;   1
2Pe 2: 1 bringing swift destruction on themselves.   2

swim

1. κολυμβάω, *kolymbaō, 3147*

Act 27:43 He ordered those who could swim   1

swim away

1. ἐκκολυμβάω, *ekkolymbaō, 1713*

Act 27:42 so that none might swim away and escape;   1

swine

1. χοῖρος, *choiros, 5956*

Mat	7: 6	and do not throw your pearls before swine	1
	8:30	Now a large herd of swine was feeding	1
	8:31	cast us out, send us into the herd of swine."	1
	8:32	"Go!" So they came out and entered the swine;	1
Mrk	5:11	the hillside a great herd of swine was feeding;	1
	5:12	"Send us into the swine; let us enter them."	1
	5:13	unclean spirits came out and entered the swine;	1
	5:16	to the demoniac and to the swine	1
Lke	8:32	on the hillside a large herd of swine was feeding;	1
	8:33	the demons…entered the swine	1

swineherd

1. βόσκω, *boskō, 1081*

Mat 8:33 The swineherds ran off, and on going into the town   1
Mrk 5:14 The swineherds ran off and told it   1
Lke 8:34 When the swineherds saw what had happened   1

swing

1. βάλλω, *ballō, 965*

Rev 14:16 the one who sat on the cloud swung his sickle   1
    14:19 So the angel swung his sickle over the earth   1

sword

1. Contextual: Not in Greek

2. μάχαιρα, *machaira, 3479*
3. ῥομφαία, *rhomphaia, 4855*

Mat	10:34	I have not come to bring peace, but a sword.	2
	26:47	with him was a large crowd with swords and clubs	2
	26:51	put his hand on his sword, drew it,	2
	26:52	"Put your sword back into its place;	2
	26:52	all who take the sword will perish by the sword.	2
	26:52	all who take the sword will perish by the sword.	2
	26:55	with swords and clubs to arrest me	2
Mrk	14:43	with him there was a crowd with swords and clubs	2
	14:47	one of those who stood near drew his sword	2
	14:48	with swords and clubs to arrest me	2
Lke	2:35	and a sword will pierce your own soul too."	3
	21:24	they will fall by the edge of the sword	2
	22:36	one who has no sword must sell his cloak	2
	22:38	They said, "Lord, look, here are two swords."	2
	22:49	should we strike with the sword?"	2
	22:52	with swords and clubs as if I were a bandit?	2
Jhn	18:10	Simon Peter, who had a sword, drew it	2
	18:11	"Put your sword back into its sheath.	2
Act	12: 2	James, the brother of John, killed with the sword.	2
	16:27	he drew his sword and was about to kill himself	2
Rom	8:35	or famine, or nakedness, or peril, or sword?	2
	13: 4	for the authority does not bear the sword in vain!	2
Eph	6:17	the sword of the Spirit, which is the word of God.	2
Heb	4:12	sharper than any two-edged sword	2
	11:34	escaped the edge of the sword	2
	11:37	they were killed by the sword;	2
Rev	1:16	from his mouth came a sharp, two-edged sword	3
	2:12	the words of him who has the sharp two-edged sword:	3
	2:16	make war against them with the sword of my mouth.	3
	6: 4	and he was given a great sword.	2
	6: 8	authority…to kill with sword, famine, and pestilence,	3
	13:10	if you kill with the sword	2
	13:10	if you kill…with the sword you must be killed.	2
	13:14	the beast that had been wounded by the sword	2
	19:15	From his mouth comes a sharp sword	3
	19:21	And the rest were killed by the sword	3
	19:21	the sword that came from his mouth;	1

sycamore tree

1. συκομορέα, *sykomorea, 5191*

Lke 19: 4 and climbed a sycamore tree   1

Sychar

1. Συχάρ, *Sychar, 5373*

Jhn 4: 5 So he came to a Samaritan city called Sychar   1

symbol

1. παραβολή, *parabolē, 4130*

Heb 9: 9 This is a symbol of the present time   1

symbol of authority

1. ἐξουσία, *exousia, 2026*

1Co 11:10 ought to have a symbol of authority on her head   1

sympathize

1. συμπαθέω, *sympatheō, 5217*

Heb 4:15 is unable to sympathize with our weaknesses   1

sympathy

1. οἰκτιρμός, *oiktirmos, 3880*
2. συμπαθής, *sympathēs, 5218*

Php 2: 1 any compassion and sympathy   1
1Pe 3: 8 Finally, all of you, have unity of spirit, sympathy   2

synagogue *See also* leader of the synagogue, official of the synagogue, put out of the synagogue

1. Contextual: Not in Greek
2. ἐκεῖθεν, *ekeithen, 1696*
3. συναγωγή, *synagōgē, 5252*

Mat	4:23	throughout Galilee, teaching in their synagogues	3
	6: 2	as the hypocrites do in the synagogues	3
	6: 5	pray in the synagogues and at the street corners	3
	9:18	suddenly a leader of the synagogue came in	1
	9:35	teaching in their synagogues, and proclaiming	3
	10:17	and flog you in their synagogues;	3
	12: 9	and entered their synagogue;	3
	13:54	began to teach the people in their synagogue	3

23: 6	They love...the best seats in the synagogues	3
23:34	some you will flog in your synagogues	3
Mrk 1:21	he entered the synagogue and taught.	3
1:23	Just then there was in their synagogue a man	3
1:29	As soon as they left the synagogue	3
1:39	proclaiming the message in their synagogues	3
3: 1	Again he entered the synagogue	3
6: 2	On the sabbath he began to teach in the synagogue	3
12:39	and to have the best seats in the synagogues	3
13: 9	you will be beaten in synagogues;	3
Lke 4:15	He began to teach in their synagogues	3
4:16	he went to the synagogue on the sabbath day,	3
4:20	The eyes of all in the synagogue were fixed on him.	3
4:28	all in the synagogue were filled with rage.	3
4:33	In the synagogue there was a man	3
4:38	leaving the synagogue	3
4:44	the message in the synagogues of Judea.	3
6: 6	he entered the synagogue and taught	3
7: 5	it is he who built our synagogue for us."	3
8:41	Jairus, a leader of the synagogue.	3
11:43	love to have the seat of honor in the synagogues	3
12:11	bring you before the synagogues, the rulers	3
13:10	in one of the synagogues on the sabbath.	3
20:46	and love...the best seats in the synagogues	3
21:12	hand you over to synagogues and prisons	3
Jhn 6:59	he was teaching in the synagogue at Capernaum.	3
18:20	always taught in synagogues and in the temple	3
Act 6: 9	who belonged to the synagogue of the Freedmen	3
9: 2	letters to the synagogues at Damascus	3
9:20	he began to proclaim Jesus in the synagogues,	3
13: 5	proclaimed the word of God in the synagogues	3
13:14	they went into the synagogue and sat down.	3
13:43	When the meeting of the synagogue broke up	3
14: 1	Paul and Barnabas went into the Jewish synagogue	3
15:21	read aloud every sabbath in the synagogues."	3
17: 1	where there was a synagogue of the Jews.	3
17:10	they went to the Jewish synagogue.	3
17:17	he argued in the synagogue with the Jews	3
18: 4	Every sabbath he would argue in the synagogue	3
18: 7	he left the synagogue and went to the house	2
18: 7	his house was next door to the synagogue.	3
18:19	but first he himself went into the synagogue	3
18:26	He began to speak boldly in the synagogue;	3
19: 8	He entered the synagogue	3
22:19	in every synagogue I imprisoned and beat	3
24:12	stirring up a crowd either in the synagogues	3
26:11	punishing them often in all the synagogues	3
Rev 2: 9	but are a synagogue of Satan.	3
3: 9	I will make those of the synagogue of Satan	3

out of the synagogue
1. ἀποσυνάγωγος, *aposynagōgos, 697*

Jhn 16: 2	They will put you out of the synagogues.	1

Syntyche
1. Συντύχη, *Syntychē, 5345*

Php 4: 2	Euodia and I urge Syntyche to be of the same mind	1

Syracuse
1. Συράκουσαι, *Syrakousai, 5352*

Act 28:12	put in at Syracuse and stayed there	1

Syria
1. Συρία, *Syria, 5353*

Mat 4:24	So his fame spread throughout all Syria	1
Lke 2: 2	while Quirinius was governor of Syria.	1
Act 15:23	the believers...in Antioch and Syria and Cilicia	1
15:41	He went through Syria and Cilicia	1
18:18	farewell to the believers and sailed for Syria	1
20: 3	He was about to set sail for Syria	1
21: 3	leaving it on our left, we sailed to Syria	1
Gal 1:21	I went into the regions of Syria and Cilicia	1

Syrian
1. Σύρος, *Syros, 5354*

Lke 4:27	except Naaman the Syrian."	1

Syrophoenician
1. Συροφοινίκισσα, *Syrophoinikissa, 5355*

Mrk 7:26	the woman was a Gentile, of Syrophoenician origin.	1

Syrtis
1. Σύρτις, *Syrtis, 5358*

Act 27:17	then, fearing that they would run on the Syrtis	1

T

Tabitha
1. Ταβιθά, *Tabitha, 5412*

Act 9:36	in Joppa there was a disciple whose name was Tabitha	1
9:40	turned to the body and said, "Tabitha, get up."	1

table   *See also* sit at table, sit at table with, take one's place at table
1. Contextual: Not in Greek
2. ἀναπίπτω, *anapiptō, 404*
3. δεῖπνον, *deipnon, 1270*
4. τράπεζα, *trapeza, 5544*

Mat 15:27	crumbs that fall from their masters' table."	4
21:12	he overturned the tables of the money changers	4
Mrk 7:28	"Sir, even the dogs under the table eat	4
11:15	he overturned the tables of the money changers	4
Lke 16:21	with what fell from the rich man's table;	4
22:21	with me, and his hand is on the table.	4
22:30	you may eat and drink at my table in my kingdom	4
Jhn 2:14	the money changers seated at their tables.	1
2:15	and overturned their tables.	4
13: 4	got up from the table, took off his outer robe	3
13:12	put on his robe, and had returned to the table	2
Act 6: 2	neglect the word of God in order to wait on tables.	4
Rom 11: 9	"Let their table become a snare and a trap,	4
1Co 10:21	You cannot partake of the table of the Lord	4
10:21	table of the Lord and the table of demons.	4
Heb 9: 2	in which were the lampstand, the table	4

at table
1. ἀνάκειμαι, *anakeimai, 367*
2. κατακλίνω, *kataklinō, 2884*

Lke 22:27	one who is at the table or the one who serves?	1
22:27	Is it not the one at the table?	1
24:30	When he was at the table with them, he took bread	2
Jhn 12: 2	Lazarus was one of those at the table with him.	1
13:28	no one at the table knew why he said this to him.	1

at table with
1. συνανάκειμαι, *synanakeimai, 5263*

Lke 7:49	But those who were at the table with him	1

tablet   *See also* writing tablet
1. Contextual: Not in Greek
2. πλάξ, *plax, 4419*

2Co 3: 3	not on tablets of stone	2
3: 3	but on tablets of human hearts.	2
3: 7	chiseled in letters on stone tablets	1
Heb 9: 4	the tablets of the covenant;	2

tackle
1. σκευή, *skeuē, 5006*

Act 27:19	own hands they threw the ship's tackle overboard.	1

tail
1. οὐρά, *oura, 4038*

Rev 9:10	They have tails like scorpions, with stingers	1
9:10	in their tails is their power to harm people	1
9:19	power...is in their mouths and in their tails;	1
9:19	their tails are like serpents, having heads;	1
12: 4	His tail swept down a third of the stars of heaven	1

take
1. Contextual: Not in Greek
2. ἄγω, *agō, 72*
3. αἴρω, *airō, 149*
4. ἀνάγω, *anagō, 343*
5. ἀναλαμβάνω, *analambanō, 377*
6. ἀπάγω, *apagō, 552*
7. ἀποφέρω, *apopherō, 708*
8. ἀφορίζω, *aphorizō, 928*
9. γίνομαι, *ginomai, 1181*

10. δέχομαι, *dechomai, 1312*
11. εἰσέρχομαι, *eiserchomai, 1656*
12. ἐπιλαμβάνομαι, *epilambanomai, 2138*
13. ἔχω, *echō, 2400*
14. κατέχω, *katechō, 2988*
15. κρατέω, *krateō, 3195*
16. κτάομαι, *ktaomai, 3227*
17. λαμβάνω, *lambanō, 3284*
18. μετάθεσις, *metathesis, 3557*
19. μεταλαμβάνω, *metalambanō, 3561*
20. μετατίθημι, *metatithēmi, 3572*
21. παραλαμβάνω, *paralambanō, 4161*
22. πιάζω, *piazō, 4389*
23. προσλαμβάνω, *proslambanō, 4689*
24. συλλαμβάνω, *syllambanō, 5197*
25. ὑπολαμβάνω, *hypolambanō, 5696*
26. φέρω, *pherō, 5770*
27. χράομαι, *chraomai, 5968*

Mat	1:20	do not be afraid to take Mary as your wife	21
	1:24	of the Lord commanded him; he took her as his wife	21
	2:13	"Get up, take the child and his mother, and flee	21
	2:14	Joseph got up, took the child and his mother	21
	2:20	"Get up, take the child and his mother, and go	21
	2:21	Joseph got up, took the child and his mother	21
	4: 5	Then the devil took him to the holy city	21
	4: 8	Again, the devil took him to a very high mountain	21
	5:40	and if anyone wants to sue you and take your coat	17
	7:13	and there are many who take it.	11
	8:17	"He took our infirmities and bore our diseases."	17
	9: 6	"Stand up, take your bed and go to your home."	3
	9:25	he went in and took her by the hand	15
	10: 9	Take no gold, or silver, or copper in your belts	16
	11:29	Take my yoke upon you, and learn from me;	3
	13:31	that someone took and sowed in his field;	17
	13:33	yeast that a woman took and mixed	17
	14:12	His disciples came and took the body	3
	14:19	Taking the five loaves and the two fish	17
	15:26	"It is not fair to take the children's food	17
	15:36	he took the seven loaves and the fish;	17
	17:25	From whom do kings of the earth take toll	17
	17:27	take the first fish that comes up	3
	17:27	take that and give it to them for you and me."	17
	20:14	Take what belongs to you and go;	3
	24:17	to take what is in the house;	3
	24:40	one will be taken and one will be left.	21
	24:41	one will be taken and one will be left.	21
	25: 1	Ten bridesmaids took their lamps	17
	25: 3	When the foolish took their lamps	17
	25: 3	they took no oil with them;	17
	25: 4	the wise took flasks of oil with their lamps.	17
	25:28	So take the talent from him	3
	26:26	While they were eating, Jesus took a loaf of bread	17
	26:26	"Take, eat; this is my body."	17
	26:27	he took a cup	17
	26:52	all who take the sword will perish by the sword.	17
	26:57	took him to Caiaphas the high priest	6
	27: 6	the chief priests, taking the pieces of silver,	17
	27: 9	"And they took the thirty pieces of silver	17
	27:24	took some water and washed his hands	17
	27:27	Then the soldiers of the governor took Jesus	21
	27:30	took the reed and struck him on the head.	17
	27:59	Joseph took the body	17
	28:15	took the money and did as they were directed.	17
Mrk	1:31	He came and took her by the hand and lifted her up.	15
	2: 9	or to say, 'Stand up and take your mat and walk'?	3
	2:11	"I say to you, stand up, take your mat and go	3
	2:12	he stood up, and immediately took the mat	3
	5:40	and took the child's father and mother	21
	5:41	He took her by the hand and said to her,	15
	6: 8	ordered them to take nothing for their journey	3
	6:29	they came and took his body, and laid it in a tomb.	3
	6:41	Taking the five loaves and the two fish	17
	7:27	for it is not fair to take the children's food	17
	8: 6	he took the seven loaves	17
	8:23	he took the blind man by the hand	12
	9:27	Jesus took him by the hand and lifted him up	15
	9:36	he took a little child and put it among them	17
	11: 6	and they allowed them to take it.	1
	13:15	or enter the house to take anything away;	3
	14:22	he took a loaf of bread, and after blessing it	17

	14:22	"Take; this is my body."	17
	14:23	he took a cup	17
	14:53	They took Jesus to the high priest;	6
	14:65	The guards also took him over and beat him.	17
	15:23	he did not take it.	17
	15:24	casting lots to decide what each should take.	3
Lke	2: 2	taken while Quirinius was governor	1
	2:28	Simeon took him in his arms and praised God,	10
	4: 9	the devil took him to Jerusalem	2
	5: 9	amazed at the catch of fish that they had taken;	24
	5:24	stand up and take your bed and go to your home."	3
	5:25	took what he had been lying on, and went	3
	6: 4	took and ate the bread of the Presence	17
	8:54	took her by the hand and called out, "Child	15
	9: 3	He said to them, "Take nothing for your journey	3
	9:16	taking the five loaves and the two fish	17
	9:47	took a little child and put it by his side	12
	13:19	that someone took and sowed in the garden;	17
	13:21	It is like yeast that a woman took and mixed	17
	14: 4	they were silent. So Jesus took him and healed him	12
	14: 9	you would start to take the lowest place.	14
	16: 6	He said to him, 'Take your bill	10
	16: 7	to him, 'Take you bill and make it eighty.'	10
	17:34	one will be taken and the other left.	21
	17:35	one will be taken and the other left."	21
	19:17	take charge of ten cities.'	13
	19:21	you take what you did not deposit	3
	19:22	a harsh man, taking what I did not deposit	3
	19:24	'Take the pound from him	3
	22:17	he took a cup, and after giving thanks he said	10
	22:17	"Take this and divide it among yourselves;	17
	22:19	he took a loaf of bread	17
	22:36	who has a purse must take it, and likewise a bag.	3
	24: 1	taking the spices that they had prepared.	26
	24:30	When he was at the table with them, he took bread	17
	24:43	he took it and ate in their presence.	17
Jhn	2: 8	draw some out, and take it to the chief steward."	26
	2: 8	to the chief steward." So they took it.	26
	2:16	the doves, "Take these things out	3
	5: 8	"Stand up, take your mat and walk."	3
	6:11	Then Jesus took the loaves	17
	6:21	they wanted to take him into the boat	17
	10:18	No one takes it from me	3
	12: 3	Mary took a pound of costly perfume	17
	12:13	they took branches of palm trees	17
	14: 3	I will come again and will take you to myself	21
	16:14	will take what is mine and declare it to you.	17
	16:15	I said that he will take what is mine	17
	16:22	no one will take your joy from you.	3
	17:15	not asking you to take them out of the world	3
	18:13	First they took him to Annas	2
	18:28	they took Jesus from Caiaphas	2
	18:31	Pilate said to them, "Take him yourselves	17
	19: 1	Pilate took Jesus and had him flogged.	17
	19: 6	Pilate said to them, "Take him yourselves	17
	19:16	to be crucified. So they took Jesus;	21
	19:23	they took his clothes and divided them	17
	19:23	They also took his tunic;	1
	19:27	the disciple took her into his own home.	17
	19:40	They took the body of Jesus	17
	20: 2	"They have taken the Lord out of the tomb	3
	21:13	Jesus came and took the bread and gave it	17
	21:18	take you where you do not wish to go."	26
Act	1: 9	a cloud took him out of their sight.	25
	1:20	'Let another take his position of overseer.'	17
	1:25	to take the place in this ministry	17
	3: 7	he took him by the right hand and raised him up;	22
	9:19	taking some food, he regained his strength.	17
	9:25	his disciples took him by night	17
	9:27	Barnabas took him, brought him to the apostles	12
	9:39	when he arrived, they took him to the room upstairs.	4
	15:14	to take from among them a people for his name.	17
	16: 3	he took him and had him circumcised	17
	16:33	At the same hour of the night he took them	21
	17: 9	after they had taken bail from Jason	17
	17:19	So they took him and brought him to the Areopagus	12
	19: 9	he left them, taking the disciples with him	8
	21:11	came to us and took Paul's belt	3
	21:26	Then Paul took the men	21
	21:32	Immediately he took soldiers and centurions	21
	22:11	took my hand and led me to Damascus.	1

23:17	"Take this young man to the tribune	6
23:18	took him, brought him to the tribune, and said	21
23:19	The tribune took him by the hand	12
23:31	according to their instructions, took Paul	5
27:17	they took measures to undergird the ship;	27
27:33	Paul urged all of them to take some food, saying	19
27:34	Therefore I urge you to take some food	19
27:35	After he had said this, he took bread;	17
27:36	were encouraged and took food for themselves.	23
28:15	Paul thanked God and took courage.	17
1Co 6: 1	instead of taking it before the saints?	1
6:15	Should I therefore take the members of Christ	3
11:23	the night when he was betrayed took a loaf of bread	17
11:25	In the same way he took the cup also, after supper,	1
16: 2	so that collections need not be taken when I come.	9
16: 3	to take your gift to Jerusalem.	7
2Co 12:16	I was crafty...I took you in by deceit.	17
12:18	Did we not take the same steps?	1
Eph 6:16	With all of these, take the shield of faith	5
6:17	Take the helmet of salvation	10
Php 2: 7	emptied himself, taking the form of a slave	17
1Ti 5:23	No longer drink only water, but take a little wine	27
Heb 5: 4	one does not presume to take this honor	17
5: 4	takes it only when called by God	1
8: 9	on the day when I took them by the hand	12
9: 7	not without taking the blood	1
9:19	he took the blood of calves and goats	17
11: 5	By faith Enoch was taken	20
11: 5	"he was not found, because God had taken him."	20
11: 5	For it was attested before he was taken away	18
Jas 3: 4	it takes strong winds to drive them,	1
5:10	As an example...beloved, take the prophets	17
Rev 5: 7	He went and took the scroll from the right hand	17
5: 8	When he had taken the scroll	17
5: 9	worthy...to take the scroll and to open its seals	17
6: 4	rider was permitted to take peace from the earth	17
8: 5	Then the angel took the censer and filled it	17
10: 8	"Go, take the scroll that is open in the hand	17
10: 9	"Take it, and eat; it will be bitter to your stomach	17
10:10	took the little scroll from the hand of the angel	17
11:17	have taken your great power and begun to reign.	17
12: 5	her child was snatched away and taken to God	1
22:17	Let anyone who wishes take the water of life	17

take a name

1. ὀνομάζω, *onomazō, 3951*

Eph 3:15	every family in heaven and on earth takes its name.	1

take a rest

1. ἀναπαύω, *anapauō, 399*

Mat 26:45	"Are you still sleeping and taking your rest?	1
Mrk 14:41	"Are you still sleeping and taking your rest?	1

take a seat

1. καθίζω, *kathizō, 2767*

Act 12:21	Herod...took his seat on the platform	1
25: 6	the next day he took his seat on the tribunal	1
25:17	but on the next day took my seat on the tribunal	1
2Th 2: 4	he takes his seat in the temple of God	1
Heb 12: 2	taken his seat at the right hand of the throne of God.	1

take a sounding

1. βολίζω, *bolizō, 1075*

Act 27:28	So they took soundings and found twenty fathoms;	1
27:28	a little farther on they took soundings again	1

take a stand

1. ἵστημι, *histēmi, 2705*
2. παρίστημι, *paristēmi, 4225*

Act 4:26	The kings of the earth took their stand	2
Rev 12:18	the dragon took his stand on the sand of the seashore.	1

take a straight course

1. εὐθυδρομέω, *euthydromeō, 2312*

Act 16:11	took a straight course to Samothrace	1

take action

1. ἀνίστημι, *anistēmi, 482*

Act 5:17	the high priest took action;	1

take advantage

1. λαμβάνω, *lambanō, 3284*
2. πλεονεκτέω, *pleonekteō, 4430*

2Co 7: 2	we have taken advantage of no one.	2
11:20	or preys upon you, or takes advantage of you	1
12:17	Did I take advantage of you	2
12:18	Titus did not take advantage of you	2

take along

1. ἀναλαμβάνω, *analambanō, 377*
2. παραλαμβάνω, *paralambanō, 4161*
3. συμπαραλαμβάνω, *symparalambanō, 5221*

Mat 18:16	not listened to, take one or two others along	2
Act 7:43	No; you took along the tent of Moloch	1
Gal 2: 1	taking Titus along with me.	3

take aside

1. ἀπολαμβάνω, *apolambanō, 655*
2. παραλαμβάνω, *paralambanō, 4161*
3. προσλαμβάνω, *proslambanō, 4689*

Mat 16:22	Peter took him aside and began to rebuke him	3
20:17	he took the twelve disciples aside by themselves	2
Mrk 7:33	took him aside in private, away from the crowd	1
8:32	Peter took him aside and began to rebuke him.	3
10:32	took the twelve aside again and began to tell	2
Lke 18:31	took the twelve aside and said to them, "See	2
Act 18:26	they took him aside and explained the Way of God	3

take away

1. ἄγω, *agō, 72*
2. αἴρω, *airō, 149*
3. ἀπαίρω, *apairō, 554*
4. ἀφαιρέω, *aphaireō, 904*
5. περιαιρέω, *periaireō, 4311*

Mat 9:15	the bridegroom is taken away from them	3
13:12	even what they have will be taken away.	2
21:43	the kingdom of God will be taken away from you	2
25:29	even what they have will be taken away.	2
Mrk 2:20	when the bridegroom is taken away from them	3
4:15	takes away the word that is sown in them.	2
4:25	even what they have will be taken away."	2
Lke 1:25	took away the disgrace I have endured	4
5:35	when the bridegroom will be taken away from them	3
6:29	from anyone who takes away your coat	2
6:30	anyone takes away your goods	2
8:12	then the devil comes and takes away the word	2
8:18	what they seem to have will be taken away."	2
10:42	which will not be taken away from her."	4
11:22	he takes away his armor in which he trusted	2
11:52	you have taken away the key of knowledge;	2
16: 3	now that my master is taking the position away	4
17:31	must not come down to take them away;	2
19:26	even what they have will be taken away.	2
Jhn 1:29	who takes away the sin of the world!	2
11:39	Jesus said, "Take away the stone."	2
11:41	they took away the stone.	2
19:38	to let him take away the body of Jesus.	2
20:13	"They have taken away my Lord	2
20:15	and I will take him away."	2
Act 8:33	For his life is taken away from the earth."	2
20:12	they had taken the boy away alive	1
Rom 11:27	covenant with them, when I take away their sins."	4
Heb 10: 4	the blood of...goats to take away sins.	4
10:11	sacrifices that can never take away sins.	5
1Jn 3: 5	You know that he was revealed to take away sins	2
Rev 22:19	if anyone takes away from the words of the book	4
22:19	God will take away that person's share in the tree	4

take away as captive

1. αἰχμαλωτίζω, *aichmalōtizō, 170*

Lke 21:24	and be taken away as captives among all nations;	1

take by force

1. ἁρπάζω, *harpazō, 773*

Mat 11:12	and the violent take it by force.	1
Jhn 6:15	and take him by force to make him king	1
Act 23:10	go down, take him by force	1

take captive

1. αἰχμαλωσία, *aichmalōsia, 168*
2. αἰχμαλωτίζω, *aichmalōtizō, 170*
3. συλαγωγέω, *sylagōgeō, 5194*

2Co 10: 5 take every thought captive to obey Christ.   2
Col   2: 8 that no one takes you captive through philosophy   3
Rev 13:10 If you are to be taken captive   1

take care

1. βλέπω, *blepō, 1063*
2. διακονέω, *diakoneō, 1354*
3. ἐπιμελέομαι, *epimeleomai, 2150*
4. ἐπισκέπτομαι, *episkeptomai, 2170*
5. ὁράω, *horaō, 3972*
6. σκοπέω, *skopeō, 5023*
7. φοβέομαι, *phobeomai, 5828*

Mat 18:10 "Take care that you do not despise   5
   25:36 I was sick and you took care of me   4
   25:44 and did not take care of you?'   2
Lke 10:34 brought him to an inn, and took care of him.   3
   10:35 'Take care of him;   3
   12:15 "Take care! Be on your guard against…greed;   5
1Co   8: 9 But take care that this liberty of yours does not   1
Gal   5:15 If…you bite and devour one another, take care   1
   6: 1 Take care that you yourselves are not tempted.   6
1Ti   3: 5 how can he take care of God's church?   3
Heb   3:12 Take care, brothers and sisters, that none of you   1
   4: 1 let us take care that none of you should seem   7

take care of needs

1. ὑπηρετέω, *hypēreteō, 5676*

Act 24:23 his friends from taking care of his needs.   1

take courage

1. θαρσέω, *tharseō, 2510*

Jhn 16:33 take courage; I have conquered the world!"   1

take down

1. καθαιρέω, *kathaireō, 2747*

Mrk 15:36 see whether Elijah will come to take him down."   1
   15:46 taking down the body, wrapped it in the linen cloth   1
Lke 23:53 he took it down, wrapped it in a linen cloth   1
Act 13:29 they took him down from the tree   1

take effect

1. βέβαιος, *bebaios, 1010*

Heb   9:17 For a will takes effect only at death   1

take heart

1. θαρσέω, *tharseō, 2510*

Mat   9: 2 he said to the paralytic, "Take heart, son;   1
   9:22 Jesus turned, and seeing her he said, "Take heart   1
   14:27 "Take heart, it is I; do not be afraid."   1
Mrk   6:50 "Take heart, it is I; do not be afraid."   1
   10:49 "Take heart; get up, he is calling you."   1

take hold

1. ἐπιλαμβάνομαι, *epilambanomai, 2138*
2. κρατέω, *krateō, 3195*

Mat 28: 9 they came to him, took hold of his feet,   2
1Ti   6:12 take hold of the eternal life   1
   6:19 take hold of the life that really is life.   1

take in one's arms

1. ἐναγκαλίζομαι, *enankalizomai, 1878*
2. συμπεριλαμβάνω, *symperilambanō, 5227*

Mrk   9:36 taking it in his arms, he said to them   1
   10:16 he took them up in his arms   1
Act 20:10 took him in his arms, and said, "Do not be alarmed   2

take leave

1. ἀποτάσσω, *apotassō, 698*

Act 18:21 but on taking leave of them, he said   1

take note

1. ἰδού, *idou, 2627*
2. σημειόω, *sēmeioō, 4957*

Mat 24:25 Take note, I have told you beforehand.   1
2Th   3:14 Take note of those who do not obey what we say   2

take notice

1. ἐπιβλέπω, *epiblepō, 2098*

Jas   2: 3 you take notice of the one wearing the fine clothes   1

take off

1. ἐκδύω, *ekdyō, 1694*
2. λύω, *lyō, 3395*
3. τίθημι, *tithēmi, 5502*

Jhn 13: 4 got up from the table, took off his outer robe   3
Act   7:33 'Take off the sandals from your feet   2
2Co   5: 3 we have taken it off we will not be found naked.   1

take offense

1. σκανδαλίζω, *skandalizō, 4997*

Mat 11: 6 blessed is anyone who takes no offense at me."   1
   13:57 they took offense at him.   1
   15:12 "Do you know that the Pharisees took offense   1
Mrk   6: 3 And they took offense at him.   1
Lke   7:23 blessed is anyone who takes no offense at me."   1

take office

1. εἰμί, *eimi, 1639*

Heb   7:20 took their office without an oath   1

take on board

1. ἀναλαμβάνω, *analambanō, 377*

Act 20:13 intending to take Paul on board there;   1
   20:14 When he met us in Assos, we took him on board   1

take one's place

1. ἀνάκειμαι, *anakeimai, 367*

Mat 26:20 he took his place with the twelve;   1
Mrk 14:18 when they had taken their places and were eating   1

take one's place at table

1. ἀναπίπτω, *anapiptō, 404*
2. κατακλίνω, *kataklinō, 2884*

Lke   7:36 and took his place at the table.   2
   11:37 so he went in and took his place at the table.   1
   17: 7 'Come here at once and take your place at the table'?   1
   22:14 he took his place at the table, and the apostles   1

take out

1. ἐκβάλλω, *ekballō, 1675*
2. ἐκφέρω, *ekpherō, 1766*
3. ἐξάγω, *exagō, 1974*

Mat   7: 4 'Let me take the speck out of your eye,'   1
   7: 5 hypocrite, first take the log out of your own eye   1
   7: 5 see clearly to take the speck out of your neighbor's eye   1
Lke   6:42 let me take out the speck in your eye,'   1
   6:42 first take the log out of your own eye   1
   6:42 you will see clearly to take the speck out   1
   10:35 The next day he took out two denarii   1
Act 16:37 Let them come and take us out themselves."   3
   16:39 And they took them out   3
1Ti   6: 7 so that we can take nothing out of it;   2

take part

1. κοινωνός, *koinōnos, 3128*
2. συγκοινωνέω, *synkoinōneō, 5170*

Mat 23:30 we would not have taken part with them   1
Eph   5:11 Take no part in the unfruitful works of darkness   2
Rev 18: 4 "Come out…so that you do not take part in her sins   2

take place

1. γίνομαι, *ginomai, 1181*
2. εἰμί, *eimi, 1639*

Mat   1:18 birth of Jesus the Messiah took place in this way.   2
   1:22 All this took place to fulfill what had been spoken   1
   18:31 reported to their lord all that had taken place.   1
   21: 4 This took place to fulfill what had been spoken   1
   24: 6 this must take place, but the end is not yet.   1
   24:34 until all these things have taken place.   1
   26:56 But all this has taken place   1
   27:54 saw the earthquake and what took place   1
Mrk 13: 7 do not be alarmed; this must take place   1
   13:29 So also, when you see these things taking place   1
   13:30 until all these things have taken place.   1

Lke 2:15 this thing that has taken place   1
    9: 7 ruler heard about all that had taken place   1
  15:14 a severe famine took place throughout that country   1
  21: 7 the sign that this is about to take place?"   1
  21: 9 these things must take place first   1
  21:28 Now when these things begin to take place   1
  21:31 So also, when you see these things taking place   1
  21:32 until all things have taken place.   1
  21:36 to escape all these things that will take place   1
  23:19 an insurrection that had taken place in the city   1
  23:47 When the centurion saw what had taken place   1
  23:48 all the crowds…saw what had taken place   1
  24:18 does not know the things that have taken place   1
  24:21 now the third day since these things took place.   1
Jhn 1:28 This took place in Bethany across the Jordan   1
  10:22 festival of the Dedication took place in Jerusalem.   1
Act 4:28 whatever…your plan had predestined to take place.   1
  8:13 saw the signs and great miracles that took place.   1
  11:19 the persecution that took place over Stephen   1
  11:28 this took place during the reign of Claudius.   1
  26:22 what…Moses said would take place: 1
2Ti 2:18 claiming that the resurrection has already taken place.   1
1Pe 4:12 fiery ordeal that is taking place among you to test you   1
Rev 1: 1 show his servants what must soon take place;   1
  1:19 what is, and what is to take place after this.   1
  4: 1 I will show you what must take place after this."   1
  22: 6 to show his servants what must soon take place."   1

take pleasure
  1. εὐδοκέω, *eudokeō, 2305*
2Th 2:12 took pleasure in unrighteousness   1
Heb 10: 6 you have taken no pleasure.   1
  10: 8 "You have neither desired nor taken pleasure in   1
  10:38 My soul takes no pleasure in anyone who shrinks back."   1

take refuge
  1. καταφεύγω, *katapheugō, 2966*
Heb 6:18 we who have taken refuge   1

take safely
  1. διασώζω, *diasōzō, 1407*
Act 23:24 and take him safely to Felix the governor."   1

take thought
  1. προνοέω, *pronoeō, 4629*
Rom 12:17 take thought for what is noble in the sight of all.   1

take to court
  1. κρίνω, *krinō, 3212*
1Co 6: 1 you dare to take it to court before the unrighteous   1

take up
  1. αἴρω, *airō, 149*
  2. ἀναλαμβάνω, *analambanō, 377*
  3. ἀνάλημψις, *analēmpsis, 378*
  4. βαστάζω, *bastazō, 1002*
  5. λαμβάνω, *lambanō, 3284*
Mat 10:38 whoever does not take up the cross and follow me   5
  14:20 took up what was left over of the broken pieces   1
  15:37 they took up the broken pieces left over   1
  16:24 let them deny themselves and take up their cross   1
Mrk 6:43 they took up twelve baskets   1
  8: 8 they took up the broken pieces left over   1
  8:34 let them deny themselves and take up their cross   1
  11:23 'Be taken up and thrown into the sea,'   1
  16:19 ⟦Jesus…was taken up into heaven⟧   2
Lke 9:23 deny themselves and take up their cross daily   1
  9:51 When the days drew near for him to be taken up   3
Jhn 5: 9 he took up his mat and began to walk.   1
  5:11 'Take up your mat and walk.' "   1
  5:12 'Take it up and walk'?"   1
  10:17 I lay down my life in order to take it up again.   5
  10:18 I have power to take it up again.   5
  10:31 The Jews took up stones again to stone him.   4
Act 1: 2 until the day when he was taken up to heaven   2
  1:11 who has been taken up from you into heaven   2
  1:22 until the day when he was taken up from us   2
  10:16 the thing was suddenly taken up to heaven.   2
Eph 6:13 Therefore take up the whole armor of God   2

1Ti 3:16 believed in throughout the world, taken up in glory.   2
Rev 18:21 Then a mighty angel took up a stone   1

take with
  1. παραλαμβάνω, *paralambanō, 4161*
  2. συμπαραλαμβάνω, *symparalambanō, 5221*
Mat 17: 1 Six days later, Jesus took with him Peter   1
  26:37 took with him Peter and the two sons of Zebedee   1
Mrk 4:36 leaving the crowd behind, they took him with them   1
  9: 2 Six days later, Jesus took with him Peter   1
  14:33 He took with him Peter and James and John   1
Lke 9:10 He took them with him and withdrew privately   1
  9:28 Jesus took with him Peter and John and James   1
Act 15:37 Barnabas wanted to take with them John   2
  15:38 Paul decided not to take with them one   2
  15:39 Barnabas took Mark with him   1

tale
  1. Contextual: Not in Greek
1Ti 4: 7 profane myths and old wives' tales.   1

idle tale
  1. λῆρος, *lēros, 3333*
Lke 24:11 these words seemed to them an idle tale   1

talent
  1. Contextual: Not in Greek
  2. τάλαντον, *talanton, 5419*
Mat 18:24 one who owed him ten thousand talents was brought   2
  25:15 to one he gave five talents, to another two   2
  25:16 had received the five talents went off at once   2
  25:16 made five more talents.   2
  25:17 who had the two talents made two more talents.   1
  25:17 who had the two talents made two more talents.   1
  25:18 the one who had received the one talent went off   1
  25:20 who had received the five talents came forward   2
  25:20 bringing five more talents, saying   2
  25:20 'Master, you handed over to me five talents;   2
  25:20 see, I have made five more talents.'   2
  25:22 the one with the two talents also came forward   2
  25:22 'Master, you handed over to me two talents;   2
  25:22 see, I have made two more talents.'   2
  25:24 had received the one talent also came forward   2
  25:25 I went and hid your talent in the ground.   2
  25:28 So take the talent from him   2
  25:28 give it to the one with the ten talents.   2

talitha
  1. ταλιθά, *talitha, 5420*
Mrk 5:41 and said to her, "Talitha cum,"   1

talk
  1. διαλέγομαι, *dialegomai, 1363*
  2. διαλογίζομαι, *dialogizomai, 1368*
  3. λαλέω, *laleō, 3281*
  4. λέγω, *legō, 3306*
  5. λόγος, *logos, 3364*
  6. ὁμιλέω, *homileō, 3917*
  7. συλλαλέω, *syllaleō, 5196*
Mat 16: 8 why are you talking about having no bread?   2
  26:70 "I do not know what you are talking about."   4
Mrk 8:17 "Why are you talking about having no bread?   2
  14:68 not know or understand what you are talking about."   4
  14:71 "I do not know this man you are talking about."   4
Lke 9:30 two men, Moses and Elijah, talking to him.   7
  22:60 "Man, I do not know what you are talking about!"   4
  24:14 talking with each other about all these things   6
  24:15 they were talking and discussing   6
  24:32 while he was talking to us on the road   3
  24:36 While they were talking about this   3
Jhn 14:30 I will no longer talk much with you   3
  16:18 We do not know what he is talking about."   3
Act 20: 9 while Paul talked still longer.   1
1Co 4:19 find out not the talk of these arrogant people   5
  4:20 For the kingdom of God depends not on talk   5
2Co 11:23 I am talking like a madman   3
Eph 4:29 Let no evil talk come out of your mouths   5
2Ti 2:17 their talk will spread like gangrene.   5
2Jn 1:12 I hope to come to you and talk with you   3

3Jn   1:14 and we will talk together face to face.   3
Rev 21:15 angel who talked to me had a measuring rod of gold   3

meaningless talk

1. ματαιολογία, *mataiologia, 3467*

1Ti   1: 6 deviated…and turned to meaningless talk   1

silly talk

1. μωρολογία, *mōrologia, 3703*

Eph   5: 4 out of place is obscene, silly, and vulgar talk   1

smooth talk

1. χρηστολογία, *chrēstologia, 5981*

Rom 16:18 and by smooth talk and flattery they deceive   1

talk about

1. διαλαλέω, *dialaleō, 1362*

Lke   1:65 all these things were talked about   1

talk back

1. ἀντιλέγω, *antilegō, 515*

Tit   2: 9 they are not to talk back   1

talk with

1. συλλαλέω, *syllaleō, 5196*
2. συνομιλέω, *synomileō, 5326*

Mat 17: 3 Moses and Elijah, talking with him.   1
Mrk   9: 4 who were talking with Jesus.   1
Act 10:27 as he talked with him   2

vulgar talk

1. εὐτραπελία, *eutrapelia, 2365*

Eph   5: 4 out of place is obscene, silly, and vulgar talk   1

idle talker

1. ματαιολόγος, *mataiologos, 3468*

Tit   1:10 idle talkers and deceivers   1

Tamar

1. Θαμάρ, *Thamar, 2500*

Mat   1: 3 Judah the father of Perez and Zerah by Tamar   1

tame

1. δαμάζω, *damazō, 1238*

Jas   3: 7 For every species of beast…can be tamed   1
       3: 7 every species…has been tamed by the human species   1
       3: 8 no one can tame the tongue—a restless evil   1

tanner

1. βυρσεύς, *byrseus, 1114*

Act   9:43 in Joppa for some time with a certain Simon, a tanner.   1
      10: 6 he is lodging with Simon, a tanner   1
      10:32 in the home of Simon, a tanner, by the sea.'   1

tap

1. πατάσσω, *patassō, 4250*

Act 12: 7 He tapped Peter on the side and woke him, saying   1

Tarsus   *See also* man of Tarsus

1. Ταρσεύς, *Tarseus, 5432*
2. Ταρσός, *Tarsos, 5433*

Act   9:30 and sent him off to Tarsus.   2
      11:25 Barnabas went to Tarsus to look for Saul   2
      21:39 Tarsus in Cilicia, a citizen of an important city;   1
      22: 3 "I am a Jew, born in Tarsus in Cilicia   2

task

1. διακονία, *diakonia, 1355*
2. ἔργον, *ergon, 2240*
3. ποιέω, *poieō, 4472*
4. χρεία, *chreia, 5970*

Lke 10:40 Martha was distracted by her many tasks;   1
Act   6: 3 whom we may appoint to this task   4
Col   3:23 Whatever your task, put yourselves into it   3
       4:17 the task that you have received in the Lord."   1
1Ti   3: 1 to the office of bishop desires a noble task.   2

taste   *See also* lose taste

1. γεύομαι, *geuomai, 1174*

Mat 16:28 some standing here who will not taste death   1
      27:34 when he tasted it, he would not drink it.   1
Mrk   9: 1 some standing here who will not taste death   1
Lke   9:27 some standing here who will not taste death   1
      14:24 who were invited will taste my dinner.' "   1
Jhn   2: 9 When the steward tasted the water   1
       8:52 will never taste death.'   1
Act 23:14 an oath to taste no food until we have killed Paul.   1
Col   2:21 "Do not handle, Do not taste, Do not touch"?   1
Heb   2: 9 so that by the grace of God he might taste death   1
       6: 4 and have tasted the heavenly gift   1
       6: 5 have tasted the goodness of the word of God   1
1Pe   2: 3 if indeed you have tasted that the Lord is good.   1

taught by God

1. θεοδίδακτος, *theodidaktos, 2531*

1Th   4: 9 taught by God to love one another;   1

taunt

1. ὀνειδίζω, *oneidizō, 3943*

Mat 27:44 The bandits…also taunted him in the same way.   1
Mrk 15:32 who were crucified with him also taunted him.   1

tax   *See also* chief tax collector, tax *booth*, tax *collector*

1. κῆνσος, *kēnsos, 3056*
2. φόρος, *phoros, 5843*

Mat 22:17 Is it lawful to pay taxes to the emperor, or not?"   1
      22:19 Show me the coin used for the tax."   1
Mrk 12:14 Is it lawful to pay taxes to the emperor, or not?   1
Lke 20:22 Is it lawful for us to pay taxes to the emperor   2
      23: 2 forbidding us to pay taxes to the emperor   2
Rom 13: 6 For the same reason you also pay taxes   2
      13: 7 Pay…due them—taxes to whom taxes are due   2
      13: 7 Pay…due them—taxes to whom taxes are due   2

temple tax

1. δίδραχμον, *didrachmon, 1440*

Mat 17:24 the collectors of the temple tax   1
      17:24 "Does your teacher not pay the temple tax?"   1

teach   *See also* taught by God

1. Contextual: Not in Greek
2. διδακτός, *didaktos, 1435*
3. διδάσκω, *didaskō, 1438*
4. διδαχή, *didachē, 1439*
5. κατηχέω, *katēcheō, 2994*
6. λαλέω, *laleō, 3281*
7. λέγω, *legō, 3306*
8. μανθάνω, *manthanō, 3443*

Mat   4:23 throughout Galilee, teaching in their synagogues   3
       5: 2 he began to speak, and taught them, saying: 3
       5:19 teaches others to do the same, will be called least   3
       5:19 whoever does them and teaches them will be called   3
       7:29 for he taught them as one having authority   3
       9:35 teaching in their synagogues, and proclaiming   3
      11: 1 from there to teach and proclaim his message   3
      13:54 began to teach the people in their synagogue   3
      15: 9 in vain…teaching human precepts as doctrines.' "   3
      21:23 came to him as he was teaching, and said   3
      22:16 teach the way of God in accordance with truth   3
      23: 3 therefore, do whatever they teach you and follow   7
      23: 3 for they do not practice what they teach   7
      26:55 Day after day I sat in the temple teaching   3
      28:20 teaching them to obey everything   3
Mrk   1:21 he entered the synagogue and taught.   3
       1:22 he taught them as one having authority   3
       2:13 crowd gathered around him, and he taught them.   3
       4: 1 Again he began to teach beside the sea.   3
       4: 2 He began to teach them many things in parables   3
       6: 2 On the sabbath he began to teach in the synagogue   3
       6: 6 he went about among the villages teaching.   3
       6:30 told him all that they had done and taught.   3
       6:34 he began to teach them many things.   3
       7: 7 teaching human precepts as doctrines.'   3
       8:31 he began to teach them that the Son of Man must   3
       9:31 for he was teaching his disciples, saying   3
      10: 1 as was his custom, he again taught them.   3
      11:17 He was teaching and saying, "Is it not written   3

	12:14	teach the way of God in accordance with truth.	3
	12:35	While Jesus was teaching in the temple, he said	3
	12:38	As he taught, he said, "Beware of the scribes	4
	14:49	I was with you in the temple teaching	3
Lke	4:15	He began to teach in their synagogues	3
	4:31	was teaching them on the sabbath.	3
	5: 3	he sat down and taught the crowds from the boat.	3
	5:17	One day, while he was teaching	3
	6: 6	he entered the synagogue and taught	3
	11: 1	teach us to pray, as John taught his disciples."	3
	11: 1	teach us to pray, as John taught his disciples."	3
	12:12	the Holy Spirit will teach you at that very hour	3
	13:10	Now he was teaching in one of the synagogues	3
	13:22	teaching as he made his way to Jerusalem.	3
	13:26	you taught in our streets.'	3
	19:47	Every day he was teaching in the temple.	3
	20: 1	as he was teaching the people in the temple	3
	20:21	that you are right in what you say and teach	3
	20:21	teach the way of God in accordance with truth.	3
	21:37	Every day he was teaching in the temple	3
	23: 5	teaching throughout all Judea	3
Jhn	6:45	'And they shall all be taught by God.'	2
	6:59	he was teaching in the synagogue at Capernaum.	3
	7:14	Jesus went up into the temple and began to teach.	3
	7:15	such learning, when he has never been taught?"	8
	7:28	Jesus cried out as he was teaching in the temple	3
	7:35	Does he intend to…teach the Greeks?	3
	8: 2	[he sat down and began to teach them.]	3
	8:20	he was teaching in the treasury of the temple	3
	9:34	and are you trying to teach us?"	3
	14:26	the Holy Spirit…will teach you everything	3
	18:20	always taught in synagogues and in the temple	3
Act	1: 1	all that Jesus did and taught from the beginning	3
	4: 2	much annoyed because they were teaching the people	3
	4:18	not to speak or teach at all in the name of Jesus.	3
	5:21	at daybreak and went on with their teaching.	3
	5:25	standing in the temple and teaching the people!"	3
	5:28	strict orders not to teach in this name	3
	5:42	they did not cease to teach	3
	11:26	and taught a great many people	3
	15: 1	were teaching the brothers	3
	15:35	taught and proclaimed the word of the Lord.	3
	18:11	teaching the word of God among them.	3
	18:25	taught accurately the things concerning Jesus	3
	20:20	teaching you publicly and from house to house	3
	21:21	you teach all the Jews living among the Gentiles	3
	21:28	This is the man who is teaching everyone everywhere	3
	28:31	teaching about the Lord Jesus Christ	3
Rom	2:21	that teach others, will you not teach yourself?	3
	2:21	that teach others, will you not teach yourself?	3
1Co	2:13	in words not taught by human wisdom	2
	2:13	taught by the Spirit	2
	4:17	as I teach them everywhere in every church.	3
	11:14	Does not nature itself teach you	3
Gal	1:12	from a human source, nor was I taught it	3
	6: 6	Those who are taught the word must share	5
Eph	4:21	have heard about him and were taught in him	3
	4:22	taught to put away your former way of life	1
Col	1:28	teaching everyone in all wisdom	3
	2: 7	just as you were taught	3
	3:16	teach and admonish one another in all wisdom;	3
2Th	2:15	hold fast to the traditions that you were taught	3
1Ti	2:12	I permit no woman to teach	3
	4:11	These are the things you must insist on and teach.	3
	6: 2	Teach and urge these duties.	3
2Ti	2: 2	who will be able to teach others as well.	3
Tit	1:11	teaching for sordid gain	3
	1:11	by teaching…what it is not right to teach.	1
	2: 1	as for you, teach what is consistent with sound doctrine.	6
Heb	5:12	you need someone to teach you again	3
	8:11	they shall not teach one another or say	3
Jas	3: 1	for you know that we who teach will be judged	1
1Jn	2:27	and so you do not need anyone to teach you.	3
	2:27	as his anointing teaches you about all things	3
	2:27	just as it has taught you, abide in him.	3
Rev	2:14	Balaam, who taught Balak to put a stumbling block	3
	2:20	Jezebel…is teaching and beguiling	3

teach different doctrine

1. ἑτεροδιδασκαλέω, *heterodidaskaleō, 2281*

| 1Ti | 1: 3 | not to teach any different doctrine | 1 |

teach otherwise

1. ἑτεροδιδασκαλέω, *heterodidaskaleō, 2281*

| 1Ti | 6: 3 | Whoever teaches otherwise | 1 |

teach what is good

1. καλοδιδάσκαλος, *kalodidaskalos, 2815*

| Tit | 2: 3 | they are to teach what is good | 1 |

teacher

1. διδάσκαλος, *didaskalos, 1437*
2. διδάσκω, *didaskō, 1438*
3. κατηχέω, *katēcheō, 2994*
4. ῥαββουνί, *rhabbouni, 4808*

Mat	8:19	"Teacher, I will follow you wherever you go."	1
	9:11	"Why does your teacher eat with tax collectors	1
	10:24	"A disciple is not above the teacher	1
	10:25	the disciple to be like the teacher	1
	12:38	"Teacher, we wish to see a sign from you."	1
	17:24	"Does your teacher not pay the temple tax?"	1
	19:16	"Teacher, what good deed must I do	1
	22:16	"Teacher, we know that you are sincere	1
	22:24	"Teacher, Moses said	1
	22:36	"Teacher, which commandment…is the greatest?"	1
	23: 8	you have one teacher, and you are all students.	1
	26:18	'The Teacher says, My time is near;	1
Mrk	4:38	"Teacher, do you not care that we are perishing?"	1
	5:35	Why trouble the teacher any further?"	1
	9:17	"Teacher, I brought you my son;	1
	9:38	"Teacher, we saw someone casting out demons	1
	10:17	"Good Teacher, what must I do	1
	10:20	"Teacher, I have kept all these since my youth."	1
	10:35	came forward to him and said to him, "Teacher	1
	10:51	"My teacher, let me see again."	4
	12:14	"Teacher, we know that you are sincere	1
	12:19	"Teacher, Moses wrote for us	1
	12:32	the scribe said to him, "You are right, Teacher;	1
	13: 1	one of his disciples said to him, "Look, Teacher	1
	14:14	'The Teacher asks, Where is my guest room	1
Lke	2:46	sitting among the teachers	1
	3:12	"Teacher, what should we do?"	1
	6:40	A disciple is not above the teacher	1
	6:40	everyone…will be like the teacher.	1
	7:40	"Teacher," he replied, "speak."	1
	8:49	do not trouble the teacher any longer."	1
	9:38	Just then a man from the crowd shouted, "Teacher	1
	10:25	"Teacher," he said, "what must I do to inherit	1
	11:45	"Teacher, when you say these things,	1
	12:13	Someone in the crowd said to him, "Teacher	1
	18:18	asked him, "Good Teacher, what must I do	1
	19:39	"Teacher, order your disciples to stop."	1
	20:21	they asked him, "Teacher	1
	20:28	asked him a question, "Teacher, Moses wrote	1
	20:39	some of the scribes answered, "Teacher	1
	21: 7	They asked him, "Teacher, when will this be	1
	22:11	to the owner of the house, 'The teacher asks you	1
Jhn	1:38	"Rabbi" (which translated means Teacher)	1
	3: 2	that you are a teacher who has come from God;	1
	3:10	Jesus answered him, "Are you a teacher of Israel	1
	8: 4	[they said to him, "Teacher, this woman]	1
	11:28	"The Teacher is here and is calling for you."	1
	13:13	You call me Teacher and Lord—and you are right	1
	13:14	I, your Lord and Teacher, have washed your feet	1
	20:16	"Rabbouni!" (which means Teacher).	1
Act	13: 1	at Antioch there were prophets and teachers:	1
Rom	2:20	a corrector of the foolish, a teacher of children	1
	12: 7	the teacher, in teaching;	2
1Co	12:28	first apostles, second prophets, third teachers;	1
	12:29	Are all teachers? Do all work miracles?	1
Gal	6: 6	share in all good things with their teacher.	3
Eph	4:11	some evangelists, some pastors and teachers	1
1Ti	2: 7	a teacher of the Gentiles in faith and truth.	1
2Ti	1:11	appointed a herald and an apostle and a teacher	1
	4: 3	will accumulate for themselves teachers	1
Heb	5:12	For though by this time you ought to be teachers	1
Jas	3: 1	Not many of you should become teachers,	1

apt teacher

1. διδακτικός, *didaktikos, 1434*

| 1Ti | 3: 2 | respectable, hospitable, an apt teacher | 1 |
| 2Ti | 2:24 | kindly to everyone, an apt teacher, patient | 1 |

false teacher

1. ψευδοδιδάσκαλος, *pseudodidaskalos, 6015*

2Pe 2: 1 just as there will be false teachers among you   1

teacher of the law

1. νομοδιδάσκαλος, *nomodidaskalos, 3791*

Lke 5:17 Pharisees and teachers of the law   1
Act 5:34 Gamaliel, a teacher of the law   1
1Ti 1: 7 desiring to be teachers of the law   1

teaching

1. διδασκαλία, *didaskalia, 1436*
2. διδαχή, *didachē, 1439*
3. λόγος, *logos, 3364*

Mat 7:28 the crowds were astounded at his teaching   2
   16:12 the teaching of the Pharisees and Sadducees.   2
   19:11 "Not everyone can accept this teaching   3
   22:33 they were astounded at his teaching.   2
Mrk 1:22 They were astounded at his teaching   2
   1:27 A new teaching—with authority! He commands   2
   4: 2 in his teaching he said to them: 2
   11:18 the whole crowd was spellbound by his teaching.   2
Lke 4:32 They were astounded at his teaching   2
Jhn 6:60 "This teaching is difficult; who can accept it?"   3
   7:16 Jesus answered them, "My teaching is not mine   2
   7:17 will know whether the teaching is from God   2
   18:19 about his disciples and about his teaching.   2
Act 2:42 devoted themselves to the apostles' teaching   2
   5:28 you have filled Jerusalem with your teaching   2
   13:12 he was astonished at the teaching about the Lord.   2
   17:19 "May we know what this new teaching is   2
Rom 6:17 form of teaching to which you were entrusted   2
   12: 7 teacher, in teaching;   1
   16:17 offenses, in opposition to the teaching   2
1Co 14: 6 knowledge or prophecy or teaching?   2
Col 2:22 simply human commands and teachings.   1
1Ti 1:10 whatever else is contrary to the sound teaching   1
   4: 1 deceitful spirits and teachings of demons   1
   4: 6 the sound teaching that you have followed.   1
   4:13 reading of scripture, to exhorting, to teaching.   1
   4:16 Pay close attention to yourself and to your teaching;   1
   5:17 those who labor in preaching and teaching;   1
   6: 1 name of God and the teaching may not be blasphemed.   1
   6: 3 the teaching that is in accordance with godliness   1
2Ti 1:13 sound teaching that you have heard from me   3
   3:10 Now you have observed my teaching, my conduct   1
   3:16 inspired by God and is useful for teaching   1
   4: 2 with the utmost patience in teaching.   2
Tit 1: 9 word that is trustworthy in accordance with the teaching   2
   2: 7 in your teaching show integrity, gravity   1
Heb 6: 1 leaving behind the basic teaching about Christ   3
   13: 9 carried away by all kinds of strange teachings;   2
2Jn 1: 9 does not abide in the teaching of Christ,   2
   1: 9 whoever abides in the teaching has both the Father   2
   1:10 comes to you and does not bring this teaching;   2
Rev 2:14 some there who hold to the teaching of Balaam   2
   2:15 some who hold to the teaching of the Nicolaitans.   2
   2:24 you in Thyatira, who do not hold this teaching   2

tear[1]

1. διαρρήγνυμι, *diarrēgnymi, 1396*
2. σχίζω, *schizō, 5387*
3. σχίσμα, *schisma, 5388*

Mat 9:16 and a worse tear is made.   3
   26:65 the high priest tore his clothes and said   1
   27:51 the curtain of the temple was torn in two   2
Mrk 2:21 the new from the old, and a worse tear is made.   3
   14:63 the high priest tore his clothes and said   1
   15:38 the curtain of the temple was torn in two   2
Lke 5:36 "No one tears a piece from a new garment   2
   5:36 otherwise the new will be torn   2
   23:45 the curtain of the temple was torn in two.   2
Jhn 19:24 they said to one another, "Let us not tear it   2
   21:11 though there were so many, the net was not torn.   2
Act 14:14 they tore their clothes   1

tear[2]

1. δάκρυον, *dakryon, 1232*
2. κλαίω, *klaiō, 3081*

Lke 7:38 and began to bathe his feet with her tears   1
   7:44 she has bathed my feet with her tears   1
Act 20:19 with all humility and with tears,   1
   20:31 not cease…to warn everyone with tears.   1
2Co 2: 4 anguish of heart and with many tears   1
Php 3:18 and now I tell you even with tears   2
2Ti 1: 4 Recalling your tears, I long to see you   1
Heb 5: 7 supplications, with loud cries and tears   1
   12:17 even though he sought the blessing with tears.   1
Rev 7:17 God will wipe away every tear from their eyes."   1
   21: 4 he will wipe every tear from their eyes.   1

tear apart

1. σχίζω, *schizō, 5387*

Mrk 1:10 he saw the heavens torn apart   1

tear down

1. καθαίρεσις, *kathairesis, 2746*
2. καταλύω, *katalyō, 2907*

2Co 10: 8 building you up and not for tearing you down   1
   13:10 for building up and not for tearing down.   1
Gal 2:18 build up again the very things that I once tore down   2

tear out

1. ἐκβάλλω, *ekballō, 1675*
2. ἐξαιρέω, *exaireō, 1975*
3. ἐξορύσσω, *exoryssō, 2021*

Mat 5:29 If your right eye causes you to sin, tear it out   2
   18: 9 if your eye causes you to stumble, tear it out   2
Mrk 9:47 if your eye causes you to stumble, tear it out;   1
Gal 4:15 torn out your eyes and given them to me.   3

tear to pieces

1. διασπάω, *diaspaō, 1400*

Act 23:10 fearing that they would tear Paul to pieces   1

tell

1. Contextual: Not in Greek
2. ἀναγγέλλω, *anangellō, 334*
3. ἀπαγγέλλω, *apangellō, 550*
4. ἀποκρίνομαι, *apokrinomai, 646*
5. γνωρίζω, *gnōrizō, 1192*
6. διαφημίζω, *diaphēmizō, 1424*
7. διηγέομαι, *diēgeomai, 1455*
8. ἐκδιηγέομαι, *ekdiēgeomai, 1687*
9. ἐκκαλέω, *eklaleō, 1718*
10. ἐξαγγέλλω, *exangellō, 1972*
11. ἐξηγέομαι, *exēgeomai, 2007*
12. κατηχέω, *katēcheō, 2994*
13. λαλέω, *laleō, 3281*
14. λέγω, *legō, 3306*

Mat 2: 5 They told him, "In Bethlehem of Judea;   14
   2:13 flee to Egypt, and remain there until I tell you;   14
   3: 9 for I tell you, God is able from these stones   14
   5:18 For truly I tell you, until heaven and earth pass   14
   5:20 For I tell you, unless your righteousness   14
   5:26 Truly I tell you, you will never get out until you   14
   6: 2 Truly I tell you, they have received their reward.   14
   6: 5 Truly I tell you, they have received their reward.   14
   6:16 Truly I tell you, they have received their reward   14
   6:25 I tell you, do not worry about your life   14
   6:29 I tell you, even Solomon in all his glory was not   14
   8:10 "Truly I tell you, in no one in Israel have I found   14
   8:11 I tell you, many will come from east and west   14
   8:33 going into the town, they told the whole   3
   10:15 Truly I tell you, it will be more tolerable   14
   10:23 for truly I tell you, you will not have gone   14
   10:27 What I say to you in the dark, tell in the light;   14
   10:42 truly I tell you, none of these will lose their reward."   14
   11: 4 "Go and tell John what you hear and see: 3
   11: 9 Yes, I tell you, and more than a prophet.   14
   11:11 Truly I tell you, among those born of women   14
   11:22 But I tell you, on the day of judgment it will be   14
   11:24 But I tell you that on the day of judgment   14
   12: 6 I tell you, something greater than the temple   14
   12:31 Therefore I tell you, people will be forgiven for   14
   12:36 I tell you, on the day of judgment   14
   12:47 Someone told him, "Look, your mother   14
   12:48 to the one who had told him this, Jesus replied   14

13: 3	he told them many things in parables, saying:	13
13:17	I tell you, many prophets and righteous people	14
13:30	at harvest time I will tell the reapers	14
13:33	He told them another parable:	13
13:34	Jesus told the crowds all these things in parables;	13
13:34	without a parable he told them nothing.	13
14: 4	because John had been telling him	14
14:12	then they went and told Jesus.	3
15: 5	you say that whoever tells father or mother	14
16:12	he had not told them to beware of the yeast	14
16:18	I tell you, you are Peter	14
16:20	sternly ordered the disciples not to tell anyone	14
16:24	Then Jesus told his disciples	14
16:28	Truly I tell you, there are some standing here	14
17: 9	"Tell no one about the vision	14
17:12	I tell you that Elijah has already come	14
17:20	For truly I tell you, if you have faith	14
18: 3	said, "Truly I tell you	14
18:10	I tell you, in heaven	14
18:13	if he finds it, truly I tell you, he rejoices	14
18:17	tell it to the church;	14
18:18	Truly I tell you, whatever you bind on earth	14
18:19	Again, truly I tell you, if two of you agree	14
18:22	"Not seven times, but, I tell you, seventy-seven	14
19:23	Jesus said to his disciples, "Truly I tell you	14
19:24	Again I tell you, it is easier for a camel	14
19:28	Jesus said to them, "Truly I tell you	14
21: 5	"Tell the daughter of Zion	14
21:21	Jesus answered them, "Truly I tell you	14
21:24	if you tell me the answer	14
21:24	then I will also tell you by what authority	14
21:27	he said to them, "Neither will I tell you	14
21:31	"Truly I tell you	14
21:43	I tell you, the kingdom of God will be taken away	14
22: 4	'Tell those who have been invited:	14
22:17	Tell us, then, what you think.	14
23:36	Truly I tell you	14
23:39	For I tell you, you will not see me again until	14
24: 2	Truly I tell you	14
24: 3	"Tell us, when will this be	14
24:34	Truly I tell you	14
24:47	Truly I tell you	14
25:12	he replied, 'Truly I tell you, I do not know you.'	14
25:40	the king will answer them, 'Truly I tell you	14
25:45	Then he will answer them, 'Truly I tell you	14
26:13	Truly I tell you	14
26:13	has done will be told in remembrance of her."	13
26:21	they were eating, he said, "Truly I tell you	14
26:29	I tell you, I will never again drink of this	14
26:34	Jesus said to him, "Truly I tell you	14
26:63	tell us if you are the Messiah, the Son of God."	14
26:64	I tell you, From now on you will see the Son	14
27:64	steal him away, and tell the people	14
28: 7	Then go quickly and tell his disciples	14
28: 8	ran to tell his disciples.	3
28:10	go and tell my brothers to go to Galilee;	3
28:11	told the chief priests everything that had happened.	3
28:13	telling them, "You must say, 'His disciples came	14
28:15	this story is still told among the Jews	6
Mrk 1:30	they told him about her at once.	14
3: 9	He told his disciples to have a boat ready	14
3:28	"Truly I tell you, people will be forgiven	14
5:14	told it in the city and in the country.	3
5:19	tell them how much the Lord has done for you	3
5:33	told him the whole truth.	14
5:43	and told them to give her something to eat.	14
6:18	John had been telling Herod, "It is not lawful	14
6:30	told him all that they had done and taught.	3
7:11	you say that if anyone tells father or mother	14
7:36	Jesus ordered them to tell no one;	14
8:12	Truly I tell you, no sign will be given	14
8:30	ordered them not to tell anyone about him.	14
9: 1	he said to them, "Truly I tell you	14
9: 9	to tell no one about what they had seen	7
9:13	I tell you that Elijah has come	14
9:41	truly I tell you, whoever gives you a cup of water	14
10:15	Truly I tell you, whoever does not receive	14
10:29	Jesus said, "Truly I tell you, there is no one	14
10:32	began to tell them what was to happen to him	14
11: 6	They told them what Jesus had said;	14
11:23	Truly I tell you, if you say to this mountain	14

11:24	So I tell you, whatever you ask for in prayer	14
11:29	tell you by what authority I do these things.	14
11:33	"Neither will I tell you by what authority	14
12:12	he had told this parable against them	14
12:43	said to them, "Truly I tell you	14
13: 4	"Tell us, when will this be, and what will be	14
13:30	Truly I tell you, this generation will not pass	14
14: 9	Truly I tell you, wherever the good news	14
14: 9	what she has done will be told in remembrance	13
14:16	found everything as he had told them;	14
14:18	"Truly I tell you, one of you will betray me	14
14:25	Truly I tell you, I will never again drink	14
14:30	Jesus said to him, "Truly I tell you	14
16: 7	tell his disciples and Peter that he is going	14
16: 7	there you will see him, just as he told you."	14
16:10	⟦She went out and told those who had been with him⟧	3
16:13	⟦they went back and told the rest⟧	3
16: S	⟦they told briefly to those around Peter⟧	10
Lke 2:17	what had been told them about this child;	13
2:18	amazed at what the shepherds told them.	13
2:20	as it had been told them.	13
3: 8	I tell you, God is able from these stones to raise	14
4:24	he said, "Truly I tell you	14
5:14	he ordered him to tell no one.	14
5:36	He also told them a parable:	14
6:39	He also told them a parable:	14
6:46	call me 'Lord, Lord,' and do not do what I tell	14
7: 9	"I tell you, not even in Israel	14
7:22	Go and tell John what you have seen and heard:	3
7:26	Yes, I tell you, and more than a prophet.	14
7:28	I tell you, among those born of women	14
7:47	I tell you, her sins, which were many	14
8:20	he was told, "Your mother and your brothers	3
8:34	told it in the city and in the country.	3
8:36	Those who had seen it told them	3
8:56	he ordered them to tell no one what had happened.	14
9:10	the apostles told Jesus all they had done.	7
9:21	He…commanded them not to tell anyone,	14
9:27	truly I tell you, there are some standing here	14
9:36	they kept silent and in those days told no one	3
10:12	I tell you, on that day it will be more tolerable	14
10:24	I tell you that many prophets and kings desired	14
10:40	Tell her then to help me."	14
11: 8	I tell you, even though he will not get up	14
11:51	Yes, I tell you, it will be charged	14
12: 4	"I tell you, my friends, do not fear those	14
12: 5	Yes, I tell you, fear him!	14
12: 8	I tell you, everyone who acknowledges me	14
12:13	tell my brother to divide the family inheritance	14
12:16	he told them a parable: "The land	14
12:22	He said to his disciples, "Therefore I tell you	14
12:27	yet I tell you, even Solomon in all his glory	14
12:37	truly I tell you, he will fasten his belt	14
12:41	are you telling this parable for us	14
12:44	Truly I tell you, he will put that one in charge	14
12:51	No, I tell you, but rather division!	14
12:59	I tell you, you will never get out	14
13: 1	who told him about the Galileans	3
13: 3	No, I tell you;	14
13: 5	No, I tell you;	14
13: 6	he told this parable: "A man had a fig tree	14
13:24	many, I tell you, will try to enter	14
13:32	He said to them, "Go and tell that fox for me,	14
13:35	I tell you, you will not see me until the time	14
14: 7	chose the places of honor, he told them a parable.	14
14:24	For I tell you, none of those who were invited	14
15: 3	So he told them this parable:	14
15: 7	Just so, I tell you, there will be more joy	14
15:10	Just so, I tell you, there is joy	14
16: 9	I tell you, make friends for yourselves	14
17:34	I tell you…there will be two in one bed;	14
18: 1	Jesus told them a parable	14
18: 8	I tell you, he will quickly grant justice to them.	14
18: 9	He also told this parable to some	14
18:14	I tell you, this man went down to his home	14
18:17	Truly I tell you, whoever does not receive	14
18:29	he said to them, "Truly I tell you,	14
18:37	They told him, "Jesus of Nazareth is passing by."	3
19:11	he went on to tell a parable	14
19:26	'I tell you	14
19:32	departed and found it as he had told them.	14

Lke 19:40 He answered, "I tell you, if these were silent | 14
20: 2 "Tell us, by what authority are you doing these | 14
20: 3 "I will also ask you a question, and you tell me: | 14
20: 8 Jesus said to them, "Neither will I tell you | 14
20: 9 He began to tell the people this parable: | 14
20:19 he had told this parable against them | 14
21: 3 He said, "Truly I tell you | 14
21:29 he told them a parable: | 14
21:32 Truly I tell you, this generation will not pass | 14
22:13 they went and found everything as he had told them; | 14
22:16 I tell you, I will not eat it until it is fulfilled | 14
22:18 I tell you that from now on I will not drink | 14
22:34 "I tell you, Peter, the cock will not crow | 14
22:37 I tell you, this scripture must be fulfilled | 14
22:67 "If you are the Messiah, tell us." | 14
22:67 He replied, "If I tell you, you will not believe; | 14
23:43 He replied, "Truly I tell you | 14
24: 6 Remember how he told you | 13
24: 9 returning from the tomb, they told all this | 3
24:10 who told this to the apostles. | 14
24:23 told us that they had indeed seen a vision | 14
24:35 Then they told what had happened on the road | 11
Jhn 1:50 "Do you believe because I said that I saw you | 14
1:51 truly, I tell you, you will see heaven opened | 14
2: 5 said to the servants, "Do whatever he tells you." | 14
2:16 He told those who were selling the doves | 14
3: 3 Jesus answered him, "Very truly, I tell you | 14
3: 5 Jesus answered, "Very truly, I tell you | 14
3:11 "Very truly, I tell you, we speak of what we know | 14
3:12 If I have told you about earthly things | 14
3:12 believe if I tell you about heavenly things? | 14
4:29 "Come and see a man who told me everything | 14
4:35 I tell you, look around you, and see how | 14
4:39 "He told me everything I have ever done." | 14
4:51 his slaves…told him that his child was alive. | 14
5:15 The man went away and told the Jews | 2
5:19 Jesus said to them, "Very truly, I tell you | 14
5:24 Very truly, I tell you | 14
5:25 "Very truly, I tell you, the hour is coming | 14
6:12 he told his disciples, "Gather up the fragments | 14
6:26 Jesus answered them, "Very truly, I tell you | 14
6:32 Jesus said to them, "Very truly, I tell you | 14
6:47 Very truly, I tell you | 14
6:53 Jesus said to them, "Very truly, I tell you | 14
6:65 he said, "For this reason I have told you | 14
8:24 I told you that you would die in your sins | 14
8:34 Jesus answered them, "Very truly, I tell you | 14
8:40 a man who has told you the truth | 13
8:45 because I tell the truth, you do not believe me. | 14
8:46 If I tell the truth, why do you not believe me? | 14
8:51 Very truly, I tell you, whoever keeps my word | 14
8:58 Jesus said to them, "Very truly, I tell you | 14
9:27 He answered them, "I have told you already | 14
9:36 Tell me, so that I may believe in him." | 1
10: 1 "Very truly, I tell you | 14
10: 7 Jesus said to them, "Very truly, I tell you | 14
10:24 If you are the Messiah, tell us plainly." | 14
10:25 Jesus answered, "I have told you | 14
11:11 After saying this, he told them | 14
11:14 Jesus told them plainly, "Lazarus is dead. | 14
11:28 called her sister Mary, and told her privately | 14
11:40 Jesus said to her, "Did I not tell you | 14
11:46 told them what he had done. | 14
12:22 Philip went and told Andrew; | 14
12:22 Andrew and Philip went and told Jesus. | 14
12:24 Very truly, I tell you | 14
12:50 I speak just as the Father has told me." | 14
13:16 Very truly, I tell you, servants are not greater | 14
13:19 I tell you this now, before it occurs | 14
13:20 Very truly, I tell you, whoever receives one | 14
13:21 I tell you, one of you will betray me." | 14
13:29 Some thought that…Jesus was telling him | 14
13:38 Very truly, I tell you, before the cock crows | 14
14: 2 If it were not so, would I have told you | 14
14:12 Very truly, I tell you | 14
14:29 now I have told you this before it occurs | 14
16: 4 you may remember that I told you about them. | 14
16: 7 Nevertheless I tell you the truth: | 14
16:20 Very truly, I tell you | 14
16:23 Very truly, I tell you | 14
16:25 tell you plainly of the Father. | 3

18: 8 Jesus answered, "I told you that I am he. | 14
18:34 did others tell you about me?" | 14
18:38 went out to the Jews again and told them | 14
19:35 he knows that he tells the truth.) | 14
20:15 tell me where you have laid him | 14
20:18 she told them that he had said these things | 1
20:25 the other disciples told him | 14
21:18 Very truly, I tell you | 14
Act 3:22 You must listen to whatever he tells you. | 13
5: 8 "Tell me whether you and your husband sold the land | 14
5:20 "Go, stand in the temple and tell the people | 13
5:38 So in the present case, I tell you | 14
9: 6 you will be told what you are to do." | 13
10: 8 after telling them everything | 11
11:12 The Spirit told me to go with them | 14
11:13 He told us how he had seen the angel standing | 3
12:17 he added, "Tell this to James and to the believers." | 3
13:41 never believe, even if someone tells you.' " | 8
15:12 as they told of all the signs and wonders | 11
15:27 who themselves will tell you the same things | 3
17:21 telling or hearing something new. | 14
19: 4 telling the people to believe | 14
21: 4 they told Paul not to go on to Jerusalem. | 14
21:21 They have been told about you | 12
21:21 tell them not to circumcise their children | 14
21:23 So do what we tell you. | 14
21:24 nothing in what they have been told about you | 12
22:10 will be told everything that has been assigned | 13
22:27 "Tell me, are you a Roman citizen?" | 14
23:16 gained entrance to the barracks and told Paul. | 3
23:18 he has something to tell you." | 13
23:22 "Tell no one that you have informed me of this." | 9
24:20 Or let these men here tell | 14
25:16 I told them that it was not the custom | 4
27:25 it will be exactly as I have been told. | 13
Rom 9:12 she was told, "The elder shall serve the younger." | 14
15: 8 For I tell you that Christ has become a servant | 14
15:21 "Those who have never been told of him shall see | 2
1Co 15:51 Listen, I will tell you a mystery! | 14
2Co 7: 7 as he told us of your longing, your mourning | 2
Gal 4:21 Tell me, you who desire to be subject to the law | 14
5: 2 Listen! I, Paul, am telling you | 14
Eph 6:21 Tychicus will tell you everything. | 5
Php 3:18 I have often told you of them, and now I tell you | 14
3:18 and now I tell you even with tears | 14
Col 4: 7 Tychicus will tell you all the news about me; | 5
4: 9 They will tell you about everything here | 5
1Th 3: 6 told us also that you always remember us kindly | 1
2Th 2: 5 I told you these things when I was still with you? | 14
1Ti 2: 7 (I am telling the truth, I am not lying) | 14
Tit 2: 2 Tell the older men to be temperate, serious, prudent | 1
2: 3 Likewise, tell the older women to be reverent | 1
2: 9 Tell slaves to be submissive to their masters | 1
Heb 9:19 For when every commandment had been told | 13
11:18 of whom he had been told | 13
11:32 time would fail me to tell of Gideon, Barak, | 7
Rev 6:11 They were each…told to rest a little longer | 14
9: 4 They were told not to damage the grass of the earth | 14
10: 9 So I went to the angel and told him to give me | 14
11: 1 I was told, "Come and measure the temple of God | 14
13:14 telling them to make an image for the beast | 14
16: 1 voice from the temple telling the seven angels | 14
17: 7 I will tell you the mystery of the woman | 14

not tell

1. ἄρρητος, *arrētos*, 777
2Co 12: 4 heard things that are not to be told | 1

tell already

1. προλέγω, *prolegō*, 4625
Mrk 13:23 alert; I have already told you everything. | 1

tell beforehand

1. προλέγω, *prolegō*, 4625
Mat 24:25 Take note, I have told you beforehand. | 1
1Th 3: 4 when we were with you, we told you beforehand | 1
4: 6 just as we have already told you beforehand | 1

tell the good news

1. εὐαγγελίζω, *euangelizō*, 2294

Lke	20: 1	he was teaching…and telling the good news	1
Act	17:18	because he was telling the good news about Jesus	1

tell the truth

1. ἀληθεύω, *alētheuō*, 238

Gal	4:16	become your enemy by telling you the truth?	1

temperate

1. νηφάλιος, *nēphalios*, 3767

1Ti	3: 2	married only once, temperate, sensible	1
	3:11	not slanderers, but temperate, faithful in all	1
Tit	2: 2	Tell the older men to be temperate, serious, prudent	1

tempest

1. θύελλα, *thyella*, 2590
2. χειμών, *cheimōn*, 5930

Act	27:20	no small tempest raged,	2
Heb	12:18	darkness, and gloom, and a tempest	1

temple *See also* officer of the temple police, rob a temple, temple *keeper*, temple *police*, temple *robber*, temple *service*, temple *tax*

1. Contextual: Not in Greek
2. ἱερόν, *hieron*, 2639
3. ναός, *naos*, 3724
4. ὅστις, *hostis*, 4015

Mat	4: 5	placed him on the pinnacle of the temple	2
	12: 5	on the sabbath the priests in the temple break	2
	12: 6	something greater than the temple is here.	2
	21:12	Jesus entered the temple	2
	21:12	all who were selling and buying in the temple	2
	21:14	The blind and the lame came to him in the temple	2
	21:15	heard the children crying out in the temple	2
	21:23	When he entered the temple	2
	24: 1	Jesus came out of the temple and was going away	2
	24: 1	point out to him the buildings of the temple.	2
	26:55	Day after day I sat in the temple teaching	2
	26:61	'I am able to destroy the temple of God	3
	27: 5	Throwing down the pieces of silver in the temple	3
	27:40	saying, "You who would destroy the temple	3
	27:51	the curtain of the temple was torn in two	3
Mrk	11:11	he entered Jerusalem and went into the temple;	2
	11:15	he entered the temple	2
	11:15	those who were buying in the temple	2
	11:16	to carry anything through the temple.	2
	11:27	As he was walking in the temple	2
	12:35	While Jesus was teaching in the temple, he said	2
	13: 1	As he came out of the temple	2
	13: 3	on the Mount of Olives opposite the temple	2
	14:49	I was with you in the temple teaching	2
	14:58	will destroy this temple that is made with hands	3
	15:29	You who would destroy the temple	3
	15:38	the curtain of the temple was torn in two	3
Lke	2:27	Guided by the Spirit, Simeon came into the temple;	2
	2:37	She never left the temple	2
	2:46	After three days they found him in the temple	2
	4: 9	placed him on the pinnacle of the temple	2
	18:10	"Two men went up to the temple to pray	2
	19:45	he entered the temple	2
	19:47	Every day he was teaching in the temple.	2
	20: 1	as he was teaching the people in the temple	2
	21: 5	speaking about the temple, how it was adorned	2
	21:37	Every day he was teaching in the temple	2
	21:38	in the morning to listen to him in the temple.	2
	22:52	officers of the temple police, and the elders	2
	22:53	I was with you day after day in the temple	2
	23:45	the curtain of the temple was torn in two.	2
	24:53	were continually in the temple blessing God.	2
Jhn	2:14	In the temple he found people selling	2
	2:15	he drove all of them out of the temple	2
	2:19	"Destroy this temple, and in three days I	3
	2:20	"This temple has been under construction for	3
	2:21	But he was speaking of the temple of his body.	3
	5:14	Later Jesus found him in the temple and said	2
	7:14	Jesus went up into the temple and began to teach.	2
	7:28	Jesus cried out as he was teaching in the temple	2
	8: 2	[Early in the morning he came again to the temple.]	2
	8:20	while he was teaching in the treasury of the temple	2
	8:59	Jesus hid himself and went out of the temple.	2
	10:23	and Jesus was walking in the temple	2

	11:56	as they stood in the temple	2
	18:20	always taught in synagogues and in the temple	2
Act	2:46	as they spent much time together in the temple	2
	3: 1	One day Peter and John were going up to the temple	2
	3: 2	People would lay him daily at the gate of the temple	2
	3: 2	could ask for alms from those entering the temple.	2
	3: 3	saw Peter and John about to go into the temple	2
	3: 8	walk, and he entered the temple with them	2
	3:10	at the Beautiful Gate of the temple;	2
	4: 1	the captain of the temple, and the Sadducees	2
	5:20	"Go, stand in the temple and tell the people	2
	5:21	they entered the temple at daybreak and went on	2
	5:24	the captain of the temple and the chief priests	2
	5:25	standing in the temple and teaching the people!"	2
	5:42	every day in the temple and at home	2
	14:13	whose temple was just outside the city	1
	19:27	the temple of the great goddess Artemis	2
	21:26	entered the temple with them, making public	2
	21:27	who had seen him in the temple	2
	21:28	he has actually brought Greeks into the temple	2
	21:29	Paul had brought him into the temple.	2
	21:30	seized Paul and dragged him out of the temple	2
	22:17	was praying in the temple	2
	24: 6	tried to profane the temple, and so we seized him.	2
	24:12	disputing with anyone in the temple	2
	24:18	in the temple, completing the rite of purification	2
	25: 8	or against the temple, or against the emperor."	2
	26:21	Jews seized me in the temple and tried to kill me.	2
1Co	3:16	Do you not know that you are God's temple	3
	3:17	If anyone destroys God's temple	3
	3:17	God's temple is holy, and you are that temple.	3
	3:17	God's temple is holy, and you are that temple.	4
	6:19	do you not know that your body is a temple	3
	9:13	get their food from the temple	2
2Co	6:16	What agreement has the temple of God with idols?	3
	6:16	we are the temple of the living God; as God said	3
Eph	2:21	grows into a holy temple in the Lord;	3
2Th	2: 4	he takes his seat in the temple of God	3
Rev	3:12	I will make you a pillar in the temple of my God,	3
	7:15	and worship him day and night within his temple	3
	11: 1	"Come and measure the temple of God and the altar	3
	11: 2	do not measure the court outside the temple;	3
	11:19	Then God's temple in heaven was opened	3
	11:19	ark of his covenant was seen within his temple;	3
	14:15	Another angel came out of the temple, calling	3
	14:17	another angel came out of the temple in heaven	3
	15: 5	temple of the tent of witness in heaven was opened	3
	15: 6	out of the temple came the seven angels	3
	15: 8	and the temple was filled with smoke	3
	15: 8	and no one could enter the temple	3
	16: 1	Then I heard a loud voice from the temple	3
	16:17	and a loud voice came out of the temple	3
	21:22	I saw no temple in the city	3
	21:22	for its temple is the Lord God the Almighty	3

temple of an idol

1. εἰδωλεῖον, *eidōleion*, 1627

1Co	8:10	see you…eating in the temple of an idol	1

temporary

1. πρόσκαιρος, *proskairos*, 4672

2Co	4:18	for what can be seen is temporary	1

tempt *See also* cannot be tempted

1. πειράζω, *peirazō*, 4279

Mat	4: 1	the wilderness to be tempted by the devil.	1
Mrk	1:13	wilderness forty days, tempted by Satan;	1
Lke	4: 2	for forty days he was tempted by the devil.	1
1Co	7: 5	come together again, so that Satan may not tempt	1
Gal	6: 1	Take care that you yourselves are not tempted.	1
1Th	3: 5	somehow the tempter had tempted you	1
Jas	1:13	No one, when tempted, should say	1
	1:13	No one…should say, "I am being tempted by God";	1
	1:13	God cannot be tempted…and…tempts no one.	1
	1:14	one is tempted by one's own desire, being lured	1

temptation

1. πειρασμός, *peirasmos*, 4280

1Ti	6: 9	those who want to be rich fall into temptation	1
Jas	1:12	Blessed is anyone who endures temptation.	1

tempter

1. πειράζω, *peirazō, 4279*

Mat 4: 3 The tempter came and said to him, "If you are   1
1Th 3: 5 somehow the tempter had tempted you   1

ten

1. δέκα, *deka, 1274*

Mat 20:24 When the ten heard it   1
    25: 1 Ten bridesmaids took their lamps   1
    25:28 give it to the one with the ten talents.   1
Mrk 10:41 When the ten heard this, they began to be angry   1
Lke 14:31 whether he is able with ten thousand to oppose   1
    15: 8 what woman having ten silver coins   1
    17:12 As he entered a village, ten lepers approached him.   1
    17:17 "Were not ten made clean? But the other nine   1
    19:13 summoned ten of his slaves   1
    19:13 ten of his slaves, and gave them ten pounds   1
    19:16 'Lord, your pound has made ten more pounds.'   1
    19:17 take charge of ten cities.'   1
    19:24 give it to the one who has ten pounds.'   1
    19:25 they said to him, 'Lord, he has ten pounds!')   1
Act 25: 6 stayed among them not more than eight or ten days   1
Rev 2:10 and for ten days you will have affliction.   1
    12: 3 great red dragon, with seven heads and ten horns   1
    13: 1 I saw a beast…having ten horns and seven heads;   1
    13: 1 a beast…and on its horns were ten diadems   1
    17: 3 and it had seven heads and ten horns.   1
    17: 7 and of the beast with seven heads and ten horns   1
    17:12 And the ten horns that you saw are ten kings   1
    17:12 And the ten horns that you saw are ten kings   1
    17:16 the ten horns that you saw, they and the beast   1

ten thousand

1. μυριάς, *myrias, 3689*
2. μύριοι, *myrioi, 3691*
3. μυρίος, *myrios, 3692*

Mat 18:24 one who owed him ten thousand talents was brought   2
1Co 4:15 you might have ten thousand guardians in Christ   3
    14:19 than ten thousand words in a tongue   3
Jde 1:14 "See, the Lord is coming with ten thousands of his holy   1

tenant

1. γεωργός, *geōrgos, 1177*

Mat 21:33 Then he leased it to tenants   1
    21:34 he sent his slaves to the tenants   1
    21:35 the tenants seized his slaves and beat one   1
    21:38 when the tenants saw the son   1
    21:40 what will he do to those tenants?"   1
    21:41 and lease the vineyard to other tenants   1
Mrk 12: 1 built a watchtower; then he leased it to tenants   1
    12: 2 he sent a slave to the tenants   1
    12: 7 those tenants said to one another   1
    12: 9 He will come and destroy the tenants   1
Lke 20: 9 planted a vineyard, and leased it to tenants   1
    20:10 he sent a slave to the tenants   1
    20:10 the tenants beat him   1
    20:14 when the tenants saw him, they discussed it   1
    20:16 He will come and destroy those tenants   1

tend

1. ποιμαίνω, *poimainō, 4477*

Jhn 21:16 Jesus said to him, "Tend my sheep."   1
1Co 9: 7 who tends a flock and does not get any…milk?   1
1Pe 5: 2 tend the flock of God that is in your charge   1

tend sheep

1. ποιμαίνω, *poimainō, 4477*

Lke 17: 7 who has just come in from plowing or tending sheep   1

tender *See also* tender *heart*

1. ἁπαλός, *hapalos, 559*
2. σπλάγχνον, *splanchnon, 5073*

Mat 24:32 as soon as its branch becomes tender   1
Mrk 13:28 as soon as its branch becomes tender   1
Lke 1:78 By the tender mercy of our God   2

tenderhearted

1. εὔσπλαγχνος, *eusplanchnos, 2359*

Eph 4:32 be kind to one another, tenderhearted   1

tenderly *See* care for tenderly

tent

1. Contextual: Not in Greek
2. σκηνή, *skēnē, 5008*
3. σκῆνος, *skēnos, 5011*

Act 7:43 No; you took along the tent of Moloch   2
    7:44 "Our ancestors had the tent of testimony   2
2Co 5: 1 For we know that if the earthly tent we live   3
    5: 2 For in this tent we groan   1
    5: 4 while we are still in this tent   3
Heb 8: 2 a minister in the sanctuary and the true tent   2
    8: 5 Moses, when he was about to erect the tent   2
    9: 2 a tent was constructed, the first one   2
    9: 3 a tent called the Holy of Holies.   2
    9: 6 the priests go continually into the first tent   2
    9: 8 as long as the first tent is still standing.   2
    9:11 then through the greater and perfect tent   2
    9:21 both the tent and all the vessels used in worship.   2
    11: 9 living in tents, as did Isaac and Jacob   2
    13:10 who officiate in the tent have no right to eat.   2
Rev 15: 5 temple of the tent of witness in heaven was opened   2

tenth *See also* give a tenth

1. δέκατος, *dekatos, 1281*

Heb 7: 2 to him Abraham apportioned "one-tenth of everything."   1
    7: 4 Abraham…gave him a tenth of the spoils.   1
Rev 11:13 great earthquake, and a tenth of the city fell;   1
    21:20 the ninth topaz, the tenth chrysoprase   1

tentmaker

1. σκηνοποιός, *skēnopoios, 5010*

Act 18: 3 by trade they were tentmakers.   1

Terah

1. Θάρα, *Thara, 2508*

Lke 3:34 son of Isaac, son of Abraham, son of Terah   1

term *See also* come to terms

1. Contextual: Not in Greek

Lke 14:32 a delegation and asks for the terms of peace.   1

human term

1. ἀνθρώπινος, *anthrōpinos, 474*

Rom 6:19 I am speaking in human terms   1

in this term

1. οὕτως, *houtōs, 4048*

Act 7: 6 God spoke in these terms   1

terrible

1. δεινῶς, *deinos, 1267*

Mat 8: 6 at home paralyzed, in terrible distress."   1

terribly

1. κακῶς, *kakōs, 2809*
2. πολύς, *polys, 4498*

Mat 17:15 and he suffers terribly;   1
Mrk 9:26 After crying out and convulsing him terribly   2

terrify

1. ἔκφοβος, *ekphobos, 1769*
2. ἔμφοβος, *emphobos, 1873*
3. πτοέω, *ptoeō, 4765*
4. ταράσσω, *tarassō, 5429*
5. φοβέομαι, *phobeomai, 5828*
6. φοβέομαι + σφόδρα, *phobeomai + sphodra, 5828 + 5379*
7. φοβέομαι + φόβος + μέγας, *phobeomai + phobos + megas, 5828 + 5832 + 3489*
8. φοβερός, *phoberos, 5829*
9. φόβος + μέγας + ἐπιπίπτω, *phobos + megas + epipiptō, 5832 + 3489 + 2158*

Mat 14:26 they were terrified, saying, "It is a ghost!"   4
    27:54 they were terrified and said   6
Mrk 6:50 for they all saw him and were terrified.   4
    9: 6 for they were terrified.   1
Lke 1:12 When Zechariah saw him, he was terrified;   4
    2: 9 and they were terrified.   7

9:34	they were terrified as they entered the cloud.	5
21: 9	do not be terrified;	3
24: 5	women were terrified and bowed their faces	2
24:37	They were startled and terrified	2
Jhn 6:19	they were terrified.	5
Heb 12:21	Indeed, so terrifying was the sight	8
Rev 11:11	and those who saw them were terrified.	9
11:13	and the rest were terrified and gave glory	2

territory

1. ὅριον, *horion, 3990*

Mat 4:13 Capernaum by the sea, in the territory of Zebulun   1

terror

1. ἔμφοβος, *emphobos, 1873*
2. τρόμος, *tromos, 5571*
3. φόβος, *phobos, 5832*

Mrk 16: 8	terror and amazement had seized them;	2
Act 10: 4	He stared at him in terror and said	1
Rom 13: 3	For rulers are not a terror to good conduct	3

Tertius

1. Τέρτιος, *Tertios, 5470*

Rom 16:22 I Tertius, the writer of this letter, greet you   1

Tertullus

1. Τέρτυλλος, *Tertyllos, 5472*

Act 24: 1	some elders and an attorney, a certain Tertullus	1
24: 2	Paul...summoned, Tertullus began to accuse him	1

test *See also* fail to meet the test, meet the test, put to the test

1. δοκιμάζω, *dokimazō, 1507*
2. δοκιμή, *dokimē, 1509*
3. δοκίμιον, *dokimion, 1510*
4. δόκιμος, *dokimos, 1511*
5. ἐκπειράζω, *ekpeirazō, 1733*
6. πειράζω, *peirazō, 4279*
7. πειρασμός, *peirasmos, 4280*

Mat 16: 1	to test Jesus they asked him to show them a sign	6
19: 3	Pharisees came to him, and to test him they asked	6
22:35	a lawyer, asked him a question to test him.	6
Mrk 8:11	asking him for a sign from heaven, to test him.	6
10: 2	Pharisees came, and to test him they asked	6
Lke 4:13	When the devil had finished every test	7
8:13	and in a time of testing fall away.	7
10:25	Just then a lawyer stood up to test Jesus.	5
11:16	to test him, kept demanding from him a sign	6
Jhn 6: 6	He said this to test him	6
8: 6	⟦They said this to test him⟧	6
1Co 3:13	fire will test what sort of work	1
10:13	No testing has overtaken you	7
10:13	not let you be tested beyond your strength	6
10:13	with the testing he will also provide	7
2Co 2: 9	I wrote for this reason: to test you	2
8: 8	I am testing the genuineness of your love	1
8:22	whom we have often tested	1
9:13	Through the testing of this ministry	2
13: 5	Test yourselves.	1
Gal 6: 4	All must test their own work;	1
1Th 2: 4	to please God who tests our hearts.	1
5:21	test everything; hold fast to what is good;	1
1Ti 3:10	let them first be tested;	1
Heb 2:18	Because he...was tested by what he suffered	6
2:18	he is able to help those who are being tested.	6
3: 8	on the day of testing in the wilderness	7
4:15	one who in every respect has been tested	6
Jas 1: 3	testing of your faith produces endurance;	3
1:12	Such a one has stood the test and will receive	4
1Pe 1: 7	gold that, though perishable, is tested by fire	1
4:12	fiery ordeal that is taking place among you to test you	7
1Jn 4: 1	test the spirits to see whether they are from God;	1
Rev 2: 2	tested those who claim to be apostles	6
2:10	throw...you into prison so that you may be tested	6
3:10	to test the inhabitants of the earth.	6

testify

1. διαμαρτύρομαι, *diamartyromai, 1371*
2. ἐπιμαρτυρέω, *epimartyreō, 2148*
3. μαρτυρέω, *martyreō, 3455*

4. μαρτύριον, *martyrion, 3457*
5. μαρτύρομαι, *martyromai, 3458*
6. μάρτυς, *martys, 3459*

Mat 23:31	Thus you testify against yourselves	3
Lke 21:13	This will give you an opportunity to testify.	4
Jhn 1: 7	He came...to testify to the light	3
1: 8	but he came to testify to the light.	3
1:15	(John testified to him and cried out	3
1:32	And John testified, "I saw the Spirit descending	3
1:34	And I myself have seen and have testified	3
2:25	and needed no one to testify about anyone;	3
3:11	and testify to what we have seen;	3
3:26	to whom you testified, here he is baptizing	3
3:32	He testifies to what he has seen and heard	3
4:44	(for Jesus himself had testified that a prophet	3
5:31	"If I testify about myself	3
5:32	There is another who testifies on my behalf	3
5:33	and he testified to the truth.	3
5:36	the very works...testify on my behalf	3
5:37	the Father...has himself testified on my behalf.	3
5:39	it is they that testify on my behalf.	3
7: 7	I testify against it that its works are evil.	3
8:13	"You are testifying on your own behalf;	3
8:14	"Even if I testify on my own behalf	3
8:18	I testify on my own behalf	3
8:18	the Father who sent me testifies on my behalf."	3
10:25	The works that I do...testify to me;	3
12:17	the crowd...continued to testify.	3
15:26	he will testify on my behalf.	3
15:27	You also are to testify	3
18:23	testify to the wrong.	3
18:37	I was born...to testify to the truth.	3
19:35	(He who saw this has testified	3
21:24	the disciple who is testifying to these	3
Act 2:40	he testified with many other arguments and exhorted	1
8:25	Now after Peter and John had testified and spoken	1
10:42	to testify that he is the one ordained by God	1
10:43	All the prophets testify about him	3
14: 3	who testified to the word of his grace	3
15: 8	God, who knows the human heart, testified to them	3
18: 5	testifying to the Jews that the Messiah was Jesus.	1
20:21	testified to both Jews and Greeks	1
20:23	the Holy Spirit testifies to me in every city	1
20:24	testify to the good news of God's grace.	1
22: 5	as...the whole council of elders can testify about me.	3
23:11	just as you have testified for me in Jerusalem	1
26: 5	if they are willing to testify	3
26:16	to appoint you to serve and testify	6
26:22	I stand here, testifying to both small and great	5
28:23	testifying to the kingdom of God	1
Rom 10: 2	I can testify that they have a zeal for God	3
1Co 15:15	we testified of God that he raised Christ	3
2Co 8: 3	as I can testify, they voluntarily gave according	3
Gal 4:15	I testify that, had it been possible	3
5: 3	Once again I testify to every man	5
Col 4:13	I testify for him that he has worked hard for you	3
Heb 2: 6	But someone has testified somewhere,	1
3: 5	to testify to the things...spoken later.	4
7: 8	one of whom it is testified that he lives.	3
10:15	the Holy Spirit also testifies to us	3
1Pe 5:12	to testify that this is the true grace of God.	2
1Jn 1: 2	and we have seen it and testify to it	3
4:14	And we have seen and do testify that	3
5: 6	the Spirit is the one that testifies	3
5: 7	There are three that testify:	3
5: 9	that he has testified to his Son.	3
3Jn 1: 3	arrived and testified to your faithfulness to the truth	3
1: 6	testified to your love before the church.	3
1:12	We also testify for him	3
Rev 1: 2	who testified to the word of God	3
22:20	The one who testifies to these things says,	3

testify against

1. καταμαρτυρέω, *katamartyreō, 2909*

Mat 26:62	What is it that they testify against you?"	1
Mrk 14:60	What is it that they testify against you?"	1

testify favorably

1. μαρτυρέω, *martyreō, 3455*

3Jn 1:12 Everyone has testified favorably about Demetrius   1

testify in advance

1. προμαρτύρομαι, *promartyromai, 4626*

1Pe 1:11 when it testified in advance to the sufferings   1

testimony *See also* add one's testimony, give false testimony

1. Contextual: Not in Greek
2. μαρτυρέω, *martyreō, 3455*
3. μαρτυρία, *martyria, 3456*
4. μαρτύριον, *martyrion, 3457*

Mat 8: 4 offer the gift...as a testimony to them."   4
      10:18 as a testimony to them and the Gentiles.   4
      24:14 as a testimony to all the nations;   4
Mrk 1:44 as a testimony to them."   4
      6:11 as a testimony against them."   4
      13: 9 as a testimony to them.   4
      14:55 looking for testimony against Jesus   3
      14:56 their testimony did not agree.   3
      14:59 even on this point their testimony did not agree.   3
Lke 5:14 your cleansing, for a testimony to them."   4
      9: 5 dust off your feet as a testimony against them."   4
      22:71 they said, "What further testimony do we need?   3
Jhn 1:19 This is the testimony given by John   3
      3:11 yet you do not receive our testimony.   3
      3:32 yet no one accepts his testimony.   3
      3:33 Whoever has accepted his testimony has certified   3
      4:39 believed in him because of the woman's testimony   2
      5:31 my testimony is not true.   3
      5:32 I know that his testimony to me is true.   3
      5:34 Not that I accept such human testimony   3
      5:36 I have a testimony greater than John's.   3
      8:13 your testimony is not valid."   3
      8:14 my testimony is valid because I know where   3
      8:17 the testimony of two witnesses is valid.   3
      19:35 His testimony is true   3
      21:24 we know that his testimony is true.   3
Act 4:33 testimony to the resurrection of the Lord Jesus   4
      7:44 the tent of testimony in the wilderness   4
      13:22 his testimony about him he said   2
      22:18 will not accept your testimony about me.'   3
1Co 1: 6 just as the testimony of Christ has been strengthened   4
2Co 1:12 the testimony of our conscience: 4
2Th 1:10 because our testimony to you was believed.   4
1Ti 6:13 in his testimony before Pontius Pilate   2
2Ti 1: 8 Do not be ashamed...of the testimony about our Lord   4
Tit 1:13 That testimony is true.   3
Heb 10:28 "on the testimony of two or three witnesses."   1
1Jn 5: 9 If we receive human testimony, the testimony of God   3
      5: 9 human testimony, the testimony of God is greater;   3
      5: 9 for this is the testimony of God   3
      5:10 Those who believe...have the testimony in their hearts.   3
      5:10 the testimony that God has given concerning his Son.   3
      5:11 the testimony: God gave us eternal life   3
3Jn 1:12 and you know that our testimony is true.   3
Rev 1: 2 testified...to the testimony of Jesus Christ   3
      1: 9 because of...the testimony of Jesus.   3
      6: 9 slaughtered...for the testimony they had given;   3
      11: 7 When they have finished their testimony   3
      12:11 conquered him...by the word of their testimony   3
      12:17 and hold the testimony of Jesus.   3
      19:10 your comrades who hold the testimony of Jesus.   3
      19:10 testimony of Jesus is the spirit of prophecy."   3
      20: 4 beheaded for their testimony to Jesus   3
      22:16 to you with this testimony for the churches.   2

false testimony

1. ψευδομαρτυρία, *pseudomartyria, 6019*

Mat 26:59 whole council were looking for false testimony   1

text

1. γράφω, *graphō, 1211*

Lke 20:17 "What then does this text mean: 'The stone   1

Thaddaeus

1. Θαδδαῖος, *Thaddaios, 2497*

Mat 10: 3 James son of Alphaeus, and Thaddaeus;   1
Mrk 3:18 Thaddaeus, and Simon the Cananaean   1

than Not Indexed

thank *See also* give thanks

1. ἐξομολογέω, *exomologeō, 2018*
2. εὐχαριστέω, *eucharisteō, 2373*
3. εὐχαριστία, *eucharistia, 2374*
4. χάρις, *charis, 5921*
5. χάρις + ἔχω, *charis + echō, 5921 + 2400*

Mat 11:25 At that time Jesus said, "I thank you, Father   1
Lke 10:21 "I thank you, Father, Lord of heaven and earth   1
      17: 9 Do you thank the slave   5
      17:16 He prostrated...and thanked him.   2
      18:11 I thank you that I am not like other people: 2
Jhn 11:41 "Father, I thank you for having heard me.   2
Act 28:15 Paul thanked God and took courage.   2
Rom 1: 8 I thank my God through Jesus Christ for all of you   2
      6:17 But thanks be to God   4
      7:25 Thanks be to God through Jesus Christ our Lord!   4
1Co 1:14 I thank God that I baptized none of you   2
      14:18 I thank God that I speak in tongues   2
      15:57 thanks be to God, who gives us the victory   4
2Co 2:14 thanks be to God   4
      8:16 thanks be to God who put in the heart of Titus   4
Php 1: 3 I thank my God every time I remember you   2
Col 1: 3 we always thank God, the Father of our Lord Jesus   2
1Th 3: 9 How can we thank God enough for you   3
Phm 1: 4 I always thank my God   2
Heb 12:28 Therefore...let us give thanks   4
Rev 4: 9 creatures give glory and honor and thanks to the one   3

thankful

1. εὐχάριστος, *eucharistos, 2375*

Col 3:15 And be thankful.   1

thankfulness

1. χάρις, *charis, 5921*

1Co 10:30 If I partake with thankfulness   1

thanks

1. χάρις, *charis, 5921*

2Co 9:15 Thanks be to God for his indescribable gift!   1

thanksgiving

1. εὐχαριστία, *eucharistia, 2374*

1Co 14:16 say the "Amen" to your thanksgiving   1
2Co 4:15 increase thanksgiving, to the glory of God.   1
      9:11 will produce thanksgiving to God through us;   1
      9:12 also overflows with many thanksgivings to God.   1
Eph 5: 4 instead, let there be thanksgiving.   1
Php 4: 6 by prayer and supplication with thanksgiving   1
Col 2: 7 abounding in thanksgiving.   1
      4: 2 keeping alert in it with thanksgiving.   1
1Ti 2: 1 thanksgivings be made for everyone   1
      4: 3 created to be received with thanksgiving   1
      4: 4 provided it is received with thanksgiving;   1
Rev 7:12 Blessing and glory and wisdom and thanksgiving   1

that *See also* at that *moment,* at that *time,* even that, more than that, not after that, see that, so that, so that not, that *moment,* that *time,* that *way*

1. διά + οὗτος, *dia + houtos, 1328 + 4047*
2. εἰ, *ei, 1623*
3. εἰς, *eis, 1650*
4. ἵνα, *hina, 2671*
5. κατά, *kata, 2848*
6. μή + πώς, *mē + pōs, 3590 + 4803*
7. ὅθεν, *hothen, 3854*
8. ὅπως, *hopōs, 3968*
9. ὅταν, *hotan, 4020*
10. ὅτι, *hoti, 4022*
11. οὕτως, *houtōs, 4048*
12. πώς, *pōs, 4803*
13. ὡς, *hōs, 6055*
14. ὥστε, *hōste, 6063*

Mat 2:16 When Herod saw that he had been tricked   10
      2:22 he heard that Archelaus was ruling over Judea   10
      4:12 Now when Jesus heard that John had been arrested   10
      5:17 not think that I have come to abolish the law   10
      5:21 heard that it was said to those of ancient times   10
      5:22 But I say to you that if you are angry   10

5:23	that your brother or sister has something against you	10	
5:27	"You have heard that it was said, 'You shall not	10	
5:28	I say to you that everyone who looks at a woman	10	
5:32	I say to you that anyone who divorces his wife	10	
5:33	heard that it was said to those of ancient times	10	
5:38	"You have heard that it was said, 'An eye for an eye	10	
5:43	"You have heard that it was said, 'You shall love	10	
6: 7	for they think that they will be heard because	10	
6:32	your heavenly Father knows that you need all these	10	
8:24	so great that the boat was being swamped by the waves;	14	
8:27	that even the winds and the sea obey him?"	10	
8:28	so fierce that no one could pass that way.	14	
9: 6	you may know that the Son of Man has authority	10	
9:28	"Do you believe that I am able to do this?"	10	
10:34	"Do not think that I have come to bring peace	10	
11:24	that on the day of judgment it will be more tolerable	10	
12: 5	read in the law that on the sabbath the priests	10	
13: 2	that he got into a boat and sat there	14	
13:13	that 'seeing they do not perceive	10	
14: 7	so much that he promised on oath to grant her	7	
14:36	that they might touch even the fringe of his cloak;	4	
15:12	"Do you know that the Pharisees took offense	10	
15:17	Do you not see that whatever goes into the mouth	10	
16:11	that I was not speaking about bread?	10	
16:12	that he had not told them to beware of the yeast	10	
16:20	not to tell anyone that he was the Messiah.	10	
16:21	that he must go to Jerusalem	10	
17:10	the scribes say that Elijah must come first?"	10	
17:12	I tell you that Elijah has already come	10	
17:13	that he was speaking to them about John the Baptist.	10	
18:14	that one of these little ones should be lost.	4	
19: 4	He answered, "Have you not read that	10	
20:21	"Declare that these two sons of mine will sit	4	
20:25	that the rulers of the Gentiles lord it over	10	
20:30	When they heard that Jesus was passing by	10	
21:45	they realized that he was speaking about them.	10	
22:16	"Teacher, we know that you are sincere	10	
22:34	heard that he had silenced the Sadducees	10	
23:31	Thus you testify against yourselves that	10	
24:20	Pray that your flight may not be in winter	4	
24:32	you know that summer is near.	10	
24:33	you know that he is near, at the very gates.	10	
25:24	'Master, I knew that you were a harsh man	10	
25:26	You knew…that I reap where I did not sow	10	
26: 2	"You know that after two days	10	
26:41	Stay awake and pray that you may not come	4	
26:53	Do you think that I cannot appeal to my Father	10	
27: 3	Judas, his betrayer, saw that Jesus was condemned	10	
27:18	For he realized that it was out of jealousy	10	
27:24	So when Pilate saw that he could do nothing	10	
28: 5	I know that you are looking for Jesus	10	
Mrk 2: 1	it was reported that he was at home.	10	
2: 2	that there was no longer room for them	14	
2: 8	that they were discussing these questions	10	
2:10	that the Son of Man has authority on earth	10	
2:16	Pharisees saw that he was eating with sinners	10	
4: 1	that he got into a boat on the sea and sat	14	
4:38	"Teacher, do you not care that we are perishing?"	10	
4:41	that even the wind and the sea obey him?"	10	
5:18	begged him that he might be with him.	4	
5:29	she felt in her body that she was healed	10	
5:43	He strictly ordered them that no one should know	4	
6:12	and proclaimed that all should repent.	4	
6:56	that they might touch even the fringe	4	
7:18	Do you not see that whatever goes into a person	10	
8:31	he began to teach them that the Son of Man must	10	
9:11	the scribes say that Elijah must come first?"	10	
9:12	that he is to go through many sufferings	4	
9:13	I tell you that Elijah has come	10	
9:25	Jesus saw that a crowd came running together	10	
10:42	"You know that among the Gentiles	10	
10:47	When he heard that it was Jesus of Nazareth	10	
11:23	believe that what you say will come to pass	10	
11:24	believe that you have received it	10	
12:12	they realized that he had told this parable	10	
12:14	we know that you are sincere, and show deference	10	
12:19	that if a man's brother dies, leaving a wife	10	
12:28	seeing that he answered them well, he asked him	10	
12:32	you have truly said that 'he is one	10	
12:34	When Jesus saw that he answered wisely	10	
12:35	say that the Messiah is the son of David?	10	

13: 4	that all these things are about to be accomplished?"	9	
13:18	Pray that it may not be in winter.	4	
13:28	you know that summer is near.	10	
13:29	you know that he is near, at the very gates.	10	
14:35	that, if it were possible, the hour might pass	4	
14:38	pray that you may not come into the time of trial;	4	
14:72	Peter remembered that Jesus had said to him	13	
15:10	For he realized that it was out of jealousy	10	
15:39	saw that in this way he breathed his last	10	
16: 4	they looked up, they saw that the stone	10	
16: 7	that he is going ahead of you to Galilee;	10	
16:11	[heard that he was alive and had been seen by her]	10	
Lke 1:22	realized that he had seen a vision in the sanctuary.	10	
1:43	that the mother of my Lord comes to me?	4	
1:45	blessed is she who believed that	10	
1:58	that the Lord had shown his great mercy to her	10	
2:49	not know that I must be in my Father's house?"	10	
5:24	you may know that the Son of Man has authority	10	
7:37	learned that he was eating	10	
7:39	who is touching him—that she is a sinner."	10	
8:25	that he commands even the winds	10	
8:47	the woman saw that she could not remain hidden	10	
8:53	they laughed at him, knowing that she was dead.	10	
9: 7	it was said by some that John had been raised	10	
9: 8	by some that Elijah had appeared	10	
9: 8	that one of the ancient prophets had arisen.	10	
9:19	that one of the ancient prophets has arisen."	10	
10:20	that the spirits submit to you	10	
10:20	rejoice that your names are written in heaven."	10	
10:24	I tell you that many prophets and kings desired	10	
10:40	do you not care that my sister has left me	10	
11:38	that he did not first wash before dinner.	10	
12:30	your Father knows that you need them.	10	
12:51	Do you think that I have come to bring peace	10	
13: 2	that because these Galileans suffered in this way	10	
13: 4	do you think that they were worse offenders	10	
16: 1	that this man was squandering his property.	13	
16: 3	now that my master is taking the position away	10	
16:25	that during your lifetime you received your good	10	
16:28	for I have five brothers—that he may warn them	8	
17:15	one of them, when he saw that he was healed	10	
18: 9	trusted in themselves that they were righteous	10	
18:11	I thank you that I am not like other people:	10	
18:15	that he might touch them;	4	
19:11	that the kingdom of God was to appear immediately.	10	
19:22	You knew, did you, that I was a harsh man	10	
20:19	that he had told this parable against them	10	
20:21	we know that you are right in what you say	10	
20:37	that the dead are raised Moses himself showed	10	
21: 7	the sign that this is about to take place?"	9	
21:20	then know that its desolation has come near.	10	
21:30	know that summer is already near.	10	
21:31	you know that the kingdom of God is near.	10	
21:36	praying that you may have the strength	4	
22: 8	the Passover meal for us that we may eat it."	4	
22:18	that from now on I will not drink of the fruit	10	
22:32	prayed for you that your own faith may not fail;	4	
22:46	pray that you may not come into the time of trial."	4	
22:70	He said to them, "You say that I am."	10	
23: 7	that he was under Herod's jurisdiction	10	
24:21	had hoped that he was the one to redeem Israel.	10	
24:39	Look at my hands and my feet; see that it is I	10	
24:44	that everything written about me in the law of Moses	10	
Jhn 1:31	that he might be revealed to Israel."	4	
1:34	testified that this is the Son of God."	10	
1:50	I told you that I saw you under the fig tree?	10	
2:17	His disciples remembered that it was written	10	
2:22	his disciples remembered that he had said this;	10	
3: 2	that you are a teacher who has come from God;	10	
3: 7	Do not be astonished that I said to you	10	
3:15	that whoever believes in him may have eternal life.	4	
3:16	God so loved the world that he gave his only Son	14	
3:19	this is the judgment, that the light has come	10	
3:21	seen that their deeds have been done in God."	10	
3:28	You yourselves are my witnesses that I said	10	
3:33	certified this, that God is true.	10	
4: 1	when Jesus learned that the Pharisees had heard	10	
4:19	"Sir, I see that you are a prophet.	10	
4:20	you say that the place where people must worship	10	
4:25	"I know that Messiah is coming"	10	
4:27	astonished that he was speaking with a woman	10	

Jhn	4:42 we know that this is truly the Savior	10
	4:44 (for Jesus himself had testified that a prophet	10
	4:47 heard that Jesus had come from Judea to Galilee	10
	4:51 his slaves…told him that his child was alive.	10
	4:53 that this was the hour when Jesus had said	10
	5: 6 and knew that he had been there a long time	10
	5:15 that it was Jesus who had made him well.	10
	5:32 I know that his testimony to me is true.	10
	5:36 testify on my behalf that the Father has sent me.	10
	5:42 I know that you do not have the love of God	10
	5:45 not think that I will accuse you before the Father;	10
	6:15 that they were about to come and take him by force	10
	6:22 saw that there had been only one boat there.	10
	6:22 also saw that Jesus had not got into the boat	10
	6:24 saw that neither Jesus nor his disciples were there	10
	6:29 that you believe in him whom he has sent."	4
	6:36 I said to you that you have seen me	10
	6:39 that I should lose nothing of all that	4
	6:40 that all who see the Son and believe in him	4
	6:46 Not that anyone has seen the Father	10
	6:61 aware that his disciples were complaining	10
	6:65 I have told you that no one can come to me	10
	6:69 and know that you are the Holy One of God."	10
	7: 7 I testify against it that its works are evil.	10
	7:26 know that this is the Messiah?	10
	7:35 that we will not find him?	10
	7:42 that the Messiah is descended from David	10
	7:52 that no prophet is to arise from Galilee."	10
	8:17 that the testimony of two witnesses is valid.	10
	8:24 I told you that you would die in your sins	10
	8:24 unless you believe that I am he."	10
	8:27 that he was speaking to them about the Father.	10
	8:28 then you will realize that I am he	10
	8:37 I know that you are descendants of Abraham;	10
	8:47 that you are not from God."	10
	8:48 that you are a Samaritan and have a demon?"	10
	8:52 "Now we know that you have a demon.	10
	8:55 if I would say that I do not know him,	10
	8:56 Abraham rejoiced that he would see my day;	4
	9: 2 who sinned…that he was born blind?"	4
	9:18 The Jews did not believe that he had been blind	10
	9:20 parents answered, "We know that this is our son	10
	9:20 this is our son, and that he was born blind;	10
	9:22 that anyone who confessed Jesus to be the Messiah	4
	9:24 We know that this man is a sinner."	10
	9:25 I do know, that though I was blind, now I see."	10
	9:29 We know that God has spoken to Moses	10
	9:31 We know that God does not listen to sinners	10
	9:32 that anyone opened the eyes of a person born blind.	10
	9:35 Jesus heard that they had driven him out	10
	9:41 now that you say, 'We see,' your sin remains.	10
	10:10 I came that they may have life	4
	10:36 you say that the one whom the Father has sanctified	10
	10:38 that the Father is in me and I am in the Father."	10
	11: 6 after having heard that Lazarus was ill	10
	11:13 they thought that he was referring merely to sleep.	10
	11:16 "Let us also go, that we may die with him."	4
	11:20 When Martha heard that Jesus was coming	10
	11:22 even now I know that God will give you whatever	10
	11:24 said to him, "I know that he will rise again	10
	11:27 I believe that you are the Messiah, the Son of God	10
	11:31 thought that she was going to the tomb to weep	10
	11:40 that if you believed, you would see the glory	10
	11:42 I knew that you always hear me	10
	11:42 so that they may believe that you sent me."	10
	11:50 You do not understand that it is better	10
	11:51 that Jesus was about to die for the nation	10
	11:57 that anyone who knew where Jesus was	4
	12: 9 great crowd of the Jews learned that he was there	10
	12:12 heard that Jesus was coming to Jerusalem.	10
	12:16 that these things had been written of him	10
	12:18 that the crowd went to meet him.	1
	12:34 that the Messiah remains forever.	10
	12:34 you say that the Son of Man must be lifted up?	10
	12:42 that they would be put out of the synagogue;	4
	12:50 I know that his commandment is eternal life.	10
	13: 1 Jesus knew that his hour had come to depart	10
	13: 3 knowing that the Father had given all things	10
	13: 3 that he had come from God and was going to God	10
	13:15 that you also should do as I have done to you.	4
	13:19 you may believe that I am he.	10

	13:29 Some thought that…Jesus was telling him	10
	13:29 that he should give something to the poor.	4
	13:34 that you love one another.	4
	13:35 everyone will know that you are my disciples	10
	14: 2 that I go to prepare a place for you?	10
	14:10 Do you not believe that I am in the Father	10
	14:11 Believe me that I am in the Father	10
	14:20 On that day you will know that I am in my Father	10
	14:22 "Lord, how is it that you will reveal yourself	10
	14:28 that I am going to the Father	10
	14:31 so that the world may know that I love the Father.	10
	15: 8 that you bear much fruit	4
	15:12 my commandment, that you love one another	4
	15:18 world hates you, be aware that it hated me	10
	16: 4 you may remember that I told you about them.	10
	16: 7 it is to your advantage that I go away	4
	16:15 I said that he will take what is mine	10
	16:19 Jesus knew that they wanted to ask him	10
	16:26 I do not say to you that I will ask the Father	10
	16:27 have believed that I came from God.	10
	16:30 Now we know that you know all things	10
	16:30 by this we believe that you came from God."	10
	17: 3 this is eternal life, that they may know you	4
	17: 7 Now they know that everything…is from you;	10
	17: 8 and know in truth that I came from you;	10
	17: 8 they have believed that you sent me.	10
	17:21 they may all be one. As you, Father, are in me	4
	17:21 the world may believe that you have sent me.	10
	17:23 that they may become completely one	4
	17:23 the world may know that you have sent me	10
	17:24 Father, I desire that those also…may be with me	4
	17:25 these know that you have sent me.	10
	18: 8 Jesus answered, "I told you that I am he.	10
	18:14 that is was better to have one person die	10
	18:37 Jesus answered, "You say that I am a king.	10
	18:39 you have a custom that I release someone	4
	19: 4 to let you know that I find no case against him."	10
	19:10 Do you not know that I have power to release you	10
	19:28 Jesus knew that all was now finished	10
	19:35 he knows that he tells the truth.)	10
	20: 9 the scripture, that he must rise from the dead.	10
	20:14 she did not know that it was Jesus.	10
	20:31 that Jesus is the Messiah, the Son of God	10
	20:31 that through believing you may have life	4
	21: 4 the disciples did not know that it was Jesus.	10
	21: 7 When Simon Peter heard that it was the Lord	10
	21:15 to him, "Yes, Lord; you know that I love you."	10
	21:16 to him, "Yes, Lord; you know that I love you."	10
	21:17 you know everything; you know that I love you."	10
	21:23 the rumor…that this disciple would not die.	10
	21:23 Jesus did not say to him that he would not die	10
	21:24 we know that his testimony is true.	10
Act	2:29 that he both died and was buried	10
	2:30 knew that God had sworn with an oath to him	10
	2:36 know with certainty that God has made him…Lord	10
	3:17 now, friends, I know that you acted in ignorance	10
	4:10 that this man is standing before you	10
	4:13 realized that they were uneducated and ordinary men	10
	4:16 that a notable sign has been done through them;	10
	5: 4 How is it that you have contrived this deed	10
	5: 9 "How is it that you have agreed together	10
	5:41 rejoiced that they were considered worthy	10
	6:14 that this Jesus of Nazareth will destroy this place	10
	7: 6 that his descendants would be resident aliens	10
	7:25 that God through him was rescuing them	10
	8:14 that Samaria had accepted the word of God	10
	8:15 that they might receive the Holy Spirit	8
	8:18 Now when Simon saw that the Spirit was given	10
	8:24 that nothing of what you have said may happen to me."	8
	9:22 by proving that Jesus was the Messiah.	10
	9:26 for they did not believe that he was a disciple.	10
	9:38 disciples, who heard that Peter was there	10
	10:28 "You yourselves know that it is unlawful for a Jew	13
	10:34 "I truly understand that God shows no partiality	10
	10:42 to testify that he is the one ordained by God	10
	10:45 that the gift…had been poured out	10
	11: 1 heard that the Gentiles had also accepted	10
	11:17 God gave them the same gift that he gave us	13
	12: 3 After he saw that it pleased the Jews	10
	12: 9 that what was happening with the angel's help was real;	10
	12:11 "Now I am sure that the Lord has sent his angel	10

13: 8	(for that is the translation of his name)	11
13:38	that through this man forgiveness of sins	10
14: 1	that a great number…became believers.	14
14: 9	and seeing that he had faith to be healed	10
15: 7	you know that in the early days God made a choice	10
15:24	that certain persons who have gone out from us	10
15:39	became so sharp that they parted company;	14
16: 3	for they all knew that his father was a Greek.	10
16:10	convinced that God had called us	10
16:19	owners saw that their hope of making money was gone	10
16:26	so violent that the foundations…were shaken;	14
16:38	when they heard that they were Roman citizens;	10
17: 3	explaining and proving that it was necessary	10
17:13	learned that the word of God had been proclaimed	10
19: 2	not even heard that there is a Holy Spirit."	2
19:16	that they fled out of the house naked and wounded.	14
19:25	"Men, you know that we get our wealth	10
19:26	You also see and hear that	10
19:26	saying that gods made with hands are not gods.	10
19:34	when they recognized that he was a Jew	10
20:23	except that the Holy Spirit testifies to me	10
20:23	that imprisonment and persecutions are waiting	10
20:25	now I know that none of you…will ever see	10
20:26	that I am not responsible for the blood of any	10
20:29	that after I have gone, savage wolves will come	10
20:31	remembering that…I did not cease night or day	10
20:34	You know for yourselves that I worked	10
20:35	that by such work we must support the weak	10
20:38	that they would not see him again.	10
21:21	They have been told about you that you teach	10
21:22	They will certainly hear that you have come.	10
21:24	Thus all will know that there is nothing	10
21:29	they supposed that Paul had brought him	10
21:31	that all Jerusalem was in an uproar.	10
22:19	I said, 'Lord, they themselves know that	10
22:29	he realized that Paul was a Roman citizen	10
22:29	and that he had bound him.	10
23: 5	"I did not realize, brothers, that he was high priest;	10
23: 6	When Paul noticed that some were Sadducees	10
23:22	"Tell no one that you have informed me of this."	10
23:27	had learned that he was a Roman citizen	10
23:34	when he learned that he was from Cilicia	10
24:14	that according to the Way, which they call a sect	10
24:26	he hoped that money would be given him by Paul	10
25:16	I told them that it was not the custom	10
26: 5	that I have belonged to the strictest sect	10
26: 8	thought incredible…that God raises the dead?	2
26:23	that the Messiah must suffer	2
26:23	that, by being the first to rise from the dead	2
26:27	I know that you believe."	10
27:10	I can see that the voyage will be with danger	10
27:25	that it will be exactly as I have been told.	10
28: 1	then learned that the island was called Malta.	10
28:22	we know that everywhere it is spoken against."	10
28:28	Let it be known to you then that this salvation	10
Rom 1: 9	that without ceasing I remember you always	13
1:13	that I have often intended to come to you	10
1:32	that those who practice such things deserve to die	10
2: 2	"We know that God's judgment on those who do such	10
2: 3	that…you will escape the judgment of God?	10
2: 4	Do you not realize that God's kindness is meant	10
3:19	Now we know that whatever the law says	10
3:26	it was to prove…that he himself is righteous	3
4:18	that he would become "the father of many nations,"	3
4:21	that God was able to do what he had promised.	10
5: 3	knowing that suffering produces endurance	10
5: 8	that while we still were sinners Christ died for us.	10
6: 3	Do you not know that all of us	10
6: 6	We know that our old self was crucified with him	10
6: 8	we believe that we will also live with him.	10
6: 9	We know that Christ…will never die again;	10
6:16	Do you not know that if you present yourselves	10
6:17	that you, having once been slaves of sin	10
7: 1	that the law is binding on a person only during	10
7:14	For we know that the law is spiritual	10
7:16	I agree that the law is good.	10
7:18	For I know that nothing good dwells within me	10
7:21	a law that when I want to do what is good,	10
8:16	bearing witness…that we are children of God	10
8:18	I consider that the sufferings of this present	10
8:21	that the creation itself will be set free	10

8:22	We know that…creation has been groaning	10
8:28	We know that all things work together for good	10
8:38	For I am convinced that neither death, nor life	10
10: 2	I can testify that they have a zeal for God	10
10: 5	that "the person who does these things will live	10
10: 9	and believe…that God raised him from the dead	10
14:14	persuaded…that nothing is unclean in itself;	10
15:14	that you yourselves are full of goodness	10
15:29	I know that when I come to you	10
15:31	that I may be rescued from the unbelievers	4
1Co 1:10	that all of you be in agreement	4
1:11	that there are quarrels among you, my brothers	10
1:12	that each of you says, "I belong to Paul,"	10
1:14	I thank God that I baptized none of you	10
1:15	so that no one can say that you were baptized	10
3:16	Do you not know that you are God's temple	10
3:20	the thoughts of the wise, that they are futile."	10
4: 2	that they be found trustworthy.	4
4: 3	that I should be judged by you or by any human court.	4
5: 6	that a little yeast leavens the whole batch of dough?	10
6: 2	know that the saints will judge the world?	10
6: 3	Do you not know that we are to judge angels	10
6: 9	Do you not know that wrongdoers will not inherit	10
6:15	know that your bodies are members of Christ?	10
6:16	know that whoever is united to a prostitute	10
6:19	do you not know that your body is a temple	10
7:17	lead the life that the Lord has assigned,	13
7:26	I think that, in view of the impending crisis	10
8: 1	we know that "all of us possess knowledge."	10
8: 4	we know that "no idol in the world really exists,"	10
8: 4	and that "there is no God but one."	10
9:13	Do you not know that those who are employed	10
9:18	Just this: that in my proclamation	4
9:22	that I might by all means save some.	4
9:24	Do you not know that in a race	10
9:24	Run in such a way that you may win it.	4
10: 1	that our ancestors were all under the cloud	10
10:19	That food sacrificed to idols is anything	10
10:19	that an idol is anything?	10
10:20	No, I imply that what pagans sacrifice	10
11: 3	understand that Christ is the head of every man	10
11:14	Does not nature itself teach you that if a man	10
11:23	that the Lord Jesus on the night	10
12: 2	You know that when you were pagans	10
12: 3	that no one speaking by the Spirit of God ever says	10
12:25	that there may be no dissension within the body	4
14: 1	especially that you may prophesy.	4
14:23	will they not say that you are out of your mind?	10
14:37	acknowledge that what I am writing to you	10
15: 3	that Christ died for our sins	10
15: 4	that he was buried, and that he was raised	10
15: 4	that he was buried, and that he was raised	10
15: 5	that he appeared to Cephas, then to the twelve.	10
15:15	we testified of God that he raised Christ	10
15:27	it is plain that this does not include the one	10
15:58	know that in the Lord your labor is not in vain	10
16:10	If Timothy comes, see that he has nothing to fear	4
16:15	know that members of the household of Stephanas	10
2Co 1: 7	we know that as you share in our sufferings	10
1: 8	that we despaired of life itself.	14
1:10	set our hope that he will rescue us again	10
1:14	that on the day of the Lord Jesus	10
1:23	it was to spare you that I did not come again	10
1:24	not mean to imply that we lord it over your faith;	10
2: 3	that my joy would be the joy of all of you.	10
3: 3	you show that you are a letter of Christ	10
3: 5	Not that we are competent of ourselves to claim	10
4:14	know that the one who raised the Lord Jesus	10
5: 1	For we know that if the earthly tent we live	10
5: 6	we know that while we are at home in the body	10
5:14	we are convinced that one has died for all;	10
7: 3	I said before that you are in our hearts	10
7: 8	I see that I grieved you with that letter	10
8: 6	that, as he had already made a beginning	4
8: 9	that though he was rich, yet for your sakes	10
8:13	I do not mean that there should be relief for others	4
9: 2	that Achaia has been ready since last year;	10
10: 7	that just as you belong to Christ, so also do we.	10
10:11	that what we say by letter when absent	10
11: 3	I am afraid that as the serpent deceived Eve	6
11:31	God…knows that I do not lie.	10

2Co	12: 8	I appealed…that it would leave me	4
	12:13	except that I myself did not burden you?	10
	12:19	that we have been defending ourselves before you?	10
	13: 2	that if I come again, I will not be lenient—	10
	13: 5	you not realize that Jesus Christ is in you?	10
	13: 6	I hope you will find out that we have not failed.	10
	13: 7	not that we may appear to have met the test	4
	13: 7	that you may do what is right	4
Gal	1: 6	I am astonished that you are so quickly deserting	10
	1:11	that the gospel that was proclaimed by me	10
	2: 7	when they saw that I had been entrusted with	10
	2: 9	agreeing that we should go to the Gentiles	4
	2:10	asked only one thing, that we remember the poor	4
	2:14	when I saw that they were not acting consistently	10
	2:16	know that a person is not justified by the works	10
	3: 8	the scripture, foreseeing that God would justify	10
	3:11	Now it is evident that no one is justified	10
	4:11	afraid that my work for you may have been wasted.	12
	4:13	You know that it was because of a physical infirmity	10
	4:15	I testify that, had it been possible	10
	4:22	For it is written that Abraham had two sons	10
	5: 2	that if you let yourselves be circumcised	10
	5: 3	that he is obliged to obey the entire law.	10
	5:10	confident…that you will not think otherwise.	10
	6:12	only that they may not be persecuted	4
Eph	1:17	I pray that the God of our Lord Jesus Christ,	4
	2:11	remember that at one time you Gentiles by birth	10
	2:12	that you were at that time without Christ	10
	2:15	that he might create in himself one new humanity	4
	3:16	I pray that, according to the riches of his glory	4
	3:18	I pray that you may have the power to comprehend	4
	4: 9	that he had also descended into the lower parts	10
	5: 5	that no fornicator or impure person	10
	6: 8	knowing that whatever good we do	10
	6: 9	you know that both of you have the same Master	10
	6:20	Pray that I may declare it boldly, as I must speak.	4
Php	1: 6	that the one who began a good work among you	10
	1: 9	my prayer, that your love may overflow more	4
	1:12	that what has happened to me has actually helped	10
	1:16	knowing that I have been put here	10
	1:18	Just this, that Christ is proclaimed in every way	10
	1:19	for I know that through your prayers	10
	1:20	my…hope that I will not be put to shame in any way	10
	1:25	convinced of this, I know that I will remain	10
	1:27	I will know that you are standing firm	10
	2:11	every tongue should confess that Jesus Christ is Lord	10
	2:16	that I can boast on the day of Christ	3
	2:16	that I did not run in vain or labor in vain.	10
	2:24	I trust…that I will also come soon.	10
	2:26	distressed because you heard that he was ill.	10
	3:12	Not that I have already obtained this	10
	4:10	that now at last you have revived your concern	10
	4:11	Not that I am referring to being in need;	10
	4:15	know that in the early days of the gospel	10
	4:17	Not that I seek the gift	10
Col	1: 9	asking that you may be filled with the knowledge	4
	3:24	know that…you will receive the inheritance	10
	4: 1	know that you also have a Master in heaven.	10
	4: 3	that God will open to us a door for the word	4
	4:13	I testify for him that he has worked hard for you	10
	4:16	see that you read also the letter from Laodicea.	4
	4:17	say to Archippus, "See that you complete the task	4
1Th	2: 1	that our coming to you was not in vain	10
	2:12	pleading that you lead a life worthy of God	3
	2:13	that when you received the word of God	10
	3: 3	know that this is what we are destined for.	10
	3: 4	that we were to suffer persecution;	10
	3: 6	told us also that you always remember us kindly	10
	3:10	that we may see you face to face	3
	3:13	that you may be blameless before our God and Father	3
	4: 1	we ask and urge you in the Lord Jesus that	4
	4:14	since we believe that Jesus died and rose again	10
	4:15	that we who are alive, who are left	10
	5: 2	you…know very well that the day of the Lord	10
2Th	1:11	that our God will make you worthy of his call	4
	2: 2	that the day of the Lord is already here.	10
	2: 5	Do you not remember that I told you these things	10
	3: 2	that we may be rescued from wicked and evil people;	4
	3: 4	that you are doing and will go on doing	10
1Ti	1: 8	Now we know that the law is good	10
	1: 9	that the law is laid down not for the innocent	10

	1:15	that Christ Jesus came into the world to save	10
	4: 1	the Spirit expressly says that in later times	10
2Ti	1:12	I am sure that he is able to guard until that day	10
	1:15	You are aware that all who are in Asia have turned away	10
	2: 8	descendant of David—that is my gospel	5
	2:23	you know that they breed quarrels.	10
	3: 1	You must understand this, that in the last days	10
Tit	2:14	who gave himself for us that he might redeem us	4
	3:11	since you know that such a person is perverted	10
Phm	1: 6	that the sharing of your faith	8
	1:21	knowing that you will do even more than I say.	10
Heb	2: 6	"What are human beings that you are mindful of them	10
	2: 6	"What are…mortals, that you care for them?	10
	3:19	So we see that they were unable to enter	10
	7: 8	one of whom it is testified that he lives.	10
	7:14	evident that our Lord was descended from Judah	10
	9:15	because a death has occurred that redeems them	3
	11: 6	must believe that he exists	10
	11:13	They confessed that they were strangers	10
	11:14	clear that they are seeking a homeland.	10
	11:19	He considered the fact that God is able even to raise	10
	12:17	You know that later…he was rejected	10
	13:18	we are sure that we have a clear conscience	10
Jas	1: 3	because you know that the testing of your faith	10
	2:19	You believe that God is one; you do well.	10
	2:20	that faith apart from works is barren?	10
	2:22	You see that faith was active…with his works	10
	2:24	You see that a person is justified by works	10
	3: 1	for you know that we who teach will be judged	10
	4: 4	Do you not know that friendship with the world	10
	4: 5	suppose that it is for nothing that the scripture says	10
	5:20	you should know that whoever brings back a sinner	10
1Pe	1:12	It was revealed to them that they were serving	10
	1:18	You know that you were ransomed	10
	2: 3	if indeed you have tasted that the Lord is good.	10
	2:15	For it is God's will that by doing right	11
	3: 9	that you might inherit a blessing.	4
2Pe	1:14	since I know that my death will come soon	10
	1:20	that no prophecy of scripture is a matter of one's own	10
	3: 3	that in the last days scoffers will come	10
	3: 5	that by the word of God heavens existed long ago	10
	3: 8	that with the Lord one day is like a thousand years	10
	3:17	beware that you are not carried away with the error	4
1Jn	1: 5	that God is light and in him there is no darkness	10
	1: 6	If we say that we have fellowship with him	10
	1: 8	If we say that we have no sin, we deceive ourselves	10
	1:10	If we say that we have not sinned, we make him a liar	10
	2: 3	by this we may be sure that we know him	10
	2: 5	By this we may be sure that we are in him:	10
	2:18	As you have heard that antichrist is coming	10
	2:18	From this we know that it is the last hour.	10
	2:19	they made it plain that none of them belongs	10
	2:21	and you know that no lie comes from the truth.	10
	2:22	the one who denies that Jesus is the Christ?	10
	2:29	If you know that he is righteous, you may be sure	10
	2:29	you may be sure that everyone who does right	10
	3: 1	that we should be called children of God;	4
	3: 1	is that it did not know him.	10
	3: 5	You know that he was revealed to take away sins	10
	3:11	that we should love one another.	4
	3:13	Do not be astonished…that the world hates you.	2
	3:14	We know that we have passed from death to life	10
	3:15	you know that murderers do not have eternal life	10
	3:16	We know love by this, that he laid down his life	10
	3:19	by this we will know that we are from the truth	10
	3:23	this is his commandment, that we should believe	4
	3:24	And by this we know that he abides in us	10
	4: 3	antichrist, of which you have heard that it is coming;	10
	4:10	In this is love, not that we loved God	10
	4:10	not that we loved God but that he loved us	10
	4:13	By this we know that we abide in him and he in us	10
	4:14	And we have seen and do testify that	10
	4:15	who confess that Jesus is the Son of God	10
	4:17	that we may have boldness on the day of judgment	4
	5: 1	Everyone who believes that Jesus is the Christ	10
	5: 2	By this we know that we love the children of God	10
	5: 3	the love of God is this, that we obey his commandments.	4
	5: 5	the one who believes that Jesus is the Son of God?	10
	5: 9	that he has testified to his Son.	10
	5:13	so that you may know that you have eternal life.	10
	5:14	that if we ask anything according to his will,	10

	5:15 if we know that he hears us in whatever we ask	10
	5:15 we know that we have obtained the requests	10
	5:16 I do not say that you should pray about that.	4
	5:18 We know that those who are born of God do not sin	10
	5:19 We know that we are God's children	10
	5:20 we know that the Son of God has come	10
2Jn	1: 6 love, that we walk according to his commandments;	4
3Jn	1:12 and you know that our testimony is true.	10
Jde	1: 5 that the Lord, who once for all saved a people	10
Rev	2: 2 I know that you cannot tolerate evildoers	10
	2: 4 that you have abandoned the love you had at first.	10
	2:23 And all the churches will know that I am the one	10
	3: 8 I know that you have but little power	10
	3: 9 and they will learn that I have loved you.	10
	3:17 not realize that you are wretched, pitiable, poor	10
	12:13 when the dragon saw that he had been thrown down	10

that is

1. δέ, *de*, 1254
2. ὅτι, *hoti*, 4022
3. ὡς, *hōs*, 6055

Rom	9:30 that is, righteousness through faith;	1
2Co	5:19 that is, in Christ God was reconciling the world	2
Gal	3:16 "And to your offspring," that is, to one person	3
Heb	12:27 what is shaken—that is, created things	3

that not

1. μήποτε, *mēpote*, 3607

Heb	3:12 that none of you may have an evil…heart	1
	4: 1 that none of you should seem to have failed	1

the   Not Indexed

theater

1. θέατρον, *theatron*, 2519

Act	19:29 people rushed together to the theater	1
	19:31 urging him not to venture into the theater.	1

theft

1. κλέμμα, *klemma*, 3092
2. κλοπή, *klopē*, 3113

Mat	15:19 murder, adultery, fornication, theft	2
Mrk	7:21 fornication, theft, murder	2
Rev	9:21 And they did not repent of…their thefts.	1

themselves   Not Indexed

then   Not Indexed; *See* even then, for then, just then, since then, so then

Theophilus

1. Θεόφιλος, *Theophilos*, 2541

Lke	1: 3 write an orderly account…most excellent Theophilus	1
Act	1: 1 In the first book, Theophilus	1

there   *See also* come there, from there, go here and there, happen to be there, over there, people there

1. αὐτός, *autos*, 899
2. ἐκεῖ, *ekei*, 1695
3. ἐκεῖθεν, *ekeithen*, 1696
4. ἐκεῖσε, *ekeise*, 1698
5. ἐν, *en*, 1877
6. ἐν + ὅς, *en + hos*, 1877 + 4005
7. ἐν + αὐτός, *en + autos*, 1877 + 899
8. ἐνθάδε, *enthade*, 1924
9. ἰδού, *idou*, 2627
10. ἵστημι, *histēmi*, 2705
11. κἀκεῖ, *kakei*, 2795
12. κεῖμαι, *keimai*, 3023
13. ὅπου, *hopou*, 3963
14. οὗ, *hou*, 4023
15. πρόκειμαι, *prokeimai*, 4618
16. τόπος, *topos*, 5536
17. ὧδε, *hōde*, 6045

Mat	2: 9 and there, ahead of them, went the star	9
	2:13 flee to Egypt, and remain there until I tell you;	2
	2:15 remained there until the death of Herod.	2
	2:22 he was afraid to go there	2

	5:24 leave your gift there before the altar and go;	2
	6:21 treasure is, there your heart will be also.	2
	12:45 and they enter and live there;	2
	13:58 he did not do many deeds of power there	2
	14:23 When evening came, he was there alone	2
	17:20 'Move from here to there,' and it will	2
	18:20 I am there among them."	2
	19: 2 and he cured them there.	2
	21:17 to Bethany, and spent the night there.	2
	22:11 a man there who was not wearing a wedding robe	2
	24:23 'Look! Here is the Messiah!' or 'There he is!'	17
	24:28 there the vultures will gather.	2
	27:36 they sat down there and kept watch over him.	2
	27:55 Many women were also there	2
	27:61 Mary Magdalene and the other Mary were there	2
	28: 7 there you will see him.'	2
	28:10 there they will see me."	11
Mrk	1:35 there he prayed.	11
	1:38 so that I may proclaim the message there also;	2
	2: 6 Now some of the scribes were sitting there	2
	3: 1 a man was there who had a withered hand.	2
	5:11 Now there on the hillside a great herd of swine	2
	6: 5 he could do no deed of power there	2
	6:10 stay there until you leave the place.	2
	6:33 they hurried there on foot from all the towns	2
	13:21 'Look! There he is!'—do not believe it.	2
	14:15 Make preparations for us there."	2
	16: 6 Look, there is the place they laid him.	13
	16: 7 there you will see him, just as he told you."	2
Lke	2: 6 While they were there	2
	5: 2 he saw two boats there at the shore of the lake;	10
	5:12 there was a man covered with leprosy.	9
	6: 6 was a man there whose right hand was withered.	2
	8:32 Now there on the hillside a large herd of swine	2
	9: 4 Whatever house you enter, stay there	2
	10: 6 if anyone is there who shares in peace	2
	10: 9 cure the sick who are there, and say to them	5
	11:26 they enter and live there;	2
	12:18 there I will store all my grain and my goods.	2
	12:34 there your heart will be also.	2
	15:13 there he squandered his property in dissolute	2
	17:21 'Look, here it is!' or 'There it is!'	2
	17:23 They will say to you, 'Look there!' or 'Look here!'	2
	17:37 there the vultures will gather."	2
	19:30 as you enter it you will find tied there a colt	6
	22:12 Make preparations for us there."	2
	23:33 they crucified Jesus there with the criminals	2
	24:18 things that have taken place in these days?"	5
Jhn	2: 1 in Cana…and the mother of Jesus was there.	2
	2: 6 Now standing there were six stone water jars	2
	2:12 and they remained there a few days.	2
	3:22 He spent some time there with them and baptized.	2
	3:23 near Salim because water was abundant there;	2
	4: 6 Jacob's well was there, and Jesus…sitting	2
	4:40 and he stayed there two days.	2
	5: 5 One man was there who had been ill	2
	5:13 disappeared in the crowd that was there.	16
	6: 3 and sat down there with his disciples.	2
	6:22 saw that there had been only one boat there.	2
	6:24 neither Jesus nor his disciples were there	2
	10:40 he remained there.	2
	10:42 many believed in him there.	2
	11: 8 are you going there again?"	2
	11:15 For your sake I am glad I was not there	2
	11:31 she was going to the tomb to weep there.	2
	12: 2 There they gave a dinner for him. Martha served	2
	12: 9 great crowd of the Jews learned that he was there	2
	12:26 where I am, there will my servant be also.	2
	18: 2 Jesus often met there with his disciples.	2
	18: 3 came there with lanterns and torches	2
	19:18 There they crucified him, and with him two others	13
	19:42 they laid Jesus there.	2
	21: 9 they saw a charcoal fire there	12
Act	7:29 Midian. There he became the father of two sons.	14
	9:33 There he found a man named Aeneas	2
	9:38 disciples, who heard that Peter was there	1
	10:18 Simon, who was called Peter, was staying there.	8
	14: 7 there they continued proclaiming the good news.	11
	18:19 they reached Ephesus, he left them there	1
	19:21 "After I have gone there, I must also see Rome."	2
	20:13 intending to take Paul on board there;	3

Act	20:22	not knowing what will happen to me there	5
	21: 3	the ship was to unload its cargo there.	4
	21: 4	and stayed there for seven days.	1
	22: 5	in order to bind those who were there	4
	22:10	there you will be told	11
	25: 9	and be tried there before me on these charges?"	2
	25:14	Since they were staying there several days	2
	25:20	be tried there on these charges.	11
	27: 6	There the centurion found an Alexandrian ship	11
	28:14	There we found believers	14
Rom	9:26	there they shall be called children of the living God."	2
1Co	7:24	there remain with God.	5
2Co	8:12	if the eagerness is there, the gift is acceptable	15
Php	3:20	from there that we are expecting a Savior, the Lord	14
Tit	3:12	I have decided to spend the winter there.	2
Jas	2: 3	while to the one who is poor you say, "Stand there,"	2
	3:16	there will also be disorder and wickedness of every kind.	2
	4:13	spend a year there, doing business and making money."	2
Rev	2:14	some there who hold to the teaching of Balaam	2
	4: 1	I looked, and there in heaven a door stood open!	9
	4: 2	I was in the spirit; and there in heaven stood a throne	9
	6: 2	I looked, and there was a white horse! Its rider	9
	6: 5	I looked, and there was a black horse! Its rider	9
	6: 8	I looked and there was a pale green horse!	9
	7: 9	After this I looked, and there was a great multitude	9
	9:12	There are still two woes to come.	9
	11: 1	the temple of God…and those who worship there	7
	12: 6	prepared by God, so that there she can be nourished	2
	14: 1	and there was the Lamb, standing on Mount Zion!	9
	14:14	Then I looked, and there was a white cloud	9
	19:11	I saw heaven opened, and there was a white horse!	9
	21:25	and there will be no night there.	2

there is

1. ἔνι, *eni, 1928*

1Co	6: 5	Can it be that there is no one among you	1
Gal	3:28	There is no longer Jew or Greek	1
	3:28	there is no longer slave or free	1
	3:28	there is no longer male and female;	1
Col	3:11	In that renewal there is no longer Greek and Jew	1
Jas	1:17	Father of lights, with whom there is no variation	1

there too

1. κἀκεῖ, *kakei, 2795*

Act	17:13	they came there too	1

thereby

1. Contextual: Not in Greek
2. ἐν, *en, 1877*

Jhn	5:18	thereby making himself equal to God.	1
Act	27:21	thereby avoided this damage and loss.	1
1Co	4: 4	I am not thereby acquitted.	2

therefore

1. Contextual: Not in Greek
2. ἀντί + ὅς, *anti + hos, 505 + 4005*
3. ἄρα, *ara, 726*
4. δέ, *de, 1254*
5. δή, *dē, 1314*
6. διά, *dia, 1328*
7. διά + οὗτος, *dia + houtos, 1328 + 4047*
8. διό, *dio, 1475*
9. διόπερ, *dioper, 1478*
10. διότι, *dioti, 1484*
11. ἐν + οὗτος, *en + houtos, 1877 + 4047*
12. ὅθεν, *hothen, 3854*
13. ὅς + χάριν, *hos + charin, 4005 + 5920*
14. οὖν, *oun, 4036*
15. τοιγαροῦν, *toigaroun, 5521*
16. ὥστε, *hōste, 6063*

Mat	3:10	every tree therefore that does not bear good	14
	5:19	Therefore, whoever breaks one of the least of these	14
	5:48	Be perfect, therefore, as your heavenly Father	14
	6:25	"Therefore I tell you, do not worry about	7
	6:31	Therefore do not worry, saying, 'What will we eat?'	14
	9:38	therefore ask the Lord of the harvest	14
	10:32	"Everyone therefore who acknowledges me before	14
	12:27	Therefore they will be your judges.	7
	12:31	Therefore I tell you, people will be forgiven for	7

	13:52	"Therefore every scribe who has been trained	7
	19: 6	Therefore what God has joined together	14
	21:43	Therefore I tell you, the kingdom of God	7
	22: 9	Go therefore into the main streets, and invite	14
	22:21	"Give therefore to the emperor	14
	23: 3	therefore, do whatever they teach you and follow	14
	23:34	Therefore I send you prophets, sages,	7
	24:42	Keep awake therefore, for you do not know	14
	24:44	Therefore you also must be ready	7
	25:13	Keep awake therefore, for you know neither	14
	27:64	Therefore command the tomb to be made secure	14
	28:19	Go therefore and make disciples of all nations	14
Mrk	10: 9	Therefore what God has joined together	14
	13:35	Therefore, keep awake—for you do not know	14
Lke	1:35	therefore the child to be born will be holy	8
	3: 9	tree therefore that does not bear good fruit	14
	7: 7	therefore I did not presume to come to you.	8
	7:47	Therefore, I tell you, her sins, which were many	13
	10: 2	therefore ask the Lord of the harvest	14
	11:19	Therefore they will be your judges.	7
	11:35	Therefore consider whether the light in you	14
	11:49	Therefore also the Wisdom of God said,	7
	12: 3	Therefore whatever you have said in the dark	2
	12:22	He said to his disciples, "Therefore I tell you	7
	13:18	said therefore, "What is the kingdom of God like?	14
	14:20	just been married, and therefore I cannot come.'	6
	14:33	So therefore, none of you can become my disciple	14
	20:33	In the resurrection, therefore, whose wife	14
	23:16	I will therefore have him flogged and release him."	14
	23:22	I will therefore have him flogged and then release	14
Jhn	5:16	Therefore the Jews started persecuting Jesus	7
	9:23	Therefore his parents said, "He is of age;	7
	11:45	Many of the Jews therefore…believed in him	14
	11:54	Jesus therefore no longer walked about openly	14
	12:50	What I speak, therefore	14
	13:24	Simon Peter therefore motioned to him to ask Jesus	14
	15:19	therefore the world hates you.	7
	19:10	Pilate therefore said to him, "Do you refuse	14
	19:11	therefore the one…guilty of a greater sin."	7
Act	2:26	therefore my heart was glad	7
	2:33	Being therefore exalted at the right hand of God	14
	2:36	Therefore let the entire house of Israel know	14
	3:19	Repent therefore, and turn to God	14
	6: 3	Therefore, friends, select…seven men	4
	8:22	Repent therefore of this wickedness of yours	14
	10:32	Send therefore to Joppa and ask for Simon	14
	10:33	Therefore I sent for you immediately	14
	13:35	Therefore he has also said in another psalm	10
	13:38	Let it be known to you therefore, my brothers	14
	13:40	Beware, therefore, that what the prophets said	14
	15:10	Now therefore why are you putting God to the test	14
	15:19	Therefore I have reached the decision	8
	15:27	We have therefore sent Judas and Silas	14
	16:36	therefore come out now and go in peace."	14
	17:12	Many of them therefore believed	14
	17:23	What therefore you worship as unknown	14
	19:38	If therefore Demetrius and the artisans with him	14
	20:26	Therefore I declare to you this day	10
	20:31	Therefore be alert	8
	24:16	Therefore I do my best always to have a clear conscience	11
	25:26	Therefore I have brought him before all of you	8
	26: 3	therefore I beg of you to listen to me patiently.	8
	27:34	Therefore I urge you to take some food	8
	28:20	For this reason therefore I have asked to see	14
Rom	1:24	Therefore God gave them up in the lusts	8
	2: 1	Therefore you have no excuse	8
	4:22	Therefore his faith "was reckoned to him	8
	5: 1	Therefore, since we are justified by faith,	14
	5:12	Therefore, just as sin came into the world	7
	5:18	Therefore…one man's trespass led to condemnation	14
	6: 4	Therefore we have been buried with him by baptism	14
	6:12	Therefore, do not let sin exercise dominion	14
	8: 1	There is therefore now no condemnation	3
	12: 1	I appeal to you therefore, brothers and sisters	14
	13: 2	Therefore whoever resists authority resists	16
	13: 5	Therefore one must be subject	8
	13:10	therefore, love is the fulfilling of the law.	14
	14:13	therefore no longer pass judgment on one another	14
	15: 7	Welcome one another, therefore	8
	15: 9	"Therefore I will confess you among the Gentiles	7
1Co	4: 5	Therefore do not pronounce judgment	16

	5: 8 Therefore, let us celebrate the festival	16
	6:15 Should I therefore take the members of Christ	14
	6:20 therefore glorify God in your body.	5
	8:13 Therefore, if food is a cause of their falling	9
	10:14 Therefore…flee from the worship of idols.	9
	11:27 Whoever, therefore, eats the bread	16
	12: 3 Therefore I want you to understand	8
	14:13 Therefore, one who speaks in a tongue should pray	8
	14:23 If, therefore, the whole church comes together	14
	15:58 Therefore, my beloved, be steadfast	16
	16:11 therefore let no one despise him.	14
2Co	4: 1 Therefore, since it is by God's mercy	7
	5:11 Therefore, knowing the fear of the Lord	14
	5:14 therefore all have died.	3
	5:16 From now on, therefore, we regard	16
	6:17 Therefore come out from them, and be separate	8
	8:24 Therefore openly before the churches,	14
	12: 7 Therefore, to keep me from being too elated.	8
	12:10 Therefore I am content with weaknesses, insults,	8
Gal	3:24 Therefore the law was our disciplinarian	16
	5: 1 Stand firm, therefore, and do not submit	14
Eph	3:13 I pray therefore that you may not lose heart	8
	4: 1 I therefore, the prisoner in the Lord, beg you	14
	4: 8 Therefore it is said, "When he ascended on high	8
	5: 1 Therefore be imitators of God, as beloved children	14
	5: 7 Therefore do not be associated with them.	14
	5:14 Therefore it says, "Sleeper, awake!	8
	6:13 Therefore take up the whole armor of God	7
	6:14 Stand therefore, and fasten the belt of truth	14
Php	2: 9 Therefore God also highly exalted him	8
	2:12 Therefore…just as you have always obeyed	16
	2:23 I hope therefore to send him	14
	2:28 I am the more eager to send him, therefore	14
	4: 1 Therefore, my brothers and sisters, whom I love	16
Col	2: 6 As you therefore have received Christ Jesus the Lord	14
	2:16 Therefore do not let anyone condemn you	14
	3: 5 Put to death, therefore, whatever in you is earthly:	14
1Th	3: 1 Therefore when we could bear it no longer	8
	4: 8 Therefore whoever rejects this	15
	4:18 Therefore encourage one another	16
	5:11 Therefore encourage one another	8
2Th	1: 4 Therefore we ourselves boast of you	16
2Ti	2:10 Therefore I endure everything	7
Heb	1: 9 therefore God, your God, has anointed you	7
	2: 1 Therefore we must pay greater attention	7
	2:14 therefore, the children share flesh and blood	14
	2:17 Therefore he had to become like his brothers and sisters	12
	3: 1 Therefore, brothers and sisters…consider that Jesus	12
	3: 7 Therefore, as the Holy Spirit says	8
	3:10 Therefore I was angry with that generation	8
	4: 1 Therefore, while the promise of entering his rest	14
	4: 6 Since therefore it remains open for some to enter it	14
	4:11 Let us therefore make every effort to enter that rest	14
	4:16 therefore approach the throne of grace with boldness	14
	6: 1 Therefore let us go on toward perfection,	8
	10:19 Therefore, my friends, since we have confidence	14
	10:35 Do not, therefore, abandon that confidence of yours;	14
	11:12 Therefore from one person, and this one as good as dead	8
	11:16 Therefore God is not ashamed	8
	12: 1 Therefore…let us also lay aside every weight	15
	12:12 Therefore lift your drooping hands	8
	12:28 Therefore…let us give thanks	8
	13:12 Therefore Jesus also suffered outside the city gate	8
Jas	1:21 Therefore rid yourselves of all sordidness	8
	4: 4 Therefore whoever wishes to be a friend of the world	14
	4: 6 But he gives all the more grace; therefore it says	8
	4: 7 Submit yourselves therefore to God.	14
	5: 7 Be patient, therefore, beloved, until the coming	14
	5:16 Therefore confess your sins to one another	14
1Pe	1:13 Therefore prepare your minds for action; discipline	8
	2: 1 Rid yourselves, therefore, of all malice.	14
	4: 1 Since therefore Christ suffered in the flesh	14
	4: 7 therefore be serious and discipline yourselves	14
	4:19 Therefore, let those suffering in accordance with	16
	5: 6 Humble yourselves therefore under…God	14
2Pe	1:10 Therefore, brothers and sisters, be all the more eager	8
	1:12 Therefore I intend to keep on reminding you	8
	3:14 Therefore, beloved, while you are waiting for these	8
	3:17 Therefore, beloved, since you are forewarned, beware	14
1Jn	4: 5 therefore what they say is from the world	7
3Jn	1: 8 Therefore we ought to support such people	14

Rev	3:18 Therefore I counsel you to buy from me gold	1
	3:19 Be earnest, therefore, and repent.	14
	18: 8 therefore her plagues will come in a single day	7

Thessalonian

1. Θεσσαλονικεύς, *Thessalonikeus, 2552*

1Th	1: 1 To the church of the Thessalonians	1
2Th	1: 1 To the church of the Thessalonians	1

Thessalonica

1. Θεσσαλονικεύς, *Thessalonikeus, 2552*
2. Θεσσαλονίκη, *Thessalonikē, 2553*

Act	17: 1 they came to Thessalonica	2
	17:11 were more receptive than those in Thessalonica	2
	17:13 when the Jews of Thessalonica learned	2
	20: 4 Aristarchus and Secundus from Thessalonica	1
	27: 2 Aristarchus, a Macedonian from Thessalonica.	1
Php	4:16 even when I was in Thessalonica, you sent me help	2
2Ti	4:10 has deserted me and gone to Thessalonica;	2

Theudas

1. Θευδᾶς, *Theudas, 2554*

Act	5:36 For some time ago Theudas rose up	1

they Not Indexed

thief

1. ἅρπαξ, *harpax, 774*
2. κλέπτης, *kleptēs, 3095*
3. κλέπτω, *kleptō, 3096*

Mat	6:19 consume and where thieves break in and steal;	2
	6:20 where thieves do not break in and steal.	2
	24:43 in what part of the night the thief was coming	2
Lke	12:33 where no thief comes near and no moth destroys.	2
	12:39 at what hour the thief was coming	2
	18:11 thieves, rogues, adulterers	1
Jhn	10: 1 in by another way is a thief and a bandit.	2
	10: 8 All who came before me are thieves and bandits;	2
	10:10 The thief comes only to steal and kill	2
	12: 6 because he was a thief;	2
1Co	6:10 thieves, the greedy, drunkards	2
Eph	4:28 Thieves must give up stealing;	3
1Th	5: 2 the day of the Lord will come like a thief	2
	5: 4 for that day to surprise you like a thief;	2
1Pe	4:15 let none of you suffer as a murderer, a thief	2
2Pe	3:10 But the day of the Lord will come like a thief	2
Rev	3: 3 If you do not wake up, I will come like a thief	2
	16:15 ("See, I am coming like a thief!	2

thigh

1. μηρός, *mēros, 3611*

Rev	19:16 and on his thigh he has a name inscribed	1

thing *See also* all things, amazing thing, astonishing thing, deadly thing, deep thing, earthly thing, evil thing, fearful thing, few things, first thing, good thing, great thing, harsh thing, heavenly thing, hidden thing, make a thing, many things, one thing, one thing more, only thing, other thing, perishable thing, present thing, right thing, same thing, set things right, shameful thing, small thing, some things, spiritual thing, strange thing, such a thing, this thing, vain thing, very small thing, what thing, wonderful thing, worthless thing

1. Contextual: Not in Greek
2. αὐτός, *autos, 899*
3. ἐκεῖνος, *ekeinos, 1697*
4. λόγος, *logos, 3364*
5. ὁ, *ho, 3836*
6. οἷος, *hoios, 3888*
7. ὅς, *hos, 4005*
8. ὅσος, *hosos, 4012*
9. οὗτος, *houtos, 4047*
10. πρᾶγμα, *pragma, 4547*
11. ῥῆμα, *rhēma, 4839*
12. σκεῦος, *skeuos, 5007*
13. τὶς, *tis, 5516*
14. ψυχή, *psychē, 6034*

Mat	16:23 setting your mind not on divine things but on human	5

Mat	16:23	your mind not on divine things but on human things	5
	22:21	the things that are the emperor's	5
	22:21	and to God the things that are God's."	5
Mrk	7:15	the things that come out are what defile."	5
	8:33	you are setting your mind not on divine things	5
	8:33	mind not on divine things but on human things	5
	12:17	to the emperor the things that are the emperor's	5
	12:17	and to God the things that are God's."	5
Lke	1: 4	the truth concerning the things	4
	1:65	all these things were talked about	11
	2:15	"Let us go now to Bethlehem and see this thing	11
	2:51	His mother treasured all these things in her heart.	11
	4:23	things that we have heard you did at Capernaum.' "	8
	9:36	told no one any of the things they had seen.	7
	11:41	give for alms those things that are within;	5
	12:20	the things you have prepared, whose will they be?'	7
	17:20	is not coming with things that can be observed;	1
	19:42	on this day the things that make for peace!	5
	19:45	drive out those who were selling things there	1
	20:25	to the emperor the things that are the emperor's	5
	20:25	to God the things that are God's."	5
	24:18	does not know the things that have taken place	5
	24:19	replied, "The things about Jesus of Nazareth	5
	24:27	he interpreted to them the things about himself	5
Jhn	16:13	will declare to you the things that are to come.	5
Act	5:32	we are witnesses to these things	11
	6:13	saying things against this holy place and the law;	11
	10:16	the thing was suddenly taken up to heaven.	12
	13:42	urged them to speak about these things again	11
	15:20	abstain only from things polluted by idols	5
	15:24	certain persons…have said things to disturb you	1
	18:25	and taught accurately the things concerning Jesus	5
	19:32	Meanwhile, some were shouting one thing,	13
	21:19	he related one by one the things that God had done	7
	21:34	Some in the crowd shouted one thing, some another;	13
	26:16	the things in which you have seen me	7
Rom	1:28	and to things that should not be done.	5
	4:17	calls into existence the things that do not exist.	5
	6:21	get from the things of which you now are ashamed?	7
	6:21	The end of those things is death.	3
	7:15	but I do the very thing I hate.	9
	8: 5	set their minds on the things of the flesh	5
	8: 5	set their minds on the things of the Spirit.	5
	15:27	to be of service to them in material things.	1
1Co	1:28	God chose…things that are not	5
	1:28	to reduce to nothing things that are	5
2Co	11:30	I will boast of the things that show my weakness.	1
	12: 4	heard things that are not to be told	11
	13:11	Put things in order, listen to my appeal	1
Gal	5:21	drunkenness, carousing, and things like these	5
Eph	1:10	things in heaven and things on earth.	5
	1:10	things in heaven and things on earth.	5
Php	2:23	as soon as I see how things go with me;	5
	4: 9	things that you have learned and received and heard	9
Col	1:16	were created, things visible and invisible	5
	3: 1	seek the things that are above, where Christ is	5
	3: 2	Set your minds on things that are above	5
	3: 2	not on things that are on earth	5
2Th	3: 4	and will go on doing the things that we command.	7
1Ti	1: 7	the things about which they make assertions.	1
2Ti	2:21	cleanse themselves of the things I have mentioned	9
	3:11	the things that happened to me in Antioch,	6
Heb	3: 5	to testify to the things…spoken later.	1
	5: 1	things pertaining to God on their behalf	5
	6: 9	better things in your case, things that belong to salvation.	5
	6:18	so that through two unchangeable things	10
	11: 1	faith is…the conviction of things not seen.	10
	11: 3	was made from things that are not visible.	5
	12:27	what is shaken—that is, created things	1
1Pe	1:12	the things that have now been announced to you	2
	1:12	things into which angels long to look!	1
1Jn	2:15	Do not love the world or the things in the world.	5
Rev	16: 3	and every living thing in the sea died.	14

not a thing

1. οὐδείς, *oudeis, 4029*

Lke	22:35	lack anything?" They said, "No, not a thing."	1

thing against

1. ἐναντίος, *enantios, 1885*

Act	26: 9	things against the name of Jesus of Nazareth.	1

thing to come

1. μέλλω, *mellō, 3516*

Rom	8:38	nor things present, nor things to come, nor powers	1

think

1. Contextual: Not in Greek
2. διαλογίζομαι, *dialogizomai, 1368*
3. διαλογισμός, *dialogismos, 1369*
4. διανόημα, *dianoēma, 1378*
5. διενθυμέομαι, *dienthymeomai, 1445*
6. δοκέω, *dokeō, 1506*
7. ἐνθυμέομαι, *enthymeomai, 1926*
8. ἐνθύμησις, *enthymēsis, 1927*
9. ἡγέομαι, *hēgeomai, 2451*
10. κρίνω, *krinō, 3212*
11. λογίζομαι, *logizomai, 3357*
12. μνημονεύω, *mnēmoneuō, 3648*
13. νομίζω, *nomizō, 3787*
14. νοῦς, *nous, 3808*
15. φρήν, *phrēn, 5856*
16. φρονέω, *phroneō, 5858*
17. ὡς, *hōs, 6055*

Mat	5:17	not think that I have come to abolish the law	13
	6: 7	for they think that they will be heard because	6
	9: 4	"Why do you think evil in your hearts?	7
	10:34	"Do not think that I have come to bring peace	13
	12:25	He knew what they were thinking and said to them	8
	17:25	"What do you think, Simon?	6
	18:12	What do you think?	6
	20:10	they thought they would receive more;	13
	21:28	"What do you think? A man had two sons;	6
	22:17	Tell us, then, what you think.	6
	22:42	"What do you think of the Messiah? Whose son	6
	26:53	Do you think that I cannot appeal to my Father	6
Mrk	6:49	they thought it was a ghost and cried out;	6
Lke	3:23	was the son (as was thought) of Joseph	13
	6: 8	he knew what they were thinking	3
	10:36	Which of these three, do you think	6
	11:17	he knew what they were thinking and said	4
	12:17	he thought to himself, 'What should I do	2
	12:51	Do you think that I have come to bring peace	6
	13: 2	He asked them, "Do you think	6
	13: 4	do you think that they were worse offenders	6
	24:37	thought that they were seeing a ghost.	6
Jhn	5:39	you think that in them you have eternal life;	6
	5:45	not think that I will accuse you before the Father;	6
	11:13	they thought that he was referring merely to sleep.	6
	11:31	thought that she was going to the tomb to weep	6
	11:56	"What do you think? Surely he will not come to	6
	13:29	Some thought that…Jesus was telling him	6
	16: 2	will think that…they are offering worship	6
Act	8:20	thought you could obtain God's gift with money!	13
	10:19	While Peter was still thinking about the vision	5
	12: 9	he thought he was seeing a vision.	6
	17:29	ought not to think that the deity is like gold	13
	26: 8	Why is it thought incredible by any of you	10
	27:13	they thought they could achieve their purpose;	6
	28:22	we would like to hear from you what you think,	16
Rom	1:21	but they became futile in their thinking	3
	12: 3	more highly than you ought to think	16
	12: 3	but to think with sober judgment	16
	14:14	it is unclean for anyone who thinks it unclean.	11
1Co	3:18	If you think that you are wise in this age	6
	4: 1	Think of us in this way, as servants	11
	4: 9	I think that God has exhibited us apostles	6
	4:18	some of you, thinking that I am not coming to you,	17
	7:26	I think that, in view of the impending crisis	13
	7:36	If anyone thinks that he is not behaving	13
	7:40	I think that I too have the Spirit of God.	6
	8: 7	think of the food they eat as food offered to an idol;	1
	10:12	So if you think you are standing, watch out	6
	12:23	members of the body that we think less honorable	6
	13:11	I thought like a child, I reasoned like a child;	16
	14:20	do not be children in your thinking;	15
	14:20	be infants in evil, but in thinking be adults.	15
2Co	9: 5	So I thought it necessary to urge the brothers	9
	10: 2	who think we are acting according to human standards.	11
	11: 5	I think that I am not in the least inferior	11
	11:16	I repeat, let no one think that I am a fool;	6

	12: 6	no one may think better of me than what is seen	11
	12:19	Have you been thinking all along	6
Gal	5:10	confident…that you will not think otherwise.	16
	6: 3	if those who are nothing think they are something	6
Php	1: 7	right for me to think this way about all of you	16
	2:25	I think it necessary to send to you	9
	3:15	if you think differently about anything	16
	4: 8	think about these things.	11
Col	2:18	puffed up without cause by a human way of thinking	14
Heb	10:29	How much worse…do you think will be deserved	6
	11:15	If they had been thinking of the land	12
Jas	1:26	If any think they are religious	6
2Pe	1:13	I think it right, as long as I am in this body	9
	3: 9	The Lord is not slow…as some think of slowness	9

think highly

    1. ὑπερφρονέω, *hyperphroneō, 5672*

Rom	12: 3	not to think of yourself more highly than you ought	1

think over

    1. νοέω, *noeō, 3783*

2Ti	2: 7	Think over what I say	1

third   *See also* third time

    1. τρίτον, *triton, 5568*
    2. τρίτος, *tritos, 5569*

Mat	16:21	and be killed, and on the third day be raised.	2
	17:23	on the third day he will be raised."	2
	20:19	on the third day he will be raised."	2
	22:26	so also the third, down to the seventh.	2
	26:44	he went away and prayed for the third time	2
	27:64	to be made secure until the third day;	2
Mrk	12:21	the third likewise;	2
Lke	9:22	be killed, and on the third day be raised."	2
	13:32	the third day I finish my work.	2
	18:33	on the third day he will rise again."	2
	20:12	he sent still a third;	2
	20:31	and the third married her	2
	24: 7	crucified, and on the third day rise again."	2
	24:21	now the third day since these things took place.	2
	24:46	rise from the dead on the third day	2
Jhn	2: 1	On the third day there was a wedding in Cana	2
	21:14	This was now the third time	1
	21:17	He said to him the third time, "Simon son of John	1
	21:17	he said to him the third time, "Do you love me?"	1
Act	10:40	God raised him on the third day	2
	27:19	the third day…they threw the ship's tackle	2
1Co	12:28	first apostles, second prophets, third teachers;	1
	15: 4	that he was raised on the third day	2
2Co	12: 2	a person in Christ…caught up to the third heaven	2
Rev	4: 7	the third living creature with a face like a human	2
	6: 5	When he opened the third seal, I heard	2
	6: 5	I heard the third living creature call out, "Come!"	2
	8: 7	and a third of the earth was burned up	2
	8: 7	and a third of the trees were burned up	2
	8: 9	A third of the sea became blood	2
	8: 9	a third of the living creatures in the sea died	2
	8: 9	and a third of the ships were destroyed.	2
	8:10	The third angel blew his trumpet, and a great star	2
	8:10	star fell…and it fell on a third of the rivers	2
	8:11	A third of the waters became wormwood	2
	8:12	blew his trumpet, and a third of the sun was struck	2
	8:12	third of the sun was struck, and a third of the moon	2
	8:12	and a third of the moon, and a third of the stars	2
	8:12	so that a third of their light was darkened;	2
	8:12	a third of the day was kept from shining	2
	9:15	angels…ready…to kill a third of humankind.	2
	9:18	By…three plagues a third of humankind was killed	2
	11:14	The third woe is coming very soon.	2
	12: 4	His tail swept down a third of the stars of heaven	2
	14: 9	Then another angel, a third, followed them, crying	2
	16: 4	The third angel poured his bowl into the rivers	2
	21:19	every jewel;…the third agate	2

thirst

    1. διψάω, *dipsaō, 1498*

Mat	5: 6	those who hunger and thirst for righteousness	1
Rev	7:16	will hunger no more, and thirst no more;	1

thirsty

    1. διψάω, *dipsaō, 1498*
    2. δίψος, *dipsos, 1499*

Mat	25:35	I was thirsty and you gave me something to drink	1
	25:37	or thirsty and gave you something to drink?	1
	25:42	I was thirsty and you gave me nothing to drink	1
	25:44	that we saw you hungry or thirsty	1
Jhn	4:13	"Everyone who drinks…will be thirsty again	1
	4:14	water that I give them will never be thirsty.	1
	4:15	give me this water, so that I may never be thirsty	1
	6:35	whoever believes in me will never be thirsty.	1
	7:37	"Let anyone who is thirsty come to me	1
	19:28	Jesus…said…"I am thirsty."	1
Rom	12:20	if they are thirsty, give them something to drink;	1
1Co	4:11	To the present hour we are hungry and thirsty	1
2Co	11:27	hungry and thirsty, often without food	2
Rev	21: 6	To the thirsty I will give water as a gift	1
	22:17	And let everyone who is thirsty come.	1

thirty

    1. τριάκοντα, *triakonta, 5558*

Mat	13: 8	some a hundredfold, some sixty, some thirty	1
	13:23	yields…in another sixty, and in another thirty	1
	26:15	They paid him thirty pieces of silver.	1
	27: 3	he repented and brought back the thirty pieces	1
	27: 9	"And they took the thirty pieces of silver	1
Mrk	4: 8	thirty and sixty and a hundredfold."	1
	4:20	thirty and sixty and a hundredfold."	1
Lke	3:23	Jesus was about thirty years old when he began	1
Gal	3:17	law, which came four hundred thirty years later	1

thirty gallons

    1. τρεῖς + μετρητής, *treis + metrētēs, 5552 + 3583*

Jhn	2: 6	jars…each holding twenty or thirty gallons.	1

thirty-eight

    1. τριάκοντα + καί + ὀκτώ, *triakonta + kai + oktō, 5558 + 2779 + 3893*

Jhn	5: 5	who had been ill for thirty-eight years.	1

this   Not Indexed; *See* all this, at this, at this *moment*, from this, in this *term*, like this, this *day*, this *point*, this very *day*, this *way*

this fellow

    1. οὗτος, *houtos, 4047*

Mat	12:24	that this fellow casts out the demons."	1
	26:61	"This fellow said, 'I am able to destroy	1
Mrk	2: 7	"Why does this fellow speak in this way?	1
Lke	15: 2	"This fellow welcomes sinners and eats with them."	1
	23:18	all shouted out together, "Away with this fellow!	1

this man

    1. ἐκεῖνος, *ekeinos, 1697*
    2. οὗτος, *houtos, 4047*

Mat	9: 3	"This man is blaspheming."	2
	13:54	"Where did this man get this wisdom	2
	13:56	Where then did this man get all this?"	2
	26:71	"This man was with Jesus of Nazareth."	2
	27:24	"I am innocent of this man's blood;	2
	27:32	they compelled this man to carry his cross.	2
	27:47	"This man is calling for Elijah."	2
	27:54	"Truly this man was God's Son!"	2
Mrk	14:69	"This man is one of them."	2
Lke	7:39	he said to himself, "If this man were a prophet	2
	16: 1	this man was squandering his property.	2
	18:14	I tell you, this man went down to his home	2
	19:14	'We do not want this man to rule over us.'	2
	22:56	and said, "This man also was with him."	2
	22:59	"Surely this man also was with him;	2
	23:41	this man has done nothing wrong."	2
	23:52	This man went to Pilate and asked for the body	2
Jhn	6:52	"How can this man give us his flesh to eat?"	2
	7:15	"How does this man have such learning	2
	7:25	this the man whom they are trying to kill?	2
	7:27	Yet we know where this man is from;	2
	7:31	will he do more signs than this man has done?"	2
	9: 2	who sinned, this man or his parents	2
	9: 3	"Neither this man nor his parents sinned;	2

Jhn	9:33	If this man were not from God, he could do nothing."	2
	10:41	everything that John said about this man was true."	2
	11:37	"Could not he…have kept this man from dying?"	2
	18: 8	So if you are looking for me, let these men go."	2
	18:30	"If this man were not a criminal	2
	18:40	shouted in reply, "Not this man, but Barabbas!"	2
	19:12	the Jews cried out, "If you release this man	2
	19:21	but, 'This man said, I am King of the Jews.' "	1
Act	1:18	this man acquired a field with the reward	2
	4:10	this man is standing before you in good health	2
	8:10	saying, "This man is the power of God	2
	13:23	Of this man's posterity	2
	13:38	through this man forgiveness of sins	2
	21:24	Join these men, go through the rite of purification	2
	25:24	you see this man	2
	27:31	"Unless these men stay in the ship	2

this person

1. οὗτος, *houtos, 4047*

Lke	14: 9	'Give this person your place,'	1
1Jn	2: 5	in this person the love of God has reached perfection.	1

this thing

1. Contextual: Not in Greek
2. αὐτός, *autos, 899*
3. ὅς, *hos, 4005*
4. οὗτος, *houtos, 4047*

Mat	7:28	Jesus had finished saying these things	4
	9:18	While he was saying these things to them	4
	11:25	because you have hidden these things from the wise	4
	13:34	Jesus told the crowds all these things in parables;	4
	19: 1	Jesus had finished saying these things	4
	21:23	"By what authority are you doing these things	4
	21:24	by what authority I do these things.	4
	21:27	by what authority I am doing these things.	4
	24:33	So also, when you see all these things	4
	24:34	until all these things have taken place.	4
Mrk	11:28	"By what authority are you doing these things?	4
	11:29	tell you by what authority I do these things.	4
	11:33	by what authority I am doing these things."	4
	13:29	So also, when you see these things taking place	4
Lke	1:20	unable to speak, until the day these things occur	4
	10:21	hidden these things from the wise	4
	11:45	"Teacher, when you say these things,	4
	12:31	these things will be given to you as well.	4
	18:34	they understood nothing about all these things;	4
	20: 2	by what authority are you doing these things?	4
	20: 8	by what authority I am doing these things."	4
	21: 6	"As for these things that you see	4
	21: 9	for these things must take place first	4
	21:28	Now when these things begin to take place	4
	21:31	So also, when you see these things taking place	4
	23:49	stood at a distance, watching these things.	4
	24:21	now the third day since these things took place.	4
	24:26	suffer these things and then enter into his glory?"	4
	24:48	You are witnesses of these things.	4
Jhn	2:16	the doves, "Take these things out	4
	3: 9	Nicodemus said to him, "How can these things be?"	4
	3:10	a teacher…yet you do not understand these things?	4
	5:34	I say these things so that you may be saved.	4
	6:59	He said these things while he was teaching	4
	7: 4	If you do these things, show yourself to the world	4
	8:28	speak these things as the Father instructed me.	4
	8:30	As he was saying these things, many believed	4
	12:16	disciples did not understand these things at first;	4
	12:16	that these things had been written of him	4
	13:17	If you know these things	4
	14:25	"I have said these things to you	4
	15:11	I have said these things to you	4
	15:21	they will do all these things to you	4
	16: 1	"I have said these things to you	4
	16: 4	I have said these things to you	4
	16: 4	"I did not say these things…from the beginning	4
	16: 6	because I have said these things to you	4
	16:25	"I have said these things to you in figures	4
	17:13	I speak these things in the world	4
	19:36	These things occurred so that the scripture	4
	19:38	After these things, Joseph of Arimathea,	4
	20:18	she told them that he had said these things	4
	21: 1	After these things Jesus showed himself again	4

	21:24	the disciple who is testifying to these things	4
Act	5:11	all who heard of these things.	4
	7: 1	high priest asked him, "Are these things so?"	4
	7:54	When they heard these things, they became enraged	4
	15:17	who has been making these things	4
	17:11	to see whether these things were so.	4
	18:17	But Gallio paid no attention to any of these things.	4
	19:21	Now after these things had been accomplished	4
	19:36	Since these things cannot be denied	4
	26:26	the king knows about these things	4
	26:26	none of these things has escaped his notice	4
Rom	8:31	What then are we to say about these things?	4
	8:37	No, in all these things we are more	4
	10: 5	"the person who does these things will live by them."	2
	13: 6	God's servants, busy with this very thing.	4
1Co	2:10	these things God has revealed to us	1
	2:13	we speak of these things in words	3
	10: 6	Now these things occurred as examples for us	4
	10:11	These things happened to them…as an example	4
2Co	2:16	Who is sufficient for these things?	4
	5: 5	He who has prepared us for this very thing is God	4
	13:10	I write these things while I am away from you	4
Eph	5: 6	for because of these things the wrath of God	4
Php	4: 8	think about these things.	4
2Th	2: 5	I told you these things when I was still with you?	4
1Ti	4:11	These are the things you must insist on and teach.	4
	4:15	Put these things into practice, devote yourself to them	4
	4:16	attention to…teaching; continue in these things	2
Tit	2:15	Declare these things;	4
	3: 8	I desire that you insist on these things	4
	3: 8	these things are excellent and profitable to everyone.	4
Heb	7:13	Now the one of whom these things are spoken	4
	9: 5	Of these things we cannot speak now in detail.	3
2Pe	1: 4	he has given us, through these things, his…promises	3
	1: 8	For if these things are yours and are increasing	4
	1: 9	For anyone who lacks these things is nearsighted	4
	1:12	I intend to keep on reminding you of these things	4
	1:15	you may be able at any time to recall these things.	4
	3:11	Since all these things are to be dissolved in this way	4
	3:14	Therefore…while you are waiting for these things	4
1Jn	1: 4	writing these things so that our joy may be complete.	4
	2: 1	I am writing these things to you so that you may not sin.	4
	2:26	I write these things to you	4
	5:13	I write these things to you who believe in the name	4
Rev	16: 5	"You are just…for you have judged these things;	4
	21: 7	Those who conquer will inherit these things	4
	22: 8	I, John, am the one who heard and saw these things.	4
	22:20	The one who testifies to these things says,	4

this woman

1. οὗτος, *houtos, 4047*

Lke	13:16	ought not this woman…be set free from this	1
Gal	4:24	these women are two covenants.	1

thistle

1. τρίβολος, *tribolos, 5560*

Mat	7:16	gathered from thorns, or figs from thistles?	1
Heb	6: 8	if it produces thorns and thistles	1

Thomas

1. Θωμᾶς, *Thōmas, 2605*

Mat	10: 3	Philip and Bartholomew; Thomas and Matthew	1
Mrk	3:18	Philip, and Bartholomew, and Matthew, and Thomas	1
Lke	6:15	Matthew, and Thomas, and James son	1
Jhn	11:16	Thomas, who was called the Twin	1
	14: 5	Thomas said to him, "Lord, we do not know	1
	20:24	But Thomas (who was called the Twin),	1
	20:26	Thomas was with them.	1
	20:27	Then he said to Thomas, "Put your finger here	1
	20:28	Thomas answered him, "My Lord and my God!"	1
	21: 2	Simon Peter, Thomas called the Twin	1
Act	1:13	Philip and Thomas, Bartholomew and Matthew	1

thong

1. Contextual: Not in Greek
2. ἱμάς, *himas, 2666*

Mrk	1: 7	untie the thong of his sandals.	2
Lke	3:16	I am not worthy to untie the thong of his sandals.	2
Jhn	1:27	I am not worthy to untie the thong of his sandal."	2
Act	13:25	to untie the thong of the sandals on his feet.'	1
	22:25	when they had tied him up with thongs	2

thorn

1. ἄκανθα, *akantha, 180*
2. ἀκάνθινος, *akanthinos, 181*
3. σκόλοψ, *skolops, 5022*

Mat	7:16	Are grapes gathered from thorns	1
	13: 7	Other seeds fell among thorns	1
	13: 7	and the thorns grew up and choked them.	1
	13:22	As for what was sown among thorns	1
	27:29	twisting some thorns into a crown, they put it	1
Mrk	4: 7	Other seed fell among thorns	1
	4: 7	the thorns grew up and choked it	1
	4:18	others are those sown among the thorns:	1
	15:17	twisting some thorns into a crown, they put it on him.	2
Lke	6:44	Figs are not gathered from thorns	1
	8: 7	Some fell among thorns	1
	8: 7	and the thorns grew with it and choked it.	1
	8:14	As for what fell among the thorns	1
Jhn	19: 2	the soldiers wove a crown of thorns	1
	19: 5	Jesus came out, wearing the crown of thorns	2
2Co	12: 7	a thorn was given me in the flesh	3
Heb	6: 8	if it produces thorns and thistles	1

more thorough

1. ἀκριβῶς, *akribōs, 209*

Act	23:15	you want to make a more thorough examination	1

thoroughly

1. πυγμή, *pygmē, 4778*

Mrk	7: 3	do not eat unless they thoroughly wash their hands	1

more thoroughly

1. ἀκριβῶς, *akribōs, 209*

Act	23:20	to inquire more thoroughly into his case	1

though *See also* as though, even though

1. Contextual: Not in Greek
2. ἀλλά, *alla, 247*
3. ἄν, *an, 323*
4. γάρ, *gar, 1142*
5. δέ, *de, 1254*
6. ἐάν, *ean, 1569*
7. εἰ, *ei, 1623*
8. εἴπερ, *eiper, 1642*
9. ἐν, *en, 1877*
10. καί, *kai, 2779*
11. καίπερ, *kaiper, 2788*
12. καίτοι, *kaitoi, 2792*
13. μέν, *men, 3525*
14. ὑπάρχω, *hyparchō, 5639*

Mat	14: 5	Though Herod wanted to put him to death	1
	26:33	"Though all become deserters because of you	7
	26:60	though many false witnesses came forward.	1
Mrk	14:29	"Even though all become deserters, I will not."	7
Lke	8:43	though she had spent all she had on physicians	1
	11: 8	even though he will not get up and give him	7
	18: 4	'Though I have no fear of God and no respect	7
	23:50	who, though a member of the council	1
Jhn	2: 9	(though the servants who had drawn the water knew)	5
	6:71	though one of the twelve, was going to betray him.	1
	8:55	though you do not know him.	1
	9:25	I do know, that though I was blind, now I see."	1
	10:33	though only a human being	1
	11: 5	Accordingly, though Jesus loved Martha and her sister	1
	13:10	you are clean, though not all of you."	2
	19:38	was a disciple of Jesus, though a secret one	5
	21:11	though there were so many, the net was not torn.	1
Act	3:13	though he had decided to release him.	1
	9: 8	though his eyes were open, he could see nothing;	1
	15:24	though with no instructions from us	1
	17:27	though indeed he is not far from each one of us.	10
	18:25	though he knew only the baptism of John.	1
	28: 4	though he has escaped from the sea	1
	28:17	though I had done nothing against our people	1
Rom	1:20	power and divine nature, invisible though they are	1
	1:21	for though they knew God, they did not honor him	1
	2:14	though not having the law, are a law to themselves.	1
	5: 7	though perhaps for a good person someone might…die.	4
	8:10	though the body is dead because of sin	13
	9:27	"Though the number of the children of Israel were	6

1Co	2: 6	though it is not a wisdom of this age	5
	4:15	For though you might have ten thousand guardians	6
	5: 3	For though absent in body, I am present in spirit;	13
	8: 5	even though there may be so-called gods in heaven	8
	9:19	For though I am free with respect to all	1
	9:20	(though I myself am not under the law)	1
	9:21	(though I am not free from God's law	1
	12:12	all the members of the body, though many, are one	1
	15: 6	though some have died.	5
	15:10	though it was not I, but the grace of God	5
2Co	5:16	even though we once knew Christ	7
	7: 8	I do not regret it (though I did regret it)	7
	7: 8	grieved you with that letter, though only briefly).	7
	8: 9	that though he was rich, yet for your sakes	1
	10: 9	seem as though I am trying to frighten you	3
	12:11	even though I am nothing.	7
	13: 7	though we may seem to have failed.	5
Gal	2: 2	(though only in a private meeting	5
	2: 3	though he was a Greek.	1
	2:14	"If you, though a Jew, live like a Gentile	14
	4: 1	though they are the owners of all the property;	1
	4:14	though my condition put you to the test	1
Php	2: 6	who, though he was in the form of God, did not regard	1
Col	2: 5	For though I am absent in body	7
1Th	2: 2	though we had already suffered	1
	2: 7	though we might have made demands	1
Phm	1: 8	For this reason, though I am bold enough in Christ	1
Heb	3: 9	though they had seen my works	10
	4: 3	though his works were finished	12
	5:12	For though by this time you ought to be teachers	1
	6: 9	Even though we speak in this way	7
	7: 5	though these also are descended from Abraham.	11
	11:39	all these, though they were commended for their faith	1
Jas	3: 4	Or look at ships: though they are so large	1
1Pe	1: 7	gold that, though perishable, is tested by fire	5
	2: 4	though rejected by mortals yet chosen and precious	13
	2:12	though they malign you as evildoers	9
	4: 6	so that, though they had been judged in the flesh	13
2Pe	1:12	though you know them already and are established	11
	2:11	angels, though greater in might and power	1
Jde	1: 5	to remind you, though you are fully informed,	1

thought *See also* take thought

1. Contextual: Not in Greek
2. διαλογισμός, *dialogismos, 1369*
3. διάνοια, *dianoia, 1379*
4. ἐνθύμησις, *enthymēsis, 1927*
5. λογισμός, *logismos, 3361*
6. μαρτυρία, *martyria, 3456*
7. νόημα, *noēma, 3784*

Mat	9: 4	Jesus, perceiving their thoughts, said	4
Lke	1:51	in the thoughts of their hearts.	3
	2:35	inner thoughts of many will be revealed	2
	9:47	Jesus, aware of their inner thoughts	2
Rom	2:15	their conflicting thoughts will accuse…them	5
	2:16	God…will judge the secret thoughts of all.	1
1Co	3:20	the thoughts of the wise, that they are futile."	2
2Co	10: 5	take every thought captive to obey Christ.	7
	11: 3	your thoughts will be led astray	7
1Ti	3: 7	Moreover, he must be well thought of by outsiders	6
Heb	4:12	able to judge the thoughts…of the heart.	4
Jas	2: 4	and become judges with evil thoughts?	2

thousand *See also* fifty thousand, five thousand, four thousand, seven thousand, ten thousand, three thousand, two thousand

1. μυριάς, *myrias, 3689*
2. χιλιάς, *chilias, 5942*
3. χίλιοι, *chilioi, 5943*

Lke	12: 1	when the crowd gathered by the thousands,	1
	14:31	whether he is able with ten thousand to oppose	2
	14:31	who comes against him with twenty thousand?	2
Act	4: 4	they numbered about five thousand.	2
	21:20	thousands of believers there are among the Jews	2
1Co	10: 8	twenty-three thousand fell in a single day.	2
2Pe	3: 8	with the Lord one day is like a thousand years	3
	3: 8	and a thousand years are like one day.	3
Rev	5:11	myriads of myriads and thousands of thousands	2
	5:11	myriads of myriads and thousands of thousands	2
	7: 4	one hundred forty-four thousand, sealed	2

Rev 7: 5 From the tribe of Judah twelve thousand sealed, 2
    7: 5 from the tribe of Reuben twelve thousand, 2
    7: 5 from the tribe of Gad twelve thousand, 2
    7: 6 from the tribe of Asher twelve thousand, 2
    7: 6 from the tribe of Naphtali twelve thousand, 2
    7: 6 from the tribe of Manasseh twelve thousand, 2
    7: 7 from the tribe of Simeon twelve thousand, 2
    7: 7 from the tribe of Levi twelve thousand, 2
    7: 7 from the tribe of Issachar twelve thousand, 2
    7: 8 from the tribe of Zebulun twelve thousand, 2
    7: 8 from the tribe of Joseph twelve thousand, 2
    7: 8 from the tribe of Benjamin twelve thousand sealed. 2
    11: 3 prophesy for one thousand two hundred sixty days 3
    11:13 seven thousand people were killed in the earthquake 2
    12: 6 nourished for one thousand two hundred sixty days 3
    14: 1 one hundred forty-four thousand who had his name 2
    14: 3 except the one hundred forty-four thousand 2
    20: 2 the dragon...and bound him for a thousand years. 3
    20: 3 until the thousand years were ended 3
    20: 4 and reigned with Christ a thousand years. 3
    20: 5 until the thousand years were ended.) 3
    20: 6 they will reign with him a thousand years. 3
    20: 7 When the thousand years are ended, 3

threat *See also* extort money by threat
    1. ἀπειλή, *apeilē, 581*
Act 4:29 now, Lord, look at their threats 1
    9: 1 Saul, still breathing threats and murder 1

threaten
    1. ἀπειλέω, *apeileō, 580*
    2. ἀπειλή, *apeilē, 581*
    3. στυγνάζω, *stygnazō, 5145*
Mat 16: 3 for the sky is red and threatening.' 3
Eph 6: 9 Stop threatening them 2
1Pe 2:23 when he suffered, he did not threaten; 1

threaten again
    1. προσαπειλέω, *prosapeileō, 4653*
Act 4:21 After threatening them again, they let them go 1

three *See also* three *floors*
    1. Contextual: Not in Greek
    2. τρεῖς, *treis, 5552*
    3. τρίς, *tris, 5565*
Mat 12:40 For just as Jonah was three days and three nights 2
    12:40 For just as Jonah was three days and three nights 2
    12:40 so for three days and three nights the Son 2
    12:40 so for three days and three nights the Son 2
    13:33 mixed in with three measures of flour 2
    15:32 because they have been with me now for three days 2
    17: 4 if you wish, I will make three dwellings here 2
    18:16 by the evidence of two or three witnesses 2
    18:20 For where two or three are gathered in my name 2
    26:61 to build it in three days.' " 2
    27:40 destroy the temple and build it in three days 2
    27:63 'After three days I will rise again.' 2
Mrk 8: 2 because they have been with me now for three days 2
    8:31 be killed, and after three days rise again. 2
    9: 5 let us make three dwellings 2
    9:31 three days after being killed, he will rise again." 2
    10:34 after three days he will rise again." 2
    14:58 in three days I will build another 2
    15:29 destroy the temple and build it in three days 2
Lke 1:56 Mary remained with her about three months 2
    2:46 After three days they found him in the temple 2
    4:25 the heaven was shut up three years and six months 2
    9:33 let us make three dwellings 2
    10:36 Which of these three, do you think 2
    11: 5 'Friend, lend me three loaves of bread; 2
    12:52 three against two and two against three; 2
    12:52 three against two and two against three; 2
    13: 7 For three years I have come looking for fruit 2
    13:21 took and mixed in with three measures of flour 2
Jhn 2:19 this temple, and in three days I will raise it up." 2
    2:20 and will you raise it up in three days?" 2
Act 5: 7 After an interval of about three hours 2
    7:20 three months he was brought up in his father's house; 2
    9: 9 For three days he was without sight 2
    10:16 This happened three times 3

    10:19 three men are searching for you. 2
    11:10 This happened three times; 3
    11:11 three men, sent to me from Caesarea, arrived 2
    17: 2 on three sabbath days argued with them 2
    19: 8 and for three months spoke out boldly 2
    20: 3 where he stayed for three months. 2
    23: 8 the Pharisees acknowledge all three.) 1
    25: 1 Three days after Festus had arrived in the province 2
    28: 7 entertained us hospitably for three days. 2
    28:11 Three months later we set sail 2
    28:12 Syracuse and stayed there for three days; 2
    28:17 Three days later he called together...leaders 2
1Co 13:13 And now faith, hope, and love abide, these three; 2
    14:27 let there be only two or at most three 2
    14:29 Let two or three prophets speak 2
2Co 13: 1 by the evidence of two or three witnesses." 2
Gal 1:18 Then after three years I did go up to Jerusalem 2
1Ti 5:19 except on the evidence of two or three witnesses. 2
Heb 10:28 "on the testimony of two or three witnesses." 2
Jas 5:17 for three years and six months it did not rain 2
1Jn 5: 7 There are three that testify: 2
    5: 8 and these three agree. 2
Rev 6: 6 and three quarts of barley for a day's pay 2
    8:13 trumpets that the three angels...blow!" 2
    9:18 By...three plagues a third of humankind was killed 2
    11: 9 For three and a half days members of the peoples 2
    11:11 after the three and a half days, the breath of life 2
    16:13 I saw three foul spirits like frogs coming from 2
    16:19 The great city was split into three parts 2
    21:13 on the east three gates, on the north three gates 2
    21:13 on the east three gates, on the north three gates 2
    21:13 on the south three gates, and on the west 2
    21:13 and on the west three gates. 2

three hundred
    1. τριακόσιοι, *triakosioi, 5559*
Mrk 14: 5 sold for more than three hundred denarii 1
Jhn 12: 5 perfume...sold for three hundred denarii 1

three in the afternoon
    1. ἔνατος + ὥρα, *enatos + hōra, 1888 + 6052*
Mat 27:45 over the whole land until three in the afternoon. 1
Mrk 15:33 over the whole land until three in the afternoon. 1
Lke 23:44 darkness came...until three in the afternoon 1

three miles
    1. εἴκοσι + πέντε + στάδιον, *eikosi + pente + stadion, 1633 + 4297 + 5084*
Jhn 6:19 When they had rowed about three or four miles 1

three months
    1. τρίμηνος, *trimēnos, 5564*
Heb 11:23 was hidden by his parents for three months 1

three o'clock
    1. ἔνατος, *enatos, 1888*
    2. ἔνατος + ὥρα, *enatos + hōra, 1888 + 6052*
Mat 20: 5 about noon and about three o'clock, 2
    27:46 about three o'clock Jesus cried 2
Mrk 15:34 At three o'clock Jesus cried out with a loud voice 2
Act 10:30 at three o'clock, I was praying in my house 1

three o'clock in the afternoon
    1. ἔνατος, *enatos, 1888*
    2. ἔνατος + ὥρα, *enatos + hōra, 1888 + 6052*
Act 3: 1 the hour of prayer, at three o'clock in the afternoon. 1
    10: 3 One afternoon at about three o'clock 2

Three Taverns
    1. Τρεῖς ταβέρναι, *Treis tabernai, 5553*
Act 28:15 as far as the Forum of Appius and Three Taverns 1

three thousand
    1. τρισχίλιοι, *trischilioi, 5567*
Act 2:41 that day about three thousand persons were added. 1

three times
    1. τρίς, *tris, 5565*
Mat 26:34 you will deny me three times." 1

26:75	you will deny me three times."	1
Mrk 14:30	you will deny me three times."	1
14:72	you will deny me three times."	1
Lke 22:34	until you have denied three times that you know me."	1
22:61	you will deny me three times."	1
Jhn 13:38	you will have denied me three times.	1
2Co 11:25	Three times I was beaten with rods.	1
11:25	Three times I was shipwrecked;	1
12: 8	Three times I appealed to the Lord about this	1

three years

1. τριετία, *trietia*, 5562

Act 20:31	for three years I did not cease night or day	1

thresh   *See also* threshing *floor*

1. Contextual: Not in Greek
2. ἀλοάω, *aloaō*, 262

1Co 9:10	threshes should thresh in hope of a share in the crop.	2
9:10	should thresh in hope of a share in the crop.	1

throat

1. λάρυγξ, *larynx*, 3296
2. πνίγω, *pnigō*, 4464

Mat 18:28	and seizing him by the throat, he said	2
Rom 3:13	"Their throats are opened graves;	1

throne

1. θρόνος, *thronos*, 2585

Mat 5:34	either by heaven, for it is the throne of God	1
19:28	Son of Man is seated on the throne of his glory	1
19:28	will also sit on twelve thrones	1
23:22	swears by the throne of God	1
25:31	then he will sit on the throne of his glory.	1
Lke 1:32	give to him the throne of his ancestor David.	1
1:52	brought down the powerful from their thrones	1
22:30	sit on thrones judging the twelve tribes	1
Act 2:30	put one of his descendants on his throne.	1
7:49	'Heaven is my throne, and the earth is my footstool.	1
Col 1:16	thrones or dominions or rulers	1
Heb 1: 8	"Your throne, O God, is forever and ever	1
4:16	therefore approach the throne of grace with boldness	1
8: 1	right hand of the throne of the Majesty in the heavens	1
12: 2	seat at the right hand of the throne of God.	1
Rev 1: 4	from the seven spirits who are before his throne	1
2:13	"I know where you are living, where Satan's throne is.	1
3:21	I will give a place with me on my throne	1
3:21	and sat down with my Father on his throne.	1
4: 2	I was in the spirit, and in heaven stood a throne	1
4: 2	in heaven stood a throne, with one seated on the throne!	1
4: 3	and around the throne is a rainbow	1
4: 4	Around the throne are twenty-four thrones	1
4: 4	Around the throne are twenty-four thrones	1
4: 4	seated on the thrones are twenty-four elders	1
4: 5	Coming from the throne are flashes of lightning	1
4: 5	in front of the throne burn seven flaming torches	1
4: 6	in front of the throne there is something like a sea	1
4: 6	Around the throne, and on each side of the throne	1
4: 6	Around the throne, and on each side of the throne	1
4: 9	thanks to the one who is seated on the throne	1
4:10	fall before the one who is seated on the throne	1
4:10	they cast their crowns before the throne, singing	1
5: 1	the one seated on the throne	1
5: 6	between the throne and the…living creatures	1
5: 7	right hand of the one who was seated on the throne.	1
5:11	the voice of many angels surrounding the throne	1
5:13	"To the one seated on the throne and to the Lamb	1
6:16	hide us from…the one seated on the throne	1
7: 9	standing before the throne and before the Lamb	1
7:10	"Salvation…to our God who is seated on the throne	1
7:11	all the angels stood around the throne	1
7:11	they fell on their faces before the throne	1
7:15	For this reason they are before the throne of God	1
7:15	one who is seated on the throne will shelter them.	1
7:17	for the Lamb at the center of the throne will be	1
8: 3	on the golden altar that is before the throne.	1
11:16	the twenty-four elders who sit on their thrones	1
12: 5	snatched away and taken to God and to his throne;	1
13: 2	the dragon gave it his power and his throne	1
14: 3	and they sing a new song before the throne	1
16:10	angel poured his bowl on the throne of the beast	1

16:17	voice came…from the throne, saying, "It is done!"	1
19: 4	worshiped God who is seated on the throne, saying	1
19: 5	And from the throne came a voice saying	1
20: 4	Then I saw thrones, and those seated on them	1
20:11	I saw a great white throne and the one who sat on it;	1
20:12	dead, great and small, standing before the throne	1
21: 3	I heard a loud voice from the throne saying	1
21: 5	And the one who was seated on the throne said,	1
22: 1	flowing from the throne of God and of the Lamb	1
22: 3	the throne of God and of the Lamb will be in it	1

through   *See also* carry through, come through, dig through, effective through, go on through, go through, go through all, go through rite of purification, go through suffering, pass through, wander through, work through

1. ἀπό, *apo*, 608
2. διά, *dia*, 1328
3. διά + ὁ + στόμα, *dia + ho + stoma*, 1328 + 3836 + 5125
4. διά + ὁ + χείρ, *dia + ho + cheir*, 1328 + 3836 + 5931
5. διά + στόμα, *dia + stoma*, 1328 + 5125
6. διά + χείρ, *dia + cheir*, 1328 + 5931
7. ἐκ, *ek*, 1666
8. ἐν, *en*, 1877
9. ἐπί, *epi*, 2093
10. κατά, *kata*, 2848
11. στόμα, *stoma*, 5125
12. σύν + χείρ, *syn + cheir*, 5250 + 5931

Mat 1:22	spoken by the Lord through the prophet:	2
2:15	spoken by the Lord through the prophet, "Out of Egypt	2
2:17	what had been spoken through the prophet Jeremiah:	2
2:23	so that what was spoken through the prophets	2
4:14	so that what had been spoken through the prophet	2
7:13	"Enter through the narrow gate; for the gate is wide	2
8:17	what had been spoken through the prophet Isaiah:	2
10:20	the Spirit of your Father speaking through you.	8
12: 1	At that time Jesus went through the grainfields	2
12:17	what had been spoken through the prophet Isaiah:	2
12:43	it wanders through waterless regions	2
13:35	to fulfill what had been spoken through the prophet:	2
19:24	for a camel to go through the eye of a needle	2
21: 4	what had been spoken through the prophet, saying	2
27: 9	what had been spoken through the prophet Jeremiah	2
Mrk 2:23	he was going through the grainfields;	2
9:29	can come out only through prayer."	8
9:30	They went on…and passed through Galilee.	2
10:25	a camel to go through the eye of a needle	2
11:16	to carry anything through the temple.	2
16: S	[afterward Jesus himself sent out through them,]	2
Lke 1:70	as he spoke the mouth of his holy prophets	2
4:14	spread through all the surrounding country.	10
4:30	passed through the midst of them and went on his way.	2
5:19	let him down with his bed through the tiles	2
6: 1	while Jesus was going through the grainfields	2
8: 1	he went on through cities and villages	10
9: 6	They departed and went through the villages	10
11:24	it wanders through waterless regions looking for	2
13:24	"Strive to enter through the narrow door;	2
17:11	through the region between Samaria and Galilee.	2
18:25	to go through the eye of a needle	2
Jhn 1: 3	All things came into being through him	2
1: 7	so that all might believe through him.	2
1:10	and the world came into being through him;	2
1:17	The law indeed was given through Moses;	2
1:17	grace and truth came through Jesus Christ.	2
3:17	that the world might be saved through him.	2
4: 4	he had to go through Samaria.	2
11: 4	the Son of God may be glorified through it."	2
14: 6	No one comes to the Father except through me.	2
17:20	those who will believe in me through their word	2
Act 1: 2	giving instructions through the Holy Spirit	2
1:16	which the Holy Spirit through David foretold	5
2:16	this is what was spoken through the prophet Joel:	2
2:22	signs that God did through him among you	2
3:16	the faith that is through Jesus	2
3:18	what he had foretold through all the prophets	5
3:21	long ago through his holy prophets.	5
4:16	a notable sign has been done through them;	2
4:25	said by the Holy Spirit through our ancestor David	11
4:30	through the name of your holy servant Jesus."	2
5:12	done…through the apostles.	4

Act	7:25	God through him was rescuing them	6
	7:35	through the angel who appeared to him in the bush.	12
	8:18	through the laying on of the apostles' hands	2
	9:25	and let him down through an opening in the wall	2
	10:43	receives forgiveness of sins through his name."	2
	13:38	through this man forgiveness of sins	2
	14: 3	granting...wonders to be done through them.	4
	14:22	saying, "It is through many persecutions	2
	15: 7	through whom the Gentiles would hear the message	3
	15:11	saved through the grace of the Lord Jesus	2
	15:12	signs and wonders that God had done through them	2
	18:27	helped those who through grace had become believers	2
	19:11	God did extraordinary miracles through Paul	4
	20: 3	he decided to return through Macedonia.	2
	20:19	that came to me through the plots of the Jews.	8
	21: 4	Through the Spirit they told Paul not to go	2
	21:19	done among the Gentiles through his ministry.	2
	28:25	saying...through the prophet Isaiah	2
Rom	1: 2	he promised beforehand through his prophets	2
	1: 5	through whom we have received grace	2
	1: 8	I thank my God through Jesus Christ for all of you	2
	1:17	revealed through faith for faith;	7
	2:16	God, through Jesus Christ, will judge the secret	2
	3: 7	But if through my falsehood God's truthfulness	8
	3:22	the righteousness of God through faith in Jesus	2
	3:24	through the redemption that is in Christ Jesus	2
	3:30	and the uncircumcised through that same faith.	2
	4:13	but through the righteousness of faith.	2
	5: 1	peace with God through our Lord Jesus Christ	2
	5: 2	through whom we have obtained access	2
	5: 5	poured into our hearts through the Holy Spirit	2
	5: 9	will we be saved through him from the wrath of God	2
	5:10	reconciled to God through the death of his Son	2
	5:11	boast in God through our Lord Jesus Christ	2
	5:11	Jesus Christ, through whom we have now received	2
	5:12	just as sin came into the world through one man	2
	5:17	death exercised dominion through that one	2
	5:17	dominion in life through the one man, Jesus Christ.	2
	5:21	grace might...exercise dominion through justification	2
	5:21	leading to eternal life through Jesus Christ our Lord.	2
	7: 4	have died to the law through the body of Christ	2
	7:11	sin...deceived me and through it killed me.	2
	7:13	sin, working death in me through what is good	2
	7:13	through the commandment might become sinful	2
	7:25	Thanks be to God through Jesus Christ our Lord!	2
	8:11	through his Spirit that dwells in you.	2
	8:37	more than conquerors through him who loved us.	2
	9: 7	through Isaac that descendants shall be named for you."	8
	9:30	attained it...righteousness through faith;	7
	11:36	and through him and to him are all things.	2
	15:18	except what Christ has accomplished through me	2
	16:26	through the prophetic writings is made known	2
	16:27	through Jesus Christ, to whom be the glory forever!	2
1Co	1:21	the world did not know God through wisdom	2
	1:21	through the foolishness of our proclamation, to save	2
	2:10	God has revealed to us through the Spirit;	2
	3: 5	Servants through whom you came to believe	2
	3:15	saved, but only as through fire.	2
	4: 6	so that you may learn through us the meaning	8
	4:15	I became your father through the gospel.	2
	7:14	made holy through his wife	8
	7:14	made holy through her husband.	8
	8: 6	through whom are all things	2
	8: 6	through whom we exist.	2
	10: 1	all passed through the sea	2
	12: 8	To one is given through the Spirit the utterance	2
	15: 2	through which also you are being saved	2
	15:57	victory through our Lord Jesus Christ.	2
2Co	1: 5	our consolation is abundant through Christ	2
	1:11	granted us through the prayers of many.	2
	1:20	it is through him that we say the "Amen,"	2
	2:14	through us spreads in every place the fragrance	2
	3: 4	that we have through Christ toward God.	2
	5:18	who reconciled us to himself through Christ	2
	5:20	God is making his appeal through us;	2
	6: 4	through great endurance, in afflictions	8
	9:11	which will produce thanksgiving to God through us;	2
	9:13	Through the testing of this ministry	2
	11:27	in toil...through many a sleepless night	8
	11:33	let down in a basket through a window in the wall	2
	12:17	through any of those whom I sent to you?	2

Gal	1: 1	through Jesus Christ and God the Father	2
	1:12	received it through a revelation of Jesus Christ.	2
	1:15	called me through his grace	2
	2:16	through faith in Jesus Christ.	2
	2:19	For through the law I died to the law	2
	3:14	receive the promise of the Spirit through faith.	2
	3:18	God granted it to Abraham through the promise.	2
	3:19	ordained through angels by a mediator.	2
	3:21	righteousness would indeed come through the law.	7
	3:22	what was promised through faith in Jesus Christ	7
	3:26	you are all children of God through faith.	2
	4: 7	if a child then also an heir through God	2
	4:23	child of the free woman, was born through the promise.	2
	5: 6	faith working through love.	2
	5:13	through love become slaves to one another.	2
Eph	1: 5	adoption as his children through Jesus Christ	2
	1: 7	In him we have redemption through his blood	2
	2: 8	For by grace you have been saved through faith	2
	2:16	reconcile both...through the cross	2
	2:16	thus putting to death that hostility through it	8
	2:18	for through him both of us have access in one Spirit	2
	3: 6	sharers in the promise...through the gospel.	2
	3:10	so that through the church the wisdom of God	2
	3:12	access to God in boldness and confidence through faith	2
	3:16	in your inner being with power through his Spirit	2
	3:17	Christ may dwell in your hearts through faith	2
	4: 6	who is above all and through all and in all.	2
Php	1:19	for I know that through your prayers	2
	4:13	I can do all things through him who strengthens me.	8
Col	1:16	all things have been created through him	2
	1:20	through him God was pleased to reconcile to himself	2
	1:20	making peace through the blood of his cross.	2
	1:22	now reconciled in his fleshly body through death	2
	2: 8	captive through philosophy and empty deceit	2
	2:12	through faith in the power of God	2
	3:17	giving thanks to God the Father through him.	2
1Th	3: 7	encouraged about you through your faith.	2
	4: 2	instructions we gave you through the Lord Jesus.	2
	4:14	through Jesus, God will bring with him those who...	2
	5: 9	for obtaining salvation through our Lord Jesus	2
2Th	2:13	through sanctification by the Spirit	8
	2:14	called...through our proclamation of the good news	2
	2:16	through grace gave us eternal comfort and good hope	8
1Ti	2:15	she will be saved through childbearing	2
	4: 2	through the hypocrisy of liars	8
	4:14	which was given to you through prophecy	2
2Ti	1: 6	within you through the laying on of my hands;	2
	1:10	been revealed through the appearing of our Savior	2
	1:10	brought life...to light through the gospel.	2
	2: 2	have heard from me through many witnesses	2
	3:15	salvation through faith in Christ Jesus.	2
	4:17	through me the message might be fully proclaimed	2
Tit	1: 3	revealed his word through the proclamation	8
	3: 5	through the water of rebirth	2
	3: 6	through Jesus Christ our Savior	2
Phm	1: 7	the saints have been refreshed through you	2
	1:22	through your prayers to be restored to you.	2
Heb	1: 2	through whom he also created the worlds.	2
	2: 2	For if the message declared through angels was valid	2
	2: 3	It was declared at first through the Lord	2
	2:10	for whom and through whom all things exist	2
	2:10	make...perfect through sufferings.	2
	2:14	so that through death he might destroy the one	2
	4: 7	saying through David much later	8
	4:11	so that no one may fall through such disobedience	8
	5: 8	he learned obedience through what he suffered;	1
	6:12	through faith and patience inherit the promises	2
	6:18	so that through two unchangeable things	2
	7: 9	Levi himself...paid tithes through Abraham	2
	7:11	attainable through the levitical priesthood	2
	7:16	become a priest, not through a legal requirement	10
	7:16	through the power of an indestructible life.	10
	7:19	a better hope, through which we approach God.	2
	7:25	to save those who approach God through him	2
	8: 6	which has been enacted through better promises.	9
	9:11	then through the greater and perfect tent	2
	9:14	who through the eternal Spirit offered himself	2
	10:10	sanctified through the offering of...Jesus	2
	10:20	through the curtain (that is, through his flesh)	2
	11: 4	Through this he received approval	2
	11: 4	through his faith he still speaks.	2

11:18	through Isaac that descendants shall be named	8
11:33	who through faith conquered kingdoms	2
12:15	through it many become defiled.	2
13:15	Through him, then, let us continually offer	2
13:21	through Jesus Christ, to whom be the glory forever	2

1Pe	1: 3	new birth…through the resurrection of Jesus	2
	1: 5	being protected by the power of God through faith	2
	1:12	through those who brought you good news	2
	1:21	Through him you have come to trust in God	2
	1:23	through the living and enduring word of God.	2
	2: 5	acceptable to God through Jesus Christ.	2
	3:20	ark, in which a few…were saved through water.	2
	3:21	through the resurrection of Jesus Christ	2
	4:11	God may be glorified in all things through Jesus Christ.	2
	5:12	Through Silvanus…I have written this short letter	2
2Pe	1: 1	through the righteousness of our God and Savior	8
	1: 3	through the knowledge of him who called us	2
	1: 4	he has given us, through these things, his…promises	2
	1: 4	promises, so that through them you may escape	2
	2:20	escaped…through the knowledge of our Lord	8
	3: 6	through which the world…perished.	2
1Jn	4: 9	so that we might live through him.	2
Jde	1:25	God our Savior, through Jesus Christ our Lord	2
Rev	22: 2	through the middle of the street of the city.	8

throughout *See also* go throughout

1. ἀπό, *apo, 608*
2. διά + ὅλος, *dia + holos, 1328 + 3910*
3. εἰς, *eis, 1650*
4. εἰς + ὅλος, *eis + holos, 1650 + 3910*
5. ἐν, *en, 1877*
6. ἐν + ὅλος, *en + holos, 1877 + 3910*
7. ἐπί + ὅλος, *epi + holos, 2093 + 3910*
8. κατά, *kata, 2848*
9. κατά + ὅλος, *kata + holos, 2848 + 3910*
10. πᾶς, *pas, 4246*

Mat	4:23	Jesus went throughout Galilee, teaching	6
	4:24	So his fame spread throughout all Syria	3
	9:26	report of this spread throughout that district.	4
	9:31	spread the news about him throughout that district.	6
	14:35	they sent word throughout the region	4
	24:14	good news…proclaimed throughout the world	6
Mrk	1:28	fame…spread throughout the surrounding region	4
	1:39	he went throughout Galilee	4
Lke	1:65	throughout the entire hill country of Judea.	5
	7:17	throughout Judea and all the surrounding country	6
	8:39	proclaiming throughout the city	9
	15:14	a severe famine took place throughout that country	8
	23: 5	teaching throughout all Judea	8
Act	7:11	came a famine throughout Egypt and Canaan	7
	8: 1	scattered throughout the countryside of Judea	8
	9:31	the church throughout Judea, Galilee, and	9
	9:42	This became known throughout Joppa	9
	10:37	That message spread throughout Judea	9
	13:49	word of the Lord spread throughout the region.	2
	24: 5	among all the Jews throughout the world	8
	24:12	stirring up a crowd…throughout the city.	8
	26:20	throughout the countryside of Judea	10
Rom	1: 8	your faith is proclaimed throughout the world.	6
2Co	1: 1	including all the saints throughout Achaia:	6
Php	1:13	throughout the whole imperial guard	5
Col	1:26	mystery that has been hidden throughout the ages	1
1Th	4:10	love all the brothers and sisters throughout Macedonia.	6
1Ti	3:16	believed in throughout the world, taken up in glory.	5

throw

1. Contextual: Not in Greek
2. βάλλω, *ballō, 965*
3. βολή, *bolē, 1074*
4. ἐκβάλλω, *ekballō, 1675*
5. πίπτω, *piptō, 4406*
6. ῥίπτω, *rhiptō, 4849*

Mat	3:10	good fruit is cut down and thrown into the fire.	2
	4: 6	"If you are the Son of God, throw yourself down;	2
	5:13	but is thrown out and trampled under foot.	2
	5:25	to the guard, and you will be thrown into prison.	2
	5:29	tear it out and throw it away; it is better	2
	5:29	than for your whole body to be thrown into hell.	2
	5:30	cut it off and throw it away; it is better	2
	6:30	alive today and tomorrow is thrown into the oven	2

	7: 6	and do not throw your pearls before swine	2
	7:19	tree…is cut down and thrown into the fire.	2
	8:12	heirs…will be thrown into the outer darkness	4
	13:42	throw them into the furnace of fire	2
	13:47	like a net that was thrown into the sea	2
	13:48	but threw out the bad.	2
	13:50	throw them into the furnace of fire	2
	15:26	and throw it to the dogs."	2
	18: 8	or your foot…cut it off and throw it away;	2
	18: 8	to be thrown into the eternal fire.	2
	18: 9	tear it out and throw it away;	2
	18: 9	have two eyes and to be thrown into the hell of fire.	2
	18:30	then he went and threw him into prison	2
	21:21	'Be lifted up and thrown into the sea,'	2
	22:13	and throw him into the outer darkness	4
	25:30	throw him into the outer darkness	4
Mrk	7:27	throw it to the dogs."	2
	9:42	you were thrown into the sea.	2
	9:45	have two feet and to be thrown into hell.	2
	9:47	have two eyes and to be thrown into hell	2
	11:23	'Be taken up and thrown into the sea,'	2
	14:35	a little farther, he threw himself on the ground	5
Lke	3: 9	tree…is cut down and thrown into the fire."	2
	4: 9	throw yourself down from here	2
	12:28	tomorrow is thrown into the oven	2
	12:58	the officer throw you in prison.	2
	14:35	they throw it away.	2
	17: 2	if…you were thrown into the sea	6
	22:41	he withdrew from them about a stone's throw	3
Jhn	3:24	John…had not yet been thrown into prison.	2
	8: 7	⟦who is without sin be the first to throw a stone⟧	2
	8:59	they picked up stones to throw at him	2
	15: 6	branches are gathered, thrown into the fire	2
Act	16:23	they threw them into prison	2
	16:37	have thrown us into prison;	2
	27:38	throwing the wheat into the sea.	4
Rev	2:10	devil is about to throw some of you into prison	2
	2:22	Beware, I am throwing her on a bed	2
	2:22	I am throwing into great distress	1
	8: 5	filled it with fire…and threw it on the earth;	2
	8: 8	something like…was thrown into the sea.	2
	12: 4	the stars of heaven and threw them to the earth.	2
	14:19	the angel…threw it into the great wine press	2
	18:19	And they threw dust on their heads, as they wept	2
	18:21	took up a stone…and threw it into the sea	2
	19:20	These two were thrown alive into the lake of fire	2
	20: 3	and threw him into the pit, and locked	2
	20:10	the devil…was thrown into the lake of fire	2
	20:14	Death and Hades were thrown into the lake of fire.	2
	20:15	was thrown into the lake of fire.	2

throw away

1. βάλλω, *ballō, 965*

Jhn	15: 6	is thrown away like a branch and withers;	1

throw down

1. βάλλω, *ballō, 965*
2. καταλύω, *katalyō, 2907*
3. ῥίπτω, *rhiptō, 4849*

Mat	24: 2	one stone…all will be thrown down."	2
	27: 5	Throwing down the pieces of silver in the temple	3
Mrk	13: 2	all will be thrown down."	2
Lke	4:35	When the demon had thrown him down before them,	3
	21: 6	all will be thrown down."	2
Rev	12: 9	The great dragon was thrown down	1
	12: 9	the deceiver…—he was thrown down to the earth	1
	12: 9	and his angels were thrown down with him.	1
	12:10	the accuser of our comrades has been thrown down	1
	12:13	when the dragon saw that he had been thrown down	1
	18:21	such violence Babylon the great city will be thrown down	1

throw off

1. ἀποβάλλω, *apoballō, 610*
2. ῥιπτέω, *rhipteō, 4848*

Mrk	10:50	throwing off his cloak, he sprang up	1
Act	22:23	they were shouting, throwing off their cloaks,	2

throw on

1. ἐπιβάλλω, *epiballō, 2095*
2. ἐπιρίπτω, *epiriptō, 2166*

Mrk 11: 7	and threw their cloaks on it;	1
Lke 19:35	throwing their cloaks on the colt	2

throw oneself on the ground

1. πίπτω + ἐπί + πρόσωπον, *piptō + epi + prosōpon, 4406 + 2093 + 4725*

Mat 26:39	he threw himself on the ground and prayed	1

throw out

1. ἐκβάλλω, *ekballō, 1675*

Mat 21:39	they seized him, threw him out of the vineyard	1
Mrk 12: 8	and threw him out of the vineyard.	1
Lke 13:28	and you yourselves thrown out.	1
20:12	this one also they wounded and threw out.	1
20:15	they threw him out of the vineyard and killed him.	1

throw overboard

1. ῥίπτω, *rhiptō, 4849*

Act 27:19	own hands they threw the ship's tackle overboard.	1

throw overboard cargo

1. ἐκβολή, *ekbolē, 1678*

Act 27:18	next day they began to throw the cargo overboard	1

thunder *See also* peal of thunder

1. βροντή, *brontē, 1103*

Mrk 3:17	the name Boanerges, that is, Sons of Thunder);	1
Jhn 12:29	heard it and said that it was thunder.	1
Rev 6: 1	call out, as with a voice of thunder, "Come!"	1
10: 3	when he shouted, the seven thunders sounded.	1
10: 4	when the seven thunders had sounded	1
10: 4	"Seal up what the seven thunders have said	1
14: 2	a voice…like the sound of loud thunder;	1

thunderpeal

1. βροντή, *brontē, 1103*

Rev 19: 6	like the sound of mighty thunderpeals, crying out	1

thus

1. Contextual: Not in Greek
2. ἄρα, *ara, 726*
3. γάρ, *gar, 1142*
4. δέ, *de, 1254*
5. εἰς, *eis, 1650*
6. ἐν + οὗτος, *en + houtos, 1877 + 4047*
7. καί, *kai, 2779*
8. ὅδε, *hode, 3840*
9. οὖν, *oun, 4036*
10. οὗτος, *houtos, 4047*
11. οὕτως, *houtōs, 4048*
12. ὡς, *hōs, 6055*
13. ὥστε, *hōste, 6063*

Mat 7:20	Thus you will know them by their fruits.	2
22:45	If David thus calls him Lord, how can he be his son?"	9
23:31	Thus you testify against yourselves	13
Mrk 7: 3	thus observing the tradition of the elders;	1
7:13	thus making void the word of God	1
7:19	(Thus he declared all foods clean.)	1
Lke 1:72	Thus he has shown the mercy promised	1
12:58	Thus, when you go with your accuser	3
18:11	The Pharisee, standing by himself, was praying thus	10
20:44	David thus calls him Lord; so how can he be his son?"	9
24:46	said to them, "Thus it is written	11
Act 13:49	Thus the word of the Lord spread	4
21:11	"Thus says the Holy Spirit	8
21:24	Thus all will know	7
Rom 4:11	who thus have righteousness reckoned to them	5
7: 2	Thus a married woman is bound by the law	3
11:14	to make…jealous, and thus save some of them.	1
14:18	one who thus serves Christ is acceptable to God	6
15:20	Thus I make it my ambition to proclaim the good news	11
1Co 8:12	thus sin against members of your family	11
15:45	Thus it is written, "The first man, Adam	11
Eph 2:15	one new humanity in place of the two, thus making peace	1
2:16	thus putting to death that hostility through it	1
1Th 2:16	Thus they have constantly been filling up the measure	5
1Ti 6:19	thus storing up for themselves the treasure	1
Heb 6:15	thus Abraham…obtained the promise.	11
9:12	thus obtaining eternal redemption.	1

9:23	Thus it was necessary…to be purified	9
Jas 2:23	Thus the scripture was fulfilled that says	7
1Pe 3: 6	Thus Sarah obeyed Abraham and called him lord.	12

thus far

1. ἄχρι + ὁ + δεῦρο, *achri + ho + deuro, 948 + 3836 + 1306*

Rom 1:13	(but thus far have been prevented)	1

thwart

1. ἀθετέω, *atheteō, 119*

1Co 1:19	the discernment of the discerning I will thwart."	1

Thyatira

1. Θυάτειρα, *Thyateira, 2587*

Act 16:14	Lydia…was from the city of Thyatira	1
Rev 1:11	seven churches…to Pergamum, to Thyatira	1
2:18	"And to the angel of the church in Thyatira write:	1
2:24	But to the rest of you in Thyatira	1

Tiberias

1. Τιβεριάς, *Tiberias, 5500*

Jhn 6: 1	Sea of Galilee, also called the Sea of Tiberias.	1
6:23	Then some boats from Tiberias came near the place	1
21: 1	Jesus showed himself…by the Sea of Tiberias;	1

Tiberius

1. Τιβέριος, *Tiberios, 5501*

Lke 3: 1	fifteenth year of the reign of Emperor Tiberius	1

tie

1. Contextual: Not in Greek
2. δέω, *deō, 1313*

Mat 21: 2	immediately you will find a donkey tied	2
Mrk 11: 2	as you enter it, you will find tied there a colt	2
11: 4	They went away and found a colt tied near a door	2
Lke 19:30	as you enter it you will find tied there a colt	2
Act 27:40	loosened the ropes that tied the steering-oars;	1

tie around

1. διαζώννυμι, *diazōnnymi, 1346*

Jhn 13: 4	tied a towel around himself.	1
13: 5	the towel that was tied around him.	1

tie up

1. δεσμεύω, *desmeuō, 1297*
2. δέω, *deō, 1313*
3. προτείνω, *proteinō, 4727*

Mat 12:29	without first tying up the strong man?	2
23: 4	They tie up heavy burdens, hard to bear	1
Mrk 3:27	without first tying up the strong man;	2
Act 22:25	when they had tied him up with thongs	3

tile

1. κέραμος, *keramos, 3041*

Lke 5:19	let him down with his bed through the tiles	1

Timaeus

1. Τιμαῖος, *Timaios, 5505*

Mrk 10:46	Bartimaeus son of Timaeus, a blind beggar	1

time[1] *See also* five times, four times as much, know a long time, lose time, one time, seven times, seventy-seven times, some time, spend much time, spend time, stay for a time, three times

1. Contextual: Not in Greek
2. αἰών, *aiōn, 172*
3. ἐπί, *epi, 2093*
4. ἤδη, *ēdē, 2453*
5. ἡμέρα, *hēmera, 2465*
6. καιρός, *kairos, 2789*
7. ὅς, *hos, 4005*
8. πάρειμι, *pareimi, 4205*
9. τότε, *tote, 5538*
10. χρόνος, *chronos, 5989*
11. ὥρα, *hōra, 6052*

Mat 1:11	at the time of the deportation to Babylon.	3
2: 1	In the time of King Herod, after Jesus was born	5
2: 7	learned from them the exact time when the star	10

	2:16	two years old or under, according to the time	10
	4:17	From that time Jesus began to proclaim,	9
	8:29	Have you come here to torment us before the time?"	6
	10:19	to say will be given to you at that time;	11
	11:25	At that time Jesus said, "I thank you, Father	6
	12: 1	At that time Jesus went through the grainfields	6
	13:30	at harvest time I will tell the reapers	6
	14: 1	At that time Herod the ruler heard	6
	14:24	by this time the boat…was far from the land	4
	16: 3	but you cannot interpret the signs of the times.	6
	18: 1	At that time the disciples came to Jesus and asked	11
	21:34	When the harvest time had come	6
	25:19	After a long time the master…came	10
	26:18	'The Teacher says, My time is near;	6
Mrk	1:15	saying, "The time is fulfilled	6
	13:11	say whatever is given you at that time	11
	13:33	for you do not know when the time will come.	6
Lke	1:10	Now at the time of the incense offering	11
	1:20	which will be fulfilled in their time.	6
	1:23	When his time of service was ended	5
	1:57	Now the time came for Elizabeth to give birth	10
	2: 6	the time came for her to deliver her child.	5
	2:21	it was time to circumcise the child;	1
	2:22	When the time came for their purification	5
	4:25	were many widows in Israel in the time of Elijah	5
	4:27	lepers in Israel in the time of the prophet Elisha	3
	7:45	from the time I came in she has not stopped	7
	8:13	and in a time of testing fall away.	6
	8:27	For a long time he had worn no clothes	10
	12:56	not know how to interpret the present time?	6
	13: 1	At that very time there were some present	6
	13:35	not see me until the time comes when you say	1
	14:17	At the time for the dinner he sent his slave	11
	19:44	you did not recognize the time of your visitation	6
	20: 9	went to another country for a long time.	10
	21: 8	'The time is near!' Do not go after them.	6
	21:24	until the times of the Gentiles are fulfilled.	6
	21:36	Be alert at all times	6
	23: 7	who was himself in Jerusalem at that time.	5
	23: 8	he had been wanting to see him for a long time	10
Jhn	5: 6	and knew that he had been there a long time	10
	7: 6	Jesus said to them, "My time has not yet come	6
	7: 6	your time is always here.	6
	7: 8	for my time has not yet fully come."	6
	14: 9	to him, "Have I been with you all this time	10
Act	1: 6	the time when you will restore the kingdom to Israel?"	10
	1: 7	"It is not for you to know the times or periods	10
	1:21	during all the time that the Lord Jesus went	10
	3:20	so that times of refreshing may come	6
	3:21	until the time of universal restoration	10
	5:36	For some time ago Theudas rose up	5
	5:37	at the time of the census	5
	7:17	as the time drew near for the fulfillment	10
	7:20	At this time Moses was born	6
	7:41	At that time they made a calf	5
	7:45	And it was there until the time of David	5
	8:11	for a long time he had amazed them with his magic.	10
	9:23	After some time had passed	5
	9:37	At that time she became ill and died.	5
	9:43	in Joppa for some time with a certain Simon, a tanner.	5
	11:27	At that time prophets came down from Jerusalem	5
	12: 1	About that time King Herod laid violent hands	6
	13:20	he gave them judges until the time of…Samuel.	1
	14: 3	So they remained for a long time	10
	14:28	stayed there with the disciples for some time.	10
	15:33	After they had been there for some time	10
	17:26	he allotted the times of their existence	6
	17:30	God has overlooked the times of human ignorance	10
	18:18	After staying there for a considerable time,	5
	18:23	After spending some time there he departed	10
	19:22	he himself stayed for some time longer in Asia.	10
	19:23	About that time no little disturbance broke out	6
	20:18	how I lived among you the entire time	10
	27: 9	Since much time had been lost	10
	27:21	they had been without food for a long time	1
	28: 6	after they had waited a long time	1
Rom	3:26	prove at the present time that he…is righteous	6
	8:18	the sufferings of this present time are not worth	6
	9: 9	the promise said, "About this time I will return	6
	11: 5	So too at the present time there is a remnant	6
	13:11	Besides this, you know what time it is	6

1Co	4: 5	do not pronounce judgment before the time	6
	7:18	Was anyone at the time of his call…circumcised?	1
	7:18	Was anyone at the time of his call uncircumcised?	1
	11:21	For when the time comes to eat,	1
	16: 7	I hope to spend some time with you	10
2Co	6: 2	"At an acceptable time I have listened to you	6
	6: 2	See, now is the acceptable time;	6
Gal	4: 4	when the fullness of time had come	10
	6: 9	we will reap at harvest time	6
Eph	1:10	as a plan for the fullness of time	6
	2:12	you were at that time without Christ	6
	5:16	making the most of the time	6
	6:18	Pray in the Spirit at all times	6
Col	4: 5	making the most of the time.	6
1Th	2:17	for a short time, we were made orphans	6
	5: 1	Now concerning the times and the seasons,	10
2Th	2: 6	so that he may be revealed when his time	6
1Ti	2: 6	this was attested at the right time.	6
	4: 1	in later times some will renounce the faith	6
	6:15	which he will bring about at the right time	6
2Ti	3: 1	in the last days distressing times will come.	6
	4: 3	For the time is coming	6
	4: 6	the time of my departure has come.	6
Tit	1: 3	in due time he revealed his word	6
Heb	5:12	For though by this time you ought to be teachers	10
	9: 9	This is a symbol of the present time	6
	9:10	imposed until the time comes to set things right.	6
	11:32	time would fail me to tell of Gideon, Barak,	10
	12:10	for a short time as seemed best to them	5
	12:11	seems painful rather than pleasant at the time	8
1Pe	1: 5	salvation ready to be revealed in the last time.	6
	1:11	inquiring about the person or time that the Spirit	6
	1:17	during the time of your exile.	10
	4: 3	You have already spent enough time in doing	10
	4:17	For the time has come for judgment to begin	6
2Pe	3: 6	the world of that time was deluged with water	9
Jde	1:18	"In the last time there will be scoffers	10
	1:25	before all time and now and forever. Amen.	2
Rev	1: 3	for the time is near.	6
	2:21	I gave her time to repent, but she refuses	10
	11:18	and the time for judging the dead	6
	12:12	because he knows that his time is short!"	6
	12:14	nourished for a time, and times, and half a time.	6
	12:14	nourished for a time, and times, and half a time.	6
	12:14	nourished for a time, and times, and half a time.	6
	22:10	for the time is near.	6

time²

1. Contextual: Not in Greek
2. ἐπί, *epi*, 2093
3. χρόνος, *chronos*, 5989

Mat	26:42	Again he went away for the second time and prayed	1
	26:44	he went away and prayed for the third time	1
Mrk	14:72	At that moment the cock crowed for the second time.	1
Lke	8:29	(For many times it had seized him;	3
Jhn	3: 4	Can one enter a second time into the mother's womb	1
	9:24	for the second time they called the man	1
	21:14	This was now the third time	1
	21:16	A second time he said to him, "Simon son of John	1
	21:17	He said to him the third time, "Simon son of John	1
	21:17	he said to him the third time, "Do you love me?"	1
Act	10:15	The voice said to him again, a second time	1
	10:16	This happened three times	2
	11: 9	a second time the voice answered from heaven	1
	11:10	This happened three times;	2

all time

1. διηνεκής, *diēnekēs*, 1457
2. παντελής, *pantelēs*, 4117
3. πάντοτε, *pantote*, 4121
4. πᾶς, *pas*, 4246

Gal	4:18	made much of for a good purpose at all times	3
Eph	5:20	giving thanks to God the Father at all times	3
2Th	3:16	Lord of peace himself give you peace at all times	4
Heb	7:25	Consequently he is able for all time to save	2
	10:12	offered for all time a single sacrifice for sins	1
	10:14	perfected for all time those who are sanctified.	1

ancient time

1. ἀρχαῖος, *archaios*, 792

Mat 5:21 heard that it was said to those of ancient times   1
        5:33 heard that it was said to those of ancient times   1

any time
    1. ἑκάστοτε, *hekastote, 1668*

2Pe   1:15 you may be able at any time to recall these things.   1

appointed time
    1. καιρός, *kairos, 2789*

1Co   7:29 the appointed time has grown short;   1

at any time
    1. ποτέ, *pote, 4537*

1Co   9: 7 at any time pays the expenses for…military service?   1

at that time
    1. τότε, *tote, 5538*

Mat 27:16 At that time they had a notorious prisoner   1
Mrk 13:21 if anyone says to you at that time, 'Look!   1
Heb 12:26 At that time his voice shook the earth;   1

due time
    1. καιρός, *kairos, 2789*

1Pe   5: 6 so that he may exalt you in due time.   1

every time
    1. πᾶς, *pas, 4246*

Php   1: 3 I thank my God every time I remember you   1

favorable time
    1. εὐκαίρως, *eukairōs, 2323*

2Ti   4: 2 be persistent whether the time is favorable   1

former time
    1. ποτέ, *pote, 4537*

1Pe   3:20 who in former times did not obey   1

harvest time
    1. καιρός, *kairos, 2789*

Mat 21:41 who will give him the produce at the harvest time."   1

in time
    1. ταχέως, *tacheōs, 5441*

Heb 13:23 if he comes in time, he will be with me when I see you.   1

long time
    1. ἄνωθεν, *anōthen, 540*

Act 26: 5 They have known for a long time   1

opportune time
    1. καιρός, *kairos, 2789*

Lke   4:13 he departed from him until an opportune time.   1

proper time
    1. καιρός, *kairos, 2789*

Mat 24:45 their allowance of food at the proper time?   1
Lke 12:42 to give them…food at the proper time?   1

right time
    1. καιρός, *kairos, 2789*

Rom   5: 6 at the right time Christ died for the ungodly.   1

same time
    1. Contextual: Not in Greek
    2. ἅμα, *hama, 275*

Act 24:26 At the same time he hoped that money   2
       27:40 At the same time they loosened the ropes   2
2Co   1:17 say "Yes, yes" and "No, no" at the same time?   1
Col   4: 3 At the same time pray for us as well   2

set time
    1. καιρός, *kairos, 2789*

1Co   7: 5 except perhaps by agreement for a set time   1

short time
    1. βραχύς, *brachys, 1099*

Act   5:34 ordered the men to be put outside for a short time.   1

that time
    1. τότε, *tote, 5538*

Mat 16:21 From that time on, Jesus began to show his disciples   1
       24:21 For at that time there will be great suffering   1
Jhn 10:22 At that time the festival of the Dedication   1
Gal   4:29 just as at that time the child who was born   1

third time
    1. τρίτον, *triton, 5568*

Mrk 14:41 He came a third time and said to them   1
Lke 23:22 A third time he said to them, "Why   1
2Co 12:14 Here I am, ready to come to you this third time.   1
       13: 1 This is the third time I am coming to you.   1

time of need
    1. εὔκαιρος, *eukairos, 2322*

Heb   4:16 find grace to help in time of need.   1

time of trial
    1. πειρασμός, *peirasmos, 4280*

Mat   6:13 do not bring us to the time of trial, but rescue us   1
       26:41 that you may not come into the time of trial;   1
Mrk 14:38 pray that you may not come into the time of trial;   1
Lke 11: 4 do not bring us to the time of trial."   1
       22:40 "Pray that you may not come into the time of trial."   1
       22:46 pray that you may not come into the time of trial."   1

unfavorable time
    1. ἀκαίρως, *akairōs, 178*

2Ti   4: 2 be persistent whether the time is…unfavorable   1

Timon
    1. Τίμων, *Timōn, 5511*

Act   6: 5 Philip, Prochorus, Nicanor, Timon   1

Timothy
    1. αὐτός, *autos, 899*
    2. οὗτος, *houtos, 4047*
    3. Τιμόθεος, *Timotheos, 5510*

Act 16: 1 where there was a disciple named Timothy   3
       16: 3 Paul wanted Timothy to accompany him;   2
       17:14 Silas and Timothy remained behind.   3
       17:15 instructions to have Silas and Timothy join him   3
       18: 5 When Silas and Timothy arrived from Macedonia   3
       19:22 sent two of his helpers, Timothy and Erastus   3
       20: 4 by Gaius from Derbe, and by Timothy   3
Rom 16:21 Timothy, my co-worker, greets you;   3
1Co   4:17 For this reason I sent you Timothy   3
       16:10 If Timothy comes, see that he has nothing to fear   3
2Co   1: 1 Paul…and Timothy our brother   3
       1:19 Silvanus and Timothy and I   3
Php   1: 1 Paul and Timothy, servants of Christ Jesus   3
       2:19 hope in the Lord Jesus to send Timothy to you soon   3
       2:22 Timothy's worth you know   1
Col   1: 1 Paul, an apostle…and Timothy our brother   3
1Th   1: 1 Paul, Silvanus, and Timothy   3
       3: 2 we sent Timothy, our brother and co-worker for God   3
       3: 6 Timothy has just now come to us from you   3
2Th   1: 1 Paul, Silvanus, and Timothy   3
1Ti   1: 2 To Timothy, my loyal child in the faith: 3
       1:18 giving you these instructions, Timothy, my child   3
       6:20 Timothy, guard what has been entrusted to you.   3
2Ti   1: 2 To Timothy, my beloved child: 3
Phm   1: 1 Paul…and Timothy our brother   3
Heb 13:23 our brother Timothy has been set free;   3

tip
    1. ἄκρον, *akron, 216*

Lke 16:24 send Lazarus to dip the tip of his finger in water   1

tire out
    1. κοπιάω, *kopiaō, 3159*

Jhn   4: 6 Jesus, tired out by his journey, was sitting   1

tithe   *See also* collect tithes, pay a tithe
    1. ἀποδεκατόω, *apodekatoō, 620*
    2. δέκατος, *dekatos, 1281*

Mat 23:23 you tithe mint, dill, and cummin   1

Lke	11:42	you tithe mint and rue and herbs of all kinds	1
Heb	7: 8	tithes are received by those who are mortal;	2
	7: 9	Levi himself, who receives tithes, paid tithes	2

Titius

1. Τίτιος, *Titios*, 5517

Act	18: 7	went to the house of a man named Titius Justus	1

title

1. ἐπιγραφή, *epigraphē*, 2107

Mat	22:20	"Whose head is this, and whose title?"	1
Mrk	12:16	"Whose head is this, and whose title?"	1
Lke	20:24	Whose head and whose title does it bear?"	1

Titus

1. Τίτος, *Titos*, 5519

2Co	2:13	because I did not find my brother Titus there.	1
	7: 6	consoled us by the arrival of Titus	1
	7:13	we rejoiced still more at the joy of Titus	1
	7:14	so our boasting to Titus has proved true	1
	8: 6	so that we might urge Titus	1
	8:16	who put in the heart of Titus the same eagerness	1
	8:23	As for Titus, he is my partner and co-worker	1
	12:18	I urged Titus to go, and sent the brother with him.	1
	12:18	Titus did not take advantage of you	1
Gal	2: 1	taking Titus along with me.	1
	2: 3	even Titus, who was with me, was not compelled	1
2Ti	4:10	Crescens has gone to Galatia, Titus to Dalmatia.	1
Tit	1: 4	To Titus, my loyal child in the faith we share:	1

to   See *also* to an *end*, to the *ground*, to the *point*

1. ἀπό, *apo*, 608
2. ἄχρι, *achri*, 948
3. διά, *dia*, 1328
4. εἰς, *eis*, 1650
5. ἐκ, *ek*, 1666
6. ἐν, *en*, 1877
7. ἐνώπιον, *enōpion*, 1967
8. ἐπί, *epi*, 2093
9. ἕως, *heōs*, 2401
10. ἵνα, *hina*, 2671
11. κατά, *kata*, 2848
12. μετά, *meta*, 3552
13. μέχρι, *mechri*, 3588
14. ὁ, *ho*, 3836
15. ὅπως, *hopōs*, 3968
16. ὅτι, *hoti*, 4022
17. περί, *peri*, 4309
18. πρός, *pros*, 4639
19. ὑπό, *hypo*, 5679
20. χάριν, *charin*, 5920
21. ὥστε, *hōste*, 6063

Mat	1:17	So all the generations from Abraham to David	9
	1:17	and from David to the deportation to Babylon	9
	1:17	Babylon to the Messiah, fourteen generations.	9
	1:22	All this took place to fulfill what had been spoken	10
	2: 1	wise men from the East came to Jerusalem	4
	2: 8	he sent them to Bethlehem, saying, "Go and search	4
	2:12	having been warned in a dream not to return to Herod	18
	2:13	take the child and his mother, and flee to Egypt	4
	2:14	his mother by night, and went to Egypt	4
	2:15	This was to fulfill what had been spoken	10
	2:20	his mother, and go to the land of Israel, for those	4
	2:21	his mother, and went to the land of Israel.	4
	2:22	he went away to the district of Galilee.	4
	3: 5	of Jerusalem and all Judea were going out to him	18
	3: 9	Do not presume to say to yourselves, 'We have	6
	3:13	Jesus came from Galilee to John at the Jordan	4
	3:14	"I need to be baptized by you, and do you come to me?"	18
	4: 5	Then the devil took him to the holy city	4
	4: 8	Again, the devil took him to a very high mountain	4
	4:12	John had been arrested, he withdrew to Galilee.	4
	5:22	'You fool,' you will be liable to the hell of fire.	4
	5:29	is better for you to lose one of your members	10
	5:30	is better for you to lose one of your members	10
	6:13	do not bring us to the time of trial, but rescue us	4
	6:27	by worrying add a single hour to your span of life?	8
	7:13	the road is easy that leads to destruction	4
	7:14	the road is hard that leads to life	4

	7:15	false prophets, who come to you	18
	8: 8	I am not worthy to have you come under my roof;	10
	8:18	he gave orders to go over to the other side.	4
	8:28	When he came to the other side	4
	8:28	to the country of the Gadarenes	4
	8:34	Then the whole town came out to meet Jesus;	4
	8:34	and when they saw him, they begged him to leave	15
	9: 1	he crossed the sea and came to his own town.	4
	9: 3	Then some of the scribes said to themselves	6
	9: 6	"Stand up, take your bed and go to your home."	4
	9: 7	he stood up and went to his home.	4
	9:21	for she said to herself, "If I only touch	6
	9:23	When Jesus came to the leader's house	4
	9:38	to send out laborers into his harvest."	15
	10: 1	authority over unclean spirits, to cast them out	21
	10: 6	go rather to the lost sheep	18
	10:13	if it is not worthy, let your peace return to you.	18
	10:17	they will hand you over to councils	4
	10:21	Brother will betray brother to death	4
	10:22	But the one who endures to the end will be saved.	4
	10:23	flee to the next;	4
	10:25	the disciple to be like the teacher	10
	10:29	Yet not one of them will fall to the ground	8
	10:34	to bring peace to the earth;	8
	11:23	you, Capernaum, will you be exalted to heaven?	9
	11:23	No, you will be brought down to Hades.	9
	11:28	"Come to me, all you that are weary and are carrying	18
	12:16	ordered them not to make him known.	10
	12:17	to fulfill what had been spoken through the prophet	10
	12:20	until he brings justice to victory.	4
	12:28	then the kingdom of God has come to you.	4
	12:44	'I will return to my house from which I came.'	4
	12:49	pointing to his disciples, he said,	8
	13:30	bind them in bundles to be burned	18
	13:35	to fulfill what had been spoken through the prophet:	15
	13:54	came to his hometown and began to teach the people	4
	14:13	withdrew from there in a boat to a deserted place	4
	14:19	he looked up to heaven, and blessed and broke	4
	14:22	and go on ahead to the other side	4
	14:28	command me to come to you on the water."	18
	14:34	they came to land at Gennesaret.	8
	15:21	and went away to the district of Tyre and Sidon.	4
	15:24	"I was sent only to the lost sheep	4
	15:33	enough bread...to feed so great a crowd?"	21
	15:39	and went to the region of Magadan.	4
	16: 7	They said to one another, "It is because	6
	16:20	sternly ordered the disciples to not tell anyone	10
	16:21	must go to Jerusalem and undergo great suffering	4
	17:12	but they did to him whatever they pleased.	6
	17:14	When they came to the crowd	18
	17:27	do not give offense to them, go to the sea	4
	19: 1	went to the region of Judea beyond the Jordan.	4
	19:14	Jesus said, "Let the little children come to me	18
	19:16	to have eternal life?"	10
	20:17	While Jesus was going up to Jerusalem	4
	20:18	"See, we are going up to Jerusalem	4
	20:19	to be mocked and flogged and crucified;	4
	20:31	The crowd sternly ordered them to be quiet;	10
	21: 4	This took place to fulfill what had been spoken	10
	21:17	He left them, went out of the city to Bethany	4
	21:18	In the morning, when he returned to the city	4
	21:19	seeing a fig tree...he went to it	8
	21:32	For John came to you in the way of righteousness	18
	21:34	he sent his slaves to the tenants	18
	21:37	Finally he sent his son to them, saying	18
	21:38	the tenants saw the son, they said to themselves	6
	22: 3	who had been invited to the wedding banquet	4
	22: 4	everything is ready; come to the wedding banquet.'	4
	22: 5	went away, one to his farm, another to his business	4
	22: 5	went away, one to his farm, another to his business	8
	22: 9	invite everyone you find to the wedding banquet.'	4
	22:16	and show deference to no one;	17
	23: 5	They do all their deeds to be seen by others;	18
	23:34	pursue from town to town	4
	23:35	to the blood of Zechariah son of Barachiah	9
	23:37	stones those who are sent to it!	18
	24: 9	"Then they will hand you over to be tortured	4
	24:13	the one who endures to the end will be saved.	4
	24:16	those in Judea must flee to the mountains;	4
	24:24	produce great signs and omens, to lead astray	21
	24:31	from one end of heaven to the other.	9

Mat 24:48	if that wicked slave says to himself	6
25: 1	went to meet the bridegroom.	4
25: 6	Here is the bridegroom! Come out to meet him.'	4
25: 9	you had better go to the dealers and buy some	18
26: 2	Son of Man will be handed over to be crucified."	4
26: 4	and they conspired to arrest Jesus	10
26:14	Judas Iscariot, went to the chief priests	18
26:16	to look for an opportunity to betray him.	10
26:18	"Go into the city to a certain man, and say	18
26:30	they went out to the Mount of Olives.	4
26:32	I will go ahead of you to Galilee."	4
26:36	Then Jesus went with them to a place	4
26:38	"I am deeply grieved, even to death;	9
26:40	he came to the disciples and found them sleeping;	18
26:45	Then he came to the disciples and said to them	18
26:57	took him to Caiaphas the high priest	18
26:71	he went out to the porch, another servant-girl	4
27: 4	"What is that to us? See to it yourself."	18
27: 8	has been called the Field of Blood to this day.	9
27:14	gave him no answer, not even to a single charge	18
27:19	his wife sent word to him	18
27:20	elders persuaded the crowds to ask for Barabbas	18
27:26	handed him over to be crucified.	10
27:31	Then they led him away to crucify him.	4
27:32	they compelled this man to carry his cross.	10
27:33	when they came to a place called Golgotha	4
27:51	torn in two, from top to bottom.	9
28: 7	indeed he is going ahead of you to Galilee;	4
28:10	go and tell my brothers to go to Galilee;	10
28:10	go and tell my brothers to go to Galilee;	4
28:14	If this comes to the governor's ears	8
28:15	story is still told among the Jews to this day.	13
28:16	Now the eleven disciples went to Galilee	4
28:16	to the mountain to which Jesus had directed	4
28:20	I am with you always, to the end of the age."	9
Mrk 1: 5	the people of Jerusalem were going out to him	18
1:14	after John was arrested, Jesus came to Galilee	4
1:21	They went to Capernaum;	4
1:32	they brought to him all who were sick	18
1:35	he got up and went out to a deserted place	4
1:38	"Let us go on to the neighboring towns	4
1:40	A leper came to him begging him, and kneeling	18
1:45	people came to him from every quarter.	18
2: 1	When he returned to Capernaum after some days	4
2: 3	people came, bringing to him a paralyzed man	18
2:11	stand up, take your mat and go to your home."	4
3: 7	Jesus departed with his disciples to the sea	18
3: 8	hearing all that he was doing, they came to him	18
3: 9	He told his disciples to have a boat ready	10
3:10	had diseases pressed upon him to touch him.	10
3:12	he sternly ordered them not to make him known.	10
3:13	they came to him.	18
3:14	he appointed twelve…to be with him	10
3:14	to be sent out to proclaim the message	10
3:31	standing outside, they sent to him and called	18
4:21	lamp brought in to be put under the bushel basket	10
4:22	there is nothing hidden, except to be disclosed;	10
4:22	nor is anything secret, except to come to light.	10
4:22	nor is anything secret, except to come to light.	4
4:35	"Let us go across to the other side."	4
4:41	and said to one another, "Who then is this	18
5: 1	They came to the other side of the sea	4
5: 1	to the country of the Gerasenes.	4
5:10	not to send them out of the country.	10
5:15	They came to Jesus and saw the demoniac sitting	18
5:16	to the demoniac and to the swine	17
5:19	"Go home to your friends	18
5:21	crossed again in the boat to the other side	4
5:38	When they came to the house	4
6: 1	left that place and came to his hometown	4
6: 8	ordered them to take nothing for their journey	10
6:25	Immediately she rushed back to the king	18
6:25	"I want you to give me at once the head of John	10
6:31	"Come away to a deserted place all by yourselves	4
6:32	in the boat to a deserted place by themselves.	4
6:41	he looked up to heaven	4
6:41	loaves…to set before the people;	10
6:45	go on ahead to the other side, to Bethsaida	4
6:45	go on ahead to the other side, to Bethsaida	18
6:50	But immediately he spoke to them and said	12
6:53	they came to land at Gennesaret	8

7:24	he set out and went away to the region of Tyre.	4
7:26	begged him to cast the demon out of her daughter.	10
7:32	they begged him to lay his hand on him.	10
7:34	looking up to heaven, he sighed and said	4
7:36	Jesus ordered them to tell no one;	10
8: 3	If I send them away hungry to their homes	4
8: 6	to his disciples to distribute;	10
8:10	went to the district of Dalmanutha.	4
8:13	he went across to the other side.	14
8:16	They said to one another, "It is because	18
8:22	They came to Bethsaida.	4
8:22	begged him to touch him.	10
8:26	he sent him away to his home, saying	4
8:27	to the villages of Caesarea Philippi;	4
8:30	ordered them not to tell anyone about him.	10
9: 9	to tell no one about what they had seen	10
9:10	So they kept the matter to themselves	18
9:14	When they came to the disciples	18
9:18	I asked your disciples to cast it out	10
9:19	must I put up with you? Bring him to me."	18
9:20	they brought the boy to him.	18
9:22	into the water, to destroy him;	10
9:30	He did not want anyone to know it;	10
9:33	they came to Capernaum;	4
9:43	to have two hands and to go to hell	4
9:43	to go to hell, to the unquenchable fire.	4
10: 1	He left that place and went to the region of Judea	4
10: 7	be joined to his wife	18
10:14	"Let the little children come to me	18
10:17	what must I do to inherit eternal life?"	10
10:26	greatly astounded and said to one another,	18
10:32	They were on the road, going up to Jerusalem	4
10:33	saying, "See, we are going up to Jerusalem	4
10:35	we want you to do for us whatever we ask of you."	10
10:37	"Grant us to sit, one at your right hand	10
10:46	They came to Jericho.	4
10:48	Many sternly ordered him to be quiet	10
10:50	he sprang up and came to Jesus.	18
11: 7	they brought the colt to Jesus	18
11:11	he went out to Bethany with the twelve.	4
11:13	When he came to it, he found nothing but leaves	8
11:15	they came to Jerusalem.	4
11:16	to carry anything through the temple.	10
11:20	they saw the fig tree withered away to its roots.	5
11:27	Again they came to Jerusalem.	4
11:27	the scribes, and the elders came to him	18
11:28	Who gave you this authority to do them?"	10
12: 2	he sent a slave to the tenants	18
12: 2	to collect from them his share of the produce	10
12: 4	again he sent another slave to them;	18
12: 6	Finally he sent him to them, saying	18
12: 7	those tenants said to one another	18
12:13	they sent to him some Pharisees	18
12:13	to trap him in what he said.	10
12:14	you are sincere, and show deference to no one;	17
12:18	Sadducees…came to him and asked him a question	18
12:43	all those who are contributing to the treasury.	4
13: 9	they will hand you over to councils;	4
13:10	good news must first be proclaimed to all nations.	4
13:12	Brother will betray brother to death	4
13:13	one who endures to the end will be saved.	4
13:14	those in Judea must flee to the mountains;	4
13:22	produce signs and omens, to lead astray	18
13:27	from the ends of the earth to the ends of heaven.	9
13:34	commands the doorkeeper to be on the watch	10
14: 4	some were there who said to one another in anger	18
14:10	went to the chief priests in order to betray him	18
14:12	the preparations for you to eat the Passover?"	10
14:16	the disciples set out and went to the city	4
14:26	they went out to the Mount of Olives.	4
14:28	I will go before you to Galilee."	4
14:32	They went to a place called Gethsemane;	4
14:34	"I am deeply grieved, even to death;	9
14:53	They took Jesus to the high priest;	18
14:55	testimony against Jesus to put him to death;	4
15:11	to have him release Barabbas for them instead.	10
15:15	he handed him over to be crucified.	10
15:20	they led him out to crucify him.	10
15:21	to carry his cross; it was Simon of Cyrene	10
15:22	they brought Jesus to the place called Golgotha	8
15:38	torn in two, from top to bottom.	9

15:41	women who had come up with him to Jerusalem.	4
15:43	went boldly to Pilate	18
16: 2	when the sun had risen, they went to the tomb.	8
16: 3	They had been saying to one another	18
16: 7	he is going ahead of you to Galilee;	4
16: S	⟦sent out through them, from east to west,⟧	2
Lke 1:13	the angel said to him, "Do not be afraid	18
1:16	turn many of the people of Israel to the Lord	8
1:17	to turn the hearts of parents to their children	8
1:17	the disobedient to the wisdom of the righteous	6
1:18	Zechariah said to the angel, "How will I know	18
1:19	I have been sent to speak to you	18
1:23	he went to his home.	4
1:26	to a town in Galilee called Nazareth	4
1:27	to a virgin engaged to a man whose name was Joseph	18
1:28	he came to her and said, "Greetings, favored one!	18
1:34	Mary said to the angel, "How can this be	18
1:39	to a Judean town in the hill country	4
1:43	that the mother of my Lord comes to me?	18
1:50	who fear him from generation to generation.	4
1:55	according to the promise he made to our ancestors	18
1:56	returned to her home.	4
1:58	the Lord had shown his great mercy to her	12
1:61	They said to her, "None of your relatives	18
1:73	the oath that he swore to our ancestor Abraham	18
1:80	until the day he appeared publicly to Israel.	18
2: 3	All went to their own towns to be registered.	4
2: 4	from the town of Nazareth in Galilee to Judea	4
2: 4	to the city of David called Bethlehem	4
2:15	the shepherds said to one another, "Let us go	18
2:15	"Let us go now to Bethlehem and see this thing	9
2:22	they brought him up to Jerusalem to present him	4
2:34	Simeon blessed them and said to his mother Mary	18
2:34	to be a sign that will be opposed	4
2:37	then as a widow to the age of eighty-four	9
2:39	they returned to Galilee, to their own town	4
2:39	they returned to Galilee, to their own town	4
2:41	Now every year his parents went to Jerusalem	4
2:45	they returned to Jerusalem to search for him.	4
2:48	his mother said to him, "Child, why have you	18
2:49	He said to them, "Why were you searching	18
2:51	he went down with them and came to Nazareth	4
3: 2	the word of God came to John son of Zechariah	8
3: 8	Do not begin to say to yourselves	6
3:13	He said to them, "Collect no more than the amount	18
3:20	added to them all by shutting up John in prison	8
4: 3	command this stone to become a loaf of bread."	10
4: 9	the devil took him to Jerusalem	4
4:14	Jesus…returned to Galilee	4
4:16	he came to Nazareth, where he had been brought up	4
4:16	he went to the synagogue on the sabbath day,	4
4:21	he began to say to them, "Today this scripture	18
4:23	He said to them, "Doubtless you will quote to me	18
4:26	yet Elijah was sent to none of them	18
4:26	to a widow at Zarephath in Sidon.	18
4:29	led him to the brow of the hill	9
4:31	He went down to Capernaum, a city in Galilee	4
4:36	were all amazed and kept saying to one another	18
4:40	brought them to him;	18
4:43	he said to them, "I must proclaim the good news	18
5: 4	When he had finished speaking, he said to Simon	18
5:10	Jesus said to Simon, "Do not be afraid;	18
5:11	When they had brought their boats to shore	8
5:16	he would withdraw to deserted places and pray.	6
5:24	stand up and take your bed and go to your home."	4
5:25	and went to his home, glorifying God.	4
5:30	their scribes were complaining to his disciples	18
5:32	I have come to call…sinners to repentance."	4
5:33	they said to him, "John's disciples,	18
5:34	Jesus said to them, "You cannot make wedding guests	18
6: 9	Jesus said to them, "I ask you	18
6:12	he went out to the mountain to pray;	4
6:34	to receive as much again.	10
6:35	he is kind to the ungrateful and the wicked.	8
6:47	someone is like who comes to me, hears my words	18
7: 3	he sent some Jewish elders to him	18
7: 3	asking him to come and heal his slave.	15
7: 4	When they came to Jesus	18
7: 6	am not worthy to have you come under my roof;	10
7: 7	therefore I did not presume to come to you.	18
7:10	those who had been sent returned to the house	4

7:11	Soon afterwards he went to a town called Nain	4
7:19	sent them to the Lord to ask, "Are you the one	18
7:20	When the men had come to him, they said	18
7:20	"John the Baptist has sent us to you to ask	18
7:24	Jesus began to speak to the crowds about John:	18
7:36	One of the Pharisees asked Jesus to eat with him	10
7:39	he said to himself, "If this man were a prophet	6
7:40	Jesus spoke up and said to him, "Simon	18
7:50	he said to the woman, "Your faith has saved you;	18
8: 4	people from town after town came to him	18
8:17	that will not become known and come to light.	4
8:19	Then his mother and his brothers came to him	18
8:21	he said to them, "My mother and my brothers	18
8:22	he said to them, "Let us go across	18
8:22	"Let us go across to the other side of the lake."	4
8:25	amazed, and said to one another	18
8:31	They begged him not to order them to go back	10
8:32	demons begged Jesus to let them enter these.	10
8:35	they came to Jesus	18
8:39	"Return to your home	4
8:41	begged him to come to his house	4
8:51	When he came to the house	4
9: 3	He said to them, "Take nothing for your journey	18
9:10	withdrew privately to a city called Bethsaida.	4
9:13	he said to them, "You give them something to eat."	18
9:14	he said to his disciples, "Make them sit down	18
9:16	he looked up to heaven, and blessed and broke them	4
9:23	he said to them all, "If any want to become	18
9:33	Peter said to Jesus, "Master, it is good	18
9:40	I begged your disciples to cast it out	10
9:43	he said to his disciples	18
9:50	Jesus said to him, "Do not stop him;	18
9:51	he set his face to go to Jerusalem.	4
9:56	Then they went on to another village.	4
9:57	going along the road, someone said to him	18
9:59	To another he said, "Follow me."	18
9:62	Jesus said to him, "No one	18
9:62	"No one who puts a hand to the plow	8
10: 1	to every town and place	4
10: 2	He said to them, "The harvest is plentiful	18
10: 2	to send out laborers into his harvest.	15
10: 6	if not, it will return to you.	8
10: 7	Do not move about from house to house.	4
10: 9	'The kingdom of God has come near to you.'	8
10:11	'Even the dust of your town that clings to our feet	4
10:15	you, Capernaum, will you be exalted to heaven?	9
10:15	No, you will be brought down to Hades.	9
10:23	Then turning to the disciples, Jesus said	18
10:26	He said to him, "What is written in the law?	18
10:30	"A man was going down from Jerusalem to Jericho	4
10:32	a Levite, when he came to the place and saw him	11
10:34	brought him to an inn, and took care of him.	4
10:40	Tell her then to help me."	10
11: 1	finished, one of his disciples said to him,	18
11: 4	do not bring us to the time of trial."	4
11: 5	he said to them, "Suppose one of you has a friend	18
11: 5	one of you has a friend, and you go to him	18
11:20	then the kingdom of God has come to you.	8
11:24	it says, 'I will return to my house	4
11:37	a Pharisee invited him to dine with him;	15
11:39	the Lord said to him, "Now you Pharisees clean	18
11:51	from the blood of Abel to the blood of Zechariah	9
12: 1	he began to speak first to his disciples	18
12:15	he said to them, "Take care!	18
12:17	he thought to himself, 'What should I do	6
12:22	He said to his disciples, "Therefore I tell you	18
12:25	add a single hour to your span of life?	8
12:45	if that slave says to himself	6
12:49	"I came to bring fire to the earth	8
12:51	that I have come to bring peace to the earth?	6
13: 7	he said to the gardener, 'See here!	18
13:22	teaching as he made his way to Jerusalem.	4
13:23	He said to them	18
13:34	stones those who are sent to it!	18
14: 1	when Jesus was going to the house of a leader	4
14: 5	he said to them, "If one of you has a child	18
14: 6	they could not reply to this.	18
14: 8	you are invited by someone to a wedding banquet	4
14:23	the master said to the slave, 'Go out	18
14:25	he turned and said to them	18
14:26	"Whoever comes to me	18

Lke	14:28	to see whether he has enough to complete it?	4
	15:13	and traveled to a distant country	4
	15:15	who sent him to his fields to feed the pigs.	4
	15:17	when he came to himself he said	4
	15:18	I will get up and go to my father	18
	15:20	he set off and went to his father.	18
	15:22	the father said to his slaves	18
	16: 1	Then Jesus said to the disciples,	18
	16: 3	the manager said to himself, 'What will I do	6
	16:24	send Lazarus to dip the tip of his finger in water	10
	16:26	who might want to pass from here to you cannot	18
	16:26	and no one can cross from there to us.'	18
	16:27	I beg you to send him to my father's house	10
	16:27	I beg you to send him to my father's house	4
	16:30	if someone goes to them from the dead	18
	17: 1	Jesus said to his disciples,	18
	17: 4	turns back to you seven times and says, 'I repent,'	18
	17:11	On the way to Jerusalem	4
	17:22	he said to the disciples, "The days are coming	18
	17:24	lights up the sky from one side to the other	4
	18: 3	there was a widow who kept coming to him	18
	18: 4	later he said to himself	6
	18: 9	He also told this parable to some	18
	18:10	"Two men went up to the temple to pray	4
	18:13	would not even look up to heaven	4
	18:14	this man went down to his home justified	4
	18:16	"Let the little children come to me, and do not	18
	18:31	took the twelve aside and said to them, "See	18
	18:31	"See, we are going up to Jerusalem.	4
	18:39	sternly ordered him to be quiet	10
	18:40	Jesus...ordered the man to be brought to him	18
	19: 4	climbed a sycamore tree to see him	10
	19: 5	When Jesus came to the place, he looked up	8
	19: 5	he looked up and said to him	18
	19: 8	Zacchaeus stood there and said to the Lord,	18
	19: 9	Jesus said to him, "Today salvation has come	18
	19:12	"A nobleman went to a distant country	4
	19:13	said to them, 'Do business with these until	18
	19:28	he went on ahead, going up to Jerusalem.	4
	19:35	they brought it to Jesus;	18
	19:39	Some of the Pharisees in the crowd said to him	18
	20: 2	said to him, "Tell us	18
	20:10	he sent a slave to the tenants	18
	20:23	he perceived their craftiness and said to them	18
	20:25	He said to them, "Then give to the emperor	18
	20:41	he said to them, "How can they say	18
	21:12	hand you over to synagogues and prisons	4
	21:13	This will give you an opportunity to testify.	4
	21:21	those in Judea must flee to the mountains	4
	22:15	He said to them, "I have eagerly desired to eat	18
	22:33	I am ready to go with you to prison and to death!"	4
	22:33	I am ready to go with you to prison and to death!"	4
	22:39	went, as was his custom, to the Mount of Olives;	4
	22:45	he got up from prayer, he came to the disciples	18
	22:52	Then Jesus said to the chief priests	18
	22:66	they brought him to their council.	4
	22:70	He said to them, "You say that I am."	18
	23: 4	Pilate said to the chief priests	18
	23: 5	from Galilee where he began even to this place."	9
	23: 7	he sent him off to Herod	18
	23:14	said to them, "You brought me this man	18
	23:15	Neither has Herod, for he sent him back to us.	18
	23:22	A third time he said to them, "Why	18
	23:28	Jesus turned to them and said	18
	23:33	they came to the place that is called The Skull	8
	24: 1	at early dawn, they came to the tomb	8
	24: 5	bowed their faces to the ground	4
	24: 5	said to them, "Why do you look for the living	18
	24: 7	must be handed over to sinners	4
	24:10	who told this to the apostles.	18
	24:11	these words seemed to them an idle tale	7
	24:12	Peter got up and ran to the tomb	8
	24:13	two of them were going to a village called Emmaus	4
	24:17	he said to them, "What are you discussing	18
	24:20	to be condemned to death and crucified him.	4
	24:24	Some of those who were with us went to the tomb	8
	24:25	he said to them, "Oh, how foolish you are,	18
	24:32	said to each other, "Were not our hearts burning	18
	24:33	That same hour they got up and returned to Jerusalem;	4
	24:44	Then he said to them, "These are my words	18
	24:44	"These are my words that I spoke to you	18

	24:47	proclaimed in his name to all nations	4
	24:52	and returned to Jerusalem with great joy;	4
Jhn	1: 7	He came as a witness to testify	10
	1: 7	He came...to testify to the light	17
	1: 8	but he came to testify to the light.	10
	1: 8	but he came to testify to the light.	17
	1:11	He came to what was his own	4
	1:15	(John testified to him and cried out	17
	1:19	priests and Levites from Jerusalem to ask him	10
	1:27	I am not worthy to untie the thong of his sandal."	10
	1:42	He brought Simon to Jesus, who looked at him	18
	1:43	The next day Jesus decided to go to Galilee.	4
	2: 2	Jesus...had also been invited to the wedding.	4
	2: 3	wine gave out, the mother of Jesus said to him,	18
	2:12	After this he went down to Capernaum	4
	2:13	and Jesus went up to Jerusalem.	4
	2:25	and needed no one to testify about anyone;	10
	3: 2	He came to Jesus by night and said to him	18
	3: 4	Nicodemus said to him, "How can anyone be born	18
	3:17	God did not send the Son...to condemn the world	10
	3:20	hate the light and do not come to the light	18
	3:21	But those who do what is true come to the light	18
	3:26	They came to John and said to him, "Rabbi	18
	3:26	here he is baptizing, and all are going to him."	18
	4: 3	he left Judea and started back to Galilee.	4
	4: 5	So he came to a Samaritan city called Sychar	4
	4: 8	(His disciples had gone to the city	4
	4: 8	had gone to the city to buy food.)	10
	4:14	a spring of water gushing up to eternal life."	4
	4:15	The woman said to him, "Sir, give me this water	18
	4:28	left her water jar and went back to the city.	4
	4:30	They left the city and were on their way to him.	18
	4:33	So the disciples said to one another	18
	4:34	"My food is to do the will of him who sent me	10
	4:40	So when the Samaritans came to him, they asked him	18
	4:43	he went from that place to Galilee	4
	4:45	he came to Galilee, the Galileans welcomed him	18
	4:45	for they too had gone to the festival.	4
	4:46	Then he came again to Cana in Galilee	4
	4:47	heard that Jesus had come from Judea to Galilee	4
	4:47	and begged him to come down and heal his son	10
	4:48	Then Jesus said to him, "Unless you see signs	18
	4:49	The official said to him, "Sir, come down	18
	4:54	after coming from Judea to Galilee.	4
	5: 1	and Jesus went up to Jerusalem.	4
	5: 7	I have no one to put me into the pool	10
	5:24	has passed from death to life.	4
	5:29	who have done good, to the resurrection of life	4
	5:29	done evil, to the resurrection of condemnation.	4
	5:32	I know that his testimony to me is true.	17
	5:33	You sent messengers to John	18
	5:36	works that the Father has given me to complete	10
	5:40	you refuse to come to me to have life.	18
	5:40	you refuse to come to me to have life.	10
	6: 5	Jesus said to Philip, "Where are we to buy bread	18
	6:15	and take him by force to make him king	10
	6:15	he withdrew again to the mountain by himself.	4
	6:16	his disciples went down to the sea	8
	6:17	started across the sea to Capernaum.	4
	6:17	and Jesus had not yet come to them.	18
	6:24	they...got into the boats and went to Capernaum	4
	6:28	they said to him, "What must we do	18
	6:28	"What must we do to perform the works of God?"	10
	6:34	said to him, "Sir, give us this bread always."	18
	6:35	Whoever comes to me will never be hungry	18
	6:37	that the Father gives me will come to me	18
	6:37	anyone who comes to me I will never drive away;	18
	6:38	come down from heaven, not to do my own will	10
	6:44	No one can come to me unless drawn	18
	6:45	Everyone who has heard...comes to me.	18
	6:65	I have told you that no one can come to me	18
	6:68	Peter answered him, "Lord, to whom can we go?	18
	7: 3	his brothers said to him, "Leave here	18
	7: 3	"Leave here and go to Judea	4
	7: 8	Go to the festival yourselves.	4
	7: 8	I am not going to this festival	4
	7:10	after his brothers had gone to the festival	4
	7:32	Pharisees sent temple police to arrest him.	10
	7:33	then I am going to him who sent me.	18
	7:35	The Jews said to one another	18
	7:35	Does he intend to go to the Dispersion	4

7:37	"Let anyone who is thirsty come to me	18
7:45	the temple police went back to the chief priests	18
7:50	Nicodemus, who had gone to Jesus before	18
8: 1	[[Jesus went to the Mount of Olives.]]	4
8: 2	[[Early in the morning he came again to the temple.]]	4
8: 2	[[All the people came to him]]	18
8:26	I declare to the world what I have heard from him."	4
8:31	Then Jesus said to the Jews who had believed	18
8:57	Then the Jews said to him	18
8:59	they picked up stones to throw at him	10
9:11	'Go to Siloam and wash.' Then I went and washed	4
9:13	They brought to the Pharisees the man	18
10:10	The thief comes only to steal and kill	10
10:25	The works that I do…testify to me;	17
10:31	The Jews took up stones again to stone him.	10
10:35	to whom the word of God came were called 'gods'	18
10:40	to the place where John had been baptizing earlier	4
10:41	Many came to him, and they were saying,	18
11: 3	the sisters sent a message to Jesus,	18
11: 7	"Let us go to Judea again."	4
11:11	I am going there to awaken him."	10
11:13	they thought that he was referring merely to sleep.	17
11:15	let us go to him."	18
11:19	many of the Jews had come to Martha and Mary	18
11:19	to console them about their brother.	10
11:21	Martha said to Jesus, "Lord, if you had been here	18
11:29	she got up quickly and went to him	18
11:30	Now Jesus had not yet come to the village	4
11:31	thought that she was going to the tomb to weep	4
11:31	thought that she was going to the tomb to weep	10
11:38	Jesus, again greatly disturbed, came to the tomb.	4
11:46	some of them went to the Pharisees	18
11:50	to have one man die for the people	10
11:52	to gather into one the dispersed children of God.	10
11:53	they planned to put him to death.	10
11:54	went from there to a town called Ephraim	4
11:55	many went up from the country to Jerusalem	4
11:55	many went up…to purify themselves.	10
11:56	Surely he will not come to the festival	4
12: 1	Jesus came to Bethany, the home of Lazarus	4
12: 9	to see Lazarus, whom he had raised from the dead.	10
12:10	planned to put Lazarus to death as well	10
12:12	great crowd that had come to the festival heard	4
12:12	heard that Jesus was coming to Jerusalem.	4
12:13	and went out to meet him	4
12:19	The Pharisees then said to one another	18
12:20	among those who went up to worship at the festival	10
12:27	for this reason that I have come to this hour.	4
12:32	I…will draw all people to myself."	18
12:38	to fulfill the word spoken by the prophet Isaiah:	10
12:47	for I came not to judge the world	10
12:47	not to judge the world, but to save the world.	10
13: 1	to depart from this world and go to the Father.	10
13: 1	he loved them to the end.	4
13: 2	put it into the heart…to betray him.	10
13: 3	he had come from God and was going to God	18
13: 6	He came to Simon Peter, who said to him, "Lord	18
13:18	to fulfill the scripture, 'The one	10
14: 3	I will come again and will take you to myself	18
14: 6	No one comes to the Father except through me.	18
14:12	because I am going to the Father.	18
14:16	another Advocate, to be with you forever.	10
14:18	not leave you orphaned; I am coming to you.	18
14:23	we will come to them and make our home with them.	18
14:28	'I am going away, and I am coming to you.'	18
14:28	that I am going to the Father	18
15: 2	he prunes to make it bear more fruit.	10
15:13	to lay down one's life for one's friends.	10
15:16	I appointed you to go and bear fruit	10
15:21	they will do all these things to you	4
15:25	to fulfill the word that is written in their law	10
16: 1	to keep you from stumbling.	10
16: 5	now I am going to him who sent me;	18
16: 7	not go away, the Advocate will not come to you	18
16: 7	if I go, I will send him to you.	18
16:10	because I am going to the Father	18
16:17	some of his disciples said to one another	18
16:17	'Because I am going to the Father'?"	18
16:28	leaving the world and am going to the Father."	18
16:30	not need to have anyone question you;	10
16:32	when you will be scattered, each one to his home	4

	17: 1	he looked up to heaven and said	4
	17: 2	to give eternal life to all	10
	17: 4	the work that you gave me to do.	10
	17:11	they are in the world, and I am coming to you.	18
	17:13	now I am coming to you	18
	17:15	not asking you to take them out of the world	10
	17:15	I ask you to protect them from the evil one.	10
	17:24	to see my glory, which you have given me	10
	18: 4	Jesus, knowing all that was to happen to him	8
	18: 9	This was to fulfill the word that he had spoken	10
	18:13	First they took him to Annas	18
	18:23	testify to the wrong.	17
	18:24	Then Annas sent him bound to Caiaphas	18
	18:28	from Caiaphas to Pilate's headquarters.	4
	18:29	Pilate went out to them and said	18
	18:32	to fulfill what Jesus had said	10
	18:36	to keep me from being handed over to the Jews.	10
	18:37	I was born…to testify to the truth.	10
	18:37	Everyone who belongs to the truth listens	5
	18:38	he went out to the Jews again	18
	19: 3	They kept coming up to him, saying, "Hail, King	18
	19: 4	to let you know that I find no case against him."	10
	19:16	he handed him over to them to be crucified.	10
	19:17	to what is called The Place of the Skull	4
	19:24	they said to one another, "Let us not tear it	18
	19:24	This was to fulfill what the scripture says,	10
	19:31	to have the legs of the crucified men broken	10
	19:33	when they came to Jesus	8
	19:38	to let them take away the body of Jesus.	10
	19:39	Nicodemus, who had at first come to Jesus by night	18
	20: 1	still dark, Mary Magdalene came to the tomb	4
	20: 2	went to Simon Peter and the other disciple	18
	20:10	the disciples returned to their homes.	18
	20:17	because I have not yet ascended to the Father.	18
	20:17	go to my brothers and say to them	18
	20:17	'I am ascending to my Father and your Father	18
	21: 6	"Cast the net to the right side of the boat	4
	21:22	what is that to you? Follow me!"	18
	21:23	what is that to you?"	18
	21:24	the disciple who is testifying to these	17
Act	1: 8	Judea and Samaria, and to the ends of the earth."	9
	1:12	Then they returned to Jerusalem from the mount	4
	1:13	they went to the room upstairs	4
	1:25	to go to his own place."	4
	1:26	he was added to the eleven apostles.	12
	2:12	were amazed and perplexed, saying to one another	18
	2:20	The sun shall be turned to darkness	4
	2:20	the moon to blood	4
	2:22	Jesus of Nazareth, a man attested to you by God	18
	2:27	you will not abandon my soul to Hades	4
	2:29	I may say to you confidently of our ancestor	18
	2:29	his tomb is with us to this day.	2
	2:31	'He was not abandoned to Hades	4
	2:37	said to Peter and to the other apostles	18
	2:38	Peter said to them, "Repent, and be baptized	18
	2:47	day by day the Lord added to their number	8
	3: 1	One day Peter and John were going up to the temple	4
	3:11	all the people ran together to them	18
	3:22	You must listen to whatever he tells you.	11
	3:25	the covenant that God gave to your ancestors	18
	3:25	saying to Abraham, 'And in your descendants	18
	4: 1	While Peter and John were speaking to the people	18
	4: 8	Peter, filled with the Holy Spirit, said to them	18
	4:17	to keep it from spreading further among the people	10
	4:23	they went to their friends	18
	4:23	the chief priests and the elders had said to them	18
	4:24	raised their voices together to God and said	18
	4:30	while you stretch out your hand to heal	4
	5: 8	Peter said to her, "Tell me	18
	5: 9	Peter said to her, "How is it that you have agreed	18
	5:21	sent to the prison to have them brought.	4
	5:35	he said to them, "Fellow Israelites,	18
	5:35	consider carefully what you propose to do to these	8
	6: 3	whom we may appoint to this task	8
	7: 3	said to him, 'Leave your country	18
	7: 3	go to the land that I will show you.'	4
	7: 4	God had him move from there to this country	4
	7:15	Jacob went down to Egypt.	4
	7:16	their bodies were brought back to Shechem	4
	7:34	Come now, I will send you to Egypt.'	4
	7:39	in their hearts they turned back to Egypt	4

Act	8: 3 committed them to prison.	4
	8: 5 Philip went down to the city of Samaria	4
	8:10 All of them, from the least to the greatest,	9
	8:14 they sent Peter and John to them.	18
	8:20 Peter said to him, "May your silver perish with you	18
	8:24 Simon answered, "Pray for me to the Lord	18
	8:24 nothing of what you have said may happen to me."	8
	8:25 they returned to Jerusalem	4
	8:26 an angel of the Lord said to Philip, "Get up and go	18
	8:26 "Get up and go toward the south to the road	8
	8:26 the road that goes down from Jerusalem to Gaza."	4
	8:27 had come to Jerusalem to worship	4
	8:32 "Like a sheep he was led to the slaughter	8
	8:36 they came to some water;	8
	8:40 until he came to Caesarea.	4
	9: 2 asked him for letters to the synagogues	18
	9: 2 he might bring them bound to Jerusalem.	4
	9: 4 He fell to the ground and heard a voice saying	8
	9:10 The Lord said to him in a vision, "Ananias."	18
	9:11 The Lord said to him, "Get up and go	18
	9:11 "Get up and go to the street called Straight	8
	9:15 the Lord said to him, "Go	18
	9:26 When he had come to Jerusalem	4
	9:27 Barnabas took him, brought him to the apostles	18
	9:30 they brought him down to Caesarea	4
	9:30 and sent him off to Tarsus.	4
	9:32 he came down also to the saints living in Lydda.	18
	9:35 saw him and turned to the Lord.	8
	9:38 disciples…sent two men to him with the request	18
	9:38 "Please come to us without delay."	9
	9:39 when he arrived, they took him to the room upstairs.	4
	9:40 turned to the body and said, "Tabitha, get up."	18
	10: 5 Now send men to Joppa	4
	10: 8 he sent them to Joppa.	4
	10:11 being lowered to the ground by its four corners.	8
	10:15 The voice said to him again, a second time	18
	10:16 the thing was suddenly taken up to heaven.	4
	10:21 Peter went down to the men and said, "I am the one	18
	10:24 The following day they came to Caesarea.	4
	10:28 he said to them, "You yourselves know	18
	10:32 Send therefore to Joppa and ask for Simon	4
	11: 2 when Peter went up to Jerusalem	4
	11: 3 saying, "Why did you go to uncircumcised men	18
	11:10 everything was pulled up again to heaven.	4
	11:11 three men, sent to me from Caesarea, arrived	18
	11:13 'Send to Joppa and bring Simon, who is called Peter;	4
	11:20 who, on coming to Antioch, spoke to the Hellenists	4
	11:20 who, on coming to Antioch, spoke to the Hellenists	18
	11:21 a great number became believers and turned to the Lord.	8
	11:22 News…came to the ears of the church in Jerusalem	4
	11:22 they sent Barnabas to Antioch.	9
	11:25 Barnabas went to Tarsus to look for Saul	4
	11:26 when he had found him, he brought him to Antioch.	4
	11:27 prophets came down from Jerusalem to Antioch.	4
	11:30 this they did, sending it to the elders	18
	12: 5 prayed fervently to God for him.	18
	12: 8 The angel said to him, "Fasten your belt	18
	12:11 Peter came to himself and said	6
	12:12 as he realized this, he went to the house of Mary	8
	12:15 They said to her, "You are out of your mind!"	18
	12:17 Then he left and went to another place.	4
	12:19 Then he went down from Judea to Caesarea	4
	12:20 they came to him in a body;	18
	12:21 Herod…delivered a public address to them	18
	12:25 Barnabas and Saul returned to Jerusalem	4
	13: 4 they went down to Seleucia;	4
	13: 4 from there they sailed to Cyprus.	4
	13:13 and came to Perga in Pamphylia.	4
	13:13 John, however, left them and returned to Jerusalem;	4
	13:14 and came to Antioch in Pisidia.	4
	13:31 came up with him from Galilee to Jerusalem	4
	13:31 they are now his witnesses to the people.	18
	13:32 what God promised to our ancestors	18
	13:34 no more to return to corruption	4
	13:46 we are now turning to the Gentiles.	4
	13:47 'I have set you to be a light for the Gentiles	4
	13:47 bring salvation to the ends of the earth.' "	9
	13:51 and went to Iconium.	4
	14: 3 who testified to the word of his grace	8
	14: 6 apostles learned of it and fled to Lystra and Derbe	4
	14:11 "The gods have come down to us in human form!"	18

14:13 brought oxen and garlands to the gates;	8
14:15 turn from these worthless things to the living God	8
14:20 The next day he went on with Barnabas to Derbe.	4
14:21 returned to Lystra, then on to Iconium and Antioch.	4
14:21 returned to Lystra, then on to Iconium and Antioch.	4
14:24 passed through Pisidia and came to Pamphylia.	4
14:25 they went down to Attalia.	4
14:26 From there they sailed back to Antioch	4
15: 2 appointed to go up to Jerusalem to discuss this	4
15: 4 When they came to Jerusalem	4
15: 7 Peter stood up and said to them, "My brothers	18
15:19 not trouble those Gentiles who are turning to God	8
15:22 send them to Antioch with Paul and Barnabas.	4
15:25 to choose representatives and send them to you	18
15:30 they were sent off and went down to Antioch.	4
15:33 sent off…to those who had sent them.	18
15:36 After some days Paul said to Barnabas, "Come	18
15:39 Barnabas…sailed away to Cyprus.	4
16: 1 Paul went on also to Derbe and to Lystra	4
16: 1 Paul went on also to Derbe and to Lystra	4
16: 8 so, passing by Mysia, they went down to Troas.	4
16: 9 "Come over to Macedonia and help us."	4
16:10 we immediately tried to cross over to Macedonia	4
16:11 took a straight course to Samothrace	4
16:11 the following day to Neapolis	4
16:12 and from there to Philippi	4
16:16 as we were going to the place of prayer	4
16:30 "Sirs, what must I do to be saved?"	10
16:36 the jailer reported the message to Paul, saying	18
16:36 "The magistrates sent word to let you go;	10
16:40 leaving the prison they went to Lydia's home;	18
17: 1 they came to Thessalonica	4
17: 5 Paul and Silas to bring them out to the assembly	4
17:10 the believers sent Paul and Silas off to Beroea;	4
17:10 they went to the Jewish synagogue.	4
17:14 the believers…sent Paul away to the coast	9
17:19 brought him to the Areopagus and asked	8
18: 1 After this Paul left Athens and went to Corinth.	4
18: 6 shook the dust from his clothes and said to them	18
18: 6 From now on I will go to the Gentiles."	4
18: 7 went to the house of a man named Titius Justus	4
18:14 Gallio said to the Jews	18
18:21 "I will return to you, if God wills."	18
18:22 and then went down to Antioch.	4
18:24 Now there came to Ephesus a Jew named Apollos	4
18:27 when he wished to cross over to Achaia	4
19: 1 through the interior regions and came to Ephesus	4
19: 2 He said to them, "Did you receive the Holy Spirit	18
19: 4 to believe in the one who was to come after him	10
19:12 had touched his skin were brought to the sick	8
19:21 resolved…to go on to Jerusalem.	4
19:22 he sent two of his helpers…to Macedonia	4
19:29 people rushed together to the theater	4
20: 2 he came to Greece	4
20:13 went ahead to the ship and set sail for Assos	8
20:14 we took him on board and went to Mitylene.	4
20:15 the day after that we came to Miletus.	4
20:17 From Miletus he sent a message to Ephesus	4
20:18 When they came to him, he said to them:	18
20:22 captive to the Spirit, I am on my way to Jerusalem	4
20:38 they brought him to the ship.	4
21: 1 we came by a straight course to Cos	4
21: 1 the next day to Rhodes…from there to Patara.	4
21: 1 the next day to Rhodes…from there to Patara.	4
21: 3 leaving it on our left, we sailed to Syria	4
21: 4 they told Paul not to go on to Jerusalem.	4
21: 8 The next day we left and came to Caesarea;	4
21:11 came to us and took Paul's belt	18
21:11 will hand him over to the Gentiles.' "	4
21:12 people there urged him not to go up to Jerusalem.	4
21:15 we got ready and started to go up to Jerusalem.	4
21:32 and ran down to them.	8
21:35 When Paul came to the steps	8
21:37 "May I say something to you?"	18
21:39 I beg you, let me speak to the people."	18
22: 5 From them I also received letters to the brothers	18
22: 5 to bring them back to Jerusalem for punishment	4
22: 7 I fell to the ground and heard a voice saying	4
22: 8 he said to me, 'I am Jesus of Nazareth	18
22:10 The Lord said to me, 'Get up and go to Damascus;	18
22:10 The Lord said to me, 'Get up and go to Damascus;	4

22:11	took my hand and led me to Damascus.	4
22:13	came to me; and standing beside me, he said	18
22:15	you will be his witness to all the world	18
22:17	"After I had returned to Jerusalem	4
22:21	he said to me, 'Go, for I will send you	18
22:21	I will send you far away to the Gentiles.' "	4
22:24	to find out the reason for this outcry against him.	10
22:25	Paul said to the centurion who was standing by	18
23: 3	Paul said to him, "God will strike you	18
23:15	must notify the tribune to bring him down	15
23:15	notify the tribune to bring him down to you	4
23:16	gained entrance to the barracks and told Paul.	4
23:17	"Take this young man to the tribune	18
23:18	took him, brought him to the tribune, and said	18
23:18	Paul...asked me to bring this young man to you;	18
23:20	to ask you to bring Paul down to the council	4
23:23	to leave by nine o'clock tonight for Caesarea	15
23:24	and take him safely to Felix the governor."	18
23:28	I had him brought to their council.	4
23:30	I sent him to you at once	18
23:31	and brought him during the night to Antipatris.	4
23:32	go on with him, while they returned to the barracks.	4
23:33	When they came to Caesarea	4
23:34	he asked what province he belonged to	5
24: 4	to detain you no further	10
24:17	to bring alms to my nation and to offer sacrifices.	4
25: 1	he went up from Caesarea to Jerusalem	4
25: 3	to have him transferred to Jerusalem.	15
25: 3	to have him transferred to Jerusalem.	4
25: 6	he went down to Caesarea;	4
25: 9	"Do you wish to go up to Jerusalem	4
25:10	Paul said, "I am appealing to the emperor's tribunal;	8
25:12	to the emperor you will go."	8
25:20	I asked whether he wished to go to Jerusalem	4
25:21	until I could send him to the emperor."	18
25:22	Agrippa said to Festus, "I would like to hear	18
26: 1	Agrippa said to Paul, "You have permission	18
26: 6	hope in the promise made by God to our ancestors	4
26:11	I pursued them even to foreign cities.	4
26:12	"With this in mind, I was traveling to Damascus	4
26:14	When we had all fallen to the ground	4
26:14	heard a voice saying to me in the Hebrew language	18
26:17	from the Gentiles—to whom I am sending you	4
26:18	they may turn from darkness to light	4
26:18	turn...from the power of Satan to God	8
26:20	they should repent and turn to God	8
26:22	To this day I have had help from God	2
26:26	to him I speak freely;	18
26:28	Agrippa said to Paul	18
26:31	as they were leaving, they said to one another	18
27: 2	set sail to the ports along the coast of Asia	4
27: 3	allowed him to go to his friends to be cared for.	18
27: 5	we came to Myra in Lycia.	4
27: 8	we came to a place called Fair Havens	4
27:42	The soldiers' plan was to kill the prisoners	10
27:44	so it was that all were brought safely to land.	8
28: 4	they said to one another	18
28: 6	saw that nothing unusual had happened to him	4
28:13	we weighed anchor and came to Rhegium.	4
28:13	on the second day we came to Puteoli.	4
28:14	so we came to Rome.	4
28:15	came as far as the Forum of Appius...to meet us.	4
28:17	When they had assembled, he said to them,	18
28:17	in Jerusalem and handed over to the Romans.	4
28:23	they came to him at his lodgings in great numbers.	18
28:25	was right in saying to your ancestors	18
28:26	'Go to this people and say, You will indeed listen	18
28:30	welcomed all who came to him	18
Rom 1:10	I may somehow at last succeed in coming to you.	18
1:11	share...some spiritual gift to strengthen you	4
1:13	that I have often intended to come to you	18
1:19	For what can be known about God is plain to them	6
1:24	God gave them up...to impurity	4
1:26	God gave them up to degrading passions.	4
1:28	God gave them up to a debased mind	4
2: 4	God's kindness is meant to lead you to repentance?	4
3: 7	if...God's truthfulness abounds to his glory	4
3:25	He did this to show his righteousness	4
3:26	it was to prove...that he himself is righteous	18
5: 2	we have obtained access to this grace	4
5:12	death spread to all because all have sinned—	4

5:14	Yet death exercised dominion from Adam to Moses	13
6:17	obedient...to the form of teaching	4
7: 5	at work in our members to bear fruit for death.	4
7: 6	dead to that which held us captive	6
7:23	making me captive to the law of sin	6
8: 7	the mind that is set on the flesh is hostile to God;	4
8:18	the glory about to be revealed to us.	4
10: 1	my heart's desire and prayer to God for them	18
10:12	and is generous to all who call on him	4
10:18	"Their voice has gone out to all the earth	4
10:18	and their words to the ends of the world."	4
10:21	my hands to a disobedient and contrary people."	18
11:36	and through him and to him are all things.	4
15:16	to be a minister of Christ Jesus to the Gentiles	4
15:16	to be a minister of Christ Jesus to the Gentiles	4
15:22	I have so often been hindered from coming to you.	18
15:23	I desire, as I have for many years, to come to you	18
15:24	when I go to Spain. For I do hope to see you	4
15:25	I am going to Jerusalem in a ministry to the saints;	4
15:28	I will set out by way of you to Spain;	4
15:29	I know that when I come to you	18
15:30	join me in earnest prayer to God on my behalf	18
15:31	that my ministry to Jerusalem may be acceptable	4
15:32	that by God's will I may come to you with joy	18
16:19	For while your obedience is known to all	4
16:26	is made known to all the Gentiles	4
1Co 1: 8	He will also strengthen you to the end	9
1:27	to shame the wise;	10
1:27	to shame the strong;	10
1:28	to reduce to nothing things that are	10
2: 1	When I came to you, brothers and sisters	18
2: 3	And I came to you in weakness and in fear	18
2:15	are themselves subject to no one else's scrutiny.	19
4: 6	I have applied all this to Apollos and myself	4
4:11	To the present hour we are hungry and thirsty	2
4:13	the dregs of all things, to this very day.	9
4:18	some of you, thinking that I am not coming to you,	18
4:19	I will come to you soon, if the Lord wills	18
4:21	you prefer? Am I to come to you with a stick	18
6: 5	I say this to your shame.	18
7: 5	to devote yourselves to prayer	10
7:15	It is to peace that God has called you.	6
7:35	not to put any restraint upon you	10
9:25	they do it to receive a perishable wreath	10
10:11	they were written down to instruct us	18
11:22	What! Do you not have homes to eat and drink in?	4
11:33	brothers and sisters, when you come together to eat	4
12: 2	and led astray to idols that could not speak	18
13:12	but then we will see face to face.	18
14: 5	to speak in tongues, but even more to prophesy.	10
14: 6	if I come to you speaking in tongues	18
14:11	the speaker a foreigner to me.	6
14:12	strive to excel in them for building up the church.	10
14:13	should pray for the power to interpret.	10
14:16	say the "Amen" to your thanksgiving	8
15:34	I say this to your shame.	18
16: 3	to take your gift to Jerusalem.	4
16:11	so that he may come to me;	18
16:12	I strongly urged him to visit you	10
16:12	he was not at all willing to come now.	10
16:15	devoted themselves to the service of the saints;	4
16:16	I urge you to put yourselves at the service	10
2Co 1:15	I wanted to come to you first	18
1:16	to come back to you from Macedonia	18
1:16	and have you send me on to Judea.	4
1:18	our word to you has not been "Yes and No."	18
1:20	that we say the "Amen," to the glory of God.	18
1:23	I did not come again to Corinth.	4
2: 4	not to cause you pain, but to let you know	10
2: 4	to let you know the abundant love that I have	10
2: 9	I wrote for this reason: to test you	10
2:12	When I came to Troas	4
2:12	to proclaim the good news of Christ	4
2:13	I said farewell to them and went on to Macedonia.	4
2:16	to the one a fragrance from death to death	4
2:16	to the other a fragrance from life to life.	4
3: 1	letters of recommendation to you or from you	18
3:13	to keep the people of Israel from gazing	18
3:14	Indeed, to this very day, when they hear	2
3:15	Indeed, to this very day whenever Moses is read	9
3:16	when one turns to the Lord, the veil is removed.	18

2Co	3:18	from one degree of glory to another;	4
	4: 2	commend ourselves to the conscience of everyone	18
	4: 3	it is veiled to those who are perishing.	6
	4: 4	to keep them from seeing the light of the gospel	4
	4:11	always being given up to death for Jesus' sake	4
	4:15	that grace, as it extends to more and more people	3
	4:15	increase thanksgiving, to the glory of God.	4
	5:11	that we are also well known to your consciences.	6
	5:19	entrusting the message of reconciliation to us.	6
	6:11	We have spoken frankly to you Corinthians;	18
	7: 3	I do not say this to condemn you	18
	7: 3	to die together and to live together.	4
	7:12	zeal...might be made known to you before God.	18
	7:14	so our boasting to Titus has proved true	8
	7:15	his heart goes out all the more to you	4
	8: 1	grace...granted to the churches of Macedonia;	6
	8: 4	sharing in this ministry to the saints—	4
	8:17	he is going to you of his own accord.	18
	9: 1	to write you about the ministry to the saints	4
	9: 4	we would be humiliated—to say nothing of you	10
	9: 5	necessary to urge the brothers to go on ahead to you	10
	9: 5	necessary to urge the brothers to go on ahead to you	4
	10: 4	they have divine power to destroy strongholds.	18
	10: 5	take every thought captive to obey Christ.	4
	11: 3	from a sincere and pure devotion to Christ.	4
	11: 6	in all things we have made this evident to you.	4
	11:12	an opportunity to be recognized as our equals	10
	11:21	To my shame, I must say, we were too weak for that!	11
	12: 1	go on to visions and revelations of the Lord.	4
	12: 2	a person in Christ...caught up to the third heaven	9
	12: 7	Therefore, to keep me from being too elated.	10
	12: 7	to torment me, to keep me from being too elated.	10
	12: 7	to torment me, to keep me from being too elated.	10
	12:14	Here I am, ready to come to you this third time.	18
	12:17	through any of those whom I sent to you?	18
	13: 1	This is the third time I am coming to you.	18
	13: 7	we pray to God that you may not do anything wrong	18
Gal	1: 4	to set us free from the present evil age	15
	1: 6	turning to a different gospel—	4
	1:16	to reveal his Son in me	6
	1:17	nor did I go up to Jerusalem	4
	1:17	to those who were already apostles before me	18
	1:17	afterwards I returned to Damascus.	4
	1:18	Then after three years I did go up to Jerusalem	4
	2: 1	I went up again to Jerusalem with Barnabas	4
	2: 8	worked through me in sending me to the Gentiles)	4
	2: 9	agreeing that we should go to the Gentiles	4
	2: 9	go to the Gentiles and they to the circumcised.	4
	2:11	when Cephas came to Antioch	4
	2:11	I opposed him to his face	11
	3:14	blessing of Abraham might come to the Gentiles	4
	3:16	"And to your offspring," that is, to one person	8
	3:17	so as to nullify the promise.	4
	4: 3	enslaved to the elemental spirits of the world.	19
	4: 9	can you turn back again to the weak and beggarly	8
	5:13	you were called to freedom, brothers and sisters;	8
	5:17	to prevent you from doing what you want.	10
	6: 8	If you sow to your own flesh,	4
	6: 8	if you sow to the Spirit	4
Eph	1: 6	to the praise of his glorious grace	4
	1:14	to the praise of his glory.	4
	2:10	God prepared beforehand to be our way of life	10
	2:18	both of us have access in one Spirit to the Father.	18
	3:21	to him be glory...to all generations	4
	4: 4	just as you were called to the one hope	6
	4:12	to equip the saints for the work of ministry	18
	4:13	until all of us come to the unity of the faith	4
	4:13	to maturity, to the measure of the full stature	4
	4:13	to the measure of the full stature of Christ.	4
	4:19	greedy to practice every kind of impurity.	4
	4:25	let all of us speak the truth to our neighbors	12
	4:32	be kind to one another, tenderhearted	4
	5:31	be joined to his wife	18
	5:32	I am applying it to Christ and the church.	4
	6: 9	masters, do the same to them.	18
	6:22	I am sending him to you for this very purpose	18
	6:22	to let you know how we are	10
Php	1:12	actually helped to spread the gospel	4
	1:23	my desire is to depart and be with Christ	4
	1:26	when I come to you again.	18
	2:11	to the glory of God the Father.	4

	2:25	I think it necessary to send to you	18
	2:30	he came close to death for the work of Christ	13
	2:30	risking his life to make up for those services	10
	3:16	Only let us hold fast to what we have attained.	4
	4: 6	let your requests be made known to God.	18
	4:11	Not that I am referring to being in need;	11
	4:17	I seek the profit that accumulates to your account.	4
Col	1: 6	that has come to you.	4
	1:11	to endure everything with patience, while joyfully	4
	1:12	has enabled you to share in the inheritance	4
	1:20	God was pleased to reconcile to himself all things	4
	1:23	been proclaimed to every creature under heaven.	6
	2:20	died to the elemental spirits of the universe	1
	2:22	All these regulations refer to things that perish	4
	3: 9	Do not lie to one another	4
	3:15	to which indeed you were called in the one body.	4
	4: 8	I have sent him to you for this very purpose	18
	4:10	if he comes to you, welcome him.	18
1Th	1: 5	message of the gospel came to you not in word only	4
	1: 9	how you turned to God from idols	18
	2: 1	our coming to you was not in vain	18
	2: 2	to declare to you the gospel of God	18
	2: 9	while we proclaimed to you the gospel of God.	18
	2:18	For we wanted to come to you	18
	3: 2	to strengthen and encourage you for the sake	4
	3: 5	I sent to find out about your faith;	4
	3: 6	Timothy has just now come to us from you	18
	3:11	our Lord Jesus direct our way to you.	18
	4: 7	God did not call us to impurity	8
	4: 8	who also gives his Holy Spirit to you.	4
	4: 9	taught by God to love one another;	4
	4:17	together with them to meet the Lord in the air;	4
	5:15	always seek to do good to one another and to all.	4
	5:15	always seek to do good to one another and to all.	4
2Th	1:10	because our testimony to you was believed.	8
	1:11	To this end we always pray for you	4
	2: 1	our being gathered together to him	8
	2: 2	not to be quickly shaken in mind or alarmed	4
	3: 5	May the Lord direct your hearts to the love of God	4
	3: 5	love of God and to the steadfastness of Christ.	4
	3: 9	in order to give you an example to imitate.	4
	3:12	to do their work quietly	10
1Ti	1: 3	as I did when I was on my way to Macedonia	4
	1: 6	deviated...and turned to meaningless talk	4
	1:12	and appointed me to his service	4
	2: 4	to come to the knowledge of the truth.	4
	3:14	I hope to come to you soon	18
	4: 3	created to be received with thanksgiving	4
	4:10	For to this end we toil and struggle	4
	4:15	Put...into practice, devote yourself to them	6
	5:21	I warn you to keep these instructions without prejudice	10
	5:24	are conspicuous and precede them to judgment	4
	6:12	the eternal life, to which you were called	4
2Ti	2:24	kindly to everyone, an apt teacher, patient	18
	2:26	having been held captive by him to do his will.	4
	3:13	impostors will go from bad to worse	8
	4: 4	will turn away...and wander away to myths.	8
	4: 9	Do your best to come to me soon	18
	4:10	has deserted me and gone to Thessalonica;	4
	4:10	Crescens has gone to Galatia, Titus to Dalmatia.	4
	4:10	Crescens has gone to Galatia, Titus to Dalmatia.	4
	4:12	I have sent Tychicus to Ephesus.	4
Tit	2:12	training us to renounce impiety	10
	3: 2	to show every courtesy to everyone.	18
	3:12	When I send Artemas to you, or Tychicus	18
	3:12	do your best to come to me at Nicopolis	18
Heb	1:13	But to which of the angels has he ever said, "Sit	18
	1:14	angels spirits in the divine service, sent to serve	4
	2: 3	it was attested to us by those who heard him	4
	2:10	in bringing many children to glory	4
	2:17	to make a sacrifice of atonement for the sins	4
	3: 5	to testify to the things...spoken later.	4
	3:14	if only we hold...firm to the end.	13
	4:13	the eyes of the one to whom we must render an account.	18
	5: 1	to offer gifts and sacrifices for sins.	10
	5: 5	but was appointed by the one who said to him	18
	5: 7	to the one who was able to save him from death	18
	5:14	to distinguish good from evil.	18
	6: 4	For it is impossible to restore again to repentance	4
	6: 8	its end is to be burned over.	4
	6:11	the full assurance of hope to the very end	2

	7:21 because of the one who said to him,	18
	7:25 since he always lives to make intercession	4
	8: 3 every high priest is appointed to offer gifts	4
	8:11 from the least of them to the greatest.	9
	9:14 from dead works to worship the living God!	4
	9:25 Nor was it to offer himself again and again	10
	9:26 to remove sin by the sacrifice of himself.	4
	9:28 Christ…offered once to bear the sins of many	4
	9:28 to save those who are eagerly waiting for him.	4
	10:19 we have confidence to enter the sanctuary	4
	10:24 let us consider how to provoke one another to love	4
	11: 4 God himself giving approval to his gifts;	8
	11: 7 built an ark to save his household;	4
	11:26 he was looking ahead to the reward.	4
	12: 2 looking to Jesus the pioneer…of our faith	4
	13:13 Let us then go to him outside the camp	18
Jas	1: 7 must not expect to receive anything from the Lord.	16
	1:19 let everyone be quick to listen, slow to speak	4
	1:19 let everyone be quick to listen, slow to speak	4
	1:19 let everyone be quick to listen…slow to anger;	4
	3: 3 to make them obey us	4
	3:14 do not be boastful and false to the truth.	11
	4:13 tomorrow we will go to such and such a town	4
1Pe	1: 2 sanctified by the Spirit to be obedient	4
	1:25 the good news that was announced to you.	4
	2: 4 Come to him, a living stone, though rejected	18
	2: 5 into a spiritual house, to be a holy priesthood,	4
	2:14 sent by him to punish those who do wrong	4
	2:21 For to this you have been called	4
	2:25 but now you have returned to the shepherd	8
	3:12 and his ears are open to their prayer.	4
	3:21 but as an appeal to God for a good conscience	4
	4: 9 Be hospitable to one another without complaining.	4
	4:12 fiery ordeal that is taking place among you to test you	18
	5:10 who has called you to his eternal glory in Christ	4
2Pe	2:12 creatures…born to be caught and killed.	4
	2:22 "The dog turns back to its own vomit,"	8
	2:22 "The sow is washed only to wallow in the mud."	4
	3: 9 but all to come to repentance.	4
	3:16 the ignorant…twist to their own destruction	18
	3:18 glory both now and to the day of eternity. Amen.	4
1Jn	3: 5 You know that he was revealed to take away sins	10
	3: 8 to destroy the works of the devil.	10
	3:14 We know that we have passed from death to life	4
	5: 9 that he has testified to his Son.	17
2Jn	1:10 welcome anyone who comes to you and does not bring	18
	1:12 I hope to come to you and talk with you	18
	1:12 I hope to…talk with you face to face	18
3Jn	1:14 and we will talk together face to face.	18
Jde	1:16 speech, flattering people to their own advantage.	20
Rev	1:11 to the seven churches, to Ephesus, to Smyrna	4
	1:11 to the seven churches, to Ephesus, to Smyrna	4
	1:11 seven churches…to Pergamum, to Thyatira	4
	1:11 seven churches…to Pergamum, to Thyatira	4
	1:11 seven churches…to Sardis, to Philadelphia	4
	1:11 seven churches…to Sardis, to Philadelphia	4
	1:11 seven churches, to Ephesus…and to Laodicea."	4
	1:12 I turned to see whose voice it was that spoke to me	12
	2:21 I gave her time to repent, but she refuses	10
	2:26 continues to do my works to the end,	2
	3: 3 you will not know at what hour I will come to you.	8
	3:18 and white robes to clothe you	10
	3:20 I will come in to you and eat with you	18
	4: 1 the first voice, which I had heard speaking to me	12
	6: 2 and he came out conquering and to conquer.	10
	6:11 They were each…told to rest a little longer	10
	6:13 the stars of the sky fell to the earth	4
	7:17 he will guide them to springs of the water of life	8
	8: 3 a great quantity of incense to offer with the prayers	10
	8: 6 angels who had…trumpets made ready to blow them.	10
	8: 7 with blood, and they were hurled to the earth;	4
	9: 1 I saw a star that had fallen from heaven to earth	4
	9: 4 They were told not to damage the grass of the earth	10
	9: 5 were allowed to torture them for five months	10
	9: 5 allowed to torture…but not to kill them	10
	9:15 angels…ready…to kill a third of humankind.	10
	10: 5 the angel…raised his right hand to heaven	4
	10: 8 the voice…from heaven spoke to me again	12
	10: 9 So I went to the angel and told him to give me	18
	11:12 they went up to heaven in a cloud	4
	12: 4 the stars of heaven and threw them to the earth.	4

	12: 5 her child was snatched away and taken to God	18
	12: 5 snatched away and taken to God and to his throne;	18
	12: 9 the deceiver…—he was thrown down to the earth	4
	12:12 for the devil has come down to you with great wrath	18
	12:13 saw that he had been thrown down to the earth	4
	12:14 wilderness, to her place where she is nourished	4
	12:15 to sweep her away with the flood.	10
	13: 6 It opened its mouth to utter blasphemies	4
	13:10 If you are to be taken captive	4
	13:13 even making fire come down from heaven to earth	4
	13:16 to be marked on the right hand or the forehead	10
	14: 6 gospel to proclaim to those who live on the earth	8
	14: 6 to every nation and tribe and language and people.	8
	16:14 who go abroad to the kings of the whole world	8
	17: 1 one of the seven angels…came and said to me	12
	17: 8 beast…is about to ascend…and go to destruction.	4
	17:11 As for the beast…it goes to destruction.	4
	18:14 your dainties and your splendor are lost to you	1
	19: 8 her it has been granted to be clothed with fine linen	10
	19: 9 those who are invited to the marriage supper	4
	19:15 a sharp sword with which to strike down the nations	10
	19:18 to eat the flesh of kings, the flesh of captains	10
	21: 9 one of the seven angels…said to me	12
	21:10 he carried me away to a great, high mountain	8
	21:15 angel who talked to me had a measuring rod of gold	12
	21:15 to measure the city and its gates and walls.	10
	21:23 the city has no need of sun or moon to shine on it	10
	22:14 they will have the right to the tree of life	8
	22:18 if anyone adds to them, God will add to that person	8
	22:18 God will add to that person the plagues	8

to [be]

1. μέλλω, *mellō, 3516*

Mat	11:14 he is Elijah who is to come.	1
	16:27 "For the Son of Man is to come with his angels	1
Mrk	10:32 began to tell them what was to happen to him	1
Lke	19:11 the kingdom of God was to appear immediately.	1
Jhn	7:39 which believers in him were to receive;	1
	12:33 to indicate the kind of death he was to die.	1
	18:32 he indicated the kind of death he was to die.)	1
Act	26: 2 I am to make my defense today	1
1Th	3: 4 that we were to suffer persecution;	1
2Ti	4: 1 who is to judge the living and the dead	1
Heb	1:14 for the sake of those who are to inherit salvation?	1
	11: 8 a place that he was to receive as an inheritance;	1
Jas	2:12 So speak and so act as those who are to be judged	1
1Pe	5: 1 one who shares in the glory to be revealed	1
Rev	1:19 what is, and what is to take place after this.	1
	10: 7 when the seventh angel is to blow his trumpet,	1
	12: 5 who is to rule all the nations with a rod of iron	1

today

1. αὐτός, *autos, 899*
2. ἡμέρα, *hēmera, 2465*
3. σήμερον, *sēmeron, 4958*

Mat	6:30 the grass of the field, which is alive today	3
	6:34 Today's trouble is enough for today.	1
	6:34 Today's trouble is enough for today.	2
	16: 3 'It will be stormy today, for the sky is red	3
	21:28 'Son, go and work in the vineyard today.'	3
	27:19 for today I have suffered a great deal	3
Lke	4:21 "Today this scripture has been fulfilled	3
	5:26 saying, "We have seen strange things today."	3
	12:28 the grass of the field, which is alive today	3
	13:32 performing cures today and tomorrow	3
	13:33 Yet today, tomorrow, and the next day	3
	19: 5 I must stay at your house today."	3
	19: 9 "Today salvation has come to this house	3
	22:61 "Before the cock crows today, you will deny me	3
	23:43 today you will be with me in Paradise."	3
Act	4: 9 if we are questioned today	3
	13:33 'You are my Son; today I have begotten you.'	3
	19:40 we are in danger of being charged with rioting today	3
	22: 3 zealous for God, just as all of you are today	3
	24:21 I am on trial before you today.' "	3
	26: 2 I am to make my defense today	3
	26:29 but also all who are listening to me today	3
	27:33 "Today is the fourteenth day	3
Heb	1: 5 "You are my Son; today I have begotten you"?	3
	3: 7 "Today, if you hear his voice	3

Heb	3:13	as long as it is called "today,"	3
	3:15	As it is said, "Today, if you hear his voice	3
	4: 7	again he sets a certain day—"today"	3
	4: 7	"Today, if you hear his voice	3
	5: 5	"You are my Son, today I have begotten you";	3
	13: 8	Jesus Christ is the same yesterday and today	3
Jas	4:13	"Today or tomorrow we will go to...a town	3

together

See also agree together, all together, bind together, build together, call together, choose together, come running together, come together, confer together, die together, gather together, grow together, hold together, join together, knit together, life together, live together, make alive together, meet together, rejoice together, run together, rush together, servant working together, shake together, sit down together, suffer together, work together

1. Contextual: Not in Greek
2. ἅμα, *hama, 275*
3. ἑαυτοῦ, *heautou, 1571*
4. ἐπί + ὁ + αὐτός, *epi + ho + autos, 2093 + 3836 + 899*
5. ὁμοθυμαδόν, *homothymadon, 3924*
6. ὁμοῦ, *homou, 3938*

Mat	22:34	they gathered together	4
Lke	17:35	There will be two women grinding meal together;	4
Jhn	4:36	so that sower and reaper may rejoice together.	6
	20: 4	The two were running together	6
Act	1:15	(together the crowd numbered about one hundred twenty	4
	2: 1	they were all together in one place.	6
	2:44	All who believed were together	4
	2:46	as they spent much time together in the temple	5
	4:24	raised their voices together to God and said	5
	4:26	the rulers have gathered together	4
	5:12	they were all together in Solomon's Portico.	5
	7:57	with a loud shout all rushed together against him.	5
	18: 3	he stayed with them, and they worked together	1
	19:29	people rushed together to the theater	5
Rom	3:12	together they have become worthless;	2
	15: 6	together you may with one voice glorify the God	5
1Co	7: 5	come together again, so that Satan may not tempt	4
	11:20	When you come together, it is not really to eat	4
	14:23	If, therefore, the whole church comes together	4
1Th	4:17	will be caught up in the clouds together with them	2
Heb	10:25	not neglecting to meet together	3

together with

1. καί, *kai, 2779*
2. μετά, *meta, 3552*
3. σύν, *syn, 5250*

Mat	18:25	together with his wife and children and all	1
Jhn	18: 3	together with police from the chief priests	1
Act	1:14	together with certain women	3
	6: 5	together with Philip, Prochorus, Nicanor, Timon	1
	18: 8	Crispus...together with all his household;	3
1Co	1: 2	together with all those who in every place	3
	16:19	together with the church in their house	3
Eph	4:31	wrangling and slander, together with all malice	3
Php	4: 3	in the work of the gospel, together with Clement	2
Rev	17:12	receive authority...together with the beast.	2

toil

1. κοπιάω, *kopiaō, 3159*
2. κόπος, *kopos, 3160*
3. μόχθος, *mochthos, 3677*

Mat	6:28	how they grow; they neither toil nor spin	1
Lke	12:27	they neither toil nor spin;	1
1Co	16:16	of everyone who works and toils with	1
2Co	11:27	in toil and hardship	2
Col	1:29	For this I toil and struggle with all the energy	1
1Th	2: 9	remember our labor and toil, brothers and sisters;	3
2Th	3: 8	with toil and labor we worked night and day	2
1Ti	4:10	For to this end we toil and struggle	1
Rev	2: 2	"I know your works, your toil and your patient	2

more tolerable

1. ἀνεκτός, *anektos, 445*

Mat	10:15	it will be more tolerable for the land of Sodom	1
	11:22	on the day of judgment it will be more tolerable	1
	11:24	on the day of judgment it will be more tolerable	1
Lke	10:12	on that day it will be more tolerable for Sodom	1

	10:14	more tolerable for Tyre and Sidon than for you	1

tolerate

1. ἀφίημι, *aphiēmi, 918*
2. βαστάζω, *bastazō, 1002*

Rev	2: 2	I know that you cannot tolerate evildoers	2
	2:20	against you: you tolerate that woman Jezebel	1

toll

1. τέλος, *telos, 5465*

Mat	17:25	From whom do kings of the earth take toll	1

tomb

1. Contextual: Not in Greek
2. μνῆμα, *mnēma, 3645*
3. μνημεῖον, *mnēmeion, 3646*
4. τάφος, *taphos, 5439*

Mat	8:28	two demoniacs coming out of the tombs met him.	3
	23:27	you are like whitewashed tombs	4
	23:29	you build the tombs of the prophets	4
	27:52	The tombs also were opened	3
	27:53	After his resurrection they came out of the tombs	3
	27:60	laid it in his own new tomb	3
	27:60	rolled a great stone to the door of the tomb	3
	27:61	sitting opposite the tomb.	4
	27:64	Therefore command the tomb to be made secure	4
	27:66	they went with the guard and made the tomb secure	4
	28: 1	the other Mary went to see the tomb.	4
	28: 8	they left the tomb quickly with fear	3
Mrk	5: 2	a man out of the tombs with an unclean spirit	3
	5: 3	He lived among the tombs;	2
	5: 5	Night and day among the tombs	2
	6:29	they came and took his body, and laid it in a tomb.	3
	15:46	laid it in a tomb	3
	15:46	rolled a stone against the door of the tomb.	3
	16: 2	when the sun had risen, they went to the tomb.	3
	16: 3	the stone for us from the entrance to the tomb?"	3
	16: 5	As they entered the tomb, they saw a young man	3
	16: 8	So they went out and fled from the tomb	3
Lke	8:27	he did not live in a house but in the tombs.	2
	11:47	For you build the tombs of the prophets	3
	11:48	they killed them, and you build their tombs.	1
	23:53	and laid it in a rock-hewn tomb	2
	23:55	The women...followed, and they saw the tomb	3
	24: 1	at early dawn, they came to the tomb	2
	24: 2	They found the stone rolled away from the tomb	3
	24: 9	returning from the tomb, they told all this	3
	24:12	Peter got up and ran to the tomb	3
	24:22	They were at the tomb early this morning	3
	24:24	Some of those who were with us went to the tomb	3
Jhn	11:17	Lazarus had already been in the tomb four days.	3
	11:31	thought that she was going to the tomb to weep	3
	11:38	Jesus, again greatly disturbed, came to the tomb.	3
	12:17	when he called Lazarus out of the tomb	3
	19:41	and in the garden there was a new tomb	3
	19:42	and the tomb was nearby	3
	20: 1	still dark, Mary Magdalene came to the tomb	3
	20: 1	the stone had been removed from the tomb.	3
	20: 2	"They have taken the Lord out of the tomb	3
	20: 3	went toward the tomb.	3
	20: 4	outran Peter and reached the tomb first.	3
	20: 6	Simon Peter came...and went into the tomb.	3
	20: 8	the other disciple, who reached the tomb first	3
	20:11	Mary stood weeping outside the tomb.	3
	20:11	she bent over to look into the tomb;	3
Act	2:29	his tomb is with us to this day.	2
	7:16	laid in the tomb that Abraham had bought	2
	13:29	took him down from the tree and laid him in a tomb.	3
Rev	11: 9	and refuse to let them be placed in a tomb;	2

tomorrow

1. αὔριον, *aurion, 892*

Mat	6:30	alive today and tomorrow is thrown into the oven	1
	6:34	"So do not worry about tomorrow	1
	6:34	for tomorrow will bring worries of its own.	1
Lke	12:28	tomorrow is thrown into the oven	1
	13:32	performing cures today and tomorrow	1
	13:33	Yet today, tomorrow, and the next day	1
Act	23:20	to bring Paul down to the council tomorrow	1
	25:22	"Tomorrow," he said, "you will hear him."	1

1Co 15:32	"Let us eat and drink, for tomorrow we die."	1
Jas 4:13	"Today or tomorrow we will go to…a town	1
4:14	Yet you do not even know what tomorrow	1

tone

1. φωνή, *phōnē, 5889*

Gal 4:20	present with you now and could change my tone	1

tongue   *See also* person of strange tongues

1. Contextual: Not in Greek
2. γλῶσσα, *glōssa, 1185*

Mrk 7:33	he spat and touched his tongue.	2
7:35	his ears were opened, his tongue was released	2
16:17	⟦they will speak in new tongues;⟧	2
Lke 1:64	his mouth was opened and his tongue freed	2
16:24	cool my tongue;	2
Act 2: 3	Divided tongues, as of fire, appeared among them,	2
2: 3	and a tongue rested on each of them.	1
2:26	my heart was glad, and my tongue rejoiced;	2
10:46	for they heard them speaking in tongues	2
19: 6	they spoke in tongues and prophesied	2
Rom 3:13	they use their tongues to deceive."	2
14:11	and every tongue shall give praise to God."	2
1Co 12:10	to another various kinds of tongues	2
12:10	to another the interpretation of tongues	2
12:28	forms of leadership, various kinds of tongues.	2
12:30	Do all speak in tongues? Do all interpret?	2
13: 1	If I speak in the tongues of mortals and of angels	2
13: 8	as for tongues, they will cease;	2
14: 2	For those who speak in a tongue do not speak	2
14: 4	Those who speak in a tongue build up themselves	2
14: 5	Now I would like all of you to speak in tongues	2
14: 5	greater than one who speaks in tongues	2
14: 6	if I come to you speaking in tongues	2
14: 9	if in a tongue you utter speech	2
14:13	who speaks in a tongue should pray for the power	2
14:14	For if I pray in a tongue, my spirit prays	2
14:18	I speak in tongues more than all of you;	2
14:19	than ten thousand words in a tongue	2
14:22	Tongues, then, are a sign not for believers	2
14:23	church comes together and all speak in tongues	2
14:26	a hymn, a lesson, a revelation, a tongue	2
14:27	If anyone speaks in a tongue	2
14:39	do not forbid speaking in tongues;	2
Php 2:11	every tongue should confess that Jesus Christ is Lord	2
Jas 1:26	If any…do not bridle their tongues	2
3: 5	So also the tongue is a small member, yet it boasts	2
3: 6	And the tongue is a fire.	2
3: 6	The tongue…among our members as a world of iniquity;	2
3: 8	no one can tame the tongue—a restless evil	2
1Pe 3:10	let them keep their tongues from evil	2
Rev 16:10	people gnawed their tongues in agony	2

tonight

1. νύξ, *nyx, 3816*

Act 23:23	to leave by nine o'clock tonight for Caesarea	1

too¹   Not Indexed

too²   *See also* have too little, have too much, too *deep* for a word, too *elated*, too *much*

1. Contextual: Not in Greek
2. παρά, *para, 4123*

2Co 11:21	To my shame, I must say, we were too weak for that!	1
Heb 11:11	even though he was too old	2

tooth

1. Contextual: Not in Greek
2. ὀδούς, *odous, 3848*

Mat 5:38	'An eye for an eye and a tooth for a tooth.'	2
5:38	'An eye for an eye and a tooth for a tooth.'	2
8:12	there will be weeping and gnashing of teeth."	2
13:42	there will be weeping and gnashing of teeth.	2
13:50	there will be weeping and gnashing of teeth.	2
22:13	there will be weeping and gnashing of teeth.'	2
24:51	there will be weeping and gnashing of teeth.	2
25:30	there will be weeping and gnashing of teeth.'	2
Mrk 9:18	he foams and grinds his teeth and becomes rigid;	2
Lke 13:28	There will be weeping and gnashing of teeth	2

Act 7:54	ground their teeth at Stephen.	2
Rev 9: 8	and their teeth like lions' teeth;	2
9: 8	and their teeth like lions' teeth;	1

top

1. ἄκρον, *akron, 216*
2. ἄνωθεν, *anōthen, 540*
3. μέγας, *megas, 3489*

Mat 27:51	torn in two, from top to bottom.	2
Mrk 5: 7	he shouted at the top of his voice	3
15:38	torn in two, from top to bottom.	2
Lke 8:28	and shouted at the top of his voice	3
Jhn 19:23	seamless, woven in one piece from the top.	2
Heb 11:21	"bowing in worship over the top of his staff."	1

topaz

1. τοπάζιον, *topazion, 5535*

Rev 21:20	the eighth beryl, the ninth topaz	1

torch

1. λαμπάς, *lampas, 3286*

Jhn 18: 3	came there with lanterns and torches	1
Rev 4: 5	in front of the throne burn seven flaming torches	1
8:10	great star fell from heaven, blazing like a torch	1

torment

1. βασανίζω, *basanizō, 989*
2. βασανισμός, *basanismos, 990*
3. βάσανος, *basanos, 992*
4. κακουχέω, *kakoucheō, 2807*
5. κακῶς, *kakōs, 2809*
6. κολαφίζω, *kolaphizō, 3139*
7. ὀχλέω, *ochleō, 4061*

Mat 8:29	Have you come here to torment us before the time?"	1
15:22	my daughter is tormented by a demon."	5
Mrk 5: 7	I adjure you by God, do not torment me."	1
Lke 8:28	I beg you, do not torment me"	1
16:23	In Hades, where he was being tormented,	3
16:28	will not also come into this place of torment.'	3
Act 5:16	those tormented by unclean spirits	7
2Co 12: 7	to torment me, to keep me from being too elated.	6
Heb 11:37	destitute, persecuted, tormented—	4
2Pe 2: 8	day after day, was tormented in his righteous soul	1
Rev 11:10	because these two prophets had been a torment	1
14:10	they will be tormented with fire and sulfur	1
14:11	smoke of their torment goes up forever and ever.	2
18: 7	give her a like measure of torment and grief.	2
18:10	they will stand far off, in fear of her torment	2
18:15	in fear of her torment, weeping and mourning	2
20:10	they will be tormented day and night forever	1

torture

1. βασανίζω, *basanizō, 989*
2. βασανισμός, *basanismos, 990*
3. βασανιστής, *basanistēs, 991*
4. ἐν + σῶμα, *en + sōma, 1877 + 5393*
5. θλῖψις, *thlipsis, 2568*
6. κακουχέω, *kakoucheō, 2807*
7. τυμπανίζω, *tympanizō, 5594*

Mat 18:34	in anger his lord handed him over to be tortured	3
24: 9	"Then they will hand you over to be tortured	5
Heb 11:35	Others were tortured, refusing to accept release	7
13: 3	Remember…those who are being tortured	6
13: 3	as though you yourselves were being tortured.	4
Rev 9: 5	were allowed to torture them for five months	1
9: 5	their torture was like the torture of a scorpion	2
9: 5	their torture was like the torture of a scorpion	2

toss

1. βάλλω, *ballō, 965*
2. ῥιπίζω, *rhipizō, 4847*

Act 22:23	their cloaks, and tossing dust into the air	1
Jas 1: 6	wave of the sea…driven and tossed by the wind;	2

toss to and fro

1. κλυδωνίζομαι, *klydōnizomai, 3115*

Eph 4:14	tossed to and fro and blown about	1

touch

1. ἀπό, *apo, 608*
2. ἅπτω, *haptō, 721*
3. θιγγάνω, *thinganō, 2566*
4. παραβάλλω, *paraballō, 4125*
5. ψηλαφάω, *psēlaphaō, 6027*

Mat	8: 3	He stretched out his hand and touched him	2
	8:15	he touched her hand, and the fever left her	2
	9:20	came up behind him and touched the fringe	2
	9:21	she said to herself, "If I only touch his cloak	2
	9:29	Then he touched their eyes and said	2
	14:36	they might touch even the fringe of his cloak;	2
	14:36	and all who touched it were healed.	2
	17: 7	Jesus came and touched them, saying	2
	20:34	Moved with compassion, Jesus touched their eyes.	2
Mrk	1:41	Jesus stretched out his hand and touched him	2
	3:10	had diseases pressed upon him to touch him.	2
	5:27	touched his cloak	2
	5:28	"If I but touch his clothes, I will be made well."	2
	5:30	"Who touched my clothes?"	2
	5:31	how can you say, 'Who touched me?' "	2
	6:56	touch even the fringe of his cloak;	2
	6:56	all who touched it were healed.	2
	7:33	he spat and touched his tongue.	2
	8:22	begged him to touch him.	2
	10:13	in order that he might touch them;	2
Lke	5:13	Jesus stretched out his hand, touched him,	2
	6:19	all in the crowd were trying to touch him	2
	7:14	he came forward and touched the bier	2
	7:39	what kind of woman this is who is touching him	2
	8:44	touched the fringe of his clothes	2
	8:45	Jesus asked, "Who touched me?"	2
	8:46	Jesus said, "Someone touched me;	2
	8:47	she declared…why she had touched him	2
	18:15	that he might touch them;	2
	22:51	he touched his ear and healed him.	2
	24:39	Touch me and see;	5
Act	19:12	aprons that had touched his skin were brought	1
	20:15	The next day we touched at Samos	4
1Co	7: 1	"It is well for a man not to touch a woman."	2
2Co	6:17	touch nothing unclean; then I will welcome you	2
Col	2:21	"Do not handle, Do not taste, Do not touch"?	3
Heb	11:28	the destroyer…would not touch the firstborn	3
	12:18	You have not come to something that can be touched	5
	12:20	"If even an animal touches the mountain	3
1Jn	1: 1	we have looked at and touched with our hands	5
	5:18	and the evil one does not touch them.	2

toward

1. Contextual: Not in Greek
2. εἰς, *eis, 1650*
3. ἐπί, *epi, 2093*
4. κατά, *kata, 2848*
5. πρός, *pros, 4639*

Mat	14:25	he came walking toward them on the sea.	5
	14:29	walking on the water, and came toward Jesus.	5
Lke	7:44	Then turning toward the woman, he said to Simon	5
	9:53	because his face was set toward Jerusalem.	2
	11:53	the Pharisees began to be very hostile toward him	1
	12:21	are not rich toward God."	2
Jhn	1:29	The next day he saw Jesus coming toward him	5
	1:47	Jesus saw Nathanael coming toward him, he said	5
	6: 5	saw a large crowd coming toward him	5
	6:21	reached the land toward which they were going.	2
	20: 3	went toward the tomb.	2
Act	1:10	he was going and they were gazing up toward heaven	2
	1:11	why do you stand looking up toward heaven?	2
	8:26	"Get up and go toward the south	4
	20:21	testified…about repentance toward God	2
	20:21	faith toward our Lord Jesus.	2
	24:16	a clear conscience toward God and all people	5
Rom	1:30	inventors of evil, rebellious toward parents	1
	11:22	severity toward those who have fallen	3
	11:22	God's kindness toward you, provided you continue	3
1Co	7:36	is not behaving properly toward his fianc,e	3
	15:10	his grace toward me has not been in vain.	2
2Co	1:12	and all the more toward you.	5
	3: 4	that we have through Christ toward God.	5
	10: 1	bold toward you when I am away!—	2
Eph	1:14	toward redemption as God's own people	2

	1:15	your love toward all the saints	2
	2: 7	in kindness toward us in Christ Jesus.	3
Php	3:14	I press on toward the goal for the prize	4
Col	4: 5	Conduct yourselves wisely toward outsiders	5
1Th	2:10	blameless our conduct was toward you believers.	1
	4:12	that you may behave properly toward outsiders	5
Phm	1: 5	your faith toward the Lord Jesus.	5
Heb	6: 1	Therefore let us go on toward perfection,	3
	6: 1	the foundation:…faith toward God	3
	8:12	For I will be merciful toward their iniquities	1

towards

1. εἰς, *eis, 1650*
2. πρός, *pros, 4639*

Mrk	6:48	he came towards them early in the morning	2
	7:31	went by way of Sidon towards the Sea of Galilee	1

towel

1. λέντιον, *lention, 3317*

Jhn	13: 4	tied a towel around himself.	1
	13: 5	to wipe them with the towel	1

tower

1. πύργος, *pyrgos, 4788*

Lke	13: 4	killed when the tower of Siloam fell on them	1
	14:28	For which of you, intending to build a tower	1

town   *See also* go from town to town

1. κωμόπολις, *kōmopolis, 3268*
2. πόλις, *polis, 4484*

Mat	2:23	he made his home in a town called Nazareth	2
	8:33	The swineherds ran off, and on going into the town	2
	8:34	Then the whole town came out to meet Jesus;	2
	9: 1	he crossed the sea and came to his own town.	2
	10: 5	and enter no town of the Samaritans	2
	10:11	Whatever town or village you enter	2
	10:14	as you leave that house or town.	2
	10:15	more tolerable…than for that town.	2
	10:23	When they persecute you in one town	2
	10:23	you will not have gone through all the towns	2
	14:13	they followed him on foot from the towns.	2
	23:34	pursue from town to town	2
	23:34	pursue from town to town	2
Mrk	1:38	"Let us go on to the neighboring towns	1
	1:45	Jesus could no longer go into a town openly	2
	6:33	they hurried there on foot from all the towns	2
Lke	1:26	to a town in Galilee called Nazareth	2
	1:39	to a Judean town in the hill country	2
	2: 3	All went to their own towns to be registered.	2
	2: 4	from the town of Nazareth in Galilee to Judea	2
	2:39	to Galilee, to their own town of Nazareth.	2
	4:29	They got up, drove him out of the town	2
	4:29	brow of the hill on which their town was built	2
	7:11	Soon afterwards he went to a town called Nain	2
	7:12	As he approached the gate of the town	2
	7:12	with her was a large crowd from the town.	2
	9: 5	as you are leaving that town shake the dust off	2
	10: 1	to every town and place	2
	10: 8	Whenever you enter a town and its people welcome	2
	10:10	whenever you enter a town	2
	10:11	'Even the dust of your town that clings to our feet	2
	10:12	more tolerable…for Sodom than for that town.	2
	13:22	Jesus went through one town and village	2
	14:21	at once into the streets and lanes of the town	2
	23:51	he came from the Jewish town of Arimathea	2
Jhn	11:54	went from there to a town called Ephraim	2
Act	5:16	gather from the towns around Jerusalem	2
	8:40	he proclaimed the good news to all the towns	2
	16: 4	As they went from town to town,	2
Tit	1: 5	appoint elders in every town, as I directed you:	2
Jas	4:13	tomorrow we will go to such and such a town	2

town after town

1. κατά + πόλις, *kata + polis, 2848 + 4484*

Lke	8: 4	people from town after town came to him	

town clerk

1. γραμματεύς, *grammateus, 1208*

Act	19:35	when the town clerk had quieted the crowd	1

trace
  1. Contextual: Not in Greek
Jas   3:17 without a trace of partiality or hypocrisy.   1

Trachonitis
  1. Τραχωνῖτις, *Trachōnitis, 5551*
Lke   3: 1 the region of Ituraea and Trachonitis   1

trade *See also* gain by trading
  1. ἐργάζομαι, *ergazomai, 2237*
  2. μέρος, *meros, 3538*
  3. περί, *peri, 4309*
  4. τέχνη, *technē, 5492*
Mat 25:16 went off at once and traded with them   1
Act   18: 3 by trade they were tentmakers.   4
     19:25 with the workers of the same trade   3
     19:27 this trade of ours may come into disrepute   2
Rev 18:17 sailors and all whose trade is on the sea   1
     18:22 an artisan of any trade will be found   4

same trade
  1. ὁμότεχνος, *homotechnos, 3937*
Act   18: 3 because he was of the same trade   1

slave trader
  1. ἀνδραποδιστής, *andrapodistēs, 435*
1Ti   1:10 fornicators, sodomites, slave traders, liars   1

tradition
  1. παράδοσις, *paradosis, 4142*
  2. παραλαμβάνω, *paralambanō, 4161*
Mat 15: 2 "Why do your disciples break the tradition   1
     15: 3 for the sake of your tradition?   1
     15: 6 for the sake of your tradition   1
Mrk   7: 3 observing the tradition of the elders;   1
     7: 4 many other traditions that they observe   2
     7: 5 according to the tradition of the elders   1
     7: 8 and hold to human tradition."   1
     7: 9 in order to keep your tradition!   1
     7:13 through your tradition that you have handed on.   1
1Co 11: 2 maintain the traditions just as I handed them on   1
Gal   1:14 zealous for the traditions of my ancestors.   1
Col   2: 8 according to human tradition   1
2Th   2:15 hold fast to the traditions that you were taught   1
     3: 6 the tradition that they received from us.   1

train
  1. γυμνάζω, *gymnazō, 1214*
  2. γυμνασία, *gymnasia, 1215*
  3. μαθητεύω, *mathēteuō, 3411*
  4. οἰκονομία, *oikonomia, 3873*
  5. παιδεία, *paideia, 4082*
  6. παιδεύω, *paideuō, 4084*
Mat 13:52 scribe...trained for the kingdom of heaven   3
1Ti   1: 4 rather than the divine training that is known by faith.   4
     4: 7 Train yourself in godliness   1
     4: 8 for, while physical training is of some value   2
2Ti   3:16 useful...for training in righteousness   5
Tit   2:12 training us to renounce impiety   6
Heb   5:14 faculties have been trained by practice   1
     12:11 those who have been trained by it.   1
2Pe   2:14 They have hearts trained in greed.   1

traitor
  1. προδότης, *prodotēs, 4595*
Lke   6:16 Judas Iscariot, who became a traitor.   1

trample
  1. καταπατέω, *katapateō, 2922*
  2. πατέω, *pateō, 4251*
Mat   7: 6 or they will trample them under foot and turn   1
Rev 11: 2 they will trample over the holy city   2

trample on
  1. καταπατέω, *katapateō, 2922*
  2. πατέω, *pateō, 4251*
Lke   8: 5 some fell on the path and was trampled on   1

     12: 1 so that they trampled on one another   1
     21:24 Jerusalem will be trampled on by the Gentiles   2

trample under foot
  1. καταπατέω, *katapateō, 2922*
Mat   5:13 thrown out and trampled under foot.   1

trance
  1. ἔκστασις, *ekstasis, 1749*
Act 10:10 while it was being prepared, he fell into a trance.   1
     11: 5 in a trance I saw a vision.   1
     22:17 praying in the temple, I fell into a trance   1

transfer
  1. μεθίστημι, *methistēmi, 3496*
  2. μεταπέμπω, *metapempō, 3569*
  3. παραδίδωμι, *paradidōmi, 4140*
Act 25: 3 to have him transferred to Jerusalem.   2
     27: 1 they transferred Paul...to a centurion   3
Col   1:13 transferred us into the kingdom of his beloved Son   1

transfigure
  1. μεταμορφόω, *metamorphoō, 3565*
Mat 17: 2 he was transfigured before them   1
Mrk   9: 2 he was transfigured before them   1

transform
  1. μεταμορφόω, *metamorphoō, 3565*
  2. μετασχηματίζω, *metaschēmatizō, 3571*
Rom 12: 2 but be transformed by the renewing of your minds   1
2Co   3:18 transformed into the same image   1
Php   3:21 He will transform the body of our humiliation   2

transgression
  1. παράβασις, *parabasis, 4126*
  2. παρανομία, *paranomia, 4175*
  3. παράπτωμα, *paraptōma, 4183*
Rom   5:14 sins were not like the transgression of Adam   1
Gal   3:19 It was added because of transgressions   1
     6: 1 friends, if anyone is detected in a transgression   3
Heb   2: 2 every transgression...received a just penalty.   1
     9:15 the transgressions under the first covenant.   1
2Pe   2:16 was rebuked for his own transgression;   2

transgressor
  1. παράβασις, *parabasis, 4126*
  2. παραβάτης, *parabatēs, 4127*
Gal   2:18 then I demonstrate that I am a transgressor.   2
1Ti   2:14 was deceived and became a transgressor.   1
Jas   2: 9 are convicted by the law as transgressors.   2
     2:11 you have become a transgressor of the law.   2

translate
  1. ἑρμηνεύω, *hermēneuō, 2257*
  2. μεθερμηνεύω, *methermēneuō, 3493*
Jhn   1:38 "Rabbi" (which translated means Teacher)   2
     1:41 the Messiah" (which is translated Anointed).   2
     1:42 be called Cephas" (which is translated Peter).   1

translation
  1. μεθερμηνεύω, *methermēneuō, 3493*
Act 13: 8 (for that is the translation of his name)   1

transparent
  1. διαυγής, *diaugēs, 1420*
Rev 21:21 street...is pure gold, transparent as glass.   ·1

trap
  1. ἀγρεύω, *agreuō, 65*
  2. ἐπιλαμβάνομαι, *epilambanomai, 2138*
  3. θήρα, *thēra, 2560*
  4. παγίς, *pagis, 4075*
Mrk 12:13 to trap him in what he said.   1
Lke 20:20 in order to trap him by what he said   2
     20:26 to trap him by what he said;   2
     21:35 like a trap. For it will come upon all   4
Rom 11: 9 "Let their table become a snare and a trap,   3
1Ti   6: 9 trapped by many senseless and harmful desires   4

travel *See also* travel *companion*

1. ἀποδημέω, *apodēmeō, 623*
2. διέρχομαι, *dierchomai, 1451*
3. ὁδεύω, *hodeuō, 3841*
4. πορεύομαι, *poreuomai, 4513*

Lke	10:33	a Samaritan while traveling came near him;	3
	15:13	and traveled to a distant country	1
Act	11:19	traveled as far as Phoenicia, Cyprus, and Antioch	2
	26:12	"With this in mind, I was traveling to Damascus	4

travel with

1. συμπορεύομαι, *symporeuomai, 5233*
2. συνέκδημος, *synekdēmos, 5292*
3. συνοδεύω, *synodeuō, 5321*

Lke	14:25	Now large crowds were traveling with him;	1
Act	9: 7	The men who were traveling with him	3
2Co	8:19	appointed by the churches to travel with us	2

traveler *See* group of travelers

treacherous

1. προδότης, *prodotēs, 4595*

2Ti	3: 4	treacherous, reckless, swollen with conceit	1

tread

1. πατέω, *pateō, 4251*

Lke	10:19	have given you authority to tread on snakes	1
Rev	14:20	the wine press was trodden outside the city	1
	19:15	will tread the wine press of the fury…of God	1

tread out grain

1. ἀλοάω, *aloaō, 262*

1Co	9: 9	not muzzle an ox while it is treading out the grain."	1
1Ti	5:18	not muzzle an ox while it is treading out the grain,"	1

treasure *See also* lay up treasure, store up treasure, treasure *chest*

1. Contextual: Not in Greek
2. διατηρέω, *diatēreō, 1413*
3. θησαυρός, *thēsauros, 2565*
4. συντηρέω, *syntēreō, 5337*

Mat	6:19	"Do not store up for yourselves treasures on earth	3
	6:20	store up for yourselves treasures in heaven	3
	6:21	For where your treasure is, there your heart will	3
	12:35	brings good things out of a good treasure	3
	12:35	brings evil things out of an evil treasure.	3
	13:44	like treasure hidden in a field	3
	13:52	master of a household who brings out of his treasure	3
	19:21	you will have treasure in heaven;	3
Mrk	10:21	you will have treasure in heaven;	3
Lke	2:19	Mary treasured all these words	4
	2:51	His mother treasured all these things in her heart.	2
	6:45	person out of the good treasure of the heart	3
	6:45	evil person out of evil treasure produces evil;	1
	12:33	an unfailing treasure in heaven	3
	12:34	where your treasure is, there your heart will be	3
	18:22	you will have treasure in heaven;	3
2Co	4: 7	we have this treasure in clay jars	3
Col	2: 3	all the treasures of wisdom and knowledge.	3
Heb	11:26	greater wealth than the treasures of Egypt	3

treasure entrusted

1. παραθήκη, *parathēkē, 4146*

2Ti	1:14	Guard the good treasure entrusted to you	1

treasurer

1. οἰκονόμος, *oikonomos, 3874*

Rom	16:23	Erastus, the city treasurer, and…greet you.	1

treasury

1. γάζα², *gaza², 1125*
2. γαζοφυλάκιον, *gazophylakion, 1126*
3. κορβανᾶς, *korbanas, 3168*

Mat	27: 6	"It is not lawful to put them into the treasury	3
Mrk	12:41	He sat down opposite the treasury	2
	12:41	the crowd putting money into the treasury.	2
	12:43	all those who are contributing to the treasury.	2
Lke	21: 1	rich people putting their gifts into the treasury;	2
Jhn	8:20	he was teaching in the treasury of the temple	2

Act	8:27	a court official…in charge of her entire treasury.	1

treat

1. Contextual: Not in Greek
2. ἀναστρέφω, *anastrephō, 418*
3. ἔχω, *echō, 2400*
4. παρέχω, *parechō, 4218*
5. ποιέω, *poieō, 4472*
6. προσφέρω, *prospherō, 4712*
7. χράομαι, *chraomai, 5968*

Mat	21:36	they treated them in the same way.	5
Lke	2:48	"Child, why have you treated us like this?	5
	15:19	treat me like one of your hired hands." '	5
Act	27: 3	Julius treated Paul kindly	7
1Co	12:23	treated with greater respect;	3
2Co	6: 8	We are treated as impostors, and yet are true;	1
Col	4: 1	Masters, treat your slaves justly and fairly	4
Heb	10:33	sometimes being partners with those so treated.	2
	12: 7	God is treating you as children;	6

treat harshly

1. πικραίνω, *pikrainō, 4393*

Col	3:19	love your wives and never treat them harshly.	1

treat with contempt

1. ἐξουδενέω, *exoudeneō, 2022*
2. ἐξουθενέω, *exoutheneō, 2024*

Mrk	9:12	many sufferings and be treated with contempt?	1
Lke	23:11	Herod…treated him with contempt	2

severe treatment

1. ἀφειδία, *apheidia, 910*

Col	2:23	humility, and severe treatment of the body	1

tree *See also* cultivated *olive* tree, fig tree, mulberry tree, olive tree, palm tree, sycamore tree, wild *olive* tree

1. δένδρον, *dendron, 1285*
2. ξύλον, *xylon, 3833*

Mat	3:10	Even now the ax is lying at the root of the trees;	1
	3:10	every tree therefore that does not bear good	1
	7:17	In the same way, every good tree bears good fruit	1
	7:17	but the bad tree bears bad fruit.	1
	7:18	A good tree cannot bear bad fruit	1
	7:18	nor can a bad tree bear good fruit.	1
	7:19	Every tree that does not bear good fruit is cut	1
	12:33	"Either make the tree good, and its fruit good;	1
	12:33	or make the tree bad, and its fruit bad;	1
	12:33	for the tree is known by its fruit.	1
	13:32	and becomes a tree	1
	21: 8	others cut branches from the trees	1
Mrk	8:24	see people, but they look like trees, walking."	1
Lke	3: 9	Even now the ax is lying at the root of the trees;	1
	3: 9	every tree…that does not bear good fruit	1
	6:43	"No good tree bears bad fruit	1
	6:43	nor again does a bad tree bear good fruit;	1
	6:44	for each tree is known by its own fruit.	1
	13:19	it grew and became a tree	1
	21:29	"Look at the fig tree and all the trees;	1
Act	5:30	whom you had killed by hanging him on a tree.	2
	10:39	They put him to death by hanging him on a tree;	2
	13:29	took him down from the tree and laid him in a tomb.	2
Gal	3:13	"Cursed is everyone who hangs on a tree"—	2
Jde	1:12	autumn trees without fruit, twice dead, uprooted;	1
Rev	2: 7	I will give permission to eat from the tree of life	2
	7: 1	blow on earth or sea or against any tree.	1
	7: 3	"Do not damage the earth or the sea or the trees	1
	8: 7	and a third of the trees were burned up	1
	9: 4	not to damage…any green growth or any tree	1
	22: 2	the tree of life with its twelve kinds of fruit	2
	22: 2	the leaves of the tree are for the healing	2
	22:14	they will have the right to the tree of life	2
	22:19	take away that person's share in the tree of life	2

tremble

1. ἔντρομος, *entromos, 1958*
2. τρέμω, *tremō, 5554*
3. τρόμος, *tromos, 5571*

Mrk	5:33	came in fear and trembling	2
Lke	8:47	she came trembling;	2

Act	7:32	Moses began to tremble and did not dare to look.	1
	16:29	he fell down trembling before Paul and Silas.	1
1Co	2: 3	in weakness and in fear and in much trembling.	3
2Co	7:15	you welcomed him with fear and trembling.	3
Eph	6: 5	obey your earthly masters with fear and trembling	3
Php	2:12	your own salvation with fear and trembling;	3
Heb	12:21	Moses said, "I tremble with fear.")	1

trespass

   1. Contextual: Not in Greek
   2. παράπτωμα, *paraptōma, 4183*

Mat	6:14	For if you forgive others their trespasses	2
	6:15	will your Father forgive your trespasses.	2
Mrk	11:25	may also forgive you your trespasses."	2
Rom	4:25	who was handed over to death for our trespasses	2
	5:15	But the free gift is not like the trespass.	2
	5:15	if the many died through the one man's trespass	2
	5:16	judgment following one trespass brought condemnation	1
	5:16	the free gift following many trespasses brings	2
	5:17	If, because of the one man's trespass, death	2
	5:18	one man's trespass led to condemnation for all	2
	5:20	with the result that the trespass multiplied;	2
2Co	5:19	not counting their trespasses against them	2
Eph	1: 7	the forgiveness of our trespasses	2
	2: 1	You were dead through the trespasses and sins	2
	2: 5	even when we were dead through our trespasses	2
Col	2:13	when you were dead in your trespasses	2
	2:13	when he forgave us all our trespasses	2

trial   *See also* bring to trial, time of trial

   1. Contextual: Not in Greek
   2. κρίνω, *krinō, 3212*
   3. πειρασμός, *peirasmos, 4280*

Lke	22:28	those who have stood by me in my trials;	3
Act	20:19	humility and with tears, enduring the trials	3
	23: 6	I am on trial concerning...the resurrection	2
Heb	12: 7	Endure trials for the sake of discipline.	1
Jas	1: 2	whenever you face trials of any kind,	3
1Pe	1: 6	you have had to suffer various trials	3
2Pe	2: 9	the Lord knows how to rescue the godly from trial	3
Rev	3:10	I will keep you from the hour of trial	3

on trial

   1. κρίνω, *krinō, 3212*

Act	24:21	I am on trial before you today.' "	1
	26: 6	now I stand here on trial on account of my hope	1

tribe   *See also* twelve tribes

   1. φυλή, *phylē, 5876*

Mat	19:28	judging the twelve tribes of Israel.	1
	24:30	then all the tribes of the earth will mourn	1
Lke	2:36	of the tribe of Asher.	1
	22:30	judging the twelve tribes of Israel.	1
Act	13:21	Saul son of Kish, a man of the tribe of Benjamin	1
Rom	11: 1	I myself am...a member of the tribe of Benjamin.	1
Php	3: 5	of the people of Israel, of the tribe of Benjamin	1
Heb	7:13	belonged to another tribe	1
	7:14	in connection with that tribe Moses said	1
Jas	1: 1	To the twelve tribes in the Dispersion:	1
Rev	1: 7	on his account all the tribes of the earth will wail.	1
	5: 5	See, the Lion of the tribe of Judah...has conquered	1
	5: 9	ransomed for God saints from every tribe and language	1
	7: 4	sealed out of every tribe of the people of Israel:	1
	7: 5	From the tribe of Judah twelve thousand sealed,	1
	7: 5	from the tribe of Reuben twelve thousand,	1
	7: 5	from the tribe of Gad twelve thousand,	1
	7: 6	from the tribe of Asher twelve thousand,	1
	7: 6	from the tribe of Naphtali twelve thousand,	1
	7: 6	from the tribe of Manasseh twelve thousand,	1
	7: 7	from the tribe of Simeon twelve thousand,	1
	7: 7	from the tribe of Levi twelve thousand,	1
	7: 7	from the tribe of Issachar twelve thousand,	1
	7: 8	from the tribe of Zebulun twelve thousand,	1
	7: 8	from the tribe of Joseph twelve thousand,	1
	7: 8	from the tribe of Benjamin twelve thousand sealed.	1
	7: 9	multitude...from every nation, from all tribes	1
	11: 9	the peoples and tribes and languages and nations	1
	13: 7	It was given authority over every tribe	1
	14: 6	to every nation and tribe and language and people.	1
	21:12	names of the twelve tribes of the Israelites;	1

tribunal

   1. βῆμα, *bēma, 1037*

Act	18:12	brought him before the tribunal.	1
	18:16	he dismissed them from the tribunal.	1
	18:17	and beat him in front of the tribunal.	1
	25: 6	the next day he took his seat on the tribunal	1
	25:10	Paul said, "I am appealing to the emperor's tribunal;	1
	25:17	but on the next day took my seat on the tribunal	1

tribune

   1. Contextual: Not in Greek
   2. χιλίαρχος, *chiliarchos, 5941*

Act	21:31	word came to the tribune of the cohort	2
	21:32	When they saw the tribune and the soldiers	2
	21:33	Then the tribune came, arrested him	2
	21:37	brought into the barracks, he said to the tribune	2
	21:37	The tribune replied, "Do you know Greek?	1
	22:24	the tribune directed	2
	22:26	he went to the tribune and said to him	2
	22:27	The tribune came and asked Paul	2
	22:28	The tribune answered, "It cost me a large sum	2
	22:29	the tribune also was afraid	2
	23:10	the tribune...ordered the soldiers to go down	2
	23:15	must notify the tribune to bring him down	2
	23:17	"Take this young man to the tribune	2
	23:18	took him, brought him to the tribune, and said	2
	23:19	The tribune took him by the hand	2
	23:22	So the tribune dismissed the young man	2
	24:22	"When Lysias the tribune comes down	2

military tribune

   1. χιλίαρχος, *chiliarchos, 5941*

Act	25:23	they entered...with the military tribunes	1

tribute

   1. κῆνσος, *kēnsos, 3056*

Mat	17:25	take toll or tribute?	1

trick

   1. ἐμπαίζω, *empaizō, 1850*

Mat	2:16	When Herod saw that he had been tricked	1

trickery

   1. δόλος, *dolos, 1515*
   2. κυβεία, *kybeia, 3235*

Eph	4:14	blown about...by people's trickery,	2
1Th	2: 3	from deceit or impure motives or trickery	1

trim

   1. κοσμέω, *kosmeō, 3175*

Mat	25: 7	trimmed their lamps.	1

triumph over

   1. θριαμβεύω, *thriambeuō, 2581*
   2. κατακαυχάομαι, *katakauchaomai, 2878*

Col	2:15	triumphing over them in it.	1
Jas	2:13	mercy triumphs over judgment.	2

triumphal   *See* lead in triumphal procession

trivial

   1. ἐλάχιστος, *elachistos, 1788*

1Co	6: 2	are you incompetent to try trivial cases?	1

Troas

   1. Τρῳάς, *Trōas, 5590*

Act	16: 8	so, passing by Mysia, they went down to Troas.	1
	16:11	We set sail from Troas	1
	20: 5	went ahead and were waiting for us in Troas;	1
	20: 6	in five days we joined them in Troas	1
2Co	2:12	When I came to Troas	1
2Ti	4:13	bring the cloak that I left with Carpus at Troas	1

troop

   1. στράτευμα, *strateuma, 5128*

Mat	22: 7	sent his troops, destroyed those murderers	1
Rev	9:16	of the troops of cavalry was two hundred million;	1

Trophimus

1. Τρόφιμος, *Trophimos, 5576*

Act 20: 4 as well as by Tychicus and Trophimus from Asia.   1
21:29 had previously seen Trophimus the Ephesian   1
2Ti   4:20 Trophimus I left ill in Miletus.   1

trouble   *See also* cause trouble

1. ἐνοχλέω, *enochleō, 1943*
2. θλῖψις, *thlipsis, 2568*
3. κακία, *kakia, 2798*
4. κόπος, *kopos, 3160*
5. κόπος + παρέχω, *kopos + parechō, 3160 + 4218*
6. παρενοχλέω, *parenochleō, 4214*
7. σκύλλω, *skyllō, 5035*
8. ταράσσω, *tarassō, 5429*

Mat   6:34 Today's trouble is enough for today.   3
13:21 and when trouble or persecution arises   2
26:10 "Why do you trouble the woman?"   5
Mrk   4:17 then, when trouble or persecution arises   2
5:35 Why trouble the teacher any further?"   7
14: 6 "Let her alone; why do you trouble her?   5
Lke   6:18 those who were troubled with unclean spirits   1
7: 6 do not trouble yourself, for I am not worthy   7
8:49 do not trouble the teacher any longer."   7
Jhn 12:27 "Now my soul is troubled. And what should I say   8
13:21 Jesus was troubled in spirit, and declared   8
14: 1 not let your hearts be troubled. Believe in God   8
14:27 Do not let your hearts be troubled   8
Act 15:19 not trouble those Gentiles who are turning to God   6
Gal   6:17 From now on, let no one make trouble for me;   4

out of trouble

1. ἀμέριμνος, *amerimnos, 291*

Mat 28:14 we will satisfy him and keep you out of trouble."   1

troublesome

1. ὀκνηρός, *oknēros, 3891*

Php   3: 1 To write the same things to you is not troublesome   1

true

1. Contextual: Not in Greek
2. ἀλήθεια, *alētheia, 237*
3. ἀληθής, *alēthēs, 239*
4. ἀληθινός, *alēthinos, 240*
5. ἄρα, *ara, 726*
6. αὐτός, *autos, 899*
7. καλῶς, *kalōs, 2822*
8. οὕτως, *houtōs, 4048*

Lke 16:11 who will entrust to you the true riches?   4
Jhn   1: 9 The true light, which enlightens everyone   4
3:21 But those who do what is true come to the light   2
3:33 certified this, that God is true.   3
4:18 What you have said is true!"   3
4:23 true worshipers will worship the Father   4
4:37 For here the saying holds true, 'One sows   4
5:31 my testimony is not true.   3
5:32 I know that his testimony to me is true.   3
6:32 my Father who gives you the true bread from heaven.   4
6:55 my flesh is true food and my blood is true drink.   3
6:55 my flesh is true food and my blood is true drink.   3
7:18 seeks the glory of him who sent him is true   3
7:28 who sent me is true, and you do not know him.   4
8:26 the one who sent me is true   3
10:41 everything that John said about this man was true."   3
15: 1 "I am the true vine   4
17: 3 they may know you, the only true God   4
19:35 His testimony is true   4
21:24 we know that his testimony is true.   3
Act 24: 9 asserting that all this was true.   8
Rom   2:28 nor is true circumcision something external   1
3: 4 Although everyone is a liar, let God be proved true   3
9: 7 of Abraham's children are his true descendants;   1
11:20 That is true. They were broken off   7
1Co 15:15 whom he did not raise if it is true   5
2Co   6: 8 We are treated as impostors, and yet are true;   3
7:14 just as everything we said to you was true   2
7:14 so our boasting to Titus has proved true   2
12:12 The signs of a true apostle were performed among you   1
Eph   4:24 in true righteousness and holiness.   2

5: 9 found in all that is good and right and true.   2
Php   1:18 whether out of false motives or true;   2
4: 8 Finally, beloved, whatever is true   3
1Th   1: 9 to serve a living and true God   4
Tit   1:13 That testimony is true.   3
Heb   8: 2 a minister in the sanctuary and the true tent   4
9:24 a mere copy of the true one   4
10: 1 not the true form of these realities   6
10:22 let us approach with a true heart   4
1Pe   5:12 to testify that this is the true grace of God.   3
2Pe   2:22 It has happened to them according to the true proverb   3
1Jn   1: 6 we lie and do not do what is true;   2
2: 8 a new commandment that is true in him and in you   3
2: 8 and the true light is already shining.   4
2:27 anointing teaches…and is true and is not a lie   3
5:20 understanding so that we may know him who is true;   4
5:20 we are in him who is true, in his Son Jesus Christ.   4
5:20 He is the true God and eternal life.   4
3Jn   1:12 and you know that our testimony is true.   4
Rev   3:14 words of the Amen, the faithful and true witness   4
6:10 "Sovereign Lord, holy and true, how long   4
15: 3 Just and true are your ways, King of the nations!   4
16: 7 Lord God…your judgments are true and just!"   4
19: 2 for his judgments are true and just;   4
19: 9 And he said to me, "These are true words of God."   4
19:11 Its rider is called Faithful and True   4
21: 5 for these words are trustworthy and true."   4
22: 6 "These words are trustworthy and true   4

true one

1. ἀληθινός, *alēthinos, 240*

Rev   3: 7 the holy one, the true one, who has the key of David   1

truly

1. Contextual: Not in Greek
2. ἀλήθεια, *alētheia, 237*
3. ἀληθῶς, *alēthōs, 242*
4. ἀμήν, *amēn, 297*
5. δέ, *de, 1254*
6. ὄντως, *ontōs, 3953*

Mat   5:18 For truly I tell you, until heaven and earth pass   4
5:26 Truly I tell you, you will never get out until you   4
6: 2 Truly I tell you, they have received their reward.   4
6: 5 Truly I tell you, they have received their reward.   4
6:16 Truly I tell you, they have received their reward   4
8:10 "Truly I tell you, in no one in Israel have I found   4
10:15 Truly I tell you, it will be more tolerable   4
10:23 for truly I tell you, you will not have gone   4
10:42 truly I tell you, none of these will lose their reward."   4
11:11 Truly I tell you, among those born of women   4
13:17 Truly I tell you   4
14:33 "Truly you are the Son of God."   3
16:28 Truly I tell you, there are some standing here   4
17:20 For truly I tell you, if you have faith   4
18: 3 said, "Truly I tell you   4
18:13 if he finds it, truly I tell you, he rejoices   4
18:18 Truly I tell you, whatever you bind on earth   4
18:19 Again, truly I tell you, if two of you agree   4
19:23 Jesus said to his disciples, "Truly I tell you   4
19:28 Jesus said to them, "Truly I tell you   4
21:21 Jesus answered them, "Truly I tell you   4
21:31 "Truly I tell you   4
23:36 Truly I tell you   4
24: 2 Truly I tell you   4
24:34 Truly I tell you   4
24:47 Truly I tell you   4
25:12 he replied, 'Truly I tell you, I do not know you.'   4
25:40 the king will answer them, 'Truly I tell you   4
25:45 Then he will answer them, 'Truly I tell you   4
26:13 Truly I tell you   4
26:21 they were eating, he said, "Truly I tell you   4
26:34 Jesus said to him, "Truly I tell you   4
27:54 "Truly this man was God's Son!"   3
Mrk   3:28 "Truly I tell you, people will be forgiven   4
8:12 Truly I tell you, no sign will be given   4
9: 1 he said to them, "Truly I tell you   4
9:41 For truly I tell you, whoever gives you a cup   4
10:15 Truly I tell you, whoever does not receive   4
10:29 Jesus said, "Truly I tell you, there is no one   4
11:23 Truly I tell you, if you say to this mountain   4

11:32	for all regarded John as truly a prophet.	6
12:32	you have truly said that 'he is one	2
12:43	said to them, "Truly I tell you	4
13:30	Truly I tell you, this generation will not pass	4
14: 9	Truly I tell you, wherever the good news	4
14:18	"Truly I tell you, one of you will betray me	4
14:25	Truly I tell you, I will never again drink	4
14:30	Jesus said to him, "Truly I tell you	4
15:39	he said, "Truly this man was God's Son!"	3

Lke	4:24	he said, "Truly I tell you	4
	9:27	truly I tell you, there are some standing here	3
	12:37	truly I tell you, he will fasten his belt	4
	12:44	Truly I tell you, he will put that one in charge	3
	18:17	Truly I tell you, whoever does not receive	4
	18:29	he said to them, "Truly I tell you,	4
	21: 3	He said, "Truly I tell you	3
	21:32	Truly I tell you, this generation will not pass	4
	23:43	He replied, "Truly I tell you	4

Jhn	1:47	"Here is truly an Israelite in whom…no deceit!"	3
	4:42	we know that this is truly the Savior	3
	8:31	you are truly my disciples;	3
Act	10:34	"I truly understand that God shows no partiality	2
Rom	9: 6	For not all Israelites truly belong to Israel	1
1Co	2:11	what human being knows what is truly human	1
	2:11	So also no one comprehends what is truly God's	1
Col	1: 6	heard it and truly comprehended the grace of God.	2
1Jn	1: 3	and truly our fellowship is with the Father	5
	2: 5	truly in this person the love of God has reached perfection.	3

very truly

1. ἀμήν + ἀμήν, *amēn + amēn, 297 + 297*

Jhn	1:51	"Very truly, I tell you, you will see heaven	1
	3: 3	Jesus answered him, "Very truly, I tell you	1
	3: 5	Jesus answered, "Very truly, I tell you	1
	3:11	"Very truly, I tell you, we speak of what we know	1
	5:19	Jesus said to them, "Very truly, I tell you	1
	5:24	Very truly, I tell you	1
	5:25	"Very truly, I tell you, the hour is coming	1
	6:26	Jesus answered them, "Very truly, I tell you	1
	6:32	Jesus said to them, "Very truly, I tell you	1
	6:47	Very truly, I tell you	1
	6:53	Jesus said to them, "Very truly, I tell you	1
	8:34	Jesus answered them, "Very truly, I tell you	1
	8:51	Very truly, I tell you, whoever keeps my word	1
	8:58	Jesus said to them, "Very truly, I tell you	1
	10: 1	"Very truly, I tell you	1
	10: 7	Jesus said to them, "Very truly, I tell you	1
	12:24	Very truly, I tell you	1
	13:16	Very truly, I tell you, servants are not greater	1
	13:20	Very truly, I tell you, whoever receives one	1
	13:21	"Very truly, I tell you, one of you will betray me."	1
	13:38	Very truly, I tell you, before the cock crows	1
	14:12	Very truly, I tell you	1
	16:20	Very truly, I tell you	1
	16:23	Very truly, I tell you	1
	21:18	Very truly, I tell you	1

trumpet *See also* blow a trumpet, sound a trumpet, sound of a trumpet, trumpet *call*

1. σάλπιγξ, *salpinx, 4894*

1Co	15:52	at the last trumpet. For the trumpet will sound	1
Heb	12:19	the sound of a trumpet	1
Rev	1:10	and I heard behind me a loud voice like a trumpet	1
	4: 1	which I had heard speaking to me like a trumpet	1
	8: 2	and seven trumpets were given to them.	1
	8: 6	Now the seven angels who had the seven trumpets	1
	8:13	woe…at the blasts of the other trumpets	1
	9:14	saying to the sixth angel who had the trumpet	1

trumpeter

1. σαλπιστής, *salpistēs, 4896*

Rev	18:22	the sound…of flutists and trumpeters	1

trust *See also* put one's trust

1. πείθω, *peithō, 4275*
2. πιστεύω, *pisteuō, 4409*
3. πιστός, *pistos, 4412*

Mat	27:43	He trusts in God; let God deliver him now	1
Lke	11:22	he takes away his armor in which he trusted	1
	18: 9	to some who trusted in themselves	1

Rom	4: 5	trusts him who justifies the ungodly	2
Php	2:24	I trust in the Lord	1
Heb	2:13	And again, "I will put my trust in him."	1
1Pe	1:21	Through him you have come to trust in God	3

trustee

1. οἰκονόμος, *oikonomos, 3874*

Gal	4: 2	they remain under guardians and trustees	1

trustworthy

1. πιστός, *pistos, 4412*

Mat	25:21	'Well done, good and trustworthy slave;	1
	25:21	you have been trustworthy in a few things	1
	25:23	'Well done, good and trustworthy slave;	1
	25:23	you have been trustworthy in a few things	1
Lke	19:17	you have been trustworthy in a very small thing	1
1Co	4: 2	that they be found trustworthy.	1
	7:25	one who by the Lord's mercy is trustworthy.	1
Tit	1: 9	have a firm grasp of the word that is trustworthy	1
Rev	21: 5	for these words are trustworthy and true."	1
	22: 6	"These words are trustworthy and true	1

truth *See also* distort truth, speak the truth, tell the truth

1. ἀλήθεια, *alētheia, 237*
2. ἀληθής, *alēthēs, 239*
3. ἀληθῶς, *alēthōs, 242*
4. ἀσφάλεια, *asphaleia, 854*

Mat	22:16	teach the way of God in accordance with truth	1
Mrk	5:33	told him the whole truth.	1
	12:14	teach the way of God in accordance with truth.	1
Lke	1: 4	so that you may know the truth	4
	4:25	the truth is, there were many widows	1
	20:21	teach the way of God in accordance with truth.	1
Jhn	1:14	of a father's only son, full of grace and truth.	1
	1:17	grace and truth came through Jesus Christ.	1
	4:23	will worship the Father in spirit and truth	1
	4:24	must worship in spirit and truth."	1
	5:33	and he testified to the truth. .	1
	8:32	you will know the truth	1
	8:32	the truth will make you free."	1
	8:40	has told you the truth that I heard from God.	1
	8:44	and does not stand in the truth	1
	8:44	because there is no truth in him.	1
	8:45	because I tell the truth, you do not believe me.	1
	8:46	If I tell the truth, why do you not believe me?	1
	14: 6	"I am the way, and the truth, and the life.	1
	14:17	This is the Spirit of truth	1
	15:26	the Spirit of truth who comes from the Father	1
	16: 7	Nevertheless I tell you the truth:	1
	16:13	When the Spirit of truth comes	1
	16:13	he will guide you into all the truth;	1
	17: 8	and know in truth that I came from you;	3
	17:17	Sanctify them in the truth; your word is truth.	1
	17:17	Sanctify them in the truth; your word is truth.	1
	17:19	so that they also may be sanctified in truth.	1
	18:37	I was born…to testify to the truth.	1
	18:37	who belongs to the truth listens to my voice."	1
	18:38	Pilate asked him, "What is truth?"	1
	19:35	he knows that he tells the truth.)	2
Act	26:25	I am speaking the sober truth.	1
Rom	1:18	those who by their wickedness suppress the truth.	1
	1:25	they exchanged the truth about God for a lie	1
	2: 2	God's judgment…is in accordance with truth	1
	2: 8	who are self-seeking and who obey not the truth	1
	2:20	in the law the embodiment of knowledge and truth	1
	9: 1	I am speaking the truth in Christ—I am not lying;	1
	15: 8	of the circumcised on behalf of the truth of God	1
1Co	5: 8	the unleavened bread of sincerity and truth.	1
	13: 6	but rejoices in the truth.	1
2Co	4: 2	by the open statement of the truth	1
	11:10	As the truth of Christ is in me	1
	12: 6	for I will be speaking the truth.	1
	13: 8	For we cannot do anything against the truth	1
	13: 8	but only for the truth.	1
Gal	2: 5	the truth of the gospel might always remain	1
	2:14	acting consistently with the truth of the gospel	1
	5: 7	who prevented you from obeying the truth?	1
Eph	1:13	you also, when you had heard the word of truth	1
	4:21	taught in him, as truth is in Jesus.	1
	4:25	let all of us speak the truth to our neighbors	1

Eph	6:14	fasten the belt of truth around your waist	1
Col	1: 5	heard of this hope...in the word of the truth	1
2Th	2:10	refused to love the truth and so be saved.	1
	2:12	so that all who have not believed the truth	1
	2:13	through belief in the truth.	1
1Ti	2: 4	to come to the knowledge of the truth.	1
	2: 7	(I am telling the truth, I am not lying)	1
	2: 7	a teacher of the Gentiles in faith and truth.	1
	3:15	the pillar and bulwark of the truth.	1
	4: 3	those who believe and know the truth.	1
	6: 5	who are depraved in mind and bereft of the truth	1
2Ti	2:15	rightly explaining the word of truth.	1
	2:18	who have swerved from the truth by claiming	1
	2:25	they will repent and come to know the truth	1
	3: 7	can never arrive at a knowledge of the truth.	1
	3: 8	these people...also oppose the truth.	1
	4: 4	will turn away from listening to the truth	1
Tit	1: 1	and the knowledge of the truth	1
	1:14	commandments of those who reject the truth.	1
Heb	10:26	after having received the knowledge of the truth	1
Jas	1:18	he gave us birth by the word of truth	1
	3:14	do not be boastful and false to the truth.	1
	5:19	if anyone among you wanders from the truth	1
1Pe	1:22	purified your souls by your obedience to the truth	1
2Pe	1:12	you know them already and are established in the truth	1
	2: 2	these teachers the way of truth will be maligned.	1
1Jn	1: 8	we deceive ourselves, and the truth is not in us.	1
	2: 4	in such a person the truth does not exist;	1
	2:21	not because you do not know the truth	1
	2:21	and you know that no lie comes from the truth.	1
	3:18	let us love, not in word...but in truth and action.	1
	3:19	by this we will know that we are from the truth	1
	4: 6	the spirit of truth and the spirit of error.	1
	5: 6	for the Spirit is the truth.	1
2Jn	1: 1	lady and her children, whom I love in the truth	1
	1: 1	and not only I but also all who know the truth	1
	1: 2	because of the truth that abides in us	1
	1: 3	from Jesus Christ...in truth and love.	1
	1: 4	to find some of your children walking in the truth	1
3Jn	1: 1	the beloved Gaius, whom I love in truth.	1
	1: 3	testified to your faithfulness to the truth	1
	1: 3	namely how you walk in the truth.	1
	1: 4	to hear that my children are walking in the truth.	1
	1: 8	so that we may become co-workers with the truth.	1
	1:12	testified favorably...so has the truth itself.	1

truthful

1. ἀλήθεια, *alētheia, 237*

2Co	6: 7	truthful speech, and the power of God;	1

truthfulness

1. ἀλήθεια, *alētheia, 237*

Rom	3: 7	if...God's truthfulness abounds to his glory	1

try¹

1. Contextual: Not in Greek
2. ἐπιχειρέω, *epicheireō, 2217*
3. ζητέω, *zēteō, 2426*
4. θέλω, *thelō, 2527*
5. πειράζω, *peirazō, 4279*
6. πειράω, *peiraō, 4281*

Mrk	9:38	tried to stop him, because he was not following us."	1
Lke	5:18	trying to bring him in and lay him before Jesus;	3
	6:19	all in the crowd were trying to touch him	3
	9: 9	he tried to see him.	3
	9:49	we tried to stop him, because he does not follow	1
	13:24	many...will try to enter and will not be able.	3
	16:16	everyone tries to enter it by force.	1
	17:33	who try to make their life secure will lose it	3
	19: 3	He was trying to see who Jesus was,	3
Jhn	7:20	Who is trying to kill you?"	3
	7:25	this the man whom they are trying to kill?	3
	7:30	they tried to arrest him	3
	8:40	now you are trying to kill me	3
	9:34	and are you trying to teach us?"	1
	10:39	they tried to arrest him again	3
	11: 8	the Jews were just now trying to stone you	3
	19:12	From then on Pilate tried to release him	3
Act	7:26	tried to reconcile them, saying	1
	13: 8	tried to turn the proconsul away	3

	16:10	we immediately tried to cross over to Macedonia	3
	18: 4	would try to convince Jews and Greeks.	1
	19:13	tried to use the name of the Lord	2
	19:33	tried to make a defense before the people.	4
	21:31	While they were trying to kill him	3
	24: 6	He even tried to profane the temple	5
	26:11	I tried to force them to blaspheme;	1
	26:21	Jews seized me in the temple and tried to kill me.	6
	27:30	the sailors tried to escape from the ship	3
	28:23	trying to convince them about Jesus	1
1Co	10:33	as I try to please everyone in everything I do	1
2Co	5:11	we try to persuade others;	1
	10: 9	as though I am trying to frighten you with my letters.	1
Gal	1:10	Or am I trying to please people?	3
	1:13	and was trying to destroy it.	1
	1:23	proclaiming the faith he once tried to destroy."	1
	6:12	try to compel you to be circumcised	1
2Pe	3: 1	in them I am trying to arouse your sincere intention	1

try²

1. Contextual: Not in Greek
2. κρίνω, *krinō, 3212*

Act	25: 9	and be tried there before me on these charges?"	2
	25:10	emperor's tribunal; this is where I should be tried.	2
	25:20	be tried there on these charges.	2
1Co	6: 2	are you incompetent to try trivial cases?	1

try out

1. δοκιμάζω, *dokimazō, 1507*

Lke	14:19	I am going to try them out;	1

try to escape

1. παραιτέομαι, *paraiteomai, 4148*

Act	25:11	I am not trying to escape death;	1

try to find out

1. δοκιμάζω, *dokimazō, 1507*

Eph	5:10	Try to find out what is pleasing to the Lord.	1

Tryphaena

1. Τρύφαινα, *Tryphaina, 5586*

Rom	16:12	workers in the Lord, Tryphaena and Tryphosa.	1

Tryphosa

1. Τρυφῶσα, *Tryphōsa, 5589*

Rom	16:12	workers in the Lord, Tryphaena and Tryphosa.	1

tunic

1. χιτών, *chitōn, 5945*

Mat	10:10	no bag for your journey, or two tunics	1
Mrk	6: 9	to wear sandals and not to put on two tunics.	1
Lke	9: 3	not even an extra tunic.	1
Jhn	19:23	They also took his tunic;	1
	19:23	now the tunic was seamless	1
Act	9:39	showing tunics and other clothing	1
Jde	1:23	hating even the tunic defiled by their bodies.	1

turmoil

1. σείω, *seiō, 4940*

Mat	21:10	the whole city was in turmoil, asking	1

turn¹

1. Contextual: Not in Greek
2. ἀπέρχομαι, *aperchomai, 599*
3. ἀποστρέφω, *apostrephō, 695*
4. ἐκτρέπω, *ektrepō, 1762*
5. ἐπιστρέφω, *epistrephō, 2188*
6. στρέφω, *strephō, 5138*

Mat	5:39	on the right cheek, turn the other also;	6
	7: 6	and turn and maul you.	6
	9:22	Jesus turned, and seeing her he said, "Take heart	6
	13:15	and turn—and I would heal them.'	5
	16:23	turned and said to Peter, "Get behind me, Satan!	6
	24:18	the one in the field must not turn back	5
Mrk	8:33	turning and looking at his disciples	5
	13:16	must not turn back to get a coat.	5
Lke	1:16	turn many of the people of Israel to the Lord	5
	1:17	to turn the hearts of parents to their children	5
	7: 9	turning to the crowd that followed him, he said	6

	7:44 Then turning toward the woman, he said to Simon	6
	9:55 he turned and rebuked them.	6
	10:23 Then turning to the disciples, Jesus said	6
	14:25 he turned and said to them	6
	17:31 likewise anyone in the field must not turn back.	5
	22:61 The Lord turned and looked at Peter.	6
	23:28 Jesus turned to them and said	6
Jhn	1:38 Jesus turned and saw them following, he said	6
	6:66 Because of this many of his disciples turned back	2
	12:40 turn—and I would heal them."	6
	20:14 said this, she turned around and saw Jesus	6
	20:16 She turned and said to him in Hebrew, "Rabbouni!"	6
	21:20 Peter turned and saw the disciple	5
Act	3:19 Repent therefore, and turn to God	5
	3:26 by turning each of you from your wicked ways."	3
	7:42 God turned away from them and handed them over	6
	9:35 saw him and turned to the Lord.	5
	9:40 turned to the body and said, "Tabitha, get up."	5
	11:21 a great number became believers and turned to the Lord.	5
	13:46 we are now turning to the Gentiles.	6
	14:15 turn from these worthless things to the living God	5
	15:19 not trouble those Gentiles who are turning to God	5
	16:18 Paul...turned and said to the spirit	5
	26:18 they may turn from darkness to light	5
	26:20 they should repent and turn to God	5
	28:27 turn—and I would heal them.'	5
2Co	3:16 when one turns to the Lord, the veil is removed.	5
Gal	1: 6 turning to a different gospel—	1
1Th	1: 9 how you turned to God from idols	5
1Ti	1: 6 deviated...and turned to meaningless talk	4
Rev	1:12 I turned to see whose voice it was that spoke to me	5
	1:12 and on turning I saw seven golden lampstands	5

turn²

1. διαδέχομαι, diadechomai, 1342
2. μέρος, meros, 3538

Act	7:45 Our ancestors in turn brought it in with Joshua	1
1Co	14:27 speaks in a tongue...and each in turn;	2

turn³

1. γίνομαι, ginomai, 1181
2. μεταστρέφω, metastrephō, 3570
3. μετατρέπω, metatrepō, 3573
4. στρέφω, strephō, 5138

Jhn	16:20 your pain will turn into joy.	1
Act	2:20 The sun shall be turned to darkness	2
Jas	4: 9 Let your laughter be turned into mourning	3
Rev	11: 6 authority over the waters to turn them into blood	4

in turn

1. καί, kai, 2779

1Co	15: 1 which you in turn received, in which also you stand	1
	15: 3 what I in turn had received:	1

turn about

1. ἐπιστρέφω, epistrephō, 2188

Mrk	5:30 Jesus turned about in the crowd and said	1

turn again

1. ἐπιστρέφω, epistrephō, 2188

Mrk	4:12 so that they may not turn again and be forgiven.' "	1

turn aside

1. ἐκκλίνω, ekklinō, 1712
2. παραβαίνω, parabainō, 4124

Act	1:25 the place...from which Judas turned aside	2
Rom	3:12 All have turned aside	1

turn away

1. ἀποστρέφω, apostrephō, 695
2. ἀφίστημι, aphistēmi, 923
3. διαστρέφω, diastrephō, 1406
4. ἐκκλίνω, ekklinō, 1712
5. ἐκτρέπω, ektrepō, 1762

Act	13: 8 to turn the proconsul away from the faith.	3
1Ti	5:15 For some have already turned away to follow Satan.	5
2Ti	1:15 all who are in Asia have turned away from me	1
	2:19 "Let everyone...turn away from wickedness."	2
	4: 4 will turn away from listening to the truth	1
Heb	3:12 evil...heart that turns away from the living God.	2

1Pe	3:11 let them turn away from evil and do good;	4

turn back

1. ἐπιστρέφω, epistrephō, 2188
2. στρέφω, strephō, 5138
3. ὑποστρέφω, hypostrephō, 5715

Lke	17: 4 turns back to you seven times and says, 'I repent,'	1
	17:15 turned back, praising God with a loud voice.	3
	22:32 when once you have turned back	1
Act	7:39 in their hearts they turned back to Egypt	2
Gal	4: 9 how can you turn back again to the weak	1
2Pe	2:21 to turn back from the holy commandment	3
	2:22 "The dog turns back to its own vomit,"	1

turn head-on

1. ἀντοφθαλμέω, antophthalmeō, 535

Act	27:15 could not be turned head-on into the wind	1

turn out

1. ἀποβαίνω, apobainō, 609
2. γίνομαι, ginomai, 1181

Php	1:19 this will turn out for my deliverance.	1
1Th	3: 4 so it turned out, as you know.	2

turn over

1. παραδίδωμι, paradidōmi, 4140
2. χαρίζομαι, charizomai, 5919

Act	25:11 no one can turn me over to them.	2
1Ti	1:20 whom I have turned over to Satan	1

turn to ashes

1. τεφρόω, tephroō, 5491

2Pe	2: 6 turning the cities of Sodom and Gomorrah to ashes	1

turn upside down

1. ἀναστατόω, anastatoō, 415

Act	17: 6 who have been turning the world upside down	1

turtledove

1. τρυγών, trygōn, 5583

Lke	2:24 "a pair of turtledoves or two young pigeons."	1

twelfth

1. δωδέκατος, dōdekatos, 1558

Rev	21:20 the eleventh jacinth, the twelfth amethyst.	1

twelve

1. δώδεκα, dōdeka, 1557

Mat	9:20 suffering from hemorrhages for twelve years	1
	10: 1 Jesus summoned his twelve disciples and gave them	1
	10: 2 These are the names of the twelve apostles:	1
	10: 5 These twelve Jesus sent out with the following	1
	11: 1 instructing his twelve disciples	1
	14:20 of the broken pieces, twelve baskets full.	1
	19:28 will also sit on twelve thrones	1
	19:28 judging the twelve tribes of Israel.	1
	20:17 he took the twelve disciples aside by themselves	1
	26:14 Then one of the twelve...Judas Iscariot	1
	26:20 he took his place with the twelve;	1
	26:47 Judas, one of the twelve, arrived,	1
	26:53 send me more than twelve legions of angels?	1
Mrk	3:14 he appointed twelve, whom he also named apostles	1
	3:16 So he appointed the twelve: Simon	1
	4:10 those who were around him along with the twelve	1
	5:25 suffering from hemorrhages for twelve years.	1
	5:42 (she was twelve years of age).	1
	6: 7 He called the twelve	1
	6:43 they took up twelve baskets	1
	8:19 They said to him, "Twelve."	1
	9:35 He sat down, called the twelve, and said	1
	10:32 took the twelve aside again and began to tell	1
	11:11 he went out to Bethany with the twelve.	1
	14:10 Then Judas Iscariot, who was one of the twelve	1
	14:17 When it was evening, he came with the twelve.	1
	14:20 He said to them, "It is one of the twelve	1
	14:43 Judas, one of the twelve, arrived;	1
Lke	2:42 when he was twelve years old	1
	6:13 called his disciples and chose twelve of them	1
	8: 1 The twelve were with him	1
	8:42 an only daughter, about twelve years old,	1

Lke	8:43	suffering from hemorrhages for twelve years;	1
	9: 1	Then Jesus called the twelve together	1
	9:12	the twelve came to him and said	1
	9:17	twelve baskets of broken pieces.	1
	18:31	took the twelve aside and said to them, "See	1
	22: 3	Judas...who was one of the twelve;	1
	22:30	judging the twelve tribes of Israel.	1
	22:47	one called Judas, one of the twelve, was leading	1
Jhn	6:13	from the fragments...they filled twelve baskets.	1
	6:67	Jesus asked the twelve	1
	6:70	"Did I not choose you, the twelve?	1
	6:71	though one of the twelve, was going to betray him.	1
	11: 9	"Are there not twelve hours of daylight?	1
	20:24	But Thomas (who was called the Twin),	1
Act	6: 2	the twelve called together the whole community	1
	7: 8	Jacob of the twelve patriarchs.	1
	19: 7	altogether there were about twelve of them.	1
	24:11	it is not more than twelve days since I went up	1
1Co	15: 5	that he appeared to Cephas, then to the twelve.	1
Jas	1: 1	To the twelve tribes in the Dispersion:	1
Rev	7: 5	From the tribe of Judah twelve thousand sealed,	1
	7: 5	from the tribe of Reuben twelve thousand,	1
	7: 5	from the tribe of Gad twelve thousand,	1
	7: 6	from the tribe of Asher twelve thousand,	1
	7: 6	from the tribe of Naphtali twelve thousand,	1
	7: 6	from the tribe of Manasseh twelve thousand,	1
	7: 7	from the tribe of Simeon twelve thousand,	1
	7: 7	from the tribe of Levi twelve thousand,	1
	7: 7	from the tribe of Issachar twelve thousand,	1
	7: 8	from the tribe of Zebulun twelve thousand,	1
	7: 8	from the tribe of Joseph twelve thousand,	1
	7: 8	from the tribe of Benjamin twelve thousand sealed.	1
	12: 1	and on her head a crown of twelve stars.	1
	21:12	It has a great, high wall with twelve gates	1
	21:12	and at the gates twelve angels	1
	21:12	names of the twelve tribes of the Israelites;	1
	21:14	And the wall of the city has twelve foundations	1
	21:14	twelve names of the twelve apostles of the Lamb.	1
	21:14	twelve names of the twelve apostles of the Lamb.	1
	21:21	And the twelve gates are twelve pearls	1
	21:21	And the twelve gates are twelve pearls	1
	22: 2	the tree of life with its twelve kinds of fruit	1

twelve tribes

1. δωδεκάφυλον, *dōdekaphylon, 1559*

Act	26: 7	a promise that our twelve tribes hope to attain	1

twenty

1. εἴκοσι, *eikosi, 1633*

Lke	14:31	who comes against him with twenty thousand?	1
Act	1:15	the crowd numbered about one hundred twenty persons)	1
	27:28	So they took soundings and found twenty fathoms;	1

twenty gallons

1. δύο + μετρητής, *dyo + metrētēs, 1545 + 3583*

Jhn	2: 6	jars...each holding twenty or thirty gallons.	1

twenty-four

1. εἴκοσι + τέσσαρες, *eikosi + tessares, 1633 + 5475*

Rev	4: 4	Around the throne are twenty-four thrones	1
	4: 4	seated on the thrones are twenty-four elders	1
	4:10	the twenty-four elders fall...and worship	1
	5: 8	the twenty-four elders fell before the Lamb	1
	11:16	the twenty-four elders who sit...before God	1
	19: 4	the twenty-four elders...fell down and worshiped	1

twenty-three

1. εἴκοσι + τρεῖς, *eikosi + treis, 1633 + 5552*

1Co	10: 8	twenty-three thousand fell in a single day.	1

twice

1. δίς, *dis, 1489*

Mrk	14:30	this very night, before the cock crows twice	1
	14:72	"Before the cock crows twice	1
Lke	18:12	I fast twice a week; I give a tenth of all	1
Jde	1:12	autumn trees without fruit, twice dead, uprooted;	1

twice as much

1. διπλοῦς, *diplous, 1487*

Mat	23:15	the new convert twice as much a child of hell	1

Twin

1. Δίδυμος, *Didymos, 1441*

Jhn	11:16	Thomas, who was called the Twin	1
	20:24	But Thomas (who was called the Twin),	1
	21: 2	Simon Peter, Thomas called the Twin	1

Twin Brothers

1. Διόσκουροι, *Dioskouroi, 1483*

Act	28:11	with the Twin Brothers as its figurehead.	1

twinkle

1. ῥιπή, *rhipē, 4846*

1Co	15:52	in a moment, in the twinkling of an eye	1

twist

1. πλέκω, *plekō, 4428*
2. στρεβλόω, *strebloō, 5137*

Mat	27:29	twisting some thorns into a crown, they put it	1
Mrk	15:17	twisting some thorns into a crown, they put it on him.	1
2Pe	3:16	which the ignorant and unstable twist	2

two *See also* saw in two

1. Contextual: Not in Greek
2. δύο, *dyo, 1545*
3. μέσος, *mesos, 3545*
4. μεταξύ, *metaxy, 3568*
5. ὅστις, *hostis, 4015*

Mat	4:18	he saw two brothers, Simon, who is called Peter	2
	4:21	went from there, he saw two other brothers	2
	6:24	"No one can serve two masters; for a slave	2
	8:28	two demoniacs coming out of the tombs met him.	2
	9:27	two blind men followed him, crying loudly	2
	10:10	no bag for your journey, or two tunics	2
	10:29	Are not two sparrows sold for a penny?	2
	14:17	"We have nothing here but five loaves and two fish."	2
	14:19	Taking the five loaves and the two fish	2
	18: 8	than to have two hands or two feet	2
	18: 8	than to have two hands or two feet	2
	18: 9	have two eyes and to be thrown into the hell of fire.	2
	18:15	point out the fault when the two of you are alone.	4
	18:16	not listened to, take one or two others along	2
	18:16	by the evidence of two or three witnesses.	2
	18:19	truly I tell you, if two of you agree on earth	2
	18:20	For where two or three are gathered in my name	2
	19: 5	and the two shall become one flesh'?	2
	19: 6	So they are no longer two, but one flesh.	2
	20:21	"Declare that these two sons of mine will sit	2
	20:24	they were angry with the two brothers.	2
	20:30	There were two blind men sitting by the roadside.	2
	21: 1	Jesus sent two disciples	2
	21:28	"What do you think? A man had two sons;	2
	21:31	Which of the two did the will of his father?"	2
	22:40	On these two commandments hang all the law	2
	24:40	Then two will be in the field;	2
	24:41	Two women will be grinding meal together;	2
	25:15	to one he gave five talents, to another two	2
	25:17	who had the two talents made two more talents.	2
	25:17	who had the two talents made two more talents.	2
	25:22	the one with the two talents also came forward	2
	25:22	'Master, you handed over to me two talents;	2
	25:22	see, I have made two more talents.'	2
	26: 2	after two days the Passover is coming	2
	26:37	took with him Peter and the two sons of Zebedee	2
	26:60	At last two came forward	2
	27:21	"Which of the two do you want me to release	2
	27:38	Then two bandits were crucified with him	2
	27:51	the curtain of the temple was torn in two	2
Mrk	6: 7	began to send them out two by two	2
	6: 7	began to send them out two by two	2
	6: 9	to wear sandals and not to put on two tunics	2
	6:38	they said, "Five, and two fish."	2
	6:41	Taking the five loaves and the two fish	2
	6:41	he divided the two fish among them all.	2
	9:43	to have two hands and to go to hell	2
	9:45	have two feet and to be thrown into hell.	2
	9:47	have two eyes and to be thrown into hell	2
	10: 8	the two shall become one flesh.'	2
	10: 8	So they are no longer two, but one flesh.	2
	11: 1	he sent two of his disciples	2

12:42	A poor widow came and put in two small copper coins	2
14: 1	It was two days before the Passover	2
14:13	he sent two of his disciples, saying to them,	2
15:27	with him they crucified two bandits	2
15:38	the curtain of the temple was torn in two	2
16:12	[he appeared in another form to two of them]	2
Lke 2:24	"a pair of turtledoves or two young pigeons."	2
3:11	"Whoever has two coats must share	2
5: 2	he saw two boats there at the shore of the lake;	2
7:18	John summoned two of his disciples	2
7:41	"A certain creditor had two debtors;	2
9:13	"We have no more than five loaves and two fish	2
9:16	taking the five loaves and the two fish	2
9:30	Suddenly they saw two men, Moses and Elijah,	2
9:32	his glory and the two men who stood with him.	2
10:35	The next day he took out two denarii	2
12: 6	Are not five sparrows sold for two pennies?	2
12:52	three against two and two against three;	2
12:52	three against two and two against three;	2
15:11	Jesus said, "There was a man who had two sons.	2
16:13	No slave can serve two masters;	2
17:34	on that night there will be two in one bed;	2
17:35	There will be two women grinding meal together;	2
18:10	"Two men went up to the temple to pray	2
19:29	he sent two of the disciples	2
21: 2	saw a poor widow put in two small copper coins.	2
22:38	They said, "Lord, look, here are two swords."	2
23:32	Two others also, who were criminals, were led away	2
23:45	the curtain of the temple was torn in two.	3
24: 4	suddenly two men in dazzling clothes stood beside	2
24:13	two of them were going to a village called Emmaus	2
Jhn 1:35	John again was standing with two of his disciples	2
1:37	The two disciples heard him say this	2
1:40	One of the two who heard John speak…was Andrew	2
4:40	and he stayed there two days.	2
4:43	the two days were over, he went from that place	2
6: 9	a boy…who has five barley loaves and two fish.	2
8:17	the testimony of two witnesses is valid.	2
11: 6	he stayed two days longer in the place	2
19:18	they crucified him, and with him two others	2
20: 4	The two were running together	2
20:12	she saw two angels in white	2
21: 2	sons of Zebedee, and two others of his disciples.	2
Act 1:10	suddenly two men in white robes stood by them.	2
1:23	they proposed two, Joseph…and Matthias.	2
1:24	Show us which one of these two you have chosen	2
7:29	Midian. There he became the father of two sons.	2
8:15	The two went down and prayed for them	5
9:38	disciples…sent two men to him with the request	2
10: 7	called two of his slaves and a devout soldier	2
12: 6	Peter, bound with two chains, was sleeping	2
12: 6	Peter…was sleeping between two soldiers	2
19:10	This continued for two years	2
19:22	he sent two of his helpers, Timothy and Erastus,	2
19:34	for about two hours all of them shouted	2
21:33	ordered him to be bound with two chains;	2
23:23	he summoned two of the centurions and said	2
1Co 6:16	it is said, "The two shall be one flesh."	2
14:27	let there be only two or at most three	2
14:29	Let two or three prophets speak	2
2Co 13: 1	by the evidence of two or three witnesses."	2
Gal 4:22	For it is written that Abraham had two sons	2
4:24	these women are two covenants.	2
Eph 2:15	create…one new humanity in place of the two	2
5:31	the two will become one flesh."	2
Php 1:23	I am hard pressed between the two:	2
1Ti 5:19	except on the evidence of two or three witnesses.	2
2Ti 3: 9	as in the case of those two men	1
Heb 6:18	so that through two unchangeable things	2
10:28	"on the testimony of two or three witnesses."	2
Rev 9:12	There are still two woes to come.	2
11: 3	I will grant my two witnesses authority to prophesy	2
11: 4	two olive trees…that stand before the Lord	2
11: 4	two lampstands that stand before the Lord	2
11:10	because these two prophets had been a torment	2
12:14	woman was given the two wings of the great eagle	2
13:11	another beast…it had two horns like a lamb	2
19:20	These two were thrown alive into the lake of fire	2

two hundred

1. διακόσιοι, *diakosioi, 1357*

Mrk 6:37	"Are we to go and buy two hundred denarii worth	1
Act 23:23	two hundred soldiers, seventy horsemen	1
23:23	seventy horsemen, and two hundred spearmen.	1
27:37	(We were in all two hundred seventy-six persons	1
Rev 11: 3	prophesy for one thousand two hundred sixty days	1
12: 6	nourished for one thousand two hundred sixty days	1

two hundred miles

1. στάδιον + χίλιοι + ἑξακόσιοι, *stadion + chilioi + hexakosioi, 5084 + 5943 + 1980*

Rev 14:20	for a distance of about two hundred miles.	1

two hundred million

1. δισμυριάς + μυριάς, *dismyrias + myrias, 1490 + 3689*

Rev 9:16	of the troops of cavalry was two hundred million;	1

two miles

1. δεκαπέντε + στάδιον, *dekapente + stadion, 1278 + 5084*

Jhn 11:18	Bethany was near Jerusalem, some two miles away	1

two thousand

1. δισχίλιοι, *dischilioi, 1493*

Mrk 5:13	herd, numbering about two thousand, rushed down	1

two years

1. διετής, *dietēs, 1453*
2. διετία, *dietia, 1454*

Mat 2:16	around Bethlehem who were two years old or under	1
Act 24:27	After two years had passed	2
28:30	He lived there two whole years at his own expense	2

two-edged

1. δίστομος, *distomos, 1492*

Heb 4:12	sharper than any two-edged sword	1
Rev 1:16	from his mouth came a sharp, two-edged sword	1
2:12	the words of him who has the sharp two-edged sword:	1

Tychicus

1. Τυχικός, *Tychikos, 5608*

Act 20: 4	as well as by Tychicus and Trophimus from Asia.	1
Eph 6:21	Tychicus will tell you everything.	1
Col 4: 7	Tychicus will tell you all the news about me;	1
2Ti 4:12	I have sent Tychicus to Ephesus.	1
Tit 3:12	When I send Artemas to you, or Tychicus	1

type

1. τύπος, *typos, 5596*

Rom 5:14	Adam, who is a type of the one who was to come.	1

Tyrannus

1. Τύραννος[1], *Tyrannos[1], 5598*

Act 19: 9	argued daily in the lecture hall of Tyrannus.	1

tyrant over

1. κατεξουσιάζω, *katexousiazō, 2980*

Mat 20:25	their great ones are tyrants over them.	1
Mrk 10:42	their great ones are tyrants over them.	1

Tyre   *See also* person of Tyre

1. Τύρος, *Tyros, 5602*

Mat 11:21	had been done in Tyre and Sidon.	1
11:22	more tolerable for Tyre and Sidon than for you.	1
15:21	and went away to the district of Tyre and Sidon.	1
Mrk 3: 8	beyond the Jordan, and the region around Tyre	1
7:24	he set out and went away to the region of Tyre.	1
7:31	Then he returned from the region of Tyre	1
Lke 6:17	Jerusalem, and the coast of Tyre and Sidon.	1
10:13	if the deeds of power…had been done in Tyre	1
10:14	more tolerable for Tyre and Sidon than for you	1
Act 21: 3	sailed to Syria and landed at Tyre	1
21: 7	When we had finished the voyage from Tyre	1

U

unable

1. μή, *mē, 3590*
2. μή + δύναμαι, *mē + dynamai, 3590 + 1538*

3. οὐ + δύναμαι, *ou + dynamai, 4024 + 1538*

Lke	1:20	you will become mute, unable to speak	2
	13:11	quite unable to stand up straight.	2
Act	13:11	be blind for a while, unable to see the sun."	1
1Co	2:14	they are unable to understand them	3
Heb	3:19	So we see that they were unable to enter	3
	4:15	is unable to sympathize with our weaknesses	2

unable to speak

1. ἄλαλος, *alalos, 228*
2. κωφός, *kōphos, 3273*

Mrk	9:17	he has a spirit that makes him unable to speak;	1
Lke	1:22	motioning to them and remained unable to speak.	2

unafraid

1. μή + φοβέομαι, *mē + phobeomai, 3590 + 5828*

Heb	11:27	unafraid of the king's anger;	1

unanimously

1. ὁμοθυμαδόν, *homothymadon, 3924*

Act	15:25	we have decided unanimously to choose	1

unapproachable

1. ἀπρόσιτος, *aprositos, 717*

1Ti	6:16	dwells in unapproachable light	1

unaware

1. ἀγνοέω, *agnoeō, 51*

1Co	10: 1	I do not want you to be unaware, brothers	1
2Co	1: 8	not want you to be unaware, brothers and sisters	1

unbearably

1. ὑπέρ + δύναμις, *hyper + dynamis, 5642 + 1539*

2Co	1: 8	we were so utterly, unbearably crushed	1

unbelief

1. ἀπιστία, *apistia, 602*

Mat	13:58	because of their unbelief.	1
Mrk	6: 6	he was amazed at their unbelief.	1
	9:24	cried out, "I believe; help my unbelief!"	1
Rom	11:20	They were broken off because of their unbelief	1
	11:23	if they do not persist in unbelief	1
1Ti	1:13	because I had acted ignorantly in unbelief	1
Heb	3:19	they were unable to enter because of unbelief.	1

unbeliever

1. ἀπειθέω, *apeitheō, 578*
2. ἄπιστος, *apistos, 603*
3. αὐτός, *autos, 899*

Rom	15:31	I may be rescued from the unbelievers in Judea	1
1Co	6: 6	before unbelievers at that?	2
	7:12	if any believer has a wife who is an unbeliever	2
	7:13	if any woman has a husband who is an unbeliever	2
	10:27	If an unbeliever invites you to a meal	2
	14:22	a sign not for believers but for unbelievers	2
	14:22	while prophecy is not for unbelievers	2
	14:23	outsiders or unbelievers enter	2
	14:24	an unbeliever or outsider who enters	2
	14:25	the secrets of the unbeliever's heart are disclosed	3
2Co	4: 4	blinded the minds of the unbelievers	2
	6:14	Do not be mismatched with unbelievers.	2
	6:15	what does a believer share with an unbeliever?	2
1Ti	5: 8	and is worse than an unbeliever.	2

unbelieving

1. ἀπειθέω, *apeitheō, 578*
2. ἀπιστία, *apistia, 602*
3. ἄπιστος, *apistos, 603*

Act	14: 2	the unbelieving Jews stirred up the Gentiles	1
1Co	7:14	For the unbelieving husband is made holy	3
	7:14	the unbelieving wife is made holy	3
	7:15	if the unbelieving partner separates,	3
Tit	1:15	to the corrupt and unbelieving nothing is pure.	3
Heb	3:12	none of you may have an evil, unbelieving heart	2

unbind

1. λύω, *lyō, 3395*

Jhn	11:44	said to them, "Unbind him, and let him go."	1

unceasing

1. ἀδιάλειπτος, *adialeiptos, 89*

Rom	9: 2	great sorrow and unceasing anguish in my heart.	1

uncertain

1. ἀπορέω, *aporeō, 679*

Jhn	13:22	uncertain of whom he was speaking.	1

uncertainty

1. ἀδηλότης, *adēlotēs, 84*

1Ti	6:17	to set their hopes on the uncertainty of riches	1

unchangeable

1. ἀμετάθετος, *ametathetos, 292*

Heb	6:17	the unchangeable character of his purpose	1
	6:18	so that through two unchangeable things	1

unchastity

1. πορνεία, *porneia, 4518*

Mat	5:32	his wife, except on the ground of unchastity	1
	19: 9	divorces his wife, except for unchastity	1

uncircumcised

1. ἀκροβυστία, *akrobystia, 213*
2. ἀπερίτμητος, *aperitmētos, 598*

Act	7:51	uncircumcised in heart and ears	2
	11: 3	saying, "Why did you go to uncircumcised men	1
Rom	2:26	if those who are uncircumcised keep the…law	1
	2:27	Then those who are physically uncircumcised	1
	3:30	and the uncircumcised through that same faith.	1
	4: 9	blessedness…also on the uncircumcised?	1
	4:11	had by faith while he was still uncircumcised.	1
1Co	7:18	Was anyone at the time of his call uncircumcised?	1
Gal	2: 7	entrusted with the gospel for the uncircumcised	1
Col	3:11	circumcised and uncircumcised, barbarian	1

uncircumcision

1. ἀκροβυστία, *akrobystia, 213*

Rom	2:25	your circumcision has become uncircumcision.	1
	2:26	uncircumcision be regarded as circumcision?	1
1Co	7:19	Circumcision…and uncircumcision is nothing;	1
Gal	5: 6	neither circumcision nor uncircumcision	1
	6:15	nor uncircumcision is anything; but a new creation	1
Eph	2:11	Gentiles by birth, called "the uncircumcision"	1
Col	2:13	the uncircumcision of your flesh	1

unclean

1. Contextual: Not in Greek
2. ἀκάθαρτος, *akathartos, 176*
3. κοινός, *koinos, 3123*

Mat	10: 1	and gave them authority over unclean spirits	2
	12:43	"When the unclean spirit has gone out of a person	2
Mrk	1:23	in their synagogue a man with an unclean spirit	2
	1:26	the unclean spirit, convulsing him and crying	2
	1:27	He commands even the unclean spirits	2
	3:11	Whenever the unclean spirits saw him	2
	3:30	for they had said, "He has an unclean spirit."	2
	5: 2	a man out of the tombs with an unclean spirit	2
	5: 8	"Come out of the man, you unclean spirit!"	2
	5:12	unclean spirits begged him, "Send us into the swine;	1
	5:13	unclean spirits came out and entered the swine;	2
	6: 7	gave them authority over the unclean spirits.	2
	7:25	woman whose little daughter had an unclean spirit	2
	9:25	he rebuked the unclean spirit, saying to it	2
Lke	4:33	a man who had the spirit of an unclean demon	2
	4:36	commands the unclean spirits, and out they come!"	2
	6:18	those who were troubled with unclean spirits	2
	8:29	commanded the unclean spirit to come out	2
	9:42	But Jesus rebuked the unclean spirit	2
	11:24	the unclean spirit has gone out of a person	2
Act	5:16	those tormented by unclean spirits	2
	8: 7	for unclean spirits…came out of many	2
	10:14	never eaten anything that is profane or unclean."	2
	10:28	I should not call anyone profane or unclean	2
	11: 8	nothing…unclean has ever entered my mouth.'	2
Rom	14:14	persuaded…that nothing is unclean in itself;	3
	14:14	it is unclean for anyone who thinks it unclean.	3
	14:14	it is unclean for anyone who thinks it unclean.	3
1Co	7:14	Otherwise, your children would be unclean	2

2Co 6:17 touch nothing unclean; then I will welcome you   2
Rev 21:27 But nothing unclean will enter it   3

unclothed
1. ἐκδύω, *ekdyō, 1694*

2Co 5: 4 we wish not to be unclothed   1

uncondemned
1. ἀκατάκριτος, *akatakritos, 185*

Act 16:37 "They have beaten us in public, uncondemned   1
    22:25 flog a Roman citizen who is uncondemned?"   1

uncover
1. ἀποκαλύπτω, *apokalyptō, 636*

Mat 10:26 nothing is covered up that will not be uncovered   1
Lke 12: 2 Nothing is covered up that will not be uncovered   1

undefiled
1. ἀμίαντος, *amiantos, 299*

Heb 7:26 such a high priest, holy, blameless, undefiled   1
    13: 4 let the marriage bed be kept undefiled;   1
Jas 1:27 Religion that is pure and undefiled before God   1
1Pe 1: 4 an inheritance that is...undefiled   1

under
See also keep under guard, put under, put under oath, run under the lee, sail under the lee, trample under foot, under *construction*, under *control*, under *guard*, under *law*, under *power*, under *punishment*, under *stress*, under the *earth*, under the *leadership*

1. εἰς, *eis, 1650*
2. ἐκ, *ek, 1666*
3. ἐν, *en, 1877*
4. ἐπί, *epi, 2093*
5. ἔχω, *echō, 2400*
6. κατά, *kata, 2848*
7. κατωτέρω, *katōterō, 3006*
8. ὑπό, *hypo, 5679*
9. ὑποκάτω, *hypokatō, 5691*

Mat 2:16 around Bethlehem who were two years old or under   7
     5:15 lighting a lamp puts it under the bushel basket   8
     7: 6 or they will trample them under foot and turn   3
     8: 8 I am not worthy to have you come under my roof;   8
     8: 9 a man under authority, with soldiers under me;   8
     8: 9 a man under authority, with soldiers under me;   8
    22:44 until I put your enemies under your feet" '?   9
    23:37 as a hen gathers her brood under her wings   8
Mrk 4:21 lamp brought in to be put under the bushel basket   8
     4:21 or under the bed, and not on the lampstand?   8
     5:26 She had endured much under many physicians   8
     7:28 "Sir, even the dogs under the table eat   9
    12:36 until I put your enemies under your feet." '   9
Lke 2:27 to do for him what was customary under the law   6
     7: 6 am not worthy to have you come under my roof;   8
     7: 8 I also am a man set under authority   8
     7: 8 set under authority, with soldiers under me;   8
     8:16 puts it under a bed   9
    13:34 as a hen gathers her brood under her wings   8
    23: 7 that he was under Herod's jurisdiction   2
    23:40 you are under the same sentence of condemnation?   3
Jhn 1:48 "I saw you under the fig tree   8
     1:50 I told you that I saw you under the fig tree?   9
     5:24 and does not come under judgment   1
Act 2: 5 devout Jews from every nation under heaven   8
     4:12 no other name under heaven given among mortals   8
    18:18 he had his hair cut, for he was under a vow.   5
    21:23 We have four men who are under a vow.   4
Rom 2:12 and all who have sinned under the law   3
     3:13 "The venom of vipers is under their lips."   8
     3:19 the law...speaks to those who are under the law   3
     6:14 since you are not under law but under grace.   8
     6:14 since you are not under law but under grace.   8
     6:15 Should we sin because we are not under law   8
     6:15 because we are not under law but under grace?   8
     7:14 I am of the flesh, sold into slavery under sin.   8
    16:20 God...will shortly crush Satan under your feet.   8
1Co 7:37 stands firm...being under no necessity   5
     9:20 To those under the law I became as one under the law 8
     9:20 To those under the law I became as one under the law 8
     9:20 (though I myself am not under the law)   8

     9:20 so that I might win those under the law.   8
    10: 1 our ancestors were all under the cloud   8
    15:25 until he has put all his enemies under his feet.   8
    15:27 all things in subjection under his feet."   8
2Co 9: 7 not reluctantly or under compulsion   2
Gal 3:10 rely on the works of the law are under a curse;   8
     3:23 we were imprisoned and guarded under the law   8
     4: 2 they remain under guardians and trustees   8
     4: 4 born of a woman, born under the law   8
     4: 5 in order to redeem those who were under the law   8
Eph 1:22 he has put all things under his feet   8
Php 3: 6 as to righteousness under the law, blameless.   3
Col 1:23 been proclaimed to every creature under heaven.   8
1Ti 6: 1 all who are under the yoke of slavery   8
Heb 2: 8 subjecting all things under their feet."   9
     7:11 for the people received the law under this priesthood 4
     9:15 the transgressions under the first covenant.   4
     9:22 under the law almost everything is purified   6
Jas 5:12 so that you may not fall under condemnation.   8
1Pe 5: 6 Humble yourselves...under the mighty hand of God   8
Rev 5: 3 no one in heaven or on earth or under the earth   9
     5:13 every creature...under the earth and in the sea   9
     6: 9 I saw under the altar the souls of those   9
    12: 1 clothed with the sun, with the moon under her feet 9

undergird
1. ὑποζώννυμι, *hypozōnnymi, 5690*

Act 27:17 they took measures to undergird the ship;   1

undergo
1. ἐπιτελέω, *epiteleō, 2200*
2. ὑπέχω, *hypechō, 5674*

1Pe 5: 9 are undergoing the same kinds of suffering.   1
Jde 1: 7 serve as an example by undergoing a punishment   2

undergo suffering
1. πάσχω, *paschō, 4248*

Mat 16:21 must go to Jerusalem and undergo great suffering   1
Mrk 8:31 the Son of Man must undergo great suffering,   1
Lke 9:22 "The Son of Man must undergo great suffering,   1

understand
See also fail to understand, hard to understand, want to understand

1. Contextual: Not in Greek
2. ἀκούω, *akouō, 201*
3. γινώσκω, *ginōskō, 1182*
4. ἐπιγινώσκω, *epiginōskō, 2105*
5. ἐπίσταμαι, *epistamai, 2179*
6. καταλαμβάνω, *katalambanō, 2898*
7. λογίζομαι, *logizomai, 3357*
8. νοέω, *noeō, 3783*
9. οἶδα, *oida, 3857*
10. οὐ + ἀγνοέω, *ou + agnoeō, 4024 + 51*
11. συνίημι, *syniēmi, 5317*

Mat 13:13 hearing they do not listen, nor do they understand.' 11
    13:14 'You will indeed listen, but never understand   11
    13:15 and understand with their heart   11
    13:19 and does not understand it   11
    13:23 hears the word and understands it   11
    13:51 "Have you understood all this?"   11
    15:10 "Listen and understand: 11
    16:12 Then they understood   11
    17:13 Then the disciples understood   11
    24:15 (let the reader understand)   8
    24:43 understand this: if the owner of the house had known 3
Mrk 4:12 and may indeed listen, but not understand;   11
     4:13 "Do you not understand this parable?   9
     4:13 Then how will you understand all the parables?   3
     6:52 for they did not understand about the loaves   11
     7:14 "Listen to me, all of you, and understand.   11
     8:17 Do you still not perceive or understand?   11
     8:21 he said to them, "Do you not yet understand?"   11
    13:14 (let the reader understand)   8
    14:68 "I do not know or understand what you are talking   5
Lke 2:50 they did not understand what he said to them   11
     8:10 listening they may not understand.'   11
    18:34 they understood nothing about all these things;   11
    24:45 to understand the scriptures   11
Jhn 3:10 a teacher...yet you do not understand these things? 3

Jhn   8:27   They did not understand   3
     8:43   Why do you not understand what I say?   3
     10: 6   they did not understand what he was saying   3
     10:38   so that you may know and understand   3
     11:50   You do not understand that it is better   7
     12:16   disciples did not understand these things at first;   3
     12:40   understand with their heart   8
     13: 7   later you will understand."   3
     20: 9   for as yet they did not understand the scripture   9
Act   7:25   He supposed that his kinsfolk would understand   11
     7:25   they did not understand.   11
     8:30   asked, "Do you understand what you are reading?"   3
     10:34   "I truly understand that God shows no partiality   6
     13:27   or understand the words of the prophets   1
     28:26   You will indeed listen, but never understand   11
     28:27   understand with their heart   11
Rom   1:20   understood and seen through the things   8
     7:15   I do not understand my own actions.   3
     10:19   Again I ask, did Israel not understand?   3
     11:25   and sisters, I want you to understand this mystery: 10
     15:21   who have never heard of him shall understand."   11
1Co   2: 8   None of the rulers of this age understood this;   3
     2:12   understand the gifts bestowed on us by God.   9
     2:14   they are unable to understand them   3
     11: 3   I want you to understand   9
     13: 2   and understand all mysteries and all knowledge   9
     14: 2   for nobody understands them,   2
2Co   1:13   what you can read and also understand;   4
     1:13   I hope you will understand until the end   4
     1:14   as you have already understood us in part   4
     10:11   Let such people understand   7
Eph   5:17   but understand what the will of the Lord is.   11
1Ti   1: 7   without understanding either what they are saying   8
     1: 9   This means understanding that the law   9
     6: 4   is conceited, understanding nothing   5
2Ti   3: 1   You must understand this, that in the last days   3
Heb   11: 3   By faith we understand…   8
Jas   1:19   You must understand this, my beloved: 9
2Pe   1:20   First of all you must understand this   3
     3: 3   First of all you must understand this   3
Jde   1:10   people slander whatever they do not understand   9

not understand

   1. ἀγνοέω, *agnoeō, 51*

Mrk   9:32   they did not understand what he was saying   1
Lke   9:45   they did not understand this saying;   1
2Pe   2:12   They slander what they do not understand   1

understanding

   1. ἀκοή, *akoē, 198*
   2. διάνοια, *dianoia, 1379*
   3. ἐπιστήμων, *epistēmōn, 2184*
   4. νοῦς, *nous, 3808*
   5. σύνεσις, *synesis, 5304*
   6. συνίημι, *syniēmi, 5317*

Mrk   12:33   and 'to love him…with all the understanding   5
Lke   2:47   who heard him were amazed at his understanding   5
Rom   3:11   there is no one who has understanding   6
Eph   3: 4   perceive my understanding of the mystery of Christ.   5
     4:18   They are darkened in their understanding   2
Php   4: 7   the peace of God, which surpasses all understanding   4
Col   1: 9   in all spiritual wisdom and understanding   5
     2: 2   may have all the riches of assured understanding   5
2Ti   2: 7   the Lord will give you understanding   5
Heb   5:11   since you have become dull in understanding.   1
Jas   3:13   Who is wise and understanding among you?   3
1Jn   5:20   the Son of God…has given us understanding   2
Rev   13:18   let anyone with understanding calculate the number   4

without understanding

   1. ἀσύνετος, *asynetos, 852*

Mat   15:16   "Are you also still without understanding?   1

undertake

   1. ἐπιχειρέω, *epicheireō, 2217*

Lke   1: 1   many have undertaken to set down an orderly account   1

undertaking

   1. ἔργον, *ergon, 2240*
   2. ὑπόστασις, *hypostasis, 5712*

Act   5:38   if this plan or this undertaking is of human origin   1
2Co   9: 4   we would be humiliated…in this undertaking   2

generous undertaking

   1. χάρις, *charis, 5921*

2Co   8: 6   also complete this generous undertaking among you.   1
     8: 7   so we want you to excel also in this generous undertaking.   1
     8:19   while we are administering this generous undertaking   1

undying

   1. ἀφθαρσία, *aphtharsia, 914*

Eph   6:24   an undying love for our Lord Jesus Christ.   1

uneducated

   1. ἀγράμματος, *agrammatos, 63*

Act   4:13   realized that they were uneducated and ordinary men   1

unexpected

   1. οὐ + δοκέω, *ou + dokeō, 4024 + 1506*

Mat   24:44   Son of Man is coming at an unexpected hour.   1
Lke   12:40   the Son of Man is coming at an unexpected hour."   1

unexpectedly

   1. αἰφνίδιος, *aiphnidios, 167*

Lke   21:34   and that day does not catch you unexpectedly   1

unfading

   1. ἀμάραντος, *amarantos, 278*

1Pe   1: 4   an inheritance that is…unfading   1

unfailing

   1. ἀνέκλειπτος, *anekleiptos, 444*

Lke   12:33   an unfailing treasure in heaven   1

unfaithful

   1. ἀπιστέω, *apisteō, 601*
   2. ἄπιστος, *apistos, 603*

Lke   12:46   and put him with the unfaithful.   2
Rom   3: 3   What if some were unfaithful?   1

unfasten

   1. ἀνίημι, *aniēmi, 479*

Act   16:26   everyone's chains were unfastened.   1

unfavorable   *See* unfavorable *time*

unfit

   1. ἀδόκιμος, *adokimos, 99*
   2. οὐ + ἱκανός, *ou + hikanos, 4024 + 2653*

1Co   15: 9   unfit to be called an apostle   2
Tit   1:16   detestable, disobedient, unfit for any good work.   1

unfruitful

   1. ἄκαρπος, *akarpos, 182*

Eph   5:11   Take no part in the unfruitful works of darkness   1
2Pe   1: 8   keep you from being ineffective and unfruitful   1

ungodliness

   1. ἀσέβεια, *asebeia, 813*

Rom   1:18   against all ungodliness and wickedness of those   1
     11:26   he will banish ungodliness from Jacob."   1
Jde   1:15   to convict…of all the deeds of ungodliness   1

ungodly   *See also* commit in an ungodly way

   1. ἀσέβεια, *asebeia, 813*
   2. ἀσεβής, *asebēs, 815*

Rom   4: 5   trusts him who justifies the ungodly   2
     5: 6   at the right time Christ died for the ungodly.   2
1Pe   4:18   what will become of the ungodly and the sinners?"   2
2Pe   2: 5   he brought a flood on a world of the ungodly;   2
     2: 6   an example of what is coming to the ungodly;   2
Jde   1: 4   ungodly, who pervert the grace of our God   2
     1:15   harsh things that ungodly sinners have spoken   2
     1:18   scoffers, indulging their own ungodly lusts."   1

ungrateful

   1. ἀχάριστος, *acharistos, 940*

Lke   6:35   he is kind to the ungrateful and the wicked.   1

2Ti 3: 2 disobedient to their parents, ungrateful, unholy 1

ungrudgingly
1. μή + ὀνειδίζω, *mē + oneidizō, 3590 + 3943*
Jas 1: 5 ask God, who gives to all…ungrudgingly 1

unhealthy
1. πονηρός, *ponēros, 4505*
Mat 6:23 your eye is unhealthy, your whole body will be full 1

unhindered
1. ἀπερισπάστως, *aperispastōs, 597*
1Co 7:35 unhindered devotion to the Lord. 1

unholy
1. ἀνόσιος, *anosios, 495*
1Ti 1: 9 law is laid down…for the unholy and profane 1
2Ti 3: 2 disobedient to their parents, ungrateful, unholy 1

uninformed
1. ἀγνοέω, *agnoeō, 51*
1Co 12: 1 I do not want you to be uninformed. 1
1Th 4:13 we do not want you to be uninformed, 1

unintentionally *See* sin committed unintentionally

unison
1. εἷς + φωνή, *heis + phōnē, 1651 + 5889*
Act 19:34 all of them shouted in unison 1

unite
1. Contextual: Not in Greek
2. εἷς + γνώμη, *heis + gnōmē, 1651 + 1191*
3. καταρτίζω, *katartizō, 2936*
4. κολλάω, *kollaō, 3140*
5. ὁμοθυμαδόν, *homothymadon, 3924*
6. συγκεράννυμι, *synkerannymi, 5166*
7. συμβιβάζω, *symbibazō, 5204*
8. σύμφυτος, *symphytos, 5242*
Act 18:12 the Jews made a united attack on Paul 5
Rom 6: 5 if we have been united with him in a death 8
    6: 5 be united with him in a resurrection like his. 1
1Co 1:10 that you be united in the same mind 3
    6:16 whoever is united to a prostitute becomes one 4
    6:17 anyone united to the Lord becomes one spirit 4
Col 2: 2 hearts to be encouraged and united in love, 7
Heb 4: 2 they were not united by faith with those who listened. 6
Rev 17:13 These are united in yielding their power 2

unity
1. ἑνότης, *henotēs, 1942*
Eph 4: 3 every effort to maintain the unity of the Spirit 1
    4:13 until all of us come to the unity of the faith 1

unity of spirit
1. ὁμόφρων, *homophrōn, 3939*
1Pe 3: 8 Finally, all of you, have unity of spirit, sympathy 1

universal
1. πᾶς, *pas, 4246*
Act 3:21 until the time of universal restoration 1

universe
1. κόσμος, *kosmos, 3180*
Col 2: 8 the elemental spirits of the universe 1
    2:20 died to the elemental spirits of the universe 1

unjust
1. ἀδικία, *adikia, 94*
2. ἄδικος, *adikos, 96*
Lke 18: 6 "Listen to what the unjust judge says.
Rom 3: 5 That God is unjust to inflict wrath on us? 2
Heb 6:10 For God is not unjust; he will not overlook your work 2

unjustly
1. ἀδίκως, *adikōs, 97*
1Pe 2:19 you endure pain while suffering unjustly. 1

unknown
1. ἀγνοέω, *agnoeō, 51*
2. ἄγνωστος, *agnōstos, 58*
Act 17:23 'To an unknown god.' 2
    17:23 What therefore you worship as unknown 1
2Co 6: 9 as unknown, and yet are well known; 1
Gal 1:22 I was still unknown by sight 1

unlawful
1. ἀθέμιτος, *athemitos, 116*
Act 10:28 "You yourselves know that it is unlawful for a Jew 1

unleavened *See also* festival of unleavened bread, unleavened *bread*
1. ἄζυμος, *azymos, 109*
1Co 5: 7 as you really are unleavened. 1

unless
1. ἐάν, *ean, 1569*
2. ἐάν + μή, *ean + mē, 1569 + 3590*
3. εἰ + μή, *ei + mē, 1623 + 3590*
4. εἰ + μήτι, *ei + mēti, 1623 + 3614*
5. ἐκτός + εἰ + μή, *ektos + ei + mē, 1760 + 1623 + 3590*
6. ἤ, *ē, 2445*
Mat 5:20 For I tell you, unless your righteousness 2
    18: 3 unless you change and become like children 2
    26:42 if this cannot pass unless I drink it 2
Mrk 7: 3 do not eat unless they thoroughly wash their hands 2
    7: 4 eat anything from the market unless they wash it 2
Lke 9:13 unless we are to go and buy food 4
    13: 3 unless you repent, you will all perish as 2
    13: 5 unless you repent, you will all perish just as 2
Jhn 4:48 "Unless you see signs and wonders 2
    6:44 unless drawn by the Father who sent me; 2
    6:53 unless you eat the flesh of the Son of Man 2
    6:65 unless it is granted by the Father." 2
    8:24 unless you believe that I am he." 2
    12:24 unless a grain of wheat falls into the earth 2
    13: 8 "Unless I wash you, you have no share with me." 2
    15: 4 unless it abides in the vine 2
    15: 4 neither can you unless you abide in me. 2
    19:11 unless it had been given you from above; 3
    20:25 "Unless I see the mark of the nails in his hands 2
Act 8:31 He replied, "How can I, unless someone guides me?" 2
    15: 1 "Unless you are circumcised 2
    24:21 unless it was this one sentence that I called out 6
    27:31 "Unless these men stay in the ship 2
Rom 10:15 how are they to proclaim him unless they are sent? 2
1Co 14: 5 unless someone interprets, so that the church 5
    14: 6 unless I speak to you in some revelation or knowledge 2
    15: 2 unless you have come to believe in vain. 5
    15:36 What you sow does not come to life unless it dies. 2
2Th 2: 3 unless the rebellion comes first 1
Rev 2: 5 and remove your lampstand…unless you repent. 2
    2:22 unless they repent of her doings; 2

unless indeed
1. εἰ + μήτι, *ei + mēti, 1623 + 3614*
2Co 13: 5 unless, indeed, you fail to meet the test! 1

unlike
1. ὥσπερ, *hōsper, 6061*
Heb 7:27 Unlike the other high priests, he has no need 1

unload
1. ἀποφορτίζομαι, *apophortizomai, 711*
Act 21: 3 the ship was to unload its cargo there. 1

unmarked
1. ἄδηλος, *adēlos, 83*
Lke 11:44 Woe to you! For you are like unmarked graves 1

unmarried
1. Contextual: Not in Greek
2. ἄγαμος, *agamos, 23*
3. παρθένος, *parthenos, 4221*
Act 21: 9 four unmarried daughters who had the gift of prophecy. 3
1Co 7: 8 To the unmarried and the widows I say 2

1Co 7: 8 it is well for them to remain unmarried as I am.   1
       7:11 if she does separate, let her remain unmarried   2

unmarried man

1. ἄγαμος, *agamos, 23*

1Co 7:32 The unmarried man is anxious about the affairs   1

unmarried woman

1. ἄγαμος, *agamos, 23*

1Co 7:34 the unmarried woman and the virgin are anxious   1

unmixed

1. ἄκρατος, *akratos, 204*

Rev 14:10 poured unmixed into the cup of his anger   1

unnatural

1. ἕτερος, *heteros, 2283*
2. παρά + φύσις, *para + physis, 4123 + 5882*

Rom 1:26 exchanged natural intercourse for unnatural   2
Jde   1: 7 indulged in sexual immorality and pursued unnatural lust   1

unproductive

1. ἄκαρπος, *akarpos, 182*

1Co 14:14 my spirit prays but my mind is unproductive.   1
Tit   3:14 so that they may not be unproductive.   1

unprofitable

1. ἀνωφελής, *anōphelēs, 543*

Tit   3: 9 for they are unprofitable and worthless.   1

unquenchable

1. ἄσβεστος, *asbestos, 812*

Mat 3:12 the chaff he will burn with unquenchable fire."   1
Mrk 9:43 to go to hell, to the unquenchable fire.   1
Lke   3:17 the chaff he will burn with unquenchable fire."   1

unreasonable

1. ἄλογος, *alogos, 263*

Act 25:27 seems to me unreasonable to send a prisoner   1

unrighteous

1. ἄδικος, *adikos, 96*

Mat 5:45 sends rain on the righteous and on the unrighteous.   1
Act 24:15 resurrection of both the righteous and the unrighteous.   1
1Co 6: 1 you dare to take it to court before the unrighteous   1
1Pe 3:18 the righteous for the unrighteous   1
2Pe 2: 9 and to keep the unrighteous under punishment   1

unrighteousness

1. ἀδικία, *adikia, 94*

2Th 2:12 took pleasure in unrighteousness   1
1Jn 1: 9 and cleanse us from all unrighteousness.   1

unroll

1. ἀναπτύσσω, *anaptyssō, 408*

Lke   4:17 He unrolled the scroll   1

unsearchable

1. ἀνεξεραύνητος, *anexeraunētos, 451*

Rom 11:33 How unsearchable are his judgments   1

as yet unseen

1. μηδέπω + βλέπω, *mēdepō + blepō, 3596 + 1063*

Heb 11: 7 warned by God about events as yet unseen   1

unsettle

1. ἀνασκευάζω, *anaskeuazō, 412*
2. ἀναστατόω, *anastatoō, 415*

Act 15:24 to disturb you and have unsettled your minds   1
Gal   5:12 who unsettle you would castrate themselves!   2

unshaken

1. βέβαιος, *bebaios, 1010*

2Co 1: 7 Our hope for you is unshaken;   1

unshrunk

1. ἄγναφος, *agnaphos, 47*

Mat 9:16 No one sews a piece of unshrunk cloth on   1

Mrk 2:21 sews a piece of unshrunk cloth on an old cloak;   1

unskilled

1. ἄπειρος, *apeiros, 586*

Heb 5:13 is unskilled in the word of righteousness.   1

unsold

1. Contextual: Not in Greek

Act 5: 4 While it remained unsold   1

unspiritual

1. ψυχικός, *psychikos, 6035*

1Co 2:14 Those who are unspiritual do not receive the gifts   1
Jas   3:15 wisdom...is earthly, unspiritual, devilish.   1

unstable

1. ἀκατάστατος, *akatastatos, 190*
2. ἀστήρικτος, *astēriktos, 844*

Jas   1: 7 being double-minded and unstable in every way,   1
2Pe 3:16 which the ignorant and unstable twist   2

unstained

1. ἄσπιλος, *aspilos, 834*

Jas   1:27 to keep oneself unstained by the world.   1

unsteady

1. ἀστήρικτος, *astēriktos, 844*

2Pe 2:14 They entice unsteady souls.   1

untie

1. λύω, *lyō, 3395*

Mat 21: 2 untie them and bring them to me.   1
Mrk 1: 7 I am not worthy to stoop down and untie   1
     11: 2 untie it and bring it.   1
     11: 4 they were untying it   1
     11: 5 "What are you doing, untying the colt?"   1
Lke   3:16 I am not worthy to untie the thong of his sandals.   1
    13:15 Does not each of you on the sabbath untie his ox   1
    19:30 Untie it and bring it here.   1
    19:31 If anyone asks you, 'Why are you untying it?'   1
    19:33 As they were untying the colt, its owners asked   1
    19:33 "Why are you untying the colt?"   1
Jhn   1:27 I am not worthy to untie the thong of his sandal."   1
Act 13:25 to untie the thong of the sandals on his feet.'   1

until

1. ἄχρι, *achri, 948*
2. ἄχρι + ὅς, *achri + hos, 948 + 4005*
3. ἄχρι + ὅς + ἄν, *achri + hos + an, 948 + 4005 + 323*
4. εἰ + μή, *ei + mē, 1623 + 3590*
5. εἰς, *eis, 1650*
6. ἐν + ὅς, *en + hos, 1877 + 4005*
7. ἕως, *heōs, 2401*
8. ἕως + ἄν, *heōs + an, 2401 + 323*
9. ἕως + ὅς, *heōs + hos, 2401 + 4005*
10. ἕως + ὅστις, *heōs + hostis, 2401 + 4015*
11. καί, *kai, 2779*
12. μετά, *meta, 3552*
13. μέχρι, *mechri, 3588*
14. μέχρι + ὅς, *mechri + hos, 3588 + 4005*
15. πρό, *pro, 4574*

Mat 1:25 no marital relations...until she had borne a son;   9
      2: 9 went the star...until it stopped over the place   7
      2:13 flee to Egypt, and remain there until I tell you;   8
      2:15 remained there until the death of Herod.   7
      5:18 For truly I tell you, until heaven and earth pass   8
      5:18 will pass from the law until all is accomplished   8
      5:26 get out until you have paid the last penny.   8
    10:11 and stay there until you leave.   8
    11:12 From the days of John the Baptist until now   7
    11:13 the prophets and the law prophesied until John   7
    11:23 it would have remained until this day.   13
    12:20 until he brings justice to victory.   8
    13:30 Let both of them grow together until the harvest;   7
    13:33 until all of it was leavened."   9
    17: 9 until after the Son of Man has been raised   7
    18:30 into prison until he would pay the debt.   7
    18:34 until he would pay his entire debt.   9

	22:44 until I put your enemies under your feet" '?	8
	23:39 you will not see me again until you say	8
	24:21 from the beginning of the world until now	7
	24:34 until all these things have taken place.	8
	24:38 until the day Noah entered the ark	2
	24:39 they knew nothing until the flood came	7
	26:29 until that day when I drink it new with you	7
	27:45 over the whole land until three in the afternoon.	7
	27:64 to be made secure until the third day;	7
Mrk	6:10 stay there until you leave the place.	8
	9: 1 until they see that the kingdom of God has come	8
	9: 9 until after the Son of Man had risen	4
	12:36 until I put your enemies under your feet." '	8
	13:19 the creation that God created until now	7
	13:30 until all these things have taken place.	14
	14:25 until that day when I drink it new in the kingdom	7
	15:33 over the whole land until three in the afternoon.	7
Lke	1:20 unable to speak, until the day these things occur	1
	1:80 until the day he appeared publicly to Israel.	7
	4:13 he departed from him until an opportune time.	1
	9:39 It convulses him until he foams at the mouth	12
	12:50 what stress I am under until it is completed!	10
	12:59 until you have paid the very last penny."	7
	13: 8 until I dig around it and put manure on	10
	13:21 until all of it was leavened."	9
	13:35 not see me until the time comes when you say	7
	15: 4 go after the one that is lost until he finds it?	7
	15: 8 search carefully until she finds it?	9
	16:16 law and the prophets were in effect until John	13
	17:27 until the day Noah entered the ark	2
	19:13 'Do business with these until I come back.'	6
	20:43 until I make your enemies your footstool." '	8
	21:24 until the times of the Gentiles are fulfilled.	2
	21:32 until all things have taken place.	8
	22:16 I will not eat it until it is fulfilled	10
	22:18 until the kingdom of God comes."	9
	22:34 until you have denied three times that you know me."	7
	23:44 darkness came...until three in the afternoon	7
	24:49 stay...until you have been clothed with power	9
Jhn	2:10 But you have kept the good wine until now."	7
	9:18 until they called the parents of the man	10
	16:24 Until now you have not asked for anything	7
	21:22 "If it is my will that he remain until I come	7
	21:23 "If it is my will that he remain until I come	7
Act	1: 2 until the day when he was taken up to heaven	1
	1:22 until the day when he was taken up from us	7
	2:35 until I make your enemies your footstool." '	8
	3:21 until the time of universal restoration	1
	4: 3 put them in custody until the next day	5
	7:18 until another king who had not known Joseph	2
	7:45 And it was there until the time of David	7
	8:40 until he came to Caesarea.	7
	13:20 he gave them judges until the time of...Samuel.	7
	20: 7 he continued speaking until midnight.	13
	20:11 continued to converse with them until dawn;	1
	23:12 until they had killed Paul.	9
	23:14 an oath to taste no food until we have killed Paul.	9
	23:21 until they kill him.	9
	25:21 until I could send him to the emperor."	9
	28:23 From morning until evening	7
Rom	8:22 whole creation has been groaning...until now;	1
	11:25 until the full number of the Gentiles has come in.	2
1Co	8: 7 have become so accustomed to idols until now	7
	11:26 you proclaim the Lord's death until he comes.	2
	15:25 until he has put all his enemies under his feet.	2
	16: 8 I will stay in Ephesus until Pentecost	7
2Co	1:13 I hope you will understand until the end	7
Gal	2:12 for until certain people came from James	15
	3:19 until the offspring would come	2
	3:23 until faith would be revealed.	5
	3:24 the law was our disciplinarian until Christ came	5
	4: 2 until the date set by the father.	1
	4:19 until Christ is formed in you	14
Eph	4:13 until all of us come to the unity of the faith	13
Php	1: 5 from the first day until now.	1
1Th	4:15 who are left until the coming of the Lord	5
2Th	2: 7 until the one who now restrains it is removed.	7
1Ti	4:13 Until I arrive, give attention to the...reading	7
	6:14 until the manifestation of our Lord Jesus Christ	13
2Ti	1:12 I am sure that he is able to guard until that day	5
Heb	1:13 until I make your enemies a footstool for your feet"?	8

	4:12 piercing until it divides soul from spirit	1
	9:10 imposed until the time comes to set things right.	13
	10:13 "until his enemies would be made a footstool	7
Jas	5: 7 Be patient...until the coming of the Lord.	7
	5: 7 until it receives the early and the late rains.	7
2Pe	1:19 until the day dawns and the morning star rises	9
	2: 4 into hell...to be kept until the judgment;	5
	2: 9 under punishment until the day of judgment	5
	3: 7 kept until the day of judgment and destruction	5
Rev	2:10 Be faithful until death	1
	2:25 only hold fast to what you have until I come.	3
	6:11 rest...until the number would be complete	7
	7: 3 until we have marked the servants of our God with a seal	1
	15: 8 until the seven plagues...were ended.	1
	16:21 until they cursed God for the plague of the hail	11
	17:17 until the words of God will be fulfilled.	1
	20: 3 until the thousand years were ended.	1
	20: 5 until the thousand years were ended.)	1

untimely   *See* bear untimely

untrained

    1. ἰδιώτης, *idiōtēs, 2626*

2Co 11: 6 I may be untrained in speech   1

unusual

    1. ἄτοπος, *atopos, 876*

    2. οὐ + ὁ + τυγχάνω, *ou + ho + tynchanō, 4024 + 3836 + 5593*

Act 28: 2 The natives showed us unusual kindness.   2
    28: 6 saw that nothing unusual had happened to him   1

unveiled

    1. ἀκατακάλυπτος, *akatakalyptos, 184*

    2. ἀνακαλύπτω, *anakalyptō, 365*

1Co 11: 5 who prays or prophesies with her head unveiled   1
    11:13 for a woman to pray to God with her head unveiled?   1
2Co 3:18 all of us, with unveiled faces, seeing the glory   2

unwashed

    1. ἄνιπτος, *aniptos, 481*

Mat 15:20 to eat with unwashed hands does not defile."   1

unwilling

    1. μή + θέλω, *mē + thelō, 3590 + 2527*

    2. οὐ + θέλω, *ou + thelō, 4024 + 2527*

Mat 1:19 Joseph...unwilling to expose her to public disgrace   1
    23: 4 are unwilling to lift a finger to move them.   2
Act 7:39 Our ancestors were unwilling to obey him;   2
2Th 3:10 Anyone unwilling to work should not eat.   2

unwise person

    1. ἄσοφος, *asophos, 831*

Eph 5:15 live, not as unwise people but as wise   1

unworthy

    1. οὐ + ἄξιος, *ou + axios, 4024 + 545*

Act 13:46 judge yourselves to be unworthy of eternal life   1

unworthy manner

    1. ἀναξίως, *anaxiōs, 397*

1Co 11:27 drinks the cup of the Lord in an unworthy manner   1

up   *See also* bear up, break up, bring up, bring up a child, build up, burn up, carry up, cast up foam, catch up, climb up, come up, come up with, cover up, dry up, eat up, fill up, gather up, get up, give up, go up, grow up, gush up, heap up empty phrases, help up, hoist up, hold up to contempt, jump up, keep up courage, lay up, lay up treasure, lead up, lift up, light up, lock up, look up, make up, make up one's mind, march up, move up, offer up, pick up, puff up, puff up with conceit, pull up, put up with, raise up, raise up with, rise up, roll up, run up, seal up, set up, shut up, sit up, speak up, spring up, stand up, stand up straight, stir up, stir up revolt, store up, store up

treasure, straighten up, sum up, swallow up, swell up, take up, tie up, wake up, wrap up
1. ἄνω, *anō, 539*
2. μέγας, *megas, 3489*

Heb 11:24 Moses, when he was grown up   2
    12:15 no root of bitterness springs up   1

up to
1. ἄχρι, *achri, 948*
2. ἕως, *heōs, 2401*

Jhn   2: 7 And they filled them up to the brim.   2
Act 22:22 Up to this point they listened to him   1
    23: 1 "Brothers, up to this day I have lived my life   1

upbraid
1. ὀνειδίζω, *oneidizō, 3943*

Mrk 16:14 ⟦he upbraided them for their lack of faith⟧   1

upbuild
1. οἰκοδομή, *oikodomē, 3869*

Rom 14:19 makes for peace and for mutual upbuilding.   1
1Co 14: 3 upbuilding and encouragement and consolation   1

uphold
1. ἵστημι, *histēmi, 2705*

Rom   3:31 By no means! On the contrary, we uphold the law.   1
    14: 4 And they will be upheld   1

uplift
1. ὑψηλός, *hypsēlos, 5734*

Act 13:17 with uplifted arm he led them out of it.   1

upon   *See also* break upon, bring upon, build upon, come upon, fall upon, lay upon, press upon, prevail upon, prey upon, put upon, spit upon
1. Contextual: Not in Greek
2. ἀντί, *anti, 505*
3. ἀπό, *apo, 608*
4. ἐπάνω, *epanō, 2062*
5. ἐπί, *epi, 2093*

Mat 10:13 If the house is worthy, let your peace come upon it;   5
    11:29 Take my yoke upon you, and learn from me;   5
    12:18 I will put my Spirit upon him   5
    23:22 by the one who is seated upon it.   4
    23:35 so that upon you may come all the righteous blood   5
    23:36 all this will come upon this generation.   5
    24: 2 not one stone will be left here upon another;   5
Mrk   4:31 when sown upon the ground, is the smallest   5
    13: 2 Not one stone will be left here upon another;   5
Lke   1:35 "The Holy Spirit will come upon you   5
    2:40 the favor of God was upon him.   5
    3:22 Holy Spirit descended upon him in bodily form   5
    4:18 "The Spirit of the Lord is upon me   5
    19:43 Indeed, the days will come upon you   5
    19:44 will not leave within you one stone upon another;   5
    21: 6 not one stone will be left upon another;   5
    21:35 For it will come upon all   5
    24:49 I am sending upon you what my Father promised;   5
Jhn   1:16 we have all received, grace upon grace.   2
    1:51 ascending and descending upon the Son of Man."   5
Act   1: 8 when the Holy Spirit has come upon you;   5
    2:17 I will pour out my Spirit upon all flesh   5
    2:18 Even upon my slaves, both men and women,   5
    2:43 Awe came upon everyone   1
    4:33 great grace was upon them all.   5
    8:16 as yet the Spirit had not come upon any of them;   5
    10:44 the Holy Spirit fell upon all who heard the word.   5
    11:15 as I began to speak, the Holy Spirit fell upon them   5
    11:15 upon them just as it had upon us at the beginning.   5
    19: 6 the Holy Spirit came upon them   5
Rom 11:25 a hardening has come upon part of Israel   3
Gal   6:16 follow this rule—peace be upon them, and mercy   5
    6:16 upon the Israel of God.   5
Eph   2:20 built upon the foundation of the apostles   5
1Th   5: 3 as labor pains come upon a pregnant woman   1
Rev 16:18 as had not occurred since people were upon the earth   5

upright
1. δίκαιος, *dikaios, 1465*

2. δικαίως, *dikaiōs, 1469*
3. ὀρθός, *orthos, 3981*

Act 10:22 a centurion, an upright and God-fearing man   1
    14:10 said in a loud voice, "Stand upright on your feet."   3
1Th   2:10 how pure, upright, and blameless   2
Tit   1: 8 lover of goodness, prudent, upright   1
    2:12 in the present age to live lives that are self-controlled,   2

uproar   *See also* set in an uproar
1. θόρυβος, *thorybos, 2573*

Act 20: 1 After the uproar had ceased   1
    21:34 because of the uproar   1

in an uproar
1. συγχέω, *syncheō, 5177*

Act 21:31 all Jerusalem was in an uproar.   1

uproot
1. ἐκριζόω, *ekrizoō, 1748*

Mat 13:29 in gathering the weeds you would uproot the wheat   1
    15:13 "Every plant...will be uprooted.   1
Lke 17: 6 'Be uprooted and planted in the sea,'   1
Jde   1:12 autumn trees without fruit, twice dead, uprooted;   1

upset
1. ἀνατρέπω, *anatrepō, 426*

2Ti   2:18 They are upsetting the faith of some.   1
Tit   1:11 since they are upsetting whole families   1

upstairs   *See* go upstairs, room upstairs

upward
1. ἄνω, *anō, 539*

Jhn 11:41 Jesus looked upward and said, "Father   1

Urbanus
1. Οὐρβανός, *Ourbanos, 4042*

Rom 16: 9 Greet Urbanus, our co-worker in Christ   1

urge
1. Contextual: Not in Greek
2. ἐρωτάω, *erōtaō, 2263*
3. παραινέω, *paraineō, 4147*
4. παρακαλέω, *parakaleō, 4151*
5. πείθω, *peithō, 4275*

Mat 15:23 And his disciples came and urged him, saying   2
Jhn   4:31 the disciples were urging him, "Rabbi, eat   2
Act 13:42 urged them to speak about these things again   4
    13:43 urged them to continue in the grace of God.   5
    16:15 she urged us, saying   4
    19:31 urging him not to venture into the theater.   4
    21:12 we and the people there urged him not to go up   4
    27:22 I urge you now to keep up your courage   3
    27:33 Paul urged all of them to take some food, saying   4
    27:34 Therefore I urge you to take some food   4
Rom 16:17 I urge you, brothers and sisters, to keep an eye   4
1Co 16:12 I strongly urged him to visit you   4
    16:16 I urge you to put yourselves at the service   1
2Co   2: 8 I urge you to reaffirm your love for him.   4
    6: 1 urge you also not to accept the grace of God   4
    8: 6 so that we might urge Titus   4
    9: 5 So I thought it necessary to urge the brothers   4
    12:18 I urged Titus to go, and sent the brother with him.   4
Php   4: 2 I urge Euodia and...Syntyche to be of the same mind   4
    4: 2 Euodia and I urge Syntyche to be of the same mind   4
1Th   2:12 urging and encouraging you and pleading   4
    4: 1 we ask and urge you in the Lord Jesus   4
    4:10 we urge you, beloved, to do so more and more   4
    5:14 we urge you, beloved, to admonish the idlers   4
1Ti   1: 3 I urge you...to remain in Ephesus   4
    2: 1 First of all, then, I urge that...   4
    6: 2 Teach and urge these duties.   4
Tit   2: 6 Likewise, urge the younger men   4
Heb 13:19 I urge you all the more to do this   4
1Pe   2:11 I urge you as aliens and exiles to abstain   4

urge on
1. συνέχω, *synechō, 5309*

2Co   5:14 For the love of Christ urges us on   1

urge solemnly
1. διαμαρτύρομαι, *diamartyromai, 1371*
2Ti   4: 1 In the presence of God...I solemnly urge you   1

urge strongly
1. παραβιάζομαι, *parabiazomai, 4128*
Lke 24:29 they urged him strongly, saying, "Stay with us   1

urgent
1. ἀναγκαῖος, *anankaios, 338*
Tit   3:14 in order to meet urgent needs   1

urgently
1. ἐπίκειμαι, *epikeimai, 2130*
Lke 23:23 they kept urgently demanding with loud shouts   1

Uriah
1. Οὐρίας, *Ourias, 4043*
Mat   1: 6 David...father of Solomon by the wife of Uriah   1

urn
1. στάμνος, *stamnos, 5085*
Heb   9: 4 in which there were a golden urn holding the manna   1

use *See also* make full use, make use, special use
1. Contextual: Not in Greek
2. ἀπόχρησις, *apochrēsis, 712*
3. διά, *dia, 1328*
4. εἰμί, *eimi, 1639*
5. ἐκ, *ek, 1666*
6. ἐν, *en, 1877*
7. ἔχω, *echō, 2400*
8. λέγω, *legō, 3306*
9. πέμπω, *pempō, 4287*
10. τίθημι, *tithēmi, 5502*
11. χράομαι, *chraomai, 5968*
Mat 22:19 Show me the coin used for the tax."   1
        27: 7 used them to buy the potter's field   5
Mrk   4:30 what parable will we use for it?   10
        16:17 ⟦by using my name they will cast out demons;⟧   6
Jhn 10: 6 Jesus used this figure of speech with them   8
Act 14: 8 a man sitting who could not use his feet   1
Rom   3:13 they use their tongues to deceive."   1
2Co 13:10 not have to be severe in using the authority   11
Gal   5:13 only do not use your freedom as an opportunity   1
Col   2:22 refer to things that perish with use;   2
2Th   2: 9 Satan, who uses all power, signs, lying wonders   6
1Ti   1: 8 law is good, if one uses it legitimately.   11
2Ti   2:20 some for special use, some for ordinary.   1
Heb   9:21 both the tent and all the vessels used in worship.   1
1Pe   2:16 do not use your freedom as a pretext for evil.   7
2Jn   1:12 I would rather not use paper and ink;   3
Rev 14:15 "Use your sickle and reap   9
        14:18 "Use your sharp sickle and gather the clusters   9
        21:17 human measurement, which the angel was using.   4

ordinary use
1. ἀτιμία, *atimia, 871*
Rom   9:21 object for special use and another for ordinary use?   1

use a name
1. ὀνομάζω, *onomazō, 3951*
Act 19:13 tried to use the name of the Lord   1

used to
1. Contextual: Not in Greek
Mrk 15: 6 he used to release a prisoner for them   1
        15:41 These used to follow him and provided for him   1
Jhn   9: 8 "Is this not the man who used to sit and beg?"   1
        12: 6 used to steal what was put into it.)   1
        21:18 were younger, you used to fasten your own belt   1
Act   3:10 the one who used to sit and ask for alms   1
        7:51 just as your ancestors used to do.   1
        24:26 for that reason he used to send for him very often   1
1Co   6:11 what some of you used to be.   1
Gal   2:12 he used to eat with the Gentiles.   1

useful
1. ἀγαθός, *agathos, 19*
2. εὔθετος, *euthetos, 2310*
3. εὔχρηστος, *euchrēstos, 2378*
4. ὠφέλιμος, *ōphelimos, 6068*
Eph   4:29 only what is useful for building up   1
2Ti   2:21 dedicated and useful to the owner of the house   3
        3:16 inspired by God and is useful for teaching   4
        4:11 for he is useful in my ministry.   3
Phm   1:11 now he is indeed useful both to you and to me.   3
Heb   6: 7 useful to those for whom it is cultivated   2

useless
1. ἄχρηστος, *achrēstos, 947*
2. ὠφελέω + οὐδείς, *ōpheleō + oudeis, 6067 + 4029*
Jhn   6:63 the flesh is useless.   2
Phm   1:11 Formerly he was useless to you   1

usual *See also* usual daily *wage*
1. ἔθος, *ethos, 1621*
Lke   2:42 they went up as usual for the festival   1

utensil
1. σκεῦος, *skeuos, 5007*
2Ti   2:20 there are utensils not only of gold and silver   1
        2:21 will become special utensils, dedicated and useful   1

utmost
1. ἅπας, *hapas, 570*
2. πᾶς, *pas, 4246*
Act 24: 3 We welcome this...with utmost gratitude.   2
2Co   8: 7 in utmost eagerness, and in our love for you   2
        12:12 with utmost patience, signs and wonders   2
1Ti   1:16 Christ might display the utmost patience   1
2Ti   4: 2 with the utmost patience in teaching.   2

utter
1. Contextual: Not in Greek
2. δίδωμι, *didōmi, 1443*
3. λαλέω, *laleō, 3281*
4. λέγω, *legō, 3306*
Mat   5:11 and persecute you and utter all kinds of evil   4
        12:36 have to give an account for every careless word   3
1Co 14: 9 if in a tongue you utter speech   2
Rev 13: 5 a mouth uttering haughty and blasphemous words   3
        13: 6 It opened its mouth to utter blasphemies   1

utter blasphemy
1. βλασφημέω, *blasphēmeō, 1059*
Mrk   3:28 whatever blasphemies they utter;   1

utterance
1. λόγος, *logos, 3364*
Lke   4:36 "What kind of utterance is this?   1
1Co 12: 8 through the Spirit the utterance of wisdom   1
        12: 8 to another the utterance of knowledge   1

utterly *See also* amaze utterly, astonish utterly, root out utterly
1. κατά + ὑπερβολή, *kata + hyperbolē, 2848 + 5651*
2. λίαν + ἐκ + περισσός, *lian + ek + perissos, 3336 + 1666 + 4356*
Mrk   6:51 they were utterly astounded   2
2Co   1: 8 we were so utterly, unbearably crushed   1

Uzziah
1. Ὀζίας, *Ozias, 3852*
Mat   1: 8 and Joram the father of Uzziah   1
        1: 9 Uzziah the father of Jotham   1

V

vacillate
1. ἐλαφρία + χράομαι, *elaphria + chraomai, 1786 + 5968*
2Co   1:17 Was I vacillating when I wanted to do this?   1

vain

1. εἰκῇ, *eikē, 1632*
2. κενός, *kenos, 3031*
3. μάτην, *matēn, 3472*

Mat 15: 9 in vain do they worship me, teaching human precepts   3
Mrk 7: 7 in vain do they worship me   3
Rom 13: 4 for the authority does not bear the sword in vain!   1
1Co 15: 2 unless you have come to believe in vain.   1
    15:10 his grace toward me has not been in vain.   2
    15:14 then our proclamation has been in vain   2
    15:14 and your faith has been in vain.   2
    15:58 in the Lord your labor is not in vain.   2
2Co 6: 1 not to accept the grace of God in vain.   2
Gal 2: 2 that I was not running, or had not run, in vain.   2
Php 2:16 I did not run in vain or labor in vain.   2
    2:16 I did not run in vain or labor in vain.   2
1Th 2: 1 our coming to you was not in vain   2
    3: 5 our labor had been in vain.   2

vain thing

1. κενός, *kenos, 3031*

Act 4:25 the peoples imagine vain things?   1

valid

1. ἀληθής, *alēthēs, 239*
2. ἀληθινός, *alēthinos, 240*
3. βέβαιος, *bebaios, 1010*

Jhn 8:13 your testimony is not valid."   1
    8:14 my testimony is valid because I know where   1
    8:16 Yet even if I do judge, my judgment is valid;   2
    8:17 the testimony of two witnesses is valid.   1
Heb 2: 2 For if the message declared through angels was valid   3

valley

1. φάραγξ, *pharanx, 5754*
2. χείμαρρος, *cheimarros, 5929*

Lke 3: 5 Every valley shall be filled   1
Jhn 18: 1 he went out…across the Kidron valley   2

valuable

1. ὠφέλιμος, *ōphelimos, 6068*

1Ti 4: 8 godliness is valuable in every way   1

more valuable

1. διαφέρω, *diapherō, 1422*

Mat 12:12 more valuable is a human being than a sheep!   1

value

1. διαφέρω, *diapherō, 1422*
2. τιμή, *timē, 5507*
3. τίμιος, *timios, 5508*
4. ὠφέλεια, *ōpheleia, 6066*
5. ὠφελέω, *ōpheleō, 6067*
6. ὠφέλιμος, *ōphelimos, 6068*

Mat 6:26 them. Are you not of more value than they?   1
Lke 12:24 Of how much more value are you than the birds!   1
Act 19:19 the value of these books was calculated   2
    20:24 I do not count my life of any value   3
Rom 2:25 Circumcision…is of value if you obey the law;   5
    3: 1 Or what is the value of circumcision?   4
Col 2:23 of no value in checking self-indulgence.   2
1Ti 4: 8 for, while physical training is of some value   6

great value

1. πολύτιμος, *polytimos, 4501*

Mat 13:46 on finding one pearl of great value   1

more value

1. διαφέρω, *diapherō, 1422*

Mat 10:31 you are of more value than many sparrows.   1
Lke 12: 7 you are of more value than many sparrows.   1

surpassing value

1. ὑπερέχω, *hyperechō, 5660*

Php 3: 8 the surpassing value of knowing Christ Jesus   1

value highly

1. ἔντιμος, *entimos, 1952*

Lke 7: 2 had a slave whom he valued highly,   1

vanish

1. ἀποχωρίζω, *apochōrizō, 714*
2. ἀφανίζω, *aphanizō, 906*

Jas 4:14 appears for a little while and then vanishes.   2
Rev 6:14 The sky vanished like a scroll rolling itself up   1

vanish from sight

1. ἄφαντος, *aphantos, 908*

Lke 24:31 he vanished from their sight.   1

variation

1. παραλλαγή, *parallagē, 4164*

Jas 1:17 Father of lights, with whom there is no variation   1

variety   *See also* rich variety

1. διαίρεσις, *diairesis, 1348*

1Co 12: 4 are varieties of gifts, but the same Spirit;   1
    12: 5 are varieties of services, but the same Lord;   1
    12: 6 there are varieties of activities   1

various   *See also* various *ways*

1. Contextual: Not in Greek
2. διάφορος, *diaphoros, 1427*
3. κατά, *kata, 2848*
4. ποικίλος, *poikilos, 4476*

Mat 4:24 those who were afflicted with various diseases   4
    24: 7 famines and earthquakes in various places: 3
Mrk 1:34 cured many who were sick with various diseases   4
    13: 8 there will be earthquakes in various places;   3
Lke 21:11 in various places famines and plagues;   3
1Co 12:10 to another various kinds of tongues   1
    12:28 forms of leadership, various kinds of tongues.   1
Tit 3: 3 slaves to various passions and pleasures   4
Heb 2: 4 by signs and wonders and various miracles   4
    9:10 food and drink and various baptisms   2
1Pe 1: 6 you have had to suffer various trials   4

various kinds

1. ποικίλος, *poikilos, 4476*

Lke 4:40 any who were sick with various kinds of diseases   1

vegetable

1. λάχανον, *lachanon, 3303*

Rom 14: 2 while the weak eat only vegetables.   1

vehemently

1. ἐκπερισσῶς, *ekperissōs, 1735*
2. εὐτόνως, *eutonōs, 2364*

Mrk 14:31 he said vehemently, "Even though I must die   1
Lke 23:10 the scribes stood by, vehemently accusing him.   2

veil   *See also* wear a veil

1. κάλυμμα, *kalymma, 2820*
2. καλύπτω, *kalyptō, 2821*
3. κατακαλύπτω, *katakalyptō, 2877*

1Co 11: 6 For if a woman will not veil herself   3
    11: 7 For a man ought not to have his head veiled   3
2Co 3:13 not like Moses, who put a veil over his face   1
    3:14 that same veil is still there   1
    3:15 a veil lies over their minds;   1
    3:16 when one turns to the Lord, the veil is removed.   1
    4: 3 even if our gospel is veiled   2
    4: 3 it is veiled to those who are perishing.   2

vengeance

1. ἐκδίκησις, *ekdikēsis, 1689*

Lke 21:22 these are days of vengeance   1
Rom 12:19 "Vengeance is mine, I will repay, says the Lord."   1
2Th 1: 8 inflicting vengeance on those who do not know   1
Heb 10:30 "Vengeance is mine, I will repay."   1

venom

1. ἰός, *ios, 2675*

Rom 3:13 "The venom of vipers is under their lips."   1

venture

1. δίδωμι, *didōmi, 1443*
2. τολμάω, *tolmaō, 5528*

Act 19:31 urging him not to venture into the theater.   1
Rom 15:18 For I will not venture to speak of anything   2

verdict *See also* give a verdict
  1. δοκέω, *dokeō, 1506*
Mat 26:66 What is your verdict?"   1

verge
  1. ἐγγύς, *engys, 1584*
Heb 6: 8 it is worthless and on the verge of being cursed;   1

very¹ *See also* annoy very much, from the very *first*, this
  very day, very *act*, very *being*, very *costly*, very *dear*, very
  great, very *hard*, very *heavy*, very *highly*, very *large*, very
  least, very *little*, very *moment*, very much *more*, very
  often, very *precious*, very *rare*, very *small*, very *small*
  thing, very *soon*, very *truly*, very *well*
  1. Contextual: Not in Greek
  2. δεινῶς, *deinōs, 1267*
  3. λίαν, *lian, 3336*
  4. ὅσος, *hosos, 4012*
  5. πᾶς, *pas, 4246*
  6. σφόδρα, *sphodra, 5379*
Mat 4: 8 the devil took him to a very high mountain   3
Mrk 1:35 In the morning, while it was still very dark   3
     6:35 a deserted place, and the hour is now very late;   1
    16: 2 very early on the first day of the week   3
    16: 4 the stone, which was very large,...rolled back.   6
Lke 11:53 the Pharisees began to be very hostile toward him   2
    18:23 he became sad; for he was very rich.   6
    23: 8 When Herod saw Jesus, he was very glad   3
Act 17:11 they welcomed the message very eagerly   5
Heb 10:37 For yet "in a very little while,   4

very²
  1. Contextual: Not in Greek
  2. αὐτός, *autos, 899*
  3. ἐκεῖνος, *ekeinos, 1697*
  4. εὐθέως, *eutheōs, 2311*
  5. καί, *kai, 2779*
  6. οὗτος, *houtos, 4047*
Mat 24:33 you know that he is near, at the very gates.   1
    26:34 this very night, before the cock crows   6
Mrk 5:15 right mind, the very man who had had the legion;   1
    13:29 you know that he is near, at the very gates.   1
    14:30 this very night, before the cock crows twice   6
Lke 12:12 the Holy Spirit will teach you at that very hour   2
    12:20 This very night your life is being demanded   6
    12:59 until you have paid the very last penny."   5
    13: 1 At that very time there were some present   2
    13:31 At that very hour some Pharisees came and said   2
    20:19 wanted to lay hands on him at that very hour   2
Jhn 5:36 the very works that I am doing   1
Act 10:30 Cornelius replied, "Four days ago at this very hour   6
    12: 6 The very night before Herod was going to bring   3
    16:18 it came out that very hour.   2
    17:10 That very night the believers sent Paul and Silas   4
    22:13 In that very hour I regained my sight and saw him.   2
Rom 2: 1 you, the judge, are doing the very same things.   1
     7:10 the very commandment that promised life   6
     7:15 but I do the very thing I hate.   1
     8:16 that very Spirit bearing witness with our spirit   2
     8:26 that very Spirit intercedes with sighs   2
     9:17 for the very purpose of showing my power in you   2
     9:26 "And in the very place where it was said to them   1
    13: 6 God's servants, busy with this very thing.   2
2Co 5: 5 He who has prepared us for this very thing is God   2
Gal 2:18 build up again the very things that I once tore down   6
Eph 6:22 I am sending him to you for this very purpose   2
Col 4: 8 I have sent him to you for this very purpose   2
1Ti 1:16 for that very reason I received mercy   1
Tit 1:12 one of them, their very own prophet, who said   1
     1:15 Their very minds and consciences are corrupted.   1
Heb 6:11 the full assurance of hope to the very end   1
1Pe 2: 7 "The stone that the builders rejected has become the very   1
     4:11 do so as one speaking the very words of God;   1
2Pe 1: 5 For this very reason, you must make every effort   2

vessel
  1. σκεῦος, *skeuos, 5007*
Heb 9:21 both the tent and all the vessels used in worship.   1

vicious
  1. κακός, *kakos, 2805*
Tit 1:12 "Cretans are always liars, vicious brutes   1

slain victim
  1. σφάγιον, *sphagion, 5376*
Act 7:42 'Did you offer to me slain victims and sacrifices   1

victory
  1. νίκη, *nikē, 3772*
  2. νῖκος, *nikos, 3777*
Mat 12:20 until he brings justice to victory.   2
1Co 15:54 "Death has been swallowed up in victory."   2
    15:55 "Where, O death, is your victory?   2
    15:57 thanks be to God, who gives us the victory   2
1Jn 5: 4 this is the victory that conquers the world   1

view *See also* point of view
  1. Contextual: Not in Greek
  2. διά, *dia, 1328*
1Co 7:26 I think that, in view of the impending crisis   2
2Ti 4: 1 in view of his appearing and his kingdom   1

village
  1. κώμη, *kōmē, 3267*
Mat 9:35 Jesus went about all the cities and villages   1
    10:11 Whatever town or village you enter   1
    14:15 into the villages and buy food for themselves."   1
    21: 2 to them, "Go into the village ahead of you   1
Mrk 6: 6 he went about among the villages teaching.   1
     6:36 may go into the surrounding country and villages   1
     6:56 wherever he went, into villages or cities or farms   1
     8:23 led him out of the village;   1
     8:26 "Do not even go into the village."   1
     8:27 to the villages of Caesarea Philippi;   1
    11: 2 said to them, "Go into the village ahead of you   1
Lke 5:17 had come from every village of Galilee and Judea   1
     8: 1 he went on through cities and villages   1
     9: 6 They departed and went through the villages   1
     9:12 so that they may go into the surrounding villages   1
     9:52 they entered a village of the Samaritans   1
     9:56 Then they went on to another village.   1
    10:38 on their way, he entered a certain village   1
    13:22 Jesus went through one town and village   1
    17:12 As he entered a village, ten lepers approached him.   1
    19:30 saying, "Go into the village ahead   1
    24:13 two of them were going to a village called Emmaus   1
    24:28 came near the village to which they were going   1
Jhn 7:42 from Bethlehem, the village where David lived?"   1
    11: 1 the village of Mary and her sister Martha.   1
    11:30 Now Jesus had not yet come to the village   1
Act 8:25 many villages of the Samaritans.   1

villainy
  1. ῥᾳδιούργημα, *rhadiourgēma, 4815*
  2. ῥᾳδιουργία, *rhadiourgia, 4816*
Act 13:10 full of all deceit and villainy   2
    18:14 a matter of crime or serious villainy   1

vindicate
  1. δικαιόω, *dikaioō, 1467*
Mat 11:19 Yet wisdom is vindicated by her deeds."   1
Lke 7:35 wisdom is vindicated by all her children."   1
1Ti 3:16 vindicated in spirit, seen by angels   1

vine
  1. ἄμπελος, *ampelos, 306*
Mat 26:29 never again drink of this fruit of the vine   1
Mrk 14:25 I will never again drink of the fruit of the vine   1
Lke 22:18 I will not drink of the fruit of the vine   1
Jhn 15: 1 "I am the true vine   1
    15: 4 unless it abides in the vine   1
    15: 5 I am the vine, you are the branches.   1
Rev 14:18 and gather the clusters of the vine of the earth   1

vinegrower

1. γεωργός, *geōrgos, 1177*

Jhn 15: 1 my Father is the vinegrower.   1

vineyard

1. ἀμπελών, *ampelōn, 308*

Mat 20: 1 to hire laborers for his vineyard.   1
20: 2 he sent them into his vineyard.   1
20: 4 he said to them, 'You also go into the vineyard   1
20: 7 He said to them, 'You also go into the vineyard.'   1
20: 8 the owner of the vineyard said to his manager   1
21:28 'Son, go and work in the vineyard today.'   1
21:33 There was a landowner who planted a vineyard   1
21:39 they seized him, threw him out of the vineyard   1
21:40 Now when the owner of the vineyard comes   1
21:41 and lease the vineyard to other tenants   1
Mrk 12: 1 "A man planted a vineyard   1
12: 2 share of the produce of the vineyard.   1
12: 8 and threw him out of the vineyard.   1
12: 9 What then will the owner of the vineyard do?   1
12: 9 give the vineyard to others.   1
Lke 13: 6 "A man had a fig tree planted in his vineyard;   1
20: 9 "A man planted a vineyard, and leased it   1
20:10 give him his share of the produce of the vineyard;   1
20:13 the owner of the vineyard said, 'What shall I do?   1
20:15 they threw him out of the vineyard and killed him.   1
20:15 will the owner of the vineyard do to them?   1
20:16 give the vineyard to others."   1
1Co 9: 7 Who plants a vineyard and does not eat   1

vintage

1. ἄμπελος, *ampelos, 306*

Rev 14:19 the angel...gathered the vintage of the earth   1

violate

1. ἀθετέω, *atheteō, 119*

1Ti 5:12 having violated their first pledge.   1
Heb 10:28 Anyone who has violated the law of Moses dies   1

violation

1. παράβασις, *parabasis, 4126*

Rom 4:15 but where there is no law, neither is there violation.   1

violation of the law

1. παρανομέω, *paranomeō, 4174*

Act 23: 3 in violation of the law you order me to be struck?"   1

violence   *See also* man of violence, suffer violence

1. βία, *bia, 1040*
2. ὅρμημα, *hormēma, 3996*

Act 5:26 brought them, but without violence   1
21:35 the violence of the mob was so great   1
Rev 18:21 "With such violence Babylon...will be thrown down   2

violent

1. βίαιος, *biaios, 1042*
2. βιαστής, *biastēs, 1043*
3. κακόω, *kakoō, 2808*
4. μέγας, *megas, 3489*
5. πλήκτης, *plēktēs, 4438*
6. πολύς, *polys, 4498*
7. τυφωνικός, *typhōnikos, 5607*

Mat 11:12 and the violent take it by force.   2
Act 2: 2 a sound like the rush of a violent wind   1
12: 1 King Herod laid violent hands upon some   3
16:26 Suddenly there was an earthquake, so violent   4
23:10 When the dissension became violent   6
27:14 soon a violent wind, called the northeaster   7
1Ti 3: 3 not a drunkard, not violent but gentle   5
Tit 1: 7 addicted to wine or violent or greedy for gain;   5
Rev 16:18 a violent earthquake, such as had not occurred   4

so violent

1. τηλικοῦτος, *tēlikoutos, 5496*

Rev 16:18 so violent was that earthquake.   1

violently

1. σφοδρῶς, *sphodrōs, 5380*

2. ὑπερβολή, *hyperbolē, 5651*

Act 27:18 We were being pounded by the storm so violently   1
Gal 1:13 I was violently persecuting the church of God   2

viper

1. ἀσπίς, *aspis, 835*
2. ἔχιδνα, *echidna, 2399*

Mat 3: 7 "You brood of vipers! Who warned you to flee   2
12:34 You brood of vipers! How can you speak good   2
23:33 You snakes, you brood of vipers!   2
Lke 3: 7 "You brood of vipers!   2
Act 28: 3 when a viper, driven out by the heat   2
Rom 3:13 "The venom of vipers is under their lips."   1

virgin

1. οὐ + γινώσκω + ἀνήρ, *ou + ginōskō + anēr, 4024 + 1182 + 467*
2. παρθένος, *parthenos, 4221*

Mat 1:23 "Look, the virgin shall conceive and bear a son   2
Lke 1:27 a virgin engaged to a man whose name was Joseph   2
1:27 The virgin's name was Mary.   2
1:34 "How can this be, since I am a virgin?"   1
1Co 7:25 Now concerning virgins, I have no command   2
7:28 if a virgin marries, she does not sin.   2
7:34 the unmarried woman and the virgin are anxious   2
2Co 11: 2 to present you as a chaste virgin to Christ.   2
Rev 14: 4 not defiled themselves...for they are virgins;   2

visible   *See also* make visible

1. ὁρατός, *horatos, 3971*
2. φαίνω, *phainō, 5743*
3. φανερός, *phaneros, 5745*
4. φανερόω, *phaneroō, 5746*

1Co 3:13 work of each builder will become visible   3
Eph 5:13 exposed by the light becomes visible   4
5:14 for everything that becomes visible is light.   4
Col 1:16 were created, things visible and invisible   1
Heb 11: 3 was made from things that are not visible.   2

vision

1. ὀπτασία, *optasia, 3965*
2. ὅραμα, *horama, 3969*
3. ὅρασις, *horasis, 3970*
4. ὁράω, *horaō, 3972*

Mat 17: 9 "Tell no one about the vision   2
Lke 1:22 realized that he had seen a vision in the sanctuary.   1
24:23 that they had indeed seen a vision of angels   1
Act 2:17 your young men shall see visions   3
9:10 The Lord said to him in a vision, "Ananias."   2
9:12 he has seen in a vision a man named Ananias come   2
10: 3 a vision in which he clearly saw an angel of God   2
10:17 what to make of the vision that he had seen,   2
10:19 While Peter was still thinking about the vision   2
11: 5 in a trance I saw a vision.   2
12: 9 he thought he was seeing a vision.   2
16: 9 During the night Paul had a vision: there stood   2
16:10 When he had seen the vision   2
18: 9 One night the Lord said to Paul in a vision   2
26:19 I was not disobedient to the heavenly vision   2
2Co 12: 1 go on to visions and revelations of the Lord.   1
Col 2:18 dwelling on visions, puffed up without cause   4
Rev 9:17 this was how I saw the horses in my vision: 3

visit   *See also* make a visit

1. Contextual: Not in Greek
2. διέρχομαι, *dierchomai, 1451*
3. εἰσέρχομαι, *eiserchomai, 1656*
4. ἐπισκέπτομαι, *episkeptomai, 2170*
5. ἔρχομαι, *erchomai, 2262*
6. ἱστορέω, *historeō, 2707*
7. πρός, *pros, 4639*
8. προσέρχομαι, *proserchomai, 4665*

Mat 25:36 I was in prison and you visited me.'   5
25:39 we saw you sick or in prison and visited you?'   5
25:43 sick and in prison and you did not visit me.'   4
Act 7:12 he sent our ancestors there on their first visit.   1
7:13 On the second visit   1
7:23 it came into his heart to visit his relatives   4
10:28 to associate with or to visit a Gentile   8

15:36	let us return and visit the believers	4
21:18	The next day Paul went with us to visit James;	7
28: 8	Paul visited him and cured him by praying	3
1Co 16: 5	I will visit you	5
16:12	I strongly urged him to visit you	5
2Co 1:16	I wanted to visit you on my way to Macedonia	2
13: 2	as I did when present on my second visit	1
Gal 1:18	I did go up to Jerusalem to visit Cephas	6

visitation

1. ἐπισκοπή, *episkopē, 2175*

Lke 19:44 recognize the time of your visitation from God."   1

visitor

1. ἐπιδημέω, *epidēmeō, 2111*

Act 2:10 visitors from Rome, both Jews and proselytes   1

voice

1. στόμα, *stoma, 5125*
2. φθόγγος, *phthongos, 5782*
3. φωνή, *phōnē, 5889*
4. φωνή + ἐκ + ὁ + στόμα, *phōnē + ek + ho + stoma, 5889 + 1666 + 3836 + 5125*

Mat 2:18	"A voice was heard in Ramah, wailing and loud	3
3: 3	"The voice of one crying out in the wilderness:	3
3:17	a voice from heaven said, "This is my Son	3
12:19	nor will anyone hear his voice in the streets.	3
17: 5	and from the cloud a voice said	3
27:46	Jesus cried with a loud voice	3
27:50	Jesus cried again with a loud voice	3
Mrk 1: 3	the voice of one crying out in the wilderness:	3
1:11	a voice came from heaven, "You are my Son,	3
1:26	convulsing him and crying with a loud voice	3
5: 7	he shouted at the top of his voice	3
9: 7	from the cloud there came a voice	3
15:34	At three o'clock Jesus cried out with a loud voice	3
Lke 3: 4	"The voice of one crying out in the wilderness:	3
3:22	a voice came from heaven	3
4:33	and he cried out with a loud voice	3
8:28	and shouted at the top of his voice	3
9:35	from the cloud came a voice that said,	3
9:36	When the voice had spoken, Jesus was found alone.	3
11:27	a woman in the crowd raised her voice and said	3
17:15	turned back, praising God with a loud voice.	3
19:37	began to praise God joyfully with a loud voice	3
23:23	their voices prevailed.	3
23:46	Jesus, crying with a loud voice, said, "Father	3
Jhn 1:23	"I am the voice of one crying out in the wilderness	3
3:29	rejoices greatly at the bridegroom's voice.	3
5:25	the dead will hear the voice of the Son of God	3
5:28	all who are in their graves will hear his voice	3
5:37	never heard his voice or seen his form	3
10: 3	the sheep hear his voice.	3
10: 4	the sheep follow him because they know his voice.	3
10: 5	because they do not know the voice of strangers."	3
10:16	they will listen to my voice.	3
10:27	My sheep hear my voice. I know them	3
11:43	When he had said this, he cried with a loud voice	3
12:28	Then a voice came from heaven	3
12:30	Jesus answered, "This voice has come for your sake	3
18:37	who belongs to the truth listens to my voice."	3
Act 2:14	Peter…raised his voice and addressed them	3
4:24	raised their voices together to God and said	3
7:31	to look, there came the voice of the Lord:	3
7:60	he knelt down and cried out in a loud voice	3
9: 4	He fell to the ground and heard a voice saying	3
9: 7	heard the voice but saw no one.	3
10:13	he heard a voice saying, "Get up, Peter; kill and eat."	3
10:15	The voice said to him again, a second time	3
11: 7	I also heard a voice saying to me, 'Get up, Peter;	3
11: 9	a second time the voice answered from heaven	3
12:14	On recognizing Peter's voice,	3
12:22	shouting, "The voice of a god, and not of a mortal!"	3
14:10	said in a loud voice, "Stand upright on your feet."	3
16:28	Paul shouted in a loud voice, "Do not harm yourself	3
22: 7	to the ground and heard a voice saying to me	3
22: 9	did not hear the voice of the one who was speaking	3
22:14	to see the Righteous One and to hear his own voice;	4
26:14	heard a voice saying to me in the Hebrew language	3
Rom 10:18	"Their voice has gone out to all the earth	2

15: 6	together you may with one voice glorify the God	1
Heb 3: 7	"Today, if you hear his voice	3
3:15	As it is said, "Today, if you hear his voice	3
4: 7	"Today, if you hear his voice	3
12:19	a voice whose words made the hearers beg	3
12:26	At that time his voice shook the earth;	3
2Pe 1:17	that voice was conveyed to him by the Majestic Glory	3
1:18	We ourselves heard this voice come from heaven	3
2:16	a speechless donkey spoke with a human voice	3
Rev 1:10	and I heard behind me a loud voice like a trumpet	3
1:12	I turned to see whose voice it was that spoke to me	3
1:15	his voice was like the sound of many waters.	3
3:20	if you hear my voice and open the door	3
4: 1	the first voice, which I had heard speaking to me	3
5: 2	a mighty angel proclaiming with a loud voice	3
5:11	I heard the voice of many angels	3
5:12	singing with full voice, "Worthy is the Lamb	3
6: 1	creatures call out, as with a voice of thunder,	3
6: 6	I heard what seemed to be a voice in the midst	3
6: 7	I heard the voice of the fourth living creature	3
6:10	they cried out with a loud voice, "Sovereign Lord	3
7: 2	he called with a loud voice to the four angels	3
7:10	cried out in a loud voice, saying, "Salvation	3
8:13	I heard an eagle crying with a loud voice	3
9:13	I heard a voice from the four horns of the…altar	3
10: 4	but I heard a voice from heaven saying	3
10: 8	voice that I had heard from heaven spoke to me	3
11:12	Then they heard a loud voice from heaven saying	3
11:15	and there were loud voices in heaven, saying	3
12:10	Then I heard a loud voice in heaven, proclaiming	3
14: 2	I heard a voice from heaven	3
14: 2	the voice I heard was like the sound of harpists	3
14: 7	He said in a loud voice, "Fear God	3
14: 9	another angel…crying with a loud voice	3
14:13	I heard a voice from heaven saying, "Write this:	3
14:15	Another angel…calling with a loud voice	3
14:18	another angel…called with a loud voice	3
16: 1	Then I heard a loud voice from the temple	3
16:17	and a loud voice came out of the temple	3
18: 2	He called out with a mighty voice	3
18: 4	Then I heard another voice from heaven saying	3
18:23	the voice of bridegroom and bride will be heard	3
19: 1	what seemed to be the loud voice of a great multitude	3
19: 5	And from the throne came a voice saying	3
19: 6	what seemed to be the voice of a great multitude	3
19:17	with a loud voice he called to all the birds	3
21: 3	I heard a loud voice from the throne saying	3

void   *See also* make void

1. καταργέω, *katargeō, 2934*

Rom 4:14 faith is null and the promise is void.   1

voluntarily

1. αὐθαίρετος, *authairetos, 882*

2Co 8: 3 they voluntarily gave according to their means   1

voluntary   *See also* voluntary *gift*

1. ἑκούσιος, *hekousios, 1730*

Phm 1:14 good deed might be voluntary and not something forced.   1

vomit

1. ἐξέραμα, *exerama, 2000*

2Pe 2:22 "The dog turns back to its own vomit,"   1

vote

1. ψῆφος, *psēphos, 6029*

Act 26:10 I also cast my vote against them   1

vow

1. εὐχή, *euchē, 2376*
2. ὅρκος, *horkos, 3992*

Mat 5:33	carry out the vows you have made to the Lord.'	2
Act 18:18	he had his hair cut, for he was under a vow.	1
21:23	We have four men who are under a vow.	1

voyage

1. πλόος, *ploos, 4452*

Act 21: 7	When we had finished the voyage from Tyre	1
27:10	I can see that the voyage will be with danger	1

vulgar   *See* vulgar *talk*

vulture

   1. ἀετός, *aetos, 108*

Mat	24:28 there the vultures will gather.	1
Lke	17:37 there the vultures will gather."	1

W

wage[1]

   1. συμβάλλω, *symballō, 5202*

Lke	14:31 what king, going out to wage war against another	1

wage[2]

   1. μισθός, *misthos, 3635*
   2. ὀψώνιον, *opsōnion, 4072*

Lke	3:14 be satisfied with your wages."	2
Jhn	4:36 The reaper is already receiving wages	1
Rom	4: 4 wages are not reckoned as a gift but as something due.	1
	6:23 For the wages of sin is death	2
1Co	3: 8 each will receive wages according to the labor	1
Jas	5: 4 The wages of the laborers who mowed your fields	1
2Pe	2:15 Balaam…who loved the wages of doing wrong	1

six months' wages

   1. διακόσιοι + δηνάριον, *diakosioi + dēnarion, 1357 + 1324*

Jhn	6: 7 "Six months' wages would not buy enough bread	1

usual daily wage

   1. δηνάριον, *dēnarion, 1324*

Mat	20: 2 for the usual daily wage	1
	20: 9 each of them received the usual daily wage.	1
	20:10 each of them also received the usual daily wage.	1
	20:13 not agree with me for the usual daily wage?	1

wage war

   1. στρατεύομαι, *strateuomai, 5129*

2Co	10: 3 we do not wage war according to human standards;	1
1Pe	2:11 desires…that wage war against the soul.	1

wail

   1. ἀλαλάζω, *alalazō, 226*
   2. θρηνέω, *thrēneō, 2577*
   3. κλαυθμός, *klauthmos, 3088*
   4. κόπτω, *koptō, 3164*
   5. ὀλολύζω, *ololyzō, 3909*

Mat	2:18 "A voice was heard in Ramah, wailing and loud	3
	11:17 we wailed, and you did not mourn.'	2
Mrk	5:38 people weeping and wailing loudly.	1
Lke	7:32 we wailed, and you did not weep.'	2
	8:52 were all weeping and wailing for her;	4
	23:27 were beating their breasts and wailing for him.	2
Jas	5: 1 weep and wail for the miseries that are coming	5
Rev	1: 7 on his account all the tribes of the earth will wail.	4
	18: 9 the kings…will weep and wail over her	4

waist

   1. ὀσφῦς, *osphys, 4019*

Mat	3: 4 leather belt around his waist, and his food was	1
Mrk	1: 6 a leather belt around his waist	1
Eph	6:14 fasten the belt of truth around your waist	1

wait[1]   *See also* lie in wait

   1. ἀναμένω, *anamenō, 388*
   2. ἀπεκδέχομαι, *apekdechomai, 587*
   3. ἀφίημι, *aphiēmi, 918*
   4. ἐκδέχομαι, *ekdechomai, 1683*
   5. μένω, *menō, 3531*
   6. περιμένω, *perimenō, 4338*
   7. προσδέχομαι, *prosdechomai, 4657*
   8. προσδοκάω, *prosdokaō, 4659*

Mat	11: 3 or are we to wait for another?"	8
	27:49 "Wait, let us see whether Elijah will come	3
Mrk	15:36 gave it to him to drink, saying, "Wait	3
Lke	1:21 the people were waiting for Zechariah	8
	7:19 or are we to wait for another?"	8
	7:20 or are we to wait for another?' "	8

	8:40 they were all waiting for him.	8
	12:36 be like those who are waiting for their master	7
Act	1: 4 to wait there for the promise of the Father.	6
	17:16 While Paul was waiting for them in Athens	4
	20: 5 went ahead and were waiting for us in Troas;	5
	20:23 imprisonment and persecutions are waiting for me.	5
	23:21 They are ready now and are waiting for your consent	7
	28: 6 after they had waited a long time	8
Rom	8:19 For the creation waits with eager longing	2
	8:23 groan inwardly while we wait for adoption	2
	8:25 if we hope…we wait for it with patience.	2
1Co	1: 7 as you wait for the revealing of our Lord Jesus	2
	11:33 come together to eat, wait for one another.	4
1Th	1:10 to wait for his Son from heaven	1
Tit	2:13 while we wait for the blessed hope	7
Heb	10:13 and since then has been waiting	4
Jas	5: 7 farmer waits for the precious crop from the earth	4
1Pe	3:20 when God waited patiently in the days of Noah	2
2Pe	3:12 waiting for…the coming of the day of God	8
	3:13 we wait for new heavens and a new earth	8
	3:14 Therefore, beloved, while you are waiting for these	8

wait[2]

   1. διακονέω, *diakoneō, 1354*

Mat	4:11 suddenly angels came and waited on him.	1
Mrk	1:13 the angels waited on him.	1
Act	6: 2 neglect the word of God in order to wait on tables.	1

wait eagerly

   1. ἀπεκδέχομαι, *apekdechomai, 587*

Gal	5: 5 we eagerly wait for the hope of righteousness.	1
Heb	9:28 to save those who are eagerly waiting for him.	1

wait expectantly

   1. προσδέχομαι, *prosdechomai, 4657*

Mrk	15:43 waiting expectantly for the kingdom of God	1
Lke	23:51 waiting expectantly for the kingdom of God.	1

wake

   1. ἐγείρω, *egeirō, 1586*

Act	12: 7 He tapped Peter on the side and woke him, saying	1
Rom	13:11 it is now the moment for you to wake from sleep.	1

wake up

   1. γρηγορέω, *grēgoreō, 1213*
   2. γρηγορέω + γίνομαι, *grēgoreō + ginomai, 1213 + 1181*
   3. διεγείρω, *diegeirō, 1444*
   4. ἐγείρω, *egeirō, 1586*
   5. ἔξυπνος, *exypnos, 2031*

Mat	8:25 they went and woke him up, saying, "Lord, save	4
Mrk	4:38 they woke him up and said to him	4
	4:39 He woke up and rebuked the wind	3
Lke	8:24 They went to him and woke him up, shouting,	3
	8:24 woke up and rebuked the wind and the raging waves;	3
Act	16:27 When the jailer woke up	5
Rev	3: 2 Wake up, and strengthen what remains	2
	3: 3 If you do not wake up, I will come like a thief	1

walk

   1. περιπατέω, *peripateō, 4344*
   2. πορεύομαι, *poreuomai, 4513*

Mat	4:18 As he walked by the Sea of Galilee, he saw two	1
	9: 5 or to say, 'Stand up and walk'?	1
	11: 5 the blind receive their sight, the lame walk	1
	14:25 he came walking toward them on the sea.	1
	14:26 when the disciples saw him walking on the sea	1
	14:29 walking on the water, and came toward Jesus.	1
	15:31 the maimed whole, the lame walking	1
Mrk	2: 9 or to say, 'Stand up and take your mat and walk'?	1
	6:48 he came towards them…walking on the sea.	1
	6:49 when they saw him walking on the sea	1
	8:24 see people, but they look like trees, walking."	1
	11:27 As he was walking in the temple	1
	16:12 ⟦as they were walking into the country.⟧	2
Lke	5:23 or to say, 'Stand up and walk'?	1
	7:22 the blind receive their sight, the lame walk	1
	11:44 people walk over them without realizing it."	1
Jhn	5: 8 "Stand up, take your mat and walk."	1
	5: 9 he took up his mat and began to walk.	1

5:11	'Take up your mat and walk.' "	1
5:12	'Take it up and walk'?"	1
6:19	they saw Jesus walking on the sea	1
8:12	Whoever follows me will never walk in darkness	1
10:23	and Jesus was walking in the temple	1
11: 9	Those who walk during the day do not stumble	1
11:10	those who walk at night stumble,	1
12:35	Walk while you have the light	1
12:35	If you walk in the darkness	1
Act 3: 6	in the name of Jesus Christ…stand up and walk."	1
3: 8	stood and began to walk, and he entered the temple	1
3: 8	walking and leaping and praising God.	1
3: 9	All the people saw him walking and praising God	1
3:12	by our own power or piety we had made him walk?	1
14: 8	never walked, for he had been crippled from birth.	1
14:10	man sprang up and began to walk.	1
Rom 6: 4	so we too might walk in newness of life.	1
8: 4	in us, who walk not according to the flesh	1
14:15	you are no longer walking in love.	1
2Co 5: 7	for we walk by faith, not by sight.	1
1Jn 1: 6	while we are walking in darkness	1
1: 7	if we walk in the light as he himself is in the light	1
2: 6	ought to walk just as he walked.	1
2: 6	ought to walk just as he walked.	1
2:11	is in the darkness, walks in the darkness	1
2Jn 1: 4	to find some of your children walking in the truth	1
1: 6	this is love, that we walk according to his commandments;	1
1: 6	this is the commandment…—you must walk in it.	1
3Jn 1: 3	namely how you walk in the truth.	1
1: 4	to hear that my children are walking in the truth.	1
Rev 2: 1	who walks among the seven golden lampstands:	1
3: 4	they will walk with me…for they are worthy.	1
9:20	idols…which cannot see or hear or walk.	1
21:24	The nations will walk by its light	1

walk about

1. περιπατέω, *peripateō, 4344*

Mrk 5:42	immediately the girl got up and began to walk about	1
Jhn 11:54	Jesus therefore no longer walked about openly	1

walk ahead

1. Contextual: Not in Greek
2. προάγω, *proagō, 4575*

Mrk 10:32	Jesus was walking ahead of them;	2
Lke 24:28	he walked ahead as if he were going on.	1

walk along

1. παράγω, *paragō, 4135*
2. περιπατέω, *peripateō, 4344*
3. προέρχομαι, *proerchomai, 4601*

Mat 9: 9	As Jesus was walking along, he saw a man	1
Mrk 2:14	walking along, he saw Levi son of Alphaeus	1
Lke 24:17	discussing with each other while you walk along?"	2
Jhn 9: 1	As he walked along, he saw a man blind from birth.	1
Act 12:10	they went outside and walked along a lane	3

walk among

1. ἐμπεριπατέω, *emperipateō, 1853*

2Co 6:16	"I will live in them and walk among them	1

walk around

1. περιπατέω, *peripateō, 4344*

Mrk 12:38	who like to walk around in long robes	1
Lke 20:46	the scribes, who like to walk around in long robes	1

walk by

1. περιπατέω, *peripateō, 4344*

Jhn 1:36	as he watched Jesus walk by, he exclaimed, "Look,	1

wall

1. τεῖχος, *teichos, 5446*
2. τοῖχος, *toichos, 5526*
3. φραγμός, *phragmos, 5850*

Act 9:25	and let him down through an opening in the wall	1
23: 3	"God will strike you, you whitewashed wall!	2
2Co 11:33	let down in a basket through a window in the wall	1
Eph 2:14	broken down the dividing wall, that is, the hostility	3
Heb 11:30	By faith the walls of Jericho fell	1
Rev 21:12	It has a great, high wall with twelve gates	1

21:14	And the wall of the city has twelve foundations	1
21:15	to measure the city and its gates and walls.	1
21:17	He also measured its wall	1
21:18	The wall is built of jasper	1
21:19	The foundations of the wall of the city	1

wallow

1. κυλισμός, *kylismos, 3243*

2Pe 2:22	"The sow is washed only to wallow in the mud."	1

wander

1. πλανάω, *planaō, 4414*
2. πλάνη, *planē, 4415*
3. πλανήτης, *planētēs, 4417*

Heb 11:38	wandered in deserts and mountains	1
Jas 5:19	if anyone among you wanders from the truth	1
5:20	brings back a sinner from wandering will save	2
Jde 1:13	wandering stars, for whom the deepest darkness	3

wander away

1. ἀποπλανάω, *apoplanaō, 675*
2. ἐκτρέπω, *ektrepō, 1762*

1Ti 6:10	some have wandered away from the faith	1
2Ti 4: 4	will turn away…and wander away to myths.	2

wander through

1. διέρχομαι, *dierchomai, 1451*

Mat 12:43	it wanders through waterless regions	1
Lke 11:24	it wanders through waterless regions looking for	1

want *See also* have all one wants

1. Contextual: Not in Greek
2. βούλομαι, *boulomai, 1089*
3. ἐπιζητέω, *epizēteō, 2118*
4. ἐπιθυμέω, *epithymeō, 2121*
5. ζητέω, *zēteō, 2426*
6. θέλημα, *thelēma, 2525*
7. θέλω, *thelō, 2527*
8. ἵνα, *hina, 2671*
9. μέλλω, *mellō, 3516*

Mat 5:40	and if anyone wants to sue you and take your coat	7
5:42	do not refuse anyone who wants to borrow	7
12:46	wanting to speak to him.	5
12:47	are standing outside, wanting to speak to you."	5
13:28	'Then do you want us to go and gather them?'	7
14: 5	Though Herod wanted to put him to death	7
15:32	I do not want to send them away hungry	7
16:24	"If any want to become my followers	7
16:25	those who want to save their life will lose it	7
20:21	he said to her, "What do you want?"	7
20:32	"What do you want me to do for you?"	7
21:46	They wanted to arrest him, but they feared	5
26:17	"Where do you want us to make the preparations	7
26:39	yet not what I want but what you want."	7
26:39	yet not what I want but what you want."	1
27:15	release a prisoner…anyone whom they wanted.	7
27:17	"Whom do you want me to release for you	7
27:21	of the two do you want me to release for you?"	7
27:43	let God deliver him now, if he wants to;	7
Mrk 3:13	called to him those whom he wanted	7
6:19	wanted to kill him. But she could not	7
6:25	"I want you to give me at once the head of John	7
6:26	he did not want to refuse her.	7
7:24	entered a house and did not want anyone to know	7
8:34	to them, "If any want to become my followers	7
8:35	those who want to save their life will lose it	7
9:30	He did not want anyone to know it;	7
9:35	"Whoever wants to be first must be last of all	7
10:35	we want you to do for us whatever we ask of you."	7
10:36	"What is it you want me to do for you?"	7
10:51	"What do you want me to do for you?"	7
12:12	they wanted to arrest him	5
14:12	"Where do you want us to go	7
14:36	yet, not what I want, but what you want."	7
14:36	yet, not what I want, but what you want."	1
15: 9	want me to release for you the King of the Jews?"	7
Lke 1:62	find out what name he wanted to give him.	7
4:42	wanted to prevent him from leaving them.	1
8:20	standing outside, wanting to see you."	7

Lke	9:23	"If any want to become my followers	7
	9:24	For those who want to save their life will lose	7
	9:54	do you want us to command fire to come down	7
	10:29	wanting to justify himself, he asked Jesus	7
	12:47	That slave who knew what his master wanted	6
	12:47	did not prepare himself or do what was wanted	6
	13:31	"Get away from here, for Herod wants to kill you."	7
	16:26	so that those who might want to pass from here	7
	18:41	"What do you want me to do for you?"	7
	19:14	'We do not want this man to rule over us.'	7
	19:27	who did not want me to be king over them	7
	20:19	wanted to lay hands on him at that very hour	5
	22: 9	"Where do you want us to make preparations for it?"	7
	23: 8	he had been wanting to see him for a long time	7
	23:20	Pilate, wanting to release Jesus, addressed them	7
Jhn	4:27	"What do you want?" or, "Why are you speaking	5
	5: 6	he said to him, "Do you want to be made well?"	7
	6:11	so also the fish, as much as they wanted.	7
	6:21	they wanted to take him into the boat	7
	7: 4	who wants to be widely known acts in secret.	5
	7:44	Some of them wanted to arrest him	7
	9:27	Why do you want to hear it again?	7
	9:27	Do you also want to become his disciples?"	7
	16:19	Jesus knew that they wanted to ask him	7
	18:39	you want me to release for you the King	2
	19:31	Jews did not want the bodies left on the cross	1
Act	5:33	they were enraged and wanted to kill them.	2
	7:28	Do you want to kill me as you killed the Egyptian	7
	10:10	He became hungry and wanted something to eat;	7
	13: 7	wanted to hear the word of God.	3
	14:13	he and the crowds wanted to offer sacrifice.	7
	15:37	Barnabas wanted to take with them John	2
	16: 3	Paul wanted Timothy to accompany him;	7
	17:18	Some said, "What does this babbler want to say?"	7
	22:30	wanted to find out what Paul was being accused of	2
	23:15	pretext that you want…a more thorough examination	9
	23:28	Since I wanted to know the charge	2
	24:27	wanted to grant the Jews a favor	7
	28:18	the Romans wanted to release me	2
Rom	1:13	I want you to know, brothers and sisters	7
	7:15	I do not do what I want	7
	7:16	Now if I do what I do not want, I agree	7
	7:19	For I do not do the good I want, but the evil	7
	7:19	but the evil I do not want is what I do.	7
	7:20	Now if I do what I do not want, it is no longer I	7
	7:21	when I want to do what is good, evil lies close	7
	11:25	and sisters, I want you to understand this mystery:	7
	16:19	I want you to be wise in what is good	7
1Co	7:32	I want you to be free from anxieties	7
	10: 1	I do not want you to be unaware, brothers	7
	10:20	I do not want you to be partners with demons.	7
	11: 3	I want you to understand	7
	12: 1	I do not want you to be uninformed.	7
	16: 7	I do not want to see you now just in passing	7
2Co	1: 8	not want you to be unaware, brothers and sisters	7
	1:15	I wanted to come to you first	2
	1:16	I wanted to visit you on my way to Macedonia	1
	1:17	Was I vacillating when I wanted to do this?	2
	8: 7	want you to excel also in this generous undertaking.	1
	10: 9	I do not want to seem as though I am trying	1
	11:12	who want an opportunity to be recognized	7
	12:14	I do not want what is yours but you;	5
Gal	1: 7	want to pervert the gospel of Christ.	7
	3: 2	The only thing I want to learn from you is this:	7
	4: 9	you want to be enslaved to them again?	7
	4:17	want to exclude you, so that you may make much	7
	5: 4	You who want to be justified by the law	1
	5:17	to prevent you from doing what you want.	7
	6:12	who want to make a good showing in the flesh	7
	6:13	they want you to be circumcised	7
Php	1:12	I want you to know, beloved	2
	3:10	I want to know Christ and the power of his resurrection	1
Col	2: 1	want you to know how much I am struggling for you	7
	2: 2	I want their hearts to be encouraged	8
1Th	2:18	For we wanted to come to you	7
	2:18	I, Paul, wanted to again and again	1
	4:13	we do not want you to be uninformed,	7
1Ti	5:11	they want to marry	7
	6: 9	those who want to be rich fall into temptation	2
2Ti	3:12	all who want to live a godly life in Christ	7
Phm	1:13	I wanted to keep him with me	2

Heb	6:11	we want each one of you to show…diligence	4
	12:17	when he wanted to inherit the blessing	7
	13:23	I want you to know…	1
Jas	2:20	Do you want to be shown, you senseless person	7
	4: 2	You want something and do not have it; so you…murder.	4
2Pe	3: 9	not wanting any to perish	2
3Jn	1:10	and even prevents those who want to do so	2
Rev	11: 5	if anyone wants to harm them, fire pours	7
	11: 5	anyone who wants to harm them must be killed	7

want to know

1. γνωρίζω, *gnōrizō, 1192*
2. ἐπιζητέω, *epizēteō, 2118*

Act	19:39	If there is anything further you want to know	2
2Co	8: 1	We want you to know…about the grace	1
Gal	1:11	I want you to know, brothers and sisters	1

want to understand

1. γνωρίζω, *gnōrizō, 1192*

1Co	12: 3	Therefore I want you to understand	1

war   *See also* make war, wage war

1. ἀντιστρατεύομαι, *antistrateuomai, 529*
2. πόλεμος, *polemos, 4483*
3. στρατεύομαι, *strateuomai, 5129*

Mat	24: 6	you will hear of wars and rumors of wars;	2
	24: 6	you will hear of wars and rumors of wars;	2
Mrk	13: 7	When you hear of wars and rumors of wars	2
	13: 7	When you hear of wars and rumors of wars	2
Lke	14:31	what king, going out to wage war against another	2
	21: 9	"When you hear of wars and insurrections	2
Rom	7:23	another law at war with the law of my mind	1
Heb	11:34	became mighty in war	2
Jas	4: 1	Do they not come from your cravings…at war within you?	3
Rev	11: 7	the beast…will make war on them and conquer	2
	12: 7	And war broke out in heaven; Michael and his angels	2
	12:17	went off to make war on the rest of her children	2
	13: 7	Also it was allowed to make war on the saints	2
	19:19	kings…with their armies gathered to make war	2

ware

1. Contextual: Not in Greek

Rev	18:15	The merchants of these wares, who gained wealth	1

warfare

1. στρατεία, *strateia, 5127*

2Co	10: 4	for the weapons of our warfare are not merely human	1

warm

1. θερμαίνω, *thermainō, 2548*

Mrk	14:54	warming himself at the fire.	1
	14:67	saw Peter warming himself, she stared at him	1
Jhn	18:18	were standing around it and warming themselves.	1
	18:18	standing with them and warming himself.	1
	18:25	Simon Peter was standing and warming himself.	1
Jas	2:16	"Go in peace; keep warm and eat your fill,"	1

warmly

1. ἀσμένως, *asmenōs, 830*
2. πολύς, *polys, 4498*

Act	21:17	the brothers welcomed us warmly.	1
1Co	16:19	greet you warmly in the Lord.	2

warn

1. Contextual: Not in Greek
2. ἀπειλέω, *apeileō, 580*
3. διαμαρτύρομαι, *diamartyromai, 1371*
4. μαρτυρέω, *martyreō, 3455*
5. νουθετέω, *noutheteō, 3805*
6. προλέγω, *prolegō, 4625*
7. ὑποδείκνυμι, *hypodeiknymi, 5683*
8. χρηματίζω, *chrēmatizō, 5976*

Mat	2:12	having been warned in a dream not to return to Herod	8
	2:22	And after being warned in a dream, he went away	8
	3: 7	"You brood of vipers! Who warned you to flee	7
Lke	3: 7	Who warned you to flee from the wrath to come?	7
	12: 5	I will warn you whom to fear:	7
	16:28	for I have five brothers—that he may warn them	3
Act	4:17	let us warn them to speak no more to anyone	2
	20:31	not cease…to warn everyone with tears.	5

2Co	13: 2	I warned those who sinned previously	6
	13: 2	I warn them now while absent	6
Gal	5:21	I am warning you, as I warned you before:	6
Col	1:28	warning everyone and teaching everyone	5
2Th	3:15	but warn them as believers.	5
1Ti	5:21	I warn you to keep these instructions without prejudice	3
2Ti	2:14	Remind them…and warn them before God	3
Heb	8: 5	Moses…about to erect the tent, was warned	8
	11: 7	warned by God about events as yet unseen	8
	11: 7	Noah…respected the warning and built an ark	1
	12:25	they refused the one who warned them on earth	8
	12:25	if we reject the one who warns from heaven!	1
Rev	22:18	I warn everyone who hears the words	4

warn before

1. προλέγω, *prolegō, 4625*

Gal 5:21 I am warning you, as I warned you before: 1

warn solemnly

1. διαμαρτύρομαι, *diamartyromai, 1371*

1Th 4: 6 just as we have already…solemnly warned you   1

warn sternly

1. ἐμβριμάομαι, *embrimaomai, 1839*

Mrk 1:43 After sternly warning him   1

wash

1. ἀπολούω, *apolouō, 666*
2. ἀπονίπτω, *aponiptō, 672*
3. βαπτίζω, *baptizō, 966*
4. βαπτισμός, *baptismos, 968*
5. λουτρόν, *loutron, 3373*
6. λούω, *louō, 3374*
7. νίπτω, *niptō, 3782*
8. πλύνω, *plynō, 4459*

Mat	6:17	when you fast, put oil on your head and wash your face	7
	15: 2	For they do not wash their hands before they eat."	7
	27:24	and washed his hands before the crowd	2
Mrk	7: 3	do not eat unless they thoroughly wash their hands	7
	7: 4	eat anything from the market unless they wash it	3
	7: 4	washing of cups, pots, and bronze kettles.)	4
Lke	5: 2	were washing their nets.	8
	11:38	he did not first wash before dinner.	3
Jhn	9: 7	saying to him, "Go, wash in the pool of Siloam"	7
	9: 7	Then he went and washed and came back able to see.	7
	9:11	'Go to Siloam and wash.' Then I went and washed	7
	9:11	Then I went and washed and received my sight."	7
	9:15	I washed, and now I see."	7
	13: 5	began to wash the disciples' feet	7
	13: 6	to him, "Lord, are you going to wash my feet?"	7
	13: 8	Peter said to him, "You will never wash my feet."	7
	13: 8	"Unless I wash you, you have no share with me."	7
	13:10	does not need to wash, except for the feet	7
	13:12	After he had washed their feet	7
	13:14	I, your Lord and Teacher, have washed your feet	7
	13:14	you also ought to wash one another's feet.	7
Act	9:37	When they had washed her	6
	16:33	he took them and washed their wounds;	6
1Co	6:11	you were washed, you were sanctified	1
Eph	5:26	cleansing her with the washing of water by the word	5
1Ti	5:10	washed the saints' feet, helped the afflicted	7
Heb	10:22	our bodies washed with pure water.	6
2Pe	2:22	"The sow is washed only to wallow in the mud."	6
Rev	7:14	they have washed their robes and made them white	8
	22:14	Blessed are those who wash their robes	8

wash away

1. ἀπολούω, *apolouō, 666*

Act 22:16 have your sins washed away, calling on his name.'   1

without washing

1. ἄνιπτος, *aniptos, 481*

Mrk 7: 2 eating with defiled hands, that is, without washing   1

waste *See also* lay waste

1. ἀπώλεια, *apōleia, 724*
2. εἰκῇ, *eikē, 1632*
3. καταργέω, *katargeō, 2934*

Mat 26: 8 they were angry and said, "Why this waste?   1

Mrk	14: 4	"Why was the ointment wasted in this way?	1
Lke	13: 7	Cut it down! Why should it be wasting the soil?'	3
Gal	4:11	afraid that my work for you may have been wasted.	2

waste away

1. διαφθείρω, *diaphtheirō, 1425*

2Co 4:16 Even though our outer nature is wasting away   1

watch *See also* keep watch over

1. βλέπω, *blepō, 1063*
2. γρηγορέω, *grēgoreō, 1213*
3. ἐμβλέπω, *emblepō, 1838*
4. θεωρέω, *theōreō, 2555*
5. ὁράω, *horaō, 3972*
6. ὀφθαλμοδουλία, *ophthalmodoulia, 4056*
7. παρατηρέω, *paratēreō, 4190*
8. φυλακή, *phylakē, 5871*

Mrk	3: 2	They watched him to see whether he would cure him	7
	12:41	watched the crowd	4
	13:34	commands the doorkeeper to be on the watch	2
Lke	2: 8	keeping watch over their flock by night.	8
	6: 7	The scribes and the Pharisees watched him	7
	10:18	He said to them, "I watched Satan fall from heaven	4
	20:20	So they watched him and sent spies	7
	23:35	the people stood by, watching;	4
	23:49	stood at a distance, watching these things.	5
Jhn	1:36	as he watched Jesus walk by, he exclaimed, "Look,	3
Act	1: 9	When he had said this, as they were watching	1
	9:24	They were watching the gates day and night	7
Eph	6: 6	not only while being watched, and in order to please	6
Col	3:22	not only while being watched and in order to please	6
Rev	11:12	went up to heaven…while their enemies watched	4

watch closely

1. παρατηρέω, *paratēreō, 4190*

Lke 14: 1 they were watching him closely.   1

watch out

1. βλέπω, *blepō, 1063*
2. ὁράω, *horaō, 3972*

Mat	16: 6	"Watch out, and beware of the yeast	2
Mrk	8:15	"Watch out—beware of the yeast of the Pharisees	2
1Co	10:12	watch out that you do not fall.	1

watchtower

1. πύργος, *pyrgos, 4788*

Mat	21:33	dug a wine press in it, and built a watchtower.	1
Mrk	12: 1	built a watchtower; then he leased it to tenants	1

water *See also* drink only water, give water, water *jar*

1. Contextual: Not in Greek
2. λουτρόν, *loutron, 3373*
3. ποτίζω, *potizō, 4540*
4. ὕδωρ, *hydōr, 5623*

Mat	3:11	"I baptize you with water for repentance, but one	4
	3:16	just as he came up from the water, suddenly	4
	8:32	into the sea and perished in the water.	4
	10:42	whoever gives even a cup of cold water to one	1
	14:28	command me to come to you on the water."	4
	14:29	walking on the water, and came toward Jesus.	4
	17:15	and often into the water.	4
	27:24	took some water and washed his hands	4
Mrk	1: 8	I have baptized you with water;	4
	1:10	just as he was coming up out of the water	4
	9:22	often cast him into the fire and into the water	4
	9:41	whoever gives you a cup of water to drink	4
	14:13	a man carrying a jar of water will meet you;	4
Lke	3:16	John answered…"I baptize you with water;	4
	5: 4	he said to Simon, "Put out into the deep water	1
	7:44	you gave me no water for my feet	4
	8:23	filling with water, and they were in danger.	1
	8:25	he commands even the winds and the water	4
	16:24	send Lazarus to dip the tip of his finger in water	4
	22:10	a man carrying a jar of water will meet you;	4
Jhn	1:26	John answered them, "I baptize with water.	4
	1:31	but I came baptizing with water for this	4
	1:33	but the one who sent me to baptize with water	4
	2: 7	Jesus said to them, "Fill the jars with water."	4
	2: 9	tasted the water that had become wine	4

Jhn	2: 9	(though the servants who had drawn the water knew)	4
	3: 5	without being born of water and Spirit.	4
	3:23	near Salim because water was abundant there;	4
	4: 7	A Samaritan woman came to draw water	4
	4:10	and he would have given you living water."	4
	4:11	Where do you get that living water?	4
	4:13	who drinks of this water will be thirsty again	4
	4:14	who drink of the water that I will give them	4
	4:14	The water that I will give will become in them	4
	4:14	a spring of water gushing up to eternal life."	4
	4:15	give me this water, so that I may never be thirsty	4
	4:15	or have to keep coming here to draw water."	1
	4:46	Cana...where he had changed the water into wine.	4
	5: 7	when the water is stirred up;	4
	7:38	shall flow rivers of living water.' "	4
	13: 5	Then he poured water into a basin	4
	19:34	at once blood and water came out.	4
Act	1: 5	for John baptized with water	4
	8:36	they came to some water;	4
	8:36	the eunuch said, "Look, here is water!	4
	8:38	Philip and the eunuch, went down into the water	4
	8:39	When they came up out of the water	4
	10:47	"Can anyone withhold the water for baptizing	4
	11:16	'John baptized with water	4
1Co	3: 6	I planted, Apollos watered	3
	3: 7	neither the one who plants nor the one who waters is	3
	3: 8	who plants and the one who waters have a common	3
Eph	5:26	cleansing her with the washing of water by the word	4
Tit	3: 5	through the water of rebirth	2
Heb	9:19	with water and scarlet wool and hyssop	4
	10:22	our bodies washed with pure water.	4
Jas	3:11	from the same opening both fresh and brackish water?	1
	3:12	No more can salt water yield fresh.	4
1Pe	3:20	ark, in which a few...were saved through water.	4
2Pe	3: 5	an earth was formed out of water and by means of water	4
	3: 5	an earth was formed out of water and by means of water	4
	3: 6	world...was deluged with water and perished.	4
1Jn	5: 6	This is the one who came by water and blood, Jesus	4
	5: 6	the one who came...not with the water only	4
	5: 6	but with the water and the blood.	4
	5: 8	the Spirit and the water and the blood,	4
Rev	1:15	his voice was like the sound of many waters.	4
	7:17	he will guide them to springs of the water of life	4
	8:10	it fell...on the springs of water.	4
	8:11	A third of the waters became wormwood	4
	8:11	died from the water, because it was made bitter.	4
	11: 6	authority over the waters to turn them into blood	4
	12:15	Then from his mouth the serpent poured water	4
	14: 2	a voice from heaven like the sound of many waters	4
	14: 7	who made...the sea and the springs of water."	4
	16: 4	into the rivers and the springs of water	4
	16: 5	And I heard the angel of the waters say	4
	16:12	its water was dried up in order to prepare the way	4
	17: 1	the great whore who is seated on many waters	4
	17:15	"The waters that you saw, where the whore is	4
	19: 6	like the sound of many waters	4
	21: 6	thirsty I will give water as a gift from the spring	1
	21: 6	as a gift from the spring of the water of life.	4
	22: 1	angel showed me the river of the water of life	4
	22:17	Let anyone who wishes take the water of life	4

waterless

1. ἄνυδρος, *anydros, 536*

Mat	12:43	it wanders through waterless regions	1
Lke	11:24	it wanders through waterless regions looking for	1
2Pe	2:17	These are waterless springs and mists	1
Jde	1:12	waterless clouds carried along by the winds;	1

wave

1. κλύδων, *klydōn, 3114*
2. κῦμα, *kyma, 3246*
3. σάλος, *salos, 4893*
4. ὕδωρ, *hydōr, 5623*

Mat	8:24	so great that the boat was being swamped by the waves;	2
	14:24	boat, battered by the waves, was far from the land	2
Mrk	4:37	the waves beat into the boat	2
Lke	8:24	woke up and rebuked the wind and the raging waves;	4
	21:25	by the roaring of the sea and the waves.	3
Act	27:41	the stern...broken up by the force of the waves.	2
Jas	1: 6	the one who doubts is like a wave of the sea	1
Jde	1:13	wild waves of the sea, casting up the foam	2

waver

1. διακρίνω, *diakrinō, 1359*

| Jde | 1:22 | And have mercy on some who are wavering; | 1 |

make waver

1. διακρίνω, *diakrinō, 1359*

| Rom | 4:20 | No distrust made him waver | 1 |

without wavering

1. ἀκλινής, *aklinēs, 195*

| Heb | 10:23 | Let us hold fast...without wavering | 1 |

way   *See also* all the way, block a way, commit in an ungodly way, give way, go on one's way, hindrance in the way, lead the way, make one's way, obstacle in the way, send on one's way, start on one's way, such a way

1. Contextual: Not in Greek
2. ἀναστροφή, *anastrophē, 419*
3. διά, *dia, 1328*
4. εἰς, *eis, 1650*
5. κατά, *kata, 2848*
6. ὁδός, *hodos, 3847*
7. ὅς, *hos, 4005*
8. οὕτως, *houtōs, 4048*
9. ποῖος, *poios, 4481*
10. πορεία, *poreia, 4512*
11. πορεύομαι, *poreuomai, 4513*
12. ποῦ, *pou, 4544*
13. πῶς, *pōs, 4802*
14. τρόπος, *tropos, 5573*
15. ὡς, *hōs, 6055*

Mat	3: 3	'Prepare the way of the Lord, make his paths	6
	5:25	accuser while you are on the way to court with him	6
	8:28	so fierce that no one could pass that way.	6
	11:10	who will prepare your way before you.'	6
	15:32	for they might faint on the way."	6
	20:17	and said to them on the way	6
	21:32	For John came to you in the way of righteousness	6
	22:16	teach the way of God in accordance with truth	6
Mrk	1: 2	who will prepare your way;	6
	1: 3	'Prepare the way of the Lord	6
	2:23	as they made their way	6
	7:31	went by way of Sidon towards the Sea of Galilee	3
	8: 3	they will faint on the way	6
	8:27	on the way he asked his disciples	6
	9:33	"What were you arguing about on the way?"	6
	9:34	for on the way they had argued with one another	6
	10:52	regained his sight and followed him on the way.	6
	11:18	they kept looking for a way to kill him;	13
	12:14	teach the way of God in accordance with truth.	6
	14: 1	way to arrest Jesus by stealth and kill him;	13
Lke	1:76	you will go before the Lord to prepare his ways	6
	1:79	to guide our feet into the way of peace."	6
	3: 4	'Prepare the way of the Lord	6
	3: 5	the rough ways made smooth;	6
	5: 3	asked him to put out a little way from the shore.	1
	5:19	no way to bring him in because of the crowd	9
	7:27	who will prepare your way before you.'	6
	12:58	on the way make an effort to settle the case	6
	13:22	teaching as he made his way to Jerusalem.	10
	17:11	On the way to Jerusalem	11
	19: 4	he was going to pass that way.	1
	19:47	leaders...kept looking for a way to kill him	1
	20:21	teach the way of God in accordance with truth.	6
	22: 2	were looking for a way to put Jesus to death	13
Jhn	1:23	'Make straight the way of the Lord,' "	6
	14: 4	you know the way to the place where I am going."	6
	14: 5	How can we know the way?"	6
	14: 6	"I am the way, and the truth, and the life.	6
Act	1:11	Jesus...will come in the same way as you saw him go	14
	2:28	You have made known to me the ways of life;	6
	4:21	they let them go, finding no way to punish them	13
	8:39	went on his way rejoicing.	6
	9: 2	found any who belonged to the Way, men or women	6
	9:17	the Lord Jesus, who appeared to you on your way	6
	14:16	allowed all the nations to follow their own ways;	6
	16:17	who proclaim to you a way of salvation."	6
	18:13	worship God in ways that are contrary to the law."	1
	18:25	He had been instructed in the Way of the Lord;	6

18:26	explained the Way of God to him more accurately	6
19: 9	spoke evil of the Way before the congregation	6
19:23	no little disturbance broke out concerning the Way.	6
22: 4	I persecuted this Way up to the point of death	6
24:14	according to the Way, which they call a sect	6
24:22	was rather well informed about the Way	6
25: 3	planning an ambush to kill him along the way.	6
Rom 3: 2	Much, in every way.	14
3: 5	(I speak in a human way.)	5
3:17	the way of peace they have not known."	6
11:33	and how inscrutable his ways!	6
15:15	written to you rather boldly by way of reminder	15
15:28	I will set out by way of you to Spain;	3
1Co 4:17	to remind you of my ways in Christ Jesus	6
7: 6	This I say by way of concession, not of command.	5
12:31	I will show you a still more excellent way.	6
13: 5	It does not insist on its own way;	1
13:11	I became an adult, I put an end to childish ways.	1
2Co 1:16	I wanted to visit you on my way to Macedonia	4
7: 9	so that you were not harmed in any way by us.	1
Eph 4:20	That is not the way you learned Christ!	8
Php 1:18	Just this, that Christ is proclaimed in every way	14
Col 2:18	puffed up without cause by a human way of thinking	1
3: 7	These are the ways you also once followed	7
1Th 3:11	our Lord Jesus direct our way to you.	6
2Th 2: 3	Let no one deceive you in any way;	14
3:16	Lord of peace himself give you peace…in all ways	14
3:17	it is the way I write.	8
Heb 3:10	and they have not known my ways.'	6
9: 8	the way into the sanctuary has not yet been disclosed	6
10:20	by the new and living way that he opened for us	6
Jas 1: 7	being double-minded and unstable in every way,	6
1Pe 1:18	you were ransomed from the futile ways	2
2Pe 2: 2	these teachers the way of truth will be maligned.	6
2:21	to have known the way of righteousness	6
1Jn 2:11	the darkness, and does not know the way to go	12
Jde 1:11	Woe to them! For they go the way of Cain	6
Rev 15: 3	Just and true are your ways, King of the nations!	6
16:12	to prepare the way for the kings from the east.	6

another way

1. ἀλλαχόθεν, *allachothen, 249*

Jhn 10: 1	but climbs in by another way	1

any way

1. πᾶς, *pas, 4246*
2. τὶς, *tis, 5516*

2Co 11: 9	continue to refrain from burdening you in any way.	1
Phm 1:18	If he has wronged you in any way, or owes you	2

every way

1. πάντη, *pantē, 4118*
2. πᾶς, *pas, 4246*

Act 24: 3	We welcome this in every way and everywhere	1
1Co 1: 5	for in every way you have been enriched in him	2
2Co 4: 8	afflicted in every way, but not crushed;	2
6: 4	we have commended ourselves in every way:	2
7: 5	we were afflicted in every way	2
9:11	You will be enriched in every way	2
11: 6	in every way…we have made this evident to you.	2
Eph 4:15	grow up in every way into him who is the head	2
1Ti 3: 4	submissive and respectful in every way	2
4: 8	godliness is valuable in every way	2
5:10	and devoted herself to doing good in every way.	2

fine way

1. καλῶς, *kalos, 2822*

Mrk 7: 9	"You have a fine way of rejecting the commandment	1

in way

1. κατά, *kata, 2848*

Act 17:22	how extremely religious you are in every way.	1

licentious way

1. ἀσέλγεια, *aselgeia, 816*

2Pe 2: 2	Even so, many will follow their licentious ways	1

many ways

1. πολυμερῶς, *polymeros, 4495*

Heb 1: 1	God spoke to our ancestors in many and various ways	1

no way

1. μηδείς, *mēdeis, 3594*
2. οὔτε, *oute, 4046*

Act 25: 8	"I have in no way committed an offense against	2
Php 1:28	in no way intimidated by your opponents.	1

on one's way

1. ἄγω, *agō, 72*
2. ἐκεῖθεν, *ekeithen, 1696*
3. ἔρχομαι, *erchomai, 2262*
4. πορεύομαι, *poreuomai, 4513*

Mat 19:15	he laid his hands on them and went on his way.	2
Lke 9:52	On their way they entered a village of the Samaritans	4
13:33	tomorrow, and the next day I must be on my way	4
Jhn 4:30	They left the city and were on their way to him.	3
14:31	Rise, let us be on our way.	1
Act 20:22	captive to the Spirit, I am on my way to Jerusalem	4
22: 6	"While I was on my way and approaching Damascus	4
1Ti 1: 3	as I did when I was on my way to Macedonia	4

same way

1. αὐτός, *autos, 899*
2. ὁμοίως, *homoiōs, 3931*
3. ὅμως, *homōs, 3940*
4. ὅς, *hos, 4005*
5. οὕτως, *houtōs, 4048*
6. ὡσαύτως, *hōsautōs, 6058*
7. ὥστε, *hōste, 6063*

Mat 5:12	for in the same way they persecuted the prophets	5
5:16	In the same way, let your light shine before others	5
7:17	In the same way, every good tree bears good fruit	5
21:36	they treated them in the same way.	6
25:17	In the same way, the one who had the two talents	6
27:41	In the same way the chief priests also,	2
27:44	The bandits…also taunted him in the same way.	1
Mrk 15:31	In the same way the chief priests	2
Lke 20:31	in the same way all seven died childless.	6
Rom 1:27	in the same way also the men	2
7: 4	In the same way…you have died to the law	7
1Co 9:14	In the same way, the Lord commanded	5
11:25	In the same way he took the cup also, after supper,	6
14: 7	It is the same way with lifeless instruments	3
Eph 5:28	In the same way, husbands should love their wives	5
Php 2:18	in the same way you also must be glad and rejoice	1
Heb 6:17	In the same way, when God desired to show	4
9:21	in the same way he sprinkled with the blood	2
Jas 1:11	the same way with the rich…they will wither away.	5
1Pe 3: 1	Wives, in the same way, accept the authority	2
3: 7	Husbands, in the same way, show consideration	2
5: 5	In the same way, you who are younger must accept	2
Jde 1: 8	Yet in the same way these…defile the flesh	2

that way

1. Contextual: Not in Greek

2Co 5:16	we know him no longer in that way.	1

this way

1. καθώς, *kathōs, 2777*
2. οὗτος, *houtos, 4047*
3. οὕτως, *houtōs, 4048*
4. τοιοῦτος, *toioutos, 5525*

Mat 1:18	birth of Jesus the Messiah took place in this way.	3
3:15	proper for us in this way to fulfill all righteousness."	3
6: 9	"Pray then in this way: Our Father in heaven	3
26:54	which say it must happen in this way?"	3
Mrk 2: 7	"Why does this fellow speak in this way?	3
14: 4	"Why was the ointment wasted in this way?	2
15:39	saw that in this way he breathed his last	3
Lke 13: 2	because these Galileans suffered in this way they	3
Jhn 21: 1	and he showed himself in this way.	3
Act 3:18	In this way God fulfilled what he had foretold	3
13:34	he has spoken in this way	3
21:11	'This is the way the Jews in Jerusalem will bind	3
1Co 4: 1	Think of us in this way, as servants	3
Gal 6: 2	in this way you will fulfill the law of Christ.	3
Php 1: 7	right for me to think this way about all of you	1
4: 1	stand firm in the Lord in this way, my beloved.	3
Heb 6: 9	Even though we speak in this way	3
11:14	for people who speak in this way make it clear	4

1Pe	3: 5	in this way long ago that the holy women	3
2Pe	1:11	For in this way, entry into the eternal kingdom	3
	3:11	Since all these things are to be dissolved in this way	3
1Jn	3:10	children of the devil are revealed in this way:	2
	4: 9	God's love was revealed among us in this way:	2

various ways

1. πολυτρόπως, *polytropōs, 4502*

Heb	1: 1	God spoke to our ancestors in many and various ways	1

way of life

1. ἀναστροφή, *anastrophē, 419*
2. βίωσις, *biōsis, 1052*
3. περιπατέω, *peripateō, 4344*

Act	26: 4	"All the Jews know my way of life from my youth	2
Eph	2:10	God prepared beforehand to be our way of life	3
	4:22	put away your former way of life, your old self	1
Heb	13: 7	consider the outcome of their way of life	1

way out

1. ἔκβασις, *ekbasis, 1676*

1Co	10:13	he will also provide the way out	1

wicked way

1. πονηρία, *ponēria, 4504*

Act	3:26	by turning each of you from your wicked ways."	1

wayward

1. πλανάω, *planaō, 4414*

Heb	5: 2	able to deal gently with the ignorant and wayward	1

we Not Indexed

weak

1. ἀδύνατος, *adynatos, 105*
2. ἀσθενέω, *astheneō, 820*
3. ἀσθενής, *asthenēs, 822*
4. παραλύω, *paralyō, 4168*

Mat	26:41	but the flesh is weak."	3
Mrk	14:38	the flesh is weak."	3
Act	20:35	by such work we must support the weak	2
Rom	5: 6	For while we were still weak…Christ died	3
	14: 1	Welcome those who are weak in faith	2
	14: 2	while the weak eat only vegetables.	2
	15: 1	ought to put up with the failings of the weak	1
1Co	1:27	God chose what is weak in the world	3
	4:10	We are weak, but you are strong.	3
	8: 7	their conscience, being weak, is defiled.	3
	8: 9	somehow become a stumbling block to the weak.	3
	8:10	might they not, since their conscience is weak	3
	8:11	So by your knowledge those weak believers	2
	8:12	wound their conscience when it is weak	2
	9:22	To the weak I became weak	3
	9:22	To the weak I became weak	3
	9:22	so that I might win the weak.	3
	11:30	many of you are weak and ill, and some have died.	3
	12:22	that seem to be weaker are indispensable	3
2Co	10:10	his bodily presence is weak	3
	11:21	To my shame, I must say, we were too weak for that!	2
	11:29	Who is weak, and I am not weak?	2
	11:29	Who is weak, and I am not weak?	2
	12:10	whenever I am weak, then I am strong.	2
	13: 3	He is not weak in dealing with you	2
	13: 4	we are weak in him	2
	13: 9	we rejoice when we are weak and you are strong.	2
Gal	4: 9	weak and beggarly elemental spirits?	3
1Th	5:14	encourage the fainthearted, help the weak	3
Heb	7:18	because it was weak and ineffectual	3
	12:12	and strengthen your weak knees	4
1Pe	3: 7	paying honor to the woman as the weaker sex	3

weaken

1. ἀσθενέω, *astheneō, 820*

Rom	4:19	He did not weaken in faith	1
	8: 3	what the law, weakened by the flesh, could not do:	1

weakness

1. ἀσθένεια, *astheneia, 819*
2. ἀσθενής, *asthenēs, 822*

Rom	8:26	Likewise the Spirit helps us in our weakness;	1
1Co	1:25	God's weakness is stronger than human strength	2
	2: 3	And I came to you in weakness and in fear	1
	15:43	It is sown in weakness, it is raised in power.	1
2Co	11:30	I will boast of the things that show my weakness.	1
	12: 5	I will not boast, except of my weaknesses.	1
	12: 9	for power is made perfect in weakness."	1
	12: 9	I will boast all the more gladly of my weaknesses	1
	12:10	I am content with weaknesses, insults, hardships	1
	13: 4	For he was crucified in weakness	1
Heb	4:15	is unable to sympathize with our weaknesses	1
	5: 2	since he himself is subject to weakness;	1
	7:28	appoints as high priests those who are subject to weakness	1
	11:34	won strength out of weakness	1

wealth *See also* gain wealth

1. εὐπορία, *euporia, 2345*
2. μαμωνᾶς, *mamōnas, 3440*
3. πλοῦτος, *ploutos, 4458*
4. τιμιότης, *timiotēs, 5509*
5. χρῆμα, *chrēma, 5975*

Mat	6:24	the other. You cannot serve God and wealth.	2
	13:22	and the lure of wealth choke the word	3
Mrk	4:19	the cares of the world, and the lure of wealth	3
	10:23	"How hard it will be for those who have wealth	5
Lke	16: 9	make friends…by means of dishonest wealth	2
	16:11	not been faithful with the dishonest wealth	2
	16:13	You cannot serve God and wealth."	2
	18:24	hard it is for those who have wealth to enter	5
Act	19:25	"Men…we get our wealth from this business.	1
2Co	8: 2	overflowed in a wealth of generosity	3
Heb	11:26	greater wealth than the treasures of Egypt	3
Rev	5:12	to receive power and wealth and wisdom and might	3
	18:17	in one hour all this wealth has been laid waste!"	3
	18:19	all who had ships at sea grew rich by her wealth!	4

weapon

1. ὅπλον, *hoplon, 3960*

Jhn	18: 3	lanterns and torches and weapons.	1
2Co	6: 7	with the weapons of righteousness	1
	10: 4	for the weapons of our warfare are not merely human	1

wear

1. ἐνδύω, *endyō, 1907*
2. ἔχω, *echō, 2400*
3. περιβάλλω, *periballō, 4314*
4. περίθεσις, *perithesis, 4324*
5. ὑποδέω, *hypodeō, 5686*
6. φορέω, *phoreō, 5841*

Mat	3: 4	Now John wore clothing of camel's hair	2
	6:25	or about your body, what you will wear.	1
	6:31	will we drink?' or 'What will we wear?'	3
	11: 8	those who wear soft robes are in royal palaces.	6
	22:11	a man there who was not wearing a wedding robe	1
Mrk	6: 9	to wear sandals and not to put on two tunics.	5
	14:51	wearing nothing but a linen cloth.	3
Lke	8:27	For a long time he had worn no clothes	1
	12:22	or about your body, what you will wear.	1
Jhn	19: 5	Jesus came out, wearing the crown of thorns	6
Jas	2: 3	you take notice of the one wearing the fine clothes	6
1Pe	3: 3	adorn yourselves outwardly by…wearing gold ornaments	4
Rev	9:17	the riders wore breastplates the color of fire	2
	11: 3	authority to prophesy…wearing sackcloth."	3
	19:14	wearing fine linen, white and pure	1

wear a veil

1. κατακαλύπτω, *katakalyptō, 2877*

1Co	11: 6	she should wear a veil.	1

wear long hair

1. κομάω, *komaō, 3150*

1Co	11:14	if a man wears long hair, it is degrading to him	1

wear out

1. παλαιόω, *palaioō, 4096*
2. ὑπωπιάζω, *hypōpiazō, 5724*

Lke	12:33	purses for yourselves that do not wear out	1
	18: 5	she may not wear me out by continually coming.' "	2
Heb	1:11	they will all wear out like clothing;	1

weary

1. ἐγκακέω, *enkakeō, 1591*
2. κοπιάω, *kopiaō, 3159*

Mat 11:28 all you that are weary and are carrying heavy burdens   2
2Th 3:13 and sisters, do not be weary in doing what is right.   1

grow weary

1. ἐγκακέω, *enkakeō, 1591*
2. κάμνω, *kamnō, 2827*
3. κοπιάω, *kopiaō, 3159*

1Co 4:12 we grow weary from the work of our own hands.   3
Gal   6: 9 let us not grow weary in doing what is right   1
Heb 12: 3 you may not grow weary or lose heart.   2
Rev   2: 3 and that you have not grown weary.   3

fair weather

1. εὐδία, *eudia, 2304*

Mat 16: 2 'It will be fair weather, for the sky is red.'   1

weave

1. πλέκω, *plekō, 4428*
2. ὑφαντός, *hyphantos, 5733*

Jhn 19: 2 the soldiers wove a crown of thorns   1
     19:23 seamless, woven in one piece from the top.   2

wedding *See also* wedding *banquet,* wedding *hall*

1. γάμος, *gamos, 1141*
2. νυμφών, *nymphōn, 3813*

Mat 9:15 Jesus said to them, "The wedding guests cannot mourn   2
     22: 8 Then he said to his slaves, 'The wedding is ready   1
     22:11 a man there who was not wearing a wedding robe   1
     22:12 how did you get in here without a wedding robe?'   1
Mrk 2:19 wedding guests cannot fast while the bridegroom   2
Lke 5:34 "You cannot make wedding guests fast   2
Jhn 2: 1 there was a wedding in Cana of Galilee   1
     2: 2 Jesus...had also been invited to the wedding.   1

weed

1. ζιζάνιον, *zizanion, 2429*

Mat 13:25 an enemy came and sowed weeds among the wheat   1
     13:26 then the weeds appeared as well.   1
     13:27 Where, then, did these weeds come from?'   1
     13:29 in gathering the weeds you would uproot the wheat   1
     13:30 Collect the weeds first and bind them in bundles   1
     13:36 the parable of the weeds of the field."   1
     13:38 the weeds are the children of the evil one   1
     13:40 as the weeds are collected and burned up   1

week

1. ὀκτώ + ἡμέρα, *oktō + hēmera, 3893 + 2465*
2. σάββατον, *sabbaton, 4879*

Mat 28: 1 as the first day of the week was dawning   2
Mrk 16: 2 very early on the first day of the week   2
     16: 9 ⟦after he rose early on the first day of the week⟧   2
Lke 18:12 I fast twice a week; I give a tenth of all   2
     24: 1 on the first day of the week, at early dawn   2
Jhn 20: 1 Early on the first day of the week   2
     20:19 the first day of the week   2
     20:26 A week later his disciples were...in the house   1
Act 20: 7 On the first day of the week   2
1Co 16: 2 On the first day of every week   2

weep

1. δακρύω, *dakryō, 1233*
2. κλαίω, *klaiō, 3081*
3. κλαυθμός, *klauthmos, 3088*

Mat 2:18 wailing and loud lamentation, Rachel weeping   2
     8:12 darkness, where there will be weeping and gnashing   3
     13:42 there will be weeping and gnashing of teeth.   3
     13:50 there will be weeping and gnashing of teeth.   3
     22:13 there will be weeping and gnashing of teeth.'   3
     24:51 there will be weeping and gnashing of teeth.   3
     25:30 there will be weeping and gnashing of teeth.'   3
     26:75 he went out and wept bitterly.   2
Mrk 5:38 people weeping and wailing loudly.   2
     5:39 "Why do you make a commotion and weep?   2
     14:72 he broke down and wept.   2
     16:10 ⟦while they were mourning and weeping.⟧   2
Lke 6:21 "Blessed are you who weep now,   2

6:25 for you will mourn and weep.   2
7:13 and said to her, "Do not weep."   2
7:32 we wailed, and you did not weep.'   2
7:38 stood behind him at his feet, weeping   2
8:52 were all weeping and wailing for her;   2
8:52 "Do not weep; for she is not dead but sleeping."   2
13:28 There will be weeping and gnashing of teeth   3
19:41 As he came near and saw the city, he wept over it   2
22:62 he went out and wept bitterly.   2
23:28 "Daughters of Jerusalem, do not weep for me   2
23:28 weep for yourselves and for your children.   2
Jhn 11:31 she was going to the tomb to weep there.   2
     11:33 When Jesus saw her weeping   2
     11:33 and the Jews who came with her also weeping   2
     11:35 Jesus began to weep.   1
     16:20 you will weep and mourn   2
     20:11 Mary stood weeping outside the tomb.   2
     20:11 As she wept, she bent over to look into the tomb;   2
     20:13 They said to her, "Woman, why are you weeping?"   2
     20:15 Jesus said to her, "Woman, why are you weeping?   2
Act 9:39 All the widows stood beside him, weeping   2
     20:37 There was much weeping among them all   3
     21:13 "What are you doing, weeping and breaking my heart?   2
Rom 12:15 weep with those who weep.   2
     12:15 weep with those who weep.   2
Jas 4: 9 Lament and mourn and weep.   2
     5: 1 weep and wail for the miseries that are coming   2
Rev 5: 4 to weep bitterly because no one was found worthy   2
     5: 5 Then one of the elders said to me, "Do not weep.   2
     18: 9 the kings...will weep and wail over her   2
     18:11 the merchants of the earth weep and mourn for her   2
     18:15 fear of her torment, weeping and mourning aloud   2
     18:19 as they wept and mourned, crying out, "Alas, alas   2

weigh

1. Contextual: Not in Greek
2. διακρίνω, *diakrinō, 1359*

Jhn 19:39 myrrh and aloes, weighing about a hundred pounds   1
1Co 14:29 let the others weigh what is said.   2
Rev 16:21 hailstones, each weighing about a hundred pounds   1

weigh anchor

1. αἴρω, *airō, 149*
2. περιαιρέω, *periaireō, 4311*

Act 27:13 they weighed anchor and began to sail past Crete   1
     28:13 we weighed anchor and came to Rhegium.   2

weigh down

1. βαρέω, *bareō, 976*

Lke 9:32 were weighed down with sleep;   1
     21:34 so that your hearts are not weighed down   1

weight

1. βάρος, *baros, 983*
2. ὄγκος, *onkos, 3839*

2Co 4:17 preparing us for an eternal weight of glory   1
Heb 12: 1 Therefore...let us also lay aside every weight   2

weighty

1. βαρύς, *barys, 987*

2Co 10:10 For they say, "His letters are weighty and strong   1

weighty matter

1. βαρύς, *barys, 987*

Mat 23:23 have neglected the weightier matters of the law: 1

welcome

1. Contextual: Not in Greek
2. ἀποδέχομαι, *apodechomai, 622*
3. ἀσπάζομαι, *aspazomai, 832*
4. δέχομαι, *dechomai, 1312*
5. εἰσδέχομαι, *eisdechomai, 1654*
6. εἴσοδος, *eisodos, 1658*
7. ἐπιδέχομαι, *epidechomai, 2110*
8. παραδέχομαι, *paradechomai, 4138*
9. προσδέχομαι, *prosdechomai, 4657*
10. προσλαμβάνω, *proslambanō, 4689*
11. συνάγω, *synagō, 5251*
12. ὑποδέχομαι, *hypodechomai, 5685*

13. χαίρω, *chairō*, 5897

Mat	10:14	If anyone will not welcome you or listen	4
	10:40	"Whoever welcomes you welcomes me	4
	10:40	"Whoever welcomes you welcomes me	4
	10:40	whoever welcomes me welcomes the one who sent me.	4
	10:40	whoever welcomes me welcomes the one who sent me.	4
	10:41	Whoever welcomes a prophet in the name of a prophet	4
	10:41	whoever welcomes a righteous person	4
	18: 5	Whoever welcomes one such child in my name	4
	18: 5	one such child in my name welcomes me.	4
	25:35	I was a stranger and you welcomed me	11
	25:38	that we saw you a stranger and welcomed you	11
	25:43	I was a stranger and you did not welcome me	11
Mrk	6:11	If any place will not welcome you	4
	9:37	"Whoever welcomes one such child in my name	4
	9:37	welcomes one such child in my name welcomes me	4
	9:37	whoever welcomes me welcomes not me	4
	9:37	whoever welcomes me welcomes not me	4
Lke	8:40	Now when Jesus returned, the crowd welcomed him	2
	9: 5	Wherever they do not welcome you	4
	9:11	he welcomed them, and spoke to them	2
	9:48	"Whoever welcomes this child in my name	4
	9:48	"Whoever welcomes this child…welcomes me	4
	9:48	whoever welcomes me welcomes the one who sent me;	4
	9:48	whoever welcomes me welcomes the one who sent me;	4
	10: 8	you enter a town and its people welcome you	4
	10:10	they do not welcome you	4
	15: 2	"This fellow welcomes sinners and eats with them."	9
	16: 4	people may welcome me into their homes.'	4
	16: 9	welcome you into the eternal homes.	4
	19: 6	down and was happy to welcome him.	12
Jhn	4:45	he came to Galilee, the Galileans welcomed him	4
Act	2:41	So those who welcomed his message were baptized	2
	15: 4	were welcomed by the church and the apostles	8
	17:11	they welcomed the message very eagerly	4
	18:27	wrote to the disciples to welcome him.	2
	21:17	the brothers welcomed us warmly.	2
	24: 3	We welcome this in every way and everywhere	2
	25:13	Agrippa…arrived at Caesarea to welcome Festus.	3
	28: 2	they kindled a fire and welcomed all of us	10
	28:30	welcomed all who came to him	2
Rom	14: 1	Welcome those who are weak in faith	10
	14: 3	for God has welcomed them.	10
	15: 7	Welcome one another, therefore	10
	15: 7	therefore, just as Christ has welcomed you	10
	16: 2	welcome her in the Lord as is fitting for the saints	9
2Co	6:17	touch nothing unclean; then I will welcome you	5
	7:15	you welcomed him with fear and trembling.	4
Gal	4:14	welcomed me as an angel of God	4
Php	2:29	Welcome him then in the Lord with all joy	9
Col	4:10	if he comes to you, welcome him.	4
1Th	1: 9	report about us what kind of welcome we had	6
Phm	1:17	welcome him as you would welcome me.	10
	1:17	welcome him as you would welcome me.	1
Jas	1:21	welcome with meekness the implanted word	4
	2:25	justified…when she welcomed the messengers	12
2Jn	1:10	Do not receive into the house or welcome	13
	1:11	for to welcome is to participate in the evil	13
3Jn	1:10	he refuses to welcome the friends	7

welcome into a home

1. ὑποδέχομαι, *hypodechomai*, 5685

Lke	10:38	a woman named Martha welcomed him into her home	1

welfare

1. περί, *peri*, 4309

Php	2:20	who will be genuinely concerned for your welfare.	1

well[1] *See also* attest well, do well, give as well, go well, know well, make well, please well, speak well

1. Contextual: Not in Greek
2. εὖ, *eu*, 2292
3. εὐοδόω, *euodoō*, 2338
4. καλός, *kalos*, 2819
5. καλῶς, *kalōs*, 2822
6. κρείττων, *kreittōn*, 3202

Mrk	7:37	"He has done everything well	5
	12:28	seeing that he answered them well, he asked him	5
Lke	6:26	"Woe to you when all speak well of you	5
	6:48	because it had been well built.	5

	13: 9	If it bears fruit next year, well and good;	1
	20:39	"Teacher, you have spoken well."	5
Act	15:29	you will do well. Farewell."	2
1Co	7: 1	"It is well for a man not to touch a woman."	4
	7: 8	it is well for them to remain unmarried as I am.	4
	7:26	it is well for you to remain as you are.	4
	7:37	to keep her as his fianc,e, he will do well.	5
	7:38	So then, he who marries his fianc,e does well;	5
	7:38	he who refrains from marriage will do better.	6
	14:17	For you may give thanks well enough	5
Gal	5: 7	You were running well;	5
Eph	6: 3	"so that it may be well with you	2
1Ti	3: 4	He must manage his own household well	5
	3: 7	Moreover, he must be well thought of by outsiders	4
	3:12	let them manage…their households well;	5
	3:13	those who serve well as deacons	5
	5:17	the elders who rule well	5
Heb	13: 9	is well for the heart to be strengthened by grace	4
Jas	2: 8	You do well if you really fulfill the royal law	5
	2:19	You believe that God is one; you do well.	5
2Pe	1:19	You will do well to be attentive to this	5
3Jn	1: 2	just as it is well with your soul.	3
	1: 6	You will do well to send them on	5

well[2]

1. δέ, *de*, 1254
2. καθώς, *kathōs*, 2777
3. καί, *kai*, 2779
4. μετά, *meta*, 3552

Mat	5:40	your coat, give your cloak as well;	3
	13:26	then the weeds appeared as well.	3
Lke	8: 2	as well as some women who had been cured	3
Jhn	12:10	planned to put Lazarus to death as well	3
Act	1:14	Mary the mother of Jesus, as well as his brothers.	3
	6:12	They stirred up the people as well as the elders	3
	7:15	He himself died there as well as our ancestors	3
	17:13	proclaimed by Paul in Beroea as well	3
	20: 4	as well as by Tychicus and Trophimus from Asia.	1
Rom	16: 2	a benefactor of many and of myself as well.	3
1Co	16:18	for they refreshed my spirit as well as yours.	3
2Co	7:14	so our boasting to Titus has proved true as well	3
Php	1:29	suffering for him as well	3
Col	4: 3	At the same time pray for us as well	3
2Th	1: 7	give relief to the afflicted as well as to us	4
1Ti	5: 7	Give these commands as well	3
2Ti	2: 2	who will be able to teach others as well.	3
Heb	5: 3	as well as for those of the people.	2
	7:12	necessarily a change in the law as well.	3
1Pe	5: 1	as well as one who shares in the glory to be	3

well[3]

1. ἰσχύω, *ischyō*, 2710
2. ὑγιαίνω, *hygiainō*, 5617
3. ὑγιής, *hygiēs*, 5618

Mat	9:12	"Those who are well have no need of a physician	1
Mrk	2:17	"Those who are well have no need of a physician	1
Lke	5:31	"Those who are well have no need of a physician	2
Jhn	5: 6	he said to him, "Do you want to be made well?"	3
	5: 9	At once the man was made well	3
	5:11	he answered them, "The man who made me well said	3
	5:14	"See, you have been made well!	3
	5:15	it was Jesus who had made him well.	3

well[4]

1. πηγή, *pēgē*, 4380
2. φρέαρ, *phrear*, 5853

Lke	14: 5	a child or an ox that has fallen into a well	2
Jhn	4: 6	Jacob's well was there, and Jesus…sitting	1
	4: 6	Jesus…was sitting by the well.	1
	4:11	you have no bucket, and the well is deep.	2
	4:12	Jacob, who gave us the well, and with his sons	2

rather well

1. ἀκριβῶς, *akribōs*, 209

Act	24:22	was rather well informed about the Way	1

very well

1. ἀκριβῶς, *akribōs*, 209
2. βελτίων, *beltiōn*, 1019
3. καλῶς, *kalōs*, 2822

Act 25:10 done no wrong to the Jews, as you very well know.   3
1Th   5: 2 you...know very well that the day of the Lord   1
2Ti   1:18 you know very well how much service he rendered   2

well off

1. περισσεύω, *perisseuō, 4355*

1Co   8: 8 and no better off if we do.   1

well-fed

1. χορτάζω, *chortazō, 5963*

Php   4:12 I have learned the secret of being well-fed   1

well-versed

1. δυνατός, *dynatos, 1543*

Act 18:24 an eloquent man, well-versed in the scriptures.   1

west

1. δύσις, *dysis, 1550*
2. δυσμή, *dysmē, 1553*

Mat   8:11 I tell you, many will come from east and west   2
     24:27 lightning...flashes as far as the west   2
Mrk 16: S ⟦sent out through them, from east to west,⟧   1
Lke 12:54 "When you see a cloud rising in the west   2
     13:29 come from east and west, from north and south   2
Rev 21:13 and on the west three gates.   2

what Not Indexed; *See* from what, teach what is good

what about

1. τίς, *tis, 5515*

Jhn 21:21 he said to Jesus, "Lord, what about him?"   1

what is done

1. ἔργον, *ergon, 2240*

Rev 20:13 and all were judged according to what they had done.   1

what kind

1. οἷος, *hoios, 3888*
2. ὁποῖος, *hopoios, 3961*
3. ποῖος, *poios, 4481*
4. ποταπός, *potapos, 4534*
5. τίς, *tis, 5515*

Lke   4:36 "What kind of utterance is this?   5
     7:39 known who and what kind of woman this is   4
Act   7:49 What kind of house will you build for me   3
1Co 15:35 With what kind of body do they come?"   3
1Th   1: 5 you know what kind of persons we proved to be   1
     1: 9 report about us what kind of welcome we had   1

what sort

1. ὁποῖος, *hopoios, 3961*
2. ποταπός, *potapos, 4534*

Mat   8:27 amazed, saying, "What sort of man is this   2
Lke   1:29 pondered what sort of greeting this might be.   2
1Co   3:13 test what sort of work each has done.   1

what sort of person

1. ποταπός, *potapos, 4534*

2Pe   3:11 what sort of persons ought you to be   1

what thing

1. ποῖος, *poios, 4481*

Lke 24:19 He asked them, "What things?"   1

whatever Not Indexed

wheat

1. σῖτος, *sitos, 4992*

Mat   3:12 clear his threshing floor and will gather his wheat   1
     13:25 sowed weeds among the wheat, and then went away.   1
     13:29 in gathering the weeds you would uproot the wheat   1
     13:30 but gather the wheat into my barn.' "   1
Lke   3:17 to gather the wheat into his granary;   1
     16: 7 He replied, 'A hundred containers of wheat.'   1
     22:31 Satan has demanded to sift all of you like wheat   1
Jhn 12:24 unless a grain of wheat falls into the earth   1
Act 27:38 throwing the wheat into the sea.   1
1Co 15:37 perhaps of wheat or of some other grain.   1

Rev   6: 6 "A quart of wheat for a day's pay   1
     18:13 wine, olive oil, choice flour and wheat, cattle and sheep   1

when Not Indexed

whenever

1. ἐάν, *ean, 1569*
2. ἡνίκα + ἄν, *hēnika + an, 2471 + 323*
3. ὅπου + ἐάν, *hopou + ean, 3963 + 1569*
4. ὅς + ἄν, *hos + an, 4005 + 323*
5. ὅταν, *hotan, 4020*
6. ὡς, *hōs, 6055*

Mat   6: 2 "So whenever you give alms, do not sound a trumpet   5
     6: 5 whenever you pray, do not be like the hypocrites;   5
     6: 6 whenever you pray, go into your room and shut the door   5
     6:16 whenever you fast, do not look dismal   5
Mrk   3:11 Whenever the unclean spirits saw him   5
     9:18 whenever it seizes him, it dashes him down;   3
     11:25 "Whenever you stand praying, forgive   5
     14: 7 you can show kindness to them whenever you wish;   5
Lke 10: 8 Whenever you enter a town and its people welcome   4
     10:10 whenever you enter a town   4
2Co   3:15 Indeed, to this very day whenever Moses is read   2
     12:10 whenever I am weak, then I am strong.   5
Gal   6:10 So then, whenever we have an opportunity   6
Jas   1: 2 My brothers and sisters, whenever you face trials   5
1Jn   3:20 whenever our hearts condemn us;   1
Rev   4: 9 whenever the living creatures give glory   5

where

1. ἐκεῖ, *ekei, 1695*
2. ἐν, *en, 1877*
3. ἐν + ὅς, *en + hos, 1877 + 4005*
4. ἐπί + ὅς, *epi + hos, 2093 + 4005*
5. ὅθεν, *hothen, 3854*
6. ὅπου, *hopou, 3963*
7. ὅς, *hos, 4005*
8. οὗ, *hou, 4023*
9. πόθεν, *pothen, 4470*
10. ποῦ, *pou, 4544*
11. ὡς, *hōs, 6055*

Mat   2: 2 "Where is the child who has been born king of the Jews?   10
     2: 4 inquired of them where the Messiah was to be born.   10
     2: 9 stopped over the place where the child was.   8
     6:19 on earth, where moth and rust consume and where   6
     6:19 where moth and rust consume and where thieves   6
     6:20 in heaven, where neither moth nor rust consumes   6
     6:20 where thieves do not break in and steal.   6
     6:21 For where your treasure is, there your heart will   6
     8:12 darkness, where there will be weeping and gnashing   1
     13: 5 where they did not have much soil   6
     13:27 Where, then, did these weeds come from?'   9
     13:42 where there will be weeping and gnashing of teeth.   1
     13:50 where there will be weeping and gnashing of teeth.   1
     13:54 "Where did this man get this wisdom   9
     13:56 Where then did this man get all this?"   9
     15:29 he went up the mountain, where he sat down.   1
     15:33 "Where are we to get enough bread in the desert   9
     18:20 For where two or three are gathered in my name   8
     22:13 where there will be weeping and gnashing of teeth.'   1
     24:51 where there will be weeping and gnashing of teeth.   1
     25:24 reaping where you did not sow   6
     25:24 gathering where you did not scatter seed;   5
     25:26 You knew...that I reap where I did not sow   6
     25:26 gather where I did not scatter?   5
     25:30 where there will be weeping and gnashing of teeth.'   1
     26:17 "Where do you want us to make the preparations   10
     28: 6 Come, see the place where he lay.   6
Mrk   4: 5 where it did not have much soil   6
     4:15 the ones on the path where the word is sown: 6
     5:40 and went in where the child was.   6
     6: 2 "Where did this man get all this?   9
     9:48 where their worm never dies   6
     13:14 set up where it ought not to be   6
     14:12 "Where do you want us to go   10
     14:14 'The Teacher asks, Where is my guest room   10
     14:14 where I may eat the Passover with my disciples?'   6
     15:47 the mother of Joses saw where the body was laid.   10
Lke   4:16 to Nazareth, where he had been brought up   8
     4:17 found the place where it was written: 8

Lke	8:25	He said to them, "Where is your faith?"	10
	10: 1	place where he himself intended to go.	8
	12:33	where no thief comes near and no moth destroys.	6
	12:34	where your treasure is, there your heart will be	6
	17:17	ten made clean? But the other nine, where are	10
	17:37	they asked him, "Where, Lord?"	10
	17:37	"Where the corpse is, there the vultures will gather."	6
	20:37	where he speaks of the Lord as the God of Abraham	11
	22: 9	"Where do you want us to make preparations for it?"	10
	22:11	"Where is the guest room	10
	22:11	where I may eat the Passover with my disciples?" '	6
	23:53	tomb where no one had ever been laid.	8
Jhn	1:28	across the Jordan where John was baptizing.	6
	1:38	to him, "Rabbi"…"where are you staying?"	10
	1:39	They came and saw where he was staying	10
	1:48	Nathanael asked him, "Where did you get to know me?"	9
	3: 8	The wind blows where it chooses	6
	3: 8	do not know where it comes from or where it goes.	10
	4:11	Where do you get that living water?	9
	4:20	place where people must worship is in Jerusalem	6
	4:46	Cana…where he had changed the water into wine.	6
	6: 5	"Where are we to buy bread for these people	9
	6:23	the place where they had eaten the bread	6
	6:62	the Son of Man ascending to where he was before?	6
	7:11	The Jews were…saying, "Where is he?"	10
	7:34	where I am, you cannot come."	6
	7:35	"Where does this man intend to go	10
	7:36	'Where I am, you cannot come'?"	6
	7:42	from Bethlehem, the village where David lived?"	6
	8:10	⟦"Woman, where are they? Has no one condemned⟧	10
	8:14	I know where I have come from and where I am going	10
	8:14	do not know where I come from or where I am going.	6
	8:19	Then they said to him, "Where is your Father?"	10
	8:21	Where I am going, you cannot come."	6
	8:22	by saying, 'Where I am going, you cannot come'?"	6
	9:12	They said to him, "Where is he?"	10
	10:40	to the place where John had been baptizing earlier	6
	11:30	still at the place where Martha had met him.	6
	11:32	When Mary came where Jesus was and saw him	6
	11:34	He said, "Where have you laid him?"	10
	11:57	orders that anyone who knew where Jesus was	10
	12:26	where I am, there will my servant be also.	6
	12:35	do not know where you are going.	10
	13:33	'Where I am going, you cannot come.'	6
	13:36	Peter said to him, "Lord, where are you going?"	10
	13:36	"Where I am going, you cannot follow me now;	6
	14: 3	so that where I am, there you may be also.	6
	14: 4	you know the way to the place where I am going."	6
	14: 5	"Lord, we do not know where you are going.	10
	16: 5	yet none of you asks me, 'Where are you going?'	10
	17:24	may be with me where I am	6
	18: 1	to a place where there was a garden	6
	18:20	where all the Jews come together.	6
	19:20	the place where Jesus was crucified	6
	19:41	a garden in the place where he was crucified	6
	20: 2	we do not know where they have laid him."	10
	20:12	sitting where the body of Jesus had been lying	6
	20:13	I do not know where they have laid him."	10
	20:15	tell me where you have laid him,	10
	20:19	the house where the disciples had met	6
	21:18	take you where you do not wish to go."	6
Act	1:13	to the room upstairs where they were staying	8
	2: 2	it filled the entire house where they were sitting.	8
	7:33	the place where you are standing is holy ground.	4
	11:11	arrived at the house where we were.	2
	12:12	the house of Mary…where many had gathered	8
	14:26	where they had been commended to the grace of God	5
	15:36	in every city where we proclaimed the word	3
	16: 1	where there was a disciple named Timothy	1
	16:13	the river, where we supposed there was	8
	17: 1	where there was a synagogue of the Jews.	6
	20: 6	Troas, where we stayed for seven days.	6
	20: 8	the room upstairs where we were meeting.	8
	25:10	emperor's tribunal; this is where I should be tried.	8
Rom	4:15	where there is no law, neither is there violation.	8
	5:20	but where sin increased, grace abounded	8
	9:26	in the very place where it was said to them	8
	15:20	not where Christ has already been named	6
1Co	1:20	Where is the one who is wise?	10
	1:20	Where is the scribe?	10
	1:20	Where is the debater of this age?	10

	12:17	whole body…an eye, where would the hearing be?	10
	12:17	where would the sense of smell be?	10
	12:19	all were a single member, where would the body be?	10
	15:55	"Where, O death, is your victory?	10
	15:55	Where, O death, is your sting?"	10
2Co	3:17	and where the Spirit of the Lord is	8
Col	3: 1	where Christ is, seated at the right hand of God.	8
Heb	3: 9	where your ancestors put me to the test	8
	6:20	where Jesus, a forerunner on our behalf, has entered	6
	9:16	Where a will is involved	6
	10:18	Where there is forgiveness of these	6
	11: 8	he set out, not knowing where he was going.	10
Jas	3:16	For where there is envy and selfish ambition	6
2Pe	3: 4	and saying, "Where is the promise of his coming?	10
	3:13	and a new earth, where righteousness is at home.	7
Rev	2:13	"I know where you are living, where Satan's throne is.	10
	2:13	"I know where you are living, where Satan's throne is.	6
	2:13	who was killed among you, where Satan lives.	6
	11: 8	great city…where also their Lord was crucified.	6
	12: 6	wilderness, where she has a place prepared by God	6
	12:14	wilderness, to her place where she is nourished	6
	17:15	"The waters…where the whore is seated	8
	18:19	"Alas, alas, the great city, where all…grew rich	2
	20:10	lake…where the beast and the false prophet	6

where from

1. πόθεν, *pothen, 4470*

Lke	13:25	'I do not know where you come from.'	1
	13:27	'I do not know where you come from; go away	1
	20: 7	they did not know where it came from.	1
Jhn	2: 9	and did not know where it came from	1
	3: 8	do not know where it comes from or where it goes.	1
	7:27	Yet we know where this man is from;	1
	7:27	no one will know where he is from."	1
	7:28	"You know me, and you know where I am from.	1
	8:14	I know where I have come from and where I am going	1
	8:14	do not know where I come from or where I am going.	1
	9:29	we do not know where he comes from."	1
	9:30	You do not know where he comes from	1
	19: 9	He…asked Jesus, "Where are you from?"	1
Jas	4: 1	and disputes among you, where do they come from?	1
Rev	7:13	"Who are these…and where have they come from?"	1

whereas

1. δέ, *de, 1254*
2. ὅπου, *hopou, 3963*

1Co	12:24	whereas our more respectable members do not need	1
2Pe	2:11	whereas angels, though greater in might	2

wherever

1. ὅπου, *hopou, 3963*
2. ὅπου + ἐάν, *hopou + ean, 3963 + 1569*
3. ὅπου + ἄν, *hopou + an, 3963 + 323*
4. ὅσος + ἄν, *hosos + an, 4012 + 323*
5. οὗ + ἐάν, *hou + ean, 4023 + 1569*

Mat	8:19	"Teacher, I will follow you wherever you go."	2
	24:28	Wherever the corpse is, there the vultures	2
	26:13	wherever this good news is proclaimed	2
Mrk	6:10	He said to them, "Wherever you enter a house,	2
	6:55	to wherever they heard he was.	1
	6:56	wherever he went, into villages or cities	3
	14: 9	wherever the good news is proclaimed	2
	14:14	wherever he enters, say to the owner	2
Lke	9: 5	Wherever they do not welcome you	4
	9:57	"I will follow you wherever you go."	2
Jhn	21:18	and to go wherever you wished.	1
1Co	16: 6	may send me on my way, wherever I go.	5
Jas	3: 4	wherever the will of the pilot directs.	1
Rev	14: 4	these follow the Lamb wherever he goes.	3

whether

1. Contextual: Not in Greek
2. ἐάν, *ean, 1569*
3. εἰ, *ei, 1623*
4. εἴτε, *eite, 1664*
5. καί, *kai, 2779*
6. μήποτε, *mēpote, 3607*
7. οὔτε, *oute, 4046*
8. πότερον, *poteron, 4538*

Mat	27:49	let us see whether Elijah will come to save him."	3
Mrk	3: 2	They watched him to see whether he would cure him	3
	11:13	whether perhaps he would find anything on it.	3
	15:36	let us see whether Elijah will come	3
	15:44	whether he had been dead for some time.	3
Lke	3:15	questioning…whether he might be the Messiah	6
	6: 7	to see whether he would cure on the sabbath	3
	11:35	consider whether the light in you is not darkness.	1
	14:28	to see whether he has enough to complete it?	3
	14:31	whether he is able with ten thousand to oppose	3
	23: 6	he asked whether the man was a Galilean.	3
Jhn	7:17	will know whether the teaching is from God	8
	7:17	whether I am speaking on my own.	1
	9:25	"I do not know whether he is a sinner.	3
Act	4:19	"Whether it is right in God's sight	3
	5: 8	"Tell me whether you and your husband sold the land	3
	10:18	ask whether Simon…was staying there.	3
	17:11	to see whether these things were so.	3
	25:20	I asked whether he wished to go to Jerusalem	3
	26:29	Paul replied, "Whether quickly or not,	5
Rom	14: 8	whether we live or whether we die, we are the Lord's.	2
	14: 8	whether we live or whether we die, we are the Lord's.	2
1Co	1:16	I do not know whether I baptized anyone else.)	3
	3:22	whether Paul or Apollos or Cephas or the world	4
	10:31	So, whether you eat or drink, or whatever you do	4
	15:11	Whether then it was I or they	4
2Co	2: 9	know whether you are obedient in everything.	3
	5: 9	So whether we are at home or away	4
	5:10	done in the body, whether good or evil.	4
	12: 2	whether in the body or out of the body	4
	12: 3	whether in the body or out of the body	4
	13: 5	to see whether you are living in the faith.	3
Eph	6: 8	whether we are slaves or free.	4
Php	1:18	whether out of false motives or true;	4
	1:20	whether by life or by death.	4
	1:27	so that, whether I come and see you or am absent	4
Col	1:16	whether thrones or dominions	4
	1:20	all things, whether on earth or in heaven	4
1Th	2: 6	whether from you or from others	7
	5:10	so that whether we are awake or asleep we may live	4
1Pe	2:13	whether of the emperor as supreme	4
1Jn	4: 1	test the spirits to see whether they are from God;	3

which   Not Indexed

while   *See also* little while, while still *dark*

1. Contextual: Not in Greek
2. δέ, *de*, 1254
3. ἐν, *en*, 1877
4. ἔτι, *eti*, 2285
5. ἕως, *heōs*, 2401
6. ἰδού, *idou*, 2627
7. καί, *kai*, 2779
8. καιρός, *kairos*, 2789
9. κατά, *kata*, 2848
10. μέν, *men*, 3525
11. μετά, *meta*, 3552
12. ὀλίγος, *oligos*, 3900
13. ὅτε, *hote*, 4021
14. οὖν, *oun*, 4036
15. πρόσκαιρος, *proskairos*, 4672
16. χρόνος, *chronos*, 5989
17. ὥρα, *hōra*, 6052
18. ὡς, *hōs*, 6055

Mat	5:25	quickly with your accuser while you are on the way	5
	7: 4	while the log is in your own eye?	6
	8:12	while the heirs…will be thrown into the…darkness	2
	13:21	but endures only for a while	15
	13:25	while everybody was asleep, an enemy came and sowed	3
	14:22	while he dismissed the crowds.	5
	22: 6	while the rest seized his slaves	5
	26:36	"Sit here while I go over there and pray."	5
	26:73	After a little while the bystanders came up	1
Mrk	2:19	while the bridegroom is with them	3
	4:17	endure only for a while;	15
	6:31	rest a while."	12
	6:45	while he dismissed the crowd.	5
	14:32	he said to his disciples, "Sit here while I pray."	5
Lke	2: 6	While they were there	3

	5: 1	while Jesus was standing beside the lake	3
	5:34	while the bridegroom is with them	3
	6: 1	One sabbath while Jesus was going through	3
	8:13	they believe only for a while	8
	9:29	while he was praying	3
	9:42	While he was coming, the demon dashed him	4
	11:27	While he was saying this	3
	11:37	While he was speaking	3
	17: 8	while I eat and drink;	5
	18: 4	For a while he refused;	16
	24: 4	While they were perplexed about this	3
	24:15	While they were talking and discussing	3
	24:32	while he was talking to us on the road	18
	24:32	while he was opening the scriptures to us?"	18
	24:51	While he was blessing them, he withdrew from them	3
Jhn	5: 7	while I am making my way, someone else steps down	3
	5:35	willing to rejoice for a while in his light.	17
	7:12	While some were saying, "He is a good man,"	10
	7:33	"I will be with you a little while longer	16
	9: 4	work the works of him who sent me while it is day;	5
	11:20	she went and met him, while Mary stayed at home.	2
	12:35	Walk while you have the light	18
	12:36	While you have the light, believe in the light	18
	14:19	In a little while the world will no longer see	4
	16:16	"A little while, and you will no longer see me	1
	16:16	again a little while, and you will see me."	1
	16:17	'A little while, and you will no longer see me	1
	16:17	again a little while, and you will see me';	1
	16:18	"What does he mean by this 'a little while'?	1
	16:19	'A little while, and you will no longer see me	1
	16:19	again a little while, and you will see me'?	1
	17:12	While I was with them, I protected them	13
Act	1:10	While he was going and they were gazing up	18
	4:30	while you stretch out your hand to heal	3
	6: 4	while we…will devote ourselves to prayer	2
	10:17	Now while Peter was greatly puzzled	18
	13:11	be blind for a while, unable to see the sun."	8
	17:30	While God has overlooked the times of…ignorance	14
	19: 1	While Apollos was in Corinth	3
	22:20	while the blood of your witness Stephen was shed	13
	24:18	While I was doing this	3
	28:24	while others refused to believe.	2
Rom	2: 8	while for those who are self-seeking	2
	4:11	had by faith while he was still uncircumcised.	3
	7: 5	While we were living in the flesh	13
	14: 2	while the weak eat only vegetables.	2
	14: 5	while others judge all days to be alike.	2
	14: 6	while those who abstain, abstain in honor	7
1Co	14:22	while prophecy is not for unbelievers	2
Gal	4: 3	So with us; while we were minors,	13
Eph	6: 6	not only while being watched, and in order to please	9
Col	1:11	to endure everything with patience, while joyfully	11
	3:22	not only while being watched and in order to please	3
1Ti	4: 8	for, while physical training is of some value	2
	5:24	while the sins of others follow them there.	2
Phm	1:15	was separated from you for a while	17
Heb	10:37	in a very little while, the one who is coming will come	1
Jas	2: 3	while to the one who is poor you say, "Stand there,"	7
1Pe	4:19	while continuing to do good.	3
1Jn	1: 6	while we are walking in darkness	7
	2: 9	Whoever says, "I am in the light," while hating	7
Rev	11:12	went up to heaven…while their enemies watched	7
	17:10	when he comes, he must remain only a little while.	1
	20: 3	After that he must be let out for a little while.	16
	21:18	while the city is pure gold, clear as glass.	7

whip

1. φραγέλλιον, *phragellion*, 5848

Jhn	2:15	Making a whip of cords, he drove all of them	1

whisper

1. εἰς + ὁ + οὖς, *eis + ho + ous*, 1650 + 3836 + 4044
2. λαλέω + πρός + ὁ + οὖς, *laleō + pros + ho + ous*, 3281 + 4639 + 3836 + 4044

Mat	10:27	what you hear whispered, proclaim	1
Lke	12: 3	what you have whispered behind closed doors	2

white   *See also* make white

1. Contextual: Not in Greek
2. λευκός, *leukos*, 3328

Mat	5:36	head, for you cannot make one hair white or black.	2
	17: 2	and his clothes became dazzling white.	2
	28: 3	his clothing white as snow.	2
Mrk	9: 3	clothes became dazzling white	2
	16: 5	they saw a young man, dressed in a white robe	2
Lke	9:29	his clothes became dazzling white.	2
Jhn	20:12	she saw two angels in white	2
Act	1:10	suddenly two men in white robes stood by them.	2
Rev	1:14	His head and his hair were white as white wool	2
	1:14	His head and his hair were white as white wool	2
	1:14	His head and his hair were…white as snow;	1
	2:17	and I will give a white stone	2
	2:17	on the white stone is written a new name	1
	3: 4	with me, dressed in white, for they are worthy.	2
	3: 5	you conquer, you will be clothed like them in white	2
	3:18	and white robes to clothe you	2
	4: 4	elders, dressed in white robes, with golden	2
	6: 2	I looked…a white horse! Its rider had a bow;	2
	6:11	They were each given a white robe and told	2
	7: 9	robed in white, with palm branches	2
	7:13	"Who are these, robed in white	2
	14:14	Then I looked, and there was a white cloud	2
	19:11	I saw heaven opened, and there was a white horse!	2
	19:14	wearing fine linen, white and pure	2
	19:14	armies of heaven…following him on white horses.	2
	20:11	I saw a great white throne and the one who sat on it;	2

whitewash

1. κονιάω, *koniaō, 3154*

Mat	23:27	you are like whitewashed tombs	1
Act	23: 3	"God will strike you, you whitewashed wall!	1

who, whoever   Not Indexed

whole   *See also* whole *armor,* whole *body,* whole burnt *offering,* whole *community,* whole *group*

1. Contextual: Not in Greek
2. ἅπας, *hapas, 570*
3. ὅλος, *holos, 3910*
4. πᾶς, *pas, 4246*
5. ὑγιής, *hygiēs, 5618*

Mat	5:29	than for your whole body to be thrown into hell.	3
	5:30	members than for your whole body to go into hell.	3
	6:22	eye is healthy, your whole body will be full of light;	3
	6:23	your eye is unhealthy, your whole body will be full	3
	8:32	suddenly, the whole herd rushed down the steep bank	4
	8:33	they told the whole story about what had happened	4
	8:34	Then the whole town came out to meet Jesus;	4
	13: 2	while the whole crowd stood on the beach.	4
	15:31	the mute speaking, the maimed whole	5
	16:26	gain the whole world but forfeit their life?	3
	21:10	the whole city was in turmoil, asking	4
	26:13	this good news is proclaimed in the whole world	3
	26:59	the chief priests and the whole council	3
	27:27	they gathered the whole cohort around him.	3
	27:45	darkness came over the whole land	4
Mrk	1: 5	people from the whole Judean countryside	4
	1:33	the whole city was gathered	3
	2:13	the whole crowd gathered around him	4
	4: 1	the whole crowd was beside the sea on the land.	4
	5:33	told him the whole truth.	4
	6:55	and rushed about that whole region	3
	8:36	to gain the whole world and forfeit their life?	3
	9:15	When the whole crowd saw him,	4
	11:18	because the whole crowd was spellbound	4
	14: 9	the good news is proclaimed in the whole world	3
	14:55	Now the chief priests and the whole council	3
	15: 1	with the elders and scribes and the whole council.	3
	15:16	they called together the whole cohort.	3
	15:33	darkness came over the whole land	3
	16:15	[proclaim the good news to the whole creation.]	4
Lke	1:10	the whole assembly of the people was praying	4
	9:25	does it profit them if they gain the whole world	3
	11:34	your whole body is full of light;	3
	11:36	If then your whole body is full of light	3
	19:37	the whole multitude of the disciples	2
	21:35	all who live on the face of the whole earth.	4
	23:44	darkness came over the whole land until three	3
Jhn	4:53	he himself believed, along with his whole household.	3
	7:23	I healed a man's whole body on the sabbath?	3

	11:50	than to have the whole nation destroyed."	3
Act	5:11	great fear seized the whole church	3
	5:20	tell the people the whole message about this life."	4
	6: 5	What they said pleased the whole community	4
	10:22	who is well spoken of by the whole Jewish nation	3
	13: 6	had gone through the whole island as far as Paphos	3
	13:44	The next sabbath almost the whole city gathered	4
	15:12	The whole assembly kept silence	4
	15:22	with the consent of the whole church, decided	3
	17:26	to inhabit the whole earth	4
	19:26	in almost the whole of Asia	4
	20:27	declaring to you the whole purpose of God.	4
	21:27	stirred up the whole crowd. They seized him	4
	22: 5	the high priest and the whole council of elders	4
	25:24	about whom the whole Jewish community petitioned	2
	28:30	He lived there two whole years at his own expense	3
Rom	3:19	the whole world may be held accountable to God.	4
	8:22	the whole creation has been groaning in labor pains	4
	11:16	If the part…is holy, then the whole batch is	1
	16:23	Gaius, who is host to me and to the whole church	3
1Co	5: 6	a little yeast leavens the whole batch of dough?	3
	12:17	If the whole body were an eye	3
	12:17	If the whole body were hearing,	3
	14:23	If, therefore, the whole church comes together	3
Gal	5: 9	A little yeast leavens the whole batch of dough.	3
	5:14	the whole law is summed up in a single commandment	4
Eph	2:21	In him the whole structure is joined together	4
	4:16	the whole body, joined and knit together	4
Php	1:13	throughout the whole imperial guard	3
Col	1: 6	bearing fruit and growing in the whole world	4
	2: 9	in him the whole fullness of deity dwells bodily	4
	2:19	the whole body, nourished and held together	4
Tit	1:11	since they are upsetting whole families	3
Jas	2:10	For whoever keeps the whole law but fails	3
	3: 2	perfect, able to keep the whole body in check	3
	3: 3	we guide their whole bodies.	3
	3: 6	The tongue…stains the whole body	3
1Jn	2: 2	but also for the sins of the whole world.	3
	5:19	the whole world lies under the power of the evil one.	3
Rev	3:10	hour of trial that is coming on the whole world	3
	12: 9	deceiver of the whole world—he was thrown down	3
	13: 3	In amazement the whole earth followed the beast.	3
	16:14	who go abroad to the kings of the whole world	3

as a whole

1. πᾶς, *pas, 4246*

Mat	27:25	the people as a whole answered, "His blood be	1

wholeheartedly

1. ἁπλότης + καρδία, *haplotēs + kardia, 605 + 2840*

Col	3:22	wholeheartedly, fearing the Lord.	1

whore

1. πόρνη, *pornē, 4520*

Rev	17: 1	I will show you the judgment of the great whore	1
	17: 5	"Babylon the great, mother of whores	1
	17:15	waters that you saw, where the whore is seated	1
	17:16	they and the beast will hate the whore;	1
	19: 2	judged the great whore who corrupted the earth	1

why

1. Contextual: Not in Greek
2. γάρ, *gar, 1142*
3. διά + ὅς + αἰτία, *dia + hos + aitia, 1328 + 4005 + 162*
4. διά + τίς, *dia + tis, 1328 + 5515*
5. εἰς + τίς, *eis + tis, 1650 + 5515*
6. ἱνατί, *hinati, 2672*
7. ὅς + τὶς, *hos + tis, 4005 + 5516*
8. ὅτι, *hoti, 4022*
9. πόθεν, *pothen, 4470*
10. πρός + τίς, *pros + tis, 4639 + 5515*
11. πῶς, *pōs, 4802*
12. τίς, *tis, 5515*
13. τίς + ἕνεκεν, *tis + heneken, 5515 + 1915*
14. τίς + λόγος, *tis + logos, 5515 + 3364*
15. τίς + ὅτι, *tis + hoti, 5515 + 4022*
16. χάριν, *charin, 5920*

Mat	6:28	And why do you worry about clothing? Consider	12
	7: 3	Why do you see the speck	12
	8:26	he said to them, "Why are you afraid	12

9: 4	"Why do you think evil in your hearts?	6
9:11	"Why does your teacher eat with tax collectors	4
9:14	"Why do we and the Pharisees fast often,	4
13:10	"Why do you speak to them in parables?"	4
14:31	"You of little faith, why did you doubt?"	5
15: 2	"Why do your disciples break the tradition	4
15: 3	"And why do you break the commandment of God	4
16: 8	why are you talking about having no bread?	12
17:10	"Why, then, do the scribes say	12
17:19	"Why could we not cast it out?"	4
19: 7	"Why then did Moses command	12
19:17	"Why do you ask me about what is good?	12
20: 6	'Why are you standing here idle all day?'	12
21:25	'Why then did you not believe him?'	4
22:18	"Why are you putting me to the test, you hypocrites?	12
26: 8	they were angry and said, "Why this waste?	5
26:10	"Why do you trouble the woman?	12
26:65	Why do we still need witnesses?	12
27:23	he asked, "Why, what evil has he done?"	2
27:46	"My God, my God, why have you forsaken me?"	6
Mrk 2: 7	"Why does this fellow speak in this way?	12
2: 8	"Why do you raise such questions in your hearts?	12
2:16	"Why does he eat with tax collectors and sinners?"	8
2:18	"Why do John's disciples…fast	4
2:24	"Look, why are they doing what is not lawful	12
4:40	"Why are you afraid? Have you still no faith?"	12
5:35	Why trouble the teacher any further?"	12
5:39	"Why do you make a commotion and weep?	12
7: 5	"Why do your disciples not live according	4
8:12	"Why does this generation ask for a sign?	12
8:17	"Why are you talking about having no bread?	12
9:11	they asked him, "Why do the scribes say	8
9:28	"Why could we not cast it out?"	8
10:18	"Why do you call me good? No one is good but God	12
11: 3	If anyone says to you, 'Why are you doing this?'	12
11:31	he will say, 'Why then did you not believe him?'	4
12:15	"Why are you putting me to the test?	12
14: 4	"Why was the ointment wasted in this way?	5
14: 6	"Let her alone; why do you trouble her?	12
14:63	"Why do we still need witnesses?	12
15:14	Pilate asked them, "Why, what evil has he done?"	1
15:34	"My God, my God, why have you forsaken me?"	5
Lke 1:43	why has this happened to me	9
2:48	"Child, why have you treated us like this?	12
2:49	to them, "Why were you searching for me?	15
5:22	"Why do you raise such questions in your hearts?	12
5:30	"Why do you eat and drink with tax collectors	4
6: 2	"Why are you doing what is not lawful	12
6:41	Why do you see the speck	12
6:46	"Why do you call me 'Lord, Lord,' and do not	12
8:47	she declared…why she had touched him	3
12:26	why do you worry about the rest?	12
12:56	why do you not know how to interpret the present	11
12:57	why do you not judge for yourselves what is right?	12
13: 7	Cut it down! Why should it be wasting the soil?'	6
18:19	"Why do you call me good? No one is good but God	12
19:23	Why then did you not put my money into the bank?	4
19:31	If anyone asks you, 'Why are you untying it?'	4
19:33	"Why are you untying the colt?"	12
20: 5	he will say, 'Why did you not believe him?'	4
22:46	he said to them, "Why are you sleeping?	12
23:22	"Why, what evil has he done?	1
24: 5	"Why do you look for the living among the dead?	12
24:38	He said to them, "Why are you frightened	12
24:38	why do doubts arise in your hearts?	4
Jhn 1:25	They asked him, "Why then are you baptizing	12
4:27	or, "Why are you speaking with her?"	12
7:19	Why are you looking for an opportunity to kill me?"	12
7:45	who asked them, "Why did you not arrest him?"	4
8:25	"Why do I speak to you at all?	7
8:43	Why do you not understand what I say?	4
8:46	If I tell the truth, why do you not believe me?	12
9:27	Why do you want to hear it again?	12
10:20	is out of his mind. Why listen to him?"	12
12: 5	"Why was this perfume not sold	4
13:28	no one at the table knew why he said this to him.	10
13:37	"Lord, why can I not follow you now?	4
18:21	Why do you ask me? Ask those who heard	12
18:23	if I have spoken rightly, why do you strike me?"	12
20:13	They said to her, "Woman, why are you weeping?"	12
20:15	Jesus said to her, "Woman, why are you weeping?	12

Act 1:11	why do you stand looking up toward heaven?	12
3:12	"You Israelites, why do you wonder at this	12
3:12	why do you stare at us	12
4:25	'Why did the Gentiles rage	6
5: 3	"why has Satan filled your heart to lie	4
7:26	you are brothers; why do you wrong each other?'	6
9: 4	"Saul, Saul, why do you persecute me?"	12
10:29	Now may I ask why you sent for me?"	14
11: 3	saying, "Why did you go to uncircumcised men	8
14:15	"Friends, why are you doing this?	12
15:10	Now therefore why are you putting God to the test	12
19:32	most of them did not know why they had come	13
22: 7	'Saul, Saul, why are you persecuting me?'	12
22:16	now why do you delay? Get up, be baptized	12
26: 8	Why is it thought incredible by any of you	12
26:14	'Saul, Saul, why are you persecuting me?'	12
Rom 3: 7	why am I still being condemned as a sinner?	12
3: 8	And why not say…"Let us do evil so that good	1
9:19	"Why then does he still find fault?	12
9:20	"Why have you made me like this?"	12
9:32	Why not? Because they did not strive for it	4
14:10	Why do you pass judgment on your brother or sister?	12
14:10	Or you, why do you despise your brother or sister?	12
1Co 4: 7	why do you boast as if it were not a gift?	12
6: 7	Why not rather be wronged?	4
6: 7	Why not rather be defrauded?	4
10:29	why should my liberty be subject to the judgment	6
10:30	why should I be denounced	12
15:29	why are people baptized on their behalf?	12
15:30	why are we putting ourselves in danger every hour?	12
2Co 11:11	why? Because I do not love you? God knows I do!	4
Gal 3:19	Why then the law?	12
5:11	why am I still being persecuted	12
Col 2:20	why do you live as if you still belonged	12
2:20	Why do you submit to regulations	1
1Jn 3:12	And why did he murder him?	16
Rev 17: 7	But the angel said to me, "Why are you so amazed?	4

wick

1. λίνον, *linon, 3351*

Mat 12:20	or quench a smoldering wick	1

wicked *See also* wicked *way*

1. ἀδικία, *adikia, 94*
2. ἄτοπος, *atopos, 876*
3. κακός, *kakos, 2805*
4. πονηρός, *ponēros, 4505*

Mat 18:32	'You wicked slave! I forgave you all that debt	4
24:48	if that wicked slave says to himself	3
25:26	his master replied, 'You wicked and lazy slave!	4
Lke 6:35	he is kind to the ungrateful and the wicked.	4
19:22	'I will judge you…you wicked slave!	4
2Th 2:10	every kind of wicked deception	1
3: 2	that we may be rescued from wicked and evil people;	2
2Ti 3:13	But wicked people…will go from bad to worse	4

wicked person

1. πονηρός, *ponēros, 4505*

1Co 5:13	"Drive out the wicked person from among you."	1

wickedness

1. ἀδικία, *adikia, 94*
2. ἀνομία, *anomia, 490*
3. κακία, *kakia, 2798*
4. πονηρία, *ponēria, 4504*
5. φαῦλος, *phaulos, 5765*

Mrk 7:22	avarice, wickedness, deceit, licentiousness	4
Lke 11:39	inside you are full of greed and wickedness.	4
Act 1:18	acquired a field with the reward of his wickedness;	1
8:22	Repent therefore of this wickedness of yours	3
8:23	you are in…the chains of wickedness."	1
Rom 1:18	against all ungodliness and wickedness of those	1
1:18	those who by their wickedness suppress the truth.	1
1:29	every…wickedness, evil, covetousness, malice.	1
2: 8	and who obey not the truth but wickedness	1
6:13	your members…as instruments of wickedness	1
2Ti 2:19	"Let everyone…turn away from wickedness."	1
Heb 1: 9	You have loved righteousness and hated wickedness;	2
Jas 1:21	all sordidness and rank growth of wickedness	3
3:16	there will also be disorder and wickedness of every kind.	5

wide *See also* open wide, wide *open*
1. μέγας, *megas, 3489*
2. πλατύς, *platys, 4426*

Mat	7:13	for the gate is wide and the road is easy	2
1Co	16: 9	for a wide door for effective work has opened	1

widely *See* know widely

widow
1. Contextual: Not in Greek
2. αὐτός, *autos, 899*
3. γυνή, *gynē, 1222*
4. χήρα, *chēra, 5939*

Mat	22:24	his brother shall marry the widow	3
	22:25	childless, leaving the widow to his brother.	3
Mrk	12:19	the man shall marry the widow and raise up children	3
	12:21	the second married the widow and died	2
	12:40	They devour widows' houses	4
	12:42	A poor widow came and put in two small copper coins	4
	12:43	this poor widow has put in more than all	4
Lke	2:37	then as a widow to the age of eighty-four	4
	4:25	were many widows in Israel in the time of Elijah	4
	4:26	to a widow at Zarephath in Sidon.	4
	7:12	was his mother's only son, and she was a widow;	4
	18: 3	In that city there was a widow who kept	4
	18: 5	yet because this widow keeps bothering me	4
	20:28	man shall marry the widow and raise up children	3
	20:47	They devour widows' houses	4
	21: 2	saw a poor widow put in two small copper coins.	4
	21: 3	this poor widow has put in more than all of them;	4
Act	6: 1	because their widows were being neglected	4
	9:39	All the widows stood beside him, weeping	4
	9:41	Then calling the saints and widows	4
1Co	7: 8	To the unmarried and the widows I say	4
1Ti	5: 3	Honor widows who are really widows.	4
	5: 3	Honor widows who are really widows.	4
	5: 4	If a widow has children or grandchildren	4
	5: 5	The real widow…has set her hope on God	4
	5: 6	but the widow who lives for pleasure is dead	1
	5: 9	Let a widow be put on the list	4
	5:11	refuse to put younger widows on the list;	4
	5:14	I would have younger widows marry, bear children	1
	5:16	woman has relatives who are really widows	4
	5:16	it can assist those who are real widows.	4
Jas	1:27	to care for orphans and widows in their distress	4
Rev	18: 7	I am no widow, and I will never see grief,'	4

width
1. πλάτος, *platos, 4424*

Rev	21:16	its length the same as its width;	1
	21:16	its length and width and height are equal.	1

wife
1. Contextual: Not in Greek
2. γυνή, *gynē, 1222*
3. ὁ, *ho, 3836*

Mat	1: 6	David…father of Solomon by the wife of Uriah	3
	1:20	do not be afraid to take Mary as your wife	2
	1:24	of the Lord commanded him; he took her as his wife	2
	5:31	"It was also said, 'Whoever divorces his wife	2
	5:32	I say to you that anyone who divorces his wife	2
	14: 3	Herodias, his brother Philip's wife	2
	18:25	his wife and children and all his possessions	2
	19: 3	lawful for a man to divorce his wife for any cause?"	2
	19: 5	and be joined to his wife	2
	19: 8	Moses allowed you to divorce your wives	2
	19: 9	I say to you, whoever divorces his wife	2
	19:10	"If such is the case of a man with his wife	2
	22:28	whose wife of the seven will she be?	2
	27:19	his wife sent word to him	2
Mrk	6:17	Herodias, his brother Philip's wife	2
	6:18	not lawful for you to have your brother's wife."	2
	10: 2	"Is it lawful for a man to divorce his wife?"	2
	10: 7	be joined to his wife	2
	10:11	"Whoever divorces his wife and marries another	2
	12:19	if a man's brother dies, leaving a wife	2
	12:23	In the resurrection whose wife will she be?	2
Lke	1: 5	His wife was a descendant of Aaron	2
	1:13	Your wife Elizabeth will bear you a son	2

	1:18	old man, and my wife is getting on in years."	2
	1:24	After those days his wife Elizabeth conceived	2
	3:19	Herodias, his brother's wife	2
	8: 3	Joanna, the wife of Herod's steward Chuza	2
	14:26	father and mother, wife and children	2
	16:18	"Anyone who divorces his wife	2
	17:32	Remember Lot's wife.	2
	18:29	there is no one who has left house or wife	2
	20:28	brother dies, leaving a wife but no children	2
	20:33	whose wife will the woman be?	2
Jhn	19:25	his mother's sister, Mary the wife of Clopas	3
Act	5: 1	Ananias, with the consent of his wife Sapphira	2
	5: 2	with his wife's knowledge	2
	5: 7	his wife came in, not knowing what had happened.	2
	18: 2	recently come from Italy with his wife Priscilla	2
	21: 5	all of them, with wives and children	2
	24:24	Felix came with his wife Drusilla	2
1Co	5: 1	a man is living with his father's wife.	2
	7: 2	each man should have his own wife	2
	7: 3	husband should give to his wife her conjugal rights	2
	7: 3	likewise the wife to her husband.	2
	7: 4	wife does not have authority over her own body	2
	7: 4	but the wife does.	2
	7:10	the wife should not separate from her husband	2
	7:11	the husband should not divorce his wife.	2
	7:12	if any believer has a wife who is an unbeliever	2
	7:14	made holy through his wife	2
	7:14	the unbelieving wife is made holy	2
	7:16	Wife, for all you know	2
	7:16	you might save your wife.	2
	7:27	Are you bound to a wife? Do not seek to be free.	2
	7:27	Are you free from a wife? Do not seek a wife.	2
	7:27	Are you free from a wife? Do not seek a wife.	2
	7:29	who have wives be as though they had none	2
	7:33	how to please his wife	2
	7:39	A wife is bound as long as her husband lives.	2
	9: 5	have the right to be accompanied by a believing wife	2
	11: 3	the husband is the head of his wife	2
Eph	5:22	Wives, be subject to your husbands as you are to the Lord.	2
	5:23	For the husband is the head of the wife	2
	5:24	so also wives ought to be, in everything	2
	5:25	Husbands, love your wives	2
	5:28	In the same way, husbands should love their wives	2
	5:28	He who loves his wife loves himself.	2
	5:31	be joined to his wife	2
	5:33	Each of you, however, should love his wife as himself	2
	5:33	a wife should respect her husband.	2
Col	3:18	Wives, be subject to your husbands	2
	3:19	Husbands, love your wives	2
1Pe	3: 1	Wives…accept the authority of your husbands	2
	3: 1	won over without a word by their wives' conduct	2
	3: 7	Husbands…show consideration for your wives	1
Rev	21: 9	I will show you the bride, the wife of the Lamb."	2

believing wife
1. ἀδελφή, *adelphē, 80*

1Co	9: 5	have the right to be accompanied by a believing wife	1

old wife
1. γραώδης, *graōdēs, 1212*

1Ti	4: 7	profane myths and old wives' tales.	1

wild *See also* fight with a wild animal, wild *animal*, wild *beast*, wild *olive* shoot, wild *olive* tree
1. ἄγριος, *agrios, 67*
2. ἔρημος, *erēmos, 2245*

Mat	3: 4	waist, and his food was locusts and wild honey.	1
Mrk	1: 6	ate locusts and wild honey.	1
Lke	8:29	be driven by the demon into the wilds.)	2
Jde	1:13	wild waves of the sea, casting up the foam	1

wilderness
1. ἐρημία, *erēmia, 2244*
2. ἔρημος, *erēmos, 2245*

Mat	3: 1	Baptist appeared in the wilderness of Judea	2
	3: 3	voice of one crying out in the wilderness: 'Prepare	2
	4: 1	led up by the Spirit into the wilderness	2
	11: 7	"What did you go out into the wilderness to look at?	2
	24:26	they say to you, 'Look! He is in the wilderness,'	2
Mrk	1: 3	the voice of one crying out in the wilderness:	2

	1: 4	John the baptizer appeared in the wilderness	2
	1:12	immediately drove him out into the wilderness.	2
	1:13	He was in the wilderness forty days	2
Lke	1:80	he was in the wilderness	2
	3: 2	John son of Zechariah in the wilderness.	2
	3: 4	"The voice of one crying out in the wilderness:	2
	4: 1	Jesus…was led by the Spirit in the wilderness	2
	7:24	did you go out into the wilderness to look at?	2
	15: 4	does not leave the ninety-nine in the wilderness	2
Jhn	1:23	"I am the voice of one crying out in the wilderness	2
	3:14	as Moses lifted up the serpent in the wilderness	2
	6:31	Our ancestors ate the manna in the wilderness;	2
	6:49	Your ancestors ate the manna in the wilderness	2
	11:54	Ephraim in the region near the wilderness;	2
Act	7:30	an angel appeared to him in the wilderness	2
	7:36	and in the wilderness for forty years.	2
	7:38	who was in the congregation in the wilderness	2
	7:42	forty years in the wilderness, O house of Israel?	2
	7:44	the tent of testimony in the wilderness	2
	8:26	(This is a wilderness road.)	2
	13:18	he put up with them in the wilderness.	2
	21:38	led…out into the wilderness?"	2
1Co	10: 5	and they were struck down in the wilderness.	2
2Co	11:26	danger in the city, danger in the wilderness	1
Heb	3: 8	on the day of testing in the wilderness	2
	3:17	who sinned, whose bodies fell in the wilderness?	2
Rev	12: 6	and the woman fled into the wilderness	2
	12:14	could fly from the serpent into the wilderness	2
	17: 3	So he carried me away…into a wilderness	2

wile

1. μεθοδεία, *methodeia, 3497*

Eph	6:11	able to stand against the wiles of the devil.	1

will¹   *See also* make [a will]

1. Contextual: Not in Greek
2. ἄν, *an, 323*
3. βούλημα, *boulēma, 1088*
4. βούλομαι, *boulomai, 1089*
5. ἑκών, *hekōn, 1776*
6. εὐδοκέω, *eudokeō, 2305*
7. θέλημα, *thelēma, 2525*
8. θέλησις, *thelēsis, 2526*
9. θέλω, *thelō, 2527*
10. κατά, *kata, 2848*
11. ὁρμή, *hormē, 3995*

Mat	6:10	Your will be done, on earth as it is in heaven.	7
	7:12	do to others as you would have them do to you	9
	7:21	who does the will of my Father in heaven.	7
	12:50	For whoever does the will of my Father in heaven	7
	18:14	it is not the will of your Father in heaven	7
	21:29	He answered, 'I will not'; but later he changed	9
	21:31	Which of the two did the will of his father?"	9
	22: 3	but they would not come.	9
	26:15	said, "What will you give me if I betray him	9
	26:42	if this cannot pass…your will be done."	7
	27:34	when he tasted it, he would not drink it.	9
Mrk	3:35	Whoever does the will of God is my brother	7
Lke	6:31	Do to others as you would have them do to you.	9
	18:13	would not even look up to heaven	9
	22:42	yet, not my will but yours be done."	7
Jhn	1:13	born, not of blood or of the will of the flesh	7
	1:13	born, not of blood…or of the will of man	7
	4:34	"My food is to do the will of him who sent me	7
	5:30	because I seek to do not my own will	7
	5:30	but the will of him who sent me.	7
	6:38	not…own will, but the will of him who sent me.	7
	6:38	not…own will, but the will of him who sent me.	7
	6:39	this is the will of him who sent me	7
	6:40	This is indeed the will of my Father	7
	7:17	Anyone who resolves to do the will of God	7
	9:31	listen to one who worships him and obeys his will.	7
	21:22	"If it is my will that he remain until I come	9
	21:23	"If it is my will that he remain until I come	9
Act	18:21	"I will return to you, if God wills."	9
	21:14	except to say, "The Lord's will be done."	7
	22:14	God of our ancestors has chosen you to know his will	7
Rom	1:10	by God's will I may somehow at last succeed	7
	2:18	know his will and determine what is best	7
	7:18	I can will what is right, but I cannot do it.	9

Rom	8:20	not of its own will but by the will of the one	5
	8:20	by the will of the one who subjected it, in hope	1
	8:27	Spirit intercedes…according to the will of God.	1
	9:16	So it depends not on human will or exertion	9
	9:19	For who can resist his will?"	3
	12: 2	so that you may discern what is the will of God	7
	15:32	that by God's will I may come to you with joy	7
1Co	1: 1	an apostle of Christ Jesus by the will of God	7
	4:19	I will come to you soon, if the Lord wills.	9
	9:17	For if I do this of my own will, I have a reward;	5
	14:19	nevertheless, in church I would rather speak	9
2Co	1: 1	Paul, an apostle of Christ Jesus by the will of God	7
	5: 8	we would rather be away from the body and at home	6
	8: 5	to the Lord and, by the will of God, to us	7
Gal	1: 4	according to the will of our God and Father	7
Eph	1: 1	Paul, an apostle of Christ Jesus by the will of God	7
	1: 5	according to the good pleasure of his will	7
	1: 9	has made known…the mystery of his will	7
	1:11	according to his counsel and will	7
	5:17	but understand what the will of the Lord is.	7
	6: 6	doing the will of God from the heart.	7
Php	2:13	both to will and to work for his good pleasure.	9
Col	1: 1	Paul, an apostle of Christ Jesus by the will of God	7
	1: 9	you may be filled with the knowledge of God's will	7
	4:12	fully assured in everything that God wills.	7
1Th	4: 3	For this is the will of God, your sanctification:	7
	5:18	for this is the will of God in Christ Jesus	7
1Ti	5:14	I would have younger widows marry, bear children	4
2Ti	1: 1	Paul, an apostle of Christ Jesus by the will of God	7
	2:26	having been held captive by him to do his will.	7
Heb	2: 4	distributed according to his will.	8
	10: 7	I said, 'See, God, I have come to do your will, O God'	7
	10: 9	he added, "See, I have come to do your will."	7
	10:10	by God's will that we have been sanctified through	7
	10:36	done the will of God, you may receive what was promised	7
	13:21	so that you may do his will	7
Jas	3: 4	wherever the will of the pilot directs.	11
1Pe	2:15	For it is God's will that by doing right	7
	3:17	to suffer…if suffering should be God's will	7
	4: 2	no longer by human desires but by the will of God.	7
	4:19	let those suffering in accordance with God's will	7
	5: 2	tend…as God would have you do it—	10
2Pe	1:21	because no prophecy ever came by human will,	7
1Jn	2:17	but those who do the will of God live forever.	7
	2:19	they would have remained with us.	2
	5:14	if we ask anything according to his will, he hears	7
2Jn	1:12	I would rather not use paper and ink;	4
3Jn	1:13	but I would rather not write with pen and ink;	9
Rev	4:11	and by your will they existed and were created."	7

will²

1. διαθήκη, *diathēkē, 1347*

Gal	3:15	once a person's will has been ratified	1
Heb	9:16	Where a will is involved	1
	9:17	For a will takes effect only at death	1

will³

1. μέλλω, *mellō, 3516*

Mat	24: 6	you will hear of wars and rumors of wars;	1
Lke	21:36	to escape all these things that will take place	1
	22:23	which one of them it could be who would do this.	1
Jhn	14:22	"Lord, how is it that you will reveal yourself	1
Act	11:28	there would be a severe famine over all the world;	1
	17:31	fixed a day on which he will have the world judged	1
	19:27	she will be deprived of her majesty	1
	20:38	that they would not see him again.	1
	23: 3	"God will strike you, you whitewashed wall!	1
	24:15	there will be a resurrection of both the righteous	1
	26:22	what…Moses said would take place:	1
	26:23	he would proclaim light…to our people	1
	27:10	I can see that the voyage will be with danger	1
Rom	4:24	It will be reckoned to us who believe in him	1
	8:13	if you live according to the flesh, you will die;	1
Gal	3:23	until faith would be revealed.	1
Heb	10:27	fire that will consume the adversaries.	1

gracious will

1. εὐδοκία, *eudokia, 2306*

Mat	11:26	yes, Father, for such was your gracious will.	1
Lke	10:21	yes, Father, for such was your gracious will.	1

not of one's will

1. ἄκων, *akōn, 220*

1Co 9:17 if not of my own will, I am entrusted with   1

willful

1. αὐθάδης, *authadēs, 881*

2Pe 2:10 Bold and willful, they are not afraid to slander   1

willfully

1. ἑκουσίως, *hekousiōs, 1731*

Heb 10:26 For if we willfully persist in sin   1

willing

1. Contextual: Not in Greek
2. βούλομαι, *boulomai, 1089*
3. θέλημα, *thelēma, 2525*
4. θέλω, *thelō, 2527*
5. πρόθυμος, *prothymos, 4609*

Mat 11:14 if you are willing to accept it, he is Elijah   4
     23:37 and you were not willing!   4
     26:41 the spirit indeed is willing   5
Mrk 14:38 the spirit indeed is willing   5
Lke 13:34 and you were not willing!   4
     22:42 if you are willing, remove this cup from me;   2
Jhn 5:35 you were willing to rejoice for a while   4
Act 26: 5 if they are willing to testify   4
1Co 16:12 he was not at all willing to come now.   3
Heb 12: 9 Should we not be even more willing to be subject   1

willing to yield

1. εὐπειθής, *eupeithēs, 2340*

Jas 3:17 wisdom from above is…gentle, willing to yield   1

willingly

1. ἑκουσίως, *hekousiōs, 1731*

1Pe 5: 2 tend…not under compulsion but willingly   1

win

1. Contextual: Not in Greek
2. εἰς, *eis, 1650*
3. καταλαμβάνω, *katalambanō, 2898*
4. κερδαίνω, *kerdainō, 3045*
5. κομίζω, *komizō, 3152*

Act 7:10 enabled him to win favor and to show wisdom   1
Rom 15:18 to win obedience from the Gentiles   2
1Co 9:19 a slave to all, so that I might win more   4
      9:20 To the Jews I became as a Jew, in order to win Jews. 4
      9:20 so that I might win those under the law.   4
      9:21 so that I might win those outside the law.   4
      9:22 so that I might win the weak.   4
      9:24 Run in such a way that you may win it.   3
1Pe 5: 4 you will win the crown of glory that never fades away. 5

win over

1. κερδαίνω, *kerdainō, 3045*
2. πείθω, *peithō, 4275*

Act 12:20 winning over Blastus, the king's chamberlain   2
     14:19 won over the crowds.   2
1Pe 3: 1 won over without a word by their wives' conduct   1

win strength

1. δυναμόω, *dynamoō, 1540*

Heb 11:34 won strength out of weakness   1

wind *See also* driven by the wind

1. ἄνεμος, *anemos, 449*
2. πνεῦμα, *pneuma, 4460*
3. πνέω, *pneō, 4463*
4. πνοή, *pnoē, 4466*

Mat 7:25 rain fell, the floods came, and the winds blew   1
      7:27 the floods came, and the winds blew and beat   1
      8:26 Then he got up and rebuked the winds and the sea;   1
      8:27 that even the winds and the sea obey him?"   1
     11: 7 A reed shaken by the wind?   1
     14:24 for the wind was against them.   1
     14:30 he noticed the strong wind, he became frightened   1
     14:32 When they got into the boat, the wind ceased.   1
     24:31 they will gather his elect from the four winds   1

Mrk 4:39 and rebuked the wind, and said to the sea   1
      4:39 the wind ceased, and there was a dead calm.   1
      4:41 that even the wind and the sea obey him?"   1
      6:48 against an adverse wind, he came towards them   1
      6:51 got into the boat with them and the wind ceased.   1
     13:27 gather his elect from the four winds   1
Lke 7:24 A reed shaken by the wind?   1
      8:24 woke up and rebuked the wind and the raging waves;   1
      8:25 he commands even the winds and the water,   1
Jhn 3: 8 The wind blows where it chooses   2
      6:18 sea became rough because a strong wind was blowing. 1
Act 2: 2 a sound like the rush of a violent wind   4
     27: 4 because the winds were against us.   1
     27: 7 and as the wind was against us   1
     27:14 soon a violent wind, called the northeaster   1
     27:15 could not be turned head-on into the wind   1
     27:40 then hoisting the foresail to the wind   3
Eph 4:14 blown about by every wind of doctrine   1
Heb 1: 7 Of the angels he says, "He makes his angels winds   2
Jas 3: 4 it takes strong winds to drive them,   1
Jde 1:12 waterless clouds carried along by the winds;   1
Rev 7: 1 angels…holding back the four winds   1
      7: 1 so that no wind could blow on earth or sea   1

south wind

1. νότος, *notos, 3803*

Lke 12:55 when you see the south wind blowing, you say   1
Act 27:13 When a moderate south wind began to blow   1
     28:13 After one day there a south wind sprang up   1

window

1. θυρίς, *thyris, 2600*

Act 20: 9 Eutychus, who was sitting in the window   1
2Co 11:33 let down in a basket through a window in the wall   1

windstorm

1. λαῖλαψ + ἄνεμος, *lailaps + anemos, 3278 + 449*
2. σεισμός, *seismos, 4939*

Mat 8:24 A windstorm arose on the sea, so great   2
Mrk 4:37 A great windstorm arose   1
Lke 8:23 A windstorm swept down on the lake   1

wine *See also* addicted to wine, pit for the wine press, wine press

1. Contextual: Not in Greek
2. οἶνος, *oinos, 3885*
3. ὄξος, *oxos, 3954*

Mat 9:17 Neither is new wine put into old wineskins;   2
      9:17 otherwise, the skins burst, and the wine is spilled 2
      9:17 but new wine is put into fresh wineskins.   2
     27:34 they offered him wine to drink, mixed with gall;   2
Mrk 2:22 no one puts new wine into old wineskins;   2
      2:22 otherwise, the wine will burst the skins   2
      2:22 the wine is lost, and so are the skins;   2
      2:22 one puts new wine into fresh wineskins."   2
     15:23 they offered him wine mixed with myrrh;   2
Lke 1:15 He must never drink wine or strong drink;   2
      5:37 no one puts new wine into old wineskins,   2
      5:37 otherwise the new wine will burst the skins   2
      5:38 new wine must be put into fresh wineskins.   2
      5:39 no one after drinking old wine desires new   1
      5:39 after drinking old wine desires new wine,   1
      7:33 has come eating no bread and drinking no wine   2
     10:34 wounds, having poured oil and wine on them   2
Jhn 2: 3 When the wine gave out, the mother of Jesus said   2
      2: 3 mother of Jesus said to him, "They have no wine."   2
      2: 9 tasted the water that had become wine   2
      2:10 said to him, "Everyone serves the good wine first   2
      2:10 inferior wine after the guests have become drunk.   1
      2:10 But you have kept the good wine until now."   2
      4:46 Cana…where he had changed the water into wine.   2
     19:29 they put a sponge full of the wine on a branch   3
     19:30 When Jesus had received the wine, he said   3
Rom 14:21 it is good not to eat meat or drink wine   2
Eph 5:18 Do not get drunk with wine, for that is debauchery; 2
1Ti 3: 8 not double-tongued, not indulging in much wine   2
      5:23 take a little wine for the sake of your stomach   2
Rev 6: 6 but do not damage the olive oil and the wine!"   2
     14: 8 drink of the wine of the wrath of her fornication." 2
     14:10 they will also drink the wine of God's wrath   2

17: 2 and with the wine of whose fornication 2
18: 3 drunk of the wine of the wrath of her fornication 2
18:13 wine, olive oil, choice flour and wheat, cattle 2
19:15 will tread the wine press of the fury...of God 2

new wine
1. γλεῦκος, *gleukos, 1183*

Act 2:13 "They are filled with new wine." 1

sour wine
1. ὄξος, *oxos, 3954*

Mat 27:48 ran and got a sponge, filled it with sour wine 1
Mrk 15:36 filled a sponge with sour wine, put it on a stick 1
Lke 23:36 coming up and offering him sour wine 1
Jhn 19:29 A jar full of sour wine was standing there. 1

wine-cup
1. ποτήριον + οἶνος, *potērion + oinos, 4539 + 3885*

Rev 16:19 gave her the wine-cup of the fury of his wrath. 1

wineskin
1. ἀσκός, *askos, 829*

Mat 9:17 Neither is new wine put into old wineskins; 1
9:17 but new wine is put into fresh wineskins 1
Mrk 2:22 no one puts new wine into old wineskins; 1
2:22 one puts new wine into fresh wineskins." 1
Lke 5:37 no one puts new wine into old wineskins; 1
5:38 new wine must be put into fresh wineskins. 1

wing
1. πτέρυξ, *pteryx, 4763*

Mat 23:37 as a hen gathers her brood under her wings 1
Lke 13:34 as a hen gathers her brood under her wings 1
Rev 4: 8 four living creatures, each...with six wings 1
9: 9 the noise of their wings was like the noise 1
12:14 woman was given the two wings of the great eagle 1

winnowing *See* winnowing *fork*

winter *See also* spend the winter, winter *fruit*
1. παραχειμάζω, *paracheimazō, 4199*
2. χειμών, *cheimōn, 5930*

Mat 24:20 in winter or on a sabbath. 2
Mrk 13:18 Pray that it may not be in winter. 2
Jhn 10:22 Dedication took place in Jerusalem. It was winter 2
Act 28:11 on a ship that had wintered at the island 1
2Ti 4:21 Do your best to come before winter. 2

wipe
1. ἐκμάσσω, *ekmassō, 1726*
2. ἐξαλείφω, *exaleiphō, 1981*

Jhn 11: 2 wiped his feet with her hair; 1
12: 3 wiped them with her hair. 1
13: 5 to wipe them with the towel 1
Rev 21: 4 he will wipe every tear from their eyes. 2

wipe away
1. ἐξαλείφω, *exaleiphō, 1981*

Rev 7:17 God will wipe away every tear from their eyes." 1

wipe off
1. ἀπομάσσω, *apomassō, 669*

Lke 10:11 dust...we wipe off in protest against you. 1

wipe out
1. ἐξαλείφω, *exaleiphō, 1981*

Act 3:19 so that your sins may be wiped out 1

wisdom
1. Contextual: Not in Greek
2. σοφία, *sophia, 5053*
3. φρόνησις, *phronēsis, 5860*

Mat 11:19 Yet wisdom is vindicated by her deeds." 2
12:42 to listen to the wisdom of Solomon 2
13:54 "Where did this man get this wisdom 2
Mrk 6: 2 What is this wisdom that has been given to him? 2
Lke 1:17 the disobedient to the wisdom of the righteous 3
2:40 grew and became strong, filled with wisdom; 2

2:52 Jesus increased in wisdom and in years 2
7:35 wisdom is vindicated by all her children." 2
11:31 to listen to the wisdom of Solomon 2
11:49 Therefore also the Wisdom of God said, 2
21:15 for I will give you words and a wisdom 2
Act 6: 3 full of the Spirit and of wisdom 2
6:10 could not withstand the wisdom and the Spirit 2
7:10 enabled him to win favor and to show wisdom 2
7:22 instructed in all the wisdom of the Egyptians 2
Rom 11:33 the riches and wisdom and knowledge of God! 2
1Co 1:17 proclaim the gospel, not with eloquent wisdom 2
1:19 "I will destroy the wisdom of the wise 2
1:20 Has not God made foolish the wisdom of the world? 2
1:21 in the wisdom of God, the world did not know God 2
1:21 the world did not know God through wisdom 2
1:22 For Jews demand signs and Greeks desire wisdom 2
1:24 Christ the power of God and the wisdom of God. 2
1:25 For God's foolishness is wiser than human wisdom 1
1:30 who became for us wisdom from God, and righteousness 2
2: 1 the mystery of God to you in lofty words or wisdom. 2
2: 4 not with plausible words of wisdom 2
2: 5 your faith might rest not on human wisdom 2
2: 6 Yet among the mature we do speak wisdom 2
2: 6 though it is not a wisdom of this age 2
2: 7 we speak God's wisdom, secret and hidden, 2
2:13 in words not taught by human wisdom 2
3:19 For the wisdom of this world is foolishness with God. 2
12: 8 through the Spirit the utterance of wisdom 2
2Co 1:12 not by earthly wisdom but by the grace of God 2
Eph 1: 8 With all wisdom and insight 2
1:17 may give you a spirit of wisdom and revelation 2
3:10 the wisdom of God in its rich variety 2
Col 1: 9 in all spiritual wisdom and understanding 2
1:28 teaching everyone in all wisdom 2
2: 3 all the treasures of wisdom and knowledge. 2
2:23 These have indeed an appearance of wisdom 2
3:16 teach and admonish one another in all wisdom; 2
Jas 1: 5 If any of you is lacking in wisdom, ask God 2
3:13 that your works are done with gentleness born of wisdom. 2
3:15 Such wisdom does not come down from above 2
3:17 wisdom from above is first pure, then peaceable 2
2Pe 3:15 Paul wrote...according to the wisdom given him 2
Rev 5:12 to receive power and wealth and wisdom and might 2
7:12 Blessing and glory and wisdom and thanksgiving 2
13:18 This calls for wisdom: 2
17: 9 "This calls for a mind that has wisdom: 2

wise
1. σοφός, *sophos, 5055*
2. φρόνιμος, *phronimos, 5861*

Mat 7:24 will be like a wise man who built his house 2
10:16 so be wise as serpents and innocent as doves. 2
11:25 these things from the wise and the intelligent 1
24:45 "Who then is the faithful and wise slave 2
25: 2 Five of them were foolish, and five were wise. 2
25: 4 the wise took flasks of oil with their lamps. 2
25: 8 The foolish said to the wise 2
25: 9 But the wise replied, 'No! 2
Lke 10:21 hidden...from the wise and the intelligent 1
Rom 1:14 both to the wise and to the foolish 1
1:22 Claiming to be wise, they became fools; 1
11:25 So that you may not claim to be wiser than you are 2
12:16 do not claim to be wiser than you are 2
16:19 I want you to be wise in what is good 1
16:27 to the only wise God, through Jesus Christ, 1
1Co 1:19 "I will destroy the wisdom of the wise 1
1:20 Where is the one who is wise? Where is the scribe? 1
1:25 For God's foolishness is wiser than human wisdom 1
1:26 not many of you were wise by human standards 1
1:27 to shame the wise; 1
3:18 If you think that you are wise in this age 1
3:18 you should become fools so that you may become wise. 1
3:19 "He catches the wise in their craftiness," 1
3:20 the thoughts of the wise, that they are futile." 1
4:10 you are wise in Christ, 2
6: 5 there is no one among you wise enough to decide 1
2Co 11:19 For you gladly put up with fools, being wise 2
Eph 5:15 live, not as unwise people but as wise 1
Jas 3:13 Who is wise and understanding among you? 1

wise man

　1. μάγος, *magos, 3407*

Mat	2: 1	wise men from the East came to Jerusalem	1
	2: 7	Then Herod secretly called for the wise men	1
	2:16	been tricked by the wise men, he was infuriated	1
	2:16	time that he had learned from the wise men.	1

wisely

　1. νουνεχῶς, *nounechōs, 3807*
　2. σοφία, *sophia, 5053*

| Mrk | 12:34 | When Jesus saw that he answered wisely | 1 |
| Col | 4: 5 | Conduct yourselves wisely toward outsiders | 2 |

wish

　1. βούλομαι, *boulomai, 1089*
　2. εὔχομαι, *euchomai, 2377*
　3. θέλημα, *thelēma, 2525*
　4. θέλω, *thelō, 2527*
　5. ὄφελον, *ophelon, 4054*

Mat	12:38	"Teacher, we wish to see a sign from you."	4
	15:28	it be done for you as you wish."	4
	17: 4	if you wish, I will make three dwellings here	4
	18:23	a king who wished to settle accounts	4
	19:17	If you wish to enter into life, keep	4
	19:21	"If you wish to be perfect, go, sell	4
	20:26	whoever wishes to be great among you	4
	20:27	whoever wishes to be first among you	4
Mrk	6:22	"Ask me for whatever you wish, and I will give it."	4
	10:43	whoever wishes to become great among you	4
	10:44	whoever wishes to be first among you	4
	14: 7	you can show kindness to them whenever you wish;	4
	15:12	"Then what do you wish me to do with the man	4
	15:15	So Pilate, wishing to satisfy the crowd	1
Lke	12:49	how I wish it were already kindled!	4
	23:25	he handed Jesus over as they wished.	3
Jhn	5:21	so also the Son gives life to whomever he wishes.	4
	6:67	"Do you also wish to go away?"	4
	7: 1	He did not wish to go about in Judea	4
	12:21	"Sir, we wish to see Jesus."	4
	15: 7	ask for whatever you wish, and it will be done	4
	21:18	and to go wherever you wished.	4
	21:18	take you where you do not wish to go."	4
Act	13:22	a man after my heart, who will carry out all my wishes.'	3
	18:15	I do not wish to be a judge of these matters."	1
	18:27	when he wished to cross over to Achaia	1
	19:30	Paul wished to go into the crowd	1
	25: 9	Festus, wishing to do the Jews a favor, asked Paul	4
	25: 9	"Do you wish to go up to Jerusalem	4
	25:20	I asked whether he wished to go to Jerusalem	1
	27:43	the centurion, wishing to save Paul	1
Rom	9: 3	For I could wish that I myself were accursed	2
	13: 3	you wish to have no fear of the authority?	4
1Co	4: 8	Indeed, wish that you had become kings,	5
	7: 7	I wish that all were as I myself am.	4
	7:36	let him marry as he wishes; it is no sin.	4
	7:39	marry anyone she wishes, only in the Lord.	4
2Co	5: 4	because we wish not to be unclothed	4
	11: 1	I wish you would bear with me	5
	12: 6	But if I wish to boast, I will not be a fool	4
	12:20	I come, I may find you not as I wish	4
	12:20	you may find me not as you wish;	4
Gal	4:20	I wish I were present with you now	4
	5:12	I wish those who unsettle you	5
Jas	4: 4	whoever wishes to be a friend of the world	1
	4:15	"If the Lord wishes, we will live and do this	4
Rev	3:15	I wish that you were either cold or hot.	5
	22:17	Let anyone who wishes take the water of life	4

with　*See also* active along with, aflame with passion, along
　with, at *table* with, bear with, bear witness with, beat with
　a rod, bring with, bury with, choose with care, citizen
　with, come down with, come up with, come with,
　compare with, covered with sores, crucify with, die with,
　dispute with one another, do away with, drag with, drink
　with, eat with, feast with, fight with a wild animal, fill with
　awe, fill with compassion, fill with expectation, get into
　with, glorify with, go with, greet with respect, grow with,
　heir with, in prison with, keep in check with a bridle, king
　with, live with, look on with favor, make with hands, make

with human hands, mark with a seal, meet with, mix with
myrrh, move with compassion, move with pity, not made
with hands, overcome with amazement, overcome with
awe, possessed with a demon, puff up with conceit, put up
with, raise up with, raise with, regard with contempt, reign
with, rejoice with, sear with a hot iron, seat with, send
with, sit at table with, sit with, stand with, stay with, suffer
with, sweep away with the flood, swell with conceit, take
with, talk with, together with, travel with, treat with
contempt, with *child*, with *consent*, with *help*, with *seven*
others, work with, worker with

　1. ἀπό, *apo, 608*
　2. διά, *dia, 1328*
　3. διά + χείρ, *dia + cheir, 1328 + 5931*
　4. εἰς, *eis, 1650*
　5. εἰς + ὁ + κόλπος, *eis + ho + kolpos, 1650 + 3836 + 3146*
　6. ἐκ, *ek, 1666*
　7. ἐν, *en, 1877*
　8. ἐνώπιον, *enōpion, 1967*
　9. ἐπί, *epi, 2093*
　10. ἔχω, *echō, 2400*
　11. καί, *kai, 2779*
　12. κατά, *kata, 2848*
　13. μετά, *meta, 3552*
　14. παρά, *para, 4123*
　15. περί, *peri, 4309*
　16. ποιέω, *poieō, 4472*
　17. πρός, *pros, 4639*
　18. προσμένω, *prosmenō, 4693*
　19. σύν, *syn, 5250*
　20. σύνειμι[1], *syneimi[1], 5289*
　21. χωρίς, *chōris, 6006*

Mat	1:23	Emmanuel," which means, "God is with us."	13
	2: 3	he was frightened, and all Jerusalem with him;	13
	2:11	entering the house, they saw the child with Mary	13
	3: 4	clothing of camel's hair with a leather belt	11
	3:11	"I baptize you with water for repentance, but one	7
	3:11	baptize you with the Holy Spirit and fire.	7
	3:17	my Son, the Beloved, with whom I am well pleased."	7
	4:21	in the boat with their father Zebedee, mending	13
	5:25	accuser while you are on the way to court with him	13
	5:28	who looks at a woman with lust has already	17
	7: 2	For with the judgment you make	7
	8: 9	a man under authority, with soldiers under me;	10
	8:11	eat with Abraham and Isaac and Jacob	13
	9:11	"Why does your teacher eat with tax collectors	13
	9:15	as long as the bridegroom is with them	13
	9:19	Jesus got up and followed him, with his disciples.	11
	11:15	Let anyone with ears listen!	10
	12:10	a man was there with a withered hand	10
	12:18	my beloved, with whom my soul is well pleased.	4
	12:30	Whoever is not with me is against me,	13
	12:30	and whoever does not gather with me scatters.	13
	12:41	rise up at the judgment with this generation	13
	12:42	at the judgment with this generation	13
	13: 9	Let anyone with ears listen!"	10
	13:20	and immediately receives it with joy;	13
	13:43	Let anyone with ears listen!	10
	13:56	are not all his sisters with us?	17
	15:30	crowds came to him, bringing with them the lame	13
	15:32	because they have been with me now for three days	18
	16:27	"For the Son of Man is to come with his angels	13
	17: 3	Moses and Elijah, talking with him.	13
	17: 5	my Son, the Beloved; with him I am well pleased;	7
	17:17	how much longer must I be with you?	13
	18:16	take one or two others along with you	13
	18:23	to settle accounts with his slaves.	13
	18:26	'Have patience with me, and I will pay you	9
	18:29	'Have patience with me, and I will pay you.'	9
	19:10	"If such is the case of a man with his wife	13
	20: 2	After agreeing with the laborers	13
	20: 8	beginning with the last and then going	1
	20:15	to do what I choose with what belongs to me?	7
	20:20	the mother...came to him with her sons	13
	20:24	they were angry with the two brothers.	15
	21: 2	a donkey tied, and a colt with her;	13
	21:25	And they argued with one another	7
	22:16	for you do not regard people with partiality	4

22:37	love the Lord your God with all your heart	7
22:37	with all your heart, and with all your soul	7
22:37	with all your soul, and with all your mind.'	7
24:30	with power and great glory.	13
24:31	send out his angels with a loud trumpet call	13
24:49	eats and drinks with drunkards	13
24:51	and put him with the hypocrites	13
25: 3	they took no oil with them;	13
25: 4	the wise took flasks of oil with their lamps.	13
25:10	who were ready went with him into the wedding	13
25:16	went off at once and traded with them	7
25:19	settled accounts with them.	13
25:27	what was my own with interest.	19
25:28	give it to the one with the ten talents.	10
25:31	all the angels with him	13
26: 7	with an alabaster jar	10
26:11	For you always have the poor with you	13
26:18	Passover at your house with my disciples.' "	13
26:20	he took his place with the twelve;	13
26:23	who has dipped his hand into the bowl with me	13
26:29	until that day when I drink it new with you	13
26:35	"Even though I must die with you, I will not deny	19
26:36	Then Jesus went with them to a place	13
26:38	remain here, and stay awake with me."	13
26:40	"So, could you not stay awake with me one hour?	13
26:47	with him was a large crowd with swords and clubs	13
26:47	with him was a large crowd with swords and clubs	13
26:51	Suddenly, one of those with Jesus	13
26:55	with swords and clubs to arrest me	13
26:58	he sat with the guards in order to see how	13
26:69	"You also were with Jesus the Galilean."	13
26:71	"This man was with Jesus of Nazareth."	13
26:72	Again he denied it with an oath	13
27:34	they offered him wine to drink, mixed with gall;	13
27:38	Then two bandits were crucified with him	19
27:44	The bandits who were crucified with him	19
27:54	Now when the centurion and those with him	13
27:66	they went with the guard and made the tomb secure	13
28: 8	they left the tomb quickly with fear	13
28:12	After the priests had assembled with the elders	13
28:20	I am with you always, to the end of the age."	13

Mrk	1: 6	with a leather belt around his waist	11
	1: 8	he will baptize you with the Holy Spirit."	7
	1:11	with you I am well pleased."	7
	1:13	and he was with the wild beasts;	13
	1:20	Zebedee in the boat with the hired men	13
	1:23	in their synagogue a man with an unclean spirit	7
	1:27	A new teaching—with authority! He commands	12
	1:29	entered the house…with James and John.	13
	2:16	Pharisees saw that he was eating with sinners	13
	2:16	"Why does he eat with tax collectors and sinners?"	13
	2:19	while the bridegroom is with them	13
	2:19	As long as they have the bridegroom with them	13
	3: 5	He looked around at them with anger;	13
	3: 6	immediately conspired with the Herodians	13
	3: 7	Jesus departed with his disciples to the sea	13
	3:14	he appointed twelve…to be with him	13
	4: 9	he said, "Let anyone with ears to hear listen!"	10
	4:16	immediately receive it with joy.	13
	4:23	Let anyone with ears to hear listen!"	10
	4:36	Other boats were with him.	13
	5: 2	a man out of the tombs with an unclean spirit	7
	5:18	begged that he might be with him.	13
	5:24	he went with him.	13
	5:40	and took…those who were with him	13
	6: 3	are not his sisters here with us?"	17
	6:51	got into the boat with them and the wind ceased.	17
	8: 2	because they have been with me now for three days	18
	8:10	he got into the boat with his disciples	13
	8:14	they had only one loaf with them in the boat.	13
	8:27	Jesus went on with his disciples	11
	8:34	He called the crowd with his disciples	19
	8:38	glory of his Father with the holy angels."	13
	9: 1	the kingdom of God has come with power."	7
	9: 4	there appeared to them Elijah with Moses	19
	9: 8	saw no one with them any more, but only Jesus.	13
	9:14	scribes arguing with them.	17
	9:16	"What are you arguing about with them?"	17
	9:34	on the way they had argued with one another	17
	9:50	be at peace with one another."	7
	10:30	children, and fields, with persecutions	13

	10:41	they began to be angry with James and John.	15
	11:11	he went out to Bethany with the twelve.	13
	11:31	They argued with one another	17
	12:14	for you do not regard people with partiality	4
	12:30	shall love the Lord your God with all your heart	6
	12:30	with all your soul, and with all your mind	6
	12:30	with all your mind, and with all your strength.'	6
	12:33	'to love him with all the heart	6
	12:33	and 'to love him…with all the understanding	6
	12:33	and 'to love him…with all the strength,'	6
	13:26	coming in clouds' with great power and glory.	13
	14: 3	a woman came with an alabaster jar of…ointment	10
	14: 7	For you always have the poor with you	13
	14:14	where I may eat the Passover with my disciples?'	13
	14:17	When it was evening, he came with the twelve.	13
	14:18	one who is eating with me."	13
	14:20	one who is dipping bread into the bowl with me.	13
	14:33	He took with him Peter and James and John	13
	14:43	with him there was a crowd with swords and clubs	13
	14:43	with him there was a crowd with swords and clubs	13
	14:48	with swords and clubs to arrest me	13
	14:49	Day after day I was with you in the temple	17
	14:54	he was sitting with the guards	13
	14:62	'coming with the clouds of heaven.' "	13
	14:67	"You also were with Jesus, the man from Nazareth."	13
	15: 1	held a consultation with the elders and scribes	13
	15: 7	a man called Barabbas was in prison with the rebels	13
	15:27	with them they crucified two bandits	19
	15:32	Those who were crucified with him also taunted	19
	16:10	⟦She went out and told those who had been with him⟧	13

Lke	1:17	With the spirit and power of Elijah he will go	7
	1:28	"Greetings, favored one! The Lord is with you."	13
	1:30	you have found favor with God.	14
	1:37	For nothing will be impossible with God."	14
	1:39	went with haste to a Judean town in the hill country	13
	1:51	He has shown strength with his arm;	7
	1:56	Mary remained with her about three months	19
	1:66	For, indeed, the hand of the Lord was with him.	13
	2: 5	registered with Mary, to whom he was engaged	19
	2:13	suddenly there was with the angel a multitude	19
	2:36	lived with her husband seven years	13
	2:51	he went down with them and came to Nazareth	13
	3:16	baptize you with the Holy Spirit and fire.	7
	3:22	my Son, the Beloved; with you I am well pleased."	7
	4:32	because he spoke with authority.	7
	4:36	For with authority and power he commands	7
	5: 9	For he and all who were with him were amazed	19
	5:17	the power of the Lord was with him to heal.	4
	5:19	let him down with his bed through the tiles	19
	5:29	and others sitting at the table with them.	13
	5:30	"Why do you eat and drink with tax collectors	13
	5:34	while the bridegroom is with them	13
	6:11	filled with fury and discussed with one another	17
	6:17	came down with them and stood on a level place	13
	6:17	with a great crowd of his disciples	11
	6:18	those who were troubled with unclean spirits	1
	7: 6	Jesus went with them	19
	7: 8	set under authority, with soldiers under me;	10
	7:12	with her was a large crowd from the town.	19
	7:36	One of the Pharisees asked Jesus to eat with him	13
	8: 1	The twelve were with him	19
	8: 8	"Let anyone with ears to hear listen!"	10
	8:13	when they hear the word, receive it with joy.	13
	8:15	and bear fruit with patient endurance.	7
	8:22	One day he got into a boat with his disciples	11
	8:38	begged that he might be with him;	19
	8:51	he did not allow anyone to enter with him	19
	9:41	how much longer must I be with you and bear	17
	9:49	stop him, because he does not follow with us."	13
	10:17	The seventy returned with joy, saying,	13
	10:27	love the Lord your God with all your heart	6
	10:27	with all your soul, and with all your strength	7
	10:27	with all your soul, and with all your strength	7
	10:27	with all your strength, and with all your mind;	7
	11: 7	and my children are with me in bed;	13
	11:23	Whoever is not with me is against me,	13
	11:23	whoever does not gather with me scatters.	13
	11:31	rise…with the people of this generation	13
	11:32	rise up at the judgment with this generation	13
	11:36	full of light, with no part of it in darkness	10

Lke	11:37	a Pharisee invited him to dine with him;	14
	12:13	to divide the family inheritance with me."	13
	12:46	and put him with the unfaithful.	13
	12:58	you go with your accuser before a magistrate	13
	13: 1	blood…had mingled with their sacrifices.	13
	13:11	a woman with a spirit that had crippled	10
	13:21	took and mixed in with three measures of flour	4
	13:26	'We ate and drank with you	8
	14:31	whether he is able with ten thousand to oppose	7
	14:31	who comes against him with twenty thousand?	13
	14:35	Let anyone with ears to hear listen!"	10
	15:16	He would gladly have filled himself with the pods	6
	15:29	so that I might celebrate with my friends.	13
	15:30	who has devoured your property with prostitutes	13
	15:31	father said to him, 'Son, you are always with me	13
	16:11	not been faithful with the dishonest wealth	7
	16:12	not been faithful with what belongs to another	7
	16:21	satisfy his hunger with what fell from…table;	1
	16:22	carried away by the angels to be with Abraham.	5
	16:23	saw Abraham far away with Lazarus by his side.	11
	17:15	turned back, praising God with a loud voice.	13
	17:20	is not coming with things that can be observed;	13
	19:23	I could have collected it with interest.'	19
	20: 1	priests and the scribes came with the elders	19
	20: 5	They discussed it with one another, saying	17
	21:27	coming in a cloud' with power and great glory.	13
	21:34	weighed down with dissipation and drunkenness	7
	22:11	where I may eat the Passover with my disciples?" '	13
	22:14	his place at the table, and the apostles with him.	19
	22:15	to eat this Passover with you before I suffer;	13
	22:21	the one who betrays me is with me, and his hand	13
	22:33	I am ready to go with you to prison and to death!"	13
	22:49	should we strike with the sword?"	7
	22:52	"Have you come out with swords and clubs	13
	22:53	I was with you day after day in the temple	13
	22:56	and said, "This man also was with him."	19
	22:59	"Surely this man also was with him;	13
	23:11	Herod with his soldiers	19
	23:12	Herod and Pilate became friends with each other;	13
	23:32	Two others…were led away to be put to death	19
	23:33	they crucified Jesus there with the criminals	11
	23:43	today you will be with me in Paradise."	13
	24:10	and the other women with them who told this	19
	24:14	talking with each other about all these things	17
	24:17	he said to them, "What are you discussing	17
	24:24	Some of those who were with us went to the tomb	19
	24:27	beginning with Moses and all the prophets	1
	24:29	they urged him strongly, saying, "Stay with us	13
	24:29	So he went in to stay with them.	19
	24:30	When he was at the table with them, he took bread	13
	24:44	while I was still with you	19
	24:52	and returned to Jerusalem with great joy;	13
Jhn	1: 1	the Word was with God, and the Word was God.	17
	1: 2	He was in the beginning with God.	17
	1:26	John answered them, "I baptize with water.	7
	1:31	but I came baptizing with water for this	7
	1:33	but the one who sent me to baptize with water	7
	1:33	is the one who baptizes with the Holy Spirit.'	7
	1:35	John again was standing with two of his disciples	11
	1:39	and they remained with him that day.	14
	2:12	with his mother, his brothers	11
	3:22	he spent some time there with them and baptized.	13
	3:26	the one who was with you across the Jordan	13
	4:12	with his sons and his flocks drank from it?"	11
	4:27	astonished that he was speaking with a woman	13
	4:27	or, "Why are you speaking with her?"	13
	4:40	they asked him to stay with them;	14
	6: 3	and sat down there with his disciples.	13
	6:66	and no longer went about with him.	13
	7:33	"I will be with you a little while longer	13
	8: 9	⟦went away, one by one, beginning with the elders;⟧	1
	8: 9	⟦Jesus was left alone with the woman⟧	11
	8:29	the one who sent me is with me; he has not left	13
	9: 6	made mud with the saliva	6
	9:37	one speaking with you is he.	13
	11:16	"Let us also go, that we may die with him."	13
	11:31	The Jews who were with her in the house	13
	11:45	the Jews therefore, who had come with Mary	17
	11:54	and he remained there with the disciples.	13
	12: 2	Lazarus was one of those at the table with him.	19
	12: 3	The house was filled with the fragrance	6

	12: 8	You always have the poor with you	13
	12:17	So the crowd that had been with him	13
	12:35	"The light is with you for a little longer.	7
	13: 8	"Unless I wash you, you have no share with me."	13
	13:33	Little children, I am with you only a little longer.	13
	14: 9	to him, "Have I been with you all this time	13
	14:16	another Advocate, to be with you forever.	13
	14:17	You know him, because he abides with you	14
	14:23	we will come to them and make our home with them.	14
	14:25	while I am still with you.	14
	14:30	I will no longer talk much with you	13
	15:27	because you have been with me from the beginning.	13
	16: 4	because I was with you.	13
	16:32	I am not alone because the Father is with me.	13
	17:12	While I was with them, I protected them	13
	17:24	may be with me where I am	13
	18: 1	he went out with his disciples	19
	18: 2	Jesus often met there with his disciples.	13
	18: 3	came there with lanterns and torches	13
	18: 5	Judas, who betrayed him, was standing with them.	13
	18:18	standing with them and warming himself.	13
	18:26	"Did I not see you in the garden with him?"	13
	19:18	they crucified him, and with him two others	13
	19:40	and wrapped it with the spices in linen cloths	13
	20: 7	the cloth…not lying with the linen wrappings	13
	20:24	Thomas…was not with them when Jesus came.	13
	20:26	Thomas was with them.	13
	21: 3	They said to him, "We will go with you."	19
	21: 9	a charcoal fire…with fish on it, and bread.	11
Act	1: 5	you will be baptized with the Holy Spirit	7
	1:18	acquired a field with the reward of his wickedness;	6
	1:22	become a witness with us to his resurrection."	19
	2:14	Peter, standing with the eleven	19
	2:28	make me full of gladness with your presence.'	13
	2:29	his tomb is with us to this day.	7
	2:46	ate their food with glad and generous hearts	7
	3: 8	walk, and he entered the temple with them	19
	4: 6	with Annas the high priest, Caiaphas, John,	11
	4:15	they discussed the matter with one another.	17
	4:27	both Herod and Pontius Pilate, with the Gentiles	19
	4:29	servants to speak your word with all boldness	13
	4:31	spoke the word of God with boldness.	13
	5:17	took action; he and all who were with him	19
	5:21	the high priest and those with him arrived	19
	5:26	captain went with the temple police and brought	19
	7: 9	but God was with him	13
	7:38	with the angel who spoke to him at Mount Sinai	13
	7:45	Our ancestors in turn brought it in with Joshua	13
	7:46	who found favor with God	8
	8:20	Peter said to him, "May your silver perish with you	19
	8:20	thought you could obtain God's gift with money!	2
	8:35	starting with this scripture	1
	9:19	he was with the disciples in Damascus	13
	9:29	He spoke and argued with the Hellenists;	17
	9:39	clothing that Dorcas made while she was with them.	13
	9:43	in Joppa for some time with a certain Simon, a tanner	14
	10: 2	devout man who feared God with all his household;	19
	10: 6	he is lodging with Simon, a tanner	14
	10:20	go down, and go with them without hesitation;	19
	10:23	The next day he got up and went with them	19
	10:38	doing good and healing…for God was with him.	13
	11:16	you will be baptized with the Holy Spirit.'	7
	11:21	The hand of the Lord was with them	13
	11:26	for an entire year they met with the church	7
	13: 7	He was with the proconsul, Sergius Paulus,	19
	13:17	with uplifted arm he led them out of it.	13
	14: 4	some sided with the Jews	19
	14: 4	some with the apostles.	19
	14: 5	both Gentiles and Jews, with their rulers	19
	14:20	The next day he went on with Barnabas to Derbe.	19
	14:23	with prayer and fasting they entrusted them	13
	14:27	related all that God had done with them	13
	14:28	stayed there with the disciples for some time.	19
	15: 2	had no small dissension and debate with them	17
	15: 2	to discuss this question with the apostles	17
	15: 4	they reported all that God had done with them.	13
	15:22	send them to Antioch with Paul and Barnabas.	19
	15:23	with the following letter:	3
	15:35	and there, with many others, they taught	13
	17:17	he argued…with those who happened to be there.	17
	17:23	I found among them an altar with the inscription	7

17:34	a woman named Damaris, and others with them.	19
18: 2	recently come from Italy with his wife Priscilla	11
18: 3	he stayed with them, and they worked	14
18:10	for I am with you, and no one will lay a hand	13
19:16	the man with the evil spirit leaped on them	7
19:25	with the workers of the same trade	11
19:26	saying that gods made with hands are not gods.	2
19:38	Demetrius and the artisans with him	19
20:19	serving the Lord with all humility	13
20:28	that he obtained with the blood of his own Son.	2
20:31	not cease...to warn everyone with tears.	13
20:36	he knelt down with them all and prayed.	19
21: 5	all of them, with wives and children	19
21: 7	stayed with them for one day.	14
21: 8	we went into the house...and stayed with him.	14
21:16	Mnason of Cyprus...with whom we were to stay.	14
21:18	The next day Paul went with us to visit James;	19
21:24	go through the rite of purification with them	19
21:26	entered the temple with them, making public	19
21:29	Trophimus the Ephesian with him in the city	19
22: 9	Now those who were with me saw the light	19
22:11	those who were with me took my hand	20
23: 9	"We find nothing wrong with this man.	7
23:27	I came with the guard and rescued him.	19
23:32	The next day they let the horsemen go on with him	19
24: 1	the high priest Ananias came down with some elders	13
24: 3	We welcome this...with utmost gratitude.	13
24:12	They did not find me disputing with anyone	17
24:24	Felix came with his wife Drusilla	19
25:12	after he had conferred with his council	13
25:19	they had certain points of disagreement with him	17
25:23	Agrippa and Bernice came with great pomp	13
25:23	they entered...with the military tribunes	19
26:12	with the authority...of the chief priests	13
27:10	I can see that the voyage will be with danger	13
27:24	God has granted safety to all...sailing with you.'	13
27:39	they noticed a bay with a beach	10
28:14	were invited to stay with them for seven days.	14
28:16	with the soldier who was guarding him.	19
28:25	they disagreed with each other;	17
28:31	teaching...with all boldness and without hindrance.	13
Rom 1: 4	declared to be Son of God with power	7
1: 9	I serve with my spirit by announcing the gospel	7
1:27	men...consumed with passion for one another.	7
1:27	Men committed shameless acts with men	7
5: 1	peace with God through our Lord Jesus Christ	17
6: 8	But if we have died with Christ, we believe	19
8:25	if we hope...we wait for it with patience.	2
8:32	will he not with him also give us everything	19
9:22	endured with much patience the objects of wrath	7
10: 9	if you confess with your lips that Jesus is Lord	7
10:19	with a foolish nation I will make you angry."	9
12: 3	but to think with sober judgment	4
12:15	Rejoice with those who rejoice	13
12:15	weep with those who weep.	13
12:16	Live in harmony with one another;	4
12:18	If it is possible...live peaceably with all.	13
12:21	but overcome evil with good.	7
13: 6	God's servants, busy with this very thing.	4
15: 5	to live in harmony with one another	7
15: 6	together you may with one voice glorify the God	7
15:10	"Rejoice, O Gentiles, with his people";	13
15:23	But now, with no further place for me	10
15:26	pleased to share their resources with the poor	4
15:32	that by God's will I may come to you with joy	7
15:33	The God of peace be with all of you. Amen.	13
16:14	Greet...the brothers and sisters who are with them.	19
16:15	Greet...all the saints who are with them.	19
16:16	Greet one another with a holy kiss.	7
16:20	The grace of our Lord Jesus Christ be with you.	13
1Co 1:17	proclaim the gospel, not with eloquent wisdom	7
2: 4	not with plausible words of wisdom	7
2: 4	with a demonstration of the Spirit and of power	7
3:13	because it will be revealed with fire	7
3:19	For the wisdom of this world is foolishness with God.	14
4:21	you prefer? Am I to come to you with a stick	7
4:21	with love in a spirit of gentleness?	7
5: 8	celebrate the festival, not with the old yeast	7
5: 8	with the unleavened bread of sincerity	7
6: 7	to have lawsuits at all with one another	13
7:12	she consents to live with him	13

7:13	he consents to live with her	13
7:24	there remain with God.	14
10: 5	God was not pleased with most of them	7
10:13	with the testing he will also provide	19
11: 4	prays or prophesies with something on his head	10
14:16	Otherwise, if you say a blessing with the spirit	7
14:36	Or did the word of God originate with you?	1
15:10	the grace of God that is with me.	19
15:32	If with merely human hopes I fought with wild animals	12
16: 3	I will send any whom you approve with letters	2
16: 6	perhaps I will stay with you	17
16: 7	I hope to spend some time with you	17
16:11	I am expecting him with the brothers.	13
16:12	to visit you with the other brothers	13
16:20	Greet one another with a holy kiss.	7
16:23	The grace of the Lord Jesus be with you.	13
16:24	My love be with all of you in Christ Jesus.	13
2Co 1: 4	with the consolation...by God	2
1:12	with frankness and godly sincerity	7
1:21	it is God who establishes us with you in Christ	19
2: 4	anguish of heart and with many tears	2
4:14	will raise us also with Jesus	19
4:14	and will bring us with you into his presence.	19
5: 8	be away from the body and at home with the Lord.	17
6: 7	with the weapons of righteousness	2
6:15	What agreement does Christ have with Beliar?	17
6:15	what does a believer share with an unbeliever?	13
6:16	What agreement has the temple of God with idols?	13
7: 8	For even if I made you sorry with my letter	7
7:15	you welcomed him with fear and trembling.	13
8:18	With him we are sending the brother who is famous	13
8:19	appointed by the churches to travel with us	19
9: 4	if some Macedonians come with me and find	19
9:12	also overflows with many thanksgivings to God.	2
9:13	your sharing with them and with all others	4
9:13	your sharing with them and with all others	4
10: 1	who am humble when face to face with you	7
10: 9	as though I am trying to frighten you with my letters.	2
10:14	all the way to you with the good news of Christ.	7
11: 9	when I was with you and was in need	17
11:23	with far greater labors, far more imprisonments	7
11:23	with countless floggings, and often near death.	7
12:10	I am content with weaknesses, insults, hardships	7
12:12	with utmost patience, signs and wonders	7
13: 4	in dealing with you we will live with him	19
13:11	the God of love and peace will be with you.	13
13:12	Greet one another with a holy kiss.	7
13:13	communion of the Holy Spirit be with all of you.	13
Gal 1: 2	all the members of God's family who are with me	19
1:18	stayed with him fifteen days;	17
2: 1	I went up again to Jerusalem with Barnabas	13
2: 3	even Titus, who was with me, was not compelled	19
2: 5	truth of the gospel might always remain with you	17
2:12	he used to eat with the Gentiles.	13
2:14	acting consistently with the truth of the gospel	17
3: 9	who believe are blessed with Abraham	19
4:18	not only when I am present with you.	17
4:20	I wish I were present with you now	17
4:30	child of the slave will not share the inheritance with	13
4:25	for she is in slavery with her children.	13
5:24	crucified the flesh with its passions	19
6:18	grace...be with your spirit, brothers and sisters.	13
Eph 1: 3	blessed us...with every spiritual blessing	7
1: 8	With all wisdom and insight	7
3:18	the power to comprehend, with all the saints	19
3:19	you may be filled with all the fullness of God.	4
4: 2	with all humility and gentleness	13
4: 2	humility and gentleness, with patience	13
4:30	with which you were marked with a seal	7
5:18	be filled with the Spirit	7
6: 2	this is the first commandment with a promise:	7
6: 5	obey your earthly masters with fear and trembling	13
6: 7	Render service with enthusiasm,	13
6: 9	with him there is no partiality.	14
6:16	With all of these, take the shield of faith	7
6:16	with which you will be able to quench...arrows	7
6:19	to make known with boldness the mystery of the gospel	7
6:23	Peace be to the whole community, and love with faith	13
6:24	Grace be with all who have an undying love	13
Php 1: 1	in Philippi, with the bishops and deacons:	19
1: 4	constantly praying with joy in...my prayers	13

Php	1: 8	I long...with the compassion of Christ Jesus.	7
	1: 9	with knowledge and full insight	7
	1:20	that by my speaking with all boldness,	7
	1:23	my desire is to depart and be with Christ	19
	2:12	work out your own salvation with fear	13
	2:22	he has served with me in the work of the gospel.	19
	2:23	as soon as I see how things go with me;	15
	2:29	Welcome him then in the Lord with all joy	13
	4: 6	by prayer and supplication with thanksgiving	13
	4: 9	the God of peace will be with you.	13
	4:11	I have learned to be content with whatever I have.	7
	4:21	The friends who are with me greet you.	19
	4:23	The grace of the Lord...be with your spirit.	13
Col	1:11	May you be made strong with all the strength	7
	1:29	For this I toil and struggle with all the energy	12
	2: 4	no one may deceive you with plausible arguments.	7
	2: 5	yet I am with you in spirit	19
	2:13	God made you alive together with him	19
	2:20	If with Christ you died to the elemental spirits	19
	3: 3	your life is hidden with Christ in God.	19
	3: 4	you also will be revealed with him in glory.	19
	3: 9	seeing that you have stripped off the old self	19
	3:16	with gratitude in your hearts sing psalms, hymns,	7
	4: 2	keeping alert in it with thanksgiving.	7
	4: 9	he is coming with Onesimus, the faithful	19
	4:18	Remember my chains. Grace be with you.	13
1Th	1: 5	in the Holy Spirit and with full conviction;	7
	1: 6	with joy inspired by the Holy Spirit	13
	2: 5	we never came with words of flattery	7
	2: 5	we never came...with a pretext for greed;	7
	3: 4	In fact, when we were with you, we told you	17
	3:13	the coming of our Lord Jesus with all his saints.	13
	4: 5	not with lustful passion	7
	4:14	God will bring with him those who have died.	19
	4:16	For the Lord himself, with a cry of command,	7
	4:16	For the Lord himself...with the archangel's call	7
	4:16	with the sound of God's trumpet, will descend	7
	4:17	will be caught up in the clouds together with them	19
	4:17	so we will be with the Lord forever.	19
	4:18	encourage one another with these words.	7
	5:10	whether we are awake or asleep we may live with him.	19
	5:14	help the weak, be patient with all of them.	17
	5:26	Greet all the brothers and sisters with a holy kiss.	7
	5:28	The grace of our Lord Jesus Christ be with you.	13
2Th	1: 7	revealed from heaven with his mighty angels	13
	2: 5	I told you these things when I was still with you?	17
	3: 7	we were not idle when we were with you	7
	3: 8	with toil and labor we worked night and day	7
	3:10	For even when we were with you	17
	3:16	The Lord be with all of you.	13
	3:18	The grace of our Lord Jesus Christ be with all of you.	13
1Ti	1:14	with the faith and love that are in Christ Jesus.	13
	2: 9	not with their hair braided, or with gold,	7
	2:10	with good works, as is proper for women	2
	2:11	woman learn in silence with full submission	7
	2:15	in faith and love and holiness, with modesty.	13
	3: 9	must hold fast...the faith with a clear conscience.	7
	4: 3	created to be received with thanksgiving	13
	4: 4	provided it is received with thanksgiving;	13
	4:14	with the laying on of hands by the...elders.	13
	5: 2	younger women as sisters—with absolute purity.	7
	6:21	Grace be with you.	13
2Ti	1: 3	God—whom I worship with a clear conscience	7
	2:10	salvation...with eternal glory.	13
	2:25	correcting opponents with gentleness.	7
	4: 2	with the utmost patience in teaching.	7
	4:11	Only Luke is with me.	13
	4:11	Get Mark and bring him with you	13
	4:13	bring the cloak that I left with Carpus at Troas	14
	4:22	The Lord be with your spirit. Grace be with you.	13
	4:22	The Lord be with your spirit. Grace be with you.	13
Tit	1: 9	be able both to preach with sound doctrine	7
	2:15	exhort and reprove with all authority.	13
	3:15	All who are with me send greetings to you.	13
	3:15	Grace be with all of you.	13
Phm	1:13	I wanted to keep him with me	17
	1:25	the Lord Jesus Christ be with your spirit.	13
Heb	4:16	therefore approach the throne of grace with boldness	13
	5: 7	supplications, with loud cries and tears	13
	7:20	This was confirmed with an oath;	21
	7:21	but this one became a priest with an oath,	13

	8: 8	a new covenant with the house of Israel	9
	8: 8	a new covenant...with the house of Judah	9
	9:12	not with the blood of goats and calves	2
	9:12	with...his own blood	2
	9:13	with the sprinkling of the ashes of a heifer	11
	9:19	with water and scarlet wool and hyssop	13
	9:22	almost everything is purified with blood	7
	9:25	enters...with blood that is not his own;	7
	10:16	"This is the covenant that I will make with them	17
	10:22	let us approach with a true heart	13
	12: 1	let us run with perseverance the race	2
	12:14	Pursue peace with everyone	13
	12:17	even though he sought the blessing with tears.	13
	12:21	Moses said, "I tremble with fear.")	11
	12:28	acceptable worship with reverence and awe;	13
	13:17	Let them do this with joy and not with sighing	13
	13:23	if he comes in time, he will be with me when I see you.	13
	13:25	Grace be with all of you.	13
Jas	1:11	For the sun rises with its scorching heat	19
	1:17	with every perfect gift, is from above	11
	1:17	Father of lights, with whom there is no variation	14
	1:21	welcome with meekness the implanted word	7
	2: 1	do you with your acts of favoritism really believe	7
	3: 9	With it we bless the Lord and Father	7
	3: 9	with it we curse those...in the likeness of God.	7
	3:13	that your works are done with gentleness born of wisdom.	7
	5: 7	waits for the...crop...being patient with it	9
1Pe	2:18	Slaves, accept the authority...with all deference	7
	3: 4	with the lasting beauty of a gentle and quiet spirit	7
	3:16	yet do it with gentleness and reverence.	13
	4:11	whoever serves must do so with the strength	6
	4:17	for judgment to begin with the household of God;	1
	4:17	if it begins with us, what will be the end for those	1
	5:14	Greet one another with a kiss of love.	7
2Pe	1:17	my Son, my Beloved, with whom I am well pleased."	4
	1:18	while we were with him on the holy mountain.	19
	2:16	a speechless donkey spoke with a human voice	7
	2:18	with licentious desires of the flesh they entice	7
	3: 8	with the Lord one day is like a thousand years	14
	3: 9	The Lord...is patient with you	4
1Jn	1: 2	the eternal life that was with the Father	17
	1: 3	so that you also may have fellowship with us;	13
	1: 3	our fellowship is with the Father	13
	1: 3	with the Father and with his Son Jesus Christ.	13
	1: 6	If we say that we have fellowship with him	13
	1: 7	we have fellowship with one another	13
	2: 1	we have an advocate with the Father, Jesus Christ	17
	2:19	they would have remained with us.	13
	5: 6	the one who came...not with the water only	7
	5: 6	but with the water and the blood.	7
2Jn	1: 2	the truth that...will be with us forever:	13
	1: 3	Grace, mercy, and peace will be with us from God	13
3Jn	1:10	And not content with those charges, he refuses	9
	1:13	but I would rather not write with pen and ink;	2
Jde	1:14	"See, the Lord is coming with ten thousands of his holy	7
	1:23	have mercy on still others with fear	7
	1:24	in the presence of his glory with rejoicing	7
Rev	1: 7	Look! He is coming with the clouds;	13
	1:16	face was like the sun shining with full force.	7
	2:16	make war against them with the sword of my mouth.	7
	2:22	those who commit adultery with her I am throwing	13
	2:27	to rule them with an iron rod	7
	3: 4	they will walk with me...for they are worthy.	13
	3:20	I will come in to you and eat with you	13
	3:20	come in to you and eat with you, and you with me.	13
	3:21	I will give a place with me on my throne	13
	3:21	and sat down with my Father on his throne.	13
	4: 2	stood a throne, with one seated on the throne!	11
	4: 4	elders...with golden crowns on their heads.	11
	4: 7	the third living creature with a face like a human	10
	4: 8	four living creatures, each...with six wings	10
	5: 2	a mighty angel proclaiming with a loud voice	7
	6: 8	name was Death, and Hades followed with him;	13
	6: 8	authority...to kill with sword, famine, and pestilence,	7
	7: 9	in white, with palm branches in their hands.	11
	8: 3	Another angel with a golden censer came and stood	10
	8: 5	took the censer and filled it with fire	6
	8: 7	there came hail and fire, mixed with blood	7
	9: 2	the sun and the air were darkened with the smoke	6
	9:10	They have tails like scorpions, with stingers	11
	9:19	their tails;...and with them they inflict harm.	7

10: 1	mighty angel...with a rainbow over his head;	11
11: 6	and to strike the earth with every kind of plague	7
12: 1	clothed with the sun, with the moon under her feet	11
12: 3	great red dragon, with seven heads and ten horns	10
12: 5	who is to rule all the nations with a rod of iron	7
12: 9	and his angels were thrown down with him.	13
12:12	for the devil has come down to you with great wrath	10
12:17	Then the dragon was angry with the woman	9
13:10	if you kill with the sword	7
13:10	if you kill...with the sword you must be killed.	7
13:18	let anyone with understanding calculate the number	10
14: 1	with him were one hundred forty-four thousand	13
14: 4	who have not defiled themselves with women	13
14: 6	another angel...with an eternal gospel to proclaim	10
14: 9	another angel...crying with a loud voice	7
14:10	they will be tormented with fire and sulfur	7
14:14	the Son of Man, with a golden crown on his head	10
14:15	Another angel...calling with a loud voice	7
15: 1	I saw...seven angels with seven plagues	10
15: 1	for with them the wrath of God is ended.	7
15: 6	came the seven angels with the seven plagues	10
15: 6	with golden sashes across their chests.	11
16: 8	and it was allowed to scorch people with fire;	7
17: 2	with whom the kings...have committed fornication	13
17: 2	and with the wine of whose fornication	6
17: 6	the woman was drunk with the blood of the saints	6
17: 7	and of the beast with seven heads and ten horns	10
17:14	those with him are called and chosen and faithful."	13
17:16	will devour her flesh and burn her up with fire.	7
18: 1	and the earth was made bright with his splendor.	6
18: 2	He called out with a mighty voice	7
18: 3	kings...have committed fornication with her,	13
18: 8	and she will be burned with fire;	7
18: 9	fornication and lived in luxury with her,	13
18:16	adorned with gold, with jewels, and with pearls!	7
19: 2	who corrupted the earth with her fornication	7
19:15	a sharp sword with which to strike down the nations	7
19:15	and he will rule them with a rod of iron;	7
19:17	with a loud voice he called to all the birds	7
19:19	kings...with their armies gathered to make war	11
19:20	beast was captured, and with it the false prophet	13
19:20	the lake of fire that burns with sulfur.	7
19:21	and all the birds were gorged with their flesh.	6
20: 4	and reigned with Christ a thousand years.	13
20: 6	they will reign with him a thousand years.	13
21: 3	He will dwell with them;	13
21: 3	and God himself will be with them;	13
21:12	It has a great, high wall with twelve gates	10
22: 2	the tree of life with its twelve kinds of fruit	16
22:12	my reward is with me, to repay according to	13
22:21	The grace of the Lord Jesus be with all	13

combine with

1. μετά, *meta*, 3552

1Ti 6: 6	great gain in godliness combined with contentment;	1

withdraw

1. ἀναχωρέω, *anachōreō*, 432
2. ἀποσπάω, *apospaō*, 685
3. διΐστημι, *diistēmi*, 1460
4. ὑποχωρέω, *hypochōreō*, 5723

Mat 4:12	John had been arrested, he withdrew to Galilee.	1
14:13	when Jesus heard this, he withdrew from there	1
Lke 5:16	he would withdraw to deserted places and pray.	4
9:10	with him and withdrew privately to a city	4
22:41	he withdrew from them about a stone's throw	2
24:51	While he was blessing them, he withdrew from them	3
Jhn 6:15	he withdrew again to the mountain by himself.	1

wither

1. ξηραίνω, *xērainō*, 3830
2. ξηρός, *xēros*, 3831

Mat 12:10	a man was there with a withered hand	2
21:19	And the fig tree withered at once.	1
21:20	"How did the fig tree wither at once?"	1
Mrk 3: 1	a man was there who had a withered hand.	1
3: 3	he said to the man who had the withered hand	2
11:21	The fig tree that you cursed has withered."	1
Lke 6: 6	was a man there whose right hand was withered.	2
6: 8	he said to the man who had the withered hand	2

8: 6	as it grew up, it withered	1
Jhn 15: 6	is thrown away like a branch and withers;	1
Jas 1:11	the sun rises...and withers the field;	1
1Pe 1:24	The grass withers, and the flower falls	1

wither away

1. μαραίνω, *marainō*, 3447
2. ξηραίνω, *xērainō*, 3830

Mat 13: 6	since they had no root, they withered away.	2
Mrk 4: 6	since it had no root, it withered away.	2
11:20	they saw the fig tree withered away to its roots.	2
Jas 1:11	in the midst of a busy life, they will wither away.	1

withhold

1. κωλύω, *kōlyō*, 3266
2. φείδομαι, *pheidomai*, 5767

Lke 6:29	do not withhold even your shirt.	1
Act 10:47	"Can anyone withhold the water for baptizing	1
Rom 8:32	He who did not withhold his own Son, but gave	2

within

1. ἐν, *en*, 1877
2. ἔνειμι, *eneimi*, 1913
3. ἔσωθεν, *esōthen*, 2277
4. κατά, *kata*, 2848

Mrk 7:21	For it is from within, from the human heart	3
7:23	All these evil things come from within	3
Lke 11: 7	he answers from within, 'Do not bother me;	3
11:41	give for alms those things that are within;	2
19:44	you and your children within you	1
19:44	will not leave within you one stone upon another;	1
24:32	"Were not our hearts burning within us	1
Rom 7:17	no longer I...but sin that dwells within me.	1
7:18	For I know that nothing good dwells within me	1
7:20	no longer I...but sin that dwells within me.	1
8:29	he might be the firstborn within a large family.	1
1Co 2:11	except the human spirit that is within?	1
6:19	a temple of the Holy Spirit within you	1
12:25	that there may be no dissension within the body	1
2Co 7: 5	disputes without and fears within.	3
10:13	keep within the field that God has assigned to us	4
Eph 3:20	by the power at work within us	1
Col 1:29	the energy that he powerfully inspires within me.	1
2Ti 1: 6	rekindle the gift of God that is within you	1
Jas 4: 1	Do they not come from your cravings...at war within you?	1
1Pe 1:11	that the Spirit of Christ within them indicated	1
Rev 7:15	and worship him day and night within his temple	1
11:19	ark of his covenant was seen within his temple;	1

without[1] *See also* without a *witness*, without any *doubt*, without being *circumcised*, without *blame*, without *blemish*, without *cause*, without *ceasing*, without *defect*, without *delay*, without *excuse*, without *father*, without *fear*, without *food*, without *fruit*, without *genealogy*, without *God*, without *hindrance*, without *honor*, without *hypocrisy*, without *knowing*, without *mercy*, without *mother*, without *objection*, without *partiality*, without *paying*, without *payment*, without *sin*, without *sound*, without *spot*, without *understanding*, without *washing*, without *wavering*

1. ἄνευ, *aneu*, 459
2. ἄτερ, *ater*, 868
3. ἐάν + μή, *ean* + *mē*, 1569 + 3590
4. μή, *mē*, 3590
5. μή + ἔχω, *mē* + *echō*, 3590 + 2400
6. μηδείς, *mēdeis*, 3594
7. οὐ, *ou*, 4024
8. οὐ + μετά, *ou* + *meta*, 4024 + 3552
9. χωρίς, *chōris*, 6006

Mat 9:36	helpless, like sheep without a shepherd.	5
12:29	without first tying up the strong man?	3
13:34	without a parable he told them nothing.	9
22:12	how did you get in here without a wedding robe?'	5
23:23	without neglecting the others.	4
Mrk 3:27	without first tying up the strong man;	3
6:34	because they were like sheep without a shepherd;	5
8: 1	again a great crowd without anything to eat	5
Lke 6:49	a house on the ground without a foundation.	9

Lke	11:42	without neglecting the others.	4
	11:44	people walk over them without realizing it."	7
	22:35	"When I sent you out without a purse, bag,	2
Jhn	1: 3	without him not one thing came into being.	9
	3: 3	see the kingdom…without being born from above."	3
	3: 5	without being born of water and Spirit.	3
	3:34	for he gives the Spirit without measure.	7
	7:51	judge people without first giving them a hearing	3
Act	5:26	brought them, but without violence	8
	9: 9	For three days he was without sight	4
	9:38	"Please come to us without delay."	4
	10:20	go down, and go with them without hesitation;	6
	25:27	without indicating the charges against him."	4
Rom	4: 5	to one who without works trusts him	4
	10:14	how are they to hear without someone to proclaim	9
1Co	11:29	who eat and drink without discerning the body	4
2Co	10:16	without boasting of work already done	7
Eph	2:12	you were at that time without Christ	9
	5:27	without a spot or wrinkle or anything of the kind	4
Php	2:14	Do all things without murmuring and arguing	9
Col	1:23	without shifting from the hope promised by the gospel	4
1Ti	1: 7	without understanding either what they are saying	4
	2: 8	lifting up holy hands without anger or argument;	9
	5:21	I warn you to keep these instructions without prejudice	9
2Ti	2: 5	without competing according to the rules.	3
Phm	1:14	I preferred to do nothing without your consent	9
Heb	4:15	who…has been tested as we are, yet without sin.	9
	7:20	took their office without an oath	9
	9: 7	not without taking the blood	9
	9:18	not even the first covenant was inaugurated without blood	9
	9:22	without the shedding of blood there is no	9
	10:28	violated the law of Moses dies without mercy	9
	11: 6	without faith it is impossible to please God	9
	11:13	without having received the promises,	4
	12:14	holiness without which no one will see the Lord.	9
Jas	2:26	For just as the body without the spirit is dead	9
	2:26	so faith without works is also dead.	9
1Pe	3: 1	won over without a word by their wives' conduct	1
	4: 9	Be hospitable to one another without complaining.	1
Rev	4: 8	Day and night without ceasing they sing	7

without²

1. ἔξωθεν, *exōthen, 2033*

2Co	7: 5	disputes without and fears within.	1

without any

1. μηδείς, *mēdeis, 3594*
2. οὐ + μετά, *ou + meta, 4024 + 3552*

Lke	4:35	he came out of him without having done him any harm.	1
Act	24:18	without any crowd or disturbance.	2
1Co	10:25	without raising any question	1
	10:27	eat…without raising any question	1

withstand

1. ἀνθίστημι, *anthistēmi, 468*

Lke	21:15	will be able to withstand or contradict.	1
Act	6:10	could not withstand the wisdom and the Spirit	1
Eph	6:13	that you may be able to withstand on that evil day	1

witness   *See also* bear false witness, bear witness, bear witness also, bear witness with

1. ἄνθρωπος, *anthrōpos, 476*
2. μαρτυρέω, *martyreō, 3455*
3. μαρτυρία, *martyria, 3456*
4. μαρτύριον, *martyrion, 3457*
5. μάρτυς, *martys, 3459*

Mat	18:16	by the evidence of two or three witnesses.	5
	26:65	Why do we still need witnesses?	5
Mrk	14:63	"Why do we still need witnesses?	5
Lke	11:48	So you are witnesses	5
	24:48	You are witnesses of these things.	5
Jhn	1: 7	He came as a witness to testify	3
	3:28	You yourselves are my witnesses that I said	2
	8:17	the testimony of two witnesses is valid.	1
Act	1: 8	you will be my witnesses in Jerusalem	5
	1:22	become a witness with us to his resurrection."	5
	2:32	of that all of us are witnesses.	5
	3:15	To this we are witnesses.	5
	5:32	we are witnesses to these things	5
	6:13	They set up false witnesses who said	5

	7:58	the witnesses laid their coats at the feet	5
	10:39	We are witnesses to all that he did	5
	10:41	to us who were chosen by God as witnesses	5
	13:31	they are now his witnesses to the people.	5
	22:15	you will be his witness to all the world	5
	22:20	while the blood of your witness Stephen was shed	5
Rom	1: 9	For God…is my witness that without ceasing	5
2Co	1:23	I call on God as witness against me:	5
	13: 1	by the evidence of two or three witnesses."	5
Php	1: 8	For God is my witness, how I long for all of you	5
1Th	2: 5	As you know and as God is our witness,	5
	2:10	You are witnesses, and God also	5
1Ti	5:19	except on the evidence of two or three witnesses.	5
	6:12	confession in the presence of many witnesses.	5
2Ti	2: 2	have heard from me through many witnesses.	5
Heb	10:28	"on the testimony of two or three witnesses."	5
	12: 1	surrounded by so great a cloud of witnesses	5
1Pe	5: 1	an elder myself and a witness of the sufferings of Christ	5
Rev	1: 5	and from Jesus Christ, the faithful witness	5
	2:13	the days of Antipas my witness, my faithful one	5
	3:14	words of the Amen, the faithful and true witness	5
	11: 3	I will grant my two witnesses authority to prophesy	5
	15: 5	temple of the tent of witness in heaven was opened	4
	17: 6	drunk with…the blood of the witnesses to Jesus.	5

false witness

1. ψευδομαρτυρία, *pseudomartyria, 6019*
2. ψευδόμαρτυς, *pseudomartys, 6020*

Mat	15:19	fornication, theft, false witness, slander.	1
	26:60	though many false witnesses came forward.	2

without a witness

1. ἀμάρτυρος, *amartyros, 282*

Act	14:17	yet he has not left himself without a witness	1

woe

1. οὐαί, *ouai, 4026*

Mat	11:21	"Woe to you, Chorazin! Woe to you, Bethsaida!	1
	11:21	"Woe to you, Chorazin! Woe to you, Bethsaida!	1
	18: 7	Woe to the world because of stumbling blocks!	1
	18: 7	woe to the one by whom the stumbling block comes!	1
	23:13	woe to you, scribes and Pharisees, hypocrites!	1
	23:15	Woe to you, scribes and Pharisees, hypocrites!	1
	23:16	"Woe to you, blind guides, who say	1
	23:23	"Woe to you, scribes and Pharisees, hypocrites!	1
	23:25	"Woe to you, scribes and Pharisees, hypocrites!	1
	23:27	"Woe to you, scribes and Pharisees, hypocrites!	1
	23:29	"Woe to you, scribes and Pharisees, hypocrites!	1
	24:19	Woe to those who are pregnant	1
	26:24	woe to that one by whom the Son of Man is betrayed!	1
Mrk	13:17	Woe to those who are pregnant	1
	14:21	woe to that one by whom the Son of Man is betrayed!	1
Lke	6:24	woe to you who are rich	1
	6:25	"Woe to you who are full now,	1
	6:25	"Woe to you who are laughing now,	1
	6:26	"Woe to you when all speak well of you	1
	10:13	"Woe to you, Chorazin! Woe to you, Bethsaida!	1
	10:13	"Woe to you, Chorazin! Woe to you, Bethsaida!	1
	11:42	woe to you Pharisees!	1
	11:43	Woe to you Pharisees!	1
	11:44	Woe to you! For you are like unmarked graves	1
	11:46	he said, "Woe also to you lawyers!	1
	11:47	Woe to you! For you build the tombs	1
	11:52	Woe to you lawyers!	1
	17: 1	woe to anyone by whom they come!	1
	21:23	Woe to those who are pregnant	1
	22:22	woe to that one by whom he is betrayed!"	1
1Co	9:16	woe to me if I do not proclaim the gospel!	1
Jde	1:11	Woe to them! For they go the way of Cain	1
Rev	8:13	"Woe, woe, woe to the inhabitants of the earth	1
	8:13	"Woe, woe, woe to the inhabitants of the earth	1
	8:13	"Woe, woe, woe to the inhabitants of the earth	1
	9:12	The first woe has passed.	1
	9:12	There are still two woes to come.	1
	11:14	The second woe has passed. The third woe	1
	11:14	The third woe is coming very soon.	1
	12:12	woe to the earth and the sea, for the devil has come	1

wolf

1. λύκος, *lykos, 3380*

Mat	7:15	but inwardly are ravenous wolves.	1
	10:16	sending you out like sheep into the midst of wolves;	1
Lke	10: 3	like lambs into the midst of wolves.	1
Jhn	10:12	sees the wolf coming and leaves the sheep	1
	10:12	the wolf snatches them and scatters them.	1
Act	20:29	savage wolves will come in among you	1

woman See also believing woman, desolate woman, divorce woman, each woman, free woman, man and woman, married woman, old woman, one woman, other woman, silly woman, slave woman, this woman, unmarried woman, young woman

1. Contextual: Not in Greek
2. αὐτός, *autos*, 899
3. γυναικεῖος, *gynaikeios*, 1221
4. γυνή, *gynē*, 1222
5. θῆλυς, *thēlys*, 2559
6. παιδίσκη, *paidiskē*, 4087

Mat	5:28	who looks at a woman with lust has already	4
	9:20	suddenly a woman who had been suffering	4
	9:22	And instantly the woman was made well.	4
	11:11	Truly I tell you, among those born of women	4
	13:33	yeast that a woman took and mixed	4
	14:21	five thousand men, besides women and children	4
	15:22	Just then a Canaanite woman from that region	4
	15:28	Jesus answered her, "Woman, great is your faith!	4
	15:38	four thousand men, besides women and children	4
	22:27	Last of all, the woman herself died.	4
	24:41	Two women will be grinding meal together;	1
	26: 7	a woman came to him	4
	26:10	"Why do you trouble the woman?	4
	27:55	Many women were also there	4
	28: 5	the angel said to the women, "Do not be afraid;	4
Mrk	5:25	Now there was a woman who had been suffering	4
	5:33	the woman, knowing what had happened to her, came	4
	7:25	woman whose little daughter had an unclean spirit	4
	7:26	the woman was a Gentile, of Syrophoenician origin.	4
	12:22	Last of all the woman herself died.	4
	14: 3	a woman came with an alabaster jar of…ointment	4
	15:40	There were also women looking on from a distance;	4
	15:41	many other women who had come up with him	1
Lke	1:42	"Blessed are you among women	4
	7:28	among those born of women no one is greater	4
	7:37	a woman in the city, who was a sinner	4
	7:39	what kind of woman this is who is touching him	4
	7:44	Then turning toward the woman, he said to Simon	4
	7:44	"Do you see this woman?	4
	7:50	he said to the woman, "Your faith has saved you;	4
	8: 2	as well as some women who had been cured	4
	8:43	Now there was a woman who had been suffering	4
	8:47	the woman saw that she could not remain hidden	4
	10:38	a woman named Martha welcomed him	4
	11:27	a woman in the crowd raised her voice and said	4
	13:11	a woman with a spirit that had crippled	4
	13:12	"Woman, you are set free from your ailment."	4
	13:21	It is like yeast that a woman took and mixed	4
	15: 8	what woman having ten silver coins	4
	16:18	whoever marries a woman divorced from her husband	1
	17:35	There will be two women grinding meal together;	1
	20:32	Finally the woman also died.	4
	20:33	whose wife will the woman be?	4
	22:57	he denied it, saying, "Woman, I do not know him."	4
	23:27	women who were beating their breasts and wailing	4
	23:49	the women who had followed him from Galilee	4
	23:55	The women who had come with him from Galilee	4
	24: 5	women were terrified and bowed their faces	2
	24:22	Moreover, some women of our group astounded us.	4
	24:24	and found it just as the women had said;	4
Jhn	2: 4	"Woman, what concern is that to you and to me?	4
	4: 7	A Samaritan woman came to draw water	4
	4: 9	The Samaritan woman said to him, "How is it	4
	4: 9	you, a Jew, ask a drink of me, a woman of Samaria?"	4
	4:11	woman said to him, "Sir, you have no bucket,	4
	4:15	The woman said to him, "Sir, give me this water	4
	4:17	The woman answered him, "I have no husband."	4
	4:19	The woman said to him, "Sir, I see	4
	4:21	"Woman, believe me, the hour is coming	4
	4:25	The woman said to him, "I know that Messiah	4
	4:27	astonished that he was speaking with a woman	4
	4:28	the woman left her water jar and went back	4

	4:39	believed in him because of the woman's testimony	4
	4:42	They said to the woman, "It is no longer	4
	8: 3	⟦The scribes and the Pharisees brought a woman⟧	4
	8: 4	⟦this woman was caught in the very act⟧	4
	8: 5	⟦in the law Moses commanded us to stone such women⟧	1
	8: 9	⟦left alone with the woman standing before him.⟧	4
	8:10	⟦"Woman, where are they? Has no one condemned you?"⟧	4
	16:21	When a woman is in labor, she has pain	4
	18:17	The woman said to Peter	6
	19:26	he said to his mother, "Woman, here is your son."	4
	20:13	They said to her, "Woman, why are you weeping?"	4
	20:15	Jesus said to her, "Woman, why are you weeping?	4
Act	1:14	certain women, including Mary the mother of Jesus	4
	5:14	great numbers of both men and women	4
	8: 3	dragging off both men and women	4
	8:12	they were baptized, both men and women.	4
	9: 2	found any who belonged to the Way, men or women	4
	13:50	the Jews incited the devout women of high standing	4
	16: 1	the son of a Jewish woman who was a believer;	4
	16:13	and spoke to the women who had gathered	4
	16:14	A certain woman named Lydia, a worshiper of God	4
	17: 4	not a few of the leading women.	4
	17:12	not a few Greek women and men of high standing.	4
	17:34	a woman named Damaris, and others with them.	4
	22: 4	both men and women and putting them in prison	4
Rom	1:26	Their women exchanged natural intercourse	5
	1:27	the men…giving up natural intercourse with women	5
	7: 2	a married woman is bound by the law to her husband	4
1Co	7: 1	"It is well for a man not to touch a woman."	4
	7:13	if any woman has a husband who is an unbeliever	4
	7:34	the unmarried woman and the virgin are anxious	4
	11: 5	any woman who prays or prophesies with her head	4
	11: 6	For if a woman will not veil herself	4
	11: 6	disgraceful for a woman to have her hair cut off	4
	11: 7	woman is the reflection of man.	4
	11: 8	man was not made from woman, but woman from man.	4
	11: 8	man was not made from woman, but woman from man.	4
	11: 9	Neither was man created for the sake of woman	4
	11: 9	the sake of woman, but woman for the sake of man.	4
	11:10	a woman ought to have a symbol of authority	4
	11:11	woman is not independent of man or man independent	4
	11:11	not independent of man or man independent of woman.	4
	11:12	just as woman came from man	4
	11:12	so man comes through woman;	4
	11:13	for a woman to pray to God with her head unveiled?	4
	11:15	if a woman has long hair, it is her glory?	4
	14:34	women should be silent in the churches.	4
	14:35	it is shameful for a woman to speak in church.	4
Gal	4: 4	born of a woman, born under the law	4
Php	4: 3	you also, my loyal companion, help these women	1
1Th	5: 3	as labor pains come upon a pregnant woman	1
1Ti	2: 9	women should dress themselves modestly	4
	2:10	as is proper for women who profess reverence for God.	4
	2:11	Let a woman learn in silence	4
	2:12	I permit no woman to teach	4
	2:14	Adam was not deceived, but the woman was deceived	4
	3:11	Women likewise must be serious	4
Heb	11:35	Women received their dead by resurrection.	4
1Pe	3: 5	the holy women who hoped in God used to adorn	4
	3: 7	paying honor to the woman as the weaker sex	3
Rev	2:20	against you: you tolerate that woman Jezebel	4
	9: 8	their hair like women's hair, and their teeth like	4
	12: 1	a woman clothed with the sun	4
	12: 4	Then the dragon stood before the woman	4
	12: 6	and the woman fled into the wilderness	4
	12:13	pursued the woman who had given birth to the male child.	4
	12:14	woman was given the two wings of the great eagle	4
	12:15	the serpent poured water…after the woman	4
	12:16	But the earth came to the help of the woman;	4
	12:17	Then the dragon was angry with the woman	4
	14: 4	who have not defiled themselves with women	4
	17: 3	and I saw a woman sitting on a scarlet beast	4
	17: 4	The woman was clothed in purple and scarlet	4
	17: 6	the woman was drunk with the blood of the saints	4
	17: 7	I will tell you the mystery of the woman	4
	17: 9	are seven mountains on which the woman is seated;	4
	17:18	The woman you saw is the great city	4

woman who guards the gate

1. θυρωρός, *thyrōros*, 2601

Jhn	18:16	spoke to the woman who guarded the gate	1

womb

1. γαστήρ, *gastēr, 1143*
2. κοιλία, *koilia, 3120*
3. μήτρα, *mētra, 3616*

Lke	1:31	you will conceive in your womb and bear a son	1
	1:41	the child leaped in her womb.	2
	1:42	blessed is the fruit of your womb.	2
	1:44	the child in my womb leaped for joy.	2
	2:21	before he was conceived in the womb.	2
	11:27	"Blessed is the womb that bore you	2
	23:29	the wombs that never bore	2
Jhn	3: 4	Can one enter a second time into the mother's womb	2
Rom	4:19	he considered the barrenness of Sarah's womb.	3

wonder

1. Contextual: Not in Greek
2. θάμβος, *thambos, 2502*
3. θαῦμα, *thauma, 2512*
4. θαυμάζω, *thaumazō, 2513*
5. τέρας, *teras, 5469*

Mrk	15:44	Pilate wondered if he were already dead;	4
Lke	1:21	wondered at his delay in the sanctuary.	4
	24:41	they were disbelieving and still wondering	4
Jhn	4:48	"Unless you see signs and wonders	5
Act	2:22	with deeds of power, wonders, and signs	5
	2:43	many wonders and signs were being done	5
	3:10	they were filled with wonder and amazement	2
	3:12	"You Israelites, why do you wonder at this	4
	4:30	signs and wonders are performed	5
	5:12	Now many signs and wonders were done	5
	5:24	wondering what might be going on.	1
	6: 8	did great wonders and signs among the people.	5
	7:36	having performed wonders and signs in Egypt	5
	14: 3	granting...wonders to be done through them.	5
	15:12	signs and wonders that God had done through them	5
Rom	15:19	by the power of signs and wonders	5
2Co	11:14	no wonder! Even Satan disguises himself	3
	12:12	patience, signs and wonders and mighty works.	5
2Th	2: 9	Satan, who uses all power, signs, lying wonders	5
Heb	2: 4	while God added his testimony by signs and wonders	5

wonderful thing

1. ἔνδοξος, *endoxos, 1902*

Lke	13:17	all the wonderful things that he was doing.	1

wood

1. ξύλινος, *xylinos, 3832*
2. ξύλον, *xylon, 3833*

Lke	23:31	if they do this when the wood is green	2
1Co	3:12	gold, silver, precious stones, wood, hay, straw—	2
2Ti	2:20	utensils...also of wood and clay	1
Rev	9:20	idols of...silver and bronze and stone and wood	1
	18:12	all kinds of scented wood, all articles of ivory	2
	18:12	articles of costly wood, bronze, iron, and marble	2

wool

1. ἔριον, *erion, 2250*

Heb	9:19	with water and scarlet wool and hyssop	1
Rev	1:14	His head and his hair were white as white wool	1

word　　*See also* bring word, dispute about words, send word,
too *deep* for a word, wrangle over words

1. Contextual: Not in Greek
2. λέγω, *legō, 3306*
3. λόγιον, *logion, 3359*
4. λόγος, *logos, 3364*
5. ῥῆμα, *rhēma, 4839*
6. στόμα, *stoma, 5125*
7. φάσις, *phasis, 5762*
8. φωνή, *phōnē, 5889*

Mat	4: 4	by bread alone, but by every word that comes	5
	5:37	Let your word be 'Yes, Yes' or 'No, No'	4
	7:24	"Everyone then who hears these words of mine	4
	7:26	And everyone who hears these words of mine	4
	8: 8	speak the word, and my servant will be healed.	4
	8:16	and he cast out the spirits with a word	4
	10:14	or listen to your words	4
	11: 2	he sent word by his disciples	1

	12:32	Whoever speaks a word against the Son of Man	4
	12:36	have to give an account for every careless word	5
	12:37	for by your words you will be justified	4
	12:37	and by your words you will be condemned."	4
	13:19	When anyone hears the word of the kingdom	4
	13:20	this is the one who hears the word	4
	13:21	persecution arises on account of the word	4
	13:22	this is the one who hears the word	4
	13:22	and the lure of wealth choke the word	4
	13:23	this is the one who hears the word	4
	15: 6	you make void the word of God.	4
	18:16	so that every word may be confirmed	5
	19:22	the young man heard this word, he went away	4
	24:35	but my words will not pass away.	4
	26:44	for the third time, saying the same words.	4
	27:19	his wife sent word to him	2
Mrk	1:45	to spread the word	4
	2: 2	he was speaking the word to them.	4
	4:14	The sower sows the word.	4
	4:15	the ones on the path where the word is sown:	4
	4:15	takes away the word that is sown in them.	4
	4:16	they hear the word, they immediately receive	4
	4:17	persecution arises on account of the word	4
	4:18	these are the ones who hear the word	4
	4:19	come in and choke the word	4
	4:20	they hear the word and accept it	4
	4:33	With many such parables he spoke the word	4
	7:13	thus making void the word of God	4
	8:38	who are ashamed of me and of my words	4
	10:24	the disciples were perplexed at these words.	4
	13:31	my words will not pass away.	4
	14:39	went away and prayed, saying the same words.	4
Lke	1: 2	eyewitnesses and servants of the word	4
	1:20	because you did not believe my words	4
	1:29	she was much perplexed by his words	4
	1:38	let it be with me according to your word."	5
	2:19	Mary treasured all these words	5
	2:29	according to your word;	5
	3: 2	the word of God came to John son of Zechariah	4
	3: 4	the book of the words of the prophet Isaiah	4
	4:22	amazed at the gracious words	4
	5: 1	pressing in on him to hear the word of God	4
	5:15	more than ever the word about Jesus spread abroad;	4
	6:47	who comes to me, hears my words, and acts on them.	4
	7: 7	speak the word, and let my servant be healed.	4
	7:17	This word about him spread	4
	8:11	the parable is this: The seed is the word of God.	4
	8:12	takes away the word from their hearts	4
	8:13	when they hear the word, receive it with joy.	4
	8:15	who, when they hear the word, hold it fast	4
	8:21	those who hear the word of God and do it."	4
	9:26	who are ashamed of me and of my words	4
	9:44	"Let these words sink into your ears:	4
	11:28	"Blessed rather are those who hear the word of God	4
	12:10	who speaks a word against the Son of Man	4
	19:22	'I will judge you by your own words	6
	21:15	for I will give you words and a wisdom	6
	21:33	my words will not pass away.	4
	22:61	Peter remembered the word of the Lord	4
	24: 8	they remembered his words	5
	24:11	these words seemed to them an idle tale	5
	24:19	a prophet mighty in deed and word before God	4
	24:44	"These are my words that I spoke to you	4
Jhn	1: 1	and the Word was with God, and the Word was God.	4
	1: 1	In the beginning was the Word	4
	1: 1	the Word was with God, and the Word was God.	4
	1:14	And the Word became flesh and lived among us	4
	2:22	believed...the word that Jesus had spoken.	4
	3:34	He whom God has sent speaks the words of God	5
	4:41	And many more believed because of his word.	4
	4:50	The man believed the word that Jesus spoke to him	4
	5:24	who hears my word and believes him who sent me	4
	5:38	you do not have his word abiding in you	4
	6:63	The words that I have spoken to you	5
	6:68	You have the words of eternal life.	5
	7:40	When they heard these words	4
	8:20	He spoke these words while he was teaching	5
	8:31	"If you continue in my word	4
	8:37	because there is no place in you for my word.	4
	8:43	It is because you cannot accept my word.	4
	8:47	Whoever is from God hears the words of God.	5

	8:51	whoever keeps my word will never see death."	4
	8:52	yet you say, 'Whoever keeps my word	4
	8:55	I do know him and I keep his word.	4
	10:19	the Jews were divided...because of these words.	4
	10:21	"These are not the words of one who has a demon.	5
	10:35	to whom the word of God came were called 'gods'	4
	12:38	to fulfill the word spoken by the prophet Isaiah:	4
	12:47	anyone who hears my words and does not keep them	5
	12:48	one who rejects me and does not receive my word	5
	12:48	the word that I have spoken will serve as judge	4
	14:10	The words that I say to you	5
	14:23	"Those who love me will keep my word	4
	14:24	Whoever does not love me does not keep my words;	4
	14:24	the word that you hear is not mine	4
	15: 3	cleansed by the word that I have spoken to you.	4
	15: 7	If you abide in me, and my words abide in you	5
	15:20	Remember the word that I said to you	4
	15:20	if they kept my word, they will keep yours also.	4
	15:25	to fulfill the word that is written in their law	4
	17: 1	After Jesus had spoken these words	1
	17: 6	gave them to me, and they have kept your word.	4
	17: 8	for the words that you gave to me I have given	5
	17:14	I have given them your word	4
	17:17	Sanctify them in the truth; your word is truth.	4
	17:20	those who will believe in me through their word	4
	18: 1	After Jesus had spoken these words	1
	18: 9	This was to fulfill the word that he had spoken	4
	19:13	When Pilate heard these words	4
Act	4: 4	many of those who heard the word believed;	4
	4:29	grant to your servants to speak your word	4
	4:31	spoke the word of God with boldness.	4
	5: 5	when Ananias heard these words	4
	5:24	when...the chief priests heard these words	4
	6: 2	neglect the word of God in order to wait on tables.	4
	6: 4	to prayer and to serving the word."	4
	6: 7	The word of God continued to spread;	4
	6:11	blasphemous words against Moses and God."	5
	7:22	was powerful in his words and deeds.	4
	8: 4	went from place to place, proclaiming the word.	4
	8:14	Samaria had accepted the word of God	4
	8:25	had testified and spoken the word of the Lord	4
	10:44	the Holy Spirit fell upon all who heard the word.	4
	11: 1	the Gentiles had also accepted the word of God.	4
	11:16	I remembered the word of the Lord, how he had said	5
	11:19	spoke the word to no one except Jews.	4
	12:24	the word of God continued to advance and gain adherents	4
	13: 5	proclaimed the word of God in the synagogues	4
	13: 7	wanted to hear the word of God.	4
	13:15	"Brothers, if you have any word of exhortation	4
	13:27	or understand the words of the prophets	8
	13:27	fulfilled those words by condemning him.	1
	13:44	gathered to hear the word of the Lord.	4
	13:46	the word of God should be spoken first to you.	4
	13:48	they were glad and praised the word of the Lord;	4
	13:49	Thus the word of the Lord spread	4
	14: 3	who testified to the word of his grace	4
	14:18	with these words, they scarcely restrained	2
	14:25	When they had spoken the word in Perga	4
	15:15	This agrees with the words of the prophets	4
	15:35	taught and proclaimed the word of the Lord.	4
	15:36	in every city where we proclaimed the word	4
	16: 6	forbidden...to speak the word in Asia.	4
	16:32	They spoke the word of the Lord to him	4
	16:38	police reported these words to the magistrates	5
	17:13	learned that the word of God had been proclaimed	4
	18: 5	Paul was occupied with proclaiming the word	4
	18:11	teaching the word of God among them.	4
	18:15	a matter of questions about words and names	4
	19:10	residents of Asia...heard the word of the Lord.	4
	19:20	word of the Lord grew mightily and prevailed.	4
	20:35	remembering the words of the Lord Jesus	4
	21:31	word came to the tribune of the cohort	7
Rom	3: 4	"So that you may be justified in your words	4
	4:23	the words...were written not for his sake alone	1
	9: 6	It is not as though the word of God had failed.	4
	10: 8	"The word is near you, on your lips and in your heart"	5
	10: 8	(that is, the word of faith that we proclaim);	4
	10:17	what is heard comes through the word of Christ.	5
	10:18	and their words to the ends of the world."	5
	13: 9	commandments...are summed up in this word	4
	15:18	obedience from the Gentiles, by word and deed	4

1Co	2: 1	the mystery of God to you in lofty words or wisdom.	4
	2: 4	not with plausible words of wisdom	4
	2:13	in words not taught by human wisdom	4
	14:19	I would rather speak five words with my mind...than	4
	14:19	than ten thousand words in a tongue	4
	14:36	Or did the word of God originate with you?	4
2Co	1:18	our word to you has not been "Yes and No."	4
	2:17	we are not peddlers of God's word like so many;	4
	4: 2	practice cunning or to falsify God's word;	4
Gal	6: 6	Those who are taught the word must share	4
Eph	1:13	you also, when you had heard the word of truth	4
	3: 3	as I wrote above in a few words	1
	4:29	so that your words may give grace	1
	5: 6	Let no one deceive you with empty words	4
	5:26	cleansing her with the washing of water by the word	5
	6:17	the sword of the Spirit, which is the word of God.	5
Php	1:14	dare to speak the word with greater boldness	4
	2:16	holding fast to the word of life	4
Col	1: 5	heard of this hope...in the word of the truth	4
	1:25	to make the word of God fully known	4
	3:16	Let the word of Christ dwell in you richly;	4
	3:17	whatever you do, in word or deed	4
	4: 3	God will open to us a door for the word	4
1Th	1: 5	message of the gospel came to you not in word only	4
	1: 6	in spite of persecution you received the word	4
	1: 8	the word of the Lord has sounded forth from you	4
	2: 5	we never came with words of flattery	4
	2:13	when you received the word of God	4
	2:13	you accepted it not as a human word	4
	2:13	but as what it really is, God's word	4
	4:15	this we declare to you by the word of the Lord	4
	4:18	encourage one another with these words.	4
2Th	2: 2	either by spirit or by word or by letter	4
	2:17	strengthen them in every good work and word.	4
	3: 1	so that the word of the Lord may spread rapidly	4
1Ti	4: 5	is sanctified by God's word and by prayer.	4
	4: 6	nourished on the words of the faith	4
	6: 3	does not agree with the sound words of our Lord	4
2Ti	2: 9	But the word of God is not chained.	4
	2:15	rightly explaining the word of truth.	4
Tit	1: 3	in due time he revealed his word	4
	1: 9	have a firm grasp of the word that is trustworthy	4
	2: 5	the word of God may not be discredited.	4
Heb	1: 3	sustains all things by his powerful word.	5
	4:12	Indeed, the word of God is living and active	4
	5:13	is unskilled in the word of righteousness.	4
	6: 5	have tasted the goodness of the word of God	5
	7:28	the word of the oath, which came later than the law	4
	11: 3	the worlds were prepared by the word of God	5
	12:19	a voice whose words made the hearers beg	5
	12:19	that not another word be spoken to them.	4
	12:24	that speaks a better word than the blood of Abel.	1
	13: 7	those who spoke the word of God to you;	4
	13:22	bear with my word of exhortation	4
Jas	1:18	he gave us birth by the word of truth	4
	1:21	welcome with meekness the implanted word	4
	1:22	But be doers of the word, and not merely hearers	4
	1:23	For if any are hearers of the word and not doers,	4
1Pe	1:23	through the living and enduring word of God.	4
	1:25	but the word of the Lord endures forever."	5
	1:25	That word is the good news that was announced	5
	2: 8	They stumble because they disobey the word	4
	3: 1	even if some of them do not obey the word	4
	3: 1	won over without a word by their wives' conduct	4
	4:11	do so as one speaking the very words of God;	3
2Pe	2: 3	they will exploit you with deceptive words.	4
	3: 2	you should remember the words spoken in the past	5
	3: 5	by the word of God heavens existed long ago	4
	3: 7	by the same word the present heavens and earth	4
1Jn	1: 1	concerning the word of life	4
	1:10	we make him a liar, and his word is not in us.	4
	2: 5	but whoever obeys his word	4
	2: 7	old commandment is the word that you have heard.	4
	2:14	and the word of God abides in you	4
	3:18	let us love, not in word or speech, but in truth	4
Rev	1: 2	who testified to the word of God	4
	1: 3	the one who reads aloud the words of the prophecy	4
	1: 9	because of the word of God	4
	2: 1	the words of him who holds the seven stars	2
	2: 8	the words of the first and the last	2
	2:12	the words of him who has the sharp two-edged sword:	2

Rev	2:18	words of the Son of God, who has eyes like a flame	2
	3: 1	the words of him who has the seven spirits of God	2
	3: 7	the words of the holy one, the true one	2
	3: 8	you have kept my word and have not denied my name.	4
	3:10	you have kept my word of patient endurance	4
	3:14	words of the Amen, the faithful and true witness	2
	6: 9	slaughtered for the word of God and for the testimony	4
	12:11	conquered him…by the word of their testimony	4
	17:17	until the words of God will be fulfilled.	4
	19: 9	And he said to me, "These are true words of God."	4
	19:13	his name is called The Word of God.	4
	20: 4	who had been beheaded…for the word of God.	4
	21: 5	for these words are trustworthy and true."	4
	22: 6	"These words are trustworthy and true	4
	22: 7	Blessed is the one who keeps the words of the prophecy	4
	22: 9	with those who keep the words of this book.	4
	22:10	"Do not seal up the words of the prophecy	4
	22:18	I warn everyone who hears the words	4
	22:19	if anyone takes away from the words of the book	4

blasphemous word

1. βλασφημία, *blasphēmia, 1060*

Rev	13: 5	a mouth uttering haughty and blasphemous words	1

many words

1. πολυλογία, *polylogia, 4494*

Mat	6: 7	that they will be heard because of their many words.	1

word already quoted

1. προλέγω, *prolegō, 4625*

Heb	4: 7	in the words already quoted	1

word of a prophet

1. προφητεία, *prophēteia, 4735*

1Th	5:20	Do not despise the words of prophets	1

word of mouth

1. λόγος, *logos, 3364*

Act	15:27	will tell you the same things by word of mouth.	1
2Th	2:15	taught…either by word of mouth or by our letter.	1

work *See also* do work, mighty work, perform work, put to work

1. Contextual: Not in Greek
2. αὐτός, *autos, 899*
3. δρόμος, *dromos, 1536*
4. ἐνέργεια, *energeia, 1918*
5. ἐνεργέω, *energeō, 1919*
6. ἐνέργημα, *energēma, 1920*
7. ἐργάζομαι, *ergazomai, 2237*
8. ἔργον, *ergon, 2240*
9. κατεργάζομαι, *katergazomai, 2981*
10. κοπιάω, *kopiaō, 3159*
11. ὁ, *ho, 3836*
12. ποιέω, *poieō, 4472*
13. πόνος, *ponos, 4506*
14. ὑπηρετέω, *hypēreteō, 5676*

Mat	5:16	so that they may see your good works and give glory	8
	14: 2	for this reason these powers are at work in him."	5
	20:12	saying, 'These last worked only one hour	12
	21:28	'Son, go and work in the vineyard today.'	7
	24:46	whom his master will find at work when he arrives.	12
Mrk	6:14	for this reason these powers are at work in him."	5
	13:34	puts his slaves in charge, each with his work	8
Lke	3:23	Jesus…thirty years old when he began his work.	1
	5: 5	"Master, we have worked all night long but	10
	12:43	his master will find at work when he arrives.	12
	13:32	the third day I finish my work.	1
Jhn	4:34	and to complete his work.	8
	5:17	Jesus answered them, "My Father is still working	7
	5:17	"My Father is still working, and I also am working."	7
	5:20	he will show him greater works than these	8
	5:36	works that the Father has given me to complete	8
	5:36	the very works that I am doing	8
	6:27	Do not work for the food that perishes	7
	6:28	"What must we do to perform the works of God?"	8
	6:29	Jesus answered them, "This is the work of God:	8
	7: 3	disciples also may see the works you are doing;	8
	7: 7	I testify against it that its works are evil.	8

	7:21	Jesus answered them, "I performed one work	8
	9: 3	so that God's works might be revealed in him.	8
	9: 4	We must work the works of him who sent me	7
	9: 4	We must work the works of him who sent me	8
	9: 4	night is coming when no one can work.	7
	10:25	The works that I do in my Father's name	8
	10:32	shown you many good works from the Father.	8
	10:33	"It is not for a good work that we…stone you	8
	10:37	If I am not doing the works of my Father	8
	10:38	believe the works	8
	14:10	the Father who dwells in me does his works.	8
	14:11	believe me because of the works themselves.	8
	14:12	believes in me will also do the works that I do	8
	14:12	will do greater works than these	1
	15:24	done among them the works that no one else did	8
	17: 4	finishing the work that you gave me	8
Act	7:41	reveled in the works of their hands.	8
	9:36	She was devoted to good works and acts of charity.	8
	13: 2	the work to which I have called them."	8
	13:25	as John was finishing his work, he said	3
	13:41	for in your days I am doing a work	8
	13:41	a work that you will never believe	8
	14:26	for the work that they had completed.	8
	15:38	and had not accompanied them in the work.	8
	18: 3	he stayed with them, and they worked	7
	20:34	worked with my own hands to support myself	14
	20:35	by such work we must support the weak	10
Rom	3:27	By what law? By that of works?	8
	3:28	by faith apart from works prescribed by the law.	8
	4: 2	For if Abraham was justified by works	8
	4: 4	Now to one who works, wages are not reckoned	7
	4: 5	to one who without works trusts him	7
	4: 6	God reckons righteousness apart from works:	8
	7: 5	sinful passions…were at work in our members	5
	7:13	sin, working death in me through what is good	9
	9:12	not by works but by his call)	8
	9:32	but as if it were based on works.	8
	11: 6	it is no longer on the basis of works	8
	13:12	Let us then lay aside the works of darkness	8
	14:20	Do not, for the sake of food, destroy the work	8
	15:17	I have reason to boast of my work for God.	11
	16: 6	Greet Mary, who has worked very hard among you.	10
	16:12	beloved Persis, who has worked hard in the Lord.	10
1Co	3:13	work of each builder will become visible	8
	3:13	test what sort of work each has done.	8
	3:15	work is burned up, the builder will suffer loss;	8
	4:12	we grow weary from the work of our own hands.	7
	9: 1	Are you not my work in the Lord?	8
	9: 6	have no right to refrain from working for a living?	7
	12:10	to another the working of miracles	6
	15:10	On the contrary, I worked harder than any of them	10
	15:58	always excelling in the work of the Lord	8
	16:10	he is doing the work of the Lord just as I am;	8
2Co	4:12	death is at work in us, but life in you.	5
	9: 8	share abundantly in every good work.	8
Gal	2:16	a person is not justified by the works of the law	8
	2:16	not by doing the works of the law	8
	2:16	no one will be justified by the works of the law.	8
	3: 2	Did you receive the Spirit by doing the works of the law	8
	3: 5	work miracles among you	5
	3: 5	by your doing the works of the law	8
	3:10	rely on the works of the law are under a curse;	8
	3:12	"Whoever does the works of the law will live by them."	2
	4:11	afraid that my work for you may have been wasted.	10
	5: 6	faith working through love.	5
	5:19	Now the works of the flesh are obvious:	8
	6: 4	All must test their own work;	8
	6: 4	then that work, rather than their neighbor's work,	1
	6: 4	then that work, rather than their neighbor's work,	1
	6:10	opportunity, let us work for the good of all	7
Eph	1:19	according to the working of his great power.	4
	2: 2	is now at work among those who are disobedient.	5
	2: 9	not the result of works, so that no one may boast.	8
	2:10	created in Christ Jesus for good works	8
	3: 7	that was given me by the working of his power.	4
	3:20	by the power at work within us	5
	4:12	to equip the saints for the work of ministry	8
	4:16	as each part is working properly	4
	4:28	labor and work honestly with their own hands	7
	5:11	Take no part in the unfruitful works of darkness	8
Php	1: 6	that the one who began a good work among you	8

	2:13 for it is God who is at work in you, enabling you	5
	2:13 both to will and to work for his good pleasure.	5
	2:30 he came close to death for the work of Christ	8
Col	1:10 bear fruit in every good work	8
	4:13 I testify for him that he has worked hard for you	13
1Th	1: 3 work of faith and labor of love	8
	2: 9 worked night and day, so that we might not burden	7
	2:13 God's word, which is also at work in you believers.	5
	4:11 to work with your hands, as we directed you	7
	5:13 esteem them…because of their work.	8
2Th	1:11 fulfill…every good resolve and work of faith	8
	2: 7 the mystery of lawlessness is already at work	5
	2: 9 apparent in the working of Satan	4
	2:17 strengthen them in every good work and word.	8
	3: 8 with toil and labor we worked night and day	7
	3:10 Anyone unwilling to work should not eat.	7
1Ti	2:10 with good works, as is proper for women	8
	5:10 she must be well attested for her good works	8
	5:25 So also good works are conspicuous;	8
	6:18 They are to do good, to be rich in good works	8
2Ti	1: 9 a holy calling, not according to our works	8
	2: 6 It is the farmer who does the work	10
	2:21 ready for every good work.	8
	3:17 equipped for every good work.	8
	4: 5 do the work of an evangelist	8
Tit	1:16 detestable, disobedient, unfit for any good work.	8
	2: 7 in all respects a model of good works	8
	3: 1 to be obedient, to be ready for every good work	8
	3: 5 not because of any works of righteousness	8
	3: 8 may be careful to devote themselves to good works;	8
	3:14 learn to devote themselves to good works	8
Heb	1:10 the heavens are the work of your hands;	8
	3: 9 though they had seen my works	8
	4: 3 though his works were finished	8
	4: 4 God rested on the seventh day from all his works."	8
	6: 1 the foundation: repentance from dead works	8
	6:10 For God is not unjust; he will not overlook your work	8
	9:14 purify our conscience from dead works	8
	13:21 working…that which is pleasing in his sight	12
Jas	2:14 if you say you have faith but do not have works?	8
	2:17 So faith by itself, if it has no works, is dead.	8
	2:18 someone will say, "You have faith and I have works."	8
	2:18 Show me your faith apart from your works	8
	2:18 and I by my works will show you my faith.	8
	2:20 that faith apart from works is barren?	8
	2:21 Was not our ancestor Abraham justified by works	8
	2:22 faith was active along with his works	8
	2:22 and faith was brought to completion by the works.	8
	2:24 You see that a person is justified by works	8
	2:25 was not Rahab the prostitute also justified by works	8
	2:26 so faith without works is also dead.	8
	3:13 your works are done with gentleness born of wisdom.	8
1Jn	3: 8 to destroy the works of the devil.	8
2Jn	1: 8 so that you do not lose what we have worked for	7
Rev	2: 2 "I know your works, your toil and your patient	8
	2: 5 repent, and do the works you did at first.	8
	2: 6 you hate the works of the Nicolaitans	8
	2:19 "I know your works—your love, faith, service,	8
	2:19 that your last works are greater than the first.	8
	2:23 I will give to each of you as your works deserve.	8
	2:26 everyone who conquers and continues to do my works	8
	3: 1 "I know your works; you have a name of being alive	8
	3: 2 for I have not found your works perfect	8
	3: 8 "I know your works.	8
	3:15 "I know your works; you are neither cold nor hot.	8
	9:20 did not repent of the works of their hands	8
	20:12 dead were judged according to their works,	8
	22:12 to repay according to everyone's work.	8

effective work
1. ἐνεργής, *energēs, 1921*

1Co	16: 9 for a wide door for effective work has opened	1

work a miracle
1. δύναμις, *dynamis, 1539*

1Co	12:29 Are all teachers? Do all work miracles?	1

work already done
1. ἕτοιμος, *hetoimos, 2289*

2Co	10:16 work already done in someone else's sphere of action.	1

work like a slave
1. δουλεύω, *douleuō, 1526*

Lke	15:29 years I have been working like a slave for you	1

work of the gospel
1. εὐαγγέλιον, *euangelion, 2295*

Php	2:22 he has served with me in the work of the gospel.	1
	4: 3 struggled beside me in the work of the gospel	1

work out
1. κατεργάζομαι, *katergazomai, 2981*

Php	2:12 work out your own salvation with fear	1

work through
1. ἐνεργέω, *energeō, 1919*

Gal	2: 8 (for he who worked through Peter	1
	2: 8 worked through me in sending me to the Gentiles)	1

work together
1. συνεργέω, *synergeō, 5300*

Rom	8:28 work together for good for those who love God	1
2Co	6: 1 work together with him, we urge you also	1

work with
1. συνεργέω, *synergeō, 5300*
2. συνεργός, *synergos, 5301*

Mrk	16:20 ⟦while the Lord worked with them⟧	1
Rom	16: 3 who work with me in Christ Jesus	2
1Co	16:16 of everyone who works and toils with them.	1

worker
1. ἐργάτης, *ergatēs, 2239*
2. κοπιάω, *kopiaō, 3159*

Act	19:25 with the workers of the same trade	1
Rom	16:12 Greet those workers in the Lord	2
2Co	11:13 such boasters are false apostles, deceitful workers	1
Php	3: 2 beware of the evil workers	1
2Ti	2:15 a worker who has no need to be ashamed	1

fellow worker
1. συνεργός, *synergos, 5301*

Phm	1:24 Aristarchus, Demas, and Luke, my fellow workers.	1

worker with
1. συνεργός, *synergos, 5301*

2Co	1:24 rather, we are workers with you for your joy	1

working   *See* servant working together

world   *See also* world *begin*
1. αἰών, *aiōn, 172*
2. ἄνθρωπος, *anthrōpos, 476*
3. κόσμος, *kosmos, 3180*
4. οἰκουμένη, *oikoumenē, 3876*

Mat	4: 8 the kingdoms of the world and their splendor;	3
	5:14 "You are the light of the world.	3
	13:22 but the cares of the world…choke the word	1
	13:35 hidden from the foundation of the world."	3
	13:38 the field is the world	3
	16:26 gain the whole world but forfeit their life?	3
	18: 7 Woe to the world because of stumbling blocks!	3
	24:14 good news…proclaimed throughout the world	4
	24:21 from the beginning of the world until now	3
	25:34 from the foundation of the world;	3
	26:13 this good news is proclaimed in the whole world	3
Mrk	4:19 the cares of the world, and the lure of wealth	1
	8:36 to gain the whole world and forfeit their life?	3
	14: 9 the good news is proclaimed in the whole world	3
	16:15 ⟦"Go into all the world and proclaim the good news⟧	3
Lke	2: 1 all the world should be registered.	4
	4: 5 in an instant all the kingdoms of the world.	4
	9:25 does it profit them if they gain the whole world	3
	11:50 blood…shed since the foundation of the world	3
	12:30 the nations of the world that strive after all	3
	21:26 foreboding of what is coming upon the world	4
Jhn	1: 9 The true light…was coming into the world.	3
	1:10 He was in the world	3
	1:10 and the world came into being through him;	3

Jhn	1:10	yet the world did not know him.	3
	1:29	who takes away the sin of the world!	3
	3:16	God so loved the world that he gave his only Son	3
	3:17	"Indeed, God did not send the Son into the world	3
	3:17	God did not send the Son…to condemn the world	3
	3:17	that the world might be saved through him.	3
	3:19	that the light has come into the world	3
	4:42	this is truly the Savior of the world."	3
	6:14	the prophet who is to come into the world."	3
	6:33	gives life to the world."	3
	6:51	bread that I will give for the life of the world	3
	7: 4	If you do these things, show yourself to the world	3
	7: 7	The world cannot hate you, but it hates me	3
	8:12	"I am the light of the world.	3
	8:23	you are of this world, I am not of this world.	3
	8:23	you are of this world, I am not of this world.	3
	8:26	I declare to the world what I have heard from him."	3
	9: 5	As long as I am in the world	3
	9: 5	I am the light of the world."	3
	9:39	Jesus said, "I came into this world for judgment	3
	10:36	the Father has sanctified and sent into the world	3
	11: 9	because they see the light of this world.	3
	11:27	the Son of God, the one coming into the world."	3
	12:19	Look, the world has gone after him!"	3
	12:25	who hate their life in this world will keep it	3
	12:31	Now is the judgment of this world;	3
	12:31	now the ruler of this world will be driven out.	3
	12:46	I have come as light into the world	3
	12:47	not to judge the world, but to save the world.	3
	12:47	not to judge the world, but to save the world.	3
	13: 1	to depart from this world and go to the Father.	3
	13: 1	Having loved his own who were in the world	3
	14:17	whom the world cannot receive	3
	14:19	In a little while the world will no longer see	3
	14:22	reveal yourself to us, and not to the world?"	3
	14:27	I do not give to you as the world gives.	3
	14:30	the ruler of this world is coming.	3
	14:31	so that the world may know that I love the Father.	3
	15:18	"If the world hates you…it hated me	3
	15:19	If you belonged to the world	3
	15:19	the world would love you as its own.	3
	15:19	Because you do not belong to the world	3
	15:19	I have chosen you out of the world	3
	15:19	therefore the world hates you.	3
	16: 8	when he comes, he will prove the world wrong	3
	16:11	the ruler of this world has been condemned.	3
	16:20	the world will rejoice;	3
	16:21	having brought a human being into the world.	3
	16:28	have come into the world;	3
	16:28	leaving the world and am going to the Father."	3
	16:33	In the world you face persecution.	3
	16:33	take courage; I have conquered the world!"	3
	17: 5	glory that I had…before the world existed.	3
	17: 6	those whom you gave me from the world.	3
	17: 9	I am not asking on behalf of the world	3
	17:11	now I am no longer in the world	3
	17:11	they are in the world, and I am coming to you.	3
	17:13	I speak these things in the world	3
	17:14	the world has hated them	3
	17:14	because they do not belong to the world	3
	17:14	just as I do not belong to the world.	3
	17:15	not asking you to take them out of the world	3
	17:16	They do not belong to the world, just as I	3
	17:16	just as I do not belong to the world.	3
	17:18	As you have sent me into the world	3
	17:18	so I have sent them into the world.	3
	17:21	the world may believe that you have sent me.	3
	17:23	the world may know that you have sent me	3
	17:24	loved me before the foundation of the world.	3
	17:25	"Righteous Father, the world does not know you	3
	18:20	"I have spoken openly to the world;	3
	18:36	answered, "My kingdom is not from this world.	3
	18:36	If my kingdom were from this world	3
	18:37	for this I came into the world	3
	21:25	the world itself could not contain the books	3
Act	11:28	there would be a severe famine over all the world;	4
	17: 6	who have been turning the world upside down	4
	17:24	The God who made the world and everything in it	3
	17:31	fixed a day on which he will have the world judged	4
	19:27	that brought all Asia and the world to worship	4
	22:15	you will be his witness to all the world	2

	24: 5	among all the Jews throughout the world	4
Rom	1: 8	your faith is proclaimed throughout the world.	3
	1:20	Ever since the creation of the world	3
	3: 6	For then how could God judge the world?	3
	3:19	the whole world may be held accountable to God.	3
	4:13	promise…that he would inherit the world	3
	5:12	just as sin came into the world through one man	3
	5:13	sin was indeed in the world before the law	3
	10:18	and their words to the ends of the world."	4
	11:12	Now if their stumbling means riches for the world	3
	11:15	is the reconciliation of the world	3
	12: 2	Do not be conformed to this world	1
1Co	1:20	Has not God made foolish the wisdom of the world?	3
	1:21	the world did not know God through wisdom	3
	1:27	God chose what is foolish in the world	3
	1:27	God chose what is weak in the world	3
	1:28	God chose what is low and despised in the world	3
	2:12	Now we have received not the spirit of the world	3
	3:19	For the wisdom of this world is foolishness with God.	3
	3:22	the world or life or death or the present	3
	4: 9	a spectacle to the world, to angels and to mortals.	3
	4:13	We have become…like the rubbish of the world	3
	5:10	not at all meaning the immoral of this world	3
	5:10	since you would then need to go out of the world.	3
	6: 2	know that the saints will judge the world?	3
	6: 2	if the world is to be judged by you	3
	7:31	those who deal with the world	3
	7:31	the present form of this world is passing away.	3
	7:33	married man is anxious about the affairs of the world	3
	7:34	married woman is anxious about the affairs of the world	3
	8: 4	we know that "no idol in the world really exists,"	3
	11:32	may not be condemned along with the world.	3
	14:10	many different kinds of sounds in the world	3
2Co	1:12	we have behaved in the world	3
	4: 4	the god of this world has blinded the minds	1
	5:19	in Christ God was reconciling the world	3
Gal	4: 3	enslaved to the elemental spirits of the world.	3
	6:14	by which the world has been crucified to me	3
	6:14	crucified to me, and I to the world.	3
Eph	1: 4	chose us in Christ before the foundation of the world	3
	2: 2	following the course of this world	3
	2:12	having no hope and without God in the world.	3
Php	2:15	in which you shine like stars in the world.	3
Col	1: 6	bearing fruit and growing in the whole world	3
	2:20	you live as if you still belonged to the world?	3
1Ti	1:15	Jesus came into the world to save sinners	3
	3:16	believed in throughout the world, taken up in glory.	3
	6: 7	for we brought nothing into the world	3
2Ti	4:10	Demas, in love with this present world	1
Heb	1: 2	through whom he also created the worlds.	1
	1: 6	when he brings the firstborn into the world	4
	2: 5	Now God did not subject the coming world	4
	4: 3	were finished at the foundation of the world.	3
	9:26	since the foundation of the world.	3
	10: 5	when Christ came into the world, he said	3
	11: 3	the worlds were prepared by the word of God	1
	11: 7	by this he condemned the world	3
	11:38	of whom the world was not worthy.	3
Jas	1:27	to keep oneself unstained by the world.	3
	2: 5	Has not God chosen the poor in the world	3
	3: 6	The tongue…among our members as a world of iniquity	3
	4: 4	friendship with the world is enmity with God?	3
	4: 4	whoever wishes to be a friend of the world	3
1Pe	1:20	destined before the foundation of the world	3
	5: 9	your brothers and sisters in all the world	3
2Pe	1: 4	escape from the corruption that is in the world	3
	2: 5	if he did not spare the ancient world	3
	2: 5	he brought a flood on a world of the ungodly;	3
	2:20	they have escaped the defilements of the world	3
	3: 6	the world of that time was deluged with water	3
1Jn	2: 2	but also for the sins of the whole world.	3
	2:15	Do not love the world or the things in the world.	3
	2:15	Do not love the world or the things in the world.	3
	2:15	love…is not in those who love the world	3
	2:16	for all that is in the world	3
	2:16	comes not from the Father but from the world.	3
	2:17	the world and its desire are passing away,	3
	3: 1	The reason the world does not know us	3
	3:13	Do not be astonished…that the world hates you.	3
	3:17	has the world's goods and sees a brother or sister in need	3
	4: 1	many false prophets have gone out into the world.	3

	4: 3	antichrist…and now it is already in the world.	3
	4: 4	greater than the one who is in the world.	3
	4: 5	They are from the world;	3
	4: 5	therefore what they say is from the world	3
	4: 5	and the world listens to them.	3
	4: 9	God sent his only Son into the world	3
	4:14	Father has sent his Son as the Savior of the world.	3
	4:17	because as he is, so are we in this world.	3
	5: 4	for whatever is born of God conquers the world.	3
	5: 4	this is the victory that conquers the world	3
	5: 5	Who is it that conquers the world	3
	5:19	the whole world lies under the power of the evil one.	3
2Jn	1: 7	Many deceivers have gone out into the world	3
Rev	3:10	hour of trial that is coming on the whole world	4
	11:15	"The kingdom of the world has become the kingdom	3
	12: 9	deceiver of the whole world—he was thrown down	4
	13: 8	written from the foundation of the world	3
	16:14	who go abroad to the kings of the whole world	4
	17: 8	written…from the foundation of the world	3

worldly

1. κοσμικός, *kosmikos, 3176*
2. κόσμος, *kosmos, 3180*

2Co	7:10	worldly grief produces death.	2
Tit	2:12	to renounce impiety and worldly passions	1

worldly person

1. ψυχικός, *psychikos, 6035*

Jde	1:19	worldly people, devoid of the Spirit	1

worm *See also* eaten by worms

1. σκώληξ, *skōlēx, 5038*

Mrk	9:48	where their worm never dies	1

wormwood

1. ἄψινθος, *apsinthos, 952*

Rev	8:11	The name of the star is Wormwood.	1
	8:11	A third of the waters became wormwood	1

worry

1. μέριμνα, *merimna, 3533*
2. μεριμνάω, *merimnaō, 3534*
3. μετεωρίζομαι, *meteōrizomai, 3577*

Mat	6:25	I tell you, do not worry about your life	2
	6:27	can any of you by worrying add a single hour	2
	6:28	And why do you worry about clothing? Consider	2
	6:31	do not worry, saying, 'What will we eat?'	2
	6:34	"So do not worry about tomorrow	2
	6:34	for tomorrow will bring worries of its own.	2
	10:19	do not worry about how you are to speak	2
Lke	10:41	you are worried and distracted by many things;	2
	12:11	do not worry about how you are to defend	2
	12:22	do not worry about your life	2
	12:25	can any of you by worrying add a single hour	2
	12:26	why do you worry about the rest?	2
	12:29	and do not keep worrying.	3
	21:34	drunkenness and the worries of this life	1
Php	4: 6	not worry about anything	2

worry beforehand

1. προμεριμνάω, *promerimnaō, 4628*

Mrk	13:11	not worry beforehand about what you are to say;	1

worship *See also* bow in worship, object of worship, offer worship

1. εὐσεβέω, *eusebeō, 2355*
2. θεοσεβής, *theosebēs, 2538*
3. θρησκεία, *thrēskeia, 2579*
4. λατρεία, *latreia, 3301*
5. λατρεύω, *latreuō, 3302*
6. λειτουργέω, *leitourgeō, 3310*
7. λειτουργία, *leitourgia, 3311*
8. προσκυνέω, *proskyneō, 4686*
9. σεβάζομαι, *sebazomai, 4933*
10. σέβω, *sebō, 4936*

Mat	4: 9	you, if you will fall down and worship me."	8
	4:10	is written, 'Worship the Lord your God	8
	14:33	those in the boat worshiped him, saying	8
	15: 9	in vain do they worship me, teaching human precepts	10
	28: 9	took hold of his feet, and worshiped him.	8
	28:17	When they saw him, they worshiped him;	8
Mrk	7: 7	in vain do they worship me	10
Lke	2:37	worshiped there with fasting and prayer	5
	4: 7	If you…worship me, it will all be yours."	8
	4: 8	"It is written, 'Worship the Lord your God	8
	24:52	they worshiped him, and returned to Jerusalem	8
Jhn	4:20	Our ancestors worshiped on this mountain	8
	4:20	place where people must worship is in Jerusalem	8
	4:21	the hour is coming when you will worship the Father	8
	4:22	You worship what you do not know;	8
	4:22	we worship what we know	8
	4:23	will worship the Father in spirit and truth	8
	4:23	the Father seeks such as these to worship him.	8
	4:24	those who worship him must worship in spirit	8
	4:24	must worship in spirit and truth."	8
	9:31	listen to one who worships him and obeys his will.	2
	9:38	He said, "Lord, I believe." And he worshiped him.	8
	12:20	among those who went up to worship at the festival	8
	16: 2	by doing so they are offering worship to God.	4
Act	7: 7	they shall come out and worship me in this place.'	5
	7:42	God…handed them over to worship the host of heaven	5
	7:43	the images that you made to worship;	8
	8:27	had come to Jerusalem to worship	8
	10:25	and falling at his feet, worshiped him.	8
	13: 2	While they were worshiping the Lord and fasting	6
	17:23	What therefore you worship as unknown	1
	18:13	worship God in ways that are contrary to the law."	10
	19:27	that brought all Asia and the world to worship	10
	24:11	since I went up to worship in Jerusalem.	8
	24:14	I admit to you…I worship the God of our ancestors	5
	26: 7	as they earnestly worship day and night.	5
	27:23	the God to whom I belong and whom I worship	5
Rom	1:25	worshiped and served the creature rather	9
	9: 4	giving of the law, the worship, and the promises;	4
	12: 1	which is your spiritual worship.	4
1Co	14:25	person will bow down before God and worship	8
Php	3: 3	worship in the Spirit of God and boast in Christ	5
Col	2:18	self-abasement and worship of angels	3
2Ti	1: 3	God—whom I worship with a clear conscience	5
Heb	1: 6	he says, "Let all God's angels worship him."	8
	9: 1	the first covenant had regulations for worship	4
	9:14	from dead works to worship the living God!	5
	9:21	both the tent and all the vessels used in worship.	7
Rev	4:10	worship the one who lives forever and ever;	8
	5:14	And the elders fell down and worshiped.	8
	7:11	they fell on their faces…and worshiped God	8
	7:15	and worship him day and night within his temple	5
	9:20	or give up worshiping demons and idols of gold	8
	11: 1	the temple of God…and those who worship there	8
	11:16	elders…fell on their faces and worshiped God	8
	13: 4	They worshiped the dragon	8
	13: 4	and they worshiped the beast, saying	8
	13: 8	all the inhabitants of the earth will worship it	8
	13:12	makes…inhabitants worship the first beast	8
	13:15	and cause those who would not worship	8
	14: 7	and worship him who made heaven and earth	8
	14: 9	"Those who worship the beast and its image	8
	14:11	those who worship the beast and its image	8
	15: 4	All nations will come and worship before you	8
	16: 2	the mark of the beast and who worshiped its image.	8
	19: 4	living creatures fell down and worshiped God	8
	19:10	Then I fell down at his feet to worship him	8
	19:10	Worship God! For the testimony of Jesus	8
	19:20	and those who worshiped its image.	8
	20: 4	They had not worshiped the beast or its image	8
	22: 3	and his servants will worship him;	5
	22: 8	I fell down to worship at the feet of the angel	8
	22: 9	who keep the words of this book. Worship God!"	8

worship of an idol

1. εἰδωλολατρία, *eidōlolatria, 1630*

1Co	10:14	my dear friends, flee from the worship of idols.	1

worshiper

1. λατρεύω, *latreuō, 3302*
2. προσκυνητής, *proskynētēs, 4687*
3. σέβω, *sebō, 4936*

Jhn	4:23	true worshipers will worship the Father	2
Act	16:14	A certain woman named Lydia, a worshiper of God	3

Act 18: 7 Titius Justus, a worshiper of God;
Heb 9: 9 cannot perfect the conscience of the worshiper   3
      10: 2 since the worshipers, cleansed once for all   1

worth

1. Contextual: Not in Greek
2. ἄξιος, *axios, 545*
3. δοκιμή, *dokimē, 1509*
4. εἰμί, *eimi, 1639*

Mrk 6:37 "Are we to go and buy two hundred denarii worth   1
      12:42 two small copper coins, which are worth a penny.   4
Rom 8:18 the sufferings...are not worth comparing   2
Php 2:22 Timothy's worth you know   3

worthless

1. ἀδόκιμος, *adokimos, 99*
2. ἀχρεῖος, *achreios, 945*
3. ἀχρειόω, *achreioō, 946*
4. μάταιος, *mataios, 3469*

Mat 25:30 this worthless slave, throw   2
Lke 17:10 say, 'We are worthless slaves;   2
Rom 3:12 together they have become worthless;   3
Tit 3: 9 for they are unprofitable and worthless.   4
Heb 6: 8 it is worthless and on the verge of being cursed;   1
Jas 1:26 deceive their hearts, their religion is worthless.   4

worthless thing

1. μάταιος, *mataios, 3469*

Act 14:15 turn from these worthless things to the living God   1

worthy   *See also* consider worthy, make worthy

1. ἄξιος, *axios, 545*
2. ἀξιόω, *axioō, 546*
3. ἀξίως, *axiōs, 547*
4. ἱκανός, *hikanos, 2653*

Mat 3: 8 Bear fruit worthy of repentance.   1
     3:11 I am not worthy to carry his sandals.   4
     8: 8 I am not worthy to have you come under my roof;   4
     10:11 find out who in it is worthy   1
     10:13 If the house is worthy, let your peace come upon it;   1
     10:13 if it is not worthy, let your peace return to you.   1
     10:37 is not worthy of me;   1
     10:37 is not worthy of me;   1
     10:38 is not worthy of me.   1
     22: 8 but those invited were not worthy.   1
Mrk 1: 7 I am not worthy to stoop down and untie   4
Lke 3: 8 Bear fruits worthy of repentance.   1
     3:16 I am not worthy to untie the thong of his sandals.   4
     7: 4 "He is worthy of having you do this for him   1
     7: 6 am not worthy to have you come under my roof;   4
     15:19 I am no longer worthy to be called your son;   1
     15:21 I am no longer worthy to be called your son.'   1
Jhn 1:27 I am not worthy to untie the thong of his sandal."   1
Act 13:25 I am not worthy to untie the thong of the sandals   1
Eph 4: 1 to lead a life worthy of the calling   3
Col 1:10 so that you may lead lives worthy of the Lord   3
1Th 2:12 pleading that you lead a life worthy of God   3
1Ti 1:15 The saying is sure and worthy of full acceptance   1
     4: 9 is sure and worthy of full acceptance.   1
     6: 1 regard their masters as worthy of all honor   1
Heb 3: 3 Yet Jesus is worthy of more glory than Moses,   2
     11:38 of whom the world was not worthy.   1
Rev 3: 4 with me, dressed in white, for they are worthy.   1
     4:11 "You are worthy, our Lord and God, to receive glory   1
     5: 2 "Who is worthy to open the scroll and break   1
     5: 4 because no one was found worthy to open the scroll   1
     5: 9 "You are worthy to take the scroll and to open   1
     5:12 "Worthy is the Lamb that was slaughtered to receive   1

worthy manner

1. ἀξίως, *axiōs, 547*

Php 1:27 life in a manner worthy of the gospel of Christ   1
3Jn 1: 6 to send them on...in a manner worthy of God;   1

worthy of praise

1. ἔπαινος, *epainos, 2047*

Php 4: 8 if there is anything worthy of praise   1

wound

1. μώλωψ, *mōlōps, 3698*
2. πληγή, *plēgē, 4435*
3. τραῦμα, *trauma, 5546*
4. τραυματίζω, *traumatizō, 5547*
5. τύπτω, *typtō, 5597*

Lke 10:34 He went to him and bandaged his wounds   3
     20:12 this one also they wounded and threw out.   4
Act 16:33 he took them and washed their wounds;   2
     19:16 they fled out of the house naked and wounded.   4
1Co 8:12 wound their conscience when it is weak   5
1Pe 2:24 by his wounds you have been healed.   1
Rev 13: 3 but its mortal wound had been healed.   2
     13:12 the first beast, whose mortal wound had been healed.   2
     13:14 the beast that had been wounded by the sword   2

wrangle

1. διαπαρατριβή, *diaparatribē, 1384*
2. ἐρίζω, *erizō, 2248*
3. κραυγή, *kraugē, 3199*

Mat 12:19 He will not wrangle or cry aloud   2
Eph 4:31 wrath and anger and wrangling and slander   3
1Ti 6: 5 wrangling among those who are depraved in mind   1

wrangle over words

1. λογομαχέω, *logomacheō, 3362*

2Ti 2:14 warn them...to avoid wrangling over words   1

wrap

1. δέω, *deō, 1313*
2. ἐνειλέω, *eneileō, 1912*
3. ἐντυλίσσω, *entylissō, 1962*
4. περιβάλλω, *periballō, 4314*
5. περιδέω, *perideō, 4317*

Mat 27:59 and wrapped it in a clean linen cloth   3
Mrk 15:46 taking down the body, wrapped it in the linen cloth   2
Lke 23:53 he took it down, wrapped it in a linen cloth   3
Jhn 11:44 his face wrapped in a cloth.   5
     19:40 and wrapped it with the spices in linen cloths   1
Rev 10: 1 coming down from heaven, wrapped in a cloud   4

wrap around

1. περιβάλλω, *periballō, 4314*

Act 12: 8 "Wrap your cloak around you and follow me."   1

wrap in bands of cloth

1. σπαργανόω, *sparganoō, 5058*

Lke 2: 7 and wrapped him in bands of cloth   1
     2:12 you will find a child wrapped in bands of cloth   1

wrap up

1. ἀπόκειμαι, *apokeimai, 641*
2. συστέλλω, *systellō, 5366*

Lke 19:20 I wrapped it up in a piece of cloth   1
Act 5: 6 The young men came and wrapped up his body   2

linen wrapping

1. ὀθόνιον, *othonion, 3856*

Jhn 20: 5 and saw the linen wrappings lying there   1
     20: 6 He saw the linen wrappings lying there   1
     20: 7 the cloth...not lying with the linen wrappings   1

wrath

1. θυμός, *thymos, 2596*
2. ὀργή, *orgē, 3973*

Mat 3: 7 Who warned you to flee from the wrath to come?   2
Lke 3: 7 Who warned you to flee from the wrath to come?   2
     21:23 and wrath against this people;   2
Jhn 3:36 but must endure God's wrath.   2
Rom 1:18 For the wrath of God is revealed from heaven   2
     2: 5 storing up wrath for yourself on the day of wrath   2
     2: 5 storing up wrath for yourself on the day of wrath   2
     2: 8 for those...there will be wrath and fury.   2
     3: 5 That God is unjust to inflict wrath on us?   2
     4:15 For the law brings wrath;   2
     5: 9 will we be saved through him from the wrath of God.   2
     9:22 What if God, desiring to show his wrath   2
     9:22 endured with much patience the objects of wrath   2

	12:19	but leave room for the wrath of God;	2
	13: 4	to execute wrath on the wrongdoer.	2
	13: 5	one must be subject, not only because of wrath	2
Eph	2: 3	we were by nature children of wrath	2
	4:31	wrath and anger and wrangling and slander	1
	5: 6	the wrath of God comes on those…disobedient	2
Col	3: 6	On account of these the wrath of God is coming	2
	3: 8	wrath, malice, slander, and abusive language	1
1Th	1:10	Jesus, who rescues us from the wrath that is coming.	2
	2:16	God's wrath has overtaken them at last.	2
	5: 9	For God has destined us not for wrath	2
Rev	6:16	hide us…from the wrath of the Lamb;	2
	6:17	for the great day of their wrath has come	2
	11:18	The nations raged, but your wrath has come	2
	12:12	for the devil has come down to you with great wrath	1
	14: 8	drink of the wine of the wrath of her fornication."	1
	14:10	they will also drink the wine of God's wrath	1
	14:19	into the great wine press of the wrath of God.	1
	15: 1	for with them the wrath of God is ended.	1
	15: 7	seven golden bowls full of the wrath of God	1
	16: 1	pour out…the seven bowls of the wrath of God."	1
	16:19	gave her the wine-cup of the fury of his wrath.	2
	18: 3	drunk of the wine of the wrath of her fornication	1
	19:15	of the fury of the wrath of God the Almighty.	2

wreath

1. στέφανος², *stephanos²*, 5109

1Co	9:25	they do it to receive a perishable wreath	1

wrench apart

1. διασπάω, *diaspaō*, 1400

Mrk	5: 4	but the chains he wrenched apart	1

wrestle

1. ἀγωνίζομαι, *agōnizomai*, 76

Col	4:12	wrestling in his prayers on your behalf	1

wretch

1. κακός, *kakos*, 2805

Mat	21:41	put those wretches to a miserable death	1

wretched

1. ταλαίπωρος, *talaipōros*, 5417

Rom	7:24	Wretched man that I am! Who will rescue me	1
Rev	3:17	not realize that you are wretched, pitiable, poor	1

wrinkle

1. ῥυτίς, *rhytis*, 4869

Eph	5:27	without a spot or wrinkle or anything of the kind	1

wrist

1. χείρ, *cheir*, 5931

Act	12: 7	the chains fell off his wrists.	1

write

1. Contextual: Not in Greek
2. γράμμα, *gramma*, 1207
3. γραπτός, *graptos*, 1209
4. γράφω, *graphō*, 1211
5. ἐγγράφω, *engraphō*, 1582
6. ἐπιγράφω, *epigraphō*, 2108
7. ἐπιστέλλω, *epistellō*, 2182
8. καταγράφω, *katagraphō*, 2863
9. ποιέω, *poieō*, 4472

Mat	2: 5	Judea; for so it has been written by the prophet:	4
	4: 4	But he answered, "It is written, 'One does not live	4
	4: 6	for it is written, 'He will command his angels	4
	4: 7	Jesus said to him, "Again it is written, 'Do not	4
	4:10	"Away with you, Satan! for it is written,	4
	11:10	This is the one about whom it is written	4
	21:13	He said to them, "It is written	4
	26:24	The Son of Man goes as it is written of him	4
	26:31	it is written, 'I will strike the shepherd	4
Mrk	1: 2	As it is written in the prophet Isaiah	4
	7: 6	as it is written, 'This people honors me	4
	9:12	How then is it written about the Son of Man	4
	9:13	as it is written about him."	4
	10: 4	allowed a man to write a certificate of dismissal	4
	10: 5	he wrote this commandment for you.	4

	11:17	He was teaching and saying, "Is it not written	4
	12:19	"Teacher, Moses wrote for us	4
	14:21	For the Son of Man goes as it is written of him	4
	14:27	it is written, 'I will strike the shepherd	4
Lke	1: 3	to write an orderly account for you	4
	1:63	for a writing tablet and wrote, "His name is John."	4
	2:23	(as it is written in the law of the Lord	4
	3: 4	as it is written in the book of…Isaiah	4
	4: 4	"It is written, 'One does not live by bread alone.' "	4
	4: 8	"It is written, 'Worship the Lord your God	4
	4:10	it is written, 'He will command his angels	4
	4:17	found the place where it was written:	4
	7:27	This is the one about whom it is written	4
	10:20	rejoice that your names are written in heaven."	5
	10:26	"What is written in the law? What do you read	4
	18:31	everything that is written about the Son of Man	4
	19:46	said, "It is written	4
	20:28	Moses wrote for us that if a man's brother dies	4
	21:22	as a fulfillment of all that is written.	4
	22:37	what is written about me is being fulfilled."	1
	24:44	everything written about me in the law of Moses	4
	24:46	said to them, "Thus it is written	4
Jhn	1:45	Moses in the law and also the prophets wrote	4
	2:17	His disciples remembered that it was written	4
	5:46	you would believe me, for he wrote about me.	4
	5:47	if you do not believe what he wrote	2
	6:31	as it is written, 'He gave them bread from heaven	4
	6:45	It is written in the prophets	4
	8: 6	⟦Jesus…wrote with his finger on the ground.⟧	8
	8: 8	⟦and wrote on the ground.⟧	4
	8:17	In your law it is written	4
	10:34	Jesus answered, "Is it not written in your law	4
	12:14	as it is written:	4
	12:16	that these things had been written of him	4
	15:25	to fulfill the word that is written in their law	4
	19:19	Pilate also had an inscription written	4
	19:20	it was written in Hebrew, in Latin, and in Greek.	4
	19:21	"Do not write, 'The King of the Jews,'	4
	19:22	"What I have written I have written."	4
	19:22	"What I have written I have written."	4
	20:30	which are not written in this book.	4
	20:31	these are written so that you may come to believe	4
	21:24	testifying to these things and has written them	4
	21:25	the books that would be written.	4
Act	1: 1	I wrote about all that Jesus did and taught	9
	1:20	"For it is written in the book of Psalms	4
	7:42	as it is written in the book of the prophets:	4
	13:29	everything that was written about him	4
	13:33	as also it is written in the second psalm	4
	15:15	the words of the prophets, as it is written,	4
	15:20	write to them to abstain only from…idols	7
	18:27	wrote to the disciples to welcome him.	4
	23: 5	it is written, 'You shall not speak evil of a leader	4
	23:25	He wrote a letter to this effect:	4
	24:14	written in the prophets.	4
	25:26	nothing definite to write to our sovereign about him.	4
	25:26	I may have something to write	4
Rom	1:17	as it is written, "The one who is righteous	4
	2:15	what the law requires is written on their hearts	3
	2:24	as it is written, "The name of God is blasphemed	4
	3: 4	let God be proved true…as it is written	4
	3:10	as it is written: "There is no one who is righteous	4
	4:17	as it is written, "I have made you the father	4
	4:23	the words…were written not for his sake alone	4
	8:36	As it is written, "For your sake we are being killed	4
	9:13	As it is written, "I have loved Jacob,	4
	9:33	as it is written, "See, I am laying in Zion	4
	10: 5	Moses writes concerning the righteousness	4
	10:15	As it is written, "How beautiful are the feet	4
	11: 8	as it is written, "God gave them a sluggish spirit	4
	11:26	so all Israel will be saved; as it is written	4
	12:19	for it is written, "Vengeance is mine, I will repay	4
	14:11	For it is written, "As I live, says the Lord	4
	15: 3	but, as it is written, "The insults of those	4
	15: 4	was written for our instruction	4
	15: 9	As it is written, "Therefore I will confess you	4
	15:15	written to you rather boldly by way of reminder	4
	15:21	as it is written, "Those who have never been told	4
1Co	1:19	it is written, "I will destroy the wisdom	4
	1:31	that, as it is written, "Let the one who boasts	4
	2: 9	But, as it is written, "What no eye has seen	4

1Co	3:19	it is written, "He catches the wise	4
	4: 6	the saying, "Nothing beyond what is written,"	4
	4:14	I am not writing this to make you ashamed	4
	5: 9	I wrote to you in my letter	4
	5:11	But now I am writing to you	4
	7: 1	concerning the matters about which you wrote:	4
	9: 9	For it is written in the law of Moses	4
	9:10	It was indeed written for our sake	4
	9:15	nor am I writing this	4
	10: 7	as it is written, "The people sat down to eat	4
	14:21	In the law it is written, "By people of strange tongues	4
	14:37	acknowledge that what I am writing to you	4
	15:45	Thus it is written, "The first man, Adam	4
	15:54	then the saying that is written will be fulfilled:	4
	16:21	I, Paul, write this greeting with my own hand.	1
2Co	1:13	we write you nothing other than what you can read	4
	2: 3	I wrote as I did, so that when I came	4
	2: 4	For I wrote you out of much distress	4
	2: 9	I wrote for this reason: to test you	4
	3: 2	written on our hearts, to be known and read by all;	5
	3: 3	written not with ink but with the Spirit	5
	7:12	So although I wrote to you	4
	8:15	As it is written, "The one who had much did not have	4
	9: 1	Now it is not necessary for me to write you	4
	9: 9	As it is written, "He scatters abroad	4
	13:10	I write these things while I am away from you	4
Gal	1:20	I am writing to you, before God, I do not lie!	4
	3:10	for it is written, "Cursed is everyone	4
	3:10	obey all the things written in the book of the law."	4
	3:13	for it is written, "Cursed is everyone who hangs	4
	4:22	For it is written that Abraham had two sons	4
	4:27	For it is written, "Rejoice, you childless one	4
	6:11	See what large letters I make when I am writing	4
Php	3: 1	To write the same things to you is not troublesome	4
Col	4:18	I, Paul, write this greeting with my own hand.	1
1Th	4: 9	you do not need to have anyone write to you	4
	5: 1	you do not need to have anything written to you.	4
2Th	3:17	I, Paul, write this greeting with my own hand.	1
	3:17	it is the way I write.	4
1Ti	3:14	I am writing these instructions to you	4
Phm	1:19	I, Paul, am writing this with my own hand: I will repay	4
	1:21	Confident of your obedience, I am writing to you	4
Heb	8:10	write them on their hearts	6
	10: 7	(in the scroll of the book it is written of me)."	4
	10:16	and I will write them on their minds,"	6
	13:22	I have written to you briefly.	7
1Pe	1:16	for it is written, "You shall be holy, for I am	4
	5:12	I have written this short letter to encourage you	4
2Pe	3: 1	This is now, beloved, the second letter I am writing	4
	3:15	So also our beloved brother Paul wrote to you	4
1Jn	1: 4	writing these things so that our joy may be complete.	4
	2: 1	I am writing these things to you so that you may not sin.	4
	2: 7	Beloved, I am writing you no new commandment	4
	2: 8	Yet I am writing you a new commandment	4
	2:12	I am writing to you, little children	4
	2:13	I am writing to you, fathers, because you know him	4
	2:13	I am writing to you, young people	4
	2:14	I write to you, children	4
	2:14	I write to you, fathers, because you know him	4
	2:14	I write to you, young people, because you are strong	4
	2:21	I write to you, not because you do not know	4
	2:26	I write…concerning those who would deceive you.	4
	5:13	I write these things to you who believe in the name	4
2Jn	1: 5	as though I were writing you a new commandment	4
	1:12	Although I have much to write to you	4
3Jn	1: 9	I have written something to the church;	4
	1:13	I have much to write to you	4
	1:13	but I would rather not write with pen and ink;	4
Jde	1: 3	Beloved, while eagerly preparing to write to you	4
	1: 3	I find it necessary to write and appeal to you	4
Rev	1: 3	who hear and who keep what is written in it;	4
	1:11	saying, "Write in a book what you see and send it	4
	1:19	Now write what you have seen	4
	2: 1	"To the angel of the church in Ephesus write:	4
	2: 8	"And to the angel of the church in Smyrna write:	4
	2:12	"And to the angel of the church in Pergamum write:	4
	2:17	on the white stone is written a new name	4
	2:18	"And to the angel of the church in Thyatira write:	4
	3: 1	"And to the angel of the church in Sardis write:	4
	3: 7	to the angel of the church in Philadelphia write:	4
	3:12	I will write on you the name of my God	4

	3:14	"And to the angel of the church in Laodicea write:	4
	5: 1	a scroll written on the inside and on the back	4
	10: 4	I was about to write, but I heard a voice	4
	13: 8	name has not been written…in the book of life	4
	14: 1	his Father's name written on their foreheads.	4
	14:13	I heard a voice from heaven saying, "Write this:	4
	17: 5	on her forehead was written a name, a mystery:	4
	17: 8	names have not been written in the book of life	4
	19: 9	And the angel said to me, "Write this:	4
	20:15	name was not found written in the book of life	4
	21: 5	"Write this, for these words are trustworthy	4
	21:27	only those…written in the Lamb's book of life.	4

write above
 1. προγράφω, *prographō, 4592*

Eph	3: 3	as I wrote above in a few words	1

write down
 1. γράφω, *graphō, 1211*

Jhn	21:25	if every one of them were written down	1
1Co	10:11	they were written down to instruct us	1
Rev	10: 4	and do not write it down."	1

write in former days
 1. προγράφω, *prographō, 4592*

Rom	15: 4	For whatever was written in former days	1

writer
 1. γράφω, *graphō, 1211*

Rom	16:22	I Tertius, the writer of this letter, greet you	1

writing
 1. γράμμα, *gramma, 1207*
 2. γραφή, *graphē, 1210*

Rom	16:26	through the prophetic writings is made known	2
2Ti	3:15	from childhood you have known the sacred writings	1

writing tablet
 1. πινακίδιον, *pinakidion, 4400*

Lke	1:63	He asked for a writing tablet and wrote, "His name	1

written code
 1. γράμμα, *gramma, 1207*

Rom	2:27	will condemn you that have the written code	1
	7: 6	we are slaves not under the old written code	1

wrong *See also* do wrong, prove wrong
 1. ἀδικέω, *adikeō, 92*
 2. ἀδικία, *adikia, 94*
 3. ἄτοπος, *atopos, 876*
 4. κακός, *kakos, 2805*
 5. πλανάω, *planaō, 4414*
 6. ὑπερβαίνω, *hyperbainō, 5648*

Mat	22:29	Jesus answered them, "You are wrong	5
Mrk	12:24	"Is not this the reason you are wrong	5
	12:27	you are quite wrong."	5
Lke	23:41	this man has done nothing wrong."	3
Jhn	18:23	testify to the wrong.	4
Act	7:24	saw one of them being wronged	1
	7:26	you are brothers; why do you wrong each other?'	1
	7:27	the man who was wronging his neighbor	1
	23: 9	"We find nothing wrong with this man.	4
	25: 5	if there is anything wrong about the man	3
	25:11	Now if I am in the wrong	1
Rom	13: 4	if you do what is wrong, you should be afraid	4
	13:10	Love does no wrong to a neighbor;	4
	14:20	but it is wrong for you to make others fall	4
1Co	6: 7	Why not rather be wronged?	1
	6: 8	you yourselves wrong and defraud	1
2Co	7: 2	we have wronged no one, we have corrupted no one	1
	7:12	nor on account of the one who was wronged	1
	12:13	Forgive me this wrong!	2
	13: 7	we pray to God that you may not do anything wrong	4
1Th	4: 6	that no one wrong or exploit a brother or sister	6
Phm	1:18	If he has wronged you in any way, or owes you anything	1

wrongdoer
 1. ἀδικέω, *adikeō, 92*
 2. ἄδικος, *adikos, 96*

3. κακός + πράσσω, *kakos + prassō, 2805 + 4556*

Rom	13: 4	to execute wrath on the wrongdoer.	3
1Co	6: 9	wrongdoers will not inherit the kingdom of God?	2
Col	3:25	For the wrongdoer will be paid back	1

wrongdoing

1. ἀδικία, *adikia, 94*

1Co	13: 6	it does not rejoice in wrongdoing	1
1Jn	5:17	All wrongdoing is sin	1

wrongly

1. κακῶς, *kakōs, 2809*

Jhn	18:23	Jesus answered, "If I have spoken wrongly	1
Jas	4: 3	You...do not receive, because you ask wrongly	1

Y

yard *See* hundred yards

year *See also* forty years, hundred years, three years, two years

1. ἐνιαυτός, *eniautos, 1929*
2. ἔτος, *etos, 2291*
3. ἡλικία, *hēlikia, 2461*
4. ἡμέρα, *hēmera, 2465*

Mat	9:20	suffering from hemorrhages for twelve years	2
Mrk	5:25	suffering from hemorrhages for twelve years.	2
	5:42	(she was twelve years of age).	2
Lke	1: 7	both were getting on in years.	4
	1:18	old man, and my wife is getting on in years."	4
	2:36	seven years after her marriage	2
	2:41	Now every year his parents went to Jerusalem	2
	2:42	when he was twelve years old	2
	2:52	Jesus increased in wisdom and in years	3
	3: 1	In the fifteenth year of the reign of...Tiberius	2
	3:23	Jesus was about thirty years old when he began	2
	4:19	to proclaim the year of the Lord's favor."	1
	4:25	the heaven was shut up three years and six months	2
	8:42	an only daughter, about twelve years old	2
	8:43	suffering from hemorrhages for twelve years;	2
	12:19	Soul, you have ample goods laid up for many years;	2
	13: 7	For three years I have come looking for fruit	2
	13: 8	He replied, 'Sir, let it alone for one more year	2
	13:11	spirit that had crippled her for eighteen years.	2
	13:16	whom Satan bound for eighteen long years	2
	15:29	'Listen! For all these years I have been working	2
Jhn	2:20	temple...under construction for forty-six years,	2
	5: 5	who had been ill for thirty-eight years.	2
	8:57	"You are not yet fifty years old	2
	11:49	Caiaphas, who was high priest that year, said	1
	11:51	being high priest that year he prophesied	1
	18:13	Caiaphas, the high priest that year.	1
Act	4:22	the man...was more than forty years old.	2
	7: 6	and mistreat them during four hundred years.	2
	7:30	"Now when forty years had passed	2
	7:36	and in the wilderness for forty years.	2
	7:42	forty years in the wilderness, O house of Israel?	2
	9:33	Aeneas, who had been bedridden for eight years	2
	11:26	for an entire year they met with the church	1
	13:20	for about four hundred fifty years.	2
	13:21	God gave them Saul...who reigned for forty years.	2
	18:11	He stayed there a year and six months	1
	19:10	This continued for two years	2
	24:10	many years you have been a judge over this nation.	2
	24:17	after some years I came to bring alms to my nation	2
Rom	15:23	I desire, as I have for many years, to come to you	2
2Co	12: 2	who fourteen years ago was caught up	2
Gal	1:18	Then after three years I did go up to Jerusalem	2
	2: 1	Then after fourteen years I went up again	2
	3:17	law, which came four hundred thirty years later	2
	4:10	days, and months, and seasons, and years.	1
1Ti	5: 9	if she is not less than sixty years old	2
Heb	1:12	you are the same, and your years will never end."	2
	3:10	for forty years. Therefore I was angry	2
	3:17	But with whom was he angry forty years?	2
	9: 7	and he but once a year	1
	9:25	as the high priest enters the Holy Place year after year	1
	10: 1	are continually offered year after year	1
	10: 3	there is a reminder of sin year after year.	1

Jas	4:13	spend a year there, doing business and making money."	1
	5:17	for three years and six months it did not rain	1
2Pe	3: 8	with the Lord one day is like a thousand years	2
	3: 8	and a thousand years are like one day.	2
Rev	9:15	ready for the hour, the day, the month, and the year	1
	20: 2	the dragon...and bound him for a thousand years.	2
	20: 3	until the thousand years were ended.	2
	20: 4	and reigned with Christ a thousand years.	2
	20: 5	until the thousand years were ended.)	2
	20: 6	they will reign with him a thousand years.	2
	20: 7	When the thousand years are ended,	2

hundred years

1. ἑκατονταετής, *hekatontaetēs, 1670*

Rom	4:19	(for he was about a hundred years old)	1

last year

1. πέρυσι, *perysi, 4373*

2Co	8:10	who began last year not only to do something	1
	9: 2	Achaia has been ready since last year;	1

next year

1. μέλλω, *mellō, 3516*

Lke	13: 9	If it bears fruit next year, well and good;	1

yearn

1. ἐπιποθέω, *epipotheō, 2160*

Jas	4: 5	"God yearns jealously for the spirit	1

yeast

1. ζύμη, *zymē, 2434*

Mat	13:33	"The kingdom of heaven is like yeast	1
	16: 6	beware of the yeast of the Pharisees	1
	16:11	Beware of the yeast of the Pharisees	1
	16:12	to beware of the yeast of bread	1
Mrk	8:15	"Watch out—beware of the yeast of the Pharisees	1
	8:15	the yeast of Herod."	1
Lke	12: 1	"Beware of the yeast of the Pharisees	1
	13:21	It is like yeast that a woman took and mixed	1
1Co	5: 6	a little yeast leavens the whole batch of dough?	1
	5: 7	Clean out the old yeast	1
	5: 8	celebrate the festival, not with the old yeast	1
	5: 8	the old yeast, the yeast of malice and evil	1
Gal	5: 9	A little yeast leavens the whole batch of dough.	1

yes

1. ἀλλά, *alla, 247*
2. γάρ, *gar, 1142*
3. γέ, *ge, 1145*
4. δέ, *de, 1254*
5. ἔτι, *eti, 2285*
6. ἴδε, *ide, 2623*
7. μᾶλλον, *mallon, 3437*
8. ναί, *nai, 3721*

Mat	5:37	Let your word be 'Yes, Yes' or 'No, No'	8
	5:37	Let your word be 'Yes, Yes' or 'No, No'	8
	9:28	They said to him, "Yes, Lord."	8
	11: 9	Yes, I tell you, and more than a prophet.	8
	11:26	yes, Father, for such was your gracious will.	8
	13:51	They answered, "Yes."	8
	15:27	"Yes, Lord, yet even the dogs eat the crumbs	8
	17:25	He said, "Yes	8
	21:16	Jesus said to them, "Yes;	8
Lke	7:26	Yes, I tell you, and more than a prophet.	8
	10:21	yes, Father, for such was your gracious will.	8
	11:51	Yes, I tell you, it will be charged	8
	12: 5	Yes, I tell you, fear him!	8
	14:26	yes, and even life itself,	5
	24:21	Yes, and besides all this, it is now the third day	3
Jhn	11:27	She said to him, "Yes, Lord, I believe	8
	16:29	"Yes, now you are speaking plainly	6
	21:15	to him, "Yes, Lord; you know that I love you."	8
	21:16	to him, "Yes, Lord; you know that I love you."	8
Act	5: 8	she said, "Yes, that was the price."	8
	22:27	are you a Roman citizen?" And he said, "Yes."	8
Rom	3:29	God of Gentiles also? Yes, of Gentiles also	8
	8:34	Christ Jesus, who died, yes, who was raised	7
2Co	1:17	say "Yes, yes" and "No, no" at the same time?	8
	1:17	say "Yes, yes" and "No, no" at the same time?	8

2Co	1:18	our word to you has not been "Yes and No."	8
	1:19	not "Yes and No"; but in him it is always "Yes."	8
	1:19	not "Yes and No"; but in him it is always "Yes."	8
	1:20	in Him every one of God's promises is a "Yes."	8
	4:15	Yes, everything is for your sake	2
	5: 8	Yes, we do have confidence	4
Eph	5:27	yes, so that she may be holy and without blemish.	1
Php	1:18	Yes, and I will continue to rejoice	1
	4: 3	Yes, and I ask you also…help these women	8
1Th	2:20	Yes, you are our glory and joy!	2
Phm	1:20	Yes, brother, let me have this benefit from you	8
Jas	5:12	let your "Yes" be yes and your "No" be no	8
	5:12	let your "Yes" be yes and your "No" be no	8
Rev	14:13	"Yes," says the Spirit	8
	16: 7	the altar respond, "Yes, O Lord God, the Almighty	8

yesterday

1. ἐχθές, *echthes, 2396*

Jhn	4:52	"Yesterday at one in the afternoon the fever left	1
Act	7:28	kill me as you killed the Egyptian yesterday?'	1
Heb	13: 8	Jesus Christ is the same yesterday and today	1

yet   *See also* as yet *unseen*

1. Contextual: Not in Greek
2. ἀλλά, *alla, 247*
3. γάρ, *gar, 1142*
4. γέ, *ge, 1145*
5. δέ, *de, 1254*
6. ἔτι, *eti, 2285*
7. καί, *kai, 2779*
8. καίτοι, *kaitoi, 2792*
9. μέντοι, *mentoi, 3530*
10. πάλιν, *palin, 4099*
11. πλήν, *plēn, 4440*

Mat	6:26	barns, and yet your heavenly Father feeds them.	7
	6:29	yet I tell you, even Solomon in all his glory was not	5
	10:29	Yet not one of them will fall to the ground	7
	11:11	yet the least in the kingdom of heaven	5
	11:19	Yet wisdom is vindicated by her deeds."	7
	12: 5	break the sabbath and yet are guiltless?	1
	13:21	yet such a person has no root	5
	14: 9	yet out of regard for his oaths	1
	15:27	"Yes, Lord, yet even the dogs eat the crumbs	3
	26:39	yet not what I want but what you want."	11
Mrk	4:32	yet when it is sown it grows up	7
	6:20	yet he liked to listen to him.	7
	6:26	yet out of regard for his oaths and for the guests	1
	7:24	Yet he could not escape notice	7
	14:36	yet, not what I want, but what you want."	2
Lke	4:26	yet Elijah was sent to none of them	7
	5: 5	Yet if you say so, I will let down the nets."	5
	7:28	yet the least in the kingdom of God	5
	10:11	Yet know this:	11
	12: 6	Yet not one of them is forgotten in God's sight.	7
	12:24	yet God feeds them.	7
	12:27	yet I tell you, even Solomon in all his glory	5
	13:33	Yet today, tomorrow, and the next day	11
	15:29	yet you have never given me even a young goat	7
	18: 5	yet because this widow keeps bothering me	4
	18: 8	yet, when the Son of Man comes	11
	22:42	yet, not my will but yours be done."	11
Jhn	1:10	yet the world did not know him.	7
	3:10	a teacher…and yet you do not understand	7
	3:11	yet you do not receive our testimony.	7
	3:32	yet no one accepts his testimony.	7
	5:40	Yet you refuse to come to me	7
	6:36	you have seen me and yet do not believe.	7
	6:70	Yet one of you is a devil."	7
	7:13	Yet no one would speak openly about him	9
	7:19	Yet none of you keeps the law.	7
	7:27	Yet we know where this man is from;	2
	7:31	Yet many in the crowd believed in him	5
	8:16	Yet even if I do judge, my judgment is valid;	7
	8:37	yet you look for an opportunity to kill me	2
	8:50	Yet I do not seek my own glory;	5
	8:52	yet you say, 'Whoever keeps my word	7
	9:30	and yet he opened my eyes.	7
	16: 5	yet none of you asks me, 'Where are you going?	7
	16:32	Yet I am not alone because the Father is with me.	7
	20:29	who have not seen and yet have come to believe."	7

	21:23	Yet Jesus did not say to him that he would not die	5
Act	5:14	Yet more than ever believers were added to the Lord	5
	5:28	yet here you have filled Jerusalem	7
	7:48	Yet the Most High does not dwell in houses	2
	7:53	received the law…and yet you have not kept it."	1
	14:17	yet he has not left himself without a witness	8
	23: 3	yet in violation of the law you order me to be struck?"	7
	28:17	yet I was arrested in Jerusalem	1
Rom	1:32	yet they not only do them but even applaud	1
	2: 3	and yet do them yourself	1
	5:14	Yet death exercised dominion from Adam to Moses	2
	7: 7	Yet, if it had not been for the law	2
1Co	2: 6	Yet among the mature we do speak wisdom	5
	7:28	Yet those who marry will experience distress	5
	8: 6	yet for us there is one God, the Father	2
	12:20	As it is, there are many members, yet one body.	5
	14:21	yet even then they will not listen to me."	7
2Co	6: 8	We are treated as impostors, and yet are true;	1
	6: 9	as unknown, and yet are well known;	1
	6: 9	as punished, and yet not killed;	1
	6:10	as sorrowful, yet always rejoicing;	5
	6:10	as poor, yet making many rich;	5
	6:10	as having nothing, and yet possessing	1
	8: 9	yet for your sakes he became poor	1
Gal	2:16	yet we know that a person is not justified by the works	5
Php	3: 7	whatever gains I had	2
Col	2: 5	yet I am with you in spirit	2
1Ti	2:15	Yet she will be saved through childbearing	5
2Ti	3:11	Yet the Lord rescued me from all of them.	7
Phm	1: 9	yet I would rather appeal to you on the basis of love	1
Heb	3: 3	Yet Jesus is worthy of more glory than Moses,	3
	3:16	who were they who heard and yet were rebellious?	1
	4:15	who…has been tested as we are, yet without sin.	1
	10:37	For yet "in a very little while,	6
	11:39	Yet all these, though…commended for their faith	7
	12:26	"Yet once more I will shake not only the earth	6
	12:27	This phrase, "Yet once more," indicates…	6
Jas	2:16	and yet you do not supply their bodily needs	1
	3: 4	yet they are guided by a very small rudder	1
	3: 5	the tongue…yet it boasts of great exploits.	7
	4:14	Yet you do not even know what tomorrow	1
1Pe	2: 4	though rejected by mortals yet chosen and precious	5
	2:16	live as free people, yet do not use your freedom	7
	3:16	yet do it with gentleness and reverence.	2
	4:16	Yet if any of you suffers as a Christian	5
1Jn	2: 8	Yet I am writing you a new commandment	10
	3:17	sees…in need and yet refuses help?	1
Jde	1: 8	Yet in the same way these…defile the flesh	9
Rev	2: 6	Yet this is to your credit: you hate…the Nicolaitans	7
	2:13	Yet you are holding fast to my name	7
	3: 4	Yet you have still a few persons in Sardis	2
	3: 8	yet you have kept my word and…not denied my name.	1
	13:14	that had been wounded by the sword and yet lived;	1

no yet

1. οὔπω, *oupō, 4037*

Jhn	7:39	as yet there was no Spirit,	1

not yet

1. μήπω, *mēpō, 3609*
2. οὐδέπω, *oudepō, 4031*
3. οὔπω, *oupō, 4037*

Mat	24: 6	this must take place, but the end is not yet.	3
Mrk	8:21	he said to them, "Do you not yet understand?"	3
Jhn	2: 4	Jesus said to her…My hour has not yet come."	3
	3:24	John…had not yet been thrown into prison.	3
	6:17	and Jesus had not yet come to them.	3
	7: 6	Jesus said to them, "My time has not yet come	3
	7: 8	for my time has not yet fully come."	3
	7:30	because his hour had not yet come.	3
	7:39	because Jesus was not yet glorified.	2
	8:20	because his hour had not yet come.	3
	8:57	"You are not yet fifty years old	3
	11:30	Now Jesus had not yet come to the village	3
	20: 9	for as yet they did not understand the scripture	2
	20:17	because I have not yet ascended to the Father.	3
Act	8:16	as yet the Spirit had not come upon any of them;	3
1Co	8: 2	does not yet have the necessary knowledge;	3
Heb	2: 8	do not yet see everything in subjection to them	3
	9: 8	the way into the sanctuary has not yet been disclosed	1

	12: 4	not yet resisted to the point of…blood.	3
1Jn	3: 2	what we will be has not yet been revealed.	3
Rev	17:10	one is living, and the other has not yet come;	3
	17:12	ten kings who have not yet received a kingdom	3

yield

1. ἀποδίδωμι, *apodidōmi, 625*
2. βλαστάνω, *blastanō, 1056*
3. γίνομαι, *ginomai, 1181*
4. δίδωμι, *didōmi, 1443*
5. ποιέω, *poieō, 4472*
6. φέρω, *pherō, 5770*

Mat	13:22	and it yields nothing.	3
	13:23	who indeed bears fruit and yields	5
Mrk	4: 7	it yielded no grain.	4
	4: 8	growing up and increasing and yielding	6
	4:19	choke the word, and it yields nothing.	3
Heb	12:11	later it yields the…fruit of righteousness	1
Jas	3:12	Can a fig tree, my brothers and sisters, yield olives	5
	3:12	No more can salt water yield fresh.	5
	5:18	and the earth yielded its harvest.	2
Rev	17:13	yielding their power and authority to the beast;	4

yoke

1. ζεῦγος, *zeugos, 2414*
2. ζυγός, *zygos, 2433*

Mat	11:29	Take my yoke upon you, and learn from me;	2
	11:30	For my yoke is easy, and my burden is light."	2
Lke	14:19	Another said, 'I have bought five yoke of oxen	1
Act	15:10	by placing on the neck of the disciples a yoke	2
Gal	5: 1	do not submit again to a yoke of slavery.	2
1Ti	6: 1	all who are under the yoke of slavery	2

you, yourself   Not Indexed

young   *See also* young *donkey,* young *goat*

1. ἐλάσσων, *elassōn, 1781*
2. μικρός, *mikros, 3625*
3. νέος, *neos, 3742*
4. νοσσός, *nossos, 3801*

Mrk	15:40	Mary the mother of James the younger and of Joses	2
Lke	2:24	"a pair of turtledoves or two young pigeons."	4
	15:12	The younger of them said to his father, 'Father	3
	15:13	the younger son gathered all he had	3
	22:26	greatest among you must become like the youngest	3
Jhn	21:18	when you were younger, you used to fasten	3
Rom	9:12	she was told, "The elder shall serve the younger."	1
1Ti	5:11	refuse to put younger widows on the list;	3
	5:14	I would have younger widows marry, bear children	3
1Pe	5: 5	who are younger must accept the authority of the elders.	3

young man

1. νεανίας, *neanias, 3733*
2. νεανίσκος, *neaniskos, 3734*
3. νέος, *neos, 3742*

Mat	19:20	The young man said to him	2
	19:22	the young man heard this word, he went away	2
Mrk	14:51	A certain young man was following him	2
	16: 5	As they entered the tomb, they saw a young man	2
Lke	7:14	he said, "Young man, I say to you, rise!"	2
Act	2:17	your young men shall see visions	2
	5: 6	The young men came and wrapped up his body	3
	5:10	When the young men came in they found her dead	2
	7:58	at the feet of a young man named Saul.	1
	20: 9	A young man named Eutychus	1
	23:17	"Take this young man to the tribune	1
	23:18	Paul…asked me to bring this young man to you;	2
	23:22	So the tribune dismissed the young man	2
1Ti	5: 1	speak…to younger men as brothers	3
Tit	2: 6	urge the younger men to be self-controlled.	3

young person

1. νεανίσκος, *neaniskos, 3734*

1Jn	2:13	I am writing to you, young people	1
	2:14	I write to you, young people, because you are strong	1

young woman

1. νέος, *neos, 3742*

1Ti	5: 2	younger women as sisters—with absolute purity.	1

Tit	2: 4	may encourage the young women to love their husbands	1

youth

1. νεότης, *neotēs, 3744*

Mrk	10:20	"Teacher, I have kept all these since my youth."	1
Lke	18:21	He replied, "I have kept all these since my youth."	1
Act	26: 4	"All the Jews know my way of life from my youth	1
1Ti	4:12	Let no one despise your youth	1

youthful

1. νεωτερικός, *neōterikos, 3754*

2Ti	2:22	Shun youthful passions	1

Z

Zacchaeus

1. Ζακχαῖος, *Zakchaios, 2405*

Lke	19: 2	A man was there named Zacchaeus;	1
	19: 5	"Zacchaeus, hurry and come down;	1
	19: 8	Zacchaeus stood there and said to the Lord,	1

Zadok

1. Σαδώκ, *Sadōk, 4882*

Mat	1:14	Azor the father of Zadok	1
	1:14	and Zadok the father of Achim	1

Zarephath

1. Σάρεπτα, *Sarepta, 4919*

Lke	4:26	to a widow at Zarephath in Sidon.	1

zeal

1. ζῆλος, *zēlos, 2419*
2. σπουδή, *spoudē, 5082*

Jhn	2:17	"Zeal for your house will consume me."	1
Rom	10: 2	I can testify that they have a zeal for God	1
	12:11	not lag in zeal, be ardent in spirit	2
2Co	7: 7	your zeal for me	1
	7:11	what longing, what zeal, what punishment!	1
	7:12	in order that your zeal for us might be made known	2
	9: 2	your zeal has stirred up most of them.	1
Php	3: 6	as to zeal, a persecutor of the church;	1

Zealot

1. ζηλωτής, *zēlōtēs, 2421*

Lke	6:15	Simon, who was called the Zealot	1
Act	1:13	James son of Alphaeus, and Simon the Zealot	1

zealous

1. ζηλωτής, *zēlōtēs, 2421*

Act	21:20	they are all zealous for the law.	1
	22: 3	zealous for God, just as all of you are today	1
Gal	1:14	for I was far more zealous for the traditions	1
Tit	2:14	who are zealous for good deeds.	1

zealously

1. περισσότερος, *perissoteros, 4358*

Mrk	7:36	the more zealously they proclaimed it.	1

Zebedee

1. Ζεβεδαῖος, *Zebedaios, 2411*

Mat	4:21	James son of Zebedee and his brother John	1
	4:21	in the boat with their father Zebedee, mending	1
	10: 2	James son of Zebedee, and his brother John;	1
	20:20	the mother of the sons of Zebedee came to him	1
	26:37	took with him Peter and the two sons of Zebedee	1
	27:56	the mother of the sons of Zebedee.	1
Mrk	1:19	James son of Zebedee and his brother John	1
	1:20	they left their father Zebedee in the boat	1
	3:17	James son of Zebedee	1
	10:35	James and John, the sons of Zebedee, came forward	1
Lke	5:10	so also were James and John, sons of Zebedee	1
Jhn	21: 2	Nathanael of Cana in Galilee, the sons of Zebedee	1

Zebulun

1. Ζαβουλών, *Zaboulōn, 2404*

Mat	4:13	in the territory of Zebulun and Naphtali	1
	4:15	"Land of Zebulun, land of Naphtali	1
Rev	7: 8	from the tribe of Zebulun twelve thousand,	1

Zechariah

1. Ζαχαρίας, *Zacharias*, 2408

Mat	23:35	to the blood of Zechariah son of Barachiah	1
Lke	1: 5	there was a priest named Zechariah	1
	1:12	When Zechariah saw him, he was terrified;	1
	1:13	angel said to him, "Do not be afraid, Zechariah	1
	1:18	Zechariah said to the angel, "How will I know	1
	1:21	the people were waiting for Zechariah	1
	1:40	she entered the house of Zechariah	1
	1:59	going to name him Zechariah after his father.	1
	1:67	Zechariah was filled with the Holy Spirit	1
	3: 2	John son of Zechariah in the wilderness.	1
	11:51	from the blood of Abel to the blood of Zechariah	1

Zenas

1. Ζηνᾶς, *Zēnas*, 2424

Tit   3:13   send Zenas the lawyer and Apollos on their way   1

Zerah

1. Ζάρα, *Zara*, 2406

Mat   1: 3   Judah the father of Perez and Zerah by Tamar   1

Zerubbabel

1. Ζοροβαβέλ, *Zorobabel*, 2431

Mat	1:12	Salathiel the father of Zerubbabel	1
	1:13	Zerubbabel the father of Abiud	1
Lke	3:27	son of Zerubbabel, son of Shealtiel	1

Zeus

1. Ζεύς, *Zeus*, 2416

Act   14:12   Barnabas they called Zeus   1
       14:13   The priest of Zeus...brought oxen and garlands   1

Zion

1. Σιών, *Siōn*, 4994

Mat	21: 5	"Tell the daughter of Zion	1
Jhn	12:15	"Do not be afraid, daughter of Zion.	1
Rom	9:33	"See, I am laying in Zion a stone	1
	11:26	it is written, "Out of Zion will come the Deliverer;	1
Heb	12:22	you have come to Mount Zion	1
1Pe	2: 6	"See, I am laying in Zion a stone, a cornerstone	1
Rev	14: 1	and there was the Lamb, standing on Mount Zion!	1

NUMBERS

1/10 *See* tenth

1/4 *See* fourth

1/3 *See* third

1/2 *See* half

1 *See* one

2 *See* two

3 *See* three

4 *See* four

5 *See* five

6 *See* six

7 *See* seven

8 *See* eight

9 *See* nine

10 *See* ten

11 *See* eleven

12 *See* twelve

14 *See* fourteen

15 *See* fifteen

18 *See* eighteen

20 *See* twenty

24 *See* twenty-four

30 *See* thirty

38 *See* thirty-eight

40 *See* forty

42 *See* forty-two

46 *See* forty-six

50 *See* fifty

60 *See* sixty

70 *See* seventy

75 *See* seventy-five

77 *See* seventy-seven times

80 *See* eighty

84 *See* eighty-four

99 *See* ninety-nine

100 *See* hundred

100 years *See* hundred years

120 *See* hundred, twenty

144 *See* hundred, forty-four

153 *See* hundred, fifty-three

200 *See* two hundred, two hundred miles

276 *See* two hundred, seventy-six

300 *See* three hundred

400 *See* four hundred

430 *See* four hundred, thirty

450 *See* four hundred, fifty

500 *See* five hundred

666 *See* six hundred, sixty-six

1,000 *See* thousand

1,260 *See* thousand, two hundred, sixty

1,500 *See* fifteen hundred miles

2,000 *See* two thousand

3,000 *See* three thousand

4,000 *See* four thousand

5,000 *See* five thousand

7,000 *See* seven thousand, seven, thousand

10,000 *See* two hundred million, ten, ten thousand, thousand

12,000 *See* twelve, thousand

20,000 *See* twenty, thousand

23,000 *See* twenty-three, thousand

50,000 *See* fifty thousand

144,000 *See* hundred, forty-four, thousand

GREEK–ENGLISH INDEX

TO THE

NEW TESTAMENT

OF THE

NEW REVISED STANDARD VERSION

2 Ἀαρών, *Aarōn*
Aaron [5]

3 Ἀβαδδών, *Abaddōn*
Abaddon [1]

4 ἀβαρής, *abarēs*
burden [1]

5 ἀββά, *abba*
Abba [3]

6 Ἅβελ, *Habel*
Abel [4]

7 Ἀβιά, *Abia*
Abijah [3]

8 Ἀβιαθάρ, *Abiathar*
Abiathar [1]

9 Ἀβιληνή, *Abilēnē*
Abilene [1]

10 Ἀβιούδ, *Abioud*
Abiud [2]

11 Ἀβραάμ, *Abraam*
Abraham [73]

12 ἄβυσσος, *abyssos*
bottomless pit [6], abyss [2], pit [1]

13 Ἅγαβος, *Hagabos*
Agabus [2]

14 ἀγαθοεργέω, *agathoergeō*
do good [2]

16 ἀγαθοποιέω, *agathopoieō*
do good [7], do right [2]

17 ἀγαθοποιία, *agathopoiia*
do good [1]

18 ἀγαθοποιός, *agathopoios*
do right [1]

19 ἀγαθός, *agathos*
good [78], good thing [8], clear [2],
generous [2], good deed [2], goods [2],
kind² [2], good man [1], good person [1],
honestly [1], kindly [1], perfect [1],
useful [1]

20 ἀγαθωσύνη, *agathōsynē*
good [2], generosity [1], goodness [1]

21 ἀγαλλίασις, *agalliasis*
gladness [2], glad [1], joy [1], rejoicing [1]

22 ἀγαλλιάω, *agalliaō*
rejoice [8], glad [2], exult [1]

23 ἄγαμος, *agamos*
unmarried [2], unmarried man [1],
unmarried woman [1]

24 ἀγανακτέω, *aganakteō*
angry [4], indignant [2], anger [1]

25 ἀγανάκτησις, *aganaktēsis*
indignation [1]

26 ἀγαπάω, *agapaō*
love [131], beloved [8], cling [1],
desire [1], long² [1], show love [1]

27 ἀγάπη, *agapē*
love [114], beloved [1], love-feast [1]

28 ἀγαπητός, *agapētos*
beloved [56], dear friend [2], dear [1],
love [1], very dear [1]

29 Ἁγάρ, *Hagar*
Hagar [2]

30 ἀγγαρεύω, *angareuō*
compel [2], force [1]

31 ἀγγεῖον, *angeion*
flask [1]

32 ἀγγελία, *angelia*
message [2]

33 ἀγγέλλω, *angellō*
announce [1]

34 ἄγγελος, *angelos*
angel [168], messenger [7]

35 ἄγγος, *angos*
basket [1]

36 ἀγέλη, *agelē*
herd [7]

37 ἀγενεαλόγητος, *agenealogētos*
without genealogy [1]

38 ἀγενής, *agenēs*
low [1]

39 ἁγιάζω, *hagiazō*
sanctify [19], make holy [3], hallow [2],
make sacred [2], dedicate [1], holy [1]

40 ἁγιασμός, *hagiasmos*
sanctification [5], holiness [4], sanctify [1]

41 ἅγιος, *hagios*
holy [155], saint [61], sanctuary [6], holy
one [5], holy place [3], holiness [2], most
holy [1]

42 ἁγιότης, *hagiotēs*
holiness [1]

43 ἁγιωσύνη, *hagiōsynē*
holiness [3]

44 ἀγκάλη, *ankalē*
arm¹ [1]

45 ἄγκιστρον, *ankistron*
hook [1]

46 ἄγκυρα, *ankyra*
anchor [4]

47 ἄγναφος, *agnaphos*
unshrunk [2]

48 ἁγνεία, *hagneia*
purity [2]

49 ἁγνίζω, *hagnizō*
purify [5], complete the rite of
purification [1], go through rite of
purification [1]

50 ἁγνισμός, *hagnismos*
purification [1]

51 ἀγνοέω, *agnoeō*
ignorant [3], not recognize [3], not
understand [3], unknown [3], not
know [2], unaware [2], uninformed [2],
ignorantly [1], not realize [1], *see 4024*
[know] [1], *see 4024* [understand] [1]

52 ἀγνόημα, *agnoēma*
sin committed unintentionally [1]

53 ἄγνοια, *agnoia*
ignorance [4]

54 ἁγνός, *hagnos*
pure [4], chaste [2], guiltless [1],
purity [1]

55 ἁγνότης, *hagnotēs*
pure [1], purity [1]

56 ἁγνῶς, *hagnōs*
sincerely [1]

57 ἀγνωσία, *agnōsia*
ignorance [1], no knowledge [1]

58 ἄγνωστος, agnōstos
unknown [1]

59 ἀγορά, agora
marketplace [10], market [1]

60 ἀγοράζω, agorazō
buy [27], redeem [2], ransom [1]

61 ἀγοραῖος, agoraios
court[2] [1], marketplace [1]

62 ἄγρα, agra
catch [2]

63 ἀγράμματος, agrammatos
uneducated [1]

64 ἀγραυλέω, agrauleō
live in a field [1]

65 ἀγρεύω, agreuō
trap [1]

66 ἀγριέλαιος, agrielaios
wild olive shoot [1], wild olive tree [1]

67 ἄγριος, agrios
wild [3]

68 Ἀγρίππας, Agrippas
Agrippa [11]

69 ἀγρός, agros
field [26], country [6], farm [2],
countryside [1], piece of land [1]

70 ἀγρυπνέω, agrypneō
keep alert [2], alert [1], keep watch
over [1]

71 ἀγρυπνία, agrypnia
sleepless night [2]

72 ἄγω, agō
bring [40], lead [6], go [5], take [3],
come [2], lead away [2], arrest [1], bring
back [1], bring to trial [1], drag [1],
entice [1], go on [1], now [1], on one's
way [1], open [1], sway [1], take away [1]

73 ἀγωγή, agōgē
conduct [1]

74 ἀγών, agōn
fight [2], struggle [2], opposition [1],
race[2] [1]

75 ἀγωνία, agōnia
anguish [1]

76 ἀγωνίζομαι, agōnizomai
fight [3], struggle [2], athlete [1],
strive [1], wrestle [1]

77 Ἀδάμ, Adam
Adam [9]

78 ἀδάπανος, adapanos
free of charge [1]

79 Ἀδδί, Addi
Addi [1]

80 ἀδελφή, adelphē
sister [25], believing wife [1]

81 ἀδελφός, adelphos
brother [136], brother and sister [102],
believer [31], friend [17], beloved [12],
neighbor [6], another [3], comrade [3],
member of the church [3], person [3],
untranslated [3], man [2], member of a
family [2], one another [2], they [2],
another disciple [1], community [1],
family [1], fellow Israelite [1],
husband [1], kindred [1], kinsfolk [1],
member [1], member of God's family [1],
one [1], other [1], relative [1], student [1],
whole community [1], see 467 [friend] [1]

82 ἀδελφότης, adelphotēs
brother and sister [1], family of
believers [1]

83 ἄδηλος, adēlos
indistinct [1], unmarked [1]

84 ἀδηλότης, adēlotēs
uncertainty [1]

85 ἀδήλως, adēlōs
aimlessly [1]

86 ἀδημονέω, adēmoneō
agitate [2], distress [1]

87 ἅδης, hadēs
Hades [10]

88 ἀδιάκριτος, adiakritos
without partiality [1]

89 ἀδιάλειπτος, adialeiptos
constantly [1], unceasing [1]

90 ἀδιαλείπτως, adialeiptōs
constantly [2], without ceasing [2]

92 ἀδικέω, adikeō
wrong [9], do wrong [5], damage [4],
harm [4], do evil [1], evildoer [1], hurt [1],
inflict harm [1], suffer[2] [1], wrongdoer [1]

93 ἀδίκημα, adikēma
crime [2], iniquity [1]

94 ἀδικία, adikia
wickedness [8], dishonest [2], do
wrong [2], iniquity [2], injustice [2],
unrighteousness [2], wrongdoing [2],
false [1], unjust [1], wicked [1],
wrong [1], see 2239 [evildoer] [1]

96 ἄδικος, adikos
unrighteous [5], dishonest [3], unjust [2],
rogue [1], wrongdoer [1]

97 ἀδίκως, adikōs
unjustly [1]

98 Ἀδμίν, Admin
Admin [1]

99 ἀδόκιμος, adokimos
fail [2], counterfeit [1], debased [1],
disqualify [1], fail to meet the test [1],
unfit [1], worthless [1]

100 ἄδολος, adolos
pure [1]

101 Ἀδραμυττηνός, Adramyttēnos
Adramyttium [1]

102 Ἀδρίας, Adrias
Adria [1]

103 ἁδρότης, hadrotēs
generous gift [1]

104 ἀδυνατέω, adynateō
impossible [2]

105 ἀδύνατος, adynatos
impossible [7], can not [2], weak [1]

106 ᾄδω, adō
sing [5]

107 ἀεί, aei
always [5], forever [1], keep on [1]

108 ἀετός, aetos
eagle [3], vulture [2]

109 ἄζυμος, azymos
unleavened bread [7], festival of
unleavened bread [1], unleavened [1]

110 Ἀζώρ, Azōr
Azor [2]

111 Ἄζωτος, Azōtos
Azotus [1]

113 ἀήρ, aēr
air [7]

114 ἀθανασία, athanasia
immortality [3]

116 ἀθέμιτος, athemitos
lawless [1], unlawful [1]

117 ἄθεος, atheos
without God [1]

118 ἄθεσμος, athesmos
lawless [2]

119 ἀθετέω, atheteō
reject [10], violate [2], annul [1],
nullify [1], refuse [1], thwart [1]

120 ἀθέτησις, athetēsis
abrogation [1], remove [1]

121 Ἀθῆναι, Athēnai
Athens [4]

122 Ἀθηναῖος, Athēnaios
Athenian [2]

123 ἀθλέω, athleō
athlete [1], compete [1]

124 ἄθλησις, athlēsis
struggle [1]

125 ἀθροίζω, athroizō
gather together [1]

126 ἀθυμέω, athymeō
lose heart [1]

127 ἀθῷος, athōos
innocent [2]

128 αἴγειος, aigeios
goat [1]

129 αἰγιαλός, aigialos
beach [5], see 2093 [ashore] [1]

130 Αἰγύπτιος, Aigyptios
Egyptian [5]

131 Αἴγυπτος, Aigyptos
Egypt [25]

132 ἀΐδιος, aidios
eternal [2]

133 αἰδώς, aidōs
modestly [1]

134 Αἰθίοψ, Aithiops
Ethiopian [2]

135 αἷμα, haima
blood [92], see 4868 [hemorrhage] [3], see
4380 [hemorrhage] [1], see 4922 [human
being] [1]

136 αἱματεκχυσία, haimatekchysia
shedding of blood [1]

137 αἱμορροέω, haimorroeō
suffer from a hemorrhage [1]

138 Αἰνέας, Aineas
Aeneas [2]

139 αἴνεσις, ainesis
praise [1]

140 αἰνέω, aineō
praise [8]

141 αἴνιγμα, ainigma
see 1877 [dimly] [1]

142 αἶνος, ainos
praise [1]

142 + 1443 αἶνος + δίδωμι, ainos +
didōmi
praise [1]

143 Αἰνών, Ainōn
Aenon [1]

145 αἱρέομαι, *haireomai*
choose [2], prefer [1]

146 αἵρεσις, *hairesis*
sect [6], faction [2], opinion [1]

147 αἱρετίζω, *hairetizō*
choose [1]

148 αἱρετικός, *hairetikos*
cause division [1]

149 αἴρω, *airō*
take [29], take away [21], take up [12],
away [5], remove [5], carry [4], pick
up [3], bear up [2], collect [2], get [2], pull
away [2], raise [2], deny [1], destroy [1],
gather up [1], hoist up [1], lift up [1], put
away [1], set¹ [1], sweep away [1], weigh
anchor [1]

149 + 3836 + 4057 αἴρω + ὁ +
ὀφθαλμός, *airō + ho + ophthalmos*
look [1]

149 + 3836 + 6034 αἴρω + ὁ + ψυχή,
airō + ho + psychē
keep in suspense [1]

149 + 5889 αἴρω + φωνή, *airō + phōnē*
call out [1]

150 αἰσθάνομαι, *aisthanomai*
perceive [1]

151 αἴσθησις, *aisthēsis*
insight [1]

152 αἰσθητήριον, *aisthētērion*
faculty [1]

153 αἰσχροκερδής, *aischrokerdēs*
greedy for gain [1], greedy for money [1]

154 αἰσχροκερδῶς, *aischrokerdōs*
sordid gain [1]

155 αἰσχρολογία, *aischrologia*
abusive language [1]

156 αἰσχρός, *aischros*
shameful [2], disgraceful [1], sordid [1]

157 αἰσχρότης, *aischrotēs*
obscene [1]

158 αἰσχύνη, *aischynē*
shame [4], disgrace [1], shameful thing [1]

159 αἰσχύνομαι, *aischynomai*
ashamed [2], put to shame [2],
disgrace [1]

160 αἰτέω, *aiteō*
ask [49], ask for [10], demand [4], beg [2],
request [2], call [1], make [1], pray [1]

161 αἴτημα, *aitēma*
request [2], demand [1]

162 αἰτία, *aitia*
reason¹ [8], case [4], charge³ [4],
cause [1], cause for a sentence [1], *see
1328* [why] [1]

162 + 5770 αἰτία + φέρω, *aitia + pherō*
charge³ [1]

165 αἴτιος, *aitios*
basis for accusation [1], cause [1], ground
for sentence [1], guilty [1], source [1]

166 αἰτίωμα, *aitiōma*
charge³ [1]

167 αἰφνίδιος, *aiphnidios*
sudden [1], unexpectedly [1]

168 αἰχμαλωσία, *aichmalōsia*
captivity [2], take captive [1]

169 αἰχμαλωτεύω, *aichmalōteuō*
make a captive [1]

170 αἰχμαλωτίζω, *aichmalōtizō*
captivate [1], make captive [1], take away
as captive [1], take captive [1]

171 αἰχμάλωτος, *aichmalōtos*
captive [1]

172 αἰών, *aiōn*
see 1650 [forever] [46], age² [28],
ever [21], *see 4024* [never] [8], world [7],
see 1650 [again] [2], course [1],
eternal [1], eternity [1], forever [1], long
ago [1], old² [1], time¹ [1], world
begin [1], *see 608* [long ago] [1], *see 1650*
[permanent] [1]

173 αἰώνιος, *aiōnios*
eternal [67], age² [2], forever [1], long¹ [1]

174 ἀκαθαρσία, *akatharsia*
impurity [8], filth [1], impure motive [1]

176 ἀκάθαρτος, *akathartos*
unclean [26], foul [4], impure person [1],
impurity [1]

177 ἀκαιρέομαι, *akaireomai*
no opportunity [1]

178 ἀκαίρως, *akairōs*
unfavorable time [1]

179 ἄκακος, *akakos*
blameless [1], simple-minded [1]

180 ἄκανθα, *akantha*
thorn [14]

181 ἀκάνθινος, *akanthinos*
thorn [2]

182 ἄκαρπος, *akarpos*
nothing [2], unfruitful [2],
unproductive [2], without fruit [1]

183 ἀκατάγνωστος, *akatagnōstos*
cannot be censured [1]

184 ἀκατακάλυπτος, *akatakalyptos*
unveiled [2]

185 ἀκατάκριτος, *akatakritos*
uncondemned [2]

186 ἀκατάλυτος, *akatalytos*
indestructible [1]

188 ἀκατάπαυστος, *akatapaustos*
insatiable [1]

189 ἀκαταστασία, *akatastasia*
disorder [3], insurrection [1], riot [1]

190 ἀκατάστατος, *akatastatos*
restless [1], unstable [1]

192 Ἁκελδαμάχ, *Hakeldamach*
Hakeldama [1]

193 ἀκέραιος, *akeraios*
innocent [2], guileless [1]

195 ἀκλινής, *aklinēs*
without wavering [1]

196 ἀκμάζω, *akmazō*
ripe [1]

197 ἀκμήν, *akmēn*
still¹ [1]

198 ἀκοή, *akoē*
hear [10], ear [2], fame [2], message [2],
rumor [2], *see 201* [listen indeed] [2],
listen [1], report [1], sound¹ [1],
understanding [1]

199 ἀκολουθέω, *akoloutheō*
follow [89], follower [1]

201 ἀκούω, *akouō*
hear [338], listen [76], accept [2],
hearer [2], report [2], come [1], come to

ear [1], give a hearing [1], understand [1],
see 201 [listen indeed] [1]

201 + 198 ἀκούω + ἀκοή, *akouō +
akoē*
listen indeed [2]

201 + 201 ἀκούω + ἀκούω, *akouō +
akouō*
listen indeed [1]

202 ἀκρασία, *akrasia*
lack of self-control [1], self-indulgence [1]

203 ἀκρατής, *akratēs*
profligate [1]

204 ἄκρατος, *akratos*
unmixed [1]

205 ἀκρίβεια, *akribeia*
strictly [1]

207 ἀκριβής, *akribēs*
strict [1]

208 ἀκριβόω, *akriboō*
learn [1], learn exact [1]

209 ἀκριβῶς, *akribōs*
accurately [1], carefully [1], diligently [1],
more accurately [1], more thorough [1],
more thoroughly [1], rather well [1], very
well [1], *see 1063* [careful] [1]

210 ἀκρίς, *akris*
locust [4]

211 ἀκροατήριον, *akroatērion*
audience hall [1]

212 ἀκροατής, *akroatēs*
hearer [4]

213 ἀκροβυστία, *akrobystia*
uncircumcised [9], uncircumcision [7],
before one is circumcised [3], without
being circumcised [1]

214 ἀκρογωνιαῖος, *akrogōniaios*
cornerstone [2]

215 ἀκροθίνιον, *akrothinion*
spoil [1]

216 ἄκρον, *akron*
end [3], other [1], tip [1], top [1]

217 Ἀκύλας, *Akylas*
Aquila [6]

218 ἀκυρόω, *akyroō*
make void [2], annul [1]

219 ἀκωλύτως, *akōlytōs*
without hindrance [1]

220 ἄκων, *akōn*
not of one's will [1]

223 ἀλάβαστρος, *alabastros*
alabaster jar [3], jar [1]

224 ἀλαζονεία, *alazoneia*
arrogance [1], pride [1]

225 ἀλαζών, *alazōn*
boaster [1], boastful [1]

226 ἀλαλάζω, *alalazō*
clang [1], wail [1]

227 ἀλάλητος, *alalētos*
too deep for a word [1]

228 ἄλαλος, *alalos*
keep from speaking [1], mute [1], unable
to speak [1]

229 ἅλας, *halas*
salt [8]

230 ἀλείφω, *aleiphō*
anoint [8], put oil on [1]

231 ἀλεκτοροφωνία, alektorophōnia
cockcrow [1]

232 ἀλέκτωρ, alektōr
cock [12]

233 Ἀλεξανδρεύς, Alexandreus
Alexandria [1], Alexandrian [1]

234 Ἀλεξανδρῖνος, Alexandrinos
Alexandrian [2]

235 Ἀλέξανδρος, Alexandros
Alexander [6]

236 ἄλευρον, aleuron
flour [2]

237 ἀλήθεια, alētheia
truth [95], true [7], truly [3], fact [1],
surely [1], truthful [1], truthfulness [1]

238 ἀληθεύω, alētheuō
speak the truth [1], tell the truth [1]

239 ἀληθής, alēthēs
true [19], valid [3], sincere [2], real [1],
truth [1]

240 ἀληθινός, alēthinos
true [26], true one [1], valid [1]

241 ἀλήθω, alēthō
grind meal [1]

241 + 1877 + 3836 + 3685 ἀλήθω + ἐν
+ ὁ + μύλος, alēthō + en + ho + mylos
grind meal [1]

242 ἀληθῶς, alēthōs
truly [10], really [3], certainly [2],
indeed [1], truth [1], see 3857 [sure] [1]

243 ἁλιεύς, halieus
fisherman [3], fish [2]

244 ἁλιεύω, halieuō
fish [1]

245 ἁλίζω, halizō
restore saltiness [1], salt [1]

246 ἁλίσγημα, alisgēma
pollute [1]

247 ἀλλά, alla
but [511], untranslated [46], rather [12],
yet [12], no [6], what [6], and [5],
instead [5], nevertheless [5], then [5],
contrary [4], indeed [3], even though [2],
now [2], only [2], yes [2], again [1],
certainly [1], even [1], however [1],
mere [1], moreover [1], so [1], though [1]

247 + 3590 ἀλλά + μή, alla + mē
except [1]

247 + 4498 + 3437 ἀλλά + πολύς +
μᾶλλον, alla + polys + mallon
contrary [1]

248 ἀλλάσσω, allassō
change [5], exchange [1]

249 ἀλλαχόθεν, allachothen
another way [1]

250 ἀλλαχοῦ, allachou
untranslated [1]

251 ἀλληγορέω, allēgoreō
allegory [1]

252 ἀλληλουϊά, hallēlouia
Hallelujah [4]

253 ἀλλήλων, allēlōn
one another [81], each other [8],
themselves [3], yourself [2],
untranslated [2], another [1], company [1],
mutual [1], other [1]

254 ἀλλογενής, allogenēs
foreigner [1]

256 ἅλλομαι, hallomai
gush up [1], leap [1], spring up [1]

257 ἄλλος, allos
other [73], another [55], more [5],
someone else [5], else [4], one [4],
some [3], also [1], any other [1], other
thing [1], otherwise [1], then [1],
untranslated [1]

258 ἀλλοτριεπίσκοπος,
allotriepiskopos
mischief maker [1]

259 ἀλλότριος, allotrios
other [4], another [2], foreign [2],
someone else [2], stranger [2], belong to
others [1], not one's own [1]

260 ἀλλόφυλος, allophylos
Gentile [1]

261 ἄλλως, allōs
not [1]

262 ἀλοάω, aloaō
tread out grain [2], thresh [1]

263 ἄλογος, alogos
irrational [2], unreasonable [1]

264 ἀλόη, aloē
aloe [1]

266 ἁλυκός, halykos
salt [1]

267 ἄλυπος, alypos
less anxious [1]

268 ἅλυσις, halysis
chain [11]

269 ἀλυσιτελής, alysitelēs
harmful [1]

270 ἄλφα, alpha
Alpha [3]

271 Ἁλφαῖος, Halphaios
Alphaeus [5]

272 ἅλων, halōn
threshing floor [2]

273 ἀλώπηξ, alōpēx
fox [3]

274 ἅλωσις, halōsis
catch [1]

275 ἅμα, hama
same time [3], together [2],
untranslated [2], along [1], besides [1],
one thing more [1]

276 ἀμαθής, amathēs
ignorant [1]

277 ἀμαράντινος, amarantinos
never fades away [1]

278 ἀμάραντος, amarantos
unfading [1]

279 ἁμαρτάνω, hamartanō
sin [38], commit an offense [1], commit
sin [1], do wrong [1], persist in sin [1],
sinful [1]

280 ἁμάρτημα, hamartēma
sin [4]

281 ἁμαρτία, hamartia
sin [171], sinful [2]

282 ἀμάρτυρος, amartyros
without a witness [1]

283 ἁμαρτωλός, hamartōlos
sinner [43], sinful [4]

285 ἄμαχος, amachos
avoid quarreling [1], not quarrelsome [1]

286 ἀμάω, amaō
mow [1]

287 ἀμέθυστος, amethystos
amethyst [1]

288 ἀμελέω, ameleō
neglect [2], have no concern [1], make
light [1]

289 ἄμεμπτος, amemptos
blameless [3], blamelessly [1],
faultless [1]

290 ἀμέμπτως, amemptōs
blameless [2]

291 ἀμέριμνος, amerimnos
free from anxiety [1], out of trouble [1]

292 ἀμετάθετος, ametathetos
unchangeable [2]

293 ἀμετακίνητος, ametakinētos
immovable [1]

294 ἀμεταμέλητος, ametamelētos
bring no regret [1], irrevocable [1]

295 ἀμετανόητος, ametanoētos
impenitent [1]

296 ἄμετρος, ametros
beyond limit [2]

297 ἀμήν, amēn
truly [50], amen [27], see 297 [very
truly] [25], untranslated [2]

297 + 297 ἀμήν + ἀμήν, amēn + amēn
very truly [25]

298 ἀμήτωρ, amētōr
without mother [1]

299 ἀμίαντος, amiantos
undefiled [4]

300 Ἀμιναδάβ, Aminadab
Aminadab [2], Amminadab [1]

302 ἄμμος, ammos
sand [4], grain of sand [1]

303 ἀμνός, amnos
lamb [4]

304 ἀμοιβή, amoibē
repayment [1]

306 ἄμπελος, ampelos
vine [7], grapevine [1], vintage [1]

307 ἀμπελουργός, ampelourgos
gardener [1]

308 ἀμπελών, ampelōn
vineyard [23]

309 Ἀμπλιᾶτος, Ampliatos
Ampliatus [1]

310 ἀμύνομαι, amynomai
defend [1]

311 ἀμφιβάλλω, amphiballō
cast a net [1]

312 ἀμφίβληστρον, amphiblēstron
net [1]

313 ἀμφιέζω, amphiezō
clothe [1]

314 ἀμφιέννυμι, amphiennymi
dress [2], clothe [1]

315 Ἀμφίπολις, Amphipolis
Amphipolis [1]

316 ἄμφοδον, amphodon
street [1]

317 ἀμφότεροι, amphoteroi
both [12], all [2]

318 ἀμώμητος, amōmētos
without blemish [1]

319 ἄμωμον, amōmon
spice [1]

320 ἄμωμος, amōmos
without blemish [4], blameless [3],
without defect [1]

322 Ἀμώς, Amōs
Amos [3]

323 ἄν, an
untranslated [45], see 4005
[whoever] [25], see 4005 [who] [17],
see 2401 [until] [16], see 4005
[whatever] [10], see 5515 [what] [5],
if [4], see 2401 [before] [4], see 3968
[so that] [4], see 4005 [any] [3], see 4005
[you] [3], see 2776 [as] [2], see 3963
[wherever] [2], see 4005 [one] [2],
see 4005 [whenever] [2], see 4015
[whoever] [2], see 4246 [whatever] [2],
see 6055 [when] [2], perhaps [1], then [1],
though [1], will[1] [1], see 608 [when] [1],
see 948 [until] [1], see 2471
[whenever] [1], see 4005 [that] [1],
see 4012 [all] [1], see 4012 [everyone] [1],
see 4012 [whatever] [1], see 4012
[wherever] [1], see 4570 [before] [1],
see 5515 [which] [1], see 6055 [as soon
as] [1]

324 ἀνά, ana
each [4], untranslated [3], in [2]

324 + 3545 ἀνά + μέσος, ana + mesos
among [1], between [1], center [1], in [1]

325 ἀναβαθμός, anabathmos
step[2] [2]

326 ἀναβαίνω, anabainō
go up [34], ascend [13], come up [7],
go [6], grow up [4], rise [4], come [3], get
into [2], arise [1], climb in [1], climb
up [1], conceive [1], get in [1], go
aboard [1], go on board [1], go
upstairs [1], march up [1]

327 ἀναβάλλω, anaballō
adjourn [1]

328 ἀναβιβάζω, anabibazō
draw[2] [1]

329 ἀναβλέπω, anablepō
look up [8], receive sight [7], regain
sight [7], see again [2], restore sight [1]

330 ἀνάβλεψις, anablepsis
recovery of sight [1]

331 ἀναβοάω, anaboaō
cry [1]

332 ἀναβολή, anabolē
lose time [1]

333 ἀνάγαιον, anagaion
room upstairs [2]

334 ἀναγγέλλω, anangellō
declare [4], tell [3], proclaim [2],
announce [1], disclose [1], proclaim the
message [1], relate [1], report [1]

335 ἀναγεννάω, anagennaō
bear anew [1], give a new birth [1]

336 ἀναγινώσκω, anaginōskō
read [28], read aloud [2], reader [2]

337 ἀναγκάζω, anankazō
compel [5], force [2], make [2]

338 ἀναγκαῖος, anankaios
necessary [4], close [1], indispensable [1],
more necessary [1], urgent [1]

339 ἀναγκαστῶς, anankastōs
compulsion [1]

340 ἀνάγκη, anankē
distress [2], hardship [2], must [2],
necessary [2], bind [1], must [2],
crisis [1], force [1], necessarily [1],
necessity [1], need [1], obligation [1]

340 + 2400 ἀνάγκη + ἔχω, anankē +
echō
must [1]

341 ἀναγνωρίζω, anagnōrizō
make known [1]

342 ἀνάγνωσις, anagnōsis
read [3]

343 ἀνάγω, anagō
set sail [9], bring up [3], put to sea [3],
lead up [2], bring back [1], bring out [1],
offer [1], put out [1], sail [1], take [1]

344 ἀναδείκνυμι, anadeiknymi
appoint [1], show [1]

345 ἀνάδειξις, anadeixis
appear publicly [1]

346 ἀναδέχομαι, anadechomai
receive [2]

347 ἀναδίδωμι, anadidōmi
deliver [1]

348 ἀναζάω, anazaō
alive again [1], revive [1]

349 ἀναζητέω, anazēteō
look for [2], search [1]

350 ἀναζώννυμι, anazōnnymi
prepare for action [1]

351 ἀναζωπυρέω, anazōpyreō
rekindle [1]

352 ἀναθάλλω, anathallō
revive [1]

353 ἀνάθεμα, anathema
accursed [4], curse [1], strictly [1]

354 ἀναθεματίζω, anathematizō
bind by oath [3], curse [1]

355 ἀναθεωρέω, anatheōreō
consider [1], look carefully [1]

356 ἀνάθημα, anathēma
gift dedicated to God [1]

357 ἀναίδεια, anaideia
persistence [1]

358 ἀναίρεσις, anairesis
kill [1]

359 ἀναιρέω, anaireō
kill [16], put to death [3], abolish [1],
adopt [1], condemn to death [1],
destroy [1], do away with [1]

360 ἀναίτιος, anaitios
guiltless [2]

361 ἀνακαθίζω, anakathizō
sit up [2]

362 ἀνακαινίζω, anakainizō
restore [1]

363 ἀνακαινόω, anakainoō
renew [2]

364 ἀνακαίνωσις, anakainōsis
renew [1], renewal [1]

365 ἀνακαλύπτω, anakalyptō
unveiled [1], untranslated [1]

366 ἀνακάμπτω, anakamptō
return [4]

367 ἀνάκειμαι, anakeimai
at table [4], guest [3], sit at table [2], take
one's place [2], recline [1], seat [1], sit at
dinner [1]

368 ἀνακεφαλαιόω, anakephalaioō
gather up [1], sum up [1]

369 ἀνακλίνω, anaklinō
eat [2], sit down [2], lay [1], sit down to
eat [1]

371 ἀνακράζω, anakrazō
cry out [3], shout [1], shout out [1]

373 ἀνακρίνω, anakrinō
examine [6], judge [3], discern [2], raise a
question [2], call to account [1],
question [1], subject to scrutiny [1]

374 ἀνάκρισις, anakrisis
examine [1]

376 ἀνακύπτω, anakyptō
straighten up [2], stand up [1], stand up
straight [1]

377 ἀναλαμβάνω, analambanō
take up [7], take [2], take on board [2],
get [1], take along [1]

378 ἀνάλημψις, analēmpsis
take up [1]

381 ἀναλογία, analogia
proportion [1]

382 ἀναλογίζομαι, analogizomai
consider [1]

383 ἄναλος, analos
lose saltiness [1]

384 ἀναλόω, analoō
consume [2]

385 ἀνάλυσις, analysis
departure [1]

386 ἀναλύω, analyō
depart [1], return [1]

387 ἀναμάρτητος, anamartētos
without sin [1]

388 ἀναμένω, anamenō
wait[1] [1]

389 ἀναμιμνῄσκω, anamimnēskō
remember [3], remind [2], recall [1]

390 ἀνάμνησις, anamnēsis
remembrance [3], reminder [1]

391 ἀνανεόομαι, ananeoomai
renew [1]

392 ἀνανήφω, ananēphō
escape [1]

393 Ἀνανίας, Hananias
Ananias [11]

394 ἀναντίρρητος, anantirrētos
cannot be denied [1]

395 ἀναντιρρήτως, anantirrētōs
without objection [1]

396 ἀνάξιος, anaxios
incompetent [1]

397 ἀναξίως, anaxiōs
unworthy manner [1]

398 ἀνάπαυσις, anapausis
rest[1] [2], resting place [2], cease [1]

399 ἀναπαύω, anapauō
rest[1] [4], refresh [3], take a rest [2], give
rest [1], relax [1], set at rest [1]

400 ἀναπείθω, anapeithō
persuade [1]

401 ἀνάπειρος, anapeiros
cripple [2]

402 ἀναπέμπω, anapempō
send back [3], send [1], send off [1]

403 ἀναπηδάω, anapēdaō
spring up [1]

404 ἀναπίπτω, anapiptō
sit down [6], take one's place at table [3],
recline [2], table [1]

405 ἀναπληρόω, anaplēroō
fulfill [2], make up [2], fill up [1], in [1]

406 ἀναπολόγητος, anapologētos
no excuse [1], without excuse [1]

408 ἀναπτύσσω, anaptyssō
unroll [1]

409 ἀνάπτω, anaptō
kindle [1], set ablaze [1]

410 ἀναρίθμητος, anarithmētos
innumerable [1]

411 ἀνασείω, anaseiō
stir up [2]

412 ἀνασκευάζω, anaskeuazō
unsettle [1]

413 ἀνασπάω, anaspaō
pull out [1], pull up [1]

414 ἀνάστασις, anastasis
resurrection [40], rise [2]

415 ἀναστατόω, anastatoō
stir up revolt [1], turn upside down [1],
unsettle [1]

416 ἀνασταυρόω, anastauroō
crucify again [1]

417 ἀναστενάζω, anastenazō
sigh deeply [1]

418 ἀναστρέφω, anastrephō
live [3], behave [2], return [2], act [1],
treat [1]

419 ἀναστροφή, anastrophē
conduct [5], life [3], way of life [2], lead a
life [1], way [1], untranslated [1]

421 ἀνατάσσομαι, anatassomai
set down [1]

422 ἀνατέλλω, anatellō
rise [6], dawn [1], descend [1], make
rise [1]

423 ἀνατίθημι, anatithēmi
lay before [2]

424 ἀνατολή, anatolē
east [6], rise [3], dawn [1]

424 + 2463 ἀνατολή + ἥλιος, anatolē
+ hēlios
east [1]

426 ἀνατρέπω, anatrepō
upset [2], overturn [1]

427 ἀνατρέφω, anatrephō
bring up [3]

428 ἀναφαίνω, anaphainō
appear [1], come in sight [1]

429 ἀναφέρω, anapherō
offer [5], bear[1] [2], lead up [2], carry
up [1]

430 ἀναφωνέω, anaphōneō
exclaim [1]

431 ἀνάχυσις, anachysis
excess [1]

432 ἀναχωρέω, anachōreō
depart [3], go away [3], leave [3],
withdraw [3], draw aside [1], go [1]

433 ἀνάψυξις, anapsyxis
refresh [1]

434 ἀναψύχω, anapsychō
refresh [1]

435 ἀνδραποδιστής, andrapodistēs
slave trader [1]

436 Ἀνδρέας, Andreas
Andrew [13]

437 ἀνδρίζομαι, andrizomai
courageous [1]

438 Ἀνδρόνικος, Andronikos
Andronicus [1]

439 ἀνδροφόνος, androphonos
murderer [1]

441 ἀνέγκλητος, anenklētos
blameless [3], irreproachable [1], prove
blameless [1]

442 ἀνεκδιήγητος, anekdiēgētos
indescribable [1]

443 ἀνεκλάλητος, aneklalētos
indescribable [1]

444 ἀνέκλειπτος, anekleiptos
unfailing [1]

445 ἀνεκτός, anektos
more tolerable [5]

446 ἀνελεήμων, aneleēmōn
ruthless [1]

447 ἀνέλεος, aneleos
without mercy [1]

448 ἀνεμίζω, anemizō
driven by the wind [1]

449 ἄνεμος, anemos
wind [28], see 3278 [windstorm] [2]

449 + 3489 ἄνεμος + μέγας, anemos +
megas
gale [1]

450 ἀνένδεκτος, anendektos
bind [1]

451 ἀνεξεραύνητος, anexeraunētos
unsearchable [1]

452 ἀνεξίκακος, anexikakos
patient [1]

453 ἀνεξιχνίαστος, anexichniastos
boundless [1], inscrutable [1]

454 ἀνεπαίσχυντος, anepaischyntos
no need to be ashamed [1]

455 ἀνεπίλημπτος, anepilēmptos
above reproach [2], without blame [1]

456 ἀνέρχομαι, anerchomai
go up [3]

457 ἄνεσις, anesis
relief [2], liberty [1], rest[1] [1]

457 + 2400 ἄνεσις + ἔχω, anesis + echō
rest[1] [1]

458 ἀνετάζω, anetazō
examine [2]

459 ἄνευ, aneu
without[1] [2], apart [1]

460 ἀνεύθετος, aneuthetos
not suitable [1]

461 ἀνευρίσκω, aneuriskō
find [1], look up [1]

462 ἀνέχομαι, anechomai
put up with [5], bear[1] [3], bear with [3],
endure [2], accept a complaint [1],
submit [1]

463 ἀνεψιός, anepsios
cousin [1]

464 ἄνηθον, anēthon
dill [1]

465 ἀνήκω, anēkō
duty [1], fitting [1], see 4024 [out of
place] [1]

466 ἀνήμερος, anēmeros
brute [1]

467 ἀνήρ, anēr
man [104], husband [48],
untranslated [30], person [5], they [4],
you [4], fellow [2], one [2], that [2],
adult [1], anyone [1], citizen [1],
friend [1], he [1], representative [1],
sir [1], some [1], see 1222 [marry] [1], see
2400 [marry] [1], see 4024 [virgin] [1]

467 + 81 ἀνήρ + ἀδελφός, anēr +
adelphos
friend [1]

467 + 1222 ἀνήρ + γυνή, anēr + gynē
marry [2]

467 + 1222 + 2400 ἀνήρ + γυνή + ἔχω,
anēr + gynē + echō
marry [1]

468 ἀνθίστημι, anthistēmi
resist [6], oppose [5], withstand [3]

469 ἀνθομολογέομαι,
anthomologeomai
praise [1]

470 ἄνθος, anthos
flower [4]

471 ἀνθρακιά, anthrakia
charcoal fire [2]

472 ἄνθραξ, anthrax
coal [1]

473 ἀνθρωπάρεσκος, anthrōpareskos
please [2]

474 ἀνθρώπινος, anthrōpinos
human [5], common to everyone [1],
human term [1]

475 ἀνθρωποκτόνος, anthrōpoktonos
murderer [3]

476 ἄνθρωπος, anthrōpos
man [200], person [75], human [50],
untranslated [34], other [24], mortal [18],
one [18], human being [15], see 4246
[everyone] [13], that [12], they [11],
anyone [10], someone [9], see 4246
[all] [8], humankind [7], self [6], you [5],
everyone [4], all [2], friend [2], human
authority [2], man and woman [2], merely
human [2], being [1], daily life [1],
doubter [1], everybody [1], fellow [1],
human inclination [1], humanity [1],
intruder [1], master [1], nature [1],
shepherd [1], we [1], who [1], whoever [1],
witness [1], world [1], see 3284 [show
partiality] [1], see 5516 [anyone] [1], see
5626 [humankind] [1], see 5626
[mortal] [1], see 5626 [person] [1]

478 ἀνθύπατος, anthypatos
proconsul [5]

479 ἀνίημι, aniēmi
leave [1], loosen [1], stop [1], unfasten [1]

481 ἄνιπτος, aniptos
unwashed [1], without washing [1]

482 ἀνίστημι, anistēmi
get up [36], stand up [14], rise [13], raise
up [10], rise again [8], rise up [6],
arise [4], raise [3], come [2], set out [2],
stand[1] [2], *untranslated* [2], help up [1],
leave [1], rule[1] [1], set off [1], take
action [1]

483 Ἄννα, Hanna
Anna [1]

484 Ἄννας, Hannas
Annas [4]

485 ἀνόητος, anoētos
foolish [5], senseless [1]

486 ἄνοια, anoia
folly [1], fury [1]

487 ἀνοίγω, anoigō
open [71], begin [1], frankly [1], wide
open [1]

487 + 3836 + 5125 ἀνοίγω + ὁ +
στόμα, anoigō + ho + stoma
speak [3]

488 ἀνοικοδομέω, anoikodomeō
rebuild [2]

489 + 3836 + 5125 ἄνοιξις + ὁ + στόμα,
anoixis + ho + stoma
speak [1]

490 ἀνομία, anomia
lawlessness [6], iniquity [2], lawless
deed [1], lawless one [1], wickedness [1],
see 490 [greater and greater iniquity] [1],
see 2237 [evildoer] [1], *see 4472*
[evildoer] [1]

490 + 1650 + 490 ἀνομία + εἰς +
ἀνομία, anomia + eis + anomia
greater and greater iniquity [1]

491 ἄνομος, anomos
outside the law [4], lawless [3], free from
law [1], lawless one [1]

492 ἀνόμως, anomōs
apart from the law [2]

494 ἀνορθόω, anorthoō
lift [1], set up [1], stand up straight [1]

495 ἀνόσιος, anosios
unholy [2]

496 ἀνοχή, anochē
forbearance [2]

497 ἀνταγωνίζομαι, antagōnizomai
struggle [1]

498 ἀντάλλαγμα, antallagma
return [2]

499 ἀνταναπληρόω, antanaplēroō
complete [1]

500 ἀνταποδίδωμι, antapodidōmi
repay [5], receive a gift in return [1],
return [1]

501 ἀνταπόδομα, antapodoma
repay [1], retribution [1]

502 ἀνταπόδοσις, antapodosis
reward [1]

503 ἀνταποκρίνομαι, antapokrinomai
argue [1], reply [1]

504 ἀντέχω, antechō
devote [2], have a firm grasp [1], help [1]

505 ἀντί, anti
for [11], instead [2], because [1],
place [1], sake [1], upon [1]

505 + 4005 ἀντί + ὅς, anti + hos
because [3], therefore [1]

505 + 4047 ἀντί + οὗτος, anti + houtos
reason[1] [1]

506 ἀντιβάλλω, antiballō
discuss [1]

507 ἀντιδιατίθημι, antidiatithēmi
opponent [1]

508 ἀντίδικος, antidikos
accuser [3], adversary [1], opponent [1]

509 ἀντίθεσις, antithesis
contradiction [1]

510 ἀντικαθίστημι, antikathistēmi
resist [1]

511 ἀντικαλέω, antikaleō
invite in return [1]

512 ἀντίκειμαι, antikeimai
opponent [3], adversary [2], oppose [2],
contrary [1]

513 ἄντικρυς, antikrys
opposite [1]

514 ἀντιλαμβάνω, antilambanō
benefit [1], help [1], support [1]

515 ἀντιλέγω, antilegō
contradict [3], contrary [1], object[2] [1],
oppose [1], say [1], say in opposition [1],
set against [1], speak against [1], talk
back [1]

516 ἀντίλημψις, antilēmpsis
assistance [1]

517 ἀντιλογία, antilogia
dispute [2], hostility [1], rebellion [1]

518 ἀντιλοιδορέω, antiloidoreō
return abuse [1]

519 ἀντίλυτρον, antilytron
ransom [1]

520 ἀντιμετρέω, antimetreō
get back measure [1]

521 ἀντιμισθία, antimisthia
penalty [1], return [1]

522 Ἀντιόχεια, Antiocheia
Antioch [18]

523 Ἀντιοχεύς, Antiocheus
Antioch [1]

524 ἀντιπαρέρχομαι, antiparerchomai
pass by on the other side [2]

525 Ἀντιπᾶς, Antipas
Antipas [1]

526 Ἀντιπατρίς, Antipatris
Antipatris [1]

527 ἀντιπέρα, antipera
opposite [1]

528 ἀντιπίπτω, antipiptō
oppose [1]

529 ἀντιστρατεύομαι, antistrateuomai
war [1]

530 ἀντιτάσσω, antitassō
oppose [3], resist [2]

531 ἀντίτυπος, antitypos
copy [1], prefigure [1]

532 ἀντίχριστος, antichristos
antichrist [5]

533 ἀντλέω, antleō
draw[2] [3], draw out [1]

534 ἄντλημα, antlēma
bucket [1]

535 ἀντοφθαλμέω, antophthalmeō
turn head-on [1]

536 ἄνυδρος, anydros
waterless [4]

537 ἀνυπόκριτος, anypokritos
genuine [3], sincere [2], without
hypocrisy [1]

538 ἀνυπότακτος, anypotaktos
disobedient [1], outside one's control [1],
rebellious [1], rebellious person [1]

539 ἄνω, anō
above [5], brim [1], heavenly [1], up [1],
upward [1]

540 ἄνωθεν, anōthen
from above [7], top [3], from the very
first [1], long time [1], *see 4099*
[again] [1]

541 ἀνωτερικός, anōterikos
interior [1]

542 ἀνώτερος, anōteros
above [1], high [1]

543 ἀνωφελής, anōphelēs
ineffectual [1], unprofitable [1]

544 ἀξίνη, axinē
ax [2]

545 ἄξιος, axios
worthy [24], deserve [12], advisable [1],
consistent [1], right[1] [1], worth [1], *see
4024* [unworthy] [1]

546 ἀξιόω, axioō
consider worthy [1], decide [1],
deserve [1], like[2] [1], make worthy [1],
presume [1], worthy [1]

547 ἀξίως, axiōs
worthy [3], worthy manner [2], fitting [1]

548 ἀόρατος, aoratos
invisible [5]

550 ἀπαγγέλλω, apangellō
tell [24], report [10], declare [5],
announce [2], proclaim [2], bring
word [1], say [1]

551 ἀπάγχω, apanchō
hang [1]

552 ἀπάγω, apagō
lead away [5], lead [3], take [3], bring [2],
lead astray [1], put to death [1]

553 ἀπαίδευτος, apaideutos
senseless [1]

554 ἀπαίρω, apairō
take away [3]

555 ἀπαιτέω, apaiteō
ask again [1], demand [1]

556 ἀπαλγέω, apalgeō
lose all sensitivity [1]

557 ἀπαλλάσσω, apallassō
free [1], leave [1], settle a case [1]

558 ἀπαλλοτριόω, apallotrioō
alien [1], alienate [1], estrange [1]

559 ἁπαλός, hapalos
tender [2]

560 ἀπαντάω, apantaō
approach [1], meet [1]

561 ἀπάντησις, apantēsis
meet [3]

562 ἅπαξ, hapax
once[1] [8], once for all [5]

562 + 2779 + 1489 ἅπαξ + καί + δίς,
hapax + kai + dis
again and again [1]

563 ἀπαράβατος, *aparabatos*
permanently [1]

564 ἀπαρασκεύαστος, *aparaskeuastos*
not ready [1]

565 ἀπαρνέομαι, *aparneomai*
deny [11]

568 ἀπαρτισμός, *apartismos*
complete [1]

569 ἀπαρχή, *aparchē*
first fruit [7], first convert [2]

570 ἅπας, *hapas*
all [20], everything [6], all things [3], whole [2], as a body [1], utmost [1], *see 4024* [none] [1]

571 ἀπασπάζομαι, *apaspazomai*
say farewell [1]

572 ἀπατάω, *apataō*
deceive [3]

573 ἀπάτη, *apatē*
lure [2], deceit [1], deceitfulness [1], deception [1], delude [1], dissipation [1]

574 ἀπάτωρ, *apatōr*
without father [1]

575 ἀπαύγασμα, *apaugasma*
reflection [1]

577 ἀπείθεια, *apeitheia*
disobedience [4], disobedient [3]

578 ἀπειθέω, *apeitheō*
disobedient [5], not obey [4], disobey [2], refuse to believe [1], unbeliever [1], unbelieving [1]

579 ἀπειθής, *apeithēs*
disobedient [5], rebellious [1]

580 ἀπειλέω, *apeileō*
threaten [1], warn [1]

581 ἀπειλή, *apeilē*
threat [2], threaten [1]

582 ἄπειμι¹, *apeimi¹*
absent [5], away [2]

583 ἄπειμι², *apeimi²*
go [1]

584 ἀπεῖπον, *apeipon*
renounce [1]

585 ἀπείραστος, *apeirastos*
cannot be tempted [1]

586 ἄπειρος, *apeiros*
unskilled [1]

587 ἀπεκδέχομαι, *apekdechomai*
wait¹ [5], wait eagerly [2], expect [1]

588 ἀπεκδύομαι, *apekdyomai*
disarm [1], strip off [1]

589 ἀπέκδυσις, *apekdysis*
put off [1]

590 ἀπελαύνω, *apelaunō*
dismiss [1]

591 ἀπελεγμός, *apelegmos*
disrepute [1]

592 ἀπελεύθερος, *apeleutheros*
free person [1]

593 Ἀπελλῆς, *Apellēs*
Apelles [1]

594 ἀπελπίζω, *apelpizō*
expect in return [1]

595 ἀπέναντι, *apenanti*
before [2], contrary [1], opposite [1], presence [1]

596 ἀπέραντος, *aperantos*
endless [1]

597 ἀπερισπάστως, *aperispastōs*
unhindered [1]

598 ἀπερίτμητος, *aperitmētos*
uncircumcised [1]

599 ἀπέρχομαι, *aperchomai*
go [51], go away [27], leave [9], go back [4], depart [3], go off [2], pass [2], pass away [2], come [1], enter [1], go across [1], go on [1], go over [1], go to [1], go up [1], pursue [1], set out [1], spread [1], start back [1], step back [1], turn¹ [1], *untranslated* [1]

599 + 3958 ἀπέρχομαι + ὀπίσω,
aperchomai + opisō
follow [1]

599 + 4099 ἀπέρχομαι + πάλιν,
aperchomai + palin
return [1]

600 ἀπέχω, *apechō*
abstain [5], be [4], receive [4], abstinence [1], enough [1], far [1], have back [1], pay [1], *untranslated* [1]

601 ἀπιστέω, *apisteō*
not believe [4], disbelieve [1], faithless [1], refuse to believe [1], unfaithful [1]

602 ἀπιστία, *apistia*
unbelief [7], distrust [1], faithlessness [1], lack of faith [1], unbelieving [1]

603 ἄπιστος, *apistos*
unbeliever [12], faithless [4], unbelieving [4], doubt [1], incredible [1], unfaithful [1]

605 ἁπλότης, *haplotēs*
generosity [4], frankness [1], sincere [1], singleness [1]

605 + 2840 ἁπλότης + καρδία,
haplotēs + kardia
wholeheartedly [1]

606 ἁπλοῦς, *haplous*
healthy [2]

607 ἁπλῶς, *haplōs*
generously [1]

608 ἀπό, *apo*
from [389], *untranslated* [61], of [37], by [22], out [15], in [12], on one's own [11], for [9], with [9], away [6], because [6], since [6], at [5], on [5], some [4], against [3], belong [2], come from [2], leave [2], off [2], separated from [2], share [2], to [2], accord [1], account¹ [1], after [1], ago [1], as [1], at one's hand [1], before [1], cut off [1], distance [1], do [1], ever since [1], part¹ [1], through [1], throughout [1], touch [1], upon [1], *see 4513* [leave] [1]

608 + 172 ἀπό + αἰών, *apo + aiōn*
long ago [1]

608 + 1651 ἀπό + εἷς, *apo + heis*
alike [1]

608 + 3427 ἀπό + μακρόθεν, *apo + makrothen*
far off [3], far away [1]

608 + 3836 + 6052 + 1697 ἀπό + ὁ + ὥρα + ἐκεῖνος, *apo + ho + hōra + ekeinos*
instantly [3]

608 + 4005 ἀπό + ὅς, *apo + hos*
since [2], ever since [1]

608 + 4005 + 323 ἀπό + ὅς + ἄν, *apo + hos + an*
when [1]

608 + 785 ἀπό + ἄρτι, *apo + arti*
again [2]

609 ἀποβαίνω, *apobainō*
give an opportunity [1], go ashore [1], go out [1], turn out [1]

610 ἀποβάλλω, *apoballō*
abandon [1], throw off [1]

611 ἀποβλέπω, *apoblepō*
look ahead [1]

612 ἀπόβλητος, *apoblētos*
reject [1]

613 ἀποβολή, *apobolē*
loss [1], rejection [1]

614 ἀπογίνομαι, *apoginomai*
free [1]

615 ἀπογραφή, *apographē*
census [1], registration [1]

616 ἀπογράφω, *apographō*
register [3], enroll [1]

617 ἀποδείκνυμι, *apodeiknymi*
attest [1], declare [1], exhibit [1], prove [1]

618 ἀπόδειξις, *apodeixis*
demonstration [1]

620 ἀποδεκατόω, *apodekatoō*
tithe [2], collect tithes [1], give a tenth [1]

621 ἀπόδεκτος, *apodektos*
acceptable [1], please [1]

622 ἀποδέχομαι, *apodechomai*
welcome [7]

623 ἀποδημέω, *apodēmeō*
go to another country [3], go away [1], go on a journey [1], travel [1]

624 ἀπόδημος, *apodēmos*
go on a journey [1]

625 ἀποδίδωμι, *apodidōmi*
give [13], pay [10], repay [7], reward [3], sell [3], give back [2], pay back [2], render [2], carry out [1], give an account [1], make a payment [1], make repayment [1], produce [1], yield [1]

626 ἀποδιορίζω, *apodiorizō*
cause division [1]

627 ἀποδοκιμάζω, *apodokimazō*
reject [9]

628 ἀποδοχή, *apodochē*
acceptance [2]

629 ἀπόθεσις, *apothesis*
removal [1]

629 + 3836 + 5013 ἀπόθεσις + ὁ + σκήνωμα, *apothesis + ho + skēnōma*
death [1]

630 ἀποθήκη, *apothēkē*
barn [4], granary [2]

631 ἀποθησαυρίζω, *apothēsaurizō*
store up treasure [1]

632 ἀποθλίβω, *apothlibō*
press in on [1]

633 ἀποθνῄσκω, *apothnēskō*
die [95], dead [10], death [3], kill [1], mortal [1], perish [1]

635 ἀποκαθίστημι, *apokathistēmi*
restore [8]

636 ἀποκαλύπτω, *apokalyptō*
reveal [23], uncover [2], make a
revelation [1]

637 ἀποκάλυψις, *apokalypsis*
revelation [11], reveal [7]

638 ἀποκαραδοκία, *apokaradokia*
eager expectation [1], eager longing [1]

639 ἀποκαταλλάσσω, *apokatallassō*
reconcile [3]

640 ἀποκατάστασις, *apokatastasis*
restoration [1]

641 ἀπόκειμαι, *apokeimai*
appoint [1], lay up [1], reserve [1], wrap
up [1]

642 ἀποκεφαλίζω, *apokephalizō*
behead [4]

643 ἀποκλείω, *apokleiō*
shut [1]

644 ἀποκόπτω, *apokoptō*
cut off [4], castrate [1], cut away [1]

645 ἀπόκριμα, *apokrima*
sentence[1] [1]

646 ἀποκρίνομαι, *apokrinomai*
answer [159], say [29], reply [25], ask [7],
give an answer [4], address [2],
untranslated [2], speak [1], speak up [1],
tell [1]

647 ἀπόκρισις, *apokrisis*
answer [4]

648 ἀποκρύπτω, *apokryptō*
hide [4]

649 ἀπόκρυφος, *apokryphos*
secret [2], hide [1]

650 ἀποκτείνω, *apokteinō*
kill [67], put to death [6], strike [1]

652 ἀποκυέω, *apokyeō*
give birth [2]

653 ἀποκυλίω, *apokyliō*
roll away [2], roll back [2]

655 ἀπολαμβάνω, *apolambanō*
receive [5], get back [2], get [1], receive
again [1], take aside [1]

656 ἀπόλαυσις, *apolausis*
enjoyment [1], pleasure [1]

657 ἀπολείπω, *apoleipō*
leave [3], remain [3], leave behind [1]

660 ἀπόλλυμι, *apollymi*
lose [35], destroy [24], perish [23],
kill [4], cause ruin [1], die [1],
perishable [1], put to death [1]

661 Ἀπολλύων, *Apollyōn*
Apollyon [1]

662 Ἀπολλωνία, *Apollōnia*
Apollonia [1]

663 Ἀπολλῶς, *Apollōs*
Apollos [10]

664 ἀπολογέομαι, *apologeomai*
make a defense [4], defend [3],
defense [1], excuse [1], say in defense [1]

665 ἀπολογία, *apologia*
defense [6], eagerness to clear [1], make a
defense [1]

666 ἀπολούω, *apolouō*
wash [1], wash away [1]

667 ἀπολύτρωσις, *apolytrōsis*
redemption [8], redeem [1], release [1]

668 ἀπολύω, *apolyō*
release [22], divorce [12], send away [10],
dismiss [7], let go [5], send off [3], set
free [3], forgive [2], divorce woman [1],
leave [1]

669 ἀπομάσσω, *apomassō*
wipe off in protest [1]

671 ἀπονέμω, *aponemō*
pay [1]

672 ἀπονίπτω, *aponiptō*
wash [1]

674 ἀποπίπτω, *apopiptō*
fall [1]

675 ἀποπλανάω, *apoplanaō*
lead astray [1], wander away [1]

676 ἀποπλέω, *apopleō*
sail [3], sail back [1]

678 ἀποπνίγω, *apopnigō*
choke [1], drown [1]

679 ἀπορέω, *aporeō*
perplex [4], loss [1], uncertain [1]

680 ἀπορία, *aporia*
confuse [1]

681 ἀπορίπτω, *aporiptō*
jump overboard [1]

682 ἀπορφανίζω, *aporphanizō*
make an orphan [1]

684 ἀποσκίασμα, *aposkiasma*
shadow [1]

685 ἀποσπάω, *apospaō*
draw[1] [1], entice [1], part[2] [1],
withdraw [1]

686 ἀποστασία, *apostasia*
forsake [1], rebellion [1]

687 ἀποστάσιον, *apostasion*
dismissal [2], certificate of divorce [1]

689 ἀποστεγάζω, *apostegazō*
remove [1]

690 ἀποστέλλω, *apostellō*
send [114], send out [10], send away [2],
send word [2], go in [1], let go [1], send a
message [1], send a messenger [1]

691 ἀποστερέω, *apostereō*
defraud [3], bereft [1], deprive [1], keep
back by fraud [1]

692 ἀποστολή, *apostolē*
apostleship [3], apostle [1]

693 ἀπόστολος, *apostolos*
apostle [75], messenger [3], *see 5663*
[super-apostle] [2]

694 ἀποστοματίζω, *apostomatizō*
cross-examine [1]

695 ἀποστρέφω, *apostrephō*
reject [2], turn away [2], banish [1],
pervert [1], put back [1], refuse [1],
turn[1] [1]

696 ἀποστυγέω, *apostygeō*
hate [1]

697 ἀποσυνάγωγος, *aposynagōgos*
put out of the synagogue [2], out of the
synagogue [1]

698 ἀποτάσσω, *apotassō*
say farewell [4], give up [1], take leave [1]

699 ἀποτελέω, *apoteleō*
grow fully [1], perform [1]

700 ἀποτίθημι, *apotithēmi*
rid [3], lay aside [2], put away [2], lay [1],
put [1]

701 ἀποτινάσσω, *apotinassō*
shake off [2]

702 ἀποτίνω, *apotinō*
repay [1]

703 ἀποτολμάω, *apotolmaō*
bold [1]

704 ἀποτομία, *apotomia*
severity [2]

705 ἀποτόμως, *apotomōs*
severe [1], sharply [1]

706 ἀποτρέπω, *apotrepō*
avoid [1]

707 ἀπουσία, *apousia*
absence [1]

708 ἀποφέρω, *apopherō*
carry away [2], bring [1], carry [1], lead
away [1], take [1]

709 ἀποφεύγω, *apopheugō*
escape [3]

710 ἀποφθέγγομαι, *apophthengomai*
ability [1], address [1], speak [1]

711 ἀποφορτίζομαι, *apophortizomai*
unload [1]

712 ἀπόχρησις, *apochrēsis*
use [1]

713 ἀποχωρέω, *apochōreō*
leave [2], go away [1]

714 ἀποχωρίζω, *apochōrizō*
part[2] [1], vanish [1]

715 ἀποψύχω, *apopsychō*
faint [1]

716 Ἄππιος, *Appios*
Appius [1]

717 ἀπρόσιτος, *aprositos*
unapproachable [1]

718 ἀπρόσκοπος, *aproskopos*
blameless [1], clear [1], no offense [1]

719 ἀπροσωπολήμπτως,
aprosōpolēmptōs
impartially [1]

720 ἄπταιστος, *aptaistos*
fall [1]

721 ἅπτω, *haptō*
touch [33], light[1] [3], handle [1], hold
on [1], kindle [1]

722 Ἀπφία, *Apphia*
Apphia [1]

723 ἀπωθέω, *apōtheō*
reject [4], push aside [2]

724 ἀπώλεια, *apōleia*
destruction [12], lose [2], waste [2],
destructive [1], *see 1650* [perish] [1]

725 ἀρά, *ara*
curse [1]

726 ἄρα, *ara*
then [20], so [12], *untranslated* [6],
therefore [2], case [1], perhaps [1],
possible [1], thus [1], true [1], *see 1623*
[perhaps] [1], *see 2075* [otherwise] [1]

726 + 1145 ἄρα + γέ, *ara + ge*
then [1]

726 + 4036 ἄρα + οὖν, *ara + oun*
accordingly [1]

727 ἄρα, *ara*
untranslated [2], then [1]

728 Ἀραβία, *Arabia*
Arabia [2]

730 Ἀράμ, *Aram*
Aram [2]

731 ἄραφος, *araphos*
seamless [1]

732 Ἄραψ, *Araps*
Arab [1]

733 ἀργέω, *argeō*
idle [1]

734 ἀργός, *argos*
idle [4], barren [1], careless [1], lazy [1],
see 4024 [ineffective] [1]

736 ἀργύριον, *argyrion*
money [9], piece of silver [5], silver [5],
silver coin [1]

737 ἀργυροκόπος, *argyrokopos*
silversmith [1]

738 ἄργυρος, *argyros*
silver [5]

739 ἀργυροῦς, *argyrous*
silver [3]

740 Ἄρειος πάγος, *Areios pagos*
Areopagus [2]

741 Ἀρεοπαγίτης, *Areopagitēs*
Areopagite [1]

742 ἀρεσκεία, *areskeia*
please [1]

743 ἀρέσκω, *areskō*
please [16], *see 3590* [displease] [1]

744 ἀρεστός, *arestos*
please [3], right[1] [1]

745 Ἀρέτας, *Haretas*
Aretas [1]

746 ἀρετή, *aretē*
goodness [3], excellence [1], mighty
act [1]

748 ἀρήν, *arēn*
lamb [1]

749 ἀριθμέω, *arithmeō*
count [3]

750 ἀριθμός, *arithmos*
number [15], all [1], numerous [1], one [1]

751 Ἀριμαθαία, *Harimathaia*
Arimathea [4]

752 Ἀρίσταρχος, *Aristarchos*
Aristarchus [5]

753 ἀριστάω, *aristaō*
breakfast [2], dine [1]

754 ἀριστερός, *aristeros*
left [3], left hand [1]

755 Ἀριστόβουλος, *Aristoboulos*
Aristobulus [1]

756 ἄριστον, *ariston*
dinner [2], luncheon [1]

757 ἀρκετός, *arketos*
enough [3]

758 ἀρκέω, *arkeō*
content [3], enough [2], satisfy [2],
sufficient [1]

759 ἄρκος, *arkos*
bear[2] [1]

761 ἅρμα, *harma*
chariot [4]

762 Ἁρμαγεδών, *Harmagedōn*
Harmagedon [1]

764 ἁρμόζω, *harmozō*
promise in marriage [1]

765 ἁρμός, *harmos*
joint [1]

766 ἀρνέομαι, *arneomai*
deny [28], reject [3], refuse [1],
renounce [1]

767 Ἀρνί, *Arni*
Arni [1]

768 ἀρνίον, *arnion*
lamb [30]

769 ἀροτριάω, *arotriaō*
plow [3]

770 ἄροτρον, *arotron*
plow [1]

771 ἁρπαγή, *harpagē*
greed [2], plunder [1]

772 ἁρπαγμός, *harpagmos*
something to exploit [1]

773 ἁρπάζω, *harpazō*
snatch [4], catch up [3], snatch away [3],
take by force [3], plunder [1]

774 ἅρπαξ, *harpax*
robber [3], ravenous [1], thief [1]

775 ἀρραβών, *arrabōn*
first installment [1], guarantee [1],
pledge [1]

777 ἄρρητος, *arrētos*
not tell [1]

779 ἄρρωστος, *arrōstos*
sick [3], ill [1], sick person [1]

780 ἀρσενοκοίτης, *arsenokoitēs*
sodomite [2]

781 ἄρσην, *arsēn*
male [6], man [3]

782 Ἀρτεμᾶς, *Artemas*
Artemas [1]

783 Ἄρτεμις, *Artemis*
Artemis [5]

784 ἀρτέμων, *artemōn*
foresail [1]

785 ἄρτι, *arti*
now [26], *see 608* [again] [2], *see 2401*
[still[1]] [2], just[1] [1], just now [1], once[2] [1],
present[3] [1], still[1] [1], this very day [1]

786 ἀρτιγέννητος, *artigennētos*
newborn [1]

787 ἄρτιος, *artios*
proficient [1]

788 ἄρτος, *artos*
bread [60], loaf [22], loaf of bread [7],
untranslated [4], food [2], live [1],
meal [1]

789 ἀρτύω, *artyō*
season[2] [2], restore saltiness [1]

790 Ἀρφαξάδ, *Arphaxad*
Arphaxad [1]

791 ἀρχάγγελος, *archangelos*
archangel [2]

792 ἀρχαῖος, *archaios*
ancient [5], ancient time [2], early [2],
old[3] [1], past [1]

793 Ἀρχέλαος, *Archelaos*
Archelaus [1]

794 ἀρχή, *archē*
beginning [32], ruler [9], first [4],
basic [2], corner [2], at all [1], early
days [1], jurisdiction [1], origin [1],
position [1], rule[1] [1]

795 ἀρχηγός, *archēgos*
pioneer [2], author [1], leader [1]

796 ἀρχιερατικός, *archieratikos*
high-priestly [1]

797 ἀρχιερεύς, *archiereus*
chief priest [64], high priest [57], high
priesthood [1]

799 ἀρχιποίμην, *archipoimēn*
chief shepherd [1]

800 Ἄρχιππος, *Archippos*
Archippus [2]

801 ἀρχισυνάγωγος, *archisynagōgos*
leader of the synagogue [4], official of the
synagogue [3], leader [2]

802 ἀρχιτέκτων, *architektōn*
master builder [1]

803 ἀρχιτελώνης, *architelōnēs*
chief tax collector [1]

804 ἀρχιτρίκλινος, *architriklinos*
steward [2], chief steward [1]

806 ἄρχω, *archō*
begin [81], start [2], be [1], rule[1] [1],
ruler [1]

807 ἄρχων, *archōn*
ruler [22], leader [10], authority [4],
magistrate [1]

808 ἄρωμα, *arōma*
spice [4]

810 ἀσάλευτος, *asaleutos*
cannot be shaken [1], immovable [1]

811 Ἀσάφ, *Asaph*
Asaph [2]

812 ἄσβεστος, *asbestos*
unquenchable [3]

813 ἀσέβεια, *asebeia*
ungodliness [3], impiety [2], ungodly [1]

814 ἀσεβέω, *asebeō*
commit in an ungodly way [1]

815 ἀσεβής, *asebēs*
ungodly [7], godless [2]

816 ἀσέλγεια, *aselgeia*
licentiousness [8], licentious [1], licentious
way [1]

817 ἄσημος, *asēmos*
see 4024 [important] [1]

818 Ἀσήρ, *Asēr*
Asher [2]

819 ἀσθένεια, *astheneia*
weakness [13], infirmity [3], ailment [2],
disease [2], cripple [1], ill [1], illness [1],
limitation [1]

820 ἀσθενέω, *astheneō*
weak [12], ill [9], sick [8], weaken [2],
invalid [1], sick man [1]

821 ἀσθένημα, *asthenēma*
fail [1]

822 ἀσθενής, *asthenēs*
weak [18], sick [6], weakness [1],
untranslated [1]

823 Ἀσία, *Asia*
Asia [18]

824 Ἀσιανός, *Asianos*
Asia [1]

825 Ἀσιάρχης, *Asiarchēs*
official of the province of Asia [1]

826 ἀσιτία, *asitia*
without food [1]

827 ἄσιτος, *asitos*
without food [1]

828 ἀσκέω, *askeō*
do one's best [1]

829 ἀσκός, *askos*
skin [6], wineskin [6]

830 ἀσμένως, *asmenōs*
warmly [1]

831 ἄσοφος, *asophos*
unwise person [1]

832 ἀσπάζομαι, *aspazomai*
greet [46], send greetings [9], give
greetings [1], salute [1], say farewell [1],
welcome [1]

833 ἀσπασμός, *aspasmos*
greeting [6], greet with respect [4]

834 ἄσπιλος, *aspilos*
without spot [2], unstained [1], without
blemish [1]

835 ἀσπίς, *aspis*
viper [1]

836 ἄσπονδος, *aspondos*
implacable [1]

837 ἀσσάριον, *assarion*
penny [2]

839 ἆσσον, *asson*
close to shore [1]

840 Ἄσσος, *Assos*
Assos [2]

841 ἀστατέω, *astateō*
homeless [1]

842 ἀστεῖος, *asteios*
beautiful [2]

843 ἀστήρ, *astēr*
star [24]

844 ἀστήρικτος, *astēriktos*
unstable [1], unsteady [1]

845 ἄστοργος, *astorgos*
heartless [1], inhuman [1]

846 ἀστοχέω, *astocheō*
deviate [1], miss the mark [1], swerve [1]

847 ἀστραπή, *astrapē*
flash of lightning [5], lightning [3], ray [1]

848 ἀστράπτω, *astraptō*
dazzle [1], flash [1]

849 ἄστρον, *astron*
star [4]

850 Ἀσύγκριτος, *Asynkritos*
Asyncritus [1]

851 ἀσύμφωνος, *asymphōnos*
disagree [1]

852 ἀσύνετος, *asynetos*
foolish [2], fail to understand [1],
senseless [1], without understanding [1]

853 ἀσύνθετος, *asynthetos*
faithless [1]

854 ἀσφάλεια, *asphaleia*
security [1], truth [1], *see 1877*
[securely] [1]

855 ἀσφαλής, *asphalēs*
definite [1], fact [1], safeguard [1],
sure [1], *untranslated* [1]

856 ἀσφαλίζω, *asphalizō*
make secure [3], fasten [1]

857 ἀσφαλῶς, *asphalōs*
certainty [1], securely [1], under guard [1]

858 ἀσχημονέω, *aschēmoneō*
not behave properly [1], rude [1]

859 ἀσχημοσύνη, *aschēmosynē*
shame [1], shameless act [1]

860 ἀσχήμων, *aschēmōn*
less respectable [1]

861 ἀσωτία, *asōtia*
debauchery [2], dissipation [1]

862 ἀσώτως, *asōtōs*
dissolute [1]

863 ἀτακτέω, *atakteō*
idle [1]

864 ἄτακτος, *ataktos*
idler [1]

865 ἀτάκτως, *ataktōs*
idleness [2]

866 ἄτεκνος, *ateknos*
childless [1], no child [1]

867 ἀτενίζω, *atenizō*
look intently [5], gaze [4], stare [3],
closely [1], fix [1]

868 ἄτερ, *ater*
not present [1], without[1] [1]

869 ἀτιμάζω, *atimazō*
dishonor [3], insult [2], degrade [1], suffer
dishonor [1]

871 ἀτιμία, *atimia*
degrade [2], dishonor [2], ordinary [1],
ordinary use [1], shame [1]

872 ἄτιμος, *atimos*
without honor [2], disrepute [1], less
honorable [1]

874 ἀτμίς, *atmis*
mist [2]

875 ἄτομος, *atomos*
moment [1]

876 ἄτοπος, *atopos*
wrong [2], unusual [1], wicked [1]

877 Ἀττάλεια, *Attaleia*
Attalia [1]

878 αὐγάζω, *augazō*
see [1]

879 αὐγή, *augē*
dawn [1]

880 Αὔγουστος, *Augoustos*
Augustus [1]

881 αὐθάδης, *authadēs*
arrogant [1], willful [1]

882 αὐθαίρετος, *authairetos*
accord [1], voluntarily [1]

883 αὐθεντέω, *authenteō*
authority over [1]

884 αὐλέω, *auleō*
play the flute [2]

884 + 2445 + 3068 αὐλέω + ἤ +
κιθαρίζω, *auleō + ē + kitharizō*
play [1]

885 αὐλή, *aulē*
courtyard [6], castle [1], court[1] [1],
fold [1], palace [1], palace courtyard [1]

885 + 3836 + 4585 αὐλή + ὁ +
πρόβατον, *aulē + ho + probaton*
sheepfold [1]

886 αὐλητής, *aulētēs*
flute player [1], flutist [1]

887 αὐλίζομαι, *aulizomai*
spend the night [2]

888 αὐλός, *aulos*
flute [1]

889 αὐξάνω, *auxanō*
grow [13], increase [5], give growth [2],
advance [1], grow up [1], spread [1]

890 αὔξησις, *auxēsis*
growth [2]

892 αὔριον, *aurion*
tomorrow [11], next day [3]

893 αὐστηρός, *austēros*
harsh [2]

894 αὐτάρκεια, *autarkeia*
contentment [1], enough [1]

895 αὐτάρκης, *autarkēs*
content [1]

896 αὐτοκατάκριτος, *autokatakritos*
self-condemned [1]

897 αὐτόματος, *automatos*
accord [1], of oneself [1]

898 αὐτόπτης, *autoptēs*
eyewitness [1]

899 αὐτός, *autos*
he [2712], they [1528], *untranslated* [371],
it [297], she [235], himself [54],
same [49], Jesus [35], you [27], that [22],
yourself [18], themselves [16], who [16],
very[2] [15], one's own [14], God [9],
myself [9], man [8], one [8], the [8], *see
2093* [together] [8], itself [7],
ourselves [7], person [7], same thing [7],
a [6], this [6], anyone [4], Christ [3],
Paul [3], child [3], city [3], herself [3],
such a person [3], there [3], believer [2],
body [2], boy [2], harmony [2], here [2],
same way [2], such [2], this thing [2],
Crete [1], I [1], Israel [1], John [1],
Lazarus [1], Levi [1], Moses [1], Saul [1],
Simeon [1], Simon [1], Stephen [1],
Timothy [1], actually [1], alike [1],
altar [1], another [1], beast [1],
blessing [1], book [1], branch [1],
builder [1], convert [1], faith [1],
firstborn [1], group [1], home [1],
host[2] [1], kingdom [1], lie[2] [1], love [1],
member [1], number [1], offender [1], one
another [1], other [1], own[2] [1],
priesthood [1], prisoner [1], proceeds [1],
prophet [1], reply [1], same kind [1],
sinner [1], slave [1], such a one [1],
thing [1], today [1], true [1],
unbeliever [1], we [1], which [1],
widow [1], woman [1], work [1], *see 1877*
[there] [1], *see 3836* [agreement] [1], *see
3836* [one place] [1]

899 + 2840 αὐτός + καρδία, *autos +
kardia*
himself [1]

900 αὐτόφωρος, *autophōros*
very act [1]

901 αὐτόχειρ, autocheir
one's own hand [1]

902 αὐχέω, aucheō
boast [1]

903 αὐχμηρός, auchmēros
dark [1]

904 ἀφαιρέω, aphaireō
take away [7], cut off [3]

905 ἀφανής, aphanēs
hide [1]

906 ἀφανίζω, aphanizō
consume [2], disfigure [1], perish [1],
vanish [1]

907 ἀφανισμός, aphanismos
disappear [1]

908 ἄφαντος, aphantos
vanish from sight [1]

909 ἀφεδρών, aphedrōn
sewer [2]

910 ἀφειδία, apheidia
severe treatment [1]

911 ἀφελότης, aphelotēs
generous [1]

912 ἄφεσις, aphesis
forgiveness [14], forgive [1], free [1],
release [1]

913 ἀφή, haphē
ligament [2]

914 ἀφθαρσία, aphtharsia
immortality [2], imperishability [2],
imperishable [2], undying [1]

915 ἄφθαρτος, aphthartos
imperishable [5], immortal [2], last² [1]

917 ἀφθορία, aphthoria
integrity [1]

918 ἀφίημι, aphiēmi
leave [48], forgive [47], let [14], allow [4],
let alone [4], divorce [3], abandon [2],
desert¹ [2], give [2], leave behind [2],
neglect [2], permit [2], wait¹ [2],
consent [1], give up [1], leave alone [1],
let go [1], tolerate [1], see 4024
[refuse] [1], see 4028 [stop] [1],
untranslated [1]

918 + 3836 + 4460 ἀφίημι + ὁ +
πνεῦμα, aphiēmi + ho + pneuma
breathe one's last [1]

919 ἀφικνέομαι, aphikneomai
know [1]

920 ἀφιλάγαθος, aphilagathos
hater·of good [1]

921 ἀφιλάργυρος, aphilargyros
free from love of money [1], not a lover of
money [1]

922 ἄφιξις, aphixis
go [1]

923 ἀφίστημι, aphistēmi
leave [4], turn away [2], depart [1],
desert¹ [1], draw back [1], fall away [1],
get to follow [1], go away [1], keep
away [1], renounce [1]

924 ἄφνω, aphnō
suddenly [2], untranslated [1]

925 ἀφόβως, aphobōs
without fear [3], nothing to fear [1]

926 ἀφομοιόω, aphomoioō
resemble [1]

927 ἀφοράω, aphoraō
look [1], see [1]

928 ἀφορίζω, aphorizō
separate [4], set apart [3], exclude [1],
keep separate [1], take [1]

929 ἀφορμή, aphormē
opportunity [6], occasion [1]

930 ἀφρίζω, aphrizō
foam [1], foam at the mouth [1]

931 ἀφρός, aphros
foam at the mouth [1]

932 ἀφροσύνη, aphrosynē
fool [2], folly [1], foolishness [1]

933 ἄφρων, aphrōn
fool [8], foolish [3]

934 ἀφυπνόω, aphypnoō
fall asleep [1]

936 ἄφωνος, aphōnos
can not speak [1], silent [1],
speechless [1], without sound [1]

937 Ἀχάζ, Achaz
Ahaz [2]

938 Ἀχαία, Achaia
Achaia [10]

939 Ἀχαϊκός, Achaikos
Achaicus [1]

940 ἀχάριστος, acharistos
ungrateful [2]

942 ἀχειροποίητος, acheiropoiētos
not make with hands [2], spiritual [1]

943 Ἀχίμ, Achim
Achim [2]

944 ἀχλύς, achlys
mist [1]

945 ἀχρεῖος, achreios
worthless [2]

946 ἀχρειόω, achreioō
worthless [1]

947 ἄχρηστος, achrēstos
useless [1]

948 ἄχρι, achri
until [15], to [7], far [3], high [2], up
to [2], all the way [1], before [1], by [1],
close [1], even in the face of [1], for [1],
in [1], just¹ [1], long¹ [1], point¹ [1]

948 + 3836 + 1306 ἄχρι + ὁ + δεῦρο,
achri + ho + deuro
thus far [1]

948 + 4005 ἄχρι + ὅς, achri + hos
until [8]

948 + 4005 + 323 ἄχρι + ὅς + ἄν, achri
+ hos + an
until [1]

949 ἄχυρον, achyron
chaff [2]

950 ἀψευδής, apseudēs
never lie [1]

952 ἄψινθος, apsinthos
wormwood [2]

953 ἄψυχος, apsychos
lifeless [1]

955 Βάαλ, Baal
Baal [1]

956 Βαβυλών, Babylōn
Babylon [12]

957 βαθμός, bathmos
standing [1]

958 βάθος, bathos
depth [6], deep [1], see 2848 [extreme] [1]

959 βαθύνω, bathynō
deeply [1]

960 βαθύς, bathys
deep [2], deep thing [1], early [1]

961 βάϊον, baion
branch [1]

962 Βαλαάμ, Balaam
Balaam [3]

963 Βαλάκ, Balak
Balak [1]

964 βαλλάντιον, ballantion
purse [4]

965 βάλλω, ballō
throw [50], put [25], cast [11], throw
down [6], lie¹ [4], pour [4], bring [3],
contribute [2], swing [2], drop [1],
hurl [1], invest [1], jump [1], lay [1], lie in
bed [1], put back [1], put into [1], rush
down [1], scatter [1], sow¹ [1], throw
away [1], toss [1], untranslated [1]

965 + 1650 + 3836 + 1565 βάλλω + εἰς
+ ὁ + δῶρον, ballō + eis + ho + dōron
contribute [1]

966 βαπτίζω, baptizō
baptize [71], baptizer [3], wash [2],
receive baptism [1]

967 βάπτισμα, baptisma
baptism [19]

968 βαπτισμός, baptismos
baptism [3], wash [1]

969 βαπτιστής, baptistēs
Baptist [12]

970 βάπτω, baptō
dip [4]

972 Βαραββᾶς, Barabbas
Barabbas [11]

973 Βαράκ, Barak
Barak [1]

974 Βαραχίας, Barachias
Barachiah [1]

975 βάρβαρος, barbaros
barbarian [2], foreigner [2], native [2]

976 βαρέω, bareō
burden [2], weigh down [2], crush [1],
heavy [1]

977 βαρέως, bareōs
hard [2]

978 Βαρθολομαῖος, Bartholomaios
Bartholomew [4]

979 Βαριησοῦς, Bariēsous
Bar-Jesus [1]

980 Βαριωνᾶ, Bariōna
son of Jonah [1]

982 Βαρναβᾶς, Barnabas
Barnabas [28]

983 βάρος, baros
burden [4], demand [1], weight [1]

984 Βαρσαββᾶς, Barsabbas
Barsabbas [2]

985 Βαρτιμαῖος, Bartimaios
Bartimaeus [1]

987 βαρύς, barys
burdensome [1], heavy [1], savage [1],
serious [1], weighty [1], weighty matter [1]

988 βαρύτιμος, barytimos
very costly [1]

989 βασανίζω, basanizō
torment [7], agony [1], batter [1],
distress [1], strain [1], torture [1]

990 βασανισμός, basanismos
torment [4], torture [2]

991 βασανιστής, basanistēs
torture [1]

992 βάσανος, basanos
torment [2], pain [1]

993 βασιλεία, basileia
kingdom [159], royal power [2]

993 + 2400 βασιλεία + ἔχω, basileia +
echō
rule[1] [1]

994 βασίλειος, basileios
royal [2]

995 βασιλεύς, basileus
king [110], Excellency [2], emperor [2],
royal [1]

996 βασιλεύω, basileuō
reign [9], exercise dominion [6], king [4],
rule[1] [2]

997 βασιλικός, basilikos
royal [2], king [1], official [1], royal
official [1]

999 βασίλισσα, basilissa
queen [4]

1000 βάσις, basis
foot [1]

1001 βασκαίνω, baskainō
bewitch [1]

1002 βαστάζω, bastazō
carry [11], bear[1] [6], bear up [1],
bearer [1], bring [1], carry away [1],
pay [1], put up with [1], steal [1],
support [1], take up [1], tolerate [1]

1003 βάτος[1], batos[1]
bush [4], bramble bush [1]

1004 βάτος[2], batos[2]
jug [1]

1005 βάτραχος, batrachos
frog [1]

1006 βατταλογέω, battalogeō
heap up empty phrases [1]

1007 βδέλυγμα, bdelygma
abomination [4], sacrilege [2]

1008 βδελυκτός, bdelyktos
detestable [1]

1009 βδελύσσομαι, bdelyssomai
abhor [1], pollute [1]

1010 βέβαιος, bebaios
confirm fully [1], firm [1], guarantee [1],
steadfast [1], take effect [1], unshaken [1],
valid [1]

1010 + 4472 βέβαιος + ποιέω, bebaios
+ poieō
confirm [1]

1011 βεβαιόω, bebaioō
strengthen [3], confirm [2], establish [2],
attest [1]

1012 βεβαίωσις, bebaiōsis
confirmation [2]

1013 βέβηλος, bebēlos
profane [4], godless person [1]

1014 βεβηλόω, bebēloō
break [1], profane [1]

1015 Βεελζεβούλ, Beelzeboul
Beelzebul [7]

1016 Βελιάρ, Beliar
Beliar [1]

1017 βελόνη, belonē
needle [1]

1018 βέλος, belos
arrow [1]

1019 βελτίων, beltiōn
very well [1]

1021 Βενιαμίν, Beniamin
Benjamin [4]

1022 Βερνίκη, Bernikē
Bernice [3]

1023 Βέροια, Beroia
Beroea [2]

1024 Βεροιαῖος, Beroiaios
Beroea [1]

1029 Βηθανία, Bēthania
Bethany [12]

1032 Βηθζαθά, Bēthzatha
Beth-zatha [1]

1033 Βηθλέεμ, Bēthleem
Bethlehem [8]

1034 Βηθσαϊδά, Bēthsaida
Bethsaida [7]

1036 Βηθφαγή, Bēthphagē
Bethphage [3]

1037 βῆμα, bēma
tribunal [6], judgment seat [3], judge's
bench [1], length [1], platform [1]

1039 βήρυλλος, bēryllos
beryl [1]

1040 βία, bia
violence [2], force [1]

1041 βιάζω, biazō
enter by force [1], suffer violence [1]

1042 βίαιος, biaios
violent [1]

1043 βιαστής, biastēs
violent [1]

1044 βιβλαρίδιον, biblaridion
little scroll [3]

1046 βιβλίον, biblion
book [19], scroll [13], certificate [2]

1047 βίβλος, biblos
book [9], account[2] [1]

1048 βιβρώσκω, bibrōskō
eat [1]

1049 Βιθυνία, Bithynia
Bithynia [2]

1050 βίος, bios
life [2], live [2], property [2],
everyday [1], goods [1], have [1],
riches [1]

1051 βιόω, bioō
live [1]

1052 βίωσις, biōsis
way of life [1]

1053 βιωτικός, biōtikos
life [1], ordinary [1], ordinary matter [1]

1054 βλαβερός, blaberos
harmful [1]

1055 βλάπτω, blaptō
do harm [1], hurt [1]

1056 βλαστάνω, blastanō
bud [1], come up [1], sprout [1], yield [1]

1058 Βλάστος, Blastos
Blastus [1]

1059 βλασφημέω, blasphēmeō
blaspheme [13], slander [5], curse [3],
deride [3], blasphemer [1], blasphemy [1],
denounce [1], discredit [1], insult [1],
malign [1], revile [1], speak evil [1], speak
of as evil [1], utter blasphemy [1]

1060 βλασφημία, blasphēmia
blasphemy [8], slander [7],
blasphemous [2], blasphemous word [1]

1061 βλάσφημος, blasphēmos
abusive [1], blasphemer [1],
blasphemous [1], slanderous [1]

1062 βλέμμα, blemma
see [1]

1063 βλέπω, blepō
see [82], beware [11], look [8], take
care [3], see 1063 [look indeed] [3],
consider [2], pay attention [2], perceive [2],
regard [2], sight [2], alert [1], choose with
care [1], expose [1], face [1], gaze [1],
notice [1], on guard [1], watch [1], watch
out [1], see 3596 [as yet unseen] [1]

1063 + 209 βλέπω + ἀκριβῶς, blepō +
akribōs
careful [1]

1063 + 1063 βλέπω + βλέπω, blepō +
blepō
look indeed [3]

1064 βλητέος, blēteos
put [1]

1065 Βοανηργές, Boanērges
Boanerges [1]

1066 βοάω, boaō
cry out [5], shout [5], cry [2]

1067 Βόες, Boes
Boaz [2]

1068 βοή, boē
cry [1]

1069 βοήθεια, boētheia
help [1], measure [1]

1070 βοηθέω, boētheō
help [7], come to help [1]

1071 βοηθός, boēthos
helper [1]

1073 βόθυνος, bothynos
pit [3]

1074 βολή, bolē
throw [1]

1075 βολίζω, bolizō
take a sounding [2]

1078 Βόος, Boos
Boaz [1]

1079 βόρβορος, borboros
mud [1]

1080 βορρᾶς, borras
north [2]

1081 βόσκω, boskō
feed [6], swineherd [3]

1082 Βοσόρ, Bosor
Bosor [1]

1083 βοτάνη, botanē
crop [1]

1084 βότρυς, botrys
cluster [1]

1085 βουλευτής, bouleutēs
member of the council [2]

1086 βουλεύω, bouleuō
plan [3], consider [1], make a plan [1], untranslated [1]

1087 βουλή, boulē
plan [5], purpose [5], counsel [1], favor [1]

1088 βούλημα, boulēma
like2 [1], plan [1], will1 [1]

1089 βούλομαι, boulomai
want [13], wish [7], desire [4], choose [3], like2 [2], will1 [2], determine [1], direct [1], intend [1], plan [1], purpose [1], willing [1]

1090 βουνός, bounos
hill [2]

1091 βοῦς, bous
ox [6], cattle [2]

1092 βραβεῖον, brabeion
prize [2]

1093 βραβεύω, brabeuō
rule1 [1]

1094 βραδύνω, bradynō
delay [1], slow [1]

1095 βραδυπλοέω, bradyploeō
sail slowly [1]

1096 βραδύς, bradys
slow [3]

1097 βραδύτης, bradytēs
slowness [1]

1098 βραχίων, brachiōn
arm1 [3]

1099 βραχύς, brachys
little [3], briefly [1], short time [1]

1099 + 5516 βραχύς + τὶς, brachys + tis
little while [2]

1100 βρέφος, brephos
child [4], infant [3], childhood [1]

1101 βρέχω, brechō
rain [3], bathe [2], fall [1], send rain [1]

1103 βροντή, brontē
thunder [7], peal of thunder [4], thunderpeal [1]

1104 βροχή, brochē
rain [2]

1105 βρόχος, brochos
restraint [1]

1106 βρυγμός, brygmos
gnash [7]

1107 βρύχω, brychō
grind [1]

1108 βρύω, bryō
pour forth [1]

1109 βρῶμα, brōma
food [14], eat [2], solid food [1]

1110 βρώσιμος, brōsimos
eat [1]

1111 βρῶσις, brōsis
food [7], rust [2], eat [1], meal [1]

1112 βυθίζω, bythizō
plunge [1], sink [1]

1113 βυθός, bythos
sea [1]

1114 βυρσεύς, byrseus
tanner [3]

1115 βύσσινος, byssinos
fine linen [5]

1116 βύσσος, byssos
fine linen [1]

1117 βωμός, bōmos
altar [1]

1119 Γαββαθᾶ, Gabbatha
Gabbatha [1]

1120 Γαβριήλ, Gabriēl
Gabriel [2]

1121 γάγγραινα, gangraina
gangrene [1]

1122 Γάδ, Gad
Gad [1]

1123 Γαδαρηνός, Gadarēnos
Gadarene [1]

1124 Γάζα1, Gaza1
Gaza [1]

1125 γάζα2, gaza2
treasury [1]

1126 γαζοφυλάκιον, gazophylakion
treasury [5]

1127 Γάϊος, Gaios
Gaius [5]

1128 γάλα, gala
milk [5]

1129 Γαλάτης, Galatēs
Galatian [1]

1130 Γαλατία, Galatia
Galatia [4]

1131 Γαλατικός, Galatikos
Galatia [2]

1132 γαλήνη, galēnē
calm [3]

1133 Γαλιλαία, Galilaia
Galilee [61]

1134 Γαλιλαῖος, Galilaios
Galilean [10], Galilee [1]

1136 Γαλλίων, Galliōn
Gallio [3]

1137 Γαμαλιήλ, Gamaliēl
Gamaliel [2]

1138 γαμέω, gameō
marry [24], marriage [1], married man [1], married woman [1]

1138 + 1222 γαμέω + γυνή, gameō + gynē
marry [1]

1139 γαμίζω, gamizō
give in marriage [5], marriage [1], marry [1]

1140 γαμίσκω, gamiskō
give in marriage [1]

1141 γάμος, gamos
wedding banquet [7], wedding [5], marriage [3], wedding hall [1]

1142 γάρ, gar
for [790], untranslated [158], indeed [32], because [18], now [6], but [5], since [5], and [4], as for [2], even [2], in fact [2], of course [2], so [2], thus [2], yes [2], yet [2], certainly [1], matter [1], no doubt [1], surely [1], though [1], what [1], why [1]

1143 γαστήρ, gastēr
see 1877 [pregnant] [5], glutton [1], womb [1], see 1877 [conceive] [1], see 1877 [with child] [1]

1145 γέ, ge
untranslated [7], indeed [3], see 1623 [otherwise] [3], at least [2], surely [2], even [1], really [1], yes [1], yet [1], see 726 [then] [1], see 1623 [for then] [1], see 1623 [perhaps] [1], see 3590 [do] [1]

1146 Γεδεών, Gedeōn
Gideon [1]

1147 γέεννα, geenna
hell [12]

1149 Γεθσημανί, Gethsēmani
Gethsemane [2]

1150 γείτων, geitōn
neighbor [4]

1151 γελάω, gelaō
laugh [2]

1152 γέλως, gelōs
laughter [1]

1153 γεμίζω, gemizō
fill [7], swamp [1]

1154 γέμω, gemō
full [11]

1155 γενεά, genea
generation [43]

1156 γενεαλογέω, genealogeō
ancestry [1]

1157 γενεαλογία, genealogia
genealogy [2]

1160 γενέσια, genesia
birthday [2]

1161 γένεσις, genesis
birth [2], genealogy [1], nature [1], see 4725 [themselves] [1]

1162 γενετή, genetē
birth [1]

1163 γένημα, genēma
fruit [3], harvest [1]

1164 γεννάω, gennaō
father [43], bear1 [42], beget [3], child [2], bear a child [1], breed [1], bring [1], conceive [1], parent [1], see 3120 [birth] [1], untranslated [1]

1165 γέννημα, gennēma
brood [4]

1166 Γεννησαρέτ, Gennēsaret
Gennesaret [3]

1168 γεννητός, gennētos
bear1 [2]

1169 γένος, genos
kind1 [4], family [3], native [3], people [3], offspring [2], race1 [2], descendant [1], different kind [1], origin [1]

1170 Γερασηνός, Gerasēnos
Gerasene [3]

1172 γερουσία, gerousia
elder [1]

1173 γέρων, gerōn
old1 [1]

1174 γεύομαι, geuomai
taste [13], eat [2]

1175 γεωργέω, geōrgeō
cultivate [1]

1176 γεώργιον, *geōrgion*
field [1]

1177 γεωργός, *geōrgos*
tenant [15], farmer [2], they [1],
vinegrower [1]

1178 γῆ, *gē*
earth [164], land[1] [35], ground[1] [21],
soil [12], country [4], *untranslated* [4],
district [2], shore [2], *see 1650*
[ashore], countryside [1], earthly
thing [1], it [1], *see 2093* [earthly] [1]

1179 γῆρας, *gēras*
old age [1]

1180 γηράσκω, *gēraskō*
grow old [2]

1181 γίνομαι, *ginomai*
be [166], become [115],
untranslated [101], come [57], take
place [37], do [31], happen [25],
make [14], occur [10], *see 3590* [by no
means] [10], arise [9], arrive [4],
begin [4], come into being [4], have [4],
bear[1] [3], perform [3], prove [3], break
out [2], bring [2], certainly [2], fall [2],
grow [2], live [2], rank [2], reach [2],
seize [2], yield [2], *see 3590* [never] [2],
accomplish [1], appear [1], apply [1],
belong [1], case [1], come to pass [1],
conduct [1], continue [1], during [1],
experience [1], fall into [1], fare [1],
finish [1], former [1], fulfill [1], gain [1],
get [1], give [1], go [1], go on [1],
grant [1], hear [1], hold [1], join [1],
look [1], marry [1], might [1],
occasion [1], one day [1], plunge [1],
receive [1], rule[1] [1], set[1] [1], speak [1],
spend [1], split [1], spread [1], stand[2] [1],
take [1], turn out [1], turn[3] [1], *see 1213*
[wake up] [1], *see 1666* [remove] [1], *see
3590* [heaven forbid] [1]

1181 + 1650 + 3836 + 4044 γίνομαι +
εἰς + ὁ + οὖς, *ginomai + eis + ho + ous*
hear [1]

1181 + 1650 + 4029 γίνομαι + εἰς +
οὐδείς, *ginomai + eis + oudeis*
disappear [1]

1182 γινώσκω, *ginōskō*
know [154], understand [17], find out [8],
learn [7], realize [7], aware [6], sure [4],
recognize [3], notice [2], comprehend [1],
decide [1], feel [1], grasp [1], have
knowledge [1], have marital relations [1],
know how [1], knowledge [1], make
known [1], news [1], see [1], show [1], *see
4024* [virgin] [1], *untranslated* [1]

1183 γλεῦκος, *gleukos*
new wine [1]

1184 γλυκύς, *glykys*
fresh [2], sweet [2]

1185 γλῶσσα, *glōssa*
tongue [40], language [9], speech [1]

1186 γλωσσόκομον, *glōssokomon*
common purse [2]

1187 γναφεύς, *gnapheus*
one [1]

1188 γνήσιος, *gnēsios*
loyal [3], genuineness [1]

1189 γνησίως, *gnēsiōs*
genuinely [1]

1190 γνόφος, *gnophos*
darkness [1]

1191 γνώμη, *gnōmē*
purpose [2], advice [1], consent [1],
decide [1], judgment [1], opinion [1], *see
1651* [agree] [1], *see 1651* [unite] [1]

1192 γνωρίζω, *gnōrizō*
make known [17], tell [3], want to
know [2], know [1], remind [1], want to
understand [1]

1194 γνῶσις, *gnōsis*
knowledge [26], know [2],
consideration [1]

1195 γνώστης, *gnōstēs*
familiar [1]

1196 γνωστός, *gnōstos*
know [12], acquaintance [1], friend [1],
notable [1]

1197 γογγύζω, *gongyzō*
complain [5], do [1], grumble [1],
mutter [1]

1198 γογγυσμός, *gongysmos*
complain [3], murmur [1]

1199 γογγυστής, *gongystēs*
grumbler [1]

1200 γόης, *goēs*
impostor [1]

1201 Γολγοθᾶ, *Golgotha*
Golgotha [3]

1202 Γόμορρα, *Gomorra*
Gomorrah [4]

1203 γόμος, *gomos*
cargo [3]

1204 γονεύς, *goneus*
parent [20]

1205 γόνυ, *gony*
knee [6], *see 5502* [kneel down] [6]

1206 γονυπετέω, *gonypeteō*
kneel [4]

1207 γράμμα, *gramma*
letter [5], bill [2], written code [2],
learning [1], literal [1], write [1],
writing [1], *see 3857* [learning] [1]

1208 γραμματεύς, *grammateus*
scribe [62], town clerk [1]

1209 γραπτός, *graptos*
write [1]

1210 γραφή, *graphē*
scripture [49], writing [1]

1211 γράφω, *graphō*
write [174], write down [3], describe [2],
inscribe [2], make [2], read [2],
scripture [2], letter [1], record [1], text [1],
writer [1]

1212 γραώδης, *graōdēs*
old wife [1]

1213 γρηγορέω, *grēgoreō*
keep awake [8], stay awake [5], alert [4],
awake [1], keep alert [1], wake up [1],
watch [1]

1213 + 1181 γρηγορέω + γίνομαι,
grēgoreō + ginomai
wake up [1]

1214 γυμνάζω, *gymnazō*
train [4]

1215 γυμνασία, *gymnasia*
train [1]

1217 γυμνιτεύω, *gymniteuō*
clothe poorly [1]

1218 γυμνός, *gymnos*
naked [13], bare [1], nothing [1]

1219 γυμνότης, *gymnotēs*
nakedness [2], naked [1]

1220 γυναικάριον, *gynaikarion*
silly woman [1]

1221 γυναικεῖος, *gynaikeios*
woman [1]

1222 γυνή, *gynē*
woman [127], wife [73], widow [4], *see
467* [marry] [3], *see 2400* [marry] [2], *see
3284* [marry] [2], bride [1], *see 1138*
[marry] [1], *untranslated* [1]

1222 + 467 γυνή + ἀνήρ, *gynē + anēr*
marry [1]

1223 Γώγ, *Gōg*
Gog [1]

1224 γωνία, *gōnia*
corner [5], *see 3051* [cornerstone] [4]

1227 δαιμονίζομαι, *daimonizomai*
demoniac [7], demon [2], possessed by a
demon [2], possessed with a demon [2]

1228 δαιμόνιον, *daimonion*
demon [61], demonic [1], divinity [1]

1229 δαιμονιώδης, *daimoniōdēs*
devilish [1]

1230 δαίμων, *daimōn*
demon [1]

1231 δάκνω, *daknō*
bite [1]

1232 δάκρυον, *dakryon*
tear[2] [10]

1233 δακρύω, *dakryō*
weep [1]

1234 δακτύλιος, *daktylios*
ring [1]

1235 δάκτυλος, *daktylos*
finger [8]

1236 Δαλμανουθά, *Dalmanoutha*
Dalmanutha [1]

1237 Δαλματία, *Dalmatia*
Dalmatia [1]

1238 δαμάζω, *damazō*
tame [3], subdue [1]

1239 δάμαλις, *damalis*
heifer [1]

1240 Δάμαρις, *Damaris*
Damaris [1]

1241 Δαμασκηνός, *Damaskēnos*
Damascus [1]

1242 Δαμασκός, *Damaskos*
Damascus [15]

1245 δάνειον, *daneion*
debt [1]

1247 δανίζω, *danizō*
lend [3], borrow [1]

1248 Δανιήλ, *Daniēl*
Daniel [1]

1250 δανιστής, *danistēs*
creditor [1]

1251 δαπανάω, *dapanaō*
spend [4], pay [1]

1252 δαπάνη, *dapanē*
cost [1]

1253 Δαυίδ, *Dauid*
David [59]

1254 δέ, de
untranslated [1130], but [818], and [414],
now [161], then [103], so [38], yet [19],
while [11], as for [9], however [9],
since [8], though [8], meanwhile [5], *see
1623* [otherwise] [5], also [4], or [4],
another [3], some [3], when [2], even [2],
for [2], indeed [2], instead [2], on the
other hand [2], once[4] [2], accordingly [1],
although [1], contrast [1], even though [1],
moreover [1], nevertheless [1], of
course[1] [1], once[1] [1], one day [1],
other [1], rather [1], still[1] [1], surely [1],
that is [1], the [1], therefore [1], thus [1],
truly [1], well[2] [1], whereas [1], yes [1],
see 1623 [for then] [1]

1255 δέησις, deēsis
prayer [10], supplication [5], pray [1]

**1255 + 4472 δέησις + ποιέω, deēsis +
poieō**
pray [2]

1256 δεῖ, dei
must [59], ought [19], have to [8],
should [6], necessary [5], be [1], due[1] [1],
need [1], right[3] [1]

1257 δεῖγμα, deigma
example [1]

1258 δειγματίζω, deigmatizō
expose to public disgrace [1], make an
example [1]

1259 δείκνυμι, deiknymi
show [31], bring about [1]

1261 δειλία, deilia
cowardice [1]

1262 δειλιάω, deiliaō
afraid [1]

1264 δειλός, deilos
afraid [2], cowardly [1]

1265 δεῖνα, deina
certain man [1]

1267 δεινῶς, deinōs
terrible [1], very[1] [1]

1268 δειπνέω, deipneō
supper [3], eat [1]

1270 δεῖπνον, deipnon
supper [6], dinner [5], banquet [4],
table [1]

1272 δεισιδαιμονία, deisidaimonia
religion [1]

1273 δεισιδαίμων, deisidaimōn
extremely religious [1]

1274 δέκα, deka
ten [24]

**1274 + 2779 + 3893 δέκα + καί +
ὀκτώ, deka + kai + oktō**
eighteen [1]

1277 δεκαοκτώ, dekaoktō
eighteen [2]

1278 δεκαπέντε, dekapente
fifteen [2]

**1278 + 5084 δεκαπέντε + στάδιον,
dekapente + stadion**
two miles [1]

1279 Δεκάπολις, Dekapolis
Decapolis [3]

1280 δεκατέσσαρες, dekatessares
fourteen [5]

1281 δέκατος, dekatos
tenth [4], tithe [2]

**1281 + 6052 δέκατος + ὥρα, dekatos +
hōra**
four o'clock in the afternoon [1]

1282 δεκατόω, dekatoō
collect tithes [1], pay a tithe [1]

1283 δεκτός, dektos
acceptable [3], accept [1], favor [1]

1284 δελεάζω, deleazō
entice [3]

1285 δένδρον, dendron
tree [25]

1287 δεξιολάβος, dexiolabos
spearman [1]

1288 δεξιός, dexios
right hand [37], right[2] [15], right side [2]

1289 δέομαι, deomai
beg [9], pray [7], ask [5], entreat [1]

1290 δέος, deos
awe [1]

1291 Δερβαῖος, Derbaios
Derbe [1]

1292 Δέρβη, Derbē
Derbe [3]

1293 δέρμα, derma
skin [1]

1294 δερμάτινος, dermatinos
leather [2]

1296 δέρω, derō
beat [10], receive a beating [2], flog [1],
give a slap [1], strike [1]

1297 δεσμεύω, desmeuō
bind [2], tie up [1]

1299 δέσμη, desmē
bundle [1]

1300 δέσμιος, desmios
prisoner [12], in prison [3], arrest [1]

1301 δεσμός, desmos
imprisonment [9], chain [6], bond [1],
bondage [1], *untranslated* [1]

1302 δεσμοφύλαξ, desmophylax
jailer [3]

1303 δεσμωτήριον, desmōtērion
prison [4]

1304 δεσμώτης, desmōtēs
prisoner [2]

1305 δεσπότης, despotēs
master [7], sovereign Lord [2], owner of
the house [1]

1306 δεῦρο, deuro
come [7], go [1], *see 948* [thus far] [1]

1307 δεῦτε, deute
come [9], come away [1]

**1307 + 3958 δεῦτε + ὀπίσω, deute +
opisō**
follow [2]

1308 δευτεραῖος, deuteraios
second [1]

1311 δεύτερος, deuteros
second [39], afterward [1], double [1],
once more [1]

**1311 + 5871 δεύτερος + φυλακή,
deuteros + phylakē**
middle of the night [1]

1312 δέχομαι, dechomai
welcome [29], receive [12], accept [8],
take [5], remain [1], *see 4024* [refuse] [1]

1313 δέω, deō
bind [29], tie [4], prison [2], restrain [2],
tie up [2], captive [1], chain [1], in
prison [1], wrap [1]

1314 δή, dē
come [1], indeed [1], now [1],
therefore [1], *untranslated* [1]

1316 δῆλος, dēlos
evident [1], plain [1]

**1316 + 4472 δῆλος + ποιέω, dēlos +
poieō**
betray [1]

1317 δηλόω, dēloō
indicate [3], disclose [1], make clear [1],
make known [1], report [1]

1318 Δημᾶς, Dēmas
Demas [3]

1319 δημηγορέω, dēmēgoreō
deliver a public address [1]

1320 Δημήτριος, Dēmētrios
Demetrius [3]

1321 δημιουργός, dēmiourgos
builder [1]

1322 δῆμος, dēmos
people [2], assembly [1], crowd [1]

1323 δημόσιος, dēmosios
public [3], publicly [1]

1324 δηνάριον, dēnarion
denarius [9], usual daily wage [4], day's
pay [2], *see 1357* [six months' wages] [1]

1327 δήπου, dēpou
clear [1]

1328 διά, dia
through [196], by [91], because [82],
for [34], sake [30], *untranslated* [23],
in [19], with [15], come through [11],
account[1] [8], since [6], during [4],
from [4], after [3], at [3], out [3],
among [2], ground[2] [2], regard [2],
way [2], about[1] [1], against [1], arouse [1],
basis [1], benefit [1], effect [1], effective
through [1], have [1], help [1], means[1] [1],
out of consideration [1], say [1], so
that [1], therefore [1], to [1], under the
leadership [1], use [1], view [1], when [1],
with help [1]

**1328 + 3836 + 5125 διά + ὁ + στόμα,
dia + ho + stoma**
through [1]

**1328 + 3836 + 5931 διά + ὁ + χείρ,
dia + ho + cheir**
through [3]

1328 + 3910 διά + ὅλος, dia + holos
throughout [1]

**1328 + 4005 + 162 διά + ὅς + αἰτία,
dia + hos + aitia**
why [1]

1328 + 4047 διά + οὗτος, dia + houtos
reason[1] [29], therefore [24], so [5],
that [1], then [1]

1328 + 4246 διά + πᾶς, dia + pas
continually [4], always [3], constantly [1],
forever [1]

1328 + 5125 διά + στόμα, dia + stoma
through [3]

1328 + 5515 διά + τίς, *dia + tis*
why [26]

1328 + 5931 διά + χείρ, *dia + cheir*
by [1], through [1], with [1]

1329 διαβαίνω, *diabainō*
come over [1], pass [1], pass through [1]

1330 διαβάλλω, *diaballō*
bring a charge [1]

1331 διαβεβαιόομαι, *diabebaioomai*
insist [1], make an assertion [1]

1332 διαβλέπω, *diablepō*
see clearly [2], look intently [1]

1333 διάβολος, *diabolos*
devil [34], slanderer [3]

1334 διαγγέλλω, *diangellō*
proclaim [2], make public [1]

1335 διαγίνομαι, *diaginomai*
lose [1], over[2] [1], pass [1]

1336 διαγινώσκω, *diaginōskō*
decide [1], make an examination [1]

1338 διάγνωσις, *diagnōsis*
decision [1]

1339 διαγογγύζω, *diagongyzō*
grumble [2]

1340 διαγρηγορέω, *diagrēgoreō*
stay awake [1]

1341 διάγω, *diagō*
lead [1], pass days [1]

1342 διαδέχομαι, *diadechomai*
turn[2] [1]

1343 διάδημα, *diadēma*
diadem [3]

1344 διαδίδωμι, *diadidōmi*
distribute [3], divide [1]

1345 διάδοχος, *diadochos*
succeed[1] [1]

1346 διαζώννυμι, *diazōnnymi*
tie around [2], put on [1]

1347 διαθήκη, *diathēkē*
covenant [30], will[2] [3]

1348 διαίρεσις, *diairesis*
variety [3]

1349 διαιρέω, *diaireō*
allot [1], divide [1]

1350 διακαθαίρω, *diakathairō*
clear [1]

1351 διακαθαρίζω, *diakatharizō*
clear [1]

1352 διακατελέγχομαι,
diakatelenchomai
refute [1]

1354 διακονέω, *diakoneō*
serve [19], provide [3], wait[2] [3],
administer [2], serve as deacon [2], do [1],
do work [1], helper [1], ministry [1],
prepare [1], render service [1], service [1],
take care [1]

1355 διακονία, *diakonia*
ministry [20], service [4], serve [3],
task [2], distribution [1], minister [1],
mission [1], relief [1], render [1]

1356 διάκονος, *diakonos*
servant [17], minister [7], deacon [4],
attendant [1]

1357 διακόσιοι, *diakosioi*
two hundred [6]

1357 + 1324 διακόσιοι + δηνάριον,
diakosioi + dēnarion
six months' wages [1]

1357 + 4388 διακόσιοι + πῆχυς,
diakosioi + pēchys
hundred yards [1]

1358 διακούω, *diakouō*
give a hearing [1]

1359 διακρίνω, *diakrinō*
doubt [5], make a distinction [3],
contend [1], criticize [1], decide [1],
discern [1], hesitation [1], interpret [1],
judge oneself [1], make waver [1], see
anything different [1], waver [1], weigh [1]

1360 διάκρισις, *diakrisis*
discernment [1], distinguish [1],
quarrel [1]

1361 διακωλύω, *diakōlyō*
prevent [1]

1362 διαλαλέω, *dialaleō*
discuss [1], talk about [1]

1363 διαλέγομαι, *dialegomai*
argue [6], dispute [2], address [1],
discuss [1], have a discussion [1], hold a
discussion [1], talk [1]

1364 διαλείπω, *dialeipō*
stop [1]

1365 διάλεκτος, *dialektos*
language [3], native language [2],
untranslated [1]

1367 διαλλάσσομαι, *diallassomai*
reconcile [1]

1368 διαλογίζομαι, *dialogizomai*
argue [3], question [3], discuss [2], raise a
question [2], say [2], talk [2], ponder [1],
think [1]

1369 διαλογισμός, *dialogismos*
thought [4], argument [2], intention [2],
think [2], argue [1], doubt [1], opinion [1],
question [1]

1370 διαλύω, *dialyō*
disperse [1]

1371 διαμαρτύρομαι, *diamartyromai*
testify [10], warn [3], urge solemnly [1],
warn solemnly [1]

1372 διαμάχομαι, *diamachomai*
contend [1]

1373 διαμένω, *diamenō*
remain [3], continue [1], stand by [1]

1374 διαμερίζω, *diamerizō*
divide [10], distribute [1]

1375 διαμερισμός, *diamerismos*
division [1]

1376 διανέμω, *dianemō*
spread [1]

1377 διανεύω, *dianeuō*
motion [1]

1378 διανόημα, *dianoēma*
think [1]

1379 διάνοια, *dianoia*
mind[1] [7], understanding [2], intention [1],
sense [1], thought [1]

1380 διανοίγω, *dianoigō*
open [6], explain [1]

1380 + 3616 διανοίγω + μήτρα,
dianoigō + mētra
firstborn [1]

1381 διανυκτερεύω, *dianyktereuō*
spend the night [1]

1382 διανύω, *dianyō*
finish [1]

1384 διαπαρατριβή, *diaparatribē*
wrangle [1]

1385 διαπεράω, *diaperaō*
cross [3], cross over [2], bound for [1]

1386 διαπλέω, *diapleō*
sail across [1]

1387 διαπονέομαι, *diaponeomai*
annoy much [1], annoy very much [1]

1388 διαπορεύομαι, *diaporeuomai*
go through [2], go by [1], go from town to
town [1], journey [1]

1389 διαπορέω, *diaporeō*
perplex [3], puzzle greatly [1]

1390 διαπραγματεύομαι,
diapragmateuomai
gain by trading [1]

1391 διαπρίω, *diapriō*
enrage [2]

1395 διαρπάζω, *diarpazō*
plunder [3]

1396 διαρρήγνυμι, *diarrēgnymi*
tear[1] [3], break [2]

1397 διασαφέω, *diasapheō*
explain [1], report [1]

1398 διασείω, *diaseiō*
extort money by threat [1]

1399 διασκορπίζω, *diaskorpizō*
scatter [5], squander [2], disperse [1],
scatter seed [1]

1400 διασπάω, *diaspaō*
tear to pieces [1], wrench apart [1]

1401 διασπείρω, *diaspeirō*
scatter [3]

1402 διασπορά, *diaspora*
dispersion [3]

1403 διαστέλλω, *diastellō*
order[3] [4], caution [1], give an order [1],
instruction [1], order sternly [1]

1404 διάστημα, *diastēma*
interval [1]

1405 διαστολή, *diastolē*
distinction [2], distinct [1]

1406 διαστρέφω, *diastrephō*
perverse [3], distort truth [1], make
crooked [1], pervert [1], turn away [1]

1407 διασῴζω, *diasōzō*
heal [2], save [2], bring safely [1],
escape [1], reach safety [1], take safely [1]

1408 διαταγή, *diatagē*
appoint [1], ordain [1]

1409 διάταγμα, *diatagma*
edict [1]

1410 διαταράσσω, *diatarassō*
perplex much [1]

1411 διατάσσω, *diatassō*
order[3] [4], command [2], direct [2], give
directions [1], give instruction [1],
instruct [1], instruction [1], make an
arrangement [1], ordain [1], prescribe [1],
rule[2] [1]

1412 διατελέω, *diateleō*
be [1]

1413 διατηρέω, diatēreō
keep [1], treasure [1]

1416 διατίθημι, diatithēmi
confer [2], make a covenant [2], make
[a will] [2], give [1]

1417 διατρίβω, diatribō
stay [5], remain [3], spend time [1]

1418 διατροφή, diatrophē
food [1]

1419 διαυγάζω, diaugazō
dawn [1]

1420 διαυγής, diaugēs
transparent [1]

1422 διαφέρω, diapherō
good [3], more value [2], value [2], carry
through [1], differ [1], drift across [1],
make a difference [1], more valuable [1],
spread [1]

1423 διαφεύγω, diapheugō
escape [1]

1424 διαφημίζω, diaphēmizō
spread [1], spread the news [1], tell [1]

1425 διαφθείρω, diaphtheirō
destroy [4], deprave [1], waste away [1]

1426 διαφθορά, diaphthora
corruption [6]

1427 διάφορος, diaphoros
more excellent [2], differ [1], various [1]

1428 διαφυλάσσω, diaphylassō
protect [1]

1429 διαχειρίζω, diacheirizō
kill [2]

1430 διαχλευάζω, diachleuazō
sneer [1]

1431 διαχωρίζω, diachōrizō
leave [1]

1434 διδακτικός, didaktikos
apt teacher [2]

1435 διδακτός, didaktos
teach [3]

1436 διδασκαλία, didaskalia
teaching [13], doctrine [7], instruction [1]

1437 διδάσκαλος, didaskalos
teacher [59]

1438 διδάσκω, didaskō
teach [94], direct [1], instruct [1],
teacher [1]

1439 διδαχή, didachē
teaching [27], instruction [1], lesson [1],
teach [1]

1440 δίδραχμον, didrachmon
temple tax [2]

1441 Δίδυμος, Didymos
Twin [3]

1442 διδῶ, didō
make [1]

1443 δίδωμι, didōmi
give [329], grant [16], put [10], allow [7],
pay [6], offer [4], make [3], produce [3],
be [2], bring forth [2], give up [2], let [2],
set¹ [2], yield [2], see 4825 [strike on the
face] [2], assign [1], bring [1], cast [1],
enable [1], give over [1], give
permission [1], grant authority [1],
have [1], inflict [1], leave [1], permit [1],
place [1], show [1], supply [1], utter [1],
venture [1], see 142 [praise] [1], see 1953

[command] [1], see 5206 [conspire] [1],
untranslated [1]

1443 + 3836 + 3635 δίδωμι + ὁ +
μισθός, didōmi + ho + misthos
reward [1]

1443 + 5401 δίδωμι + σωτηρία, didōmi
+ sōtēria
rescue [1]

1444 διεγείρω, diegeirō
wake up [3], arouse [1], refresh [1],
rough [1]

1445 διενθυμέομαι, dienthymeomai
think [1]

1447 διέξοδος, diexodos
main street [1]

1449 διερμηνευτής, diermēneutēs
interpret [1]

1450 διερμηνεύω, diermēneuō
interpret [5], in Greek [1]

1451 διέρχομαι, dierchomai
go through [12], pass through [9],
pass [3], come [2], go about [2], go
across [2], wander through [2], cross
over [1], go [1], go from place to
place [1], go here and there [1], go on [1],
pierce [1], spread [1], spread abroad [1],
travel [1], visit [1], untranslated [1]

1452 διερωτάω, dierōtaō
ask [1]

1453 διετής, dietēs
two years [1]

1454 διετία, dietia
two years [2]

1455 διηγέομαι, diēgeomai
describe [3], tell [3], declare [1], report [1]

1456 διήγησις, diēgēsis
orderly account [1]

1457 διηνεκής, diēnekēs
all time [2], see 1650 [continually] [1], see
1650 [forever] [1]

1458 διθάλασσος, dithalassos
see 5536 [reef] [1]

1459 διϊκνέομαι, diikneomai
pierce [1]

1460 διΐστημι, diistēmi
farther [1], late [1], withdraw [1]

1462 διϊσχυρίζομαι, diischyrizomai
insist [2]

1464 δικαιοκρισία, dikaiokrisia
righteous judgment [1]

1465 δίκαιος, dikaios
righteous [43], just² [9], right¹ [7],
righteous one [5], righteous person [5],
righteous man [3], innocent [2],
upright [2], honest [1], innocent man [1],
justly [1]

1466 δικαιοσύνη, dikaiosynē
righteousness [74], right¹ [7], justice [3],
justification [3], untranslated [2], it [1],
justify [1], piety [1]

1467 δικαιόω, dikaioō
justify [31], vindicate [3], free [2],
acknowledge justice [1], acquit [1], set
free [1]

1468 δικαίωμα, dikaiōma
regulation [3], act of righteousness [1],
decree [1], judgment [1], just
requirement [1], justification [1],
requirement [1], righteous deed [1]

1469 δικαίως, dikaiōs
justly [2], upright [2], right¹ [1]

1470 δικαίωσις, dikaiōsis
justification [2]

1471 δικαστής, dikastēs
judge [2]

1472 δίκη, dikē
punishment [2], justice [1]

1473 δίκτυον, diktyon
net [12]

1474 δίλογος, dilogos
double-tongued [1]

1475 διό, dio
therefore [37], so [7], reason¹ [5], so
then [3], consequently [1]

1476 διοδεύω, diodeuō
go on through [1], pass through [1]

1477 Διονύσιος, Dionysios
Dionysius [1]

1478 διόπερ, dioper
therefore [2]

1479 διοπετής, diopetēs
fall from heaven [1]

1480 διόρθωμα, diorthōma
reform [1]

1481 διόρθωσις, diorthōsis
set things right [1]

1482 διορύσσω, dioryssō
break in [2], break into [2]

1483 Διόσκουροι, Dioskouroi
Twin Brothers [1]

1484 διότι, dioti
because [10], for [10], therefore [2],
reason¹ [1]

1485 Διοτρέφης, Diotrephēs
Diotrephes [1]

1487 διπλοῦς, diplous
double [3], twice as much [1]

1488 διπλόω, diploō
repay [1]

1489 δίς, dis
twice [4], more [1], see 562 [again and
again] [1]

1490 + 3689 δισμυριάς + μυριάς,
dismyrias + myrias
two hundred million [1]

1491 διστάζω, distazō
doubt [2]

1492 δίστομος, distomos
two-edged [3]

1493 δισχίλιοι, dischilioi
two thousand [1]

1494 διϋλίζω, diylizō
strain out [1]

1495 διχάζω, dichazō
set against [1]

1496 διχοστασία, dichostasia
dissension [2]

1497 διχοτομέω, dichotomeō
cut in pieces [2]

1498 διψάω, dipsaō
thirsty [14], thirst [2]

1499 δίψος, dipsos
thirsty [1]

1500 δίψυχος, dipsychos
double-minded [2]

1501 διωγμός, *diōgmos*
persecution [10]

1502 διώκτης, *diōktēs*
persecutor [1]

1503 διώκω, *diōkō*
persecute [28], pursue [9], press on [2],
strive [2], extend [1], persecutor [1],
seek [1], set off in pursuit [1]

1504 δόγμα, *dogma*
decree [2], decision [1], legal demand [1],
ordinance [1]

1505 δογματίζω, *dogmatizō*
submit to regulation [1]

1506 δοκέω, *dokeō*
think [32], seem [7], suppose [4],
decide [3], acknowledge [2], claim [2],
seem good [2], *see 4024* [unexpected] [2],
convince [1], dispose [1], have [1],
leader [1], presume [1], recognize [1],
regard [1], verdict [1]

1507 δοκιμάζω, *dokimazō*
test [10], approve [3], determine [2],
interpret [2], discern [1], examine [1], see
fit [1], try out [1], try to find out [1]

1508 δοκιμασία, *dokimasia*
untranslated [1]

1509 δοκιμή, *dokimē*
character [2], test [2], ordeal [1], proof [1],
worth [1]

1510 δοκίμιον, *dokimion*
genuineness [1], test [1]

1511 δόκιμος, *dokimos*
approve [3], approval [1], genuine [1],
meet the test [1], test [1]

1512 δοκός, *dokos*
log [6]

1513 δόλιος, *dolios*
deceitful [1]

1514 δολιόω, *dolioō*
deceive [1]

1515 δόλος, *dolos*
deceit [7], stealth [2], guile [1],
trickery [1]

1516 δολόω, *doloō*
falsify [1]

1517 δόμα, *doma*
gift [4]

1518 δόξα, *doxa*
glory [149], glorious [5], glorious one [2],
honor [2], praise [2], reflection [2],
splendor [2], another [1], brightness [1]

1519 δοξάζω, *doxazō*
glorify [45], praise [10], glory [2],
honor [2], give glory [1], glorious [1]

1520 Δορκάς, *Dorkas*
Dorcas [2]

1521 δόσις, *dosis*
act of giving [1], give [1]

1522 δότης, *dotēs*
giver [1]

1524 δουλαγωγέω, *doulagōgeō*
enslave [1]

1525 δουλεία, *douleia*
slavery [4], bondage [1]

1526 δουλεύω, *douleuō*
serve [14], slave [5], enslave [3], render
service [1], slavery [1], work like a
slave [1]

1527 δούλη, *doulē*
servant [2], slave woman [1]

1528 δοῦλος[1], *doulos*[1]
slave [95], servant [27], slave man [1],
slavery [1]

1529 δοῦλος[2], *doulos*[2]
slave [2]

1530 δουλόω, *douloō*
enslave [3], slave [3], bind [1], make a
slave [1]

1531 δοχή, *dochē*
banquet [2]

1532 δράκων, *drakōn*
dragon [13]

1533 δράσσομαι, *drassomai*
catch [1]

1534 δραχμή, *drachmē*
coin [1], silver coin [1], they [1]

1535 δρέπανον, *drepanon*
sickle [8]

1536 δρόμος, *dromos*
course [1], race[2] [1], work [1]

1537 Δρούσιλλα, *Drousilla*
Drusilla [1]

1538 δύναμαι, *dynamai*
can [102], *see 4024* [cannot] [47],
able [38], *see 3590* [cannot] [6], *see 3590*
[unable] [3], enable [2], ready [2], *see
4024* [unable] [2], *see 4028* [cannot] [2],
may [1], might [1], power [1],
strength [1], *see 4046* [cannot] [1],
untranslated [1]

1539 δύναμις, *dynamis*
power [88], deed of power [13],
miracle [5], means[2] [2], ability [1], full
force [1], meaning [1], mighty [1], mighty
work [1], powerful [1], powerfully [1],
rage [1], strength [1], work a miracle [1],
see 5642 [unbearably] [1]

1540 δυναμόω, *dynamoō*
make strong [1], win strength [1]

1541 δυνάστης, *dynastēs*
court official [1], powerful [1],
sovereign [1]

1542 δυνατέω, *dynateō*
able [2], powerful [1]

1543 δυνατός, *dynatos*
possible [11], able [6], power [3],
strong [3], can [2], mighty [2],
powerful [2], authority [1], well-
versed [1], *see 4024* [impossible] [1]

1544 δύνω, *dynō*
set[2] [1]

1544 + 3836 + 2463 δύνω + ὁ + ἥλιος,
dynō + ho + hēlios
sundown [1]

1545 δύο, *dyo*
two [126], *untranslated* [3], *see 5477*
[forty-two] [2], extra [1], pair [1],
second [1]

1545 + 3583 δύο + μετρητής, *dyo +
metrētēs*
twenty gallons [1]

1546 δυσβάστακτος, *dysbastaktos*
hard to bear [2]

1548 δυσεντέριον, *dysenterion*
dysentery [1]

1549 δυσερμήνευτος, *dysermēneutos*
hard [1]

1550 δύσις, *dysis*
west [1]

1551 δύσκολος, *dyskolos*
hard [1]

1552 δυσκόλως, *dyskolōs*
hard [3]

1553 δυσμή, *dysmē*
west [5]

1554 δυσνόητος, *dysnoētos*
hard to understand [1]

1555 δυσφημέω, *dysphēmeō*
slander [1]

1556 δυσφημία, *dysphēmia*
ill repute [1]

1557 δώδεκα, *dōdeka*
twelve [74], *see 5084* [fifteen hundred
miles] [1]

1558 δωδέκατος, *dōdekatos*
twelfth [1]

1559 δωδεκάφυλον, *dōdekaphylon*
twelve tribes [1]

1560 δῶμα, *dōma*
housetop [5], roof [2]

1561 δωρεά, *dōrea*
gift [9], free gift [2]

1562 δωρεάν, *dōrean*
gift [3], without payment [2], free of
charge [1], nothing [1], without cause [1],
without paying [1]

1563 δωρέομαι, *dōreomai*
give [2], grant [1]

1564 δώρημα, *dōrēma*
free gift [1], gift [1]

1565 δῶρον, *dōron*
gift [15], give to God [1], offering to
God [1], present[1] [1], *see 965*
[contribute] [1]

1568 ἔα, *ea*
let alone [1]

1569 ἐάν, *ean*
if [188], *see 4005* [whatever] [17],
untranslated [10], *see 3963*
[wherever] [7], *see 4005* [whoever] [7],
see 5516 [whoever] [7], *see 4005*
[anyone] [6], *see 4005* [who] [5], *see 5516*
[anyone] [5], when [4], *see 5516*
[who] [4], even if [3], *see 4012*
[whatever] [3], provided [2], though [2],
whether [2], *see 4005* [that] [2], *see 4006*
[often] [2], *see 4012* [who] [2], *see 4246*
[whatever] [2], as [1], case [1], even
though [1], except [1], suppose [1],
unless [1], what [1], whenever [1], *see
2471* [when] [1], *see 3963* [whenever] [1],
see 4005 [any] [1], *see 4005* [what] [1],
see 4012 [everyone] [1], *see 4015*
[who] [1], *see 4015* [whoever] [1], *see
4023* [wherever] [1], *see 6055* [like[1]] [1]

1569 + 3590 ἐάν + μή, *ean + mē*
unless [25], without[1] [6], apart [1], but [1],
but only [1], except [1]

1569 + 5516 ἐάν + τὶς, *ean + tis*
whatever [1]

1570 ἐάνπερ, *eanper*
if [2], if only [1]

1571 ἑαυτοῦ, *heautou*
himself [56], themselves [52],
yourself [34], *untranslated* [32], one's
own [30], he [20], one another [20],
they [17], ourselves [16], itself [12],

you [11], herself [3], she [3], we [3],
oneself [2], each other [1], heart [1],
person [1], such a person [1], that [1],
the [1], together [1]

1572 ἐάω, eaō
allow [4], let [4], leave [1], no more [1],
set[1] [1]

1573 ἑβδομήκοντα, hebdomēkonta
seventy [3]

**1573 + 1971 ἑβδομήκοντα + ἕξ,
hebdomēkonta + hex**
seventy-six [1]

**1573 + 4297 ἑβδομήκοντα + πέντε,
hebdomēkonta + pente**
seventy-five [1]

**1574 + 2231 ἑβδομηκοντάκις + ἑπτά,
hebdomēkontakis + hepta**
seventy-seven times [1]

1575 ἕβδομος, hebdomos
seventh [8]

**1575 + 6052 ἕβδομος + ὥρα,
hebdomos + hōra**
one in the afternoon [1]

1576 Ἔβερ, Eber
Eber [1]

1578 Ἑβραῖος, Hebraios
Hebrew [4]

1579 Ἑβραΐς, Hebrais
Hebrew [3]

1580 Ἑβραϊστί, Hebraisti
Hebrew [7]

1581 ἐγγίζω, engizō
come near [15], approach [11], near [5],
draw near [4], at hand [3], come [2],
arrive [1], come close [1]

1582 ἐγγράφω, engraphō
write [3].

1583 ἔγγυος, engyos
guarantee [1]

1584 ἐγγύς, engys
near [28], nearby [1], soon [1], verge [1]

1586 ἐγείρω, egeirō
raise [71], get up [21], rise [11], raise
up [10], stand up [10], arise [3], come [3],
appear [2], awake [2], lift up [2], wake [2],
wake up [2], increase [1], lift out [1],
make [1], rise again [1], rise up [1]

1587 ἔγερσις, egersis
resurrection [1]

1588 ἐγκάθετος, enkathetos
spy [1]

1589 ἐγκαίνια, enkainia
festival of the Dedication [1]

1590 ἐγκαινίζω, enkainizō
inaugurate [1], open [1]

1591 ἐγκακέω, enkakeō
lose heart [4], grow weary [1], weary [1]

1592 ἐγκαλέω, enkaleō
accuse [3], bring a charge against [2],
accusation [1], charge[3] [1]

1593 ἐγκαταλείπω, enkataleipō
forsake [4], abandon [2], desert[1] [2],
leave [1], neglect [1]

1594 ἐγκατοικέω, enkatoikeō
live [1]

1595 ἐγκαυχάομαι, enkauchaomai
boast [1]

1596 ἐγκεντρίζω, enkentrizō
graft in [3], graft into [2], graft [1]

1598 ἔγκλημα, enklēma
charge[3] [2]

1599 ἐγκομβόομαι, enkomboomai
clothe [1]

1600 ἐγκοπή, enkopē
obstacle in the way [1]

1601 ἐγκόπτω, enkoptō
hinder [2], block a way [1], detain [1],
prevent [1]

1602 ἐγκράτεια, enkrateia
self-control [4]

1603 ἐγκρατεύομαι, enkrateuomai
exercise self-control [1], practice self-
control [1]

1604 ἐγκρατής, enkratēs
self-controlled [1]

1605 ἐγκρίνω, enkrinō
classify [1]

1606 ἐγκρύπτω, enkryptō
mix [1], mix in [1]

1607 ἔγκυος, enkyos
expect a child [1]

1608 ἐγχρίω, enchriō
anoint [1]

1609 ἐγώ, egō
I [1667], we [850], untranslated [27],
myself [4], I am [2], ourselves [1]

1609 + 1639 ἐγώ + εἰμί, egō + eimi
I am [30]

1609 + 6034 ἐγώ + ψυχή, egō + psychē
I [2]

1610 ἐδαφίζω, edaphizō
crush to the ground [1]

1611 ἔδαφος, edaphos
ground[1] [1]

1612 ἑδραῖος, hedraios
steadfast [2], firm [1]

1613 ἑδραίωμα, hedraiōma
bulwark [1]

1614 Ἑζεκίας, Hezekias
Hezekiah [2]

1615 ἐθελοθρησκία, ethelothrēskia
self-imposed piety [1]

1616 ἐθίζω, ethizō
customary [1]

1617 ἐθνάρχης, ethnarchēs
governor [1]

1618 ἐθνικός, ethnikos
Gentile [3], non-believer [1]

1619 ἐθνικῶς, ethnikōs
like a Gentile [1]

1620 ἔθνος, ethnos
Gentile [94], nation [61], people [5],
pagan [2]

1621 ἔθος, ethos
custom [10], habit [1], usual [1]

1623 εἰ, ei
if [300], untranslated [57], whether [19],
though [10], that [5], or [4], not [3],
since [3], for [2], when [2], see 1760
[unless] [2], although [1], as [1],
chance [1], even if [1], even though [1], if
only [1], no [1], only [1], provided [1], see
1760 [except] [1]

**1623 + 726 + 1145 εἰ + ἄρα + γέ, ei +
ara + ge**
perhaps [1]

**1623 + 1254 + 3590 εἰ + δέ + μή, ei +
de + mē**
otherwise [2]

**1623 + 1254 + 3590 + 1145 εἰ + δέ +
μή + γέ, ei + de + mē + ge**
otherwise [3], for then [1]

1623 + 3590 εἰ + μή, ei + mē
except [35], but [22], only [7], but
only [2], however [1], unless [1], until [1]

**1623 + 3590 + 3667 εἰ + μή + μόνον,
ei + mē + monon**
except [2]

1623 + 3614 εἰ + μήτι, ei + mēti
except [1], unless [1], unless indeed [1]

1623 + 4803 εἰ + πώς, ei + pōs
order[2] [1], somehow [1]

**1623 + 5593 εἰ + τυγχάνω, ei +
tynchanō**
doubtless [1], perhaps [1]

1624 εἰδέα, eidea
appearance [1]

1626 εἶδος, eidos
form [3], appearance [1], sight [1]

1627 εἰδωλεῖον, eidōleion
temple of an idol [1]

1628 εἰδωλόθυτος, eidōlothytos
food sacrificed to an idol [5], food offered
to an idol [2], sacrifice to idol [2]

1629 εἰδωλολάτρης, eidōlolatrēs
idolater [7]

1630 εἰδωλολατρία, eidōlolatria
idolatry [3], worship of an idol [1]

1631 εἴδωλον, eidōlon
idol [11]

1632 εἰκῇ, eikē
nothing [2], vain [2], waste [1], without
cause [1]

1633 εἴκοσι, eikosi
twenty [3]

**1633 + 4297 + 5084 εἴκοσι + πέντε +
στάδιον, eikosi + pente + stadion**
three miles [1]

**1633 + 5475 εἴκοσι + τέσσαρες, eikosi
+ tessares**
twenty-four [6]

**1633 + 5552 εἴκοσι + τρεῖς, eikosi +
treis**
twenty-three [1]

**1634 + 3836 + 5717 εἴκω + ὁ +
ὑποταγή, eikō + ho + hypotagē**
submit [1]

1635 εἰκών, eikōn
image [19], head [3], form [1]

1636 εἰλικρίνεια, eilikrineia
sincerity [3]

1637 εἰλικρινής, eilikrinēs
pure [1], sincere [1]

1639 εἰμί, eimi
be [2063], untranslated [186], see 1609 [I
am] [30], have [28], come [20],
belong [18], become [13], mean[1] [12],
do [7], exist [7], live [7], make [6], I
am [5], remain [4], rest[1] [3], stand[1] [3],
alive [2], bind [2], consist [2],
continue [2], endure [2], find [2], get [2],

happen [2], keep [2], number [2],
show [2], as [1], assume [1], commit [1],
devote [1], dwell [1], existence [1],
give [1], go on [1], go out [1], grow [1],
hold [1], involve [1], life [1], meet [1],
own[1] [1], put [1], refer [1], say [1],
seem [1], set[1] [1], side [1], stay [1], take
office [1], take place [1], use [1], what [1],
who [1], worth [1], you [1]

1639 + 5250 εἰμί + σύν, *eimi + syn*
accompany [1]

1641 εἵνεκεν, *heineken*
because [2]

1642 εἴπερ, *eiper*
since [2], for indeed [1], if [1], if in
fact [1], though [1]

1644 εἰρηνεύω, *eirēneuō*
peace [2], live in peace [1], live
peaceably [1]

1645 εἰρήνη, *eirēnē*
peace [89], reconciliation [1], safe [1],
untranslated [1]

1646 εἰρηνικός, *eirēnikos*
peaceable [1], peaceful [1]

1647 εἰρηνοποιέω, *eirēnopoieō*
make peace [1]

1648 εἰρηνοποιός, *eirēnopoios*
peacemaker [1]

1650 εἰς, *eis*
to [544], into [311], *untranslated* [205],
in [176], for [143], at [39], on [35],
as [30], so that [21], against [18],
with [14], among [13], toward [12], lead
to [9], so [9], until [8], *see 4024*
[never] [8], that [7], of [6], *see 2262*
[enter] [6], make [4], order[2] [4],
about[1] [3], deal [3], purpose [3],
before [2], bring [2], bring about [2],
come [2], concerning [2], sake [2], the [2],
thus [2], to an end [2], by [1], cause [1],
close [1], connection [1], destine for [1],
grant [1], gratify [1], help [1], intend [1],
lead [1], obtain [1], over[1] [1], place [1],
promise [1], result [1], service [1],
throughout [1], to the point [1],
towards [1], under [1], way [1], win [1],
see 490 [greater and greater iniquity] [1],
see 965 [contribute] [1], *see 1181*
[disappear] [1], *see 1181* [hear] [1], *see*
2848 [beyond all measure] [1], *see 3357*
[scorn] [1], *see 4024* [nothing] [1], *see*
5377 [receive a death-blow] [1]

1650 + 172 εἰς + αἰών, *eis + aiōn*
forever [2]

1650 + 724 εἰς + ἀπώλεια, *eis + apōleia*
perish [1]

1650 + 3836 + 172 εἰς + ὁ + αἰών, *eis*
+ ho + aiōn
forever [43], again [2], permanent [1]

1650 + 3545 εἰς + μέσος, *eis + mesos*
before [1]

1650 + 3836 + 1178 εἰς + ὁ + γῆ, *eis +*
ho + gē
ashore [2]

1650 + 3836 + 1457 εἰς + ὁ +
διηνεκής, *eis + ho + diēnekēs*
continually [1], forever [1]

1650 + 3836 + 1869 εἰς + ὁ +
ἔμπροσθεν, *eis + ho + emprosthen*
ahead [1]

1650 + 3836 + 3146 εἰς + ὁ + κόλπος,
eis + ho + kolpos
with [1]

1650 + 3836 + 3545 εἰς + ὁ + μέσος,
eis + ho + mesos
among [2], before [1], forward [1],
here [1]

1650 + 3836 + 3958 εἰς + ὁ + ὀπίσω,
eis + ho + opisō
back [5], around [1]

1650 + 3836 + 4044 εἰς + ὁ + οὖς, *eis*
+ ho + ous
whisper [1]

1650 + 3836 + 4117 εἰς + ὁ +
παντελής, *eis + ho + pantelēs*
quite [1]

1650 + 3910 εἰς + ὅλος, *eis + holos*
throughout [4]

1650 + 4005 εἰς + ὅς, *eis + hos*
purpose [1]

1650 + 4047 εἰς + οὗτος, *eis + houtos*
purpose [5], reason[1] [2]

1650 + 4246 + 3836 + 172 εἰς + πᾶς +
ὁ + αἰών, *eis + pas + ho + aiōn*
forever [1]

1650 + 4353 εἰς + περισσεία, *eis +*
perisseia
greatly [1]

1650 + 5465 εἰς + τέλος, *eis + telos*
continually [1]

1650 + 5515 εἰς + τίς, *eis + tis*
why [4]

1651 εἷς, *heis*
one [246], a [15], *untranslated* [14],
single [11], first [9], one man [7], one
thing [6], once[1] [4], alone [3], other [3],
someone [3], one person [2], agree [1],
another [1], anything [1], common
purpose [1], each [1], every one [1],
man [1], one party [1], one woman [1],
some [1], *see 608* [alike] [1], *see 1651*
[each] [1], *see 2848* [individually] [1], *see*
2848 [one by one] [1], *see 3590* [none] [1]

1651 + 1191 εἷς + γνώμη, *heis + gnōmē*
agree [1], unite [1]

1651 + 1667 εἷς + ἕκαστος, *heis +*
hekastos
everyone [1], one by one [1]

1651 + 1667 + 4246 εἷς + ἕκαστος +
πᾶς, *heis + hekastos + pas*
everyone [1]

1651 + 2848 + 1651 εἷς + κατά + εἷς,
heis + kata + heis
each [1]

1651 + 5889 εἷς + φωνή, *heis + phōnē*
unison [1]

1652 εἰσάγω, *eisagō*
bring into [7], bring in [4]

1653 εἰσακούω, *eisakouō*
hear [4], listen [1]

1654 εἰσδέχομαι, *eisdechomai*
welcome [1]

1655 εἴσειμι, *eiseimi*
go into [2], enter [1], go [1]

1656 εἰσέρχομαι, *eiserchomai*
enter [122], go into [13], come in [12], go
in [11], come [7], come into [7], go to [5],
go [3], come to [2], arise [1], arrival [1],
gain entrance [1], get in [1], go inside [1],

go through [1], reach [1], take [1],
visit [1], *see 4028* [stop] [1]

1656 + 3552 + 5082 εἰσέρχομαι +
μετά + σπουδή, *eiserchomai + meta*
+ spoudē
rush back [1]

1656 + 4099 εἰσέρχομαι + πάλιν,
eiserchomai + palin
return [1]

1657 εἰσκαλέομαι, *eiskaleomai*
invite [1]

1658 εἴσοδος, *eisodos*
come [2], enter [1], entry [1], welcome [1]

1659 εἰσπηδάω, *eispēdaō*
rush in [1]

1660 εἰσπορεύομαι, *eisporeuomai*
enter [9], go in [3], go into [3], come
in [1], come to [1], go to [1]

1661 εἰστρέχω, *eistrechō*
run in [1]

1662 εἰσφέρω, *eispherō*
bring [2], bring in [2], bring into [2], bring
to [1], *untranslated* [1]

1663 εἶτα, *eita*
then [14], moreover [1]

1664 εἴτε, *eite*
or [29], whether [15], *untranslated* [8],
if [7], as for [4], either [1], such [1]

1665 εἴωθα, *eiōtha*
custom [3], accustom [1]

1666 ἐκ, *ek*
from [338], of [156], out [82],
untranslated [68], by [52], at [26],
with [19], belong [17], in [15], come
from [13], some [11], for [10], on [9],
among [8], origin [8], from among [5],
through [4], because [3], part[1] [3],
since [3], to [3], according [2],
adherent [2], any [2], as [2], basis [2],
child [2], depend on [2], follow [2],
member [2], under [2], about[1] [1],
after [1], against [1], away [1], base[1] [1],
bear[1] [1], before [1], between [1],
come [1], descend [1], do [1], father [1],
ground[2] [1], have [1], means[1] [1], off [1],
on one's own [1], proceed from [1],
question [1], rely [1], respect[2] [1],
result [1], send from [1], share [1],
source [1], spring from [1], use [1], *see*
3336 [utterly] [1], *see 5889* [voice] [1]

1666 + 2702 ἐκ + Ἰσραήλ, *ek + Israēl*
Israelite [1]

1666 + 3120 + 3613 ἐκ + κοιλία +
μήτηρ, *ek + koilia + mētēr*
birth [1]

1666 + 3383 ἐκ + λύπη, *ek + lypē*
reluctantly [1]

1666 + 3538 ἐκ + μέρος, *ek + meros*
individually [1], partial [1]

1666 + 3545 ἐκ + μέσος, *ek + mesos*
from [2], aside [1]

1666 + 3545 + 1181 ἐκ + μέσος +
γίνομαι, *ek + mesos + ginomai*
remove [1]

1666 + 4041 ἐκ + οὐρανός, *ek + ouranos*
heavenly [1]

1666 + 5065 ἐκ + σπέρμα, *ek + sperma*
descend from [1]

1666 + 5882 ἐκ + φύσις, *ek + physis*
physically [1]

1667 ἕκαστος, hekastos
each [49], each one [7], all [5], everyone [3], one [3], every one [2], you [2], *see 1651* [everyone] [2], *untranslated* [2], all people [1], another [1], each man [1], each woman [1], every [1], we [1], *see 1651* [one by one] [1]

1668 ἑκάστοτε, hekastote
any time [1]

1669 ἑκατόν, hekaton
hundred [13], hundredfold [4]

1670 ἑκατονταετής, hekatontaetēs
hundred years [1]

1671 ἑκατονταπλασίων, hekatontaplasiōn
hundredfold [3]

1672 ἑκατοντάρχης, hekatontarchēs
centurion [20]

1674 ἐκβαίνω, ekbainō
leave behind [1]

1675 ἐκβάλλω, ekballō
cast out [34], drive out [11], take out [7], throw out [5], bring out [4], throw [4], put outside [3], send out [3], bring [1], discharge [1], drag out [1], drive away [1], expel [1], go out [1], leave out [1], send away [1], tear out [1]

1675 + 3836 + 3950 + 6055 + 4505 ἐκβάλλω + ὁ + ὄνομα + ὡς + πονηρός, ekballō + ho + onoma + hōs + ponēros
defame [1]

1676 ἔκβασις, ekbasis
outcome [1], way out [1]

1678 ἐκβολή, ekbolē
throw overboard cargo [1]

1681 ἔκγονος, ekgonos
grandchildren [1]

1682 ἐκδαπανάω, ekdapanaō
spend [1]

1683 ἐκδέχομαι, ekdechomai
wait[1] [4], expect [1], look forward [1]

1684 ἔκδηλος, ekdēlos
plain [1]

1685 ἐκδημέω, ekdēmeō
away [3]

1686 ἐκδίδωμι, ekdidōmi
lease [4]

1687 ἐκδιηγέομαι, ekdiēgeomai
report [1], tell [1]

1688 ἐκδικέω, ekdikeō
avenge [3], grant justice [2], punish [1]

1689 ἐκδίκησις, ekdikēsis
vengeance [4], justice [2], punish [1], punishment [1], *see 4472* [avenge] [1]

1690 ἔκδικος, ekdikos
avenger [1], execute [1]

1691 ἐκδιώκω, ekdiōkō
drive out [1]

1692 ἔκδοτος, ekdotos
hand over [1]

1693 ἐκδοχή, ekdochē
prospect [1]

1694 ἐκδύω, ekdyō
strip [4], take off [1], unclothed [1]

1695 ἐκεῖ, ekei
there [76], where [8], *untranslated* [6],

behind [1], bystander [1], in [1], other [1], over there [1]

1696 ἐκεῖθεν, ekeithen
from there [10], place [8], *untranslated* [5], on one's way [1], synagogue [1], there [1], *see 1949* [either side] [1]

1697 ἐκεῖνος, ekeinos
that [141], he [41], they [18], *untranslated* [13], this [5], same [4], one [3], she [3], *see 608* [instantly] [3], himself [2], who [2], anyone [1], father [1], land[1] [1], other [1], thing [1], this man [1], very[2] [1], *see 1877* [just then] [1]

1698 ἐκεῖσε, ekeise
there [2]

1699 ἐκζητέω, ekzēteō
seek [4], charge[3] [2], make careful search [1]

1700 ἐκζήτησις, ekzētēsis
speculation [1]

1701 ἐκθαμβέω, ekthambeō
alarm [2], distress [1], overcome with awe [1]

1702 ἔκθαμβος, ekthambos
astonish utterly [1]

1703 ἐκθαυμάζω, ekthaumazō
amaze utterly [1]

1704 ἔκθετος, ekthetos
abandon [1]

1705 ἐκκαθαίρω, ekkathairō
clean out [1], cleanse [1]

1706 ἐκκαίω, ekkaiō
consume [1]

1708 ἐκκεντέω, ekkenteō
pierce [2]

1709 ἐκκλάω, ekklaō
break off [3]

1710 ἐκκλείω, ekkleiō
exclude [2]

1711 ἐκκλησία, ekklēsia
church [108], assembly [4], congregation [2]

1712 ἐκκλίνω, ekklinō
avoid [1], turn aside [1], turn away [1]

1713 ἐκκολυμβάω, ekkolymbaō
swim away [1]

1714 ἐκκομίζω, ekkomizō
carry out [1]

1716 ἐκκόπτω, ekkoptō
cut down [5], cut off [3], cut [1], deny [1]

1717 ἐκκρεμάννυμι, ekkremannymi
spellbind [1]

1718 ἐκλαλέω, eklaleō
tell [1]

1719 ἐκλάμπω, eklampō
shine [1]

1720 ἐκλανθάνομαι, eklanthanomai
forget [1]

1721 ἐκλέγομαι, eklegomai
choose [21], make a choice [1]

1722 ἐκλείπω, ekleipō
fail [2], end [1], go [1]

1723 ἐκλεκτός, eklektos
elect [12], choose [7], chosen one [3]

1724 ἐκλογή, eklogē
choose [3], election [3], elect [1]

1725 ἐκλύω, eklyō
faint [2], give up [1], lose heart [1]

1725 + 3836 + 6034 ἐκλύω + ὁ + ψυχή, eklyō + ho + psychē
lose heart [1]

1726 ἐκμάσσω, ekmassō
wipe [3], dry [2]

1727 ἐκμυκτηρίζω, ekmyktērizō
ridicule [1], scoff [1]

1728 ἐκνεύω, ekneuō
disappear [1]

1729 ἐκνήφω, eknēphō
come to a sober mind [1]

1730 ἑκούσιος, hekousios
voluntary [1]

1731 ἑκουσίως, hekousiōs
willfully [1], willingly [1]

1732 ἔκπαλαι, ekpalai
long ago [2]

1733 ἐκπειράζω, ekpeirazō
put to the test [3], test [1]

1734 ἐκπέμπω, ekpempō
send off [1], send out [1]

1735 ἐκπερισσῶς, ekperissōs
vehemently [1]

1736 ἐκπετάννυμι, ekpetannymi
hold out [1]

1737 ἐκπηδάω, ekpēdaō
rush out [1]

1738 ἐκπίπτω, ekpiptō
fall [2], run [2], adrift [1], fail [1], fall away [1], fall off [1], lose [1], run aground [1]

1739 ἐκπλέω, ekpleō
sail [2], sail away [1]

1740 ἐκπληρόω, ekplēroō
fulfill [1]

1741 ἐκπλήρωσις, ekplērōsis
completion [1]

1742 ἐκπλήσσω, ekplēssō
astound [10], astonish [2], spellbind [1]

1743 ἐκπνέω, ekpneō
breathe one's last [3]

1744 ἐκπορεύομαι, ekporeuomai
come out [11], go out [5], come [4], come from [4], leave [3], flow [1], go [1], go abroad [1], pour from [1], reach [1], set out [1]

1745 ἐκπορνεύω, ekporneuō
indulge in sexual immorality [1]

1746 ἐκπτύω, ekptyō
despise [1]

1748 ἐκριζόω, ekrizoō
uproot [4]

1749 ἔκστασις, ekstasis
amazement [3], trance [3], *see 2014* [overcome with amazement] [1]

1750 ἐκστρέφω, ekstrephō
pervert [1]

1752 ἐκταράσσω, ektarassō
disturb [1]

1753 ἐκτείνω, ekteinō
stretch out [11], lay on [1], put [1], put out [1], reach out [1]

1753 + 3836 + 5931 ἐκτείνω + ὁ + χείρ, ekteinō + ho + cheir
point[2] [1]

1754 ἐκτελέω, *ekteleō*
finish [2]

1755 ἐκτένεια, *ekteneia*
earnestly [1]

1756 ἐκτενής, *ektenēs*
constant [1]

1757 ἐκτενῶς, *ektenōs*
deeply [1], fervently [1], more
earnestly [1]

1758 ἐκτίθημι, *ektithēmi*
explain [3], abandon [1]

1759 ἐκτινάσσω, *ektinassō*
shake off [4]

1760 ἐκτός, *ektos*
outside [2], but [1], not include [1], out [1]

1760 + 1623 + 3590 ἐκτός + εἰ + μή,
ektos + ei + mē
unless [2], except [1]

1761 ἕκτος, *hektos*
sixth [7]

1761 + 6052 ἕκτος + ὥρα, *hektos +
hōra*
noon [7]

1762 ἐκτρέπω, *ektrepō*
avoid [1], put out of joint [1], turn¹ [1],
turn away [1], wander away [1]

1763 ἐκτρέφω, *ektrephō*
bring up [1], nourish [1]

1765 ἔκτρωμα, *ektrōma*
bear untimely [1]

1766 ἐκφέρω, *ekpherō*
carry out [4], bring out [1], lead out [1],
produce [1], take out [1]

1767 ἐκφεύγω, *ekpheugō*
escape [7], flee out [1]

1768 ἐκφοβέω, *ekphobeō*
frighten [1]

1769 ἔκφοβος, *ekphobos*
fear [1], terrify [1]

1770 ἐκφύω, *ekphyō*
put forth [2]

1772 ἐκχέω, *ekcheō*
pour [8], pour out [7], shed [3], spill [2],
abandon [1], gush out [1]

1773 ἐκχύννομαι, *ekchynnomai*
pour out [3], shed [2]

1774 ἐκχωρέω, *ekchōreō*
leave [1]

1775 ἐκψύχω, *ekpsychō*
die [3]

1776 ἑκών, *hekōn*
will¹ [2]

1777 ἐλαία, *elaia*
olive [10], olive tree [3]

1778 ἔλαιον, *elaion*
oil [8], olive oil [3]

1779 ἐλαιών, *elaiōn*
olive [2], Olivet [1]

1780 Ἐλαμίτης, *Elamitēs*
Elamite [1]

1781 ἐλάσσων, *elassōn*
inferior [2], less [1], young [1]

1782 ἐλαττονέω, *elattoneō*
have too little [1]

1783 ἐλαττόω, *elattoō*
make low [2], decrease [1]

1785 ἐλαύνω, *elaunō*
drive [3], oar [1], row [1]

1786 + 5968 ἐλαφρία + χράομαι,
elaphria + chraomai
vacillate [1]

1787 ἐλαφρός, *elaphros*
light² [1], slight [1]

1788 ἐλάχιστος, *elachistos*
least [6], very little [2], very small
thing [2], small thing [1], trivial [1], very
least [1], very small [1]

1789 Ἐλεάζαρ, *Eleazar*
Eleazar [2]

1790 ἐλεάω, *eleaō*
have mercy [2], show mercy [1]

1791 ἐλεγμός, *elegmos*
reproof [1]

1792 + 2400 ἔλεγξις + ἔχω, *elenxis +
echō*
rebuke [1]

1793 ἔλεγχος, *elenchos*
conviction [1]

1794 ἐλέγχω, *elenchō*
convict [3], expose [3], rebuke [3],
reprove [3], convince [1], point out a
fault [1], prove wrong [1], punish [1],
refute [1]

1795 ἐλεεινός, *eleeinos*
pitiable [1], pity most [1]

1796 ἐλεέω, *eleeō*
have mercy [17], receive mercy [7],
mercy [2], compassionate [1],
merciful [1], show mercy [1]

1797 ἐλεημοσύνη, *eleēmosynē*
alms [12], act of charity [1]

1798 ἐλεήμων, *eleēmōn*
merciful [2]

1799 ἔλεος, *eleos*
mercy [26], show mercy [1]

1800 ἐλευθερία, *eleutheria*
freedom [8], liberty [3]

1801 ἐλεύθερος, *eleutheros*
free [17], free woman [4], free person [1],
freedom [1]

1802 ἐλευθερόω, *eleutheroō*
set free [4], make free [2], free [1]

1803 ἔλευσις, *eleusis*
come [1]

1804 ἐλεφάντινος, *elephantinos*
ivory [1]

1806 Ἐλιακίμ, *Eliakim*
Eliakim [3]

1808 Ἐλιέζερ, *Eliezer*
Eliezer [1]

1809 Ἐλιούδ, *Elioud*
Eliud [1]

1810 Ἐλισάβετ, *Elisabet*
Elizabeth [9]

1811 Ἐλισαῖος, *Elisaios*
Elisha [1]

1813 ἑλίσσω, *helissō*
roll up [2]

1814 ἕλκος, *helkos*
sore [3]

1815 ἑλκόω, *helkoō*
covered with sores [1]

1816 ἑλκύω, *helkyō*
drag [3], draw² [2], haul [2], draw¹ [1]

1817 Ἑλλάς, *Hellas*
Greece [1]

1818 Ἕλλην, *Hellēn*
Greek [25]

1819 Ἑλληνικός, *Hellēnikos*
Greek [1]

1820 Ἑλληνίς, *Hellēnis*
Gentile [1], Greek [1]

1821 Ἑλληνιστής, *Hellēnistēs*
Hellenist [3]

1822 Ἑλληνιστί, *Hellēnisti*
Greek [2]

1823 ἐλλογάω, *ellogaō*
charge to an account [1]

1824 ἐλλογέω, *ellogeō*
reckon [1]

1825 Ἐλμαδάμ, *Elmadam*
Elmadam [1]

1827 ἐλπίζω, *elpizō*
hope [24], set one's hope [6], expect [1]

1828 ἐλπίς, *elpis*
hope [53]

1829 Ἐλύμας, *Elymas*
Elymas [1]

1830 ἐλωΐ, *elōi*
eloi [2]

1831 ἐμαυτοῦ, *emautou*
I [19], myself [16], *untranslated* [2]

1832 ἐμβαίνω, *embainō*
get into [16]

1833 ἐμβάλλω, *emballō*
cast into [1]

1835 ἐμβάπτω, *embaptō*
dip [2]

1836 ἐμβατεύω, *embateuō*
dwell [1]

1837 ἐμβιβάζω, *embibazō*
put on board [1]

1838 ἐμβλέπω, *emblepō*
look at [5], look [3], see [2], stare [1],
watch [1]

1839 ἐμβριμάομαι, *embrimaomai*
disturb greatly [2], order sternly [1],
scold [1], warn sternly [1]

1840 ἐμέω, *emeō*
spit [1]

1841 ἐμμαίνομαι, *emmainomai*
enrage [1]

1842 Ἐμμανουήλ, *Emmanouēl*
Emmanuel [1]

1843 Ἐμμαοῦς, *Emmaous*
Emmaus [1]

1844 ἐμμένω, *emmenō*
continue [2], live [1], observe² [1]

1846 Ἐμμώρ, *Hemmōr*
Hamor [1]

1847 ἐμός, *emos*
I [74]

1847 + 6034 ἐμός + ψυχή, *emos +
psychē*
I [1]

1848 ἐμπαιγμονή, *empaigmonē*
scoff [1]

1849 ἐμπαιγμός, empaigmos
mock [1]

1850 ἐμπαίζω, empaizō
mock [11], ridicule [1], trick [1]

1851 ἐμπαίκτης, empaiktēs
scoffer [2]

1853 ἐμπεριπατέω, emperipateō
walk among [1]

1855 ἐμπίμπλημι, empimplēmi
fill [2], enjoy company [1], full [1],
satisfy [1]

1856 ἐμπίμπρημι, empimprēmi
burn [1]

1860 ἐμπίπτω, empiptō
fall into [5], fall [2]

1861 ἐμπλέκω, emplekō
entangle [1], get entangled [1]

1862 ἐμπλοκή, emplokē
braid [1]

1863 ἐμπνέω, empneō
breathe [1]

1864 ἐμπορεύομαι, emporeuomai
do business [1], exploit [1]

1865 ἐμπορία, emporia
business [1]

1866 ἐμπόριον, emporion
marketplace [1]

1867 ἔμπορος, emporos
merchant [5]

1869 ἔμπροσθεν, emprosthen
before [29], ahead [5], front [4], at [2],
presence [2], untranslated [2], lie
ahead [1], of [1], out [1], see 1650
[ahead] [1]

1870 ἐμπτύω, emptyō
spit upon [3], spit on [2], spit [1]

1871 ἐμφανής, emphanēs
appear [1], show [1]

1872 ἐμφανίζω, emphanizō
appear [2], inform [2], reveal [2], give a
report [1], make clear [1], notify [1],
report a case [1]

1873 ἔμφοβος, emphobos
terrify [3], frighten [1], terror [1]

1874 ἐμφυσάω, emphysaō
breathe on [1]

1875 ἔμφυτος, emphytos
implant [1]

1877 ἐν, en
in [1582], untranslated [193], with [153],
by [137], on [111], at [108], among [107],
when [34], to [30], through [22], of [21],
while [19], for [18], during [17],
within [17], as [16], into [8], because [6],
about¹ [5], under [5], against [4], have [4],
there [4], before [3], throughout [3],
after [2], bear¹ [2], case [2], include [2],
over¹ [2], spite [2], suffer² [2], use [2],
where [2], accordance [1], according [1],
across [1], along [1], any [1], behind [1],
belong [1], besides [1], charge¹ [1], come
in [1], do [1], fill [1], follow [1], from [1],
guide [1], inwardly [1], just as [1],
midst [1], near [1], out [1], place [1],
promote [1], put on [1], regard [1],
relation [1], share [1], start [1],
thereby [1], though [1], under power [1],
see 241 [grind meal] [1], see 2400
[acknowledge] [1], see 4725 [face to
face] [1], see 5502 [ponder] [1]

1877 + 141 ἐν + αἴνιγμα, en + ainigma
dimly [1]

1877 + 899 ἐν + αὐτός, en + autos
there [1]

1877 + 1143 + 2400 ἐν + γαστήρ +
ἔχω, en + gastēr + echō
pregnant [5], conceive [1], with child [1]

1877 + 1697 + 3836 + 6052 ἐν +
ἐκεῖνος + ὁ + ὥρα, en + ekeinos + ho
+ hōra
just then [1]

1877 + 2465 ἐν + ἡμέρα, en + hēmera
when [2]

1877 + 2990 ἐν + κατηγορία, en +
katēgoria
accuse [1]

1877 + 3364 ἐν + λόγος, en + logos
at length [1]

1877 + 3545 ἐν + μέσος, en + mesos
among [13], before [2], around [1],
between [1], inside [1]

1877 + 3836 + 3146 ἐν + ὁ + κόλπος,
en + ho + kolpos
next [1]

1877 + 3836 + 3220 ἐν + ὁ + κρυπτός,
en + ho + kryptos
inwardly [1]

1877 + 3836 + 3568 ἐν + ὁ + μεταξύ,
en + ho + metaxy
meanwhile [1]

1877 + 3836 + 5745 ἐν + ὁ + φανερός,
en + ho + phaneros
external [1], outwardly [1]

1877 + 3910 ἐν + ὅλος, en + holos
throughout [7]

1877 + 4005 ἐν + ὅς, en + hos
when [4], in mind [1], meanwhile [1],
there [1], until [1], where [1]

1877 + 4047 ἐν + οὗτος, en + houtos
here [2], therefore [1], thus [1]

1877 + 4246 + 854 ἐν + πᾶς +
ἀσφάλεια, en + pas + asphaleia
securely [1]

1877 + 4922 ἐν + σάρξ, en + sarx
physical [1]

1877 + 5393 ἐν + σῶμα, en + sōma
torture [1]

1877 + 5443 ἐν + τάχος, en + tachos
quickly [3], soon [3], shortly [2]

1877 + 5515 ἐν + τίς, en + tis
how [4]

1877 + 5931 ἐν + χείρ, en + cheir
by [1]

1878 ἐναγκαλίζομαι, enankalizomai
take in one's arms [2]

1879 ἐνάλιος, enalios
sea creature [1]

1882 ἔναντι, enanti
before [2]

1883 ἐναντίον, enantion
before [4], presence [1]

1885 ἐναντίος, enantios
against [2], face [1], opponent [1],
oppose [1], thing against [1]

1887 ἐνάρχομαι, enarchomai
begin [1], start [1]

1888 ἔνατος, enatos
ninth [1], three o'clock [1], three o'clock
in the afternoon [1]

1888 + 6052 ἔνατος + ὥρα, enatos +
hōra
three in the afternoon [3], three
o'clock [3], three o'clock in the
afternoon [1]

1890 ἐνδεής, endeēs
needy [1]

1891 ἔνδειγμα, endeigma
evidence [1]

1892 ἐνδείκνυμι, endeiknymi
show [9], display [1], do [1]

1893 ἔνδειξις, endeixis
evidence [1], proof [1], prove [1],
show [1]

1894 ἕνδεκα, hendeka
eleven [6]

1895 ἑνδέκατος, hendekatos
eleventh [1], five o'clock [1]

1895 + 6052 ἑνδέκατος + ὥρα,
hendekatos + hōra
five o'clock [1]

1896 ἐνδέχομαι, endechomai
see 4024 [impossible] [1]

1897 ἐνδημέω, endēmeō
home [3]

1898 ἐνδιδύσκω, endidyskō
clothe [1], dress [1]

1899 ἔνδικος, endikos
deserve [1], just² [1]

1901 ἐνδοξάζομαι, endoxazomai
glorify [2]

1902 ἔνδοξος, endoxos
fine [1], hold in honor [1], splendor [1],
wonderful thing [1]

1903 ἔνδυμα, endyma
clothing [6], robe [2]

1904 ἐνδυναμόω, endynamoō
strengthen [2], strong [2], give
strength [1], grow strong [1], powerful [1]

1905 ἐνδύνω, endynō
make one's way [1]

1906 ἔνδυσις, endysis
fine [1]

1907 ἐνδύω, endyō
put on [14], clothe [7], wear [5], robe [1]

1908 ἐνδώμησις, endōmēsis
build [1]

1909 ἐνέδρα, enedra
ambush [2]

1910 ἐνεδρεύω, enedreuō
lie in ambush [1], lie in wait [1]

1912 ἐνειλέω, eneileō
wrap [1]

1913 ἔνειμι, eneimi
within [1]

1915 ἕνεκεν, heneken
sake [12], account¹ [4], because [3],
reason¹ [3], order² [1], see 5515 [why] [1]

1916 + 1933 ἐνενήκοντα + ἐννέα,
enenēkonta + ennea
ninety-nine [4]

1917 ἐνεός, eneos
speechless [1]

1918 ἐνέργεια, *energeia*
work [4], power [2], energy [1], powerful [1]

1919 ἐνεργέω, *energeō*
work [12], activate [2], work through [2], accomplish [1], effective [1], experience [1], inspire [1], put to work [1]

1920 ἐνέργημα, *energēma*
activity [1], work [1]

1921 ἐνεργής, *energēs*
active [1], effective [1], effective work [1]

1922 ἐνευλογέω, *eneulogeō*
bless [2]

1923 ἐνέχω, *enechō*
grudge [1], hostile [1], submit [1]

1924 ἐνθάδε, *enthade*
here [6], back [1], there [1]

1925 ἔνθεν, *enthen*
from here [1], here [1]

1926 ἐνθυμέομαι, *enthymeomai*
resolve [1], think [1]

1927 ἐνθύμησις, *enthymēsis*
thought [2], imagination [1], think [1]

1928 ἔνι, *eni*
there is [6]

1929 ἐνιαυτός, *eniautos*
year [14]

1931 ἐνίστημι, *enistēmi*
present³ [3], come [1], here already [1], impending [1], present thing [1]

1932 ἐνισχύω, *enischyō*
give strength [1], regain strength [1]

1933 ἐννέα, *ennea*
see 1916 [ninety-nine] [4], nine [1]

1935 ἐννεύω, *enneuō*
motion [1]

1936 ἔννοια, *ennoia*
intention [2]

1937 ἔννομος, *ennomos*
regular [1], under law [1]

1939 ἔννυχος, *ennychos*
while still dark [1]

1940 ἐνοικέω, *enoikeō*
live [2], dwell [1], dwell in [1], live in [1]

1941 ἐνορκίζω, *enorkizō*
command solemnly [1]

1942 ἑνότης, *henotēs*
unity [2]

1943 ἐνοχλέω, *enochleō*
cause trouble [1], trouble [1]

1944 ἔνοχος, *enochos*
liable [4], deserve [2], accountable [1], answerable [1], guilty [1], hold [1]

1945 ἔνταλμα, *entalma*
precept [2], command [1]

1946 ἐνταφιάζω, *entaphiazō*
burial [2]

1947 ἐνταφιασμός, *entaphiasmos*
burial [2]

1948 ἐντέλλω, *entellō*
command [10], give instruction [2], give a command [1], ordain [1], order³ [1]

1949 ἐντεῦθεν, *enteuthen*
from here [2], here [2], *untranslated* [2], out of here [1], *see 1949* [either side] [1]

1949 + 2779 + 1696 ἐντεῦθεν + καί + ἐκεῖθεν, *enteuthen + kai + ekeithen*
either side [1]

1949 + 2779 + 1949 ἐντεῦθεν + καί + ἐντεῦθεν, *enteuthen + kai + enteuthen*
either side [1]

1950 ἔντευξις, *enteuxis*
intercession [1], prayer [1]

1952 ἔντιμος, *entimos*
precious [2], more distinguished [1], value highly [1]

1952 + 2400 ἔντιμος + ἔχω, *entimos + echō*
honor [1]

1953 ἐντολή, *entolē*
commandment [58], command [3], instruction [2], order³ [1], requirement [1]

1953 + 1443 ἐντολή + δίδωμι, *entolē + didōmi*
command [1]

1953 + 3284 ἐντολή + λαμβάνω, *entolē + lambanō*
command [1]

1954 ἐντόπιος, *entopios*
people there [1]

1955 ἐντός, *entos*
among [1], inside [1]

1956 ἐντρέπω, *entrepō*
respect¹ [6], ashamed [1], make ashamed [1], put to shame [1]

1957 ἐντρέφω, *entrephō*
nourish [1]

1958 ἔντρομος, *entromos*
tremble [3]

1959 ἐντροπή, *entropē*
shame [2]

1960 ἐντρυφάω, *entryphaō*
revel [1]

1961 ἐντυγχάνω, *entynchanō*
intercede [2], make intercession [1], petition [1], plead [1]

1962 ἐντυλίσσω, *entylissō*
wrap [2], roll up [1]

1963 ἐντυπόω, *entypoō*
chisel [1]

1964 ἐνυβρίζω, *enybrizō*
outrage [1]

1965 ἐνυπνιάζομαι, *enypniazomai*
dream [1], dreamer [1]

1966 ἐνύπνιον, *enypnion*
dream [1]

1967 ἐνώπιον, *enōpion*
before [48], presence [18], sight [16], *untranslated* [4], behalf [2], front [2], with [2], to [1]

1967 + 4246 ἐνώπιον + πᾶς, *enōpion + pas*
publicly [1]

1968 Ἐνώς, *Enōs*
Enos [1]

1969 ἐνωτίζομαι, *enōtizomai*
listen [1]

1970 Ἐνώχ, *Henōch*
Enoch [3]

1971 ἕξ, *hex*
six [10], *see 1573* [seventy-six] [1], *see*

2008 [sixty-six] [1], *see 5477* [forty-six] [1]

1972 ἐξαγγέλλω, *exangellō*
proclaim [1], tell [1]

1973 ἐξαγοράζω, *exagorazō*
make the most [2], redeem [2]

1974 ἐξάγω, *exagō*
lead out [8], bring out [2], take out [2]

1975 ἐξαιρέω, *exaireō*
rescue [5], tear out [2], set free [1]

1976 ἐξαίρω, *exairō*
drive out [1]

1977 ἐξαιτέω, *exaiteō*
demand [1]

1978 ἐξαίφνης, *exaiphnēs*
suddenly [4], all at once [1]

1979 ἐξακολουθέω, *exakoloutheō*
follow [3]

1980 ἑξακόσιοι, *hexakosioi*
six hundred [1], *see 5084* [two hundred miles] [1]

1981 ἐξαλείφω, *exaleiphō*
blot out [1], erase [1], wipe [1], wipe away [1], wipe out [1]

1982 ἐξάλλομαι, *exallomai*
jump up [1]

1983 ἐξανάστασις, *exanastasis*
resurrection [1]

1984 ἐξανατέλλω, *exanatellō*
spring up [2]

1985 ἐξανίστημι, *exanistēmi*
raise up [2], stand up [1]

1987 ἐξαπατάω, *exapataō*
deceive [6]

1988 ἐξάπινα, *exapina*
suddenly [1]

1989 ἐξαπορέω, *exaporeō*
despair [1], drive to despair [1]

1990 ἐξαποστέλλω, *exapostellō*
send [6], send away [5], send off [1], send out [1]

1992 ἐξαρτίζω, *exartizō*
end [1], equip [1]

1993 ἐξαστράπτω, *exastraptō*
dazzle [1]

1994 ἐξαυτῆς, *exautēs*
immediately [2], once² [2], soon [1], very moment [1]

1995 ἐξεγείρω, *exegeirō*
raise [1], raise up [1]

1996 ἔξειμι¹, *exeimi¹*
leave [2], go out [1], make for [1]

1999 ἐξέλκω, *exelkō*
lure [1]

2000 ἐξέραμα, *exerama*
vomit [1]

2001 ἐξεραυνάω, *exeraunaō*
make inquiry [1]

2002 ἐξέρχομαι, *exerchomai*
go out [72], come out [50], leave [22], go [11], come [10], come from [6], set out [5], spread [5], depart [4], get out [4], go away [4], go on [4], go ashore [2], go outside [2], step out [2], come forward [1], cross over [1], drive out [1], escape [1], flow [1], get away [1], go forth [1], go

from [1], journey [1], know [1],
originate [1], proceed [1], return [1]

2002 + 3836 + 4019 ἐξέρχομαι + ὁ +
ὀσφῦς, *exerchomai + ho + osphys*
descend [1]

2002 + 5250 ἐξέρχομαι + σύν,
exerchomai + syn
accompany [1]

2003 ἔξεστι, *exesti*
lawful [25], may [2], permit [2], allow [1],
legal [1]

2004 ἐξετάζω, *exetazō*
ask [1], find out [1], search [1]

2007 ἐξηγέομαι, *exēgeomai*
tell [3], relate [2], make known [1]

2008 ἐξήκοντα, *hexēkonta*
sixty [7]

2008 + 1971 ἐξήκοντα + ἕξ, *hexēkonta
+ hex*
sixty-six [1]

2008 + 5084 ἐξήκοντα + στάδιον,
hexēkonta + stadion
seven miles [1]

2009 ἑξῆς, *hexēs*
next [4], soon afterwards [1]

2010 ἐξηχέω, *exēcheō*
sound forth [1]

2011 ἕξις, *hexis*
practice [1]

2014 ἐξίστημι, *existēmi*
amaze [10], astound [4], beside [1], go out
of one's mind [1]

2014 + 1749 ἐξίστημι + ἔκστασις,
existēmi + ekstasis
overcome with amazement [1]

2015 ἐξισχύω, *exischyō*
power [1]

2016 ἔξοδος, *exodos*
departure [2], exodus [1]

2017 ἐξολεθρεύω, *exolethreuō*
root out utterly [1]

2018 ἐξομολογέω, *exomologeō*
confess [6], thank [2], consent [1], give
praise [1]

2019 ἐξορκίζω, *exorkizō*
put under oath [1]

2020 ἐξορκιστής, *exorkistēs*
exorcist [1]

2021 ἐξορύσσω, *exoryssō*
dig through [1], tear out [1]

2022 ἐξουδενέω, *exoudeneō*
treat with contempt [1]

2024 ἐξουθενέω, *exoutheneō*
despise [5], contemptible [1], no
standing [1], regard with contempt [1],
reject [1], scorn [1], treat with
contempt [1]

2026 ἐξουσία, *exousia*
authority [70], power [15], right[3] [9],
charge[1] [2], control [1], disposal [1],
jurisdiction [1], liberty [1], rightful
claim [1], symbol of authority [1]

2027 ἐξουσιάζω, *exousiazō*
authority over [3], dominate [1]

2029 ἐξοχή, *exochē*
prominent [1]

2030 ἐξυπνίζω, *exypnizō*
awake [1]

2031 ἔξυπνος, *exypnos*
wake up [1]

2032 ἔξω, *exō*
out [29], outside [24], away [3],
outsider [2], *untranslated* [2], foreign [1],
outer [1]

2033 ἔξωθεν, *exōthen*
outside [9], out [1], outsider [1],
outwardly [1], without[2] [1]

2034 ἐξωθέω, *exōtheō*
drive out [1], run ashore [1]

2035 ἐξώτερος, *exōteros*
outer [3]

2036 ἔοικα, *eoika*
like[1] [2]

2037 ἑορτάζω, *heortazō*
celebrate the festival [1]

2038 ἑορτή, *heortē*
festival [25]

2039 ἐπαγγελία, *epangelia*
promise [50], consent [1], *untranslated* [1]

2040 ἐπαγγέλλομαι, *epangellomai*
promise [11], make a promise [2],
profess [2]

2041 ἐπάγγελμα, *epangelma*
promise [2]

2042 ἐπάγω, *epagō*
bring on [3]

2043 ἐπαγωνίζομαι, *epagōnizomai*
contend [1]

2044 ἐπαθροίζω, *epathroizō*
increase [1]

2045 Ἐπαίνετος, *Epainetos*
Epaenetus [1]

2046 ἐπαινέω, *epaineō*
commend [5], praise [1]

2047 ἔπαινος, *epainos*
praise [7], approval [1],
commendation [1], famous [1], worthy of
praise [1]

2048 ἐπαίρω, *epairō*
lift up [3], raise [3], hoist [1], lift
against [1], put on airs [1], raise up [1]

2048 + 3836 + 4057 ἐπαίρω + ὁ +
ὀφθαλμός, *epairō + ho + ophthalmos*
look up [6], look around [1]

2048 + 3836 + 5889 ἐπαίρω + ὁ +
φωνή, *epairō + ho + phōnē*
shout [2]

2049 ἐπαισχύνομαι, *epaischynomai*
ashamed [11]

2050 ἐπαιτέω, *epaiteō*
beg [2]

2051 ἐπακολουθέω, *epakoloutheō*
follow [2], accompany [1], devote [1]

2052 ἐπακούω, *epakouō*
listen [1]

2053 ἐπακροάομαι, *epakroaomai*
listen [1]

2054 ἐπάν, *epan*
when [2], if [1]

2055 ἐπάναγκες, *epanankes*
essential [1]

2056 ἐπανάγω, *epanagō*
put out [2], return [1]

2057 ἐπαναμιμνῄσκω, *epanamimnēskō*
reminder [1]

2058 ἐπαναπαύομαι, *epanapauomai*
rely on [1], rest on [1]

2059 ἐπανέρχομαι, *epanerchomai*
come back [1], return [1]

2060 ἐπανίστημι, *epanistēmi*
rise against [2]

2061 ἐπανόρθωσις, *epanorthōsis*
correction [1]

2062 ἐπάνω, *epanō*
on [6], over[1] [6], above [2], more than [2],
of [1], upon [1], *untranslated* [1]

2063 ἐπάρατος, *eparatos*
accursed [1]

2064 ἐπαρκέω, *eparkeō*
assist [2], help [1]

2065 ἐπαρχεία, *eparcheia*
province [2]

2068 ἔπαυλις, *epaulis*
homestead [1]

2069 ἐπαύριον, *epaurion*
next day [15], following day [2]

2071 Ἐπαφρᾶς, *Epaphras*
Epaphras [3]

2072 ἐπαφρίζω, *epaphrizō*
cast up foam [1]

2073 Ἐπαφρόδιτος, *Epaphroditos*
Epaphroditus [2]

2074 ἐπεγείρω, *epegeirō*
stir up [2]

2075 ἐπεί, *epei*
since [13], because [5], otherwise [5],
then [2]

2075 + 726 ἐπεί + ἄρα, *epei + ara*
otherwise [1]

2076 ἐπειδή, *epeidē*
since [5], for [3], after [1], because [1]

2077 ἐπειδήπερ, *epeidēper*
since [1]

2078 ἐπεῖδον, *epeidon*
look [1], look on favorably [1]

2079 ἔπειμι, *epeimi*
next [2], follow [1], following [1], that [1]

2081 ἐπεισαγωγή, *epeisagōgē*
introduction [1]

2082 ἐπεισέρχομαι, *epeiserchomai*
come upon [1]

2083 ἔπειτα, *epeita*
then [15], next [1]

2084 ἐπέκεινα, *epekeina*
beyond [1]

2085 ἐπεκτείνομαι, *epekteinomai*
strain forward [1]

2086 ἐπενδύομαι, *ependyomai*
clothe [1], clothe further [1]

2087 ἐπενδύτης, *ependytēs*
clothes [1]

2088 ἐπέρχομαι, *eperchomai*
come upon [3], happen [2], attack [1],
come [1], come there [1], come to [1]

2089 ἐπερωτάω, *eperōtaō*
ask [45], ask a question [9], question [2]

2090 ἐπερώτημα, *eperōtēma*
appeal [1]

2091 ἐπέχω, epechō
fix attention on [1], hold fast [1], notice [1], pay close attention [1], stay [1]

2092 ἐπηρεάζω, epēreazō
abuse [2]

2093 ἐπί, epi
on [282], to [81], in [70], *untranslated* [66], over[1] [55], at [49], against [39], for [38], upon [31], before [23], of [20], by [14], about[1] [10], with [8], into [6], toward [6], because [5], after [4], from [4], above [3], during [3], under [3], when [3], accordance [2], account[1] [2], among [2], around [2], time[1] [2], time[2] [2], as [1], base[1] [1], beside [1], charge[1] [1], concerning [1], deal [1], evidence [1], give [1], help [1], in addition [1], oppose [1], side [1], still[1] [1], through [1], *see 2095* [arrest] [1], *see 2158* [embrace] [1], *see 2158* [put arms around] [1], *see 2879* [bedridden] [1], *see 4406* [bow down] [1], *see 4406* [prostrate] [1], *see 4406* [throw oneself on the ground] [1]

2093 + 2330 ἐπί + εὐλογία, epi + eulogia
bountifully [2]

2093 + 3545 ἐπί + μέσος, epi + mesos
on [1]

2093 + 3836 + 129 ἐπί + ὁ + αἰγιαλός, epi + ho + aigialos
ashore [1]

2093 + 3836 + 899 ἐπί + ὁ + αὐτός, epi + ho + autos
together [8]

2093 + 3836 + 1178 ἐπί + ὁ + γῆ, epi + ho + gē
earthly [1]

2093 + 3836 + 2498 ἐπί + ὁ + θάλασσα, epi + ho + thalassa
coast [1]

2093 + 3836 + 3131 ἐπί + ὁ + κοιτών, epi + ho + koitōn
chamberlain [1]

2093 + 3836 + 5111 ἐπί + ὁ + στῆθος, epi + ho + stēthos
next [2]

2093 + 3910 ἐπί + ὅλος, epi + holos
throughout [1]

2093 + 4005 ἐπί + ὅς, epi + hos
because [2], where [1]

2093 + 4012 ἐπί + ὅσος, epi + hosos
just as [2], inasmuch [1], long[1] [1]

2093 + 4012 + 5989 ἐπί + ὅσος + χρόνος, epi + hosos + chronos
long[1] [2]

2093 + 4047 ἐπί + οὗτος, epi + houtos
just then [1], purpose [1]

2093 + 4725 ἐπί + πρόσωπον, epi + prosōpon
to the ground [1]

2093 + 5536 + 4434 ἐπί + τόπος + πλέω, epi + topos + pleō
seafarer [1]

2094 ἐπιβαίνω, epibainō
arrive [1], embark [1], go on [1], go on board [1], mount[2] [1], set foot [1]

2095 ἐπιβάλλω, epiballō
lay on [5], sew on [2], beat [1], belong [1],

break down [1], lay upon [1], put to [1], put upon [1], throw on [1]

2095 + 2093 + 3836 + 5931 ἐπιβάλλω + ἐπί + ὁ + χείρ, epiballō + epi + ho + cheir
arrest [1]

2095 + 3836 + 5931 ἐπιβάλλω + ὁ + χείρ, epiballō + ho + cheir
arrest [2], seize [1]

2096 ἐπιβαρέω, epibareō
burden [2], exaggerate [1]

2097 ἐπιβιβάζω, epibibazō
put on [1], ride [1], set on [1]

2098 ἐπιβλέπω, epiblepō
look at [1], look on with favor [1], take notice [1]

2099 ἐπίβλημα, epiblēma
piece [4]

2101 ἐπιβουλή, epiboulē
plot [4]

2102 ἐπιγαμβρεύω, epigambreuō
marry [1]

2103 ἐπίγειος, epigeios
earthly [4], earthly thing [2], earth [1]

2104 ἐπιγίνομαι, epiginomai
spring up [1]

2105 ἐπιγινώσκω, epiginōskō
know [11], recognize [11], learn [5], realize [3], understand [3], find out [2], know fully [2], perceive [2], acknowledge [1], aware [1], comprehend [1], give recognition [1], know well [1]

2106 ἐπίγνωσις, epignōsis
knowledge [15], know [2], enlighten [1], perceive [1], *see 2400* [acknowledge] [1]

2107 ἐπιγραφή, epigraphē
title [3], inscription [2]

2108 ἐπιγράφω, epigraphō
write [2], inscribe [1], inscription [1], read [1]

2109 ἐπιδείκνυμι, epideiknymi
show [6], point out [1]

2110 ἐπιδέχομαι, epidechomai
acknowledge [1], welcome [1]

2111 ἐπιδημέω, epidēmeō
live [1], visitor [1]

2112 ἐπιδιατάσσομαι, epidiatassomai
add [1]

2113 ἐπιδίδωμι, epididōmi
give [6], deliver [1], give to [1], give way [1]

2114 ἐπιδιορθόω, epidiorthoō
put in order [1]

2115 ἐπιδύω, epidyō
go down [1]

2116 ἐπιείκεια, epieikeia
gentleness [1], graciousness [1]

2117 ἐπιεικής, epieikēs
gentle [4], gentleness [1]

2118 ἐπιζητέω, epizēteō
seek [4], ask for [2], look for [2], strive [2], search [1], want [1], want to know [1]

2119 ἐπιθανάτιος, epithanatios
sentence to death [1]

2120 ἐπίθεσις, epithesis
lay on [4]

2121 ἐπιθυμέω, epithymeō
long[2] [5], covet [3], desire [3], want [2], do [1], gladly [1], lust [1]

2122 ἐπιθυμητής, epithymētēs
desire [1]

2123 ἐπιθυμία, epithymia
desire [19], lust [7], passion [6], long[2] [2], covet [1], covetousness [1], eagerly [1], lustful [1]

2125 ἐπικαθίζω, epikathizō
sit on [1]

2126 ἐπικαλέω, epikaleō
call [8], appeal [6], call on [6], invoke [4], other name [2], call over [1], give a name [1], know [1], pray [1]

2127 ἐπικάλυμμα, epikalymma
pretext [1]

2128 ἐπικαλύπτω, epikalyptō
cover [1]

2129 ἐπικατάρατος, epikataratos
curse [2]

2130 ἐπίκειμαι, epikeimai
impose [1], lay on [1], lie against [1], on [1], press in on [1], rage [1], urgently [1]

2131 ἐπικέλλω, epikellō
run aground [1]

2134 Ἐπικούρειος, Epikoureios
Epicurean [1]

2135 ἐπικουρία, epikouria
help [1]

2137 ἐπικρίνω, epikrinō
give a verdict [1]

2138 ἐπιλαμβάνομαι, epilambanomai
take [7], seize [4], take hold [2], trap [2], arrest [1], catch [1], come to help [1], *untranslated* [1]

2140 ἐπιλανθάνομαι, epilanthanomai
forget [5], neglect [2], overlook [1]

2141 ἐπιλέγω, epilegō
call [1], choose [1]

2142 ἐπιλείπω, epileipō
fail [1]

2143 ἐπιλείχω, epileichō
lick [1]

2144 ἐπιλησμονή, epilēsmonē
forget [1]

2145 ἐπίλοιπος, epiloipos
rest[2] [1]

2146 ἐπίλυσις, epilysis
interpretation [1]

2147 ἐπιλύω, epilyō
explain [1], settle[2] [1]

2148 ἐπιμαρτυρέω, epimartyreō
testify [1]

2149 ἐπιμέλεια, epimeleia
care[2] [1]

2150 ἐπιμελέομαι, epimeleomai
take care [3]

2151 ἐπιμελῶς, epimelōs
carefully [1]

2152 ἐπιμένω, epimenō
stay [7], continue [5], keep on [1], persist [1], remain [1], spend [1]

2153 ἐπινεύω, epineuō
see 4024 [decline] [1]

2154 ἐπίνοια, epinoia
intent [1]

2155 ἐπιορκέω, epiorkeō
swear falsely [1]

2156 ἐπίορκος, epiorkos
perjurer [1]

2157 ἐπιούσιος, epiousios
daily [2]

2158 ἐπιπίπτω, epipiptō
fall upon [2], bend over [1], come
upon [1], fall [1], overwhelm [1], press
upon [1], *see 5832* [terrify] [1]

**2158 + 2093 + 3836 + 5549 ἐπιπίπτω
+ ἐπί + ὁ + τράχηλος, epipiptō + epi
+ ho + trachēlos**
embrace [1], put arms around [1]

**2158 + 5832 ἐπιπίπτω + φόβος,
epipiptō + phobos**
awestruck [1]

2159 ἐπιπλήσσω, epiplēssō
speak harshly [1]

2160 ἐπιποθέω, epipotheō
long[2] [8], yearn [1]

2161 ἐπιπόθησις, epipothēsis
long[2] [2]

2162 ἐπιπόθητος, epipothētos
long[2] [1]

**2163 + 2400 ἐπιποθία + ἔχω,
epipothia + echō**
desire [1]

2164 ἐπιπορεύομαι, epiporeuomai
come to [1]

2165 ἐπιράπτω, epiraptō
sew on [1]

2166 ἐπιρίπτω, epiriptō
cast [1], throw on [1]

2168 ἐπίσημος, episēmos
notorious [1], prominent [1]

2169 ἐπισιτισμός, episitismos
provision [1]

2170 ἐπισκέπτομαι, episkeptomai
visit [3], care[2] [2], look favorably [2],
break upon [1], look on favorably [1],
select [1], take care [1]

2171 ἐπισκευάζομαι, episkeuazomai
get ready [1]

2172 ἐπισκηνόω, episkēnoō
dwell in [1]

2173 ἐπισκιάζω, episkiazō
overshadow [4], fall on [1]

2174 ἐπισκοπέω, episkopeō
exercise oversight [1], see [1]

2175 ἐπισκοπή, episkopē
come to judge [1], office of bishop [1],
position of overseer [1], visitation [1]

2176 ἐπίσκοπος, episkopos
bishop [3], guardian [1], overseer [1]

2177 ἐπισπάομαι, epispaomai
remove mark of circumcision [1]

2178 ἐπισπείρω, epispeirō
sow[1] [1]

2179 ἐπίσταμαι, epistamai
know [12], understand [2]

2180 ἐπίστασις, epistasis
pressure [1]

**2180 + 4472 ἐπίστασις + ποιέω,
epistasis + poieō**
stir up [1]

2181 ἐπιστάτης, epistatēs
master [7]

2182 ἐπιστέλλω, epistellō
write [2], send a letter [1]

2184 ἐπιστήμων, epistēmōn
understanding [1]

2185 ἐπιστηρίζω, epistērizō
strengthen [4]

2186 ἐπιστολή, epistolē
letter [24]

2187 ἐπιστομίζω, epistomizō
silence [1]

2188 ἐπιστρέφω, epistrephō
turn[1] [22], return [6], turn back [4], bring
back [2], turn about [1], turn again [1]

2189 ἐπιστροφή, epistrophē
conversion [1]

2190 ἐπισυνάγω, episynagō
gather [6], gather together [2]

2191 ἐπισυναγωγή, episynagōgē
gather together [1], meet [1]

2192 ἐπισυντρέχω, episyntrechō
come running together [1]

2195 ἐπισφαλής, episphalēs
dangerous [1]

2196 ἐπισχύω, epischyō
insistent [1]

2197 ἐπισωρεύω, episōreuō
accumulate [1]

2198 ἐπιταγή, epitagē
command [6], authority [1]

2199 ἐπιτάσσω, epitassō
command [5], order[3] [5]

2200 ἐπιτελέω, epiteleō
complete [3], bring to completion [1],
carry out [1], end [1], erect [1], finish [1],
make perfect [1], undergo [1]

2201 ἐπιτήδειος, epitēdeios
need [1]

2202 ἐπιτίθημι, epitithēmi
lay on [22], put on [6], give [3], add [2],
impose on [1], place on [1], put [1], put on
board [1], *see 4435* [beat] [1]

**2202 + 5931 ἐπιτίθημι + χείρ,
epitithēmi + cheir**
ordain [1]

2203 ἐπιτιμάω, epitimaō
rebuke [18], order sternly [6], order[3] [3],
speak sternly [2]

2204 ἐπιτιμία, epitimia
punishment [1]

2205 ἐπιτρέπω, epitrepō
let [5], allow [4], give permission [4],
permit [4], permission [1]

2207 ἐπιτροπή, epitropē
commission [1]

2208 ἐπίτροπος, epitropos
guardian [1], manager [1], steward [1]

2209 ἐπιτυγχάνω, epitynchanō
obtain [5]

2210 ἐπιφαίνω, epiphainō
appear [3], give light [1]

2211 ἐπιφάνεια, epiphaneia
appear [3], manifestation [3]

2212 ἐπιφανής, epiphanēs
glorious [1]

2213 ἐπιφαύσκω, epiphauskō
shine on [1]

2214 ἐπιφέρω, epipherō
bring [1], inflict [1]

2215 ἐπιφωνέω, epiphōneō
shout [3], outcry [1]

2216 ἐπιφώσκω, epiphōskō
begin [1], dawn [1]

2217 ἐπιχειρέω, epicheireō
attempt [1], try[1] [1], undertake [1]

2219 ἐπιχέω, epicheō
pour on [1]

2220 ἐπιχορηγέω, epichorēgeō
supply [2], nourish [1], provide [1],
support [1]

2221 ἐπιχορηγία, epichorēgia
equip [1], help [1]

2222 ἐπιχρίω, epichriō
spread on [2]

2224 ἐποικοδομέω, epoikodomeō
build on [4], build up [2], build upon [1]

2226 ἐπονομάζω, eponomazō
call [1]

2227 ἐποπτεύω, epopteuō
see [2]

2228 ἐπόπτης, epoptēs
eyewitness [1]

2229 ἔπος, epos
untranslated [1]

2230 ἐπουράνιος, epouranios
heavenly [8], heavenly place [5],
heaven [4], heavenly thing [2]

2231 ἑπτά, hepta
seven [86], seventh [1], *see 1574* [seventy-
seven times] [1]

2232 ἑπτάκις, heptakis
seven times [4]

2233 ἑπτακισχίλιοι, heptakischilioi
seven thousand [1]

2235 Ἔραστος, Erastos
Erastus [3]

2236 ἐραυνάω, eraunaō
search [5], inquire [1]

2237 ἐργάζομαι, ergazomai
work [18], do [7], do work [3],
perform [3], produce [2], trade [2],
administer [1], commit [1], employ [1],
perform work [1], put [1]

**2237 + 490 ἐργάζομαι + ἀνομία,
ergazomai + anomia**
evildoer [1]

2238 ἐργασία, ergasia
business [2], effort [1], make money [1],
money [1], practice [1]

2239 ἐργάτης, ergatēs
laborer [11], worker [4]

**2239 + 94 ἐργάτης + ἀδικία, ergatēs +
adikia**
evildoer [1]

2240 ἔργον, ergon
work [114], deed [29], do [8], action [2],
labor [2], service [2], what [2],
untranslated [2], act [1], attack [1],
conduct [1], effect [1], require [1],
task [1], undertaking [1], what is done [1]

2241 ἐρεθίζω, erethizō
provoke [1], stir up [1]

2242 ἐρείδω, ereidō
stick[2] [1]

2243 ἐρεύγομαι, ereugomai
proclaim [1]

2244 ἐρημία, erēmia
desert[2] [3], wilderness [1]

2245 ἔρημος, erēmos
wilderness [34], desert[1] [9], desolate [2],
desolate woman [1], wild [1]

2245 + 5536 ἔρημος + τόπος, erēmos
+ topos
country [1]

2246 ἐρημόω, erēmoō
lay waste [3], desert[2] [1], desolate [1]

2247 ἐρήμωσις, erēmōsis
desolate [2], desolation [1]

2248 ἐρίζω, erizō
wrangle [1]

2249 ἐριθεία, eritheia
selfish ambition [4], quarrel [1], self-
seeking [1], selfishness [1]

2250 ἔριον, erion
wool [2]

2251 ἔρις, eris
quarrel [4], dissension [2], strife [2],
rivalry [1]

2252 ἐρίφιον, eriphion
goat [1]

2253 ἔριφος, eriphos
goat [1], young goat [1]

2254 Ἑρμᾶς, Hermas
Hermas [1]

2255 ἑρμηνεία, hermēneia
interpretation [2]

2257 ἑρμηνεύω, hermēneuō
mean[1] [2], translate [1]

2258 Ἑρμῆς, Hermēs
Hermes [2]

2259 Ἑρμογένης, Hermogenēs
Hermogenes [1]

2260 ἑρπετόν, herpeton
reptile [4]

2261 ἐρυθρός, erythros
red [2]

2262 ἔρχομαι, erchomai
come [520], go [49], arrive [7],
untranslated [7], reach [6], come back [4],
visit [4], return [3], become [2], come
up [2], join [2], alight [1], bring in [1],
come by [1], come in [1], come one [1],
come out [1], fall [1], gather [1], go
back [1], grow [1], happen [1], help [1],
make a visit [1], make one's way [1],
next [1], on one's way [1], pass [1],
start [1]

2262 + 1650 ἔρχομαι + εἰς, erchomai
+ eis
enter [6]

2262 + 3958 ἔρχομαι + ὀπίσω,
erchomai + opisō
follow [1]

2262 + 5250 ἔρχομαι + σύν, erchomai
+ syn
accompany [1]

2263 ἐρωτάω, erōtaō
ask [46], beg [4], question [4], invite [2],

please [2], urge [2], appeal [1], pray [1],
say [1]

2264 ἐσθής, esthēs
clothes [5], robe [3]

2266 ἐσθίω, esthiō
eat [145], food [3], *see 3590* [abstain] [3],
consume [1], devour [1], do [1], earn [1],
get [1], get food [1], *see 4024* [abstain] [1]

2268 Ἑσλί, Hesli
Esli [1]

2269 ἔσοπτρον, esoptron
mirror [2]

2270 ἑσπέρα, hespera
evening [3]

2272 Ἑσρώμ, Hesrōm
Hezron [3]

2273 ἐσσόομαι, hessoomai
bad off [1]

2274 ἔσχατος, eschatos
last[1] [42], end [3], last state [3], low [2],
finally [1], last of all [1]

2275 ἐσχάτως, eschatōs
point of death [1]

2276 ἔσω, esō
inside [3], inner [2], house [1], inmost [1],
into [1], *see 2401* [right[4]] [1]

2277 ἔσωθεν, esōthen
inside [7], within [4], inwardly [1]

2278 ἐσώτερος, esōteros
inner [1], innermost [1]

2279 ἑταῖρος, hetairos
friend [3]

2280 ἑτερόγλωσσος, heteroglōssos
person of strange tongues [1]

2281 ἑτεροδιδασκαλέω,
heterodidaskaleō
teach different doctrine [1], teach
otherwise [1]

2282 ἑτεροζυγέω, heterozygeō
mismatch [1]

2283 ἕτερος, heteros
other [39], another [36], different [3],
else [3], next [3], some [3], change [1],
foreigner [1], former [1], neighbor [1], one
another [1], one thing [1], other
person [1], second [1], someone else [1],
unnatural [1], *untranslated* [1]

2284 ἑτέρως, heterōs
differently [1]

2285 ἔτι, eti
still[1] [45], more [17], long[1] [4], yet [3],
untranslated [3], even [2], for [2],
further [2], while [2], again [1], any
further [1], any longer [1], any more [1],
anymore [1], before [1], go on [1], more
than that [1], moreover [1], only [1],
other [1], yes [1], *see 4024* [never] [1]

2286 ἑτοιμάζω, hetoimazō
prepare [27], make preparation [5], make
ready [4], equip [1], get ready [1], hold
ready [1], ready [1]

2288 ἑτοιμασία, hetoimasia
make ready [1]

2289 ἕτοιμος, hetoimos
ready [15], here [1], work already done [1]

2290 ἑτοίμως, hetoimōs
ready [3]

2291 ἔτος, etos
year [48], age[1] [1]

2292 εὖ, eu
do well [2], well[1] [2], kindness [1]

2293 Εὕα, Heua
Eve [2]

2294 εὐαγγελίζω, euangelizō
proclaim the good news [13], bring good
news [12], proclaim [11], proclaim the
gospel [8], tell the good news [2],
announce [1], announce good news [1],
announce the gospel [1], bring the
news [1], good news come [1], preach [1],
proclamation [1], receive the good
news [1]

2295 εὐαγγέλιον, euangelion
gospel [48], good news [18], message of
the gospel [2], proclaim the good
news [2], proclaim the gospel [2], work of
the gospel [2], announce the gospel [1],
proclamation of good news [1]

2296 εὐαγγελιστής, euangelistēs
evangelist [3]

2297 εὐαρεστέω, euaresteō
please [3]

2298 εὐάρεστος, euarestos
please [4], acceptable [3], acceptable
duty [1], give satisfaction [1]

2299 εὐαρέστως, euarestōs
acceptable [1]

2300 Εὔβουλος, Euboulos
Eubulus [1]

2301 εὖγε, euge
do well [1]

2302 εὐγενής, eugenēs
more receptive [1], noble birth [1],
nobleman [1]

2304 εὐδία, eudia
fair weather [1]

2305 εὐδοκέω, eudokeō
please well [6], please [5], take
pleasure [4], decide [2], content [1],
determine [1], good pleasure [1], will[1] [1]

2306 εὐδοκία, eudokia
good pleasure [3], gracious will [2],
desire [1], favor [1], good resolve [1],
goodwill [1]

2307 εὐεργεσία, euergesia
do a good deed [1], service [1]

2308 εὐεργετέω, euergeteō
do good [1]

2309 εὐεργέτης, euergetēs
benefactor [1]

2310 εὔθετος, euthetos
fit [2], useful [1]

2311 εὐθέως, eutheōs
immediately [22], once[2] [6], at that
moment [2], as soon as [1], quickly [1],
soon [1], suddenly [1], very[2] [1],
untranslated [1]

2312 εὐθυδρομέω, euthydromeō
straight course [1], take a straight
course [1]

2313 εὐθυμέω, euthymeō
keep up courage [2], cheerful [1]

2314 εὔθυμος, euthymos
encourage [1]

2315 εὐθύμως, euthymōs
cheerfully [1]

2316 εὐθύνω, euthynō
make straight [1], pilot [1]

2317 εὐθύς¹, euthys¹
immediately [32], once² [9], as soon as [2], just as [2], at that moment [1], at this [1], just then [1], quickly [1], suddenly [1], when [1]

2318 εὐθύς², euthys²
straight [7], right¹ [1]

2319 εὐθύτης, euthytēs
righteous [1]

2320 εὐκαιρέω, eukaireō
leisure [1], opportunity [1], spend time [1]

2321 εὐκαιρία, eukairia
opportunity [2]

2322 εὔκαιρος, eukairos
opportunity [1], time of need [1]

2323 εὐκαίρως, eukairōs
favorable time [1], opportunity [1]

2324 εὔκοπος, eukopos
easy [7]

2325 εὐλάβεια, eulabeia
reverence [1], reverent submission [1]

2326 εὐλαβέομαι, eulabeomai
respect¹ [1]

2327 εὐλαβής, eulabēs
devout [4]

2328 εὐλογέω, eulogeō
bless [35], praise [2], blessing [1], invoke a blessing [1], say a blessing [1], *untranslated* [1]

2329 εὐλογητός, eulogētos
bless [7], blessed one [1]

2330 εὐλογία, eulogia
blessing [11], *see 2093* [bountifully] [2], bountiful gift [1], flattery [1], voluntary gift [1]

2331 εὐμετάδοτος, eumetadotos
generous [1]

2332 Εὐνίκη, Eunikē
Eunice [1]

2333 εὐνοέω, eunoeō
come to terms [1]

2334 εὔνοια, eunoia
enthusiasm [1]

2335 εὐνουχίζω, eunouchizō
make a eunuch [2]

2336 εὐνοῦχος, eunouchos
eunuch [8]

2337 Εὐοδία, Euodia
Euodia [1]

2338 εὐοδόω, euodoō
earn extra [1], go well [1], succeed² [1], well¹ [1]

2339 εὐπάρεδρος, euparedros
devotion [1]

2340 εὐπειθής, eupeithēs
willing to yield [1]

2342 εὐπερίστατος, euperistatos
cling so closely [1]

2343 εὐποιία, eupoiia
do good [1]

2344 εὐπορέω, euporeō
ability [1]

2345 εὐπορία, euporia
wealth [1]

2346 εὐπρέπεια, euprepeia
beauty [1]

2347 εὐπρόσδεκτος, euprosdektos
acceptable [5]

2349 εὐπροσωπέω, euprosōpeō
make a good showing [1]

2350 εὐρακύλων, eurakylōn
northeaster [1]

2351 εὑρίσκω, heuriskō
find [166], come upon [2], be [1], disclose [1], gain [1], get [1], meet [1], obtain [1], prove [1], recognize [1]

2353 εὐρύχωρος, eurychōros
easy [1]

2354 εὐσέβεια, eusebeia
godliness [13], piety [1], religion [1]

2355 εὐσεβέω, eusebeō
religious duty [1], worship [1]

2356 εὐσεβής, eusebēs
devout [1], devout man [1], godly [1]

2357 εὐσεβῶς, eusebōs
godly [1], godly life [1]

2358 εὔσημος, eusēmos
intelligible [1]

2359 εὔσπλαγχνος, eusplanchnos
tender heart [1], tenderhearted [1]

2361 εὐσχημόνως, euschēmonōs
decently [1], honorably [1], properly [1]

2362 εὐσχημοσύνη, euschēmosynē
respect¹ [1]

2363 εὐσχήμων, euschēmōn
high standing [2], good order [1], more respectable [1], respect¹ [1]

2364 εὐτόνως, eutonōs
powerfully [1], vehemently [1]

2365 εὐτραπελία, eutrapelia
vulgar talk [1]

2366 Εὔτυχος, Eutychos
Eutychus [1]

2367 εὐφημία, euphēmia
good repute [1]

2368 εὔφημος, euphēmos
commendable [1]

2369 εὐφορέω, euphoreō
produce abundantly [1]

2370 εὐφραίνω, euphrainō
celebrate [5], rejoice [4], feast [1], glad [1], make glad [1], merry [1], revel [1]

2371 Εὐφράτης, Euphratēs
Euphrates [2]

2372 εὐφροσύνη, euphrosynē
gladness [1], joy [1]

2373 εὐχαριστέω, eucharisteō
give thanks [28], thank [10]

2374 εὐχαριστία, eucharistia
thanksgiving [12], thank [2], gratitude [1]

2375 εὐχάριστος, eucharistos
thankful [1]

2376 εὐχή, euchē
vow [2], prayer [1]

2377 εὔχομαι, euchomai
pray [6], wish [1]

2378 εὔχρηστος, euchrēstos
useful [3]

2379 εὐψυχέω, eupsycheō
cheer [1]

2380 εὐωδία, euōdia
aroma [1], fragrant [1], *see 4011* [fragrant] [1]

2381 εὐώνυμος, euōnymos
left [8], left hand [1]

2383 ἐφάλλομαι, ephallomai
leap [1]

2384 ἐφάπαξ, ephapax
once for all [4], one time [1]

2386 Ἐφέσιος, Ephesios
Ephesian [4], Ephesus [1]

2387 Ἔφεσος, Ephesos
Ephesus [16]

2388 ἐφευρετής, epheuretēs
inventor [1]

2389 ἐφημερία, ephēmeria
priestly order [1], section [1]

2390 ἐφήμερος, ephēmeros
daily [1]

2391 ἐφικνέομαι, ephikneomai
reach [1], reach out [1]

2392 ἐφίστημι, ephistēmi
come [5], stand by [2], stand beside [2], appear [1], arrive [1], attack [1], begin [1], catch [1], come to [1], come upon [1], confront suddenly [1], persistent [1], stand¹ [1], stand before [1], stand near [1]

2394 Ἐφραίμ, Ephraim
Ephraim [1]

2395 ἐφφαθά, ephphatha
ephphatha [1]

2396 ἐχθές, echthes
yesterday [3]

2397 ἔχθρα, echthra
enmity [2], hostility [2], enemy [1], hostile [1]

2398 ἐχθρός, echthros
enemy [29], foe [2], hostile [1]

2399 ἔχιδνα, echidna
viper [5]

2400 ἔχω, echō
have [447], be [40], with [30], *untranslated* [28], *see 5970* [need] [24], hold [15], possess [5], *see 1877* [pregnant] [5], can [4], get [4], receive [4], regard [4], *see 3590* [without¹] [4], keep [3], stand¹ [3], able [2], accept [2], bear¹ [2], bring [2], give [2], next [2], obtain [2], own¹ [2], under [2], wear [2], *see 2809* [sick] [2], *see 3590* [childless] [2], *see 3644* [remember] [2], after [1], away [1], become [1], begin [1], belong [1], come [1], come from [1], consider [1], credit [1], do [1], engage [1], enjoy [1], experience [1], face [1], find [1], guilty [1], hold fast [1], in hand [1], incur [1], leave [1], live with [1], maintain [1], make [1], marry [1], means² [1], meet [1], neighbor [1], possession [1], reap [1], seize [1], subject [1], suffer² [1], take [1], treat [1], use [1], *see 340* [must] [1], *see 457* [rest¹] [1], *see 467* [marry] [1], *see 993* [rule¹] [1], *see 1792* [rebuke] [1], *see 1877* [conceive] [1], *see 1877* [with child] [1], *see 1952* [honor] [1], *see 2163* [desire] [1], *see 2822* [recover] [1], *see 2998* [live] [1], *see 3130* [conceive children] [1], *see 3538* [share] [1], *see 3590* [devoid] [1], *see 3590* [lack] [1], *see 3786* [spread] [1], *see 3950* [call] [1], *see 4024* [cannot] [1], *see*

4411 [believe] [1], *see 5921* [grateful] [1], *see 5921* [thank] [1], *see 5970* [needy] [1]

2400 + 1222 ἔχω + γυνή, echō + gynē
marry [2]

2400 + 1877 + 2106 ἔχω + ἐν + ἐπίγνωσις, echō + en + epignōsis
acknowledge [1]

2400 + 3836 + 467 ἔχω + ὁ + ἀνήρ, echō + ho + anēr
marry [1]

2400 + 6034 ἔχω + ψυχή, echō + psychē
live [1]

2401 ἕως, heōs
until [39], to [32], *untranslated* [8], while [7], far [5], even [2], down [1], down to [1], for [1], go to [1], many [1], up to [1], when [1]

2401 + 323 ἕως + ἄν, heōs + an
until [16], before [4]

2401 + 785 ἕως + ἄρτι, heōs + arti
still[1] [2]

2401 + 2276 ἕως + ἔσω, heōs + esō
right[4] [1]

2401 + 4005 ἕως + ὅς, heōs + hos
until [12]

2401 + 4015 ἕως + ὅστις, heōs + hostis
until [4]

2401 + 4536 ἕως + πότε, heōs + pote
how long [7]

2404 Ζαβουλών, Zaboulōn
Zebulun [3]

2405 Ζακχαῖος, Zakchaios
Zacchaeus [3]

2406 Ζάρα, Zara
Zerah [1]

2408 Ζαχαρίας, Zacharias
Zechariah [11]

2409 ζάω, zaō
live [111], alive [19], come to life [4], life [2], bring to life [1], get a living [1], lifetime [1], living one [1]

2411 Ζεβεδαῖος, Zebedaios
Zebedee [12]

2412 ζεστός, zestos
hot [3]

2414 ζεῦγος, zeugos
pair [1], yoke [1]

2415 ζευκτηρία, zeuktēria
rope [1]

2416 Ζεύς, Zeus
Zeus [2]

2417 ζέω, zeō
ardent [1], burn [1]

2418 ζηλεύω, zēleuō
earnest [1]

2419 ζῆλος, zēlos
jealousy [7], zeal [6], envy [2], fury [1]

2420 ζηλόω, zēloō
make much [3], jealous [2], strive [2], covet [1], eager [1], envious [1], feel jealousy [1]

2421 ζηλωτής, zēlōtēs
zealous [4], Zealot [2], eager [2]

2422 ζημία, zēmia
loss [4]

2423 ζημιόω, zēmioō
forfeit [3], suffer loss [2], harm [1]

2424 Ζηνᾶς, Zēnas
Zenas [1]

2426 ζητέω, zēteō
look for [32], seek [22], search [18], try[1] [18], want [7], ask for [4], strive [4], desire [2], require [2], demand [1], discuss [1], effort [1], grope for [1], insist [1], look [1], seek out [1]

2427 ζήτημα, zētēma
question [3], controversy [1], point of disagreement [1]

2428 ζήτησις, zētēsis
controversy [3], debate [2], discussion [1], investigate [1]

2429 ζιζάνιον, zizanion
weed [8]

2431 Ζοροβαβέλ, Zorobabel
Zerubbabel [3]

2432 ζόφος, zophos
deep darkness [4], gloom [1]

2433 ζυγός, zygos
yoke [5], pair of scales [1]

2434 ζύμη, zymē
yeast [13]

2435 ζυμόω, zymoō
leaven [4]

2436 ζωγρέω, zōgreō
catch [1], hold captive [1]

2437 ζωή, zōē
life [133], lifetime [1], living thing [1]

2438 ζώνη, zōnē
belt [6], sash [2]

2439 ζώννυμι, zōnnymi
fasten belt [2], fasten belt around [1]

2441 ζωογονέω, zōogoneō
give life [1], keep one's life [1], *see 3590* [die] [1]

2442 ζῷον, zōon
living creature [20], animal [3]

2443 ζωοποιέω, zōopoieō
give life [6], make alive [3], come to life [1], life-giving [1]

2445 ἤ, ē
or [257], than [36], *untranslated* [31], *see 4570* [before] [5], and [3], either [3], rather [2], but [1], nor [1], or else [1], surely [1], unless [1], *see 884* [play] [1]

2448 ἡγεμονεύω, hēgemoneuō
governor [2]

2449 ἡγεμονία, hēgemonia
reign [1]

2450 ἡγεμών, hēgemōn
governor [19], ruler [1]

2451 ἡγέομαι, hēgeomai
regard [8], leader [5], consider [4], think [4], ruler [2], chief [1], count [1], esteem [1], judge [1], *see 3123* [profane] [1]

2452 ἡδέως, hēdeōs
gladly [2], delight [1], like[2] [1], most gladly [1]

2453 ἤδη, ēdē
already [32], now [17], *see 4020* [as soon as] [3], when [2], *untranslated* [2], about[3] [1], as [1], just[1] [1], time[1] [1]

2453 + 4537 ἤδη + πότε, ēdē + pote
last[1] [1]

2454 ἡδονή, hēdonē
pleasure [4], crave [1]

2455 ἡδύοσμον, hēdyosmon
mint [2]

2456 ἦθος, ēthos
moral [1]

2457 ἥκω, hēkō
come [25], here [1]

2458 ἡλί[1], ēli[1]
Eli [2]

2459 Ἡλί[2], Ēli[2]
Heli [1]

2460 Ἡλίας, Ēlias
Elijah [29]

2461 ἡλικία, hēlikia
age[1] [2], span of life [2], stature [2], year [1], *see 2789* [old[1]] [1]

2462 ἡλίκος, hēlikos
great [1], how much [1], small [1]

2463 ἥλιος, hēlios
sun [30], *see 424* [east] [1], *see 1544* [sundown] [1]

2464 ἧλος, hēlos
nail [2]

2465 ἡμέρα, hēmera
day [334], time[1] [16], *see 2848* [daily] [5], morning [4], *see 2848* [day after day] [3], *see 2848* [every day] [3], daybreak [2], festival [2], year [2], *see 1877* [when] [2], *see 2848* [day by day] [2], afternoon [1], age[1] [1], another [1], court[2] [1], daily [1], daylight [1], daytime [1], today [1], *see 3545* [midday] [1], *see 3893* [week] [1], *see 4246* [always] [1], *see 4574* [recently] [1], *see 5569* [nine o'clock in the morning] [1], *untranslated* [1]

2466 ἡμέτερος, hēmeteros
we [6], person [1]

2467 ἡμιθανής, hēmithanēs
half dead [1]

2468 ἥμισυς, hēmisys
half [5]

2469 ἡμιώριον, hēmiōrion
half an hour [1]

2471 + 323 ἡνίκα + ἄν, hēnika + an
whenever [1]

2471 + 1569 ἡνίκα + ἐάν, hēnika + ean
when [1]

2472 ἤπερ, ēper
than [1]

2473 ἤπιος, ēpios
kindly [1]

2474 Ἤρ, Ēr
Er [1]

2475 ἤρεμος, ēremos
quiet [1]

2476 Ἡρῴδης, Hērōdēs
Herod [43]

2477 Ἡρῳδιανοί, Hērōdianoi
Herodian [3]

2478 Ἡρῳδιάς, Hērōdias
Herodias [6]

2479 Ἡρῳδίων, Hērōdiōn
Herodion [1]

2480 Ἡσαΐας, Ēsaias
Isaiah [22]

2481 Ἠσαῦ, Ēsau
Esau [3]

2482 ἥσσων, hēssōn
bad [1], less [1]

2483 ἡσυχάζω, hēsychazō
silent [2], live quietly [1], rest[1] [1],
silence [1]

2484 ἡσυχία, hēsychia
quiet [1], quietly [1], silence [1], silent [1]

2485 ἡσύχιος, hēsychios
peaceable [1], quiet [1]

2486 ἤτοι, ētoi
either [1]

2487 ἡττάομαι, hēttaomai
master [1], overpower [1]

2488 ἥττημα, hēttēma
defeat [2]

2490 ἠχέω, ēcheō
noisy [1]

2491 ἦχος[1], ēchos[1]
sound[1] [2], report [1]

2492 ἦχος[2], ēchos[2]
roar [1]

2497 Θαδδαῖος, Thaddaios
Thaddaeus [2]

2498 θάλασσα, thalassa
sea [87], seashore [1], seaside [1], see
2093 [coast] [1], see 5927 [seashore] [1]

2499 θάλπω, thalpō
care for tenderly [2]

2500 Θαμάρ, Thamar
Tamar [1]

2501 θαμβέω, thambeō
amaze [2], perplex [1]

2502 θάμβος, thambos
amaze [1], wonder [1]

2502 + 4321 θάμβος + περιέχω,
thambos + periechō
amaze [1]

2503 θανάσιμος, thanasimos
deadly thing [1]

2504 θανατηφόρος, thanatēphoros
deadly [1]

2505 θάνατος, thanatos
death [103], see 4639 [mortal] [4], die [3],
mortal [2], pestilence [2], see 5462 [die
surely] [2], dead [1], death penalty [1],
peril [1], see 5377 [receive a death-
blow] [1]

2506 θανατόω, thanatoō
put to death [7], kill [2], bring about
death [1], die [1]

2507 θάπτω, thaptō
bury [11]

2508 Θάρα, Thara
Terah [1]

2509 θαρρέω, tharreō
have confidence [2], bold [1],
confidence [1], confident [1], show
boldness [1]

2510 θαρσέω, tharseō
take heart [5], keep up courage [1], take
courage [1]

2511 θάρσος, tharsos
courage [1]

2512 θαῦμα, thauma
wonder [1], untranslated [1]

2513 θαυμάζω, thaumazō
amaze [26], astonish [9], wonder [4],
amazement [1], flatter [1], marvel [1]

2514 θαυμάσιος, thaumasios
amazing thing [1]

2515 θαυμαστός, thaumastos
amazing [4], astonishing thing [1],
marvelous [1]

2516 θεά, thea
goddess [1]

2517 θεάομαι, theaomai
see [19], look at [3]

2518 θεατρίζω, theatrizō
expose publicly [1]

2519 θέατρον, theatron
theater [2], spectacle [1]

2520 θεῖον, theion
sulfur [7]

2521 θεῖος, theios
divine [2], deity [1]

2522 θειότης, theiotēs
divine nature [1]

2523 θειώδης, theiōdēs
sulfur [1]

2525 θέλημα, thelēma
will[1] [55], desire [2], want [2], wish [2],
willing [1]

2526 θέλησις, thelēsis
will[1] [1]

2527 θέλω, thelō
want [90], wish [34], desire [18],
will[1] [16], choose [15], see 4024
[refuse] [6], willing [5], untranslated [4],
like[2] [3], please [3], see 4024
[unwilling] [3], intend [2], prefer [2],
decide [1], deliberately [1], dispose [1],
insist [1], resolve [1], try[1] [1], see 3590
[unwilling] [1]

2528 θεμέλιον, themelion
foundation [1]

2529 θεμέλιος, themelios
foundation [14], untranslated [1]

2530 θεμελιόω, themelioō
found [2], establish [1], establish
securely [1], ground[2] [1]

2531 θεοδίδακτος, theodidaktos
taught by God [1]

2534 θεομάχος, theomachos
fight against God [1]

2535 θεόπνευστος, theopneustos
inspired by God [1]

2536 θεός, theos
God [1284], god [15], divine [7], he [4],
see 2848 [godly] [3], goddess [1],
godly [1], see 5828 [God-fearing] [1],
untranslated [1]

2537 θεοσέβεια, theosebeia
reverence for God [1]

2538 θεοσεβής, theosebēs
worship [1]

2539 θεοστυγής, theostygēs
God-hater [1]

2540 θεότης, theotēs
deity [1]

2541 Θεόφιλος, Theophilos
Theophilus [2]

2542 θεραπεία, therapeia
cure [1], healing [1], slave [1]

2543 θεραπεύω, therapeuō
cure [40], heal [2], serve [1]

2544 θεράπων, therapōn
servant [1]

2545 θερίζω, therizō
reap [18], reaper [2], harvester [1]

2546 θερισμός, therismos
harvest [13]

2547 θεριστής, theristēs
reaper [2]

2548 θερμαίνω, thermainō
warm [6]

2549 θέρμη, thermē
heat [1]

2550 θέρος, theros
summer [3]

2552 Θεσσαλονικεύς, Thessalonikeus
Thessalonian [2], Thessalonica [2]

2553 Θεσσαλονίκη, Thessalonikē
Thessalonica [5]

2554 Θευδᾶς, Theudas
Theudas [1]

2555 θεωρέω, theōreō
see [52], watch [4], look [1], look on [1]

2556 θεωρία, theōria
spectacle [1]

2557 θήκη, thēkē
sheath [1]

2558 θηλάζω, thēlazō
nurse an infant [3], nurse [1], nursing
baby [1]

2559 θῆλυς, thēlys
female [3], woman [2]

2560 θήρα, thēra
trap [1]

2561 θηρεύω, thēreuō
catch [1]

2562 θηριομαχέω, thēriomacheō
fight with a wild animal [1]

2563 θηρίον, thērion
beast [39], creature [2], animal [1], beast
of prey [1], brute [1], wild animal [1],
wild beast [1]

2564 θησαυρίζω, thēsaurizō
store up [3], lay up [1], lay up treasure [1],
reserve [1], save [1], store up treasure [1]

2565 θησαυρός, thēsauros
treasure [16], treasure chest [1]

2566 θιγγάνω, thinganō
touch [3]

2567 θλίβω, thlibō
afflict [6], crush [1], hard [1],
persecute [1], suffer persecution [1]

2568 θλῖψις, thlipsis
affliction [13], suffer[1] [10],
persecution [9], distress [5], anguish [2],
trouble [2], hardship [1], ordeal [1],
pressure [1], torture [1]

2569 θνήσκω, thnēskō
dead [6], die [2], dead man [1]

2570 θνητός, thnētos
mortal [6]

2571 θορυβάζω, thorybazō
distract [1]

2572 θορυβέω, *thorybeō*
make a commotion [2], alarm [1], set in an uproar [1]

2573 θόρυβος, *thorybos*
riot [3], uproar [2], commotion [1], disturbance [1]

2575 θραύω, *thrauō*
oppress [1]

2576 θρέμμα, *thremma*
flock [1]

2577 θρηνέω, *thrēneō*
wail [3], mourn [1]

2579 θρησκεία, *thrēskeia*
religion [3], worship [1]

2580 θρῆσκος, *thrēskos*
religious [1]

2581 θριαμβεύω, *thriambeuō*
lead in triumphal procession [1], triumph over [1]

2582 θρίξ, *thrix*
hair [15]

2583 θροέω, *throeō*
alarm [3]

2584 θρόμβος, *thrombos*
great drop [1]

2585 θρόνος, *thronos*
throne [62]

2587 Θυάτειρα, *Thyateira*
Thyatira [4]

2588 θυγάτηρ, *thygatēr*
daughter [27], descendant [1]

2589 θυγάτριον, *thygatrion*
little daughter [2]

2590 θύελλα, *thyella*
tempest [1]

2591 θύϊνος, *thyinos*
scent [1]

2592 θυμίαμα, *thymiama*
incense [5], incense offering [1]

2593 θυμιατήριον, *thymiatērion*
altar of incense [1]

2594 θυμιάω, *thymiaō*
offer incense [1]

2595 θυμομαχέω, *thymomacheō*
angry [1]

2596 θυμός, *thymos*
wrath [10], anger [3], fury [3], rage [1]

2596 + 4441 θυμός + πλήρης, *thymos + plērēs*
enrage [1]

2597 + 3336 θυμόω + λίαν, *thymoō + lian*
infuriate [1]

2598 θύρα, *thyra*
door [29], gate [9], entrance [1]

2599 θυρεός, *thyreos*
shield [1]

2600 θυρίς, *thyris*
window [2]

2601 θυρωρός, *thyrōros*
doorkeeper [1], gatekeeper [1], woman who guards the gate [1], *untranslated* [1]

2602 θυσία, *thysia*
sacrifice [28]

2603 θυσιαστήριον, *thysiastērion*
altar [22], sacrifice on an altar [1]

2604 θύω, *thyō*
kill [6], sacrifice [5], offer sacrifice [2], slaughter [1]

2605 Θωμᾶς, *Thōmas*
Thomas [11]

2606 θώραξ, *thōrax*
breastplate [4], scale [1]

2608 Ἰάϊρος, *Iairos*
Jairus [2]

2609 Ἰακώβ, *Iakōb*
Jacob [27]

2610 Ἰάκωβος, *Iakōbos*
James [42]

2611 ἴαμα, *iama*
healing [3]

2612 Ἰαμβρῆς, *Iambrēs*
Jambres [1]

2613 Ἰανναί, *Iannai*
Jannai [1]

2614 Ἰάννης, *Iannēs*
Jannes [1]

2615 ἰάομαι, *iaomai*
heal [24], cure [1], healing [1]

2616 Ἰάρετ, *Iaret*
Jared [1]

2617 ἴασις, *iasis*
cure [1], heal [1], healing [1]

2618 ἴασπις, *iaspis*
jasper [4]

2619 Ἰάσων, *Iasōn*
Jason [5]

2620 ἰατρός, *iatros*
physician [6], doctor [1]

2623 ἴδε, *ide*
here [9], look [9], see [9], *untranslated* [3], listen [2], note[1] [1], yes [1]

2625 ἴδιος, *idios*
one's own [48], own[2] [11], he [7], they [7], *see 2848* [privately] [7], home [4], themselves [4], each [2], friend [2], himself [2], private [2], right[1] [2], you [2], *untranslated* [2], due[2] [1], harvest [1], individually [1], itself [1], particular [1], private ownership [1], proper [1], relative [1], the [1], who [1], yourself [1], *see 2848* [private meeting] [1]

2626 ἰδιώτης, *idiōtēs*
outsider [3], ordinary [1], untrained [1]

2627 ἰδού, *idou*
untranslated [43], see [40], look [30], suddenly [20], there [12], here [10], listen [9], now [8], just then [7], indeed [5], surely [4], beware [2], appear [1], at that moment [1], at this moment [1], how [1], in fact [1], remember [1], see here [1], take note [1], while [1]

2628 Ἰδουμαία, *Idoumaia*
Idumea [1]

2629 ἱδρώς, *hidrōs*
sweat [1]

2630 Ἰεζάβελ, *Iezabel*
Jezebel [1]

2631 Ἱεράπολις, *Hierapolis*
Hierapolis [1]

2632 ἱερατεία, *hierateia*
priesthood [1], priestly office [1]

2633 ἱεράτευμα, *hierateuma*
priesthood [2]

2634 ἱερατεύω, *hierateuō*
serve as priest [1]

2635 Ἰερεμίας, *Ieremias*
Jeremiah [3]

2636 ἱερεύς, *hiereus*
priest [31]

2637 Ἰεριχώ, *Ierichō*
Jericho [7]

2638 ἱερόθυτος, *hierothytos*
offer in sacrifice [1]

2639 ἱερόν, *hieron*
temple [71]

2640 ἱεροπρεπής, *hieroprepēs*
reverent [1]

2641 ἱερός, *hieros*
sacred [2], temple service [1]

2643 Ἱεροσολυμίτης, *Hierosolymitēs*
person of Jerusalem [2]

2644 ἱεροσυλέω, *hierosyleō*
rob a temple [1]

2645 ἱερόσυλος, *hierosylos*
temple robber [1]

2646 ἱερουργέω, *hierourgeō*
priestly service [1]

2647 Ἱερουσαλήμ, *Ierousalēm*
Jerusalem [139]

2648 ἱερωσύνη, *hierōsynē*
priesthood [3]

2649 Ἰεσσαί, *Iessai*
Jesse [5]

2650 Ἰεφθάε, *Iephthae*
Jephthah [1]

2651 Ἰεχονίας, *Iechonias*
Jechoniah [2]

2652 Ἰησοῦς, *Iēsous*
Jesus [906], he [4], Joshua [3], *untranslated* [2], who [1]

2653 ἱκανός, *hikanos*
long[1] [5], worthy [5], some [4], large [3], many [3], enough [2], great many [2], much [2], number [2], able [1], bail [1], competent [1], considerable [1], considerable number [1], continue [1], great [1], large sum [1], sufficient [1], *see 4024* [unfit] [1]

2653 + 4472 ἱκανός + ποιέω, *hikanos + poieō*
satisfy [1]

2654 ἱκανότης, *hikanotēs*
competence [1]

2655 ἱκανόω, *hikanoō*
enable [1], make competent [1]

2656 ἱκετηρία, *hiketēria*
supplication [1]

2657 ἱκμάς, *ikmas*
moisture [1]

2658 Ἰκόνιον, *Ikonion*
Iconium [6]

2659 ἱλαρός, *hilaros*
cheerful [1]

2660 ἱλαρότης, *hilarotēs*
cheerfulness [1]

2661 ἱλάσκομαι, *hilaskomai*
make a sacrifice of atonement [1], merciful [1]

2662 ἱλασμός, *hilasmos*
atoning sacrifice [2]

2663 ἱλαστήριον, *hilastērion*
mercy seat [1], sacrifice of atonement [1]

2664 ἵλεως, *hileōs*
God forbid [1], merciful [1]

2665 Ἰλλυρικόν, *Illyrikon*
Illyricum [1]

2666 ἱμάς, *himas*
thong [4]

2667 ἱματίζω, *himatizō*
clothe [2]

2668 ἱμάτιον, *himation*
cloak [19], clothes [17], robe [9],
clothing [6], coat [5], garment [2],
clothe [1], outer robe [1]

2669 ἱματισμός, *himatismos*
clothing [3], clothes [2]

2671 ἵνα, *hina*
so that [288], to [178], that [84],
untranslated [45], order² [37], for [7],
so [7], let [2], when [2], aim [1], if [1],
or [1], ready [1], result [1], see that [1],
then [1], want [1]

2671 + 3590 ἵνα + μή, *hina + mē*
or [3], rather [1]

2671 + 3607 ἵνα + μήποτε, *hina +
mēpote*
otherwise [1]

2672 ἱνατί, *hinati*
why [6]

2673 Ἰόππη, *Ioppē*
Joppa [10]

2674 Ἰορδάνης, *Iordanēs*
Jordan [15]

2675 ἰός, *ios*
poison [1], rust [1], venom [1]

2677 Ἰουδαία, *Ioudaia*
Judea [43]

2678 ἰουδαΐζω, *ioudaizō*
live like a Jew [1]

2679 Ἰουδαϊκός, *Ioudaikos*
Jewish [1]

2680 Ἰουδαϊκῶς, *Ioudaikōs*
like a Jew [1]

2681 Ἰουδαῖος, *Ioudaios*
Jew [175], Jewish [16], Judea [4]

2682 Ἰουδαϊσμός, *Ioudaismos*
Judaism [2]

2683 Ἰούδας, *Ioudas*
Judas [32], Judah [10], Jude [1], Judea [1]

2684 Ἰουλία, *Ioulia*
Julia [1]

2685 Ἰούλιος, *Ioulios*
Julius [2]

2687 Ἰουνιᾶς, *Iounias*
Junia [1]

2688 Ἰοῦστος, *Ioustos*
Justus [3]

2689 ἱππεύς, *hippeus*
horseman [2]

2690 ἱππικός, *hippikos*
cavalry [1]

2691 ἵππος, *hippos*
horse [17]

2692 Ἶρις, *iris*
rainbow [2]

2693 Ἰσαάκ, *Isaak*
Isaac [20]

2694 ἰσάγγελος, *isangelos*
like an angel [1]

2697 Ἰσκαριώτης, *Iskariōtēs*
Iscariot [11]

2698 ἴσος, *isos*
equal [3], agree [2], equality [1],
much [1], same [1]

2699 ἰσότης, *isotēs*
fair balance [2], fairly [1]

2700 ἰσότιμος, *isotimos*
as precious [1]

2701 ἰσόψυχος, *isopsychos*
like¹ [1]

2702 Ἰσραήλ, *Israēl*
Israel [63], *see 5626* [Israelite] [4], *see
1666* [Israelite] [1]

2703 Ἰσραηλίτης, *Israēlitēs*
Israelite [9]

2704 Ἰσσαχάρ, *Issachar*
Issachar [1]

2705 ἵστημι, *histēmi*
stand¹ [108], stand still [5], make
stand [4], put [4], bystander [3], stop [3],
establish [2], keep [2], place [2], set
up [2], stand by [2], stand firm [2], set
up [2], uphold [2], appeal [1], confirm [1],
fix [1], hold against [1], pay [1],
propose [1], stand fast [1], stay [1],
sustain [1], take a stand [1], there [1]

2707 ἱστορέω, *historeō*
visit [1]

2708 ἰσχυρός, *ischyros*
strong [9], mighty [8], strong man [5],
more powerful [3], loud [1], mighty
man [1], powerful [1], severe [1]

2709 ἰσχύς, *ischys*
might [4], strength [4], power [2]

2710 ἰσχύω, *ischyō*
can [9], able [7], well³ [2], count [1],
do [1], force [1], good [1], overpower [1],
powerful [1], prevail [1], strength [1],
strong [1], *see 4024* [defeat] [1]

2711 ἴσως, *isōs*
perhaps [1]

2712 Ἰταλία, *Italia*
Italy [4]

2713 Ἰταλικός, *Italikos*
Italian [1]

2714 Ἰτουραῖος, *Itouraios*
Ituraea [1]

2715 ἰχθύδιον, *ichthydion*
small fish [2]

2716 ἰχθύς, *ichthys*
fish [20]

2717 ἴχνος, *ichnos*
step¹ [2], example [1]

2718 Ἰωαθάμ, *Iōatham*
Jotham [2]

2720 Ἰωανάν, *Iōanan*
Joanan [1]

2721 Ἰωάννα, *Iōanna*
Joanna [2]

2722 Ἰωάννης, *Iōannēs*
John [135]

2724 Ἰώβ, *Iōb*
Job [1]

2725 Ἰωβήδ, *Iōbēd*
Obed [3]

2726 Ἰωδά, *Iōda*
Joda [1]

2727 Ἰωήλ, *Iōēl*
Joel [1]

2729 Ἰωνάμ, *Iōnam*
Jonam [1]

2731 Ἰωνᾶς, *Iōnas*
Jonah [9]

2732 Ἰωράμ, *Iōram*
Joram [2]

2733 Ἰωρίμ, *Iōrim*
Jorim [1]

2734 Ἰωσαφάτ, *Iōsaphat*
Jehoshaphat [2]

2736 Ἰωσῆς, *Iōsēs*
Joses [3]

2737 Ἰωσήφ, *Iōsēph*
Joseph [35]

2738 Ἰωσήχ, *Iōsēch*
Josech [1]

2739 Ἰωσίας, *Iōsias*
Josiah [2]

2740 ἰῶτα, *iōta*
letter [1]

2743 κἀγώ, *kagō*
and I [33], I [29], I also [15], I too [3],
myself [2], then I [1], *untranslated* [1]

2745 καθά, *katha*
as [1]

2746 καθαίρεσις, *kathairesis*
tear down [2], destroy [1]

2747 καθαιρέω, *kathaireō*
take down [4], destroy [2], bring down [1],
deprive [1], pull down [1]

2748 καθαίρω, *kathairō*
prune [1]

2749 καθάπερ, *kathaper*
as [4], just as [4], like¹ [2], for [1], so [1],
untranslated [1]

2750 καθάπτω, *kathaptō*
fasten [1]

2751 καθαρίζω, *katharizō*
cleanse [12], make clean [11], purify [4],
clean [3], declare clean [1]

2752 καθαρισμός, *katharismos*
purification [4], cleanse [3]

2754 καθαρός, *katharos*
pure [13], clean [7], clear [3], cleanse [1],
innocent [1], not responsible [1],
untranslated [1]

2755 καθαρότης, *katharotēs*
purify [1]

2756 καθέδρα, *kathedra*
seat [3]

2757 καθέζομαι, *kathezomai*
sit [6], stay [1]

2759 καθεξῆς, *kathexēs*
after [1], orderly account [1], place to
place [1], soon afterwards [1], step by
step [1]

2761 καθεύδω, *katheudō*
sleep [14], asleep [6], fall asleep [1],
sleeper [1]

2762 καθηγητής, *kathēgētēs*
instructor [2]

2763 καθήκω, *kathēkō*
allow [1], should [1]

2764 κάθημαι, *kathēmai*
sit [50], seat [25], rider [9], sit down [3], live [2], rule[1], *untranslated* [1]

2766 καθημερινός, *kathēmerinos*
daily [1]

2767 καθίζω, *kathizō*
sit down [17], sit [12], take a seat [5], seat [4], ride [2], stay [2], appoint as judge [1], place [1], put [1], rest[1] [1]

2768 καθίημι, *kathiēmi*
let down [2], lower [2]

2770 καθίστημι, *kathistēmi*
put in charge [7], appoint [5], make [4], become [1], conduct [1], keep [1], place [1], set[1] [1]

2771 καθό, *katho*
according [2], as [1], insofar [1]

2773 καθόλου, *katholou*
at all [1]

2774 καθοπλίζω, *kathoplizō*
arm fully [1]

2775 καθοράω, *kathoraō*
see [1]

2776 καθότι, *kathoti*
because [4]

2776 + 323 καθότι + ἄν, *kathoti + an*
as [2]

2777 καθώς, *kathōs*
as [103], just as [51], according [4], so [3], *untranslated* [3], even as [2], how [2], like[1] [2], since [2], as equal [1], custom [1], for [1], in [1], really [1], this [1], this way [1], well[2] [1], what [1], whatever [1]

2778 καθώσπερ, *kathōsper*
just as [1]

2779 καί, *kai*
and [5802], *untranslated* [2024], also [334], then [258], but [132], even [97], so [93], or [37], yet [32], with [27], both [24], now [22], indeed [19], well[2] [17], too[1] [16], while [6], even though [5], include [5], when [5], as [4], as for [4], the [3], together with [3], for [2], from [2], in fact [2], in turn [2], nor [2], once[4] [2], only [2], though [2], thus [2], *see 1949* [either side] [2], *see 5477* [forty-two] [2], actually [1], along with [1], besides [1], by [1], certainly [1], even so [1], furthermore [1], likewise [1], meanwhile [1], more [1], nevertheless [1], next [1], similar [1], until [1], very[2] [1], whether [1], *see 562* [again and again] [1], *see 1274* [eighteen] [1], *see 4922* [human being] [1], *see 5477* [forty-six] [1], *see 5558* [thirty-eight] [1]

2780 Καϊάφας, *Kaiaphas*
Caiaphas [9]

2782 Κάϊν, *Kain*
Cain [3]

2783 Καϊνάμ, *Kainam*
Cainan [2]

2785 καινός, *kainos*
new [39], fresh [3]

2786 καινότης, *kainotēs*
new [1], newness [1]

2788 καίπερ, *kaiper*
even though [2], though [2], although [1]

2789 καιρός, *kairos*
time[1] [61], season[1] [6], opportunity [3], age[2] [2], proper time [2], while [2], appointed time [1], due time [1], harvest time [1], opportune time [1], period [1], right time [1], set time [1], *see 3814* [present[3]] [1]

2789 + 2461 καιρός + ἡλικία, *kairos + hēlikia*
old[1] [1]

2790 Καῖσαρ, *Kaisar*
emperor [29]

2791 Καισάρεια, *Kaisareia*
Caesarea [17]

2792 καίτοι, *kaitoi*
though [1], yet [1]

2793 καίτοιγε, *kaitoige*
although [1]

2794 καίω, *kaiō*
burn [7], blaze [2], light[1] [2]

2795 κἀκεῖ, *kakei*
there [6], and there [2], there too [1], *untranslated* [1]

2796 κἀκεῖθεν, *kakeithen*
from there [8], outside [1], then [1]

2797 κἀκεῖνος, *kakeinos*
they [7], he [3], other [2], that [2], *untranslated* [2], also [1], and that [1], and this [1], even that [1], he also [1], this [1]

2798 κακία, *kakia*
malice [6], evil [2], wickedness [2], trouble [1]

2799 κακοήθεια, *kakoētheia*
craftiness [1]

2800 κακολογέω, *kakologeō*
speak evil [4]

2801 κακοπάθεια, *kakopatheia*
suffer[1] [1]

2802 κακοπαθέω, *kakopatheō*
endure suffering [1], suffer[1] [1], suffer hardship [1]

2803 κακοποιέω, *kakopoieō*
do evil [2], do harm [2]

2804 κακοποιός, *kakopoios*
criminal [1], do wrong [1], evildoer [1]

2805 κακός, *kakos*
evil [30], wrong [6], bad [2], harm [2], evil thing [1], evildoer [1], foul [1], vicious [1], wicked [1], wretch [1], *see 3357* [resentful] [1]

2805 + 4472 κακός + ποιέω, *kakos + poieō*
criminal [1]

2805 + 4556 κακός + πράσσω, *kakos + prassō*
harm [1], wrongdoer [1]

2806 κακοῦργος, *kakourgos*
criminal [4]

2807 κακουχέω, *kakoucheō*
torment [1], torture [1]

2808 κακόω, *kakoō*
harm [2], force [1], mistreat [1], poison [1], violent [1]

2809 κακῶς, *kakōs*
sick [7], wrongly [2], evil [1], ill [1], miserable [1], terribly [1], torment [1]

2809 + 2400 κακῶς + ἔχω, *kakōs + echō*
sick [2]

2810 κάκωσις, *kakōsis*
mistreatment [1]

2811 καλάμη, *kalamē*
straw [1]

2812 κάλαμος, *kalamos*
reed [6], rod [2], stick[1] [2], measuring rod [1], pen [1]

2813 καλέω, *kaleō*
call [110], invite [17], name [4], summon [3], designate [1], give [1], give a name [1], guest [1], have [1], host[2] [1], say [1]

2813 + 3836 + 3950 καλέω + ὁ + ὄνομα, *kaleō + ho + onoma*
name [6]

2813 + 3950 καλέω + ὄνομα, *kaleō + onoma*
name [1]

2814 καλλιέλαιος, *kallielaios*
cultivated olive tree [1]

2815 καλοδιδάσκαλος, *kalodidaskalos*
teach what is good [1]

2816 Καλοὶ λιμένες, *Kaloi limenes*
Fair Havens [1]

2818 καλοποιέω, *kalopoieō*
do right [1]

2819 καλός, *kalos*
good [70], right[1] [5], well[1] [5], excellent [2], fair [2], noble [2], *untranslated* [2], beautiful [1], clear [1], fine [1], good purpose [1], good thing [1], goodness [1], honest [1], honorable [1], honorably [1], right thing [1], sound[2] [1]

2819 + 3437 καλός + μᾶλλον, *kalos + mallon*
good [1]

2820 κάλυμμα, *kalymma*
veil [4]

2821 καλύπτω, *kalyptō*
cover [3], veil [2], cover up [1], hide [1], swamp [1]

2822 καλῶς, *kalōs*
well[1] [17], right[1] [5], rightly [3], good [2], fine way [1], good purpose [1], honorably [1], kind enough [1], kind[2] [1], please [1], readily enough [1], true [1], very well [1]

2822 + 2400 καλῶς + ἔχω, *kalōs + echō*
recover [1]

2823 κάμηλος, *kamēlos*
camel [6]

2825 κάμινος, *kaminos*
furnace [4]

2826 καμμύω, *kammyō*
shut [2]

2827 κάμνω, *kamnō*
grow weary [1], sick [1]

2828 κάμπτω, *kamptō*
bow[1] [3], bend [1]

2829 κἄν, *kan*
if [5], even though [3], even if [2], and [1], but [1], even [1], if even [1], or [1], then [1], *untranslated* [1]

2830 Κανά, *Kana*
Cana [4]

2831 Καναναῖος, *Kananaios*
Cananaean [2]

2833 Κανδάκη, *Kandakē*
Candace [1]

2834 κανών, *kanōn*
sphere of action [2], rule[2] [1],
untranslated [1]

2836 καπηλεύω, *kapēleuō*
peddler [1]

2837 καπνός, *kapnos*
smoke [12], smoky [1]

2838 Καππαδοκία, *Kappadokia*
Cappadocia [2]

2840 καρδία, *kardia*
heart [141], mind[1] [5], inner [2],
untranslated [2], devotion [1], himself [1],
resolve [1], *see 605* [wholeheartedly] [1],
see 899 [himself] [1], *see 5502* [ponder] [1]

2841 καρδιογνώστης, *kardiognōstēs*
know the heart [1], know the human
heart [1]

2842 Κάρπος, *Karpos*
Carpus [1]

2843 καρπός, *karpos*
fruit [42], grain [5], harvest [5],
produce [4], crop [3], advantage [2],
collect [1], fruitful [1], profit [1],
untranslated [1]

2843 + 3836 + 4019 καρπός + ὁ +
ὀσφῦς, *karpos + ho + osphys*
descendant [1]

2844 καρποφορέω, *karpophoreō*
bear fruit [7], produce [1]

2845 καρποφόρος, *karpophoros*
fruitful [1]

2846 καρτερέω, *kartereō*
persevere [1]

2847 κάρφος, *karphos*
speck [6]

2848 κατά, *kata*
according [91], against [49],
untranslated [41], in [35], by [31], as [19],
accordance [14], after [7], of [7],
every [6], on [6], to [6], about[3] [5], at [5],
for [5], through [5], throughout [5],
along [3], before [3], down [3], each [3],
like[1] [3], off [3], oppose [3], various [3],
with [3], authority [2], belong [2],
case [2], follow [2], from [2], point of
view [2], regard [2], respect[2] [2], sake [2],
toward [2], under [2], way [2], about[1] [1],
according to the likeness [1],
accordingly [1], along the coast [1],
among [1], apparent [1], attack [1],
basis [1], because [1], but [1], come [1],
conform [1], deserve [1], during [1],
example [1], happen [1], how [1], in
way [1], match [1], near [1], one after
another [1], one's own [1], only [1],
opposite [1], origin [1], over[1] [1], relying
on [1], require [1], response [1], rest[1] [1],
simply [1], suit [1], that [1], while [1],
will[1] [1], within [1], *see 1651* [each] [1],
see 4513 [indulge] [1]

2848 + 958 κατά + βάθος, *kata +
bathos*
extreme [1]

2848 + 1651 κατά + εἷς, *kata + heis*
individually [1], one by one [1]

2848 + 2465 κατά + ἡμέρα, *kata +
hēmera*
daily [5], day after day [3], every day [3],
day by day [2]

2848 + 2536 κατά + θεός, *kata + theos*
godly [3]

2848 + 2625 κατά + ἴδιος, *kata + idios*
privately [7], private meeting [1]

2848 + 3364 κατά + λόγος, *kata + logos*
justify [1]

2848 + 3668 κατά + μόνος, *kata +
monos*
alone [2]

2848 + 3836 + 3875 κατά + ὁ + οἶκος,
kata + ho + oikos
house after house [1]

2848 + 3875 κατά + οἶκος, *kata + oikos*
house to house [1]

2848 + 3910 κατά + ὅλος, *kata + holos*
throughout [4]

2848 + 4005 + 5573 κατά + ὅς +
τρόπος, *kata + hos + tropos*
just as [1]

2848 + 4012 κατά + ὅσος, *kata + hosos*
just as [2]

2848 + 4484 κατά + πόλις, *kata + polis*
town after town [1]

2848 + 4725 κατά + πρόσωπον, *kata +
prosōpon*
face to face [2]

2848 + 4922 κατά + σάρξ, *kata + sarx*
earthly [2]

2848 + 5515 κατά + τίς, *kata + tis*
how [1]

2848 + 5651 κατά + ὑπερβολή, *kata +
hyperbolē*
utterly [1]

2848 + 5651 + 1650 + 5651 κατά +
ὑπερβολή + εἰς + ὑπερβολή, *kata +
hyperbolē + eis + hyperbolē*
beyond all measure [1]

2849 καταβαίνω, *katabainō*
come down [37], go down [22],
descend [12], bring down [2], fall [2],
down [1], drop [1], fall down [1], get
out [1], step down [1], sweep down [1]

2850 καταβάλλω, *kataballō*
lay [1], strike down [1]

2851 καταβαρέω, *katabareō*
burden [1]

2852 καταβαρύνω, *katabarynō*
very heavy [1]

2853 κατάβασις, *katabasis*
path down [1]

2856 καταβολή, *katabolē*
foundation [10]

2856 + 5065 καταβολή + σπέρμα,
katabolē + sperma
procreation [1]

2857 καταβραβεύω, *katabrabeuō*
disqualify [1]

2858 καταγγελεύς, *katangeleus*
proclaimer [1]

2859 καταγγέλλω, *katangellō*
proclaim [16], advocate [1], predict [1]

2860 καταγελάω, *katagelaō*
laugh [3]

2861 καταγινώσκω, *kataginōskō*
condemn [2], self-condemned [1]

2862 κατάγνυμι, *katagnymi*
break [4]

2863 καταγράφω, *katagraphō*
write [1]

2864 κατάγω, *katagō*
bring down [5], bring [2], put in [2]

2865 καταγωνίζομαι, *katagōnizomai*
conquer [1]

2866 καταδέω, *katadeō*
bandage [1]

2867 κατάδηλος, *katadēlos*
obvious [1]

2868 καταδικάζω, *katadikazō*
condemn [5]

2869 καταδίκη, *katadikē*
sentence against [1]

2870 καταδιώκω, *katadiōkō*
hunt [1]

2871 καταδουλόω, *katadouloō*
enslave [1], make a slave [1]

2872 καταδυναστεύω, *katadynasteuō*
oppress [2]

2873 κατάθεμα, *katathema*
accursed [1]

2874 καταθεματίζω, *katathematizō*
curse [1]

2875 καταισχύνω, *kataischynō*
put to shame [5], disgrace [3],
humiliate [2], shame [2], disappoint [1]

2876 κατακαίω, *katakaiō*
burn [6], burn up [6]

2877 κατακαλύπτω, *katakalyptō*
veil [2], wear a veil [1]

2878 κατακαυχάομαι, *katakauchaomai*
boast [1], boast over [1], boastful [1],
triumph over [1]

2879 κατάκειμαι, *katakeimai*
lie[1] [3], eat [2], sit at table [2], in bed [1],
lie in bed [1], lie on [1], sit at dinner [1]

2879 + 2093 + 3187 κατάκειμαι + ἐπί
+ κράβαττος, *katakeimai + epi +
krabattos*
bedridden [1]

2880 κατακλάω, *kataklaō*
break [2]

2881 κατακλείω, *katakleiō*
lock up [1], shut up [1]

2883 κατακληρονομέω,
kataklēronomeō
give as an inheritance [1]

2884 κατακλίνω, *kataklinō*
make sit down [2], at table [1], sit
down [1], take one's place at table [1]

2885 κατακλύζω, *kataklyzō*
deluge [1]

2886 κατακλυσμός, *kataklysmos*
flood [4]

2887 κατακολουθέω, *katakoloutheō*
follow [2]

2888 κατακόπτω, *katakoptō*
bruise [1]

2889 κατακρημνίζω, *katakrēmnizō*
hurl off a cliff [1]

2890 κατάκριμα, *katakrima*
condemnation [3]

2891 κατακρίνω, *katakrinō*
condemn [18]

2892 κατάκρισις, *katakrisis*
condemn [1], condemnation [1]

2893 κατακύπτω, *katakyptō*
bend down [1]

2894 κατακυριεύω, *katakyrieuō*
lord it over [3], master [1]

2895 καταλαλέω, *katalaleō*
speak evil [3], malign [2]

2896 καταλαλιά, *katalalia*
slander [2]

2897 κατάλαλος, *katalalos*
slanderer [1]

2898 καταλαμβάνω, *katalambanō*
make one's own [3], catch [2], attain [1],
comprehend [1], find [1], overcome [1],
overtake [1], realize [1], seize [1],
surprise [1], understand [1], win [1]

2899 καταλέγω, *katalegō*
put on a list [1]

2901 καταλείπω, *kataleipō*
leave [20], keep [1], neglect [1], open [1],
see 4024 [childless] [1]

2902 καταλιθάζω, *katalithazō*
stone [1]

2903 καταλλαγή, *katallagē*
reconciliation [4]

2904 καταλλάσσω, *katallassō*
reconcile [6]

2905 κατάλοιπος, *kataloipos*
other [1]

2906 κατάλυμα, *katalyma*
guest room [2], inn [1]

2907 καταλύω, *katalyō*
destroy [7], throw down [3], abolish [2],
fail [1], guest [1], lodge [1], overthrow [1],
tear down [1]

2908 καταμανθάνω, *katamanthanō*
consider [1]

2909 καταμαρτυρέω, *katamartyreō*
testify against [2], make an accusation
against [1]

2910 καταμένω, *katamenō*
stay [1]

2914 καταναλίσκω, *katanaliskō*
consume [1]

2915 καταναρκάω, *katanarkaō*
burden [3]

2916 κατανεύω, *kataneuō*
signal [1]

2917 κατανοέω, *katanoeō*
consider [5], look at [3], notice [3],
look [2], perceive [1]

2918 καταντάω, *katantaō*
come [4], arrive [3], reach [3], attain [2],
go on [1]

2919 κατάνυξις, *katanyxis*
sluggish [1]

2920 κατανύσσομαι, *katanyssomai*
cut [1]

2921 καταξιόω, *kataxioō*
consider worthy [2], make worthy [1]

2922 καταπατέω, *katapateō*
trample on [2], spurn [1], trample [1],
trample under foot [1]

2923 κατάπαυσις, *katapausis*
rest[1] [9]

2924 καταπαύω, *katapauō*
cease [1], give rest [1], rest[1] [1],
restrain [1]

2925 καταπέτασμα, *katapetasma*
curtain [6]

2927 καταπίνω, *katapinō*
swallow [2], swallow up [2], devour [1],
drown [1], overwhelm [1]

2928 καταπίπτω, *katapiptō*
fall [2], drop [1]

2929 καταπλέω, *katapleō*
arrive [1]

2930 καταπονέω, *kataponeō*
distress greatly [1], oppressed man [1]

2931 καταποντίζω, *katapontizō*
drown [1], sink [1]

2932 κατάρα, *katara*
curse [5], accursed [1]

2933 καταράομαι, *kataraomai*
curse [4], accursed [1]

2934 καταργέω, *katargeō*
destroy [5], set aside [4], come to an
end [3], abolish [2], discharge [2],
nullify [2], annihilate [1], cut off [1],
doom to perish [1], overthrow [1], put an
end [1], reduce to nothing [1], remove [1],
void [1], waste [1]

2935 καταριθμέω, *katarithmeō*
number [1]

2936 καταρτίζω, *katartizō*
prepare [3], restore [3], mend [2],
make [1], make complete [1], put in
order [1], qualify fully [1], unite [1]

2937 κατάρτισις, *katartisis*
perfect [1]

2938 καταρτισμός, *katartismos*
equip [1]

2939 κατασείω, *kataseiō*
motion [1]

2939 + 3836 + 5931 κατασείω + ὁ +
χείρ, *kataseiō + ho + cheir*
motion for silence [2], gesture [1]

2940 κατασκάπτω, *kataskaptō*
demolish [1], ruins [1]

2941 κατασκευάζω, *kataskeuazō*
prepare [4], build [3], builder [2],
construct [1], make preparation [1]

2942 κατασκηνόω, *kataskēnoō*
make a nest [3], live [1]

2943 κατασκήνωσις, *kataskēnōsis*
nest [2]

2944 κατασκιάζω, *kataskiazō*
overshadow [1]

2945 κατασκοπέω, *kataskopeō*
spy [1]

2946 κατάσκοπος, *kataskopos*
spy [1]

2947 κατασοφίζομαι, *katasophizomai*
deal craftily [1]

2948 καταστέλλω, *katastellō*
quiet [2]

2949 κατάστημα, *katastēma*
behavior [1]

2950 καταστολή, *katastolē*
clothing [1]

2951 καταστρέφω, *katastrephō*
overturn [2]

2952 καταστρηνιάω, *katastrēniaō*
sensual desires alienate [1]

2953 καταστροφή, *katastrophē*
extinction [1], ruin [1]

2954 καταστρώννυμι, *katastrōnnymi*
strike down [1]

2955 κατασύρω, *katasyrō*
drag [1]

2956 κατασφάζω, *katasphazō*
slaughter [1]

2958 κατασφραγίζω, *katasphragizō*
seal [1]

2959 κατάσχεσις, *kataschesis*
dispossess [1], possession [1]

2960 κατατίθημι, *katatithēmi*
do [1], grant [1]

2961 κατατομή, *katatomē*
mutilate the flesh [1]

2963 κατατρέχω, *katatrechō*
run down [1]

2965 καταφέρω, *katapherō*
bring against [1], cast against [1],
overcome [1], sink off [1]

2966 καταφεύγω, *katapheugō*
flee [1], take refuge [1]

2967 καταφθείρω, *kataphtheirō*
corrupt [1]

2968 καταφιλέω, *kataphileō*
kiss [6]

2969 καταφρονέω, *kataphroneō*
despise [6], disregard [1],
disrespectful [1], show contempt [1]

2970 καταφρονητής, *kataphronētēs*
scoffer [1]

2972 καταχέω, *katacheō*
pour [1], pour on [1]

2973 καταχθόνιος, *katachthonios*
under the earth [1]

2974 καταχράομαι, *katachraomai*
deal [1], make full use [1]

2976 καταψύχω, *katapsychō*
cool [1]

2977 κατείδωλος, *kateidōlos*
full of idols [1]

2978 κατέναντι, *katenanti*
ahead [3], opposite [2], presence [2],
before [1]

2979 κατενώπιον, *katenōpion*
before [2], presence [1]

2980 κατεξουσιάζω, *katexousiazō*
tyrant over [2]

2981 κατεργάζομαι, *katergazomai*
do [7], produce [6], prepare [2],
accomplish [1], action [1], bring [1],
commit [1], perform [1], work [1], work
out [1]

2982 κατέρχομαι, *katerchomai*
come down [6], go down [5], come [2],
land[2] [2], arrive [1]

2983 κατεσθίω, katesthiō
devour [5], consume [3], eat up [3], eat [2], prey upon [1]

2985 κατευθύνω, kateuthynō
direct [2], guide [1]

2986 κατευλογέω, kateulogeō
bless [1]

2987 κατεφίσταμαι, katephistamai
make an attack [1]

2988 κατέχω, katechō
hold fast [3], hold firm [2], restrain [2], hold captive [1], hold firmly [1], keep [1], maintain [1], make for [1], possess [1], possession [1], prevent [1], suppress [1], take [1]

2989 κατηγορέω, katēgoreō
accuse [14], bring a charge against [4], accusation [1], accuser [1], charge against [1], charge3 [1], make an accusation [1]

2990 κατηγορία, katēgoria
accusation [2], see 1877 [accuse] [1]

2991 κατήγορος, katēgoros
accuser [4]

2992 κατήγωρ, katēgōr
accuser [1]

2993 κατήφεια, katēpheia
dejection [1]

2994 κατηχέω, katēcheō
instruct [4], tell [2], teach [1], teacher [1]

2995 κατιόω, katioō
rust [1]

2996 κατισχύω, katischyō
prevail [2], strength [1]

2997 κατοικέω, katoikeō
live [17], inhabitant [10], resident [6], dwell [5], make one's home [2], at home [1], inhabit [1], settle1 [1], they [1]

2998 + 2400 κατοίκησις + ἔχω, katoikēsis + echō
live [1]

2999 κατοικητήριον, katoikētērion
dwelling place [2]

3000 κατοικία, katoikia
place one lives [1]

3001 κατοικίζω, katoikizō
make dwell [1]

3002 κατοπτρίζω, katoptrizō
see reflected in a mirror [1]

3004 κάτω, katō
below [4], down [3], bottom [2]

3005 κατώτερος, katōteros
low [1]

3006 κατωτέρω, katōterō
under [1]

3007 Καῦδα, Kauda
Cauda [1]

3008 καῦμα, kauma
heat [1], scorching heat [1]

3009 καυματίζω, kaumatizō
scorch [4]

3011 καῦσις, kausis
burn over [1]

3012 καυσόω, kausoō
fire [2]

3013 καυστηριάζω, kaustēriazō
sear with a hot iron [1]

3014 καύσων, kausōn
scorching heat [3]

3016 καυχάομαι, kauchaomai
boast [36], boastful [1]

3017 καύχημα, kauchēma
boast [6], ground for boasting [2], pride [2], something to boast about [1]

3018 καύχησις, kauchēsis
boast [7], reason to boast [2], boastful [1], pride [1]

3019 Καφαρναούμ, Kapharnaoum
Capernaum [16]

3020 Κεγχρεαί, Kenchreai
Cenchreae [2]

3022 Κεδρών, Kedrōn
Kidron [1]

3023 κεῖμαι, keimai
lie1 [12], stand1 [3], destine [2], lay [2], build [1], lay down [1], lay up [1], put [1], there [1]

3024 κειρία, keiria
strip of cloth [1]

3025 κείρω, keirō
cut off hair [2], cut [1], shearer [1]

3026 κέλευσμα, keleusma
cry of command [1]

3027 κελεύω, keleuō
order3 [18], command [4], give an order [2], direct [1]

3029 κενοδοξία, kenodoxia
conceit [1]

3030 κενόδοξος, kenodoxos
conceited [1]

3031 κενός, kenos
vain [10], empty [3], empty-handed [3], senseless [1], vain thing [1]

3032 κενοφωνία, kenophōnia
chatter [2]

3033 κενόω, kenoō
deprive [1], empty [1], empty of power [1], null [1], prove empty [1]

3034 κέντρον, kentron
sting [2], goad [1], stinger [1]

3035 κεντυρίων, kentyriōn
centurion [3]

3036 κενῶς, kenōs
nothing [1]

3037 κεραία, keraia
stroke of a letter [2]

3038 κεραμεύς, kerameus
potter [3]

3039 κεραμικός, keramikos
clay [1]

3040 κεράμιον, keramion
jar [2]

3041 κέραμος, keramos
tile [1]

3042 κεράννυμι, kerannymi
mix [2], pour [1]

3043 κέρας, keras
horn [10], mighty [1]

3044 κεράτιον, keration
pod [1]

3045 κερδαίνω, kerdainō
win [5], gain [4], make [4], avoid [1], make money [1], regain [1], win over [1]

3046 κέρδος, kerdos
gain [3]

3047 κέρμα, kerma
coin [1]

3048 κερματιστής, kermatistēs
money changer [1]

3049 κεφάλαιον, kephalaion
main point [1], sum of money [1]

3051 κεφαλή, kephalē
head [69], hair [1], untranslated [1]

3051 + 1224 κεφαλή + γωνία, kephalē + gōnia
cornerstone [4]

3052 κεφαλιόω, kephalioō
beat over the head [1]

3053 κεφαλίς, kephalis
scroll [1]

3055 κημόω, kēmoō
muzzle [1]

3056 κῆνσος, kēnsos
tax [3], tribute [1]

3057 κῆπος, kēpos
garden [5]

3058 κηπουρός, kēpouros
gardener [1]

3060 κήρυγμα, kērygma
proclamation [8], message [1]

3061 κῆρυξ, kēryx
herald [3]

3062 κηρύσσω, kēryssō
proclaim [49], proclaim the message [5], preach [3], proclaim the good news [2], announce [1], make a proclamation [1]

3063 κῆτος, kētos
sea monster [1]

3064 Κηφᾶς, Kēphas
Cephas [9]

3066 κιβωτός, kibōtos
ark [6]

3067 κιθάρα, kithara
harp [4]

3068 κιθαρίζω, kitharizō
play [1], see 884 [play] [1]

3069 κιθαρῳδός, kitharōdos
harpist [2]

3070 Κιλικία, Kilikia
Cilicia [8]

3073 κινδυνεύω, kindyneuō
danger [4]

3074 κίνδυνος, kindynos
danger [8], peril [1]

3075 κινέω, kineō
move [2], remove [2], shake [2], arouse [1]

3075 + 5087 κινέω + στάσις, kineō + stasis
agitator [1]

3077 κιννάμωμον, kinnamōmon
cinnamon [1]

3078 Κίς, Kis
Kish [1]

3079 κίχρημι, kichrēmi
lend [1]

3080 κλάδος, klados
branch [11]

3081 κλαίω, *klaiō*
weep [37], mourn [2], tear² [1]

3082 κλάσις, *klasis*
break [2]

3083 κλάσμα, *klasma*
broken piece [6], fragment [2], basket [1]

3086 Κλαυδία, *Klaudia*
Claudia [1]

3087 Κλαύδιος, *Klaudios*
Claudius [3]

3088 κλαυθμός, *klauthmos*
weep [8], wail [1]

3089 κλάω, *klaō*
break [14]

3090 κλείς, *kleis*
key [6]

3091 κλείω, *kleiō*
shut [9], lock [5], shut up [1]

3091 + 3836 + 5073 κλείω + ὁ +
σπλάγχνον, *kleiō + ho + splanchnon*
refuse help [1]

3092 κλέμμα, *klemma*
theft [1]

3093 Κλεοπᾶς, *Kleopas*
Cleopas [1]

3094 κλέος, *kleos*
credit [1]

3095 κλέπτης, *kleptēs*
thief [16]

3096 κλέπτω, *kleptō*
steal [10], steal away [2], thief [1]

3097 κλῆμα, *klēma*
branch [4]

3098 Κλήμης, *Klēmēs*
Clement [1]

3099 κληρονομέω, *klēronomeō*
inherit [17], share inheritance [1]

3100 κληρονομία, *klēronomia*
inheritance [12], family inheritance [1],
heritage [1]

3101 κληρονόμος, *klēronomos*
heir [14], inherit [1]

3102 κλῆρος, *klēros*
lot [6], share [2], charge¹ [1],
inheritance [1], place [1]

3103 κληρόω, *klēroō*
obtain an inheritance [1]

3104 κλῆσις, *klēsis*
call [10], condition [1]

3105 κλητός, *klētos*
call [10]

3106 κλίβανος, *klibanos*
oven [2]

3107 κλίμα, *klima*
region [3]

3108 κλινάριον, *klinarion*
cot [1]

3109 κλίνη, *klinē*
bed [8], *untranslated* [1]

3110 κλινίδιον, *klinidion*
bed [2]

3111 κλίνω, *klinō*
bow¹ [2], lay [2], draw to a close [1],
nearly over [1], put to flight [1]

3112 κλισία, *klisia*
group [1]

3113 κλοπή, *klopē*
theft [2]

3114 κλύδων, *klydōn*
rage [1], wave [1]

3115 κλυδωνίζομαι, *klydōnizomai*
toss to and fro [1]

3116 Κλωπᾶς, *Klōpas*
Clopas [1]

3117 κνήθω, *knēthō*
itch [1]

3118 Κνίδος, *Knidos*
Cnidus [1]

3119 κοδράντης, *kodrantēs*
penny [2]

3120 κοιλία, *koilia*
womb [7], stomach [6], belly [2],
appetite [1], heart [1], *see 1666* [birth] [1]

3120 + 3613 κοιλία + μήτηρ, *koilia +
mētēr*
birth [2], bear¹ [1]

3120 + 3613 + 1164 κοιλία + μήτηρ +
γεννάω, *koilia + mētēr + gennaō*
birth [1]

3121 κοιμάω, *koimaō*
die [12], fall asleep [3], sleep [2],
asleep [1]

3122 + 5678 κοίμησις + ὕπνος,
koimēsis + hypnos
mere sleep [1]

3123 κοινός, *koinos*
unclean [4], profane [3], common [2],
defile [2], share [2]

3123 + 2451 κοινός + ἡγέομαι, *koinos
+ hēgeomai*
profane [1]

3124 κοινόω, *koinoō*
defile [12], call profane [2]

3125 κοινωνέω, *koinōneō*
share [5], participate [2], contribute [1]

3126 κοινωνία, *koinōnia*
share [9], fellowship [8], communion [1],
resource [1]

3127 κοινωνικός, *koinōnikos*
ready to share [1]

3128 κοινωνός, *koinōnos*
partner [6], share [2], participant [1], take
part [1]

3130 κοίτη, *koitē*
bed [1], debauchery [1], marriage bed [1]

3130 + 2400 κοίτη + ἔχω, *koitē + echō*
conceive children [1]

3131 κοιτών, *koitōn*
see 2093 [chamberlain] [1]

3132 κόκκινος, *kokkinos*
scarlet [6]

3133 κόκκος, *kokkos*
seed [6], grain [1]

3134 κολάζω, *kolazō*
punish [1], under punishment [1]

3135 κολακεία, *kolakeia*
flattery [1]

3136 κόλασις, *kolasis*
punishment [2]

3139 κολαφίζω, *kolaphizō*
beat [2], strike [2], torment [1]

3140 κολλάω, *kollaō*
join [5], unite [2], associate [1], cling [1],
heap [1], hire out [1], hold fast [1]

3141 κολλούριον, *kollourion*
salve [1]

3142 κολλυβιστής, *kollybistēs*
money changer [3]

3143 κολοβόω, *koloboō*
cut short [4]

3145 Κολοσσαί, *Kolossai*
Colossae [1]

3146 κόλπος, *kolpos*
bay [1], heart [1], lap [1], side [1], *see
1650* [with] [1], *see 1877* [next] [1]

3147 κολυμβάω, *kolymbaō*
swim [1]

3148 κολυμβήθρα, *kolymbēthra*
pool [3]

3149 κολωνία, *kolōnia*
Roman colony [1]

3150 κομάω, *komaō*
long hair [1], wear long hair [1]

3151 κόμη, *komē*
hair [1]

3152 κομίζω, *komizō*
receive [4], bring [1], pay back [1], receive
again [1], receive back [1], receive
recompense [1], win [1]

3153 κομψότερον, *kompsoteron*
recover [1]

3154 κονιάω, *koniaō*
whitewash [2]

3155 κονιορτός, *koniortos*
dust [5]

3156 κοπάζω, *kopazō*
cease [3]

3157 κοπετός, *kopetos*
lamentation [1]

3158 κοπή, *kopē*
defeat [1]

3159 κοπιάω, *kopiaō*
work [7], labor [6], toil [5], grow
weary [2], tire out [1], weary [1],
worker [1]

3160 κόπος, *kopos*
labor [10], toil [3], trouble [1]

3160 + 4218 κόπος + παρέχω, *kopos +
parechō*
bother [2], trouble [2]

3161 κοπρία, *kopria*
manure pile [1]

3162 κόπριον, *koprion*
manure [1]

3164 κόπτω, *koptō*
wail [3], cut [2], mourn [2], beat [1]

3165 κόραξ, *korax*
raven [1]

3166 κοράσιον, *korasion*
girl [7], little girl [1]

3167 κορβᾶν, *korban*
corban [1]

3168 κορβανᾶς, *korbanas*
treasury [1]

3169 Κόρε, *Kore*
Korah [1]

3170 κορέννυμι, korennymi
have all one wants [1]

3170 + 5575 κορέννυμι + τροφή, korennymi + trophē
satisfy hunger [1]

3171 Κορίνθιος, Korinthios
Corinthian [2]

3172 Κόρινθος, Korinthos
Corinth [6]

3173 Κορνήλιος, Kornēlios
Cornelius [8]

3174 κόρος, koros
container [1]

3175 κοσμέω, kosmeō
adorn [4], put in order [2], decorate [1], dress [1], ornament [1], trim [1]

3176 κοσμικός, kosmikos
earthly [1], worldly [1]

3177 κόσμιος, kosmios
respectable [1], suitable [1]

3179 κοσμοκράτωρ, kosmokratōr
cosmic power [1]

3180 κόσμος, kosmos
world [182], universe [2], adorn [1], worldly [1]

3181 Κούαρτος, Kouartos
Quartus [1]

3182 κούμ, koum
cum [1]

3184 κουστωδία, koustōdia
guard [2], guard of soldiers [1]

3185 κουφίζω, kouphizō
lighten [1]

3186 κόφινος, kophinos
basket [5], broken piece [1]

3187 κράβαττος, krabattos
mat [10], see 2879 [bedridden] [1]

3189 κράζω, krazō
shout [19], cry out [18], cry [4], call [3], call out [3], shout out [2], cry aloud [1], give a shout [1], howl [1], shout loudly [1], shriek [1], untranslated [1]

3190 κραιπάλη, kraipalē
dissipation [1]

3191 κρανίον, kranion
skull [4]

3192 κράσπεδον, kraspedon
fringe [5]

3193 κραταιός, krataios
mighty [1]

3194 κραταιόω, krataioō
strong [3], strengthen [1]

3195 κρατέω, krateō
arrest [13], hold fast [6], hold [5], seize [5], take [5], keep [2], observe² [2], retain [2], achieve [1], catch hold [1], cling [1], hold back [1], lay hold [1], restrain [1], take hold [1]

3196 κράτιστος, kratistos
Excellency [2], most excellent [2]

3197 κράτος, kratos
power [5], dominion [2], strength [2], great [1], might [1], mightily [1]

3198 κραυγάζω, kraugazō
shout [5], cry out [2], cry [1], cry aloud [1]

3199 κραυγή, kraugē
cry [3], clamor [1], shout [1], wrangle [1]

3200 κρέας, kreas
meat [2]

3202 κρείττων, kreittōn
good [15], superior [2], good thing [1], well¹ [1]

3203 κρεμάννυμι, kremannymi
hang [6], fasten [1]

3204 κρημνός, krēmnos
steep bank [3]

3205 Κρής, Krēs
Cretan [2]

3206 Κρήσκης, Krēskēs
Crescens [1]

3207 Κρήτη, Krētē
Crete [5]

3208 κριθή, krithē
barley [1]

3209 κρίθινος, krithinos
barley [2]

3210 κρίμα, krima
judgment [13], condemnation [8], authority to judge [1], condemn [1], lawsuit [1], penalty [1], sentence of condemnation [1]

3210 + 3284 κρίμα + λαμβάνω, krima + lambanō
judge [1]

3211 κρίνον, krinon
lily [2]

3212 κρίνω, krinō
judge [69], condemn [11], decide [6], pass judgment [5], try² [3], on trial [2], pronounce judgment [2], reach a decision [2], convince [1], determine [1], give judgment [1], go to court [1], judgment [1], make judgment [1], make up one's mind [1], resolve [1], serve as judge [1], subject to judgment [1], sue [1], take to court [1], think [1], trial [1]

3213 κρίσις, krisis
judgment [38], justice [5], condemnation [3], sentence¹ [1]

3214 Κρίσπος, Krispos
Crispus [2]

3215 κριτήριον, kritērion
case [2], court² [1]

3216 κριτής, kritēs
judge [19]

3217 κριτικός, kritikos
judge [1]

3218 κρούω, krouō
knock [9]

3219 κρύπτη, kryptē
cellar [1]

3220 κρυπτός, kryptos
secret [11], hide [3], hidden thing [1], inner [1], see 1877 [inwardly] [1]

3221 κρύπτω, kryptō
hide [16], remain hidden [1], secret [1]

3222 κρυσταλλίζω, krystallizō
clear as crystal [1]

3223 κρύσταλλος, krystallos
crystal [2]

3224 κρυφαῖος, kryphaios
secret [2]

3225 κρυφῆ, kryphē
secretly [1]

3227 κτάομαι, ktaomai
acquire [1], control [1], cost [1], gain [1], income [1], obtain [1], take [1]

3228 κτῆμα, ktēma
possession [3], piece of property [1]

3229 κτῆνος, ktēnos
animal [2], cattle [1], mount² [1]

3230 κτήτωρ, ktētōr
own¹ [1]

3231 κτίζω, ktizō
create [12], creator [2], make [1]

3232 κτίσις, ktisis
creation [15], creature [3], institution [1]

3233 κτίσμα, ktisma
creature [3], create [1]

3234 κτίστης, ktistēs
creator [1]

3235 κυβεία, kybeia
trickery [1]

3236 κυβέρνησις, kybernēsis
leadership [1]

3237 κυβερνήτης, kybernētēs
pilot [1], shipmaster [1]

3238 κυκλεύω, kykleuō
surround [1]

3239 κυκλόθεν, kyklothen
around [2], all around [1]

3240 κυκλόω, kykloō
surround [2], encircle [1], gather around [1]

3241 κύκλω, kyklō
surround [3], around [2], among [1], on each side [1], untranslated [1]

3243 κυλισμός, kylismos
wallow [1]

3244 κυλίω, kyliō
roll about [1]

3245 κυλλός, kyllos
maim [4]

3246 κῦμα, kyma
wave [5]

3247 κύμβαλον, kymbalon
cymbal [1]

3248 κύμινον, kyminon
cummin [1]

3249 κυνάριον, kynarion
dog [4]

3250 Κύπριος, Kyprios
Cyprus [3]

3251 Κύπρος, Kypros
Cyprus [5]

3252 κύπτω, kyptō
bend [1], stoop down [1]

3254 Κυρηναῖος, Kyrēnaios
Cyrene [5], Cyrenian [1]

3255 Κυρήνη, Kyrēnē
Cyrene [1]

3256 Κυρήνιος, Kyrēnios
Quirinius [1]

3257 κυρία, kyria
dear lady [1], lady [1]

3258 κυριακός, kyriakos
Lord [2]

3259 κυριεύω, kyrieuō
dominion over [2], lord it over [2], Lord [1], bind [1], lord [1]

3261 κύριος, *kyrios*
Lord [631], master [43], sir [17], lord [14], owner [9], sovereign [1], *untranslated* [1]

3262 κυριότης, *kyriotēs*
authority [2], dominion [2]

3263 κυρόω, *kyroō*
ratify [1], reaffirm [1]

3264 κύων, *kyōn*
dog [5]

3265 κῶλον, *kōlon*
body [1]

3266 κωλύω, *kōlyō*
stop [7], prevent [5], forbid [4], hinder [3], withhold [2], keep from [1], restrain [1]

3267 κώμη, *kōmē*
village [27]

3268 κωμόπολις, *kōmopolis*
town [1]

3269 κῶμος, *kōmos*
revel [2], carouse [1]

3270 κώνωψ, *kōnōps*
gnat [1]

3271 Κῶς, *Kōs*
Cos [1]

3272 Κωσάμ, *Kōsam*
Cosam [1]

3273 κωφός, *kōphos*
mute [8], deaf [3], deaf man [1], keep from hearing [1], unable to speak [1]

3275 λαγχάνω, *lanchanō*
allot [1], cast lots [1], choose by lot [1], receive [1]

3276 Λάζαρος, *Lazaros*
Lazarus [15]

3277 λάθρα, *lathra*
privately [1], quietly [1], secret [1], secretly [1]

3278 λαῖλαψ, *lailaps*
storm [1]

3278 + 449 λαῖλαψ + ἄνεμος, *lailaps + anemos*
windstorm [2]

3279 λακάω, *lakaō*
burst open [1]

3280 λακτίζω, *laktizō*
kick [1]

3281 λαλέω, *laleō*
speak [196], say [46], tell [19], declare [8], talk [8], sound[1] [2], speaker [2], utter [2], *untranslated* [1], announce [1], give a message [1], make a promise [1], present[2] [1], repeat [1], sing [1], speech [1], teach [1], *see 6022* [lie[2]] [1]

3281 + 4639 + 3836 + 4044 λαλέω + πρός + ὁ + οὖς, *laleō + pros + ho + ous*
whisper [1]

3282 λαλιά, *lalia*
say [2], accent [1]

3284 λαμβάνω, *lambanō*
receive [110], take [78], seize [10], accept [9], *untranslated* [5], bring [4], marry [4], get [3], take up [3], collect [2], gather [2], *see 5206* [confer together] [2], be [1], catch [1], choose [1], collector [1], devise [1], do [1], follow [1], gift [1], give [1], incur [1], obtain [1], overtake [1], put on [1], share [1], show [1], take advantage [1], *see 1953* [command] [1], *see 3210* [judge] [1], *see 3330*

[forgetful] [1], *see 4278* [suffer[2]] [1], *see 5206* [conspire] [1], *see 5206* [plot] [1], *see 5704* [remind] [1]

3284 + 1222 λαμβάνω + γυνή, *lambanō + gynē*
marry [2]

3284 + 4725 + 476 λαμβάνω + πρόσωπον + ἄνθρωπος, *lambanō + prosōpon + anthrōpos*
show partiality [1]

3285 Λάμεχ, *Lamech*
Lamech [1]

3286 λαμπάς, *lampas*
lamp [6], torch [3]

3287 λαμπρός, *lampros*
bright [4], fine [2], dazzle [1], elegant [1], splendor [1]

3288 λαμπρότης, *lamprotēs*
bright [1]

3289 λαμπρῶς, *lamprōs*
sumptuously [1]

3290 λάμπω, *lampō*
shine [5], give light [1], light up [1]

3291 λανθάνω, *lanthanō*
escape notice [2], ignore [2], hide [1], without knowing [1]

3292 λαξευτός, *laxeutos*
rock-hewn [1]

3293 Λαοδίκεια, *Laodikeia*
Laodicea [6]

3294 Λαοδικεύς, *Laodikeus*
Laodicean [1]

3295 λαός, *laos*
people [141], *untranslated* [1]

3296 λάρυγξ, *larynx*
throat [1]

3297 Λασαία, *Lasaia*
Lasea [1]

3300 λατομέω, *latomeō*
hew [2]

3301 λατρεία, *latreia*
worship [4], ritual duty [1]

3302 λατρεύω, *latreuō*
worship [11], serve [5], offer worship [2], worshiper [2], officiate [1]

3303 λάχανον, *lachanon*
shrub [2], herb [1], vegetable [1]

3305 λεγιών, *legiōn*
legion [4]

3306 λέγω, *legō*
say [1511], *untranslated* [279], tell [265], speak [69], ask [59], call [46], reply [23], answer [13], word [9], sing [6], declare [5], call out [4], claim [4], mean[1] [4], talk [4], be [3], command [3], order[3] [3], add [2], cry [2], give [2], message [2], point[3] [2], refer [2], so-called [2], state [2], teach [2], affirm [1], apply [1], comment [1], cry out [1], exclaim [1], explain [1], heap [1], know [1], loudly [1], make [1], make a statement [1], mention [1], proclaim [1], quote [1], respond [1], shout [1], use [1], utter [1], *see 3836* [agreement] [1]

3306 + 3590 λέγω + μή, *legō + mē*
forbid [1]

3306 + 4099 λέγω + πάλιν, *legō + palin*
repeat [2]

3306 + 4819 λέγω + ῥακά, *legō + rhaka*
insult [1]

3307 λεῖμμα, *leimma*
remnant [1]

3308 λεῖος, *leios*
smooth [1]

3309 λείπω, *leipō*
lack [5], remain [1]

3310 λειτουργέω, *leitourgeō*
service [2], worship [1]

3311 λειτουργία, *leitourgia*
ministry [2], service [2], offering [1], worship [1]

3312 λειτουργικός, *leitourgikos*
divine service [1]

3313 λειτουργός, *leitourgos*
minister [3], servant [2]

3316 λεμά, *lema*
lema [2]

3317 λέντιον, *lention*
towel [2]

3318 λεπίς, *lepis*
scale [1]

3319 λέπρα, *lepra*
leprosy [4]

3320 λεπρός, *lepros*
leper [9]

3321 λεπτός, *leptos*
small copper coin [2], penny [1]

3322 Λευί, *Leui*
Levi [8]

3324 Λευίτης, *Leuitēs*
Levite [3]

3325 Λευιτικός, *Leuitikos*
Levitical [1]

3326 λευκαίνω, *leukainō*
bleach [1], make white [1]

3328 λευκός, *leukos*
white [24], ripe [1]

3329 λέων, *leōn*
lion [9]

3330 + 3284 λήθη + λαμβάνω, *lēthē + lambanō*
forgetful [1]

3331 λῆμψις, *lēmpsis*
receive [1]

3332 ληνός, *lēnos*
wine press [4], press [1]

3333 λῆρος, *lēros*
idle tale [1]

3334 ληστής, *lēstēs*
bandit [10], robber [5]

3336 λίαν, *lian*
very[1] [4], *see 5897* [overjoyed] [2], greatly [1], so [1], strongly [1], *see 2597* [infuriate] [1], *see 5118* [dazzle] [1]

3336 + 1666 + 4356 λίαν + ἐκ + περισσός, *lian + ek + perissos*
utterly [1]

3337 λίβανος, *libanos*
frankincense [2]

3338 λιβανωτός, *libanōtos*
censer [2]

3339 Λιβερτῖνος, *Libertinos*
freedman [1]

3340 Λιβύη, Libyē
Libya [1]

3342 λιθάζω, lithazō
stone [7], receive a stoning [1], stone to death [1]

3343 λίθινος, lithinos
stone [3]

3344 λιθοβολέω, lithoboleō
stone [6], stone to death [1]

3345 λίθος, lithos
stone [46], another [4], untranslated [2], jewel [1]

3345 + 3683 λίθος + μυλικός, lithos + mylikos
millstone [1]

3345 + 5508 λίθος + τίμιος, lithos + timios
jewel [4]

3346 λιθόστρωτος, lithostrōtos
stone pavement [1]

3347 λικμάω, likmaō
crush [1]

3348 λιμήν, limēn
harbor [2]

3349 λίμνη, limnē
lake [11]

3350 λιμός, limos
famine [10], hunger [1], hungry [1]

3351 λίνον, linon
linen [1], wick [1]

3352 Λίνος, Linos
Linus [1]

3353 λιπαρός, liparos
dainty [1]

3354 λίτρα, litra
pound [2]

3355 λίψ, lips
southwest [1]

3356 λογεία, logeia
collection [2]

3357 λογίζομαι, logizomai
reckon [13], think [6], consider [5], count [3], understand [2], account² [1], claim [1], count against [1], hold [1], imagine [1], reason² [1], regard [1], untranslated [1]

3357 + 1650 + 4029 λογίζομαι + εἰς + οὐδείς, logizomai + eis + oudeis
scorn [1]

3357 + 3836 + 2805 λογίζομαι + ὁ + κακός, logizomai + ho + kakos
resentful [1]

3357 + 4099 λογίζομαι + πάλιν, logizomai + palin
remind [1]

3358 λογικός, logikos
spiritual [2]

3359 λόγιον, logion
oracle [3], word [1]

3360 λόγιος, logios
eloquent [1]

3361 λογισμός, logismos
argument [1], thought [1]

3362 λογομαχέω, logomacheō
wrangle over words [1]

3363 λογομαχία, logomachia
dispute about words [1]

3364 λόγος, logos
word [211], message [17], say [16], speech [10], saying [9], account² [8], talk [4], teaching [4], what [4], untranslated [4], matter [3], question [3], speak [3], utterance [3], hear [2], word of mouth [2], accountable [1], all [1], answer [1], appearance [1], argument [1], at all [1], book [1], charge³ [1], commandment [1], complaint [1], eloquent [1], encouragement [1], ground² [1], justify [1], mean¹ [1], news [1], point¹ [1], preach [1], rumor [1], sentence¹ [1], speaker [1], story [1], thing [1], see 1877 [at length] [1], see 2848 [justify] [1], see 4472 [count] [1], see 5515 [why] [1]

3365 λόγχη, lonchē
spear [1]

3366 λοιδορέω, loidoreō
revile [2], abuse [1], insult [1]

3367 λοιδορία, loidoria
abuse [2], revile [1]

3368 λοίδορος, loidoros
reviler [2]

3369 λοιμός, loimos
pestilent fellow [1], plague [1]

3370 λοιπός, loipos
rest² [18], other [16], finally [6], from now on [3], other thing [2], still¹ [2], beyond [1], else [1], everyone else [1], last¹ [1], other woman [1], remain [1], since then [1], see 6045 [moreover] [1]

3371 Λουκᾶς, Loukas
Luke [3]

3372 Λούκιος, Loukios
Lucius [2]

3373 λουτρόν, loutron
wash [1], water [1]

3374 λούω, louō
wash [4], bathe [1]

3375 Λύδδα, Lydda
Lydda [3]

3376 Λυδία, Lydia
Lydia [2]

3377 Λυκαονία, Lykaonia
Lycaonia [1]

3378 Λυκαονιστί, Lykaonisti
Lycaonian language [1]

3379 Λυκία, Lykia
Lycia [1]

3380 λύκος, lykos
wolf [6]

3381 λυμαίνω, lymainō
ravage [1]

3382 λυπέω, lypeō
grieve [8], cause pain [4], distress [4], grief [3], feel hurt [1], have pain [1], injure [1], make sorry [1], pain [1], sorrowful [1], suffer² [1]

3383 λύπη, lypē
pain [5], sorrow [4], grief [3], painful [2], another [1], see 1666 [reluctantly] [1]

3384 Λυσανίας, Lysanias
Lysanias [1]

3385 Λυσίας, Lysias
Lysias [2]

3386 λύσις, lysis
free [1]

3387 λυσιτελέω, lysiteleō
good [1]

3388 Λύστρα, Lystra
Lystra [6]

3389 λύτρον, lytron
ransom [2]

3390 λυτρόω, lytroō
redeem [2], ransom [1]

3391 λύτρωσις, lytrōsis
redemption [2]

3391 + 4472 λύτρωσις + ποιέω, lytrōsis + poieō
redeem [1]

3392 λυτρωτής, lytrōtēs
liberator [1]

3393 λυχνία, lychnia
lampstand [12]

3394 λύχνος, lychnos
lamp [14]

3395 λύω, lyō
untie [13], release [5], break [4], loose [4], dissolve [3], free [3], break up [2], destroy [2], annul [1], break down [1], let out [1], set free [1], take off [1], unbind [1]

3396 Λωΐς, Lōis
Lois [1]

3397 Λώτ, Lōt
Lot [4]

3399 Μάαθ, Maath
Maath [1]

3400 Μαγαδάν, Magadan
Magadan [1]

3402 Μαγδαληνή, Magdalēnē
Magdalene [12]

3404 μαγεία, mageia
magic [1]

3405 μαγεύω, mageuō
practice magic [1]

3407 μάγος, magos
wise man [4], magician [2]

3408 Μαγώγ, Magōg
Magog [1]

3409 Μαδιάμ, Madiam
Midian [1]

3411 μαθητεύω, mathēteuō
make disciples [2], disciple [1], train [1]

3412 μαθητής, mathētēs
disciple [261]

3413 μαθήτρια, mathētria
disciple [1]

3414 Μαθθαῖος, Maththaios
Matthew [5]

3415 Μαθθάτ, Maththat
Matthat [2]

3416 Μαθθίας, Maththias
Matthias [2]

3417 Μαθουσαλά, Mathousala
Methuselah [1]

3419 μαίνομαι, mainomai
out of one's mind [5]

3420 μακαρίζω, makarizō
call blessed [2]

3421 μακάριος, makarios
bless [49], fortunate [1]

3422 μακαρισμός, makarismos
blessedness [2], goodwill [1]

3423 Μακεδονία, *Makedonia*
Macedonia [22]

3424 Μακεδών, *Makedōn*
Macedonian [3], Macedonia [1], person of Macedonia [1]

3425 μάκελλον, *makellon*
meat market [1]

3426 μακράν, *makran*
far [5], far off [4], distance [1]

3427 μακρόθεν, *makrothen*
distance [8], *see 608* [far off] [3], far off [1], great distance [1], *see 608* [far away] [1]

3428 μακροθυμέω, *makrothymeō*
patient [6], have patience [2], delay long [1], endure patiently [1]

3429 μακροθυμία, *makrothymia*
patience [13], patiently [1]

3430 μακροθύμως, *makrothymōs*
patiently [1]

3431 μακρός, *makros*
distant [2], long[1] [2]

3432 μακροχρόνιος, *makrochronios*
live long [1]

3433 μαλακία, *malakia*
sickness [3]

3434 μαλακός, *malakos*
soft robe [2], male prostitute [1], soft [1]

3435 Μαλελεήλ, *Maleleēl*
Mahaleleel [1]

3436 μάλιστα, *malista*
especially [11], above all [1]

3437 μᾶλλον, *mallon*
more [33], rather [19], all the more [4], instead [4], more surely [4], more than ever [4], even more [2], actually [1], especially [1], good [1], less [1], more increasingly [1], still[1] [1], yes [1], *see 247* [contrary] [1], *see 2819* [good] [1], *see 4498* [far] [1], *see 5539* [instead] [1]

3438 Μάλχος, *Malchos*
Malchus [1]

3439 μάμμη, *mammē*
grandmother [1]

3440 μαμωνᾶς, *mamōnas*
wealth [4]

3441 Μαναήν, *Manaēn*
Manaen [1]

3442 Μανασσῆς, *Manassēs*
Manasseh [3]

3443 μανθάνω, *manthanō*
learn [22], instruct [1], know [1], teach [1]

3444 μανία, *mania*
insane [1]

3445 μάννα, *manna*
manna [4]

3446 μαντεύομαι, *manteuomai*
fortune-telling [1]

3447 μαραίνω, *marainō*
wither away [1]

3448 μαράνα θά, *marana tha*
our Lord come [1]

3449 μαργαρίτης, *margaritēs*
pearl [9]

3450 Μάρθα, *Martha*
Martha [13]

3451 Μαρία, *Maria*
Mary [54]

3453 Μᾶρκος, *Markos*
Mark [8]

3454 μάρμαρος, *marmaros*
marble [1]

3455 μαρτυρέω, *martyreō*
testify [52], speak well [4], testimony [4], attest [3], receive approval [2], attest well [1], bear witness [1], commend [1], declare [1], give [1], give approval [1], good standing [1], testify favorably [1], warn [1], witness [1], *untranslated* [1]

3456 μαρτυρία, *martyria*
testimony [35], thought [1], witness [1]

3457 μαρτύριον, *martyrion*
testimony [14], testify [2], attest [1], evidence [1], witness [1]

3458 μαρτύρομαι, *martyromai*
testify [2], declare [1], insist [1], plead [1]

3459 μάρτυς, *martys*
witness [34], testify [1]

3460 μασάομαι, *masaomai*
gnaw [1]

3463 μαστιγόω, *mastigoō*
flog [6], chastise [1]

3464 μαστίζω, *mastizō*
flog [1]

3465 μάστιξ, *mastix*
disease [3], flog [2], plague [1]

3466 μαστός, *mastos*
breast [2], chest [1]

3467 ματαιολογία, *mataiologia*
meaningless talk [1]

3468 ματαιολόγος, *mataiologos*
idle talker [1]

3469 μάταιος, *mataios*
futile [3], worthless [2], worthless thing [1]

3470 ματαιότης, *mataiotēs*
futility [2], nonsense [1]

3471 ματαιόω, *mataioō*
futile [1]

3472 μάτην, *matēn*
vain [2]

3474 Ματθάν, *Matthan*
Matthan [2]

3477 Ματταθά, *Mattatha*
Mattatha [1]

3478 Ματταθίας, *Mattathias*
Mattathias [2]

3479 μάχαιρα, *machaira*
sword [29]

3480 μάχη, *machē*
dispute [2], quarrel [2]

3481 μάχομαι, *machomai*
dispute [1], engage in dispute [1], quarrel [1], quarrelsome [1]

3483 μεγαλεῖος, *megaleios*
deed of power [1]

3484 μεγαλειότης, *megaleiotēs*
majesty [2], greatness [1]

3485 μεγαλοπρεπής, *megaloprepēs*
majestic [1]

3486 μεγαλύνω, *megalynō*
enlarge [1], exalt [1], extol [1], great [1], hold in high esteem [1], long[1] [1], magnify [1], praise [1]

3487 μεγάλως, *megalōs*
greatly [1]

3488 μεγαλωσύνη, *megalōsynē*
majesty [3]

3489 μέγας, *megas*
great [114], loud [38], large [8], severe [3], dead [2], great one [2], top [2], violent [2], fearful [1], fierce [1], full [1], great solemnity [1], great thing [1], greatly [1], haughty [1], heavy [1], high [1], huge [1], not [quickly] [1], overcome [1], strange [1], strong [1], too much [1], up [1], wide [1], *see 449* [gale] [1], *see 5774* [exclaim] [1], *see 5828* [terrify] [1], *see 5832* [terrify] [1], *see 5897* [overwhelm] [1], *untranslated* [1]

3490 μέγεθος, *megethos*
greatness [1]

3491 μεγιστάν, *megistan*
magnate [2], courtier [1]

3492 μέγιστος, *megistos*
very great [1]

3493 μεθερμηνεύω, *methermēneuō*
mean[1] [5], translate [2], translation [1]

3494 μέθη, *methē*
drunkenness [3]

3496 μεθίστημι, *methistēmi*
remove [2], dismiss [1], draw away [1], transfer [1]

3497 μεθοδεία, *methodeia*
scheme [1], wile [1]

3499 μεθύσκω, *methyskō*
get drunk [3], drunk [2]

3500 μέθυσος, *methysos*
drunkard [2]

3501 μεθύω, *methyō*
drunk [4], drunkard [1]

3502 μείγνυμι, *meignymi*
mix [3], mingle [1]

3505 μείζων, *meizōn*
great [43], all the more [1], elder [1], great thing [1], large [1], more [1]

3506 μέλας, *melas*
black [3], ink [3]

3507 Μελεά, *Melea*
Melea [1]

3508 μέλει, *melei*
care[1] [5], concern [2], show deference [2], pay attention [1]

3509 μελετάω, *meletaō*
imagine [1], put into practice [1]

3510 μέλι, *meli*
honey [4]

3514 Μελίτη, *Melitē*
Malta [1]

3516 μέλλω, *mellō*
about[2] [27], to [be] [17], will[3] [17], come [14], intend [8], go [7], *untranslated* [5], future [3], point[1] [2], almost [1], before [1], close [1], delay [1], next year [1], propose [1], soon [1], thing to come [1], want [1]

3517 μέλος, *melos*
member [30], *untranslated* [3], whatever [1]

3518 Μελχί, Melchi
Melchi [2]

3519 Μελχισέδεκ, Melchisedek
Melchizedek [8]

3521 μεμβράνα, membrana
parchment [1]

3522 μέμφομαι, memphomai
find fault [2]

3523 μεμψίμοιρος, mempsimoiros
malcontent [1]

3525 μέν, men
untranslated [157], indeed [9], though [4], one [2], certainly [1], in fact [1], not only [1], on the one hand [1], one case [1], some [1], while [1]

3527 Μεννά, Menna
Menna [1]

3528 μενοῦν, menoun
rather [1]

3529 μενοῦνγε, menounge
indeed [2], more than that [1]

3530 μέντοι, mentoi
untranslated [3], but [2], yet [2], really [1]

3531 μένω, menō
abide [37], remain [33], stay [18], continue [6], endure [5], live [5], last[2] [3], have a place [2], still[1] [2], wait[1] [2], alive [1], dwell [1], leave [1], permanent [1], survive [1]

3532 μερίζω, merizō
divide [10], assign [3], apportion [1]

3533 μέριμνα, merimna
care[1] [3], anxiety [2], worry [1]

3534 μεριμνάω, merimnaō
worry [13], anxious [4], care[1] [1], concern [1]

3535 μερίς, meris
part[1] [2], share [2], district [1]

3536 μερισμός, merismos
distribute [1], divide [1]

3537 μεριστής, meristēs
arbitrator [1]

3538 μέρος, meros
part[1] [12], district [4], untranslated [4], share [3], extent [2], region [2], case [1], detail [1], group [1], little [1], observe[2] [1], one [1], piece [1], place [1], side [1], some point [1], trade [1], turn[2] [1], see 1666 [individually] [1], see 1666 [partial] [1]

3538 + 2400 μέρος + ἔχω, meros + echō
share [1]

3540 μεσημβρία, mesēmbria
noon [1], south [1]

3541 μεσιτεύω, mesiteuō
guarantee [1]

3542 μεσίτης, mesitēs
mediator [6]

3543 μεσονύκτιον, mesonyktion
midnight [4]

3544 Μεσοποταμία, Mesopotamia
Mesopotamia [2]

3545 μέσος, mesos
see 1877 [among] [13], midst [8], middle [4], among [3], between [2], see 1650 [among] [2], see 1650 [before] [2], see 1666 [from] [2], see 1877 [before] [2], untranslated [2], company [1], front [1], two [1], see 324 [among] [1], see 324

[between] [1], see 324 [center] [1], see 324 [in] [1], see 1650 [forward] [1], see 1650 [here] [1], see 1666 [aside] [1], see 1666 [remove] [1], see 1877 [around] [1], see 1877 [between] [1], see 1877 [inside] [1], see 2093 [on] [1]

3545 + 2465 μέσος + ἡμέρα, mesos + hēmera
midday [1]

3545 + 3816 μέσος + νύξ, mesos + nyx
midnight [1]

3545 + 3836 + 3816 μέσος + ὁ + νύξ, mesos + ho + nyx
midnight [1]

3546 μεσότοιχον, mesotoichon
divide [1]

3547 μεσουράνημα, mesouranēma
midheaven [3]

3548 μεσόω, mesoō
middle [1]

3549 Μεσσίας, Messias
Messiah [2]

3550 μεστός, mestos
full [9]

3551 μεστόω, mestoō
fill [1]

3552 μετά, meta
with [292], after [79], late [15], untranslated [12], to [10], among [8], companion [7], against [6], on [5], along with [4], in [4], together with [2], afterward [1], along [1], as [1], before [1], behind [1], between [1], by [1], combine with [1], from now [1], near [1], over[2] [1], presence [1], promise [1], subsequent [1], until [1], well[2] [1], while [1], see 1656 [rush back] [1], see 4024 [without any] [1], see 4024 [without[1]] [1]

3552 + 4024 + 4498 μετά + οὐ + πολύς, meta + ou + polys
soon [1]

3552 + 4047 μετά + οὗτος, meta + houtos
late [1]

3552 + 4498 + 4155 μετά + πολύς + παράκλησις, meta + polys + paraklēsis
earnestly [1]

3552 + 5915 μετά + χαρά, meta + chara
cheerfully [1]

3553 μεταβαίνω, metabainō
leave [5], move [2], pass [2], depart [1], go on [1], move about [1]

3554 μεταβάλλω, metaballō
change one's mind [1]

3555 μετάγω, metagō
guide [2]

3556 μεταδίδωμι, metadidōmi
share [4], giver [1]

3557 μετάθεσις, metathesis
change [1], removal [1], take [1]

3558 μεταίρω, metairō
leave [2]

3559 μετακαλέω, metakaleō
ask [1], ask to meet [1], invite [1], send for [1]

3560 μετακινέω, metakineō
shift [1]

3561 μεταλαμβάνω, metalambanō
share [2], take [2], eat [1], have [1], receive [1]

3562 μετάλημψις, metalēmpsis
receive [1]

3563 μεταλλάσσω, metallassō
exchange [2]

3564 μεταμέλομαι, metamelomai
change one's mind [3], regret [2], repent [1]

3565 μεταμορφόω, metamorphoō
transfigure [2], transform [2]

3566 μετανοέω, metanoeō
repent [33], repentance [1]

3567 μετάνοια, metanoia
repentance [20], repent [2]

3568 μεταξύ, metaxy
between [5], conflict [1], next [1], two [1], see 1877 [meanwhile] [1]

3569 μεταπέμπω, metapempō
send for [7], bring [1], transfer [1]

3570 μεταστρέφω, metastrephō
pervert [1], turn[3] [1]

3571 μετασχηματίζω, metaschēmatizō
disguise [3], apply [1], transform [1]

3572 μετατίθημι, metatithēmi
take [2], bring back [1], change [1], desert[1] [1], pervert [1]

3573 μετατρέπω, metatrepō
turn[3] [1]

3575 μετέπειτα, metepeita
late [1]

3576 μετέχω, metechō
partake [3], share [3], belong [1], live [1]

3577 μετεωρίζομαι, meteōrizomai
worry [1]

3578 μετοικεσία, metoikesia
deportation [4]

3579 μετοικίζω, metoikizō
move [1], remove [1]

3580 μετοχή, metochē
partnership [1]

3581 μέτοχος, metochos
partner [3], share [2], companion [1]

3582 μετρέω, metreō
measure [7], give a measure [3], get a measure [1]

3583 μετρητής, metrētēs
see 5552 [thirty gallons] [1], see 1545 [twenty gallons] [1]

3584 μετριοπαθέω, metriopatheō
deal gently [1]

3585 μετρίως, metriōs
little [1]

3586 μέτρον, metron
measure [10], field [1], measurement [1], properly [1], untranslated [1]

3587 μέτωπον, metōpon
forehead [8]

3588 μέχρι, mechri
until [6], to [4], point[1] [3], at [1], far [1]

3588 + 4005 μέχρι + ὅς, mechri + hos
until [2]

3590 μή, mē
not [552], no [70], untranslated [58], see 4024 [not] [45], see 1623 [except] [37], see 4024 [never] [32], see 1569

[unless] [25], *see 1623* [but] [22], without[1] [11], nothing [10], keep from [9], *see 4024* [no] [9], never [8], *see 1623* [only] [7], from [6], *see 1569* [without[1]] [6], cannot [5], none [5], *see 1623* [otherwise] [5], no one [4], or [4], neither [3], *see 2671* [or] [3], avoid [2], refrain [2], refuse [2], *see 1623* [but only] [2], *see 1760* [unless] [2], *see 4024* [by no means] [2], *see 4033* [never again] [2], afraid [1], against [1], except [1], fail [1], fear [1], give up [1], keep [1], no longer [1], no more [1], nor [1], not any longer [1], nowhere [1], or else [1], prevent [1], stop [1], than [1], unable [1], *see 247* [except] [1], *see 1569* [apart] [1], *see 1569* [but only] [1], *see 1569* [but] [1], *see 1569* [except] [1], *see 1623* [for then] [1], *see 1623* [however] [1], *see 1623* [unless] [1], *see 1623* [until] [1], *see 1760* [except] [1], *see 2671* [rather] [1], *see 3306* [forbid] [1], *see 4024* [before] [1], *see 4024* [none] [1], *see 4024* [nothing] [1], *see 4049* [not] [1].

3590 + 743 μή + ἀρέσκω, *mē + areskō*
displease [1]

3590 + 1145 μή + γέ, *mē + ge*
do [1]

3590 + 1181 μή + γίνομαι, *mē + ginomai*
by no means [10], never [2], heaven forbid [1]

3590 + 1538 μή + δύναμαι, *mē + dynamai*
cannot [6], unable [3]

3590 + 1651 μή + εἷς, *mē + heis*
none [1]

3590 + 2266 μή + ἐσθίω, *mē + esthiō*
abstain [3]

3590 + 2400 μή + ἔχω, *mē + echō*
without[1] [4], devoid [1], lack [1]

3590 + 2400 + 5065 μή + ἔχω + σπέρμα, *mē + echō + sperma*
childless [1]

3590 + 2400 + 5451 μή + ἔχω + τέκνον, *mē + echō + teknon*
childless [1]

3590 + 2441 μή + ζωογονέω, *mē + zōogoneō*
die [1]

3590 + 2527 μή + θέλω, *mē + thelō*
unwilling [1]

3590 + 3943 μή + ὀνειδίζω, *mē + oneidizō*
ungrudgingly [1]

3590 + 4024 μή + οὐ, *mē + ou*
not [5]

3590 + 4205 μή + πάρειμι, *mē + pareimi*
lack [1]

3590 + 4246 μή + πᾶς, *mē + pas*
no [2]

3590 + 4661 μή + προσεάω, *mē + proseaō*
against [1]

3590 + 4803 μή + πώς, *mē + pōs*
perhaps [2], otherwise [1], so that not [1], that [1]

3590 + 5516 μή + τὶς, *mē + tis*
nothing [3], none [1]

3590 + 5828 μή + φοβέομαι, *mē + phobeomai*
unafraid [1]

3592 μηδαμῶς, *mēdamōs*
by no means [2]

3593 μηδέ, *mēde*
or [29], not [10], and not [6], not even [5], nor [3], and no [1], no longer [1], refuse [1], *untranslated* [1]

3594 μηδείς, *mēdeis*
no one [25], nothing [20], no [13], not anyone [8], not [5], anyone [3], not any [3], without any [3], any [2], anything [2], never [2], no way [1], not anything [1], not in the least [1], without[1] [1]

3595 μηδέποτε, *mēdepote*
never [1]

3596 + 1063 μηδέπω + βλέπω, *mēdepō + blepō*
as yet unseen [1]

3597 Μῆδος, *Mēdos*
Mede [1]

3600 μηκέτι, *mēketi*
no longer [11], no more [2], no ever [2], any longer [1], give up [1], never again [1], no further [1], not [1], not again [1], not any more [1]

3601 μῆκος, *mēkos*
length [3]

3602 μηκύνω, *mēkynō*
grow [1]

3603 μηλωτή, *mēlōtē*
sheep [1]

3604 μήν[1], *mēn[1]*
month [18]

3605 μήν[2], *mēn[2]*
surely [1]

3606 μηνύω, *mēnyō*
inform [2], know [1], show [1]

3607 μήποτε, *mēpote*
so that not [7], or [4], in case [3], for [2], that not [2], no [1], not [1], otherwise [1], perhaps [1], whether [1], *see 2671* [otherwise] [1], *untranslated* [1]

3609 μήπω, *mēpō*
before [1], not yet [1]

3611 μηρός, *mēros*
thigh [1]

3612 μήτε, *mēte*
or [13], nor [8], neither [5], either [4], and no [1], and not [1], no [1], not even [1]

3613 μήτηρ, *mētēr*
mother [77], *see 3120* [birth] [3], *see 1666* [birth] [1], *see 3120* [bear[1]] [1]

3614 μήτι, *mēti*
untranslated [8], surely not [3], not [2], cannot [1], *see 1623* [except] [1], *see 1623* [unless] [1], *see 1623* [unless indeed] [1]

3615 μήτιγε, *mētige*
nothing [1]

3616 μήτρα, *mētra*
womb [1], *see 1380* [firstborn] [1]

3618 μητρολῴας, *mētrolōas*
kill one's mother [1]

3620 μιαίνω, *miainō*
corrupt [2], defile [2], ritual defilement [1]

3621 μίασμα, *miasma*
defilement [1]

3622 μιασμός, *miasmos*
deprave [1]

3623 μίγμα, *migma*
mixture [1]

3625 μικρός, *mikros*
little [24], small [9], least [5], little one [5], little while [1], short [1], young [1]

3626 Μίλητος, *Milētos*
Miletus [3]

3627 μίλιον, *milion*
mile [1]

3628 μιμέομαι, *mimeomai*
imitate [4]

3629 μιμητής, *mimētēs*
imitator [6]

3630 μιμνήσκομαι, *mimnēskomai*
remember [20], mindful [1], recall [1], remembrance [1]

3631 μισέω, *miseō*
hate [39], hateful [1]

3632 μισθαποδοσία, *misthapodosia*
reward [2], penalty [1]

3633 μισθαποδότης, *misthapodotēs*
reward [1]

3634 μίσθιος, *misthios*
hired hand [2]

3635 μισθός, *misthos*
reward [18], wage[2] [5], pay [3], gain [1], penalty [1], *see 1443* [reward] [1]

3636 μισθόω, *misthoō*
hire [2]

3637 μίσθωμα, *misthōma*
expense [1]

3638 μισθωτός, *misthōtos*
hired hand [2], hired man [1]

3639 Μιτυλήνη, *Mitylēnē*
Mitylene [1]

3640 Μιχαήλ, *Michaēl*
Michael [2]

3641 μνᾶ, *mna*
pound [9]

3643 Μνάσων, *Mnasōn*
Mnason [1]

3644 μνεία, *mneia*
remember [1]

3644 + 2400 μνεία + ἔχω, *mneia + echō*
remember [2]

3644 + 4472 μνεία + ποιέω, *mneia + poieō*
remember [3], mention [1]

3645 μνῆμα, *mnēma*
tomb [8]

3646 μνημεῖον, *mnēmeion*
tomb [36], grave [3]

3647 + 4472 μνήμη + ποιέω, *mnēmē + poieō*
recall [1]

3648 μνημονεύω, *mnēmoneuō*
remember [19], make mention [1], think [1]

3649 μνημόσυνον, *mnēmosynon*
remembrance [2], memorial [1]

3650 μνηστεύω, *mnēsteuō*
engage [3]

3652 μογιλάλος, mogilalos
impediment in speech [1]

3653 μόγις, mogis
scarcely [1]

3654 μόδιος, modios
bushel basket [2], untranslated [1]

3655 μοιχαλίς, moichalis
adulterous [3], adulteress [2],
adulterer [1], adultery [1]

3656 μοιχάω, moichaō
commit adultery [4]

3657 μοιχεία, moicheia
adultery [3]

3658 μοιχεύω, moicheuō
commit adultery [14], adultery [1]

3659 μοιχός, moichos
adulterer [3]

3660 μόλις, molis
difficulty [2], scarcely [2], hard [1],
rarely [1]

3661 Μολόχ, Moloch
Moloch [1]

3662 μολύνω, molynō
defile [2], soil [1]

3663 μολυσμός, molysmos
defilement [1]

3664 μομφή, momphē
complaint [1]

3665 μονή, monē
dwelling place [1], home [1]

3666 μονογενής, monogenēs
only [5], only son [3], only child [1]

3667 μόνον, monon
only [54], alone [2], even [2], merely [2],
see 1623 [except] [2], all [1], at all [1],
only thing [1], see 4024 [more than] [1]

3668 μόνος, monos
alone [20], only [19], oneself [2], see 2848
[alone] [2], any [1], apart [1], single [1],
untranslated [1]

3669 μονόφθαλμος, monophthalmos
one eye [2]

3670 μονόω, monoō
leave alone [1]

3671 μορφή, morphē
form [3]

3672 μορφόω, morphoō
form [1]

3673 μόρφωσις, morphōsis
embodiment [1], outward form [1]

3674 μοσχοποιέω, moschopoieō
make a calf [1]

3675 μόσχος, moschos
calf [5], ox [1]

3676 μουσικός, mousikos
minstrel [1]

3677 μόχθος, mochthos
hardship [1], labor [1], toil [1]

3678 μυελός, myelos
marrow [1]

3679 μυέω, myeō
learn the secret [1]

3680 μῦθος, mythos
myth [5]

3681 μυκάομαι, mykaomai
roar [1]

3682 μυκτηρίζω, myktērizō
mock [1]

3683 μυλικός, mylikos
see 3345 [millstone] [1]

3684 μύλινος, mylinos
millstone [1]

3685 μύλος, mylos
millstone [2], see 241 [grind meal] [1]

3685 + 3948 μύλος + ὀνικός, mylos +
onikos
great millstone [1]

3688 Μύρα, Myra
Myra [1]

3689 μυριάς, myrias
myriad [2], thousand [2], innumerable [1],
ten thousand [1], see 1490 [two hundred
million] [1]

3689 + 4297 μυριάς + πέντε, myrias +
pente
fifty thousand [1]

3690 μυρίζω, myrizō
anoint [1]

3691 μύριοι, myrioi
ten thousand [1]

3692 μυρίος, myrios
ten thousand [2]

3693 μύρον, myron
ointment [9], perfume [4], myrrh [1]

3695 Μυσία, Mysia
Mysia [2]

3696 μυστήριον, mystērion
mystery [24], secret [4]

3697 μυωπάζω, myōpazō
nearsighted [1]

3698 μώλωψ, mōlōps
wound [1]

3699 μωμάομαι, mōmaomai
blame [1], find fault [1]

3700 μῶμος, mōmos
blemish [1]

3701 μωραίνω, mōrainō
lose taste [2], fool [1], make foolish [1]

3702 μωρία, mōria
foolishness [5]

3703 μωρολογία, mōrologia
silly talk [1]

3704 μωρός, mōros
foolish [5], fool [4], stupid [2],
foolishness [1]

3707 Μωϋσῆς, Mōysēs
Moses [80]

3709 Ναασσών, Naassōn
Nahshon [3]

3710 Ναγγαί, Nangai
Naggai [1]

3714 Ναζαρέθ, Nazareth
Nazareth [12]

3716 Ναζαρηνός, Nazarēnos
Nazareth [5], man from Nazareth [1]

3717 Ναζωραῖος, Nazōraios
Nazareth [11], Nazarene [1], Nazorean [1]

3718 Ναθάμ, Natham
Nathan [1]

3720 Ναθαναήλ, Nathanaēl
Nathanael [6]

3721 ναί, nai
yes [31], so [1], surely [1]

3722 Ναιμάν, Naiman
Naaman [1]

3723 Ναΐν, Nain
Nain [1]

3724 ναός, naos
temple [35], sanctuary [8], shrine [2]

3725 Ναούμ, Naoum
Nahum [1]

3726 νάρδος, nardos
nard [2]

3727 Νάρκισσος, Narkissos
Narcissus [1]

3728 ναυαγέω, nauageō
shipwreck [1], suffer shipwreck [1]

3729 ναύκληρος, nauklēros
owner of the ship [1]

3730 ναῦς, naus
ship [1]

3731 ναύτης, nautēs
sailor [3]

3732 Ναχώρ, Nachōr
Nahor [1]

3733 νεανίας, neanias
young man [3]

3734 νεανίσκος, neaniskos
young man [9], young person [2]

3735 Νέα πολις, Nea polis
Neapolis [1]

3738 νεκρός, nekros
dead [122], corpse [2], dead man [2],
death [2]

3739 νεκρόω, nekroō
dead [2], put to death [1]

3740 νέκρωσις, nekrōsis
barrenness [1], death [1]

3741 νεομηνία, neomēnia
new moon [1]

3742 νέος, neos
new [11], young [7], young man [3],
young woman [2]

3744 νεότης, neotēs
youth [4]

3745 νεόφυτος, neophytos
recent convert [1]

3748 νεύω, neuō
motion [2]

3749 νεφέλη, nephelē
cloud [25]

3750 Νεφθαλίμ, Nephthalim
Naphtali [3]

3751 νέφος, nephos
cloud [1]

3752 νεφρός, nephros
mind[1] [1]

3753 νεωκόρος, neōkoros
temple keeper [1]

3754 νεωτερικός, neōterikos
youthful [1]

3755 νή, nē
certain [1]

3756 νήθω, nēthō
spin [2]

3757 νηπιάζω, nēpiazō
infant [1]

3758 νήπιος, nēpios
child [6], infant [5], minor [2],
childish [1], gentle [1]

3759 Νηρεύς, Nēreus
Nereus [1]

3760 Νηρί, Nēri
Neri [1]

3761 νησίον, nēsion
small island [1]

3762 νῆσος, nēsos
island [9]

3763 νηστεία, nēsteia
fast [3], hunger [1], without food [1]

3764 νηστεύω, nēsteuō
fast [20]

3765 νῆστις, nēstis
hungry [2]

3767 νηφάλιος, nēphalios
temperate [3]

3768 νήφω, nēphō
discipline [3], sober [3]

3769 Νίγερ, Niger
Niger [1]

3770 Νικάνωρ, Nikanōr
Nicanor [1]

3771 νικάω, nikaō
conquer [23], overcome [3],
overpower [1], prevail [1]

3772 νίκη, nikē
victory [1]

3773 Νικόδημος, Nikodēmos
Nicodemus [5]

3774 Νικολαΐτης, Nikolaitēs
Nicolaitan [2]

3775 Νικόλαος, Nikolaos
Nicolaus [1]

3776 Νικόπολις, Nikopolis
Nicopolis [1]

3777 νῖκος, nikos
victory [4]

3780 Νινευΐτης, Nineuitēs
person of Nineveh [2], Nineveh [1]

3781 νιπτήρ, niptēr
basin [1]

3782 νίπτω, niptō
wash [17]

3783 νοέω, noeō
understand [6], perceive [4], see [2],
imagine [1], think over [1]

3784 νόημα, noēma
mind[1] [3], thought [2], design [1]

3785 νόθος, nothos
illegitimate [1]

3786 νομή, nomē
pasture [1]

3786 + 2400 νομή + ἔχω, nomē + echō
spread [1]

3787 νομίζω, nomizō
think [8], suppose [5], assume [1],
imagine [1]

3788 νομικός, nomikos
lawyer [8], law [1]

3789 νομίμως, nomimōs
according to the rules [1], legitimately [1]

3790 νόμισμα, nomisma
coin [1]

3791 νομοδιδάσκαλος,
nomodidaskalos
teacher of the law [3]

3792 νομοθεσία, nomothesia
giving of the law [1]

3793 νομοθετέω, nomotheteō
enact [1], receive the law [1]

3794 νομοθέτης, nomothetēs
lawgiver [1]

3795 νόμος, nomos
law [193], legal [1]

3796 νοσέω, noseō
morbid craving [1]

3798 νόσος, nosos
disease [11]

3799 νοσσιά, nossia
brood [1]

3800 νοσσίον, nossion
brood [1]

3801 νοσσός, nossos
young [1]

3802 νοσφίζω, nosphizō
keep back [2], pilfer [1]

3803 νότος, notos
south [4], south wind [3]

3804 νουθεσία, nouthesia
admonition [1], instruct [1], instruction [1]

3805 νουθετέω, noutheteō
admonish [4], warn [3], instruct [1]

3807 νουνεχῶς, nounechōs
wisely [1]

3808 νοῦς, nous
mind[1] [21], understanding [2], think [1]

3809 Νύμφαν, Nymphan
Nympha [1]

3811 νύμφη, nymphē
bride [5], daughter-in-law [3]

3812 νυμφίος, nymphios
bridegroom [16]

3813 νυμφών, nymphōn
wedding [3]

3814 νῦν, nyn
now [126], present[3] [10], as it is [5],
as [1], just[1] [1], just now [1], present
case [1], untranslated [1]

3814 + 2789 νῦν + καιρός, nyn + kairos
present[3] [1]

3815 νυνί, nyni
now [15], as it is [2], in fact [2],
present[3] [1]

3816 νύξ, nyx
night [56], see 3545 [midnight] [2], see
5480 [early in the morning] [2],
tonight [1]

3817 νύσσω, nyssō
pierce [1]

3818 νυστάζω, nystazō
asleep [1], drowsy [1]

3819 νυχθήμερον, nychthēmeron
night and a day [1]

3820 Νῶε, Nōe
Noah [8]

3821 νωθρός, nōthros
dull [1], sluggish [1]

3822 νῶτος, nōtos
back [1]

3825 ξενία, xenia
guest room [1], lodging [1]

3826 ξενίζω, xenizō
stay [3], entertain [2], surprise [2], give
lodging [1], lodge [1], strange [1]

3827 ξενοδοχέω, xenodocheō
show hospitality [1]

3828 ξένος, xenos
stranger [8], foreigner [2], foreign [1],
host[2] [1], something strange [1],
strange [1]

3829 ξέστης, xestēs
pot [1]

3830 ξηραίνω, xērainō
wither [8], wither away [3], dry up [1],
fully ripe [1], rigid [1], stop [1]

3831 ξηρός, xēros
wither [4], dry [2], land[1] [1], paralyze [1]

3832 ξύλινος, xylinos
wood [2]

3833 ξύλον, xylon
tree [9], club [5], wood [4], cross [1],
stocks [1]

3834 ξυράω, xyraō
shave [3]

3836 ὁ, ho
untranslated [9146], the [8101],
who [735], that [320], he [287],
what [188], they [172], a [125], son [87],
you [82], whoever [71], this [50], we [45],
see 1650 [forever] [45], thing [37],
she [31], anyone [30], I [29], it [23],
which [17], everyone [13], one [12],
some [10], other [9], see 2093
[together] [8], see 4024 [never] [8],
person [7], see 2048 [look up] [6], see
2813 [name] [6], see 5502 [kneel
down] [6], see 1650 [back] [5], affair [4],
see 1328 [through] [4], Jesus [3],
family [3], interest[1] [3], mother [3],
such [3], whatever [3], see 487 [speak] [3],
see 608 [instantly] [3], see 2095
[arrest] [3], Joseph [2], all [2], and [2],
gift [2], someone [2], wife [2], see 1650
[again] [2], see 1650 [among] [2], see
1650 [ashore] [2], see 2048 [shout] [2],
see 2093 [next] [2], see 2939 [motion for
silence] [2], see 5480 [early in the
morning] [2], God [1], anything [1],
being [1], everything [1], father [1],
friend [1], goods [1], house [1], news [1],
something [1], to [1], work [1], see 149
[keep in suspense] [1], see 149 [look] [1],
see 241 [grind meal] [1], see 489
[speak] [1], see 629 [death] [1], see 885
[sheepfold] [1], see 918 [breathe one's
last] [1], see 948 [thus far] [1], see 965
[contribute] [1], see 1181 [hear] [1], see
1443 [reward] [1], see 1544
[sundown] [1], see 1634 [submit] [1], see
1650 [ahead] [1], see 1650 [around] [1],
see 1650 [before] [1], see 1650
[continually] [1], see 1650 [forward] [1],
see 1650 [here] [1], see 1650
[permanent] [1], see 1650 [quite] [1], see
1650 [whisper] [1], see 1650 [with] [1],
see 1675 [defame] [1], see 1725 [lose
heart] [1], see 1753 [point[2]] [1], see 1877
[external] [1], see 1877 [inwardly] [1], see
1877 [just then] [1], see 1877
[meanwhile] [1], see 1877 [next] [1], see

1877 [outwardly] [1], *see 2002*
[descend] [1], *see 2048* [look around] [1],
see 2093 [ashore] [1], *see 2093*
[chamberlain] [1], *see 2093* [coast] [1],
see 2093 [earthly] [1], *see 2095*
[seize] [1], *see 2158* [embrace] [1], *see*
2158 [put arms around] [1], *see 2400*
[marry] [1], *see 2843* [descendant] [1], *see*
2848 [house after house] [1], *see 2939*
[gesture] [1], *see 3091* [refuse help] [1],
see 3281 [whisper] [1], *see 3357*
[resentful] [1], *see 3545* [midnight] [1],
see 4024 [extraordinary] [1], *see 4024*
[unusual] [1], *see 4246* [always] [1], *see*
4322 [dress for action] [1], *see 4328*
[blindfold] [1], *see 4447* [self-
indulgence] [1], *see 4574* [recently] [1],
see 4725 [themselves] [1], *see 5502*
[ponder] [1], *see 5569* [nine o'clock in the
morning] [1], *see 5626* [person] [1], *see*
5774 [exclaim] [1], *see 5828* [God-
fearing] [1], *see 5889* [voice] [1], *see 5927*
[seashore] [1]

3836 + 899 ὁ + αὐτός, *ho + autos*
  one place [1]

3836 + 899 + 3306 ὁ + αὐτός + λέγω,
ho + autos + legō
  agreement [1]

3837 ὀγδοήκοντα, *ogdoēkonta*
  eighty [1]

3837 + 5475 ὀγδοήκοντα + τέσσαρες,
ogdoēkonta + tessares
  eighty-four [1]

3838 ὄγδοος, *ogdoos*
  eighth [4], with seven others [1]

3839 ὄγκος, *onkos*
  weight [1]

3840 ὅδε, *hode*
  this [6], she [1], such and such [1],
  thus [1], *untranslated* [1]

3841 ὁδεύω, *hodeuō*
  travel [1]

3842 ὁδηγέω, *hodēgeō*
  guide [5]

3843 ὁδηγός, *hodēgos*
  guide [5]

3844 ὁδοιπορέω, *hodoiporeō*
  journey [1]

3845 ὁδοιπορία, *hodoiporia*
  journey [2]

3847 ὁδός, *hodos*
  way [56], road [23], path [8], journey [6],
  roadside [3], *untranslated* [3], street [2]

3848 ὀδούς, *odous*
  tooth [12]

3849 ὀδυνάω, *odynaō*
  agony [2], great anxiety [1], grieve [1]

3850 ὀδύνη, *odynē*
  anguish [1], pain [1]

3851 ὀδυρμός, *odyrmos*
  lamentation [1], mourn [1]

3852 Ὀζίας, *Ozias*
  Uzziah [2]

3853 ὄζω, *ozō*
  stench [1]

3854 ὅθεν, *hothen*
  where [3], from which [2], hence [2],
  therefore [2], after [1], and [1],
  consequently [1], from this [1], that [1],
  untranslated [1]

3855 ὀθόνη, *othonē*
  sheet [2]

3856 ὀθόνιον, *othonion*
  linen wrapping [3], linen cloth [1]

3857 οἶδα, *oida*
  know [285], understand [8], know
  how [7], realize [5], aware [3], inform [2],
  be [1], can [1], have knowledge [1],
  regard [1], respect[1] [1], *untranslated* [1]

3857 + 242 οἶδα + ἀληθῶς, *oida +*
alēthōs
  sure [1]

3857 + 1207 οἶδα + γράμμα, *oida +*
gramma
  learning [1]

3858 οἰκεῖος, *oikeios*
  family [1], family member [1], member of
  the household [1]

3859 οἰκετεία, *oiketeia*
  household [1]

3860 οἰκέτης, *oiketēs*
  slave [3], servant [1]

3861 οἰκέω, *oikeō*
  dwell [7], live [2]

3862 οἴκημα, *oikēma*
  cell [1]

3863 οἰκητήριον, *oikētērion*
  dwelling [2]

3864 οἰκία, *oikia*
  house [81], home [5], household [5],
  house to house [1], live [1]

3865 οἰκιακός, *oikiakos*
  household [1], member of the
  household [1]

3866 οἰκοδεσποτέω, *oikodespoteō*
  manage a household [1]

3867 οἰκοδεσπότης, *oikodespotēs*
  owner of the house [6], landowner [3],
  householder [1], master of a
  household [1], master of the house [1]

3868 οἰκοδομέω, *oikodomeō*
  build [25], build up [9], builder [4],
  encourage [1], under construction [1]

3869 οἰκοδομή, *oikodomē*
  build up [10], build [3], building [2],
  upbuild [2], structure [1]

3871 οἰκοδόμος, *oikodomos*
  builder [1]

3872 οἰκονομέω, *oikonomeō*
  manager [1]

3873 οἰκονομία, *oikonomia*
  commission [3], plan [2], management [1],
  manager [1], position [1], train [1]

3874 οἰκονόμος, *oikonomos*
  manager [4], steward [4], treasurer [1],
  trustee [1]

3875 οἶκος, *oikos*
  house [66], home [25], household [16],
  family [2], palace [1], sanctuary [1], *see*
  2848 [house after house] [1], *see 2848*
  [house to house] [1], *untranslated* [1]

3876 οἰκουμένη, *oikoumenē*
  world [15]

3877 οἰκουργός, *oikourgos*
  good manager of household [1]

3880 οἰκτιρμός, *oiktirmos*
  mercy [3], sympathy [1], *see 5073*
  [compassion] [1]

3881 οἰκτίρμων, *oiktirmōn*
  merciful [3]

3882 οἰκτίρω, *oiktirō*
  have compassion [2]

3884 οἰνοπότης, *oinopotēs*
  drunkard [2]

3885 οἶνος, *oinos*
  wine [32], *see 4539* [wine-cup] [1]

3885 + 4498 οἶνος + πολύς, *oinos +*
polys
  drink [1]

3886 οἰνοφλυγία, *oinophlygia*
  drunkenness [1]

3887 οἴομαι, *oiomai*
  expect [1], intend [1], suppose [1]

3888 οἷος, *hoios*
  as [4], such [4], what [2], that [1],
  thing [1], what kind [1], *untranslated* [1]

3890 ὀκνέω, *okneō*
  delay [1]

3891 ὀκνηρός, *oknēros*
  lag [1], lazy [1], troublesome [1]

3892 ὀκταήμερος, *oktaēmeros*
  eighth day [1]

3893 ὀκτώ, *oktō*
  eight [5], *see 1274* [eighteen] [1], *see*
  5558 [thirty-eight] [1]

3893 + 2465 ὀκτώ + ἡμέρα, *oktō +*
hēmera
  week [1]

3897 ὄλεθρος, *olethros*
  destruction [3], ruin [1]

3898 ὀλιγοπιστία, *oligopistia*
  little faith [1]

3899 ὀλιγόπιστος, *oligopistos*
  little faith [5]

3900 ὀλίγος, *oligos*
  few [13], little [9], few things [3], little
  while [3], short [3], small [3], quickly [2],
  light[2] [1], some [1], while [1], *see 4024*
  [some] [1]

3901 ὀλιγόψυχος, *oligopsychos*
  fainthearted [1]

3902 ὀλιγωρέω, *oligōreō*
  regard lightly [1]

3903 ὀλίγως, *oligōs*
  just[1] [1]

3904 ὀλοθρευτής, *olothreutēs*
  destroyer [1]

3905 ὀλοθρεύω, *olothreuō*
  destroyer [1]

3906 ὁλοκαύτωμα, *holokautōma*
  burnt offering [2], whole burnt offering [1]

3907 ὁλοκληρία, *holoklēria*
  perfect health [1]

3908 ὁλόκληρος, *holoklēros*
  complete [1], sound[2] [1]

3909 ὀλολύζω, *ololyzō*
  wail [1]

3910 ὅλος, *holos*
  whole [46], all [37], *see 1877*
  [throughout] [7], entire [4], *see 1650*
  [throughout] [4], *see 2848*
  [throughout] [4], entirely [2], full [2], one
  piece [1], *see 1328* [throughout] [1], *see*
  2093 [throughout] [1]

3911 ὁλοτελής, *holotelēs*
entirely [1]

3912 Ὀλυμπᾶς, *Olympas*
Olympas [1]

3913 ὄλυνθος, *olynthos*
winter fruit [1]

3914 ὅλως, *holōs*
at all [3], actually [1]

3915 ὄμβρος, *ombros*
rain [1]

3916 ὁμείρομαι, *homeiromai*
care for deeply [1]

3917 ὁμιλέω, *homileō*
converse [2], talk [2]

3918 ὁμιλία, *homilia*
company [1]

3920 ὁμίχλη, *homichlē*
mist [1]

3921 ὄμμα, *omma*
eye [2]

3923 ὀμνύω, *omnyō*
swear [23], swear an oath [3]

3924 ὁμοθυμαδόν, *homothymadon*
together [6], body [1], constantly [1], one
accord [1], unanimously [1], unite [1]

3926 ὁμοιοπαθής, *homoiopathēs*
just like [1], like[1] [1]

3927 ὅμοιος, *homoios*
like[1] [42], as [1], look like [1], same [1]

3928 ὁμοιότης, *homoiotēs*
as [1], resemble [1]

3929 ὁμοιόω, *homoioō*
compare [8], like[1] [5], form [1], make
like [1]

3930 ὁμοίωμα, *homoiōma*
like[1] [2], likeness [2], appearance [1],
resemble [1]

3931 ὁμοίως, *homoiōs*
likewise [11], same way [8], so [3],
same [2], *untranslated* [2], as [1], just
as [1], like[1] [1], like manner [1]

3932 ὁμοίωσις, *homoiōsis*
likeness [1]

3933 ὁμολογέω, *homologeō*
confess [15], acknowledge [5], admit [1],
declare [1], make a confession [1], make a
promise [1], profess [1], promise [1]

3934 ὁμολογία, *homologia*
confession [6]

3935 ὁμολογουμένως,
homologoumenōs
without any doubt [1]

3937 ὁμότεχνος, *homotechnos*
same trade [1]

3938 ὁμοῦ, *homou*
together [3], gather together [1]

3939 ὁμόφρων, *homophrōn*
unity of spirit [1]

3940 ὅμως, *homōs*
nevertheless [1], once[4] [1], same way [1]

3941 ὄναρ, *onar*
dream [6]

3942 ὀνάριον, *onarion*
young donkey [1]

3943 ὀνειδίζω, *oneidizō*
revile [3], taunt [2], insult [1],

reproach [1], upbraid [1], *see 3590*
[ungrudgingly] [1]

3944 ὀνειδισμός, *oneidismos*
abuse [3], disgrace [1], insult [1]

3945 ὄνειδος, *oneidos*
disgrace [1]

3946 Ὀνήσιμος, *Onēsimos*
Onesimus [2]

3947 Ὀνησίφορος, *Onēsiphoros*
Onesiphorus [2]

3948 ὀνικός, *onikos*
great [1], *see 3685* [great millstone] [1]

3949 ὀνίνημι, *oninēmi*
benefit [1]

3950 ὄνομα, *onoma*
name [211], *see 2813* [name] [7], call [3],
untranslated [3], person [2], Christ [1],
sake [1], *see 1675* [defame] [1]

3950 + 2400 ὄνομα + ἔχω, *onoma +
echō*
call [1]

3951 ὀνομάζω, *onomazō*
name [5], bear the name [1], call on a
name [1], mention [1], take a name [1],
use a name [1]

3952 ὄνος, *onos*
donkey [5]

3953 ὄντως, *ontōs*
indeed [3], really [3], real [2],
certainly [1], truly [1]

3954 ὄξος, *oxos*
sour wine [4], wine [2]

3955 ὀξύς, *oxys*
sharp [7], swift [1]

3956 ὀπή, *opē*
hole [1], opening [1]

3957 ὄπισθεν, *opisthen*
behind [5], after [1], back [1]

3958 ὀπίσω, *opisō*
after [9], *see 1650* [back] [5], behind [4],
follow [4], *untranslated* [3], follower [2],
see 1307 [follow] [2], back [1], lie
behind [1], *see 599* [follow] [1], *see 1650*
[around] [1], *see 2262* [follow] [1], *see
4513* [indulge] [1]

3959 ὁπλίζω, *hoplizō*
arm[2] [1]

3960 ὅπλον, *hoplon*
weapon [3], instrument [2], armor [1]

3961 ὁποῖος, *hopoios*
what [2], as [1], what kind [1], what
sort [1]

3963 ὅπου, *hopou*
where [59], wherever [3], there [2],
which [2], above [1], home [1], house [1],
in [1], long[1] [1], whereas [1]

3963 + 323 ὅπου + ἄν, *hopou + an*
wherever [2]

3963 + 1569 ὅπου + ἐάν, *hopou + ean*
wherever [7], whenever [1]

3964 ὀπτάνομαι, *optanomai*
appear [1]

3965 ὀπτασία, *optasia*
vision [4]

3966 ὀπτός, *optos*
broil [1]

3967 ὀπώρα, *opōra*
fruit [1]

3968 ὅπως, *hopōs*
so that [25], to [10], that [4], how [3],
order[2] [2], *untranslated* [2], purpose [1],
so [1], this [1]

3968 + 323 ὅπως + ἄν, *hopōs + an*
so that [4]

3969 ὅραμα, *horama*
vision [11], sight [1]

3970 ὅρασις, *horasis*
look [2], vision [2]

3971 ὁρατός, *horatos*
visible [1]

3972 ὁράω, *horaō*
see [381], appear [21], look [21],
experience [6], perceive [4], must [2],
notice [2], take care [2], watch out [2],
come [1], consider [1], have [1],
observe[1] [1], vision [1], watch [1], *see
3972* [see surely] [1]

3972 + 3972 ὁράω + ὁράω, *horaō +
horaō*
see surely [1]

3973 ὀργή, *orgē*
wrath [27], anger [9]

3974 ὀργίζω, *orgizō*
angry [5], anger [1], enrage [1], rage [1]

3975 ὀργίλος, *orgilos*
quick-tempered [1]

3976 ὀργυιά, *orgyia*
fathom [2]

3977 ὀρέγω, *oregō*
aspire [1], desire [1], eagerness [1]

3978 ὀρεινός, *oreinos*
hill country [2]

3979 ὄρεξις, *orexis*
passion [1]

3980 ὀρθοποδέω, *orthopodeō*
act consistently [1]

3981 ὀρθός, *orthos*
straight [1], upright [1]

3982 ὀρθοτομέω, *orthotomeō*
explain rightly [1]

3983 ὀρθρίζω, *orthrizō*
early in the morning [1]

3984 ὀρθρινός, *orthrinos*
early in the morning [1]

3986 ὄρθρος, *orthros*
daybreak [1], early dawn [1], early in the
morning [1]

3987 ὀρθῶς, *orthōs*
right[1] [2], plainly [1], rightly [1]

3988 ὁρίζω, *horizō*
determine [2], allot [1], appoint [1],
declare [1], definite [1], ordain [1], set[1] [1]

3990 ὅριον, *horion*
region [8], neighborhood [2], around [1],
territory [1]

3991 ὁρκίζω, *horkizō*
adjure [2]

3992 ὅρκος, *horkos*
oath [9], vow [1]

3993 ὁρκωμοσία, *horkōmosia*
oath [4]

3994 ὁρμάω, *hormaō*
rush [5]

3995 ὁρμή, *hormē*
attempt [1], will[1] [1]

3996 ὅρμημα, hormēma
violence [1]

3997 ὄρνεον, orneon
bird [3]

3998 ὄρνις, ornis
hen [2]

3999 ὁροθεσία, horothesia
boundary [1]

4001 ὄρος, oros
mountain [41], mount[18], hill [2], hillside [2]

4002 ὀρύσσω, oryssō
dig [2], dig a hole [1]

4003 ὀρφανός, orphanos
orphan [2]

4004 ὀρχέομαι, orcheomai
dance [4]

4005 ὅς, hos
who [304], that [215], untranslated [151], what [140], which [135], he [91], they [44], this [30], one [16], some [13], see 2401 [until] [12], it [11], see 948 [until] [9], anyone [8], another [7], the [7], whoever [7], other [6], thing [6], man [4], she [4], whatever [4], when [4], you [4], see 1877 [when] [4], all [3], this thing [3], see 505 [because] [3], as [2], gospel [2], hope [2], life [2], see 608 [since] [2], see 2093 [because] [2], see 3588 [until] [2], Christ [1], God [1], I [1], Jesus [1], Paul [1], after [1], answer [1], be [1], boast [1], book [1], conscience [1], death [1], foundation [1], include [1], lawless one [1], mystery [1], power [1], promise [1], regulation [1], same way [1], so [1], someone [1], spirit [1], such a person [1], time[1], way [1], we [1], where [1], see 505 [therefore] [1], see 608 [ever since] [1], see 608 [when] [1], see 1328 [why] [1], see 1650 [purpose] [1], see 1877 [in mind] [1], see 1877 [meanwhile] [1], see 1877 [there] [1], see 1877 [until] [1], see 1877 [where] [1], see 2093 [where] [1], see 2848 [just as] [1], see 4246 [whatever] [1]

4005 + 323 ὅς + ἄν, hos + an
whoever [25], who [17], whatever [6], any [3], you [3], one [2], whenever [2], that [1]

4005 + 1569 ὅς + ἐάν, hos + ean
whatever [15], whoever [7], anyone [6], who [5], that [2], any [1], what [1]

4005 + 5516 ὅς + τὶς, hos + tis
why [1]

4005 + 5516 + 323 ὅς + τὶς + ἄν, hos + tis + an
whatever [4]

4005 + 5516 + 1569 ὅς + τὶς + ἐάν, hos + tis + ean
whatever [2]

4005 + 5573 ὅς + τρόπος, hos + tropos
as [2]

4005 + 5920 ὅς + χάριν, hos + charin
therefore [1]

4006 ὁσάκις, hosakis
often [1]

4006 + 1569 ὁσάκις + ἐάν, hosakis + ean
often [2]

4008 ὅσιος, hosios
holy [4], holy one [3], devout [1]

4009 ὁσιότης, hosiotēs
holiness [2]

4010 ὁσίως, hosiōs
pure [1]

4011 ὀσμή, osmē
fragrance [4], offering [1]

4011 + 2380 ὀσμή + εὐωδία, osmē + euōdia
fragrant [1]

4012 ὅσος, hosos
all [17], whatever [15], that [12], untranslated [9], who [8], how much [7], as [4], many [4], see 4246 [whatever] [4], see 2093 [long] [3], what [2], see 2093 [just as] [2], see 2848 [just as] [2], degree [1], even to all [1], every one [1], long[1], more [1], much [1], only [1], same [1], thing [1], very[1], see 2093 [inasmuch] [1]

4012 + 323 ὅσος + ἄν, hosos + an
all [1], everyone [1], whatever [1], wherever [1]

4012 + 1569 ὅσος + ἐάν, hosos + ean
whatever [3], who [2], everyone [1]

4014 ὀστέον, osteon
bone [3], burial [1]

4015 ὅστις, hostis
who [50], they [23], that [15], which [10], untranslated [10], this [9], see 2401 [until] [4], anyone [3], it [3], whoever [3], all [2], she [2], man [1], since [1], temple [1], two [1], whatever [1], you [1]

4015 + 323 ὅστις + ἄν, hostis + an
whoever [2]

4015 + 1569 ὅστις + ἐάν, hostis + ean
who [1], whoever [1]

4017 ὀστράκινος, ostrakinos
clay [2]

4018 ὄσφρησις, osphrēsis
sense of smell [1]

4019 ὀσφῦς, osphys
waist [3], loin [1], see 2002 [descend] [1], see 2843 [descendant] [1], see 4322 [dress for action] [1], untranslated [1]

4020 ὅταν, hotan
when [98], whenever [10], after [4], that [2], untranslated [2], as soon as [1], before [1], if [1], long[1] [1]

4020 + 2453 ὅταν + ἤδη, hotan + ēdē
as soon as [3]

4021 ὅτε, hote
when [87], after [6], while [4], untranslated [4], before [1], long[1] [1]

4022 ὅτι, hoti
that [544], untranslated [293], for [220], because [189], say [9], how [8], since [7], as [4], why [4], by [2], indeed [2], as though [1], as to [1], but [1], ground[2] [1], hence [1], if [1], of course [1], so that [1], surely [1], that is [1], to [1], what [1], when [1], see 5515 [why] [1]

4023 οὗ, hou
where [19], there [3], which [2]

4023 + 1569 οὗ + ἐάν, hou + ean
wherever [1]

4024 οὐ, ou
not [1121], no [156], untranslated [44], nothing [14], neither [13], never [11], none [9], no one [7], no longer [6], nor [6], fail [5], or [5], see 3590 [not] [5], without[1] [4], refuse [3], at all [2],

cannot [2], from [2], rather [2], see 4033 [never again] [2], before [1], except [1], instead [1], lose [1], more than [1], no more [1], not even [1], than [1], see 3552 [soon] [1]

4024 + 51 οὐ + ἀγνοέω, ou + agnoeō
know [1], understand [1]

4024 + 465 οὐ + ἀνήκω, ou + anēkō
out of place [1]

4024 + 545 οὐ + ἄξιος, ou + axios
unworthy [1]

4024 + 570 οὐ + ἄπας, ou + hapas
none [1]

4024 + 734 οὐ + ἀργός, ou + argos
ineffective [1]

4024 + 817 οὐ + ἄσημος, ou + asēmos
important [1]

4024 + 918 οὐ + ἀφίημι, ou + aphiēmi
refuse [1]

4024 + 1182 + 467 οὐ + γινώσκω + ἀνήρ, ou + ginōskō + anēr
virgin [1]

4024 + 1312 οὐ + δέχομαι, ou + dechomai
refuse [1]

4024 + 1506 οὐ + δοκέω, ou + dokeō
unexpected [2]

4024 + 1538 οὐ + δύναμαι, ou + dynamai
cannot [47], unable [2]

4024 + 1543 οὐ + δυνατός, ou + dynatos
impossible [1]

4024 + 1650 + 3836 + 172 οὐ + εἰς + ὁ + αἰών, ou + eis + ho + aiōn
never [1]

4024 + 1896 οὐ + ἐνδέχομαι, ou + endechomai
impossible [1]

4024 + 2153 οὐ + ἐπινεύω, ou + epineuō
decline [1]

4024 + 2266 οὐ + ἐσθίω, ou + esthiō
abstain [1]

4024 + 2400 οὐ + ἔχω, ou + echō
cannot [1]

4024 + 2527 οὐ + θέλω, ou + thelō
refuse [6], unwilling [3]

4024 + 2653 οὐ + ἱκανός, ou + hikanos
unfit [1]

4024 + 2710 οὐ + ἰσχύω, ou + ischyō
defeat [1]

4024 + 2901 + 5451 οὐ + καταλείπω + τέκνον, ou + kataleipō + teknon
childless [1]

4024 + 3552 οὐ + μετά, ou + meta
without[1] [1], without any [1]

4024 + 3590 οὐ + μή, ou + mē
not [45], never [22], no [9], by no means [2], before [1], none [1]

4024 + 3590 + 1650 + 3836 + 172 οὐ + μή + εἰς + ὁ + αἰών, ou + mē + eis + ho + aiōn
never [7]

4024 + 3590 + 1650 + 4246 οὐ + μή + εἰς + πᾶς, ou + mē + eis + pas
nothing [1]

4024 + 3590 + 2285 οὐ + μή + ἔτι, *ou + mē + eti*
never [1]

4024 + 3590 + 4537 οὐ + μή + ποτέ, *ou + mē + pote*
never [1]

4024 + 3590 + 4799 οὐ + μή + πώποτε, *ou + mē + pōpote*
never [1]

4024 + 3667 οὐ + μόνον, *ou + monon*
more than that [1]

4024 + 3836 + 5593 οὐ + ὁ + τυγχάνω, *ou + ho + tynchanō*
extraordinary [1], unusual [1]

4024 + 3900 οὐ + ὀλίγος, *ou + oligos*
some [1]

4024 + 4246 οὐ + πᾶς, *ou + pas*
no [7], no one [2], none [2], nothing [1]

4024 + 4246 + 4839 οὐ + πᾶς + ῥῆμα, *ou + pas + rhēma*
nothing [1]

4024 + 4498 οὐ + πολύς, *ou + polys*
few [2]

4024 + 4544 οὐ + ποῦ, *ou + pou*
nowhere [2]

4024 + 5515 οὐ + τίς, *ou + tis*
nothing [1]

4024 + 5516 οὐ + τὶς, *ou + tis*
nothing [1]

4025 οὐά, *oua*
aha [1]

4026 οὐαί, *ouai*
woe [40], alas [6]

4027 οὐδαμῶς, *oudamōs*
by no means [1]

4028 οὐδέ, *oude*
nor [35], or [30], not [22], not even [17], neither [13], no [6], *untranslated* [4], and no [3], and [2], and not [2], then not [2], no even [1], no one [1]

4028 + 918 + 1656 οὐδέ + ἀφίημι + εἰσέρχομαι, *oude + aphiēmi + eiserchomai*
stop [1]

4028 + 1538 οὐδέ + δύναμαι, *oude + dynamai*
cannot [2]

4028 + 4246 οὐδέ + πᾶς, *oude + pas*
no one [1]

4028 + 5516 οὐδέ + τὶς, *oude + tis*
nothing [1]

4029 οὐδείς, *oudeis*
no one [101], nothing [54], no [28], none [12], not any [6], anyone [4], not [4], *untranslated* [4], not anything [3], no any [3], no anything [2], no at all [1], no existence [1], nobody [1], not a single one [1], not a thing [1], not another [1], not anyone [1], not at all [1], not one [1], *see 1181* [disappear] [1], *see 3357* [scorn] [1], *see 6067* [useless] [1]

4029 + 4799 οὐδείς + πώποτε, *oudeis + pōpote*
never [1]

4030 οὐδέποτε, *oudepote*
never [14], never even [1], nothing ever [1]

4031 οὐδέπω, *oudepō*
not yet [3], no ever [1]

4033 οὐκέτι, *ouketi*
no longer [31], not any more [3], no more [2], not again [2], anymore [1], never again [1], no further [1], not [1], not after that [1], not any longer [1]

4033 + 4024 + 3590 οὐκέτι + οὐ + μή, *ouketi + ou + mē*
never again [2]

4033 + 4246 οὐκέτι + πᾶς, *ouketi + pas*
none ever [1]

4034 οὐκοῦν, *oukoun*
so [1]

4036 οὖν, *oun*
then [149], *untranslated* [115], so [102], therefore [84], now [22], since [5], and [3], but [3], thus [3], meanwhile [2], as [1], hence [1], however [1], in fact [1], indeed [1], reason¹ [1], so that [1], so then [1], the [1], while [1], *see 726* [accordingly] [1]

4037 οὔπω, *oupō*
not yet [18], still not [2], never [1], no ever [1], no yet [1], not [1], still no [2], still to come [1]

4038 οὐρά, *oura*
tail [5]

4039 οὐράνιος, *ouranios*
heavenly [8], heaven [1]

4040 οὐρανόθεν, *ouranothen*
from heaven [2]

4041 οὐρανός, *ouranos*
heaven [252], air [9], sky [8], heavenly [1], heavenly thing [1], *see 1666* [heavenly] [1], *untranslated* [1]

4042 Οὐρβανός, *Ourbanos*
Urbanus [1]

4043 Οὐρίας, *Ourias*
Uriah [1]

4044 οὖς, *ous*
ear [32], hear [1], *see 1181* [hear] [1], *see 1650* [whisper] [1], *see 3281* [whisper] [1]

4045 οὐσία, *ousia*
property [2]

4046 οὔτε, *oute*
nor [27], neither [16], or [16], *untranslated* [8], not [4], no [3], and [2], either [2], and no [1], no more [1], no way [1], none [1], refuse [1], whether [1]

4046 + 1538 οὔτε + δύναμαι, *oute + dynamai*
cannot [1]

4046 + 4537 οὔτε + ποτέ, *oute + pote*
never [1]

4046 + 4799 οὔτε + πώποτε, *oute + pōpote*
never [1]

4047 οὗτος, *houtos*
this [831], *untranslated* [113], this thing [95], that [54], he [52], this man [39], they [35], *see 1328* [reason] [29], *see 1328* [therefore] [24], she [11], it [9], one [6], very² [6], this fellow [5], *see 1328* [so] [5], *see 1650* [purpose] [5], same [4], this way [4], what [4], thing [3], who [3], Jesus [3], as [2], matter [2], present³ [2], sometimes [2], such [2], such a person [2], such a thing [2], this person [2], this woman [2], *see 1650* [reason] [2], *see 1877* [here] [2], Christ [1], Timothy [1], faith [1], follow [1], last¹ [1], life [1], man [1], one's own [1], other [1], person¹ [1], reason¹ [1], then [1], thus [1], *see 505* [reason] [1], *see 1328* [that] [1], *see 1328* [then] [1], *see 1877* [therefore] [1], *see 1877* [thus] [1], *see 2093* [just then] [1], *see 2093* [purpose] [1], *see 3552* [late] [1], *see 4574* [recently] [1]

4047 + 5920 οὗτος + χάριν, *houtos + charin*
reason¹ [2]

4048 οὕτως, *houtōs*
so [99], *untranslated* [23], this way [17], like this [6], same way [6], such [6], this [6], as [5], thus [5], even so [2], how [2], just so [2], only [2], same [2], such a way [2], that [2], then [2], way [2], as follows [1], different kind [1], enough [1], even then [1], exactly [1], hence [1], in this term [1], kind¹ [1], like¹ [1], manner [1], match [1], point¹ [1], so much [1], such a thing [1], they [1], this point [1], true [1]

4049 οὐχί, *ouchi*
not [44], no [7], instead [1], *untranslated* [1]

4049 + 3590 οὐχί + μή, *ouchi + mē*
not [1]

4050 ὀφειλέτης, *opheiletēs*
debtor [3], owe [2], obliged [1], offender [1]

4051 ὀφειλή, *opheilē*
debt [1], due¹ [1], right³ [1]

4052 ὀφείλημα, *opheilēma*
debt [1], due¹ [1]

4053 ὀφείλω, *opheilō*
ought [14], owe [7], must [3], should [3], bind by oath [2], debt [2], have to [2], indebted [1], need [1]

4054 ὄφελον, *ophelon*
wish [4]

4055 ὄφελος, *ophelos*
good [2], gain [1]

4056 ὀφθαλμοδουλία, *ophthalmodoulia*
watch [2]

4057 ὀφθαλμός, *ophthalmos*
eye [88], *see 2048* [look up] [6], sight [1], *see 149* [look] [1], *see 2048* [look around] [1], *untranslated* [1]

4057 + 4505 ὀφθαλμός + πονηρός, *ophthalmos + ponēros*
envious [1], envy [1]

4058 ὄφις, *ophis*
serpent [9], snake [5]

4059 ὀφρῦς, *ophrys*
brow [1]

4061 ὀχλέω, *ochleō*
torment [1]

4062 ὀχλοποιέω, *ochlopoieō*
form a mob [1]

4063 ὄχλος, *ochlos*
crowd [165], multitude [4], people [4], many [1], mob [1]

4065 ὀχύρωμα, *ochyrōma*
stronghold [1]

4066 ὀψάριον, *opsarion*
fish [5]

4067 ὀψέ, opse
evening [2], after [1]

4068 ὀψία, opsia
evening [14]

4069 ὄψιμος, opsimos
late [1]

4070 ὄψιος, opsios
late [1]

4071 ὄψις, opsis
face [2], appearance [1]

4072 ὀψώνιον, opsōnion
wage[2] [2], expense [1], support [1]

4074 παγιδεύω, pagideuō
entrap [1]

4075 παγίς, pagis
snare [3], trap [2]

4077 πάθημα, pathēma
suffer[1] [14], passion [2]

4078 παθητός, pathētos
suffer[1] [1]

4079 πάθος, pathos
passion [3]

4080 παιδαγωγός, paidagōgos
disciplinarian [2], guardian [1]

4081 παιδάριον, paidarion
boy [1]

4082 παιδεία, paideia
discipline [5], train [1]

4083 παιδευτής, paideutēs
corrector [1], discipline [1]

4084 παιδεύω, paideuō
discipline [5], flog [2], correct [1],
educate [1], instruct [1], learn [1],
punish [1], train [1]

4085 παιδιόθεν, paidiothen
childhood [1]

4086 παιδίον, paidion
child [41], little child [9], little boy [1],
she [1]

4087 παιδίσκη, paidiskē
servant-girl [4], slave [4], slave woman [2],
maid [1], slave-girl [1], woman [1]

4089 παίζω, paizō
play [1]

4090 παῖς, pais
servant [13], child [5], boy [4], slave [1],
slave man [1]

4091 παίω, paiō
strike [4], sting [1]

4093 πάλαι, palai
long ago [4], all along [1], past [1], some
time [1]

4094 παλαιός, palaios
old[3] [19]

4095 παλαιότης, palaiotēs
old[3] [1]

4096 παλαιόω, palaioō
wear out [2], make obsolete [1],
obsolete [1]

4097 πάλη, palē
struggle [1]

4098 παλιγγενεσία, palingenesia
rebirth [1], renewal [1]

4099 πάλιν, palin
again [115], untranslated [5], back [4],
once more [2], see 3306 [repeat] [2],
afterwards [1], also [1], another [1], fall

back [1], now [1], once again [1],
return [1], then [1], yet [1], see 599
[return] [1], see 1656 [return] [1], see
3357 [remind] [1]

**4099 + 540 πάλιν + ἄνωθεν, palin +
anōthen**
again [1]

4101 παμπληθεί, pamplēthei
all together [1]

4103 Παμφυλία, Pamphylia
Pamphylia [5]

4106 πανδοχεῖον, pandocheion
inn [1]

4107 πανδοχεύς, pandocheus
innkeeper [1]

4108 πανήγυρις, panēgyris
festal gathering [1]

4109 πανοικεί, panoikei
entire household [1]

4110 πανοπλία, panoplia
whole armor [2], armor [1]

4111 πανουργία, panourgia
craftiness [3], cunning [2]

4112 πανοῦργος, panourgos
crafty [1]

4114 πανταχῇ, pantachē
everywhere [1]

4116 πανταχοῦ, pantachou
everywhere [6], untranslated [1]

4117 παντελής, pantelēs
all time [1], see 1650 [quite] [1]

4118 πάντη, pantē
every way [1]

4119 πάντοθεν, pantothen
all sides [1], every quarter [1], every
side [1]

4120 παντοκράτωρ, pantokratōr
almighty [10]

4121 πάντοτε, pantote
always [36], all time [2], constantly [2],
forever [1]

4122 πάντως, pantōs
at all [2], all [1], by all means [1],
certainly [1], doubtless [1], entirely [1],
must [1]

4123 παρά, para
from [59], with [21], untranslated [14],
by [13], than [13], at [9], for [7], on [6],
among [4], beside [4], contrary [4], of [4],
presence [3], along [2], any less [2],
before [2], beyond [2], do [2], in [2],
rather [2], sight [2], aside [1], better
than [1], by one's side [1], come from [1],
family [1], have [1], minus [1], more
than [1], near [1], opposition [1], part[1] [1],
provide [1], send [1], shore [1], speak [1],
too[2] [1]

**4123 + 5882 παρά + φύσις, para +
physis**
unnatural [1]

4124 παραβαίνω, parabainō
break [2], turn aside [1]

4125 παραβάλλω, paraballō
touch [1]

4126 παράβασις, parabasis
transgression [4], break [1],
transgressor [1], violation [1]

4127 παραβάτης, parabatēs
transgressor [3], break [2]

4128 παραβιάζομαι, parabiazomai
prevail upon [1], urge strongly [1]

4129 παραβολεύομαι, paraboleuomai
risk [1]

4130 παραβολή, parabolē
parable [45], lesson [2], proverb [1], speak
figuratively [1], symbol [1]

4132 παραγγελία, parangelia
instruction [4], strict order [1]

4133 παραγγέλλω, parangellō
order[3] [13], command [9], give a
command [3], instruction [2], charge[2] [1],
direct [1], give an order [1], insist [1],
instruct [1]

4134 παραγίνομαι, paraginomai
come [18], arrive [10], go [2], appear [1],
arrival [1], come forward [1], come
here [1], come to support [1], present[4] [1],
return [1]

4135 παράγω, paragō
pass away [3], walk along [3], go on [1],
pass along [1], pass by [1], passer-by [1]

4136 παραδειγματίζω, paradeigmatizō
hold up to contempt [1]

4137 παράδεισος, paradeisos
paradise [3]

4138 παραδέχομαι, paradechomai
accept [4], adopt [1], welcome [1]

4140 παραδίδωμι, paradidōmi
hand over [43], betray [37], give up [8],
hand on [6], betrayer [5], entrust [4],
arrest [2], commend [2], commit [2],
abandon [1], deliver [1], give [1], give
over [1], pass on [1], put [1], ripe [1],
risk [1], transfer [1], turn over [1]

4141 παράδοξος, paradoxos
strange thing [1]

4142 παράδοσις, paradosis
tradition [13]

4143 παραζηλόω, parazēloō
make jealous [3], provoke to jealousy [1]

4144 παραθαλάσσιος, parathalassios
by the sea [1]

4145 παραθεωρέω, paratheōreō
neglect [1]

4146 παραθήκη, parathēkē
entrust [2], treasure entrusted [1]

4147 παραινέω, paraineō
advise [1], urge [1]

4148 παραιτέομαι, paraiteomai
refuse [3], nothing to do [2], regret [2],
ask [1], beg [1], make an excuse [1],
nothing more to do [1], try to escape [1]

4149 παρακαθέζομαι, parakathezomai
sit [1]

4151 παρακαλέω, parakaleō
urge [25], beg [17], encourage [15],
appeal [14], console [9], exhort [6],
comfort [4], plead [4], invite [2],
apologize [1], ask [1], exhortation [1],
exhorter [1], find comfort [1], give
encouragement [1], listen to an appeal [1],
make an appeal [1], preach [1],
request [1], speak [1], speak kindly [1],
untranslated [1]

4152 παρακαλύπτω, parakalyptō
conceal [1]

4154 παράκειμαι, parakeimai
can [1], lie close at hand [1]

4155 παράκλησις, *paraklēsis*
consolation [11], encouragement [6], exhortation [5], appeal [2], comfort [2], encourage [1], exhort [1], *see 3552* [earnestly] [1]

4156 παράκλητος, *paraklētos*
advocate [5]

4157 παρακοή, *parakoē*
disobedience [3]

4158 παρακολουθέω, *parakoloutheō*
accompany [1], follow [1], investigate [1], observe[2] [1]

4159 παρακούω, *parakouō*
refuse to listen [2], overhear [1]

4160 παρακύπτω, *parakyptō*
look [2], bend down [1], bend over [1]

4161 παραλαμβάνω, *paralambanō*
take [20], receive [11], take with [8], take aside [3], accept [1], bring [1], bring along [1], join [1], learn [1], take along [1], tradition [1]

4162 παραλέγομαι, *paralegomai*
sail past [2]

4163 παράλιος, *paralios*
coast [1]

4164 παραλλαγή, *parallagē*
variation [1]

4165 παραλογίζομαι, *paralogizomai*
deceive [2]

4166 παραλυτικός, *paralytikos*
paralytic [7], paralyzed man [2], paralyze [1]

4168 παραλύω, *paralyō*
paralyze [4], weak [1]

4169 παραμένω, *paramenō*
continue [2], persevere [1], stay [1]

4170 παραμυθέομαι, *paramytheomai*
console [2], encourage [2]

4171 παραμυθία, *paramythia*
consolation [1]

4172 παραμύθιον, *paramythion*
consolation [1]

4174 παρανομέω, *paranomeō*
violation of the law [1]

4175 παρανομία, *paranomia*
transgression [1]

4176 παραπικραίνω, *parapikrainō*
rebellious [1]

4177 παραπικρασμός, *parapikrasmos*
rebellion [2]

4178 παραπίπτω, *parapiptō*
fall away [1]

4179 παραπλέω, *parapleō*
sail past [1]

4180 παραπλήσιος, *paraplēsios*
nearly [1]

4181 παραπλησίως, *paraplēsiōs*
likewise [1]

4182 παραπορεύομαι, *paraporeuomai*
pass by [3], go through [1], pass through [1]

4183 παράπτωμα, *paraptōma*
trespass [16], stumble [2], transgression [1]

4184 παραρρέω, *pararreō*
drift away [1]

4185 παράσημος, *parasēmos*
figurehead [1]

4186 παρασκευάζω, *paraskeuazō*
ready [2], get ready [1], prepare [1]

4187 παρασκευή, *paraskeuē*
day of Preparation [4], preparation [2]

4189 παρατείνω, *parateinō*
continue [1]

4190 παρατηρέω, *paratēreō*
watch [4], observe[2] [1], watch closely [1]

4191 παρατήρησις, *paratērēsis*
observe[1] [1]

4192 παρατίθημι, *paratithēmi*
set before [6], entrust [4], distribute [3], commend [2], put before [2], give [1], prove [1]

4193 παρατυγχάνω, *paratynchanō*
happen to be there [1]

4194 παραυτίκα, *parautika*
momentary [1]

4195 παραφέρω, *parapherō*
remove [2], carry along [1], carry away [1]

4196 παραφρονέω, *paraphroneō*
madman [1]

4197 παραφρονία, *paraphronia*
madness [1]

4199 παραχειμάζω, *paracheimazō*
spend the winter [3], winter [1]

4200 παραχειμασία, *paracheimasia*
spend the winter [1]

4202 παραχρῆμα, *parachrēma*
immediately [13], once[2] [3], at that moment [1], without delay [1]

4203 πάρδαλις, *pardalis*
leopard [1]

4204 παρεδρεύω, *paredreuō*
serve [1]

4205 πάρειμι, *pareimi*
come [8], present[4] [8], here [3], be [1], have [1], here in presence [1], time[1] [1], *see 3590* [lack] [1]

4206 παρεισάγω, *pareisagō*
bring in secretly [1]

4207 παρείσακτος, *pareisaktos*
bring in secretly [1]

4208 παρεισδύω, *pareisdyō*
steal in [1]

4209 παρεισέρχομαι, *pareiserchomai*
come in [1], slip in [1]

4210 παρεισφέρω, *pareispherō*
make [1]

4211 παρεκτός, *parektos*
except [2], other thing [1]

4212 παρεμβάλλω, *paremballō*
set up [1]

4213 παρεμβολή, *parembolē*
barrack [6], camp [3], army [1]

4214 παρενοχλέω, *parenochleō*
trouble [1]

4215 παρεπίδημος, *parepidēmos*
exile [2], foreigner [1]

4216 παρέρχομαι, *parerchomai*
pass away [13], pass [5], pass by [3], already [1], come [1], come here [1], disappear [1], disobey [1], go by [1], late [1], neglect [1]

4217 πάρεσις, *paresis*
pass over [1]

4218 παρέχω, *parechō*
bring [2], show [2], *see 3160* [bother] [2], *see 3160* [trouble] [2], become [1], do [1], give [1], make [1], offer [1], promote [1], provide [1], treat [1]

4219 παρηγορία, *parēgoria*
comfort [1]

4220 παρθενία, *parthenia*
marriage [1]

4221 παρθένος, *parthenos*
virgin [8], bridesmaid [3], fianc‚e [3], unmarried [1]

4222 Πάρθοι, *Parthoi*
Parthian [1]

4223 παρίημι, *pariēmi*
droop [1], neglect [1]

4225 παρίστημι, *paristēmi*
present[2] [14], bystander [4], stand before [3], stand by [3], stand[1] [2], stand beside [2], stand near [2], stand nearby [2], bring close [1], bring into one's presence [1], come [1], help [1], prove [1], provide [1], send [1], show [1], take a stand [1]

4226 Παρμενᾶς, *Parmenas*
Parmenas [1]

4227 πάροδος, *parodos*
pass [1]

4228 παροικέω, *paroikeō*
stay for a time [1], stranger [1]

4229 παροικία, *paroikia*
exile [1], stay [1]

4230 πάροικος, *paroikos*
alien [2], resident alien [2]

4231 παροιμία, *paroimia*
figure of speech [3], figure [1], proverb [1]

4232 πάροινος, *paroinos*
addicted to wine [1], drunkard [1]

4233 παροίχομαι, *paroichomai*
past [1]

4234 παρομοιάζω, *paromoiazō*
like[1] [1]

4235 παρόμοιος, *paromoios*
like[1] [1]

4236 παροξύνω, *paroxynō*
distress deeply [1], irritable [1]

4237 παροξυσμός, *paroxysmos*
provoke [1], sharp disagreement [1]

4239 παροργίζω, *parorgizō*
make angry [1], provoke to anger [1]

4240 παροργισμός, *parorgismos*
anger [1]

4241 παροτρύνω, *parotrynō*
incite [1]

4242 παρουσία, *parousia*
come [21], presence [2], arrival [1]

4243 παροψίς, *paropsis*
plate [1]

4244 παρρησία, *parrēsia*
boldness [13], confidence [4], openly [4], plainly [4], boast [1], bold [1], confidently [1], know widely [1], public [1], quite openly [1]

4245 παρρησιάζομαι, *parrēsiazomai*
speak boldly [5], courage [1], declare boldly [1], freely [1], speak out boldly [1]

4246 πᾶς, pas
all [675], every [122], all things [89], everything [74], everyone [72], whole [32], any [15], *untranslated* [12], every way [10], all kinds [8], entire [8], *see 4024* [no] [7], every kind [6], whatever [6], full [5], anyone [4], utmost [4], *see 1328* [continually] [4], all people [3], always [3], anything [3], *see 1328* [always] [3], *see 4024* [nothing] [3], complete [2], fully [2], that [2], whoever [2], *see 3590* [no] [2], *see 4024* [no one] [2], *see 4024* [none] [2], a [1], absolute [1], all mortals [1], all time [1], altogether [1], any kind [1], any way [1], as a whole [1], every time [1], great [1], none [1], nothing but [1], one [1], someone [1], throughout [1], universal [1], very[1] [1], who [1], whole body [1], you [1], *see 1328* [constantly] [1], *see 1328* [forever] [1], *see 1650* [forever] [1], *see 1651* [everyone] [1], *see 1877* [securely] [1], *see 1967* [publicly] [1], *see 4028* [no one] [1], *see 4033* [none ever] [1], *see 5082* [eagerly] [1]

4246 + 476 πᾶς + ἄνθρωπος, pas + anthrōpos
everyone [12], all [8]

4246 + 3836 + 2465 πᾶς + ὁ + ἡμέρα, pas + ho + hēmera
always [1]

4246 + 4005 + 5516 + 1569 πᾶς + ὅς + τὶς + ἐάν, pas + hos + tis + ean
whatever [1]

4246 + 4012 πᾶς + ὅσος, pas + hosos
whatever [1]

4246 + 4012 + 323 πᾶς + ὅσος + ἄν, pas + hosos + an
whatever [1]

4246 + 4012 + 1569 πᾶς + ὅσος + ἐάν, pas + hosos + ean
whatever [1]

4246 + 4547 πᾶς + πρᾶγμα, pas + pragma
anything [1]

4246 + 4922 πᾶς + σάρξ, pas + sarx
one [1]

4246 + 6034 πᾶς + ψυχή, pas + psychē
everyone [3]

4246 + 6034 + 476 πᾶς + ψυχή + ἄνθρωπος, pas + psychē + anthrōpos
everyone [1]

4247 πάσχα, pascha
passover [22], passover meal [4], passover lamb [2], paschal lamb [1]

4248 πάσχω, paschō
suffer[1] [35], undergo suffering [3], endure [1], endure suffering [1], experience [1], go through suffering [1]

4249 Πάταρα, Patara
Patara [1]

4250 πατάσσω, patassō
strike [6], strike down [3], tap [1]

4251 πατέω, pateō
tread [3], trample [1], trample on [1]

4252 πατήρ, patēr
father [350], ancestor [55], parent [4], patriarch [3], *untranslated* [1]

4253 Πάτμος, Patmos
Patmos [1]

4255 πατριά, patria
family [3]

4256 πατριάρχης, patriarchēs
patriarch [3], ancestor [1]

4257 πατρικός, patrikos
ancestor [1]

4258 πατρίς, patris
hometown [5], country [1], homeland [1], one's own country [1]

4259 Πατροβᾶς, Patrobas
Patrobas [1]

4260 πατρολῴας, patrolōas
kill one's father [1]

4261 πατροπαράδοτος, patroparadotos
inherit from ancestor [1]

4262 πατρῷος, patrōos
ancestor [2], ancestral [1]

4263 Παῦλος, Paulos
Paul [157], Paulus [1]

4264 παύω, pauō
cease [8], finish [3], stop [3], keep [1]

4265 Πάφος, Paphos
Paphos [2]

4266 παχύνω, pachynō
grow dull [2]

4267 πέδη, pedē
shackle [3]

4268 πεδινός, pedinos
level [1]

4269 πεζεύω, pezeuō
go by land [1]

4270 πεζῇ, pezē
on foot [2]

4272 πειθαρχέω, peitharcheō
obey [2], listen [1], obedient [1]

4273 πειθός, peithos
plausible [1]

4275 πείθω, peithō
convince [8], persuade [8], confident [6], trust [5], sure [4], obey [3], follow [2], win over [2], certain [1], confidence [1], feel confident [1], have confidence [1], make confident [1], pay attention [1], persuasively [1], reason for confidence [1], reassure [1], rely [1], satisfy [1], seek approval [1], urge [1], *untranslated* [1]

4277 πεινάω, peinaō
hungry [17], famish [2], go hungry [2], hunger [2]

4278 πεῖρα, peira
attempt [1]

4278 + 3284 πεῖρα + λαμβάνω, peira + lambanō
suffer[2] [1]

4279 πειράζω, peirazō
test [15], tempt [10], put to the test [6], attempt [2], tempter [2], do [1], examine [1], try[1] [1]

4280 πειρασμός, peirasmos
test [6], time of trial [6], trial [6], temptation [2], put to the test [1]

4281 πειράω, peiraō
try[1] [1]

4282 πεισμονή, peismonē
persuasion [1]

4283 πέλαγος, pelagos
depth [1], sea [1]

4284 πελεκίζω, pelekizō
behead [1]

4286 πέμπτος, pemptos
fifth [4]

4287 πέμπω, pempō
send [76], use [2], exchange [1]

4288 πένης, penēs
poor [1]

4289 πενθερά, penthera
mother-in-law [6]

4290 πενθερός, pentheros
father-in-law [1]

4291 πενθέω, pentheō
mourn [10]

4292 πένθος, penthos
mourn [3], grief [2]

4293 πενιχρός, penichros
poor [1]

4294 πεντάκις, pentakis
five times [1]

4295 πεντακισχίλιοι, pentakischilioi
five thousand [6]

4296 πεντακόσιοι, pentakosioi
five hundred [2]

4297 πέντε, pente
five [35], *see 1573* [seventy-five] [1], *see 1633* [three miles] [1], *see 3689* [fifty thousand] [1]

4298 πεντεκαιδέκατος, pentekaidekatos
fifteenth [1]

4299 πεντήκοντα, pentēkonta
fifty [6]

4299 + 5552 πεντήκοντα + τρεῖς, pentēkonta + treis
fifty-three [1]

4300 πεντηκοστή, pentēkostē
Pentecost [3]

4301 πεποίθησις, pepoithēsis
confidence [3], reason for confidence [1], sure [1], *untranslated* [1]

4304 περαιτέρω, peraiterō
further [1]

4305 πέραν, peran
other side [13], across [6], beyond [4]

4306 πέρας, peras
end [4]

4307 Πέργαμος, Pergamos
Pergamum [2]

4308 Πέργη, Pergē
Perga [3]

4309 περί, peri
about[1] [113], for [50], of [28], *untranslated* [27], concerning [25], behalf [15], around [14], to [12], about[3] [7], against [3], as for [3], case [3], how [3], on [3], with [3], at [2], because [2], by [2], in [2], offering [2], regard [2], about[4] [1], as to [1], charge[3] [1], companion [1], deal [1], discuss [1], from [1], neighborhood [1], respect[2] [1], surround [1], trade [1], welfare [1]

4310 περιάγω, periagō
go about [3], accompany [1], cross [1], go throughout [1]

4311 περιαιρέω, periaireō
abandon [1], cast off [1], remove [1], take away [1], weigh anchor [1]

4312 περιάπτω, periaptō
kindle [1]

4313 περιαστράπτω, periastraptō
flash around [1], shine about [1]

4314 περιβάλλω, periballō
clothe [9], dress [3], give clothing [3],
wear [3], put on [1], wrap [1], wrap
around [1]

4314 + 5124 περιβάλλω + στολή,
periballō + stolē
robe [2]

4315 περιβλέπω, periblepō
look around [5], look [1], look all
around [1]

4316 περιβόλαιον, peribolaion
cloak [1], cover [1]

4317 περιδέω, perideō
wrap [1]

4318 περιεργάζομαι, periergazomai
busybody [1]

4319 περίεργος, periergos
busybody [1], magic art [1]

4320 περιέρχομαι, perierchomai
gad about [1], go about [1], itinerant [1]

4321 περιέχω, periechō
stand¹ [1], see 2502 [amaze] [1]

4322 περιζώννυμι, perizōnnymi
across [2], fasten belt [1], fasten belt
around [1], put on an apron [1]

4322 + 3836 + 4019 περιζώννυμι + ὁ +
ὀσφῦς, perizōnnymi + ho + osphys
dress for action [1]

4324 περίθεσις, perithesis
wear [1]

4325 περιΐστημι, periistēmi
avoid [2], stand¹ [1], surround [1]

4326 περικάθαρμα, perikatharma
rubbish [1]

4328 περικαλύπτω, perikalyptō
blindfold [1], overlay [1]

4328 + 3836 + 4725 περικαλύπτω + ὁ
+ πρόσωπον, perikalyptō + ho +
prosōpon
blindfold [1]

4329 περίκειμαι, perikeimai
bind [1], hang [1], hang around [1],
subject [1], surround [1]

4330 περικεφαλαία, perikephalaia
helmet [2]

4331 περικρατής, perikratēs
under control [1]

4332 περικρύβω, perikrybō
remain in seclusion [1]

4333 περικυκλόω, perikykloō
surround [1]

4334 περιλάμπω, perilampō
shine around [2]

4335 περιλείπομαι, perileipomai
leave [2]

4337 περίλυπος, perilypos
grieve deeply [3], sad [1], untranslated [1]

4338 περιμένω, perimenō
wait¹ [1]

4339 πέριξ, perix
around [1]

4340 περιοικέω, perioikeō
neighbor [1]

4341 περίοικος, perioikos
neighbor [1]

4342 περιούσιος, periousios
own² [1]

4343 περιοχή, periochē
passage [1]

4344 περιπατέω, peripateō
walk [51], live [15], go about [4], lead a
life [4], behave [2], conduct [2],
observe² [2], walk about [2], walk
around [2], act [1], do [1], follow [1],
go [1], live a life [1], practice [1], prowl
around [1], walk along [1], walk by [1],
way of life [1], untranslated [1]

4345 περιπείρω, peripeirō
pierce [1]

4346 περιπίπτω, peripiptō
face [1], fall into [1], strike [1]

4347 περιποιέω, peripoieō
gain [1], make secure [1], obtain [1]

4348 περιποίησις, peripoiēsis
obtain [2], own² [2]

4348 + 6034 περιποίησις + ψυχή,
peripoiēsis + psychē
save [1]

4351 περιρήγνυμι, perirēgnymi
strip [1]

4352 περισπάω, perispaō
distract [1]

4353 περισσεία, perisseia
abundance [1], abundant [1], rank
growth [1], see 1650 [greatly] [1]

4354 περίσσευμα, perisseuma
abundance [4], leave over [1]

4355 περισσεύω, perisseuō
abound [6], excel [4], leave over [4],
abundance [3], overflow [3], abundant [2],
do much [2], have plenty [2], increase [2],
abundantly [1], enough and to spare [1],
exceed [1], have abundance [1], have an
abundance [1], have more than enough [1],
lavish [1], leave [1], provide in
abundance [1], share abundantly [1], well
off [1]

4356 περισσός, perissos
more [2], abundantly [1], advantage [1],
not necessary [1], see 3336 [utterly] [1]

4358 περισσότερος, perissoteros
great [5], more [4], even more [1],
excessive [1], hard [1], more clearly [1],
much more [1], too much [1],
zealously [1]

4359 περισσοτέρως, perissoterōs
all the more [3], great [3], far more [2],
more [2], abundant [1], far greater [1]

4360 περισσῶς, perissōs
all the more [2], greatly [1], so [1]

4361 περιστερά, peristera
dove [9], pigeon [1]

4362 περιτέμνω, peritemnō
circumcise [16], circumcision [1]

4363 περιτίθημι, peritithēmi
put on [5], put around [2], clothe [1]

4364 περιτομή, peritomē
circumcision [21], circumcise [14],
circumcision faction [1]

4365 περιτρέπω, peritrepō
drive [1]

4366 περιτρέχω, peritrechō
rush about [1]

4367 περιφέρω, peripherō
blow about [1], bring [1], carry [1]

4368 περιφρονέω, periphroneō
look down [1]

4369 περίχωρος, perichōros
surrounding country [4], region [2], region
along [1], region around [1], surrounding
region [1]

4370 περίψημα, peripsēma
dregs [1]

4371 περπερεύομαι, perpereuomai
boastful [1]

4372 Περσίς, Persis
Persis [1]

4373 πέρυσι, perysi
last year [2]

4374 πετεινόν, peteinon
bird [14]

4375 πέτομαι, petomai
fly [5]

4376 πέτρα, petra
rock [15]

4377 Πέτρος, Petros
Peter [155]

4378 πετρώδης, petrōdēs
rocky ground [4]

4379 πήγανον, pēganon
rue [1]

4380 πηγή, pēgē
spring [8], well⁴ [2]

4380 + 135 πηγή + αἷμα, pēgē + haima
hemorrhage [1]

4381 πήγνυμι, pēgnymi
set up [1]

4382 πηδάλιον, pēdalion
rudder [1], steering-oar [1]

4383 πηλίκος, pēlikos
how great [1], large [1]

4384 πηλός, pēlos
mud [5], clay [1]

4385 πήρα, pēra
bag [6]

4388 πῆχυς, pēchys
hour [2], cubit [1], see 1357 [hundred
yards] [1]

4389 πιάζω, piazō
arrest [6], catch [2], seize [2], capture [1],
take [1]

4390 πιέζω, piezō
press down [1]

4391 πιθανολογία, pithanologia
plausible argument [1]

4393 πικραίνω, pikrainō
make bitter [2], bitter [1], treat harshly [1]

4394 πικρία, pikria
bitterness [4]

4395 πικρός, pikros
bitter [1], brackish [1]

4396 πικρῶς, pikrōs
bitterly [2]

4397 Πιλᾶτος, Pilatos
Pilate [54], he [1]

4398 πίμπλημι, *pimplēmi*
fill [18], come [3], end [1], fulfillment [1],
pass [1]

4399 πίμπρημι, *pimprēmi*
swell up [1]

4400 πινακίδιον, *pinakidion*
writing tablet [1]

4402 πίναξ, *pinax*
platter [4], dish [1]

4403 πίνω, *pinō*
drink [73]

4404 πιότης, *piotēs*
rich [1]

4405 πιπράσκω, *pipraskō*
sell [8], sell into slavery [1]

4406 πίπτω, *piptō*
fall [69], fall down [8], bow to the
ground [1], come [1], drop [1], end [1],
kneel [1], kneel down [1], strike [1],
throw [1]

**4406 + 2093 + 4725 πίπτω + ἐπί +
πρόσωπον, *piptō + epi + prosōpon***
bow down [1], prostrate [1], throw oneself
on the ground [1]

4407 Πισιδία, *Pisidia*
Pisidia [1]

4408 Πισίδιος, *Pisidios*
Pisidia [1]

4409 πιστεύω, *pisteuō*
believe [205], believer [22], entrust [8],
faith [4], put one's trust [1], trust [1]

4410 πιστικός, *pistikos*
pure [1], *untranslated* [1]

4411 πίστις, *pistis*
faith [231], believe [4], faithfulness [2],
assurance [1], belief [1], fidelity [1],
pledge [1], *untranslated* [1]

4411 + 2400 πίστις + ἔχω, *pistis + echō*
believe [1]

4412 πιστός, *pistos*
faithful [37], trustworthy [10], believer [6],
believe [5], sure [5], believing woman [1],
faithful one [1], promise [1], trust [1]

4413 πιστόω, *pistoō*
believe firmly [1]

4414 πλανάω, *planaō*
deceive [17], lead astray [8], go astray [6],
wrong [3], wander [2], beguile [1],
deceiver [1], wayward [1]

4415 πλάνη, *planē*
error [5], deceit [1], deceitful [1],
deception [1], delusion [1], wander [1]

4417 πλανήτης, *planētēs*
wander [1]

4418 πλάνος, *planos*
deceiver [2], impostor [2], deceitful [1]

4419 πλάξ, *plax*
tablet [3]

4420 πλάσμα, *plasma*
mold [1]

4421 πλάσσω, *plassō*
form [1], mold [1]

4422 πλαστός, *plastos*
deceptive [1]

4423 πλατεῖα, *plateia*
street [9]

4424 πλάτος, *platos*
breadth [2], width [2]

4425 πλατύνω, *platynō*
open wide [2], make broad [1]

4426 πλατύς, *platys*
wide [1]

4427 πλέγμα, *plegma*
braided hair [1]

4428 πλέκω, *plekō*
twist [2], weave [1]

4429 πλεονάζω, *pleonazō*
increase [4], abound [1], accumulate [1],
extend [1], have too much [1], multiply [1]

4430 πλεονεκτέω, *pleonekteō*
take advantage [3], exploit [1], outwit [1]

4431 πλεονέκτης, *pleonektēs*
greedy [4]

4432 πλεονεξία, *pleonexia*
greed [6], avarice [1], covetousness [1],
extortion [1], greedy [1]

4433 πλευρά, *pleura*
side [5]

4434 πλέω, *pleō*
sail [3], bound for [1], set sail [1], *see
2093* [seafarer] [1]

4435 πληγή, *plēgē*
plague [13], wound [4], beat [2], flog [2]

**4435 + 2202 πληγή + ἐπιτίθημι, *plēgē
+ epitithēmi***
beat [1]

4436 πλῆθος, *plēthos*
multitude [6], assembly [4], many [4],
number [3], community [2],
congregation [2], crowd [2], great
number [2], bundle [1], people [1],
resident [1], whole community [1], whole
group [1], *untranslated* [1]

4437 πληθύνω, *plēthynō*
abundance [3], multiply [3], increase [2],
increase in number [2], gain adherent [1],
untranslated [1]

4438 πλήκτης, *plēktēs*
violent [2]

4439 πλήμμυρα, *plēmmyra*
flood [1]

4440 πλήν, *plēn*
but [12], yet [5], only [3], except [2],
nevertheless [2], besides [1], however [1],
in any case [1], instead [1], just[1] [1],
so [1], than [1]

4441 πλήρης, *plērēs*
full [12], cover [1], devote [1], fill [1], *see
2596* [enrage] [1]

4442 πληροφορέω, *plērophoreō*
convince fully [2], assure fully [1], carry
out fully [1], fulfill [1], proclaim fully [1]

4443 πληροφορία, *plērophoria*
full assurance [2], assure [1],
conviction [1]

4444 πληρόω, *plēroō*
fulfill [37], fill [18], complete [9],
pass [3], accomplish [2], finish [2], make
complete [2], satisfy fully [2], be [1],
come fully [1], come to fullness [1], fill
up [1], full [1], make full [1], make fully
known [1], perfect [1], proclaim fully [1],
produce [1], sum up [1]

4445 πλήρωμα, *plērōma*
fullness [8], full [3], patch [2], fulfill [1],
full inclusion [1], full number [1], fullness
of God [1]

4446 πλησίον, *plēsion*
neighbor [16], near [1]

**4447 + 3836 + 4922 πλησμονή + ὁ +
σάρξ, *plēsmonē + ho + sarx***
self-indulgence [1]

4448 πλήσσω, *plēssō*
strike [1]

4449 πλοιάριον, *ploiarion*
boat [5]

4450 πλοῖον, *ploion*
boat [45], ship [22]

4452 πλόος, *ploos*
voyage [2], sail [1]

4454 πλούσιος, *plousios*
rich [22], rich person [4], rich man [2]

4455 πλουσίως, *plousiōs*
richly [4]

4456 πλουτέω, *plouteō*
rich [7], grow rich [2], gain wealth [1],
generous [1], prosper [1]

4457 πλουτίζω, *ploutizō*
enrich [2], make rich [1]

4458 πλοῦτος, *ploutos*
riches [16], wealth [6]

4459 πλύνω, *plynō*
wash [3]

4460 πνεῦμα, *pneuma*
spirit [364], breath [3], ghost [2],
mind[1] [2], wind [2], enthusiasm [1],
spiritual [1], spiritual gift [1],
spiritually [1], *see 918* [breathe one's
last] [1], *untranslated* [1]

4461 πνευματικός, *pneumatikos*
spiritual [15], one who is spiritual [2],
spiritual gift [2], receive the Spirit [1],
spiritual blessing [1], spiritual force [1],
spiritual good [1], spiritual person [1],
spiritual power [1], spiritual thing [1]

4462 πνευματικῶς, *pneumatikōs*
prophetically [1], spiritually [1]

4463 πνέω, *pneō*
blow [6], wind [1]

4464 πνίγω, *pnigō*
choke [1], drown [1], throat [1]

4465 πνικτός, *pniktos*
strangle [3]

4466 πνοή, *pnoē*
breath [1], wind [1]

4468 ποδήρης, *podērēs*
long robe [1]

4470 πόθεν, *pothen*
where from [15], where [8], how [2],
untranslated [2], from what [1], why [1]

4472 ποιέω, *poieō*
do [317], make [88], bear[1] [13], give [11],
perform [11], act [8], commit [8],
practice [6], show [6], keep [5], cause [4],
obey [4], work [4], *untranslated* [4],
appoint [3], be [3], carry out [3],
claim [3], execute [3], treat [3], yield [3],
see 3644 [remember] [3], bring [2],
create [2], exercise [2], follow [2],
grant [2], join [2], prepare [2],
produce [2], put [2], spend [2], *see 1255*
[pray] [2], accomplish [1], adrift [1],
become [1], begin [1], change [1],
divide [1], guilty [1], hold [1], marry [1],
observe[2] [1], plan [1], promote [1],
provide [1], put forth [1], see [1],
share [1], stay [1], task [1], with [1],

write [1], *see 1010* [confirm] [1], *see 1316* [betray] [1], *see 2180* [stir up] [1], *see 2653* [satisfy] [1], *see 2805* [criminal] [1], *see 3391* [redeem] [1], *see 3644* [mention] [1], *see 3647* [recall] [1], *see 4533* [sweep away with the flood] [1], *see 5618* [heal] [1]

4472 + 490 ποιέω + ἀνομία, *poieō + anomia*
evildoer [1]

4472 + 1689 ποιέω + ἐκδίκησις, *poieō + ekdikēsis*
avenge [1]

4472 + 3364 ποιέω + λόγος, *poieō + logos*
count [1]

4473 ποίημα, *poiēma*
make [1], make a thing [1]

4474 ποίησις, *poiēsis*
do [1]

4475 ποιητής, *poiētēs*
doer [5], poet [1]

4476 ποικίλος, *poikilos*
various [5], all kinds [2], any kind [1], manifold [1], various kinds [1]

4477 ποιμαίνω, *poimainō*
rule[1] [3], shepherd [3], tend [3], feed [1], tend sheep [1]

4478 ποιμήν, *poimēn*
shepherd [17], pastor [1]

4479 ποίμνη, *poimnē*
flock [4], it [1]

4480 ποίμνιον, *poimnion*
flock [5]

4481 ποῖος, *poios*
what [21], which [4], kind[1] [3], what kind [2], way [1], what thing [1], *untranslated* [1]

4482 πολεμέω, *polemeō*
make war [3], fight [2], conflict [1], fight back [1]

4483 πόλεμος, *polemos*
war [12], battle [5], conflict [1]

4484 πόλις, *polis*
city [121], town [40], *see 2848* [town after town] [1]

4485 πολιτάρχης, *politarchēs*
city authority [1], city official [1]

4486 πολιτεία, *politeia*
citizenship [1], commonwealth [1]

4487 πολίτευμα, *politeuma*
citizenship [1]

4488 πολιτεύομαι, *politeuomai*
live a life [2]

4489 πολίτης, *politēs*
citizen [3], another [1]

4490 πολλάκις, *pollakis*
often [12], again and again [3], frequent [1], many [1], repeatedly [1]

4491 πολλαπλασίων, *pollaplasiōn*
very much more [1]

4494 πολυλογία, *polylogia*
many words [1]

4495 πολυμερῶς, *polymerōs*
many ways [1]

4497 πολυποίκιλος, *polypoikilos*
rich variety [1]

4498 πολύς, *polys*
many [187], great [53], much [36], more [24], large [13], many things [11], most [8], long[1] [6], *untranslated* [5], even [3], further [3], great deal [3], hard [3], often [3], severe [3], greatly [2], large sum [2], majority [2], plentiful [2], several [2], very large [2], *see 4024* [few] [2], abundant [1], ample [1], bitterly [1], considerable [1], earnestly [1], enough [1], freely [1], full [1], generously [1], great number [1], great quantity [1], how much [1], late [1], loud [1], loudly [1], many in number [1], more acceptable [1], more and more people [1], more than ever [1], much heavy [1], numerous [1], quite [1], repeatedly [1], solemnly [1], some [1], sternly [1], strictly [1], strongly [1], terribly [1], too much [1], very hard [1], violent [1], warmly [1], *see 247* [contrary] [1], *see 3552* [earnestly] [1], *see 3552* [soon] [1], *see 3885* [drink] [1], *see 5084* [far] [1], *see 6052* [late] [1]

4498 + 3437 πολύς + μᾶλλον, *polys + mallon*
far [1]

4498 + 5989 πολύς + χρόνος, *polys + chronos*
long[1] [1]

4499 πολύσπλαγχνος, *polysplanchnos*
compassionate [1]

4500 πολυτελής, *polytelēs*
expensive [1], very costly [1], very precious [1]

4501 πολύτιμος, *polytimos*
costly [1], great value [1], more precious [1]

4502 πολυτρόπως, *polytropōs*
various ways [1]

4503 πόμα, *poma*
drink [2]

4504 πονηρία, *ponēria*
evil [3], wickedness [2], malice [1], wicked way [1]

4505 πονηρός, *ponēros*
evil [40], evil one [12], wicked [5], bad [3], evil thing [3], more evil [2], base[2] [1], crime [1], evildoer [1], false [1], not healthy [1], painful [1], ruffian [1], serious [1], unhealthy [1], wicked person [1], *see 1675* [defame] [1], *see 4057* [envious] [1], *see 4057* [envy] [1]

4506 πόνος, *ponos*
pain [2], agony [1], work [1]

4507 Ποντικός, *Pontikos*
Pontus [1]

4508 Πόντιος, *Pontios*
Pontius [3]

4510 Πόντος, *Pontos*
Pontus [2]

4511 Πόπλιος, *Poplios*
Publius [2]

4512 πορεία, *poreia*
busy life [1], way [1]

4513 πορεύομαι, *poreuomai*
go [109], go on one's way [5], on one's way [5], *untranslated* [4], go away [3], live [3], go on [2], go out [2], indulge [2], leave [2], depart [1], follow [1], go along [1], go off [1], proceed on a journey [1], ride along [1], set[1] [1], set

out [1], start on one's way [1], travel [1], walk [1], way [1]

4513 + 608 πορεύομαι + ἀπό, *poreuomai + apo*
leave [1]

4513 + 2848 πορεύομαι + κατά, *poreuomai + kata*
indulge [1]

4513 + 3958 πορεύομαι + ὀπίσω, *poreuomai + opisō*
indulge [1]

4513 + 5250 πορεύομαι + σύν, *poreuomai + syn*
accompany [1]

4514 πορθέω, *portheō*
destroy [2], make havoc [1]

4516 πορισμός, *porismos*
gain [1], means of gain [1]

4517 Πόρκιος, *Porkios*
Porcius [1]

4518 πορνεία, *porneia*
fornication [18], sexual immorality [3], unchastity [2], illegitimate [1], *untranslated* [1]

4519 πορνεύω, *porneuō*
commit fornication [3], practice fornication [2], do [1], fornicator [1], indulge in sexual immorality [1]

4520 πόρνη, *pornē*
prostitute [7], whore [5]

4521 πόρνος, *pornos*
fornicator [6], immoral [1], immoral person [1], sexually immoral [1], sexually immoral person [1]

4522 πόρρω, *porrō*
far [2], far away [1], on [1]

4523 πόρρωθεν, *porrōthen*
distance [2]

4525 πορφύρα, *porphyra*
purple [4]

4527 πορφυρόπωλις, *porphyropōlis*
dealer in purple cloth [1]

4528 πορφυροῦς, *porphyrous*
purple [4]

4529 ποσάκις, *posakis*
how often [3]

4530 πόσις, *posis*
drink [3]

4531 πόσος, *posos*
how much [13], how many [11], how [1], how great [1], what [1]

4532 ποταμός, *potamos*
river [15], flood [2]

4533 + 4472 ποταμοφόρητος + ποιέω, *potamophorētos + poieō*
sweep away with the flood [1]

4534 ποταπός, *potapos*
large [2], what sort [2], what [1], what kind [1], what sort of person [1]

4536 πότε, *pote*
when [11], *see 2401* [how long] [7], *untranslated* [1]

4537 ποτέ, *pote*
once[3] [11], ever [4], formerly [3], actually [1], at any time [1], early [1], former time [1], last[1] [1], long ago [1], one time [1], when [1], *see 2453*

[last[1]] [1], see 4024 [never] [1], see 4046 [never] [1]

4538 πότερον, poteron
whether [1]

4539 ποτήριον, potērion
cup [30]

4539 + 3885 ποτήριον + οἶνος, potērion + oinos
wine-cup [1]

4540 ποτίζω, potizō
give drink [4], give to drink [3], water [3], make drink [2], feed [1], give [1], give water [1]

4541 Ποτίολοι, Potioloi
Puteoli [1]

4542 πότος, potos
carouse [1]

4543 πού, pou
about[3] [1], place [1], somewhere [1], untranslated [1]

4544 ποῦ, pou
where [41], what [3], see 4024 [nowhere] [2], place [1], way [1]

4545 Πούδης, Poudēs
Pudens [1]

4546 πούς, pous
foot [86], untranslated [4], leg [1], they [1]

4547 πρᾶγμα, pragma
matter [2], thing [2], deed [1], event [1], grievance [1], kind[1] [1], reality [1], see 4246 [anything] [1], untranslated [1]

4548 πραγματεία, pragmateia
affair [1]

4549 πραγματεύομαι, pragmateuomai
do business [1]

4550 πραιτώριον, praitōrion
headquarters [5], governor's headquarters [2], imperial guard [1]

4551 πράκτωρ, praktōr
officer [2]

4552 πρᾶξις, praxis
practice [2], action [1], deed [1], do [1], function [1]

4555 πρασιά, prasia
see 4555 [group] [1]

4555 + 4555 πρασιά + πρασιά, prasia + prasia
group [1]

4556 πράσσω, prassō
do [25], practice [4], act [2], collect [2], commit [1], deed [1], mind[2] [1], obey [1], see 2805 [harm] [1], see 2805 [wrongdoer] [1]

4557 πραϋπαθία, praupathia
gentleness [1]

4558 πραΰς, praus
gentle [2], humble [1], meek [1]

4559 πραΰτης, prautēs
gentleness [7], meekness [3], courtesy [1]

4560 πρέπω, prepō
proper [4], fitting [2], consistent [1]

4561 πρεσβεία, presbeia
delegation [2]

4563 πρεσβεύω, presbeuō
ambassador [2]

4564 πρεσβυτέριον, presbyterion
council of elders [2], assembly of the elders [1]

4565 πρεσβύτερος, presbyteros
elder [62], old man [2], ancestor [1], old woman [1]

4566 πρεσβύτης, presbytēs
old man [3]

4567 πρεσβῦτις, presbytis
old woman [1]

4568 πρηνής, prēnēs
headlong [1]

4569 πρίζω, prizō
saw in two [1]

4570 πρίν, prin
before [8]

4570 + 2445 πρίν + ἤ, prin + ē
before [4]

4570 + 2445 + 323 πρίν + ἤ + ἄν, prin + ē + an
before [1]

4571 Πρίσκα, Priska
Prisca [3], Priscilla [3]

4574 πρό, pro
before [30], above [2], ago [2], at [2], ahead [1], front [1], just outside [1], until [1]

4574 + 4047 + 3836 + 2465 πρό + οὗτος + ὁ + ἡμέρα, pro + houtos + ho + hēmera
recently [1]

4574 + 4725 πρό + πρόσωπον, pro + prosōpon
ahead [5], before [1]

4575 προάγω, proagō
go ahead [7], bring out [2], go on ahead [2], bring [1], bring before [1], early [1], front [1], go before [1], go beyond [1], make earlier [1], precede [1], walk ahead [1]

4576 προαιρέω, proaireō
make up [1]

4577 προαιτιάομαι, proaitiaomai
charge already [1]

4578 προακούω, proakouō
hear before [1]

4579 προαμαρτάνω, proamartanō
sin previously [1]

4580 προαύλιον, proaulion
forecourt [1]

4581 προβαίνω, probainō
get on [2], go [1], go far [1], great [1]

4582 προβάλλω, proballō
push forward [1], sprout leaves [1]

4583 προβατικός, probatikos
Sheep Gate [1]

4585 πρόβατον, probaton
sheep [38], see 885 [sheepfold] [1]

4586 προβιβάζω, probibazō
prompt [1]

4587 προβλέπω, problepō
provide [1]

4588 προγίνομαι, proginomai
commit previously [1]

4589 προγινώσκω, proginōskō
foreknow [2], destine [1], forewarn [1], know a long time [1]

4590 πρόγνωσις, prognōsis
destine [1], foreknowledge [1]

4591 πρόγονος, progonos
ancestor [1], parent [1]

4592 προγράφω, prographō
designate [1], exhibit publicly [1], write above [1], write in former days [1]

4593 πρόδηλος, prodēlos
conspicuous [2], evident [1]

4594 προδίδωμι, prodidōmi
give a gift [1]

4595 προδότης, prodotēs
betrayer [1], traitor [1], treacherous [1]

4596 πρόδρομος, prodromos
forerunner [1]

4598 προελπίζω, proelpizō
set one's hope first [1]

4599 προενάρχομαι, proenarchomai
begin [1], make a beginning [1]

4600 προεπαγγέλλω, proepangellō
promise [1], promise beforehand [1]

4601 προέρχομαι, proerchomai
go ahead [2], go far [2], arrive ahead [1], go before [1], go on ahead [1], lead [1], walk along [1]

4602 προετοιμάζω, proetoimazō
prepare beforehand [2]

4603 προευαγγελίζομαι, proeuangelizomai
declare the gospel beforehand [1]

4604 προέχω, proechō
any better off [1]

4605 προηγέομαι, proēgeomai
outdo [1]

4606 πρόθεσις, prothesis
purpose [6], presence [4], aim in life [1], steadfast [1]

4607 προθεσμία, prothesmia
date set [1]

4608 προθυμία, prothymia
eagerness [3], eagerly [1], goodwill [1]

4609 πρόθυμος, prothymos
willing [2], eagerness [1]

4610 προθύμως, prothymōs
eagerly [1]

4611 πρόϊμος, proimos
early [1]

4613 προΐστημι, proistēmi
manage [3], devote [2], charge[1] [1], leader [1], rule[1] [1]

4614 προκαλέω, prokaleō
compete [1]

4615 προκαταγγέλλω, prokatangellō
foretell [2]

4616 προκαταρτίζω, prokatartizō
arrange in advance [1]

4618 πρόκειμαι, prokeimai
set before [3], serve [1], there [1]

4619 προκηρύσσω, prokēryssō
proclaim already [1]

4620 προκοπή, prokopē
progress [2], spread [1]

4621 προκόπτω, prokoptō
advance [1], go [1], go far [1], increase [1], lead [1], make progress [1]

4622 πρόκριμα, prokrima
prejudice [1]

4623 προκυρόω, prokyroō
ratify previously [1]

4624 προλαμβάνω, prolambanō
beforehand [1], detect [1], go ahead [1]

4625 προλέγω, prolegō
tell beforehand [3], warn [3], say
before [2], foretell [1], predict [1],
prediction [1], speak in the past [1], tell
already [1], warn before [1], word already
quoted [1]

4626 προμαρτύρομαι, promartyromai
testify in advance [1]

4627 προμελετάω, promeletaō
prepare in advance [1]

4628 προμεριμνάω, promerimnaō
worry beforehand [1]

4629 προνοέω, pronoeō
intend [1], provide [1], take thought [1]

4630 πρόνοια, pronoia
foresight [1], provision [1]

4632 προοράω, prooraō
foresee [2], see before [1], see
previously [1]

4633 προορίζω, proorizō
predestine [3], destine [2], decree [1]

4634 προπάσχω, propaschō
suffer already [1]

4635 προπάτωρ, propatōr
ancestor [1]

4636 προπέμπω, propempō
send on one's way [4], send [2], bring [1],
escort [1], send on [1]

4637 προπετής, propetēs
rash [1], reckless [1]

4638 προπορεύομαι, proporeuomai
go before [1], lead the way [1]

4639 πρός, pros
to [423], untranslated [65], with [44],
for [36], against [20], at [18], toward [12],
before [8], in [8], among [7], around [7],
of [7], so that [4], about[1] [3], beside [3],
because [2], make [2], near [2], order[2] [2],
almost [1], and [1], answer [1], by [1],
check [1], compare with [1], front [1],
give [1], go to [1], lead [1], make for [1],
need [1], on [1], pertain [1], promote [1],
provision [1], realize [1], service [1],
towards [1], visit [1], see 3281
[whisper] [1]

4639 + 2505 πρός + θάνατος, pros +
thanatos
mortal [4]

4639 + 5515 πρός + τίς, pros + tis
why [1]

4640 προσάββατον, prosabbaton
day before the sabbath [1]

4641 προσαγορεύω, prosagoreuō
designate [1]

4642 προσάγω, prosagō
bring [2], bring before [1], near [1]

4643 προσαγωγή, prosagōgē
access [3]

4644 προσαιτέω, prosaiteō
beg [1]

4645 προσαίτης, prosaitēs
beggar [2]

4646 προσαναβαίνω, prosanabainō
move up [1]

4649 προσαναλόω, prosanaloō
spend [1]

4650 προσαναπληρόω, prosanaplēroō
supply [2]

4651 προσανατίθημι, prosanatithēmi
confer [1], contribute [1]

4653 προσαπειλέω, prosapeileō
threaten again [1]

4655 προσδαπανάω, prosdapanaō
spend more [1]

4656 προσδέομαι, prosdeomai
need [1]

4657 προσδέχομαι, prosdechomai
accept [3], wait[1] [3], welcome [3], look
forward [2], wait expectantly [2], look
for [1]

4659 προσδοκάω, prosdokaō
wait[1] [9], expect [5], fill with
expectation [1], suspense [1]

4660 προσδοκία, prosdokia
expect [1], forebode [1]

4661 προσεάω, proseaō
see 3590 [against] [1]

4664 προσεργάζομαι, prosergazomai
make more [1]

4665 προσέρχομαι, proserchomai
come [25], come to [23], approach [9], go
to [8], come up [7], come forward [6],
go [2], agree [1], come near [1], go
over [1], go to see [1], go up [1], visit [1]

4666 προσευχή, proseuchē
prayer [34], pray [1], see 4667 [pray
fervently] [1]

4667 προσεύχομαι, proseuchomai
pray [78], prayer [4], say a prayer [2]

4667 + 4666 προσεύχομαι + προσευχή,
proseuchomai + proseuchē
pray fervently [1]

4668 προσέχω, prosechō
beware [8], listen eagerly [4], pay
attention [3], on guard [2], attentive [1],
consider carefully [1], give attention [1],
indulge [1], keep watch over [1],
occupy [1], serve [1]

4669 προσηλόω, prosēloō
nail [1]

4670 προσήλυτος, prosēlytos
proselyte [2], convert [1], convert to
Judaism [1]

4672 πρόσκαιρος, proskairos
while [2], fleeting [1], temporary [1]

4673 προσκαλέω, proskaleō
call [14], summon [7], call to [5], call
for [1], call in [1], call together [1]

4674 προσκαρτερέω, proskartereō
devote [4], busy [1], persevere [1],
ready [1], serve [1], spend much time [1],
stay constantly [1]

4675 προσκαρτέρησις, proskarterēsis
persevere [1]

4676 προσκεφάλαιον, proskephalaion
cushion [1]

4677 προσκληρόω, prosklēroō
join [1]

4679 προσκλίνω, prosklinō
join [1]

4680 πρόσκλισις, prosklisis
partiality [1]

4681 προσκολλάω, proskollaō
join [2]

4682 πρόσκομμα, proskomma
make stumble [2], stumbling block [2],
make fall [1], stumble [1]

4683 προσκοπή, proskopē
obstacle in the way [1]

4684 προσκόπτω, proskoptō
stumble [4], dash [2], beat against [1],
make stumble [1]

4685 προσκυλίω, proskyliō
roll [2]

4686 προσκυνέω, proskyneō
worship [48], kneel [4], pay homage [3],
bow down [2], bow in worship [1],
homage [1], knee [1]

4687 προσκυνητής, proskynētēs
worshiper [1]

4688 προσλαλέω, proslaleō
speak [2]

4689 προσλαμβάνω, proslambanō
welcome [6], take aside [3], eat [1],
help [1], take [1]

4691 πρόσλημψις, proslēmpsis
acceptance [1]

4693 προσμένω, prosmenō
continue [2], with [2], remain [1], remain
faithful [1], stay [1]

4694 προσορμίζω, prosormizō
moor a boat [1]

4695 προσοφείλω, prosopheilō
owe [1]

4696 προσοχθίζω, prosochthizō
angry [2]

4698 πρόσπεινος, prospeinos
hungry [1]

4699 προσπήγνυμι, prospēgnymi
crucify [1]

4700 προσπίπτω, prospiptō
fall down before [5], beat on [1], bow
down [1], fall down [1]

4701 προσποιέω, prospoieō
as if [1]

4702 προσπορεύομαι, prosporeuomai
come forward [1]

4703 προσρήγνυμι, prosrēgnymi
burst against [2]

4705 προστάσσω, prostassō
command [5], existence [1], order[3] [1]

4706 προστάτις, prostatis
benefactor [1]

4707 προστίθημι, prostithēmi
add [7], give as well [2], another [1], bring
to [1], give still more [1], go on [1],
increase [1], lay [1], proceed [1], still[1] [1],
untranslated [1]

4708 προστρέχω, prostrechō
run up [2], run forward [1]

4709 προσφάγιον, prosphagion
fish [1]

4710 πρόσφατος, prosphatos
new [1]

4711 προσφάτως, prosphatōs
recently [1]

4712 προσφέρω, *prospherō*
offer [21], bring [10], bring to [4], offer up [3], offering [3], carry [1], hold to [1], make a sacrifice [1], make an offering [1], offer sacrifice [1], treat [1]

4713 προσφιλής, *prosphilēs*
please [1]

4714 προσφορά, *prosphora*
offering [7], offer sacrifice [1], sacrifice [1]

4715 προσφωνέω, *prosphōneō*
address [3], call [2], call over [1], call to [1]

4717 πρόσχυσις, *proschysis*
sprinkle [1]

4718 προσψαύω, *prospsauō*
ease [1]

4719 προσωπολημπτέω, *prosōpolēmpteō*
show partiality [1]

4720 προσωπολήμπτης, *prosōpolēmptēs*
partiality [1]

4721 προσωπολημψία, *prosōpolēmpsia*
partiality [3], favoritism [1]

4725 πρόσωπον, *prosōpon*
face [32], presence [8], *untranslated* [6], *see 4574* [ahead] [5], appearance [2], face to face [2], partiality [2], person [2], *see 2848* [face to face] [2], before [1], before openly [1], deference [1], eye [1], outward appearance [1], sight [1], *see 2093* [to the ground] [1], *see 3284* [show partiality] [1], *see 4328* [blindfold] [1], *see 4406* [bow down] [1], *see 4406* [prostrate] [1], *see 4406* [throw oneself on the ground] [1], *see 4574* [before] [1]

4725 + 1877 + 4922 πρόσωπον + ἐν + σάρξ, *prosōpon + en + sarx*
face to face [1]

4725 + 3836 + 1161 πρόσωπον + ὁ + γένεσις, *prosōpon + ho + genesis*
themselves [1]

4727 προτείνω, *proteinō*
tie up [1]

4728 πρότερος, *proteros*
before [3], first [3], formerly [3], early [1], former [1]

4729 προτίθημι, *protithēmi*
intend [1], put forward [1], set forth [1]

4730 προτρέπω, *protrepō*
encourage [1]

4731 προτρέχω, *protrechō*
outrun [1], run ahead [1]

4732 προϋπάρχω, *prouparchō*
before [1], previously [1]

4733 πρόφασις, *prophasis*
appearance [2], pretext [2], excuse [1], false motive [1]

4734 προφέρω, *propherō*
produce [2]

4735 προφητεία, *prophēteia*
prophecy [16], prophesy [1], prophetic power [1], word of a prophet [1]

4736 προφητεύω, *prophēteuō*
prophesy [26], have the gift of prophecy [1], prophecy [1]

4737 προφήτης, *prophētēs*
prophet [144]

4738 προφητικός, *prophētikos*
prophetic [2]

4739 προφῆτις, *prophētis*
prophet [2]

4740 προφθάνω, *prophthanō*
speak first [1]

4741 προχειρίζω, *procheirizō*
appoint [2], choose [1]

4742 προχειροτονέω, *procheirotoneō*
choose [1]

4743 Πρόχορος, *Prochoros*
Prochorus [1]

4744 πρύμνα, *prymna*
stern [3]

4745 πρωΐ, *prōi*
morning [6], early [3], early in the morning [2], dawn [1]

4746 πρωΐα, *prōia*
daybreak [1], morning [1]

4748 πρωϊνός, *prōinos*
morning [2]

4749 πρῷρα, *prōra*
bow³ [2]

4750 πρωτεύω, *prōteuō*
first place [1]

4751 πρωτοκαθεδρία, *prōtokathedria*
good seat [3], seat of honor [1]

4752 πρωτοκλισία, *prōtoklisia*
place of honor [5]

4754 πρῶτον, *prōton*
first [52], begin [2], first place [2], before [1], early [1], first of all [1], once⁴ [1]

4755 πρῶτος, *prōtos*
first [81], leader [4], before [2], foremost [2], lead [2], leading man [2], first thing [1], good [1]

4756 πρωτοστάτης, *prōtostatēs*
ringleader [1]

4757 πρωτοτόκια, *prōtotokia*
birthright [1]

4758 πρωτότοκος, *prōtotokos*
firstborn [8]

4759 πρώτως, *prōtōs*
first [1]

4760 πταίω, *ptaiō*
make a mistake [2], stumble [2], fail [1]

4761 πτέρνα, *pterna*
heel [1]

4762 πτερύγιον, *pterygion*
pinnacle [2]

4763 πτέρυξ, *pteryx*
wing [5]

4764 πτηνός, *ptēnos*
bird [1]

4765 πτοέω, *ptoeō*
startle [1], terrify [1]

4766 πτόησις, *ptoēsis*
fear [1]

4767 Πτολεμαΐς, *Ptolemais*
Ptolemais [1]

4768 πτύον, *ptyon*
winnowing fork [2]

4769 πτύρω, *ptyrō*
intimidate [1]

4770 πτύσμα, *ptysma*
saliva [1]

4771 πτύσσω, *ptyssō*
roll up [1]

4772 πτύω, *ptyō*
spit [2], put saliva [1]

4773 πτῶμα, *ptōma*
body [3], dead body [2], corpse [1], they [1]

4774 πτῶσις, *ptōsis*
fall [2]

4775 πτωχεία, *ptōcheia*
poverty [3]

4776 πτωχεύω, *ptōcheuō*
poor [1]

4777 πτωχός, *ptōchos*
poor [30], poor man [2], beggarly [1], poor person [1]

4778 πυγμή, *pygmē*
thoroughly [1]

4780 πύθων, *pythōn*
divination [1]

4781 πυκνός, *pyknos*
frequent [1], frequently [1], very often [1]

4782 πυκτεύω, *pykteuō*
box [1]

4783 πύλη, *pylē*
gate [9], city gate [1]

4784 πυλών, *pylōn*
gate [16], outer [1], porch [1]

4785 πυνθάνομαι, *pynthanomai*
ask [7], inquire [4], learn [1]

4786 πῦρ, *pyr*
fire [68], burn [2], flame [1]

4787 πυρά, *pyra*
fire [2]

4788 πύργος, *pyrgos*
tower [2], watchtower [2]

4789 πυρέσσω, *pyressō*
fever [2]

4790 πυρετός, *pyretos*
fever [6]

4791 πύρινος, *pyrinos*
color of fire [1]

4792 πυρόω, *pyroō*
refine [2], aflame with passion [1], flame [1], indignant [1], set ablaze [1]

4793 πυρράζω, *pyrrazō*
red [2]

4794 πυρρός, *pyrros*
bright red [1], red [1]

4795 Πύρρος, *Pyrros*
Pyrrhus [1]

4796 πύρωσις, *pyrōsis*
burn [2], fiery ordeal [1]

4797 πωλέω, *pōleō*
sell [21], dealer [1]

4798 πῶλος, *pōlos*
colt [12]

4799 πώποτε, *pōpote*
ever [2], never [1], *see 4024* [never] [1], *see 4029* [never] [1], *see 4046* [never] [1]

4800 πωρόω, *pōroō*
harden [5]

4801 πώρωσις, *pōrōsis*
hardness [2], harden [1]

4802 πῶς, *pōs*
how [86], what [6], *untranslated* [5],
way [4], how much [1], why [1]

4803 πώς, *pōs*
somehow [4], *see 3590* [perhaps] [2],
order[2] [1], so that [1], that [1], *see 1623*
[order[2]] [1], *see 1623* [somehow] [1], *see
3590* [otherwise] [1], *see 3590* [so that
not] [1], *see 3590* [that] [1],
untranslated [1]

4805 Ῥαάβ, *Rhaab*
Rahab [2]

4806 ῥαββί, *rhabbi*
rabbi [15]

4808 ῥαββουνί, *rhabbouni*
Rabbouni [1], teacher [1]

4810 ῥαβδίζω, *rhabdizō*
beat with a rod [2]

4811 ῥάβδος, *rhabdos*
staff [5], rod [4], scepter [2], stick[1] [1]

4812 ῥαβδοῦχος, *rhabdouchos*
police [2]

4814 Ῥαγαύ, *Rhagau*
Reu [1]

4815 ῥαδιούργημα, *rhadiourgēma*
villainy [1]

4816 ῥαδιουργία, *rhadiourgia*
villainy [1]

4818 Ῥαιφάν, *Rhaiphan*
Rephan [1]

4819 ῥακά, *rhaka*
see 3306 [insult] [1]

4820 ῥάκος, *rhakos*
cloth [2]

4821 Ῥαμά, *Rhama*
Ramah [1]

4822 ῥαντίζω, *rhantizō*
sprinkle [4]

4823 ῥαντισμός, *rhantismos*
sprinkle [2]

4824 ῥαπίζω, *rhapizō*
slap [1], strike [1]

4825 ῥάπισμα, *rhapisma*
beat [1]

4825 + 1443 ῥάπισμα + δίδωμι,
rhapisma + didōmi
strike on the face [2]

4827 ῥαφίς, *rhaphis*
needle [2]

4829 Ῥαχάβ, *Rhachab*
Rahab [1]

4830 Ῥαχήλ, *Rhachēl*
Rachel [1]

4831 Ῥεβέκκα, *Rhebekka*
Rebecca [1]

4832 ῥέδη, *rhedē*
chariot [1]

4835 ῥέω, *rheō*
flow [1]

4836 Ῥήγιον, *Rhēgion*
Rhegium [1]

4837 ῥῆγμα, *rhēgma*
ruin [1]

4838 ῥήγνυμι, *rhēgnymi*
burst [3], burst into song [1], dash
down [1], dash to the ground [1], maul [1]

4839 ῥῆμα, *rhēma*
word [37], thing [7], say [6], saying [4],
untranslated [4], message [3], what [3],
charge[3] [2], statement [1], *see 4024*
[nothing] [1]

4840 Ῥησά, *Rhēsa*
Rhesa [1]

4842 ῥήτωρ, *rhētōr*
attorney [1]

4843 ῥητῶς, *rhētōs*
expressly [1]

4844 ῥίζα, *rhiza*
root [17]

4845 ῥιζόω, *rhizoō*
root [2]

4846 ῥιπή, *rhipē*
twinkle [1]

4847 ῥιπίζω, *rhipizō*
toss [1]

4848 ῥιπτέω, *rhipteō*
throw off [1]

4849 ῥίπτω, *rhiptō*
throw down [2], helpless [1], let down [1],
put [1], throw [1], throw overboard [1]

4850 Ῥοβοάμ, *Rhoboam*
Rehoboam [2]

4851 Ῥόδη, *Rhodē*
Rhoda [1]

4852 Ῥόδος, *Rhodos*
Rhodes [1]

4853 ῥοιζηδόν, *rhoizēdon*
loud noise [1]

4855 ῥομφαία, *rhomphaia*
sword [7]

4857 Ῥουβήν, *Rhoubēn*
Reuben [1]

4858 Ῥούθ, *Rhouth*
Ruth [1]

4859 Ῥοῦφος, *Rhouphos*
Rufus [2]

4860 ῥύμη, *rhymē*
lane [2], street [2]

4861 ῥύομαι, *rhyomai*
rescue [15], deliver [1], deliverer [1]

4862 ῥυπαίνω, *rhypainō*
filthy [1]

4864 ῥυπαρία, *rhyparia*
sordidness [1]

4865 ῥυπαρός, *rhyparos*
dirty [1], filthy [1]

4866 ῥύπος, *rhypos*
dirt [1]

4868 + 135 ῥύσις + αἷμα, *rhysis +
haima*
hemorrhage [3]

4869 ῥυτίς, *rhytis*
wrinkle [1]

4871 Ῥωμαῖος, *Rhōmaios*
Roman citizen [7], Roman [4], Rome [1]

4872 Ῥωμαϊστί, *Rhōmaisti*
Latin [1]

4873 Ῥώμη, *Rhōmē*
Rome [8]

4874 ῥώννυμι, *rhōnnymi*
farewell [1]

4876 σαβαχθάνι, *sabachthani*
sabachthani [2]

4877 Σαβαώθ, *Sabaōth*
host[1] [2]

4878 σαββατισμός, *sabbatismos*
sabbath rest [1]

4879 σάββατον, *sabbaton*
sabbath [59], week [9]

4880 σαγήνη, *sagēnē*
net [1]

4881 Σαδδουκαῖος, *Saddoukaios*
Sadducee [14]

4882 Σαδώκ, *Sadōk*
Zadok [2]

4883 σαίνω, *sainō*
shake [1]

4884 σάκκος, *sakkos*
sackcloth [3]

4884 + 5570 σάκκος + τρίχινος,
sakkos + trichinos
sackcloth [1]

4885 Σαλά, *Sala*
Sala [1], Shelah [1]

4886 Σαλαθιήλ, *Salathiēl*
Salathiel [2], Shealtiel [1]

4887 Σαλαμίς, *Salamis*
Salamis [1]

4888 σαλεύω, *saleuō*
shake [13], shake together [1], stir up [1]

4889 Σαλήμ, *Salēm*
Salem [2]

4890 Σαλίμ, *Salim*
Salim [1]

4891 Σαλμών, *Salmōn*
Salmon [2]

4892 Σαλμώνη, *Salmōnē*
Salmone [1]

4893 σάλος, *salos*
wave [1]

4894 σάλπιγξ, *salpinx*
trumpet [8], bugle [1], sound of a
trumpet [1], trumpet call [1]

4895 σαλπίζω, *salpizō*
blow a trumpet [8], blow [2], sound a
trumpet [2]

4896 σαλπιστής, *salpistēs*
trumpeter [1]

4897 Σαλώμη, *Salōmē*
Salome [2]

4899 Σαμάρεια, *Samareia*
Samaria [9], Samaritan [2]

4901 Σαμαρίτης, *Samaritēs*
Samaritan [9]

4902 Σαμαρῖτις, *Samaritis*
Samaria [1], Samaritan [1]

4903 Σαμοθράκη, *Samothrakē*
Samothrace [1]

4904 Σάμος, *Samos*
Samos [1]

4905 Σαμουήλ, *Samouēl*
Samuel [3]

4907 Σαμψών, *Sampsōn*
Samson [1]

4908 σανδάλιον, *sandalion*
sandal [2]

4909 σανίς, sanis
plank [1]

4910 Σαούλ, Saoul
Saul [9]

4911 σαπρός, sapros
bad [7], evil [1]

4912 Σάπφιρα, Sapphira
Sapphira [1]

4913 σάπφιρος, sapphiros
sapphire [1]

4914 σαργάνη, sarganē
basket [1]

4915 Σάρδεις, Sardeis
Sardis [3]

4917 σάρδιον, sardion
carnelian [2]

4918 σαρδόνυξ, sardonyx
onyx [1]

4919 Σάρεπτα, Sarepta
Zarephath [1]

4920 σαρκικός, sarkikos
flesh [3], earthly [1], material [1], material
benefit [1], merely human [1]

4921 σάρκινος, sarkinos
flesh [1], human [1], person of the
flesh [1], physical descent [1]

4922 σάρξ, sarx
flesh [104], body [7], human standard [6],
human [4], one [3], human being [2],
people [2], see 2848 [2],
untranslated [2], bear¹ [1], condition [1],
earthly [1], fleshly [1], life [1], lust [1],
natural [1], person [1], physical [1], self-
indulgence [1], see 1877 [physical] [1],
see 4246 [one] [1], see 4447 [self-
indulgence] [1], see 4725 [face to face] [1]

4922 + 2779 + 135 σάρξ + καί + αἷμα,
sarx + kai + haima
human being [1]

4924 σαρόω, saroō
sweep [3]

4925 Σάρρα, Sarra
Sarah [4]

4926 Σαρών, Sarōn
Sharon [1]

4928 Σατανᾶς, Satanas
Satan [36]

4929 σάτον, saton
measure [2]

4930 Σαῦλος, Saulos
Saul [15]

4931 σβέννυμι, sbennymi
quench [5], go out [1]

4932 σεαυτοῦ, seautou
yourself [33], you [9], self [1]

4933 σεβάζομαι, sebazomai
worship [1]

4934 σέβασμα, sebasma
object of worship [2]

4935 σεβαστός, sebastos
imperial majesty [2], Augustan [1]

4936 σέβω, sebō
worship [4], devout [3], worshiper [2],
devout person [1]

4937 σειρά, seira
chain [1]

4939 σεισμός, seismos
earthquake [13], windstorm [1]

4940 σείω, seiō
shake [4], turmoil [1]

4941 Σεκοῦνδος, Sekoundos
Secundus [1]

4942 Σελεύκεια, Seleukeia
Seleucia [1]

4943 σελήνη, selēnē
moon [9]

4944 σεληνιάζομαι, selēniazomai
epileptic [2]

4946 Σεμεΐν, Semein
Semein [1]

4947 σεμίδαλις, semidalis
choice flour [1]

4948 σεμνός, semnos
serious [3], honorable [1]

4949 σεμνότης, semnotēs
dignity [1], gravity [1], respectful [1]

4950 Σέργιος, Sergios
Sergius [1]

4952 Σερούχ, Serouch
Serug [1]

4953 Σήθ, Sēth
Seth [1]

4954 Σήμ, Sēm
Shem [1]

4955 σημαίνω, sēmainō
indicate [4], make known [1], predict [1]

4956 σημεῖον, sēmeion
sign [73], portent [3], mark [1]

4957 σημειόω, sēmeioō
take note [1]

4958 σήμερον, sēmeron
today [30], this day [8], this very day [3]

4960 σήπω, sēpō
rot [1]

4962 σής, sēs
moth [3]

4963 σητόβρωτος, sētobrōtos
moth-eaten [1]

4964 σθενόω, sthenoō
strengthen [1]

4965 σιαγών, siagōn
cheek [2]

4967 σιγάω, sigaō
silent [5], finish speaking [1], keep
secret [1], keep silence [1], keep silent [1],
quiet [1]

4968 σιγή, sigē
hush [1], silence [1]

4970 σίδηρος, sidēros
iron [1]

4971 σιδηροῦς, sidērous
iron [5]

4972 Σιδών, Sidōn
Sidon [9]

4973 Σιδώνιος, Sidōnios
Sidon [1], person of Sidon [1]

4974 σικάριος, sikarios
assassin [1]

4975 σίκερα, sikera
strong drink [1]

4976 Σίλας, Silas
Silas [12]

4977 Σιλουανός, Silouanos
Silvanus [4]

4978 Σιλωάμ, Silōam
Siloam [3]

4980 σιμικίνθιον, simikinthion
apron [1]

4981 Σίμων, Simōn
Simon [74], he [1]

4982 Σινά, Sina
Sinai [4]

4983 σίναπι, sinapi
mustard [5]

4984 σινδών, sindōn
linen cloth [6]

4985 σινιάζω, siniazō
sift [1]

4986 σιρικός, sirikos
silk [1]

4988 σιτευτός, siteutos
fatted [3]

4989 σιτίον, sition
grain [1]

4990 σιτιστός, sitistos
fat calf [1]

4991 σιτομέτριον, sitometrion
allowance of food [1]

4992 σῖτος, sitos
wheat [12], grain [2]

4994 Σιών, Siōn
Zion [7]

4995 σιωπάω, siōpaō
silent [6], quiet [2], mute [1], peace [1]

4997 σκανδαλίζω, skandalizō
cause to stumble [6], desert¹ [5], take
offense [5], fall away [3], cause to fall [2],
cause to sin [2], put a stumbling block [2],
give offense [1], make stumble [1],
offend [1], stumble [1]

4998 σκάνδαλον, skandalon
stumbling block [6], make fall [2],
occasion for stumbling [2], offense [2],
cause for stumbling [1], cause of sin [1],
hindrance in the way [1]

4999 σκάπτω, skaptō
dig [3]

5002 σκάφη, skaphē
boat [2], ship's boat [1]

5003 σκέλος, skelos
leg [3]

5004 σκέπασμα, skepasma
clothing [1]

5005 Σκευᾶς, Skeuas
Sceva [1]

5006 σκευή, skeuē
tackle [1]

5007 σκεῦος, skeuos
jar [3], object¹ [3], article [2], property [2],
something [2], utensil [2], anything [1],
belonging [1], body [1], instrument [1],
pot [1], sea anchor [1], sex [1], thing [1],
vessel [1]

5008 σκηνή, skēnē
tent [13], dwelling [5], home [2]

5009 σκηνοπηγία, skēnopēgia
booth [1]

5010 σκηνοποιός, skēnopoios
tentmaker [1]

5011 σκῆνος, skēnos
tent [2]

5012 σκηνόω, skēnoō
dwell [3], live [1], shelter [1]

5013 σκήνωμα, skēnōma
body [1], dwelling place [1], see 629 [death] [1]

5014 σκιά, skia
shadow [6], shade [1]

5015 σκιρτάω, skirtaō
leap [2], leap for joy [1]

5016 σκληροκαρδία, sklērokardia
hard-hearted [1], hardness of heart [1], stubbornness [1]

5017 σκληρός, sklēros
difficult [1], harsh [1], harsh thing [1], hurt [1], strong [1]

5018 σκληρότης, sklērotēs
hard [1]

5019 σκληροτράχηλος, sklērotrachēlos
stiff-necked [1]

5020 σκληρύνω, sklērynō
harden [4], harden the heart [1], stubbornly [1]

5021 σκολιός, skolios
crooked [2], corrupt [1], harsh [1]

5022 σκόλοψ, skolops
thorn [1]

5023 σκοπέω, skopeō
look [2], consider [1], keep an eye on [1], observe¹ [1], take care [1]

5024 σκοπός, skopos
goal [1]

5025 σκορπίζω, skorpizō
scatter [4], scatter abroad [1]

5026 σκορπίος, skorpios
scorpion [5]

5027 σκοτεινός, skoteinos
darkness [2], full of darkness [1]

5028 σκοτία, skotia
darkness [12], dark [4]

5029 σκοτίζομαι, skotizomai
darken [5]

5030 σκότος, skotos
darkness [31]

5031 σκοτόω, skotoō
darken [2], darkness [1]

5032 σκύβαλον, skybalon
rubbish [1]

5033 Σκύθης, Skythēs
Scythian [1]

5034 σκυθρωπός, skythrōpos
dismal [1], look sad [1]

5035 σκύλλω, skyllō
trouble [3], harass [1]

5036 σκῦλον, skylon
plunder [1]

5037 σκωληκόβρωτος, skōlēkobrōtos
eaten by worms [1]

5038 σκώληξ, skōlēx
worm [1]

5039 σμαράγδινος, smaragdinos
emerald [1]

5040 σμάραγδος, smaragdos
emerald [1]

5043 σμύρνα¹, smyrna¹
myrrh [2]

5044 Σμύρνα², Smyrna²
Smyrna [2]

5046 σμυρνίζω, smyrnizō
mix with myrrh [1]

5047 Σόδομα, Sodoma
Sodom [9]

5048 Σολομών, Solomōn
Solomon [12]

5049 σορός, soros
bier [1]

5050 σός, sos
you [27]

5051 σουδάριον, soudarion
cloth [2], handkerchief [1], piece of cloth [1]

5052 Σουσάννα, Sousanna
Susanna [1]

5053 σοφία, sophia
wisdom [50], wisely [1]

5054 σοφίζω, sophizō
devise cleverly [1], instruct [1]

5055 σοφός, sophos
wise [18], sage [1], skilled [1]

5056 Σπανία, Spania
Spain [2]

5057 σπαράσσω, sparassō
convulse [3]

5058 σπαργανόω, sparganoō
wrap in bands of cloth [2]

5059 σπαταλάω, spatalaō
live for pleasure [1], live in pleasure [1]

5060 σπάω, spaō
draw¹ [2]

5061 σπεῖρα, speira
cohort [5], detachment of soldiers [1], soldier [1]

5062 σπείρω, speirō
sow¹ [45], sower [7]

5063 σπεκουλάτωρ, spekoulatōr
soldier of the guard [1]

5064 σπένδω, spendō
pour out as a libation [2]

5065 σπέρμα, sperma
descendant [17], seed [8], child [7], offspring [5], descend [1], posterity [1], survivor [1], see 1666 [descend from] [1], see 2856 [procreation] [1], see 3590 [childless] [1]

5066 σπερμολόγος, spermologos
babbler [1]

5067 σπεύδω, speudō
hurry [3], eager [1], haste [1], hasten [1]

5068 σπήλαιον, spēlaion
cave [3], den [3]

5069 σπιλάς, spilas
blemish [1]

5070 σπίλος, spilos
blot [1], spot [1]

5071 σπιλόω, spiloō
defile [1], stain [1]

5072 σπλαγχνίζομαι, splanchnizomai
have compassion [6], move with pity [2],

fill with compassion [1], have pity [1], move with compassion [1], out of pity [1]

5073 σπλάγχνον, splanchnon
heart [4], compassion [2], affection [1], bowels [1], tender [1], see 3091 [refuse help] [1]

5073 + 3880 σπλάγχνον + οἰκτιρμός, splanchnon + oiktirmos
compassion [1]

5074 σπόγγος, spongos
sponge [3]

5075 σποδός, spodos
ash [3]

5076 σπορά, spora
seed [1]

5077 σπόριμος, sporimos
grainfield [3]

5078 σπόρος, sporos
seed [6]

5079 σπουδάζω, spoudazō
do one's best [4], make every effort [3], eager [2], eagerness [1], strive [1]

5080 σπουδαῖος, spoudaios
more eager [2], eager [1]

5081 σπουδαίως, spoudaiōs
eagerly [1], earnestly [1], make every effort [1], more eager [1]

5082 σπουδή, spoudē
diligence [2], eagerness [2], earnestness [2], zeal [2], effort [1], haste [1], see 1656 [rush back] [1]

5082 + 4246 σπουδή + πᾶς, spoudē + pas
eagerly [1]

5083 σπυρίς, spyris
basket [5]

5084 στάδιον, stadion
race² [1], see 1278 [two miles] [1], see 1633 [three miles] [1], see 2008 [seven miles] [1], see 5558 [four miles] [1]

5084 + 1557 + 5942 στάδιον + δώδεκα + χιλιάς, stadion + dōdeka + chilias
fifteen hundred miles [1]

5084 + 4498 στάδιον + πολύς, stadion + polys
far [1]

5084 + 5943 + 1980 στάδιον + χίλιοι + ἑξακόσιοι, stadion + chilioi + hexakosioi
two hundred miles [1]

5085 στάμνος, stamnos
urn [1]

5086 στασιαστής, stasiastēs
rebel [1]

5087 στάσις, stasis
dissension [3], insurrection [3], riot [1], stand¹ [1], see 3075 [agitator] [1]

5088 στατήρ, statēr
coin [1]

5089 σταυρός, stauros
cross [27]

5090 σταυρόω, stauroō
crucify [46]

5091 σταφυλή, staphylē
grape [3]

5092 στάχυς¹, stachys¹
head of grain [3], head [2]

5093 Στάχυς², *Stachys²*
Stachys [1]

5094 στέγη, *stegē*
roof [3]

5095 στέγω, *stegō*
bear[1] [3], endure [1]

5096 στεῖρα, *steira*
barren [4], childless [1]

5097 στέλλω, *stellō*
intend [1], keep away [1]

5098 στέμμα, *stemma*
garland [1]

5099 στεναγμός, *stenagmos*
groan [1], sigh [1]

5100 στενάζω, *stenazō*
groan [3], sigh [2], grumble [1]

5101 στενός, *stenos*
narrow [3]

5102 στενοχωρέω, *stenochōreō*
crush [1], restriction [1], *untranslated* [1]

5103 στενοχωρία, *stenochōria*
calamity [2], distress [2]

5104 στερεός, *stereos*
solid [2], firm [1], steadfast [1]

5105 στερεόω, *stereoō*
make strong [2], strengthen [1]

5106 στερέωμα, *stereōma*
firmness [1]

5107 Στεφανᾶς, *Stephanas*
Stephanas [3]

5108 Στέφανος[1], *Stephanos[1]*
Stephen [7]

5109 στέφανος², *stephanos²*
crown [17], wreath [1]

5110 στεφανόω, *stephanoō*
crown [3]

5111 στῆθος, *stēthos*
breast [2], *see 2093* [next] [2], chest [1]

5112 στήκω, *stēkō*
stand firm [6], stand[1] [3]

5113 στηριγμός, *stērigmos*
stability [1]

5114 στηρίζω, *stērizō*
strengthen [9], establish [1], fix [1], set[1] [1], support [1]

5115 στιβάς, *stibas*
leafy branch [1]

5116 στίγμα, *stigma*
brand mark [1]

5117 + 5989 στιγμή + χρόνος, *stigmē + chronos*
instant [1]

5118 + 3336 στίλβω + λίαν, *stilbō + lian*
dazzle [1]

5119 στοά, *stoa*
portico [4]

5121 Στοϊκός, *Stoikos*
Stoic [1]

5122 στοιχεῖον, *stoicheion*
elemental spirit [4], element [3]

5123 στοιχέω, *stoicheō*
follow [2], guide [1], hold fast [1], observe² [1]

5124 στολή, *stolē*
robe [5], long robe [2], *see 4314* [robe] [2]

5125 στόμα, *stoma*
mouth [50], face [4], *see 1328* [through] [4], lip [3], *see 487* [speak] [3], edge [2], evidence [2], speak [2], word [2], say [1], through [1], voice [1], *see 489* [speak] [1], *see 5889* [voice] [1], *untranslated* [1]

5126 στόμαχος, *stomachos*
stomach [1]

5127 στρατεία, *strateia*
fight [1], warfare [1]

5128 στράτευμα, *strateuma*
army [3], soldier [2], troop [2], guard [1]

5129 στρατεύομαι, *strateuomai*
wage war [2], do military service [1], fight [1], serve in the army [1], soldier [1], war [1]

5130 στρατηγός, *stratēgos*
magistrate [5], captain [3], officer of the temple police [2]

5131 στρατιά, *stratia*
host[1] [2]

5132 στρατιώτης, *stratiōtēs*
soldier [26]

5133 στρατολογέω, *stratologeō*
enlist [1]

5136 στρατόπεδον, *stratopedon*
army [1]

5137 στρεβλόω, *strebloō*
twist [1]

5138 στρέφω, *strephō*
turn[1] [17], bring back [1], change [1], turn back [1], turn³ [1]

5139 στρηνιάω, *strēniaō*
live in luxury [1], live luxuriously [1]

5140 στρῆνος, *strēnos*
luxury [1]

5141 στρουθίον, *strouthion*
sparrow [4]

5143 στρωννύω, *strōnnyō*
spread [3], furnish [2], make a bed [1]

5144 στυγητός, *stygētos*
despicable [1]

5145 στυγνάζω, *stygnazō*
shock [1], threaten [1]

5146 στῦλος, *stylos*
pillar [4]

5148 σύ, *sy*
you [2793], *untranslated* [84], yourself [24], *see 6034* [you] [1]

5149 συγγένεια, *syngeneia*
relative [3]

5150 συγγενής, *syngenēs*
relative [9], kin [1], kindred [1]

5151 συγγενίς, *syngenis*
relative [1]

5152 συγγνώμη, *syngnōmē*
concession [1]

5153 συγκάθημαι, *synkathēmai*
seat with [1], sit with [1]

5154 συγκαθίζω, *synkathizō*
seat with [1], sit down together [1]

5155 συγκακοπαθέω, *synkakopatheō*
join in suffering [1], share in suffering [1]

5156 συγκακουχέομαι, *synkakoucheomai*
share ill-treatment [1]

5157 συγκαλέω, *synkaleō*
call together [8]

5158 συγκαλύπτω, *synkalyptō*
cover up [1]

5159 συγκάμπτω, *synkamptō*
bend [1]

5160 συγκαταβαίνω, *synkatabainō*
come down with [1]

5161 συγκατάθεσις, *synkatathesis*
agreement [1]

5163 συγκατατίθημι, *synkatatithēmi*
agree [1]

5164 συγκαταψηφίζομαι, *synkatapsēphizomai*
add [1]

5166 συγκεράννυμι, *synkerannymi*
arrange [1], unite [1]

5167 συγκινέω, *synkineō*
stir up [1]

5168 συγκλείω, *synkleiō*
imprison [2], catch [1], guard [1]

5169 συγκληρονόμος, *synklēronomos*
fellow heir [1], heir also [1], heir with [1], joint heir [1]

5170 συγκοινωνέω, *synkoinōneō*
take part [2], share [1]

5171 συγκοινωνός, *synkoinōnos*
share [4]

5172 συγκομίζω, *synkomizō*
bury [1]

5173 συγκρίνω, *synkrinō*
compare [2], interpret [1]

5174 συγκύπτω, *synkyptō*
bend over [1]

5175 συγκυρία, *synkyria*
chance [1]

5176 συγχαίρω, *synchairō*
rejoice with [4], rejoice [2], rejoice together [1]

5177 συγχέω, *syncheō*
bewilder [1], confound [1], confusion [1], in an uproar [1], stir up [1]

5178 συγχράομαι, *synchraomai*
share in common [1]

5180 σύγχυσις, *synchysis*
confusion [1]

5182 συζάω, *syzaō*
live with [2], live together [1]

5183 συζεύγνυμι, *syzeugnymi*
join together [2]

5184 συζητέω, *syzēteō*
argue [5], ask [2], discuss [1], dispute with one another [1], question [1]

5186 συζητητής, *syzētētēs*
debater [1]

5187 σύζυγος, *syzygos*
companion [1]

5188 συζωοποιέω, *syzōopoieō*
make alive together [2]

5189 συκάμινος, *sykaminos*
mulberry tree [1]

5190 συκῆ, *sykē*
fig tree [16]

5191 συκομορέα, *sykomorea*
sycamore tree [1]

5192 σῦκον, *sykon*
fig [4]

5193 συκοφαντέω, *sykophanteō*
defraud [1], false accusation [1]

5194 συλαγωγέω, *sylagōgeō*
take captive [1]

5195 συλάω, *sylaō*
rob [1]

5196 συλλαλέω, *syllaleō*
confer [2], talk with [2], say [1], talk [1]

5197 συλλαμβάνω, *syllambanō*
arrest [5], conceive [5], seize [3], help [2],
take [1]

5198 συλλέγω, *syllegō*
gather [4], collect [3], put [1]

5199 συλλογίζομαι, *syllogizomai*
discuss [1]

5200 συλλυπέω, *syllypeō*
grieve [1]

5201 συμβαίνω, *symbainō*
happen [6], come to [1], have to [1]

5202 συμβάλλω, *symballō*
debate [1], discuss [1], help [1], meet [1],
ponder [1], wage[1] [1]

5203 συμβασιλεύω, *symbasileuō*
king with [1], reign with [1]

5204 συμβιβάζω, *symbibazō*
convince [1], give instruction [1], hold
together [1], instruct [1], knit together [1],
prove [1], unite [1]

5205 συμβουλεύω, *symbouleuō*
advise [1], conspire [1], counsel [1],
plot [1]

5206 συμβούλιον, *symboulion*
consultation [1], council [1], plan [1]

5206 + 1443 συμβούλιον + δίδωμι,
symboulion + didōmi
conspire [1]

5206 + 3284 συμβούλιον + λαμβάνω,
symboulion + lambanō
confer together [2], conspire [1], plot [1]

5207 σύμβουλος, *symboulos*
counselor [1]

5208 Συμεών, *Symeōn* ·
Simeon [7]

5209 συμμαθητής, *symmathētēs*
fellow disciple [1]

5210 συμμαρτυρέω, *symmartyreō*
bear witness also [1], bear witness
with [1], confirm [1]

5211 συμμερίζομαι, *symmerizomai*
share [1]

5212 συμμέτοχος, *symmetochos*
associate [1], sharer [1]

5213 συμμιμητής, *symmimētēs*
imitate [1]

5214 συμμορφίζω, *symmorphizō*
like[1] [1]

5215 σύμμορφος, *symmorphos*
conform [2]

5217 συμπαθέω, *sympatheō*
have compassion [1], sympathize [1]

5218 συμπαθής, *sympathēs*
sympathy [1]

5219 συμπαραγίνομαι, *symparaginomai*
gather [1]

5220 συμπαρακαλέω, *symparakaleō*
encourage mutually [1]

5221 συμπαραλαμβάνω,
symparalambanō
take with [2], bring with [1], take
along [1]

5223 συμπάρειμι, *sympareimi*
present[4] [1]

5224 συμπάσχω, *sympaschō*
suffer together [1], suffer with [1]

5225 συμπέμπω, *sympempō*
send with [2]

5227 συμπεριλαμβάνω,
symperilambanō
take in one's arms [1]

5228 συμπίνω, *sympinō*
drink with [1]

5229 συμπίπτω, *sympiptō*
fall [1]

5230 συμπληρόω, *symplēroō*
come [1], draw near [1], fill [1]

5231 συμπνίγω, *sympnigō*
choke [4], press in on [1]

5232 συμπολίτης, *sympolitēs*
citizen with [1]

5233 συμπορεύομαι, *symporeuomai*
go with [2], gather [1], travel with [1]

5235 συμπόσιον, *symposion*
see *5235* [group] [1]

5235 + 5235 συμπόσιον + συμπόσιον,
symposion + symposion
group [1]

5236 συμπρεσβύτερος, *sympresbyteros*
elder oneself [1]

5237 συμφέρω, *sympherō*
good [7], beneficial [2], advantage [1],
appropriate [1], collect [1], common
good [1], gain [1], helpful [1]

5238 σύμφημι, *symphēmi*
agree [1]

5239 σύμφορος, *symphoros*
advantage [1], benefit [1]

5241 συμφυλέτης, *symphyletēs*
compatriot [1]

5242 σύμφυτος, *symphytos*
unite [1]

5243 συμφύω, *symphyō*
grow with [1]

5244 συμφωνέω, *symphōneō*
agree [4], agree together [1], match [1]

5245 συμφώνησις, *symphōnēsis*
agreement [1]

5246 συμφωνία, *symphōnia*
music [1]

5247 σύμφωνος, *symphōnos*
agreement [1]

5248 συμψηφίζω, *sympsēphizō*
calculate [1]

5249 σύμψυχος, *sympsychos*
full accord [1]

5250 σύν, *syn*
with [97], companion [5], together with [5],
along with [3], and [3], beside [2], with
consent [2], accompany [1], along [1],
as [1], besides [1], include [1], present[4] [1],
see *1639* [accompany] [1], see *2002*

[accompany] [1], see *2262* [accompany] [1],
see *4513* [accompany] [1]

5250 + 5931 σύν + χείρ, *syn + cheir*
through [1]

5251 συνάγω, *synagō*
gather [29], gather together [6],
assemble [5], gather around [3], meet [3],
welcome [3], call together [2], gather
up [2], store [2], call a meeting [1],
catch [1], meet together [1], meet with [1]

5252 συναγωγή, *synagōgē*
synagogue [55], assembly [1]

5253 συναγωνίζομαι, *synagōnizomai*
join [1]

5254 συναθλέω, *synathleō*
strive side by side [1], struggle beside [1]

5255 συναθροίζω, *synathroizō*
gather [1], gather together [1]

5256 συναίρω, *synairō*
settle[2] [2], reckon [1]

5257 συναιχμάλωτος, *synaichmalōtos*
fellow prisoner [2], in prison with [1]

5258 συνακολουθέω, *synakoloutheō*
follow [3]

5259 συναλίζω, *synalizō*
stay with [1]

5261 συναλλάσσω, *synallassō*
reconcile [1]

5262 συναναβαίνω, *synanabainō*
come up with [2]

5263 συνανάκειμαι, *synanakeimai*
guest [2], sit with [2], at table with [1],
dinner guest [1], sit at table with [1]

5264 συναναμείγνυμι,
synanameignymi
associate [2], do [1]

5265 συναναπαύομαι, *synanapauomai*
refresh in company [1]

5267 συναντάω, *synantaō*
meet [5], happen [1]

5269 συναντιλαμβάνομαι,
synantilambanomai
help [2]

5270 συναπάγω, *synapagō*
associate [1], carry away [1], lead
astray [1]

5271 συναποθνήσκω, *synapothnēskō*
die with [2], die together [1]

5272 συναπόλλυμι, *synapollymi*
perish [1]

5273 συναποστέλλω, *synapostellō*
send with [1]

5274 συναρμολογέω, *synarmologeō*
join together [2]

5275 συναρπάζω, *synarpazō*
seize [2], catch [1], drag with [1]

5277 συναυξάνω, *synauxanō*
grow together [1]

5278 σύνδεσμος, *syndesmos*
bind together [1], bond [1], chain [1],
sinew [1]

5279 συνδέω, *syndeō*
in prison with [1]

5280 συνδοξάζω, *syndoxazō*
glorify with [1]

5281 σύνδουλος, *syndoulos*
fellow servant [5], fellow slave [5]

5282 συνδρομή, *syndromē*
rush together [1]

5283 συνεγείρω, *synegeirō*
raise with [2], raise up with [1]

5284 συνέδριον, *synedrion*
council [22]

5287 συνείδησις, *syneidēsis*
conscience [28], aware [1],
consciousness [1]

5289 σύνειμι[1], *syneimi*[1]
near [1], with [1]

5290 σύνειμι[2], *syneimi*[2]
gather [1]

5291 συνεισέρχομαι, *syneiserchomai*
get into with [1], go with [1]

5292 συνέκδημος, *synekdēmos*
travel companion [1], travel with [1]

5293 συνεκλεκτός, *syneklektos*
choose together [1]

5296 συνεπιμαρτυρέω, *synepimartyreō*
add one's testimony [1]

5298 συνεπιτίθημι, *synepitithēmi*
join in a charge [1]

5299 συνέπομαι, *synepomai*
accompany [1]

5300 συνεργέω, *synergeō*
work together [2], work with [2], active
along with [1]

5301 συνεργός, *synergos*
co-worker [9], fellow worker [1], servant
working together [1], work with [1],
worker with [1]

5302 συνέρχομαι, *synerchomai*
come together [11], gather [4],
accompany [3], assemble [3], come
with [3], go with [2], meet [2], come
along [1], live together [1]

5303 συνεσθίω, *synesthiō*
eat with [5]

5304 σύνεσις, *synesis*
understanding [6], discernment [1]

5305 συνετός, *synetos*
intelligent [3], discern [1]

5306 συνευδοκέω, *syneudokeō*
approve [3], consent [2], applaud [1]

5307 συνευωχέομαι, *syneuōcheomai*
feast [1], feast with [1]

5308 συνεφίστημι, *synephistēmi*
join [1]

5309 συνέχω, *synechō*
afflict [1], cover [1], hem in [1], hold [1],
occupy [1], press hard [1], seize [1],
sick [1], suffer[1] [1], surround [1], under
stress [1], urge on [1]

5310 συνήδομαι, *synēdomai*
delight [1]

5311 συνήθεια, *synētheia*
custom [2], accustom [1]

5312 συνηλικιώτης, *synēlikiōtēs*
same age [1]

5313 συνθάπτω, *synthaptō*
bury with [2]

5314 συνθλάω, *synthlaō*
break to pieces [1]

5315 συνθλίβω, *synthlibō*
press in on [2]

5316 συνθρύπτω, *synthryptō*
break [1]

5317 συνίημι, *syniēmi*
understand [24], show good sense [1],
understanding [1]

5319 συνίστημι, *synistēmi*
commend [9], prove [2], demonstrate [1],
form [1], hold together [1], serve to
confirm [1], stand with [1]

5321 συνοδεύω, *synodeuō*
travel with [1]

5322 συνοδία, *synodia*
group of travelers [1]

5323 σύνοιδα, *synoida*
aware [1], knowledge [1]

5324 συνοικέω, *synoikeō*
life together [1]

5325 συνοικοδομέω, *synoikodomeō*
build together [1]

5326 συνομιλέω, *synomileō*
talk with [1]

5327 συνομορέω, *synomoreō*
next door [1]

5328 συνοράω, *synoraō*
learn [1], realize [1]

5330 συνοχή, *synochē*
anguish [1], distress [1]

5332 συντάσσω, *syntassō*
direct [2], command [1]

5333 συντέλεια, *synteleia*
end [6]

5334 συντελέω, *synteleō*
accomplish [1], complete [1], establish [1],
finish [1], over[2] [1], quickly [1]

5335 συντέμνω, *syntemnō*
decisively [1]

5337 συντηρέω, *syntēreō*
preserve [1], protect [1], treasure [1]

5338 συντίθημι, *syntithēmi*
agree [3]

5339 συντόμως, *syntomōs*
briefly [2]

5340 συντρέχω, *syntrechō*
hurry [1], join [1], run together [1]

5341 συντρίβω, *syntribō*
break [1], break in pieces [1], break
open [1], bruise [1], crush [1], maul [1],
shatter [1]

5342 σύντριμμα, *syntrimma*
ruin [1]

5343 σύντροφος, *syntrophos*
member of the court [1]

5344 συντυγχάνω, *syntynchanō*
reach [1]

5345 Συντύχη, *Syntychē*
Syntyche [1]

5347 συνυποκρίνομαι, *synypokrinomai*
join in hypocrisy [1]

5348 συνυπουργέω, *synypourgeō*
join in helping [1]

5349 συνωδίνω, *synōdinō*
labor pains [1]

5350 συνωμοσία, *synōmosia*
conspiracy [1]

5352 Συράκουσαι, *Syrakousai*
Syracuse [1]

5353 Συρία, *Syria*
Syria [8]

5354 Σύρος, *Syros*
Syrian [1]

5355 Συροφοινίκισσα, *Syrophoinikissa*
Syrophoenician [1]

5358 Σύρτις, *Syrtis*
Syrtis [1]

5359 σύρω, *syrō*
drag [3], drag off [1], sweep down [1]

5360 συσπαράσσω, *sysparassō*
convulse [1], convulsion [1]

5361 σύσσημον, *syssēmon*
sign [1]

5362 σύσσωμος, *syssōmos*
member of the same body [1]

5364 συστατικός, *systatikos*
recommendation [1]

5365 συσταυρόω, *systauroō*
crucify with [5]

5366 συστέλλω, *systellō*
grow short [1], wrap up [1]

5367 συστενάζω, *systenazō*
groan [1]

5368 συστοιχέω, *systoicheō*
correspond [1]

5369 συστρατιώτης, *systratiōtēs*
fellow soldier [2]

5370 συστρέφω, *systrephō*
gather [2]

5371 συστροφή, *systrophē*
commotion [1], conspiracy [1]

5372 συσχηματίζω, *syschēmatizō*
conform [2]

5373 Συχάρ, *Sychar*
Sychar [1]

5374 Συχέμ, *Sychem*
Shechem [2]

5375 σφαγή, *sphagē*
slaughter [3]

5376 σφάγιον, *sphagion*
slain victim [1]

5377 σφάζω, *sphazō*
slaughter [7], murder [2]

5377 + 1650 + 2505 σφάζω + εἰς +
θάνατος, *sphazō + eis + thanatos*
receive a death-blow [1]

5379 σφόδρα, *sphodra*
greatly [5], very[1] [2], overcome [1], so [1],
see 5828 [terrify] [1], *see* 5897
[overwhelm] [1]

5380 σφοδρῶς, *sphodrōs*
violently [1]

5381 σφραγίζω, *sphragizō*
seal [6], mark with a seal [3], seal up [2],
certify [1], deliver [1], put a seal on [1],
set seal [1]

5382 σφραγίς, *sphragis*
seal [15], inscription [1]

5383 σφυδρόν, *sphydron*
ankle [1]

5385 σχεδόν, *schedon*
almost [3]

5386 σχῆμα, *schēma*
form [2]

5387 σχίζω, schizō
tear[1] [7], divide [2], split [1], tear apart [1]

5388 σχίσμα, schisma
division [3], divide [2], tear[1] [2], dissension [1]

5389 σχοινίον, schoinion
cord [1], rope [1]

5390 σχολάζω, scholazō
devote [1], empty [1]

5391 σχολή, scholē
lecture hall [1]

5392 σώζω, sōzō
save [92], make well [9], heal [4], all right [1]

5393 σῶμα, sōma
body [136], bodily [2], corpse [1], slave [1], substance [1], see 1877 [torture] [1]

5394 σωματικός, sōmatikos
bodily [1], physical [1]

5395 σωματικῶς, sōmatikōs
bodily [1]

5396 Σώπατρος, Sōpatros
Sopater [1]

5397 σωρεύω, sōreuō
heap [1], overwhelm [1]

5398 Σωσθένης, Sōsthenēs
Sosthenes [2]

5399 Σωσίπατρος, Sōsipatros
Sosipater [1]

5400 σωτήρ, sōtēr
savior [24]

5401 σωτηρία, sōtēria
salvation [37], save [5], deliverance [1], savior [1], survive [1], see 1443 [rescue] [1]

5402 σωτήριον, sōtērion
salvation [4]

5403 σωτήριος, sōtērios
salvation [1]

5404 σωφρονέω, sōphroneō
right mind [3], self-controlled [1], serious [1], sober judgment [1]

5405 σωφρονίζω, sōphronizō
encourage [1]

5406 σωφρονισμός, sōphronismos
self-discipline [1]

5407 σωφρόνως, sōphronōs
self-controlled [1]

5408 σωφροσύνη, sōphrosynē
decently [1], modesty [1], sober [1]

5409 σώφρων, sōphrōn
prudent [2], self-controlled [1], sensible [1]

5412 Ταβιθά, Tabitha
Tabitha [2]

5413 τάγμα, tagma
order[1] [1]

5414 τακτός, taktos
appoint [1]

5415 ταλαιπωρέω, talaipōreō
lament [1]

5416 ταλαιπωρία, talaipōria
misery [2]

5417 ταλαίπωρος, talaipōros
wretched [2]

5418 ταλαντιαῖος, talantiaios
hundred pounds [1]

5419 τάλαντον, talanton
talent [14]

5420 ταλιθά, talitha
talitha [1]

5421 ταμεῖον, tameion
behind closed doors [1], inner room [1], room[1] [1], storehouse [1]

5423 τάξις, taxis
order[1] [7], duty [1], morale [1]

5424 ταπεινός, tapeinos
humble [4], lowly [3], downcast [1]

5425 ταπεινοφροσύνη, tapeinophrosynē
humility [6], self-abasement [1]

5426 ταπεινόφρων, tapeinophrōn
humble mind [1]

5427 ταπεινόω, tapeinoō
humble [12], have little [1], make low [1]

5428 ταπείνωσις, tapeinōsis
humiliation [2], bring low [1], lowliness [1]

5429 ταράσσω, tarassō
trouble [4], terrify [3], confuse [2], disturb [2], frighten [2], incite [1], intimidate [1], move deeply [1], stir up [1]

5431 τάραχος, tarachos
commotion [1], disturbance [1]

5432 Ταρσεύς, Tarseus
Tarsus [1], man of Tarsus [1]

5433 Ταρσός, Tarsos
Tarsus [3]

5434 ταρταρόω, tartaroō
cast into hell [1]

5435 τάσσω, tassō
set[1] [2], appoint [1], assign [1], destine [1], devote [1], direct [1], institute [1]

5436 ταῦρος, tauros
bull [2], ox [2]

5438 ταφή, taphē
place to bury [1]

5439 τάφος, taphos
tomb [6], grave [1]

5440 τάχα, tacha
perhaps [2]

5441 ταχέως, tacheōs
quickly [5], soon [4], hastily [1], in time [1], once[2] [1], soon as possible [1], very soon [1], untranslated [1]

5442 ταχινός, tachinos
soon [1], swift [1]

5443 τάχος, tachos
see 1877 [quickly] [3], see 1877 [soon] [3], see 1877 [shortly] [2]

5444 ταχύς, tachys
quickly [5], soon [5], quick [1], soon afterward [1], very soon [1]

5445 τέ, te
untranslated [92], and [72], both [30], then [7], also [3], but [2], since [2], as [1], even [1], from [1], not only [1], or [1], so [1], the [1]

5446 τεῖχος, teichos
wall [9]

5447 τεκμήριον, tekmērion
convincing proof [1]

5448 τεκνίον, teknion
little child [8]

5449 τεκνογονέω, teknogoneō
bear a child [1]

5450 τεκνογονία, teknogonia
childbearing [1]

5451 τέκνον, teknon
child [89], son [6], daughter [1], little child [1], see 3590 [childless] [1], see 4024 [childless] [1]

5452 τεκνοτροφέω, teknotropheō
bring up a child [1]

5454 τέκτων, tektōn
carpenter [2]

5455 τέλειος, teleios
perfect [9], mature [6], adult [1], complete [1], full [1], maturity [1]

5456 τελειότης, teleiotēs
perfect harmony [1], perfection [1]

5457 τελειόω, teleioō
make perfect [7], perfect [4], finish [3], complete [2], reach perfection [2], bring to completion [1], completely [1], end [1], fulfill [1], reach a goal [1]

5458 τελείως, teleiōs
all [1]

5459 τελείωσις, teleiōsis
fulfillment [1], perfection [1]

5460 τελειωτής, teleiōtēs
perfecter [1]

5461 τελεσφορέω, telesphoreō
mature [1]

5462 τελευτάω, teleutaō
die [6], dead man [1], death [1], end of life [1]

5462 + 2505 τελευτάω + θάνατος, teleutaō + thanatos
die surely [2]

5463 τελευτή, teleutē
death [1]

5464 τελέω, teleō
finish [10], end [5], fulfill [4], pay [2], accomplish [1], carry out [1], complete [1], go through all [1], gratify [1], keep [1], make perfect [1]

5465 τέλος, telos
end [30], revenue [2], aim [1], finally [1], fulfill [1], last[1] [1], outcome [1], purpose [1], toll [1], see 1650 [continually] [1]

5467 τελώνης, telōnēs
tax collector [21]

5468 τελώνιον, telōnion
tax booth [3]

5469 τέρας, teras
wonder [13], omen [2], portent [1]

5470 Τέρτιος, Tertios
Tertius [1]

5472 Τέρτυλλος, Tertyllos
Tertullus [2]

5475 τέσσαρες, tessares
four [30], see 1633 [twenty-four] [6], see 5477 [forty-four] [4], see 3837 [eighty-four] [1]

5476 τεσσαρεσκαιδέκατος, tessareskaidekatos
fourteenth [2]

5477 τεσσεράκοντα, tesserakonta
forty [15]

5477 + 2779 + 1545 τεσσεράκοντα + καί + δύο, *tesserakonta + kai + dyo*
forty-two [2]

5477 + 2779 + 1971 τεσσεράκοντα + καί + ἕξ, *tesserakonta + kai + hex*
forty-six [1]

5477 + 5475 τεσσεράκοντα + τέσσαρες, *tesserakonta + tessares*
forty-four [4]

5478 τεσσερακονταετής, *tesserakontaetēs*
forty years [2]

5479 τεταρταῖος, *tetartaios*
four days [1]

5480 τέταρτος, *tetartos*
fourth [7], four [1]

5480 + 5871 + 3836 + 3816 τέταρτος + φυλακή + ὁ + νύξ, *tetartos + phylakē + ho + nyx*
early in the morning [2]

5481 τετράγωνος, *tetragōnos*
foursquare [1]

5482 τετράδιον, *tetradion*
squad [1]

5483 τετρακισχίλιοι, *tetrakischilioi*
four thousand [5]

5484 τετρακόσιοι, *tetrakosioi*
four hundred [4]

5485 τετράμηνος, *tetramēnos*
four months [1]

5487 τετραπλοῦς, *tetraplous*
four times as much [1]

5488 τετράπους, *tetrapous*
four-footed animal [2], four-footed creature [1]

5489 τετραρχέω, *tetrarcheō*
ruler [3]

5490 τετράρχης, *tetrarchēs*
ruler [4]

5491 τεφρόω, *tephroō*
turn to ashes [1]

5492 τέχνη, *technē*
trade [2], art [1]

5493 τεχνίτης, *technitēs*
artisan [3], architect [1]

5494 τήκομαι, *tēkomai*
melt [1]

5495 τηλαυγῶς, *tēlaugōs*
clearly [1]

5496 τηλικοῦτος, *tēlikoutos*
deadly [1], large [1], so great [1], so violent [1]

5498 τηρέω, *tēreō*
keep [41], obey [8], protect [4], keep watch over [3], keep in custody [2], refrain [2], reserve [2], be [1], do [1], follow [1], guard [1], hold [1], keep safe [1], maintain [1], observe² [1]

5499 τήρησις, *tērēsis*
custody [1], obey [1], prison [1]

5500 Τιβεριάς, *Tiberias*
Tiberias [3]

5501 Τιβέριος, *Tiberios*
Tiberius [1]

5502 τίθημι, *tithēmi*
lay [30], put [19], lay down [10], make [8], appoint [6], set¹ [3], deposit [2], destine [2], place [2], *untranslated* [2], arrange [1], contrive [1], entrust [1], make up [1], resolve [1], serve [1], sink [1], take off [1], use [1]

5502 + 1877 + 3836 + 2840 τίθημι + ἐν + ὁ + καρδία, *tithēmi + en + ho + kardia*
ponder [1]

5502 + 3836 + 1205 τίθημι + ὁ + γόνυ, *tithēmi + ho + gony*
kneel down [6]

5503 τίκτω, *tiktō*
bear¹ [7], give birth [6], bear a child [2], deliver a child [1], labor [1], produce [1]

5504 τίλλω, *tillō*
pluck [3]

5505 Τιμαῖος, *Timaios*
Timaeus [1]

5506 τιμάω, *timaō*
honor [18], set a price [2], bestow [1]

5507 τιμή, *timē*
honor [27], price [3], proceeds [3], special [2], value [2], money [1], precious [1], special use [1], sum [1]

5508 τίμιος, *timios*
precious [4], *see 3345* [jewel] [4], costly [1], hold in honor [1], respect¹ [1], value [1], very rare [1]

5509 τιμιότης, *timiotēs*
wealth [1]

5510 Τιμόθεος, *Timotheos*
Timothy [24]

5511 Τίμων, *Timōn*
Timon [1]

5512 τιμωρέω, *timōreō*
punish [1], punishment [1]

5513 τιμωρία, *timōria*
punishment [1]

5514 τίνω, *tinō*
suffer² [1]

5515 τίς, *tis*
what [248], who [140], why [67], *see 1328* [why] [26], which [19], *untranslated* [10], how [8], *see 1650* [why] [4], *see 1877* [how] [4], one [3], all [2], any [2], anything [2], something [2], anyone [1], each [1], he [1], how great [1], person [1], what about [1], what kind [1], *see 2848* [how] [1], *see 4024* [nothing] [1], *see 4639* [why] [1]

5515 + 323 τίς + ἄν, *tis + an*
what [5], which [1]

5515 + 1915 τίς + ἕνεκεν, *tis + heneken*
why [1]

5515 + 3364 τίς + λόγος, *tis + logos*
why [1]

5515 + 4022 τίς + ὅτι, *tis + hoti*
why [1]

5516 τὶς, *tis*
some [101], anyone [58], a [54], *untranslated* [47], one [39], anything [35], any [33], someone [27], certain [18], something [15], man [8], you [8], whoever [7], *see 4005* [whatever] [6], certain person [4], that [4], other [3], several [3], some person [3], what [3], *see 3590* [nothing] [3], another [2], builder [2], it [2], person [2], thing [2], whatever [2], *see 1099* [little while] [2], acknowledged leader [1], all [1], any way [1], certain individual [1], certain man [1], favor [1], kind¹ [1], little [1], matter [1], none [1], piece [1], rather [1], some things [1], somebody [1], somewhat [1], they [1], who [1], *see 1569* [whatever] [1], *see 3590* [none] [1], *see 4005* [why] [1], *see 4024* [nothing] [1], *see 4028* [nothing] [1], *see 4246* [whatever] [1]

5516 + 476 τὶς + ἄνθρωπος, *tis + anthrōpos*
anyone [1]

5516 + 1569 τὶς + ἐάν, *tis + ean*
whoever [7], anyone [5], who [4]

5517 Τίτιος, *Titios*
Titius [1]

5518 τίτλος, *titlos*
inscription [2]

5519 Τίτος, *Titos*
Titus [13]

5521 τοιγαροῦν, *toigaroun*
therefore [2]

5523 τοίνυν, *toinyn*
then [2], so [1]

5524 τοιόσδε, *toiosde*
that [1]

5525 τοιοῦτος, *toioutos*
such [21], such a person [9], such a thing [6], such a one [3], kind¹ [2], so [2], this [2], *untranslated* [2], as [1], he [1], man [1], same [1], such a case [1], such a fellow [1], that [1], this way [1], what [1], who [1]

5526 τοῖχος, *toichos*
wall [1]

5527 τόκος, *tokos*
interest² [2]

5528 τολμάω, *tolmaō*
dare [13], boldly [1], boldness [1], venture [1]

5529 τολμηρός, *tolmēros*
rather boldly [1]

5532 τολμητής, *tolmētēs*
bold [1]

5533 τομός, *tomos*
sharp [1]

5534 τόξον, *toxon*
bow² [1]

5535 τοπάζιον, *topazion*
topaz [1]

5536 τόπος, *topos*
place [79], room² [3], region [2], chance [1], need [1], opportunity [1], port [1], position [1], there [1], *see 2093* [seafarer] [1], *see 2245* [country] [1], *untranslated* [1]

5536 + 1458 τόπος + διθάλασσος, *topos + dithalassos*
reef [1]

5537 τοσοῦτος, *tosoutos*
many [4], all [3], much [2], such [2], all this [1], enough [1], great [1], like measure [1], price [1], so great [1], so much [1], such and such [1], *untranslated* [1]

5538 τότε, *tote*
then [137], *untranslated* [7], that time [4], at that time [3], when [3], time¹ [2], at this [1], formerly [1], so [1], that moment [1]

5539 τοὐναντίον, *tounantion*
contrary [2]

5539 + 3437 τοὐναντίον + μᾶλλον,
tounantion + mallon
instead [1]

5540 τοὔνομα, *tounoma*
name [1]

5543 τράγος, *tragos*
goat [4]

5544 τράπεζα, *trapeza*
table [13], bank [1], food [1]

5545 τραπεζίτης, *trapezitēs*
banker [1]

5546 τραῦμα, *trauma*
wound [1]

5547 τραυματίζω, *traumatizō*
wound [2]

5548 τραχηλίζω, *trachēlizō*
lay bare [1]

5549 τράχηλος, *trachēlos*
neck [5], *see 2158* [embrace] [1], *see 2158*
[put arms around] [1]

5550 τραχύς, *trachys*
rock [1], rough [1]

5551 Τραχωνῖτις, *Trachōnitis*
Trachonitis [1]

5552 τρεῖς, *treis*
three [65], *see 1633* [twenty-three] [1], *see*
4299 [fifty-three] [1]

5552 + 3583 τρεῖς + μετρητής, *treis +*
metrētēs
thirty gallons [1]

5553 Τρεῖς ταβέρναι, *Treis tabernai*
Three Taverns [1]

5554 τρέμω, *tremō*
tremble [2], afraid [1]

5555 τρέφω, *trephō*
feed [2], nourish [2], bring up [1], depend
on for food [1], fatten [1], give food [1],
nurse [1]

5556 τρέχω, *trechō*
run [14], compete [1], exertion [1],
runner [1], rush [1], spread rapidly [1]

5557 τρῆμα, *trēma*
eye [1]

5558 τριάκοντα, *triakonta*
thirty [9]

5558 + 2779 + 3893 τριάκοντα + καί +
ὀκτώ, *triakonta + kai + oktō*
thirty-eight [1]

5558 + 5084 τριάκοντα + στάδιον,
triakonta + stadion
four miles [1]

5559 τριακόσιοι, *triakosioi*
three hundred [2]

5560 τρίβολος, *tribolos*
thistle [2]

5561 τρίβος, *tribos*
path [3]

5562 τριετία, *trietia*
three years [1]

5563 τρίζω, *trizō*
grind [1]

5564 τρίμηνος, *trimēnos*
three months [1]

5565 τρίς, *tris*
three times [10], three [2]

5566 τρίστεγον, *tristegon*
three floors [1]

5567 τρισχίλιοι, *trischilioi*
three thousand [1]

5568 τρίτον, *triton*
third [4], third time [4]

5569 τρίτος, *tritos*
third [43]

5569 + 5871 τρίτος + φυλακή, *tritos +*
phylakē
near dawn [1]

5569 + 6052 τρίτος + ὥρα, *tritos + hōra*
nine o'clock [2], nine o'clock in the
morning [1]

5569 + 6052 + 3836 + 2465 τρίτος +
ὥρα + ὁ + ἡμέρα, *tritos + hōra + ho +*
hēmera
nine o'clock in the morning [1]

5570 τρίχινος, *trichinos*
see 4884 [sackcloth] [1]

5571 τρόμος, *tromos*
tremble [4], terror [1]

5572 τροπή, *tropē*
change [1]

5573 τρόπος, *tropos*
way [5], as [3], *see 4005* [as] [2], life [1],
manner [1], *see 2848* [just as] [1]

5574 τροποφορέω, *tropophoreō*
put up with [1]

5575 τροφή, *trophē*
food [14], allowance of food [1], *see 3170*
[satisfy hunger] [1]

5576 Τρόφιμος, *Trophimos*
Trophimus [3]

5577 τροφός, *trophos*
nurse [1]

5579 τροχιά, *trochia*
path [1]

5580 τροχός, *trochos*
cycle [1]

5581 τρύβλιον, *tryblion*
bowl [2]

5582 τρυγάω, *trygaō*
gather [2], pick [1]

5583 τρυγών, *trygōn*
turtledove [1]

5584 τρυμαλιά, *trymalia*
eye [1]

5585 τρύπημα, *trypēma*
eye [1]

5586 Τρύφαινα, *Tryphaina*
Tryphaena [1]

5587 τρυφάω, *tryphaō*
live in luxury [1]

5588 τρυφή, *tryphē*
luxury [1], revel [1]

5589 Τρυφῶσα, *Tryphōsa*
Tryphosa [1]

5590 Τρῳάς, *Trōas*
Troas [6]

5592 τρώγω, *trōgō*
eat [6]

5593 τυγχάνω, *tynchanō*
obtain [3], be [1], enjoy [1], have [1],

perhaps [1], place [1], *see 1623*
[doubtless] [1], *see 1623* [perhaps] [1], *see*
4024 [extraordinary] [1], *see 4024*
[unusual] [1]

5594 τυμπανίζω, *tympanizō*
torture [1]

5595 τυπικῶς, *typikōs*
serve as an example [1]

5596 τύπος, *typos*
example [6], mark [2], pattern [2],
effect [1], form [1], image [1], model [1],
type [1]

5597 τύπτω, *typtō*
beat [6], strike [6], wound [1]

5598 Τύραννος[1], *Tyrannos[1]*
Tyrannus [1]

5601 Τύριος, *Tyrios*
person of Tyre [1]

5602 Τύρος, *Tyros*
Tyre [11]

5603 τυφλός, *typhlos*
blind [35], blind man [10], blind
person [4], another [1]

5604 τυφλόω, *typhloō*
blind [2], bring on blindness [1]

5605 τυφόομαι, *typhoomai*
conceited [1], puff up with conceit [1],
swell with conceit [1]

5606 τύφω, *typhō*
smolder [1]

5607 τυφωνικός, *typhōnikos*
violent [1]

5608 Τυχικός, *Tychikos*
Tychicus [5]

5610 ὑακίνθινος, *hyakinthinos*
sapphire [1]

5611 ὑάκινθος, *hyakinthos*
jacinth [1]

5612 ὑάλινος, *hyalinos*
glass [3]

5613 ὕαλος, *hyalos*
glass [2]

5614 ὑβρίζω, *hybrizō*
insult [2], mistreat [2], mistreat
shamefully [1]

5615 ὕβρις, *hybris*
damage [1], danger [1], insult [1]

5616 ὑβριστής, *hybristēs*
insolent [1], man of violence [1]

5617 ὑγιαίνω, *hygiainō*
sound[2] [8], good health [2], safe and
sound [1], well[3] [1]

5618 ὑγιής, *hygiēs*
well[3] [5], sound[2] [2], good health [1],
heal [1], whole [1]

5618 + 4472 ὑγιής + ποιέω, *hygiēs +*
poieō
heal [1]

5619 ὑγρός, *hygros*
green [1]

5620 ὑδρία, *hydria*
water jar [2], jar [1]

5621 ὑδροποτέω, *hydropoteō*
drink only water [1]

5622 ὑδρωπικός, *hydrōpikos*
dropsy [1]

5623 ὕδωρ, *hydōr*
water [75], wave [1]

5624 ὑετός, *hyetos*
rain [5]

5625 υἱοθεσία, *huiothesia*
adoption [3], adoption as a child [2]

5626 υἱός, *huios*
son [305], child [37], people [8],
descendant [5], guest [3], that [3],
exorcist [2], belong [1], destine [1],
foal [1], heir [1], one destined [1],
share [1], *untranslated* [1]

5626 + 476 υἱός + ἄνθρωπος, *huios +
anthrōpos*
humankind [1], mortal [1]

5626 + 2702 υἱός + Ἰσραήλ, *huios +
Israēl*
Israelite [4]

5626 + 3836 + 476 υἱός + ὁ +
ἄνθρωπος, *huios + ho + anthrōpos*
person [1]

5627 ὕλη, *hylē*
forest [1]

5628 Ὑμέναιος, *Hymenaios*
Hymenaeus [2]

5629 ὑμέτερος, *hymeteros*
you [11]

5630 ὑμνέω, *hymneō*
sing a hymn [3], praise [1]

5631 ὕμνος, *hymnos*
hymn [2]

5632 ὑπάγω, *hypagō*
go [71], go away [3], get [2], away [1],
desert¹ [1], go on one's way [1]

5633 ὑπακοή, *hypakoē*
obedience [11], obedient [3], obey [1]

5634 ὑπακούω, *hypakouō*
obey [18], obedient [2], answer [1]

5635 ὕπανδρος, *hypandros*
marry [1]

5636 ὑπαντάω, *hypantaō*
meet [7], go and meet [1], go to meet [1],
oppose [1]

5637 ὑπάντησις, *hypantēsis*
meet [3]

5638 ὕπαρξις, *hyparxis*
goods [1], possess [1]

5639 ὑπάρχω, *hyparchō*
be [35], possession [10], *untranslated* [5],
property [3], belong [2], have [1], help [1],
live [1], resource [1], though [1]

5640 ὑπείκω, *hypeikō*
submit [1]

5641 ὑπεναντίος, *hypenantios*
adversary [1], against [1]

5642 ὑπέρ, *hyper*
for [84], sake [14], behalf [13], about¹ [7],
above [4], more than [4], than [4],
beyond [3], good [2], of [2], over¹ [2],
as [1], as for [1], because [1], by [1],
concerning [1], favor [1], in [1], in one's
place [1], more [1], *untranslated* [1]

5642 + 1539 ὑπέρ + δύναμις, *hyper +
dynamis*
unbearably [1]

5643 ὑπεραίρομαι, *hyperairomai*
too elated [2], exalt [1]

5644 ὑπέρακμος, *hyperakmos*
strong passion [1]

5645 ὑπεράνω, *hyperanō*
far above [2], above [1]

5647 ὑπεραυξάνω, *hyperauxanō*
grow abundantly [1]

5648 ὑπερβαίνω, *hyperbainō*
wrong [1]

5649 ὑπερβαλλόντως, *hyperballontōs*
countless [1]

5650 ὑπερβάλλω, *hyperballō*
immeasurable [2], surpass [2], great [1]

5651 ὑπερβολή, *hyperbolē*
see 2848 [beyond all measure] [2], beyond
measure [1], exceptional [1],
extraordinary [1], more excellent [1],
violently [1], *see 2848* [utterly] [1]

5654 ὑπερέκεινα, *hyperekeina*
land beyond [1]

5655 ὑπερεκπερισσοῦ,
hyperekperissou
abundantly [1], earnestly [1], very
highly [1]

5657 ὑπερεκτείνω, *hyperekteinō*
overstep [1]

5658 ὑπερεκχύννω, *hyperekchynnō*
run over [1]

5659 ὑπερεντυγχάνω,
hyperentynchanō
intercede [1]

5660 ὑπερέχω, *hyperechō*
good [1], govern [1], supreme [1],
surpass [1], surpassing value [1]

5661 ὑπερηφανία, *hyperēphania*
pride [1]

5662 ὑπερήφανος, *hyperēphanos*
proud [3], arrogant [1], haughty [1]

5663 + 693 ὑπερλίαν + ἀπόστολος,
hyperlian + apostolos
super-apostle [2]

5664 ὑπερνικάω, *hypernikaō*
more than conqueror [1]

5665 ὑπέρογκος, *hyperonkos*
bombastic [2]

5666 ὑπεροράω, *hyperoraō*
overlook [1]

5667 ὑπεροχή, *hyperochē*
high position [1], lofty [1]

5668 ὑπερπερισσεύω, *hyperperisseuō*
abound all the more [1]

5668 + 5915 ὑπερπερισσεύω + χαρά,
hyperperisseuō + chara
overjoyed [1]

5669 ὑπερπερισσῶς, *hyperperissōs*
beyond measure [1]

5670 ὑπερπλεονάζω, *hyperpleonazō*
overflow [1]

5671 ὑπερυψόω, *hyperypsoō*
exalt highly [1]

5672 ὑπερφρονέω, *hyperphroneō*
think highly [1]

5673 ὑπερῷον, *hyperōon*
room upstairs [4]

5674 ὑπέχω, *hypechō*
undergo [1]

5675 ὑπήκοος, *hypēkoos*
obedient [2], obey [1]

5676 ὑπηρετέω, *hypēreteō*
serve [1], take care of needs [1], work [1]

5677 ὑπηρέτης, *hypēretēs*
police [6], guard [4], temple police [4],
servant [2], assist [1], attendant [1],
follower [1], serve [1]

5678 ὕπνος, *hypnos*
sleep [5], *see 3122* [mere sleep] [1]

5679 ὑπό, *hypo*
by [135], under [39], *untranslated* [24],
from [5], at [3], of [3], subject [3], in [2],
to [2], under power [2], in power [1],
side [1]

5680 ὑποβάλλω, *hypoballō*
instigate secretly [1]

5681 ὑπογραμμός, *hypogrammos*
example [1]

5682 ὑπόδειγμα, *hypodeigma*
example [3], sketch [2], as [1]

5683 ὑποδείκνυμι, *hypodeiknymi*
warn [3], show [2], give an example [1]

5685 ὑποδέχομαι, *hypodechomai*
welcome [2], entertain as a guest [1],
welcome into a home [1]

5686 ὑποδέω, *hypodeō*
put on [1], put on shoes [1], wear [1]

5687 ὑπόδημα, *hypodēma*
sandal [10]

5688 ὑπόδικος, *hypodikos*
accountable [1]

5689 ὑποζύγιον, *hypozygion*
donkey [2]

5690 ὑποζώννυμι, *hypozōnnymi*
undergird [1]

5691 ὑποκάτω, *hypokatō*
under [10], on [1]

5693 ὑποκρίνομαι, *hypokrinomai*
pretend [1]

5694 ὑπόκρισις, *hypokrisis*
hypocrisy [5], insincerity [1]

5695 ὑποκριτής, *hypokritēs*
hypocrite [17]

5696 ὑπολαμβάνω, *hypolambanō*
suppose [2], reply [1], support [1], take [1]

5698 ὑπόλειμμα, *hypoleimma*
remnant [1]

5699 ὑπολείπω, *hypoleipō*
leave [1]

5700 ὑπολήνιον, *hypolēnion*
pit for the wine press [1]

5701 ὑπολιμπάνω, *hypolimpanō*
leave [1]

5702 ὑπομένω, *hypomenō*
endure [13], patient [1], remain [1], show
endurance [1], stay behind [1]

5703 ὑπομιμνήσκω, *hypomimnēskō*
remind [5], call attention [1],
remember [1]

5704 ὑπόμνησις, *hypomnēsis*
memory [1], remind [1]

5704 + 3284 ὑπόμνησις + λαμβάνω,
hypomnēsis + lambanō
remind [1]

5705 ὑπομονή, *hypomonē*
endurance [14], steadfastness [6], patient

endurance [5], endure patiently [2],
patience [2], endure [1], patiently [1],
perseverance [1]

5706 ὑπονοέω, hyponoeō
expect [1], suppose [1], suspect [1]

5707 ὑπόνοια, hyponoia
suspicion [1]

5709 ὑποπλέω, hypopleō
sail under the lee [2]

5710 ὑποπνέω, hypopneō
blow moderately [1]

5711 ὑποπόδιον, hypopodion
footstool [6], foot [1]

5712 ὑπόστασις, hypostasis
confidence [2], assurance [1],
undertaking [1], very being [1]

5713 ὑποστέλλω, hypostellō
shrink [2], draw back [1], shrink back [1]

5714 ὑποστολή, hypostolē
shrink back [1]

5715 ὑποστρέφω, hypostrephō
return [33], turn back [2]

5716 ὑποστρωννύω, hypostrōnnyō
spread [1]

5717 ὑποταγή, hypotagē
obedience [1], submission [1],
submissive [1], see 1634 [submit] [1]

5718 ὑποτάσσω, hypotassō
subject [15], accept authority [5],
submit [5], put in subjection [4], make
subject [2], submissive [2], obedient [1],
put at the service [1], put under [1],
subjection [1], subordinate [1]

5719 ὑποτίθημι, hypotithēmi
put before [1], risk [1]

5720 ὑποτρέχω, hypotrechō
run under the lee [1]

5721 ὑποτύπωσις, hypotypōsis
example [1], standard [1]

5722 ὑποφέρω, hypopherō
endure [3]

5723 ὑποχωρέω, hypochōreō
withdraw [2]

5724 ὑπωπιάζω, hypōpiazō
punish [1], wear out [1]

5725 ὗς, hys
sow² [1]

5727 ὕσσωπος, hyssōpos
hyssop [2]

5728 ὑστερέω, hystereō
lack [4], inferior [3], need [3], bad off [1],
destitute [1], fail to obtain [1], fail to
reach [1], fall short [1], give out [1]

5729 ὑστέρημα, hysterēma
need [4], lack [2], absence [1], not [1],
poverty [1]

5730 ὑστέρησις, hysterēsis
need [1], poverty [1]

5731 ὕστερος, hysteros
late [5], finally [2], last¹ [2], after [1],
afterward [1], afterwards [1]

5733 ὑφαντός, hyphantos
weave [1]

5734 ὑψηλός, hypsēlos
high [6], exalt above [1], prize [1],
uplift [1]

5734 + 5858 ὑψηλός + φρονέω,
hypsēlos + phroneō
haughty [1], proud [1]

5735 ὑψηλοφρονέω, hypsēlophroneō
haughty [1]

5736 ὕψιστος, hypsistos
most high [9], high heaven [4]

5737 ὕψος, hypsos
high [3], height [2], raise up [1]

5738 ὑψόω, hypsoō
exalt [13], lift up [6], make great [1]

5739 ὕψωμα, hypsōma
height [1], proud [1]

5741 φάγος, phagos
glutton [2]

5742 φαιλόνης, phailonēs
cloak [1]

5743 φαίνω, phainō
appear [10], shine [9], see [3], look [2],
show [2], become [1], decision [1],
flash [1], seem [1], visible [1]

5744 Φάλεκ, Phalek
Peleg [1]

5745 φανερός, phaneros
know [5], disclose [2], light¹ [2],
obvious [2], clear [1], plain [1], reveal [1],
see [1], visible [1], see 1877 [external] [1],
see 1877 [outwardly] [1]

5746 φανερόω, phaneroō
reveal [19], appear [6], disclose [5],
show [5], know well [2], make known [2],
make visible [2], visible [2], make
evident [1], plain [1], reveal clearly [1],
see [1], see clearly [1], spread [1]

5747 φανερῶς, phanerōs
clearly [1], openly [1], publicly [1]

5748 φανέρωσις, phanerōsis
manifestation [1], open statement [1]

5749 φανός, phanos
lantern [1]

5750 Φανουήλ, Phanouēl
Phanuel [1]

5751 φαντάζω, phantazō
sight [1]

5752 φαντασία, phantasia
pomp [1]

5753 φάντασμα, phantasma
ghost [2]

5754 φάραγξ, pharanx
valley [1]

5755 Φαραώ, Pharaō
Pharaoh [5]

5756 Φαρές, Phares
Perez [3]

5757 Φαρισαῖος, Pharisaios
Pharisee [98]

5758 φαρμακεία, pharmakeia
sorcery [2]

5760 φάρμακον, pharmakon
sorcery [1]

5761 φάρμακος, pharmakos
sorcerer [2]

5762 φάσις, phasis
word [1]

5763 φάσκω, phaskō
assert [2], claim [1]

5764 φάτνη, phatnē
manger [4]

5765 φαῦλος, phaulos
evil [4], bad [1], wickedness [1]

5766 φέγγος, phengos
light¹ [2]

5767 φείδομαι, pheidomai
spare [7], lenient [1], refrain [1],
withhold [1]

5768 φειδομένως, pheidomenōs
sparingly [2]

5770 φέρω, pherō
bring [33], bear¹ [9], take [4], carry [2],
come [2], drive [2], endure [2], convey [1],
establish [1], get [1], go [1], lead [1],
move [1], put [1], reach out [1], rush [1],
sustain [1], yield [1], see 162 [charge³] [1]

5771 φεύγω, pheugō
flee [16], run off [4], escape [3], shun [3],
flee away [1], run [1], run away [1]

5772 Φῆλιξ, Phēlix
Felix [8], untranslated [1]

5773 φήμη, phēmē
report [2]

5774 φημί, phēmi
say [52], reply [6], untranslated [3],
answer [1], ask [1], imply [1], mean¹ [1]

5774 + 3489 + 3836 + 5889 φημί +
μέγας + ὁ + φωνή, phēmi + megas +
ho + phōnē
exclaim [1]

5776 Φῆστος, Phēstos
Festus [13]

5777 φθάνω, phthanō
come [3], attain [1], overtake [1],
precede [1], succeed in fulfilling [1]

5778 φθαρτός, phthartos
perishable [4], mortal [1], perishable
thing [1]

5779 φθέγγομαι, phthengomai
speak [3]

5780 φθείρω, phtheirō
destroy [4], corrupt [3], lead astray [1],
ruin [1]

5781 φθινοπωρινός, phthinopōrinos
autumn [1]

5782 φθόγγος, phthongos
note² [1], voice [1]

5783 φθονέω, phthoneō
envy [1]

5784 φθόνος, phthonos
envy [6], jealousy [2], jealously [1]

5785 φθορά, phthora
corruption [3], perishable [2], decay [1],
destroy [1], kill [1], perish [1]

5786 φιάλη, phialē
bowl [12]

5787 φιλάγαθος, philagathos
lover of goodness [1]

5788 Φιλαδέλφεια, Philadelpheia
Philadelphia [2]

5789 φιλαδελφία, philadelphia
mutual affection [3], mutual love [2], love
of the brother and sister [1]

5790 φιλάδελφος, philadelphos
love for one another [1]

5791 φίλανδρος, philandros
love a husband [1]

5792 φιλανθρωπία, *philanthrōpia*
kindness [1], loving kindness [1]

5793 φιλανθρώπως, *philanthrōpōs*
kindly [1]

5794 φιλαργυρία, *philargyria*
love of money [1]

5795 φιλάργυρος, *philargyros*
lover of money [2]

5796 φίλαυτος, *philautos*
lover of self [1]

5797 φιλέω, *phileō*
love [22], kiss [3]

5798 φιλήδονος, *philēdonos*
lover of pleasure [1]

5799 φίλημα, *philēma*
kiss [7]

5800 Φιλήμων, *Philēmōn*
Philemon [1]

5801 Φίλητος, *Philētos*
Philetus [1]

5802 φιλία, *philia*
friendship [1]

5803 Φιλιππήσιος, *Philippēsios*
Philippian [1]

5804 Φίλιπποι, *Philippoi*
Philippi [4]

5805 Φίλιππος, *Philippos*
Philip [34], Philippi [2]

5806 φιλόθεος, *philotheos*
lover of God [1]

5807 Φιλόλογος, *Philologos*
Philologus [1]

5808 φιλονεικία, *philoneikia*
dispute [1]

5809 φιλόνεικος, *philoneikos*
contentious [1]

5810 φιλοξενία, *philoxenia*
hospitality to a stranger [1], show
hospitality to a stranger [1]

5811 φιλόξενος, *philoxenos*
hospitable [3]

5812 φιλοπρωτεύω, *philoprōteuō*
like to put first [1]

5813 φίλος, *philos*
friend [28], friendly [1]

5814 φιλοσοφία, *philosophia*
philosophy [1]

5815 φιλόσοφος, *philosophos*
philosopher [1]

5816 φιλόστοργος, *philostorgos*
love [1]

5817 φιλότεκνος, *philoteknos*
love a child [1]

5818 φιλοτιμέομαι, *philotimeomai*
aspire [1], make one's aim [1], make one's
ambition [1]

5819 φιλοφρόνως, *philophronōs*
hospitably [1]

5821 φιμόω, *phimoō*
silence [2], silent [1], muzzle [1],
speechless [1], still[2] [1]

5823 Φλέγων, *Phlegōn*
Phlegon [1]

5824 φλογίζω, *phlogizō*
set on fire [2]

5825 φλόξ, *phlox*
flame [7]

5826 φλυαρέω, *phlyareō*
spread [1]

5827 φλύαρος, *phlyaros*
gossip [1]

5828 φοβέομαι, *phobeomai*
afraid [43], fear [39], fill with awe [2],
terrify [2], alarm [1], frighten [1],
respect[1] [1], stand in awe [1], take
care [1], *see 3590* [unafraid] [1]

5828 + 3836 + 2536 φοβέομαι + ὁ +
θεός, *phobeomai + ho + theos*
God-fearing [1]

5828 + 5379 φοβέομαι + σφόδρα,
phobeomai + sphodra
terrify [1]

5828 + 5832 + 3489 φοβέομαι + φόβος
+ μέγας, *phobeomai + phobos +
megas*
terrify [1]

5829 φοβερός, *phoberos*
fearful [1], fearful thing [1], terrify [1]

5831 φόβητρον, *phobētron*
dreadful portent [1]

5832 φόβος, *phobos*
fear [32], awe [3], reverence [3],
respect[1] [2], alarm [1], deference [1],
reverent fear [1], terror [1], *see 2158*
[awestruck] [1], *see 5828* [terrify] [1]

5832 + 3489 + 2158 φόβος + μέγας +
ἐπιπίπτω, *phobos + megas +
epipiptō*
terrify [1]

5833 Φοίβη, *Phoibē*
Phoebe [1]

5834 Φοινίκη, *Phoinikē*
Phoenicia [3]

5836 φοῖνιξ[1], *phoinix*[1]
palm branch [1], palm tree [1]

5837 Φοῖνιξ[2], *Phoinix*[2]
Phoenix [1]

5838 φονεύς, *phoneus*
murderer [7]

5839 φονεύω, *phoneuō*
murder [11], commit murder [1]

5840 φόνος, *phonos*
murder [8], *untranslated* [1]

5841 φορέω, *phoreō*
bear[1] [3], wear [3]

5842 φόρον, *phoron*
forum [1]

5843 φόρος, *phoros*
tax [5]

5844 φορτίζω, *phortizō*
carry heavy burdens [1], load [1]

5845 φορτίον, *phortion*
burden [3], cargo [1], load [1], they [1]

5847 Φορτουνᾶτος, *Phortounatos*
Fortunatus [1]

5848 φραγέλλιον, *phragellion*
whip [1]

5849 φραγελλόω, *phragelloō*
flog [2]

5850 φραγμός, *phragmos*
fence [2], lane [1], wall [1]

5851 φράζω, *phrazō*
explain [1]

5852 φράσσω, *phrassō*
silence [2], shut [1]

5853 φρέαρ, *phrear*
shaft [4], well[4] [3]

5854 φρεναπατάω, *phrenapataō*
deceive [1]

5855 φρεναπάτης, *phrenapatēs*
deceiver [1]

5856 φρήν, *phrēn*
think [2]

5857 φρίσσω, *phrissō*
shudder [1]

5858 φρονέω, *phroneō*
think [7], mind[1] [5], set one's mind [5],
concern [2], live [2], observe[2] [2],
agree [1], *see 5734* [haughty] [1], *see
5734* [proud] [1]

5859 φρόνημα, *phronēma*
mind[1] [4]

5860 φρόνησις, *phronēsis*
insight [1], wisdom [1]

5861 φρόνιμος, *phronimos*
wise [11], more shrewd [1], prudent [1],
sensible person [1]

5862 φρονίμως, *phronimōs*
shrewdly [1]

5863 φροντίζω, *phrontizō*
careful [1]

5864 φρουρέω, *phroureō*
guard [2], imprison [1], protect [1]

5865 φρυάσσω, *phryassō*
rage [1]

5866 φρύγανον, *phryganon*
brushwood [1]

5867 Φρυγία, *Phrygia*
Phrygia [3]

5869 Φύγελος, *Phygelos*
Phygelus [1]

5870 φυγή, *phygē*
flight [1]

5871 φυλακή, *phylakē*
prison [34], haunt [3], imprisonment [3],
see 5480 [early in the morning] [2],
cell [1], guard [1], part of the night [1],
watch [1], *see 1311* [middle of the
night] [1], *see 5569* [near dawn] [1]

5872 φυλακίζω, *phylakizō*
imprison [1]

5873 φυλακτήριον, *phylaktērion*
phylactery [1]

5874 φύλαξ, *phylax*
guard [3]

5875 φυλάσσω, *phylassō*
keep [11], guard [9], beware [2], keep
under guard [2], obey [2], abstain [1],
keep watch over [1], observance [1], on
guard [1], save [1]

5876 φυλή, *phylē*
tribe [31]

5877 φύλλον, *phyllon*
leaf [6]

5878 φύραμα, *phyrama*
batch [2], batch of dough [2], lump [1]

5879 φυσικός, *physikos*
natural [2], instinct [1]

5880 φυσικῶς, *physikōs*
instinct [1]

5881 φυσιόω, *physioō*
arrogant [4], puff up [3]

5882 φύσις, *physis*
nature [6], natural [2], species [2],
birth [1], instinctively [1], *see 1666*
[physically] [1], *see 4123* [unnatural] [1]

5883 φυσίωσις, *physiōsis*
conceit [1]

5884 φυτεία, *phyteia*
plant [1]

5885 φυτεύω, *phyteuō*
plant [11]

5886 φύω, *phyō*
grow [1], grow up [1], spring up [1]

5887 φωλεός, *phōleos*
hole [2]

5888 φωνέω, *phōneō*
call [20], crow [12], call out [4],
summon [3], cry [2], invite [1], shout [1]

5889 φωνή, *phōnē*
voice [101], sound[1] [14], rumbling [4],
shout [3], noise [2], *see 2048* [shout] [2],
untranslated [2], blast [1], call [1], cry [1],
sentence[2] [1], shriek [1], tone [1],
word [1], *see 149* [call out] [1], *see 1651*
[unison] [1], *see 5774* [exclaim] [1]

5889 + 1666 + 3836 + 5125 φωνή + ἐκ
+ ὁ + στόμα, *phōnē + ek + ho + stoma*
voice [1]

5890 φῶς, *phōs*
light[1] [69], dazzle [1], fire [1],
firelight [1], *untranslated* [1]

5891 φωστήρ, *phōstēr*
radiance [1], star [1]

5892 φωσφόρος, *phōsphoros*
morning star [1]

5893 φωτεινός, *phōteinos*
full of light [2], light[1] [2], bright [1]

5894 φωτίζω, *phōtizō*
enlighten [4], bring to light [2], light[1] [2],
give light [1], make bright [1], make
see [1]

5895 φωτισμός, *phōtismos*
light[1] [2]

5897 χαίρω, *chairō*
rejoice [45], glad [6], greeting [6],
hail[2] [3], please greatly [2], welcome [2],
farewell [1], feel [1], gloat [1], happy [1],
joyfully [1], shout for joy [1]

5897 + 3336 χαίρω + λίαν, *chairō +
lian*
overjoyed [2]

5897 + 3489 + 5379 χαίρω + μέγας +
σφόδρα, *chairō + megas + sphodra*
overwhelm [1]

5897 + 5915 χαίρω + χαρά, *chairō +
chara*
rejoice greatly [1]

5898 χάλαζα, *chalaza*
hail[1] [3], hailstone [1]

5899 χαλάω, *chalaō*
let down [4], lower [3]

5900 Χαλδαῖος, *Chaldaios*
Chaldean [1]

5901 χαλεπός, *chalepos*
distress [1], fierce [1]

5902 χαλιναγωγέω, *chalinagōgeō*
bridle [1], keep in check with a bridle [1]

5903 χαλινός, *chalinos*
bit [1], bridle [1]

5906 χαλκεύς, *chalkeus*
coppersmith [1]

5907 χαλκηδών, *chalkēdōn*
agate [1]

5908 χαλκίον, *chalkion*
bronze kettle [1]

5909 χαλκολίβανον, *chalkolibanon*
burnished bronze [2]

5910 χαλκός, *chalkos*
money [2], bronze [1], copper [1],
gong [1]

5911 χαλκοῦς, *chalkous*
bronze [1]

5912 χαμαί, *chamai*
ground[1] [2]

5913 Χανάαν, *Chanaan*
Canaan [2]

5914 Χαναναῖος, *Chananaios*
Canaanite [1]

5915 χαρά, *chara*
joy [53], joyfully [1], overjoyed [1],
pleasant [1], *see 3552* [cheerfully] [1], *see
5668* [overjoyed] [1], *see 5897* [rejoice
greatly] [1]

5916 χάραγμα, *charagma*
mark [7], image [1]

5917 χαρακτήρ, *charaktēr*
exact imprint [1]

5918 χάραξ, *charax*
rampart [1]

5919 χαρίζομαι, *charizomai*
forgive [10], give [4], cancel a debt [2],
grant [2], bestowed gift [1], grant privilege
graciously [1], hand over [1], restore [1],
turn over [1]

5920 χάριν, *charin*
see 4047 [reason] [2], because [1], for [1],
reason[1] [1], to [1], why [1], *see 4005*
[therefore] [1], *untranslated* [1]

5921 χάρις, *charis*
grace [116], favor [9], thank [6], credit [4],
generous undertaking [3], gift [2],
gracious [2], approval [1], blessing [1],
generous act [1], goodwill [1], gracious
gift [1], grateful [1], gratitude [1],
privilege [1], thankfulness [1], thanks [1]

5921 + 2400 χάρις + ἔχω, *charis +
echō*
grateful [1], thank [1]

5922 χάρισμα, *charisma*
gift [12], free gift [3], blessing [1],
spiritual gift [1]

5923 χαριτόω, *charitoō*
bestow freely [1], favor [1]

5924 Χαρράν, *Charran*
Haran [2]

5925 χάρτης, *chartēs*
paper [1]

5926 χάσμα, *chasma*
chasm [1]

5927 χεῖλος, *cheilos*
lip [6]

5927 + 3836 + 2498 χεῖλος + ὁ +
θάλασσα, *cheilos + ho + thalassa*
seashore [1]

5928 χειμάζω, *cheimazō*
pounded by a storm [1]

5929 χείμαρρος, *cheimarros*
valley [1]

5930 χειμών, *cheimōn*
winter [4], stormy [1], tempest [1]

5931 χείρ, *cheir*
hand [153], *see 1328* [through] [4],
untranslated [4], *see 2095* [arrest] [3], *see
2939* [motion for silence] [2], finger [1],
wrist [1], *see 1328* [by] [1], *see 1328*
[with] [1], *see 1753* [point[2]] [1], *see 1877*
[by] [1], *see 2095* [seize] [1], *see 2202*
[ordain] [1], *see 2939* [gesture] [1], *see
5250* [through] [1]

5932 χειραγωγέω, *cheiragōgeō*
lead by the hand [2]

5933 χειραγωγός, *cheiragōgos*
someone to lead by the hand [1]

5934 χειρόγραφον, *cheirographon*
record [1]

5935 χειροποίητος, *cheiropoiētos*
make by human hands [3], make with
hands [2], make with human hands [1]

5936 χειροτονέω, *cheirotoneō*
appoint [2]

5937 χείρων, *cheirōn*
bad [11]

5938 Χερούβ, *Cheroub*
cherub [1]

5939 χήρα, *chēra*
widow [26]

5941 χιλίαρχος, *chiliarchos*
tribune [16], officer [2], captain [1],
general [1], military tribune [1]

5942 χιλιάς, *chilias*
thousand [22], *see 5084* [fifteen hundred
miles] [1]

5943 χίλιοι, *chilioi*
thousand [10], *see 5084* [two hundred
miles] [1]

5944 Χίος, *Chios*
Chios [1]

5945 χιτών, *chitōn*
tunic [7], coat [2], clothes [1], shirt [1]

5946 χιών, *chiōn*
snow [2]

5948 χλαμύς, *chlamys*
robe [2]

5949 χλευάζω, *chleuazō*
scoff [1]

5950 χλιαρός, *chliaros*
lukewarm [1]

5951 Χλόη, *Chloē*
Chloe [1]

5952 χλωρός, *chlōros*
green [2], green growth [1], pale green [1]

5954 χοϊκός, *choikos*
dust [4]

5955 χοῖνιξ, *choinix*
quart [2]

5956 χοῖρος, *choiros*
swine [10], pig [2]

5957 χολάω, cholaō
angry [1]

5958 χολή, cholē
gall [2]

5960 Χοραζίν, Chorazin
Chorazin [2]

5961 χορηγέω, chorēgeō
supply [2]

5962 χορός, choros
dance [1]

5963 χορτάζω, chortazō
fill [9], feed [3], eat one's fill [1],
gorge [1], satisfy hunger [1], well-fed [1]

5964 χόρτασμα, chortasma
food [1]

5965 χόρτος, chortos
grass [10], field [2], hay [1], plant [1],
stalk [1]

5966 Χουζᾶς, Chouzas
Chuza [1]

5967 χοῦς, chous
dust [2]

5968 χράομαι, chraomai
make use [3], take [2], use [2], act [1],
deal [1], treat [1], see 1786 [vacillate] [1]

5970 χρεία, chreia
need [21], dependent [1], support [1],
task [1]

5970 + 2400 χρεία + ἔχω, chreia +
echō
need [24], needy [1]

5971 χρεοφειλέτης, chreopheiletēs
debtor [2]

5973 χρή, chrē
ought [1]

5974 χρῄζω, chrēzō
need [4], require [1]

5975 χρῆμα, chrēma
money [4], wealth [2]

5976 χρηματίζω, chrēmatizō
warn [5], call [2], direct [1], reveal [1]

5977 χρηματισμός, chrēmatismos
divine reply [1]

5978 χρήσιμος, chrēsimos
do good [1]

5979 χρῆσις, chrēsis
intercourse [2]

5980 χρηστεύομαι, chrēsteuomai
kind2 [1]

5981 χρηστολογία, chrēstologia
smooth talk [1]

5982 χρηστός, chrēstos
good [3], kind2 [2], easy [1], kindness [1]

5983 χρηστότης, chrēstotēs
kindness [9], goodness [1]

5984 χρῖσμα, chrisma
anoint [3]

5985 Χριστιανός, Christianos
Christian [3]

5986 Χριστός, Christos
Christ [463], Messiah [64], anoint [1],
he [1]

5987 χρίω, chriō
anoint [5]

5988 χρονίζω, chronizō
delay [5]

5989 χρόνος, chronos
time1 [32], long1 [4], while [3], age2 [2],
begin [2], see 2093 [long1] [2], delay [1],
during [1], late [1], life [1], old1 [1],
time2 [1], see 4498 [long1] [1], see 5117
[instant] [1], untranslated [1]

5990 χρονοτριβέω, chronotribeō
spend time [1]

5992 χρυσίον, chrysion
gold [12]

5993 χρυσοδακτύλιος, chrysodaktylios
gold ring [1]

5994 χρυσόλιθος, chrysolithos
chrysolite [1]

5995 χρυσόπρασος, chrysoprasos
chrysoprase [1]

5996 χρυσός, chrysos
gold [10]

5997 χρυσοῦς, chrysous
golden [15], gold [3]

5998 χρυσόω, chrysoō
adorn [2]

5999 χρώς, chrōs
skin [1]

6000 χωλός, chōlos
lame [13], cripple [1]

6001 χώρα, chōra
country [12], region [8], countryside [3],
field [2], land1 [2], untranslated [1]

6003 χωρέω, chōreō
accept [2], come [1], contain [1], enter [1],
hold [1], make room [1], place [1],
room2 [1], untranslated [1]

6004 χωρίζω, chōrizō
separate [9], leave [3], so [1]

6005 χωρίον, chōrion
land1 [4], field [3], place [2], plot of
ground [1]

6006 χωρίς, chōris
without1 [19], apart [10], besides [3],
independent [2], not [2], beyond [1], by
oneself [1], except [1], out [1], with [1]

6008 χῶρος, chōros
northwest [1]

6010 ψάλλω, psallō
sing praise [3], make melody [1], sing
songs of praise [1]

6011 ψαλμός, psalmos
psalm [6], hymn [1]

6012 ψευδάδελφος, pseudadelphos
false believer [1], false brother and
sister [1]

6013 ψευδαπόστολος, pseudapostolos
false apostle [1]

6014 ψευδής, pseudēs
false [2], liar [1]

6015 ψευδοδιδάσκαλος,
pseudodidaskalos
false teacher [1]

6016 ψευδολόγος, pseudologos
liar [1]

6017 ψεύδομαι, pseudomai
lie2 [9], false [1], falsely [1], prove
false [1]

6018 ψευδομαρτυρέω, pseudomartyreō
bear false witness [3], give false
testimony [2]

6019 ψευδομαρτυρία, pseudomartyria
false testimony [1], false witness [1]

6020 ψευδόμαρτυς, pseudomartys
false witness [1], misrepresent [1]

6021 ψευδοπροφήτης,
pseudoprophētēs
false prophet [11]

6022 ψεῦδος, pseudos
lie2 [5], falsehood [3], false [1]

6022 + 3281 ψεῦδος + λαλέω, pseudos
+ laleō
lie2 [1]

6023 ψευδόχριστος, pseudochristos
false messiah [2]

6024 ψευδώνυμος, pseudōnymos
call falsely [1]

6025 ψεῦσμα, pseusma
falsehood [1]

6026 ψεύστης, pseustēs
liar [10]

6027 ψηλαφάω, psēlaphaō
touch [3], grope for [1]

6028 ψηφίζω, psēphizō
calculate [1], estimate [1]

6029 ψῆφος, psēphos
stone [2], vote [1]

6030 ψιθυρισμός, psithyrismos
gossip [1]

6031 ψιθυριστής, psithyristēs
gossip [1]

6033 ψιχίον, psichion
crumb [2]

6034 ψυχή, psychē
life [44], soul [33], person [4], see 4246
[everyone] [4], mind1 [3], see 1609 [I] [2],
all [1], being [1], heart [1], self [1],
themselves [1], thing [1], yourself [1], see
149 [keep in suspense] [1], see 1725 [lose
heart] [1], see 1847 [I] [1], see 2400
[live] [1], see 4348 [save] [1]

6034 + 5148 ψυχή + σύ, psychē + sy
you [1]

6035 ψυχικός, psychikos
physical [3], unspiritual [2], worldly
person [1]

6036 ψῦχος, psychos
cold [3]

6037 ψυχρός, psychros
cold [4]

6038 ψύχω, psychō
grow cold [1]

6039 ψωμίζω, psōmizō
feed [1], give away [1]

6040 ψωμίον, psōmion
piece of bread [4]

6041 ψώχω, psōchō
rub [1]

6042 ˀΩ1, Ō1
Omega [3]

6043 ὦ2, ō2
untranslated [11], you [4], O [1], oh [1]

6045 ὧδε, hōde
here [52], call [4], case [1], place [1],
there [1], untranslated [1]

6045 + 3370 ὧδε + λοιπός, hōde +
loipos
moreover [1]

6046 ᾠδή, *ōdē*
song [7]

6047 ὠδίν, *ōdin*
birth pang [2], labor pains [1],
untranslated [1]

6048 ὠδίνω, *ōdinō*
birth pang [1], endure birth pangs [1], pain
of childbirth [1]

6049 ὦμος, *ōmos*
shoulder [2]

6050 ὠνέομαι, *ōneomai*
buy [1]

6051 ᾠόν, *ōon*
egg [1]

6052 ὥρα, *hōra*
hour [67], *see 1761* [noon] [6], time[1] [5],
moment [4], *see 1888* [three in the
afternoon] [3], *see 1888* [three
o'clock] [3], *see 608* [instantly] [3],
while [2], *see 5569* [nine o'clock] [2], *see
5569* [nine o'clock in the morning] [2],
briefly [1], short [1], *see 1281* [four
o'clock in the afternoon] [1], *see 1575*
[one in the afternoon] [1], *see 1761*
[noon] [1], *see 1877* [just then] [1], *see
1888* [three o'clock in the afternoon] [1],
see 1895 [five o'clock] [1],
untranslated [1]

6052 + 4498 ὥρα + πολύς, *hōra + polys*
late [1]

6053 ὡραῖος, *hōraios*
beautiful [4]

6054 ὠρύομαι, *ōryomai*
roar [1]

6055 ὡς, *hōs*
as [183], like[1] [119], when [45],
untranslated [22], about[3] [19], as
though [18], how [15], just as [12], as
if [7], that [6], while [6], after [5],
seem [5], since [4], according [3],
what [3], order[2] [2], size [2], that is [2],
and [1], appear [1], as soon as [1],
effect [1], even as [1], even though [1], if
only [1], in [1], likewise [1], might [1],
on [1], pretext [1], same [1], some [1],
think [1], thus [1], way [1], whenever [1],
where [1], which [1], who [1], *see 1675*
[defame] [1]

6055 + 323 ὡς + ἄν, *hōs + an*
when [2], as soon as [1]

6055 + 1569 ὡς + ἐάν, *hōs + ean*
like[1] [1]

6057 ὡσαννά, *hōsanna*
Hosanna [6]

6058 ὡσαύτως, *hōsautōs*
likewise [6], same [4], same way [4], just
as [1], so [1], *untranslated* [1]

6059 ὡσεί, *hōsei*
about[3] [12], like[1] [6], as [2],
untranslated [1]

6060 Ὡσηέ, *Hōsēe*
Hosea [1]

6061 ὥσπερ, *hōsper*
just as [15], as [14], like[1] [3], as if [1], in
fact [1], unlike [1], *untranslated* [1]

6062 ὡσπερεί, *hōsperei*
as [1]

6063 ὥστε, *hōste*
so that [31], so [16], therefore [12],
that [11], to [3], so then [2], and [1],
for [1], now [1], order[2] [1], reason[1] [1],
same way [1], then [1], thus [1]

6064 ὠτάριον, *ōtarion*
ear [2]

6065 ὠτίον, *ōtion*
ear [3]

6066 ὠφέλεια, *ōpheleia*
advantage [1], value [1]

6067 ὠφελέω, *ōpheleō*
benefit [4], profit [3], do [2], support [2],
gain [1], good [1], value [1]

6067 + 4029 ὠφελέω + οὐδείς,
ōpheleō + oudeis
useless [1]

6068 ὠφέλιμος, *ōphelimos*
profitable [1], useful [1], valuable [1],
value [1]